GREEK-ENGLISH LEXICON

OF THE

NEW TESTAMENT

BASED ON
SEMANTIC DOMAINS

Volume 1
Introduction
&
Domains

Johannes P. Louw
Editor

Eugene A. Nida
Editor

Rondal B. Smith
Part-time editor

Karen A. Munson
Associate editor

United Bible Societies

GREEK-ENGLISH
LEXICON
of the
New Testament
based on
Semantic Domains

Volume 1

First edition 1988
Second impression 1988
Third impression 1989

© United Bible Societies 1988

All rights reserved.
No part of this book may be translated or reproduced
in any form without the written permission of the
United Bible Societies.

Published by the United Bible Societies, 1865 Broadway,
New York, NY 10023, USA

Library of Congress Cataloging-in-Publication Data

· Greek-English lexicon of the New Testament: based on semantic domains/
Johannes P. Louw, editor; Eugene A. Nida, editor;
Rondal B. Smith, part-time editor; Karen A. Munson, associate editor.
p. cm.
Bibliography: v. 1, p.
Includes indices.
Contents: v. 1. Introduction & Domains – v. 2. Indices.
ISBN 0-8267-0340-2 (set). ISBN 0-8267-0341-0 (v. 1). ISBN 0-8267-0342-9 (v. 2)
1. Greek language, Biblical – Glossaries, vocabularies, etc.
2. Greek language, Biblical – Dictionaries – English.
3. Greek language, Biblical – Semantics.
4. Bible. N.T.–Language, style.
I. Louw, Johannes Petrus, 1932–. II. Nida, Eugene Albert, 1914–.
PA881.G68 1988
487'.4–dc 19
87-36866
CIP

© Maps – United Bible Societies, EPF,
used by kind permission

ISBN 0 8267-0341-0 (Volume 1)
ISBN 0 8267-0340-2 (2 Volume Set)

Printed by National Book Printers, Goodwood, Cape
Type 11/11 Plantin

ABS - 1989 - 3M - 7.5M - 56496

CONTENTS

PREFACE

This Greek New Testament lexicon based on semantic domains has been designed primarily for translators of the New Testament in various languages, but biblical scholars, pastors, and theological students will no doubt also find this lexicon of particular value, since it focuses on the related meanings of different words. This focus is clearly a major concern of all theological studies. In addition, a number of linguists and lexicographers are likely to be interested in view of the distinctive approach and methodology employed in this lexicon.

The approach to the problems of the meaning of lexical units (words and idioms) in this dictionary is the outgrowth of field experience, which has included helping Bible translators in some 200 different languages in the world, but both the orientation and the methodology reflect a body of important relevant research, including the work of Lounsbury (1964), Conklin (1962), Goodenough (1956), Nida (1975), and Lehrer (1974).

Initial work on this lexicon began in the summer of 1972, and the editorial team consisted of Johannes P. Louw of the University of Pretoria in South Africa, Eugene A. Nida of the American Bible Society and the United Bible Societies, and Rondal B. Smith, then of Lincoln Christian College and at present with the Pioneer Bible Translators. In view of other commitments, however, Professor Smith was not able to continue until the end of the editorial processes. Karen A. Munson, who made important contributions to the editorial procedures of the Greek New Testament published by the United Bible Societies, has served throughout the project as an associate editor.

The procedures employed in the development of this Greek New Testament lexicon have been of four principal types: (1) the classification of meanings of the New Testament vocabulary into domains and subdomains, based on a dictionary published by the United Bible Societies and edited by Barclay M. Newman; (2) a verification of these meanings, as well as the addition of other meanings of lexical units based on a careful study of Greek New Testament concordances and dictionaries; (3) the preparation of definitions and notes (both those for translators, included in the text, and for linguists and lexicographers, in footnotes); and (4) final editing, cross referencing, and indexing, as well as proofreading. Responsibility for the first procedure rested with the editorial committee of Louw, Nida, and Smith, while the second procedure was carried out by Louw and Smith, with major responsibility resting with Louw. The third procedure was carried out by Nida in close consultation with Louw, and the fourth procedure was the responsibility of Louw and his staff (in particular Stienie Venter, Willem Oliver and Tienie Bosman assisted by Wessel Venter) at the University of Pretoria, with additional assistance from Karen Munson, who has been responsible for the preparation of the manuscript at various stages.

In a publication as extensive and complex as this Greek New Testament lexicon, it is inevitable that certain matters will be overlooked and some mistakes will be made. Accordingly, plans have been made for the publication in subsequent editions of both errata and addenda. Since the dictionary is computerized, corrections can be readily introduced.

The editors will be particularly thankful for help from any person using this lexicon who can provide assistance in noting mistakes and oversights.

The editors sincerely hope that this lexicon will be of real service to biblical scholars, students, and New Testament translators, as well as to semanticists and lexicographers, since this is the first time that such a large body of lexical data has been submitted to careful analysis and organization into semantic domains.

1987   Johannes P. Louw and Eugene A. Nida

INTRODUCTION

This introduction to the Greek New Testament lexicon has two principal purposes: (1) to help persons make the most effective use of the lexicon and (2) to help persons understand the principles which have been employed in this lexicon. Accordingly, the introduction is divided into four principal sections: (1) the significant features of the lexicon, (2) reasons for this new type of Greek lexicon, (3) how to use the lexicon, and (4) basic principles employed in the preparation of the lexicon.

Significant Features of the Lexicon

The data base for this Greek New Testament lexicon consists of the entire vocabulary of the third edition (both text and apparatus) of the Greek New Testament published by the United Bible Societies. The vocabulary, including both individual words and idioms, consists of some 5 000 lexical items, with more than 25 000 meanings in all.

In a number of respects this lexicon is a unique type of dictionary, primarily because it is based on the concept of semantic domains, and secondly because of the manner in which the domains are organized and the data presented. The primary distinction in the classification of the meanings of words and idioms is between unique referents, class referents, and markers. Words with unique referents are simply proper names (Domain 93), which are divided into personal names and place names. Words with class referents are so-called common words, and the meanings may be described as designating a class of entities, events, or abstracts. The markers consist of words (usually prepositions and particles) which serve primarily to mark the relationships between content words, phrases, and clauses. These markers are often spoken of as 'function words,' and a number of these are described in Domain 89 *Relations* and in Domain 91 *Discourse Markers*. A typical example of a discourse marker is the conjunction καί, which often does not serve to coordinate clauses or sentences but simply indicates the fact that a new sentence is to begin. This use of καί as a discourse marker is very frequent in the Gospel of Mark. The same situation occurs with respect to the conjunction δέ, which likewise often does not serve to mark a coordinate contrast but simply indicates that there is some loosely defined connection between clauses or sentences.

Lexical items which designate class referents belong to three principal classes: (1) objects or entities, (2) events, and (3) abstracts, including relationals. Lexical items relating to object referents occur primarily in Domains 1-12; those designating events occur in Domains 13-57; and abstracts are in Domains 58-91. Domain 92 *Discourse Referentials* includes pronominal and deictic expressions, which point primarily to (or substitute for) objects and to a lesser extent to events and abstracts.

The basis for the various semantic domains and subdomains consists of three major classes of semantic features: shared, distinctive, and supplementary. The shared features are those elements of the meaning of lexical items which are held in common by a set of lexical items. The distinctive features are those which separate meanings one from another, and the supplementary features are those which may be relevant in certain contexts or may play primarily a connotative or associative role. In Domain 19 *Physical Impact,* for example, κολαφίζω[a] (19.7), ῥαβδίζω (19.8), and μαστίζω and μαστιγόω[a] (19.9) all share the features of physical impact involving hitting or striking. They differ, however, in certain distinctive features in that κολαφίζω[a] designates striking or beating with the fist, ῥαβδίζω designates beating or striking with a stick or rod, and μαστίζω and μαστιγόω[a] designate beating with a whip. The terms μαστίζω and μαστιγόω[a] also differ from κολαφίζω[a] and ῥαβδίζω in that they normally refer to officially sanctioned punishment.

Within any domain or subdomain, those meanings which are first treated tend to be of a more generic nature, while more specific meanings follow. For example, in Domain 19 *Physical Impact* the first item (19.1) includes τύπτω[a], πληγή[a], πλήσσω, and παίω[a], all of which may occur with the generic meaning of "to strike or hit an object, one or more times," but without specifying the particular manner in which the hitting or striking takes place. The meanings of these terms are then followed by other less generic expressions, until finally one encounters a term such as κεφαλιόω (19.13), which designates the act of beating someone on the head. There is, however, no way in which one can move step by step from highly generic to specifically limited or restricted areas of meaning, nor is it possible to set up strict logical structures of binary contrasts as a way of classifying large sets of meanings. In fact, meanings relate to one another in diverse ways and involve a number of different dimensions, so that they constitute complex clusters or constellations. In a sense; such meanings relate to one another in a manner similar to diverse dialects of the same language.

Another important feature of this lexicon is the fact that irregular forms are noted if these are in any way connected with meaning or if the form is so diverse as to cause difficulty for a person identifying the morphological base, whether in the case of nouns, the nominative singular, or in the case of verbs, the first person singular present indicative. If, for example, the meaning of a so-called middle form of the verb cannot be derived regularly from the active, then both the active and the middle forms are listed as separate entries. Note, for example, ἀποπλανάω (31.11) "to cause someone to definitely go astray in one's beliefs or views" and ἀποπλανάομαι (31.67) in the meaning of "to stray from the truth." Also, when a term only occurs in the New Testament as a deponent in the middle form, it is listed under the middle and not under the active. Note, for example, ἀποτίθεμαι[a] (85.44). All of the important irregular forms of ἀποτίθεμαι[a] are also listed in the Greek-English Index.

One of the very noteworthy advantages of this lexicon is the fact that each distinct meaning of a term is clearly marked by a superscript letter of the alphabet. In the case of ἀφίημι, there are as many as twelve meanings (a to l), but in general, words denote far fewer distinctive lexical meanings. For the most part, the most common or 'unmarked' meaning is listed first, that is to say, with the superscript 'a,' and other less common or peripheral meanings follow, somewhat in order of specificity, but as in the case of the sets of related meanings of different terms, the relationships between the meanings of the same term form a multidimensional constellation. As such, the order of the listing is not significant.

For many persons the most distinctive and helpful feature of this lexicon is the fact that meanings are indicated by definitions and not simply by glosses, as in most dictionaries. The definitions are based upon the distinctive features of meaning of a particular term, and the glosses only suggest ways in which such a term with a particular meaning may be represented in English, but the definitions are the significant elements. For example, ἐρημόο-

μαι (20.41) is defined as "to suffer destruction, with the implication of being deserted and abandoned," but in English one may readily gloss such a term as 'to be destroyed' or 'to suffer destruction' or 'to suffer desolation.' Similarly, κίνδυνος (21.1) may be defined as "a state of dangerous and threatening circumstances" and glosses may include 'danger,' 'peril,' and 'risk.'

Without definitions, some glosses may be quite misleading. For example, one may gloss παρίστα-μαι[a] (17.3) as 'to stand near.' In Jn 19.26, however, there is a friendly intent, but in Ac 4.26 there is clearly a hostile intent, and so a definition should read "to stand near or alongside of someone, either with a friendly or hostile intent." In the case of Ac 4.26, therefore, there is a further statement in 17.3 to indicate that in some instances it may be relevant to translate part of this verse as "the kings of earth prepared themselves" or even "the kings of earth armed themselves."

In some instances, an accurate definition of a meaning may require a somewhat lengthy description of distinctive features, and even a statement about how the meaning of a term differs from the meanings of other terms. Note, for example, the definition of πόλις[b] in 1.89: "a population center of relatively greater importance (in contrast with κώμη[a] 'village,' 1.92, and κωμόπολις 'town,' 1.91), due to its size, economic significance, or political control over a surrounding area (it is possible that fortification of walls and gates also entered into the system of classification of a πόλις[b], in contrast with other terms for population centers)." All of these actual and possible features may be important in establishing certain contrasts in meaning.

In order to point out clearly the relationship of definitions and glosses to particular meanings, at least one illustrative example is given for each entry. Often there are several examples, especially if the meaning has a relatively wide range of referents. Thus, in the case of οὐρανός[b] (1.11), normally glossed as 'heaven,' there are three context examples, namely, Mt 18.10, 2 Cor 5.1, and Lk 11.13. In Domain 20.56 there are two context examples illustrating how κατασκάπτω can be used of relatively larger or smaller objects.

As will be readily noted in a glance at the lexicon, there are a number of so-called 'multiple entries,' that is to say, together in one numbered entry, there are several different terms with closely related meanings. Note, for example, 1.13, in which are listed ὕψος[b], ὑψηλός[b], ὕψιστος[a], and ὕψωμα[a]. The meaning of these terms is given as "a location above the earth and associated with supernatural events or beings," and the glosses are 'high, world above, sky, heaven, on high.' The fact that four different forms are listed together in 1.13 does not mean that they have exactly the same meaning; in fact, complete synonyms probably never occur. For practical purposes close synonyms can and should be listed together, especially where there is not sufficient evidence either in biblical contexts or in extra-biblical contexts to define specifically the distinctions in denotative or connotative meaning.

In a number of instances the lexicon contains suggestions which may be relevant for translators, especially when an object or action may have quite a different symbolic significance in diverse cultures. For example, the action of "beating the breast" in Lk 18.13 is symbolic in the Scriptures of repentance and contrition, but in many other languages this expression is a symbol of pride or self-flattery. In some languages, therefore, the equivalent of the biblical expression would be "to strike the head" or "to grasp the abdomen." Such notes do not cover all of the possibilities which a translator might encounter, but they at least alert translators as to some of the difficulties which are to be found in certain instances.

In order to employ this type of lexicon, it is essential to have three kinds of indices. The first and the most important index is the one from Greek to English, in which each Greek term is listed, and then with the appropriate designation of the superscript letter, a typical gloss is indicated, so that one may find the domain, subdomain, and entry at which this meaning is discussed. There is also an English to Greek index, but not all possible glosses are listed, since this would be not only voluminous but could in many instances be misleading. The focus of this index from English to Greek is therefore on the domains and subdomains, and frequently the reference is to an inclusive set of entries, since the English gloss covers a considerable semantic range. A third index indicates all of the passages in the New Testament which are cited.

Reasons For a New Type of Greek New Testament Lexicon

The principal reason for a new type of Greek New Testament lexicon is the inadequacy of most existing dictionaries, which for the most part are limited in indicating meanings, since they depend principally upon a series of glosses. For example, in the Greek-English Lexicon of the New Testament by Walter Bauer, as translated and revised by Gingrich and Danker, the first meaning of καταλαμβάνω is given as simply 'seize, win, attain, make one's own,' but in the illustrative examples of this first meaning, additional translational glosses occur, namely, 'grasp,' 'overcome,' and 'suppress.' The lack of a satisfactory definition of καταλαμβάνω leads to the confusion which occurs when so many different glosses representing diverse meanings are lumped together.

A more serious problem with some dictionaries is the unsystematic manner in which various meanings are treated. Note, for example, the treatment of λόγος in the Greek-English Lexicon of the New Testament by Walter Bauer. The meanings are classified and may be summarized as follows: "1. *speaking* -a. gener. -α. *word.* β. The expression may take any one of many different forms, so that the exact transl. of λ. depends on the context: *what you say, statement, question, prayer, pastoral counselling, preaching, prophecy, command, report, story, appearance, proverb, proclamation, instruction, teaching, message, speech.* γ. of a statement of definite content: *assertion, declaration, speech, statement.* δ. the pl. (οἱ) λόγοι is used (1) either of words uttered on various occasions, of speeches made here and there. ε. *the subject* under discussion, *matter, thing.* ζ. of written words and speeches: of the separate books of a work: *treatise, word.* b. *of revelation by God* -α. of God's word, command, commission. β. of the divine revelation through Christ and his messengers: *Christian message, the gospel.* 2. *computation, reckoning* -a. *account, accounts, reckoning, accounting.* b. *settlement (of an account).* c. *with respect to, with regard to, for the sake of.* d. *reason, motive.* e. *to reckon.* f. *concern for.* 3. *the Logos* (the independent, personified 'Word' of God)."

This type of classification of the meanings of λόγος is not only unsystematic but misleading, for it is based essentially upon a diversity of criteria. The meanings should have been grouped on the basis of λόγος as (1) the act of communication, (2) the verbal form of the communication, and (3) the content of the communication. These basic distinctions in meaning are then distinct from the λόγος as a title for Christ and the meaning of "reason" as a relation between events. It certainly is not particularly helpful to toss together so many different meanings and uses as occur in 1.a.β., nor is it at all clear as to how one may distinguish between 1.a.α. and 1.a.γ. One problem is the tendency to divide not along semantic lines but along theological lines. This, for example, forms the distinction between 1.a and 1.b, but the fundamental problem in this classification is the failure to distinguish between meaning and reference. (See Introduction, pp xvi-xvii.)

A further inadequacy of many existing lexicons is the lack of a systematic treatment of idioms. For example, βρόχος in the Bauer dictionary has the gloss 'noose,' and βρόχον ἐπιβάλλειν τινί is explained as "put or throw a noose on someone to catch or restrain him." Only at the end of the paragraph is there an indication that the expression is "figurative." It would seem much better, as in 37.2 of this Greek New Testament lexicon, to list βρόχον ἐπιβάλλω as an idiom (and give its literal meaning "to throw a bridle on") and then to define its figurative meaning as "to place restrictions upon someone's behavior," that is to say, 'to restrict, to control, to impose restrictions.' What the user of a dictionary needs is not merely the statement that an expression is used figuratively, but some indication as to what that figurative meaning involves.

In the Bauer dictionary the phrase δίδωμι δόξαν τῷ θεῷ is listed under the glosses 'fame, renown, honor,' and though it is identified as an adjuration with the meaning of "give God the praise by telling the truth," there is no specific indication that this is actually an idiom, and as such, a formula used in placing someone under oath to tell the truth, so that in Jn 9.24 the meaning is essentially "promise before God to tell the truth" or "swear to tell the truth."

Some scholars have given attention to the problem of producing a dictionary based on semantic domains, but in general the proposed classifications have been more philosophical and theological than semantic. Roget's *Thesaurus* has been suggested as one basis for classification, but it does not group meanings primarily in terms of related sets of distinctive semantic features. Note, for example, the major divisions in terms of abstract relations, space, matter, intellect, volition, and affections. Friedrich (1973) discusses several different attempts toward a conceptual lexicon and then proposes his own in terms of the unseen world, the physical world, mankind in the world, and God and the world. Such a classification obviously reflects a dogmatic orientation rather than one based on more general principles of shared and distinctive semantic features. A further discussion of some of the basic problems of classification and organization of related meanings is to be found in the final section of this introduction, in which basic principles of lexicography are treated.

The most important reason for a new approach to a Greek New Testament lexicon is the necessity of bringing together those meanings which are most closely related in semantic space, that is to say, those meanings which are often regarded as partial synonyms because the ranges of their meaning tend to overlap. One may also describe some of the problems of such closely related meanings as consisting of fuzzy boundaries, especially in view of the connotative factors involved.

In general, the different meanings of a single word are relatively far apart in semantic space. For example, the principal meanings of πνεῦμα are: (1) the Holy Spirit, (2) a non-material being (spirit), (3) an evil, non-material being (demon, evil spirit), (4) an apparition of an animate being (ghost), (5) a human psychological faculty (inner being), (6) a particular mode of intellectual activity (way of thinking, attitude), (7) atmospheric air in movement (wind), and (8) air coming from the lungs (breath).

Most diverse meanings of the same lexical item are relatively far apart in semantic space, that is to say, they differ appreciably in certain distinctive features and often belong to quite different major semantic domains. Such diversities of meaning of a single lexical unit are necessary if communication is to be effective, for the context must readily signal which of various meanings may be involved. If all the related meanings of a single lexical item were very close in semantic space, then the context could not readily point to one or another meaning; in other words, there would be great obscurity and ambivalence in an utterance. On the other hand, there are a number of instances in every language in which the related meanings of different words are very close in semantic space. Note, for example, the meanings of Greek νοῦς, καρδία, ψυχή, συνείδησις, φρήν, and πνεῦμα as psychological faculties in Domain 26:

νοῦς[a] (26.14): the psychological faculty of understanding, reasoning, thinking, and deciding.

καρδία[a] (26.3): the causative source of a person's psychological life in its various aspects, but with special emphasis upon thoughts.

ψυχή[a] (26.4): the essence of life in terms of thinking, willing, and feeling.

συνείδησις[b] (26.13): the psychological faculty which can distinguish between right and wrong.

φρήν (26.15): the psychological faculty of thoughtful planning, often with the implication of being wise and provident.

πνεῦμα[e] (26.9): the non-material, psychological faculty which is potentially sensitive and responsive to God.

These psychological faculties should not be regarded as distinct parts of human personality, but as different aspects or modes of human personality which may be viewed from different perspectives. There is considerable overlapping between νοῦς[a] and καρδία[a], especially since in a number of contexts καρδία reflects Hebrew *leb* (literally, 'heart'), which was regarded as primarily the center of intellectual rather than emotional life. The primary value of a lexicon based upon semantic domains is that it forces the reader to recognize some of the subtle distinctions which exist between lexical items whose meanings are closely related and which in certain contexts overlap.

Another advantage of an approach to lexical problems based on semantic domains is that different parts of speech may be classified together. For example, εὐχαριστέω[a] and εὐχαριστία (33.349) both mean "to express gratitude for benefits or blessing" and may be translated, depending on contexts, 'to thank, thanksgiving, thankfulness.' One form is a verb and the other a noun, but they both denote the event of giving thanks.

In grouping meanings on the basis of shared features, it is essential that derivatives be treated as closely as possible to their semantic bases. Accordingly, ὕβρις[c] (33.391) "the content of an insulting statement" and ὑβριστής[b] (33.392) "one who insults in an arrogant manner" immediately follow ὑβρίζω[b] (33.390), which is the base event. Derivative semantic relationships are pointed out even when the base does not occur in the New Testament. For example, διάβολος[c] (33.397) is a derivative of διαβάλλω 'to slander,' which does not happen to occur in the New Testament.

A further value to be gained in an approach to semantic problems based on domain relationships is that positives and negatives are placed in the same domain, since they share a number of fundamental features and only differ in certain positive and negative aspects. In Domain 65 *Value*, all of the subdomains contain both positive and negative elements. For example, in Subdomain C the contrast is between *Good* and *Bad*. Accordingly, positive features such as ἀγαθός[b] (65.20), καλός[b] (65.22), and χρηστός[a] (65.25) contrast with κακός[b] (65.26) and πονηρός[b] (65.27). Similarly, in Subdomain D *Useful, Useless*, χρήσιμος (65.30), εὔχρηστος (65.31), and εὔθετος[b] (65.32) contrast with ἀχρεῖος[a] (65.33), ἄκαρπος[b] (65.34), ἀνεύθετος (65.35), and ἀργός[d] (65.36). It is particularly important for translators to be aware of these positive/negative contrasts.

By clearly identifying different meanings of lexical units on the basis of their distinctive features, it is possible to highlight differences of interpretation of an expression in a particular verse by the process of cross referencing. For example, ὕβρις[b] (20.19) designates "the condition resulting from violence or mistreatment" and may be rendered in English as 'harm, damage, injury,' but in 2 Cor 12.10 it is also possible to interpret ὕβρις either as 'insults' (33.391) or as 'insolent mistreatment' (88.131). At each of these two entries, the fact of other meanings for ὕβρις in 2 Cor 12.10 is carefully noted. This not only helps a translator recognize the fact that the same term may have several different meanings in a particular context, but also provides a ready reference to possible alternative renderings to be included in marginal notes of a text.

In some instances a different interpretation is possible but not very probable, and this likewise is recognized, but two distinct entries are not employed. For example, ἐξολεθρεύω (20.35) is best understood in the sense of "to destroy and thus eliminate," but it is possible that in Ac 3.23 ἐξολεθρεύω relates to a type of severe ostracism.

In order to use this type of distinct lexicon of the Greek New Testament vocabulary, it is essential to understand the basic principles and purpose for which it has been prepared. A statement of these principles is included in this introduction, but there are a number of very helpful footnotes which also aid the reader in understanding the basic implications of these principles at various points in the text. For example, footnote 1 of Domain 33 *Communication* provides a brief description of some of the groupings of subdomains and indicates the basis for the arrangement. Footnote 2 indicates why there is a distinction between γραφή[a] (33.10) and γραφή[b] (33.53), since γραφή[a] is the more generic reference to any unit of a discourse and γραφή[b] designates a particular Old Testament Scripture passage. From time to time, there are also notes indicating different connotative or associative values of words. For example, in footnote 5 of Domain 33 the suggestion is made that δημηγορέω probably implies greater formality than διαλέγομαι[b], despite the fact that it is impossible to determine this on the basis of New Testament usage.

How To Use the Lexicon

There are three principal approaches to the use of this lexicon: (1) beginning with the Greek word, (2) beginning with an English word, and (3) beginning with a passage of Scripture. If someone has in mind a Greek word for which the meaning or meanings are the subject of discussion or inquiry, then the first step is to look up the Greek word in the Greek-English index. Immediately following the Greek term is a list of those forms which indicate the declension and gender for nouns, the two or one alternative forms for adjectives, and any irregular forms for verbs. Immediately following this listing are the selected glosses which point to the meaning or meanings of the word or idiom. If, for example, a word such as λογομαχέω has only one meaning in the New Testament, then a typical gloss (whether a single word or phrase) is listed together with the numerical marker of the domain, followed by the numbered entry. For example, for λογομαχέω the glossed phrase is 'argue about words,' and this is followed by the number 33.454, which indicates that this is the thirty-third domain and that λογομαχέω is listed as entry 454 within that domain.

For παρακαλέω all the irregular forms are listed immediately following the verb, and then there are four different meanings, listed a, b, c, d, corresponding to the superscripts used with παρακαλέω to identify the meanings in question. Most of the meanings are to be found in Domain 33 *Communication*, but the meaning of 'to encourage' occurs in Domain 25 *Attitudes and Emotions*.

For ὀφθαλμός there are only three meanings: 'eye,' 'sight,' and 'understanding,' but ὀφθαλμός occurs in eight different idioms, and these are listed both in Greek as well as with glosses to indicate their meanings. In each case the entry for these units is listed together with the unit, so that one can immediately determine the domain and the entry which are relevant for further study or consideration.

It would be a mistake, however, to consider that the glosses employed in identifying the various meanings are adequate to determine what a lexical unit may mean in a particular context. Only by carefully reading the entry, and hopefully those entries which immediately precede and follow, can one fully appreciate the referential range of any meaning.

In addition to noting the meanings of lexical items which may immediately precede or follow an individual entry, it is often useful to glance over an entire subdomain. It may also be useful to look at the outline of subdomains which occurs at the beginning of each domain. This will provide a good deal of insight as to the way in which different meanings relate to one another.

Whenever important so-called 'content words' occur in an idiomatic unit it is usually identified under one or more of these content words, and the superscript letter identifying the idiom is placed at the end of the idiom, but this does not always mean that the idiom is listed under the word which has the superscript. Idioms themselves may, of course, have more than one meaning. For example, ὀφθαλμὸς πονηρός may be understood in certain contexts as 'jealousy' and in others as 'stinginess' (see 88.165 and 57.108). Idioms are always identified in the text immediately following the form of the Greek expression, and a literal translation of the idiom is given in parentheses. This is immediately followed by a definition and then by one or more possible glosses.

If one begins with a particular English word, one must first look up the entry in the English-Greek index, but this index differs significantly from the Greek-English index in that it does not list all of the Greek words which may occur in the lexicon with a particular gloss. To have done this would have resulted in an index so bulky as to not be really helpful. Accordingly, clues as to the respective Greek terms are identified by the domains and the specific entry or set of entries in which the gloss in question is likely to represent a central or a core meaning. Note, for example, the following typical series from the English index:

today 67.205, 206

toil 42.41-50

If one is concerned primarily with the lexical values to be found in words of a particular passage of Scripture, then obviously the place to begin is with the biblical index. This index is exhaustive in that it lists all of the domains and entries where a specific verse of Scripture is treated in any way. This means that by using the biblical index one can ultimately find out everything which is said about a particular verse, but not all of the verses of the New Testament are to be found in the index, since the lexicon itself is not exhaustive of all the occurrences of every term. The choice of biblical passages to illustrate the range of meaning of any lexical item is based upon two factors: (1) the clarity and particularity of the passage and (2) the importance of the passage for exegesis. No attempt has been made to sidestep semantic problems, as will be noted by the numerous instances in which more than one meaning of a term is listed for a particular context.

In addition to the major features of the lexicon which have already been listed, one will soon recognize certain additional characteristics which can prove to be highly useful. If a term occurs only in a particular form, this is clearly noted. For example, σπλάγχνα occurs only in the plural. Even when some manuscripts have alternative spellings, this is noted if it sheds some light on meaningful relations. For example, γένεσις[a] (23.46) is followed by a statement that in some manuscripts the spelling is γέννησις. When the forms of words are radically different, then both forms are listed and one is instructed by the cross referencing to go to the base form. For example, both ὁράω and εἶδον are listed, and at the entry for εἶδον the reader is told to refer to ὁράω. All such suppletive sets are treated in this way.

Most readers will have no difficulty recognizing that certain verbs and corresponding nouns have essentially the same meaning. For example, in 33.400 βλασφημέω and βλασφημία[a] are given the same meaning, namely, "to speak against someone in such a way as to harm or injure his or her reputation." Whether a writer employs a verb or a noun depends largely upon the syntactic structure and the stylistic features of a passage. In 33.69 λέγω[a] and φημί[a] are listed as the same entry and given the meaning of "to speak or talk, with apparent focus upon the content of what is said." A native speaker of Hellenistic Greek might have been able to point out certain subtle distinctions in associative or connotative meaning of these two terms, but on the basis of existing data in the New Testament, it is not possible to distinguish meanings, particularly on the level of denotation or designation. The verb λαλέω occurs in 33.70, and the definition is given as "to speak or talk, with the possible implication of more informal usage (though this cannot be clearly and consistently shown from NT contexts)." This means that λαλέω has not been put together with λέγω[a] and φημί[a], but it also means that the three verbs are *very* closely related in meaning, and to insist upon a clear distinction in meaning is to read into the text something which one cannot consistently justify.

There is often a problem of deponency, especially with the so-called -μι verbs. For example, the middle form ἀνίσταμαι[d] (23.93) is listed as having the meaning of "to come back to life after having once died," but the second aorist active (ἀνέστην) also carries this meaning, and this type of information is always listed for those verbs which exhibit this particular characteristic. See ἀνίσταμαι and ἀνίστημι in the Greek-English Index. See also ἀνέστην in the same index. As already noted, the problems of relations in meaning between λέγω[a], φημί[a], and λαλέω are not particularly complex, but in some instances there are a number of terms which seem to have either essentially the same meaning, or their meanings cannot be distinguished on the basis of the limited number of contexts occurring in the New Testament or even in supplementary Hellenistic literature. Note, for example, 23.93, in which are listed ζάω[b], ἀναζάω[a], ἀνίσταμαι[d], ἀνάστασις[a], ἐξανάστασις, and ἔγερσις. All are given the meaning of "to come back to life after having once died." Undoubtedly, these different terms had certain subtle distinctions of meaning in Hellenistic Greek, but we are not able to recover the distinguishing data. At the same time, this does not mean that all of these terms have identical meanings; it is only that in certain contexts they may be employed to refer to essentially the same event.

In some instances the definition of the meaning of a term may seem unduly long and involved. For example, in the case of λέπρα (23.161) the definition is given as "a dreaded condition of the skin, including what is now regarded as leprosy, as well as certain other types of infectious skin diseases, resulting in a person's being regarded as ceremonially unclean and thus excluded from normal relations with other people." The various features of this definition are essential if one is to understand clearly the meaning of the Greek term in biblical times. In addition to the identification of the disease, it is also important to indicate the ritual significance of the disease and thus to help a translator understand the cultural relevance of certain passages, in which Jesus touched lepers and thus by contact made himself ceremonially unclean in order to minister to their needs.

In contrast with the highly specific definition of λέπρα, the definition of σκεῦος[a] (6.1) is extremely general, for example, "any kind of instrument, tool, weapon, equipment, container, or property," and the glosses 'object, thing' are given.

In a few instances, however, no definition is given, but simply a gloss which serves the function of a definition. For example, for ἄγκιστρον (6.10) the lexicon lists only the gloss 'fish hook.' It would be possible to devise a descriptive definition of a fish hook, but this would seem to be unnecessarily repetitive.

The identification of a term as having a meaning within a particular domain implies a number of highly generic distinctive features. One must assume that in Domain 6 *Artifacts* the referents are countables (unless masses are specified), that they are manufactured, and that they are movable in contrast with Domain 7 *Constructions*. Technically, of course, constructions such as houses, fortresses, inns, and sanctuaries are also artifacts, but in view of the popular usage of the term *artifact* and the grouping of related semantic features, it seems more practical to set up two related domains.

A good deal of important information is contained in three different types of notes. At the beginning of some domains and certain subdomains there are notes to explain the subdomain structure and some of the reasons for the distinctions which follow. Note, for example, that at the beginning of Domain 12 *Supernatural Beings and Powers* there is an important statement explaining the basic distinction. There is, however, also an additional footnote indicating that in certain respects the distinction between 'beings' and 'powers' is artificial, especially since some of the so-called 'impersonal powers' seem to have aspects of personality. The footnote also calls attention to the fact that it is difficult to determine the distinctive features of various items in this domain, since the referents are conceptual rather than perceptual, and some of the referents are unique members of a class.

At the beginning of Subdomain B *Supernatural Powers* (12.43-12.50), there is a note which heads the section and identifies these supernatural powers as ones which were believed to be active as elemental spirits exercising control over people's fate. The note goes on to say that these various supernatural powers are organized into various grades in extrabiblical literature of the time, but for the New Testament there seems to be no basis for clearly establishing gradations of power or influence.

The most common notes are those which immediately follow the discussion of meaning and illustrative examples, and are designed primarily to help translators deal with some of the frequently recurring difficulties. In some instances these notes for translators may appear at first to be trivial, but they can be extremely important from the standpoint of finding satisfactory equivalents in other languages. For example, πέτρα (2.21) designates bedrock, rocky crags, or mountain ledges in contrast with separate pieces of rock, normally referred to as λίθος[a] (2.23). Since many languages make a clear distinction between bedrock (either exposed or lying just below the surface), rocks in cliffs or crags, and separate pieces of hewn rock (primarily used in building) and field stone, it is important to note that in certain contexts one must use an expression which will clearly identify the appropriate referent. For example, in Re 6.16, "they said to the mountains and to the rocks, 'Fall on us,' " the rocks must be cliffs and certainly not bedrock, nor should the reference be to field rocks presumably jumping up into the air and falling down upon people.

As stated in footnote 3 of Domain 2 *Natural Substances*, πέτρα and λίθος occur in parallel statements in Ro 9.33 and 1 Pe 2.8 in a quotation coming from Is 8.14. On the basis of this usage, one might argue that πέτρα and λίθος are completely synonymous, at least in this context, but parallelism does not mean identity of meaning; in fact, parallelism (in contrast with tautology) normally implies certain slight differences of meaning in corresponding lexical items.

As already noted, some of the footnotes are designed primarily for lexicographers and those who may be particularly interested in some of the underlying reasons for certain classifications. Footnote 1 of Domain 2 *Natural Substances* is typical of this more technical supplementary information. It reads as follows: "From the standpoint of presuppositions of the ancient world as reflected in the NT, the most relevant way in which to classify the basic elements is in terms of air, fire, water, and earth (including soil, mud, clay, rock, precious and semiprecious stones, and metals). But for the convenience of those using this dictionary this fourth category has been subdivided into three subdomains. The Greek term ἀήρ 'air' occurs in the NT with the meaning of substance only in an idiomlike expression in 1 Cor 9.26; elsewhere it is used to designate space (see 1.6). At no point in the NT are air, fire, water, and earth specifically described as constituting the basic elements (Greek στοιχεῖα), but the occurrence of στοιχεῖα in 2 Pe 3.10 (see 2.1) appears to be a clear reference to these natural substances."

The problem of translational equivalence becomes extremely acute in the case of πνεῦμα[a] (12.18), used as a title for the third person of the Trinity. First of all, a translator must understand the basic distinction between gods and spirits, and he must also deal with the use of πνεῦμα as the nature of a supernatural being, as in 'God is spirit' and the relation of this to the expression 'the Spirit of God.' In many languages the seeming equivalent of Greek πνεῦμα[a] is a term which refers only to that part of a person which is active after death. One must obviously avoid, therefore, an expression for 'Spirit of God' which would mean that God had died. Various problems involved in finding an equivalent for πνεῦμα[a] take up almost an entire page of the lexicon.

The most serious mistake which people make in dealing with the meanings of Greek terms is to presume some kind of one-to-one correspondence in meaning. This may be due to the fact that when people first learn the meanings of Greek words, they tend to latch on to only one meaning, so that for the Greek term σάρξ, most people assume that it simply means 'flesh.' This wrong impression gained from initial contact with such a word is often reinforced by word studies which try to derive all related meanings from this so-called 'underlying meaning' of 'flesh.' In order to avoid such misconceptions of the meaning or meanings of terms, this lexicon highlights the distinct meanings, first by convenient listing in the index and secondly by the constant reminder of superscript letters, which call attention to the fact that the meaning in question is only one of several meanings of the term. For example, in the index for σάρξ there are the following:

a	flesh	8.63
b	body	8.4
c	people	9.11
d	human	9.12
e	nation	10.1
f	human nature	26.7
g	physical nature	58.10
h	life	23.90

These glosses should *not* be understood as definitions; they are only clues to various areas of meaning, but such a listing should dispel forever the idea that σάρξ simply means 'flesh.' A glance at the various meanings as defined in the lexicon shows clearly that there are quite distinct areas of meaning. Note, for example, the meaning of σάρξ[a] in Re 19.17-18, in which reference is made to the flesh of both humans and animals. σάρξ[b] designates the human body, as in 1 Tm 3.16, and σάρξ[c] designates "humans as physical beings," so that in 1 Pe 1.24 one may render πᾶσα σὰρξ ὡς χόρτος as 'all people are like grass,' and in Jn 1.14 ὁ λόγος σὰρξ ἐγένετο may be rendered as 'the Word became a human being.' On the other hand, σάρξ[d] designates "human nature with emphasis upon the physical aspects," so that in He 12.9 εἶτα τοὺς μὲν τῆς σαρκὸς ἡμῶν πατέρας may be rendered as 'in the case of our human fathers,' but σάρξ[e] designates an ethnic group and in Ro 11.14 it may be translated as 'race.' In 1 Cor 1.26, however, σάρξ[f] designates human nature, but seen from the perspective of the psychological dimension, not merely from the standpoint of the physical nature as in σάρξ[d]. But physical nature as a class entity is yet another meaning of σάρξ and is found in Ga 4.23 as σάρξ[g] in the phrase κατὰ σάρκα γεγέννηται which may be rendered as 'born like people are normally born.' In He 5.7, however, σάρξ[h] designates physical life. In addition to these eight meanings of σάρξ, the index contains several idioms in which σάρξ occurs.

Rather than regarding σάρξ as meaning 'flesh' with certain semantic aberrations, it is much better to recognize the fact that σάρξ is simply a lexical item which serves to designate a cluster of related meanings. By focusing attention on a cluster or constellation of meanings, one is inevitably forced to look more closely at those distinctive features of meaning which are relevant for the different meanings signaled by a single word or idiom.

It is important, however, to go beyond thinking in terms of the clusters of meaning of a single lexical item. In order to explore satisfactorily the areas of meaning, one must be concerned with both domains and subdomains. For the translator it is the tightly organized subdomain which is of particular significance. Note, for example, Subdomain X' *Dispute, Debate* in Domain 33 *Communication*. The first term, συμβάλλω[c] (33.439), has a generic meaning, which may be defined as "to express differences of opinion in a forceful way, involving alternative opportunities for presenting contrasting viewpoints." Such a meaning may be glossed in English as either 'to debate' or 'to discuss,' but in entry 33.440 there are several terms, συζητέω[a], συζήτησις, ζήτημα, and ζήτησις[b], which designate the expression of "forceful differences of opinion without necessarily having a presumed goal of seeking a solution." Accordingly, a relevant gloss for this meaning may be 'to dispute.' The noun συζητητής (33.441) is derived from συζητέω[a] and designates "a person who is skilled in or likely to be involved in expressing strong differences of opinion," and accordingly may be frequently translated as 'debater' or 'disputer.'

The derived noun ἐκζήτησις[b] (33.442) designates "a dispute involving empty speculation," while διακατελέγχομαι (33.443) designates the process of refuting a viewpoint in a debate. In entry 33.444, διακρίνομαι[b] and διάκρισις[b] may be defined as "to dispute with someone on the basis of different judgments," and ἀντιλογία[a] (33.445) focuses upon a dispute involving opposite opinions and even contradictory statements.

It may be useful to compare this Subdomain X' *Dispute, Debate* with Subdomain C *Accusation* in Domain 56 *Courts and Legal Procedures*. In this subdomain, αἰτία[b] (56.4) serves as a technical, legal term to designate "the basis of or grounds for an accusation in court," while αἰτίωμα and αἰτία[c] (56.5) designate "the content of legal charges brought against someone," and ἔγκλημα (56.6) is the technical, legal term for "a formal indictment or accusation brought against someone." λόγος[j] (56.7) is very similar in meaning to ἔγκλημα, but it is more generic in meaning, with focus on the process of accusation.

In this same subdomain is to be found ἐμφανίζω[d] (56.8), "the process of making a formal report before authorities on a judicial matter." ἐκζητέω[b] (56.9) designates "the process of bringing charges against someone for a crime or offense," but ἐκζητέω[b] has somewhat broader connotations than mere court procedures.

The phrase κατὰ λόγον ἀνέχομαι (56.10) is an idiom meaning "to accept a complaint against someone for a legal review," while ἀντίδικος[a] (56.11) designates "a person who brings an accusation against someone." A helpful footnote for this subdomain states that it is not possible to determine accurately some of the subtle distinctions in meaning (particularly on a connotative level) between several of these terms, namely, αἰτία[b], αἰτίωμα, αἰτία[c], ἔγκλημα, and λόγος[j].

Basic Principles of Semantic Analysis and Classification

The first principle of semantic analysis of lexical items is that there are "no synonyms," in the sense that no two lexical items ever have completely the same meanings in all of the contexts in which they might occur. Even if two lexical items seem not to be distinguishable in their designative or denotative meanings, they do differ in terms of their connotative or associative meanings. This principle of "no synonyms" may also be stated in terms of the fact that no two closely related meanings ever occur with exactly the same range of referents, much less the same set of connotative or associative features.

The principle of "no synonyms" does not rule out, however, variation for the sake of rhetorical purposes. For the sake of stylistic variation, there may be alternations between ὁράω and βλέπω, between λέγω and λαλέω, and in John 21, even between ἀγαπάω and φιλέω, but alternation for the sake of rhetorical variety does not mean that the two terms are completely identical in meaning, even though they may refer to the same event or state of being. Furthermore, even though in this lexicon two or more expressions may be included under the same entry, this does not mean that the terms are completely synonymous. It simply means that on the basis of the data available in the New Testament or in supplementary Greek literature, one cannot define the differences of meaning, either on the level of denotation or of connotation.

The second basic principle of semantic analysis is that differences in meaning are marked by context, either textual or extratextual. The textual context may consist of the immediate sentence or paragraph, a larger section of a discourse, the discourse as a whole, other writings by the same author, other documents of more or less the same literary genre, and any text in the same language which deals with similar concepts or vocabulary. The extratextual contexts are essentially historical and may shed light upon the referents, either from historical documentation or from archaeology.

Since any differences of meaning are marked by context, it follows that the correct meaning of any term is that which fits the context best. In other words, this principle maximizes the coherence of meaning within the context. For example, the Greek adjective ταπεινός, in both Classical and extrabiblical Hellenistic Greek, normally designates that which is weak, mean, base, and low, but clearly in Mt 11.29, in the expression ταπεινὸς τῇ καρδίᾳ, the value of ταπεινός is positive, not negative, for Jesus admonishes his followers to take his yoke upon themselves and to learn from him, because he is both "gentle and humble in spirit." However, though the Greek New Testament contains some examples of specialized meanings of lexical items, the Greek of the New Testament should not be regarded as a distinct form of Greek, but rather as typical Hellenistic Greek.

A third principle of semantic analysis states that the meaning is defined by a set of distinctive features (something which has already been noted at various points in this introduction). By means of a set of distinctive features, one may define the limits of the range of referents which may be designated by a particular verbal form. For example, the meaning of πατήρ^a 'father' (10.14) may be defined by contrast with the set μήτηρ^a (10.16), υἱός^a (10.42), and θυγάτηρ^a (10.46) (as members of the same subdomain) as having the distinctive features of direct lineage (either biological or legal), one generation prior to the reference person, and male,

but πατήρ^b (always in the plural; 10.18) includes both male and female and therefore may be glossed as 'parents.' πατήρ^c (10.20) is both male and direct lineage, but is normally several generations separated from the reference person and therefore is usually translated as 'ancestor.' πατήρ^d (12.12), however, as a title for God, does not share features of direct lineage, generation, or biological gender. The use of πατήρ in addressing God or referring to him is based upon certain supplementary features of πατήρ^a, namely, authority and provident care. πατήρ^e (87.48), as a title of status, contains the feature of being male and perhaps suggests greater age than the speaker, but the focus is upon rank, as in Mt 23.9. The term πατήρ is thus described as having several different meanings because there are significantly different sets of distinctive features.

How many different meanings there are for a particular term depends to a considerable extent on the fineness of the semantic grid, that is to say, the extent to which one tends to lump or to split differences. The ultimate criteria for such lumping or splitting depend upon the entire semantic system, and the ultimate objective is to obtain a statement of meanings which reflects the greatest overall coherence within the system. Unfortunately, one can really never know what is the best for any detail until one knows everything about everything, and likewise, one cannot know the whole until all the parts have been analyzed. This, however, is the fundamental problem in any classificatory system on any level of scientific analysis. What is essential is that one does not confuse the meaning of a term with the particular reference which a term has in a specific context. For example, ὄρνις (4.38) may be defined as "any kind of bird, wild or domestic," but in Mt 23.37 (the only occurrence of ὄρνις in the New Testament) it probably refers to a hen, and therefore may be translated as such. But the meaning of ὄρνις is not 'hen' but "a bird of any kind, either wild or domesticated," since it is used in Hellenistic and Classical Greek with precisely such a broad range of reference.

In a similar fashion, θήκη (6.119) may be translated in Jn 18.11 as 'sheath,' since the context refers to putting a sword in its container. This does not mean that θήκη *means* 'sheath,' for θήκη designates "any receptacle into which an object is customarily placed for safe keeping."

A somewhat more complex problem with regard to meaning and reference occurs with the verb αἰτέω, which may be glossed as 'to ask for, to pray, to demand,' but the question is: Does αἰτέω have one meaning or three meanings? In Mt 5.42 αἰτέω is perhaps best translated as 'to ask for,' but in Ac 13.28 a more appropriate rendering would be 'to demand.' In a number of contexts God is the one addressed and hence the appropriate equivalent in English would be 'pray' (for example, in Jn 14.14, Jn 16.23, Col 1.9, Jas 1.5, 1 Jn 3.22).

In all those cases in which one can perhaps best translate αἰτέω as 'to demand,' the context itself indicates the intensity of the action, while in those contexts in which one can best translate αἰτέω as 'to pray,' God is the person addressed. Actually, αἰτέω (or αἰτέομαι, for there is seemingly no difference in meaning between the active and middle forms) may be defined as "to ask for with urgency, even to the point of demanding" (33.163). In particular contexts there may be varying degrees of urgency and obviously different persons addressed, but these factors are part of the range of applicability of αἰτέω, and they do not constitute distinct meanings, even though they may be translated in various languages in different ways, depending upon the contexts. One may speak of the various types of reference of αἰτέω, for example, 'to ask for,' 'to demand,' 'to pray to,' but the meaning of αἰτέω simply includes a range which happens to overlap in English with these three types of reference.

Proper names are supposed to have only reference, since theoretically they designate only unique entities, but some proper names, for example, Barnabas and Peter, may be said to have 'motivated' designative meanings (for example, 'son of consolation' and 'rock') and as such certainly have associative or connotative features. This is particularly true of such proper names as Satan and Beelzebul.

Identifying those features which constitute the connotative or associative meanings of lexical items is even more complex than identifying the denotative or designative ones. In the case of designative factors, one can readily compare the different referents within the range of any one designative meaning, but associative meanings depend upon quite different types of factors: the persons who typically employ such terms, the physical contexts in which they are used (time, place, and institutions), the literary contexts from which such expressions are derived (the typically biblical associations of phrases such as 'thus saith the Lord' and 'verily, verily'), and the nature of the referent (for example, the associations of ναός 'tabernacle,' κύων 'dog,' and χοῖρος 'pig'). This means that in determining associative meanings there are a number of dimensions: levels of formality (ritual, formal, informal, casual, and intimate), time (archaic, obsolete, obsolescent, contemporary, modern), social class (highbrow to vulgar), sex (men's versus women's speech), age (adults, youth, children), and education (highly educated to illiterate). By analyzing the reactions of people to various expressions in terms of these dimensions, one can normally obtain a relatively satisfactory profile of the associative meaning of any term used by a particular constituency. Such meanings are by no means as idiosyncratic as many people assume; in fact, the judgments of different people within a constituency agree about associative meanings almost to the same extent as they agree about designative meanings.

A fourth principle of semantic analysis states that figurative meanings differ from their bases with respect to three fundamental factors: diversity in domains, differences in the degree of awareness of the relationship between literal and figurative meanings, and the extent of conventional usage. When Jesus speaks of Herod Antipas as ἀλώπηξ 'fox,' there is clearly a marked difference in domains between fox as an animal and Herod as a person. Similarly, in the case of such biblical idioms as 'straining out a gnat and swallowing a camel' and 'heaping coals of fire on the head,' the differences between the literal and the figurative meanings imply very different semantic domains. In fact, it is this radical distinctiveness in semantic domains which is in a sense the essence of metaphorical meaning. In the case of metonymies, such differences are not usually as extreme. The use of the term 'name,' when one is really referring to the person, or the use of 'hand,' when the reference is to the activity of a person, seems not to be such a factor and therefore normally provides less impact.

Since one of the essential elements of figurative meaning is the tension which exists between the literal and the figurative meanings, there must be some awareness of these two poles if a figurative meaning is to be psychologically relevant. In the case of 'hungering and thirsting for righteousness'

(Mt 5.6), there is a shift between a physical state and an emotional state, and there is obvious awareness of this difference, but in Lk 15.17, εἰς ἑαυτὸν δὲ ἐλθών 'coming to himself,' the shift between a physical movement and a psychological change seems not to be so drastic, and hence many persons do not even recognize this as figurative.

One reason for the failure to recognize or become aware of the figurative nature of an expression such as 'coming to oneself' is the fact that it has become so conventional in English. The more a figurative expression is employed, the less impact it carries, so that figurative expressions lose their impact almost entirely, and they become 'dead figures of speech.' This poses a real problem for a lexicographer, for it is not always possible to know whether a figurative meaning has become conventional in the language and thus may be defined as an established figure, or whether the expression is completely innovative and thus represents 'figurative usage' rather than an established 'figurative meaning.'

In dealing with the New Testament it is almost impossible to determine the precise status of conventionality in many figurative expressions. In the case of νέφος (literally, 'cloud'), as used in He 12.1 in the sense of 'a large group' or 'a crowd,' there is evidence for this usage even in Classical Greek, but in 2 Pe 2.17 people are likened to ὀμίχλαι 'mists (driven by the wind),' and there is no evidence that ὀμίχλαι has an established figurative meaning pertaining to people. ὀμίχλη is included in the lexicon, but under the category of *Atmospheric Objects* (1.35) and defined as "a cloud-like mass of moisture close to the earth's surface," but the statement is made that ὀμίχλη is used in the New Testament only in a figurative sense, and then the passage in 2 Pe 2.17 is cited, and a further statement is made that in many languages this metaphorical usage must be marked as a simile and translated as 'these men . . . are like mists which the storm blows along.'

The fifth principle of semantic analysis is that both the different meanings of the same word and the related meanings of different words tend to be multidimensional and are only rarely orthogonal in structure, that is to say, the different meanings tend to form irregularly shaped constellations rather than neatly organized structures. It is true that certain restricted subdomains may exhibit a neat set of relations, for example, kinship terms, colors, common foods, and certain species of plants and animals, but most taxonomies are irregular in shape and often have conspicuous holes in the structure.

As already noted, there has been a tendency among some lexicographers to find in the different meanings of the same lexical item a type of underlying meaning which is to be found in all occurrences of such a term. This type of meaning has often been called a *'Grundbedeutung'* (literally, 'ground meaning'). But it is usually impossible to set up any one meaning which is either shared by all the meanings of a term or which has any relevance in explaining all the meanings. The various meanings of the Greek New Testament term χάρις well illustrate this basic problem. χάρις may, for example, have the meaning of attractiveness, as in Lk 4.22, and in this context may actually be rendered as 'eloquence.' More frequently, however, χάρις has either the meaning of favorable disposition on the part of the one who grants a favor or benefit, or the meaning of the act of granting such a favor. In some instances, however, the focus may be upon the actual benefit or favor which has been received. Closely linked to this meaning is the meaning of a state of grace enjoyed by one who has been the beneficiary of the act of grace, and lastly, χάρις may mean thankfulness or even the expression of thanks by the one who is the beneficiary of some undeserved favor. In this series of meanings one can readily note a developmental process and certain logical connections, but it would be wrong to assume that a series of logical developments are necessarily a one-to-one correspondence in the historical development, nor is it wise or even especially helpful to set up some abstract generic meaning (such as 'goodness') and try to relate all of these meanings to one core concept.

In dealing with the related meanings of different words, one can to some extent set up certain basic types based on diverse relations between shared features. Some sets of terms form clusters in which there are certain highly significant distinctive features, for example, πατήρ, μήτηρ, υἱός, and θυγάτηρ, as already noted. In other instances there are overlapping sets, as in the case of ἀγαπάω, φιλέω, and στέργω (though στέργω does not occur in the New Testament). Included sets are simply taxonomies based upon various hierarchies of generic/specific meanings. Compare, for example, ζῷον[a] (4.2), θηρίον[b] (4.4), and ὑποζύγιον (4.7), which represent three levels in a hierarchy, since every ὑποζύγιον would be regarded as θηρίον[b], and every θηρίον[b] would be regarded as ζῷον[a].

Series of opposites include such antonyms as ἀγαθός/κακός, and such reversives of roles as in πωλέω 'to sell' (57.186) in contrast with ἀγοράζω[a] 'to buy' (57.188). Finally, there are series, such as numbers, days of the week, months of the year, and watches of the night.

For New Testament Greek the various sets of terms having related meanings are often quite unsystematic, due both to the limitation in the corpus of the New Testament as well as to the nature of the content. It is precisely for this reason that no attempt has been made in this lexicon to try to describe all of these sets, something which might be interesting to lexicographers and semanticists, but which would not be particularly useful to translators.

In connection with statements about the nature of this lexicon, a good deal has already been said about the classificatory principles, namely, that these are based primarily upon the shared, distinctive, and supplementary features of meaning. In a few instances, however, the relations of part to whole have been employed, particularly in the domains of *Constructions* (Domain 7), *Body, Body Parts, and Body Products* (Domain 8), and domains covering specialized activities (Domains 43-57).

Because of the type of content in the New Testament and the relative limitation of the total corpus, some domains are quite large and others very small. Compare, for example, Domain 33 *Communication*, with 489 entries, with Domain 80 *Space*, having only seven entries. It would have been possible to have combined all intellectual activities into a single domain, but in view of certain distinct features of various intellectual activities and the fact that combining all of these into a single domain would have meant considerable subclassification, it has seemed better to divide these meanings into a significant cluster of domains, namely, 26 *Psychological Faculties*, 27 *Learn*, 28 *Know*, 29 *Memory and Recall*, 30 *Think*, 31 *Hold a View, Believe, Trust* and 32 *Understand*.

For some persons it may seem strange that derivatives are classed together with their bases. For example, ἀργυροκόπος (2.52), defined as "one who makes objects out of silver," is to be found in Domain 2 *Natural Substances*, Subdomain G *Metals*, even though ἀργυροκόπος clearly designates a person and may be best translated in English as 'silversmith.' One could argue that the semantic base of ἀργυροκόπος is really -κοπος, but the structural element -κοπος, meaning "one who does something with something," is so highly productive (though it has various forms) that it seems far better to treat ἀργυροκόπος as an extended derivative of ἄργυρος. Compare also χαλκός[a] 'bronze, brass, copper' (2.54) and χαλκεύς "one who makes objects out of brass, bronze, copper, or other metals" (2.55).

In general, the order which has been selected for domains proceeds from generic to specific. Note, for example, that Domain 42 *Perform, Do* is highly generic and is then followed by a number of specific types of specialized activities (namely, Domains 43-57). Similarly, Domain 58 heads up the section of abstracts in that it deals with such highly abstract features as kind, class, and nature. Domain 58 is then followed by a number of abstract domains, starting with *Quantity, Number, Sequence*, and *Arrange, Organize* and then proceeding later to such domains as *Time, Aspect, Degree*, etc. Within any domain, the subdomains are likewise arranged primarily on the basis of varying degrees of specificity. Note, for example, the outline of the subdomains in Domain 30 *Think*:

A To Think, Thought
B To Think About, with the Implied Purpose of Responding Appropriately
C To Think Concerning Future Contingencies
D To Intend, To Purpose, To Plan
E To Decide, To Conclude
F To Choose, To Select, To Prefer
G To Distinguish, To Evaluate, To Judge

Such a set is not strictly in a hierarchical arrangement of generic to specific, but it does constitute a cluster of subdomains which are related to one another largely in terms of greater degrees of specificity.

For those preparing a lexicon in any language, and especially for those dealing with a form of language used some 2 000 years ago, there are a host of problems resulting from indeterminacy in the range of referents, fuzzy boundaries, incomplete sets of related meanings, limitations in the corpus and background data, and specialization of meaning due to the uniqueness of the message. In the preparation of this lexicon, these problems have constituted real challenges, and the editors are not at all sure that they have found fully satisfactory solutions to many of these difficulties, even as the footnotes suggest. But despite these limitations, the editors sincerely trust that translators and others will find significant help and insights leading to further analyses in the critical areas of lexical semantics.

For more information on the theory and practice of this lexicon, see under *Louw* and *Nida* in the Bibliography.

BIBLIOGRAPHY

Adrados F R, Gangutia E, Facal J L, Serrano C *Introducción a la Lexicografía Griega* Madrid 1977.

Al-Kasimi A M *Linguistics and Bilingual Dictionaries* Brill 1977.

Apresjan J D 'Regular polysemy' *Linguistics* 142, 1974, 5-32.

Arndt W F, Gingrich F W *A Greek-English Lexicon of the New Testament and Other Early Christian Literature* 2nd ed rev and augm from W Bauer *Griechisch-Deutsches Wörterbuch zu den Schriften des Neuen Testaments und die übrigen urchristliche Literatur* 5th ed 1958, by F W Gingrich and F W Danker, University of Chicago Press 1979.

Bailey R W 'Review of the American Heritage Dictionary' *Language Sciences* 10, 1970, 23-29.

Barr J *The Semantics of Biblical Language* Oxford Univ Press 1961.

Barzun J 'What is a dictionary?' *American Scholar* 32, 1963, 176-181.

Bauer W – see Arndt W F, etc.

Bendix E H 'Componential analysis of general vocabulary: the semantic structure of a set of verbs in English, Hindi, and Japanese' *International Journal of American Linguistics* 32/2, 1966.

Bolinger D 'The atomization of meaning' *Language* 41, 1965, 555-573.

Bolinger D *Meaning and Form* Longman 1977.

Brekle H E *Semantik* Fink 1972.

Burling R 'Cognition and componential analysis' *American Antropologist* 1, 1964, 20-28.

Campbell B 'Linguistic meaning' *Linguistics* 33, 1967, 5-33.

Cassidy F G 'A descriptive approach to the lexicon' in *Approaches in Linguistic Methodology* ed by I Rauch and C T Scott, University of Wisconson Press 1967, 9-15.

Chafe W L *Meaning and the Structure of Language* University of Chicago Press 1970.

Chapin P G 'Linguistic semantics today' *English Record* 20, 1970, 49-66.

Conklin H C 'Lexicographical treatment of folk taxonomies' in F Householder and S Saporta *Problems in Lexicography* Indiana Univ Press 1967.

Cook D 'A Point of Lexicographical Method' in H B Allen *Readings in Applied English Linguistics* Meredith 1964, 450-456.

Coseriu E 'Bedeutung und Bezeichnung im Lichte der strukturellen Semantik' in P Hartmann and H Vernay *Sprachwissenschaft und Übersetzen* Max Hueber 1970, 104-121.

Cruse D A *Lexical Semantics* Cambridge Univ Press 1986.

Davidson D and Harmon G eds *Semantics of Natural Language* Reidel 1972.

Droste F G 'Semantics as a dynamic device: redundancy rules in the lexicon' *Linguistics* 182, 1976, 5-33.

Drysdale P 'Lexicography: statics and dynamics' *Canadian Journal of Linguistics* 14, 1969, 108-122.

Dubois J 'Recherches lexicographiques: esquisse d'un dictionnaire structural' *Etudes de Linguistique Appliquée* 1, 1962, 43-48.

Fillmore C J 'Types of lexical information' in *Working Papers in Linguistics* No. 2 by C J Fillmore and I Lehiste, Ohio State University 1968, 65-103.

Fillmore C J 'Verbs of judging: an exercise in semantic description' in *Studies in Linguistic Semantics* ed by C J Fillmore and D T Langendoen. Holt, Rinehart and Winston 1971.

Fowler R 'A note on some uses of the term "meaning" in descriptive linguistics' *Word* 21, 1965, 411-420.

Friedrich G 'Semasiologie und Lexicologie' *Theologische Literaturzeitung* 94 (11), 1969, 801-816.

Friedrich G 'Das bisher noch fehlende Begriffslexikon zum Neuen Testament' *New Testament Studies* 19, 1973, 127-152.

Gleason H A Jr. 'What is a dictionary?' Paper given to the Conference on Lexicography, LSA, Columbus, Ohio, July 23, 1970.

Goodenough W H 'Componential analysis and the study of meaning' *Language* 32, 1956, 195-216.

Gove P B 'Linguistic advances and lexicography' *Word Study* 1961, 3-8.

Gove P B 'Usage in the dictionary' *College English* 27, 1966, 285-292.

Grice H P 'Utterer's meaning, sentence-meaning, and word-meaning' *Foundations of Language* 4, 1968, 225-242.

Gumpel L 'The structure of idioms: a phenomenological approach' *Semiotica* 12, 1974, 1-40.

Haensch G, Wolf L, Ettinger S, Werner R *La Lexicografía: de la Lingüística teórica a la Lexicografía práctica* Madrid 1982.

Hartmann R R K 'Semantics applied to English-

German lexical structures' *Folia Linguistica* 7, 1975, 357-370.

Hartmann R R K *Lexicography: Principles and Practice* Academic Press 1983.

Hill A A 'Some thoughts on segmentation of lexical meaning' *Annals of the New York Academy of Sciences* 211, 1973, 269-278.

Hill D *Greek Words and Hebrew Meanings* Cambridge Univ Press 1967.

Hiorth F 'Arrangement of meanings in lexicography' *Lingua* 4, 1955, 413-424.

Householder F and Saporta S *Problems in Lexicography* Indiana Univ Press 1967.

Iannucci J E 'Meaning discrimination in bilingual dictionaries: a new lexicographical technique' *Modern Language Journal* 41, 1957, 272-281 and 42, 1958, 232-234.

Jacobs J 'Dictionary making in the United States' *Neuphilologische Mitteilungen* 51, 1950, 145-51.

Joos M 'Semantic axiom number one' *Language* 48, 1972, 257-265.

Katz J J and Fodor J A 'The structure of a semantic theory' *Language* 39, 1963, 170-210.

Katz J J *Semantic Theory* Harper and Row 1972.

Keesing R M 'Linguistic knowledge and cultural knowledge: some doubts and speculations' *American Anthropologist* 81, 1979, 14-36.

Kurath H 'The semantic patterning of words' *Monograph Series on Language and Linguistics* 14, 1961, 91-94.

Landau S A *Dictionaries: The Art and Craft of Lexicography* Scribners 1984.

Lehrer A *Semantic Fields and Lexical Structure* North-Holland Publishing Company 1974.

Lounsbury F G 'The Varieties of Meaning' *Georgetown University Monograph Series on Languages and Linguistics* 8, 1955, 158-164.

Lounsbury F G 'The structural analysis of kinship semantics' *Proceedings of the International Congress of Linguists* 8, 1964, 1073-1093.

Louw J P 'Betekenis en Vertaalekwivalent' *Akroterion* 21, 1976, 30-34.

Louw J P ed *Lexicography and Translation* Bible Society of South Africa, Cape Town 1985.

Lyons J *Semantics* 2 Vols, Cambridge Univ Press 1977.

Malkiel Y 'Distinctive features in lexicography: a typological approach to dictionaries exemplified in Spanish' *Romance Philology* 12, 1959, 366-399; 13, 1960, 111-155.

Malkiel Y 'Lexicography' in *The Learning of Language* ed by E Reed. Appleton 1971, 363-387.

Marckwardt A H 'Dictionaries and the English Language' *English Journal* 52, 1963, 336-345.

Marckwardt A H 'The new Webster dictionary: a critical appraisal' in *Readings in Applied English Linguistics* ed by H B Allen. Meredith 1964, 476-485.

Mathiot M 'The place of the dictionary in linguistic description' *Language* 43, 1967, 703-724.

Mathiot M 'Quelques problèmes fondamentaux dans l'analyse du lexique' *Meta* 18, 1973, 19-34.

Merrell F 'Of metaphor and metonymy' *Semiotica* 31, 1980, 289-307.

Miller G A 'Semantic relations among words' in Morris H, Bresnan J and Miller G A eds *Linguistic Theory and Psychological Reality* MIT Press, 1978, 60-118.

Morris W 'The making of a dictionary' *College Composition and Communication* 20, 1969, 198-203.

Mower M L and Le Roy B 'Which are the most important dictionary skills?' *Elementary English* 45, 1968, 468-471.

Nida E A 'Analysis of meaning and dictionary making' *International Journal of American Linguistics* 24, 1958, 279-292.

Nida E A *Componential Analysis of Meaning* Mouton 1975.

Nida E A *Exploring Semantic Structures* Fink 1975.

Nida E A, Louw J P, Smith R B 'Semantic Domains and Componential analysis of Meaning' in *Current Issues in Linquistic Theory* ed by R W Cole. Indiana Univ Press 1977, 139-167.

Osgood C E, Suci G J and Tannenbaum P H *The Measurement of Meaning* University of Illinois Press 1957.

Osgood C E, May W H and Miron M S *Cross-Cultural Universals of Affective Meaning* University of Illinois Press 1975.

Pos H J 'The foundation of word-meanings, different approaches' *Lingua* 1, 1948, 281-291.

Pottier B 'La définition sémantique dans les dictionnaires' *Travaux de Linguistique et de Littérature* 3, 1965, 33-39.

Pyles T 'Dictionaries and usage' in *Linguistics Today* ed by A Hill. Basic Books Publishers 1969, 127-136.

Read A W 'Approaches to lexicography and semantics' in *Current Trends in Linguistics* ed T A Sebeok, Vol 10, *Linguistics in North America* Mouton 1972.

Rey-Debove J ed *La Lexicographie* Larousse 1970.

Rey-Debove J 'Le domaine du dictionnaire' *Languages* 19, 1970, 3-34.

Robinson D F *Manual for Bilingual Dictionaries* 3 Vols, Summer Institute of Linguistics 1969.

Siertsema B 'Language and World View' *The Bible Translator* 20, 1969, 3-21.

Sledd J and Ebbitt W R eds *Dictionaries and that Dictionary* Scott, Foresman 1962.

Sommerfelt A, 'Semantique et lexicographie. Remarques sur la tâche du lexicographie' in *Diachronic and Synchronic Aspects of Language* ed by A Sommerfelt. Mouton 1962, 273-276.

Starness De W T *Robert Estienne's Influence on Lexicography* University of Texas Press 1963.

Steinberg D and Jakobovits L A ed *Semantics* Cambridge Univ Press 1971.

Ullmann S *Semantics: Introduction to the Science of Meaning* Barnes and Noble 1962.

Vassilyev L M 'The theory of semantic fields: a survey' *Linguistics* 137, 1974, 79-93.

Wahrig G N *Neue Wege in der Wörterbucharbeit* Hamburg Verlag 1968.

Warfel V R 'Dictionaries and Linguistics' in H S Allen *Readings in Applied English Linguistics* Meredith 1964, 444-449.

Weinbrot H D *Aspects of Lexicography* Carbondale 1972.

Weinreich U 'Lexicology' *Current Trends in Linguistics* Vol 1 ed by T A Sebeok. Mouton 1963, 60-93.

Weinreich U 'Webster's Third: a critique of its semantics' *International Journal of American Linguistics* 30, 1964, 405-409.

Wierzbicka A *Semantic Primitives* Athenäum 1972.

Wotjak G *Untersuchungen zur Struktur der Bedeutung* Max Heuber 1971.

Zgusta L *Manual of Lexicography* Mouton 1971.

Zgusta L *Theory and Method in Lexicography* Hornbeam Press 1980.

TABLE OF DOMAINS

1 Geographical Objects and Features[1]

Outline of Subdomains

A   Universe, Creation (1.1-1.4)
B   Regions Above the Earth (1.5-1.16)
C   Regions Below the Surface of the Earth (1.17-1.25)
D   Heavenly Bodies (1.26-1.33)
E   Atmospheric Objects (1.34-1.38)
F   The Earth's Surface (1.39-1.45)
G   Elevated Land Formations (1.46-1.50)
H   Depressions and Holes (1.51-1.59)
I   Land in Contrast With the Sea (1.60-1.68)
J   Bodies of Water (1.69-1.78)
K   Sociopolitical Areas (1.79-1.81)
L   Governmental Administrative Areas (1.82-1.85)
M   Areas Which Are Uninhabited or Only Sparsely Populated (1.86-1.87)
N   Population Centers (1.88-1.94)
O   Pastures and Cultivated Lands (1.95-1.98)
P   Thoroughfares: Roads, Streets, Paths, etc. (1.99-1.105)

A   Universe, Creation (1.1-1.4)

1.1 κόσμος[a], ου *m*: the universe as an ordered structure – 'cosmos, universe.' ὁ θεὸς ὁ ποιήσας τὸν κόσμον καὶ πάντα τὰ ἐν αὐτῷ 'God who made the universe and everything in it' Ac 17.24. In many languages there is no specific term for the universe. The closest equivalent may simply be 'all that exists.' In other instances one may use a phrase such as 'the world and all that is above it' or 'the sky and the earth.' The concept of the totality of the universe may be expressed in some languages only as 'everything that is on the earth and in the sky.'

1 The semantic domain entitled *Geographical Objects and Features* includes certain lexical units which refer to objects not perceptually evident, for example, 'heaven' and 'hell,' but from the manner in which the meanings of these terms are employed in NT Greek, the reference is clearly to spatially defined objects or regions rather than to psychological states.

1.2 αἰών[b], ῶνος *m* (always occurring in the plural): the universe, perhaps with some associated meaning of 'eon' or 'age' in the sense of the transitory nature of the universe (but this is doubtful in the contexts of He 1.2 and 11.3) – 'universe.' δι' οὗ καὶ ἐποίησεν τοὺς αἰῶνας 'through whom (God) made the universe' He 1.2. In He 1.2 it may be essential in a number of languages to translate 'he is the one through whom God created everything,' though in some instances a more idiomatic and satisfactory way of rendering the meaning would involve a phrase such as '. . . created both the earth and the sky' or '. . . the heavens and the earth.'

1.3 ὁ οὐρανὸς καὶ ἡ γῆ: (a more or less fixed phrase equivalent to a single lexical unit) the totality of God's creation – 'heaven and earth, universe.' ὁ οὐρανὸς καὶ ἡ γῆ παρελεύσονται, οἱ δὲ λόγοι μου οὐ μὴ παρελεύσονται 'heaven and earth shall pass away, but my words shall not pass away' Mk 13.31. There may be certain complications involved in rendering ὁ οὐρανὸς καὶ ἡ γῆ as 'heaven and earth,' since 'heaven' might be interpreted in some languages as referring only to the dwelling place of God himself. The referents in this passage are 'the sky and the earth,' in other words, all of physical existence, but not the dwelling place of God, for the latter would not be included in what is destined to pass away.

1.4 κτίσις[c], εως *f*: the universe as the product of God's activity in creation – 'universe, creation, what was made.' τῇ γὰρ ματαιότητι ἡ κτίσις ὑπετάγη 'for the creation was condemned to become worthless' Ro 8.20.

The meaning of κτίσις[c] might very well be treated as a simple derivative of the verb κτίζω 'to create' (42.35), since the reference is to the result of God's creative act. However, in a number of contexts, the process of creation is no longer focal, and what is in focus is the total physical universe. In some languages the meaning may be best expressed as 'the world and all that is in it' or even 'everything that exists.'

1

B Regions Above the Earth[2] (1.5-1.16)

1.5 οὐρανός[a], **οῦ** *m* (either singular or plural without distinction in meaning): space above the earth, including the vault arching high over the earth from one horizon to another, as well as the sun, moon, and stars – 'sky.' ἄνδρες εὐλαβεῖς ἀπὸ παντὸς ἔθνους τῶν ὑπὸ τὸν οὐρανόν 'godly men from every nation under the sky' Ac 2.5; καθὼς τὰ ἄστρα τοῦ οὐρανοῦ τῷ πλήθει 'as numerous as the stars of the sky' He 11.12; ἐπισυνάξουσιν τοὺς ἐκλεκτοὺς αὐτοῦ . . . ἀπ' ἄκρων οὐρανῶν ἕως τῶν ἄκρων αὐτῶν 'they will gather his chosen ones . . . from one end of the earth to the other' (literally '. . . from the ends of sky unto their ends') Mt 24.31.

In Ac 2.5 the expression 'under the sky' is better translated in a number of languages as 'on earth,' and in He 11.12 'the stars of the sky' is effectively rendered in many instances as 'the stars up above,' though in many languages 'up above' is not only redundant, but misleading, since it might suggest stars that would not be 'up above.' The area described by the phrase ἀπ' ἄκρων οὐρανῶν ἕως τῶν ἄκρων αὐτῶν in Mt 24.31 refers to the limits of the horizon regarded as the limits of the sky, but in many languages the equivalent is an expression dealing with the limits of the earth.

In some contexts οὐρανός[a] 'sky' designates areas which in other languages are referred to by terms specifying only a part of the area above the earth. For example, a literal translation of ἐμβλέψατε εἰς τὰ πετεινὰ τοῦ οὐρανοῦ 'look at the birds of the sky' (Mt 6.26) would in some languages refer only to those birds which fly particularly high in the sky, for example, eagles, vultures, and falcons. The Greek expression τὰ πετεινὰ τοῦ οὐρανοῦ simply designates wild birds in contrast with domestic fowl, such as chickens. Therefore, in translating 'the birds of the sky,' one may wish to use a general designation for all wild birds. See also 4.41.

The sky (οὐρανός[a]) is also represented in the Scriptures as a dwelling place of certain supernatural beings, for the various stars and constellations were associated with supernatural forces (see στρατιὰ τοῦ οὐρανοῦ, literally 'the army of heaven,' in Ac 7.42: ὁ θεὸς . . . παρέδωκεν αὐτοὺς λατρεύειν τῇ στρατιᾷ τοῦ οὐρανοῦ 'God . . . gave them over to worship the stars of the heaven'). In some languages, however, there is a problem with the rendering 'stars of heaven,' since such an expression might imply that there are types of stars which do not exist in the sky. Therefore, it is often more appropriate to translate στρατιὰ τοῦ οὐρανοῦ as simply 'the stars.' At the same time it is often advisable to introduce a marginal note to indicate that the stars were regarded as symbols of supernatural beings. One may also translate στρατιὰ τοῦ οὐρανοῦ as 'supernatural beings in the sky' or 'powers that dwell in the sky' (see 12.45).

The semantic equivalent of οὐρανός[a] is in some instances merely an adverb meaning 'up' or 'above.' In other languages the various areas referred to by οὐρανός[a] must be designated by more specific terms or phrases, for example, 'the region of the stars,' 'the place of the clouds,' or 'where the wind blows,' as a way of designating at least three different areas which may be significant in certain types of contexts.

In Ac 26.19 the adjective οὐράνιος could be interpreted as being related simply to the meaning of οὐρανός[a] 'sky,' but it seems preferable to regard οὐράνιος in this context as

2 For certain of the lexical items included in Subdomain B *Regions Above the Earth,* there is no specific spatial orientation which requires their being regarded as being 'up' or 'high.' This relates, for example, to the meanings of such lexical items as δόξα[h] (1.15) and κόλπος Ἀβραάμ (1.16), but since the referents of these terms are equated with other celestial regions, one is justified in combining them into this subdomain.

In biblical times the regions above the earth were often regarded as consisting of various strata, and these views seem to be reflected in a number of NT contexts. Paul, for example, speaks of τρίτος οὐρανός 'the third heaven' as being the παράδεισος τοῦ θεοῦ, that is 'God's paradise' (ἁρπαγέντα τὸν τοιοῦτον ἕως τρίτου οὐρανοῦ . . . ἡρπάγη εἰς τὸν παράδεισον 'this man was snatched up into the third heaven . . . he was caught up into paradise' 2 Cor 12.2-4). Another significant stratum in the heavens seems to be the area in which the stars, sun, and moon existed. A third region may be regarded as 'the air,' that is to say, the region where birds fly. It is, however, impossible to insist upon a rigid boundary between such areas, for such ancient beliefs were not based upon fixed classifications or distinctions.

meaning simply 'from heaven' or 'heavenly' (1.12).

1.6 ἀήρ[a], **ἔρος** *m*: the space immediately above the earth's surface, and not including the dome arching over the earth – 'air.' ἔσεσθε γὰρ εἰς ἀέρα λαλοῦντες 'for you will be talking into the air' 1 Cor 14.9. The expression εἰς ἀέρα λαλοῦντες, literally 'talking into the air,' may be regarded as a type of idiom meaning 'talking to no purpose' or 'talking without anyone understanding.' Accordingly, ἔσεσθε γὰρ εἰς ἀέρα λαλοῦντες may be rendered as 'you will be talking, but no one will understand' or 'you will be talking, but your words will not enter anyone.' In Ac 22.23, κονιορτὸν βαλλόντων εἰς τὸν ἀέρα 'throwing dust into the air,' it may be more appropriate in a number of languages to say 'throwing dust above themselves' or simply 'throwing dust up.' A literal rendering of 'throwing dust into the air' might suggest in some languages that the air was some kind of a container in which the dust remained.

The Greek term ἀήρ in Re 9.2 (ἐσκοτώθη ὁ ἥλιος καὶ ὁ ἀὴρ ἐκ τοῦ καπνοῦ τοῦ φρέατος 'the sun and the air were darkened by the smoke from the pit') may very well be translated as 'air,' but since it is a reference primarily to space rather than to substance, it is more natural in a number of languages to say 'the sky was darkened by the smoke from the pit.'

1.7 ἀήρ[c], **ἔρος** *m*: the space above the earth inhabited by and under the control of certain supernatural powers – 'air, sky.'[3] κατὰ τὸν ἄρχοντα τῆς ἐξουσίας τοῦ ἀέρος literally 'according to the ruler of the power of the air,' but more satisfactorily rendered as 'the ruler of powers in the sky' or '. . . in space' Eph 2.2. In the

---

3 It would be possible to combine the meanings of ἀήρ[a] (1.6) and ἀήρ[c] (1.7) under a single generic definition of space above the earth. One could then leave it to the context to specify the particular area referred to. However, because of the relationship of ἀήρ[a] to the meaning of οὐρανός[a] (1.5) and the fact that in so many languages a distinct contrast in meaning is preserved for expressions designating the sky in contrast with the area immediately above the surface of the earth, it seems better to make a distinction at this point.

context of Eph 2.2 ἐξουσία is best understood as a collective and thus referring to the various supernatural powers regarded as inhabiting the area above the earth and thus controlling in many respects both the behavior and the fate of people. See also 12.44.

1.8 ἐπουράνιος[a], **ον**: (derivative of οὐρανός[a] 'sky,' 1.5) related to or located in the sky – 'in the sky, celestial.' σώματα ἐπουράνια, καὶ σώματα ἐπίγεια 'there are celestial bodies and there are terrestrial bodies' 1 Cor 15.40. For ἐπουράνιος as part of an idiom, see 1.26.

1.9 οὐρανόθεν: the sky as a source or as a location from which implied movement takes place – 'from the sky.' οὐρανόθεν ὑμῖν ὑετοὺς διδοὺς καὶ καιροὺς καρποφόρους 'he gives you rain from the sky and crops at the right time' Ac 14.17; οὐρανόθεν ὑπὲρ τὴν λαμπρότητα τοῦ ἡλίου περιλάμψαν με φῶς 'a light from the sky brighter than the sun shone around me' Ac 26.13.

οὐρανόθεν in Ac 14.17 and Ac 26.13 is somewhat ambiguous, for both events may be regarded as involving a semantic derivative of οὐρανός[b] 'heaven' (1.11) rather than οὐρανός[a] 'sky' (1.5). In Ac 14.17 one might very well translate 'he gives rain from heaven,' since obviously the agent is God. Similarly, in Ac 26.13 the light might come 'from heaven,' since the light is presumably regarded as a supernatural phenomenon.

1.10 μεσουράνημα, τος *n*: a point or region of the sky directly above the earth – 'high in the sky, midpoint in the sky, directly overhead, straight above in the sky.' εἶδον, καὶ ἤκουσα ἑνὸς ἀετοῦ πετομένου ἐν μεσουρανήματι 'I looked, and I heard an eagle that was flying overhead in the sky' Re 8.13.

1.11 οὐρανός[b], **οῦ** *m* (singular or plural; there seems to be no semantic distinction in NT literature between the singular and plural forms): the supernatural dwelling place of God and other heavenly beings (οὐρανός[b] also contains a component denoting that which is 'above' or 'in the sky,' but the element of 'abode' is evidently more significant than location above the earth) – 'heaven.' οἱ ἄγγέλοι αὐτῶν ἐν οὐρανοῖς διὰ παντὸς βλέπουσι τὸ πρόσωπον τοῦ πατρός μου τοῦ ἐν οὐρανοῖς 'their angels in heaven are always in the presence of my Father in heaven' Mt 18.10; οἰκοδομὴν ἐκ θεοῦ ἔχομεν οἰκίαν ἀχειροποίητον αἰώνιον ἐν τοῖς οὐρανοῖς 'we will have a dwelling from God, a home in heaven, eternal and not made by hands' 2 Cor 5.1; ὁ πατὴρ ὁ ἐξ οὐρανοῦ 'the Father in heaven' Lk 11.13.

In a number of languages precisely the same term is used to designate both 'sky' and 'heaven' (as the abode of God). But in many instances a completely separate term must be employed in speaking of the dwelling place of God, for example, 'where God lives' or 'where God is' or 'from where God governs.' In some languages the term referring to 'heaven' is simply 'the home above,' and in one instance a designation of heaven refers primarily to a state, for example, 'the life above.'

The phrase τρίτος οὐρανός 'the third heaven' is a fixed phrase referring to the abode of God (ἁρπαγέντα τὸν τοιοῦτον ἕως τρίτου οὐρανοῦ '(a man) who was caught up as far as the third heaven' 2 Cor 12.2), but in a number of languages it is extremely difficult to speak of 'the third heaven,' especially if one uses a term for 'heaven' which is 'the abode of God.' Therefore, in many instances τρίτος οὐρανός is translated as 'heaven' or 'the abode of God,' and if necessary, a footnote may be added in order to indicate the literal meaning of the Greek expression. If a literal rendering is employed, it is usually equivalent to 'the third sky' or 'above two degrees of sky.'

1.12 οὐράνιος, ον; ἐπουράνιος[b], ον: (derivatives of οὐρανός[b] 'heaven,' 1.11) related to or located in heaven – 'heavenly, in heaven, pertaining to heaven.'

οὐράνιος: ὡς ὁ πατὴρ ὑμῶν ὁ οὐράνιος τέλειός ἐστιν 'as your Father in heaven is perfect' Mt 5.48.

ἐπουράνιος[b]: προσεληλύθατε . . . πόλει θεοῦ ζῶντος, Ἰερουσαλὴμ ἐπουρανίῳ 'you have come . . . to the city of the living God, the Jerusalem in heaven' He 12.22; οὐκ ἔστιν ἡμῖν ἡ πάλη πρὸς αἷμα καὶ σάρκα, ἀλλὰ . . . πρὸς τὰ πνευματικὰ τῆς πονηρίας ἐν τοῖς ἐπουρανίοις 'for we are not fighting against human beings, but

. . . against the wicked spiritual forces in the heavenly realms' Eph 6.12.[4]

The derivatives οὐράνιος and ἐπουράνιος[b] are essentially equivalent to semantic compounds in that they combine a semantic element of 'heaven' as a celestial abode with another semantic element specifying location or relationship. Frequently such terms are translated as 'in heaven' or 'from heaven' or 'belonging to heaven.'

1.13 ὕψος[b], ους n; ὑψηλός[b], ή, όν; ὕψιστος[a], η, ον; ὕψωμα[a], τος n: a location above the earth and associated with supernatural events or beings – 'high, world above, sky, heaven, on high.'

ὕψος[b] (there is no difference in meaning between the singular and plural forms): ἀναβὰς εἰς ὕψος ᾐχμαλώτευσεν αἰχμαλωσίαν 'when he ascended on high, he led a host of captives' Eph 4.8; ἕως οὗ ἐνδύσησθε ἐξ ὕψους δύναμιν 'until the power from on high comes down on you' Lk 24.49. In Lk 24.49 ὕψος refers to heaven as a type of substitute reference for God, and in many languages it is advisable to translate 'until the power from God comes down on you.' In Eph 4.8 the phrase ἀναβὰς εἰς ὕψος may be rendered literally as 'when he went up to the heights,' but it is preferable in a number of languages to translate 'when he went up to heaven,' for a literal rendering of 'heights' might imply only a high building or a mountain.

ὑψηλός[b]: ἐκάθισεν ἐν δεξιᾷ τῆς μεγαλωσύνης ἐν ὑψηλοῖς 'he sat down in heaven at the right side of God' He 1.3.

ὕψιστος[a]: ἐν οὐρανῷ εἰρήνη καὶ δόξα ἐν ὑψίστοις 'let there be peace in heaven and glory in the world above' Lk 19.38. The parallelism in the phrases 'peace in heaven' and 'glory in the world above' indicates quite clearly the equivalence in reference, though not in meaning, between οὐρανός[b] (1.11) and ὕψιστος[a].

---

4 It is possible that the adjectival derivative ἐπουράνιος in Eph 6.12 should be interpreted as a designation for the area of the sky in which wicked spiritual forces were presumed to be located. However, the supernatural aspects of these wicked forces and the challenge which such forces were regarded as posing for God and his hosts may justify relating such forces to the 'heavenly world' rather than merely to the sky.

In Mt 21.9 the phrase ὡσαννὰ ἐν τοῖς ὑψίστοις, literally 'hosanna in the highest,' has been interpreted as a plea for salvation or deliverance from God who is in heaven. However, it seems preferable to understand ὡσαννά as simply being a shout of exclamation or praise and therefore to interpret the phrase ὡσαννὰ ἐν τοῖς ὑψίστοις as meaning 'praise to God.' In Lk 19.38 a parallel expression, καὶ δόξα ἐν ὑψίστοις, literally 'and glory in the highest,' is usually understood as an acclamation of glory to God and therefore may be so rendered. See 33.357.

ὕψωμαᵃ: οὔτε ὕψωμα οὔτε βάθος 'neither the world above nor the world below' Ro 8.39. There are differences of scholarly opinion as to whether ὕψωμα in Ro 8.39 is to be understood as a dimension of space (and as such, related to certain Pythagorean or Neo-Platonic concepts of elemental forces) or as 'the world above' (as the location of alien demonic forces). For another interpretation of ὕψωμα in Ro 8.39, see 12.46.

In contexts in which these expressions refer clearly to 'heaven' or 'the sky,' it is better to use terms meaning 'heaven' or 'sky' rather than terms meaning 'height' or 'that which is high.'

1.14 παράδεισος, ου *m*: a dwelling place of the righteous dead in a state of blessedness (generally equated with οὐρανόςᵇ 'heaven,' 1.11) – 'paradise.' σήμερον μετ' ἐμοῦ ἔσῃ ἐν τῷ παραδείσῳ 'today you will be with me in paradise/heaven' Lk 23.43. In some languages 'paradise' has been translated by a borrowed term, but more often than not it is rendered by an expression which is roughly equivalent to 'that wonderful place' or even 'that wonderful place in heaven.'

In Re 2.7 ἐν τῷ παραδείσῳ τοῦ θεοῦ 'in the paradise of God,' the reference may reflect somewhat more closely the historical background of this term, which is derived from an Old Persian word meaning 'enclosure,' and thus was applied to a 'garden' or 'park.' For that reason, a number of commentators have believed that in Re 2.7, it is appropriate to translate 'the garden of God,' especially since in the context the reference is to the fruit of the tree of life.

1.15 δόξαʰ, ης *f*: a place which is glorious and as such, a reference to heaven – 'glory, heaven.' ἀνελήμφθη ἐν δόξῃ 'he was taken up to heaven' 1 Tm 3.16. Some scholars, however, interpret δόξα in 1 Tm 3.16 as an abstract and thus translate ἐν δόξῃ as 'in a glorious way' or 'in a wonderful way' or 'in a way that revealed his glory.'

1.16 κόλπος Ἀβραάμ: (an idiom, literally 'Abraham's bosom') the heavenly abode, with the implication of close interpersonal relations – 'Abraham's bosom, heaven.' ἀπενεχθῆναι αὐτὸν ὑπὸ τῶν ἀγγέλων εἰς τὸν κόλπον Ἀβραάμ 'he was borne by angels to Abraham's bosom' or '. . . heaven' Lk 16.22.

A literal rendering of κόλπος Ἀβραάμ as 'the bosom of Abraham' or 'the lap of Abraham' is often misleading. In some languages it may even suggest homosexuality, and in other cases it implies that Lazarus was either a baby or was changed into a baby in heaven. Since κόλπος Ἀβραάμ is generally interpreted as a reference to the eschatological heavenly feast,[5] one may be justified in rendering Lk 16.22 as in TEV "the poor man died and was carried by the angels to sit beside Abraham at the feast in heaven." In some languages κόλπος Ἀβραάμ in this context is translated as 'he was carried by the angels to Abraham's side' or '. . . to be with Abraham.'

C Regions Below the Surface of the Earth (1.17-1.25)

1.17 καταχθόνιος, ον: pertaining to being below the surface of the earth – 'the world below, what is beneath the earth, under the earth.' ἵνα ἐν τῷ ὀνόματι Ἰησοῦ πᾶν γόνυ κάμψῃ ἐπουρανίων καὶ ἐπιγείων καὶ καταχθονίων 'that at the name of Jesus every knee should bow, of those in heaven and those on earth and

---

5 According to ancient Jewish tradition, the end of the age would be characterized by a heavenly feast to be enjoyed by the righteous. This would be presided over by Abraham, and therefore to go to 'Abraham's bosom' would be equivalent to being an honored guest at this celestial banquet.

those under the earth' Php 2.10.[6] In Php 2.10 καταχθονίων is probably a reference to the dead, generally regarded as inhabiting a dark region under the ground.

1.18 βάθος[d], ους *n*: a place or region which is low – 'the world below.' οὔτε ὕψωμα οὔτε βάθος 'neither the world above nor the world below' Ro 8.39. As in the case of ὕψωμα[a] (1.13), βάθος may be interpreted as a supernatural force (see 12.47).

The phrase κατώτερα μέρη τῆς γῆς 'the lower parts of the earth' may likewise refer to 'the world below' as in εἰς τὰ κατώτερα μέρη τῆς γῆς 'down into the lower parts of the earth' Eph 4.9 (see 83.54). Some scholars, however, understand this expression as being a reference to the earth which is low in contrast with heaven. On the basis of such an interpretation one may render Eph 4.9 as 'he came down to the earth itself.'

1.19 ᾅδης[a], ου *m*: a place or abode of the dead, including both the righteous and the unrighteous (in most contexts ᾅδης[a] is equivalent to the Hebrew term Sheol) – 'the world of the dead, Hades.' οὔτε ἐγκατελείφθη εἰς ᾅδην 'he was not abandoned in the world of the dead' Ac 2.31. There are several problems involved in rendering ᾅδης[a] as 'world of the dead,' since in some languages this may be interpreted as suggesting that there are two different earths, one for the living and another for the dead. In such cases, ᾅδης[a] may be more satisfactorily rendered as 'where the dead are' or 'where the dead remain.'

In Lk 16.23 ᾅδης[a] obviously involves torment and punishment. These aspects are important supplementary features of the word ᾅδης[a] but are not integral elements of the meaning. In Lk 16.23, however, it may be appropriate to use a term which is equivalent to Greek γέεννα meaning 'hell' (see 1.21). It is indeed possible that in addressing a Greco-Roman audience Luke would have used ᾅδης

in a context implying punishment and torment, since this was a typical Greco-Roman view of the next world. But since Luke also uses γέεννα, as in Lk 12.5, it is possible that the choice of ᾅδης in Lk 16.23 reflects Luke's intent to emphasize the fact that ᾅδης[a] includes both the unrighteous and the righteous.

1.20 ἄβυσσος, ου *f*: (a figurative extension of meaning of ἄβυσσος 'pit,' not occurring in the NT) a location of the dead and a place where the Devil is kept (Re 20.3), the abode of the beast as the antichrist (Re 11.7), and of Abaddon, as the angel of the underworld (Re 9.11) – 'abyss, abode of evil spirits, very deep place.' τίς καταβήσεται εἰς τὴν ἄβυσσον; τοῦτ' ἔστιν Χριστὸν ἐκ νεκρῶν ἀναγαγεῖν 'who can go down to the abyss? that is, to bring Christ up from the dead' Ro 10.7; καὶ ἔβαλεν αὐτὸν εἰς τὴν ἄβυσσον 'and he threw him into the abyss' Re 20.3.

ἄβυσσος is sometimes rendered as 'a very deep hole'; in other instances, 'a hole without a bottom' or 'the deepest hole in the earth.'

1.21 γέεννα, ης *f*: a place of punishment for the dead – 'Gehenna, hell.' φοβήθητε τὸν μετὰ τὸ ἀποκτεῖναι ἔχοντα ἐξουσίαν ἐμβαλεῖν εἰς τὴν γέενναν 'fear rather him who has the authority to throw (you) into hell after killing you' Lk 12.5.

The Greek term γέεννα is derived from a Hebrew phrase meaning 'Valley of Hinnom,' a ravine running along the south side of Jerusalem and a place where the rubbish from the city was constantly being burned. According to late Jewish popular belief, the last judgment was to take place in this valley, and hence the figurative extension of meaning from 'Valley of Hinnom' to 'hell.' In most languages γέεννα is rendered as 'place of punishment' or 'place where the dead suffer' or 'place where the dead suffer because of their sins.'

6 There are two basic problems involved in the translation of Php 2.10. For example, the phrase *at the name of Jesus* may mean 'when the name of Jesus is proclaimed' or 'when the presence of Jesus is announced.' The phrase *every knee* means 'every person,' since *knee* is a figurative substitute for a person (see 9.16).

1.22 λίμνη τοῦ πυρὸς (καὶ θείου): (an idiom, literally 'lake of fire (and sulfur),' occurring in some slightly different forms six times in Revelation, three times with the addition of θεῖον 'sulfur') a place of eternal punishment and destruction – 'lake of fire, hell.'[7] καὶ ὁ διάβολος ὁ πλανῶν αὐτοὺς ἐβλήθη εἰς τὴν λίμνην τοῦ πυρὸς καὶ θείου 'then the Devil, who deceived them, was thrown into the lake of fire and sulfur' Re 20.10.

In a number of languages it is impossible to translate literally 'lake of fire,' since water and fire seem to be so contradictory that a lake of fire is not even imaginable. It may be possible in some instances to speak of 'a place that looks like a lake that is on fire,' but in other languages the closest equivalent may simply be 'a great expanse of fire.' In some parts of the world people are fully familiar with the type of boiling magma in the cone of volcanoes, and terms for such a place may be readily adapted in speaking of 'a lake of fire,' since volcanic activity would seem to be the basis for this particular biblical expression.

1.23 τὸ σκότος τὸ ἐξώτερον: (an idiom, literally 'the outer darkness') a place or region which is both dark and removed (presumably from the abode of the righteous) and serving as the abode of evil spirits and devils – 'outer darkness, darkness outside.' ἐκβληθήσονται εἰς τὸ σκότος τὸ ἐξώτερον 'they will be thrown into outer darkness' Mt 8.12. In a number of languages this expression in Mt 8.12 must be rendered as 'they will be thrown outside where it is dark.'

1.24 ὁ ζόφος τοῦ σκότους: (an idiom, literally 'the gloom of darkness') the dark, gloomy nature of hell as a place of punishment – 'gloomy hell, black darkness.' ἀστέρες πλανῆται οἷς ὁ ζόφος τοῦ σκότους εἰς αἰῶνα τετήρηται 'wandering stars for whom the darkness of hell has been reserved forever' Jd 13.

1.25 ταρταρόω: (derivative of τάρταρος 'Tartarus, hell,' as a place of torture or torment, not occurring in the NT) to cast into or to cause to remain in Tartarus – 'to hold in Tartarus, to cast into hell.' ἀλλὰ σειραῖς ζόφου ταρταρώσας 'but held them in Tartarus by means of chains of darkness' or 'cast them into hell where they are kept chained in darkness' 2 Pe 2.4. In many cases it is confusing to add still another term for a designation of hell by transliterating the Greek τάρταρος, and so most translators have preferred to render ταρταρόω as either 'to cast into hell' or 'to keep in hell,' thus using for 'hell' the same term as is employed for a rendering of the Greek term γέεννα (1.21).

D Heavenly Bodies (1.26-1.33)

1.26 σῶμα ἐπουράνιον:[8] (an idiom, literally 'heavenly body,' occurring in the NT only in the plural) the luminous objects in the sky: sun, moon, and other planets and stars – 'heavenly body.' σώματα ἐπουράνια, καὶ σώματα ἐπίγεια· ἀλλὰ ἑτέρα μὲν ἡ τῶν ἐπουρανίων δόξα, ἑτέρα δὲ ἡ τῶν ἐπιγείων 'there are heavenly bodies and earthly bodies; there is a beauty that belongs to heavenly bodies, and another kind of beauty that belongs to earthly bodies' 1 Cor 15.40. See also 1.8.

The phrase σῶμα ἐπουράνιον is a highly generic expression which in the plural is sometimes translatable as 'lights in the sky,' but more often than not it may be necessary to identify the various heavenly bodies as 'sun, moon, and stars.' In certain contexts one may also wish to identify the planets, often spoken of as 'wandering stars' or 'moving stars' (reflecting the etymology of the English word *planet*, which is derived from a Greek word

---

7 It is possible that λίμνη τοῦ πυρός 'lake of fire' does not belong in this class of regions below the earth, but since it is so closely associated with other places of destruction and punishment, it is probably better treated here rather than elsewhere. If the figurative language is derived from a knowledge of volcanic activity, this could lend support to the classification of λίμνη τοῦ πυρός at this point, since it would coincide very closely with related concepts of 'pit' and 'abyss.'

8 It is difficult to say whether the phrase σῶμα ἐπουράνιον should be treated as a fixed phrase with a shifted meaning for the head word σῶμα and thus a type of idiom, or whether it should be considered a semantically endocentric expression and thus not a so-called lexical unit. The treatment of σῶμα ἐπουράνιον as semantically endocentric can certainly be justified by the highly generic meaning of σῶμα as 'body, object,' but one may also argue that the restriction in reference to the sun, moon, planets, and stars provides a basis for regarding it as semantically exocentric.

meaning 'wanderer'). These are, of course, not to be confused with shooting stars and comets in the sky.

1.27 φωστήρ[a], ῆρος *m*: any light-producing object in the sky, such as the sun, moon, and other planets and stars – 'light, luminary, star.' ἐν οἷς φαίνεσθε ὡς φωστῆρες ἐν κόσμῳ 'you shine among them like stars in the sky' (literally '. . . universe') Php 2.15. Though φωστήρ[a] may refer to any light-producing object, it is used especially of the heavenly bodies and more specifically of stars, as in Php 2.15, the one NT context in which φωστήρ[a] occurs. A focal component of this meaning is the light-giving characteristic.

1.28 ἥλιος, ου *m* – 'the sun.' ἡλίου δὲ ἀνατείλαντος ἐκαυματίσθη 'but when the sun rose, they were burned' Mt 13.6; ὁ ἥλιος σκοτισθήσεται 'the sun will become dark' Mk 13.24. Translators have relatively few difficulties in obtaining a satisfactory term for the sun, though there may be a tendency in some languages to add some kind of honorific title to the word, for example, 'our father the sun.' Translators' problems occur, however, with verbs describing the action or effect of the sun. For example, in Mt 13.6, instead of speaking of 'the sun rising,' it may be more satisfactory to speak of 'the sun shining' or, in this particular context, possibly 'when the sun was overhead' or 'by the time the sun had reached the sky.' In Mk 13.24 one can perhaps best render the meaning as 'the sun will no longer shine' or '. . . will cease shining.'

1.29 σελήνη, ης *f* – 'the moon.' ἔσονται σημεῖα ἐν ἡλίῳ καὶ σελήνῃ καὶ ἄστροις 'there will be signs in the sun and moon and stars' Lk 21.25. As in the case of ἥλιος 'the sun' (1.28), there are relatively few difficulties involved in obtaining a satisfactory word for σελήνη 'the moon,' though there may also be a tendency to add some kind of honorific or title, for example, 'mother moon.' At the same time, certain difficulties may occur in some passages. For example, in Lk 21.25 it may be misleading to speak of signs occurring 'in the moon,' for this might mean 'inside the moon.' TEV has resolved the problem somewhat by

translating "there will be strange things happening to the sun, the moon, and the stars." One may also translate 'the sun, the moon, and the stars will cause signs in the heavens' or '. . . portents in the sky.'

1.30 ἀστήρ, έρος *m*; ἄστρον[a], ου *n*: a star or a planet – 'star, planet.'

ἀστήρ: ἰδοὺ ὁ ἀστὴρ ὃν εἶδον ἐν τῇ ἀνατολῇ 'they saw the star – the same one they had seen in the east' Mt 2.9; ἀστέρες πλανῆται οἷς ὁ ζόφος τοῦ σκότους εἰς αἰῶνα τετήρηται 'wandering stars for whom is reserved forever a place of gloomy darkness' Jd 13. Since in Jd 13 godless people are likened to 'wandering stars' or 'planets,' it may be best to introduce this expression by a simile, for example, 'they are like wandering stars.' In some languages there is a serious difficulty involved in translating ἀστὴρ πλανήτης as 'planet,' since the planets or their courses through the heavens are regarded as beneficial. In Jd 13 the focal meaning is upon the heretical nature of these godless persons who do not keep on the right course. It may therefore be necessary to translate ἀστέρες πλανῆται in Jd 13 as 'stars that do not stay where they should stay' or '. . . do not remain in their right places.' See also 15.26.

ἄστρον[a]: καθὼς τὰ ἄστρα τοῦ οὐρανοῦ τῷ πλήθει 'as numerous as the stars in the sky' He 11.12. In selecting a term for 'star,' it is important to avoid an expression which may relate to only one set of stars, that is to say, a particular constellation, since there may be connotations associated with such a constellation which can radically alter the intent of a particular passage. Some constellations, for example, may be regarded as kindly disposed toward mankind, while others may be regarded as hostile.

1.31 ἄστρον[b], ου *n*: a group of stars – 'constellation.' ἀνελάβετε τὴν σκηνὴν τοῦ Μόλοχ καὶ τὸ ἄστρον τοῦ θεοῦ ὑμῶν 'Ραιφάν 'it was the tent of the god Moloch that you carried, and the image of the constellation of your god Rephan' Ac 7.43. Normally a constellation may be described as 'a group of stars' or 'a family of stars' or 'stars that travel together' or even 'stars that live together.' It is possible, however, to interpret the occurrence of ἄστρον in Ac 7.43 as being a reference to a particular planet (namely, Saturn) rather than a constellation.

1.32 φωσφόρος, ου *m*: a light-producing heavenly body, probably the morning star (a planet), but possibly the sun – 'morning star.' ἕως οὗ ἡμέρα διαυγάσῃ καὶ φωσφόρος ἀνατείλῃ ἐν ταῖς καρδίαις ὑμῶν 'until the day dawns and the light of the morning star shines in your hearts' 2 Pe 1.19. The literal meaning of φωσφόρος is 'that which bears light,' but it is a conventional reference to the morning star, which in reality is not a star, but one of the brighter planets, usually Venus, but also Jupiter, Mars, Mercury, or even Saturn. In the one occurrence of this word in the NT, namely, 2 Pe 1.19, φωσφόρος is an indirect figurative reference to Jesus and his redemptive work, but it is extremely difficult in a number of languages to speak of 'the light of the morning star shining in your hearts.' One may sometimes say '. . . shines upon your hearts' or possibly '. . . shines upon you and causes you to have new hearts' or '. . . and illumines your minds.'

1.33 ἀστὴρ πρωϊνός: (an idiom, literally 'morning star') a planet which is conspicuous in the morning sky (usually either Venus or Mars) – 'morning star, bright star in the morning sky.' δώσω αὐτῷ τὸν ἀστέρα τὸν πρωϊνόν 'I will give them the morning star' Re 2.28. In Re 2.28 the singular pronoun αὐτῷ refers to any and all of the persons in Thyatira, and therefore it is usually best rendered as plural. A literal rendering of Re 2.28 may be confusing, since it would suggest that God would be handing over the morning star to persons in Thyatira. A more satisfactory rendering may be 'I will cause the morning star to shine upon them' or possibly 'I will bring light into their hearts.'

E Atmospheric Objects[9] **(1.34-1.38)**

1.34 νεφέλη, ης *f* – 'cloud.' ὅταν ἴδητε τὴν νεφέλην ἀνατέλλουσαν ἐπὶ δυσμῶν 'when you

see a cloud coming up in the west' Lk 12.54. In many languages it would be difficult to speak of 'a cloud coming up in the west,' for this would seem to imply that a cloud was actually rising from below the earth. In some languages it is better to speak of 'a cloud getting larger' or, in the specific context of Lk 12.54, one may translate 'when you see a cloud coming to you from the west.'

1.35 ὁμίχλη, ης *f*: a cloud-like mass of moisture close to the earth's surface – 'fog, mist.' In the NT ὁμίχλη is used only figuratively: οὗτοί εἰσιν πηγαὶ ἄνυδροι καὶ ὁμίχλαι ὑπὸ λαίλαπος ἐλαυνόμεναι 'these men are dried up springs or mists blown along by a storm' 2 Pe 2.17. The metaphorical usage in 2 Pe 2.17 must be marked in a number of languages as a simile, for example, 'these men are like springs that have dried up and are like mists which the storm blows along.'

1.36 ἀτμίς, ίδος *f*: a hot steamy vapor – 'steam.' σημεῖα ἐπὶ τῆς γῆς κάτω, αἷμα καὶ ἀτμίδα καπνοῦ 'signs on the earth below; there will be blood and fire and steam' Ac 2.19. ἀτμίς is also used figuratively: ἀτμὶς γάρ ἐστε ἡ πρὸς ὀλίγον φαινομένη 'for you are a vapor which appears for a moment' Jas 4.14.

An important connotation in the use of the term ἀτμίς is the fact that it disappears so readily. This is a particularly significant element in Jas 4.14. The closest equivalent of ἀτμίς is normally a term which refers to the steam rising from a boiling pot or cauldron.

1.37 καπνός, οῦ *m* – 'smoke.' ἀνέβη καπνὸς ἐκ τοῦ φρέατος ὡς καπνὸς καμίνου μεγάλης 'smoke poured out of it, like the smoke from a great furnace' Re 9.2. Translators may very well encounter two quite distinct terms for smoke, one meaning the smoke of a relatively small,

---

9 The atmospheric objects in this subdomain may also be regarded as atmospheric phenomena, and in terms of our present-day perspective, they would be regarded as events. However, from the standpoint of a classification presumably valid for biblical times, the phenomena would more likely be regarded as objects rather than as events, and it is for this reason that they are classified at this point in the general category of *Geographical Objects and Features*.

controlled fire, and another meaning billowing smoke coming from a forest fire or volcano. It would be this latter meaning which would be relevant in Re 9.2.

1.38 ἶρις, ιδος *f*: a circular or semicircular band of light, whether colored or not – 'rainbow' or 'halo.'[10] ἶρις χυχλόθεν τοῦ θρόνου 'all around the throne there was a rainbow' or '. . . circle of light' Re 4.3. In Re 4.3 and Re 10.1 (the only occurrences of ἶρις in the NT) the reference may be either to a rainbow or to a halo. The meaning of 'rainbow' may be expressed in some languages as 'a bow of light' or 'a curve of light' or even 'a ribbon of light.' The meaning of 'halo' is usually expressed as 'a circle of light' or 'a wreath of light' or 'a band of light encircling,' followed by the object which the band of light encircles.

F The Earth's Surface (1.39-1.45)

1.39 γῆᵃ, γῆς *f*; οἰκουμένη ᵃ, ης *f*; χόσμος ᵇ, ου *m*: the surface of the earth as the dwelling place of mankind, in contrast with the heavens above and the world below – 'earth, world.'[11]
γῆᵃ: οὐαὶ τοὺς χατοιχοῦντας ἐπὶ τῆς γῆς 'how horrible it will be for all who live on earth!' Re 8.13.
οἰκουμένηᵃ: ἔδειξεν αὐτῷ πάσας τὰς βασιλείας τῆς οἰκουμένης 'he showed him all the kingdoms of the world' Lk 4.5.
χόσμοςᵇ: δείχνυσιν αὐτῷ πάσας τὰς βασιλείας τοῦ χόσμου 'he showed him all the kingdoms of the world' Mt 4.8.
  In He 2.5 there is a reference to τὴν οἰχουμένην τὴν μέλλουσαν 'the world to come, the future world.' This has generally been interpreted as being equivalent to 'the coming age,' but the use of οἰχουμένη would seem to imply an inhabited world.

1.40 χοσμικόςᵃ, ή, όν: pertaining to the earth – 'earthly, on earth.' εἶχε μὲν οὖν καὶ ἡ πρώτη δικαιώματα λατρείας τό τε ἅγιον χοσμικόν 'the first (covenant) had rules for correct worship and a holy place on earth' or '. . . a sanctuary on earth' He 9.1.

1.41 ἐπίγειοςᵃ, ον: pertaining to being located on the earth – 'on the earth, in the world.' πᾶν γόνυ κάμψῃ ἐπουρανίων καὶ ἐπιγείων καὶ καταχθονίων 'all beings in heaven, and on earth, and in the world below will fall on their knees' Php 2.10.

1.42 χοϊκόςᵇ, ή, όν: pertaining to having the nature of earthly existence in contrast with that which is heavenly or of heaven – 'of earth, earthly, made of earth.' ὁ πρῶτος ἄνθρωπος ἐχ γῆς χοϊκός 'the first man made of earth comes from the earth' 1 Cor 15.47. It may even be possible in rendering χοϊκός in 1 Cor 15.47 to say 'created out of earth' or 'made from dust' (see 2.16).

1.43 ὑπὸ τὸν οὐρανόν: (an idiom, literally 'under the sky') pertaining to being on the earth – 'on earth.' τοῦ χηρυχθέντος ἐν πάσῃ κτίσει τῇ ὑπὸ τὸν οὐρανόν 'it was preached to all people on earth' Col 1.23. ὑπὸ τὸν οὐρανόν is essentially equivalent in reference to ἐπίγειοςᵃ 'on the earth' (1.41).

1.44 ἔδαφος, ους *n*: the surface of the earth – 'ground.' ἔπεσά τε εἰς τὸ ἔδαφος 'then I fell to the ground' Ac 22.7.

1.45 χαμαί: a location on the surface of the earth – 'on the ground, to the ground.' ἔπτυσεν χαμαί 'he spat on the ground' Jn 9.6.

---

10 It would also be possible to classify ἶρις 'rainbow' or 'halo' as being an event rather than an object, but in view of the relatively fixed *Gestalt* of this phenomenon, it is probably more satisfactory from the standpoint of an emic classification to regard ἶρις as an object.
11 The occurrences of γῆᵃ, οἰκουμένηᵃ, and χόσμοςᵇ relate specifically to the known inhabited areas of the earth, which in the NT period included the countries bordering on the Mediterranean, the Fertile Crescent as far as the Indus Valley, and as far north in Europe as England and Scandinavia. This was the total known earth or world. Such a restriction to a known area of the earth is also true of terms used in some receptor languages, though the referents are obviously different. What is important is not the particular area of the earth, but the corresponding concept of the surface of the earth as the place of human habitation.
  It is possible that οἰκουμένηᵃ differs slightly in meaning from γῆᵃ and χόσμοςᵇ in view of a somewhat greater emphasis or focus upon the civilized part of earth.

G Elevated Land Formations (1.46-1.50)

1.46 ὄρος, ους *n*: a relatively high elevation of land, in contrast with βουνός 'hill' (1.48), which is by comparison somewhat lower – 'mountain.' ἐπὶ ἐρημίαις πλανώμενοι καὶ ὄρεσιν καὶ σπηλαίοις καὶ ταῖς ὀπαῖς τῆς γῆς 'they wandered like refugees in the deserts and mountains, living in caves and holes in the ground' He 11.38; πᾶν ὄρος καὶ βουνὸς ταπεινωθήσεται 'every mountain and hill shall be made low' Lk 3.5.

Terms referring to mountains, hills, or mounds inevitably reflect the nature of the surrounding landscape. For example, in the flat marshlands of the Central Sudan, an elevation called Doleib Hill is only some three or four feet above the surrounding area, but in the Himalayas elevations of land some ten or twelve thousand feet are still regarded as hills in contrast with the mountains. In the choice of receptor language terms for ὄρος and βουνός (1.48), one must seek expressions which suggest corresponding differences. What is important is relative size, not an exact correspondence to biblical geography. It may, however, be necessary in some instances to introduce a footnote to describe the approximate height of certain biblical mountains or hills.

1.47 ὀρεινός, ή, όν: pertaining to an area characterized by mountains or hills – 'mountainous region, hill country.' ἐπορεύθη εἰς τὴν ὀρεινήν 'she went into the hill country' Lk 1.39.

1.48 βουνός, οῦ *m*: a relatively low elevated land formation, in contrast with ὄρος 'mountain' (1.46), which refers to something higher – 'hill, mound.' τότε ἄρξονται λέγειν τοῖς ὄρεσιν, πέσετε ἐφ᾽ ἡμᾶς, καὶ τοῖς βουνοῖς, Καλύψατε ἡμᾶς 'then they will start crying to the mountains, Fall on us, and to the hills, Cover us up' Lk 23.30.

1.49 ὀφρῦς, ύος *f*: (a figurative extension of meaning of ὀφρῦς 'brow,' not occurring in the NT) the upper portion of a precipitous or steep contour of a hill or mountain – 'cliff, brow of a hill.' ἤγαγον αὐτὸν ἕως ὀφρύος τοῦ ὄρους ἐφ᾽ οὗ ἡ πόλις ᾠκοδόμητο 'they led him to a cliff of the hill on which the city was built' Lk 4.29.

1.50 χρημνός, οῦ *m* – 'steep slope, steep side of a hill.' ὥρμησεν πᾶσα ἡ ἀγέλη κατὰ τοῦ χρημνοῦ 'the entire herd rushed down the steep slope' Mt 8.32.

H Depressions and Holes (1.51-1.59)

1.51 φάραγξ, αγγος *f* – 'ravine, narrow steep-sided valley.' πᾶσα φάραγξ πληρωθήσεται 'every ravine will be filled' Lk 3.5. φάραγξ, as 'a narrow valley,' differs from 'a broad valley' in the sense that one does not expect agriculture to be practiced at the bottom of a φάραγξ, while in the case of a broad valley, agriculture would be an assumed feature.

1.52 χείμαρρος[b], ου *m* or **χειμάρρους**: a ravine or narrow valley in which a stream flows during the rainy season, but which is normally dry during the dry season – 'ravine, wady.' Ἰησοῦς ἐξῆλθεν σὺν μαθηταῖς αὐτοῦ πέραν τοῦ χειμάρρου τοῦ Κεδρών 'Jesus left with his disciples and crossed over the ravine of the Kidron' Jn 18.1.

In desert areas of the world designations for such ravines or valleys are common enough; in fact, there may be several different terms to describe different types of wadies, but for tropical areas and for most temperate parts of the world, it may seem incredible that rivers would regularly dry up during part of the year. What is important, however, in the biblical context in which χείμαρρος[b] occurs is not the intermittent nature of the stream so much as the fact that this is a relatively narrow valley (compare χείμαρρος[a] 'a seasonal stream,' 1.77).

1.53 ὀπή, ῆς *f*: an opening or hole in the ground, either large as in He 11.38 or relatively small as in Jas 3.11 – 'hole, opening.' ἐπὶ ἐρημίαις πλανώμενοι καὶ ὄρεσιν καὶ σπηλαίοις καὶ ταῖς ὀπαῖς τῆς γῆς 'they wandered like refugees in the deserts and hills, living in caves and holes in the earth' He 11.38; μήτι ἡ πηγὴ ἐκ τῆς αὐτῆς ὀπῆς βρύει τὸ γλυκὺ καὶ τὸ πικρόν; 'no spring from the same hole gives a flow of fresh water and salty at the same time, does it?' Jas 3.11.

Holes would differ from caves (He 11.38) in that holes would be vertical openings into the ground, while caves would be more or less horizontal openings into cliffs or sides of hills. In Jas 3.11 it may be quite unnecessary, and in fact confusing, to try to translate ὀπῆς, since ἐκ τῆς αὐτῆς ὀπῆς 'from the same opening' would seem to be redundant with ἡ πηγή 'spring,' since a spring would presumably only flow from a hole or opening in the ground.

1.54 χάσμα, τος *n*: (a figurative extension of meaning of χάσμα 'yawning,' not occurring in the NT) a deep, unbridgeable valley or trough between two points – 'chasm.' καὶ ἐν πᾶσι τούτοις μεταξὺ ἡμῶν καὶ ὑμῶν χάσμα μέγα ἐστήρικται 'but this is not all; between us and you there has been fixed a great chasm' Lk 16.26. In this only NT occurrence of χάσμα the reference is to the impassable space between two parts of the supernatural abode of the dead. Translators frequently use a descriptive phrase such as 'a deep valley which no one may cross' or 'a space which cannot be crossed.'

1.55 βόθυνος, ου *m*: a hole, trench, or pit, natural or dug – 'pit, ditch, hole.' ἐμπέσῃ τοῦτο τοῖς σάββασιν εἰς βόθυνον 'it falls into a ditch on the Sabbath' Mt 12.11. In a number of languages a distinction is made between ditches dug by people for presumably agricultural purposes and those which are natural depressions in the ground. There is no way to determine from the NT contexts which type of ditch is involved.

1.56 φωλεός, οῦ *m*: a hole, typically occupied by an animal as a den or lair – 'hole, den, lair.' αἱ ἀλώπεκες φωλεοὺς ἔχουσιν 'foxes have holes' Lk 9.58. In most languages it is important to make a distinction between φωλεός as in Lk 9.58 and ὀπή 'hole' (1.53), for φωλεός is normally some type of hole serving as a typical habitation or place of escape for an animal, while ὀπή in He 11.38 would not be a place of normal habitation.

1.57 σπήλαιον, ου *n*: a cave or den generally large enough for at least temporary occupation by persons (since such places were often used for habitation or refuge by those who were refugees or thieves, σπήλαιον has in certain contexts the connotation of a 'hideout') – 'cave, den, hideout.' ὑμεῖς δὲ αὐτὸν ποιεῖτε σπήλαιον λῃστῶν 'you make it a den of thieves' Mt 21.13; ἔκρυψαν ἑαυτοὺς εἰς τὰ σπήλαια 'they hid themselves in caves' Re 6.15. In Re 6.15 the reference of σπήλαιον is literal, since people actually hid themselves in such caves. In Mt 21.13, however, the reference is to the Temple, which has been made a kind of 'cave' or 'den,' and since the connotation of the term suggests a 'hideout,' this is obviously a reflection upon the activities and motivations of those who had commercialized the Temple in Jerusalem.

1.58 φρέαρ[b]**, ατος** *n*: a relatively deep pit or shaft in the ground – 'deep pit.' ἐσκοτώθη ὁ ἥλιος καὶ ὁ ἀὴρ ἐκ τοῦ καπνοῦ τοῦ φρέατος 'the sunlight and air were made dark by the smoke from the pit' Re 9.2. In this occurrence of φρέαρ[b] (Re 9.1-2), the reference is essentially equivalent to that of ἄβυσσος 'abyss' (1.20).

1.59 σιρός, οῦ *m* or **σειρός** – 'pit, deep hole.' ἀλλὰ σιροῖς ζόφου ταρταρώσας παρέδωκεν εἰς κρίσιν τηρουμένους 'but cast them into hell and committed them to the pits of intense gloom to be kept until the judgment' 2 Pe 2.4 (apparatus; the text of 2 Pe 2.4 reads σειρά 'chain,' 6.15). In this one occurrence of σιρός in the NT, the pit in question is a place of imprisonment until the time of judgment. The expression 'the pits of intense gloom' may be translated as 'pits where it is extremely dark.'

Though most scholars have interpreted σιρός as being equivalent to ἄβυσσος (1.20), others see a distinction. But there is a danger in attempting to make too many fine distinctions between the meanings of such biblical terms. There is little evidence that biblical writers used such expressions with the same degree of differentiation which some persons would like to find.

I Land in Contrast With the Sea (1.60-1.68)

1.60 γῆ[b], γῆς *f*; χώρα[a], ας *f*; ξηρά, ᾶς *f*: dry land, in contrast with the sea – 'land.'

γῆ[b]: τὸ δὲ πλοῖον ἤδη σταδίους πολλοὺς ἀπὸ τῆς γῆς ἀπεῖχεν 'the boat was already far away from the land' Mt 14.24.

χώρα[a]: κατὰ μέσου τῆς νυκτὸς ὑπενόουν οἱ ναῦται προσάγειν τινὰ αὐτοῖς χώραν 'about midnight the sailors began to suspect that we were getting close to some land' Ac 27.27.

ξηρά: περιάγετε τὴν θάλασσαν καὶ τὴν ξηρὰν ποιῆσαι ἕνα προσήλυτον 'you cross sea and land to make one convert' Mt 23.15.

In a number of languages a clear distinction is made between terms which designate land in contrast with water and those which designate cultivated land. Even in English the normal term for land close to water is 'shore' or 'coast,' and therefore one may translate Mt 14.24 as 'the boat was already far away from the shore.' Similarly, in Ac 27.27 one may translate 'we were getting close to shore.'

1.61 παράλιος, ου *f*: a territory bordering on the sea, in contrast with an inland area (compare ἀνωτερικός, 1.65) – 'coastal region.' πλῆθος πολὺ τοῦ λαοῦ ἀπὸ . . . τῆς παραλίου Τύρου καὶ Σιδῶνος 'a great crowd of people from . . . the coastal region of Tyre and Sidon' Lk 6.17. Frequently παράλιος must be translated by a phrase, for example, 'the land along the seaside' or 'the countries bordering on the sea.'

1.62 χεῖλος[a], ους *n*: (a figurative extension of meaning of χεῖλος 'lip,' not occurring in the NT, except as a metonymy for speech; see 33.74) the strip of land close to a body of water – 'shore.' ὡς ἡ ἄμμος ἡ παρὰ τὸ χεῖλος τῆς θαλάσσης ἡ ἀναρίθμητος 'as innumerable as the sand on the shore of the sea' He 11.12. In the NT contexts in which παράλιος (1.61), χεῖλος, and αἰγιαλός (1.63) occur, it is possible to say that χεῖλος 'shore' probably involves a somewhat narrower strip of land than παράλιος 'a coastal region,' but χεῖλος evidently denotes a somewhat wider area than αἰγιαλός 'beach, shore.'

1.63 αἰγιαλός, οῦ *m*: a strip of land immediately bordering the edge of a body of water and gradually sloping down into the water – 'beach, shore.' κόλπον δέ τινα κατενόουν ἔχοντα αἰγιαλόν 'they noticed a bay with a beach' Ac 27.39.

1.64 ἄμμος[b], ου *f*: a sandy beach or shore – 'beach.' ἐστάθη ἐπὶ τὴν ἄμμον τῆς θαλάσσης 'he stood on the shore of the sea' Re 12.18.[12] ἄμμος[b] evidently involves a particular type of αἰγιαλός (1.63) which is sandy. For languages spoken by persons living along a seacoast, there are usually few if any problems involved in distinguishing various types of land bordering the sea, but for persons living in inland areas, it may be necessary to employ a descriptive phrase such as 'land along the sea' and use such a phrase for various occurrences of different terms.

1.65 ἀνωτερικός, ή, όν: pertaining to an inland or higher area, presumably away from the shoreline – 'inland, upland, interior.' Παῦλον διελθόντα τὰ ἀνωτερικὰ μέρη 'Paul going through the inland districts' Ac 19.1.

1.66 νῆσος, ου *f*: an area of land completely surrounded by water – 'island.' ἐπέγνωμεν ὅτι Μελίτη ἡ νῆσος καλεῖται 'we learned that the island was called Malta' Ac 28.1. In some languages an island can only be designated by a description, for example, 'a small country in the sea' or 'some land surrounded by water.'

1.67 νησίον, ου *n* – 'a small island.' νησίον δέ τι ὑποδραμόντες καλούμενον Καῦδα 'running under the shelter of a small island called Cauda' Ac 27.16.

1.68 τόπος διθάλασσος: a bar or reef produced in an area where two currents meet – 'sandbar, reef.' περιπεσόντες δὲ εἰς τόπον διθάλασσον ἐπέκειλαν τὴν ναῦν 'but the ship ran into a sandbank and went aground' Ac 27.41. (It is, however, possible to understand τόπος

---

12 It would be possible to regard ἡ ἄμμος τῆς θαλάσσης, literally 'the sand of the sea,' as a type of idiom meaning 'beach.' Compare, for example, the meaning of ἄμμος[a] (2.28).

διθάλασσος in Ac 27.41 as a place of cross-currents; see 14.32.) In some languages it may be necessary to construct a descriptive equivalent for 'sandbank,' for example, 'a hill of sand just beneath the surface of the water' or 'a ridge of sand hidden by the water.'

J   Bodies of Water (1.69-1.78)

1.69 θάλασσα[a], ης f: a generic collective term for all bodies of water (in this sense θάλασσα[a] is contrasted with the sky and the land) – 'the sea.' ἐπιστρέφειν ἐπὶ θεὸν ζῶντα ὃς ἐποίησεν τὸν οὐρανὸν καὶ τὴν γῆν καὶ τὴν θάλασσαν καὶ πάντα τὰ ἐν αὐτοῖς 'turn to the living God who made heaven, earth, the sea, and all that is in them' Ac 14.15. This generic sense of θάλασσα[a] may be expressed in some languages as 'extensions of water' or simply as 'water.' In other instances it may be necessary to employ a phrase such as 'lakes and oceans,' while in certain languages a term for 'ocean' also has a generic sense of any extensive area of water.

1.70 θάλασσα[b], ης f: a particular body of water, normally rather large – 'sea, lake.' τὴν θάλασσαν τῆς Γαλιλαίας 'the lake of Galilee' Mt 4.18; ᾧ ἐστιν οἰκία παρὰ θάλασσαν 'whose house was beside the sea' Ac 10.6; ποιήσας τέρατα καὶ σημεῖα ἐν γῇ Αἰγύπτῳ καὶ ἐν Ἐρυθρᾷ Θαλάσσῃ 'performing wonders and signs in the land of Egypt and in the Red Sea' Ac 7.36.

The use of θάλασσα[b] to refer to a lake such as the Lake of Galilee (Mt 4.18; Mk 1.16) or the Lake of Tiberias (Jn 21.1) reflects Semitic usage, in which all bodies of water from oceans to pools could be referred to by a single term. Normal Greek usage would employ λίμνη 'lake, pool' (1.72).

Many languages make a clear distinction between different types of bodies of water. The three principal bases for differentiation are (1) fresh, brackish, or salty, (2) relative size, that is, large versus small bodies of water, and (3) existence of an outlet. On the basis of this third type of distinction, a term to designate the Sea of Galilee would need to be different from that used in speaking of the Dead Sea, since the Sea of Galilee has an outlet while the Dead Sea does not. Considerable care must be exercised in the choice of terms for such bodies of water, since failure to select the right terms may result in serious distortion of geography and therefore considerable misunderstanding of the geographical setting of biblical events.

1.71 παραθαλάσσιος, α, ον: pertaining to being located beside the sea or along the shore – 'by the seaside, by the lake.' Καφαρναοὺμ τὴν παραθαλασσίαν 'Capernaum by the lake' Mt 4.13.

1.72 λίμνη, ης f: a relatively small body of water either natural or artificial, surrounded by land – 'lake, pool.' αὐτὸς ἦν ἑστὼς παρὰ τὴν λίμνην Γεννησαρέτ 'he was standing on the shore of Lake Gennesaret' Lk 5.1. The use of λίμνη to refer to the Lake of Galilee (also called the Lake of Gennesaret) normally poses no special difficulty, but in the expression 'lake of fire' (Re 20.10) there are complications, as already noted in 1.22.

1.73 πέλαγος, ους n; πόντος, ου m; βυθός, οῦ m: the relatively deep area of the sea or ocean sufficiently far from land as to be beyond the range of any protection from the seacoast – 'open sea, high sea, the deep, ocean.'
πέλαγος: τό τε πέλαγος τὸ κατὰ τὴν Κιλικίαν καὶ Παμφυλίαν διαπλεύσαντες 'when we had sailed across the sea which is off Cilicia and Pamphylia' Ac 27.5.
πόντος: πᾶς ὁ ἐπὶ πόντον πλέων 'everyone sailing on the sea' Re 18.17 (apparatus).
βυθός: νυχθήμερον ἐν τῷ βυθῷ πεποίηκα 'I spent a day and a night in the open sea' 2 Cor 11.25.

In order to designate the high sea or the ocean, it may be necessary in some instances to speak of 'the sea far from land' or 'the sea out of sight of land.' People who live near the ocean and are seafaring frequently have quite distinct terms for different conditions of the sea, whether, for example, it is stormy, moderately rough, or relatively calm. Languages may also use different terms in speaking of different areas of the sea or ocean. Note, for example, in English the use of China Sea, North Sea, Bering Sea, in contrast with Indian Ocean, Pacific Ocean, Atlantic Ocean. In English this contrast is relatively fixed, but it does reflect a gradation of size, since *sea* is used normally in speaking of smaller areas than is the case with *ocean*.

1.74 κόλποςc**, ου** *m*: a part of the sea which is partially enclosed by land – 'bay, gulf.' κόλπον δέ τινα κατενόουν ἔχοντα αἰγιαλόν 'they noticed a bay with a beach' Ac 27.39. A 'bay' may be described as 'a protected area of the sea' or 'a part of the sea protected by land.'

1.75 λιμήν, ένος *m*: a relatively small area of the sea which is well protected by land but deep enough for ships to enter and moor – 'harbor.' ἀνευθέτου δὲ τοῦ λιμένος ὑπάρχοντος πρὸς παραχειμασίαν 'since the harbor was not convenient for spending the winter' Ac 27.12. λιμήν may be rendered in some languages by a descriptive phrase, 'a place where ships are safe from the storm' or 'a place where ships are never damaged' or 'a place where ships may stay.' In Ac 27.12 it is difficult to know whether the reference of λιμήν is to the harbor as a convenient place for the ships to stay during the winter, or to the port (that is to say, the town at the harbor) as a convenient place for people to stay during the winter. Some languages make a clear distinction between the area where ships stay and where people may stay waiting to continue their voyage.

1.76 ποταμός, οῦ *m*: a river or stream normally flowing throughout the year (in contrast with χείμαρρος**a** 'winter stream,' 1.77) – 'river, stream.' ἐβαπτίζοντο ἐν τῷ Ἰορδάνῃ ποταμῷ ὑπ' αὐτοῦ 'they were baptized in the Jordan river by him' Mt 3.6.

1.77 χείμαρροςa**, ου** *m* or **χείμαρρους**: a stream or river which flows only during the rainy season (in Palestine this would be during the winter months) or when melting snow from the mountains provides running water for a relatively short period of time – 'brook, winter stream, rainy-season stream.' Ἰησοῦς ἐξῆλθεν σὺν τοῖς μαθηταῖς αὐτοῦ πέραν τοῦ χειμάρρου τοῦ Κεδρών 'Jesus left with his disciples and went across the brook Kidron' Jn 18.1 (but the reference in Jn 18.1 is probably to the narrow valley, not to the stream itself, as noted in 1.52).

1.78 πηγήa**, ῆς** *f*: a source of water flowing onto the surface or into a pool somewhat below ground level – 'spring.' ἔπεσεν ἐπὶ τὸ τρίτον τῶν ποταμῶν καὶ ἐπὶ τὰς πηγὰς τῶν ὑδάτων 'it fell on a third of all the rivers and springs' Re 8.10. πηγή**a** 'spring' differs from φρέαρ**a** and πηγή**b** 'well' (see 7.57) in that a πηγή**a** is normally a natural source of water, in contrast with φρέαρ**a** and πηγή**b**, which are dug and into which a πηγή**a** may be said to flow.

K Sociopolitical Areas (1.79-1.81)

1.79 γῆd**, γῆς** *f*; **χώρα**b**, ας** *f*; **κλίμα, τος** *n*; **ὅριον, ου** *n* (always plural); **μέρος**c**, ους** *n* (always plural): region or regions of the earth, normally in relation to some ethnic group or geographical center, but not necessarily constituting a unit of governmental administration – 'region, territory, land' (and even 'district,' though this might imply too precisely a governmental area).[13] The meanings of γῆ**d**, χώρα**b**, κλίμα, ὅριον, and μέρος**c** are not to be regarded as completely synonymous, but in certain of their NT usages they are largely overlapping in reference.
γῆ**d**: γῆ Ζαβουλὼν καὶ γῆ Νεφθαλίμ, ὁδὸν θαλάσσης 'land of Zebulun, land of Naphtali, the road to the sea' Mt 4.15.
χώρα**b**: πάντες δὲ διεσπάρησαν κατὰ τὰς χώρας τῆς Ἰουδαίας καὶ Σαμαρείας πλὴν τῶν ἀποστόλων 'all the believers, except the apostles, were scattered throughout the regions of Judea and Samaria' Ac 8.1.
κλίμα: ἔπειτα ἦλθον εἰς τὰ κλίματα τῆς Συρίας καὶ τῆς Κιλικίας 'then I went to the regions of Syria and Cilicia' Ga 1.21.
ὅριον: πάλιν ἐξελθὼν ἐκ τῶν ὁρίων Τύρου ἦλθεν διὰ Σιδῶνος εἰς τὴν θάλασσαν τῆς Γαλιλαίας 'he

---

13 The overlapping features of meaning in γῆ**d**, χώρα**b**, κλίμα, ὅριον, and μέρος**c** may be readily illustrated by the comparable overlapping of English terms such as *region, territory,* and *land*. For example, in the case of Mt 15.21 it would be possible to speak of *the region of Tyre and Sidon, the territory of Tyre and Sidon, the land of Tyre and Sidon,* and even *the district of Tyre and Sidon*. The English terms *region, territory, land,* and *district* do differ in certain nuances of meaning reflecting primarily supplementary components which are largely connotative.

then left the territory of Tyre and went through Sidon to Lake Galilee' Mk 7.31; ἐν Βηθλέεμ καὶ ἐν πᾶσι τοῖς ὁρίοις αὐτῆς 'in Bethlehem and in all the region around there' Mt 2.16.

μέρος^c: ὁ Ἰησοῦς ἀνεχώρησεν εἰς τὰ μέρη Τύρου καὶ Σιδῶνος 'Jesus departed for the regions of Tyre and Sidon' Mt 15.21.

1.80 περίχωρος, ου *f*: an area or region around or near some central or focal point – 'surrounding region.' ἀπέστειλαν εἰς ὅλην τὴν περίχωρον ἐκείνην 'and they sent into all the surrounding region' Mt 14.35. In certain contexts, however, περίχωρος may include not only the surrounding region but also the point of reference, for example, τῆς περιχώρου τῶν Γερασηνῶν 'the Gerasenes and the people living around them' Lk 8.37. In a context such as Mt 3.5, ἡ περίχωρος τοῦ Ἰορδάνου, it is difficult to speak of 'the area surrounding the Jordan River,' since a river is not like a city which would constitute a center. Accordingly, one must often translate ἡ περίχωρος τοῦ Ἰορδάνου as 'the land on both sides of the River Jordan.'

1.81 πατρίς, ίδος *f*: the region or population center from which a person comes, that is to say, the place of one's birth or childhood or the place from which one's family has come – 'homeland, hometown.' ἔρχεται εἰς τὴν πατρίδα αὐτοῦ 'he came to his hometown' Mk 6.1.

In some languages a very clear distinction is made between three different references of a term such as πατρίς: (1) the place from which one's family has come, (2) the place where one is born, and (3) the place where one normally resides. Special care, therefore, must be exercised in translating a passage such as Mk 6.1.

L Governmental Administrative Areas (1.82-1.85)

1.82 βασιλεία^b, ας *f*: an area or district ruled by a king – 'kingdom.' ὅ τι ἐάν με αἰτήσῃς δώσω σοι ἕως ἡμίσους τῆς βασιλείας μου 'whatever you ask me for, I will give it to you, up to half of my kingdom' Mk 6.23. Since in many areas of the world kingship is not

known (that is to say, the succession of rulers within a family and by inheritance), it may not be possible to find a technical term meaning 'kingdom.' Usually, however, one may employ an expression which is roughly equivalent in meaning to 'domain,' so that, for example, the last part of Mk 6.23 may be rendered as 'up to a half of the region which I rule.'

1.83 οἰκουμένη^b, ης *f*: the Roman Empire, including its inhabitants (οἰκουμένη^b differs from οἰκουμένη^a 'earth,' 1.39, in that those outside of the Roman Empire are specifically excluded, that is to say, no census was to be taken of the barbarians, but only of the inhabitants of the Empire) – 'empire, people of the empire.' ἐξῆλθεν δόγμα παρὰ Καίσαρος Αὐγούστου ἀπογράφεσθαι πᾶσαν τὴν οἰκουμένην 'Emperor Augustus sent out an order for all the people of the empire to register themselves for the census' Lk 2.1.¹⁴ In order to represent accurately the meaning of οἰκουμένη^b in Lk 2.1 it may be possible to translate 'Emperor Augustus sent out an order that all the people over whom he ruled should register themselves for the census.'

1.84 ἐπαρχεία, ας *f*: a part of the Roman Empire (usually acquired by conquest) and constituting an administrative unit ruled over by an ἔπαρχος selected by the Roman Senate – 'province, region.' ἐπερωτήσας ἐκ ποίας ἐπαρχείας ἐστίν 'asked what province he was from' Ac 23.34.

1.85 μερίς^b, ίδος *f*: an administrative district – 'district.' κἀκεῖθεν εἰς Φιλίππους, ἥτις ἐστὶν πρώτης μερίδος τῆς Μακεδονίας πόλις 'and from there into Philippi which is a city in the first district of Macedonia' Ac 16.12. In Ac 16.12 (the only occurrence of μερίς^b in the NT) the Greek New Testament published by the United Bible Societies has adopted a conjectural emendation, since the more tradi-

14 In Lk 2.1 οἰκουμένη^b refers specifically to the inhabitants of the empire, though the meaning of οἰκουμένη^b is simply the Roman Empire as a region, a governmental entity, and a population.

tional text, πρώτη τῆς μερίδος, literally 'first of the district,' is not only misleading in meaning but does not reflect the historical fact that Philippi was a city in one of the four districts of Macedonia but was not a capital city.

M Areas Which Are Uninhabited or Only Sparsely Populated (1.86-1.87)

1.86 ἐρημία, ας f; ἔρημος[b], ον (τόπος): a largely uninhabited region, normally with sparse vegetation (in contrast with πόλις[a] 'a population center,' 1.88) – 'desert, wilderness, lonely place.'
ἐρημία: κινδύνοις ἐν ἐρημίᾳ 'dangers in the desert' 2 Cor 11.26.
ἔρημος[b] (with or without τόπος): ὁ Ἰησοῦς ἀνεχώρησεν ἐκεῖθεν ἐν πλοίῳ εἰς ἔρημον τόπον κατ' ἰδίαν 'Jesus left that place in a boat and went to a lonely place by himself' Mt 14.13; ἐὰν οὖν εἴπωσιν ὑμῖν, Ἰδοὺ ἐν τῇ ἐρήμῳ ἐστίν 'if then they say to you, Look, he is in the desert' Mt 24.26.

The phrase ἄνυδρος τόπος (Mt 12.43, Lk 11.24), literally 'waterless place,' is a set phrase equivalent to ἐρημία and may be translated as 'wilderness' or 'uninhabited country.'

Throughout the NT ἐρημία and ἔρημος[b] focus primarily upon the lack of population rather than upon sparse vegetation, though the two features are closely related ecologically in the Middle East.

In most languages the most satisfactory equivalent of ἐρημία and ἔρημος[b] is a word or phrase suggesting a place where few if any people live. Such expressions are generally far better than a word meaning 'a bare place' or 'a place of sand,' since in some languages such expressions could mean only a clearing in the forest or a sandy beach along a river bank. In the case of translations being made for people living in jungle areas, it may, however, be necessary to describe in a footnote the nature of an ἐρημία in NT times.

1.87 χώρα[c], ας f; ἀγρός[b], οῦ m: a rural area in contrast with a population center – 'countryside, fields, rural area.'
χώρα[c]: οἱ ἐν ταῖς χώραις μὴ εἰσερχέσθωσαν εἰς αὐτήν 'those in the country must not go into it (the city)' Lk 21.21.
ἀγρός[b]: ἀπήγγειλαν εἰς τὴν πόλιν καὶ εἰς τοὺς ἀγρούς 'they announced it in the city and in the countryside' Mk 5.14.

A rural area is often identified by a term or phrase meaning 'extension of fields' or 'place of field after field' or 'area of farms.'

N Population Centers (1.88-1.94)

1.88 πόλις[a], εως f: a population center, in contrast with a rural area or countryside and without specific reference to size – 'city, town.' ἀκούσαντες οἱ ὄχλοι ἠκολούθησαν αὐτῷ πεζῇ ἀπὸ τῶν πόλεων 'people heard about it, left their towns, and followed him by land' Mt 14.13; τότε ἤρξατο ὀνειδίζειν τὰς πόλεις ἐν αἷς ἐγένοντο αἱ πλεῖσται δυνάμεις αὐτοῦ . . . οὐαί σοι, Βηθσαϊδά 'then he began to reproach the cities where he had performed most of his miracles . . . how terrible it will be for you too, Bethsaida!' Mt 11.20-21.[15]

1.89 πόλις[b], εως f: a population center of relatively greater importance (in contrast with κώμη[a] 'village,' 1.92, and κωμόπολις 'town,' 1.91), due to its size, economic significance, or political control over a surrounding area (it is possible that fortification of walls and gates also entered into the system of classification of a πόλις[b], in contrast with other terms for population centers) – 'city.' περιῆγεν ὁ Ἰησοῦς τὰς πόλεις πάσας καὶ τὰς κώμας 'Jesus went about all the cities and towns' Mt 9.35; ἀσπάζεται ὑμᾶς Ἔραστος ὁ οἰκονόμος τῆς πόλεως 'Erastus, the city treasurer, sends you greetings' Ro 16.23. Most languages spoken by people in urbanized and industrialized

15 In contrast with Mt 11.21 in which Bethsaida is spoken of as a πόλις, in Mk 8.23 and 26 Bethsaida is specifically referred to as a κώμη (1.92). This diversity may simply reflect a difference of usage between two authors. A similar distinction, however, exists also in the case of Bethlehem. In Jn 7.42 Bethlehem is called a κώμη, and in Lk 2.4, a πόλις. These differences can probably be attributed to differences in individual usage; that is to say, the distinctions in size between a πόλις and a κώμη were not fixed, or one author used πόλις in the generic sence in contrast with the specific sense. This does not affect the generic meaning of πόλις[a] as a population center in contrast with a rural area.

societies have a number of terms for different types of population centers, for example, metropolis, city, town, village, hamlet, etc. For so-called tribal languages the primary means for making gradations consists of added attributives, for example, 'a very large village,' 'a large village,' 'a village,' 'a small village.' A translator must simply attempt to be as consistent as possible in referring to different types of population centers mentioned in the Scriptures.

1.90 κολωνία, ας *f*: a city or town with special privileges in that the inhabitants of such a town were regarded as Roman citizens (such towns were originally colonized by citizens of Rome) – 'colony.' εἰς Φιλίππους . . . κολωνία 'to Philippi . . . a colony' Ac 16.12. A translational equivalent of 'colony' is frequently a phrase, for example, 'a city where people were Romans' or 'a city of people who regarded Rome as their hometown.'

1.91 κωμόπολις, εως *f*: a city that had the status of a κώμη (1.92) as far as its legal standing or constitution was concerned – 'town, market town.' ἄγωμεν ἀλλαχοῦ εἰς τὰς ἐχομένας κωμοπόλεις 'let us go elsewhere to the nearby towns' Mk 1.38.

1.92 κώμηᵃ, **ης** *f*: a relatively unimportant population center (in contrast with πόλιςᵇ 'city,' 1.89) – 'village.' ἐξήνεγκεν αὐτὸν ἔξω τῆς κώμης 'he led him outside of the village' Mk 8.23.

1.93 ἀγρόςᶜ, **οῦ** *m*: a relatively small village, possibly merely a cluster of farms – 'farm settlement, hamlet.' ὅπου ἂν εἰσεπορεύετο εἰς κώμας ἢ εἰς πόλεις ἢ εἰς ἀγροὺς ἐν ταῖς ἀγοραῖς ἐτίθεσαν τοὺς ἀσθενοῦντας 'wherever he would go in the villages or cities or farm settlements, they would lay the sick in the markets' Mk 6.56.

1.94 παρεμβολήᵃ, **ῆς** *f*: a temporary population center consisting of an encampment – 'camp.' τούτων τὰ σώματα κατακαίεται ἔξω τῆς παρεμβολῆς 'but the bodies of the animals are burned outside the camp' He 13.11. The

equivalent of 'camp' in the context of He 13.11 is often 'a city of tents' or 'where people lived only for a short time.'[16]

O Pastures and Cultivated Lands (1.95-1.98)

1.95 χώραᵈ, **ας** *f*; **χωρίον, ου** *n*; **ἀγρός**ᵃ, **οῦ** *m*: land under cultivation or used for pasture – 'field, land.'
χώραᵈ: θεάσασθε τὰς χώρας ὅτι λευκαί εἰσιν πρὸς θερισμόν 'look, the fields are white, ready to be harvested' Jn 4.35.
χωρίον: ἐκτήσατο χωρίον 'he bought a field' Ac 1.18.
ἀγρόςᵃ: ὁ εἰς τὸν ἀγρὸν μὴ ἐπιστρεφάτω εἰς τὰ ὀπίσω ἆραι τὸ ἱμάτιον αὐτοῦ 'the man in the field must not even go back for his cloak' Mk 13.16.

1.96 γεώργιον, ου *n*: cultivated land, normally restricted to tilled fields or orchards, in contrast with pasture land (in the NT γεώργιον is used only figuratively of people whom God cares for and nurtures) – 'field.' θεοῦ γεώργιον, θεοῦ οἰκοδομή ἐστε 'you are God's field, you are God's building' 1 Cor 3.9.

1.97 κῆπος, ου *m*: a field used for the cultivation of herbs, fruits, flowers, or vegetables – 'garden, orchard.' ἔβαλεν εἰς κῆπον ἑαυτοῦ 'he plants in his garden' Lk 13.19.

1.98 νομήᵃ, **ῆς** *f*: pasture land in contrast with cultivated fields – 'pasture.' ἐξελεύσεται καὶ νομὴν εὑρήσει 'he will go out and find pasture' Jn 10.9. 'Pastures' are often designated as 'grass land' or 'cattle land.'

P Thoroughfares: Roads, Streets, Paths, etc. (1.99-1.105)

1.99 ὁδόςᵃ, **οῦ** *f*: a general term for a thoroughfare, either within a population center or between two such centers – 'road, highway, street, way.' δι' ἄλλης ὁδοῦ ἀνεχώρησαν 'they

16 Compare the meaning of παρεμβολήᵇ (7.22) as a construction consisting of barracks for soldiers.

went back another way' or '. . . by another road' Mt 2.12.

1.100 τρίβος, ου f: a well-worn path or thoroughfare – 'path, beaten path.' εὐθείας ποιεῖτε τὰς τρίβους αὐτοῦ 'make the paths he travels on straight' Mk 1.3.

1.101 ἄμφοδον, ου n: a thoroughfare within a city – 'city street.' εὗρον πῶλον δεδεμένον πρὸς θύραν ἔξω ἐπὶ τοῦ ἀμφόδου 'they found a colt tied at a door outside on the street' Mk 11.4.

1.102 διέξοδος, ου f: possibly a street crossing, but more probably the place where a principal thoroughfare crosses a city boundary and extends into the open country – 'where a main street leaves the city' (possibly at the city wall). πορεύεσθε οὖν ἐπὶ τὰς διεξόδους τῶν ὁδῶν 'go then to where the main streets leave the city' Mt 22.9.

1.103 πλατεῖα, ας f: a wide street within a city – 'avenue, wide street.' οὐδὲ ἀκούσει τις ἐν ταῖς πλατείαις τὴν φωνὴν αὐτοῦ 'nor will anyone hear his voice in the wide streets' Mt 12.19.

1.104 ῥύμη, ης f: a city thoroughfare which is relatively narrow – 'narrow street, lane, alley.' προῆλθον ῥύμην μίαν 'they walked down a narrow street' Ac 12.10.

1.105 φραγμός[b], οῦ m: a path or area along a fence, wall, or hedge (where desperately poor people might stay) – 'byway, path.' ἔξελθε εἰς τὰς ὁδοὺς καὶ φραγμούς 'go out into the highways and byways' Lk 14.23.

2 Natural Substances[1]

Outline of Subdomains

A   Elements (2.1)
B   Air (2.2)
C   Fire (2.3-2.6)
D   Water (2.7-2.13)
E   Earth, Mud, Sand, Rock (2.14-2.28)
F   Precious and Semiprecious Stones and Substances (2.29-2.48)
G   Metals (2.49-2.62)

1 From the standpoint of presuppositions of the ancient world as reflected in the NT, the most relevant way in which to classify the basic elements is in terms of air, fire, water, and earth (including soil, mud, clay, rock, precious and semiprecious stones, and metals), but for the convenience of those using this dictionary this fourth category has been subdivided into three subdomains. The Greek term ἀήρ 'air' occurs in the NT with the meaning of substance only in an idiom-like expression in 1 Cor 9.26; elsewhere it is used to designate space (see 1.6). At no point in the NT are air, fire, water, and earth specifically described as constituting the basic elements (Greek στοιχεῖα), but the occurrence of στοιχεῖα in 2 Pe 3.10 (see 2.1) appears to be a clear reference to these natural substances.

A   Elements (2.1)

2.1 στοιχεῖα[a], ων n (always occurring in the plural): the materials of which the world and the universe are composed – 'elements, natural substances.' στοιχεῖα δὲ καυσούμενα λυθήσεται 'the elements will be destroyed by burning' 2 Pe 3.10. In many languages the closest equivalent of στοιχεῖα is 'the things of which the world is made' or 'what the world is made of' or 'the substances of which the universe consists.'

B   Air (2.2)

2.2 ἀήρ[b], έρος m: air as an elemental substance – 'air.' οὕτως πυκτεύω ὡς οὐκ ἀέρα δέρων 'I do not box like someone hitting the air' 1 Cor 9.26. In some languages it may be quite impossible to translate literally 'hitting the air,' for since the air is not regarded as a kind of material substance, it is impossible to hit it. The closest equivalent may be 'hitting nothing' or possibly 'as though hitting something.'

C Fire (2.3-2.6)

2.3 πῦρᵃ, ός *n* – 'fire.' οἱ δὲ νῦν οὐρανοὶ καὶ ἡ γῆ τῷ αὐτῷ λόγῳ τεθησαυρισμένοι εἰσὶν πυρί 'but the heavens and earth that now exist are being preserved by the same word (of God) for destruction by fire' 2 Pe 3.7. Though the ancient view of the elements would lead to classification of this occurrence of πῦρ as referring to a natural substance, the fact that the reference is to a particular event means that in many languages one must speak of a 'burning,' and this must be expressed frequently by a verb or participle rather than by a noun, for example, 'for destruction by being burned up.'

2.4 φλόξ, φλογός *f*: the burning vapor surrounding an object on fire – 'flame.' ὤφθη αὐτῷ ἐν τῇ ἐρήμῳ τοῦ ὄρους Σινᾶ ἄγγελος ἐν φλογὶ πυρὸς βάτου 'an angel appeared to him in the flames of a burning bush in the desert near Mount Sinai' Ac 7.30. As in the case of πῦρᵃ 'fire' (2.3), the term φλόξ 'flame' is likewise frequently rendered by a verb rather than by a noun. Accordingly, in a passage such as Ac 7.30 'in the flames of a burning bush' becomes 'where the burning bush was flaming up' or 'where flames were burning a bush.' In some languages 'flames' are referred to as 'the tongues of the fire' or 'the banner of the fire.' In a number of languages, however, no distinction is made between 'fire' and 'flame.'

2.5 πυρά, ᾶς *f*; πῦρᵇ, ός *n*; φῶςᵇ, φωτός *n*: a pile or heap of burning material – 'fire, bonfire.'

πυρά: ἅψαντες γὰρ πυρὰν προσελάβοντο πάντας ἡμᾶς 'for they kindled a fire and welcomed us all' Ac 28.2.

πῦρᵇ: περιαψάντων δὲ πῦρ ἐν μέσῳ τῆς αὐλῆς 'a fire had been lit in the center of the courtyard' Lk 22.55.

φῶςᵇ: ὁ Πέτρος . . . ἦν συγκαθήμενος μετὰ τῶν ὑπηρετῶν καὶ θερμαινόμενος πρὸς τὸ φῶς 'Peter . . . was sitting together with the guards and was warming himself at the fire' Mk 14.54.

The Greek phrase ἅψαντες . . . πυρὰν 'to kindle a fire' is best rendered in a number of languages by a single verb meaning 'to make a fire,' and in some languages it is strange to speak of a 'fire' without indicating the type of material which is being burned. Hence, in Ac 28.2 the appropriate equivalent would be 'they caused some sticks to burn.'

In some languages a very important distinction is made between two functionally different kinds of fire, one used for getting rid of refuse and the other used for warming oneself. Fire as a destructive agent, mentioned frequently in the book of Revelation (Re 8.5 and 20.9), may require quite a different term from what is used in speaking of a fire for the purpose of warming a person or heating an object.

2.6 ἀνθρακιά, ᾶς *f* – 'charcoal fire.' οἱ δοῦλοι καὶ οἱ ὑπηρέται ἀνθρακιὰν πεποιηκότες 'the servants and officers had made a charcoal fire' Jn 18.18. The occurrence of ἀνθρακιά 'charcoal fire' in Jn 18.18 fits the context well, since a charcoal fire provides a maximum of heat with a minimum of smoke. The making and use of charcoal is widespread throughout the world, and there is generally no difficulty in obtaining a satisfactory term for 'charcoal.' However, where such a term does not exist, it is possible to speak of 'a wood fire' or simply 'a fire.'

D Water (2.7-2.13)

2.7 ὕδωρ, ὕδατος *n* – 'water.' γῆ ἐξ ὕδατος καὶ δι' ὕδατος συνεστῶσα . . . δι' ὧν ὁ τότε κόσμος ὕδατι κατακλυσθεὶς ἀπώλετο 'the earth was formed out of water, and by water . . . and it was by water also, the water of the Flood, that the old world was destroyed' 2 Pe 3.5-6. In 2 Pe 3.5 the Greek expression is admittedly both strange and obscure. ἐξ ὕδατος presumably refers to the fact that the land emerged from the water, or at least was separated from the water. The phrase δι' ὕδατος, literally 'through water,' may be locative, that is to say, it may refer to a place, but it is more likely to have some reference to water as an instrument which contributed to the act of producing the heavens and earth. However, the active instrument for this creation was τῷ τοῦ θεοῦ λόγῳ 'the word of God.' Since the dative case ὕδατι 'by water' is clearly instrumental in verse 6, it may be that ἐξ ὕδατος καὶ δι' ὕδατος in verse 5 refers in a spatial sense to the formation of the heavens and the dry land 'from water and through a watery area.'

Even more complex, however, than the interpretation of 'water' in 2 Pe 3.5-6 is the fact that in a number of languages there are quite different terms for ὕδωρ depending upon the type of water, its location, and its function. For example, water in some kind of bowl or container (and thus most likely used for drinking or cooking) may be referred to by one term, while water in a lake, stream, or ocean may be identified by quite a different term. Similarly, an important distinction may be made between salt water and fresh water, and an even further distinction may be introduced in the case of brackish water, that is to say, water which is partially salty. Some languages make a distinction between water which collects in pools and water which is flowing in streams or rivers. Accordingly, careful attention must be paid to contexts in order to select the appropriate term for ὕδωρ (see also 8.64 on Jn 19.34).

2.8 ἄνυδρος, ον: pertaining to the absence of water or moisture – 'waterless, dry.' νεφέλαι ἄνυδροι ὑπὸ ἀνέμων παραφερόμεναι 'they are clouds that give no rain, driven by the winds' Jd 12. See also 1.86 for ἄνυδρος τόπος 'lonely place.'

In the NT ἄνυδρος occurs in the figurative expressions 'waterless springs' (2 Pe 2.17) and 'waterless clouds.' A phrase such as 'waterless springs' may be rendered simply as 'springs in which there is no water,' but in some languages such a phrase would seem to be a complete contradiction, since a term for 'spring' would imply the existence of water. It may therefore be necessary to translate 'waterless springs' as 'springs which have ceased to produce water.' 'Waterless clouds' are often best rendered as 'clouds which will not produce rain' or 'clouds from which no rain will fall.' In Jd 12 the phrase 'waterless clouds' is a description of persons whose teaching and behavior are of no value in building up the faith of believers. Such a metaphor must often be changed into a simile, for example, 'they are like clouds which do not produce rain.'

2.9 ἰκμάς, άδος f – 'moisture.' ἐξηράνθη διὰ τὸ μὴ ἔχειν ἰκμάδα 'it dried up because it did not have moisture' Lk 8.6. 'It did not have moisture' may be expressed as 'there was no water in the soil' or 'the ground was not wet.'

2.10 ὑετός[a], οῦ m – 'rain, rain water.' γῆ γὰρ ἡ πιοῦσα τὸν ἐπ' αὐτῆς ἐρχόμενον πολλάκις ὑετόν 'the ground absorbs the rain that often falls on it' He 6.7. Though ὑετός, which means rain as a substance (for 'the event of raining,' see 14.10), generally occurs in contexts in which the focus is upon the event of raining as supplied by a verb (for example, Ac 14.17, Jas 5.18, and Re 11.6), in He 6.7 the focus is clearly upon the substance. Though the Greek text of He 6.7 speaks literally of the ground 'drinking the rain,' this figurative expression can rarely be reproduced. Sometimes one can use an expression such as 'soaks up,' the type of term which might be employed in speaking of a sponge soaking up moisture, but in a number of instances one can only speak of 'the rain disappearing into the earth' or 'the earth causing the rain to disappear into it.'

Translators may be confronted with several problems in selecting an appropriate term for 'rain,' since some languages make important distinctions in terms for 'rain' depending upon the season of the year and the quantity of rain. For example, rain falling in the dry season may be called by quite a different term from that which falls in the rainy season. Similarly, a series of distinctions may be made in terms for rain depending upon whether one is speaking of a torrential rainstorm or an average rain or a continuous mist.

2.11 κρύσταλλος[b], ου m: frozen water – 'ice.' ἔδειξέν μοι ποταμὸν ὕδατος ζωῆς λαμπρὸν ὡς κρύσταλλον 'showed me the river of the water of life, sparkling like ice' Re 22.1. In both Re 4.6 and 22.1 (the only two passages in which κρύσταλλος occurs in the NT) the meaning may, however, be 'rock crystal' rather than 'ice' (see 2.46).

Though in the Arctic regions people may have a number of different terms for various kinds and forms of ice, there are many areas in the world in which there is no existing local term for 'ice.' Sometimes a descriptive phrase such as 'hardened water' is employed, and in a number of languages a term is simply borrowed from a dominant language of the region. However, in Re 4.6 and 22.1 it is possible to focus upon the brilliance of color rather than the particular substance and thus to speak of λαμπρὸς ὡς κρύσταλλος as 'that which is sparkling white' or '. . . bright white.'

2.12 χιών, όνος f – 'snow.' λευκὸν ὡς χιών 'white as snow' Mt 28.3 (see also 79.27). In the NT χιών occurs only as a symbol of complete whiteness, and hence in those cases in which a receptor language may not have any term for snow, it is possible to use a nonfigurative expression such as 'very, very white.' In a number of languages, however, there may not be a specific term for snow but a type of descriptive phrase reflecting people's knowledge about snow, even though the substance may not occur in their immediate vicinity. For example, in some instances snow is spoken of as 'volcano frost.' In certain parts of the world, however, the translator's problem is not in finding a term for snow but in distinguishing between a number of different terms which designate distinct types of snow and snow formations. Under such circumstances one can simply use for 'snow' an expression which suggests the whitest variety or that form of snow which is most commonly referred to.

2.13 χάλαζα, ης f: frozen rain – 'hail.' ἐγένετο χάλαζα καὶ πῦρ μεμιγμένα ἐν αἵματι 'there was hail and fire mixed with blood' Re 8.7. In Re 8.7 and 16.21 it is possible that χάλαζα is better interpreted as referring to a 'hailstorm.'

In a number of languages hail is described as 'frozen rain,' but it may be referred to by more idiomatic expressions such as 'cloud stones' or 'ice stones.'

E Earth, Mud, Sand, Rock (2.14-2.28)

2.14 γῆ[c], γῆς f – 'soil, ground.'[2] ἔπεσεν ἐπὶ τὰ πετρώδη ὅπου οὐκ εἶχεν γῆν πολλήν 'some fell on rocky ground where there was not much

soil' Mt 13.5. The meaning of γῆ[c] may be expressed in some instances as 'soil for planting' or 'ground for plants.'

2.15 χοῦς, χοός, acc. χοῦν m; κονιορτός, οῦ m – 'dust, soil' (see also 2.16).
χοῦς: ἐκτινάξατε τὸν χοῦν τὸν ὑποκάτω ποδῶν ὑμῶν 'shake the dust from your feet' Mk 6.11. κονιορτός: ἐκτινάξατε τὸν κονιορτὸν τῶν ποδῶν ὑμῶν 'shake the dust from your feet' Mt 10.14.

'Shake the dust from your feet' may be expressed as 'kick the dust from your feet.' In some instances, however, the more appropriate equivalent would be 'get rid of the dust from your feet' or even 'remove the dust from your feet and leave it there.'

2.16 χοϊκός[a], ή, όν: (derivative of χοῦς 'dust,' 2.15) pertaining to being made or consisting of dust or soil – 'made of dust, made of soil.' ὁ πρῶτος ἄνθρωπος ἐκ γῆς χοϊκός 'the first man was made of the dust of the earth' 1 Cor 15.47. Though in general χοῦς and the derivative χοϊκός would seem to refer to dry dust, they may also refer to dirt or soil. In 1 Cor 15.47 it is more appropriate to speak of the creation of Adam as 'made from the ground' or 'formed out of soil.' For another interpretation of χοϊκός in 1 Cor 15.47, see 1.42.

2.17 βόρβορος, ου m: watery mud, with an additional feature of filth and uncleanness – 'mud, mire.' ὗς λουσαμένη εἰς κυλισμὸν βορβόρου 'a pig that has been washed goes back to roll in the mud' 2 Pe 2.22.

2.18 πηλός, οῦ m: moistened earth of a clay consistency – 'mud, clay.' ἔπτυσεν χαμαὶ καὶ ἐποίησεν πηλὸν ἐκ τοῦ πτύσματος 'he spat on the ground and made some mud with the spittle' Jn 9.6. πηλός contrasts with βόρβορος 'watery mud' (2.17) and refers to moist earth with a consistency of clay. It may be translated in some languages as 'sticky soil' or 'clay-like mud' or 'moist dirt.'

---

2 Although in the NT γῆ does not occur as a reference to all solid substances in contrast with fire, air, and water, it does so occur in Classical and Hellenistic Greek. This generic meaning of γῆ as an element is thus not part of the lexical inventory of the NT, but γῆ[c], a designation for 'soil, ground,' does occur.

In Ro 9.21 (ἢ οὐκ ἔχει ἐξουσίαν ὁ κεραμεὺς τοῦ πηλοῦ 'or doesn't the man who makes the pots have the right to use the clay as he wishes') the reference is specifically ·to potter's clay. The meaning of πηλός, therefore, may be defined as any kind of moist earth with clay consistency. πηλός includes the area of meaning of κέραμος 'potter's clay' (a meaning not occurring in the NT).

Since pottery is so widely known throughout the world, there is normally no difficulty in obtaining a term which refers to potter's clay. Even when the making of pottery is not known, it is usually possible to obtain a satisfactory term for such clay, for example, 'mud that can be molded' or 'mud for shaping pots.'

2.19 κεραμικός, ή, όν: (derivative of κέραμος 'potter's clay,' not occurring in the NT) pertaining to being made of potter's clay – 'made of clay, clay.' ὡς τὰ σκεύη τὰ κεραμικὰ συντρίβεται 'they shall be broken like clay pots' Re 2.27. In some languages it may seem unduly repetitious to speak of 'clay pots,' since a term for pot may refer only to objects made of clay. In biblical times, however, some σκεύη were of metal and others were of stone and wood. It may be possible to translate this expression in Re 2.27 as 'they shall be broken like pots' or '. . . like dishes.'

2.20 ὀστράκινος, η, ον: pertaining to being made of baked clay – 'earthenware, clay.' σκεύη χρυσᾶ καὶ ἀργυρᾶ ἀλλὰ καὶ ξύλινα καὶ ὀστράκινα 'vessels of gold and silver but also of wood and clay' 2 Tm 2.20.

2.21 πέτρα, ας f: bedrock (possibly covered with a thin layer of soil), rocky crags, or mountain ledges, in contrast with separate pieces of rock normally referred to as λίθος[a] (see 2.23) – 'rock, bedrock.'[3] ὁμοιωθήσεται ἀνδρὶ φρονίμῳ, ὅστις ᾠκοδόμησεν αὐτοῦ τὴν οἰκίαν ἐπὶ τὴν πέτραν 'he is like a wise man who built his house on bedrock' Mt 7.25; ἔθηκεν αὐτὸν ἐν

μνημείῳ ὃ ἦν λελατομημένον ἐκ πέτρας 'they then put him in a grave which had been hewn from rock' Mk 15.46; λέγουσιν τοῖς ὄρεσιν καὶ ταῖς πέτραις, Πέσετε ἐφ' ἡμᾶς 'they said to the mountains and to the rock cliffs, Fall on us' Re 6.16. In these three contexts πέτρα must be translated in some languages by three quite different terms. Bedrock, that is to say, the rock which lies horizontally and often just below the surface, may be referred to by one term, while rock with an exposed face into which a tomb could be hewn would be quite different. Similarly, the rocks which would be called upon to fall upon people would be rendered by a term referring to 'cliffs' or 'precipices.'

In Lk 8.6 the term πέτρα in ἕτερον κατέπεσεν ἐπὶ τὴν πέτραν 'other (seed) fell on rocky ground' refers to bedrock which may be covered with a thin layer of soil. One may translate such an expression as 'thin ground over rock' or 'just a little soil on top of rock.'

In those passages which involve a play on words with the name Πέτρος 'Peter,' πέτρα refers to bedrock, that is to say, the rock on which a foundation may be placed.

2.22 πετρῶδες, ους n: (derivative of πέτρα 'bedrock,' 2.21) a rocky substance or bedrock covered by a thin layer of earth – 'rocky ground.' ἄλλα δὲ ἔπεσεν ἐπὶ τὰ πετρώδη ὅπου οὐκ εἶχεν γῆν πολλήν 'some fell on the rocky ground where it did not have much earth' Mt 13.5.

2.23 λίθος[a], ου m: stone as a substance – 'stone.'[4] οὐκ ὀφείλομεν νομίζειν χρυσῷ ἢ ἀργύρῳ ἢ λίθῳ, χαράγματι τέχνης καὶ ἐνθυμήσεως

---

3 In Ro 9.33 and 1 Pe 2.8 πέτρα occurs in parallelism with λίθος 'stone,' as a quotation from Is 8.14. On the basis of this usage one might argue that λίθος and πέτρα are completely synonymous, at least in this context. One would then have to describe πέτρα as having two dif-

ferent meanings, one 'rock' and another 'stone.' Parallelism, however, does not mean identity of meaning. In fact, parallelism (in contrast with tautology) normally implies slight differences of meaning in corresponding lexical units.

4 A distinction is made here between λίθος[a] 'stone as a substance' (2.23) and λίθος[b] 'stone as a particular piece of rock' (2.24). It would be possible to combine these two meanings, since in so many instances there is an almost automatic shift between a substance and an object consisting of such a substance. Since, however, a number of languages make clear distinctions between terms for substances and those referring to corresponding objects, this difference in meaning is retained in the case of λίθος and in most instances of similar semantic associations.

ἀνθρώπου, τὸ θεῖον εἶναι ὅμοιον 'we should not think that God is like an image of gold or silver or stone made by human skill and imagination' Ac 17.29.

2.24 λίθος[b], **ου** *m*: a piece of rock, whether shaped or natural – 'stone.' εἰπὲ ἵνα οἱ λίθοι οὗτοι ἄρτοι γένωνται 'order these stones to turn into bread' Mt 4.3.

Some languages make an important distinction between 'stone' as a substance (as in Ac 17.29) and 'stones' as individual pieces of rock (as in Mt 4.3). The term λίθος in the NT may be employed in speaking of rather large stones, for example, the stone placed in front of the tomb of Jesus (Mt 27.60) and the stones of the foundation of the Temple buildings (Mt 24.2). In all such contexts, however, the reference is to stones which have been moved into position or which are capable of being moved, even though with some difficulty.

In some languages an important distinction is made between stones which are shaped for use in building and stones which occur in a natural form, for example, 'field stones.' In each instance the biblical context must be studied to determine what type of expression should be used.

2.25 λίθινος, η, ον: (derivative of λίθος[a] 'stone,' 2.23) pertaining to being made of or consisting of stone – 'stone, made out of stone.' ἦσαν δὲ ἐκεῖ λίθιναι ὑδρίαι ἓξ κατὰ τὸν καθαρισμὸν τῶν Ἰουδαίων κείμεναι 'there were six stone water jars used for Jewish ceremonial cleansings' Jn 2.6. In speaking of objects 'made of stone' it may be necessary in some languages to indicate more precisely the manner in which such objects have been formed, for example, 'hewn out of stone' or 'made from stone by chipping.'

2.26 θεῖον[b], **ου** *n* – 'sulfur, brimstone.' ἔβρεξεν πῦρ καὶ θεῖον ἀπ' οὐρανοῦ 'fire and sulfur rained down from heaven' Lk 17.29. In the NT θεῖον is always associated in some way with fire and refers to the kinds of burning hot rocks involved in volcanic eruptions. The closest equivalent in a number of languages is 'burning stones' or 'fiery hot stones' or 'fiery red stones.'

2.27 ψῆφος, ου *f* – 'pebble, small stone.' τῷ νικῶντι . . . δώσω αὐτῷ ψῆφον λευκὴν καὶ ἐπὶ τὴν ψῆφον ὄνομα καινὸν γεγραμμένον 'I will give . . . to the one who is victorious . . . a white stone upon which is written a new name' Re 2.17. A number of different suggestions have been made as to the reference of ψῆφος in this context. Some scholars believe that the white ψῆφος indicates a vote of acquittal in court. Others contend that it is simply a magical amulet; still others, a token of Roman hospitality; and finally, some have suggested that it may represent a ticket to the gladiatorial games, that is to say, to martyrdom. The context, however, suggests clearly that this is something to be prized and a type of reward for those who have 'won the victory.'

2.28 ἄμμος[a], **ου** *f* – 'sand.' ἐὰν ᾖ ὁ ἀριθμὸς τῶν υἱῶν Ἰσραὴλ ὡς ἡ ἄμμος τῆς θαλάσσης 'even if the people of Israel are as many as the grains of sand by the sea' Ro 9.27. ἄμμος[a] is primarily used in the NT in a figurative sense referring to things which cannot be counted. In such contexts, therefore, what is important is the abundance of sand and not its particular occurrence beside the sea. Therefore, in many contexts it is possible to say 'as numerous as the grains of sand.' In this way one need not specify the particular location if the meaning of innumerable quantity is fully evident.

ὁμοιωθήσεται ἀνδρὶ μωρῷ, ὅστις ᾠκοδόμησεν αὐτοῦ τὴν οἰκίαν ἐπὶ τὴν ἄμμον 'he will be like a foolish man who built his house on the sand' Mt 7.26. In some areas of the world there is little or no sand, and therefore it may be necessary to render sand in Mt 7.26 as 'loose soil' or 'unpacked dirt.'

F Precious and Semiprecious Stones and Substances (2.29-2.48)

2.29 λίθος τίμιος: valuable stones and hard substances, especially gems and jewels – 'precious stone, gem.' εἰ δέ τις ἐποικοδομεῖ ἐπὶ τὸν θεμέλιον χρυσόν, ἄργυρον, λίθους τιμίους 'some will use gold, or silver, or precious stones in building upon the foundation' 1 Cor 3.12. For another interpretation of τίμιος in 1 Cor 3.12, see 65.2.

Precious stones are often distinguished on

the basis of cost, appearance, or function, for example, 'stones that cost much' or 'stones that are beautiful' or 'stones that are worn for decoration.'

A number of precious and semiprecious stones (see 2.30-2.43) are mentioned in one NT passage, namely Re 21.19-21, and though there are certain differences of opinion among scholars as to the precise reference of certain of these terms, there is more or less general agreement as to the color of the stones in question.

In languages in which terms such as 'jasper,' 'sapphire,' 'agate,' etc. exist, one may simply borrow such terms and explain their color in a glossary or word list. For languages in which such terms are not known, translators normally borrow the names from a dominant language of the area and likewise provide an explanation of the color in a glossary. Some translators have attempted to introduce the corresponding color terms in the text of Re 21.19-21, but this often results in a rather extended and somewhat awkward set of descriptive expressions.

2.30 ἴασπις, ιδος f – 'jasper,' probably green in color (see 2.29).

2.31 σάπφιρος, ου f – 'sapphire,' usually blue in color (see 2.29).

2.32 χαλκηδών, όνος m – 'agate, chalcedony,' usually milky or gray in color (see 2.29).

2.33 σμάραγδος, ου m – 'emerald,' green in color (see 2.29).

2.34 σμαράγδινος, η, ον (derivative of σμάραγδος 'emerald,' 2.33) – 'consisting of emerald, emerald-like,' Re 4.3 (see 2.29).

2.35 σαρδόνυξ, υχος m – 'onyx, sardonyx,' of varying colors (see 2.29).

2.36 σάρδιον, ου n – 'carnelian' or 'cornelian,' usually red in color (see 2.29).

2.37 χρυσόλιθος, ου m – 'chrysolite' (yellow quartz or yellow topaz), golden yellow in color (see 2.29).

2.38 βήρυλλος, ου m and f – 'beryl,' usually bluish green or green in color (see 2.29).

2.39 τοπάζιον, ου n – 'topaz,' usually yellow in color (see 2.29).

2.40 χρυσόπρασος, ου m – 'chrysoprase,' a greenish type of quartz (see 2.29).

2.41 ὑάκινθος, ου m – 'jacinth' or 'hyacinth,' probably blue in color (see 2.29).

2.42 ἀμέθυστος, ου f – 'amethyst,' usually purple or violet in color (see 2.29).

2.43 μαργαρίτης, ου m: a smooth, rounded concretion formed within the shells of certain mollusks and valued as a gem because of its lustrous color – 'pearl' (see 2.29). οἱ δώδεκα πυλῶνες δώδεκα μαργαρῖται 'the twelve gates were twelve pearls' Re 21.21; μηδὲ βάλητε τοὺς μαργαρίτας ὑμῶν ἔμπροσθεν τῶν χοίρων 'do not throw your pearls before pigs' Mt 7.6.

In general there is little difficulty involved in obtaining a satisfactory term for 'pearl,' since such objects are relatively well known throughout the world. However, in some languages there is no term for 'pearl,' and therefore one may use in the case of Re 21.21 'beautiful white stones,' and in Mt 7.6 it may be appropriate to translate 'do not throw your valuable jewels to pigs.'

2.44 ἐλεφάντινος, η, ον: (derivative of ἐλέφας 'elephant,' not occurring in the NT) pertaining to consisting of the tusks of elephants – 'consisting of ivory, made of ivory.' πᾶν σκεῦος ἐλεφάντινον 'all kinds of objects made of ivory' Re 18.12.

Since ivory, whether of elephant or walrus tusks, is well known throughout the world, there are usually few problems involved in finding a satisfactory term. However, where a term for 'ivory' is not known, one can always speak of 'beautiful bone.'

2.45 μάρμαρος, ου m: a colorful, relatively hard form of limestone which may be polished to a lustrous finish (especially valued as material for building or for sculpture) – 'marble.' πᾶν σκεῦος ἐκ ξύλου τιμιωτάτου καὶ χαλκοῦ καὶ σιδήρου καὶ μαρμάρου 'all kinds of objects made of precious wood and bronze, iron and marble' Re 18.12. Where there is no technical term for 'marble,' one may use an expression such as 'beautiful rock' or 'valuable stone.'

2.46 κρύσταλλοςᵃ, **ου** *m*; **ὕαλος**ᵇ, **ου** *f*: a very hard, translucent, and usually transparent type of quartz – 'crystal.'
κρύσταλλοςᵃ: ἐνώπιον τοῦ θρόνου ὡς θάλασσα ὑαλίνη ὁμοία κρυστάλλῳ 'in front of the throne there was what looked like a sea of glass, clear as crystal' Re 4.6. Some scholars, however, interpret κρύσταλλος in Re 4.6 as being a reference to ice (see 2.11).
ὕαλοςᵇ: ἡ πλατεῖα τῆς πόλεως χρυσίον καθαρὸν ὡς ὕαλος διαυγής 'the street of the city was made of pure gold, as transparent as crystal' Re 21.21. Some scholars, however, interpret ὕαλος in Re 21.21 as 'glass' (see 6.222).

The equivalent of 'crystal' is often a descriptive phrase such as 'a brilliant stone' or 'a shining stone' or 'a glass-like stone.' In developing a satisfactory term for crystal, it is important to avoid possible confusion with diamond.

2.47 κρυσταλλίζω: (derivative of κρύσταλλοςᵃ 'crystal,' 2.46) to shine in the same way that crystal shines – 'to shine like crystal, to shine brightly.' ὡς λίθῳ ἰάσπιδι κρυσταλλίζοντι 'like a jasper shining clear as crystal' Re 21.11.

2.48 διοπετές, οῦ *n*: a stone which has fallen from heaven or the sky (originally employed in referring to images of the gods) – 'stone from heaven, stone fallen from the sky.' τίς γάρ ἐστιν ἀνθρώπων ὃς οὐ γινώσκει τὴν Ἐφεσίων πόλιν νεωκόρον οὖσαν τῆς μεγάλης Ἀρτέμιδος καὶ τοῦ διοπετοῦς; 'for what sort of person is there who does not know that the city of Ephesus is the keeper of the temple of the great Artemis and the stone which fell down from heaven?' Ac 19.35. The object referred to by τοῦ διοπετοῦς in Ac 19.35 was probably a stone meteorite regarded as a sacred supernatural object.

G Metals (2.49-2.62)

2.49 χρυσίονᵃ, **ου** *n*; **χρυσός**ᵃ, **οῦ** *m* – 'gold'

(the most highly valued metal in the ancient world).
χρυσίονᵃ: τὴν κιβωτὸν τῆς διαθήκης περικεκαλυμμένην πάντοθεν χρυσίῳ 'the covenant box all covered with gold' He 9.4.
χρυσόςᵃ: ὃ δ' ἂν ὀμόσῃ ἐν τῷ χρυσῷ τοῦ ναοῦ 'whoever swears by the gold of the Temple' Mt 23.16.

Terms for gold are widespread throughout the world even as the presence of gold or knowledge about gold is likewise almost universal. Therefore, there is usually no difficulty involved in obtaining a satisfactory term for 'gold.'

2.50 χρυσοῦς, ῆ, οῦν: (derivative of χρυσόςᵃ 'gold,' 2.49) pertaining to being made or consisting of gold – 'golden, made of gold.' σκεύη χρυσᾶ καὶ ἀργυρᾶ 'vessels made of gold and silver' 2 Tm 2.20.

2.51 ἄργυροςᵃ, **ου** *m*; **ἀργύριον**ᵃ, **ου** *n* – 'silver' (after gold, the next most highly valued metal in the ancient world).
ἄργυροςᵃ: εἰ δέ τις ἐποικοδομεῖ ἐπὶ τὸν θεμέλιον χρυσόν, ἄργυρον 'if anyone builds on the foundation with gold, silver' 1 Cor 3.12.
ἀργύριονᵃ: οὐ φθαρτοῖς, ἀργυρίῳ ἢ χρυσίῳ 'not with things that perish such as silver and gold' 1 Pe 1.18.

As in the case of 'gold' (2.49), there is usually no difficulty involved in obtaining a satisfactory term for 'silver' in most languages. In 1 Pe 1.18, however, there is a problem in speaking of silver and gold that 'perish,' or even as something that can be 'destroyed,' since in reality one does not destroy such elements, and silver and gold do not really 'perish.' On the other hand, silver and gold can become oxidized and lose their value, especially if they are impure (see 2.60). Therefore, it seems far better to emphasize the lack of value in translating 1 Pe 1.18. A suitable rendering may then be 'not with things that can lose their value as silver and gold.'

2.52 ἀργυροκόπος, ου *m*: one who makes objects out of silver (especially jewelry and fine utensils) – 'silversmith.' Δημήτριος γάρ τις ὀνόματι, ἀργυροκόπος, ποιῶν ναοὺς ἀργυροῦς

'Αρτέμιδος 'a silversmith named Demetrius made silver models of the temple of Artemis' Ac 19.24.

2.53 ἀργυροῦς, ᾶ, οῦν: (derivative of ἄργυρος[a] 'silver,' 2.51) pertaining to being made or consisting of silver — 'of silver, made of silver.' σκεύη χρυσᾶ καὶ ἀργυρᾶ 'vessels made of gold and silver' 2 Tm 2.20.

2.54 χαλκός[a], οῦ m: generally bronze (an alloy of copper and tin), but in some contexts apparently brass (an alloy of copper and zinc) and perhaps in a few instances copper — 'bronze, brass, copper.' πᾶν σκεῦος ἐκ ξύλου τιμιωτάτου καὶ χαλκοῦ 'every kind of object made of precious wood and bronze' Re 18.12.

Most archaeological objects of the Middle East containing copper consist of bronze, and therefore the most accurate translation of χαλκός[a] is in most instances a term for bronze, which is harder than brass and much harder than pure copper. Many languages have technical terms for bronze, brass, and copper, but some simply designate bronze as 'brown metal,' brass as 'bright metal,' and copper as 'red metal.'

2.55 χαλκεύς, έως m: (derivative of χαλκός[a] 'bronze, brass, copper,' 2.54) one who makes objects out of brass, bronze, copper, or other metals — 'coppersmith, metalworker.' Ἀλέξανδρος ὁ χαλκεὺς πολλά μοι κακὰ ἐνεδείξατο 'Alexander, the coppersmith, did me great harm' 2 Tm 4.14.

2.56 χαλκοῦς, ῆ, οῦν: (derivative of χαλκός[a] 'bronze, brass, copper,' 2.54) pertaining to being made or consisting of bronze, brass, or copper — 'made of bronze (brass or copper).' ἵνα μὴ προσκυνήσουσιν τὰ δαιμόνια καὶ τὰ εἴδωλα τὰ χρυσᾶ, καὶ τὰ ἀργυρᾶ καὶ τὰ χαλκᾶ 'lest they stop worshiping the demons and idols made of gold, silver, and bronze' Re 9.20.

2.57 χαλκολίβανον, ου n (also χαλκολίβανος, ου m): a particularly valuable or fine type of bronze or brass, possibly even an alloy containing some gold — 'fine bronze, fine brass.' οἱ πόδες αὐτοῦ ὅμοιοι χαλκολιβάνῳ 'his feet are like fine bronze' Re 2.18. In the two references with χαλκολίβανον in the NT (Re 1.15 and Re 2.18) the emphasis is upon the lustrous appearance of the metal. A satisfactory equivalent may be 'bright bronze' or 'shining metal.'

2.58 σίδηρος, ου m — 'iron.' πᾶν σκεῦος . . . σιδήρου 'every object . . . made of iron' Re 18.12. Since at the present time iron in some form is almost universal throughout the world, there is usually no difficulty involved in obtaining a satisfactory term for it. In some instances, in fact, it is such a dominant metal that it is known simply as 'the metal.'

2.59 σιδηροῦς, ᾶ, οῦν: (derivative of σίδηρος 'iron,' 2.58) pertaining to being made or consisting of iron — 'made of iron.' ἦλθαν ἐπὶ τὴν πύλην τὴν σιδηρᾶν τὴν φέρουσαν εἰς τὴν πόλιν 'they came to the iron gate that opens into the city' Ac 12.10.

2.60 ἰός[b], οῦ m: the substance resulting from the slow oxidation of metals (rust in the case of iron and tarnish in the case of gold and silver) — 'rust, tarnish.' ὁ χρυσὸς ὑμῶν καὶ ὁ ἄργυρος κατίωται, καὶ ὁ ἰὸς αὐτῶν εἰς μαρτύριον ὑμῖν ἔσται 'your gold and silver will be covered with tarnish, and the tarnish will serve as a witness against you' Jas 5.3.

Pure gold is not affected significantly by oxidation, but much of the gold of the ancient world was not pure, and therefore oxidation and resulting tarnish did take place. However, in most languages it is inappropriate to speak of 'rust' as occurring with gold and silver. If there is no satisfactory term to indicate the deterioration in gold and silver resulting in extreme tarnish, it may be possible to translate Jas 5.3 as 'your gold and silver will be ruined and this will serve as a witness against you.'

2.61 κατιόομαι: to undergo the process of oxidation of metals — 'to become rusty, to become tarnished, to corrode.' ὁ χρυσὸς ὑμῶν καὶ ὁ ἄργυρος κατίωται 'your gold and silver are tarnished' Jas 5.3. See discussion at 2.60.

2.62 βρῶσις[e], εως f: the process of producing rust or tarnish by oxidation – ʼrusting, tarnishing, corrosion.'⁵ μὴ θησαυρίζετε ὑμῖν

5 The term βρῶσιςᵉ is included at this point since it is essentially similar in meaning to κατιόομαι (2.61) and is probably to be understood as a figurative extension of meaning of βρῶσιςᵃ 'eating' (23.3).

θησαυροὺς ἐπὶ τῆς γῆς, ὅπου σὴς καὶ βρῶσις ἀφανίζει 'don't lay up treasures for yourselves on earth where moths and corrosion destroy' Mt 6.19. Though in Mt 6.19 βρῶσις has been generally understood to mean 'corrosion,' it might actually refer to a type of insect, as it does in the Septuagint of Mal 3.11.

3 Plants[1]

Outline of Subdomains[2]

A Plants (General Meaning) (3.1)
B Trees (3.2-3.12)
C Plants That Are Not Trees (3.13-3.32)
D Fruit Parts of Plants (3.33-3.46)
E Non-Fruit Parts of Plants (3.47-3.59)
F Wood and Wood Products (3.60-3.67)

A Plants (General Meaning) (3.1)

3.1 φυτεία, ας *f*: any kind of plant, whether tree, bush, or herb – 'plant.' πᾶσα φυτεία ἣν οὐκ ἐφύτευσεν ὁ πατήρ μου ὁ οὐράνιος 'every plant which my Father in heaven did not plant' Mt 15.13.

The principal translational difficulty with

1 For information on specific plants mentioned in the NT, as well as certain problems relating to the adequate choice of equivalent terms in other languages, see *Fauna and Flora of the Bible* in the series of Helps for Translators published by the United Bible Societies.
2 The major non-generic subdivisions of this domain are B *Trees* and C *Plants That Are Not Trees* (a distinction which has practical implications for a number of receptor languages), followed by D *Fruit Parts of Plants* and E *Non-Fruit Parts of Plants*. The final section is F *Wood and Wood Products*.
Certain of these subdomains involve a measure of overlapping with other domains. For example, the fruit part of plants is closely related to the domain of *Food* (5), but the meanings associated with the terms in this domain focus more upon fruit as the product of plants than upon fruit as food. Similarly, the meaning of 'flower' may be classified in the domain of *Physiological Processes* (23), since it may be regarded as the result of flowering or blossoming, but NT usage seems to focus primarily upon flowers as distinctive parts of plants. Likewise, ἄνθραξ 'charcoal' (3.67) could be treated under *Artifacts* (6). However, practical considerations make it useful to include it here within the subdomain of *Wood Products*.

φυτεία is that in so many languages there is no term with such a generic meaning. Sometimes the closest equivalent is a descriptive phrase 'green things' or 'leafy things.'

Classifications of plants vary greatly from one language to another. Principal distinctions are based upon size, woodiness, perennials versus annuals, and food-producing in contrast with non-food-producing.

B Trees (3.2-3.12)

3.2 δένδρον, ου *n*: any kind of relatively large woody plant – 'tree, bush.' πᾶν δένδρον ἀγαθὸν καρποὺς καλοὺς ποιεῖ 'every healthy tree bears good fruit' Mt 7.17.

In rendering δένδρον 'tree' it is important in a number of contexts to determine whether or not the trees in question produce edible fruit, since in a number of languages this distinction is reflected in the use of quite different terms.

3.3 ὕληᵃ, ης *f*: a dense growth of trees covering a relatively large area – 'forest.' ἡλίκον πῦρ ἡλίκην ὕλην ἀνάπτει 'a small fire sets a large forest ablaze' Jas 3.5. In Jas 3.5 it is also possible to interpret ὕλη as wood which has been cut up, either firewood or wood used for construction (see ὕληᵇ 'wood, pile of wood,' 3.64).

In some languages spoken by people living in tropical forest areas the equivalent of 'forest' is simply the expression 'where no one lives,' based upon the fact that people live in clearings and everything else is forest. Such a rendering, however, may not lead to a satisfactory translation of Jas 3.5 (the only occurrence of ὕλη in the NT), in which case one is better advised to interpret ὕλη in the sense of 'pile of wood' (3.64).

3.4 ξύλονᶜ, ου *n* – 'tree.' εἰ ἐν τῷ ὑγρῷ ξύλῳ ταῦτα ποιοῦσιν, ἐν τῷ ξηρῷ τί γένηται; 'if they do these things to a green tree, what will happen in the case of a dry one?' Lk 23.31. It is also possible to understand ξύλον in Lk 23.31 as 'firewood.' One may therefore translate the first part of this conditional sentence as 'if they do these things to firewood which has recently been cut' or 'if they do these things to firewood which hasn't dried out' (see 3.61).

In Re 2.7 and 22.2 ξύλον τῆς ζωῆς 'tree of life' may cause certain complications if the passage is translated more or less literally 'I will give him to eat of the tree of life.' In some languages a literal rendering would mean 'to gnaw on the tree of life,' that is to say, to eat the wood or the bark. It may therefore be necessary to translate 'to eat the fruit of the tree of life' or '. . . the fruit from the tree that causes life' or '. . . causes people to live.'

3.5 συκῆ, ῆς *f* – 'fig tree.' ἀπὸ δὲ τῆς συκῆς μάθετε τὴν παραβολήν 'from the fig tree learn the meaning of the parable' Mt 24.32.

In Palestine the fig tree occurs in both wild and cultivated forms and the latter is greatly valued for its sweet, edible fruit. It normally produces two crops each year: early figs ripening in June (late spring) and late ones in August and September (early fall).

For languages in which a term for 'fig tree' is not known, one can often employ a borrowed term with a so-called 'classifier,' for example, 'a tree called fig' or 'a fruit tree producing fruit called figs.' In many tropical areas of the world there are forest trees belonging to the botanical family of fig trees, but such trees generally produce inedible fruit. It may, however, be possible for a translator to use the term for such a forest tree but with the added explanation as to the fruit-bearing quality of the trees mentioned in the Bible.

3.6 συκάμινος, ου *f* – 'mulberry tree,' a deciduous fruit tree growing to the height of some 6 meters (about 20 feet) and bearing black berries containing a sweet reddish juice.

ἐλέγετε ἂν τῇ συκαμίνῳ ταύτῃ 'if you should say to this mulberry tree' Lk 17.6.

For languages which have no specific term for 'mulberry tree,' one can often employ a generic expression followed by a type of classifier, for example, 'the tree called mulberry' (in which case the term 'mulberry' may be borrowed from a dominant language of the area) or 'a tree producing berries'; but in Lk 17.6 the focus is upon the tree as a large object and not upon the type of fruit which it produced. One can, therefore, say simply 'this tree.'

3.7 συκομορέα, ας *f* – 'sycamore-fig tree,' a broad, heavy tree reaching a height of some 15 meters (about 50 feet), with large, strong branches growing out from the trunk low down on the tree (the fruit has the appearance of a small fig but its taste is relatively unpleasant). προδραμὼν εἰς τὸ ἔμπροσθεν ἀνέβη ἐπὶ συκομορέαν ἵνα ἴδῃ αὐτόν 'he ran ahead and climbed a sycamore tree in order to see him' Lk 19.4.

As in the case of other specific trees for which no local term in the receptor language is available, one can borrow a word such as 'sycamore' from a dominant language in the area and add a classifier, for example, 'tree called sycamore,' but in a number of languages it may be appropriate to render συκομορέα in Lk 19.4 simply as 'a big tree' or 'a wild fig tree.'

3.8 φοῖνιξᵃ or φοίνιξ, ικος *m* – 'palm tree.' ἔλαβον τὰ βαΐα τῶν φοινίκων 'they took palm branches' Jn 12.13. See discussion at 3.53.

3.9 ἐλαίαᵃ, ας *f* – 'olive tree.' ἦλθον εἰς Βηθφαγὴ εἰς τὸ Ὄρος τῶν Ἐλαιῶν 'they came to Bethphage at the Mount of Olives' Mt 21.1.

As in the case of other terms for trees which may not be identified by specific receptor-language terms, one can employ a generic expression followed by a borrowed term, for example, 'a tree producing fruit called olives.' In the context of Mt 21.1 and similar passages it is important that 'Mount of Olives' not be rendered in such a way as to suggest that it was a mountain consisting of olives or even a mountain consisting of olive trees. A more appropriate expression in some languages is 'a mountain known for its olive trees' or 'a mountain on which many olive trees grow.' In a number of languages, however, it is important to employ a term such as 'hill' rather than 'mountain,' since the Mount of Olives near Jerusalem would be regarded in most receptor languages as a 'hill' not a 'mountain.'

3.10 καλλιέλαιος, ου *f* – 'cultivated olive tree.' καὶ παρὰ φύσιν ἐνεκεντρίσθης εἰς καλλιέλαιον 'and contrary to nature you were grafted into the cultivated olive tree' Ro 11.24.

3.11 ἀγριέλαιος, ου *f* – 'wild olive tree,' a tree regarded by some (though probably wrongly) as the ancestor of the domestic olive tree. σὺ δὲ ἀγριέλαιος ὢν ἐνεκεντρίσθης ἐν αὐτοῖς 'and you being a wild olive have been grafted into them' Ro 11.17. This reference in Ro 11.17 is intentionally strange because the usual course of action was to graft cultivated branches into wild trees.

In speaking of the wild olive tree as 'an uncultivated olive tree,' it is important to make clear that it is not the matter of neglect which produces the wild tree, but the fact that such a tree is essentially different from the cultivated one. A marginal note to this effect may be useful in the context of Ro 11.17. The precise identification of the 'wild olive tree' cannot be made with certainty. It may be possible in some instances to speak of such a tree as an 'uncultivated olive tree' in contrast with a 'cultivated olive tree.' It may also be possible to speak of the wild olive tree as 'the olive tree producing bitter fruit,' although in reality all olives are bitter before they are cured.

3.12 ἐλαιών, ῶνος *m*: (derivative of ἐλαία[a] 'olive tree,' 3.9) a number of olive trees planted in a garden or grove – 'olive grove, olive orchard.' ἀπὸ ὄρους τοῦ καλουμένου Ἐλαιῶνος 'from the hill called The Olive Grove' Ac 1.12. In Ac 1.12, however, it may be well to employ the more common designation for the hill in question, namely, 'Hill of Olives' or 'Mount of Olives' (see 3.9).

C Plants That Are Not Trees (3.13-3.32)

3.13 χλωρόν, οῦ *n* (derivative of χλωρός[a], ά, όν 'green,' 79.34) – 'plant.' ἵνα μὴ ἀδικήσουσιν τὸν χόρτον τῆς γῆς οὐδὲ πᾶν χλωρὸν οὐδὲ πᾶν δένδρον 'not to harm the grass of the earth, nor any green plant, nor any tree' Re 9.4.[3] In a number of languages it would seem redundant to speak of 'green plants,' since all plants are regarded as being green. It may therefore be more satisfactory to employ a rendering such as 'nor any plant,' referring in this instance to larger annual plants or bushes, in contrast with both grass and trees.

3.14 βοτάνη, ης *f*: any of the smaller green plants (in Hellenistic Greek often used in contexts referring to plants as fodder for animals) – 'plant, grass.' τίκτουσα βοτάνην εὔθετον 'growing useful plants' He 6.7. (βοτάνη is more generic in meaning than χόρτος[a], 3.15.)

3.15 χόρτος[a], ου *m*: small green plants (and in NT contexts referring primarily to green grass in a field or meadow) – 'small plants, grass.' ὅτε δὲ ἐβλάστησεν ὁ χόρτος 'and when the small plants sprout' Mt 13.26; ἐπέταξεν αὐτοῖς ἀνακλῖναι . . . ἐπὶ τῷ χλωρῷ χόρτῳ 'he commanded them to sit down . . . on the green grass' Mk 6.39.

In referring to small green plants, a number of languages employ two quite different terms, one indicating specifically grass (with leaves having parallel veins) and the other designating all other types of annual plants (those having branching veins in the leaves). In Mt 13.26 it is important to employ a term which would include grass and other plants with parallel veins, since the weeds in this passage imitate the appearance of wheat, which does have parallel veins in the leaves.

3.16 βάτος, ου *m* and *f*: any type of thorn bush or shrub – 'thorn bush, bush.' Μωϋσῆς

---

3 The Greek term χλωρόν (as a substantive) also occurs in non-New Testament contexts with a generic meaning of any kind of plant, thus being roughly equivalent to the meaning of φυτεία (3.1), but in Re 9.4 χλωρόν contrasts with χόρτον 'grass' and δένδρον 'tree' and thus evidently refers to larger annuals and smaller perennial plants.

ἐμήνυσεν ἐπὶ τῆς βάτου 'Moses proved it clearly in the passage about the bush' Lk 20.37. The reference to the passage of Scripture is supplied from the context.

Except for Lk 6.44, all occurrences of βάτος in the NT are to the burning bush of Ex 3.2, in which the reference may very well be to a 'burning thorn bush.'

3.17 ἄκανθα, ης f; τρίβολος, ου m: any kind of thorny plant – 'thorn plant, thistle, brier.' μήτι συλλέγουσιν ἀπὸ ἀκανθῶν σταφυλὰς ἢ ἀπὸ τριβόλων σῦκα 'thorn bushes do not bear grapes and briers do not bear figs' Mt 7.16. Since plants having thorny projections are almost worldwide in distribution, there is no difficulty in obtaining a satisfactory term for such plants. In some instances, however, a descriptive equivalent may be necessary, for example, 'plants with piercing points' or 'plants that stick into one's flesh.'

3.18 ἀκάνθινος, η, ον: (derivative of ἄκανθα 'thorn plant,' 3.17) pertaining to being made or consisting of thorns – 'thorny, of thorns.' ἀκάνθινον στέφανον 'a crown of thorns' Mk 15.17. It may be necessary to indicate that this crown of thorns is one made of 'branches of a thorny bush,' for the crown did not consist merely of thorns but of thorny vines or branches.

3.19 κάλαμος*, ου m: a tall-growing grass or sedge – 'reed.' κάλαμον ὑπὸ ἀνέμου σαλευόμενον 'a reed bending in the wind' Mt 11.7.

3.20 σίναπι, εως n – 'mustard plant,' a large herb noted for its very small seeds and in some instances growing to a height of 3 meters (about 10 feet). κόκκῳ σινάπεως . . . ὅταν δὲ αὐξηθῇ μεῖζον τῶν λαχάνων ἐστίν 'mustard seed . . . and when it grows it becomes the largest of the plants' Mt 13.31-32. Note that in Mt 13.31-32 (and in the parallel passage Lk 13.19) σίναπι is actually spoken of as a δένδρον 'tree,' evidently a type of rhetorical hyperbole.

Though the mustard plant may not be known in certain areas of the world, the use of mustard as a condiment is widely known, and therefore it is often possible to speak of 'a plant that produces mustard' or 'the plant used in making mustard.' In order, however, to make the parable meaningful, it may be necessary to have some explanation of this plant in a footnote or glossary.

3.21 ἄψινθος*, ου m and f: a particularly bitter herb with medicinal value – 'wormwood.' τὸ ὄνομα τοῦ ἀστέρος λέγεται ὁ ἄψινθος 'the name of the star is called Wormwood' Re 8.11. In Re 8.11 it may be better to speak of the star as 'bitterness,' for example, 'the name of the star is Bitter' or '. . . Bitterness.' It is, of course, also possible to speak of the star as 'Bitter Plant' or 'Bitter Herb.' A rendering of ἄψινθος as 'wormy wood' would be completely misleading and would provide no basis for understanding the second part of verse 11, for which see 79.43. (The English term *wormwood* is derived from the use of the plant as a medicine to kill intestinal worms.)

3.22 πήγανον, ου n: an evergreen aromatic plant used for seasoning – 'rue.' ἀποδεκατοῦτε τὸ ἡδύοσμον καὶ τὸ πήγανον καὶ πᾶν λάχανον 'you tithe such seasoning herbs as mint and rue and all other herbs' Lk 11.42. In the parallel passage (Mt 23.23) ἄνηθον 'dill' and κύμινον 'cummin' occur (see 3.24-25).

In designating 'rue' as well as 'mint,' 'dill,' and 'cummin' (which immediately follow in this subdomain), it is probably wise to borrow a term and use a classifier, for example, 'a seasoning herb called rue.'

3.23 ἡδύοσμον, ου n – 'mint' (see 3.22).

3.24 ἄνηθον, ου n – 'dill' (see 3.22).

3.25 κύμινον, ου n – 'cummin' (see 3.22).

3.26 ὕσσωπος, ου m and f or ὕσσωπον, ου n – 'hyssop,' a small aromatic bush, the branches of which were often used by the Jews in religious ceremonies. σπόγγον οὖν μεστὸν τοῦ ὄξους ὑσσώπῳ περιθέντες 'they put a sponge soaked in sour wine on a branch of hyssop' Jn 19.29.

The hyssop bush may reach a height of 1 meter (3 feet) and has a number of woody stems.

In some translations a term for 'hyssop' is borrowed with a classifier such as 'plant,' for example, 'a branch of a plant called hyssop.'

In Jn 19.29 some translators have simply used 'a twig' or 'a branch,' but this may not be adequate, since some persons see a good deal of symbolism in the use of the term 'hyssop' because of its relationship to ritual uses in the OT.

According to an old conjecture, the text of Jn 19.29 could have contained the term ὑσσός 'javelin' (6.35) rather than ὕσσωπος 'hyssop' (this reading is actually found in one eleventh century minuscule manuscript), and this has been followed by the NEB translation ("they soaked a sponge with the wine, fixed it on a javelin . . ."), but this form of the text has very little support and is not recommended.

3.27 ἄμπελος, ου *f* – 'grapevine.' ἐγώ εἰμι ἡ ἄμπελος ἡ ἀληθινή 'I am the true grapevine' Jn 15.1.

A rendering of ἄμπελος as 'vine' rather than as 'grapevine' in Jn 15.1 may cause serious misunderstanding, since it might refer merely to a vine which does not produce fruit. Accordingly, if there is no particular expression for 'grapevine,' it may be more satisfactory in Jn 15.1 to speak of 'fruit bush' or 'fruit plant.' A term in Jn 15.1 which would indicate only jungle vines would also result in complete misunderstanding of the function of pruning (see 43.12), since such jungle vines are never pruned and in fact are only useful when they have been cut down and used for building purposes.

In some languages a grapevine may be referred to as 'a bush producing grapes,' and in certain other languages it is called 'the wine plant.'

3.28 ἀμπελών, ῶνος *m*: (derivative of ἄμπελος 'grapevine,' 3.27) a number of grapevines growing in a garden or field – 'vineyard, orchard of grapevines.' ἐξῆλθεν ἅμα πρωΐ μισθώσασθαι ἐργάτας εἰς τὸν ἀμπελῶνα αὐτοῦ 'he went out very early to hire workers for his vineyard' Mt 20.1. In some instances a vineyard may be described as 'a farm with grapevines' or 'a garden for grapes.'

3.29 λάχανον, ου *n*: any one of the smaller plants cultivated in a garden, for example, herbs and vegetables – 'garden plant.' μεῖζον τῶν λαχάνων ἐστίν 'it is larger than the garden plants' Mt 13.32.

3.30 ζιζάνιον, ου *n*: a particularly undesirable weed resembling wheat and possessing a seed which is poisonous – 'darnel.' ἐπέσπειρεν ζιζάνια ἀνὰ μέσον τοῦ σίτου 'he sowed darnel in the midst of the wheat' Mt 13.25.

In this one passage in which ζιζάνιον occurs in the NT, it is possible to use an expression such as 'poisonous weed' or 'bad weed.'

3.31 σῖτος[b], ου *m*: the plant of wheat – 'wheat.' ὁ κόκκος τοῦ σίτου 'the seed of wheat' Jn 12.24. Elsewhere in the NT σῖτος, when used alone, refers to wheat as grain, but even in Jn 12.24 τοῦ σίτου may be interpreted as a so-called 'appositional genitive,' that is, 'seed which is wheat' or 'wheat seed.'

While in some parts of the world wheat as a grain or as a plant is not known, in almost all instances people are acquainted with wheat flour, and therefore it is often possible to translate 'wheat' as 'flour plant' or 'plant the grain of which is used to make flour.' In some languages, however, the only possible equivalent is 'rice-like plant' in which 'rice-like' means essentially 'grass-like,' while at the same time indicating edible grain.

3.32 κρίνον, ου *n*: any one of several types of flowers, usually uncultivated – 'wild flower.' καταμάθετε τὰ κρίνα τοῦ ἀγροῦ πῶς αὐξάνουσιν 'consider the lilies of the field, how they grow' Mt 6.28. Though traditionally κρίνον has been regarded as a type of lily, scholars have suggested several other possible references, including an anemone, a poppy, a gladiolus, and a rather inconspicuous type of daisy.

D Fruit Parts of Plants (3.33-3.46)

3.33 καρπός[a], οῦ *m*: any fruit part of plants, including grain as well as pulpy fruit – 'fruit.' πᾶν δένδρον ἀγαθὸν καρποὺς καλοὺς ποιεῖ 'every good tree produces good fruit' Mt 7.17.

A number of languages distinguish carefully between different kinds of fruit. One common type of four-way distinction involves (1) nuts, (2) grain, (3) pulpy fruit surrounding a seed (the type of fruit primarily referred to in contexts containing χαρπός[a]), and (4) fruit such as bananas, in which there is no noticeable seed. It is important in each instance to choose a term which will be applicable to the particular context.

3.34 ὀπώρα, ας *f*: the mature fruit of plants (that is, fruit which is ready for use) – 'ripe fruit.' ἡ ὀπώρα σου τῆς ἐπιθυμίας τῆς ψυχῆς 'the ripe fruit for which you longed' Re 18.14. In this one occurrence of ὀπώρα in the NT, 'ripe fruit' is to be understood in a figurative sense of 'good things.'

3.35 κόκκος, ου *m*; σπέρμα[a], τος *n*; σπόρος, ου *m*: the kernel part of fruit – 'seed.'
κόκκος: σπείρεις . . . γυμνὸν κόκκον εἰ τύχοι σίτου 'you sow . . . the bare seed, like that of wheat' 1 Cor 15.37.
σπέρμα[a]: καλὸν σπέρμα ἔσπειρας ἐν τῷ ἀγρῷ 'you sowed good seed in your field' Mt 13.27.
σπόρος: καὶ ὁ σπόρος βλαστᾷ 'and the seed sprouts' Mk 4.27 (see also 10.23 for σπορά 'seed' used figuratively of descendants).

A number of languages make distinctions between two quite different types of seed: (1) those produced by grasses (that is to say, grains) and (2) those produced by other types of plants, for example, beans, squash, apples, etc. In all passages employing the Greek terms cited here, it is best to use some expression referring to 'grain.'

3.36 σῦκον, ου *n*: the fruit of the fig tree – 'fig.' ὁ γὰρ καιρὸς οὐκ ἦν σύκων 'it was not the season for figs' Mk 11.13. As in the case of the corresponding term for the fig tree (3.5), it may be best to borrow a term for fig and add a classifier, for example, 'fruit called fig.'

3.37 ὄλυνθος, ου *m*: a fig produced late in the summer season (and often falling off before it ripens) – 'late fig.' ὡς συκῆ βάλλει τοὺς ὀλύνθους αὐτῆς ὑπὸ ἀνέμου μεγάλου σειομένη 'as the fig tree sheds its late figs when shaken by a great wind' Re 6.13. In the only context in which ὄλυνθος occurs in the NT (Re 6.13), one may employ an expression such as 'unripe fig' or 'fig which ripens late.'

3.38 βότρυς, υος *m*; σταφυλή, ῆς *f*: the fruit of grapevines (see 3.27) – 'grape, bunch of grapes.' τρύγησον τοὺς βότρυας τῆς ἀμπέλου τῆς γῆς, ὅτι ἤκμασαν αἱ σταφυλαὶ αὐτῆς 'cut the grapes from the vineyard of the earth because its grapes are ripe' Re 14.18. Some scholars have contended that βότρυς means primarily a bunch of grapes, while σταφυλή designates individual grapes. In Re 14.18 this difference might seem plausible, but there is scarcely any evidence for such a distinction, since both words may signify grapes as well as bunches of grapes.

In some languages it is necessary to borrow a term for 'grapes' from a dominant language and then employ some kind of classifier, for example, 'fruit called grapes.' In other languages grapes may be known as 'wine fruit,' since wine may be more widely known than a term for grapes.

3.39 ἐλαία[b], ας *f*: the fruit of the olive tree – 'olive.' μὴ δύναται . . . συκῆ ἐλαίας ποιῆσαι 'a fig tree . . . cannot . . . bear olives' Jas 3.12.

Since in some languages a term for 'olive oil' (ἔλαιον, 6.202) is better known than the fruit itself, one may employ a descriptive phrase such as 'the fruit of olive oil' or 'the fruit that produces olive oil.' In certain instances olives are actually known as 'the cooking-oil fruit.'

3.40 στάχυς, υος *m*: the dense spiky cluster in which the seeds of grain such as wheat and barley grow (restricted in NT contexts to references to wheat) – 'ear of wheat, head of wheat.' τίλλοντες τοὺς στάχυας 'picking the heads of wheat' Mk 2.23.

In some languages it is impossible to speak of 'a head of wheat' or 'an ear of wheat,' since terms referring to 'head' and 'ear' have no such figurative extensions of meaning. In certain instances the equivalent may be 'the point of the wheat' or 'the brush of the wheat,' referring to the spike-like objects which extend from each grain.

3.41 σῖτος[a], ου *m*: any kind of edible grain,

though generally referring to wheat – 'grain, wheat.' συνάξει τὸν σῖτον αὐτοῦ εἰς τὴν ἀποθήκην 'he will gather his grain into his barn' Mt 3.12.

3.42 σιτίον^a, ου *n*: (a diminutive form of σῖτος^a 'grain,' 3.41, but not diminutive in meaning, occurring in the NT only in Ac 7.12 in a plural form) any grain, but with the evident implication of its relevance as food – 'grain, food' (see also 5.2). ἀκούσας δὲ Ἰακὼβ ὄντα σιτία εἰς Αἴγυπτον 'and when Jacob heard that there was grain in Egypt' Ac 7.12. On the basis of this one NT occurrence it is impossible to know whether the meaning of σιτία is 'grain' or 'food,' since in the phrase σιτία καὶ ποτά 'food and drink' (an expression occurring in a number of extrabiblical contexts), the term σιτίον contrasts solid with liquid nourishment.

3.43 ἅλων^b, ος *f*: (a figurative extension of meaning of ἅλων^a 'threshing floor,' 7.65) grain in the process of being threshed – 'threshed grain.' οὗ τὸ πτύον ἐν τῇ χειρὶ αὐτοῦ, καὶ διακαθαριεῖ τὴν ἅλωνα αὐτοῦ 'he has his winnowing shovel with him, and will clean his threshed grain' Mt 3.12. ἅλων in Mt 3.12 may also be interpreted as a threshing floor (see 7.65).

3.44 κριθή, ῆς *f*: a grain somewhat similar to wheat, but regarded as less desirable for food – 'barley.' τρεῖς χοίνικες κριθῶν δηναρίου 'three measures of barley for a denarius' Re 6.6.

In a number of languages there is no specific term for barley, and therefore it may be useful simply to borrow a term from a dominant language. In certain instances, however, translators have used an expression such as 'wheat-like grain.' It may even be useful to have a footnote to explain something of the nature of barley, but the fact that it was cheaper than wheat is clear from Re 6.6.

3.45 κρίθινος, η, ον: (derivative of κριθή 'barley,' 3.44) pertaining to being made or consisting of barley – 'of barley.' ἔστιν παιδάριον ὧδε ἔχει πέντε ἄρτους κριθίνους καὶ δύο ὀψάρια 'here is a boy who has five barley loaves and two fish' Jn 6.9.

3.46 κεράτιον, ου *n*: (a diminutive derivative of κέρας^a 'horn,' 8.17) the pod of the carob tree (which closely resembles a small horn) – 'carob pod.' ἐπεθύμει χορτασθῆναι ἐκ τῶν κερατίων ὧν ἤσθιον οἱ χοῖροι 'he wished he could eat the carob pods that the pigs ate' Lk 15.16. Carob pods were commonly used for fattening swine and were employed as an article of food by poor people. In translating Lk 15.16 it is not necessary, however, to identify specifically carob pods. In most languages some such expression as 'edible pods' is probably more satisfactory, since carob trees are unlikely to be known.

E   Non-Fruit Parts of Plants (3.47-3.59)

3.47 ῥίζα^a, ης *f*: the underground part of a plant – 'root.' τὴν συκῆν ἐξηραμμένην ἐκ ῥιζῶν 'the fig tree had withered away to the roots' Mk 11.20. A literal translation of 'withered away to the roots' may be misunderstood, since the expression might suggest that the tree had withered only as far down as the roots but that the roots had not withered. The Greek text, however, indicates that the entire tree including the roots had withered and was completely dead.

3.48 χόρτος^b, ου *m*: the young growth of a plant arising from a germinating seed – 'sprout, blade.'[4] ἡ γῆ καρποφορεῖ, πρῶτον χόρτον, εἶτα στάχυν 'the earth produces, first a green blade, then the head' Mk 4.28. In a number of languages a clear distinction is made between different kinds of 'sprouts.' Certain sprouts have only a single blade (for example, grass), while others are double (as in the case of beans). In Mk 4.28 the reference is to a grass-like plant with a single blade.

3.49 κλάδος, ου *m* – 'branch' (of a tree or woody shrub). ἄλλοι δὲ ἔκοπτον κλάδους ἀπὸ

4 It would be possible to combine χόρτος^b (3.48) with χόρτος^a 'small plant, grass' (3.15), since the meaning of χόρτος^a would seem to include the meaning of 'sprout.' On the other hand, the semantic focus of Mk 4.28 appears to be upon the tender sprout, rather than upon the full-size plant, and since this distinction is lexically important in a number of languages, the term χόρτος has been divided into χόρτος^a and χόρτος^b.

τῶν δένδρων καὶ ἐστρώννυον ἐν τῇ ὁδῷ 'others cut branches from the trees and spread them on the road' Mt 21.8. Some languages distinguish carefully between two major types of branches: those which are essentially leaves (as in the case of palms) and those which have a number of buds or potential branches. Other languages may make a distinction between branches of a plant which is woody (a perennial) and those which are relatively soft and flexible, typical of an annual plant.

3.50 κλῆμα, τος *n*: a more or less tender, flexible branch, as of a vine – 'branch' (principally of grapevines). πᾶν κλῆμα ἐν ἐμοὶ μὴ φέρον καρπόν 'every branch of mine that does not bear fruit' Jn 15.2.

3.51 φύλλον, ου *n* – 'leaf.' ἰδὼν συκῆν ἀπὸ μακρόθεν ἔχουσαν φύλλα 'when he saw from a distance a fig tree which had leaves' Mk 11.13. Some languages make a clear distinction between various kinds of leaves, especially a difference between leaves which have parallel veins and those which have branching veins. In Mk 11.13 what is important is that the fig tree was 'in leaf,' that is to say, the leaves had already come out after the winter season. In a number of languages a tree in this state may be referred to as 'a tree which is green.'

3.52 στιβάς, άδος *f* – 'leafy branch.' ἄλλοι δὲ στιβάδας κόψαντες ἐκ τῶν ἀγρῶν 'and others cut leafy branches in the fields' Mk 11.8.

3.53 βάϊον, ου *n*; φοῖνιξ[b] or φοίνιξ, ικος *m* – 'palm branch.'[5]
βάϊον: ἔλαβον τὰ βαΐα τῶν φοινίκων 'they took palm branches' Jn 12.13.
φοῖνιξ[b]: ὄχλος πολύς . . . ἑστῶτες . . . φοίνικες ἐν ταῖς χερσὶν αὐτῶν 'a great crowd . . . stood there . . . holding palm branches in their hands' Re 7.9.
βάϊον is a technical term meaning 'palm branch,' and in Jn 12.13 τῶν φοινίκων 'of palm

trees' may have been added redundantly, since the term βάϊον may not have been regarded as sufficiently well known to readers.

In the contexts in which φοῖνιξ[a] (Jn 12.13; see 3.8) and φοῖνιξ[b] (Re 7.9) occur in the NT, it is important to obtain a satisfactory term for 'branch,' since in a number of languages a very important distinction is made between branches of palm trees, which are often called 'leaves' (technically they are), and branches of most other trees (often spoken of idiomatically as 'arms of the trees').

3.54 σκόλοψ, οπος *m*: a sharp projection of a woody plant (though possibly a splinter of wood) with the implication of its causing injury and discomfort – 'thorn, splinter.' ἐδόθη μοι σκόλοψ τῇ σαρκί 'I was given a thorn in the flesh' 2 Cor 12.7. In the NT σκόλοψ occurs only in the figurative expression σκόλοψ τῇ σαρκί 'thorn in the flesh,' and this expression has been subject to a number of different interpretations (see 22.20).

3.55 κάλαμος[b], ου *m*: the stalk of a reed plant – 'reed.' ἔτυπτον αὐτοῦ τὴν κεφαλὴν καλάμῳ 'they hit him over the head with a reed' Mk 15.19. In some discussions of κάλαμος[b] the meaning is given as 'cane,' but the term 'cane' must not be confused with the meaning of 'walking stick.' In Mk 15.19 it may be important in some languages to use a phrase such as 'heavy reed' or 'strong reed,' in order to avoid the impression that the instrument used in striking Jesus was some flimsy or fragile stalk of a plant.

3.56 ἄνθος, ους *n*: the blossom of a plant – 'flower.' ὡς ἄνθος χόρτου παρελεύσεται 'will pass away like the flower of a plant' Jas 1.10. In some languages it may be difficult to use generic expressions such as 'flower' or 'plant.' One may therefore be obliged to use a more specific designation of a type of flower which lasts for only a day or so. It is the fragile and temporary nature of the blossom which is important in this figurative context.

3.57 ἄχυρον, ου *n*: the husks of grain – 'chaff.' τὸ δὲ ἄχυρον κατακαύσει πυρὶ ἀσβέστῳ 'he will burn the chaff in a fire that never goes

---

5 Though in English it is generally the custom to speak of what in Greek is βάϊον or φοῖνιξ (3.53) as a 'palm branch,' technically it is only a very large leaf, for there are no buds on these so-called 'branches.'

out' Mt 3.12. Chaff may be referred to in some languages as 'the empty part of the grain' or 'the leaves of the grain' or 'the refuse of the grain.'

3.58 καλάμη, ης *f*: the dry stalks of grain – 'straw, thatch.' ξύλα, χόρτον, καλάμην 'wood, grass, straw' 1 Cor 3.12. It is difficult in 1 Cor 3.12 to know precisely the distinction between χόρτον 'grass' and καλάμην 'straw.' It would seem clear that καλάμην would be less valuable than χόρτον, and this might be a reference to the use of straw as a very poor thatching material. On the other hand, it could be understood as a reference to the use of straw in place of grass in the making of sun-dried bricks.

3.59 πιότης[a], ητος *f*: a nutritionally rich, fatty quality – 'fatness, rich quality.' συγκοινωνὸς τῆς ῥίζης τῆς πιότητος τῆς ἐλαίας ἐγένου 'you have come to share the fatness of the root of the olive tree' Ro 11.17. The text of Ro 11.17 is strange, for literally it reads 'of the root of the richness.' As may be easily understood, a number of scribal variations occur in different manuscripts.

Since the reference in Ro 11.17 is to the olive tree, the fruit of which produces so much oil, one can readily understand the basis for the extension of meaning. Some translations render πιότης simply as 'sap' (New English Bible), while others abandon completely the figure of speech, for example, TEV which has "you share the strong spiritual life."[6] For another treatment of πιότης in Ro 11.17, see 65.7.

F Wood and Wood Products (3.60-3.67)

3.60 ξύλον[a], ου *n*: wood as a substance – 'wood.' πᾶν σκεῦος ἐκ ξύλου τιμιωτάτου 'all kinds of objects made of valuable wood' Re 18.12.

---

6 πιότης occurs in non-biblical Greek in the figurative sense of 'wealth' and 'riches,' and it may be that in Ro 11.17 there is a blend of the conventional figurative meaning of 'wealth' with the more specific quality of fatness as exemplified by the fruit of the olive tree. See also 65.7 and footnote 3 in Domain 65.

A number of languages make a clear distinction between wood as a substance used in artifacts and constructions and wood used for heating or cooking. A further distinction may be made between durable wood (not readily subject to rot or to the effects of termites and borers) and less durable and therefore relatively unsatisfactory wood.

3.61 ξύλον[b], ου *n*: wood as a substance used to burn for heat – 'firewood.' εἰ ἐν τῷ ὑγρῷ ξύλῳ ταῦτα ποιοῦσιν, ἐν τῷ ξηρῷ τί γένηται; 'if they do these things to moist firewood, what will happen in the case of dry firewood?' Lk 23.31. ξύλον in Lk 23.31 may also be interpreted as a live green tree (see 3.4). If one assumes that the meaning here is 'firewood,' then it may be necessary to translate 'wood which has not had an opportunity to dry out' or 'wood which is still green' or '. . .which is still wet with sap.'

3.62 ξύλινος, η, ον: (derivative of ξύλον[a] 'wood,' 3.60) pertaining to being made or consisting of wood – 'of wood, wooden.' καὶ ἀργυρᾶ ἀλλὰ καὶ ξύλινα καὶ ὀστράκινα 'some are made of silver, some of wood, and some of clay' 2 Tm 2.20.

3.63 θύϊνος, η, ον: pertaining to being made or consisting of citron wood (that is, from a citron tree) – 'of citron wood.' καὶ πᾶν ξύλον θύϊνον καὶ πᾶν σκεῦος ἐλεφάντινον 'and all kinds of things made of citron wood and all kinds of objects made of ivory' Re 18.12. The citron tree belongs to the citrus family of plants, and it produces a pale yellow fruit somewhat larger than a lemon, the rind of which is often candied. In Re 18.12, however, the focus is upon the fine quality of the wood, and since citron trees are not known in many parts of the world, it may be useful to translate πᾶν ξύλον θύϊνον simply as 'all kinds of valuable wood.'

3.64 ὕλη[b], ης *f*: the woody part of trees or bushes – 'wood, pile of wood.' ἡλίκον πῦρ ἡλίκην ὕλην ἀνάπτει 'a small fire sets a large pile of wood ablaze' Jas 3.5. In Jas 3.5 ὕλη may be interpreted as a forest (see 3.3).

As already noted in the case of ξύλον[a] (3.60),

a number of languages make a distinction between wood used as building material and wood employed in heating or cooking.

3.65 φρύγανον, ου *n*: dry branches of trees or shrubs broken or cut into suitable lengths for use as firewood – 'dry wood, firewood, sticks.' συστρέψαντος δὲ τοῦ Παύλου φρυγάνων τι πλῆθος καὶ ἐπιθέντος ἐπὶ τὴν πυράν 'Paul had gathered a bundle of sticks and put them on the fire' Ac 28.3.

3.66 κάρφος, ους *n*: a small piece of wood, chaff, or even straw – 'speck, splinter.' τί δὲ βλέπεις τὸ κάρφος τὸ ἐν τῷ ὀφθαλμῷ τοῦ ἀδελφοῦ σου 'why do you see the speck in your brother's eye' Mt 7.3.

3.67 ἄνθραξ, ακος *m* – 'charcoal.' ἄνθραξ occurs in the NT only in Ro 12.20 in the adage ἄνθρακας πυρὸς σωρεύσεις ἐπὶ τὴν κεφαλὴν αὐτοῦ 'heap coals of fire on his head.' This idiomatic expression probably refers to making someone blush with shame and remorse (see 25.199).

In rendering ἄνθρακας πυρός it is not necessary to use a word which specifically refers to 'flaming charcoal.' What is important is that the embers be understood as 'fiery embers' or 'hot ashes' or 'burning ashes.'

4 Animals[1]

Outline of Subdomains[2]

A   Animals (4.1-4.37)
B   Birds (4.38-4.46)
C   Insects (4.47-4.50)
D   Reptiles and Other 'Creeping Things' (4.51-4.57)
E   Fishes and Other Sea Creatures (4.58-4.61)

A   Animals (4.1-4.37)

4.1 ψυχὴ ζωῆς: (an idiom, literally 'living soul') any living creature, whether animal or human – 'living creature.' καὶ πᾶσα ψυχὴ ζωῆς ἀπέθανεν, τὰ ἐν τῇ θαλάσσῃ 'and every creature in the sea died' Re 16.3. Though the phrase ψυχὴ ζωῆς is highly generic in meaning, its specific reference in Re 16.3 is to creatures of the sea, and therefore in most languages one must translate simply 'fish' or 'that which lives in the sea.'

4.2 ζῷον[a], ου *n*: any living creature, whether wild or domesticated (in contrast with plants) – 'living creature, animal.' εἰσφέρεται ζῴων τὸ αἷμα περὶ ἁμαρτίας 'the blood of animals is brought as a sacrifice for sins' He 13.11; οὗτοι δέ, ὡς ἄλογα ζῷα γεγεννημένα φυσικὰ εἰς ἅλωσιν καὶ φθοράν 'they are like dumb animals born to be captured and killed' 2 Pe 2.12.

In a number of languages the equivalent of 'living things' or 'living creatures' is simply 'those which are alive' or 'those that move about.' ζῷον[a], therefore, includes essentially quadrupeds, fish, birds, and insects, and is not used in the NT to designate human beings. In several passages in the book of Revelation, ζῷον[b] 'a living being' (12.32) is employed to refer to supernatural beings at God's throne (note Re 4.6-9 which in many ways is similar to the description of 'living creatures' in Eze 1.5f).

4.3 θηρίον[a], ου *n*: any living creature, not including man – 'animal.' ὡς δὲ εἶδον οἱ βάρβαροι κρεμάμενον τὸ θηρίον ἐκ τῆς χειρὸς αὐτοῦ 'and when the native people saw the animal hanging from his hand' (a reference to a snake) Ac 28.4;[3] καὶ ἦν μετὰ τῶν θηρίων 'and

---

1 For information with regard to the characteristics of a number of specific animals mentioned in the New Testament, as well as certain problems relating to the adequate choice of equivalent terms in other languages, see *Fauna and Flora of the Bible* in the series of Helps for Translators published by the United Bible Societies.

2 The subdomains in Domain 4 *Animals* are based on the generally accepted ancient taxonomy.

3 θηρίον[a] (4.3) in Ac 28.4 includes reptiles and is thus more highly generic in meaning than θηρίον[b] (4.4) which

he lived there among the animals' (a reference to wild animals) Mk 1.13.

4.4 θηρίον^b, ου *n*; **τετράπουν, ποδός** *n*: any four-footed animal, either wild or domesticated – 'animal, quadruped.'

θηρίον^b: πᾶσα γὰρ φύσις θηρίων τε καὶ πετεινῶν ἑρπετῶν τε καὶ ἐναλίων δαμάζεται 'people can tame any wild animal, bird, reptile, or fish' Jas 3.7.[3]

τετράπουν: ἐν ᾧ ὑπῆρχεν πάντα τὰ τετράποδα 'in it were all kinds of four-footed animals' Ac 10.12.

A high percentage of languages appear to have no generic term to identify all kinds of quadrupeds whether wild or domesticated. Rather, they tend to make quite clear distinctions between wild and domesticated animals, and therefore it may be necessary to indicate both types in those contexts where the reference is to both wild as well as domesticated animals. For example, one may sometimes speak of 'animals of the grass and animals of the forest' or 'animals of the barn and animals of the mountains.'

In Ac 10.12 the reference is primarily to wild animals, since for the most part wild animals would be those designated as unclean. However, swine were also regarded as unclean, and they were domesticated.

In Re 13.1ff two visionary creatures are referred to by the term θηρίον 'beast.' Despite their strange symbolic appearance, they would no doubt be included within the potential range of reference of θηρίον^b.

4.5 θρέμμα, τος *n*: domesticated four-footed animals, primarily livestock – 'livestock, cattle.' τὰ θρέμματα αὐτοῦ 'his livestock' Jn 4.12. τὰ θρέμματα in Jn 4.12 would include cattle (bulls, cows, oxen), sheep, goats, donkeys, and possibly camels. It is difficult, however, to obtain in certain languages an expression which is sufficiently generic as to include all such domesticated animals. Sometimes, however, one can use a phrase such as 'animals that people take care of' or 'animals that are herded' or even 'animals that are owned.'

4.6 κτῆνος, ους *n*: a larger type of domesticated animal, primarily one used for riding or carrying loads – 'beast of burden, riding animal, cattle.' κτήνη τε παραστῆσαι 'and provided riding animals' Ac 23.24; ἐπιβιβάσας δὲ αὐτὸν ἐπὶ τὸ ἴδιον κτῆνος 'he put the man on his own riding animal' Lk 10.34; κτήνη καὶ πρόβατα 'cattle and sheep' Re 18.13.

In 1 Cor 15.39 (ἄλλη δὲ σὰρξ κτηνῶν, ἄλλη δὲ σὰρξ πτηνῶν, ἄλλη δὲ ἰχθύων 'another is the flesh of animals, another the flesh of birds, and another the flesh of fish') one might argue that κτηνῶν is simply a highly generic expression for all kinds of animals, but in view of its meaning in so many other contexts, it probably applies even in 1 Cor 15.39 to large domesticated animals.

As in so many instances, the translator must render passages in terms of expressions which are appropriate to particular contexts. For example, in Ac 23.24 a translation such as 'horses' would be appropriate, while in Lk 10.34 the term 'donkey' would be fitting, and in Re 18.13 κτήνη (in which κτῆνος contrasts with πρόβατα 'sheep') would perhaps best be translated as 'cattle.'

4.7 ὑποζύγιον, ου *n*: an animal which can be used to carry a burden or can be ridden – 'pack animal, beast of burden, riding animal.' ἐπιβεβηκὼς ἐπὶ ὄνον, καὶ ἐπὶ πῶλον υἱὸν ὑποζυγίου 'and rides on a donkey, and on a colt, the foal of a beast of burden' Mt 21.5. In Mt 21.5 it may not actually be necessary to translate 'the offspring of a beast of burden' (υἱὸν ὑποζυγίου), since this may be regarded as being completely redundant after speaking of a donkey and her colt. In some languages it may be necessary in certain contexts to indicate the sex of a donkey. In 2 Pe 2.16 the

---

in Jas 3.7 involves a contrast between (1) quadrupeds and (2) birds, reptiles, and fish.

In a number of contexts it is quite impossible to determine whether θηρίον^a or θηρίον^b refers to wild or to domesticated animals. For example, in He 12.20 the reference would seem to be to domesticated animals that might wander over to the holy mountain, but in Jas 3.7 the context points clearly to wild animals, since the reference is to the taming of such animals. But whether the reference is to wild or domesticated animals depends primarily upon the context, and there seems to be no way in which one can clearly distinguish two different meanings of θηρίον, based on wild versus domesticated distinctions.

reference of ὑποζύγιον is a female donkey, as indicated in the Hebrew text of Nu 22.22.

4.8 ἀγέλη, ης *f*: collective for a group of animals – 'herd.' ἀγέλη χοίρων πολλῶν βοσκομένη 'a herd of many pigs was feeding' Mt 8.30.

In a number of languages a 'herd' must be translated merely as 'many,' since there is frequently no corresponding collective term which would be applicable only or even primarily to pigs. In some languages, however, there are highly specific terms for various types of groups of animals, so that a distinctive collective expression may be used for pigs, sheep, horses, camels, etc.

4.9 υἱός[d], οῦ *m*: the male offspring of an animal (occurring in the NT only with ὑποζύγιον 'beast of burden,' 4.7) – 'foal, offspring.' καὶ ἐπὶ πῶλον υἱὸν ὑποζυγίου 'and upon a colt, the offspring of a beast of burden' Mt 21.5. See the discussion of Mt 21.5 in 4.7.

4.10 ἀλώπηξ[a], εκος *f* – 'fox.' αἱ ἀλώπεκες φωλεοὺς ἔχουσιν 'foxes have holes' Lk 9.58. Though the Greek term ἀλώπηξ and the corresponding Hebrew terms used in the OT may refer to either a fox or a jackal, ἀλώπηξ in the NT seems to refer primarily to a fox (see *Fauna and Flora of the Bible*, pp. 31-32 for certain significant distinctions between foxes and jackals).

In areas of the world where the fox is not known, one can sometimes speak of 'a small wild dog' or 'an animal like a small wild dog.' In other instances translators have borrowed the term 'fox' from a dominant language in the area and have then explained the appearance and habits of the animal in a glossary.

For ἀλώπηξ in a figurative sense as applied by Jesus to Herod Antipas, see 88.120.

4.11 λύκος[a], ου *m* – 'wolf.' ὁ λύκος ἁρπάζει 'the wolf snatches' Jn 10.12. In areas of the world in which wolves are not known, some translators have rendered λύκος[a] by the local equivalent of 'leopard' or 'jaguar.' This may be satisfactory for initial translations of the Scriptures, but such shifts in reference are normally rejected at a later stage by those readers who become more acquainted with the types of animals which exist in other parts of the world. In most instances in which local terms for 'wolf' do not exist, translators have used descriptive phrases such as 'wild dog' or 'fierce, wild dog,' or they may have borrowed a term from a dominant language in the area and have added a qualifying phrase, for example, 'a wild animal called wolf.' One may, of course, simply use a more generic expression with some kind of qualifier. For example, in Ac 20.29 it is possible to use 'fierce, wild animals,' for the meaning of the passage is primarily figurative, and a specific designation of wolf is not required.

4.12 ἄρκος, ου *m* and *f* – 'bear.' οἱ πόδες αὐτοῦ ὡς ἄρκου 'his feet were like those of a bear' Re 13.2. The term ἄρκος 'bear' occurs in the NT only in Re 13.2 as a description of the apocalyptic beast. In languages where a term for bear is not known, it is probably best to borrow a word and describe the referent in a footnote or glossary. In Re 13.2 a somewhat descriptive phrase is sometimes employed, for example, 'with large feet having claws like those of an animal called bear.' By this means the information about the bear's feet has been incorporated into the text, but usually it is better to leave such information to a marginal note.

4.13 πάρδαλις, εως *f* – 'leopard.' τὸ θηρίον ὃ εἶδον ἦν ὅμοιον παρδάλει 'a beast whose appearance was like a leopard' Re 13.2. As in the case of the term for 'bear' (4.12), this reference to a leopard occurs in the NT only in Re 13.2 and is likewise used as a means of describing the apocalyptic beast. A term referring to a local type of leopard or jaguar would be perfectly appropriate, and in some languages a term referring to a mountain lion has been employed. In other instances the equivalent expression is based upon a phrase meaning 'fierce, large, cat-like animal.' A borrowed term may also be employed with a descriptive classifier, for example, 'an animal called leopard.'

4.14 λέων, οντος *m* – 'lion.' ὁ ἀντίδικος ὑμῶν διάβολος ὡς λέων ὠρυόμενος περιπατεῖ 'our adversary the Devil walks about as a roaring lion' 1 Pe 5.8. In some languages it may be important to use a descriptive phrase such as 'a very large cat-like animal,' though it will be important to try to make some distinction between 'lion' and 'leopard' (4.13). If necessary, some more extensive identification by description may be employed in a glossary.

4.15 βοῦς, βοός *m* and *f* – (masc.) 'bull' or 'ox' (a castrated bull); (fem.) 'cow'; (plural) 'cattle.' εὗρεν ἐν τῷ ἱερῷ τοὺς πωλοῦντας βόας 'he found those in the Temple selling cattle' Jn 2.14; οὐ κημώσεις βοῦν ἀλοῶντα 'do not muzzle the ox when it treads out grain' 1 Cor 9.9. In most contexts βοῦς (masc. gender) would seem to refer to an ox (in contrast with ταῦρος 'bull,' 4.16). In the plural form βοῦς may be translated simply as a collective 'cattle.'

Though in a number of languages a very special distinction is made between 'bulls' and 'oxen' (or 'steers'), no such marked difference occurs in NT usage, and there appears to be no need of introducing any artificial distinction in particular passages.

4.16 ταῦρος, ου *m* – 'bull.' ὅ τε ἱερεὺς τοῦ Διὸς . . . ταύρους καὶ στέμματα ἐπὶ τοὺς πυλῶνας ἐνέγκας 'the priest of Zeus . . . brought bulls and flowers to the gates' Ac 14.13.

In a number of languages the equivalent of 'bull' is simply a generic term for cattle to which is added a specific designation such as 'male.'

4.17 μόσχος, ου *m*: the young of cattle – 'calf.' φέρετε τὸν μόσχον τὸν σιτευτόν 'bring the fatted calf' Lk 15.23. In Greek outside of the NT μόσχος is either masculine or feminine, but in the NT the forms are either masculine (Lk 15.23, 27, 30) or the distinction is not indicated by the accompanying grammatical forms (He 9.12).

In languages spoken by cattle-raising people, the major difficulty is in finding a satisfactory generic expression, since the tendency is to be very specific in matters of age, sex, color, size, etc. Under such circumstances one can only select terms with more or less generic meaning or employ more specific expressions which seem to fit particular contexts.

4.18 δάμαλις, εως *f*: the young female of cattle – 'heifer.' σποδὸς δαμάλεως 'ashes of a heifer' He 9.13. A δάμαλις 'heifer' would be older and bigger than a calf but younger than a cow, since 'heifer' refers to a cow before she has been impregnated or given birth to her first calf.

4.19 ἔριφος, ου *m*; ἐρίφιον, ου *n* (the diminutive of ἔριφος but without special diminutive meaning)[4] – 'kid, he-goat' in the singular and 'goats' in the plural (in the plural form both male and female goats are included in the reference).

ἔριφος: ὁ ποιμὴν ἀφορίζει τὰ πρόβατα ἀπὸ τῶν ἐρίφων 'the shepherd separates the sheep from the goats' Mt 25.32; ἐμοὶ οὐδέποτε ἔδωκας ἔριφον 'you never gave me a kid' Lk 15.29.

ἐρίφιον: στήσει τὰ μὲν πρόβατα ἐκ δεξιῶν αὐτοῦ τὰ δὲ ἐρίφια ἐξ εὐωνύμων 'he will place the sheep on his right hand but the goats on the left' Mt 25.33.

Since goats are so widely distributed throughout the world, there is usually little or no difficulty involved in finding a satisfactory term. The difficulty arises, however, in the connotations of the term for goat, especially in contrast with sheep. In contrast with usage in the Bible, in many parts of the tropical world goats are much more highly prized than sheep, because they can forage well for themselves and are appreciated for their meat. Sheep, on the other hand, are often regarded as scavengers and are much less valued. One should not reverse biblical statements about sheep and goats, but marginal notes and a fuller explanation of cultural differences in a glossary are important.

4.20 αἴγειος, α, ον: (derivative of αἴξ 'goat,' not occurring in the NT) pertaining to or

---

4 With a number of diminutive forms for animals there may be connotative meanings of endearment or special appreciation, but it is difficult to establish such values in the case of most contexts.

consisting of a goat – 'of a goat.' ἐν αἰγείοις δέρμασιν 'clothed in goat skins' He 11.37.[5]

4.21 τράγος, ου *m* – 'he-goat.' οὐδὲ δι' αἵματος τράγων καὶ μόσχων 'not through the blood of he-goats and calves' He 9.12. A number of languages have special terms for 'he-goat' and 'she-goat,' and frequently there is no formal relationship between the respective terms any more than there is in English between *billy* and *nanny* or between the corresponding terms for sheep, namely, *ram* and *ewe*.

4.22 πρόβατον[a], ου *n* – 'sheep.' ἐρριμμένοι ὡσεὶ πρόβατα μὴ ἔχοντα ποιμένα 'they were helpless like sheep without a shepherd' Mt 9.36.

Since the distribution of sheep throughout the world is somewhat less than that of goats, there may be more difficulties involved in finding an adequate term. In some instances terms for sheep are actually based upon a term for goat. For example, among Eskimos goats are well known because there are wild goats in the mountains, and sheep are accordingly called in some dialects 'woolly goats' or 'goats that have wool.' Among the Maya in Yucatan sheep were introduced by the Spanish and were first described as being 'cotton deer,' and the name still persists.[6] In some areas where sheep are not known at all, the meat of sheep is known, and accordingly sheep may be called by the name of the meat, for example, 'mutton animals.' But in most places where sheep are not indigenous, there is nevertheless some term for them, usually based upon a borrowing from a dominant language.

For the translator, however, there are often problems involving the connotations of the term for sheep and for related expressions concerning their behavior and the ways in which

they are 'led.' As already noted under the discussion of goats (4.19), sheep are frequently less prized than goats, and therefore it may seem strange in biblical texts to find sheep being given a preferential rating. What may appear even more difficult to understand is the suggestion that sheep are led by a shepherd rather than being driven. This fact may require some type of marginal note to accompany the text if people are to understand the basis for a number of similes and metaphors of the Scriptures. Furthermore, if the experience which people have of sheep is only their knowledge about wild sheep, then obviously references to the helplessness of sheep will be either meaningless or even contradictory. Again, a marginal note is in order.

4.23 προβατικός, ή, όν: (derivative of πρόβατον 'sheep,' 4.22) pertaining to sheep – 'of sheep.' ἐπὶ τῇ προβατικῇ 'at the Sheep Gate' Jn 5.2. The phrase ἐπὶ τῇ προβατικῇ is an elliptical expression in which the noun for 'gate' (which is feminine in gender) is omitted. The phrase 'at the Sheep Gate' may be rendered in some languages as 'close to the gate of the city through which sheep entered' or '. . . were driven' or '. . .were led.'

4.24 ἀρήν, ἀρνός *m*; ἀμνός, οῦ *m*: the young of sheep – 'lamb.'
ἀρήν: ἀποστέλλω ὑμᾶς ὡς ἄρνας ἐν μέσῳ λύκων 'I am sending you like lambs among wolves' Lk 10.3.
ἀμνός: ὡς ἀμνὸς ἐναντίον τοῦ κείραντος αὐτὸν ἄφωνος 'he was like a lamb making no sound when its wool is cut off' Ac 8.32.

In a number of languages a clear distinction is made between male and female lambs. It is therefore essential in any figurative reference to male persons to employ an appropriate term for lamb. In a number of languages, of course, a lamb is simply referred to as a 'young sheep' or 'child sheep.'

Perhaps the most widespread story about cultural differences in Bible translation is the one which refers to the translation of 'lamb' as 'little seal of God' in an Eskimo language. However, there is no evidence that this type of rendering was ever used, since in matters of appearance, habitat, and behavior, lambs and

---

5 The base of αἴγειος (namely, αἴξ 'goat') is essentially the same in meaning as that of ἔριφος and ἐρίφιον (4.19). The derivative suffix simply makes possible the use of this term in different syntactic constructions.
6 Since the sheep were approximately the same size as forest deer and since they had a fleece closely resembling wild cotton, they could quite logically be called 'cotton deer.'

little seals have practically nothing in common. Furthermore, Eskimo languages have terms for 'lamb' and in some instances, at least, use the expression 'young, woolly goat,' since wild goats are well known and wool is well known as an imported product.

4.25 ἀρνίον[a], ου *n*: (derivative of ἀρήν 'lamb,' 4.24) a sheep of any age – 'lamb, sheep, ram.' εἶχεν κέρατα δύο ὅμοια ἀρνίῳ 'he had two horns like those of a ram' Re 13.11. In the one context in the NT, namely Re 13.11, in which ἀρνίον refers literally to a sheep, it is used in a phrase referring to the horns of an ἀρνίον. In such a context the reference is undoubtedly to a 'ram,' that is to say, the adult male of sheep.

4.26 ἀρνίον[c], ου *n* – 'Lamb,' a title for Christ. ἄξιόν ἐστιν τὸ ἀρνίον τὸ ἐσφαγμένον 'worthy is the Lamb that has been slain' Re 5.12. ἀρνίον[c] as a title of Jesus Christ occurs only in the book of Revelation, but it is used there more than twenty times. In contrast with ἀρνίον[b] in βόσκε τὰ ἀρνία μου 'feed my lambs' (Jn 21.15; see 11.29), designating people who need care and help, the supplementary components of meaning in ἀρνίον[c] involve the atoning sacrifice of Jesus Christ on the cross. Some persons have wanted to eliminate the notion of 'lamb' in this title, especially in the case of languages in which sheep are looked down on as relatively worthless scavengers (as is the case in certain tropical areas of the world), but in view of the significance of the symbolism of 'lamb' in terms of OT sacrificial practices, it is wrong to avoid a term meaning 'lamb.' A marginal note, however, may be necessary to explain the significance of this title.

4.27 πάσχα[c] *n*: a specially selected lamb (or a collective for all such lambs) killed and eaten during the festival commemorating the departure of Israel from Egypt – 'Passover lamb.' ᾗ ἔδει θύεσθαι τὸ πάσχα 'when the Passover lamb/lambs had to be killed' Lk 22.7.

The term πάσχα (a borrowing from Hebrew) has three different meanings which refer to three different aspects of the Passover. In a context which speaks of 'the Passover taking place' (Mt 26.2), the meaning is the festival (51.6). With a term such as

ἑτοιμάζειν 'to prepare' (Mt 26.19), the term πάσχα means the Passover meal, that is to say, 'to prepare the Passover meal' (51.7). But with a term meaning 'to kill' or 'to sacrifice' (Lk 22.7), the meaning is the Passover lamb. These different meanings in Greek reflect similar uses in Hebrew.

It is often impossible, however, to use a phrase such as 'Passover lamb,' since a literal rendering may suggest 'a lamb that passes over' or 'a lamb that someone has passed over,' either in the sense of 'ridden over' or 'neglected.' It is therefore necessary in many languages to expand the phrase 'the Passover lamb' to read 'the lamb that is eaten at the Passover Festival' or 'the lamb associated with the Festival that celebrates the passing over.' It may even be necessary to expand the phrase 'passing over' to refer specifically to the passing over of the angel of death, and in certain instances one cannot even employ a literal rendering such as 'passing over,' since this might mean merely 'flying above.' Therefore, it may be necessary to use an expression roughly equivalent to 'passing by.' It may, however, be better to use a short, though somewhat obscure, expression in the text and provide a full explanation in a marginal note or glossary.

4.28 ποίμνη[a], ης *f*: a collective for a group of sheep and/or goats – 'flock.' φυλάσσοντες φυλακὰς τῆς νυκτὸς ἐπὶ τὴν ποίμνην αὐτῶν 'keeping watch over their flock at night' Lk 2.8; διασκορπισθήσονται τὰ πρόβατα τῆς ποίμνης 'the sheep of the flock will be scattered' Mt 26.31. In instances in which the reference is to a flock of sheep or goats, one can normally employ a designation for any group of animals, though there are often distinct terms for groups of domesticated animals in contrast with groups of wild animals. And in many languages there are a number of different terms for such groupings of animals depending upon the particular animals in question, for example, in English *swarm, school, drove, pack,* and *bevy.*

4.29 ἵππος, ου *m* – 'horse.' εἰ δὲ τῶν ἵππων τοὺς χαλινοὺς εἰς τὰ στόματα βάλλομεν 'if we put bits into the mouths of horses' Jas 3.3.

Since horses are widely distributed in the world (at least knowledge about them is widespread), it is rarely difficult to obtain a satisfactory term. In some instances, however, expressions designating horses may seem rather strange. For example, in Sediq, a language spoken in Taiwan, a horse is literally 'a soldier's cow.'

4.30 κάμηλος, ου *m* and *f* – 'camel.' ὁ Ἰωάννης εἶχεν τὸ ἔνδυμα αὐτοῦ ἀπὸ τριχῶν καμήλου 'John wore a garment of camel's hair' Mt 3.4; εὐκοπώτερόν ἐστιν κάμηλον διὰ τρυπήματος ῥαφίδος διελθεῖν 'it is easier for a camel to go through the eye of a needle' Mt 19.24.

In most areas where camels are not known, a term for 'camel' has been borrowed from a dominant language. In other instances people may have constructed descriptive phrases. For example, in Timorese the first two expressions suggested for camel were 'the horse with a crooked back' or 'the long-legged horse,' but finally people settled upon a more satisfactory rendering, namely, 'the horse of the desert.' In a number of languages a camel is simply called 'the big humped animal.' In a number of cases, however, it may be useful to have some kind of a description of a camel in a glossary or word list.

In referring to the camel's hair garment worn by John the Baptist, there are two problems. In the first place, it is important to translate the phrase 'garment of camel's hair' in such a way as to indicate that the garment was made of cloth woven out of camel's hair and did not consist of the entire skin nor of camel's hair stuck onto John the Baptist's body. In the second place, it is important to indicate that this camel's hair garment was a kind of rough garment, since in a number of languages an expression such as 'camel's hair coat' would refer to an expensive, luxury garment. See also 6.216.

4.31 ὄνος, ου *m* and *f* – 'donkey, ass.' ὁ βασιλεύς σου ἔρχεται, καθήμενος ἐπὶ πῶλον ὄνου 'your king is coming sitting on the foal of a donkey' Jn 12.15. In this context the reference is obviously to a female donkey.

In languages in which there is no word for 'donkey,' it is usually best to borrow a term from a dominant language rather than attempting some type of descriptive equivalent. For example, in one language a descriptive designation, namely, 'a long-eared animal,' was understood by the people as referring to a rabbit. In some languages donkey is referred to as 'a kind of small horse' or 'a small horse-like animal.'

Though in Greek the article and/or other attributives to the noun ὄνος indicate by their forms whether ὄνος is to be understood as masculine or feminine, in a number of languages quite different terms are employed for a male or female donkey.

4.32 ὀνικός, ή, όν: (derivative of ὄνος 'donkey,' 4.31) pertaining to a donkey – 'of a donkey.' μύλος ὀνικός 'a millstone turned by a donkey' Mt 18.6. In rendering Mt 18.6 it is important to avoid the impression that a donkey would turn the millstone in the same way that a person would. Sometimes a general causative expression may be used, for example, 'a millstone that a donkey causes to go round (rotate),' but it may actually be necessary to say '. . . which a donkey causes to go round (rotate) by pulling on a shaft.' In fact, a marginal note may be necessary in order to avoid serious misunderstanding and to emphasize the fact that such a millstone was large and heavy.

4.33 πῶλος, ου *m*; ὀνάριον, ου *n*: the young of a donkey – 'foal, colt.' εὑρὼν δὲ ὁ Ἰησοῦς ὀνάριον ἐκάθισεν ἐπ᾽ αὐτό, καθώς ἐστιν γεγραμμένον . . . ὁ βασιλεύς σου ἔρχεται, καθήμενος ἐπὶ πῶλον ὄνου 'Jesus found a donkey and sat on it; as it is written . . . your king comes sitting on the foal of a donkey' Jn 12.14-15. As in the case of ὄνος 'donkey' (4.31), a number of languages make a distinction either in form or in terms for the young of a donkey based upon distinctions in sex.

4.34 κύων[a], κυνός, dat pl. κυσί *m* – 'dog,' either a street dog or a watch dog. οἱ κύνες ἐρχόμενοι ἐπέλειχον τὰ ἕλκη αὐτοῦ 'the dogs would come and lick his sores' Lk 16.21. In Greek outside the NT, κύων may be either masculine or feminine and in the plural may refer to both male and female dogs.

4.35 κυνάριον, ου *n* (diminutive of κύων[a] 'dog,' 4.34, but in the NT the diminutive force may have become lost, though a component of emotive attachment or affection is no doubt retained and thus the reference is presumably to a house dog) – 'house dog, little dog.' τὰ κυνάρια ἐσθίει ἀπὸ τῶν ψιχίων τῶν πιπτόντων ἀπὸ τῆς τραπέζης 'the dogs eat the crumbs falling from the table' Mt 15.27.

4.36 χοῖρος, ου *m* – 'pig.' ἀγέλη χοίρων πολλῶν βοσκομένη 'a herd of many pigs was feeding' Mt 8.30.

Though references to pigs in the OT frequently involve very strong connotations of uncleanness and disgust, references in the NT are somewhat more neutral. However, in the story of the Prodigal Son (Lk 15.15) the reference to the task of feeding swine certainly indicates the desperate condition of the younger brother. Some translators have found it necessary to indicate such a fact by a marginal note, since the language into which the translation is being made may reflect a very different cultural attitude from that which occurs in the Scriptures. For example, in certain areas of New Guinea, one who is responsible for taking care of pigs is an individual with relatively high social status.

4.37 ὗς, ὑός *f*: a female pig – 'sow.' ὗς λουσαμένη εἰς κυλισμὸν βορβόρου 'a sow that has bathed herself only to roll in the mud again' 2 Pe 2.22.

B Birds (4.38-4.46)

4.38 πετεινόν, οῦ *n*; **πτηνόν, οῦ** *n*; **ὄρνις, ιθος** *f*; **ὄρνεον, ου** *n*: any kind of bird, wild or domestic – 'bird.'
πετεινόν: ἦλθεν τὰ πετεινὰ καὶ κατέφαγεν αὐτό 'the birds came and ate it' Mk 4.4.[7]
πτηνόν: ἄλλη δὲ σὰρξ κτηνῶν, ἄλλη δὲ σὰρξ πτηνῶν 'another is the flesh of animals, another the flesh of birds' 1 Cor 15.39.
ὄρνις: ὄρνις ἐπισυνάγει τὰ νοσσία αὐτῆς ὑπὸ τὰς

---

7 In Ro 1.23, Ac 11.6, and Jas 3.7 πετεινόν may possibly include insects, but this is not likely. The classifications in these contexts do not necessarily reflect exhaustive distinctions.

πτέρυγας 'a hen gathers her young birds under her wings' Mt 23.37. In this only NT occurrence, ὄρνις probably designates a hen.
ὄρνεον: λέγων πᾶσιν τοῖς ὀρνέοις τοῖς πετομένοις ἐν μεσουρανήματι 'calling to all the birds which fly in midair' Re 19.17. In the NT occurrences of ὄρνεον, the reference is to unclean birds, either birds of prey or scavengers.

All languages have at least some terms for birds, but there may be no generic term which identifies birds while excluding all other creatures which fly. For example, in some languages a term which includes all kinds of birds also includes flying insects and bats. However, since in most instances such a term has birds as its primary reference, it can usually be employed in contexts in which birds are more or less readily identified by other expressions in the passage. In other languages generic terms for birds may identify only certain classes of birds, for example, birds of prey, water birds, and birds of the forest.

4.39 νοσσίον, ου *n*; **νοσσός, οῦ** *m*: the young of any bird – 'young bird.'
νοσσίον: ὄρνις ἐπισυνάγει τὰ νοσσία αὐτῆς ὑπὸ τὰς πτέρυγας 'a hen gathers her young birds under her wings' Mt 23.37.
νοσσός: ζεῦγος τρυγόνων ἢ δύο νοσσοὺς περιστερῶν 'a pair of doves or two young pigeons' Lk 2.24.

4.40 νοσσιά, ᾶς *f*: a collective for the young of birds – 'brood.' ὄρνις τὴν ἑαυτῆς νοσσιὰν ὑπὸ τὰς πτέρυγας 'a hen (gathers) her brood under her wings' Lk 13.34.

4.41 πετεινὰ τοῦ οὐρανοῦ: (an idiom, literally 'birds of the sky') wild birds in contrast with domesticated birds such as chickens – 'birds, wild birds.' ἐμβλέψατε εἰς τὰ πετεινὰ τοῦ οὐρανοῦ 'look at the wild birds' Mt 6.26.

A literal rendering of πετεινὰ τοῦ οὐρανοῦ, either as 'birds of the air' or 'birds of the sky,' may be misleading, since 'birds of the air' might imply that these are birds made out of air, and 'birds of the sky' might suggest they are birds which remain always in the sky. In some languages the equivalent expression is 'birds of the trees' or 'birds of the winds.'

4.42 ἀετός, οῦ *m* – 'eagle, vulture.' ἐδόθησαν τῇ γυναικὶ αἱ δύο πτέρυγες τοῦ ἀετοῦ τοῦ μεγάλου 'they gave the woman two wings of a large eagle' Re 12.14; ὅπου ἐὰν ᾖ τὸ πτῶμα, ἐκεῖ συναχθήσονται οἱ ἀετοί 'wherever there is a dead body, there the vultures will gather' Mt 24.28.

In Re 12.14 the emphasis is upon strength and speed, and therefore a term meaning 'eagle' is probably more satisfactory, but in Mt 24.28 (and the parallel passages in Lk 17.37) the reference is to the eating of dead flesh, and therefore a word meaning 'vultures' is more appropriate.

The basic distinction between eagles and vultures is that the former either capture their prey or feed upon dead carcasses, while vultures only feed upon dead carcasses. Only in the Western Hemisphere are there two distinct families of birds: (1) birds of prey, which also feed upon dead bodies (eagles) and (2) vultures, which never take live prey, but only feed upon carcasses.

4.43 κόραξ, ακος *m* – 'crow, raven.' Crows and ravens belong to the same family of birds, but they differ in size, ravens being somewhat larger and being more inclined to feed on dead bodies. κατανοήσατε τοὺς κόρακας ὅτι οὐ σπείρουσιν οὐδὲ θερίζουσιν 'you know about crows, that they do not spin nor gather into barns' Lk 12.24.

In some languages one must be especially sensitive to connotations relating to terms for 'crow' or 'raven,' since these birds may be either particularly disliked or may be regarded as symbols of death and sickness. If such is the case, it may be preferable to simply use a more generic term for birds.

4.44 περιστερά, ᾶς *f*; τρυγών, όνος *f* – 'dove, pigeon.'
περιστερά: γίνεσθε οὖν φρόνιμοι ὡς οἱ ὄφεις καὶ ἀκέραιοι ὡς αἱ περιστεραί 'be as wise as serpents and as harmless as doves' Mt 10.16. τρυγών: ζεῦγος τρυγόνων ἢ δύο νοσσοὺς περιστερῶν 'a pair of doves or two young pigeons' Lk 2.24.

Though in English a relatively clear distinction is made between 'doves' (which have pointed tails) and 'pigeons' (which have squared off tails), there seems to be no such distinction in the use of περιστερά and τρυγών in the Greek of the New Testament.

There are, however, certain problems involved in the connotations of terms relating to pigeons or doves. According to ancient zoology, the dove was thought to have no bile, and consequently, therefore, to be a very peaceful and clean bird. It thus became a symbol of Christian virtue and of gentleness (as in Mt 10.16). In reality, however, doves and pigeons are quite aggressive, and a group of pigeons are frequently known to peck an injured bird to death. Therefore, in some societies pigeons or doves are not regarded as gentle or peaceful, but rather as wicked and harmful. In fact, in some cultures doves are thought to be symbols of death and of evil. Under such circumstances it is important, therefore, to have some marginal note so as to indicate clearly the symbolic significance of such birds in biblical contexts.

4.45 ἀλέκτωρ, ορος *m*: a male chicken – 'rooster, cock.' πρὶν ἀλέκτορα φωνῆσαι τρὶς ἀπαρνήσῃ με 'before the rooster crows, you will deny me three times' Mt 26.34.

4.46 στρουθίον, ου *n* – 'sparrow.' οὐχὶ δύο στρουθία ἀσσαρίου πωλεῖται 'for only a penny you can buy two sparrows' Mt 10.29.

The Greek term στρουθίον no doubt refers to the so-called 'house sparrow,' which almost always builds its nests near human habitation. In the Orient a similar type of sparrow exists, and a term designating such a sparrow can be used in all contexts in which the Greek term στρουθίον is employed.

C Insects (4.47-4.50)

4.47 ἀκρίς, ίδος *f* – 'locust.' ἐσθίων ἀκρίδας καὶ μέλι ἄγριον 'eating locusts and wild honey' Mk 1.6; ἐξῆλθον ἀκρίδες εἰς τὴν γῆν 'locusts came on the earth' Re 9.3.

The four NT contexts in which ἀκρίς occurs refer to locusts, either as being edible (Mt 3.4; Mk 1.6) or as being very destructive (Re 9.3, 7). In general, locusts should be carefully distinguished from so-called grasshoppers, since the latter are rarely eaten by people, while in a number of different parts of the world the former are regarded as an important source of food.

Some persons have assumed that the reference to locusts being eaten by John the Baptist should be understood not as the insects but as carob pods, but there is neither linguistic nor cultural evidence to support such an interpretation.

In a number of parts of the world there are different kinds of locusts, some of which are edible, and others which are not edible. It is therefore important in the contexts of Mt 3.4 and Mk 1.6 to select a term which designates edible locusts.

4.48 κώνωψ, ωπος *m* – 'gnat, mosquito.' διϋλίζοντες τὸν κώνωπα τὴν δὲ κάμηλον καταπίνοντες 'straining out a gnat but swallowing a camel' Mt 23.24. The straining of liquids referred to in Mt 23.24 is based on the regulations in Leviticus 11, in which the gnat is the smallest of the unclean creatures and the camel the largest.

For the only occurrence of κώνωψ in the NT, one may use a term which refers to any small flying insect which might fall into a beverage and thus have to be strained out.

4.49 σής, σητός *m* – 'moth.' ὅπου σὴς καὶ βρῶσις ἀφανίζει 'where moth and rust destroy' Mt 6.19.

In the NT the Greek term σής is used only in reference to the larvae of moths, and therefore it is frequently necessary to employ a term in the receptor language for the larvae rather than for the flying insect. This means that frequently an appropriate equivalent is 'the worms of moths,' but often one can employ an expression which means simply 'cloth worms' or 'cloth eaters.'

In Mt 6.19, 20 and in Lk 12.33 the effect of the larvae of moths is combined with rust as agents for the destruction of valuable objects. It is rare, however, that one can speak of the destruction caused by moths in the same way as one can describe the effects of rust or tarnish. It may therefore be necessary to talk about 'moths eating cloth,' while 'tarnish ruins precious metal.'

4.50 μελίσσιος, ον: (derivative of μέλισσα 'bee,' not occurring in the NT) pertaining to bees – 'of bees.'

In the Textus Receptus of Lk 24.42 μελίσσιος occurs in a phrase meaning 'from honeycomb of bees.' This reference to the honeycomb occurs only in the apparatus of the UBS Greek New Testament.

D Reptiles and Other 'Creeping Things' (4.51-4.57)

4.51 ἑρπετόν, οῦ *n* – 'creeping animal, reptile, snake.' ἐν ᾧ ὑπῆρχεν πάντα τὰ τετράποδα καὶ ἑρπετά 'in it were all kinds of quadrupeds and creeping things' Ac 10.12.

Though ἑρπετόν is often interpreted as referring only to snakes, it also includes in biblical contexts (as the result of the influence of classifications based on Hebrew terminology, as in Gn 1.25, 26, and 30) a number of small four-footed animals as well as snakes, for example, rats, mice, frogs, toads, salamanders, and lizards. However, in the various NT contexts (for example Ac 10.12, 11.6; Ro 1.23; and Jas 3.7 where 'creeping things' are contrasted with birds, animals, and fish) it is probably more satisfactory to use a term which designates primarily snakes. In a number of languages a very important distinction is made between four-footed reptiles (such as lizards) and snakes. If such a distinction is made, it is then probably better to use a term which designates only snakes, since a term for 'animals' will probably also include lizards.

4.52 ὄφις[a]**, εως** *m* – 'reptile, snake.' δέδωκα ὑμῖν τὴν ἐξουσίαν τοῦ πατεῖν ἐπάνω ὄφεων 'I gave you authority to step on snakes' Lk 10.19.

Though ὄφις[a] may refer to any kind of snake, in Lk 10.19 it is obviously a reference to a poisonous snake that would harm a person who stepped on it. In translating Lk 10.19 it is essential to avoid an expression which will mean merely 'to walk on snakes' as though one were to walk for some distance over a mass of swarming snakes. The implication of this context is simply that one is able to step on snakes without being harmed.

4.53 ἀσπίς, ίδος *f*; ἔχιδνα[a], ης *f*: species of poisonous snakes – 'asp, cobra, viper.'
ἀσπίς: ἰὸς ἀσπίδων ὑπὸ τὰ χείλη αὐτῶν 'the poison of asps is under their lips' Ro 3.13.
ἔχιδνα[a]: ἔχιδνα ἀπὸ τῆς θέρμης ἐξελθοῦσα καθῆψεν τῆς χειρὸς αὐτοῦ 'a viper came out because of the heat and fastened itself to his hand' Ac 28.3.

The terms ἀσπίς and ἔχιδνα[a] may be used to refer to almost any kind of poisonous snake, and since at least some type of poisonous snake occurs in practically all parts of the world, there is usually little difficulty involved in finding an appropriate term. One can, however, always employ a descriptive expression, for example, 'a snake whose bite causes death.'

4.54 δράκων, οντος *m*: a legendary animal, usually regarded as being a kind of monstrous winged serpent or lizard – 'dragon.' δράκων μέγας πυρρός, ἔχων κεφαλὰς ἑπτά 'a great red dragon with seven heads' Re 12.3.

All references to δράκων in the NT occur in the book of Revelation (chapters 12, 13, 16, and 20), where the term is used as a descriptive epithet for the Devil. In a sense, therefore, the connotative values of the term 'dragon' are to some extent even more important than the specific denotation. In most areas of the world a term for dragon would imply something fearsome, but in certain parts of the Orient the dragon is regarded as the symbol of prosperity and good fortune, and it is necessary, therefore, in translating into certain languages in the Orient to employ (1) a somewhat different expression, for example, 'terrible reptile' or 'fearsome snake' or (2) a marginal note which will explain the differences in connotation.

4.55 βάτραχος, ου *m* – 'frog.' εἶδον . . . πνεύματα τρία ἀκάθαρτα ὡς βάτραχοι 'I saw . . . three unclean spirits like frogs' Re 16.13. In this only reference to frogs in the NT, the connotation is of something unclean and abhorrent. In a number of societies, however, frogs are regarded as very valuable and worthwhile animals, since they are often an important source of food. On the other hand, in such areas there are usually certain types of frogs or toads which are particularly poisonous and whose names, therefore, do carry bad connotations.

4.56 σκορπίος, ου *m* – 'scorpion.' ὁ βασανισμὸς αὐτῶν ὡς βασανισμὸς σκορπίου 'their torture was like the torture of (the sting of) a scorpion' Re 9.5. In the two NT occurrences of σκορπίος (Re 9.5, 10), the emphasis is upon the stinging capacity of the scorpion, and if in a particular area of the world scorpions are not known, it is possible to use a descriptive phrase such as 'a fierce, stinging, little creature.'

4.57 σκώληξ, ηκος *m* – 'maggot, worm.' ὅπου ὁ σκώληξ αὐτῶν οὐ τελευτᾷ 'where their worm does not die' Mk 9.48. In Mk 9.48 the reference is clearly to the type of maggots which feed on refuse.

In a number of languages a very important distinction is made between three different types of worms: (1) maggots, (2) worms that live in the ground, so-called 'earthworms,' and (3) intestinal worms. It is essential that an appropriate term be employed in order to avoid meaninglessness or misunderstanding.

E Fishes and Other Sea Creatures (4.58-4.61)

4.58 ἐνάλιον, ου *n*: any creature living in the sea – 'sea creature, fish.' πᾶσα γὰρ φύσις θηρίων τε καὶ πετεινῶν ἑρπετῶν τε καὶ ἐναλίων δαμάζεται 'man can tame any wild animal, bird, reptile, or creature of the sea' Jas 3.7. In Jas 3.7 one may, of course, simply employ 'fish,' since these are the most prominent examples of creatures in the sea.

4.59 ἰχθύς, ύος *m* – 'fish.' ἢ καὶ ἰχθὺν αἰτήσει 'if he asks for a fish' Mt 7.10.

Though all languages have terms to designate at least certain kinds of fish, there are frequently important distinctions between varieties. In a number of instances distinctions are made between fish which have scales and those which do not (an important distinction in the OT, since it constituted the basis for distinguishing between 'clean' or 'unclean' varieties). In other languages the distinction may be made between fresh water and salt water fish, while in still other languages a clear distinction is made between edible and inedible fish.

Some languages also distinguish between fish which are still alive in the water and those which have been caught and are in various stages of preparation for being eaten. In Mt 7.10 ἰχθύς may refer to a piece of fish ready to be eaten.

4.60 ἰχθύδιον, ου *n*: (diminutive of ἰχθύς 'fish,' 4.59) any kind of relatively small fish – 'little fish.' εἶχον ἰχθύδια ὀλίγα 'they had a few little fish' Mk 8.7.

4.61 κῆτος, ους *n*: any large sea monster – 'big fish, huge fish.' ὥσπερ γὰρ ἦν Ἰωνᾶς ἐν τῇ κοιλίᾳ τοῦ κήτους 'for as Jonah was in the belly of the big fish' Mt 12.40.

5 Foods and Condiments[1]

Outline of Subdomains

A Food (5.1-5.22)
B Condiments (5.23-5.28)

A Food (5.1-5.22)

5.1 χόρτασμα, τος *n*; ἐπισιτισμός, οῦ *m*; ἄρτος[b], ου *m*; τροφή, ῆς *f*; διατροφή, ῆς *f*; βρῶμα[a], τος *n*; βρῶσις[c], εως *f*: any kind of food or nourishment – 'food.'[2]

χόρτασμα: λιμὸς . . . καὶ οὐχ ηὕρισκον χορτάσματα 'there was a famine . . . and they did not find food' Ac 7.11.[3]

ἐπισιτισμός: ἀπόλυσον τὸν ὄχλον, ἵνα . . . εὕρωσιν ἐπισιτισμόν 'send the people away so that . . . they can find food' Lk 9.12.

ἄρτος[b]: τὸν ἄρτον ἡμῶν τὸν ἐπιούσιον δὸς ἡμῖν σήμερον 'give us today the food we need' Mt 6.11.

τροφή: ἄξιος γὰρ ὁ ἐργάτης τῆς τροφῆς αὐτοῦ 'a worker is worthy of his food' Mt 10.10.[4]

διατροφή: ἔχοντες δὲ διατροφὰς καὶ σκεπάσματα, τούτοις ἀρκεσθησόμεθα 'if we have food and clothes, that should be enough for us' 1 Tm 6.8.[4]

βρῶμα[a]: ἀγοράσωσιν ἑαυτοῖς βρώματα 'that they may buy themselves some food' Mt 14.15.

βρῶσις[c]: ἐργάζεσθε μὴ τὴν βρῶσιν τὴν ἀπολλυμένην 'do not work for food that spoils' Jn 6.27.

Almost all languages have at least a few general terms for food, though these may be derived from verbal expressions meaning essentially 'that which is eaten.' In some instances a distinction may be made between 'that which is chewed' and 'that which is drunk,' and it may therefore be important in certain contexts to speak of food in general by a phrase meaning 'that which is either chewed or drunk.' If one fails to include both types of food, the reader might interpret a passage

---

1 Foods are variously classified in different languages. For example, a number of languages make a basic distinction between solid foods and liquid foods; others distinguish between so-called 'hot foods' and 'cold foods,' though in these languages this distinction has nothing to do with the temperature of the food at the time it is eaten, but is dependent upon concepts relating to whether the food in question is propitious for being eaten when the body is 'warm' or when the body is 'cool.' In other languages distinctions are made between vegetable products and animal products, though items such as eggs, cheese, and milk may be classified variously, in some instances as animal products and in other instances as vegetable products.

2 There are no doubt certain subtle differences of meaning in the various terms listed here as meaning 'food,' but it is impossible to determine such distinctions in meaning from NT contexts. Perhaps τροφή and διατροφή are somewhat more generic in meaning and may suggest a greater emphasis upon nourishment (see footnote 4). At the same time, βρῶσις[c] and βρῶμα[a] may imply solid substantive food, but it is difficult, if not impossible, to argue for such subtle connotative distinctions in meanings which are essentially generic.

3 Although in Hellenistic Greek χόρτασμα normally

refers to the food of animals and is regularly rendered as 'fodder,' in Ac 7.11 the reference is to food for people.

4 It is possible that τροφή and διατροφή focus primarily upon the meaning of food as nourishment, and in both Mt 10.10 and 1 Tm 6.8 it would be perfectly appropriate to use a translation meaning 'nourishment' rather than merely 'food.'

such as Mt 6.11 as requesting only solid foods.

In the place of a general term or phrase such as 'that which is eaten' or 'that which is consumed,' some languages generalize the meaning of a particular term. For example, in certain parts of the Orient the term meaning specifically 'rice' also refers to 'food' in general. In fact, some persons will declare, 'I have not eaten!' if they have not had rice as part of a meal. A similar type of meaning has developed in English with respect to 'bread.' For example, in rendering Lk 4.4 (οὐκ ἐπ' ἄρτῳ μόνῳ ζήσεται ὁ ἄνθρωπος 'man shall not live by bread alone') it would be wrong to employ a strictly literal rendering, since this might mean simply that people should not live on a diet consisting solely of bread. The meaning of Lk 4.4 is, of course, 'to live means more than merely eating.'

5.2 σιτίον[b], ου *n*: (diminutive of σῖτος[a] 'wheat, grain,' 3.41, but without diminutive meaning and occurring primarily in the plural) food consisting principally of grain products – 'food, grain.' ἀκούσας δὲ Ἰακὼβ ὄντα σιτία εἰς Αἴγυπτον 'and when Jacob heard that there was food in Egypt' Ac 7.12. It is, of course, possible in Ac 7.12 to understand the plural form as grain (see 3.42), but the reference is probably to food made from grain, a common meaning of this term in Classical Greek.

5.3 σιτομέτριον, ου *n*: an appropriate portion or ration of food (a type of food allowance) – 'a due amount of food rations.' τοῦ διδόναι ἐν καιρῷ τὸ σιτομέτριον 'to give them the due amount of food at the right time' Lk 12.42. It is possible to interpret σιτομέτριον in Lk 12.42 as 'the proper amount of food' or 'the food that was due them' or 'the food that should be given (to the servants).' Since σιτομέτριον is a semantically complex term consisting of two quite distinct components, it is usually necessary to employ a phrase as a proper equivalent.

5.4 ψωμίον, ου *n*: a small piece or bit of bread – 'a piece of bread, a bit of bread.' ἐγὼ βάψω τὸ ψωμίον καὶ δώσω αὐτῷ 'I will dip a piece of bread and give it to him' Jn 13.26. In

Jn 13.26, 27, 30 it may be necessary to use a phrase such as 'a broken-off piece of bread'; otherwise the inference might be that the ψωμίον was simply a scrap or crumb of bread. In some languages the appropriate equivalent of ψωμίον in this type of context is 'a bite of bread.'

5.5 ψιχίον, ου *n*; ψίξ, ψιχός *f*: a small piece of food (normally bread) – 'scrap, crumb.' ψιχίον: τὰ κυνάρια ἐσθίει ἀπὸ τῶν ψιχίων τῶν πιπτόντων ἀπὸ τῆς τραπέζης 'the dogs eat the crumbs falling from the table' Mt 15.27. ψίξ: ἐπιθυμῶν χορτασθῆναι ἀπὸ τῶν πιπτόντων ἀπὸ τῆς τραπέζης 'being glad to eat the scraps that fall from the table' Lk 16.21 (apparatus).

In Mt 15.27, Mk 7.28, and Lk 16.21 (apparatus) the reference is to small crumbs or pieces of food that might fall from the table. In some languages an equivalent is 'a small bit of food' or 'a tiny bite of food.'

5.6 πόσις[a], εως *f*; πόμα, τος *n*: liquids used for nourishment or to satisfy thirst – 'a drink.' πόσις[a]: τὸ αἷμά μου ἀληθής ἐστιν πόσις 'my blood is true drink' Jn 6.55. πόμα: μόνον ἐπὶ βρώμασιν καὶ πόμασιν 'these relate only to food and drink' He 9.10.

Though in many languages the equivalent of πόσις and πόμα would be a verbal derivative meaning basically 'that which is drunk,' in other languages the equivalent may be 'watery food' or 'liquid food.'

In some languages, however, one cannot refer to 'blood' (Jn 6.55) as being 'drink,' since blood is classified as food rather than as drink. On the other hand, it may be possible to translate 'my blood is the real drink' as 'my blood is real nourishment.' The expression 'food and drink' (He 9.10) may be better rendered in some languages as 'all kinds of food.'

5.7 βρῶμα[b], τος *n*; βρῶσις[d], εως *f*: any type of solid food, particularly meat – 'solid food, meat, flesh.' βρῶμα[b]: γάλα ὑμᾶς ἐπότισα, οὐ βρῶμα 'I gave you milk to drink, not solid food' 1 Cor 3.2; ἀπέχεσθαι βρωμάτων 'to abstain from meat' 1 Tm 4.3. βρῶσις[d]: οὐ γάρ ἐστιν ἡ βασιλεία τοῦ θεοῦ βρῶσις καὶ πόσις 'the kingdom of God is not a matter of food and drink' Ro 14.17.[5]

5.8 ἄρτος[a]**, ου** *m*: a relatively small and generally round loaf of bread (considerably smaller than present-day typical loaves of bread and thus more like 'rolls' or 'buns') – 'loaf of bread.' οὐκ ἔχομεν ὧδε εἰ μὴ πέντε ἄρτους 'we have here only five loaves of bread' Mt 14.17.

5.9 ἄλευρον, ου *n* – 'wheat flour.' ἢν . . . γυνὴ ἐνέκρυψεν εἰς ἀλεύρου σάτα τρία 'which . . . a woman hid in three measures of wheat flour' Mt 13.33. In some languages wheat flour is described as 'ground wheat' or 'powdered wheat.'

5.10 σεμίδαλις, εως *f*: a fine grade of wheat flour – 'fine flour.' οἶνον καὶ ἔλαιον καὶ σεμίδαλιν καὶ σῖτον 'wine and oil and fine flour and wheat' Re 18.13. In some languages 'fine flour' may be best expressed as 'expensive flour.' Such a rendering fits well the context of Re 18.13.

5.11 ζύμη, ης *f*: leaven employed in making bread rise – 'yeast.' μικρὰ ζύμη ὅλον τὸ φύραμα ζυμοῖ 'a little yeast leavens the whole lump' 1 Cor 5.6. In some languages yeast is described simply as 'that which makes bread rise,' but frequently yeast is described in terms of some characteristic or on the basis of its source, for example, 'sour froth' or 'beer foam.'

5.12 ζυμόω: (derivative of ζύμη 'yeast,' 5.11) to employ yeast in the process of making bread rise – 'to use yeast.' ἐνέκρυψεν εἰς ἀλεύρου σάτα τρία ἕως οὗ ἐζυμώθη ὅλον 'she put yeast in three measures of wheat flour until the whole lump had risen' Mt 13.33.

5.13 ἄζυμος, ον: pertaining to the absence of yeast – 'without yeast, not having yeast, unleavened.' ἦσαν δὲ αἱ ἡμέραι τῶν ἀζύμων 'this was during the days of Unleavened Bread' Ac 12.3.

The phrase 'unleavened bread' may be rendered as 'bread made without yeast' or 'bread which does not rise.' Perhaps a more difficult problem is involved in the relationship of 'days' to 'unleavened bread,' and accordingly, the expression 'the days of Unleavened Bread' may be rendered as 'the days when people ate bread that had no yeast.' Except for 1 Cor 5.7-8, in which ἄζυμος occurs in a highly figurative passage referring to pure and true life, this term is used exclusively in reference to the feast or festival of Unleavened Bread.

5.14 κρέας, κρέατος and κρέως, acc. pl. **κρέα** *n*: the flesh of animals used as food – 'meat.' μὴ φαγεῖν κρέα μηδὲ πιεῖν οἶνον 'not to eat meat nor drink wine' Ro 14.21. In some languages a distinction is made between the meat of wild animals and meat of domesticated animals. In Ro 14.21 and 1 Cor 8.13 it is the latter which is involved.

5.15 εἰδωλόθυτον, ου *n*: the meat of animals which have been sacrificed to idols – 'sacrificial meat, meat of animals sacrificed to an idol.' περὶ δὲ τῶν εἰδωλοθύτων, οἴδαμεν ὅτι πάντες γνῶσιν ἔχομεν 'concerning sacrificial meat, we know that we all have knowledge' 1 Cor 8.1. εἰδωλόθυτον is a semantically complex word meaning literally 'that which has been sacrificed to idols.' There is no specific element meaning 'meat,' but the stem meaning 'sacrifice' implies 'meat.' Part of the sacrifice was normally burned on the altar, part was eaten during a ritual meal in a temple, and part was sold in the public market. According to Jewish tradition this meat was unclean and therefore forbidden. εἰδωλόθυτον is normally translated by a phrase, for example, 'meat which had been offered to idols' or 'meat of an animal which had been sacrificed to idols' or 'meat of animals killed in honor of false gods.'

5.16 ὀψάριον, ου *n*: fish intended for food or the flesh of fish as food – 'fish.' ἔστιν παιδάριον ὧδε ὃς ἔχει πέντε ἄρτους κριθίνους καὶ δύο ὀψάρια 'there is a boy here who has five barley

---

5 It would also be possible to classify βρῶσις καὶ πόσις in Ro 14.17 as referring to the events of eating and drinking. The meanings of βρῶσις and πόσις (5.6) would then be classified under Domain 23A.

loaves and two fish' Jn 6.9. In Greek the usual meaning of ὀψάριον is a tidbit of food eaten with bread, but it occurs in later Greek in the meaning of fish, and in the NT this meaning occurs only in the fourth Gospel (compare the usage in Jn 6.9 with ἰχθύς in parallel passages).

Many languages distinguish clearly between terms for fish while still living in the water and fish which have been caught and presumably are to be used for food.

5.17 προσφάγιον, ου *n*: the flesh of fish as food – 'fish.' παιδία, μή τι προσφάγιον ἔχετε; 'children, have you any fish?' Jn 21.5. In literature outside the NT, προσφάγιον normally refers to some type of relish eaten with bread, but in Jn 21.5 (the only occurrence in the NT) the reference is to the flesh of fish.[6]

5.18 ᾠόν, οῦ *n*: any kind of egg, but primarily a chicken egg – 'egg, chicken egg.' ἢ καὶ αἰτήσει ᾠόν, ἐπιδώσει αὐτῷ σκορπίον; 'or if he asks for an egg, will you give him a scorpion?' Lk 11.12. In some languages a distinction is made between eggs produced by birds and those produced by such other animals as reptiles and amphibians. In this one NT context the reference is, of course, to the egg of a hen.[7]

5.19 γάλα, γάλακτος *n* – 'milk.' γάλα ὑμᾶς ἐπότισα, οὐ βρῶμα 'I fed you milk, not solid food' 1 Cor 3.2. The term γάλα may refer to any type of milk, whether produced by humans or by certain domesticated animals, for example, cow, sheep, goat, camel. In a number of languages two distinct terms are used for milk, one identifying the human milk and another term specifying milk from animals. In the context of 1 Cor 3.2 it is probably the latter reference which is important,

though the passage is highly figurative and the emphasis is upon food for babies.[7]

5.20 μέλι, ιτος *n* – 'honey' (produced by bees). ἀλλ' ἐν τῷ στόματί σου ἔσται γλυκὺ ὡς μέλι 'but it will be as sweet as honey in your mouth' Re 10.9. Though honey may be regarded by some as a vegetable product, since flowers constitute its source, it is more specifically associated with bees and in some languages is actually called 'bee urine.' μέλι ἄγριον, literally 'wild honey,' refers to bee honey gathered in the fields and not the result of keeping bees in hives. In the ancient world bee keeping was a highly developed industry, since honey was a principal source of sweetening. The equivalent of wild honey in a number of languages is 'forest honey' or 'tree honey.'

5.21 κηρίον, ου *n* – 'honeycomb.' οἱ δὲ ἐπέδωκαν αὐτῷ . . . ἀπὸ μελισσίου κηρίου 'and they gave him . . . some honeycomb' Lk 24.42 (apparatus); see 4.50. In rendering κηρίον it is important to employ an expression which will include both the honey and the comb. A literal rendering of 'honeycomb' might refer only to the wax container without the honey, but for many languages a term meaning simply 'honey' also refers to the honeycomb.

5.22 μάννα *n*: the miraculous food given by God to the Israelites during their journey through the wilderness – 'manna.' στάμνος χρυσῆ ἔχουσα τὸ μάννα καὶ ἡ ῥάβδος 'Ααρών 'a gold jar containing the manna and Aaron's rod' He 9.4. In most languages μάννα is rendered by a transliteration as 'manna' or 'mana.' One must, however, be very careful about the transliteration of this term, since it may correspond to an indigenous expression having quite a different meaning. Although in the OT it may be useful to have a marginal note explaining the play on words involved in the derivation of this term, in the NT one can

---

6 One may argue that the meaning of προσφάγιον in Jn 21.5 is 'relish,' and that it is only the specialized context which makes possible the reference to fish. On the other hand, one may also argue that, as in the case of ὀψάριον (5.16), the term προσφάγιον has undergone a specialization of meaning, so that it no longer refers to any type of relish eaten with bread, but has the more specific meaning of fish as food.

7 The meanings of ᾠόν 'egg' (5.18) and γάλα 'milk' (5.19) could be classified under *Body Products* in Domain 8, but in the NT contexts the focus is upon these products as food and not upon the physiological processes involved in producing such products.

usually use an expression such as 'food called manna.'

B   Condiments (5.23-5.28)

5.23 ἄμωμον, ου *n*: a generic term for any kind of spice, though often a specific reference to amomum, an Indian type of spice – 'spice, amomum.' κιννάμωμον καὶ ἄμωμον καὶ θυμιάματα 'cinnamon and spice and incense' Re 18.13. In most translations ἄμωμον is interpreted as spice in general, and though in all languages some types of herb-derivative condiments are employed, there may be no general term for such spices. One may, however, in some instances use a descriptive phrase, for example, 'good-tasting herbs' or 'flavoring leaves.'

5.24 κιννάμωμον, ου *n*: a type of spice derived from the bark of certain aromatic plants – 'cinnamon.' κιννάμωμον καὶ ἄμωμον καὶ θυμιάματα 'cinnamon and spice and incense' Re 18.13. In most languages κιννάμωμον is simply borrowed in a transliterated form. However, it is also possible to use a type of descriptive phrase, for example, 'good-tasting bark' or 'flavoring bark.'

5.25 ἅλς, ἁλός *m*; ἅλας, ατος *n* (there is no distinction of meaning between these two terms; ἅλας is merely a later spelling) – 'salt.' ὑμεῖς ἐστε τὸ ἅλας τῆς γῆς ἐὰν δὲ τὸ ἅλας μωρανθῇ, ἐν τίνι ἁλισθήσεται; 'you are the salt of the earth, but if the salt becomes tasteless, how will it be made salty again?' Mt 5.13.

Since salt is a universal condiment, there is no difficulty involved in finding an adequate expression for it, but there is a difficulty in Mt 5.13, since pure salt cannot lose its taste. In the ancient world, however, what was often sold as salt was highly adulterated and the sodium chloride could leach out in humid weather, in which case the residue (normally a form of lime) would be useless. It may, therefore, be important in some languages to provide a marginal note explaining the basis for the biblical statement concerning salt losing its flavor; otherwise, the parable may appear to be either meaningless or misleading.

5.26 ἁλυκός, ή, όν: (derivative of ἅλς 'salt,' 5.25) consisting of or pertaining to salt – 'salty.' οὔτε ἁλυκὸν γλυκὺ ποιῆσαι ὕδωρ 'nor can a salty spring produce sweet water' Jas 3.12. It may be difficult in some languages to speak of 'a salty spring'; rather, it may be necessary to say 'a spring that produces water that tastes salty.' In other instances one may have to say 'a spring that flows from salty ground.'

5.27 ἄναλος, ον: pertaining to a lack of salt – 'without salt, saltless.' ἐὰν δὲ τὸ ἄναλον γένηται 'if the salt has become saltless' Mk 9.50. In some languages one may render 'if the salt has become saltless' as 'if the salt no longer tastes like salt,' but for a discussion of some of the basic problems involved in a rendering of Mk 9.50, see 5.25.

5.28 ἁλίζω: (a causative derivative of ἅλς 'salt,' 5.25) to cause something to taste salty – 'to apply salt to something, to restore the flavor to salt.' ἐὰν δὲ τὸ ἅλας μωρανθῇ, ἐν τίνι ἁλισθήσεται; 'but if the salt becomes tasteless, how will it be made salty again?' Mt 5.13; πᾶς γὰρ πυρὶ ἁλισθήσεται 'for everyone will be salted with fire' Mk 9.49.[8]

In Mt 5.13 one may employ a causative such as 'how will the salt be made salty again' or 'how can one cause the salt to return.' In Mk 9.49 the meaning is particularly obscure. According to OT requirements sacrifices were to be salted (Lv 2.13), and it may be that in Mk 9.49 the fire is regarded as an equivalent of salt and as a symbol of suffering and sacrifice by which the disciple is tested.

---

8 It would be possible to analyze the occurrence of ἁλίζω in Mt 5.13 and Mk 9.49 as representing two quite distinct meanings, in the first instance 'to restore the taste of salt,' and in the second instance 'to cause something to taste salty.' However, this type of distinction does not seem to be necessary, for one may define the meaning of ἁλίζω as 'to cause something to taste salty.' This would then apply either to salt itself which has previously lost its salty flavor or to a sacrifice which needs to be salted. However, as already noted, the meaning of ἁλίζω in Mk 9.49 is extremely obscure and can only be understood in a highly figurative sense.

6 Artifacts[1]

1 The domain of *Artifacts* is particularly complex, for there are a number of relations between subsets of this class, and the very limitation of vocabulary in the NT results in a significant number of gaps.

Artifacts may be classified on the basis of three different sets of features: (1) materials of which the object is made, (2) the form of the object, and (3) the function or use of the object. The third basis of classification has been generally employed in setting up the following subdomains of *Artifacts*, since use and function are so important for the translator and more often than not constitute the basis for determining adequate equivalents between languages. Function is not, however, a fully satisfactory basis for classification, since the same object may have more than one function. For example, 'stocks' may be instruments either (1) for fastening or binding and/or (2) for punishment. The meanings of the terms τρῆμα, τρύπημα, and τρυμαλιά 'hole' (6.216) should theoretically be treated in a larger domain of openings and apertures, but in the NT these terms are only used to refer to a hole in a needle, and hence for the convenience of translators these terms are treated together with the term for needle, since they refer specifically to a particular kind of a hole. The corresponding expressions in various receptor languages are often highly specific and frequently involve idiomatic equivalences.

2 Because of the many different types of artifacts in this domain and the rather conspicuous gaps which occur because of the limited corpus of documents in the NT, it is not possible to arrange the subdomains in a strictly logical sequence or in an outline with several layers of logical distinctions. There are, however, a number of clusters of subdomains which may be significant for translators, for example, Subdomains B *Instruments Used in Agriculture and Husbandry* and C *Instruments Used in Fishing*. There is also a significant relationship between Subdomain D *Instruments Used in Binding and Fastening* and Subdomain E *Traps, Snares*. Note also the relationship between Subdomain T *Medicines* and Subdomain U *Perfumes and Incense*.

A   Artifacts (General Meaning) (6.1-6.3)

6.1 σκεῦος[a], **ους** *n*: any kind of instrument, tool, weapon, equipment, container, or property – 'object, thing.' οὐκ ἤφιεν ἵνα τις διενέγκῃ σκεῦος διὰ τοῦ ἱεροῦ 'he would not let anyone carry anything through the Temple courts' Mk 11.16; δύναταί τις εἰσελθεῖν εἰς τὴν οἰκίαν τοῦ ἰσχυροῦ καὶ τὰ σκεύη αὐτοῦ ἁρπάσαι 'one can break into a strong man's house and take away his things' Mt 12.29.

The manner in which σκεῦος[a] is translated depends in many instances upon the specific context. It may, of course, be rendered by a highly generic expression such as English 'things,' but wherever the context refers to some particular type of object, it is preferable to employ a specific referent. In Ac 27.17, for example, the reference of σκεῦος is generally understood to be the mainsail.

6.2 σκευή, **ῆς** *f*: a collective for any kind of artifact which may be referred to by σκεῦος[a] 'object, thing' (6.1) – 'things, equipment.' αὐτόχειρες τὴν σκευὴν τοῦ πλοίου ἔρριψαν 'they threw the ship's equipment overboard with

3 Rather than multiply the subdomains to fit a number of meanings of artifacts when there would be normally only one meaning for each subdomain, it seems much better to lump them together under a subdomain marked *Miscellaneous*.

their own hands' Ac 27.19. Wherever possible, it is useful to employ a rather specific term if this is well known in a receptor language. For example, instead of 'things of a ship' one may use 'ship's gear' or 'ship's rigging.'

6.3 ὅπλον^a, ου *n*: any type of tool or instrument – 'tool, instrument, means.' μηδὲ παριστάνετε τὰ μέλη ὑμῶν ὅπλα ἀδικίας 'do not yield your members as instruments of unrighteousness' Ro 6.13. In Ro 6.13 ὅπλον is generally interpreted as being used figuratively as a reference to parts of the body which may be instruments for doing evil.

B Instruments Used in Agriculture and Husbandry (6.4-6.9)

6.4 ἄροτρον, ου *n* – 'plow.' ἐπιβαλὼν τὴν χεῖρα ἐπ᾽ ἄροτρον 'putting one's hand to the plow' Lk 9.62. In most parts of the world at least some type of plow is known, and in ancient Palestine the plow was not a turning plow, but one which simply dug a relatively shallow furrow, but in doing so, loosened the soil. Where plows are not known or used, it is possible to employ a descriptive phrase such as 'a tool for preparing the ground for sowing.' For ἄροτρον as part of a Semitic idiom in Lk 9.62, see 68.6.

6.5 δρέπανον, ου *n*: a large, curved knife employed in cutting ripe grain – 'sickle.' ὅταν δὲ παραδοῖ ὁ καρπός, εὐθὺς ἀποστέλλει τὸ δρέπανον 'but when the grain is ripe, he starts cutting it with a sickle' Mk 4.29. Where there is no receptor language term for sickle, one may often employ a descriptive phrase such as 'a knife for harvesting grain' or 'a curved knife for cutting grain.'

6.6 πτύον, ου *n*: a fork-like shovel for throwing threshed grain into the air so that the wind may separate the chaff from the grain – 'a winnowing shovel.' τὸ πτύον ἐν τῇ χειρὶ αὐτοῦ 'a winnowing shovel is in his hand' Mt 3.12. Where there is no receptor-language term for a winnowing shovel, one may use a descriptive phrase, for example, 'a tool for throwing threshed grain into the air in order to let the chaff blow away.'

6.7 χαλινός, οῦ *m*: the bit and the bridle used to control the actions of a horse – 'bit, bridle.' τῶν ἵππων τοὺς χαλινοὺς εἰς τὰ στόματα βάλλομεν 'we put bits in the mouths of horses' Jas 3.3. In languages in which a bit or bridle as a piece of harness is not known, one can employ a descriptive phrase, 'something to guide a horse with' or 'something to put in the mouth of a horse to guide it.'

In Re 14.20 the reference to a bit and bridle is merely an indication of measurement, that is to say, the height of the bit and bridle from the ground, and one may reinterpret this measurement as 'about a meter and a half' or 'about five feet.'

6.8 ζυγός^a, οῦ *m*: a bar or frame of wood by which two draft animals are joined at the head or neck in order to work together effectively in pulling a plow, harrow, or wagon – 'yoke.' ἐπιθεῖναι ζυγὸν ἐπὶ τὸν τράχηλον τῶν μαθητῶν 'to put a yoke upon the neck of the disciples' Ac 15.10. ζυγός^a occurs in the NT only in figurative contexts. In a sense, this means that ζυγός is itself figurative in meaning, but the figure of speech is an extended figure in which case individual components are normally regarded as having a literal meaning.

6.9 κέντρον^b, ου *n*: a pointed stick used in driving draft animals – 'goad.' In the NT κέντρον^b occurs only in the idiom πρὸς κέντρον λακτίζειν 'to kick against the goad' (Ac 26.14), meaning to hurt oneself by active resistance.[4] See 39.19.

C Instruments Used in Fishing (6.10-6.13)

6.10 ἄγκιστρον, ου *n* – 'fish hook.' βάλε ἄγκιστρον καὶ τὸν ἀναβάντα πρῶτον ἰχθὺν ἆρον 'throw a hook and take the first fish that comes up' Mt 17.27.

A literal rendering of Mt 17.27 could be quite misleading, since it would imply that only the hook was thrown into the water. What was thrown into the water was a line

---

4 κέντρον also occurs in the meaning of a sharp pointed object (typically a sting, stinger) which may cause pain and even death (see 8.45).

with a baited hook on the end, and it may be necessary to be explicit in some languages in order to avoid misunderstanding.

6.11 δίκτυον, ου *n*: any kind of net, but in the NT referring only to nets used for catching fish – 'net, fishnet.' οἱ δὲ εὐθέως ἀφέντες τὰ δίκτυα ἠκολούθησαν αὐτῷ 'immediately they left their nets and followed him' Mt 4.20.

6.12 ἀμφίβληστρον, ου *n*: a round casting-net used in fishing – 'casting-net.' βάλλοντας ἀμφίβληστρον εἰς τὴν θάλασσαν 'throwing a casting-net into the sea' Mt 4.18.

An ἀμφίβληστρον had small weights attached to the outer border, and it was normally thrown in such a manner as to encircle fish. In trying to obtain a satisfactory equivalent expression in another language, it is not necessary to try to duplicate all the details of form. What is important is that such a net was thrown rather than being dragged.

6.13 σαγήνη, ης *f*: a long seine net used in fishing – 'seine net.' σαγήνη βληθείση εἰς τὴν θάλασσαν καὶ ἐκ παντὸς γένους συναγαγούση 'a net which has been lowered into the sea and caught all kinds of fish' Mt 13.47. The σαγήνη was a long net hanging vertically in the water with floats at the upper edge and weights at the lower. It was drawn in by men working in boats or from shore. In Mt 13.47 the actual form of the net is not so important. What is significant is that the net was sufficiently large to catch a large number of different kinds of fish.

D Instruments Used in Binding and Fastening (6.14-6.22)

6.14 δεσμός[a], οῦ *m* (but neuter in the plural): any instrument or means of binding or tying – 'bonds, chains, fetters.' πάντων τὰ δεσμὰ ἀνέθη 'their fetters became unfastened' Ac 16.26. In translating one may often use a descriptive phrase, for example, 'those things that bound them' or 'things with which they were tied.' It is generally more satisfactory, however, to employ wherever possible a more specific referent, for example, 'ropes,' 'chains' or 'fetters.'

6.15 σειρά (also σιρά), ᾶς *f*: a pliable instrument of binding – 'chain' (made of metal) or 'rope' (made of fiber). ἀλλὰ σειραῖς ζόφου ταρταρώσας 'but he threw them into hell, chained in darkness' 2 Pe 2.4. In a number of languages a term for 'chain' is simply 'metal rope.' In other languages it may be described as 'linked rope' in contrast with 'twisted rope,' that is, a rope made out of some kind of fiber.

The phrase σειραῖς ζόφου is admittedly a strange expression, and in some manuscripts this gave rise to a slight change in orthography (σιροῖς; see 1.59) with the resulting meaning being 'in pits of darkness.' If, however, one adopts the text ἀλλὰ σειραῖς ζόφου ταρταρώσας, it may be possible to interpret the entire expression as 'but he chained them in the darkness of hell.'

6.16 ἄλυσις[a], εως *f*: a linked, metal instrument for binding – 'chain.' ἐκέλευσεν δεθῆναι ἀλύσεσι δυσί 'he ordered them to be tied up with two chains' Ac 21.33. In some languages a distinction is made between terms for a chain used in tying up a person and one employed in agricultural or industrial work.

6.17 πέδη, ης *f*: a shackle for the feet – 'fetter, shackle.' αὐτὸν πολλάκις πέδαις καὶ ἀλύσεσιν δεδέσθαι 'he was bound many times with shackles and chains' Mk 5.4. These shackles would normally have consisted of chains with special links prepared to go around the ankles. The equivalent in some languages is simply 'chains on the feet.'

6.18 σχοινίον, ου *n*: cord or rope made of fiber – 'cord, rope.' ἀπέκοψαν οἱ στρατιῶται τὰ σχοινία τῆς σκάφης 'the soldiers cut the ropes of the boat' Ac 27.32. The ropes mentioned in Ac 27.32 would obviously have been rather thick, while in Jn 2.15 the whip which Jesus made in driving the animals and merchants out of the Temple would probably have consisted of strong cords.

6.19 ζευκτηρία, ας *f*: an instrument for joining together objects (normally two) – 'bands.' ἀνέντες τὰς ζευκτηρίας τῶν πηδαλίων 'loosening the bands of the rudders' Ac 27.40. In Ac 27.40 ζευκτηρία refers to ropes employed in linking two rudders of a boat. In most languages, however, one would simply use a term for 'rope.'

6.20 ἱμάς[a], άντος *m*: leather strap or thong (used in binding sandals or shoes and as thongs in a whip) – 'strap, thong.' λύσω αὐτοῦ τὸν ἱμάντα τοῦ ὑποδήματος 'I might untie his sandal straps' Jn 1.27. In a number of languages ἱμάς[a] may be translated as 'leather string' or 'strip of leather.' In Jn 1.27 the term may be absorbed within the total expression, for example, 'worthy to untie his sandals' (implying the untying of the straps with which the sandals were bound).

In Ac 22.25 the clause ὡς δὲ προέτειναν αὐτὸν τοῖς ἱμᾶσιν may be interpreted as 'they tied him up with thongs' or as 'they tied him up for whipping,' in which case ἱμᾶσιν would refer to an event, not to an object (see 19.9).

6.21 ξύλον[c], ου *n*: an instrument consisting of heavy blocks of wood through which the legs were placed and then securely fastened – 'stocks.' τοὺς πόδας ἠσφαλίσατο αὐτῶν εἰς τὸ ξύλον 'he fastened their feet in stocks' Ac 16.24. Stocks were employed primarily as an instrument for imprisonment, but also as a means of punishment.

6.22 ἧλος, ου *m* – 'nail' (in the NT used only in connection with nails employed in the crucifixion). ἐὰν μὴ ἴδω ἐν ταῖς χερσὶν αὐτοῦ τὸν τύπον τῶν ἥλων 'unless I see the print of the nails in his hands' Jn 20.25. In a number of languages a distinction is made between relatively small nails and larger spikes; the latter would be appropriate in speaking of crucifixion.

E Traps, Snares (6.23-6.25)

6.23 παγίς[a], ίδος *f*: an object used for trapping or snaring, principally of birds – 'trap, snare.' καὶ ἐπιστῇ ἐφ' ὑμᾶς αἰφνίδιος ἡ ἡμέρα ἐκείνη ὡς παγίς 'and that day will come suddenly upon you like a snare' Lk 21.34-35. Since snares or traps for capturing birds are almost universal, there should be no difficulty involved in obtaining an appropriate term, though in this context the function of παγίς is

figurative and clearly marked as a simile. It may be necessary in some instances to expand the simile somewhat as 'as a snare is used to catch birds.'

6.24 θήρα[a], ας *f*: an instrument used for trapping, especially of animals other than birds – 'trap, snare.' γενηθήτω ἡ τράπεζα αὐτῶν εἰς παγίδα καὶ εἰς θήραν 'let their table become a snare and a trap' Ro 11.9.[5]

6.25 σκάνδαλον[a], ου *n*: a trap, probably of the type which has a stick which when touched by an animal causes the trap to shut – 'trap.' γενηθήτω ἡ τράπεζα αὐτῶν . . . εἰς σκάνδαλον 'let their table become . . . a trap' Ro 11.9.[5] In Ro 11.9 παγίς (6.23), θήρα (6.24), and σκάνδαλον would all seem to be completely parallel in structure and meaning. As a result, in a number of languages the three terms are reduced often to two, for example, 'snare' and 'trap.' If there are three different kinds of traps, then, of course, three terms can be used. In some cases, however, it may be preferable to use verbs to express the catching and trapping, and thus one may translate γενηθήτω ἡ τράπεζα αὐτῶν εἰς παγίδα καὶ εἰς θήραν καὶ εἰς σκάνδαλον as in TEV, "may they be caught and trapped at their feasts; may they fall."

F Instruments Used in Punishment and Execution (6.26-6.28)

6.26 φραγέλλιον, ου *n*: a whip consisting of either a single or multiple thongs with or without weighted tips on the ends – 'whip.' ποιήσας φραγέλλιον ἐκ σχοινίων 'making a whip of cords' Jn 2.15. The weighted tips of a φραγέλλιον would normally have been made of metal so as to increase the force of the blow and to inflict more severe punishment.

6.27 σταυρός, οῦ *m*: a pole stuck into the ground in an upright position with a crosspiece attached to its upper part so that it was shaped like a ⊤ or like a † – 'cross.'

---

5 In Ro 11.9 παγίς (6.23), θήρα (6.24), and σκάνδαλον (6.25) are all treated as having literal meanings, whereas the passage as a whole is figurative.

εἱστήκεισαν δὲ παρὰ τῷ σταυρῷ 'they stood near the cross' Jn 19.25. In Mt 27.32 (τοῦτον ἠγγάρευσαν ἵνα ἄρῃ τὸν σταυρὸν αὐτοῦ 'they forced him to carry Jesus' cross') the reference is probably to the crosspiece of the cross, which normally would have been carried by a man condemned to die.

Because of the symbolism associated with the cross, translations of the NT in all languages preserve some expression which will identify the cross, not only as a means of capital punishment, but as having a particular form, namely, an upright pole with a crossbeam. In some receptor languages the term for a cross means simply 'crossbeam.' In other instances it is composed of a phrase meaning 'crossed poles.' It is important, however, to avoid an expression which will suggest crossed sticks in the form of X rather than a cross consisting of an upright with a horizontal beam. If at all possible one should employ a term or phrase which may be used in an extended sense, since in so many contexts the term 'cross' refers not only to the instrument of Christ's death, but to the event of execution. It also becomes a symbol of the message of forgiveness and of reconciliation. Because of these extended meanings, it is important to choose a form which can, if at all possible, support these additional meanings.

6.28 ξύλονᶠ, ου *n*: (a figurative extension of meaning of ξύλονᵃ 'wood,' 3.60) an instrument of execution – 'cross.' Outside the NT ξύλονᶠ often refers to a gallows, but in the NT contexts speaking of capital punishment, the reference is to the cross on which Jesus was crucified. Ἰησοῦν, ὃν ὑμεῖς διεχειρίσασθε κρεμάσαντες ἐπὶ ξύλου 'Jesus, whom you had killed by nailing him to a cross' Ac 5.30.

G Weapons and Armor (6.29-6.40)

6.29 ὅπλονᵇ, ου *n*: an instrument used in fighting, whether offensive or defensive – 'weapon.' Ἰούδας . . . ἔρχεται ἐκεῖ μετὰ φανῶν καὶ λαμπάδων καὶ ὅπλων 'Judas . . . came there with torches and lanterns and weapons' Jn 18.3. In the NT ὅπλονᵇ also occurs in the figurative sense of non-material means of fighting: διὰ τῶν ὅπλων τῆς δικαιοσύνης τῶν δε-

ξιῶν καὶ ἀριστερῶν 'we have righteousness as our weapon both to attack and to defend ourselves' 2 Cor 6.7.[6]

6.30 πανοπλία, ας *f*: a complete set of instruments used in defensive or offensive warfare (usually, however, with emphasis upon defensive armament, including helmet, shield, breastplate) – 'weapons and armor.' τὴν πανοπλίαν αὐτοῦ αἴρει ἐφ' ᾗ ἐπεποίθει 'he carried away all the weapons and armor the owner was depending on' Lk 11.22.

πανοπλία is also used figuratively in the NT as a reference to the virtues of Christian character used in the strife against evil: ἐνδύσασθε τὴν πανοπλίαν τοῦ θεοῦ πρὸς τὸ δύνασθαι ὑμᾶς στῆναι πρὸς τὰς μεθοδείας τοῦ διαβόλου 'put on all the armor that God gives you, so that you will stand up against the Devil's evil tricks' Eph 6.11.

Since certain ancient types of armor are no longer used to any extent in fighting, it may be necessary to employ descriptive expressions in order to make clear the types of weapons and/or instruments which were involved. Offensive weapons are often spoken of as 'tools with which one kills or harms an enemy,' while defensive armor may be described as 'what one wears to defend oneself when fighting.' The complete sense of πανοπλία may then be described in some languages as 'tools with which one fights against the enemy and what one uses to defend oneself' or '. . . to protect oneself.'

6.31 ξύλονᵈ, ου *n*: a heavy stick used in fighting – 'club.' ὄχλος μετὰ μαχαιρῶν καὶ ξύλων 'a crowd with swords and clubs' Mk 14.43.

6.32 ῥομφαίαᵃ, ας *f*: a large, broad sword used for both cutting and piercing – 'sword.'

---

6 In 2 Cor 6.7 ὅπλον occurs in a highly figurative context, but it is better under such circumstances to regard ὅπλον as referring to an instrument used in fighting and then to assign the figurative meaning to the entire expression. In some languages it may be necessary to translate ὅπλων in 2 Cor 6.7 as 'means' or simply 'instruments.' For the understanding of the phrase τῶν δεξιῶν καὶ ἀριστερῶν as referring to offensive and defensive weapons, see 82.7.

ὁ ἔχων τὴν ῥομφαίαν τὴν δίστομον τὴν ὀξεῖαν 'he who has the sharp, two-edged sword' Re 2.12.

In a number of languages the term for 'sword' is simply 'a large knife,' but in some regions it may be called 'a machete for killing.'

6.33 μάχαιρα[a], ης *f*: a relatively short sword (or even dagger) used for cutting and stabbing – 'sword, dagger.' ὡς ἐπὶ λῃστὴν ἐξήλθατε μετὰ μαχαιρῶν καὶ ξύλων συλλαβεῖν με 'you did (not have to) come with swords and clubs to capture me as though I were an outlaw' Mt 26.55.

The phrase στόμα μαχαίρης (literally 'mouth of the sword') refers to the event of killing or slaughter: ἔφυγον στόματα μαχαίρης 'they escaped being killed by the sword' He 11.34. See 79.109.

6.34 λόγχη, ης *f*: a long weapon with sharpened end used for piercing by thrusting or as a projectile by hurling – 'spear' (or possibly in Jn 19.34 'spear point'). εἷς τῶν στρατιωτῶν λόγχῃ αὐτοῦ τὴν πλευρὰν ἔνυξεν 'one of the soldiers pierced his side with his spear' Jn 19.34.

6.35 ὑσσός, οῦ *m*: a type of short spear – 'javelin.' ὑσσός is a possible variant reading in Jn 19.29, where in place of ὑσσώπος 'hyssop,' the reading ὑσσός 'javelin' has been recommended by some scholars, but rejected by most (see 3.26).

6.36 βέλος, ους *n*: a missile, including arrows (propelled by a bow) or darts (hurled by hand) – 'arrow, dart.' In the NT βέλος occurs only in a highly figurative context, τὰ βέλη . . . πεπυρωμένα 'flaming arrows (or darts)' Eph 6.16, and refers to temptations by the Devil.

6.37 τόξον, ου *n*: an instrument for propelling an arrow – 'bow.' ὁ καθήμενος ἐπ' αὐτὸν ἔχων τόξον 'the one riding on it had a bow' Re 6.2.

6.38 περικεφαλαία, ας *f*: protective armor covering the head – 'helmet.' τὴν περικεφαλαί-αν τοῦ σωτηρίου δέξασθε 'accept the helmet of salvation' or 'accept salvation, which is like a

protection for the head' Eph 6.17. For languages having no term for helmet, one may use a descriptive equivalent such as 'a protection for the head' or 'a covering for the head in fighting.' The phrase τὴν περικεφαλαίαν τοῦ σωτηρίου δέξασθε may then be translated as 'accept salvation as something like a protection for the head.'

6.39 θώραξ[a], ακος *m*: a piece of armor covering the chest to protect it against blows and arrows – 'breastplate.' εἶχον θώρακας ὡς θώρακας σιδηροῦς 'their chests were covered with what looked like iron breastplates' Re 9.9 (but see 8.38 for the meaning of θώραξ[b]). θώραξ[a] is also used figuratively in the NT to indicate the protective values of certain Christian virtues: ἐνδυσάμενοι θώρακα πίστεως καὶ ἀγάπης 'we must wear faith and love as a breastplate' 1 Th 5.8.

6.40 θυρεός, οῦ *m*: a long, oblong shield – 'shield.' ἀναλαβόντες τὸν θυρεὸν τῆς πίστεως 'taking the shield of faith' Eph 6.16. In some languages 'shield' is described as 'protection one carries when one fights' or 'protection carried to prevent blows from the enemy.' The phrase ἀναλαβόντες τὸν θυρεὸν τῆς πίστεως may thus be rendered as 'take hold of faith as a protection against the enemy' or 'regard your faith as a protection to prevent the attacks of the enemy.'

H Boats and Parts of Boats (6.41-6.51)

6.41 πλοῖον, ου *n*: any kind of boat, from small fishing boats as on Lake Galilee to large seagoing vessels – 'boat, ship.' εἶδεν δύο πλοῖα ἑστῶτα παρὰ τὴν λίμνην 'he saw two boats on the shore of the lake' Lk 5.2; ἡμεῖς δὲ προελθόντες ἐπὶ τὸ πλοῖον ἀνήχθημεν ἐπὶ τὴν Ἆσσον 'we went ahead to the ship and sailed for Assos' Ac 20.13. It may be very important to distinguish clearly between small fishing boats and larger ships or vessels. In a number of languages the distinction is based upon whether or not such vessels have decks. For the fishing boats on Lake Galilee there was probably no deck structure, while vessels going for long distances on the Mediterranean would certainly have had decks. See 6.42.

6.42 πλοιάριον, ου *n* (a diminutive form of πλοῖον 'boat, ship,' 6.41, but in some contexts it is possible that the diminutive aspect of πλοιάριον is not relevant) – 'small boat.' ἵνα πλοιάριον προσκαρτερῇ αὐτῷ διὰ τὸν ὄχλον 'so that a small boat could be made ready for him on account of the crowd' Mk 3.9. Receptor language terms to be employed for πλοιάριον, πλοῖον (6.41), and ναῦς (6.43) depend largely upon the contextual equivalents in each receptor language.

6.43 ναῦς, acc. ναῦν *f*: a larger ocean-going vessel – 'ship.' ἐπέκειλαν τὴν ναῦν 'they ran the ship aground' Ac 27.41. The term ναῦς occurs in the NT only in Ac 27.41, where it refers to the ship which was wrecked at Malta. See 6.42.

6.44 κιβωτός[a]**, οῦ** *f*: a large box-like structure (the vessel built by Noah) – 'boat, ship, the ark.' ὅτε ἀπεξεδέχετο ἡ τοῦ θεοῦ μακροθυμία ἐν ἡμέραις Νῶε κατασκευαζομένης κιβωτοῦ 'when God waited patiently during the days that Noah was building the ark' 1 Pe 3.20. The central meaning of κιβωτός is 'box' or 'chest,' but it was apparently applied to Noah's ark in view of the type of construction and the fact that Noah's ark resembled more a barge than a seagoing vessel. However, in view of the size of Noah's ark, it is probably best in most languages to speak of it as a 'ship.'

6.45 σκάφη, ης *f*: a small boat which was normally kept aboard a larger ship and used by sailors in placing anchors, repairing the ship, or saving lives in the case of storms – 'small boat, skiff.' ἰσχύσαμεν μόλις περικρατεῖς γενέσθαι τῆς σκάφης 'with some difficulty we were able to make the ship's boat secure' Ac 27.16. In some languages σκάφη is equivalent to 'rowboat' or 'lifeboat.'

6.46 πρῷρα, ης *f*: the forepart of a boat – 'bow.' ἐκ πρῴρης ἀγκύρας μελλόντων 'intending to lay anchors from the bow' Ac 27.30. In a number of languages there are rather technical terms for the bow and stern of a boat, but where such terms are lacking, one can speak of 'the front of a boat' for πρῷρα and 'the back of the boat' for πρύμνα (6.47).

6.47 πρύμνα, ης *f*: the back part of a boat – 'stern.' αὐτὸς ἦν ἐν τῇ πρύμνῃ ἐπὶ τὸ προσκεφάλαιον καθεύδων 'he was in the stern, sleeping with his head on a pillow' Mk 4.38. See translation suggestion at 6.46.

6.48 ἄγκυρα, ας *f*: a heavy object attached to a boat by a rope or chain and dropped to the bottom of a body of water in order to prevent or restrict the movement of the boat – 'anchor.' ἐκ πρύμνης ῥίψαντες ἀγκύρας τέσσαρας 'they lowered four anchors from the back of the ship' Ac 27.29. For languages having no term for 'anchor,' one may use a descriptive equivalent, for example, 'heavy weights on ropes to keep a boat from moving.'

6.49 ἀρτέμων, ωνος *m*: a cloth attached above a boat in such a way as to catch the wind and thus propel the boat through the water – 'sail.' ἐπάραντες τὸν ἀρτέμωνα τῇ πνεούσῃ 'hoisting the foresail to the wind' Ac 27.40. In Ac 27.40 (the only occurrence of ἀρτέμων in the NT) the reference may be to the foresail, that is, a relatively small sail toward the prow of the ship. A sail may be described in some languages as 'a piece of cloth to make the ship move' or 'cloth on the ship to catch the wind.'

6.50 πηδάλιον, ου *n*: a large plank at the stern of a ship used to direct its course – 'rudder.' μετάγεται ὑπὸ ἐλαχίστου πηδαλίου ὅπου ἡ ὁρμὴ τοῦ εὐθύνοντος βούλεται 'it is guided by a very small rudder wherever the pilot wishes' Jas 3.4. For some ships the rudder may have been simply a large steering paddle. For languages which have no technical term, a rudder may be described as 'an instrument for steering the ship' or 'an instrument for making the ship go the way one wants it to go.'

6.51 παράσημον, ου *n*: an identifying emblem, possibly a carved figurehead at the prow of a ship – 'emblem, figurehead.' ἀνήχθημεν ἐν πλοίῳ παρακεχειμακότι ἐν τῇ νήσῳ Ἀλεξανδρίνῳ, παρασήμῳ Διοσκούροις 'we sailed away in a ship from Alexandria which had spent the winter in the island and which had the emblem of the Twin Gods' Ac 28.11. In translating the expression 'emblem of the

Twin Gods' it may be possible to use a phrase such as 'a carving of the Twin Gods' or 'a statue of the Twin Gods.' For παράσημος as an adjective, see 33.479.

I Vehicles (6.52-6.53)

6.52 ἅρμα, τος *n*: a vehicle used in war or for traveling − 'chariot.' φωνὴ ἁρμάτων ἵππων πολλῶν τρεχόντων εἰς πόλεμον 'the sound of many horse-drawn chariots rushing into battle' Re 9.9. In Re 9.9 the reference is to war chariots drawn by horses, while in Ac 8.28, 38 the reference is to a traveling chariot in which the Ethiopian official was riding. In languages which have no technical term for chariot, it is possible to speak of a war chariot as 'a war carriage' or 'a horse-drawn cart for fighting.' A traveling chariot may be described as 'a traveling carriage' or 'a horse-drawn vehicle.' A further description of such chariots may be given in a glossary.

6.53 ῥέδη, ης *f*: a four-wheeled carriage or wagon used for travel or the transportation of loads − 'carriage, wagon.' The term ῥέδη occurs only in Re 18.13 in a list of products bought and sold by merchants.

J Instruments Used in Marking and Writing (6.54-6.67)

6.54 σφραγίς[a], ῖδος *f*: an engraved object used to make a mark denoting ownership, approval, or closure of something (normally done by pressing into heated wax and usually attached to a document or letter) − 'seal, signet.' ἄγγελον . . . ἔχοντα σφραγῖδα θεοῦ 'an angel . . . who had God's signet' Re 7.2. In some languages the closest equivalent to 'seal' or 'signet' is the mark made by the seal, for example, 'the symbol of his name' or 'the mark of his ownership.' In certain contexts one may employ a phrase such as 'the instrument by which a mark is made.'

6.55 σφραγίζω[a]; κατασφραγίζω: to use a seal to close or to make something secure − 'to seal, to put a seal on, to make secure.' σφραγίζω[a]: ἠσφαλίσαντο τὸν τάφον σφραγίσαντες τὸν λίθον 'they made the tomb secure by putting a seal on the stone' Mt 27.66; ἔβαλεν αὐτὸν εἰς τὴν ἄβυσσον καὶ ἔκλεισεν καὶ ἐσφράγισεν ἐπάνω αὐτοῦ 'he threw him into the abyss, locked it, and sealed it' Re 20.3.

κατασφραγίζω: κατεσφραγισμένον σφραγῖσιν ἑπτά 'sealed with seven seals' Re 5.1. From the immediate context of Re 5.1 it is not possible to determine whether the scroll in question had seven seals on the outside or whether the scroll was sealed at seven different points. However, since according to chapter six of Revelation the seals were broken one after another, it would appear as though the scroll had been sealed at seven different places as it had been rolled up.

For a discussion of some of the translational problems involved with 'seal,' see 6.54.

6.56 κάλαμος[c], ου *m*: a reed especially cut for making marks with ink on writing material − 'pen.' οὐ θέλω διὰ μέλανος καὶ καλάμου σοι γράφειν 'I do not want to write to you with pen and ink' 3 Jn 13.

6.57 μέλαν, ανος *n*: a dark liquid used in writing or marking − 'ink.' ἐστὲ ἐπιστολὴ Χριστοῦ διακονηθεῖσα ὑφ' ἡμῶν, ἐγγεγραμμένη οὐ μέλανι 'you are a letter from Christ delivered by us, written not with ink' 2 Cor 3.3. The use of ink is so universal at the present time that some term or expression for it is almost inevitable in all languages. However, in some cases the equivalent is essentially a descriptive phrase, for example, 'black stain' or 'writing stain.'

6.58 χάρτης, ου *m*: a sheet of papyrus used for writing − 'a sheet of paper.' οὐκ ἐβουλήθην διὰ χάρτου καὶ μέλανος 'I do not wish to use paper and ink' 2 Jn 12.

6.59 μεμβράνα[a], ης *f*: a sheet of specially prepared animal skin on which one could write with pen and ink − 'parchment.' φέρε, καὶ τὰ βιβλία, μάλιστα τὰς μεμβράνας 'bring also the books, especially the parchments' 2 Tm 4.13. In 2 Tm 4.13 the reference may be to documents written on parchment or to blank sheets of parchment. Sheets of parchment were either sewn together in long scrolls or, in later developments, bound together into book form (see 6.66).

6.60 πινακίδιον, ου *n*: a small writing tablet (normally made of wood) – 'tablet.' αἰτήσας πινακίδιον ἔγραφεν λέγων, Ἰωάννης ἐστὶν ὄνομα αὐτοῦ 'he asked for a tablet and wrote, John is his name' Lk 1.63.

6.61 πλάξ, πλακός *f*: a flat stone on which inscriptions could be made – 'tablet.' αἱ πλάκες τῆς διαθήκης 'the tablets of the covenant' He 9.4. In the NT πλάξ is used to refer to the tablets of the Law given to Moses on Mount Sinai.

6.62 σφραγίς[b], ιδος *f*: the substance which bears the imprint of a seal or signet (see σφραγίς[a], 6.54), used for sealing a document or for showing ownership or endorsement – 'seal.' τίς ἄξιος ἀνοῖξαι τὸ βιβλίον καὶ λῦσαι τὰς σφραγῖδας αὐτοῦ; 'who is worthy to open the scroll and break the seal?' Re 5.2. In Re 5.2 one may speak of 'the wax that keeps the scroll closed,' but in some languages it may be better to use a more general statement, for example, 'the substance with which the scroll is sealed' or 'the substance that kept the scroll closed.'

6.63 ἐπιστολή[a], ῆς *f*; γράμμα[c], τος *n*: an object containing writing addressed to one or more persons – 'letter' (normally written on papyrus).
ἐπιστολή[a]: ἀναδόντες τὴν ἐπιστολὴν τῷ ἡγεμόνι παρέστησαν καὶ τὸν Παῦλον αὐτῷ 'they delivered the letter to the governor and turned Paul over to him' Ac 23.33.
γράμμα[c]: ἡμεῖς οὔτε γράμματα περὶ σοῦ ἐδεξάμεθα ἀπὸ τῆς Ἰουδαίας 'we have not received any letters from Judea about you' Ac 28.21.[7]
In some languages it may be necessary to try to distinguish between a letter as an object and a letter as content or message. In Ac 23.33 the focus seems to be upon the letter as an object, not necessarily upon the contents of

the document. In most contexts, however, it is impossible to distinguish between a letter as a material object and a letter as a message (see 33.48).

6.64 βιβλίον[a], ου *n*; βίβλος[a], ου *f*: a document consisting of a scroll or book – 'scroll, roll, book.'
βιβλίον[a]: ἐπεδόθη αὐτῷ βιβλίον τοῦ προφήτου Ἡσαΐου, καὶ ἀναπτύξας τὸ βιβλίον εὗρεν τὸν τόπον οὗ ἦν γεγραμμένον 'he was handed the book of the prophet Isaiah. He unrolled the scroll and found the passage where it is written' Lk 4.17.
βίβλος[a]: ἱκανοὶ δὲ τῶν τὰ περίεργα πραξάντων συνενέγκαντες τὰς βίβλους κατέκαιον ἐνώπιον πάντων 'many of those who practiced magic brought their books together and burned them in the presence of everyone' Ac 19.19. The books referred to in Ac 19.19 consisted of sheets of parchment or of papyrus sewn together in the form of long scrolls or bound in the form of a book.

6.65 βιβλαρίδιον, ου *n* (a diminutive derivative of βίβλος[a], 6.64) – 'a little scroll.' ἔλαβον τὸ βιβλαρίδιον ἐκ τῆς χειρὸς τοῦ ἀγγέλου 'I took the little scroll from the angel's hand' Re 10.10.

6.66 μεμβράνα[b], ης *f* – 'books (or scrolls) made of parchment.' φέρε, καὶ τὰ βιβλία, μάλιστα τὰς μεμβράνας 'bring also the books, especially the books made of parchment' 2 Tm 4.13. As noted in 6.59, μεμβράνα may have the meaning of parchment sheets (μεμβράνα[a]) or of books written on parchment (μεμβράνα[b]).

6.67 κεφαλίς, ίδος *f*: section of a scroll or of a long composition – 'section, scroll.' ἐν κεφαλίδι βιβλίου γέγραπται περὶ ἐμοῦ 'just as it has been written of me in a scroll of the book of the Law' He 10.7. Long compositions often involved several scrolls, and a κεφαλίς would form one section or scroll of such a composition.
In the case of practically all terms for documents (for example, 'letter,' 'book,' 'scroll') the meaning involves not only the object on which the writing was done, but also

---

7 γράμμα[c] may also be classified as a derivative of γράφω 'to write' (33.61) and mean 'anything that is written'; see 33.50.

the contents of the writing. In some languages a distinction must be made between these two aspects of such objects, and one must make certain that the particular expression used in a receptor language will at least include the contents and not refer merely to the materials on which the words may have been written.

K Money and Monetary Units (6.68-6.82)

The following terms for money and monetary units are divided primarily into two major classes: (1) those which refer to coins in general or to coins made of particular substances and (2) monetary units having specific values. In general, it is best to relate monetary values to the denarius (6.75), since we know something of the relative value of the denarius in terms of wages and buying power. Using the denarius as a basic unit greatly facilitates the finding of satisfactory monetary equivalents in other languages, whether these are expressed in the text or in marginal notes.

6.68 χρῆμα^b, τος *n*: a generic term for currency, occurring mostly in the plural – 'money' (normally a reference to actual coins). ὑπάρχοντος αὐτῷ ἀγροῦ πωλήσας ἤνεγκεν τὸ χρῆμα 'he sold a field he owned and brought the money' Ac 4.37. It would also be possible to translate ἤνεγκεν τὸ χρῆμα in Ac 4.37 as 'he brought the proceeds from the sale.' In Ac 8.18 (προσήνεγκεν αὐτοῖς χρήματα 'he offered them money') the reference of χρήματα would appear to be cash.

6.69 ἀργύριον καὶ χρυσίον: (an idiom, literally 'silver and gold') a generic expression for currency – 'money.' ἀργυρίου ἢ χρυσίου ἢ ἱματισμοῦ οὐδενὸς ἐπεθύμησα 'I have not coveted anyone's money or clothing' Ac 20.33.

6.70 νόμισμα, τος *n*: common and official currency – 'coin.' ἐπιδείξατέ μοι τὸ νόμισμα τοῦ κήνσου 'show me a coin used in the payment of taxes' Mt 22.19.

6.71 κέρμα, τος *n*: coins of lesser value – 'coin, change.' τῶν κολλυβιστῶν ἐξέχεεν τὸ κέρμα 'he scattered· the coins of the money-changers' Jn 2.15.

6.72 χαλκός^b, οῦ *m*: coins of bronze or copper, and hence of little value – 'copper coins, bronze money.'[8] μὴ κτήσησθε χρυσὸν μηδὲ ἄργυρον μηδὲ χαλκὸν εἰς τὰς ζώνας ὑμῶν 'do not carry any gold, silver, or copper money in your belts' Mt 10.9; ἐθεώρει πῶς ὁ ὄχλος βάλλει χαλκὸν εἰς τὸ γαζοφυλάκιον 'he watched the people as they dropped their copper coins into the Temple's treasury' Mk 12.41.

6.73 ἄργυρος^b, ου *m*; ἀργύριον^b, ου *n* – 'silver money, silver coin.'[8]
ἄργυρος^b: μὴ κτήσησθε χρυσὸν μηδὲ ἄργυρον μηδὲ χαλκὸν εἰς τὰς ζώνας ὑμῶν 'do not carry any gold, silver, or copper money in your belts' Mt 10.9.
ἀργύριον^b: οἱ δὲ ἔστησαν αὐτῷ τριάκοντα ἀργύρια 'so they counted out thirty silver coins and gave them to him' Mt 26.15.

6.74 χρυσός^b, οῦ *m* – 'gold money, gold coin.'[8] μὴ κτήσησθε χρυσὸν μηδὲ ἄργυρον μηδὲ χαλκὸν εἰς τὰς ζώνας ὑμῶν 'do not carry gold, silver, or copper money in your belts' Mt 10.9.

6.75 δηνάριον, ου *n*: a Roman silver coin equivalent to a day's wage of a common laborer – 'denarius.' ὃς ὤφειλεν αὐτῷ ἑκατὸν δηνάρια 'who owed him a hundred denarii' Mt 18.28.

The practice of translating terms for coins with specific monetary values has differed widely in different languages at different times and in different contexts. One of the most serious problems has been the recent rapid inflation which has taken place in many parts of the world and which has thus made traditional renderings relatively meaningless

---

8 Except for the occurrence of ἀργύριον in the plural (Mt 26.15), it would be possible to derive all of these references to copper (bronze), silver, and gold coins as direct and predictable metonymic correspondences of the respective terms for substances (see 2.54, 51, 49). Since, however, some languages employ clear distinctions between metals as substances and metals when manufactured into the form of coins, the present classification would seem to be more useful.

or even absurd. For a number of years the silver content in an ancient denarius was equivalent to twenty cents U.S., but the value of silver has changed appreciably within recent times, and therefore any calculation based upon the value of silver content in ancient coins is misleading. Furthermore, in ancient times silver coins had proportionately far more buying power than the equivalent amount of silver would have today. Therefore, a number of translators have attempted in some measure to relate coinage to buying power, or perhaps better, to earning power. For example, in Mk 6.37 the reference to 'two hundred denarii' is sometimes translated as 'the equivalent of 200 days' wages' or even 'eight months of a laborer's wages.'

In Mt 18.28 the reference to 'a hundred denarii' is designed primarily to indicate the contrast between the enormous sum owed by one servant in contrast with the very small amount owed by the fellow servant. In this instance the contrast may be expressed in terms of 'thousands of denarii' in contrast with a 'few denarii.' In such a case the equivalent coinage may be turned into a local currency, for example, 'thousands of dollars' in contrast with a 'few dollars.' In a number of cases translators have attempted to avoid any specific reference to a particular coin and have simply spoken of 'silver coins' or 'gold coins' without indicating particular values. Under such circumstances a marginal note is sometimes employed in order to indicate the relative value of the currency.

6.76 δραχμή, ῆς *f*: a Greek silver coin with approximately the same value as the denarius – 'drachma.' εὗρον τὴν δραχμὴν ἣν ἀπώλεσα 'I have found the coin which I lost' Lk 15.9.

6.77 ἀσσάριον, ου *n*: a Roman copper coin worth 1/16 of a denarius – 'assarion, penny.' οὐχὶ δύο στρουθία ἀσσαρίου πωλεῖται; 'are not two sparrows bought for a penny?' Mt 10.29. See 6.79.

6.78 κοδράντης, ου *m*: a Roman copper coin worth 1/4 of an assarion or 1/64 of a denarius – 'quadrans, penny.' ἕως ἂν ἀποδῷς τὸν ἔσχα-

τον κοδράντην 'until you pay the last penny' Mt 5.26. See 6.79.

6.79 λεπτόν, οῦ *n*: a copper (or bronze) coin worth 1/2 of a quadrans or 1/128 of a denarius – 'lepton, tiny coin.' μία χήρα πτωχὴ ἔβαλεν λεπτὰ δύο 'one poor widow put in two small coins' Mk 12.42. In practically all instances, references to ἀσσάριον (6.77), κοδράντης (6.78), or λεπτόν may be made in terms of 'a very small coin' or 'a coin with very little value' or 'money that was not worth very much.'

6.80 στατήρ, ῆρος *m*: a silver coin worth two didrachma or approximately four denarii – 'stater, coin.' εὑρήσεις στατῆρα 'you will find a coin' Mt 17.27.

6.81 μνᾶ, ᾶς *f*: a Greek monetary unit worth 100 denarii – 'a quantity of money, one hundred denarii.' καλέσας δὲ δέκα δούλους ἑαυτοῦ ἔδωκεν αὐτοῖς δέκα μνᾶς 'he called his ten servants and gave each of them one thousand denarii' Lk 19.13.

6.82 τάλαντον, ου *n*: a Greek monetary unit (also a unit of weight) with a value which fluctuated, depending upon the particular monetary system which prevailed at a particular period of time (a silver talent was worth approximately 6 000 denarii with gold talents worth at least thirty times that much) – 'talent.' ᾧ μὲν ἔδωκεν πέντε τάλαντα 'to whom he gave five talents' Mt 25.15.

In Mt 25.15-28 what is important is the relative number of talents or sums of money. In a number of translations the respective amounts are stated in terms of local currency. For example, in English one may speak of $5 000 as equivalent to five talents, though in terms of buying power, five talents would be worth much more than $5 000. What is important, however, in this story is not the precise sums of money but the relative amount which was given to the different servants.

The 'ten thousand talents' referred to in Mt 18.24 would be equivalent to millions of denarii. The sum in this parable is perhaps greatly exaggerated, precisely in order to emphasize the vast differences between the two debts. It is also true, of course, that in ancient times persons with extensive mercantile businesses sometimes became slaves as a result of defeat in war, and they were purchased by business syndicates together with their business enterprises, which they would continue to manage.

L Musical Instruments (6.83-6.95)

6.83 κιθάρα, ας *f*: a small stringed harp-like instrument held in the hands and plucked – 'lyre, harp.' ἔχοντες ἕκαστος κιθάραν 'each having a lyre' Re 5.8. The closest equivalent to a κιθάρα is in most instances a small harp.

6.84 κιθαρίζω (derivative of κιθάρα 'lyre, harp,' 6.83) – 'to play a lyre, to play a harp.' πῶς γνωσθήσεται τὸ αὐλούμενον ἢ τὸ κιθαριζόμενον; 'how will one know what is being played on the flute or on the lyre?' 1 Cor 14.7.

6.85 κιθαρῳδός, οῦ *m*: (derivative of κιθαρίζω 'to play a lyre,' 6.84) one who plays the lyre or harp – 'harpist.' ἡ φωνὴ ἣν ἤκουσα ὡς κιθαρῳδῶν κιθαριζόντων ἐν ταῖς κιθάραις αὐτῶν 'the sound which I heard was like that of harpists playing music on their harps' Re 14.2.

6.86 αὐλός, οῦ *m*: a musical wind instrument consisting of a tube with a series of finger holes used to alter the tone – 'flute.' εἴτε αὐλὸς εἴτε κιθάρα 'whether a flute or a lyre' 1 Cor 14.7.

6.87 αὐλέω (derivative of αὐλός 'flute,' 6.86) – 'to play a flute.' ηὐλήσαμεν ὑμῖν καὶ οὐκ ὠρχήσασθε 'we played the flute for you and you did not dance' Mt 11.17.

6.88 αὐλητής, οῦ *m*: (derivative of αὐλέω 'to play a flute,' 6.87) one who plays the flute – 'flutist.' ἐλθὼν ὁ Ἰησοῦς εἰς τὴν οἰκίαν τοῦ ἄρχοντος καὶ ἰδὼν τοὺς αὐλητάς 'Jesus went into the house of the ruler and saw the flutists' Mt 9.23.

6.89 σάλπιγξ[a], ιγγος *f*: a wind instrument, frequently used in signaling, especially in connection with war – 'trumpet.' ἐὰν ἄδηλον σάλπιγξ φωνὴν δῷ 'if the trumpet gives an

unclear sound' 1 Cor 14.8. The present-day equivalent of the σάλπιγξ is the bugle.

6.90 σαλπίζω[a] (derivative of σάλπιγξ[a] 'trumpet,' 6.89) – 'to play the trumpet.' ὅταν οὖν ποιῇς ἐλεημοσύνην, μὴ σαλπίσῃς ἔμπροσθέν σου 'and so whenever you give alms, do not sound the trumpet in front of you' Mt 6.2. It is possible, of course, in Mt 6.2 to interpret σαλπίζω as a type of causative and thus to say 'to cause someone to blow the trumpet' or 'to have the trumpet blown.'

6.91 σαλπιστής, οῦ *m*: (derivative of σαλπίζω[a] 'to play the trumpet,' 6.90) one who plays the trumpet – 'trumpeter.' φωνὴ κιθαρῳδῶν . . . καὶ σαλπιστῶν οὐ μὴ ἀκουσθῇ ἐν σοὶ ἔτι 'the sound of harpists . . . and trumpeters will never be heard in you again' Re 18.22.

6.92 σαλπίζω[b]: to produce the sound of a trumpet (without specification of an agent) – 'to sound a trumpet, a trumpet sounds.' ἐν τῇ ἐσχάτῃ σάλπιγγι· σαλπίσει γάρ 'at the last trump; for trumpet will sound' 1 Cor 15.52. In a number of languages it may be best to render σαλπίσει in 1 Cor 15.52 as 'people will hear the sound of the trumpet' or 'the sound of the trumpet will be heard.'

6.93 σάλπιγξ[b], ιγγος *f*: (derivative of σαλπίζω[a] 'to play the trumpet,' 6.90) the sound made by a trumpet – 'trumpet blast, trumpet sound.'[9] ἐν ῥιπῇ ὀφθαλμοῦ, ἐν τῇ ἐσχάτῃ σάλπιγγι 'in a blinking of the eye, at the last trump' 1 Cor 15.52; καὶ ἀποστελεῖ τοὺς ἀγγέλους αὐτοῦ μετὰ σάλπιγγος μεγάλης 'and he will send out his angels after the great trumpet blast' or '. . . with the great trumpet blast' Mt 24.31. With both σαλπίζω[b] (6.92) and σάλπιγξ[b], it may be necessary to introduce an agent, even though indefinite. For example, ἐν τῇ ἐσχάτῃ σάλπιγγι may be translated as

---

9 Though it would seem logical to regard σάλπιγξ[b] as a derivative of σάλπιγξ[a] (6.89) in view of the formal similarity, nevertheless from the standpoint of the semantic components involved, σάλπιγξ[b] is actually related to the verb σαλπίζω[a] meaning 'to play the trumpet' (6.90) or possibly σαλπίζω[b] 'to sound a trumpet' (6.92). σάλπιγξ[b] definitely relates to the result of an event, not simply to the instrument employed in such an event.

'when someone blows the trumpet for the last time,' and σαλπίσει may be rendered as 'when someone sounds the trumpet' or 'when someone produces a noise on the trumpet.' However, any term for 'noise' should imply a meaningful sound.

6.94 κύμβαλον, ου *n*: a percussion instrument consisting of two metal discs which were struck together in order to make a shrill, clashing sound – 'cymbals.' γέγονα χαλκὸς ἠχῶν ἢ κύμβαλον ἀλαλάζον 'I have become a noisy brass gong or clanging cymbals' 1 Cor 13.1. The equivalent of κύμβαλον is in many instances a phrase such as 'loud metal.'

6.95 χαλκὸς ἠχῶν: (an idiom, literally 'echoing brass' or 'resounding brass') a gong made of brass – 'brass gong.' γέγονα χαλκὸς ἠχῶν ἢ κύμβαλον ἀλαλάζον 'I have become a noisy brass gong or clanging cymbals' 1 Cor 13.1. In a number of languages the equivalent of gong is 'noisy metal' or 'reverberating metal' or 'echoing metal,' but frequently translators have simply used an expression meaning 'loud bell.'

M Images and Idols (6.96-6.101)

6.96 εἰκών[a], όνος *f*; τύπος[b], ου *m*; χάραγμα[b], τος *n*: an object (not necessarily three-dimensional) which has been formed to resemble a person, god, animal, etc. – 'likeness, image' (see 58.35).
εἰκών[a]: τίνος ἡ εἰκὼν αὕτη 'whose likeness is this?' Mt 22.20; εἰκόνος φθαρτοῦ ἀνθρώπου καὶ πετεινῶν 'likeness of mortal man and birds' Ro 1.23.
τύπος[b]: τοὺς τύπους οὓς ἐποιήσατε προσκυνεῖν αὐτοῖς 'idols that you made to worship' Ac 7.43.
χάραγμα[b]: οὐκ ὀφείλομεν νομίζειν χρυσῷ ἢ ἀργύρῳ ἢ λίθῳ, χαράγματι τέχνης καὶ ἐνθυμήσεως ἀνθρώπου, τὸ θεῖον εἶναι ὅμοιον 'we should not think that the divine nature is like a gold, silver, or stone image fashioned by the skill and art of man' Ac 17.29.

In certain contexts the referents of εἰκών[a], τύπος[b], and χάραγμα[b] may have special religious significance in that they may refer to idols, but the focal component for the translator is that of a likeness or resemblance. In contexts such as Mt 22.20 an equivalent translation may be simply 'a picture,' but in Ro 1.23 and Ac 7.43 one may use the same expression as is employed to render εἴδωλον[a] 'idol' (6.97).

6.97 εἴδωλον[a], ου *n*: an object which resembles a person, animal, god, etc. and which is an object of worship – 'idol, (image).'[10] οἴδατε ὅτι ὅτε ἔθνη ἦτε πρὸς τὰ εἴδωλα τὰ ἄφωνα ὡς ἂν ἤγεσθε ἀπαγόμενοι 'you know that while you were still heathen you were controlled by dead idols, who led you astray' 1 Cor 12.2.

The technical distinction between an image and an idol is that an image may merely represent a supernatural being, while an idol not only represents such a being but is believed to possess certain inherent supernatural powers. Images often become idols when they are assumed to possess such powers in and of themselves rather than being mere representations of some supernatural entity. If, for example, various images of a particular supernatural being are supposed to have different healing powers, then what began merely as images or representations of a supernatural power have become idols, in that the different images themselves have acquired special efficacy.

Though the existence of idols and corresponding terms for them are widespread, idols are by no means universal, and therefore it may be necessary in some languages to employ some type of descriptive equivalent, for example, 'objects that are made to look like gods' or 'carved statues that are considered to be gods.'

6.98 κατείδωλος, ον: (derivative of εἴδωλον[a] 'idol,' 6.97) pertaining to numerous idols – 'full of idols.' θεωροῦντος κατείδωλον οὖσαν τὴν πόλιν 'he saw that the city was full of idols' Ac 17.16. In place of the traditional rendering 'how full of idols their city was,' one may have 'how many idols there were in their city'

---

10 In the NT εἴδωλον[a] is restricted in meaning to 'idol' in contrast with 'image,' as noted in the discussion of 6.97.

or 'how many idols the people worshiped there in their city.'

6.99 χερούβ, pl. χερουβίν *n*: in the NT the image of the winged creature that stood over the covenant box (but in certain OT contexts, supernatural winged creatures) – 'winged creature.' ὑπεράνω δὲ αὐτῆς χερουβὶν δόξης 'above it were the glorious winged creatures' He 9.5.

Since it is difficult to employ a satisfactory descriptive equivalent of χερούβ, most translators have simply employed a borrowed term and have described the appearance of the χερούβ in a glossary or marginal note. In English, however, it is impossible to use 'cherub,' since cherubs are known simply as 'baby angels' (typical of Valentine cards). In some English translations the plural form of χερούβ, namely 'cherubim,' has been employed, but for some persons *cherubim* is a singular with an analogically formed plural *cherubims*. In general, for χερούβ one can best employ a phrase, either 'the image of a winged creature' or 'a winged creature.'

6.100 ναός[b], οῦ *m*: a small replica or model of a temple or shrine – 'replica temple, model of a shrine.'[11] ποιῶν ναοὺς ἀργυροῦς Ἀρτέμιδος 'a maker of silver shrines of Artemis' Ac 19.24. In Ac 19.24 the term ναός refers only to a small replica of the temple of Artemis. An equivalent of ναός[b] in Ac 19.24 is in some languages 'tiny temples of Artemis,' or, in other instances, it is 'souvenir temples of Artemis.'

6.101 μοσχοποιέω: to make an idol in the form of a calf – 'to make a calf-idol, to shape an idol in the form of a calf.' καὶ ἐμοσχοποίησαν ἐν ταῖς ἡμέραις ἐκείναις 'in those days they made an idol in the form of a calf' Ac 7.41. In order not to appear to contradict

11 It would be possible to define ναός[a] 'temple, sanctuary' (7.15) in such a way as to include both sanctuaries as well as replicas of such buildings, but in view of the widespread diminutive derivations in Greek and the clear distinctions which many languages make between originals and souvenir replicas, there seem to be both theoretical as well as practical reasons for this distinction between ναός[a] and ναός[b].

the corresponding OT passage (Ex 32.4-6), one may wish to translate this clause in Ac 7.41 as 'they made an idol in the form of a bull calf.'

N Lights and Light Holders (6.102-6.105)

6.102 λαμπάς[a], άδος *f*; φῶς[c], φωτός *n*: a stick or bundle of sticks carried about as a light – 'torch.'
λαμπάς[a]: ἔρχεται ἐκεῖ μετὰ φανῶν καὶ λαμπάδων καὶ ὅπλων 'he came there with lanterns and torches and weapons' Jn 18.3.
φῶς[c]: αἰτήσας δὲ φῶτα εἰσεπήδησεν 'and calling for a torch, he rushed in' Ac 16.29. It is, of course, possible that in Ac 16.29 the meaning of φῶς is a lamp (see 6.104).

6.103 φανός, οῦ *m*: a small fire which was carried about for the sake of its light and which had some type of protection from wind and weather – 'lantern.' ἔρχεται ἐκεῖ μετὰ φανῶν καὶ λαμπάδων καὶ ὅπλων 'he came there with lanterns and torches and weapons' Jn 18.3. Though φανός in earlier Greek meant a torch, by NT times it appears to have been used primarily to identify a type of lamp used outdoors.

6.104 λαμπάς[b], άδος *f*; λύχνος, ου *m*: a light made by burning a wick saturated with oil contained in a relatively small vessel – 'lamp.'
λαμπάς[b]: δέκα παρθένοις αἵτινες λαβοῦσαι τὰς λαμπάδας ἑαυτῶν ἐξῆλθον εἰς ὑπάντησιν τοῦ νυμφίου 'ten girls who took their oil lamps and went out to meet the bridegroom' Mt 25.1.
λύχνος: μήτι ἔρχεται ὁ λύχνος ἵνα ὑπὸ τὸν μόδιον τεθῇ ἢ ὑπὸ τὴν κλίνην; 'does anyone ever bring in a lamp and put it under a bowl or under the bed?' (literally 'does a lamp come to be put . . .') Mk 4.21.

In some languages the closest equivalent of λαμπάς[b] and λύχνος is a kerosene lamp. What is to be avoided is a word which suggests a flashlight, which would of course be highly anachronistic.

6.105 λυχνία, ας *f*: a stand designed to hold a single lamp or a series of lamps – 'lampstand.' οὐδὲ καίουσιν λύχνον καὶ τιθέασιν αὐτὸν ὑπὸ τὸν μόδιον ἀλλ' ἐπὶ τὴν λυχνίαν 'neither do people light a lamp and place it under a bowl, but on a lampstand' Mt 5.15. One may translate 'lampstand' as 'something on which a lamp could be placed' or 'a place for putting lamps.'

O Furniture (6.106-6.117)

6.106 κλίνη, ης *f*: any piece of furniture employed for reclining or lying on – 'bed, couch, cot, stretcher, bier.' προσέφερον αὐτῷ παραλυτικὸν ἐπὶ κλίνης βεβλημένον 'they brought him a paralyzed man, lying on a stretcher' Mt 9.2. In Mt 9.2 a rendering such as 'stretcher' or 'cot' is certainly more advisable than the traditional rendering 'bed,' which might imply a large piece of furniture. In each passage one must employ a term which is most likely to identify the type of object which fits the context.

6.107 κλινίδιον, ου *n*; κλινάριον, ου *n*; κράβαττος, ου *m*: a relatively small and often temporary type of object on which a person may lie or recline – 'cot, pallet, stretcher.' κλινίδιον: καθῆκαν αὐτὸν σὺν τῷ κλινιδίῳ εἰς τὸ μέσον ἔμπροσθεν τοῦ Ἰησοῦ 'they let him down on a stretcher in the middle (of the crowd) before Jesus' Lk 5.19. κλινάριον: εἰς τὰς πλατείας ἐκφέρειν τοὺς ἀσθενεῖς καὶ τιθέναι ἐπὶ κλιναρίων καὶ κραβάττων 'they carried the sick people into the streets and put them on cots and pallets' Ac 5.15. κράβαττος: χαλῶσι τὸν κράβαττον ὅπου ὁ παραλυτικὸς κατέκειτο 'they let down the pallet on which the paralyzed man lay' Mk 2.4.

In a number of contexts the terms κλινίδιον, κλινάριον, and κράβαττος refer to cots or stretchers on which sick or convalescent persons might be resting or on which they could be transported. There is no NT context in which these terms refer to couches on which people reclined while eating.

6.108 κοίτη ᵃ, ης *f*: a piece of furniture used for sleeping – 'bed.' τὰ παιδία μου μετ' ἐμοῦ εἰς τὴν κοίτην εἰσίν 'my children are in bed with me' Lk 11.7. It is not necessary to understand Lk 11.7 to mean that the children were in the

same bed with the man, but it is, of course, possible that the reference here is to a relatively humble house in which all the members of the family would sleep on a single raised platform. See also 10.37.

6.109 σορός, οῦ *f*: a stretcher or plank used for carrying a corpse to a place of burial – 'bier.' προσελθὼν ἥψατο τῆς σοροῦ 'he came and touched the bier' Lk 7.14.

6.110 προσκεφάλαιον, ου *n*: an object on which one may lay one's head – 'cushion, pillow.' αὐτὸς ἦν ἐν τῇ πρύμνῃ ἐπὶ τὸ προσκεφάλαιον καθεύδων 'he was in the stern, sleeping with his head on a cushion' Mk 4.38. In rendering Mk 4.38 it is important to avoid a translation which would suggest that Jesus was so small or coiled up as to be able to sleep on a single pillow.

6.111 καθέδρα, ας *f* – 'seat, stool, chair.' τὰς καθέδρας τῶν πωλούντων τὰς περιστερὰς κατέστρεφεν 'he overturned the chairs of those who were selling doves' Mk 11.15.

6.112 θρόνος ᵃ, ου *m*: a relatively large and elaborate seat upon which a ruler sits on official occasions – 'throne.' εἶδον ἐπὶ τὴν δεξιὰν τοῦ καθημένου ἐπὶ τοῦ θρόνου βιβλίον 'I saw a book in the right hand of the one sitting on the throne' Re 5.1. In some languages 'throne' is rendered as 'the seat of judging' or 'the seat of decision-making for a ruler.'

6.113 τράπεζα ᵃ, ης *f*: a generic expression for any type of table – 'table.' ἐπιθυμῶν χορτασθῆναι ἀπὸ τῶν πιπτόντων ἀπὸ τῆς τραπέζης τοῦ πλουσίου 'he hoped to fill himself with the bits of food that fell from the rich man's table' Lk 16.21; τὰς τραπέζας ἀνέτρεψεν 'he overturned the tables' Jn 2.15.

6.114 θυσιαστήριον, ου *n*: any type of altar or object where gifts may be placed and ritual observances carried out in honor of supernatural beings – 'altar' (in the NT θυσιαστήριον is employed to refer to a number of different types of altars, including the altar for burnt offerings in the Temple, the altar of incense, the altar which Abraham built, and the heavenly altar mentioned in the book of Revelation). ἐὰν οὖν προσφέρῃς τὸ δῶρόν σου ἐπὶ τὸ θυσιαστήριον 'so if you are offering your gift at the altar' Mt 5.23; ὤφθη δὲ αὐτῷ ἄγγελος κυρίου ἑστὼς ἐκ δεξιῶν τοῦ θυσιαστηρίου τοῦ θυμιάματος 'an angel of the Lord appeared to him standing at the right of the altar of incense' Lk 1.11.

A descriptive equivalent of 'altar' occurs in some languages as 'a place where offerings are made to God' or 'a place where gifts are given to God.' In some contexts it may be necessary to add phrases such as 'where sacrifices are burned to God' or 'where incense is burned to honor God.'

6.115 βωμός, οῦ m: an altar with a base or pedestal – 'altar.' βωμὸν ἐν ᾧ ἐπεγέγραπτο, Ἀγνώστῳ θεῷ 'an altar on which was inscribed, To An Unknown God' Ac 17.23. In this only reference in the NT in which βωμός occurs, the altar to the Unknown God may be spoken of as 'a place for offerings to a god whom people do not know' or '. . . god whose name is not known.'

6.116 θυμιατήριον, ου n: an altar used for burning incense – 'incense altar.' χρυσοῦν ἔχουσα θυμιατήριον καὶ τὴν κιβωτὸν τῆς διαθήκης 'having the golden altar of incense and the box of the covenant' He 9.4. θυμιατήριον may be rendered in some languages as 'place where incense is burned in worship of God.' One must avoid a rendering which would imply that the altar was made of incense.

6.117 ὑποπόδιον, ου n: a piece of furniture on which one may rest one's feet – 'footstool.' ὑποπόδιον occurs only in a figurative context in the NT: ὅτι ὑποπόδιόν ἐστιν τῶν ποδῶν αὐτοῦ 'for it is a footstool for his feet' Mt 5.35. Since footstools are a common cultural feature in many parts of the world, it is rarely necessary to use a descriptive phrase. One can, however, use an expression such as 'a thing on which to rest one's feet.' In some languages the functional equivalent of a footstool is a 'footstick,' that is to say, a stick on which one normally places the feet in order to raise them from the relatively damp dirt floor of a typical house or hut.

P Containers (6.118-6.151)

6.118 σκεῦος[b], ους n: a highly generic term for any kind of jar, bowl, basket, or vase – 'vessel, container.' ὡς τὰ σκεύη τὰ κεραμικὰ συντρίβεται 'he will break them like clay pots' Re 2.27; οὐδεὶς δὲ λύχνον ἅψας καλύπτει αὐτὸν σκεύει 'no one lights a lamp and puts it under a bowl' Lk 8.16. In Ac 10.11 and 16 σκεῦος[b] refers to a 'sheet' (as a container) which was let down from heaven in Peter's vision.

In a number of languages there is no relatively high generic term which may be used to refer to any type of vessel or container, and therefore one must employ more specific terms depending upon the context, even as in the case of most English translations in Ac 10.11, Re 2.27, and Lk 8.16.

6.119 θήκη, ης f: a receptacle into which an object is customarily placed for safekeeping – 'receptacle, chest, sheath.' βάλε τὴν μάχαιραν εἰς τὴν θήκην 'put the sword in the sheath' Jn 18.11.[12] In this one occurrence of θήκη in the NT, the reference is to a 'sheath' for a sword, which may be rendered in some languages as 'a leather bag for a sword' or 'a covering for a sword' or 'something in which a sword is carried.'

6.120 ἀγγεῖον, ου n; ἄγγος, ους n: a container, primarily for liquids or wet objects – 'container, vessel.'
ἀγγεῖον: αἱ δὲ φρόνιμοι ἔλαβον ἔλαιον ἐν τοῖς ἀγγείοις μετὰ τῶν λαμπάδων ἑαυτῶν 'and the wise ones took oil in vessels with their lamps' Mt 25.4. The vessels referred to in this context would have been relatively small, containing probably not more than a liter (about a quart).
ἄγγος: συνέλεξαν τὰ καλὰ εἰς ἄγγη 'they collected the good (fish) in vessels' Mt 13.48. The vessels referred to in this context would no doubt have been rather large, containing perhaps some 16 to 20 liters (or about four to five gallons).

---

12 It would be possible to treat θήκη as a semantic derivative of τίθημι[a] (85.32), but certain specializations of meaning justify its occurrence in this domain of *Artifacts*.

6.121 ποτήριον, ου *n*: an object from which one may drink – 'cup.' ὃς γὰρ ἂν ποτίσῃ ὑμᾶς ποτήριον ὕδατος 'anyone who gives you a cup of water' Mk 9.41. In place of the expression 'cup of water' (in which cup not only identifies the container but indicates the quantity of water), some languages would use the expression 'water in a cup,' but it is even more likely that the typical equivalent of 'cup of water' would be 'a drink of water.' In some parts of the world a term such as 'cup' would suggest something rather strange and foreign; therefore, one might find that an expression 'a gourd of water' would not only be more natural, but would be the semantic equivalent of 'drink of water.'

6.122 νιπτήρ, ῆρος *m*: a basin used for washing – 'washbasin.' βάλλει ὕδωρ εἰς τὸν νιπτῆρα 'he placed water in the washbasin' Jn 13.5.

6.123 ἄντλημα, τος *n*: a container or vessel for drawing water – 'bucket.' οὔτε ἄντλημα ἔχεις καὶ τὸ φρέαρ ἐστὶν βαθύ 'you do not have a bucket, and the well is deep' Jn 4.11.

6.124 φιάλη, ης *f*: a broad, shallow bowl, normally used for cooking or for serving liquids – 'bowl.' φιάλας χρυσᾶς γεμούσας θυμιαμάτων 'golden bowls filled with incense' Re 5.8.

6.125 στάμνος, ου *f*: a jar regularly used for wine, but in the NT it refers to the jar in which manna was kept permanently – 'jar.' στάμνος χρυσῆ ἔχουσα τὸ μάννα 'a golden jar containing the manna' He 9.4.

6.126 ξέστης, ου *m*: (a borrowing based on Latin *sextarius*, a Roman measure equal to about a half liter, one pint) a kind of small pitcher or jar – 'pitcher, jar.' βαπτισμοὺς ποτηρίων καὶ ξεστῶν 'the washing of cups and pitchers' Mk 7.4.

6.127 ὑδρία, ας *f*: a container for water – 'pitcher, water jar.' ἦσαν δὲ ἐκεῖ λίθιναι ὑδρίαι ἕξ 'there were six stone water jars there' Jn 2.6.

6.128 κεράμιον, ου *n*: an earthenware container – 'jar, vessel.' ἀπαντήσει ὑμῖν ἄνθρωπος κεράμιον ὕδατος βαστάζων 'a man carrying a vessel with water will meet you' Mk 14.13.

6.129 κεραμεύς, έως *m*: (derivative of κεράμιον 'earthenware vessel,' 6.128) one who makes earthenware vessels – 'potter.' οὐκ ἔχει ἐξουσίαν ὁ κεραμεὺς τοῦ πηλοῦ ἐκ τοῦ αὐτοῦ φυράματος ποιῆσαι ὃ μὲν εἰς τιμὴν σκεῦος, ὃ δὲ εἰς ἀτιμίαν; 'doesn't the potter have the right to make from the same lump of clay an expensive vessel or one for ordinary use?' Ro 9.21; ἠγόρασαν ἐξ αὐτῶν τὸν ἀγρὸν τοῦ κεραμέως 'with the money they bought the Potter's Field' Mt 27.7.

6.130 χαλκίον, ου *n*: a container or object made of copper, brass, or bronze – 'bronze vessel.' βαπτισμοὺς ποτηρίων καὶ ξεστῶν καὶ χαλκίων 'the washing of cups, pitchers, and bronze vessels' Mk 7.4. In a number of languages the most natural equivalent of χαλκίον is 'metal vessel' or 'kettle.'

6.131 ἀλάβαστρον, ου *n*: a jar made of alabaster stone – 'alabaster jar.' ἦλθεν γυνὴ ἔχουσα ἀλάβαστρον μύρου νάρδου 'a woman came with an alabaster jar of ointment' Mk 14.3. An alabaster jar normally had a rather long neck which was broken off for the contents to be used. It served primarily as a container for precious substances such as perfumes.

In translating 'alabaster jar' many translators have simply used a term meaning 'jar' or 'flask' and have either employed a descriptive qualifier, for example, 'made of alabaster stone' or 'made of valuable stone' or 'made of valuable stone called alabaster.'

6.132 ἀσκός, οῦ *m*: a bag made of skin or leather (in the NT used only of wineskins) – 'wineskin.' οὐδὲ βάλλουσιν οἶνον νέον εἰς ἀσκοὺς παλαιούς 'they do not place new wine in old wineskins' Mt 9.17. A number of translators have attempted to substitute 'bottles' for 'wineskins,' but this has not been satisfactory, since fermenting wine does not normally break glass bottles, while it would break old wineskins. In circumstances in which the use of wineskins is not known, it may be necessary to employ some type of descriptive phrase (for example, 'a container made of skin' or 'a closed bag of skin' or 'a goat skin like a bottle') and a fuller explanation in the margin.

6.133 σπόγγος, ου *m* – 'sponge.' λαβὼν σπόγγον πλήσας τε ὄξους 'taking a sponge he filled it with sour wine' Mt 27.48. In the only type of NT context in which σπόγγος occurs (Mt 27.48; Mk 15.36; Jn 19.29), it serves as a container for cheap wine offered to Jesus on the cross.

6.134 πίναξ, ακος *f*: a relatively flat, large dish – 'plate, platter.' δός μοι, φησίν, ὧδε ἐπὶ πίνακι τὴν κεφαλὴν Ἰωάννου τοῦ βαπτιστοῦ 'she said, Give me here the head of John the Baptist on a plate' Mt 14.8.

6.135 παροψίς, ίδος *f*: a relatively flat dish, probably somewhat smaller than a πίναξ (6.134) – 'plate, dish.' καθαρίζετε τὸ ἔξωθεν τοῦ ποτηρίου καὶ τῆς παροψίδος 'you cleanse the outside of the cup and dish' Mt 23.25. In this one NT context in which παροψίς occurs, it seems to refer to any kind of plate or dish, though in contexts outside the NT, παροψίς is often employed to refer to a dish used for serving certain choice foods and delicacies.

6.136 τρύβλιον, ου *n*: a relatively deep bowl or dish – 'bowl, dish.' ὁ ἐμβάψας μετ' ἐμοῦ τὴν χεῖρα ἐν τῷ τρυβλίῳ 'he who dips his hand in the dish with me' Mt 26.23. In the two NT occurrences (Mt 26.23; Mk 14.20) τρύβλιον can be understood as a part of an idiom (literally 'to dip one's hands into the bowl with someone') meaning 'to share a meal with someone.' If, however, the idiom is to be translated literally (and this is normally the case), there are certain difficulties involved, since a literal rendering of 'to dip one's hand into a bowl' might mean literally putting one's fingers or hand into a bowl rather than dipping in food which one holds in the hand. An idiomatic interpretation of 'sharing a meal with someone' or 'eating together with' may be preferable. But if one does translate the idiom somewhat literally, it is important in some languages to render this phrase as 'to dip food into a bowl together with someone' or 'to jointly dip food into sauce.'

6.137 φάτνη[a], ης *f*: a box or crib where animals feed – 'feed box, manger, crib' (or possibly even an open feeding place under the sky). ἀνέκλινεν αὐτὸν ἐν φάτνῃ 'she placed him in a manger' Lk 2.7.

φάτνη[a] occurs only in Lk 2.7, 12, 16, and it may be important in some languages to distinguish clearly between various alternatives. The term 'crib' normally refers to the place where an animal stands when it feeds. The 'manger' is a relatively large box or rack containing hay, and a 'feed box' is a much smaller container, usually for grain. There is, of course, no way of knowing precisely where the baby Jesus was placed, but it would be very appropriate for the baby to have been placed in the feed box or in the manger. See also 7.64.

6.138 λιβανωτός, οῦ *m*: a bowl in which incense is burned – 'censer.' ἄγγελος . . . ἔχων λιβανωτὸν χρυσοῦν 'an angel . . . with a golden censer' Re 8.3.

6.139 κιβωτός[b], οῦ *f*: any box-like container, whether plain or elaborate – 'box, chest, coffer.' τὴν κιβωτὸν τῆς διαθήκης περικεκαλυμμένην πάντοθεν χρυσίῳ 'the Covenant Box all covered with gold' He 9.4. In the NT κιβωτός[b] occurs only in the phrase κιβωτὸς τῆς διαθήκης 'the box of the covenant,' which was placed in the Holy of Holies of the Temple in Jerusalem and referred to also as being in the heavenly temple (Re 11.19).

In the case of English some persons object to speaking of the so-called 'ark of the Covenant' as 'the Covenant Box,' since they assume that the English word 'ark' has some special meaning equivalent to the corresponding Greek or Hebrew terms. However, the term 'ark' in Old English and Middle English is simply a borrowing of Latin *arca* meaning 'box, chest, coffer.' In present-day English the term ark is known primarily from the context of 'Noah's ark.'

6.140 θησαυρός[b], οῦ *m* – 'treasure box.' ἀνοίξαντες τοὺς θησαυροὺς αὐτῶν προσήνεγκαν αὐτῷ δῶρα 'they opened their treasure boxes and offered him presents' Mt 2.11. A 'treasure box' may be referred to as 'a box with valuable objects' or 'a box with objects costing a great deal of money.'

6.141 γαζοφυλάκιον^b, ου *n*: a large box in which offerings were placed – 'offering box.' εἶδεν τοὺς βάλλοντας εἰς τὸ γαζοφυλάκιον τὰ δῶρα αὐτῶν πλουσίους 'he saw rich men dropping their gifts in the offering box' Lk 21.1. The offering box in the Temple was also referred to as δῶρον^b (6.142).

6.142 δῶρον^b, ου *n*: a place for making gifts or offerings – 'offering box' (see 6.141). πάντες γὰρ οὗτοι ἐκ τοῦ περισσεύοντος αὐτοῖς ἔβαλον εἰς τὰ δῶρα 'for all of these put some of their abundance into the offering boxes' Lk 21.4.

According to tradition there were thirteen such offering boxes in the Temple and the receptacles leading down to the boxes were made in the form of trumpets. As a result, the sound of coins falling into the boxes was rather conspicuous.

In Lk 21.4 it is possible to interpret εἰς τὰ δῶρα not as 'into the offering boxes' but as 'for their gifts,' thus reflecting a more common meaning of δῶρον^a 'gift' (57.84).

6.143 γλωσσόκομον, ου *n*: a box in which money was kept – 'money box.' ἐπεὶ τὸ γλωσσόκομον εἶχεν Ἰούδας 'since Judas was in charge of the money box' Jn 13.29. It may be useful, however, in rendering Jn 13.29 to say simply 'Judas had charge of the money' or 'Judas was the treasurer of the group,' since the Greek expression may be understood as an idiom.

6.144 βαλλάντιον, ου *n*: a bag or purse for carrying money – 'purse, money bag.' μὴ βαστάζετε βαλλάντιον, μὴ πήραν 'do not carry a purse or a bag' Lk 10.4.

6.145 πήρα, ας *f*: a bag used by travelers (or beggars) to carry possessions – 'traveler's bag.' μὴ πήραν εἰς ὁδὸν μηδὲ δύο χιτῶνας 'do not take a traveler's bag for the journey or two shirts' Mt 10.10. It is possible that in Mt 10.10 (and parallel passages) the reference is specifically to a 'beggar's bag' used to collect food or money.

6.146 κατασκήνωσις, εως *f*: a construction built by birds in connection with brooding and raising their young – 'nest.'[13] αἱ ἀλώπεκες φωλεοὺς ἔχουσιν καὶ τὰ πετεινὰ τοῦ οὐρανοῦ κατασκηνώσεις 'foxes have holes and birds have nests' Mt 8.20. It is, however, possible to understand κατασκήνωσις in Mt 8.20 as simply a sheltered place, but the most natural interpretation would appear to be 'nest.'

6.147 κατασκηνόω: (derivative of κατασκήνωσις 'nest,' 6.146) to make a nest (or possibly to find shelter) – 'to nest.' ὥστε ἐλθεῖν τὰ πετεινὰ τοῦ οὐρανοῦ καὶ κατασκηνοῦν ἐν τοῖς κλάδοις αὐτοῦ 'so that the birds come and nest in its branches' Mt 13.32.

6.148 σαργάνη, ης *f* – 'basket.'[14] ἐν σαργάνῃ ἐχαλάσθην 'I was let down in a basket' 2 Cor 11.33. In the one context in which σαργάνη occurs (2 Cor 11.33), the basket was evidently rather large, since it was used to let Paul down from an opening in the wall of Damascus. It may very well have been made of braided ropes. In 2 Cor 11.33 the basket is called σαργάνη, while in Ac 9.25 the same basket is referred to as σπυρίς (6.149).

6.149 σπυρίς, ίδος *f*: a basket which is presumably somewhat larger than a κόφινος (6.150) – 'large basket.'[14] τὸ περισσεῦον τῶν κλασμάτων ἦραν, ἑπτὰ σπυρίδας πλήρεις 'they took up seven baskets full of the pieces that remained' Mt 15.37.

6.150 κόφινος, ου *m*: a relatively large basket used primarily for food or produce – 'large basket.'[14] ἦραν τὸ περισσεῦον τῶν κλασμάτων δώδεκα κοφίνους πλήρεις 'they took up twelve

---

13 κατασκήνωσις in the sense of 'nest' is the only artifact in this domain which is not made by humans, but this in no way precludes it from being classified in this domain.

14 Neither from NT contexts nor from extrabiblical usage can one determine precisely the differences in meaning between these three terms for baskets: σαργάνη (6.148), σπυρίς (6.149), and κόφινος (6.150).

baskets full of the pieces that remained' Mt 14.20. Translators often find it difficult to obtain satisfactory equivalents of σπυρίς (6.149) and κόφινος, since in various receptor languages there are highly specific terms for particular kinds of baskets depending upon type of construction and size. Unfortunately, there is no way of determining from the Greek text precisely the size or type of baskets involved in references to σπυρίς and κόφινος.

6.151 μόδιος, ου *m*: a container for dry matter with a capacity of about eight liters (about two gallons) – 'basket, box.' οὐδὲ καίουσιν λύχνον καὶ τιθέασιν αὐτὸν ὑπὸ τὸν μόδιον 'no one lights a lamp and puts it under a basket' Mt 5.15. A μόδιος is variously translated as 'basket,' 'bucket,' 'box,' and 'bowl.'

Q Cloth, Leather, and Objects Made of Such Materials (6.152-6.187)

6.152 ῥάκος, ους *n*: a piece of cloth – 'patch.' οὐδεὶς δὲ ἐπιβάλλει ἐπίβλημα ῥάκους ἀγνάφου ἐπὶ ἱματίῳ παλαιῷ 'no one puts a patch of new cloth on an old garment' Mt 9.16.

6.153 ὀθόνη, ης *f*: a large piece of cloth, probably of linen – 'sheet, linen sheet.' τι ὡς ὀθόνην μεγάλην 'something like a large sheet' Ac 10.11.

6.154 ὀθόνιον, ου *n*: a piece of linen cloth – 'linen cloth.' ἔδησαν αὐτὸ ὀθονίοις μετὰ τῶν ἀρωμάτων 'they bound it in linen cloths with the spices' Jn 19.40. In the NT ὀθόνιον occurs only in reference to strips of cloth used in preparing a corpse for burial.

6.155 σινδών, όνος *f*: linen cloth of good quality – 'linen cloth.' λαβὼν τὸ σῶμα ὁ Ἰωσὴφ ἐνετύλιξεν αὐτὸ ἐν σινδόνι καθαρᾷ 'Joseph took the body and wrapped it in a clean linen cloth' Mt 27.59; περιβεβλημένος σινδόνα ἐπὶ γυμνοῦ 'wearing a linen cloth on his body' Mk 14.51. In a number of languages there is no term for 'linen,' and though a word for 'linen' may be borrowed, what is important in the NT contexts in which σινδών occurs is primarily the quality of the cloth, not the material of which it was made. According-

ly, many translators have used an expression such as 'fine cloth' or 'good cloth.'

6.156 κειρία, ας *f* – 'band of cloth, strip of cloth.' δεδεμένος τοὺς πόδας καὶ τὰς χεῖρας κειρίαις 'bound hand and foot with strips of cloth' Jn 11.44. In Jn 11.44 one may translate 'the strips of cloth that had been put around the body of Lazarus.'

6.157 ἐπίβλημα, τος *n*: a piece of cloth sewed on clothing to repair a hole or tear – 'patch.' οὐδεὶς δὲ ἐπιβάλλει ἐπίβλημα ῥάκους ἀγνάφου ἐπὶ ἱματίῳ 'no one puts a patch of new cloth on an old garment' Mt 9.16. The statement in Mt 9.16 that 'no one puts a patch of new cloth on an old garment' seems almost preposterous or incredible in some societies, since people habitually repair old clothing by putting on patches of new cloth, sometimes to the point where it is difficult to determine what was the original fabric. In Mt 9.16 the phrase ῥάκους ἀγνάφου, often translated 'new cloth,' is literally 'unshrunken cloth,' in other words, cloth which has not been washed one or more times and thus has been shrunken in the process. In biblical times there was no technique for preshrinking cloth.

6.158 λίνον[b], ου *n*: a linen cord in a lamp that draws up the oil – 'wick.' λίνον τυφόμενον οὐ σβέσει 'he will not extinguish a smoldering wick' Mt 12.20. A wick may often be referred to as 'a small strip of cloth.'

6.159 σουδάριον, ου *n*: a small piece of cloth used as a towel, napkin, or face cloth – 'towel, napkin, handkerchief, face cloth.' ὥστε καὶ ἐπὶ τοὺς ἀσθενοῦντας ἀποφέρεσθαι ἀπὸ τοῦ χρωτὸς αὐτοῦ σουδάρια ἢ σιμικίνθια 'even handkerchiefs and aprons he had used were taken to the sick' Ac 19.12; ἡ ὄψις αὐτοῦ σουδαρίῳ περιεδέδετο 'his face was covered with a face cloth' Jn 11.44.

6.160 καταπέτασμα, τος *n*: a hanging of cloth over an opening – 'drape, curtain, veil.' τὸ καταπέτασμα τοῦ ναοῦ ἐσχίσθη ἀπ' ἄνωθεν ἕως κάτω εἰς δύο 'then the drape hanging in the Temple was torn in two from top to bottom' Mt 27.51.

The χαταπέτασμα of the Temple has been traditionally called in English a 'veil,' but a literal correspondence of 'veil' would be misleading, since it would suggest something which merely covers the face. At the same time a typical correspondence of 'curtain' could be misleading, since it would suggest something which covers a window. In some languages the most appropriate equivalent for χαταπέτασμα in the context of Mt 27.51 is 'drape,' but frequently it is necessary to use some kind of descriptive equivalent, for example, 'a large piece of cloth hanging down from the ceiling' or 'a large piece of cloth covering the entrance.'

6.161 λέντιον, ου *n*: a piece of cloth (probably made of linen) used primarily for drying – 'towel.' λαβὼν λέντιον διέζωσεν ἑαυτόν 'he took a towel and tied it around himself' Jn 13.4.

6.162 ἔνδυμα, τος *n*; ἐσθής, ῆτος *f*; ἱματισμός, οῦ *m*; ἱμάτιον ᵃ, ου *n*; χιτών ᵇ, ῶνος *m* (in the plural): any kind of clothing – 'clothing, apparel.'

ἔνδυμα: περὶ ἐνδύματος τί μεριμνᾶτε; 'why worry about clothing?' Mt 6.28.

ἐσθής: ἄνδρες δύο ἐπέστησαν αὐταῖς ἐν ἐσθῆτι ἀστραπτούσῃ 'two men stood before them in shining clothing' Lk 24.4.

ἱματισμός: ἀργυρίου ἢ χρυσίου ἢ ἱματισμοῦ οὐδενὸς ἐπεθύμησα 'I have not wanted anyone's silver or gold or clothing' or '. . . anyone's money (see 6.69) or clothing' Ac 20.33.

ἱμάτιον ᵃ: διεμερίσαντο τὰ ἱμάτια αὐτοῦ 'they divided his clothes among them' Mt 27.35.

χιτών ᵇ: ὁ δὲ ἀρχιερεὺς διαρρήξας τοὺς χιτῶνας αὐτοῦ 'the high priest tore his clothes' Mk 14.63.

6.163 περιβόλαιον ᵃ, ου *n*; σκέπασμα, τος *n*: clothing as a covering – 'clothing, apparel.' ¹⁵

περιβόλαιον ᵃ: ἡ κόμη ἀντὶ περιβολαίου δέδοται αὐτῇ 'her long hair has been given her as clothing' 1 Cor 11.15.

σκέπασμα: ἔχοντες δὲ διατροφὰς καὶ σκεπάσματα, τούτοις ἀρκεσθησόμεθα 'if we have food and clothing, we should be content with them' 1 Tm 6.8.

6.164 σάκκος, ου *m*: a heavy material normally used for making sacks, but worn by persons in mourning and as a sign of repentance – 'sackcloth.' ἂν ἐν σάκκῳ καὶ σποδῷ μετενόησαν 'they would have repented in sackcloth and ashes' Mt 11.21. In most languages sackcloth is described as 'coarse cloth' and sometimes as 'heavy cloth.'

6.165 λίνον ᵃ, ου *n*: linen cloth, normally in the form of a garment – 'linen, linen garment.' ¹⁶ ἐνδεδυμένοι λίνον καθαρὸν λαμπρόν 'they dressed in clean, bright, linen garments' Re 15.6. Linen garments may be described as 'clothing made out of linen cloth.' What is important in Re 15.6 is the quality of the garments, not so much the fact that they were made of linen.

6.166 βύσσος, ου *f* – 'fine linen.' ¹⁶ ἐνεδιδύσκετο πορφύραν καὶ βύσσον 'he was clothed in purple garments and fine linen' Lk 16.19.

6.167 βύσσινον, ου *n*: (derivative of βύσσος 'fine linen,' 6.166) cloth consisting of fine linen – 'cloth of fine linen.' μαργαριτῶν καὶ βυσσίνου καὶ πορφύρας 'pearls and cloth of fine linen and purple' Re 18.12. ¹⁷

6.168 σιρικόν, οῦ *n* – 'silk cloth.' βυσσίνου καὶ πορφύρας καὶ σιρικοῦ 'fine linen and purple and silk' Re 18.12. ¹⁷

16 It would be possible to treat λίνον ᵃ 'linen cloth' (6.165) and βύσσος 'fine linen' (6.166) as meaning 'linen garments' and 'fine linen garments' respectively. However, there is no need for setting up such a separate meaning for NT usage, especially since in both Re 15.6 and Lk 16.19 the semantic element of 'garment' or 'clothing' is a significant compound of the verb meaning 'to dress,' and thus the referents would naturally be garments. The same applies to πορφύρα (6.169) in Lk 16.19.

17 From the context of Re 18.12 it is impossible to determine whether the referents of βύσσινον (6.167), σιρικόν (6.168), and πορφύρα (6.169) are cloth or garments made of linen, silk, and purple cloth respectively.

15 περιβόλαιον ᵃ and σκέπασμα could also be treated as derivatives based on their respective corresponding events involving the covering of an object. The derivatives would then be merely instruments for covering. Since, however, in the NT these two terms are so closely associated with clothing as covering, they are here treated in this subdomain.

6.169 πορφύρα, ας *f*; πορφυροῦν, οῦ *n*: a reddish-purple cloth dyed with a substance obtained from the murex shellfish – 'purple cloth.'

πορφύρα: βυσσίνου καὶ πορφύρας καὶ σιρικοῦ 'fine linen and purple and silk' Re 18.12.[17]

πορφυροῦν: περιβεβλημένη πορφυροῦν 'dressed in purple cloth' Re 17.4.

In a number of languages there is no special color term for reddish-purple, since the color in question is sometimes classified as a kind of blue and in other instances it is related to black. However, in all languages it is possible to be somewhat more precise about color terms by likening the color to that of a local flower or bird.

6.170 κόκκινον, ου *n* – 'scarlet cloth.' περιβεβλημένη πορφυροῦν καὶ κόκκινον 'dressed in purple and scarlet cloth' Re 17.4.

6.171 ἔριον[b], ου *n*: the processed hair of sheep – 'wool.' μετὰ ὕδατος καὶ ἐρίου κοκκίνου καὶ ὑσσώπου 'with water and red wool and hyssop' He 9.19. See also ἔριον[a] in 8.15.

6.172 ἐπενδύτης, ου *m*; ἱμάτιον[b], ου *n*; περιβόλαιον[b], ου *n*; φαιλόνης, ου *m*: any type of outer garment – 'cloak, coat, robe.'[18]

ἐπενδύτης: τὸν ἐπενδύτην διεζώσατο 'he put on his outer garment' Jn 21.7.

ἱμάτιον[b]: ἄφες αὐτῷ καὶ τὸ ἱμάτιον 'let him have your coat as well' Mt 5.40.

περιβόλαιον[b]: ὡσεὶ περιβόλαιον ἐλίξεις αὐτούς 'you will roll them up like a cloak' He 1.12.

φαιλόνης: τὸν φαιλόνην ὃν ἀπέλιπον ἐν Τρῳάδι 'the cloak which I left in Troas' 2 Tm 4.13.

The choice of an equivalent for these terms relating to 'outer garments' will depend largely upon the specific context and the usage in each receptor language. The most common equivalent is a term meaning 'coat.'

---

18 There are no doubt certain minor distinctions in meaning for the four terms in 6.172, but it is impossible to determine the distinctive features on the basis of existing contexts. There are considerable differences of opinion about φαιλόνης, regarded by many as a loan word from Latin *paenula*.

6.173 χλαμύς, ύδος *f*: a loose outer garment worn by Roman soldiers and travelers – 'cloak.' χλαμύδα κοκκίνην περιέθηκαν αὐτῷ 'they put a red cloak on him' Mt 27.28. In some parts of the world the closest equivalent of χλαμύς is a poncho.

6.174 στολή, ῆς *f*: a long, flowing robe – 'long robe.' νεανίσκον καθήμενον ἐν τοῖς δεξιοῖς περιβεβλημένον στολὴν λευκήν 'a young man sitting on the right and wearing a long white robe' Mk 16.5; τῶν θελόντων ἐν στολαῖς περιπατεῖν 'who like to walk around in long robes' Mk 12.38. The cultural significance of 'long robe' would be high social status and dignified occupation or activity.

6.175 ποδήρης, ους *m*: a long robe reaching to the feet – 'a robe reaching to the feet, long robe.' ἐνδεδυμένον ποδήρη 'dressed in a robe reaching to the feet' Re 1.13.

6.176 χιτών[a], ῶνος *m*: a garment worn under the ἱμάτιον[b] 'cloak' (6.172) – 'tunic, shirt.' τῷ θέλοντί σοι κριθῆναι καὶ τὸν χιτῶνά σου λαβεῖν, ἄφες αὐτῷ καὶ τὸ ἱμάτιον 'if someone takes you to court to sue you for your shirt, let him have your coat as well' Mt 5.40.

6.177 κάλυμμα, τος *n*: a piece of thin material worn over the face – 'veil.' οὐ καθάπερ Μωϋσῆς ἐτίθει κάλυμμα ἐπὶ τὸ πρόσωπον αὐτοῦ 'not like Moses who put a veil over his face' 2 Cor 3.13. The cloth of a veil would be sufficiently thin that the wearer would be able to see through it, but others would find it difficult to recognize the features through the veil.

6.178 ζώνη, ης *f*: a band of leather or cloth worn around the waist outside of one's clothing – 'belt, girdle.' ζώνην δερματίνην περὶ τὴν ὀσφὺν αὐτοῦ 'a leather belt around his waist' Mt 3.4. A ζώνη was normally quite wide and could be readily folded. As such, it was often used to carry money (see Mt 10.9).

6.179 σιμικίνθιον, ου *n*: an apron, normally worn by workmen – 'apron.' ὥστε καὶ ἐπὶ τοὺς ἀσθενοῦντας ἀποφέρεσθαι ἀπὸ τοῦ χρωτὸς αὐτοῦ σουδάρια ἢ σιμικίνθια 'even towels and aprons he had used were taken to the sick' Ac 19.12.

A σιμικίνθιον may be called in some languages 'a workman's cloth' or 'a workman's cloth to protect clothing.'

6.180 χράσπεδον[a], ου *n*: the border of a garment – 'fringe.'[19] ἵνα κἂν τοῦ χρασπέδου τοῦ ἱματίου αὐτοῦ ἅψωνται 'so that they might touch the fringe of his cloak' Mk 6.56. The edge of the garment designated by χράσπεδον[a] could have been plain or decorated. In Mt 23.5 χράσπεδον denotes the tassels worn at the four corners of the outer garment (see 6.194). It is also possible that in all instances in which χράσπεδον is used in reference to Jesus' clothing, the reference may be specifically to the tassels and not merely to the fringe or edge of the garment. The interpretation of such passages depends upon how strictly Jesus may have followed the Mosaic law and the manner in which the authors may have understood the meaning of χράσπεδον.

6.181 χόλπος[b], ου *m*: the fold of a garment forming a type of pocket or container – 'fold.' μέτρον χαλὸν . . . δώσουσιν εἰς τὸν χόλπον ὑμῶν 'they will give you good measure . . . in the fold of your garment' Lk 6.38.

6.182 ὑπόδημα, τος *n*: any type of footwear – 'sandal, shoe' (though ordinarily the reference would be to a sandal rather than to a shoe). οὐκ εἰμὶ ἱκανὸς χύψας λῦσαι τὸν ἱμάντα τῶν ὑποδημάτων αὐτοῦ 'I am not worthy to stoop down and untie his sandal straps' Mk 1.7.

6.183 σανδάλιον, ου *n*: a type of footwear consisting of a sole made of leather (or possibly wood) tied to the foot by means of thongs or straps – 'sandal.' ζῶσαι καὶ ὑπόδησαι τὰ σανδάλιά σου 'get dressed and put on your sandals' Ac 12.8.

6.184 δέρμα, τος *n*: skin of an animal, normally including attached hair and sometimes tanned – 'skin, hide.' περιῆλθον ἐν μηλωταῖς, ἐν αἰγείοις δέρμασιν 'they traveled about in sheepskins and in goatskins' or '. . . in skins of sheep and goats' He 11.37. In a number of languages it is important to distinguish clearly between tanned and untanned skins or hides. Furthermore, one must often make a distinction between a skin which still has the hair on it and that which does not. In He 11.37 the likelihood is that these skins were tanned and still retained the hair as extra protection.

6.185 δερμάτινος, η, ον: (derivative of δέρμα 'skin,' 6.184) pertaining to being made of skin or leather – 'leather, of leather.' ζώνην δερματίνην περὶ τὴν ὀσφὺν αὐτοῦ 'a leather belt around his waist' Mt 3.4.

6.186 βυρσεύς, έως *m*: one who tans hides to make leather – 'tanner, maker of leather.' ἐγένετο δὲ ἡμέρας ἱκανὰς μεῖναι ἐν Ἰόππῃ παρά τινι Σίμωνι βυρσεῖ 'he stayed in Joppa many days with a tanner named Simon' Ac 9.43.[20]

6.187 μηλωτή, ῆς *f*: the tanned hide of sheep with the hair adhering – 'sheepskin, fleece.' περιῆλθον ἐν μηλωταῖς 'they traveled about in sheepskins' He 11.37. In some languages it is important to distinguish clearly between sheepskin which has the fur on it (the meaning of μηλωτή) and a sheepskin from which the fur has been removed and thus equivalent, if properly prepared, to parchment.

R Adornments (6.188-6.196)

6.188 χόσμος[f], ου *m*: an object which serves to adorn or beautify – 'adornment.'[21] ὧν ἔστω

---

19 It would be possible to treat χράσπεδον[a] simply as an abstract of shape; however, since both biblical and extrabiblical uses of χράσπεδον seem primarily associated with cloth and garments, there is some justification for treating χράσπεδον[a] in this subdomain.

20 It is possible that βυρσεύς in Ac 9.43 should be interpreted as the surname of Simon, a Christian in Joppa, that is to say, the name of Simon would be Simon Berseus or 'Simon Tanner.'

21 χόσμος[f] may be regarded as a highly generic term for any and all kinds of decorations and adornments; or it may be considered as the process whereby people may adorn themselves (see 79.12). χόσμος[f] is semantically complex, since it involves not only certain artifacts and the use of such artifacts, but also an abstract component of 'attractive appearance.'

οὐχ ὁ ἔξωθεν ἐμπλοκῆς τριχῶν καὶ περιθέσεως χρυσίων ἢ ἐνδύσεως ἱματίων κόσμος 'you should not use outward adornment to make yourselves beautiful as in the way you fix your hair or in the jewelry you put on or in the dresses you wear' 1 Pe 3.3. Adornments may be described as 'things to make one look beautiful' or 'things with which one tries to appear attractive.' For another interpretation of κόσμος in 1 Pe 3.3, see 79.12.

6.189 χρυσίον[b], ου *n*: object or objects made of gold — 'gold jewelry, gold ornaments.'[22] ἡ γυνὴ ἦν περιβεβλημένη πορφυροῦν καὶ κόκκινον, καὶ κεχρυσωμένη χρυσίῳ 'the woman was dressed in purple and scarlet, covered with gold ornaments' Re 17.4. Gold jewelry may be referred to as 'pretty things made out of gold,' but rather than say that the woman was 'covered with gold ornaments' (Re 17.4), it may be far more appropriate to say 'she wore many gold ornaments' or 'many gold ornaments were fastened to her clothes.'

6.190 δακτύλιος, ου *m*: a ring for the finger, normally made of gold or silver and usually containing the signet of the owner by which he could mark ownership and seal documents — 'ring.' δότε δακτύλιον εἰς τὴν χεῖρα αὐτοῦ 'put a ring on his finger' Lk 15.22.

6.191 χρυσοδακτύλιος, ον: pertaining to the wearing of a gold ring — 'wearing a gold ring.' ἐὰν γὰρ εἰσέλθῃ εἰς συναγωγὴν ὑμῶν ἀνὴρ χρυσοδακτύλιος ἐν ἐσθῆτι λαμπρᾷ 'suppose a rich man wearing a gold ring and fine clothes comes into your meeting' Jas 2.2.

6.192 στέφανος[a], ου *m*: a wreath consisting either of foliage or of precious metals formed to resemble foliage and worn as a symbol of honor, victory, or as a badge of high office — 'wreath, crown.' ἵνα φθαρτὸν στέφανον λάβωσιν 'in order to be crowned with a wreath that will not last' 1 Cor 9.25. It may be important in some contexts to indicate clearly the significance of the wreath worn on the head, for example, 'a wreath to show victory.' To describe a 'wreath' merely as 'a circle of leaves' would hardly be sufficient to indicate its cultural significance. In order to do justice to the cultural relevance of such a wreath, it may be important to add some type of marginal note (compare διάδημα 'diadem crown,' 6.196).

6.193 στέμμα, τος *n*: a wreath of wool to which leaves and flowers might be added and either wound around a staff or woven into a garland to be worn on the head — 'garland, wreath.' ὅ τε ἱερεὺς τοῦ Διὸς . . . ταύρους καὶ στέμματα ἐπὶ τοὺς πυλῶνας ἐνέγκας 'the priest of Zeus . . . brought bulls and garlands to the gates' Ac 14.13. Garlands were an important part of the ritual involved in the worship of pagan gods in the ancient world. Such a garland may be described as 'a circle of leaves' or 'a ring of flowers' or 'a wreath of flowers.'

6.194 κράσπεδον[b], ου *n*: the tassels which Jews were obliged to wear on the four corners of the outer garment (see Nu 15.37-41) — 'tassel.' μεγαλύνουσιν τὰ κράσπεδα 'they make the tassels big' Mt 23.5. In some languages tassels may be described as 'decorated corners' or 'ribbons at the corners.' See the discussion at 6.180.

6.195 φυλακτήριον, ου *n*: a small leather case containing OT scripture verses and worn on the arm and forehead by Jews, especially when praying — 'phylactery.' πλατύνουσιν γὰρ τὰ φυλακτήρια αὐτῶν 'they make their phylacteries broad' Mt 23.5.

The Greek word φυλακτήριον, both before and during NT times, referred to an object used as a means of protection from evil forces. As such, it constituted a kind of amulet, but in Mt 23.5 φυλακτήριον is a reference to what was called in Aramaic *tephillin*, meaning 'prayers.' The two phylacteries, one worn on the head and the other on the left arm, were bound on during daily morning prayers. Just

---

22 It would be possible to interpret χρυσίον in Re 17.4 as being merely a natural substance and thus classified with χρυσίον[a] (2.49), but χρυσίον[b] seems to have acquired certain specializations of meaning and even in the singular to be a collective for objects made of gold. It is for that reason that χρυσίον in Re 17.4 is classified in this domain.

what their function seems to have been is not certain. In Mt 23.5, Jesus does not condemn the use of such phylacteries, but he does denounce their ostentatious use.

6.196 διάδημα, τος *n*: a type of crown employed as a symbol of the highest ruling power in a particular area and therefore often associated with kingship – 'diadem crown.' καὶ ἐπὶ τὰς κεφαλὰς αὐτοῦ ἑπτὰ διαδήματα 'and upon his heads seven diadems' Re 12.3. In the NT διάδημα occurs only in Re 12.3, 13.1, and 19.12, and such a crown may be described as 'symbol of his power, worn on his head.'

S Plant Products (6.197-6.202)

6.197 οἶνος, ου *m*: a fermented beverage made from the juice of grapes – 'wine.'[23] μὴ μεθύσκεσθε οἴνῳ 'do not get drunk with wine' Eph 5.18.

Though some persons have argued that whenever mention is made of Jesus either making or drinking wine, one must assume that this was only unfermented grape juice, there is no real basis for such a conclusion. Only where οἶνος νέος 'new wine' (6.198) is mentioned can one assume that this is unfermented grape juice or grape juice in the initial stages of fermentation.

In a number of languages there is no indigenous term for wine, and some expression may simply be borrowed from a dominant language. On the other hand, it is sometimes possible to employ a descriptive phrase, for example, 'fermented fruit juice.' In some languages the equivalent for 'wine' is more specifically 'palm wine,' that is to say, a wine made from the sap of certain palm trees. Such a term may also have a more generic meaning and be applicable to any kind of wine.

There are a number of passages in the NT where one must be particularly careful in the selection of terms to translate wine. For example, in Eph 5.18 a literal translation of 'do not get drunk with wine' could be interpreted to mean that it is permissible for one to get drunk on other types of intoxicating liquors. It may, therefore, be necessary in some languages to render Eph 5.18 as simply 'do not get drunk.'

In Lk 10.34 (κατέδησεν τὰ τραύματα αὐτοῦ ἐπιχέων ἔλαιον καὶ οἶνον 'he poured on olive oil and wine and bandaged his wounds') it is important to recognize the medicinal value of oil and wine. In some instances translators have indicated the purpose of such an activity by translating 'to cleanse and heal his wounds he poured wine and oil on them and bandaged them.' It may also be possible to add in a marginal note information as to the antiseptic quality of the wine and the value of the oil in the healing process.[24]

6.198 οἶνος νέος: a set phrase referring to newly pressed grape juice, unfermented or in the initial stages of fermentation – 'new wine, grape juice.' οὐδεὶς βάλλει οἶνον νέον εἰς ἀσκοὺς παλαιούς 'no one puts new wine into old wineskins' Mk 2.22.

6.199 γλεῦκος, ους *n*: a new, sweet wine in process of fermentation – 'sweet wine.' γλεύκους μεμεστωμένοι εἰσίν 'they are filled with sweet wine' Ac 2.13.

6.200 σίκερα *n*: an intoxicating drink made from grain – 'beer.' οἶνον καὶ σίκερα οὐ μὴ πίῃ 'he must not drink wine or beer' Lk 1.15. Though σίκερα may have a generic meaning and thus refer to any type of intoxicating drink, in the NT it occurs only in Lk 1.15, where it contrasts with wine and refers to intoxicating beverages made from grain. Distill-

---

23 It is possible that the phrase γένημα τῆς ἀμπέλου 'product of the grapevine' (Mt 26.29) should be classified as a fixed phrase meaning 'wine,' but it is also possible to treat this phrase as semantically endocentric (that is, non-idiomatic), in which case the reference could potentially be either 'grapes' or 'wine.'

24 Though the various terms for wine and olive oil might very well be treated simply in the category of *Food* (Domain 5), they obviously served other functions as well, for wine was used medicinally as an antiseptic and olive oil was used not only for food but also for illumination in lamps. Since both the production of wine and olive oil involved relatively elaborate processes, it therefore seems best to classify them as artifacts rather than subsume them under various functional categories.

ed alcoholic beverages, such as whiskey, gin, and vodka, were not known in the ancient world.

6.201 ὄξος, ους *n*: a cheap, sour wine (evidently a favorite beverage of poorer people and relatively effective in quenching thirst) – 'sour wine.' λαβὼν σπόγγον πλήσας τε ὄξους 'he took a sponge and soaked it with sour wine' Mt 27.48. 'Sour wine' is sometimes rendered as 'bitter wine' or 'sour juice.'

6.202 ἔλαιον, ου *n*: oil extracted from the fruit of olive trees – 'olive oil' (used as food, medicine, for burning in lamps, and as perfume when mixed with sweet-smelling substances).[24] οὐκ ἔλαβον μεθ' ἑαυτῶν ἔλαιον 'they did not take any olive oil with them' Mt 25.3; κατέδησεν τὰ τραύματα αὐτοῦ ἐπιχέων ἔλαιον καὶ οἶνον 'he bound up his wounds, pouring in oil and wine' Lk 10.34. See discussion of translational problems in 6.197.

T   Medicines (6.203-6.204)

6.203 κολλούριον, ου *n*: an ointment for the eyes – 'eye salve.' κολλούριον ἐγχρῖσαι τοὺς ὀφθαλμούς σου ἵνα βλέπῃς 'eye salve to anoint your eyes so that you might see' Re 3.18. κολλούριον may often be rendered simply as 'a medicine for the eyes.'

6.204 ἐσμυρνισμένος οἶνος:[25] wine drugged with myrrh and used as a stupefying potion – 'myrrhed wine.' ἐδίδουν αὐτῷ ἐσμυρνισμένον οἶνον 'they gave him myrrhed wine' Mk 15.23. In general, ἐσμυρνισμένος οἶνος must be rendered by means of a phrase or a clause, for example, 'wine which has been mixed with a drug called myrrh' or 'wine mixed with a drug to reduce pain.' It is, of course, also possible to use an abbreviated phrase such as 'myrrhed wine' and then to place the explanation of its function in a marginal note.

---

25 The phrase ἐσμυρνισμένος οἶνος may be treated as semantically endocentric (σμυρνίζω 'to flavor with myrrh' and οἶνος 'wine'), but because of its particular function in Mk 15.23, it has been noted in this domain.

U   Perfumes and Incense (6.205-6.212)

6.205 μύρον, ου *n*: a strongly aromatic and expensive ointment – 'perfume, perfumed oil.' βαλοῦσα γὰρ αὕτη τὸ μύρον τοῦτο ἐπὶ τοῦ σώματός μου πρὸς τὸ ἐνταφιάσαι με ἐποίησεν 'she has prepared me for burial by pouring this perfume on my body' Mt 26.12; ἡτοίμασαν ἀρώματα καὶ μύρα 'they prepared aromatic oils and perfumes' Lk 23.56. μύρον as a 'perfume' may be rendered as 'sweet-smelling oil' or 'fragrant oil.' In Lk 23.56 one may use a descriptive phrase such as 'perfumed oil for preserving the body' or '. . . to keep the body from rotting.'

6.206 μυρίζω: (derivative of μύρον 'perfume,' 6.205) to anoint with perfumed oil or ointment, often in connection with burial – 'to anoint with perfume, to anoint for burial.' προέλαβεν μυρίσαι τὸ σῶμά μου εἰς τὸν ἐνταφιασμόν 'she undertook in advance to anoint my body for burial' Mk 14.8.

6.207 ἄρωμα, τος *n*; σμῆγμα, τος *n* (alt. form σμίγμα): aromatic oils or salves used especially in embalming the dead – 'aromatic salves, perfumed ointment.'
ἄρωμα: ἠγόρασαν ἀρώματα ἵνα ἐλθοῦσαι ἀλείψωσιν αὐτόν 'they bought aromatic salves so that they could go and anoint him' Mk 16.1. In some languages the equivalent of ἄρωμα is 'sweet-smelling herbs' or 'good-smelling leaves' or 'perfumed oil.'
σμῆγμα: φέρων σμῆγμα σμύρνης καὶ ἀλόης 'bringing perfumed ointment of myrrh and aloes' Jn 19.39 (apparatus).

6.208 σμύρνα, ης *f*: the aromatic resin of certain bushes – 'myrrh.' προσήνεγκαν αὐτῷ δῶρα, χρυσὸν καὶ λίβανον καὶ σμύρναν 'they brought him gifts: gold and frankincense and myrrh' Mt 2.11; μίγμα σμύρνης καὶ ἀλόης 'a mixture of myrrh and aloes' Jn 19.39. Myrrh was used as one of the ingredients involved in the process of embalming a corpse. Most translators borrow a term for myrrh and then use some kind of marginal note to explain that myrrh was a valuable aromatic substance often used in preserving a corpse. See 6.204.

6.209 ἀλόη, ης *f*: an aromatic resin of a lily-like plant, often used for embalming a corpse – 'aloes.' μίγμα σμύρνης καὶ ἀλόης 'a mixture of myrrh and aloes' Jn 19.39. As in the case of σμύρνα 'myrrh' (6.208), translators normally borrow a term for 'aloes' and then employ some kind of marginal note to indicate the nature of the substance.

6.210 νάρδος, ου *f*: an aromatic oil extracted from a plant called nard – 'oil of nard, perfume of nard.' ἦλθεν γυνὴ ἔχουσα ἀλάβαστρον μύρου νάρδου 'a woman came with an alabaster jar of perfume of nard' Mk 14.3. Translators normally borrow the term 'nard' but employ some type of classifier, for example, 'a perfume called nard' or 'a sweet-smelling substance, nard.'

6.211 θυμίαμα[a], τος *n*: any aromatic substance (usually a resin) burned for its pleasing aroma – 'incense.' φιάλας χρυσᾶς γεμούσας θυμιαμάτων 'golden bowls full of incense' Re 5.8.

Since some form of incense is almost universal, there is normally no difficulty involved in finding some term to designate 'incense.' However, it is always possible to employ a descriptive phrase, for example, 'a substance which gives off a sweet-smelling smoke' or '. . . a good-smelling smoke.'

6.212 λίβανος, ου *m*: the aromatic resin of certain trees – 'frankincense.' προσήνεγκαν αὐτῷ δῶρα, χρυσὸν καὶ λίβανον καὶ σμύρναν 'they brought him gifts: gold and frankincense and myrrh' Mt 2.11. Translators may either borrow a term such as 'frankincense' or use a descriptive equivalent, for example, 'a sweet-smelling incense' or 'a valuable, sweet incense.'

V   Instruments for Measuring (6.213-6.214)

6.213 κάλαμος[d], ου *m*: a rod (possibly a reed) used for measuring – 'measuring rod.' ὁ λαλῶν μετ' ἐμοῦ εἶχεν μέτρον κάλαμον χρυσοῦν, ἵνα μετρήσῃ τὴν πόλιν 'the one who spoke to me had a gold measuring stick to measure the city' Re 21.15. There is no indication as to the particular length of κάλαμος[d], but it could have been as much as two meters (about seven feet), since this would not have been an unusual length for a reed. The equivalent of κάλαμος[d] may be simply 'a measuring stick' or 'a stick with which to count the distance.'

6.214 ζυγός[b], οῦ *m*: an instrument for weighing objects – 'balance scale.' ὁ καθήμενος ἐπ' αὐτὸν ἔχων ζυγὸν ἐν τῇ χειρὶ αὐτοῦ 'the rider on the horse held a balance scale in his hand' Re 6.5. A balance scale may be described in some languages as 'a tool for weighing' or 'an instrument for knowing how much something weighs.' Ancient balance scales often consisted of a rod held by a cord in the middle and with pans attached to both ends. Weights could be placed in one pan, while the item to be weighed would be placed in the other.

W   Miscellaneous[26] (6.215-6.225)

6.215 ῥαφίς, ίδος *f*; βελόνη, ης *f*: a small, slender instrument, pointed on one end and with a hole at the other end, used in passing thread through cloth in sewing – 'needle.' ῥαφίς: εὐκοπώτερόν ἐστιν κάμηλον διὰ τρυπήματος ῥαφίδος διελθεῖν 'it is easier for a camel to go through the eye of a needle' Mt 19.24. βελόνη: εὐκοπώτερον γάρ ἐστιν κάμηλον διὰ τρήματος βελόνης εἰσελθεῖν 'it is easier for a camel to go through the eye of a needle' Lk 18.25.

There is no convincing evidence that the expression 'eye of a needle' in Mt 19.24 and Lk 18.25 is a figurative name for a narrow gate. The reference to a camel passing through the eye of a needle is a case of rhetorical hyperbole, that is to say, a purposeful exaggeration to point out the extreme difficulty of the event referred to.

6.216 τρῆμα, τος *n* (Lk 18.25); τρύπημα, ατος *n* (Mt 19.24); τρυμαλιά, ᾶς *f* (Mk 10.25)

---

26 The various artifacts in this subdomain entitled *Miscellaneous* belong to a number of subdomains, but rather than multiply such subdomains, it seems more practical to include various of these items under the category of *Miscellaneous*.

– 'hole'[27] (used in the NT only with reference to the so-called 'eye' of a needle). εὐκοπώτερόν ἐστιν κάμηλον διὰ τρυπήματος ῥαφίδος διελθεῖν 'it is easier for a camel to go through the eye of a needle' Mt 19.24. The hole in a needle is variously referred to in different languages, for example, 'the nostril of the needle,' 'the ear of the needle,' 'the mouth of the needle,' and even 'the anus of the needle.'

6.217 ἀξίνη, ης f: an instrument with a sharp-edged head and a handle, used in chopping wood – 'axe.' ἤδη δὲ ἡ ἀξίνη πρὸς τὴν ῥίζαν τῶν δένδρων κεῖται 'already the axe is laid to the root of the trees' or 'the axe is ready to be used to cut down the trees at the roots' Mt 3.10.

6.218 ῥάβδος[a], ου f – 'stick, rod.' μηδὲν αἴρωσιν εἰς ὁδὸν εἰ μὴ ῥάβδον μόνον 'don't take anything with you on your trip except a walking stick' Mk 6.8. A ῥάβδος[a] could be used for a number of different purposes, such as an aid to walking, herding animals, or beating people.

6.219 κλῆρος[a], ου m: a specially marked pebble, piece of pottery, or stick employed in making decisions based upon chance – 'lot.' διαμεριζόμενοι δὲ τὰ ἱμάτια αὐτοῦ ἔβαλον κλήρους 'they divided his clothes among themselves by casting lots' Lk 23.34. Both in form as well as in function, the closest equivalent of κλῆρος[a] is frequently a term which refers to 'dice.' In Lk 23.34 a term for 'dice' would be particularly appropriate.

It is not possible to know the particular method employed in 'choosing by lot,' for

27 As already noted in footnote 1 of Domain 6, the terms τρῆμα, τρύπημα, and τρυμαλιά actually belong theoretically to a domain of openings, holes, and apertures, but since these terms in the NT are associated so closely with a needle, it seems far more satisfactory to treat them together with ῥαφίς and βελόνη 'needle' (6.215).

evidently various devices were used. In Ac 1.26 (ἔδωκαν κλήρους αὐτοῖς 'they drew lots,' literally 'they gave them lots'), it is probable that small sticks were handed out. See also footnote 19 in Domain 30.

6.220 κλείς[a], κλειδός f: an instrument used for locking and unlocking doors and gates – 'key.' ἐδόθη αὐτῷ ἡ κλεὶς τοῦ φρέατος τῆς ἀβύσσου 'the key to the abyss was given to him' Re 9.1. In rendering Re 9.1 it may not be possible to speak of 'the key to the abyss,' but rather 'the key to the entrance to the abyss' or 'the key used in opening or closing the gate to the abyss.'

6.221 ἔσοπτρον, ου n: a flat piece of highly polished metal used to reflect an image – 'mirror.' οὗτος ἔοικεν ἀνδρὶ κατανοοῦντι τὸ πρόσωπον τῆς γενέσεως αὐτοῦ ἐν ἐσόπτρῳ 'he is like a man observing his natural face in a mirror' Jas 1.23.

6.222 ὕαλος[a], ου f – 'glass' (it is also possible that ὕαλος should be interpreted as 'crystal'; see 2.46). ὑάλῳ καθαρῷ 'pure glass' Re 21.18. In Re 21.18 and 21 the emphasis is upon the transparency of the glass.

6.223 ὑάλινος, η, ον: (derivative of ὕαλος[a] 'glass,' 6.222) consisting of or pertaining to glass – 'of glass, glassy.' θάλασσα ὑαλίνη ὁμοία κρυστάλλῳ 'a sea of glass like crystal' Re 4.6.

6.224 κέραμος, ου m: a thin slab or bent piece of baked clay – 'tile, roof tile.' διὰ τῶν κεράμων καθῆκαν αὐτόν 'they let him down through the roof tiles' Lk 5.19.

6.225 σκύβαλον, ου n: worthless or unwanted material that is rejected and normally thrown out – 'rubbish, litter, trash.' καὶ ἡγοῦμαι σκύβαλα ἵνα Χριστὸν κερδήσω 'I consider it all rubbish in order that I may gain Christ' Php 3.8.

7 Constructions[1]

Outline of Subdomains

A Constructions (General Meaning) (7.1)
B Buildings (7.2-7.25)
C Parts and Areas of Buildings (7.26-7.53)
D Open Constructions (7.54-7.56)
E Constructions for Holding Water (7.57-7.58)
F Walls and Fences (7.59-7.62)
G Miscellaneous Constructions (7.63-7.76)
H Building Materials (7.77-7.79)

A Constructions (General Meaning) (7.1)

7.1 οἰκοδομή[a], **ῆς** *f*: any type of building or structure which encloses an area, but the area may be open to the sky, as in the case of amphitheaters – 'building, structure.'[2] ποταποὶ λίθοι καὶ ποταπαὶ οἰκοδομαί 'what wonderful stones and buildings' Mk 13.1.

B Buildings[3] (7.2-7.25)

7.2 οἶκος[a], **ου** *m*: a building consisting of one or more rooms and normally serving as a dwelling place (οἶκος[a] also includes certain public buildings, for example, a temple) – 'house, temple, sanctuary.' (The extension of οἶκος[a] to include temples may be the result of speaking of a temple as the dwelling place of the deity.) ἠκούσθη ὅτι ἐν οἴκῳ ἐστίν 'it was reported that he was at home' Mk 2.1;[4] τοῦ ἀπολομένου μεταξὺ τοῦ θυσιαστηρίου καὶ τοῦ οἴκου 'who perished between the altar and the Temple' Lk 11.51. For a discussion of certain translational problems related to οἶκος[a], see 7.3.

7.3 οἰκία[a], **ας** *f*: a building or place where one dwells – 'house, home, dwelling, residence.' ἡ δὲ οἰκία ἐπληρώθη ἐκ τῆς ὀσμῆς τοῦ μύρου 'the sweet smell of perfume filled the whole house' Jn 12.3.

The size of an οἰκία[a] or of an οἶκος[a] (7.2) may differ greatly. For example, the house referred to in Lk 7.10 would no doubt have been relatively elaborate, and in Mt 11.8 οἶκος[a] refers to the palace in which Herod lived. In a number of languages it is important to distinguish clearly between various types of dwellings depending upon their size and presumed importance. Accordingly, in rendering οἰκία[a] or οἶκος[a] it is necessary to use a number of different terms roughly equivalent to the English series 'cottage,' 'house,' 'official residence,' 'palace,' 'temple,' etc.

In a number of languages one must distinguish carefully between a house and a home. A term meaning 'house' would be used in referring to any dwelling as a construction, while a term meaning 'home' would be used in referring to the more or less permanent dwelling of a particular person. In Mk 2.1, for example, it is significant to indicate that Jesus was dwelling in the house through the roof of which the paralyzed man was let down.

7.4 ἔπαυλις, **εως** *f*: property in which a person was expected to reside, either as the result of ownership or legal contract – 'homestead,

---

1 The domain of *Constructions* (7) differs from *Artifacts* (6) in that the *Constructions* are larger and generally not moved from place to place. Because of important elements of association (and not primarily because of series of shared components involving shape, size, and function) parts of constructions (for example, windows, doors, walls, rooms, etc.) and certain principal construction materials (for example, beams, planks, etc.) are also included in this domain.

2 οἰκοδομή[a] may be interpreted as a derivative of οἰκοδομέω[a] 'to construct' (45.1), or the latter may be interpreted as a causative derivative of οἰκοδομή[a], with the meaning 'to cause a building to exist.' In view of the highly generic nature of οἰκοδομή[a], it is perhaps better to interpret it as a derivative of the corresponding event expression (45.1) since this seems to be the predominant pattern of derivative correspondences. But because of the obvious material form of constructions as buildings, οἰκοδομή[a] is introduced into Domain 7 as a generic for all the other meanings.

3 The subdomain *Buildings* differs from the more generic subdomain *Constructions* (A) in that the buildings in question entirely enclose at least some three-dimensional space and have certain areas which consist of a room or rooms.

4 The Greek phrase ἐν οἴκῳ is the normal expression meaning 'at home,' that is, being in a dwelling which a person owns or rents. The statement in Mk 2.1 would indicate that Jesus had moved from Nazareth.

house, residence.' γενηθήτω ἡ ἔπαυλις αὐτοῦ ἔρημος 'may his place become deserted' Ac 1.20. In the NT ἔπαυλις occurs only in Ac 1.20 as a quotation of Ps 69.25. The immediate reference is to a person's traditional residence, but the entire passage must be interpreted figuratively as a reference to a person's expected position or place of service. The phrase γενηθήτω ἡ ἔπαυλις αὐτοῦ ἔρημος may be rendered as 'may his house become empty' or 'may his home be deserted.'

7.5 βασίλειον, ου *n*: the dwelling of a king or ruler – 'palace.' οἱ ἐν ἱματισμῷ ἐνδόξῳ καὶ τρυφῇ ὑπάρχοντες ἐν τοῖς βασιλείοις εἰσίν 'those who dress like that and live in luxury are found in palaces' Lk 7.25. In Lk 7.25 βασίλειον may be rendered as 'the home of a king' or 'the home of a ruler.'

7.6 αὐλή[b], ῆς *f*: any dwelling having an interior courtyard (often a relatively elaborate structure) – 'dwelling, palace, mansion.' συνήχθησαν . . . εἰς τὴν αὐλὴν τοῦ ἀρχιερέως 'they gathered . . . in the palace of the high priest' Mt 26.3; ὅταν ὁ ἰσχυρὸς καθωπλισμένος φυλάσσῃ τὴν ἑαυτοῦ αὐλήν 'when a fully armed strong man guards his own dwelling' Lk 11.21.

7.7 πραιτώριον[a], ου *n*: a governor's official residence – 'palace, fortress.' παραλαβόντες τὸν Ἰησοῦν εἰς τὸ πραιτώριον 'taking Jesus into the palace/fortress' Mt 27.27. There are differences of opinion as to the particular πραιτώριον mentioned in Jerusalem. It may have been either the palace of Herod in the western part of the city or the fortress Antonia northwest of the Temple area. The πραιτώριον in Caesarea was the palace built by Herod the Great (see Ac 23.35).

In the Gospels it is satisfactory to translate πραιτώριον[a] as 'the palace where the governor lived' or 'the large dwelling where the ruler lived.' In a number of languages a term for 'palace' often suggests a military fortification, and this would accordingly be quite appropriate for NT usage.

7.8 σκήνωμα[a], τος *n*: a dwelling, with the implication of temporary duration – 'dwell-

ing.' εὑρεῖν σκήνωμα τῷ θεῷ Ἰακώβ (θεῷ from apparatus) 'to provide a dwelling for the God of Jacob' Ac 7.46. In Ac 7.46 there is a complex textual problem in which the critical text has οἴκῳ 'house' (but in the figurative sense of 'people'), but the Byzantine text reads θεῷ 'God.' It is only with this latter form of the text that σκήνωμα would mean an actual construction or dwelling. If one adopts the form of the critical text, then σκήνωμα would point to 'a place to dwell,' in other words, an area or region (see 85.77).

7.9 σκηνή[a], ῆς *f*: a portable dwelling of cloth and/or skins, held up by poles and fastened by cords to stakes – 'tent.' ἐν σκηναῖς κατοικήσας μετὰ Ἰσαὰκ καὶ Ἰακώβ 'he lived in tents with Isaac and Jacob' He 11.9. In a number of languages 'tent' is simply 'a house made of cloth.' One should avoid terms which would imply a military tent or a temporary shelter used only on vacations or holidays. In OT times such tents were permanent dwellings of nomadic groups and were moved from place to place as livestock were transferred from one pasture area to another.

7.10 σκηνοποιός, οῦ *m*: one who makes tents as an occupation – 'tentmaker.' ἔμενεν παρ' αὐτοῖς καὶ ἠργάζετο· ἦσαν γὰρ σκηνοποιοὶ τῇ τέχνῃ 'he stayed and worked with them, for they were tentmakers by trade' Ac 18.3.

7.11 κατάλυμα[a], τος *n*; πανδοχεῖον, ου *n*; ταβέρνη, ης *f*: a place for the lodging of travelers – 'inn.'
κατάλυμα[a]: διότι οὐκ ἦν αὐτοῖς τόπος ἐν τῷ καταλύματι 'since there was no room for them in the inn' Lk 2.7.
πανδοχεῖον: ἤγαγεν αὐτὸν εἰς πανδοχεῖον καὶ ἐπεμελήθη αὐτοῦ 'he took him to an inn, where he took care of him' Lk 10.34.
ταβέρνη occurs in the NT only as a part of a place name, Τριῶν Ταβερνῶν 'Three Taverns' (Ac 28.15).

7.12 πανδοχεύς, έως *m*: one who manages an inn as a place where people may obtain board and room at a price – 'innkeeper, manager of a hotel.' ἔδωκεν δύο δηνάρια τῷ πανδοχεῖ καὶ εἶπεν, Ἐπιμελήθητι αὐτοῦ 'he gave two coins to the innkeeper and said, Take care of the man' Lk 10.35. In some languages it may be necessary to describe the role of an inn or hotel as 'a place where people could stay overnight and get something to eat' or even 'a place where people could pay in order to stay overnight and get something to eat.'

7.13 ἀκροατήριον, ου *n*: a relatively large building normally used for legal hearings, though possibly also employed for more general purposes – 'audience hall, auditorium.' Ἀγρίππα καὶ τῆς Βερνίκης . . . εἰσελθόντων εἰς τὸ ἀκροατήριον 'Agrippa and Bernice . . . entered the audience hall' Ac 25.23. In a number of languages ἀκροατήριον may be rendered as 'a large hall' or 'a place where many people could gather together' or 'a building where many people could sit to listen.'

7.14 σχολή, ῆς *f*: a building where teachers and students met for study and discussion – 'lecture hall, school.' καθ' ἡμέραν διαλεγόμενος ἐν τῇ σχολῇ Τυράννου 'every day he held discussions in the lecture hall of Tyrannus' Ac 19.9. In Ac 19.9 it is better to use a translation such as 'lecture hall' rather than 'school,' since one does not wish to give the impression of the typical classroom situation characteristic of present-day schools. One may translate the relevant context of Ac 19.9 as 'every day Paul discussed with people in the lecture hall which belonged to Tyrannus' or '. . . in a hall where Tyrannus often taught' or '. . . lectured.'

7.15 ναός[a], οῦ *m*: a building in which a deity is worshiped (in the case of the Temple in Jerusalem, a place where God was also regarded as dwelling) – 'temple, sanctuary.' ὃν ἐφονεύσατε μεταξὺ τοῦ ναοῦ καὶ τοῦ θυσιαστηρίου 'whom you murdered between the sanctuary and the altar' Mt 23.35.

ναός[a] may often be rendered as 'the house of God' or 'the place where God dwells' or 'God's building.' In some languages it is most naturally referred to as 'the holy house' or 'the holy place.' See also 7.16.

ναός is used figuratively in Jn 2.21 (ἐκεῖνος δὲ ἔλεγεν περὶ τοῦ ναοῦ τοῦ σώματος αὐτοῦ 'but he spoke of the temple of his body' or '. . . of his body as a temple') and in 1 Cor 6.19, where the believer's body is spoken of as ναός τοῦ ἐν ὑμῖν ἁγίου πνεύματος 'the temple of the Holy Spirit within you.'

7.16 ἱερόν, οῦ *n*: a temple or sanctuary (ναός[a], 7.15) and the surrounding consecrated area – 'temple.' περιεπάτει ὁ Ἰησοῦς ἐν τῷ ἱερῷ ἐν τῇ στοᾷ τοῦ Σολομῶνος 'Jesus was walking in Solomon's porch in the Temple' Jn 10.23; ἐξέβαλεν πάντας τοὺς πωλοῦντας καὶ ἀγοράζοντας ἐν τῷ ἱερῷ 'he drove out all those who bought and sold in the Temple' Mt 21.12; οὐκ οἴδατε ὅτι οἱ τὰ ἱερὰ ἐργαζόμενοι τὰ ἐκ τοῦ ἱεροῦ ἐσθίουσιν 'surely you know that the men who are engaged in holy work get their food from the Temple' 1 Cor 9.13. With the exception of ἱερόν in Ac 19.27 (a reference to the temple of Artemis in Ephesus), ἱερόν in the NT refers to the Temple in Jerusalem, including the entire Temple precinct with its buildings, courts, and storerooms.

In a number of languages ἱερόν is rendered normally as 'the house of God,' or, as in Ac 19.27, 'the house of the goddess Artemis.' In a number of languages, however, there are technical terms for 'temple,' and these are often carefully distinguished from an expression designating a central sanctuary in which the deity is thought to dwell (ναός[a]). Though in a number of contexts it is not necessary to distinguish between ἱερόν and ναός, in Mt 21.12 (and parallel passages: Mk 11.15, Lk 19.45, and Jn 2.14) it is important to indicate this distinction, so as not to leave the impression that sacrificial animals were actually being sold inside the central sanctuary.

7.17 σκηνή[b], ῆς *f*: the relatively large tent used as a central place of worship by the Jews prior to the building of the Temple – 'tent, tabernacle tent.' ἡ σκηνὴ τοῦ μαρτυρίου ἦν τοῖς πατράσιν ἡμῶν ἐν τῇ ἐρήμῳ 'our ancestors had the tent of God's presence with them in the desert' Ac 7.44. In a number of languages σκηνή[b] may be rendered as 'the largest tent in which God lived' or 'the large tent for worshiping God' or 'the holy tent.' In selecting a proper designation for σκηνή^b, it is important to indicate that the function of σκηνή^b was essentially the same as that of the Temple; it was only a different type of construction and not a difference of use or of religious relevance.

Since σκηνή^b refers to one unique object, it is essentially equivalent to a title.

7.18 ἅγιον, ου *n*; ἅγια^a, ων *n*: (derivatives of ἅγιος^a 'holy,' 88.24) the tabernacle or the Temple in Jerusalem as a consecrated place – 'sanctuary.' See also 7.35.

ἅγιον: εἶχε μὲν οὖν καὶ ἡ πρώτη δικαιώματα λατρείας τό τε ἅγιον κοσμικόν 'the first covenant also had its laws governing worship, and its sanctuary was on earth' He 9.1.
ἅγια^a: οὐ γὰρ εἰς χειροποίητα εἰσῆλθεν ἅγια Χριστός 'it is not as though Christ had entered a man-made sanctuary' He 9.24. ἅγιον and ἅγια^a should be translated in essentially the same way as ναός^a (7.15).

The phrase ἅγιος τόπος (literally 'holy place') is a title for the sanctuary and is equivalent to ναός^a: ὁ ἄνθρωπος οὗτος οὐ παύεται λαλῶν ῥήματα κατὰ τοῦ τόπου τοῦ ἁγίου τούτου καὶ τοῦ νόμου 'this man is always talking against the Temple and the Law of Moses' Ac 6.13.

7.19 εἰδωλεῖον, ου *n*: a temple or sanctuary which houses an idol – 'temple of an idol.' ἐὰν γάρ τις ἴδῃ σὲ τὸν ἔχοντα γνῶσιν ἐν εἰδωλείῳ κατακείμενον 'for if a person sees you who have knowledge banqueting in the temple of an idol' 1 Cor 8.10.[5] The term εἰδωλεῖον may be rendered as 'the building in which an idol is placed' or 'a large house in which an idol is worshiped.' Since 'idol' is often rendered as 'the statue of a god,' εἰδωλεῖον may be rendered as 'the building in which there is a statue of a god' or 'a building in which a statue of a god is worshiped.'

7.20 συναγωγή^c, ῆς *f*: a building of assembly, associated with religious activity (normally a building in which Jewish worship took place and in which the Law was taught, but in Jas 2.2 a Christian assembly place) – 'synagogue' or 'Christian assembly place.' τὴν συναγωγὴν αὐτὸς ᾠκοδόμησεν ἡμῖν 'he himself built our synagogue for us' Lk 7.5; ἐὰν γὰρ εἰσέλθῃ εἰς συναγωγὴν ὑμῶν ἀνὴρ χρυσοδακτύλιος ἐν ἐσθῆτι λαμπρᾷ 'if a man comes into your Christian assembly place beautifully dressed and with a gold ring on' Jas 2.2. It is also possible to interpret συναγωγή in Jas 2.2 as a reference to an assembly of believers rather than to a building (see 11.44).

It is important to distinguish clearly between συναγωγή^c and ναός^a (7.15) or ἱερόν (7.16). There were many synagogues, but only one Temple in Jerusalem, and it is not enough to speak of synagogues merely as 'small temples.' It is better either to borrow a term for synagogue or employ a descriptive equivalent such as 'places where Jewish people worshiped God' or 'buildings for worshiping God.'

It is also important to distinguish in translating between a term for 'synagogue' and for 'church,' whether as a reference to the congregation or to the building.

7.21 ὀχύρωμα, τος *n*: a strong military fortification – 'stronghold, fortress.' δυνατὰ τῷ θεῷ πρὸς καθαίρεσιν ὀχυρωμάτων – λογισμοὺς καθαιροῦντες 'God's powerful weapons for tearing down strongholds – tearing down false arguments' 2 Cor 10.4. The term ὀχύρωμα occurs in the NT only in 2 Cor 10.4, where it is used figuratively of the strength of false arguments. In a number of languages it may be more satisfactory to render ὀχύρωμα as a kind of simile so as to mark this figurative usage, for example, 'powerful weapons with which to destroy false arguments in the same way that people would destroy fortresses.' In some languages a 'fortress' may be described in terms of its function, for example, 'a place for protection' or 'a place to defend oneself.' Often, however, a fortress is described in terms of its construction, for example, 'a strong-walled place.'

5 It is possible that the statement about 'banqueting in the temple of an idol' should be understood as a process by which a person would symbolically identify himself with the deity in question. This would accordingly provide a problem for an individual who was weak in his conscience.

7.22 παρεμβολή[b], ῆς *f*: a camp or barracks for soldiers[6] – 'soldiers' quarters, barracks.' ἐκέλευσεν ὁ χιλίαρχος εἰσάγεσθαι αὐτὸν εἰς τὴν παρεμβολήν 'the chiliarch ordered his men to take him into the soldiers' quarters' Ac 22.24. In the NT παρεμβολή[b] is used to refer to the place where Roman troops were housed in Jerusalem and to the place in Rome where soldiers who accompanied Paul were quartered. Though many languages have a set phrase or technical expression for soldiers' barracks, it may be necessary in some cases to use a descriptive phrase, for example, 'where soldiers lived' or 'where soldiers lived together.'

7.23 πύργος, ου *m*: a tall structure with a lookout at the top – 'tower, watchtower.' ἐκεῖνοι οἱ δεκαοκτὼ ἐφ' οὓς ἔπεσεν ὁ πύργος ἐν τῷ Σιλωὰμ καὶ ἀπέκτεινεν αὐτούς 'the tower in Siloam fell on those eighteen men and killed them' Lk 13.4; οἰκοδεσπότης ὅστις ἐφύτευσεν ἀμπελῶνα . . . καὶ ᾠκοδόμησεν πύργον 'a landowner who planted a vineyard . . . and built a watchtower' Mt 21.33. In the NT πύργος may designate any type of tower, whether employed for military purposes or used by watchmen protecting a harvest.

Some scholars have suggested that in Lk 14.28 the reference to πύργος is some kind of farm building, but this suggestion has been rejected by others.

In a number of languages a word for 'tower' is simply 'a high building' (though of course not a skyscraper). In other instances a tower may be more appropriately described as 'a high platform' or 'a high lookout place.'

7.24 δεσμωτήριον, ου *n*; φυλακή[a], ῆς *f*; τήρησις[b], εως *f*: a place of detention – 'jail, prison.'
δεσμωτήριον: τὸ δεσμωτήριον εὕρομεν κεκλεισμένον ἐν πάσῃ ἀσφαλείᾳ 'we found the prison locked most securely' Ac 5.23.
φυλακή[a]: ἀπεκεφάλισεν τὸν Ἰωάννην ἐν τῇ φυλακῇ 'he had John beheaded in prison' Mt 14.10.

---

6 παρεμβολή[b] 'barracks' differs from παρεμβολή[a] 'camp' (1.94) in that the latter is a temporary population center and not the actual construction of barracks or soldiers' quarters.

τήρησις[b]: ἔθεντο αὐτοὺς ἐν τηρήσει δημοσίᾳ 'they placed them in the common prison' Ac 5.18.

Practically all languages have terms for a jail or a prison, though in some instances a descriptive phrase is employed, 'a place where people are tied up' or 'a place to be chained.' In some instances, highly idiomatic expressions are used, 'a place for eating iron' or 'a room with rats.'

7.25 ἀποθήκη, ης *f*: a building for storage – 'barn, storehouse.' συνάξει τὸν σῖτον αὐτοῦ εἰς τὴν ἀποθήκην 'he will gather his wheat into the storehouse' Mt 3.12. In a number of languages an important distinction is made between buildings used to store farm produce and those which may be warehouses for other types of material.

C Parts and Areas of Buildings (7.26-7.53)

7.26 οἴκημα, τος *n*: a room or quarters where one may stay (normally a part of a house) – 'room, quarters.' φῶς ἔλαμψεν ἐν τῷ οἰκήματι 'a light shone in his quarters' Ac 12.7. In Ac 12.7 οἴκημα is used to refer to a prison cell, and in this context it is best translated as 'room' or 'room in the prison.'

7.27 ἀνάγαιον, ου *n*; ὑπερῷον, ου *n*: a room on the level above the ground floor (second story in American usage and first story in most other languages) – 'upstairs room.'
ἀνάγαιον: αὐτὸς ὑμῖν δείξει ἀνάγαιον μέγα 'he will show you a large upstairs room' Mk 14.15.
ὑπερῷον: λούσαντες δὲ ἔθηκαν αὐτὴν ἐν ὑπερῴῳ 'they washed (her body) and placed it in an upper room' Ac 9.37. In Ac 1.13; 9.37, 39; 20.8 the term ὑπερῷον may refer to the kind of rooms often built on the flat-roofed Middle East housetops.

7.28 ταμεῖον[a], ου *n*: a room in the interior of a house, normally without windows opening to the outside – 'inner room.' ὃ πρὸς τὸ οὖς ἐλαλήσατε ἐν τοῖς ταμείοις κηρυχθήσεται ἐπὶ τῶν δωμάτων 'whatever you whispered in (people's) ears in the inner room will be shouted in public' Lk 12.3. In Lk 12.3 the emphasis is upon the strictly private location of the inner room. In such a context one may translate 'a strictly private room' or 'a small room in the center of the house.'

7.29 κοιτών, ῶνος *m*: a room for sleeping – 'bedroom.' Βλάστον τὸν ἐπὶ τοῦ κοιτῶνος τοῦ βασιλέως literally, 'Blastus, who was in charge of the king's bedroom' Ac 12.20. It would be wrong to render the expression 'who was in charge of the king's bedroom' as meaning simply one who kept the bedroom clean. A person such as Blastus would have been a highly respected person with considerable responsibility for the king's living quarters and personal affairs. The expression may be adequately rendered in Ac 12.20 by speaking of Blastus as 'a high official.'

7.30 κατάλυμα[b], τος *n*: a room in a relatively large structure (possibly an inn; see 7.11), which could serve as a dining room – 'room, quarters, dining room.' ποῦ ἐστιν τὸ κατάλυμα ὅπου τὸ πάσχα μετὰ τῶν μαθητῶν μου φάγω; 'where is the dining room where I may eat the Passover with my disciples?' Lk 22.11.

7.31 ξενία[a], ας *f*: a place of temporary lodging for a person away from home – 'guestroom, lodging for guest, place to stay in.' ἡμέραν ἦλθον πρὸς αὐτὸν εἰς τὴν ξενίαν πλείονες 'a large number of them came that day to him where he was staying' Ac 28.23; ἑτοίμαζέ μοι ξενίαν 'prepare a room for me to stay in' or '. . . a place for me to stay in' Phm 22.[7]

7.32 ταμεῖον[b], ου *n*; **θησαυρός[a], οῦ** *m*: a room for the storage of valuables – 'storeroom, treasure room.'
ταμεῖον[b]: οἷς οὐκ ἔστιν ταμεῖον οὐδὲ ἀποθήκη 'they don't have a storeroom or barn' Lk 12.24.
θησαυρός[a]: ἐκβάλλει ἐκ τοῦ θησαυροῦ αὐτοῦ καινὰ καὶ παλαιά 'he takes out of his storeroom new and old things' Mt 13.52.

ταμεῖον[b] and θησαυρός[a] may often be ren-

dered by descriptive phrases, for example, 'a room where valuable things are kept' or 'a place where valuables are stored.'

In Mt 12.35 θησαυρός[a] is used figuratively (ὁ ἀγαθὸς ἄνθρωπος ἐκ τοῦ ἀγαθοῦ θησαυροῦ ἐκβάλλει ἀγαθά 'a good man draws good things from his good storehouse,' meaning '. . . storehouse of good things') to describe the heart as a kind of storehouse or treasure.

7.33 κορβανᾶς, ᾶ *m*; **γαζοφυλάκιον[a], ου** *n*: a room in the Temple used as a treasury – 'treasury, Temple treasury.'
κορβανᾶς: οὐκ ἔξεστιν βαλεῖν αὐτὰ εἰς τὸν κορβανᾶν, ἐπεὶ τιμὴ αἵματός ἐστιν 'this is blood money, and it is against our Law to put it in the Temple treasury' Mt 27.6.
γαζοφυλάκιον[a]: ταῦτα τὰ ῥήματα ἐλάλησεν ἐν τῷ γαζοφυλακίῳ διδάσκων ἐν τῷ ἱερῷ 'he spoke these words in the treasury, while teaching in the Temple' Jn 8.20. It is possible that in Jn 8.20 γαζοφυλάκιον designates the offering boxes rather than the treasury itself (see γαζοφυλάκιον[b], 6.141). If one interprets γαζοφυλάκιον in Jn 8.20 as the offering boxes, then one may translate 'he spoke these words near where the offering boxes were.'

7.34 νυμφών, ῶνος *m*; **γάμος[c], ου** *m*: a relatively large room, often serving as a place for a wedding – 'wedding hall.' ἐπλήσθη ὁ γάμος ἀνακειμένων 'the wedding hall was filled with guests' Mt 22.10. In Mt 22.10 a number of manuscripts read νυμφών rather than γάμος.[8]
υἱοὶ τοῦ νυμφῶνος, literally 'sons of the wedding hall,' is an idiom denoting the bridegroom's friends or the wedding guests (see 11.7).

7.35 ἅγια[b], ων *n*: the interior (either the outer or the inner of the two rooms) of the sanctuary of the Jerusalem Temple or of the earlier tabernacle or of a corresponding 'spiritual holy place,' perhaps regarded as being in heaven – 'the holy place.' σκηνὴ γὰρ κατεσκευάσθη ἡ πρώτη . . . ἥτις λέγεται Ἅγια

---

7 It is also possible to interpret ξενία in both Ac 28.23 and Phm 22 as hospitality or the activity involved in receiving a guest (see 34.57). This is the more common meaning of ξενία, but it fits less well in the two contexts in which ξενία occurs in the NT.

8 Though the meaning of νυμφών and γάμος[c] in Mt 22.10 is basically the same, νυμφών may still carry semantic associations relating to the bride, while γάμος[c] may have semantic associations which point more specifically to the celebration of a wedding.

'a tent was constructed, the outer one . . . which was called the Holy Place' He 9.2; εἰσῆλθεν ἐφάπαξ εἰς τὰ ἅγια 'he entered once and for all into the Holy Place' He 9.12. The inner room was more specifically identified by the phrase ἅγια ἁγίων, literally 'holy of holies' He 9.3, a Hebrew idiom indicating superlative degree. The inner sanctuary could also be referred to as 'within the curtain' (τὸ ἐσώτερον τοῦ καταπετάσματος He 6.19). See ἅγιος^a (88.24) and 7.18.

The outer room of the sanctuary may be referred to in some languages as simply 'the first room of the Holy Temple' or 'the first holy room of the Temple.' The 'holy of holies' may be referred to as 'the most holy place' or 'the second holy room of the Temple' or 'the interior holy room of the Temple.' What is important here is the degree of holiness, not so much the actual location within the Temple. It is for this reason that for the 'holy of holies' many translators use 'the most sacred place' or 'the very, very sacred room.' In this type of context the term 'sacred' may be rendered as 'dedicated especially to God' or 'consecrated to God.'

7.36 τρίστεγον, ου *n*: the third story of a building, that is, the second story above ground level – 'second story' (British usage), 'third story' (American usage). κατενεχθεὶς ἀπὸ τοῦ ὕπνου ἔπεσεν ἀπὸ τοῦ τριστέγου κάτω 'he became very sleepy and fell down from the third story' Ac 20.9.

7.37 προαύλιον, ου *n*: the area in front of an entrance to a building – 'gateway, forecourt.' ἐξῆλθεν ἔξω εἰς τὸ προαύλιον 'he went out into the gateway' Mk 14.68. προαύλιον may be rendered as 'in front of the building.'

7.38 πυλών^b, ῶνος *m*: the area associated with the entrance into a house or building – 'gateway, entrance, vestibule.' κρούσαντος δὲ αὐτοῦ τὴν θύραν τοῦ πυλῶνος 'when he was knocking at the door of the vestibule' Ac 12.13; ἐξελθόντα δὲ εἰς τὸν πυλῶνα εἶδεν αὐτὸν ἄλλη 'he went out to the vestibule where another (servant girl) saw him' Mt 26.71.

The phrase τὰ πρὸς τὴν θύραν (see 7.39) is essentially equivalent to πυλών^b: συνήχθησαν

πολλοὶ ὥστε μηκέτι χωρεῖν μηδὲ τὰ πρὸς τὴν θύραν 'so many people came together that there was no room left, not even out in the entrance' Mk 2.2.

7.39 θύρα^b, ας *f*: the entranceway into a building or structure – 'entrance, entranceway, portal.' τίς ἀποκυλίσει ἡμῖν τὸν λίθον ἐκ τῆς θύρας τοῦ μνημείου; 'who will roll away the stone from the entrance to the grave for us?' Mk 16.3.

In Jn 10.9 θύρα^b is used figuratively to refer to Jesus as the means of access to salvation: ἐγώ εἰμι ἡ θύρα· δι᾽ ἐμοῦ ἐάν τις εἰσέλθῃ σωθήσεται 'I am the door; whoever comes in by me will be saved.' In Jn 10.9 the emphasis is upon the door as a passageway and not as an object closing off an entrance. Literal translations of 'I am the door' may often lead to misinterpretation, since the term used for 'door' is likely to refer to a literal door rather than to the entranceway, thus suggesting that Jesus Christ functions primarily to prevent passage rather than making entrance possible.

7.40 στοά, ᾶς *f*: a covered colonnade, open normally on one side, where people could stand, sit, or walk, protected from the weather and the heat of the sun – 'porch, portico.' κολυμβήθρα . . . πέντε στοὰς ἔχουσα 'a pool . . . which has five porches' Jn 5.2. Also see comments at 7.58.

In many parts of the world the closest equivalent to a στοά would be a veranda, an extensive type of porch. Such a porch may be described as 'a long outside room' or 'a room made with pillars and open.'

7.41 θεμέλιος^a, ου *m*; θεμέλιον^a, ου *n*;[9] ἐνδώμησις^b, εως *f*: that on which a structure is built – 'foundation.'
θεμέλιος^a: ὅμοιός ἐστιν ἀνθρώπῳ οἰκοδομήσαντι οἰκίαν ἐπὶ τὴν γῆν χωρὶς θεμελίου 'he is like a man who built a house on the ground without laying a foundation' Lk 6.49.
θεμέλιον^a: σεισμὸς ἐγένετο μέγας ὥστε σαλευθῆ-

---

9 In Greek literature θεμέλιος (masc.) and θεμέλιον (neuter) occur in the meaning of 'foundation,' but in the NT θεμέλιον in the sense of foundation happens to occur only in the plural form (Ac 16.26).

ναι τὰ θεμέλια τοῦ δεσμωτηρίου 'there was a violent earthquake which shook the foundations of the prison' Ac 16.26.

ἐνδώμησις[b]: ἡ ἐνδώμησις τοῦ τείχους αὐτῆς ἴασπις 'the foundation of its wall was made of jasper' Re 21.18. A number of scholars, however, prefer to understand ἐνδώμησις in this context as the material of which the wall was made, rather than to the foundation of the wall (see ἐνδώμησις[a], 7.77).

In some languages it is possible to describe a typical foundation in ancient times as 'large stones underneath the walls.' In other languages, however, this may seem to be quite a meaningless type of expression, since foundations are only made secure by driving stakes deep into the ground. Therefore, it may be best to describe the function of a foundation by 'what keeps the walls firm' or 'how the walls are made not to move' or 'what goes beneath the walls.'

7.42 θεμελιόω[a]: to lay or construct a foundation – 'to lay a foundation, to found something upon.' καὶ οὐκ ἔπεσεν, τεθεμελίωτο γὰρ ἐπὶ τὴν πέτραν 'and it did not fall, for it was founded upon rock' Mt 7.25.

7.43 θεμέλιος[b], ου m: a stone used in the construction of a foundation – 'foundation stone.'[10] τὸ τεῖχος τῆς πόλεως ἔχων θεμελίους δώδεκα 'the city's wall was built on twelve foundation stones' Re 21.14. Such foundation stones may be described as 'stones beneath the walls' or 'stones beneath the walls to make the walls strong.'

7.44 ἀκρογωνιαῖος, ου m; κεφαλὴ γωνίας: the cornerstone or capstone of a building, essential to its construction – 'cornerstone, important stone' (ἀκρογωνιαῖος and κεφαλὴ γωνίας occur in the NT only figuratively in reference to Christ).

ἀκρογωνιαῖος: ἐποικοδομηθέντες ἐπὶ τῷ θεμελίῳ τῶν ἀποστόλων καὶ προφητῶν, ὄντος ἀκρογωνιαίου αὐτοῦ Χριστοῦ Ἰησοῦ 'you, too, are built upon the foundation laid by the apostles and prophets, the cornerstone being Christ Jesus himself' Eph 2.20. Some scholars have assumed that ἀκρογωνιαῖος would refer to the capstone occurring at the high point of a peaked roof, but in the NT ἀκρογωνιαῖος would probably refer to the type of stone which would have been used in the Temple in Jerusalem, and therefore it is far more likely to understand ἀκρογωνιαῖος as a cornerstone rather than a capstone of a peaked roof. It would not have referred to the keystone of an arch. Since, however, in many societies the use of 'cornerstone' is not known and in others it may have an entirely different function, it may be more satisfactory to use an expression such as 'the most important stone' or 'the very important stone.' This serves to describe the function and significance of the cornerstone without trying to indicate precisely its location or form.

κεφαλὴ γωνίας: λίθος ὃν ἀπεδοκίμασαν οἱ οἰκοδομοῦντες οὗτος ἐγενήθη εἰς κεφαλὴν γωνίας 'the stone which the builders rejected turned out to be the most important stone' 1 Pe 2.7. Though some scholars have thought that κεφαλὴ γωνίας refers to a keystone of an arch or the lintel stone over a door, it is highly probable that κεφαλὴ γωνίας has essentially the same meaning as ἀκρογωνιαῖος.

7.45 στῦλος[a], ου m: an upright shaft or structure used as a building support – 'pillar, column.' ποιήσω αὐτὸν στῦλον ἐν τῷ ναῷ τοῦ θεοῦ μου 'I will make him a pillar in the sanctuary of my God' Re 3.12.

στῦλος is also used in speaking of the leaders of the Jerusalem church (Ga 2.9; see 36.7). In Ga 2.9 the focus is upon the important role of such persons in supporting and maintaining the church. In a number of languages such a figurative meaning may be expressed as 'very important persons in the church.'

In a number of languages pillars may be described as 'those poles which support the house' or 'those logs which hold up the roof.' Usually, however, there are rather specific terms to designate these important parts in the construction of houses or halls.

7.46 τοῖχος, ου m: wall of a house or enclosure – 'wall.' τοῖχος occurs in the NT only

---

10 λίθος in the sense of 'building stone' (that is, a shaped stone in contrast with a field stone) is treated in Domain 2 *Natural Substances* (2.24).

in the phrase τοῖχε κεχονιαμένε 'whitewashed wall,' an invective used against hypocrites (Ac 23.3). A literal translation of the phrase 'whitewashed wall' is rarely meaningful. Sometimes one can use a descriptive phrase such as 'a dirty wall which is made to look white' or '... to look clean.' In other instances one may wish to focus upon the function suggested by the idiom 'whitewashed wall' and employ a phrase such as 'one who has been made to look good but really isn't.'

7.47 θυρίς, ίδος *f*: an opening in a wall for the entrance of light and air and for the purpose of seeing in or out – 'window.' καθεζόμενος δέ τις νεανίας ὀνόματι Εὔτυχος ἐπὶ τῆς θυρίδος 'a young man named Eutychus was sitting in the window' Ac 20.9. In some languages a distinction is made between windows which may be closed with glass or shutters and those which are simply openings. It is probably the latter type which is involved in Ac 20.9 and 2 Cor 11.33.

7.48 πύλη, ης *f*; πυλών^a, ῶνος *m*: doors or gates used to close off entranceways – 'door, gate.' πύλη and πυλών^a may refer to house doors and gates or to large doors and gates such as were used in a palace, temple, or in a city wall.
πύλη: ἦλθαν ἐπὶ τὴν πύλην τὴν σιδηρᾶν τὴν φέρουσαν εἰς τὴν πόλιν 'they came to the iron gate that opens into the city' Ac 12.10.
πυλών^a: ὅ τε ἱερεὺς τοῦ Διὸς . . . ταύρους καὶ στέμματα ἐπὶ τοὺς πυλῶνας ἐνέγκας 'the priest of the god Zeus . . . brought bulls and garlands to the gate' Ac 14.13. Note, however, that in Ac 14.13 the reference may not be specifically to the gates as objects, but to the entranceway into the city.

7.49 θύρα^a, ας *f*: the door to a house or building (often occurring in plural form and designating double doors or gates) – 'door, gate.' κρούσαντος δὲ αὐτοῦ τὴν θύραν τοῦ πυλῶνος 'when he was knocking at the door of the vestibule' Ac 12.13.

7.50 στέγη, ης *f*: the roof or top of a house – 'roof.' ἀπεστέγασαν τὴν στέγην ὅπου ἦν 'they made a hole in the roof above the place where

he was' Mk 2.4. In general, the types of roofs referred to in the NT are flat-top, made of pounded dirt, sometimes mixed with lime or stone, and supported by heavy beams. In view of the various types of activities described as taking place on the housetop, it may be important in some languages to indicate either in the text or in a marginal note the fact that such housetops were flat and that there was usually easy access to such roofs.

7.51 δῶμα, τος *n*: the area on the top of a flat-roof house – 'housetop.' ὁ ἐπὶ τοῦ δώματος μὴ καταβάτω 'one who is on top of the house must not go down' Mt 24.17. The phrase κηρύξατε ἐπὶ τῶν δωμάτων 'proclaim from the housetops' (Mt 10.27) is an idiom meaning 'to proclaim publicly' (see 28.64). See 7.50 for comments relating to translational problems.

7.52 ἀναβαθμός, οῦ *m*: in the singular, a step in a flight of steps, and in the plural, a series of steps – 'step, flight of steps, stairs.' ὅτε δὲ ἐγένετο ἐπὶ τοὺς ἀναβαθμούς 'and when he came to the stairs' Ac 21.35.

7.53 πτερύγιον, ου *n*: the tip or high point of a building – 'pinnacle, summit (of the Temple).'[11] καὶ ἔστησεν αὐτὸν ἐπὶ τὸ πτερύγιον τοῦ ἱεροῦ 'and he set him on the pinnacle of the Temple' Mt 4.5.

D Open Constructions (7.54-7.56)

7.54 θέατρον^a, ου *n*: a rather large, normally semicircular open structure capable of seating several thousand people and often used for public assemblies – 'theater.' ὥρμησάν τε ὁμοθυμαδὸν εἰς τὸ θέατρον 'they rushed with one mind to the theater' Ac 19.29. The emphasis in Ac 19.29 is upon the theater as a place for assembly and not as a place for dramas. In some languages the most appropriate equivalent is actually 'meeting place.' In other instances one may use a term which designates an 'enclosure.'

11 The precise meaning of πτερύγιον in Mt 4.5 and Lk 4.9 is uncertain. Some scholars have proposed 'lintel' or 'superstructure of the gate of the Temple.'

7.55 στάδιον, ου *n*: an open, oval area (frequently including a racetrack) around which was built an enclosed series of tiers of seats for those who came to watch the spectacles – 'arena, stadium.' οἱ ἐν σταδίῳ τρέχοντες πάντες μὲν τρέχουσιν, εἷς δὲ λαμβάνει τὸ βραβεῖον 'all the runners in the stadium are trying to win, but only one gets the prize' 1 Cor 9.24. In 1 Cor 9.24 the important feature is not the stadium as a construction, but as a place where races were conducted. Accordingly, 'all the runners in the stadium' may very well be rendered as 'all the runners who are racing.' The focus here is upon the competition rather than upon the type of place in which the competition took place.

7.56 αὐλή ª, ῆς *f*: a walled enclosure either to enclose human activity or to protect livestock – 'courtyard' or 'sheepfold.' τὴν αὐλὴν τὴν ἔξωθεν τοῦ ναοῦ ἔκβαλε ἔξωθεν 'omit the courtyard outside the sanctuary' Re 11.2; ἄλλα πρόβατα ἔχω ἃ οὐκ ἔστιν ἐκ τῆς αὐλῆς ταύτης 'there are other sheep that belong to me that are not of this sheepfold' Jn 10.16. A sheepfold may be described in some languages as 'a place for sheep with a wall built around it' or 'a corral for sheep' or 'a place for protecting sheep.'

E Constructions for Holding Water (7.57-7.58)

7.57 πηγή ᵇ, ῆς *f*; φρέαρ ª, ατος *n*: deep constructions, often walled with stone, at the bottom of which was a pool of water – 'well.' πηγή ᵇ: ἦν δὲ ἐκεῖ πηγὴ τοῦ Ἰακώβ 'and Jacob's well was there' Jn 4.6. φρέαρ ª: βοῦς εἰς φρέαρ πεσεῖται 'an ox will fall into a well' Lk 14.5.

If there was a relatively ready flow of water, a well could very appropriately be called a πηγή ª 'spring,' 1.78 (and this may be the reason for πηγή in Jn 4.6), but if water only gradually seeped into the well from surrounding areas or was collected in the well from surface drainage, it would be more appropriately called φρέαρ ª. However, both terms are used interchangeably in certain contexts; compare, for example, πηγή in Jn 4.6 and φρέαρ in Jn 4.11, both referring to Jacob's well at Sychar.

7.58 κολυμβήθρα, ας *f*: a relatively large construction for impounding water – 'pool' (primarily used for bathing). κολυμβήθρα ἡ ἐπιλεγομένη Ἑβραϊστὶ Βηθζαθά 'a pool called Bethzatha in Hebrew' Jn 5.2. The term κολυμβήθρα occurs in the NT only in Jn 5.2, 4, 7, and refers to a pool having five porches, one on each of four sides and another porch which went across the middle of the pool.

F Walls and Fences (7.59-7.62)

7.59 φραγμός ª, οῦ *m*: a structure for enclosing an open area – 'fence, wall.' ἐφύτευσεν ἀμπελῶνα καὶ φραγμὸν αὐτῷ περιέθηκεν 'he planted a vineyard and put a fence around it' Mt 21.33. In practically all societies there is some type of fence, wall, or barrier employed to surround fields. In some instances this may consist of piled up logs or sticks; in other instances the wall may be made of packed dirt or of laid-up stone. What is important, however, is not the form, but the function, and therefore one may often use a descriptive expression, for example, 'a barrier to surround a field,' sometimes described as 'a barrier to keep animals out of the field.'

φραγμός ª is also used figuratively of the Law, which constituted a barrier between Jews and Gentiles: τὸ μεσότοιχον τοῦ φραγμοῦ 'a wall of separation' or 'barrier' Eph 2.14. In Eph 2.14 φραγμός ª may be rendered as 'a wall to keep apart' or 'a wall to divide' (see 34.39).

7.60 χάραξ, ακος *m*: a fence of poles or stakes used to fortify entrenchments – 'palisade, barricade.' παρεμβαλοῦσιν οἱ ἐχθροί σου χάρακά σοι 'your enemies will surround you with barricades' Lk 19.43. In Lk 19.43 barricades may be rendered in some instances as 'thick walls' or 'strong fences.'

7.61 τεῖχος, ους *n*: a particularly strong wall, primarily the wall of a city – 'city wall.' διὰ τοῦ τείχους καθῆκαν αὐτὸν χαλάσαντες ἐν σπυρίδι 'placing him in a basket, they let him down over the wall' Ac 9.25.

In a number of languages a translator must make a clear distinction between a wall of a house and a city wall. The wall of a house may be called 'a side of a house' and an inner wall 'a partition in a house,' while a city wall is often related to terms such as 'barricade' or 'fence.' Hence, a city wall may be called 'a fortified fence around a city.'

7.62 μεσότοιχον, ου *n*: a wall or fence which separates one area from another – 'dividing wall.' In the NT μεσότοιχον is used figuratively in reference to the partition in the Temple in Jerusalem, which set off the court of the Gentiles from the rest of the Temple area. ὁ ποιήσας τὰ ἀμφότερα ἓν καὶ τὸ μεσότοιχον τοῦ φραγμοῦ λύσας 'who made both one people by breaking down the wall that separated them' Eph 2.14. Such a 'dividing wall' may be rendered as 'barrier' or 'fence which separates.'

G Miscellaneous Constructions (7.63-7.76)

7.63 βῆμα, τος *n*: a raised platform mounted by steps and usually furnished with a seat, used by officials in addressing an assembly, often on judicial matters – 'judgment seat, judgment place.' ἐκάθισεν ἐπὶ βήματος εἰς τόπον λεγόμενον Λιθόστρωτον 'he sat down on the judge's seat in the place called The Stone Pavement' Jn 19.13. The association of a βῆμα with judicial procedures means that there is almost always an important component of judicial function associated with this term. Therefore in translating βῆμα, it is often best to use a phrase such as 'a place where a judge decides' or 'a place where decisions are made' or 'a judge's seat.' The focus upon judgment is particularly important in those passages which refer to the judgment seat of God (Ro 14.10) and of Christ (2 Cor 5.10).

7.64 φάτνη[b], ης *f*: a stall where animals are fed – 'stall.' ἕκαστος ὑμῶν . . . οὐ λύει τὸν βοῦν αὐτοῦ ἢ τὸν ὄνον ἀπὸ τῆς φάτνης; 'would anyone of you . . . not untie his ox or his donkey from the stall?' Lk 13.15. φάτνη[b] may designate a part of a barn, or it may simply refer to a customary place where an animal is fed outside, often in a semi-enclosure (see 6.137).

7.65 ἅλων[a], ος *f*: a surface of hard ground or stone where grain was threshed out, either by

beating or having animals trample upon it – 'threshing floor.' διακαθαριεῖ τὴν ἅλωνα αὐτοῦ 'he will clean up his threshing floor' Mt 3.12. The meaning of ἅλων as 'threshing floor' forms the basis for the figurative extension of meaning (a metonymy) referring to the threshed grain still lying on the threshing floor (see 3.43). The meaning may be made clear by rendering 'to thresh out completely all of the grain.' On the other hand, it is possible to interpret ἅλων in Mt 3.12 in a literal sense and translate 'he will clean up his threshing floor,' that is, by gathering up the grain and getting rid of the straw and chaff.

7.66 ληνός, οῦ *f*: an instrument for pressing out the juice of grapes for the making of wine – 'wine press.' ἐφύτευσεν ἀμπελῶνα . . . καὶ ὤρυξεν ἐν αὐτῷ ληνόν 'he planted a vineyard . . . and dug a wine press in it' Mt 21.33. Ancient wine presses consisted of large vats into which grapes were placed and then trampled on in order to extract the juice. Accordingly, a descriptive equivalent of wine press may be 'a place where the juice of grapes was squeezed out' or '. . . pressed out.'

7.67 ὑπολήνιον, ου *n*: a trough placed beneath the wine press to receive the grape juice pressed out – 'wine trough.' ἀμπελῶνα ἄνθρωπος ἐφύτευσεν . . . καὶ ὤρυξεν ὑπολήνιον 'a man planted a vineyard . . . and dug a wine trough' or '. . . dug a place where the juice of the grapes could be collected' Mk 12.1.

7.68 μύλος[a], ου *m*: a construction of two flat stones between which grain was ground into flour by rotating the top stone – 'mill.' φωνὴ μύλου οὐ μὴ ἀκουσθῇ ἐν σοὶ ἔτι 'the sound of the mill will no longer be heard in you' Re 18.22.

Some mills were relatively small and operated by hand and could well be considered as artifacts. Others, however, were quite large, and animals were used to rotate the upper stone.

In almost all parts of the world grain is ground in one way or another. Quite frequently mills are of the same general structure as those used in ancient times, in which two relatively large, round, flat stones were placed one on top of the other, and the grain was ground between the two stones. Grain entered the mill through a round hole in the upper stone, and the flour gradually emerged from around the edges of the two stones. In other parts of the world, however, grain is prepared by means of grinding stones called metates. In still other parts of the world, a mortar and pestle are used for the grinding or preparation of grain. In most contexts, what is important is either the large size of the stones or the function of grinding grain, not necessarily the particular form. However, in contexts which speak about tying a millstone to a man's neck (see 7.69) and his being thrown into the depths of the sea, it is important to refer to relatively large stones which would cause a person to sink immediately. In such a context the use of a term for 'mortar,' especially one of wood, would hardly be appropriate since it would normally float. Frequently μύλος may be rendered as 'stones for grinding grain.' In other instances, even a more generic expression may be used, for example, 'a large stone.'

7.69 μύλος[b], ου *m*: a large, round, flat stone, either upper or lower, used in grinding grain − 'millstone.' συμφέρει αὐτῷ ἵνα κρεμασθῇ μύλος ὀνικὸς περὶ τὸν τράχηλον αὐτοῦ 'it would be better for such a person to have a large millstone tied around his neck' Mt 18.6. μύλος[a] 'mill' (7.68) denotes a mill as a whole, while μύλος[b] denotes only one of the large flat stones of a mill. For a discussion of some of the translational problems involved in rendering μύλος[b] 'millstone,' see the discussion on μύλος[a] (7.68).

7.70 μυλικός, ή, όν; μύλινος, η, ον: (derivatives of μύλος[a] 'mill,' 7.68) pertaining to a stone mill for grinding grain − 'of a mill.' μυλικός: εἰ λίθος μυλικὸς περίκειται περὶ τὸν τράχηλον αὐτοῦ 'if a millstone were placed around his neck' Lk 17.2. μύλινος: λίθον ὡς μύλινον μέγαν 'a stone like a large millstone' Re 18.21. The translation of such adjectival forms depends upon specific contexts. There is, of course, no need to translate an adjectival form by a corresponding adjective in a receptor

language, especially when a noun would be more appropriate.

7.71 λιθόστρωτον, ου *n*: an area in Jerusalem, paved with flat blocks of stone and forming a kind of courtyard (not a thoroughfare) − 'The Stone Pavement.' ἐκάθισεν ἐπὶ βήματος εἰς τόπον λεγόμενον Λιθόστρωτον 'he sat down on the judge's seat in the place called The Stone Pavement' Jn 19.13.

In some languages one may describe 'The Stone Pavement' as 'a court covered with large blocks of flat stone' or 'a stone-paved courtyard.' See 93.437.

7.72 ἀφεδρών, ῶνος *m* − 'latrine, toilet.' εἰς ἀφεδρῶνα ἐκβάλλεται 'it is cast out into the latrine' Mt 15.17. The term ἀφεδρών occurs only in Mt 15.17 and Mk 7.19 and may be rendered in a number of languages as 'place of defecation.' In some languages, however, a reference to a toilet may seem inappropriate for the Scriptures, and it is possible to translate a passage such as Mt 15.17 as 'goes into the stomach and then passes on out.' The meaning is thus clear without a specific reference to a latrine or toilet.

7.73 κάμινος, ου *f*: a construction used for the smelting of ore and burning of ceramic ware − 'furnace, kiln.' οἱ πόδες αὐτοῦ ὅμοιοι χαλκολιβάνῳ ὡς ἐν καμίνῳ πεπυρωμένης 'his feet were like polished brass that had been refined in a furnace' Re 1.15. In Mt 13.42 and 50 κάμινος is used figuratively of hell.

In rendering the meaning of κάμινος, the emphasis should be upon the extreme heat, rather than upon the particular type of construction.

7.74 κλίβανος, ου *m*: a dome-like structure made of clay, in which wood and dried grass were burned, and then after being heated, was used for baking bread − 'oven.' τὸν χόρτον τοῦ ἀγροῦ σήμερον ὄντα καὶ αὔριον εἰς κλίβανον βαλλόμενον 'the grass of the field which is alive today and tomorrow is cast into the oven' Mt 6.30.

The function of κλίβανος may be described as 'a place heated for baking bread,' and it may be useful in some instances to employ a more extensive description of a κλίβανος in a glossary, but this is rarely necessary since function is far more important than form.

7.75 τάφος, ου *m*; μνῆμα, τος *n*; μνημεῖον ᵃ, ου *n*:[12] a construction for the burial of the dead – 'grave, tomb.'
τάφος: οἰκοδομεῖτε τοὺς τάφους τῶν προφητῶν καὶ κοσμεῖτε τὰ μνημεῖα τῶν δικαίων 'you make fine graves for the prophets and decorate the tombs of those who live good lives' Mt 23.29. It is also possible to translate μνημεῖα in Mt 23.29 as 'monuments to the dead' (see 7.76).
μνῆμα: ἔθηκεν αὐτὸν ἐν μνήματι λαξευτῷ 'he laid him in a tomb hewn out of a rock' Lk 23.53.
μνημεῖον ᵃ: ὑπήντησεν αὐτῷ ἐκ τῶν μνημείων ἄνθρωπος ἐν πνεύματι ἀκαθάρτῳ 'a man with an unclean spirit came from the tombs and met him' Mk 5.2.
    In a number of languages it is important to distinguish clearly between a grave (a hole in the ground in which a corpse is placed) and a tomb (a construction built above the surface of the ground for housing a corpse). In some contexts, however, it may be better to use a more generic expression, for example, 'places where people are buried' or 'places where corpses are placed.' In Mk 5.2 it is important to avoid a term which would designate merely

───

12 It is possible that μνῆμα and μνημεῖον ᵃ differ in meaning from τάφος in that they contain a semantic component of 'memorial,' that is, a reminder to people of someone who has died.

graves, for the demoniac who met Jesus was not living down in graves in the ground, but had found some habitation either in burial caves or in tombs constructed above ground.

7.76 μνημεῖον ᵇ, ου *n*: a monument built as a memorial to someone who has died – 'monument, memorial.' οἰκοδομεῖτε τὰ μνημεῖα τῶν προφητῶν 'you build memorials to the prophets' Lk 11.47. Constructions such as those mentioned in Lk 11.47 could also serve as tombs for the individuals in question. For a discussion of μνημεῖον in Mt 23.29, see 7.75.

H Building Materials (7.77-7.79)

7.77 ἐνδώμησις ᵃ, εως *f*: material used in the construction of buildings – 'building material.' ἡ ἐνδώμησις τοῦ τείχους αὐτῆς ἴασπις 'the material of its wall was jasper' Re 21.18. It is also possible to understand ἐνδώμησις in the sense of 'foundation' (see ἐνδώμησις ᵇ, 7.41).

7.78 δοκός, οῦ *f*: beam of wood – 'beam.' τὴν δὲ ἐν τῷ σῷ ὀφθαλμῷ δοκὸν οὐ κατανοεῖς 'you do not notice the beam in your own eye' Mt 7.3. The contrast between 'splinter' and 'beam' in this context is a purposeful exaggeration, and can usually be reproduced, though in some instances a marginal note may be helpful.

7.79 σανίς, ίδος *f*: large board or plank of wood – 'plank.' οὓς μὲν ἐπὶ σανίσιν 'some holding on to planks' Ac 27.44.

8 Body, Body Parts, and Body Products

Outline of Subdomains

A Body (8.1-8.8)
B Parts of the Body (8.9-8.69)
C Physiological Products of the Body[1] (8.70-8.77)

───

1 The Subdomain *Physiological Products of the Body* could be treated together with *Physiological Processes and States* (Domain 23), but since such body products are so closely associated with animate bodies, it has seemed

A Body (8.1-8.8)

8.1 σῶμα ᵃ, τος *n*: the physical body of persons, animals, or plants,[2] either dead or alive

more practical to include them together with *Body* and *Body Parts*.
2 The use of σῶμα ᵃ in connection with plants is quite rare in extrabiblical Greek and perhaps only occurs in 1 Cor 15.37 because of the analogy between plants and persons in treating the theme of the resurrection body.

– 'body.' πάντα δὲ τὰ μέλη τοῦ σώματος πολλὰ ὄντα ἕν ἐστιν σῶμα 'though all the parts of the body are many, it is still one body' 1 Cor 12.12; ὅπου τὸ σῶμα, ἐκεῖ καὶ οἱ ἀετοὶ ἐπισυναχθήσονται 'where there is a body, the vultures will gather' Lk 17.37; οὐ τὸ σῶμα τὸ γενησόμενον σπείρεις 'you do not sow the body of the plant which is to be' 1 Cor 15.37.

In a number of languages a clear distinction must be made between the body of a living person and a dead body (or corpse). Other languages distinguish between the bodies of persons and the bodies of animals, and frequently the term for a body of a plant is distinct from those referring to persons or animals. Often a term for body consists of a phrase, for example, 'flesh and bones,' and in a number of languages a reference to the body is made primarily by referring to the person himself. For example, in Mt 26.12 ('has poured this ointment on my body') the appropriate equivalent may be 'has poured this ointment on me.' In certain instances 'body' may be rendered as something which is experienced. For example, in 1 Cor 6.20 'glorify God through your body' may be rendered as 'glorify God through what you do' or '. . . do in your body.'

8.2 σωματικός, ή, όν; σωματικῶς^a: (derivatives of σῶμα^a 'body,' 8.1) pertaining to a physical body – 'bodily, physical, bodily form.'
σωματικός: ἡ γὰρ σωματικὴ γυμνασία πρὸς ὀλίγον ἐστὶν ὠφέλιμος 'for bodily training is of some value' 1 Tm 4.8; καταβῆναι τὸ πνεῦμα τὸ ἅγιον σωματικῷ εἴδει ὡς περιστερὰν ἐπ' αὐτόν 'the Holy Spirit descended upon him in bodily form like a dove' Lk 3.22.
σωματικῶς^a: ἐν αὐτῷ κατοικεῖ πᾶν τὸ πλήρωμα τῆς θεότητος σωματικῶς 'in him all the fullness of deity dwells bodily' or '. . . in physical form' Col 2.9. It is also possible to interpret σωματικῶς in Col 2.9 as meaning 'in reality,' that is to say, 'not symbolically' (see 70.7).

8.3 ὁ ἔξω ἄνθρωπος: (an idiom, literally 'the outside person') the physical nature or aspect of a person – 'body, physical form.' ἀλλ' εἰ καὶ ὁ ἔξω ἡμῶν ἄνθρωπος διαφθείρεται 'but if indeed our bodies perish' 2 Cor 4.16. The

phrase ὁ ἔξω ἄνθρωπος is to be understood in direct contrast with ὁ ἔσω (ἄνθρωπος) in the same verse, which refers to the psychological or spiritual nature of human personality (see 26.1).

8.4 σάρξ^b, σαρκός f: a living body – 'body, physical body.'³ ὃς ἐφανερώθη ἐν σαρκί 'who appeared in a physical body' 1 Tm 3.16. Though the reference of σάρξ in 1 Tm 3.16 is to the physical body, it may be necessary in some instances to translate this as 'a human being' or 'a person,' that is to say, 'Christ appeared as a human being' or 'Christ became a person.' Otherwise, the reader might assume that Christ took on the body of someone else or merely indwelt some miraculous human form rather than actually became a human being.

8.5 σκῆνος, ους n; σκήνωμα^c, τος n: (figurative extensions of meaning of σκῆνος 'tent,' not occurring in the NT, and σκήνωμα^a 'temporary dwelling,' 7.8) temporary habitation in the human body – 'body.'
σκῆνος: ἐὰν ἡ ἐπίγειος ἡμῶν οἰκία τοῦ σκήνους καταλυθῇ 'if our earthly house, our body, is torn down' 2 Cor 5.1.
σκήνωμα^c: ταχινή ἐστιν ἡ ἀπόθεσις τοῦ σκηνώματός μου 'I shall soon put off this body of mine' 2 Pe 1.14. It is also possible to interpret σκήνωμα in 2 Pe 1.14 as meaning a temporary habitation, though referring, of course, to the human body (see 85.77).

Only rarely can one preserve in translation the figurative meanings suggested by the terms σκῆνος and σκήνωμα. What is significant in such contexts is the temporary nature of the dwelling, and therefore the relatively brief time which the body is to serve the person who dwells in it. In some cases it may be relevant, therefore, to have a footnote to point out the temporal aspects of this figurative usage of σκῆνος and σκήνωμα^c.

8.6 σκεῦος^c, ους n: (a figurative extension of meaning of σκεῦος^a 'object, thing, instru-

---

3 It is possible that σάρξ^b differs in meaning from σῶμα^a (8.1) in focusing somewhat more upon the physical nature.

ment,' 6.1, or of σκεῦος^b 'vessel,' 6.118) the human body – 'body.' ἕκαστον ὑμῶν τὸ ἑαυτοῦ σκεῦος κτᾶσθαι 'each one of you should learn to gain mastery over his own body' 1 Th 4.4. It is also possible to interpret σκεῦος in 1 Th 4.4 as meaning 'wife,' and for a discussion of this meaning and some of the problems involved in translation, see 10.55. A further alternative meaning, and one closely related to the meaning of 'body' is 'sexual life,' so that this expression in 1 Th 4.4 might be rendered as 'each of you must gain mastery over his sexual life' or, in the form τὸ ἑαυτοῦ σκεῦος κτᾶσθαι ἐν ἁγιασμῷ καὶ τιμῇ, 'your sexual life should be holy and honorable' (see 23.63).

8.7 πτῶμα, τος *n*: a dead body, whether of an animal or a human being – 'dead body, corpse.' ἦραν τὸ πτῶμα αὐτοῦ καὶ ἔθηκαν αὐτὸ ἐν μνημείῳ 'they took his dead body and buried it' Mk 6.29; ὅπου ἐὰν ᾖ τὸ πτῶμα, ἐκεῖ συναχθήσονται οἱ ἀετοί 'wherever there is a corpse, the vultures will gather' Mt 24.28. In the parallel passage of Lk 17.37, the term σῶμα (8.1) occurs. Since in some languages one must distinguish varying degrees of decomposition of a corpse, it may be important in certain contexts to indicate whether the body is of a person or an animal which has recently died or one which has undergone considerable decomposition.

8.8 κῶλον, ου *n*: the dead body of a person, especially one which is still unburied[4] – 'dead body, corpse.' ὧν τὰ κῶλα ἔπεσεν ἐν τῇ ἐρήμῳ 'whose dead bodies fell in the wilderness' He 3.17. Though in He 3.17 the Greek text reads literally 'whose dead bodies fell in the wilderness,' it would normally be a mistake to translate this clause literally, since it might suggest that the people died while they were still standing, and that only the corpses fell. A more natural equivalent is 'they died in the wilderness' or 'they died and their bodies lay in the wilderness.'

B Parts of the Body[5] (8.9-8.69)

8.9 μέλος^a, ους *n*: a part of the body – 'body part, member.'[6] καθάπερ γὰρ ἐν ἑνὶ σώματι πολλὰ μέλη ἔχομεν 'as we have many members in one body' Ro 12.4. In some languages an equivalent of μέλος is simply 'division,' and in a few languages an even more generic expression such as 'things' is used, so that 'the parts of the body' may be rendered by an expression meaning literally 'things of the body.'

In different languages the various parts of the body are classified in a number of diverse ways. In some languages the sensory organs of seeing, hearing, smelling, and tasting (those related to the head) are often set off from other types of organs, while in other languages special terms may be employed for those organs involving movement, for example, the joints, arms, legs, etc. Other languages make extensive subclassifications of body parts on the basis of whether they are external or internal, though such classifications often appear to be arbitrary, since teeth and tongue may be regarded as either external or internal.

8.10 κεφαλή^a, ῆς *f* – 'head.' θέλω ἵνα ἐξαυτῆς δῷς μοι ἐπὶ πίνακι τὴν κεφαλὴν Ἰωάννου τοῦ βαπτιστοῦ 'I want you to give me the head of John the Baptist on a plate' Mk 6.25. In some languages it may be necessary to distinguish clearly between the head which is still a part of a body and a severed head. It is this latter meaning which is obviously involved in Mk 6.25.

In rendering 1 Cor 11.4, πᾶς ἀνὴρ προσευχόμενος ἢ προφητεύων κατὰ κεφαλῆς ἔχων 'any man who prays or prophesies with his head covered,' it may be important to indicate

---

4 In earlier Greek κῶλον designated a 'limb,' but in the NT it occurs only in the plural and means corpses.

5 Though the terms for certain body parts, namely, καρδία 'heart', νεφρός 'kidney,' βραχίων 'arm,' ὀφρῦς 'brow,' and χεῖλος 'lip,' occur in the NT, they do so only in figurative senses, and hence these meanings are treated under the various domains to which they belong.

6 One may also classify the meaning of μέλος in Domain 63 *Whole, Unite, Part, Divide* and consider its reference to body parts as only an instance of an even more generic meaning, namely, 'part' (63.17). On the other hand, its frequent association with the body in absolute contexts may justify its classification here as a generic for body parts.

that the covering is not one which is designed to cover the entire head including the face, but only the top of the head. The same applies, of course, to 1 Cor 11.5 and 7.

8.11 κρανίον, ου *n*: the bony framework of the head, especially the upper portion – 'skull' (in the NT κρανίον is used only as a name for the hill of Golgotha). τόπον λεγόμενον Γολγοθᾶ, ὅ ἐστιν Κρανίου Τόπος λεγόμενος 'a place called Golgotha which is called The Place of a Skull' Mt 27.33. In rendering κρανίου τόπος 'place of the skull,' it may be necessary to indicate clearly the relationship between 'place' and 'skull.' A literal rendering of such a phrase might simply mean 'a place where there was a skull.' However, the meaning of Golgotha has been interpreted generally as 'a hill resembling a skull,' and therefore κρανίου τόπος may be more satisfactorily rendered as 'a place resembling a skull' or 'a hill looking like a skull.' See 93.453.

8.12 θρίξ, τριχός *f*: hair, either of a person or of an animal – 'hair.' τὸ ἔνδυμα αὐτοῦ ἀπὸ τριχῶν καμήλου 'his garment was of camel's hair' Mt 3.4 (see note at 4.30); αἱ τρίχες τῆς κεφαλῆς πᾶσαι 'all the hairs of (your) head' Mt 10.30.

In a number of languages important distinctions are made between the hair of animals and the hair of humans. Further distinctions may also be made between the hair of the head, the hair of the beard, and general body hair. In certain instances special terms are also used for pubic hair.

8.13 τρίχινος, η, ον: (derivative of θρίξ 'hair,' 8.12) pertaining to or consisting of hair – 'of hair, hairy.' ὁ ἥλιος ἐγένετο μέλας ὡς σάκκος τρίχινος 'the sun became dark as hairy sackcloth' Re 6.12.

8.14 κόμη, ης *f*: hair of the head of human beings – 'hair.' ἡ κόμη ἀντὶ περιβολαίου δέδοται αὐτῇ 'her hair has been given to her for a covering' 1 Cor 11.15.

8.15 ἔριον[a]**, ου** *n*: the curly hair that forms the fleece of sheep – 'wool.' ἡ δὲ κεφαλὴ αὐτοῦ καὶ αἱ τρίχες λευκαὶ ὡς ἔριον λευκόν 'his head

and his hair were as white as white wool' Re 1.14. ἔριον in Re 1.14 and He 9.19 may also mean unspun wool; hence ἔριον as 'processed wool' has been classified as an artifact (6.171).

8.16 μέτωπον, ου *n*: the front part of the head above the eyes – 'forehead.' οἵτινες οὐκ ἔχουσι τὴν σφραγῖδα τοῦ θεοῦ ἐπὶ τῶν μετώπων 'who did not have the seal of God upon their foreheads' Re 9.4. Though in most languages there is a specific term to designate the forehead, it may be necessary in some instances to speak of 'the upper face' or 'the face above the eyes.'

8.17 κέρας[a]**, ατος** *n*: the hard bony outgrowth on the heads of certain animals – 'horn.' ἀρνίον . . . ἔχων κέρατα ἑπτά 'a lamb . . . with seven horns' Re 5.6. Finding a term for 'horn' is usually not at all difficult. The problem arises when a term for 'horn' is already employed in a receptor language as a euphemistic expression for the male genital organ. It may therefore be necessary in Re 5.6 to speak of 'a lamb with seven horns on his head.'

In speaking of the horn-shaped corners of the altar (Re 9.13), it is often better not to use a term meaning literally 'horn,' since this might imply that the altar had the horns of animals stuck on to the corners. One can normally say 'corners of the altar shaped like horns' or '. . . looking like horns' or 'projections on the corners of the altar.' See 79.105.

8.18 πρόσωπον[a]**, ου** *n*; **ὄψις**[a]**, εως** *f*: the front part of the human head – 'face.'
πρόσωπον[a]: ἔλαμψεν τὸ πρόσωπον αὐτοῦ ὡς ὁ ἥλιος 'his face shone like the sun' Mt 17.2.
ὄψις[a]: ἡ ὄψις αὐτοῦ ὡς ὁ ἥλιος φαίνει 'his face was shining like the sun' Re 1.16.

8.19 στόμα[a]**, τος** *n* – 'mouth.' ἐπέταξεν τοῖς παρεστῶσιν αὐτῷ τύπτειν αὐτοῦ τὸ στόμα 'he ordered the ones standing there to strike him on the mouth' Ac 23.2. In some languages a distinction is made between terms used for the mouth when it is open and when it is closed. In Ac 23.2 presumably the mouth was closed.

The term στόμα also occurs in a number of phrases associated with speech, but while in some languages one can say 'to speak with the mouth,' it may be more appropriate to say 'to speak with the lips' or 'to speak with the tongue.' In a number of contexts, however, it may be better simply to say 'to speak,' since the addition of 'with the lips' or 'with the tongue' or 'with the mouth' may appear to be unnecessarily redundant.

8.20 ὀδούς, ὀδόντος *m* – 'tooth.' οἱ ὀδόντες αὐτῶν ὡς λεόντων ἦσαν 'their teeth were as the teeth of lions' Re 9.8. There are several problems involved in the rendering of ὀδούς. Even in the case of Re 9.8 it may be necessary to use two different terms for teeth, since human teeth may be referred to by expressions quite different from those used in referring to the teeth of animals. In Ac 7.54 the idiom 'to grind one's teeth' denotes anger (88.184), but a literal rendering of 'to grind the teeth' may mean in some languages merely 'to be nervous.' The expression βρυγμὸς τῶν ὀδόντων 'gnashing of the teeth' is used in connection with the tortures of hell (Lk 13.28), but a literal rendering of such a phrase can be quite misleading, since it may refer merely to the eating of some hard substance. See 23.41.

8.21 γλῶσσα ᵃ, ης *f* – 'tongue.' ἡ γλῶσσα μικρὸν μέλος ἐστίν 'the tongue is a small member of the body' Jas 3.5. Though in Jas 3.5 the tongue is referred to as a part of the body, it is used essentially as a symbol for speech, and since in some languages the tongue is not regarded as an organ of speech, but simply as a part of the mouth, it may be necessary to change the expression to read 'the mouth is a small member of the body' or 'speaking is only a small part of one's life.' It is obviously not the tongue as an organ which corrupts the whole person, but the capacity for speech which has such a corrupting effect.

8.22 σιαγών, όνος *f*: the fleshy part on either side of the face – 'cheek.' ὅστις σε ῥαπίζει εἰς τὴν δεξιὰν σιαγόνα σου 'whoever strikes you on your right cheek' Mt 5.39. Though in many languages there is a specific term for 'cheek,' in some instances it may be necessary to use a phrase meaning 'the side of the head' or 'the side of the face.'

8.23 ὀφθαλμός ᵃ, οῦ *m*; ὄμμα, τος *n* – 'eye' (normally including the eyelids).
ὀφθαλμός ᵃ: τότε ἥψατο τῶν ὀφθαλμῶν αὐτῶν 'then he touched their eyes' Mt 9.29.
ὄμμα: ὁ Ἰησοῦς ἥψατο τῶν ὀμμάτων αὐτῶν 'Jesus touched their eyes' Mt 20.34.

In a number of languages an important distinction is made between the eyes consisting of the eyeballs and the eyes covered or partially covered by the eyelids. In Mt 9.29 and 20.34, Jesus apparently touched the eyelids, not the eyeballs.

8.24 οὖς ᵃ, ὠτός *n*; ὠτίον, ου *n*; ὠτάριον, ου *n* – 'ear.' [7]
οὖς ᵃ: ὁ ἔχων ὦτα ἀκουέτω 'he who has ears, let him hear' Mt 11.15.
ὠτίον: οὗ ἀπέκοψεν Πέτρος τὸ ὠτίον 'whose ear Peter had cut off' Jn 18.26.
ὠτάριον: ἀπέκοψεν αὐτοῦ τὸ ὠτάριον τὸ δεξιόν 'he cut off his right ear' Jn 18.10.

8.25 τράχηλος, ου *m* – 'neck.' κρεμασθῇ μύλος ὀνικὸς περὶ τὸν τράχηλον αὐτοῦ 'a great millstone fastened around his neck' Mt 18.6.

τράχηλος also occurs in the NT in certain idiomatic expressions, for example, 'to fall on the neck of someone' (Lk 15.20 and Ac 20.37) in the sense of 'to embrace' (34.64), and 'to put down their necks' (Ro 16.4) meaning 'to risk their lives' (21.8). It is rare indeed that one can translate such idioms literally, since 'to fall on the neck of someone' may readily suggest a murderous attack, and 'to risk one's neck' may be simply meaningless, since the custom of beheading as a means of execution may be relatively unknown.

8.26 λάρυγξ, γγος *m* – 'throat.' τάφος ἀνεῳγμένος ὁ λάρυγξ αὐτῶν 'their throat is an open tomb' Ro 3.13. The context of Ro 3.13 is highly figurative, and in a number of languages it may be necessary either to change the metaphor into a simile, for example, 'their throat is like an open tomb,' or to employ a somewhat altered equivalent, for example, 'their speech is full of deadly deceit.'

---

7 ὠτίον and ὠτάριον are formally diminutive derivatives of οὖς, but how much diminutive meaning is involved is questionable.

8.27 ὦμος, ου *m* – 'shoulder.' ἐπιτίθησιν ἐπὶ τοὺς ὤμους αὐτοῦ 'he places it on his shoulders' Lk 15.5. In rendering Lk 15.5 the reference to the shoulder is often incorporated into the verb expression itself, that is to say, in a number of languages there are different verbs indicating the manner of carrying, for example, in the hands, on the shoulders, on the head, on the back, etc.

8.28 ἀγκάλη, ης *f*: the arm bent as in a position to receive or hold something – 'bent arm.' αὐτὸς ἐδέξατο αὐτὸ εἰς τὰς ἀγκάλας 'he took him up in his arms' Lk 2.28. In a number of languages it is not necessary to speak of 'bent arms' in translating Lk 2.28, since the context itself indicates the presumed position of the arms.

8.29 πτέρυξ, υγος *f*: a wing of any flying creature – 'wing.' ὄρνις ἐπισυνάγει τὰ νοσσία αὐτῆς ὑπὸ τὰς πτέρυγας 'a hen gathers her brood under her wings' Mt 23.37. In Re 9.9, in which the apocalyptic locusts are mentioned, the expression ἡ φωνὴ τῶν πτερύγων may require a distinct term for 'wings,' since the wings of insects may be referred to by terms different from those employed in speaking of the wings of birds.

8.30 χείρ ᵃ, χειρός *f*: a hand or any relevant portion of the hand, including, for example, the fingers – 'hand, finger.' ἐκτείνας τὴν χεῖρα ἥψατο αὐτοῦ 'he stretched out his hand and touched him' Mt 8.3. In rendering Mt 8.3 it would be inappropriate in some languages to translate literally 'he stretched out his hand,' since this would imply some kind of miracle of extending the hand itself. A correct rendering may be 'he extended his arm and touched him with his hand.'

In Lk 15.22 χείρ refers to the finger, not to the hand, and therefore it is necessary to translate in most languages 'put a ring on his finger.'

8.31 αὐτόχειρ, ος: of a person's own hands – 'one's own hands.' αὐτόχειρες τὴν σκευὴν τοῦ πλοίου ἔρριψαν 'they threw the ship's tackle overboard with their own hands' Ac 27.19. But in rendering Ac 27.19, it may be some-what superfluous or even misleading to speak about throwing over the ship's tackle 'with their own hands.' The emphasis is not upon the hands so much as the activity of the people aboard the ship. Therefore, one may better translate Ac 27.19 as 'they themselves threw the ship's tackle overboard.' Obviously, more than the hands were employed in this activity.

8.32 δεξιά ᵃ, ᾶς *f* – 'right hand.' μὴ γνώτω ἡ ἀριστερά σου τί ποιεῖ ἡ δεξιά σου 'do not let your left hand know what your right hand is doing' Mt 6.3. This expression is idiomatic and means not letting others know about the good which one does (see 28.74). The right hand is often spoken of idiomatically as 'the good hand' or 'the strong hand.' Sometimes it is called 'the mouth hand,' that is to say, the hand which one uses in eating.

For δεξιά in the idiom δεξιὰς δίδωμι 'to give the right hand' (Ga 2.9), see 34.42.

8.33 ἀριστερά, ᾶς *f* – 'left hand.' μὴ γνώτω ἡ ἀριστερά σου τί ποιεῖ ἡ δεξιά σου 'do not let your left hand know what your right hand is doing' Mt 6.3. The left hand is designated in a number of languages by an idiomatic phrase which normally contrasts with expressions for the right hand. For example, one may often speak of the left hand as 'the bad hand' or 'the weak hand,' and in some instances as 'the anus hand,' since this is the hand used in cleansing the body after defecation. See also 8.32.

8.34 δάκτυλος ᵃ, ου *m* – 'finger.' ὁ δὲ Ἰησοῦς κάτω κύψας τῷ δακτύλῳ κατέγραφεν εἰς τὴν γῆν 'Jesus bent down and wrote with his finger on the ground' Jn 8.6. Though it may seem quite logical to speak of 'writing with the finger,' in some languages one is required to speak of 'writing with the hand.' Similarly, in Mt 23.4 the idiom 'to lift a finger' is more satisfactorily expressed as 'to lift a hand.' Expressions such as 'to lift the hand' and 'to lift the finger' must be carefully studied for their idiomatic significance, for 'to lift the hand' may mean 'to release something,' while 'to lift the finger' may be a lewd gesture. In a number of languages the expression 'to lift a finger' (Mt

23.4) may be best rendered as 'to do a thing to help' or 'to help in any way.' For δάκτυλος θεοῦ 'the finger of God' (Lk 11.20), see 76.3.

8.35 πυγμή, ῆς f: the clenched hand – 'fist.' οἱ γὰρ Φαρισαῖοι . . . ἐὰν μὴ πυγμῇ νίψωνται τὰς χεῖρας οὐκ ἐσθίουσιν 'the Pharisees . . . do not eat unless they wash their hands with the fist' Mk 7.3. In the NT πυγμή occurs only in this very problematic expression in Mk 7.3. Some manuscripts omit πυγμῇ, while others read πυκνά 'often.' A number of translators have attempted to solve the interpretative problem in Mk 7.3 by translating 'unless they wash in the proper manner' or '. . . thoroughly.'

8.36 στῆθος, ους n: the trunk of the body from the neck to the abdomen – 'chest.' περιεζωσμένοι περὶ τὰ στήθη ζώνας χρυσᾶς 'they had gold bands tied around their chests' Re 15.6. In some languages one must distinguish clearly between a term which refers to the entire upper part of the human trunk and that which designates primarily the surface as in Re 15.6.

8.37 μαστός, οῦ m: the breast of both humans and animals, with special reference to the mammary glands – 'breast.' μακαρία ἡ κοιλία ἡ βαστάσασά σε καὶ μαστοὶ οὓς ἐθήλασας 'blessed is the womb that bore you and the breasts which you sucked' Lk 11.27; περιεζωσμένον πρὸς τοῖς μαστοῖς ζώνην χρυσᾶν 'wearing a gold band around his breast' Re 1.13. In Re 1.13 the phrase πρὸς τοῖς μαστοῖς is a reference to the particular location of the gold band which went around the chest and not to the mammary glands as such. In some languages, therefore, it is often preferable to use a phrase such as 'around his chest' rather than trying to be more specific, for example, 'a gold band around his chest at the location of his breasts.'

In translating Lk 11.27 it is important to use an expression which will be perfectly natural, for example, 'the breasts that gave you milk' or 'the breasts from which you obtained milk.' In some instances, however, a specific reference to breasts as the source of milk may seem somewhat vulgar, and therefore it may be better to speak of 'happy is your mother who nursed you.'

8.38 θώραξ [b], ακος m: the portion of the upper trunk covered by the breastplate – 'chest.' εἶχον θώρακας ὡς θώρακας σιδηροῦς 'they had (on) their chests breastplates of iron' or '. . . what looked like breastplates of iron' Re 9.9. Note, however, that in Re 9.9 it is possible to understand the first occurrence of θώραξ in the sense of 'breastplate,' the meaning which it normally has in other biblical contexts (for example, Eph 6.14 and 1 Th 5.8). The passage could then be translated as 'their breastplates were iron breastplates' (see 6.39).

8.39 κόλπος [a], ου m: the region of the body extending from the breast to the legs, especially when a person is in a seated position – 'bosom, lap.' ὁρᾷ 'Αβραὰμ ἀπὸ μακρόθεν καὶ Λάζαρον ἐν τοῖς κόλποις αὐτοῦ 'he saw Abraham far off and Lazarus in his lap' Lk 16.23.

The term κόλπος occurs in several idiomatic phrases in the NT. For example, the expression 'who was in the bosom of the Father' in Jn 1.18 denotes an association of intimacy and affection (see 34.18). In a context referring to the position of a person at a meal (as in Jn 13.23), κόλπος indicates an honored place (see 17.25). In Lk 16.22 κόλπος 'Αβραάμ signifies the heavenly abode (see 1.16).

8.40 νῶτος, ου m: the back part of the body from the neck to the pelvis – 'back.' καὶ τὸν νῶτον αὐτῶν διὰ παντὸς σύγκαμψον 'and bend their backs forever' Ro 11.10. The phrase τὸν νῶτον . . . συγκάμπτειν may be regarded as an idiom, since its meaning may be to suffer oppression and trouble. An equivalent expression for 'and bend their backs forever' (Ro 11.10) may be 'to make them slaves forever' or 'to make them toil hard forever' (see 24.94).

8.41 πλευρά, ᾶς f: either side of the trunk of the body – 'side of the body.' λόγχη αὐτοῦ τὴν πλευρὰν ἔνυξεν 'with his spear he pierced the side' Jn 19.34. In a number of languages it is necessary to be quite specific with regard to the side of the body, since terms differ depending on whether the area involves (1) the ribs, (2) the area between the ribs and the pelvic bone, or (3) the area of the hip, from the fleshy mid-part of the trunk to the leg.

8.42 ὀσφῦς^a, ύος *f*: the part of the human body above the hips and below the ribs, the customary place for tying a belt – 'waist.' ζώνην δερματίνην περὶ τὴν ὀσφὺν αὐτοῦ 'a leather belt around his waist' Mt 3.4. In a number of languages the equivalent of 'waist' is a term meaning literally 'the middle.'

8.43 ὀσφῦς^b, ύος *f*: the male genital organs ('loins' in traditional English translations) – 'genitals, loins.' γὰρ ἐν τῇ ὀσφύϊ τοῦ πατρὸς ἦν 'he was still in the loins of his father' (that is, he was not yet born) He 7.10. A literal rendering of 'he was still in the genitals of his father' (He 7.10) might be regarded in a number of languages as being excessively specific and even vulgar. It is possible to render this passage as simply 'he was not as yet born' or 'his father had not yet caused him to be conceived.' In Ac 2.30 (καρποῦ τῆς ὀσφύος αὐτοῦ 'the fruit of his loins') it may be best to translate 'one of his descendants' (see 10.34).

8.44 οὐρά, ᾶς *f*: tail of an animal or insect – 'tail.' ἔχουσιν οὐρὰς ὁμοίας σκορπίοις 'they have tails like scorpions' Re 9.10. In some languages it may be important to distinguish clearly between the tail of a mammal, a fish, and a creature such as the scorpion.

8.45 κέντρον^a, ου *n*: a sharp, pointed projection used in stinging – 'sting, stinger.' καὶ ἔχουσιν οὐρὰς ὁμοίας σκορπίοις καὶ κέντρα 'and they have tails like scorpions and stingers' Re 9.10.

8.46 σκέλος, ους *n* – 'leg.' ἵνα κατεαγῶσιν αὐτῶν τὰ σκέλη καὶ ἀρθῶσιν 'if they could break their legs and bring them down' Jn 19.31.

8.47 γόνυ^a, γόνατος *n* – 'knee.' προσέπεσεν τοῖς γόνασιν Ἰησοῦ 'he fell on his knees before Jesus' (literally 'he fell at the knees of Jesus') Lk 5.8. In Lk 5.8 the phrase 'fell on his knees before Jesus' should normally not be rendered literally since it might imply accidental stumbling. A more satisfactory equivalent may be 'knelt down before,' as a sign of worship or gratitude.

The term γόνυ occurs in a number of idiomatic phrases in the NT. For example, in He 12.12 the command 'to strengthen the weak knees' should normally not be translated literally, but by an expression meaning 'to strengthen determination' or 'to give courage to' (see 25.152). The 'bending of the knees' in Mk 15.19 was a sign of mock respect, and in such a context the term for 'knee' is often semantically absorbed into an expression meaning literally 'bow down before' (see 53.61).

8.48 μηρός, οῦ *m*: the part of the leg above the knee – 'thigh.' ἐπὶ τὸν μηρὸν αὐτοῦ ὄνομα γεγραμμένον 'a name is inscribed on his thigh' Re 19.16.

8.49 πούς, ποδός *m*; βάσις, εως *f* – 'foot.'
πούς: οὐκ εἰμὶ ἄξιος τὸ ὑπόδημα τῶν ποδῶν λῦσαι 'I am not good enough to take his sandals off his feet' Ac 13.25.
βάσις: ἐστερεώθησαν αἱ βάσεις αὐτοῦ 'his feet became strong' Ac 3.7. βάσις is a more technical term for the foot than is πούς.

In Re 10.1 (οἱ πόδες αὐτοῦ ὡς στῦλοι πυρός 'his feet were like pillars of fire') it is possible that πούς refers to the leg since the context of Re 10.1 would seem to favor this interpretation, but the meaning of 'foot' should not be excluded, especially since this passage refers to an image as part of a supernatural vision, and one cannot be certain of the specific intent.

8.50 πεζῇ: (derivative of πεζός 'on foot,' not occurring in the NT) pertaining to travel by foot overland – 'on foot, by land.' οἱ ὄχλοι ἠκολούθησαν αὐτῷ πεζῇ 'the crowds followed him by land' or '. . . on foot' Mt 14.13. In some languages a more appropriate rendering might be 'followed him by walking.'[8]

8.51 σφυδρόν, οῦ *n*: the joint connecting the foot to the leg – 'ankle.' ἐστερεώθησαν αἱ βάσεις αὐτοῦ καὶ τὰ σφυδρά 'his feet and ankles became strong' Ac 3.7.

---

8 Though the more specific reference of πεζῇ is the feet as a means of movement, it would be possible to classify πεζῇ as a particular type of movement in Domain 15 *Linear Movement*.

8.52 πτέρνα, ης *f* – 'heel.' πτέρνα occurs in the NT only in Jn 13.18 (ὁ τρώγων μου τὸν ἄρτον ἐπῆρεν ἐπ' ἐμὲ τὴν πτέρναν αὐτοῦ 'the one eating my bread has raised his heel against me') in an idiomatic expression denoting antagonism and opposition (see 39.3).

8.53 χρώς, χρωτός *m*: skin or surface of the human body – 'skin, surface of the body.' ἐπὶ τοὺς ἀσθενοῦντας ἀποφέρεσθαι ἀπὸ τοῦ χρωτὸς αὐτοῦ σουδάρια ἢ σιμικίνθια 'handkerchiefs or aprons from his body were carried to the sick' Ac 19.12. In a number of languages a clear distinction must be made between the skin of an animal and the skin of a human being. A further distinction is often made between skin as a part of a living animal or human and skin which has been removed from the body and presumably made into leather (see δέρμα, 6.184).

8.54 ῥυτίς, ίδος *f*: lines or creases in the skin – 'wrinkle.'[9] μὴ ἔχουσαν σπίλον ἢ ῥυτίδα 'not having a spot or wrinkle' Eph 5.27. In Eph 5.27 ῥυτίς is used symbolically as a type of imperfection, but in some languages wrinkles can be an evidence of age and therefore of seniority and even wisdom.

8.55 στίγμα[a], τος *n*: a permanent mark or scar on the body, especially the type of 'brand' used to mark ownership of slaves – 'scar, brand.'[10] ἐγὼ γὰρ τὰ στίγματα τοῦ Ἰησοῦ ἐν τῷ σώματί μου βαστάζω 'for I bear the marks of Jesus in my body' Ga 6.17. In Ga 6.17 Paul is most likely alluding to scars resulting from wounds received in the service of Jesus, but στίγμα may also imply ownership and hence suggest that such scars served as brands (see 8.56). For other interpretations of στίγμα in Ga 6.17, see 33.481 and 90.84.

8.56 τύπος[a], ου *m*: a visible impression or trace made as the result of a blow or pressure

– 'scar, wound.'[10] ἐὰν μὴ ἴδω ἐν ταῖς χερσὶν αὐτοῦ τὸν τύπον τῶν ἥλων 'if I do not see the scars of the nails in his hands' Jn 20.25.

Though both στίγμα[a] (8.55) and τύπος[a] may mean scars, there are significant differences in meaning. στίγμα[a] bears the connotation of brand or mark of ownership, while τύπος[a] indicates a wound or scar resulting from the shape and form of some object, for example, nails in the case of Jn 20.25.

8.57 λεπίς, ίδος *f*: a thin layer or peel, especially of skin – 'flake, scale.'[11] ἀπέπεσαν αὐτοῦ ἀπὸ τῶν ὀφθαλμῶν ὡς λεπίδες 'something like scales fell from his eyes' Ac 9.18. In rendering Ac 9.18 it is possible to say 'there fell from his eyes something which looked like a fish scale' or '. . . a small flake of skin.'

8.58 σπλάγχνα[a], ων *n* (only in the plural): the inner parts of the body, especially the intestines – 'intestines.' ἐξεχύθη πάντα τὰ σπλάγχνα αὐτοῦ 'all of his intestines gushed out' Ac 1.18.

8.59 ἀρμός, οῦ *m*: a part of the body which joins two parts together – 'joint.' διϊκνούμενος ἄχρι μερισμοῦ . . . ἀρμῶν τε καὶ μυελῶν 'piercing to the separation . . . of joints and marrow' He 4.12. In the use of ἀρμός the emphasis is not upon the joints as a moving part of the body but as a means by which different parts of the body are effectively joined together. Accordingly, ἀρμός overlaps in meaning with ἀφή (8.60) and σύνδεσμος[a] (18.17). For problems in translating He 4.12, see 8.62.

8.60 ἀφή, ῆς *f*: part of the joints of the body which binds the different parts together – 'ligament, that which binds together.' τὸ σῶμα συναρμολογούμενον καὶ συμβιβαζόμενον διὰ πάσης ἀφῆς 'the body joined and held together

---

9 It would also be possible to classify ῥυτίς 'wrinkle' in Domain 79 *Features of Objects*.

10 Properly speaking, στίγμα[a] (8.55) and τύπος[a] (8.56) are not body parts, but may refer to features of the body which result from some external force or object and could accordingly be classified in Domain 19 *Physical*

Impact. They are, however, included at this point because they may refer to types of scars, which become a permanent feature of the body.

11 On the basis of the extrabiblical usage of λεπίς, one could classify its meaning in Domain 79 *Features of Objects.*

with every ligament' Eph 4.16. In some languages the ligaments may be spoken of as 'the ropes of the body' or 'the strings of the body.'

8.61 ὀστοῦν, οῦ *n* or ὀστέον, ου *n* – 'bone.' ὅτι πνεῦμα σάρκα καὶ ὀστέα οὐκ ἔχει 'because a spirit does not have flesh and bones' Lk 24.39.

In some languages a distinction is made between bones as a part of a living body and bones from which the meat has been removed, for example, the bones of a skeleton. Note, for example, the reference to τὰ ὀστέα as the bones of Joseph in He 11.22.

8.62 μυελός, οῦ *m*: the soft material that fills the cavity in the bones – 'marrow.' δι-ϊκνούμενος ἄχρι μερισμοῦ . . . ἁρμῶν τε καὶ μυελῶν 'piercing to the separation . . . of joints and marrow' or 'piercing to where the joints and marrow come together' He 4.12. There are certain problems, however, involved in the rendering of He 4.12, for strictly speaking there is no one point at which joints and marrow may be separated. Similarly, the expression 'to where joints and marrow come together' seems rather anomalous, since the joints bring together various bones, but they are not joined together with marrow. This passage in He 4.12 is essentially figurative in that it is speaking of the word of God being sharper than a two-edged sword cutting all the way through to where soul and spirit meet, and this is described as being parallel to where 'joints and marrow come together.' Perhaps one can best state this in some languages as 'to where the joints and the marrow are,' thus suggesting that part of the human body farthest from the surface.

8.63 σάρξ ᵃ, σαρκός *f*: the flesh of both animals and human beings – 'flesh.' δεῦτε . . . ἵνα φάγητε σάρκας βασιλέων . . . καὶ σάρκας ἵππων 'come . . . and eat the flesh of kings . . . and the flesh of horses' Re 19.17-18. Some languages, however, make an important distinction between the flesh of a living person and the flesh of someone who has been killed or who has died. It would be this latter sense which should be reflected in Re 19.18.

In Ro 2.28 the reference to 'circumcision in the flesh' (ἐν σαρκὶ περιτομή) would, however, require the first sense, namely, the flesh of a living person.

8.64 αἷμα ᵃ, τος *n* – 'blood.' γυνὴ οὖσα ἐν ῥύσει αἵματος δώδεκα ἔτη 'a woman who had had a flow of blood for twelve years' Mk 5.25. In Mk 5.25 it may be important to use a special term for blood, since this passage is a reference to the hemorrhaging of menstruation.

In Jn 19.34 (ἐξῆλθεν εὐθὺς αἷμα καὶ ὕδωρ 'then blood and water came out') it may be necessary to use a term which can refer to the lymph fluid rather than to water itself; otherwise the reader might understand the water as being urine (with the spear having pierced the bladder) or even possibly water that Jesus had presumably drunk and was still in his stomach. The real reference of ὕδωρ in Jn 19.34 is to the lymph fluid and not to water as such. It is simply a colorless fluid which was mixed with blood.

In Re 8.8 (καὶ ἐγένετο τὸ τρίτον τῆς θαλάσσης αἷμα 'and a third of the sea became blood') and Re 11.6 (καὶ ἐξουσίαν ἔχουσιν ἐπὶ τῶν ὑδάτων στρέφειν αὐτὰ εἰς αἷμα 'and they had power over the waters to turn them into blood') the reference may not be to blood as a substance but to the blood-like color of the objects in question.

8.65 θρόμβος, ου *m*: a small amount of blood in coagulated form – 'clot of blood, drop of blood.' καὶ ἐγένετο ὁ ἱδρὼς αὐτοῦ ὡσεὶ θρόμβοι αἵματος 'and his sweat became like clots of blood' Lk 22.44.

8.66 στόμαχος, ου *m*: the upper part of the digestive tract, especially the stomach – 'stomach.' οἴνῳ ὀλίγῳ χρῶ διὰ τὸν στόμαχον 'take a little wine for the sake of your stomach' 1 Tm 5.23. In 1 Tm 5.23 it may, however, be useful in some languages to translate 'a little wine for the sake of your digestion' or '. . . in order to help your digestion.'

8.67 κοιλία ᵃ, ας *f*: the entire digestive apparatus, including stomach and intestines – 'belly, internal organs.' τὰ βρώματα τῇ κοιλίᾳ καὶ ἡ κοιλία τοῖς βρώμασιν 'food is for the belly, and the belly for food' 1 Cor 6.13.

8.68 γαστήρᵃ, **τρός** f: the inward parts of the body, either the digestive system (as in γαστέρες ἀργαί, literally 'lazy bellies,' but meaning 'gluttons' Tt 1.12) or the womb (in set phrases such as συλλαμβάνω ἐν γαστρί 'to conceive' Lk 1.31; ἐν γαστρὶ ἔχω 'be pregnant' Mt 1.18 and elsewhere) – 'belly, stomach, womb.' See also 23.19, 23.49, and 23.50.

8.69 κοιλίαᵇ, **ας** f; **μήτρα, ας** f: the uterus – 'womb.'
κοιλίαᵇ: μὴ δύναται εἰς τὴν κοιλίαν τῆς μητρὸς αὐτοῦ δεύτερον εἰσελθεῖν 'he cannot enter into his mother's womb a second time' Jn 3.4.
μήτρα: πᾶν ἄρσεν διανοῖγον μήτραν 'every male that opens the womb' Lk 2.23. For the total expression as an idiom, see 10.45. Rarely can one translate literally Lk 2.23 as 'every male that opens the womb,' since this is likely to refer to an adult male who first has sexual intercourse with a woman. The reference in Lk 2.23 is, of course, to the first male child which is born to a woman, and therefore an appropriate equivalent in many languages is 'a woman's first baby if it is a boy.'

C Physiological Products of the Body (8.70-8.77)

8.70 ἐξέραμα, τος n: the contents of the stomach ejected through the mouth – 'vomit.' κύων ἐπιστρέψας ἐπὶ τὸ ἴδιον ἐξέραμα 'a dog goes back to its own vomit' 2 Pe 2.22. In a number of languages the equivalent of 'vomit' is a descriptive phrase based upon a verb describing the process of vomiting, for example, 'that which is vomited' or 'food that flows out of the mouth from the stomach.'

8.71 πτύσμα, τος n: the watery fluid in the mouth – 'spit, saliva.' ἔπτυσεν χαμαὶ ἐποίησεν πηλὸν ἐκ τοῦ πτύσματος 'he spat on the ground and made mud from the saliva' Jn 9.6.

8.72 ἱδρώς, ῶτος m: the watery fluid excreted through the pores of the skin – 'sweat.' ἐγένετο ὁ ἱδρὼς αὐτοῦ ὡσεὶ θρόμβοι αἵματος 'his sweat was like drops of blood' Lk 22.44.

8.73 δάκρυον, ου n: the watery fluid which flows from the eye – 'tear.' ἐξαλείψει ὁ θεὸς πᾶν δάκρυον ἐκ τῶν ὀφθαλμῶν αὐτῶν 'God shall wipe away every tear from their eyes' Re 7.17.

8.74 ἰός, οῦ m: the poisonous secretion of some animals – 'venom, poison' (used especially of the venom of snakes). ἰὸς ἀσπίδων ὑπὸ τὰ χείλη αὐτῶν 'the poison of asps is under their lips' Ro 3.13.

8.75 χολή, ῆς f: the bitter yellowish liquid secreted by the liver and stored in the gall bladder – 'gall.' οἶνον μετὰ χολῆς μεμιγμένον 'wine mixed with gall' Mt 27.34. It is possible, however, that in Mt 27.34 the reference is not specifically to gall but to a substance with an especially unpleasant taste.

8.76 κόπριον, ου n: fecal matter used as agricultural fertilizer – 'manure, dung.' σκάφω περὶ αὐτὴν καὶ βάλω κόπρια 'I will dig around it and put on manure' Lk 13.8. In some languages a distinction is made in terminology between fresh dung and manure which has been piled up in order to mature properly as fertilizer. It would no doubt be this latter meaning which would be involved in Lk 13.8.

8.77 κοπρία, ας f: (derivative of κόπριον 'manure,' 8.76) a pile or heap of manure – 'manure pile, dung heap.' οὔτε εἰς γῆν οὔτε εἰς κοπρίαν εὔθετόν ἐστιν 'it is of no use to the soil, not even to the dung heap' Lk 14.35.

9 People[1]

Outline of Subdomains

A Human Beings (9.1-9.23)
B Males (9.24-9.33)
C Females (9.34-9.40)
D Children (9.41-9.45)
E Persons For Whom There Is Affectionate Concern (9.46-9.48)

A Human Beings (9.1-9.23)

9.1 ἄνθρωπος^a, ου *m*; ἀνήρ^b, ἀνδρός *m*: a human being (normally an adult) – (in the singular) 'person, human being, individual,' (in the plural) 'people, persons, mankind.'
ἄνθρωπος^a: σὺ ἄνθρωπος ὢν ποιεῖς σεαυτὸν θεόν 'you are only a human being, but you make yourself God' Jn 10.33; κρίνει ὁ θεὸς τὰ κρυπτὰ τῶν ἀνθρώπων 'God will judge the secret thoughts of people' Ro 2.16.
ἀνήρ^b: μακάριος ἀνὴρ οὗ οὐ μὴ λογίσηται κύριος ἁμαρτίαν 'happy is the person to whom the Lord does not reckon sin' Ro 4.8. The parallelism in this quotation from Ps 32.1-2 indicates clearly that the reference of ἀνήρ is not a particular male but any person.
In Mt 14.35 (ἐπιγνόντες αὐτὸν οἱ ἄνδρες τοῦ τόπου ἐκείνου 'when the people of that place recognized him') one may argue that οἱ ἄνδρες refers specifically to males, but the context would seem to indicate that the reference is to people in general. In translation a pronominal expression may frequently be employed when ἀνήρ^b occurs in the text, for example, 'when those who lived in that place recognized him.'
It is not uncommon in languages for a term which is often used to refer to an adult male to be employed also in a generic sense of 'person.' This is especially true when such terms are used in the plural form.

1 The domain of *People* includes all those meanings which are used to refer to individuals, while groups and members of groups are considered in Domain 11. The domain of *People* is divided into a generic Subdomain *Human Beings,* followed by Subdomains *Males, Females, Children,* and *Persons For Whom There Is Affectionate Concern.* In general, sex and age grading are the most conspicuous distinctions employed in differentiating meanings relating to human beings.

In a number of instances, generic meanings of receptor languages have not been recognized as such, since translators have assumed that such receptor-language terms refer only to members of a particular tribe or group (because they have been found only in specific contexts), while in reality such terms often designate people in general. One must, however, be on the alert for seemingly generic terms which refer only to the so-called 'ingroup,' that is to say, members of a particular tribe, society, or community.

9.2 υἱοὶ τῶν ἀνθρώπων: (a Semitic idiom, literally 'sons of men') human beings (equivalent in denotative meaning to ἄνθρωπος^a, 9.1) – 'people, mankind.' πάντα ἀφεθήσεται τοῖς υἱοῖς τῶν ἀνθρώπων τὰ ἁμαρτήματα 'people will be forgiven all their sins' Mk 3.28. It is rare indeed that one can reproduce literally the Semitic phrase 'sons of men,' since the expression is likely to be interpreted as relating only to the male offspring of fathers.

9.3 υἱὸς τοῦ ἀνθρώπου: a title with Messianic implications used by Jesus concerning himself – 'Son of Man.' ὁ δὲ υἱὸς τοῦ ἀνθρώπου οὐκ ἔχει ποῦ τὴν κεφαλὴν κλίνη 'but the Son of Man does not have a place to lay down his head' Mt 8.20; ὥστε κύριός ἐστιν ὁ υἱὸς τοῦ ἀνθρώπου καὶ τοῦ σαββάτου 'so that the Son of Man is Lord even over the Sabbath' Mk 2.28. This title 'Son of Man' served not only to affirm but also to hide Christ's Messianic role.
In a number of languages there are serious complications involved in a literal translation of υἱὸς τοῦ ἀνθρώπου 'Son of Man.' In the first place, this is likely to be understood in a more or less literal sense of 'son of a man' and thus a denial of the virgin birth. Such is particularly true in languages which have two words for 'son,' one meaning 'son of a man' and the other, 'son of a woman.' Under such circumstances, a literal translation would be a clear denial of the virgin birth.

9.4 υἱός^e . . . (followed by the genitive of class or kind): a person of a class or kind, specified by the following genitive construction – 'son of ..., person of ..., one who is ...' οἱ υἱοὶ ὑμῶν 'your sons' (referring to those like the Pharisees) Mt 12.27; υἱὲ διαβόλου 'you son of the Devil' Ac 13.10; οἱ υἱοὶ τοῦ αἰῶνος τούτου 'sons of this age' Lk 16.8; υἱὸν γεέννης 'son of Gehenna' Mt 23.15; υἱοὶ βροντῆς 'sons of thunder' Mk 3.17. For a discussion of υἱὸς τοῦ θεοῦ, see 12.15.

In most languages it is difficult, if not impossible, to represent adequately the meaning of such expressions consisting of the formula 'son of ...' without making some significant adjustments. For example, 'your sons' in Mt 12.27 may be rendered as 'your followers.' In Ac 13.10 'son of the Devil' may be rendered as 'you are like the Devil,' while in Lk 16.8 'sons of this age' may be readily translated as 'people who are typical of this age.' In Mt 23.15 'son of Gehenna' may be rendered as 'you who deserve to go to hell,' and in Mk 3.17 'sons of thunder' may be rendered as 'men who are like thunder' or 'thunderous persons.' For idiomatic expressions involving 'sons of ...,' see 11.13, 11.14, and 11.16.

9.5 χεὶρ ἀνθρωπίνη: (an idiom, literally 'human hand') a human being as a means of accomplishing something – 'person, people.' οὐδὲ ὑπὸ χειρῶν ἀνθρωπίνων θεραπεύεται προσδεόμενός τινος 'he does not need anything that people can supply by working for him' Ac 17.25.

9.6 ἀνθρώπινος, η, ον: (derivative of ἄνθρωπος[a] 'people,' 9.1) pertaining to being a person – 'human, of people.' λαλοῦμεν οὐκ ἐν διδακτοῖς ἀνθρωπίνης σοφίας λόγοις 'we do not speak in words taught by human wisdom' 1 Cor 2.13. Many languages, however, lack an adjectival form equivalent to 'human,' and therefore one may speak of 'human wisdom' as being 'wisdom that people have.' At the same time, languages may actually lack an abstract term such as 'wisdom,' and therefore it may be necessary to translate 'taught by human wisdom' as 'taught by those people who are wise.'

9.7 ἐπίγειος, ον: pertaining to human, earthly activity (primarily in contrast with divine activity) – 'human, of people.' οὐκ ἔστιν αὕτη ἡ σοφία ἄνωθεν κατερχομένη, ἀλλὰ ἐπίγειος 'this kind of wisdom does not come from God; it is characteristic of people' or 'this is the kind of wisdom that people produce' Jas 3.15.

9.8 σῶμα[b], τος n: (a figurative extension of meaning of σῶμα[a] 'body,' 8.1) a person as a physical being, including natural desires – 'self, physical being.'[2] ἵνα καταργηθῇ τὸ σῶμα τῆς ἁμαρτίας 'in order that our physical beings, which are prone to sin, might be rendered powerless' Ro 6.6.

9.9 πρόσωπον[b], ου n (a figurative extension of meaning of πρόσωπον[a] 'face,' 8.18) – 'person, individual.' ἵνα ἐκ πολλῶν προσώπων ... εὐχαριστηθῇ ὑπὲρ ἡμῶν 'in order that ... thanksgiving for us may be expressed ... by many people' or 'in order that many ... may express thanks to God for us' 2 Cor 1.11.

9.10 τέλειος[f], α, ον: pertaining to an adult human being – 'grown person, adult.' τελείων δέ ἐστιν ἡ στερεὰ τροφή 'but solid food is for adults' He 5.14. Though in He 5.14 τέλειος is to be understood in a literal sense, the context as a whole is figurative.

9.11 σάρξ[c], σαρκός f: (a figurative extension of meaning of σάρξ[a] 'flesh,' 8.63) humans as physical beings – 'people, human being.' πᾶσα σὰρξ ὡς χόρτος 'all people are like grass' 1 Pe 1.24; ὁ λόγος σὰρξ ἐγένετο 'the Word became a human being' Jn 1.14.

9.12 σάρξ[d], σαρκός f: (a figurative extension of meaning of σάρξ[a] 'flesh,' 8.63) human nature, with emphasis upon the physical aspects – 'physical nature, human.' εἶτα τοὺς μὲν τῆς σαρκὸς ἡμῶν πατέρας 'in the case of our human fathers' He 12.9. In a number of languages it would seem strange, if not totally redundant, to speak of 'physical fathers' or 'human fathers,' since the term 'fathers'

---

2 σῶμα[b] is very similar in meaning to σάρξ[f] (26.7) in that both denote human nature. There are, however, certain connotative differences in meaning in that σάρξ[f] seems to focus more upon the purely physical desires of human nature, with the possible implication of greater emphasis upon normal sexual impulses.

would suffice, and any addition would be misleading. In some instances, however, one might use an expression such as 'our own fathers,' so as to provide an implied contrast with the heavenly Father. Where it is necessary to qualify the term 'fathers,' one may use an expression such as 'fathers which caused us to be conceived.'

9.13 σάρκινοςᵃ, η, ον: (derivative of σάρξᶜ 'people,' 9.11) pertaining to physical human beings – 'human, of people.' ὃς οὐ κατὰ νόμον ἐντολῆς σαρκίνης γέγονεν 'he was not made (a priest) by the rules of human regulations' He 7.16. In He 7.16 the phrase 'human regulations' can be rendered as 'regulations made by people.' For another interpretation of σάρκινος in He 7.16, see 26.8.

9.14 σὰρξ καὶ αἷμα: (an idiom, literally 'flesh and blood') a human being in contrast with a divine being – 'person, human being.' σὰρξ καὶ αἷμα οὐκ ἀπεκάλυψέν σοι 'it was not revealed to you by any human being' or 'no person ever revealed it to you' Mt 16.17.

9.15 κοινωνέω αἵματος καὶ σαρκός: (an idiom, literally 'to share blood and flesh') to have the characteristics and nature of a human being – 'to be a person, to be a physical being.' ἐπεὶ οὖν τὰ παιδία κεχοινώνηκεν αἵματος καὶ σαρκός 'since then the children are human beings' He 2.14.

9.16 γόνυᵇ, γόνατος n: (a figurative extension of meaning of γόνυᵃ 'knee,' 8.47) a person in the attitude or position of one worshiping or submitting to authority – 'person, individual.' ἐν τῷ ὀνόματι Ἰησοῦ πᾶν γόνυ κάμψῃ 'at the name of Jesus every person shall bow' Php 2.10.

9.17 χείρᵇ, χειρός f: (a figurative extension of meaning of χείρᵃ 'hand,' 8.30) a human as an agent in some activity – 'person, agent.' οὐχὶ ἡ χείρ μου ἐποίησεν ταῦτα πάντα; 'did not I myself make all these things?' Ac 7.50.

9.18 γλῶσσαᵍ, ης f: (a figurative extension of meaning of γλῶσσαᵃ 'tongue,' 8.21) a person as one who utters something – 'person, indi-

vidual.'[3] καὶ πᾶσα γλῶσσα ἐξομολογήσηται ὅτι κύριος Ἰησοῦς Χριστός 'and every person will confess that Jesus Christ is Lord' Php 2.11.

9.19 ὄνομαᵇ, τος n: (a figurative extension of meaning of ὄνομαᵃ 'name,' 33.126) a person, with the possible implication of existence or relevance as individuals – 'person, people.' ὄχλος ὀνομάτων ἐπὶ τὸ αὐτὸ ὡσεὶ ἑκατὸν εἴκοσι 'a gathering of about one hundred and twenty people' Ac 1.15. In some instances ἄνθρωποςᵃ 'people' (9.1) occurs together with ὄνομαᵇ without any significant distinction in meaning: ὀνόματα ἀνθρώπων χιλιάδες ἑπτά 'seven thousand people' Re 11.13.[4] See also 9.20.

9.20 ψυχήᶜ, ῆς f: (a figurative extension of meaning of ψυχήᵃ 'inner self, mind,' 26.4) a person as a living being – 'person, people.' ψυχαὶ ὡσεὶ τρισχίλιαι 'about three thousand people' Ac 2.41. As in the case of ὄνομαᵇ (9.19), ἄνθρωποςᵃ (9.1) may occur with ψυχήᶜ: πᾶσαν ψυχὴν ἀνθρώπου 'every person' Ro 2.9.

9.21 σκεῦοςᵈ, ους n: (a figurative extension of meaning of σκεῦοςᵃ 'object, instrument, thing,' 6.1) a person in relation to a particular function or role – 'person.' πορεύου, ὅτι σκεῦος ἐκλογῆς ἐστίν μοι οὗτος 'go, for he is a person I have chosen' or '. . . a person whom I have chosen for a particular task' Ac 9.15.

9.22 οἰκουμένηᶜ, ης f; **γῆ**ᶜ, γῆς f: (figurative extensions of meaning of οἰκουμένηᵃ 'inhabited earth,' 1.39, and of γῆᵃ 'earth,' 1.39, respectively) all people who dwell on the earth – 'people, all mankind.'
οἰκουμένηᶜ: ἔστησεν ἡμέραν ἐν ᾗ μέλλει κρίνειν τὴν οἰκουμένην 'he has fixed a day in which he will judge all mankind' Ac 17.31.
γῆᶜ: ὑμεῖς ἐστε τὸ ἅλας τῆς γῆς 'you are like salt for all mankind' Mt 5.13.

---

3 In this subdomain (*Human Beings*) a number of expressions referring to people are based upon metonymies involving terms for parts or aspects of persons. Such metonymic figures of speech are involved in σὰρξ καὶ αἷμα (9.14), γόνυᵇ (9.16), χείρᵇ (9.17), γλῶσσαᵍ (9.18), ὄνομαᵇ (9.19), and ψυχήᶜ (9.20).
4 In Re 11.13 ἀνθρώπων may be regarded as a type of semantic classifier.

9.23 κόσμος^d, ου *m*: (a figurative extension of meaning of κόσμος^a 'cosmos, universe,' 1.1) people associated with a world system and estranged from God – 'people of the world.' οὐκ οἴδατε ὅτι οἱ ἅγιοι τὸν κόσμον κρινοῦσιν 'don't you know that God's people will judge the people of the world' 1 Cor 6.2.[5]

B Males (9.24-9.33)

Languages employ a number of different terms for the age-grading of males. Some of the most common distinctions involve the following: (1) male baby boys up to the time of weaning; (2) boys from the age of weaning to the time of puberty rites, when they are recognized as being sexually capable; (3) from puberty to the time of marriage; (4) from marriage until they cease to engage in normal military or work pursuits; and (5) old age, from the time of retirement from active responsibilities and work until the time of death.

9.24 ἄνθρωπος^b, ου *m*; ἀνήρ^a, ἀνδρός *m*: an adult male person of marriageable age – 'man.'[6]

ἄνθρωπος^b: ἄνθρωπον κατὰ τοῦ πατρὸς αὐτοῦ καὶ θυγατέρα κατὰ τῆς μητρὸς αὐτῆς 'a man against his father and a daughter against her mother' Mt 10.35; εἰ οὕτως ἐστὶν ἡ αἰτία τοῦ ἀνθρώπου μετὰ τῆς γυναικός 'if this is how it is between a man and his wife' Mt 19.10.

ἀνήρ^a: ὅτε γέγονα ἀνήρ, κατήργηκα τὰ τοῦ νηπίου 'now that I am a man, I am finished with childish things' 1 Cor 13.11. In some languages the equivalent of 'now that I am a man' is 'now that I am grown' or 'now that I have become strong.'

9.25 εὐνοῦχος^a, ου *m*: a castrated male person – 'eunuch.'[7] εἰσὶν εὐνοῦχοι οἵτινες εὐνουχίσ-θησαν ὑπὸ τῶν ἀνθρώπων 'there are eunuchs who have been made eunuchs by people' Mt 19.12b.

In the ancient Middle East eunuchs were frequently in charge of royal harems and sometimes rose to high positions of state. The reference to the eunuch in Ac 8.34 is best interpreted as 'court official' (see 37.85).

Since in many societies castration of human males is not known, any attempt to employ a descriptive explanation within the text might seem unnecessarily crude and even vulgar. A number of translators have therefore preferred to borrow a term for eunuch and then place the explanation of its meaning in a glossary or word list.

9.26 εὐνουχίζω^a: (derivative of εὐνοῦχος^a 'eunuch,' 9.25) to cause a person to be a eunuch – 'to make a eunuch, to castrate.' οἵτινες εὐνουχίσθησαν ὑπὸ τῶν ἀνθρώπων 'men who have been castrated by people' Mt 19.12. Sometimes one may render εὐνουχίζω as 'to cause a person not to be able to have marital relations.'

In a number of languages the castration of a man is referred to by a term very different from what is employed in the case of the castration of an animal.

9.27 εὐνουχίζω^b (used with a reflexive pronoun): to live without engaging in sexual relations – 'to be celibate, to live without marrying.' οἵτινες εὐνούχισαν ἑαυτοὺς διὰ τὴν βασιλείαν τῶν οὐρανῶν 'there are men who do not marry for the sake of the kingdom of heaven' Mt 19.12.

9.28 εὐνοῦχος^b, ου *m*: a human male who without being castrated is by nature incapable of sexual intercourse – 'impotent male.'[7] εἰσὶν γὰρ εὐνοῦχοι οἵτινες ἐκ κοιλίας μητρὸς ἐγεννήθησαν οὕτως 'for there are impotent males who have been so from birth' Mt 19.12.

---

5 It is possible to understand κόσμος in 1 Cor 6.2 as referring to all mankind, but in view of certain contrasts which are implied in this context, it seems more satisfactory to understand κόσμος in a more limited sense of 'people of the world.'
6 It is possible that ἄνθρωπος^b differs somewhat from ἀνήρ^a in connotation, since ἄνθρωπος^b would perhaps be somewhat more generic in implications.
7 It would be possible to treat εὐνοῦχος^{a, b, c} (9.25, 28, 29) as identifying various physiological states resulting from the different processes or states referred to by the verb εὐνουχίζω (9.26 and 9.27), but since εὐνοῦχος is frequently used absolutely in various senses, these three meanings seem best classified under the subdomain of *Males*.

9.29 εὐνοῦχος ᶜ, ου *m*: a male person who abstains from marriage without being necessarily impotent – 'celibate.'[7] εἰσὶν εὐνοῦχοι οἵτινες εὐνούχισαν ἑαυτοὺς διὰ τὴν βασιλείαν τῶν οὐρανῶν 'there are men who are celibate who do not marry for the sake of the kingdom of heaven' Mt 19.12.

9.30 γέρων, οντος *m*: an adult male, with emphasis upon relatively advanced age – 'grown man, old man.' πῶς δύναται ἄνθρωπος γεννηθῆναι γέρων ὤν 'how can a man be born when he is an old man' Jn 3.4.

9.31 πρεσβύτης, ου *m*; πρεσβύτερος ᵃ, ου *m*: an adult male advanced in years – 'old man.'[8]
πρεσβύτης: ἐγὼ γάρ εἰμι πρεσβύτης καὶ ἡ γυνή μου προβεβηκυῖα ἐν ταῖς ἡμέραις αὐτῆς 'I am an old man and my wife also is advanced in years' Lk 1.18.
πρεσβύτερος ᵃ: οἱ πρεσβύτεροι ὑμῶν ἐνυπνίοις ἐνυπνιασθήσονται 'your old men will dream dreams' Ac 2.17.

9.32 νεανίσκος, ου *m*; νεανίας, ου *m*: a young man beyond the age of puberty, but normally before marriage – 'young man.'
νεανίσκος: νεανίσκος τις συνηκολούθει αὐτῷ περιβεβλημένος σινδόνα 'a young man dressed in a linen cloth was following Jesus' Mk 14.51.
νεανίας: καθεζόμενος δέ τις νεανίας ὀνόματι Εὔτυχος ἐπὶ τῆς θυρίδος 'a young man named Eutychus was sitting in the window' Ac 20.9. The person referred to as a νεανίας in Ac 20.9 is called a παῖς 'boy' (see 9.41) in Ac 20.12. This should not be understood as identity in meaning, since the person concerned could have been of such an age that either 'young man' or 'boy' was a possible denotation. In other words, the age reference of νεανίας and παῖς overlaps in Greek. In a number of languages, however, there is a much more specific and clear-cut distinction in age grading.

9.33 παρθένος ᵇ, ου *m*: an adult male who has not engaged in sexual relations with a woman

– 'virgin, chaste.' οὗτοί εἰσιν οἳ μετὰ γυναικῶν οὐκ ἐμολύνθησαν, παρθένοι γάρ εἰσιν 'these are men who have not defiled themselves with women, for they are virgins' Re 14.4. It is very rare that the same term can be applied to a man who has not engaged in sexual relations with a woman as is used in speaking of a woman who has not had sexual relations with a man. In fact, in English the use of 'virgin' as applied to a man seems strange. In many languages there is simply no term for a man who is a virgin, since such a state is regarded as being rather unthinkable. However, the first part of this statement in Re 14.4 indicates clearly the state of the persons in question. But if one does attempt to find a satisfactory term, it is important to determine whether such a word implies homosexuality, for this tends to be the case in some languages. See also comments at 9.39.

C Females (9.34-9.40)

In most languages terms for the age-grading of females parallel quite closely those relating to males. The principal distinctions in age include (1) girl babies before the age of weaning; (2) from weaning to puberty; (3) from puberty to marriage; (4) from marriage to menopause; and (5) after menopause.

9.34 γυνή ᵃ, αικός *f*: an adult female person of marriageable age – 'woman.' δεσμεύων καὶ παραδιδοὺς εἰς φυλακὰς ἄνδρας τε καὶ γυναῖκας 'I arrested men and women and threw them into prison' Ac 22.4. In some languages it may be awkward to speak of 'arresting men and women,' since it is normal in such languages to speak of 'men and women' simply as 'people.' However, where the distinction of 'men and women' can be employed, it should be done, since the arresting of women for presumed heresy in NT times would seem far less justified than the arresting of men, who were supposed to take a more active part in new movements and thus were more likely to be arraigned before authorities.

As a form of address, γυνή was used in Koine Greek in speaking politely to a female person: ὦ γύναι, μεγάλη σου ἡ πίστις 'Lady, your faith is great' Mt 15.28. In Jn 2.4 Jesus

---

8 πρεσβύτης and πρεσβύτερος ᵃ may differ somewhat in connotation from γέρων 'grown man' (9.30) in the implication of greater status or dignity.

uses γυνή to address his mother courteously. In a number of languages it would be totally impossible to have Jesus address his mother merely as 'woman.' To do so in some languages would imply that Jesus was denying that Mary was his mother. In other languages, such an expression would imply that Jesus was calling his mother a prostitute or evil person. Accordingly, in a number of languages there is simply no other way in which Jesus could address his mother than as 'mother' or 'my mother.'

9.35 γυναικάριον, ου *n*: (a diminutive, pejorative derivative of γυνή[a] 'woman,' 9.34) an adult woman of foolish and/or frivolous character – 'foolish woman, frivolous woman.' εἰσιν οἱ ἐνδύνοντες εἰς τὰς οἰκίας καὶ αἰχμαλωτίζοντες γυναικάρια 'they go into homes and get control over frivolous women' 2 Tm 3.6.

9.36 γυναικεῖος, α, ον: (derivative of γυνή[a] 'woman,' 9.34) pertaining to being a woman – 'woman, female, of women.' ὡς ἀσθενεστέρῳ σκεύει τῷ γυναικείῳ ἀπονέμοντες τιμήν 'giving honor to the female as the weaker sex' 1 Pe 3.7.

9.37 πρεσβῦτις, ιδος *f*: an adult female advanced in years – 'old woman.' πρεσβύτιδας ὡσαύτως ἐν καταστήματι ἱεροπρεπεῖς 'the older women also should lead a holy life' Tt 2.3.

9.38 γραώδης, ες: (derivative of γραῦς 'old woman,' not occurring in the NT) characteristic of old women – 'like old women say, like old women do.' τοὺς δὲ βεβήλους καὶ γραώδεις μύθους παραιτοῦ 'keep away from godless myths such as old women are likely to tell' or 'keep away from godless and useless legends' 1 Tm 4.7.

9.39 παρθένος[a], ου *f*: a female person beyond puberty but not yet married and a virgin (though in some contexts virginity is not a focal component of meaning) – 'virgin, young woman.' ἡ παρθένος ἐν γαστρὶ ἕξει 'a virgin will conceive' Mt 1.23.

In Ac 21.9 (τούτῳ δὲ ἦσαν θυγατέρες τέσσαρες παρθένοι 'he had four virgin daughters') the emphasis seems to be upon the fact that the daughters were not as yet married. (See 34.77). Similarly, in Mt 25.1-11 the ten παρθένοι are unmarried girls desirous of participating in a wedding party, and the emphasis would seem to be more upon their being unmarried rather than upon their being virgins.

In obtaining a satisfactory term for 'virgin,' there are often a number of difficulties. For example, a term which designates a virgin may also imply participation in a particular set of ritual or cult practices consisting of puberty rites, in which ritual sexual intercourse is an integral element. In some languages a term which technically means 'virgin' is also employed with unacceptable connotations in that it may suggest that the woman in question has a queer personality or unattractive appearance and therefore is to be sexually avoided. In some instances a term which in some contexts may be equivalent to 'virgin' may also refer to a homosexual female who has not had relations with a man but who does engage in sexual relations with women.

9.40 κοράσιον, ου *n*: (a diminutive derivative of κόρη 'girl,' not occurring in the NT, but seemingly having lost the diminutive feature of meaning) a girl about the age of puberty – 'girl.' τὸ κοράσιον, σοὶ λέγω, ἔγειρε 'Girl, I say to you, Get up' Mk 5.41. In Mk 5.41 κοράσιον is equated in meaning with the Aramaic term ταλιθα (see 9.48), and in Mk 5.42 this girl is identified as being twelve years of age. Compare also ἠνέχθη ἡ κεφαλὴ αὐτοῦ ἐπὶ πίνακι καὶ ἐδόθη τῷ κορασίῳ 'his head was brought in on a plate and given to the girl' (Mt 14.11). It is impossible to determine the age of Herodias's daughter, but in view of her role as an attractive dancer, she was probably of the age of puberty.

D Children (9.41-9.45)

The terms for children may refer to immediate offspring, that is, a person's own children, in which case they are discussed in the domain of *Kinship Terms* (10). The following terms are used for any child without any distinction as to sex.

9.41 παῖς ª, παιδός *m* and *f*: a young person, normally below the age of puberty and without distinction as to sex − 'child.' ἰδόντες δὲ . . . τοὺς παῖδας τοὺς κράζοντας ἐν τῷ ἱερῷ 'and when they saw . . . the children shouting in the Temple' Mt 21.15.

The term παῖς may occur with either masculine or feminine articles and corresponding adjectival attributes. These gender distinctions indicate whether the person referred to is male or female. With the masculine article or attributives one may translate παῖς ª as 'boy,' and similarly with female attributives one may translate παῖς ª as 'girl.'

9.42 παιδίον ª, ου *n*; παιδάριον, ου *n*: (diminutives of παῖς ª 'child,' 9.41, but in the NT παιδίον ª and παιδάριον have seemingly lost at least most of this diminutive force, but may have retained some implications of affectionate concern or interest) a child, normally below the age of puberty − 'child.'
παιδίον ª: ὁμοία ἐστὶν παιδίοις καθημένοις ἐν ταῖς ἀγοραῖς ἃ προσφωνοῦντα τοῖς ἑτέροις 'it is like children sitting in the marketplace and shouting to their companions' Mt 11.16; εἶδον τὸ παιδίον μετὰ Μαρίας τῆς μητρὸς αὐτοῦ 'they saw the child with Mary his mother' Mt 2.11. παιδάριον: ἔστιν παιδάριον ὧδε ὃς ἔχει πέντε ἄρτους κριθίνους 'there is a little boy here who has five loaves of barley bread' Jn 6.9. Note that παιδάριον in Jn 6.9 denotes merely a child; it is the referential pronoun ὅς which indicates masculine gender, and therefore one may translate 'boy.' It is also possible that in this context the diminutive παιδάριον carries some connotation of endearment.

9.43 νήπιος, α, ον: a small child above the age of a helpless infant but probably not more than three or four years of age − 'small child.' ἐκ στόματος νηπίων καὶ θηλαζόντων κατηρτίσω αἶνον 'from the mouth of small children and infants you have brought forth perfect praise' or 'you have trained children and babies to offer perfect praise' Mt 21.16. In Ro 2.20 the Greek expression διδάσκαλον νηπίων, literally 'teacher of little children,' may be better understood in a sense of 'teacher of the ignorant' or 'teacher of the unlearned.'

9.44 νηπιάζω: to be or to become like a child − 'to be as a child, to be childlike.' μὴ παιδία γίνεσθε ταῖς φρεσίν, ἀλλὰ τῇ κακίᾳ νηπιάζετε 'do not be children in your thinking, but be like children as far as evil is concerned' 1 Cor 14.20.

9.45 βρέφος ª, ους *n*: a very small child, even one still unborn − 'baby, infant, fetus.' εὑρήσετε βρέφος ἐσπαργανωμένον καὶ κείμενον ἐν φάτνῃ 'you will find a baby wrapped in cloths and lying in a manger' Lk 2.12; ἐσκίρτησεν τὸ βρέφος ἐν τῇ κοιλίᾳ αὐτῆς 'the baby moved within her womb' Lk 1.41.

In a number of languages one must make a clear distinction between a baby after its birth and one before birth, that is, a fetus. Hence, in such languages the term employed in Lk 1.41 must be quite different from the term used in Lk 2.12.

E Persons For Whom There Is Affectionate Concern (9.46-9.48)

9.46 παιδίον ᶜ, ου *n*; τέκνον ᵈ, ου *n*; τεκνίον, ου *n*; υἱός ᵇ, οῦ *m*: (extensions of meaning of παιδίον ª 'child,' 9.42; τέκνον ª 'child, offspring,' 10.36; υἱός ª 'son,' 10.42, respectively) a person of any age for whom there is a special relationship of endearment and association − 'my child, my dear friend, my dear man, my dear one, my dear lad.'
παιδίον ᶜ: λέγει οὖν αὐτοῖς ὁ Ἰησοῦς, Παιδία, μή τι προσφάγιον ἔχετε; 'Jesus said to them, My children, do you have some fish to eat?' Jn 21.5. In a number of languages παιδία in Jn 21.5 is better rendered as 'my good friends' or 'my dear friends' or 'my dear comrades.' In this context, not age, but the connotation of affection and endearment is in focus.
τέκνον ᵈ: εἶπεν τῷ παραλυτικῷ, Θάρσει, τέκνον 'he said to the paralyzed man, Courage, my dear man' Mt 9.2. In a number of languages it is impossible to translate τέκνον in Mt 9.2 as 'child,' since this might immediately suggest that Jesus was declaring himself to be the father of this man. Furthermore, the paralytic was evidently an adult male. A more satisfactory equivalent would be 'my dear man' or 'my dear fellow.'
τεκνίον: τεκνία, μηδεὶς πλανάτω ὑμᾶς 'my

children, let no one deceive you' 1 Jn 3.7. It may be impossible to translate τεκνία literally as 'my children,' since this might suggest a kinship relationship between the author of 1 John and the people to whom he is addressing his letter. A more satisfactory equivalent in some languages is often 'my dear friends' or 'my dear ones.'

υἱός[b]: καὶ Μᾶρκος ὁ υἱός μου 'and so does my son Mark' 1 Pe 5.13. This usage of υἱός reflects the relationship between a spiritual father or teacher and a follower.

9.47 θυγάτηρ[b], τρός f: (a figurative extension of meaning of θυγάτηρ[a] 'daughter,' 10.46) a woman for whom there is some affectionate concern – 'daughter, lady, woman.' ἰδὼν αὐτὴν εἶπεν, Θάρσει, θύγατερ· ἡ πίστις σου σέ-σωχέν σε 'he saw her and said, Courage, my daughter! Your faith has made you well' Mt 9.22. In a number of languages it is impossible to translate θυγάτηρ[b] literally as 'daughter,' since this would imply that Jesus was acknowledging that the woman was in fact his own daughter. An obvious adjustment must be made in such instances, and therefore one may use such expressions as 'lady' or 'my dear woman.'

9.48 ταλιθα: (an Aramaic word in an emphatic form) the designation for a little girl, probably implying affectionate concern – 'girl, little girl.' ταλιθα κουμ, ὅ ἐστιν μεθερμηνευόμενον Τὸ κοράσιον, σοὶ λέγω, ἔγειρε 'talitha koum, which interpreted means, Little girl, I say to you, get up' Mk 5.41.

10 Kinship Terms

Many of the problems relating to correspondence in kinship terms derive from quite different categories employed in other languages. Societies, for example, which have a matrilineal system of reckoning kinship ties tend to have quite different sets of terms from those based on a patrilineal system such as occurs in the Bible. A number of languages also make distinctions in terms depending on whether the kin is older or younger than the so-called 'reference person.' For example, an older brother may be called by a term which is completely different from one which designates a younger brother.

In a number of instances there are different sets of terms depending upon the sex of the reference person. For example, a boy may call his brother by the same term that a sister calls her sister, and similarly a brother may call his sister by the same term that a sister uses in speaking of her brother. That is to say, the basic distinction is whether the sibling in question is of the same sex or of a different sex.

There are also a number of languages which make distinctions in so-called 'cross cousins.' For example, the child of one's mother's brother or of one's father's sister would be called by a different term from the one used to designate the child of one's father's brother or of one's mother's sister.

A still further complication in some kinship systems is the distinction made between vocative and nonvocative forms. When one is speaking about one's mother, one form may be used, but when one is speaking to one's mother, a completely different form may be required. There may also be differences depending on whether a person is speaking about his own mother or speaking about someone else's mother. These distinctions are by no means all of the basic classificatory differences, but they do reflect some of the more common problems which result from very different ways of speaking about kinship relations.

A translator of the Bible should avoid making isolated decisions with regard to individual kinship terms, but should analyze the kinship system as a whole. Only in this way can one be relatively certain that the appropriate corresponding terms have been satisfactorily employed.

Outline of Subdomains

A Groups and Members of Groups of Persons Regarded as Related by Blood but without Special Reference to Successive Generations (10.1-10.13)
B Kinship Relations Involving Successive Generations (10.14-10.48)
C Kinship Relations of the Same Generation (10.49-10.52)
D Kinship Relations Based upon Marriage (10.53-10.61)

A Groups and Members of Groups of Persons Regarded as Related by Blood but without Special Reference to Successive Generations (10.1-10.13)

10.1 γένος^b, ους *n*; σάρξ^e, σαρκός *f*: a relatively large group of persons regarded as being biologically related – 'race, ethnic group, nation.'[1]

γένος^b: ἡ δὲ γυνὴ ἦν Ἑλληνίς, Συροφοινίκισσα τῷ γένει 'the woman was Greek in culture, of the Syrophoenician race' Mk 7.26.

σάρξ^e: εἴ πως παραζηλώσω μου τὴν σάρκα 'perhaps I can make the people of my own race jealous' Ro 11.14.

It may be difficult in some languages to clearly distinguish between culture and race as in Mk 7.26. Sometimes this difference can be indicated by saying 'the woman lived like a Greek, but she was a Syrophoenician' or '. . . her parents were from Syrophoenicia.' In translating 'people of my own race' in Ro 11.14, it may be necessary to say 'all my fellow Jews' or 'all those people of whom I am a part' or 'those people who are my roots' or '. . . my trunk,' based on the analogy of a tree trunk and branches.

10.2 φυλή^a, ῆς *f*: a subgroup of a nation which is regarded as being more closely

related biologically than the entire nation – 'tribe.' ἦν Ἅννα προφῆτις . . . ἐκ φυλῆς Ἀσήρ 'Anna, a prophetess, was there . . . from the tribe of Asher' Lk 2.36.

In a number of societies there are only three well-defined biologically related groups: (1) the nuclear family (that is to say, the immediate family); (2) the extended family (often referred to as 'the clan'); and (3) the tribe or nation as a whole. Under such circumstances it may be necessary to speak of the twelve tribes of Israel as being 'twelve large clans.' This would emphasize their biological relationships and at the same time would suggest that they constituted part of a larger ethnic unit, namely, the nation. On the other hand, a number of so-called 'primitive societies' have a great many designations for different sets of biologically related persons. These may designate an individual family, an extended family, the clan, a grouping of clans, a division of a tribe into two interacting units (called moieties), and finally the tribe as a whole, equivalent in larger societies to a nation. The choice of appropriate terms for various groups of biologically related persons becomes particularly complex in certain passages in the OT.

10.3 δωδεκάφυλον, ου *n*: the twelve tribes of Israel as a designation of the entire ethnic unit – 'the twelve tribes, the people of Israel.' τὸ δωδεκάφυλον ἡμῶν ἐν ἐκτενείᾳ νύκτα καὶ ἡμέραν λατρεῦον 'our twelve tribes earnestly worshiping day and night' Ac 26.7.

10.4 γενεά^b, ᾶς *f*: an ethnic group exhibiting cultural similarities – 'people of the same kind.' οἱ υἱοὶ τοῦ αἰῶνος τούτου φρονιμώτεροι ὑπὲρ τοὺς υἱοὺς τοῦ φωτὸς εἰς τὴν γενεὰν τὴν ἑαυτῶν εἰσιν 'the people of this world are more prudent in dealing with these of their own kind than are the people who belong to the light' or '. . . in dealing with people like themselves . . .' Lk 16.8. Compare γενεά^a 'those of the same time' (11.4).

10.5 συγγένεια, ας *f*: the group of persons who are members of an extended family – 'relatives, kinfolks.' οὐδείς ἐστιν ἐκ τῆς συγγενείας σου ὃς καλεῖται τῷ ὀνόματι τούτῳ 'but you

---

1 πατριά^b and φυλή^b 'nation, people' (11.56) focus attention upon a particular people as a socially functioning unit, while the feature of biological descent is largely secondary. But in the case of γένος^b and σάρξ^e, the feature of biological descent is focal, while group functioning is largely secondary.

don't have a single relative with that name'
Lk 1.61. This clause in Lk 1.61 may also be
translated in some languages as 'but you do
not have anyone in your clan who has that
name' or 'no one in your family has ever had
that name' or 'none of your ancestors has ever
had that name.'

10.6 συγγενής ᵃ, οὖς, dat. pl. συγγενεῦσιν *m*:
a person who belongs to the same extended
family or clan – 'relative, kinsman.' ἀνεζήτουν
αὐτὸν ἐν τοῖς συγγενεῦσιν καὶ τοῖς γνωστοῖς
'they started looking for him among their
relatives and friends' Lk 2.44.

10.7 συγγενίς, ίδος *f*: a female member of an
extended family or clan – 'relative, kinswoman.' Ἐλισάβετ ἡ συγγενίς σου 'Elizabeth,
your kinswoman' Lk 1.36.

10.8 οἶκος ᵇ, ου *m*; οἰκία ᵇ, ας *f*: the family
consisting of those related by blood and marriage, as well as slaves and servants, living in
the same house or homestead – 'family,
household.'
οἶκος ᵇ: ἐβάπτισα δὲ καὶ τὸν Στεφανᾶ οἶκον 'and
I also baptized Stephanas and his family'
1 Cor 1.16. In Ac 7.10 οἶκος can mean the
household over which Joseph was placed, or it
can mean the property of Pharaoh (see 57.21).
οἰκία ᵇ: οὐκ ἔστιν προφήτης ἄτιμος εἰ μὴ ἐν τῇ
πατρίδι αὐτοῦ καὶ ἐν τοῖς συγγενεῦσιν αὐτοῦ καὶ
ἐν τῇ οἰκίᾳ αὐτοῦ 'there is no prophet without
honor except in his own hometown, among
his own relatives, and among the members of
his own family' Mk 6.4.
   In a number of languages the equivalent of
οἶκος ᵇ or οἰκία ᵇ would be 'those who live
together' or 'those who have the same fence'
(this being a reference to a group of huts surrounded by a fence and thus constituting a
single so-called 'family unit').

10.9 οἱ παρ' αὐτοῦ: (an idiom, literally 'those
beside him') the associates of a person, including family, neighbors, and friends – 'his
family.' ἀκούσαντες οἱ παρ' αὐτοῦ ἐξῆλθον
κρατῆσαι αὐτόν 'when his family heard about
this, they set out to get him' Mk 3.21. In some
languages the idiom οἱ παρ' αὐτοῦ is matched
by other idiomatic expressions such as 'those
who share the same fire' or 'those who eat
from the same pot.'

10.10 πανοικεί: consisting of all those who
belong to the same family or household – 'together with an entire household.' ἠγαλλιάσατο
πανοικεὶ πεπιστευκὼς τῷ θεῷ 'he together with
his entire household were filled with joy
because they now believed in God' Ac 16.34.

10.11 οἰκεῖος, ου *m*; οἰκιακός, οῦ *m*:
(derivatives of οἶκος ᵇ 'family,' 10.8) one who
belongs to a particular household or extended
family – 'member of a family, relative.'
οἰκεῖος: εἰ δέ τις τῶν ἰδίων καὶ μάλιστα οἰκείων
οὐ προνοεῖ 'but if someone does not take care
of his own relatives, especially members of his
own family' 1 Tm 5.8.
οἰκιακός: ἐχθροὶ τοῦ ἀνθρώπου οἱ οἰκιακοὶ αὐτοῦ
'a man's enemies are those of his family' Mt
10.36.

10.12 οἱ ἴδιοι: persons who in some sense
belong to a so-called 'reference person' – 'his
own people.' οἱ ἴδιοι αὐτὸν οὐ παρέλαβον 'his
own people did not receive him' Jn 1.11.

10.13 μονόομαι: to be left without a family –
'to be without a family, to be without relatives.' ἡ δὲ ὄντως χήρα καὶ μεμονωμένη ἤλπικεν
ἐπὶ θεόν 'a woman who is really a widow and
without any family puts her hope in God'
1 Tm 5.5. In 1 Tm 5.5 χήρα would mean that
the woman's husband had died, but μεμονωμένη would imply that she had no relatives
who would be in a position to help her.

B Kinship Relations Involving Succes-
sive Generations (10.14-10.48)

10.14 πατήρ ᵃ, πατρός *m*: one's biological or
adoptive male parent – 'father.' [2] εἶτα τοὺς μὲν
τῆς σαρκὸς ἡμῶν πατέρας εἴχομεν παιδευτὰς καὶ
ἐνετρεπόμεθα 'in the case of our human fathers, they punished us, and we respected
them' He 12.9; ὁ πατήρ σου κἀγὼ ὀδυνώμενοι
ἐζητοῦμέν σε 'your father and I have been terribly worried trying to find you' Lk 2.48.

2 The Aramaic word αββα meaning 'father' occurs in
the NT only as a title for God (see 12.12).

In some languages it may be necessary to distinguish clearly between a term for one's biological father and an expression which refers to one's legal father.

10.15 ἀπάτωρ, ορος: a person for whom there is no record of a male parent or who has never had a male parent or whose father has died – 'without father.' ἀπάτωρ, ἀμήτωρ 'without record of father or mother' He 7.3.[3]

10.16 μήτηρ[a], τρός *f*: one's biological or adoptive female parent – 'mother.' γάμος ἐγένετο ἐν Κανὰ τῆς Γαλιλαίας, καὶ ἦν ἡ μήτηρ τοῦ Ἰησοῦ ἐκεῖ 'there was a marriage in Cana of Galilee and Jesus' mother was there' Jn 2.1. μήτηρ[a] is sometimes used figuratively to refer to persons who are not biological parents but who are in some respects closely associated with the reference person: μήτηρ μου καὶ ἀδελφοί μου οὗτοί εἰσιν οἱ τὸν λόγον τοῦ θεοῦ ἀκούοντες καὶ ποιοῦντες 'my mother and my brothers are those who hear God's word and act accordingly' Lk 8.21. For a discussion of Lk 8.21, see 10.49.

10.17 ἀμήτωρ, ορος: a person for whom there is no record of a female parent or who has never had a female parent or whose mother has died – 'without mother.' ἀπάτωρ, ἀμήτωρ 'without record of father or mother' He 7.3.[3]

10.18 γονεύς, έως *m*; πατήρ[b], πατρός *m* (always in the plural): biological or legal parents – 'parents.'
γονεύς: ὑπέμεινεν Ἰησοῦς ὁ παῖς ἐν Ἰερουσαλήμ, καὶ οὐκ ἔγνωσαν οἱ γονεῖς αὐτοῦ 'the boy Jesus remained in Jerusalem, but his parents didn't know it' Lk 2.43.
πατήρ[b]: Μωϋσῆς γεννηθεὶς ἐκρύβη τρίμηνον ὑπὸ τῶν πατέρων αὐτοῦ 'after Moses was born he was hidden for three months by his parents' He 11.23. In a number of instances it may be

necessary to translate 'parents' as simply 'father and mother.'

10.19 μάμμη, ης *f*: the mother of one's own mother or father (with a possible connotation of affection) – 'grandmother.' ἥτις ἐνῴκησεν πρῶτον ἐν τῇ μάμμῃ σου Λωΐδι 'which dwelt first in your grandmother Lois' 2 Tm 1.5.
In a number of languages it is necessary to distinguish between the grandmother on one's father's side and the grandmother on one's mother's side. There is no positive indication in 2 Tm 1.5 as to the particular relationship involved, but one may assume that the grandmother Lois was the mother of Eunice, and therefore it would be the grandmother on the mother's side.

10.20 προπάτωρ, ορος *m*; πρόγονος, ου *m* or *f*; πατήρ[c], πατρός *m*: a person several preceding generations removed from the reference person – 'ancestor, forefather.'
προπάτωρ: τί οὖν ἐροῦμεν εὑρηκέναι Ἀβραὰμ τὸν προπάτορα ἡμῶν κατὰ σάρκα; 'what then shall we say that Abraham, our forefather by birth, has found?' Ro 4.1.
πρόγονος: χάριν ἔχω τῷ θεῷ, ᾧ λατρεύω ἀπὸ προγόνων ἐν καθαρᾷ συνειδήσει 'I thank God, whom I serve with a clear conscience the way my ancestors did' 2 Tm 1.3.
πατήρ[c]: ὁ θεὸς τῶν πατέρων ἡμῶν ἐδόξασεν τὸν παῖδα αὐτοῦ Ἰησοῦν 'the God of our ancestors has given divine glory to his servant Jesus' Ac 3.13.
In a number of languages one's forefathers may be referred to simply as 'fathers who have long since died.' In other languages they may be referred to as 'fathers of other generations' or 'fathers of ancient times.'

10.21 πατρῷος, α, ον; πατρικός, ή, όν: (derivatives of πατήρ[c] 'ancestor, forefather,' 10.20) pertaining to one's ancestors – 'of the ancestors, of the forefathers.'
πατρῷος: πεπαιδευμένος κατὰ ἀκρίβειαν τοῦ πατρῴου νόμου 'educated according to the strictness of the law of our ancestors' Ac 22.3.
πατρικός: περισσοτέρως ζηλωτὴς ὑπάρχων τῶν πατρικῶν μου παραδόσεων 'I was very zealous for the traditions of my forefathers' Ga 1.14.

---

3 Though it is possible to understand ἀπάτωρ, ἀμήτωρ in He 7.3 as referring to some type of supernatural theophany as in the case of the stories of certain Greek gods and goddesses, it is unlikely that this is the meaning. The focus of attention in He 7.3 seems to be upon the legitimacy of succession in which the priesthood of Christ is contrasted with that of the descendants of Levi.

10.22 πατριάρχης, ου *m*: a particularly noted male ancestor (either because of his role in initiating an ethnic group or groups, for example, Abraham, Isaac, Jacob and the twelve sons of Jacob, or because of important exploits and accomplishments, for example, David) – 'patriarch.' Ἰακὼβ τοὺς δώδεκα πατριάρχας 'the twelve sons of Jacob, the famous ancestors (of our race)' Ac 7.8; ἐξὸν εἰπεῖν μετὰ παρρησίας πρὸς ὑμᾶς περὶ τοῦ πατριάρχου Δαυίδ 'it is appropriate to speak plainly to you concerning your forefather David' Ac 2.29. The equivalent expression for patriarch in a number of languages is merely 'important forefather' or 'famous forefather' or 'great ancestor.'

10.23 σπορά, ᾶς *f*: (a figurative extension of meaning of σπορά 'sowing of seed,' not occurring in the NT) the instrumental means of birth – 'parentage.' ἀναγεγεννημένοι οὐκ ἐκ σπορᾶς φθαρτῆς ἀλλὰ ἀφθάρτου 'you have been born again of parentage which is immortal, not mortal' 1 Pe 1.23.[4]

10.24 γένεσις[b], εως *f*; οἶκος[c], ου *m*; πατριά[a], ᾶς *f*: persons of successive generations who are related by birth – 'lineage, family line.' γένεσις[b]: βίβλος γενέσεως Ἰησοῦ Χριστοῦ υἱοῦ Δαυὶδ υἱοῦ Ἀβραάμ 'the book of the lineage of Jesus Christ, David's son, who was Abraham's son' Mt 1.1.

In biblical times the reckoning of a lineage was somewhat complex in view of certain distinctions between legal and biological relations. The focus of meaning in γένεσις[b], οἶκος[c], and πατριά[a] is not, however, the list of ancestors, but the lineage of successively related persons to which the reference person belongs. Some scholars, however, interpret γένεσις in Mt 1.1 as being part of what is essentially a title for the book of Matthew and thus would render the introductory phrase as

'the book of the history of Jesus Christ' (see γένεσις[c] 'history,' 33.19).

οἶκος[c]; πατριά[a]: διὰ τὸ εἶναι αὐτὸν ἐξ οἴκου καὶ πατριᾶς Δαυίδ 'because he was from David's lineage and family line' Lk 2.4. In Lk 2.4 there appears to be no significant difference in meaning between οἶκος and πατριά, and in some receptor languages it would be sufficient to use a single term essentially equivalent to 'lineage.' The two terms appear to simply reinforce their shared meaning.

In some languages a successive series of ancestors is called 'the forefathers' or 'those to whom one looks back' or 'those who have gone ahead.' In other languages a lineage is referred to as 'a person's root' or 'a man's trunk' (referring to the trunk of a tree).

10.25 γενεαλογέομαι: to have descended from a particular lineage – 'to be in the lineage of, to be descended from.' ὁ δὲ μὴ γενεαλογούμενος ἐξ αὐτῶν 'who was not descended from them' He 7.6. The meaning of He 7.6 may also be expressed as 'they were not his forefathers.'

10.26 γενεαλογία, ας *f*: (derivative of γενεαλογέομαι 'to be descended from,' 10.25) a list of direct descendants or ascendants – 'genealogy.' γενεαλογίαις ἀπεράντοις 'those endless lists of ancestors' 1 Tm 1.4.

10.27 ἀγενεαλόγητος, ον: pertaining to one for whom there is no record of ancestors – 'with no record of ancestors.' ἀπάτωρ, ἀμήτωρ, ἀγενεαλόγητος 'without record of father or mother or ancestors' He 7.3.

10.28 γενεά[c], ᾶς *f*; τέκνον[b], ου *n*: successive following generations of those who are biologically related to a reference person – 'posterity, descendants, offspring.' γενεά[c]: τὴν γενεὰν αὐτοῦ τίς διηγήσεται 'no one will be able to tell about his descendants' Ac 8.33.

τέκνον[b] (always in the plural): ὑμῖν γάρ ἐστιν ἡ ἐπαγγελία καὶ τοῖς τέκνοις ὑμῶν 'for the promise is to you and to your descendants' Ac 2.39.

In the case of γενεά[c], τέκνον[b], and σπέρμα[b] (10.29), the reference is not to one's im-

---

4 It is also possible to understand σπορά in 1 Pe 1.23 as referring to the process of procreation as being analogical to the 'sowing of seed,' but the attributives φθαρτῆς and ἀφθάρτου would seem to shift the meaning of σπορά to 'parentage.' It is possible that this use of σπορά in 1 Pe 1.23 represents a case of figurative usage rather than conventionalized figurative meaning.

mediate descendants or offspring (that is to say, to one's sons or daughters) but to a successive series of such persons, one's descendants. In some languages such descendants may be called merely 'the children of one's children,' and in other languages one may refer to descendants as 'those who follow one' or 'those who come later.'

10.29 σπέρμα^b, τος *n*: (a figurative extension of meaning of σπέρμα^a 'seed,' 3.35) posterity, with emphasis upon the ancestor's role in founding the lineage – 'posterity, descendants, offspring.' ἐν τῷ σπέρματί σου ἐνευλογηθήσονται πᾶσαι αἱ πατριαὶ τῆς γῆς 'through your posterity I will bless all people' Ac 3.25. See discussion at 10.28.

10.30 υἱός^c, οῦ *m*: (an extended meaning of υἱός^a 'son,' 10.42) a non-immediate male descendant (possibly involving a gap of several generations) – 'male descendant.'[5] Ἰωσὴφ υἱὸς Δαυίδ, μὴ φοβηθῇς παραλαβεῖν Μαρίαν τὴν γυναῖκά σου 'Joseph, descendant of David, do not be afraid to take Mary to be your wife' Mt 1.20. Though υἱός^c is often translated as 'son,' speaking, for example, of 'Joseph son of David,' this may be very misleading in some languages, since readers would assume that a 'son' belonged to an immediately following generation. In some instances a term such as 'great grandson' is generalized to mean any individual in the third or in any one of a number of succeeding generations. In place of a phrase such as 'descendant of David,' it is sometimes necessary to invert the expression to read 'David was one of his ancestors.'

10.31 θυγάτηρ^c, τρός *f*: (an extended meaning of θυγάτηρ^a 'daughter,' 10.46) a non-immediate female descendant (possibly involving a gap of several generations) – 'female

---

5 The shift of meaning from υἱός^a 'son' (10.42) to υἱός^c 'male descendant' bears an interesting shift in the distinctive feature of generational succession, for in the case of υἱός^a the denotation is of one who is one following generation removed from the reference person, while in the case of υἱός^c the individual is several generations separated from the reference person.

descendant.' ταύτην δὲ θυγατέρα Ἀβραὰμ οὖσαν 'now here is this female descendant of Abraham' Lk 13.16. See discussion at 10.30 and the corresponding footnote.

10.32 γένος^a, ους *n*: a non-immediate descendant (possibly involving a gap of several generations), either male or female – 'descendant, offspring.' ἐγώ εἰμι ἡ ῥίζα καὶ τὸ γένος Δαυίδ 'I am the root and descendant of David' Re 22.16. Here ῥίζα^b (10.33) and γένος^a are very similar in meaning, and it is often best to coalesce the two terms into a single expression, for example, 'I am a descendant of David' or 'I belong to the lineage of David.'

10.33 ῥίζα^b, ης *f*: (a figurative extension of meaning of ῥίζα^a 'root,' 3.47) a descendant, with probable connotations of continuing relation – 'descendant, offspring.' ἔσται ἡ ῥίζα τοῦ Ἰεσσαί 'a descendant of Jesse will come' Ro 15.12.

10.34 καρπὸς τῆς ὀσφύος: (an idiom, literally 'fruit of the genitals') descendant, as the result of the male role in procreation – 'descendant, offspring.' ὅρκῳ ὤμοσεν αὐτῷ ὁ θεὸς ἐκ καρποῦ τῆς ὀσφύος αὐτοῦ καθίσαι ἐπὶ τὸν θρόνον αὐτοῦ 'God had sworn him an oath to make one of his descendants succeed him on the throne' Ac 2.30 (see 8.43).

10.35 ἀνατέλλω^c: (a figurative extension of meaning of ἀνατέλλω^a 'to rise' as of the sun, 15.104) to be an important descendant, presumably of a distinguished ancestor, normally with a number of intervening generations – 'be a descendant, offspring.' πρόδηλον γὰρ ὅτι ἐξ Ἰούδα ἀνατέταλκεν ὁ κύριος ἡμῶν 'now it is clear that our Lord is a descendant of Judah' He 7.14.

10.36 τέκνον^a, ου *n*; παῖς^b, παιδός *m* and *f*: one's immediate offspring, but without specific reference to sex or age – 'child, offspring.'
τέκνον^a: οὐκ ἦν αὐτοῖς τέκνον 'they had no children' Lk 1.7.
παῖς^b (marked as masculine or feminine by attributives): οἱ δοῦλοι αὐτοῦ ὑπήντησαν αὐτῷ λέγοντες ὅτι ὁ παῖς αὐτοῦ ζῇ 'his servants met

him with the news, Your boy is going to live' Jn 4.51.

In languages in which there is no generic term for 'child' or 'offspring,' one may use 'son' or 'daughter' or 'son and daughter,' singular or plural, depending upon the context.

10.37 παιδίον[b], **ου** *n*: (diminutive of παῖς[b] 'child,' 10.36, but with the loss of at least most of the diminutive meaning) one's immediate offspring – 'child, offspring.' τὰ παιδία μου μετ' ἐμοῦ εἰς τὴν κοίτην εἰσίν 'my children are in bed with me' Lk 11.7. One need not assume in Lk 11.7 that the children were in the same bed with their father. One may render this passage simply as 'I have gone to bed and so have my children' or 'I am already in bed and so are my children,' but see 6.108.

10.38 καρπὸς τῆς κοιλίας: (an idiom, literally 'fruit of the womb') the child of a woman – 'child, baby.' εὐλογημένος ὁ καρπὸς τῆς κοιλίας σου 'blessed is your child' Lk 1.42.

10.39 νόθος, η, ον: pertaining to someone who is born out of wedlock and is thus without legal status or rights – 'illegitimate, bastard.' ἄρα νόθοι καὶ οὐχ υἱοί ἐστε 'then you are bastards and not sons' He 12.8. There may, however, be some serious problems involved in translating νόθοι in He 12.8, especially if νόθοι must be rendered in some languages as 'sons whose parents are not married,' for νόθοι occurs here in a highly figurative passage speaking of God as one's parent. It may, therefore, be necessary to employ an expression such as 'this means you are not his real sons' or '. . . not sons who truly belong to him.'

10.40 ὀρφανός[a], **οῦ** *m* or *f*: an offspring whose parents either are no longer alive or no longer function as parents (as the result of having abandoned their offspring) – 'orphan.' ἐπισκέπτεσθαι ὀρφανοὺς καὶ χήρας ἐν τῇ θλίψει αὐτῶν 'to take care of orphans and widows in their suffering' Jas 1.27.

Some languages make a distinction in terms for 'orphan' by indicating whether the child has been abandoned or whether one or both of the parents are dead. In languages where some indication of relative age must be introduced in speaking of 'orphans,' it is preferable in Jas 1.27 to use a term which pertains to young children.

10.41 ἄτεκνος, ον: pertaining to being without offspring – 'childless, having no children.' ἐάν τινος ἀδελφὸς ἀποθάνῃ ἔχων γυναῖκα, καὶ οὗτος ἄτεκνος ᾖ 'if a man's brother dies having a wife but no children' Lk 20.28.

10.42 υἱός[a], **οῦ** *m*: an immediate male offspring – 'son.' γέγραπται γὰρ ὅτι 'Αβραὰμ δύο υἱοὺς ἔσχεν 'the Scriptures say that Abraham had two sons' Ga 4.22.

10.43 πρωτότοκος[a], **ον**: pertaining to being a firstborn child (normally in contexts speaking of people but also used in reference to domestic animals) – 'firstborn.' ἔτεκεν τὸν υἱὸν αὐτῆς τὸν πρωτότοκον 'she gave birth to her firstborn son' Lk 2.7.

In Jewish society the rights and responsibilities of being a firstborn son resulted in considerable prestige and status. The firstborn son, for example, received twice as much in inheritance as any other offspring.

The use of πρωτότοκος 'firstborn' does not imply in Greek that other children were also born to a woman, though in a number of languages one would never use 'firstborn' unless other children followed. Such an individual would be spoken of merely as 'the only child.' It is also frequently necessary to employ an appropriate qualifier for 'firstborn' in order to mark clearly the fact that it is 'a firstborn son' rather than 'a firstborn daughter.'

The figurative meaning of πρωτότοκος in the messianic title πρωτότοκος πάσης κτίσεως 'firstborn of all creation' (Col 1.15) may be interpreted as 'existing before all creation' (see 13.79) or 'existing superior to all creation' (see 87.47).

10.44 πρωτοτόκια, ων *n*: rights associated with being the firstborn – 'birthright, rights of being the firstborn.' 'Ησαῦ, ὃς ἀντὶ βρώσεως μιᾶς ἀπέδετο τὰ πρωτοτόκια ἑαυτοῦ 'Esau, who for the sake of a single meal sold his rights as the firstborn' He 12.16.

10.45 ἄρσην διανοίγων μήτραν: (an idiom, literally 'male that opens the womb,' and closely related in meaning to πρωτότοκος[a] 'firstborn,' 10.43) the first male offspring of a female – 'firstborn son, firstborn male.' πᾶν ἄρσεν διανοῖγον μήτραν ἅγιον τῷ κυρίῳ κληθήσεται 'every firstborn male shall be dedicated to the Lord' Lk 2.23.[6]

A literal translation of the idiom 'male that opens the womb' may be extremely misleading in some languages, since it may refer to the first act of sexual intercourse and not to the birth of the first, male child.

10.46 θυγάτηρ[a], τρός f: immediate female offspring – 'daughter.' ὁ φιλῶν υἱὸν ἢ θυγατέρα ὑπὲρ ἐμὲ οὐκ ἔστιν μου ἄξιος 'whoever loves his son or daughter more than me is not worthy of me' Mt 10.37.

A literal rendering of Mt 10.37, namely, 'whoever loves his son or daughter more than me,' may be misleading, since in some languages it could refer to only one particular son or daughter. A more indefinite expression may therefore be preferable, namely, 'any one of his sons or daughters.'

10.47 θυγάτριον, ου n (a diminutive derivative of θυγάτηρ[a] 'daughter,' 10.46, with possible emphasis upon young age and probable implication of affection) – 'little daughter, dear daughter.' τὸ θυγάτριόν μου ἐσχάτως ἔχει 'my dear daughter is at the point of death' Mk 5.23.

In Mk 5.23 the text indicates specifically that the daughter was twelve years of age, and it may very well be that in Mk 7.25 (the only other passage in which θυγάτριον occurs in the NT) the daughter may have been of approximately the same age. In languages in which some indication of relative age is obligatory, one could employ a term identifying a girl about the age of puberty.

10.48 ἔκγονον, ου n: the offspring of one's children – 'grandchild.' εἰ δέ τις χήρα τέκνα ἢ ἔκγονα ἔχει 'but if a widow has children or grandchildren' 1 Tm 5.4.

6 This idiom is also discussed in 8.69 in connection with the meaning of μήτρα.

In the one passage in which ἔκγονος occurs in the NT (namely, 1 Tm 5.4), the reference is to adult grandchildren, and in some languages this element in the meaning must be made explicit. In languages in which there is no generic term to include both 'grandsons' and 'granddaughters,' it may be necessary to translate ἔκγονος in 1 Tm 5.4 as 'grandsons or granddaughters.'

C Kinship Relations of the Same Generation (10.49-10.52)

10.49 ἀδελφός[a], οῦ m: a male having the same father and mother as the reference person – 'brother.' εἶδεν δύο ἀδελφούς, Σίμωνα τὸν λεγόμενον Πέτρον καὶ Ἀνδρέαν τὸν ἀδελφὸν αὐτοῦ 'he saw two brothers, Simon, called Peter, and his brother Andrew' Mt 4.18. In a number of languages it is necessary to indicate the difference between older and younger brothers, and this can usually be done on the basis of Semitic usage, since the older brother was normally named first. Therefore, in Mt 4.18 one may translate 'Simon and his younger brother Andrew.'

The interpretation of ἀδελφός[a] in such passages as Mt 12.46; Mk 3.31; and Jn 2.12 as meaning 'cousins' (on the basis of a corresponding Hebrew term, which is used in certain cases to designate masculine relatives of various degrees) is not attested in Greek nor affirmed in the Greek-English lexicon edited by Arndt, Gingrich, and Danker. Such an interpretation depends primarily on ecclesiastical tradition.

Though the plural of ἀδελφός[a] (namely, ἀδελφοί) can mean both 'brothers and sisters,' there is no reason to believe that in Mt 12.46; Mk 3.31; Jn 2.12; 7.3, 5; and Ac 1.14 the reference is to both brothers and sisters.

In Lk 8.21 (μήτηρ μου καὶ ἀδελφοί μου οὗτοί εἰσιν οἱ τὸν λόγον τοῦ θεοῦ ἀκούοντες καὶ ποιοῦντες 'my mother and my brothers are those who hear the word of God and act accordingly') ἀδελφοί is used figuratively as a qualification of Jesus' followers. In some languages, however, it is necessary to make more evident the qualifying relationship, for example, 'those who hear the word and act accordingly are my mother and my brothers' or

'. . . are just like a mother and brothers to me.'

10.50 ἀδελφήᵃ, ῆς *f*: a female having the same father and mother as the reference person – 'sister.' οὐκ εἰσὶν αἱ ἀδελφαὶ αὐτοῦ ὧδε πρὸς ἡμᾶς; 'aren't his sisters living here among us?' Mk 6.3.

A number of languages make a distinction in relative age of sisters, paralleling the usage of distinct terms for 'brother' (see 10.49). The order of names in the NT normally suggests relative age, and therefore in speaking of Martha and Mary in such languages, one may designate Mary as the younger sister, since the order is normally first Martha and then Mary, though in Jn 11.1 the order is reversed.

For a discussion of ἀδελφή**ᵃ** in the possible meaning of 'cousin,' see the discussion under ἀδελφός**ᵃ** (10.49).

10.51 σύντροφοςᵃ, ου *m*: a person offered parental care and/or adoption along with the reference person, though not related by blood – 'foster brother' or 'foster sister.' Μαναήν τε Ἡρῴδου τοῦ τετραάρχου σύντροφος 'Manaen who was a foster brother of Governor Herod' Ac 13.1. It is possible, however, that σύντροφος in Ac 13.1 has the meaning of 'a close friend from childhood' (see 34.15).

In some languages 'a foster brother' may be referred to as 'a person who becomes a brother by being adopted' or 'a person who grows up just as though he were a brother.'

10.52 ἀνεψιός, οῦ *m*: the child of one's uncle and aunt, either on the father's side or the mother's side – 'cousin.' Μᾶρκος ὁ ἀνεψιὸς Βαρναβᾶ 'Marcus, the cousin of Barnabas' Col 4.10.

Some languages make a clear distinction between so-called 'parallel cousins' and 'cross cousins.' Parallel cousins would be the off-spring of one's father's brother or of one's mother's sister, while cross cousins would be the offspring of one's father's sister or of one's mother's brother. There is no way of knowing from the context of Col 4.10 what the specific relationship is between Mark and Barnabas, but for languages which have no general term for cousins, but only specific terms for

parallel cousins or cross cousins, it is necessary to select one or another of these specific terms in speaking of Mark. By means of a footnote one can indicate that the Greek text does not specify which type of cousin is involved.

D Kinship Relations Based upon Marriage (10.53-10.61)

10.53 ἄνθρωποςᶜ, ου *m*; **ἀνήρ**ᶜ, **ἀνδρός** *m*: a man who is married to a woman – 'husband.' ἄνθρωπος**ᶜ**: εἰ οὕτως ἐστὶν ἡ αἰτία τοῦ ἀνθρώπου μετὰ τῆς γυναικός 'if that is the relation between a husband and a wife' Mt 19.10. ἀνήρ**ᶜ**: ἀπεκρίθη ἡ γυνὴ καὶ εἶπεν αὐτῷ, Οὐκ ἔχω ἄνδρα. λέγει αὐτῇ ὁ Ἰησοῦς, Καλῶς εἶπας ὅτι Ἄνδρα οὐκ ἔχω· πέντε γὰρ ἄνδρας ἔσχες, καὶ νῦν ὃν ἔχεις οὐκ ἔστιν σου ἀνήρ 'the woman answered and said to him, I do not have a husband. Jesus said to her, You have said well that you do not have a husband, for you have had five husbands and the man you now have is not your husband' Jn 4.17-18. ἀνήρ in the meaning of 'husband' is normally clearly marked by context, usually involving a so-called 'possessive marker,' though in some contexts such as Jn 4.17-18 and Mt 19.10, the distinctions in meaning are quite clear, but it is only from each individual context that one can determine whether ἀνήρ means simply 'man' (see 9.24) or 'husband.' See also discussion at 10.54.

10.54 γυνήᵇ, αικός *f*: a woman who is married to a man – 'wife.' ὃς ἂν ἀπολύσῃ τὴν γυναῖκα αὐτοῦ, δότω αὐτῇ ἀποστάσιον 'whoever divorces his wife must give her a certificate of divorce' Mt 5.31. The distinctions in meaning of γυνή**ᵃ** 'woman' (9.34) and γυνή**ᵇ** 'wife' parallel those involving ἀνήρ**ᶜ** and ἄνθρωπος**ᶜ** (see 10.53). A number of languages, however, employ essentially the same usage as Greek in that a wife is simply called 'his woman,' 'my woman,' etc. The contexts normally indicate clearly which meaning of γυνή is involved.

10.55 σκεῦοςᶠ, ους *n*: (a figurative extension of meaning of σκεῦος**ᵇ** 'vessel,' 6.118) a woman married to a man, with focus upon the sexual relation – 'wife.' εἰδέναι ἕκαστον ὑμῶν τὸ ἑαυτοῦ σκεῦος κτᾶσθαι ἐν ἁγιασμῷ καὶ τιμῇ 'that each one of you know how to take a wife for himself in holiness and honor' 1 Th 4.4. The interpretation of σχεῦος in 1 Th 4.4 has given rise to serious divisions of opinion as noted in 8.6, where σχεῦος is interpreted as designating a person's own body. The interpretation of σχεῦος as 'wife' is based upon a number of considerations. In the first place, the verb χτᾶσθαι 'to get, to acquire' (57.58) does not normally go with 'body,' while it fits well with the meaning of 'wife.' On the other hand, σχεῦος meaning 'wife' is nowhere else attested in Greek but is assumed in 1 Th 4.4 to refer to a wife primarily on the strength of the particular interpretation of the context, in which πορνεία 'immorality' (88.271) in verse 3 and ἐν πάθει ἐπιθυμίας 'with a lustful desire' (25.30) in verse 5 are assumed to point to the meaning of σχεῦος as 'wife.' In ancient Jewish literature a wife was euphemistically called a 'vessel' in contexts relating to sexual relations, and 'vessel' is a very common meaning of σχεῦος in Greek. If, therefore, one assumes a Semitic background for this Greek text, the statement in 1 Th 4.4 would refer to the need for sexual life to be both holy and honorable (see 23.63).

10.56 νυμφίος, ου *m*: a man who is about to be married or has just been married – 'bridegroom.' ἐξῆλθον εἰς ὑπάντησιν τοῦ νυμφίου 'they came out to meet the bridegroom' Mt 25.1. In a number of languages a term for bridegroom must indicate explicitly whether the marriage is about to take place or has just taken place. Therefore, one may have to employ some such phrase as 'a man who is going to be married soon' or 'a man who has just been married.' A corresponding type of expression may be required for 'bride' (see 10.57).

10.57 νύμφη[a], ης *f*: a woman who is about to be married or who has just been married – 'bride.' ὁ ἔχων τὴν νύμφην νυμφίος ἐστίν 'the bridegroom is the one to whom the bride belongs' Jn 3.29.

As in the case of 'bridegroom' (10.56), it may be necessary in some languages to indicate with 'bride' whether the person has just been married or is about to be married.

10.58 πενθερός, οῦ *m*: the father of one's spouse – 'father-in-law.' ἦν γὰρ πενθερὸς τοῦ Καϊάφα 'for he was the father-in-law of Caiaphas' Jn 18.13. In a number of languages one must indicate explicitly the various components of meaning in 'father-in-law.' For example, πενθερός in Jn 18.13 may be rendered as 'Caiaphas had married the daughter of Annas' or 'the daughter of Annas had become the wife of Caiaphas.'

10.59 πενθερά, ᾶς *f*: the mother of one's spouse – 'mother-in-law.' ἡ δὲ πενθερὰ Σίμωνος κατέχειτο πυρέσσουσα 'the mother-in-law of Simon was lying sick with a fever' Mk 1.30. In a number of languages the semantic components of 'mother-in-law' must be made explicit. For example, in Mk 1.30 one may translate 'the mother-in-law of Simon' as 'the mother of Simon's wife.'

10.60 νύμφη[b], ης *f*: the wife of one's son – 'daughter-in-law.' διαμερισθήσονται . . . πενθερὰ ἐπὶ τὴν νύμφην αὐτῆς καὶ νύμφη ἐπὶ τὴν πενθεράν 'mothers-in-law will be against their daughters-in-law, and daughters-in-law against their mothers-in-law' Lk 12.53. For languages which do not have specific terms for 'mother-in-law' and 'daughter-in-law' it may be possible to render Lk 12.53 by translating 'women will be against the wives of their sons, and young women will be against the mothers of their husbands.'

10.61 χήρα, ας *f*: a woman whose husband has died – 'widow.' ἐλθοῦσα μία χήρα πτωχὴ ἔβαλεν λεπτὰ δύο 'a poor widow came along and dropped in two little copper coins' Mk 12.42. In rendering Mk 12.42 'poor widow' may be translated as 'poor woman whose husband had died.'

11 Groups and Classes of Persons and Members of Such Groups and Classes

The domain of *Groups and Classes of Persons and Members of Such Groups and Classes* may be subdivided in several different ways, but the division into *General, Socio-Religious, Socio-Political, Ethnic-Cultural,* and *Philosophical* seems the most practical, even though there are several instances of overlapping.

Outline of Subdomains

A General (11.1-11.11)
B Socio-Religious (11.12-11.54)
C Socio-Political (11.55-11.89)
D Ethnic-Cultural (11.90-11.95)
E Philosophical (11.96-11.97)

A General[1] (11.1-11.11)

11.1 ὄχλος[a], ου *m*; πλῆθος[b], ους *n*; λαός[c], οῦ *m*; ὅμιλος, ου *m*: a casual non-membership group of people, fairly large in size and assembled for whatever purpose – 'crowd, multitude.'[2]
ὄχλος[a]: ἐκάθητο περὶ αὐτὸν ὄχλος 'a crowd was sitting around him' Mk 3.32.
πλῆθος[b]: γενομένης δὲ τῆς φωνῆς ταύτης συνῆλθεν τὸ πλῆθος 'when they heard this noise, a crowd gathered' Ac 2.6.
λαός[c]: ἀποκριθεὶς πᾶς ὁ λαὸς εἶπεν 'the whole crowd answered back and said' Mt 27.25.
ὅμιλος: πᾶς ἐπὶ τῶν πλοίων ὁ ὅμιλος 'all the crowd in ships' Re 18.17 (apparatus).
In a number of languages there is no term corresponding to 'crowd.' One may, however, usually speak of such a group of people as 'many people' or 'many men and women.' Depending on the context, it may be necessary to indicate some relative difference in size, for example, 'very large crowd' or 'many, many people.' If the crowd is relatively small, one may sometimes speak of 'just some people.'

11.2 ὀχλοποιέω: to cause a crowd to gather – 'to gather a crowd' or 'to cause a crowd to form.' ὀχλοποιήσαντες ἐθορύβουν τὴν πόλιν 'they gathered a crowd and set the whole city in an uproar' Ac 17.5. The context of Ac 17.5 indicates clearly that the crowd was an unruly and undisciplined gathering of people, and therefore one may often employ an expression equivalent to 'they gathered together a mob.'

11.3 νέφος, ους *n*: (a figurative extension of meaning of νέφος 'cloud,' not occurring in the NT) a large crowd of people – 'large crowd.' τοσοῦτον ἔχοντες περικείμενον ἡμῖν νέφος μαρτύρων 'we have this large crowd of witnesses around us' He 12.1. In He 12.1 a possible supplementary component of 'heavenly' is applicable, since the reference is to the heroes of faith mentioned in chapter 11. In general one cannot preserve the figure of speech, nor even a term meaning 'crowd,' since the persons in chapter 11 did not form a crowd historically. A more common equivalent of 'large crowd of witnesses' is 'many, many witnesses.'

11.4 γενεά[a], ᾶς *f*: people living at the same time and belonging to the same reproductive age-class – 'those of the same time, those of the same generation.' ἐκζητηθήσεται ἀπὸ τῆς γενεᾶς ταύτης 'the people of this generation will be punished' Lk 11.51.
The expression 'the people of this generation' may also be expressed as 'the people living now' or 'the people of this time.' Successive generations may be spoken of as 'groups of people who live one after the other' or 'successions of parents and children.'

11.5 κλισία, ας *f*; συμπόσιον, ου *n*: a group of persons engaged in eating together – 'a group eating together.'

---

1 The term 'General' in the heading of this subdomain should be understood as referring to classes or members of classes which are not subsumed under any of the following categories.
2 In this set of terms referring to a crowd or a multitude, it is possible that πλῆθος[b] denotes a somewhat larger group of persons than the other terms and that λαός[c] suggests a crowd made up of common people, but one cannot be certain of these distinctions from existing contexts.

κλισία: κατακλίνατε αὐτοὺς κλισίας ὡσεὶ ἀνὰ πεντήκοντα 'make the people sit down in groups of about fifty each' Lk 9.14.

συμπόσιον: ἐπέταξεν αὐτοῖς ἀνακλῖναι πάντας συμπόσια συμπόσια ἐπὶ τῷ χλωρῷ χόρτῳ 'he ordered them to have all the people sit down in groups on the green grass' Mk 6.39.[3]

Note that Luke employs κλισίας in essentially the same type of context in which Mark uses συμπόσια.

11.6 πρασιά, ᾶς f: (a figurative extension of meaning of πρασιά 'garden plot,' not occurring in the NT) a group of persons arranged in an orderly fashion – 'group.' ἀνέπεσαν πρασιαὶ πρασιαὶ κατὰ ἑκατὸν καὶ κατὰ πεντήκοντα 'the people sat down in groups of a hundred and groups of fifty' Mk 6.40.

A comparison of πρασιαὶ πρασιαί in Mk 6.40 with συμπόσια συμπόσια (see 11.5) in Mk 6.39 indicates clearly that the reference in both instances is essentially the same, but in Mk 6.39 συμπόσια συμπόσια points to the grouping of people with the intent of eating, while in Mk 6.40 πρασιαὶ πρασιαί marks the orderly arrangement of the persons. One may therefore translate Mk 6.40 as 'the people sat down in orderly groups of a hundred and of fifty' or 'the people sat down in rows by groups of a hundred and groups of fifty.'

11.7 υἱοὶ τοῦ νυμφῶνος: (an idiom, literally 'sons of the wedding hall') guests at a wedding, or more specifically, friends of the bridegroom participating in wedding festivities – 'wedding guests' or 'friends of the bridegroom.' μὴ δύνανται οἱ υἱοὶ τοῦ νυμφῶνος πενθεῖν 'the friends of the bridegroom are not able to weep' Mt 9.15. A literal rendering of the idiom 'sons of the wedding hall' has often been seriously misunderstood, for example, the bride's children born prior to the marriage.

11.8 μέρος[d], ους n: a group of people having specific membership and forming a part of a

larger constituency – 'party, group.' τινὲς τῶν γραμματέων τοῦ μέρους τῶν Φαρισαίων διεμάχοντο 'some of the teachers of the Law who belonged to the party of the Pharisees protested strongly' Ac 23.9.

In the NT μέρος[d] occurs only in the expression μέρος τῶν Φαρισαίων 'the party of the Pharisees,' and though the Pharisees constituted a socio-religious group, the use of μέρος[d] does not focus upon this socio-religious aspect of the Pharisees' relationship to the Jewish nation as a whole, but merely upon their identity as a part of a larger constituency. The expression 'the party of the Pharisees' may be rendered in some languages as 'the group to which the Pharisees belonged' or 'those who were counted as Pharisees' or 'the division called Pharisees.' In selecting a word for 'party' or 'group,' it is important to avoid a term which would be essentially political in meaning. If there is no general term for 'party,' it may be necessary to use one with a socio-religious denotation, since that would be the most accurate way of identifying the Pharisees in their relationship to other distinctive groups in the Jewish nation.

11.9 σύσσωμος, ον: a person who is a member of a group, with emphasis upon his coordinate relation to other members of the group – 'co-member.' τὰ ἔθνη . . . σύσσωμα καὶ συμμέτοχα τῆς ἐπαγγελίας 'the Gentiles . . . are co-members (with the Jews) and share along with them in the promise' Eph 3.6.

The concept of 'being a co-member' may be expressed in some languages as 'a person who is counted along with others,' so that in Eph 3.6 one may translate 'the Gentiles are counted along with the Jews in sharing in the promise' or even 'the Gentiles along with the Jews share in the promise.'

11.10 ὁ ἔξω (a figurative extension of meaning of ἔξω[a] 'outside,' 83.20); ὁ ἔξωθεν (a figurative extension of meaning of ἔξωθεν[a] 'from outside,' 84.15): a person who is not a member of a particular in-group – 'outsider.' ὁ ἔξω: τί γάρ μοι τοὺς ἔξω κρίνειν; οὐχὶ τοὺς ἔσω ὑμεῖς κρίνετε; 'why should I judge outsiders? should you not judge the insiders?' 1 Cor 5.12. See also 11.11.

---

3 In Mk 6.39 the repetition of συμπόσια indicates a distributive plural, in other words, a series of groups distributed over an area. Note the same kind of distributive plural in connection with πρασιαί in Mk 6.40 (see 11.6).

ὁ ἔξωθεν: δεῖ δὲ καὶ μαρτυρίαν καλὴν ἔχειν ἀπὸ τῶν ἔξωθεν 'he should be a man who is respected by the outsiders' 1 Tm 3.7. In a number of languages it may be appropriate to render 1 Tm 3.7 as 'he should be a man who is respected by those who are not believers' or '. . . by those who are not followers of Christ.'

11.11 ὁ ἔσωᵃ: (a figurative extension of meaning of ἔσω 'inside,' 83.13) a person belonging to a so-called 'in-group' (in other words, not being a member of the out-group in question) – 'insider.' τί γάρ μοι τοὺς ἔξω κρίνειν; οὐχὶ τοὺς ἔσω ὑμεῖς κρίνετε; 'why should I judge outsiders? should you not judge the insiders?' 1 Cor 5.12. See also 11.10.

In the rendering of 1 Cor 5.12 it may be necessary to be quite specific about those who constitute outsiders and insiders, for example, 'why should I judge those who are not believers? should you not judge the believers?' Note the rendering of TEV for 1 Cor 5.12-13: "After all, it is none of my business to judge outsiders. God will judge them. But should you not judge the members of your own fellowship? As the scripture says, 'Remove the evil man from your group.' "

B Socio-Religious (11.12-11.54)

11.12 λαόςᵇ, **οῦ** *m*: a collective for people who belong to God (whether Jews or Christians) – 'people of God.' ἔσται δὲ πᾶσα ψυχὴ ἥτις ἐὰν μὴ ἀκούσῃ τοῦ προφήτου ἐκείνου ἐξολεθρευθήσεται ἐκ τοῦ λαοῦ 'anyone who does not listen to what that prophet says will be separated from God's people and destroyed' Ac 3.23.

The phrase 'people of God' may be rendered in some languages as 'the people who belong to God' or 'the people whom God possesses,' but in a number of languages the relationship between the people and God must be expressed in terms of reverence or worship, for example, 'the people who worship God' or 'the people who reverence God.' See also 11.27.

11.13 υἱοὶ τῆς βασιλείας: (an idiom, literally 'sons of the kingdom') people who should

properly be or were traditionally regarded as a part of the kingdom of God – 'people of God's kingdom, God's people.' οἱ δὲ υἱοὶ τῆς βασιλείας ἐκβληθήσονται εἰς τὸ σκότος τὸ ἐξώτερον 'but those who should be God's people will be thrown out into the darkness outside' Mt 8.12.

In a number of languages a literal rendering of 'sons of the kingdom' would be relatively meaningless. It is normally possible to use a descriptive phrase in contexts such as Mt 8.12, for example, 'those who should be a part of the kingdom of God' or 'those over whom God should be ruling.' In this context, as well as in most others, the Greek term traditionally rendered 'kingdom' (in speaking of 'the kingdom of God') points essentially to the rule of God rather than to any place or time. See also 37.64.

11.14 υἱοὶ τοῦ φωτός; υἱοὶ τῆς ἡμέρας; τέκνα φωτός: (idioms, literally 'sons of the light,' 'sons of the day,' and 'children of light,' respectively) persons to whom the truth of God has been revealed and who are presumably living according to such truth – 'sons of the light, children of the light, people of God.' See also 9.4 and 12.15.

υἱοὶ τοῦ φωτός: ὡς τὸ φῶς ἔχετε, πιστεύετε εἰς τὸ φῶς, ἵνα υἱοὶ φωτὸς γένησθε 'believe in the light then, while you have it, so that you will be God's people' Jn 12.36.

υἱοὶ τῆς ἡμέρας: πάντες γὰρ ὑμεῖς υἱοὶ φωτός ἐστε καὶ υἱοὶ ἡμέρας 'for all of you are people of the light and people of the day' 1 Th 5.5. Though there are two expressions, υἱοὶ φωτός and υἱοὶ ἡμέρας, in 1 Th 5.5, there does not seem to be any significant difference in meaning. The two phrases simply supplement and reinforce each other.

τέκνα φωτός: ὡς τέκνα φωτὸς περιπατεῖτε 'you must live like people who belong to God' Eph 5.8.

In a number of languages it is difficult to speak of 'light' in the metaphorical sense of the truth that comes from God. Such truth is not to be equated with knowledge, but with the principles and practices of right moral behavior. Because of these difficulties in speaking of 'truth' as 'light,' a number of translators have preferred to use the expression 'people of God' for the phrases υἱοὶ τοῦ φωτός, υἱοὶ τῆς ἡμέρας, and τέκνα φωτός. In some instances, however, it is possible to employ 'light,' if this is described as 'light that comes from God' or even 'the true light from God.'

11.15 αἱ δώδεκα φυλαί: (a set phrase, literally 'the twelve tribes,' but used in a figurative sense) all of the people of God as a possible reference to the new Israel – 'all God's people.' Ἰάκωβος θεοῦ καὶ κυρίου Ἰησοῦ Χριστοῦ δοῦλος ταῖς δώδεκα φυλαῖς ταῖς ἐν τῇ διασπορᾷ χαίρειν 'James, a servant of God and of the Lord Jesus Christ, to all the people of God scattered over the world, Greetings' Jas 1.1. It is possible to understand Jas 1.1 as containing a salutation to the twelve tribes of Israel scattered throughout the Diaspora, but this literal interpretation has generally been rejected for a reference to all of God's people scattered throughout the known world. If one elects to follow a literal translation of this passage, it would be important to introduce a marginal note indicating the alternative meaning and vice versa.

11.16 υἱοὶ τοῦ αἰῶνος τούτου: (an idiom, literally 'sons of this age') persons who hold to the value system of the world – 'non-religious people, people of this world, people of this age.' οἱ υἱοὶ τοῦ αἰῶνος τούτου φρονιμώτεροι ὑπὲρ τοὺς υἱοὺς τοῦ φωτὸς εἰς τὴν γενεὰν τὴν ἑαυτῶν εἰσιν 'the people of this world are much more shrewd in handling their affairs than the people who serve God' Lk 16.8; οἱ υἱοὶ τοῦ αἰῶνος τούτου γαμοῦσιν καὶ γαμίσκονται 'people of this age marry and are given in marriage' Lk 20.34.

In some instances 'the people of this world' may be rendered as 'the people who live like most people in the world' or 'the people who are concerned only about what people say.' Sometimes the identification with the world is expressed in contrast with people's attitude concerning God, for example, 'people who have no use for God.'

11.17 πιστή [b], ῆς f: one who is included among the faithful followers of Christ – 'believer, Christian, follower.' υἱὸς γυναικὸς Ἰουδαίας πιστῆς 'the son of a Jewish woman who was a believer' Ac 16.1.[4]

11.18 τέλειος [g], α, ον: one who is initiated into a religious community of faith (a meaning which reflects the occurrence of τέλειος as a technical term for persons initiated into the mystery religions) – 'initiated.' ὅσοι οὖν τέλειοι, τοῦτο φρονῶμεν 'all of us who are initiated into this faith should have this same attitude' Php 3.15; ἵνα παραστήσωμεν πάντα ἄνθρωπον τέλειον ἐν Χριστῷ 'in order that we might bring everyone into a state of being initiated in Christ' Col 1.28. In a number of languages 'initiated' may be best expressed as 'to become a member of' or 'to become a believer in.' It is possible, however, to interpret τέλειος in Php 3.15 and Col 1.28 as mature spirituality or a state of being spiritually mature (see 88.100).

11.19 ἄπιστος [b], ου m: a person who does not belong to the group of believers in Christ – 'non-Christian.' εἰ δὲ ὁ ἄπιστος χωρίζεται, χωριζέσθω 'if the one who is not a Christian wants to leave, let him do so' 1 Cor 7.15.[5]

In 1 Cor 7.15 it may be necessary to indicate the so-called goal of belief or trust, for example, 'if one who is not a believer in Christ' or 'if the one who is not a follower of Christ.'

11.20 ἄδικος, ου m: a person who is not a member of the Christian community and by implication possibly unjust or not in a right relation with God – 'unbeliever, not a follower of Christ.' τολμᾷ τις ὑμῶν πρᾶγμα ἔχων πρὸς τὸν ἕτερον κρίνεσθαι ἐπὶ τῶν ἀδίκων 'if one of you has a dispute with the other, how dare he go to law before unbelievers' 1 Cor 6.1.

11.21 νεόφυτος, ου m: (a figurative extension of meaning of νεόφυτος 'newly planted,' not

---

4 πιστή may also be regarded as a derivative of πιστεύω [c] 'to be a believer' (31.102), but NT usage in a passage such as Ac 16.1 seems to focus more upon group adherence than upon the actual state of believing. See also 31.103, fn 16.

5 The problems of classifying ἄπιστος are essentially similar to those involving πιστή [b] (11.17 and footnote 4 above).

occurring in the NT) an individual who has recently become a member of a religious group – 'recent convert.' μὴ νεόφυτον, ἵνα μὴ τυφωθείς 'not a recent convert, in order that he may not swell up with pride' 1 Tm 3.6. A 'recent convert' may be rendered as 'one who has only recently begun to believe in Christ' or 'one who has just begun to trust Christ.'

11.22 ἀδελφότης, ητος *f*: an association of persons having a strong sense of unity – 'brotherhood, fellow believers.' τὴν ἀδελφότητα ἀγαπᾶτε 'love the brethren' 1 Pe 2.17. It is often quite impossible to speak of fellow Christians as 'the brothers,' since a number of receptor languages do not permit this type of extension of meaning from an underlying base meaning 'brother' or 'brothers.' Therefore, it may be necessary to speak of 'fellow believers' or 'those who believe together with others' or 'those who likewise believe.' See also discussion at 11.23.

11.23 ἀδελφός [b], οῦ *m*: a close associate of a group of persons having a well-defined membership (in the NT ἀδελφός [b] refers specifically to fellow believers in Christ) – 'fellow believer, (Christian) brother.' ἀδελφοί μου, χαίρετε ἐν κυρίῳ 'my fellow believers, be joyful in your union with the Lord' Php 3.1. The masculine form ἀδελφός [b] may include both men and women, but see also 11.24.

Though in a number of languages it is possible to use a corresponding term meaning 'brother' or 'brothers' in the sense of fellow believers, in some languages this cannot be done, and one must employ other types of expressions. In some instances it is possible to generalize a term meaning 'relative' and therefore to address or to speak of fellow Christians as 'relatives' rather than specifically 'brothers and sisters.' In most instances, however, one may only employ a phrase such as 'those who also believe' or 'those who believe in Christ even as we do.'

11.24 ἀδελφή [b], ῆς *f*: a close female associate of a group with well-defined membership (in the NT referring specifically to fellow believers in Christ) – 'fellow believer, sister in Christ, sister in the faith.' ἐὰν ἀδελφὸς ἢ

ἀδελφὴ γυμνοὶ ὑπάρχωσιν 'if there is a brother or sister who needs clothes' Jas 2.15.

Though in a number of languages it is possible to use a term meaning 'sister' in the sense of a fellow believer, in some languages this cannot be done. As in the case of ἀδελφός [b] (see 11.23), it may be possible to use a term such as 'relative,' but more often than not, it may be necessary to use a phrase such as 'one who also believes' or 'one who believes in Christ even as we do.'

11.25 ἀδελφός [c], οῦ *m*: a person belonging to the same socio-religious entity and being of the same age group as the so-called reference person – 'brother, fellow countryman, fellow Jew, associate.' ἀδελφοὶ καὶ πατέρες, ἀκούσατέ μου τῆς πρὸς ὑμᾶς νυνὶ ἀπολογίας 'brothers and fathers, listen to me as I now make my defense before you' Ac 22.1. [6]

11.26 πατήρ [f], πατρός *m*: a member of a well-defined socio-religious entity and representing an older age group than the so-called reference person – 'father, elder.' ἀδελφοὶ καὶ πατέρες, ἀκούσατέ μου τῆς πρὸς ὑμᾶς νυνὶ ἀπολογίας 'brothers and fathers, listen to me as I now make my defense before you' Ac 22.1. [6]

11.27 οἱ ἅγιοι (occurring in the plural as a substantive): persons who belong to God, and as such constitute a religious entity – 'God's people.' κλητοῖς ἁγίοις 'to the ones called to be God's people' 1 Cor 1.2.

In rendering οἱ ἅγιοι it is important to avoid an expression which means 'sanctified,' for the focus is not upon a particular state of holiness, but upon a special relationship with God. Those who are spoken of as οἱ ἅγιοι may also be admonished to become sanctified.

In a number of respects, οἱ ἅγιοι is similar in meaning to λαός [b] 'people of God' (11.12) and to ἀδελφός [b] 'fellow believer' (11.23).

11.28 ἐπικαλέομαι τὸ ὄνομά τινος ἐπί τινα: (an idiom, literally 'to have someone's name

---

6 In Ac 22.1, as noted in 11.25 and 11.26, the use of ἀδελφοί focuses more upon identification of the speaker with the persons addressed, while πατέρες implies respect accorded those representing an older generation.

called upon someone') to be acknowledged as belonging to the one whose name is called upon such an individual – 'to be one of (God's) people, to be the people of.' δῆσαι πάντας τοὺς ἐπικαλουμένους τὸ ὄνομά σου 'to put in prison all those who are your people' (literally 'all those upon whom your name is called') Ac 9.14; πάντα τὰ ἔθνη ἐφ' οὓς ἐπικέκληται τὸ ὄνομά ἐπ' αὐτούς literally 'all the nations upon whom my name has been called,' meaning 'all the nations who belong to me' or 'all the nations whom I have called to be my own' Ac 15.17.

This interpretation of the expression ἐπικαλέομαι τὸ ὄνομά τινος ἐπί τινα is based upon well attested OT usage, and though it is quite different from traditional interpretations of Ac 9.14 and Ac 15.17, it should be followed as reflecting a more satisfactory and accurate interpretation of the passive form of ἐπικαλέω.

11.29 ἀρνίον[b], ου *n*: (a figurative extension of meaning of ἀρνίον[a] 'lamb,' 4.25) a follower of Christ, with the implication of helplessness and dependence – 'a person who is like a lamb.' βόσκε τὰ ἀρνία μου 'take care of my people, who are like lambs' Jn 21.15. Compare 11.30 and 11.31.

11.30 πρόβατον[b], ου *n*: (a figurative extension of meaning of πρόβατον[a] 'sheep,' 4.22) a follower of Christ, with the implication of needing care and guidance – 'a person who is like a sheep.' ποίμαινε τὰ πρόβατά μου 'take care of my people, who are like sheep' Jn 21.16. Compare 11.29 and 11.31.

11.31 ποίμνιον, ου *n* (a figurative extension of meaning of ποίμνιον 'flock,' not occurring in the NT); ποίμνη[b], ης *f* (a figurative extension of meaning of ποίμνη[a] 'flock,' 4.28): the followers of Christ constituting a well-defined membership group – 'people who are like a flock.'
ποίμνιον: προσέχετε ἑαυτοῖς καὶ παντὶ τῷ ποιμνίῳ 'keep watch over yourselves and over all my people, who are like a flock' Ac 20.28.
ποίμνη[b]: γενήσονται μία ποίμνη, εἷς ποιμήν 'there will be one flock and one shepherd' Jn 10.16.

It is often impossible to reproduce the figurative values of ἀρνίον[b] (11.29), πρόβατον[b] (11.30), ποίμνιον, and ποίμνη[b], since such metaphors cannot be employed in areas of the world in which sheep serve primarily as scavengers around villages (something which is generally true in many parts of the tropics). It may be possible in some instances to preserve something of the metaphorical value of these four terms by translating in some such manner as 'take care of my people as you would sheep' or 'take care of my people, who are like sheep,' or 'take care of my helpless people,' but frequently one can only translate as 'take care of my people.'

11.32 ἐκκλησία[a], ας *f*: a congregation of Christians, implying interacting membership – 'congregation, church.' τῇ ἐκκλησίᾳ τοῦ θεοῦ τῇ οὔσῃ ἐν Κορίνθῳ 'to the church of God which is in Corinth' 1 Cor 1.2; ἀσπάζονται ὑμᾶς αἱ ἐκκλησίαι πᾶσαι τοῦ Χριστοῦ 'all the churches of Christ greet you' Ro 16.16.

Though some persons have tried to see in the term ἐκκλησία a more or less literal meaning of 'called-out ones,' this type of etymologizing is not warranted either by the meaning of ἐκκλησία in NT times or even by its earlier usage. The term ἐκκλησία was in common usage for several hundred years before the Christian era and was used to refer to an assembly of persons constituted by well-defined membership. In general Greek usage it was normally a socio-political entity based upon citizenship in a city-state (see ἐκκλησία[c], 11.78) and in this sense is parallel to δῆμος (11.78). For the NT, however, it is important to understand the meaning of ἐκκλησία[a] as 'an assembly of God's people.'

In the rendering of ἐκκλησία[a] a translator must beware of using a term which refers primarily to a building rather than to a congregation of believers. In many contexts ἐκκλησία[a] may be readily rendered as 'gathering of believers' or 'group of those who trust in Christ.' Sometimes, as in 1 Cor 1.2, it is possible to translate 'Paul writes to the believers in Christ who live in Corinth.' Such a translation does, however, omit a significant element in the term ἐκκλησία[a], in that the sense of corporate unity is not specified.

11.33 ἐκκλησία^b, ας *f*: the totality of congregations of Christians – 'church.' σὺ εἶ Πέτρος, καὶ ἐπὶ ταύτῃ τῇ πέτρᾳ οἰκοδομήσω μου τὴν ἐκκλησίαν 'you are Peter, and upon this rock I will build my church' Mt 16.18.

11.34 σῶμα^c, τος *n*: (a figurative extension of meaning of σῶμα^a 'body,' 8.1) believers in Christ who are joined together as a group, with the implication of each having a distinctive function within the group – 'congregation, Christian group, church.' εἰς οἰκοδομὴν τοῦ σώματος τοῦ Χριστοῦ 'to build up the church of Christ which is like a body' Eph 4.12.
Though in some languages it may seem relatively strange to speak of an organization of persons as a 'body,' it is important to try to preserve in one way or another this figurative meaning of σῶμα, since it plays such an important role in various phases of Paul's teaching. It is frequently necessary, however, to change the metaphor into a simile, as has already been suggested in the translation of Eph 4.12.

11.35 Χριστιανός, οῦ *m*: one who is identified as a believer in and follower of Christ – 'Christian.' χρηματίσαι τε πρώτως ἐν Ἀντιοχείᾳ τοὺς μαθητὰς Χριστιανούς 'it was at Antioch that the believers were first called Christians' Ac 11.26.

11.36 ψευδάδελφος, ου *m*: an individual who pretends to be a close member of a socio-religious group but is not (see 11.22, 11.23, and 11.24) – 'false brother, one who only pretends to be a fellow believer in Christ.' ὁδοιπορίαις πολλάκις, κινδύνοις ποταμῶν . . . λῃστῶν . . . ἐν ψευδαδέλφοις 'in my many travels I have been in danger from floods . . . robbers . . . and false brothers' 2 Cor 11.26. It is frequently necessary to make explicit the full implications of 'false brother' by translating 'one who pretends to be a fellow believer in Christ but is not.'

11.37 τὰ ἔθνη (occurring only in the plural): (an extended meaning of ἔθνος 'nation,' 11.55) those who do not belong to the Jewish or Christian faith – 'heathen, pagans.' μηκέτι ὑμᾶς περιπατεῖν καθὼς καὶ τὰ ἔθνη 'do not any longer live like the heathen' Eph 4.17.
Though in a number of instances τὰ ἔθνη may be rendered as 'those who do not believe in God,' it is often more appropriate to render τὰ ἔθνη in terms of belief in other gods or in false gods. For example, Eph 4.17 may be rendered as 'do not any longer live like those who believe in idols' or '. . . in gods who are not really God.'

11.38 ἐθνικός, ή, όν: (derivative of ἔθνος 'nation,' 11.55) pertaining to one who is not a Jew – 'Gentile, heathen, pagan.' ἐὰν ἀσπάσησθε τοὺς ἀδελφοὺς ὑμῶν μόνον, τί περισσὸν ποιεῖτε; οὐχὶ καὶ οἱ ἐθνικοὶ τὸ αὐτὸ ποιοῦσιν 'if you greet only your friends, have you done anything out of the ordinary? Even the Gentiles do that' Mt 5.47.

11.39 ἐθνικῶς: (derivative of ἔθνος 'nation,' 11.55) pertaining to being like or similar to one who is not a Jew – 'like a Gentile, as a heathen, similar to a pagan.' εἰ σὺ Ἰουδαῖος ὑπάρχων ἐθνικῶς καὶ οὐχὶ Ἰουδαϊκῶς ζῇς 'if you are a Jew and live like a Gentile and not like a Jew' Ga 2.14. In Ga 2.14 one cannot use some such expression as 'like those who do not believe in God' (compare τὰ ἔθνη, 11.37), since here the contrast is between two types of believers, Jews and non-Jews. Frequently there is no specific term for 'Gentile' in contrast with Jews, and therefore it may be important to speak of 'Gentiles' as 'those who are not Jews.' Ga 2.14 may then be rendered as 'you are a Jew, but you have been living like those who are not Jews.'

11.40 Ἕλλην^b, ηνος *m*: (an extended meaning of Ἕλλην^a 'Greek,' 11.90) a person who is a Gentile in view of being a Greek – 'Gentile, non-Jew, Greek.' μὴ εἰς τὴν διασπορὰν τῶν Ἑλλήνων μέλλει πορεύεσθαι καὶ διδάσκειν τοὺς Ἕλληνας; 'he is not likely, is he, to go to the Jews scattered among the Greeks and to teach the Greeks?' Jn 7.35. Though the occurrence of Ἕλλην in Jn 7.35 could be interpreted as merely a reference to Greeks, it is probably a reference to Greeks as being Gentiles, and therefore Ἕλλην^b is classified here in the subdomain of socio-religious groups. The occurrence of "Ελλην in Ac 14.1 (ὥστε πιστεῦσαι Ἰουδαίων τε καὶ Ἑλλήνων πολὺ πλῆθος 'so that a large number of Jews and Gentiles believed') is another instance of "Ελλην referring primarily to a socio-religious group rather than merely to Greeks as a nation.

11.41 Ἑλληνίς^b, ίδος f: (an extended meaning of Ἑλληνίς^a 'Greek woman,' 11.91) a female who is a Gentile in view of being a Greek – 'Gentile woman, non-Jew, Greek.' πολλοὶ μὲν οὖν ἐξ αὐτῶν ἐπίστευσαν, καὶ τῶν Ἑλληνίδων γυναικῶν τῶν εὐσχημόνων 'as a result many of them believed, including Greek women of high social standing' Ac 17.12. Though one may translate Ἑλληνίς in Ac 17.12 as 'Greek,' the focus is probably upon these women as being Gentiles rather than merely Greeks, for it is the Gentile status of these persons which seems to have been particularly aggravating to some of the Jews in that region.

11.42 ἄνομος, ου m: a non-Jew who lives completely without reference to the Jewish Law – 'Gentile, heathen, pagan.' τοῖς ἀνόμοις ὡς ἄνομος . . . ἵνα κερδάνω τοὺς ἀνόμους 'for the sake of the Gentiles I live like a Gentile . . . in order to win Gentiles' 1 Cor 9.21. For another interpretation of ἄνομος in 1 Cor 9.21, see 33.57.

In a number of contexts, it may be best to speak of 'Gentiles' as 'those who are not Jews.' In some languages the equivalent of 'Gentiles' is simply 'foreigners,' but one must be very certain that the use of a term meaning 'foreigners' will actually designate non-Jews rather than those people who do not speak the particular receptor language.

It would be a serious mistake to render ἄνομος as 'lawless' on the basis of its etymology. To speak of a 'lawless person' is to imply that he transgresses existing laws rather than being one who is not subject to the Mosaic Law.

11.43 ἀλλόφυλος, ου m: a person not belonging to the ethnic group in question (from the specifically Jewish point of view, one who is not a Jew, but a Gentile) – 'foreigner, Gentile, heathen, pagan.' ἀθέμιτόν ἐστιν ἀνδρὶ Ἰουδαίῳ κολλᾶσθαι ἢ προσέρχεσθαι ἀλλοφύλῳ 'a Jew is not allowed to visit or associate with a Gentile' or '. . . with a person who is not a Jew' Ac 10.28.[7]

11.44 συναγωγή^a, ῆς f: an assembled group of worshipers or members of such a group – 'assembly, congregation.' ἀλλὰ συναγωγὴ τοῦ Σατανᾶ 'but a congregation of Satan' Re 2.9; ἐὰν γὰρ εἰσέλθῃ εἰς συναγωγὴν ὑμῶν ἀνήρ 'if a man comes into your assembly' Jas 2.2. In Jas 2.2 συναγωγή may indicate the place of gathering, rather than the assembled group (see συναγωγή^c, 7.20).

In translating Jas 2.2 it is possible to render the conditional clause as 'if a person comes into your church' or '. . . into your congregation.'

11.45 συναγωγή^b, ῆς f: a congregation of Jews – 'synagogue, congregation.' ᾐτήσατο παρ' αὐτοῦ ἐπιστολὰς εἰς Δαμασκὸν πρὸς τὰς συναγωγάς 'he asked for letters of introduction to the synagogues at Damascus' Ac 9.2.

Since the borrowed term 'synagogue' in receptor languages so frequently refers only to a building rather than to a congregation, it may be necessary in Ac 9.2 to say 'he asked for letters of introduction to leaders of the synagogues' or '. . . leaders of the congregations of Jews.'

11.46 ἀποσυνάγωγος, ον: a state of having been excommunicated from membership in a synagogue – 'expelled from a synagogue.' ἐάν τις αὐτὸν ὁμολογήσῃ Χριστόν, ἀποσυνάγωγος γένηται 'if anyone professed him to be the Messiah, he would be put out of the synagogue' Jn 9.22.

In rendering Jn 9.22 it is important to indicate clearly that this is not a matter of an individual merely being forced outside of a synagogue building, but excluded from membership and thus from worship in the synagogue. In some languages this is made explicit by saying 'his name will be erased from the

---

7 Though ἀλλόφυλος in its more general meaning belongs to a class of socio-political terms, its specific usage in the NT justifies the classification of its meaning as socio-religious.

list of those belonging to the synagogue' or 'he will no longer be able to enter a synagogue' or 'he will be rejected as a member of the synagogue.'

11.47 ἐφημερία, ας *f*: a class or division of persons who perform certain daily duties (in the one NT occurrence, a reference to a group of priests performing certain functions in the Temple at Jerusalem) – 'work group, division.' ἱερεύς τις ὀνόματι Ζαχαρίας ἐξ ἐφημερίας Ἀβιά 'there was a priest named Zechariah who belonged to the work group of Abijah' Lk 1.5.

It may be necessary to expand somewhat the expression 'the work group of Abijah' to read 'a work group known as the division of Abijah.' Otherwise, one might get the impression that this was a work group under the command of Abijah or a group of persons who belonged specifically to the person named Abijah. If it is difficult to obtain a satisfactory expression for 'work group,' one can of course translate the final clause of Lk 1.5 as simply 'who belonged to a group of priests known as the group of Abijah.'

11.48 Σαδδουκαῖος, ου *m* (always occurring in the plural): a member of a politically influential Jewish party in Jerusalem at the time of Jesus and the apostles. The Sadducees were a smaller group than the Pharisees (see 11.49), but were often in control of important political and religious positions. Their denial of the resurrection of the dead and their acceptance of only the first five books of the OT are important elements in some of the important differences which arose between the Sadducees and the Pharisees – 'Sadducee.' ὁ ἀρχιερεὺς καὶ πάντες οἱ σὺν αὐτῷ, ἡ οὖσα αἵρεσις τῶν Σαδδουκαίων 'the high priest and all of those associated with him being members of the party of the Sadducees' Ac 5.17.

11.49 Φαρισαῖος, ου *m*: a member of an important religious and political Jewish party at the time of Jesus and the apostles. The Pharisees constituted a significantly larger group than the Sadducees (see 11.48) and differed with them on certain doctrines and patterns of behavior. The Pharisees were strict and jealous adherents to the laws of the OT and to numerous additional traditions – 'Pharisee.' διὰ τί ἡμεῖς καὶ οἱ Φαρισαῖοι νηστεύομεν πολλά; 'why is it that we and the Pharisees fast often?' Mt 9.14.

Translators have generally found it both wise and necessary to simply transliterate in one form or another Σαδδουκαῖος (11.48) and Φαρισαῖος, but some background information concerning these two parties is particularly important in a glossary; otherwise, certain passages of Scripture become extremely difficult to understand satisfactorily.

11.50 αἵρεσις[a], εως *f*: a division or group based upon different doctrinal opinions and/or loyalties and hence by implication in certain contexts an unjustified party or group (applicable in the NT to religious parties) – 'religious party, sect.' τὴν ἀκριβεστάτην αἵρεσιν τῆς ἡμετέρας θρησκείας 'the strictest party of our religion' Ac 26.5; τὴν ὁδὸν ἣν λέγουσιν αἵρεσιν 'the way which they say is a false party' Ac 24.14. Compare αἵρεσις[b] in 33.241 where it means the content of false doctrines or teaching.

It is often difficult to find a term in a receptor language which designates primarily a religious party. Normally one must employ some type of phrase in which the various components of αἵρεσις[a] are somewhat redistributed. For example, in Ac 26.5 'the strictest party of our religion' may be rendered as 'those who have the strictest rules about the way they should worship God.' Similarly, the wrong kind of religious party in Ac 24.14 may be rendered as 'the group of those who worship God in the wrong way.'

11.51 οἱ ἐκ περιτομῆς: (a set phrase, literally 'those of circumcision') those who insisted on circumcising Gentiles if they were to be regarded as true believers in Jesus Christ – 'those of the circumcision' or 'those who insisted on circumcision.' διεκρίνοντο πρὸς αὐτὸν οἱ ἐκ περιτομῆς 'those who were in favor of circumcising Gentiles criticized him' Ac 11.2.

11.52 ἀκροβυστία[a], ας *f*: a state of being uncircumcised by not having the foreskin of the penis cut off – 'being uncircumcised, the foreskin not cut off.'[8] εἰσῆλθες πρὸς ἄνδρας ἀκροβυστίαν ἔχοντας καὶ συνέφαγες αὐτοῖς 'you went as a guest with men who are uncircumcised and you ate with them' Ac 11.3.

11.53 ἀκροβυστία[b], ας *f*: a collective for those who are uncircumcised – 'uncircumcised, Gentiles, the Gentile world.' ἰδόντες ὅτι πεπίστευμαι τὸ εὐαγγέλιον τῆς ἀκροβυστίας καθὼς Πέτρος τῆς περιτομῆς 'seeing that I was entrusted with the good news to the Gentiles even as Peter was entrusted with the good news to the circumcised' Ga 2.7.

In translating Ga 2.7 it is essential in some languages to avoid the impression that there are two gospels, one for the Jews and another for the Gentiles. One may, therefore, render Ga 2.7 as 'I had been entrusted with the good news to the uncircumcised, just as Peter had been for the circumcised' or even 'God had given me and Peter the task of preaching the good news; I to the Gentiles and Peter to the Jews.'

11.54 προσήλυτος, ου *m*: a Gentile who had converted to Judaism – 'Jewish convert, proselyte.' Ἰουδαῖοί τε καὶ προσήλυτοι 'both Jews and proselytes' Ac 2.11.

C Socio-Political (11.55-11.89)

11.55 ἔθνος, ους *n*; λαός[a], οῦ *m*: the largest unit into which the people of the world are divided on the basis of their constituting a socio-political community – 'nation, people.' ἔθνος: καθελὼν ἔθνη ἑπτὰ ἐν γῇ Χανάαν 'he destroyed seven nations in the land of Canaan' Ac 13.19. λαός[a]: ὃ ἡτοίμασας κατὰ πρόσωπον πάντων τῶν λαῶν 'which you have made ready in the presence of all peoples' Lk 2.31.

In a number of languages a term meaning basically 'tribe' has been extended in meaning to identify 'nations.' In other instances dif-

ferent nations are spoken of simply as 'different peoples.' In certain cases distinct nations are classified primarily in terms of their diverse languages, for example, 'those people who speak different languages.' Such an expression should not, however, be used if it only refers to multilingual persons.

11.56 πατριά[b], ᾶς *f*; φυλή[b], ῆς *f*: a relatively large unit of people who constitute a socio-political group, sharing a presumed biological descent (in many contexts πατριά[b] and φυλή[b] are very similar in meaning to ἔθνος and λαός[a], 11.55) – 'nation, people.' πατριά[b]: ἐν τῷ σπέρματί σου ἐνευλογηθήσονται πᾶσαι αἱ πατριαὶ τῆς γῆς 'through your descendants I will bless all the peoples on earth' Ac 3.25. φυλή[b]: τότε κόψονται πᾶσαι αἱ φυλαὶ τῆς γῆς 'then all the nations on earth will mourn' Mt 24.30.

11.57 συμφυλέτης, ου *m*; συγγενής[b], οῦς, dat. pl. συγγενεῦσιν *m*; ἀδελφός[d], οῦ *m*: a person who is a member of the same πατριά[b] or φυλή[b] 'nation' (11.56) – 'fellow countryman.' συμφυλέτης: τὰ αὐτὰ ἐπάθετε καὶ ὑμεῖς ὑπὸ τῶν ἰδίων συμφυλετῶν καθὼς καὶ αὐτοὶ ὑπὸ τῶν Ἰουδαίων 'you suffered the same persecution from your countrymen that they suffered from the Jews' 1 Th 2.14. συγγενής[b]: ἀσπάσασθε Ἀνδρόνικον καὶ Ἰουνιᾶν τοὺς συγγενεῖς μου 'greetings to Andronicus and Junias, my fellow countrymen' Ro 16.7. ἀδελφός[d]: ἀνέβη ἐπὶ τὴν καρδίαν αὐτοῦ ἐπισκέψασθαι τοὺς ἀδελφοὺς αὐτοῦ τοὺς υἱοὺς Ἰσραήλ 'he decided to visit his countrymen, the people of Israel' Ac 7.23.

The term ἄνδρες is often added to ἀδελφοί[d], constituting a lexical unit having essentially the same meaning as ἀδελφοί[d], but with the connotation of greater formality: ἄνδρες ἀδελφοί, ἐξὸν εἰπεῖν μετὰ παρρησίας πρὸς ὑμᾶς 'fellow countrymen, I can speak to you quite plainly' Ac 2.29.

συμφυλέτης, συγγενής[b], and ἀδελφός[d] may often be translated by a phrase, for example, 'a person of the same country' or 'a man who belongs to the same nation' or 'one who is part of the same tribe.'

---

8 The term ἀκροβυστία as a designation of a state of being uncircumcised belongs technically to a domain of physiological states (Domain 23). Since, however, its significance for the NT text is only in connection with the socio-religious character of people, ἀκροβυστία is classified here in Domain 11 (see also 11.53).

11.58 οἶκος Ἰσραήλ; υἱοὶ Ἰσραήλ: (idioms, literally 'house of Israel' and 'sons of Israel' respectively) the people of Israel as an ethnic entity – 'the people of Israel, the nation of Israel.'

οἶκος Ἰσραήλ: ἀσφαλῶς οὖν γινωσκέτω πᾶς οἶκος Ἰσραήλ 'all the people of Israel, then, are to know for sure' Ac 2.36.

υἱοὶ Ἰσραήλ: ἀνέβη ἐπὶ τὴν καρδίαν αὐτοῦ ἐπισκέψασθαι τοὺς ἀδελφοὺς αὐτοῦ τοὺς υἱοὺς Ἰσραήλ 'he decided to visit his countrymen, the people of Israel' Ac 7.23.

In translating the expression 'the people of Israel' it may be necessary to use an appositional phrase, for example, 'the people, namely, Israel' or a relative clause which also serves an appositional function, for example, 'the people who are Israel.' In some languages it may be preferable to use a term such as 'nation' followed by some expression which will indicate that Israel is simply the name of the nation, for example, 'the nation called Israel.'

11.59 τόπος[f], ου *m*: the inhabitants of a place – 'place, people.'[9] ὃς ἂν τόπος μὴ δέξηται ὑμᾶς 'whatever place does not welcome you' or 'whatever people do not welcome you' or 'if the people of any town do not welcome you' Mk 6.11.

In a number of languages it is impossible to use a term meaning 'place' as a reference to the people of such a place.

11.60 ἐντόπιος, ου *m*: the inhabitants of a particular place – 'local people.' παρεκαλοῦμεν ἡμεῖς τε καὶ οἱ ἐντόπιοι τοῦ μὴ ἀναβαίνειν αὐτὸν εἰς Ἱερουσαλήμ 'we and the local people begged him not to go to Jerusalem' Ac 21.12. A typical rendering of 'the local people' is sim-

9 It is possible that in the case of such meanings as τόπος[f] (11.59), πόλις[c] (11.61), κώμη[b] (11.62), and χώρα[e] (11.64) one should count on certain more or less automatic semantic 'rules' by which the meaning of inhabitants could be derived by metonymy from expressions of place. Since, however, such metonymic developments are far from universal, the distinct meanings are listed here as a practical guide to translators. The same type of problem occurs with Ἱεροσόλυμα 'Jerusalem,' Ἰουδαία 'Judea,' and περίχωρος 'region' in Mt 3.5.

ply 'the people who lived there' or 'those who inhabited that place.'

11.61 πόλις[c], εως *f*: the inhabitants of a city – 'city, inhabitants of a city.'[9] σχεδὸν πᾶσα ἡ πόλις συνήχθη 'nearly the whole city gathered together' or 'almost everyone living in that city came together' Ac 13.44.

11.62 κώμη[b], ης *f*: the inhabitants of a village – 'the people there, the people of a village.'[9] πολλάς τε κώμας τῶν Σαμαριτῶν εὐηγγελίζοντο 'they announced the good news to people in many villages of the Samaritans' Ac 8.25. Though in English it may seem perfectly appropriate to speak of 'announcing the good news to a town' or '. . . a village,' in a number of languages this is simply not possible, for any announcement of good news must be directed to people and not to a place or area.

11.63 τέκνον[c], ου *n* (only in the plural): (a figurative extension of meaning of τέκνον[a] 'child,' 10.36) inhabitants of a particular place – 'persons of, people of.' Ἱερουσαλήμ . . . ποσάκις ἠθέλησα ἐπισυνάξαι τὰ τέκνα σου ὃν τρόπον ὄρνις τὴν ἑαυτῆς νοσσιάν 'Jerusalem . . . how many times I wanted to gather your people just as a hen does her chicks' Lk 13.34.

Only rarely can one preserve the figurative significance of τέκνον[c] as a designation of the inhabitants of an area. Readers are too likely to understand such a reference as applicable only to children who live in a particular place. Even the use of a simile does not assist appreciably, since it would be interpreted as likening the inhabitants of an area to children, probably in the sense of their being immature or incapable. For example, the expression 'the people of Jerusalem like children' would probably lead to serious misunderstanding.

11.64 χώρα[e], ας *f*: the inhabitants of a region – 'region, inhabitants of a region.'[9] ἐξεπορεύετο πρὸς αὐτὸν πᾶσα ἡ Ἰουδαία χώρα 'the whole region of Judea went out to him' or 'everyone living in the region of Judea went out to him' Mk 1.5.

In a number of languages it is quite impossible to speak of 'a region going out,' since the term for 'region' cannot substitute for 'the people of the region.' Therefore, all such references must be made personal.

11.65 θυγάτηρ^d, τρός *f*: (a figurative extension of meaning of θυγάτηρ^a 'daughter,' 10.46) a female inhabitant of a place – 'woman of.' θυγατέρες Ἰερουσαλήμ, μὴ κλαίετε ἐπ' ἐμέ 'women of Jerusalem, do not weep for me' Lk 23.28.

11.66 θυγάτηρ Σιών: (an idiom, literally 'daughter of Zion') the inhabitants of Jerusalem – 'people of Zion, people of Jerusalem.' εἴπατε τῇ θυγατρὶ Σιών, ἰδοὺ ὁ βασιλεύς σου ἔρχεταί σοι 'tell the people of Zion, Behold your king is coming to you' Mt 21.5.

11.67 πολιτεία^b, ας *f*: a group of people constituting a socio-political unit – 'state, people.' ἀπηλλοτριωμένοι τῆς πολιτείας τοῦ Ἰσραήλ 'you were excluded from the people of Israel' Eph 2.12.

It is possible that in Eph 2.12 the use of πολιτεία suggests not merely a socio-political but also a socio-religious grouping. Such a conclusion would, in a sense, be true of any and all designations of a Jewish constituency, since religion and ethnic identification were so inextricably bound together.

11.68 πολίτης, ου *m*: a person having full status as a member of a socio-political unit of people – 'citizen.' ἐκολλήθη ἑνὶ τῶν πολιτῶν τῆς χώρας ἐκείνης 'he went to work for one of the citizens of that country' Lk 15.15.

In a number of languages a citizen may be described as 'a person who belongs to that country' or 'one who is a part of the people of that country' or 'one who is counted as a person of that country,' but one could be a citizen of a country without necessarily living in such a geographical area.

In He 8.11 (καὶ οὐ μὴ διδάξωσιν ἕκαστος τὸν πολίτην αὐτοῦ 'none of them will have to teach his fellow citizen') πολίτης occurs with the possessive pronoun αὐτοῦ and hence is therefore equivalent to συμπολίτης (11.72) in meaning.

11.69 υἱός^g, οῦ *m*: a member of a socio-political group with some presumed ethnic

relationship – 'citizen.' ἀπὸ τίνων λαμβάνουσιν τέλη ἢ κῆνσον; ἀπὸ τῶν υἱῶν αὐτῶν ἢ ἀπὸ τῶν ἀλλοτρίων; 'from whom do they collect tribute or taxes? from the citizens of that country or from foreigners?' Mt 17.25.

11.70 πολιτεία^a, ας *f*: the right to be a citizen of a particular socio-political entity (see 11.67 and 11.68) – 'citizenship.' ἐγὼ πολλοῦ κεφαλαίου τὴν πολιτείαν ταύτην ἐκτησάμην 'I acquired this citizenship with a large sum of money' Ac 22.28. In some languages Ac 22.28 may be rendered as 'I obtained the right to be counted as a citizen' or 'I became a person who belongs to that nation.'

11.71 πολίτευμα, τος *n*: the place or location in which one has the right to be a citizen – 'state, commonwealth, place of citizenship.' ἡμῶν γὰρ τὸ πολίτευμα ἐν οὐρανοῖς ὑπάρχει 'our place of citizenship is in heaven' Php 3.20.

11.72 συμπολίτης, ου *m*: a fellow member of a socio-political unit – 'fellow citizen.' ἐστὲ συμπολῖται τῶν ἁγίων 'you are fellow citizens with God's people' Eph 2.19. The expression in Eph 2.19 may also be rendered as 'you join with God's people as fellow citizens together with them' or 'you and God's people are all persons who belong to the same place' or as in some languages, '. . . people of God's country.'

11.73 ξένος^a, ου *m*: a person belonging to a socio-political group other than the reference group – 'stranger, foreigner.' ξένος ἤμην καὶ συνηγάγετέ με 'I was a stranger and you welcomed me in your homes' Mt 25.35.

Terms for 'stranger' or 'foreigner' are often based upon geographical differences or upon lack of previous knowledge. For example, 'I was a stranger' may be rendered as 'I came from another country' or 'I was not known to any of you.'

11.74 ἀλλότριος^b, α, ον: a person from another geographical or cultural region and/or one not known to members of the socio-political group in question – 'stranger, foreigner.' ἀλλοτρίῳ δὲ οὐ μὴ ἀκολουθήσουσιν 'they will certainly not follow a stranger' Jn 10.5. In

Jn 10.5 the most satisfactory rendering of 'stranger' is often 'someone who is not known,' in other words, 'they will not follow someone whom they do not know' or '. . . recognize.'

11.75 ἀπαλλοτριόομαι: (derivative of ἀλλότριος[b] 'stranger, foreigner,' 11.74) to be a stranger or foreigner – 'to be a stranger, to be a foreigner.' ἀπηλλοτριωμένοι τῆς πολιτείας τοῦ Ἰσραήλ 'you were foreigners not belonging to the people of Israel' Eph 2.12.

11.76 ἀλλογενής, οῦς m: a person belonging to a different socio-political group, with the implication of lack of kinship ties – 'foreigner.' οὐχ εὑρέθησαν ὑποστρέψαντες δοῦναι δόξαν τῷ θεῷ εἰ μὴ ὁ ἀλλογενὴς οὗτος; 'why is this foreigner the only one who came back to give thanks to God?' Lk 17.18.

11.77 πάροικος, ου m; παρεπίδημος, ου m: (derivatives of παροικέω[b] and ἐπιδημέω 'to live as a foreigner,' 85.78, respectively) a person who for a period of time lives in a place which is not his normal residence – 'alien, stranger, temporary resident.'
πάροικος: ἔσται τὸ σπέρμα αὐτοῦ πάροικον ἐν γῇ ἀλλοτρίᾳ 'his descendants will live as strangers in a foreign country' Ac 7.6.
παρεπίδημος: ἐκλεκτοῖς παρεπιδήμοις διασπορᾶς Πόντου 'to God's chosen people who live as aliens scattered throughout Pontus' 1 Pe 1.1.
In Ac 7.6 the expression 'as strangers in a foreign country' may be rendered 'as strangers living in a country which was not their own.' Similarly, 'who live as aliens' may also be rendered as 'who live in countries not their own' or 'who live with people to whose nation they do not belong.'

11.78 ἐκκλησία[c], ας f; δῆμος, ου m: a group of citizens assembled for socio-political activities – 'assembly, gathering.'
ἐκκλησία[c]: ἐν τῇ ἐννόμῳ ἐκκλησίᾳ ἐπιλυθήσεται 'it will have to be settled in the legal assembly' Ac 19.39.
δῆμος: ὁ δὲ Ἀλέξανδρος . . . ἤθελεν ἀπολογεῖσθαι τῷ δήμῳ 'but Alexander . . . wanted to make a speech before the assembly of the citizens' Ac 19.33.

It is possible that in ἐκκλησία[c] there is somewhat more focus upon the people being together as a legal assembly, while in the case of δῆμος the emphasis is merely upon a meeting of citizens. But in the NT one cannot distinguish clearly between the meanings of these two words.
ἐκκλησία[c] and δῆμος may be rendered in some languages as 'a meeting of the people who belonged to that place' or '. . . who were inhabitants of that town' or '. . . whose homes were in that town.'

11.79 συνέδριον[a], ου n: a socio-political group acting as a judicial council – 'city council, council of judges.' παραδώσουσιν γὰρ ὑμᾶς εἰς συνέδρια 'they will take you (for judgment) to the local city councils' Mt 10.17. There are certain problems involved in the rendering of συνέδριον[a] as 'city council,' since in so many parts of the world a group which would be designated as a 'city council' would be primarily legislative rather than judicial in function. It is for that reason that συνέδριον[a] may be better translated in a number of instances as 'the council which will judge you' or 'before a group of men who will decide whether you have done right or wrong.'

11.80 συνέδριον[b], ου n: the highest Jewish council, exercising jurisdiction in civil and religious matters, but having no power over life and death or over military actions or taxation – 'Sanhedrin, the council of the Jews.' συνήγαγον οὖν οἱ ἀρχιερεῖς καὶ οἱ Φαρισαῖοι συνέδριον 'then the chief priests and the Pharisees called together a meeting of the Sanhedrin' Jn 11.47.
In a number of languages συνέδριον[b] can be rendered by a descriptive phrase, for example, 'the most important council of the Jews' or 'the council that made decisions for the Jewish people.'

11.81 Ἄρειος Πάγος[b] m: an advisory council of Athens dealing with ethical, cultural, and religious matters – 'council of the Areopagus.' σταθεὶς δὲ ὁ Παῦλος ἐν μέσῳ τοῦ Ἀρείου Πάγου 'Paul stood up in the midst of the council of the Areopagus' Ac 17.22. It is also possible to understand τοῦ Ἀρείου Πάγου as referring to the location rather than to the council (see 93.412).

It is probably wise in translating Ἄρειος Πάγος[b] to simply transliterate the expression, since it has the status of a proper name. On the other hand, it is extremely important that some footnote be employed so as to indicate something of the significance of this advisory council of Athens.

11.82 Ἀρεοπαγίτης, ου *m*: a member of the council of the Areopagus – 'a member of the council, a member of the Areopagus.' τινὲς δὲ ἄνδρες κολληθέντες αὐτῷ ἐπίστευσαν, ἐν οἷς καὶ Διονύσιος ὁ Ἀρεοπαγίτης 'but some men joined him and believed; one of them was Dionysius, a member of the Areopagus' Ac 17.34.

11.83 γερουσία, ας *f*; πρεσβυτέριον[a], ου *n*: the highest council of the Jews (see also συνέδριον[b] 'Sanhedrin, the council of the Jews,' 11.80) but with the implication of the maturity and relative advanced age of those constituting the membership of such a council – 'Sanhedrin, high council of the Jews.'[10]
γερουσία: ὁ ἀρχιερεὺς καὶ οἱ σὺν αὐτῷ συνεκάλεσαν τὸ συνέδριον καὶ πᾶσαν τὴν γερουσίαν τῶν υἱῶν Ἰσραήλ 'the High Priest and his companions called together the Sanhedrin, that is, the whole council of elders of the Jewish people' Ac 5.21.
πρεσβυτέριον[a]: ὁ ἀρχιερεὺς μαρτυρεῖ μοι καὶ πᾶν τὸ πρεσβυτέριον 'the High Priest and all the council of elders can witness on my behalf' Ac 22.5.

11.84 πρεσβυτέριον[b], ου *n*: a council of elders, with emphasis upon maturity of judgment more than mere age – 'group of elders, elders.' ὃ ἐδόθη σοι διὰ προφητείας μετὰ ἐπιθέσεως τῶν χειρῶν τοῦ πρεσβυτερίου 'which he gave you when the prophets spoke and

when the elders laid their hands on you' 1 Tm 4.14.

11.85 βουλευτής, οῦ *m*: a councilor as a member of the Sanhedrin (see 11.80) – 'a member of the Sanhedrin, a member of the council.' Ἰωσὴφ ὁ ἀπὸ Ἀριμαθαίας εὐσχήμων βουλευτής 'Joseph of Arimathea, a respected member of the council' or '. . . of the Sanhedrin' Mk 15.43.

11.86 συμβούλιον[b], ου *n*: an advisory council – 'council.' τότε ὁ Φῆστος συλλαλήσας μετὰ τοῦ συμβουλίου ἀπεκρίθη 'then Festus answered after conferring with his council' Ac 25.12. In Ac 25.12 it is possible to render 'council' as 'those persons who gave him their opinions' or 'those who were his advisors' or even 'those who said what should be done' or '. . . what was best to do.'

11.87 Ἡρῳδιανοί, ῶν *m*: the political followers and adherents to Herod the Great and his family – 'the followers of Herod, Herodians.' ἀποστέλλουσιν αὐτῷ τοὺς μαθητὰς αὐτῶν μετὰ τῶν Ἡρῳδιανῶν 'they sent to him their disciples together with the followers of Herod' Mt 22.16.

11.88 ζηλωτής[b], οῦ *m*; Καναναῖος, ου *m* (the Aramaic equivalent of ζηλωτής[b] and not in any way related to the geographical terms Cana or Canaan): a member of a Jewish nationalistic group seeking independence from Rome – 'zealot, nationalist.'
ζηλωτής[b]: Σίμωνα τὸν καλούμενον Ζηλωτήν 'Simon called the Zealot' Lk 6.15.
Καναναῖος: Σίμων ὁ Καναναῖος καὶ Ἰούδας ὁ Ἰσκαριώτης 'Simon the Zealot and Judas Iscariot' Mt 10.4.

It is possible that ζηλωτής in Lk 6.15 and Καναναῖος in Mt 10.4 function not so much as a designation of an individual belonging to the particular Jewish nationalistic party (according to some scholars such a party may not have been organized at that time), but of one who is simply zealous for national independence (see ζηλωτής[a] 'enthusiast, zealous person,' 25.77). Therefore, one might speak of Simon as 'Simon the patriot' (the same applies

---

10 Though γερουσία and πρεσβυτέριον[a] refer to the same council of the Jews as the term συνέδριον[b] (11.80), this does not mean that the three terms are completely identical in meaning. The focus upon maturity of age and judgment as well as presumed social standing are more significant factors in γερουσία and πρεσβυτέριον[a] than in συνέδριον[b].

to Ac 1.13, the only other occurrence of ζηλωτής[b] in the NT). To render ζηλωτής[b] as 'armed insurrectionist' or 'guerilla fighter' (as some translators have suggested) would be reading into the text more than is specifically warranted.

11.89 γείτων, ονος *m* and *f*; περίοικος, ου *m*; πλησίον[b]; ἀδελφός[c], οῦ *m*: a person who lives close beside others and who thus by implication is a part of a so-called 'in-group,' that is, the group with which an individual identifies both ethnically and culturally – 'neighbor, brother.'

γείτων: εὑροῦσα συγκαλεῖ τὰς φίλας καὶ γείτονας λέγουσα, Συγχάρητέ μοι 'when she finds it, she calls her friends and neighbors together and says, Rejoice with me' Lk 15.9.

περίοικος: ἤκουσαν οἱ περίοικοι καὶ οἱ συγγενεῖς αὐτῆς ὅτι ἐμεγάλυνεν κύριος τὸ ἔλεος αὐτοῦ μετ' αὐτῆς 'her neighbors and relatives heard how wonderfully good the Lord had been to her' Lk 1.58.

πλησίον[b]: ἀγαπήσεις . . . τὸν πλησίον σου ὡς σεαυτόν 'you must love . . . your neighbor as yourself' Lk 10.27.

ἀδελφός[c]: ὃς δ' ἂν εἴπῃ τῷ ἀδελφῷ αὐτοῦ, Ῥακά 'whoever says to his brother, Fool' Mt 5.22; τί δὲ βλέπεις τὸ κάρφος τὸ ἐν τῷ ὀφθαλμῷ τοῦ ἀδελφοῦ σου 'and why do you pay attention to the speck that is in the eye of your brother' Lk 6.41. Though in Mt 5.22 and Lk 6.41 one may translate ἀδελφός as 'brother,' the evident meaning is not a reference to a sibling, but to a close associate or neighbor, so that the denotation of ἀδελφός is very similar to that of γείτων, περίοικος, and πλησίον[b].

It may be that of the three terms γείτων, περίοικος, and πλησίον[b], the last is somewhat broader in meaning. At least πλησίον is used in Lk 10.27 in a somewhat extended sense of 'fellow man,' while ἀδελφός[c] probably suggests a more intimate or close relationship.

The translation of πλησίον[b] as a singular in Lk 10.27 may pose a problem in understanding, since the singular may be understood in a specific rather than in a generic sense, that is to say, 'love your neighbor as yourself' might immediately give rise to the question 'which neighbor?' Therefore, one must often translate Lk 10.27 as 'you must love your neigh-

bors as you love yourselves' or 'you must love other people as you love yourselves.'

D Ethnic-Cultural (11.90-11.95)

11.90 Ἕλλην[a], ηνος *m*: a person who participates in Greek culture and in so doing would speak the Greek language, but not necessarily a person of Greek ethnic background – 'civilized, Greek.' Ἕλλησίν τε καὶ βαρβάροις, σοφοῖς τε καὶ ἀνοήτοις 'both to the civilized and to the barbarians, to the educated and to the ignorant' Ro 1.14. In Ro 1.14 it is possible that the contrast Ἕλλησίν τε καὶ βαρβάροις may be interpreted as 'to the Greek-speaking persons and to those who do not speak Greek,' but the entire context of Ro 1.14 points to a somewhat broader designation.

11.91 Ἑλληνίς[a], ίδος *f*: a woman of Greek culture and language – 'Greek woman.' ἡ δὲ γυνὴ ἦν Ἑλληνίς, Συροφοινίκισσα τῷ γένει 'the woman was Greek, but Syrophoenician in race' Mk 7.26. It is possible that in Mk 7.26 Ἑλληνίς is to be understood in the sense of Gentile (see 11.41), for the account seems to focus upon the fact that this woman who was not a Jewess nevertheless displayed remarkable faith and confidence in Jesus' ability to help.

11.92 Ἑλληνικός, ή, όν: pertaining to what is Greek – 'Greek.' ἐν τῇ Ἑλληνικῇ ὄνομα ἔχει Ἀπολλύων 'in Greek the name is Apollyon' Re 9.11. In rendering this expression in Re 9.11 it is often necessary to say 'in the language spoken by the Greeks' or 'in the Greek language.' Ἑλληνικός as an adjective does not denote the Greek language as such, but in the feminine form the reference would be to γλῶσσα 'language.'

11.93 Ἑλληνιστής, οῦ *m*: a Greek-speaking Jew in contrast to one speaking a Semitic language – 'Greek-speaking Jew.' ἐγένετο γογγυσμὸς τῶν Ἑλληνιστῶν πρὸς τοὺς Ἑβραίους 'a quarrel arose between the Greek-speaking Jews and the native Jews' Ac 6.1; συνεζήτει πρὸς τοὺς Ἑλληνιστάς 'he argued with the Greek-speaking Jews' Ac 9.29. The Greek-speaking Jews were basically Jewish in culture and religion, but they had adopted certain customs typical of the larger Greco-Roman world in which many of them lived. This inevitably resulted in certain suspicions and misunderstandings.

11.94 βάρβαρος [b], ον: the native people of an area in which a language other than Greek or Latin was spoken (such persons would be regarded as being outside the civilized world of NT times) – 'native people, uncivilized, foreigners.' οἵ τε βάρβαροι παρεῖχον οὐ τὴν τυχοῦσαν φιλανθρωπίαν ἡμῖν 'the native people there were very friendly to us' Ac 28.2. In rendering this expression in Ac 28.2 it would be possible in some languages to translate 'the people there who spoke a strange language were friendly to us' or 'the local inhabitants of that island were kind to us.' ἔσομαι τῷ λαλοῦντι βάρβαρος καὶ ὁ λαλῶν ἐν ἐμοὶ βάρβαρος 'I will be a foreigner to the one who speaks, and the one who speaks will be a foreigner to me' 1 Cor 14.11. In 1 Cor 14.11 βάρβαρος implies being a foreigner from a country outside of the so-called civilized world.

11.95 βάρβαρος [a], ον: a person not participating in Greek culture and civilization (βάρβαρος contrasts with Ἕλλην [a] 'Greek,' 11.90, with the focus on culture rather than on language; see 1 Cor 14.11 at 11.94) – 'non-Greek.' Ἕλλησίν τε καὶ βαρβάροις . . . ὀφειλέτης εἰμί 'I have an obligation . . . to those of Greek culture and to those without' Ro 1.14.

It would be a mistake in the case of Ro 1.14

to speak merely of 'Greeks and barbarians' or 'Greeks and savages.' By NT times Ἕλλην (see 11.90) would have included most of those who participated in one way or another in the culture of the Greco-Roman world. Accordingly, one may render the contrast in Ro 1.14 as 'the civilized and the uncivilized.'

E   Philosophical (11.96-11.97)

11.96 Ἐπικούρειος, η, ον: pertaining to the philosophical system of the Greek philosopher Epicurus, who taught that the world is a series of fortuitous combinations of atoms and that the highest good is pleasure – 'Epicurean, a follower of Epicurus.' τινὲς δὲ καὶ τῶν Ἐπικουρείων καὶ Στοϊκῶν φιλοσόφων συνέβαλλον αὐτῷ 'and some of the Epicurean and Stoic philosophers debated with him' Ac 17.18. In most instances translators have found it more satisfactory to simply transliterate the terms Ἐπικούρειος and Στοϊκός (11.97), but some supplementary note to identify the teachings of the Epicureans and Stoics is important.

11.97 Στοϊκός, ή, όν: pertaining to the philosophical system of the Greek philosopher Zeno, who taught that people should be free from excessive joy or grief and submit without complaint to necessity – 'Stoic, one who adheres to Stoic philosophy.' τινὲς δὲ καὶ τῶν Ἐπικουρείων καὶ Στοϊκῶν φιλοσόφων συνέβαλλον αὐτῷ 'and some of the Epicurean and Stoic philosophers debated with him' Ac 17.18. For comments on some translational problems, see 11.96.

12 Supernatural Beings and Powers

The domain of *Supernatural Beings and Powers* includes all those lexical units whose meanings involve both beings and powers (whether good or bad) which are regarded as possessing supernatural characteristics. The two principal subclasses within this domain are (1) *Supernatural Beings,* for example, God,

Holy Spirit, angel, devil, demon, ghost, and (2) *Supernatural Powers.* [1]

---

1 In certain respects the distinction between 'beings' and 'powers' is artificial, since some of the so-called 'impersonal powers' seem to have certain aspects of personality. Similarly, some of the supernatural beings

Outline of Subdomains

A   Supernatural Beings (12.1-12.42)
B   Supernatural Powers (12.43-12.50)

A   Supernatural Beings[2] (12.1-12.42)

12.1 θεός[a], οῦ *m*: the one supreme super-natural being as creator and sustainer of the universe – 'God.' ὁ θεὸς ὁ ποιήσας τὸν κόσμον καὶ πάντα τὰ ἐν αὐτῷ 'God who made the world and everything in it' Ac 17.24.

The componential features of θεός involve a basic, underlying ambivalence. On the one hand, θεός is regarded as unique to the exclusion of all other gods: οὐδεὶς θεὸς εἰ μὴ εἷς 'there is no God but one' 1 Cor 8.4. This is strictly a monotheistic view of θεός. On the other hand, there occur such expressions as εἴπερ εἰσὶν λεγόμενοι θεοί 'even if there are so-called gods' (1 Cor 8.5), and in the OT the Lord is described as being 'far above all gods' (Ps 97.9), 'the God of gods' (Ps 136.2), and the 'great King above all gods' (Ps 95.3), which is essentially a henotheistic view of θεός. Fundamentally, however, the NT view may be most succinctly reflected in Ga 4.8, τοῖς φύσει μὴ οὖσιν θεοῖς 'those who by nature are not really gods.' In other words, the gods of the pagans (see 12.22) are not to be viewed in the same category as θεός[a].

A further semantic problem is involved in the use of θεός[a] in reference to Christ. In Jn 1.1, 'the Word was God,' the meaning of θεός may be described on the basis that all the com-ponential features of θεός[a] are applied to the referent λόγος, which is in turn identified with 'Christ.' This is not to be interpreted as indicating that the two referents are identical (which was, of course, the position of those who maintained the so-called patropassian heresy), but that the distinctive features of θεός[a] are also fully applicable to another referent, namely, the λόγος or Christ; that is to say, it is legitimate to interpret Jn 1.1 as 'the Word was God' but not as 'God was the Word.'

Translational equivalents of 'God' are of three major types: (1) proper names, (2) descriptive titles, and (3) borrowed terms. There are a number of problems involved in each of these types of translational equiv-alents.

If translators wish to employ in the biblical text a proper name in the receptor language, it is essential that the characteristics of the referent of such a name be sufficiently close to those which characterize the biblical God, so that the message may not be unduly distorted. In fact, the equivalent should be sufficiently close that ready identification can be made. The essential features of such a receptor language term should include (1) benevolent disposition and behavior, (2) creative and sus-taining activity in the world, and (3) supreme power. In most instances it has not been found necessary for such a term to refer to a strictly monotheistic view (that is to say, hav-ing an existence which precludes the ex-istence of any other gods), but it is essential that the name apply to a referent who is regarded as supreme over all others.

There may, however, be a number of dif-ficulties involved in the use of an indigenous expression for θεός[a], since the views concern-ing such a god may involve such factors as (1) psychological distance (the idea that such a god, though all powerful, is still very remote from mankind) and (2) the necessity for con-stant propitiation (as though such a god needs to be constantly entreated or sustained by means of gifts in order to make him favorably disposed toward mankind).

In some instances problems have arisen in the use of an indigenous term for God because such a name may be perfectly ap-propriate in one area in which a language is

would in some contexts be equivalent to supernatural. forces.

It is extremely difficult to determine the precise com-ponential features of the items in this domain of *Super-natural Beings and Powers*, since the referents are con-ceptual rather than perceptual, and some of the referents are unique members of a class. Furthermore, different NT writers seem to use certain terms with somewhat diverse sets of distinctive features.

2 The meanings of this domain are classified as 'per-sons' or 'beings' not because of certain intrinsic character-istics of the referents, but because the meanings of the corresponding terms combine in syntagmatic relations with events and abstracts in essentially the same way as do the meanings of those lexical units which refer to animate beings.

spoken, but have quite a different meaning or value in another part of the language area. For example, in one area of East Africa the name for 'God' in one tribe is the name for the devil in a nearby, closely related tribe.

Descriptive titles for God (which often become essentially names) may focus upon a number of different features or characteristics. In some instances such descriptive titles are traditional for certain receptor languages. In other instances they have been constructed by translators on the basis of indigenous models. The following are illustrative examples of various types of descriptive titles: 'he who made us,' 'the supreme powerful one,' 'the one who performs miracles,' 'the owner of all,' 'he who is sufficient,' 'our great father,' 'the highest one,' 'the great spirit,' 'the unending spirit,' 'the commanding spirit,' 'the great chief,' 'the self-existing one,' and 'the truly sacred one.'

Some Bible translators have attempted to avoid semantic complications by borrowing a term from a dominant language. In Latin America, for example, many early missionaries borrowed the Spanish term *Dios,* but in explaining the meaning of *Dios* as the great and all-powerful creator, they simply provided another name for what people already understood to be the sun. The difficulty with borrowed proper names is that they are essentially zero in meaning, that is to say, they are words with a significant absence of meaning which must be filled in one way or another, and this is usually done merely by equating the meaning of such a zero term with already existing concepts. Hence, rather than avoiding wrong views of God, borrowed terms often perpetuate wrong views indirectly.

There may also be additional complications in the use of a borrowed term, since it may not provide a basis for certain syntactic or morphological modifications. For example, some missionaries have borrowed the term *Allah* for 'God,' but in speaking of 'gods' they have attempted to add a plural to the underlying form *Allah.* In most instances this procedure has resulted in something which is not only conceptually and grammatically impossible, but also highly offensive to receptors.

One special problem involving θεός[a] results

from the occurrence of 'God' in expressions of possession, for example, 'my God' or 'our God.' In a number of languages one simply cannot say 'my God,' for one cannot 'possess God.' Rather, one must say 'the God whom I worship' or 'the God in whom I trust.' Similarly, it may be impossible to speak of 'the God of Abraham' without implying that such a God would only be an idol, that is to say, 'the God that Abraham personally possessed.' Under such circumstances it may be necessary to translate 'the God of Abraham' as 'the God in whom Abraham trusted.'

Ideally, one should employ a well known receptor-language term for 'God' which would be applicable not only to the one supreme being, but could also refer to the 'gods of the heathen,' that is to say, a rendering of θεός[a] should be a generic expression which could be made particular and even exclusive by some such qualifier as 'the' or 'the one' or 'the unique.' Sometimes this can only be done by a qualifier such as 'the great' or even 'the supreme.'

12.2 ἄθεος, ον: pertaining to being without any relationship to God – 'being without God.' ἐλπίδα μὴ ἔχοντες καὶ ἄθεοι ἐν τῷ κόσμῳ 'having no hope in this world and being without God' Eph 2.12.

12.3 ηλι (a Hebrew term meaning 'my God'); ελωι (an Aramaic term meaning 'my God') – 'my God.'
ηλι: ηλι ηλι λεμα σαβαχθανι; 'my God, my God, why have you forsaken me?' Mt 27.46.
ελωι: ελωι ελωι λεμα σαβαχθανι; 'my God, my God, why have you forsaken me?' Mk 15.34.
For certain problems involved in rendering an expression such as 'my God,' see the discussion in 12.1.

12.4 ὕψιστος[b], ου m:[3] (a title for God, literally 'highest') one who is supreme, primarily a

---

3 Items 12.4-12.8, (12.9) and 12.12 in this domain are titles for θεός[a] 'God' (12.1). As titles, they have precisely the same reference as θεός[a], but they each contribute distinctive meanings which are legitimate qualifications of the referent in question.

reference to status – 'the Most High, the Highest, the Supreme One.' υἱὸς ὑψίστου κληθήσεται 'he will be called Son of the Most High' Lk 1.32.

In some languages the concept of height is entirely unrelated to the idea of importance, and therefore it may be necessary to translate 'the Most High' as 'the Most Important' or even 'the Greatest.'

12.5 μεγαλωσύνη[b], ης *f*: (a title for God, literally 'majesty') one who is characterized by majesty and greatness – 'the Majesty, the Majestic One.' ἐν δεξιᾷ τῆς μεγαλωσύνης 'at the right hand of the Majesty' He 1.3.

The use of 'Majesty' as a title for God may be rendered in some languages as 'the one who is truly great' or '. . . truly important.' In other instances a more satisfactory equivalent is 'the one who is truly wonderful.'

12.6 μεγαλοπρεπὴς δόξα: (a title for God, literally 'majestic glory') – 'Sublime Glory, Majestic Glory.' φωνῆς ἐνεχθείσης αὐτῷ τοιᾶσδε ὑπὸ τῆς μεγαλοπρεποῦς δόξης 'when such a voice came to him from the Sublime Glory' 2 Pe 1.17. It is rare that one can use a literal rendering of μεγαλοπρεπὴς δόξα as a title for God, since 'Sublime Glory' is a quality and not normally a reference to a person or supernatural being. It is also possible, however, to use a descriptive phrase such as 'the one who is supremely glorious' or 'the one who is glorious above all others' or 'God who is supremely glorious.' See 79.14.

12.7 παντοκράτωρ, ορος *m*: (a title for God, literally 'all powerful') – 'the Almighty, the One who has all power.' κύριος ὁ θεὸς ἡμῶν ὁ παντοκράτωρ 'the Lord, our God, the all-powerful One' Re 19.6; ὁ παντοκράτωρ, ὁ ἦν καὶ ὁ ὢν καὶ ὁ ἐρχόμενος 'the Almighty, who was and is and will be' Re 4.8. In some languages the Almighty as a title for God may be expressed as 'the one who controls everything' or 'the one who commands all things and all people.'

12.8 Σαβαώθ: (a Greek transliteration of a Hebrew word meaning 'armies' and used with κύριος[a] 'Lord,' 12.9, as a title for God) per-taining to one who has overwhelming power – 'Almighty, All Powerful, One who is powerful over all.' εἰ μὴ κύριος Σαβαώθ ἐγκατέλιπεν ἡμῖν σπέρμα 'if the Lord Almighty had not left us some descendants' Ro 9.29.

12.9 κύριος[a], ου *m*: (a title for God and for Christ) one who exercises supernatural authority over mankind – 'Lord, Ruler, One who commands' (see also 37.51). ἄγγελος κυρίου κατ' ὄναρ ἐφάνη αὐτῷ 'the angel of the Lord appeared to him in a dream' Mt 1.20; χάρις ὑμῖν καὶ εἰρήνη ἀπὸ θεοῦ πατρὸς ἡμῶν καὶ κυρίου Ἰησοῦ Χριστοῦ 'grace to you and peace from God our Father and the Lord Jesus Christ' 1 Cor 1.3.

The most common equivalent of 'Lord' is a term meaning 'chief' or 'leader,' but frequently this cannot be employed as a title for 'God.' One may, however, combine such an expression with a term for 'God' and employ a phrase meaning 'God our leader' or 'God our chief.' In some instances, however, a term for 'Lord' is related to a verb meaning 'to command' or 'to order,' and therefore 'Lord' is rendered as 'the one who commands us' and combined with 'God' may form a phrase such as 'God, the one who commands us.'

12.10 κυριακός, ή, όν: (derivative of κύριος[a] 'Lord,' 12.9) pertaining to the Lord – 'belonging to the Lord, Lord's.' συνερχομένων οὖν ὑμῶν ἐπὶ τὸ αὐτὸ οὐκ ἔστιν κυριακὸν δεῖπνον φαγεῖν 'when you meet together as a group, you do not come to eat the Lord's Supper' 1 Cor 11.20. A strictly literal rendering of 'the Lord's Supper' might simply mean 'the supper which the Lord ate,' implying that no one else participated. Therefore, it may be necessary in some languages to translate 'the meal at which the Lord presided' or 'the meal which the Lord had for his disciples' or 'the meal which the Lord ate with his followers.'

12.11 μαρανα (an Aramaic expression) – 'our Lord.' μαρανα θα 'our Lord, come' 1 Cor 16.22. The expression μαρανα θα in 1 Cor 16.22 is an Aramaic formula evidently associated with early Christian liturgy. It must have been widely used, since it occurs in

1 Cor 16.22 without explanation. See also Domain 15, footnote 18.

12.12 πατήρ[d], πατρός *m*; αββα (a Greek transliteration of an Aramaic word meaning 'father'): (titles for God, literally 'father') one who combines aspects of supernatural authority and care for his people – 'Father.'

πατήρ[d]: καθὼς γινώσκει με ὁ πατὴρ κἀγὼ γινώσκω τὸν πατέρα 'just as the Father knows me, so I know the Father' Jn 10.15.

αββα: αββα ὁ πατήρ, πάντα δυνατά σοι 'Abba Father, you can do all things' Mk 14.36. Though there is a widespread tendency to preserve the Aramaic transliteration in the form of either abba or aba, there are frequent dangers in doing so, since the transliterated form may actually correspond to another word in a receptor language and thus provide an obstacle to proper understanding. In general, there is no point in a translation of αββα, since the resulting expression would simply be 'Father Father.' Accordingly, in many languages the combination of 'Abba, Father' is simply reduced to 'Father.' In a number of languages, however, a vocative form (that is to say, a form used in direct address) is different from a form used in speaking about God as Father. It is, of course, essential to employ the appropriate grammatical form.

In a number of languages it is necessary to distinguish clearly between 'Father' when referring to the heavenly Father and 'father' as a reference to a human father. The use of capitalization is quite satisfactory for the individual who is reading a text but not for one who is hearing it read, and since more people hear a text read than read it for themselves, it is essential that the reference of 'Father' be clear. In order to identify the use of 'Father' as a title for God, it is possible in many languages to use 'Father in heaven' or 'Father above' or 'Father God.'

In some languages it may even be necessary to identify the 'Father' as the creator and therefore employ a phrase such as 'our Father who created us.'

A particularly complicating factor involved in the use of 'Father' as a title for God is its occurrence without a pronominal reference as to whose father is involved. For example, in a number of languages one cannot speak of 'father' without indicating whose father, because a person does not become a father except by some relationship to another individual. Therefore, one must always speak of 'my father' or 'his father' and never simply 'the father.' In passages in which Jesus is speaking of 'the Father' in relationship to himself, it is necessary usually to employ a phrase such as 'my Father.' When, however, 'Father' is used as a title for 'God' in his relationship to people generally, then one may speak of 'our Father' (normally with an inclusive first person plural pronoun if the language in question makes a distinction between inclusive and exclusive first person plural pronoun referents).

12.13 θεότης, ητος *f*; θειότης, ητος *f*; θεῖον[a], ου *n*: (derivatives of θεός[a] 'God,' 12.1) the nature or state of being God – 'deity, divine nature, divine being.'

θεότης: ἐν αὐτῷ κατοικεῖ πᾶν τὸ πλήρωμα τῆς θεότητος σωματικῶς 'in him dwells all the fullness of divine nature in bodily form' Col 2.9.

θειότης: ἀΐδιος αὐτοῦ δύναμις καὶ θειότης 'his eternal power and deity' Ro 1.20.

θεῖον[a]: νομίζειν χρυσῷ ἢ ἀργύρῳ . . . τὸ θεῖον εἶναι ὅμοιον 'think . . . that the deity is like . . . gold or silver' Ac 17.29.

The expression 'divine nature' may be rendered in a number of languages as 'just what God is like' or 'how God is' or 'what God is.' In Ro 1.20 'deity' may sometimes be expressed as 'the fact that he is God' or '. . . is truly God.'

In 2 Pe 1.4 'to share in the very being of God,' one may speak of 'to share in what God is like' or 'to become in a measure like God.' It is important, of course, to avoid the implication that people can become completely God.

12.14 θεῖος, α, ον: pertaining to having the nature of God – 'divine, of God.' πάντα ἡμῖν τῆς θείας δυνάμεως αὐτοῦ τὰ πρὸς ζωὴν καὶ εὐσέβειαν δεδωρημένης 'his divine power has given us everything needed for a devout life' or '. . . for a truly religious life' 2 Pe 1.3.

12.15 υἱὸς τοῦ θεοῦ: (a title applied to Jesus, literally 'son of God'; parallel in semantic structure to phrases consisting of υἱός followed by the genitive of class or kind; compare 9.4) one who has the essential characteristics and nature of God – 'Son of God.' εἰ υἱὸς εἶ τοῦ θεοῦ, βάλε σεαυτὸν κάτω 'if you are the Son of God, throw yourself down on the ground' Mt 4.6.

Before adopting a translation of υἱὸς τοῦ θεοῦ such as 'Son of God,' one must always investigate the extent to which such an expression might already be used in a particular language. For example, in the Tarahumara language of Mexico mankind is divided into two classes: (1) 'sons of God,' who are Tarahumaras and (2) 'sons of the devil,' all other people. In these circumstances it is necessary in translating υἱὸς τοῦ θεοῦ to use an expression which will identify 'the unique Son of God' or 'the one who is truly the Son of God.'

12.16 οὐρανός^c, οῦ *m*: (a figurative extension of meaning of οὐρανός^b 'heaven,' 1.11) a reference to God based on the Jewish tendency to avoid using a name or direct term for God – 'God.' ἥμαρτον εἰς τὸν οὐρανὸν καὶ ἐνώπιόν σου 'I have sinned against God and against you' Lk 15.18, 21.

A translation such as 'I have sinned against God' would seem to be so much simpler than 'I have sinned against heaven,' but in reality it is not easy to find a satisfactory expression for 'sinning against God.' It is, of course, possible to speak of 'fighting against a person,' but 'to sin against a person' involves a very complex relationship which often needs to be more clearly explained, for example, 'I have sinned against what God has said' or 'I have sinned by doing what displeases God.' In some languages a strictly literal rendering of 'I have sinned against God' might be understood in the sense of committing some kind of sin with God.

12.17 ἐπουράνιος^c, ον: (derivative of οὐρανός^c 'God,' 12.16) pertaining to being derived from God – 'from God.' κλήσεως ἐπουρανίου μέτοχοι 'those who share in the calling from God' He 3.1.

Though it is possible to interpret He 3.1 as a 'calling which comes from heaven,' it seems more appropriate in terms of the frequent references to 'calling' to recognize that the use of ἐπουράνιος in this context is simply a substitute for a direct reference to God. Accordingly, the passage may be effectively rendered as 'those who have been called by God' or 'those whom God has called.'

12.18 πνεῦμα^a, τος *n* (a title for the third person of the Trinity, literally 'spirit') – 'Spirit, Spirit of God, Holy Spirit.' τὸ πνεῦμα αὐτὸν ἐκβάλλει εἰς τὴν ἔρημον 'the Spirit made him go into the desert' Mk 1.12.

In many religious systems the significant difference between the gods and the spirits is that the gods are regarded as supernatural beings which control certain aspects of natural phenomena, while the spirits are supernatural beings, often impersonal, which indwell or inhabit certain places, including rivers, streams, mountains, caves, animals, and people. Spirits are often regarded as being primarily evil, though it may be possible to induce them to be favorable to people.

It is extremely difficult to find in some languages a fully satisfactory term to speak of the Spirit of God. If one uses a term which normally identifies local supernatural beings, there is a tendency to read into the term the meaning of evil or mischievous character. If, however, one uses a term which may identify the spirit of a person, the problems may even be greater, since according to many systems of religious belief, the spirit of an individual does not become active until the individual dies. Therefore, the activity of the Spirit of God would presumably suggest that God himself had died. However, if one uses a term which means 'heart' or 'soul' (and thus the Spirit of God would be literally equivalent to 'the heart of God'), there may be complications since this aspect of human personality is often regarded as not being able to act on its own.

The solutions to the problem of 'Spirit' have been varied. In some languages the term for Spirit is essentially equivalent to 'the unseen one,' and therefore the Spirit of God is essentially equivalent to 'the invisibleness of

God.' In a number of languages the closest equivalent for Spirit is 'breath,' and in a number of indigenous religious systems, the 'breath' is regarded as having a kind of independent existence. In other languages the term for Spirit is equivalent to what is often translated as 'the soul,' that is to say, the immaterial part of a person. There is, of course, always the difficulty of employing a term meaning 'soul' or 'life,' since it often proves to be impersonal and thus provides no basis for speaking of the Spirit of God as being a person or a personal manifestation of God.

In quite a few languages the equivalent of Spirit is literally 'shadow,' since the 'shadow' of a person is regarded as the immaterial part of the individual. Moreover, in many systems of religious thought the shadow is regarded as having some significant measure of independent existence.

In a few cases the term for Spirit is literally 'wind,' but there are frequently difficulties involved in this type of terminology since a term for wind often suggests calamity or evil intent. One meaning of Spirit which must be clearly avoided is that of 'apparition' or 'ghost.'

Frequently it is not possible to find a fully satisfactory term for 'Spirit,' and therefore in all contexts some characterizing feature is added, for example, either 'of God' or 'holy,' in the sense of 'divine.' This may be particularly necessary in a passage such as Mk 1.12 where the average reader might assume that a spirit which would make Jesus go out into the desert would be an evil rather than a good spirit.

Often the Holy Spirit is named by phrases which explain something of the nature and activity of the Spirit: πνεῦμα (ἐκ τοῦ) θεοῦ 'Spirit of God,' πνεῦμα ἅγιον 'Holy Spirit,' πνεῦμα αἰώνιον 'the Eternal Spirit' (often called 'the unending spirit' or 'the spirit that never ceases'), πνεῦμα τῆς ἀληθείας 'the Spirit of Truth,' that is, 'the Spirit who communicates truth' (sometimes rendered as 'the Spirit that communicates the truth about God'); πνεῦμα τῆς δόξης 'Spirit of glory,' that is, 'the glorious Spirit' or 'the wonderful Spirit'; πνεῦμα τῆς ζωῆς 'the Spirit of life,' that is, 'the Spirit who brings life' or 'the Spirit that causes people to live'; πνεῦμα υἱοθεσίας 'the Spirit of sonship,' that is, 'the Spirit who makes us sons of God' or 'the Spirit that causes us to become God's sons'; πνεῦμα τῆς χάριτος 'Spirit of grace,' that is, 'the Spirit who bestows kindness' or 'the Spirit who shows kindness to us'; πνεῦμα σοφίας καὶ ἀποκαλύψεως 'Spirit of wisdom and revelation,' that is, 'the Spirit who gives wisdom and who reveals God' or 'the Spirit who causes us to become wise and who shows us what God is like' (or '. . . who God truly is'). The phrase πνεῦμα κυρίου, 'Spirit of the Lord,' is ambiguous because κύριος may either refer to God the Father or to Jesus Christ, but the Spirit in either case is the same: τί ὅτι συνεφωνήθη ὑμῖν πειράσαι τὸ πνεῦμα κυρίου; 'why did you decide to put the Lord's Spirit to the test?' Ac 5.9.

12.19 παράκλητος[a], ου *m*: (a title for the Holy Spirit) one who helps, by consoling, encouraging, or mediating on behalf of – 'Helper, Encourager, Mediator.' ὁ δὲ παράκλητος, τὸ πνεῦμα τὸ ἅγιον ὃ πέμψει ὁ πατὴρ ἐν τῷ ὀνόματί μου 'the Helper, the Holy Spirit whom the Father will send in my name' Jn 14.26.

The principal difficulty encountered in rendering παράκλητος is the fact that this term covers potentially such a wide area of meaning. The traditional rendering of 'Comforter' is especially misleading because it suggests only one very limited aspect of what the Holy Spirit does. A term such as 'Helper' is highly generic and can be particularly useful in some languages. In certain instances, for example, the concept of 'Helper' is expressed idiomatically, for example, 'the one who mothers us' or, as in one language in Central Africa, 'the one who falls down beside us,' that is to say, an individual who upon finding a person collapsed along the road, kneels down beside the victim, cares for his needs, and carries him to safety.

A rendering based upon the concept of legal advocate seems in most instances to be too restrictive. Furthermore, there may be quite unsatisfactory connotations associated with any word which suggests a lawyer, especially since in so many societies, a lawyer is thought of primarily as one who 'bribes the judges' or 'can speak two truths' or, as in one language, is 'a professional liar.' See also 35.16 and especially footnote 4 in Domain 35.

12.20 πνευματικός, οῦ *m*: (derivative of πνεῦμα[a] 'Spirit,' 12.18) one who has received God's Spirit and presumably lives in accordance with this relationship – 'one who is spiritual, one who has received the Spirit.' πνευματικοῖς πνευματικὰ συγκρίνοντες 'explaining spiritual truths to those who possess the Spirit' 1 Cor 2.13. In a number of languages it is not possible to speak of 'possessing the Spirit,' but one can often say 'to be possessed by the Spirit' or 'those whom the Spirit possesses' or '. . . owns' or '. . . controls.'

12.21 πνευματικός[a], ή, όν; πνευματικῶς[a]: (derivatives of πνεῦμα[a] 'Spirit,' 12.18) pertaining to being derived from or being about the Spirit – 'spiritual, from the Spirit' (in reference to such matters as gifts, benefits, teachings, blessings, and religious songs).
πνευματικός[a]: περὶ δὲ τῶν πνευματικῶν, ἀδελφοί, οὐ θέλω ὑμᾶς ἀγνοεῖν 'brothers, I do not want you to be ignorant about spiritual gifts' or '. . . gifts which come from the Spirit' 1 Cor 12.1; πνευματικοῖς πνευματικὰ συγκρίνοντες 'explaining spiritual truths to spiritual persons' 1 Cor 2.13. In 1 Cor 2.13 πνευματικά may perhaps be best rendered in some languages as 'truths revealed by the Spirit' or possibly 'truths about the Spirit.' Some persons would insist, however, that in 1 Cor 2.13 πνευματικά refers to teachings which are of particular benefit or relevance to people's spirits.
ὁ εὐλογήσας ἡμᾶς ἐν πάσῃ εὐλογίᾳ πνευματικῇ 'who has blessed us with every spiritual blessing' or '. . . with every blessing which comes from the Spirit' Eph 1.3; ἵνα τι μεταδῶ χάρισμα ὑμῖν πνευματικὸν εἰς τὸ στηριχθῆναι ὑμᾶς 'in order to share a spiritual blessing with you to make you strong' Ro 1.11. The occurrence of πνευματικός in Eph 1.3 and Ro 1.11 could be understood as referring to the human spirit, but the contexts would seem to point more clearly to the involvement of the Spirit of God. See 26.10.
λαλοῦντες ἑαυτοῖς ἐν ψαλμοῖς καὶ ὕμνοις καὶ

ᾠδαῖς πνευματικαῖς 'speak to one another in the words of psalms, hymns, and songs inspired by the Spirit' Eph 5.19. It is also possible that in Eph 5.19 πνευματικαῖς means merely 'spiritual,' and as such pertains to what is 'sacred' or 'religious.' One can, therefore, translate ᾠδαῖς πνευματικαῖς as 'songs used in worship' or 'songs used in worship of God.' For a discussion of certain related problems involving the rendering of πνευματικός, see 26.10.
πνευματικῶς[a]: ὅτι πνευματικῶς ἀνακρίνεται 'because it is judged in terms of the Spirit' 1 Cor 2.14 . The reference in 1 Cor 2.14 may be interpreted to mean that the unspiritual person cannot receive the gifts of the Spirit; neither can such a person understand them because they can only be judged or evaluated on the basis of their being derived from the Spirit of God. For another interpretation of πνευματικῶς in 1 Cor 2.14, see 26.10.

12.22 θεός[b], οῦ *m*: any one of many different supernatural beings regarded as having authority or control over some aspect of the universe or human activity – 'god.' θεωρούντων μηδὲν ἄτοπον εἰς αὐτὸν γινόμενον . . . ἔλεγον αὐτὸν εἶναι θεόν 'when they saw that nothing unusual happened to him . . . they said, He is a god!' Ac 28.6.
Some translators have made a practice of trying to render the meaning of θεός[b] by terms which mean essentially 'demons' or 'evil spirits,' but this is a mistake, for though the gods of the ancient pagans may be regarded as having had no existence at all, nevertheless, the NT does not speak of them as being evil.
In those languages in which there is no contrast between 'gods' and 'spirits,' that is to say, in instances in which people believe only in indwelling spirits rather than in supernatural beings who have control over natural phenomena, it may be possible to distinguish 'gods' by speaking of them as 'powerful spirits.' In certain instances, therefore, the equivalent of 'God' (12.1) is 'the all-powerful Spirit.'

12.23 εἴδωλον[b], ου *n*: (a figurative extension of meaning of εἴδωλον[a] 'idol,' 6.97) an unreal supernatural being – 'false god.' φυλάξατε ἑαυτὰ ἀπὸ τῶν εἰδώλων 'keep yourselves away from false gods' 1 Jn 5.21. A 'false god' may be rendered as 'that which seems to be a god.' In 1 Jn 5.21 one may speak of 'those that seem to be gods but really are not.' It is also possible, however, to interpret εἴδωλον in 1 Jn 5.21 as being simply an idol.

12.24 ὁ θεὸς τοῦ αἰῶνος τούτου: (a title for the Devil, literally 'the god of this world') one who has power or authority over this world (or this age) and is so recognized by people of the world – 'the god of this world, the Devil.' ὁ θεὸς τοῦ αἰῶνος τούτου ἐτύφλωσεν τὰ νοήματα τῶν ἀπίστων 'the god of this world has blinded the minds of the unbelievers' 2 Cor 4.4.

The expression 'the god of this world' may be understood in two senses: (1) the god who rules over this world or (2) the god whom the people of this world trust or worship. Though many persons have traditionally interpreted 'the god of this world' as the one who rules over this world, it is the second meaning which probably fits more accurately in the context of 2 Cor 4.4.

12.25 θεά, ᾶς f; θεός ᶜ, οῦ f: a female deity – 'goddess.'
θεά: τὸ τῆς μεγάλης θεᾶς Ἀρτέμιδος ἱερόν 'the temple of the great goddess Artemis' Ac 19.27.
θεός ᶜ: ἠγάγετε γὰρ τοὺς ἄνδρας τούτους . . . οὔτε βλασφημοῦντας τὴν θεὸν ἡμῶν 'you have brought these men here . . . who have not insulted our goddess' Ac 19.37.

In some languages it may seem quite strange to attribute female sex to a divine being. However, one can almost always say 'a woman god' or 'a spirit like a woman' or 'a spirit thought of as being like a woman.'

12.26 δαιμόνιον ᵇ, ου n: a supernatural being of somewhat lesser status than θεός ᵇ 'god' (12.22) – 'god, lesser god.' ξένων δαιμονίων δοκεῖ καταγγελεὺς εἶναι 'he seems to be talking about foreign gods' Ac 17.18 . The expression 'foreign gods' may be rendered as 'gods whom the foreigners worshiped' or 'gods of the foreigners.' It would be wrong to render

'foreign gods' by a phrase which would mean 'the gods are foreigners.'

12.27 δίκη ᵇ, ης f: (a figurative extension of meaning of δίκη 'justice,' not occurring in the NT) a goddess who personifies justice in seeking out and punishing the guilty – 'the goddess Justice.' ἡ δίκη ζῆν οὐκ εἴασεν 'the goddess Justice would not let him live' Ac 28.4. The expression 'the goddess Justice' may be relatively meaningless if translated literally. It may therefore be necessary to say 'the goddess that demands justice' or 'the goddess that makes people suffer for the evil they have done' or 'the goddess that punishes people because of their bad deeds.'

12.28 ἄγγελος ᵇ, ου m: a supernatural being that attends upon or serves as a messenger of a superior supernatural entity – 'angel.' ἄγγελος κυρίου κατ' ὄναρ ἐφάνη αὐτῷ 'an angel of the Lord appeared to him in a dream' Mt 1.20; τῷ διαβόλῳ καὶ τοῖς ἀγγέλοις αὐτοῦ 'for the Devil and his angels' Mt 25.41.

In many languages a term for 'angels' is borrowed from another dominant language, but in other instances a somewhat descriptive phrase may be employed. The most common expressions for the 'angels of God' are 'messengers' and 'messengers from heaven.' Sometimes these angels are called 'spirit messengers' and even 'flying messengers.' In some instances they have been called 'the holy servants of God,' but an expression such as 'servants of God' or even 'messengers of God' tends to overlap in meaning with expressions used to characterize the role and function of the prophets who were sent as messengers from God. In some languages a term for 'angels' is contrasted with that for 'prophets' by calling angels 'messengers from heaven' and prophets 'messengers from God.' The 'angels of the Devil' are often called 'the Devil's servants.'

One cannot avoid problems involved in the rendering of 'angel' merely by borrowing a term. In some instances such a borrowing may already exist in the language and with a different meaning. For example, in one instance *angel* had already been borrowed but with a meaning of babies who died at child-birth or shortly thereafter.

12.29 ἰσάγγελος, ον: pertaining to one who is like or similar to an angel – 'like an angel.' ἰσάγγελοι γάρ εἰσιν, καὶ υἱοί εἰσιν θεοῦ 'for they are like angels and are sons of God' Lk 20.36.

12.30 στρατιὰ οὐράνιος: (an idiom, literally 'heavenly army') a large group or throng of angels – 'throng of angels, ranks of angels.' ἐγένετο σὺν τῷ ἀγγέλῳ πλῆθος στρατιᾶς οὐρανίου 'and there was with the angel a multitude of the angels of heaven' Lk 2.13.
There may be distinct objections to speaking of στρατιὰ οὐράνιος as being a 'heavenly army,' though undoubtedly in earlier times the thought of angels being God's military force would have been quite appropriate. Therefore, in place of some expression which may refer to an army or military unit, it may be possible to translate στρατιὰ οὐράνιος as simply 'many, many angels' or 'row after row of angels.'

12.31 ἀρχάγγελος, ου m: a chief or highly important angel – 'archangel.' ὁ κύριος ἐν κελεύσματι, ἐν φωνῇ ἀρχαγγέλου . . . καταβήσεται ἀπ' οὐρανοῦ 'with a shout of command and the cry of the archangel the Lord . . . will descend from heaven' 1 Th 4.16.
An archangel may be described as 'one who commands other angels' or 'a leading angel' or 'a chief angel.'

12.32 ζῷον b, ου n: a supernatural being surrounding the throne of God in visions of the book of Revelation – 'a living being.' ὅταν δώσουσιν τὰ ζῷα δόξαν καὶ τιμήν 'whenever the living beings give glory and honor' Re 4.9.
The OT parallel for the ζῷον in Revelation is to be found in Eze 1.5-14.

12.33 πνεῦμα b, τος n: a supernatural non-material being – 'spirit.' πνεῦμα ὁ θεός 'God is spirit' Jn 4.24; Σαδδουκαῖοι μὲν γὰρ λέγουσιν μὴ εἶναι ἀνάστασιν μήτε ἄγγελον μήτε πνεῦμα 'for the Sadducees affirm there is no resurrection, nor an angel, nor a spirit being' Ac 23.8. πνεῦμα in Jn 4.24 and Ac 23.8 is highly

generic. There is no implication of such a spirit being either good or evil, nor is πνεῦμα in such contexts to be regarded as merely an aspect of some other being. The reference is simply to a supernatural and non-material entity. In rendering Ac 23.8, one may speak of the Sadducees' rejection of the existence of spirits as 'they say . . . there is nothing which isn't physical' or '. . . everything that exists is physical.'

12.34 διάβολος a, ου m (a title for the Devil, literally 'slanderer'); Σατανᾶς a, ᾶ m (a borrowing from Aramaic; a title for the Devil, literally 'adversary'): the principal supernatural evil being – 'Devil, Satan.'[4]
διάβολος a: ἐκράτησεν τὸν δράκοντα . . . ὅς ἐστιν Διάβολος καὶ ὁ Σατανᾶς 'he seized the dragon . . . that is, the Devil or Satan' Re 20.2; πειρασθῆναι ὑπὸ τοῦ διαβόλου 'to be tried by the Devil' or 'to be tested by the Devil' Mt 4.1.
Σατανᾶς a: πῶς δύναται Σατανᾶς Σατανᾶν ἐκβάλλειν; 'how can Satan cast out Satan?' or 'how can Satan get rid of Satan?' Mk 3.23. See also Re 20.2 above.
In a number of languages there is a well known proper name for the Devil as the chief of all demons. In other instances, however, he is given a descriptive name, for example, 'the ruler of the evil spirits,' 'the chief of the demons,' 'the truly bad one,' 'the left-handed one' (as the one who is opposed to all which is right or correct), 'the no-good one,' 'the avaricious one.' In some instances a term for the Devil may be highly idiomatic as, for example, 'the barking one,' a reference to the Devil's presumed activity in animal guise.
Some translators have attempted to construct a term for Devil on the basis of the meaning of the Greek term διάβολος as 'slanderer.' This, however, has rarely been advisable, largely because in practically all

---

4 The terms διάβολος and Σατανᾶς appear to function both as titles and as proper names. This results from the fact that the referent in each instance is unique. In the text of the Greek NT Σατανᾶς was traditionally written with an initial capital letter, while διάβολος was normally written with a lower case initial letter, except for the occurrences of Διάβολος in Re 12.9 and Re 20.2.

languages there is a far more relevant way of speaking about the Devil. Other translators have attempted to render the term Devil by simply borrowing the form of the word from a dominant language, but this may also introduce complications, since one cannot always control the manner in which such a term will be understood. In one language, for example, the borrowed term 'devil' was identified simply as a small spirit that spreads fever among people, while in another area the borrowed term ended up meaning only a spirit which induces insanity. In this latter instance, the translators finally used an expression for the Devil which meant literally 'the lord of all sin.'

Some translators have employed for 'Devil' the proper name *Satan,* but this is often not a satisfactory solution. In one language in West Africa, for example, the term Satan had already been borrowed but was understood in the sense of the culture hero of the people and not as a designation for the chief of demons.

12.35 ὁ πονηρός: (a title for the Devil, literally 'the evil one') the one who is essentially evil or in a sense personifies evil – 'the Evil One, He who is evil.' ἀλλὰ ῥῦσαι ἡμᾶς ἀπὸ τοῦ πονηροῦ 'but rescue us from the Evil One' Mt 6.13.

12.36 ὁ πειράζων: (a title for the Devil, literally 'one who tempts') one who tempts or tries people with the intent of making them sin – 'Tempter.' καὶ προσελθὼν ὁ πειράζων εἶπεν αὐτῷ 'and the Tempter came and said to him' Mt 4.3. A common equivalent of ὁ πειράζων is 'one who tries to make people sin' or 'one who tries to cause people to sin.'

12.37 πνεῦμα^c, τος *n*; **δαιμόνιον^a, ου** *n*; **δαίμων, ονος** *m*; **διάβολος^b, ου** *m*: an evil supernatural being or spirit – 'demon, evil spirit.'
πνεῦμα^c: προσήνεγκαν αὐτῷ δαιμονιζομένους πολλούς· καὶ ἐξέβαλεν τὰ πνεύματα 'they brought to him many who were demon possessed and he drove out the evil spirits' Mt 8.16.
δαιμόνιον^a: δαιμόνια πολλὰ ἐξέβαλεν 'he drove out many demons' Mk 1.34.

δαίμων: οἱ δὲ δαίμονες παρεκάλουν αὐτόν 'the evil spirits begged him' Mt 8.31.
διάβολος^b: ἐξ ὑμῶν εἷς διάβολός ἐστιν 'one of you is a demon' Jn 6.70. For another interpretation of διάβολος in Jn 6.70, see 88.124.

While in a number of languages the Devil may be spoken of as 'the chief of the demons,' sometimes the demons are simply called 'the spirits of the Devil' or 'the servants of the Devil.'

In a number of languages the difficulty in terminology for demons is not the absence of a term, but the abundance of different terms for different kinds of demons, each one of which may be responsible for particular kinds of human behavior, for example, insanity, depression, epilepsy, sex perversion, and violent assault. Sometimes demons are classified as 'those of the home' and 'those of the forest,' in which case the latter are normally regarded as more violent and virulent. When there is an abundance of different terms for demons and no generic term for all types of demons, one can usually select a class of demons which parallels most closely the descriptions of demon activity in the NT and use such a term with appropriate contextual qualifications so as to suggest that such a term is to be understood in a general sense.

12.38 πνεῦμα πονηρόν: (a fixed phrase equivalent in reference to πνεῦμα^c 'demon,' 12.37, but with specific emphasis upon evil) a supernatural evil being – 'demon, evil spirit.' ἐθεράπευσεν πολλοὺς ἀπὸ ... πνευμάτων πονηρῶν 'he healed many from ... their evil spirits' Lk 7.21.

There are a number of translational problems involved in rendering 'evil spirits.' In the first place, one must make certain that any characterization of 'spirits' as 'wicked' or 'evil' or 'unclean' will not be misunderstood as unduly restrictive. For example, if the term for 'spirits' itself indicates an evil supernatural being, then 'evil spirits' might suggest that there were both 'evil demons' as well as 'good demons.' The same would be true of an expression such as 'unclean spirits.'

12.39 πνεῦμα ἀκάθαρτον: an evil supernatural spirit which is ritually unclean and which causes persons to be ritually unclean – 'unclean spirit.' ἐπετίμησεν τῷ πνεύματι τῷ ἀκαθάρτῳ 'he rebuked the unclean spirit' Mk 9.25. It is important in rendering a term such as 'unclean' to avoid the implication that one is merely speaking of 'dirty demons.' What is important about the term 'unclean' is that the possession of such a spirit makes the individual ritually or ceremonially unclean. Accordingly, 'an unclean spirit' is equivalent in a number of languages to 'a contaminating spirit.'

12.40 δαιμονιώδης, ες: (derivative of δαιμόνιονᵃ 'demon,' 12.37) pertaining to a demon – 'demonic, devilish.' ἐπίγειος, ψυχική, δαιμονιώδης 'earthly, physical, demonic' Jas 3.15. In some languages δαιμονιώδης may be rendered as 'typical of the way a demon acts' or 'the way in which demons behave.'

12.41 δαιμονίζομαι: (derivative of δαιμόνιονᵃ 'demon,' 12.37) to be possessed by a demon – 'to be demon possessed.' προσήνεγκαν αὐτῷ δαιμονιζομένους πολλούς 'they brought to him many who were possessed by demons' Mt 8.16.
In a number of languages one cannot speak of a person 'being possessed by a demon.' A more appropriate expression may be 'the person possesses a demon.' In other instances an idiomatic phrase is employed, 'the demon rides the person' or 'the demon commands the person' or even 'the demon is the person.'

12.42 πνεῦμαᵈ, τος _n_; φάντασμα, τος _n_: an apparition – 'ghost.'
πνεῦμαᵈ: ἔμφοβοι γενόμενοι ἐδόκουν πνεῦμα θεωρεῖν 'they were full of terror and thought they were seeing a ghost' Lk 24.37.
φάντασμα: ἐταράχθησαν λέγοντες ὅτι Φάντασμά ἐστιν 'they were terrified and said, It's a ghost' Mt 14.26.
Most languages have quite satisfactory terms for 'ghosts' or 'apparitions,' since the psychological phenomena associated with such appearances are apparently universal. In some languages the equivalent of 'ghost' is simply 'shadow.' In other instances it may be literally 'breath.' In some instances the meaning of 'ghost' is incorporated within a verb expression, for example, 'they saw, as it were, through him.'

B Supernatural Powers (12.43-12.50)

The NT contains a number of lexical items (12.43-12.47) referring to supernatural powers believed to be active as elemental spirits exercising control over man's fate. Though these may have certain special features associated with them and though in extrabiblical literature they may represent various grades of supernatural power, there seems to be no way in which they can be clearly distinguished on the basis of their NT usage. Appropriate equivalent expressions in other languages are extremely difficult to find, primarily because other religious systems usually have completely different beliefs relative to supernatural powers. In many languages it is simply not possible to speak of such supernatural powers without in some way identifying them with various kinds of spirits.

12.43 στοιχεῖαᵇ, ων _n_ (always occurring in the plural): the supernatural powers or forces regarded as having control over the events of this world – 'the supernatural powers over this world.' εἰ ἀπεθάνετε σὺν Χριστῷ ἀπὸ τῶν στοιχείων τοῦ κόσμου 'now that you have died with Christ and are free from the supernatural powers ruling over this world' Col 2.20. In a number of languages there is no way of speaking of 'supernatural powers' or 'supernatural forces.' Reference can only be made to such powers in terms of kinds of spirit beings; therefore, one may render στοιχεῖαᵇ in Col 2.20 as 'those spirits that have power' or 'those spirits which control.'

12.44 αἰὼν τοῦ κόσμου τούτου; ἄρχων τῆς ἐξουσίας τοῦ ἀέρος; ἀρχήᶠ, ῆς _f_; ἐξουσίαᵍ, ας _f_; κοσμοκράτωρᵇ, ορος _m_; τὰ πνευματικὰ τῆς πονηρίας ἐν τοῖς ἐπουρανίοις; δύναμιςᶜ, εως _f_; κυριότηςᵇ, ητος _f_; θρόνοςᶜ, ου _m_ (a figurative extension of meaning of θρόνοςᵃ 'throne,' 6.112): (titles for supernatural forces and powers) a supernatural power having some particular role in controlling the destiny and activities of human beings – 'power, authority, lordship, ruler, wicked force.'

ἐν αἷς ποτε περιεπατήσατε κατὰ τὸν αἰῶνα τοῦ κόσμου τούτου, κατὰ τὸν ἄρχοντα τῆς ἐξουσίας τοῦ ἀέρος, τοῦ πνεύματος τοῦ νῦν ἐνεργοῦντος ἐν τοῖς υἱοῖς τῆς ἀπειθείας 'at that time you lived according to the supernatural forces of this world, according to the ruler of the supernatural powers in space, the spiritual power who now controls the people disobeying God' Eph 2.2; ἔστιν ἡμῖν ἡ πάλη . . ., πρὸς τὰς ἀρχάς, πρὸς τὰς ἐξουσίας, πρὸς τοὺς κοσμοκράτορας τοῦ σκότους τούτου, πρὸς τὰ πνευματικὰ τῆς πονηρίας ἐν τοῖς ἐπουρανίοις 'we are fighting against the rulers, authorities, the cosmic powers of this dark age, against the wicked spiritual forces in the heavenly world' Eph 6.12; ὑπεράνω πάσης ἀρχῆς καὶ ἐξουσίας καὶ δυνάμεως καὶ κυριότητος '(Christ rules) above all rulers, authorities, powers, and forces' Eph 1.21; ἐκτίσθη τὰ πάντα . . . εἴτε θρόνοι εἴτε κυριότητες 'he created everything . . . including spiritual powers, lords' Col 1.16. See also 37.52, 37.70, and 37.73.

Some scholars have believed that it is possible to reconstruct at least in part some of the hierarchy represented by these various supernatural forces and powers, on the basis of the neoplatonic system of nine such powers arranged in three orders of three each. NT terminology and usage does not, however, lend itself to such a classification, and it is difficult, if not impossible, to determine what are the significant differences between these supernatural powers and forces.

For the most part, translators have endeavored to render the various terms in somewhat different ways, for example, ἐξουσία as 'authority'; δύναμις as 'power'; κυριότης as 'ruler'; and phrases such as τὰ πνευματικὰ τῆς πονηρίας ἐν τοῖς ἐπουρανίοις as 'wicked spiritual forces in the heavenly world.' In a number of languages, however, there are simply not enough terms to designate various kinds of powers, authorities, and forces which could be employed in speaking of such supernatural impersonal powers. Accordingly, some translators have simply used a phrase such as 'any and all kinds of supernatural powers.' Where it is possible to make certain lexical distinctions between terms and phrases, this,

of course, should be done, but in a number of contexts this may be impossible, and accordingly, some explanation in a marginal note may be required if the reader is to understand satisfactorily the intent of the passages in question.

In some instances a measure of meaning may be obtained by somewhat paraphrastic expressions. For example, Eph 2.2 is rendered in some languages as 'at that time you lived in the way in which the spirit that governs this world dictated you should live. This is the way the one who rules over the power in space commanded you to live. This is the very spirit that now commands the people who disobey God.'

In the case of Eph 1.21 some scholars apply the terms in question both to the supernatural and to the human sphere, thus emphasizing the totality of Christ's rule. This has a considerable measure of justification in view of the concepts held by persons in the ancient world, since various earthly powers were supposed to reflect corresponding supernatural powers.

12.45 στρατιὰ τοῦ οὐρανοῦ: (an idiom, literally 'army of heaven') the stars of heaven as symbols of various supernatural powers – 'the stars of heaven.' ὁ θεὸς καὶ παρέδωκεν αὐτοὺς λατρεύειν τῇ στρατιᾷ τοῦ οὐρανοῦ 'God gave them over to worship the stars of heaven' Ac 7.42. Since 'the stars of heaven' serve primarily as symbols of certain heavenly supernatural powers, it may be appropriate in some languages to speak of 'the spirits of the stars in the sky.' See also 1.5.

12.46 ὕψωμα[b], τος n: (a figurative extension of meaning of ὕψωμα[a] 'world above,' 1.13) supernatural powers in the region above the earth – 'powers of the world above.' πέπεισμαι γὰρ ὅτι . . . οὔτε ὕψωμα οὔτε βάθος . . . δυνήσεται ἡμᾶς χωρίσαι ἀπὸ τῆς ἀγάπης τοῦ θεοῦ 'I am certain that . . . neither powers in the world above nor powers in the world below . . . will be able to separate us from the love of God' Ro 8.38-39. For another interpretation of ὕψωμα in Ro 8.39, see 1.13.

It is possible that ὕψωμα in Ro 8.39 should be interpreted merely as a reference to the distance which a person might be separated from God.

12.47 βάθος ͨ, ους *n*: (a figurative extension of meaning of βάθος ͣ 'depth,' 81.8) supernatural powers in the region below the earth – 'powers of the world below.' See 12.46 for an illustrative passage in Ro 8.38-39. For another interpretation of βάθος in Ro 8.39, see 1.18.

As in the case of ὕψωμα ͤ (12.46), βάθος ͨ has been interpreted by some as indicating merely the distance which a person might be separated from God, but most scholars assume that the reference here is to 'the powers of the world below.'

12.48 πύθων, ωνος *m*: a supernatural power of divination known as 'Python' – 'spirit of divination.' παιδίσκην τινὰ ἔχουσαν πνεῦμα πύθωνα ὑπαντῆσαι ἡμῖν 'we were met by a slave girl who had a spirit of divination in her' or '. . . a demon that spoke through her' Ac 16.16. For πύθων as part of an idiom, see 33.285.

In most languages there seems to be no reason to borrow the term 'Python,' since it may be readily misunderstood. It is both more meaningful and to some extent more accurate to translate 'a spirit of divination' or 'the spirit which caused her to foretell the future' or '. . . to tell what was going to happen.'

12.49 δόξα ᵍ, ης *f*: a benevolent supernatural power deserving respect and honor – 'glorious power, wonderful being.' αὐθάδεις, δόξας οὐ τρέμουσιν 'arrogant people showing no respect for the glorious powers above' 2 Pe 2.10.

If one can employ a phrase such as 'wonderful beings above,' this is fine, but in a number of languages such a phrase would refer to believers who have died. Since the reference is apparently to certain types of supernatural powers, it may be more satisfactory in some languages to speak of 'the glorious spirits above.'

12.50 πύλαι ᾅδου: (an idiom, literally 'gates of Hades') death as an impersonal supernatural power – 'death.' πύλαι ᾅδου οὐ κατισχύσουσιν αὐτῆς 'the gates of Hades will not prevail against it' or 'death will never be able to overcome it' Mt 16.18. Some scholars, however, understand πύλαι ᾅδου to mean Satanic powers of evil.

13 Be, Become, Exist, Happen[1]

Outline of Subdomains

A   State (13.1-13.47)
B   Change of State (13.48-13.68)
C   Exist (13.69-13.103)
D   Happen (13.104-13.163)

A   State[2] (13.1-13.47)

13.1 εἰμί ͣ: to possess certain characteristics, whether inherent or transitory – 'to be.' πραΰς εἰμι καὶ ταπεινὸς τῇ καρδίᾳ 'I am gentle and

for overlapping with Domain 90 *Case*, Domain 68 *Aspect*, and Domain 71 *Mode*, for in addition to the highly generic meanings of *Be*, *Become*, *Exist*, and *Happen*, there are often associated meanings which tend to parallel those of *Aspect* and *Mode* and which tend to serve certain functions expressed by verbs which mark case relations. This will become evident in the discussion of a number of the meanings which are placed toward the end of the respective subdomains.

2 Subdomain A *State* includes not only terms which mean essentially 'to be,' but also those which indicate 'to cause to be in a state,' 'to attain a state,' 'to remain in a state,' 'to cause to continue in a state,' and finally 'to cease to be in a state.' There are, however, no rigid demarcations between such groupings. These meanings relating to a state of being contrast significantly with similar meanings involving aspects, in which one may speak of 'continuing,' 'causing to cease,' or 'initiating' certain activities (see Domain 68, items 68.16, 68.17, and 68.38).

1 Domain 13 *Be, Become, Exist, Happen* is a highly generic domain indicating various aspects of states, existence, and events. To some extent there is a tendency

humble in spirit' Mt 11.29; ὅτι πρῶτός μου ἦν 'because he was before me' Jn 1.15; ἵνα ἡ χαρὰ ἡμῶν ᾖ πεπληρωμένη 'in order that our joy might be complete' 1 Jn 1.4; τοῦτο γὰρ εὐάρεστόν ἐστιν ἐν κυρίῳ 'for this is well pleasing to the Lord' Col 3.20; μακάριοι οἱ δοῦλοι ἐκεῖνοι 'truly fortunate are those servants' Lk 12.37.[3]

13.2 ἔχω[g]**; φορέω**[b]: to be in a particular state or condition – 'to be, to bear.'
ἔχω[g]: εἶπεν δὲ ὁ ἀρχιερεύς, Εἰ ταῦτα οὕτως ἔχει; 'the high priest asked him, Is this really so?' Ac 7.1; πάντας τοὺς κακῶς ἔχοντας ἐθεράπευσεν 'he healed all who were sick' Mt 8.16.
φορέω[b]: καθὼς ἐφορέσαμεν τὴν εἰκόνα τοῦ χοϊκοῦ 'as we are in the likeness of the earthly' or 'as we bear the likeness of the earthly' 1 Cor 15.49.

13.3 γίνομαι[b]: to possess certain characteristics, with the implication of their having been acquired – 'to be.' γίνεσθε οὖν φρόνιμοι ὡς οἱ ὄφεις 'therefore be wise as serpents' Mt 10.16; διότι ἀγαπητοὶ ἡμῖν ἐγενήθητε 'because you are dear to us' 1 Th 2.8.

13.4 εἰμί[b]**; ὑπάρχω**[b]: to be identical with – 'to be.'
εἰμί[b]: σὺ εἶ ὁ υἱὸς τοῦ θεοῦ 'you are the Son of God' Mk 3.11; οὗτός ἐστιν ὁ ἀντίχριστος 'this one is the antichrist' 1 Jn 2.22; αὕτη ἐστὶν ἡ ἐπαγγελία 'this is the promise' 1 Jn 2.25.
ὑπάρχω[b]: οὗτος ἄρχων τῆς συναγωγῆς ὑπῆρχεν 'this man was the leader of the synagogue' Lk 8.41.[4]

13.5 ὑπάρχω[a]: to be in a state, normally with the implication of a particular set of circumstances – 'to be.' καὶ πραθὲν ἐν τῇ σῇ ἐξουσίᾳ ὑπῆρχεν 'after you sold it, it was under your control' Ac 5.4; ἀκούω σχίσματα ἐν ὑμῖν ὑπάρχειν 'I hear there are divisions among you'

1 Cor 11.18; μηδενὸς αἰτίου ὑπάρχοντος 'there being no reason' Ac 19.40; ὑπάρχων ἐν βασάνοις 'being in torment' Lk 16.23.

13.6 περίκειμαι[d]: to be in a state involving various aspects – 'to be in various ways, to be in many ways.' ἐπεὶ καὶ αὐτὸς περίκειται ἀσθένειαν 'since he himself was weak in many ways' He 5.2.

13.7 εὑρίσκομαι: to be in a state which has not been anticipated – 'to be found to be, to discover to be, to turn out to be.'[5] μήποτε καὶ θεομάχοι εὑρεθῆτε 'that you may not be found to be fighting against God' Ac 5.39; εὑρέθη μοι ἡ ἐντολὴ ἡ εἰς ζωὴν αὕτη εἰς θάνατον 'this commandment which was for the purpose of life was found in my case to be one which produced death' Ro 7.10.

13.8 ἐν[c]: a marker of a state or condition – 'in, with.' ἐν μαλακοῖς ἠμφιεσμένον 'dressed in soft clothes' Mt 11.8; ὑπάρχων ἐν βασάνοις 'being in torment' Lk 16.23; σπείρεται ἐν φθορᾷ, ἐγείρεται ἐν ἀφθαρσίᾳ 'it is sown in a state of being mortal, and it rises in a state of being immortal' 1 Cor 15.42.

13.9 ποιέω[c]**; τίθημι**[f]**; καθίστημι**[b]**; ἐργάζομαι**[d]**; κατεργάζομαι**[c]**; ἐπάγω; ἐνεργέω**[c]: to cause a state to be – 'to cause to be, to make to be, to make, to result in, to bring upon, to bring about.'[6]
ποιέω[c]: πᾶς ὁ βασιλέα ἑαυτὸν ποιῶν ἀντιλέγει τῷ Καίσαρι 'everyone who makes himself king opposes the emperor' Jn 19.12.
τίθημι[f]: καιροὺς οὓς ὁ πατὴρ ἔθετο ἐν τῇ ἰδίᾳ ἐξουσίᾳ 'times which the Father has caused to be on his own authority' or '. . . established on his own authority' Ac 1.7; πατέρα πολλῶν

---

3 The ellipsis of εἰμί[a] in this type of construction may be regarded as a zero actualization, that is, a significant omission.
4 Despite the fact that ἄρχων is anarthrous, the context would seem to imply clearly that the reference is definite rather than indefinite. With ὑπάρχω, however, there may be an implication of particular circumstances which are relevant to the context (see ὑπάρχω[a], 13.5).

5 εὑρίσκομαι in the sense of 'to be found to be' is typical of a complex semantic structure which involves not only intellectual discovery but a type of semantic equational relation.
6 Any meaning involving 'to cause to be' implies some change in state, and therefore one could classify these meanings under Subdomain B *Change of State.* However, the focus seems to be primarily upon the changed state rather than upon the process of moving from one state to another. The fact that a change of state has taken place seems to be semantically incidental.

ἐθνῶν τέθεικά σε 'I have made you father of many nations' Ro 4.17.

καθίστημι^b: διὰ τῆς παρακοῆς τοῦ ἑνὸς ἀνθρώπου ἁμαρτωλοὶ κατεστάθησαν οἱ πολλοί 'through the disobedience of one man, many were made sinners' Ro 5.19.

ἐργάζομαι^d: οἱ ἐργαζόμενοι τὴν ἀνομίαν 'those who cause wickedness' Mt 7.23. It is also possible to interpret ἐργάζομαι in Mt 7.23 as ἐργάζομαι^c (see 90.47).

κατεργάζομαι^c: ὁ γὰρ νόμος ὀργὴν κατεργάζεται 'for the Law brings about (God's) anger' or '. . . punishment' Ro 4.15; μετὰ φόβου καὶ τρόμου τὴν ἑαυτῶν σωτηρίαν κατεργάζεσθε 'with fear and trembling effect your salvation' Php 2.12.

ἐπάγω: ἐπάγοντες ἑαυτοῖς ταχινὴν ἀπώλειαν 'they brought upon themselves quick destruction' 2 Pe 2.1.

ἐνεργέω^c: θεὸς γάρ ἐστιν ὁ ἐνεργῶν ἐν ὑμῖν καὶ τὸ θέλειν 'for God is causing you to be willing' Php 2.13.

13.10 περιτίθημι^b: to cause a state with regard to some object – 'to cause to have, to assign to.' τούτοις τιμὴν περισσοτέραν περιτίθεμεν 'we assigned greater honor to these' 1 Cor 12.23.

13.11 παρίστημι^b or παριστάνω: to cause something to be or to serve as – 'to cause to be, to cause to serve as, to make something be.' παραστῆσαι ὑμᾶς ἁγίους καὶ ἀμώμους καὶ ἀνεγκλήτους κατενώπιον αὐτοῦ 'to make you holy, pure and faultless in his presence' Col 1.22; μηδὲ παριστάνετε τὰ μέλη ὑμῶν ὅπλα ἀδικίας 'do not cause any part of yourselves to serve as an instrument for doing wrong' Ro 6.13.

13.12 ἀποκυέω^a: to cause a state, with focus upon the process – 'to cause, to give rise to, to give birth to.' ἡ δὲ ἁμαρτία ἀποτελεσθεῖσα ἀποκύει θάνατον 'and when sin has run its course, it causes death' Jas 1.15.

13.13 τάσσω^b: to cause someone to be in a state involving an order or arrangement – 'to cause to be, to be placed.' καὶ γὰρ ἐγὼ ἄνθρωπός εἰμι ὑπὸ ἐξουσίαν τασσόμενος 'for I am a person who is under authority' Lk 7.8.

13.14 βάλλω^f: to cause a state or condition, with focus upon the suddenness or force of the action – 'to cause, to bring about.' οὐκ ἦλθον βαλεῖν εἰρήνην ἀλλὰ μάχαιραν 'I did not come to bring about peace but conflict' Mt 10.34.

13.15 προτίθεμαι^b: to cause a manifest state or condition of someone or something – 'to cause to be, to bring forth, to offer.' ὃν προέθετο ὁ θεὸς ἱλαστήριον 'whom God brought forth as a means of forgiveness' or 'whom God caused to be a means of forgiveness' Ro 3.25.

13.16 φθάνω^c; κατανταω^b: to attain or arrive at a particular state – 'to come to be, to attain, to achieve.'[7]

φθάνω^c: Ἰσραὴλ δὲ διώκων νόμον δικαιοσύνης εἰς νόμον οὐκ ἔφθασεν 'and Israel, while seeking a law that would put them right with God, did not attain it' Ro 9.31. Though grammatically it is the law which is not attained, semantically it is, of course, the state of righteousness which was the ultimate goal, and hence it was this particular state which was not attained.

κατανταω^b: μέχρι καταντήσωμεν οἱ πάντες εἰς τὴν ἑνότητα τῆς πίστεως 'until we all attain to the oneness of faith' Eph 4.13.

13.17 εὑρίσκω^c: to attain a state, with the supplementary implication of discovery – 'to attain to, to discover.' ὁ εὑρὼν τὴν ψυχὴν αὐτοῦ 'he who tries to attain his own life' Mt 10.39;[8] μετανοίας γὰρ τόπον οὐχ εὗρεν 'for he did not find a place of repentance' or '. . . a way to change what he had done' He 12.17.

13.18 τελειόω^g: to attain a state as a goal – 'to attain, to become.' ἵνα ὦσιν τετελειωμένοι εἰς ἕν 'in order that they might in the end become one' Jn 17.23.

13.19 ζητέω^f: to attempt to attain some state or condition – 'to attempt, to find, to try to

---

7 In the case of meanings involving 'to attain to a state,' there is obviously a change in state implied, but the focus seems to be primarily on the end point, and hence these meanings are classified in this subdomain rather than in the following subdomain.

8 The implication of 'to try to' is derived from the form of the present participle.

be.' καὶ ἀπὸ τότε ἐζήτει εὐκαιρίαν ἵνα αὐτὸν παραδῷ 'and from then on he attempted to find favorable circumstances in order to betray him' Mt 26.16.

13.20 ἐπεκτείνομαι[b]: to attempt energetically to attain a state or condition – 'to seek strongly to, to try hard to.' τοῖς δὲ ἔμπροσθεν ἐπεκτεινόμενος 'doing one's best to attain those things that are ahead' Php 3.13.

13.21 ὑστερέω[d]: to fail in some measure to attain some state or condition – 'to fail to attain, to not attain, to be behind in.' ὥστε ὑμᾶς μὴ ὑστερεῖσθαι ἐν μηδενὶ χαρίσματι 'so that you have not failed to attain a single blessing' 1 Cor 1.7.

13.22 ἥττημα, τος n: a lack of attaining a desirable state or condition – 'to fail, to lack, failure.' ἤδη μὲν οὖν ὅλως ἥττημα ὑμῖν ἐστιν ὅτι κρίματα ἔχετε μεθ' ἑαυτῶν 'the fact that you have legal disputes among yourselves is indeed evidence of your complete failure' 1 Cor 6.7; τὸ ἥττημα αὐτῶν πλοῦτος ἐθνῶν 'their failure brought rich blessings to the Gentiles' Ro 11.12.

13.23 ἀναθάλλω: (a figurative extension of meaning of ἀναθάλλω 'to bloom again,' not occurring in the NT) to be in a state identical with a previous state – 'to be again in a position to, to be as one was formerly.' ὅτι ἤδη ποτὲ ἀνεθάλετε τὸ ὑπὲρ ἐμοῦ φρονεῖν 'that after so long a time you again were in a position to show your concern for me' Php 4.10.

13.24 ὑποστρέφω[c]: to be again in a former state – 'to return to again, to again be in.' μηκέτι μέλλοντα ὑποστρέφειν εἰς διαφθοράν 'never again to be in a state of disintegration' or '. . . rotting' Ac 13.34.

13.25 ἀναπαύομαι[c]; ἐπαναπαύομαι[a]: to continue to be in a state in or on someone, with the implication of beneficent result – 'to remain on, to continue to be on.' ἀναπαύομαι[c]: τὸ τοῦ θεοῦ πνεῦμα ἐφ' ὑμᾶς ἀναπαύεται 'the Spirit of God continues on you' or 'the Spirit of God continues to be with you' 1 Pe 4.14.

ἐπαναπαύομαι[a]: ἐπαναπαήσεται ἐπ' αὐτὸν ἡ εἰρήνη ὑμῶν 'your greeting of peace will remain on him' or '. . . continue to be with him' Lk 10.6.

13.26 παρέχω[a]: to maintain a state or condition – 'to continue to be, to keep on being.' παρέσχον ἡσυχίαν 'they kept silent' Ac 22.2.

13.27 διατελέω: to continue in a particular state or condition unto the end – 'to remain, to continue to the end.' ἄσιτοι διατελεῖτε 'you continue to be without food' Ac 27.33.

13.28 ἐκδέχομαι[c]; ἀπεκδέχομαι[b]: to continue to remain in a state until an expected event – 'to remain until, to wait until.' ἐκδέχομαι[c]: ἐκδεχόμενος ἕως τεθῶσιν οἱ ἐχθροὶ αὐτοῦ ὑποπόδιον τῶν ποδῶν αὐτοῦ 'waiting until his enemies are put under his feet' He 10.13.
ἀπεκδέχομαι[b]: ὅτε ἀπεξεδέχετο ἡ τοῦ θεοῦ μακροθυμία ἐν ἡμέραις Νῶε 'when the patience of God continued in the days of Noah' 1 Pe 3.20.

13.29 ἵσταμαι[f] (and 2nd aorist, perfect, and pluperfect active): to continue firmly or well-established in a particular state – 'to firmly remain, to continue steadfastly.' εἰς τὴν χάριν ταύτην ἐν ᾗ ἑστήκαμεν 'into this grace in which we firmly remain' Ro 5.2; καὶ ἐν τῇ ἀληθείᾳ οὐκ ἔστηκεν 'and he has not remained in the truth' or 'and he has never been on the side of truth' Jn 8.44; ὃ καὶ παρελάβετε, ἐν ᾧ καὶ ἑστήκατε 'which you received and in which you continue firm' 1 Cor 15.1.

13.30 στήκω[b]: to continue in a state, with a possible implication of acceptability – 'to continue to be, to stand.' τῷ ἰδίῳ κυρίῳ στήκει ἢ πίπτει 'stand or fall to the advantage or disadvantage of his own master' or 'whether he stands or falls is a concern of his own master' Ro 14.4. For a discussion of στήκω as part of an idiom in Ro 14.4, see 87.56.

13.31 ἀσάλευτος[b], ον: (a figurative extension of meaning of ἀσάλευτος[a] 'immovable,' 15.4) pertaining to occurring in an unchangeable state – 'unchangeable, enduring.' βασιλείαν ἀσάλευτον παραλαμβάνοντες 'having received an enduring kingdom' He 12.28. In a number of languages it may be better to express the concept of 'enduring' as 'not ending,' and accordingly one might translate this phrase in He 12.28 as 'God's ruling over us will never end.'

13.32 τηρέω^a: to cause a state to continue – 'to cause to continue, to retain, to keep.' καὶ τοῦτο κέκρικεν ἐν τῇ ἰδίᾳ καρδίᾳ, τηρεῖν τὴν ἑαυτοῦ παρθένον 'and has already decided in his mind to keep his girl unmarried' 1 Cor 7.37. In 1 Cor 7.37 the reference to 'girl' may be either a man's daughter or a man's fiancée. Because of the ambiguity of this statement in 1 Cor 7.37 and in view of the cultural complications involved, especially because of differences of customs in different parts of the world, it is important that translators add a note at this point explaining the difference of interpretation and some of the cultural implications.

13.33 συντηρέω^a: to cause something to continue along with something else – 'to keep together, to preserve both.' ἀλλὰ βάλλουσιν οἶνον νέον εἰς ἀσκοὺς καινούς, καὶ ἀμφότεροι συντηροῦνται 'but new wine is poured into fresh wineskins, and both are preserved' Mt 9.17.

13.34 κρατέω^d: to cause a state to continue, on the basis of some authority or power – 'to hold, to keep, to cause to continue.' ἄν τινων κρατῆτε κεκράτηνται 'if you hold (people's sins) against them, they are held' Jn 20.23. In this expression in Jn 20.23 it is the state of being guilty of sin which is caused to continue. (See also discussion at 40.8.)

13.35 φέρωⁱ: to cause to continue by sustaining or maintaining a state – 'to sustain, to maintain.' φέρων τε τὰ πάντα τῷ ῥήματι τῆς δυνάμεως αὐτοῦ 'sustaining all things by his powerful word' He 1.3. In some languages, however, the closest equivalent of this expression in He 1.3 may be 'causing everything to continue to be as it is by his powerful word.' It is also possible to interpret φέρω in He 1.3 as 'to cause to continue to exist,' in which case it may be classified after 13.89. However, the focus seems to be on the state of being.

13.36 ἀθέτησις^b, εως f: the process of causing something not to continue – 'removal of, to cause not to continue.' εἰς ἀθέτησιν τῆς ἁμαρτίας 'to remove sin' or 'to remove the guilt of sin' He 9.26.

13.37 ἀφίημι^j: to cease, of a state – 'to cease, to stop, to leave.' καὶ ἀφῆκεν αὐτήν 'and (the fever) stopped' or 'and (the fever) left her' Lk 4.39.⁹

13.38 ἀφαιρέω^c; περιαιρέω^c; καθαιρέω^c; λύω^g: to cause a state to cease – 'to do away with, to remove, to eliminate.'¹⁰
ἀφαιρέω^c: ὅταν ἀφέλωμαι τὰς ἁμαρτίας αὐτῶν 'when I take away their sins' Ro 11.27.
περιαιρέω^c: αἵτινες οὐδέποτε δύνανται περιελεῖν ἁμαρτίας 'which are not ever able to take away sins' He 10.11.
καθαιρέω^c: καθαιρεῖσθαι τῆς μεγαλειότητος αὐτῆς 'and to have her greatness done away with' Ac 19.27.
λύω^g: λύσας τὰς ὠδῖνας τοῦ θανάτου 'having removed the pains of death' Ac 2.24.

13.39 ἐκλείπω^d: to cease, of a state, with the implication of nothing of the state continuing to exist – 'to cease, to die out, to come to an end.' καὶ τὰ ἔτη σου οὐκ ἐκλείψουσιν 'and your years will not come to an end' He 1.12.

13.40 ἀπαλλάσσομαι^b: to cease as of a state, with a significant element of change of state involved – 'to cease, to stop, to depart.' ἀπαλλάσσεσθαι ἀπ' αὐτῶν τὰς νόσους 'their diseases were driven from them' or 'they no longer suffered from their diseases' Ac 19.12.

13.41 ἐπιλείπω: to begin to cease – 'to begin to come to the end, to fail, to run out.' ἐπιλείψει με γὰρ διηγούμενον ὁ χρόνος περὶ Γεδεών

9 ἀφίημι^j differs somewhat from the other meanings in this subdomain in that it is not an individual who ceases to be involved in a particular state, but it is the state itself which ceases. At the same time, however, one may interpret this expression in Lk 4.39 semantically as 'she ceased to be in a state of fever.'
10 There are undoubtedly some significant differences of meaning in this series in 13.38, but it is not possible to determine the distinctive differences on the basis of existing contexts.

'time is running out for me to speak of Gideon' He 11.32. In some languages this reference to time in He 11.32 must be shifted to one of space, for example, 'there is not space enough for me to write about Gideon.'

13.42 μετακινέω: to cause a state to cease, with the implication of force – 'to cause to cease, to be shaken from.' μὴ μετακινούμενοι ἀπὸ τῆς ἐλπίδος 'not to be shaken from the hope (you have)' Col 1.23.

13.43 καταπίνωᶜ: (a figurative extension of meaning of καταπίνωᵃ 'to swallow,' 23.45) to cause the complete cessation of a state – 'to cause the end of, to swallow up.' κατεπόθη ὁ θάνατος εἰς νῖκος 'death was swallowed up in victory' or 'death turned into victory' 1 Cor 15.54; ἵνα καταποθῇ τὸ θνητὸν ὑπὸ τῆς ζωῆς 'in order that death might be swallowed up by life' or 'in order that the power of death might end and life take over' or 'in order that there might be life, not death' 2 Cor 5.4.

13.44 ἀποκτείνωᵇ: (a figurative extension of meaning of ἀποκτείνωᵃ 'to kill,' 20.61) to cause a state to cease, with the implication of strong emphasis and forceful action – 'to do away with, to eliminate.' ἀποκτείνας τὴν ἔχθραν '(Christ) did away with the hatred' Eph 2.16. In Eph 2.16 there is a subtle rhetorical device employed in ascribing to Christ the activity of 'killing,' when in reality he was the one who was killed on the cross in order to make life possible.

13.45 βάλλωᵍ; ἀποβάλλωᵇ: to cause a state to cease by force and with the implication of elimination – 'to remove, to drive out, to do away with.'
βάλλωᵍ: ἡ τελεία ἀγάπη ἔξω βάλλει τὸν φόβον 'perfect love drives out fear' 1 Jn 4.18. In a number of languages it is extremely difficult to speak of states such as love and fear as being respectively agent and affected element. Therefore, it may be necessary to shift significantly the semantic structure so as to translate this expression in 1 Jn 4.18 as 'if one completely loves, he does not at all fear.'
ἀποβάλλωᵇ: μὴ ἀποβάλητε οὖν τὴν παρρησίαν ὑμῶν 'do not cause your courage to cease' or 'do not let your courage cease' He 10.35.

13.46 διαστρέφωᶜ: to cause a state to cease by a diversion to some other state, usually with the implication of a wrong state – 'to turn away from, to divert from.' ζητῶν διαστρέψαι τὸν ἀνθύπατον ἀπὸ τῆς πίστεως 'he tried to turn the governor away from the faith' Ac 13.8.

13.47 ἀκατάλυτος, ον: pertaining to that which cannot be caused to cease – 'cannot be brought to an end, cannot be caused to finish.' ἀλλὰ κατὰ δύναμιν ζωῆς ἀκαταλύτου 'but through the power of a life that cannot be brought to an end' He 7.16.

B Change of State (13.48-13.68)

13.48 γίνομαιᶜ: to come to acquire or experience a state – 'to become.' ὁ λόγος σὰρξ ἐγένετο 'the Word became a human being' or 'the Word became a person' Jn 1.14; ὅπως γένησθε υἱοὶ τοῦ πατρὸς ὑμῶν τοῦ ἐν οὐρανοῖς 'in order that you may become the sons of your Father in heaven' Mt 5.45; πάντας τοὺς ἀκούοντάς μου σήμερον γενέσθαι τοιούτους ὁποῖος καὶ ἐγώ εἰμι 'that those who hear me might become this day such as I am' Ac 26.29. In some languages there is no convenient lexical item meaning simply 'to become,' but in all instances there are certain paraphrastic expressions which may be employed, for example, 'to arrive at being' or 'to cease being one thing and be another' or 'to change to be.' One must, however, beware in the case of Jn 1.14 not to employ some expression which would suggest that Christ had lost his divine nature in becoming a person or that he only appeared to be human (docetism).

13.49 γένημα, τος n: (derivative of γίνομαιᶜ 'to become,' 13.48) that which is a product or result of becoming – 'product, yield, what is produced by.' οὐ μὴ πίω ἀπ' ἄρτι ἐκ τούτου τοῦ γενήματος τῆς ἀμπέλου ἕως τῆς ἡμέρας ἐκείνης 'from now I will not drink of this product of the vine until that day' or 'I will never again drink this wine until the day' Mt 26.29.

13.50 ἔρχομαι^c: to come into a particular state or condition, implying a process – 'to become.' μηδὲν ὠφεληθεῖσα ἀλλὰ μᾶλλον εἰς τὸ χεῖρον ἐλθοῦσα 'she did not improve in health, but rather became worse' Mk 5.26.

13.51 μεταβαίνω^b; εἰμὶ εἰς (an idiom, literally 'to be into'): to change from one state to another – 'to change, to become.'
μεταβαίνω^b: εἰς κρίσιν οὐκ ἔρχεται ἀλλὰ μεταβέβηκεν ἐκ τοῦ θανάτου εἰς τὴν ζωήν 'he will not be judged, but has already changed from death to life' Jn 5.24.
εἰμὶ εἰς: καὶ ἔσται τὰ σκολιὰ εἰς εὐθείαν 'and the crooked ways will become straight' Lk 3.5.

13.52 μετάθεσις^b, εως f: a change from one state to another – 'change, transformation.' ἐξ ἀνάγκης καὶ νόμου μετάθεσις γίνεται 'there is also necessarily a change of the law' He 7.12.

13.53 μεταμορφόομαι^a: to change the essential form or nature of something – 'to become, to change, to be changed into, to be transformed.' ἀλλὰ μεταμορφοῦσθε τῇ ἀνακαινώσει τοῦ νοός 'but be transformed by the renewing of your thinking' Ro 12.2. In a number of languages the equivalent of μεταμορφόομαι in Ro 12.2 may be 'become completely different' or 'become different from what you are.'

13.54 ὑπάγω^e: to undergo a significant change – 'to undergo, to go to.' καὶ εἰς ἀπώλειαν ὑπάγει 'and he goes to destruction' or 'he is destroyed' Re 17.8. It is also possible to interpret ὑπάγω in Re 17.8 as 'to experience a state' (Domain 90M), and there may be in the context of Re 17.8 some aspect of movement (Domain 15).

13.55 ἀναγεννάω: (a figurative extension of meaning of ἀναγεννάω 'to be physically born again,' not occurring in the NT) to cause to be changed as a form of spiritual rebirth – 'to cause to be born again, to be given new birth.' ὁ . . . ἀναγεννήσας ἡμᾶς εἰς ἐλπίδα ζῶσαν 'who . . . has caused us to be born again to a living hope' 1 Pe 1.3.
In a number of languages the use of ἀναγεννάω in the sense of 'to be born again spiritually' is extremely difficult for people to understand, even as it was in biblical times. However, the concept is such an integral element in so much NT thought and teaching that the expression should be retained, though it may very well require some brief marginal explanation or at least significant cross referencing.
In its NT usage ἀναγεννάω, of course, has nothing to do with birth as such, but refers to a radical change in personality, with the attendant change in state, and it is for that reason that ἀναγεννάω is here classified in Domain 13. See also 41.53.

13.56 γεννάω^c: (a figurative extension of meaning of γεννάω^b 'to give birth,' 23.52) to cause to experience a radical change, with the implication of involvement of the total personality – 'to cause to be born, to be born of.' ἐὰν μή τις γεννηθῇ ἐξ ὕδατος καὶ πνεύματος 'unless someone is born of water and the Spirit' Jn 3.5. The phrase γεννηθῇ ἐξ ὕδατος has been interpreted by some as a literal reference to physical birth (see 23.52). Others, however, interpret this phrase as referring to baptism by water. In a parallel fashion, the expression γεννηθῇ ἐξ . . . πνεύματος would refer to baptism by the Spirit or rebirth made possible by the Spirit.

13.57 προκόπτω^a; προκοπή, ῆς f: to change one's state for the better by advancing and making progress – 'to advance, to progress, to change for the better, advancement.'
προκόπτω^a: προέκοπτον ἐν τῷ Ἰουδαϊσμῷ 'I advanced in Judaism' Ga 1.14.
προκοπή: ἵνα σου ἡ προκοπὴ φανερὰ ᾖ πᾶσιν 'in order that your progress may be seen by all' 1 Tm 4.15.

13.58 φέρομαι^b: (a figurative extension of meaning of φέρομαι^a 'to move from one place to another,' 15.11) to change from one state to another, with the implication of progressive development – 'to change to, to move on to, to progress.' ἐπὶ τὴν τελειότητα φερώμεθα 'let us move on to mature teaching' He 6.1.

13.59 πίπτω^h; πτῶσις^c, εως f; ἐκπίπτω^d: to change for the worse, with emphasis upon extent and suddenness – 'to fall from, to worsen.'

πίπτω[h]: μνημόνευε οὖν πόθεν πέπτωκας 'remember from where you have fallen' Re 2.5.

πτῶσις[c]: οὗτος κεῖται εἰς πτῶσιν καὶ ἀνάστασιν πολλῶν ἐν τῷ Ἰσραήλ 'this one is set for the fall and rise of many in Israel' Lk 2.34. For somewhat different interpretations of πτῶσις in Lk 2.34, see 20.50 and 87.75.

ἐκπίπτω[d]: ἵνα μὴ τῇ τῶν ἀθέσμων πλάνῃ συναπαχθέντες ἐκπέσητε τοῦ ἰδίου στηριγμοῦ 'that you will not be led away by the errors of lawless men and fall from your secure position' 2 Pe 3.17.

13.60 ἀνάστασις[c], εως f: a change for the better – 'rising up.' οὗτος κεῖται εἰς πτῶσιν καὶ ἀνάστασιν πολλῶν ἐν τῷ Ἰσραήλ 'this one is set for the fall and rise of many in Israel' Lk 2.34. For another interpretation of ἀνάστασις in Lk 2.34, see 87.39.

13.61 ἀπαράβατος, ον; ἀμετάθετος, ον: pertaining to that which does not change from one state to another – 'not changing, unchanging, never to change.'

ἀπαράβατος: ὁ δὲ διὰ τὸ μένειν αὐτὸν εἰς τὸν αἰῶνα ἀπαράβατον ἔχει τὴν ἱερωσύνην 'and because he lives forever, his priesthood never changes' He 7.24.

ἀμετάθετος: ἐπιδεῖξαι τοῖς κληρονόμοις τῆς ἐπαγγελίας τὸ ἀμετάθετον τῆς βουλῆς αὐτοῦ 'to show those who were to receive what he has promised that his plan is unchanging' or '. . . never changes' He 6.17.

13.62 ἀπό . . . εἰς; εἰς[k]: markers of a change of state – 'from . . . to, to, for.'

ἀπό . . . εἰς: ἀπὸ τῆς δουλείας τῆς φθορᾶς εἰς τὴν ἐλευθερίαν τῆς δόξης 'from slavery of decay to glorious freedom' Ro 8.21.

εἰς[k]: καὶ ἐγένετο εἰς δένδρον 'and it became a tree' Lk 13.19; καὶ ἔσονται οἱ δύο εἰς σάρκα μίαν 'and the two will become one flesh' or '. . . one person' Mt 19.5 (see 9.11); καὶ ἐλογίσθη αὐτῷ εἰς δικαιοσύνην 'and it was reckoned to him for righteousness' Ro 4.3.

13.63 στρέφω[b]; ἀποστρέφω[d]: to cause something to turn into or to become something else – 'to change, to turn into, to remove from.'

στρέφω[b]: ἐξουσίαν ἔχουσιν ἐπὶ τῶν ὑδάτων στρέφειν αὐτὰ εἰς αἷμα 'they have authority over the waters to turn them into blood' Re 11.6.

ἀποστρέφω[d]: ἀποστρέψει ἀσεβείας ἀπὸ Ἰακώβ 'he will remove wickedness from Jacob' Ro 11.26.

13.64 μεταστρέφω; μετατρέπω; περιτρέπω; μετατίθημι[b]; μεθίστημι[b]: to cause a change of state, with emphasis upon the difference in the resulting state – 'to change to, to turn into, to cause to be different from, to transform.'[11]

μεταστρέφω: ὁ ἥλιος μεταστραφήσεται εἰς σκότος 'the sun will be changed to darkness' Ac 2.20.

μετατρέπω: ὁ γέλως ὑμῶν εἰς πένθος μετατραπήτω 'let your laughter be turned into crying' Jas 4.9.

περιτρέπω: τὰ πολλά σε γράμματα εἰς μανίαν περιτρέπει 'your considerable learning has caused you to become mad' or '. . . has made you insane' Ac 26.24.

μετατίθημι[b]: τὴν τοῦ θεοῦ ἡμῶν χάριτα μετατιθέντες εἰς ἀσέλγειαν 'who turned the grace of our God into indecency' Jd 4.

μεθίστημι[b]: ὅταν μετασταθῶ ἐκ τῆς οἰκονομίας 'when I have been changed from my responsibility as manager' or 'when I have lost my job' Lk 16.4 (but see also 68.38); καὶ μετέστησεν εἰς τὴν βασιλείαν τοῦ υἱοῦ τῆς ἀγάπης αὐτοῦ 'and transformed (us) into the kingdom of his beloved Son' Col 1.13.

13.65 ἀποκαθίστημι[a]; ἀποκατάστασις, εως f; ἐγείρω[f]: to change to a previous good state – 'to restore, to cause again to be, restoration.'

ἀποκαθίστημι[a]: ἐξέτεινεν, καὶ ἀπεκατεστάθη ἡ χεὶρ αὐτοῦ 'he stretched out his hand and it was restored' or '. . . it was healed' Mk 3.5. A rendering of ἀποκαθίστημι in Mk 3.5 as 'was healed' is justified on the basis that at a previous time the hand was crippled, but ἀποκαθίστημι in and of itself does not mean 'to be healed.' Note, however, a contrasting situation in ἰάομαι[b] (13.66).

ἀποκατάστασις: ἄχρι χρόνων ἀποκαταστάσεως

---

11 There are undoubtedly certain significant differences of meaning in this series in 13.64, but it is impossible to determine this on the basis of existing contexts.

πάντων ὧν ἐλάλησεν ὁ θεός 'till the times of restoring all things of which God spoke' or 'until the time of making all things new of which God spoke' Ac 3.21.
ἐγείρω^f: καὶ ἐν τρισὶν ἡμέραις ἐγερῶ αὐτόν 'and in three days I will restore it' (a reference to the Temple) Jn 2.19.

13.66 ἰάομαι^b: (a figurative extension of meaning of ἰάομαι^a 'to heal,' 23.136) to cause something to change to an earlier, correct, or appropriate state – 'to renew, to heal.' καὶ ἐπιστρέψωσιν, καὶ ἰάσομαι αὐτούς 'and they might turn to me, and I would renew them' Mt 13.15.

13.67 ἀνακαινίζω; ἀνακαινόω^b: to cause a change to a previous, preferable state – 'to renew, to restore, to bring back.'
ἀνακαινίζω: ἀδύνατον ... πάλιν ἀνακαινίζειν εἰς μετάνοιαν 'it is impossible ... to bring them back to repent again' He 6.4-6.
ἀνακαινόω^b: ἀλλ' ὁ ἔσω ἡμῶν ἀνακαινοῦται ἡμέρᾳ καὶ ἡμέρᾳ 'yet our spiritual being is renewed day after day' 2 Cor 4.16.

13.68 ἐκβάλλω^f: to cause a significant change of state by decisive action – 'to cause to be, to make become.' ἕως ἂν ἐκβάλῃ εἰς νῖκος τὴν κρίσιν 'until he makes justice to triumph' or 'until he causes justice to prevail' Mt 12.20. In some languages, however, it may be extremely difficult to speak of 'justice prevailing.' The closest equivalent may be 'until he causes all people to be treated justly' or 'until authorities treat all people in a just manner.'

C Exist (13.69-13.103)

13.69 εἰμί^c: to exist, in an absolute sense – 'to be, to exist.' πιστεῦσαι ... ὅτι ἔστιν 'must have faith ... that (God) exists' He 11.6; πρὸ τοῦ τὸν κόσμον εἶναι 'before the world existed' Jn 17.5; καλοῦντος τὰ μὴ ὄντα ὡς ὄντα 'whose command brings into being what did not exist' Ro 4.17; ἐν αὐτῷ γὰρ ζῶμεν καὶ κινούμεθα καὶ ἐσμέν 'in whom we live and move about and have our existence' Ac 17.28.

13.70 ἔνι (a short form of ἔνεστι, in the NT only with negative): to exist, with respect to

particular circumstances – 'to be, to exist.' παρ' ᾧ οὐκ ἔνι παραλλαγή 'with whom there is no variation' Jas 1.17; οὕτως οὐκ ἔνι ἐν ὑμῖν οὐδείς ... 'surely there exists among you at least one person who ...' 1 Cor 6.5; οὐκ ἔνι Ἰουδαῖος οὐδὲ Ἕλλην 'there exists no difference between Jews and Gentiles' Ga 3.28.

13.71 γένεσις^d, εως f: the state of existence – 'existence.' φλογίζουσα τὸν τροχὸν τῆς γενέσεως 'set on fire the course of existence' Jas 3.6; οὗτος ἔοικεν ἀνδρὶ κατανοοῦντι τὸ πρόσωπον τῆς γενέσεως αὐτοῦ ἐν ἐσόπτρῳ 'this one is like a man who sees the face of his existence in a mirror' Jas 1.23. In Jas 1.23 the term γένεσις is largely redundant, for the reference could only be to a person's own face.

13.72 στάσις^c, εως f: the state of existence, with the implication of being in a place or position – 'existence, to be in existence.' ἔτι τῆς πρώτης σκηνῆς ἐχούσης στάσιν 'as long as the outside tent is still in existence' He 9.8.

13.73 κεῖμαι^c; ἐπίκειμαι^e; ἀπόκειμαι^b: to exist, with the implication of having been established and thus having continuity and purpose – 'to exist, to exist for, to be set.'
κεῖμαι^c: δικαίῳ νόμος οὐ κεῖται, ἀνόμοις δὲ καὶ ἀνυποτάκτοις 'laws do not exist for good people, but for lawbreakers and criminals' 1 Tm 1.9; ἰδοὺ οὗτος κεῖται εἰς πτῶσιν καὶ ἀνάστασιν πολλῶν 'behold, he exists (or 'he is set') for the fall and rise of many' Lk 2.34.
ἐπίκειμαι^e: δικαιώματα σαρκὸς μέχρι καιροῦ διορθώσεως ἐπικείμενα 'these are outward rules which exist until the time when (God) will reform all things' He 9.10. For another interpretation of ἐπίκειμαι in He 9.10, see 76.17.
ἀπόκειμαι^b: διὰ τὴν ἐλπίδα τὴν ἀποκειμένην ὑμῖν ἐν τοῖς οὐρανοῖς 'based on the hope which exists for you in heaven' Col 1.5. In Col 1.5 'the hope' is 'the hope for reality,' not a mere human feeling.

13.74 ἀπολείπομαι: to continue to exist, with the implication of being a part of a larger whole – 'to continue, to continue to exist.'

οὐκέτι περὶ ἁμαρτιῶν ἀπολείπεται θυσία 'there no longer exists any sacrifice that will take away sins' He 10.26.

13.75 πρόκειμαι[a]: to exist in an evident manner – 'to exist openly, to exist clearly.' πρόκεινται δεῖγμα πυρὸς αἰωνίου δίκην ὑπέχουσαι 'they exist as an example of the suffering of punishment by eternal fire' Jd 7.

13.76 πρόκειμαι[b]: to exist subsequent to some temporal reference point – 'to exist later, to lie before (someone), to lie ahead.' ὃς ἀντὶ τῆς προκειμένης αὐτῷ χαρᾶς ὑπέμεινεν σταυρόν 'who for the sake of the joy that lay ahead of him endured the cross' He 12.2.

13.77 ὑπάρχω[c]: to exist, particularly in relation to ownership – 'to exist, to belong to.' ἐν δὲ τοῖς περὶ τὸν τόπον ἐκεῖνον ὑπῆρχεν χωρία τῷ πρώτῳ τῆς νήσου ὀνόματι Ποπλίῳ 'near that place there were some fields belonging to Publius, the chief of the island' Ac 28.7.

13.78 προϋπάρχω: to exist prior to some temporal reference point – 'to exist formerly, to be formerly.' ἀνὴρ δέ τις ὀνόματι Σίμων προϋπῆρχεν ἐν τῇ πόλει 'there was formerly in the city a man whose name was Simon' Ac 8.9.

13.79 πρωτότοκος[b], ον: pertaining to existing prior to something else – 'existing first, existing before.' πρωτότοκος πάσης κτίσεως 'existing before all creation' or 'existing before anything was created' Col 1.15. It is possible to understand πρωτότοκος in Col 1.15 as 'superior in status,' see 87.47. See also discussion at 10.43.

13.80 γίνομαι[a]: to come into existence – 'to be formed, to come to exist.' πάντα δι' αὐτοῦ ἐγένετο 'everything came into existence through him' Jn 1.3; πρὶν Ἀβραὰμ γενέσθαι ἐγὼ εἰμί 'before Abraham came into existence, I existed' Jn 8.58.

13.81 ἀνίσταμαι[c] (and 2nd aorist active): to come into existence, with the implication of assuming a place or position – 'to come into existence, to appear, to arise.' τίς ἔτι χρεία . . .

ἕτερον ἀνίστασθαι ἱερέα 'what need would there have been . . . for a new priest to come into existence' He 7.11; ἄχρι οὗ ἀνέστη βασιλεὺς ἕτερος ἐπ' Αἴγυπτον 'at length another king arose in Egypt' Ac 7.18.

13.82 συνίσταμαι[b] (and perfect active): to come into existence, with the implication of acquiring form and substance – 'to come into existence, to be formed.' γῆ ἐξ ὕδατος καὶ δι' ὕδατος συνεστῶσα τῷ τοῦ θεοῦ λόγῳ 'by the word of God the earth was formed out of water and by water' 2 Pe 3.5.

13.83 ἐγείρω[d]; **ἐξεγείρω**[b]; **παρίστημι**[c]: to cause to come into existence – 'to cause to exist, to provide, to raise up.'
ἐγείρω[d]: δύναται ὁ θεὸς ἐκ τῶν λίθων τούτων ἐγεῖραι τέκνα τῷ Ἀβραάμ 'God can raise up descendants for Abraham from these rocks' Lk 3.8; οὐκ ἐγήγερται ἐν γεννητοῖς γυναικῶν μείζων Ἰωάννου τοῦ βαπτιστοῦ 'from those born of women there has not arisen one greater than John the Baptist' Mt 11.11.
ἐξεγείρω[b]: εἰς αὐτὸ τοῦτο ἐξήγειρά σε 'for this purpose I caused you to be what you are' Ro 9.17. For another interpretation of ἐξεγείρω in Ro 9.17, see 87.38.
παρίστημι[c]: ἵνα παραστήσῃ αὐτὸς ἑαυτῷ ἔνδοξον τὴν ἐκκλησίαν 'in order that he might raise up for himself the church in all its glory' Eph 5.27.

13.84 ἐγκαινίζω: to cause something to go into effect, with the implication of something being newly established – 'to put into effect, to put into force, to establish.' ὅθεν οὐδὲ ἡ πρώτη χωρὶς αἵματος ἐγκεκαίνισται 'that is why even the first (covenant) went into effect only by (the shedding of) blood' or 'the first (covenant) did not go into effect without (the shedding of) blood' He 9.18.

13.85 προφέρω: to cause to exist in an evident manner – 'to cause to exist clearly, to bring forth, to produce.' ὁ ἀγαθὸς ἄνθρωπος ἐκ τοῦ ἀγαθοῦ θησαυροῦ τῆς καρδίας προφέρει τὸ ἀγαθόν 'the good person from the good treasure of the heart brings forth that which is good' or '. . . causes to exist that which is good' Lk 6.45.

13.86 ποιέω καρπόν^b (an idiom, literally 'to make fruit'); καρποφορέω^b: to cause results to exist – 'to produce results, to cause results.'
ποιέω καρπόν^b: ποιήσατε οὖν καρπὸν ἄξιον τῆς μετανοίας 'therefore produce results worthy of repentance' or 'do that which shows that you have turned from your sins' Mt 3.8.
καρποφορέω^b: ἐν παντὶ ἔργῳ ἀγαθῷ καρποφοροῦντες 'producing all kinds of good deeds' Col 1.10.

13.87 ἀποκυέω^b: (a figurative extension of meaning of ἀποκυέω 'to give birth to,' not occurring in the NT) to be brought into being as something newly created – 'to bring into being, to cause to exist.' βουληθεὶς ἀπεκύησεν ἡμᾶς λόγῳ ἀληθείας 'by his own will he brought us into being through the word of truth' Jas 1.18.

13.88 συντελέω^b: to cause to exist by virtue of its having been finally accomplished – 'to cause to exist, to accomplish.' συντελέσω ἐπὶ τὸν οἶκον Ἰσραὴλ καὶ ἐπὶ τὸν οἶκον Ἰούδα διαθήκην καινήν 'I will bring into existence a new covenant with the people of Israel and Judah' He 8.8.

13.89 μένω^c; διαμένω^c: to continue to exist – 'to remain, to continue, to continue to exist, to still be in existence.'[12]
μένω^c: εἰ ἐν Σοδόμοις ἐγενήθησαν αἱ δυνάμεις αἱ γενόμεναι ἐν σοί, ἔμεινεν ἂν μέχρι τῆς σήμερον 'if the miracles which were performed in you had been performed in Sodom, it would still be in existence today' Mt 11.23.
διαμένω^c: αὐτοὶ ἀπολοῦνται, σὺ δὲ διαμένεις 'they will all disappear, but you will continue to exist' He 1.11.

13.90 ἵσταμαι^c: to continue to exist, with the probable implication of some resistance involved – 'to continue, to continue to be, to keep on existing.' πᾶσα πόλις ἢ οἰκία μερισθεῖσα καθ' ἑαυτῆς οὐ σταθήσεται 'every city or household divided against itself will not continue to exist' Mt 12.25. In a number of languages, however, it may be preferable to

translate ἵσταμαι in Mt 12.25 as 'will come to ruin' or 'will be destroyed.'

13.91 ὑπολιμπάνω: to cause to continue to exist subsequent to some temporal reference point – 'to cause to remain after, to leave behind.' ὑμῖν ὑπολιμπάνων ὑπογραμμὸν ἵνα ἐπακολουθήσητε τοῖς ἴχνεσιν αὐτοῦ 'leaving behind for you an example in order that you might follow in his footsteps' 1 Pe 2.21.[13]

13.92 καταλείπω^c; ἐγκαταλείπω^a: to cause to continue to exist, normally referring to a small part of a larger whole – 'to cause to remain, to leave to exist, to leave.'
καταλείπω^c: καταλειπομένης ἐπαγγελίας 'a promise having been left (with us by God)' He 4.1.
ἐγκαταλείπω^a: εἰ μὴ κύριος Σαβαὼθ ἐγκατέλιπεν ἡμῖν σπέρμα 'if the Lord Almighty had not left us some descendants' Ro 9.29.

13.93 παράγω^c; παρέρχομαι^d; ἀπέρχομαι^b; ἐξέρχομαι^b: to go out of existence – 'to cease to exist, to pass away, to cease.'
παράγω^c: ὁ κόσμος παράγεται 'the world passes away' 1 Jn 2.17.
παρέρχομαι^d: ὁ οὐρανὸς καὶ ἡ γῆ παρελεύσεται, οἱ δὲ λόγοι μου οὐ μὴ παρέλθωσιν 'heaven and earth will pass away, but my words will not pass away' Mt 24.35.
ἀπέρχομαι^b: ἡ οὐαὶ ἡ μία ἀπῆλθεν 'the first horror ceased' Re 9.12; εὐθὺς ἀπῆλθεν ἀπ' αὐτοῦ ἡ λέπρα 'at once the leprosy left him' Mk 1.42.
ἐξέρχομαι^b: ἰδόντες δὲ οἱ κύριοι αὐτῆς ὅτι ἐξῆλθεν ἡ ἐλπὶς τῆς ἐργασίας αὐτῶν 'when her owners realized that their chance of making money no longer existed' or '. . . was gone' Ac 16.19.

13.94 μαραίνομαι: to go out of existence gradually – 'to fade away.' ὁ πλούσιος ἐν ταῖς πορείαις αὐτοῦ μαρανθήσεται 'the rich man will fade away while busy conducting his affairs' Jas 1.11. In many languages it is simply not

12 It is possible that διαμένω^c is somewhat more emphatic in meaning than μένω^c.

13 It is difficult to know in the case of ὑπολιμπάνω whether one should assume a strictly figurative meaning of the term in 1 Pe 2.21, or whether in reality this type of meaning had become a standardized peripheral meaning of the term in question.

possible to speak of a 'rich man fading away.'
Colors may fade, but not a person, and
therefore it may be necessary to shift the
figure of speech, for example, 'the rich man
will end up being no one' or 'the rich man
will finally count for nothing.'

13.95 φεύγω^c: to cease rapidly to exist – 'to
cease quickly, to disappear rapidly.' καὶ πᾶσα
νῆσος ἔφυγεν 'and every island quickly disappeared' Re 16.20. For another interpretation of φεύγω in Re 16.20, see 24.6.

13.96 ἀπόλλυμαι^b: to cease to exist, with a
possible implication of violent means – 'to
cease to exist, to no longer exist, to come to an
end, to disappear.' αὐτοὶ ἀπολοῦνται, σὺ δὲ
διαμένεις 'these will cease to exist, but you will
remain' He 1.11; ἵνα τὸ δοκίμιον ὑμῶν τῆς
πίστεως πολυτιμότερον χρυσίου τοῦ ἀπολλυμένου
'in order that the genuineness of your faith
may be more valuable than gold which may
cease to exist' or '... which can disappear'
1 Pe 1.7.[14]

13.97 πίπτωⁱ: to cease to exist in a particular
post or position – 'to cease, to come to an end,
to fall.' οἱ πέντε ἔπεσαν 'the five (kings) came
to an end' Re 17.10.

13.98 ἀφανίζομαι^b; ἀφανισμός, οῦ *m*: to
cease to exist, with the implication of no
longer being evident or visible – 'to cease to
exist, to disappear, to die, disappearance.'
ἀφανίζομαι^b: ἴδετε, οἱ καταφρονηταί, καὶ θαυμά-
σατε καὶ ἀφανίσθητε 'look, you scoffers, marvel
and die' Ac 13.41.
ἀφανισμός: τὸ δὲ παλαιούμενον καὶ γηράσκον
ἐγγὺς ἀφανισμοῦ 'that which becomes old and
worn out will soon cease to exist' or '... will
soon disappear' He 8.13.

13.99 ἀνέκλειπτος, ον: pertaining to what
will not go out of existence – 'unfailing, inex-
haustible, never decrease.' θησαυρὸν ἀνέκλειπ-
τον ἐν τοῖς οὐρανοῖς 'treasure in heaven which

will never fail' or 'treasure in heaven which
can never decrease' Lk 12.33.

13.100 λύω^h; καταλύω^c; καταργέω^a: to
cause to cease to exist – 'to cause to come to
an end, to cause to become nothing, to put an
end to.'
λύω^h: ἵνα λύσῃ τὰ ἔργα τοῦ διαβόλου 'in order
to put an end to the works of the Devil' 1 Jn
3.8.[15]
καταλύω^c: ἐὰν ᾖ ἐξ ἀνθρώπων ἡ βουλὴ αὕτη ἢ τὸ
ἔργον τοῦτο, καταλυθήσεται 'if what has been
planned and done is of human origin, it will
be caused to come to nothing' or '... it will
be put to an end' Ac 5.38.
καταργέω^a: ὁ δὲ θεὸς καὶ ταύτην καὶ ταῦτα
καταργήσει 'but God will put an end to both'
1 Cor 6.13.

13.101 ἐκκόπτω^b: (a figurative extension of
meaning of ἐκκόπτω^a 'to cut off,' 19.18) to
cause to cease by removing – 'to do away
with, to eliminate.' ἵνα ἐκκόψω τὴν ἀφορμὴν
... ἐν ᾧ καυχῶνται 'to do away with any opportunity ... for them to boast' 2 Cor 11.12.

13.102 ἐξαλείφω^b: (a figurative extension of
meaning of ἐξαλείφω^a 'to wipe off, to wipe
away,' 47.18) to cause something to cease by
obliterating any evidence – 'to eliminate, to
do away with, to wipe out.' ἐξαλείψας τὸ καθ'
ἡμῶν χειρόγραφον τοῖς δόγμασιν ὃ ἦν ὑπεναντίον
ἡμῖν 'he will wipe out the record of our debts
which were against us' Col 2.14; εἰς τὸ
ἐξαλειφθῆναι ὑμῶν τὰς ἁμαρτίας 'in order that
your sins may be wiped out' Ac 3.19.

13.103 ἀποβολή^b, ῆς *f*: the event of ceasing
to exist – 'loss, destruction.' ἀποβολὴ γὰρ
ψυχῆς οὐδεμία ἔσται ἐξ ὑμῶν πλὴν τοῦ πλοίου

---

[14] It is possible that ἀπόλλυμαι in 1 Pe 1.7 should be
understood as 'to be destroyed' (see ἀπόλλυμι^a 'to
destroy,' 20.31), but in this context it appears to have a
more generic meaning.

[15] The phrase τὰ ἔργα τοῦ διαβόλου 'the works of the
Devil' may be regarded either as something which the
Devil has done and therefore something which exists (in
which case the meaning of λύω is appropriately in Domain 13), or the phrase could mean 'what the Devil is
doing,' and accordingly λύω could be interpreted as a
type of aspect, that is to say, it would mean 'causing an
activity to cease.' There are a number of such problems
involved in meanings which may be interpreted as fitting either into Domain 13 or into Domain 68 *Aspect*.

'for there will be no loss of life among you, only the loss of the ship' Ac 27.22.

D Happen (13.104-13.163)

13.104 εἰμί^d: to occur, of an event – 'to be, to happen.' μὴ ἐν τῇ ἑορτῇ, μήποτε ἔσται θόρυβος τοῦ λαοῦ 'we must not do it during the feast in order that there may not be a riot' Mk 14.2.

13.105 πρᾶγμα^a, τος *n*: that which happens – 'happening, event.' περὶ τῶν πεπληροφορημένων ἐν ἡμῖν πραγμάτων 'concerning the events that took place among us' Lk 1.1.

13.106 πληροφορέω^a; πληρόω^g; ἐκπληρόω; ἀναπληρόω^c; πίμπλημι^b: to cause to happen, with the implication of fulfilling some purpose – 'to cause to happen, to make happen, to fulfill.'[16]

πληροφορέω^a: περὶ τῶν πεπληροφορημένων ἐν ἡμῖν πραγμάτων 'concerning the events that took place among us' Lk 1.1.

πληρόω^g: τοῦτο δὲ ὅλον γέγονεν ἵνα πληρωθῇ τὸ ῥηθὲν ὑπὸ κυρίου διὰ τοῦ προφήτου 'all this happened in order to fulfill what was spoken by the Lord through the prophet' Mt 1.22.

ἐκπληρόω: ὅτι ταύτην ὁ θεὸς ἐκπεπλήρωκεν τοῖς τέκνοις αὐτῶν ἡμῖν 'God did this for us who are their offspring' Ac 13.33.

ἀναπληρόω^c: καὶ ἀναπληροῦται αὐτοῖς ἡ προφητεία Ἡσαΐου 'and the prophecy of Isaiah applies to them' Mt 13.14.

πίμπλημι^b: τοῦ πλησθῆναι πάντα τὰ γεγραμμένα 'in order to fulfill those things that have been written' Lk 21.22.

13.107 γίνομαι^d; ἐπιγίνομαι: to happen, with the implication that what happens is different from a previous state – 'to happen, to occur, to come to be.'[17]

γίνομαι^d: γίνεται λαῖλαψ μεγάλη ἀνέμου 'a strong wind came up' Mk 4.37.

ἐπιγίνομαι: μετὰ μίαν ἡμέραν ἐπιγενομένου

16 There are undoubtedly certain subtle differences of meaning in this set of terms in 13.106, but the distinctive features cannot be determined from existing contexts.

17 This meaning of γίνομαι and ἐπιγίνομαι reflects only a slight shift of focus from the meaning of γίνομαι in 13.48, in which the focus is upon the change.

νότου 'the next day a wind came up from the south' Ac 28.13.

13.108 ἐπιτελέω^b: to cause to happen, with the purpose of some end result – 'to accomplish, to bring about.' εἰδότες τὰ αὐτὰ τῶν παθημάτων τῇ ἐν τῷ κόσμῳ ὑμῶν ἀδελφότητι ἐπιτελεῖσθαι 'knowing that these same experiences are happening to your fellow believers in the world' 1 Pe 5.9.

13.109 ἐνίσταμαι^a: to happen, with the implication of there being a particular set of circumstances – 'to happen, to come about.' ἐν ἐσχάταις ἡμέραις ἐνστήσονται καιροὶ χαλεποί 'difficult times will come about in the last days' 2 Tm 3.1.

13.110 εἰσέρχομαι^b: to happen, with the focus upon the initial aspect – 'to happen, to come into.' ἡ ἁμαρτία εἰς τὸν κόσμον εἰσῆλθεν 'sin came into the world' Ro 5.12. In some languages, however, it may be impossible to speak of 'sin coming,' and therefore one may have to restructure the relationships, for example, 'people began to sin.'

13.111 συμβαίνω^b: to happen, with the implication of occurring in connection with other events – 'to happen.' αὐτοὶ ὡμίλουν πρὸς ἀλλήλους περὶ πάντων τῶν συμβεβηκότων τούτων 'they were talking to each other about all the things that had happened' Lk 24.14.

13.112 ἥκω^c: to have come or to be present, with respect to some temporal reference point – 'to happen, to have happened.' καὶ τότε ἥξει τὸ τέλος 'and then the end will come' Mt 24.14; ἥξει δὲ ἡμέρα κυρίου ὡς κλέπτης 'the day of the Lord will come as a thief' 2 Pe 3.10; οὐ μὴ ἴδητέ με ἕως ἥξει 'you will not see me until it happens' or '. . . until it will have happened' Lk 13.35.

13.113 παρακολουθέω^c; ἐπακολουθέω^b: to happen in conjunction with some other happening – 'to happen along with, to happen at the same time, to accompany.'

παρακολουθέω^c: σημεῖα δὲ τοῖς πιστεύσασιν ταῦτα παρακολουθήσει 'and these miracles will accompany those who believed' Mk 16.17.

ἐπακολουθέω^b: τοῦ κυρίου συνεργοῦντος καὶ τὸν λόγον βεβαιοῦντος διὰ τῶν ἐπακολουθούντων σημείων 'the Lord worked with them and confirmed their preaching by the accompanying signs' Mk 16.20.

13.114 προάγω^d; προγίνομαι: to happen or occur previous to some point of time – 'to happen previously, to occur formerly, to happen before.'
προάγω^d: κατὰ τὰς προαγούσας ἐπὶ σὲ προφητείας 'according to the words of prophecy spoken before about you' 1 Tm 1.18.
προγίνομαι: διὰ τὴν πάρεσιν τῶν προγεγονότων ἁμαρτημάτων 'by overlooking their former sins' Ro 3.25.

13.115 λόγος^h, ου *m*; ῥῆμα^c, τος *n*: a happening to which one may refer – 'matter, thing, event.'
λόγος^h: οὐκ ἔστιν σοι μερὶς οὐδὲ κλῆρος ἐν τῷ λόγῳ τούτῳ 'you have no part or share in this thing' Ac 8.21.
ῥῆμα^c: ἐπὶ στόματος δύο μαρτύρων ἢ τριῶν σταθῇ πᾶν ῥῆμα 'every matter may be upheld by the testimony of two or three witnesses' Mt 18.16.

13.116 συγκυρία, ας *f*: an unexpected coincidence of events – 'by coincidence, it so happened that.' κατὰ συγκυρίαν δὲ ἱερεύς τις κατέβαινεν ἐν τῇ ὁδῷ ἐκείνῃ 'it so happened that a priest was going down that road' Lk 10.31.

13.117 ἔρχομαι^d: to happen, with the implication of the event being directed to someone or something – 'to happen to.' τὰ κατ' ἐμὲ μᾶλλον εἰς προκοπὴν τοῦ εὐαγγελίου ἐλήλυθεν 'the things that have happened to me really helped the progress of the gospel' Php 1.12.

13.118 ποῦ φανεῖται: (an idiom, literally 'where will it appear') a question as to what may have happened to someone or something – 'what will happen to, what may become of.' ὁ ἀσεβὴς καὶ ἁμαρτωλὸς ποῦ φανεῖται; 'what will happen to the godless sinner?' 1 Pe 4.18.

13.119 ἐπέρχομαι^c; ἐπεισέρχομαι; ἐφίσταμαι^c; καταλαμβάνομαι^b: to happen to someone or something, with the implication of an event which is undesirable – 'to happen to, to come upon, to overtake.'
ἐπέρχομαι^c: βλέπετε οὖν μὴ ἐπέλθῃ τὸ εἰρημένον ἐν τοῖς προφήταις 'take care, then, that what the prophets said may not come upon you' Ac 13.40.
ἐπεισέρχομαι: ἐπεισελεύσεται γὰρ ἐπὶ πάντας τοὺς καθημένους ἐπὶ πρόσωπον πάσης τῆς γῆς 'for it will surely come upon all people over the whole earth' Lk 21.35.
ἐφίσταμαι^c: τότε αἰφνίδιος αὐτοῖς ἐφίσταται ὄλεθρος 'then sudden destruction comes upon them' 1 Th 5.3.
καταλαμβάνομαι^b: ἵνα ἡ ἡμέρα ὑμᾶς ὡς κλέπτης καταλάβῃ 'in order that the day may come upon you as a thief' 1 Th 5.4.

13.120 συναντάω: to happen, with the implication of that which one meets up with – 'to come upon, to happen to.' πορεύομαι εἰς Ἰερουσαλήμ, τὰ ἐν αὐτῇ συναντήσοντά μοι μὴ εἰδώς 'I am going to Jerusalem not knowing what will come upon me there' or '. . . what I will meet up with there' Ac 20.22.

13.121 καταντάω^c: to happen to, with the implication of something definitive and final –'to come upon.' εἰς οὓς τὰ τέλη τῶν αἰώνων κατήντηκεν 'on whom the end of the ages is about to come' or '. . . has come' 1 Cor 10.11.

13.122 πίπτω^g; ἐπιπίπτω^b: to happen suddenly to, with the connotation of something bad and adverse – 'to happen to, to fall upon.'
πίπτω^g: παραχρῆμά τε ἔπεσεν ἐπ' αὐτὸν ἀχλὺς καὶ σκότος 'suddenly a dark mist came upon him' Ac 13.11. In this particular context it may be necessary to be somewhat more specific concerning the blindness that Elymas experienced. For example, one may render this expression as 'suddenly a dark mist covered his eyes' or 'suddenly the eyes of Elymas became dark and misty' (see 24.40).
ἐπιπίπτω^b: οἱ ὀνειδισμοὶ τῶν ὀνειδιζόντων σε ἐπέπεσαν ἐπ' ἐμέ 'the insults which they used in insulting you happened to me' Ro 15.3. In a number of languages it is difficult to speak of 'insults happening.' Therefore, it may be necessary to restructure this expression in Ro 15.3 as 'they began insulting me in the same way they used to insult you.'

13.123 φθάνω^d: to happen to someone prior to a particular point in time – 'to happen to already, to come upon, to come upon already.' ἄρα ἔφθασεν ἐφ' ὑμᾶς ἡ βασιλεία τοῦ θεοῦ 'so the kingdom of God has already come upon you' Mt 12.28.

13.124 ἐνεργής, ές: pertaining to being effective in causing something to happen – 'effective, able to bring about.' ὅπως ἡ κοινωνία τῆς πίστεώς σου ἐνεργὴς γένηται ἐν ἐπιγνώσει παντὸς ἀγαθοῦ τοῦ ἐν ἡμῖν εἰς Χριστόν 'in order that our fellowship of faith with you may be effective in understanding every blessing which is ours in Christ' Phm 6; ζῶν γὰρ ὁ λόγος τοῦ θεοῦ καὶ ἐνεργής 'for the word of God is alive and effective' or '. . . able to make things happen' He 4.12.

13.125 συγκλείω^b: (a figurative extension of meaning of συγκλείω 'to enclose,' not occurring in the NT) to cause to happen, with the implication of significant restrictions – 'to cause to occur, to restrict.' συνέκλεισεν γὰρ ὁ θεὸς τοὺς πάντας εἰς ἀπείθειαν 'for God caused all to be guilty of disobedience' Ro 11.32.

13.126 τελέω^c; τελειόω^f; τελείωσις^b, εως f: to cause to happen for some end result – 'to make happen, to fulfill, to bring to fruition, to accomplish, fulfillment.'
τελέω^c: καὶ ἐπιθυμίαν σαρκὸς οὐ μὴ τελέσητε 'and you will not accomplish what the flesh desires' or '. . . the desires of the body' Ga 5.16.
τελειόω^f: ἵνα τελειωθῇ ἡ γραφή 'in order that the writing might be fulfilled' or 'in order that the Scripture might be fulfilled' or 'in order that what was written in the Scripture might happen' Jn 19.28.
τελείωσις^b: καὶ μακαρία ἡ πιστεύσασα ὅτι ἔσται τελείωσις τοῖς λελαλημένοις αὐτῇ παρὰ κυρίου 'happy is the one who believes that what has been spoken to her by the Lord will happen' or '. . . will be made to happen' Lk 1.45.

13.127 παρέχω^b: to cause something to happen to someone – 'to cause to happen.' τί κόπους παρέχετε τῇ γυναικί; 'why do you cause the woman trouble?' Mt 26.10; ἄξιός ἐστιν ᾧ παρέξῃ τοῦτο 'he is worthy to have you do this for him' (literally 'to have you cause this for

him to happen') Lk 7.4. In some languages it may be more appropriate to translate 'he deserves this favor from you' or 'he deserves your help.' See also 90.91.

13.128 δίδωμι^b: to cause to happen, used particularly in relationship to physical events – 'to make, to cause, to give, to produce.'[18] καὶ ὁ οὐρανὸς ὑετὸν ἔδωκεν 'and the sky produces rain' Jas 5.18; δώσω τέρατα ἐν τῷ οὐρανῷ ἄνω 'I will produce omens in the sky above' Ac 2.19; καὶ ἡ σελήνη οὐ δώσει τὸ φέγγος αὐτῆς 'and the moon will not produce its light' Mt 24.29.

13.129 γεννάω^d: to cause to happen, with the implication of the result of existing circumstances – 'to cause, to produce, to give rise to.' εἰδὼς ὅτι γεννῶσιν μάχας 'knowing that they give rise to quarrels' or '. . . produce quarreling' 2 Tm 2.23.

13.130 καταρτίζω^b: to cause to happen by means of some arrangement – 'to produce, to arrange for, to cause to happen.' ἐκ στόματος νηπίων καὶ θηλαζόντων κατηρτίσω αἶνον 'I will produce praise from the mouths of children and infants' Mt 21.16.

13.131 ἐνδείκνυμαι^d: to do something to someone, normally with the implication of something bad or unfortunate – 'to do to.' Ἀλέξανδρος ὁ χαλκεὺς πολλά μοι κακὰ ἐνεδείξατο 'Alexander the coppersmith did me a great deal of harm' 2 Tm 4.14.

13.132 παρεισάγω: to cause something to happen by introducing factors from outside – 'to bring in, to cause from outside.' οἵτινες παρεισάξουσιν αἱρέσεις ἀπωλείας 'who will bring in destructive divisions' or 'who will cause destructive divisions' or 'who will cause divisions which will greatly harm people' 2 Pe 2.1.

13.133 φέρω^f; καταφέρω: to cause something adverse to happen to someone, usually in connection with accusations or condemna-

---

18 In this meaning δίδωμι serves primarily as a so-called 'empty verb.' The event is to be found in the so-called object of the verb.

tions – 'to bring against, to cause to happen to, to bring about.'

φέρω^f: τίνα κατηγορίαν φέρετε κατὰ τοῦ ἀνθρώπου τούτου; 'what charge do you bring against this man?' Jn 18.29.

καταφέρω: πολλὰ καὶ βαρέα αἰτιώματα καταφέροντες ἃ οὐκ ἴσχυον ἀποδεῖξαι 'they brought many serious accusations which they were not able to prove' Ac 25.7.

13.134 ὁράω^g; βλέπω^f: to take responsibility for causing something to happen – 'to see to it that something happens, to arrange for something to happen.'

ὁράω^g: ὑμεῖς ὄψεσθε 'you see to it' Mt 27.24.
βλέπω^f: βλέπετε ἵνα ἀφόβως γένηται πρὸς ὑμᾶς 'see to it that he is at ease with you' or 'be sure to make him feel welcome among you' 1 Cor 16.10.

13.135 θησαυρίζω^b: (a figurative extension of meaning of θησαυρίζω^a 'to treasure up,' 65.11) to cause something of a more extensive nature to happen in the future – 'to make even greater, to cause to happen more intensely or more extensively.' θησαυρίζεις σεαυτῷ ὀργὴν ἐν ἡμέρᾳ ὀργῆς 'you are making your punishment even greater on the day of judgment' or 'you are accumulating even more judgment for yourself for the day of judgment' Ro 2.5.

13.136 ἀποδίδωμι^c: to cause to happen what has been promised, often in relation to vows or oaths – 'to cause to happen, to do, to pay back.' ἀποδώσεις δὲ τῷ κυρίῳ τοὺς ὅρκους σου 'do what you have promised the Lord you would do' or 'pay back to the Lord your vows' Mt 5.33.

13.137 κερδαίνω^b: to cause a loss not to happen – 'to avoid, to cause not to occur.'[19] κερδῆσαί τε τὴν ὕβριν ταύτην καὶ τὴν ζημίαν 'and to avoid this damage and loss' Ac 27.21.

13.138 ἐάω; ἐπιτρέπω: to allow someone to do something – 'to allow, to let, to permit.'

---

[19] κερδαίνω normally has the meaning of 'to gain' or 'to make a profit' (see κερδαίνω^a, 57.189); however, the avoidance of a loss may also be regarded as a gain.

ἐάω: ὃς ἐν ταῖς παρῳχημέναις γενεαῖς εἴασεν πάντα τὰ ἔθνη πορεύεσθαι ταῖς ὁδοῖς αὐτῶν 'in the past he allowed all people to go their own way' Ac 14.16; οὐκ εἴασεν αὐτοὺς τὸ πνεῦμα Ἰησοῦ 'the Spirit of Jesus did not allow them to go' or 'the Spirit of Jesus prevented them from going' Ac 16.7.

ἐπιτρέπω: ἐπέτρεψεν Μωϋσῆς βιβλίον ἀποστασίου γράψαι καὶ ἀπολῦσαι 'Moses allowed (a man) to write a divorce notice and send (his wife) away' Mk 10.4.

13.139 προσεάω: to allow to go beyond what is expected – 'to allow to go farther.' μὴ προσεῶντος ἡμᾶς τοῦ ἀνέμου 'the wind would not let us go any farther' Ac 27.7.

13.140 ἀφίημι^k; ἀπολείπω^c: to leave it to someone to do something, with the implication of distancing oneself from the event – 'to let, to allow, to leave it to.'

ἀφίημι^k: ἄφες ἐκβάλω τὸ κάρφος ἐκ τοῦ ὀφθαλμοῦ σου 'let me take out the speck from your eye' Mt 7.4; ἀφεῖς τὴν γυναῖκα Ἰεζάβελ, ἡ λέγουσα ἑαυτὴν προφῆτιν, καὶ διδάσκει 'who let the woman Jezebel, who calls herself a prophetess, to teach' Re 2.20.

ἀπολείπω^c: ἐπεὶ οὖν ἀπολείπεται τινὰς εἰσελθεῖν εἰς αὐτήν 'since, therefore, it allows some to enter into it' (referring to 'rest') He 4.6.

13.141 συγγνώμη, ης f: permission to do something (implying some type of concession) – 'permission, concession, to be allowed to.' τοῦτο δὲ λέγω κατὰ συγγνώμην, οὐ κατ' ἐπιταγήν 'I say this as a matter of permission and not as an order' 1 Cor 7.6.

13.142 δίδωμι^c; παραδίδωμι^d: to grant someone the opportunity or occasion to do something – 'to grant, to allow.'

δίδωμι^c: τοῦ δοῦναι ἡμῖν ἀφόβως . . . λατρεύειν αὐτῷ 'to allow us . . . to serve him without fear' Lk 1.73-74.

παραδίδωμι^d: ὅταν δὲ παραδοῖ ὁ καρπός 'when the condition of the crop allows' Mk 4.29.

13.143 ἐκκλείω^a: to cause something to be excluded or not allowed – 'to eliminate, to not allow, to exclude.' ποῦ οὖν ἡ καύχησις; ἐξεκλείσθη 'where, then, is boasting? It is not allowed' Ro 3.27. It is also possible to understand ἐκκλείω in Ro 3.27 as meaning that there is no basis for boasting; in other words, there is nothing that one can boast about.

13.144 ἀθέμιτος[a], ον: pertaining to what is not allowed – 'not allowed, forbidden.' ὑμεῖς ἐπίστασθε ὡς ἀθέμιτόν ἐστιν ἀνδρὶ Ἰουδαίῳ κολλᾶσθαι ἢ προσέρχεσθαι ἀλλοφύλῳ 'you yourselves know very well that a Jew is not allowed by his religion to visit or associate with Gentiles' Ac 10.28.

13.145 παρίημι: to allow not to do – 'to avoid, to overlook doing.' ταῦτα δὲ ἔδει ποιῆσαι κἀκεῖνα μὴ παρεῖναι 'but it was necessary to do these things and not to overlook doing those' Lk 11.42.

13.146 κωλύω; διακωλύω: to cause something not to happen – 'to prevent, to hinder.'[20] κωλύω: ἄφετε τὰ παιδία καὶ μὴ κωλύετε αὐτὰ ἐλθεῖν πρός με 'let the children come to me and do not prevent them' Mt 19.14; μήτι τὸ ὕδωρ δύναται κωλῦσαί τις τοῦ μὴ βαπτισθῆναι τούτους; 'can anyone forbid water from being used in baptizing these?' or 'can anyone prevent these from being baptized by water?' Ac 10.47.
διακωλύω: ὁ δὲ Ἰωάννης διεκώλυεν αὐτόν 'but John tried to prevent him' Mt 3.14.

13.147 ἐγκόπτω[a]: (a figurative extension of meaning of ἐγκόπτω 'to knock in' or 'to incise,' not occurring in the NT) to use strong measures in causing someone not to do something – 'to prevent, to hinder, to stop someone from.' ἐνεκοπτόμην τὰ πολλὰ τοῦ ἐλθεῖν πρὸς ὑμᾶς 'many times I have been prevented from coming to you' Ro 15.22.

13.148 ἐγκοπή, ῆς f: (derivative of ἐγκόπτω[a] 'to prevent,' 13.147) that which prevents or hinders the occurrence of an event – 'obstacle, hindrance.' ἵνα μή τινα ἐγκοπὴν δῶμεν τῷ εὐαγγελίῳ τοῦ Χριστοῦ 'in order not to put any

___

20 διακωλύω may be somewhat stronger in meaning than κωλύω, but this cannot be determined on the basis of existing contexts.

obstacle in the way of the good news about Christ' 1 Cor 9.12.

13.149 ὄγκος, ου m: that which serves to hinder or prevent someone from doing something – 'hindrance, impediment.' ὄγκον ἀποθέμενοι πάντα 'setting aside everything that serves as a hindrance' He 12.1.

13.150 κατέχω[a]: to prevent someone from doing something by restraining or hindering – 'to prevent, to hinder, to restrain, to keep from.' ἀνθρώπων τῶν τὴν ἀλήθειαν ἐν ἀδικίᾳ κατεχόντων 'the people whose evil ways keep the truth from being known' Ro 1.18.

13.151 ἀκωλύτως: pertaining to not being prevented – 'without hindrance, freely, without restriction.' διδάσκων τὰ περὶ τοῦ κυρίου Ἰησοῦ Χριστοῦ μετὰ πάσης παρρησίας ἀκωλύτως 'preaching those things concerning the Lord Jesus Christ with complete openness and without restriction' Ac 28.31.

13.152 φείδομαι[b]: to keep oneself from doing something – 'to avoid, to refrain from, to keep oneself from.' φείδομαι δέ 'but I will avoid boasting' (καυχήσασθαι is to be understood from the first part of verse 6) 2 Cor 12.6.

13.153 διατηρέω: to keep oneself from doing something, with the implication of duration – 'to avoid, to keep from doing.' ἐξ ὧν διατηροῦντες ἑαυτοὺς εὖ πράξετε 'if you keep yourselves from doing these things, you will do well' Ac 15.29.

13.154 φυλάσσομαι: to make a distinct effort to keep oneself from doing something – 'to be careful not to, to make an effort not to, to seriously avoid, to keep from.' φυλάσσεσθε ἀπὸ πάσης πλεονεξίας 'keep yourself from all kinds of greed' Lk 12.15; κρίναντες φυλάσσεσθαι αὐτοὺς τό τε εἰδωλόθυτον καὶ αἷμα καὶ πνικτὸν καὶ πορνείαν 'having decided that they must keep themselves from food offered to idols, from blood, from an animal that has been strangled, and from sexual immorality' Ac 21.25.

13.155 ἐκτρέπομαι[b]: to avoid becoming involved in some type of activity – 'to avoid, to not become involved.' ἐκτρεπόμενος τὰς βεβήλους κενοφωνίας 'avoiding profane, empty talk' 1 Tm 6.20.

13.156 ἀπολέγομαι[a]: to be determined to avoid doing something – 'to renounce, to put aside, to reject.' ἀλλὰ ἀπειπάμεθα τὰ κρυπτὰ τῆς αἰσχύνης 'but we reject secret and shameful deeds' or 'we refuse to become involved in secret and shameful deeds' or '. . . in doing what is secret and shameful' 2 Cor 4.2. For another interpretation of ἀπολέγομαι in 2 Cor 4.2, see 33.220.

13.157 περιΐσταμαι: to keep oneself away from being involved in some activity – 'to avoid, to keep oneself from doing.' ἔρεις καὶ μάχας νομικὰς περιΐστασο 'avoid quarrels and fights about the law' Tt 3.9.

13.158 ἀπέχομαι: to keep on avoiding doing something – 'to restrain from, to not do, to avoid doing, to keep from doing.' ἀπέχεσθαι εἰδωλοθύτων 'to keep from eating food which has been offered to idols' Ac 15.29.

13.159 στέλλομαι: to keep oneself away from some activity – 'to avoid doing.' στελλόμενοι τοῦτο μή τις ἡμᾶς μωμήσηται 'avoiding this so that no one will blame you' 2 Cor 8.20.

13.160 ὑποστέλλω[a]: to hold oneself back from doing something, with the implication of some fearful concern – 'to hold back from, to shrink from, to avoid.' οὐ γὰρ ὑπεστειλάμην τοῦ μὴ ἀναγγεῖλαι πᾶσαν τὴν βουλὴν τοῦ θεοῦ ὑμῖν 'for I have not held back from announcing to you the whole purpose of God' Ac 20.27. For another interpretation of ὑποστέλλω in Ac 20.27, see 68.53.

13.161 φεύγω[d]: (a figurative extension of meaning of φεύγω[a] 'to flee,' 15.61) to avoid doing something, with the evident purpose of attempting to avoid danger – 'to avoid.' τὰς δὲ νεωτερικὰς ἐπιθυμίας φεῦγε 'avoid the evil desires of youth' 2 Tm 2.22; φεύγετε τὴν πορνείαν 'avoid immoral sexual behavior' 1 Cor 6.18.

13.162 καταργέομαι[b]: to cease to happen – 'to no longer take place, to cease.' εἴτε δὲ προφητεῖαι, καταργηθήσονται 'if there are prophecies, they shall cease' 1 Cor 13.8.

13.163 καταργέω[b]: to cause to cease to happen – 'to put a stop to.' ὅτε γέγονα ἀνήρ, κατήργηκα τὰ τοῦ νηπίου 'when I became a man, I put a stop to those things of a child' 1 Cor 13.11; καταργήσαντος μὲν τὸν θάνατον 'putting an end to death' 2 Tm 1.10.

14 Physical Events and States[1]

Outline of Subdomains

A   Weather[2] (14.1-14.3)

14.1 εὐδία, ας f: sunny, mild weather without strong winds – 'fair weather.' ὀψίας

1 As will be readily noted, the domain of *Physical Events and States* includes a number of nouns and verbs with closely related meanings. There is a 'class meaning' distinction between the noun πνεῦμα[g] 'wind' (14.4) and the verb πνέω 'to blow' (14.4), but the denotative components of these two forms are essentially the same. See the statement on Principles and Procedures in the Introduction.

2 It would be possible to include under the category of *Weather* various features of weather such as wind, rain,

γενομένης λέγετε, Εὐδία, πυρράζει γὰρ ὁ οὐρανός 'when the sun is setting, you say, We are going to have fair weather because the sky is red' Mt 16.2. Fair weather may be referred to by a number of different expressions, for example, 'growing weather' or 'cloudless skies' or 'happy weather.' The variety of expressions depends largely upon the type of activity associated with weather or the atmospheric conditions typical of what people regard as fair weather. In a number of languages fair weather is expressed as a negative of bad weather, that is to say, 'a not stormy day' or 'a not windy day.'

14.2 χειμών^b, ῶνος *m*: stormy weather involving strong wind, overcast sky, and often cold temperature; thunder and lightning may also be present – 'bad weather, stormy weather.' χειμῶνός τε οὐκ ὀλίγου ἐπικειμένου 'the stormy weather did not abate in the least' or 'the violent storm continued' Ac 27.20.

The principal difficulty involved in translating χειμών^b is the fact that in so many languages there are quite distinct terms for various kinds of bad weather or storms. Furthermore, the location of such bad weather will also influence significantly the terms which may be used. For example, stormy weather over the open sea may require quite a different term from what would be used in speaking of a similar kind of storm over the land. In addition, storms which are accompanied by rain may also be referred to by different terms from those which involve wind without rain. Accordingly, one must carefully examine each biblical context in which χειμών^b is employed and determine what would be the most satisfactory expression in the receptor language. For example, in Mt 16.3 the reference is to a windstorm accompanied by clouds and moving over land, while in Ac 27.20 the reference is to a storm of long duration which takes place over a body of water.

storm, and certain movements of liquids. However, rather than combine a number of subordinate categories, it seems preferable to set up a series of separate subdomains and to indicate clearly their relationship by juxtaposition and by definitions relating to shared components.

14.3 χειμάζομαι: to be overtaken by or to experience stormy weather – 'to undergo bad weather, to be in a storm.' σφοδρῶς δὲ χειμαζομένων ἡμῶν 'we were caught in a very bad storm' Ac 27.18. In some languages it may be appropriate to translate χειμάζομαι in an idiomatic form, for example, 'the wind and rain caught us' or 'the storm trapped us.'

B Wind (14.4-14.9)

14.4 ἄνεμος, ου *m*; πνεῦμα^g, τος *n*; πνοή^a, ῆς *f*; πνέω: air in relatively rapid movement, but without specification as to the force of the movement – 'wind, blowing, to blow.'
ἄνεμος: ἵνα μὴ πνέῃ ἄνεμος ἐπὶ τῆς γῆς 'so that no wind should blow on earth' Re 7.1.
πνεῦμα^g: ὁ ποιῶν τοὺς ἀγγέλους αὐτοῦ πνεύματα 'he makes his angels winds' He 1.7. In Ps 104.4 the Hebrew actually means 'you use the winds as your messengers.' The form cited here in He 1.7 reflects the Septuagint translation. It may be relevant in some translations to call attention to the reason for this difference, since it may not be easy to make the Greek form of this expression fully meaningful, for literally 'to turn his angels into winds' may seem like purposeless magic. Some translators must employ a phrase such as 'he makes his angels like winds.'
πνοή^a: ἦχος ὥσπερ φερομένης πνοῆς βιαίας 'a sound as of a strong wind blowing' Ac 2.2.
πνέω: ὅταν νότον πνέοντα 'when the south wind is blowing' Lk 12.55.

As in the case of English (which has, for example, such terms as *breeze, zephyr, gust, storm, whirlwind, cyclone, tornado,* etc.), other languages likewise normally have a number of different terms depending upon the strength of the wind and whether the wind may be carrying substances such as sand or dust. In some languages there may also be a problem involved in the use of terms for 'wind,' since some of these may have meanings of malicious or malevolent spirits, or they may imply a disease-bringing event.

14.5 ὑποπνέω: a gentle blowing of the wind – 'to blow gently.' ὑποπνεύσαντος δὲ νότου 'the south wind was blowing gently' Ac 27.13. In some instances a gentle wind may be described as 'the air was just moving' or 'the air could just barely be felt' or 'the wind was just touching the skin.'

14.6 θύελλα, ης *f*; λαῖλαψ, απος *f*: sudden and violent gusts of winds, often from varied directions – 'windstorm, whirlwind, squall.'[3] θύελλα: οὐ γὰρ προσεληλύθατε . . . γνόφῳ καὶ ζόφῳ καὶ θυέλλῃ 'you did not experience . . . the darkness and the gloom and the strong wind' or 'you have not come to . . .' He 12.18. λαῖλαψ: γίνεται λαῖλαψ μεγάλη 'a strong wind blew up' Mk 4.37. In a number of languages a strong wind which causes the waves or a storm on water must be referred to by a special term. Compare, for example, the English term *squall*; this would mean a wind of relatively short duration but sufficiently intense so as to create relatively high waves.

14.7 τυφωνικός, ή, όν: (derivative of τυφῶν 'Typhon,' the legendary father of the winds, not occurring in the NT) pertaining to a very strong wind – 'of a violent, strong wind.' ἔβαλεν κατ' αὐτῆς ἄνεμος τυφωνικός 'a violent wind blew down from it (the island)' Ac 27.14.

Expressions for strong winds often differ on the basis of two important features: (1) the strength or violence of the wind and (2) the duration of the wind. For example, in English terms such as *squall* and *tornado* indicate violent but short periods of blowing, while *hurricane* or *typhoon* indicates a storm which takes a much longer period of time to pass. In Ac 27.14 the reference is obviously to the latter type of storm, called typhoon, hurricane, or monsoon, depending upon the region in which such violent and protracted storms occur.

14.8 νότος[b], ου *m*: a wind which blows from the south – 'south wind.' μετὰ μίαν ἡμέραν

ἐπιγενομένου νότου 'the next day a wind began to blow from the south' Ac 28.13.

A number of languages have terms for winds coming from or going toward different directions. In a number of cases, however, directional expressions are not included in the terms for such winds. For example, a north wind may be simply called 'a cold wind,' and a south wind might be called 'a wind from the sea.' Such expressions depend upon local geographical features. Even in the instance in which a south wind is described in terms of direction, it may be necessary to use a somewhat expanded phrase, for example, 'a wind from the right of the rising sun.' Such an expression is based upon the experience of a person facing the rising sun and determining the south in terms of the right side of the person.

14.9 Εὐρακύλων, ωνος *m*: (a hybrid formation from Greek and Latin, meaning literally either 'east wind' or 'broad wind') a strong storm wind blowing from the northeast – 'a Northeaster.' ἄνεμος τυφωνικὸς ὁ καλούμενος Εὐρακύλων 'a very strong wind, called Euraquilo' or '. . . called a Northeaster' Ac 27.14.[4]

It is, of course, possible to use the form Εὐρακύλων as a proper name, but this is probably much less meaningful than employing a term such as 'strong northeast wind' or 'a strong storm coming from the northeast.' In instances in which languages do not readily and easily distinguish between north and northeast or between east and northeast, it may be satisfactory simply to use a term such as 'east,' but frequently one can use a designation for 'northeast' such as 'between the north and the east' or 'a little to the north of east.'

C Rain (14.10-14.14)

14.10 ὑετός[b], οῦ *m*; βροχή, ῆς *f*; βρέχω[a]: rain, whether light or torrential – 'rain, to rain.'

---

3 It may very well be that θύελλα and λαῖλαψ differ somewhat with respect to the suddenness of wind or the force of the wind. In certain contexts outside of the NT, λαῖλαψ would appear to be a somewhat stronger wind than θύελλα, but this is by no means certain, and for the NT there is no way to determine whether such a distinction is relevant.

4 Some manuscripts read Εὐροκλύδων, explained as 'an east wind that stirs up waves.' Another form is Εὐρυκλύδων 'the wind that stirs up broad waves.' These two forms, however, are regarded by most scholars as being scribal errors.

ὑετός[b]: οὐρανόθεν ὑμῖν ὑετοὺς διδούς 'giving you rain from heaven' Ac 14.17.

βροχή: κατέβη ἡ βροχή 'the rain poured down' Mt 7.25.

βρέχω[a]: οὐκ ἔβρεξεν ἐπὶ τῆς γῆς ἐνιαυτοὺς τρεῖς καὶ μῆνας ἕξ 'it did not rain on the earth for three years and six months' Jas 5.17.

Though most languages have a general term for rain, the event of raining is more frequently referred to by a verb rather than by a noun, since rain is something which takes place and is not regarded as a thing or mass, unless, of course, one is referring to the water which comes down as rain, that is to say, 'rain water' (see 2.10). In some languages the event of raining is generally expressed idiomatically as 'God is urinating.' This might appear unduly crude and anthropomorphic, but to the speakers of such a language the expression is often quite acceptable and has no undesirable connotations.

Though in English one may use an impersonal subject with the verb 'to rain,' for example, 'it is raining,' many languages require some kind of personal agent, for example, 'God is raining,' or an impersonal agent such as 'the sky is raining' or 'the clouds are raining.'

14.11 βρέχω[b]: to cause rain to fall – 'to send rain, to cause it to rain.' βρέχει ἐπὶ δικαίους καὶ ἀδίκους 'he sends rain to those who do right and those who do wrong' Mt 5.45. In a number of languages one cannot say literally 'to send rain,' for this would seem to imply that someone was carrying the rain to some destination. It may be more appropriate, therefore, to speak of 'causing rain to fall' or 'causing rain to come down.' It may be necessary, however, in some languages to indicate whether the occurrence of rain is for the detriment or the benefit of persons involved, and therefore it may be necessary to say in some instances 'to cause rain to come down upon for the benefit of'; otherwise the reader might infer that the rain was some kind of punishment.

14.12 ὄμβρος, ου m: a heavy rain, either in length of occurrence or in force, as in the case of a thunderstorm (thus differing from ὑετός[b], βροχή, and βρέχω[a] in 14.10) – 'rainstorm, thunderstorm.' λέγετε ὅτι Ὄμβρος ἔρχεται 'you say that a rainstorm is coming' Lk 12.54. In some languages a rainstorm is simply 'a rain with wind,' but it may also be expressed as 'rain that hurts' or 'rain that floods.'

14.13 ὄψιμος, ου m: (derivative of ὄψιος 'late,' 67.76, and used absolutely of 'late rain') a rain that comes late in the season, that is to say, in April or May after the normal rains of the winter season have passed – 'late rain, spring rain.' ἕως λάβῃ πρόϊμον καὶ ὄψιμον 'until he receives the early and late rains' Jas 5.7. See πρόϊμος 'early rain' (14.14) for a discussion of problems involving 'late rain' and 'early rain.'

14.14 πρόϊμος, ου m: a rain occurring early in the autumn, September or October, in contrast with normal rains occurring in the middle of the winter season – 'early rain, autumn rain.' ἕως λάβῃ πρόϊμον καὶ ὄψιμον 'until he receives the early and late rains' Jas 5.7 (see 14.13).

In Palestine the rainy season differs appreciably from what it is in many other parts of the world. In tropical regions north of the Equator, the rains occur primarily from May through October, and in the tropical regions below the Equator, the rains normally occur from November through April. The other seasons of the year are normally quite dry. In Palestine, however, rains occur primarily during the months of November through March, and the summer months are often without rain. Because of this significant difference in the time of rainfall, it may be important to relate the early and late rains not to particular times of the year but to the normal period for rain. For example, the early rains could be 'rain coming before it is normally expected' or 'rain at the beginning of the rainy season,' and late rains are 'rains which come later than what one expects' or 'rain at the end of the rainy season.' On the other hand, the contrast may be expressed as 'rain coming before it should' or 'rain coming later than it should.' It is difficult to relate early and late rains to so-called 'growing seasons,' since in the Middle East grains grow primarily during the rainy season and are harvested early in the spring, while fruits and vegetables are grown in the spring and summer with extensive use made of irrigation.

D Thunder and Lightning (14.15-14.16)

14.15 βροντή, ῆς *f*: the loud sound that accompanies a flash of lightning – 'thunder.' ἀκούσας ἔλεγεν βροντὴν γεγονέναι 'they heard the voice and said, It thundered' Jn 12.29. See ἀστραπή[a] 'lightning' (14.16) for further discussion.

14.16 ἀστραπή[a], ῆς *f*: the flash of lightning – 'lightning.' ὥσπερ γὰρ ἡ ἀστραπὴ ἐξέρχεται ἀπὸ ἀνατολῶν 'as lightning comes out of the east' Mt 24.27.

Terms referring to thunder and lightning often have important taboo connotations. The specific terms for thunder and lightning may be avoided and figurative expressions employed in their place in order to avoid danger which might occur from being struck by lightning or frightened by a thunderstorm. One can, therefore, expect in some languages a number of different terms, and it is important to avoid expressions which might have wrong connotations.

E Events Involving Liquids and Dry Masses[5] (14.17-14.35)

14.17 ῥέω; ῥύσις, εως *f*: the movement of a liquid in some direction – 'to flow, a flow.'[6]

ῥέω: καθὼς εἶπεν ἡ γραφή, ποταμοὶ ἐκ τῆς κοιλίας αὐτοῦ ῥεύσουσιν ὕδατος ζῶντος 'as the scripture says, Streams of living water will flow from his heart' Jn 7.38. In the NT ῥέω occurs only in the figurative context of Jn 7.38.

ῥύσις: γυνὴ οὖσα ἐν ῥύσει αἵματος δώδεκα ἔτη 'the woman had had a hemorrhage for twelve years' Mk 5.25.

In a number of languages a term referring to the flow of liquid may also be applied to the movement of any object, so that a literal rendering might be 'the liquid moved.' However, terms for 'flow' or 'pour' often differ substantially on the basis of the direction of the flow. For example, if the flow is relatively horizontal, and therefore slow, it may have one term, while if it is quite fast, another expression may be used, and if the flow is almost perpendicular (as in the case of pouring), a still different term is employed.

14.18 ἐκχέομαι[a]: to flow out of a container – 'to flow out, to pour out.'[7] καὶ ὁ οἶνος ἐκχεῖται καὶ οἱ ἀσκοὶ ἀπόλλυνται 'and the wine pours out and the wineskins are ruined' Mt 9.17; καὶ ἐξεχύθη πάντα τὰ σπλάγχνα αὐτοῦ 'and all his entrails poured out' Ac 1.18.

14.19 ὑπερεκχύννομαι: to pour or run out over, either of a liquid or a dry mass – 'to overflow, to flow over, to run over.' μέτρον καλὸν πεπιεσμένον σεσαλευμένον ὑπερεκχυννόμενον 'a good measure pressed down, shaken, and pouring out over' or '. . . running over' Lk 6.38.

---

5 Meanings included in the Subdomain *Events Involving Liquids and Dry Masses* (contrast Domain 47) do not include 'rain,' since this seems more specifically related to events of weather, wind, and storm.

There are some terms which involve the action of liquids which are not, however, specifically restricted to liquids as instruments, and since they cannot be used in a completely absolute sense of the action of liquids, they are not included in this subdomain. For example, προσρήγνυμι (or προσρήσσω) is employed in describing the action of a river in flood which bursts upon a house and breaks it to pieces (Lk 6.48), but this action of a river in flood can be subsumed under the general meaning of προσρήγνυμι (or προσρήσσω) in the sense of 'to strike against, to burst against' (19.6). There is accordingly no need to set up a separate meaning.

6 It is possible to regard ῥέω 'to flow' and ῥύσις 'a flow' or 'a flowing' as being semantically distinct on the basis

that one refers only to the event of flowing, while the second particularizes the event by assuming a specific beginning and end point and thus making it possible to speak of a number of such events. In English this type of semantic derivation is almost automatic between verbs and nouns, and it is widespread in Greek, though with obvious morphological differences. In a number of other languages, however, there is no corresponding noun form, and in order to speak of a series of events, one must simply say 'it flowed several times.'

7 Verbs employing the stem -χεο- differ from ῥέω 'to flow' (14.17), are less generic in meaning, and frequently imply a more restricted quantity of liquid. In classical Greek ῥέω and related derivatives were employed more in poetic discourse.

14.20 διεγείρομαι^b: (a figurative extension of meaning of διεγείρομαι^a 'to become awake from sleep,' 23.74) to become rough, in reference to a surface of water – 'to become rough, to become stormy.' ἥ τε θάλασσα ἀνέμου μεγάλου πνέοντος διεγείρετο 'by now a strong wind was blowing and the sea was getting rough' Jn 6.18.

In describing a rough surface of a body of water, one may say in some languages 'there were many waves' or 'the waves were very big.' In other languages one may speak of a rough surface of a body of water by an idiomatic expression, for example, 'the face of the water was foaming' or 'the water was angry.'

14.21 ἐπιβάλλω^c: to strike upon and into (with special reference to the action of waves) – 'to splash into.' καὶ τὰ κύματα ἐπέβαλλεν εἰς τὸ πλοῖον 'and the waves splashed into the boat' Mk 4.37.[8]

14.22 σεισμός^b, οῦ *m*: a violent action of the surface of a body of water as the result of high waves caused by a strong wind – 'storm on the sea.' καὶ ἰδοὺ σεισμὸς μέγας ἐγένετο ἐν τῇ θαλάσσῃ 'and there was a great storm on the sea' Mt 8.24.

Though the term σεισμός^b obviously implies the strong action of the wind, the focus is upon the violent motion caused by the waves. It might, therefore, be more appropriate to translate Mt 8.24 as 'there were huge waves on the sea' or '. . . on the lake.' Such a translation would then be appropriate for the following clause.

14.23 γαλήνη, ης *f*: a calm or unruffled surface of a body of water – 'a calm' (in contrast with a storm over water). ἐκόπασεν ὁ ἄνεμος, καὶ ἐγένετο γαλήνη μεγάλη 'the wind died down and there was a great calm' Mk 4.39.

A calm after a storm may be referred to figuratively in some languages as 'the water

lay down' or 'the waves sank down again' or 'the water became like a table top.'

14.24 σιωπάω^c: (a figurative extension of meaning of σιωπάω^a 'to be silent,' 33.117) the process of becoming calm after a storm – 'to become calm, to become still.' εἶπεν τῇ θαλάσσῃ, Σιώπα 'he said to the sea, Be still' Mk 4.39. In a number of languages it is not possible to translate σιωπάω^c literally as 'be still' since this might imply 'continue to remain still.' Since there is a change in state, it may be necessary to say 'become still' or 'cease to be stormy.'

14.25 κῦμα, τος *n*; κλύδων, ωνος *m*: a moving ridge or succession of swells on the surface of a body of water – 'wave, billow, surge.'
κῦμα: ὥστε τὸ πλοῖον καλύπτεσθαι ὑπὸ τῶν κυμάτων 'so that the waves were breaking right over the boat' (literally 'so that the boat was covered by the waves') Mt 8.24.
κλύδων: ἐπετίμησεν τῷ ἀνέμῳ καὶ τῷ κλύδωνι τοῦ ὕδατος 'he rebuked the wind and the waves' Lk 8.24.

14.26 σάλος, ου *m*: the tossing motion of large waves on a body of water – 'surging waves.' ἤχους θαλάσσης καὶ σάλου 'sound of the sea and of the tossing waves' Lk 21.25.

14.27 ἀφρός, οῦ *m*: (derivative of ἀφρίζω 'to cause foaming of a liquid,' 14.28) a frothy, foaming mass or substance – 'foam.' σπαράσσει αὐτὸν μετὰ ἀφροῦ 'it convulses him and causes him to foam at the mouth' Lk 9.39. Though ἀφρός may refer to any type of foam or frothy substance, in Lk 9.39 the reference is clearly to frothy saliva coming out of the mouth, something which is typical of persons experiencing an epileptic seizure. A number of languages have quite specific terms for this type of foaming or frothing at the mouth, expressed literally in some instances as 'his saliva was bubbling out of his mouth' or 'the water of his mouth came out in bubbles.'

14.28 ἀφρίζω: to cause or to produce the foaming up of a liquid (restricted in the NT to the foaming at the mouth of a person expe-

---

8 It would be possible to analyze the meaning of ἐπιβάλλω^c as merely a matter of impact, but it is the evident action of the waves, not only in striking the boat but filling it with water, that would seem to justify setting up a separate meaning.

riencing an epileptic seizure) – 'to foam up, to foam at the mouth.' πεσὼν ἐπὶ τῆς γῆς ἐκυλίετο ἀφρίζων 'so that he fell on the ground and rolled around, foaming at the mouth' Mk 9.20.

Since foaming at the mouth is so characteristic of epileptic seizures, there should be no difficulty in finding a rather specific term to identify this type of event.

14.29 ἐπαφρίζω: to cause foam to occur on the surface of a liquid – 'to cause to foam up.' κύματα . . . ἐπαφρίζοντα τὰς ἑαυτῶν αἰσχύνας 'waves . . . causing their shameless deeds to foam up' Jd 13.

ἐπαφρίζω occurs in the NT only in Jd 13 in a figurative context. It probably differs from ἀφρίζω (14.28) in emphasizing the greater degree or extent of foam on the surface.

In some languages the type of foam which would be referred to in Jd 13 is called 'the saliva of the waves' or 'the whiteness of the waves.' Since foaming at the mouth is also regarded as a sign of anger, it is possible to speak in some languages of the foam of the waves as being 'the anger of the waves.' In other languages one may speak simply of 'the whiteness of the waves.'

14.30 ἅλλομαι[b]: the action of water forming bubbles and welling up from underneath the ground – 'to bubble up, to well up.' πηγὴ ὕδατος ἁλλομένου εἰς ζωὴν αἰώνιον 'a spring of water bubbling up to eternal life' Jn 4.14. In the NT ἅλλομαι[b] occurs only in the figurative context of Jn 4.14.

In some languages expressions referring to the flowing of water from a spring depend upon the extent or continuity of such a flow. If the spring is a perennial one, that is to say, if it flows all the time, it may be designated by one term, while if it is intermittent, that is, flows only during the rainy season, it may be referred to by quite a different term. There may also be distinctions as to whether the water flows out and then down or whether it actually comes up from below the surface. In Jn 4.14 the direction of flow is not important, but it is important to use a term which would indicate continuous flowing.

14.31 βρύω: to cause a forceful and abundant supply of a liquid – 'to cause to pour out, to cause to gush out.' μήτι ἡ πηγὴ ἐκ τῆς αὐτῆς ὀπῆς βρύει τὸ γλυκὺ καὶ τὸ πικρόν 'a spring cannot cause to gush out of its opening both sweet and bitter water' Jas 3.11. This flow from a spring may be referred to in some languages as 'to cause to come out' or 'to cause to flow out.'

14.32 διθάλασσος, ον: two currents which meet in a body of water – 'cross-currents.' περιπεσόντες δὲ εἰς τόπον διθάλασσον 'encountering cross-currents' Ac 27.41. Other scholars, however, interpret διθάλασσος together with τόπος as being a reef, a sandbar, or even a headland (see 1.68).

Cross-currents may be spoken of as 'streams in the sea' or 'rivers in the sea' or 'two rivers that meet in the sea.' It would be wrong, however, to use the expression 'two rivers that meet in the sea' if this meant merely two rivers which meet at the coastline as they flow from the interior. In this context 'rivers' can only refer to 'rivers of the sea,' in other words, 'currents.'

14.33 πλήμμυρα, ης f: the overflowing of the banks by a river or stream – 'flood, high water.' πλημμύρης δὲ γενομένης προσέρηξεν ὁ ποταμὸς τῇ οἰκίᾳ ἐκείνῃ 'and when a flood came, the river broke against that house' Lk 6.48. One might very well render Lk 6.48 as 'when the river overflowed its banks, it burst against the house.' In some instances it may not be possible to use a term which would be more or less literally 'to burst against,' but one can say 'tried to cause the house to collapse' or 'tried to destroy the house.'

14.34 κατακλύζω; κατακλυσμός, οῦ m: a large flood with destructive force (more intense and extensive than πλήμμυρα 'flood,' 14.33) – 'flood, deluge.' κατακλύζω: κόσμος ὕδατι κατακλυσθεὶς ἀπώλετο 'the world was destroyed by being flooded with water' 2 Pe 3.6. κατακλυσμός: κατακλυσμὸν κόσμῳ ἀσεβῶν ἐπάξας 'brought the flood on the world of godless people' 2 Pe 2.5.

In the NT κατακλύζω and κατακλυσμός occur only in 2 Peter and are used exclusively of the catastrophic flood in the time of Noah. Such a flood may be spoken of as 'a flood that destroys' or 'much water which destroys.'

14.35 πίνω^b: (a figurative extension of meaning of πίνω^a 'to drink,' 23.34) the action of a material which soaks up a liquid – 'to absorb, to soak up.' γῆ γὰρ ἡ πιοῦσα τὸν ἐπ' αὐτῆς ἐρχόμενον πολλάκις ὑετόν 'the ground absorbs the rain which frequently falls upon it' He 6.7. Instead of speaking about 'the ground absorbing the rain' or '. . . drinking up the rain,' it is often more natural to describe the event as 'the rain disappearing into the ground' or 'the rain flowing into the ground.'

F   Light⁹ (14.36-14.52)

14.36 φῶς^a, φωτός *n*; φέγγος, ους *n*: light, in contrast with darkness (σκότος^a, σκοτία^a, 14.53), usually in relationship to some source of light such as the sun, moon, fire, lamp, etc. – 'light.'¹⁰
φῶς^a: ὅτι ὁ θεὸς ὁ εἰπών, Ἐκ σκότους φῶς λάμψει 'the God who said, Out of darkness the light shall shine' 2 Cor 4.6.
φέγγος: ἡ σελήνη οὐ δώσει τὸ φέγγος αὐτῆς 'the moon will not give its light' Mt 24.29.
Terms for 'light' often differ on the basis of whether there is a specific source of light, for example, a fire, lamps, sun, moon, etc., or whether the light is simply generalized, in the sense of daylight apart from the actual shining of the sun (for example, as in the interior of a room). Some languages also make distinctions between terms for light depending on whether the light comes from a fire or lamp or from a heavenly body.
In a number of languages there is no noun

for 'light,' but only verbs are employed, since the fact of light is spoken of as something which happens and is hence regarded as an event.

14.37 λάμπω; φαίνω: to shine or to produce light, as in the case of heavenly bodies, lightning, candles, torches, etc. – 'to shine, to give light, to bring light.'
λάμπω: ἡ ἀστραπὴ . . . ἐκ τῆς ὑπὸ τὸν οὐρανὸν εἰς τὴν ὑπ' οὐρανὸν λάμπει 'the lightning . . . shines from one part of the sky to the other' Lk 17.24.
φαίνω: ὡς λύχνω φαίνοντι ἐν αὐχμηρῷ τόπῳ 'for it is like a lamp shining in a dark place' 2 Pe 1.19.
Terms for 'shining, giving light' often differ depending upon the type of source. There may be, for example, a contrast between the shining of a heavenly body in contrast with some source on earth. There may also be a difference between a continuous shining such as of the sun and the moon and a brief flash, as in the case of lightning or sparks from a fire.

14.38 ἐκλάμπω: to shine forth from a source (occurring only in Mt 13.43 in a figurative context) – 'to shine forth.' οἱ δίκαιοι ἐκλάμψουσιν ὡς ὁ ἥλιος ἐν τῇ βασιλείᾳ τοῦ πατρὸς αὐτῶν 'God's people will shine forth like the sun in their Father's kingdom' Mt 13.43.

14.39 φωτίζω^a; ἐπιφαίνω; ἐπιφαύσκω: to cause light to shine upon some object, in the sense of illuminating it – 'to illuminate, to shine upon.'
φωτίζω^a: ὡς ὅταν ὁ λύχνος τῇ ἀστραπῇ φωτίζῃ σε 'as when a lamp shines on you brightly' Lk 11.36.
ἐπιφαίνω: ἐπιφᾶναι τοῖς ἐν σκότει καὶ σκιᾷ θανάτου καθημένοις 'to shine upon those seated in darkness and the shadow of death' Lk 1.79.
ἐπιφαύσκω (occurring only in Eph 5.14 as an instance of figurative usage): καὶ ἐπιφαύσει σοι ὁ Χριστός 'and Christ will shine upon you' Eph 5.14.
Expressions involving the causing of light to shine upon an object often involve explicit causative elements, for example, 'to cause light to shine upon' or 'to cause to shine' or

---

9 In this subdomain are included the meanings of light, either as a physical event or as a resulting condition.
10 It is possible that there is some contrast between φῶς^a and φέγγος in that φῶς^a may suggest a somewhat stronger source of light, since φῶς^a is so frequently associated with the light of the sun while φέγγος is typically related to the light of the moon. In contexts outside the Scriptures there are, however, a number of instances in which there seems to be considerable overlapping of meaning.

'to cause to be bright' or 'to cause to be in the light.'

14.40 ἡμέρα^d, ας *f*: the light of the day in contrast with the darkness of night (see νύξ^b 'night,' 14.59) – 'daylight.'[11] γενομένης δὲ ἡμέρας ἐξελθὼν ἐπορεύθη 'when daylight came, he left (town)' Lk 4.42. In order to focus attention upon the beginning of daylight, one may translate Lk 4.42 as 'when the sun began to shine' or 'when the sky began to become light' or even 'when it was no longer night.'

In some languages there is no noun for either 'day' or 'daylight,' but a verb expression may be employed which may be rendered literally as 'to day' or 'to become day.'

14.41 ἀνατέλλω^b; ἐπιφώσκω: to change from darkness to light in the early morning hours – 'to dawn, to become light.' ἀνατέλλω^b: φῶς ἀνέτειλεν αὐτοῖς 'the light dawned upon them' Mt 4.16. ἐπιφώσκω: τῇ ἐπιφωσκούσῃ εἰς μίαν σαββάτων 'as it was dawning on the first day of the week' Mt 28.1.

In some languages dawning is divided into more than one aspect or period of time. The first may be only a glimmering of light in the east; the second period makes visibility quite easy; and the third period involves shafts of light or colored clouds visible in the sky immediately before sunrise. Usually an expression for one of these periods of time is more generalized in usage, and therefore it is probably satisfactory to adopt such an expression for any transition from darkness to light.

14.42 ἀνατολὴ ἐξ ὕψους: (an idiom, literally 'dawning from on high') the bright dawn of salvation (or possibly to be understood as a title for the Messiah) – 'the dawn from on high.' ἐπισκέψεται ἡμᾶς ἀνατολὴ ἐξ ὕψους 'the dawn of salvation will come upon us' Lk 1.78.

The expression ἀνατολὴ ἐξ ὕψους occurs in a highly poetic liturgical passage in Lk 1, and many translators have preferred to retain the more or less literal rendering. Others, however, have interpreted this as the dawning of salvation and have therefore translated ἐπισκέψεται ἡμᾶς ἀνατολὴ ἐξ ὕψους as 'salvation will dawn upon us from heaven' or 'from heaven salvation will come to us as the dawn does.' If one wishes to employ ἀνατολὴ ἐξ ὕψους as simply a title for the Messiah, one can translate 'the Messiah will come to us,' but it is normally better to preserve the figurative expression and relate it to the coming of the Messiah as 'the Messiah will come to us even as the dawn does from on high.' One may also treat the problem of interpretation in a footnote.

14.43 διαυγάζω: to shine through, with special reference to dawn, and possibly implying the shining of the sun through clouds or overcast sky – 'to shine through, to dawn upon.' ἕως οὗ ἡμέρα διαυγάσῃ 'until the day dawns' 2 Pe 1.19. In some languages it may be more satisfactory to say 'until it becomes light' or 'until that day happens.' This expression is generally regarded as applying to the second coming of Christ.

14.44 περιλάμπω: to illuminate an area surrounding an object – 'to shine around.' οὐρανόθεν ὑπὲρ τὴν λαμπρότητα τοῦ ἡλίου περιλάμψαν με φῶς 'a light much brighter than the sun shone around me from the sky' Ac 26.13.

There may be difficulties involved in expressing the concept of 'to shine around,' since a more or less literal rendering might suggest a particular circle of light moving around an object. A more satisfactory way of dealing with this problem of 'to shine around' is to say 'it was light there' or 'light shone upon me.' In the case of Ac 26.13, one may translate 'I saw a light from the sky there where I was.'

14.45 περιαστράπτω: to shine very brightly on an area surrounding an object – 'to shine brightly around, to flash around.' ἐξαίφνης τε αὐτὸν περιήστραψεν φῶς ἐκ τοῦ οὐρανοῦ 'suddenly a light from the sky flashed around him' Ac 9.3. See the discussion in 14.44.

---

11 ἡμέρα^d 'daylight' overlaps considerably in meaning with ἡμέρα^b 'daylight period' (67.178). In Lk 4.42, for example, one could interpret ἡμέρα as a period of time rather than as light associated with daytime. See also 14.59.

14.46 ἀστραπή^b, ῆς *f*: shafts or beams of light radiating from a source – 'bright beam.' ὡς ὅταν ὁ λύχνος τῇ ἀστραπῇ φωτίζῃ σε 'as when a lamp shines upon you brightly' Lk 11.36. It is often better to render ἀστραπή^b as a type of qualifying adverb, for example, 'brightly.'

14.47 στίλβω; ἀστράπτω; ἐξαστράπτω: to give off or to reflect a very bright light – 'to glisten, to dazzle, to gleam, to flash.'[12]
στίλβω: τὰ ἱμάτια αὐτοῦ ἐγένετο στίλβοντα λευκά 'his clothes became dazzling white' Mk 9.3.
ἀστράπτω: ἐπέστησαν αὐταῖς ἐν ἐσθῆτι ἀστραπτούσῃ 'they stood by them in gleaming clothes' Lk 24.4.
ἐξαστράπτω: ὁ ἱματισμὸς αὐτοῦ λευκὸς ἐξαστράπτων 'his clothes became dazzling white' Lk 9.29.

14.48 ἀπαύγασμα, τος *n*: shining, either in the sense of radiance from a source or the reflection of a source of light – 'radiance, reflection.' ὃς ὢν ἀπαύγασμα τῆς δόξης 'who is the reflection of (God's) glory' or 'who is the radiance of (God's) glory' He 1.3.
It is impossible to determine whether ἀπαύγασμα should be interpreted in an active sense and therefore 'radiance,' or in a passive sence and therefore as 'reflection.' If the meaning is 'radiance,' then one may translate this phrase in He 1.3 as 'he shines with God's glory' or even 'God's glory shines through him.' If one understands the meaning of ἀπαύγασμα as being 'reflection,' then one may often say 'God's glory shines back from him.'

14.49 λαμπρότης, ητος *f*; δόξα^b, ης *f*; φωστήρ^b, ῆρος *m*: the state of brightness or shining – 'brightness, shining, radiance.'
λαμπρότης: οὐρανόθεν ὑπὲρ τὴν λαμπρότητα τοῦ ἡλίου περιλάμψαν με φῶς 'a light much brighter than the sun shone around me from the sky' Ac 26.13.

[12] It may be that ἐξαστράπτω differs from ἀστράπτω either in emphasizing the source or in suggesting greater intensity of brightness, but NT usage does not provide a clear indication for such a distinction.

δόξα^b: οὐκ ἐνέβλεπον ἀπὸ τῆς δόξης τοῦ φωτός 'I could not see because of the brightness of the light' Ac 22.11. In Re 15.8 (καὶ ἐγεμίσθη ὁ ναὸς καπνοῦ ἐκ τῆς δόξης τοῦ θεοῦ 'and the temple was filled with smoke from the brightness of God') the reference is evidently to the Shekinah. The Shekinah, which filled the Temple when it was first constructed (1 Kgs 8.11), was regarded as a bright, cloud-like object which represented the personal presence of God.
φωστήρ^b: ὁ φωστὴρ αὐτῆς ὅμοιος λίθῳ τιμιωτάτῳ 'its radiance is like a most valuable stone' Re 21.11.
In a number of languages a clear distinction is made between some object which is bright in and of itself (that is to say, the source of brightness or radiance) and objects which are bright because they reflect light from some source. In the case of Mt 17.5 (which is generally regarded as a reference to the Shekinah presence of God), the cloud would not be merely reflecting light but would be a source of light (see 14.50).

14.50 λαμπρός^a, ά, όν; λευκός^b, ή, όν; φωτεινός^b, ή, όν: pertaining to being bright or shining, either of a source or of an object which is illuminated by a source – 'bright, shining, radiant.'
λαμπρός^a: ὁ ἀστὴρ ὁ λαμπρὸς ὁ πρωϊνός 'the bright morning star' Re 22.16.
λευκός^b: τὰ δὲ ἱμάτια αὐτοῦ ἐγένετο λευκὰ ὡς τὸ φῶς 'his clothes became bright as light' Mt 17.2.
φωτεινός^b: ἔτι αὐτοῦ λαλοῦντος ἰδοὺ νεφέλη φωτεινὴ ἐπεσκίασεν αὐτούς 'while he was talking, a shining cloud came over them' Mt 17.5.

14.51 φωτεινός^a, ή, όν: pertaining to being well lighted – 'full of light, well lighted.' ἐὰν οὖν ᾖ ὁ ὀφθαλμός σου ἁπλοῦς, ὅλον τὸ σῶμά σου φωτεινὸν ἔσται 'if your eyes are clear, your whole body will be full of light' Mt 6.22. In a number of languages one cannot speak of an object being 'full of light,' for light is not spoken of as a substance. It is, of course, normally possible to speak of something as 'having light inside' (for example, the occurrence of light within a room). However, rather than speaking positively of the occurrence of light, it is sometimes more satisfactory to indicate the absence of darkness, for example, 'there was no darkness there' or, as in Mt 6.22, 'your whole body will have no darkness in it.'

14.52 κατοπτρίζομαι^b: to reflect light or visual patterns coming from some source – 'to reflect.' ἡμεῖς δὲ πάντες ἀνακεκαλυμμένῳ προσώπῳ τὴν δόξαν κυρίου κατοπτριζόμενοι 'all of us, then, reflect the glory of the Lord with uncovered faces' 2 Cor 3.18. In order to speak of a reflection of light, it may be necessary to say 'to throw back the light' or 'to shine back the form.' Sometimes it is necessary to stipulate a type of object which reflects such light, for example, 'we are a shining object that shows back the glory of the Lord.' For another interpretation of κατοπτρίζομαι in 2 Cor 3.18, see 24.44.

G Darkness (14.53-14.62)

14.53 σκότος^a, ους *n*; **σκοτία**^a, ας *f*; **γνόφος, ου** *m*: a condition resulting from the partial or complete absence of light (see 14.36) – 'darkness.'
σκότος^a: σκότος ἐγένετο ἐφ' ὅλην τὴν γῆν ἕως ὥρας ἐνάτης 'darkness covered the whole country until three o'clock' (literally . . . 'the ninth hour') Lk 23.44.
σκοτία^a: Μαρία ἡ Μαγδαληνὴ ἔρχεται πρωῒ σκοτίας ἔτι οὔσης 'Mary Magdalene went early while it was still dark' Jn 20.1.
γνόφος: γνόφῳ καὶ ζόφῳ καὶ θυέλλῃ 'the darkness, the gloom, and the storm' He 12.18.

In a number of languages it is impossible to speak of 'darkness' as being an agent in the sense of Lk 23.44 'darkness covered the whole country.' Accordingly, one must say 'throughout the whole country it was dark' or 'it darkened over the whole country.' In some languages darkness may be characterized as being a quality of the night, for example, 'it was like night.'

14.54 σκοτεινός, ή, όν: pertaining to being in a state of darkness – 'dark, in darkness.' μὴ ἔχον μέρος τι σκοτεινόν 'not having any part dark' Lk 11.36. In some languages 'dark' may

be most satisfactorily expressed as 'without light.'

14.55 σκοτόομαι^a; **σκοτίζομαι**^a: (derivatives of σκότος^a and σκοτία^a 'darkness,' 14.53) to change from a condition of being light to one of being dark – 'to become dark.'
σκοτόομαι^a: ἐσκοτώθη ὁ ἥλιος καὶ ὁ ἀήρ 'the sun and the air became dark' Re 9.2.
σκοτίζομαι^a: ὁ ἥλιος σκοτισθήσεται 'the sun will become dark' Mt 24.29.

In Re 9.2 it may not be difficult to speak of 'the air becoming dark,' since this would mean the space above the earth, but it may be difficult to speak of 'the sun becoming dark.' In the latter instance, for both Re 9.2 and Mt 24.29, one may say 'the sun will no longer shine' or 'the sun will not give its light.'

In place of 'the air became dark,' it is also possible to speak of 'the sky will become dark.'

14.56 στυγνάζω^a: to become both dark and gloomy, with the implication of threatening – 'to become dark and gloomy.' πυρράζει γὰρ στυγνάζων ὁ οὐρανός 'for the sky is red and gloomy' Mt 16.3.

In order to combine the components of στυγνάζω, which involve not only darkness but also gloom and threatening, it may be possible to translate as 'dark and threatening' or 'so dark as to cause one to be afraid.'

14.57 ζόφος, ου *m*: a condition of darkness associated with feelings of despair and foreboding – 'gloom, darkness.' γνόφῳ καὶ ζόφῳ καὶ θυέλλῃ 'the darkness and the gloom and the storm' He 12.18. In He 12.18 γνόφος 'darkness' (14.53) and ζόφος may be combined to form a phrase such as 'fearful darkness' or 'darkness that causes fear' or 'fear because of darkness.'

14.58 αὐχμηρός, ά, όν: pertaining to being not only dark, but also dirty and miserable – 'dark and miserable.' ὡς λύχνῳ φαίνοντι ἐν αὐχμηρῷ τόπῳ 'like a lamp shining in a dark and miserable place' 2 Pe 1.19. In 2 Pe 1.19 αὐχμηρός may also suggest moral degradation, and in English the phrase 'filthy darkness' could suggest this type of meaning.

14.59 νύξ^b, νυκτός *f*: darkness of the night in contrast with daylight (see 14.40) – 'night.' νὺξ οὐκ ἔσται ἔτι 'there will be no more night' Re 22.5. It is also possible to interpret νύξ in Re 22.5 as a period of time rather than as darkness (see 67.192). See also 14.40 and footnote 11.

14.60 σκιά^a, ᾶς *f*: shade, as a shelter from light and the heat associated with light – 'shade.' ὥστε δύνασθαι ὑπὸ τὴν σκιὰν αὐτοῦ τὰ πετεινὰ τοῦ οὐρανοῦ κατασκηνοῦν 'so that birds will be able to nest in its shade' Mk 4.32.

A term for 'shade' as an area sheltered from the direct rays of the sun usually differs from a term for 'shadow,' which is cast by a particular object blocking rays of light (see 14.61).

14.61 σκιά^b, ᾶς *f*; ἀποσκίασμα, τος *n*: the shape or shade cast by an object which blocks rays of light – 'shadow.'

σκιά^b: ἐρχομένου Πέτρου κἂν ἡ σκιὰ ἐπισκιάσῃ τινὶ αὐτῶν 'when Peter walked by, at least his shadow might pass over one of them' or '. . . touch one of them' or '. . . fall on one of them' Ac 5.15.

ἀποσκίασμα: παρ' ᾧ οὐκ ἔνι παραλλαγὴ ἢ τροπῆς ἀποσκίασμα 'in whom there is no change or shifting shadow' Jas 1.17. In Jas 1.17 one may translate 'shifting shadow' as 'a shadow which constantly changes.'

In Lk 1.79 (τοῖς ἐν σκότει καὶ σκιᾷ θανάτου καθημένοις 'those living in the darkness and shadow of death'), σκιά may be interpreted as being used figuratively of a shadow cast by impending death, that is to say, death is personified in such a way as to suggest that it casts a shadow because of its nearness. One may, therefore, translate τοῖς ἐν σκότει καὶ σκιᾷ θανάτου καθημένοις as 'those who live in the darkness of impending death,' in which case σκιά becomes essentially equivalent to an expression of time.

In a number of languages a term for 'shadow' has a number of very important meanings. In some instances it is regarded as a part of personality which goes on to the next world, since a dead person no longer 'casts a shadow.' The shadow may also be regarded as a kind of counterpart of the personality, a

type of alter ego. In cases of severe illness one may say 'his shadow has walked away,' and in many parts of the world the shadow of a person is an important element in the practice of black magic, for to damage a shadow may be regarded as a means of causing harm to a person.

14.62 ἐπισκιάζω; κατασκιάζω: to cause a shadow by interposing something between an object and a source of light – 'to cast a shadow upon.'

ἐπισκιάζω: κἂν ἡ σκιὰ ἐπισκιάσῃ τινὶ αὐτῶν 'at least his shadow might fall on one of them' Ac 5.15; νεφέλη φωτεινὴ ἐπεσκίασεν αὐτούς 'a shining cloud overshadowed them' Mt 17.5. In Ac 5.15 there is a semantic duplication of the element of 'shadow' in view of the noun σκιά and the verb ἐπισκιάζω. In Mt 17.5 the shining cloud would not produce the same kind of shadow as in the case of Ac 5.15, but it would be interposed between (1) the sun and (2) Jesus and his disciples. In Mt 17.5 the shining cloud may thus be more like a covering than a shadow. The reference to this shining cloud in Mt 17.5 as the Shekinah of God is discussed in 14.49, 50.

In Lk 1.35 ἐπισκιάζω is used figuratively in speaking of the agency of the Holy Spirit in causing Mary to conceive: πνεῦμα ἅγιον ἐπελεύσεται ἐπὶ σέ, καὶ δύναμις ὑψίστου ἐπισκιάσει σοι 'the Holy Spirit will come upon you and the power of the Most High will overshadow you.' In a number of languages it is not possible, however, to translate ἐπισκιάζω literally as 'overshadow.' It may therefore be necessary to use some such expression as 'the power of the Most High will come to you' or 'God's power will come upon you.' A strictly literal rendering of ἐπισκιάζω in Lk 1.35 could be interpreted in some languages as being a rather crude reference to sexual intercourse, and this interpretation should be avoided.

κατασκιάζω: χερουβὶν δόξης κατασκιάζοντα τὸ ἱλαστήριον 'the cherubim of glory overshadowing the place of atonement' He 9.5. It is possible in He 9.5 to regard the action of the cherubim as being one of protection, but it is also possible to regard this as an expression of overshadowing in view of the position of the cherubim whose wings covered the top of the Covenant Box.

H Burning (14.63-14.73)

14.63 καίω[a]; καυσόομαι; καῦσις, εως *f*; πυρόομαι[a]; πύρωσις[a], εως *f*: the process of burning – 'to burn, burning, to be on fire.'

καίω[a]: καὶ οἱ λύχνοι καιόμενοι 'and lamps burning' or 'and lamps alight' Lk 12.35.

καυσόομαι: στοιχεῖα καυσούμενα τήκεται 'the elements will be melted by burning' 2 Pe 3.12.

καῦσις: ἧς τὸ τέλος εἰς καῦσιν 'whose end will come about by burning' He 6.8.

πυρόομαι[a]: οὐρανοὶ πυρούμενοι λυθήσονται 'the heavens will be destroyed by burning' 2 Pe 3.12. In a number of languages it is extremely difficult to indicate burning as means simply by a phrase such as 'by burning.' Normally, burning can only be referred to by means of an expression referring to fire. Accordingly, 2 Pe 3.12 may be rendered as 'a great fire will destroy the sky and will cause the elements to melt'; likewise, in He 6.8 one may translate 'in the end a great fire will destroy the earth.'

πύρωσις[a]: βλέποντες τὸν καπνὸν τῆς πυρώσεως αὐτῆς 'when they see the smoke of her burning' Re 18.18. It is important to indicate that in the phrase 'her burning' she is the one who is burned. One may therefore render this part of Re 18.18 as 'when they see the smoke of the fire that burns her up.'

In a number of languages important distinctions are made in the use of terms for burning. For example, the burning of a substance for light, as in the case of a lamp or candle, may be indicated by a term quite different from an expression indicating the destruction or burning up of something. Similarly, the burning of wood for cooking may require still another term. The extent or size of the fire involved may also require some distinctions in terms for burning.

14.64 τύφομαι: the process of burning slowly, with accompanying smoke and relatively little glow – 'to smolder, to flicker.' λίνον τυφόμενον οὐ σβέσει 'he will not put out the smoldering flax wick' Mt 12.20. In Mt 12.20 the burning of the wick may be described as 'to burn very slowly' or 'to burn just a little,' but it may be more satisfactory to render τύφομαι in terms of the amount of light which is shown, for example, 'causing just a little light' or 'shining only a little as it burns.'

14.65 ἅπτω; περιάπτω; ἀνάπτω; φλογίζω; καίω[b]; ἐμπί(μ)πρημι: to cause the process of burning to begin – 'to ignite, to kindle, to set ablaze, to start a fire, to light a lamp.'

ἅπτω: ἅψαντες γὰρ πυρὰν προσελάβοντο πάντας ἡμᾶς 'so they built a fire and made us all welcome' Ac 28.2.

περιάπτω: περιαψάντων δὲ πῦρ ἐν μέσῳ τῆς αὐλῆς 'when they had lit a fire in the center of the courtyard' Lk 22.55. It is possible that περιάπτω, in view of the prefix περι-, adds a component of 'round about,' suggesting that the blaze or fire was for the benefit of those who encircled the fire.

ἀνάπτω: ἰδοὺ ἡλίκον πῦρ ἡλίκην ὕλην ἀνάπτει 'just think how large a forest can be set on fire by a tiny flame' Jas 3.5. It is possible that ἀνάπτω differs from ἅπτω either in the intensity of the activity or with special emphasis upon the initial phase of setting something on fire.

φλογίζω: καὶ φλογίζουσα τὸν τροχὸν τῆς γενέσεως 'and set on fire the entire course of existence' Jas 3.6.

καίω[b]: οὐδὲ καίουσιν λύχνον 'they do not light a lamp' Mt 5.15. In a number of languages one must not speak of 'a lamp burning' or 'to burn a lamp,' for this would imply burning up a lamp or destroying it. It may therefore be necessary to say 'to cause the wick of a lamp to burn' or 'to light the wick of a lamp,' and instead of saying 'the lamp burns,' one may say 'the lamp gives light' or 'the lamp shows a flame.'

ἐμπί(μ)πρημι: τὴν πόλιν αὐτῶν ἐνέπρησεν 'he set their city on fire' Mt 22.7. ἐμπί(μ)πρημι refers specifically to the process of setting something on fire, but obviously the implication in Mt 22.7 is that the city was burned down. A number of translations, therefore, follow the implied component of ἐμπί(μ)πρημι and translate 'he burned down their city.' In some languages it may seem strange to speak of 'burning down a city.' A more natural expression would be 'to burn down all the buildings of the city.'

As already noted in the series of terms listed in 14.63, languages differ appreciably in terms employed for different phases and results of burning. For example, to set something on fire for the sake of providing warmth may be expressed by quite a different term from that which is used in speaking of the process of setting something on fire in order to destroy it.

14.66 κατακαίω; καταπίμπρημι: to destroy something by burning – 'to burn something down, to burn something up, to reduce to ashes.'

κατακαίω: συνενέγκαντες τὰς βίβλους κατέκαιον ἐνώπιον πάντων 'they brought their books together and burned them in the presence of everyone' Ac 19.19.

καταπίμπρημι: πόλεις Σοδόμων καὶ Γομόρρας τεφρώσας κατέπρησεν 'he burned down the cities of Sodom and Gomorrah, reducing them to ashes' 2 Pe 2.6 (apparatus).

See comments on terms for burning in 14.63 and 14.65.

14.67 καύσων, ωνος *m*; **καῦμα, τος** *n*: heat sufficiently intense to cause suffering or burning – 'heat, scorching heat.'

καύσων: ἀνέτειλεν γὰρ ὁ ἥλιος σὺν τῷ καύσωνι 'for the sun rises with its scorching heat' Jas 1.11.

καῦμα: οὐδὲ μὴ πέσῃ ἐπ' αὐτοὺς ὁ ἥλιος οὐδὲ πᾶν καῦμα 'neither sun nor any scorching heat will burn them' Re 7.16.

In some languages the effect of heat may be described simply as 'heat will not scorch them' or 'they will not suffer because of heat.' Such expressions, however, may be ambiguous because they might mean that the individuals involved would be able to easily withstand the heat. The meaning of the biblical passage, however, is that there would be no heat to cause them harm.

14.68 καυματίζω: to cause to suffer because of intense heat – 'to harm by heat, to scorch.' ἡλίου δὲ ἀνατείλαντος ἐκαυματίσθη καὶ διὰ τὸ μὴ ἔχειν ῥίζαν ἐξηράνθη 'when the sun had come up, they were scorched and withered

because they did not have roots' Mt 13.6; καὶ ἐκαυματίσθησαν οἱ ἄνθρωποι καῦμα μέγα 'and the people were burned with the great heat' Re 16.9.

14.69 σβέννυμαι: to cease burning, either because of lack of material to be burned or because the fire has been forcibly extinguished – 'to stop burning.' δότε ἡμῖν ἐκ τοῦ ἐλαίου ὑμῶν, ὅτι αἱ λαμπάδες ἡμῶν σβέννυνται 'let us have some of your oil, because our lamps are going out' Mt 25.8. The expression 'our lamps are going out' may be rendered as 'our lamps will soon not be burning' or 'our lamps will burn only a little bit more.' It may, however, be misleading to speak of 'lamps burning' (see discussion in 14.65), and accordingly, it may be much better to translate 'our lamps will show light only a little bit more' or 'the oil in our lamps will burn only a little bit more.'

14.70 σβέννυμι[a]: to cause a fire to be extinguished – 'to extinguish a fire, to put out a fire.' ἔσβεσαν δύναμιν πυρός 'they put out fierce fires' (literally 'they put out the fury of fire') He 11.34. 'To put out fierce fires' may be expressed as 'to cause fierce fires no longer to burn' or 'to make large fires stop burning.' In order to speak of 'fierce fires' it may be necessary in some languages to speak of 'large, hot fires.'

14.71 ἄσβεστος, ον: pertaining to a fire that cannot be put out – 'unquenchable.' ἀπελθεῖν εἰς τὴν γέενναν, εἰς τὸ πῦρ τὸ ἄσβεστον 'to go to Gehenna, to the fire which cannot be put out' Mk 9.43. It may be necessary in some languages to render 'unquenchable' by an active equivalent, for example, 'a fire that no one can put out.'

14.72 τεφρόω: (derivative of τέφρα 'ashes,' not occurring in the NT) to destroy by reducing something to ashes – 'to reduce to ashes.' πόλεις Σοδόμων καὶ Γομόρρας τεφρώσας καταστροφῇ κατέκρινεν '(God) condemned the cities of Sodom and Gomorrah to destruction, reducing them to ashes' 2 Pe 2.6. It is possible to render 'to reduce to ashes' as 'to burn up completely' or 'to destroy by fire and leave only ashes.'

14.73 σποδός, οῦ *f*: the residue from a burned substance – 'ashes.'[13] σποδὸς δαμάλεως 'ashes of a heifer' He 9.13. It may be important in rendering σποδὸς δαμάλεως to indicate that the ashes are the result of the animal having been burned as a sacrifice, for example, 'the ashes of a heifer burned as a sacrifice.' Otherwise, the relationship between 'ashes' and 'heifer' may be difficult, if not impossible, for readers to understand.

I Sound (14.74-14.86)

14.74 φωνή[a], ῆς *f*; φθόγγος[a], ου *m*: any type of sound, including human speech, but normally a distinctive type of sound as opposed to confused noise – 'sound.'
φωνή[a]: γὰρ ὡς ἐγένετο ἡ φωνὴ τοῦ ἀσπασμοῦ σου εἰς τὰ ὦτά μου 'for as soon as I heard the sound of your greeting' Lk 1.44.
φθόγγος[a]: ἐὰν διαστολὴν τοῖς φθόγγοις μὴ δῷ 'unless the notes are sounded distinctly' 1 Cor 14.7.
In many languages an important distinction is made between verbal sounds, that is to say, the sounds of speech, and non-verbal sounds. In some languages musical sounds also require a very special type of terminology, often with distinctions made depending upon the type of instrument involved.

14.75 ἦχος[a], either ου *m* or ους *n*: any type of sound, tone, or noise other than human speech – 'sound, noise.' ἐγένετο ἄφνω ἐκ τοῦ οὐρανοῦ ἦχος 'suddenly there was a noise from the sky' Ac 2.2; σάλπιγγος ἤχῳ 'with the sound of a trumpet' He 12.19; ἐν ἀπορίᾳ ἤχους θαλάσσης 'afraid of the sound of the sea' Lk 21.25.
In a number of languages it will be essential to make a clear distinction between various types of sound referred to by ἦχος[a]. The sounds of a cymbal, a trumpet, and the sea are very frequently referred to by entirely different terms.

---

13 It would be possible to classify σποδός as a natural substance (see Domain 2), since it is the result of a natural process and occurs in circumstances not involving artifacts.

14.76 φωνέω[c]: to produce a sound – 'to sound.' πρὶν ἀλέκτορα φωνῆσαι τρὶς ἀπαρνήσῃ με 'before the rooster crows, you will say three times that you do not know me' Mt 26.75. Though in Mt 26.75 one may wish to use a more specific term such as 'crows,' the meaning of φωνέω[c] is simply 'to produce a sound.'

14.77 μυκάομαι: to produce a loud, roaring, or bellowing noise, typically of oxen, but also applicable to other large animals – 'to bellow, to roar.' ἔκραξεν φωνῇ μεγάλῃ ὥσπερ λέων μυκᾶται 'he called out with a loud voice which sounded like the roar of lions' Re 10.3.

14.78 ὠρύομαι: to produce a howling or roaring sound, typically of wolves, but also applicable to lions – 'to roar, to howl.' ὡς λέων ὠρυόμενος περιπατεῖ 'he walks around like a roaring lion' 1 Pe 5.8. For languages spoken by people who are acquainted with the behavior of lions in the wild, there should be no difficulty in obtaining a specific term applicable to lions. In the case of other languages, one can often use a more generic expression such as 'to make a great noise.'

14.79 θόρυβος[a], ου *m*: noise or clamor marked by confusion – 'clamor, noise.' μὴ δυναμένου δὲ αὐτοῦ γνῶναι τὸ ἀσφαλὲς διὰ τὸν θόρυβον 'there was such a confused clamor that (the commander) could not find out exactly what had happened' Ac 21.34. In some languages it may be legitimate to translate θόρυβος in Ac 21.34 as 'so much noise from so many people shouting' or 'because so many people were shouting different things.'

14.80 ἠχέω: to produce a sound or noise not involving human speech – 'to produce a sound, to make noise.' χαλκὸς ἠχῶν 'noisy brass' or 'noisy gong' 1 Cor 13.1. In translating χαλκὸς ἠχῶν it is usually desirable to employ a term which will more specifically refer to the sound of brass cymbals, for example, 'resounding cymbal' or 'clanging cymbal.'

14.81 προσαχέω (an alternative form of προσηχέω, not occurring in the NT): to reflect back a sound – 'to resound.' προσαχέω occurs only in the first hand of the Vaticanus manuscript of Ac 27.27, where the best textual authorities read προσάγειν in the phrase ὑπενόουν οἱ ναῦται προσάγειν τινὰ αὐτοῖς χώραν 'the sailors suspected that they were getting close to land.' With the verb προσαχεῖν the meaning would be 'the sailors suspected that there was an echoing sound coming from the land.'

14.82 ἀλαλάζω[a]: to make a loud, reverberating sound – 'to clang.' κύμβαλον ἀλαλάζον 'clanging cymbal' or 'reverberating cymbal' 1 Cor 13.1.

14.83 συμφωνία, ας *f*: melodic and rhythmic sound, produced either by several instruments or by a single instrument – 'music.' ἤκουσεν συμφωνίας καὶ χορῶν 'he heard the music and dancing' Lk 15.25.[14] In view of the combination of music and dancing, it will be necessary in some languages to choose a term for music which will fit this type of context, that is to say, music which would be normally employed for a dance.

14.84 μουσικός, οῦ *m*: one who produces music – 'musician, singer.' φωνὴ κιθαρῳδῶν καὶ μουσικῶν 'the sound of harpists and musi-

---

14 In Lk 15.25 there are differences of opinion as to the meaning of συμφωνία. Some scholars contend that the reference is to music produced by several instruments, while others insist that this is music produced by a single instrument, possibly a double flute or a kind of bagpipe.

cians' Re 18.22. In Re 18.22 μουσικῶν probably refers to singers.

14.85 ῥοιζηδόν: (derivative of ῥοῖζος 'the noise made by something passing swiftly through the air,' not occurring in the NT) pertaining to a sudden noise made by swift movement – 'with a shrill noise, with a rushing noise.' οἱ οὐρανοὶ ῥοιζηδὸν παρελεύσονται 'the heavens will disappear with a rushing noise' 2 Pe 3.10. The expression 'with a rushing noise' may be rendered as 'suddenly and with a roar' or 'quickly and with a lot of noise.'

14.86 φιμόω[c]: to cause to cease to make a sound – 'to stop making a sound, to become quiet.' πεφίμωσο 'become still' or 'become quiet' Mk 4.39.

J Movement of the Earth (14.87)

14.87 σεισμός[a], οῦ *m*: a sudden and severe movement of the earth – 'earthquake.' ἄφνω δὲ σεισμὸς ἐγένετο μέγας 'and suddenly there was a strong earthquake' Ac 16.26.

Since earthquakes are universal in occurrence, there is normally no difficulty involved in finding some way of speaking about them. However, in a number of languages idiomatic expressions are used, for example, 'the devil rolled over' or 'mother earth belched.'

In Ac 16.26 the earthquake is regarded as the cause of the prison foundations shaking, and it may be better to restructure the relationships expressed in Ac 16.26 as 'the prison shook because of the earthquake.'

15 Linear Movement

The domain of *Linear Movement* (15) is complex, with a number of subdomains related to one another in various ways. As will be readily noted, there are a number of relevant subgroupings of the subdomains. Subdomains A and B, for example, are without any special reference to a point in space, but Subdomains C-L can be described in terms of some point.

The same is somewhat true of Subdomains M and N, but in these instances there is multiple movement toward or away from a particular point. Subdomains O-U involve potentially moving points with more than one object moving in space. The same is somewhat true of Subdomains V-Y, but there are significant causative relationships. Subdomain Z is likewise causative, but the causative agent does not move but causes something else to move. Subdomains A' and B' are highly specialized in meaning, while Subdomains C'-I' refer primarily to particular means or manner of movement.

Outline of Subdomains

A Move, Come/Go (15.1-15.17)

15.1 κινέω[a]; γίνομαι[e]: to make a change of location in space (a highly generic meaning) – 'to move, to come, to go.'

κινέω[a]: ἐν αὐτῷ γὰρ ζῶμεν καὶ κινούμεθα καὶ ἐσμέν 'in him we live, move about, and exist' Ac 17.28. A strictly literal translation of κινέω in Ac 17.28 might imply merely moving from one place to another. The meaning, however, is generalized movement and activity; therefore, it may be possible to translate κινούμεθα as 'we come and go' or 'we move about' or even 'we do what we do.'

γίνομαι[e]: γενομένου μου εἰς Ἱεροσόλυμα 'when I came to Jerusalem' Ac 25.15; μόλις γενόμενοι κατὰ τὴν Κνίδον 'with difficulty we came to Cnidus' Ac 27.7. Though the meaning of γίνομαι is often given as 'to become,' it is clear that in contexts such as Ac 25.15 and 27.7 it would be impossible to render γίνομαι by traditional expressions such as 'to become.' In these contexts movement is clearly indicated, and therefore one must frequently employ an expression such as 'to come to,' 'to arrive at,' or even 'to travel to.'

15.2 μεταβαίνω[a]; μετατίθημι[a]; μετάθεσις[a], εως f: to effect a change of location in space, with the implication that the two locations are significantly different – 'to move from one place to another, to change one's location, to depart, departure.'

μεταβαίνω[a]: μεταβὰς ἐκεῖθεν εἰσῆλθεν εἰς οἰκίαν τινὸς ὀνόματι Τιτίου Ἰούστου 'so he moved from that place and went to the house of Titius Justus' Ac 18.7.

μετατίθημι[a]: καὶ μετετέθησαν εἰς Συχὲμ καὶ ἐτέθησαν ἐν τῷ μνήματι 'and they were moved to Shechem and buried in a grave' Ac 7.16.

μετάθεσις[a]: πρὸ γὰρ τῆς μεταθέσεως μεμαρτύρηται εὐαρεστηκέναι τῷ θεῷ 'because before his departure it was witnessed that he was pleasing to God' He 11.5. In view of the specific reference of μετάθεσις in He 11.5, it is possible to speak of 'being taken up,' but the meaning is clearly a significant change of location from one place to another, that is to say, from earth to heaven.

15.3 κινέω[b]: to cause something to be moved

from a place – 'to move, to remove.' καὶ κινήσω τὴν λυχνίαν σου ἐκ τοῦ τόπου αὐτῆς 'and I will remove your lampstand from its place' Re 2.5. It is also possible to translate κινέω in Re 2.5 as 'I will take away.'

15.4 ἀσάλευτος[a], ον: pertaining to that which cannot be moved – 'immovable, not able to move.' καὶ ἡ μὲν πρῶρα ἐρείσασα ἔμεινεν ἀσάλευτος 'and the prow got stuck and remained immovable' or '. . . got stuck and could not be moved' Ac 27.41.

15.5 ἐρείδω: to become not able to be moved – 'to become fixed, to jam fast.' ἡ μὲν πρῶρα ἐρείσασα ἔμεινεν ἀσάλευτος 'the prow became jammed fast and remained immovable' or 'the front part of the ship got stuck and could not be moved' Ac 27.41.

15.6 συναρπάζω[b]: to cause something to be moved off course – 'to force off course, to cause to go off course.' συναρπασθέντος δὲ τοῦ πλοίου 'the ship having been forced off course' Ac 27.15.

15.7 ἔρχομαι[a]: to move from one place to another, either coming or going – 'to come, to go.'[1] ἦλθεν εἰς πᾶσαν τὴν περίχωρον τοῦ Ἰορδάνου 'so he went throughout the whole territory of the Jordan River' Lk 3.3; μήτι ἔρχεται ὁ λύχνος ἵνα ὑπὸ τὸν μόδιον τεθῇ ἢ ὑπὸ τὴν κλίνην; 'a lamp certainly doesn't come in order to be put under a bowl or a bed, does it?' Mk 4.21. Note that in Mk 4.21 the subject of ἔρχεται is not something that would normally move by its own force but would need to be brought. Accordingly, in a number of languages it is necessary to say 'no one brings a lamp . . .'

15.8 ἄπειμι[a]: to move away from one place to another – 'to come, to go, to arrive.' οἵτινες παραγενόμενοι εἰς τὴν συναγωγὴν τῶν Ἰουδαίων ἀπῄεσαν 'when they arrived, they went to the Jewish synagogue' Ac 17.10.[2]

15.9 μεθίστημι[a] and μεθιστάνω: to cause something to be moved from one place to another – 'to cause to move, to remove.' μεταστήσας αὐτὸν ἤγειρεν τὸν Δαυὶδ αὐτοῖς εἰς βασιλέα 'having removed him, he raised up David to be their king' Ac 13.22; ἐὰν ἔχω πᾶσαν τὴν πίστιν ὥστε ὄρη μεθιστάναι 'if I have complete faith so as to remove mountains' 1 Cor 13.2. It is not possible to determine whether in 1 Cor 13.2 one should understand 'remove mountains' in the sense of 'causing them to disappear' or 'to cause a mountain to change its location,' that is to say, to move a mountain from one place to another.

15.10 πορεύομαι[a]: to move from one place to another, with the possible implication of continuity and distance – 'to move, to go.'[3] ὅταν τὰ ἴδια πάντα ἐκβάλῃ, ἔμπροσθεν αὐτῶν πορεύεται 'when he has brought his own (sheep) out, he goes ahead of them' Jn 10.4; ἐὰν δὲ ἄξιον ᾖ τοῦ κἀμὲ πορεύεσθαι, σὺν ἐμοὶ πορεύσονται 'if it seems worthwhile for me to go, then they will go along with me' 1 Cor 16.4.

15.11 φέρομαι[a]: to move from one place to another, with the possible implication of causing the movement of some other object or objects – 'to move, to come, to blow.' ὥσπερ φερομένης πνοῆς βιαίας 'like a strong wind coming' or '. . . blowing' Ac 2.2. It is possible that in Ac 2.2 φέρομαι should be understood in an idiomatic sense of 'blowing,' since it is

---

1 ἔρχομαι[a] involves a highly generic meaning of movement from one place to another, either coming or going. In this sense ἔρχομαι[a] contrasts with the meaning of ἔρχομαι[b] 'to come' (15.81), which in turn contrasts in certain contexts with ὑπάγω[b] 'to go away from' (15.35). In other words, ἔρχομαι occurs on two taxonomic levels in the domain of *Linear Movement:* (1) generic, including both coming and going, and (2) 'to come,' in contrast with 'to go.' This type of analysis seems far more legitimate than trying to set up highly complex series of shifts in so-called 'perspective viewpoint.' See also footnote 16.

2 Despite the fact that ἄπειμι[a] is morphologically derived from ἀπό 'from' and εἶμι 'to come' or 'to go,' there are certain contexts, such as in Ac 17.10, in which there appears to be no meaning of separation or departure, but merely generalized movement. ἄπειμι[a], however, seems to be not as generalized in meaning of movement as in the case of κινέω[a], γίνομαι[c], and μεταβαίνω[a] (15.1, 2).

3 πορεύομαι[a] seems to contrast with πορεύομαι[b] 'to travel, to journey' (15.18) as well as with πορεύομαι[c] 'to go away, to leave' (15.34). In general, however, the meaning of πορεύομαι[a] is more frequently rendered as 'to go' than as 'to move' or 'to come.'

combined with the noun for 'wind' (πνοή ᵃ, 14.4). In any event, one must often translate φέρομαι ᵃ as 'blowing,' since this is frequently the appropriate type of term to use in speaking of the movement of wind.

15.12 διΐσταμαι ᵃ (and 2nd aorist active): to continue to move on – 'to move on, to go on.' βραχὺ δὲ διαστήσαντες 'when they had gone a little farther' Ac 27.28.

15.13 χωρέω ᵃ: to move on from one place to another – 'to move on, to advance.' πᾶν τὸ εἰσπορευόμενον εἰς τὸ στόμα εἰς τὴν κοιλίαν χωρεῖ 'anything that goes into a person's mouth moves on into his stomach' Mt 15.17. In translating Mt 15.17 it may be necessary to add an element which suggests swallowing, since something which enters a person's mouth does not automatically go into the stomach. Accordingly, it may be necessary to translate 'anything that goes into a person's mouth and is swallowed goes on then into his stomach.' It would also be possible to say 'anything that goes into one's throat goes on then into a person's stomach.'

In Jn 8.37 χωρέω ᵃ appears to be used figuratively in the statement ὁ λόγος ὁ ἐμὸς οὐ χωρεῖ ἐν ὑμῖν 'my word makes no progress in you,' but it is also possible to interpret χωρέω in this context as referring to a fitting place, for example, 'my word finds no room in you' (see 80.4).

15.14 ἀποχωρίζομαι ᵃ: to move away from a normal location, with the implication of disappearing – 'to move away, to disappear.' καὶ ὁ οὐρανὸς ἀπεχωρίσθη 'and the sky disappeared' Re 6.14. It would be difficult to translate ἀποχωρίζομαι in Re 6.14 as meaning literally 'to go away,' for this would seem strange in a reference to the sky. If, however, one employs an expression meaning 'to disappear,' it may be necessary to say literally 'could no longer be seen.' For another interpretation of ἀποχωρίζομαι in Re 6.14, see 63.30.

15.15 παράγω ᵃ; ὑπάγω ᵃ: to continue to move along – 'to move along, to go along.' παράγω ᵃ: παράγων ὁ Ἰησοῦς ἐκεῖθεν εἶδεν ἄνθρωπον καθήμενον ἐπὶ τὸ τελώνιον 'as Jesus

was moving along from the place, he saw a man sitting in his tax office' Mt 9.9. ὑπάγω ᵃ: ἐν δὲ τῷ ὑπάγειν αὐτὸν οἱ ὄχλοι συνέπνιγον αὐτόν 'as he went along, the people were crowding around him from every side' Lk 8.42.

15.16 προβαίνω; προέρχομαι ᵃ: to continue to move forward – 'to move on, to go on, to go ahead.' ⁴
προβαίνω: προβὰς ὀλίγον εἶδεν Ἰάκωβον 'he went a little farther on and saw James' Mk 1.19.
προέρχομαι ᵃ: προελθὼν μικρὸν ἔπεσεν ἐπὶ πρόσωπον αὐτοῦ 'he went a little farther on and fell face down to the ground' Mt 26.39.

15.17 διέρχομαι ᵃ: to complete movement in a particular direction – 'to move on to, to go on to.' οἱ μὲν οὖν διασπαρέντες ἀπὸ τῆς θλίψεως τῆς γενομένης ἐπὶ Στεφάνῳ διῆλθον ἕως Φοινίκης '(the believers) who were scattered by the persecution which took place when Stephen was killed, went as far as Phoenicia' Ac 11.19. It would also be possible to translate διέρχομαι in Ac 11.19 as 'arrived' or 'finally reached.'

B Travel, Journey (15.18-15.26)

15.18 πορεύομαι ᵇ; πορεία ᵃ, ας f: to move a considerable distance, either with a single destination or from one destination to another in a series – 'to travel, to journey, to be on one's way.'
πορεύομαι ᵇ: ἐν δὲ τῷ πορεύεσθαι αὐτοὺς αὐτὸς εἰσῆλθεν εἰς κώμην τινά 'as they went on their way, he came to a certain village' Lk 10.38.
πορεία ᵃ: πορείαν ποιούμενος εἰς Ἰεροσόλυμα 'he was making his way to Jerusalem' Lk 13.22.

15.19 ὁδεύω; ὁδός ᵇ, οῦ f: to be in the process of travelling, presumably for some distance – 'to travel, to be on a journey, journey.'

---

4 It is possible to analyze προβαίνω and προέρχομαι ᵃ as involving a reference point in space, in that the person's initial position could constitute such a point. But it is equally possible to interpret the movement as being primarily related to the direction in which a person has already been moving.

ὁδεύω: Σαμαρίτης δέ τις ὁδεύων ἦλθεν κατ' αὐτόν 'but a Samaritan who was travelling came upon him' Lk 10.33.

ὁδός[b]: παρήγγειλεν αὐτοῖς ἵνα μηδὲν αἴρωσιν εἰς ὁδόν 'he ordered them, Don't take anything with you as you travel' Mk 6.8; παρέλαβεν τοὺς δώδεκα μαθητὰς κατ' ἰδίαν, καὶ ἐν τῇ ὁδῷ εἶπεν αὐτοῖς 'on the way he took the twelve disciples aside and spoke to them privately' Mt 20.17. Note that ὁδός[b] may also refer to a particular journey, as in Lk 2.44, ἦλθον ἡμέρας ὁδόν 'they made a day's trip.'

15.20 ὁδοιπορέω; ὁδοιπορία, ας *f*: to be on a journey, presumably with the focus upon being en route – 'to travel, to be en route, journey, trip.'
ὁδοιπορέω: τῇ δὲ ἐπαύριον ὁδοιπορούντων ἐκείνων καὶ τῇ πόλει ἐγγιζόντων 'the next day as they were on their way coming near the city' Ac 10.9.
ὁδοιπορία: Ἰησοῦς κεκοπιακὼς ἐκ τῆς ὁδοιπορίας ἐκαθέζετο 'Jesus, tired out by the trip, sat down' Jn 4.6.

15.21 διοδεύω; διαπορεύομαι[a]; διέρχομαι[b]: to travel around through an area, with the implication of both extensive and thorough movement throughout an area – 'to travel around through, to journey all through.'
διοδεύω: αὐτὸς διώδευεν κατὰ πόλιν καὶ κώμην κηρύσσων 'he travelled through the towns and villages preaching' Lk 8.1.
διαπορεύομαι[a]: ὡς δὲ διεπορεύοντο τὰς πόλεις 'as they went through the towns' Ac 16.4; διεπορεύετο κατὰ πόλεις καὶ κώμας διδάσκων 'he went through towns and villages teaching' Lk 13.22.
διέρχομαι[b]: διήρχοντο κατὰ τὰς κώμας εὐαγγελιζόμενοι 'they travelled around throughout the villages preaching the good news' Lk 9.6; διελθόντες δὲ ὅλην τὴν νῆσον ἄχρι Πάφου 'when they had travelled throughout the entire island, they came to Paphos' Ac 13.6.
  In order to express the meaning of διοδεύω, διαπορεύομαι[a], and διέρχομαι[b] in these types of contexts, it may be necessary in some languages to say 'he went from one town to another' or, as in Ac 13.6, 'he travelled to all the places on the island' or '. . . to the various towns on the island.'

15.22 διαπορεύομαι[b]: to go completely through an area – 'to pass through, to go by.' ἀκούσας δὲ ὄχλου διαπορευομένου 'hearing that a crowd was passing through' or '. . . passing by' Lk 18.36.

15.23 περιάγω[a]; περιέρχομαι[a]: to move about from place to place, with significant changes in direction – 'to travel about, to wander about.'
περιάγω[a]: περιάγετε τὴν θάλασσαν καὶ τὴν ξηρὰν ποιῆσαι ἕνα προσήλυτον 'you travel about over land and sea to make a single proselyte' Mt 23.15; περιάγων ἐζήτει χειραγωγούς 'he went around trying to find someone to lead him by the hand' Ac 13.11.
περιέρχομαι[a]: ἅμα δὲ καὶ ἀργαὶ μανθάνουσιν, περιερχόμεναι τὰς οἰκίας 'they learn to waste their time in going around from house to house' 1 Tm 5.13; περιῆλθον ἐν μηλωταῖς 'they wandered around clothed in skins of sheep' He 11.37.
  In order to communicate the meaning of 'to wander about' or 'to travel about,' it may be necessary to be rather specific, for example, 'they first go in one direction and then in another' or 'they first go to one place and then off to another.'

15.24 πλανάομαι[a]: to move about, without definite destination or particular purpose – 'to wander about.' ἐπὶ ἐρημίαις πλανώμενοι καὶ ὄρεσιν 'they wandered in the deserts and hills' He 11.38.

15.25 ἀστατέω[a]: to be without a permanent residence and thus engaged in travelling from one place to another – 'to be homeless, to wander from place to place, to be constantly going from place to place.' κολαφιζόμεθα καὶ ἀστατοῦμεν 'we are beaten and we wander from place to place' 1 Cor 4.11. For another interpretation of ἀστατέω in 1 Cor 4.11, see 85.80.

15.26 πλανήτης, ου *m*: (derivative of πλανάομαι[a] 'to wander about,' 15.24) one who or that which wanders about or around – 'wanderer.' ἀστέρες πλανῆται οἷς ὁ ζόφος τοῦ σκότους εἰς αἰῶνα τετήρηται 'they are like wandering stars, for whom God has reserved a place forever in the deepest darkness' Jd 13. In Jd 13 there appears to be a double-entendre in that πλανήτης may also suggest the meaning of πλανάω 'to deceive, to cause to be mistaken' (see 31.8). Therefore, such persons may be described not only as 'wanderers,' but as 'deceivers.' For a further discussion of πλανήτης in Jd 13, see 1.30.

C Pass, Cross Over, Go Through, Go Around⁵ (15.27-15.33)

15.27 προέρχομαι^b: to move continuously along a particular path or route – 'to pass along, to go along.' ἐξελθόντες προῆλθον ῥύμην μίαν 'they went out and passed along a street' Ac 12.10. It is also possible to interpret ῥύμην μίαν in Ac 12.10 as referring to a particular section or block in a street; therefore, one may translate 'they went one street further.'

15.28 παρέρχομαι^a; παραπορεύομαι; παράγω^b: to move past a reference point – 'to pass by, to go by.'⁶
παρέρχομαι^a: Ἰησοῦς ὁ Ναζωραῖος παρέρχεται 'Jesus of Nazareth is passing by' Lk 18.37.
παραπορεύομαι: οἱ δὲ παραπορευόμενοι ἐβλασφήμουν αὐτόν 'those who passed by hurled insults at him' Mt 27.39.
παράγω^b: ἀκούσαντες ὅτι Ἰησοῦς παράγει, ἔκραξαν 'when they heard that Jesus was passing by, they began to shout' Mt 20.30.

15.29 πάροδος, ου f: to pass by some point of reference as one travels – 'to pass by, to travel on through, to travel past.' οὐ θέλω γὰρ ὑμᾶς ἄρτι ἐν παρόδῳ ἰδεῖν 'I do not want to see you just briefly as I travel past' 1 Cor 16.7. A strictly literal translation of 1 Cor 16.7 in the form 'I do not want to see you just briefly as I

---

⁵ Subdomain C involves a reference to a fixed point, but the relationships are quite varied, either beside, beyond, or around such a point.
⁶ It is possible that there are slight distinctions in meaning between παρέρχομαι^a, παραπορεύομαι, and παράγω^b in view of certain distinctions of meaning in ἔρχομαι, πορεύομαι, and ἄγω (especially in the sense of ὑπάγω). παρέρχομαι^a may therefore be judged to be more generic in meaning, while παραπορεύομαι may refer specifically to walking along, and παράγω^b may involve primarily the act of passing beyond a particular point.

---

travel past' may be misleading, for it might imply that Paul simply did not want to have a glance at the people as he travelled past. In fact, the negative in this expression may result in serious misunderstanding, and therefore it may be better to translate 'I want to have an opportunity to talk with you as I travel on through' or 'I wish to visit you at least for a while as I journey on.'

15.30 ἀντιπαρέρχομαι: to pass by a point of reference on the opposite side – 'to pass by on the opposite side.' ἰδὼν αὐτὸν ἀντιπαρῆλθεν 'seeing him, he went by on the other side' Lk 10.31. There may, however, be a number of problems involved in rendering ἀντιπαρέρχομαι in Lk 10.31, for in many languages it is difficult to conceive of a road having an 'opposite side.' One can often render this phrase in Lk 10.31 as 'having seen him he went on past, staying as far away from him as he could.'

15.31 διαπεράω; διαβαίνω; διέρχομαι^c: to move from one side to another of some geographical object (for example, body of water, chasm, valley, etc.) – 'to cross over, to go over.'
διαπεράω: μηδὲ ἐκεῖθεν πρὸς ἡμᾶς διαπερῶσιν 'nor can anyone cross over to us from where you are' Lk 16.26.
διαβαίνω: ὅπως οἱ θέλοντες διαβῆναι ἔνθεν πρὸς ὑμᾶς μὴ δύνωνται 'so that those who want to cross over from here to you cannot do it' Lk 16.26.
διέρχομαι^c: διέλθωμεν εἰς τὸ πέραν τῆς λίμνης 'let's go to the other side of the lake' Lk 8.22.

15.32 διϊκνέομαι; διέρχομαι^d: to move through a three-dimensional space – 'to go through, to penetrate through.'
διϊκνέομαι: διϊκνούμενος ἄχρι μερισμοῦ ψυχῆς καὶ πνεύματος, ἁρμῶν τε καὶ μυελῶν 'it penetrates all the way through to where soul and spirit meet, to where joints and marrow come together' He 4.12.
διέρχομαι^d: σοῦ δὲ αὐτῆς τὴν ψυχὴν διελεύσεται ῥομφαία 'your own heart will be pierced with a sword' Lk 2.35; διελθόντες δὲ πρώτην φυλακὴν 'they passed through the first guard station' Ac 12.10. The use of διέρχομαι in Ac 12.10 would suggest that the guard station

was some kind of enclosure where guards stayed to control passage.

15.33 περιέρχομαι^b: to move or go around some object or point of reference – 'to go around, to sail around.' ὅθεν περιελθόντες κατηντήσαμεν εἰς Ῥήγιον 'from there we sailed around and arrived at Rhegium' Ac 28.13 (apparatus).

D Leave, Depart, Flee, Escape, Send[7] (15.34-15.74)

15.34 πορεύομαι^c; ἄγω^c: to move away from a reference point – 'to go away, to leave.'
πορεύομαι^c: πορευθεὶς εἰς θάλασσαν βάλε ἄγκιστρον 'so go to the lake and throw in a hook and line' Mt 17.27.[8]
ἄγω^c: ἄγωμεν εἰς τὴν Ἰουδαίαν πάλιν 'let us go to Judea again' or 'let us go off to Judea again' Jn 11.7. It would also be possible to translate ἄγωμεν in Jn 11.7 as 'let us depart for.'

15.35 ὑπάγω^b; μεταίρω: to move away from a reference point, perhaps more definitively than in the case of πορεύομαι^c and ἄγω^c (15.34) – 'to go, to go away from, to depart, to leave.'
ὑπάγω^b: ἦσαν γὰρ οἱ ἐρχόμενοι καὶ οἱ ὑπάγοντες πολλοί 'there were so many people coming and going' Mk 6.31.
μεταίρω: μετῆρεν ἀπὸ τῆς Γαλιλαίας καὶ ἦλθεν εἰς τὰ ὅρια τῆς Ἰουδαίας πέραν τοῦ Ἰορδάνου 'he

---

7 There are a number of problems of analysis and classification in the case of verbs involving motion away from some reference point. In a number of instances the verbs themselves suggest motion away from, and this may be further emphasized by certain prefixes, for example, ἀπό and ἐκ. One might assume that preference should be given in any classification to the treatment of all verbs having a particular prepositional prefix or to all occurrences of a particular verb occurring with different prefixes. This, however, is not a satisfactory solution, since a number of combinations of verbs of motion plus prefixes develop various specialized meanings which cannot be readily determined merely by adding together the literal meanings of the constituent parts. In some instances, prefixes are semantically quite separable in meaning, for example, in ἐκβαίνω 'to go out of' (15.40), but in ὑπάγω^b and μεταίρω 'to go away from' (15.35), there is complete semantic coalescence.
8 It would also be possible to treat πορεύομαι in Mt 17.27 as being a case of πορεύομαι^a 'to move, to go' (15.10).

left Galilee and went to the territory of Judea beyond the Jordan River' Mt 19.1.

15.36 ἀνίσταμαι^b (and 2nd aorist active): to move away from a reference point, with the possible implication of 'getting up and leaving' – 'to depart, to go away from, to leave.' ἀναστὰς δὲ ἀπὸ τῆς συναγωγῆς εἰσῆλθεν εἰς τὴν οἰκίαν Σίμωνος 'he left the synagogue and went to Simon's home' Lk 4.38.

15.37 ἀπέρχομαι^a; ἄφιξις, εως *f*: motion away from a reference point with emphasis upon the departure, but without implications as to any resulting state of separation or rupture – 'to go away, to depart, to leave.'[9]
ἀπέρχομαι^a: ἀπῆλθεν καὶ ἤρξατο κηρύσσειν ἐν τῇ Δεκαπόλει 'he left and went all through the ten towns telling . . .' Mk 5.20; ὡς οὖν εἶπεν αὐτοῖς, Ἐγώ εἰμι, ἀπῆλθον εἰς τὰ ὀπίσω καὶ ἔπεσαν χαμαί 'when he said to them, I am he, they moved back and fell to the ground' Jn 18.6.
ἄφιξις: ἐγὼ οἶδα ὅτι εἰσελεύσονται μετὰ τὴν ἄφιξίν μου λύκοι βαρεῖς εἰς ὑμᾶς 'I know that after I leave, fierce wolves will come among you' Ac 20.29.

15.38 ἀπολύομαι: to depart from a place or set of circumstances, with perhaps an implication of finality or significant separation or rupture being involved – 'to go away, to depart, to leave.' ἀσύμφωνοι δὲ ὄντες πρὸς ἀλλήλους ἀπελύοντο 'so they left, disagreeing among themselves' Ac 28.25.

15.39 ἀποβαίνω: to get off or to depart, as from a ship – 'to disembark, to get off.' οἱ δὲ ἁλιεῖς ἀπ' αὐτῶν ἀποβάντες ἔπλυνον τὰ δίκτυα 'the fishermen had gotten out of their boats and were washing the nets' Lk 5.2.

15.40 ἐκπορεύομαι; ἐξέρχομαι^a; ἐκβαίνω; ἔξειμι: to move out of an enclosed or well-defined two or three-dimensional area – 'to go out of, to depart out of, to leave from within.'

---

9 ἀπέρχομαι^a and ἄφιξις differ in meaning from πορεύομαι^c, ἄγω^c, ὑπάγω^b, and μεταίρω (15.34, 35) in marking the departure more specifically and overtly by the prefixial forms ἀπ- and ἀφ-.

ἐκπορεύομαι: ἐκπορευομένου αὐτοῦ ἐκ τοῦ ἱεροῦ 'when he had gone out of the Temple' Mk 13.1; ἐξεπορεύετο πρὸς αὐτὸν πᾶσα ἡ Ἰουδαία χώρα 'all the people of Judea went out (of their villages and cities) to him' Mk 1.5. In some contexts one may interpret occurrences of ἐκπορεύομαι as being used figuratively or as part of an idiomatic phrase, but ἐκπορεύομαι also implies some type of movement out from a defined or enclosed area. Note, for example, the occurrences of ἐκπορεύομαι in the following contexts: τὸ ἐκπορευόμενον ἐκ τοῦ στόματος τοῦτο κοινοῖ τὸν ἄνθρωπον 'that which comes from a man's mouth causes him to be defiled' Mt 15.11; ἐξεπορεύετο ἦχος περὶ αὐτοῦ εἰς πάντα τόπον τῆς περιχώρου 'the report about him went out into all parts of the surrounding region' Lk 4.37; τά τε πνεύματα τὰ πονηρὰ ἐκπορεύεσθαι 'the evil spirits would go out of them' Ac 19.12. In a number of languages, however, it may be necessary to translate the meaning of ἐκπορεύομαι in quite different ways. For example, in Mt 15.11 it may be necessary to translate 'that which a man says causes him to be defiled,' and in Lk 4.37 it may be necessary to translate 'more and more people in all parts of the surrounding region heard about Jesus,' and for Ac 19.12 it may be necessary to say 'the evil spirits would no longer ride them' or '. . . control them.'

ἐξέρχομαιᵃ: πᾶσα ἡ πόλις ἐξῆλθεν εἰς ὑπάντησιν τῷ Ἰησοῦ 'all the people of the city went out to meet Jesus' Mt 8.34; ἐξῆλθεν ἀπ' αὐτοῦ τὸ δαιμόνιον 'the demon came out of him' Mt 17.18; ἐξῆλθεν ἡ ἀκοὴ αὐτοῦ εὐθὺς πανταχοῦ 'then, word about him went out everywhere' Mk 1.28.

ἐκβαίνω: εἰ μὲν ἐκείνης ἐμνημόνευον ἀφ' ἧς ἐξέβησαν 'they didn't think back to the country from which they had departed' He 11.15.

ἔξειμι: λαβόντες ἐντολὴν πρὸς τὸν Σιλᾶν καὶ τὸν Τιμόθεον ἵνα ὡς τάχιστα ἔλθωσιν πρὸς αὐτὸν ἐξῄεσαν 'they departed after being instructed that Silas and Timothy were to come to him as quickly as possible' Ac 17.15.[10]

15.41 ἐκχωρέω: to move out of or away from a place, with a possible implication of a considerable distance separating a person from the earlier location – 'to depart, to leave, to go out of.' οἱ ἐν μέσῳ αὐτῆς ἐκχωρείτωσαν 'those who are in (the city) must leave' Lk 21.21.

15.42 ἔξοδοςᵃ, ου f: motion from or out of a region (in He 11.22, the only occurrence of ἔξοδοςᵃ in the NT, the reference is to Israel's departure from Egypt) – 'departure, the Exodus, the departure (of Israel from Egypt).' πίστει Ἰωσὴφ τελευτῶν περὶ τῆς ἐξόδου τῶν υἱῶν Ἰσραὴλ ἐμνημόνευσεν 'it was faith that made Joseph, when he was about to die, speak of the departure of the Israelites (from Egypt)' He 11.22.

15.43 ἀπολύωᵃ; ἀφίημιᵃ: to cause (or permit) a person or persons to leave a particular location – 'to let go away, to dismiss.'[11] ἀπολύωᵃ: ἀπόλυσον τοὺς ὄχλους 'let the people leave' or 'dismiss the crowds' Mt 14.15. ἀφίημιᵃ: τότε ἀφεὶς τοὺς ὄχλους 'then having dismissed the crowds' Mt 13.36.

15.44 ἐκβάλλωᵇ: to cause to go out or leave, often, but not always, involving force – 'to send away, to drive out, to expel.' καὶ νῦν λάθρα ἡμᾶς ἐκβάλλουσιν 'and now they want to send us away secretly' Ac 16.37; ἤρξατο ἐκβάλλειν τοὺς πωλοῦντας καὶ τοὺς ἀγοράζοντας ἐν τῷ ἱερῷ 'he began to drive out all those who bought and sold in the Temple' Mk 11.15; ἐξέβαλεν τὰ πνεύματα λόγῳ 'he drove out the (evil) spirits with a word' Mt 8.16. In referring to exorcism of evil spirits, it may be necessary in some languages to use figurative expressions, for example, 'to pull out,' 'to cause to to dismount,' or 'to cause one's heart to return.'

15.45 ἐξωθέωᵃ: to force someone or something to leave – 'to expel, to drive away.' τῶν

_____

10 In Ac 27.43 one might assume that ἐξιέναι in the phrase ἐπὶ τὴν γῆν ἐξιέναι would mean 'to head for land,' but it seems quite clear from the context that one should interpret ἐξιέναι as meaning 'to leave the boat and go to shore.'

11 It is possible that ἀπολύωᵃ and ἀφίημιᵃ differ somewhat in meaning in that ἀπολύωᵃ may suggest more permission and ἀφίημιᵃ more dismissal, but this cannot be determined from NT usage.
In Ac 15.30, however, οἱ . . . ἀπολυθέντες implies clearly 'being sent' (see ἀπολύωᵇ, 15.66).

ἐθνῶν ὧν ἐξῶσεν ὁ θεὸς ἀπὸ προσώπου τῶν πατέρων ἡμῶν 'the nations whom God drove out before our ancestors' Ac 7.45. In some languages it may be necessary to indicate more explicitly the factors involved in driving out the nations, for example, 'the nations whom God forced to leave their land as our ancestors came in.'

15.46 ἀπωθέομαι[a]: to use force in pushing or thrusting someone or something away or aside – 'to push away, to thrust aside.' ὁ δὲ ἀδικῶν τὸν πλησίον ἀπώσατο αὐτόν 'the one who was mistreating the other pushed him aside' Ac 7.27.

15.47 ἀποδημέω: to journey away from one's home or home country, implying for a considerable period of time and at quite a distance – 'to leave home on a journey, to be away from home on a journey.' ὁ νεώτερος υἱὸς ἀπεδήμησεν εἰς χώραν μακράν 'the younger son went on a journey to a distant country' Lk 15.13.

15.48 ἀφίημι[b]: to move away from, with the implication of resulting separation – 'to leave, to depart from.'[12] οὐχὶ ἀφήσει τὰ ἐνενήκοντα ἐννέα; 'does he not leave the other ninety-nine?' Mt 18.12; ἀφῆκεν τὴν Ἰουδαίαν καὶ ἀπῆλθεν πάλιν εἰς τὴν Γαλιλαίαν 'he left Judea and departed again for Galilee' Jn 4.3.

15.49 χωρίζω[c]: to separate from, as the result of motion away from – 'to depart, to leave.' παρήγγειλεν αὐτοῖς ἀπὸ Ἱεροσολύμων μὴ χωρίζεσθαι 'he commanded them not to depart from Jerusalem' Ac 1.4; μετὰ ταῦτα χωρισθεὶς ἐκ τῶν Ἀθηνῶν 'after this, he left Athens' Ac 18.1.

15.50 διαχωρίζομαι; διΐσταμαι[b] (and 2nd aorist active): to move away from, with the possible implication of definitiveness of separation (particularly in contexts relating to persons) – 'to depart from, to leave.'

διαχωρίζομαι: ἐν τῷ διαχωρίζεσθαι αὐτοὺς ἀπ' αὐτοῦ 'as they were parting from him' Lk 9.33. διΐσταμαι[b]: ἐν τῷ εὐλογεῖν αὐτὸν αὐτοὺς διέστη ἀπ' αὐτῶν 'as he was blessing them, he departed from them' Lk 24.51; βραχὺ δὲ διαστήσαντες καὶ πάλιν βολίσαντες 'departing a little way off, again they dropped a line with a weight tied to it' Ac 27.28. Since the movement in Ac 27.28 is by boat, it may be necessary to specify this, for example, 'going a little way further in a boat' or 'sailing a little further.'

15.51 ἀποχωρέω; ἀφίσταμαι[a] (and 2nd aorist active): to move away from, with emphasis upon separation and possible lack of concern for what has been left – 'to go away, to depart, to leave.'
ἀποχωρέω: ἀποχωρεῖτε ἀπ' ἐμοῦ οἱ ἐργαζόμενοι τὴν ἀνομίαν 'depart from me, you evildoers' Mt 7.23; Ἰωάννης δὲ ἀποχωρήσας ἀπ' αὐτῶν ὑπέστρεψεν εἰς Ἱεροσόλυμα 'John left them there and returned to Jerusalem' Ac 13.13.
ἀφίσταμαι[a]: οὐκ ἀφίστατο τοῦ ἱεροῦ 'she never left the Temple' Lk 2.37; εὐθέως ἀπέστη ὁ ἄγγελος ἀπ' αὐτοῦ 'suddenly the angel left him' Ac 12.10.

15.52 ὑπάγω[c]: to depart from someone's presence, with the implication of a changed relation – 'to depart, to leave, to go away.' ὕπαγε, Σατανᾶ 'go away, Satan' Mt 4.10; μὴ καὶ ὑμεῖς θέλετε ὑπάγειν; 'do you, too, want to go away?' Jn 6.67.[13]

15.53 ἀναχωρέω[a]; **ὑποχωρέω**: to move away from a location, implying a considerable distance – 'to withdraw, to retire, to go off, to go away.'
ἀναχωρέω[a]: ἀκούσας δὲ ὁ Ἰησοῦς ἀνεχώρησεν ἐκεῖθεν ἐν πλοίῳ εἰς ἔρημον τόπον κατ' ἰδίαν 'when Jesus heard the news, he withdrew from that place in a boat to a lonely place by himself' Mt 14.13.
ὑποχωρέω: αὐτὸς δὲ ἦν ὑποχωρῶν ἐν ταῖς ἐρήμοις 'he would go away to lonely places' Lk 5.16.

---

12 ἀφίημι[b] involves two principal semantic components: (1) movement away from and (2) resulting separation. It would appear from most contexts that the focal component of ἀφίημι[b] is resulting separation.

13 It is possible to interpret ὑπάγω in Mt 4.10 and Jn 6.67 as being simply a matter of 'going' and therefore equivalent to ὑπάγω[b] (15.35).

15.54 ἀποσπάομαι: to draw oneself away from, suggesting that the movement was not sudden – 'to leave, to go off, to withdraw.' καὶ αὐτὸς ἀπεσπάσθη ἀπ' αὐτῶν ὡσεὶ λίθου βολήν 'then, he withdrew from them, about the distance one can throw a stone' Lk 22.41; ὡς δὲ ἐγένετο ἀναχθῆναι ἡμᾶς ἀποσπασθέντας ἀπ' αὐτῶν 'we took our leave from them and set sail' Ac 21.1.[14]

15.55 ἀποτάσσομαι[b]: to say goodbye and to leave – 'to take leave of, to say goodbye.' ἀποταξάμενος ἐξέπλει εἰς τὴν Συρίαν 'taking leave, he sailed off for Syria' Ac 18.18. In a number of languages the equivalent of 'to take leave of' or 'saying goodbye' is highly idiomatic, for example, 'to snap fingers as one leaves,' 'to raise one's hands together,' 'to clasp one's hands before leaving,' or 'to bow to one another as one leaves.'

15.56 ἀπελαύνω: to cause to move away from a point by threat or by force – 'to drive away, to force to leave.' ἀπήλασεν αὐτοὺς ἀπὸ τοῦ βήματος 'he drove them out of court' Ac 18.16. A strictly literal translation of Ac 18.16 as 'he drove them out of court' might imply that Gallio personally and physically forced them out of the court; probably, he simply caused them to be driven out of the court by court officials. Therefore, it may be necessary in some languages to indicate this causative relationship by 'he ordered them to leave the court' or 'he ordered the officials to force them out of the court.'

15.57 καταλείπω[a]: to leave or depart, with emphasis on the finality of the action – 'to leave, to leave from, to go away from.' καταλιπὼν τὴν Ναζαρὰ ἐλθὼν κατῴκησεν εἰς Καφαρναούμ 'leaving Nazareth, he came to live in Capernaum' Mt 4.13; πίστει κατέλιπεν Αἴγυπτον 'by faith he left Egypt' He 11.27.

15.58 ἐκλείπω[b]: to depart out of a place – 'to depart out of, to leave from.' κἀκείνους κατέ-λειπεν ἐκεῖ καὶ ἔκλειπεν 'he left them behind there and departed' Ac 18.19 (apparatus).

15.59 ἀπολείπω[b]: to depart from a point definitively, with the possible implication of abandoning or deserting – 'to leave, to abandon, to desert.' ἀπολιπόντας τὸ ἴδιον οἰκητήριον 'they deserted their own dwelling place' Jd 6.

15.60 ἐκνεύω: to depart from a place without being noticed – 'to withdraw quietly, to slip out.' ὁ γὰρ Ἰησοῦς ἐξένευσεν ὄχλου ὄντος ἐν τῷ τόπῳ 'for Jesus slipped out since there was a crowd in that place' Jn 5.13. In rendering ἐκνεύω in Jn 5.13 one may say 'Jesus left and no one saw him' or 'no one saw Jesus departing.'

15.61 φεύγω[a]; φυγή, ῆς f: to move quickly from a point or area in order to avoid presumed danger or difficulty – 'to run away, to flee, flight.'
φεύγω[a]: τότε οἱ ἐν τῇ Ἰουδαίᾳ φευγέτωσαν εἰς τὰ ὄρη 'then those who are in Judea must run away to the hills' Mt 24.16.
φυγή: προσεύχεσθε δὲ ἵνα μὴ γένηται ἡ φυγὴ ὑμῶν χειμῶνος 'pray that your flight will not be in the winter' or '. . . in the cold season' Mt 24.20.

15.62 καταφεύγω[a]: to flee from an area, with probably greater intensity than in the case of φεύγω[a] and φυγή (15.61) – 'to flee, to flee for safety.' συνιδόντες κατέφυγον εἰς τὰς πόλεις τῆς Λυκαονίας 'when they learned about it, they fled to the cities in Lycaonia' Ac 14.6.

15.63 ἐκφεύγω[a]: to flee from or out of – 'to flee out of, to flee from, to escape.' ὥστε γυμνοὺς καὶ τετραυματισμένους ἐκφυγεῖν ἐκ τοῦ οἴκου ἐκείνου 'so that they fled from that house naked and wounded' Ac 19.16; νομίζων ἐκπεφευγέναι τοὺς δεσμίους 'thinking that the prisoners had fled' Ac 16.27.

15.64 διαφεύγω: to succeed in fleeing from – 'to flee successfully, to escape by fleeing, to escape.' μή τις ἐκκολυμβήσας διαφύγῃ 'in order that no one would swim out and escape' Ac 27.42.

---

14 It is possible to interpret ἀποσπάομαι in Ac 21.1 as referring to the act of saying goodbye, and thus being equivalent to ἀποτάσσομαι[b] (15.55).

15.65 κλίνω[b]: to cause to flee or run away from – 'to cause to run away, to put to flight, to rout.' παρεμβολὰς ἔκλιναν ἀλλοτρίων 'they routed the armies of foreigners' He 11.34.

15.66 πέμπω[a]; ἀποστέλλω[a]; ἀπολύω[b]: to cause someone to depart for a particular purpose – 'to send.'

πέμπω[a]: ἔδοξε . . . ἐκλεξαμένους ἄνδρας ἐξ αὐτῶν πέμψαι εἰς Ἀντιόχειαν σὺν τῷ Παύλῳ καὶ Βαρναβᾷ 'decided . . . to choose some men from the group and send them to Antioch with Paul and Barnabas' Ac 15.22; ἐλπίζω δὲ ἐν κυρίῳ Ἰησοῦ Τιμόθεον ταχέως πέμψαι ὑμῖν 'I trust in the Lord Jesus that I will be able to send Timothy to you soon' Php 2.19.

ἀποστέλλω[a]: ἀποστέλλει δύο τῶν μαθητῶν αὐτοῦ 'he sends two of his disciples' Mk 11.1; ἀπέστειλέν με . . . εὐαγγελίζεσθαι 'he sent me . . . to tell the good news' 1 Cor 1.17.

ἀπολύω[b]: οἱ μὲν οὖν ἀπολυθέντες κατῆλθον εἰς Ἀντιόχειαν 'then those who were sent arrived in Antioch' Ac 15.30.

15.67 πέμπω[c]; ἀποστέλλω[b]; ἐξαποστέλλω[b]: to send a message, presumably by someone – 'to send a message, to send word.'[15]

πέμπω[c]: πέμψαντες πρὸς αὐτὸν παρεκάλουν μὴ δοῦναι ἑαυτὸν εἰς τὸ θέατρον 'they sent word to him to urge him not to present himself in the theater' Ac 19.31.

ἀποστέλλω[b]: ὅτι τοῖς ἔθνεσιν ἀπεστάλη τοῦτο τὸ σωτήριον τοῦ θεοῦ 'because this salvation from God was sent to the Gentiles' Ac 28.28.

ἐξαποστέλλω[b]: ἡμῖν ὁ λόγος τῆς σωτηρίας ταύτης ἐξαπεστάλη 'the message about this salvation was sent to us' Ac 13.26.

15.68 ἐκπέμπω; ἐξαποστέλλω[a]; ἐκβάλλω[c]: to send out or away from, presumably for some purpose – 'to send, to send out, to send forth.'

ἐκπέμπω: οἱ δὲ ἀδελφοὶ εὐθέως διὰ νυκτὸς ἐξέπεμψαν τόν τε Παῦλον καὶ τὸν Σιλᾶν εἰς Βέροιαν 'the Christian brothers sent out Paul and Silas to Beroea, as soon as night came' Ac 17.10.

ἐξαποστέλλω[a]: εὐθέως δὲ τότε τὸν Παῦλον

---

15 πέμπω, ἀποστέλλω, and ἐξαποστέλλω in the contexts in 15.67 could be classified as a type of communication in Domain 33.

ἐξαπέστειλαν οἱ ἀδελφοὶ πορεύεσθαι ἕως ἐπὶ τὴν θάλασσαν 'at once the Christian brothers sent Paul away to the coast' Ac 17.14.

ἐκβάλλω[c]: δεήθητε οὖν τοῦ κυρίου τοῦ θερισμοῦ ὅπως ἐκβάλῃ ἐργάτας εἰς τὸν θερισμὸν αὐτοῦ 'pray to the owner of the harvest that he will send out workers to gather his harvest' Mt 9.38.

15.69 συμπέμπω; συναποστέλλω: to send someone together with someone else – 'to send with, to send together.'

συμπέμπω: συνεπέμψαμεν δὲ αὐτοῖς τὸν ἀδελφὸν ἡμῶν 'we have sent our Christian brother with them' 2 Cor 8.22.

συναποστέλλω: παρεκάλεσα Τίτον καὶ συναπέστειλα τὸν ἀδελφόν 'I begged Titus to go and sent the other Christian brother with him' 2 Cor 12.18.

In some languages it may be difficult to express in a succinct way the meaning of 'to send with.' For example, in 2 Cor 8.22 it may be necessary to translate 'they are going and so we are causing our Christian brother to go with them,' and in 2 Cor 12.18 one may translate 'I begged Titus to go, and I caused the other Christian brother to go with him.'

15.70 ἀναπέμπω[a]: to send back to a previous location – 'to send back.' ὃν ἀνέπεμψά σοι 'I have sent him back to you' Phm 12.

15.71 ἀναπέμπω[b]: to send on or up to some higher or appropriate authority – 'to send on, to send up.' ἐκέλευσα τηρεῖσθαι αὐτὸν ἕως οὗ ἀναπέμψω αὐτὸν πρὸς Καίσαρα 'so I gave orders for him to be kept under guard until I could send him on to the Emperor' Ac 25.21.

15.72 προπέμπω[a]: to send someone on in the direction in which he has already been moving, with the probable implication of providing help – 'to send on one's way, to help on one's way.' ἐλπίζω γὰρ διαπορευόμενος θεάσασθαι ὑμᾶς καὶ ὑφ' ὑμῶν προπεμφθῆναι ἐκεῖ 'I would like to see you on my way (to Spain) and be helped by you on my way there' Ro 15.24.

15.73 μεταπέμπομαι: to send someone to obtain something or someone – 'to send for, to summon.' μετάπεμψαι Σίμωνά τινα ὃς ἐπικαλεῖται Πέτρος 'summon a certain Simon who is called Peter' Ac 10.5. In some languages it may be important to make somewhat more explicit some of the implied events or relationships in this phrase in Ac 10.5, for example, 'ask a certain Simon called Peter to come' or 'deliver a message to a certain Simon called Peter asking him to come.'

15.74 ἀποκαθίστημι[b]: to send someone back to a place where one has been before – 'to send back, to cause to go back.' ἵνα τάχιον ἀποκατασταθῶ ὑμῖν 'in order that I may quickly send back to you' He 13.19.

E Come Near, Approach (15.75-15.80)

15.75 ἐγγίζω[a]: to move nearer to a reference point – 'to draw near, to come near, to approach.' ὅπου κλέπτης οὐκ ἐγγίζει 'where no thief can get near it' Lk 12.33; ἐγγίσαντος δὲ αὐτοῦ ἐπηρώτησεν αὐτόν 'when he came near, he questioned him' Lk 18.40. In a number of languages it is not possible to merely say 'to come near,' for it is necessary to specify the reference point, in other words, 'near to what?' One may accordingly translate this expression in Lk 18.40 as 'when he came near to Jesus, Jesus asked him.'

15.76 συντυγχάνω: to come near to or to reach, with the implication of some type of association – 'to reach, to get near to.' καὶ οὐκ ἠδύναντο συντυχεῖν αὐτῷ διὰ τὸν ὄχλον 'and they were not able to get near to him because of the crowd' Lk 8.19.

15.77 προσεγγίζω; προσάγω[b]; προσπορεύομαι; προσέρχομαι[a]; προσανέχω: to move toward a reference point, with a possible implication in certain contexts of a reciprocal relationship between the person approaching and the one who is approached – 'to move toward, to approach, to come near to.'
προσεγγίζω: κατὰ μέσον τῆς νυκτὸς ὑπενόουν οἱ ναῦται προσεγγίζειν τινὰ αὐτοῖς χώραν 'in the middle of the night the sailors sensed that they were approaching some land' Ac 27.27 (apparatus).
προσάγω[b]: κατὰ μέσον τῆς νυκτὸς ὑπενόουν οἱ

ναῦται προσάγειν τινὰ αὐτοῖς χώραν 'in the middle of the night the sailors sensed that they were approaching some land' Ac 27.27.
προσπορεύομαι: προσπορεύονται αὐτῷ Ἰάκωβος καὶ Ἰωάννης 'James and John approached him' Mk 10.35.
προσέρχομαι[a]: οὗτοι οὖν προσῆλθον Φιλίππῳ 'these men then approached Philip' Jn 12.21.
προσανέχω: ὑπενόουν οἱ ναῦται προσανέχειν τινὰ αὐτοῖς χώραν 'the sailors sensed that they were approaching some land' Ac 27.27 (apparatus).

15.78 ἀπαντάω; ἀπάντησις, εως f; ὑπαντάω[a]; ὑπάντησις, εως f: to come near to and to meet, either in a friendly or hostile sense – 'to draw near, to meet, to meet up with.'
ἀπαντάω: ἀπήντησαν αὐτῷ δέκα λεπροὶ ἄνδρες 'the ten lepers met him' Lk 17.12.
ἀπάντησις: ἁρπαγησόμεθα ἐν νεφέλαις εἰς ἀπάντησιν τοῦ κυρίου εἰς ἀέρα 'we will be snatched up in the clouds to meet the Lord in the air' 1 Th 4.17.
ὑπαντάω[a]: ὑπήντησαν αὐτῷ δύο δαιμονιζόμενοι 'two demon-possessed persons met him' Mt 8.28.
ὑπάντησις: πᾶσα ἡ πόλις ἐξῆλθεν εἰς ὑπάντησιν τῷ Ἰησοῦ 'all the people of the city came out to meet Jesus' Mt 8.34.
In a number of languages it is necessary to specify clearly by the choice of terms whether the meeting is friendly or hostile.

15.79 συμβάλλω[d]: to meet and join up with, with either friendly or hostile intent – 'to join up with, to meet.' συνέβαλλεν ἡμῖν εἰς τὴν Ἆσσον 'he joined up with us in Assos' Ac 20.14; τίς βασιλεὺς πορευόμενος ἑτέρῳ βασιλεῖ συμβαλεῖν εἰς πόλεμον 'what king going out to meet another king in battle' Lk 14.31. In instances in which meeting up with someone may be either friendly or hostile, it is frequently necessary to select terms which will indicate clearly the relation or intention of the participants. In most languages a purely neutral term of 'meeting' would be misleading.

15.80 ἀπρόσιτος, ον: pertaining to not being capable of being approached – 'unapproachable, that which cannot be approached.' ὁ μόνος ἔχων ἀθανασίαν, φῶς οἰκῶν ἀπρόσιτον 'he alone is immortal and lives in the light that cannot be approached by anyone' 1 Tm 6.16. It may be necessary to indicate, either in the text or in a marginal note, the reason why the light cannot be approached, for one could interpret this passage to mean that the light was either so small as not to be generally visible or so far away that it could not be reached. If, however, one uses a term for 'light' which implies extreme intensity of light, then the context should indicate the basis for its being unapproachable.

F   Come, Come To, Arrive (15.81-15.87)

15.81 ἔρχομαι[b]; ἔλευσις, εως *f*: to move toward or up to the reference point of the viewpoint character or event – 'to come, coming.'[16]

ἔρχομαι[b]: σὺ εἶ ὁ ἐρχόμενος ἢ ἕτερον προσδοκῶμεν; 'are you the one who was going to come, or should we expect another?' Mt 11.3; μὴ νομίσητε ὅτι ἦλθον βαλεῖν εἰρήνην ἐπὶ τὴν γῆν 'don't think I came to bring peace on the earth' Mt 10.34.

ἔλευσις: ἀπέκτειναν τοὺς προκαταγγείλαντας περὶ τῆς ἐλεύσεως τοῦ δικαίου 'they killed those who long ago announced the coming of the righteous one' Ac 7.52.[17]

15.82 θα (an Aramaic word): to move to or toward a reference point of the viewpoint character or event – 'to come.'[18] μαρανα θα '(our) Lord, come' 1 Cor 16.22.

15.83 ἐπέρχομαι[a]; ἐπιπορεύομαι; ἐπιβαίνω[a]: to move to or onto, generally with the implication of having arrived – 'to come to, to arrive.'

ἐπέρχομαι[a]: ἐπῆλθαν δὲ ἀπὸ Ἀντιοχείας καὶ Ἰκονίου Ἰουδαῖοι 'some Jews came from An-

tioch (of Pisidia) and from Iconium' Ac 14.19; πνεῦμα ἅγιον ἐπελεύσεται ἐπὶ σέ 'the Holy Spirit will come upon you' Lk 1.35. In the rendering of Lk 1.35 it is important to avoid the kind of literal translation which might suggest sexual relations.

ἐπιπορεύομαι: τῶν κατὰ πόλιν ἐπιπορευομένων πρὸς αὐτόν 'when people kept coming to him from one town after another' Lk 8.4.

ἐπιβαίνω[a]: ὑμεῖς ἐπίστασθε ἀπὸ πρώτης ἡμέρας ἀφ' ἧς ἐπέβην εἰς τὴν Ἀσίαν 'you know that since the first day that I came to Asia' Ac 20.18.

15.84 ἐφικνέομαι; φθάνω[a]; κατανπάω[a]; ἥκω[a]: to move toward and to arrive at a point – 'to come to, to reach, to arrive.'[19]

ἐφικνέομαι: οὐ γὰρ ὡς μὴ ἐφικνούμενοι εἰς ὑμᾶς 'for it is not as though we had not come to you' 2 Cor 10.14.

φθάνω[a]: ἄχρι γὰρ καὶ ὑμῶν ἐφθάσαμεν ἐν τῷ εὐαγγελίῳ τοῦ Χριστοῦ 'for we did come to you with the gospel of Christ' 2 Cor 10.14.

κατανπάω[a]: κατήντησαν δὲ εἰς Ἔφεσον, κἀκείνους κατέλιπεν αὐτοῦ 'they reached Ephesus and he left them there' Ac 18.19.

ἥκω[a]: Ἰησοῦς ἥκει ἐκ τῆς Ἰουδαίας εἰς τὴν Γαλιλαίαν 'Jesus came from Judea to Galilee' Jn 4.47; ἐγὼ γὰρ ἐκ τοῦ θεοῦ ἐξῆλθον καὶ ἥκω 'for I came from God and arrived here' Jn 8.42.[20]

15.85 περιπίπτω[a]: to move to and strike against, involving both movement and impact – 'to run into, to hit against, to strike.' περιπεσόντες δὲ εἰς τόπον διθάλασσον 'striking against a sandbank' Ac 27.41. Since the context of Ac 27.41 involves a ship, it is important to select terms which will be appropriate for such an event.

15.86 παρέρχομαι[b]; παραγίνομαι[a]; πάρειμι[b]; παρουσία[b], ας *f*; παρίσταμαι[e] (and 2nd aorist active): to come to be present at a

---

16 ἔρχομαι[b] 'to come' or 'to come to' is a more restricted or specific meaning than ἔρχομαι[a], which means either 'to come' or 'to go,' that is to say, simply to move from one place to another without specifying any viewpoint character or place (see 15.7). See also Domain 15, footnote 1.

17 ἔλευσις also occurs as a reference to the second coming of Christ in a textual variant of Lk 23.42, μνήσθητί μου ἐν τῇ ἡμέρᾳ τῆς ἐλεύσεως σου 'remember me in the day of your coming.'

18 In the Didache (10,6) and in some NT manuscripts the expression reads μαραν αθα '(our) Lord has come.'

19 There are no doubt certain subtle distinctions of meaning in ἐφικνέομαι, φθάνω[a], κατανπάω[a], and ἥκω[a], but it is not possible to determine what the distinctive features are on the basis of existing contexts.

20 In a context such as Jn 8.42, it is possible to understand ἥκω in the sense of being in a particular location rather than having moved to such a point (see 85.10).

particular place – 'to come, to arrive, to come to be present.'

παρέρχομαι[b]: παρελθὼν διακονήσει αὐτοῖς 'when he arrives, he will serve them' Lk 12.37.

παραγίνομαι[a]: ὄρθρου δὲ πάλιν παρεγένετο εἰς τὸ ἱερόν 'early in the morning he came again to the Temple' Jn 8.2; Χριστὸς δὲ παραγενόμενος ἀρχιερεὺς τῶν γενομένων ἀγαθῶν 'Christ came as the high priest of the good things to come' He 9.11.

πάρειμι[b]: οὗτοι καὶ ἐνθάδε πάρεισιν 'these men have come here' Ac 17.6; ὁμοθυμαδὸν δὲ παρῆσαν πρὸς αὐτόν 'so in a group they came to him' Ac 12.20.

παρουσία[b]: παρεκάλεσεν ἡμᾶς ὁ θεὸς ἐν τῇ παρουσίᾳ Τίτου 'but God, who encouraged us with the coming of Titus' 2 Cor 7.6; τί τὸ σημεῖον τῆς σῆς παρουσίας καὶ συντελείας τοῦ αἰῶνος 'what will happen to show that it is the time for your coming and the end of the age' Mt 24.3.[21]

παρίσταμαι[c]: παρέστη γάρ μοι ταύτῃ τῇ νυκτὶ τοῦ θεοῦ οὗ εἰμι ἐγώ, ᾧ καὶ λατρεύω, ἄγγελος 'for last night an angel of the God to whom I belong and whom I worship came to me' or '. . . appeared to me' Ac 27.23.

15.87 εἴσοδος[a], ου f: to come to or to arrive at the scene of action – 'coming, arrival.' προκηρύξαντος Ἰωάννου πρὸ προσώπου τῆς εἰσόδου αὐτοῦ βάπτισμα μετανοίας παντὶ τῷ λαῷ Ἰσραήλ 'before (Jesus') coming, John preached ahead of time to all the people of Israel that they should repent and be baptized' Ac 13.24.

G Return (15.88-15.92)

15.88 ὑποστρέφω[a]: to move back to a point from which one has previously departed – 'to return, to go back, to come back.' πάλιν ὑπέστρεφα εἰς Δαμασκόν 'then I returned to Damascus' Ga 1.17.

15.89 ἀνακάμπτω[a]; ἀναστρέφω; ἀναλύω[a]; ἀναχωρέω[b]: to move back to a point or area

from which one has previously departed, but with more explicit emphasis upon the return (compare ὑποστρέφω[a], 15.88) – 'to move back, to return.'

ἀνακάμπτω[a]: χρηματισθέντες κατ' ὄναρ μὴ ἀνακάμψαι πρὸς Ἡρώδην 'they were warned in a dream not to return to Herod' Mt 2.12; εἰ δὲ μή γε, ἐφ' ὑμᾶς ἀνακάμψει 'if not, it will come back to you' Lk 10.6. In Lk 10.6 ἀνακάμπτω[a] occurs in a somewhat figurative context, but it is difficult to determine precisely to what extent the use of this term suggests actual movement.[22]

ἀναστρέφω: ἀναστρέψαντες δὲ ἀπήγγειλαν 'they returned (to the council) and reported' Ac 5.22.

ἀναλύω[a]: ὑμεῖς ὅμοιοι ἀνθρώποις προσδεχομένοις τὸν κύριον ἑαυτῶν πότε ἀναλύσῃ ἐκ τῶν γάμων 'you will be like servants who are waiting for their master to come back from a wedding feast' Lk 12.36.

ἀναχωρέω[b]: δι' ἄλλης ὁδοῦ ἀνεχώρησαν εἰς τὴν χώραν αὐτῶν 'they returned to their own country by another way' Mt 2.12.[23]

15.90 ἐπιστρέφω[a]: to return to a point or area where one has been before, with probable emphasis on turning about – 'to return to, to go back to.' ἐπέστρεψαν εἰς τὴν Γαλιλαίαν 'they returned to Galilee' Lk 2.39.

15.91 ἐπανέρχομαι; ἐπανάγω[a]: to go back toward or to some point or area (perhaps somewhat more emphatic than the series in 15.89 in view of the prepositional prefix ἐπ-) – 'to return to, to go back to, to go back again to.'

ἐπανέρχομαι: ἐγὼ ἐν τῷ ἐπανέρχεσθαί με ἀποδώσω σοι 'when I return to you, I will give you . . .' Lk 10.35.

ἐπανάγω[a]: πρωῒ δὲ ἐπανάγων εἰς τὴν πόλιν ἐπείνασεν 'in the morning as he returned again to the city, he was hungry' Mt 21.18.

---

21 παρουσία was often used in contexts referring to the arrival or appearance of an important person or supernatural being. In later ecclesiastical Greek, ἡ παρουσία occurs in an absolute sense as a specific reference to the second coming of Christ.

22 In 2 Pe 2.21 ἀνακάμπτω occurs in an apparatus variant in a figurative sense of returning to a previous state with regard to divine revelation.

23 It is possible that ἀναχωρέω in Mt 2.12 means only 'to depart, to withdraw,' and is thus equivalent to ἀναχωρέω[a] (15.53), but it is also possible that ἀναχωρέω[b] differs from the other verbs in this series (15.89) by focusing attention upon the distance involved.

15.92 ἀπέρχομαι πρὸς ἑαυτόν: (an idiom, literally 'to return to oneself') to go back to one's place or abode – 'to go back home, to go back to one's place.' ἀπῆλθεν πρὸς ἑαυτόν 'he went back to where he was staying' Lk 24.12. It would be possible to translate 'he went back home,' but probably Peter did not have a home in Jerusalem, and so such a rendering could be misleading in the case of Lk 24.12.

H Come/Go Into (15.93-15.96)

15.93 εἰσέρχομαι[a]; εἰσπορεύομαι; εἴσειμι: to move into a space, either two-dimensional or three-dimensional – 'to move into, to come into, to go into, to enter.'

εἰσέρχομαι[a]: εἰσῆλθεν εἰς Καφαρναούμ 'he came into Capernaum' Lk 7.1. In a number of contexts the area or structure which is entered is not specified, for example, ὅτε εἰσῆλθον, εἰς τὸ ὑπερῷον ἀνέβησαν 'when they entered (the house), they went up into the upper room' Ac 1.13; τολμήσας εἰσῆλθεν πρὸς τὸν Πιλᾶτον 'he went in bravely to the presence of Pilate' Mk 15.43.

εἰσέρχομαι[a] is also used in the NT in speaking of the entrance of demons or Satan into animate beings, for example, λέγοντες, Πέμψον ἡμᾶς εἰς τοὺς χοίρους, ἵνα εἰς αὐτοὺς εἰσέλθωμεν 'saying, Send us into the swine so we may enter them' Mk 5.12. In a number of languages one cannot speak of such supernatural beings 'entering' an object. It may be necessary to use such expressions as 'to grab' or 'to control' or 'to command.'

εἰσπορεύομαι: εἰσπορεύεται ὅπου ἦν τὸ παιδίον 'they entered (the room) where the child was' Mk 5.40; πᾶν τὸ εἰσπορευόμενον εἰς τὸ στόμα εἰς τὴν κοιλίαν χωρεῖ 'everything which goes into the mouth moves on into the stomach' Mt 15.17.

εἴσειμι: ὃς ἰδὼν Πέτρον καὶ Ἰωάννην μέλλοντας εἰσιέναι εἰς τὸ ἱερόν 'he saw Peter and John about to enter the Temple' Ac 3.3.

15.94 ἐνδύνω: to enter secretly and with ulterior motives – 'to enter in secretly, to slip into.' ἐκ τούτων γάρ εἰσιν οἱ ἐνδύνοντες εἰς τὰς οἰκίας 'some of them slip into homes' 2 Tm 3.6. In order to render the meaning of ἐνδύνω in 2 Tm 3.6, it may be necessary in some languages to be somewhat more explicit, for example, 'they enter into houses without being seen' or 'they enter into houses without people knowing what they really intend to do.'

15.95 ἐμβαίνω[a]: to go into or onto, as in the case of a boat – 'to embark, to get into a boat.' ἐμβὰς εἰς πλοῖον διεπέρασεν 'he got into the boat and went back across (the lake)' Mt 9.1. In certain contexts ἐμβαίνω[a] occurs without a specific indication of a ship or boat in the immediate context, for example, πάλιν ἐμβὰς ἀπῆλθεν εἰς τὸ πέραν 'again embarking, he left for the other side' Mk 8.13. In a number of languages it is necessary to introduce into the context some specific reference to a boat or ship.

15.96 ἐμβιβάζω: to cause someone to go into, as in the case of a boat – 'to cause to go aboard, to cause to embark.' ἐνεβίβασεν ἡμᾶς εἰς αὐτό 'he had us go aboard' Ac 27.6. The causative in this type of context may be expressed simply as 'he commanded us,' or the causative may be somewhat weakened to a form such as in English 'he had us go aboard.'

I Come/Go Onto (15.97-15.100)

15.97 ἐπιβαίνω[b]: to move up onto some object – 'to embark, to go onto, to mount.' ἐπιβάντες ἀνήχθημεν 'so we went aboard and sailed away' Ac 21.2; ἐπιβεβηκὼς ἐπὶ ὄνον 'he is mounted on a donkey' Mt 21.5. In a high percentage of languages it is necessary to use quite distinct terms in speaking of boarding a ship in contrast with mounting a donkey. A wrong choice in such a context can be seriously misleading.

15.98 ἐπιβιβάζω: to cause to mount, as in the case of an animal – 'to cause to mount.' ἐπιβιβάσας δὲ αὐτὸν ἐπὶ τὸ ἴδιον κτῆνος 'he had him get on his own riding animal' Lk 10.34. In Lk 10.34 it is difficult to know whether the causative aspect of the verb includes 'helping him get on' or 'having him get on.'

15.99 ἀναβαίνω[b]: to move up onto an object, with specialization of meaning in reference to boats – 'to go aboard, to embark.' ἀναβάντων

195

αὐτῶν εἰς τὸ πλοῖον ἐκόπασεν ὁ ἄνεμος 'when they got up into the boat, the wind died down' Mt 14.32.

15.100 ἀναλαμβάνω^c: to cause or permit someone to move up onto an object, used especially in relation to boats, but with the possible associated meaning of welcoming or receiving – 'to receive aboard, to take aboard.' ἀνήχθημεν ἐπὶ τὴν ˮΑσσον, ἐκεῖθεν μέλλοντες ἀναλαμβάνειν τὸν Παῦλον 'we sailed off to Assos, where we were going to take Paul aboard' Ac 20.13.

J Come/Go Up, Ascend (15.101-15.106)

15.101 ἀναβαίνω^a; ἀνέρχομαι: to move up – 'to come up, to go up, to ascend.' The upward movement may be of almost any gradient, for example, in going up a road to Jerusalem (Ga 1.17) or in going up into a tree (Lk 19.4) or in ascending into heaven (Ac 2.34).
ἀναβαίνω^a: ὅτε εἰσῆλθον, εἰς τὸ ὑπερῷον ἀνέβησαν 'when they entered, they went up into the upper room' Ac 1.13; ἰδὼν δὲ τοὺς ὄχλους ἀνέβη εἰς τὸ ὄρος 'he saw the crowds and went up a mountain' Mt 5.1; ἄνθρωποι δύο ἀνέβησαν εἰς τὸ ἱερὸν προσεύξασθαι 'two men went up into the Temple to pray' Lk 18.10.
ἀνέρχομαι: οὐδὲ ἀνῆλθον εἰς Ἱεροσόλυμα πρὸς τοὺς πρὸ ἐμοῦ ἀποστόλους 'neither did I go up to Jerusalem to those who were apostles before me' Ga 1.17.

15.102 ὑπολαμβάνω^a: to cause to ascend – 'to make ascend, to take up.' καὶ νεφέλη ὑπέλαβεν αὐτὸν ἀπὸ τῶν ὀφθαλμῶν αὐτῶν 'and a cloud took him up and away from their sight' Ac 1.9.

15.103 ἀνάλημψις, εως f: the process of being taken up – 'to be taken up into, assumption, ascension.' ἐγένετο δὲ ἐν τῷ συμπληροῦσθαι τὰς ἡμέρας τῆς ἀναλήμψεως αὐτοῦ 'and as the days drew near for him to be taken up' or 'when the time was fulfilled for him to be received up (into heaven)' Lk 9.51.

15.104 ἀνατέλλω^a; ἀνατολή^a, ῆς f: to move up, especially of the upward movement of the sun, stars, or clouds – 'to come up, to move upward, to rise.'
ἀνατέλλω^a: ἀνέτειλεν γὰρ ὁ ἥλιος σὺν τῷ καύσωνι καὶ ἐξήρανεν τὸν χόρτον 'the sun rises in its blazing heat and burns the plant' Jas 1.11; ὅταν ἴδητε τὴν νεφέλην ἀνατέλλουσαν ἐπὶ δυσμῶν 'when you see a cloud coming up in the west' Lk 12.54.
ἀνατολή^a: εἴδομεν γὰρ αὐτοῦ τὸν ἀστέρα ἐν τῇ ἀνατολῇ 'we saw his star when it arose' Mt 2.2. It is also possible to understand ἀνατολή in Mt 2.2 as meaning 'the east' (see ἀνατολή^b, 82.1).

15.105 ἐπαίρω: to cause to move up – 'to raise.' ἐπαίροντας ὁσίους χεῖρας 'raising up holy hands' 1 Tm 2.8. In a number of languages one cannot speak of 'raising hands,' since this would imply something that was detached from the body. It may therefore be necessary to say 'extending hands upwards.'

15.106 προσαναβαίνω: to move up to a point (with the possible implication of higher status) – 'to move up to, to come up to, to go up to.' φίλε, προσανάβηθι ἀνώτερον 'friend, come up higher' Lk 14.10. It may be necessary in some languages to translate this expression in Lk 14.10 as 'come up to a higher place' or 'come up to a better seat' or 'come up to a more important place.'

K Come/Go Down, Descend (15.107-15.117)

15.107 καταβαίνω; κατέρχομαι^a: to move down, irrespective of the gradient – 'to move down, to come down, to go down, to descend.'
καταβαίνω: οἱ γραμματεῖς οἱ ἀπὸ Ἱεροσολύμων καταβάντες 'some of the teachers of the Law who had come down from Jerusalem' Mk 3.22; κατέβη ἡ βροχή 'the rain descended' Mt 7.25; καταβαῖνον ἀπὸ τοῦ πατρὸς τῶν φώτων 'it comes down from the Father of lights' Jas 1.17; καταβὰς ἀπὸ τοῦ πλοίου ὁ Πέτρος περιεπάτησεν ἐπὶ τὰ ὕδατα 'Peter got out of the boat and walked on the water' Mt 14.29.
κατέρχομαι^a: κατῆλθεν εἰς Καφαρναούμ 'he came down to Capernaum' Lk 4.31.
In a number of languages there is a series of terms for going down or descending, depend-

ing upon the gradient and the rapidity with which someone or something descends. There may also be distinct terms depending upon the extent of the descent. Rain coming down would be regarded as an extensive descent, while getting out of a boat to walk on the water would be a very limited descent.

Movement downward may, of course, involve more than physical objects, for example, οὐκ ἔστιν αὕτη ἡ σοφία ἄνωθεν κατερχομένη 'this is not the wisdom that comes down from above' Jas 3.15. Since in Jas 3.15 ἄνωθεν is a substitute for God, it may be necessary to restructure this statement as 'this wisdom does not come from God' or 'God is not the source of this wisdom.'

15.108 καταβιβάζω: (occurring only in three variant readings in the NT text) to cause to move down – 'to bring down, to make go down.' ἐκ δὲ τοῦ ὄχλου κατεβίβασαν Ἀλέξανδρον, προβαλόντων αὐτὸν τῶν Ἰουδαίων 'some of the crowd brought Alexander down, since he had been put forward by the Jews' Ac 19.33 (apparatus); ἕως ᾅδου καταβιβασθήσῃ 'you will be brought down to hell' Mt 11.23 (apparatus). See also Lk 10.15 (apparatus).

15.109 κατάβασις, εως *f*: (derivative of καταβαίνω 'to move down, to descend,' 15.107) the slope or declivity of an object which one may descend – 'slope, descent.' ἐγγίζοντος δὲ αὐτοῦ ἤδη πρὸς τῇ καταβάσει τοῦ Ὄρους τῶν Ἐλαιῶν 'he was already approaching the slope of the Mount of Olives' or 'he was already approaching the descent of the Mount of Olives' Lk 19.37. The latter translation could represent the means of descent, namely, 'the road leading down from the Mount of Olives.'

15.110 καθαιρέω[a]: to cause something or someone to be lowered or brought down – 'to bring down, to lower.' ἴδωμεν εἰ ἔρχεται Ἠλίας καθελεῖν αὐτόν 'let us see if Elijah will come and lower him' Mk 15.36. For another interpretation of καθαιρέω in Mk 15.36, see 15.199.

15.111 χαλάω; καθίημι: to cause something to move down gradually – 'to let down, to lower.'

χαλάω: διὰ θυρίδος ἐν σαργάνῃ ἐχαλάσθην διὰ τοῦ τείχους '(but) I was let down in a basket, through an opening in the wall' 2 Cor 11.33. καθίημι: καθῆκαν αὐτὸν σὺν τῷ κλινιδίῳ εἰς τὸ μέσον ἔμπροσθεν τοῦ Ἰησοῦ 'they let him down on his bed into the middle of the group in front of Jesus' Lk 5.19.

15.112 βάλλω[c]: to move down suddenly and quickly – 'to sweep down, to rush down.' μετ' οὐ πολὺ δὲ ἔβαλεν κατ' αὐτῆς ἄνεμος τυφωνικός 'but soon a very strong wind swept down from there' Ac 27.14. In a number of languages, however, it may be more appropriate to speak of a strong wind 'blowing down from the island.'

15.113 δύνω: to move or sink down, especially of the sun sinking below the horizon – 'to sink, to set, to go down.' ὀψίας δὲ γενομένης, ὅτε ἔδυ ὁ ἥλιος 'when evening came, after the sun had set' Mk 1.32.

15.114 ἐπιδύω: to go down or to sink down, especially of the sun in relationship to some event or state – 'to go down, to go down upon.' ὁ ἥλιος μὴ ἐπιδυέτω ἐπὶ τῷ παροργισμῷ ὑμῶν 'don't let the sun go down while you are still angry' or '. . . upon your anger' Eph 4.26.

In a number of languages it may seem very strange to speak of 'the sun going down upon one's anger.' A more natural and more meaningful equivalent may be 'do not be angry all day long' or 'do not be angry even until sundown.'

15.115 βυθίζω[a]: to cause to go down into water or other liquid substance – 'to sink.' ἔπλησαν ἀμφότερα τὰ πλοῖα ὥστε βυθίζεσθαι αὐτά 'they filled both the boats so full (of fish) that they were about to sink' Lk 5.7.

15.116 καταποντίζομαι: to sink down into deep water – 'to sink.' ἀρξάμενος καταποντίζεσθαι ἔκραξεν 'beginning to sink, he cried out' Mt 14.30.

15.117 καταποντίζω: to cause something or someone to sink into deep water – 'to sink, to drown.' καὶ καταποντισθῇ ἐν τῷ πελάγει τῆς θαλάσσης 'and be drowned in the depths of the sea' Mt 18.6.

L   Fall (15.118-15.122)

15.118 πίπτω[a]; καταπίπτω[a]: to fall from one level to another – 'to fall.'[24]

πίπτω[a]: ἔπεσεν ἀπὸ τοῦ τριστέγου κάτω 'he fell from the third story' Ac 20.9.

καταπίπτω[a]: καὶ ἕτερον κατέπεσεν ἐπὶ τὴν πέτραν 'and another fell upon the stony ground' Lk 8.6.

15.119 πίπτω[b]; καταπίπτω[b]: to fall from a standing or upright position down to the ground or surface – 'to fall, to fall down.'[24]

πίπτω[b]: τὰ τείχη Ἰεριχὼ ἔπεσαν 'the walls of Jericho fell' He 11.30.

καταπίπτω[b]: πάντων τε καταπεσόντων ἡμῶν εἰς τὴν γῆν 'we all fell to the ground' Ac 26.14; καταπίπτειν ἄφνω νεκρόν 'to suddenly fall down dead' Ac 28.6.

15.120 ἀποπίπτω; ἐκπίπτω[a]: to fall from a particular point or location – 'to fall, to fall from, to fall off.'

ἀποπίπτω: καὶ εὐθέως ἀπέπεσαν αὐτοῦ ἀπὸ τῶν ὀφθαλμῶν ὡς λεπίδες 'and immediately there fell from his eyes something like scales' Ac 9.18.

ἐκπίπτω[a]: καὶ τὸ ἄνθος ἐξέπεσεν 'and the flower falls' 1 Pe 1.24.

15.121 ἐμπίπτω[a]: to fall into a particular point or location – 'to fall in(to).' καὶ ἐὰν ἐμπέσῃ τοῦτο τοῖς σάββασιν εἰς βόθυνον 'and if it falls on the Sabbath into a pit' Mt 12.11.

15.122 βάλλω[b]: to cause or to let fall down – 'to let fall, to drop.' ὡς συκῆ βάλλει τοὺς ὀλύνθους αὐτῆς 'as when a fig tree drops its unripe figs' Re 6.13.

M   Gather, Cause To Come Together (15.123-15.134)

15.123 συνάγομαι; συνέρχομαι[a]; συμπορεύ-

ομαι[b]; σύνειμι[a]; συστρέφομαι; συμπαραγίνομαι: the movement of two or more objects to the same location – 'to gather together, to come together, to go together, to meet, to assemble.'[25]

συνάγομαι: οὗ γάρ εἰσιν δύο ἢ τρεῖς συνηγμένοι εἰς τὸ ἐμὸν ὄνομα 'where two or three have come together in my name' Mt 18.20.

συνέρχομαι[a]: ἐν τῷ ἱερῷ, ὅπου πάντες οἱ Ἰουδαῖοι συνέρχονται 'in the Temple where all the Jews assemble' Jn 18.20.

συμπορεύομαι[b]: συμπορεύονται πάλιν ὄχλοι πρὸς αὐτόν 'crowds gathered around him again' Mk 10.1.

σύνειμι[a]: συνιόντος δὲ ὄχλου πολλοῦ . . . εἶπεν 'when a crowd gathered . . . he spoke' Lk 8.4.

συστρέφομαι: συστρεφομένων δὲ αὐτῶν ἐν τῇ Γαλιλαίᾳ 'when they were assembled in Galilee' Mt 17.22.

συμπαραγίνομαι: πάντες οἱ συμπαραγενόμενοι ὄχλοι 'when the people had all gathered together' Lk 23.48.

In a number of languages important distinctions are made in terms referring to gathering or assembling of animate beings. The distinctions are usually based upon the number of individuals, the distance which they have come, and whether or not the individuals in question constitute a membership group or whether they are merely a loose aggregation. In view of these types of distinctions, it is likely that quite different terms will be required for the various contexts listed for this set of related meanings.

15.124 ἐπισυνάγομαι: to come or gather together to, toward, or at a particular location – 'to gather (at), to come together (to).' ἦν ὅλη ἡ πόλις ἐπισυνηγμένη πρὸς τὴν θύραν 'all the people of the town had gathered at the door' Mk 1.33.

15.125 συνάγω[a]; συστρέφω; συμφέρω[a]: to cause to come together, whether of animate or inanimate objects – 'to gather together, to call together.'

---

24 In both instances (15.118 and 15.119) καταπίπτω may be somewhat more emphatic in meaning than πίπτω in view of the prefixial form κατα-.

25 There are no doubt a number of subtle distinctions in meaning in this series of expressions meaning 'to gather together,' but the precise distinctions in meaning cannot be determined from existing NT contexts.

συνάγω[a]: συναγαγὼν πάντας τοὺς ἀρχιερεῖς καὶ γραμματεῖς τοῦ λαοῦ 'he gathered together all the chief priests and teachers of the people' Mt 2.4.

συστρέφω: συστρέψαντος δὲ τοῦ Παύλου φρυγάνων τι πλῆθος 'and when Paul had gathered quite a few sticks' Ac 28.3.

συμφέρω[a]: συνενέγκαντες τὰς βίβλους κατέκαιον ἐνώπιον πάντων 'when they had gathered together the books, they burned them in front of everyone' Ac 19.19.

15.126 ἐπισυνάγω; ἐπισυναγωγή[a], ῆς f: to cause to come together to, toward, or at a particular location – 'to cause to come together, to gather together.'

ἐπισυνάγω: ποσάκις ἠθέλησα ἐπισυναγαγεῖν τὰ τέκνα σου 'how often I wanted to gather your people together' Mt 23.37.

ἐπισυναγωγή[a]: ὑπὲρ τῆς παρουσίας τοῦ κυρίου ἡμῶν Ἰησοῦ Χριστοῦ καὶ ἡμῶν ἐπισυναγωγῆς ἐπ᾽ αὐτόν 'concerning the coming of our Lord Jesus Christ and our being gathered together to be with him' 2 Th 2.1.

15.127 προσλαμβάνομαι[d]: to gather together to oneself a group of persons – 'to gather together, to form a group.' προσλαβόμενοι τῶν ἀγοραίων ἄνδρας τινὰς πονηροὺς καὶ ὀχλοποιήσαντες 'gathering together some worthless men from the streets and forming a mob' Ac 17.5. It is also possible that προσλαμβάνομαι in Ac 17.5 means 'to take along in addition to oneself' (see 15.167).

15.128 ἐπισυναγωγή[b], ῆς f: (derivative of ἐπισυνάγομαι 'to gather at,' 15.124) the gathering together of a group (in the active rather than in the passive sense of ἐπισυναγωγή[a], 15.126) – 'gathering, assembling.' μὴ ἐγκαταλείποντες τὴν ἐπισυναγωγὴν ἑαυτῶν, καθὼς ἔθος τισίν 'do not neglect your assembling as some are doing' He 10.25.

15.129 ἀθροίζομαι: to assemble together, with the possible implication of compactness or solidarity – 'to gather together, to come together.' εὗρον ἠθροισμένους τοὺς ἔνδεκα καὶ τοὺς σὺν αὐτοῖς 'they found the eleven disciples gathered together with the others' Lk 24.33.

15.130 συναθροίζομαι: to assemble together, with emphasis on the element of togetherness (compare ἀθροίζομαι, 15.129) – 'to gather together.' οὗ ἦσαν ἱκανοὶ συνηθροισμένοι καὶ προσευχόμενοι 'many people had gathered together there and were praying' Ac 12.12.

15.131 συναθροίζω: to cause to gather together (compare συναθροίζομαι, 15.130) – 'to cause to come together, to gather together, to call together.' οὓς συναθροίσας καὶ τοὺς περὶ τὰ τοιαῦτα ἐργάτας 'so he called them together, with others whose work was like theirs' Ac 19.25.

15.132 ἐπαθροίζομαι: to gather together in addition to or besides – 'to gather together more, to collect (as of crowds).' τῶν δὲ ὄχλων ἐπαθροιζομένων 'when the crowds had gathered even more' Lk 11.29. In Lk 11.29 it may be more satisfactory to translate ἐπαθροίζομαι as 'having gotten larger' or 'becoming more and more.'

15.133 συντρέχω[a]; συνδρομή, ῆς f: to come together quickly to form a crowd – 'to rush together, to run together, to assemble quickly.' συντρέχω[a]: συνέδραμεν πᾶς ὁ λαὸς πρὸς αὐτούς 'all the people ran together to them' Ac 3.11. συνδρομή: ἐγένετο συνδρομὴ τοῦ λαοῦ 'the people rushed together' Ac 21.30.

15.134 ἐπισυντρέχω: to come together hurriedly to, toward, or at a particular location – 'to rush together to a place, to throng to.' ἰδὼν δὲ ὁ Ἰησοῦς ὅτι ἐπισυντρέχει ὄχλος ἐπετίμησεν τῷ πνεύματι τῷ ἀκαθάρτῳ 'Jesus noticed that the crowd was thronging toward him, so he gave a command to the evil spirit' Mk 9.25.

N Disperse, Scatter (15.135-15.140)

15.135 σκορπίζω[a]: to cause a group or a gathering to disperse or scatter – 'to scatter, to cause to disperse.' ὁ λύκος ἁρπάζει αὐτὰ καὶ σκορπίζει 'the wolf snatches them (the sheep) and scatters (the flock)' Jn 10.12; ἵνα σκορπισθῆτε ἕκαστος εἰς τὰ ἴδια 'so each of you will be scattered, each to his own home' Jn 16.32.

15.136 διασκορπίζω^a; διασπείρω; διαλύω:
to cause a group or gathering to disperse or
scatter, with possible emphasis on the distributive nature of the scattering (that is to say,
each going in a different direction) – 'to scatter, to cause to disperse.'

διασκορπίζω^a: πατάξω τὸν ποιμένα, καὶ τὰ
πρόβατα διασκορπισθήσονται 'I will strike the
shepherd and the flock will be scattered' Mk
14.27; συνάγων ὅθεν οὐ διεσκόρπισας 'gathering
where you have not scattered' Mt 25.24. In
Mt 25.24 it may be important to indicate
clearly what was scattered. This could not be
a reference to sowing, since sowing has already been mentioned in the previous statement. The reference in this verse may therefore be to chaff or to manure.

διασπείρω: πάντες δὲ διεσπάρησαν κατὰ τὰς
χώρας τῆς Ἰουδαίας καὶ Σαμαρείας πλὴν τῶν
ἀποστόλων 'all of them, except the apostles,
were scattered throughout the provinces of
Judea and Samaria' Ac 8.1.

διαλύω: ὃς ἀνῃρέθη, καὶ πάντες ὅσοι ἐπείθοντο
αὐτῷ διελύθησαν 'but he was killed and all his
followers were scattered' Ac 5.36.

15.137 διασπορά, ᾶς f: (derivative of διασπείρω 'to scatter,' 15.136) the region or area in
which persons have been scattered (particularly a reference to the nation of Israel which had
been scattered throughout the ancient world)
– 'region in which people are scattered, diaspora.' μὴ εἰς τὴν διασπορὰν τῶν Ἑλλήνων
μέλλει πορεύεσθαι 'will he go to the diaspora
among the Greeks?' Jn 7.35; ταῖς δώδεκα
φυλαῖς ταῖς ἐν τῇ διασπορᾷ χαίρειν 'greetings to
all God's people (literally 'the twelve tribes')
who are in the diaspora' Jas 1.1. For the most
part, the phrase ταῖς δώδεκα φυλαῖς in Jas 1.1
has been interpreted as a reference to believers in Christ. In translating, one may render the term διασπορά as 'in all the regions
where they have been scattered,' thus rendering this expression in Jas 1.1 as 'greetings to
all of God's people in all of the regions in
which they have been scattered.'

15.138 ἐκχέω^b: to scatter a substance or
mass – 'to scatter.' καὶ τῶν κολλυβιστῶν ἐξέχεεν τὸ κέρμα 'and he scattered the money of the
moneychangers' Jn 2.15.

15.139 λύω^d: to cause a gathering to be dismissed or dispersed – 'to dismiss, to disperse.'
λυθείσης δὲ τῆς συναγωγῆς 'when the gathering
had been dispersed' or 'when the meeting had
been dismissed' Ac 13.43. In some languages
it may be more appropriate to render this expression in Ac 13.43 as 'when most of the
people had left' or 'when the meeting was
over.'

15.140 διαμερίζομαι: to disperse, on the
basis of having been divided up – 'to spread
out, to disperse.' καὶ ὤφθησαν αὐτοῖς διαμεριζόμεναι γλῶσσαι ὡσεὶ πυρός 'and there appeared to them dispersing tongues as of fire'
or '. . . tongues as of fire spreading out' Ac
2.3. There are, however, serious questions as
to the precise meaning of διαμερίζομαι in Ac
2.3; the meaning could be 'tongues as of fire
dispersing one to each person,' but it is also
possible that the individual tongues of fire
were divided (see 63.23).

O Come/Go Prior To (15.141-15.142)

15.141 φθάνω^b; προέρχομαι^c: to come/go
prior to some other event, normally one in-
volving a similar type of movement – 'to
come/go prior to, to come/go beforehand, to
precede.'

Though the movement referred to by
φθάνω^b and προέρχομαι^c may involve movement which is spacially ahead of someone
else, nevertheless the focus of meaning is not
a spacial relationship but a temporal one.

φθάνω^b: ἡμεῖς οἱ ζῶντες οἱ περιλειπόμενοι εἰς
τὴν παρουσίαν τοῦ κυρίου οὐ μὴ φθάσωμεν τοὺς
κοιμηθέντας 'we who are left alive on the day
the Lord comes will not go before those who
have died' 1 Th 4.15.

προέρχομαι^c: ἀναγκαῖον οὖν ἡγησάμην παρακαλέσαι τοὺς ἀδελφοὺς ἵνα προέλθωσιν εἰς ὑμᾶς
'thus I thought it necessary to urge the fellow
believers to come to you beforehand' 2 Cor
9.5; αὐτὸς προελεύσεται ἐνώπιον αὐτοῦ ἐν
πνεύματι καὶ δυνάμει Ἠλίου 'he will go ahead
of him in the spirit and power of Elijah' Lk
1.17.

15.142 προάγω^a: to go prior to someone
else's going – 'to go prior to, to go away

beforehand.' εὐθὺς ἠνάγκασεν τοὺς μαθητὰς αὐτοῦ ἐμβῆναι εἰς τὸ πλοῖον καὶ προάγειν . . . πρὸς Βηθσαϊδάν 'at once he made his disciples get into the boat and go ahead of him . . . to Bethsaida' Mk 6.45.

P Come/Go In Front Of (15.143)

15.143 προάγω[b]; προπορεύομαι[a]: to move in front of or ahead of, with the implication that both parties are moving in the same direction – 'to go in front of, to precede.'
προάγω[b]: οἱ προάγοντες καὶ οἱ ἀκολουθοῦντες ἔκραζον 'the people who went in front and those who followed behind shouted' Mk 11.9.
προπορεύομαι[a]: προπορεύσῃ γὰρ ἐνώπιον κυρίου ἑτοιμάσαι ὁδοὺς αὐτοῦ 'you will go on before the Lord to prepare the way for him' Lk 1.76.[26]

Q Come/Go Behind (15.144-15.145)

15.144 ἀκολουθέω[a]: to come/go behind or after someone else – 'to follow, to come behind, to go behind.' ἠκολούθει γὰρ τὸ πλῆθος τοῦ λαοῦ κράζοντες, Αἶρε αὐτόν 'for the crowd of people followed him screaming, Away with him' Ac 21.36; οἱ προάγοντες καὶ οἱ ἀκολουθοῦντες ἔκραζον 'those going ahead of him and those following him shouted' Mk 11.9.

15.145 κατακολουθέω: to come/go behind or after, with the possible implication of continual and determined action – 'to follow along behind, to keep on following.' αὕτη κατακολουθοῦσα τῷ Παύλῳ καὶ ἡμῖν ἔκραζεν 'she kept following Paul and us and was shouting' Ac 16.17.

R Go Around, Surround (15.146-15.147)

15.146 κυκλόω[a]: to move around an object – 'to go around.' τὰ τείχη Ἰεριχὼ ἔπεσαν κυκλωθέντα ἐπὶ ἑπτὰ ἡμέρας 'the walls of Jericho fell, having been gone around for seven days' He 11.30. A strictly literal translation of the Greek text of He 11.30 may be extremely difficult, since it is usually necessary to employ

an active form involving movement so as to specify what entities go around. Therefore, it may be preferable to translate 'the walls of Jericho fell after the Israelites had gone around them for seven days.'

15.147 κυκλεύω; κυκλόω[b]; περικυκλόω: to move in such a way as to encircle an object – 'to surround, to be around.'[27]
κυκλεύω: ἐκύκλευσαν τὴν παρεμβολὴν τῶν ἁγίων καὶ τὴν πόλιν τὴν ἠγαπημένην 'they surrounded the camp of the people of God and the beloved city' Re 20.9.
κυκλόω[b]: ἐκύκλωσαν οὖν αὐτὸν οἱ Ἰουδαῖοι 'so the Jews surrounded him' Jn 10.24.
περικυκλόω: καὶ περικυκλώσουσίν σε καὶ συνέξουσίν σε πάντοθεν 'and they will surround you and press you in from every side' Lk 19.43.

S Come/Go With, Travel With (15.148-15.155)

15.148 συνέρχομαι[b]; συμπορεύομαι[a]: to come/go together with one or more other persons – 'to come with, to go with, to accompany.'
συνέρχομαι[b]: Ἰησοῦς οὖν ὡς εἶδεν αὐτὴν κλαίουσαν καὶ τοὺς συνελθόντας αὐτῇ Ἰουδαίους κλαίοντας 'when Jesus saw her crying and the Jews who were accompanying her also crying' Jn 11.33.
συμπορεύομαι[a]: συνεπορεύοντο αὐτῷ οἱ μαθηταὶ αὐτοῦ καὶ ὄχλος πολύς 'his disciples and a large crowd went with him' Lk 7.11.

15.149 συνοδεύω: to travel together with – 'to travel with.' οἱ δὲ ἄνδρες οἱ συνοδεύοντες αὐτῷ εἱστήκεισαν ἐνεοί 'the men who were travelling with him had stopped, not saying a word' Ac 9.7. In a number of languages it may be necessary in speaking of 'travelling' to indicate whether a single journey is involved or whether one is going from place to place. In Ac 9.7 it is evidently a single journey.

15.150 συνοδία, ας f: (derivative of συνοδεύω 'to travel with,' 15.149) a group of persons travelling together – 'a group of travellers, a

---

26 It is possible that προπορεύομαι in Lk 1.76 should be interpreted as temporal rather than as spacial.

27 It is possible that περικυκλόω is somewhat more emphatic than κυκλόω[b] and κυκλεύω in emphasizing the fact of being surrounded.

group of those travelling with.' νομίσαντες δὲ αὐτὸν εἶναι ἐν τῇ συνοδίᾳ 'they thought that he was in the group of those travelling with them' Lk 2.44.

15.151 συνέκδημος, ου *m*: one who is away from home on a journey with someone else – 'travelling companion.' Γάϊον καὶ Ἀρίσταρχον Μακεδόνας, συνεκδήμους Παύλου 'Gaius and Aristarchus, the Macedonians (who were) travelling companions of Paul' Ac 19.29.

15.152 συνεισέρχομαι: to come/go into together with – 'to go in with, to enter with.' συνεισῆλθεν τῷ Ἰησοῦ εἰς τὴν αὐλὴν τοῦ ἀρχιερέως 'he entered into the courtyard of the high priest with Jesus' Jn 18.15.

15.153 συναναβαίνω: to accompany in going up to – 'to go or come up together with, to travel with, to accompany.' ὃς ὤφθη ἐπὶ ἡμέρας πλείους τοῖς συναναβᾶσιν αὐτῷ ἀπὸ τῆς Γαλιλαίας εἰς Ἰερουσαλήμ 'for many days he was seen by those who had come up with him from Galilee to Jerusalem' Ac 13.31.

15.154 συγκαταβαίνω: to accompany in going down to – 'to go or come down together with, to travel with, to accompany.' οἱ οὖν ἐν ὑμῖν, φησίν, δυνατοὶ συγκαταβάντες εἴ τί ἐστιν ἐν τῷ ἀνδρὶ ἄτοπον κατηγορείτωσαν αὐτοῦ 'let your leaders, he said, go down (to Caesarea) with me and accuse the man, if he has done anything wrong' Ac 25.5.

15.155 προπέμπω^b: to accompany a person for a short distance at the beginning of a journey – 'to escort, to accompany.' προέπεμπον δὲ αὐτὸν εἰς τὸ πλοῖον 'they escorted him to the boat' Ac 20.38.

T Follow, Accompany (15.156-15.157)

15.156 ἀκολουθέω^b: to follow or accompany someone who takes the lead in determining direction and route of movement – 'to accompany as a follower, to follow, to go along with.' ἠκολούθησαν αὐτῷ ὄχλοι πολλοὶ ἀπὸ τῆς Γαλιλαίας 'a great crowd from Galilee followed him' Mt 4.25. ἀκολουθέω^b differs from ἀκολουθέω^a (15.144) in that it specifies a factor

of accompaniment rather than merely going behind.

15.157 συνακολουθέω; συνέπομαι: to accompany someone, with explicit marking of association – 'to accompany, to follow.' συνακολουθέω: οὐκ ἀφῆκεν οὐδένα μετ' αὐτοῦ συνακολουθῆσαι εἰ μὴ τὸν Πέτρον 'he permitted no one to accompany him except Peter' Mk 5.37.
συνέπομαι: συνείπετο δὲ αὐτῷ Σώπατρος Πύρρου Βεροιαῖος 'Sopater, the son of Pyrrhus, from Beroea, accompanied him' Ac 20.4.

U Pursue, Follow (15.158-15.159)

15.158 διώκω^a: to follow with haste, and presumably with intensity of effort, in order to catch up with, for friendly or hostile purpose – 'to run after, to chase after, to pursue.' μὴ ἀπέλθητε μηδὲ διώξητε 'do not go and chase after them' Lk 17.23; ἐδίωξεν τὴν γυναῖκα ἥτις ἔτεκεν τὸν ἄρσενα 'he pursued the woman who had given birth to the boy' Re 12.13; διώξετε ἀπὸ πόλεως εἰς πόλιν 'you will pursue them from town to town' Mt 23.34.

15.159 ἐκδιώκω^a: to pursue to the point of driving out – 'to pursue and drive out.' καὶ ἡμᾶς ἐκδιωξάντων 'and pursuing us to the point of driving us out' 1 Th 2.15. ἐκδιώκω in 1 Th 2.15 may also be understood in the sense of 'to persecute' (see 39.45).

V Drive Along, Carry Along²⁸ (15.160-15.164)

15.160 φέρω^c: to cause an object to move by means of a force – 'to drive along, to carry along.' χαλάσαντες τὸ σκεῦος, οὕτως ἐφέροντο 'having lowered the sails, they were thus carried along (by the wind)' Ac 27.17.

15.161 ἐλαύνω: to cause an object to move by means of a strong force or vigorous action

---

28 Subdomain V *Drive Along, Carry Along* differs from Subdomains W and Y in that the agent is a force rather than an animate being. This distinction seems to be relevant as far as the Greek semantic structure is concerned, and it corresponds to a number of lexical distinctions in other languages.

– 'to drive along, to carry along.' ὁμίχλαι ὑπὸ λαίλαπος ἐλαυνόμεναι 'like mists driven by a storm' 2 Pe 2.17; ὑπὸ ἀνέμων σκληρῶν ἐλαυνόμενα '(the ships) can be driven by strong winds' Jas 3.4; ἰδὼν αὐτοὺς βασανιζομένους ἐν τῷ ἐλαύνειν 'he saw that they were having great difficulty in rowing' Mk 6.48.[29]

In Lk 8.29 ἐλαύνω occurs in the statement ἠλαύνετο ὑπὸ τοῦ δαιμονίου εἰς τὰς ἐρήμους 'he was driven into the desert by the demon.' In this context it would appear that the demon was regarded as a type of force, parallel perhaps to wind.

15.162 παραφέρω[a]: to cause to move along continually in the same direction as the force involved – 'to drive along, to carry along.' νεφέλαι ἄνυδροι ὑπὸ ἀνέμων παραφερόμεναι 'clouds carried along by the wind and bringing no rain' Jd 12.

15.163 διαφέρω[b]: to cause to move in various directions by means of a force – 'to drive about, to carry about.' ὡς δὲ τεσσαρεσκαιδεκάτη νὺξ ἐγένετο διαφερομένων ἡμῶν ἐν τῷ Ἀδρίᾳ 'it was the fourteenth night, and we were being carried about on the Adriatic Sea' Ac 27.27.

15.164 ἀνεμίζομαι: to be caused to move by the wind – 'to be driven or carried about by the wind.' ὁ γὰρ διακρινόμενος ἔοικεν κλύδωνι θαλάσσης ἀνεμιζομένῳ καὶ ῥιπιζομένῳ 'whoever doubts is like a wave in the sea that is driven by the wind and tossed about' Jas 1.6.[30]

W Lead, Bring, Take[31] (15.165-15.186)

15.165 ἄγω[a]: to direct or guide the movement of an object, without special regard to point of departure or goal – 'to lead, to bring.' ἤγαγον τὴν ὄνον καὶ τὸν πῶλον 'they led the

donkey and the colt' Mt 21.7; Μᾶρκον ἀναλαβὼν ἄγε μετὰ σεαυτοῦ 'get Mark and bring him with you' 2 Tm 4.11.

The Spirit of God is also regarded as an agent in leading or directing the movement of a person, for example, ἤγετο ἐν τῷ πνεύματι ἐν τῇ ἐρήμῳ 'he was led by the Spirit into the desert' Lk 4.1.

ἄγω[a] also occurs in contexts in which the leading involves force: ὅταν ἄγωσιν ὑμᾶς παραδιδόντες 'whenever you are taken into custody and turned over to the courts' Mk 13.11; ἤγοντο δὲ καὶ ἕτεροι κακοῦργοι δύο σὺν αὐτῷ ἀναιρεθῆναι 'they led two others off also, both of them criminals, to be put to death with him' Lk 23.32.

15.166 φέρω[b]: to cause to move to a place, with a possible implication of assistance or firm control – 'to take, to carry, to bring.' φέρουσιν αὐτὸν ἐπὶ τὸν Γολγοθᾶν τόπον 'they brought him to a place called Golgotha' Mk 15.22.

15.167 προσλαμβάνομαι[b]: to take or bring along in addition to oneself – 'to bring along, to take along.' καὶ προσλαβόμενοι τῶν ἀγοραίων ἄνδρας τινὰς πονηρούς 'and bringing along some worthless men from the streets' Ac 17.5. It is also possible to interpret προσλαμβάνομαι in Ac 17.5 as meaning 'to gather together' (see 15.127).

15.168 παραλαμβάνω[a]; **ἀναλαμβάνω**[b]: to take or bring someone along with – 'to take along, to bring along.'
παραλαμβάνω[a]: παραλαβὼν Πέτρον καὶ Ἰωάννην καὶ Ἰάκωβον ἀνέβη εἰς τὸ ὄρος προσεύξασθαι 'he took Peter, John, and James with him and went up into the mountain to pray' Lk 9.28.
ἀναλαμβάνω[b]: ἀναλαβόντες τὸν Παῦλον ἤγαγον διὰ νυκτὸς εἰς τὴν Ἀντιπατρίδα 'taking Paul along, they brought him to Antipatris during the night' Ac 23.31.

15.169 συμπαραλαμβάνω: to take along with, with emphasis upon accompaniment – 'to take along, to bring along with.' συμπαραλαβὼν καὶ Τίτον 'taking Titus along with (me)' Ga 2.1.

---

29 In Mk 6.48 the specific reference of ἐλαύνω is to rowing, though the meaning of ἐλαύνω in its more general sense involves simply moving an object by means of force.

30 It is also possible to classify ἀνεμίζομαι as a derivative of ἄνεμος 'wind' and thus classify it in Domain 14.

31 Subdomain W *Lead, Bring, Take* involves the movement of at least two entities, in which one determines the movement of the other.

15.170 περιάγω^b: to take along or to bring along on a journey or as one travels about – 'to take along, to bring along on a trip.' μὴ οὐκ ἔχομεν ἐξουσίαν ἀδελφὴν γυναῖκα περιάγειν; 'don't I have the right to take a Christian wife with me on my trips?' 1 Cor 9.5.

15.171 προάγω^c: to lead or bring forward or forth – 'to bring forward, to lead forth.' ἐζήτουν αὐτοὺς προαγαγεῖν εἰς τὸν δῆμον 'they tried to find them and bring them forth to the people' Ac 17.5; διὸ προήγαγον αὐτὸν ἐφ' ὑμῶν 'so I brought him on here before you' Ac 25.26.

15.172 προσάγω^a; προσφέρω^b: to bring or lead into the presence of someone – 'to lead before, to bring into the presence of, to bring to.'
προσάγω^a: προσαγαγόντες αὐτοὺς τοῖς στρατηγοῖς 'they brought them before the Roman officials' Ac 16.20; προσάγαγε ὧδε τὸν υἱόν σου 'bring your son here (to me)' Lk 9.41.
προσφέρω^b: προσηνέγκατέ μοι τὸν ἄνθρωπον τοῦτον ὡς ἀποστρέφοντα τὸν λαόν 'you brought this man to me, as one who was misleading the people' Lk 23.14.

15.173 εἰσάγω^a: to bring or lead into – 'to lead into, to take into.' εἶπεν τῇ θυρωρῷ καὶ εἰσήγαγεν τὸν Πέτρον 'he spoke to the girl at the gate and brought Peter inside' Jn 18.16.

15.174 ἐξάγω; ἐκφέρω^b; ἐκβάλλω^d: to lead or bring out of a structure or area – 'to lead out, to bring forth.'
ἐξάγω: ὃς ἐξήγαγεν ἡμᾶς ἐκ γῆς Αἰγύπτου 'who brought us out of Egypt' Ac 7.40.
ἐκφέρω^b: ἐξήνεγκεν αὐτὸν ἔξω τῆς κώμης 'he led him out of the village' Mk 8.23.
ἐκβάλλω^d: εὐθὺς τὸ πνεῦμα αὐτὸν ἐκβάλλει εἰς τὴν ἔρημον 'immediately, the Spirit led him out into the desert' Mk 1.12;³² ὅταν τὰ ἴδια πάντα ἐκβάλῃ 'when he has led all of his own people out' Jn 10.4.

15.175 κατάγω^a; καθιστάνω: to lead or to bring down – 'to bring down, to lead down.'
κατάγω^a: ἐπιγνόντες δὲ οἱ ἀδελφοὶ κατήγαγον αὐτὸν εἰς Καισάρειαν 'when the Christian brothers found out about this, they brought him down to Caesarea' Ac 9.30.
καθιστάνω: οἱ δὲ καθιστάνοντες τὸν Παῦλον ἤγαγον ἕως Ἀθηνῶν 'the men who were bringing Paul down went with him as far as Athens' Ac 17.15.

15.176 ἀνάγω^a; ἀναφέρω^a: to bring or lead up – 'to bring up, to lead up.'
ἀνάγω^a: ὃν παραγενόμενον ἀνήγαγον εἰς τὸ ὑπερῷον 'when he arrived, they led him up to the upstairs room' Ac 9.39; βουλόμενος μετὰ τὸ πάσχα ἀναγαγεῖν αὐτὸν τῷ λαῷ 'planning to bring him up for a public trial after the Passover' Ac 12.4.³³
ἀναφέρω^a: ἀναφέρει αὐτοὺς εἰς ὄρος ὑψηλὸν κατ' ἰδίαν μόνους 'he led them up a high mountain alone' Mk 9.2.

15.177 ἀπάγω^a; ἀπολαμβάνω^c; ἀποφέρω^b; ἀπαίρω: to lead or take away from a particular point – 'to lead off, to lead away, to take away, to take aside.'
ἀπάγω^a: ἕκαστος ὑμῶν τῷ σαββάτῳ οὐ λύει τὸν βοῦν αὐτοῦ ἢ τὸν ὄνον ἀπὸ τῆς φάτνης καὶ ἀπαγαγὼν ποτίζει 'anyone of you would untie his ox or his donkey from the stall and lead it off to give it water on the Sabbath' Lk 13.15; κρατήσατε αὐτὸν καὶ ἀπάγετε ἀσφαλῶς 'arrest him and take him away under guard' Mk 14.44; ἀπήγαγον αὐτὸν εἰς τὸ σταυρῶσαι 'they led him off to nail him to the cross' Mt 27.31.³⁴
ἀπολαμβάνω^c: ἀπολαβόμενος αὐτὸν ἀπὸ τοῦ ὄχλου κατ' ἰδίαν 'he took the man off by himself, away from the crowd' Mk 7.33.
ἀποφέρω^b: δήσαντες τὸν Ἰησοῦν ἀπήνεγκαν 'they put Jesus in chains and took him away' Mk 15.1.
ἀπαίρω: ἐλεύσονται δὲ ἡμέραι ὅταν ἀπαρθῇ ἀπ'

---

32 It would be possible to understand ἐκβάλλω in Mk 1.12 as meaning 'to force out' (see 15.44) and thus to translate 'the Spirit forced him out into the desert,' but this meaning does not apply to Jn 10.4, where the meaning of 'to lead' would be the appropriate rendering.

33 One may assume from the use of ἀνάγω in Ac 12.4 that the prison was probably an underground prison, and Peter would then be led up to a courtroom which would be higher than the prison.

34 ἀπάγω^a is frequently used in contexts referring to persons being led off to trial or to execution, but there seems to be no reason for setting up a separate meaning.

αὐτῶν ὁ νυμφίος 'the time will come when the bridegroom will be taken away from them' Mt 9.15.[35]

15.178 σύρω[b]; ἕλκω[b]: to drag or pull by physical force, often implying resistance – 'to drag, to lead by force.'

σύρω[b]: ἔσυρον Ἰάσονα καί τινας ἀδελφοὺς ἐπὶ τοὺς πολιτάρχας 'they dragged Jason and some other fellow believers to the city authorities' Ac 17.6.

ἕλκω[b]: ἐπιλαβόμενοι τὸν Παῦλον καὶ τὸν Σιλᾶν εἵλκυσαν εἰς τὴν ἀγορὰν ἐπὶ τοὺς ἄρχοντας 'they grabbed Paul and Silas and dragged them to the authorities in the public square' Ac 16.19.

15.179 κατασύρω: to drag or lead, with emphasis upon forceful and thorough action – 'to drag off forcefully, to lead away.' μήποτε κατασύρῃ σε πρὸς τὸν κριτήν 'so he won't drag you before the judge' Lk 12.58.

15.180 παραλαμβάνω[b]; προσλαμβάνομαι[c]: to take or lead off to oneself – 'to lead aside, to take aside.'

παραλαμβάνω[b]: παρέλαβεν τοὺς δώδεκα μαθητὰς κατ' ἰδίαν 'he took the twelve disciples aside privately' Mt 20.17.

προσλαμβάνομαι[c]: προσλαβόμενος ὁ Πέτρος αὐτὸν ἤρξατο ἐπιτιμᾶν αὐτῷ 'Peter took him aside and began to rebuke him' Mk 8.32.

15.181 προέρχομαι[d]; προπορεύομαι[b]: to go in front of, in order to show the way – 'to lead, to show the way to.'

προέρχομαι[d]: ὁ λεγόμενος Ἰούδας εἷς τῶν δώδεκα προήρχετο αὐτούς 'Judas, one of the twelve (disciples), was leading them' Lk 22.47.

προπορεύομαι[b]: ποίησον ἡμῖν θεοὺς οἳ προπορεύσονται ἡμῶν 'make us some gods who will go in front to lead us' Ac 7.40.

15.182 ὁδηγέω[a]: to guide or to direct, with the implication of making certain that people reach an appropriate destination – 'to lead, to guide.' τυφλὸς δὲ τυφλὸν ἐὰν ὁδηγῇ, ἀμφότεροι εἰς βόθυνον πεσοῦνται 'if one who is blind tries to guide another who is blind, they will both fall into a ditch' Mt 15.14; ὁδηγήσει αὐτοὺς ἐπὶ ζωῆς πηγὰς ὑδάτων 'he shall lead them to living springs of water' Re 7.17.

15.183 ὁδηγός[a], οῦ m: (derivative of ὁδηγέω[a] 'to guide,' 15.182) one who guides – 'guide, leader.' περὶ Ἰούδα τοῦ γενομένου ὁδηγοῦ τοῖς συλλαβοῦσιν Ἰησοῦν 'concerning Judas who became the guide for those who arrested Jesus' Ac 1.16.

15.184 χειραγωγέω: to lead or guide by taking by the hand – 'to lead someone by the hand, to take by the hand.' χειραγωγοῦντες δὲ αὐτὸν εἰσήγαγον εἰς Δαμασκόν 'they led him by the hand and took him into Damascus' Ac 9.8.

15.185 χειραγωγός, οῦ m: (derivative of χειραγωγέω 'to lead by the hand,' 15.184) a person who leads another by the hand – 'a guide, one who leads by the hand.' περιάγων ἐζήτει χειραγωγούς 'he went around seeking for people to lead him by the hand' Ac 13.11.

15.186 μετάγω: to cause to move from one place to another by bringing or leading – 'to direct, to steer, to guide.' εἰ δὲ τῶν ἵππων τοὺς χαλινοὺς εἰς τὰ στόματα βάλλομεν εἰς τὸ πείθεσθαι αὐτοὺς ἡμῖν, καὶ ὅλον τὸ σῶμα αὐτῶν μετάγομεν 'if we put bits into the mouths of horses in order to make them obey us, we can guide them' (literally 'their whole body') Jas 3.3; μετάγεται ὑπὸ ἐλαχίστου πηδαλίου '(the ship) can be steered by means of a very small rudder' Jas 3.4.

X Carry, Bear[36] (15.187-15.211)

15.187 φέρω[a]: to bear or carry something from one place to another – 'to carry, to bear, to take along.' ἐπέθηκαν αὐτῷ τὸν σταυρὸν φέρειν ὄπισθεν τοῦ Ἰησοῦ 'they put the cross on

---

35 There may be an implication of force in ἀπαίρω in some contexts, but this is not a distinctive feature of ἀπαίρω.

36 In Subdomain X *Carry, Bear* both types of participants are in motion and one is carrying or bearing the other. The agent participant is normally an animate being, while the affected participant is an inanimate object or an animate being.

him and made him carry it behind Jesus' Lk
23.26; ἔφερον τὰς τιμὰς τῶν πιπρασκομένων
'they would bring the money from the sale'
Ac 4.34.

15.188 βαστάζω[a]: to bear or carry a relatively heavy or burdensome object – 'to carry, to
bear.' ἀπαντήσει ὑμῖν ἄνθρωπος κεράμιον ὕδατος
βαστάζων 'a man carrying a water jar will
meet you' Mk 14.13.

15.189 σφραγίζω[d]: (a figurative extension of
meaning of σφραγίζω[a] 'to seal,' 6.55) to deliver
something safely to a destination – 'to take
safely to, to deliver safely.' σφραγισάμενος
αὐτοῖς τὸν καρπὸν τοῦτον 'having delivered to
them what has been raised' (literally '. . . this
harvest,' used figuratively) Ro 15.28. It is also
possible that σφραγισάμενος in Ro 15.28 serves
to confirm the significance of the collection
which has been raised. For a somewhat different interpretation of σφραγίζω in Ro 15.28,
see 57.87.

15.190 περιφέρω: to carry around from one
place to another – 'to carry around, to carry
about.' ἤρξαντο ἐπὶ τοῖς κραβάττοις τοὺς κακῶς
ἔχοντας περιφέρειν ὅπου ἤκουον ὅτι ἐστίν 'they
began to carry the sick about on mats to
wherever they heard he was' Mk 6.55.
περιφέρω may also be used in figurative contexts, as in 2 Cor 4.10, πάντοτε τὴν νέκρωσιν
τοῦ Ἰησοῦ ἐν τῷ σώματι περιφέροντες 'we
always carry around in our body the death of
Jesus.'

15.191 κομίζω[a]: to carry or bring something
to someone, usually implying a transfer – 'to
carry to, to bring (to).' κομίσασα ἀλάβαστρον
μύρου 'she brought an alabaster jar of perfume' Lk 7.37.

15.192 προσφέρω[a]: to carry or bring something into the presence of someone, usually
implying a transfer of something to that person – 'to carry to, to bring (to).' οἱ δὲ προσήνεγκαν αὐτῷ δηνάριον 'they brought him a
coin' Mt 22.19.

15.193 πέμπω[b]: to cause someone to carry
something to some destination – 'to send

something, to send by someone.' τῶν δὲ
μαθητῶν καθὼς εὐπορεῖτό τις ὥρισαν ἕκαστος
αὐτῶν εἰς διακονίαν πέμψαι τοῖς κατοικοῦσιν ἐν
τῇ Ἰουδαίᾳ ἀδελφοῖς 'the disciples decided that
each of them would send as much as he could
to help their Christian brothers who lived in
Judea' Ac 11.29.[37]

15.194 εἰσφέρω; εἰσάγω[b]: to carry or bring
something into an area or structure – 'to bring
in, to carry in.'
εἰσφέρω: ὧν γὰρ εἰσφέρεται ζῴων τὸ αἷμα περὶ
ἁμαρτίας εἰς τὰ ἅγια διὰ τοῦ ἀρχιερέως 'the
Jewish high priest brings the blood of the
animals into the Most Holy Place to offer it as
a sacrifice for sins' He 13.11.
εἰσάγω[b]: εἰσήγαγον διαδεξάμενοι οἱ πατέρες
ἡμῶν μετὰ Ἰησοῦ 'having received (the tabernacle), our fathers under Joshua brought it in
(with them)' Ac 7.45.

15.195 στρέφω[c]: to carry something back to
a point where it had been formerly – 'to bring
back, to carry back to, to take back to.'
μεταμεληθεὶς ἔστρεψεν τὰ τριάκοντα ἀργύρια
τοῖς ἀρχιερεῦσιν καὶ πρεσβυτέροις 'he repented
and took back the thirty silver coins to the
chief priests and the elders' Mt 27.3. It is also
possible to interpret στρέφω in Mt 27.3 as
'pay back' or 'giving back money' (see
57.157).

15.196 διαφέρω[a]: to carry or take something
through an area or structure – 'to carry
through, to take through.' οὐχ ἤφιεν ἵνα τις
διενέγκῃ σκεῦος διὰ τοῦ ἱεροῦ 'he didn't permit
anyone to carry anything through the temple
courts' Mk 11.16.

15.197 ἐκφέρω[a]: to carry something out of a
structure or area – 'to carry out, to take out, to
bring out.' ταχὺ ἐξενέγκατε στολὴν τὴν πρώτην
καὶ ἐνδύσατε αὐτόν 'quickly, bring the best
robe out and put it on him' Lk 15.22.

15.198 ἐκκομίζω: to carry or bring out,
especially of a corpse for burial –'to carry out
for burial.' ἐξεκομίζετο τεθνηκὼς μονογενὴς

37 The participant who actually carries the substance
in question may be merely implicit.

υἱὸς τῇ μητρὶ αὐτοῦ, καὶ αὐτὴ ἦν χήρα 'a dead person was being carried out who was the only son of his mother, who was also a widow' Lk 7.12.

15.199 καθαιρέω^b: to bring something down from one point to another – 'to bring down, to take down.' ἴδωμεν εἰ ἔρχεται ᾿Ηλίας καθελεῖν αὐτόν 'let us see if Elijah will come and take him down' Mk 15.36. For another interpretation of καθαιρέω in Mk 15.36, see 15.110.

15.200 συστέλλω^b: to remove from a place by taking away or carrying away – 'to remove, to take away.' ἀναστάντες δὲ οἱ νεώτεροι συνέστειλαν αὐτὸν καὶ ἐξενέγκαντες ἔθαψαν 'the young men came in and taking him away they carried him out for burial' Ac 5.6. In Ac 5.6 συστέλλω may also be interpreted as meaning 'to wrap up' (see 79.119).

15.201 βαστάζω^b: to carry away from a place, with the probable implication of something that is relatively heavy – 'to remove, to carry away, to take away.' κύριε, εἰ σὺ ἐβάστασας αὐτόν, εἰπέ μοι ποῦ ἔθηκας αὐτόν 'sir, if you have carried him away, tell me where you placed him' Jn 20.15.

15.202 ἀποφέρω^a: to carry something away from a point – 'to carry away, to take away.' καὶ ἐπὶ τοὺς ἀσθενοῦντας ἀποφέρεσθαι ἀπὸ τοῦ χρωτὸς αὐτοῦ σουδάρια ἢ σιμικίνθια 'even handkerchiefs and aprons he had used were taken away to the sick' Ac 19.12.

15.203 αἴρω^a; **ἀναλαμβάνω**^a: to lift up and carry (away) – 'to carry (away), to carry off, to remove, to take (away).'
αἴρω^a: οἱ μαθηταὶ αὐτοῦ ἦλθον καὶ ἦραν τὸ πτῶμα αὐτοῦ καὶ ἔθηκαν αὐτὸ ἐν μνημείῳ 'his disciples came, took his body, and placed it in a tomb' Mk 6.29; ἄρατε ταῦτα ἐντεῦθεν 'take these away from here' Jn 2.16; οὐκ ἔγνωσαν ἕως ἦλθεν ὁ κατακλυσμὸς καὶ ἦρεν ἅπαντας 'yet they didn't know what was happening until the flood came and carried them all away' Mt 24.39.
ἀναλαμβάνω^a: ἀνελάβετε τὴν σκηνὴν τοῦ Μόλοχ 'it was the tent of the god Moloch that you carried' Ac 7.43.

15.204 περιαιρέω^a: to remove something which is around something else – 'to take from around, to remove.' τὰς ἀγκύρας περιελόντες 'removing the anchors' Ac 27.40; περιαιρεῖται τὸ κάλυμμα 'the veil is removed' 2 Cor 3.16.

15.205 ποταμοφόρητος, ον: pertaining to being carried away by river or flood –'carried off by a flood.' ἵνα αὐτὴν ποταμοφόρητον ποιήσῃ 'so that he might cause her to be carried away by a flood of water' Re 12.15.

15.206 ἀναφέρω^b: to be carried or borne upward – 'to carry up.' καὶ ἀνεφέρετο εἰς τὸν οὐρανόν 'and he was carried up into heaven' Lk 24.51.

15.207 φορτίζω: to cause to carry or bear a load – 'to cause to carry, to cause to bear a load.' φορτίζετε τοὺς ἀνθρώπους φορτία δυσβάστακτα 'you make men carry heavy loads' Lk 11.46.³⁸

15.208 φορτίον, ου n (derivative of φορτίζω 'to cause to carry a load,' 15.207); **γόμος, ου** m (derivative of γέμω 'to be laden,' not occurring in the NT): a relatively heavy object which is carried – 'load, burden, cargo (as of a ship).'
φορτίον: μετὰ ὕβρεως καὶ πολλῆς ζημίας οὐ μόνον τοῦ φορτίου καὶ τοῦ πλοίου ἀλλὰ καὶ τῶν ψυχῶν ἡμῶν 'there will be great damage to the cargo and to the ship and loss of life as well' Ac 27.10.
γόμος: ἐκεῖσε γὰρ τὸ πλοῖον ἦν ἀποφορτιζόμενον τὸν γόμον 'for there the ship was to unload the cargo' Ac 21.3.

15.209 ἀποφορτίζομαι: to cause a load to be carried off – 'to unload, to discharge cargo.' ἐκεῖσε γὰρ τὸ πλοῖον ἦν ἀποφορτιζόμενον τὸν γόμον 'for there the ship was to unload the cargo' Ac 21.3.

15.210 ἄγω^b: to carry or bring, especially animate beings – 'to carry, to bring.' ἅπαντες ὅσοι εἶχον ἀσθενοῦντας νόσοις ποικίλαις ἤγαγον αὐτοὺς πρὸς αὐτόν 'all who had friends who

---

38 In the NT, φορτίζω occurs only in figurative contexts.

were sick with various diseases brought them to him' Lk 4.40.[39]

15.211 ἀνάγω[b]: to bring an offering to – 'to offer to, to present to.' καὶ ἀνήγαγον θυσίαν τῷ εἰδώλῳ 'and they presented a sacrifice to the idol' Ac 7.41.[40]

Y Pull, Draw, Drag[41] **(15.212-15.214)**

15.212 σύρω[a]; ἕλκω[a]; σπάομαι: to pull or drag, requiring force because of the inertia of the object being dragged – 'to pull, to drag, to draw.'

σύρω[a]: λιθάσαντες τὸν Παῦλον ἔσυρον ἔξω τῆς πόλεως 'they stoned Paul and dragged him out of town' Ac 14.19; ἡ οὐρὰ αὐτοῦ σύρει τὸ τρίτον τῶν ἀστέρων τοῦ οὐρανοῦ 'with his tail he dragged a third of the stars out of the sky' Re 12.4; σύροντες τὸ δίκτυον τῶν ἰχθύων 'they pulled the net full of fish' Jn 21.8.

ἕλκω[a]: οὐκέτι αὐτὸ ἑλκύσαι ἴσχυον 'they could not pull the net back in' Jn 21.6; Σίμων οὖν Πέτρος ἔχων μάχαιραν εἵλκυσεν αὐτήν 'Simon Peter had a sword and drew it' Jn 18.10.

σπάομαι: εἷς δέ τις τῶν παρεστηκότων σπασάμενος τὴν μάχαιραν 'one of those standing by drew a sword' Mk 14.47.

15.213 ἀνασπάω; ἀναβιβάζω: to pull or draw something in an upward direction – 'to pull up, to draw up.'

ἀνασπάω: οὐκ εὐθέως ἀνασπάσει αὐτὸν ἐν ἡμέρᾳ τοῦ σαββάτου; 'would you not immediately pull him up (out of the well) on the Sabbath

itself?' Lk 14.5; ἀνεσπάσθη πάλιν ἅπαντα εἰς τὸν οὐρανόν 'finally the whole thing was drawn back up into heaven' Ac 11.10.

ἀναβιβάζω: ἣν ὅτε ἐπληρώθη ἀναβιβάσαντες ἐπὶ τὸν αἰγιαλόν 'when it was full, they pulled it up onto the shore' Mt 13.48.

In a number of languages clear distinctions are made on the basis of the means by which something is pulled or drawn. For example, to pull something by means of a rope may be entirely different from a term indicating that the object itself has been seized and is being drawn or dragged.

15.214 ἀποσπάω[a]: to pull or draw away from or out of – 'to pull out, to draw out, to drag.' εἷς τῶν μετὰ Ἰησοῦ . . . ἀπέσπασεν τὴν μάχαιραν αὐτοῦ 'one of those who were with Jesus . . . drew his sword' Mt 26.51.

Z Throw, Hurl[42] **(15.215-15.221)**

15.215 βάλλω[a] – 'to throw.' ἔκκοψον αὐτὴν καὶ βάλε ἀπὸ σοῦ 'cut it off and throw it from you' Mt 5.30.

15.216 βολή, ῆς f: (derivative of βάλλω[a] 'to throw,' 15.215) the distance which one would normally throw some object – 'a (stone's) throw, the distance one might throw.' αὐτὸς ἀπεσπάσθη ἀπ' αὐτῶν ὡσεὶ λίθου βολήν 'he withdrew from them about a stone's throw' or '. . . about the distance that a person might throw a stone' Lk 22.41.

15.217 ῥίπτω[a]: to throw with considerable force – 'to throw, to hurl.' τὴν σκευὴν τοῦ πλοίου ἔρριψαν 'they threw out the tackle of the ship' Ac 27.19.

15.218 ἐπιβάλλω[a]: to throw something on – 'to throw on.'[43] ἐπιβάλλουσιν αὐτῷ τὰ ἱμάτια

---

[39] ἄγω[b], in speaking of the relationship of persons to one another, normally means 'to bring' or 'to lead,' with the implication that the individual who is brought is able to walk or move on his own power, but in some contexts ἄγω[b] indicates that the person is actually carried, and thus ἄγω[b] parallels the use of φέρω[a] (15.187) or φορτίζω (15.207) in the sense of to carry or bring an object.

[40] Though the Greek term ἀνάγω means literally 'to lead up' (see 15.176), it is not necessary in translating to always introduce the element of height or to translate it by some expression meaning 'up.' In ancient temples the idol or god was often on an elevated platform, and so one can readily understand how a term meaning 'to bring up' or 'to carry up' could readily acquire the meaning of 'to carry up to' or 'to present to.'

[41] This subdomain involves the movement of passive objects.

[42] Subdomain Z *Throw, Hurl* involves actions in which an agent causes something to move through space by means of an initial force.

[43] The meanings of ἐπιβάλλω[a] (15.218) and ἐπιρίπτω (15.219) parallel to a certain extent the distinction in βάλλω[a] (15.215) and ῥίπτω[a] (15.217) in that βάλλω[a] suggests a more deliberate action, while ῥίπτω[a] suggests an action characterized by being quicker, more energetic, and often somewhat more impetuous.

αὐτῶν 'they throw their garments on it' Mk 11.7.

15.219 ἐπιρίπτω: to throw or hurl something upon something else – 'to throw on, to hurl on.'[43] ἐπιρίψαντες αὐτῶν τὰ ἱμάτια ἐπὶ τὸν πῶλον 'they threw their garments on the donkey' Lk 19.35.

15.220 ἐκβάλλω[a]; ἐκβολή, ῆς f: to throw out of an area or object – 'to throw out, to jettison (from a boat).'
ἐκβάλλω[a]: αὐτὸν ἐξέβαλον ἔξω τοῦ ἀμπελῶνος 'they threw him out of the vineyard' Mt 21.39. It may be that ἐκβάλλω in Mt 21.39 is a type of hyperbole for causing to go out, but at the same time it is possible that the term ἐκβάλλω is to be understood in a literal sense.
ἐκβολή: τῇ ἑξῆς ἐκβολὴν ἐποιοῦντο 'on the next day, they threw out the cargo (of the boat)' Ac 27.18.

15.221 κατακρημνίζω: to throw someone or something down a cliff – 'to throw down a cliff.' ὥστε κατακρημνίσαι αὐτόν 'in order to throw him down a cliff' Lk 4.29.

A' Movement with Speed (15.222)

15.222 ὁρμάω: a fast movement from one place to another – 'to rush, to run.' ὥρμησεν ἡ ἀγέλη κατὰ τοῦ κρημνοῦ εἰς τὴν λίμνην 'the herd rushed down the side of the cliff into the lake' Lk 8.33.

B' Goal-Oriented Movement (15.223)

15.223 διώκω[b]: to move quickly and energetically toward some objective – 'to hasten, to run, to press forward, to press on.' κατὰ σκοπὸν διώκω εἰς τὸ βραβεῖον 'so I run straight toward the goal in order to win the prize' Php 3.14. In Php 3.14 διώκω is to be understood in a literal sense, though the entire context is figurative. For interpreting the expression κατὰ σκοπὸν διώκω as an idiom, see 89.56.

C' Walk, Step (15.224-15.229)

15.224 πεζεύω: to travel by foot – 'to go by foot, to go by land.' οὕτως γὰρ διατεταγμένος

ἦν μέλλων αὐτὸς πεζεύειν 'he told us to do this, because he was going there by land' Ac 20.13.[44]

15.225 ἐμβαίνω[b]: to step into some area – 'to go into, to step into.' ὁ οὖν πρῶτος ἐμβὰς μετὰ τὴν ταραχὴν τοῦ ὕδατος ὑγιὴς ἐγίνετο 'the first one to go into (the pool) after the water was stirred up was healed' Jn 5.4 (apparatus).

15.226 πατέω[a]: to step on something – 'to step on, to tread on.' δέδωκα ὑμῖν τὴν ἐξουσίαν τοῦ πατεῖν ἐπάνω ὄφεων καὶ σκορπίων 'I have given you authority, so that you can step on snakes and scorpions' Lk 10.19. It is possible to interpret πατέω in Lk 10.19 as meaning 'to trample,' with emphasis upon the impact of the feet upon the snakes (see 19.51). It is important in rendering Lk 10.19 not to give the impression that someone is to merely walk on a mass of snakes; this is simply a matter of accidentally stepping on a poisonous snake or scorpion.

15.227 περιπατέω[a]: to walk along or around – 'to walk, to go.' περιπατῶν δὲ παρὰ τὴν θάλασσαν τῆς Γαλιλαίας 'as he walked by Lake Galilee' Mt 4.18.

15.228 προσκόπτω[b]: to strike one's foot against something as one walks and in this way to lose one's balance temporarily – 'to stumble.' ἐάν τις περιπατῇ ἐν τῇ ἡμέρᾳ, οὐ προσκόπτει 'so if a man walks in broad daylight, he does not stumble' Jn 11.9.

15.229 πρόσκομμα[a], τος n: that which causes someone to stumble – 'stumbling stone.' προσέκοψαν τῷ λίθῳ τοῦ προσκόμματος 'they stumbled on the stone which caused stumbling' Ro 9.32.

D' Run (15.230-15.237)

15.230 τρέχω[a]: to run, with emphasis upon relative speed in contrast with walking – 'to run, to rush.' δραμὼν ἐπέπεσεν ἐπὶ τὸν τράχηλον αὐτοῦ καὶ κατεφίλησεν αὐτόν 'he ran and

---

44 It is possible that πεζεύω in Ac 20.13 can mean merely 'to travel by land' and not necessarily by foot.

threw his arms around him and kissed him' Lk 15.20; ἡ φωνὴ τῶν πτερύγων αὐτῶν ὡς φωνὴ ἁρμάτων ἵππων πολλῶν τρεχόντων εἰς πόλεμον 'the sound made by their wings was like the noise of many horses drawing chariots running into war' Re 9.9.

τρέχω[a] also occurs in figurative contexts: δι' ὑπομονῆς τρέχωμεν τὸν προκείμενον ἡμῖν ἀγῶνα 'let us run with determination the race that is before us' He 12.1.

15.231 περιτρέχω: to run or go hurriedly about – 'to run about.' περιέδραμον ὅλην τὴν χώραν ἐκείνην 'they ran throughout the whole region' Mk 6.55.

15.232 εἰστρέχω – 'to run in, to run into.' εἰσδραμοῦσα δὲ ἀπήγγειλεν ἑστάναι τὸν Πέτρον πρὸ τοῦ πυλῶνος 'she ran back in and told them that Peter was standing at the gate' Ac 12.14.

15.233 κατατρέχω – 'to run down to.' ὃς ἐξαυτῆς παραλαβὼν στρατιώτας καὶ ἑκατοντάρχας κατέδραμεν ἐπ' αὐτούς 'at once he took some officers and soldiers and ran down to them' Ac 21.32.

15.234 προστρέχω: to run into the presence of someone – 'to run up to, to run into the presence of.' προστρέχοντες ἠσπάζοντο αὐτόν 'they ran up to him and greeted him' Mk 9.15.

15.235 προτρέχω: to run ahead of someone else, with the implication of arriving at a destination sooner – 'to run in front of, to run ahead of.' προδραμὼν εἰς τὸ ἔμπροσθεν 'so he ran ahead to the front of (the crowd)' Lk 19.4; ὁ ἄλλος μαθητὴς προέδραμεν τάχιον τοῦ Πέτρου καὶ ἦλθεν πρῶτος εἰς τὸ μνημεῖον 'the other disciple ran faster than Peter and reached the tomb first' Jn 20.4.

15.236 ἐκπηδάω: to run or rush out quickly – 'to run out, to rush out.' διαρρήξαντες τὰ ἱμάτια αὐτῶν ἐξεπήδησαν εἰς τὸν ὄχλον 'they tore their clothes and rushed out into the middle of the crowd' Ac 14.14.

15.237 εἰσπηδάω: to run or rush quickly in-to – 'to run into, to rush into.' αἰτήσας δὲ φῶτα εἰσεπήδησεν 'and he called for a light and rushed in' Ac 16.29.

E' Jump, Leap (15.238-15.243)

15.238 ἅλλομαι[a]: to leap or to jump into the air – 'to leap, to jump.' εἰσῆλθεν σὺν αὐτοῖς εἰς τὸ ἱερὸν περιπατῶν καὶ ἁλλόμενος καὶ αἰνῶν τὸν θεόν 'then he went into the Temple with them, walking and jumping and praising God' Ac 3.8.

15.239 ἐφάλλομαι: to leap or jump onto a place or object – 'to jump on, to leap upon.' ἐφαλόμενος ὁ ἄνθρωπος ἐπ' αὐτούς 'the man jumped on them' Ac 19.16.

15.240 ἐξάλλομαι: to leap up to a standing position – 'to jump up, to leap up.' ἐξαλλόμενος ἔστη ·καὶ περιεπάτει 'he jumped up, stood on his feet, and started walking around' Ac 3.8. It is possible that in Ac 3.8 the paralyzed man actually jumped up from the ground, but it is more likely that the reference is to the rapidity with which he got onto his feet.

15.241 ἀναπηδάω: to leap or spring up, presumably from a seated position – 'to leap up, to jump up.' ἀναπηδήσας ἦλθεν πρὸς τὸν Ἰησοῦν 'he jumped up and came to Jesus' Mk 10.50.

15.242 ἀπορίπτω: to throw oneself off from some object (as from a ship) – 'to jump off, to leap overboard.' ἐκέλευσέν τε τοὺς δυναμένους κολυμβᾶν ἀπορίψαντας 'he ordered those who could swim to jump overboard' Ac 27.43.

15.243 σκιρτάω[a]: to leap or jump, as a possible expression of joy and happiness – 'to jump for joy, to leap for joy' (for a difference of semantic focus, see 25.134). χάρητε ἐν ἐκείνῃ τῇ ἡμέρᾳ καὶ σκιρτήσατε 'be glad when that happens (literally '. . . on that day') and jump for joy' Lk 6.23. In Lk 1.41 σκιρτάω may be regarded as an instance of figurative usage: ἐσκίρτησεν τὸ βρέφος ἐν τῇ κοιλίᾳ αὐτῆς 'the baby leaped for joy in her womb.'

Though it may seem quite natural to speak

of 'leaping for joy,' in some cultures this would not be a meaningful combination of words, for leaping might suggest anger, ritual exorcism (driving out demons), or preparation for war. It may, therefore, be necessary in some languages to translate 'jump for joy' merely as 'be exceedingly glad.' It may be particularly awkward to speak of a fetus jumping in the womb, for obviously it would simply be a rapid movement of the limbs and not actual change of location. Therefore, it may be better to translate in some instances 'moved quickly to show joy' or '. . . as a sign of happiness.'

F' Dance (15.244)

15.244 ὀρχέομαι; χορός, οῦ *m*: patterned rhythmic movements of the whole and/or parts of the body, normally to the accompaniment of music – 'to dance, dancing.'
ὀρχέομαι: ηὐλήσαμεν ὑμῖν καὶ οὐκ ὠρχήσασθε 'we played the flute for you, but you would not dance' Mt 11.17.
χορός: ἤκουσεν συμφωνίας καὶ χορῶν 'he heard music and dancing' Lk 15.25.
In a number of languages there are highly specific terms for various types of dancing, and one must make certain that the appropriate expression is used. Some terms for dancing may refer only to erotic dances; others, to highly ritualized performances in drama or religious practice; and still others may refer to personal expressions of happiness, joy, or grief. Special care must be exercised in selecting a term which will fit the context.

G' Fly (15.245)

15.245 πέτομαι: movement of an object through the air by means of wings – 'to fly.'
ἤκουσα ἑνὸς ἀετοῦ πετομένου ἐν μεσουρανήματι

'I heard an eagle that was flying high in the air' Re 8.13.
In some languages a clear distinction is made in verbs meaning 'to fly' depending on whether it is a bird or an insect.

H' Swim (15.246-15.247)

15.246 κολυμβάω: movement through water by the use of limbs – 'to swim.' ἐκέλευσέν τε τοὺς δυναμένους κολυμβᾶν ἀπορίψαντας 'he ordered those who could swim to jump overboard' Ac 27.43. A number of languages have several different terms for 'swim' depending on whether it is a person, an animal, a fish, or an eel (or a snake). Care must be exercised in choosing the appropriate term for this context.

15.247 ἐκκολυμβάω: to swim out of or away from a structure or area – 'to swim away, to swim from.' μή τις ἐκκολυμβήσας διαφύγῃ 'so that none would swim away and escape' Ac 27.42.

I' Roll (15.248-15.249)

15.248 ἀποκυλίω: to cause to roll away from a particular point – 'to cause to roll away, to roll away.' ἀπεκύλισεν τὸν λίθον καὶ ἐκάθητο ἐπάνω αὐτοῦ 'he rolled the stone away, and sat on it' Mt 28.2.

15.249 προσκυλίω: to cause something to roll up to or against – 'to roll up to, to roll against.' προσεκύλισεν λίθον ἐπὶ τὴν θύραν τοῦ μνημείου 'then he rolled a stone against the entrance to the grave' Mk 15.46.
In some languages it may be necessary to distinguish in verbs for 'roll' whether the object in question is ball-shaped or disc-shaped. The stone at the tomb is more likely to have been disc-shaped.

16 Non-Linear Movement[1]

16.1 κίνησις, εως *f*: the motion of a solid or mass, without indication of movement in space – 'to be in motion, to move, movement.' ἐκδεχομένων τὴν τοῦ ὕδατος κίνησιν 'waiting for the water to move' Jn 5.3 (apparatus). In a number of languages it may be necessary to indicate clearly the kind of motion which would be implied in Jn 5.3. Perhaps the most satisfactory rendering would involve the kind of motion resulting from the bubbling up of water, but not with the implication of being caused by heat. It would be inappropriate to use a term meaning merely 'to shake,' since this might suggest an earthquake.

16.2 κινέωᶜ: to set something in motion, with the nature of the movement dependent upon the object in question – 'to shake (as of the head).' οἱ παραπορευόμενοι ἐβλασφήμουν αὐτὸν κινοῦντες τὰς κεφαλὰς αὐτῶν 'people passing by shook their heads and hurled insults at him' Mk 15.29. In Mk 15.29 the shaking of the head signifies derision and scorn, but in some languages this meaning is expressed by quite different gestures, for example, pointing with the finger, throwing back the head, or shrugging the shoulders. In fact, in some languages shaking the head from side to side means assent, while nodding shows opposition.

16.3 ταράσσωᵃ: to cause movement, usually as the result of shaking or stirring – 'to cause to move, to stir up.' ἄγγελος γὰρ κυρίου κατὰ καιρὸν κατέβαινεν ἐν τῇ κολυμβήθρᾳ καὶ ἐταράσσετο τὸ ὕδωρ 'from time to time an angel of the Lord would come down in the pool and cause the water to move' Jn 5.4 (apparatus).

16.4 ταραχήᵃ, **ῆς** *f*: the motion resulting from a mass being stirred up or shaken – 'movement, motion.' ὁ οὖν πρῶτος ἐμβὰς μετὰ τὴν ταραχὴν τοῦ ὕδατος ὑγιὴς ἐγίνετο 'the first person to go into (the pool) after the water had been moved was healed' Jn 5.4 (apparatus).

16.5 ῥιπή, ῆς *f*: a rapid motion, especially of the eye – 'blinking.' ἐν ῥιπῇ ὀφθαλμοῦ, ἐν τῇ ἐσχάτῃ σάλπιγγι 'in the blinking of an eye, at the last trumpet sound' 1 Cor 15.52. For ῥιπή as part of an idiom, see 67.114.

16.6 τρέμωᵃ; **τρόμος, ου** *m*; **ἔντρομος**ᵃ, **ον**; **σείομαι**: to shake or tremble, often with the implication of fear and/or consternation – 'to tremble, trembling, to quiver, to shake.'
τρέμω ᵃ: ἰδοῦσα δὲ ἡ γυνὴ ὅτι οὐκ ἔλαθεν, τρέμουσα ἦλθεν 'and when the woman saw that she could not escape notice, she came trembling' Lk 8.47.
τρόμος: ἐν ἀσθενείᾳ καὶ ἐν φόβῳ καὶ ἐν τρόμῳ πολλῷ ἐγενόμην πρὸς ὑμᾶς 'I came to you in weakness and with fear and great trembling' 1 Cor 2.3.
ἔντρομος ᵃ: ἔντρομος δὲ γενόμενος Μωϋσῆς οὐκ ἐτόλμα κατανοῆσαι 'Moses trembled and dared not look' Ac 7.32.
σείομαι: ἀπὸ δὲ τοῦ φόβου αὐτοῦ ἐσείσθησαν οἱ τηροῦντες καὶ ἐγενήθησαν ὡς νεκροί 'the guards were so afraid that they trembled and became like dead men' Mt 28.4.

In a number of languages there are two distinct terms for trembling, one relating to illness (as in the case of epileptic seizures or the chills and fever associated with malaria) and the other associated with fear.

16.7 σείωᵃ; **σαλεύω**ᵃ: to cause something to move back and forth rapidly, often violently – 'to shake.'
σείω ᵃ: ἔτι ἅπαξ ἐγὼ σείσω οὐ μόνον τὴν γῆν ἀλλὰ καὶ τὸν οὐρανόν 'yet once more I will shake not only the earth but also the sky' He 12.26; ὡς συκῆ βάλλει τοὺς ὀλύνθους αὐτῆς ὑπὸ ἀνέμου μεγάλου σειομένη 'like unripe figs falling from the tree when it is shaken by a strong wind' Re 6.13.
σαλεύω ᵃ: οὗ ἡ φωνὴ τὴν γῆν ἐσάλευσεν τότε 'his voice shook the earth at that time' He 12.26; μέτρον καλὸν πεπιεσμένον σεσαλευμένον ὑπερεκχυννόμενον δώσουσιν 'they will give a full measure, pressed down, shaken together, and

---

1 The domain of *Non-Linear Movement* involves primarily non-linear motion of an object which for the most part remains in the same place, though there may be minor displacements in space in the case of κυλίομαι 'to roll about, to wallow' (16.17).

running over' Lk 6.38. It is possible to interpret σαλεύω in Mt 24.29 (αἱ δυνάμεις τῶν οὐρανῶν σαλευθήσονται 'the hosts of heaven will be shaken') as meaning literal shaking, but it may be used figuratively in the sense of deposing the hosts of heaven from their positions of power.

In some languages there are quite distinct terms for shaking, depending upon the vigor of the motion and/or the objects which are shaken. Accordingly, one must exercise care in selecting terms which will accurately and adequately represent the nature of the shaking in the various contexts. For example, in He 12.26 the shaking would presumably involve some kind of reverberation, but in Re 6.13 the action of the wind suggests whipping something back and forth.

16.8 ἀποτινάσσω; ἐκτινάσσω: to shake something out or off, in order to get rid of an object or a substance – 'to shake off, to shake out, to shake from.'
ἀποτινάσσω: ὁ μὲν οὖν ἀποτινάξας τὸ θηρίον εἰς τὸ πῦρ ἔπαθεν οὐδὲν κακόν 'but he shook the snake off into the fire without being harmed at all' Ac 28.5; ἐξερχόμενοι ἀπὸ τῆς πόλεως ἐκείνης τὸν κονιορτὸν ἀπὸ τῶν ποδῶν ὑμῶν ἀποτινάσσετε εἰς μαρτύριον ἐπ' αὐτούς 'leave that town and shake the dust off your feet as a warning to them' Lk 9.5.
ἐκτινάσσω: ἐκπορευόμενοι ἐκεῖθεν ἐκτινάξατε τὸν χοῦν τὸν ὑποκάτω τῶν ποδῶν ὑμῶν εἰς μαρτύριον αὐτοῖς 'leave that place and shake the dust off your feet as a witness against them' Mk 6.11; ἀντιτασσομένων δὲ αὐτῶν καὶ βλασφημούντων ἐκτιναξάμενος τὰ ἱμάτια 'when they opposed him and said evil things about him, he protested by shaking the dust from his clothes' Ac 18.6.
In a number of languages quite different terms for shaking will be required for the contexts of Ac 28.5 and Lk 9.5, since in the first instance it is an animate being which clings, and in the second instance it is simply a substance that adheres. In a number of languages, however, the symbolic meaning of 'shaking dust off one's feet' is not at all clear, so that it may be necessary to add a type of classifier to indicate that such an action symbolizes the breaking off of association. It is for

this reason that the expression ἐκτιναξάμενος τὰ ἱμάτια in Ac 18.6 is often translated as 'he protested by shaking the dust from his clothes.'

16.9 ἀπομάσσομαι: to wipe off, as a means of getting rid of some adhering substance – 'to wipe off, to wipe away.' καὶ τὸν κονιορτὸν τὸν κολληθέντα ἡμῖν ἐκ τῆς πόλεως ὑμῶν εἰς τοὺς πόδας ἀπομασσόμεθα ὑμῖν 'even the dust from your town which sticks to our feet we wipe off against you' Lk 10.11. Since the action of wiping off the dust from one's feet was a symbolic act of denunciation, it may be necessary in some languages to translate this expression in Lk 10.11 as 'we wipe off as a way of denouncing you' or 'we wipe off as a way of showing how bad you are.'

16.10 ῥίπτω^c: to wave or possibly to throw something into the air – 'to wave, to throw into the air.' ῥιπτούντων τὰ ἱμάτια 'waving (their) garments' or possibly 'throwing (their) garments into the air' Ac 22.23. This symbolic action of throwing garments into the air or waving them violently was a means of indicating strong protest by an angry mob. In a number of languages, however, such an expression would be interpreted as a sign of joyous agreement. One cannot change the nature of the event, but it may be essential to have some type of explanatory note to indicate the meaning of such an action.

16.11 ῥιπίζομαι: to be forcibly tossed back and forth – 'to be tossed about.'[2] ὁ γὰρ διακρινόμενος ἔοικεν κλύδωνι θαλάσσης ἀνεμιζομένῳ καὶ ῥιπιζομένῳ 'whoever doubts, is like a wave in the sea that is driven by the wind and tossed about' Jas 1.6.

16.12 κλυδωνίζομαι: to be tossed back and forth by the motion of waves – 'to be tossed about by waves.' ἵνα μηκέτι ὦμεν νήπιοι, κλυδωνιζόμενοι καὶ περιφερόμενοι παντὶ ἀνέμῳ τῆς διδασκαλίας 'then we shall no longer be

---

2 Though with ῥιπίζομαι there is some movement in space, there is no linear movement from one place to another, but only the back and forth movement which results in the object remaining more or less in the same place.

children tossed about by the waves and carried about by every wind of teaching' Eph
4.14. The imagery in Eph 4.14 is based upon
a person in a boat being tossed about by the
waves. It may, therefore, be necessary to
introduce a boat or ship in the context.

16.13 στρέφομαι^a; ἐπιστρέφομαι: to turn
around to or toward – 'to turn around, to turn
toward.'
στρέφομαι^a: ὁ δὲ Ἰησοῦς στραφεὶς καὶ ἰδὼν
αὐτήν 'Jesus turned and saw her' Mt 9.22.
ἐπιστρέφομαι: ἐπιστραφεὶς ἐν τῷ ὄχλῳ ἔλεγεν
'turning around in the crowd, he said' Mk
5.30.

16.14 στρέφω^a: to cause something to turn –
'to turn.' στρέφον αὐτῷ καὶ τὴν ἄλλην 'turn to
him the other (cheek)' Mt 5.39.

16.15 τροπή, ῆς f: the process of turning,
with the implication of variation and change
– 'turning, variation.' παρ' ᾧ οὐκ ἔνι παραλλαγὴ ἢ τροπῆς ἀποσκίασμα 'for whom there is
no change or shadow cast by turning' Jas
1.17. It is difficult to know precisely the significance of the phrase τροπῆς ἀποσκίασμα. It
probably had a technical sense which has been
lost, but clearly it is parallel in meaning to
παραλλαγή 'change, alteration' (58.44). In
some languages it may be best to translate this
expression in Jas 1.17 as 'in whom there is no
change or variation.'

16.16 κλίνω^a: to cause something to incline
– 'to bow down (the head), to incline.' κλίνας
τὴν κεφαλήν 'he bowed his head' Jn 19.30. See
also 23.83.

16.17 κυλίομαι; κυλισμός, οῦ m: the motion
of an object rolling back and forth or rolling
about – 'to roll about, to wallow.'[3]
κυλίομαι: πεσὼν ἐπὶ τῆς γῆς ἐκυλίετο ἀφρίζων
'he fell on the ground and rolled around,
foaming at the mouth' Mk 9.20.

---

[3] It is, of course, impossible for an object to roll without some movement in space; however, the focus here is
not upon the linear movement of an object from one
place to another by means of rolling, but simply the motion in and of itself, and any movement in space is irrelevant.

κυλισμός: ὗς λουσαμένη εἰς κυλισμὸν βορβόρου
'a pig that has been washed goes back to roll
about in the mud' 2 Pe 2.22.
    It is rare that one can use in a language the
same or related terms for the rolling of a person in an epileptic fit and the wallowing of a
pig in the mud. The first is chaotic and uncontrolled, while the second is both purposeful and slower.

16.18 ἀνατρέπω^a; καταστρέφω: to cause
something to be completely overturned – 'to
turn over, to upset, to overturn.'
ἀνατρέπω^a: καὶ τὰς τραπέζας ἀνέτρεψεν 'and he
overturned the tables' Jn 2.15.
καταστρέφω: καὶ τὰς τραπέζας τῶν κολλυβιστῶν
κατέστρεψεν 'and he overturned the tables of
the moneychangers' Mt 21.12.

16.19 ἐκτείνω; ἐκπετάννυμι: to cause an
object to extend in space (for example, by becoming straight, unfolded, or uncoiled) – 'to
stretch out, to extend, to reach out.'[4]
ἐκτείνω: ἐξέτεινεν, καὶ ἀπεκατεστάθη ἡ χεὶρ
αὐτοῦ 'he stretched his hand out and it became
well again' Mk 3.5; ὡς ἐκ πρῴρης ἀγκύρας
μελλόντων ἐκτείνειν 'as if they were extending
the anchors from the front of the ship' Ac
27.30.
ἐκπετάννυμι: ὅλην τὴν ἡμέραν ἐξεπέτασα τὰς
χεῖράς μου πρὸς λαὸν ἀπειθοῦντα καὶ ἀντιλέ-
γοντα 'I held out my hands the whole day long
to a disobedient and rebellious people' Ro
10.21.

16.20 ἐπεκτείνομαι^a: to reach out or stretch
out toward some goal – 'to reach out, to
stretch toward.' τὰ μὲν ὀπίσω ἐπιλανθανόμενος
τοῖς δὲ ἔμπροσθεν ἐπεκτεινόμενος 'to forget
what is behind me and to reach out to what is
ahead' Php 3.13. In Php 3.13 ἐπεκτείνομαι is

---

[4] With ἐκτείνω and ἐκπετάννυμι there is a type of
movement in space, but only a movement of an extremi-
ty, not of the base from which the extension takes place.
There is a sense in which the occurrence of 'hand' with
ἐκτείνω and ἐκπετάννυμι involves the motion of a body
part (see Domain 18 *Attachment*), but since the same
terms may be used not only of body parts but of any object which may be extended, it seems more satisfactory
to classify all of these related meanings together.

used figuratively to suggest intense effort as well as firm purpose.[5]

16.21 προτείνω: to stretch out or to spread out an object – 'to stretch out.' ὡς δὲ προέτειναν αὐτὸν τοῖς ἱμᾶσιν 'when they had stretched him out to be whipped' Ac 22.25.

5 There is no evidence that the figurative meaning of ἐπεκτείνομαι had become conventionalized by NT times. Accordingly, in Php 3.13 the occurrence of ἐπεκτείνομαι involves figurative usage rather than figurative meaning.
  It is rare that one can use a word meaning 'to stretch out' or 'to reach toward' in this context of Php 3.13. It may be far better to use an expression such as 'to earnestly seek those things that are ahead' or 'to do one's best to reach what is ahead' or 'to strongly desire to experience what is ahead of me' or '. . . what lies in the future.'

In a number of languages one would not speak of a person being 'stretched out' in order to be whipped, but merely 'tied up' or 'tied in a stretched-out position.'

16.22 στρώννυμι[a]: to spread something out – 'to spread, to spread out.' ὁ δὲ πλεῖστος ὄχλος ἔστρωσαν ἑαυτῶν τὰ ἱμάτια ἐν τῇ ὁδῷ 'the large crowd spread their garments on the road' Mt 21.8.

16.23 ὑποστρωννύω: to spread out something underneath – 'to spread out, to spread out under.' πορευομένου δὲ αὐτοῦ ὑπεστρώννυον τὰ ἱμάτια αὐτῶν ἐν τῇ ὁδῷ 'as he went along, they spread their garments on the road' Lk 19.36.

17 Stances and Events Related to Stances[1]

Outline of Subdomains

A   Stand (17.1-17.11)
B   Sit (17.12-17.18)
C   Kneel (17.19)
D   Prostrate (17.20)
E   Prostrate as an Act of Reverence or Supplication (17.21-17.22)
F   Recline (to eat) (17.23-17.25)
G   Lie (17.26-17.28)
H   Bend Over, Straighten Up (17.29-17.33)

1 It would be possible to classify Domain 17 *Stances and Events Related to Stances* as being a set of abstracts and events related to such abstracts. In other words, *Stances* could be treated as abstracts of body position, and the events involved in taking such a position could be treated simply as derivatives of such abstracts. However, it seems better to regard *Stances* as being essentially states of being and the accompanying events as being closely related features of such states. Accordingly, the classification of stances together with events and states seems more relevant.
  For this domain there are several sets of contrastive semantic features, for example, maintenance of a stance versus taking such a stance, and an original position in contrast with direction of motion. There are also a number of purposes implied in such stances, for example, 'sitting down to teach' (the normal stance of a rabbi when teaching) and 'reclining' as a metonym for eating or dining.

A   Stand[2] (17.1-17.11)

17.1 ἵσταμαι[a] (and 2nd aorist, perfect, pluperfect active); στήκω[a]: to be in a standing position – 'to stand.'[3]
ἵσταμαι[a]: ἐν τῷ ἱερῷ ἑστῶτες καὶ διδάσκοντες τὸν λαόν 'standing in the Temple and teaching the people' Ac 5.25.
στήκω[a]: ἔξω στήκοντες ἀπέστειλαν πρὸς αὐτόν 'standing outside, they sent (a message) for him' Mk 3.31.

17.2 συνίσταμαι[a] (and perfect active): to stand together with someone – 'to stand with.' τοὺς δύο ἄνδρας τοὺς συνεστῶτας αὐτῷ 'the two men who were standing with him' Lk 9.32. It is, of course, essential to avoid the idiomatic meaning of 'to stand with' in a sense of 'to support.' In this context the emphasis is simply upon being present with.

2 In the following set of meanings, there are important and clear distinctions between those which refer to maintaining a standing position and those which indicate a change of stance to a standing position.
3 ἵσταμαι[a] and στήκω[a] would seem to differ only in terms of linguistic level or register, since στήκω was a new formation and probably somewhat more colloquial.

17.3 παρίσταμαι[a] (and 2nd aorist, perfect, pluperfect active): to stand near or alongside of someone, either with friendly or hostile intent – 'to stand near.' καὶ τὸν μαθητὴν παρεστῶτα ὃν ἠγάπα 'and the disciple whom he loved standing nearby' Jn 19.26; παρέστησαν οἱ βασιλεῖς τῆς γῆς 'the kings of the earth were there' Ac 4.26. To indicate merely that the kings of the earth were present may not be sufficient to communicate satisfactorily the hostile intent implied by the context of Ac 4.26. It may therefore be important to translate 'the kings of earth prepared themselves' or even 'the kings of earth armed themselves.'

17.4 περιΐστημι: to stand around someone or to encircle – 'to stand around, to be around.' περιέστησαν αὐτὸν . . . Ἰουδαῖοι 'the Jews . . . stood around him' Ac 25.7; διὰ τὸν ὄχλον τὸν περιεστῶτα εἶπον 'I say this because of the people standing around here' Jn 11.42.

17.5 ἐφίσταμαι[a] (and 2nd aorist, perfect active): to stand at a particular place, often with the implication of suddenness – 'to stand by, to stand at.' καὶ ἐπιστὰς ἐπάνω αὐτῆς ἐπετίμησεν τῷ πυρετῷ 'and standing by her, he rebuked the fever' Lk 4.39; ἰδοὺ ἄνδρες δύο ἐπέστησαν αὐταῖς ἐν ἐσθῆτι ἀστραπτούσῃ 'then, suddenly two men in bright shining clothes stood by them' Lk 24.4. For another interpretation of ἐφίσταμαι in Lk 24.4, see 85.13.

17.6 ἵσταμαι[b] (and 2nd aorist, perfect, pluperfect active); ἀνίσταμαι[a] (and 2nd aorist active): to assume a standing position – 'to stand up.'
ἵσταμαι[b]: εἱστήκει ὁ Ἰησοῦς καὶ ἔκραξεν λέγων 'Jesus stood up and said in a loud voice' Jn 7.37. In the context of Jn 7.37 Jesus has been teaching and thus would be presumably in the seated position of a rabbi, but the unusual declaration which follows this introductory statement is made somewhat more emphatic not only by Jesus standing but by his proclamation in a loud voice.
ἀνίσταμαι[a]: ἀνέστη ἀναγνῶναι 'he stood up to read (the Scriptures)' Lk 4.16.

17.7 ἀνίστημι[a]: to cause someone to stand up – 'to cause to stand, to raise up.' δοὺς δὲ

αὐτῇ χεῖρα ἀνέστησεν αὐτήν 'taking her by the hand, he raised her up' Ac 9.41.

17.8 κουμ (an Aramaic expression): to stand up from a reclining position – 'to stand up.' λέγει αὐτῇ, Ταλιθα κουμ, ὅ ἐστιν μεθερμηνευόμενον Τὸ κοράσιον, σοὶ λέγω, ἔγειρε 'he said to her, Talitha koum, which means, Little girl, I tell you, get up' Mk 5.41. Note that κουμ is translated in Mk 5.41 by ἐγείρω (see 17.9).

17.9 ἐγείρομαι[a]; ἐγείρω[b]: to get up, normally from a lying or reclining position but possibly from a seated position (in some contexts with the implication of some degree of previous incapacity) – 'to get up, to stand up.'
ἐγείρομαι[a]: ἐγείρεται ἐκ τοῦ δείπνου καὶ τίθησιν τὰ ἱμάτια 'he got up from the table and put off his outer garment' Jn 13.4; ἠγέρθη δὲ Σαῦλος ἀπὸ τῆς γῆς 'Saul got up from the ground' Ac 9.8.
ἐγείρω[b]: τὸ κοράσιον, σοὶ λέγω, ἔγειρε 'little girl, I tell you, get up' Mk 5.41.

17.10 ἐγείρω[a]: to cause to stand up, with a possible implication of some previous incapacity – 'to get up, to cause to stand up.' οὐχὶ κρατήσει αὐτὸ καὶ ἐγερεῖ 'will he not take hold of it and get it on its feet' (implying, no doubt, up and out of the ditch or hole) Mt 12.11.[4]

17.11 ἐξανίσταμαι (and 2nd aorist active): to stand up in a manner distinct from someone else – 'to stand up.' ἐξανέστησαν δέ τινες τῶν ἀπὸ τῆς αἱρέσεως τῶν Φαρισαίων πεπιστευκότες 'and some of the believers from the party of the Pharisees stood up' Ac 15.5.

B Sit (17.12-17.18)

17.12 καθέζομαι; κάθημαι[a]; καθίζω[a]: to be in a seated position or to take such a position – 'to sit, to sit down, to be seated, sitting.'[5]
καθέζομαι: καθεζομένους . . . ὅπου ἔκειτο τὸ σῶμα τοῦ Ἰησοῦ 'sitting . . . where the body of

---

4 It is possible that ἐγείρω in Mt 12.11 should be understood only in the sense of 'to lift up.'
5 There are certain technical problems involved in

Jesus had been' Jn 20.12; ὁ οὖν Ἰησοῦς κεκοπιακὼς ἐκ τῆς ὁδοιπορίας ἐκαθέζετο οὕτως ἐπὶ τῇ πηγῇ 'Jesus, tired out from the trip, thus sat down by the well' Jn 4.6.

κάθημαι^a: ὁ πρὸς τὴν ἐλεημοσύνην καθήμενος ἐπὶ τῇ Ὡραίᾳ Πύλῃ 'the one who sat begging at the Temple's Beautiful Gate' Ac 3.10; κάθου ὑπὸ τὸ ὑποπόδιόν μου 'sit down here on the floor by my feet' Jas 2.3.

καθίζω^a: ἀνέβη εἰς τὸ ὄρος· καὶ καθίσαντος 'he went up on a hill, and sitting down. . .' Mt 5.1.

17.13 συγκάθημαι; συγκαθίζω^a: to sit down with someone or to be seated with someone – 'to sit down with, to be seated with, sitting with.'[5]

συγκάθημαι: καὶ οἱ συγκαθήμενοι αὐτοῖς 'and those that were sitting with them' Ac 26.30; καὶ ἦν συγκαθήμενος μετὰ τῶν ὑπηρετῶν 'there he sat down with the guards' Mk 14.54.

συγκαθίζω^a: συγκαθισάντων ἐκάθητο ὁ Πέτρος μέσος αὐτῶν 'Peter sat down in the midst of those who were seated together' Lk 22.55.

17.14 παρακαθέζομαι: to sit down near or beside someone – 'to sit down by, to sit down near.' ἣ καὶ παρακαθεσθεῖσα πρὸς τοὺς πόδας τοῦ κυρίου 'who sat down at the feet of the Lord' Lk 10.39.

17.15 ἐπικαθίζω: to sit down upon something – 'to sit upon, to mount, to get on.' καὶ ἐπεκάθισεν ἐπάνω αὐτῶν 'and he sat down on them' Mt 21.7. In Mt 21.7 the pronominal form αὐτῶν is ambiguous in reference, for it may refer either to the garments or to the donkey and colt. The closest noun reference is τὰ ἱμάτια 'the garments,' but in view of Matthew's quotation and evident interpretation of

treating the series καθέζομαι, κάθημαι^a, καθίζω^a (17.12) and συγκάθημαι, συγκαθίζω^a (17.13), since there appears to be an alternation in meaning between (1) being in a position and (2) assuming such a position. It would be possible to set up two distinct meanings or to assume that the respective forms are essentially ambiguous. In general, however, the participial forms indicate a state of being, while the non-participial forms imply assuming a particular position of being seated. However, there are certain subtle differences in the tenses of the participial forms, and hence one cannot determine precisely what are the referential distinctions.

the reference to Zechariah 9.9, both the donkey and the colt may be the substantive referents, though being seated upon two animals at the same time poses real problems of understanding.

17.16 ἀνακαθίζω: to sit up from a reclining or lying position – 'to sit up.' ἀνεκάθισεν ὁ νεκρὸς καὶ ἤρξατο λαλεῖν 'the dead man sat up and began to talk' Lk 7.15.

17.17 καθίζω^b: to cause someone to sit or to be in a seated position – 'to cause to sit down, to seat.' καὶ καθίσας ἐν δεξιᾷ αὐτοῦ ἐν τοῖς ἐπουρανίοις 'and seated him at his right hand in the heavenly world' Eph 1.20. For καθίζω as part of an idiom in Eph 1.20, see 87.36.

17.18 συγκαθίζω^b: to cause someone to sit down with someone – 'to seat with, to cause to sit down with.' καὶ συνεκάθισεν ἐν τοῖς ἐπουρανίοις 'and seated us with him in the heavenly places' Eph 2.6.

C Kneel (17.19)

17.19 γονυπετέω; τίθημι τὰ γόνατα (an idiom, literally 'to place the knees,' a Latinism): to kneel down before, with the implication of an act of reverence or of supplication – 'to kneel down, to kneel.'

γονυπετέω: προσῆλθεν αὐτῷ ἄνθρωπος γονυπετῶν αὐτόν 'a man came to him and knelt down before him' Mt 17.14.

τίθημι τὰ γόνατα: καὶ τιθέντες τὰ γόνατα προσεκύνουν αὐτῷ 'and kneeling, they prostrated themselves before him' Mk 15.19.

In a number of cultures, kneeling does not imply either reverence for or an act of supplication. In some instances translators have used a functional substitute involving a similar type of stance, namely, 'to bow low before,' but it may be necessary to use a more or less literal description of 'kneeling before' and then to place in a marginal note an indication of the implications of such an act.

D Prostrate (17.20)

17.20 πρηνής, ές, gen. **οῦς:** pertaining to being stretched out in a position facedown and headfirst – 'prostrate, headlong, headfirst.' πρηνὴς γενόμενος 'falling headlong' Ac 1.18.

It is also possible that in Ac 1.18 πρηνής could have the meaning of 'swollen' or 'distended,' a meaning which is linguistically possible, but not widely witnessed to (see apparatus).

E Prostrate as an Act of Reverence or Supplication (17.21-17.22)

17.21 προσκυνέω[b]; κλίνω τὸ πρόσωπον εἰς τὴν γῆν (an idiom, literally 'to incline the face to the ground'): to prostrate oneself before someone as an act of reverence, fear, or supplication – 'to prostrate oneself before.'[6]
προσκυνέω[b]: καὶ προσκυνήσουσιν ἐνώπιον τῶν ποδῶν σου 'and they will prostrate themselves before your feet' Re 3.9; τιθέντες τὰ γόνατα προσεκύνουν αὐτῷ 'kneeling down, they prostrated themselves before him' Mk 15.19. προσκυνέω[b] is semantically very complex in that it indicates not only a body position but also an attitude and activity of reverence or honor. In many contexts it is not necessary to specify both semantic elements, but one or the other may be selected depending upon what seems to be the focus of attention. For example, in Mk 15.19 one may either translate 'they knelt before him and worshiped him in a mocking way' or 'they knelt before him and prostrated themselves before him.'
κλίνω τὸ πρόσωπον εἰς τὴν γῆν: ἐμφόβων δὲ γενομένων αὐτῶν καὶ κλινουσῶν τὰ πρόσωπα εἰς τὴν γῆν 'they were fearful and prostrated themselves on the ground' or '. . . bowed down to the ground' Lk 24.5.

17.22 πίπτω[c]; προσπίπτω[a]: to prostrate oneself before someone, implying supplication – 'to prostrate oneself before, to fall down before.'[7]

πίπτω[c]: καὶ πεσόντες προσεκύνησαν αὐτῷ 'and prostrating themselves, they worshiped him' Mt 2.11.
προσπίπτω[a]: προσέπεσεν πρὸς τοὺς πόδας αὐτοῦ 'she prostrated herself at his feet' Mk 7.25.

A strictly literal translation of προσπίπτω[a] or πίπτω[c], namely, 'to fall down before,' can be entirely misleading in that it may suggest an accident caused by stumbling or tripping. It may therefore be necessary in a number of languages to translate 'to bow down low before' or 'to bow down to the ground before.'

F Recline (to eat)[8] (17.23-17.25)

17.23 ἀνάκειμαι[a]; ἀνακλίνομαι; κατάκειμαι[b]; κατακλίνομαι; ἀναπίπτω: to be in a reclining position as one eats (with the focus either upon the position or the act of eating) – 'to recline, to eat, to be at table, to eat, to dine, to sit down to eat.'
ἀνάκειμαι[a]: καὶ ἀνακειμένων αὐτῶν καὶ ἐσθιόντων ὁ Ἰησοῦς εἶπεν 'while they were at table eating, Jesus said' Mk 14.18; οὐδεὶς ἔγνω τῶν ἀνακειμένων 'none of those dining understood' Jn 13.28.
ἀνακλίνομαι: ἀνακλιθήσονται μετὰ Ἀβραὰμ καὶ Ἰσαὰκ καὶ Ἰακὼβ ἐν τῇ βασιλείᾳ τῶν οὐρανῶν 'they will dine with Abraham, Isaac, and Jacob in the kingdom of heaven' Mt 8.11.
κατάκειμαι[b]: κατακειμένου αὐτοῦ 'while he was reclining at table' Mk 14.3. For the interpre-

upon the actual position rather than upon the intent of showing reverence or making supplication. προσκυνέω[b] is the more formal term and focuses more upon the attitude of reverence or honor.

8 The meanings in this subdomain are semantically complex in that they indicate not only a position but a particular activity of eating or dining. Reclining was not the only position which people took in eating, for it seems quite clear that people also had a practice of being seated to eat. In fact, the position of reclining on a couch or cushions to eat would suggest a somewhat elaborate meal. However, terms meaning literally 'to recline' were often used so extensively in the context of eating that they are used absolutely in the sense of 'to eat' or 'to dine' without reference to the position of the person eating (see 23.21). Because of the complex semantic features in this subdomain, it is often preferable for a translator to focus upon the semantic element of eating rather than upon the position of the persons. This is particularly true in cultures where reclining to eat would be misinterpreted as suggesting laziness or a sensual activity.

---

6 προσκυνέω may involve the meaning of 'worship' without reference to a prostrate position. For example, in He 11.21, προσεκύνησεν ἐπὶ τὸ ἄκρον τῆς ῥάβδου αὐτοῦ 'he leaned on the top of his walking stick and worshiped God,' there is evidently no suggestion of a prostrate position, and this particular meaning of προσκυνέω is treated under *Religious Activities* (see 53.56).

7 πίπτω[c] and προσπίπτω[a] (17.22) differ to some extent from προσκυνέω[b] (17.21) in that they focus primarily

tation of ἀνάκειμαι and κατάκειμαι focusing upon eating, see 23.21.

κατακλίνομαι: εἰσελθὼν . . . κατεκλίθη 'he came in . . . and sat down to eat' Lk 7.36.

ἀναπίπτω: εἰσελθὼν δὲ ἀνέπεσεν 'and he came in and sat down to eat' Lk 7.37.

17.24 ἀνακλίνω[b]; κατακλίνω: to cause someone to assume a reclining (or possibly sitting) position as part of the process of eating – 'to cause to recline to eat, to have someone sit down to eat.'

ἀνακλίνω[b]: ἀνακλινεῖ αὐτούς 'have them sit down' Lk 12.37; κελεύσας τοὺς ὄχλους ἀνακλιθῆναι ἐπὶ τοῦ χόρτου 'he ordered the people to sit down on the grass' Mt 14.19.

κατακλίνω: κατακλίνατε αὐτοὺς κλισίας ὡσεὶ ἀνὰ πεντήκοντα 'have them sit down to eat in groups of about fifty' Lk 9.14.

17.25 ἀνάκειμαι ἐν τῷ κόλπῳ; ἀναπίπτω ἐπὶ τὸ στῆθος: (idioms, literally 'to recline on the bosom') to take the place of honor at a meal – 'to dine in the place of honor.'

ἀνάκειμαι ἐν τῷ κόλπῳ: ἦν ἀνακείμενος εἷς ἐκ τῶν μαθητῶν αὐτοῦ ἐν τῷ κόλπῳ τοῦ Ἰησοῦ, ὃν ἠγάπα ὁ Ἰησοῦς 'one of Jesus' disciples whom he loved was dining in the place of honor next to Jesus' Jn 13.23.

ἀναπίπτω ἐπὶ τὸ στῆθος: ἀναπεσὼν οὖν ἐκεῖνος οὕτως ἐπὶ τὸ στῆθος τοῦ Ἰησοῦ 'the one who was dining in the place of honor next to Jesus' Jn 13.25. This expression (ἀναπεσὼν ἐπὶ τὸ στῆθος) in Jn 13.25 (following on ἀνακείμενος . . . ἐν τῷ κόλπῳ in Jn 13.23) seems to be typical of the tendency of the Gospel of John to employ relatively close synonyms with essentially the same meaning. It is possible, however, in view of the aorist participle in Jn 13.25 that the phrase ἀναπεσὼν ἐπὶ τὸ στῆθος could also be understood in a more literal sense to mean 'to move closer to the side (of Jesus).'

These expressions in Jn 13.23 and 25 would mean that the so-called 'beloved disciple' would be at the right of Jesus, since guests at a meal would be reclining on the left side so as to permit freedom of the right hand in dining. It may, of course, be that the same expression could be used of persons sitting at a table rather than reclining on couches.

Literal translations of ἀνάκειμαι ἐν τῷ κόλπῳ and ἀναπίπτω ἐπὶ τὸ στῆθος can result in serious misunderstanding, since they might imply overt homosexuality. There is no justification for reading into such idioms this type of implication.

G Lie (17.26-17.28)

17.26 κεῖμαι[a]: to be in a lying or reclining position – 'to lie, to recline.' βρέφος . . . κείμενον ἐν φάτνῃ 'a baby . . . lying in a manger' Lk 2.12; ἴδετε τὸν τόπον ὅπου ἔκειτο 'see the place where he lay' Mt 28.6.[9]

17.27 κατάκειμαι[a]: to lie down, often with the implication of some degree of incapacity – 'to lie, lying down.' ἐν ταύταις κατέκειτο πλῆθος τῶν ἀσθενούντων 'a large crowd of sick people were lying in these (porches)' Jn 5.3; ἐγένετο δὲ τὸν πατέρα τοῦ Ποπλίου πυρετοῖς καὶ δυσεντερίῳ συνεχόμενον κατακεῖσθαι 'and it happened that the father of Publius was lying sick with fever and dysentery' Ac 28.8.

17.28 ἀνακλίνω[a]: to cause someone to lie down – 'to lay down, to lay.' καὶ ἀνέκλινεν αὐτὸν ἐν φάτνῃ 'and laid him in a manger' Lk 2.7.

H Bend Over, Straighten Up (17.29-17.33)

17.29 κύπτω: to bend over into a stooping position – 'to bend down, to stoop down.' οὗ οὐκ εἰμὶ ἱκανὸς κύψας λῦσαι τὸν ἱμάντα τῶν ὑποδημάτων αὐτοῦ 'I am not good enough to bend down and untie his sandals' Mk 1.7.

17.30 κατακύπτω: to bend over and stoop down, with perhaps greater emphasis on the position being 'down' than in the case of κύπτω (17.29) – 'to bend down, to bend over, to stoop down.' πάλιν κατακύψας ἔγραφεν εἰς τὴν γῆν 'he bent over again and wrote on the ground' Jn 8.8.

---

9 It is also possible to interpret κεῖμαι in Lk 2.12 and Mt 28.6 as indicating merely 'to be in a particular location' (see 85.3).

17.31 παρακύπτω[a]: to bend over or stoop down, with the implication of looking into something – 'to bend over, to stoop down.' παρέκυψεν εἰς τὸ μνημεῖον 'she bent over and looked in the tomb' Jn 20.11.[10]

17.32 συγκύπτω: to be bent over in a doubled up position – 'to be bent over, to be dou-

bled up.' ἦν συγκύπτουσα καὶ μὴ δυναμένη ἀνακύψαι εἰς τὸ παντελές 'she was bent over and could not straighten up at all' Lk 13.11.

17.33 ἀνορθόω[b]; ἀνακύπτω: to straighten up from a bent over position – 'to straighten up.' ἀνορθόω[b]: παραχρῆμα ἀνωρθώθη 'at once she straightened herself up' Lk 13.13. ἀνακύπτω: μὴ δυναμένη ἀνακύψαι εἰς τὸ παντελές 'she was not able to straighten up at all' Lk 13.11.[11]

---

10 In παρακύπτω[a] there appear to be two coordinate semantic elements: 'to stoop down' and 'to look into.' It is possible, of course, to understand the second element as implying the purpose for the first, but in translation it is essential that both elements, especially in the context of Jn 20.11, be adequately noted. The fact that there are two significant elements of meaning in παρακύπτω[a] means that this term is essentially a member of two different domains at the same time, namely, Domain 17 dealing with *Stances* and Domain 24 *Sensory Events and States*.

11 It is possible that ἀνακύπτω differs to some extent in meaning from ἀνορθόω[b] in that the focus of ἀνακύπτω is upon the reversal of a process. This is linguistically possible since ἀνα- may mean not only 'up' but also may refer to the reversal of an event, for example, ἀνάγω 'to restore' and ἀνακαλύπτω 'to uncover.'

---

18 Attachment

Outline of Subdomains

A   Grasp, Hold (18.1-18.11)
B   Fasten, Stick To (18.12-18.23)

A   Grasp, Hold (18.1-18.11)

18.1 λαμβάνω[a]; δέχομαι[d]: to take hold of something or someone, with or without force – 'to take hold of, to grasp, to grab.' λαμβάνω[a]: εἴπας δὲ ταῦτα καὶ λαβὼν ἄρτον εὐχαρίστησεν τῷ θεῷ ἐνώπιον πάντων 'after saying these things, he took some bread and gave thanks to God before all of them' Ac 27.35; λαβόντες αὐτὸν ἐξέβαλον ἔξω τοῦ ἀμπελῶνος καὶ ἀπέκτειναν 'so they grabbed him, threw him out of the vineyard, and killed him' Mt 21.39. δέχομαι[d]: δεξάμενος ποτήριον εὐχαριστήσας 'then he took the cup and gave thanks (to God)' Lk 22.17.[1]

A number of languages differ radically in terms for 'taking hold of,' depending upon whether force is employed, whether the object is a thing or an animate being, and whether

---

1 It is possible that δέχομαι in Lk 22.17 may mean 'to receive' (see 57.125).

the language incorporates into a verb of 'taking hold of' a classification as to the objects involved, for example, long and thin, round and flat, ball-like, angular, or lumpy.

18.2 προσλαμβάνομαι[a]; ἐπιλαμβάνομαι[a]: to take hold of or grasp, with focus upon the goal of the motion – 'to take hold of, to grasp.' προσλαμβάνομαι[a]: καὶ αὐτοὶ προσελάβοντο τροφῆς 'and they took some food' Ac 27.36. The phrase προσλαμβάνομαι τροφῆς may be interpreted as an idiom meaning 'to eat' (see footnote 3 in 23.2). ἐπιλαμβάνομαι[a]: ἐπιλαβόμενος τῆς χειρὸς τοῦ τυφλοῦ ἐξήνεγκεν αὐτὸν ἔξω τῆς κώμης 'he took the blind man by the hand and led him out of the village' Mk 8.23; εὐθέως δὲ ὁ Ἰησοῦς ἐκτείνας τὴν χεῖρα ἐπελάβετο αὐτοῦ 'at once Jesus reached out and took hold of him' Mt 14.31.

In a number of languages quite different terms must be employed if one is to take someone by the hand in order to lead him or take someone by the hand in order to rescue him. The difference implied in the presumed force or strength required frequently results in quite different words being used.

18.3 πιάζω[a]: to take hold of firmly and with a considerable measure of force – 'to take hold of, to seize, to catch, to grasp firmly.' καὶ πιάσας αὐτὸν τῆς δεξιᾶς χειρὸς ἤγειρεν αὐτόν 'and having grasped his right hand firmly, he raised him up' Ac 3.7; καὶ ἐπιάσθη τὸ θηρίον 'and the beast was seized' Re 19.20.

18.4 ἁρπάζω[a]: to grab or seize by force, with the purpose of removing and/or controlling – 'to seize, to snatch away, to take away.' ἐκέλευσεν τὸ στράτευμα καταβὰν ἁρπάσαι αὐτὸν ἐκ μέσου αὐτῶν 'he ordered soldiers to go down (into the group) and snatch him away from them' Ac 23.10; ἔρχεται ὁ πονηρὸς καὶ ἁρπάζει τὸ ἐσπαρμένον ἐν τῇ καρδίᾳ αὐτοῦ 'the Evil One comes and snatches away the seed that was sown in his heart' Mt 13.19. In Mt 13.19 the context as a whole is figurative, but a more or less literal rendering of 'snatches' or 'seizes' is probably satisfactory.

18.5 συναρπάζω[a]: to seize or snatch by force and to take away with – 'to seize, to take off with.' ἐπιστάντες συνήρπασαν αὐτὸν καὶ ἤγαγον εἰς τὸ συνέδριον 'they came to him, seized him, and took him before the council' Ac 6.12; συναρπασθέντος δὲ τοῦ πλοίου 'when the ship had been seized and carried off (by the wind)' Ac 27.15. In a number of languages, one must distinguish carefully between seizure by an animate being and seizure by a force such as the wind.

18.6 κρατέω[a]; ἔχω[b]; ἅπτομαι[a]: to hold on to an object – 'to hold on to, to retain in the hand, to seize.'
κρατέω[a]: τάδε λέγει ὁ κρατῶν τοὺς ἑπτὰ ἀστέρας ἐν τῇ δεξιᾷ αὐτοῦ 'this is the message from the one who holds the seven stars in his right hand' Re 2.1.
ἔχω[b]: ὁ καθήμενος ἐπ' αὐτὸν ἔχων ζυγὸν ἐν τῇ χειρὶ αὐτοῦ 'its rider held a pair of scales in his hand' Re 6.5.
ἅπτομαι[a]: μή μου ἅπτου 'do not hold on to me' Jn 20.17.[2]

18.7 καθάπτω: to seize and fasten on to – 'to

seize, to fasten on to.' καθῆψεν τῆς χειρὸς αὐτοῦ '(a snake) fastened on to his hand' Ac 28.3. In some languages it may be necessary to translate this expression in Ac 28.3 as 'a snake bit his hand and did not let go.'

18.8 ἄγρα, ας f: the act of catching something – 'to catch, a catch.' χαλάσατε τὰ δίκτυα ὑμῶν εἰς ἄγραν 'put in your nets for a catch' Lk 5.4. Though in Greek the term ἄγρα may be used to refer to the catching of a wide variety of objects, in the context of Lk 5.4 the reference is to fish, and one must make certain that the appropriate term in the receptor language is employed, depending, for example, whether one catches fish, animals, or people.

18.9 τίλλω: to pluck or pick by pulling off or out of – 'to pluck, to pick.' οἱ μαθηταὶ αὐτοῦ ἤρξαντο ὁδὸν ποιεῖν τίλλοντες τοὺς στάχυας 'as his disciples walked along with him, they began to pick off the heads of wheat' Mk 2.23.

18.10 συλλέγω: to pluck or pick by pulling off or out of, with the intent of gathering together – 'to pick, to pluck.' οὐ γὰρ ἐξ ἀκανθῶν συλλέγουσιν σῦκα 'people do not pick figs from thorn bushes' Lk 6.44. (See footnote 3 in 43.18.)

18.11 προσψαύω[b]: to touch something, with the intent of doing something about it – 'to touch, to touch to help.' καὶ αὐτοὶ ἑνὶ τῶν δακτύλων ὑμῶν οὐ προσψαύετε τοῖς φορτίοις 'and you yourselves will not touch these burdens with one of your fingers' Lk 11.46. In employing a term for 'touch' in Lk 11.46, it is important to use an expression which will imply 'touching in order to relieve the burden.' This may be done in some instances by translating 'to help by touching' or 'to touch with a finger in order to help a little.' For another interpretation of προσψαύω in Lk 11.46, see 24.75.

B Fasten, Stick To (18.12-18.23)

18.12 ἀσφαλίζω[b]: to fasten something securely – 'to fasten, to tie.' τοὺς πόδας ἠσφαλίσατο αὐτῶν εἰς τὸ ξύλον 'they fastened their feet to a

---

2 ἅπτομαι in Jn 20.17 may also be interpreted as 'to touch' (see 24.73).

block of wood' Ac 16.24. It is possible that in Ac 16.24 τὸ ξύλον designates 'stocks,' namely, two pieces of wood through which the feet could be placed so as to make a prisoner immobile (see 6.21).

18.13 δέω[a]: to tie objects together – 'to tie, to tie together, to tie up.' δήσατε αὐτὰ εἰς δέσμας 'tie these into bundles' Mt 13.30.

18.14 περιδέω: to tie or wrap an object around something – 'to tie around, to wrap up, to wrap around.' ἡ ὄψις αὐτοῦ σουδαρίῳ περιεδέδετο 'a cloth wrapped around his face' (literally 'his face tied around with cloth') Jn 11.44.

18.15 δεσμεύω: to bind or tie on – 'to bind, to tie.' δεσμεύουσιν δὲ φορτία βαρέα 'but they bind on heavy burdens' Mt 23.4. Note, however, that the context of Mt 23.4 is figurative.

18.16 δέσμη, ης *f*: (derivative of δεσμεύω 'to bind,' 18.15) that which has been tied up or tied together – 'bundle.' δήσατε αὐτὰ εἰς δέσμας πρὸς τὸ κατακαῦσαι αὐτά 'tie these into bundles in order to burn them' Mt 13.30.

18.17 σύνδεσμος[a], **ου** *m*: that which ties something together – 'bindings, bonds, that which ties together.' πᾶν τὸ σῶμα διὰ τῶν ἁφῶν καὶ συνδέσμων ἐπιχορηγούμενον καὶ συμβιβαζόμενον 'the whole body supported and held together by ligaments and those things

which tie it together' Col 2.19. The context of Col 2.19 is, however, highly figurative.

18.18 λύω[a]: to reverse the result of tying by untying – 'to untie, to loosen.' οὐκ εἰμὶ ἱκανὸς κύψας λῦσαι τὸν ἱμάντα τῶν ὑποδημάτων αὐτοῦ 'I am not worthy to stoop down and untie the thongs of his sandals' Mk 1.7.

18.19 ἀνίημι[a]: to cause something to become loose – 'to loosen, to unfasten.' πάντων τὰ δεσμὰ ἀνέθη 'the bonds of all (the prisoners) were loosened' Ac 16.26.

18.20 προσηλόω: to cause something to be fixed in place by means of nails – 'to nail onto, to nail fast to.' προσηλώσας αὐτὸ τῷ σταυρῷ 'nailing it to the cross' Col 2.14.

18.21 κολλάομαι[b]: to stick or cling to something – 'to cling to, to stick to.' τὸν κονιορτὸν τὸν κολληθέντα ἡμῖν 'dust that sticks to us' Lk 10.11.

18.22 κρέμαμαι[a]: to hang down from some point – 'to hang from, to hang down from.' ὡς δὲ εἶδον οἱ βάρβαροι κρεμάμενον τὸ θηρίον ἐκ τῆς χειρὸς αὐτοῦ 'when the natives saw the serpent hanging from his hand' Ac 28.4.

18.23 κρεμάννυμι: to cause to hang down from – 'to make to hang, to be hung from.' συμφέρει αὐτῷ ἵνα κρεμασθῇ μύλος ὀνικὸς περὶ τὸν τράχηλον αὐτοῦ 'it would be better for him to have a large millstone hung around his neck' Mt 18.6.

19 Physical Impact[1]

Outline of Subdomains

A Hit, Strike (19.1-19.13)
B Pierce, Cut (19.14-19.26)
C Split, Tear (19.27-19.33)
D Break, Break Through (19.34-19.42)
E Press (19.43-19.54)
F Dig (19.55)

A Hit, Strike (19.1-19.13)

19.1 τύπτω[a]; **πληγή**[a], **ῆς** *f*; **πλήσσω**; **παίω**[a]: to strike or hit an object, one or more times – 'to hit, to strike, to beat.'

1 Though Domain 20 *Violence, Harm, Destroy, Kill* involves varying aspects of physical impact, it seems far better to make a significant distinction between physical impact as such (Domain 19) and the results of such impact as are described in Domain 20.

τύπτω[a]: ἔτυπτον αὐτοῦ τὴν κεφαλὴν καλάμῳ 'they beat him over the head with a reed' Mk 15.19. Note that the imperfect tense may be used of a repeated action, and therefore the translation 'beat.' ἔτυπτεν τὸ στῆθος αὐτοῦ 'he beat his breast' Lk 18.13. The action of 'beating the breast' in Lk 18.13 is symbolic in that it has the meaning of repentance and contrition. In other languages, however, the expression 'to beat the breast' may constitute a symbol of pride or self-flattery. In some languages the equivalent of the biblical expression 'to beat the breast' is 'to strike the head' or 'to grasp the abdomen.'

πληγή[a]: (in the plural indicating repeated blows) ποιήσας δὲ ἄξια πληγῶν 'doing something which deserves beating' Lk 12.48. One may also render this expression in Lk 12.48 as 'does something for which he should be beaten.'

πλήσσω: καὶ ἐπλήγη τὸ τρίτον τοῦ ἡλίου 'and a third of the sun was struck' Re 8.12. In Re 8.12 the emphasis seems to be upon the damage caused to the sun rather than the actual fact of a blow, but the use of πλήσσω seems to indicate that the damage is the result of some type of blow.

παίω[a]: περικαλύψαντες αὐτὸν ἐπηρώτων λέγοντες, Προφήτευσον, τίς ἐστιν ὁ παίσας σε; 'they blindfolded him and said, Tell us! Who hit you?' Lk 22.64.

19.2 δέρω: to strike or beat repeatedly – 'to strike, to beat, to whip.' ἐκεῖνος δὲ ὁ δοῦλος ὁ γνοὺς τὸ θέλημα τοῦ κυρίου αὐτοῦ καὶ μὴ ἑτοιμάσας ἢ ποιήσας πρὸς τὸ θέλημα αὐτοῦ δαρήσεται πολλάς 'the servant who knows what his master wants him to do, but does not get himself ready and do what his master wants, will be punished with a hard beating' Lk 12.47.

19.3 πατάσσω[a]: to strike a heavy blow, implying severe damage – 'to strike a blow.' ἐπάταξεν εἷς τις ἐξ αὐτῶν τοῦ ἀρχιερέως τὸν δοῦλον καὶ ἀφεῖλεν τὸ οὖς αὐτοῦ τὸ δεξιόν 'one of them struck the high priest's slave and cut off his right ear' Lk 22.50. The context indicates that a sword was used in striking the blow.

19.4 ῥαπίζω; ῥάπισμα, τος *n*: to hit or strike with the open hand, the fist, or an instrument (for example, club, rod, or whip) – 'to slap, to hit, to whip, to beat.'
ῥαπίζω: ὅστις σε ῥαπίζει εἰς τὴν δεξιὰν σιαγόνα σου, στρέφον αὐτῷ καὶ τὴν ἄλλην 'if anyone slaps you on the right cheek, let him slap your left cheek too' (literally 'turn to him also the other') Mt 5.39.
ῥάπισμα: εἷς παρεστηκὼς τῶν ὑπηρετῶν ἔδωκεν ῥάπισμα τῷ Ἰησοῦ 'one of the guards standing there slapped Jesus' Jn 18.22; οἱ ὑπηρέται ῥαπίσμασιν αὐτὸν ἔλαβον 'the guards took him and beat him' Mk 14.65.

19.5 προσκόπτω[a]: to strike against something, with the implication of resistance or damage – 'to strike against.' μήποτε προσκόψῃς πρὸς λίθον τὸν πόδα σου 'so that you will not even strike your foot on a stone' Mt 4.6. The focus in Mt 4.6 is upon the result of striking a foot against a stone, and therefore one may translate 'to hurt your foot by striking it against a stone.'

19.6 προσρήγνυμι or προσρήσσω: to strike suddenly and with force – 'to strike against, to burst against.' προσέρηξεν ὁ ποταμὸς τῇ οἰκίᾳ ἐκείνῃ 'the river struck against that house' Lk 6.48. It is also possible to understand προσρήγνυμι in Lk 6.48 as meaning 'to overflow the stream bed,' but in view of the occurrence of τῇ οἰκίᾳ ἐκείνῃ, the meaning of 'strike against' seems more justified.

19.7 κολαφίζω[a]: to strike or beat with the fist, either once or repeatedly – 'to strike with the fist, to beat with the fist.' τότε ἐνέπτυσαν εἰς τὸ πρόσωπον αὐτοῦ καὶ ἐκολάφισαν αὐτόν 'then they spat in his face and beat him with their fists' Mt 26.67.

19.8 ῥαβδίζω: to beat or strike repeatedly with a stick or rod – 'to beat with a stick or rod.' οἱ στρατηγοὶ περιρήξαντες αὐτῶν τὰ ἱμάτια ἐκέλευσον ῥαβδίζειν 'the officials tore off their clothes and ordered them to be beaten' Ac 16.22.

19.9 φραγελλόω; μαστίζω; μαστιγόω[a]; μάστιξ[a], ιγος *f*; ἱμάς[b], άντος *m*: to beat severely with a whip – 'to whip, to beat with a whip, whipping, flogging.'

φραγελλόω: παρέδωκεν τὸν Ἰησοῦν φραγελλώσας ἵνα σταυρωθῇ 'he had Jesus whipped and handed him over to be crucified' Mk 15.15.

μαστίζω: εἰ ἄνθρωπον Ῥωμαῖον καὶ ἀκατάκριτον ἔξεστιν ὑμῖν μαστίζειν; 'is it lawful for you to whip a Roman citizen who hasn't been tried for any crime?' Ac 22.25.

μαστιγόω[a]: ἔλαβεν ὁ Πιλᾶτος τὸν Ἰησοῦν καὶ ἐμαστίγωσεν 'Pilate took Jesus and had him whipped' Jn 19.1.

μάστιξ[a]: ἕτεροι δὲ ἐμπαιγμῶν καὶ μαστίγων πεῖραν ἔλαβον 'some were ridiculed and others underwent flogging' He 11.36.

ἱμάς[b]: ὡς δὲ προέτειναν αὐτὸν τοῖς ἱμᾶσιν 'but when they had tied him up to be whipped' Ac 22.25. It is also possible to interpret ἱμάς in Ac 22.25 as the thongs with which Paul was tied up (see 6.20).

19.10 καταβάλλω[a]: to hit or strike with sufficient impact so as to knock an object down – 'to knock down.' καταβαλλόμενοι ἀλλ' οὐκ ἀπολλύμενοι 'though we get knocked down at times, we are not destroyed' 2 Cor 4.9. It is possible, however, to interpret καταβάλλω in 2 Cor 4.9 as meaning 'to hurt badly' (see 20.21).

19.11 προσπίπτω[b]: to strike against some object – 'to strike against, to hit against.' ἔπνευσαν οἱ ἄνεμοι καὶ προσέπεσαν τῇ οἰκίᾳ ἐκείνῃ 'the winds blew and struck against that house' Mt 7.25.

19.12 κρούω: to knock on a door, as a means of signaling one's presence to those inside – 'to knock.' κρούετε, καὶ ἀνοιγήσεται ὑμῖν 'knock and the door will be opened to you' Mt 7.7.[2] A literal rendering of κρούω in Mt 7.7 may be misleading in a number of languages, since in some areas only thieves knock on doors. This is done in order to determine whether anyone is at home, in which case, of course, the thief runs off. The more general

practice for signaling one's presence may be to cough, to clap the hands, or to call out one's name.

19.13 κεφαλιόω: to beat someone on the head, implying repeated blows – 'to beat on the head.' κἀκεῖνον ἐκεφαλίωσαν 'and another they beat on the head' Mk 12.4.

B Pierce, Cut (19.14-19.26)

19.14 ἐκκεντέω: to pierce with a pointed instrument – 'to pierce.' ὄψονται εἰς ὃν ἐξεκέντησαν 'they will look on the one whom they have pierced' Jn 19.37.

19.15 νύσσω – 'to prick, to pierce' (normally not as serious a wound as is implied by ἐκκεντέω, 19.14). εἷς τῶν στρατιωτῶν λόγχῃ αὐτοῦ τὴν πλευρὰν ἔνυξεν 'one of the soldiers pierced his side with a spear' Jn 19.34. Though νύσσω in Jn 19.34 and ἐκκεντέω in Jn 19.37 refer to the same event, this does not necessarily mean that the two words have precisely the same meaning. This shift in close synonyms is characteristic of Johannine style.

19.16 παίω[b]: to sting (as of a scorpion) – 'to sting, to strike.' ὁ βασανισμὸς αὐτῶν ὡς βασανισμὸς σκορπίου, ὅταν παίσῃ ἄνθρωπον 'the sharp pain they caused is like the pain caused by a scorpion when it stings a person' Re 9.5.[3]

19.17 κόπτω: to cut, by means of a sharp-edged instrument (for example, knife, sword, or ax) – 'to cut.' ἄλλοι δὲ στιβάδας κόψαντες ἐκ τῶν ἀγρῶν 'others cut branches in the fields' Mk 11.8. In a number of languages important distinctions are made for various types of cutting. For example, terms referring to the cutting of flesh may be different from those involving wood or stone. Similarly, important distinctions may be made as to whether there is simply an incision by cutting or whether a particular object is cut in two or cut off.

---

2 In view of the fact that κρούω in Mt 7.7 involves an act of communication, it would be possible to classify this meaning of κρούω in Domain 33 *Communication*, but since the action of κρούω involves physical impact, it is listed here in Domain 19.

3 It is possible that παίω in Re 9.5 should be understood in the more generic sense of 'to strike' (see παίω[a], 19.1). It is difficult to tell, especially in apocalyptic literature, precisely what particular meaning fits a context.

19.18 ἐκκόπτωᵃ; ἀποκόπτω: to cut in such a way as to cause separation – 'to cut down, to cut off, to cut in two.'

ἐκκόπτωᵃ: πᾶν οὖν δένδρον μὴ ποιοῦν καρπὸν καλὸν ἐκκόπτεται καὶ εἰς πῦρ βάλλεται 'every tree that does not bear good fruit will be cut down and thrown in the fire' Mt 3.10.
ἀποκόπτω: ἀπέκοψαν οἱ στρατιῶται τὰ σχοινία τῆς σκάφης καὶ εἴασαν αὐτὴν ἐκπεσεῖν 'the soldiers cut the ropes that held the boat and let it go' Ac 27.32.[4]

19.19 διχοτομέωᵃ: to cut an object into two parts – 'to cut in two.' διχοτομήσει αὐτὸν καὶ τὸ μέρος αὐτοῦ μετὰ τῶν ἀπίστων θήσει '(the master) will cut him in two and make him share the fate of the disobedient' Lk 12.46. It is also possible to interpret διχοτομέω in Lk 12.46 as severe punishment (see διχοτομέωᵇ, 38.12).

19.20 πρίζω: to cut an object in two with a saw – 'to cut in two with a saw, to saw in two.' ἐλιθάσθησαν, ἐπρίσθησαν 'they were stoned, they were sawed in two' He 11.37.

19.21 κατακόπτω: to cut severely with some sharp instrument or object – 'to cut.' ἐν τοῖς μνήμασιν καὶ ἐν τοῖς ὄρεσιν ἦν κράζων καὶ κατακόπτων ἑαυτὸν λίθοις '(he wandered) among the graves and through the hills, screaming and cutting himself with stones' Mk 5.5. Some have interpreted κατακόπτω in Mk 5.5 as meaning 'to bruise severely' on the basis that stones would only bruise rather than cut, but this inference seems unnecessary.

19.22 κατατομή, ῆς f: to mutilate by severe cutting (occurring in Php 3.2 as an exaggerated reference to περιτομή 'circumcision,' see 53.51) – 'to mutilate, mutilation.' βλέπετε τὴν κατατομήν 'beware of the mutilation' Php 3.2. It is possible that κατατομή in Php 3.2 means 'those who practice mutilation' (as a hyperbole for circumcision) in the same way that περιτομή in some contexts means 'those who circumcise.'

4 In Ga 5.12 ἀποκόπτω probably refers to severe mutilation of the penis or possibly to castration.

19.23 κείρω: to cut the hair of a person or animal – 'to cut hair, to shear.' εἰ γὰρ οὐ κατακαλύπτεται γυνή, καὶ κειράσθω 'if the woman does not cover her head, she might as well cut her hair' 1 Cor 11.6; ὡς ἀμνὸς ἐναντίον τοῦ κείραντος αὐτὸν ἄφωνος 'he was like a lamb that makes no sound when its wool is cut off' Ac 8.32.

19.24 ξυράω: to shave the head or beard – 'to shave.' ἓν γάρ ἐστιν καὶ τὸ αὐτὸ τῇ ἐξυρημένῃ 'for it is one and the same as for a woman who has her head shaved' 1 Cor 11.5.

19.25 λατομέω: to shape rock by cutting, either internally or externally – 'to cut rock, to hew out rock.' ἔθηκεν αὐτὸ ἐν τῷ καινῷ αὐτοῦ μνημείῳ ὃ ἐλατόμησεν ἐν τῇ πέτρᾳ 'he placed it in his own new tomb which he had cut in the rock' Mt 27.60. In some languages important distinctions are made in terms for cutting rock depending upon the type of activity, for example, shaping of rock by cutting, the quarrying of rock from an outcrop, or the hewing of an area inside of an outcropping of rock (a cave-like structure hewn into rock).

19.26 λαξευτός, ή, όν: pertaining to having been hewn out of rock – 'hewn out of rock.' ἔθηκεν αὐτὸν ἐν μνήματι λαξευτῷ 'he placed him in a grave which had been hewn out of rock' Lk 23.53. In Lk 23.53 'rock' must be understood as a basic outcropping of rock, so that the grave would have been a cave-like structure cut into a rock outcropping.

C Split, Tear (19.27-19.33)

19.27 σχίζωᵃ: to split or to tear an object into at least two parts – 'to split, to tear.' εὐθὺς ἀναβαίνων ἐκ τοῦ ὕδατος εἶδεν σχιζομένους οὐρανούς 'as soon as he came up from the water he saw the sky split open' Mk 1.10. In some languages the meaning of σχίζω in Mk 1.10 may be best expressed as 'the sky tore' or 'there was a slit in the sky' or possibly 'there was suddenly an opening in the sky.' The adverb 'suddenly' may provide some of the implications of the splitting involved in the verb σχίζω.

19.28 σχίσμα^a. τος *n*: (derivative of σχίζω^a 'to split, to tear,' 19.27) the condition resulting from the splitting or tearing – 'tear.' αἴρει τὸ πλήρωμα ἀπ᾽ αὐτοῦ τὸ καινὸν τοῦ παλαιοῦ, καὶ χεῖρον σχίσμα γίνεται 'the new patch will tear off some of the old cloth, making an even greater tear' Mk 2.21. The separation indicated by σχίσμα^a may be quite different in languages, depending upon the substance involved, for example, cloth, leather, paper, and clouds.

19.29 διασπάω: to pull or tear an object apart – 'to pull apart, to tear apart.' διεσπάσθαι ὑπ᾽ αὐτοῦ τὰς ἁλύσεις 'he tore apart the chains' (literally 'the chains were torn apart by him') Mk 5.4.

19.30 λακάω: to burst open, probably from internal pressure – 'to burst open.' ἐλάκησεν μέσος 'he burst open in the middle' or 'his belly burst open' Ac 1.18.

19.31 ῥήγνυμι^a: to tear, rip, or burst, either from internal or external forces, with the implication of sudden and forceful action – 'to tear, to rip, to burst.' ῥήξει ὁ οἶνος ὁ νέος τοὺς ἀσκούς 'the new wine will burst the skins' Lk 5.37.

19.32 διαρρήγνυμι or διαρήσσω: to tear or rip in two (as of clothing) – 'to tear, to rip.'[5] διαρρήξαντες τὰ ἱμάτια αὐτῶν ἐξεπήδησαν εἰς τὸν ὄχλον 'they tore their clothes and ran into the middle of the crowd' Ac 14.14.

In the NT tearing of clothing was a symbol of horror associated with sacrilege. In many cultures, however, the tearing of clothing may be associated only with insanity. It may therefore be important to add a phrase in describing 'the tearing of clothing' in order to mark the significance, for example, 'to show horror' Mt 26.65, Ac 14.14. (In the case of the OT, 'to show mourning' Gn 37.34, Jdg 11.35).

19.33 περιρήγνυμι: to tear off or to strip off, as of clothing – 'to tear off, to strip off.' οἱ στρατηγοὶ περιρήξαντες αὐτῶν τὰ ἱμάτια 'the officials tore off their clothes' Ac 16.22.

---

5 διαρρήγνυμι differs from ῥήγνυμι^a (19.31) in that it specifies a more decisive and thorough action.

D Break, Break Through (19.34-19.42)

19.34 κλάω; κλάσις, εως *f*: to break an object into two or more parts (in the NT κλάω and κλάσις are used exclusively for breaking bread) – 'to break, to break bread.'
κλάω: κλάσας ἔδωκεν τοῖς μαθηταῖς τοὺς ἄρτους 'he broke the loaves and gave them to the disciples' Mt 14.19.
κλάσις: ὡς ἐγνώσθη αὐτοῖς ἐν τῇ κλάσει τοῦ ἄρτου 'how they recognized him when he broke bread' Lk 24.35.

In some languages important distinctions are made for terms meaning 'to break' depending on the substance involved. For example, the breaking of a stick or a bone would require quite a different term from that used in speaking of breaking bread. Furthermore, the action of breaking bread would probably imply breaking into several pieces rather than a single break. Such a distinction may likewise require a special term.

19.35 κατάγνυμι: to break or to shatter a rigid object – 'to break.' ἠρώτησαν τὸν Πιλᾶτον ἵνα κατεαγῶσιν αὐτῶν τὰ σκέλη 'they asked Pilate to allow them to break the legs of the men' Jn 19.31; κάλαμον συντετριμμένον οὐ κατεάξει 'he will not break a crushed reed' Mt 12.20.

19.36 ἐκκλάω: to break off a part – 'to break off.' εἰ δέ τινες τῶν κλάδων ἐξεκλάσθησαν 'but if some of the branches have been broken off' Ro 11.17.

19.37 θρύπτω: to break into a number of relatively small pieces – 'to break into pieces.' τοῦτό μού ἐστιν τὸ σῶμα τὸ ὑπὲρ ὑμῶν θρυπτόμενον 'this is my body which is broken into pieces for you' 1 Cor 11.24 (apparatus).

19.38 κατακλάω: to break into pieces, implying thoroughness of the activity (in contrast with κλάω, 19.34) – 'to break into pieces.' κατέκλασεν τοὺς ἄρτους 'he broke the loaves into pieces' Mk 6.41.

19.39 συντρίβω^a; συνθλάω: to break or shatter a solid object into pieces, with the implication of destruction – 'to break into pieces, to shatter.'

συντρίβω[a]: συντρίψασα τὴν ἀλάβαστρον κατέχεεν αὐτοῦ τῆς κεφαλῆς 'breaking the alabaster jar, she anointed his head' Mk 14.3.

συνθλάω: ὁ πεσὼν ἐπὶ τὸν λίθον τοῦτον συνθλασθήσεται 'whoever falls on this stone will be broken to pieces' Mt 21.44.

19.40 κλάσμα, τος *n*: (derivative of κλάω 'to break,' 19.34) a fragment or piece resulting from the action of breaking – 'fragment, piece.' ἐγέμισαν δώδεκα κοφίνους κλασμάτων ἐκ τῶν πέντε ἄρτων τῶν κριθίνων 'they filled twelve baskets with pieces from the five loaves of barley bread' Jn 6.13.

19.41 διορύσσω: to break through a wall or barrier, normally by the process of digging through (usually implying a wall made of sun-dried brick) – 'to break through, to break in, to break into.' οὐκ ἂν ἀφῆκεν διορυχθῆναι τὸν οἶκον αὐτοῦ 'he would not have permitted his house to have been broken into' Lk 12.39.

19.42 ἐξορύσσω: to break something loose, usually by digging out and opening up an area – 'to break loose, to take out, to dig out an opening.' καὶ ἐξορύξαντες χαλῶσι τὸν κράβατ-τον ὅπου ὁ παραλυτικὸς κατέκειτο 'and having dug out an opening, they let down the pallet on which the paralytic was lying' Mk 2.4.

E Press (19.43-19.54)

19.43 ἐπίκειμαι[b]; ἐπιπίπτω[a]: to press or push against – 'to press against, to push against.'
ἐπίκειμαι[b]: ἐγένετο δὲ ἐν τῷ τὸν ὄχλον ἐπικεῖσθαι αὐτῷ καὶ ἀκούειν τὸν λόγον τοῦ θεοῦ 'while the people pushed their way to him to listen to the word of God' Lk 5.1.
ἐπιπίπτω[a]: ὥστε ἐπιπίπτειν αὐτῷ ἵνα αὐτοῦ ἅψωνται ὅσοι εἶχον μάστιγας 'so that all the sick kept pressing toward him in order to touch him' Mk 3.10.

19.44 θλίβω[a]; ἀποθλίβω: to crowd in hard against – 'to press against, to crowd against.'[6]

6 ἀποθλίβω may be somewhat more emphatic than θλίβω[a].

θλίβω[a]: ἵνα μὴ θλίβωσιν αὐτόν 'so that the people would not crowd against him' Mk 3.9.
ἀποθλίβω: οἱ ὄχλοι συνέχουσίν σε καὶ ἀποθλίβουσιν 'the crowds are pressing in from all sides and crowding against you' Lk 8.45.

19.45 συνθλίβω; συνέχω[c]: to press in hard from all sides – 'to press in, to crowd around.'
συνθλίβω: καὶ συνέθλιβον αὐτόν 'and they were crowding him from every side' Mk 5.24.
συνέχω[c]: οἱ ὄχλοι συνέχουσίν σε καὶ ἀποθλίβουσιν 'the crowds are pressing in from all sides and crowding against you' Lk 8.45.

19.46 συντρίβω[b]: to cause damage to an object by crushing – 'to crush, to bruise.'
κάλαμον συντετριμμένον οὐ κατεάξει 'he will not break off a crushed reed' Mt 12.20; μόγις ἀποχωρεῖ ἀπ' αὐτοῦ συντρῖβον αὐτόν 'he continues to crush him and will hardly let him go' Lk 9.39. It is difficult to know precisely what the reference is in the use of συντρίβω in Lk 9.39. The obvious result is severe pain, but it is not possible to tell precisely what symptoms are involved in what is described as being crushed by the demon.

19.47 λικμάω: to crush by a destructive amount of vertical pressure – 'to crush.' ἐφ' ὃν δ' ἂν πέσῃ, λικμήσει αὐτόν 'if (that stone) falls on someone, it will crush him' Lk 20.18.

19.48 συμπνίγω[b]: to crowd around to the point that one can hardly breathe – 'to crowd around, to press against' (a very emphatic form). ἐν δὲ τῷ ὑπάγειν αὐτὸν οἱ ὄχλοι συνέπνιγον αὐτόν 'as he went along, the people were crowding around him from every side' Lk 8.42.

19.49 πιέζω: to press down, in order to make more compact – 'to press down.' μέτρον καλὸν πεπιεσμένον σεσαλευμένον 'good measure, pressed down, shaken' Lk 6.38.

19.50 ψώχω: to rub something under pressure to make it smaller – 'to rub.' τοὺς στάχυας ψώχοντες ταῖς χερσίν 'rubbing the heads of wheat with their hands' Lk 6.1. By rubbing the heads of wheat, the disciples were able to remove the chaff and the so-called 'beards,' the stiff projections arising from each kernel. This process would be equivalent to threshing and would thus be condemned by the Pharisees as work on the Sabbath.

19.51 πατέω[b]: to step down on, with the possible implication of continuous or repeated action – 'to trample.' αὐτὸς πατεῖ τὴν ληνὸν τοῦ οἴνου τοῦ θυμοῦ τῆς ὀργῆς τοῦ θεοῦ 'he tramples the wine press of the wine of the wrath of the anger of God' Re 19.15. The occurrence of πατέω in the figurative context of Re 19.15 is based upon the practice of persons squeezing out the juice from grapes by trampling on the grapes in a large vat or container which had an opening at the bottom through which the grape juice could flow.

19.52 καταπατέω[a]: to step down forcibly upon, often with the implication of destruction or ruin – 'to trample on.' μήποτε καταπατήσουσιν αὐτοὺς ἐν τοῖς ποσὶν αὐτῶν 'so that they do not trample them with their feet' Mt 7.6.

19.53 πνίγω[a]: to apply pressure around the neck in order to harm or kill – 'to choke.' κρατήσας αὐτὸν ἔπνιγεν 'he grabbed him and started choking him' Mt 18.28.

19.54 πνικτός, ή, όν: pertaining to being choked or strangled – 'choked, strangled.' ἐπιστεῖλαι αὐτοῖς τοῦ ἀπέχεσθαι ... τοῦ πνικτοῦ 'to write them to abstain ... (from eating) what has been strangled' Ac 15.20.

F Dig (19.55)

19.55 ὀρύσσω; σκάπτω[a]: to make a hole in the ground and to remove earth with some sharp-edged intrument (for example pick or spade) – 'to dig, to excavate.'
ὀρύσσω: ἐφύτευσεν ἀμπελῶνα ... καὶ ὤρυξεν ἐν αὐτῷ ληνόν 'he planted a vineyard ... and dug a wine press in it' Mt 21.33.
σκάπτω[a]: ἔσκαψεν καὶ ἐβάθυνεν καὶ ἔθηκεν θεμέλιον ἐπὶ τὴν πέτραν 'he dug and went down deep and laid the foundation on the rock' Lk 6.48; σκάπτειν οὐκ ἰσχύω 'I am not strong enough to dig (ditches)' Lk 16.3. For another interpretation of σκάπτω in Lk 16.3, see 43.3.

20 Violence, Harm, Destroy, Kill[1]

Outline of Subdomains

A Violence (20.1-20.11)
B Harm, Wound (20.12-20.30)
C Destroy (20.31-20.60)
D Kill (20.61-20.88)

A Violence (20.1-20.11)

20.1 βία, ας *f*: a strong, destructive force – 'force, violence.' οὐ μετὰ βίας, ἐφοβοῦντο γὰρ τὸν λαόν 'not with violence, for they were afraid of the people' Ac 5.26; ἡ δὲ πρύμνα ἐλύετο ὑπὸ τῆς βίας τῶν κυμάτων 'and the stern was destroyed by the violence of the waves' Ac 27.41. In some languages it is difficult, if not impossible, to find a term such as 'violence,' but one may describe the effects of violence by expressions which indicate the harm that is done. For example, Ac 5.26 may be translated 'they did not wish to harm anyone, for they were afraid of the people,' and similarly in Ac 27.41, one may translate 'the waves did great damage to the stern.'

20.2 χαλεπός[b]**, ή, όν**: pertaining to one who is inclined to violent and dangerous activity – 'dangerous, fierce.' δαιμονιζόμενοι ... χαλεποὶ λίαν 'they were demon possessed ... and were very fierce' Mt 8.28.

1 Domain 20 *Violence, Harm, Destroy, Kill* focuses upon physical harm in contrast with psychological harm, which may be caused either by persons or circumstances. In this domain of physical harm the causative agents may likewise be either animate beings or inanimate forces.

20.3 σκληρόςª, ά, όν: pertaining to being harsh and violent – 'harsh, strong, violent.' ὑπὸ ἀνέμων σκληρῶν ἐλαυνόμενα 'driven by strong winds' Jas 3.4. For another interpretation of σκληρός in Jas 3.4, see 76.15.

20.4 ἅρπαξª, αγος: pertaining to being destructively vicious – 'vicious, destructive.' ἔσωθεν δέ εἰσιν λύκοι ἅρπαγες 'but they are like vicious wolves on the inside' Mt 7.15.

20.5 ἀνήμερος, ον: pertaining to fierceness, in the sense of being wild and untamed – 'fierce, vicious, untamed.' ἔσονται γὰρ οἱ ἄνθρωποι . . . ἀκρατεῖς, ἀνήμεροι, ἀφιλάγαθοι 'for people will be . . . lacking in self-control, they will be fierce and hate the good' 2 Tm 3.2-3.

20.6 ἄγριος, α, ον: (a figurative extension of meaning of ἄγριος 'wild, savage,' not occurring in the NT) pertaining to what is violent and uncontrolled – 'violent, stormy.' κύματα ἄγρια θαλάσσης 'stormy waves of the sea' Jd 13. This expression in Jd 13, however, is applied to people, and therefore it may be necessary to make the figurative reference clear, for example, 'they are like stormy waves of the sea' or '. . . wild waves of the sea.'

20.7 βαρύςᵈ, εῖα, ύ: pertaining to one who is vicious and cruel – 'fierce, vicious, cruel.' ἐγὼ οἶδα ὅτι εἰσελεύσονται μετὰ τὴν ἄφιξίν μου λύκοι βαρεῖς εἰς ὑμᾶς 'I know that after I leave, cruel wolves will come among you' Ac 20.29. In a number of languages a strictly literal translation of Ac 20.29 might be misunderstood. It may therefore be important to translate the last part of this expression as 'people like cruel wolves will come among you.'

20.8 βίαιος, α, ον: pertaining to the use of violent or strong force – 'violent, forcible.' ἐγένετο ἄφνω ἐκ τοῦ οὐρανοῦ ἦχος ὥσπερ φερομένης πνοῆς βιαίας 'and suddenly there was a sound like a violent wind from heaven' Ac 2.2.

20.9 βιάζομαιª: to experience a violent attack – 'to be attacked with violence, to suffer violent attacks.' ἡ βασιλεία τῶν οὐρανῶν βιάζεται 'the kingdom of heaven suffers violent attacks' Mt 11.12. In many languages it may be difficult, if not impossible, to speak of the kingdom of heaven 'suffering violent attacks,' but generally some active form may be employed, for example, 'and violently attack the kingdom of heaven' or '. . . the rule of God.' See comment at 20.10.

20.10 βιάζομαιᵇ: to employ violence in doing harm to someone or something – 'to use violence.' πᾶς εἰς αὐτὴν βιάζεται 'everyone uses violence in entering it' (referring to the kingdom of God) Lk 16.16. Since there are a number of different interpretations of this expression (πᾶς εἰς αὐτὴν βιάζεται) in Lk 16.16 as well as for the parallel expression in Mt 11.12 (ἡ βασιλεία τῶν οὐρανῶν βιάζεται; see 20.9), it is important to consult various commentaries before undertaking a translation. Probably the most widely held interpretation of these difficult expressions is based on the fact that many people did not hesitate to employ violence or military force in order to establish what they regarded as the rule of God on earth.

20.11 βιαστής, οῦ *m*: (derivative of βιάζομαιᵇ 'to use violence,' 20.10) a person who employs violence in order to accomplish his purpose – 'violent person.' βιασταὶ ἁρπάζουσιν αὐτήν 'violent men take it by force' Mt 11.12. See the comment at 20.10 for a discussion of some of the problems involved in the interpretation of this type of expression.

B Harm, Wound (20.12-20.30)

20.12 κακόω; κάκωσις, εως *f*; **κακοποιέω**ᵇ; **βλάπτω**: to cause harm or injury to someone or something (a highly generic meaning involving a wide range of harm and injury) – 'to harm, to hurt, to injure.'
κακόω: οὗτος κατασοφισάμενος τὸ γένος ἡμῶν ἐκάκωσεν τοὺς πατέρας ἡμῶν 'he deceived our people and did harm to our ancestors' Ac 7.19.
κάκωσις: εἶδον τὴν κάκωσιν τοῦ λαοῦ μου τοῦ ἐν Αἰγύπτῳ 'I have seen the harming of my people in Egypt' Ac 7.34. In some languages it may be necessary to translate this expression

in Ac 7.34 as passive, for example, 'I have seen the harm done to my people in Egypt' or, in the active form, 'I have seen how the people in Egypt harmed my people.'

κακοποιέω^b: ἔξεστιν τοῖς σάββασιν ἀγαθὸν ποιῆσαι ἢ κακοποιῆσαι 'what is permissible for us to do on the Sabbath? To help (literally 'to do good') or to harm?' Mk 3.4. For another interpretation of κακοποιέω in Mk 3.4, see 88.112.

βλάπτω: ἐξῆλθεν ἀπ' αὐτοῦ μηδὲν βλάψαν αὐτόν '(the demon) went out of him without doing him any harm' Lk 4.35.

In translating terms meaning 'to harm' or 'to injure,' it may be necessary to specify suffering, for example, 'to cause people to suffer' or 'to cause people t⁻ have pain.'

20.13 βλαβερός, ά, όν: pertaining to that which causes harm – 'harmful.' ἐπιθυμίας πολλὰς ἀνοήτους καὶ βλαβεράς 'many senseless and harmful desires' 1 Tm 6.9. There is no indication in 1 Tm 6.9 as to the specific nature of the harm, but the extent of it is made clear in the following clause which speaks of 'complete destruction.' This could be physical, moral, and/or spiritual.

20.14 σαπρός^b, ά, όν: pertaining to that which is harmful in view of its being unwholesome and corrupting – 'harmful, unwholesome.' πᾶς λόγος σαπρὸς ἐκ τοῦ στόματος ὑμῶν μὴ ἐκπορευέσθω 'let no harmful word go out of your mouth' Eph 4.29. In Eph 4.29 σαπρός is in contrast with that which is ἀγαθός 'good' for building up what is necessary. In such a context ἀγαθός may be interpreted as that which is helpful, and by contrast σαπρός may be understood to mean 'harmful.'

20.15 τύπτω^b: (a figurative extension of meaning of τύπτω^a 'to strike, to beat,' 19.1) to cause serious harm to, in a psychological sense – 'to harm, to injure.' τύπτοντες αὐτῶν τὴν συνείδησιν ἀσθενοῦσαν 'harming their weak consciences' or 'causing spiritual injury to those whose consciences are weak' 1 Cor 8.12.

20.16 ἅπτομαι^c: to cause some relatively light physical, moral, and/or spiritual harm to – 'to harm.' ὁ πονηρὸς οὐχ ἅπτεται αὐτοῦ 'and the Evil One does not harm him at all' or 'and

the Evil One doesn't so much as touch him' 1 Jn 5.18.

20.17 καταστροφή^a, ῆς f: to do serious harm to, with the implication of misleading – 'to cause harm, to cause ruin to.' μὴ λογομαχεῖν, ἐπ' οὐδὲν χρήσιμον, ἐπὶ καταστροφῇ τῶν ἀκουόντων 'not to fight over words; it does no good but rather harms those who hear' 2 Tm 2.14.

20.18 κακός^c, ή, όν; κακῶς^b: pertaining to having experienced harm – 'harmed, harm, injured.'

κακός^c: ὁ μὲν οὖν ἀποτινάξας τὸ θηρίον εἰς τὸ πῦρ ἔπαθεν οὐδὲν κακόν 'but he shook the snake off into the fire without being harmed at all' Ac 28.5. In some languages Ac 28.5 may be rendered as 'but Paul shook the snake off into the fire, and it did not cause him pain at all.'

κακῶς^b: καὶ κακῶς πάσχει 'and he suffers harm' Mt 17.15. The phrase κακῶς πάσχει in Mt 17.15 may be a reference to a type of epileptic seizure.

20.19 ὕβρις^b, εως f: the condition resulting from violence or mistreatment – 'harm, damage, injury.' μετὰ ὕβρεως καὶ πολλῆς ζημίας οὐ μόνον τοῦ φορτίου καὶ τοῦ πλοίου 'with damage and much loss not only to the cargo and the ship' Ac 27.10; εὐδοκῶ ἐν ἀσθενείαις, ἐν ὕβρεσιν 'I am content with weaknesses, injuries . . .' 2 Cor 12.10. It is possible to interpret ὕβρις in 2 Cor 12.10 as 'insults' (see 33.391) or as 'insolent mistreatment' (see 88.131).

20.20 σητόβρωτος, ον: pertaining to that which has been damaged by the larvae of moths – 'moth-eaten, ruined by moths.' τὰ ἱμάτια ὑμῶν σητόβρωτα 'your garments are motheaten' Jas 5.2. This expression in Jas 5.2 may often be rendered as 'your garments have been eaten by worms' or 'your garments are full of holes.'

20.21 καταβάλλω^b: to cause someone to suffer considerable pain or injury – 'to hurt badly, to cause to suffer considerably.' καταβαλλόμενοι ἀλλ' οὐκ ἀπολλύμενοι 'though badly hurt at times, we are not destroyed' 2 Cor 4.9.

It is possible, however, that in 2 Cor 4.9 κατα-βάλλω should be understood as 'to knock 'own' (see 19.10).

20.22 πατέω^c: (a figurative extension of meaning of πατέω^b 'to trample,' 19.51) to harm severely by subjugation – 'to trample on, to subdue by force.' τὴν πόλιν τὴν ἁγίαν πατήσουσιν μῆνας τεσσεράκοντα καὶ δύο 'they will trample upon the holy city for forty-two months' Re 11.2; καὶ Ἰερουσαλὴμ ἔσται πατουμένη ὑπὸ ἐθνῶν 'and Jerusalem will be trampled on by the Gentiles' Lk 21.24. For another interpretation of πατέω in Lk 21.24, see 39.54.

20.23 φθείρω^b: to cause harm to someone – 'to cause harm, to ruin.' οὐδένα ἐφθείραμεν 'we have ruined no one' 2 Cor 7.2. It may be possible to translate this expression in 2 Cor 7.2 (referring to financial ruin) as 'we have not caused anyone to suffer a loss,' but φθείρω in 2 Cor 7.2 may also refer to the undermining of faith.

20.24 λυμαίνομαι^a: to cause injury or harm by maltreatment – 'to injure severely, to maltreat.' Σαῦλος δὲ ἐλυμαίνετο τὴν ἐκκλησίαν 'Saul then was causing great harm to the church' Ac 8.3. It is also possible that λυμαίνομαι in Ac 8.3 may mean 'to destroy' (see 20.31).

20.25 ἀδικέω^a: to hurt or to harm, with the implication of doing something which is wrong and undeserved – 'to harm, to hurt.' οὐδὲν ὑμᾶς οὐ μὴ ἀδικήσῃ 'nothing will hurt you' Lk 10.19.

20.26 δάκνω: (a figurative extension of meaning of δάκνω 'to bite,' not occurring in the NT) to cause personal harm to someone – 'to harm.' εἰ δὲ ἀλλήλους δάκνετε 'you are harming one another' Ga 5.15.

20.27 κολαφίζω^b: (a figurative extension of meaning of κολαφίζω^a 'to beat with the fist,' 19.7) to cause injury or weakness or possibly a circumstantial difficulty – 'to cause harm to.' ἐδόθη μοι σκόλοψ τῇ σαρκί, ἄγγελος Σατανᾶ, ἵνα με κολαφίζῃ, ἵνα μὴ ὑπεραίρωμαι 'there was

given me a thorn in my flesh, a messenger of Satan, to cause me harm lest I become conceited' 2 Cor 12.7.

Though differences of interpretation exist concerning the meaning of 'a thorn in my flesh,' especially since some scholars have felt that this must refer to some kind of physical disability, it seems more likely to assume that it refers to some special personal circumstance such as the opposition Paul encountered in preaching the gospel, a reference suggested by 2 Cor 12.10. See also 22.20. Without some clear understanding of the reference of 'a thorn in my flesh,' it is difficult to determine precisely how κολαφίζω is to be interpreted in 2 Cor 12.7.

20.28 τραυματίζω: to hurt or wound, normally resulting in some mark or permanent scar on the body – 'to hurt, to wound.' οἱ δὲ καὶ τοῦτον τραυματίσαντες ἐξέβαλον 'they wounded him, too, and threw him out' Lk 20.12.

20.29 τραῦμα, τος *n*; **μώλωψ, ωπος** *m*; **πληγή**^b, **ῆς** *f*: the condition resulting from being severely hurt or wounded – 'wound.'[2] τραῦμα: προσελθὼν κατέδησεν τὰ τραύματα αὐτοῦ 'he went to him and bandaged his wounds' Lk 10.34.
μώλωψ: οὗ τῷ μώλωπι ἰάθητε 'because he was wounded, you were healed' 1 Pe 2.24.[3]
πληγή^b: παραλαβὼν αὐτοὺς ἐν ἐκείνῃ τῇ ὥρᾳ τῆς νυκτὸς ἔλουσεν ἀπὸ τῶν πληγῶν 'at that very hour of the night he took them and washed off their wounds' Ac 16.33.

20.30 φράσσω στόμα^b: (an idiom, literally 'to shut the mouth') to prevent harm or injury being done (in the one context in the NT, He 11.33, a reference to lions) – 'to stop the mouth of, to keep from harming.' ἔφραξαν στόματα λεόντων 'they shut the mouths of

2 These expressions for 'wound' normally do not imply a mortal wound. It is possible, however, to speak of a mortal wound by the phrase ἡ πληγὴ τοῦ θανάτου as in Re 13.3, 12.
3 μώλωψ appears to be a welt or bruise caused specifically by blows or beating, but the context of 1 Pe 2.24 appears to be highly generic.

lions' or 'they kept lions from doing harm' He 11.33. The particular historical reference of this phrase in He 11.33 is not clear. In the account in Dn 6.22 it is the angel of God which shut the mouths of the lions.

C Destroy⁴ (20.31-20.60)

20.31 ἀπόλλυμιᵃ; ἀπώλειαᵃ, ας f; λυμαίν-ομαιᵇ: to destroy or to cause the destruction of persons, objects, or institutions – 'to ruin, to destroy, destruction.'

ἀπόλλυμιᵃ: οἱ ἀσκοὶ ἀπολοῦνται 'the wineskins will be ruined' Lk 5.37; ὁ κλέπτης οὐκ ἔρχεται εἰ μὴ ἵνα κλέψῃ καὶ θύσῃ καὶ ἀπολέσῃ 'the thief comes only in order to steal, kill, and destroy' Jn 10.10; φοβεῖσθε δὲ μᾶλλον τὸν δυνάμενον καὶ ψυχὴν καὶ σῶμα ἀπολέσαι ἐν γεέννῃ 'but fear rather the one who is able to destroy soul and body in hell' Mt 10.28.

ἀπώλειαᵃ: σκεύη ὀργῆς κατηρτισμένα εἰς ἀπώλειαν 'objects of his wrath destined for destruction' Ro 9.22; εἰ μὴ ὁ υἱὸς τῆς ἀπωλείας 'except the one who is bound for destruction' Jn 17.12.

λυμαίνομαιᵇ: Σαῦλος δὲ ἐλυμαίνετο τὴν ἐκκλησίαν 'Saul then worked for the destruction of the church' Ac 8.3. It is also possible that λυμαίνομαι in Ac 8.3 may mean 'to injure severely' (see 20.24).

In a number of languages it is difficult to find a general term for 'destruction.' What has often happened is the extension of meaning from a more specific type of reference, for example, 'to smash,' to a more generic meaning of 'to destroy,' and whether one understands the specific or more generic meaning depends largely upon the context. Accordingly, in Ac 8.3 one may find a figurative usage of a term meaning 'to smash' (though understood in a more generic sense), for example, 'Saul then worked in order to smash the church.'

20.32 συναπόλλυμαι: to be destroyed together with someone or something else – 'to be destroyed with, to perish with.' Ῥαὰβ ἡ πόρνη οὐ συναπώλετο τοῖς ἀπειθήσασιν 'Rahab the harlot did not perish with those who were disobedient' He 11.31. In a number of languages one must translate συναπόλλυμαι in He 11.31 as 'to die,' for example, 'Rahab the harlot did not die with those who were disobedient.'

20.33 ὄλεθροςᵃ, ου m: a state of utter ruin or destruction – 'ruin, destruction.'⁵ αἵτινες βυθίζουσιν τοὺς ἀνθρώπους εἰς ὄλεθρον 'which cause people to sink into ruin' or 'which ruin people' 1 Tm 6.9.

20.34 ὀλοθρεύω; ὄλεθροςᵇ, ου m: to cause the complete destruction or ruin of someone or something – 'to destroy, to ruin, destruction.'⁶

ὀλοθρεύω: ἵνα μὴ ὁ ὀλοθρεύων τὰ πρωτότοκα θίγῃ αὐτῶν 'in order that the Destroyer might not cause the death of their firstborn' He 11.28.

ὄλεθροςᵇ: παραδοῦναι τὸν τοιοῦτον τῷ Σατανᾷ εἰς ὄλεθρον τῆς σαρκός 'to hand such a person over to Satan for the destruction of the body' 1 Cor 5.5.

20.35 ἐξολεθρεύω: to destroy and thus eliminate – 'to destroy, to destroy and remove.' ἔσται δὲ πᾶσα ψυχὴ ἥτις ἐὰν μὴ ἀκούσῃ τοῦ προφήτου ἐκείνου ἐξολεθρευθήσεται ἐκ τοῦ λαοῦ 'anyone who does not obey that prophet shall be destroyed and so removed from the people' Ac 3.23. It is possible in Ac 3.23 that ἐξολεθρεύω refers to a type of severe ostracism.

20.36 ὀλοθρευτής, οῦ m: (derivative of ὀλοθρεύω 'to destroy, to ruin,' 20.34) one who causes destruction – 'destroyer.' καὶ ἀπώλοντο ὑπὸ τοῦ ὀλοθρευτοῦ 'and they were destroyed

---

4 The subdomain entitled *Destroy* includes those meanings which involve the destruction or termination of a structure or object and not merely the cessation of some function. To this extent the meanings in this subcategory differ from those involving merely harm or damage.

5 ὄλεθροςᵃ suggests a type of ruin or destruction which is somewhat more violent and extensive than in the case of φθοράᵃ (20.38).

6 The meaning of ὀλοθρεύω and ὄλεθροςᵇ in 20.34 is considerably stronger and more 'intense' than the meanings in 20.31.

by the destroyer' 1 Cor 10.10. In 1 Cor 10.10 ὀλοθρευτής may serve as a title referring to a destroying angel or even to Satan.

20.37 πορθέω: to attack with the intent or result of destroying – 'to attack, to destroy.' οὐχ οὗτός ἐστιν ὁ πορθήσας εἰς Ἰερουσαλήμ τοὺς ἐπικαλουμένους τὸ ὄνομα τοῦτο 'isn't this the man who in Jerusalem was destroying those who call on this name' Ac 9.21; τὴν ἐκκλησίαν τοῦ θεοῦ καὶ ἐπόρθουν 'I attacked with the purpose of destroying the church of God' Ga 1.13.

20.38 φθορά ª, ᾶς f: a state of ruin or destruction, with the implication of disintegration – 'ruin, destruction.' ἅ ἐστιν πάντα εἰς φθορὰν τῇ ἀποχρήσει 'all such things are ruined by use' Col 2.22; ὡς ἄλογα ζῷα γεγεννημένα φυσικὰ εἰς ἅλωσιν καὶ φθοράν 'like wild animals born to be captured and destroyed' 2 Pe 2.12. In 2 Pe 2.12 it may be more appropriate in a number of languages to translate '. . . to be killed.'

20.39 φθείρω ª: to ruin or destroy something, with the implication of causing something to be corrupt and thus to cease to exist – 'to destroy.' εἴ τις τὸν ναὸν τοῦ θεοῦ φθείρει, φθερεῖ τοῦτον ὁ θεός 'so if anyone destroys God's temple, God will destroy him' 1 Cor 3.17.

20.40 διαφθείρω ª: to cause the complete destruction of someone or something – 'to destroy utterly.' τὸ τρίτον τῶν πλοίων διεφθάρησαν 'a third of the ships were completely destroyed' Re 8.9; διαφθεῖραι τοὺς διαφθείροντας τὴν γῆν 'to destroy those who deprave the earth' Re 11.18. In Re 11.18 there is a play on the two meanings of διαφθείρω. In the first instance the meaning is destroy, but in the second instance the meaning is 'to deprave' (see 88.266.)

20.41 ἐρημόομαι; ἐρήμωσις, εως f: to suffer destruction, with the implication of being deserted and abandoned – 'to be destroyed, to suffer destruction, to suffer desolation.' ἐρημόομαι: μιᾷ ὥρᾳ ἠρημώθη ὁ τοσοῦτος πλοῦτος 'such great wealth has been destroyed within a single hour' Re 18.17.

ἐρήμωσις: ὅταν δὲ ἴδητε κυκλουμένην ὑπὸ στρατοπέδων Ἰερουσαλήμ, τότε γνῶτε ὅτι ἤγγικεν ἡ ἐρήμωσις αὐτῆς 'when you see Jerusalem surrounded by armies, then you will know that she will soon be destroyed' Lk 21.20.

20.42 καθαιρέω ᵈ: to destroy by conquering and overpowering – 'to destroy, to conquer.' καθελὼν ἔθνη ἑπτὰ ἐν γῇ Χανάαν 'he destroyed seven nations in the land of Canaan' Ac 13.19.

20.43 αἴρω ᵇ: to destroy, with the implication of removal and doing away with – 'to destroy, to do away with.' ἐλεύσονται οἱ Ῥωμαῖοι καὶ ἀροῦσιν ἡμῶν καὶ τὸν τόπον καὶ τὸ ἔθνος 'the Roman authorities will take action and destroy our Temple (literally 'our place') and our nation' Jn 11.48.

20.44 ἐσθίω ᵇ: (a figurative extension of meaning of ἐσθίω ª 'to eat,' 23.1) to destroy, with the implication of doing away with all traces of an object – 'to destroy, to consume.' κρίσεως καὶ πυρὸς ζῆλος ἐσθίειν μέλλοντος τοὺς ὑπεναντίους 'the judgment and the fierce fire which will destroy those who oppose (God)' He 10.27.

20.45 κατεσθίω ᵇ: (a figurative extension of meaning of κατεσθίω ª 'to eat up,' 23.11) to destroy completely (in a sense more emphatic than ἐσθίω ᵇ, 20.44) – 'to destroy utterly, to consume completely.' πῦρ ἐκπορεύεται ἐκ τοῦ στόματος αὐτῶν καὶ κατεσθίει τοὺς ἐχθροὺς αὐτῶν 'the fire will come out of their mouths and utterly destroy their enemies' Re 11.5.

20.46 ἀφανίζω ª: to destroy the value or use of something – 'to destroy, to completely ruin.' θησαυροὺς ἐπὶ τῆς γῆς, ὅπου σὴς καὶ βρῶσις ἀφανίζει 'treasures on earth where moth and tarnish destroy' Mt 6.19. See 4.49.

20.47 ἀναλίσκω or ἀναλόω: to destroy, with the possible implication of something being used up – 'to destroy.' κύριε, θέλεις εἴπωμεν πῦρ καταβῆναι ἀπὸ τοῦ οὐρανοῦ καὶ ἀναλῶσαι αὐτούς 'Lord, do you want us to call fire down from heaven and destroy them' Lk 9.54. In contexts such as Lk 9.54 it is always possible to translate a term such as ἀναλίσκω as 'to cause to die.'

20.48 καταναλίσκω: to destroy completely, with the possible implication of something being used up or consumed – 'to destroy completely, to consume completely.' γὰρ ὁ θεὸς ἡμῶν πῦρ καταναλίσκον 'for our God is indeed a consuming fire' He 12.29.

20.49 καταστροφή[b], ῆς f: a state of total ruin or destruction – 'complete ruin, destruction.' καὶ πόλεις Σοδόμων καὶ Γομόρρας τεφρώσας καταστροφῇ κατέκρινεν 'and he condemned the cities of Sodom and Gomorrah to complete destruction by reducing them to ashes' 2 Pe 2.6.

20.50 πτῶσις[a], εως f: (a figurative extension of meaning of πτῶσις 'fall,' not occurring in the NT) to suffer destruction or ruin, with the implication of having formerly held a position of eminence – 'destruction.' κεῖται εἰς πτῶσιν καὶ ἀνάστασιν πολλῶν 'set for the destruction and rise of many' Lk 2.34. In rendering εἰς πτῶσιν καὶ ἀνάστασιν πολλῶν in Lk 2.34 it is important to indicate clearly that some are to be destroyed and others are to rise. If one translates literally 'for the destruction and rise of many,' it might imply that certain individuals are to be destroyed and then to rise again. For other interpretations of this passage, see 13.59 and 87.75.

20.51 συμπίπτω: to fall together in a heap – 'to collapse.' καὶ εὐθὺς συνέπεσεν, καὶ ἐγένετο τὸ ῥῆγμα τῆς οἰκίας ἐκείνης μέγα 'and it immediately collapsed, and the crash of that house was terrible' Lk 6.49.

20.52 καταπίνω[b]: (a figurative extension of meaning of καταπίνω[a] 'to swallow,' 23.45) to cause the complete and sudden destruction of someone or something – 'to destroy, to ruin completely.' ὁ ἀντίδικος ὑμῶν διάβολος ὡς λέων ὠρυόμενος περιπατεῖ ζητῶν τινα καταπιεῖν 'your enemy, the Devil, roams around like a roaring lion, looking for someone to destroy' 1 Pe 5.8.

20.53 λύω[c]: to destroy or reduce something to ruin by tearing down or breaking to pieces – 'to destroy, to tear down, to break to pieces.' ἡ δὲ πρύμνα ἐλύετο ὑπὸ τῆς βίας τῶν κυμάτων 'the back part of the ship was being broken to pieces by the violence of the waves' Ac 27.41; τὸ μεσότοιχον τοῦ φραγμοῦ λύσας, τὴν ἔχθραν, ἐν τῇ σαρκὶ αὐτοῦ 'with his own body he broke down the wall that separated them and kept them enemies' Eph 2.14.

In some languages there may be an important distinction in terms meaning 'to destroy,' depending upon whether the destruction is purposeful or not. A still further distinction may arise on the basis of beneficial or non-beneficial results. In Eph 2.14 the destruction is regarded as beneficial, while in Ac 27.41 the opposite is the case.

20.54 καταλύω[a]; καθαιρέω[c]; καθαίρεσις[a], εως f: to destroy completely by tearing down and dismantling – 'to destroy, to tear down, destruction.'
καταλύω[a]: οὐκ ἀφεθήσεται λίθος ἐπὶ λίθῳ ὃς οὐ καταλυθήσεται 'there will not be one stone left on another which will not be torn down' Lk 21.6.
καθαιρέω[c]: καθελῶ μου τὰς ἀποθήκας καὶ μείζονας οἰκοδομήσω 'I will tear my barns down and build bigger ones' Lk 12.18. It may be important in rendering Lk 12.18 to indicate clearly that there is purpose in tearing down the barns, and that presumably materials resulting from the dismantling of the barns would be used in building bigger ones.
καθαίρεσις[a]: ἀλλὰ δυνατὰ τῷ θεῷ πρὸς καθαίρεσιν ὀχυρωμάτων 'but God's powerful weapons, with which to tear down strongholds' 2 Cor 10.4.

20.55 καταλύω[b]: to destroy completely the efforts or work of someone else – 'to destroy, to ruin utterly.' μὴ ἕνεκεν βρώματος κατάλυε τὸ ἔργον τοῦ θεοῦ 'for the sake of meat, do not destroy the work of God' Ro 14.20. In Ro 14.20 the work of God involves the building up of the community of faith.

20.56 κατασκάπτω: (a figurative extension of meaning of κατασκάπτω 'to dig down,' not occurring in the NT) to tear down or destroy by digging down into or under – 'to tear down, to destroy.' κύριε, τοὺς προφήτας σου ἐπέκτειναν, τὰ θυσιαστήριά σου κατέσκαφαν 'Lord, they have killed your prophets and torn down your altars' Ro 11.3; καὶ τὰ κατεσκαμμένα αὐτῆς ἀνοικοδομήσω 'I will build up again its ruins' or '. . . those buildings which have been torn down' Ac 15.16.

20.57 ἐδαφίζω[a]: (a derivative of ἔδαφος 'ground,' 1.44) to destroy or tear down, by causing something to be brought down to the level of the ground – 'to raze, to tear down, to destroy.' ἐδαφιοῦσίν σε 'they will raze you to the ground' Lk 19.44. In Lk 19.44 the pronoun σε 'you' refers to the city of Jerusalem.

20.58 ῥῆγμα, τος *n*: the event of destruction, involving splitting open and breaking – 'destruction, crash.' ἐγένετο τὸ ῥῆγμα τῆς οἰκίας ἐκείνης μέγα 'the crash of that house was terrible' Lk 6.49. Though the noun ῥῆγμα with the derivative suffix -μα might lead one to assume that the reference is to a state of ruin or destruction, the context points to the actual event of destruction, and therefore the translation of 'crash' or 'destruction.'

20.59 σύντριμμα, τος *n*: a state of destruction and ruin – 'ruin, destruction.' σύντριμμα καὶ ταλαιπωρία ἐν ταῖς ὁδοῖς αὐτῶν 'they leave ruin and misery wherever they go' Ro 3.16. In some languages it is impossible to speak of 'leaving ruin' except in the sense of going off from ruin. Accordingly, it may be necessary to render this expression in Ro 3.16 as 'they cause ruin and misery wherever they go.'

20.60 πίπτω[d]: to suffer or experience destruction – 'to experience destruction, to be destroyed.' καὶ τὸ δέκατον τῆς πόλεως ἔπεσεν 'and a tenth of the city was destroyed' Re 11.13.

D Kill (20.61-20.88)

20.61 ἀποκτείνω[a] or ἀποκτέννω: to cause someone's death, normally by violent means, with or without intent and with or without legal justification – 'to kill.'[7] ἢ ἐκεῖνοι οἱ δεκα-

οκτὼ ἐφ' οὓς ἔπεσεν ὁ πύργος ἐν τῷ Σιλωὰμ καὶ ἀπέκτεινεν αὐτούς 'what about those eighteen in Siloam who were killed when the tower fell on them' Lk 13.4; θέλων αὐτὸν ἀποκτεῖναι ἐφοβήθη τὸν ὄχλον 'though he wanted to kill him, he was afraid of the people' Mt 14.5.

20.62 διαχειρίζομαι: to lay hands on someone and kill – 'to seize and kill, to arrest and cause the death of.' ὃν ὑμεῖς διεχειρίσασθε 'whom you seized and killed' Ac 5.30; ἐν τῷ ἱερῷ ἐπειρῶντο διαχειρίσασαι 'in the Temple they tried to arrest and kill (me)' Ac 26.21.

20.63 καταστρώννυμι: (a figurative extension of meaning of καταστρώννυμι 'to spread out,' not occurring in the NT) to cause the death of a number of persons, with the implication of bodies spread out over an area – 'to kill.' κατεστρώθησαν γὰρ ἐν τῇ ἐρήμῳ 'for they were killed in the desert' 1 Cor 10.5. It is also possible to understand this expression in 1 Cor 10.5 as meaning that the individuals died and that their bodies were strewn over the desert.

20.64 ἐδαφίζω[b]: (a figurative extension of meaning of ἐδαφίζω[a] 'to raze, to tear down,' 20.57) to destroy or kill a population – 'to kill.' ἐδαφιοῦσίν σε καὶ τὰ τέκνα σου ἐν σοί 'they will raze you to the ground and kill those who live in you' Lk 19.44. The verb ἐδαφίζω in relationship to the pronoun σε (referring to Jerusalem) means 'to raze to the ground' (see 20.57), but in reference to τὰ τέκνα σου ἐν σοί the meaning is 'to kill.' Accordingly, ἐδαφίζω must be regarded as having two different meanings within the same context: (1) 'to raze to the ground' and (2) 'to kill.'

---

7 Though some semanticists have analyzed terms meaning 'to kill' as being simply a causative relating to death, that is, 'to cause to die' or 'to cause to no longer live,' this does not seem to be a satisfactory manner in which to treat the essential semantic components of expressions meaning 'to kill, to murder, to execute, etc.' Though from the standpoint of propositional logic the results of the activities are essentially the same, nevertheless, the manner in which the death is produced is certainly different. The meaning of 'to kill' involves unnatural death, normally a degree of violence, and often evil intent.

20.65 αἴρω^c; θανατόω^a; ἀπάγω^c: to deprive a person of life, with the implication of this being the result of condemnation by legal or quasi-legal procedures – 'to kill, to execute.'
αἴρω^c: ἀνέκραγον δὲ παμπληθεὶ λέγοντες, Αἶρε τοῦτον 'the whole crowd cried out, Kill him' Lk 23.18.
θανατόω^a: ὡς παιδευόμενοι, καὶ μὴ θανατούμενοι 'although punished, we are not killed' 2 Cor 6.9.
ἀπάγω^c: τοὺς φύλακας ἐκέλευσεν ἀπαχθῆναι 'he commanded the guards to be executed' Ac 12.19. For another interpretation of ἀπάγω in Ac 12.19, see 56.38.

20.66 ζητέω τὴν ψυχήν: (an idiom, literally 'to seek the life') to desire or intend to kill – 'to want to kill, to desire to kill.' οἱ ζητοῦντες τὴν ψυχὴν τοῦ παιδίου 'those who sought to kill the child' Mt 2.20.

20.67 μάρτυς^b, μάρτυρος, dat. pl. μάρτυσιν m: a person who has been deprived of life as the result of bearing witness to his beliefs – 'martyr.' καὶ ἐκ τοῦ αἵματος τῶν μαρτύρων Ἰησοῦ 'and the blood of those who were killed because they had been loyal to Jesus' Re 17.6. A strictly literal translation of the Greek expression in Re 17.6 (ἐκ τοῦ αἵματος τῶν μαρτύρων Ἰησοῦ 'of the blood of the martyrs of Jesus') is likely to result in considerable misunderstanding, for it could mean that these were individuals who had been martyred by Jesus rather than those who had been deprived of their lives because of their relationship to Jesus. It would be possible to render τῶν μαρτύρων Ἰησοῦ as 'those who had been killed because they belonged to Jesus,' but one should avoid any expression which would suggest slave ownership.

20.68 μάχαιρα^c, ης f: (a figurative extension of meaning of μάχαιρα^a 'sword,' 6.33) death by violence or execution – 'death, being killed.' γυμνότης ἢ κίνδυνος ἢ μάχαιρα 'poverty or danger or death' Ro 8.35.

20.69 κέντρον^c, ου n: (a figurative extension of meaning of κέντρον^a 'sting,' 8.45) the power or ability to kill or destroy – 'power to kill, power to destroy.' ποῦ σου, θάνατε, τὸ κέντρον;

'where, death, is your power to kill?' 1 Cor 15.55. For another interpretation of κέντρον in 1 Cor 15.55, see 24.86.

20.70 σπεκουλάτωρ^b, ορος m: one who carries out official executions on the basis of orders from military or government officials – 'executioner.' εὐθὺς ἀποστείλας ὁ βασιλεὺς σπεκουλάτορα ἐπέταξεν ἐνέγκαι τὴν κεφαλὴν αὐτοῦ 'the king sent off the executioner at once with orders to bring his head' Mk 6.27. It is also possible to interpret σπεκουλάτωρ (a borrowing from Latin) as meaning 'courier,' possibly a soldier who had special duties to carry messages of a confidential nature (see 33.196).

20.71 ἀναιρέω^a; ἀναίρεσις, εως f: to get rid of someone by execution, often with legal or quasi-legal procedures – 'to kill, to execute, killing.'
ἀναιρέω^a: ἐθυμώθη λίαν, καὶ ἀποστείλας ἀνεῖλεν πάντας τοὺς παῖδας τοὺς ἐν Βηθλέεμ 'he was furious and gave orders to kill all the boys in Bethlehem' Mt 2.16.
ἀναίρεσις: Σαῦλος δὲ ἦν συνευδοκῶν τῇ ἀναιρέσει αὐτοῦ 'Saul approved of their killing him' Ac 8.1.

20.72 θύω^b; σφάζω; κατασφάζω; σφαγή, ῆς f: to slaughter, either animals or persons; in contexts referring to persons, the implication is of violence and mercilessness – 'to slaughter, to kill.'[8]
θύω^b: ὁ κλέπτης οὐκ ἔρχεται εἰ μὴ ἵνα κλέψῃ καὶ θύσῃ καὶ ἀπολέσῃ 'the thief comes only in order to steal, slaughter, and destroy' Jn 10.10; φέρετε τὸν μόσχον τὸν σιτευτόν, θύσατε 'go get the prize calf and kill it' Lk 15.23.
σφάζω: αἷμα . . . πάντων τῶν ἐσφαγμένων ἐπὶ τῆς γῆς 'the blood . . . of all those who have been slaughtered on earth' Re 18.24; ἀρνίον ἑστηκὸς ὡς ἐσφαγμένον 'the lamb appeared to have been killed' Re 5.6.
κατασφάζω: ἐπ' αὐτοὺς ἀγάγετε ὧδε καὶ κατασφάξατε αὐτοὺς ἔμπροσθέν μου 'bring them here and kill them before me' Lk 19.27.
σφαγή: ἐλογίσθημεν ὡς πρόβατα σφαγῆς 'we are

8 It is possible that κατασφάζω is somewhat more emphatic in connotation than σφάζω.

reckoned to be like sheep that are to be slaughtered' Ro 8.36.

20.73 πατάσσω^b: to slay by means of a mortal blow or disease – 'to slay, to strike down.' πατάξας τὸν Αἰγύπτιον 'he slew the Egyptian' Ac 7.24; παραχρῆμα δὲ ἐπάταξεν αὐτὸν ἄγγελος κυρίου 'at once the angel of the Lord struck him down' Ac 12.23.

20.74 κοπή, ῆς f: a violent and extensive slaughter, especially associated with armed conflicts – ·'to kill, to slaughter, to defeat.' ὑποστρέφοντι ἀπὸ τῆς κοπῆς τῶν βασιλέων 'returning from the defeat of the kings' He 7.1.

20.75 θιγγάνω^b: (a figurative extension of meaning of θιγγάνω^a 'to touch,' 24.74) to cause the death of someone, perhaps suggesting some supernatural or mysterious means – 'to kill, to slay, to cause the death of.' ἵνα μὴ ὁ ὀλοθρεύων τὰ πρωτότοκα θίγῃ αὐτῶν 'in order that the Destroyer might not cause the death of their firstborn' He 11.28.

20.76 σταυρόω; προσπήγνυμι; κρεμάννυμι ἐπὶ ξύλου (an idiom, literally 'to hang on a tree'): to execute by nailing to a cross – 'to crucify.'
σταυρόω: ὅπου αὐτὸν ἐσταύρωσαν 'there they nailed him to the cross' Jn 19.18. It is rare that one can find in receptor languages a technical term or phrase meaning specifically 'to crucify.' In general, a phrase must be employed, since this type of execution is no longer practiced. One can, for example, use such expressions as 'to nail to a cross bar' or 'to nail up on wood' or even 'to nail up high.'
προσπήγνυμι: διὰ χειρὸς ἀνόμων προσπήξαντες ἀνείλατε 'you killed him by letting sinful men crucify him' Ac 2.23.⁹
κρεμάννυμι ἐπὶ ξύλου: Ἰησοῦν, ὃν ὑμεῖς διεχειρίσασθε κρεμάσαντες ἐπὶ ξύλου 'Jesus, whom you seized and killed by crucifying' Ac 5.30. It is possible to understand ξύλου in Ac 5.30 as

ξύλον^f 'cross' (6.28) and to interpret the expression literally as '. . . you seized and killed by hanging him on a cross.'

20.77 ἀνασταυρόω: to cause to die on a cross a second time – 'to crucify again.' ἀνασταυροῦντας ἑαυτοῖς τὸν υἱὸν τοῦ θεοῦ 'because in their case they are crucifying the Son of God again' He 6.6. In extrabiblical Greek ἀνασταυρόω is essentially equivalent in meaning to σταυρόω (20.76), but in He 6.6 ἀνασταυρόω is used figuratively of believers whose sin causes Christ to be crucified again in the sense of exposing Christ to public shame by virtue of the misdeeds of his professed followers. Some scholars, however, interpret ἀνασταυρόω in He 6.6 as referring simply to the original crucifixion and thus interpret ἀνασταυρόω as being essentially synonymous with σταυρόω.

20.78 συσταυρόω: to crucify someone at the same time that another person is being crucified – 'to crucify together with.' τὸ δ' αὐτὸ καὶ οἱ λῃσταὶ οἱ συσταυρωθέντες σὺν αὐτῷ ὠνείδιζον αὐτόν 'even the bandits who had been crucified with him insulted him in the same way' Mt 27.44.

20.79 λιθάζω; καταλιθάζω; λιθοβολέω: to kill or attempt to kill by means of hurling stones, normally carried out by angry mobs – 'to stone to death.'¹⁰
λιθάζω: ἐλιθάσθησαν, ἐπρίσθησαν 'they were stoned to death, they were sawed in two' He 11.37; πείσαντες τοὺς ὄχλους καὶ λιθάσαντες τὸν Παῦλον ἔσυρον ἔξω τῆς πόλεως 'they won the crowds to their side, stoned Paul, and dragged him out of town' Ac 14.19.
καταλιθάζω: ὁ λαὸς ἅπας καταλιθάσει ἡμᾶς 'this whole crowd here will stone us' Lk 20.6.
λιθοβολέω: καὶ ἐκβαλόντες ἔξω τῆς πόλεως ἐλιθοβόλουν 'and driving him out of the city, they stoned him to death' Ac 7.58.

20.80 πελεκίζω (derivative of πέλεκυς 'axe,' not occurring in the NT); ἀποκεφαλίζω: to

---

9 It is possible to consider προσπήγνυμι as meaning merely 'to nail to something.' However, in Ac 2.23 it is used in an absolute sense of 'to crucify,' and therefore can be considered as essentially equivalent in meaning to σταυρόω.

10 It is possible that καταλιθάζω is somewhat more emphatic than λιθάζω, but it is difficult to determine this from existing contexts.

kill by beheading, normally an act of capital punishment – 'to cut the head off, to behead.'

πελεκίζω: τὰς ψυχὰς τῶν πεπελεκισμένων 'the souls of those who had been beheaded' Re 20.4.

ἀποκεφαλίζω: πέμψας ἀπεκεφάλισεν τὸν Ἰωάννην ἐν τῇ φυλακῇ 'he sent and had John the Baptist beheaded in prison' Mt 14.10.

20.81 ἀπάγχομαι: to cause one's own death by hanging – 'to hang oneself, to commit suicide.' καὶ ἀπελθὼν ἀπήγξατο 'and he went out and hung himself' Mt 27.5.

20.82 φονεύω; φόνος, ου *m*: to deprive a person of life by illegal, intentional killing – 'to murder, to commit murder.'

φονεύω: ὃς δ' ἂν φονεύσῃ, ἔνοχος ἔσται τῇ κρίσει 'anyone who commits murder will be brought before the judge' (literally 'will be brought to judgment') Mt 5.21.

φόνος: ὁ δὲ Σαῦλος, ἔτι ἐμπνέων ἀπειλῆς καὶ φόνου εἰς τοὺς μαθητὰς τοῦ κυρίου 'in the meantime Saul kept up his violent threats of murder against the disciples of the Lord' Ac 9.1.

20.83 αἷμα^c, τος *n*: (a figurative extension of meaning of αἷμα^a 'blood,' 8.64) to deprive a person of life by violent means – 'to kill, killing, to commit murder.' οὐκ ἂν ἤμεθα αὐτῶν κοινωνοὶ ἐν τῷ αἵματι τῶν προφητῶν 'we would not have done what they did in murdering the prophets' Mt 23.30.

20.84 αἷμα ἐκχέω or ἐκχύννω: (an idiom, literally 'to pour out blood') to cause the death of someone by violent means – 'to murder, to kill.' ὀξεῖς οἱ πόδες αὐτῶν ἐκχέαι αἷμα 'they are quick to murder' Ro 3.15; ὅπως ἔλθῃ ἐφ' ὑμᾶς πᾶν αἷμα δίκαιον ἐκχυννόμενον 'as a result responsibility for the death of every innocent person will fall upon you' Mt 23.35. The phrase πᾶν αἷμα δίκαιον ἐκχυννόμενον in Mt 23.35 may be literally translated as 'all innocent blood that is poured out.'

20.85 φονεύς, έως *m*; ἀνδροφόνος, ου *m*; ἀνθρωποκτόνος, ου *m*: a person who murders another person – 'murderer.'

φονεύς: ἀπώλεσεν τοὺς φονεῖς ἐκείνους 'he destroyed those murderers' Mt 22.7.

ἀνδροφόνος: πατρολῴαις καὶ μητρολῴαις, ἀνδροφόνοις 'murderers of fathers, murderers of mothers, and murderers of people' 1 Tm 1.9.

ἀνθρωποκτόνος: ἀνθρωποκτόνος ἦν ἀπ' ἀρχῆς 'he was a murderer from the beginning' Jn 8.44.

20.86 σικάριος, ου *m*: one who kills someone with intent and as a part of a plot – 'assassin, terrorist.' ἐξαγαγὼν εἰς τὴν ἔρημον τοὺς τετρακισχιλίους ἄνδρας τῶν σικαρίων 'he led into the wilderness four thousand terrorists' Ac 21.38.

20.87 μητρολῴας, ου *m* – 'one who murders his mother.' μητρολῴαις 'those who murder their mothers' 1 Tm 1.9.

20.88 πατρολῴας, ου *m* – 'one who murders his father.' πατρολῴαις 'those who murder their fathers' 1 Tm 1.9.

21 Danger, Risk, Safe, Save

Outline of Subdomains

A Danger (21.1-21.5)

21.1 κίνδυνος, ου *m*: a state of dangerous and

threatening circumstances – 'danger, peril, risk.' κινδύνοις ποταμῶν, κινδύνοις λῃστῶν 'dangers from rivers, dangers from robbers' 2 Cor 11.26; γυμνότης ἢ κίνδυνος ἢ μάχαιρα 'poverty or danger or death' Ro 8.35.

21.2 κινδυνεύω[a]: to be in dangerous circumstances – 'to be in danger.' τί καὶ ἡμεῖς κινδυνεύομεν πᾶσαν ὥραν; 'why, indeed, should we be in danger all the time?' 1 Cor 15.30.

21.3 ἐπισφαλής, ές: pertaining to that which poses danger – 'dangerous.' ὄντος ἤδη ἐπισφαλοῦς τοῦ πλοός 'the voyage already being dangerous' Ac 27.9.

21.4 παγίς[b], ίδος f: (a figurative extension of meaning of παγίς[a] 'trap,' 6.23) that which brings or is a means of sudden danger – 'danger, trap.' οἱ δὲ βουλόμενοι πλουτεῖν ἐμπίπτουσιν εἰς πειρασμὸν καὶ παγίδα καὶ ἐπιθυμίας πολλὰς ἀνοήτους 'those who want to get rich fall into temptation and danger and many foolish and harmful desires' 1 Tm 6.9. Though in 1 Tm 6.9 παγίδα and ἐπιθυμίας πολλάς are syntactically coordinate, the semantic relationship involves dependency, since the danger consists of the many foolish and harmful desires. One could translate, therefore, 'the danger of many foolish and harmful desires' or 'the danger of being trapped by many foolish and harmful desires.' In this way, something of the literal as well as the figurative meaning of παγίς may be retained.

21.5 σπιλάς[a], άδος f: (a figurative extension of meaning of σπιλάς 'a rock or reef washed by the sea,' not occurring in the NT) an unrecognized source of danger or peril – 'unseen danger, hidden danger.' οὗτοί εἰσιν οἱ ἐν ταῖς ἀγάπαις ὑμῶν σπιλάδες 'these are the hidden dangers in your fellowship meals' Jd 12. σπιλάς in Jd 12 may also be understood as meaning 'spot' or 'stain' (see 79.57).

B Expose Oneself to Danger (21.6-21.8)

21.6 κινδυνεύω[b]: to expose oneself to danger – 'to run a risk.' γὰρ κινδυνεύομεν ἐγκαλεῖσθαι

στάσεως 'for we run the risk of being accused of engaging in a riot' Ac 19.40.

21.7 παραβολεύομαι; παραδίδωμι τὴν ψυχήν (an idiom, literally 'to hand over life'): to expose oneself willingly to a danger or risk – 'to risk, to risk one's life.'
παραβολεύομαι: παραβολευσάμενος τῇ ψυχῇ 'risking his life' Php 2.30.
παραδίδωμι τὴν ψυχήν: ἀνθρώποις παραδεδωκόσι τὰς ψυχὰς αὐτῶν ὑπὲρ τοῦ ὀνόματος τοῦ κυρίου ἡμῶν Ἰησοῦ Χριστοῦ 'men who have risked their lives on behalf of the name of our Lord Jesus Christ' Ac 15.26.
  In a number of languages the equivalent of 'risking one's life' is 'exposing oneself to death' or 'showing that one is willing to die' or 'walking into the danger of dying.'

21.8 τράχηλον ὑποτίθημι: (an idiom, literally 'to put down the neck') willingly and purposely to expose oneself to extreme danger and risk – 'to risk one's life.' οἵτινες ὑπὲρ τῆς ψυχῆς μου τὸν ἑαυτῶν τράχηλον ὑπέθηκαν 'who risked their lives on my behalf' or 'who risked their necks to save my life' Ro 16.4. In some instances one can translate this expression in Ro 16.4 as 'who showed they were willing to die in order that I could live' or 'in order to help me continue to live, they almost died.'

C Safe, Free from Danger (21.9-21.13)

21.9 ἀσφάλεια[a], ας f: a state of safety and security, implying a complete lack of danger – 'safety, security.' ὅταν λέγωσιν, Εἰρήνη καὶ ἀσφάλεια 'when they say, Peace and security' 1 Th 5.3. In some languages safety or security is expressed in a negative way, for example, 'without any danger' or 'without anything that might possibly harm.'

21.10 ἀσφαλής[a], ές; ἀσφαλῶς[a]: pertaining to a state of safety and security, and hence free from danger – 'safe, safely, secure, securely.'
ἀσφαλής[a]: τὰ αὐτὰ γράφειν ὑμῖν ἐμοὶ μὲν οὐκ ὀκνηρόν, ὑμῖν δὲ ἀσφαλές 'to write these things to you is not burdensome to me, but it is a matter of safety for you' Php 3.1.
ἀσφαλῶς[a]: παραγγείλαντες τῷ δεσμοφύλακι ἀσφαλῶς τηρεῖν αὐτούς 'ordering the jailer to

keep them securely' Ac 16.23. In Ac 16.23 ἀσφαλῶς does not refer to the safety of the prisoners but to the security with which they were guarded, hence eliminating any danger of their escaping.

21.11 ἀσφαλίζω[a]: to cause something to be secure in the sense of something which could not be tampered with or opened – 'to make secure, to be guarded.' κέλευσον οὖν ἀσφαλισθῆναι τὸν τάφον ἕως τῆς τρίτης ἡμέρας 'therefore command the tomb to be made secure until the third day' or 'then command the tomb to be guarded until the third day' Mt 27.64.

21.12 κρύπτω[a]; ὑπερασπίζω (a figurative extension of meaning of ὑπερασπίζω 'to hold a shield over,' not occurring in the NT): to cause to be safe or protected by hiding, in some contexts with the intent of not being found – 'to keep safe, to cause to be protected, to protect, to hide.'
κρύπτω[a]: ἔκρυψεν τὸ ἀργύριον τοῦ κυρίου αὐτοῦ 'he hid his master's money' Mt 25.18; θησαυρῷ κεκρυμμένῳ ἐν τῷ ἀγρῷ 'a treasure hidden in the field' Mt 13.44; καὶ ἡ ζωὴ ὑμῶν κέκρυπται σὺν τῷ Χριστῷ 'your life is kept safe with Christ' Col 3.3. Since κρύπτω also means 'to make invisible,' some scholars believe that this statement in Col 3.3 means that 'your life is concealed in Christ' or '. . . hidden from view . . .' (see 24.30). For another interpretation of κρύπτω in Mt 13.44, see 24.29.
ὑπερασπίζω: ὑπερασπίζειν αὐτοὺς ἀπὸ τοῦ κόσμου 'to keep them safe from the world' Jas 1.27 (apparatus).

21.13 στηριγμός[a], οῦ m: a state of security and safety – 'place of safety, position of safety.' ἵνα μὴ τῇ τῶν ἀθέσμων πλάνῃ συναπαχθέντες ἐκπέσητε τοῦ ἰδίου στηριγμοῦ 'in order that you may not be led away by the errors of lawless people and fall from your safe position' or '. . . no longer be safe' 2 Pe 3.17. For another interpretation of στηριγμός in 2 Pe 3.17, see 74.20.

D Become Safe, Free from Danger (21.14-21.16)

21.14 φεύγω[b]; ἐκφεύγω[b]; ἀποφεύγω: to be-

come safe from danger by avoiding or escaping – 'to escape, to avoid.'[1]
φεύγω[b]: ἔφυγον στόματα μαχαίρης 'they escaped being killed' (literally 'escaped the mouths of the sword') He 11.34 (see 79.109); πῶς φύγητε ἀπὸ τῆς κρίσεως τῆς γεέννης; 'how can you escape being condemned to Gehenna?' Mt 23.33.
ἐκφεύγω[b]: ὅτι σὺ ἐκφεύξῃ τὸ κρίμα τοῦ θεοῦ 'that you will be able to escape the judgment of God' Ro 2.3. The meaning of this part of Ro 2.3 is 'to become free from the danger of being judged by God.' ἵνα κατισχύσητε ἐκφυγεῖν ταῦτα πάντα τὰ μέλλοντα γίνεσθαι 'in order that you may be able to escape all of these things that are going to happen' Lk 21.36. In Ro 2.3 and Lk 21.36 ἐκφεύγω should not be understood in the literal sense of running away from (see 15.63). The meaning is simply not to become involved in such danger.
ἀποφεύγω: ἀποφυγόντες τῆς ἐν τῷ κόσμῳ ἐν ἐπιθυμίᾳ φθορᾶς 'escaping from the corruption in the world because of evil desire' 2 Pe 1.4.

21.15 καταφεύγω[b]: to become safe by taking refuge – 'to flee to safety, to take refuge.' ἰσχυρὰν παράκλησιν ἔχωμεν οἱ καταφυγόντες κρατῆσαι τῆς προκειμένης ἐλπίδος 'that we who have taken refuge might have strong encouragement to seize the hope which lies before us' He 6.18.

21.16 ἔκβασις[c], εως f: a means by which one may escape from some danger or difficulty – 'a means of escape, a way of escape.' ἀλλὰ ποιήσει σὺν τῷ πειρασμῷ καὶ τὴν ἔκβασιν τοῦ δύνασθαι ὑπενεγκεῖν 'but with the temptation he provides also a means of escape in being able to bear up' 1 Cor 10.13. In this context πειρασμός may mean either 'temptation' or 'testing.'

---

1 It is possible that ἐκφεύγω[b] and ἀποφεύγω differ somewhat in meaning from φεύγω[b] and from each other, but it is not possible to determine from existing contexts what the distinctive features might be, except perhaps to indicate that ἐκφεύγω[b] and ἀποφεύγω may be connotatively somewhat more emphatic than φεύγω[b]. Note, also, that in this series of terms meaning 'to escape,' there is no special indication of movement, but simply the fact of not having to experience some particular difficulty or danger.

E Cause to be Safe, Free from Danger (21.17-21.24)

21.17 ἐξαιρέομαι[a]: to rescue or set someone free from danger – 'to set free, to rescue, to deliver.' καὶ κατέβην ἐξελέσθαι αὐτούς 'and I came down to rescue them' Ac 7.34; ἐξαπέστειλεν ὁ κύριος τὸν ἄγγελον αὐτοῦ καὶ ἐξείλατό με 'the Lord sent his angel and rescued me' Ac 12.11.

21.18 σῴζω[a]; **σωτηρία**[a], **ας** *f*: to rescue from danger and to restore to a former state of safety and well being – 'to deliver, to rescue, to make safe, deliverance.'[2]

σῴζω[a]: καὶ ἀρξάμενος καταποντίζεσθαι ἔκραξεν λέγων, Κύριε, σῶσόν με 'and as he began to sink, he shouted, Lord, rescue me' Mt 14.30. σωτηρία[a]: ἐνόμιζεν δὲ συνιέναι τοὺς ἀδελφοὺς αὐτοῦ ὅτι ὁ θεὸς διὰ χειρὸς αὐτοῦ δίδωσιν σωτηρίαν αὐτοῖς 'and he thought that his own people would recognize that God would provide for their deliverance through him' Ac 7.25; διὸ παρακαλῶ ὑμᾶς μεταλαβεῖν τροφῆς, τοῦτο γὰρ πρὸς τῆς ὑμετέρας σωτηρίας ὑπάρχει 'therefore, I urge you to take some food, for this is important for your deliverance' or '. . . for your survival' Ac 27.34.

21.19 διασῴζω[a]: to rescue completely from danger – 'to save, to rescue.' κιβωτοῦ, εἰς ἣν ὀλίγοι, τοῦτ᾽ ἔστιν ὀκτὼ ψυχαί, διεσώθησαν δι᾽ ὕδατος 'an ark, in which a few, that is eight persons, were saved through water' 1 Pe 3.20;[3] ὁ ἄνθρωπος οὗτος ὃν διασωθέντα ἐκ τῆς θαλάσσης 'this man who was rescued from the sea' Ac 28.4.

21.20 κτάομαι τὴν ψυχήν: (an idiom, literally 'to acquire one's soul' or 'to acquire one's life') to save oneself from grave danger or death – 'to save oneself, to protect oneself.' ἐν τῇ ὑπομονῇ ὑμῶν κτήσασθε τὰς ψυχὰς ὑμῶν 'by your steadfastness you will save yourselves' or 'stand firm and you will save yourselves' Lk 21.19.

21.21 διαφυλάσσω: to guard or protect something in order to keep it safe or free from harm – 'to guard, to protect, to keep safe.' τοῖς ἀγγέλοις αὐτοῦ ἐντελεῖται περὶ σοῦ τοῦ διαφυλάξαι σε 'he will order his angels to keep you safe' or '. . . to protect you' Lk 4.10.

21.22 σωτήρ[a], **ῆρος** *m*: (derivative of σῴζω[a] 'to rescue, to save,' 21.18) one who rescues or saves – 'deliverer, rescuer, savior.' καὶ ἠγαλλίασεν τὸ πνεῦμά μου ἐπὶ τῷ θεῷ τῷ σωτῆρί μου 'and my spirit rejoices in God my Deliverer' Lk 1.47.

21.23 ῥύομαι: to rescue from danger, with the implication that the danger in question is severe and acute – 'to rescue, to deliver.' πέποιθεν ἐπὶ τὸν θεόν, ῥυσάσθω νῦν εἰ θέλει αὐτόν 'he put his confidence in God; therefore let God rescue him if he wants to' Mt 27.43; τίς με ῥύσεται ἐκ τοῦ σώματος τοῦ θανάτου τούτου; 'who will rescue me from this body which is causing my death?' Ro 7.24.

21.24 τὴν ψυχὴν αὐτοῦ περιποιέομαι: (an idiom, literally 'to do something with regard to one's life') to save or preserve one's own life – 'to save one's life, to save oneself.' ὃς ἐὰν ζητήσῃ τὴν ψυχὴν αὐτοῦ περιποιήσασθαι ἀπολέσει αὐτήν 'whoever seeks to save his own life will lose it' Lk 17.33.

F Save in a Religious Sense[4] (21.25-21.32)

21.25 σωτηρία[b], **ας** *f*: a state of having been saved – 'salvation.' ἡ γὰρ κατὰ θεὸν λύπη

---

2 The meanings of σῴζω[a] and σωτηρία[a] in this subdomain differ from the meaning of ἐξαιρέομαι[a] (21.17) in implying not only a rescue from danger but a restoration to a former state of safety and well being. It is this aspect of the terms σῴζω and σωτηρία which provides such an excellent basis for their use in denoting 'religious salvation' (see footnote 4).

3 In 1 Pe 3.20 it is possible that the phrase δι᾽ ὕδατος, literally 'through water,' may mean 'by means of water.' This has been interpreted by some as an indirect reference to and a prototype of baptism.

4 Meanings of terms in this subdomain are essentially figurative extensions of meaning of the alternative stems σωζ- and σωτ-, meaning either 'to rescue from physical danger' (see 21.18) or 'to heal, to make whole' (see 23.136). In most instances translators have preferred to employ a figurative equivalent based on the concept of

μετάνοιαν εἰς σωτηρίαν ἀμεταμέλητον ἐργάζεται 'for the sadness that is used by God brings repentance that leads to salvation, in which there is no regret' 2 Cor 7.10; κομιζόμενοι τὸ τέλος τῆς πίστεως ὑμῶν σωτηρίαν ψυχῶν 'receiving the purpose of your faith, that is, the salvation of your souls' 1 Pe 1.9.

21.26 σωτηρία[c], ας *f*: the process of being saved – 'salvation.' ἡμῖν ὁ λόγος τῆς σωτηρίας ταύτης ἐξαπεστάλη 'the message about this salvation has been sent to us' Ac 13.26.

Although it is difficult and sometimes impossible to determine whether σωτηρία refers to the state of being saved (21.25) or the process of being saved, in some languages it is obligatory to choose one or the other meaning.

21.27 σῴζω[b]: to cause someone to experience divine salvation – 'to save.' εὐδόκησεν ὁ θεὸς . . . σῶσαι τοὺς πιστεύοντας 'God decided . . . to save those who believe' 1 Cor 1.21; τοῖς πᾶσιν γέγονα πάντα, ἵνα πάντως τινὰς σώσω 'so I became all things to all people that I might save at least some' 1 Cor 9.22; χάριτί ἐστε σεσωσμένοι 'you have been saved by grace' Eph 2.5.

'to rescue' or 'to deliver.' Increasingly, however, translators are employing figurative meanings based on the concept of 'healing' or 'making whole' and thus have used such expressions as 'to give new life to' or 'to cause to have a new heart.' These latter equivalences attempt to combine both the physical and the moral implications. Some translators, however, have employed highly generic equivalents meaning essentially 'to restore' or 'to re-create.'

21.28 σωτήριος, ον: pertaining to divine salvation – 'saving, bringing salvation.' ἐπεφάνη γὰρ ἡ χάρις τοῦ θεοῦ σωτήριος πᾶσιν ἀνθρώποις 'the saving grace of God has appeared to all people' or 'the grace of God has appeared bringing salvation to all people' Tt 2.11.

21.29 σωτήριον[a], ου *n*: the means by which people experience divine salvation – 'salvation, the way of saving, the manner of saving.' ὄψεται πᾶσα σὰρξ τὸ σωτήριον τοῦ θεοῦ 'all will see the way God saves' Lk 3.6.

21.30 σωτήριον[b], ου *n*: the message about God saving people – 'the message of salvation, the message about being saved.' ὅτι τοῖς ἔθνεσιν ἀπεστάλη τοῦτο τὸ σωτήριον τοῦ θεοῦ αὐτοὶ καὶ ἀκούσονται 'that this message about God saving people has been sent to the Gentiles and they will listen' Ac 28.28.

21.31 σωτήρ[b], ῆρος *m*: (derivative of σῴζω[b] 'to save,' 21.27) one who saves – 'Savior.' τοῦ σωτῆρος ἡμῶν θεοῦ 'God our Savior' 1 Tm 2.3; ἐξ οὗ καὶ σωτῆρα ἀπεκδεχόμεθα κύριον Ἰησοῦν Χριστόν 'from where we wait for (our) Savior the Lord Jesus Christ' Php 3.20.

21.32 ἀπόλλυμαι[c]: to be lost, in the religious or spiritual sense – 'to be lost, to perish.' ὁ λόγος γὰρ ὁ τοῦ σταυροῦ τοῖς μὲν ἀπολλυμένοις μωρία ἐστίν 'for the message about the cross is foolishness to those who are perishing' 1 Cor 1.18.

22 Trouble, Hardship, Relief, Favorable Circumstances

Outline of Subdomains

A Trouble, Hardship, Distress (22.1-22.14)

22.1 ἀνάγκη[a], ης *f*: a general state of distress and trouble – 'trouble, distress, troublous times.' ἔσται γὰρ ἀνάγκη μεγάλη ἐπὶ τῆς γῆς 'for there will be great trouble upon the earth'

Lk 21.23; νομίζω οὖν τοῦτο καλὸν ὑπάρχειν διὰ τὴν ἐνεστῶσαν ἀνάγκην 'therefore I think this is better in view of the present troublous times' 1 Cor 7.26. In a number of languages there is no term meaning a general state of distress or trouble, but one can usually speak of such trouble by a verb phrase or clause, for example, 'that which causes trouble,' 'what is hard to live with,' or 'what makes people suffer much.'

22.2 θλῖψις, εως f: trouble involving direct suffering – 'trouble and suffering, suffering, persecution.' οἱ μὲν οὖν διασπαρέντες ἀπὸ τῆς θλίψεως τῆς γενομένης ἐπὶ Στεφάνῳ 'therefore those who were scattered as a result of the trouble and suffering which took place at the time of Stephen's (death)' Ac 11.19; ἔσται γὰρ τότε θλῖψις μεγάλη οἵα οὐ γέγονεν ἀπ' ἀρχῆς κόσμου 'and there will be at that time great suffering such as has not taken place since the beginning of the world' Mt 24.21. For a number of languages 'trouble and suffering' may be expressed as 'that which causes pain.'

22.3 ἀσθενής [d], ές: pertaining to a state of helplessness in view of circumstances – 'helpless, helpless condition.' ἔτι γὰρ Χριστὸς ὄντων ἡμῶν ἀσθενῶν ἔτι κατὰ καιρὸν ὑπὲρ ἀσεβῶν ἀπέθανεν 'for while we were still helpless, Christ died at the right time for the wicked' Ro 5.6. The meaning of 'helpless' may be expressed in some languages as 'when we could not do anything about it.' For another interpretation of ἀσθενής in Ro 5.6, see 88.117.

22.4 βάρος [a], ους n: hardship which is regarded as particularly burdensome and exhausting – 'hardship, burden.' ἴσους ἡμῖν αὐτοὺς ἐποίησας τοῖς βαστάσασι τὸ βάρος τῆς ἡμέρας 'you treated them the same as you treated us who bore the hardship of the day' Mt 20.12. In Mt 20.12 βάρος refers not to difficulties in general but to the specific hardship of working for the entire day. In a number of languages hardship resulting from work may be expressed in terms of the effect upon the workers, for example, 'to get tired from working' or 'to become weak as the result of working.'

22.5 κακία [b], ας f: a state involving difficult and distressing circumstances – 'difficulties, evil.' ἀρκετὸν τῇ ἡμέρᾳ ἡ κακία αὐτῆς 'sufficient for each day is its own evil' or '. . . are its own hardships' Mt 6.34. It may be quite difficult to find a way of translating this adage in a literal way, but one can use some such expression as 'each day has its own way of causing trouble' or 'each day makes us suffer in a special way.'

22.6 λοιμός [b], οῦ m: (a figurative extension of meaning of λοιμός [a] 'plague,' 23.158) one who causes all sorts of trouble – 'troublemaker, pest.' εὑρόντες γὰρ τὸν ἄνδρα τοῦτον λοιμόν 'for we have found this man to be a troublemaker' Ac 24.5.

22.7 κόπος [b], ου m: a state characterized by troubling circumstances – 'trouble, distress.' τί κόπους παρέχετε τῇ γυναικί; 'why are you troubling the woman?' Mt 26.10.

22.8 ὀκνηρός [b], ά, όν: pertaining to being bothersome – 'bothersome, to be a bother, to not mind (in combination with οὐκ).' τὰ αὐτὰ γράφειν ὑμῖν ἐμοὶ μὲν οὐκ ὀκνηρόν 'to write these things to you is not a bother to me' or 'I do not mind writing these things to you' Php 3.1.

22.9 οὐαί f: a state of intense hardship or distress – 'disaster, horror.' ἡ οὐαὶ ἡ μία ἀπῆλθεν ἰδοὺ ἔρχεται ἔτι δύο οὐαὶ μετὰ ταῦτα 'the first disaster came; after this there are still two more disasters to come' Re 9.12; πλὴν οὐαὶ ὑμῖν τοῖς πλουσίοις 'how disastrous it will be for you who are rich' Lk 6.24; οὐαὶ γάρ μοί ἐστιν ἐὰν μὴ εὐαγγελίσωμαι 'how terrible it would be for me if I did not preach the good news' 1 Cor 9.16. In some languages there may not be a noun for 'disaster,' but one can express the meaning of the Greek term οὐαί as 'how greatly one will suffer' or 'what terrible pain will come to one.'

22.10 στενοχωρία, ας f: a set of difficult circumstances, implying certain restrictions – 'distress, difficulty.' θλῖψις καὶ στενοχωρία ἐπὶ πᾶσαν ψυχὴν ἀνθρώπου τοῦ κατεργαζομένου τὸ κακόν 'there will be suffering and distress for all those who do what is evil' Ro 2.9.

'Distress' may be expressed in some languages as 'people will be in trouble' or in an idiomatic expression, 'the world will fall on people.'

22.11 ταλαιπωρία, ας *f*: hardship resulting in wretchedness – 'hardship, wretchedness.' σύντριμμα καὶ ταλαιπωρία ἐν ταῖς ὁδοῖς αὐτῶν 'they leave destruction and wretchedness in their way' or '. . . wherever they go' Ro 3.16. 'Wretchedness' may be expressed idiomatically in some languages as 'to have nothing' or 'to have even one's shirt in rags.'

22.12 ταλαίπωρος, ον: pertaining to being in a wretched state, either mentally or physically – 'wretched, pathetic.' ταλαίπωρος ἐγὼ ἄνθρωπος 'wretched person that I am' Ro 7.24.

22.13 πληγή[d], ῆς *f*: (a figurative extension of meaning of πληγή[c] 'plague,' 23.158) a type of trouble or distress causing widespread and/or intense suffering – 'plague, great suffering, distress.' ἀπὸ τῶν τριῶν πληγῶν τούτων ἀπεκτάνθησαν τὸ τρίτον τῶν ἀνθρώπων 'a third of mankind was killed as a result of these three plagues' Re 9.18; καὶ ἐκ τῶν πληγῶν αὐτῆς ἵνα μὴ λάβητε 'so that you will not receive the severe sufferings that are coming upon her' or 'so that you may not share in her severe sufferings' Re 18.4. One may also render Re 18.4 as 'so that you will not suffer as she is going to suffer.'

22.14 προσκοπή[a], ῆς *f*: an obstacle or difficulty which may be encountered – 'obstacle, trouble, difficulty.' μηδεμίαν ἐν μηδενὶ διδόντες προσκοπήν 'not putting any obstacle in the way of anyone' or 'not causing trouble for anyone' 2 Cor 6.3. For other interpretations of προσκοπή in 2 Cor 6.3, see 25.183 and 88.307.

B Experience Trouble, Hardship[1] (22.15-22.20)

22.15 θλίβομαι: to experience trouble or hardship – 'to suffer hardship, to be

troubled.' εἴτε δὲ θλιβόμεθα, ὑπὲρ τῆς ὑμῶν παρακλήσεως καὶ σωτηρίας 'if we suffer hardship, it is for your help and salvation' 2 Cor 1.6; ὑστερούμενοι, θλιβόμενοι, κακουχούμενοι 'poor, suffering, and mistreated' He 11.37.

22.16 σκύλλομαι: to suffer trouble or harassment – 'to be troubled, to be harassed, to be bothered.' ἰδὼν δὲ τοὺς ὄχλους ἐσπλαγχνίσθη περὶ αὐτῶν ὅτι ἦσαν ἐσκυλμένοι καὶ ἐρριμμένοι ὡσεὶ πρόβατα μὴ ἔχοντα ποιμένα 'seeing the crowds, he had pity upon them because they were harassed and helpless like sheep without a shepherd' Mt 9.36; κύριε, μὴ σκύλλου, οὐ γὰρ ἱκανός εἰμι 'master, do not be bothered, for I am not worthy' Lk 7.6. In Lk 7.6 σκύλλου can perhaps be best rendered in some languages by supplying a pronoun, for example, 'do not bother yourself' or 'do not trouble yourself' or even 'do not cause yourself difficulty.'

22.17 ἐνοχλέομαι: to undergo hardship from continual annoyance – 'to be afflicted, to suffer.' καὶ οἱ ἐνοχλούμενοι ἀπὸ πνευμάτων ἀκαθάρτων ἐθεραπεύοντο 'and those who suffered from unclean spirits were healed' Lk 6.18.

22.18 βαρέομαι: to experience difficulty by burdensome and troublous obligations – 'to be burdened, to be troubled.' καθ' ὑπερβολὴν ὑπὲρ δύναμιν ἐβαρήθημεν 'we were burdened completely beyond our strength' 2 Cor 1.8.

22.19 στενοχωρέομαι[b]: to be in serious circumstances, with the implication of no escape or way out – 'to be in great trouble, to be hemmed in with difficulty.' ἐν παντὶ θλιβόμενοι ἀλλ' οὐ στενοχωρούμενοι 'often suffering but not completely crushed' or 'often in difficulty but never completely overwhelmed' 2 Cor 4.8.

22.20 σκόλοψ τῇ σαρκί: (an idiom, literally 'thorn in the flesh') something which causes

---

1 For a number of meanings in this subdomain, *Experience Trouble, Hardship*, there are close parallels in

Domain 24, Subdomain F *Pain, Suffering* (24.77-24.94). In Domain 22, however, the focus seems to be upon the circumstances which cause the suffering and not primarily upon the pain or suffering itself.

serious trouble and difficulty – 'trouble, woe, suffering, serious inconvenience, thorn in the flesh.' ἐδόθη μοι σκόλοψ τῇ σαρκί 'there was given me a thorn in the flesh' or 'there was given to me serious trouble' 2 Cor 12.7. There are a number of different interpretations of σκόλοψ τῇ σαρκί in 2 Cor 12.7, see 20.27.

C Cause Trouble, Hardship (22.21-22.28)

22.21 θλίβω[b]: to cause someone to suffer trouble or hardship – 'to cause trouble to, to persecute, to cause to suffer hardship.' ἀνταποδοῦναι τοῖς θλίβουσιν ὑμᾶς θλῖψιν 'to bring suffering on those who make you suffer' 2 Th 1.6; στενὴ ἡ πύλη καὶ τεθλιμμένη ἡ ὁδός 'the gate is narrow and the way is difficult (to travel)' Mt 7.14.

22.22 θραύω; καταδυναστεύω; συμπνίγω[c] (a figurative extension of meaning employing the base πνίγω[a] 'to choke,' 19.53): to cause serious trouble to, with the implication of dire consequences and probably a weakened state – 'to cause severe hardship, to oppress, to overwhelm.'
θραύω: ἀποστεῖλαι τεθραυσμένους ἐν ἀφέσει 'to set free the oppressed' or '. . . the downtrodden' Lk 4.18.
καταδυναστεύω: καὶ ἰώμενος πάντας τοὺς καταδυναστευομένους ὑπὸ τοῦ διαβόλου 'and healing all who were oppressed by the Devil' Ac 10.38.
συμπνίγω[c]: ὑπὸ μεριμνῶν καὶ πλούτου καὶ ἡδονῶν τοῦ βίου πορευόμενοι συμπνίγονται 'as they go on living, they are overwhelmed by the worries and riches and pleasures of daily life' Lk 8.14.

22.23 σκύλλω: to cause trouble or harassment – 'to trouble, to harass, to bother.' τί ἔτι σκύλλεις τὸν διδάσκαλον 'why should you bother the Teacher any longer?' Mk 5.35.

22.24 ὀχλέω; ἐνοχλέω: to cause hardship by continual annoyance – 'to afflict, to cause suffering.'
ὀχλέω: φέροντες ἀσθενεῖς καὶ ὀχλουμένους ὑπὸ πνευμάτων ἀκαθάρτων 'bringing the sick and those who were afflicted by unclean spirits' Ac 5.16.
ἐνοχλέω: μή τις ῥίζα πικρίας ἄνω φύουσα ἐνοχλῇ 'that no one becomes like a bitter plant that grows up and causes trouble' He 12.15.

22.25 παρενοχλέω: to cause extra difficulty and hardship by continual annoyance – 'to cause extra difficulty.' διὸ ἐγὼ κρίνω μὴ παρενοχλεῖν τοῖς ἀπὸ τῶν ἐθνῶν ἐπιστρέφουσιν ἐπὶ τὸν θεόν 'therefore I think that we should not cause extra difficulty for those among the Gentiles who are turning to God' Ac 15.19.

22.26 καταβαρέω: to overburden someone by causing undue hardship – 'to overburden, to cause undue hardship.' ἐγὼ οὐ κατεβάρησα ὑμᾶς 'I did not overburden you' 2 Cor 12.16. The meaning of 'to cause undue hardship' or 'to overburden someone' may be expressed in some languages as 'to cause more trouble to someone than that person should have' or 'to cause more suffering than what is right.'

22.27 ἐπιτίθημι ζυγὸν ἐπὶ τὸν τράχηλον: (an idiom, literally 'to put a yoke upon the neck') to cause difficulty to someone by requiring conformity to rules and regulations – 'to load down with obligations, to place a burden on the backs of.' νῦν οὖν τί πειράζετε τὸν θεόν, ἐπιθεῖναι ζυγὸν ἐπὶ τὸν τράχηλον τῶν μαθητῶν 'why do you now want to put God to the test by laying a load on the backs of the believers' or '. . . by causing the believers so much trouble' Ac 15.10.

22.28 φείδομαι[a]: to cause someone not to be troubled – 'to spare, to prevent trouble happening to someone.' φειδόμενος ὑμῶν οὐκέτι ἦλθον εἰς Κόρινθον 'in order to spare you, I have as yet not gone to Corinth' 2 Cor 1.23.

D Difficult, Hard (22.29-22.34)

22.29 χαλεπός[a], ή, όν: pertaining to that which causes trouble and hardship, with an implication of violence – 'troublous, distressful, violent.' ἐν ἐσχάταις ἡμέραις ἐνστήσονται καιροὶ χαλεποί 'in the last days there will be troublous times' 2 Tm 3.1. It may be very difficult in some languages to speak of 'troublous times,' for 'trouble' seems to relate to human experience and not to circumstances. Therefore, this expression in 2 Tm 3.1 can perhaps be best rendered in some languages as 'in the last days, people will suffer very much.'

22.30 βαρύς[b], εῖα, ύ: pertaining to that which is difficult in view of its being burdensome – 'burdensome, troublous.' καὶ αἱ ἐντολαὶ αὐτοῦ βαρεῖαι οὐκ εἰσίν 'and his commandments are not burdensome' 1 Jn 5.3. In rendering 'his commandments are not burdensome,' it may be necessary in some languages to translate 'it is not difficult to do what he has commanded.'

22.31 δεινός, ή, όν: pertaining to that which is severe or hard, with the implication of fear – 'difficult, hard, severe.' ἀλλὰ ἐγγίζει ἄλλα δεινά 'but other severe (afflictions) are near' Mk 16.14-15 (apparatus).

22.32 δύσκολος, ον; δυσκόλως: pertaining to that which is difficult to accomplish or do – 'difficult, hard, with difficulty.'
δύσκολος: πῶς δύσκολόν ἐστιν εἰς τὴν βασιλείαν τοῦ θεοῦ εἰσελθεῖν 'how hard it is to enter the kingdom of God' Mk 10.24.
δυσκόλως: λέγω ὑμῖν ὅτι πλούσιος δυσκόλως εἰσελεύσεται εἰς τὴν βασιλείαν τῶν οὐρανῶν 'I tell you that a rich person will enter in the kingdom of heaven only with difficulty' Mt 19.23. In some languages it may be difficult to render concisely the expression 'only with difficulty.' To express this contrastive element in connection with entering the kingdom of heaven, one must often translate as 'a rich person will be able to enter into the kingdom of heaven, but it will be very difficult for him to do so.'

22.33 μόλις[b]: pertaining to that which can be accomplished only with difficulty – 'with difficulty.' καὶ ταῦτα λέγοντες μόλις κατέπαυσαν τοὺς ὄχλους τοῦ μὴ θύειν αὐτοῖς 'even with these words, they could only with difficulty keep the crowds from offering a sacrifice to them' Ac 14.18. Because of the complications involved in rendering the expression 'only with difficulty,' it may be necessary to recast

the translation of Ac 14.18 as 'with these words they were able to keep the crowds from offering a sacrifice to them, but it was extremely difficult for them to accomplish this' or '. . . but they had to try very hard to keep the crowds from doing so.' For another interpretation of μόλις in Ac 14.18, see 78.41.

22.34 δυσβάστακτος, ον: pertaining to that which is difficult to bear or endure – 'difficult, hard to bear.' φορτίζετε τοὺς ἀνθρώπους φορτία δυσβάστακτα 'you place upon men burdens that are difficult to bear' Lk 11.46.[2]

E Relief from Trouble (22.35-22.37)

22.35 ἀνάψυξις[a], εως f: relief from distressful, burdensome circumstances – 'relief, breathing space.' ὅπως ἂν ἔλθωσιν καιροὶ ἀναψύξεως ἀπὸ προσώπου τοῦ κυρίου 'so that times of relief may come from the Lord' Ac 3.20. In Ac 3.20 the phrase καιροὶ ἀναψύξεως is generally regarded as a reference to the Messianic age.
In a number of languages it may be extremely difficult to speak of 'relief coming from the Lord.' It is easy enough to speak of animate beings 'coming,' but to have a state of relief 'coming' may be semantically impossible. However, the entire expression in Ac 3.20 may be restructured as 'so that the Lord may cause you to have relief from trouble' or '. . . cause you to no longer be troubled.' For another interpretation of ἀνάψυξις in Ac 3.20, see 25.148.

22.36 ἄνεσις[a], εως f: relief as a cessation or suspension of trouble and difficulty – 'relief.' οὐ γὰρ ἵνα ἄλλοις ἄνεσις, ὑμῖν θλῖψις 'for this is not for the purpose of relief for others while constituting suffering for you' 2 Cor 8.13; καὶ ὑμῖν τοῖς θλιβομένοις ἄνεσιν 'and relief to you who suffer' 2 Th 1.7. In rendering 'relief to you who suffer,' it may be necessary to restructure the semantic relations, for example, 'to cause you who suffer not to have to suffer

2 It is sometimes possible to render δυσβάστακτος as 'difficult to carry,' provided the receptor language term for 'burdens' in Lk 11.46 may refer to religious obligations.

longer' or 'to cause you to no longer have to suffer.'

22.37 ἀνάπαυσις^d, εως *f*: relief from trouble and related anxiety — 'relief.' καὶ εὑρήσετε ἀνάπαυσιν ταῖς ψυχαῖς ὑμῶν 'and you will find relief for yourselves' or 'you will find for yourselves relief from trouble' Mt 11.29.

F Easy, Light (22.38-22.41)

22.38 ἐλαφρός^c, ά, όν: pertaining to that which is easy to bear or endure — 'light, easy.' τὸ φορτίον μου ἐλαφρόν ἐστιν 'my burden is easy to bear' or '. . . not difficult' Mt 11.30. It is possible to render ἐλαφρός in Mt 11.30 as 'light,' in the sense of 'light in weight' (see 86.2). However, if 'burden' in Mt 11.30 is understood figuratively, ἐλαφρός can generally also be understood in a figurative sense.

22.39 εὔκοπος, ον: (occurring only in the comparative form in the NT) pertaining to that which is easy, in the sense of not requiring great effort or work — 'easy, without trouble.' εὐκοπώτερόν ἐστιν κάμηλον διὰ τρυπήματος ῥαφίδος διελθεῖν 'it is easier for a camel to go through the eye of a needle' Mt 19.24. In some languages it is difficult to render in a succinct manner an expression such as 'easier to do,' for a comparative expression involving degree of effort may require complex restructuring. Accordingly, one can often translate the first part of this expression in Mt 19.24 as 'a camel does not have to struggle as much to go through the eye of a needle as . . .'

22.40 χρηστός^d, ή, όν: pertaining to that which is pleasant or easy, with the implication of suitability — 'pleasant, easy.' ὁ γὰρ ζυγός μου χρηστός 'for my yoke is easy' Mt 11.30. In a number of languages it is necessary to translate χρηστός by a negativized equivalent, for example, 'it is not difficult to bear.'

22.41 ἐν ὀλίγῳ^b: pertaining to that which is accomplished easily or without difficulty — 'easily, without much trouble, without difficulty.' ἐν ὀλίγῳ με πείθεις Χριστιανὸν ποιῆσαι 'you think you will easily make me a Chris-

tian' Ac 26.28. For another, more probable, interpretation of ἐν ὀλίγῳ in Ac 26.28, see 67.106.

G Favorable Circumstances or State (22.42-22.47)

22.42 εἰρήνη^a, ης *f*: a set of favorable circumstances involving peace and tranquility — 'peace, tranquility.' εἰ ἔγνως ἐν τῇ ἡμέρᾳ ταύτῃ καὶ σὺ τὰ πρὸς εἰρήνην 'if you knew in this day those things related to peace' Lk 19.42; προπέμψατε δὲ αὐτὸν ἐν εἰρήνη 'send him on his way in peace' 1 Cor 16.11. The meaning of 'peace' or 'tranquility' may be expressed in some languages in a negative form, for example, 'to be without trouble' or 'to have no worries' or 'to sit down in one's heart.'

22.43 ἡσυχία^a, ας *f*: a state of undisturbed quietness and calm — 'quiet circumstances, undisturbed life.' ἵνα μετὰ ἡσυχίας ἐργαζόμενοι τὸν ἑαυτῶν ἄρτον ἐσθίωσιν 'in order that they may live calmly and work to earn their living' 2 Th 3.12. 'To earn their own living' is a rendering of an idiom which is literally 'to eat their own bread,' see 57.190. For another interpretation of ἡσυχία in 2 Th 3.12 focusing on personal behavior, see 88.103.

22.44 εὐπρόσδεκτος^b, ον: pertaining to that which is particularly favorable or propitious — 'truly favorable.' νῦν καιρὸς εὐπρόσδεκτος, ἰδοὺ νῦν ἡμέρα σωτηρίας 'now is the truly favorable time; behold, now is the day of salvation' 2 Cor 6.2.

22.45 καιρός^d, οῦ *m*: a favorable opportunity or occasion in view of propitious circumstances — 'opportunity, good occasion.' καιρὸν δὲ μεταλαβὼν μετακαλέσομαί σε 'when I have an opportunity, I will call you' Ac 24.25. It is possible to interpret καιρός in Ac 24.25 merely as an 'occasion,' see 67.1. In fact, one may translate simply as 'and when I have time, I will call you.'

22.46 ἀφορμή^a, ῆς *f*: a set of circumstances favorable for a particular activity or endeavor — 'favorable circumstances, opportunity, occasion.' ἀφορμὴν δὲ λαβοῦσα ἡ ἁμαρτία διὰ τῆς ἐντολῆς 'sin grasping an opportunity through the commandment' Ro 7.8; μόνον μὴ τὴν ἐλευθερίαν εἰς ἀφορμὴν τῇ σαρκί 'only do not let your freedom constitute a favorable opportunity for the flesh' Ga 5.13; μηδεμίαν ἀφορμὴν διδόναι τῷ ἀντικειμένῳ λοιδορίας χάριν 'to provide no opportunity for a person opposed to us of speaking evil concerning us' 1 Tm 5.14. In a number of languages it may be necessary to translate ἀφορμή 'opportunity' in different ways depending upon the context. For example, in Ro 7.8 ἀφορμή may be rendered as 'a

good chance to . . .' In Ga 5.13 ἀφορμή may be rendered as 'a good way for . . .,' and in 1 Tm 5.14 ἀφορμή may be rendered as 'a good reason for . . .'

22.47 εὐοδόομαιᵃ: to experience and enjoy favorable circumstances – 'to get along well, to succeed.' περὶ πάντων εὔχομαί σε εὐοδοῦσθαι 'I pray that everything may go well with you' 3 Jn 2. In a number of languages εὐοδόομαι in 3 Jn 2 is expressed idiomatically, for example, 'to always eat well' or 'to live under the shade' or 'to live always with laughter and song.'

23 Physiological Processes and States[1]

Outline of Subdomains

A   Eat, Drink (23.1-23.39)
B   Processes Involving the Mouth, Other Than Eating and Drinking (23.40-23.45)
C   Birth, Procreation (23.46-23.60)
D   Sexual Relations (23.61-23.65)
E   Sleep, Waking (23.66-23.77)
F   Tire, Rest (23.78-23.87)
G   Live, Die (23.88-23.128)
H   Health, Vigor, Strength (23.129-23.141)
I   Sickness, Disease, Weakness (23.142-23.184)
J   Breathe, Breath (23.185-23.187)
K   Grow, Growth (23.188-23.196)
L   Ripen, Produce Fruit, Bear Seed (23.197-23.204)
M   Rot, Decay (23.205)

1 The domain of *Physiological Processes and States* includes such events as eating, drinking, giving birth, sleeping, resting, living, dying, breathing, growing, being healthy or sick, and a number of physiological processes particularly characteristic of plants. As in the case of practically all domains, it is possible to classify some meanings in two or more different ways. This is particularly true of some of the physiological processes and states. For example, the meanings of 'banquet' and 'feast' could be classified under *Festivals* (51). Similarly, certain meanings classified now under *Sensory Events and States* (24) could be regarded as examples of physiological states. These problems of classification simply emphasize the multi-dimensional character of semantic structures. However, the classification conforms to the features of meaning that seem to be more focal.

A   Eat, Drink[2] (23.1-23.39)

23.1 ἐσθίωᵃ: to consume food, usually solids, but also liquids – 'to eat, to drink, to consume food, to use food.' ἤρξαντο τίλλειν στάχυας καὶ ἐσθίειν 'they began to pick heads of wheat and eat (the grain)' Mt 12.1; τίς ποιμαίνει ποίμνην καὶ ἐκ τοῦ γάλακτος τῆς ποίμνης οὐκ ἐσθίει; 'who will tend a flock without drinking the milk from his sheep?' or '. . . without using the milk from his sheep?' 1 Cor 9.7.

As noted in the contexts of Mt 12.1 and 1 Cor 9.7, ἐσθίωᵃ is generic in the sense that it includes the consumption of both solid foods and liquids, but ἐσθίω is not employed in referring to the drinking of alcoholic bev-

2 In some languages a very fundamental distinction is made between terms referring to the consumption of solid foods in contrast with liquids (either beverages or soups). For the most part, however, a term meaning 'eat' is more generic than one meaning 'drink,' since the former is frequently employed to describe the consumption of any type of nourishment, while a term meaning 'drink' refers only to beverages or very thin soups or broths.

Still further important distinctions are made in some languages between the consumption of so-called 'cold foods' and 'hot foods.' This distinction is not, however, based upon the temperature of the food itself but upon the physiological effect which such foods are supposed to have upon the body in causing coolness or heat. A further important distinction may be made with respect to terms referring to animals eating in contrast with humans eating.

erages (see μεθύω[b] 'to drink freely of wine or beer,' 23.37).

In some languages an important distinction is made in terms for 'eating' depending upon whether the eating is done by an adult or by a very small child, who in most instances must be helped to eat. Other distinctions in terminology for eating may involve the quantities of food (whether small or extensive), the rapidity with which one eats (gulping or mincing), the state of what is eaten (raw, fresh, cooked), or the type of food, for example, meat, cereal, fruit, or leafy vegetable.

23.2 μετέχω[b]: (normally occurring together with a term specifying the particular food in question, but also occurring absolutely in contexts relating to food. μετέχω[b] is probably more formal than ἐσθίω[a], 23.1) to partake of or to consume food, whether solid or liquid – 'to eat, to eat food, to drink.' εἰ ἐγὼ χάριτι μετέχω 'if I give thanks for the food I eat' 1 Cor 10.30; πᾶς γὰρ ὁ μετέχων γάλακτος 'everyone who drinks milk' He 5.13.[3] In contexts in which μετέχω occurs, it may be important to select a term for the eating which will go specifically with the type of food in question. For various types of distinctions made in terms for eating, see the discussion at 23.1 and footnote 2.

23.3 τρώγω; γεύομαι[b]; βιβρώσκω; βρῶσις[a], εως f: to consume solid food – 'to eat, eating.' τρώγω: ἦσαν . . . τρώγοντες καὶ πίνοντες 'people ate and drank' Mt 24.38. γεύομαι[b]: ἐγένετο δὲ πρόσπεινος καὶ ἤθελεν γεύσασθαι 'he became hungry and wanted to eat' Ac 10.10. βιβρώσκω: ἐκ τῶν πέντε ἄρτων τῶν κριθίνων ἃ

3 It is possible to interpret μετέχω[b] as simply an instance of μετέχω[a] 'to have a share in' or 'to partake of' (57.6), and in He 5.13 μετέχων could be interpreted in this sense. In 1 Cor 10.30, however, μετέχω may be interpreted as being used in an absolute sense and thus meaning 'to partake of food.' But it is also possible that even in 1 Cor 10.30 one should recognize the ellipsis of an expression for food which could be supplied from the wider context.

Note that προσλαμβάνομαι occurs with specific terms for food in Ac 27.36, but in such contexts there is no need to assign a meaning to this verb other than the more general meaning of 'to take hold of' (see 18.2).

ἐπερίσσευσαν τοῖς βεβρωκόσιν 'from the five barley loaves of bread which the people had eaten' Jn 6.13.
βρῶσις[a]: περὶ τῆς βρώσεως οὖν τῶν εἰδωλοθύτων 'concerning the eating of meat sacrificed to idols' 1 Cor 8.4.

23.4 βρώσιμος, ον: (derivative of βρῶσις[a] 'eating,' 23.3) pertaining to what can be eaten – 'eatable.' ἔχετέ τι βρώσιμον ἐνθάδε 'do you have anything to eat here?' Lk 24.41.

23.5 ψωμίζω[a]: to cause someone to eat – 'to feed, to give to eat.' ἐὰν πεινᾷ ὁ ἐχθρός σου, ψώμιζε αὐτόν 'if your enemy is hungry, give him something to eat' Ro 12.20.

23.6 τρέφω[a]; ἐκτρέφω[a]: to provide food for, with the implication of a considerable period of time and the food being adequate nourishment – 'to provide food for, to give food to someone to eat.'[4]
τρέφω[a]: πότε σε εἴδομεν πεινῶντα καὶ ἐθρέψαμεν 'when did we ever see you hungry and give you food to eat?' Mt 25.37.
ἐκτρέφω[a]: οὐδεὶς γάρ ποτε τὴν ἑαυτοῦ σάρκα ἐμίσησεν, ἀλλὰ ἐκτρέφει καὶ θάλπει αὐτήν 'no one ever hates his own body; instead he feeds it and takes care of it' Eph 5.29.

23.7 θηλάζω[a]: the activity of a baby feeding at the breast – 'to nurse (of a baby), to suck, to feed on.' μακαρία . . . μαστοὶ οὓς ἐθήλασας 'fortunate . . . are the breasts you sucked' or '. . . you fed on' Lk 11.27. In a number of languages there are highly specific terms for the manner in which babies nurse, including 'to suck upon' or 'to pull at the breasts.' There may also be distinctions in terminology depending upon whether the child in question is a helpless infant held in the arms or a small child capable of moving about. See also discussion at 23.8.

23.8 θηλάζω[b]: to cause a baby to feed at the breast – 'to nurse a baby.' οὐαὶ . . . ταῖς θηλαζούσαις ἐν ἐκείναις ταῖς ἡμέραις 'how terrible

4 It is possible that ἐκτρέφω[a] is somewhat more emphatic in meaning than τρέφω[a], but this cannot be determined from existing contexts.

it will be . . . for women who are nursing infants in those days' Mt 24.19. In many languages entirely distinct terms are employed for the causative and noncausative meanings of 'to nurse.' Still additional distinctions may be employed depending upon the age of the child. One term may be used in speaking of helpless infants, while another may be used of small children who are able to walk around, but who still are nursed from time to time.

23.9 βόσκομαι: eating by animals – 'to graze, to feed.' ἀγέλη χοίρων πολλῶν βοσκομένη 'a large herd of pigs was feeding' Mt 8.30. In some languages a distinction is made in terms relating to eating by animals on the basis of the type of food involved, for example, animals which graze on grass in contrast with those who eat refuse, roots, acorns, etc. An additional distinction is sometimes made in the case of animals which are largely meat-eating in contrast with those that are predominantly plant-eating.

23.10 βόσκω[a]: to cause animals to eat, particularly pasturing animals – 'to feed, to cause to eat.' λέγει αὐτῷ, Βόσκε τὰ ἀρνία μου 'he said to him, Feed my lambs' Jn 21.15. It is possible to interpret βόσκω in Jn 21.15 as meaning 'to tend' or 'to take care of,' especially since βόσκω occurs in a figurative context referring to people. Such an interpretation may be classified in Domain 35 D as a figurative meaning. However, it seems more likely that βόσκω in Jn 21.15 should be understood as an instance of figurative usage, and as such it may also be interpreted as βόσκω[b] 'to take care of,' 44.1.

23.11 κατεσθίω[a]: to devour something completely – 'to eat up.' τὰ πετεινὰ κατέφαγεν αὐτά 'the birds ate it up' Mt 13.4. In some languages a distinction is made in terms referring to eating by birds in contrast with eating by animals or people.

23.12 συνεσθίω: to eat together with others – 'to eat together.' εἰσῆλθες πρὸς ἄνδρας ἀκροβυστίαν ἔχοντας καὶ συνέφαγες αὐτοῖς 'you were a guest in the home of uncircumcised Gentiles, and you even ate with them' Ac 11.3.

In a number of languages a term meaning 'to eat together with others' is completely distinct from an expression referring to eating by one person. Furthermore, a term meaning basically 'to eat together' may focus primarily on conviviality and feasting rather than merely on the process of eating. In Ac 11.3 there is no indication of 'feasting.'

23.13 συναλίζομαι[a]: eating together, with emphasis upon fellowship during the process – 'to eat with.' καὶ συναλιζόμενος παρήγγειλεν αὐτοῖς 'and while he was at table with them, he commanded them' Ac 1.4.

συναλίζομαι in Ac 1.4 is interpreted by some as being συναλίζομαι[b] 'to stay with' (41.37) on the assumption that the occurrence in Ac 1.4 is simply an alternative spelling for συναυλίζομαι 'to stay with.' This latter reading is supported by some manuscripts.

23.14 συνευωχέομαι: to join with others in eating elaborate meals or banquets – 'to feast together.' οὗτοί εἰσιν οἱ ἐν ταῖς ἀγάπαις ὑμῶν σπιλάδες συνευωχούμενοι ἀφόβως 'they are like dirty spots in your fellowship meals, for they feast together shamelessly' Jd 12. 'To feast together' may be expressed in some languages merely as 'to eat a great deal together with others' or 'to join with others in filling one's stomach' or 'to eat with others more than one should.'

23.15 χορτάζομαι[a]: to eat, resulting in a state of being satisfied – 'to eat one's fill.' ἐφάγετε ἐκ τῶν ἄρτων καὶ ἐχορτάσθητε 'you ate the bread and were satisfied' Jn 6.26. One may render 'were satisfied' as 'had all you wanted to eat' or 'did not want to eat any more.'

23.16 χορτάζω: to cause to eat so as to become satisfied – 'to cause to eat one's fill, to satisfy with food.' πόθεν ἡμῖν ἐν ἐρημίᾳ ἄρτοι τοσοῦτοι ὥστε χορτάσαι ὄχλον τοσοῦτον; 'where will we find enough food in this lonely place to satisfy such a large crowd?' Mt 15.33. In some languages one may translate χορτάζω in Mt 15.33 as 'to cause to have as much as they wanted' or 'to give them food so that they didn't want any more.'

In Mt 5.6 (ὅτι αὐτοὶ χορτασθήσονται 'because they will be satisfied') the occurrence of χορτάζω should be interpreted as figurative, for it does not have specific reference to being satisfied with food (see 25.82).

23.17 ἐμπί(μ)πλημι or ἐμπιπλάω (two different forms of the same base; compare 23.18): to cause someone to be satisfied as the result of food which has been provided in sufficient quantity – 'to satisfy with food, to fill with food.' πεινῶντας ἐνέπλησεν ἀγαθῶν 'he filled the hungry with good things' Lk 1.53. It is possible that in Lk 1.53 the reference is to God's providence in general rather than merely to feeding the hungry.

A strictly literal rendering of ἐμπίμπλημι or ἐμπιπλάω in the sense of 'to fill with food' might carry the wrong implication, namely, 'to stuff with food' to the point of making someone extremely uncomfortable. It may therefore be important to divide somewhat the complex semantic components of meaning and to translate 'to cause to eat much and to become happy' or 'to cause to eat enough and as a result to be content.'

23.18 ἐμπί(μ)πλαμαι[a] or ἐμπιπλάομαι (two different forms of the same base; compare 23.17): to be satisfied with food on the basis of having eaten enough – 'to be satisfied, to have one's fill.' ὡς δὲ ἐνεπλήσθησαν 'and when they were satisfied (with food)' Jn 6.12; οὐαὶ ὑμῖν, οἱ ἐμπεπλησμένοι νῦν, ὅτι πεινάσετε 'woe to you who are now well satisfied (with food) because you will be hungry' Lk 6.25. See also comments at 23.17.

23.19 γαστήρ[b], τρός f (a figurative extension of meaning of γαστήρ[a] 'belly,' 8.68); φάγος, ου m (derivative of the stem φαγ- 'to eat,' the aorist of ἐσθίω[a], 23.1): a person who habitually eats excessively – 'glutton.'
γαστήρ[b]: Κρῆτες . . . γαστέρες ἀργαί 'the Cretans . . . are lazy gluttons' Tt 1.12.
φάγος: ἄνθρωπος φάγος καὶ οἰνοπότης 'he is a glutton and drunkard' Mt 11.19.

A glutton is often spoken of idiomatically, for example, 'a large belly' or 'a person who is only a stomach' or 'a professional eater.'

23.20 ἀριστάω[a]; δειπνέω; ἄρτον κλάω (an idiom, literally 'to break bread'): to eat a meal, without reference to any particular time of the day or to the type of food involved – 'to eat a meal, to have a meal.'
ἀριστάω[a]: ἐρωτᾷ αὐτὸν Φαρισαῖος ὅπως ἀριστήσῃ παρ' αὐτῷ 'a Pharisee invited him to have a meal with him' Lk 11.37.
δειπνέω: εἰσελεύσομαι πρὸς αὐτὸν καὶ δειπνήσω μετ' αὐτοῦ 'I will come into his house and eat a meal with him' Re 3.20.
ἄρτον κλάω: κλῶντές τε κατ' οἶκον ἄρτον 'eating (together) in their homes' or 'having meals (together) in their homes' Ac 2.46. The implication of 'eating together' comes from the total context. ἐν δὲ τῇ μιᾷ τῶν σαββάτων συνηγμένων ἡμῶν κλάσαι ἄρτον 'on the first day of the week we gathered together for a meal' Ac 20.7. No doubt the reference in Ac 20.7 is to the 'fellowship meal,' called 'agape,' which constituted the early Christian form of the 'Lord's Supper.' See 23.28.

In some languages it is impossible to speak of 'having a meal' without indicating the time of day or the nature of the food consumed.

23.21 ἀνάκειμαι[b]; κατάκειμαι[c]: to eat a meal, with possible reference to the fact of the people reclining to eat – 'to eat a meal.'[5]
ἀνάκειμαι[b]: ἀνακειμένοις αὐτοῖς τοῖς ἕνδεκα ἐφανερώθη 'as they were eating, he appeared to the eleven' Mk 16.14.
κατάκειμαι[c]: ἐπιγνοῦσα ὅτι κατάκειται 'she knew that he was having a meal' Lk 7.37.

In biblical times there were apparently three different positions involved in the eating of a meal. People might, for example, (1) be

---

5 One would assume that ἀνάκειμαι[b] and κατάκειμαι[c] would have almost opposite meanings in view of the prefixes ἀνα- and κατα-. It is, of course, possible that ἀνάκειμαι[b] refers to being propped up on a couch where one was eating and κατάκειμαι[c] refers specifically to reclining, that is to say, 'lying down,' but the contexts in which these two expressions occur do not provide a clear basis for such a distinction in meaning. In fact, the two are largely generalized to simply mean 'to eat a meal,' though their etymological history may be significantly different. See also Domain 17, footnote 8.

seated on cushions around a low table or (2) be seated on chairs around a table or (3) recline on couches facing a table. Meals which involved reclining on couches would normally have been more elaborate, but the verbs ἀνάκειμαι[b] and κατάκειμαι[c] have been generalized in meaning to denote the eating of a meal without necessarily specifying the particular reclining position of those who participated in the meal.

For the translator, it may be extremely awkward to speak of 'reclining to eat,' since this may have connotations of people who are too lazy to sit up at the table or who are too sick to partake of an ordinary meal. It is for that reason that instead of rendering ἀνάκειμαι[b] or κατάκειμαι[c] as 'to recline to eat,' translators use expressions such as 'to sit down to eat' or 'to eat a meal.'

23.22 ἄριστον[a], ου *n*; δεῖπνον[a], ου *n*; βρῶσις[b], εως *f*: a meal whether simple or elaborate (this generic meaning of ἄριστον and δεῖπνον is in contrast with the more specific meanings of ἄριστον[b], 23.23, and δεῖπνον[b], 23.25) – 'a meal, a banquet, a feast.'
ἄριστον[a]: ὅτι οὐ πρῶτον ἐβαπτίσθη πρὸ τοῦ ἀρίστου 'because he did not wash before the meal' Lk 11.38; ἰδοὺ τὸ ἄριστόν μου ἡτοίμακα 'see now, the feast I have prepared (for you is ready)' Mt 22.4.
δεῖπνον[a]: Ἡρῴδης τοῖς γενεσίοις αὐτοῦ δεῖπνον ἐποίησεν 'Herod gave a banquet for his officials' Mk 6.21.
βρῶσις[b]: ὃς ἀντὶ βρώσεως μιᾶς ἀπέδετο τὰ πρωτοτόκια ἑαυτοῦ 'who for the sake of one meal gave up his rights as the older son' He 12.16.

Though ἄριστον[a], δεῖπνον[a], and βρῶσις[b] are highly generic in this usage, it is not necessary to translate these terms by a corresponding generic term in another language, since a more specific term may fit the context more satisfactorily. In fact, a generic term might be quite inappropriate in that it would suggest in the case of Mk 6.21 that Herod was quite stingy in simply providing an ordinary meal for his officials.

23.23 ἄριστον[b], ου *n*: a less important meal, normally in the earlier or middle part of the day – 'noon meal, lunch.' ὅταν ποιῇς ἄριστον ἢ δεῖπνον 'whenever you give a lunch or a dinner' Lk 14.12.

23.24 ἀριστάω[b]: to eat the earlier meal of the day – 'to have breakfast.' λέγει αὐτοῖς ὁ Ἰησοῦς, Δεῦτε ἀριστήσατε 'Jesus said to them, Come, have breakfast' Jn 21.12. Some scholars, however, interpret ἀριστάω in Jn 21.12 as meaning any kind of meal (see ἀριστάω[a], 23.20), and therefore one would translate as 'Jesus said to them, Come have something to eat' or '. . . have a meal.'

In a number of languages the earlier meal of the day may be spoken of as 'the morning meal' or 'the first meal.' In some languages it is actually called 'the leftovers meal,' but see the discussion on meals at different times of the day at 23.25.

23.25 δεῖπνον[b], ου *n*: the principal meal of the day, usually in the evening – 'supper, main meal.' καὶ δείπνου γινομένου 'and they were at supper' Jn 13.2.

Though in the so-called Western world there is a tendency to have three meals each day, breakfast, lunch, and dinner (or supper), in many parts of the world there are only two principal meals: one eaten around nine or ten o'clock in the morning, and another at four or five o'clock in the afternoon.

In some languages there is a very important distinction made between a more or less formal meal and the relatively informal times of eating which might be called 'snacks.' These would be occasions on which one would eat only one kind of food and possibly in relatively small quantities.

23.26 τράπεζα[b], ης *f*: (a figurative extension of meaning of τράπεζα[a] 'table,' 6.113) a meal, with possible emphasis upon its being relatively bountiful – 'a meal.' ἀναγαγών τε αὐτοὺς εἰς τὸν οἶκον παρέθηκεν τράπεζαν 'he invited them into his house and served them a meal' Ac 16.34.

23.27 δοχή, ῆς *f*: an elaborate meal – 'banquet, feast.' ὅταν δοχὴν ποιῇς, κάλει πτωχούς 'when you give a banquet, invite the poor' Lk 14.13.

23.28 ἀγάπη^b, ης *f*: a special type of communal meal having particular significance for early Christians as an expression of their mutual affection and concern – 'fellowship meal.' οὗτοί εἰσιν οἱ ἐν ταῖς ἀγάπαις ὑμῶν σπιλάδες συνευωχούμενοι ἀφόβως 'they are like dirty spots in your fellowship meals, for they feast together shamelessly' Jd 12. The meaning of ἀγάπη^b may be rendered in some languages as 'meals in which you show your love for one another as you eat together' or 'your eating together as the result of your love for one another.'

23.29 πεινάω^a: to be in a state of hunger, without any implications of particular contributing circumstances – 'to be hungry, to have hunger.' ἐπείνασα γὰρ καὶ ἐδώκατέ μοι φαγεῖν 'for I was hungry and you gave me something to eat' Mt 25.35. Hunger is often spoken of in an idiomatic manner, for example, 'my stomach is crying,' 'my throat has been cut' (implying that one has not been able to swallow food for a long time), or 'my stomach is a deep hole.'

23.30 πρόσπεινος, ον: pertaining to a state of hunger – 'hungry.' ἐγένετο δὲ πρόσπεινος καὶ ἤθελεν γεύσασθαι 'he became hungry and wanted to eat' Ac 10.10.

23.31 νῆστις, ιδος, acc. pl. νήστεις *m* and *f*; νηστεία^b, ας *f*; λιμός^b, οῦ *m* and *f*: the state of being very hungry, presumably for a considerable period of time and as the result of necessity rather than choice (compare νηστεία^a 'fasting,' 53.65) – 'to be quite hungry, considerable hunger, lack of food.'
νῆστις: ἀπολῦσαι αὐτοὺς νήστεις οὐ θέλω 'I do not want to send them away really hungry' Mt 15.32.
νηστεία^b: ἐν νηστείαις 'we have gone hungry' 2 Cor 6.5.
λιμός^b: ἐν λιμῷ καὶ δίψει 'hungry and thirsty' 2 Cor 11.27.
Terms referring to hunger often distinguish varying degrees of hunger and whether the hunger is by necessity or by choice.

23.32 ἀσιτία, ας *f*; ἄσιτος, ον: a state of having been without food, frequently with the implication of being caused by a lack of appetite – 'without food, without desiring food.'
ἀσιτία: πολλῆς τε ἀσιτίας ὑπαρχούσης τότε σταθεὶς ὁ Παῦλος ἐν μέσῳ αὐτῶν εἶπεν 'after they had gone a long time without (desiring) food, Paul stood before them and said' Ac 27.21.
ἄσιτος: τεσσαρεσκαιδεκάτην σήμερον ἡμέραν προσδοκῶντες ἄσιτοι διατελεῖτε 'you have been waiting for fourteen days now and all this time you have not wanted to eat a thing' Ac 27.33.

23.33 λιμός^a, οῦ *m* and *f*: a widespread lack of food over a considerable period of time and resulting in hunger for many people – 'famine, hunger.'[6] ἐγένετο λιμὸς μέγας ἐπὶ πᾶσαν τὴν γῆν 'there was a great famine throughout the whole land' Lk 4.25.
In a number of languages the only way of talking about a famine is to say 'many people were very hungry for a long time' or 'many people had to go for days without anything to eat.' It is important to distinguish clearly between a famine and voluntary abstinence from food for the sake of fasting. (See Domain 53H.)

23.34 πίνω^a (also πίννω in some manuscripts); πόσις^b, εως *f*: to consume liquids, particularly water and wine – 'to drink, drinking.'
πίνω^a: πᾶς ὁ πίνων ἐκ τοῦ ὕδατος τούτου διψήσει πάλιν 'he who drinks from this water will become thirsty again' Jn 4.13.
πόσις^b: μὴ οὖν τις ὑμᾶς κρινέτω ἐν βρώσει καὶ ἐν πόσει 'let no one judge you about eating or drinking' Col 2.16.
In a number of languages a clear distinction is made between drinking water and drinking alcoholic beverages. Still other terms may be employed in speaking of drinking soups or broths.

23.35 ποτίζω^a: to cause to drink – 'to give to drink.' ἐδίψησα καὶ ἐποτίσατέ με 'I was thirsty and you gave me something to drink' Mt

---

6 λιμός^a could be classified as a physical event, since a famine results from lack of rainfall or some natural disaster causing crops to fail. However, since a famine is so specifically related to people's experience of hunger, it seems best to classify λιμός^a together with other expressions involving lack of food.

25.35. In some languages it is impossible to avoid a reference to what is drunk. Therefore, one may translate Mt 25.35 as 'I was thirsty and you gave me water to drink.'

23.36 συμπίνω: to drink together with others – 'to drink together.' οἵτινες συνεφάγομεν καὶ συνεπίομεν αὐτῷ 'we who ate and drank with him' Ac 10.41. In rendering Ac 10.41 it may be necessary to restructure somewhat the expression of joint activity, for example, 'we and he drank together' or 'he was one with us in drinking together.' In some languages it may seem strange to speak of 'eating and drinking,' since both of these activities are often subsumed under a term for 'dining.' It may therefore be preferable in some languages to translate 'we dined together with him' or 'we had our meals together with him.'

23.37 μεθύω[b]: to drink wine or beer (distilled alcoholic beverages were not known in the ancient world), usually with emphasis upon drinking relatively large quantities – 'to drink freely, to drink a great deal, to get drunk.' πρῶτον τὸν καλὸν οἶνον τίθησιν, καὶ ὅταν μεθυσθῶσιν τὸν ἐλάσσω 'he serves the best wine first, and after they have drunk a lot, he serves the ordinary wine' Jn 2.10.

23.38 ὑδροποτέω – 'to drink water.' μηκέτι ὑδροπότει 'do not drink water only' 1 Tm 5.23. In a number of languages 'to drink water' is expressed by a single term which combines the components of drinking and of water. In other instances a verb meaning simply 'to drink' normally means to drink water unless otherwise specified. In Greek almost the opposite situation exists. For example, Mt 11.18 (ἦλθεν γὰρ Ἰωάννης μήτε ἐσθίων μήτε πίνων 'for John came neither eating nor drinking') implies a reference to drinking alcoholic beverages.

23.39 διψάω[a]; δίψος, ους n: the state resulting from not having drunk anything for a period of time – 'to be thirsty, thirst.' διψάω[a]: ἐδίψησα καὶ ἐποτίσατέ με 'I was thirsty and you gave me something to drink' Mt 25.35. δίψος: ἐν λιμῷ καὶ δίψει 'hungry and thirsty' 2 Cor 11.27.

B Processes Involving the Mouth, Other Than Eating and Drinking (23.40-23.45)

23.40 μασάομαι: to bite with the teeth – 'to bite.' ἐμασῶντο τὰς γλώσσας αὐτῶν ἐκ τοῦ πόνου 'they bit their tongues because of their pain' Re 16.10.

In some languages it is important to distinguish clearly between three different kinds of biting: the biting of food, the biting of one's own lips or tongue, and the biting of a person in a fight or quarrel.

23.41 τρίζω τοὺς ὀδόντας; βρύχω τοὺς ὀδόντας[a]; βρυγμὸς τῶν ὀδόντων: the grinding or the gnashing of the teeth, whether involuntary as in the case of certain illnesses, or as an expression of an emotion such as anger or of pain and suffering – 'to grind the teeth, to gnash the teeth, gnashing of teeth.' τρίζω τοὺς ὀδόντας: ἀφρίζει καὶ τρίζει τοὺς ὀδόντας καὶ ξηραίνεται 'he foams at the mouth, grinds his teeth, and becomes stiff all over' Mk 9.18. The action of grinding one's teeth in the case of an epileptic fit is so widespread that it is normally not difficult to find some way of expressing this type of action. βρύχω τοὺς ὀδόντας[a]: ἔβρυχον τοὺς ὀδόντας ἐπ' αὐτόν 'they ground their teeth at him' Ac 7.54. In translating 'they ground their teeth at him' it may be necessary to indicate the type of emotion which is involved in such an action, for example, 'in anger they ground their teeth at him' or 'they showed their anger by grinding their teeth.' It is essential to avoid an expression such as 'to grit the teeth,' which in English is a symbol of determination, not of anger.[7] βρυγμὸς τῶν ὀδόντων: ἐκεῖ ἔσται ὁ κλαυθμὸς καὶ ὁ βρυγμὸς τῶν ὀδόντων 'there will be crying and gnashing of teeth there' Lk 13.28. Though it is possible to interpret βρυγμὸς τῶν ὀδόντων as an idiom denoting suffering, it is probably better to understand this in a some-

7 It is possible to interpret the phrase βρύχω τοὺς ὀδόντας as being simply an idiom meaning 'to show anger against,' but the context suggests that the persons actually did grind their teeth as a symbol of their anger. See also 88.184.

what more literal sense (especially in view of biblical views current at that time concerning the next world). It may be important, however, to suggest the significance of this symbolic action, namely, 'gnashing their teeth in suffering' or 'to suffer so much as to gnash the teeth.' As in the case of Ac 7.54, it is important to avoid an expression for 'gnashing the teeth' which will suggest 'gritting the teeth' in the sense of determination or courageous resistance.

23.42 ἐπιλείχω: to lick an object with the tongue – 'to lick.' οἱ κύνες ἐρχόμενοι ἐπέλειχον τὰ ἕλκη αὐτοῦ 'the dogs came and licked his sores' Lk 16.21. It may be necessary in some languages to be somewhat more specific in the expression 'licked his sores' so that the text may read 'licked the pus from his sores.'

23.43 πτύω; ἐμπτύω: to spit on or at something or someone – 'to spit.'[8]

πτύω: ἔπτυσεν χαμαὶ καὶ ἐποίησεν πηλὸν ἐκ τοῦ πτύσματος 'he spat on the ground and made some mud with the spittle' Jn 9.6.
ἐμπτύω: ἐνέπτυσαν εἰς τὸ πρόσωπον αὐτοῦ καὶ ἐκολάφισαν αὐτόν 'they spat in his face and beat him' Mt 26.67.
In some societies spitting has quite a different symbolic meaning than it has in the Western world. In fact, in some societies in Africa, to spit upon a person's head is to confer a blessing. It may therefore be necessary in the case of Mt 26.67 to translate 'they spat in his face' as 'they spat in his face to dishonor him' or '. . . to show their anger against him.'

23.44 ἐμέω – 'to vomit.' ὅτι χλιαρὸς εἶ καὶ οὔτε ζεστὸς οὔτε ψυχρός, μέλλω σε ἐμέσαι ἐκ τοῦ στόματός μου 'because you are barely warm, neither hot nor cold, I will vomit you out of my mouth' Re 3.16.
Since a term meaning 'to vomit' often carries somewhat vulgar connotations, ἐμέω in Re 3.16 has frequently been translated as 'to

spit out of my mouth.' It is also possible to interpret 'to vomit out of the mouth' as an idiom meaning 'to reject.'[9]

23.45 καταπίνω[a]: to cause something to pass through the mouth and into the stomach – 'to swallow.' οἱ διϋλίζοντες τὸν κώνωπα τὴν δὲ κάμηλον καταπίνοντες 'you strain a fly out of your drink, but you swallow a camel' Mt 23.24. The saying about 'straining out a fly and swallowing a camel' refers to gross unawareness of inconsistencies in one's behavior, but in translating it is far better to preserve the intentional hyperbole, since it is one which can be readily grasped. As an aid to the reader, one can refer to the fact that in the list of unclean animals in Lv 11, the fly or gnat is the smallest and the camel is the largest.

C Birth, Procreation (23.46-23.60)

23.46 γένεσις[a], εως *f* (γέννησις in some manuscripts); γενετή, ῆς *f*: coming into existence by birth – 'be born, birth.'

γένεσις[a]: τοῦ δὲ Ἰησοῦ ἡ γένεσις οὕτως ἦν 'this is the way that Jesus Christ was born'. Mt 1.18. A literal translation of Mt 1.18 as 'this is the way that Jesus Christ was born' might be misleading, since it would imply a description of the actual process of his birth rather than an account of those circumstances and events which took place in connection with his birth. It may, therefore, be better to translate Mt 1.18 as 'this is what happened when Jesus Christ was born' or 'these things happened at the time of Jesus Christ's birth.'
γενετή: εἶδεν ἄνθρωπον τυφλὸν ἐκ γενετῆς 'he saw a man who was blind from the time he was born' Jn 9.1. In some languages 'from the time he was born' may be best rendered as 'from the time he was a small baby.' One may also render this expression of time as 'a man who had always been blind' or 'a man who had never been able to see.'

---

8 It is possible that a distinction in meaning should be made between πτύω and ἐμπτύω, in which case the latter term would emphasize the spitting in or upon an object. However, there are insufficient contrasts in contexts to warrant making such a distinction.

9 Though it is possible to understand the expression 'vomit out of the mouth' as being an idiom meaning 'to reject,' it is probably better to assume that this expression (ἐμέω ἐκ τοῦ στόματος) is simply used figuratively rather than being a conventionalized idiom.

23.47 γεννητός, ή, όν: (derivative of γεννάω[b] 'to give birth,' 23.52) pertaining to having been born – 'one born, one who has been born, person.' οὐκ ἐγήγερται ἐν γεννητοῖς γυναικῶν μείζων Ἰωάννου τοῦ βαπτιστοῦ 'among those born of women, no one is greater than John the Baptist' or 'among those who have lived, no one is greater than John the Baptist' Mt 11.11.

In some languages a literal rendering of γεννητοῖς γυναικῶν 'born of women' could be misleading, for it might suggest that there are persons who have not been born of women. It is for that reason that γεννητοῖς γυναικῶν may be rendered in some instances as 'of all those persons who have ever lived.' However, this reference to the preeminence of John the Baptist is difficult, and the implications of it go far beyond the matter of translational equivalence.

23.48 ἀρτιγέννητος, ον: pertaining to having been born recently – 'newly born, recently born.' ὡς ἀρτιγέννητα βρέφη 'like newly born babies' or 'like those who are just babies' 1 Pe 2.2. 'Newly born babies' may be rendered as 'babies who have just been born' or 'babies who have just begun to live.'

23.49 συλλαμβάνω[b]; καταβολὴ σπέρματος (an idiom, literally 'sowing of seed') – 'to conceive, to become pregnant.'
συλλαμβάνω[b]: συνέλαβεν Ἐλισάβετ ἡ γυνὴ αὐτοῦ 'Elizabeth his wife became pregnant' Lk 1.24. The phrases ἐν γαστρί (Lk 1.31) and ἐν τῇ κοιλίᾳ (Lk 2.21), meaning 'in the womb,' may be added to συλλαμβάνω without significant alteration of its meaning.
καταβολὴ σπέρματος: πίστει – καὶ αὐτὴ Σάρρα στεῖρα – δύναμιν εἰς καταβολὴν σπέρματος ἔλαβεν 'by faith – Sarah herself was not able to conceive – she received the power to conceive' He 11.11. There are a number of textual problems involved in this expression in He 11.11, and many scholars have concluded that the reference is not to Sarah's conceiving but to Abraham's being able to become a father (see Today's English Version).

In many languages the process of becoming pregnant is expressed in different ways: 'to begin to become large,' 'to receive sperm,' 'to

let a child enter,' or 'to stop bleeding' (a reference to the cessation of menstrual periods).

23.50 ἔγκυος, ον; κοίτην ἔχω (an idiom, literally 'to have bed,' though in combination with ἔχω, κοίτη early acquired the metonymic meaning of sexual relations); ἐν γαστρὶ ἔχω (an idiom, literally 'to have in the womb'): to be in a state of pregnancy – 'pregnant, to be pregnant.' These expressions contrast with the meaning of συλλαμβάνω[b], 23.49, in that they seem to focus more upon the state of pregnancy rather than the event of conception.
ἔγκυος: σὺν Μαριὰμ τῇ ἐμνηστευμένῃ αὐτῷ, οὔσῃ ἐγκύῳ 'with Mary, who was promised in marriage to him, and who was pregnant' Lk 2.5.
κοίτην ἔχω: Ῥεβέκκα ἐξ ἑνὸς κοίτην ἔχουσα 'Rebecca was pregnant by one man' Ro 9.10.
ἐν γαστρὶ ἔχω: οὐαὶ δὲ ταῖς ἐν γαστρὶ ἐχούσαις . . . ἐν ἐκείναις ταῖς ἡμέραις 'how terrible it will be . . . in those days . . . for women who are pregnant' Mt 24.19.

It is impossible to determine whether in Mt 1.23 (ἐν γαστρὶ ἕξει καὶ τέξεται υἱόν 'she will be pregnant and bear a son') the focus is upon the state of pregnancy or the fact of conception, 23.49.

23.51 ἡ κοιλία βαστάζει: (an idiom, literally 'the womb carries') to experience the process of pregnancy – 'to be pregnant with, to carry in the womb.' μακαρία ἡ κοιλία ἡ βαστάσασά σε 'fortunate is the womb that carried you' or 'fortunate is the woman who was pregnant with you' Lk 11.27. It may, however, be necessary in some languages to render Lk 11.27 as 'fortunate is the woman who gave you birth,' since a literal reference to carrying in the womb may seem unduly crude.

23.52 τίκτω[a]; γεννάω[b]; τεκνογονέω; τεκνογονία, ας f: to give birth to a child – 'to bear, to give birth.'[10]
τίκτω[a]: ἐν γαστρὶ ἕξει καὶ τέξεται υἱόν 'she will

---

10 It is possible that τεκνογονέω and τεκνογονία differ somewhat in connotation from τίκτω[a] and γεννάω[b] in being stylistically more formal, but there seems to be no significant denotative distinction in meaning.

become pregnant and give birth to a son' Mt 1.23.

γεννάω[b]: ἡ γυνή σου Ἐλισάβετ γεννήσει υἱόν σοι 'your wife Elizabeth will bear you a son' Lk 1.13; ἐπυνθάνετο παρ' αὐτῶν ποῦ ὁ Χριστὸς γεννᾶται 'they asked them where the Messiah would be born' Mt 2.4. γεννάω also occurs together with ἐξ αἱμάτων (Jn 1.13) and ἐκ τῆς σαρκός (Jn 3.6) in reference to physical birth. In Jn 3.5, γεννηθῇ ἐξ ὕδατος has likewise been interpreted by some scholars as referring to physical birth (compare Jn 3.6), but others understand this as referring to baptism. Certainly the occurrence of γεννηθῇ with πνεύματος in Jn 3.5 is a reference to religious rebirth, in which case γεννάω would involve a radical change of state (see 13.56). The use of the same word with two different meanings or referents is typical of the style of the Gospel of John.

τεκνογονέω: βούλομαι οὖν νεωτέρας γαμεῖν, τεκνογονεῖν 'I would rather that the younger widows get married and have children' 1 Tm 5.14.

τεκνογονία: σωθήσεται δὲ διὰ τῆς τεκνογονίας 'she will be saved through having children' 1 Tm 2.15.

All languages have expressions for human birth, though these are frequently in idiomatic forms, for example, 'to drop a child' or 'to cause a baby to pass between the legs.' A number of languages have a variety of terms referring to giving birth, and some of these may involve unfortunate connotations. One must therefore be careful about the selection of appropriate expressions.

23.53 γέννημα[a], τος *n*: (derivative of γεννάω[b] 'to give birth,' 23.52) that which has been produced or born of a living creature – 'offspring, brood, child.' γεννήματα ἐχιδνῶν 'brood of vipers' Mt 3.7. In some languages it may be possible to translate this phrase in Mt 3.7 more or less literally, for example, 'the offspring of vipers,' in which 'vipers' means poisonous snakes, but in other languages this would be impossible, and one must therefore use 'little snakes.' For another interpretation of γέννημα in Mt 3.7, see 58.26.

23.54 ὠδίνω[a]; ὠδίν[a], ῖνος *f*: to experience pains associated with giving birth – 'to have birth pains, to suffer pain in connection with giving birth, birth pains.'

ὠδίνω[a]: κράζει ὠδίνουσα καὶ βασανιζομένη τεκεῖν 'she cried out in her birth pangs and suffering to give birth' Re 12.2.

ὠδίν[a]: ὥσπερ ἡ ὠδὶν τῇ ἐν γαστρὶ ἐχούσῃ 'it will be like the birth pains that come upon a pregnant woman' 1 Th 5.3.

23.55 ἔκτρωμα, τος *n*: an untimely or premature birth – 'untimely birth.' ἔσχατον δὲ πάντων ὡσπερεὶ τῷ ἐκτρώματι ὤφθη κάμοί 'last of all he appeared also to me, even though I was like one who was born at the wrong time' 1 Cor 15.8.

There is a certain fundamental problem involved in the rendering of ἔκτρωμα in 1 Cor 15.8. Here Paul refers to himself, but the event in question is the appearance of Jesus to Paul, evidently on the road to Damascus. The reference, therefore, would seem to be to his being born as a Christian. This spiritual birth, however, would appear to be rather late in the process rather than premature. It is for this reason that it may be wise to translate ἔκτρωμα in some instances as 'untimely birth' or 'born at the wrong time,' rather than indicating that he was 'born too soon.'

23.56 στεῖρα, ας *f*: the state of not being able to conceive and bear children – 'barren, not able to bear children.' οὐκ ἦν αὐτοῖς τέκνον, καθότι ἦν ἡ Ἐλισάβετ στεῖρα 'they had no children because Elizabeth could not have any' Lk 1.7.

23.57 νέκρωσις[b], εως *f*: (a figurative extension of meaning of νέκρωσις[a] 'death,' 23.99) the state of not being able to bear children as the result of having passed through menopause – 'barrenness.' καὶ τὴν νέκρωσιν τῆς μήτρας Σάρρας 'and of the fact that Sarah could not have children' (literally 'and the barrenness of Sarah's womb') Ro 4.19.

23.58 γεννάω[a]: the male role in causing the conception and birth of a child – 'to be the father of, to procreate, to beget.' Ἀβραὰμ ἐγέννησεν τὸν Ἰσαάκ 'Abraham was the father of Isaac' Mt 1.2.

23.59 ἀνίστημι σπέρμα or ἐξανίστημι σπέρμα: (idioms meaning literally 'to raise up seed') the male role in begetting children – 'to beget, to procreate, to become the father of.' ἀνίστημι σπέρμα: ἀναστήσει σπέρμα τῷ ἀδελφῷ αὐτοῦ 'he will have to beget children for his brother' Mt 22.24 (Mk 12.19 and Lk 20.28 have ἐξανίστημι). In contexts such as Mt 22.24, Mk 12.19, and Lk 20.28 it may be important to add a note concerning levirate responsibilities, that is to say, the requirement for a younger brother to beget children by a deceased older brother's wife and the reckoning of such an offspring as being the descendant of the older deceased brother.

23.60 ἐξέρχομαι ἐκ τῆς ὀσφύος: (an idiom, literally 'to come out from the loins, genitals') to be born as the result of the male role in begetting an offspring – 'to be born of, to be begotten by.' καίπερ ἐξεληλυθότας ἐκ τῆς ὀσφύος Ἀβραάμ 'even though Abraham had been their father' He 7.5.

In a number of languages it is more satisfactory to speak of the male role in procreation in terms of 'being the father of' rather than employing a term which may have undesirable connotations of sexual relations.

D Sexual Relations[11] (23.61-23.65)

23.61 γινώσκω[f] (a figurative extension of meaning of γινώσκω[a] 'to know,' 28.1); συνέρχομαι[c] (a figurative extension of meaning of συνέρχομαι[a] 'to come together,' 15.123) – 'to have sexual intercourse with.' γινώσκω[f]: πῶς ἔσται τοῦτο, ἐπεὶ ἄνδρα οὐ γινώσκω 'how can this happen, for I have not had sexual intercourse with a man' Lk 1.34. συνέρχομαι[c]: πρὶν ἢ συνελθεῖν αὐτοὺς εὑρέθη ἐν γαστρὶ ἔχουσα 'before they had sexual intercourse, she was found to be pregnant' Mt 1.18.

---

11 It would be possible to classify the various meanings of this subdomain as involving primarily interpersonal relations (Domain 34) rather than physiological processes and states, since in at least certain contexts the emphasis seems to be upon the manner in which people relate to one another rather than upon the physiological state or activity involved in such relations.

In almost all languages there are euphemistic ways of speaking about sexual intercourse, and the use of γινώσκω[f] and συνέρχομαι[c] is illustrative of this in the Greek NT. It is possible to translate γινώσκω[f] in Lk 1.34 as simply 'for I am not married to a man,' and likewise, συνέρχομαι[c] in Mt 1.18 may be rendered as 'before they were married.' In some languages one may use such expressions as 'before they were joined' or 'before they slept together' or 'before they discovered one another.'

23.62 κοίτη[b], ης f: (a figurative extension of meaning of κοίτη[a] 'bed,' 6.108) to have sexual relations – 'sexual activity, sexual life, marriage relations.' τίμιος ὁ γάμος ἐν πᾶσιν καὶ ἡ κοίτη ἀμίαντος 'marriage should be honored by all, and sexual life should be undefiled' He 13.4. In some languages one may speak of 'sexual life' as 'the way one lives with one's wife' or 'how one treats one's wife.'

23.63 σκεῦος κτάομαι: (an idiom, literally 'to possess a vessel') a euphemistic manner of referring to sexual relations – 'sexual life.' τὸ ἑαυτοῦ σκεῦος κτᾶσθαι ἐν ἁγιασμῷ καὶ τιμῇ 'each one's sexual life should be holy and honorable' 1 Th 4.4. It is also possible to understand σκεῦος in 1 Th 4.4 as one's wife (see 10.55). σκεῦος in 1 Th 4.4 may also be understood as one's body, and therefore the phrase τὸ ἑαυτοῦ σκεῦος κτᾶσθαι may be rendered as 'to control his own body' (see 8.6).

23.64 παρθενία, ας f: the state of a person who has not had sexual intercourse (in the NT referring only to females; compare 9.33, 39) – 'virginity.' ἀπὸ τῆς παρθενίας αὐτῆς 'since the time she was a virgin' or 'since the time of her marriage' Lk 2.36. See also discussion at 9.39.

23.65 χρῆσις, εως f: the sexual function or use of the same or opposite sex – 'sexual function, sexual use.' αἵ τε γὰρ θήλειαι αὐτῶν μετήλλαξαν τὴν φυσικὴν χρῆσιν εἰς τὴν παρὰ φύσιν, ὁμοίως τε καὶ οἱ ἄρσενες ἀφέντες τὴν φυσικὴν χρῆσιν τῆς θηλείας 'for the women pervert the natural sexual function for that which is contrary to nature, and likewise men give up the natural sexual function of a woman' Ro 1.26-27. It is often possible to refer to 'natural sexual function' as 'sexual relations with the opposite sex' or 'men having sexual relations with women.' 'That which is contrary to nature' may be expressed often as 'men having sexual relations with men' and 'women having sexual relations with women.' In many societies homosexuality is almost unknown, but there are always ways of speaking about such relations in a euphemistic manner.

E Sleep, Waking (23.66-23.77)

23.66 καθεύδωᵃ; κοιμάομαιᵃ; κοίμησις, εως f; ὕπνος, ου m: the state of being asleep – 'to sleep, to be asleep, sleep.'
καθεύδωᵃ: τὸ παιδίον οὐκ ἀπέθανεν ἀλλὰ καθεύδει 'the child is not dead; she sleeps' Mk 5.39.
κοιμάομαιᵃ: ἔκλεψαν αὐτὸν ἡμῶν κοιμωμένων 'they stole his body while we were asleep' Mt 28.13.
κοίμησις: ἔδοξαν ὅτι περὶ τῆς κοιμήσεως τοῦ ὕπνου λέγει 'they thought he meant natural sleep' Jn 11.13. In Jn 11.13 κοίμησις is combined with ὕπνος apparently to stress the fact that the sleep was an ordinary or natural sleep.
ὕπνος: ἐγερθεὶς δὲ ὁ Ἰωσὴφ ἀπὸ τοῦ ὕπνου 'when Joseph woke up from his sleep' Mt 1.24.

In some languages sleep is expressed by an idiom, for example, 'his soul had wandered away' or 'his eyes had disappeared.' Though an expression such as 'his soul had wandered away' might appear in some languages to have misleading theological implications, it really means only 'to sleep.'

23.67 νυστάζω: the process of becoming sleepy – 'to grow drowsy.' χρονίζοντος δὲ τοῦ νυμφίου ἐνύσταξαν πᾶσαι καὶ ἐκάθευδον 'the bridegroom was late in coming, so all grew drowsy and fell asleep' Mt 25.5. 'To grow drowsy' may be rendered in some languages as 'to begin to nod' or 'their heads fell' or 'their eyes gradually closed.'

In 2 Pe 2.3 νυστάζω occurs in a highly figurative context: καὶ ἡ ἀπώλεια αὐτῶν οὐ νυστάζει, literally 'and their destruction is not drowsy,' meaning either 'their destruction is imminent' or 'their Destroyer has been wide awake' (see Today's English Version).

23.68 καταφέρομαι ὕπνῳ: (an idiom, literally 'to be carried away by sleep') to become increasingly more sleepy – 'to get sleepier, to become more and more sleepy.' καταφερόμενος ὕπνῳ βαθεῖ διαλεγομένου τοῦ Παύλου ἐπὶ πλεῖον, κατενεχθεὶς ἀπὸ τοῦ ὕπνου 'as Paul kept on talking (Eutychus) got sleepier and sleepier (literally '. . . became exceedingly sleepier) until he finally went sound asleep' Ac 20.9. See 23.71.[12]

23.69 ἦσαν οἱ ὀφθαλμοὶ βεβαρημένοι; ἦσαν οἱ ὀφθαλμοὶ καταβαρυνόμενοι: (idioms, literally 'their eyes were weighed down') to become excessively or exceedingly sleepy – 'to have become very sleepy, to be very sleepy.'
ἦσαν οἱ ὀφθαλμοὶ βεβαρημένοι: εὗρεν αὐτοὺς καθεύδοντας ἦσαν γὰρ αὐτῶν οἱ ὀφθαλμοὶ βεβαρημένοι 'he found them asleep, for they were very sleepy' Mt 26.43.
ἦσαν οἱ ὀφθαλμοὶ καταβαρυνόμενοι: ἦσαν γὰρ αὐτῶν οἱ ὀφθαλμοὶ καταβαρυνόμενοι 'they were exceedingly sleepy' Mk 14.40.

In some languages the equivalent of ἦσαν οἱ ὀφθαλμοὶ βεβαρημένοι (or καταβαρυνόμενοι) would be 'they could no longer keep their eyes open' or 'they could not drive sleep away.'

23.70 ἀφυπνόω: to begin to sleep – 'to fall asleep.' πλεόντων δὲ αὐτῶν ἀφύπνωσεν 'as they were sailing, he fell asleep' Lk 8.23. It would obviously be a mistake to try to imitate the English idiom 'to fall asleep,' for this might be understood as 'to go to sleep and as a result fall down' or even 'to fall down and then remain unconscious.'

23.71 βαρέομαι ὕπνῳ (an idiom, literally 'to be burdened by sleep'); καταφέρομαι ἀπὸ τοῦ ὕπνου (an idiom, literally 'to be carried away

12 The differences in meaning between καταφερόμενος ὕπνῳ (23.68) and κατενεχθεὶς ἀπὸ τοῦ ὕπνου (23.71) in Ac 20.9 depend upon aspectual distinctions. The first phrase marks a process, while the second indicates a final state.

from sleep'): to be in a state of deep sleep – 'to be sound asleep, to be completely asleep.'

βαρέομαι ὕπνῳ: ὁ δὲ Πέτρος καὶ οἱ σὺν αὐτῷ ἦσαν βεβαρημένοι ὕπνῳ 'Peter and his companions were sound asleep' Lk 9.32.

καταφέρομαι ἀπὸ τοῦ ὕπνου: διαλεγομένου τοῦ Παύλου ἐπὶ πλεῖον, κατενεχθεὶς ἀπὸ τοῦ ὕπνου 'as Paul kept on talking (Eutychus) went sound asleep' Ac 20.9. See 23.68.[12]

23.72 γρηγορέω[a]: to remain awake because of the need to continue alert – 'to stay awake, to be watchful.' εἰ ᾔδει ὁ οἰκοδεσπότης ποίᾳ φυλακῇ ὁ κλέπτης ἔρχεται, ἐγρηγόρησεν ἄν 'if the man of the house knew the time when the thief would come, he would stay awake' Mt 24.43. In some languages γρηγορέω in Mt 24.43 may be rendered as 'his eyes would be open' or 'he would surely see what was happening.'

23.73 ἀγρυπνία, ας f: the state of remaining awake because of not being able to go to sleep, whether from anxiety or because of external circumstances – 'sleeplessness.' ἐν κόποις, ἐν ἀγρυπνίαις, ἐν νηστείαις 'from overwork, from sleeplessness, from lack of food' 2 Cor 6.5.

In the two occurrences of ἀγρυπνία in the NT (2 Cor 6.5; 11.27), failure to sleep was evidently the result of external circumstances which prevented normal sleep. It may therefore be possible to translate ἀγρυπνία as 'it was not possible to sleep' or 'there was no way to sleep.'

23.74 ἐγείρομαι[b]; διεγείρομαι[a]: to become awake after sleeping – 'to wake up, to become awake.'

ἐγείρομαι[b]: ὅτι ὥρα ἤδη ὑμᾶς ἐξ ὕπνου ἐγερθῆναι 'because it is already time for you to awaken from sleep' Ro 13.11. The context of this clause in Ro 13.11 is figurative, and it may be necessary in some languages to translate 'now it is time for you to be alert to what is happening.'

διεγείρομαι[a]: διεγερθεὶς ἐπετίμησεν τῷ ἀνέμῳ 'he woke up and commanded the wind' Mk 4.39.

23.75 ἔξυπνος, ον: pertaining to having awakened – 'having awakened, awake after

having slept.' ἔξυπνος δὲ γενόμενος ὁ δεσμοφύλαξ 'when the keeper of the prison had awakened' Ac 16.27. In some languages the process of waking up is described idiomatically as 'when his mind came back to him' or 'when his eyes opened.'

23.76 διαγρηγορέω: to awaken completely from sleep – 'to become fully awake.' διαγρηγορήσαντες δὲ εἶδον τὴν δόξαν αὐτοῦ 'they became fully awake and saw his glory' Lk 9.32.

23.77 διεγείρω[a]; ἐξυπνίζω; ἐγείρω[c]: to cause someone to awaken – 'to cause to wake up, to awaken someone, to wake up someone.' διεγείρω[a]: προσελθόντες δὲ διήγειραν αὐτόν 'they came to him and woke him up' Lk 8.24. ἐξυπνίζω: Λάζαρος . . . κεκοίμηται, ἀλλὰ πορεύομαι ἵνα ἐξυπνίσω αὐτόν 'Lazarus . . . has fallen asleep, but I will go and wake him up' Jn 11.11. ἐγείρω[c]: πατάξας δὲ τὴν πλευρὰν τοῦ Πέτρου ἤγειρεν αὐτόν 'he shook Peter by the shoulder and woke him up' Ac 12.7.

F Tire, Rest (23.78-23.87)

23.78 κοπιάω[b]: to be tired or weary, as the result of hard or difficult endeavor – 'to be tired, to be weary.' δεῦτε πρός με πάντες οἱ κοπιῶντες καὶ πεφορτισμένοι 'come to me all of you who are tired from carrying heavy loads' Mt 11.28. It is also possible, however, to interpret κοπιάω in Mt 11.28 as κοπιάω[a] 'to work hard' (see 42.47). ὁ οὖν Ἰησοῦς κεκοπιακὼς ἐκ τῆς ὁδοιπορίας ἐκαθέζετο 'Jesus became tired because of the trip and sat down' Jn 4.6.

23.79 ἐκλύομαι[a]: to become so tired and weary as to give out (possibly even to faint from exhaustion) – 'to become extremely weary, to give out, to faint from exhaustion.' μήποτε ἐκλυθῶσιν ἐν τῇ ὁδῷ 'lest they faint on the road' Mt 15.32. A number of languages make a clear distinction between (1) fainting as the result of surprise, astonishment, or fear and (2) fainting from physical exhaustion.

23.80 ἀναπαύομαι[a]; ἀνάπαυσις[b], εως f: to become physically refreshed after ceasing activity or work – 'rest, to rest.'

ἀναπαύομαι^a: δεῦτε . . . εἰς ἔρημον τόπον καὶ ἀναπαύσασθε ὀλίγον 'let's go . . . to a quiet place and you can rest awhile' Mk 6.31. ἀνάπαυσις^b: εὑρήσετε ἀνάπαυσιν ταῖς ψυχαῖς ὑμῶν 'you will find rest for yourselves' Mt 11.29.

In the use of ἀναπαύομαι^a and ἀνάπαυσις^b, the focus of meaning seems to be upon the restorative character of rest rather than mere cessation of activity (see 68.34).

23.81 καταπαύω^a; κατάπαυσις, εως f: to cease one's work or activity, resulting in a period of rest − 'to rest, to cease from work.' καταπαύω^a and κατάπαυσις appear to differ in meaning from ἀναπαύομαι^a and ἀνάπαυσις^b (23.80) in that the emphasis of καταπαύω^a and κατάπαυσις is more upon the cessation of activity resulting in rest rather than upon the mere restorative character of rest. καταπαύω^a: αὐτὸς κατέπαυσεν ἀπὸ τῶν ἔργων αὐτοῦ 'he will rest from his work' He 4.10. κατάπαυσις: τίσιν δὲ ὤμοσεν μὴ εἰσελεύσεσθαι εἰς τὴν κατάπαυσιν αὐτοῦ 'he made this solemn promise that they will never come in and rest with him' He 3.18.

23.82 ἡσυχάζω^a: to be at rest, that is, not to be engaged in some activity − 'to rest.' τὸ μὲν σάββατον ἡσύχασαν κατὰ τὴν ἐντολήν 'on the Sabbath day they rested as the Law commanded' Lk 23.56.

23.83 τὴν κεφαλὴν κλίνω: (an idiom, literally 'to lay down the head') to experience the rest which comes from sleep − 'to lie down to rest, to lie down to sleep.' ὁ δὲ υἱὸς τοῦ ἀνθρώπου οὐκ ἔχει ποῦ τὴν κεφαλὴν κλίνῃ 'the Son of Man has no place to lie down to rest' Mt 8.20, implying that Jesus possessed no permanent home. In Jn 19.30 this same expression must be understood not as an idiom but as a case of literally bowing the head (see 16.16).

23.84 ἀναπαύω: to cause someone to become physically refreshed as the result of resting from work − 'to cause to rest, to give rest.' δεῦτε πρός με . . . κἀγὼ ἀναπαύσω ὑμᾶς 'come to me . . . and I will give you rest' Mt 11.28. In some languages it may be difficult to speak

of 'causing someone to become refreshed by resting.' Normally this would be accomplished simply by causing a person not to have to work. Accordingly, Mt 11.28 may be expressed in some languages as 'I will make it possible for you no longer to have to work' or '. . . to toil hard.' This, however, must not be understood merely in the sense of 'to give a person a vacation' or 'to make it possible for someone to live without working.'

23.85 καταπαύω^b: to cause someone to cease from activity and as a result to enjoy a period of rest − 'to cause to rest.' εἰ γὰρ αὐτοὺς Ἰησοῦς κατέπαυσεν, οὐκ ἂν περὶ ἄλλης ἐλάλει μετὰ ταῦτα ἡμέρας 'if Joshua had given them rest, he would not have spoken later of another day' He 4.8.

23.86 συναναπαύομαι: to experience restorative rest together with someone else (see ἀναπαύομαι^a 'to rest,' 23.80) − 'to rest together with someone else, to rest with.' συναναπαύσωμαι ὑμῖν 'that I may rest with you' Ro 15.32.

23.87 ἀνάπαυσις^c, εως f: (derivative of ἀναπαύομαι^a 'to rest,' 23.80) a location for resting − 'a place to rest.' διέρχεται δι' ἀνύδρων τόπων ζητοῦν ἀνάπαυσιν 'it travels over dry country looking for a place to rest' Mt 12.43. It is possible, however, to treat ἀνάπαυσις in Mt 12.43 as not being a place of rest, but simply a state of rest as in ἀνάπαυσις^b (23.80). Compare Mt 11.29, in which ἀνάπαυσις appears to refer to a state rather than to a location.

G Live, Die (23.88-23.128)

23.88 ζάω^a; ζωή, ῆς f; ψυχή^b, ῆς f − 'to be alive, to live, life.' ζάω^a: ὁ νόμος κυριεύει τοῦ ἀνθρώπου ἐφ' ὅσον χρόνον ζῇ 'the law rules over a person as long as he or she lives' Ro 7.1. ζωή: μήτε ἀρχὴν ἡμερῶν μήτε ζωῆς τέλος ἔχων 'without beginning of days or the end of life' He 7.3.

In some figurative expressions ζάω^a and ζωή may involve serious complications in reference. For example, in Jn 6.51 the expression ἐγώ εἰμι ὁ ἄρτος ὁ ζῶν 'I am the living bread' may be understood in some languages as bread which has some living objects in it, namely, bread which is being eaten by worms or weevils. It may therefore be necessary to say 'I am that bread which gives life.'[13]

In Mk 10.30 καὶ ἐν τῷ αἰῶνι τῷ ἐρχομένῳ ζωὴν αἰώνιον 'and in the age to come (he will receive) eternal life' there are significant differences of opinion as to whether the emphasis is primarily upon duration or upon the quality of life which is to be characteristic of the coming age. Since in some languages life can only be spoken of as a verb meaning literally 'to live,' then 'eternal life' might be expressed merely as 'living without dying,' but this can be misunderstood to mean that Christians will never die physically. Some translators have thus spoken of 'eternal life' as being 'real life that never ends.' In this way a qualitative distinction is introduced so that readers will not think merely in terms of the prolongation of earthly life, something which in some parts of the world would be regarded as being a terrible punishment rather than a blessing.

ψυχή[b]: καὶ ζητοῦσιν τὴν ψυχήν μου 'and they seek my life' Ro 11.3. In rendering ψυχή in Ro 11.3 it may be necessary to indicate more precisely the relationship between 'to seek' and 'life,' for example, 'they seek to destroy my life' or 'they seek to cause me no longer to live.'

In a number of languages there is no noun-like word for 'life.' It may therefore be necessary to change all passages which speak of 'life' into a corresponding expression using a verb-like form meaning 'to live.'

23.89 ζωογονέω[a]: to cause to continue to live – 'to keep alive, to preserve alive.' τοῦ ποιεῖν τὰ βρέφη ἔκθετα αὐτῶν εἰς τὸ μὴ ζωογονεῖσθαι 'to expose their infants so that they could not be kept alive' Ac 7.19. 'So that they could not be kept alive' may be rendered as 'so that they would not continue to live' or 'so that they would die.'

---

13 The phrase ὁ ἄρτος ὁ ζῶν is probably best interpreted as a type of transform of the phrase ὁ ἄρτος τῆς ζωῆς in Jn 6.48 and accordingly may be best translated as 'bread that gives life' or 'bread that causes life.'

23.90 σάρξ[h], σαρκός f: (a figurative extension of meaning of σάρξ[a] 'flesh,' 8.63) physical life – 'life.' ὃς ἐν ταῖς ἡμέραις τῆς σαρκὸς αὐτοῦ 'during his life' He 5.7.

23.91 ἐνδημέω ἐν τῷ σώματι (an idiom, literally 'to be at home in the body'); εἶναι ἐν σκηνώματι (an idiom, literally 'to be in a dwelling,' see 7.8): to be alive, with special emphasis upon physical existence on earth – 'to be alive.'
ἐνδημέω ἐν τῷ σώματι: ὅτι ἐνδημοῦντες ἐν τῷ σώματι 'as long as we are alive here on earth' 2 Cor 5.6.
εἶναι ἐν σκηνώματι: ἐφ' ὅσον εἰμὶ ἐν τούτῳ τῷ σκηνώματι 'as long as I am alive' 2 Pe 1.13.

Most languages have rather generic expressions for 'life' or 'to live,' but sometimes there are idiomatic expressions which may readily fit the types of contexts illustrated by 2 Cor 5.6 and 2 Pe 1.13, for example, 'to have strength,' 'to have one's eyes,' and 'to walk about on the earth.'

23.92 ζωογονέω[b]; ζωοποιέω: to cause to live – 'to give life to, to make live.'
ζωογονέω[b]: τοῦ θεοῦ τοῦ ζωογονοῦντος τὰ πάντα 'God who gives life to all things' 1 Tm 6.13.
ζωοποιέω: θεοῦ τοῦ ζωοποιοῦντος τοὺς νεκρούς 'God who is able to make alive the dead' Ro 4.17; ἐν τῷ Χριστῷ πάντες ζωοποιηθήσονται 'all will be raised to life because of their union with Christ' 1 Cor 15.22.

23.93 ζάω[b]; ἀναζάω[a]; ἀνίσταμαι[d] (and 2nd aorist active); ἀνάστασις[a], εως f; ἐξανάστασις, εως f; ἔγερσις, εως f: to come back to life after having once died – 'to come back to life, to live again, to be resurrected, resurrection.'
ζάω[b]: Χριστὸς ἀπέθανεν καὶ ἔζησεν 'Christ died and rose to life again' Ro 14.9.
ἀναζάω[a]: Χριστὸς καὶ ἀπέθανεν καὶ ἀνέστη καὶ ἀνέζησεν 'Christ also died, rose, and lives again' Ro 14.9 (apparatus). In Lk 15.24, ὅτι οὗτος ὁ υἱός μου νεκρὸς ἦν καὶ ἀνέζησεν 'because this son of mine was dead and he has come back to life,' the figurative hyperbole may reflect the practice of referring to a person as dead and then coming back to life if he has been completely separated for a time from all

family relations, but then has later been discovered alive and well. It is possible, of course, that in Lk 15.24 the expression is an idiom, but it is more likely to be simply a figurative usage.

ἀνίσταμαι[d]: προφήτης τις τῶν ἀρχαίων ἀνέστη 'one of the prophets of long ago came back to life' Lk 9.8.

ἀνάστασις[a]: Σαδδουκαῖοι, λέγοντες μὴ εἶναι ἀνάστασιν 'the Sadducees say that there is no resurrection' Mt 22.23. One may also translate 'there is no resurrection' as 'people will not live again.'

ἐξανάστασις: εἴ πως καταντήσω εἰς τὴν ἐξανάστασιν τὴν ἐκ νεκρῶν 'if in some way I might attain to the resurrection from among the dead' Php 3.11. The phrase 'the resurrection from among the dead' may be rendered as 'to live again' or 'to live again after having died.'

ἔγερσις: μετὰ τὴν ἔγερσιν αὐτοῦ 'after his resurrection' or 'after he rose from death' Mt 27.53.

In a number of languages there is a difficulty involved in formulating some expression for 'resurrection' or 'living again,' since such a phrase may refer to what is technically known as metempsychosis, that is to say, the rebirth of the soul in another existence, a belief which is widely held in a number of areas of south Asia. This problem may be avoided in some languages by speaking of 'his body will live again' or 'his body will come back to life' or 'he will be the same person when he lives again.'

23.94 ἐγείρω[e]; ἐξεγείρω[a]; ἀνίστημι[b]: to cause someone to live again after having once died – 'to raise to life, to make live again.'
ἐγείρω[e]: οὐκ ἔστιν ὧδε, ἠγέρθη 'he is not here; he has been raised' Mt 28.6. In some languages it may be important to indicate in Mt 28.6 who is the agent, and one may therefore translate 'he is not here; God has caused him to live again.'
ἐξεγείρω[a]: ὁ δὲ θεὸς καὶ τὸν κύριον ἤγειρεν καὶ ἡμᾶς ἐξεγερεῖ διὰ τῆς δυνάμεως αὐτοῦ 'God raised up the Lord and will raise us up through his power' or 'God caused the Lord to live again and he will cause us to live through his power' 1 Cor 6.14.

ἀνίστημι[b]: ἀλλὰ ἀναστήσω αὐτὸ ἐν τῇ ἐσχάτῃ ἡμέρᾳ 'but that I should raise them to life on the last day' Jn 6.39.

23.95 συνεγείρω; συζωοποιέω: to cause to live again together with others – 'to raise to life together with.'
συνεγείρω: εἰ οὖν συνηγέρθητε τῷ Χριστῷ 'since you have been raised to life with Christ' Col 3.1.
συζωοποιέω: συνεζωοποίησεν τῷ Χριστῷ 'he brought to life with Christ' or 'he caused to live again together with Christ' Eph 2.5.

There are serious semantic difficulties involved in a literal translation of συνεγείρω or συζωοποιέω, for a literal rendering could either be interpreted as 'to be raised to life at the same time with' or 'to be raised to life in the same way as,' but the reference in Col 3.1 and Eph 2.5 is to a spiritual existence more than to a literal resurrection of the body. This means that both συνεγείρω and συζωοποιέω must be understood as highly figurative. Hence, in Col 3.1 it may be necessary to translate εἰ οὖν συνηγέρθητε τῷ Χριστῷ as 'since you have been raised to life, so to speak, with Christ' or 'since, as it were, you have been raised to life with Christ.' In this way one may point to the fact of a figurative element involved.

23.96 συζάω: to live in association with or together with someone else – 'to live together with, to live with.' ἐν ταῖς καρδίαις ἡμῶν ἐστε εἰς τὸ συναποθανεῖν καὶ συζῆν 'you are so dear to us whether we die together or live together' 2 Cor 7.3. In 2 Cor 7.3 it is important to note that συζάω should not be understood in the sense of inhabiting the same house with someone else. The reference here is the sense of unity and comradeship rather than dwelling in the same place.

23.97 γρηγορέω[c]: (a figurative extension of meaning of γρηγορέω[a] 'to stay awake,' 23.72) to remain fully alive and alert – 'to remain alive, to be alive.' εἴτε γρηγορῶμεν εἴτε καθεύδωμεν 'whether we are alive or dead' 1 Th 5.10.

23.98 ἄψυχος, ον: pertaining to a state of not having life – 'lifeless, inanimate.' ὅμως τὰ ἄψυχα φωνὴν διδόντα, εἴτε αὐλὸς εἴτε κιθάρα 'even lifeless musical instruments like the flute and the harp giving their sound' 1 Cor 14.7. In some translations it may seem strange or even meaningless to speak of 'musical instruments' as being 'lifeless' or 'not alive,' since everyone would obviously know such a fact. It may therefore be necessary to translate as 'even musical instruments like the flute and the harp, which are obviously not alive, nevertheless produce a sound.'

23.99 ἀποθνήσκω[a]; θνήσκω; θάνατος[a], ου m; νέκρωσις[a], εως f; ἐκψύχω: the process of dying – 'to die, death.'

ἀποθνήσκω[a]: ὁ πιστεύων εἰς ἐμὲ κἂν ἀποθάνῃ ζήσεται 'whoever believes in me will live even though he dies' Jn 11.25; ἵνα τις ἐξ αὐτοῦ φάγῃ καὶ μὴ ἀποθάνῃ 'so that if anyone eats of it, he will not die' Jn 6.50. In Jn 6.50 ἀποθνήσκω must be understood in a spiritual rather than in a strictly literal sense. This bold figurative language is characteristic of the Gospel of John and should not be eliminated, though in some languages a strictly literal translation may be understood only in a literal sense and thus lead to misinterpretation. In some instances, therefore, it may be necessary to suggest the metaphorical significance by translating 'he will not, as it were, die.'

θνήσκω: τεθνήκασιν γὰρ οἱ ζητοῦντες τὴν ψυχὴν τοῦ παιδίου 'for those who tried to kill the child have died' Mt 2.20.

θάνατος[a]: οὐδὲν ἄξιον θανάτου ἐστὶν πεπραγμένον αὐτῷ 'there is nothing this man has done to deserve death' or '... to deserve to die' Lk 23.15.

νέκρωσις[a]: πάντοτε τὴν νέκρωσιν τοῦ Ἰησοῦ ἐν τῷ σώματι περιφέροντες 'at all times we carry in our bodies the death of Jesus' 2 Cor 4.10. This first clause of 2 Cor 4.10 is highly elliptical, for it evidently refers to the fact that Paul was constantly in danger of dying in the same manner in which Jesus died, that is to say, by violence. One may render 2 Cor 4.10 as 'at all times we live in the constant threat of being killed as Jesus was.'

ἐκψύχω: ἀκούων δὲ ὁ Ἀνανίας τοὺς λόγους τούτους πεσὼν ἐξέψυξεν 'when Ananias heard these words, he fell down and died' Ac 5.5.

In a number of languages clear distinctions are made in the use of terms for dying on the basis of the manner or circumstances of death. For example, one term may refer to death primarily as the result of old age, while another term may refer to death caused by sickness, and still other terms may be used for death caused by violence. Careful distinctions must be used in determining the choice of terms based on particular contexts.

23.100 δίδωμι ψυχήν: (an idiom, literally 'to give one's life') to die willingly, with the implication of being for some purpose – 'to die for, to lay down one's life, to give one's life.' καὶ δοῦναι τὴν ψυχὴν αὐτοῦ λύτρον ἀντὶ πολλῶν 'and to give his life as a ransom on behalf of many' Mt 20.28. In a number of languages, however, one cannot speak of 'giving one's life.' It may therefore be necessary to translate 'to permit oneself to be killed' or 'to allow others to kill oneself.'

23.101 ἀναλύω[b] (a figurative extension of meaning of ἀναλύω 'to depart,' not occurring in the NT); ἀνάλυσις, εως f (a figurative extension of meaning of ἀνάλυσις 'loosing, releasing,' not occurring in the NT); ἔξοδος[b], ου f (a figurative extension of meaning of ἔξοδος[a] 'departure,' 15.42); ὑπάγω[d] (a figurative extension of meaning of ὑπάγω[b] 'to depart,' 15.35); πορεύομαι[e] (a figurative extension of meaning of πορεύομαι[c] 'to go away,' 15.34): to depart from life, as a euphemistic expression for death – 'to leave this life, to die, death, departure.'[14]

ἀναλύω[b]: τὴν ἐπιθυμίαν ἔχων εἰς τὸ ἀναλῦσαι 'I want very much to leave this life' Php 1.23.

ἀνάλυσις: ὁ καιρὸς τῆς ἀναλύσεώς μου 'the time of my death' 2 Tm 4.6.

ἔξοδος[b]: ἔλεγον τὴν ἔξοδον αὐτοῦ ... ἐν Ἰερουσαλήμ 'they talked about his dying ... in Jerusalem' Lk 9.31; μετὰ τὴν ἐμὴν ἔξοδον 'after my death' 2 Pe 1.15.

ὑπάγω[d]: ὁ μὲν υἱὸς τοῦ ἀνθρώπου ὑπάγει καθὼς

---

14 Expressions occurring in numbered items 23.101-23.105 involve euphemistic expressions for death. These, however, have been subdivided here on the basis of certain significant features of the underlying bases, as will be noted in the following discussions.

γέγραπται περὶ αὐτοῦ 'the Son of Man will die as the Scriptures say about him' Mk 14.21. πορεύομαιᶜ: ὅτι ὁ υἱὸς μὲν τοῦ ἀνθρώπου κατὰ τὸ ὡρισμένον πορεύεται 'for the Son of Man will die as was decided' Lk 22.22.

23.102 τελευτάω; τελευτή, ῆς *f*: (figurative extensions of meaning of τελευτάω 'to end' and τελευτή 'end,' not occurring in the NT) to come to the end of one's life, as a euphemistic expression for death – 'to die, death.'
τελευτάω: τελευτήσαντος δὲ τοῦ Ἡρῴδου 'after Herod had died' Mt 2.19.
τελευτή: ἦν ἐκεῖ ἕως τῆς τελευτῆς Ἡρῴδου 'he remained there until the death of Herod' Mt 2.15.

23.103 ἐκπνέω: (a figurative extension of meaning of ἐκπνέω 'to breathe out,' not occurring in the NT) to engage in the final act of dying – 'to die, to breathe out one's last.' ὁ δὲ Ἰησοῦς ἀφεὶς φωνὴν μεγάλην ἐξέπνευσεν 'then Jesus gave a loud cry and died' Mk 15.37.

23.104 καθεύδωᵇ; κοιμάομαιᵇ: (figurative extensions of meaning of καθεύδωᵃ and κοιμάομαιᵃ, respectively, 'to sleep,' 23.66) to sleep, as a euphemistic expression for the state of being dead – 'to be dead, to have died.'
καθεύδωᵇ: εἴτε γρηγορῶμεν εἴτε καθεύδωμεν 'whether we are alive or dead' 1 Th 5.10.
κοιμάομαιᵇ: ἡμεῖς οἱ ζῶντες . . . οὐ μὴ φθάσωμεν τοὺς κοιμηθέντας 'we who are alive . . . will not go ahead of those who have died' 1 Th 4.15.
Some translators have attempted to preserve the figure of speech in καθεύδωᵇ and κοιμάομαιᵇ by translating 'to sleep' rather than 'to have died' or 'to be dead.' Such a practice, however, has resulted in misunderstanding in a number of instances, and has sometimes led to the doctrine of so-called 'soul-sleep.'

23.105 πίπτωᵉ: (a figurative extension of meaning of πίπτωᵃ 'to fall,' 15.118) to fall down, as a euphemistic expression for a violent death – 'to die.' ἔπεσαν μιᾷ ἡμέρᾳ εἴκοσι τρεῖς χιλιάδες 'in one day twenty-three thousand died' 1 Cor 10.8. It is rare that one can employ a literal meaning of πίπτω as a euphemistic expression for 'dying,' since receptors are too likely to understand 'to fall' in a purely literal sense.

23.106 ἀπόλλυμαιᵃ: to die, with the implication of ruin and destruction – 'to die, to perish.' πάντες γὰρ οἱ λαβόντες μάχαιραν ἐν μαχαίρῃ ἀπολοῦνται 'for all those who take the sword will die by the sword' Mt 26.52; ἐγὼ δὲ λιμῷ ὧδε ἀπόλλυμαι 'but I am dying here of hunger' Lk 15.17. It is possible to understand ἀπόλλυμαι in Lk 15.17 as involving a measure of exaggeration.

23.107 αἷμαᵇ, τος *n*: (a figurative extension of meaning of αἷμαᵃ 'blood,' 8.64) the death of a person, generally as the result of violence or execution – 'death, violent death.' τὸ αἷμα αὐτοῦ ἐφ' ἡμᾶς 'the responsibility for his death be upon us' Mt 27.25.
It is possible to interpret αἷμα in Ro 5.9 (δικαιωθέντες νῦν ἐν τῷ αἵματι αὐτοῦ 'by his death we are put right with God') as primarily a reference to physiological death. But in such contexts in which αἷμα is used in speaking of the death of Christ, there is no doubt an additional component derived from the occurrence of αἷμα in contexts speaking of atoning sacrifice. Therefore, one may analyze the meaning of αἷμα in such contexts as meaning 'sacrificial death' and not merely physiological death. In Ro 5.9 and similar contexts, a number of translators have preferred to preserve an often recurring phrase such as 'the shedding of his blood.' However, in English this can be somewhat ambiguous in that 'the shedding of blood' normally refers to the killing of someone else and not to experiencing death. See also 23.112.

23.108 ᾅδηςᵇ, ου *m* (a figurative extension of meaning of ᾅδηςᵃ 'Hades,' 1.19, as a personification of the power of Hades as the place of the dead) – 'death, power of death.' ποῦ σου, ᾅδη, τὸ νῖκος; 'death, where is your victory?' 1 Cor 15.55 (apparatus). In 1 Cor 15.55 ᾅδη is a variant reading of θάνατε 'death' (23.99).
In some languages it is extremely difficult to personify death except as a reference to

some demon which may cause death, but this, of course, is not the reference in this passage. The closest equivalent in some languages is 'how can death be victorious?' or 'death cannot be victorious.' In some instances it may be necessary to represent the personification as 'you who cause death,' and thus this expression in 1 Cor 15.55 may be translated as 'you who cause death will not always be victorious' or '. . . will not in the end be victorious.'

23.109 ἀφίημι τὸ πνεῦμα (an idiom, literally 'to send away the spirit,' interpreted by some as implying voluntarily laying down one's life, but such an inference is not justified by normal Greek usage) – 'to die.' ὁ δὲ Ἰησοῦς πάλιν κράξας φωνῇ μεγάλῃ ἀφῆκεν τὸ πνεῦμα 'Jesus again gave a loud cry and died' Mt 27.50.

23.110 παραδίδωμι τὸ πνεῦμα: (an idiom, literally 'to give over the spirit') to die, with the possible implication of a willing or voluntary act – 'to die.' καὶ κλίνας τὴν κεφαλὴν παρέδωκεν τὸ πνεῦμα 'and bowing his head, he gave up his spirit' or '. . . he died' Jn 19.30.

23.111 ἀπόθεσις τοῦ σκηνώματος (an idiom, literally 'putting off of the dwelling,' 7.8); ἐκδημέω ἐκ τοῦ σώματος (an idiom, literally 'to leave home from the body'): euphemistic expressions for dying – 'to die.' ἀπόθεσις τοῦ σκηνώματος: ταχινή ἐστιν ἡ ἀπόθεσις τοῦ σκηνώματός μου 'I shall soon die' 2 Pe 1.14.
ἐκδημέω ἐκ τοῦ σώματος: εὐδοκοῦμεν μᾶλλον ἐκδημῆσαι ἐκ τοῦ σώματος καὶ ἐνδημῆσαι πρὸς τὸν κύριον 'we would much prefer to die and be at home with the Lord' 2 Cor 5.8.

23.112 ἐκχύννεται τὸ αἷμα: (an idiom, literally 'the blood pours out') to die, with the implication of a sacrificial purpose – 'to die as a sacrifice, sacrificial death.' τὸ αἷμά μου . . . τὸ περὶ πολλῶν ἐκχυννόμενον εἰς ἄφεσιν ἁμαρτιῶν 'my death . . . as a sacrifice for many unto the forgiveness of sins' Mt 26.28. The relations between the various elements in this clause in Mt 26.28 must in some instances be made somewhat more specific, for example, 'by my dying, I am like a sacrifice for many

for the purpose of their sins being forgiven.' See also 23.107.

23.113 τὴν ψυχὴν τίθημι: (an idiom, literally 'to lay down one's life') to die, with the implication of voluntary or willing action – 'to die voluntarily, to die willingly.' τὴν ψυχήν σου ὑπὲρ ἐμοῦ θήσεις; 'are you ready to die for me?' Jn 13.38. Though in English the phrases 'to lay down one's life' or 'to give one's life' do suggest a voluntary dying, a literal rendering of such expressions in other languages would not necessarily imply the same. It may therefore be necessary to use such expressions as 'to die willingly' or 'to die without resisting.' In some languages 'willingly' is expressed primarily as a negation of objecting, for example, 'I will not object to dying.'

23.114 ἀπόλλυμι τὴν ψυχήν (an idiom, literally 'to suffer the destruction of one's life' or 'to have one's life destroyed') – 'to experience the loss of life, to die.' ὁ ἀπολέσας τὴν ψυχὴν αὐτοῦ ἕνεκεν ἐμοῦ εὑρήσει αὐτήν 'he who dies for my sake will gain his life' Mt 10.39. In Mt 10.39 some scholars see in the use of ψυχή a reference not to physical life but to a particular quality of life. This is difficult to justify except in terms of the total context, and it may be that in Mt 10.39 there is a degree of intentional ambiguity with respect to the meaning of ψυχή.

23.115 θανάσιμον, ου n (derivative of θάνατος[a] 'death,' 23.99); θανατηφόρος, ον: that which causes or produces death – 'deadly.'
θανάσιμον: κἂν θανάσιμόν τι πίωσιν 'if they drink anything deadly' Mk 16.18.
θανατηφόρος: μεστὴ ἰοῦ θανατηφόρου 'full of deadly poison' Jas 3.8. The phrase 'deadly poison' may be rendered as 'that which can cause death' or 'that which causes people to die.'

23.116 ἐπιθανάτιος, ον: (a derivative involving the base θάνατος[a] 'death,' 23.99) pertaining to having been condemned to death – 'doomed to die, sentenced to die.' ὁ θεὸς ἡμᾶς τοὺς ἀποστόλους ἐσχάτους ἀπέδειξεν ὡς ἐπιθανατίους 'God has given us apostles the very last place, like men doomed to die' 1 Cor 4.9. The phrase 'like men doomed to die' may be rendered in some languages as 'like men who will soon be killed' or '. . . will soon be executed.'

23.117 ἀποθνῄσκω^b; (εἰμὶ) ἐν θανάτοις (an idiom, literally 'to be in death'): to be in imminent danger of dying – 'to face death, to be likely to die.'
ἀποθνῄσκω^b: καθ' ἡμέραν ἀποθνῄσκω 'I face death day by day' 1 Cor 15.31. It would also be possible to render καθ' ἡμέραν ἀποθνῄσκω in 1 Cor 15.31 as 'I am in danger of being killed each day.'
ἐν θανάτοις: ἐν θανάτοις πολλάκις 'often in danger of death' 2 Cor 11.23.

23.118 συναποθνῄσκω: to experience death along with others – 'to die together with.' ἐὰν δέῃ με συναποθανεῖν σοι, οὐ μή σε ἀπαρνήσομαι 'I will never say I do not know you, even if I have to die with you' Mk 14.31.

23.119 πνίγομαι; ἀποπνίγομαι: to die as the result of drowning – 'to drown.'[15]
πνίγομαι: ἐπνίγοντο ἐν τῇ θαλάσσῃ 'they were drowned in the lake' Mk 5.13.
ἀποπνίγομαι: ὥρμησεν ἡ ἀγέλη κατὰ τοῦ κρημνοῦ εἰς τὴν λίμνην καὶ ἀπεπνίγη 'the herd rushed down the cliff into the lake and were drowned' Lk 8.33.

23.120 πνίγω^b; ἀποπνίγω; συμπνίγω^a: (figurative extensions of meaning employing the base πνίγω^a 'to choke,' 19.53) to cause the death of plants by other plants crowding them out and/or overshadowing them – 'to cause plants to die.'[16]
πνίγω^b: ἀνέβησαν αἱ ἄκανθαι καὶ ἔπνιξαν αὐτά 'the thorns grew up and caused them to die' Mt 13.7.
ἀποπνίγω: ἕτερον ἔπεσεν ἐν μέσῳ τῶν ἀκανθῶν, καὶ συμφυεῖσαι αἱ ἄκανθαι ἀπέπνιξαν αὐτό 'other (seeds) fell among the thorns and the thorns

grew up with the plants and caused them to die' Lk 8.7.
συμπνίγω^a: ἀνέβησαν αἱ ἄκανθαι καὶ συνέπνιξαν αὐτό 'the thorns grew up and caused them to die' Mk 4.7.

23.121 νεκρός^a, ά, όν: pertaining to being dead – 'lifeless, dead.' τὸ σῶμα χωρὶς πνεύματος νεκρόν ἐστιν 'the body without the spirit is dead' Jas 2.26. In some languages it may be difficult or even impossible to speak of 'the body without the spirit,' for this would be equivalent to the meaning of 'corpse,' and obviously a 'corpse' is 'dead.' It may therefore be necessary to translate this expression in Jas 2.26 as 'if a person does not have a spirit, he is dead.'

23.122 ἡμιθανής, ές: the state of being somewhere between life and death – 'half dead, nearly dead.' λῃσταῖς περιέπεσεν, οἳ καὶ ἐκδύσαντες αὐτὸν καὶ πληγὰς ἐπιθέντες ἀπῆλθον ἀφέντες ἡμιθανῆ 'robbers attacked him, stripped him, and beat him up, leaving him half dead' Lk 10.30. One may render 'half dead' as 'almost dead' or 'about to die.'

23.123 δὶς ἀποθάνων: (an idiom, literally 'dying twice') the state of being completely dead – 'completely dead.' δὶς ἀποθανόντα 'completely dead' Jd 12. The phrase δὶς ἀποθανόντα in Jd 12 refers specifically to trees, but figuratively to persons. It is possible that δὶς ἀποθανόντα is applicable to trees (1) on the basis that they die while still standing and (2) that death is fully confirmed by their being rooted up, but in view of the figurative context, it is better to translate δὶς ἀποθανόντα as simply 'completely dead.'

23.124 θνητός, ή, όν: pertaining to being liable to death (that which will eventually die) – 'mortal.' μὴ οὖν βασιλευέτω ἡ ἁμαρτία ἐν τῷ θνητῷ ὑμῶν σώματι 'sin must no longer rule in your mortal bodies' Ro 6.12. The phrase 'mortal bodies' may be rendered as 'bodies which will die.'

23.125 φθαρτός, ή, όν: pertaining to that which is bound to disintegrate and die – 'perishable, mortal.' ἤλλαξαν τὴν δόξαν τοῦ ἀφθάρτου θεοῦ ἐν ὁμοιώματι εἰκόνος φθαρτοῦ

---

15 It is possible that ἀποπνίγομαι differs from πνίγομαι in being somewhat more intensive in meaning, but this cannot be determined with accuracy on the basis of existing contexts.

16 It is possible that ἀποπνίγω and συμπνίγω^a are somewhat more intensive in meaning than πνίγω^b, but this is difficult, if not impossible, to determine on the basis of NT usage.

ἀνθρώπου 'they changed the glory of immortal God for the likeness of a mortal human being' Ro 1.23.

23.126 ἀθανασία, ας f: the state of not being subject to death (that which will never die) – 'immortality.' ὁ βασιλεὺς τῶν βασιλευόντων καὶ κύριος τῶν κυριευόντων, ὁ μόνος ἔχων ἀθανασίαν 'the King of kings and Lord of lords, who alone is immortal' 1 Tm 6.15-16. The clause 'who alone is immortal' may be expressed in some languages as simply 'he is the only one who never dies' or 'he is the only one who always exists.'

23.127 ἀφθαρσία[a], ας f: the state of not being subject to decay, leading to death – 'immortal, immortality.' ἐγείρεται ἐν ἀφθαρσίᾳ 'it will be raised immortal' 1 Cor 15.42. It is possible to translate this clause as 'it will be raised and will never again die.'

In rendering 'immortality' it may be necessary to employ an entire clause, for example, 'that people will not die.' However, in 2 Tm 1.10 'life and immortality' may be best understood as a phrase in which 'immortality' is a qualification of 'life,' and therefore one may translate 'revealing immortal life through the gospel' or 'revealing by means of the good news the life that does not end.'

23.128 ἄφθαρτος, ον: pertaining to being not subject to decay and death – 'imperishable, immortal.' καὶ οἱ νεκροὶ ἐγερθήσονται ἄφθαρτοι 'and the dead will be raised immortal' 1 Cor 15.52; ἐν τῷ ἀφθάρτῳ τοῦ πραέως καὶ ἡσυχίου πνεύματος 'in the immortal character of a gentle and quiet spirit' 1 Pe 3.4.

H Health, Vigor, Strength (23.129-23.141)

23.129 ὑγιαίνω[a]; ὑγιής[a], ές, acc. ὑγιῆ; καλῶς ἔχω (an idiom, literally 'to have well'): the state of being healthy, well (in contrast with sickness) – 'to be well, to be healthy.' ὑγιαίνω[a]: οὐ χρείαν ἔχουσιν οἱ ὑγιαίνοντες ἰατροῦ ἀλλὰ οἱ κακῶς ἔχοντες 'people who are well do not need a doctor, but (only) those who are sick' Lk 5.31. ὑγιής[a]: γνοὺς ὅτι πολὺν ἤδη χρόνον ἔχει, λέγει

αὐτῷ, Θέλεις ὑγιὴς γενέσθαι 'he knew that the man had been sick for a long time, so he said to him, Do you want to get well?' Jn 5.6. καλῶς ἔχω: ἐπὶ ἀρρώστους χεῖρας ἐπιθήσουσιν καὶ καλῶς ἕξουσιν 'they will place their hands on the sick and they will be well' Mk 16.18.

In a number of languages health is expressed only in terms of strength, for 'to be well' is 'to be strong.' In other languages, however, to be well or to be healthy is a negation of illness or sickness, so that in Mk 16.18 one may translate 'they will place their hands on those who are sick and these people will become not sick.'

23.130 ἰσχύω[c]: a state of being healthy, with the implication of robustness and vigor – 'to be healthy.' οὐ χρείαν ἔχουσιν οἱ ἰσχύοντες ἰατροῦ ἀλλ' οἱ κακῶς ἔχοντες 'people who are healthy do not need a doctor, but (only) those who are sick' Mk 2.17.

23.131 ὁλοκληρία, ας f: a state of complete health or soundness in all parts of the body – 'complete health, perfect health.' ἡ πίστις . . . ἔδωκεν αὐτῷ τὴν ὁλοκληρίαν ταύτην 'faith . . . has given him this complete health' Ac 3.16. In some languages it may be possible to translate ὁλοκληρίαν as 'very healthy' or 'all parts of his body are healthy' or '. . . strong.'

23.132 ἁπλοῦς[a], ῆ, οῦν: pertaining to being healthy, with the implication of sound, proper functioning (in the NT with particular reference to the eyes) – 'to be healthy, to be sound.' ὅταν ὁ ὀφθαλμός σου ἁπλοῦς ᾖ, καὶ ὅλον τὸ σῶμά σου φωτεινόν ἐστιν 'when your eyes are sound, your whole body is full of light' Lk 11.34. For another interpretation of ἁπλοῦς in Lk 11.34, see 57.107. See also 23.149.

23.133 ῥώννυμαι[a]: (derivative of a base meaning literally 'to be strong, to be well,' but used in the NT only as a formula for the ending of letters) to be well and to fare well – 'to fare well.'[17] ἔρρωσθε 'may you fare well' Ac

---

17 The analysis of ῥώννυμαι in its epistolary usage is similar to the use of the term 'dear' in English, used at the beginning of a letter. It may actually represent an affectionate greeting, but it is more likely to occur simply as a greeting formula.

15.29. The occurrence of ῥώννυμαι as an epistolary formula may be understood in two different senses: either as a sincere expression of the wish that the person involved may fare well or merely as a device to indicate that the letter is complete. This second sense of ῥώννυμαι is treated in 33.24.

23.134 κραταιόομαιᵃ: to become strong and healthy, with the implication of physical vigor – 'to become strong.' τὸ δὲ παιδίον ηὔξανεν καὶ ἐκραταιοῦτο 'the child grew up and became strong' Lk 2.40. In employing an expression to translate 'to become strong,' it is important to avoid the impression of 'to become muscular.' The emphasis is upon total physical vigor, not mere muscular strength.

23.135 κομψότερον: the state of being in better health after a previous state of relative lack of health – 'to be better, to be in better health.' ἐπύθετο οὖν τὴν ὥραν παρ' αὐτῶν ἐν ᾗ κομψότερον ἔσχεν 'he asked them what time it was when (his son) got better' Jn 4.52.

23.136 ἰάομαιᵃ; **ἴασις, εως** f; **σῴζω**ᶜ; **διασῴζω**ᵇ: to cause someone to become well again after having been sick – 'to heal, to cure, to make well, healing.'[18]
ἰάομαιᵃ: ἦλθον ἀκοῦσαι αὐτοῦ καὶ ἰαθῆναι ἀπὸ τῶν νόσων αὐτῶν 'they came to hear him and to be healed of their diseases' Lk 6.18.
ἴασις: ἐτῶν γὰρ ἦν πλειόνων τεσσεράκοντα ὁ ἄνθρωπος ἐφ' ὃν γεγόνει τὸ σημεῖον τοῦτο τῆς ἰάσεως 'the man on whom this miracle of healing had been performed was over forty years old' Ac 4.22.
σῴζωᶜ: ὅσοι ἂν ἥψαντο αὐτοῦ ἐσῴζοντο 'all who touched him were made well' Mk 6.56.
διασῴζωᵇ: ἐρωτῶν αὐτὸν ὅπως ἐλθὼν διασώσῃ τὸν δοῦλον αὐτοῦ 'he asked him to come and heal his servant' Lk 7.3.
In a number of languages there are different terms for 'healing' depending upon the type of sickness or illness which is involved.

18 It is possible that διασῴζωᵇ is somewhat more emphatic in meaning than σῴζωᶜ. It is also possible that in a number of contexts σῴζωᶜ and διασῴζωᵇ may have the added implication of having rescued such persons from a state of illness.

23.137 καθαρίζωᶜ: to heal a person of a disease which has caused ceremonial uncleanness – 'to heal and make ritually pure, to heal and to make ritually acceptable.' ἐὰν θέλῃς δύνασαί με καθαρίσαι 'if you want to, you can heal me and make me ritually clean' Mt 8.2. Since καθαρίζωᶜ implies two changes of state, (1) the healing of a disease and (2) the making of a person ritually pure or acceptable, it may be necessary in some languages, and particularly in certain contexts, to render καθαρίζωᶜ in a relatively explicit manner, namely, 'to heal and to make ritually acceptable' or '. . . ceremonially clean.'

23.138 ἴαμα, τος n: (derivative of ἰάομαιᵃ 'to cause to be well again, to heal,' 23.136) the capacity to cause someone to become healed or cured – 'the power to heal, the capacity to heal.' ἄλλῳ δὲ χαρίσματα ἰαμάτων ἐν τῷ ἑνὶ πνεύματι 'and to another man the same Spirit gives the power to heal' 1 Cor 12.9. In some languages it may be difficult to speak of 'giving the power to heal.' A more natural form of expression is 'cause to be able to heal.'

23.139 θεραπεύωᵃ; **θεραπεία, ας** f: to cause someone to recover health, often with the implication of having taken care of such a person – 'to heal, to cure, to take care of, healing.'
θεραπεύωᵃ: ἔδωκεν αὐτοῖς ἐξουσίαν . . . θεραπεύειν πᾶσαν νόσον 'he gave them authority . . . to heal every disease' Mt 10.1.
θεραπείαᵃ: τοὺς χρείαν ἔχοντας θεραπείας ἰᾶτο 'he cured those who needed healing' Lk 9.11.

23.140 ἐγείρωᵍ: (a figurative extension of meaning of ἐγείρωᵃ 'to cause to stand up,' 17.10) to restore a person to health and vigor (somewhat equivalent to the English idiom 'to get him on his feet again') – 'to restore to health, to heal.' ἡ εὐχὴ τῆς πίστεως σώσει τὸν κάμνοντα, καὶ ἐγερεῖ αὐτὸν ὁ κύριος 'prayer made in faith will make the sick man well, and the Lord will restore him to health' Jas 5.15.

23.141 ἰατρός, οῦ m: one who causes someone to be healed – 'physician, doctor, healer.' οὐ χρείαν ἔχουσιν οἱ ἰσχύοντες ἰατροῦ 'people who are well do not need a doctor' Mt 9.12.

I   Sickness, Disease, Weakness (23.142-23.184)

23.142 κάμνω: to be ill, with a possible implication of being worn-out or wasting away – 'to be sick, to be very sick.' ἡ εὐχὴ τῆς πίστεως σώσει τὸν κάμνοντα 'prayer made in faith will make the sick man well' Jas 5.15.

As in the case of expressions for health and vigor, it may also be necessary in some languages to specify more precisely the nature of the illness, disease, or weakness. Often the context provides a clue, but in some instances this is not possible, in which case it is important to try to employ a term for sickness or illness which will be the most generalized.

23.143 ἀσθένεια[b], ας *f*: the state of being ill and thus incapacitated in some manner – 'illness, disability, weakness.' αὐτὸς τὰς ἀσθενείας ἡμῶν ἔλαβεν καὶ τὰς νόσους ἐβάστασεν 'he took our illnesses and carried away our diseases' Mt 8.17. It may be extremely difficult in some languages to speak of 'taking illness' or 'carrying away diseases.' A strictly literal rendering of such an expression might suggest immediately that Jesus was a type of medicine man who healed others by taking upon himself precisely the same kinds of diseases (a widespread shamanistic practice). It may therefore be necessary in some languages to translate Mt 8.17 as 'he caused us to no longer have illness and disease.' In this way, one may avoid a specific type of shamanistic practice which would be inappropriate in this context.

23.144 ἀσθενέω[b]: to be sick and, as a result, in a state of weakness and incapacity – 'to be sick, to be ill, to be disabled.' ἀσθενοῦντας νόσοις ποικίλαις ἤγαγον αὐτοὺς πρὸς αὐτόν . . . ἐθεράπευεν αὐτούς 'they brought those who were sick with various diseases to him . . . he healed them' Lk 4.40.

23.145 ἀσθενής[c], ές: pertaining to being ill and, as a result, weak and incapacitated – 'sick, ill, weak, disabled.' ἀσθενὴς καὶ ἐν φυλακῇ καὶ οὐκ ἐπεσκέψασθέ με 'I was sick and in prison, but you would not take care of me' Mt 25.43.

23.146 διαφθείρω[c]: to become gradually incapacitated – 'to lose one's strength, to waste away.' εἰ καὶ ὁ ἔξω ἡμῶν ἄνθρωπος διαφθείρεται 'even if our physical being is gradually wasting away' or '. . . becoming weak' or '. . . is gradually being destroyed' 2 Cor 4.16.

23.147 ἄρρωστος, ον: to be sick or ill, as a state of powerlessness – 'to be sick, sick, ill.' ἐθεράπευσεν τοὺς ἀρρώστους αὐτῶν 'he healed their sick' Mt 14.14.

23.148 κακῶς ἔχω: (an idiom, literally 'to have badly' or 'to fare badly') to be in a bad state, to be ill – 'to be ill, to be sick' (to some extent equivalent to the English idiom 'to be bad off,' in speaking of ill health). οὐ χρείαν ἔχουσιν οἱ ἰσχύοντες ἰατροῦ ἀλλ' οἱ κακῶς ἔχοντες 'people who are well do not need a doctor, but (only) those who are sick' Mt 9.12.

23.149 πονηρός[d], ά, όν: (a figurative extension of meaning of πονηρός[a] 'evil,' 88.110) a state of being sickly or diseased (in the NT with special reference to the eyes) – 'to be sick, to be diseased.' ὁ λύχνος τοῦ σώματός ἐστιν ὁ ὀφθαλμός σου . . . ἐπὰν δὲ πονηρὸς ᾖ, καὶ τὸ σῶμά σου σκοτεινόν 'your eyes are like a lamp for the body . . . when your eyes are sick, your whole body will be in darkness' Lk 11.34. For other interpretations of πονηρός with ὀφθαλμός, see 57.108 and 88.165. See also 23.132.

23.150 εἰς τὸ χεῖρον ἔρχομαι: (an idiom, literally 'to come to the worse') to become increasingly more sick – 'to get worse, to become more sick.' μηδὲν ὠφεληθεῖσα ἀλλὰ μᾶλλον εἰς τὸ χεῖρον ἐλθοῦσα 'she did not benefit, but instead became more sick' Mk 5.26.

23.151 ἐσχάτως ἔχω: (an idiom, literally 'to be at an extreme') to be very sick, with the implication of imminent death – 'to be very sick, to be about to die.' τὸ θυγάτριόν μου ἐσχάτως ἔχει 'my little daughter is very sick' Mk 5.23.

23.152 βάλλω εἰς κλίνην: (an idiom, literally 'to throw on a bed') to cause someone to become very ill – 'to cause illness, to make sick.' ἰδοὺ βάλλω αὐτὴν εἰς κλίνην . . . εἰς θλῖψιν μεγάλην 'look, I will make her sick . . . and she will suffer terribly' Re 2.22.

23.153 μάστιξᵇ, ιγος *f*: a state of disease, often implying divine punishment – 'to be diseased, to be sick, disease.' ὥστε ἐπιπίπτειν αὐτῷ ἵνα αὐτοῦ ἅψωνται ὅσοι εἶχον μάστιγας 'and all who had diseases kept pushing their way to him in order to touch him' Mk 3.10.

23.154 μαλακία, ας *f*: a state of weakness resulting from disease – 'disease, sickness.'[19] θεραπεύων πᾶσαν νόσον καὶ πᾶσαν μαλακίαν ἐν τῷ λαῷ 'healing people from every kind of disease and sickness' Mt 4.23.

23.155 νόσος, ου *f*; νόσημα, τος *n*: the state of being diseased – 'diseased, disease, sickness.'
νόσος: προσήνεγκαν αὐτῷ πάντας τοὺς κακῶς ἔχοντας ποικίλαις νόσοις 'they brought to him all those who were sick with all kinds of diseases' Mt 4.24.
νόσημα: ὑγιὴς ἐγίνετο οἵῳ δήποτ' οὖν κατείχετο νοσήματι 'was healed from whatever disease he had' Jn 5.4 (apparatus).

23.156 δεσμόςᶜ, οῦ *m*: (a figurative extension of meaning of δεσμόςᵃ 'bond,' 6.14) a state of physical incapacity or illness, usually as the result of some controlling supernatural force (in Lk 13.16, the result of the activity of Satan) – 'illness.' ἣν ἔδησεν ὁ Σατανᾶς ἰδοὺ δέκα καὶ ὀκτὼ ἔτη, οὐκ ἔδει λυθῆναι ἀπὸ τοῦ δεσμοῦ τούτου 'whom Satan has kept physically incapacitated for eighteen years, should she not be freed from this illness' Lk 13.16.

23.157 δέωᶠ: to cause physical incapacity for someone – 'to cause physical hardship, to cause illness.' ἣν ἔδησεν ὁ Σατανᾶς ἰδοὺ δέκα καὶ ὀκτὼ ἔτη 'whom Satan has kept physically incapacitated for eighteen years' or 'for whom Satan has caused physical hardship for eighteen years' Lk 13.16.

23.158 λοιμόςᵃ, οῦ *m*; πληγήᶜ, ῆς *f*; θάνατοςᵇ, ου *m*: a widespread contagious disease, often associated with divine retribution – 'plague, pestilence.'
λοιμόςᵃ: σεισμοί τε μεγάλοι καὶ κατὰ τόπους λιμοὶ καὶ λοιμοὶ ἔσονται 'there will be terrible earthquakes, famines, and plagues everywhere' Lk 21.11.
πληγήᶜ: πατάξαι τὴν γῆν ἐν πάσῃ πληγῇ ὁσάκις ἐὰν θελήσωσιν 'to strike the earth with every kind of plague as often as they wish' Re 11.6. It is also possible to interpret πληγή in Re 11.6 as being somewhat more generic in meaning, that is to say, trouble or distress causing widespread suffering (see 22.13).
θάνατοςᵇ: ἀποκτεῖναι ἐν ῥομφαίᾳ καὶ ἐν λιμῷ καὶ ἐν θανάτῳ 'to kill with the sword, famine and pestilence' Re 6.8.

23.159 πυρέσσω; πυρετός, οῦ *m*; πίμπραμαιᵃ: to be sick with a fever – 'to have a fever, fever.'
πυρέσσω: ἡ δὲ πενθερὰ Σίμωνος κατέκειτο πυρέσσουσα 'Simon's mother-in-law was in bed with a fever' Mk 1.30.
πυρετός: πενθερὰ δὲ τοῦ Σίμωνος ἦν συνεχομένη πυρετῷ μεγάλῳ 'Simon's mother-in-law was confined with a high fever' Lk 4.38.
πίμπραμαιᵃ: οἱ δὲ προσεδόκων αὐτὸν μέλλειν πίμπρασθαι 'they waited for him to burn with a fever' Ac 28.6. It is also possible to understand πίμπραμαι in Ac 28.6 as a process of swelling up (see 23.163).
Though in a number of languages one can say 'a person has a fever,' in some languages the reverse expression is used, for example, 'the fever has a person.' Similarly, instead of saying 'a person has a disease,' it is 'the disease which grabs a person.' One may often speak of a fever as 'to become hot' or 'to burn' or 'to be sick with burning.'

23.160 δυσεντέριον, ου *n*: an infectious disease of the intestinal tract, usually involving severe pain and diarrhea – 'dysentery.' πυρετοῖς καὶ δυσεντερίῳ συνεχόμενον κατακεῖσθαι 'he was in bed with fever and dysentery' Ac 28.8. In some languages one may speak of dysentery as 'a watery discharge' or 'pain and discharge.'

23.161 λέπρα, ας *f*: a dreaded condition of the skin, including what is now regarded as

---

19 It is possible that μαλακία should be regarded as essentially synonymous with ἀσθένειαᵇ (23.143).

leprosy, as well as certain other types of infectious skin diseases, resulting in a person's being regarded as ceremonially unclean and thus excluded from normal relations with other people – 'leprosy, dread skin disease.'[20] ἀνὴρ πλήρης λέπρας . . . ἐδεήθη αὐτοῦ . . . καθαρίσαι 'a man covered with a dread skin disease . . . asked him (Jesus) . . . to heal him' Lk 5.12.

23.162 λεπρός, οῦ *m*: (derivative of λέπρα 'dread skin disease,' 23.161) a person suffering from a dread skin disease – 'leper, one having a dread skin disease.' ἀσθενοῦντας θεραπεύετε . . . λεπροὺς καθαρίζετε 'heal the sick . . . cure those who have a dread skin disease' Mt 10.8.

23.163 πίμπραμαι[b] – 'to swell up.' οἱ δὲ προσεδόκων αὐτὸν μέλλειν πίμπρασθαι 'they waited for him to swell up' Ac 28.6. It is also possible to understand πίμπραμαι in Ac 28.6 as being sick with a fever (see 23.159).

23.164 ὑδρωπικός, ή, όν: pertaining to swelling resulting from the accumulation of lymph in the body tissues – 'suffering from dropsy.' ἄνθρωπός τις ἦν ὑδρωπικὸς ἔμπροσθεν αὐτοῦ 'a man who was suffering from dropsy came to him' Lk 14.2.

23.165 γάγγραινα, ης *f*: a disease involving severe inflammation and possibly a cancerous spread of ulcers which eat away the flesh and bones – 'ulcers, gangrene, cancer.' ὁ λόγος αὐτῶν ὡς γάγγραινα νομὴν ἕξει 'what they teach will spread like cancer' 2 Tm 2.17.

23.166 σκωληκόβρωτος, ον: pertaining to being eaten by worms (a reference to the occurrence of worms in ulcerous tissue) – 'to be

eaten by worms.' γενόμενος σκωληκόβρωτος ἐξέψυξεν 'he was eaten by worms and died' Ac 12.23. In some languages it is important to make a clear distinction between intestinal parasites and the grubs of flies which feed on ulcerous tissue.

23.167 σπαράσσω; συσπαράσσω: to cause a person to shake violently in convulsions – 'to throw into convulsions, to throw into a fit.' σπαράσσω: σπαράξαν αὐτὸν τὸ πνεῦμα τὸ ἀκάθαρτον καὶ φωνῆσαν φωνῇ μεγάλῃ ἐξῆλθεν ἐξ αὐτοῦ 'the evil spirit threw him into a fit, gave a loud scream and came out of him' Mk 1.26. συσπαράσσω: ἔρρηξεν αὐτὸν τὸ δαιμόνιον καὶ συνεσπάραξεν 'the demon knocked him to the ground and threw him into a convulsion' Lk 9.42.

23.168 ῥήγνυμι[d] or ῥήσσω: to cause to fall to the ground in convulsions – 'to throw down in convulsions, to throw into a fit.' ἔρρηξεν αὐτὸν τὸ δαιμόνιον καὶ συνεσπάραξεν 'the demon threw him down to the ground and convulsed him' Lk 9.42. ῥήγνυμι seemingly refers to the first stage in the process of throwing a person into convulsions; this would mean to cause someone to fall down in convulsions. In Lk 9.42 ῥήγνυμι is followed by συσπαράσσω (23.167) which indicates the violent shaking in convulsions. ὅπου ἐὰν αὐτὸν καταλάβῃ ῥήσσει αὐτόν 'whenever (the spirit) attacks him, it throws him to the ground in convulsions' Mk 9.18.

23.169 σεληνιάζομαι: to suffer epileptic seizures (associated in ancient times with the supernatural power of the moon) – 'to suffer epileptic seizures, to be an epileptic.' σεληνιάζεται καὶ κακῶς πάσχει 'he is an epileptic and suffers terribly' Mt 17.15.

23.170 παραλύομαι: to suffer paralysis in one or more limbs, especially in the leg or foot – 'to be paralyzed, to be lame.' φέροντες ἐπὶ κλίνης ἄνθρωπον ὃς ἦν παραλελυμένος 'they carried a paralyzed man on a bed' Lk 5.18.

In He 12.12 παραλύομαι occurs in a highly figurative context: τὰ παραλελυμένα γόνατα ἀνορθώσατε 'straighten up the paralyzed knees.' It is often better in this context to

---

20 There are significant differences of opinion with regard to the nature of λέπρα as mentioned in the NT. Some authorities insist that this type of disease is not in any way related to so-called Hansen's disease, while others assume that it does include Hansen's disease as well as a number of other skin ailments, including psoriasis, seborrhea, and pinto (a white, spotted discoloration of the skin). From the standpoint of the biblical text, the factor of ritual uncleanness or impurity was even more important than the physical malady.

speak of 'strengthening the weak knees,' but in any event, the reference to the physical situation of the individual is merely a way of speaking about a psychological state, as in 25.152.

23.171 παραλυτικός, ή, όν: pertaining to being lame and/or paralyzed – 'lame, paralyzed.' προσέφερον αὐτῷ παραλυτικὸν ἐπὶ κλίνης βεβλημένον 'they brought him a paralytic lying on a bed' Mt 9.2. It is often best to speak of a paralytic as 'one who cannot walk.'

23.172 ξηραίνομαι[c]: (a figurative extension of meaning of ξηραίνομαι[a] 'to dry up,' 79.81) to become stiff to the point of not being able to move – 'to be stiff, to be paralyzed.' τρίζει τοὺς ὀδόντας καὶ ξηραίνεται 'he grits his teeth and becomes stiff all over' Mk 9.18. In some languages one may express the meaning of 'to be stiff all over' as 'not able to move any part of the body.'

23.173 ξηρός[b], ά, όν: (a figurative extension of meaning of ξηρός[a] 'dry, withered,' 79.80) pertaining to a shrunken, withered, and hence immobile part of the body – 'withered, paralyzed.' ἄνθρωπος χεῖρα ἔχων ξηράν 'a man who had a hand that was shrunken and paralyzed' Mt 12.10.

23.174 παρίεμαι: to suffer weakness or disability in some part of the body – 'to be weak, to be weakened.' τὰς παρειμένας χεῖρας καὶ τὰ παραλελυμένα γόνατα ἀνορθώσατε 'lift up your weak hands and straighten your paralyzed knees' He 12.12. In some languages 'weak hands' may be expressed as 'hands that cannot hold anything' or 'hands that cannot do anything.'

23.175 χωλός, ή, όν: pertaining to a disability that involves the imperfect function of the lower limbs – 'lame, one who is lame.' τυφλοὶ ἀναβλέπουσιν καὶ χωλοὶ περιπατοῦσιν 'the blind can see, the lame can walk' Mt 11.5.

23.176 κυλλός, ή, όν: pertaining to a disability in one or more limbs, especially the leg or foot, often as the result of some deformity

– 'crippled.' προσῆλθον αὐτῷ ὄχλοι πολλοὶ ἔχοντες μεθ᾽ ἑαυτῶν χωλούς, τυφλούς, κυλλούς, κωφούς 'large crowds came to him bringing with them the lame, the blind, the crippled, and the dumb' Mt 15.30.

23.177 ἀνάπειρος, ον: pertaining to a state of being maimed or mutilated, resulting in a crippling condition – 'maimed, mutilated, crippled.' ὅταν δοχὴν ποιῇς, κάλει πτωχούς, ἀναπείρους, χωλούς, τυφλούς 'when you give a feast, invite the poor, the cripples, the lame, and the blind' Lk 14.13.

23.178 ἐκτρέπω: to wrench or sprain the ligaments of a joint, especially in the legs and feet – 'to sprain, to wrench.' τροχιὰς ὀρθὰς ποιεῖτε τοῖς ποσὶν ὑμῶν, ἵνα μὴ τὸ χωλὸν ἐκτραπῇ 'keep walking on straight paths so that the lame foot may not be wrenched' He 12.13. It is often possible to speak of 'being wrenched' as 'being twisted.'

23.179 ἕλκος, ους n: a painful, ulcerated sore resulting from infection – 'sore, ulcer.' οἱ κύνες ἐρχόμενοι ἐπέλειχον τὰ ἕλκη αὐτοῦ 'the dogs would come and lick his sores' Lk 16.21.

23.180 ἑλκόομαι: (derivative of ἕλκος 'sore, ulcer,' 23.179) to have sores on the body – 'to have sores, to have ulcers, to be full of sores.' πτωχὸς δέ τις ὀνόματι Λάζαρος ἐβέβλητο πρὸς τὸν πυλῶνα αὐτοῦ εἱλκωμένος 'there was a poor man by the name of Lazarus who was lying at his door and was full of sores' or '. . . whose body was covered with sores' or '. . . who had many sores on his body' Lk 16.20.

23.181 αἱμορροέω: to experience or suffer a loss of blood – 'to bleed.'[21] γυνὴ αἱμορροοῦσα δώδεκα ἔτη 'there was a woman who suffered bleeding for twelve years' Mt 9.20.

---

21 The expressions in 23.181 and 23.182 all refer to a menstrual flow of blood, but the phrases πηγὴ αἵματος and ῥύσις αἵματος seem to be restricted primarily to this meaning, while αἱμορροέω in non-biblical contexts means simply 'to suffer a loss of blood' or 'to bleed,' but it may, of course, refer to menstrual bleeding. Because of the wider range of reference in αἱμορροέω, this term has been listed separately.

23.182 πηγὴ αἵματος (an idiom, literally 'a fountain of blood'); ῥύσις αἵματος (a set phrase, literally 'flow of blood'): the loss of blood through menstrual bleeding – 'loss of blood, menstrual flow, bleeding.'[21]
πηγὴ αἵματος: εὐθὺς ἐξηράνθη ἡ πηγὴ τοῦ αἵματος αὐτῆς 'immediately her bleeding stopped' Mk 5.29.
ῥύσις αἵματος: καὶ γυνὴ οὖσα ἐν ῥύσει αἵματος δώδεκα ἔτη 'and the woman suffered from menstrual bleeding for twelve years' Mk 5.25.

23.183 αἱματεκχυσία, ας f: the process of causing blood to flow out – 'to cause bleeding, to cause blood to flow, the flow of blood.' χωρὶς αἱματεκχυσίας οὐ γίνεται ἄφεσις 'sins were forgiven only if blood was caused to flow' He 9.22. It may be important in translating He 9.22 to introduce some statement with regard to sacrifice, for example, 'if the blood of the sacrifice did not flow' or 'if there was no sacrifice involving blood' or simply 'if there was no sacrifice,' but because of the symbolic value of 'blood' in the ritual, some reference to blood should be retained.

23.184 ἀποψύχω[a]: to lose one's consciousness temporarily – 'to faint.' ἀποψυχόντων ἀνθρώπων ἀπὸ φόβου 'people fainting from fear' Lk 21.26. It is possible that ἀποψύχω in Lk 21.26 refers primarily to a psychological experience rather than a physiological one. Some scholars, however, have interpreted ἀποψύχω in this context as meaning 'to die.' For another interpretation of ἀποψύχω in Lk 21.26, see 25.293.

J   Breathe, Breath (23.185-23.187)

23.185 ἐμφυσάω: to breathe upon something – 'to breathe on.' ἐνεφύσησεν καὶ λέγει αὐτοῖς, Λάβετε πνεῦμα ἅγιον 'then he breathed on them and said, Receive the Holy Spirit' Jn 20.22. The process of breathing on someone may have very important symbolic implications. In some instances this can be related to a blessing, as in Jn 20.22, but in some languages the act of breathing on a person almost inevitably suggests some harmful influence, often connected with the use of black magic. It may therefore be important to select some less specific term so as to avoid a symbolic meaning which would considerably distort the significance of this one passage in which ἐμφυσάω occurs in the NT.

23.186 πνεῦμα[h], τος n: a breath of air coming from the lungs – 'breath.' ὃν ὁ κύριος Ἰησοῦς ἀνελεῖ τῷ πνεύματι τοῦ στόματος αὐτοῦ 'the Lord Jesus will kill him by the breath of his mouth' 2 Th 2.8. In this figurative context, πνεῦμα[h] refers to a single breath of air. It does not refer to the process of breathing (see πνοή[b] 'breath,' 23.187). The use of 'breath' to kill a person may immediately suggest in some languages the power of sorcery. It would be difficult indeed to avoid this connotation in view of the total context, but it may be necessary to have some type of marginal note explaining the symbolic significance.

23.187 πνοή[b], ῆς f: the process of breathing – 'breath, capacity to breathe.' αὐτὸς διδοὺς πᾶσι ζωὴν καὶ πνοήν 'it is he himself who gives life and breath to all people' Ac 17.25. Rather than rendering Ac 17.25 as 'gives life and breath to all people,' it may be better to say 'causes all people to live and breathe.' In some languages, however, 'to breathe' is synonymous with 'life,' and therefore to say 'to live and to breathe' is to be both redundant and repetitious. One may therefore translate 'who causes all people to live.'

K   Grow, Growth (23.188-23.196)

23.188 αὐξάνω[c]; αὔξησις, εως f: to grow, to increase in size, whether of animate beings or of plants – 'to grow, growth.'
αὐξάνω[c]: κατανοήσατε τὰ κρίνα πῶς αὐξάνει 'look how the wild flowers grow' Lk 12.27; τὸ δὲ παιδίον ηὔξανεν 'the child grew' Lk 2.40.
αὔξησις: πᾶν τὸ σῶμα . . . αὔξει τὴν αὔξησιν τοῦ θεοῦ 'the whole body . . . grows as God wants it to grow' Col 2.19. In Col 2.19 αὔξησις is used figuratively in the sense that the reference of 'body' is the church rather than a physical body. Normally a term for 'growth' would imply not only size but also number, that is to say, the growth of the church would be in terms of the increase of members of the

church, though it might refer to spiritual maturity. In some instances, however, it may be necessary to specify 'growth in numbers' so as to avoid the implication which might be derived from the context, namely that the church is simply a building which gets bigger and bigger.

In a number of languages one must make a clear distinction in the choice of terms referring to the growth of an animate being (animal or human) and the growth of plants.

23.189 ἀναβαίνω^d: to grow taller (restricted in the NT to the growth of plants) – 'to grow up.' καὶ ἀνέβησαν αἱ ἄκανθαι 'and the thorn plants grew up' Mt 13.7.

23.190 μηκύνομαι: to increase in length, restricted in the NT to the growth of plants – 'to grow.' ὁ σπόρος βλαστᾷ καὶ μηκύνηται 'the seeds are sprouting and growing' Mk 4.27.

23.191 φύω^a: to grow (of plants) – 'to grow.' φυὲν ἐποίησεν καρπόν '(the plants) grew and bore grain' Lk 8.8.

In He 12.15 φύω occurs in an extended figurative context which may be better treated as a simile. Compare, for example, a literal translation of μή τις ῥίζα πικρίας ἄνω φύουσα 'lest any root of bitterness grow up' with the treatment of this expression as a type of simile, 'in order that no one becomes like a bitter plant that grows up.'

23.192 συναυξάνομαι: to become larger together with, in the sense of growing in essentially the same area and at the same time (compare συμφύομαι, 23.193) – 'to grow with, to grow together.' ἄφετε συναυξάνεσθαι ἀμφότερα ἕως τοῦ θερισμοῦ 'let both grow together until harvest' Mt 13.30.

23.193 συμφύομαι: to grow together with, in reference to plants – 'to grow together with.' συμφυεῖσαι αἱ ἄκανθαι ἀπέπνιξαν αὐτό 'the thorns grew up with (the plants) and choked them' Lk 8.7.

In rendering συναυξάνομαι (23.192) and συμφύομαι, it is important to avoid an expression which will imply that two plants grew together to become a single plant. The mean-

ing is that two or more plants grew in the same general area and at approximately the same time.

23.194 τίκτω^b; ἐκφέρω^c: to cause the growth and production of plants – 'to grow, to produce.'
τίκτω^b: γῆ . . . τίκτουσα βοτάνην εὔθετον 'the earth . . . produces plants that are useful' He 6.7.
ἐκφέρω^c: ἐκφέρουσα δὲ ἀκάνθας καὶ τριβόλους ἀδόκιμος 'if it grows thorns and weeds, it is worth nothing' He 6.8.

23.195 βλαστάνω or βλαστάω; ἐκφύω; προβάλλω; ἐξανατέλλω: to begin vegetative growth, with special emphasis upon the sprouting of leaves – 'to sprout, to sprout leaves.'
βλαστάνω: ἡ ῥάβδος Ἀαρὼν ἡ βλαστήσασα 'the rod of Aaron had sprouted leaves' He 9.4.
ἐκφύω: ὅταν ἤδη ὁ κλάδος αὐτῆς γένηται ἀπαλὸς καὶ τὰ φύλλα ἐκφύῃ 'when its branch becomes tender and it starts putting out leaves' Mt 24.32.
προβάλλω: ὅταν προβάλωσιν ἤδη, βλέποντες ἀφ' ἑαυτῶν 'when you see their leaves begin to appear' Lk 21.30.
ἐξανατέλλω: εὐθὺς ἐξανέτειλεν '(the plants) soon sprouted' Mk 4.5.

The initial stages of growth, either of a plant as a whole or in the renewal of foliage after a winter or dry season, may be expressed in a number of ways, for example, 'to become green again,' 'to show leaves,' 'to see leaves begin,' or 'when leaves unfold.'

23.196 ἀναβαίνω^c: to grow, as of plants, from the time of sprouting to mature size – 'to sprout and grow.' ἀνέβησαν αἱ ἄκανθαι καὶ συνέπνιξαν αὐτό 'the thorn bushes sprouted and grew and choked the plants' Mk 4.7.[22]

---

22 It would be possible to treat the meaning of ἀναβαίνω in Mk 4.7 as being somewhat more generic, that is to say, 'to come up' or 'to increase by extension,' but in view of the absolute use of ἀναβαίνω with the subject αἱ ἄκανθαι 'thorn bushes,' one is seemingly justified in attributing to ἀναβαίνω a more specific meaning in this context.

L   Ripen, Produce Fruit, Bear Seed (23.197-23.204)

23.197 ἀκμάζω: to become or to be ripe – 'to ripen, to be ripe.' ἤκμασαν αἱ σταφυλαὶ αὐτῆς 'her bunches of grapes have ripened' Re 14.18. In some languages the equivalent of 'to ripen' is 'to become sweet' or 'to become edible.'

23.198 ξηραίνομαι[b]: (derivative of ξηρός[a] 'dry,' 79.80) to become ripe, with reference to grain which dries in the process of ripening – 'to become ripe, to be ripe.' ἐξηράνθη ὁ θερισμὸς τῆς γῆς 'the harvest of the earth is ripe' Re 14.15.

23.199 καρποφορέω[a]; καρπὸν βλαστάνω; καρπὸν φέρω; φέρω[m]; καρπὸν δίδωμι; καρπὸν ἀποδίδωμι; ποιέω καρπόν[a]: to produce fruit or seed (of plants) – 'to bear fruit, to produce fruit, to produce seed, to yield.'[23]
καρποφορέω[a]: ὁ δὲ ἐπὶ τὴν καλὴν γῆν σπαρείς . . . ὃς δὴ καρποφορεῖ 'the seed sown in the good soil . . . indeed bears fruit' Mt 13.23.
καρπὸν βλαστάνω: ἡ γῆ ἐβλάστησεν τὸν καρπὸν αὐτῆς 'the earth produced its fruit' Jas 5.18.
καρπὸν φέρω: ἐὰν δὲ ἀποθάνῃ, πολὺν καρπὸν φέρει 'if (the grain of wheat) dies, it yields much fruit' Jn 12.24.
φέρω[m]: καὶ ἔφερεν ἐν τριάκοντα καὶ ἐν ἑξήκοντα καὶ ἐν ἑκατόν 'and produced some thirty, some sixty, and some one hundredfold' or '. . . thirty times, and sixty times, and a hundred times what was planted' Mk 4.8.
καρπὸν δίδωμι: καὶ καρπὸν οὐκ ἔδωκεν 'and it did not produce fruit' or '. . . grain' or 'it produced nothing' Mk 4.7.
καρπὸν ἀποδίδωμι: κατὰ μῆνα ἕκαστον ἀποδιδοῦν τὸν καρπὸν αὐτοῦ 'once every month it yields its fruit' Re 22.2.
ποιέω καρπόν[a]: ἐποίησεν καρπὸν ἑκατονταπλασίονα 'produced a hundred times (what was planted)' Lk 8.8.

[23] By setting up certain highly generic meanings for βλαστάνω, δίδωμι, ἀποδίδωμι, and ποιέω, it would be possible to treat the 'phrase compounds' in this series as being semantically endocentric. However, it seems more satisfactory to regard them as what might be called 'low-grade idioms' with specialized meanings of the semantically head expressions.

23.200 καρπὸς παραδίδωσι: (an idiom, literally 'fruit gives') the ripening of fruit as a sign for the harvest to begin – 'the harvest is ripe, the fruit is ripe, the harvest time has come.' ὅταν δὲ παραδοῖ ὁ καρπός, εὐθὺς ἀποστέλλει τὸ δρέπανον 'and when the harvest is ripe, (the man) starts working with his sickle' Mk 4.29.

23.201 καρποφόρος, ον: (derivative of καρποφορέω[a] 'to produce seed,' 23.199) pertaining to producing seed or harvest – 'fruitful, to be fruitful.' οὐρανόθεν ὑμῖν ὑετοὺς διδοὺς καὶ καιροὺς καρποφόρους 'he gives you rain from heaven and fruitful seasons' Ac 14.17. In some instances it may be useful to translate 'fruitful seasons' as 'seasons when crops become ripe' or even 'the time of the year when there is always plenty to eat.'

23.202 ἄκαρπος[a], ον: pertaining to not producing seed, fruit, or harvest – 'without fruit, bearing no fruit, producing no harvest.' δένδρα φθινοπωρινὰ ἄκαρπα 'trees that bear no fruit, even in autumn' Jd 12. In Jd 12 a literal rendering of 'even in autumn' might be misleading in some areas in which autumn as a calendrical term might not be the period for bearing fruit. Therefore, it might be better to translate Jd 12 as 'trees that bear no fruit even in the season when they should.'

23.203 τελεσφορέω: to produce completely mature fruit – 'to produce ripe fruit, to bear mature fruit.' συμπνίγονται καὶ οὐ τελεσφοροῦσιν 'they are choked and their fruit never matures' or '. . . never ripens' Lk 8.14.

23.204 εὐφορέω: to produce an abundance of good fruit or grain – 'to yield plenty of fruit, to produce a good harvest.' ἀνθρώπου τινὸς πλουσίου εὐφόρησεν ἡ χώρα 'a rich man had land which yielded plenty of fruit' Lk 12.16. In some languages it may be difficult, if not impossible, to speak of the ground producing crops. Therefore, one may employ such expressions as 'good crops grew on the ground' or 'the plants produced plenty of fruit' or '. . . plenty of grain.'

M Rot, Decay (23.205)

23.205 σήπω; φθορά^b, ᾶς *f*; διαφθορά, ᾶς *f*: to rot or decay, in reference to organic matter – 'to rot, to decay, decay.'

σήπω: ὁ πλοῦτος ὑμῶν σέσηπεν 'your riches have rotted away' Jas 5.2. There may be problems involved in a literal rendering of Jas 5.2 because it may seem strange to speak of 'riches rotting,' since a term for 'riches' is likely to refer primarily to money. It may

therefore be necessary to translate 'the things that make you rich' or 'all the things you have as a rich person.'

φθορά^b: αὐτὴ ἡ κτίσις ἐλευθερωθήσεται ἀπὸ τῆς δουλείας τῆς φθορᾶς 'the creation itself will be set free from the slavery to decay' or '. . . the inevitable tendency to decay' Ro 8.21.

διαφθορά: ἐκοιμήθη καὶ προσετέθη πρὸς τοὺς πατέρας αὐτοῦ καὶ εἶδεν διαφθοράν 'he died and was buried beside his ancestors and suffered decay' Ac 13.36.

24 Sensory Events and States[1]

Outline of Subdomains

A See (24.1-24.51)
B Hear (24.52-24.70)
C Smell (24.71)
D Taste (24.72)
E Touch, Feel (24.73-24.76)
F Pain, Suffering (24.77-24.94)
G General Sensory Perception (24.95)

A See[2] (24.1-24.51)

24.1 ὁράω^a; εἶδος^b, ους *n* – 'to see, sight, seeing.'[3]

ὁράω^a: ἔπειτα ὤφθη ἐπάνω πεντακοσίοις ἀδελφοῖς ἐφάπαξ 'then he was seen by more than five hundred of the brothers at the same time' 1 Cor 15.6. As in a number of other contexts, ἀδελφοῖς in 1 Cor 15.6 may be rendered as 'fellow believers' or simply 'believers.'

εἶδος^b: διὰ πίστεως γὰρ περιπατοῦμεν οὐ διὰ εἴδους 'our life is a matter of faith and not of seeing' 2 Cor 5.7. It is also possible to interpret εἶδος in 2 Cor 5.7 as meaning 'what is seen' (see 24.2).

24.2 ὅραμα^a, τος *n*: (derivative of ὁράω^a 'to see,' 24.1) that which is seen – 'something seen, sight.'[4] ὁ δὲ Μωϋσῆς ἰδὼν ἐθαύμαζεν τὸ ὅραμα 'Moses was amazed by what he saw' Ac 7.31.[5]

24.3 ὁρατός, ή, όν: pertaining to that which can be seen – 'what can be seen, visible.' ἐν αὐτῷ ἐκτίσθη τὰ πάντα . . . τὰ ὁρατὰ καὶ τὰ ἀόρατα 'all things were created by him . . . both visible and invisible' Col 1.16. In a number of languages it may be wise to render

---

1 Domain 24 *Sensory Events and States* includes meanings in which any one of the five senses or certain combinations of these are involved. It is, of course, impossible to distinguish clearly and definitively between sensory events and certain psychological events involving cognitive interpretation of sensory input. However, when the context seems to focus upon the involvement of the specific senses, the meanings are included in this domain, but in a number of instances there is obviously a tendency for overlapping with certain cognitive activities (Domains 26-32) and *Communication* (Domain 33).

2 The Subdomain *See* involves not only the active event of seeing and the corresponding passive 'to be seen,' but also the faculty of seeing and the lack of such a faculty. In addition, there are certain derivatives such as 'visible' and 'invisible,' as well as meanings involving 'coming into a range of vision,' in other words, 'to appear.'

3 As in the case of other so-called 'semantic primitives,' there seems to be no reason for setting up an

artificial kind of definition, since the corresponding glosses serve quite satisfactorily to indicate the semantic content.

4 ὅραμα may also occur in the meaning of 'vision,' a type of non-verbal communication in 33.488, *Communication.*

5 It may seem strange to have in the same expression ἰδών and τὸ ὅραμα, for these would seem to be redundant. However, this expression in Ac 7.31 may be rendered as 'as Moses looked, he was amazed by what he saw.'

'visible and invisible' as an active expression with 'people' as the subject, for example, 'all things were created by him . . . both those things which people can see and those things which people cannot see' or '. . . what people can see and what they cannot see.'

24.4 ἀόρατος, ον: pertaining to that which cannot be seen – 'what cannot be seen, invisible.' ἐν αὐτῷ ἐκτίσθη τὰ πάντα . . . τὰ ὁρατὰ καὶ τὰ ἀόρατα 'all things were created by him . . . both visible and invisible' Col 1.16. See translation note at 24.3.

24.5 προοράω^a: to have seen something or someone beforehand or prior to an event in question – 'to see beforehand,' to have seen previously.' ἦσαν γὰρ προεωρακότες Τρόφιμον τὸν Ἐφέσιον 'for they had previously seen Trophimus the Ephesian' Ac 21.29. In some languages an adverb such as 'previously' must be represented by a clause, for example, 'before this happened,' so that one might translate the expression in Ac 21.29 as 'for they had seen Trophimus the Ephesian even before this happened.'

24.6 φεύγω^e: (a figurative extension of meaning of φεύγω^a 'to flee,' 15.61) to disappear quickly from sight – 'to disappear, to become invisible.' καὶ πᾶσα νῆσος ἔφυγεν 'and every island suddenly disappeared' Re 16.20. For another interpretation of φεύγω in Re 16.20, see 13.95.

24.7 βλέπω^a: to see, frequently in the sense of becoming aware of or taking notice of something – 'to see, to become aware of, to notice, to glance at.'⁶ τῇ ἐπαύριον βλέπει τὸν Ἰησοῦν ἐρχόμενον πρὸς αὐτόν 'the next day he saw Jesus coming to him' Jn 1.29.

24.8 βλέμμα, τος n: (derivative of βλέπω^a 'to see,' 24.7) that which is seen or that which one becomes aware of – 'what is seen.' βλέμματι γὰρ καὶ ἀκοῇ ὁ δίκαιος . . . ἐβασάνιζεν 'by

what he saw and heard the righteous man (Lot) . . . was tormented' 2 Pe 2.8.

24.9 ἐμβλέπω^a: to direct one's vision and attention to a particular object – 'to look straight at, to look directly at.' στραφεὶς ὁ κύριος ἐνέβλεψεν τῷ Πέτρῳ 'the Lord turned around and looked straight at Peter' Lk 22.61. In Jn 1.36 ἐμβλέπω may not differ significantly in meaning from βλέπω in Jn 1.29 (see 24.7).

24.10 ἀναβλέπω^a: to direct one's vision upward – 'to look up.' ἀναβλέψας δὲ εἶδεν τοὺς βάλλοντας εἰς τὸ γαζοφυλάκιον τὰ δῶρα αὐτῶν πλουσίους 'as he looked up, he saw the rich putting their gifts into the temple treasury' Lk 21.1.

24.11 περιβλέπομαι: to look or to glance around, though not necessarily in a complete circle – 'to look around, to glance around.' περιβλεψάμενος τοὺς περὶ αὐτὸν κύκλῳ καθημένους 'looking around at those who were seated around him' Mk 3.34; περιβλεψάμενος πάντα 'when he had looked around at everything' Mk 11.11. In a number of languages the equivalent of 'to look around' would be 'to look in one direction and then in another' or 'to keep on looking in different directions.'

24.12 ἐπιβλέπω^a: to notice and pay special attention to – 'to notice especially.'⁷ ἐπιβλέψητε δὲ ἐπὶ τὸν φοροῦντα τὴν ἐσθῆτα τὴν λαμπράν 'you especially notice (or '. . . pay special attention to') a person who is well-dressed' Jas 2.3. In the case of ἐπιβλέπω in Jas 2.3, there is obviously a considerable measure of cognitive involvement, for not only sight but evaluation is also involved. For another interpretation of ἐπιβλέπω in Jas 2.3, see 87.17.

24.13 παρακύπτω^b: to look into something by stooping down – 'to stoop and look into.' παρέκυψεν εἰς τὸ μνημεῖον 'she stooped down and looked into the tomb' Jn 20.11.⁸

---

6 On the basis of existing contexts, it is not possible to distinguish clearly between the meanings of ὁράω^a (24.1) and βλέπω^a (24.7). Especially in the Gospel of John, the two terms are used in some instances for what appears to be merely stylistic variation.

7 In a number of contexts, ἐπιβλέπω involves not only sight but a considerable focus upon an accompanying mental activity, so that one may classify ἐπιβλέπω not only as meaning 'sight' but as indicating 'paying attention to' or even 'concerning oneself with' (see 30.45).

8 Since παρακύπτω, particularly in the context of

24.14 θεωρέω^a; θεάομαι^a: to observe something with continuity and attention, often with the implication that what is observed is something unusual – 'to observe, to be a spectator of, to look at.'

θεωρέω^a: θεωρῶ τοὺς οὐρανοὺς διηνοιγμένους 'I see the heavens opened' Ac 7.56.

θεάομαι^a: ὅτι τοῖς θεασαμένοις αὐτὸν ἐγηγερμένον οὐκ ἐπίστευσαν 'because they did not believe those who had seen him after he had risen' Mk 16.14.

24.15 θεωρία, ας *f*; θέατρον^b, ου *n*: (derivatives of θεωρέω^a 'to observe,' 24.14) an unusual object or event which is observed – 'spectacle, unusual sight.'

θεωρία: πάντες οἱ συμπαραγενόμενοι ὄχλοι ἐπὶ τὴν θεωρίαν ταύτην 'all the crowds that had gathered for this spectacle' (or '. . . to see this spectacle') Lk 23.48.

θέατρον^b: ὅτι θέατρον ἐγενήθημεν τῷ κόσμῳ 'because we became a spectacle for the world' 1 Cor 4.9.

24.16 ὀφθαλμός^b, οῦ *m*: (a figurative extension of meaning of ὀφθαλμός^a 'eye,' 8.23) the capacity to see – 'seeing, sight.' νεφέλη ὑπέλαβεν αὐτὸν ἀπὸ τῶν ὀφθαλμῶν αὐτῶν 'a cloud hid him from their sight' Ac 1.9; εἰ ὅλον τὸ σῶμα ὀφθαλμός, ποῦ ἡ ἀκοή; 'if the whole body were a matter of sight, where would the hearing be?' 1 Cor 12.17.[9]

24.17 ὀπτάνομαι: to be seen by or to be visible to, in the sense of being within the range of sight – 'to be seen by, to be visible to.' δι' ἡμερῶν τεσσεράκοντα ὀπτανόμενος αὐτοῖς 'he was seen by them for forty days' Ac 1.3.

Jn 20.11, involves two quite distinct semantic features, namely 'to stoop down' and 'to look into,' it may be classified either as a particular stance (17.31) with the added element of seeing, or one may classify παρακύπτω as here, in the sensory subdomain of seeing, with an adjunct feature of 'stooping down.' See also 17.31 and footnote 10 in Domain 17.

9 It would, of course, be possible to interpret ὀφθαλμός in 1 Cor 12.17 as meaning simply 'eye,' and therefore one might translate as 'if the whole body were an eye.' But the following terms such as ἀκοή (24.53) and ὄσφρησις (24.71) indicate quite clearly that it is the sensory faculty or capacity which is involved.

24.18 φαίνομαι^a: to become visible to someone – 'to appear, to become visible.' ἄγγελος κυρίου κατ' ὄναρ ἐφάνη αὐτῷ 'an angel of the Lord appeared to him in a dream' Mt 1.20. In a number of languages the equivalent of 'appeared to' would simply be 'came to' or 'arrived at.' In other languages the equivalent is '. . . he saw in a dream.'

24.19 φανερόω^a; ἐμφανίζω^a: to cause to become visible – 'to make appear, to make visible, to cause to be seen.'

φανερόω^a: μετὰ ταῦτα ἐφανέρωσεν ἑαυτὸν πάλιν ὁ Ἰησοῦς τοῖς μαθηταῖς 'after this, Jesus appeared (literally '. . . made himself visible . . .') once more to his disciples' Jn 21.1. In a number of languages the meaning of 'appeared to' must be expressed as two closely related events, so that in Jn 21.1 it may be necessary to translate 'Jesus came and was seen once more by his disciples' or 'Jesus came and once more his disciples saw him.'

ἐμφανίζω^a: καὶ ἐνεφανίσθησαν πολλοῖς 'and they were seen by many people' Mt 27.53.

24.20 φανερός^c, ά, όν; φανερῶς^b: (derivatives of the stem φαν- 'to appear,' 24.18,19) pertaining to that which appears clear or evident – 'clear, evident, clearly.'

φανερός^c: οὐδὲ ἡ ἐν τῷ φανερῷ ἐν σαρκὶ περιτομή 'and not the evident circumcision in the flesh' Ro 2.28. In view of the contrast which exists in Ro 2.28-29 between ἐν τῷ φανερῷ and ἐν τῷ κρυπτῷ, it is, of course, possible to translate ἐν τῷ φανερῷ as 'that which is external' and ἐν τῷ κρυπτῷ as 'that which is internal,' but it would seem better to preserve the contrast as 'that which can be seen' and 'that which cannot be seen.' (See 24.29.)

φανερῶς^b: εἶδεν ἐν ὁράματι φανερῶς 'he saw clearly in a vision' Ac 10.3.

24.21 ἐπιφαίνομαι; ἐπιφάνεια, ας *f*: to appear to someone or at some place – 'to appear, appearance, appearing.'

ἐπιφαίνομαι: μήτε δὲ ἡλίου μήτε ἄστρων ἐπιφαινόντων ἐπὶ πλείονας ἡμέρας 'for many days neither sun nor stars appeared' Ac 27.20.

ἐπιφάνεια: καὶ πᾶσι τοῖς ἠγαπηκόσι τὴν ἐπιφάνειαν αὐτοῦ 'and to all those who love his appearing' 2 Tm 4.8.

24.22 ἐμφανής[a], ές: (derivative of ἐμφανίζω[a] 'to make visible,' 24.19) pertaining to that which has been made visible – 'visible, seen.' καὶ ἔδωκεν αὐτὸν ἐμφανῆ γενέσθαι 'and caused him to be seen' Ac 10.40.

24.23 ἀναφαίνομαι: to come to a point of being visible, with focus upon the process of becoming seen – 'to come to be seen, to appear, to come into view.' ὅτι παραχρῆμα μέλλει ἡ βασιλεία τοῦ θεοῦ ἀναφαίνεσθαι 'that soon the kingdom of God would appear' Lk 19.11. In a number of languages there may be difficulties involved in speaking of 'the kingdom of God appearing.' It may not be difficult to speak of a 'person appearing,' because an individual may 'show himself' or 'cause himself to be seen.' It may therefore be necessary to render this expression in Lk 19.11 as 'that soon people will be seeing the kingdom of God' or '. . . experiencing the kingdom of God' or '. . . become aware of the kingdom of God.'

24.24 πρόσωπον[d], ου *n*: the form or characteristics of something as seen – 'appearance.' τὸ μὲν πρόσωπον τοῦ οὐρανοῦ γινώσκετε διακρίνειν 'you know how to judge the appearance of the sky' or '. . . what the sky looks like' or even '. . . what the sky is trying to say' Mt 16.3; ἡ εὐπρέπεια τοῦ προσώπου αὐτοῦ ἀπώλετο 'the beauty of its appearance is destroyed' Jas 1.11.

24.25 ἐπιδείκνυμι[a]: to cause to be seen – 'to show.' πορευθέντες ἐπιδείξατε ἑαυτοὺς τοῖς ἱερεῦσιν 'go show yourselves to the priests' Lk 17.14.

24.26 φαντάζομαι: to become visible, implying an extraordinary and startling appearance – 'sight, spectacle.' φοβερὸν ἦν τὸ φανταζόμενον 'the sight was terrifying' He 12.21.

24.27 ἀφανίζομαι[a]: to become such as not to be seen – 'to become invisible' (in the passive, 'to disappear, to vanish'). ἀτμὶς γάρ ἐστε ἡ πρὸς ὀλίγον φαινομένη, ἔπειτα καὶ ἀφανιζομένη 'you are like a mist that appears for a moment and then vanishes' Jas 4.14. In a number of instances one can best render 'vanishes' as 'cannot be seen' or 'suddenly people cannot see it.'

24.28 ἄφαντος, ον: (derivative of ἀφανίζομαι[a] 'to become invisible' 24.27) pertaining to that which becomes invisible – 'invisible, unseen.' καὶ αὐτὸς ἄφαντος ἐγένετο ἀπ' αὐτῶν 'and he became invisible to them' or 'he disappeared from their sight' Lk 24.31.

24.29 κρύπτω[b]: to cause something to be invisible, with the intent of its being not found – 'to make invisible, to hide.' θησαυρῷ κεκρυμμένῳ ἐν τῷ ἀγρῷ 'a treasure hidden in a field' Mt 13.44. For another interpretation of κρύπτω in Mt 13.44, see 21.12.

24.30 κρύπτω[c]: to cause something to be invisible (in the sense of being hidden), but for the purpose of safekeeping and protection – 'to hide, to make invisible, to make hidden and safe.' ἡ ζωὴ ὑμῶν κέκρυπται σὺν τῷ Χριστῷ ἐν τῷ θεῷ 'your life has been hidden with Christ in God' Col 3.3. The evident implication of this statement in Col 3.3 is to emphasize the fact that the true life of the believer is not some material, visible object or happening, but something spiritual and thus only visible to those spiritually enlightened or concerned. For another interpretation of κρύπτω in Col 3.3, see 21.12.

24.31 ὅρασις[b], εως *f*: that which appears or is seen – 'appearance.' καὶ ὁ καθήμενος ὅμοιος ὁράσει λίθῳ ἰάσπιδι 'and the one who sat (upon it) was similar in appearance to a jasper stone' Re 4.3. ὅρασις[b] may be rendered in some languages as 'as seen' or 'to the eyes' or 'to look at,' for example, 'and he who sat upon it was similar to a jasper stone to look at' or 'to look at the one who sat on it was like looking at a jasper stone.'

24.32 σκοπέω[a]: to continue to regard closely – 'to watch, to notice carefully.' σκοπεῖν τοὺς τὰς διχοστασίας καὶ τὰ σκάνδαλα παρὰ τὴν διδαχὴν ἣν ὑμεῖς ἐμάθετε ποιοῦντας 'take careful notice of those who cause divisions and upset people's faith contrary to the teaching which you have received' Ro 16.17. It is also possible to understand σκοπέω in Ro 16.17 as being predominantly a mental process of paying close attention in order to be prepared to respond appropriately (see 27.58).

24.33 ἐπέχωc: to direct one's attention to a particular object or event – 'to notice, to watch.' ἐπέχων πῶς τὰς πρωτοκλισίας ἐξελέγοντο 'noticing how they chose the best places' Lk 14.7.

24.34 ἐπαίρω τοὺς ὀφθαλμούς: (an idiom, literally 'to lift up the eyes') to direct one's attention to something by looking closely at – 'to notice, to look.' ἐπάραντες δὲ τοὺς ὀφθαλμοὺς αὐτῶν οὐδένα εἶδον 'when they looked up, they saw no one' Mt 17.8.

24.35 διαβλέπω: to be able to see clearly or plainly – 'to see clearly, to be able to distinguish clearly.' καὶ τότε διαβλέψεις ἐκβαλεῖν τὸ κάρφος ἐκ τοῦ ὀφθαλμοῦ τοῦ ἀδελφοῦ σου 'and then you will be able to see clearly to take the speck out of your brother's eye' Mt 7.5.

24.36 τηλαυγῶς: pertaining to a particularly clear or plain visual image – 'clearly, distinctly, plainly.' καὶ ἐνέβλεπεν τηλαυγῶς ἅπαντα 'then he saw everything clearly' Mk 8.25. In Mk 8.25 both διέβλεψεν (24.35) and ἐνέβλεπεν (24.9) occur. Some scholars assume that the two expressions are essentially equivalent in meaning, but others believe that διέβλεψεν is to be understood as 'to look intently' or 'to focus one's eyes upon.'

24.37 αἴνιγμαb, **τος** n: an indirect or indistinct visual image – 'dim image, reflected image, dimly.' βλέπομεν γὰρ ἄρτι δι' ἐσόπτρου ἐν αἰνίγματι 'for now we see dimly in a mirror' or 'for now we see a dim reflected image in a mirror' 1 Cor 13.12. For another interpretation of αἴνιγμα in 1 Cor 13.12, see 32.21.

24.38 τυφλόςa, **ή, όν:** pertaining to being unable to see – 'unable to see, blind.' εἶδεν ἄνθρωπον τυφλὸν ἐκ γενετῆς 'he saw a man who had been born blind' Jn 9.1.

24.39 μονόφθαλμος, ον: pertaining to one who has only one eye with which he can see (in other words, one who is blind in one eye)

– 'one-eyed, blind in one eye.' καλόν σοί ἐστιν μονόφθαλμον εἰς τὴν ζωὴν εἰσελθεῖν 'it is better for you to enter into life with only one eye' Mt 18.9.

24.40 ἀχλὺς καὶ σκότος πίπτει: (a possible idiom, literally 'mistiness and darkness fall') a serious impairment of sight, possibly involving total blindness – 'dark mistiness occurs (to someone), to become blind.' παραχρῆμά τε ἔπεσεν ἐπ' αὐτὸν ἀχλὺς καὶ σκότος 'immediately mistiness and darkness came over him' or 'immediately he became blind' Ac 13.11.

24.41 βλέπωb: to have the faculty of sight – 'to be able to see.' ἦν ἡμέρας τρεῖς μὴ βλέπων 'for three days he was not able to see' Ac 9.9.

24.42 ἀναβλέπωb; **ἀνάβλεψις, εως** f: to become able to see, whether for the first time or again – 'to gain sight, to be able to see, to regain one's sight, gaining of sight.'
ἀναβλέπωb: τυφλοὶ ἀναβλέπουσιν 'the blind become able to see' Lk 7.22. There is nothing in the statement of Lk 7.22 to indicate whether this is a matter of being able to see for the first time or being able to regain one's lost sight. It is, however, better to assume that it is a matter of regaining sight unless the context specifies 'being blind from birth' or 'always blind.'
ἀνάβλεψις: ἀπέσταλκέν με κηρύξαι αἰχμαλώτοις ἄφεσιν καὶ τυφλοῖς ἀνάβλεψιν 'he has sent me to proclaim liberty to the captives and the gaining of sight to the blind' Lk 4.18.

24.43 ἀνοίγω τοὺς ὀφθαλμούς: (an idiom, literally 'to open the eyes') to cause someone to be able to see – 'to open the eyes, to cause a blind person to see.' καὶ ἠνεῴχθησαν αὐτῶν οἱ ὀφθαλμοί 'and their eyes were opened' or 'they became able to see' Mt 9.30. A strictly literal translation of ἀνοίγω τοὺς ὀφθαλμούς 'to open the eyes' may be entirely misleading since it would imply simply opening the eyelids. It is accordingly much better to translate as 'to cause to see.'

24.44 κατοπτρίζομαιa: to see indirectly or by reflection as in a mirror – 'to see as in a mirror, to see by reflection.' ἡμεῖς δὲ πάντες ἀνα-

κεκαλυμμένῳ προσώπῳ τὴν δόξαν κυρίου κατοπτριζόμενοι 'and we all with uncovered faces behold the glory of the Lord as in a mirror' or
'. . . by reflection' 2 Cor 3.18. The phrase 'as
in a mirror' may be translated in some languages as 'as though we were looking into a
mirror' or 'as though what we saw was in a
mirror.' In some languages, however, one
does not say 'in a mirror' but 'through a mirror' or 'by means of a mirror.' For another
interpretation of κατοπτρίζομαι in 2 Cor 3.18,
see 14.52.

24.45 ἐποπτεύω: to observe something, implying both continuity and intent – 'to observe, to see, to watch.' ἐποπτεύσαντες τὴν ἐν
φόβῳ ἁγνὴν ἀναστροφὴν ὑμῶν 'for they will observe how pure and reverent your conduct is'
1 Pe 3.2. The phrase 'they will observe' may
be expressed in some languages as 'they will
constantly see' or 'they will always see.'

24.46 αὐτόπτης, ου m; ἐπόπτης, ου m: one
who has personally seen an event and thus has
personal knowledge and can be expected to at-
test to the occurrence of such an event –
'eyewitness, personal witness.'
αὐτόπτης: καθὼς παρέδοσαν ἡμῖν οἱ ἀπ' ἀρχῆς
αὐτόπται καὶ ὑπηρέται γενόμενοι τοῦ λόγου
'(they wrote) what we have been told by those
who saw these things from the beginning and
proclaimed the message' Lk 1.2.
ἐπόπτης: ἐπόπται γενηθέντες τῆς ἐκείνου
μεγαλειότητος 'with our own eyes we saw his
greatness' 2 Pe 1.16.

24.47 ἀναθεωρέω: to observe closely and
give serious consideration to, suggesting the
possibility of something unusual – 'to observe, to notice.' διερχόμενος γὰρ καὶ ἀναθεωρῶν τὰ σεβάσματα ὑμῶν 'for as I walked
around and observed your objects of worship'
Ac 17.23. In Ac 17.23 ἀναθεωρέω implies considerable mental activity, for Paul was not
merely looking at the objects of worship but
was undoubtedly thinking about the implications of them. In fact, in some languages it
may be necessary to specify the elements of
seeing and thinking by translating 'for as I
walked around and saw your objects of worship and thought about them.'

24.48 παρατηρέω; παρατήρησις, εως f: to
watch closely or diligently – 'to watch closely,
to guard.'
παρατηρέω: παρετηροῦντο δὲ καὶ τὰς πύλας
ἡμέρας τε καὶ νυκτὸς ὅπως αὐτὸν ἀνέλωσιν 'day
and night they watched the city gates in order
to kill him' Ac 9.24.
παρατήρησις: οὐκ ἔρχεται ἡ βασιλεία τοῦ θεοῦ
μετὰ παρατηρήσεως 'the kingdom of God
doesn't come in such a way that it can be
closely watched' Lk 17.20.

24.49 ἀτενίζω: to fix one's eyes on some
object continually and intensely – 'to look
straight at, to stare at, to keep one's eyes fixed
on.' μὴ δύνασθαι ἀτενίσαι τοὺς υἱοὺς Ἰσραὴλ εἰς
τὸ πρόσωπον Μωϋσέως 'the people of Israel
could not keep their eyes fixed on Moses'
face' 2 Cor 3.7. The expression 'could not
keep their eyes fixed on' may be rendered as
'could not keep looking at' or 'could not continue to look at.'

24.50 κατασκοπέω: to watch or observe secretly and with presumed evil intent – 'to
observe secretly, to spy out.' οἵτινες παρεισῆλθον κατασκοπῆσαι τὴν ἐλευθερίαν ἡμῶν 'these
men slipped in to spy out our freedom' Ga
2.4. The phrase 'to spy out our freedom' may
be rendered as 'to observe how free we are as
spies would do.'

24.51 κατανοέω: to discover something
through direct observation, with the implication of also thinking about it – 'to notice, to
discover.' κόλπον δέ τινα κατενόουν ἔχοντα
αἰγιαλόν 'they noticed a bay with a beach' Ac
27.39. For another interpretation of κατανοέω
in Ac 27.39, see 30.43.

B Hear[10] **(24.52-24.70)**
24.52 ἀκούω; ἀκοή, ῆς f – 'to hear, hearing.'[11]
ἀκούω: φωνὴ κιθαρῳδῶν καὶ μουσικῶν καὶ

10 Various meanings in Subdomain B *Hear* obviously
involve the acquisition of information and therefore are
closely related to Domain 27 *Learn* and Domain 33
Communication.
11 As in the case of other so-called semantic
derivatives, it seems best in this instance likewise to
employ only evident glosses. One could, of course,

αὐλητῶν καὶ σαλπιστῶν οὐ μὴ ἀκουσθῇ ἐν σοὶ ἔτι 'the sound of harpists and musicians and flute players and trumpeters will never again be heard in you' Re 18.22.

ἀκοή[a]: ἀλλ' οὐκ ὠφέλησεν ὁ λόγος τῆς ἀκοῆς ἐκείνους 'but the message which they heard did not do them any good' He 4.2.

24.53 ἀκοή[b], ῆς f: the faculty of hearing – 'ability to hear, hearing.' εἰ ὅλον τὸ σῶμα ὀφθαλμός, ποῦ ἡ ἀκοή; 'if the whole body were the faculty of sight, where would the hearing be?' 1 Cor 12.17. In some languages it may be better to speak about the organs involved rather than the related faculties, for example, 'if the whole body were an eye, what about the ears?'

24.54 οὖς[b], ὠτός n: (a figurative extension of meaning of οὖς[a] 'ear,' 8.24) the activity of hearing – 'to hear, hearing.' σήμερον πεπλήρωται ἡ γραφὴ αὕτη ἐν τοῖς ὠσὶν ὑμῶν 'today this scripture is fulfilled in your hearing' or '. . . as you hear' Lk 4.21.

24.55 εἰσφέρω εἰς τὰς ἀκοάς[a]: (an idiom, literally 'to bring into the ears') to cause someone to hear – 'to cause to hear, to make hear.' ξενίζοντα γάρ τινα εἰσφέρεις εἰς τὰς ἀκοὰς ἡμῶν 'you cause us to hear some strange things' Ac 17.20. In a number of languages, however, it is awkward to speak of 'to cause to hear'; rather, it seems far better to use an expression of 'speaking,' for example, 'what we hear you say is strange.' For another interpretation of this idiom in Ac 17.20, see 33.92.

24.56 ἀκροατής, οῦ m: (derivative of ἀκροάομαι 'to hear,' not occurring in the NT) one who hears – 'hearer.' οὐ γὰρ οἱ ἀκροαταὶ νόμου δίκαιοι παρὰ τῷ θεῷ 'for not the hearers of the Law are righteous in God's sight' Ro 2.13. In rendering Ro 2.13, it may be necessary to specify certain limitations with regard to being 'hearers,' for example, 'for not just those who listen to the Law are righteous in God's

sight' or 'for those who merely listen to the Law are not the ones who are righteous in God's sight.'

24.57 ἀκοή[c], ῆς f: (derivative of ἀκούω[a] 'to hear,' 24.52) that which is heard by someone – 'what is heard, message.' τίς ἐπίστευσεν τῇ ἀκοῇ ἡμῶν; 'who has believed what was heard from us?' or '. . . our message?' Ro 10.16. In a number of languages the closest equivalent of 'message' would be 'that which is said' rather than 'that which is heard,' and accordingly, one may perhaps best translate Ro 10.16 as 'who has believed what we said.'

24.58 ἀκούω[b]: to have the faculty of hearing in contrast with being deaf – 'to be able to hear, faculty of hearing.'[12] κωφοὶ ἀκούουσιν 'the deaf are able to hear' Mt 11.5.

24.59 ἔχω οὖς: (an idiom, literally 'to have ear') to be able to hear, with the implication of being expected to hear or having the obligation to hear (with a further implication of related mental activity) – 'to be able to hear, can hear.' ὁ ἔχων οὖς ἀκουσάτω τί τὸ πνεῦμα λέγει ταῖς ἐκκλησίαις 'if you can hear, listen to what the Spirit is saying to the churches' Re 2.7. In rendering the idiom ἔχω οὖς in Re 2.7, the implication is that the individuals involved ought to be able to hear and pay attention.

24.60 εἰσακούω[a]; ἐπακούω: to listen to someone, with the implication of heeding and responding to what is heard – 'to listen to, to heed, to pay attention to what is said.'
εἰσακούω[a]: εἰσηκούσθη σου ἡ προσευχή 'he has listened to your prayer' (literally 'your prayer has been listened to' or '. . . has been heard') Ac 10.31.
ἐπακούω: καιρῷ δεκτῷ ἐπήκουσά σου 'at the right time I have listened to you' 2 Cor 6.2.

24.61 ἐπακροάομαι: to listen to, with the probable implication of one's own interest –

---

define the process of hearing as 'perceiving by means of the ears,' but such a definition would be unnecessarily artificial.

12 ἀκούω[b] in 24.58 differs significantly from ἀκούω[a] 'to hear' (24.52) in that ἀκούω[b] indicates the ability to do something, not merely the activity involved.

'to listen to.' ἐπηκροῶντο δὲ αὐτῶν οἱ δέσμιοι 'the (other) prisoners were listening to them' Ac 16.25.

24.62 ἐνωτίζομαι: to listen carefully to and pay attention – 'to listen carefully to, to mark someone's words.' ἐνωτίσασθε τὰ ῥήματά μου 'listen carefully to my words' or 'pay attention to what I am going to say' Ac 2.14.

24.63 ἀκοῇ ἀκούω: (a Semitic idiom, literally 'to hear with hearing') to listen intently and with presumed continuity – 'to listen carefully, to listen and listen.' ἀκοῇ ἀκούσετε καὶ οὐ μὴ συνῆτε, καὶ βλέποντες βλέψετε καὶ οὐ μὴ ἴδητε 'you will listen and listen but not understand; you will look and look but not perceive' Ac 28.26.

24.64 τίθεμαι εἰς τὰ ὦτα^[a]: (an idiom, literally 'to put into the ears') to listen carefully to, with the implication of not forgetting – 'to listen carefully to.' θέσθε ὑμεῖς εἰς τὰ ὦτα ὑμῶν τοὺς λόγους τούτους 'listen carefully to what I am about to tell you' (literally '. . . to these words') Lk 9.44. For another interpretation of this idiom in Lk 9.44, see 29.5.

24.65 προακούω: to hear before or previously to an event in question – 'to hear before.' τὴν ἐλπίδα . . . ἣν προηκούσατε 'the hope . . . about which you have heard before' Col 1.5.

24.66 παρακούω^[b]: to hear something without the speaker's knowledge or intent – 'to overhear.' ὁ δὲ Ἰησοῦς παρακούσας τὸν λόγον λαλούμενον 'Jesus overheard what they said' Mk 5.36. Some scholars, however, understand παρακούω in Mk 5.36 as meaning 'to ignore' or 'to overlook' (see 30.37).

24.67 ἀκούω εἰς τὸ οὖς: (an idiom, literally 'to hear into the ear') to hear something in a secret setting – 'to hear in secret.' καὶ ὃ εἰς τὸ οὖς ἀκούετε, κηρύξατε ἐπὶ τῶν δωμάτων 'and what you hear in secret, announce from the housetops' Mt 10.27. In some languages the equivalent of 'what you hear in secret' may be 'what you hear when no one else is around' or 'what you hear whispered to you.'

24.68 κωφός^[b], ή, όν: pertaining to being unable to hear – 'deaf.' φέρουσιν αὐτῷ κωφόν 'they brought him a man who was deaf' Mk 7.32. In a number of languages the equivalent of 'deaf' is an idiom, for example, 'his ears are closed' or 'he has no ears' or 'his ears are stone.'

24.69 ἀνοίγουσιν αἱ ἀκοαί: (an idiom, literally 'ears open' or possibly 'hearing opens') to become able to hear – 'to regain one's hearing, to have one's hearing restored.'^[13] ἠνοίγησαν αὐτοῦ αἱ ἀκοαί 'his hearing was restored' or 'he was again able to hear' Mk 7.35. In some languages it may be relatively meaningless to translate literally 'his ears were opened,' since this might mean nothing more than the removal of some wax from the ear channel. It may therefore be necessary to translate 'his ears were made so that he could hear again' or 'his lack of hearing was healed.'

24.70 συνέχω τὰ ὦτα: (an idiom, literally 'hold the ears closed') to refuse to listen to what is being said – 'to refuse to listen, to refuse to pay attention.' κράξαντες δὲ φωνῇ μεγάλῃ συνέσχον τὰ ὦτα αὐτῶν 'they shouted loudly and refused to listen' Ac 7.57. In some languages the refusal to hear may be expressed idiomatically as 'they put their hands over their ears' or 'they closed their ears' or 'the words never entered their heads.'

C Smell (24.71)

24.71 ὄσφρησις, εως f: the capacity or ability to smell – 'sense of smell.' εἰ ὅλον ἀκοή, ποῦ ἡ ὄσφρησις; 'if the hearing were everything, where would the sense of smell be?' or '. . . how could one smell?' 1 Cor 12.17.

D Taste (24.72)

24.72 γεύομαι^[a] – 'to taste.' ἐγεύσατο ὁ ἀρχιτρίκλινος τὸ ὕδωρ οἶνον γεγενημένον 'the head steward tasted the water which had turned to wine' Jn 2.9.

---

13 The plural form αἱ ἀκοαί probably refers primarily to the inner ear or the faculty of hearing rather than to the outer ears as body parts.

E Touch, Feel (24.73-24.76)

24.73 ἅπτομαι[b]: to touch, with the implication of relatively firm contact – 'to touch.' ἥψατο τῆς γλώσσης αὐτοῦ 'he touched the man's tongue' Mk 7.33; προσελθὼν ἥψατο τῆς σοροῦ 'he walked over and touched the coffin' Lk 7.14.

24.74 θιγγάνω[a]: to come in contact with – 'to touch.' κἂν θηρίον θίγῃ τοῦ ὄρους, λιθοβοληθήσεται 'if even an animal touches the mountain, it must be stoned to death' He 12.20; ἵνα μὴ ὁ ὀλοθρεύων τὰ πρωτότοκα θίγῃ αὐτῶν 'in order that he who destroyed the firstborn might not touch them' He 11.28. It is also possible in He 11.28 that θιγγάνω is to be understood in the sense of 'to kill' (see 20.75).

24.75 προσψαύω[a]: to touch something lightly, normally with the finger or hand – 'to touch.' αὐτοὶ ἑνὶ τῶν δακτύλων ὑμῶν οὐ προσψαύετε τοῖς φορτίοις 'you yourselves won't even touch these burdens with one of your fingers' Lk 11.46. For another interpretation of προσψαύω in Lk 11.46, see 18.11. Note that προσψαύω[a] differs in meaning from προσψαύω[b] 'to touch' (18.11) in that it is understood in a hyperbolic sense of 'to merely touch,' while προσψαύω[b] implies 'doing something to help' or 'doing something about it.'

24.76 ψηλαφάω[a]: to touch by feeling and handling, implying movement over a surface – 'to touch, to feel, to handle, to feel around for.' καὶ αἱ χεῖρες ἡμῶν ἐψηλάφησαν 'and our hands have handled it' 1 Jn 1.1. There are a number of problems involved in the rendering of 1 Jn 1.1, for there are several radical shifts in figurative meaning. The specific reference is to 'the Word of life' which seems like a purposely ambiguous reference to Jesus Christ. The statement about 'hearing the Word' would seem to refer to a message, but the reference to 'seeing' implies some type of object. To emphasize the concrete nature of such an object (namely, the person of Christ), this statement about 'touching' is included, but in some languages a reference to 'feeling and handling' might imply quite a wrong connotation or even improper activity, particularly if the object involved is specifically a person.

F Pain, Suffering[14] (24.77-24.94)

24.77 πόνος[a], ου *m*: the experience of pain, normally involving both continuity and intensity – 'pain, suffering.' ὁ θάνατος οὐκ ἔσται ἔτι, οὔτε πένθος οὔτε κραυγὴ οὔτε πόνος οὐκ ἔσται ἔτι 'there will be no more death, no more grief, crying or pain' Re 21.4. In a number of languages it may not be possible, or at least it may not be natural, to use nouns for 'death,' 'grief,' 'crying,' or 'pain.' Corresponding verb expressions may, however, be employed, for example, 'people will no longer die, will no longer grieve, will no longer cry, and will no longer be in pain' or '. . . suffer pain.'

24.78 πάσχω[a]; πάθημα[a], τος *n*: to suffer pain – 'pain, suffering, to suffer, to be in pain.'
πάσχω[a]: ἐπιθυμίᾳ ἐπεθύμησα τοῦτο τὸ πάσχα φαγεῖν μεθ' ὑμῶν πρὸ τοῦ με παθεῖν 'I wanted so much to eat this Passover meal with you before my suffering' Lk 22.15.
πάθημα[a]: τῶν αὐτῶν παθημάτων ὧν καὶ ἡμεῖς πάσχομεν 'the same experiences of suffering which we suffer' 2 Cor 1.6.[15] In 1 Pe 4.13 the phrase τοῖς τοῦ Χριστοῦ παθήμασιν 'in the sufferings of Christ' may mean 'the sufferings experienced at the time of the Messiah,' that is to say, 'the Messianic woes.' See also 24.87.

24.79 προπάσχω: to suffer beforehand or previous to an event in question – 'to suffer already, to suffer before.' ἀλλὰ προπαθόντες καὶ ὑβρισθέντες καθὼς οἴδατε ἐν Φιλίπποις 'but you know how we had already suffered and been insulted in Philippi' 1 Th 2.2. In order

---

14 Almost all aspects of pain involve sensory, physiological, and psychological aspects. Furthermore, there is also a cognitive awareness of pain. The source of pain can be internal, that is to say, from the body organs, or external, as the result of severe impact or prolonged hardship.

15 It is also possible to interpret πάσχομεν in 2 Cor 1.6 as being essentially a marker of a case relationship meaning 'to experience' (see 90.66).

to render 'already' in the expression 'how we had already suffered,' it may be necessary in some languages to use the equivalent of a clause, for example, 'how we had suffered even before that happened.'

24.80 συμπαθέω[a]: to suffer along with someone else – 'to suffer with, to share in the sufferings of.' καὶ γὰρ τοῖς δεσμίοις συνεπαθήσατε 'for you also shared the sufferings of prisoners' He 10.34. It is, however, possible to interpret συμπαθέω in He 10.34 as referring primarily to sympathy rather than actual sharing or suffering.

24.81 πίνω ποτήριον: (an idiom, literally 'to drink a cup') to undergo a trying, difficult experience – 'to undergo a difficult experience, to drink the cup, to suffer.' τὸ ποτήριον ὃ δέδωκέν μοι ὁ πατὴρ οὐ μὴ πίω αὐτό; 'shall I not drink the cup which the Father has given me?' or 'shall I not suffer in the way in which the Father has indicated to me?' Jn 18.11; δύνασθε πιεῖν τὸ ποτήριον ὃ ἐγὼ πίνω; 'are you able to drink the cup of suffering that I must drink?' or 'are you able to suffer as I must suffer?' Mk 10.38.

In a number of languages it is not possible to use the phrase 'to drink the cup,' since this will almost inevitably refer to the drinking of a poison cup as a means of proving innocence in an ordeal. Even if one uses a literal rendering of the idiom 'to drink the cup,' it is usually necessary to have some explanation as to the significance of the idiom.

24.82 βάπτισμα βαπτίζομαι: (an idiom, literally 'to be baptized with a baptism') to be overwhelmed by some difficult experience or ordeal – 'to suffer, to undergo.' βάπτισμα δὲ ἔχω βαπτισθῆναι, καὶ πῶς συνέχομαι ἕως ὅτου τελεσθῇ 'I have a baptism to undergo, and how constrained I am until it is over' or 'I must undergo an ordeal, and how constrained I am until the ordeal is over' Lk 12.50.

It is usually not possible to employ the general term for 'baptism' to indicate a difficult trial or ordeal. On the other hand, there may be a serious problem involved in using a technical term for 'ordeal,' since such an ex-

pression may imply merely a 'proof of innocence.' In a number of languages, therefore, one can best translate the idiom simply as 'to suffer greatly.'

24.83 αἴρω τὸν σταυρόν; λαμβάνω τὸν σταυρόν; βαστάζω τὸν σταυρόν: (a productive series of idiomatic expressions, literally 'to take up one's cross,' 'to take one's cross,' or 'to carry one's cross') to be prepared to endure severe suffering, even to the point of death – 'to be prepared to suffer even unto death, to take up one's cross.'

αἴρω τὸν σταυρόν: ἀπαρνησάσθω ἑαυτὸν καὶ ἀράτω τὸν σταυρὸν αὐτοῦ καὶ ἀκολουθείτω μοι 'he must forget himself, be prepared to endure suffering and even death, and follow me' Mk 8.34.

λαμβάνω τὸν σταυρόν: ὃς οὐ λαμβάνει τὸν σταυρὸν αὐτοῦ καὶ ἀκολουθεῖ ὀπίσω μου 'whoever does not take up his cross and follow me' Mt 10.38.

βαστάζω τὸν σταυρόν: ὅστις οὐ βαστάζει τὸν σταυρὸν ἑαυτοῦ καὶ ἔρχεται ὀπίσω μου 'whoever does not carry his own cross and come after me' Lk 14.27.

The idiom 'to carry one's cross' or 'to take up one's cross' involves a number of important features of meaning. Unfortunately, this expression is frequently not understood correctly by many people who hear it or even use it. One reason for this is the actual absence of crucifixion in modern society. If a literal translation is to be employed, then some marginal note will probably be necessary in order to indicate clearly the full implications of such a statement.

24.84 συμπάσχω; συγκακουχέομαι; συγκακοπαθέω: to undergo the same type of suffering as others do – 'to join in suffering, to assume one's share of suffering, to suffer together.'

συμπάσχω: συμπάσχει πάντα τὰ μέλη 'all the parts of the body suffer together' 1 Cor 12.26.

συγκακουχέομαι: ἑλόμενος συγκακουχεῖσθαι τῷ λαῷ τοῦ θεοῦ 'he chose to suffer with the people of God' He 11.25.

συγκακοπαθέω: συγκακοπάθησον ὡς καλὸς στρατιώτης Χριστοῦ Ἰησοῦ 'join in suffering as a good soldier of Jesus Christ' 2 Tm 2.3.

24.85 παθητός, ή, όν: pertaining to being subject to suffering − 'subject to suffering.' εἰ παθητὸς ὁ Χριστός 'if Christ was subject to suffering' Ac 26.23.

24.86 κέντρον[d], ου n: (a figurative extension of meaning of κέντρον[a] 'sting,' 8.45) the means or capacity to cause severe suffering − 'means to hurt, power to cause suffering.' ποῦ σου, θάνατε, τὸ κέντρον; 'where, death, is your power to hurt?' 1 Cor 15.55. For another interpretation of κέντρον in 1 Cor 15.55, see 20.69.

24.87 ὠδίνω[b]; ὠδίν[b], ῖνος f: (figurative extensions of meaning of ὠδίνω[a] and ὠδίν[a] 'to suffer birth pain,' 23.54) to suffer intensely (similar to birth pain) − 'to suffer greatly, great pain.'
ὠδίνω[b]: οὓς πάλιν ὠδίνω μέχρις οὗ μορφωθῇ Χριστὸς ἐν ὑμῖν 'for whom again I suffer until Christ is formed in you' Ga 4.19.
ὠδίν[b]: πάντα δὲ ταῦτα ἀρχὴ ὠδίνων 'all these things are simply the beginning of great suffering' Mt 24.8, a reference to the so-called 'Messianic woes' (see 24.78).

24.88 συνωδίνω: to suffer great anguish or pain together, with the implication of an important and creative event − 'to suffer together.' πᾶσα ἡ κτίσις συστενάζει καὶ συνωδίνει ἄχρι τοῦ νῦν 'the whole creation moans and suffers together until the present time' Ro 8.22.

24.89 κακοπαθέω; κακοπάθεια, ας f: to suffer physical pain, hardship and distress − 'to suffer distress, to suffer pain, suffering hardship.'
κακοπαθέω: ἐν ᾧ κακοπαθῶ μέχρι δεσμῶν ὡς κακοῦργος 'because of which I suffer as a criminal to the point of being chained' 2 Tm 2.9; σὺ δὲ νῆφε ἐν πᾶσιν, κακοπάθησον, ἔργον ποίησον εὐαγγελιστοῦ 'but in everything exhibit self-control, endure suffering, and do the work of one who preaches the good news' 2 Tm 4.5. In rendering 'endure suffering,' one must often expand somewhat the number of lexical units in order to convey the correct meaning, for example, 'continue doing what you should even though you are suffering' or 'remain firm even though people cause you suffering.'
κακοπάθεια: ὑπόδειγμα λάβετε, ἀδελφοί, τῆς κακοπαθείας καὶ τῆς μακροθυμίας τοὺς προφήτας 'fellow believers, consider the prophets as examples of suffering hardship with patience' Jas 5.10.

24.90 βάσανος, ου f; βασανισμός, οῦ m: severe pain associated with torture and torment − 'torment, severe pain, severe suffering.'
βάσανος: προσήνεγκαν αὐτῷ πάντας τοὺς κακῶς ἔχοντας ποικίλαις νόσοις καὶ βασάνοις συνεχομένους 'they brought to him all those who were suffering from various diseases and torments' or '. . . severe pain' Mt 4.24.
βασανισμός: καὶ ὁ καπνὸς τοῦ βασανισμοῦ αὐτῶν 'and the smoke of their severe suffering' Re 14.11. A strictly literal translation of ὁ καπνὸς τοῦ βασανισμοῦ αὐτῶν may be seriously misleading, for it might imply that it is the smoke which causes the suffering, but it is clearly the fire which torments them (as indicated in Re 14.10). Therefore, it may be necessary to translate 'and the smoke of the fire that torments them.'

24.91 πύρωσις[b], εως f: (a figurative extension of meaning of πύρωσις[a] 'to burn,' 14.63) the experience of painful suffering − 'to suffer pain, to experience severe suffering, painful suffering.' μὴ ξενίζεσθε τῇ ἐν ὑμῖν πυρώσει 'do not be surprised at the painful suffering you are experiencing' 1 Pe 4.12. For another interpretation of πύρωσις in 1 Pe 4.12, see 78.37.

24.92 ὀδυνάομαι[a]: to be in severe or great pain − 'to suffer greatly, to be in great pain.' ὀδυνῶμαι ἐν τῇ φλογὶ ταύτῃ 'I am in great pain in this fire' or 'I am suffering terribly in this fire' Lk 16.24. In a number of languages 'the fire' must be more clearly marked as the causative agent, so that this expression in Lk 16.24 may be restructured as 'this fire is causing me great pain.'

24.93 πίπτω ἐπί τινα: (an idiom, literally 'to fall upon someone') to cause someone suffering or harm − 'to cause to suffer, to cause pain to.' οὐδὲ μὴ πέσῃ ἐπ' αὐτοὺς ὁ ἥλιος 'nor will the sun ever cause them to suffer' or 'nor will the heat of the sun ever make them suffer' Re 7.16. It is rare indeed that this idiom can ever be produced literally in other languages, though it may be possible to preserve some of the figurative impact by translating 'nor will the heat of the sun ever cause them to suffer.'

24.94 συγκάμπτω τὸν νῶτον: (an idiom, literally 'to bend the back') to undergo particularly difficult hardships, possibly implying forced labor – 'to be overwhelmed with trouble, to be bent down with difficulties.' καὶ τὸν νῶτον αὐτῶν διὰ παντὸς σύγκαμψον 'and make them bend under their troubles at all times' Ro 11.10.

G General Sensory Perception [16] (24.95)

24.95 ἄδηλος, ον: pertaining to not being perceived – 'not evident, not perceived, unseen, unmarked.' ὅτι ἐστὲ ὡς τὰ μνημεῖα τὰ ἄδηλα 'because you are like unmarked graves' Lk 11.44. Though in Greek ἄδηλος may designate anything which is unperceived by any of the senses, in Lk 11.44 the most evident sense involved would be sight, and therefore one may translate 'because you are like graves that cannot be seen.'

---

16 The Subdomain *General Sensory Perception* includes meanings (though only one occurs in the NT) which do not depend upon any one sense but involve a combination of sensory stimuli.

25 Attitudes and Emotions[1,2]

Outline of Subdomains

1 Domain 25 *Attitudes and Emotions* is very closely related to a number of domains, including *Think* (30), *Psychological Faculties* (26), *Sensory Events and States* (24), *Behavior and Related States* (41), and *Moral and Ethical Qualities and Related Behavior* (88). For some of the emotions in Domain 25 there are significant physiological aspects. Within Domain 25 one will immediately note a number of clusters of related subdomains. For example, Subdomains A, B, D, E, and F involve future orientation, and some of these share significant elements of 'desire.' Subdomains G, I, J, and K involve 'pleasure' and 'happiness,' and Subdomain C in certain ways links these two groups of subdomains. Subdomains T, U, and V involve varying degrees of 'astonishment,' 'anxiety,' and 'fear.'

Certain meanings may be regarded as generic features of attitudes and emotions, but these are treated primarily in Domain 26 *Psychological Faculties* and in Domain 90 *Case*, which includes meanings dealing with experiencing events and states.

2 Of all the semantic domains, *Attitudes and Emotions* (25) is most likely to consist of numerous idiomatic and figurative expressions. The reason for this is that atti-

tudes and emotions are essentially subjective events and states, and there is a marked tendency in languages to describe such subjective experiences in terms of figurative expressions or idioms, which for the most part employ terms for body parts in the viscera. This is, of course, the result of reactions of the so-called sympathetic nervous system.

Those organs which are most frequently employed in expressions of attitudes and emotions are the liver, the diaphragm, the heart, and the stomach. In a number of languages in Africa, one encounters such expressions as 'to have a liver,' meaning 'to be brave,' and 'to have a diaphragm,' meaning 'to have a guilty conscience.' 'To have a heart,' may, however, mean 'to be patient,' and 'to have a cool stomach' often means 'to be happy.'

In a number of languages there may be a whole series of expressions based on some one particular internal organ. For example, in the Conob language of Guatemala (a Mayan language) a 'mixed-up stomach' signifies 'astonishment,' while a 'stomach that dies' means 'love,' and a 'stomach that rises' signifies 'hate.' A 'dried-up stomach' denotes 'sadness,' and 'to cry in the stomach' means 'to take pity on someone.'

J   Enjoy, Take Pleasure In, Be Fond of Doing (25.102-25.115)
K   Happy, Glad, Joyful (25.116-25.134)
L   Laugh, Cry, Groan (25.135-25.145)
M Encouragement, Consolation (25.146-25.155)
N   Courage, Boldness (25.156-25.166)
O   Patience, Endurance, Perseverance (25.167-25.178)
P   Offend, Be Offended (25.179-25.185)
Q   Abhor (25.186-25.188)
R   Shame, Disgrace, Humiliation (25.189-25.202)
S   Pride (legitimate) (25.203-25.205)
T   Surprise, Astonish (25.206-25.222)
U   Worry, Anxiety, Distress, Peace (25.223-25.250)
V   Fear, Terror, Alarm (25.251-25.269)
W Sorrow, Regret (25.270-25.287)
X   Discouragement (25.288-25.296)

A Desire, Want, Wish (25.1-25.11)

25.1 θέλω^c; θέλησις, εως f: to desire to have or experience something – 'to desire, to want, to wish.'
θέλω^c: τί θέλεις; 'what do you want?' Mt 20.21; οἷς πάλιν ἄνωθεν δουλεύειν θέλετε; 'do you wish to be enslaved by them all over again?' Ga 4.9; ὁ θεὸς ἔθετο τὰ μέλη . . . ἐν τῷ σώματι καθὼς ἠθέλησεν 'God has arranged the

In Africa there is a tendency to build a number of idioms on a term for 'liver.' In the Anuak language of the Sudan (a Nilotic language) there are the following expressions which employ in one way or another the term for 'liver': 'my liver is sweet' ('I am happy'); 'my liver is bitter' ('I am completely unsociable'); 'a heavy liver' ('to be sad'); 'a shallow liver' ('a tendency to get angry quickly'); 'a bad liver' ('unhappy'); 'a large liver' ('greedy'); 'a light-colored liver' ('well-disposed, sociable'); 'a cold liver' ('not emotionally upset'); 'a hot liver' ('passionately upset'); 'a black liver' ('unsociable'); 'to light up the liver' ('to be lonely for'); 'the liver falls' ('to be sorry'); 'the liver floats' ('to be uncertain'); 'the liver jumps up' ('to be angry quickly').

Some translators have hesitated to use terms meaning 'liver' or 'stomach,' since they regard such expressions as being psychologically and physiologically inappropriate, but they are no more inappropriate or anomalous than the English use of 'heart,' and in many instances it simply is not possible to speak of various attitudes and emotions without using these terms which refer to various internal organs.

parts . . . of the body just as he wanted them' 1 Cor 12.18.
θέλησις: πνεύματος ἁγίου μερισμοῖς κατὰ τὴν αὐτοῦ θέλησιν 'distributed by the Holy Spirit just as he wanted them' He 2.4.

As may be noted, in translating θέλησις, θέλημα^a (25.2), βούλημα^a (25.4), and εὐδοκία^b (25.8), there is a tendency to employ verbs rather than nouns. This is true especially in languages outside the Indo-European family of languages. Wanting, desiring, and wishing are essentially psychological events or states and accordingly are most frequently expressed in languages by verbs.

25.2 θέλημα^a, τος n: (derivative of θέλω^c 'to desire,' 25.1) that which is desired or wished for – 'wish, desire.' εἰς τὸ μηκέτι ἀνθρώπων ἐπιθυμίαις ἀλλὰ θελήματι θεοῦ τὸν ἐπίλοιπον ἐν σαρκὶ βιῶσαι χρόνον 'you must live the rest of your earthly lives controlled by what God desires and not by human passions' 1 Pe 4.2.

25.3 βούλομαι^a: to desire to have or experience something, with the implication of some reasoned planning or will to accomplish the goal – 'to desire, to want, to will.' ἐβουλόμην καὶ αὐτὸς τοῦ ἀνθρώπου ἀκοῦσαι 'I would like to hear this man myself' Ac 25.22; γινώσκειν δὲ ὑμᾶς βούλομαι 'I want you to know' Php 1.12.

25.4 βούλημα^a, τος n: (derivative of βούλομαι^a 'to desire,' 25.3) that which is desired, with the implication of accompanying planning and will – 'desire, want, will.' ἀρκετὸς γὰρ ὁ παρεληλυθὼς χρόνος τὸ βούλημα τῶν ἐθνῶν κατειργάσθαι 'you have spent enough time in the past doing what the heathen desire to do' 1 Pe 4.3.

25.5 ἀξιόω^c: to desire something on the basis of its evident worth or value – 'to desire, to want, to like.' ἀξιοῦμεν δὲ παρὰ σοῦ ἀκοῦσαι ἃ φρονεῖς 'we would like to hear from you what your ideas are' Ac 28.22.

25.6 εὔχομαι^b: to desire something, with the implication of a pious wish – 'to desire, to wish.' ηὐχόμην γὰρ ἀνάθεμα εἶναι αὐτὸς ἐγὼ ἀπὸ τοῦ Χριστοῦ 'I could wish that I myself were under a curse and separated from Christ' Ro 9.3.[3]

25.7 δοκέω[b]: to be disposed to some desire or intent – 'to be disposed to, to want to.' εἰ δέ τις δοκεῖ φιλόνεικος εἶναι 'if anyone is disposed to quarrel' 1 Cor 11.16. For another interpretation of δοκέω in 1 Cor 11.16, see 30.96.

25.8 εὐδοκία[b], **ας** *f*: (derivative of εὐδοκέω[c] 'to prefer,' 30.97) that which is desired on the basis of its appearing to be beneficial – 'desire, what is wished for.' ἡ μὲν εὐδοκία τῆς ἐμῆς καρδίας 'what I wish for with all my heart' Ro 10.1.

25.9 ζητέω[c]; **ἐπιζητέω**[b]: to desire to have or experience something, with the probable implication of making an attempt to realize one's desire – 'to desire, to want to.'[4] ζητέω[c]: ἐν ταῖς ἡμέραις ἐκείναις ζητήσουσιν οἱ ἄνθρωποι τὸν θάνατον καὶ οὐ μὴ εὑρήσουσιν αὐτόν 'in those days people will want to die and not be able to do so' Re 9.6; τί ζητεῖτε; 'what do you want?' Jn 1.38. ἐπιζητέω[b]: οὐχ ὅτι ἐπιζητῶ τὸ δόμα 'it is not that I just want to receive the gift' Php 4.17; ἐπεζήτησεν ἀκοῦσαι τὸν λόγον τοῦ θεοῦ 'he wanted to hear the word of God' Ac 13.7.

25.10 νοσέω: to have an unhealthy or morbid desire for something – 'to desire in an unhealthy manner, to have a morbid desire.' ἀλλὰ νοσῶν περὶ ζητήσεις καὶ λογομαχίας 'but he has an unhealthy desire for controversies and arguments' 1 Tm 6.4. In some languages the closest equivalent of 'an unhealthy desire' would be 'to desire something that one should not desire.'

25.11 κνήθομαι τὴν ἀκοήν: (an idiom, literally 'to itch with respect to hearing') to have one's ears tickled by what is heard – 'to have itching ears, to desire to hear what one wants to hear, to be desirous of hearing.'

ἐπισωρεύσουσιν διδασκάλους κνηθόμενοι τὴν ἀκοήν 'they will heap up for themselves teachers, since they desire simply to hear what they want to hear' 2 Tm 4.3.[5]

B Desire Strongly[6] (25.12-25.32)

25.12 ἐπιθυμέω[a]; **ἐπιθυμία**[a], **ας** *f*: to greatly desire to do or have something – 'to long for, to desire very much.' ἐπιθυμέω[a]: ἐπιθυμοῦμεν δὲ ἕκαστον ὑμῶν τὴν αὐτὴν ἐνδείκνυσθαι σπουδήν 'we desire very much that each of you demonstrate the same eagerness' He 6.11; ἐλεύσονται ἡμέραι ὅτε ἐπιθυμήσετε μίαν τῶν ἡμερῶν τοῦ υἱοῦ τοῦ ἀνθρώπου ἰδεῖν 'the time will come when you will long to see one of the days of the Son of Man' Lk 17.22. ἐπιθυμία[a]: αἱ περὶ τὰ λοιπὰ ἐπιθυμίαι εἰσπορευόμεναι συμπνίγουσιν τὸν λόγον 'desires for other things will come and choke out the message' Mk 4.19; ἐπιθυμίᾳ ἐπεθύμησα τοῦτο τὸ πάσχα φαγεῖν μεθ' ὑμῶν 'I have greatly desired to eat this Passover with you' Lk 22.15. The phrase ἐπιθυμίᾳ ἐπεθύμησα may be regarded as a type of Semitic idiom.

25.13 ἐπιθυμητής, οῦ *m*: (derivative of ἐπιθυμέω[a] 'to desire very much,' 25.12) one who very much desires something, whether good or bad – 'one who greatly desires.' εἰς τὸ μὴ εἶναι ἡμᾶς ἐπιθυμητὰς κακῶν 'in order that we might not desire evil things' 1 Cor 10.6.

25.14 πλησμονή, ῆς *f*: the process of indulging in or procuring the satisfaction of certain desires or needs – 'gratification, indulgence.'

---

3 It is possible, but not very probable, that εὔχομαι in Ro 9.3 could mean 'to pray' (see 33.178).
4 It is possible that ἐπιζητέω[b] focuses somewhat more upon the goal, but such a distinction does not hold for all contexts.

5 The idiom κνήθομαι τὴν ἀκοήν involves two quite distinct semantic features. One is the desire to be pleased, and the second is the means of such gratification, namely, what is heard. It would be possible to classify this idiom either under *Sensory Events and States* (Domain 24) or here in the domain of *Attitudes and Emotions*. Since in 2 Tm 4.3 the latter seems the more focal feature of meaning, the idiom is included at this point.
6 Subdomain B *Desire Strongly* includes meanings which are ethically neutral, ethically valued, and those which are ethically disvalued, in the sense of being that which is not moral. Items 25.19-25.28 are typical of such desires, but rather than set these up as a special category in Domain 88, it seems better to treat them together with all other expressions of desire and wanting.

οὐκ ἐν τιμῇ τινι πρὸς πλησμονὴν τῆς σαρκός '(these are) of no value for the indulgence of physical desires' Col 2.23. There have been extensive differences of opinion with regard to the precise meaning of πλησμονή and of σάρξ in Col 2.23. Some early Greek exegetes understood this passage to involve 'gratification of physical needs,' but since σάρξ seemingly needs to be understood in a bad sense, the meaning of 'indulgence' seems to be more appropriate. The meaning of 'indulgence' can be expressed in some languages as 'to give in to' or 'to surrender to' or 'to permit oneself to enjoy.'

25.15 ὀρέγομαι: to eagerly desire to accomplish some goal or purpose – 'to strive to attain, to aspire to, to eagerly long for.' εἴ τις ἐπισκοπῆς ὀρέγεται 'if anyone aspires to be an overseer' 1 Tm 3.1; νῦν δὲ κρείττονος ὀρέγονται 'instead, they are eagerly longing for a better (country)' He 11.16.[7]

25.16 ἐκκαίομαι ἐν τῇ ὀρέξει: (an idiom, literally 'to burn with intense desire') to have a strong, intense desire for something – 'to be inflamed with passion, to have a strong lust for, to be inflamed with lust.' ἐξεκαύθησαν ἐν τῇ ὀρέξει αὐτῶν εἰς ἀλλήλους '(men) were inflamed with lust for one another' Ro 1.27. In some languages the equivalent idiom is 'to boil with desire,' 'to feel hot in the genitals,' or 'to prefer to die rather than to do.'

25.17 διψάω[b]; πεινάω[b]: (figurative extensions of meaning of διψάω[a] 'to thirst,' 23.39, and πεινάω[a] 'to hunger,' 23.29) to have a strong desire to attain some goal, with the implication of an existing lack – 'to desire strongly.' μακάριοι οἱ πεινῶντες καὶ διψῶντες τὴν δικαιοσύνην 'happy are those who desire intensely to do what God requires' or '. . . to see right prevail' Mt 5.6. In Mt 5.6 the two terms διψάω and πεινάω mutually reinforce the meaning of great desire.

25.18 ἐπιποθέω[a]; ἐπιποθία, ας f; ἐπιπόθησις, εως f: to long for something, with the

implication of recognizing a lack – 'to long for, to deeply desire, deep desire.'

ἐπιποθέω[a]: πρὸς φθόνον ἐπιποθεῖ τὸ πνεῦμα ὃ κατῴκισεν ἐν ἡμῖν 'the spirit which he has placed in us longs jealously' or 'the spirit that he placed in us is filled with jealous desire' Jas 4.5.

ἐπιποθία: ἐπιποθίαν δὲ ἔχων τοῦ ἐλθεῖν πρὸς ὑμᾶς ἀπὸ πολλῶν ἐτῶν 'since I have been longing for so many years to come to (see) you' Ro 15.23.

ἐπιπόθησις: ἀναγγέλλων ἡμῖν τὴν ὑμῶν ἐπιπόθησιν 'he told us how much you long (to see me)' 2 Cor 7.7.

25.19 θυμός[b], οῦ m: an intense, passionate desire of an overwhelming and possibly destructive character – 'intense desire, overwhelming passion.' ἐκ τοῦ οἴνου τοῦ θυμοῦ τῆς πορνείας αὐτῆς 'from the wine of her passionate lust' Re 14.8.

25.20 ἐπιθυμέω[b]; ἐπιθυμία[b], ας f: to strongly desire to have what belongs to someone else and/or to engage in an activity which is morally wrong – 'to covet, to lust, evil desires, lust, desire.'

ἐπιθυμέω[b]: ἀργυρίου ἢ χρυσίου ἢ ἱματισμοῦ οὐδενὸς ἐπεθύμησα 'I have not coveted anyone's silver, gold, or clothing' Ac 20.33; ὁ βλέπων γυναῖκα πρὸς τὸ ἐπιθυμῆσαι αὐτὴν 'anyone who looks at a woman lustfully' Mt 5.28.

ἐπιθυμία[b]: ἐπιθυμίας πολλὰς ἀνοήτους 'many foolish desires' 1 Tm 6.9; νεωτερικὰς ἐπιθυμίας 'youthful desires' 2 Tm 2.22; ταῖς πρότερον ἐν τῇ ἀγνοίᾳ ὑμῶν ἐπιθυμίαις 'the former desires when you were ignorant' 1 Pe 1.14; ἐπιθυμίαν σαρκὸς οὐ μὴ τελέσητε 'do not gratify the desires of the body' Ga 5.16.

25.21 ζηλόω[c]: to set one's heart on something that belongs to someone else – 'to covet.' φονεύετε καὶ ζηλοῦτε, καὶ οὐ δύνασθε ἐπιτυχεῖν 'you kill and covet, but you cannot have what you want' Jas 4.2. It is, of course, also possible to render ζηλόω in Jas 4.2 as meaning 'to be envious' or 'to be jealous' (see 88.163).

25.22 πλεονεξία[a], ας f: a strong desire to acquire more and more material possessions or

---

7 The meaning of ὀρέγομαι normally involves greater intensity of feeling than the meaning of ἐπιθυμέω[a] and ἐπιθυμία[a] (25.12).

to possess more things than other people have, all irrespective of need – 'greed, avarice, covetousness.' καὶ τὴν πλεονεξίαν ἥτις ἐστὶν εἰδωλολατρία 'and greed, which is idolatry' Col 3.5; καρδίαν γεγυμνασμένην πλεονεξίας ἔχοντες 'they are experts in greed' 2 Pe 2.14.

25.23 πλεονέκτης, ου *m*: (derivative of πλεονεξία[a] 'greed,' 25.22) one who is greedy or covetous – 'greedy person, covetous person.' οὐ πάντως τοῖς πόρνοις τοῦ κόσμου τούτου ἢ τοῖς πλεονέκταις καὶ ἅρπαξιν 'now I do not mean people of this world who are immoral or greedy or are thieves' 1 Cor 5.10.

25.24 ἁρπαγή[c], ῆς *f*: a state of strong desire to gain things and, if necessary, by violent means – 'grasping, violent greed.' τὸ δὲ ἔσωθεν ὑμῶν γέμει ἁρπαγῆς καὶ πονηρίας 'but inside you are full of violent greed and wickedness' Lk 11.39.

25.25 ἅρπαξ[b], αγος (adj.): pertaining to being violently greedy – 'violently greedy.' ὅτι οὐκ εἰμὶ ὥσπερ οἱ λοιποὶ τῶν ἀνθρώπων, ἅρπαγες, ἄδικοι, μοιχοί 'that I am not like other people, violently greedy, unjust, adulterers' Lk 18.11. In Lk 18.11 ἅρπαξ may also be interpreted as a noun, see 57.239.

25.26 αἰσχροκερδής, ές; αἰσχροκερδῶς: pertaining to being shamefully greedy for material gain or profit – 'shamefully greedy, greedily.'
αἰσχροκερδής: διακόνους . . . μὴ αἰσχροκερδεῖς 'deacons . . . who are not shamefully greedy for material gain' 1 Tm 3.8.
αἰσχροκερδῶς: ποιμάνατε . . . μηδὲ αἰσχροκερδῶς ἀλλὰ προθύμως 'be shepherds . . . not greedy for money, but eager to serve' 1 Pe 5.2.

25.27 ἡδονή[b], ῆς *f*: desire for physical pleasure, often sexual – 'desire, passion, desire for pleasure.' ἐκ τῶν ἡδονῶν ὑμῶν τῶν στρατευομένων ἐν τοῖς μέλεσιν ὑμῶν 'from the desires for pleasure that battle within you' Jas 4.1.

25.28 κοιλία[d], ας *f*: desire for gratification of the body – 'physical desires, desires of the body.' οἱ γὰρ τοιοῦτοι τῷ κυρίῳ ἡμῶν Χριστῷ οὐ δουλεύουσιν ἀλλὰ τῇ ἑαυτῶν κοιλίᾳ 'for those who do such things are not serving Christ our Lord, but their own physical desires' Ro 16.18. It is also possible that κοιλία in Ro 16.18 refers to Jewish dietary laws and regulations.

25.29 σαρκὸς θέλημα: (an idiom, literally 'desire of the flesh') desire for sexual gratification – 'sexual desire, physical desire.' οἳ οὐκ ἐξ αἱμάτων οὐδὲ ἐκ θελήματος σαρκὸς οὐδὲ ἐκ θελήματος ἀνδρὸς ἀλλ' ἐκ θεοῦ ἐγεννήθησαν 'who were born not from a human father or because of sexual desire or by a man's will but of God himself' Jn 1.13.

25.30 πάθος, ους *n*; πάθημα[b], τος *n*; καταστρηνιάω: to experience strong physical desires, particularly of a sexual nature – 'passion, lust, lustful desire, to have lust.'
πάθος: παρέδωκεν αὐτοὺς ὁ θεὸς εἰς πάθη ἀτιμίας 'God gave them over to shameful passions' Ro 1.26; μὴ ἐν πάθει ἐπιθυμίας καθάπερ καὶ τὰ ἔθνη 'not with lustful desires, like the heathen' 1 Th 4.5.
πάθημα[b]: τὰ παθήματα τῶν ἁμαρτιῶν τὰ διὰ τοῦ νόμου ἐνηργεῖτο ἐν τοῖς μέλεσιν ἡμῶν 'the sinful passions aroused by the Law were at work in our bodies' Ro 7.5; τὴν σάρκα ἐσταύρωσαν σὺν τοῖς παθήμασιν καὶ ταῖς ἐπιθυμίαις 'they have crucified their sinful nature with its passions and desires' Ga 5.24.
καταστρηνιάω: νεωτέρας δὲ χήρας παραιτοῦ· ὅταν γὰρ καταστρηνιάσωσιν . . . 'but do not accept younger widows; for when they experience strong physical desires . . .' 1 Tm 5.11.

25.31 πυρόομαι[c]: to experience intense sexual desire – 'to burn with passion, to be sexually aroused.' κρεῖττον γάρ ἐστιν γαμῆσαι ἢ πυροῦσθαι 'for it is better to marry than to burn with sexual passion' 1 Cor 7.9.

25.32 ὁμοιοπαθής, ές: pertaining to having the same kinds of feelings or desires – 'same kinds of feelings, same kinds of desires.' ἡμεῖς ὁμοιοπαθεῖς ἐσμεν ὑμῖν ἄνθρωποι 'we are human beings who have the same kinds of feelings that you do' Ac 14.15.

C Love, Affection, Compassion (25.33-25.58)

25.33 φιλέω^a; φιλία, ας *f*: to have love or affection for someone or something based on association – 'to love, to have affection for.' See the discussion of the meaning of φιλέω^a and φιλία in 25.43.

φιλέω^a: ὁ φιλῶν πατέρα ἢ μητέρα ὑπὲρ ἐμὲ οὐκ ἔστιν μου ἄξιος 'the person who loves his father or mother more than me is not worthy of me' Mt 10.37.

φιλία: ἡ φιλία τοῦ κόσμου ἔχθρα τοῦ θεοῦ ἐστιν 'affection for the world is hostility toward God' Jas 4.4. In a number of languages it may be difficult if not impossible to speak of 'affection . . . is hostility.' Frequently it is necessary to relate such emotional attitudes to individuals, so that this expression in Jas 4.4 may be rendered in some languages as 'people who love the things in the world are against God.'

25.34 φιλαδελφία, ας *f*: affection for one's fellow believer in Christ – 'love for one's fellow believer, affection for a fellow believer.' περὶ δὲ τῆς φιλαδελφίας οὐ χρείαν ἔχετε γράφειν ὑμῖν 'there is no need to write you about affection for your fellow believers' 1 Th 4.9; ἡ φιλαδελφία μενέτω 'keep on loving one another as fellow believers' He 13.1.

In the NT the terms φιλαδελφία and φιλάδελφος (25.35) have acquired highly specialized meanings which restrict the range of reference to fellow believers. In nonbiblical contexts these terms would refer to affection or love for persons belonging to a so-called 'in-group,' but in the NT this in-group is defined in terms of Christian faith.

25.35 φιλάδελφος, ον: pertaining to love or affection for fellow believers – 'one who loves fellow believers, loving one another as brothers.' τὸ δὲ τέλος πάντες ὁμόφρονες, συμπαθεῖς, φιλάδελφοι 'in conclusion, you must all have the same attitude and the same feelings, loving one another as Christian brothers' or '. . . as fellow believers' 1 Pe 3.8. See discussion at 25.34.

25.36 φιλανθρωπία^a, ας *f*: affection for people in general – 'love of mankind, affection for people.' ὅτε δὲ ἡ χρηστότης καὶ ἡ φιλανθρωπία ἐπεφάνη τοῦ σωτῆρος ἡμῶν θεοῦ 'when God our Savior showed his kindness and affection for mankind' Tt 3.4.

25.37 φίλανδρος: pertaining to having affection for a husband – 'having love for one's husband, having affection for one's husband.' ἵνα σωφρονίζωσιν τὰς νέας φιλάνδρους εἶναι 'in order to train the young women to have affection for their husbands' Tt 2.4.

25.38 φιλότεκνος, ον: pertaining to having affection for one's own offspring – 'loving one's own children, one who loves children.' ἵνα σωφρονίζωσιν τὰς νέας φιλάνδρους εἶναι, φιλοτέκνους 'in order to train the young women to love their husbands and children' Tt 2.4.

25.39 φίλαυτος, ον: pertaining to self-centered love or concern for one's own self – 'selfish love, self-centered love.' ἔσονται γὰρ οἱ ἄνθρωποι φίλαυτοι 'for people will be lovers of themselves' 2 Tm 3.2.

25.40 φιλόθεος, ον: pertaining to love for God – 'loving God, having affection for God.' φιλήδονοι μᾶλλον ἢ φιλόθεοι 'they are persons who love pleasure rather than loving God' 2 Tm 3.4.

25.41 φιλόστοργος, ον: pertaining to love or affection for those closely related to one, particularly members of one's immediate family or in-group – 'very loving, warmly devoted to, very affectionate.' τῇ φιλαδελφίᾳ εἰς ἀλλήλους φιλόστοργοι 'love one another affectionately as fellow believers' Ro 12.10.

25.42 ἄστοργος, ον: pertaining to a lack of love or affection for close associates or family – 'without normal human affection, without love for others.' ἔσονται γὰρ οἱ ἄνθρωποι . . . ἄστοργοι 'for they will be people . . . who will lack human affection' 2 Tm 3.2-3.

25.43 ἀγαπάω^a; ἀγάπη^a, ης *f*: to have love for someone or something, based on sincere appreciation and high regard – 'to love, to regard with affection, loving concern, love.'

ἀγαπάω[a]: ἐντολὴν καινὴν δίδωμι ὑμῖν, ἵνα ἀγαπᾶτε ἀλλήλους 'I give you a new commandment, that you love one another' Jn 13.34; γὰρ τὸν ἕνα μισήσει καὶ τὸν ἕτερον ἀγαπήσει 'for he will hate the one and love the other' Lk 16.13; ὁ πατὴρ ἀγαπᾷ τὸν υἱόν 'the Father loves the Son' Jn 3.35; ὅτι αὐτὸς πρῶτος ἠγάπησεν ἡνᾶς 'for he loved us first' 1 Jn 4.19.

ἀγάπη[a]: ἡ ἀγάπη οὐδέποτε πίπτει 'love does not fail' 1 Cor 13.8; ἡ ἀγάπη τῷ πλησίον κακὸν οὐκ ἐργάζεται 'a person who loves doesn't do evil to his neighbor' Ro 13.10.

Though some persons have tried to assign certain significant differences of meaning between ἀγαπάω[a], ἀγάπη[a] and φιλέω[a], φιλία (25.33), it does not seem possible to insist upon a contrast of meaning in any and all contexts. For example, the usage in Jn 21.15-17 seems to reflect simply a rhetorical alternation designed to avoid undue repetition. There is, however, one significant clue to possible meaningful differences in at least some contexts, namely, the fact that people are never commanded to love one another with φιλέω or φιλία, but only with ἀγαπάω and ἀγάπη. Though the meanings of these terms overlap considerably in many contexts, there are probably some significant differences in certain contexts; that is to say, φιλέω and φιλία are likely to focus upon love or affection based upon interpersonal association, while ἀγαπάω and ἀγάπη focus upon love and affection based on deep appreciation and high regard. On the basis of this type of distinction, one can understand some of the reasons for the use of ἀγαπάω and ἀγάπη in commands to Christians to love one another. It would, however, be quite wrong to assume that φιλέω and φιλία refer only to human love, while ἀγαπάω and ἀγάπη refer to divine love. Both sets of terms are used for the total range of loving relations between people, between people and God, and between God and Jesus Christ.

25.44 ἀγαπάω[b]: to demonstrate or show one's love – 'to show one's love, to demonstrate one's love.' μὴ ἀγαπῶμεν λόγῳ μηδὲ τῇ γλώσσῃ ἀλλὰ ἐν ἔργῳ 'let us show our love, but not by just word and talk, but by means of action' 1 Jn 3.18.

25.45 ἀγαπητός[a], ή, όν: (derivative of ἀγαπάω[a] 'to love,' 25.43) pertaining to one who or that which is loved – 'object of one's affection, one who is loved, beloved, dear.' ἰδοὺ ὁ παῖς μου ὃν ᾑρέτισα, ὁ ἀγαπητός μου εἰς ὃν εὐδόκησεν ἡ ψυχή μου 'here is my servant, whom I have chosen, the one I love, with whom I am well pleased' Mt 12.18. It is also possible to understand ἀγαπητός in Mt 12.18 as 'the only beloved one' (see 58.53), and the meaning may, in fact, be simply 'only' or 'unique.' This meaning has evidently arisen because of the association of ἀγαπητός with μονογενής 'unique, only' (58.52).

25.46 ζηλόω[b]; ζῆλος[a], ου *m* and ους *n*: to have a deep concern for or devotion to someone or something – 'to have a deep concern for, to be devoted to, earnest concern.' ζηλόω[b]: ζηλοῦσιν ὑμᾶς οὐ καλῶς 'they have a deep concern for you, but it is not good' Ga 4.17. The Judaizers referred to in Ga 4.17 may have been sincere, but they were misguided in their zeal. ζῆλος[a]: μαρτυρῶ γὰρ αὐτοῖς ὅτι ζῆλον θεοῦ ἔχουσιν 'for I witness for them that they are deeply devoted to God' Ro 10.2; τὸν ὑμῶν ζῆλον ὑπὲρ ἐμοῦ 'your earnest concern on my behalf' 2 Cor 7.7.

25.47 ἐπιποθέω[b]; ὀμείρομαι: to experience a yearning affection for someone – 'to have a great affection for, to have a yearning love for.' ἐπιποθέω[b]: αὐτῶν δεήσει ὑπὲρ ὑμῶν ἐπιποθούντων ὑμᾶς 'they will pray for you with great affection' 2 Cor 9.14. ὀμείρομαι: οὕτως ὀμειρόμενοι ὑμῶν εὐδοκοῦμεν μεταδοῦναι ὑμῖν 'because of our great affection for you, we were ready to share with you' 1 Th 2.8.

The nominal phrases with the English term 'affection' can and must be expressed in a number of languages by verb phrases or clauses. For example, in 2 Cor 9.14 one may translate 'they love you very much and will pray for you.' In 1 Th 2.8 one may translate 'because we love you so much, we were ready to share with you.'

25.48 ἐπιπόθητος, ον: pertaining to yearning affection for someone – 'yearningly affectionate, longed for, very dear.' ἀδελφοί μου ἀγαπητοὶ καὶ ἐπιπόθητοι 'my fellow believers whom I love and long for' Php 4.1.

25.49 σπλαγχνίζομαι; σπλάγχνα^c, ων *n* (only in the plural): to experience great affection and compassion for someone – 'to feel compassion for, to have great affection for, love, compassion.'
σπλαγχνίζομαι: Σαμαρίτης δέ τις ὁδεύων ἦλθεν κατ' αὐτὸν καὶ ἰδὼν ἐσπλαγχνίσθη 'but a certain Samaritan who was travelling that way came upon him, and when he saw the man, he felt compassion for him' Lk 10.33.
σπλάγχνα^c: ὡς ἐπιποθῶ πάντας ὑμᾶς ἐν σπλάγχνοις Χριστοῦ Ἰησοῦ 'how I long for you all because of the compassion of Christ Jesus himself' Php 1.8.
In Php 1.8 the phrase ἐν σπλάγχνοις Χριστοῦ Ἰησοῦ is ambiguous. It may mean 'because of the compassion which Christ Jesus himself has for you' or '. . . for me.' On the other hand, it may be interpreted as characterizing the kind of love which Paul has for the believers, for example, 'how I long for all of you, even with the kind of love Christ Jesus himself has for you.'

25.50 σπλάγχνα^d, ων *n*: one for whom one has deep affection or compassion – 'object of affection.' ὃν ἀνέπεμψά σοι, αὐτόν, τοῦτ' ἔστιν τὰ ἐμὰ σπλάγχνα 'whom I am sending back to you, this one for whom I have such deep affection' Phm 12.

25.51 εὔσπλαγχνος, ον: pertaining to being affectionate and compassionate – 'compassionate.' γίνεσθε δὲ εἰς ἀλλήλους χρηστοί, εὔσπλαγχνοι 'instead, be kind and compassionate to one another' Eph 4.32.

25.52 πολύσπλαγχνος, ον: pertaining to great affection and compassion – 'very compassionate, with much affection.' ὅτι πολύσπλαγχνός ἐστιν ὁ κύριος καὶ οἰκτίρμων 'for the Lord is full of mercy and very compassionate' Jas 5.11.

25.53 πλατύνω τὴν καρδίαν: (an idiom, literally 'to broaden the heart') to make evident that one has affection for someone – 'to show affection for, to open one's heart to.' ἡ καρδία ἡμῶν πεπλάτυνται 'our heart is open' 2 Cor 6.11.

25.54 στενοχωρέομαι ἐν τοῖς σπλάγχνοις: (an idiom, literally 'to be restricted in the bowels') to restrict one's affection for someone – 'to not respond with affection to someone, to close one's heart to.' οὐ στενοχωρεῖσθε ἐν ἡμῖν, στενοχωρεῖσθε δὲ ἐν τοῖς σπλάγχνοις ὑμῶν 'it is not we who have closed our hearts to you, but it is you who have closed your hearts to us' 2 Cor 6.12. In 2 Cor 6.12 it is also possible to understand στενοχωρέομαι as meaning 'to live with severe restrictions' (see 37.18), and σπλάγχνα may be interpreted as a psychological faculty of intent and feeling (see 26.11).

25.55 κλείω τὰ σπλάγχνα: (an idiom, literally 'to close the bowels') to refuse to show compassion – 'to not have compassion for, to close one's heart toward.' καὶ θεωρῇ τὸν ἀδελφὸν αὐτοῦ χρείαν ἔχοντα καὶ κλείσῃ τὰ σπλάγχνα αὐτοῦ ἀπ' αὐτοῦ 'and sees his brother in need and refuses to show him compassion' 1 Jn 3.17.

25.56 ἐμβριμάομαι^c: to have an intense, strong feeling of concern, often with the implication of indignation – 'to feel strongly, to be indignant.' Ἰησοῦς οὖν ὡς εἶδεν αὐτὴν κλαίουσαν καὶ τοὺς συνελθόντας αὐτῇ Ἰουδαίους κλαίοντας, ἐνεβριμήσατο τῷ πνεύματι 'then when Jesus saw her weeping and saw those Jews who were with her weeping, his feeling was intense' or '. . . he was indignant' Jn 11.33.

25.57 συμπαθέω^b: to share someone's feeling in the sense of being sympathetic with – 'to be sympathetic toward, to have sympathy for.' οὐ γὰρ ἔχομεν ἀρχιερέα μὴ δυνάμενον συμπαθῆσαι ταῖς ἀσθενείαις ἡμῶν 'our high priest is not one who cannot feel sympathy for our weaknesses' He 4.15. In a number of languages the closest equivalent of 'being sympathetic with' may be 'to understand completely how one feels' or 'to feel in one's heart just like someone else feels.'

25.58 συμπαθής, ές: pertaining to feeling sympathy for someone or something – 'sympathetic.' τὸ δὲ τέλος πάντες ὁμόφρονες, συμπαθεῖς 'and in conclusion, all should have the same attitude and be sympathetic' 1 Pe 3.8.

D Hope, Look Forward To[8] (25.59-25.64)

25.59 ἐλπίζω^a; ἐλπίς^a, ίδος f: to look forward with confidence to that which is good and beneficial – 'to hope, to hope for, hope.' ἐλπίζω^a: ἡμεῖς δὲ ἠλπίζομεν ὅτι αὐτός ἐστιν ὁ μέλλων λυτροῦσθαι τὸν Ἰσραήλ 'and we had hoped that he would be the one who was going to redeem Israel' Lk 24.21; ὅτι ἠλπίκαμεν ἐπὶ θεῷ ζῶντι 'because we have placed our hope in the living God' 1 Tm 4.10. ἐλπίς^a: περὶ ἐλπίδος καὶ ἀναστάσεως νεκρῶν ἐγὼ κρίνομαι 'I am on trial (here) because I hope that the dead will rise to life' Ac 23.6; ἵνα διὰ τῆς ὑπομονῆς καὶ διὰ τῆς παρακλήσεως τῶν γραφῶν τὴν ἐλπίδα ἔχωμεν 'in order that through patience and encouragement given by the Scriptures we might have hope' Ro 15.4.

25.60 προελπίζω: to hope in a prior manner, either beforehand or prior to someone else – 'to hope beforehand, to be the first to hope.' εἰς τὸ εἶναι ἡμᾶς εἰς ἔπαινον δόξης αὐτοῦ τοὺς προηλπικότας ἐν τῷ Χριστῷ 'let us then, who are the first to hope in Christ, praise God's glory' Eph 1.12.

25.61 ἐλπίς^b, ίδος f: (derivative of ἐλπίζω^a 'to hope,' 25.59) that which is hoped for – 'what is hoped for, hope.' διὰ τὴν ἐλπίδα τὴν ἀποκειμένην ὑμῖν ἐν τοῖς οὐρανοῖς 'because of the hope which is stored up for you in heaven' Col 1.5; ἐλπὶς δὲ βλεπομένη οὐκ ἔστιν ἐλπίς 'when what is hoped for is seen, there is no longer any need to hope' Ro 8.24.

8 Subdomain D *Hope, Look Forward To* involves three important features of meaning: a future orientation, a desire, and a benefit. Accordingly, in a number of languages expressions of 'hope' involve phrases such as 'looking forward to what is good' or 'waiting expectantly for what is good.'

25.62 ἐλπίς^c, ίδος f: (derivative of ἐλπίζω^a 'to hope,' 25.59) that which constitutes the cause or reason for hoping – 'the basis for hope, the reason for hope.' τίς γὰρ ἡμῶν ἐλπὶς ἢ χαρά; 'for who is the basis for our hope or joy?' 1 Th 2.19. This expression in 1 Th 2.19 may be rendered in some languages as 'for who is the one who causes us to hope and to have joy' or '. . . to be happy.'

25.63 ἀπεκδέχομαι^a: to await eagerly or expectantly for some future event – 'to look forward eagerly, to await expectantly.' ἐκ δευτέρου . . . ὀφθήσεται τοῖς αὐτὸν ἀπεκδεχομένοις εἰς σωτηρίαν 'he shall appear yet . . . a second time . . . to save those who are eagerly expecting him' He 9.28; ἡ γὰρ ἀποκαραδοκία τῆς κτίσεως τὴν ἀποκάλυψιν τῶν υἱῶν τοῦ θεοῦ ἀπεκδέχεται 'for creation awaits with eager expectation for God to reveal his sons' Ro 8.19.

25.64 ἀποκαραδοκία, ας f: that which one looks forward to with eagerness and desire – 'what one eagerly expects, eager expectancy, eager desire.' κατὰ τὴν ἀποκαραδοκίαν καὶ ἐλπίδα μου ὅτι ἐν οὐδενὶ αἰσχυνθήσομαι 'my eager desire and hope is that I shall be ashamed in nothing' Php 1.20. In Ro 8.19 (see 25.63) ἀποκαραδοκία serves in some respects to reinforce the meaning of ἀπεκδέχομαι, but it appears to add a significant component of desire.

E Be Willing (25.65-25.67)

25.65 ἑκούσιος, α, ον; ἑκών, οῦσα, όν; ἑκουσίως^a: pertaining to being willing to do something without being forced or pressured – 'willing, willingly, of one's own free will.' ἑκούσιος: ἵνα μὴ ὡς κατὰ ἀνάγκην τὸ ἀγαθόν σου ᾖ ἀλλὰ κατὰ ἑκούσιον 'in order that your help may not be a matter of necessity, but of your own free will' Phm 14. ἑκών: εἰ γὰρ ἑκὼν τοῦτο πράσσω, μισθὸν ἔχω 'for if I do this out of willingness, I have a reward' 1 Cor 9.17. ἑκουσίως^a: ἐπισκοποῦντες μὴ ἀναγκαστῶς ἀλλὰ ἑκουσίως κατὰ θεόν 'look after it willingly, as God wants you to, and not unwillingly' 1 Pe 5.2.

In a number of languages 'willingness' to perform some action is expressed negatively, for example, 'not having to' or 'not being forced to' or 'not being told one must.' A positive expression of 'willingness' may be indicated idiomatically by a phrase such as 'my heart approves.'

25.66 αὐθαίρετος, ον: pertaining to being willing, with the implication of choice – 'willing, of one's own free will.' αὐθαίρετοι μετὰ πολλῆς παρακλήσεως δεόμενοι ἡμῶν 'of their own free will they begged us and pleaded' 2 Cor 8.3-4.

25.67 ἄκων, ἄκουσα, ἄκον: pertaining to not being willing to do something – 'not willing, not of one's own free will, not a matter of free choice.' εἰ δὲ ἄκων, οἰκονομίαν πεπίστευμαι 'if (I do my work) not as a matter of free choice, I am (simply) discharging the trust committed to me' 1 Cor 9.17. Expressions of 'not being willing to do something' may often be rendered as 'being forced to do something' or 'doing something because one has to.'

F Be Eager, Be Earnest, In a Devoted Manner (25.68-25.79)

25.68 προθυμία, ας f: eagerness to engage in some activity or event – 'eagerness, desire.' πρὸς τὴν αὐτοῦ τοῦ κυρίου δόξαν καὶ προθυμίαν ἡμῶν 'for the sake of the glory of the Lord himself and for the sake of showing our desire (to help)' 2 Cor 8.19; οἵτινες ἐδέξαντο τὸν λόγον μετὰ πάσης προθυμίας 'who received the message with all eagerness' Ac 17.11. A phrase such as 'with all eagerness' must often be expressed as a clause, for example, 'and were very eager.'

25.69 πρόθυμος, ον; προθύμως: pertaining to being eager to do something – 'eager, eagerly, willing, willingly.' πρόθυμος: τὸ μὲν πνεῦμα πρόθυμον ἡ δὲ σὰρξ ἀσθενής 'the spirit is eager, but the flesh is weak' Mk 14.38; οὕτως τὸ κατ' ἐμὲ πρόθυμον καὶ ὑμῖν τοῖς ἐν Ῥώμῃ εὐαγγελίσασθαι 'so I am eager to preach the gospel to you also who are in Rome' Ro 1.15. προθύμως: ἐπισκοποῦντες . . . μηδὲ αἰσχροκερ-

δῶς ἀλλὰ προθύμως 'look after it . . . not for pay, but from a real eagerness to serve' 1 Pe 5.2.

It would be wrong to equate the meaning of πρόθυμος and προθύμως with ἑκούσιος, ἑκών, and ἑκουσίως (25.65), for πρόθυμος and προθύμως imply far more desire and eagerness, though both sets of terms are often translated in English as 'willing' or 'willingly.'

25.70 ἐκτένεια, ας f: a state of eagerness involving perseverance over a period of time – 'earnestness, eager perseverance.' εἰς ἣν τὸ δωδεκάφυλον ἡμῶν ἐν ἐκτενείᾳ νύκτα καὶ ἡμέραν λατρεῦον ἐλπίζει καταντῆσαι 'this is the promise our twelve tribes are hoping to receive as they earnestly serve God night and day' Ac 26.7.

25.71 ἐκτενής[b], ές; ἐκτενῶς[b]: pertaining to being eager to persevere in some state or activity – 'eager, eagerly, earnest, earnestly.' ἐκτενής[b]: πρὸ πάντων τὴν εἰς ἑαυτοὺς ἀγάπην ἐκτενῆ ἔχοντες 'above everything, love one another earnestly' 1 Pe 4.8. For another interpretation of ἐκτενής in 1 Pe 4.8, see 68.12. ἐκτενῶς[b]: ἀλλήλους ἀγαπήσατε ἐκτενῶς 'love one another earnestly' 1 Pe 1.22; προσευχὴ δὲ ἦν ἐκτενῶς γινομένη ὑπὸ τῆς ἐκκλησίας πρὸς τὸν θεὸν περὶ αὐτοῦ 'the church was earnestly praying to God for him' Ac 12.5. For another interpretation of ἐκτενῶς in Ac 12.5, see 68.12.

25.72 εὔνοια, ας f: a state of zeal based upon a desire to be involved in some activity or state – 'zeal, eagerness, wholeheartedness.' μετ' εὐνοίας δουλεύοντες, ὡς τῷ κυρίῳ 'serve wholeheartedly, as if you were serving the Lord' Eph 6.7. An equivalent of 'serve wholeheartedly' may be expressed in some languages as 'serve because you really want to' or 'serve because that is what you really desire to do.'

25.73 ζέω τῷ πνεύματι: (an idiom, literally 'to boil in the spirit') to show great eagerness toward something – 'to show enthusiasm, to commit oneself completely to.' ζέων τῷ πνεύματι ἐλάλει καὶ ἐδίδασκεν ἀκριβῶς τὰ περὶ τοῦ Ἰησοῦ 'with great enthusiasm he spoke and taught correctly the facts about Jesus' Ac

18.25. In some languages it may be difficult to find an appropriate equivalent of the phrase 'with great enthusiasm.' In some instances an equivalent expression may be 'he showed how much he liked to do' or 'he showed how he did so with all his heart.'

25.74 σπεύδω^c; σπουδάζω^c; σπουδή^c, ῆς *f*: to be eager to do something, with the implication of readiness to expend energy and effort – 'to be eager, eagerness, devotion.'

σπεύδω^c: ἔσπευδεν γὰρ εἰ δυνατὸν εἴη αὐτῷ τὴν ἡμέραν τῆς πεντηκοστῆς γενέσθαι εἰς Ἱεροσόλυμα 'he was eager to arrive in Jerusalem, if at all possible, by the day of Pentecost' Ac 20.16. For another interpretation of σπεύδω in Ac 20.16, see 68.79.

σπουδάζω^c: ὃ καὶ ἐσπούδασα αὐτὸ τοῦτο ποιῆσαι 'which is the very thing I have been eager to do' Ga 2.10.

σπουδή^c: ἕνεκεν τοῦ φανερωθῆναι τὴν σπουδὴν ὑμῶν τὴν ὑπὲρ ἡμῶν πρὸς ὑμᾶς 'in order to make plain to you how deep is your devotion to us' 2 Cor 7.12.

25.75 σπουδαῖος, α, ον; σπουδαίως^b: pertaining to being earnest and diligent in undertaking an activity – 'eager, eagerly, earnest, earnestly.'

σπουδαῖος: σπουδαιότερος δὲ ὑπάρχων αὐθαίρετος ἐξῆλθεν πρὸς ὑμᾶς 'he was so eager that of his own free will he decided to go to you' 2 Cor 8.17.

σπουδαίως^b: σπουδαιοτέρως οὖν ἔπεμψα αὐτόν 'I am all the more eager to send him (to you)' Php 2.28.

In a number of languages eagerness can only be expressed in terms of desire. Hence, for Php 2.28 one must sometimes translate 'I am all the more desirous of sending him to you.'

25.76 ζηλόω^a; ζηλεύω: to be deeply committed to something, with the implication of accompanying desire – 'to be earnest, to set one's heart on, to be completely intent upon.'

ζηλόω^a: ζηλοῦτε δὲ τὰ χαρίσματα τὰ μείζονα 'set your hearts, then, on the more important gifts' 1 Cor 12.31. It is also possible to understand ζηλοῦτε in 1 Cor 12.31 as being indicative and therefore translated as 'you set your hearts on the more important gifts.'

ζηλεύω: ζήλευε οὖν καὶ μετανόησον 'be earnest, then, and repent' Re 3.19.

25.77 ζηλωτής^a, οῦ *m*: one who is deeply committed to something and therefore zealous – 'enthusiast, zealous person.' ζηλωτὴς ὑπάρχων τοῦ θεοῦ καθὼς πάντες ὑμεῖς ἐστε σήμερον 'being deeply committed to God even as all of you are today' Ac 22.3.

25.78 φιλοτιμέομαι: to earnestly aspire to something, implying strong ambition for some goal – 'to aspire to, to make something one's ambition to.' φιλοτιμεῖσθαι ἡσυχάζειν 'earnestly aspire to live the quiet life' 1 Th 4.11. An equivalent of φιλοτιμεῖσθαι ἡσυχάζειν in 1 Th 4.11 may be in some languages 'do everything you can to live the quiet life.'

25.79 ἀντιλαμβάνομαι^b; ἐπακολουθέω^a: to give or commit oneself wholeheartedly to something – 'to devote oneself to, to give oneself to.'

ἀντιλαμβάνομαι^b: οἱ τῆς εὐεργεσίας ἀντιλαμβανόμενοι 'those who are devoted to doing kind things' 1 Tm 6.2. It is also possible to understand ἀντιλαμβάνομαι in 1 Tm 6.2 in the sense of 'to be benefited' (see 65.48).

ἐπακολουθέω^a: παντὶ ἔργῳ ἀγαθῷ ἐπηκολούθησεν 'she devoted herself to all kinds of good deeds' 1 Tm 5.10.

In a number of languages the concept of 'devoting oneself to' or 'giving oneself wholly to' is often expressed as 'to do with one's whole heart' or 'to want to do nothing else but.'

G Content, Satisfied (25.80-25.84)

25.80 κορέννυμι^a: to be happy or content with what one has, with the implication of its being abundant – 'to be content, to be satisfied.' ἤδη κεκορεσμένοι ἐστέ 'already you are satisfied' 1 Cor 4.8. Note that in this statement in 1 Cor 4.8 there is evidently a significant element of irony, and it is for that reason that some translations employ a question, for example, 'do you already have everything you need?' For another interpretation of κορέννυμι in 1 Cor 4.8, see 57.22.

25.81 ἀρκέομαι: to be happy or content as the result of having what one desires or needs – 'to be content, to be satisfied.' ἀρκεῖσθε τοῖς ὀψωνίοις ὑμῶν 'be content with your pay' Lk 3.14. In a number of languages 'to be content' is expressed negatively, for example, 'to not complain.' In other instances, one may be forced to employ a type of direct or indirect discourse, for example, 'to acknowledge that it is enough' or 'to say, It is all that is needed.'

25.82 χορτάζομαι[b]: (a figurative extension of meaning of χορτάζομαι[a] 'to eat one's fill,' 23.15) to be satisfied or content with some object or state – 'to be satisfied, to be content with.' ὅτι αὐτοὶ χορτασθήσονται 'because they will be satisfied' Mt 5.6.

25.83 αὐτάρκεια[a], ας f: the state of being content with one's circumstances or lot in life – 'self-content, contentment, contentment with what one has.' ἔστιν δὲ πορισμὸς μέγας ἡ εὐσέβεια μετὰ αὐταρκείας 'and religion is a source of great wealth if it is accompanied by contentment with what one has' 1 Tm 6.6.

25.84 αὐτάρκης, ες: pertaining to being happy or content with what one has – 'content with what one has, content with the circumstances in which one exists.' ἐγὼ γὰρ ἔμαθον ἐν οἷς εἰμι αὐτάρκης εἶναι 'for I have learned to be content with whatever circumstances I am in' Php 4.11.

H Acceptable To, To Be Pleased With (25.85-25.98)

25.85 δεκτός[a], ή, όν; ἀπόδεκτος, ον: pertaining to that which is pleasing in view of its being acceptable – 'pleasing, acceptable.'
δεκτός[a]: ὁ φοβούμενος αὐτὸν καὶ ἐργαζόμενος δικαιοσύνην δεκτὸς αὐτῷ ἐστιν 'whoever worships him and does what is right is acceptable to him' Ac 10.35.
ἀπόδεκτος: τοῦτο καλὸν καὶ ἀπόδεκτον ἐνώπιον τοῦ σωτῆρος ἡμῶν θεοῦ 'this is good and it pleases God our Savior' 1 Tm 2.3.
In a number of languages it is necessary to restructure expressions containing 'acceptable to' or 'pleasing to.' For example, in Ac 10.35 it may be necessary to translate 'God accepts

whoever worships him and does what is right' or 'God is pleased with whoever worships him and does what is right.' Similarly, in 1 Tm 2.3 one may translate 'this is good, and God our Savior likes it' or '. . . is happy because of it.'

25.86 εὐπρόσδεκτος[a], ον: pertaining to that which is particularly acceptable, and hence quite pleasing – 'very acceptable, quite pleasing.' ἵνα γένηται ἡ προσφορὰ τῶν ἐθνῶν εὐπρόσδεκτος 'in order that the Gentiles may be an offering very acceptable (to God)' Ro 15.16. In some languages the statement 'an offering very acceptable to God' must be rendered as 'an offering with which God is very pleased' or 'an offering which pleases God very much.'

25.87 εὐδοκέω[a]: to be pleased with something or someone, with the implication of resulting pleasure – 'to be pleased with, to take pleasure in.' οὗτός ἐστιν ὁ υἱός μου ὁ ἀγαπητός, ἐν ᾧ εὐδόκησα 'this is my dear Son; I am very pleased with him' Mt 3.17.

25.88 εὐδοκία[a], ας f: that which pleases someone – 'what pleases.' καὶ τὸ ἐνεργεῖν ὑπὲρ τῆς εὐδοκίας 'to do according to what pleases him' Php 2.13; ὅτι οὕτως εὐδοκία ἐγένετο ἔμπροσθέν σου 'because this was what pleased you' Lk 10.21.

25.89 χάρις[d], ιτος f: a favorable attitude toward someone or something – 'favor, good will.' ἔχοντες χάριν πρὸς ὅλον τὸν λαόν 'having the good will of all the people' or 'all the people were pleased with them' Ac 2.47; εὗρες γὰρ χάριν παρὰ τῷ θεῷ 'for you have found favor with God' or 'for God is pleased with you' Lk 1.30.
In the expressions ἔχοντες χάριν πρὸς ὅλον τὸν λαόν (Ac 2.47) and εὗρες γὰρ χάριν παρὰ τῷ θεῷ (Lk 1.30) it would appear on the basis of superficial examination that the subject of the participle or the verb is in some respects an active agent. Semantically, however, the subject is actually the recipient of the good will, and in these contexts it is either the people or God who takes pleasure in or is pleased by the grammatical subjects in question. These expressions are typical of situations in which the

semantic relationships are almost completely the reverse of the syntactic relationships.

25.90 ἀρέσκω: to cause someone to be pleased with someone or something – 'to please.' ἤρεσεν ὁ λόγος ἐνώπιον παντὸς τοῦ πλήθους 'this proposal pleased the whole group' Ac 6.5; ἕκαστος ἡμῶν τῷ πλησίον ἀρεσκέτω 'each of us should please his neighbor' Ro 15.2. In a number of languages the equivalent of 'to cause someone to be pleased with something' is expressed as 'to cause someone to be happy about' or 'to cause someone to feel good about.'

25.91 ἀρεσκεία, ας *f*: that which causes someone to be pleased with something – 'means of favor, that which pleases.' περιπατῆσαι ἀξίως τοῦ κυρίου εἰς πᾶσαν ἀρεσκείαν 'to live worthily of the Lord so as to please him in everything' Col 1.10.

25.92 ἀρεστός[a], ή, όν: pertaining to that which pleases someone – 'pleasing.' ὅτι ἐγὼ τὰ ἀρεστὰ αὐτῷ ποιῶ πάντοτε 'because I always do those things that please him' Jn 8.29; ἰδὼν δὲ ὅτι ἀρεστόν ἐστιν τοῖς Ἰουδαίοις 'when he saw that this pleased the Jews' Ac 12.3. In some languages the equivalent of 'this pleased the Jews' is 'this caused the Jews to be happy' or even 'this caused the Jews to say, That's fine.'

25.93 εὐαρεστέω: to cause someone to be well-disposed toward or to be pleased with someone – 'to cause to be pleased, to please.' πρὸ γὰρ τῆς μεταθέσεως μεμαρτύρηται εὐαρεστηκέναι τῷ θεῷ 'for it says that before being taken up, he had pleased God' He 11.5.

25.94 εὐάρεστος, ον; εὐαρέστως: pertaining to that which causes someone to be pleased – 'pleasing to, pleasingly.' εὐάρεστος: τὸ ἀγαθὸν καὶ εὐάρεστον καὶ τέλειον 'what is good and is pleasing to him and is perfect' Ro 12.2. εὐαρέστως: ἔχωμεν χάριν, δι' ἧς λατρεύωμεν εὐαρέστως τῷ θεῷ 'let us be grateful and worship God in a way that pleases him' He 12.28.

25.95 ἐπιστρέφω καρδίας ἐπί: (an idiom, literally 'to turn hearts to') to cause a change of attitude in a positive and acceptable direction – 'to make well-disposed toward, to make friendly toward, to cause to become acceptable.' ἐπιστρέψαι καρδίας πατέρων ἐπὶ τέκνα καὶ ἀπειθεῖς ἐν φρονήσει δικαίων 'he will cause fathers to be well-disposed to their children and he will cause disobedient people to accept the way of thinking of the righteous' Lk 1.17.

25.96 ποιέω τὸ ἱκανόν: (an idiom, literally 'to do what is enough') to cause someone to be pleased by doing what will satisfy – 'to act in a pleasing manner, to please.' ὁ δὲ Πιλᾶτος βουλόμενος τῷ ὄχλῳ τὸ ἱκανὸν ποιῆσαι 'Pilate wanted to please the crowd' Mk 15.15.

25.97 προσφιλής, ές: pertaining to that which causes people to be pleased with something – 'pleasing, lovely.' ὅσα προσφιλῆ . . . λογίζεσθε 'whatever things are pleasing . . . think about' Php 4.8.

25.98 ἀνθρωπάρεσκος, ον: pertaining to causing people to be pleased, with the implication of being in contrast to God or at the sacrifice of some principle – 'pleasing people, men-pleaser.' μὴ . . . ὡς ἀνθρωπάρεσκοι ἀλλ' ὡς δοῦλοι Χριστοῦ 'not . . . as men-pleasers, but as servants of Christ' Eph 6.6. The expression 'men-pleasers' may often be rendered as 'those who are just trying to make people like them.'

I Thankful, Grateful[9] (25.99-25.101)

25.99 εὐχάριστος[a], ον: pertaining to being thankful for what has been done to or for someone – 'thankful.' καὶ εὐχάριστοι γίνεσθε 'and become thankful' Col 3.15. Expressions for 'thankfulness' are frequently idiomatic, for example, 'to have a full heart' or 'to speak from the heart' or even 'to say, You are very kind.' For another interpretation of εὐχάριστος in Col 3.15, see 33.352.

25.100 εὐχαριστέω[b]: to be thankful on the basis of some received benefit – 'to be

---

9 In Subdomain I *Thankful, Grateful* the meanings involve attitudes or emotional states, while in Domain 33 (33.349, 352, 353) the focus is upon the communication of such an attitude by expressing thankfulness.

thankful, to be grateful.' οἷς οὐκ ἐγὼ μόνος εὐ-χαριστῶ ἀλλὰ καὶ πᾶσαι αἱ ἐκκλησίαι τῶν ἐθνῶν 'not I alone, but all the churches among the Gentiles are thankful to them' Ro 16.4.

25.101 ἀχάριστος ᵃ, ον: pertaining to a complete lack of thankfulness – 'unthankful, ungrateful.' ὅτι αὐτὸς χρηστός ἐστιν ἐπὶ τοὺς ἀχαρίστους 'because he is good to the ungrateful' Lk 6.35. For another interpretation of ἀχάριστος in Lk 6.35, see 33.353.

J Enjoy, Take Pleasure In, Be Fond of Doing (25.102-25.115)

25.102 θέλω ᵈ: to take pleasure in something in view of its being desirable – 'to like, to enjoy.' τῶν γραμματέων τῶν θελόντων ἐν στολαῖς περιπατεῖν 'the teachers of the Law who like to walk around in long robes' Mk 12.38.

25.103 φιλέω ᵇ: to particularly like or enjoy doing something – 'to like to, to love to.' φιλοῦσιν ἐν ταῖς συναγωγαῖς καὶ ἐν ταῖς γωνίαις τῶν πλατειῶν ἑστῶτες προσεύχεσθαι 'they love to stand up and pray in the synagogues and on the street corners' Mt 6.5; φιλοῦσιν δὲ τὴν πρωτοκλισίαν ἐν τοῖς δείπνοις 'they love to sit in the best places at feasts' Mt 23.6.

25.104 ἀγαπάω ᶜ: to like or love something on the basis of a high regard for its value or importance – 'to love to, to like to, to take pleasure in.' ἠγάπησαν γὰρ τὴν δόξαν τῶν ἀνθρώπων μᾶλλον ἤπερ τὴν δόξαν τοῦ θεοῦ 'they loved the approval of men rather than the approval of God' Jn 12.43.

25.105 φιλάγαθος, ον: pertaining to liking or loving what is good – 'liking what is good, loving what is good.' δεῖ γὰρ τὸν ἐπίσκοπον . . . φιλάγαθον 'for a bishop must be one . . . who loves what is good' Tt 1.7-8.

25.106 ἀφιλάγαθος, ον: pertaining to not loving what is good – 'not loving what is good, being an enemy to what is good, being against what is good.' ἔσονται γὰρ οἱ ἄνθρωποι . . . ἀφιλάγαθοι 'there will be people . . . who will not love what is good' 2 Tm 3.2-3.

25.107 φιλαργυρία, ας f: the state of loving money or wealth – 'love of wealth, love of money.' ῥίζα γὰρ πάντων τῶν κακῶν ἐστιν ἡ φιλαργυρία 'for the love of money is the source of all kinds of evil' 1 Tm 6.10.

25.108 φιλάργυρος, ον: pertaining to the love of wealth or money – 'loving wealth, lover of riches.' οἱ Φαρισαῖοι φιλάργυροι ὑπάρχοντες 'the Pharisees being lovers of wealth' Lk 16.14.

25.109 ἀφιλάργυρος, ον: pertaining to not being desirous or greedy for money – 'not loving wealth, one who does not love money.' μὴ πάροινον, μὴ πλήκτην, ἀλλὰ ἐπιεικῆ, ἄμαχον, ἀφιλάργυρον 'one who is not a drunkard or a violent man, but gentle and peaceful, not a lover of money' 1 Tm 3.3.

25.110 φιλοπρωτεύω: to like or love to be first in rank or position – 'to desire to be first, to desire to order others.' ἀλλ' ὁ φιλοπρωτεύων αὐτῶν Διοτρέφης οὐκ ἐπιδέχεται ἡμᾶς 'but Diotrephes, who always wants to order others, will not pay any attention to us' 3 Jn 9.

25.111 ἡδονή ᵃ, ῆς f: that which someone is fond of doing, in that it produces enjoyment – 'that which is pleasurable, pleasure.' ἡδονὴν ἡγούμενοι τὴν ἐν ἡμέρᾳ τρυφήν 'that which is pleasurable for them is to satisfy their bodily desires during the day' or 'they enjoy satisfying their bodily desires during the day' 2 Pe 2.13.

25.112 φιλήδονος, ον: pertaining to being fond of pleasure and enjoyment – 'given over to pleasure, lover of pleasure, loving pleasure.' φιλήδονοι μᾶλλον ἢ φιλόθεοι 'they are lovers of pleasure rather than lovers of God' 2 Tm 3.4.

25.113 εὐδοκέω ᵇ: to take pleasure in something in that it fulfills one's desires – 'to enjoy.' ἀλλὰ εὐδοκήσαντες τῇ ἀδικίᾳ 'but they enjoy sinning' 2 Th 2.12. In some languages the equivalent of 'to enjoy' is 'to make someone happy' or 'to make one feel good.' This expression in 2 Th 2.12 may be rendered as 'but when they are sinning, they feel good' or 'but to sin makes them happy.'

25.114 ἐμπί(μ)πλαμαι[b] or ἐμπιπλάομαι[b]: to enjoy something fully and completely, with the implication of satisfying one's desires – 'to enjoy.' ἐὰν ὑμῶν πρῶτον ἀπὸ μέρους ἐμπλησθῶ 'after I have enjoyed your (company) for a while' or '. . . enjoyed (visiting) you for a while' Ro 15.24.

25.115 ἀπόλαυσις, εως *f*: enjoyment based upon the satisfaction of one's desires – 'enjoyment.' θεῷ τῷ παρέχοντι ἡμῖν πάντα πλουσίως εἰς ἀπόλαυσιν 'God, who generously gives us everything to enjoy' 1 Tm 6.17; ἢ πρόσκαιρον ἔχειν ἁμαρτίας ἀπόλαυσιν 'rather than enjoy sin for a little while' He 11.25.

K Happy, Glad, Joyful (25.116-25.134)

25.116 ἱλαρότης, ητος *f*: a state of happiness characterized by being cheerful – 'happiness, cheerfulness.' ὁ ἐλεῶν ἐν ἱλαρότητι 'whoever shows kindness must do it with cheerfulness' Ro 12.8. In some languages 'cheerfulness' may be expressed idiomatically as 'one's heart is laughing' or 'one's eyes are dancing.'

25.117 ἱλαρός, ά, όν: pertaining to being cheerfully happy – 'happy, cheerful, one who is happy.' ἱλαρὸν γὰρ δότην ἀγαπᾷ ὁ θεός 'for God loves the one who is cheerful as he gives' 2 Cor 9.7.

25.118 μακαρισμός, οῦ *m*: a state of happiness, implying favorable circumstances – 'happiness.' ποῦ οὖν ὁ μακαρισμὸς ὑμῶν; 'where, then, is that happiness of yours?' Ga 4.15. In Ga 4.15 μακαρισμός clearly refers to a state of happiness which occurred in the past but which was no longer evident. It may therefore be necessary to indicate that the happiness in question is past, and accordingly, one may translate 'you were so happy! What has happened?' or 'then you were so happy! What has happened to you now?'

25.119 μακάριος, α, ον: pertaining to being happy, with the implication of enjoying

favorable circumstances – 'happy.' μακάριοι οἱ ἐλεήμονες, ὅτι αὐτοὶ ἐλεηθήσονται 'happy are those who show mercy, for God will be merciful to them' Mt 5.7. This passive construction in Greek (ἐλεηθήσονται) is generally regarded as a so-called 'passive of avoidance,' that is to say, the use of a passive form in order to avoid a direct reference to God.

25.120 μακαρίζω: to regard someone as happy or fortunate in view of favorable circumstances – 'to regard as happy, to regard as fortunate.' μακαρίζομεν τοὺς ὑπομείναντας 'we regard as fortunate those who have endured' Jas 5.11; μακαριοῦσίν με πᾶσαι αἱ γενεαί 'all generations of people will regard me as fortunate' Lk 1.48.

25.121 εὐφροσύνη, ης *f*: a state of joyful happiness – 'joyfulness, rejoicing.' πληρώσεις με εὐφροσύνης 'you will make me very joyful' Ac 2.28.

25.122 εὐφραίνομαι[a]: to rejoice as an expression of happiness – 'to rejoice.' εὐφράνθητε, ἔθνη, μετὰ τοῦ λαοῦ αὐτοῦ 'rejoice, Gentiles, together with his people' Ro 15.10; εὐφραίνοντο ἐν τοῖς ἔργοις τῶν χειρῶν αὐτῶν 'they rejoiced because of what they had made' Ac 7.41; διὰ τοῦτο ηὐφράνθη ἡ καρδία μου 'therefore, my heart rejoices' Ac 2.26. In some languages it may be necessary to translate εὐφραίνομαι in Ac 2.26 in an idiomatic manner, for example, 'my heart sings' or 'my heart shouts because it is happy.' For another interpretation of εὐφραίνομαι in Ac 7.41, see 51.3.

25.123 χαρά[a], ᾶς *f*: a state of joy and gladness – 'joy, gladness, great happiness.' ἀπελθοῦσαι ταχὺ ἀπὸ τοῦ μνημείου μετὰ φόβου καὶ χαρᾶς μεγάλης 'and quickly leaving the tomb, fearful and (at the same time) very joyful' Mt 28.8. In a number of languages 'joy' is expressed idiomatically, for example, 'my heart is dancing' or 'my heart shouts because I am happy.'

25.124 χαρά[b], ᾶς *f*: that which is the cause of joy or gladness – 'cause of joy, reason for gladness.' τίς γὰρ ἡμῶν ἐλπὶς ἢ χαρά 'for who is the basis for our hope or the reason for our joy' 1 Th 2.19.

25.125 χαίρω[a]: to enjoy a state of happiness and well-being – 'to rejoice, to be glad.' χαίρω ἐν τοῖς παθήμασιν ὑπὲρ ὑμῶν 'I rejoice as I suffer for you' Col 1.24; ὡς λυπούμενοι ἀεὶ δὲ χαίροντες 'although saddened, we are always rejoicing' 2 Cor 6.10.

25.126 συγχαίρω: to enjoy a state of happiness or well-being together with someone else – 'to enjoy with, to rejoice with.' συγχάρητέ μοι 'rejoice with me' Lk 15.6; εἴτε δοξάζεται ἓν μέλος, συγχαίρει πάντα τὰ μέλη 'if one part is honored, every part rejoices with it' 1 Cor 12.26.

25.127 συνήδομαι: to be happy as the result of the pleasure derived from some experience or state – 'to rejoice in, to delight in.' συνήδομαι γὰρ τῷ νόμῳ τοῦ θεοῦ κατὰ τὸν ἔσω ἄνθρωπον 'my inner being delights in the law of God' Ro 7.22. In a number of languages one may speak of 'one's inner being' as 'one's liver' or 'one's heart' or 'one's abdomen' (employing a reference to one of the organs of the body as a focal element of the personality). But in some languages a more figurative and idiomatic expression may be employed, for example, 'one's inner counterpart' or 'the little one who stands inside of a person.' It is often this central or crucial aspect of the personality which must be referred to in contexts speaking of the type of pleasure or delight which one might have in the law of God.

25.128 ἀσμένως: pertaining to experiencing happiness, implying ready and willing acceptance – 'happily, gladly.' ἀσμένως ἀπεδέξαντο ἡμᾶς οἱ ἀδελφοί 'the fellow believers welcomed us gladly' Ac 21.17.

25.129 ἡδέως; ἥδιστα (superlative): pertaining to experiencing happiness, based primarily upon the pleasure derived – 'gladly, happily.'
ἡδέως: ἡδέως γὰρ ἀνέχεσθε τῶν ἀφρόνων φρόνιμοι ὄντες 'you yourselves are so wise and so you gladly tolerate fools' 2 Cor 11.19.
ἥδιστα: ἐγὼ δὲ ἥδιστα δαπανήσω καὶ ἐκδαπανηθήσομαι ὑπὲρ τῶν ψυχῶν ὑμῶν 'I will most gladly spend all I have and myself as well in order to help you' 2 Cor 12.15.

25.130 ἀσπάζομαι[b]: to be happy about something, on the basis that it would prove particularly welcome (thus implying a type of future orientation) – 'to be happy about, to anticipate with pleasure.' ἀλλὰ πόρρωθεν αὐτὰς ἰδόντες καὶ ἀσπασάμενοι 'but from a long way off they saw them (the promises) and anticipated them with pleasure' He 11.13. In order to render the future implications of ἀσπάζομαι in He 11.13, one may be able to translate 'and looked forward with happiness to what was going to happen.' For another interpretation of ἀσπάζομαι in He 11.13, see 34.55.

25.131 εὐφραίνω: to cause someone to be or become happy or glad – 'to make glad, to cheer up, to cause to be happy.' εἰ γὰρ ἐγὼ λυπῶ ὑμᾶς, καὶ τίς ὁ εὐφραίνων με; 'for if I were to make you sad, who would be left to cheer me up?' 2 Cor 2.2.

25.132 ἀγαλλίασις, εως f: a state of intensive joy and gladness, often implying verbal expression and body movement (for example, jumping, leaping, dancing) – 'to be extremely joyful, to rejoice greatly, extreme gladness.' ἐσκίρτησεν ἐν ἀγαλλιάσει τὸ βρέφος ἐν τῇ κοιλίᾳ μου 'my yet unborn child jumped with great gladness' Lk 1.44.

25.133 ἀγαλλιάω: to experience a state of great joy and gladness, often involving verbal expression and appropriate body movement – 'to be extremely joyful, to be overjoyed, to rejoice greatly.' ἠγαλλίασεν τὸ πνεῦμά μου ἐπὶ τῷ θεῷ τῷ σωτῆρί μου 'my soul rejoices greatly because of God my Savior' Lk 1.47; ἠγαλλιάσατο ἡ γλῶσσά μου 'my tongue rejoices' Ac 2.26. In Ac 2.26 it may be impossible to say 'my tongue rejoices.' One may, however, translate in some languages as 'I shout because I am so happy.'

25.134 σκιρτάω[b]: (a figurative extension of meaning of σκιρτάω[a] 'to jump for joy,' 15.243) to be extremely happy, possibly implying in some contexts actually leaping or dancing for joy – 'to be extremely joyful, to dance for joy.' χάρητε ἐν ἐκείνῃ τῇ ἡμέρᾳ καὶ σκιρτήσατε 'be glad when that happens and dance for joy'

Lk 6.23, but see also 15.243 for a different semantic focus. The phrase 'for joy' clearly expresses 'reason,' and therefore it may be useful to translate 'dance for joy' as 'dance because I am so joyful' or '. . . so happy.'

L Laugh, Cry, Groan (25.135-25.145)

25.135 γελάω; γέλως, ωτος *m* – 'to laugh, laughter.'
γελάω: μακάριοι οἱ κλαίοντες νῦν, ὅτι γελάσετε 'happy are you who weep now, for you will laugh' Lk 6.21.
γέλως: ὁ γέλως ὑμῶν εἰς πένθος μετατραπήτω 'let your laughter be changed into sorrow' Jas 4.9.

A number of languages distinguish clearly between various types of laughter: (1) laughter directed against some person as a form of ridicule; (2) laughter resulting from seeing some humorous event or as the result of listening to a humorous account; and (3) laughter which reflects happiness and joy. In Lk 6.21 and Jas 4.9 it is this third type of laughter which is relevant to the contexts.

25.136 ταλαιπωρέω: to be sorrowful and complain, presumably on the basis of wretched circumstances – 'to be sorrowful, to lament.' ταλαιπωρήσατε καὶ πενθήσατε καὶ κλαύσατε 'be sorrowful, grieve, and weep' Jas 4.9.

25.137 δακρύω: to weep, with the clear implication of shedding tears – 'to weep, to cry.' ἐδάκρυσεν ὁ Ἰησοῦς 'Jesus wept' Jn 11.35. In a number of languages a clear distinction is made between weeping which results from sorrow and grief and weeping caused by physical suffering. Without careful attention to such a distinction, a translator may seriously distort the meaning of the text.

25.138 κλαίω; κλαυθμός, οῦ *m*; κραυγή[b], ῆς *f*: to weep or wail, with emphasis upon the noise accompanying the weeping – 'to weep, to wail, to lament, weeping, crying.'
κλαίω: ἐξελθὼν ἔξω ἔκλαυσεν πικρῶς 'he went out and wept bitterly' Mt 26.75; ταλαιπωρήσατε καὶ πενθήσατε καὶ κλαύσατε 'be sorrowful, grieve, and weep' Jas 4.9. In Mt 2.18 κλαίω occurs with a so-called 'direct object,' for ex-

ample, Ῥαχὴλ κλαίουσα τὰ τέκνα αὐτῆς . . . ὅτι οὐκ εἰσίν 'Rachel weeps for her children . . . because they are all dead.' The so-called direct object is, however, the cause of the weeping, and the so-called transitive usage of κλαίω does not alter the meaning.
κλαυθμός: ἱκανὸς δὲ κλαυθμὸς ἐγένετο πάντων, καὶ ἐπιπεσόντες ἐπὶ τὸν τράχηλον τοῦ Παύλου κατεφίλουν αὐτόν 'they were all crying as they hugged Paul and kissed him goodbye' Ac 20.37.
κραυγή[b]: οὔτε πένθος οὔτε κραυγή . . . ἔσται ἔτι 'there will be . . . no more grief, no more crying' Re 21.4.

25.139 ἀλαλάζω[b]: to cry or weep intensely and with wailing – 'to weep loudly, to wail.' θεωρεῖ θόρυβον καὶ κλαίοντας καὶ ἀλαλάζοντας πολλά 'he saw the confusion and (heard) all the crying and loud weeping' Mk 5.38. In a number of languages the equivalent of ἀλαλάζω[b] is a term or phrase referring to ritual or ceremonial weeping or wailing. This would not necessarily imply lack of sincerity, but it would be typical of what would frequently occur in many societies in the case of the type of presumed death reported in Mk 5.38.

25.140 ὀλολύζω: to make a loud cry as an expression of either joy or sorrow – 'to make a loud cry, to cry aloud.' κλαύσατε ὀλολύζοντες ἐπὶ ταῖς ταλαιπωρίαις ὑμῶν ταῖς ἐπερχομέναις 'weep and cry aloud over the miseries that are coming upon you' Jas 5.1. In a number of languages the equivalent of 'cry aloud' would simply be 'scream.' In this one occurrence of ὀλολύζω in the NT, the context refers to desperate circumstances, and one must often select an expression for 'screaming' or 'crying' which will be in keeping with this context referring to the threat of future misery.

25.141 θρηνέω[a]: to weep or cry, especially in mourning for the dead – 'to wail, to lament.'[10] κλαύσετε καὶ θρηνήσετε ὑμεῖς 'you will cry and

---

10 It is possible that θρηνέω[a] should be classified only in Domain 52 *Funerals and Burial*, in view of the fact that θρηνέω[a] may in many contexts suggest a formal type of ritual expression.

wail' Jn 16.20; καὶ γυναικῶν αἳ ἐκόπτοντο καὶ ἐθρήνουν αὐτόν 'some women who were mourning and wailing for him' Lk 23.27. For another interpretation of θρηνέω in Lk 23.27, see 52.2.

Mourning and wailing for the dead are frequently expressed by a term very different from expressions employed in referring to events not involving death.

25.142 πενθέω; πένθος, ους *n*: to experience sadness or grief as the result of depressing circumstances or the condition of persons – 'to be sad, to grieve for, to weep for, sorrow, grief.'
πενθέω: πενθήσω πολλοὺς τῶν προημαρτηκότων 'I will grieve for many who sinned in the past' 2 Cor 12.21; μακάριοι οἱ πενθοῦντες 'happy are those who grieve' Mt 5.4. The reference in Mt 5.4 is not to grieving or mourning for the dead but rather sadness and grief because of wickedness and oppression.
πένθος: ὁ γέλως ὑμῶν εἰς πένθος μετατραπήτω 'let your laughter be turned into grief' or 'instead of laughing, grieve' Jas 4.9.

25.143 στενάζω[a]; στεναγμός, οῦ *m*: to groan or sigh as the result of deep concern or stress – 'to groan, to sigh, groan, sigh.'
στενάζω[a]: καὶ ἀναβλέψας εἰς τὸν οὐρανὸν ἐστέναξεν 'and looking up into heaven, he sighed' Mk 7.34.
στεναγμός: εἶδον τὴν κάκωσιν τοῦ λαοῦ μου τοῦ ἐν Αἰγύπτῳ, καὶ τοῦ στεναγμοῦ αὐτῶν ἤκουσα 'I have seen the suffering of my people in Egypt and have heard their groans' Ac 7.34.

To groan or to sigh may be the result of quite different circumstances, and in a number of languages a clear distinction must be made in any term for groaning or sighing, depending upon the reason or basis for such an expression of emotion. In Mk 7.34 the sigh or groan would seem to be an expression of sympathy for the deaf-mute, but in Ac 7.34 the groans would be caused by severe misery and oppression.

25.144 ἀναστενάζω: to groan or to sigh deeply or intensely – 'to groan deeply, to sigh deeply.' ἀναστενάξας τῷ πνεύματι αὐτοῦ λέγει, Τί ἡ γενεὰ αὕτη ζητεῖ σημεῖον; 'he sighed deep-

ly and said, Why do the people of this day ask for a miracle?' Mk 8.12.

25.145 συστενάζω: to groan or to sigh together with someone else – 'to groan together, to sigh together.' οἴδαμεν γὰρ ὅτι πᾶσα ἡ κτίσις συστενάζει . . . ἄχρι τοῦ νῦν 'we know that . . . up to the present . . . all of creation groans together' Ro 8.22. In Ro 8.22 συστενάζω is used figuratively. It may be difficult to speak of 'all of creation groans together,' since the phrase 'all of creation' would seem to be a total unit. It may therefore be necessary to translate 'all of creation groans together' as 'all parts of the creation groan together' or 'everything that has been created is groaning at the same time.'

M Encouragement, Consolation (25.146-25.155)

25.146 εὐψυχέω; εὐθυμέω: to be or to become encouraged and hence cheerful – 'to be encouraged, to take courage, to become encouraged.'
εὐψυχέω: ἵνα κἀγὼ εὐψυχῶ γνοὺς τὰ περὶ ὑμῶν 'so that I may be encouraged by news about you' Php 2.19.
εὐθυμέω: καὶ τὰ νῦν παραινῶ ὑμᾶς εὐθυμεῖν 'but now I beg you, take courage' Ac 27.22.

In some languages the equivalent of 'to become encouraged' is 'to have one's heart return' or 'to have one's liver stand up again' or 'to have one's heart become hard again.'

25.147 εὔθυμος, ον; εὐθύμως: pertaining to being encouraged – 'encouraged.'
εὔθυμος: εὔθυμοι δὲ γενόμενοι πάντες καὶ αὐτοὶ προσελάβοντο τροφῆς 'they were all encouraged and took some nourishment' Ac 27.36.
εὐθύμως: εὐθύμως τὰ περὶ ἐμαυτοῦ ἀπολογοῦμαι 'I am encouraged as I make my defense' Ac 24.10.

25.148 ἀνάψυξις[b], εως *f*: a state of cheer and encouragement after a period of having been troubled or upset – 'refreshing, encouragement, recovery of happiness.' ὅπως ἂν ἔλθωσιν καιροὶ ἀναψύξεως ἀπὸ προσώπου τοῦ κυρίου 'so that times of encouragement will come from the presence of the Lord' Ac 3.20. For another interpretation of ἀνάψυξις in Ac 3.20, see 22.35.

25.149 ἀναψύχω: to cause someone to recover a state of cheer or encouragement after a time of anxiety and trouble – 'to encourage, to cheer up.' ὅτι πολλάκις με ἀνέψυξεν 'because many times he cheered me up' 2 Tm 1.16. ἀναψύχω may be rendered idiomatically in a number of instances, for example, 'to give one's heart back to a person' or 'to make one's heart feel strong again.'

25.150 παρακαλέω[d]; παράκλησις[a], εως f: to cause someone to be encouraged or consoled, either by verbal or non-verbal means – 'to encourage, to console, encouragement.'[11]
παρακαλέω[d]: ἵνα γνῶτε τὰ περὶ ἡμῶν καὶ παρακαλέσῃ τὰς καρδίας ὑμῶν 'that you may know how we are and that he may encourage you' Eph 6.22.
παράκλησις[a]: εἴ τίς ἐστιν ἐν ὑμῖν λόγος παρακλήσεως πρὸς τὸν λαόν 'if you have any message of encouragement for the people' Ac 13.15; εἴ τις οὖν παράκλησις ἐν Χριστῷ 'if then there is any encouragement in Christ' Php 2.1.

25.151 συμπαρακαλέομαι: to be encouraged at the same time with someone else – 'to be encouraged together, to be encouraged at the same time.' τοῦτο δέ ἐστιν συμπαρακληθῆναι ἐν ὑμῖν διὰ τῆς ἐν ἀλλήλοις πίστεως ὑμῶν τε καὶ ἐμοῦ 'what I mean is that both you and I will be encouraged at the same time, you by my faith and I by yours' Ro 1.12.

25.152 τὰ παραλελυμένα γόνατα ἀνορθόω: (an idiom, literally 'straighten paralyzed knees') to gain encouragement by a strong resolve – 'to become encouraged, to encourage oneself by determination.' τὰ παραλελυμένα γόνατα ἀνορθώσατε 'strengthen your weak knees' or rather 'become more determined and encouraged' He 12.12.

25.153 παραμυθέομαι: to cause someone to become consoled – 'to console, to comfort, to encourage.' παραμυθούμενοι αὐτήν 'those who were comforting her' Jn 11.31; παραμυθεῖσθε

τοὺς ὀλιγοψύχους 'encourage those who are losing heart' 1 Th 5.14.

25.154 παραμύθιον, ου n; παραμυθία, ας f: (derivatives of παραμυθέομαι 'to comfort,' 25.153) that which causes or constitutes the basis for consolation and encouragement – 'consolation, encouragement.'
παραμύθιον: εἴ τι παραμύθιον ἀγάπης 'if there is any consolation of love' or 'if his love consoles you' or '. . . encourages you' Php 2.1.
παραμυθία: ὁ δὲ προφητεύων ἀνθρώποις λαλεῖ οἰκοδομὴν καὶ παράκλησιν καὶ παραμυθίαν 'the one who declares God's message to people speaks of that which builds up and encourages and consoles' 1 Cor 14.3.

25.155 παρηγορία[a], ας f: a means of providing comfort or consolation – 'comfort, consolation.' ἐγενήθησάν μοι παρηγορία 'they have become a comfort to me' Col 4.11. It is also possible to understand παρηγορία in Col 4.11 as meaning 'help' (see 35.14).

N Courage, Boldness (25.156-25.166)

25.156 θαρρέω or θαρσέω (alternative dialectal forms, with θαρσέω occurring in the NT only in the imperative): to have confidence and firmness of purpose in the face of danger or testing – 'to be courageous, to have courage, to be bold.' θαρροῦντες οὖν πάντοτε 'therefore always being full of courage' 2 Cor 5.6; ὃς κατὰ πρόσωπον μὲν ταπεινὸς ἐν ὑμῖν, ἀπὼν δὲ θαρρῶ εἰς ὑμᾶς 'I who am meek when face to face with you, but full of courage when away' 2 Cor 10.1; ἐν τῷ κόσμῳ θλῖψιν ἔχετε, ἀλλὰ θαρσεῖτε 'in the world you will have trouble, but have courage' Jn 16.33. In a number of languages 'courage' is rendered by an idiomatic expression, for example, 'to not move,' 'to be deaf to threats,' and 'to have a heart like iron.'

25.157 λαμβάνω θάρσος: (an idiom, literally 'to take courage') to become confident or courageous in the face of real or possible danger – 'to become confident, to take courage.' οὓς ἰδὼν ὁ Παῦλος εὐχαριστήσας τῷ θεῷ ἔλαβε θάρσος 'when Paul saw them, he thanked God and became confident' Ac 28.15.

---

11 The term παράκλητος, when used as a title for the Holy Spirit, is treated in 12.19.

25.158 παρρησία, ας *f*: a state of boldness and confidence, sometimes implying intimidating circumstances – 'boldness, courage.' προσερχώμεθα οὖν μετὰ παρρησίας τῷ θρόνῳ τῆς χάριτος 'let us boldly approach the throne of grace' He 4.16; μὴ ἀποβάλητε οὖν τὴν παρρησίαν ὑμῶν, ἥτις ἔχει μεγάλην μισθαποδοσίαν 'do not lose your courage which brings a great reward' He 10.35.

25.159 παρρησιάζομαι[b]: to have courage or boldness in the face of danger or opposition – 'to be bold, to have courage.' ἐπαρρησιασάμεθα ἐν τῷ θεῷ ἡμῶν λαλῆσαι πρὸς ὑμᾶς τὸ εὐαγγέλιον τοῦ θεοῦ ἐν πολλῷ ἀγῶνι 'and even though there was much opposition, our God gave us the courage to tell you the good news of God' 1 Th 2.2.

25.160 ἐπαίρω τὴν κεφαλήν: (an idiom, literally 'to raise up the head') to demonstrate courage in the face of danger or adversity – 'to have courage, to lift the head.' ἐπάρατε τὰς κεφαλὰς ὑμῶν 'lift up your heads' Lk 21.28. A literal rendering of ἐπαίρω τὴν κεφαλήν 'to lift up the head' can be misleading in some languages, since the expression may be an idiom meaning 'to be proud' or 'to try to take precedence over others.' A more satisfactory equivalent in some languages may be 'to look up.'

25.161 τολμάω: to be so bold as to challenge or defy possible danger or opposition – 'to dare.' τολμήσας εἰσῆλθεν πρὸς τὸν Πιλᾶτον 'he dared to go in to see Pilate' Mk 15.43; καὶ οὐδεὶς οὐκέτι ἐτόλμα αὐτὸν ἐπερωτῆσαι 'and from that time, no one dared to ask him any more questions' Mk 12.34; οὐκ ἐτόλμησεν κρίσιν ἐπενεγκεῖν βλασφημίας 'he did not dare to bring an accusation involving insulting words' Jd 9.

25.162 τολμηρότερον: (comparative adverb of τολμηρός 'bold, daring,' not occurring in the NT) pertaining to an activity involving unusual boldness or daring – 'boldly.' τολμηρότερον δὲ ἔγραψα ὑμῖν ἀπὸ μέρους 'I have written to you boldly about certain subjects' Ro 15.15.

25.163 ἀποτολμάω: to be particularly bold or daring in what one does – 'to be very bold, to be very daring.' Ἡσαΐας δὲ ἀποτολμᾷ καὶ λέγει 'and Isaiah was very bold and said' Ro 10.20.

25.164 τολμητής, οῦ *m*: one who is particularly bold and daring – 'daring person.' τολμηταί, αὐθάδεις 'bold, arrogant' 2 Pe 2.10.

25.165 ἀνδρίζομαι: (a figurative extension of meaning of ἀνδρίζομαι 'to be manly' or 'to become a man,' not occurring in the NT) to exhibit courage in the face of danger – 'to be brave, to be courageous.' στήκετε ἐν τῇ πίστει, ἀνδρίζεσθε, κραταιοῦσθε 'stand firm in the faith; be brave; be strong' 1 Cor 16.13.

25.166 πείθω τὴν καρδίαν: (an idiom, literally 'to convince the heart') to exhibit confidence and assurance in a situation which might otherwise cause dismay or fear – 'to be confident, to be assured.' καὶ ἔμπροσθεν αὐτοῦ πείσομεν τὴν καρδίαν ἡμῶν 'and we will be confident in his presence' 1 Jn 3.19.

O Patience, Endurance, Perseverance (25.167-25.178)

25.167 μακροθυμία, ας *f*: a state of emotional calm in the face of provocation or misfortune and without complaint or irritation – 'patience.' μιμηταὶ δὲ τῶν διὰ πίστεως καὶ μακροθυμίας κληρονομούντων τὰς ἐπαγγελίας 'but imitators of those who through faith and patience inherited the promises' He 6.12; ὑπόδειγμα λάβετε, ἀδελφοί, τῆς κακοπαθείας καὶ τῆς μακροθυμίας τοὺς προφήτας 'fellow believers, take the prophets as an example of suffering and patience' or '. . . patience in the face of suffering' Jas 5.10. In a number of languages 'patience' is expressed idiomatically, for example, 'to remain seated in one's heart' or 'to keep one's heart from jumping' or 'to have a waiting heart.'

25.168 μακροθυμέω[a]: (derivative of μακροθυμία 'patience,' 25.167) to demonstrate patience despite difficulties – 'to be patient, to remain patient, to wait patiently.' καὶ οὕτως μακροθυμήσας ἐπέτυχεν τῆς ἐπαγγελίας 'and so after waiting patiently, he received what was promised' He 6.15; μακροθύμησον ἐπ' ἐμοί, καὶ πάντα ἀποδώσω σοι 'be patient with me and I will repay you everything' Mt 18.26.

25.169 μακροθύμως: (derivative of μακροθυμία 'patience,' 25.167) pertaining to being patient – 'patiently.' διὸ δέομαι μακροθύμως ἀκοῦσαί μου 'therefore I beg you to listen to me patiently' Ac 26.3. In Ac 26.3 it may be necessary in some languages to spell out the implications of μακροθύμως, for example, 'therefore I beg you to listen to me without interrupting' or '. . . without stopping me.'

25.170 ἀνεξίκακος, ον: pertaining to enduring difficulties without becoming angry or upset – 'tolerant, patient.' ἀλλὰ ἤπιον εἶναι πρὸς πάντας, διδακτικόν, ἀνεξίκακον 'but be kind to all, a good teacher, and patient' 2 Tm 2.24.

25.171 ἀνέχομαιᵃ; ἀνοχή, ῆς f: to be patient with, in the sense of enduring possible difficulty – 'to be patient with, to have patience, patience.'
ἀνέχομαιᵃ: ἀνεχόμενοι ἀλλήλων ἐν ἀγάπῃ 'be patient with one another in love' Eph 4.2.
ἀνοχή: τῆς ἀνοχῆς καὶ τῆς μακροθυμίας καταφρονεῖς; 'do you despise (his) patience and longsuffering?' Ro 2.4.

25.172 ἀνεκτός, όν: pertaining to what can be borne or endured – 'bearable, endurable, tolerable.' Τύρῳ καὶ Σιδῶνι ἀνεκτότερον ἔσται ἐν ἡμέρᾳ κρίσεως ἢ ὑμῖν 'it will be more tolerable for Tyre and Sidon on the day of judgment than for you' Mt 11.22. In some languages the expression 'more tolerable' in Mt 11.22 may be satisfactorily expressed as 'will be easier to bear' or 'the suffering will be less.'

25.173 τροποφορέω: to put up with someone or something, implying extensive patience – 'to bear with, to put up with, to be very patient with.' ὡς τεσσερακονταετῆ χρόνον ἐτροποφόρησεν αὐτοὺς ἐν τῇ ἐρήμῳ 'for forty years he put up with them in the desert' Ac 13.18.

25.174 ὑπομονή, ῆς f: capacity to continue to bear up under difficult circumstances – 'endurance, being able to endure.' τῆς ὑπομονῆς

τῆς ἐλπίδος τοῦ κυρίου ἡμῶν Ἰησοῦ Χριστοῦ 'endurance inspired by hope in our Lord Jesus Christ' 1 Th 1.3.

25.175 ὑπομένωᵈ (derivative of ὑπομονή 'endurance,' 25.174); ὑποφέρω: to continue to bear up despite difficulty and suffering – 'to endure, to bear up, to demonstrate endurance, to put up with.'
ὑπομένωᵈ: διὰ τοῦτο πάντα ὑπομένω διὰ τοὺς ἐκλεκτούς 'so I endured everything for the sake of God's chosen people' 2 Tm 2.10.
ὑποφέρω: οἵους διωγμοὺς ὑπήνεγκα 'the kinds of persecutions I endured' 2 Tm 3.11.

25.176 στέγω; φέρωˡ: to put up with annoyance or difficulty – 'to put up with, to endure.'
στέγω: ἀλλὰ πάντα στέγομεν ἵνα μή τινα ἐγκοπὴν δῶμεν τῷ εὐαγγελίῳ τοῦ Χριστοῦ 'on the contrary, we put up with everything rather than hinder the gospel of Christ' 1 Cor 9.12; διὰ τοῦτο κἀγὼ μηκέτι στέγων ἔπεμψα εἰς τὸ γνῶναι τὴν πίστιν ὑμῶν 'for this reason, when I could not any longer endure it, I sent to find out about your faith' 1 Th 3.5.
φέρωˡ: ἤνεγκεν ἐν πολλῇ μακροθυμίᾳ σκεύη ὀργῆς 'he was very patient in enduring those who were objects of his anger' Ro 9.22.

25.177 βαστάζωᶜ: (similar in meaning to ὑποφέρω 'to endure,' 25.175, but probably somewhat more emphatic in meaning) to continue to bear up under unusually trying circumstances and difficulties – 'to endure, to bear up under.' ὃν οὔτε οἱ πατέρες ἡμῶν οὔτε ἡμεῖς ἰσχύσαμεν βαστάσαι 'which neither our forefathers nor we were able to bear up under' Ac 15.10.

25.178 καρτερέω: to continue to persist in any undertaking or state – 'to persevere, to persist.' τὸν γὰρ ἀόρατον ὡς ὁρῶν ἐκαρτέρησεν 'he persevered as if he saw him who is invisible' He 11.27.

P Offend, Be Offended (25.179-25.185)

25.179 σκανδαλίζωᶜ: to cause someone to experience anger and/or shock because of what has been said or done – 'to cause someone to be offended, to offend.' ἵνα δὲ μὴ σκανδαλίσωμεν αὐτούς 'in order that we might not cause them to be offended' Mt 17.27. See discussion at 25.180.

25.180 σκανδαλίζομαι^c: to be offended because of some action – 'to be offended, to take offense.' οἶδας ὅτι οἱ Φαρισαῖοι ἀκούσαντες τὸν λόγον ἐσκανδαλίσθησαν; 'do you know that the Pharisees were offended when they heard this?' Mt 15.12. In a number of languages the equivalent of 'to be offended' is expressed idiomatically, for example, 'to be bitter against' or 'to be stung in the heart.' In some languages, however, the closest equivalent for some contexts is simply 'to be angered.'

25.181 σκάνδαλον^c, ου *n*: that which causes offense and thus arouses opposition – 'what causes offense, offense.' Χριστὸν ἐσταυρωμένον, Ἰουδαίοις μὲν σκάνδαλον 'Christ crucified, an offense to the Jews' 1 Cor 1.23; τὸ σκάνδαλον τοῦ σταυροῦ 'the offense of the cross' or 'the offense caused by preaching about the crucifixion of Jesus' Ga 5.11.

25.182 προσκόπτω^c: to take offense, with the implication of a feeling of repugnance or rejection – 'to take offense, to be offended.' ἐν ᾧ ὁ ἀδελφός σου προσκόπτει 'by means of which your Christian brother takes offense' or '. . . your fellow believer takes offense' Ro 14.21. This expression in Ro 14.21 may, however, be restructured and translated as 'which will cause your brother to become offended' or 'which will cause your brother to feel repugnance (because of what you have done).' In some instances the closest equivalent of προσκόπτω may be 'to feel bad against.'

25.183 προσκοπή^b, ῆς *f*; πρόσκομμα^b, τος *n*: an occasion or reason for taking offense – 'something to cause offense, what causes someone to be offended, offense.' προσκοπή^b: μηδεμίαν ἐν μηδενὶ διδόντες προσκοπήν 'in nothing providing an occasion for someone to take offense' 2 Cor 6.3. For other interpretations of προσκοπή in 2 Cor 6.3, see 22.14 and 88.307. πρόσκομμα^b: τὸ μὴ τιθέναι πρόσκομμα τῷ ἀδελφῷ 'to not provide an occasion for a Christian brother to take offense' Ro 14.13.

25.184 ἀπρόσκοπος^b, ον: pertaining to not causing offense – 'without causing offense, without causing trouble.' ἀπρόσκοποι καὶ Ἰουδαίοις γίνεσθε καὶ Ἕλλησιν καὶ τῇ ἐκκλησίᾳ τοῦ θεοῦ 'live in such a way as not to cause offense to the Jews and to the Greeks and to the church of God' 1 Cor 10.32.

25.185 ἐγκόπτω^b: to cause an offense to someone – 'to offend, to irritate, to trouble.' ἵνα δὲ μὴ ἐπὶ πλεῖόν σε ἐγκόπτω 'in order that I might not trouble you more' Ac 24.4.

Q Abhor[12] (25.186-25.188)

25.186 βδελύσσομαι: to strongly detest something on the basis that it is abominable – 'to abhor, to abominate.' ὁ βδελυσσόμενος τὰ εἴδωλα ἱεροσυλεῖς; 'you who abominate idols, do you rob temples?' Ro 2.22; ἀπίστοις καὶ ἐβδελυγμένοις καὶ φονεῦσιν 'traitors and the abominable and murderers' Re 21.8. It is possible that in Re 21.8 ἐβδελυγμένοις refers to sexual perverts.

25.187 βδέλυγμα, τος *n*: (derivative of βδελύσσομαι 'to abhor,' 25.186) that which is utterly detestable and abhorrent – 'what is detestable, what is abhorrent.' τὸ ἐν ἀνθρώποις ὑψηλὸν βδέλυγμα ἐνώπιον τοῦ θεοῦ 'that which is of great value to people is abhorrent in God's sight' Lk 16.15; καὶ ὁ ποιῶν βδέλυγμα καὶ ψεῦδος 'and anyone who does what is abhorrent and false' Re 21.27.

25.188 βδελυκτός, ή, όν: pertaining to one who or that which is or should be detested or regarded as abhorrent – 'detested, detestable, abominable, abhorrent.' βδελυκτοὶ ὄντες καὶ ἀπειθεῖς 'they are detestable and disobedient' Tt 1.16. In some languages 'detestable' may be rendered as 'thought to be extremely bad' or even 'that which should never even be seen.'

---

[12] The Subdomain *Abhor* (Q) may be regarded as essentially an intensive form of hate, involving both strong dislike and revulsion.

R Shame, Disgrace, Humiliation (25.189-25.202)

25.189 αἰσχύνη[a], ης *f*: a painful feeling due to the consciousness of having done or experienced something disgraceful – 'shame, disgrace.' τότε ἄρξῃ μετὰ αἰσχύνης τὸν ἔσχατον τόπον κατέχειν 'and then you will be ashamed and begin to take the lowest place' Lk 14.9. In some languages 'shame' may be referred to by a descriptive expression, for example, 'the feeling of being caught doing something bad' or 'the feeling of being seen while sinning.' In other languages 'shame' is expressed idiomatically as 'to hang the head' or 'to turn away the eyes' or 'to hide from people's stares.'

25.190 αἰσχύνομαι: (derivative of αἰσχύνη[a] 'shame,' 25.189) to feel shame or disgrace because of having done something wrong or something beneath one's dignity or social status – 'to be ashamed, to feel disgraced.' σκάπτειν οὐκ ἰσχύω, ἐπαιτεῖν αἰσχύνομαι 'I am not strong enough to dig (ditches), and I would be ashamed to beg' Lk 16.3.

25.191 αἰσχύνη[b], ης *f*: that which is or should be the source of shame or disgrace – 'that which causes shame.' ἡ δόξα ἐν τῇ αἰσχύνῃ αὐτῶν 'they glory in what they should be ashamed of' Php 3.19.

25.192 ἀνεπαίσχυντος, ον: pertaining to having no reason or need for being ashamed or feeling disgrace – 'unashamed, not feeling disgrace.' ἐργάτην ἀνεπαίσχυντον 'a workman who has no need to feel ashamed' 2 Tm 2.15.

25.193 ἐπαισχύνομαι: to experience or feel shame or disgrace because of some particular event or activity – 'to be ashamed of.'[13] τίνα οὖν καρπὸν εἴχετε τότε ἐφ᾽ οἷς νῦν ἐπαισχύνεσθε; 'what did you gain from doing the things that you are now ashamed of?' Ro 6.21; μὴ οὖν ἐπαισχυνθῇς τὸ μαρτύριον τοῦ κυρίου ἡμῶν 'then do not be ashamed of witnessing for our Lord'

or '. . . of the witness the Lord gave' 2 Tm 1.8.

25.194 καταισχύνω: to cause someone to be much ashamed – 'to humiliate, to disgrace, to put to shame.' τὰ μωρὰ τοῦ κόσμου ἐξελέξατο ὁ θεὸς ἵνα καταισχύνῃ τοὺς σοφούς 'God purposely chose what the world considers nonsense in order to put wise men to shame' 1 Cor 1.27.

25.195 ἐντροπή, ῆς *f*: a state of embarrassment resulting from what one has done or failed to do – 'embarrassment, shame.'[14] πρὸς ἐντροπὴν ὑμῖν λαλῶ 'I say this to your shame' or 'I say this in order to make you feel ashamed' 1 Cor 15.34.

25.196 ἐντρέπω: to cause someone to be embarrassed or ashamed – 'to shame, to embarrass.' οὐκ ἐντρέπων ὑμᾶς γράφω ταῦτα 'I do not write this to embarrass you' 1 Cor 4.14; μὴ συναναμίγνυσθαι αὐτῷ, ἵνα ἐντραπῇ 'have nothing to do with him, so that he will be ashamed' 2 Th 3.14.

25.197 ἀπαλγέω: to lose the capacity to feel shame or embarrassment – 'to lose a feeling of shame, to become calloused.' οἵτινες ἀπηλγηκότες ἑαυτοὺς παρέδωκαν τῇ ἀσελγείᾳ 'some, having lost all feeling of shame, gave themselves over to vice' Eph 4.19.

25.198 ταπεινόω[e]: to cause someone to become disgraced and humiliated, with the implication of embarrassment and shame – 'to humiliate, to put to shame.' ταπεινώσῃ με ὁ θεός μου πρὸς ὑμᾶς 'God will humiliate me in your presence' 2 Cor 12.21.

25.199 σωρεύω ἄνθρακας πυρὸς ἐπὶ τὴν κεφαλήν: (an idiom, literally 'to heap coals of fire on the head,' but the historical background of this idiom is not known, and hence to some extent the meaning is uncertain) to treat someone in such a positive manner as to cause that person to be ashamed or em-

---

13 ἐπαισχύνομαι appears to differ somewhat in meaning from αἰσχύνομαι (25.190) in that attention is focused upon that which causes shame.

14 ἐντροπή and ἐντρέπω (25.196) differ from αἰσχύνη[a] (25.189) and αἰσχύνομαι (25.190) in seeming to focus upon the embarrassment which is involved in the feeling of shame.

barrassed – 'to cause to be ashamed, to make ashamed.' ἀλλὰ ἐὰν πεινᾷ ὁ ἐχθρός σου, ψώμιζε αὐτόν· ἐὰν διφᾷ, πότιζε αὐτόν· τοῦτο γὰρ ποιῶν ἄνθρακας πυρὸς σωρεύσεις ἐπὶ τὴν κεφαλὴν αὐτοῦ 'but if your enemy is hungry, give him something to eat; if he is thirsty, give him something to drink; for in doing this, you will make him ashamed' Ro 12.20.

25.200 δειγματίζω; παραδειγματίζω: to cause someone to suffer public disgrace or shame – 'to disgrace in public, to put to shame.'
δειγματίζω: καὶ μὴ θέλων αὐτὴν δειγματίσαι 'and he did not want to disgrace her in public' Mt 1.19.
παραδειγματίζω: ἀνασταυροῦντας ἑαυτοῖς τὸν υἱὸν τοῦ θεοῦ καὶ παραδειγματίζοντας 'because they are crucifying again the Son of God and exposing him to public shame' He 6.6.
The expression 'to disgrace in public' may be rendered in some languages as 'to cause everyone to think bad about' or 'to cause everyone to speak in whispers about.'

25.201 θεατρίζω: to cause someone to be publicly exhibited as an object of shame or disgrace – 'to shame publicly.' τοῦτο μὲν ὀνειδισμοῖς τε καὶ θλίψεσιν θεατριζόμενοι 'you were at times exhibited as an object of shame by insults and mistreatment' He 10.33.

25.202 ἀσχημοσύνη^b, ης f: a state which is or should be regarded as causing shame – 'shameful state, shameful condition.' ἵνα μὴ γυμνὸς περιπατῇ καὶ βλέπωσιν τὴν ἀσχημοσύνην αὐτοῦ 'in order that he may not be naked and people see his shameful condition' Re 16.15.

S Pride (legitimate) (25.203-25.205)

25.203 καύχημα^d, τος n: the basis for or the content of one's feeling of legitimate pride – 'basis of pride, reason for being proud.' ἵνα τὸ καύχημα ὑμῶν περισσεύῃ ἐν Χριστῷ Ἰησοῦ ἐν ἐμοὶ 'in order that you may have every reason to be proud of me in your union with Christ Jesus' Php 1.26; καύχημα ὑμῶν ἐσμεν καθάπερ καὶ ὑμεῖς ἡμῶν 'that we may be the reason for your pride even as you are the reason for ours' or 'that you will be as proud of us as we shall be of you' 2 Cor 1.14. For another interpretation of καύχημα in 2 Cor 1.14, see 33.371.

25.204 καύχησις^c, εως f: the state of being rightfully proud – 'pride, to be proud.' πολλή μοι καύχησις ὑπὲρ ὑμῶν 'I am so proud of you' 2 Cor 7.4.

25.205 δόξα^i, ης f: the reason or basis for legitimate pride – 'pride.' ὑμεῖς γάρ ἐστε ἡ δόξα ἡμῶν καὶ ἡ χαρά 'for you are our pride and joy' 1 Th 2.20.

T Surprise, Astonish (25.206-25.222)

25.206 ξενίζομαι: (compare ξένος 'unknown, surprising,' 28.34) to experience a sudden feeling of unexpected wonder – 'to be surprised.' μὴ ξενίζεσθε τῇ ἐν ὑμῖν πυρώσει πρὸς πειρασμὸν ὑμῖν 'do not be surprised at the painful testing you are suffering' 1 Pe 4.12. The experience of 'surprise' may be expressed idiomatically in some languages, for example, 'to be left with one's mouth open' or 'to have one's eyes made wide open.'

25.207 μέγας^c, μεγάλη, μέγα: pertaining to being surprising in view of being important – 'surprising, strange.' οὐ μέγα οὖν εἰ καὶ οἱ διάκονοι αὐτοῦ μετασχηματίζονται ὡς διάκονοι δικαιοσύνης 'therefore it isn't surprising if his servants make themselves out to be servants of righteousness' 2 Cor 11.15; μέγα εἰ ἡμεῖς ὑμῶν τὰ σαρκικὰ θερίσομεν; 'is it strange if we reap material benefits from you?' 1 Cor 9.11.

25.208 θάμβος, ους n: a state of astonishment due to both the suddenness and the unusualness of the phenomenon and with either a positive or a negative reaction – 'astonishment, alarm.' θάμβος γὰρ περιέσχεν αὐτὸν καὶ πάντας τοὺς σὺν αὐτῷ ἐπὶ τῇ ἄγρᾳ τῶν ἰχθύων 'he and all those with him were astonished at the catch of fish' Lk 5.9.

25.209 θαμβέομαι: (derivative of θάμβος 'astonishment,' 25.208) to experience astonishment as the result of some unusual event – 'to be astonished, to be startled, to be amazed.' ἐθαμβήθησαν ἅπαντες, ὥστε συζητεῖν πρὸς ἑαυτοὺς λέγοντας 'the people were all so astonished that they started saying to one another . . .' Mk 1.27; ἐθαμβοῦντο, οἱ δὲ ἀκολουθοῦντες ἐφοβοῦντο 'they were astonished, while those who followed were afraid' Mk 10.32.

25.210 ἐκθαμβέομαι: to be greatly astounded, with either positive or negative reactions – 'to be amazed, to be astounded, to be alarmed.' καὶ εὐθὺς πᾶς ὁ ὄχλος ἰδόντες αὐτὸν ἐξεθαμβήθησαν 'and immediately when all the crowd saw him, they were astounded' Mk 9.15; εἶδον νεανίσκον καθήμενον ἐν τοῖς δεξιοῖς περιβεβλημένον στολὴν λευκήν, καὶ ἐξεθαμβήθησαν 'they saw a young man seated at the right wearing a white robe, and they were alarmed' Mk 16.5. In the meaning of 'alarmed,' ἐκθαμβέομαι may often be rendered simply as 'to be afraid.'

25.211 ἔκθαμβος, ον: pertaining to being astonished or alarmed – 'amazed, utterly astonished, alarmed.' συνέδραμεν πᾶς ὁ λαὸς πρὸς αὐτοὺς ἐπὶ τῇ στοᾷ τῇ καλουμένῃ Σολομῶντος ἔκθαμβοι 'all the people were astounded and ran to them on the porch that was called Solomon's Porch' Ac 3.11.

25.212 θαῦμα[a], τος n: a state of wonderment or amazement, usually with the implication of marveling – 'wonder, amazement.' ἐθαύμασα ἰδὼν αὐτὴν θαῦμα μέγα 'when I saw her, I wondered with great amazement' Re 17.6.

25.213 θαυμάζω: (derivative of θαῦμα[a] 'wonder, amazement,' 25.212) to wonder or marvel at some event or object – 'to wonder, to be amazed, to marvel' (whether the reaction is favorable or unfavorable depends on the context). ἐθαυμάσθη ὅλη ἡ γῆ ὀπίσω τοῦ θηρίου 'the whole earth marveled and followed the beast' Re 13.3; ὁ δὲ Μωϋσῆς ἰδὼν ἐθαύμαζεν τὸ ὅραμα 'Moses was amazed by what he saw' Ac 7.31.

25.214 ἐκθαυμάζω: to wonder greatly or to be very much amazed – 'to be very amazed.' καὶ ἐξεθαύμαζον ἐπ' αὐτῷ 'they were very much amazed at him' Mk 12.17.

25.215 θαυμάσιος, α, ον; θαυμαστός, ή, όν: (derivatives of θαυμάζω 'to be amazed,'

25.213) pertaining to that which causes or is worthy of amazement and wonder – 'wonderful, remarkable, marvelous.'

θαυμάσιος: ἰδόντες δὲ οἱ ἀρχιερεῖς καὶ οἱ γραμματεῖς τὰ θαυμάσια ἃ ἐποίησεν 'the chief priests and scribes saw the wonderful things he was doing' Mt 21.15.

θαυμαστός: μεγάλα καὶ θαυμαστὰ τὰ ἔργα σου 'great and marvelous are your works' Re 15.3.

25.216 θαῦμα[b], τος n: an event which causes someone to wonder or marvel – 'wonder, miracle, something to be wondered at.' καὶ οὐ θαῦμα, αὐτὸς γὰρ ὁ Σατανᾶς μετασχηματίζεται εἰς ἄγγελον φωτός 'and this is nothing to be wondered at, for Satan himself changes himself into an angel of light' 2 Cor 11.14.

25.217 ἔκστασις[a], εως f: a state of intense amazement, to the point of being beside oneself with astonishment – 'amazement, astonishment.' ἐξέστησαν εὐθὺς ἐκστάσει μεγάλῃ 'then they were beside themselves with astonishment' (literally 'they were astonished with big astonishment') Mk 5.42; ἔκστασις ἔλαβεν ἅπαντας 'astonishment seized all of them' Lk 5.26. In many languages it is simply impossible to speak of 'being beside oneself with astonishment' or 'having astonishment seize someone.' Though such expressions may seem quite appropriate in English, literal renderings of such statements may be almost totally meaningless in other languages. In Mk 5.42, for example, one may readily translate 'they were extremely astonished' or in Lk 5.26, 'they were all very much astonished.' In a number of languages, of course, astonishment is expressed in an idiomatic manner, for example, 'they had to look three times' or 'they looked but they couldn't believe.'

25.218 ἐξίσταμαι[a] (and 2nd aorist active): to be so astonished as to almost fail to comprehend what one has experienced – 'to be greatly astonished, to be astounded.' ἐξίσταντο δὲ πάντες οἱ ἀκούοντες αὐτοῦ ἐπὶ τῇ συνέσει 'all who heard him were greatly astonished at his understanding' Lk 2.47.

25.219 ἐκπλήσσομαι: to be so amazed as to be practically overwhelmed – 'to be greatly astounded.' ἐκπλησσόμενος ἐπὶ τῇ διδαχῇ τοῦ κυρίου 'for he was greatly astounded at the teaching of the Lord' Ac 13.12.

25.220 ἐξίστημι or ἐξιστάνω: to cause someone to be so astounded as to be practically overwhelmed – 'to astonish greatly, to greatly astound, to astound completely.' γυναῖκές τινες ἐξ ἡμῶν ἐξέστησαν ἡμᾶς 'some of the women of our group completely astounded us' Lk 24.22; ἐξιστάνων τὸ ἔθνος τῆς Σαμαρείας 'he astounded the people of Samaria' Ac 8.9.

25.221 συγχέω or συγχύννω: (figurative extensions of meaning of συγχέω or συγχύννω 'to pour together, to mix,' not occurring in the NT) to cause such astonishment as to bewilder and dismay – 'to cause consternation, to confound.' συνέχυννεν τοὺς Ἰουδαίους τοὺς κατοικοῦντας ἐν Δαμασκῷ 'he caused consternation among the Jews living in Damascus' Ac 9.22; συνέχεον πάντα τὸν ὄχλον 'they threw the whole crowd into consternation' Ac 21.27. It is also possible to render this expression in Ac 21.27 as 'they stirred up the whole crowd.'

25.222 στυγνάζωᶜ: to experience an emotional state of great surprise because of something which appears incredible and alarming – 'to be shocked, to be appalled.' ὁ δὲ στυγνάσας ἐπὶ τῷ λόγῳ ἀπῆλθεν λυπούμενος 'he was appalled at what was said and went away sad' Mk 10.22. For a different interpretation of στυγνάζω in Mk 10.22, see 25.286.

U Worry, Anxiety, Distress, Peace (25.223-25.250)

25.223 μέλειᵇ (only impersonal in the New Testament): to be particularly concerned about something, with the implication of some apprehension – 'to be of concern, to be anxious about.' δοῦλος ἐκλήθης; μή σοι μελέτω 'were you a slave when you were called? Don't let that concern you' 1 Cor 7.21; οὐδὲν τούτων τῷ Γαλλίωνι ἔμελεν 'none of these things were of any concern to Gallio' Ac 18.17. In a number of languages the equivalent of 'to be concerned about' may be simply 'to think about,' and the negative might be merely 'not to let something enter one's head.'

25.224 μέριμνα, ης f: a feeling of apprehension or distress in view of possible danger or misfortune – 'anxiety, worry, anxious concern.' ἡ μέριμνα πασῶν τῶν ἐκκλησιῶν 'anxious concern for all the churches' 2 Cor 11.28; πᾶσαν τὴν μέριμναν ὑμῶν ἐπιρίψαντες ἐπ' αὐτόν 'cast all your worry upon him' or 'leave all your worries with him' 1 Pe 5.7.[15] For μέριμνα as part of an idiom in 1 Pe 5.7, see 25.250.

The term μέριμνα may refer to either unnecessary worry or legitimate concern. The equivalent of 'worry' may be expressed in some languages in an idiomatic manner, for example, 'to be killed by one's mind' or 'to be pained by thinking.'

25.225 μεριμνάω: (derivative of μέριμνα 'worry,' 25.224) to have an anxious concern, based on apprehension about possible danger or misfortune – 'to be worried about, to be anxious about.' τίς δὲ ἐξ ὑμῶν μεριμνῶν δύναται ἐπὶ τὴν ἡλικίαν αὐτοῦ προσθεῖναι πῆχυν; 'can any of you live a bit longer by worrying about it?' Lk 12.25; μὴ μεριμνήσητε πῶς ἢ τί λαλήσητε 'do not worry about how or what you are going to say' Mt 10.19.

25.226 ἀμέριμνος, ον: pertaining to not being concerned or anxious – 'without worry, unworried, free from concern.' θέλω δὲ ὑμᾶς ἀμερίμνους εἶναι 'I would like you to be free from concern' 1 Cor 7.32; ὑμᾶς ἀμερίμνους ποιήσομεν 'you will have nothing to be concerned about' or 'you will not have to be worried' (literally 'we will cause you not to be worried') Mt 28.14.

25.227 προμεριμνάω: to be worried or anxious beforehand or in advance – 'to worry beforehand.' μὴ προμεριμνᾶτε τί λαλήσητε 'do not worry beforehand about what to say' Mk 13.11.

25.228 προσδοκάωᵃ: to await with apprehension concerning impending danger or trouble – 'to wait with apprehension, to wait with anxiety.' τεσσαρεσκαιδεκάτην σήμερον ἡμέραν

---

15 It is possible to interpret μέριμνα in 1 Pe 5.7 as being the context of what one worries about.

προσδοκῶντες 'having waited with apprehension for fourteen days' Ac 27.33.[16]

25.229 πυρόομαι[b]: (a figurative extension of meaning of πυρόομαι[a] 'to burn,' 14.63) to be upset, with great concern and anxiety – 'to be greatly worried, to be very distressed, to be worried and distressed.' τίς σκανδαλίζεται, καὶ οὐκ ἐγὼ πυροῦμαι; 'who is led into sin without me being worried and distressed?' or 'when someone is led into sin, I am worried and distressed' 2 Cor 11.29.

25.230 καταπονέομαι: to be distressed, with the implication of being worn out by such an experience – 'to be distressed.' Λὼτ καταπονούμενον ὑπὸ τῆς τῶν ἀθέσμων ἐν ἀσελγείᾳ ἀναστροφῆς 'Lot was distressed by the immoral conduct of lawless people' 2 Pe 2.7.

25.231 ἀνασκευάζω: to cause someone distress and worry – 'to distress, to upset.' ἐτάραξαν ὑμᾶς λόγοις ἀνασκευάζοντες τὰς ψυχὰς ὑμῶν 'they troubled and upset you by what they said' Ac 15.24.

25.232 μετεωρίζομαι: to be very concerned about, with the implication of placing too much value upon something – 'to be anxious about, to be concerned about.' καὶ ὑμεῖς μὴ ζητεῖτε τί φάγητε καὶ τί πίητε, καὶ μὴ μετεωρίζεσθε 'and do not seek (or 'attempt to find') what you will eat or what you will drink; don't be concerned about it' Lk 12.29.

25.233 σείω[b]: (a figurative extension of meaning of σείω[a] 'to shake,' 16.7) to cause extreme anxiety and apprehension, implying accompanying movement – 'to stir up, to cause an uproar, to cause great anxiety.' καὶ εἰσελθόντος αὐτοῦ εἰς Ἱεροσόλυμα ἐσείσθη πᾶσα ἡ πόλις 'and when he came into Jerusalem, the whole city was thrown into an uproar' Mt 21.10.

16 In Ac 27.33 προσδοκάω includes two significant semantic features: (1) waiting over a period of time and (2) apprehension and worry with regard to the outcome of the severe storm. It would be possible to classify προσδοκάω as simply continuing in a state over a period of time, but particularly in the context of Ac 27.33 the element of apprehension and worry seems to be dominant.

25.234 θορυβέομαι; θορυβάζομαι; τυρβάζομαι: to be emotionally upset by a concern or anxiety – 'to be troubled, to be distressed, to be upset.'
θορυβέομαι: μὴ θορυβεῖσθε, ἡ γὰρ ψυχὴ αὐτοῦ ἐν αὐτῷ ἐστιν 'don't be upset; he is still alive' Ac 20.10. It is also possible to interpret θορυβέομαι in Ac 20.10 as referring to the evident commotion caused by the fall of Eutychus from a window. Accordingly, one may translate as 'stop this commotion; he is still alive.'
θορυβάζομαι: Μάρθα Μάρθα, μεριμνᾷς καὶ θορυβάζῃ περὶ πολλά 'Martha, Martha, you are worried and troubled about many things' Lk 10.41. In Lk 10.41 the meanings of μεριμνάω (25.225) and θορυβάζομαι reinforce each other.
τυρβάζομαι: μεριμνᾷς καὶ τυρβάζῃ 'you are worried and troubled' Lk 10.41 (apparatus).

25.235 ὀδύνη, ης f: (a figurative extension of meaning of ὀδύνη 'physical pain,' not occurring in the NT) a state of severe emotional anxiety and distress – 'great distress, intense anxiety.' καὶ ἀδιάλειπτος ὀδύνη τῇ καρδίᾳ μου 'great distress in my heart is endless' Ro 9.2.

25.236 ὀδυνάομαι[b]: (derivative of ὀδύνη 'great distress,' 25.235) to experience great distress or anxiety – 'to be very much distressed, to be terribly worried.' ὁ πατήρ σου κἀγὼ ὀδυνώμενοι ἐζητοῦμέν σε 'your father and I have been terribly worried trying to find you' Lk 2.48.

25.237 ἐξαπορέομαι: to be in extreme despair, implying both anxiety and fear – 'to be in utter despair, to despair completely.' ὥστε ἐξαπορηθῆναι ἡμᾶς καὶ τοῦ ζῆν 'so that we despaired even of living' or 'so that we totally despaired of our lives' 2 Cor 1.8.

25.238 περισπάομαι: (a figurative extension of meaning of περισπάομαι 'to be drawn off from around,' not occurring in the NT) to be so overburdened by various distractions as to be worried and anxious – 'to be overburdened and worried, to be distracted and anxious.' ἡ δὲ Μάρθα περιεσπᾶτο περὶ πολλὴν διακονίαν 'Martha was overburdened and worried about so much work' or '. . . about all the work she had to do' Lk 10.40.

25.239 ἐπίστασις ᵃ, εως *f*: a state of prolonged concern and anxiety – 'pressure, concern, burden.' χωρὶς τῶν παρεκτὸς ἡ ἐπίστασίς μοι ἡ καθ' ἡμέραν, ἡ μέριμνα πασῶν τῶν ἐκκλησιῶν 'apart from other things, my daily pressure, my anxiety about all the churches' 2 Cor 11.28. For another interpretation of ἐπίστασις in 2 Cor 11.28, see 35.42.

25.240 συνοχή, ῆς *f*: a state of mental distress, involving acute anxiety – 'distress.' καὶ ἐπὶ τῆς γῆς συνοχὴ ἐθνῶν 'and upon the earth great distress of nations' Lk 21.25; ἐκ γὰρ πολλῆς θλίψεως καὶ συνοχῆς καρδίας ἔγραφα ὑμῖν 'for out of great trouble and distress of heart, I wrote to you' 2 Cor 2.4.

25.241 συνέχομαι ᵇ: to experience great psychological pressure and anxiety – 'to be distressed, to be troubled.' πῶς συνέχομαι ἕως ὅτου τελεσθῇ 'how distressed I am until it is over' Lk 12.50.

25.242 σαλεύομαι: (a figurative extension of meaning of σαλεύω 'to shake,' 16.7) to become emotionally unsettled and distraught – 'to become unsettled, to be deeply distressed, to be upset.' εἰς τὸ μὴ ταχέως σαλευθῆναι ὑμᾶς ἀπὸ τοῦ νοός 'in order that you may not be completely upset in your thinking' 2 Th 2.2; ἐκ δεξιῶν μού ἐστιν ἵνα μὴ σαλευθῶ 'he is at my right side so that I will not be upset' Ac 2.25.

25.243 τάραχος ᵇ, ου *m*: a state of acute distress and great anxiety, with the additional possible implications of dismay and confusion – 'great distress, extreme anxiety.' γενομένης δὲ ἡμέρας ἦν τάραχος οὐκ ὀλίγος ἐν τοῖς στρατιώταις, τί ἄρα ὁ Πέτρος ἐγένετο 'when morning came, there was great distress among the guards as to what had happened to Peter' Ac 12.18. Since τάραχος refers to the type of extreme anxiety which borders on fear, it may be possible in some languages to use a double expression, 'were greatly distressed and afraid.'

25.244 ταράσσω ᵇ: (a figurative extension of meaning of ταράσσω ᵃ 'to stir up,' 16.3) to cause acute emotional distress or turbulence – 'to cause great mental distress.' ἐνεβριμή-

σατο τῷ πνεύματι καὶ ἐτάραξεν ἑαυτόν 'he was deeply moved in his spirit and greatly distressed' Jn 11.33; τὸν δὲ φόβον αὐτῶν μὴ φοβηθῆτε, μηδὲ ταραχθῆτε 'do not be afraid of them and do not be distressed' 1 Pe 3.14.

25.245 ὑπωπιάζω ᵃ: to cause great annoyance to and thus to wear someone out – 'to annoy and wear out, to wear someone down by annoying.' ἵνα μὴ εἰς τέλος ἐρχομένη ὑπωπιάζῃ με 'in order that she may not keep on coming and in the end wear me out by annoying me' Lk 18.5.

25.246 διαταράσσομαι: (similar in meaning to ταράσσω ᵇ 'to cause acute distress,' 25.244, but probably somewhat more emphatic) to be mentally disturbed and thus deeply troubled – 'to be deeply troubled, to be very much upset.' ἡ δὲ ἐπὶ τῷ λόγῳ διεταράχθη 'she was deeply troubled by the (angel's) message' Lk 1.29.

25.247 ἀδημονέω: to be distressed and troubled, with the probable implication of anguish – 'to be troubled, to be upset, to be distressed.' ἀδημονῶν διότι ἠκούσατε ὅτι ἠσθένησεν 'he was very upset because you heard he was sick' Php 2.26.

25.248 εἰρήνη ᵇ, ης *f*: a state of freedom from anxiety and inner turmoil – 'peace, freedom from worry.'¹⁷ ὁ δὲ θεὸς τῆς ἐλπίδος πληρώσαι ὑμᾶς πάσης χαρᾶς καὶ εἰρήνης 'may the God of hope fill you with all joy and peace' Ro 15.13; ὁ δὲ καρπὸς τοῦ πνεύματός ἐστιν ἀγάπη, χαρά, εἰρήνη 'the fruit of the Spirit is love, joy, peace' Ga 5.22. 'Peace' in the sense of 'freedom from worry' is often expressed by means of an idiom, for example, 'to sit down in the heart,' 'to rest in the liver,' 'to be quiet in one's inner self.'

25.249 εἰρηνικός, ή, όν: pertaining to freedom from anxiety and inner turmoil – 'peaceful, free from worry.' ὕστερον δὲ καρπὸν εἰρηνικὸν τοῖς δι' αὐτῆς γεγυμνασμένοις ἀποδί-

---

17 εἰρήνη in Domain 25 pertains to a psychological state and not to a set of circumstances which may lead to peace and tranquility (see 22.42).

δωσιν δικαιοσύνης 'later those who have been disciplined by it reap the peaceful reward of a righteous life' He 12.11.

25.250 τὴν μέριμναν ἐπιρίπτω ἐπί: (an idiom, literally 'to cast cares upon') to stop worrying and to put one's trust in someone – 'to put one's cares upon, to leave one's worries to.' πᾶσαν τὴν μέριμναν ὑμῶν ἐπιρίψαντες ἐπ' αὐτόν 'put all of your cares upon him' or 'give all of your worries to him' or 'stop worrying and trust him completely' 1 Pe 5.7. For another explanation of this expression in 1 Pe 5.7 taking only ἐπιρίπτω ἐπί as an idiom, see 90.18.

V Fear, Terror, Alarm [18] (25.251-25.269)

25.251 φόβος[a], ου m: a state of severe distress, aroused by intense concern for impending pain, danger, evil, etc., or possibly by the illusion of such circumstances – 'fear.' ἀπελθοῦσαι ταχὺ ἀπὸ τοῦ μνημείου μετὰ φόβου καὶ χαρᾶς μεγάλης 'with fear and great joy they quickly left the tomb' Mt 28.8; ἐν παντὶ θλιβόμενοι – ἔξωθεν μάχαι, ἔσωθεν φόβοι 'troubled in every way, conflicts without and fears within' 2 Cor 7.5. In a number of languages there is no noun-like word for 'fear.' Accordingly, expressions containing such a noun in Greek must often be restructured so that the corresponding semantic unit may be expressed by a verb. Therefore, instead of 'fear,' one may have expressions such as 'be afraid' or 'to fear.' Instead of 'fears within' (2 Cor 7.5), one may translate 'in our hearts we were afraid.'

25.252 φοβέομαι[a]: (derivative of φόβος[a] 'fear,' 25.251) to be in a state of fearing – 'to fear, to be afraid.' καὶ ἀκούσαντες οἱ μαθηταὶ ἔπεσαν ἐπὶ πρόσωπον αὐτῶν καὶ ἐφοβήθησαν σφόδρα 'when the disciples heard this, they fell face down-

ward and were extremely afraid' Mt 17.6; καὶ μὴ φοβεῖσθε ἀπὸ τῶν ἀποκτεννόντων τὸ σῶμα 'and do not fear those who are able to kill the body' Mt 10.28; ἐφοβοῦντο γὰρ τὸν λαόν, μὴ λιθασθῶσιν 'they were afraid that the people might stone them' Ac 5.26.

25.253 ἀφόβως[a]: pertaining to being without fear – 'fearlessly, without fear, not afraid.' ἀφόβως ἐκ χειρὸς ἐχθρῶν ῥυσθέντας λατρεύειν αὐτῷ 'having been rescued from our enemies to serve him without fear' Lk 1.74; τολμᾶν ἀφόβως τὸν λόγον λαλεῖν 'dare to preach the message fearlessly' Php 1.14. An adverb such as ἀφόβως often corresponds to a clause in other languages. Accordingly, 'dare to preach the message fearlessly' must be rendered in some languages as 'dare to preach the message without being afraid of anyone.'

25.254 φόβος[b], ου m: the occasion or source of fear – 'something to be feared.' οἱ γὰρ ἄρχοντες οὐκ εἰσὶν φόβος τῷ ἀγαθῷ ἔργῳ ἀλλὰ τῷ κακῷ 'for the rulers are not a source of fear to those who do good but to those who do what is bad' Ro 13.3. φόβος in the sense of 'source of fear' is essentially a causative, so that Ro 13.3 may often be rendered as 'for the rulers do not cause those who do good to fear but cause those who do what is bad to fear.'

25.255 φοβερός, ά, όν: pertaining to something or someone who causes fear – 'fearful, causing fear.' φοβερὸν τὸ ἐμπεσεῖν εἰς χεῖρας θεοῦ ζῶντος 'it is a fearful thing to fall into the hands of the living God' He 10.31.

25.256 ἔκφοβος, ον; ἔμφοβος, ον: pertaining to being extremely afraid – 'very frightened, terrified, very much afraid.' [19]
ἔκφοβος: οὐ γὰρ ᾔδει τί ἀποκριθῇ, ἔκφοβοι γὰρ ἐγένοντο 'they were so afraid that they didn't know what to say' Mk 9.6.
ἔμφοβος: ὁ δὲ ἀτενίσας αὐτῷ καὶ ἔμφοβος γενόμενος 'he stared at (the angel) and became very much afraid' Ac 10.4.

---

18 Though in so many meanings involving worry, anxiety, and distress, there is an element of fear and apprehension (see Subdomain U, 25.223-25.250), in Subdomain V *Fear, Terror, Alarm* the focus is upon the fear and not the state of anxious worry. In Subdomain V the emotional state is significantly more acute than in the previous subdomain.

19 It is possible that ἔκφοβος and ἔμφοβος differ slightly in the intensity of fear, but this cannot be determined from existing contexts.

25.257 ἐκφοβέω: to cause someone to become terrified or very much afraid – 'to terrify, to greatly frighten.' ὡς ἂν ἐκφοβεῖν ὑμᾶς διὰ τῶν ἐπιστολῶν 'as though I am trying to terrify you with my letters' 2 Cor 10.9.

25.258 φόβητρον, ου *n*: (derivative of φόβος[a] 'fear,' 25.251) an object, event, or condition which causes fear – 'dreadful sight, terrifying happening, fearful thing.' φόβητρά τε καὶ ἀπ' οὐρανοῦ σημεῖα μεγάλα ἔσται 'there will be dreadful happenings and great signs from heaven' Lk 21.11.

25.259 τρέμω[b]: (a figurative extension of meaning of τρέμω[a] 'to tremble,' 16.6) to be so afraid as to tremble, often with the implication of awe – 'to fear, to have awesome respect for.'[20] δόξας οὐ τρέμουσιν βλασφημοῦντες 'they have no fear of the glorious beings; they slander them' 2 Pe 2.10. For another interpretation of τρέμω in 2 Pe 2.10, see 87.14.

25.260 φρίσσω: to be so afraid as to shudder or tremble – 'to shudder with fear, to be extremely afraid.'[20] τὰ δαιμόνια πιστεύουσιν καὶ φρίσσουσιν 'the demons believe and tremble with fear' Jas 2.19.

25.261 ἔντρομος[b], ον: pertaining to extreme terror or fear, often accompanied by trembling – 'trembling with fear, extremely fearful.' ἔντρομος γενόμενος προσέπεσεν τῷ Παύλῳ 'he fell trembling with fear at Paul's feet' Ac 16.29; ἔκφοβός εἰμι καὶ ἔντρομος 'I am fearful and trembling' He 12.21. In He 12.21 the meanings of ἔκφοβος (25.256) and ἔντρομος serve to reinforce each other.

25.262 θροέομαι: to be in a state of fear associated with surprise – 'to be startled.' μηδὲ θροεῖσθαι μήτε διὰ πνεύματος μήτε διὰ λόγου

20 It is possible to regard τρέμω[b] (25.259) and φρίσσω (25.260) as belonging simultaneously to two quite distinct semantic domains, the one being physiological, that is to say, a type of uncontrolled physical response because of fear or great awe, and a psychological experience of fear or terror. Since, however, it is the latter which gives rise to the former, one would seem to be more justified in treating these meanings as matters of emotive responses rather than as physiological events.

μήτε δι' ἐπιστολῆς ὡς δι' ἡμῶν, ὡς ὅτι ἐνέστηκεν ἡ ἡμέρα τοῦ κυρίου 'don't be alarmed by some prophecy, report, or letter supposed to have come from us saying that the day of the Lord has already come' 2 Th 2.2. (For the reference of διὰ πνεύματος in 2 Th 2.2, see commentaries.)

25.263 πτύρομαι: to be fearful as the result of being intimidated – 'to be afraid, to be scared, to be intimidated.' μὴ πτυρόμενοι ἐν μηδενὶ ὑπὸ τῶν ἀντικειμένων 'don't be intimidated in anything by your enemies' Php 1.28. The expression 'don't be intimidated' may be rendered in some languages as 'don't let yourself be frightened' or 'don't let anyone cause you to be afraid.'

25.264 πτοέομαι: to be terrified as the result of something which startles or alarms – 'to be very frightened, to be terrified, to be alarmed.' ὅταν δὲ ἀκούσητε πολέμους καὶ ἀκαταστασίας, μὴ πτοηθῆτε 'don't be alarmed when you hear of wars and revolutions' Lk 21.9; πτοηθέντες δὲ καὶ ἔμφοβοι γενόμενοι ἐδόκουν πνεῦμα θεωρεῖν 'they were alarmed and fearful, thinking they had seen a ghost' Lk 24.37.

25.265 πτόησις, εως *f*: (derivative of πτοέομαι 'to be terrified,' 25.264) an object, event, or condition that causes terror or alarm – 'something fearful, something alarming, something that causes one to be afraid.' μὴ φοβούμεναι μηδεμίαν πτόησιν 'don't be frightened by anything alarming' 1 Pe 3.6.

25.266 δειλία, ας *f*: a state of fear because of a lack of courage or moral strength – 'cowardice, timidity.' οὐ γὰρ ἔδωκεν ἡμῖν ὁ θεὸς πνεῦμα δειλίας 'for God has not given us a spirit of timidity' or '. . . a spirit of cowardice' 2 Tm 1.7. 'Cowardice' is often rendered by means of an idiom, for example, 'to have a fallen heart,' 'to have a soft heart,' or 'one's heart has disappeared.'

25.267 δειλιάω: to be fearful and cowardly – 'to be cowardly, to lack courage.' μὴ ταρασσέσθω ὑμῶν ἡ καρδία μηδὲ δειλιάτω 'do not let your heart be anxious; do not be cowardly' Jn 14.27.

25.268 δειλός, ή, όν: pertaining to being cowardly – 'cowardly, coward.' τοῖς δὲ δειλοῖς καὶ ἀπίστοις . . . τὸ μέρος αὐτῶν ἐν τῇ λίμνῃ τῇ καιομένῃ πυρὶ καὶ θείῳ 'but for cowards and traitors . . . the place for them is the lake burning with fire and brimstone' Re 21.8. In some languages a 'coward' is 'one who always runs' or 'one who runs away at nothing.'

25.269 ἀσθένεια^c, ας f: (a figurative extension of meaning of ἀσθένεια^a 'weakness,' 74.23) a state of timidity resulting from a lack of confidence – 'timidity, being fearful.' κἀγὼ ἐν ἀσθενείᾳ καὶ ἐν φόβῳ καὶ ἐν τρόμῳ πολλῷ ἐγενόμην πρὸς ὑμᾶς 'so when I came to you I was timid and trembling with fear' 1 Cor 2.3.

W Sorrow, Regret (25.270-25.287)

25.270 μεταμέλομαι^a: to feel regret as the result of what one has done – 'to regret, to feel sad about, to feel sorry because of.' ὅτι εἰ καὶ ἐλύπησα ὑμᾶς ἐν τῇ ἐπιστολῇ, οὐ μεταμέλομαι 'for even if that letter of mine made you sad, I do not regret (having written it)' or 'for even if I made you sad by my letter . . .' 2 Cor 7.8.

25.271 ἀμεταμέλητος, ον: (derivative of μεταμέλομαι^a 'to regret,' 25.270, with a negative prefix) pertaining to not feeling regret as the result of what one has done – 'not regretful, not feeling sorry about.' ἡ γὰρ κατὰ θεὸν λύπη μετάνοιαν εἰς σωτηρίαν ἀμεταμέλητον ἐργάζεται 'for the sadness that is used by God brings repentance leading to salvation; and there is no regret in that' 2 Cor 7.10.

25.272 λύπη^a, ης f: a state of unhappiness marked by regret as a result of what has been done – 'unhappiness, regret, sadness.' ἕκαστος καθὼς προῄρηται τῇ καρδίᾳ, μὴ ἐκ λύπης ἢ ἐξ ἀνάγκης 'each one should do as he has decided in his heart, not with regret or because of compulsion' 2 Cor 9.7.

25.273 λύπη^b, ης f: a state of mental pain and anxiety – 'sadness, sorrow, distress.' τοὺς μαθητὰς εὗρεν κοιμωμένους αὐτοὺς ἀπὸ τῆς λύπης 'he found the disciples asleep, (worn out) by their distress' Lk 22.45.

25.274 λυπέομαι: to be sad as the result of what has happened or what one has done – 'to be sad, to be distressed.' ἀλλ᾽ ὅτι ἐλυπήθητε εἰς μετάνοιαν 'but you were sad to the point of repenting' 2 Cor 7.9; ἀπῆλθεν λυπούμενος 'he left, greatly distressed' Mk 10.22.

25.275 λυπέω^b: (derivative of λύπη^b 'state of sadness,' 25.273) to cause someone to be sad, sorrowful, or distressed – 'to make sad, to sadden.' εἰ δέ τις λελύπηκεν 'if anyone has made someone sad' 2 Cor 2.5; μὴ λυπεῖτε τὸ πνεῦμα τὸ ἅγιον τοῦ θεοῦ 'don't make God's Holy Spirit sad' Eph 4.30.

25.276 συλλυπέομαι: to feel sorrow or grief together with someone or at the same time – 'to feel sorry for.' συλλυπούμενος ἐπὶ τῇ πωρώσει τῆς καρδίας αὐτῶν 'at the same time he felt sorry for them because of their willful stubbornness' Mk 3.5.

25.277 περίλυπος, ον: pertaining to being very sad or deeply distressed – 'very sad, sorrowful.' περίλυπός ἐστιν ἡ ψυχή μου ἕως θανάτου 'I am so sorrowful as to almost die' Mt 26.38.

25.278 ἀλυπότερος, α, ον: pertaining to no longer experiencing sorrow or anxiety – 'relieved of anxiety, no longer sorrowful.' ἵνα ἰδόντες αὐτὸν πάλιν χαρῆτε κἀγὼ ἀλυπότερος ὦ 'in order that seeing him you may again be joyful and I will be relieved of anxiety' Php 2.28.

25.279 τὴν ψυχὴν διέρχεται ῥομφαία: (an idiom, literally 'a sword goes through one's soul') to feel the intense pain of sorrow – 'to feel pain and sorrow, to be sorrowful and distressed.' καὶ σοῦ δὲ αὐτῆς τὴν ψυχὴν διελεύσεται ῥομφαία 'and sorrow like a sharp sword will pierce your own heart' or 'and you will feel the pain of sorrow as though a sword were piercing your heart' Lk 2.35.

25.280 ψυχὴν βασανίζω: (an idiom, literally 'to be tormented in soul') to experience mental torment involving sorrow mixed with anger – 'to experience anguish, to be tormented in one's heart.' ψυχὴν δικαίαν ἀνόμοις ἔργοις ἐβασάνιζεν 'his righteous heart was tormented by their evil deeds' (literally 'he tormented his righteous soul by their evil deeds') 2 Pe 2.8.[21]

25.281 κατανύσσομαι τὴν καρδίαν: (an idiom, literally 'to pierce the heart') to experience acute emotional distress, implying both concern and regret – 'to be greatly troubled, to be acutely distressed.' ἀκούσαντες δὲ κατενύγησαν τὴν καρδίαν 'when they heard this, they were deeply troubled' Ac 2.37.

25.282 συνθρύπτω τὴν καρδίαν: (an idiom, literally 'to break the heart') to cause great sorrow and grief – 'to make grieve, to break one's heart.' τί ποιεῖτε κλαίοντες καὶ συνθρύπτοντές μου τὴν καρδίαν; 'what are you doing, crying and breaking my heart?' Ac 21.13. It is rare that one can reproduce in a literal form the idiom συνθρύπτω τὴν καρδίαν. A frequent equivalent of 'to break one's heart' is 'to cause one to cry.' In some languages one may even have 'to cause one's heart to cry.'

25.283 ἀγωνία, ας f: a state of great mental and emotional grief and anxiety – 'anguish, intense sorrow.' ἐν ἀγωνίᾳ ἐκτενέστερον προσηύχετο 'in anguish he prayed even more fervently' Lk 22.44.

25.284 πικρῶς: pertaining to feeling mental agony – 'bitterly, with agony.' ἐξελθὼν ἔξω ἔκλαυσεν πικρῶς 'he went out and wept bitterly' Mt 26.75.

25.285 καταπίνομαι λύπῃ: (an idiom, literally 'to be swallowed up by grief') to be so overcome with grief as to despair – 'to grieve to the point of giving up, to grieve and despair.' [22] μή πως τῇ περισσοτέρᾳ λύπῃ καταποθῇ ὁ τοιοῦτος 'in order that somehow he may not so despair as to give up completely' 2 Cor 2.7.

---

21 Though the Greek term ψυχή is usually glossed as 'soul,' it is often more equivalent in meaning to 'heart' in English. In 2 Pe 2.8 the subject is Lot as a righteous person.

22 In view of the element of despair in the idiom καταπίνομαι λύπῃ, it would be possible to classify this meaning under Subdomain X *Discouragement*.

25.286 στυγνάζω[b]: to experience an emotional state of both grief and discouragement, as evidenced in the appearance of one's face – 'to be downcast, to look gloomy.' ὁ δὲ στυγνάσας ἐπὶ τῷ λόγῳ ἀπῆλθεν λυπούμενος 'because of that statement, he was downcast and went away sad' Mk 10.22. It is also possible to understand στυγνάζω in Mk 10.22 as meaning 'to be shocked, to be appalled' (see 25.222).

25.287 σκυθρωπός, ή, όν: pertaining to being sad and discouraged – 'sad, gloomy.' μὴ γίνεσθε ὡς οἱ ὑποκριταὶ σκυθρωποί 'do not put on a gloomy face as the hypocrites do' Mt 6.16.

X Discouragement (25.288-25.296)

25.288 ἐγκακέω; ἐκλύομαι[b]: to lose one's motivation to accomplish some valid goal – 'to become discouraged, to lose heart, to give up.'
ἐγκακέω: μὴ ἐγκακήσητε καλοποιοῦντες 'don't be discouraged in doing good' 2 Th 3.13; διὸ αἰτοῦμαι μὴ ἐγκακεῖν ἐν ταῖς θλίψεσίν μου ὑπὲρ ὑμῶν 'as I suffer difficulties on your behalf, I ask you not to give up' Eph 3.13. In place of a negative expression such as 'not to give up,' it may be better in some languages to use a positive equivalent, for example, 'to keep on' or 'to continue.'
ἐκλύομαι[b]: καιρῷ γὰρ ἰδίῳ θερίσομεν μὴ ἐκλυόμενοι 'for if we do not give up, the time will come when we will harvest' Ga 6.9; μηδὲ ἐκλύου ὑπ' αὐτοῦ ἐλεγχόμενος 'do not be discouraged when he rebukes you' He 12.5.

25.289 κοπιάω[c]: (a figurative extension of meaning of κοπιάω[b] 'to be tired,' 23.78) to become emotionally fatigued and discouraged – 'to give up, to lose heart.' ἐβάστασας διὰ τὸ ὄνομά μου, καὶ οὐ κεκοπίακες 'you have suffered for my sake and have not given up' Re 2.3.

25.290 ὀλιγόψυχος, ον: pertaining to having limited or diminished motivation for the attainment of some goal – 'fainthearted, discouraged, losing heart.' παραμυθεῖσθε τοὺς ὀλιγοψύχους 'encourage those who are losing heart' 1 Th 5.14. The expression 'those who are losing heart' is semantically negative, but can be expressed in a more specifically negative form in some languages, for example, 'those who do not have courage' or 'those whose hearts are not strong.'

25.291 κάμνω τῇ ψυχῇ: (an idiom, literally 'to become tired in spirit') to gradually lose one's motivation to accomplish some goal – 'to become discouraged, to become tired of.' μὴ κάμητε ταῖς ψυχαῖς ὑμῶν ἐκλυόμενοι 'do not let yourselves become discouraged or give up' He 12.3.

25.292 ἀθυμέω: to be or to become disheartened and hence lack motivation – 'to become discouraged, to be disheartened.' οἱ πατέρες, μὴ ἐρεθίζετε τὰ τέκνα ὑμῶν, ἵνα μὴ ἀθυμῶσιν 'parents, do not irritate your children, or they will become disheartened' Col 3.21.

25.293 ἀποψύχω[b]: (a figurative extension of meaning of ἀποψύχω[a] 'to faint,' 23.184) to become totally disheartened and thus ready to give up – 'to be totally disheartened, to be completely discouraged, to lose heart.' ἀπο-ψυχόντων ἀνθρώπων ἀπὸ φόβου 'people giving up because of fear' Lk 21.26. For another interpretation of ἀποψύχω in Lk 21.26, see 23.184.

25.294 ῥίπτομαι: (a figurative extension of meaning of ῥίπτω[a] 'to throw,' 15.217) to be or to become dejected, with a possible implication of loss of hope – 'to be dejected, to be discouraged.' ἦσαν ἐσκυλμένοι καὶ ἐρριμμένοι 'they were harassed and dejected' Mt 9.36.[23]

25.295 ταπεινός[a], ή, όν: (compare ταπεινός[c] 'of low status,' 87.61) pertaining to being discouraged and lacking in hope, with the possible implication of some association with low social status – 'dejected, downhearted, downcast.' ἀλλ' ὁ παρακαλῶν τοὺς ταπεινοὺς παρεκάλεσεν ἡμᾶς ὁ θεός 'but God who encourages the downhearted has encouraged us' 2 Cor 7.6.

25.296 κατήφεια, ας f: a state of mental gloominess and dejection – 'gloom, depression.' ὁ γέλως ὑμῶν εἰς πένθος μετατραπήτω καὶ ἡ χαρὰ εἰς κατήφειαν 'change your laughter into mourning and your joy into gloom' Jas 4.9. In a number of languages it may be extremely difficult to speak of 'changing' one activity into another or one state into another, and so this expression in Jas 4.9 must often be rendered as 'instead of laughing, mourn, and instead of being happy, become sad.'

23 It is also possible to understand ἐρριμμένοι in Mt 9.36 as meaning 'helpless.'

26 Psychological Faculties

26.1 ὁ ἔσω (ἄνθρωπος); ὁ ἐν τῷ κρυπτῷ (ἄνθρωπος): (idioms, literally 'the inner person' and 'the hidden person') the psychological faculty, including intellectual, emotional, and spiritual aspects, in contrast with the purely physical aspects of human existence – 'the inner being, the inmost being, inwardly.'
ὁ ἔσω (ἄνθρωπος): συνήδομαι γὰρ τῷ νόμῳ τοῦ θεοῦ κατὰ τὸν ἔσω ἄνθρωπον 'for in my inner being I delight in God's law' Ro 7.22; ἀλλ' εἰ καὶ ὁ ἔξω ἡμῶν ἄνθρωπος διαφθείρεται, ἀλλ' ὁ ἔσω ἡμῶν ἀνακαινοῦται ἡμέρα καὶ ἡμέρα 'but if our physical being is decaying, yet our inner being is renewed day by day' 2 Cor 4.16.
ὁ ἐν τῷ κρυπτῷ (ἄνθρωπος): ἀλλ' ὁ ἐν τῷ κρυπτῷ Ἰουδαῖος 'but he is a Jew who is one inwardly' or '. . . in the heart' Ro 2.29. A strictly literal rendering of ἀλλ' ὁ ἐν τῷ κρυπτῷ Ἰουδαῖος might be misunderstood in Ro 2.29 to refer only to the fact of circumcision, which would be something which would normally not be evident.
In a number of languages it is quite impossible to speak of the psychological faculty of a person as being merely 'that which is within.' It is frequently necessary to refer to a particular organ of the body, for example, 'the

heart' or 'the liver' or 'the spleen.' In some languages, however, one may refer to this faculty as being 'the person who stands inside' or 'the real person' or even 'the other person.'

In Lk 17.21 the phrase ἐντὸς ὑμῶν in the statement ἰδοὺ γὰρ ἡ βασιλεία τοῦ θεοῦ ἐντὸς ὑμῶν ἐστιν 'look, God's reign is within you' may constitute a reference to the same inner being designated by the phrases ὁ ἔσω and ὁ ἐν τῷ κρυπτῷ. On this basis some scholars have suggested that the phrase ἐντὸς ὑμῶν can be interpreted as a potentiality for participation and hence be translated 'within your grasp,' but it is more likely that one should understand the phrase ἐντὸς ὑμῶν in Lk 17.21 as a spacial relationship, for example, 'in your midst' or 'among you' (see 83.9).

26.2 ἔσωθεν ᶜ: (a figurative extension of meaning of ἔσωθεν ᵃ 'from inside,' 84.14) the inner being of a person as the source or agent of thought or behavior – 'a person's inner self, the inner being, within oneself.' πάντα ταῦτα τὰ πονηρὰ ἔσωθεν ἐκπορεύεται καὶ κοινοῖ τὸν ἄνθρωπον 'all these evil things come from one's inner being and make that person unclean' Mk 7.23; ἔσωθεν δέ εἰσιν λύκοι ἅρπαγες 'but in their inner being they are like vicious wolves' Mt 7.15.

A literal translation of ἔσωθεν δέ εἰσιν λύκοι ἅρπαγες in Mt 7.15 as 'on the inside they are ravaging wolves' could be seriously misleading, since in some cultures certain people are regarded as actually being animals but disguised as human beings. It may therefore be necessary to make some adjustments in this passage and to translate as 'but what they want to do makes them like wild wolves' or 'but their minds are like the minds of wild wolves.' On the other hand, one could employ a strictly literal translation and then have a footnote indicating that this statement in the Scriptures does not confirm local beliefs concerning animals disguised as humans.

26.3 καρδία ᵃ, ας f: (a figurative extension of meaning of καρδία 'heart,' not occurring in the NT in its literal sense) the causative source of a person's psychological life in its various aspects, but with special emphasis upon thoughts – 'heart, inner self, mind.'[1] ἀγαπήσεις κύριον τὸν θεόν σου ἐν ὅλῃ τῇ καρδίᾳ σου 'you shall love the Lord your God with your whole heart' Mt 22.37; τὰ κρυπτὰ τῆς καρδίας αὐτοῦ φανερὰ γίνεται 'the secret thoughts of his heart will be brought into the open' 1 Cor 14.25; ἕκαστος καθὼς προῄρηται τῇ καρδίᾳ 'each person (should give) what he has decided in his heart' 2 Cor 9.7; κατὰ δὲ τὴν σκληρότητά σου καὶ ἀμετανόητον καρδίαν θησαυρίζεις σεαυτῷ ὀργὴν ἐν ἡμέρᾳ ὀργῆς 'because of your stubbornness and your unrepentant heart, you are storing up wrath against yourself for the day of wrath' Ro 2.5.

It is often possible to render καρδία ᵃ by a number of different terms depending upon the immediate context, for example, 'mind,' 'intention,' 'purpose,' or 'desire.' In many languages it is quite impossible to use a term meaning 'heart,' since such a term may not lend itself to figurative extension in meaning. Often the equivalent of καρδία is 'liver,' while in a number of languages it is 'stomach' or 'bowels.'

26.4 ψυχή ᵃ, ῆς f: the essence of life in terms of thinking, willing, and feeling – 'inner self, mind, thoughts, feelings, heart, being.' μιᾷ ψυχῇ συναθλοῦντες τῇ πίστει τοῦ εὐαγγελίου 'with one mind, struggling together for the faith of the gospel' Php 1.27. It is also possible to render ψυχή in Php 1.27 as 'purpose' or 'desire,' for ψυχή focuses upon the total psychological being involved in struggling for the faith.

ψυχή ᵃ is often glossed as 'heart' or 'desire.' Compare the following: περίλυπός ἐστιν ἡ ψυχή μου ἕως θανάτου 'my heart is sorrowful even to the point of death' Mt 26.38; ἵνα μὴ κάμητε ταῖς ψυχαῖς ὑμῶν ἐκλυόμενοι 'so do not let your hearts become discouraged and give up' He 12.3 (for ψυχή in the idiom κάμνω τῇ ψυχῇ, see 25.291); ἀλλ' ὡς δοῦλοι Χριστοῦ ποιοῦντες τὸ θέλημα τοῦ θεοῦ ἐκ ψυχῆς 'but

---

1 Though in English the term 'heart' focuses primarily upon the emotive aspects of life, in the Greek NT the emphasis is more upon the result of thought, particularly in view of the relationship of καρδία to the Hebrew term *lēb*, which, though literally meaning 'heart,' refers primarily to the mind.

with all your heart, do what God wants, as slaves of Christ' Eph 6.6. In these passages, however, ψυχή refers really to the entire being of a person, so that Mt 26.38 may very well be rendered as 'my sorrow is so great it almost kills me.' He 12.3 may also be rendered as 'so do not let yourselves become discouraged and give up,' and Eph 6.6 may be appropriately rendered as 'but with your whole being, do what God wants, as slaves of Christ.'

The meaning of ψυχή in the sense of the person as an individual is treated under ψυχή^c (9.20) as, for example, in Mt 11.29 (εὑρήσετε ἀνάπαυσιν ταῖς ψυχαῖς ὑμῶν 'you will find rest for yourselves').

Even in those contexts in which ψυχή refers to existence beyond death, it may be referring figuratively to the person. For example, in Ac 2.27 (οὐκ ἐγκαταλείψεις τὴν ψυχήν μου εἰς ᾅδην) one may translate 'you will not abandon my soul to Hades' or 'you will not abandon me to the grave.'

It is important to distinguish ψυχή^a, signifying a psychological faculty, from ψυχή^b, meaning 'physical life, life principle' (23.88). Note, for example, the occurrence of ψυχή^b in He 4.12 (διϊκνούμενος ἄχρι μερισμοῦ ψυχῆς καὶ πνεύματος 'it cuts all the way through to where physical life and spirit meet'). Note also the occurrence of ψυχή^b in 1 Th 5.23 (αὐτὸς δὲ ὁ θεὸς τῆς εἰρήνης ἁγιάσαι ὑμᾶς ὁλοτελεῖς, καὶ ὁλόκληρον ὑμῶν τὸ πνεῦμα καὶ ἡ ψυχὴ καὶ τὸ σῶμα ἀμέμπτως ἐν τῇ παρουσίᾳ τοῦ κυρίου ἡμῶν Ἰησοῦ Χριστοῦ τηρηθείη 'may the God who gives us peace make you holy in every way and keep your whole being – spirit, life, and body – free from all fault at the coming of our Lord Jesus Christ').

In certain contexts ψυχή would appear to be in contrast with καρδία (26.3) and διάνοια (26.14) as, for example, in Mt 22.37 (ἀγαπήσεις κύριον τὸν θεόν σου ἐν ὅλῃ τῇ καρδίᾳ σου καὶ ἐν ὅλῃ τῇ ψυχῇ σου καὶ ἐν ὅλῃ τῇ διανοίᾳ σου 'you shall love the Lord your God with all your heart and soul and mind'). Because of the three terms, some have insisted that there must be at least three quite different parts of human personality. Others, however, have concluded that instead of being three parts of personality, these are only three different perspectives which one may employ in thinking

about or describing human personality. Still others would contend that the use of the three terms, καρδία, ψυχή, and διάνοια, only emphasizes the totality of human personality, and no clear-cut distinctions can possibly be made. Certainly the referents involve considerable overlapping. One could translate with complete justification Mt 22.37 as 'you shall love the Lord your God with all your heart and life and mind.' In fact, in many languages it is impossible to distinguish satisfactorily between καρδία, ψυχή, and διάνοια, and therefore it may be necessary to translate as 'you shall love the Lord your God with all that you desire and with all that you think' or 'you must love the Lord your God with all your being.'

26.5 ἰσόψυχος, ον: pertaining to being of the same mind or attitude – 'having the same mind, similarly minded, of the same attitude.' οὐδένα γὰρ ἔχω ἰσόψυχον ὅστις γνησίως τὰ περὶ ὑμῶν μεριμνήσει 'for I have no one of the same mind who really is concerned for you' Php 2.20. In a number of languages ἰσόψυχος may be rendered as 'one who thinks the same way' or possibly 'one who has the same feelings about.' In the latter instance, 'feelings' would be the equivalent of 'attitude.'

26.6 σύμψυχος, ον: pertaining to similarity of attitude and spirit – 'harmonious, united in spirit, being one in spirit.' τὴν αὐτὴν ἀγάπην ἔχοντες, σύμψυχοι 'having the same love and being one in spirit' Php 2.2.

26.7 σάρξ^f, σαρκός f: the psychological aspect of human nature which contrasts with the spiritual nature; in other words, that aspect of human nature which is characterized by or reflects typical human reasoning and desires in contrast with those aspects of human thought and behavior which relate to God and the spiritual life – 'human nature, human aspects, natural, human.' οὐ πολλοὶ σοφοὶ κατὰ σάρκα 'few of you were wise from a human point of view' 1 Cor 1.26; φανερὰ δέ ἐστιν τὰ ἔργα τῆς σαρκός 'what human nature does is quite plain' Ga 5.19; ὁ σπείρων εἰς τὴν σάρκα ἑαυτοῦ 'he who plants in the area of his human, natural desire' Ga 6.8.

Some scholars understand the meaning of

σάρξ[f] as being a person's 'lower nature' rather than simply 'human nature,' but the distinction between lower nature and higher nature seems to be primarily one arising out of typical Greek thought rather than out of the Semitic background which seems to be so pervasive in the use of the term σάρξ in such contexts in the NT. There are, of course, contexts in which σάρξ does refer to that psychological factor in man which serves as a willing instrument of sin and is subject to sin.

26.8 σαρκικός[a], ή, όν; σάρκινος[b], η, ον: pertaining to what is human or characteristic of human nature – 'human, natural.'
σαρκικός[a]: οὐκ ἐν σοφίᾳ σαρκικῇ ἀλλ' ἐν χάριτι θεοῦ 'not with human wisdom, but by the grace of God' 2 Cor 1.12.
σάρκινος[b]: ὃς οὐ κατὰ νόμον ἐντολῆς σαρκίνης γέγονεν ἀλλὰ κατὰ δύναμιν ζωῆς ἀκαταλύτου 'who became (a priest) not by human rules and regulations but by the power of a life which never ends' He 7.16. For another interpretation of σάρκινος in He 7.16, see 9.13.

26.9 πνεῦμα[e], τος *n*: the non-material, psychological faculty which is potentially sensitive and responsive to God (πνεῦμα[e] contrasts with σάρξ[f], 26.7, as an expression of the divine in contrast with the purely human) – 'spirit, spiritual, spiritual nature, inner being.' ἐν δὲ ταῖς Ἀθήναις ἐκδεχομένου αὐτοὺς τοῦ Παύλου, παρωξύνετο τὸ πνεῦμα αὐτοῦ ἐν αὐτῷ θεωροῦντος κατείδωλον οὖσαν τὴν πόλιν 'while Paul was waiting for them in Athens, his spirit was greatly distressed to see that the city was full of idols' Ac 17.16; εὐθὺς ἐπιγνοὺς ὁ Ἰησοῦς τῷ πνεύματι αὐτοῦ ὅτι οὕτως διαλογίζονται ἐν ἑαυτοῖς 'immediately Jesus knew in his spirit that this is what they were thinking in themselves' Mk 2.8; τίς γὰρ οἶδεν ἀνθρώπων τὰ τοῦ ἀνθρώπου εἰ μὴ τὸ πνεῦμα τοῦ ἀνθρώπου τὸ ἐν αὐτῷ 'as for a man, it is his own spirit within him that knows all about him' 1 Cor 2.11; εἰ γὰρ καὶ τῇ σαρκὶ ἀλλὰ τῷ πνεύματι σὺν ὑμῖν εἰμι 'for even though I am absent in body, yet I am with you in spirit' Col 2.5; παραδοῦναι τὸν τοιοῦτον τῷ Σατανᾷ εἰς ὄλεθρον τῆς σαρκός, ἵνα τὸ πνεῦμα σωθῇ ἐν τῇ ἡμέρᾳ τοῦ κυρίου 'you are to hand this man over to Satan for his body to be destroyed, so that his spirit may be saved in the day of the Lord' 1 Cor 5.5.

A special problem is posed by the phrase πνεῦμα ἁγιωσύνης in Ro 1.4. Some persons have assumed that this phrase is merely a lexical alternative for πνεῦμα ἅγιον 'Holy Spirit,' but this hardly seems to be the case, especially since κατὰ πνεῦμα ἁγιωσύνης is in structural contrast with κατὰ σάρκα (Ro 1.3). The phrase κατὰ σάρκα seems to be best interpreted as referring to the humanity of Jesus, and therefore in contrast κατὰ πνεῦμα ἁγιωσύνης may perhaps be best interpreted as his 'divine holiness' or rather his 'holy spiritual being.' Accordingly, the relevant elements in Ro 1.3b-4 may be rendered as 'as to his humanity, he was born a descendant of David, but as to his divine nature, he was shown with great power to be the Son of God by being raised from death.'

There are often a number of serious problems involved in obtaining a satisfactory term for translating πνεῦμα[e]. In a few instances one can use a more or less literal equivalent, namely 'breath,' and in other instances the appropriate equivalent is a derived term meaning 'that which doesn't die.' In some instances the equivalent is 'the person who isn't seen,' meaning that part of the person which is never visible. In order to emphasize the non-material aspects of πνεῦμα[e], some persons have used terms which actually refer to ghosts, but this should be avoided. In a number of languages a clear distinction is made between (1) the spirit that dwells within a person during one's lifetime and (2) that spirit which leaves a person and passes on into the next world. In a number of contexts one must make certain that the appropriate term is used; otherwise, there is not only extreme confusion but serious misunderstanding.

26.10 πνευματικός[b], ή, όν; πνευματικῶς[b]: pertaining to the spiritual nature or being of a person – 'spiritual, of the spirit, on a spiritual basis, in a spiritual manner.'
πνευματικός[b]: ὁ εὐλογήσας ἡμᾶς ἐν πάσῃ εὐλογίᾳ πνευματικῇ 'who blessed us with every spiritual blessing' Eph 1.3. It is also possible to interpret πνευματικός in Eph 1.3 as referring to 'the Holy Spirit,' that is to say, these

blessings would be those which come from the Spirit of God (see 12.21).

In Ro 15.27 (εἰ γὰρ τοῖς πνευματικοῖς αὐτῶν ἐκοινώνησαν τὰ ἔθνη, ὀφείλουσιν καὶ ἐν τοῖς σαρχικοῖς λειτουργῆσαι αὐτοῖς) πνευματικός stands in contrast to σαρχικός[b] 'material' (79.1) and may therefore focus upon non-material or spiritual aspects of human personality or life in contrast with the physical aspects. Accordingly, one may translate Ro 15.27 as 'if the Gentiles shared in their spiritual benefits, they ought to help them with material things.' It is also possible, however, to understand πνευματικός in Ro 15.27 as referring to those blessings which come from the Holy Spirit (see 12.21) rather than those blessings which are for the human spirit. The terms πνευματικός, ψυχικός, σαρχικός, and σάρχινος reflect considerable overlapping in meaning; see also 26.8 and 79.1-79.6.

πνευματικῶς[b]: μωρία γὰρ αὐτῷ ἐστιν, καὶ οὐ δύναται γνῶναι, ὅτι πνευματικῶς ἀνακρίνεται 'they are foolishness to him and he cannot understand (them), because they can be judged only on a spiritual basis' or '. . . in a spiritual manner' 1 Cor 2.14. For another interpretation of πνευματικῶς in 1 Cor 2.14, see 12.21.

26.11 σπλάγχνα[b], ων n; κοιλία[c], ας f; νεφρός, οῦ m: (figurative extensions of meaning of σπλάγχνα[a] 'intestines,' 8.58; κοιλία[a] 'belly,' 8.67; and νεφρός 'kidney,' not occurring in its literal meaning in the NT) the psychological faculty of desire, intent, and feeling – 'heart, feelings, desires.'[2]

σπλάγχνα[b]: ἐνδύσασθε . . . σπλάγχνα οἰκτιρμοῦ 'you must clothe yourselves . . . with a capacity for compassion' or '. . . ability to feel compassion' Col 3.12.

κοιλία[c]: ποταμοὶ ἐκ τῆς κοιλίας αὐτοῦ ῥεύσουσιν ὕδατος ζῶντος 'streams of living water will pour out of his heart' Jn 7.38.

νεφρός: ἐγώ εἰμι ὁ ἐραυνῶν νεφροὺς καὶ καρδίας 'I am he who searches people's feelings and desires' Re 2.23.

Though some persons have attempted to distinguish between σπλάγχνα[b], κοιλία[c], and νεφρός, it is extremely doubtful whether this is really possible or practical. The semantic focus in the use of these terms is clearly the deeper and more intimate feelings and emotions. In some languages one can use a term which literally means 'belly' or 'bowels,' but more often than not, these emotions are associated with some particular organ of the body such as heart, spleen, liver, etc. Rather, however, than attempting to employ a figurative expression which may or may not be fully equivalent, it is often preferable to refer to the emotional content by using terms such as 'feelings,' 'intents,' 'desires,' or 'compassion,' depending upon the context.

26.12 ὁρμή, ῆς f: (a figurative extension of meaning of ὁρμή 'rushing motion,' not occurring in the NT) the psychological faculty of will and impulse – 'will, impulse, desire.' ὅπου ἡ ὁρμὴ τοῦ εὐθύνοντος βούλεται 'wherever the will of the pilot wants it' Jas 3.4. This clause in Jas 3.4 may also be rendered simply as 'wherever the pilot wants it to go.'

26.13 συνείδησις[b], εως f: (contrast συνείδησις[a] 'knowledge about something,' 28.4) the psychological faculty which can distinguish between right and wrong – 'moral sensitivity, conscience.' συμμαρτυρούσης αὐτῶν τῆς συνειδήσεως καὶ μεταξὺ ἀλλήλων τῶν λογισμῶν κατηγορούντων ἢ καὶ ἀπολογουμένων 'their consciences also show that this is true, since their thoughts sometimes accuse them and sometimes defend them' Ro 2.15.

In some languages συνείδησις[b] may be rendered as 'the inner voice' or 'the voice in one's heart' or 'how one knows right from wrong.' In some instances συνείδησις[b] may be equivalent to some organ of the body, for example, heart or liver, but generally some descriptive phrase proves to be the most satisfactory equivalent.

26.14 νοῦς[a], νοός, νοΐ, νοῦν m; νόημα[a], τος n; διάνοια[a], ας f: the psychological faculty

---

2 It would be possible to treat σπλάγχνα[b], κοιλία[c], and νεφρός in this figurative sense in Domain 25 *Attitudes and Emotions,* but these meanings have been assigned to this domain of *Psychological Faculties* since the meanings involve aspects of personality which function as agents or presumed locations of psychological dispositions.

of understanding, reasoning, thinking, and deciding – 'mind.'

νοῦς^a: ἐὰν γὰρ προσεύχωμαι γλώσσῃ, τὸ πνεῦμά μου προσεύχεται, ὁ δὲ νοῦς μου ἄκαρπός ἐστιν 'for if I pray in a strange tongue, my spirit indeed prays, but my mind has no part in it' 1 Cor 14.14; αὐτὸς ἐγὼ τῷ μὲν νοΐ δουλεύω νόμῳ θεοῦ 'by myself I can serve God's law with my mind' Ro 7.25.

νόημα^a: φοβοῦμαι δὲ . . . φθαρῇ τὰ νοήματα ὑμῶν 'I am afraid that . . . your minds will be corrupted' 2 Cor 11.3; ἡ εἰρήνη τοῦ θεοῦ ἡ ὑπερέχουσα πάντα νοῦν φρουρήσει τὰς καρδίας ὑμῶν καὶ τὰ νοήματα ὑμῶν ἐν Χριστῷ Ἰησοῦ 'God's peace which is far beyond all human capacity for understanding will keep your hearts and minds safe in Christ Jesus' Php 4.7.

διάνοια^a: ἐσκοτωμένοι τῇ διανοίᾳ ὄντες 'whose minds are in the dark' Eph 4.18.

In some languages there is no noun such as English *mind*, and therefore one must use a verb expression meaning 'to think,' 'to reason,' or 'to understand,' depending upon the particular context. In some languages the closest equivalent of 'mind' may be a figurative extension of a term meaning 'head,' but more often than not, thinking is regarded as being in some other part of the body, for example, 'heart' or 'liver.'

26.15 φρήν, φρενός *f*; φρόνησις^a, εως *f*; φρόνημα, τος *n*: the psychological faculty of thoughtful planning, often with the implication of being wise and provident – 'thoughtful planning, way of thinking, outlook.'

φρήν: ἀδελφοί, μὴ παιδία γίνεσθε ταῖς φρεσίν 'do not be like children in the way you think, Christian brothers' 1 Cor 14.20.

φρόνησις^a: ἐπιστρέψαι . . . ἀπειθεῖς ἐν φρονήσει δικαίων 'he will turn . . . the disobedient people back to the way of thinking of righteous people' Lk 1.17.

φρόνημα: τὸ γὰρ φρόνημα τῆς σαρκὸς θάνατος 'for to those whose outlook is formed by their human nature, death is the result' Ro 8.6.

26.16 φρονέω^a: (derivative of the base φρον- 'thoughtful planning,' 26.15) to employ one's faculty for thoughtful planning, with emphasis upon the underlying disposition or attitude – 'to have an attitude, to think in a particular manner.' τοῦτο φρονεῖτε ἐν ὑμῖν ὃ καὶ ἐν Χριστῷ Ἰησοῦ 'the attitude you should have is the one that Christ Jesus had' Php 2.5. In some instances it may be appropriate to render Php 2.5 as 'you should think the way Christ Jesus did' or 'how Jesus Christ thought about things is the way you should think about them' (in which a term meaning 'things' would refer to events and not simply to material objects). It is also possible to understand φρονέω in Php 2.5 as referring specifically to the attitude of people to one another.

27 Learn[1]

Outline of Subdomains

A   Learn (27.1-27.26)

27.1 εὑρίσκω^b: to learn something previously not known, frequently involving an element of surprise – 'to learn, to find out, to discover.' ζητεῖν τὸν θεὸν εἰ ἄρα γε ψηλαφήσειαν

1 In English the term *learn* is used in two principal senses: (1) to acquire information and (2) to acquire understanding. This latter area of meaning is treated in Domain 32 *Understand*.

αὐτὸν καὶ εὕροιεν 'to seek God and perhaps find him as they were groping around for him' Ac 17.27; συνεψήφισαν τὰς τιμὰς αὐτῶν καὶ εὗρον ἀργυρίου μυριάδας πέντε 'they calculated their value and discovered that they had been worth fifty thousand (drachmas)' Ac 19.19; οὐχ εὕρισκον τὸ τί ποιήσωσιν 'but they could not find out how to do it' Lk 19.48.

27.2 γινώσκω[b]: to acquire information by whatever means, but often with the implication of personal involvement or experience – 'to learn, to find out.' καὶ γνόντες λέγουσιν, Πέντε 'and when they found out, they told him, Five (loaves)' Mk 6.38.

27.3 διαγινώσκω[a]: to obtain accurate and thorough information about – 'to learn about accurately, to get detailed information, to examine thoroughly.'[2] ὅπως καταγάγῃ αὐτὸν εἰς ὑμᾶς ὡς μέλλοντας διαγινώσκειν ἀκριβέστερον τὰ περὶ αὐτοῦ 'that he may bring him down to you on the basis that you want to obtain more accurate information about him' Ac 23.15.

27.4 εἰς ἐπίγνωσιν ἔρχομαι[a]: (an idiom, literally 'to come into knowledge') to acquire information about something, with emphasis upon the process involved – 'to learn about, to find out, to come to know.' ὃς πάντας ἀνθρώπους θέλει σωθῆναι καὶ εἰς ἐπίγνωσιν ἀληθείας ἐλθεῖν 'who wants all people to be saved and to learn the truth' 1 Tm 2.4. It is also possible to treat the phrase εἰς ἐπίγνωσιν ἔρχομαι as meaning 'to come to know' in the sense of 'to come to understand' (see 32.17).

27.5 ὁράω[f]; **συνοράω**[a]: to acquire information, with focus upon the event of perception – 'to learn about, to find out about.'
ὁράω[f]: ἐραύνησον καὶ ἴδε ὅτι ἐκ τῆς Γαλιλαίας προφήτης οὐκ ἐγείρεται 'search and learn that from Galilee no prophet ever arises' Jn 7.52.
συνοράω[a]: συνιδόντες κατέφυγον εἰς τὰς πόλεις τῆς Λυκαονίας 'when they learned about it, they fled to cities in Lycaonia' Ac 14.6.

27.6 ἀφοράω[b]: to acquire information, with focus presumably upon the source of such information – 'to learn about, to find out about.' τοῦτον μὲν οὖν ἐλπίζω πέμψαι ὡς ἂν ἀφίδω τὰ περὶ ἐμὲ ἐξαυτῆς 'I hope to send him (to you), then, as soon as I can learn how things are going to turn out for me' Php 2.23.

27.7 καθοράω: to acquire definite information, and with focus upon the process of perception – 'to learn about, to perceive clearly.' τὰ γὰρ ἀόρατα αὐτοῦ ἀπὸ κτίσεως κόσμου τοῖς ποιήμασιν νοούμενα καθορᾶται 'for since the creation of the world, his invisible qualities have been clearly perceived, being understood from what has been made' Ro 1.20.[3]

27.8 ἐπιγινώσκω[c]: to acquire information, probably in a somewhat more exact or detailed form and perhaps with focus upon what is learned (compare 27.2) – 'to learn about, to find out about.' ἐπιγνοῦσα ὅτι κατάκειται ἐν τῇ οἰκίᾳ τοῦ Φαρισαίου 'she found out that he was eating in the Pharisee's house' Lk 7.37; ἐπέγνωμεν ὅτι Μελίτη ἡ νῆσος καλεῖται 'then we learned that the island was called Malta' Ac 28.1.

ἐπιγινώσκω[c] also occurs in legal contexts referring to careful investigation and interrogation: εἴπας μάστιξιν ἀνετάζεσθαι αὐτὸν ἵνα ἐπιγνῷ δι' ἣν αἰτίαν οὕτως ἐπεφώνουν αὐτῷ 'he told them to whip him to ascertain why they (the Jews) were screaming like this against him' Ac 22.24; βουλόμενός τε ἐπιγνῶναι τὴν αἰτίαν δι' ἣν ἐνεκάλουν αὐτῷ κατήγαγον εἰς τὸ συνέδριον αὐτῶν 'I wanted to find out what they were accusing him of, so I took him down to their Council' Ac 23.28.[4]

---

2 διαγινώσκω[a] probably differs in meaning from γινώσκω[b] (27.2) in implying more thorough and detailed information being obtained.

3 Some persons might insist that καθοράω refers primarily to the sensory act of perception, but since the qualities spoken of in Ro 1.20 are invisible, obviously the perception is a mental one and not a sensory one. Furthermore, the process of learning about these invisible qualities must be distinguished from the process of understanding, which is introduced in Ro 1.20 by a form of the verb νοέω (see 32.2).

4 Though ἐπιγινώσκω does occur in certain legal contexts, it still means essentially 'to acquire more exact or detailed information,' and therefore it does not seem necessary to set up a distinct meaning for ἐπιγινώσκω merely because of its use in such contexts.

27.9 ἀκριβόω: to acquire information in an exact and accurate manner or to acquire information which is exact and accurate – 'to learn exactly, to find out accurately, to ascertain.' τότε Ἡρῴδης λάθρᾳ καλέσας τοὺς μάγους ἠκρίβωσεν παρ᾽ αὐτῶν τὸν χρόνον τοῦ φαινομένου ἀστέρος 'so Herod called the visitors from the east to a secret meeting and from them found out exactly what time the star had appeared' Mt 2.7.

27.10 καταλαμβάνομαι[a]: to acquire definite information, with the possible implication of effort – 'to learn about, to find, to find out about, to discover.' ἐγὼ δὲ κατελαβόμην μηδὲν ἄξιον αὐτὸν θανάτου πεπραχέναι 'but I could not find that he had done anything for which he deserved the death sentence' Ac 25.25.

27.11 πυνθάνομαι[b]; διερωτάω: to acquire information by questioning – 'to learn about, to find out about by inquiry.'
πυνθάνομαι[b]: πυθόμενος ὅτι ἀπὸ Κιλικίας 'when he found out he was from Cilicia' Ac 23.34.
διερωτάω: ἰδοὺ οἱ ἄνδρες οἱ ἀπεσταλμένοι ὑπὸ τοῦ Κορνηλίου διερωτήσαντες τὴν οἰκίαν τοῦ Σίμωνος ἐπέστησαν ἐπὶ τὸν πυλῶνα 'meanwhile, the men sent by Cornelius had learned where Simon's house was and were now standing at the gate' Ac 10.17.[5]
Since πυνθάνομαι[b] and διερωτάω imply quite distinct semantic components, namely 'to acquire information' and 'by the process of questioning,' it may be appropriate in many languages to use two verbs meaning 'to ask' and 'to find out.' Accordingly, this expression in Ac 10.17 may be rendered as 'meanwhile, men sent by Cornelius asked and learned where Simon's house was.'

27.12 μανθάνω[a]: to acquire information as the result of instruction, whether in an informal or formal context – 'to learn, to be instructed, to be taught.' δύνασθε γὰρ καθ᾽ ἕνα πάντες προφητεύειν, ἵνα πάντες μανθάνωσιν καὶ

πάντες παρακαλῶνται 'all of you may speak God's message, one by one, so that all will learn and be encouraged' 1 Cor 14.31; παρὰ τὴν διδαχὴν ἣν ὑμεῖς ἐμάθετε 'against the teaching which you learned' Ro 16.17; τοῦτο μόνον θέλω μαθεῖν ἀφ᾽ ὑμῶν 'this one thing I want to learn from you' Ga 3.2; πῶς οὗτος γράμματα οἶδεν μὴ μεμαθηκώς; 'how does this man know so much when he has never had formal instruction?' Jn 7.15. See also 27.21. A translation of Jn 7.15 which merely says 'when he has never been to school' gives quite a wrong impression, for Jesus undoubtedly did attend a local synagogue school where he learned to read and write and studied the Scriptures. What is implied in Jn 7.15 is that Jesus was not the disciple of a particular rabbi nor did he have formal or advanced instruction under a recognized rabbi.

27.13 παραλαμβάνω[c]: to acquire information from someone, implying the type of information passed on by tradition – 'to learn from someone, to learn about a tradition, to learn by tradition.' παρέδωκα γὰρ ὑμῖν . . . ὃ καὶ παρέλαβον 'for I passed on to you . . . what also I had learned from another' 1 Cor 15.3; ἄλλα πολλά ἐστιν ἃ παρέλαβον κρατεῖν 'they follow many other rules which they have learned by tradition' Mk 7.4; καθὼς παρελάβετε παρ᾽ ἡμῶν τὸ πῶς δεῖ ὑμᾶς περιπατεῖν καὶ ἀρέσκειν θεῷ 'as you learned from us how you should live in order to be pleasing to God' 1 Th 4.1.

27.14 μυέομαι: to learn the secret of something through personal experience or as the result of initiation – 'to learn a secret.' ἐν παντὶ καὶ ἐν πᾶσιν μεμύημαι καὶ χορτάζεσθαι καὶ πεινᾶν 'I have learned the secret (of being content) in any and every situation, whether well-fed or hungry' Php 4.12.

27.15 μανθάνω[b]: to learn from experience, often with the implication of reflection – 'to learn, to come to realize.' καίπερ ὢν υἱός ἔμαθεν ἀφ᾽ ὧν ἔπαθεν τὴν ὑπακοήν 'but even though he was (God's) Son, he learned to be obedient by means of his suffering' He 5.8; πορευθέντες δὲ μάθετε τί ἐστιν, Ἔλεος θέλω καὶ οὐ θυσίαν 'go and learn what this (scripture)

---

5 It is also possible to interpret διερωτάω as meaning 'to ask questions' or 'to inquire about,' in which case the meaning of διερωτάω may be treated under Domain 33 *Communication*.

means, I do not want animal sacrifices, but kindness' Mt 9.13.

27.16 μαθητής[b], οῦ *m*: (derivative of μανθάνω[a] 'to learn, to be instructed,' 27.12) a person who learns from another by instruction, whether formal or informal – 'disciple, pupil.'[6] οὐκ ἔστιν μαθητὴς ὑπὲρ τὸν διδάσκαλον, κατηρτισμένος δὲ πᾶς ἔσται ὡς ὁ διδάσκαλος αὐτοῦ 'no pupil is greater than his teacher; but every pupil, when he has completed his training, will be like his teacher' Lk 6.40.

27.17 ὁδηγέω[b]: (a figurative extension of meaning of ὁδηγέω[a] 'to lead, to guide,' 15.182) to guide someone in acquiring information – 'to lead someone to know, to guide someone in learning.'[7] ὅταν δὲ ἔλθῃ ἐκεῖνος, τὸ πνεῦμα τῆς ἀληθείας, ὁδηγήσει ὑμᾶς ἐν τῇ ἀληθείᾳ πάσῃ 'but when the Spirit of truth comes, he will lead you to complete truth' Jn 16.13.

27.18 γινώσκω[c]: to learn to know a person through direct personal experience, implying a continuity of relationship – 'to know, to become acquainted with, to be familiar with.' καὶ ἐν τούτῳ γινώσκομεν ὅτι ἐγνώκαμεν αὐτόν 'then we are sure that we know him' 1 Jn 2.3; ἵνα γινώσκωσιν σὲ τὸν μόνον ἀληθινὸν θεόν 'for people to know you, the only true God' Jn 17.3. In translating γινώσκω in Jn 17.3, it is important to avoid an expression which will mean merely 'to learn about.' Here the emphasis must be on the interpersonal relationship which is experienced.

27.19 σπερμολόγος[a], ου *m*: (a figurative extension of meaning of a term based on the

---

6 μαθητής[b] 'disciple, pupil' differs from μαθητής[a], which has the sense of being a disciple or follower of someone (see 36.38).

7 Meanings which involve acquisition of information by formal or informal instruction overlap to a considerable extent with the domain of *Communication* (33). In some contexts the focus seems to be upon the fact of verbal communication, while in other contexts, it is learning which appears to be in focus. It is for that reason that a number of these related meanings are included in this domain of *Learn*, for example, μανθάνω[a] (27.12), μανθάνω[b] (27.15), μαθητής[b] (27.16), and ὁδηγέω[b] (27.17).

practice of birds in picking up seeds) one who acquires bits and pieces of relatively extraneous information and proceeds to pass them on with pretense and show – 'ignorant show-off, charlatan.' τινες ἔλεγον, Τί ἂν θέλοι ὁ σπερμολόγος οὗτος λέγειν; 'some said, What is this ignorant show-off trying to say?' Ac 17.18. The term σπερμολόγος is semantically complex in that it combines two quite distinct phases of activity: (1) the acquiring of information and (2) the passing on of such information. Because of the complex semantic structure of σπερμολόγος, it may be best in some languages to render it as 'one who learns lots of trivial things and wants to tell everyone about his knowledge,' but in most languages there is a perfectly appropriate idiom for 'a pseudo-intellectual who insists on spouting off.' For a different focus on the meaning of σπερμολόγος in Ac 17.18, see 33.381.

27.20 λόγιος[b], α, ον: pertaining to one who has learned a great deal of the intellectual heritage of a culture – 'learned, cultured.' Ἰουδαῖος δέ τις Ἀπολλῶς ὀνόματι, Ἀλεξανδρεὺς τῷ γένει, ἀνὴρ λόγιος 'now a certain Jew by the name of Apollos, born in Alexandria, who was a learned man' Ac 18.24. It is also possible to understand λόγιος in Ac 18.24 as meaning 'eloquent' (see 33.32).

27.21 γράμματα, των *n*: the body of information acquired in school or from the study of writings – 'learning, education, scholarship.' πῶς οὗτος γράμματα οἶδεν μὴ μεμαθηκώς; 'how does this man know so much (literally 'know learning') when he has never had formal instruction?' Jn 7.15; τὰ πολλά σε γράμματα εἰς μανίαν περιτρέπει 'your great learning is driving you mad' Ac 26.24. For a discussion of problems involved in translating Jn 7.15, see μανθάνω[a] (27.12).

27.22 γραμματεύς[b], έως *m*: a person who has acquired a high level of education in a certain body of literature or discipline – 'scholar, teacher.' ποῦ σοφός; ποῦ γραμματεύς; ποῦ συζητητὴς τοῦ αἰῶνος τούτου; 'where (does this leave) the philosopher? Or the scholar? Or the skillful debater of this world?' 1 Cor 1.20; διὰ τοῦτο πᾶς γραμματεὺς μαθητευθεὶς τῇ βασιλείᾳ τῶν οὐρανῶν ὅμοιός ἐστιν ἀνθρώπῳ οἰκοδεσπότῃ 'this means, then, that every teacher (of the Law) who becomes a disciple in the kingdom of heaven is like a homeowner' Mt 13.52.

In traditional translations γραμματεύς in contexts such as 1 Cor 1.20 and Mt 13.52 has been rendered as 'scribe,' but this generally is misleading since the term 'scribe' is usually restricted in meaning to one who writes or copies documents. A γραμματεύς in Jewish life of Bible times would have been an expert in the Law or a scholar in the Holy Scriptures and not a mere copier of manuscripts.

27.23 ἀγράμματος, ον: pertaining to one who has not acquired a formal education (referring primarily to formal training) – 'uneducated, unlearned.' θεωροῦντες δὲ τὴν τοῦ Πέτρου παρρησίαν καὶ Ἰωάννου, καὶ καταλαβόμενοι ὅτι ἄνθρωποι ἀγράμματοί εἰσιν καὶ ἰδιῶται 'the members of the Council were amazed to see how bold Peter and John were, and to realize that they were ordinary men with no education' Ac 4.13. Some persons have assumed that ἀγράμματος in Ac 4.13 means 'illiterate' in the sense of not being able to read or write, but this is highly unlikely in view of the almost universal literacy in NT times, and especially as the result of extensive synagogue schools. Evidently, ἀγράμματος in Ac 4.13 refers to a lack of formal rabbinic training.

27.24 ἀμαθής, ές: pertaining to one who has not acquired a formal education, and hence with the implication of being stupid and ignorant – 'uneducated, unlearned, ignorant.'[8] ἐν αἷς ἐστιν δυσνόητά τινα, ἃ οἱ ἀμαθεῖς καὶ ἀστήρικτοι στρεβλοῦσιν 'there are some difficult things in his letters which ignorant and unstable people explain falsely' 2 Pe 3.16.

27.25 ἀπαίδευτος, ον: pertaining to that which or one who fails to reflect formal instruction or training – 'uneducated, foolish, ignorant.' τὰς δὲ μωρὰς καὶ ἀπαιδεύτους ζη-

τήσεις παραιτοῦ 'but stay away from foolish and ignorant arguments' 2 Tm 2.23.

27.26 ἰδιώτης, ου m: a person who has not acquired systemic information or expertise in some field of knowledge or activity – 'layman, ordinary person, amateur.' εἰ δὲ καὶ ἰδιώτης τῷ λόγῳ, ἀλλ' οὐ τῇ γνώσει 'perhaps I am an amateur in speaking, but certainly not in knowledge' 2 Cor 11.6.

In 1 Cor 14.16 ἰδιώτης is used to refer to a class of persons who were neither unbelievers nor fully instructed Christians, but who were inquirers or catechumens. In such a context, ἰδιώτης may be rendered as 'ordinary, uninitiated' (ἐπεὶ ἐὰν εὐλογῇς ἐν πνεύματι, ὁ ἀναπληρῶν τὸν τόπον τοῦ ἰδιώτου πῶς ἐρεῖ τὸ Ἀμήν ἐπὶ τῇ σῇ εὐχαριστίᾳ 'when you give thanks to God in spirit only, how can an ordinary, uninitiated person taking part in the meeting say "Amen" to your prayer of thanksgiving').

B Learn the Location of Something (27.27-27.29)

27.27 εὑρίσκω[a]: to learn the location of something, either by intentional searching or by unexpected discovery – 'to learn the whereabouts of something, to find, to discover, to come upon, to happen to find.' ὃν εὑρὼν ἄνθρωπος ἔκρυψεν 'a man happens to find it, so he covers it up (again)' Mt 13.44.

27.28 ἀνευρίσκω: to learn the location of something by intentional searching – 'to find by searching, to look for and find.' ἀνεῦραν τήν τε Μαριὰμ καὶ τὸν Ἰωσὴφ καὶ τὸ βρέφος κείμενον ἐν τῇ φάτνῃ 'they found Mary and Joseph and the baby lying in the manger' Lk 2.16.

27.29 ἀπόλλυμι[d]: to become unaware of the location of something – 'to lose, to no longer know where something is.'[9] τίς ἄνθρωπος ἐξ ὑμῶν ἔχων ἑκατὸν πρόβατα καὶ ἀπολέσας ἐξ αὐτῶν ἕν 'suppose one of you has a hundred

---

8 It is also possible to understand ἀμαθής as meaning 'a person who has not been taught or instructed,' and accordingly, such a meaning would be classified under *Communication* (33).

9 ἀπόλλυμι[d] may be regarded as a type of semantic reversive of εὑρίσκω[a] 'to find' (27.27). In other words, εὑρίσκω[a] means 'to learn the location of something' and ἀπόλλυμι[d] would mean 'to come to no longer know the location of something.'

sheep and loses one of them' Lk 15.4. It is also possible to interpret ἀπόλλυμι in Lk 15.4 as meaning a loss of possession (see 57.68).

C   Learn Something Against Someone (27.30-27.33)

27.30 ἀγρεύω; παγιδεύω; θηρεύω: (figurative extensions of meaning of terms meaning literally 'to hunt, to trap,' not occurring in the NT) to acquire information about an error or fault, with the purpose of causing harm or trouble – 'to trap, to catch off guard, to catch in a mistake.'

ἀγρεύω: ἀποστέλλουσιν πρὸς αὐτόν τινας τῶν Φαρισαίων καὶ τῶν Ἡρῳδιανῶν ἵνα αὐτὸν ἀγρεύσωσιν λόγῳ 'some Pharisees and some members of Herod's party were sent to him to trap him with questions' Mk 12.13.

παγιδεύω: τότε πορευθέντες οἱ Φαρισαῖοι συμβούλιον ἔλαβον ὅπως αὐτὸν παγιδεύσωσιν ἐν λόγῳ 'the Pharisees went off and made a plan to trap him with questions' Mt 22.15.

θηρεύω: ἐνεδρεύοντες αὐτὸν θηρεῦσαί τι ἐκ τοῦ στόματος αὐτοῦ 'they were plotting against him to catch him in something (wrong) he might say' Lk 11.54.

In a number of languages it is possible to retain the figurative meaning of 'trap' or 'catch,' but in a number of instances other figures are used, for example, 'to cause to trip,' 'to cause to fall,' 'to hear wrong words from his mouth,' or 'to use his words against him.'

27.31 πειράζω[b]; ἐκπειράζω[b]: to obtain information to be used against a person by trying to cause someone to make a mistake – 'to try to trap, to attempt to catch in a mistake.'

πειράζω[b]: προσελθόντες οἱ Φαρισαῖοι καὶ Σαδδουκαῖοι πειράζοντες ἐπηρώτησαν αὐτὸν σημεῖον ἐκ τοῦ οὐρανοῦ ἐπιδεῖξαι αὐτοῖς 'the Pharisees and Sadducees came and tried to trap him by asking him to show them a sign from heaven' Mt 16.1.

ἐκπειράζω[b]: νομικός τις ἀνέστη ἐκπειράζων αὐτόν 'an expert in the Law stood up to try and trap him' Lk 10.25.

It is also possible to interpret πειράζω and ἐκπειράζω in Mt 16.1 and Lk 10.25 as 'the process of testing or examining,' see 27.46. See also 88.308.

27.32 ἐπιλαμβάνομαι[c]; δράσσομαι: (figurative extensions of meaning of ἐπιλαμβάνομαι[a] 'to grasp,' 18.2, and δράσσομαι 'to catch, to seize,' not occurring in the NT) to learn something about someone, with the purpose of seizing, arresting, or overcoming – 'to catch, to trap, to seize, to learn in order to seize.'

ἐπιλαμβάνομαι[c]: οὐκ ἴσχυσαν ἐπιλαβέσθαι αὐτοῦ ῥήματος ἐναντίον τοῦ λαοῦ 'they could not catch him in a thing he said before the people' Lk 20.26.

δράσσομαι: ὁ δρασσόμενος τοὺς σοφοὺς ἐν τῇ πανουργίᾳ αὐτῶν 'he traps the wise men in their cleverness' 1 Cor 3.19.

27.33 προλαμβάνω[a]: to learn something by surprise – 'to detect, to surprise, to catch, to be discovered.' ἐὰν καὶ προλημφθῇ ἄνθρωπος ἔν τινι παραπτώματι 'if someone is caught in any kind of wrongdoing' Ga 6.1. It is possible that προλαμβάνω in Ga 6.1 refers to actual seizing or arresting, but it seems more likely to refer to the fact that someone becomes aware of wrongdoing, and therefore the wrongdoer is surprised by being detected or discovered. It is, of course, also possible to render προλαμβάνω in Ga 6.1 as 'to be involved in.' Compare Domain 90 K.

D   Try to Learn (27.34-27.47)

27.34 ἐραυνάω; ζητέω[b]; ζήτησις[a], εως f: to attempt to learn something by careful investigation or searching – 'to try to learn, to search, to try to find out, to seek information.'

ἐραυνάω: ἐραύνησον καὶ ἴδε ὅτι ἐκ τῆς Γαλιλαίας προφήτης οὐκ ἐγείρεται 'search (the Scriptures) and you will learn that no prophet ever comes from Galilee' Jn 7.52; ὁ δὲ ἐραυνῶν τὰς καρδίας οἶδεν τί τὸ φρόνημα τοῦ πνεύματος 'he who searches the heart knows what the thought of the Spirit is' Ro 8.27. An equivalent of 'search' in the expression 'search the Scriptures' may be in some languages simply 'read carefully' or 'study well.'

ζητέω[b]: Ἰουδαῖοι σημεῖα αἰτοῦσιν καὶ Ἕλληνες σοφίαν ζητοῦσιν 'Jews ask for signs and Greeks are searching for wisdom' 1 Cor 1.22; ἐζήτουν πῶς αὐτὸν ἀπολέσωσιν 'they began searching for some way to kill him' Mk 11.18.

ζήτησις^a: ἀπορούμενος δὲ ἐγὼ τὴν περὶ τούτων ζήτησιν 'I was undecided about how I could get information on these matters' Ac 25.20. The clause 'about how I could get information on these matters' may also be rendered as 'about how I should try to find out about these matters' or 'about how I could learn about these matters.'

27.35 ἐκζητέω^a; ἐξεραυνάω: to exert considerable effort and care in learning something — 'to make a careful search, to seek diligently to learn, to make an examination.'
ἐκζητέω^a: ὅπως ἂν ἐκζητήσωσιν οἱ κατάλοιποι τῶν ἀνθρώπων τὸν κύριον 'so all other people will seek the Lord' Ac 15.17.
ἐξεραυνάω: περὶ ἧς σωτηρίας ἐξεζήτησαν καὶ ἐξηραύνησαν προφῆται 'it was concerning this salvation that the prophets made a careful search and investigation' 1 Pe 1.10.

27.36 σκοπέω^c: to exert effort in continually acquiring information regarding some matter, with the implication of concern as to how to respond appropriately — 'to be aware of, to be concerned about, to consider.' μὴ τὰ ἑαυτῶν ἕκαστος σκοποῦντες, ἀλλὰ καὶ τὰ ἑτέρων ἕκαστοι 'each of you should be continually concerned about not only your own interests, but also the interests of others' Php 2.4.

27.37 ἐξετάζω^a: to engage in a careful search in order to acquire information, though primarily by inquiry — 'to try to find out, to make a diligent effort to learn.' πορευθέντες ἐξετάσατε ἀκριβῶς περὶ τοῦ παιδίου 'go and carefully find out all about the child' Mt 2.8.

27.38 παρακολουθέω^b: (a figurative extension of meaning of παρακολουθέω 'to follow,' not occurring in the NT) to make an extensive effort to learn the details and truth about something — 'to trace, to investigate carefully, to diligently check out.' κἀμοὶ παρηκολουθηκότι ἄνωθεν πᾶσιν ἀκριβῶς 'since I myself have carefully investigated everything from the beginning' Lk 1.3.

27.39 παρακύπτω^c: (a figurative extension of meaning of παρακύπτω^b 'to stoop and look into,' 24.13) to make considerable effort in order to try to find out something — 'to try to learn, to desire to learn.' εἰς ἃ ἐπιθυμοῦσιν ἄγγελοι παρακύψαι 'things which (even) the angels desire to learn about' 1 Pe 1.12.

27.40 ψηλαφάω^b: (a figurative extension of meaning of ψηλαφάω^a 'to touch, to feel,' 24.76) to make an effort, despite difficulties, to come to know something, when the chances of success in such an enterprise are not particularly great — 'to feel around for, to grope for, to try to find.' εἰ ἄρα γε ψηλαφήσειαν αὐτόν 'as they felt around for him' Ac 17.27.

27.41 ζητέω^a: to try to learn the location of something, often by movement from place to place in the process of searching — 'to try to learn where something is, to look for, to try to find.' πάντες ζητοῦσίν σε 'everyone is trying to find you' Mk 1.37.

27.42 ἀναζητέω; ἐπιζητέω^a: to try to learn the location of something by searching for it (presumably somewhat more emphatic or goal-directed than in the case of ζητέω^a 'to try to learn where something is,' 27.41) — 'to seek, to search, to try to find out by looking for.'
ἀναζητέω: ἐξῆλθεν δὲ εἰς Ταρσὸν ἀναζητῆσαι Σαῦλον 'then he went to Tarsus to look for Saul' Ac 11.25.
ἐπιζητέω^a: Ἡρῴδης δὲ ἐπιζητήσας αὐτὸν καὶ μὴ εὑρών 'Herod searched for him, but he could not find him' Ac 12.19.

27.43 καταδιώκω: to try to learn the location of an object by diligently following after or tracking down — 'to seek for, to search, to go looking for diligently.' κατεδίωξεν αὐτὸν Σίμων καὶ οἱ μετ' αὐτοῦ 'but Simon and his companions went out diligently searching for him' Mk 1.36.

27.44 ἀνακρίνω^a: to try to learn the nature or truth of something by the process of careful study, evaluation and judgment — 'to examine carefully, to investigate, to study thoroughly.' καθ' ἡμέραν ἀνακρίνοντες τὰς γραφὰς εἰ ἔχοι ταῦτα οὕτως 'every day they carefully examined the Scriptures to see if what he said was really true' Ac 17.11.

27.45 δοκιμάζωᵃ; **δοκιμή**ᵃ, **ῆς** *f*; **δοκίμιον**ᵃ, **ου** *n*; **δοκιμασία, ας** *f*: to try to learn the genuineness of something by examination and testing, often through actual use – 'to test, to examine, to try to determine the genuineness of, testing.'

δοκιμάζω ᵃ: ζεύγη βοῶν ἠγόρασα πέντε καὶ πορεύομαι δοκιμάσαι αὐτά 'I bought five pairs of oxen and am on my way to test them out' Lk 14.19; δοκιμαζέτω δὲ ἄνθρωπος ἑαυτόν, καὶ οὕτως ἐκ τοῦ ἄρτου ἐσθιέτω καὶ ἐκ τοῦ ποτηρίου πινέτω 'everyone should examine himself, and then eat the bread and drink from the cup' 1 Cor 11.28.

δοκιμή ᵃ: ἐν πολλῇ δοκιμῇ θλίψεως 'being tested severely by the troubles' 2 Cor 8.2.

δοκίμιον ᵃ: τὸ δοκίμιον ὑμῶν τῆς πίστεως κατεργάζεται ὑπομονήν 'the testing of your faith produces endurance' Jas 1.3.

δοκιμασία: οὗ ἐπείρασαν οἱ πατέρες ὑμῶν ἐν δοκιμασίᾳ 'when your fathers tested and tried (me)' He 3.9.

27.46 πειράζωᵃ; **πειρασμός**ᵃ, **οῦ** *m*; **ἐκπειράζω**ᵃ: to try to learn the nature or character of someone or something by submitting such to thorough and extensive testing – 'to test, to examine, to put to the test, examination, testing.'

πειράζω ᵃ: ἑαυτοὺς πειράζετε εἰ ἐστὲ ἐν τῇ πίστει 'put yourselves to the test as to whether you are in the faith (or not)' 2 Cor 13.5; προσελθόντες οἱ Φαρισαῖοι καὶ Σαδδουκαῖοι πειράζοντες ἐπηρώτησαν αὐτὸν σημεῖον ἐκ τοῦ οὐρανοῦ ἐπιδεῖξαι αὐτοῖς 'the Pharisees and Sadducees came, and to test him they asked if he would show them a sign from heaven' Mt 16.1.

πειρασμός ᵃ: μὴ ξενίζεσθε τῇ ἐν ὑμῖν πυρώσει πρὸς πειρασμὸν ὑμῖν γινομένῃ 'don't be surprised at the painful testing you are experiencing' 1 Pe 4.12; ὅταν πειρασμοῖς περιπέσητε ποικίλοις 'when you undergo all kinds of testing' Jas 1.2.

ἐκπειράζω ᵃ: οὐκ ἐκπειράσεις κύριον τὸν θεόν σου 'you shall not put the Lord your God to the test' Lk 4.12; νομικός τις ἀνέστη ἐκπειράζων αὐτόν 'an expert in the Law stood up to test him' Lk 10.25.

It is also possible to understand πειράζω and ἐκπειράζω in Mt 16.1 and Lk 10.25 as meaning 'to try to trap,' see 27.31. See also 88.308.

27.47 κατάσκοπος, ου *m* (derivative of κατασκοπέω 'to observe secretly,' 24.50); **ἐγκάθετος, ου** *m* (derivative of ἐγκάθημαι 'to lie in a crouched position,' not occurring in the NT): one whose task it is to obtain information surreptitiously – 'spy, secret agent.'

κατάσκοπος: δεξαμένη τοὺς κατασκόπους μετ' εἰρήνης 'she gave the (Israelite) spies a friendly welcome' He 11.31.

ἐγκάθετος: ἀπέστειλαν ἐγκαθέτους ὑποκρινομένους ἑαυτοὺς δικαίους εἶναι 'they sent some spies who pretended to be sincere' Lk 20.20.

E Be Willing to Learn (27.48-27.54)

27.48 εὐγενήςᵇ, **ές**: a willingness to learn and evaluate something fairly – 'willingness to learn, to be open-minded, to be noble-minded.' οὗτοι δὲ ἦσαν εὐγενέστεροι τῶν ἐν Θεσσαλονίκῃ 'the people there were more open-minded than the people in Thessalonica' Ac 17.11.

27.49 διανοίγω τὸν νοῦν; **διανοίγω τὴν καρδίαν**: (idioms, literally 'to open the mind' and 'to open the heart') to cause someone to be willing to learn and evaluate fairly – 'to open someone's mind, to cause someone to be open-minded.'

διανοίγω τὸν νοῦν: τότε διήνοιξεν αὐτῶν τὸν νοῦν τοῦ συνιέναι τὰς γραφάς 'then he opened their minds to understand the Scriptures' Lk 24.45.

διανοίγω τὴν καρδίαν: ἧς ὁ κύριος διήνοιξεν τὴν καρδίαν προσέχειν τοῖς λαλουμένοις ὑπὸ τοῦ Παύλου 'the Lord opened her mind to pay attention to what Paul was saying' Ac 16.14.

It is rare that one can speak literally of 'opening the mind' or 'opening the heart.' It is sometimes possible to use an expression such as 'to cause the mind to see' or 'to cause the heart to know' or '. . . to recognize.' In some languages, however, 'to open the mind' or 'to open the heart' may refer to murderous violence.

27.50 καμμύω τοὺς ὀφθαλμούς: (an idiom, literally 'to close the eyes') to be unwilling to learn and to evaluate something fairly – 'to refuse to learn, to refuse to recognize.' τοὺς ὀφθαλμοὺς αὐτῶν ἐκάμμυσαν· μήποτε ἴδωσιν τοῖς ὀφθαλμοῖς 'they have closed their eyes; otherwise, their eyes would see' Ac 28.27. In a number of languages there is a problem involved in a literal rendering of 'to close the eyes,' since this may be understood in a strictly literal sense or as denoting death.

27.51 πωρόω: (a figurative extension of meaning of πωρόω 'to harden,' not occurring in the NT) to cause someone to be completely unwilling to learn and to accept new information – 'to cause to be completely unwilling to learn, to cause the mind to be closed.' καὶ ἐπώρωσεν αὐτῶν τὴν καρδίαν 'and he closed their minds' Jn 12.40; οἱ δὲ λοιποὶ ἐπωρώθησαν 'the rest were made completely unwilling to learn' Ro 11.7; ἀλλὰ ἐπωρώθη τὰ νοήματα αὐτῶν 'but their minds were closed' 2 Cor 3.14. In 2 Cor 3.14 and in Jn 12.40 νόημα and καρδία function syntactically as so-called 'accusatives of specification.'

27.52 πώρωσις, εως f: stubborn unwillingness to learn – 'unwillingness to learn, mental stubbornness, closed mind.' πώρωσις ἀπὸ μέρους τῷ Ἰσραὴλ γέγονεν 'the stubbornness of Israel is for a time' Ro 11.25.

27.53 πηρόω τὴν καρδίαν: (an idiom, literally 'to maim the heart') to cause someone to be unwilling to learn – 'to close someone's mind, to make someone unable to learn.' πεπήρωκεν αὐτῶν τὴν καρδίαν 'he has made their hearts unable to learn' Jn 12.40 (apparatus).

27.54 καυστηριάζομαι τὴν συνείδησιν: (an idiom, literally 'to be seared in the conscience' or '. . . as to one's conscience') to be unwilling to learn from one's conscience – 'to refuse to listen to one's conscience, to be completely insensitive to.' κεκαυστηριασμένων τὴν ἰδίαν συνείδησιν 'their own consciences are seared' or 'they refuse to listen to their consciences' 1 Tm 4.2.

F   Be Ready to Learn, Pay Attention (27.55-27.60)

27.55 ἀναζώννυμαι τὰς ὀσφύας τῆς διανοίας: (an idiom, literally 'to bind up the loins of the mind') to prepare oneself for learning and thinking – 'to get one's mind ready for action, to be ready to learn and to think, to be alert.' διὸ ἀναζωσάμενοι τὰς ὀσφύας τῆς διανοίας ὑμῶν 'so then, have your minds ready for action' 1 Pe 1.13.

27.56 γρηγορέω[b]: (a figurative extension of meaning of γρηγορέω[a] 'to stay awake,' 23.72) to be in continuous readiness and alertness to learn – 'to be alert, to be watchful, to be vigilant.' γρηγορεῖτε, στήκετε ἐν τῇ πίστει 'be alert, stand fast in the faith' 1 Cor 16.13.

27.57 ἀγρυπνέω[a]: (a figurative extension of meaning of ἀγρυπνέω 'to keep oneself awake,' not occurring in the NT) to make an effort to learn of what might be a potential future threat – 'to be alert, to be on the lookout for, to be vigilant.' βλέπετε ἀγρυπνεῖτε· οὐκ οἴδατε γὰρ πότε ὁ καιρός ἐστιν 'be on watch, be alert, for you do not know when the time will be' Mk 13.33; εἰς αὐτὸ ἀγρυπνοῦντες ἐν πάσῃ προσκαρτερήσει καὶ δεήσει περὶ πάντων τῶν ἁγίων 'for this reason be alert and always keep on praying for all God's people' Eph 6.18.

27.58 βλέπω[c]; σκοπέω[b]: (figurative extensions of meaning of βλέπω[a] 'to see,' 24.7, and σκοπέω[a] 'to notice carefully,' 24.32) to be ready to learn about future dangers or needs, with the implication of preparedness to respond appropriately – 'to beware of, to watch out for, to pay attention to.'
βλέπω[c]: βλέπετε τί ἀκούετε 'pay attention to what you hear' Mk 4.24; βλέπετε τοὺς κακοὺς ἐργάτας 'watch out for those who do evil things' Php 3.2.
σκοπέω[b]: σκοπῶν σεαυτόν, μὴ καὶ σὺ πειρασθῇς 'watch yourself, so that you too will not be tempted' Ga 6.1.

27.59 προσέχω[a]; ἐπέχω[a]: to be in a continuous state of readiness to learn of any future danger, need, or error, and to respond appropriately – 'to pay attention to, to keep on the lookout for, to be alert for, to be on one's guard against.'
προσέχω[a]: προσέχετε δὲ τὴν δικαιοσύνην ὑμῶν μὴ ποιεῖν ἔμπροσθεν τῶν ἀνθρώπων 'make certain that you do not perform your religious duties in public' Mt 6.1.

ἐπέχω[a]: ἔπεχε σεαυτῷ καὶ τῇ διδασκαλίᾳ 'watch yourself and watch your teaching' 1 Tm 4.16.

27.60 παραιτέομαι[b]: to not pay attention to – 'to refuse to pay attention to, to avoid, to pay no attention to.' τοὺς δὲ βεβήλους καὶ γραώδεις μύθους παραιτοῦ 'pay no attention to the godless legends such as old women tell' 1 Tm 4.7.

G Recognize (27.61-27.62)

27.61 ἐπιγινώσκω[d]: to identify newly ac-

quired information with what had been previously learned or known – 'to recognize.' ἐπιγνοῦσα τὴν φωνὴν τοῦ Πέτρου 'she recognized Peter's voice' Ac 12.14; οἱ δὲ ὀφθαλμοὶ αὐτῶν ἐκρατοῦντο τοῦ μὴ ἐπιγνῶναι αὐτόν 'they saw him, but somehow did not recognize him' Lk 24.16.

27.62 ἀναγνωρίζομαι: to cause oneself to be recognized or to be known again – 'to make recognized, to make known again.' ἀνεγνωρίσθη Ἰωσὴφ τοῖς ἀδελφοῖς αὐτοῦ 'Joseph made himself known to his brothers again' Ac 7.13.

28 Know

Outline of Subdomains

A Know[1] (28.1-28.16)

28.1 γινώσκω[a]; οἶδα[a]; γνωρίζω[a]; γνῶσις[a], εως f: to possess information about – 'to know, to know about, to have knowledge of, to be acquainted with, acquaintance.'
γινώσκω[a]: διότι γνόντες τὸν θεὸν οὐκ ὡς θεὸν ἐδόξασαν 'since, although they knew about God, they did not honor him as God' or '. . . they did not give him the honor that belongs to him' Ro 1.21; ὑμεῖς ἐστε οἱ δικαιοῦντες ἑαυτοὺς ἐνώπιον τῶν ἀνθρώπων, ὁ δὲ θεὸς

γινώσκει τὰς καρδίας ὑμῶν 'you are the ones who make yourselves look right in people's sight, but God knows your hearts' Lk 16.15.[2]
οἶδα[a]: γρηγορεῖτε οὖν, ὅτι οὐκ οἴδατε τὴν ἡμέραν οὐδὲ τὴν ὥραν 'watch out, then, because you do not know the day or hour' Mt 25.13; τὰς ἐντολὰς οἶδας 'you know the commandments' Mk 10.19.
γνωρίζω[a]: τί αἱρήσομαι οὐ γνωρίζω 'which I shall choose, I do not know' Php 1.22.
γνῶσις[a]: τοῦ δοῦναι γνῶσιν σωτηρίας τῷ λαῷ αὐτοῦ 'to let his people know that they will be saved' Lk 1.77.

28.2 ἐπιγινώσκω[a]; ἐπίγνωσις[a], εως f: to possess more or less definite information about, possibly with a degree of thoroughness or competence – 'to know about, to know definitely about, knowledge about.'
ἐπιγινώσκω[a]: οὐδεὶς ἐπιγινώσκει τὸν υἱὸν εἰ μὴ ὁ πατήρ, οὐδὲ τὸν πατέρα τις ἐπιγινώσκει εἰ μὴ ὁ υἱός 'no one knows the Son except the Father, and no one knows the Father except the Son' Mt 11.27; ἃ ὁ θεὸς ἔκτισεν εἰς μετάλημψιν μετὰ εὐχαριστίας τοῖς πιστοῖς καὶ ἐπεγνωκόσι τὴν ἀλήθειαν 'which things God created to be

---

1 The meanings in Domain 28 *Know* are rarely expressed or represented by figurative lexical units, since expressions for 'know, known, make known' are fundamentally semantic primitives. In some languages, however, the 'eye' is regarded as the organ of knowledge, and to know something may be literally 'to hold in the eye.' A few languages also employ a term for 'liver' in idiomatic expressions relating to knowing and knowledge.

2 In Jn 8.23 (γνώσεσθε τὴν ἀλήθειαν, καὶ ἡ ἀλήθεια ἐλευθερώσει ὑμᾶς 'you will know the truth and the truth will make you free'), it is also possible to understand γινώσκω as 'to find out' or 'to learn' (27.2).

received with thanksgiving by those who believe and know the truth' 1 Tm 4.3.

ἐπίγνωσις^a: αἰτούμενοι ἵνα πληρωθῆτε τὴν ἐπίγνωσιν τοῦ θελήματος αὐτοῦ 'we are asking (God) to fill you by letting you know what he wants' Col 1.9; ἐν ἐπιγνώσει παντὸς ἀγαθοῦ τοῦ ἐν ἡμῖν εἰς Χριστόν 'so that you will know every blessing that we receive in Christ' Phm 6; καὶ καθὼς οὐκ ἐδοκίμασαν τὸν θεὸν ἔχειν ἐν ἐπιγνώσει 'and because they refused to keep in mind knowledge about God' or '. . . to think about God' Ro 1.28. It is also possible to render ἐπίγνωσις in Ro 1.28 as 'true knowledge.' For another interpretation of ἐπίγνωσις as part of an idiom in Ro 1.28, see 31.28.

28.3 ἐπίσταμαι^a: to possess information about, with the implication of an understanding of the significance of such information – 'to know.'[3] τὸν Παῦλον ἐπίσταμαι 'I know about Paul' Ac 19.15; ὑμεῖς ἐπίστασθε ὅτι ἀφ' ἡμερῶν ἀρχαίων ἐν ὑμῖν ἐξελέξατο ὁ θεός 'you know that a long time ago God chose (me) from among you' Ac 15.7.

28.4 σύνοιδα^a; συνείδησις^a, εως *f*: to be aware of information about something – 'to know, to be conscious of, to be aware of.' σύνοιδα^a: οὐδὲν γὰρ ἐμαυτῷ σύνοιδα 'I am aware of nothing against myself' 1 Cor 4.4. συνείδησις^a: εἰ διὰ συνείδησιν θεοῦ ὑποφέρει τις λύπας πάσχων ἀδίκως 'if you endure the pain of undeserved suffering because you are conscious of God's will' 1 Pe 2.19.

28.5 σύνοιδα^b: to share information or knowledge with – 'to know something together with someone else.' ἐνοσφίσατο ἀπὸ τῆς τιμῆς, συνειδυίης καὶ τῆς γυναικός 'he kept part of the money for himself, his wife sharing in knowledge of that too' Ac 5.2. The sharing of information may be expressed in Ac 5.2 as 'his wife also knew about it.'

28.6 προγινώσκω^a; πρόγνωσις^a, εως *f*; προοράω^b: to know about something prior to some temporal reference point, for example,

to know about an event before it happens – 'to know beforehand, to know already, to have foreknowledge.'

προγινώσκω^a: προγινώσκοντές με ἄνωθεν, ἐὰν θέλωσι μαρτυρεῖν 'they have already known me beforehand, if they are willing to testify' Ac 26.5; προεγνωσμένου μὲν πρὸ καταβολῆς κόσμου 'known already before the world was made' 1 Pe 1.20. It is also possible to understand προγινώσκω in 1 Pe 1.20 as meaning 'chosen beforehand' (see 30.100).

πρόγνωσις^a: τοῦτον τῇ ὡρισμένῃ βουλῇ καὶ προγνώσει τοῦ θεοῦ ἔκδοτον 'God, in his own will and foreknowledge, had already decided that this one would be handed over to (you)' Ac 2.23.

προοράω^b: προϊδὼν ἐλάλησεν περὶ τῆς ἀναστάσεως τοῦ Χριστοῦ 'knowing ahead of time, he spoke about the resurrection of the Christ' Ac 2.31.[4]

28.7 οἶδα^b: to have the knowledge as to how to perform a particular activity or to accomplish some goal – 'to know how to.' εἰ οὖν ὑμεῖς πονηροὶ ὄντες οἴδατε δόματα ἀγαθὰ διδόναι τοῖς τέκνοις ὑμῶν 'if you, then, though you are evil, know how to give good gifts to your children' Mt 7.11.

28.8 σοφία^c, ας *f*: knowledge which makes possible skillful activity or performance – 'specialized knowledge, skill.' ἀπέστειλέν με Χριστός . . . εὐαγγελίζεσθαι, οὐκ ἐν σοφίᾳ λόγου 'Christ sent me . . . to preach the good news not with skillful speech' 1 Cor 1.17. It is also possible to interpret σοφία in 1 Cor 1.17 as wisdom which makes possible correct understanding (see 32.32).

28.9 σοφός^a, ή, όν: pertaining to specialized knowledge resulting in the skill for accomplishing some purpose – 'skillful, expert.' ὡς

---

3 The implicational meaning in ἐπίσταμαι^a may very well be due to the frequent use of ἐπίσταμαι in the sense of 'to understand' (32.3).

4 It is possible to understand προοράω in Ac 2.31 as meaning 'to learn ahead of time' or 'to become aware of ahead of time' or even 'to understand ahead of time.'

In Ga 3.8 προοράω is used with the Scripture as the subject, in which case it would be the personified Scripture as 'knowing beforehand,' but it is also possible to understand προοράω in Ga 3.8 as meaning 'to cause something to be known ahead of time.'

σοφὸς ἀρχιτέκτων θεμέλιον ἔθηκα 'I did the work like an expert builder and laid the foundation' 1 Cor 3.10. In some languages one may render the phrase 'expert builder' as 'one who knew just how to build best.'

28.10 σοφίζομαι: (derivative of σοφία^c 'specialized knowledge, skill,' 28.8) to have specialized knowledge involving the capacity to produce what is cleverly or skillfully made – 'to know how to create skillfully, to know how to contrive cleverly.' οὐ γὰρ σεσοφισμένοις μύθοις ἐξακολουθήσαντες ἐγνωρίσαμεν ὑμῖν 'it was not any cleverly contrived myth that we were repeating when we brought you knowledge' 2 Pe 1.16.

28.11 γνώστης, ου m: (derivative of γινώσκω^a 'to know,' 28.1) one who knows, with the usual implication of to know well – 'one who knows, expert.' μάλιστα γνώστην ὄντα σε πάντων τῶν κατὰ Ἰουδαίους ἐθῶν 'especially because you are an expert in all the Jewish customs' or '. . . because you know so well all the Jewish customs' Ac 26.3.

28.12 καρδιογνώστης, ου m: one who knows what someone else thinks (literally 'to know what is in the heart') – 'one who knows the hearts of, one who knows what people think.' σὺ κύριε, καρδιογνῶστα πάντων 'Lord, you know the hearts of all' Ac 1.24. In a number of languages one may render this phrase in Ac 1.24 as 'Lord, you know what all people are thinking.'

28.13 ἀγνοέω^a; ἄγνοια, ας f: to not have information about – 'to not know, to be unaware of, to be ignorant of, ignorance.' ἀγνοέω^a: οὐ θέλομεν δὲ ὑμᾶς ἀγνοεῖν, ἀδελφοί 'I do not wish for you to be unaware, fellow believers' 1 Th 4.13; οὐ γὰρ αὐτοῦ τὰ νοήματα ἀγνοοῦμεν 'for we are not ignorant of what his plans are' 2 Cor 2.11.
ἄγνοια: οἶδα ὅτι κατὰ ἄγνοιαν ἐπράξατε 'I know that what you did was because of your ignorance' Ac 3.17; τοὺς μὲν οὖν χρόνους τῆς ἀγνοίας ὑπεριδὼν ὁ θεός 'God has overlooked the times when people did not know' Ac 17.30.

28.14 λανθάνω^c: to not have knowledge about or to be unaware of something, with the implication that something can readily escape notice or be hidden – 'to be unaware of, to not know.' διὰ ταύτης γὰρ ἔλαθόν τινες ξενίσαντες ἀγγέλους 'there are some who did it and welcomed angels without knowing it' (literally 'for by this some welcomed . . .') He 13.2.

28.15 ἄπειρος, ον: pertaining to the lack of knowledge or capacity to do something – 'inexperienced in, unacquainted with.' ἄπειρος λόγου δικαιοσύνης 'without any experience in the matter of what is right' He 5.13.

28.16 ἀγνωσία^a, ας f: the state of lacking knowledge – 'to lack knowledge, to have no knowledge, ignorance.' ἀγνωσίαν γὰρ θεοῦ τινες ἔχουσιν 'some have no knowledge about God' 1 Cor 15.34 (for another interpretation of ἀγνωσία in 1 Cor 15.34, see 32.7); ἀγαθοποιοῦντας φιμοῦν τὴν τῶν ἀφρόνων ἀνθρώπων ἀγνωσίαν 'to silence the talk of foolish people who have no knowledge of the good things you do' 1 Pe 2.15. In 1 Pe 2.15, ἀγνωσία may involve lack of understanding (see 32.8).

B Known (the content of knowledge) (28.17-28.27)

Subdomain B *Known* implies in many contexts a process of communication, since there is an implication of the acquisition or lack of acquisition of information. In a sense, this subdomain also touches closely the domain of *Learn* (27), since to make something become known is indirectly a process of causing someone to learn.

28.17 γνῶσις^b, εως f: the content of what is known – 'knowledge, what is known.' ἔχοντα τὴν μόρφωσιν τῆς γνώσεως καὶ τῆς ἀληθείας ἐν τῷ νόμῳ 'because you have in the Law the embodiment of knowledge and truth' Ro 2.20; οἴδαμεν ὅτι πάντες γνῶσιν ἔχομεν 'we know that we all have knowledge' 1 Cor 8.1.

28.18 ἐπίγνωσις^b, εως f: the content of what is definitely known – 'what is known, definite knowledge, full knowledge, knowledge.' μαρτυρῶ γὰρ αὐτοῖς ὅτι ζῆλον θεοῦ ἔχουσιν, ἀλλ' οὐ κατ' ἐπίγνωσιν 'for I can testify about them that they are zealous for God, but (their zeal is) not based on knowledge' Ro 10.2.

28.19 γνῶσιςᶜ, εως *f*: esoteric knowledge (primarily philosophical and religious), with the implication of its being heretical and contrary to the gospel – 'esoteric knowledge.' ἐκτρεπόμενος τὰς βεβήλους κενοφωνίας καὶ ἀντιθέσεις τῆς ψευδωνύμου γνώσεως 'avoid the godless talk and foolish arguments of "Knowledge," as some people wrongly call it' 1 Tm 6.20. In 1 Tm 6.20, ψευδωνύμου γνώσεως may be rendered as 'that which is falsely called knowledge' or 'knowledge which people think is true but is really false.'

28.20 πρόγνωσιςᵇ, εως *f*: (derivative of προγινώσκωᵃ 'to know beforehand,' 28.6) that which is known ahead of time or before a particular temporal reference – 'foreknowledge, what is known beforehand.' ἐκλεκτοῖς . . . κατὰ πρόγνωσιν θεοῦ πατρός 'to those who have been chosen . . . according to what God the Father had known beforehand' 1 Pe 1.1-2.[5]

28.21 γνωστόςᵃ, ή, όν: pertaining to that which is known – 'what is known, information.' περὶ μὲν γὰρ τῆς αἱρέσεως ταύτης γνωστὸν ἡμῖν ἐστιν ὅτι πανταχοῦ ἀντιλέγεται 'it is known to us that everywhere people speak against this party' Ac 28.22; λέγει κύριος ποιῶν ταῦτα γνωστὰ ἀπ' αἰῶνος 'so says the Lord, who made this known long ago' Ac 15.17-18.

28.22 ὀνομάζομαι: (a figurative extension of meaning of ὀνομάζωᵇ 'to call a name,' 33.133) to be caused to be made known – 'to be known.' οὕτως δὲ φιλοτιμούμενον εὐαγγελίζεσθαι οὐχ ὅπου ὠνομάσθη Χριστός 'my ambition has always been to proclaim the good news in places where Christ is not known' Ro 15.20. It would be possible, however, to interpret ὀνομάζομαι in Ro 15.20 in a more literal sense, so that one could translate the final part of the verse as 'where the name of Christ had not been used' or 'where no one had spoken the name of Christ.'

28.23 ἀφικνέομαι: (a figurative extension of meaning of ἀφικνέομαι 'to move up to a point,' not occurring in the NT) to become known as the result of information reaching its destination – 'to become known.' ἡ γὰρ ὑμῶν ὑπακοὴ εἰς πάντας ἀφίκετο 'for (the report of) your obedience has become known to everyone' Ro 16.19.[6]

28.24 διανέμομαι: (a figurative extension of meaning of διανέμομαι 'to spread out,' not occurring in the NT) to become known as the result of information spreading abroad – 'to become known, to spread.' ἵνα μὴ ἐπὶ πλεῖον διανεμηθῇ εἰς τὸν λαόν 'to keep (this matter) from spreading any further among the people' Ac 4.17.

28.25 λόγος τρέχει: (an idiom, literally 'word runs') a message which becomes widely and rapidly known – 'for a message to spread rapidly, to be known quickly.' ἵνα ὁ λόγος τοῦ κυρίου τρέχῃ 'so that the Lord's message may spread rapidly' or '. . . come to be known quickly' 2 Th 3.1.

28.26 γνωρίζωᵇ: to cause information to be known by someone – 'to make known.' πάντα ἃ ἤκουσα παρὰ τοῦ πατρός μου ἐγνώρισα ὑμῖν 'I have made known to you everything I heard from my Father' Jn 15.15.[7]

28.27 ἄγνωστος, ον: pertaining to not being known – 'not known, unknown.' εὗρον καὶ βωμὸν ἐν ᾧ ἐπεγέγραπτο, Ἀγνώστῳ θεῷ 'I

---

[6] It would be possible to treat ἀφικνέομαι in Ro 16.19 as simply a matter of the movement of information. It would also be possible to handle ἀφικνέομαι in the domain of *Communication* (33), involving the reception of information or messages. This is a typical instance of semantic overlapping, depending upon the degree to which one wishes to recognize figurative extensions of meaning.

[7] It would also be possible to treat γνωρίζω in Jn 15.15 as a matter of communication (Domain 33), but the focal component of meaning in γνωρίζωᵇ, as in this context, would seem to be upon the resulting knowledge, not upon the communicative process.

[5] One should not understand πρόγνωσις in 1 Pe 1.2 as being merely equivalent to ἐκλεκτοῖς (see 30.93).

found also an altar on which is written, To An Unknown God' Ac 17.23. In Ac 17.23 the phrase 'Unknown God' may be simply rendered as 'the god whom no one knows about,' but in a number of languages the closest equivalent is 'the god who has no name.'

C Well Known, Clearly Shown, Revealed (28.28-28.56)

The Subdomain *Well Known, Clearly Shown, Revealed* overlaps considerably with the domain of *Communication* (33), for there is always the implication of some kind of prior activity by which information is made known. But since in a majority of contexts the focus of attention seems to be upon the resulting knowledge, this subdomain is included in Domain 28 *Know*.

28.28 φανερός[a], ά, όν: pertaining to being widely and well known – 'well known, widely known.' φανερὸν γὰρ ἐγένετο τὸ ὄνομα αὐτοῦ 'his reputation became widely known' Mk 6.14. In some languages it may be necessary in translating Mk 6.14 to reverse certain roles, for example, 'people everywhere came to know about Jesus.'

28.29 ἐν παρρησίᾳ: (an idiom, literally 'in boldness') in an evident or publicly known manner – 'publicly, in an evident manner, well known.' οὐδεὶς γάρ τι ἐν κρυπτῷ ποιεῖ καὶ ζητεῖ αὐτὸς ἐν παρρησίᾳ εἶναι 'no one does anything in secret but seeks to be well known' Jn 7.4.

28.30 γνωστός[b], ή, όν: pertaining to being well known or well acquainted with – 'acquaintance, well known.' ἀνεζήτουν αὐτὸν ἐν τοῖς συγγενεῦσιν καὶ τοῖς γνωστοῖς 'then they started looking for him among relatives and acquaintances' Lk 2.44. It may also be possible to understand γνωστός in Lk 2.44 as meaning 'friend' (see 34.17).

28.31 ἐπίσημος, ον: pertaining to being well known or outstanding, either because of positive or negative characteristics – 'outstanding, famous, notorious, infamous.' εἰσιν ἐπίσημοι ἐν τοῖς ἀποστόλοις 'they are outstanding among the apostles' Ro 16.7; εἶχον δὲ τότε δέσμιον ἐπίσημον λεγόμενον Ἰησοῦν Βαραββᾶν 'at that time there was a notorious prisoner named Jesus Barabbas' Mt 27.16.

In Ro 16.7 the meaning of 'outstanding' may be rendered in some instances as 'well known for being important,' while 'notorious' in Mt 27.16 may be rendered in some languages as 'well known for being bad.'

28.32 γνωστός[d], ή, όν: pertaining to being well known or famous because of some outstanding quality – 'well known, remarkable.' ὅτι μὲν γὰρ γνωστὸν σημεῖον γέγονεν δι' αὐτῶν πᾶσιν τοῖς κατοικοῦσιν Ἰερουσαλὴμ φανερόν 'it is clear to everyone living in Jerusalem that this remarkable miracle has been performed by them' Ac 4.16. For another interpretation of γνωστός in Ac 4.16, see 58.55.

28.33 καινός[c], ή, όν: pertaining to not being well known previously but being significant – 'previously unknown, previously unheard of, new.' τί ἐστιν τοῦτο; διδαχὴ καινὴ κατ' ἐξουσίαν 'what is this? Some kind of new teaching with authority!' Mk 1.27.[8]

28.34 ξένος, η, ον: pertaining to not being previously known and hence unheard of and unfamiliar – 'unknown, unheard of, unfamiliar, surprising.' ὡς ξένου ὑμῖν συμβαίνοντος 'as though something unknown before were happening to you' 1 Pe 4.12.

28.35 ἐμφανής[b], ές: pertaining to not having been known before but having become evident – 'well known, evident.' ἐμφανὴς ἐγενόμην τοῖς ἐμὲ μὴ ἐπερωτῶσιν 'I became well known to those who were not asking for me' Ro 10.20.

28.36 φανερόω[b]; ἐμφανίζω[b]; φαίνομαι[b]; φωτίζω[b]; φανέρωσις, εως *f*; φωτισμός[b], οῦ *m*: to cause something to be fully known by

---

8 It is possible to treat καινός in Mk 1.27 as meaning 'different' and therefore related to Subdomain F *Different Kind or Class* in Domain 58. The phrase κατ' ἐξουσίαν in Mk 1.27 may be related to the following statement about commanding unclean spirits.

revealing clearly and in some detail – 'to make known, to make plain, to reveal, to bring to the light, to disclose, revelation.'[9]

φανερόω[b]: θεῷ δὲ πεφανερώμεθα 'we are fully known by God' 2 Cor 5.11; τὴν ὀσμὴν τῆς γνώσεως αὐτοῦ φανεροῦντι δι' ἡμῶν ἐν παντὶ τόπῳ 'making known the knowledge about him in every place like a sweet aroma' 2 Cor 2.14; νυνὶ δὲ χωρὶς νόμου δικαιοσύνη θεοῦ πεφανέρωται 'but now, God's way of putting people right with himself has been made known apart from the Law' Ro 3.21; εἰ ταῦτα ποιεῖς, φανέρωσον σεαυτὸν τῷ κόσμῳ 'since you are doing these things, make yourself known to the world' Jn 7.4.

ἐμφανίζω[b]: κἀγὼ ἀγαπήσω αὐτὸν καὶ ἐμφανίσω αὐτῷ ἐμαυτόν 'I, too, will love him and reveal myself to him' Jn 14.21;[10] μηδενὶ ἐκλαλῆσαι ὅτι ταῦτα ἐνεφάνισας πρός με 'do not tell anyone that you have disclosed this to me' Ac 23.22. For another interpretation of ἐμφανίζω in Ac 23.22, see 33.208.

φαίνομαι[b] (and φαν-): ἵνα φανῇ ἁμαρτία 'so that its true nature as sin can be made fully and clearly known' Ro 7.13.

φωτίζω[b]: φωτίσαι πάντας τίς ἡ οἰκονομία τοῦ μυστηρίου 'to make known to everyone what is the secret plan to be put into effect' Eph 3.9.

φανέρωσις: ἑκάστῳ δὲ δίδοται ἡ φανέρωσις τοῦ πνεύματος πρὸς τὸ συμφέρον 'the Spirit's presence is made clearly known in each one of us, for the good of all' 1 Cor 12.7.

φωτισμός[b]: πρὸς φωτισμὸν τῆς γνώσεως τῆς δόξης τοῦ θεοῦ ἐν προσώπῳ Ἰησοῦ Χριστοῦ 'in order to make known the knowledge of God's glory, shining in the face of Jesus Christ' 2 Cor 4.6.

28.37 αὐγάζω: to cause something to be clearly evident – 'to cause to be seen, to cause to be clear to.' εἰς τὸ μὴ αὐγάσαι τὸν φωτισμὸν τοῦ εὐαγγελίου τῆς δόξης τοῦ Χριστοῦ 'so that

the light of the gospel of the glory of Christ would not be evident (to them)' or 'so that they would not see the light of the good news about the glory of Christ' 2 Cor 4.4.

28.38 ἀποκαλύπτω; ἀποκάλυψις, εως *f*: (figurative extensions of meaning of ἀποκαλύπτω and ἀποκάλυψις 'to uncover, to take out of hiding,' not occurring in the NT) to cause something to be fully known – 'to reveal, to disclose, to make fully known, revelation.'
ἀποκαλύπτω: ὅπως ἂν ἀποκαλυφθῶσιν ἐκ πολλῶν καρδιῶν διαλογισμοί 'and so the thoughts of many will be fully known' Lk 2.35; τότε ἀποκαλυφθήσεται ὁ ἄνομος 'then the Wicked One will be revealed' 2 Th 2.8.
ἀποκάλυψις: κατὰ ἀποκάλυψιν μυστηρίου χρόνοις αἰωνίοις σεσιγημένου 'according to the disclosure of the secret truth which was hidden for long ages in the past' Ro 16.25; ἡ γὰρ ἀποκαραδοκία τῆς κτίσεως τὴν ἀποκάλυψιν τῶν υἱῶν τοῦ θεοῦ ἀπεκδέχεται 'all of creation waits with eager longing for God to reveal his sons' Ro 8.19.

28.39 χρηματίζω[a]: to make known a divine revelation – 'to make known God's message, to reveal a message from God.' εἰ γὰρ ἐκεῖνοι οὐκ ἐξέφυγον ἐπὶ γῆς παραιτησάμενοι τὸν χρηματίζοντα 'for if those who refused to hear the one who made the divine message known on earth did not escape' He 12.25; ἦν αὐτῷ κεχρηματισμένον ὑπὸ τοῦ πνεύματος τοῦ ἁγίου μὴ ἰδεῖν θάνατον 'it had been made known to him by the Holy Spirit that he would not die . . .' Lk 2.26.

28.40 χρηματισμός, οῦ *m*: (derivative of χρηματίζω[a] 'to make known a divine revelation,' 28.39) the content of a divine revelation or utterance – 'divine revelation, revelation from God.'[11] ἀλλὰ τί λέγει αὐτῷ ὁ χρημα-

---

9 All of these meanings involve a shift from the sensory domain of seeing, causing to see, or giving light to, to the cognitive domain of making something fully known, evident, and clear.

10 In Jn 14.21 it is difficult to know precisely the manner or extent of the revealing represented by the verb ἐμφανίζω. It would seem that cognitive awareness or knowledge about is far more likely than any physical or visual appearance.

11 It is also possible to understand χρηματισμός as primarily focusing upon the communication rather than the aspect of revelation which makes known information from a divine source. Accordingly, χρηματισμός (28.40) and χρηματίζω[a] (28.39) can be regarded as typical instances of semantic overlap between the process of revelation (that is, 'making known') and communication (Domain 33).

τισμός; 'but what did the divine revelation say to him?' Ro 11.4.

28.41 ἐξηγέομαι^b: to make something fully known by careful explanation or by clear revelation – 'to make fully and clearly known.' μονογενὴς θεὸς . . . ἐκεῖνος ἐξηγήσατο 'the only One who is the same as God . . . has made him fully and clearly known' Jn 1.18. For another interpretation of ἐξηγέομαι in Jn 1.18, see 33.201.

28.42 δηλόω^a: to make something known by making evident what was either unknown before or what may have been difficult to understand – 'to make known, to make plain, to reveal.' ἡ γὰρ ἡμέρα δηλώσει 'the day will make it clearly known' 1 Cor 3.13; ὁ καὶ δηλώσας ἡμῖν τὴν ἀγάπην ἐν πνεύματι 'the one who made known to us the love which the Spirit has given you' Col 1.8; ἐδηλώθη γάρ μοι περὶ ὑμῶν 'it was made plain to me about you' 1 Cor 1.11.

28.43 βέβαιος^c, α, ον: pertaining to that which is known with certainty – 'known to be true, certain, verified.'[12] εἰ γὰρ ὁ δι' ἀγγέλων λαληθεὶς λόγος ἐγένετο βέβαιος 'for if the message given by angels was known to be true' or '. . . shown to be true' He 2.2. For another interpretation of βέβαιος in He 2.2, see 31.90.

28.44 βεβαιόω^b; βεβαίωσις, εως *f*: to cause something to be known as certain – 'to confirm, to verify, to prove to be true and certain, confirmation, verification.'[12]
βεβαιόω^b: τοῦ κυρίου συνεργοῦντος καὶ τὸν λόγον βεβαιοῦντος 'the Lord worked with them and verified that their preaching was true' Mk 16.20. For another interpretation of βεβαιόω in Mk 16.20, see 31.91.
βεβαίωσις: πάσης αὐτοῖς ἀντιλογίας πέρας εἰς

---

[12] The meanings of βέβαιος^c (28.43), βεβαιόω^b and βεβαίωσις (28.44) involve two quite distinct sets of semantic features. There is the obvious element of that which is confirmed, verified, and true (meanings which could be classified in Domain 72 *True, False*) as well as the process of making such information known. These meanings could therefore be treated in either domain.

βεβαίωσιν ὁ ὅρκος 'an oath, by making known that something is true and certain, brings an end to all disputes among them' He 6.16; ἐν τῇ ἀπολογίᾳ καὶ βεβαιώσει τοῦ εὐαγγελίου 'for a defense and confirmation of the gospel' Php 1.7. In Php 1.7 βεβαίωσις may denote either the process of making known something in such a way as to confirm its truth or to the process of causing people to think about something and to accept it as trustworthy, in which case βεβαίωσις might also be classified in Domain 31, Subdomain G.

28.45 τεκμήριον, ου *n*: that which causes something to be known as verified or confirmed – 'evidence, proof, convincing proof.' παρέστησεν ἑαυτὸν ζῶντα μετὰ τὸ παθεῖν αὐτὸν ἐν πολλοῖς τεκμηρίοις 'by many convincing proofs he showed himself alive after his death' Ac 1.3. In a number of languages 'convincing proof' is rendered as 'that which causes one to know for sure' or '. . . with certainty.'

28.46 συμβιβάζω^c: to cause something to be known as certain and therefore dependable – 'to show for certain, to prove.' συμβιβάζων ὅτι οὗτός ἐστιν ὁ Χριστός 'he showed for certain that this one is the Christ' Ac 9.22. In a number of languages one may express certainty by a negative phrase, for example, 'so that no one could ever doubt.' In other instances, an idiomatic expression may be used, for example, 'with heavy words' or 'with words that speak to the heart' or 'with words that are like rocks.'

28.47 δείκνυμι^a or δεικνύω; ὑποδείκνυμι^a: to make known the character or significance of something by visual, auditory, gestural, or linguistic means – 'to make known, to demonstrate, to show.'[13]
δείκνυμι^a: δειξάτω ἐκ τῆς καλῆς ἀναστροφῆς τὰ ἔργα αὐτοῦ 'let him demonstrate his deeds by his good life' Jas 3.13; ἔτι καθ' ὑπερβολὴν ὁδὸν ὑμῖν δείκνυμι 'I will make known to you a more excellent way' 1 Cor 12.31. For another

---

[13] It is possible that ὑποδείκνυμι^a is somewhat more emphatic or intensive in connotation than δείκνυμι^a, but this cannot be shown from existing contexts.

interpretation of δείκνυμι in 1 Cor 12.31, see 33.150.

ὑποδείκνυμι^a: πάντα ὑπέδειξα ὑμῖν ὅτι οὕτως κοπιῶντας 'in everything I did, I showed you that by working hard in this way . . .' Ac 20.35. In some languages it may be useful to translate ὑποδείκνυμι in Ac 20.35 as 'I showed you by example' or 'I demonstrated by example' or 'I showed you by what I did.'

28.48 δεῖγμα, τος *n*: (derivative of δείκνυμι^a 'to make known,' 28.47) the means by which the nature of something is made known, particularly as an example of what is to be avoided – 'example (such as to warn), means by which something is known.' πρόκεινται δεῖγμα πυρὸς αἰωνίου δίκην ὑπέχουσαι 'they exist as an example of undergoing the punishment of eternal fire' or 'they suffer the punishment of eternal fire, as an example (to us all)' Jd 7.

28.49 συνίστημι^b or συνιστάνω: to cause something to be known by action – 'to make known by action, to demonstrate, to show.' συνίστησιν δὲ τὴν ἑαυτοῦ ἀγάπην εἰς ἡμᾶς ὁ θεός 'but God has shown us how much he loves us' Ro 5.8; ἐν παντὶ συνίσταντες ἑαυτοὺς ὡς θεοῦ διάκονοι 'in everything showing ourselves to be servants of God' 2 Cor 6.4. In a number of languages the expression 'to show oneself to be' may best be rendered as 'to cause people to know that one is,' and therefore this expression in 2 Cor 6.4 may be rendered as 'in everything causing people to know by what we do that we are servants of God.'

28.50 ἀποδείκνυμι^a: to cause something to be known as genuine, with possible focus upon the source of such knowledge – 'to demonstrate, to show, to make clearly known.' Ἰησοῦν τὸν Ναζωραῖον, ἄνδρα ἀποδεδειγμένον ἀπὸ τοῦ θεοῦ εἰς ὑμᾶς δυνάμεσι 'Jesus of Nazareth was a man whose divine mission was clearly shown to you by miracles' Ac 2.22.

28.51 ἐνδείκνυμαι^a: to cause to be made known, with possible emphasis upon the means – 'to cause to be known, to show, to demonstrate.' εἰ δὲ θέλων ὁ θεὸς ἐνδείξασθαι τὴν ὀργήν 'if God wanted to demonstrate his wrath' Ro 9.22.

28.52 ἔνδειξις, εως *f*; ἔνδειγμα, τος *n* (derivatives of ἐνδείκνυμαι^a 'to show, to demonstrate,' 28.51); ἀπόδειξις, εως *f* (derivatives of ἀποδείκνυμι^a 'to demonstrate, to show,' 28.50): the means by which one knows that something is a fact – 'proof, evidence, verification, indication.'^{14, 15}

ἔνδειξις: ἥτις ἐστὶν αὐτοῖς ἔνδειξις ἀπωλείας 'this is a clear indication of their destruction' Php 1.28.

ἔνδειγμα: ἔνδειγμα τῆς δικαίας κρίσεως τοῦ θεοῦ 'this is the evidence of God's righteous judgment' 2 Tm 1.5.

ἀπόδειξις: ἀλλ' ἐν ἀποδείξει πνεύματος καὶ δυνάμεως 'but with evidence of the Spirit and of power' or 'but with evidence of the power of the Spirit' 1 Cor 2.4.

28.53 σφραγίζω^e: (derivative of σφραγίς^e 'validation,' 73.9) to demonstrate by authentic proof the truth or validity of something – 'to make known, to confirm, to show clearly.' ὁ λαβὼν αὐτοῦ τὴν μαρτυρίαν ἐσφράγισεν ὅτι ὁ θεὸς ἀληθής ἐστιν 'and he who accepts his message makes known the fact that God is truthful' or '. . . shows clearly . . .' Jn 3.33.

28.54 ἀναδείκνυμι^a; ἀνάδειξις εως *f*: to make known that which has presumably been hidden or unknown previously – 'to make known, to show, to reveal, to make clear, revelation.'

ἀναδείκνυμι^a: ἀνάδειξον ὃν ἐξελέξω ἐκ τούτων τῶν δύο ἕνα 'show us which one of these two you have chosen' Ac 1.24.

ἀνάδειξις: ἦν ἐν ταῖς ἐρήμοις ἕως ἡμέρας ἀναδείξεως αὐτοῦ πρὸς τὸν Ἰσραήλ 'he lived in the

---

14 It is possible that ἀπόδειξις should be classified as having a meaning somewhat distinct from ἔνδειξις and ἔνδειγμα and thus be more closely related to ἀποδείκνυμι^a (28.50), but there is no clear evidence of this in existing contexts.

15 As in the case of βέβαιος^c (28.43), βεβαιόω^b and βεβαίωσις (28.44), there are two distinct sets of semantic features in the series ἔνδειξις, ἔνδειγμα, and ἀπόδειξις. The element of 'showing' or 'demonstrating' implies clearly 'making something known,' but that which is made known is done in a clear, convincing, and confirming manner and therefore 'shown to be certain or true.' This double set of semantic features is contained in such terms as 'proof,' 'evidence' and 'confirmation.'

desert until the day he made himself known to the people of Israel' Lk 1.80.

28.55 φαίνομαι^c: to make known only the superficial and not the real character of something – 'to appear to be (something), to give an impression of.' ὑμεῖς ἔξωθεν μὲν φαίνεσθε τοῖς ἀνθρώποις δίκαιοι 'on the outside you appear to everybody as good' Mt 23.28. In order to do justice to φαίνομαι in Mt 23.28, it may be necessary in some languages to translate as follows: 'on the outside you appear to people to be good, but you really are not' or '. . . you only appear to people to be good' or '. . . you make people think you are good, but you are not.'

28.56 ἐπικάλυμμα, τος *n*: that which causes something to be known as or appear to be other than it really is, thus causing its true nature to be unknown – 'means of hiding, pretext, means of covering up the true nature of something.' μὴ ὡς ἐπικάλυμμα ἔχοντες τῆς κακίας τὴν ἐλευθερίαν 'never using your freedom as a means of covering up your evil deeds' 1 Pe 2.16.

D Able To Be Known (28.57-28.67)

28.57 γνωστός^c, ή, όν: pertaining to being able to be known – 'what can be known, what is evident, what can be clearly seen.' διότι τὸ γνωστὸν τοῦ θεοῦ φανερόν ἐστιν ἐν αὐτοῖς 'because what can be known about God is plain to them' Ro 1.19. In a number of languages the phrase 'can be known,' expressing a capacity relating to a passive state, must be restructured in an active form. This may often be done by rendering Ro 1.19 as 'because what people can know about God is clearly evident to these persons' or 'they can clearly comprehend what they can know about God' or 'because they can clearly see what people can know about God.'

28.58 δῆλος, η, ον; φανερός^b, ά, όν: pertaining to being clearly and easily able to be known – 'clearly known, easily known, evident, plain, clear.'
δῆλος: δῆλον ὅτι ἐκτὸς τοῦ ὑποτάξαντος αὐτῷ τὰ πάντα 'it is clear that the one who subjected all

things to him is excluded' 1 Cor 15.27; ὅτι δὲ ἐν νόμῳ οὐδεὶς δικαιοῦται παρὰ τῷ θεῷ δῆλον 'now it is evident that no one is put right with God by means of the Law' Ga 3.11.
φανερός^b: διότι τὸ γνωστὸν τοῦ θεοῦ φανερόν ἐστιν ἐν αὐτοῖς 'because what can be known about God is plain to them' Ro 1.19. For some of the problems involved in the rendering of Ro 1.19, see the discussion under γνωστός^c (28.57).

28.59 ἔκδηλος, ον: pertaining to being very easily known – 'easily known, very evident, quite obvious.'[16] ἡ γὰρ ἄνοια αὐτῶν ἔκδηλος ἔσται πᾶσιν 'their folly will be very obvious to everyone' 2 Tm 3.9.

28.60 πρόδηλος, ον: pertaining to being easily seen and known by the public – 'very easily known, very clear, very obvious.' τινῶν ἀνθρώπων αἱ ἁμαρτίαι πρόδηλοί εἰσιν 'the sins of some people are very obvious' 1 Tm 5.24.

28.61 τραχηλίζομαι: (a figurative extension of meaning of τραχηλίζω 'to have the neck of a sacrificial victim twisted and thus exposed for slaughter,' not occurring in the NT) that which can readily be known as the result of being exposed – 'to be easily known, to be exposed.' οὐκ ἔστιν κτίσις ἀφανὴς ἐνώπιον αὐτοῦ, πάντα δὲ γυμνὰ καὶ τετραχηλισμένα τοῖς ὀφθαλμοῖς αὐτοῦ 'there is no creature hidden from him, but all are naked and exposed to his eyes' He 4.13.

28.62 γυμνός^b, ή, όν: (a figurative extension of meaning of γυμνός^a 'naked,' 49.22) easily able to be known in view of the fact that nothing is hidden – 'not hidden, easily known, naked.' οὐκ ἔστιν κτίσις ἀφανὴς ἐνώπιον αὐτοῦ, πάντα δὲ γυμνὰ καὶ τετραχηλισμένα τοῖς ὀφθαλμοῖς αὐτοῦ 'there is no creature hidden from him, but all are naked and exposed to his eyes' He 4.13. It is rare that one can employ in translating a term which literally means 'naked,' but it is possible to retain something of the metaphorical value by using a phrase

---

16 ἔκδηλος apparently differs somewhat in force from δῆλος (28.58).

such as 'with nothing to cover' or 'with nothing which can be used to hide.'

28.63 φανερῶς[a]: pertaining to the manner by which something can easily be known by the public, with the implication that the related events take place in the open – 'publicly, openly.' τότε καὶ αὐτὸς ἀνέβη, οὐ φανερῶς ἀλλὰ ὡς ἐν κρυπτῷ 'he also went; however, he did not go openly, but secretly' Jn 7.10. The expression 'he did not go openly' may often be rendered as 'he did not go about where people could see him' or 'people did not see where he was.'

28.64 ἐν τῷ φωτί; ἐπὶ τῶν δωμάτων: (idioms, literally 'in the light' and 'on the housetops') pertaining to being widely known in view of the events in question having taken place in public – 'in public, publicly.'[17]
ἐν τῷ φωτί: ὃ λέγω ὑμῖν ἐν τῇ σκοτίᾳ, εἴπατε ἐν τῷ φωτί 'what I tell you secretly, you must tell publicly' Mt 10.27.
ἐπὶ τῶν δωμάτων: ὃ εἰς τὸ οὖς ἀκούετε, κηρύξατε ἐπὶ τῶν δωμάτων 'what you hear in private, proclaim publicly' Mt 10.27.

28.65 ἀποδείκνυμι[b]: to cause something to be known publicly – 'to show publicly, to demonstrate publicly.' δοκῶ γάρ, ὁ θεὸς ἡμᾶς τοὺς ἀποστόλους ἐσχάτους ἀπέδειξεν ὡς ἐπιθανατίους 'for it seems to me that God has shown publicly that we apostles are last, like persons condemned to die' 1 Cor 4.9.

28.66 δημόσιος, α, ον: pertaining to being able to be known by the public – 'public, open.' εὐτόνως γὰρ τοῖς Ἰουδαίοις διακατηλέγχετο δημοσίᾳ 'he vigorously refuted the Jews in public debate' Ac 18.28. The rendering of διακατηλέγχετο in Ac 18.28 provides the verbal correspondences 'he ... refuted ... in ... debate.' The term δημοσίᾳ indicates that the debates took place in public so that everyone could know or did know what was said and proven. It is, of course, possible to understand δημοσίᾳ only in the sense of 'public setting,' but in Ac 18.28 something more than mere setting seems to be implied.

28.67 κατ' ἰδίαν: (an idiom, literally 'according to that which is private') pertaining to what occurs in a private context or setting, in the sense of not being made known publicly – 'privately.'[18] κατ' ἰδίαν δὲ τοῖς δοκοῦσιν 'and in private with the leaders' Ga 2.2.

E Not Able To Be Known, Secret (28.68-28.83)

28.68 ἀφανής, ές: pertaining to not being able to be seen or known, and thus to be hidden – 'hidden, unknown.' οὐκ ἔστιν κτίσις ἀφανὴς ἐνώπιον αὐτοῦ 'there is nothing that can be hidden from him' He 4.13. It is possible to render 'that can be hidden from him' as 'that people can keep God from seeing' or 'that people can prevent God from knowing about.'

28.69 κρυπτός, ή, όν: pertaining to not being able to be known, in view of the fact that it has been kept secret – 'secret, hidden, not able to be made known.' οὐδὲν ... κρυπτὸν ὃ οὐ γνωσθήσεται 'there is nothing ... secret which will not be made known' Mt 10.26. In a number of languages there may be complications involved in what could be regarded as a triple negation in the sense that 'nothing,' 'secret' (in the sense of 'not known'), and 'not be made known' are all semantic negations. It may therefore be better to render Mt 10.26 as 'everything that is now not known will be made known.' In a number of languages 'secret' is regularly expressed as 'not known' or 'what is kept from being known.'

28.70 ἀπόκρυφος, ον: pertaining to not being able to be known and thus secret, possibly in

---

17 It is very possible that the two idioms in 28.64 differ somewhat in meaning, or at least in connotation, but it is difficult, if not impossible, to show this from existing contexts.

18 It is possible to interpret κατ' ἰδίαν as being primarily an element of setting, that is to say, 'without the presence of other persons,' but in some contexts the focus seems to shift from setting to the fact that such events take place without the general knowledge of the public. Depending therefore upon the context, one may render κατ' ἰδίαν by such expressions as 'without others knowing' or 'without other people being present.'

view of something being separate – 'secret, not able to be known.' ἐν ᾧ εἰσιν πάντες οἱ θησαυροὶ τῆς σοφίας καὶ γνώσεως ἀπόκρυφοι 'in whom are all the secret treasures of wisdom and knowledge' Col 2.3; οὐδὲ ἀπόκρυφον ὃ οὐ μὴ γνωσθῇ 'there is nothing secret which shall not be known' Lk 8.17. The triple negation in Lk 8.17 may lead to some shift in a number of languages, for example, 'everything which is secret now will be known.'

28.71 κρυφῇ; λάθρᾳ; ἐν τῇ σκοτίᾳ (an idiom, literally 'in the darkness'); ἐν (τῷ) κρυπτῷ (an idiom, literally 'in the hidden'): pertaining to not being able to be known by the public but known by some in-group or by those immediately involved – 'in secret, in private, secretly, privately.'
κρυφῇ: τὰ γὰρ κρυφῇ γινόμενα ὑπ' αὐτῶν αἰσχρόν ἐστιν καὶ λέγειν 'it is really too shameful even to talk about the things they do in secret' Eph 5.12.
λάθρᾳ: καὶ νῦν λάθρᾳ ἡμᾶς ἐκβάλλουσιν 'and now they want to send us away secretly' Ac 16.37.
ἐν τῇ σκοτίᾳ: ὃ λέγω ὑμῖν ἐν τῇ σκοτίᾳ, εἴπατε ἐν τῷ φωτί 'what I am telling you secretly, you must report openly' Mt 10.27.
ἐν (τῷ) κρυπτῷ: ὅπως ᾖ σου ἡ ἐλεημοσύνη ἐν τῷ κρυπτῷ 'so that your giving will be done secretly' Mt 6.4; οὐ φανερῶς ἀλλὰ ὡς ἐν κρυπτῷ 'not openly, but secretly' Jn 7.10.

28.72 κρυφαῖος, α, ον: pertaining to being secret as a result of people not knowing – 'in secret, privately.' καὶ ὁ πατήρ σου ὁ βλέπων ἐν τῷ κρυφαίῳ ἀποδώσει σοι 'and your Father who sees in secret will reward you' Mt 6.18.

28.73 εἰς τὸ οὖς; πρὸς τὸ οὖς: (idioms, literally 'into the ear' and 'to the ear') pertaining to what is known only by those who hear a particular message in private – 'in secret, in private, privately.'
εἰς τὸ οὖς: ὃ εἰς τὸ οὖς ἀκούετε, κηρύξατε ἐπὶ τῶν δωμάτων 'whatever you hear in secret, proclaim publicly' Mt 10.27. A phrase such as 'whatever you hear in secret' may be rendered as 'whatever you hear when no one else is listening.'
πρὸς τὸ οὖς: ὃ πρὸς τὸ οὖς ἐλαλήσατε ἐν τοῖς ταμείοις κηρυχθήσεται ἐπὶ τῶν δωμάτων 'whatever you say privately in the inner room will be proclaimed publicly' Lk 12.3. For another treatment of the phrase πρὸς τὸ οὖς λαλέω, see 33.91.

28.74 μὴ γνώτω ἡ ἀριστερά σου τί ποιεῖ ἡ δεξιά σου: (an idiom, probably an adage or traditional saying, literally 'do not let your left hand know what your right hand is doing') an admonition to do something without letting people know about it – 'to do something secretly, to do something without letting the public know.' σοῦ δὲ ποιοῦντος ἐλεημοσύνην μὴ γνώτω ἡ ἀριστερά σου τί ποιεῖ ἡ δεξιά σου 'but when you help a needy person, do it in such a way that others will not know about it' Mt 6.3. It is rare that one can preserve this idiom, since in its literal form it may seem absurd. For many English-speaking people the meaning has already been twisted by common usage to mean 'be sure to not let anyone know if you are performing something that is shady or illegal.' Today's English Version attempts to represent something of the impact of this idiom by translating "do it in such a way that even your closest friend will not know about it."

28.75 τὰ κρυπτά: the content of what is not able to be known – 'secret information, secret knowledge, secrets.' τὰ κρυπτὰ τῆς καρδίας αὐτοῦ φανερὰ γίνεται 'the secrets of his heart will be brought out in the open' 1 Cor 14.25.

28.76 τὰ βαθέα; τὰ βάθη: (figurative extensions of meaning of βαθύς 'deep,' 81.10, and βάθος 'depth,' 81.8) the content of knowledge which is very difficult to know – 'deep secrets, secrets difficult to find out about.'
τὰ βαθέα: οἵτινες οὐκ ἔγνωσαν τὰ βαθέα τοῦ Σατανᾶ, ὡς λέγουσιν '(you) who have not learned what others call the deep secrets of Satan' Re 2.24.
τὰ βάθη: τὸ γὰρ πνεῦμα πάντα ἐραυνᾷ, καὶ τὰ βάθη τοῦ θεοῦ 'the Spirit searches everything, even the deep secrets of God' 1 Cor 2.10.
Only rarely can one use a literal rendering of τὰ βαθέα or τὰ βάθη in referring to secrets. In some instances it may be possible to use an expression such as 'far away' or 'distant,' and

in other cases one can use expressions meaning 'hard' or 'difficult.' More often than not, however, the closest equivalent of τὰ βαθέα and τὰ βάθη in this type of context is either an expression of degree using a term such as 'very' (for example, 'that which is very secret') or an expression implying 'that which is hidden' or 'that which is difficult to discover.'

28.77 μυστήριον, ου *n*: the content of that which has not been known before but which has been revealed to an in-group or restricted constituency – 'secret, mystery.' ὑμῖν δέδοται γνῶναι τὰ μυστήρια τῆς βασιλείας τῶν οὐρανῶν 'the knowledge of the secrets of the kingdom of heaven has been given to you' Mt 13.11. There is a serious problem involved in translating μυστήριον by a word which is equivalent to the English expression 'mystery,' for this term in English refers to a secret which people have tried to uncover but which they have failed to understand. In many instances μυστήριον is translated by a phrase meaning 'that which was not known before,' with the implication of its being revealed at least to some persons.

28.78 κρύπτη, ης *f*: (locative derivative of κρυπτός 'secret, hidden,' 28.69) a place which is secret or hidden and thus not generally known, possibly referring to a structure built underground for hiding or storing objects – 'secret place, hidden place, cellar.'[19] οὐδεὶς λύχνον ἅψας εἰς κρύπτην τίθησιν 'no one lights a lamp and then puts it in a secret place' Lk 11.33.

28.79 κρύπτω[d]; καλύπτω[b]; περικρύβω: to cause something not to be known – 'to hide, to keep secret, to conceal.'[20]
κρύπτω[d]: ὅτι ἔκρυψας ταῦτα ἀπὸ σοφῶν καὶ

συνετῶν καὶ ἀπεκάλυψας αὐτὰ νηπίοις 'because you have hidden these things from the wise and learned and have revealed them to the unlearned' Mt 11.25. In a number of languages, the causative relationships involved in Mt 11.25 must be made somewhat more explicit, for example, 'because you have kept the wise and learned people from knowing and have caused the unlearned to know.' In Mt 11.25 νήπιος is used figuratively in reference to unlearned people.
καλύπτω[b]: οὐδὲν γάρ ἐστιν κεκαλυμμένον ὃ οὐκ ἀποκαλυφθήσεται 'there is nothing which is hidden which shall not be made known' or 'what has been kept secret shall be made known' Mt 10.26.
περικρύβω: περιέκρυβεν ἑαυτὴν μῆνας πέντε 'she hid herself for five months' Lk 1.24.

28.80 ἀποκρύπτω: to cause something to remain unknown, with the implication of concealment and inaccessibility – 'to keep secret, to conceal.'[21] λαλοῦμεν θεοῦ σοφίαν ἐν μυστηρίῳ, τὴν ἀποκεκρυμμένην 'we speak of God's secret wisdom which has been concealed' 1 Cor 2.7. The passive expression 'concealed' may be rendered in an active form as 'God has kept people from knowing about this wisdom.'

28.81 συγκαλύπτω: to cause something to remain unknown by means of purposeful concealment – 'to keep secret, to hide, to conceal.'[21] οὐδὲν δὲ συγκεκαλυμμένον ἐστὶν ὃ οὐκ ἀποκαλυφθήσεται 'there is nothing which is hidden which shall not be made known' Lk 12.2.

28.82 παρακαλύπτω: to cause something to be unknown or to be known only with great difficulty – 'to cause to not be known, to hide, to conceal, to make secret.' οἱ δὲ ἠγνόουν τὸ ῥῆμα τοῦτο, καὶ ἦν παρακεκαλυμμένον ἀπ'

---

19 It would also be possible to classify κρύπτη in Domain 24 *Sensory Events and States* as 'a place which cannot be seen.'
20 The series of meanings in 28.79 differs significantly from the meaning of ἐγκρύπτω in 85.50. In 28.79 the focus in concealment is upon preventing knowledge about something, while in 85.50 the concealment focuses upon something being in a place where it is no longer visible.

21 It is not easy to distinguish clearly between ἀποκρύπτω (28.80) and συγκαλύπτω (28.81), but ἀποκρύπτω, particularly in passive forms, may imply concealment on the basis of the nature of the object itself, while συγκαλύπτω would appear, at least in certain contexts, to imply a greater measure of intent or purpose.

αὐτῶν 'they did not know what this meant; it was a secret' or '. . . it was hidden from them' Lk 9.45.

28.83 λανθάνω[a]: to cause oneself to not be known, with the implication of concealment and secrecy – 'to escape notice, to remain hid-

den.' καὶ οὐκ ἠδυνήθη λαθεῖν 'and he was not able to escape notice' or '. . . to remain un-noticed' Mk 7.24. In some languages this expression in Mk 7.24 may be rendered as 'he was not able to keep people from knowing where he was' or 'he was not able to keep secret where he was.'

29 Memory and Recall

Outline of Subdomains

A   Storing of Information (29.1-29.5)
B   Recalling from Memory (29.6-29.12)
C   Not Remembering, Forgetting (29.13-29.15)
D   Recalling and Responding with Appropriate Action (29.16-29.18)

As the above outline clearly indicates, the Domain *Memory and Recall* involves four significant aspects of memory which are closely related. *Storing of Information* involves primarily paying special attention to information for the sake of ready recall. Subdomain B *Recalling from Memory* does not, however, imply necessarily that one has forgotten information. It is only that the information may not be a matter of constant awareness. Subdomain C *Not Remembering, Forgetting* is simply a negation of Subdomain B, while Subdomain D *Recalling and Responding with Appropriate Action* involves a variety of events directly implied by the use of terms, the central meaning of which involves remembering or forgetting, but to which have been added important elements of behavior.

A   Storing of Information (29.1-29.5)

29.1 συντηρέω[b]: to exert mental effort in storing information so as to have continual access and use of it – 'to cause oneself to be fully aware of, to keep in mind, to remember.' ἡ δὲ Μαριὰμ πάντα συνετήρει τὰ ῥήματα ταῦτα συμβάλλουσα ἐν τῇ καρδίᾳ αὐτῆς 'Mary kept all these things in mind and thought deeply about them' Lk 2.19. An equivalent of 'to

keep in mind' may be 'to keep thinking about' or 'to continue to think about' or even 'not to stop thinking about.'

29.2 τίθεμαι ἐν τῇ καρδίᾳ: (an idiom, literally 'to place in the heart') to store information in the mind, with the implication of its being valuable – 'to treasure up in the heart, to store in the mind as valuable.' ἔθεντο πάντες οἱ ἀκούσαντες ἐν τῇ καρδίᾳ αὐτῶν 'everyone who heard it treasured it in their hearts' Lk 1.66.

29.3 σημειόομαι: to pay special attention to something for the sake of a future recall and response – 'to take note of, to pay special attention to.' τοῦτον σημειοῦσθε, μὴ συναναμίγνυσθαι αὐτῷ 'take note of him and have nothing to do with him' 2 Th 3.14.

29.4 λογίζομαι[b]: to keep a mental record of events for the sake of some future action – 'to keep a record, to remember, to bear in mind.' οὐ λογίζεται τὸ κακόν '(love) doesn't keep a record of evil' 1 Cor 13.5; μὴ λογιζόμενος αὐτοῖς τὰ παραπτώματα αὐτῶν 'he did not keep their sins in mind' 2 Cor 5.19. 'To keep a mental record of something' may be rendered as 'to add up in one's mind' or 'to make a list in one's heart.'

29.5 τίθεμαι εἰς τὰ ὦτα[b]: (an idiom, literally 'to place in the ears') to continue to bear something in mind – 'to bear in mind, to remember well, to not forget.' θέσθε ὑμεῖς εἰς τὰ ὦτα ὑμῶν τοὺς λόγους τούτους 'bear in mind these words' Lk 9.44. For another interpretation of the idiom τίθεμαι εἰς τὰ ὦτα in Lk 9.44, see 24.64.

B Recalling from Memory (29.6-29.12)

29.6 οἶδα^d: to be able to recall from memory
– 'to remember, to recall, to recollect.' λοιπὸν
οὐκ οἶδα εἴ τινα ἄλλον ἐβάπτισα 'for the rest, I
do not remember if I baptized any other person' 1 Cor 1.16.

29.7 μνημονεύω^a; μιμνῄσκομαι^a; μνήμη,
ης *f*; μνεία^a, ας *f*: to recall information from
memory, but without necessarily the implica-
tion that persons have actually forgotten – 'to
remember, to recall, to think about again,
memory, remembrance.'
μνημονεύω^a: μνημονεύετε γάρ, ἀδελφοί, τὸν κόπον ἡμῶν καὶ τὸν μόχθον 'surely you remem-
ber, fellow believers, how we worked and toil-
ed' 1 Th 2.9; μνημονεύετε τῶν ἡγουμένων
ὑμῶν, οἵτινες ἐλάλησαν ὑμῖν τὸν λόγον τοῦ θεοῦ
'remember your (former) leaders, who spoke
God's message to you' He 13.7.
μιμνῄσκομαι^a: μνησθῆναι τῶν προειρημένων
ῥημάτων ὑπὸ τῶν ἁγίων προφητῶν '(I want
you) to remember the words that were spoken
long ago by the holy prophets' 2 Pe 3.2; ἐμνήσ-
θησαν οἱ μαθηταὶ αὐτοῦ ὅτι γεγραμμένον ἐστίν,
Ὁ ζῆλος τοῦ οἴκου σου καταφάγεταί με 'his
disciples remembered that the Scripture says,
My devotion to your house will consume me'
Jn 2.17.
μνήμη: σπουδάσω δὲ καὶ ἑκάστοτε ἔχειν ὑμᾶς
μετὰ τὴν ἐμὴν ἔξοδον τὴν τούτων μνήμην
ποιεῖσθαι 'I will do my best, then, to provide a
way for you to remember these matters at all
times after my death' 2 Pe 1.15.
μνεία^a: ὅτι ἔχετε μνείαν ἡμῶν ἀγαθὴν πάντοτε
'that you remember us well at all times' 1 Th
3.6; ἐπὶ πάσῃ τῇ μνείᾳ ὑμῶν 'every time I think
of you' Php 1.3.

In some languages the process of remembering is expressed idiomatically, for example, 'to find one's thoughts again' or 'to see
again in one's heart' or 'to have one's liver
repeat the words.'

29.8 μνημονεύω^b: (compare μνημονεύω^a 'to
remember, to recall,' 29.7) to keep on recall-
ing and thinking about again and again – 'to
keep thinking about, to think about again and
again.' εἰ μὲν ἐκείνης ἐμνημόνευον ἀφ' ἧς
ἐξέβησαν, εἶχον ἂν καιρὸν ἀνακάμψαι 'if they

had kept thinking of that (country) which they
had left behind, they could have gone back'
He 11.15; οὐκέτι μνημονεύει τῆς θλίψεως διὰ
τὴν χαρὰν ὅτι ἐγεννήθη ἄνθρωπος εἰς τὸν κόσμον
'she no longer keeps thinking about her suffering because she is happy that a child
(literally 'human being') has been born into
the world' Jn 16.21.

29.9 ἀναμιμνῄσκομαι; ὑπομιμνῄσκομαι: to
cause oneself to remember or to be caused to
remember – 'to recall, to remember.'
ἀναμιμνῄσκομαι: τὰ σπλάγχνα αὐτοῦ περισσοτέρως εἰς ὑμᾶς ἐστιν ἀναμιμνησκομένου τὴν
πάντων ὑμῶν ὑπακοήν 'so his love for you
grows stronger, as he remembers how all of
you were ready to obey' 2 Cor 7.15.
ὑπομιμνῄσκομαι: στραφεὶς ὁ κύριος ἐνέβλεψεν
τῷ Πέτρῳ, καὶ ὑπεμνήσθη ὁ Πέτρος τοῦ ῥήματος
τοῦ κυρίου 'the Lord turned around and looked straight at Peter, and Peter remembered
the Lord's words' Lk 22.61.

29.10 ἀναμιμνῄσκω; ἐπαναμιμνῄσκω; ὑπομιμνῄσκω; ὑπόμνησις, εως *f*: to cause to recall and to think about again – 'to remind, to
cause to remember, to cause to think about
again.'[1]
ἀναμιμνῄσκω: δι' ἣν αἰτίαν ἀναμιμνῄσκω σε
ἀναζωπυρεῖν τὸ χάρισμα τοῦ θεοῦ 'for this
reason I remind you to keep alive the gift that
God gave to you' 2 Tm 1.6.
ἐπαναμιμνῄσκω: τολμηρότερον δὲ ἔγραψα ὑμῖν
ἀπὸ μέρους, ὡς ἐπαναμιμνῄσκων ὑμᾶς 'but in
this letter I have been quite bold about certain
subjects of which I have reminded you again'
Ro 15.15.
ὑπομιμνῄσκω: ἐκεῖνος ὑμᾶς διδάξει πάντα καὶ
ὑπομνήσει ὑμᾶς πάντα ἃ εἶπον ὑμῖν ἐγώ 'he will
teach you everything and remind you of
everything I've said to you' Jn 14.26; ἐὰν
ἔλθω, ὑπομνήσω αὐτοῦ τὰ ἔργα ἃ ποιεῖ 'when I
come, I will remind him of everything he has
done' 3 Jn 10.
ὑπόμνησις: διεγείρειν ὑμᾶς ἐν ὑπομνήσει 'to stir
you up by reminding you' 2 Pe 1.13. It is also
possible to interpret ὑπόμνησις in 2 Pe 1.13 as

---

1 It is possible that ἐπαναμιμνῄσκω differs somewhat in
meaning from ἀναμιμνῄσκω in focusing attention upon
the particular information which is recalled, but it is impossible to determine this from existing contexts.

meaning simply 'to remember,' and therefore one may translate as 'to stir you up as you remember.'

In 2 Tm 1.5 the phrase ὑπόμνησιν λαμβάνω may be interpreted as a causative passive phrase (compare λαμβάνω in 90.63 and 90.85), for example, ὑπόμνησιν λαβὼν τῆς ἐν σοὶ ἀνυποκρίτου πίστεως 'I have been reminded of your sincere faith,' but it may also be appropriately rendered as an instance of active remembering and accordingly translated as 'I remember the sincere faith that you have.'

29.11 ἀνάμνησις, εως *f*: (derivative of ἀναμιμνήσκω 'to cause to remember,' 29.10) the means for causing someone to remember – 'means of remembering, reminder.' ἀλλ' ἐν αὐταῖς ἀνάμνησις ἁμαρτιῶν κατ' ἐνιαυτόν 'but in those (sacrifices) there is a yearly reminder of sins' or '. . . that people have sinned' He 10.3.

29.12 μνημόσυνον, ου *n*: (derivative of μνημονεύω[a] 'to think about again, to remember,' 29.7) an instrument or means designed to cause to remember – 'memorial, in memory of, something to cause people to remember.' ὅπου ἐὰν κηρυχθῇ τὸ εὐαγγέλιον τοῦτο ἐν ὅλῳ τῷ κόσμῳ, λαληθήσεται καὶ ὃ ἐποίησεν αὕτη εἰς μνημόσυνον αὐτῆς 'wherever this gospel is preached, all over the world, what she has done will be told in memory of her' Mt 26.13; αἱ προσευχαί σου καὶ αἱ ἐλεημοσύναι σου ἀνέβησαν εἰς μνημόσυνον ἔμπροσθεν τοῦ θεοῦ 'your prayers and acts of charity have gone up as a memorial before God' or '. . . as a means of reminding . . .' Ac 10.4. In translating Ac 10.4 it is important to avoid implying that God had forgotten; the implication is simply that prayers and acts of charity are means by which God becomes aware and thus responds to such events. It is also possible to restructure the meaningful components of this statement as in the case of TEV, "God is pleased with your prayers and works of charity."

C Not Remembering, Forgetting (29.13-29.15)

29.13 λανθάνω[b]; λήθη, ης *f*: to not recall information and thus to lose sight of its signifi-

cance – 'to forget, to not remember, to lose sight of, to ignore.'

λανθάνω[b]: ἓν δὲ τοῦτο μὴ λανθανέτω ὑμᾶς, ἀγαπητοί 'but do not forget this one thing, dear friends' 2 Pe 3.8; λανθάνει γὰρ αὐτοὺς τοῦτο θέλοντας, ὅτι οὐρανοὶ ἦσαν ἔκπαλαι . . . τῷ τοῦ θεοῦ λόγῳ 'for when they maintain this, they forget that . . . by the word of God . . . the heavens existed long ago' 2 Pe 3.5.

λήθη: λήθην λαβὼν τοῦ καθαρισμοῦ τῶν πάλαι αὐτοῦ ἁμαρτιῶν 'he has lost sight of the fact that his past sins have been washed away' 2 Pe 1.9.

In a number of languages the fact of 'forgetting' or 'not remembering' is expressed idiomatically, for example, 'to lose out of one's heart,' 'to have one's thoughts walk away,' or 'to have words disappear from one's liver.'

29.14 ἐπιλανθάνομαι[a]; ἐπιλησμονή, ῆς *f*: to not recall information concerning some particular matter – 'to forget, to not recall.'

ἐπιλανθάνομαι[a]: ἓν δέ, τὰ μὲν ὀπίσω ἐπιλανθανόμενος 'the one thing (I do), however, is to forget what is behind me' Php 3.13.

ἐπιλησμονή: οὐκ ἀκροατὴς ἐπιλησμονῆς γενόμενος 'do not be one who hears and then forgets' Jas 1.25.

29.15 ἐκλανθάνομαι: to forget completely or thoroughly – 'to forget entirely, to not remember at all.' ἐκλέλησθε τῆς παρακλήσεως, ἥτις ὑμῖν ὡς υἱοῖς διαλέγεται 'you have entirely forgotten the exhortation which addresses you as sons' He 12.5.

D Recalling and Responding with Appropriate Action (29.16-29.18)

29.16 μνημονεύω[c]; μιμνήσκομαι[b]: to recall or be aware of information, and as a result to respond in an appropriate manner (for example, punishing, helping, honoring, etc., depending upon the context) – 'to recall, to remember.'

μνημονεύω[c]: ἐμνημόνευσεν ὁ θεὸς τὰ ἀδικήματα αὐτῆς 'God has remembered her crimes' Re 18.5; μόνον τῶν πτωχῶν ἵνα μνημονεύωμεν 'all they asked was that we should remember the needy of their group' (literally 'alone that we . . .') Ga 2.10. μνημονεύω in Re 18.5 implies much more than God's mental state in remembering the crimes of Babylon. The reference is clearly to God's both remembering and punishing. Similarly, in Ga 2.10 μνημονεύω refers to more than mere mental awareness of those in need, for the process of recall involves doing something about the needy (contrast 29.7). In a number of languages it may be necessary to make this implication quite specific, for example, 'all they asked was that we should be concerned for the needy of their group.'

μιμνῄσκομαι^b: ἐπαινῶ δὲ ὑμᾶς ὅτι πάντα μου μέμνησθε 'I praise you because you always remember me' 1 Cor 11.2. In 1 Cor 11.2 the occurrence of μιμνῄσκομαι would seem to imply more than merely a mental state of recalling the presence of Paul in Corinth. The implication may very well be to the mention of Paul in prayer.

29.17 ἐπιλανθάνομαι^b: to not recall and thus to fail to do something – 'to forget to do, to neglect, to overlook.' οὐχὶ πέντε στρουθία πωλοῦνται ἀσσαρίων δύο; καὶ ἓν ἐξ αὐτῶν οὐκ ἔστιν ἐπιλελησμένον ἐνώπιον τοῦ θεοῦ 'aren't five sparrows sold for two pennies? Yet, not a single one of them is forgotten by God' Lk 12.6.

29.18 μνημονεύω^d; μνεία^b, ας f: to recall and to respond by making mention of – 'to remember and mention, to remember to mention.'[2]

μνημονεύω^d: μνημονεύοντες ὑμῶν τοῦ ἔργου τῆς πίστεως . . . ἔμπροσθεν τοῦ θεοῦ καὶ πατρὸς ἡμῶν 'for we remember and mention . . . (in our prayers) to our God and Father . . . how you put your faith to work' 1 Th 1.3.

μνεία^b: ὡς ἀδιαλείπτως μνείαν ὑμῶν ποιοῦμαι πάντοτε ἐπὶ τῶν προσευχῶν μου 'how I always remember to mention you every time I pray' Ro 1.9-10; ἀδιάλειπτον ἔχω τὴν περὶ σοῦ μνείαν ἐν ταῖς δεήσεσίν μου νυκτὸς καὶ ἡμέρας 'I remember to mention you always in my prayers, night and day' 2 Tm 1.3.

---

2 μνημονεύω^d and μνεία^b overlap with the domain of *Communication* (33), since the meaning involves not only remembering but making mention of a person in prayer. It is possible, however, that the prayer would be inaudible, that is to say, 'silent prayer.'

30 Think

Outline of Subdomains

While the Domain *Know* (28) involves the possession of information and the Domain *Learn* (27) involves the acquisition of information, the Domain *Think* (30) involves essentially the processing and manipulation of information, often leading to decision and choice. The Domain *Hold a View, Believe, Trust* (31) is closely related to Domain 30 *Think*, but in general it is more static than procedural and manipulative. Thinking does, of course, also relate closely to the process of comprehension and understanding, but these latter meanings are treated in a separate domain, *Understanding* (32).

A   To Think, Thought (30.1-30.38)

30.1 ἐνθυμέομαι; βλέπω^d; ἐμβλέπω^b: to process information by giving consideration to various aspects – 'to think about, to consider.'[1]

ἐνθυμέομαι: ταῦτα δὲ αὐτοῦ ἐνθυμηθέντος 'while he was thinking about these things' Mt 1.20; ἱνατί ἐνθυμεῖσθε πονηρὰ ἐν ταῖς καρδίαις ὑμῶν; 'why are you thinking (such) evil things in your hearts?' Mt 9.4.

βλέπω[d]: βλέπετε γὰρ τὴν κλῆσιν ὑμῶν, ἀδελφοί 'think about (what you were), fellow believers, when (God) called you' 1 Cor 1.26.

ἐμβλέπω[b]: ἐμβλέψατε εἰς τὰ πετεινὰ τοῦ οὐρανοῦ 'consider the birds which fly in the sky' Mt 6.26.[2]

In a number of languages the concept of thinking is closely related to terms referring to perception. For example, in some languages one may speak of thinking as 'to see with the heart' or 'to look at with the liver.'

30.2 διενθυμέομαι: to think about something thoroughly and/or seriously – 'to think seriously about, to ponder.' τοῦ δὲ Πέτρου διενθυμουμένου περὶ τοῦ ὁράματος εἶπεν αὐτῷ τὸ πνεῦμα 'while Peter was still thinking seriously about the vision, the Spirit spoke to him' Ac 10.19. In a number of languages the equivalent of 'thinking thoroughly or seriously about something' is merely 'to think very much about,' but if possible, the focus should be upon intensity rather than mere quantity.

30.3 νοέω[b]: to think over a matter with care – 'to think about carefully, to consider well.' ὁ ἀναγινώσκων νοείτω 'let the reader think carefully' or 'note to the reader: carefully think about what this means' Mk 13.14; νόει ὃ λέγω 'think carefully about what I am saying' 2 Tm 2.7.

30.4 κατανοέω[a]: to give very careful consideration to some matter – 'to think about very carefully, to consider closely.'[3] κατανο-

---

1 It is possible that ἐμβλέπω[b] differs somewhat in meaning from βλέπω[d] in focusing the thought processes on some particular object or matter, but it is difficult to determine this on the basis of existing contexts.

2 It is possible to regard ἐμβλέπω in Mt 6.26 as involving a combination of seeing (see 24.9) plus intellectual activity.

3 κατανοέω[a] seems to differ from νοέω[b] (30.3) in the intensity of the mental activity, but this is not evident from all contexts.

ήσατε τὸν ἀπόστολον καὶ ἀρχιερέα τῆς ὁμολογίας ἡμῶν Ἰησοῦν 'consider Jesus, whom (God) sent to be the High Priest of (the faith) we confess' He 3.1; κατενόησεν τὸ ἑαυτοῦ σῶμα ἤδη νενεκρωμένον 'he carefully considered his body, which was already practically dead' Ro 4.19. For another interpretation of κατανοέω in Ro 4.19, see 32.12.

30.5 νοῦς[b], νοός, νοΐ, νοῦν m; διάνοια[b], ας f; ἔννοια[a], ας f: a particular manner or way of thinking – 'way of thinking, disposition, manner of thought, attitude.'

νοῦς[b]: εἰκῇ φυσιούμενος ὑπὸ τοῦ νοὸς τῆς σαρκὸς αὐτοῦ '(such a person is) puffed up, for no reason at all, by his human way of thinking' Col 2.18.

διάνοια[b]: ὑμᾶς ποτε ὄντας ἀπηλλοτριωμένους καὶ ἐχθροὺς τῇ διανοίᾳ ἐν τοῖς ἔργοις τοῖς πονηροῖς 'at that time you were strangers and enemies because of the manner in which you thought and the evil things you did' Col 1.21.

ἔννοια[a]: ὑμεῖς τὴν αὐτὴν ἔννοιαν ὁπλίσασθε 'you too must strengthen yourselves with the same way of thinking' 1 Pe 4.1.

In a number of languages it may be necessary to render 'way of thinking' by a clause, for example, 'how people think.' In the case of 1 Pe 4.1, it may be necessary to translate 'you too must strengthen yourselves by thinking just like Christ thought.'

30.6 πνεῦμα[f], τος n: (compare πνεῦμα[e] 'inner being,' 26.9) an attitude or disposition reflecting the way in which a person thinks about or deals with some matter – 'disposition, attitude, way of thinking.' ὑμεῖς οἱ πνευματικοὶ καταρτίζετε τὸν τοιοῦτον ἐν πνεύματι πραΰτητος 'those of you who are spiritual should set him right, but in an attitude of gentleness' Ga 6.1. In some languages πνεῦμα[f] may be regarded as implicit in the context itself, so that the last part of Ga 6.1 may well be translated as 'but do it with gentleness.'

30.7 συμβάλλω[a]; ἐπιβάλλω[c]: to give careful consideration to various implications of an issue – 'to reflect on, to think about seriously, to think deeply about.'

συμβάλλω[a]: ἡ δὲ Μαριὰμ πάντα συνετήρει τὰ ῥήματα ταῦτα συμβάλλουσα ἐν τῇ καρδίᾳ αὐτῆς 'Mary remembered all these things and thought deeply about them' Lk 2.19.

ἐπιβάλλω[c]: καὶ ἐπιβαλὼν ἔκλαιεν 'and as he thought seriously about this, he cried' Mk 14.72. For another interpretation of ἐπιβάλλω in Mk 14.72, see 68.5.

30.8 βουλεύομαι[b]: to think over carefully in an attempt to make a decision – 'to think about carefully, to deliberate.' βουλεύσεται εἰ δυνατός ἐστιν . . . ὑπαντῆσαι τῷ . . . ἐρχομένῳ ἐπ' αὐτόν 'he will deliberate as to whether he is strong enough . . . to face the one . . . coming against him' Lk 14.31.

30.9 λογίζομαι[a]; λογισμός[a], οῦ m: to think about something in a detailed and logical manner – 'to think about, to reason about, to ponder, reasoning.'
λογίζομαι[a]: ὅτε ἤμην νήπιος . . . ἐλογιζόμην ὡς νήπιος 'when I was a child . . . I reasoned as a child' 1 Cor 13.11.
λογισμός[a]: συμμαρτυρούσης αὐτῶν τῆς συνειδήσεως καὶ μεταξὺ ἀλλήλων τῶν λογισμῶν κατηγορούντων ἢ καὶ ἀπολογουμένων 'their consciences also show that this is true, since in their reasoning within themselves, they either accuse or excuse themselves' Ro 2.15.

30.10 διαλογίζομαι[a]; διαλογισμός[a], οῦ m; ἀναλογίζομαι: to think or reason with thoroughness and completeness – 'to think out carefully, to reason thoroughly, to consider carefully, to reason, reasoning.'[4]
διαλογίζομαι[a]: διελογίζετο ἐν ἑαυτῷ 'he began to reason about this in himself' Lk 12.17; διελογίζετο ποταπὸς εἴη ὁ ἀσπασμὸς οὗτος 'she carefully considered what the greeting meant' Lk 1.29.
διαλογισμός[a]: ἐματαιώθησαν ἐν τοῖς διαλογισμοῖς αὐτῶν 'their reasoning became futile' (literally 'they became futile in their reasoning') Ro 1.21.

---

4 διαλογίζομαι[a] and διαλογισμός[a] appear to differ from λογίζομαι[a] and λογισμός[a] (30.9) in reflecting a greater degree of thoroughness or completeness, but this contrast is not evident in all contexts.
It is possible that ἀναλογίζομαι differs somewhat from διαλογίζομαι[a], but this is not evident from existing contexts.

ἀναλογίζομαι: ἀναλογίσασθε γὰρ τὸν τοιαύτην ὑπομεμενηκότα ὑπὸ τῶν ἁμαρτωλῶν εἰς ἑαυτὸν ἀντιλογίαν 'consider carefully the one who endured such opposition from sinners against himself' He 12.3.

30.11 λογισμός[b], οῦ m: fallacious and deceptive reasoning and, by implication, based on evil intentions – 'false reasoning, false arguments.' δυνατὰ τῷ θεῷ πρὸς καθαίρεσιν ὀχυρωμάτων, λογισμοὺς καθαιροῦντες 'God's powerful weapons, with which to destroy strongholds, that is, to destroy false arguments' 2 Cor 10.4. It may be difficult in some languages to speak of 'false arguments,' especially if the equivalent of 'arguments' is a verb meaning 'to argue' or 'to discuss against someone.' One can, however, express the semantic content of 'false arguments' (as reflected in λογισμός[b]) by translating as 'what people say when they argue, but their words are not true' or 'they argue with words that are not true.'

30.12 ἄλογος[a], ον: pertaining to a lack of capacity to reason or think properly – 'without reason, not able to reason.' ὡς ἄλογα ζῷα γεγεννημένα 'having become like creatures unable to reason' 2 Pe 2.12. In rendering 2 Pe 2.12 one may translate 'creatures unable to reason' as 'wild animals,' for this is clearly the reference of the phrase ἄλογα ζῷα.

30.13 λόγος[i], ου m: that which is thought to be true but is not necessarily so – 'appearance, to seem to be.' ἅτινά ἐστιν λόγον μὲν ἔχοντα σοφίας 'things have the appearance of being based on wisdom' or 'which things seem to be a matter of wisdom' Col 2.23.

30.14 ὄψις[b], εως f: that which is thought to be true but is not necessarily so, since it is based upon mere appearance and external form – 'outward appearance, external form.' μὴ κρίνετε κατ' ὄψιν 'do not judge according to external appearance' or 'do not judge according to what merely seems to be so' Jn 7.24.

30.15 ἐνθύμησις, εως f; νόημα[b], τος n; διάνοια[c], ας f; διανόημα, τος n: the content of thinking and reasoning – 'thought, what is thought, opinion.'

ἐνθύμησις: ἰδὼν ὁ Ἰησοῦς τὰς ἐνθυμήσεις αὐτῶν 'Jesus knew what they were thinking' Mt 9.4; χαράγματι τέχνης καὶ ἐνθυμήσεως ἀνθρώπου 'formed by the skill and thought of people' Ac 17.29.

νόημα[b]: αἰχμαλωτίζοντες πᾶν νόημα εἰς τὴν ὑπακοὴν τοῦ Χριστοῦ 'we take every thought captive and make it obey Christ' 2 Cor 10.5. It may be difficult in some languages to speak of 'taking every thought captive,' but one can often say 'to control every thought' or 'to make oneself think as one should.'

διάνοια[c]: διεσκόρπισεν ὑπερηφάνους διανοίᾳ καρδίας αὐτῶν 'he scatters the proud in the thoughts of their hearts' or '. . . what they have thought in their hearts' Lk 1.51.

διανόημα: αὐτὸς δὲ εἰδὼς αὐτῶν τὰ διανοήματα 'but he knew their thoughts' Lk 11.17.

In a number of languages it is simply not possible to find noun-like words for thinking or reasoning. Therefore, it may be necessary to use a verb equivalent throughout. For example, in Lk 11.17 one may translate as 'but Jesus knew what they were thinking.'

30.16 διαλογισμός[b], οῦ *m*: the content or result of one's thorough reasoning – 'what is reasoned, reasoning.' ὅπως ἂν ἀποκαλυφθῶσιν ἐκ πολλῶν καρδιῶν διαλογισμοί 'and so he will reveal what they have reasoned out in their hearts' (literally 'so that the reasoning from many hearts will be revealed') Lk 2.35.

30.17 ἀναβαίνω ἐπὶ καρδίαν: (an idiom, literally 'to arise in the heart') to begin to think about something – 'to begin to think, to think, to have a thought occur to someone.' ἐπὶ καρδίαν ἀνθρώπου οὐκ ἀνέβη 'what no one ever thought could happen' 1 Cor 2.9.

30.18 συνέχομαι ἐκ: (an idiom, literally 'to be held together from') to be in a mental state between two alternatives – 'to be pulled in two directions, to be betwixt and between, to have conflicting thoughts.' συνέχομαι δὲ ἐκ τῶν δύο 'I have conflicting thoughts' or 'I am in the middle between two sets of thoughts' Php 1.23. In a number of languages the rendering of this expression in Php 1.23 must be expressed idiomatically, for example, 'my mind is pulling me in two directions' or 'my

thoughts are going in two different directions' or 'my heart is speaking two different words to me.'

30.19 κατάνυξις, εως *f*: a state of not being able to think satisfactorily because of complete bewilderment and stupor – 'not being able to think, bewilderment.' ἔδωκεν αὐτοῖς ὁ θεὸς πνεῦμα κατανύξεως 'God gave them a spirit of bewilderment' or 'God caused them to be completely bewildered' or 'God made them unable to think' Ro 11.8.

30.20 φρονέω[b]; φροντίζω; σκοπέω[d]; μελετάω[a]: to keep on giving serious consideration to something – 'to ponder, to let one's mind dwell on, to keep thinking about, to fix one's attention on.'

φρονέω[b]: τὰ ἄνω φρονεῖτε 'let your mind dwell on the things which are above' Col 3.2.

φροντίζω: ἵνα φροντίζωσιν καλῶν ἔργων προΐστασθαι οἱ πεπιστευκότες θεῷ 'in order that those who believe in God may fix their attention on being concerned with good works' or '. . . on being active in doing good works' Tt 3.8.

σκοπέω[d]: μὴ σκοπούντων ἡμῶν τὰ βλεπόμενα ἀλλὰ τὰ μὴ βλεπόμενα 'we let our minds dwell not on the things that are seen but on the things that are not seen' 2 Cor 4.18.

μελετάω[a]: ταῦτα μελέτα 'keep thinking carefully about these things' 1 Tm 4.15. It is also possible to understand μελετάω in 1 Tm 4.15 as meaning 'to do' or 'to practice,' as noted in 68.20.

30.21 ὁμόφρων, ον: pertaining to being of the same mind or having the same thoughts as someone else – 'like-minded, with similar thoughts.' τὸ δὲ τέλος πάντες ὁμόφρονες 'in conclusion, all should be like-minded' 1 Pe 3.8. In some languages it may be better to speak of 'having the same attitudes' or, idiomatically, 'having thoughts that follow the same path.'

30.22 σωφρονέω[a]: to be able to reason and think properly and in a sane manner – 'to be in one's right mind, to be sane, to think straight, to reason correctly.' εἴτε γὰρ ἐξέστημεν, θεῷ· εἴτε σωφρονοῦμεν, ὑμῖν 'are we really out of our minds? It is for God's sake. Or are we sane? It is for your sake' 2 Cor 5.13; εὗρον καθήμενον τὸν ἄνθρωπον ἀφ' οὗ τὰ δαιμόνια ἐξῆλθεν ἱματισμένον καὶ σωφρονοῦντα παρὰ τοὺς πόδας τοῦ Ἰησοῦ 'they found the man from whom the demons had gone out sitting at the feet of Jesus; he was clothed and in his right mind' Lk 8.35. The meaning of σωφρονέω[a] is often expressed idiomatically, for example, 'to have right thoughts,' 'to have one's head,' 'to have straight thoughts,' or 'to have thoughts that do not wander.'

30.23 εὐνοέω[a]: to consider a view favorably, with the intention of finding a solution – 'to consider someone's views in a favorable light, to consider how to solve.' εὐνοῶν τῷ ἀντιδίκῳ σου ταχύ 'consider how to resolve matters with your adversary quickly' Mt 5.25. For other interpretations of εὐνοέω in Mt 5.25, see 31.20 and 56.3.

30.24 μαίνομαι; μανία, ας f; παραφρονέω; παραφρονία, ας f; ἐξίσταμαι[b]: to think or reason in a completely irrational manner – 'to not be in one's right mind, to be insane, to be mad, to be out of one's mind, insanity, madness.'[5]
μαίνομαι: ὁ δὲ Παῦλος, Οὐ μαίνομαι, φησίν, κράτιστε Φῆστε 'Paul answered, I am not out of my mind, most excellent Festus' Ac 26.25.
μανία: τὰ πολλά σε γράμματα εἰς μανίαν περιτρέπει 'your great learning is driving you mad' Ac 26.24. In some languages μανία is best rendered by an idiomatic expression, for example, 'thoughts that never return,' 'distorted thoughts,' 'senseless thoughts,' or 'thoughts that cannot be understood.'
παραφρονέω: παραφρονῶν λαλῶ 'I am speaking like an insane person' 2 Cor 11.23.
παραφρονία: ὑποζύγιον ἄφωνον ἐν ἀνθρώπου φωνῇ φθεγξάμενον ἐκώλυσεν τὴν τοῦ προφήτου παραφρονίαν 'the dumb donkey spoke with a human voice and prevented the prophet from

---

5 It is possible that there are some significant differences in meaning between the set μαίνομαι, μανία and the set παραφρονέω, παραφρονία, but the difference is likely to be more connotative than denotative, as, for example, the distinction in English between 'crazy' and 'insane.'

carrying out his unwise idea' or '. . . and stopped the prophet's insane action' 2 Pe 2.16. It may be necessary in some languages to restructure the expression 'stopped the prophet's insane action.' This can often be done by saying 'prevented the prophet from acting like a crazy person.' In other languages παραφρονία is best rendered by an idiomatic expression such as 'wandering thoughts' or 'twisted thoughts.'
ἐξίσταμαι[b]: ἔλεγον γὰρ ὅτι ἐξέστη 'people were saying, He is insane' Mk 3.21.

30.25 νήφω[a]: (a figurative extension of meaning of νήφω 'to be sober, to not be drunk,' probably not occurring in the NT; see 88.86) to be in control of one's thought processes and thus not be in danger of irrational thinking – 'to be sober-minded, to be well composed in mind.' ἀλλὰ γρηγορῶμεν καὶ νήφωμεν 'but we should be awake and sober-minded' 1 Th 5.6. It is also possible to understand νήφω in 1 Th 5.6 as meaning 'self-control,' as a characteristic of moral behavior (see 88.86).

30.26 ἐκνήφω: to change to a state of control over one's thought processes – 'to come to one's right senses, to change to a proper state of mind.' ἐκνήψατε δικαίως καὶ μὴ ἁμαρτάνετε 'come back to your right senses and stop your sinful ways' 1 Cor 15.34. The equivalent of 'to come to one's senses' may be in some languages 'to think again as one should think' or 'to no longer have crazy ideas.'

30.27 ἀνανήφω: to return to a proper state of mind – 'to return to one's right senses, to come back to one's senses.' ἀνανήψωσιν ἐκ τῆς τοῦ διαβόλου παγίδος 'they will return to their senses (and escape) from the trap of the Devil' 2 Tm 2.26. 'To return to one's senses' may be rendered as 'to again think right' or 'to no longer think wrong thoughts.'

30.28 ἀναθεωρέω[b]: to continue to think back upon – 'to reflect upon, to think back on.' ἀναθεωροῦντες τὴν ἔκβασιν τῆς ἀναστροφῆς 'keep thinking back on the results of their lives' He 13.7. In a number of instances the equivalent of 'think back on' is 'think about what happened' or 'reflect about what happened some time ago.'

30.29 πληρόω τὴν καρδίαν (an idiom, literally 'to fill the heart'); βάλλω εἰς τὴν καρδίαν (an idiom, literally 'to throw into the heart'): to cause someone to think in a particular manner, often as a means of inducing some behavior – 'to make think, to fill the heart, to cause to decide.'
πληρόω τὴν καρδίαν: διὰ τί ἐπλήρωσεν ὁ Σατανᾶς τὴν καρδίαν σου ψεύσασθαί σε τὸ πνεῦμα τὸ ἅγιον; 'why did Satan cause you to think as you did so as to lie to the Holy Spirit?' Ac 5.3. It is also possible to see in this expression in Ac 5.3 an element of assent on the part of Ananias. Accordingly, one may translate 'why did you let Satan cause you to plan to lie to the Holy Spirit?' ἡ λύπη πεπλήρωκεν ὑμῶν τὴν καρδίαν 'grief has caused you to think as you do' Jn 16.6.
βάλλω εἰς τὴν καρδίαν: τοῦ διαβόλου ἤδη βεβληκότος εἰς τὴν καρδίαν ἵνα παραδοῖ αὐτὸν Ἰούδας 'the Devil having already put into the heart of Judas to betray him' Jn 13.2.

30.30 καταμανθάνω: to think about, with the purpose of ultimate understanding – 'to consider, to observe, to think about.' καταμάθετε τὰ κρίνα τοῦ ἀγροῦ πῶς αὐξάνουσιν 'consider how the wild flowers grow' Mt 6.28.

30.31 ἀποβλέπω; ἀφοράω[a]: to keep thinking about, without having one's attention distracted – 'to think about, to fix one's attention on.'
ἀποβλέπω: ἀπέβλεπεν γὰρ εἰς τὴν μισθαποδοσίαν 'because he fixed his attention on the future reward' He 11.26.
ἀφοράω[a]: ἀφορῶντες εἰς τὸν . . . Ἰησοῦν 'let us fix our attention on . . . Jesus' He 12.2.

30.32 εὐπερίσπαστος, ον: pertaining to easily distracting one's thinking – 'easily distracting, that which keeps one from continuing to think about something.' τὴν εὐπερίσπαστον ἁμαρτίαν 'the sin that so easily distracts us' He 12.1 (apparatus).

30.33 ἀπερισπάστως: pertaining to not causing someone to be distracted – 'without distraction, not distracting.' πρὸς τὸ . . .

εὐπάρεδρον τῷ κυρίῳ ἀπερισπάστως 'so that your devoted service to the Lord (may be) without distraction' or 'so that you might give yourselves completely to the Lord's service without anything distracting you' 1 Cor 7.35. In a number of instances it is possible to render ἀπερισπάστως simply as 'without beginning to think about something else' or 'without beginning to be concerned about something else.'

30.34 ἐκκρέμαμαι[a]: (a figurative extension of meaning of ἐκκρέμαμαι 'to hang out from,' not occurring in the NT) to pay unusually close attention to what is being said – 'to pay close attention to, to consider seriously.' ὁ λαὸς γὰρ ἅπας ἐξεκρέματο αὐτοῦ ἀκούων 'for all the people paid close attention as they listened to him' Lk 19.48. For another interpretation of ἐκκρέμαμαι in Lk 19.48, see 68.15.

30.35 προσέχω[b]: to pay close attention to something, with the possible implication of agreement – 'to pay close attention to, to consider carefully.' προσεῖχον δὲ οἱ ὄχλοι τοῖς λεγομένοις ὑπὸ τοῦ Φιλίππου 'the crowds paid close attention to what was being said by Philip' Ac 8.6.

30.36 αἴρω τὴν ψυχήν τινος: (an idiom, literally 'to lift up the soul of someone') to keep someone in suspense so that one cannot come to a conclusion in one's thinking – 'to keep in suspense, to keep someone from being able to form a conclusion about something.' ἕως πότε τὴν ψυχὴν ἡμῶν αἴρεις; 'how long will you keep us in suspense?' Jn 10.24.

30.37 παρακούω[c]: to not pay attention to something – 'to pay no attention to, to ignore.' ὁ δὲ Ἰησοῦς παρακούσας τὸν λόγον λαλούμενον 'Jesus paid no attention to what was being said' Mk 5.36. Some scholars, however, understand παρακούω in Mk 5.36 as meaning 'to overhear' (see 24.66).

30.38 ἀγνοέω[b]: to refuse to think about or pay attention to – 'to pay no attention to, to ignore.' εἰ δέ τις ἀγνοεῖ, ἀγνοεῖται 'but if he does not pay attention to this, pay no attention to him' 1 Cor 14.38.

B To Think About, with the Implied Purpose of Responding Appropriately[6] (30.39-30.52)

30.39 μέλει[a] (only impersonal in the NT): to think about something in such a way as to make an appropriate response – 'to think about, to be concerned about.' μὴ τῶν βοῶν μέλει τῷ θεῷ; 'now, is God concerned about oxen?' 1 Cor 9.9. It may be possible to render 'is God concerned about oxen' as 'is God thinking about doing something about oxen.'

30.40 ἐπιμελέομαι[b]: to give proper consideration to some issue or matter – 'to think about, to be concerned about, to give attention so as to respond.' εἰ δέ τις τοῦ ἰδίου οἴκου προστῆναι οὐκ οἶδεν, πῶς ἐκκλησίας θεοῦ ἐπιμελήσεται; 'if a man does not know how to manage his own family, how can he give proper consideration to (the needs of) God's church?' 1 Tm 3.5.

30.41 ἐπιμελῶς: (derivative of ἐπιμελέομαι[b] 'to think about,' 30.40) pertaining to the manner of giving thoughtful concern to an activity – 'carefully, thoroughly.' ζητεῖ ἐπιμελῶς ἕως οὗ εὕρῃ 'she looks carefully everywhere until she finds it' Lk 15.8.

30.42 ἐπιλαμβάνομαι[e]: to be concerned about, with the implication of possible help – 'to be concerned about, to be concerned for.' οὐ γὰρ δήπου ἀγγέλων ἐπιλαμβάνεται 'for it is evident that he is not concerned about angels' He 2.16. For another interpretation of ἐπιλαμβάνομαι in He 2.16, see 35.1.[7]

---

6 Meanings in Subdomain B not only involve thought, but imply that the thought is directed toward some kind of meaningful response, so that the meanings tend to shade off into the area of 'to be concerned about.' In this subdomain are also included the polar opposite meanings involving 'disregard, overlooking' and 'purposely paying no attention to.' There is obviously a very clear connection between Subdomains A and B, and in a number of instances the area of meaning shades from one subdomain into the other.

7 It is difficult to know whether ἐπιλαμβάνομαι in a context such as He 2.16 refers principally or even in a significant measure to the intellectual concern rather than the more practical implication of giving help. It is specifically for that reason that ἐπιλαμβάνομαι is classified in both Domain 30 and Domain 35.

30.43 κατανοέω[b]: to give proper and decisive thought about something – 'to consider carefully, to be concerned about.' τὴν δὲ δοκὸν τὴν ἐν τῷ ἰδίῳ ὀφθαλμῷ οὐ κατανοεῖς 'but you are not concerned about the beam in your own eye' Lk 6.41; κόλπον δέ τινα κατενόουν ἔχοντα αἰγιαλόν 'they were concerned about a bay that had a beach' Ac 27.39. It is also possible that κατανοέω in Ac 27.39 means simply 'to notice' (see 24.51), but there seems to be more involved than mere seeing.

30.44 ἀργός[c], ή, όν: pertaining to not giving careful consideration to something – 'careless, without thought.' πᾶν ῥῆμα ἀργὸν ὃ λαλήσουσιν οἱ ἄνθρωποι ἀποδώσουσιν περὶ αὐτοῦ λόγον ἐν ἡμέρᾳ κρίσεως 'people will have to give account in the day of judgment for every careless word they have spoken' Mt 12.36. For another interpretation of ἀργός in Mt 12.36, see 72.21. It is also possible that ἀργός in Mt 12.36 means 'useless' (see 65.36).

30.45 ἐπιβλέπω[b]; ἐφοράω; ὁράω[b]: to take special notice of something, with the implication of concerning oneself – 'to take notice of, to consider, to pay attention to, to concern oneself with.'
ἐπιβλέπω[b]: ὅτι ἐπέβλεψεν ἐπὶ τὴν ταπείνωσιν τῆς δούλης αὐτοῦ 'for he has paid attention to his humble servant' (literally '. . . to the humbleness of his servant') Lk 1.48; διδάσκαλε, δέομαί σου ἐπιβλέψαι ἐπὶ τὸν υἱόν μου, ὅτι μονογενής μοί ἐστιν 'teacher, I beg you, please take note of my son, my only son' or '. . . because he is my only son' Lk 9.38. For another interpretation of ἐπιβλέπω in Lk 9.38, see 35.8.
ἐφοράω: οὕτως μοι πεποίηκεν κύριος ἐν ἡμέραις αἷς ἐπεῖδεν 'thus the Lord has done to me in the days when he concerned himself with me' or 'now at last the Lord has concerned himself with me in this way' Lk 1.25; τὰ νῦν, κύριε, ἔπιδε ἐπὶ τὰς ἀπειλὰς αὐτῶν 'now, Lord, take notice of the threats they made' Ac 4.29.
ὁράω[b]: ὁρᾶτε μηδεὶς γινωσκέτω 'see to it that no one knows about this' or 'be sure you tell no one' Mt 9.30.

Though the terms ἐπιβλέπω, ἐφοράω, and ὁράω suggest as a result of their central meanings some measure of visual perception, what is involved in these specific contexts is much more than visual perception. The focus is actually upon intellectual activity and concern.

30.46 ἐπισκοπέω[b]: to give careful consideration to something, with the implication of guarding against – 'to give careful attention to, to consider carefully, to guard against.' ἐπισκοποῦντες μή τις ὑστερῶν ἀπὸ τῆς χάριτος τοῦ θεοῦ 'guard against turning back from the grace of God' or 'being concerned in order that no one will fail in respect to the grace of God' He 12.15. For another interpretation of ἐπισκοπέω in He 12.15, see 35.39. Some scholars have seen in the occurrence of ἐπισκοπέω in He 12.15 a meaning at least somewhat similar to that which occurs in ἐπισκοπέω[c] 'to be responsible, to care for' (53.70).

30.47 προνοέω[a]; πρόνοια, ας f: to think about something ahead of time, with the implication that one can then respond appropriately – 'to give attention beforehand, to have in mind to do, foresight.' προνοέω[a]: προνοούμενοι καλὰ ἐνώπιον πάντων ἀνθρώπων 'give attention to doing what everyone considers good' Ro 12.17. πρόνοια: διορθωμάτων γινομένων τῷ ἔθνει τούτῳ διὰ τῆς σῆς προνοίας 'your foresight has brought many reforms to our (literally 'this') nation' Ac 24.2; τῆς σαρκὸς πρόνοιαν μὴ ποιεῖσθε εἰς ἐπιθυμίας 'stop planning ahead so as to satisfy the desires of your sinful nature' Ro 13.14.

30.48 παραθεωρέω: to fail to consider something sufficiently, and as a result fail to respond appropriately – 'to overlook, to neglect, to disregard.' ὅτι παρεθεωροῦντο ἐν τῇ διακονίᾳ τῇ καθημερινῇ αἱ χῆραι αὐτῶν 'because their widows were being overlooked in the daily distribution of funds' Ac 6.1. It may be important to restructure this statement in Ac 6.1 to read 'because when help was being given out each day, their widows got nothing.'

30.49 ὑπεροράω; πάρεσις, εως f: to intentionally not regard or be concerned about certain objects or events – 'to overlook, to purposely pay no attention to, disregard.' ὑπεροράω: τοὺς μὲν οὖν χρόνους τῆς ἀγνοίας ὑπεριδὼν ὁ θεός 'God has overlooked the times when people did not know' Ac 17.30. πάρεσις: εἰς ἔνδειξιν τῆς δικαιοσύνης αὐτοῦ διὰ τὴν πάρεσιν τῶν προγεγονότων ἁμαρτημάτων 'as evidence of his righteousness by overlooking past sins' Ro 3.25.

30.50 ἀμελέω: to not think about, and thus not respond appropriately to – 'to neglect, to disregard, to pay no attention to.' οἱ δὲ ἀμελήσαντες ἀπῆλθον 'but they paid no attention and left' Mt 22.5; μὴ ἀμέλει τοῦ ἐν σοὶ χαρίσματος 'do not neglect the spiritual gift that is in you' 1 Tm 4.14; πῶς ἡμεῖς ἐκφευξόμεθα τηλικαύτης ἀμελήσαντες σωτηρίας; 'how shall we escape if we neglect such a great salvation?' He 2.3.

30.51 καταλείπω[d]: to give up or neglect one's concern for something – 'to no longer be concerned about, to neglect, to give up one's concern for.' οὐκ ἀρεστόν ἐστιν ἡμᾶς καταλείψαντας τὸν λόγον τοῦ θεοῦ διακονεῖν τραπέζαις 'it is not right for us to neglect preaching God's word in order to take care of finances' Ac 6.2.

30.52 ἀρνέομαι[d]; ἀπαρνέομαι[b]: to refuse to give thought to or express concern for – 'to disregard, to pay no attention to, to say No to.'[8] ἀρνέομαι[d]: ἀρνησάσθω ἑαυτὸν καὶ ἀράτω τὸν σταυρὸν αὐτοῦ καθ' ἡμέραν 'he must say "No" to himself and take up his cross every day' Lk 9.23. ἀπαρνέομαι[b]: ἀπαρνησάσθω ἑαυτὸν καὶ ἀράτω τὸν σταυρὸν αὐτοῦ 'he must say "No" to himself and take up his cross' Mk 8.34. There are a number of problems involved in rendering appropriately ἀρνέομαι[d] and ἀπαρνέομαι[b] as in Lk 9.23 and Mk 8.34. In a number of languages it simply makes no sense to translate 'to say No to oneself,' nor is it possible in many instances to use an expression such as 'to deny oneself,' since it almost always implies to deny oneself something. Sometimes the meaning may be expressed in a

---

8 ἀπαρνέομαι[b] appears to be somewhat more forceful in meaning than ἀρνέομαι[d].

figurative or idiomatic manner, for example, 'to refuse to pay attention to what one's own desires are saying' or 'to refuse to think about what one just wants for oneself.' In certain instances other kinds of idioms may be employed, for example, 'to put oneself at the end of the line' or even 'to say to one's heart, Keep quiet.'

C To Think Concerning Future Contingencies (30.53-30.55)

30.53 ἐκδέχομαι[b]; ἐκδοχή, ῆς f: to expect something to happen, often implying waiting – 'to expect, expectation.'

ἐκδέχομαι[b]: ἐκδέχομαι γὰρ αὐτόν 'for I am expecting him' 1 Cor 16.11.

ἐκδοχή: φοβερὰ δέ τις ἐκδοχὴ κρίσεως 'and some fearful expectation of judgment' He 10.27.

The closest equivalent of 'to expect' is usually 'to think that it will happen that.'

30.54 ἐλπίζω[b]; ἀπελπίζω: to expect, with the implication of some benefit – 'to expect, to hope.'

ἐλπίζω[b]: καὶ ἐὰν δανίσητε παρ' ὧν ἐλπίζετε λαβεῖν 'and if you lend to those from whom you expect to receive' Lk 6.34.

ἀπελπίζω: δανίζετε μηδὲν ἀπελπίζοντες 'lend expecting nothing in return' Lk 6.35.[9]

30.55 προσδοκάω[b]; προσδοκία, ας f: to expect something to happen, whether good or bad – 'to expect, to anticipate, expectation.'

προσδοκάω[b]: ἥξει ὁ κύριος τοῦ δούλου ἐκείνου ἐν ἡμέρᾳ ᾗ οὐ προσδοκᾷ 'the master of that servant will come at a time when he (the servant) is not expecting him' Mt 24.50.

προσδοκία: ἀποψυχόντων ἀνθρώπων ἀπὸ φόβου καὶ προσδοκίας τῶν ἐπερχομένων τῇ οἰκουμένῃ 'people will lose heart because of fear and expectation of those things that are coming upon the world' Lk 21.26.

---

9 It is possible that ἀπελπίζω differs from ἐλπίζω[b] in focusing upon 'an expectation of something coming back' or 'expecting something in return,' but the shift from ἐλπίζω to ἀπελπίζω may be merely a matter of stylistic variation.

D To Intend, To Purpose, To Plan (30.56-30.74)

30.56 βούλομαι[b]; βουλεύομαι[a]: to think, with the purpose of planning or deciding on a course of action – 'to purpose, to plan, to intend.'

βούλομαι[b]: ἐβουλήθη λάθρᾳ ἀπολῦσαι αὐτήν 'he intended to divorce her secretly' Mt 1.19; ταύτῃ τῇ πεποιθήσει ἐβουλόμην πρότερον πρὸς ὑμᾶς ἐλθεῖν 'I was so sure of this that I planned at first to visit you' or 'because of this confidence I planned . . .' 2 Cor 1.15; βουλόμενος μετὰ τὸ πάσχα ἀναγαγεῖν αὐτὸν τῷ λαῷ 'he planned to put him on trial in public after the Passover' Ac 12.4.

βουλεύομαι[a]: οἱ δὲ ἀκούσαντες διεπρίοντο καὶ ἐβουλεύσαντο ἀνελεῖν αὐτούς 'but when they heard this they were furious, for they were planning to put them to death' Ac 5.33 (apparatus); ἢ ἃ βουλεύομαι κατὰ σάρκα βουλεύομαι; 'or do I make my plans in a worldly manner?' 2 Cor 1.17.

In a number of languages there are two quite distinct sets of terms for planning depending upon the purpose involved in such planning. If the planning is constructive, either for oneself or someone else, one set of terms is likely to be used, while if the planning is harmful (usually against someone else), another set of terms would be used.

30.57 βούλημα[b], τος n; βουλή, ῆς f: (derivatives of βούλομαι[b] and βουλεύομαι[a] 'to purpose, to plan, to intend,' 30.56) that which has been purposed and planned – 'plan, intention, purpose.'

βούλημα[b]: ἐκώλυσεν αὐτοὺς τοῦ βουλήματος 'he kept them from carrying out their plan' Ac 27.43; τῷ γὰρ βουλήματι αὐτοῦ τίς ἀνθέστηκεν; 'who can resist his plan?' Ro 9.19.[10]

βουλή: τῶν δὲ στρατιωτῶν βουλὴ ἐγένετο ἵνα τοὺς δεσμώτας ἀποκτείνωσιν 'there was a plan by the soldiers to kill the prisoners' Ac 27.42.

30.58 θέλω[a]: to purpose, generally based upon a preference and desire – 'to purpose.'

ἠθέλησεν ὁ θεὸς γνωρίσαι τί τὸ πλοῦτος τῆς

---

10 It is also possible to understand βούλημα in Ro 9.19 as what God desires or wills (see 25.4).

δόξης τοῦ μυστηρίου τούτου ἐν τοῖς ἔθνεσιν 'God purposed to make known among the Gentiles the glorious riches of this mystery' Col 1.27. It is also possible that θέλω in Col 1.27 focuses more upon 'desire' (see 25.1).

30.59 θέλημα[b], τος *n*: (derivative of θέλω[a] 'to purpose,' 30.58) that which is purposed, intended, or willed – 'will, intent, purpose, plan.' προορίσας ἡμᾶς εἰς υἱοθεσίαν διὰ Ἰησοῦ Χριστοῦ εἰς αὐτόν, κατὰ τὴν εὐδοκίαν τοῦ θελήματος αὐτοῦ 'he had already decided that through Jesus Christ he would bring us to himself as his sons – this was his pleasure and purpose' Eph 1.5; γενηθήτω τὸ θέλημά σου, ὡς ἐν οὐρανῷ καὶ ἐπὶ γῆς 'may your will be done on earth as it is in heaven' Mt 6.10.[11]

30.60 μελετάω[b]: to think seriously about a particular course of action – 'to plan to act, to plot.' λαοὶ ἐμελέτησαν κενά; 'why do the people plot in vain?' Ac 4.25.

30.61 προμελετάω: to plan ahead of time, with considerable thought and attention – 'to plan ahead of time, to plan in advance.' θέτε οὖν ἐν ταῖς καρδίαις ὑμῶν μὴ προμελετᾶν ἀπολογηθῆναι 'decide that you will not plan your defense ahead of time' Lk 21.14.

30.62 προτίθεμαι[a]: to formulate a future course of action – 'to plan beforehand, to purpose, to intend.'[12] πολλάκις προεθέμην ἐλθεῖν πρὸς ὑμᾶς 'many times I have planned to visit you' Ro 1.13; κατὰ τὴν εὐδοκίαν αὐτοῦ ἣν προέθετο ἐν αὐτῷ 'according to his good pleasure which he planned beforehand in (Christ)' Eph 1.9.

30.63 πρόθεσις, εως *f*: (derivative of προτίθεμαι[a] 'to plan in advance,' 30.62) that which is planned or purposed in advance – 'plan, proposal, purpose.' παρεκάλει πάντας τῇ

---

11 It is possible that in both Eph 1.5 and Mt 6.10 τὸ θέλημα means 'wish' or 'desire,' but this is not probable.
12 προτίθεμαι[a] is similar in meaning to βούλομαι[b] and βουλεύομαι[a] (30.56) with perhaps, however, some additional emphasis upon prior planning. βούλομαι[b] and βουλεύομαι[a] also imply some prior thought by virtue of their meaning 'to plan.'

προθέσει τῆς καρδίας προσμένειν τῷ κυρίῳ 'he urged them all to remain true to the Lord in the purposes of their hearts' Ac 11.23; ἐν ᾧ καὶ ἐκληρώθημεν προορισθέντες κατὰ πρόθεσιν 'in whom we were also chosen, having been predetermined according to his purpose' Eph 1.11.

30.64 ἑκουσίως[b]: pertaining to being deliberately intentional – 'intentionally, purposely, deliberately.' ἑκουσίως γὰρ ἁμαρτανόντων ἡμῶν μετὰ τὸ λαβεῖν τὴν ἐπίγνωσιν τῆς ἀληθείας 'if we purposely go on sinning after the truth has been made known to us' He 10.26.

30.65 ἀδήλως: pertaining to being without a special goal or purpose – 'without purpose, unintentionally, aimlessly.' ἐγὼ τοίνυν οὕτως τρέχω ὡς οὐκ ἀδήλως 'I, then, do not run like a man running aimlessly' 1 Cor 9.26. In a number of languages 'aimlessly' may be rendered simply as 'without having some goal' or 'without some reason' or 'without trying to accomplish something.'

30.66 ἔννοια[b], ας *f*; ἐπίνοια, ας *f*: that which is intended or purposed as the result of thinking – 'intention, purpose.'
ἔννοια[b]: κριτικὸς ἐνθυμήσεων καὶ ἐννοιῶν καρδίας 'it judges the thoughts and purposes of the heart' He 4.12.
ἐπίνοια: εἰ ἄρα ἀφεθήσεταί σοι ἡ ἐπίνοια τῆς καρδίας σου 'perhaps he will forgive you for having such a purpose in your heart' Ac 8.22.

30.67 γνώμη[a], ης *f*: that which is purposed or intended, with the implication of judgment or resolve – 'purpose, intention.' οὗτοι μίαν γνώμην ἔχουσιν 'these have the same purpose' Re 17.13.

30.68 οἰκονομία[b], ας *f*: a plan which involves a set of arrangements (referring in the NT to God's plan for bringing salvation to mankind within the course of history) – 'purpose, scheme, plan, arrangement.' αἵτινες ἐκζητήσεις παρέχουσιν μᾶλλον ἢ οἰκονομίαν θεοῦ τὴν ἐν πίστει 'these promote controversies rather than God's plan, which is by faith' 1 Tm 1.4; φωτίσαι πάντας τίς ἡ οἰκονομία τοῦ μυστηρίου 'to make all people see what his secret plan is' Eph 3.9.

30.69 ἐφευρετής, οῦ *m*: one who thinks up schemes or plans of action – 'contriver, inventor, one who thinks up.' ἐφευρετὰς κακῶν 'they think up ways of doing evil' Ro 1.30.

30.70 ἐνεδρεύω[b]: (a figurative extension of meaning of ἐνεδρεύω[a] 'to lie in ambush, to lie in wait in order to attack,' 39.51) to plan, with the specific purpose of harming – 'to plot, to make plans against.' ἐνεδρεύοντες αὐτὸν θηρεῦσαί τι ἐκ τοῦ στόματος αὐτοῦ 'they were plotting against him to catch him in something (wrong) he might say' Lk 11.54.

30.71 ἐπιβουλή, ῆς *f*: a plan for treacherous activity against someone – 'plot, plan, scheme.' ἐπιβουλῆς αὐτῷ ὑπὸ τῶν Ἰουδαίων 'because the Jews had made a plot against him' Ac 20.3; ἐγνώσθη δὲ τῷ Σαύλῳ ἡ ἐπιβουλὴ αὐτῶν 'but Saul learned of their plot against him' Ac 9.24.

30.72 συστροφή[b], ῆς *f*: a plan devised by a number of persons who agree to act against someone or some institution – 'plot, scheme, conspiracy.' ποιήσαντες συστροφὴν οἱ Ἰουδαῖοι 'some Jews formed a conspiracy' Ac 23.12. See 30.73, footnote 13.

30.73 συνωμοσία, ας *f*: a plan for taking secret action against someone or some institution, with the implication of an oath binding the conspirators – 'conspiracy, plot.' ἦσαν δὲ πλείους τεσσεράκοντα οἱ ταύτην τὴν συνωμοσίαν ποιησάμενοι 'there were more than forty of them who formed this conspiracy' Ac 23.13.[13]

30.74 συμβουλεύομαι; συμβούλιον[a], ου *n*: to engage in joint planning so as to devise a course of common action, often one with a harmful or evil purpose – 'to confer, to consult, to plot, to make plans against.' συμβουλεύομαι: συνεβουλεύσαντο ἵνα τὸν Ἰη-

σοῦν δόλῳ κρατήσωσιν 'they plotted together to arrest Jesus secretly' Mt 26.4. συμβούλιον[a]: συμβούλιον ἐδίδουν κατ' αὐτοῦ ὅπως αὐτὸν ἀπολέσωσιν 'they made plans against him to kill him' Mk 3.6.

E To Decide, To Conclude (30.75-30.85)

30.75 κρίνω[a]; ἐπικρίνω: to come to a conclusion in the process of thinking and thus to be in a position to make a decision – 'to come to a conclusion, to decide, to make up one's mind.'[14]
κρίνω[a]: οὐ γὰρ ἔκρινά τι εἰδέναι ἐν ὑμῖν εἰ μὴ Ἰησοῦν Χριστὸν καὶ τοῦτον ἐσταυρωμένον 'for I made up my mind to know nothing while I was with you except Jesus Christ and him crucified' 1 Cor 2.2; ἠρνήσασθε κατὰ πρόσωπον Πιλάτου, κρίναντος ἐκείνου ἀπολύειν 'you rejected him in Pilate's presence, even after he had decided to set him free' Ac 3.13; τοῦτο κέκρικεν ἐν τῇ ἰδίᾳ καρδίᾳ 'he has already decided in his own heart (or 'in his own mind') what to do' 1 Cor 7.37.
ἐπικρίνω: Πιλᾶτος ἐπέκρινεν γενέσθαι τὸ αἴτημα αὐτῶν 'Pilate decided to grant their demand' Lk 23.24.
   In some languages the process of 'deciding' is expressed idiomatically, for example, 'to come to the end in one's thinking' or 'to choose in one's mind' or 'the mind sees its goal.'

30.76 τίθημι ἐν τῇ καρδίᾳ; τίθεμαι ἐν τῷ πνεύματι: (idioms, literally 'to place in the heart, or mind,' and 'to place in the spirit, or mind') to engage in the process of deciding – 'to make up one's mind, to decide.'
τίθημι ἐν τῇ καρδίᾳ: τί ὅτι ἔθου ἐν τῇ καρδίᾳ σου τὸ πρᾶγμα τοῦτο; 'why, then, did you make up your mind that you would do such a thing?' Ac 5.4; θέτε οὖν ἐν ταῖς καρδίαις ὑμῶν μὴ προμελετᾶν ἀπολογηθῆναι 'decide not to plan ahead of time how you will defend yourselves' Lk 21.14.
τίθεμαι ἐν τῷ πνεύματι: ἔθετο ὁ Παῦλος ἐν τῷ πνεύματι διελθὼν τὴν Μακεδονίαν 'Paul made

---

13 It is possible that συνωμοσία (30.73) in Ac 23.13 is only a stylistic variant for συστροφή (30.72) in Ac 23.12. Obviously the reference in both instances is to the same event.

14 It is possible that ἐπικρίνω differs from κρίνω[a] in focusing greater attention upon what is decided.

up his mind to travel through Macedonia' Ac 19.21. It is also possible to interpret the phrase ἐν τῷ πνεύματι in Ac 19.21 as being a reference to the Holy Spirit and accordingly, the passage may be translated as 'Paul, led by the Spirit, decided to travel through Macedonia.'

30.77 γίνομαι γνώμης: (an idiom, literally 'to become of a mind') to make up one's mind, with emphasis upon the process of coming to such a decision – 'to decide, to make up one's mind.'[15] ἐγένετο γνώμης τοῦ ὑποστρέφειν διὰ Μακεδονίας 'he decided to go back through Macedonia' Ac 20.3.

30.78 ὁρμὴ γίνομαι: (an idiom, literally 'an impulse happens') to make a decision to carry out some action, but with emphasis upon the impulse involved – 'to make up one's mind, to decide, to determine.' ὡς δὲ ἐγένετο ὁρμὴ τῶν ἐθνῶν τε καὶ Ἰουδαίων σὺν τοῖς ἄρχουσιν αὐτῶν ὑβρίσαι καὶ λιθοβολῆσαι αὐτούς 'then the Gentiles and the Jews, together with their leaders, determined to mistreat and to stone them' Ac 14.5.

30.79 πρόκριμα, τος n: to make a decision based upon unjustified preference, with the implication of prejudging – 'to show partiality, to decide unfairly, to judge prejudicially, partiality, prejudice.' ἵνα ταῦτα φυλάξῃς χωρὶς προκρίματος 'obey these (instructions) without showing any partiality' 1 Tm 5.21. It may be necessary in some languages to define the implications of 'prejudice' by saying 'to decide against someone without any reason' or 'to decide against someone without knowing what is true.'

30.80 στηρίζω τὸ πρόσωπον: (a Semitic idiom, literally 'to fix one's face') to make a decision, with emphasis upon finality – 'to decide firmly, to resolve, to make up one's mind definitely.' αὐτὸς τὸ πρόσωπον ἐστήρισεν τοῦ

πορεύεσθαι εἰς Ἰερουσαλήμ 'he made up his mind and set out for Jerusalem' Lk 9.51. In order to express the meaning of 'to decide firmly,' it may be useful in some instances to translate 'to decide and to refuse to change one's mind' or 'to decide and not to change.'

30.81 ἐπιλύω[b]: (a figurative extension of meaning of ἐπιλύω 'to untie, to loose,' not occurring in the NT) to come to a conclusion concerning a presumably difficult or complex matter – 'to resolve (a dispute), to settle (a problem), to come to a decision.' ἐν τῇ ἐννόμῳ ἐκκλησίᾳ ἐπιλυθήσεται 'it will have to be settled in a legal meeting of the citizens' Ac 19.39.[16]

30.82 συμβιβάζω[b]: (a figurative extension of meaning of συμβιβάζω[a] 'to bring together, to unite, to combine,' 63.5) to come to a solution or a decision, implying a process of putting together different aspects of related information – 'to conclude, to decide, to infer.' συμβιβάζοντες ὅτι προσκέκληται ἡμᾶς ὁ θεός 'concluding that God had called us' Ac 16.10.

30.83 ὁρίζω[a]: (a figurative extension of meaning of ὁρίζω 'to set limits on,' not occurring in the NT) to come to a definite decision or firm resolve – 'to decide, to determine, to resolve.' τῶν δὲ μαθητῶν καθὼς εὐπορεῖτό τις ὥρισαν ἕκαστος αὐτῶν εἰς διακονίαν πέμψαι τοῖς κατοικοῦσιν ἐν τῇ Ἰουδαίᾳ ἀδελφοῖς 'the disciples decided that each of them would send as much as he could to help their fellow believers who lived in Judea' Ac 11.29.

30.84 προορίζω; προαιρέομαι: to come to a decision beforehand – 'to decide beforehand, to determine ahead of time, to decide upon ahead of time.'
προορίζω: προορίσας ἡμᾶς εἰς υἱοθεσίαν διὰ Ἰησοῦ Χριστοῦ εἰς αὐτόν 'he had already decided that through Jesus Christ he would bring us to himself as his sons' Eph 1.5; οὓς δὲ

---

15 γίνομαι γνώμης is similar to τίθημι ἐν τῇ καρδίᾳ and τίθεμαι ἐν τῷ πνεύματι (30.76). All relate to the process of decision making, but it is possible that the idioms in 30.76 indicate greater initiative and purpose.

16 ἐπιλύω[b] in Ac 19.39 involves several different semantic features, but since the focus is upon the final resolution of the issues, the meaning of ἐπιλύω in Ac 19.39 can perhaps be best treated in this subdomain.

προώρισεν, τούτους καὶ ἐκάλεσεν 'those whom he decided upon ahead of time, these he called' Ro 8.30.

προαιρέομαι: ἕκαστος καθὼς προῄρηται τῇ καρδίᾳ 'each person (should give) in the way he has decided beforehand in his heart (to do)' 2 Cor 9.7.

30.85 τακτός, ή, όν: pertaining to that which has been decided upon in advance – 'determined, chosen, fixed.' τακτῇ δὲ ἡμέρᾳ ὁ Ἡρῴδης ἐνδυσάμενος ἐσθῆτα βασιλικήν 'on a chosen day Herod put on his royal robes' or 'on the day that had been determined in advance . . .' Ac 12.21.

F To Choose, To Select, To Prefer (30.86-30.107)

30.86 ἐκλέγομαιª; αἱρέομαιª; λαμβάνωᵉ: to make a choice of one or more possible alternatives – 'to choose, to select, to prefer.'

ἐκλέγομαιª: ἐντειλάμενος τοῖς ἀποστόλοις διὰ πνεύματος ἁγίου οὓς ἐξελέξατο 'he gave instructions by the power of the Holy Spirit to the men whom he had chosen as his apostles' Ac 1.2; οὐχ ὁ θεὸς ἐξελέξατο τοὺς πτωχοὺς τῷ κόσμῳ; 'has not God chosen the poor in this world?' Jas 2.5.

αἱρέομαιª: τί αἱρήσομαι οὐ γνωρίζω 'I do not know which I should prefer' Php 1.22; μᾶλλον ἑλόμενος συγκακουχεῖσθαι τῷ λαῷ τοῦ θεοῦ ἢ πρόσκαιρον ἔχειν ἁμαρτίας ἀπόλαυσιν 'he chose to suffer with God's people rather than enjoy sin for a little while' He 11.25.

λαμβάνωᵉ: πᾶς γὰρ ἀρχιερεὺς ἐξ ἀνθρώπων λαμβανόμενος ὑπὲρ ἀνθρώπων καθίσταται τὰ πρὸς τὸν θεόν 'every high priest is chosen from his fellowmen and appointed to serve God on their behalf' He 5.1. It is also possible to interpret λαμβάνω in He 5.1 as meaning 'to acquire, to obtain' (see λαμβάνωᵇ, 57.55).

In a number of languages the choice of terms or expressions for 'choosing' or 'selecting' often depends upon either (1) what is chosen or selected or (2) the purpose for such a choice, for example, personal pleasure, rational evaluation, or outright prejudice.

30.87 ἵστημιᵉ: to propose or put forward a particular selection – 'to select, to choose.'

ἔστησαν δύο, Ἰωσήφ . . . καὶ Μαθθίαν 'so they selected two men: Joseph . . . and Matthias' Ac 1.23. For another interpretation of ἵστημι in Ac 1.23, see 33.343.

30.88 ἐπιλέγομαι: to choose for a particular purpose – 'to choose, to select.' Παῦλος δὲ ἐπιλεξάμενος Σιλᾶν ἐξῆλθεν 'Paul chose Silas and left' Ac 15.40.

30.89 προχειρίζομαι; προχειροτονέω: to choose for a particular purpose in advance – 'to choose in advance, to select beforehand, to designate in advance.'

προχειρίζομαι: ὁ θεὸς τῶν πατέρων ἡμῶν προεχειρίσατό σε γνῶναι τὸ θέλημα αὐτοῦ 'the God of our ancestors has already chosen you to know his will' Ac 22.14; ἀποστείλῃ τὸν προκεχειρισμένον ὑμῖν Χριστόν 'that he might send him, who is the Messiah he has already chosen for you' Ac 3.20.

προχειροτονέω: οὐ παντὶ τῷ λαῷ ἀλλὰ μάρτυσιν τοῖς προκεχειροτονημένοις ὑπὸ τοῦ θεοῦ, ἡμῖν 'not to all the people, but only to us who are the witnesses that God has already chosen' Ac 10.41.

30.90 ἐξαιρέομαιᵇ: to choose out from among – 'to choose.' ἐξαιρούμενός σε ἐκ τοῦ λαοῦ 'I have chosen you from among the people' Ac 26.17. It is also possible to interpret ἐξαιρέομαι in Ac 26.17 as meaning 'to rescue from' (see 21.17).

30.91 αἱρέομαιᵇ; αἱρετίζω: to choose or select for the purpose of showing special favor to or concern for – 'to choose, to select.'

αἱρέομαιᵇ: εἵλατο ὑμᾶς ὁ θεὸς ἀπαρχὴν εἰς σωτηρίαν 'God chose you as the first to be saved' 2 Th 2.13.

αἱρετίζω: ἰδοὺ ὁ παῖς μου ὃν ᾑρέτισα 'here is my servant, whom I have chosen' Mt 12.18.

30.92 ἐκλέγομαιᵇ; ἐκλογήª, ῆς f: to make a special choice based upon significant preference, often implying a strongly favorable attitude toward what is chosen – 'to choose, choice.'

ἐκλέγομαιᵇ: οὗτός ἐστιν ὁ υἱός μου ὁ ἐκλελεγμένος 'this is my Son, whom I have chosen' Lk

9.35;[17] ὁ θεὸς τοῦ λαοῦ τούτου Ἰσραὴλ ἐξελέξατο τοὺς πατέρας ἡμῶν 'the God of this people of Israel chose our ancestors' Ac 13.17.[18]

ἐκλογή[a]: ἵνα ἡ κατ' ἐκλογὴν πρόθεσις τοῦ θεοῦ μένῃ 'in order that God's purpose according to his choice might remain' or 'in order that God's choice (of one son) might be completely the result of his own purpose' Ro 9.11; κατὰ δὲ τὴν ἐκλογὴν ἀγαπητοί 'because of (God's) choice, they are his friends' Ro 11.28; πορεύου, ὅτι σκεῦος ἐκλογῆς ἐστίν μοι οὗτος τοῦ βαστάσαι τὸ ὄνομά μου ἐνώπιον ἐθνῶν 'go, because I have chosen him to serve me, to make my name known to Gentiles' Ac 9.15.

30.93 ἐκλεκτός, ή, όν; ἐκλογή[b], ῆς f: (derivatives of ἐκλέγομαι[b] and ἐκλογή[a] 'to choose, choice,' 30.92) that which has been chosen – 'chosen.'
ἐκλεκτός: ὑμεῖς δὲ γένος ἐκλεκτόν 'you are the chosen race' 1 Pe 2.9; διὰ τοὺς ἐκλεκτοὺς οὓς ἐξελέξατο ἐκολόβωσεν τὰς ἡμέρας 'for the sake of his chosen people whom he chose, he has reduced those days' Mk 13.20.
ἐκλογή[b]: ὃ ἐπιζητεῖ Ἰσραήλ, τοῦτο οὐκ ἐπέτυχεν, ἡ δὲ ἐκλογὴ ἐπέτυχεν 'what Israel sought so eagerly it did not gain, but those whom he chose did' Ro 11.7.

30.94 συνεκλεκτός, ή, όν: pertaining to being selected together with – 'one who is also chosen, what is chosen together with.' ἀσπάζεται ὑμᾶς ἡ ἐν Βαβυλῶνι συνεκλεκτή 'the (church) in Babylon also chosen (by God) greets you' 1 Pe 5.13.

As indicated in some of the renderings of terms expressing choice and selection, it is often preferable, and frequently necessary, to indicate who does the choosing. Therefore, it is often advisable or necessary to indicate the agent, whether in an active or passive construction.

30.95 ἀξιόω[b]: to make a choice on the basis of greater worth – 'to choose, to decide in favor of, to prefer.' Παῦλος δὲ ἠξίου . . . μὴ συμπαραλαμβάνειν τοῦτον 'but Paul preferred . . . not to take him along with (them)' Ac 15.38.

30.96 δοκέω[c]: to make a choice on the basis of something being better or superior – 'to choose, to decide to prefer, to choose as superior.' εἰ δέ τις δοκεῖ φιλόνεικος εἶναι 'if anyone chooses to be contentious' 1 Cor 11.16. It would also be possible to translate the "if" clause in 1 Cor 11.16 as 'if anyone is disposed to be contentious' or 'if anyone wants to quarrel about it' (see δοκέω[b], 25.7).

30.97 εὐδοκέω[c]: to think of something as being good, better, or preferable – 'to choose as better, to prefer, to seem good to.' εὐδοκοῦμεν μᾶλλον ἐκδημῆσαι ἐκ τοῦ σώματος καὶ ἐνδημῆσαι πρὸς τὸν κύριον 'rather we prefer to be away from the body and at home with the Lord' 2 Cor 5.8; ὅτι ἐν αὐτῷ εὐδόκησεν πᾶν τὸ πλήρωμα κατοικῆσαι 'because it seemed good to him to have all his fullness dwell in him' Col 1.19.

30.98 δοκιμάζω[b]: to regard something as being worthwhile or appropriate – 'to regard as worthwhile, to think of as appropriate.' καθὼς οὐκ ἐδοκίμασαν τὸν θεὸν ἔχειν ἐν ἐπιγνώσει 'since they did not think it worthwhile to retain the knowledge of God' or '. . . to acknowledge God' Ro 1.28. For another interpretation of δοκιμάζω in Ro 1.28, see 30.114.

30.99 κρίνω[b]; διακρίνω[b]: to judge something to be better than something else, and hence, to prefer – 'to prefer, to judge as superior, to regard as more valuable.'
κρίνω[b]: ὃς μὲν γὰρ κρίνει ἡμέραν παρ' ἡμέραν 'one person thinks a certain day is better than other days' (literally '. . . than another day') Ro 14.5.
διακρίνω[b]: τίς γάρ σε διακρίνει; 'who judges you to be superior?' 1 Cor 4.7. Superiority is often expressed in terms of 'being better,' but in some languages it is designated by means of a phrase meaning 'to surpass,' so that the question in 1 Cor 4.7 may be rendered as 'who judges that you surpass others?'

---

17 The occurrence of ἐκλελεγμένος in Lk 9.35 is paralleled by ἀγαπητός or ἀγαπητός, ἐν ᾧ εὐδόκησα in Mark and Matthew, respectively.
18 In Ac 13.17 ἐκλέγομαι[b] parallels closely the meaning of χάρις[b] (57.103) in referring to God's special favor or grace.

30.100 προβλέπομαι[b]; προγινώσκω[b]: to choose or select in advance of some other event – 'to choose beforehand, to select in advance.'

προβλέπομαι[b]: τοῦ θεοῦ περὶ ἡμῶν κρεῖττόν τι προβλεψαμένου 'because God had chosen ahead of time an even better plan for us' He 11.40. It is also possible to understand προβλέπομαι in He 11.40 as meaning 'to decide in advance' (compare the meanings in 30.84) or 'to provide for' (35.35).

προγινώσκω[b]: οὓς προέγνω, καὶ προώρισεν συμμόρφους τῆς εἰκόνος τοῦ υἱοῦ αὐτοῦ 'those whom he had chosen beforehand, he had already decided should become like his Son' Ro 8.29. In Ro 8.29 προγινώσκω may also be understood as meaning 'to know beforehand' (28.6).

30.101 χειροτονέω[a]: to choose or select, presumably by a group and possibly by the actual raising of the hand – 'to choose, to elect, to select.' χειροτονηθεὶς ὑπὸ τῶν ἐκκλησιῶν συνέκδημος ἡμῶν 'he has been chosen by the churches to travel with us' 2 Cor 8.19.

30.102 ἐπισκέπτομαι[a]: to choose or select on the basis of having investigated carefully – 'to select carefully, to choose after careful investigation.' ἐπισκέψασθε δέ, ἀδελφοί, ἄνδρας ἐξ ὑμῶν μαρτυρουμένους ἑπτὰ πλήρεις πνεύματος 'so then, fellow believers, carefully select seven men among you who are known to be full of the Holy Spirit' Ac 6.3.

30.103 καταφέρω ψῆφον: (an idiom, literally 'to bring a pebble against someone,' a reference to a white or black pebble used in voting for or against someone) to make known one's choice against someone – 'to vote against.' ἀναιρουμένων τε αὐτῶν κατήνεγκα ψῆφον 'when they were sentenced to death, I also voted against them' Ac 26.10.

30.104 λαγχάνω[b]: to choose by lot, probably by the use of marked pebbles or pieces of pottery – 'to choose by lot, to decide by gambling.' μὴ σχίσωμεν αὐτόν, ἀλλὰ λάχωμεν περὶ αὐτοῦ τίνος ἔσται 'let us not tear it, but let us throw lots to determine to whom it will belong' Jn 19.24. In a number of languages the closest equivalent to 'casting lots,' par-

ticularly for this type of context, is 'to gamble.'

30.105 κληρόω: (a figurative extension of meaning of κληρόω 'to be chosen by lot,' not occurring in the NT) to choose, with the implication of supernatural or divine intervention or guidance – 'to choose in accordance with the will of God.' ἐν ᾧ καὶ ἐκληρώθημεν 'in him we also were chosen' Eph 1.11.[19]

30.106 λαγχάνω[c]: to be selected by a decision based on the casting of lots, with the possible implication of reflecting divine choice – 'to be chosen by lot, to be selected by lot.' ἔλαχε τοῦ θυμιᾶσαι εἰσελθὼν εἰς τὸν ναὸν τοῦ κυρίου 'he was selected by lot to go into the sanctuary of the Lord to offer incense' Lk 1.9.

30.107 ὁ κλῆρος πίπτει ἐπί τινα: (an idiom, literally 'the lot falls upon someone') the process of choosing, with the probable implication of discerning God's will in this manner – 'to choose by lot, to select by lot.' ἔπεσεν ὁ κλῆρος ἐπὶ Μαθθίαν, καὶ συγκατεψηφίσθη μετὰ τῶν ἕνδεκα ἀποστόλων 'the name chosen was that of Matthias and he was added to the group of the eleven apostles' Ac 1.26. In some societies the closest natural equivalents of deciding by lot are procedures involving 'drawing straws' or 'throwing dice' or 'throwing down sticks' or 'dropping pebbles.'

G To Distinguish, To Evaluate, To Judge[20,21] (30.108-30.122)

30.108 κρίνω[c]: to make a judgment based upon the correctness or value of something –

---

19 The phrases δίδωμι κλήρους in Ac 1.26 and βάλλω κλήρους in Lk 23.34 (βάλλω κλῆρον in Mt 27.35) refer to choosing someone by means of casting lots, but these expressions may be interpreted in a strictly literal sense and thus are not treated here as idioms (see 6.219).

20 Subdomain G *To Distinguish, To Evaluate, To Judge* involves essentially the process of deciding the correctness, meaning, truth, or value of something or someone. This process normally implies careful thinking about various alternatives and then deciding what is to be regarded as more justified. The meanings in this subdomain are the final result of the process of thinking.

21 The preposition παρά and the so-called 'improper

'to evaluate, to judge.'[22] ὡς φρονίμοις λέγω· κρίνατε ὑμεῖς ὅ φημι 'I speak to you as sensible people; judge for yourselves what I say' 1 Cor 10.15; εἰ δίκαιόν ἐστιν ἐνώπιον τοῦ θεοῦ ὑμῶν ἀκούειν μᾶλλον ἢ τοῦ θεοῦ, κρίνατε 'you yourselves judge which is right in God's sight, to obey you or to obey God' Ac 4.19.

30.109 ἀνακρίνω[d]; διακρίνω[a]: to make a judgment on the basis of careful and detailed information – 'to judge carefully, to evaluate carefully.'[22]

ἀνακρίνω[d]: ὁ δὲ πνευματικὸς ἀνακρίνει τὰ πάντα 'the spiritual person makes careful judgments about all things' 1 Cor 2.15.

διακρίνω[a]: προφῆται δὲ δύο ἢ τρεῖς λαλείτωσαν, καὶ οἱ ἄλλοι διακρινέτωσαν 'two or three who are given God's message should speak, while the others evaluate carefully (what is said)' 1 Cor 14.29; τὸ μὲν πρόσωπον τοῦ οὐρανοῦ γινώσκετε διακρίνειν 'you know how to judge the appearance of the sky' Mt 16.3.

30.110 κρίσις[g], εως f; κρίμα[f], τος n: (derivatives of κρίνω[c] 'to judge,' 30.108) the content of the process of judging – 'judgment, decision, evaluation.'

κρίσις[g]: μὴ κρίνετε κατ' ὄψιν, ἀλλὰ τὴν δικαίαν κρίσιν κρίνετε 'do not judge according to appearance, but pronounce a righteous judgment' or '. . . deliver a righteous judgment' Jn 7.24. It may also be possible to translate ἀλλὰ τὴν δικαίαν κρίσιν κρίνετε as 'judge in a righteous manner' or 'judge according to true standards.'

κρίμα[f]: ὡς ἀνεξεραύνητα τὰ κρίματα αὐτοῦ 'how impossible it is to understand his judgments' or '. . . his decisions' Ro 11.33.

30.111 κρίσις[h], εως f: the basis for rendering a judgment – 'basis of judging, basis for judg-

ment.' αὕτη δέ ἐστιν ἡ κρίσις, ὅτι τὸ φῶς ἐλήλυθεν εἰς τὸν κόσμον καὶ ἠγάπησαν οἱ ἄνθρωποι μᾶλλον τὸ σκότος ἢ τὸ φῶς 'this is the basis for judging, namely, that light has come into the world and people love darkness rather than light' Jn 3.19. It is also possible to render κρίσις in Jn 3.19 as 'how judgment works' or 'the reason for God judging.'

30.112 διάκρισις[a], εως f: (derivative of διακρίνω[a] 'to evaluate carefully,' 30.109) the ability to evaluate and judge – 'to be able to judge, ability to make judgments, ability to decide.' ἄλλῳ δὲ διακρίσεις πνευμάτων 'to another is given the ability to judge the genuineness of gifts that come from the Spirit and those that do not' 1 Cor 12.10. In rendering 1 Cor 12.10 it is essential to recognize that the process of judging must have both positive and negative aspects, so that πνευμάτων must imply gifts which are genuinely from the Spirit of God and those which are not.

30.113 διακρίνω[c]: to judge that there is a difference or distinction – 'to make a distinction, to judge that there is a difference.' καὶ οὐθὲν διέκρινεν μεταξὺ ἡμῶν τε καὶ αὐτῶν 'he made no distinction between us and them' Ac 15.9. In some languages it may be best to render this statement in Ac 15.9 as 'he did not think that we and they are different.'

30.114 δοκιμάζω[c]: to regard something as genuine or worthy on the basis of testing – 'to judge to be genuine, to judge as good, to approve.' μακάριος ὁ μὴ κρίνων ἑαυτὸν ἐν ᾧ δοκιμάζει 'happy is the man who doesn't cause himself to be condemned by what he judges to be good' Ro 14.22; καθὼς οὐκ ἐδοκίμασαν τὸν θεὸν ἔχειν ἐν ἐπιγνώσει 'since they did not approve of retaining the knowledge of God' or '. . . to acknowledge God' Ro 1.28. For another interpretation of δοκιμάζω in Ro 1.28, see 30.98.

30.115 δόκιμος[a], ον: (derivative of δοκιμάζω[c] 'to judge to be genuine,' 30.114) pertaining to being judged worthy on the basis of testing – 'considered good, regarded as worthy.' οὐ γὰρ ὁ ἑαυτὸν συνιστάνων, ἐκεῖνός ἐστιν δόκιμος,

prepositions' ἔμπροσθεν, ἐναντίον, ἔναντι, κατέναντι, ἐνώπιον, and κατενώπιον all involve the meaning of 'judgment' or 'opinion' and are often translated as 'in the judgment of' or 'in the opinion of,' but these are essentially markers of participants in events and accordingly are treated in 90.20.

22 The meanings of κρίνω[c] (30.108), ἀνακρίνω[d] and διακρίνω[a] (30.109) are all closely related to the process of learning and of understanding, and in some contexts the meanings shade one into the other.

ἀλλὰ ὃν ὁ κύριος συνίστησιν 'for it is not the person who commends himself who is considered worthy, but the person whom the Lord commends' 2 Cor 10.18.

30.116 ἀποδιορίζω^b: to judge that there is a significant distinction between two or more objects or events – 'to make a distinction between, to draw a line between, to separate one from another.' οὗτοί εἰσιν οἱ ἀποδιορίζοντες, ψυχικοί, πνεῦμα μὴ ἔχοντες 'these draw a line between (spiritual and unspiritual persons), worldly people who are themselves without the Spirit' Jd 19. In Jd 19 the specific distinction between 'spiritual and unspiritual persons' comes from the context, as suggested in the New English Bible. For another interpretation of ἀποδιορίζω in Jd 19, see 39.16.

30.117 ἀποδοκιμάζω: to judge someone or something as not being worthy or genuine and thus something to be rejected – 'to regard as not worthy, to reject.' δεῖ τὸν υἱὸν τοῦ ἀνθρώπου πολλὰ παθεῖν καὶ ἀποδοκιμασθῆναι ὑπὸ τῶν πρεσβυτέρων 'the Son of Man must suffer much and be rejected by the elders' Mk 8.31.

30.118 καταγινώσκω: to judge something to be bad – 'to condemn.' ἐὰν καταγινώσκῃ ἡμῶν ἡ καρδία 'if our hearts condemn us' or 'if our hearts say to us that we have done wrong' 1 Jn 3.20.

30.119 αὐτοκατάκριτος, ον: pertaining to one who is condemned as the result of his own actions – 'condemned by one's own actions.' ὅτι ἐξέστραπται ὁ τοιοῦτος καὶ ἁμαρτάνει, ὢν αὐτοκατάκριτος 'that such a man is twisted and sinful, being condemned by what he himself has done' Tt 3.11.

30.120 βλέπω εἰς πρόσωπον: (an idiom, literally 'to see into the face') to judge on the basis of external appearances – 'to judge on the basis of appearance, to render a superficial judgment, to pay no attention to a person's status, to judge on the basis of reputation.' οὐ γὰρ βλέπεις εἰς πρόσωπον ἀνθρώπων 'for you do not judge a person on the basis of outward appearance' Mt 22.16. In some languages an equivalent of this expression in Mt 22.16 may be 'when you judge, you look into a man's heart' or 'when you judge you see more than a person's face' or 'when you judge a person, who he appears to be doesn't count.'

30.121 καταβραβεύω: to judge as a referee that someone is not worthy to receive a prize – 'to disqualify, to condemn, to judge as not worthy of a reward, to deprive of a reward.' μηδεὶς ὑμᾶς καταβραβευέτω 'let no one disqualify you' or 'let no one judge that you should not receive the prize' Col 2.18.

30.122 ἐξουσία^h, ας f: the right to judge on the basis of having the potential to evaluate – 'right, freedom of choice, freedom of action, power to evaluate.' βλέπετε δὲ μή πως ἡ ἐξουσία ὑμῶν αὕτη πρόσκομμα γένηται τοῖς ἀσθενέσιν 'but see to it that your freedom of choice does not become a cause of offense to those who are weak (in the faith)' 1 Cor 8.9.

31 Hold a View, Believe, Trust

Outline of Subdomains

A Have an Opinion, Hold a View (31.1-31.7)

31.1 φρονέω^c; κρίνω^d; λογίζομαι^c; ἡγέομαι^a; ἔχω^c: to hold a view or have an opinion with regard to something – 'to hold a view, to have an opinion, to consider, to regard.'

φρονέω^c: ἐγὼ πέποιθα εἰς ὑμᾶς ἐν κυρίῳ ὅτι οὐδὲν ἄλλο φρονήσετε 'our union in the Lord makes me confident that you will not take a different view' Ga 5.10.

κρίνω^d: διὸ ἐγὼ κρίνω μὴ παρενοχλεῖν τοῖς ἀπὸ τῶν ἐθνῶν ἐπιστρέφουσιν ἐπὶ τὸν θεόν 'it is my opinion that we should not trouble the Gentiles who are turning to God' Ac 15.19.

λογίζομαι^c: τοὺς λογιζομένους ἡμᾶς ὡς κατὰ σάρκα περιπατοῦντας 'who are of the opinion that we live by worldly standards' 2 Cor 10.2; καὶ μετὰ ἀνόμων ἐλογίσθη 'and he was considered to be one of the criminals' Lk 22.37.

ἡγέομαι^a: ἀναγκαῖον δὲ ἡγησάμην Ἐπαφρόδιτον τὸν ἀδελφὸν . . . πέμψαι πρὸς ὑμᾶς 'I have thought it necessary to send you our Christian brother, Epaphroditus' Php 2.25.

ἔχω^c: ὅτι ὡς προφήτην αὐτὸν εἶχον 'because they considered him to be a prophet' Mt 14.5; ἔχε με παρῃτημένον 'consider me excused' Lk 14.19.

31.2 λόγου ποιέομαι: (an idiom, literally 'to make of reason') to have an opinion based on some reason – 'to consider, to regard, to hold a view, to be of the opinion.' ἀλλ' οὐδενὸς λόγου ποιοῦμαι τὴν ψυχὴν τιμίαν ἐμαυτῷ 'but I regard my life to be worth nothing to me' Ac 20.24.[1]

31.3 γνώμη^b, ης f: that which is regarded or considered to be the case – 'what is considered, opinion.' κατὰ τὴν ἐμὴν γνώμην, δοκῶ δὲ κἀγὼ πνεῦμα θεοῦ ἔχειν 'according to my opinion, and I think that I too have God's Spirit' 1 Cor 7.40; χωρὶς δὲ τῆς σῆς γνώμης οὐδὲν ἠθέλησα ποιῆσαι 'but I would not want to do anything without having your opinion on the matter' Phm 14. It is also possible to under-

stand γνώμη in Phm 14 as 'agreement' or 'consent' (see 31.14).

31.4 θέλω^b: to have a particular view or opinion about something – 'to be of an opinion, to think something is so.' λανθάνει γὰρ αὐτοὺς τοῦτο θέλοντας 'for it has escaped the notice of those who hold this view' 2 Pe 3.5. Since θέλω in 2 Pe 3.5 is the only NT occurrence with this meaning, a number of scholars prefer to interpret θέλω in this context as referring to intention or evident purpose, in which case the meaning would be related to θέλω^a (30.58).

31.5 λέγω ἐν ἑαυτῷ: (an idiom, literally 'to speak to oneself') to think about something without communicating the content to others – 'to think to oneself, to say to oneself' (often used to introduce a direct quotation of one's thoughts). ἰδού τινες τῶν γραμματέων εἶπαν ἐν ἑαυτοῖς, Οὗτος βλασφημεῖ 'then some of the teachers of the Law thought to themselves, This man is talking against God' Mt 9.3; ἔλεγεν γὰρ ἐν ἑαυτῇ, Ἐὰν μόνον ἅψωμαι τοῦ ἱματίου αὐτοῦ σωθήσομαι 'she thought to herself, If only I touch his cloak, I will get well' Mt 9.21.

31.6 νοέω^c: to be able to form some idea about – 'to be able to form an idea, to imagine.' ὑπερεκπερισσοῦ ὧν . . . νοοῦμεν 'far beyond what . . . we imagine' Eph 3.20. It is also possible to understand νοέω in Eph 3.20 as meaning merely 'to hold a particular view' (compare 31.1), and therefore one may translate 'far beyond what we think to be the case.'

31.7 ἵσταμαι ἐν τῇ καρδίᾳ: (an idiom, literally 'to stand at the heart') to continue to have an opinion – 'to keep on being of an opinion, to remain with an opinion, to continue in one's views.' ὃς δὲ ἕστηκεν ἐν τῇ καρδίᾳ αὐτοῦ ἑδραῖος 'whoever is firmly of the opinion' or 'who is firmly convinced of his views' 1 Cor 7.37.

B Hold a Wrong View, Be Mistaken (31.8-31.13)

31.8 πλανάω; πλάνη^a, ης f: (figurative extensions of meaning of πλανάω 'to cause to

---

1 In Ac 20.24 the negation οὐδενός has been syntactically combined with λόγου rather than with τιμίαν, with which it is semantically more closely connected. Compare English *I didn't think he would go* in contrast with *I thought he would not go*.

wander off the path,' not occurring in the NT) to cause someone to hold a wrong view and thus be mistaken – 'to mislead, to deceive, deception, to cause to be mistaken.'[2]

πλανάω: βλέπετε μή τις ὑμᾶς πλανήσῃ 'watch out, and do not let anyone deceive you' Mt 24.4; πλανῶντες καὶ πλανώμενοι 'deceiving others and being deceived themselves' 2 Tm 3.13.

πλάνη[a]: ἐκ τούτου γινώσκομεν τὸ πνεῦμα τῆς ἀληθείας καὶ τὸ πνεῦμα τῆς πλάνης 'this is the way we know the difference between the Spirit which leads to truth and the spirit that misleads us' or '. . . causes us to hold a wrong view' or '. . . causes us to be mistaken' 1 Jn 4.6.

To mislead people as to proper views which they should have may often be expressed idiomatically, for example, 'to twist people's thoughts,' 'to cause what is false to seem like what is true,' 'to make a lie appear true,' 'to dig away the truth,' or 'to cover the eyes with lies.'

31.9 πλάνος, ον: pertaining to causing someone to be mistaken – 'causing someone to be mistaken, deceitful, that which deceives.'[2] προσέχοντες πνεύμασιν πλάνοις καὶ διδασκαλίαις δαιμονίων 'they will believe spirits which deceive and the teachings of demons' 1 Tm 4.1.

31.10 πλάνη[b], ης f: (derivative of πλάνη[a] 'to deceive,' 31.8) the content of that which misleads or deceives – 'misleading belief, deceptive belief, error, mistaken view.'[2] ἵνα μὴ τῇ τῶν ἀθέσμων πλάνῃ συναπαχθέντες 'so that you will not be led astray by the error of lawless people' 2 Pe 3.17.

31.11 ἀποπλανάω: to cause someone to definitely go astray in one's beliefs or views – 'to deceive, to mislead, to cause to have completely wrong views.'[2] δώσουσιν σημεῖα καὶ τέρατα πρὸς τὸ ἀποπλανᾶν, εἰ δυνατόν, τοὺς ἐκλεκτούς 'they will perform signs and miracles in order to mislead the elect, if possible' Mk 13.22.

31.12 ἀπατάω; ἐξαπατάω; φρεναπατάω; ἀπάτη, ης f: to cause someone to have misleading or erroneous views concerning the truth – 'to mislead, to deceive, deception.'[3] ἀπατάω: μηδεὶς ὑμᾶς ἀπατάτω κενοῖς λόγοις 'let no one mislead you with foolish words' Eph 5.6. ἐξαπατάω: διὰ τῆς χρηστολογίας καὶ εὐλογίας ἐξαπατῶσιν τὰς καρδίας τῶν ἀκάκων 'by their fine words and flattering speech they mislead the minds of naive people' Ro 16.18. φρεναπατάω: εἰ γὰρ δοκεῖ τις εἶναί τι μηδὲν ὤν, φρεναπατᾷ ἑαυτόν 'if a person thinks he is something when he really is nothing, he is only deceiving himself' Ga 6.3. ἀπάτη: ἡ ἀπάτη τοῦ πλούτου 'being misled by riches' Mk 4.19.

31.13 φρεναπάτης, ου m: (derivative of φρεναπατάω 'to lead astray,' 31.12) one who misleads people concerning the truth – 'person who misleads, deceiver.' εἰσὶν γὰρ πολλοὶ καὶ ἀνυπότακτοι, ματαιολόγοι καὶ φρεναπάται 'there are many disorderly people, empty talkers, and deceivers' Tt 1.10. In some languages the equivalent of φρεναπάτης is 'one who leads along the wrong path' or 'one who says wrong is right.'

C Agree, Consent (31.14-31.25)

31.14 γνώμη[c], ης f: agreement based on knowledge – 'agreement, consent.' χωρὶς δὲ τῆς σῆς γνώμης οὐδὲν ἠθέλησα ποιῆσαι 'I did not wish to do anything without your agreement' Phm 14. This interpretation of γνώμη in Phm 14 is less likely than the meaning of γνώμη as 'opinion' (see 31.3).

---

2 The meanings of πλανάω and πλάνη[a] (31.8), πλάνος (31.9), πλάνη[b] (31.10), and ἀποπλανάω (31.11) focus primarily upon the misleading or deceptive views which people are caused to have, but these same terms may refer to more than mere mistaken ideas or opinions. They may involve deception of a behavioral nature, and therefore these same meanings could be in Domain 88, Subdomain U.

3 This series of meanings containing the stem ἀπατ- overlaps considerably in meaning with the previous series containing the stem πλαν- (31.8-31.11). Both sets of terms involve deception and erroneous views. It is difficult to determine the precise implications of differences in meaning, but it may be that terms with the stem πλαν- are somewhat more related to general deceptive behavior rather than primarily to misconceptions.

31.15 συμφωνέω[a]; συμφώνησις, εως *f*; σύμφωνον, ου *n*: to come to an agreement with, often implying a type of joint decision – 'to agree with, agreement.'

συμφωνέω[a]: συμφωνήσας δὲ μετὰ τῶν ἐργατῶν ἐκ δηναρίου 'he came to an agreement with the workmen for a denarius' Mt 20.2.

συμφώνησις: τίς δὲ συμφώνησις Χριστοῦ πρὸς Βελιάρ 'do Christ and Beliar agree on anything?' 2 Cor 6.15.

σύμφωνον: μὴ ἀποστερεῖτε ἀλλήλους, εἰ μήτι ἂν ἐκ συμφώνου πρὸς καιρόν 'do not deny yourselves to each other, unless you agree to do so for a while' 1 Cor 7.5.

31.16 σύμφημι: to give assent to a particular proposition – 'to agree with, to assent to.' σύμφημι τῷ νόμῳ ὅτι καλός 'I agree with the Law, that it is good' Ro 7.16. In a number of languages the equivalent of 'to give assent to' is simply 'to say Yes to.' In other instances it may be important to introduce direct discourse, for example, 'to say, I agree.'

31.17 συνευδοκέω: to decide with someone else that something is preferable or good – 'to agree to, to consent to.' εἴ τις ἀδελφὸς γυναῖκα ἔχει ἄπιστον, καὶ αὕτη συνευδοκεῖ οἰκεῖν μετ' αὐτοῦ, μὴ ἀφιέτω αὐτήν 'if a Christian man has a wife who is an unbeliever, and she agrees to go on living with him, he must not divorce her' 1 Cor 7.12.

31.18 συντίθεμαι; συγκατατίθεμαι; συγκατάθεσις, εως *f*: to work out a joint arrangement – 'to agree on, to arrange together, joint agreement, joint arrangement, mutual agreement.'

συντίθεμαι: οἱ Ἰουδαῖοι συνέθεντο τοῦ ἐρωτῆσαί σε ὅπως αὔριον τὸν Παῦλον καταγάγῃς εἰς τὸ συνέδριον 'the Jewish authorities have agreed to ask you tomorrow to take Paul down to the Council' Ac 23.20.

συγκατατίθεμαι: οὗτος οὐκ ἦν συγκατατεθειμένος τῇ βουλῇ καὶ τῇ πράξει αὐτῶν 'he had not agreed with their plan and the action they took' Lk 23.51.

συγκατάθεσις: τίς δὲ συγκατάθεσις ναῷ θεοῦ μετὰ εἰδώλων; 'how can God's temple come to a mutual agreement with pagan idols?' 2 Cor 6.16.

31.19 προσέρχομαι[c]: (a figurative extension of meaning of προσέρχομαι[a] 'to move toward,' 15.77) to come to a position of holding the same opinion as someone else – 'to come to an opinion with, to agree with.' εἴ τις ἑτεροδιδασκαλεῖ καὶ μὴ προσέρχεται ὑγιαίνουσιν λόγοις, τοῖς τοῦ κυρίου ἡμῶν Ἰησοῦ Χριστοῦ 'whoever teaches a different doctrine and does not agree with the true words of our Lord Jesus Christ' 1 Tm 6.3.

31.20 εὐνοέω[b]: to come to an agreement with someone – 'to agree to, to agree with.' ἴσθι εὐνοῶν τῷ ἀντιδίκῳ σου ταχύ 'go and agree with your accuser quickly' Mt 5.25. For other interpretations of εὐνοέω in Mt 5.25, see 30.23 and 56.3.

31.21 μεσιτεύω: to bring about a mutually accepted agreement between two or more parties, with the probable additional component of making something certain – 'to bring about an agreement, to cause an agreement.' ἐμεσίτευσεν ὅρκῳ 'so he used a vow to help bring about the agreement and make it certain' He 6.17. Since one who was a μεσίτης (31.22) often acted as one who provided the surety or guarantee of an agreement or arrangement, there is a significant component of certainty involved in μεσιτεύω. Hence, one may understand this as implying not only the agreement but the guarantee of its validity.

31.22 μεσίτης[a], ου *m*: (derivative of μεσιτεύω 'to bring about an agreement,' 31.21) one who causes or helps parties to come to an agreement, with the implication of guaranteeing the certainty of the arrangement – 'go-between, mediator.' διαταγεὶς δι' ἀγγέλων ἐν χειρὶ μεσίτου '(the Law) was put into effect through angels by a mediator' Ga 3.19.

31.23 ὁμοθυμαδόν: pertaining to mutual consent or agreement – 'with one mind, by common consent, unanimously.' οὗτοι πάντες ἦσαν προσκαρτεροῦντες ὁμοθυμαδὸν τῇ προσευχῇ 'all these continued in prayer with one mind' Ac 1.14. In a number of languages 'with one mind' would need to be rendered as 'prayed for the same things' or 'said the same in their prayers.' ἔδοξεν ἡμῖν γενομένοις ὁμοθυμαδὸν ἐκλεξαμένοις ἄνδρας πέμψαι πρὸς ὑμᾶς 'we unanimously agreed to choose some messengers to send to you' Ac 15.25. The expression 'we unanimously agreed' may also be rendered as 'we were in agreement that.'

31.24 ἀσύμφωνος, ον: pertaining to not being able to come to some agreement – 'to be in disagreement, to not agree with, to be unable to agree.' ἀσύμφωνοι δὲ ὄντες πρὸς ἀλλήλους ἀπελύοντο 'so they left, being unable to agree among themselves' Ac 28.25.

31.25 ἀρνέομαι^c: to refuse to agree or consent to something – 'to refuse to agree to, to not consent to.' πίστει Μωϋσῆς μέγας γενόμενος ἠρνήσατο λέγεσθαι υἱὸς θυγατρὸς Φαραώ 'it was faith that made Moses, when he was grown, refuse to be called the son of Pharaoh's daughter' He 11.24.

D Acknowledge[4] (31.26-31.28)

31.26 ἀποδέχομαι^c: to recognize or acknowledge the truth of something, normally implying something good – 'to acknowledge, to recognize, to think about favorably.' πάντῃ τε καὶ πανταχοῦ ἀποδεχόμεθα, κράτιστε Φῆλιξ, μετὰ πάσης εὐχαριστίας 'most excellent Felix, we acknowledge this anywhere and everywhere with complete thankfulness' Ac 24.3. See 83.8.

31.27 γινώσκω^e; ἐπιγινώσκω^e: to indicate that one does know – 'to acknowledge.'
γινώσκω^e: εἰ δέ τις ἀγαπᾷ τὸν θεόν, οὗτος ἔγνωσται ὑπ' αὐτοῦ 'if anyone loves God, such a person is acknowledged by him' 1 Cor 8.3. It is also possible that in 1 Cor 8.3 γινώσκω means only 'to know' (28.1).

---

4 In a number of contexts the meanings in Subdomain D *Acknowledge* imply not only the processes of intellectual recognition, but in some instances the evidence of this recognition by some type of communication. The focal element seems to be the mental recognition, but since in some contexts the verbalization or other means of communication may be important, it may be useful to make this explicit, for example, 'to recognize the truth of and to say so.' In such contexts the meanings in this subdomain overlap with the domain of *Communication* (33).

ἐπιγινώσκω^e: ἐπιγινώσκετε οὖν τοὺς τοιούτους 'therefore you should acknowledge these persons' 1 Cor 16.18. It may also be possible to translate this expression in 1 Cor 16.18 as 'you should give these people due recognition' in the sense of 'causing to be recognized' or 'causing to be acknowledged.'

31.28 ἔχω ἐν ἐπιγνώσει: (an idiom, literally 'to have in recognition') to recognize something as being what it truly is – 'to acknowledge.' καὶ καθὼς οὐκ ἐδοκίμασαν τὸν θεὸν ἔχειν ἐν ἐπιγνώσει 'because they did not think it worthwhile to acknowledge God' Ro 1.28. For another interpretation of ἐπίγνωσις in Ro 1.28, see 28.2.

E Suppose, Think Possible (31.29-31.34)

31.29 οἶμαι; νομίζω; δοκέω^a; ὑπολαμβάνω^d: to regard something as presumably true, but without particular certainty – 'to suppose, to presume, to assume, to imagine, to believe, to think.'
οἶμαι: μὴ γὰρ οἰέσθω ὁ ἄνθρωπος ἐκεῖνος ὅτι λήμψεταί τι παρὰ τοῦ κυρίου 'for that man must not suppose that he will receive anything from the Lord' Jas 1.7; οὐδ' αὐτὸν οἶμαι τὸν κόσμον χωρῆσαι τὰ γραφόμενα βιβλία 'I imagine that the whole world could not hold the books that would be written' Jn 21.25.
νομίζω: οὗ ἐνομίζομεν προσευχὴν εἶναι 'where we presumed there would be a place of prayer' Ac 16.13.
δοκέω^a: εἴ τις δοκεῖ σοφὸς εἶναι ἐν ὑμῖν ἐν τῷ αἰῶνι τούτῳ 'if anyone among you thinks that he is a wise person by this world's standards' 1 Cor 3.18.
ὑπολαμβάνω^d: οὐ γὰρ ὡς ὑμεῖς ὑπολαμβάνετε οὗτοι μεθύουσιν 'these men are not drunk as you suppose' Ac 2.15; ὑπολαμβάνω ὅτι ᾧ τὸ πλεῖον ἐχαρίσατο 'I suppose the one to whom the most was forgiven' Lk 7.43.

In some languages the equivalent of 'to suppose' or 'to presume' is 'to think somewhat' or 'to think perhaps' or 'to think a little.' In some instances the lack of certainty is spelled out clearly as 'to think, but not with certainty' or 'to think, but not to know' or 'to think, but not to be sure.'

31.30 δοκεῖ (impersonal form): to hold an opinion based upon appearances which may be significantly different from reality – 'to seem, to appear, to assume, to think.' τίς τούτων τῶν τριῶν πλησίον δοκεῖ σοι γεγονέναι; 'which one of these three seems to you to have been a neighbor?' Lk 10.36; τί σοι δοκεῖ; 'what do you think?' Mt 17.25.

31.31 τὰ κατὰ πρόσωπον: (an idiom, literally 'those things according to the face') that which seems to be so – 'outward appearance, what things seem to be.' τὰ κατὰ πρόσωπον βλέπετε 'you look at outward appearances' 2 Cor 10.7.

31.32 ὑπονοέω; ὑπόνοια, ας f: to have an opinion based on scant evidence, often with the implication of regarding a false opinion as true – 'to imagine, to conjecture, to suspect, to falsely suspect, to be suspicious, suspicion.' ὑπονοέω: περὶ οὗ σταθέντες οἱ κατήγοροι οὐδεμίαν αἰτίαν ἔφερον ὧν ἐγὼ ὑπενόουν πονηρῶν 'when the accusers stood up, they brought no charge in his case of such evils as I had suspected' Ac 25.18.
ὑπόνοια: ἐξ ὧν γίνεται . . . ὑπόνοιαι πονηραί 'this causes . . . people to suspect evil' or '. . . to suspect falsely' or '. . . be suspicious' 1 Tm 6.4.

31.33 ἐκζήτησις, εως f: to form ideas which are unrelated to reality, normally with a negative connotation – 'speculation, worthless speculation, imaginings.' αἵτινες ἐκζητήσεις παρέχουσιν 'these promote worthless speculations' 1 Tm 1.4. It is also possible to understand ἐκζήτησις in 1 Tm 1.4 as meaning 'controversies' or 'arguments' (see 33.442).

31.34 ἄκακος[b], ον: pertaining to being unsuspecting or naive with regard to possible deception – 'unsuspecting, naive.' διὰ τῆς χρηστολογίας καὶ εὐλογίας ἐξαπατῶσιν τὰς καρδίας τῶν ἀκάκων 'by their fine words and flattering speech they deceive the minds of naive people' Ro 16.18. It may be possible to spell out the implications of ἄκακος in Ro 16.18 by translating 'the minds of people who do not suspect lies.'

F Believe To Be True (31.35-31.49)

31.35 πιστεύω[a]: to believe something to be true and, hence, worthy of being trusted – 'to believe, to think to be true, to regard as trustworthy.'[5] ἀκούω σχίσματα ἐν ὑμῖν ὑπάρχειν, καὶ μέρος τι πιστεύω 'I have been told that there are opposing groups among you, and this I believe is partly true' 1 Cor 11.18; ἀνθ' ὧν οὐκ ἐπίστευσας τοῖς λόγοις μου 'but you have not believed my message' Lk 1.20; ἐάν τις ὑμῖν εἴπῃ, Ἰδοὺ ὧδε ὁ Χριστός, . . . μὴ πιστεύσητε 'if anyone says to you, Here is the Christ, . . . do not believe them' Mt 24.23; σὺ πιστεύεις ὅτι εἷς ἐστιν ὁ θεός; 'do you believe that there is only one God?' Jas 2.19.

In a number of languages the equivalent of πιστεύω[a] is simply 'to think to be true' or 'to regard as true,' but in some languages an idiomatic expression is employed, for example, 'to think in the heart' or 'to think in the liver' or 'to hold in the heart.'

31.36 πιστόομαι: to come to believe something to be true – 'to come to believe.' σὺ δὲ μένε ἐν οἷς ἔμαθες καὶ ἐπιστώθης 'but as for you, continue in what you were taught and firmly came to believe' 2 Tm 3.14.

31.37 διακρίνομαι[a]; διαλογισμός[d], οῦ m; διστάζω: to think that something may not be true or certain – 'to doubt, to be uncertain about, doubt.'
διακρίνομαι[a]: πορεύου σὺν αὐτοῖς μηδὲν διακρινόμενος 'go with them, with no doubts at all'

---

5 πιστεύω[a] differs from φρονέω[c], κρίνω[d], λογίζομαι[c], ἡγέομαι[a], and ἔχω[c] 'to hold a view' (31.1) because of the added component of trustworthiness. There is also a greater certainty in πιστεύω[a] than in οἶμαι, νομίζω, δοκέω[a], and ὑπολαμβάνω[d] 'to suppose' (31.29), and though for certain contexts there may be a somewhat less degree of certainty than in the case of γινώσκω[a] and οἶδα[a] 'to know' (28.1), there is the component of confidence and trustworthiness which is a focal element in this subdomain.
πιστεύω[a] in the sense of 'believing information' differs from πιστεύω[b] and πίστις[b] 'to trust or rely on' (31.85). There is also a contrast with πιστεύω[c] and πίστις[d] (31.102), which are essentially equivalent in meaning to 'becoming a Christian,' since the belief and trust is specifically in salvation through Jesus Christ with the resulting new relationship to God.

Ac 10.20; αἰτείτω δὲ ἐν πίστει, μηδὲν διακρι-νόμενος 'but you must believe when you pray, and not doubt at all' Jas 1.6.

διαλογισμός^d: διὰ τί διαλογισμοὶ ἀναβαίνουσιν ἐν τῇ καρδίᾳ ὑμῶν; 'why are you beginning to doubt?' (literally 'why do doubts arise in your mind?') Lk 24.38.

διστάζω: ὀλιγόπιστε, εἰς τί ἐδίστασας; 'how little faith you have; why did you doubt?' Mt 14.31.

In a number of languages 'doubt' is express-ed by means of idioms, for example, 'to have two thoughts' or 'to think only perhaps' or 'to believe only a little' or 'to question one's heart about.'

31.38 δίψυχος, ον: pertaining to being uncer-tain about the truth of something – 'double-minded, doubting, doubter.' καὶ ἁγνίσατε καρ-δίας, δίψυχοι 'and consecrate your hearts, you doubters' Jas 4.8.

31.39 ἀπιστέω^a: to believe that something is not true – 'to not believe, to disbelieve, to not think to be true.' ἀκούσαντες ὅτι ζῇ καὶ ἐθεάθη ὑπ' αὐτῆς ἠπίστησαν 'when they heard her say that he was alive and that she had seen him, they did not believe her' Mk 16.11.

31.40 ἄπιστος^a, ον: (derivative of ἀπιστέω^a 'to not believe,' 31.39) pertaining to not being believable – 'unbelievable, impossible to be believed.' τί ἄπιστον κρίνεται παρ' ὑμῖν εἰ ὁ θεὸς νεκροὺς ἐγείρει; 'why do you consider it im-possible to believe that God raises the dead?' Ac 26.8.

31.41 ἀσφάλεια^b, ας f: a state of certainty with regard to a belief – 'certainty, being without doubt.' ἵνα ἐπιγνῷς περὶ ὧν κατηχήθης λόγων τὴν ἀσφάλειαν 'so that you will know the certainty of those things that you have been taught' Lk 1.4. It is also possible to render Lk 1.4 as 'so that you may know that those things that you have been taught are certainly true.'

31.42 ἀσφαλής^b, ές; ἀσφαλῶς^b: pertaining to being certain and thus completely believ-able – 'worthy of being believed, certainly true, completely believable.'

ἀσφαλής^b: μὴ δυναμένου δὲ αὐτοῦ γνῶναι τὸ ἀσφαλὲς διὰ τὸν θόρυβον 'because of the con-fusion he was not able to find out what was certain' or '. . . what had really happened' Ac 21.34.

ἀσφαλῶς^b: ἀσφαλῶς οὖν γινωσκέτω πᾶς οἶκος Ἰσραήλ 'all the people of Israel, then, are to know with certainty' Ac 2.36.

31.43 πίστις^a, εως f: that which is complete-ly believable – 'what can be fully believed, that which is worthy of belief, believable evidence, proof.' πίστιν παρασχὼν πᾶσιν ἀναστήσας αὐτὸν ἐκ νεκρῶν 'having provided proof to all by raising him from the dead' Ac 17.31.

31.44 παράδοξος^a, ον: pertaining to being difficult to be believed – 'difficult to believe, unusual, incredible.' εἴδομεν παράδοξα σήμε-ρον 'we have seen incredible signs today' Lk 5.26. It would also be possible to translate εἴ-δομεν παράδοξα σήμερον as 'we have seen today things we can hardly believe' or even '. . . things which people would scarcely believe.' For another interpretation of παράδοξος in Lk 5.26, see 58.56.

31.45 πληροφορέομαι; πληροφορία, ας f: to be completely certain of the truth of some-thing – 'to be absolutely sure, to be certain, complete certainty.'

πληροφορέομαι: πληροφορηθεὶς ὅτι ὃ ἐπήγ-γελται δυνατός ἐστιν καὶ ποιῆσαι 'he was abso-lutely sure that (God) would be able to do what he had promised' Ro 4.21.

πληροφορία: ὅτι τὸ εὐαγγέλιον ἡμῶν οὐκ ἐγενήθη εἰς ὑμᾶς ἐν λόγῳ μόνον ἀλλὰ καὶ ἐν δυνάμει καὶ ἐν πνεύματι ἁγίῳ καὶ ἐν πληροφορίᾳ πολλῇ 'for we brought the good news to you, not with words only, but also with power and the Holy Spirit, and with complete certainty' 1 Th 1.5. The phrase 'with complete certain-ty' may be expressed in some languages as 'you may surely believe it' or 'there is no reason at all for you to doubt.'

31.46 πείθομαι^c: to come to believe the cer-tainty of something on the basis of being con-vinced – 'to be certain, to be sure, to be con-vinced.' πειθόμεθα γὰρ ὅτι καλὴν συνείδησιν ἔχομεν 'we are sure that we have a clear conscience' He 13.18; οὐδ' ἐάν τις ἐκ νεκρῶν ἀναστῇ πεισθήσονται 'neither will they be convinced if someone rises from the dead' Lk 16.31; πέπεισμαι γὰρ ὅτι οὔτε θάνατος οὔτε ζωή . . . δυνήσεται ἡμᾶς χωρίσαι ἀπὸ τῆς ἀγάπης τοῦ θεοῦ 'for I am certain that neither death nor life . . . can separate us from the love of God' Ro 8.38-39; πεποιθὼς αὐτὸ τοῦτο, ὅτι ὁ ἐναρξάμενος ἐν ὑμῖν ἔργον ἀγαθὸν ἐπιτελέσει ἄχρι ἡμέρας Χριστοῦ Ἰησοῦ 'I am sure of this: that he who began his good work in you will carry it on until it is finished in the day of Christ Jesus' Php 1.6.

31.47 ἐπέχω[b]; προσέχω[c]: to hold firmly to a particular belief – 'to hold firmly to, to continue to believe.'

ἐπέχω[b]: λόγον ζωῆς ἐπέχοντες 'as you continue to hold to the word of life' Php 2.16. It is also possible to understand ἐπέχω in Php 2.16 as meaning 'to offer.'

προσέχω[c]: μηδὲ προσέχειν μύθοις καὶ γενεαλογίαις ἀπεράντοις 'to no longer hold on to legends and long lists of ancestors' 1 Tm 1.4; διὰ τοῦτο δεῖ περισσοτέρως προσέχειν ὑμᾶς τοῖς ἀκουσθεῖσιν 'that is why we must hold on all the more firmly to what we have heard' He 2.1.

The equivalent of ἐπέχω[b] and προσέχω[c] may be simply 'to continue to strongly believe' or 'to not give up at all to believe.'

31.48 κατέχω[b]: to continue to believe, with the implication of acting in accordance with such belief – 'to continue to believe and practice, to continue to follow.' καθὼς παρέδωκα ὑμῖν τὰς παραδόσεις κατέχετε 'you continue to believe and practice the traditions as I passed them on to you' 1 Cor 11.2; δι' οὗ καὶ σῴζεσθε . . . εἰ κατέχετε 'by which you are saved . . . if you continue to believe and practice it' 1 Cor 15.2.

31.49 ἀντέχομαι[b]: to hold fast to a particular belief, with the implication of acting accordingly – 'to hold fast to, to cling to, to hold firmly to.' ἀντεχόμενον τοῦ κατὰ τὴν διδαχὴν πιστοῦ λόγου 'holding firmly to the message which can be trusted and which is in accordance with the teaching' Tt 1.9.

G Accept As True[6] (31.50-31.57)

31.50 λαμβάνω[f]: to come to believe something and to act in accordance with such a belief – 'to accept, to receive, to come to believe.' ὁ ἀθετῶν ἐμὲ καὶ μὴ λαμβάνων τὰ ῥήματά μου ἔχει τὸν κρίνοντα αὐτόν 'whoever rejects me and does not accept my message has one who will judge him' Jn 12.48.

31.51 δέχομαι[c]: to readily receive information and to regard it as true – 'to receive readily, to accept, to believe.' οἳ ὅταν ἀκούσωσιν μετὰ χαρᾶς δέχονται τὸν λόγον 'those who hear the message receive it gladly' Lk 8.13; ἀκούσαντες δὲ οἱ ἐν Ἱεροσολύμοις ἀπόστολοι ὅτι δέδεκται ἡ Σαμάρεια τὸν λόγον τοῦ θεοῦ 'the apostles in Jerusalem heard that the people of Samaria had received the word of God' Ac 8.14; εὐαγγέλιον ἕτερον ὃ οὐκ ἐδέξασθε καλῶς ἀνέχεσθε 'you tolerate a gospel different from what you received' 2 Cor 11.4.

31.52 ἀποδέχομαι[b]; ἀποδοχή, ῆς f; παραδέχομαι[a]: to come to believe something to be true and to respond accordingly, with some emphasis upon the source – 'to accept, to receive, acceptance, reception.'

ἀποδέχομαι[b]: οἱ μὲν οὖν ἀποδεξάμενοι τὸν λόγον αὐτοῦ ἐβαπτίσθησαν 'many of them accepted his message and were baptized' Ac 2.41.

ἀποδοχή: πιστὸς ὁ λόγος καὶ πάσης ἀποδοχῆς ἄξιος 'this is a true saying and is worthy of being fully received' 1 Tm 1.15.

παραδέχομαι[a]: διότι οὐ παραδέξονταί σου μαρτυρίαν περὶ ἐμοῦ 'because the people will not accept your witness about me' Ac 22.18; κατὰ πρεσβυτέρου κατηγορίαν μὴ παραδέχου, ἐκτὸς εἰ μὴ ἐπὶ δύο ἢ τριῶν μαρτύρων 'do not accept an accusation against an elder unless there are two or three witnesses' 1 Tm 5.19.

31.53 προσδέχομαι[a]: to accept a message for oneself and to act accordingly – 'to accept, to

---

6 Subdomain G *Accept As True* involves not only belief but also corresponding behavior. Acting in accordance with one's belief is not merely an implication of the belief but a crucial semantic component in the meanings in this subdomain, for 'to accept or receive something as true' implies in the NT context acting in accordance with such a belief.

receive, to hold.' ἐλπίδα ἔχων εἰς τὸν θεόν, ἣν καὶ αὐτοὶ προσδέχονται 'I have the (same) hope in God that these themselves have accepted' Ac 24.15.

31.54 ἀνέχομαιᵇ: to continue to accept as valid or true – 'to accept, to receive.' ἔσται γὰρ καιρὸς ὅτε τῆς ὑγιαινούσης διδασκαλίας οὐκ ἀνέξονται 'for there will be a time when they will not accept sound teaching' 2 Tm 4.3.

31.55 βαστάζωᶠ; **φέρω**ᵏ: to accept, but with the implication of the truth being difficult to comprehend or to respond to properly – 'to accept, to receive.'
βαστάζωᶠ: ἀλλ' οὐ δύνασθε βαστάζειν ἄρτι 'but you are not able to accept it now' Jn 16.12.
φέρωᵏ: οὐκ ἔφερον γὰρ τὸ διαστελλόμενον 'they could not accept the order' He 12.20.

31.56 ἀκούωᵈ; **ἀκοή**ᵉ, **ῆς** *f*: to believe something and to respond to it on the basis of having heard – 'to accept, to listen to, to listen and respond, to pay attention and respond, to heed.'
ἀκούωᵈ: ἐάν σου ἀκούσῃ, ἐκέρδησας τὸν ἀδελφόν σου 'if he listens to you, you have won your brother back' Mt 18.15;⁷ γνωστὸν οὖν ἔστω ὑμῖν ὅτι τοῖς ἔθνεσιν ἀπεστάλη τοῦτο τὸ σωτήριον τοῦ θεοῦ· αὐτοὶ καὶ ἀκούσονται 'you are to know for sure, then, that God's message of salvation has been sent to the Gentiles; they will accept it' Ac 28.28.
ἀκοήᵉ: καὶ ἀπὸ μὲν τῆς ἀληθείας τὴν ἀκοὴν ἀποστρέφουσιν 'and they will turn away from heeding the truth' 2 Tm 4.4.

31.57 χωρέωᶜ: to be able to accept a message and respond accordingly – 'to be able to accept, to receive.' οὐ πάντες χωροῦσιν τὸν λόγον τοῦτον, ἀλλ' οἷς δέδοται 'not everyone is able to accept this teaching, but only those to whom he has given it' Mt 19.11. It is possible to understand χωρέω in Mt 19.11 as meaning 'to be able to understand.'

---

7 It is obvious that in the use of ἀκούω in Mt 18.15 there is more than mere sensory perception. There is acceptance of the truth of what is said and the evident willingness to respond appropriately. These two elements are much more in focus than the sensory process of listening.

H Change an Opinion Concerning Truth (31.58-31.81)

31.58 μεταβάλλομαι: to change one's thinking about something – 'to change one's mind, to alter an opinion.' μεταβαλόμενοι ἔλεγον αὐτὸν εἶναι θεόν 'they changed their minds and said, He is a god' Ac 28.6. In Ac 28.6 μεταβάλλομαι may often be expressed as 'to no longer think as they did' or 'to think differently now.'

31.59 μεταμέλομαιᵇ: to change one's mind about something, with the probable implication of regret – 'to change one's mind, to think differently.' ὑμεῖς δὲ ἰδόντες οὐδὲ μετεμελήθητε ὕστερον τοῦ πιστεῦσαι αὐτῷ 'even when you saw this, you did not change your minds later on and believe him' Mt 21.32; ὤμοσεν κύριος, καὶ οὐ μεταμεληθήσεται 'the Lord has made a vow and will not change his mind' He 7.21.

31.60 στρέφομαιᵇ; **ἐπιστρέφω**ᵇ; **ἐπιστροφή**ᵃ, **ῆς** *f*: to change one's belief, with focus upon that to which one turns – 'to turn to, to come to believe, to come to accept.'
στρέφομαιᵇ: ἐὰν μὴ στραφῆτε καὶ γένησθε ὡς τὰ παιδία 'unless you change and become like children' Mt 18.3 (for another interpretation of στρέφομαι in Mt 18.3, see 41.50); μὴ . . . στραφῶσιν, καὶ ἰάσομαι αὐτούς 'they would not turn to me for me to heal them' Jn 12.40; ἐστράφησαν ἐν ταῖς καρδίαις αὐτῶν εἰς Αἴγυπτον 'they turned back to Egypt in their hearts' Ac 7.39.
ἐπιστρέφωᵇ: πῶς ἐπιστρέφετε πάλιν ἐπὶ τὰ ἀσθενῆ καὶ πτωχὰ στοιχεῖα; 'how is it that you want to turn back again to those weak and pitiful ruling spirits?' Ga 4.9; ἐπεστράφητε νῦν ἐπὶ τὸν ποιμένα 'now you have returned to the Shepherd' 1 Pe 2.25.
ἐπιστροφήᵃ: ἐκδιηγούμενοι τὴν ἐπιστροφὴν τῶν ἐθνῶν 'they reported how the Gentiles had turned (to God)' Ac 15.3. For another interpretation of ἐπιστροφή in Ac 15.3, see 41.51.
In analyzing the meaning of στρέφομαιᵇ, ἐπιστρέφωᵇ, and ἐπιστροφήᵃ in such passages as have been cited above, it is difficult to determine the extent to which belief or behavior is primarily in focus. In the case of 1 Pe 2.25,

one could certainly argue that the emphasis is upon the interpersonal relationship. It is therefore essential in rendering these terms not to narrow the meaning too much, for in this way one would certainly do violence to certain crucial semantic features.

31.61 ἐπιστρέφω^c: to cause a person to change belief, with focus upon that to which one turns – 'to cause to change belief, to cause to turn to.' πολλοὺς τῶν υἱῶν Ἰσραὴλ ἐπιστρέψει ἐπὶ κύριον τὸν θεὸν αὐτῶν 'he will cause many of the people of Israel to turn to the Lord their God' Lk 1.16.

31.62 ἀποστρέφομαι^a: to no longer continue to believe as one has and hence to turn away from or to reject a previous set of beliefs – 'to turn away from, to reject.' ἐντολαῖς ἀνθρώπων ἀποστρεφομένων τὴν ἀλήθειαν 'commandments of men who reject the truth' Tt 1.14.

31.63 ἀπωθέομαι^b (a figurative extension of meaning of ἀπωθέομαι^a 'to push away,' 15.46); ἀφίημι^h: to no longer pay attention to previous beliefs – 'to refuse to listen to, to reject.'
ἀπωθέομαι^b: ἔχων πίστιν καὶ ἀγαθὴν συνείδησιν, ἥν τινες ἀπωσάμενοι 'keeping your faith and a clear conscience, which some have refused to listen to' 1 Tm 1.19.
ἀφίημι^h: ἀφέντες τὴν ἐντολὴν τοῦ θεοῦ κρατεῖτε τὴν παράδοσιν τῶν ἀνθρώπων 'having rejected the commandment of God, you abide by the tradition of people' Mk 7.8.

31.64 ὑποστρέφω^b (a figurative extension of meaning of ὑποστρέφω^a 'to return,' 15.88); ἀνακάμπτω^b (a figurative extension of meaning of ἀνακάμπτω^a 'to return,' 15.89): to turn back to a previous belief – 'to turn back again to, to change to a former belief, to turn back from.'
ὑποστρέφω^b: ἢ ἐπιγνοῦσιν ὑποστρέψαι ἐκ τῆς παραδοθείσης αὐτοῖς ἁγίας ἐντολῆς 'than to know it and then turn back from the sacred command that was given to them' 2 Pe 2.21.
ἀνακάμπτω^b: ἢ ἐπιγνοῦσιν εἰς τὰ ὀπίσω ἀνακάμψαι ἀπὸ τῆς παραδοθείσης αὐτοῖς ἁγίας ἐντολῆς 'than to know it and turn back to things in the past from the sacred command that was given to them' 2 Pe 2.21 (apparatus).[8]

31.65 ἐκτρέπομαι^a: (a figurative extension of meaning of ἐκτρέπομαι 'to turn from,' not occurring in the NT) to turn away from the truth and to believe something which is different – 'to go astray, to stray after, to turn from and to follow.' ἐπὶ δὲ τοὺς μύθους ἐκτραπήσονται 'they will stray after legends' 2 Tm 4.4.

31.66 σαίνομαι: to be so emotionally disturbed as to give up one's beliefs – 'to give up one's beliefs, shaken in one's beliefs, to turn back from one's beliefs.' τὸ μηδένα σαίνεσθαι ἐν ταῖς θλίψεσιν ταύταις 'so that no one might turn back from his beliefs because of these persecutions' 1 Th 3.3.

31.67 πλανάομαι^b; ἀποπλανάομαι: to no longer believe what is true, but to start believing what is false – 'to stray from the truth, to wander from the truth, to go astray from.'[9]
πλανάομαι^b: ἐάν τις ἐν ὑμῖν πλανηθῇ ἀπὸ τῆς ἀληθείας 'if anyone among you should stray from the truth' Jas 5.19.
ἀποπλανάομαι: ἀπεπλανήθησαν ἀπὸ τῆς πίστεως 'they have wandered from the faith' 1 Tm 6.10.
Though in some languages one can preserve the figurative meaning of 'to wander' or 'to go astray' in connection with truth, it is not possible to do so in many languages, and therefore it may be necessary to spell out in some detail precisely what is involved, for example, 'to stop believing what is true and to start believing what is false.'

31.68 ἀστοχέω: to go astray as the result of departing from the truth – 'to abandon the truth, to lose one's way.' οἵτινες περὶ τὴν ἀλήθειαν ἠστόχησαν 'some have lost their way with regard to the truth' 2 Tm 2.18.

8 The substitution of ἀνακάμπτω for ὑποστρέφω in certain manuscripts of 2 Pe 2.21 would indicate clearly how closely these terms seem to be related in meaning. Any distinctions of meaning which they may have had would evidently be connotative.
9 It is possible that ἀποπλανάομαι differs slightly from πλανάομαι^b in emphasizing the departure from truth.

31.69 παραρρέω: (a figurative extension of meaning of παραρρέω 'to flow from alongside,' not occurring in the NT) to gradually give up one's belief in the truth – 'to give up a belief, to drift away from a belief.' μήποτε παραρυῶμεν 'so that we will not drift away (from the faith)' He 2.1. It is also possible to render μήποτε παραρυῶμεν in He 2.1 as 'so that we will not gradually give up believing what we have believed in the past.'

31.70 ἀποστρέφω[a]: to cause someone to turn away from a previous belief – 'to cause to turn away from, to cause to change one's belief, to mislead.' ἐν τῷ ἀποστρέφειν ἕκαστον ἀπὸ τῶν πονηριῶν ὑμῶν 'by causing each of you to turn away from your wicked ways' Ac 3.26 (for another interpretation of ἀποστρέφω in Ac 3.26, see 68.44); προσηνέγκατέ μοι τὸν ἄνθρωπον τοῦτον ὡς ἀποστρέφοντα τὸν λαόν 'you brought this man to me and said he was misleading the people' or '. . . causing the people to turn away from their beliefs' Lk 23.14. For another interpretation of ἀποστρέφω in Lk 23.14, see 88.264.

31.71 διαστρέφω[a]: to cause someone to believe something that is quite different – 'to cause someone to turn away from a belief, to mislead.'[10] ἤρξαντο δὲ κατηγορεῖν αὐτοῦ λέγοντες, Τοῦτον εὕραμεν διαστρέφοντα τὸ ἔθνος ἡμῶν 'then they began to accuse him, saying, We caught this man misleading our people' Lk 23.2. For another interpretation of διαστρέφω in Lk 23.2, see 88.264.

31.72 ἀνατρέπω[b]: (a figurative extension of meaning of ἀνατρέπω[a] 'to overturn,' 16.18) to cause serious difficulty or trouble with regard to someone's belief – 'to upset belief.' οἵτινες ὅλους οἴκους ἀνατρέπουσιν διδάσκοντες ἃ μὴ δεῖ 'who upset the faith of entire households by teaching what they should not' Tt 1.11.

31.73 μεθίστημι[c]: (a figurative extension of meaning of μεθίστημι[a] 'to cause to move,'

15.9) to cause a complete change in someone's beliefs, normally in the unfavorable sense of causing someone to turn away from a previous belief and hence to be misled – 'to turn away, to mislead.' ὁ Παῦλος οὗτος πείσας μετέστησεν ἱκανὸν ὄχλον 'this Paul persuaded and misled many people' Ac 19.26.

31.74 ἀποσπάω[b]; ἐξέλκω: (figurative extensions of meaning of ἀποσπάω[a] 'to pull out, to drag,' 15.214, and ἐξέλκω 'to pull, to draw out,' not occurring in the NT) to cause a change of belief so as to correspond more with the beliefs of the person or factor causing the change – 'to draw away, to lead away, to lure away to.'
ἀποσπάω[b]: τοῦ ἀποσπᾶν τοὺς μαθητὰς ὀπίσω αὐτῶν 'in order to draw away disciples after them' Ac 20.30.[11]
ἐξέλκω: πειράζεται ὑπὸ τῆς ἰδίας ἐπιθυμίας ἐξελκόμενος καὶ δελεαζόμενος 'but a person is tempted when he is drawn away and trapped by his own desires' Jas 1.14.

31.75 παραφέρω[b]: (a figurative extension of meaning of παραφέρω[a] 'to carry along,' 15.162) to cause someone to depart from an earlier belief, with the implication of accepting a belief which is false – 'to mislead, to lead astray, to carry off.' διδαχαῖς ποικίλαις καὶ ξέναις μὴ παραφέρεσθε 'do not be led astray by all kinds of strange teachings' He 13.9.

31.76 συναπάγομαι[a]: to cause someone else in addition to change from belief in what is true to belief in what is false – 'to cause to go astray together, to deceive in addition, to lead astray with.' ἵνα μὴ τῇ τῶν ἀθέσμων πλάνῃ συναπαχθέντες 'so that you will not be led astray by the error of lawless people' 2 Pe 3.17; Βαρναβᾶς συναπήχθη αὐτῶν τῇ ὑποκρίσει 'Barnabas was led astray with them by their hypocrisy' Ga 2.13.

31.77 σκανδαλίζομαι[a]: (a figurative extension of meaning of σκανδαλίζομαι 'to fall into a

---

10 διαστρέφω[a] apparently differs somewhat in meaning from ἀποστρέφω[a] (31.70) in emphasizing the effectiveness or thoroughness of the manner in which someone changes the belief of someone else.

11 In view of the interpersonal relationship implied in the occurrence of ἀποσπάω in Ac 20.30, it would be possible to classify this meaning under the domain of *Association* (34).

trap,' not occurring in the NT) to give up believing what is right and let oneself believe what is false – 'to cease believing, to give up believing.' γενομένης δὲ θλίψεως ἢ διωγμοῦ διὰ τὸν λόγον εὐθὺς σκανδαλίζεται 'when trouble or persecution comes because of the message, he quickly gives up believing' Mt 13.21. It is also possible to understand σκανδαλίζομαι in Mt 13.21 as meaning 'to let oneself be led into sin' or 'to fall into sin as the result of unbelief.'

31.78 σκανδαλίζω[a]: to cause someone to no longer believe – 'to cause to give up believing, to make someone no longer believe.' τοῦτο ὑμᾶς σκανδαλίζει; 'does this cause you to no longer believe?' Jn 6.61. It is also possible to understand σκανδαλίζω in Jn 6.61 as meaning 'to cause offense' (see 25.179).

31.79 ἀστήρικτος, ον: pertaining to the tendency to change and waver in one's views and attitudes – 'unstable.' δελεάζοντες ψυχὰς ἀστηρίκτους 'leading astray unstable persons' 2 Pe 2.14.

31.80 ἀκλινής, ές: pertaining to being without change or wavering in one's faith – 'without wavering, firmly.' κατέχωμεν τὴν ὁμολογίαν τῆς ἐλπίδος ἀκλινῆ 'let us hold on without wavering to the hope which we profess' He 10.23.

31.81 ἀμετακίνητος, ον: pertaining to not being readily shaken in one's opinions or beliefs – 'firm, unshaken, steady.' ἑδραῖοι γίνεσθε, ἀμετακίνητοι 'be steady, unshaken' or '. . . not wavering in belief' 1 Cor 15.58.

I   Trust, Rely (31.82-31.101)

31.82 πείθω[b] (perf stem only); πεποίθησις, εως f: to believe in something or someone to the extent of placing reliance or trust in or on – 'to rely on, to trust in, to depend on, to have (complete) confidence in, confidence, trust.' πείθω[b]: τὴν πανοπλίαν αὐτοῦ αἴρει ἐφ' ᾗ ἐπεποίθει 'he will take away his weapons on which he depended' Lk 11.22; ἵνα μὴ πεποιθότες ὦμεν ἐφ' ἑαυτοῖς 'lest we rely on ourselves' 2 Cor 1.9.

πεποίθησις: πεποίθησιν δὲ τοιαύτην ἔχομεν διὰ τοῦ Χριστοῦ πρὸς τὸν θεόν 'we have such confidence in God through Christ' 2 Cor 3.4; καίπερ ἐγὼ ἔχων πεποίθησιν καὶ ἐν σαρκί 'I could, of course, put my trust in physical matters' Php 3.4.

In a number of languages trust or reliance is expressed idiomatically, for example, 'to lean one's weight on' or 'to hang upon' or 'to place oneself in the hands of.'

31.83 ἐπαναπαύομαι: (a figurative extension of meaning of ἐπαναπαύομαι 'to remain upon something or someone,' not occurring in the NT) to continue to believe firmly in someone or something and thus to rely upon – 'to rely on, to depend on, to put one's trust in.' σὺ Ἰουδαῖος ἐπονομάζῃ καὶ ἐπαναπαύῃ νόμῳ 'you call yourself a Jew and you depend on the Law' Ro 2.17. The concept of dependence or reliance upon something may be expressed in a number of different ways. For example, the phrase ἐπαναπαύῃ νόμῳ in Ro 2.17 may be rendered in some languages as 'you believe that all you need is the Law' or 'you believe the Law will help you in every way.'

31.84 ὑπόστασις[b], εως f: that which provides the basis for trust and reliance – 'trust, confidence, assurance.' καταισχυνθῶμεν ἡμεῖς, ἵνα μὴ λέγω ὑμεῖς, ἐν τῇ ὑποστάσει ταύτῃ 'how ashamed we would be – not to speak of your shame – for we had such confidence in you' 2 Cor 9.4; ἐάνπερ τὴν ἀρχὴν τῆς ὑποστάσεως μέχρι τέλους βεβαίαν κατάσχωμεν 'if we hold on firmly to the end to the trust we had at the beginning' He 3.14.

31.85 πιστεύω[b]; πίστις[b], εως f: to believe to the extent of complete trust and reliance – 'to believe in, to have confidence in, to have faith in, to trust, faith, trust.' πιστεύω[b]: ὃς δ' ἂν σκανδαλίσῃ ἕνα τῶν μικρῶν τούτων τῶν πιστευόντων εἰς ἐμέ 'if anyone should cause one of these little ones to turn away from his faith in me' Mt 18.6; ἐπίστευσεν δὲ Ἀβραὰμ τῷ θεῷ 'Abraham trusted in God' Ro 4.3; ὁ πιστεύων ἐπ' αὐτῷ οὐ μὴ καταισχυνθῇ 'whoever believes in him will not be disappointed' 1 Pe 2.6.
πίστις[b]: ἔχετε πίστιν θεοῦ 'you have faith in

God' Mk 11.22; ἤκουσεν αὐτοῦ περὶ τῆς εἰς Χριστὸν Ἰησοῦν πίστεως 'he listened to him (as he talked) about faith in Christ Jesus' Ac 24.24; ὁ δὲ δίκαιος ἐκ πίστεως ζήσεται 'he who is righteous because of his faith shall live' Ro 1.17; ἀκούσαντες τὴν πίστιν ὑμῶν ἐν Χριστῷ Ἰησοῦ 'we heard about your faith in Christ Jesus' Col 1.4.

In rendering πιστεύω[b] and πίστις[b] it would be wrong to select a term which would mean merely 'reliance' or 'dependency' or even 'confidence,' for there should also be a significant measure of 'belief,' since real trust, confidence, and reliance can only be placed in someone who is believed to have the qualities attributed to such a person.

31.86 πιστός[a], ή, όν: (derivative of πιστεύω[b] 'to trust,' 31.85) pertaining to trusting – 'one who trusts in, trusting.' ὥστε οἱ ἐκ πίστεως εὐλογοῦνται σὺν τῷ πιστῷ Ἀβραάμ 'so those who believe are blessed with Abraham, the one who trusted' or 'Abraham trusted (in God) and was blessed; so all who believe are blessed as he was' Ga 3.9.

31.87 πιστός[b], ή, όν: (derivative of πιστεύω[b] 'to trust,' 31.85) pertaining to being trusted – 'faithful, trustworthy, dependable, reliable.' δοῦλε ἀγαθὲ καὶ πιστέ 'good and faithful servant' Mt 25.21; ταῦτα παράθου πιστοῖς ἀνθρώποις 'pass these on to reliable men' 2 Tm 2.2; πιστὸς ὁ λόγος 'this word can be trusted' 2 Tm 2.11. Since πιστός[b] is a type of passive derivative of πιστεύω[b], it may be necessary in a number of languages to render this passive relationship in an active form. For example, the phrase δοῦλε ἀγαθὲ καὶ πιστέ in Mt 25.21 may be rendered as 'good servant and one whom I can trust.' In 2 Tm 2.11 the phrase πιστὸς ὁ λόγος may be rendered as 'this is a saying we can have confidence in' or '. . . that we can trust.'

31.88 πίστις[c], εως f: the state of being someone in whom complete confidence can be placed – 'trustworthiness, dependability, faithfulness.' μὴ ἡ ἀπιστία αὐτῶν τὴν πίστιν τοῦ θεοῦ καταργήσει 'that doesn't mean that their lack of faithfulness annuls the faithfulness of God' Ro 3.3.

31.89 ἀπιστία[a], ας f: the state of being someone in whom confidence cannot be placed – 'lacking in trustworthiness, unfaithfulness.' μὴ ἡ ἀπιστία αὐτῶν τὴν πίστιν τοῦ θεοῦ καταργήσει 'that doesn't mean that their lack of faithfulness annuls the faithfulness of God' Ro 3.3. The occurrence of both ἀπιστία and πίστις (31.88) in this expression in Ro 3.3 may cause certain difficulties in appropriately rendering the meaning in other languages. It may therefore be necessary to spell out in some detail the fuller implications of ἀπιστία and πίστις. Moreover, the question implies a negative response, but the question (since it is rhetorical) can easily be rendered as a strong negative statement, for example, 'the fact that they were persons who could not be trusted does not mean that God cannot be trusted.'

31.90 βέβαιος[b], α, ον: pertaining to being able to be relied on or depended on – 'dependable, reliable, trustworthy.' ἡ ἐλπὶς ἡμῶν βεβαία ὑπὲρ ὑμῶν 'we are able to rely on our hope for you' 2 Cor 1.7; ἔχομεν βεβαιότερον τὸν προφητικὸν λόγον 'so we are able to trust even more the message proclaimed by the prophets' 2 Pe 1.19; εἰ γὰρ ὁ δι' ἀγγέλων λαληθεὶς λόγος ἐγένετο βέβαιος 'for if the message given by angels was trustworthy' He 2.2. For another interpretation of βέβαιος in He 2.2, see 28.43.

31.91 βεβαιόω[a]: (derivative of βέβαιος[b] 'dependable, reliable,' 31.90) to cause someone to be firm or established in belief – 'to cause to believe, to establish in belief.' ὑπὸ τῶν ἀκουσάντων εἰς ἡμᾶς ἐβεβαιώθη 'those who heard him caused us to be able to believe it' He 2.3; τοῦ κυρίου συνεργοῦντος καὶ τὸν λόγον βεβαιοῦντος διὰ τῶν ἐπακολουθούντων σημείων 'the Lord worked with them and caused people to believe their preaching was true by the signs that followed' or '. . . by giving them the signs (of power)' or '. . . by the signs that were performed' Mk 16.20. For another interpretation of βεβαιόω in Mk 16.20, see 28.44.

31.92 ἑδραῖος, α, ον: pertaining to being firmly established in one's position or opinions – 'firm, steadfast, unwavering.' ἀδελφοί μου ἀγαπητοί, ἑδραῖοι γίνεσθε 'my dear fellow believers, be firmly established' 1 Cor 15.58; εἴ γε ἐπιμένετε τῇ πίστει τεθεμελιωμένοι καὶ ἑδραῖοι 'if, indeed, you remain well founded and established in the faith' Col 1.23.

31.93 ἑδραίωμα, τος *n*: that which provides the basis or foundation for belief or practice – 'support, foundation, basis.' στῦλος καὶ ἑδραίωμα τῆς ἀληθείας 'pillar and support of the truth' 1 Tm 3.15.

31.94 θεμελιόω*b*: to provide a firm basis for belief or practice – 'to provide a basis for, to provide a foundation for, to cause to be steadfast in.' εἴ γε ἐπιμένετε τῇ πίστει τεθεμελιωμένοι 'if, indeed, you remain well founded in the faith' Col 1.23.

31.95 ὀλιγοπιστία, ας *f*: the state of having little or inadequate faith – 'to not have enough faith, to have limited faith.' διὰ τὴν ὀλιγοπιστίαν ὑμῶν 'it was because you do not have enough faith' Mt 17.20.

31.96 ὀλιγόπιστος, ον: pertaining to having relatively little faith – 'of little faith, of insufficient faith.' λέγει αὐτοῖς, Τί δειλοί ἐστε, ὀλιγόπιστοι; 'he answered, Why are you so frightened? What little faith you have!' Mt 8.26.

31.97 ἀπιστέω*b*; ἀπιστία*b*, ας *f*: to refuse to put one's trust or reliance in something or someone – 'to not believe (in), to refuse to believe, to not trust in, unbelief.'[12]
ἀπιστέω*b*: ὁ δὲ ἀπιστήσας κατακριθήσεται 'whoever refuses to believe shall be condemned' Mk 16.16.
ἀπιστία*b*: τῇ ἀπιστίᾳ ἐξεκλάσθησαν 'they were broken off because they refused to believe' Ro 11.20.
One of the serious problems involved in rendering 'to believe' or 'to refuse to believe' is that so frequently the NT text does not indicate precisely the goal or object of such belief. In a number of languages, however, the syntactic requirements are such that some clear goal must be in the immediate context. For example, in Mk 16.16 it may be possible to translate 'whoever refuses to believe the good news shall be condemned.'

31.98 ἄπιστος*b*, ον: (derivative of ἀπιστέω*b* 'to not believe (in),' 31.97) pertaining to not believing, with the implication of refusing to believe – 'to be unbelieving, to be lacking in trust.' ὦ γενεὰ ἄπιστος, ἕως πότε πρὸς ὑμᾶς ἔσομαι; 'how unbelieving you people are; how long must I stay with you?' Mk 9.19.

31.99 ἐκκλίνω*b*: (a figurative extension of meaning of ἐκκλίνω*a* 'to avoid,' 34.41) to no longer put one's trust or confidence in someone – 'to turn away from.' πάντες ἐξέκλιναν 'all have turned away (from God)' Ro 3.12.

31.100 ἀθετέω*a*: (a figurative extension of meaning of ἀθετέω 'to set aside,' not occurring in the NT) to believe that something or someone cannot be trusted or relied on and hence to reject – 'to not rely on, to set aside, to reject.' ὁ ἀθετῶν ὑμᾶς ἐμὲ ἀθετεῖ 'whoever rejects you, rejects me' Lk 10.16.[13]

31.101 μοιχαλίς, ί (adjectival form): (a figurative extension of meaning of the substantive μοιχαλίς 'adulteress,' 88.278) pertaining to being unfaithful to one's earlier and true beliefs – 'unfaithful, adulterous.' γενεὰ πονηρὰ καὶ μοιχαλὶς σημεῖον ἐπιζητεῖ 'this evil and unfaithful generation seeks a sign' Mt 12.39; μοιχαλίδες, οὐκ οἴδατε ὅτι ἡ φιλία τοῦ κόσμου ἔχθρα τοῦ θεοῦ ἐστιν; 'you unfaithful people, do you not know that being friendly to the world means being enemies of God?' Jas 4.4.[14]

---

13 It would also be possible to classify ἀθετέω*a* in the sense of 'to reject' in Domain 34, involving interpersonal relations, but in Lk 10.16 the focal element in the rejection is a matter of belief or confidence, and it is for that reason that ἀθετέω*a* is included in this subdomain.

14 It would be possible to classify μοιχαλίς in Jas 4.4 as being a substantive and thus having a meaning different from μοιχαλίς in Mt 12.39, where it occurs as an adjective. However, the regular use of adjectives in the role of substantives does not warrant setting up separate meanings, especially since the adjectival form may be regarded as being attributive to a syntactically implied substantive.

---

12 In contrast with ἀπιστέω*a* (31.39) meaning 'to not believe that something is true,' ἀπιστέω*b* (and ἀπιστία*b*) involve a refusal to put one's trust, reliance, or belief in something or someone. ἀπιστέω*b* thus has a number of significant added components of meaning.

J   Be a Believer, Christian Faith[15] (31.102-31.107)

31.102 πιστεύω^c; πίστις^d, εως *f*: to believe in the good news about Jesus Christ and to become a follower – 'to be a believer, to be a Christian, Christian faith.'

πιστεύω^c: τοῦ δὲ πλήθους τῶν πιστευσάντων ἦν καρδία καὶ ψυχὴ μία 'the group of those who were believers was one in heart and mind' Ac 4.32; δύναμις γὰρ θεοῦ ἐστιν εἰς σωτηρίαν παντὶ τῷ πιστεύοντι 'for it is God's power to save everyone who is a believer' Ro 1.16.

πίστις^d: ἡ πίστις ὑμῶν καταγγέλλεται ἐν ὅλῳ τῷ κόσμῳ 'the whole world is hearing that you have faith' Ro 1.8; τῇ γὰρ χάριτί ἐστε σεσωσμένοι διὰ πίστεως 'for it is by his grace that you have been saved because you have faith' Eph 2.8.

31.103 πιστή^a, ῆς *f*: (derivative of πιστεύω^c 'to be a believer,' 31.102) one who believes in Jesus Christ – 'believer, Christian, one who has Christian faith.'[16] υἱὸς γυναικὸς Ἰουδαίας πιστῆς 'the son of a Jewish woman who was a believer' Ac 16.1.

31.104 πίστις^e, εως *f*: (semantic derivative of πίστις^d 'to be a believer, Christian faith,' 31.102) the content of what Christians believe – 'the faith, beliefs, doctrine.' ἐπαγωνίζεσθαι τῇ ἅπαξ παραδοθείσῃ τοῖς ἁγίοις πίστει 'fight on for the faith which once and for all God has given to his people' Jd 3; ὁ διώκων ἡμᾶς ποτε

νῦν εὐαγγελίζεται τὴν πίστιν ἥν ποτε ἐπόρθει 'the man who used to persecute us is now preaching the faith he once tried to destroy' Ga 1.23. It is also possible to interpret πίστις in Jd 3 and Ga 1.23 as the act of believing and placing confidence in Jesus Christ (see 31.102).

31.105 ἀπιστέω^c; ἀπιστία^c, ας *f*: to not believe in the good news about Jesus Christ and hence not become a follower – 'to not be a believer, to be a non-Christian, to be an infidel, not believing, to be a pagan.'[17]

ἀπιστέω^c: ἀπιστοῦσιν δέ 'but for those who are unbelievers' 1 Pe 2.7.

ἀπιστία^c: ὅτι ἀγνοῶν ἐποίησα ἐν ἀπιστίᾳ 'because as an unbeliever, I did not know what I was doing' 1 Tm 1.13.

31.106 ἄπιστος^a, ου *m*: one who does not believe the good news about Jesus Christ – 'one who is not a believer, unbeliever.' ἔστιν ἀπίστου χείρων 'he is worse than an unbeliever' 1 Tm 5.8. It is clearly not enough in most languages to render ἄπιστος in 1 Tm 5.8 as merely 'one who does not believe,' for it is the specific content of what is not believed which is crucial. In this connection, one should compare the context of ἄπιστος^b in Mk 9.19 (see 31.98).

31.107 ἀπειθέω^b; ἀπείθεια^b, ας *f*: to refuse to believe the Christian message – 'to refuse to be a believer, to reject the Christian message, to refuse to believe.'

ἀπειθέω^b: οἱ δὲ ἀπειθήσαντες Ἰουδαῖοι ἐπήγειραν 'but the Jews who would not believe stirred up (the Gentiles)' Ac 14.2.

ἀπείθεια^b: τοῦ πνεύματος τοῦ νῦν ἐνεργοῦντος ἐν τοῖς υἱοῖς τῆς ἀπειθείας 'the spirit that works in those who refuse to believe' Eph 2.2. It is also possible to interpret ἀπείθεια in Eph 2.2 as overt disobedience to God (see 36.23).

---

15 It would be possible to classify the meanings in this subdomain as being essentially a part of the preceding Subdomain I *Trust, Rely*. The meanings in Subdomain J, however, have an added semantic component of believing a particular set of truths or trusting a particular person, namely, Christ. Especially in absolute or semi-absolute contexts, it seems far better to treat these meanings as a separate category rather than employing elaborate ellipses. There is also a sense in which the meanings in Subdomain J relate closely to Domain 34 *Association*, since adherence to a particular set of beliefs implies a special interpersonal relation to God or Christ.

16 πιστή has also been treated in 11.17 as a name for a member of the Christian constituency. This is a good instance of complete overlapping in that the same term may be classified in two quite distinct ways, one based on group membership and the other based upon the type of belief which results in such membership. It would be

possible, therefore, to indicate that in the case of πιστή^b in 11.17 there is an added component of group identification, but one may also argue that such a feature of meaning is derived essentially from the context.

17 The same factors apply to the classification of ἀπιστέω^c and ἀπιστία^c as apply to the classification of πιστεύω^c and πίστις^d (31.102), in view of the fact that a set of specific beliefs or relationships is clearly implied.

32 Understand[1]

Outline of Subdomains

A Understand (32.1-32.10)
B Come to Understand (32.11-32.18)
C Ease or Difficulty in Understanding (32.19-32.23)
D Capacity for Understanding (32.24-32.41)
E Lack of Capacity for Understanding (32.42-32.61)

A Understand[2] (32.1-32.10)

32.1 ἀκούω[f]: to hear and understand a message – 'to understand, to comprehend.'[3] ἐλάλει αὐτοῖς τὸν λόγον, καθὼς ἠδύναντο ἀκούειν 'he spoke the word to them to the extent they could understand' Mk 4.33; ὁ γὰρ λαλῶν γλώσσῃ οὐκ ἀνθρώποις λαλεῖ ἀλλὰ θεῷ, οὐδεὶς γὰρ ἀκούει 'the one who speaks in strange tongues does not speak to people but to God, because no one understands him' 1 Cor 14.2.

---

1 All the domains and subdomains relating to intellectual activity (Domains 24-32) involve considerable overlapping and multi-dimensional relationships. Domain *Know* (28) involves essentially the possession of information, while *Learn* (27) treats the acquisition of information. The Domain *Think* (30) involves primarily the manipulation of information, while *Understand* (32) refers to a process by which information is used in order to arrive at a correct comprehension or evaluation. However, no one aspect of these intellectual activities is completely devoid of other aspects, and thus, to a certain extent, any attempt to classify various aspects of these activities or states inevitably results in what mathematicians call 'fuzzy sets,' that is to say, classes of items which show considerable overlapping and indeterminate borders.
In the Domain *Understand*, the first set of subdomains (A to C) deals essentially with the process of comprehension, while Subdomains D and E focus upon the capacity for understanding, and accordingly, meanings such as 'foolish,' 'senseless,' 'wise,' and 'intelligent' are included.
2 In a number of languages the equivalent of 'understand' consists of a more generic term for mental activity plus some kind of qualifier; hence, 'to understand' may be literally 'to really know' or 'to think right about' or 'to perceive clearly' or 'to see with the mind.'
3 The meaning of ἀκούω[f] is an excellent example of a meaning which overlaps two domains, but since the focal element is not hearing but comprehending, ἀκούω[f] is classified in this subdomain.

32.2 νοέω[a]: to comprehend something on the basis of careful thought and consideration – 'to perceive, to gain insight into, to understand, to comprehend.' θέλοντες εἶναι νομοδιδάσκαλοι, μὴ νοοῦντες μήτε ἃ λέγουσιν 'they want to be teachers of the law, but they do not understand what they are talking about' 1 Tm 1.7; πίστει νοοῦμεν κατηρτίσθαι τοὺς αἰῶνας ῥήματι θεοῦ 'by faith we understand that the universe was formed by the word of God' He 11.3.

32.3 ἐπίσταμαι[b]: to have or gain insight, with focus upon the process – 'to understand, to be aware of, to really know.' τετύφωται, μηδὲν ἐπιστάμενος 'he is conceited and understands nothing' 1 Tm 6.4.

32.4 οἶδα[c]: to comprehend the meaning of something, with focus upon the resulting knowledge – 'to understand, to comprehend.' οὐκ οἴδαμεν τί λαλεῖ 'we don't understand what he is saying' Jn 16.18; ἐλάβομεν ἀλλὰ τὸ πνεῦμα τὸ ἐκ τοῦ θεοῦ, ἵνα εἰδῶμεν τὰ ὑπὸ τοῦ θεοῦ χαρισθέντα ἡμῖν 'but we received the Spirit from God so that we might understand those things graciously given to us by God' 1 Cor 2.12; πῶς ἐρεῖ τὸ Ἀμήν . . . ἐπειδὴ τί λέγεις οὐκ οἶδεν; 'how can he say, Amen, . . . if he doesn't understand what you are saying?' 1 Cor 14.16.

32.5 συνίημι[a] or **συνίω:** to employ one's capacity for understanding and thus to arrive at insight – 'to understand, to comprehend, to perceive, to have insight into.' ἀκούοντες ἀκούωσιν καὶ μὴ συνιῶσιν 'they may listen and listen, yet not understand' Mk 4.12; ἐνόμιζεν δὲ συνιέναι τοὺς ἀδελφοὺς αὐτοῦ ὅτι ὁ θεὸς διὰ χειρὸς αὐτοῦ δίδωσιν σωτηρίαν αὐτοῖς 'he thought his own people would understand that God was using him to rescue them' Ac 7.25.

32.6 σύνεσις[a], εως [f]: (derivative of συνίημι[a] 'to understand,' 32.5) that which is understood or comprehended – 'understanding, what is understood.' δύνασθε . . . νοῆσαι τὴν σύνεσίν μου ἐν τῷ μυστηρίῳ τοῦ Χριστοῦ 'you can . . . perceive what I understand about the secret of Christ' Eph 3.4.

32.7 ἀγνοέω^c; ἀγνωσία^b, ας *f*: to not understand, with the implication of a lack of capacity or ability – 'not to understand, to fail to understand.'

ἀγνοέω^c: οἱ δὲ ἠγνόουν τὸ ῥῆμα 'but they did not understand what he said' Mk 9.32; ἐν οἷς ἀγνοοῦσιν βλασφημοῦντες 'but they speak against God in matters they do not understand' 2 Pe 2.12.

ἀγνωσία^b: ἀγνωσίαν γὰρ θεοῦ τινες ἔχουσιν 'some (of you) do not understand anything about God' 1 Cor 15.34. It is also possible to interpret ἀγνωσία in 1 Cor 15.34 as meaning 'to not know about' (see 28.16).

32.8 ἀγνωσία^c, ας *f*: that which is not understood or comprehended, implying a lack of capacity – 'what is not understood.' φιμοῦν τὴν τῶν ἀφρόνων ἀνθρώπων ἀγνωσίαν 'silence the talk of foolish people who do not understand those things' 1 Pe 2.15.[4] For another interpretation of ἀγνωσία in 1 Pe 2.15, see 28.16.

32.9 ἀπορέω; ἀπορία, ας *f*: to be in perplexity, with the implication of serious anxiety – 'to be at a loss, to be uncertain, to be anxious, to be in doubt, consternation.'

ἀπορέω: οἱ μαθηταὶ ἀπορούμενοι περὶ τίνος λέγει 'the disciples were at a loss to understand what he meant' Jn 13.22.

ἀπορία: καὶ ἐπὶ τῆς γῆς συνοχὴ ἐθνῶν ἐν ἀπορίᾳ 'and upon the earth despair among nations, with consternation' or '. . . and great anxiety' Lk 21.25.

32.10 διαπορέω: to be thoroughly perplexed – 'to be very perplexed, to not know what to do, to be very confused.' διηπόρει διὰ τὸ λέγεσθαι ὑπό τινων ὅτι Ἰωάννης ἠγέρθη ἐκ νεκρῶν 'he was thoroughly perplexed because

some people were saying that John had risen from the dead' Lk 9.7.

B Come to Understand[5] (32.11-32.18)

32.11 θεωρέω^b; βλέπω^c; ὁράω^c: to come to understand as the result of perception – 'to understand, to perceive, to see, to recognize.'

θεωρέω^b: κατὰ πάντα ὡς δεισιδαιμονεστέρους ὑμᾶς θεωρῶ 'I perceive that in every way you are very religious' Ac 17.22; θεωρεῖτε δὲ πηλίκος οὗτος 'you understand, then, how great this man was' He 7.4.

βλέπω^c: βλέπω δὲ ἕτερον νόμον ἐν τοῖς μέλεσίν μου 'I perceive another law at work in my members' Ro 7.23.

ὁράω^c: ὁρᾶτε ὅτι ἐξ ἔργων δικαιοῦται ἄνθρωπος 'you can understand then that a person is justified by what he does' Jas 2.24.

32.12 κατανοέω^c: to come to a clear and definite understanding of something – 'to understand completely, to perceive clearly.' κατανοήσας δὲ αὐτῶν τὴν πανουργίαν 'he clearly perceived their tricks' Lk 20.23; κατενόησεν τὸ ἑαυτοῦ σῶμα ἤδη νενεκρωμένον 'he was thoroughly aware that his body was as good as dead' Ro 4.19. For another interpretation of κατανοέω in Ro 4.19, see 30.4.

32.13 συνοράω^b: to come to understand clearly on the basis of perceived information – 'to understand clearly, to realize fully, to become fully aware of.' συνιδών τε ἦλθεν ἐπὶ τὴν οἰκίαν τῆς Μαρίας 'when he fully realized this, he went to Mary's house' Ac 12.12.

32.14 μανθάνω^c: to come to understand as the result of a process of learning – 'to understand.' ἵνα ἐν ἡμῖν μάθητε τὸ Μὴ ὑπὲρ ἃ γέγραπται 'so that you may understand from our example what the saying means, Don't go beyond what has been written' 1 Cor 4.6. It is possible to understand μανθάνω in 1 Cor 4.6 as meaning simply 'to learn' (see 27.12).

---

4 The semantic structure of φιμοῦν τὴν τῶν ἀφρόνων ἀνθρώπων ἀγνωσίαν is extremely complex, since φιμοῦν 'to silence' would normally be related to 'foolish people,' and it is clearly these who are the ones talking about things 'which they do not understand.'

5 The meanings in Subdomain B *Come To Understand* obviously imply capacity, but this particular element is not focal; rather, it is the process by which one arrives at understanding which seems to be semantically dominant in the meanings of this series.

32.15 ψηφίζω^b: to come to understand the meaning of something by figuring it out – 'to come to understand, to interpret, to figure out.' ὁ ἔχων νοῦν ψηφισάτω τὸν ἀριθμὸν τοῦ θηρίου 'whoever is intelligent, let him understand the meaning of the number of the beast' Re 13.18. The third person imperative form ψηφισάτω in Re 13.18 is extremely difficult to render in some languages, and even in English the expression 'let him understand' is quite misleading, since it might imply permission rather than polite command. In some languages the equivalent of this third person imperative is an expression such as 'should understand' or 'ought to be able to understand.' For another interpretation of ψηφίζω in Re 13.18, see 60.4.

32.16 γινώσκω^d; γνῶσις^d, εως *f*; ἐπιγινώσκω^b: to come to an understanding as the result of ability to experience and learn – 'to come to understand, to perceive, to comprehend.'⁶

γινώσκω^d: σὺ εἶ ὁ διδάσκαλος τοῦ Ἰσραὴλ καὶ ταῦτα οὐ γινώσκεις; 'are you a teacher in Israel and don't understand these things?' Jn 3.10; τὴν ἁμαρτίαν οὐκ ἔγνων εἰ μὴ διὰ νόμου 'I wouldn't have understood sin without the help of the Law' Ro 7.7; ὑμῖν δέδοται γνῶναι τὰ μυστήρια τῆς βασιλείας '(God) will enable you to understand the secrets of the kingdom' Mt 13.11. It is also possible to interpret γινώσκω in Mt 13.11 as meaning 'to know about' (see 28.1).
γνῶσις^d: ἤρατε τὴν κλεῖδα τῆς γνώσεως 'you have taken away the means by which people are able to understand' Lk 11.52.
ἐπιγινώσκω^b: οὐ γὰρ ἄλλα γράφομεν ὑμῖν ἀλλ' ἢ ἃ ἀναγινώσκετε ἢ καὶ ἐπιγινώσκετε 'we write to you only what you can read and understand' 2 Cor 1.13.

32.17 εἰς ἐπίγνωσιν ἔρχομαι^b: (an idiom, literally 'to come into knowledge') to come to understand the meaning of something, with special emphasis upon the process – 'to come to understand, to come to know.' πάντοτε μανθάνοντα καὶ μηδέποτε εἰς ἐπίγνωσιν ἀληθείας ἐλθεῖν δυνάμενα 'they are always learning but never able to (really) come to understand the truth' 2 Tm 3.7. One may also interpret εἰς ἐπίγνωσιν ἔρχομαι as meaning 'to come to have knowledge of, to come to know' (see 27.4).

32.18 καταλαμβάνω^e: (a figurative extension of meaning of καταλαμβάνω^d 'to overcome,' 37.19)⁷ to come to understand something which was not understood or perceived previously – 'to understand, to realize, to grasp, to comprehend.' ἐπ' ἀληθείας καταλαμβάνομαι ὅτι οὐκ ἔστιν προσωπολήμπτης ὁ θεός 'I (now) understand how true it is that God does not show favoritism' Ac 10.34; καὶ καταλαβόμενοι ὅτι ἄνθρωποι ἀγράμματοί εἰσιν 'and realized that they were uneducated men' Ac 4.13; καὶ ἡ σκοτία αὐτὸ οὐ κατέλαβεν 'and the darkness did not comprehend it' Jn 1.5. It is also possible to understand καταλαμβάνω in Jn 1.5 in the sense of 'to overcome' (see 37.19). It is possible that in Jn 1.5 a word play involving both meanings may be intended, something which is typical of Johannine style.

C Ease or Difficulty in Understanding (32.19-32.23)

32.19 εὔσημος, ον: pertaining to being easily understood – 'intelligible, easily understandable.' διὰ τῆς γλώσσης ἐὰν μὴ εὔσημον λόγον δῶτε, πῶς γνωσθήσεται τὸ λαλούμενον; 'unless you speak intelligible words with your tongue, how will anyone know what you are saying?' 1 Cor 14.9.

32.20 κατάδηλος, ον: pertaining to being clearly evident and hence easily understood – 'easily understood, very evident, very clear.' περισσότερον ἔτι κατάδηλόν ἐστιν 'the matter becomes very easy to understand' He 7.15.

---

6 It is possible that ἐπιγινώσκω^b differs somewhat in meaning from γινώσκω^d in focusing attention on what is understood or indicating that the process of understanding is somewhat more emphatic, but such a distinction cannot be determined from existing contexts.

7 It is difficult to determine the extent to which καταλαμβάνω^e should be classified as a figurative extension of meaning. The average Greek speaker would probably be no more aware of this figurative significance of καταλαμβάνω than an English speaker would be aware of the figurative background in the term *understand*.

32.21 αἴνιγμα[a], **τος** *n*: that which is difficult or impossible to understand – 'that which is puzzling, that which is difficult to understand, puzzle, riddle.' βλέπομεν γὰρ ἄρτι δι' ἐσόπτρου ἐν αἰνίγματι 'now we see only puzzling reflections in a mirror' 1 Cor 13.12. In 1 Cor 13.12 the term αἴνιγμα may be interpreted as lack of clarity in perception, so that the meaning would be 'that which is difficult to see clearly,' but the general usage of αἴνιγμα would seem to point to the meaning of difficulty in understanding and comprehension rather than in visual perception. For another interpretation of αἴνιγμα in 1 Cor 13.12, see 24.37.

32.22 δυσνόητος, ον: pertaining to being understandable, but only with great effort – 'difficult to understand, not easily understood.' ἐν αἷς ἐστιν δυσνόητά τινα 'in which there are some things difficult to understand' 2 Pe 3.16.

32.23 ἀνεξεραύνητος, ον; ἀνεξιχνίαστος, ον: pertaining to being impossible to understand on the basis of careful examination or investigation – 'impossible to understand, unfathomable, impossible to comprehend.' ὡς ἀνεξεραύνητα τὰ κρίματα αὐτοῦ καὶ ἀνεξιχνίαστοι αἱ ὁδοὶ αὐτοῦ 'how impossible it is to understand his decisions and to comprehend his ways' Ro 11.33.[8]

D Capacity for Understanding (32.24-32.41)

32.24 ὀφθαλμός[c], **οῦ** *m*: (a figurative extension of meaning of ὀφθαλμός[a] 'eye,' 8.23) capacity to understand as the result of perception – 'to be able to understand, to come to perceive, understanding.' νῦν δὲ ἐκρύβη ἀπὸ ὀφθαλμῶν σου 'but now it is hidden from your understanding' (literally '. . . from your eyes') Lk 19.42; πεφωτισμένους τοὺς ὀφθαλμοὺς τῆς

---

8 It is possible that ἀνεξεραύνητος and ἀνεξιχνίαστος are somewhat different in meaning, but they appear to be used in Ro 11.33 as very close synonyms. From a semotactic standpoint, however, it is easy to see why ἀνεξεραύνητα would be combined with κρίματα and ἀνεξιχνίαστοι would be combined with ὁδοί.

καρδίας ὑμῶν εἰς τὸ εἰδέναι ὑμᾶς τίς ἐστιν ἡ ἐλπὶς τῆς κλήσεως αὐτοῦ 'the understanding of your mind has been enlightened so that you can know what is the hope of your calling' Eph 1.18. In both Lk 19.42 and Eph 1.18 ὀφθαλμός designates a faculty of understanding and is not a reference merely to perception. In Eph 1.18 καρδία denotes the mind (see 26.3), so that the phrase 'the eyes of the mind' really means 'the capacity for understanding which the mind has.'

32.25 τυφλόω τοὺς ὀφθαλμούς: (an idiom, literally 'to blind the eyes') to cause someone to no longer have the capacity for understanding – 'to cause to not understand, to make unable to comprehend.' τετύφλωκεν αὐτῶν τοὺς ὀφθαλμούς 'he has made it impossible for them to understand' (literally 'he has blinded their eyes') Jn 12.40; ἡ σκοτία ἐτύφλωσεν τοὺς ὀφθαλμοὺς αὐτοῦ 'the darkness has made it impossible for him to understand' (literally 'the darkness has blinded his eyes') 1 Jn 2.11. Though in some languages there is a close relationship between the eyes and comprehension, in many languages it is simply impossible to use the idiom 'to blind the eyes' in speaking of 'causing someone not to understand.' The problem becomes particularly difficult in speaking of 'darkness blinding the eyes' as in 1 Jn 2.11. People can understand how 'bright light would blind the eyes,' but it would be strange indeed to think of 'darkness' having such an effect. In the context of 1 Jn 2.11, the darkness is, of course, not literal darkness but a state of sinfulness. Therefore, in some languages it may be necessary to translate 'their sinfulness has made it impossible for them to understand' or 'because they sin, they cannot understand.'

32.26 συνίημι[b] or **συνίω; σύνεσις**[b], **εως** *f*: to be able to understand and evaluate – 'to be able to comprehend, to understand, to be intelligent, insight, intelligence.'
συνίημι[b]: οὐκ ἔστιν ὁ συνίων 'there is no one who is able to understand' Ro 3.11.
σύνεσις[b]: δώσει γάρ σοι ὁ κύριος σύνεσιν ἐν πᾶσιν 'because the Lord will give you the ability to understand all things' 2 Tm 2.7.

32.27 συνετός, ή, όν; ἐπιστήμων, ον (derivative of ἐπίσταμαι[b] 'to understand,' 32.3): pertaining to being able to understand and evaluate – 'intelligent, insightful, understanding.'
συνετός: Σεργίῳ Παύλῳ, ἀνδρὶ συνετῷ 'Sergius Paulus, an intelligent man' Ac 13.7; τὴν σύνεσιν τῶν συνετῶν ἀθετήσω 'I will frustrate the intelligence of those who are intelligent' 1 Cor 1.19.
ἐπιστήμων: τίς σοφὸς καὶ ἐπιστήμων ἐν ὑμῖν; 'who is wise and understanding among you?' Jas 3.13.

32.28 αἰσθάνομαι; αἴσθησις, εως f; αἰσθητήριον, ου n: to have the capacity to perceive clearly and hence to understand the real nature of something – 'to be able to perceive, to have the capacity to understand, understanding.'
αἰσθάνομαι: ἦν παρακεκαλυμμένον ἀπ᾽ αὐτῶν ἵνα μὴ αἴσθωνται αὐτό 'it had been hidden from them so that they could not understand it' Lk 9.45.
αἴσθησις: ἡ ἀγάπη ὑμῶν ἔτι μᾶλλον καὶ μᾶλλον περισσεύῃ ἐν ἐπιγνώσει καὶ πάσῃ αἰσθήσει 'your love will keep on growing more and more together with your knowledge and complete capacity for understanding' Php 1.9.
αἰσθητήριον: τὰ αἰσθητήρια γεγυμνασμένα ἐχόντων πρὸς διάκρισιν καλοῦ τε καὶ κακοῦ 'those whose capacity to understand has been disciplined by exercise to distinguish between good and bad' He 5.14.

32.29 νουνεχῶς: pertaining to ability to reason and hence understand – 'with understanding, wisely.' ἰδὼν αὐτὸν ὅτι νουνεχῶς ἀπεκρίθη 'recognizing that he had answered wisely' or '. . . with understanding' Mk 12.34.

32.30 φρόνησις[b], εως f: the ability to understand, as the result of insight and wisdom – 'capacity to understand, wisdom, being wise.' ἐν πάσῃ σοφίᾳ καὶ φρονήσει 'using all wisdom and ability to understand' Eph 1.8.

32.31 φρόνιμος, ον; φρονίμως: pertaining to understanding resulting from insight and wisdom – 'wise, wisely, with understanding, with insight.'

φρόνιμος: ὅστις ἀκούει μου τοὺς λόγους τούτους καὶ ποιεῖ αὐτοὺς ὁμοιωθήσεται ἀνδρὶ φρονίμῳ 'everyone who hears these words of mine and obeys them is like one who has understanding' Mt 7.24.
φρονίμως: ἐπήνεσεν ὁ κύριος τὸν οἰκονόμον τῆς ἀδικίας ὅτι φρονίμως ἐποίησεν 'the master praised the unjust steward because he had acted wisely' Lk 16.8.

32.32 σοφία[a], ας f: the capacity to understand and, as a result, to act wisely – 'to be prudent, wisdom.' ἐν σοφίᾳ περιπατεῖτε πρὸς τοὺς ἔξω 'act with wisdom toward those who are not believers' Col 4.5.

32.33 σοφός[b], ή, όν: pertaining to understanding resulting in wisdom – 'prudent, wise, understanding.' περιπατεῖτε, μὴ ὡς ἄσοφοι ἀλλ᾽ ὡς σοφοί 'don't live like ignorant people, but like people who are wise' Eph 5.15.

32.34 σωφρονέω[b]; σωφρονισμός[a], οῦ m; σωφροσύνη[a], ης f: to have understanding about practical matters and thus be able to act sensibly – 'to have sound judgment, to be sensible, to use good sense, sound judgment.'
σωφρονέω[b]: τοὺς νεωτέρους ὡσαύτως παρακάλει σωφρονεῖν 'in the same way urge the young men to be wise and sensible' Tt 2.6; φρονεῖν εἰς τὸ σωφρονεῖν 'be sensible in your thinking' Ro 12.3.
σωφρονισμός[a]: ἀλλὰ δυνάμεως καὶ ἀγάπης καὶ σωφρονισμοῦ 'instead (his Spirit fills us) with power, love, and the ability to understand how to make wise decisions' 2 Tm 1.7. It is also possible to understand σωφρονισμός in 2 Tm 1.7 as moderation and sensible behavior (see 88.93).
σωφροσύνη[a]: οὐ μαίνομαι, φησίν, κράτιστε Φῆστε, ἀλλὰ ἀληθείας καὶ σωφροσύνης ῥήματα ἀποφθέγγομαι 'he said, I am not mad, most excellent Festus! The words I speak are true and sensible' Ac 26.25.

32.35 σοφός, οῦ m: a person of professional or semi-professional status who is regarded as particularly capable in understanding the philosophical aspects of knowledge and experience – 'one who is wise, wise man.' ποῦ σοφός; ποῦ γραμματεύς; 'where is the man who is wise? where is the scholar?' 1 Cor 1.20.[9]

32.36 σοφίζω: to cause a person to have wisdom and understanding – 'to cause to understand, to cause to be wise, to make wise.' τὰ δυνάμενά σε σοφίσαι εἰς σωτηρίαν 'which is able to make you wise unto salvation,' that is, '. . . cause you to have the wisdom that leads to salvation' 2 Tm 3.15.

32.37 σοφία[b], ας f: the content of what is known by those regarded as wise – 'wisdom, insight, understanding.' ἐπαιδεύθη Μωϋσῆς ἐν πάσῃ σοφίᾳ Αἰγυπτίων 'Moses learned all the wisdom of the Egyptians' Ac 7.22; σοφίαν δὲ λαλοῦμεν ἐν τοῖς τελείοις 'yet, we have wisdom to tell those who are spiritually mature' 1 Cor 2.6.

32.38 φιλοσοφία, ας f: human understanding or wisdom and, by implication, in contrast with divinely revealed knowledge – 'human understanding, human wisdom, philosophy.' μή τις ὑμᾶς ἔσται ὁ συλαγωγῶν διὰ τῆς φιλοσοφίας καὶ κενῆς ἀπάτης 'lest anyone make you captive by means of human understanding and worthless deceit' or '. . . by means of the worthless deceit of human wisdom' Col 2.8. In Col 2.8 φιλοσοφία may be rendered in some languages as 'the way in which people are wise' or 'the way in which people understand things' or 'the manner in which people reason.'

32.39 φιλόσοφος, ου m: a person of professional or semi-professional status regarded as having particular capacity or competence in understanding the meaning or significance of human experience – 'philosopher, scholar.' τινὲς δὲ καὶ τῶν Ἐπικουρείων καὶ Στοϊκῶν φιλοσόφων συνέβαλλον αὐτῷ 'certain Epicurean and Stoic philosophers also debated with him' Ac 17.18. In some instances φιλόσοφος in Ac 17.18 may be translated simply as

'teacher,' since such a word would normally designate a professional or semi-professional person involved in scholarly activities.

32.40 μάγος[a], ου m: a person noted for unusual capacity of understanding based upon astrology (such persons were regarded as combining both secular and religious aspects of knowledge and understanding) – 'a wise man and priest, a magus.' ἰδοὺ μάγοι ἀπὸ ἀνατολῶν παρεγένοντο εἰς Ἰεροσόλυμα 'soon afterward, some magi came from the East to Jerusalem' Mt 2.1. In Mt 2.1 μάγοι may be translated as 'men of wisdom who studied the stars.'[10]

32.41 σοφία[d], ας f: a document or book containing wise sayings (as in the phrase ἡ σοφία τοῦ θεοῦ 'the Wisdom of God,' Lk 11.49, a possible reference to the OT or to apocryphal wisdom literature, possibly even a book which has been lost) – 'Wisdom.' διὰ τοῦτο καὶ ἡ σοφία τοῦ θεοῦ εἶπεν 'for this reason the Wisdom of God said' Lk 11.49. If one understands ἡ σοφία τοῦ θεοῦ as being a reference to a book, one could translate the statement in Lk 11.49 as 'for this reason, the book entitled The Wisdom of God has the words: . . .' On the other hand, the phrase ἡ σοφία τοῦ θεοῦ in Lk 11.49 may mean merely 'God's wisdom' (32.32), and therefore this expression in Lk 11.49 may be rendered as 'God in his wisdom said' or 'God, who is wise, said.'

E   Lack of Capacity for Understanding (32.42-32.61)

32.42 τυφλός[b], ή, όν: (a figurative extension of meaning of τυφλός[a] 'unable to see, blind,' 24.38) pertaining to not being able to understand – 'unable to understand, incapable of comprehending, blind.' τυφλοί εἰσιν ὁδηγοί 'they are guides who themselves do not

---

9 It is possible to interpret σοφός in 1 Cor 1.20 as meaning merely 'wise' and thus referring to someone who is particularly wise in behavior, but in combination with the term γραμματεύς, σοφός would appear to have a more highly specialized meaning.

10 It would also be possible to classify μάγος in Domain 28 *Know*, in view of the highly specialized knowledge involved. Because of the religious implications of the role of a μάγος, this term could also be classified under Domain 53 *Religious Activities*, but the dominant semantic feature of μάγος would seem to be reputed wisdom, and therefore μάγος is treated in this domain, *Understand* (32).

understand' Mt 15.14; σὺ εἶ . . . τυφλὸς καὶ γυμνός 'you are . . . blind and naked' Re 3.17. In a number of languages it is possible to preserve the figurative meaning of 'blind'; in certain instances, however, part of the figurative meaning may be retained by translating 'not able to see how to live' or 'not able to see the truth.'

32.43 τυφλόω: (a causative derivative of τυφλός[b] 'unable to understand,' 32.42) to cause someone not to be able to understand – 'to make someone not understand, to remove someone's understanding.' ἐτύφλωσεν τὰ νοήματα τῶν ἀπίστων 'he made unbelievers unable to understand' or 'he made unbelievers' minds unable to comprehend' 2 Cor 4.4.

32.44 σκοτίζομαι[b]; σκοτόομαι[b]: (figurative extensions of meaning of σκοτίζομαι[a] and σκοτόομαι[a] 'to become dark,' 14.55) to become unable to perceive and thus unable to understand – 'to be incapable of perceiving, to not be able to understand.'
σκοτίζομαι[b]: ἐσκοτίσθη ἡ ἀσύνετος αὐτῶν καρδία 'their foolish minds became unable to perceive the truth' or '. . . were darkened' Ro 1.21; σκοτισθήτωσαν οἱ ὀφθαλμοὶ αὐτῶν 'may they become unable to perceive' (literally 'may their understanding become unable to understand') Ro 11.10.
σκοτόομαι[b]: ἐσκοτωμένοι τῇ διανοίᾳ ὄντες 'their minds were darkened' Eph 4.18.
It is rare that one can combine the concept of 'becoming dark' with incapacity to understand or comprehend. Sometimes a parallel figure of speech may be employed by using an expression such as 'to not be able to see.' For example, in Ro 1.21 it is sometimes possible to translate 'their foolish minds became unable to see the truth,' and in Eph 4.18 it is sometimes possible to translate 'they were not able to see with their minds.'

32.45 παχύνομαι: (a figurative extension of meaning of παχύνομαι 'to become thick,' not occurring in the NT) to become unable to understand or comprehend as the result of being mentally dull or spiritually insensitive – 'to be unable to understand, to be mentally dull.' ἐπαχύνθη γὰρ ἡ καρδία τοῦ λαοῦ τούτου 'for the heart of this people has become unable to understand' or '. . . incapable of understanding' Mt 13.15.

32.46 τοῖς ὠσὶν βαρέως ἀκούω: (an idiom, literally 'to hear heavily with the ears') to be mentally slow or dull in comprehending – 'to be slow to understand, to be mentally dull.' καὶ τοῖς ὠσὶν βαρέως ἤκουσαν 'and they were slow to understand' Ac 28.27.

32.47 νωθρὸς ταῖς ἀκοαῖς: (an idiom, literally 'lazy as to one's ears') to be slow to understand, with an implication of laziness – 'slow to understand.' ἐπεὶ νωθροὶ γεγόνατε ταῖς ἀκοαῖς 'because you have been slow to understand' He 5.11.

32.48 μυωπάζω: (a figurative extension of meaning of μυωπάζω 'to be shortsighted,' not occurring in the NT) to be extremely limited in one's understanding – 'to fail to understand, to be restricted in understanding, to be shortsighted.' τυφλός ἐστιν μυωπάζων 'being so limited in understanding as to not realize' or '. . . as to not comprehend' 2 Pe 1.9.

32.49 ἀσύνετος, ον: pertaining to a lack of capacity for insight and understanding – 'without understanding, senseless, foolish.' ἀκμὴν καὶ ὑμεῖς ἀσύνετοί ἐστε; 'are you still without understanding?' Mt 15.16; ἐσκοτίσθη ἡ ἀσύνετος αὐτῶν καρδία 'their foolish hearts are filled with darkness' Ro 1.21. Care must be exercised in the rendering of ἀσύνετος in Mt 15.16 and Ro 1.21, since a lack of capacity for understanding may result from mental deficiencies or from a lack of the proper use of mental capacity. It is, of course, this latter meaning which is involved in the use of ἀσύνετος in these contexts.

32.50 ἀνόητος, ον: pertaining to unwillingness to use one's mental faculties in order to understand – 'foolish, stupid, without understanding.' σοφοῖς τε καὶ ἀνοήτοις ὀφειλέτης εἰμί 'I am obligated to both wise and foolish men' Ro 1.14; ὦ ἀνόητοι Γαλάται 'oh, foolish Galatians' Ga 3.1. As in the case of ἀσύνετος (32.49) the meaning of ἀνόητος is that people presumably would not use their capacity for understanding and as a result, thought and behaved foolishly. ἀνόητος does not imply the mental state of being an idiot or imbecile.

32.51 ἄνοια[a], ας *f*: the state of being devoid of understanding – 'to lack understanding, absence of understanding.' ἡ γὰρ ἄνοια αὐτῶν ἔκδηλος ἔσται πᾶσιν 'their lack of understanding will be evident to everyone' 2 Tm 3.9. ἄνοια does not imply in 2 Tm 3.9 that people are incapable of understanding, but that they evidently are unwilling to understand.

32.52 ἄφρων, ον: pertaining to not employing one's understanding, particularly in practical matters – 'foolish, senseless, unwise.' μὴ γίνεσθε ἄφρονες, ἀλλὰ συνίετε τί τὸ θέλημα τοῦ κυρίου 'do not be foolish, but understand what the Lord's will is' Eph 5.17; ἀγαθοποιοῦντας φιμοῦν τὴν τῶν ἀφρόνων ἀνθρώπων ἀγνωσίαν 'by the good things you do, silence the ignorant talk of foolish men' 1 Pe 2.15.

It is possible that ἄφρων in Ro 2.20 (παιδευτὴν ἀφρόνων 'instructor of the foolish') refers to people who are simply uninstructed or ignorant, since ἀφρόνων could be parallel with νηπίων, occurring in the same verse. On the other hand, there appears to be a contrast in the meanings of ἀφρόνων and νηπίων because of the distinctiveness in meanings of παιδευτήν and διδάσκαλον. Therefore, ἄφρων in Ro 2.20 is better understood as referring to those who act foolishly because they do not use their potential for understanding.

32.53 ἀφροσύνη, ης *f*: the state of not using one's capacity for understanding – 'to be a fool, foolishness.' ὃ λαλῶ οὐ κατὰ κύριον λαλῶ, ἀλλ' ὡς ἐν ἀφροσύνῃ 'what I am saying is not what the Lord would have me say, but is a matter of foolishness on my part' or '. . . but is, as it were, foolishness' or '. . . but is, as it were, being like a fool' 2 Cor 11.17; ἀσέλγεια, ὀφθαλμὸς πονηρός, βλασφημία, ὑπερηφανία, ἀφροσύνη 'lewdness, envy, slander, arrogance, and foolishness' Mk 7.22.

32.54 ἄσοφος, ον: pertaining to not being wise – 'foolish, unwise.' περιπατεῖτε, μὴ ὡς ἄσοφοι ἀλλ' ὡς σοφοί 'do not live like unwise people, but like wise people' Eph 5.15.

32.55 μωρός[a], ά, όν: pertaining to being extremely unwise and foolish – 'unwise, foolish, fool.' πᾶς ὁ ἀκούων μου τοὺς λόγους τούτους καὶ μὴ ποιῶν αὐτοὺς ὁμοιωθήσεται ἀνδρὶ μωρῷ, ὅστις ᾠκοδόμησεν αὐτοῦ τὴν οἰκίαν ἐπὶ τὴν ἄμμον 'everyone who hears these words of mine and does not obey them is like a foolish man who built his house on the sand' Mt 7.26; ἡμεῖς μωροὶ διὰ Χριστόν, ὑμεῖς δὲ φρόνιμοι ἐν Χριστῷ 'we are fools for Christ's sake, but you are wise in Christ' 1 Cor 4.10. In rendering μωρός in 1 Cor 4.10 it is essential to recognize the rhetorical exaggeration. Paul is not stating that he and his colleagues actually act unwisely or foolishly, and so it may be necessary in some languages to translate 'we are fools for Christ's sake' as 'we are regarded as fools for Christ's sake' or 'it might seem that we are fools in order to serve Christ.'

32.56 μωραίνομαι[a]: (derivative of μωρός[a] 'unwise, foolish,' 32.55) to become one who does not employ a capacity to understand and thus acts very foolishly – 'to become foolish, to act more foolishly.' φάσκοντες εἶναι σοφοὶ ἐμωράνθησαν 'saying they are wise, they became fools' or '(the more) they claim they are wise men, (the more) foolish they became' Ro 1.22.

32.57 μωρία, ας *f*: the content of foolish thought – 'foolishness, nonsense, what is thought to be foolish.' ὁ λόγος γὰρ ὁ τοῦ σταυροῦ τοῖς μὲν ἀπολλυμένοις μωρία ἐστίν 'for the message of the cross is foolishness to those who are being destroyed' 1 Cor 1.18. In rendering 1 Cor 1.18 it is important to recognize that 'foolishness' must be defined in terms of the relationship that it has to those who 'are being destroyed.' Therefore, it may be important to translate 1 Cor 1.18 as 'those who are being destroyed think that the message concerning the cross is nonsense' or '. . . makes no sense' or '. . . simply cannot be understood.'

32.58 μωρός[b], ά, όν: (derivative of μωρία 'foolishness,' 32.57) pertaining to thoughts devoid of understanding and therefore foolish – 'foolish, nonsensical, to be nonsense.' ἀλλὰ τὰ μωρὰ τοῦ κόσμου ἐξελέξατο ὁ θεὸς ἵνα καταισχύνῃ τοὺς σοφούς 'God (purposely) chose what the world considered to be nonsense in order to put wise men to shame' 1 Cor 1.27. Some translators have endeavored to render μωρός[b] in the sense of 'nonsense' as 'that which cannot be understood,' but this could refer to some type of deep mystery. Accordingly, the expression 'what the world considered to be nonsense' can often be better rendered as 'what the world thinks makes no sense' or 'what so many people think is foolishness.'

32.59 μωραίνω: (causative derivative of μωρία 'foolishness,' 32.57) to cause the content of certain thoughts to become devoid of meaning – 'to cause to become nonsense.' οὐχὶ ἐμώρανεν ὁ θεὸς τὴν σοφίαν τοῦ κόσμου; 'did not God cause the world's wisdom to become nonsense?' 1 Cor 1.20. In 1 Cor 1.20 the focus is upon the content of wisdom and non-sense, and it may be necessary to make this explicit, for example, 'the people of the world thought that what they understood was wise, but God showed that their thoughts were foolish' or '. . . their way of thinking was foolish.'

32.60 κενός[b], ή, όν: (a figurative extension of meaning of κενός[a] 'empty,' 57.42) pertaining to a complete lack of understanding and insight – 'foolish, stupid.' θέλεις δὲ γνῶναι, ὦ ἄνθρωπε κενέ, ὅτι ἡ πίστις χωρὶς τῶν ἔργων ἀργή ἐστιν; 'you fool! Do you want to be shown that faith without works is useless?' Jas 2.20.

32.61 ῥακά (a borrowing from Aramaic): one who is totally lacking in understanding – 'numskull, fool.' ὃς δ' ἂν εἴπῃ τῷ ἀδελφῷ αὐτοῦ, Ῥακά, ἔνοχος ἔσται τῷ συνεδρίῳ 'whoever says to his brother, You fool, will be brought before the Council' Mt 5.22.

33 Communication

Outline of Subdomains[1]

A Language (33.1-33.8)
B Word, Passage (33.9-33.10)
C Discourse Types (33.11-33.25)
D Language Levels (33.26-33.34)
E Written Language (33.35-33.68)
F Speak, Talk (33.69-33.108)
G Sing, Lament (33.109-33.116)
H Keep Silent (33.117-33.125)
I Name (33.126-33.133)
J Interpret, Mean, Explain (33.134-33.155)

1 As may be readily noted from the Outline of Subdomains, there are a number of ways in which the subdomains are related to one another. Unfortunately, this cannot be made clear by an outline. Noting distinctive features by means of a matrix or a comparison of formulae based on a calculus of meanings would reveal certain important relations, but all of the semantic features and interrelations of meaning could never be satisfactorily diagrammed in view of the multi-dimensional sets of relations. Thus, the order and arrangement of the subdomains is bound to seem somewhat artificial and arbitrary. It may, however, be useful to point out some of the related sets. For example, Subdomains A-E are largely metalinguistic. Subdomains L, M, and N involve requests and presumed responses, while Subdomains O, P, and Q are primarily informative in nature. Subdomains R-V contain an important factor of implied truth and the relationship of the speaker to such truth. Subdomains X-F' have an element of future orientation, while Subdomains P'-W' involve adverse content, and Subdomains X'-Z' involve opposition. Finally, Subdomains A''-C'' involve certain supernatural elements.

These particular groupings of subdomains are, of course, not the only subclasses, but they are some of the more conspicuous ones. It would, however, be possible to organize the subdomains in quite different ways. For example, reciprocal involvement in communication could include Subdomains K, W, X', Y', and Z'. A factor of imposition of the speaker upon a presumed hearer could include B', E', F', G', S', and T'. These multidimensional relations will, of course, be even more obvious as one studies the detailed distinctions given in the definitions of the various meanings under each subdomain.

K Converse, Discuss (33.156-33.160)
L Ask For, Request (33.161-33.177)
M Pray (33.178-33.179)
N Question, Answer (33.180-33.188)
O Inform, Announce (33.189-33.217)
P Assert, Declare (33.218-33.223)
Q Teach (33.224-33.250)
R Speak Truth, Speak Falsehood
   (33.251-33.255)
S Preach, Proclaim (33.256-33.261)
T Witness, Testify (33.262-33.273)
U Profess Allegiance (33.274)
V Admit, Confess, Deny (33.275-33.277)
W Agree (33.278-33.280)
X Foretell, Tell Fortunes
   (33.281-33.285)
Y Promise (33.286-33.290)
Z Threaten (33.291-33.293)
A' Advise (33.294-33.298)
B' Urge, Persuade (33.299-33.306)
C' Call (33.307-33.314)
D' Invite (33.315-33.318)
E' Insist (33.319-33.322)
F' Command, Order (33.323-33.332)
G' Law, Regulation, Ordinance
   (33.333-33.342)
H' Recommend, Propose (33.343-33.346)
I' Intercede (33.347-33.348)
J' Thanks (33.349-33.353)
K' Praise (33.354-33.364)
L' Flatter (33.365-33.367)
M' Boast (33.368-33.373)
N' Foolish Talk (33.374-33.381)
O' Complain (33.382-33.386)
P' Insult, Slander (33.387-33.403)
Q' Gossip (33.404-33.405)
R' Mock, Ridicule (33.406-33.411)
S' Criticize (33.412-33.416)
T' Rebuke (33.417-33.422)
U' Warn (33.423-33.425)
V' Accuse, Blame (33.426-33.434)
W' Defend, Excuse (33.435-33.438)
X' Dispute, Debate (33.439-33.445)
Y' Argue, Quarrel (33.446-33.454)
Z' Oppose, Contradict (33.455-33.458)
A" Prophesy (33.459-33.462)
B" Swear, Put Under Oath, Vow
   (33.463-33.469)
C" Bless, Curse (33.470-33.475)
D" Non-Verbal Communication
   (33.476-33.489)

A Language (33.1-33.8)

33.1 φωνή[d], ῆς *f*; διάλεκτος, ου *f*: a verbal code, whether oral or written, as a basic means of communication – 'language.'

φωνή[d]: τοσαῦτα εἰ τύχοι γένη φωνῶν εἰσιν ἐν κόσμῳ 'there are so many different languages in the world' 1 Cor 14.10; ὑποζύγιον ἄφωνον ἐν ἀνθρώπου φωνῇ φθεγξάμενον 'a donkey, incapable of speech, spoke in a human language' 2 Pe 2.16. It is possible to interpret φωνή in 2 Pe 2.16 as 'voice' (see 33.103).

διάλεκτος: ἤκουον εἷς ἕκαστος τῇ ἰδίᾳ διαλέκτῳ λαλούντων αὐτῶν 'each one heard them talking in his own language' Ac 2.6. It is possible, though perhaps not probable, that διάλεκτος in Ac 2.6 may be understood not only as a language as such, but as a particular form of such a language, and hence would have a meaning of 'manner of speaking' or even 'accent' (see 33.102).

33.2 γλῶσσα[b], ης *f*: a language, with the possible implication of its distinctive form – 'language, dialect, speech.' ἤρξαντο λαλεῖν ἑτέραις γλώσσαις 'they began to talk in other languages' Ac 2.4. The miracle described in Ac 2.4 may have been a miracle of speaking or a miracle of hearing, but at any rate people understood fully, and therefore it seems appropriate in this context to speak of 'languages' in contrast with 1 Cor 14.2, in which case people required an interpreter if they were to receive the presumed content of the speech (see 33.3).

33.3 γλῶσσα[c], ης *f*: an utterance having the form of language but requiring an inspired interpreter for an understanding of the content – 'ecstatic language, tongue, ecstatic speech.' ὁ γὰρ λαλῶν γλώσσῃ οὐκ ἀνθρώποις λαλεῖ ἀλλὰ θεῷ 'he who speaks in a tongue does not speak to people but to God' 1 Cor 14.2. Most scholars assume that the phenomena described in Ac 2.4 (see 33.2) and in 1 Cor 14.2 are significantly different in that in one instance people understood in their own regional language or dialect and in the other instance an interpreter was required. It is for that reason that many interpret γλῶσσα in 1 Cor 14.2 as ecstatic speech, which was also an element in

Hellenistic religions and constituted a symbol of divine inspiration.

33.4 ἑτερόγλωσσος, ον: pertaining to being a different or strange language – 'speaking in a strange language, in a strange language.' ἐν ἑτερογλώσσοις καὶ ἐν χείλεσιν ἑτέρων λαλήσω τῷ λαῷ τούτῳ 'I will speak to this people through those who speak strange languages and through the lips of foreigners' 1 Cor 14.21.

33.5 Ἑλληνιστί — 'in the Greek language, in Greek.' καὶ ἦν γεγραμμένον Ἑβραϊστί, Ῥωμαϊστί, Ἑλληνιστί 'and it was written in Hebrew, in Latin, in Greek' Jn 19.20.

33.6 Ἑβραϊστί – 'in the Hebrew language, in Hebrew.' εἰς τόπον λεγόμενον Λιθόστρωτον, Ἑβραϊστὶ δὲ Γαββαθα 'to a place called Pavement and in Hebrew Gabbatha' Jn 19.13.

33.7 Ῥωμαϊστί – 'in the Latin language, in Latin.' καὶ ἦν γεγραμμένον Ἑβραϊστί, Ῥωμαϊστί, Ἑλληνιστί 'and it was written in Hebrew, in Latin, in Greek' Jn 19.20.

33.8 Λυκαονιστί – 'in the Lycaonian language, in Lycaonian.' οἵ τε ὄχλοι ἰδόντες ὃ ἐποίησεν Παῦλος ἐπῆραν τὴν φωνὴν αὐτῶν Λυκαονιστί 'when the crowds saw what Paul did, they shouted in the Lycaonian language' Ac 14.11.

B Word, Passage (33.9-33.10)

33.9 ῥῆμαᵃ, τος n: a minimal unit of discourse, often a single word – 'word, saying.' οὐκ ἀπεκρίθη αὐτῷ πρὸς οὐδὲ ἓν ῥῆμα 'he refused to answer him a single word' Mt 27.14. In place of a rendering such as 'refused to answer a single word,' it may be more idiomatic to say 'said nothing' or 'refused to speak.'

33.10 τόποςᵇ, ου m; περιοχή, ῆς f; γραφήᵃ, ῆς f: a particular portion or unit of discourse – 'passage, part of document, part of Scripture.'
τόποςᵇ: ἀναπτύξας τὸ βιβλίον εὗρεν τὸν τόπον οὗ

ἦν γεγραμμένον 'he unrolled the scroll and found the passage where it is written' Lk 4.17.
περιοχή: ἡ δὲ περιοχὴ τῆς γραφῆς ἣν ἀνεγίνωσκεν ἦν αὕτη 'the passage of Scripture which he was reading was this' Ac 8.32.
γραφήᵃ: σήμερον πεπλήρωται ἡ γραφὴ αὕτη ἐν τοῖς ὠσὶν ὑμῶν 'this passage has come true today as you heard it (being read)' Lk 4.21.[2]

In rendering τόποςᵇ, περιοχή, or γραφήᵃ, it is often possible to use a rather general term such as 'the place' or 'the part.' In other instances one may wish to use a term meaning 'the words.' Accordingly, Lk 4.21 may be rendered as 'these words have come true today as you have heard them being read.'

C Discourse Types (33.11-33.25)

33.11 διήγησις, εως f: a discourse consisting of an orderly exposition or narration – 'account, report, narration.' πολλοὶ ἐπεχείρησαν ἀνατάξασθαι διήγησιν περὶ τῶν πεπληροφορημένων ἐν ἡμῖν πραγμάτων 'many have undertaken to write an account of the things that have taken place among us' Lk 1.1.

In a number of languages it may be necessary to represent the meaning of διήγησις by qualifying the type of writing, for example, 'many have undertaken to write carefully about what has taken place among us.' Other equivalent expressions might be 'to write in detail.'

33.12 κεφάλαιονᵃ, ου n: a brief statement of the main point of a previously given discourse – 'main point, summary.' κεφάλαιον δὲ ἐπὶ τοῖς λεγομένοις 'here is a summary of what we are saying' He 8.1.

33.13 μῦθος, ου m: a legendary story or account, normally about supernatural beings, events, or cultural heroes, and in the NT always with an unfavorable connotation –

---

2 γραφήᵃ in 33.10 differs significantly in meaning from γραφήᵇ (33.53) in that the latter denotes specifically some OT Scripture passage, while γραφήᵃ is a more generic reference to any unit of discourse, though in Lk 4.21 it happens to refer to an OT section.

'legend, myth, tale, story, fable.' οὐ γὰρ σεσοφισμένοις μύθοις ἐξακολουθήσαντες ἐγνωρίσαμεν ὑμῖν τὴν τοῦ κυρίου ἡμῶν Ἰησοῦ Χριστοῦ δύναμιν καὶ παρουσίαν 'we have not depended on cleverly contrived myths in making known to you the mighty coming of our Lord Jesus Christ' 2 Pe 1.16. The term μῦθος may often be translated simply as 'untrue stories' or 'false tales.'

33.14 παροιμία[a], ας *f*: a short saying of a fixed form, emphasizing some general truth – 'proverb, saying.' συμβέβηκεν αὐτοῖς τὸ τῆς ἀληθοῦς παροιμίας, Κύων ἐπιστρέφας ἐπὶ τὸ ἴδιον ἐξέραμα 'what happened to them shows that the saying is true: A dog goes back to what he has vomited' 2 Pe 2.22. In a context such as 2 Pe 2.22 one may render 'saying' as 'what people so often say' or 'what is often said.'

33.15 παραβολή[a], ῆς *f*; παροιμία[b], ας *f*: a relatively short narrative with symbolic meaning – 'parable, figure, allegory, figure of speech.'
παραβολή[a]: ἐλάλησεν αὐτοῖς πολλὰ ἐν παραβολαῖς 'he spoke to them about many things using parables' Mt 13.3.
παροιμία[b]: ταῦτα ἐν παροιμίαις λελάληκα ὑμῖν 'I have told you these things by means of figures of speech' Jn 16.25.
In almost all languages there is some way of speaking about parables or allegories. The equivalent in some languages may be 'a likeness story' or 'a story that teaches' or 'a story that points the way' or 'words that have another meaning' or 'words that are saying something else important.'
Some scholars have insisted that in the NT παραβολή is used only in the sense of a story with one level of symbolic meaning, but in some contexts παραβολή is also used to identify allegories in which each element of the account has a symbolic significance. It is therefore extremely difficult to make a rigid distinction between parables and allegories.

33.16 παρατίθημι τὴν παραβολήν (an idiom, literally 'to place alongside a parable') – 'to tell a parable, to utter a parable.' ἄλλην παρα-

βολὴν παρέθηκεν αὐτοῖς 'he told them another parable' Mt 13.24.[3]

33.17 ἐν παραβολῇ; πνευματικῶς[c]: pertaining to expressions which are not to be understood literally, but symbolically or figuratively – 'symbolically, allegorically, figuratively, so to speak.'
ἐν παραβολῇ: ὅθεν αὐτὸν καὶ ἐν παραβολῇ ἐκομίσατο 'from where he received him back, so to speak' He 11.19.
πνευματικῶς[c]: ἥτις καλεῖται πνευματικῶς Σόδομα 'that city is figuratively called Sodom' Re 11.8.
In a number of languages it may be more satisfactory to translate ἐν παραβολῇ and πνευματικῶς[c] by a negative expression, for example, 'not literally' or 'not really.' The expression in Re 11.8 might be translated as 'that city might be called Sodom, but it isn't really Sodom.'

33.18 ἀλληγορέω: to employ an analogy or likeness in communicating – 'to speak allegorically, to employ an analogy, to use a likeness.' ἅτινά ἐστιν ἀλληγορούμενα· αὗται γάρ εἰσιν δύο διαθῆκαι 'this incident can be taken as a kind of likeness: the two women stand for two covenants' Ga 4.24.

33.19 γένεσις[c], εως *f*: an account of the origin and life of someone – 'history.' βίβλος γενέσεως Ἰησοῦ Χριστοῦ υἱοῦ Δαυὶδ υἱοῦ Ἀβραάμ 'book of the history of Jesus Christ, the son of David, the son of Abraham' Mt 1.1. For the most part, however, scholars understand the phrase βίβλος γενέσεως in Mt 1.1 as referring to the list of ancestors which immediately follows. Therefore, βίβλος γενέσεως is more often interpreted as 'the record of the ancestors' or 'the birth record of . . .' (see 10.24).[4]

3 It would be possible to interpret παρατίθημι τὴν παραβολήν as meaning 'to put a parable to,' in other words, 'to address a parable to someone.' This interpretation is possible in view of the following participle λέγων, but the occurrence of such a participle to introduce direct discourse is frequent with expressions of speaking.
4 See 33.38, where Mt 1.1 is the illustrative example for βίβλος[c] 'written statement, record.' See 23.46 for γένεσις[a] 'birth.'

33.20 ἀσπάζομαι[a]; ἀσπασμός, οῦ *m*: to employ certain set phrases as a part of the process of greeting, whether communicated directly or indirectly – 'to greet, to send greetings.'

ἀσπάζομαι[a]: προστρέχοντες ἠσπάζοντο αὐτόν 'they ran to him and greeted him' Mk 9.15; ἀσπάζονται ὑμᾶς οἱ ἀδελφοὶ πάντες 'all the Christian brothers (here) send greetings to you' 1 Cor 16.20. It is possible that in some contexts ἀσπάζομαι[a] could be interpreted as 'to visit,' so that in Ac 18.22 one may render ἀσπασάμενος τὴν ἐκκλησίαν as 'visiting the church' rather than as 'greeting the church.'

ἀσπασμός: τῶν θελόντων ἐν στολαῖς περιπατεῖν καὶ ἀσπασμοὺς ἐν ταῖς ἀγοραῖς 'who like to walk around in long robes and be greeted in the marketplace' Mk 12.38.

33.21 ἀπασπάζομαι: to say goodbye – 'to bid goodbye to, to take leave of.' ἀπησπασάμεθα ἀλλήλους, καὶ ἀνέβημεν εἰς τὸ πλοῖον 'we bid goodbye to one another and went aboard the ship' Ac 21.6; ἀσπασάμενος ἐξῆλθεν πορεύεσθαι εἰς Μακεδονίαν 'he said goodbye, then left and went on to Macedonia' Ac 20.1.

33.22 χαίρω[b]: to employ a formalized expression of greeting, implying a wish for happiness on the part of the person greeted – 'hail, greetings.' ἤρξαντο ἀσπάζεσθαι αὐτόν, Χαῖρε, βασιλεῦ τῶν Ἰουδαίων 'they began to greet him, Hail, King of the Jews' Mk 15.18. The functional equivalent of χαίρω[b] in Spanish would be *que viva*. In traditional English one might employ an expression such as 'long live!'

33.23 ἀποτάσσομαι[a]: to employ formalized expressions appropriate to leaving or saying farewell to someone, possibly involving the communication of final arrangements for leaving – 'to say goodbye.' πρῶτον δὲ ἐπίτρεφόν μοι ἀποτάξασθαι τοῖς εἰς τὸν οἶκόν μου 'first let me go and say goodbye to my family' Lk 9.61.

33.24 ἔρρωσθε (ἐρρώσσω in some manuscripts): (a formula derived from the verb ῥώνυμαι meaning literally 'to be strong') to end a letter by means of the expression ἔρρωσθε, always having a favorable connotation – 'goodbye.' ἐξ ὧν διατηροῦντες ἑαυτοὺς εὖ πράξετε. Ἔρρωσθε 'you will do well if you keep yourselves from doing these things. Goodbye' Ac 15.29. Since in Ac 15.29 ἔρρωσθε ends a letter, it may be necessary in some languages to employ a typical letter-ending formula which will at the same time be favorable, for example, 'with best wishes' or 'with sincere greetings.' It would be quite wrong to use literally an expression such as 'goodbye' if this would be employed only or principally in direct address rather than at the end of a letter. For another interpretation of ἔρρωσθε in Ac 15.29, see 23.133.

33.25 ποιητής[b], οῦ *m*: one who produces literary texts, normally in poetic form – 'poet, writer.' ὡς καί τινες τῶν καθ' ὑμᾶς ποιητῶν εἰρήκασιν 'it is as some of your poets have said' Ac 17.28.

D Language Levels (33.26-33.34)

33.26 διαλέγομαι[b]; δημηγορέω: to speak in a somewhat formal setting and probably implying a more formal use of language – 'to address, to make a speech.'[5]

διαλέγομαι[b]: συνηγμένων ἡμῶν κλάσαι ἄρτον ὁ Παῦλος διελέγετο αὐτοῖς 'we gathered together for the fellowship meal and Paul spoke to the people' Ac 20.7.

δημηγορέω: ὁ Ἡρῴδης ἐνδυσάμενος ἐσθῆτα βασιλικὴν καὶ καθίσας ἐπὶ τοῦ βήματος ἐδημηγόρει πρὸς αὐτούς 'Herod put on his royal robes, sat on his throne, and made a speech to the people' Ac 12.21.

33.27 προσφωνέω[a]: to address an audience, with possible emphasis upon loudness – 'to address, to speak out to.' πολλῆς δὲ σιγῆς γενομένης προσεφώνησεν τῇ Ἑβραΐδι διαλέκτῳ 'when they were quiet, he addressed them in Hebrew' Ac 21.40.

33.28 ἀποκρίνομαι[b]: to introduce or continue a somewhat formal discourse (occurring

---

5 It is possible that δημηγορέω implies somewhat greater formality than διαλέγομαι[b], but it is impossible to determine this on the basis of NT usage.

regularly with λέγω[a] 'to say,' 33.69) – 'to speak, to declare, to say.'[6] ἐν ἐκείνῳ τῷ καιρῷ ἀποκριθεὶς ὁ Ἰησοῦς εἶπεν 'at that time Jesus said' Mt 11.25. A literal translation such as 'at that time Jesus spoke and said' may sound redundant in many languages.

33.29 ἀνοίγω τὸ στόμα; ἄνοιξις τοῦ στόματος: (Semitic idioms, literally 'to open the mouth' and 'the opening of the mouth') to begin to speak in a somewhat formal and systematic manner – 'to address, to start speaking, to begin to speak, to utter.'
ἀνοίγω τὸ στόμα: ἀνοίξας δὲ Πέτρος τὸ στόμα 'then Peter began to address them' Ac 10.34. ἄνοιξις τοῦ στόματος: ἵνα μοι δοθῇ λόγος ἐν ἀνοίξει τοῦ στόματός μου 'in order that a message may be given to me to utter' or '. . . to announce' Eph 6.19.

33.30 χρηστολογία, ας f: eloquent and attractive speech involving pleasing rhetorical devices – 'attractive speech, fine language.' διὰ τῆς χρηστολογίας καὶ εὐλογίας ἐξαπατῶσιν τὰς καρδίας τῶν ἀκάκων 'by their fine words and flattering speech they deceive the minds of innocent people' Ro 16.18.

33.31 πιθανολογία, ας f: plausible, but false, speech resulting from the use of well-constructed, probable arguments – 'convincing speech, plausible language.' ἵνα μηδεὶς ὑμᾶς παραλογίζηται ἐν πιθανολογίᾳ 'do not let anyone fool you with plausible but false language' Col 2.4.

33.32 λόγιος[a], α, ον: pertaining to attractive and convincing speech – 'eloquent.' ἀνὴρ λόγιος . . . δυνατὸς ὢν ἐν ταῖς γραφαῖς 'he was an eloquent speaker . . . and had a thorough knowledge of the Scriptures' Ac 18.24. It is also possible to understand λόγιος in Ac 18.24 as meaning 'learned' (see 27.20).

33.33 αἰσχρολογία, ας f: obscene, shameful speech involving culturally disapproved themes – 'vulgar speech, obscene speech, dirty talk.' ἀπόθεσθε . . . βλασφημίαν, αἰσχρολογίαν ἐκ τοῦ στόματος ὑμῶν 'get rid of . . . slander and dirty talk that ever came from your lips' Col 3.8.

33.34 εὐτραπελία, ας f: coarse jesting involving vulgar expressions and indecent content – 'vulgar speech, indecent talk.' καὶ αἰσχρότης καὶ μωρολογία ἢ εὐτραπελία, ἃ οὐκ ἀνῆκεν 'nor is it fitting for you to use shameful, foolish, or vulgar language' Eph 5.4.

E Written Language (33.35-33.68)

33.35 γράμμα[a], τος n: a letter of the Greek alphabet – 'letter.'[7] ἴδετε πηλίκοις ὑμῖν γράμμασιν ἔγραψα 'see what big letters I make as I write to you' Ga 6.11.

33.36 ἰῶτα n: the smallest letter of the Greek alphabet (corresponding to the 'yod' of the Hebrew alphabet) – 'iota, smallest letter, small mark.' ἰῶτα ἓν ἢ μία κεραία οὐ μὴ παρέλθῃ ἀπὸ τοῦ νόμου 'not one small letter or part of a letter shall pass away from the Law' Mt 5.18. See discussion in 33.37.

33.37 κεραία, ας f: a part of a letter of the alphabet – 'stroke, short mark, short line of a letter, part of a letter.' ἰῶτα ἓν ἢ μία κεραία οὐ μὴ παρέλθῃ ἀπὸ τοῦ νόμου 'not one small letter or part of a letter shall pass away from the Law' Mt 5.18.
The reference of ἰῶτα (33.36) and κεραία is to the small details of the Law, and therefore it may be appropriate in many languages to translate Mt 5.18 as 'not one of the smallest parts of the Law will be done away with' or '. . . will become null and void.'

33.38 βίβλος[c], ου f; βιβλίον[c], ου n: relatively short statements in written form – 'written statement, certificate, notice, record.' βίβλος[c]: βίβλος γενέσεως Ἰησοῦ Χριστοῦ 'the

---

6 ἀποκρίνομαι[b] (33.28) apparently differs from ἀνοίγω τὸ στόμα and ἄνοιξις τοῦ στόματος (33.29) in focusing primarily upon the content of the discourse, while the idioms in 33.29 appear to relate more to the formal aspects of the presentation.

7 α, β, and γ, the first three letters of the Greek alphabet, are used as ordinal numbers (first, second, and third) in connection with the titles of books of the NT. See Domain 60 *Number*.

birth record of Jesus Christ' or 'a list of the ancestors of Jesus Christ' Mt 1.1.

βιβλίον^c: ἐπέτρεψεν Μωϋσῆς βιβλίον ἀποστασίου γράψαι καὶ ἀπολῦσαι 'Moses allowed (a man) to write a divorce notice and to send (his wife) away' Mk 10.4.

33.39 γράμμα^d, τος *n*: a written statement of financial accounts, especially of debts – 'account, record of debts.' δέξαι σου τὰ γράμματα καὶ καθίσας ταχέως γράψον πεντήκοντα 'here is your account; sit down quickly and write fifty on it' Lk 16.6. In place of the expression 'here is your account,' one may say 'here is a list of what you owe.'

33.40 χειρόγραφον, ου *n*: a handwritten statement, especially a record of financial accounts (similar in meaning to γράμμα^d 'account,' 33.39, but perhaps with emphasis upon the handwritten nature of the document) – 'account, record of debts.' ἐξαλείψας τὸ καθ' ἡμῶν χειρόγραφον 'he canceled the record of our debts' Col 2.14.

33.41 ἀποστάσιον, ου *n*: a written statement prepared by a husband and given to a wife as evidence of a legal divorce – 'written notice of divorce.' ὃς ἂν ἀπολύσῃ τὴν γυναῖκα αὐτοῦ, δότω αὐτῇ ἀποστάσιον 'anyone who divorces his wife must give her a written notice of divorce' Mt 5.31.[8]

33.42 ἀπογράφω: to register someone, often in connection with taking a census – 'to register, to put on a census list.' ἐπορεύοντο πάντες ἀπογράφεσθαι, ἕκαστος εἰς τὴν ἑαυτοῦ πόλιν 'everyone went to be registered, each to his own town' Lk 2.3. In a number of languages the equivalent of ἀπογράφω is simply 'to have one's name put in a book' or 'to have one's name put in a list of those living in a particular place.'

In He 12.23 (καὶ ἐκκλησίᾳ πρωτοτόκων ἀπογεγραμμένων ἐν οὐρανοῖς 'and at the gathering of the first-born, whose names are written in heaven') ἀπογράφω is used in a figurative sense, but it is usually translated more or less literally.

33.43 ἀπογραφή, ῆς *f*: the event of registering persons in connection with taking a census – 'census.' αὕτη ἀπογραφὴ πρώτη ἐγένετο 'when the first census took place' Lk 2.2. One may construct a descriptive equivalent of 'census' by speaking of 'when everyone's name is taken down and he is counted' or 'a time when the government writes down everyone's name on a list' or '. . . in books.'

33.44 καταλέγω: to enroll a person as a member of a group – 'to put one's name on a list, to enter someone on a list.' χήρα καταλεγέσθω μὴ ἔλαττον ἐτῶν ἑξήκοντα γεγονυῖα 'do not put any widow on the list unless she is more than sixty years old' 1 Tm 5.9.

33.45 ἐλλογέω^a: to keep a record of something – 'to record, to list.' ἁμαρτία δὲ οὐκ ἐλλογεῖται μὴ ὄντος νόμου 'but where there is no law, no account is kept of sins' Ro 5.13. There may be difficulties involved in changing the passive expression 'no account is kept of sins' in Ro 5.13 to 'God doesn't keep an account of sins,' for this might imply that God was unconcerned about sin. It is sometimes possible to avoid this difficulty by rendering 'no account is kept of sins' as 'a sin is not listed as a sin.'

33.46 τίτλος, ου *m*; **ἐπιγραφή, ῆς** *f*: a brief notice used primarily for identification – 'inscription, writing.'
τίτλος: ἔγραψεν δὲ καὶ τίτλον ὁ Πιλᾶτος καὶ ἔθηκεν ἐπὶ τοῦ σταυροῦ 'Pilate wrote an inscription and had it put on the cross' Jn 19.19.
ἐπιγραφή: τίνος ἡ εἰκὼν αὕτη καὶ ἡ ἐπιγραφή; 'whose image and inscription is this (on the coin)?' Mt 22.20; ἦν ἡ ἐπιγραφὴ τῆς αἰτίας αὐτοῦ ἐπιγεγραμμένη, Ὁ βασιλεὺς τῶν Ἰουδαίων 'the inscription of the charge against him read (literally 'was written'), The King of the Jews' Mk 15.26.

33.47 σφραγίς^d, ῖδος *f*: the mark or impression made by a seal or stamp – 'mark, inscription.' θεμέλιος . . . ἔχων τὴν σφραγῖδα ταύτην

---

[8] In Mt 19.7 and Mk 10.4 ἀποστάσιον occurs together with βιβλίον^c 'notice' (33.38), but in Mt 5.31 ἀποστάσιον occurs in the absolute sense and denotes both the document and its particular contents.

'the foundation . . . which had this inscription on it' 2 Tm 2.19.

33.48 ἐπιστολή[b], ῆς *f*: a written communication, usually from one person to one or more persons – 'letter.'[9] γράψας ἐπιστολὴν ἔχουσαν τὸν τύπον τοῦτον 'then he wrote a letter that went like this' Ac 23.25. It is also possible to understand ἐπιστολή in Ac 23.25 not as a content or message, but as an object, see 6.63.

33.49 ἐπιστέλλω: to communicate with someone by means of a letter – 'to write a letter, to send a letter to.' ἐπιστεῖλαι αὐτοῖς τοῦ ἀπέχεσθαι τῶν ἀλισγημάτων 'we should write a letter telling them not to eat any food that is unclean' Ac 15.20.

33.50 γράμμα[b], τος *n*: any kind of written document, whether in book or manuscript form, with focus upon the content – 'writing, what has been written.' εἰ δὲ τοῖς ἐκείνου γράμμασιν οὐ πιστεύετε, πῶς τοῖς ἐμοῖς ῥήμασιν πιστεύσετε; 'but since you do not believe his writings, how will you believe my words?' Jn 5.47.

33.51 λόγος[d], ου *m*: a relatively formal and systematic treatment of a subject – 'treatise, book, account.'[10] τὸν μὲν πρῶτον λόγον ἐποιησάμην περὶ πάντων 'in my first book I wrote about all the things that . . .' Ac 1.1.

33.52 βίβλος[b], ου *f*; βιβλίον[b], ου *n*: the contents of a book – 'book.'[11] βίβλος[b]: αὐτὸς γὰρ Δαυὶδ λέγει ἐν βίβλῳ ψαλμῶν 'David himself says in the book of the Psalms' Lk 20.42.

---

9 ἐπιστολή may occur either in the sense of the physical object (see 6.63) which is used as a means of communication or as the content of what is written (33.48), but in some contexts it is difficult, if not impossible, to distinguish between these two phases of the meaning of ἐπιστολή.

10 λόγος[d] appears to differ from γράμμα[b] (33.50) in denoting a somewhat more formal treatment of the subject matter.

11 As noted in the case of ἐπιστολή[b] (33.48), there is an intimate semantic relationship between letter, document, and book as physical objects and the contents of such writings. For 'book' as an object, see βίβλος[a] and βιβλίον[a] (6.64).

βιβλίον[b]: πολλὰ μὲν οὖν καὶ ἄλλα σημεῖα ἐποίησεν ὁ Ἰησοῦς . . . ἃ οὐκ ἔστιν γεγραμμένα ἐν τῷ βιβλίῳ τούτῳ 'Jesus did many other works . . . which are not written down in this book' Jn 20.30.

33.53 γραφή[b], ῆς *f*: a particular passage of the OT – 'Scripture, Scripture passage.'[12] λέγει γὰρ ἡ γραφή, Πᾶς ὁ πιστεύων ἐπ᾽ αὐτῷ οὐ καταισχυνθήσεται 'for the Scripture says, Whoever believes in him will not be disappointed' Ro 10.11.

33.54 γραφαί, ῶν *f* (the plural form): the sacred writings of the OT – 'the Scriptures, the holy writings.' πλανᾶσθε μὴ εἰδότες τὰς γραφάς 'you are wrong because you do not know the Scriptures' Mk 12.24.

Some translators have mistakenly attempted to use the rendering 'Bible' when translating αἱ γραφαί 'the Scriptures' in the NT. The reference is to the OT and not to the entire Bible, including both New and Old Testaments. It is also a mistake to translate αἱ γραφαί as 'God's writings,' for this would give the impression that God himself wrote the words.

33.55 νόμος[b], ου *m*: the first five books of the OT called the Torah (often better rendered as 'instruction') – 'the Law.' ἄχρι γὰρ νόμου ἁμαρτία ἦν ἐν κόσμῳ 'before the Law (was given), there was sin in the world' Ro 5.13. In a number of languages it is not possible to use a singular expression such as 'the Law,' for since the Torah consisted of five books and included a number of regulations and instructions, it is necessary in many languages to use 'the laws.' Furthermore, to distinguish this body of laws from common, ordinary customs or legal regulations, it may be necessary to employ a phrase such as 'the laws given to Moses' or simply 'the laws of Moses.'

33.56 νόμος[c], ου *m*: the sacred writings of the OT – 'holy writings, Scriptures, sacred writings.' οὐκ ἔστιν γεγραμμένον ἐν τῷ νόμῳ ὑμῶν ὅτι Ἐγὼ εἶπα, Θεοί ἐστε; 'is it not written in your Scriptures, "I said, You are

---

12 For γραφή in the more generic sense, see 33.10 and footnote 2.

gods"?' Jn 10.34. It is clear from the content of the quotation in Jn 10.34 that the reference of νόμος is not restricted to the first five books of the OT, for the passage comes from the Psalms.

33.57 ἄνομος[b], ον; ἀνόμως: pertaining to being without the Law (specifically the first five books of the OT) – 'without the Law.'
ἄνομος[b]: τοῖς ἀνόμοις ὡς ἄνομος 'to those who are without the Law, I am like one who is without the Law' 1 Cor 9.21. For another interpretation of ἄνομος in 1 Cor 9.21, see 11.42.
ἀνόμως: ὅσοι γὰρ ἀνόμως ἥμαρτον, ἀνόμως καὶ ἀπολοῦνται 'as many as sin without the Law, perish without the Law' Ro 2.12.
Even from the two contexts of 1 Cor 9.21 and Ro 2.12, it should be clear that ἄνομος[b] and ἀνόμως carry quite different implications in different contexts. In 1 Cor 9.21 a phrase such as 'without the Law' must be understood in the sense of 'not being under obligation to the Law' or 'not being bound by the Law,' and so 1 Cor 9.21 must be translated in a number of languages as 'with those who are not bound by the Law, I live as one who is not bound by the Law,' referring in these instances to the Law of Moses. It is important, however, in rendering the expression 'not bound by the Law' to avoid a phrase which would mean 'lawless' or 'heedless of the Law.' In the case of Ro 2.12, the phrase 'without the Law' must refer to those who are ignorant of the Law and thus are not bound by it, and so Ro 2.12 must be rendered in some languages as 'those who sin without knowing anything about the Law are lost, but quite apart from any relationship to the Law.'

33.58 ὁ νόμος καὶ οἱ προφῆται: (an idiom, literally 'the Law and the Prophets') all of the sacred writings of the OT, including the Law, the Prophets, and the Writings – 'the sacred writings, the Law and the Prophets.'[13] μὴ νομίσητε ὅτι ἦλθον καταλῦσαι τὸν νόμον ἢ τοὺς προφήτας 'do not think I have come to do away with the sacred writings' Mt 5.17.

33.59 Μωϋσῆς[b], ἕως m: the Law given through Moses, as formulated in the first five books of the OT – 'the Law, the Law of Moses, the Law given through Moses, Moses.' ἡνίκα ἂν ἀναγινώσκηται Μωϋσῆς 'whenever the Law of Moses is read' or 'whenever Moses is read' 2 Cor 3.15.
In a number of languages it is quite appropriate to refer to the writings of a person by simply mentioning the author, but in many languages this cannot be done. Furthermore, in 2 Cor 3.15 it may be necessary to employ an active expression, so that one must translate 'whenever people read the laws which God gave through Moses.' The use of Μωϋσῆς as a reference to the Law of Moses also occurs in the phrase 'Moses and the prophets' as a reference to the sacred writings (compare ὁ νόμος καὶ οἱ προφῆται 'the sacred writings,' 33.58).

33.60 προφῆται, ων m (occurring in the plural as a collective): the writings of the prophets, including both the earlier and the later prophets – 'the writings of the prophets, the Prophets.' τοῖς ἐν τοῖς προφήταις γεγραμμένοις 'those things written in the Prophets' Ac 24.14.[14] It is quite impossible, however, in many languages to speak of 'the Prophets' in reference to the writings of the prophets, and therefore one must often say 'what the prophets wrote' or 'the books containing the words of the prophets.'

33.61 γράφω – 'to write.' ὃν ἔγραψεν Μωϋσῆς ἐν τῷ νόμῳ 'the one of whom Moses wrote in the Law' Jn 1.45. Since the knowledge of writing is almost universal, there is usually no difficulty in obtaining a satisfactory term for writing. In some instances in which languages are only now being reduced to writing, a

---

13 The phrase ὁ νόμος καὶ οἱ προφῆται is classified as an idiom, since the meaning of this fixed phrase is really different from the total of the constituent parts, in that more is included than merely 'the Law and the Prophets.'

14 It is possible that προφῆται may have an even wider range of meaning, as in Lk 24.25 (ὦ ἀνόητοι καὶ βραδεῖς τῇ καρδίᾳ τοῦ πιστεύειν ἐπὶ πᾶσιν οἷς ἐλάλησαν οἱ προφῆται 'how foolish you are and how slow you are to believe everything the prophets said').

phrase is often employed, for example, 'to make marks on paper' or 'to talk with lines' or 'to speak with paper.'

33.62 ἐγγράφω – 'to write in, to record.' χαίρετε δὲ ὅτι τὰ ὀνόματα ὑμῶν ἐγγέγραπται ἐν τοῖς οὐρανοῖς 'be glad because your names are recorded in heaven' Lk 10.20.

33.63 καταγράφω: to write something down – 'to write down, to record.' τῷ δακτύλῳ κατέγραφεν εἰς τὴν γῆν 'he wrote on the ground with his finger' Jn 8.6. It is possible to interpret καταγράφω in Jn 8.6 as implying only the position of Jesus writing something down on the ground, but in view of the total context, one can also interpret it in the sense of writing down an accusation.

33.64 γραπτός, ή, όν: pertaining to being written – 'written.' οἵτινες ἐνδείκνυνται τὸ ἔργον τοῦ νόμου γραπτὸν ἐν ταῖς καρδίαις αὐτῶν 'their conduct shows that what the Law commands is written in their hearts' Ro 2.15.

33.65 ἐπιγράφω: to write on a surface – 'to write on.' εὗρον καὶ βωμὸν ἐν ᾧ ἐπεγέγραπτο, Ἀγνώστῳ θεῷ 'I found also an altar on which is written, To An Unknown God' Ac 17.23.

33.66 προγράφωᵃ: to write in advance or in anticipation of – 'to write beforehand.' ὅσα γὰρ προεγράφη, εἰς τὴν ἡμετέραν διδασκαλίαν ἐγράφη 'for everything written formerly was written to teach us' Ro 15.4.

33.67 ἐντυπόω: to cut or incise letters or designs – 'to cut, to carve, to engrave.' ἡ διακονία τοῦ θανάτου ἐν γράμμασιν ἐντετυπωμένη λίθοις 'the ministry of death carved in letters on stone tablets' 2 Cor 3.7.

33.68 ἀναγινώσκω; ἀνάγνωσις, εως f: to read something written, normally done aloud and thus involving verbalization – 'to read, reading.'[15] ἀναγινώσκω: οὐδέποτε ἀνέγνωτε τί ἐποίησεν

Δαυίδ 'have you never read what David did' Mk 2.25.
ἀνάγνωσις: τὸ αὐτὸ κάλυμμα ἐπὶ τῇ ἀναγνώσει τῆς παλαιᾶς διαθήκης μένει 'the same veil remains unlifted when they read from the Old Testament' 2 Cor 3.14.

In areas where literacy is a relatively new factor in the culture, idiomatic expressions are often employed for reading, for example, 'to let paper speak' or 'to mouth the marks on paper' or 'to see speech.'

F Speak, Talk (33.69-33.108)

33.69 λέγωᵃ; φημίᵃ: to speak or talk, with apparent focus upon the content of what is said – 'to say, to talk, to tell, to speak.'
λέγωᵃ: ἄγγελος κυρίου κατ᾽ ὄναρ ἐφάνη αὐτῷ λέγων 'an angel of the Lord appeared to him in a dream and said' Mt 1.20.
φημίᵃ: Σίμων, ἔχω σοί τι εἰπεῖν. ὁ δέ, Διδάσκαλε, εἰπέ, φησίν 'Simon, I have something to tell you. And he said, Teacher, tell me' Lk 7.40.

33.70 λαλέω: to speak or talk, with the possible implication of more informal usage (though this cannot be clearly and consistently shown from NT contexts) – 'to speak, to say, to talk, to tell.' ἐλάλησεν αὐτοῖς πολλὰ ἐν παραβολαῖς 'he used parables to tell them many things' or 'he spoke to them about many things using parables' Mt 13.3; τότε ὁ Ἰησοῦς ἐλάλησεν τοῖς ὄχλοις καὶ τοῖς μαθηταῖς αὐτοῦ 'then Jesus spoke to the crowds and to his disciples' Mt 23.1.

33.71 προσλαλέω – 'to speak to, to address.' οἵτινες προσλαλοῦντες αὐτοῖς ἔπειθον αὐτοὺς προσμένειν τῇ χάριτι τοῦ θεοῦ 'they spoke to them and encouraged them to keep on living in the grace of God' Ac 13.43.[16]

33.72 προσαγωγή, ῆς f: the right or opportunity to address someone, implying higher status of the person addressed – 'approach, access.' ἐν ᾧ ἔχομεν τὴν παρρησίαν καὶ προσ-

---

15 ἀναγινώσκω and ἀνάγνωσις are placed here as a type of semantic converse of γράφω (33.61) and related terms meaning 'to write.'

16 It is possible that in Ac 13.43 προσλαλέω implies some degree of reciprocal response, in view of the prepositional prefix προσ-.

ἀγωγὴν ἐν πεποιθήσει 'because of him we have boldness to address him with confidence' Eph 3.12.

33.73 ἐκλαλέω: to speak out about something – 'to tell, to inform, to report on.' μηδενὶ ἐκλαλῆσαι ὅτι ταῦτα ἐνεφάνισας πρός με 'don't inform anyone that you have reported this to me' or 'don't tell anyone that . . .' Ac 23.22.

33.74 στόμα^b, τος *n*; γλῶσσα^d, ης *f*; χεῖλος^b, ους *n*: (figurative extensions of meaning of στόμα^a 'mouth,' 8.19; γλῶσσα^a 'tongue,' 8.21; and χεῖλος 'lip,' not occurring in the NT) to communicate orally – 'speech, to speak.'
στόμα^b: ἣν προεῖπεν τὸ πνεῦμα τὸ ἅγιον διὰ στόματος Δαυίδ 'which the Holy Spirit spoke beforehand by means of what David said' Ac 1.16.
γλῶσσα^d: ἠγαλλιάσατο ἡ γλῶσσά μου 'my speech exulted' Ac 2.26.
χεῖλος^b: τοῦτ' ἔστιν καρπὸν χειλέων ὁμολογούντων τῷ ὀνόματι αὐτοῦ 'which is the offering of our lips confessing his name' He 13.15.

33.75 στόμα^c, τος *n*; γλῶσσα^c, ης *f*: (figurative extensions of meaning of στόμα^a 'mouth,' 8.19; and γλῶσσα^a 'tongue,' 8.21) the faculty or capacity for speech – 'speech, ability to speak.' ἀνεῴχθη δὲ τὸ στόμα αὐτοῦ παραχρῆμα καὶ ἡ γλῶσσα αὐτοῦ 'and immediately his speech was restored' Lk 1.64. In Lk 1.64 στόμα and γλῶσσα appear to have the same referent and therefore may be regarded as essentially synonymous.

33.76 φθέγγομαι; ἀποφθέγγομαι: to speak, with focus upon verbal sound rather than upon content – 'to speak, to utter.'
φθέγγομαι: παρήγγειλαν τὸ καθόλου μὴ φθέγγεσθαι 'they ordered them not to speak at all' Ac 4.18.
ἀποφθέγγομαι: ἤρξαντο λαλεῖν ἑτέραις γλώσσαις καθὼς τὸ πνεῦμα ἐδίδου ἀποφθέγγεσθαι αὐτοῖς 'they began to talk in other languages, as the Spirit enabled them to speak' Ac 2.4.

33.77 φωνέω^b; ἀναφωνέω; ἐπιφωνέω: to speak with considerable volume or loudness –

'to cry out, to shout, to call out, to speak loudly.'[17]
φωνέω^b: αὐτὸς δὲ κρατήσας τῆς χειρὸς αὐτῆς ἐφώνησεν 'he took her by the hand and called out' Lk 8.54.
ἀναφωνέω: ἀνεφώνησεν κραυγῇ μεγάλῃ 'he spoke in a loud voice' Lk 1.42.
ἐπιφωνέω: ἄλλοι δὲ ἄλλο τι ἐπεφώνουν ἐν τῷ ὄχλῳ 'some in the crowd shouted one thing; others, something else' Ac 21.34.

33.78 ἐπαίρω φωνήν: (an idiom, literally 'to raise the voice') to increase the volume with which one speaks, so as to overcome existing noise or the speech of someone else – 'to raise the voice, to cry out, to speak loudly.' ἐπάρασά τις φωνὴν γυνή 'a woman raised her voice' or '. . . cried out' Lk 11.27.

33.79 προσφωνέω^b: to call out, with the probable implication of seeking some response – 'to call out to.' ὅμοιοί εἰσιν παιδίοις τοῖς . . . προσφωνοῦσιν ἀλλήλοις 'they are like children who . . . call out to one another' Lk 7.32.[18]

33.80 φωνή^c, ῆς *f*: the sound of a cry or shout – 'cry, shout.' φωνὴ ἐν Ῥαμὰ ἠκούσθη 'a cry was heard in Ramah' Mt 2.18.

33.81 βοάω; ἀναβοάω: to cry or shout with unusually loud volume – 'to cry out, to scream, to shout.'
βοάω: βοῶντες μὴ δεῖν αὐτὸν ζῆν μηκέτι 'they scream that he should not live any longer' Ac 25.24.
ἀναβοάω: περὶ δὲ τὴν ἐνάτην ὥραν ἀνεβόησεν ὁ Ἰησοῦς φωνῇ μεγάλῃ 'at about three o'clock, Jesus cried out with a loud shout' Mt 27.46.

33.82 βοή, ῆς *f*: the sound of shouting or crying out – 'cry, shout.' αἱ βοαὶ τῶν θερισάν-

17 It is possible that ἀναφωνέω implies somewhat greater volume of sound than φωνέω^b and that ἐπιφωνέω focuses more upon the content or upon the person or persons to whom a message is directed, but these distinctions cannot be readily determined on the basis of available contexts.
18 In view of the occurrence of the prefix προσ- in a reciprocal sense in a number of contexts, particularly in Classical Greek, it may very well be that in the use of προσφωνέω in Lk 7.32 there is a measure of reciprocity implied in addition to the reciprocal pronoun.

τῶν εἰς τὰ ὦτα κυρίου Σαβαὼθ εἰσεληλύθασιν 'the cries of the harvesters have reached the ears of the Lord Almighty' Jas 5.4.

33.83 κράζω; ἀνακράζω; κραυγάζω: to shout or cry out, with the possible implication of the unpleasant nature of the sound – 'to shout, to scream.'[19]
κράζω: ἠκολούθησαν αὐτῷ δύο τυφλοὶ κράζοντες καὶ λέγοντες, Ἐλέησον ἡμᾶς 'two blind men followed him and shouted, Have mercy on us' Mt 9.27.
ἀνακράζω: ἔδοξαν ὅτι φάντασμά ἐστιν, καὶ ἀνέκραξαν 'they thought that it was a ghost and screamed' Mk 6.49.
κραυγάζω: οἱ δὲ Ἰουδαῖοι ἐκραύγασαν λέγοντες 'the Jews shouted and said' Jn 19.12.

33.84 κραυγή[a], ῆς f: the sound of a loud scream or shout – 'cry, shout, scream.' μέσης δὲ νυκτὸς κραυγὴ γέγονεν 'and when it was midnight, a cry rang out' Mt 25.6.

33.85 ῥήγνυμι[b]: to suddenly break out into shouting – 'to begin to shout, to shout.' ῥῆξον καὶ βόησον 'shout and cry (with joy)' Ga 4.27. In Ga 4.27 the combination ῥῆξον καὶ βόησον may be analyzed either as two expressions for shouting, for example, 'break into shouting and shout,' or ῥῆξον may function primarily as an aspectual qualifier of βόησον, so that the meaning of the expression ῥῆξον καὶ βόησον may be 'break into shouting' or 'begin to shout,' but the beginning of shouting would imply considerable energy, spontaneity, and suddenness. For this interpretation of ῥήγνυμι in Ga 4.27, see 68.81.

33.86 προλέγω[a]: to speak beforehand or in advance – 'to say already' or, in written discourse, 'to quote above.' καθὼς προείρηται 'as has been said above' He 4.7.

33.87 πολυλογία, ας f: to speak for a long time or much – 'many words, long speaking.' δοκοῦσιν γὰρ ὅτι ἐν τῇ πολυλογίᾳ αὐτῶν εἰσακουσθήσονται 'for they think that they will be heard because of their many words' Mt 6.7.

33.88 βατταλογέω[a]: to speak much or extensively, with a possible added implication of meaningless words – 'to use many words, to speak for a long time.' προσευχόμενοι δὲ μὴ βατταλογήσητε ὥσπερ οἱ ἐθνικοί 'and when you pray, do not use many words like the heathen' Mt 6.7. For another interpretation of βατταλογέω in Mt 6.7, see 33.89.[20]

33.89 βατταλογέω[b]: to utter senseless sounds or to speak indistinctly and incoherently – 'to babble.' προσευχόμενοι δὲ μὴ βατταλογήσητε ὥσπερ οἱ ἐθνικοί 'and when you pray, do not babble like the heathen' Mt 6.7. For another interpretation of βατταλογέω in Mt 6.7, see 33.88.
In some languages the equivalent of 'to babble' is 'to speak like a baby' or 'to speak sounds that make no sense.'

33.90 παρρησιάζομαι[a]: (derivative of παρρησία 'boldness,' 25.158) to speak openly about something and with complete confidence – 'to speak boldly, to speak openly.' εἰσελθὼν δὲ εἰς τὴν συναγωγὴν ἐπαρρησιάζετο 'he went into the synagogue and spoke boldly' Ac 19.8. In some languages the equivalent of 'to speak boldly' is 'to speak regardless of who is listening' or 'to speak without fearing' or 'to speak without worrying.'

33.91 πρὸς τὸ οὖς λαλέω: (an idiom, literally 'to speak to the ear') to speak quietly and presumably to a restricted audience – 'to whisper, to speak quietly.' ὃ πρὸς τὸ οὖς ἐλαλήσατε ἐν τοῖς ταμείοις κηρυχθήσεται ἐπὶ τῶν δωμάτων 'whatever you have whispered in the inner room will be shouted from the housetops' Lk 12.3. For another treatment of the phrase πρὸς τὸ οὖς, see 28.73.

---

19 It is possible that ἀνακράζω suggests a somewhat louder and more piercing cry than κράζω. In Ac 24.21 ἐκέκραξα may be understood as a reduplicated aorist of κοάζω.

20 βατταλογέω in the sense of 'to babble' or 'to utter senseless sounds' is treated in 33.89. The justification for βατταλογέω in the sense of 'to speak much' is probably to be found in the context of Mt 6.7, where the term πολυλογία (33.87) appears to be an explanation of the meaning of βατταλογέω.

33.92 εἰσφέρω εἰς τὰς ἀκοάς[b]: (an idiom, literally 'to bring into the ears') to bring something to the attention of people by means of speech, but probably not in a formal or open manner – 'to bring to the attention of, to speak about to.' ξενίζοντα γάρ τινα εἰσφέρεις εἰς τὰς ἀκοὰς ἡμῶν 'you speak to us about strange things' Ac 17.20. For another interpretation of this idiom in Ac 17.20, see 24.55.

33.93 ὀνομάζω[c]: to speak of something by mentioning the name of it – 'to mention, to speak about.' πλεονεξία μηδὲ ὀνομαζέσθω ἐν ὑμῖν 'greed should not even be mentioned among you' Eph 5.3. There may, however, be certain problems involved in translating ὀνομάζω in Eph 5.3, for the text does not mean that one should never use a term such as πλεονεξία 'greed' (25.22). The meaning is simply that there should never be a reason for having to speak about greed, since the people should not themselves be guilty of such behavior.

33.94 ῥητῶς: pertaining to what is spoken or has been spoken – 'thusly, just as said, in so many words.' τὸ δὲ πνεῦμα ῥητῶς λέγει 'the Spirit speaks thusly' or 'this is exactly what the Spirit says' 1 Tm 4.1.

33.95 ἄρρητος, ον: pertaining to what cannot or must not be spoken – 'what cannot be spoken.' ἤκουσεν ἄρρητα ῥήματα 'he heard things that cannot be put into words' 2 Cor 12.4.

33.96 ἀλάλητος, ον; ἀνεκλάλητος, ον: pertaining to what cannot be uttered or expressed – 'what cannot be expressed in words.'[21]
ἀλάλητος: αὐτὸ τὸ πνεῦμα ὑπερεντυγχάνει στεναγμοῖς ἀλαλήτοις 'the Spirit himself intercedes with groans that cannot be expressed in words' Ro 8.26.
ἀνεκλάλητος: ἀγαλλιᾶσθε χαρᾷ ἀνεκλαλήτῳ καὶ δεδοξασμένῃ 'you rejoice with a glorious joy which words cannot express' 1 Pe 1.8.

21 It is possible that ἀνεκλάλητος is somewhat more forceful in meaning than ἀλάλητος, but this cannot be determined from NT usage.

33.97 λόγια, ων [n] (only in the plural): the content of various utterances – 'sayings, oracles, message.' χρείαν ἔχετε τοῦ διδάσκειν ὑμᾶς τινὰ τὰ στοιχεῖα τῆς ἀρχῆς τῶν λογίων τοῦ θεοῦ 'you need someone to teach you the first lessons about the message of God' He 5.12; ὃς ἐδέξατο λόγια ζῶντα δοῦναι ἡμῖν 'who received the living oracles to give to us' Ac 7.38.

33.98 ῥῆμα[b], τος [n]; λόγος[a], ου [m] (derivative of λέγω[a] 'to say,' 33.69): that which has been stated or said, with primary focus upon the content of the communication – 'word, saying, message, statement, question.'
ῥῆμα[b]: ἀλλ' ἐπὶ παντὶ ῥήματι ἐκπορευομένῳ διὰ στόματος θεοῦ 'but by every word that comes from the mouth of God' Mt 4.4.
λόγος[a]: πολλῷ πλείους ἐπίστευσαν διὰ τὸν λόγον αὐτοῦ 'many more believed because of what he said' Jn 4.41. In Mt 21.24 λόγος may be rendered as 'question' in view of the preceding ἐρωτάω, but the meaning of 'question' is, of course, derived essentially from the verb ἐρωτάω[a] 'to ask' (33.180).
Any difference of meaning between λόγος[a] and ῥῆμα[b] would be only a matter of stylistic usage.

33.99 λόγος[b], ου [m]: the act of speaking – 'speaking, speech.' ἐκάλουν . . . Παῦλον Ἑρμῆν, ἐπειδὴ αὐτὸς ἦν ὁ ἡγούμενος τοῦ λόγου 'they gave . . . Paul the name Hermes, because he took the lead in speaking' Ac 14.12.

33.100 λόγος[e], οῦ [m]: a title for Jesus in the Gospel of John as a reference to the content of God's revelation and as a verbal echo of the use of the verbs meaning 'to speak' in Genesis 1 and in many utterances of the prophets – 'Word, Message.' ὁ λόγος σὰρξ ἐγένετο καὶ ἐσκήνωσεν ἐν ἡμῖν 'the Word became a human being and lived among us' Jn 1.14.

33.101 λαλιά[a], ᾶς [f] (derivative of λαλέω 'to speak,' 33.70); στόμα[d], τος [n] (derivative of στόμα[b] 'speech,' 33.74); γλῶσσα[f], ης [f] (derivative of γλῶσσα[d] 'speech,' 33.74): that which has been spoken or uttered – 'what is said, talk, utterance.'
λαλιά[a]: οὐκέτι διὰ τὴν σὴν λαλιὰν πιστεύομεν· αὐτοὶ γὰρ ἀκηκόαμεν 'we believe now, not

because of what you said, but because we ourselves have heard him' Jn 4.42.

στόμα[d]: λέγει αὐτῷ, Ἐκ τοῦ στόματός σου κρινῶ σε, πονηρὲ δοῦλε 'he said to him, You bad servant! I will condemn you by your own words' Lk 19.22.

γλῶσσα[f]: μὴ ἀγαπῶμεν λόγῳ μηδὲ τῇ γλώσσῃ 'our love should not be just words and talk' 1 Jn 3.18.

33.102 λαλιά[b], ᾶς f: a particular manner of speech – 'accent, the way one speaks.' ἡ λαλιά σου δῆλόν σε ποιεῖ 'the way you speak gives you away' or 'your accent makes it clear who you are' Mt 26.73.

33.103 φωνή[b], ῆς f: the human voice as an instrument of communication – 'voice.' φωνὴ ἐγένετο ἐκ τῆς νεφέλης λέγουσα 'a voice said from the cloud' Lk 9.35.

In a number of languages one cannot speak of a voice without identifying who is speaking, and since the context indicates clearly that this is God, one can only say 'God's voice came from the cloud' or 'God spoke from a cloud.'

33.104 φθόγγος[b], ου m: (derivative of φθέγγομαι 'to utter,' 33.76) an utterance, with possible focus upon the clarity of the verbal sounds – 'utterance, message, what is uttered.' εἰς πᾶσαν τὴν γῆν ἐξῆλθεν ὁ φθόγγος αὐτῶν 'their message went out to all the world' Ro 10.18.

33.105 δίδωμι στόμα: (an idiom, literally 'to give mouth') to cause someone to have something to say – 'to help someone to say something, to give someone something to say.' ἐγὼ γὰρ δώσω ὑμῖν στόμα 'I will give you something to say' Lk 21.15.

33.106 κωφός[a], ή, όν; ἄφωνος[a], ον; ἄλαλος, ον: pertaining to not being able to speak or talk – 'dumb, mute, unable to speak, incapable of talking.'
κωφός[a]: ἦν ἐκβάλλων δαιμόνιον, καὶ αὐτὸ ἦν κωφόν 'he drove out a demon that could not talk' Lk 11.14.
ἄφωνος[a]: ὑποζύγιον ἄφωνον 'a mute beast of burden' 2 Pe 2.16.

ἄλαλος: τοὺς κωφοὺς ποιεῖ ἀκούειν καὶ τοὺς ἀλάλους λαλεῖν 'he makes the deaf to hear and the dumb to speak' Mk 7.37.

33.107 μογιλάλος, ον: pertaining to being almost mute – 'hardly able to speak, having difficulty in speaking.' φέρουσιν αὐτῷ κωφὸν καὶ μογιλάλον 'they brought him a man who was deaf and could hardly speak' Mk 7.32.[22] In translating μογιλάλος it may be necessary in some instances to use a descriptive phrase, for example, 'when he spoke, people could hardly understand' or 'he spoke in such a way that people had difficulty in understanding.'

33.108 ἐνεός, ά, όν: pertaining to incapacity to speak, whether temporary or permanent, but in the NT only temporary and associated with fright or amazement – 'speechless, dumbfounded.' οἱ δὲ ἄνδρες οἱ συνοδεύοντες αὐτῷ εἱστήκεισαν ἐνεοί 'the men who were travelling with him stood there, speechless' Ac 9.7.

G Sing, Lament (33.109-33.116)

33.109 ᾄδω: to utter words in a melodic pattern – 'to sing.' ᾄδουσιν ὡς ᾠδὴν καινὴν ἐνώπιον τοῦ θρόνου 'they stood facing the throne and sang a new song' Re 14.3.

33.110 ᾠδή, ῆς f: a particular melodic pattern with verbal content – 'song.' ᾄδουσιν ὡς ᾠδὴν καινὴν ἐνώπιον τοῦ θρόνου 'they stood facing the throne and sang a new song' Re 14.3. In a number of languages it is impossible to use a combination such as 'to sing a new song.' One can, however, often use an expression such as 'to sing with new words' or 'to utter a new song.'

In employing terms for 'to sing' or 'song,' it is important to avoid an expression which will apply only to some restricted type of music, for example, translated hymns using melodies from Western Europe.

---

22 Some have interpreted μογιλάλος in Mk 7.32 as meaning 'not able to speak,' but the context (especially Mk 7.35) seems to confirm the meaning of 'to speak with difficulty' or 'to be scarcely able to speak.'

33.111 ψάλλω: to sing songs of praise, with the possible implication of instrumental accompaniment (in the NT often related to the singing of OT psalms) – 'to sing, to sing a psalm, to sing a song of praise, to sing praises.' τῷ ὀνόματί σου ψαλῶ 'I will sing praises to your name' or 'I will sing praises to you' Ro 15.9.

33.112 ψαλμός, οῦ m: a song of praise (in the NT probably a reference to an OT psalm) – 'song of praise, psalm.' νουθετοῦντες ἑαυτοὺς ψαλμοῖς, ὕμνοις, ᾠδαῖς πνευματικαῖς 'instruct each other to sing psalms, hymns, and sacred songs' Col 3.16.

33.113 ὑμνέω: to sing a song associated with religion and worship – 'to sing a hymn, to sing a song of praise.' καὶ ὑμνήσαντες ἐξῆλθον εἰς τὸ Ὄρος τῶν Ἐλαιῶν 'then they sang a hymn and went out to the Mount of Olives' Mt 26.30.[23]

33.114 ὕμνος, ου m: a song with religious content – 'hymn.' λαλοῦντες ἑαυτοῖς ἐν ψαλμοῖς καὶ ὕμνοις καὶ ᾠδαῖς πνευματικαῖς 'speak to one another in psalms, hymns, and sacred songs' Eph 5.19.

33.115 θρηνέω[b]: to sing or chant expressions of mourning – 'to sing funeral songs, to chant a dirge.' ἐθρηνήσαμεν καὶ οὐκ ἐκλαύσατε 'we sang funeral songs, but you would not cry' Lk 7.32.

33.116 θρῆνος, ου m: a song expressing grief and mourning – 'song of grief, dirge.' θρῆνος καὶ κλαυθμός 'a song of grief and wailing' Mt 2.18 (apparatus).

H Keep Silent (33.117-33.125)

33.117 σιωπάω[a]: to refrain from speaking or talking – 'to keep quiet, to be silent.' ὁ δὲ ἐσιώπα καὶ οὐκ ἀπεκρίνατο οὐδέν 'he kept quiet and made no reply' Mk 14.61.

---

23 It is possible that the reference of ὑμνέω in Mt 26.30 is to the second part of the Hallel (Psalms 115-118). Accordingly, one could translate 'then they sang The Hymn . . .'

33.118 σιωπάω[b]: to lose or not have the ability to speak – 'to not be able to speak.' ἔσῃ σιωπῶν καὶ μὴ δυνάμενος λαλῆσαι ἄχρι ἧς ἡμέρας γένηται ταῦτα 'you will lose the ability to speak and will not be able to say anything until the day these things take place' Lk 1.20. It is possible, however, that σιωπάω in Lk 1.20 means only 'to say nothing' or 'to remain silent' (33.117) in which case it would probably be better to reverse somewhat the order and translate 'and you will not be able to speak but will remain silent until the day these things happen.'

33.119 ἡσυχάζω[c]; ἡσυχία[b], ας f: to maintain a state of silence, with a possible focus upon the attitude involved – 'to say nothing, to remain quiet.'
ἡσυχάζω[c]: ὁ Ἰησοῦς εἶπεν . . . Ἔξεστιν τῷ σαββάτῳ θεραπεῦσαι ἢ οὔ; οἱ δὲ ἡσύχασαν 'Jesus asked . . . Is healing allowed on the Sabbath or not? But they would not say a thing' Lk 14.3-4.
ἡσυχία[b]: ἀκούσαντες δὲ ὅτι τῇ Ἑβραΐδι διαλέκτῳ προσεφώνει αὐτοῖς μᾶλλον παρέσχον ἡσυχίαν 'when they heard him speaking to them in Hebrew, they were even quieter' Ac 22.2.

33.120 σιγή, ῆς f: the absence of noise – 'silence.' ἐγένετο σιγὴ ἐν τῷ οὐρανῷ ὡς ἡμιώριον 'and there was silence in heaven for half an hour' Re 8.1. It is possible that σιγή in Re 8.1 does not refer to verbal silence.

33.121 σιγάω: to keep quiet, with the implication of preserving something which is secret – 'to keep quiet about, to say nothing about.' αὐτοὶ ἐσίγησαν καὶ οὐδενὶ ἀπήγγειλαν 'they kept quiet (about all this) and told no one' Lk 9.36.

33.122 φιμοῦμαι: to have nothing to say, with the implication of being prevented from speaking (compare φιμός 'muzzle,' not occurring in the NT) – 'to have nothing to say, to say nothing.' λέγει αὐτῷ, Ἑταῖρε, πῶς εἰσῆλθες ὧδε μὴ ἔχων ἔνδυμα γάμου; ὁ δὲ ἐφιμώθη 'he asked him, Friend, how did you get in here without wedding clothes? But he had nothing to say' Mt 22.12.

33.123 φιμόω[b]: to cause someone to have nothing to say – 'to silence.' οἱ δὲ Φαρισαῖοι ἀκούσαντες ὅτι ἐφίμωσεν τοὺς Σαδδουκαίους 'when the Pharisees heard that he had silenced the Sadducees' Mt 22.34.

33.124 ἐπιστομίζω: to cause someone to stop talking – 'to silence, to keep someone from speaking.' οὓς δεῖ ἐπιστομίζειν, οἵτινες ὅλους οἴκους ἀνατρέπουσιν 'it is necessary to silence them, for they are upsetting whole families' Tt 1.11.

33.125 στόμα φράσσω[a]: (an idiom, literally 'to block the mouth') to cause someone not to have anything to say – 'to silence, to remove any reason to speak.' ἵνα πᾶν στόμα φραγῇ 'in order to stop everyone from having anything to say' Ro 3.19.

I Name (33.126-33.133)

33.126 ὄνομα[a], **τος** *n*: the proper name of a person or object – 'name.' τῶν δὲ δώδεκα ἀποστόλων τὰ ὀνόματά ἐστιν ταῦτα 'these are the names of the twelve apostles' Mt 10.2.

33.127 χρηματίζω[b]; **προσαγορεύω; ὀνομάζω**[a]: to give a name or title to – 'to call, to give a name to, to give a title to.'
χρηματίζω[b]: χρηματίσαι τε πρώτως ἐν Ἀντιοχείᾳ τοὺς μαθητὰς Χριστιανούς 'it was at Antioch that the disciples were first called Christians' Ac 11.26.
προσαγορεύω: προσαγορευθεὶς ὑπὸ τοῦ θεοῦ ἀρχιερεύς 'God called him high priest' He 5.10.
ὀνομάζω[a]: οὓς καὶ ἀποστόλους ὠνόμασεν 'whom he called apostles' Mk 3.14; Σίμωνα, ὃν καὶ ὠνόμασεν Πέτρον 'Simon, to whom he also gave the name Peter' Lk 6.14.

33.128 ἐπιτίθημι ὄνομα: (an idiom, literally 'to place a name') to give a name to, with the possible implication of an additional name – 'to name, to give a name to.' ἐπέθηκεν ὄνομα τῷ Σίμωνι Πέτρον 'to Simon, he gave the name Peter' Mk 3.16.[24]

---

24 In Lk 6.14, which is parallel to Mk 3.16, Luke uses ὀνομάζω meaning simply 'to name' (see 33.127).

33.129 καλέω[a]; **λέγω**[b]; **ἐπιλέγω**: to speak of a person or object by means of a proper name – 'to call, to name.'
καλέω[a]: εἰς πόλιν Δαυὶδ ἥτις καλεῖται βηθλέεμ 'to the town of David, which is called Bethlehem' Lk 2.4.
λέγω[b]: οὐχ ἡ μήτηρ αὐτοῦ λέγεται Μαριάμ 'isn't his mother called Mary' Mt 13.55.
ἐπιλέγω: κολυμβήθρα ἡ ἐπιλεγομένη Ἑβραϊστὶ Βηθζαθά 'a pool called Bethzatha in the Hebrew language' Jn 5.2.

33.130 ψευδώνυμος, ον: pertaining to being falsely or wrongly called by a name – 'falsely called, falsely named.' ἀντιθέσεις τῆς ψευδωνύμου γνώσεως 'arguments of what is wrongly called knowledge' 1 Tm 6.20.

33.131 καλέω[b]; **λέγω**[c]; **φωνέω**[c]; **ἐπικαλέω**: to use an attribution in speaking of a person – 'to call, to name.'
καλέω[b]: φίλος θεοῦ ἐκλήθη 'he was called the friend of God' Jas 2.23; καλέσουσιν τὸ ὄνομα αὐτοῦ Ἐμμανουήλ 'they will call his name Emmanuel' Mt 1.23.
λέγω[c]: αὐτὸς Δαυὶδ λέγει αὐτὸν κύριον 'David himself called him Lord' Mk 12.37.
φωνέω[c]: ὑμεῖς φωνεῖτέ με Ὁ διδάσκαλος 'you call me Teacher' Jn 13.13.
ἐπικαλέω: εἰ τὸν οἰκοδεσπότην Βεελζεβοὺλ ἐπεκάλεσαν 'if they have called the head of the family Beelzebul' Mt 10.25.

It is not always possible to determine from the context whether the act involved is an initial naming of a person or simply calling a person by a particular name. Likewise in the case of attributions or titles, it is not always possible to determine whether it is a matter of giving an attribution or title to a person or simply a matter of speaking of or to a person by means of such an attribution or title. In some instances the giving of a title may be made indirect. For example, in Mt 1.23 the statement 'and they will call his name Emmanuel' suggests the giving of a title, but the process is stated in terms of how people will speak of this person.

33.132 ἐπονομάζομαι: to classify oneself by means of a name, title, or attribution – 'to call oneself, to regard oneself.' εἰ δὲ σὺ Ἰουδαῖος ἐπονομάζῃ 'and if you call yourself a Jew' Ro 2.17.

33.133 ὀνομάζω[b]: to utter a name in a ritual context (without directly referring to the person or speaking about the person in question) – 'to pronounce a name, to call out a name.' ὀνομάζειν ἐπὶ τοὺς ἔχοντας τὰ πνεύματα τὰ πονηρὰ τὸ ὄνομα τοῦ κυρίου Ἰησοῦ 'to call out the name of the Lord Jesus over those who had evil spirits' Ac 19.13.

J   Interpret, Mean, Explain[25] (33.134-33.155)

33.134 δύναμις[f], εως *f*: the meaning or significance of a word or statement – 'meaning, what is intended.' ἐὰν οὖν μὴ εἰδῶ τὴν δύναμιν τῆς φωνῆς 'if I do not know the meaning of the language' 1 Cor 14.11. It is, of course, also possible to translate 1 Cor 14.11 as 'if I cannot understand what has been said.'

33.135 ἄφωνος[b], ον: pertaining to being without meaning – 'without meaning, meaningless.' καὶ οὐδὲν ἄφωνον 'yet not one is without meaning' 1 Cor 14.10. Rather than use a double negative expression in rendering this phrase in 1 Cor 14.10, it may be better in many languages to use a positive expression, for example, 'yet all can be understood' or 'yet all have meaning.'

33.136 θέλει εἶναι: (an idiom, literally 'it wishes to be') something which is to mean or to be understood in a particular manner – 'it means, this is to be understood as.' διηπόρουν, ἄλλος πρὸς ἄλλον λέγοντες, Τί θέλει τοῦτο εἶναι; 'they were confused and kept asking each other, What does this mean?' Ac 2.12. The question in Ac 2.12 does not refer to the immediate meaning of the particular expression but rather to its broader implications, so

that the question may very well be rendered as 'what does this say' or 'what does this imply?'

33.137 ἄφες τοὺς νεκροὺς θάψαι τοὺς ἑαυτῶν νεκρούς: (an idiom, possibly an adage, literally 'let the dead bury their dead') the matter in question is not the real issue – 'that is not what I mean, that is not the issue, that is not the point.' εἶπεν δὲ αὐτῷ, Ἄφες τοὺς νεκροὺς θάψαι τοὺς ἑαυτῶν νεκρούς, σὺ δὲ ἀπελθὼν διάγγελλε τὴν βασιλείαν τοῦ θεοῦ 'but he said to him, That is not the issue; you go and announce the kingdom of God' Lk 9.60. Some scholars, however, understand this expression as merely a figurative reference to various types of people and thus translate 'let those who are spiritually dead take care of their own dead.'

33.138 λέγω[d]: to mark the correspondence in the meaning of foreign expressions – 'to mean.' μαθήτρια ὀνόματι Ταβιθά, ἣ διερμηνευομένη λέγεται Δορκάς 'a disciple named Tabitha, which interpreted means Dorcas' Ac 9.36. The meaning of λέγω[d] must often be expressed in rather specific ways, for example, 'which says in our language' or 'what is the same as what we say in our language.'

33.139 ὡς ἔπος εἰπεῖν: (an idiom, literally 'as to speak a word') an expression used to introduce an alternative form of expression as an interpretation of what has been said – 'that is, that is to say, so to speak, in a sense.' καὶ ὡς ἔπος εἰπεῖν, δι' Ἀβραὰμ καὶ Λευὶ ὁ δεκάτας λαμβάνων δεδεκάτωται 'and in a sense, through Abraham even Levi who receives the tenth, paid the tenth' He 7.9.

33.140 φημί[b]; λέγω[e]: to say something in order to explain more fully the implications or intent of what has been said – 'to mean, to imply.' φημί[b]: τοῦτο δέ φημι, ἀδελφοί, ὁ καιρὸς συνεσταλμένος ἐστίν 'this is what I mean, fellow believers; there is not much time left' 1 Cor 7.29. λέγω[e]: τοῦτο δὲ λέγω 'but this is what I mean' Ga 3.17.

---

25 As will be readily noted, a number of meanings in Subdomain J *Interpret, Mean, Explain* parallel closely or overlap with such domains as *Know* (28), especially in the meaning of 'to cause to know,' and *Understand* (32), likewise in the meaning of 'to cause to understand.' In Subdomain J, however, the focus is on communicating the significance of something.

33.141 ἐπιλύω[a]; ἐπίλυσις, εως *f*; φράζω: to explain the meaning of something, with the implication that the text in question is difficult or complex – 'to explain, meaning, explanation.'

ἐπιλύω[a]: κατ᾽ ἰδίαν δὲ τοῖς ἰδίοις μαθηταῖς ἐπέλυεν πάντα 'but when he was alone with his disciples, he would explain everything' Mk 4.34.

ἐπίλυσις: πᾶσα προφητεία γραφῆς ἰδίας ἐπιλύσεως οὐ γίνεται 'no one can explain by himself a prophecy in the Scriptures' 2 Pe 1.20. In 2 Pe 1.20 ἐπίλυσις clearly involves the interpretation, not the formulation, of a text.

φράζω: φράσον ἡμῖν τὴν παραβολὴν ταύτην 'explain to us what this parable means' Mt 15.15.

33.142 διανοίγω[b]: to explain something which has been previously hidden or obscure – 'to explain, to open up, to make evident.' διήνοιγεν ἡμῖν τὰς γραφάς 'he explained the Scriptures to us' Lk 24.32.

33.143 διασαφέω[a]: to make an obscurity clear by a thorough explanation – 'to make clear, to make evident, to explain.' διασάφησον ἡμῖν τὴν παραβολὴν τῶν ζιζανίων τοῦ ἀγροῦ 'explain to us what the parable of the weeds in the field means' Mt 13.36.

33.144 πληρόω[f]: to give the true or complete meaning to something – 'to give the true meaning to, to provide the real significance of.' οὐκ ἦλθον καταλῦσαι ἀλλὰ πληρῶσαι 'I did not come to destroy but to give true meaning to' Mt 5.17; ὁ γὰρ πᾶς νόμος ἐν ἑνὶ λόγῳ πεπλήρωται, ἐν τῷ Ἀγαπήσεις τὸν πλησίον σου ὡς σεαυτόν 'for the whole Law has its true meaning in one expression, Love your neighbor as yourself' Ga 5.14. In speaking of 'true meaning,' it may be useful in some languages to use a phrase meaning 'real intent' or 'real purpose.'

33.145 ἑρμηνεύω; μεθερμηνεύω; διερμηνεύω[a]: to translate from one language to another – 'to translate, to interpret.'

ἑρμηνεύω: Σιλωάμ (ὃ ἑρμηνεύεται Ἀπεσταλμένος) 'Siloam (which is interpreted Sent)' Jn 9.7; Μελχισέδεκ ... ἑρμηνευόμενος βασιλεὺς δικαιοσύνης 'Melchizedek ... translated king of righteousness' He 7.1-2.

μεθερμηνεύω: Ταλιθα κουμ, ὅ ἐστιν μεθερμηνευόμενον Τὸ κοράσιον, σοὶ λέγω, ἔγειρε 'Talitha koum, which in translation is, Girl, I say to you, Arise' Mk 5.41.

διερμηνεύω[a]: Ταβιθά, ἣ διερμηνευομένη λέγεται Δορκάς 'Tabitha, which in translation means Dorcas' Ac 9.36.

In a number of languages the equivalent of 'to translate' or 'to interpret' is an idiomatic expression, for example, 'it comes out in our language as' or 'in our words it means' or 'in our mouths it says.'

33.146 διερμηνευτής, οῦ *m*: (derivative of διερμηνεύω[a] 'to translate,' 33.145) a person who interprets or translates – 'interpreter, translator.' ἐὰν δὲ μὴ ᾖ διερμηνευτής, σιγάτω 'and if there is no interpreter present, no one should speak' 1 Cor 14.28.

33.147 ἑρμηνεία, ας *f*: capacity or ability to interpret or translate – 'translating, interpreting, interpretation.' ἄλλῳ δὲ ἑρμηνεία γλωσσῶν 'but to another, the interpretation of tongues' 1 Cor 12.10.

33.148 διερμηνεύω[b]: to explain on a more extensive and formal level the meaning of something which is particularly obscure or difficult to comprehend – 'to explain, to interpret.' διερμήνευσεν αὐτοῖς ἐν πάσαις ταῖς γραφαῖς τὰ περὶ ἑαυτοῦ 'he interpreted to them what was said about him in all the Scriptures' Lk 24.27.

33.149 δυσερμήνευτος, ον: pertaining to being difficult to explain or interpret – 'difficult to explain, hard to interpret.' περὶ οὗ πολὺς ἡμῖν ὁ λόγος καὶ δυσερμήνευτος λέγειν 'I have much to say about the matter, but it is difficult to explain it (to you)' He 5.11.

33.150 δείκνυμι[b]; ὑποδείκνυμι[b]: to explain the meaning or significance of something by demonstration – 'to show, to explain, to make clear.'[26]

---

[26] There may very well be a slight difference of meaning between δείκνυμι[b] and ὑποδείκνυμι[b], but this cannot be determined from existing contexts.

δείκνυμιᵇ: ἔτι καθ' ὑπερβολὴν ὁδὸν ὑμῖν δείκνυμι 'I will show you a still more excellent way' 1 Cor 12.31. For another interpretation of δείκνυμι in 1 Cor 12.31, see 28.47.²⁷

ὑποδείκνυμιᵇ: ὑποδείξω ὑμῖν τίνι ἐστὶν ὅμοιος 'I will show you what he is like' Lk 6.47.

33.151 τίθημιᵈ; ἐκτίθεμαι; ἀνατίθεμαι: to explain something, presumably by putting forward additional or different information – 'to explain, to make clear.'

τίθημιᵈ: ἐν τίνι αὐτὴν παραβολῇ θῶμεν; 'what parable shall we use to explain it?' Mk 4.30.

ἐκτίθεμαι: ἀκριβέστερον αὐτῷ ἐξέθεντο τὴν ὁδὸν τοῦ θεοῦ 'they explained to him the way of God more accurately' Ac 18.26.

ἀνατίθεμαι: καὶ ἀνεθέμην αὐτοῖς τὸ εὐαγγέλιον ὃ κηρύσσω ἐν τοῖς ἔθνεσιν 'and I made clear to them the gospel which I was announcing to the Gentiles' Ga 2.2.

33.152 δηλόωᵇ: to make something evident or clear by explanation – 'to make clear, to make evident.' τὸ δέ, "Ἔτι ἅπαξ δηλοῖ 'the words "once more" make clear that . . .' He 12.27.

33.153 σημαίνω: to cause something to be both specific and clear – 'to indicate clearly, to make clear.' ἄλογον γάρ μοι δοκεῖ πέμποντα δέσμιον μὴ καὶ τὰς κατ' αὐτοῦ αἰτίας σημᾶναι 'for it seems unreasonable to me to send a prisoner without clearly indicating the charges against him' Ac 25.27.

33.154 συγκρίνωᵇ: to explain, primarily by means of comparison – 'to explain, to make clear.' πνευματικοῖς πνευματικὰ συγκρίνοντες 'we explain spiritual truths by means of

spiritual matters' 1 Cor 2.13. The expression πνευματικοῖς πνευματικὰ συγκρίνοντες in 1 Cor 2.13 is highly ambiguous and may mean, in addition to the rendering given here, 'we explain spiritual truths to those who have the Spirit' or 'we explain spiritual truths with words given by the Spirit.'

33.155 στρεβλόω: to distort the meaning of something in communicating to others – 'to distort, to misinterpret, to change the meaning of, to explain falsely.' δυσνόητά τινα, ἃ οἱ ἀμαθεῖς καὶ ἀστήρικτοι στρεβλοῦσιν 'difficult things to understand, which ignorant and unstable persons distort' or '. . . explain in a false manner' 2 Pe 3.16.

K Converse, Discuss²⁸ (33.156-33.160)

33.156 ὁμιλέω: to speak with someone, with the implication of a reversal of roles in communication – 'to talk (with), to speak (with).' αὐτοὶ ὡμίλουν πρὸς ἀλλήλους περὶ πάντων τῶν συμβεβηκότων τούτων 'they were talking to each other about all the things that had happened' Lk 24.14;²⁹ πυκνότερον αὐτὸν μεταπεμπόμενος ὡμίλει αὐτῷ 'frequently he sent for him and talked with him' Ac 24.26.

33.157 συνομιλέω; συλλαλέω; συλλογίζομαι; συζητέωᵇ: to converse with someone, including a clear implication as to reciprocal response – 'to talk with, to speak with, to converse.'

συνομιλέω: συνομιλῶν αὐτῷ εἰσῆλθεν '(Peter) kept on talking with him as he went in' Ac 10.27.

συλλαλέω: ὤφθη αὐτοῖς Ἠλίας σὺν Μωϋσεῖ, καὶ ἦσαν συλλαλοῦντες τῷ Ἰησοῦ 'they saw Elijah and Moses talking with Jesus' Mk 9.4.

συλλογίζομαι: οἱ δὲ συνελογίσαντο πρὸς ἑαυτούς 'they discussed the matter among themselves' Lk 20.5.

συζητέωᵇ: ἐθαμβήθησαν ἅπαντες, ὥστε συζητεῖν

---

27 The 'more excellent way' referred to in 1 Cor 12.31 consists of a verbal statement occurring in 1 Corinthians 13, so that in this context δείκνυμι refers to an oral communication, but the content of 1 Corinthians 13 involves far more than oral communication, so that in the context of 1 Cor 12.31, one is perfectly justified in analyzing the meaning as being essentially 'causing to know.' It is obviously very difficult to determine in the case of δείκνυμιᵇ and ὑποδείκνυμιᵇ whether the focus is upon the act of communication or upon the resulting knowledge or understanding of the receptors. The same type of difficulty occurs in the meanings listed in 33.151-33.154.

28 As the title of Subdomain K *Converse, Discuss* suggests, the meanings in this subdomain involve multiple participants in communication, both those who speak and those who are spoken to.

29 The reciprocity expressed in Lk 24.14 is indicated directly by the reciprocal pronouns.

πρὸς ἑαυτούς 'the people were amazed, so that they discussed among themselves' Mk 1.27.

33.158 διαλαλέω; διαλογίζομαι^b: to engage in some relatively detailed discussion of a matter – 'to converse, to discuss.'
διαλαλέω: διελάλουν πρὸς ἀλλήλους τί ἂν ποιήσαιεν τῷ Ἰησοῦ 'they were discussing among themselves what they could do to Jesus' Lk 6.11.
διαλογίζομαι^b: διελογίζοντο πρὸς ἀλλήλους 'they discussed the matter among themselves' Mk 8.16.

33.159 συμβάλλω^b: to confer, implying a series of proposals – 'to confer.' συνέβαλλον πρὸς ἀλλήλους 'they were conferring with each other' Ac 4.15. In some languages the equivalent of 'to confer' is 'to discuss what should be done' or 'to talk about plans.'

33.160 ἀντιβάλλω: to discuss, implying conflicting opinions – 'to discuss, to argue about.'
τίνες οἱ λόγοι οὗτοι οὓς ἀντιβάλλετε πρὸς ἀλλήλους περιπατοῦντες; 'what were you discussing as you walked along?' (literally 'what were the sayings you argued about with one another as you walked along?') Lk 24.17.

L Ask For, Request (33.161-33.177)

33.161 ἐρωτάω^b; ἐπερωτάω^b: to ask for, usually with the implication of an underlying question – 'to ask for, to request.'[30]
ἐρωτάω^b: ἠρώτα αὐτὸν ἵνα τὸ δαιμόνιον ἐκβάλῃ ἐκ τῆς θυγατρὸς αὐτῆς 'she asked him to drive the demon out of her daughter' Mk 7.26. See also footnote 33.
ἐπερωτάω^b: πειράζοντες ἐπηρώτησαν αὐτὸν σημεῖον 'they wanted to trap him, so they asked him (to perform) a miracle' Mt 16.1.

33.162 ἐπερώτημα, τος n: (derivative of ἐπερωτάω^b 'to ask for,' 33.161) that which is asked for – 'request, appeal.' βάπτισμα . . . ἀλλὰ συνειδήσεως ἀγαθῆς ἐπερώτημα εἰς θεόν

'but baptism . . . is a request to God for a good conscience' 1 Pe 3.21. It is also possible to interpret ἐπερώτημα in 1 Pe 3.21 as meaning 'pledge' or 'promise,' in which case it may be classified under 33.288. Accordingly, the phrase συνειδήσεως ἀγαθῆς ἐπερώτημα εἰς θεόν may be rendered as 'a promise made to God from a good conscience.'

33.163 αἰτέω; παραιτέομαι^a: to ask for with urgency, even to the point of demanding – 'to ask for, to demand, to plead for.'[31]
αἰτέω: αἴτησόν με ὃ ἐὰν θέλῃς, καὶ δώσω σοι 'ask me anything you want and I will give it to you' Mk 6.22; ᾐτήσατο τὸ σῶμα τοῦ Ἰησοῦ 'he asked for the body of Jesus' Mt 27.58; παντὶ τῷ αἰτοῦντι ὑμᾶς λόγον περὶ τῆς ἐν ὑμῖν ἐλπίδος 'to anyone who asks you for an account of your hope' or '. . . to give a reason for your hope' 1 Pe 3.15. See also footnote 33.
παραιτέομαι^a: κατὰ δὲ ἑορτὴν ἀπέλυεν αὐτοῖς ἕνα δέσμιον ὃν παρῃτοῦντο 'at every Passover Feast he would set free any prisoner the people asked for' Mk 15.6.

33.164 αἴτημα, τος n: (derivative of αἰτέω 'to ask for,' 33.163) that which is being asked for – 'request, demand, what was being asked for.' Πιλᾶτος ἐπέκρινεν γενέσθαι τὸ αἴτημα αὐτῶν 'Pilate passed the sentence that they were asking for' Lk 23.24.

33.165 ἀπαιτέω: to ask for something to be returned – 'to ask back.' ἀπὸ τοῦ αἴροντος τὰ σὰ μὴ ἀπαίτει 'when someone takes what is yours, do not ask for it back' Lk 6.30. In some languages it may be necessary to be quite specific and detailed in rendering ἀπαιτέω in Lk 6.30, for example, 'when someone takes from you what is yours, do not ask that he give it back to you.'

33.166 ἐξαιτέομαι: to ask for something and to receive what one has asked for – 'to ask for with success, to ask and to receive.' ὁ Σατανᾶς ἐξῃτήσατο ὑμᾶς τοῦ σινιάσαι ὡς τὸν σῖτον 'Satan

---

30 ἐπερωτάω^b may be somewhat more intensive in meaning than ἐρωτάω^b, but both seem to be somewhat weaker in urgency than αἰτέω and παραιτέομαι^a (33.163).

31 It is possible that παραιτέομαι^a differs somewhat from αἰτέω, both in intensity as well as in focusing upon the source from which the grant is to be made.

asked and received permission to sift you like wheat' Lk 22.31.

33.167 ζητέω^d: to ask for something which is being especially sought – 'to ask earnestly for, to demand.' ζητοῦντες παρ' αὐτοῦ σημεῖον 'they demanded that he perform a miracle' Mk 8.11. For another interpretation of ζητέω in Mk 8.11, see 57.59.

33.168 παρακαλέω^a; παράκλησις^b, εως *f*: to ask for something earnestly and with propriety – 'to ask for (earnestly), to request, to plead for, to appeal to, earnest request, appeal.'
παρακαλέω^a: διὰ ταύτην οὖν τὴν αἰτίαν παρεκάλεσα ὑμᾶς ἰδεῖν καὶ προσλαλῆσαι 'that is why I have earnestly asked to see you and to talk to you' Ac 28.20. It is also possible to interpret παρακαλέω in Ac 28.20 as meaning 'to call together' (see 33.310).
παράκλησις^b: μετὰ πολλῆς παρακλήσεως δεόμενοι ἡμῶν 'with an earnest appeal, they begged us' 2 Cor 8.4.

33.169 ἐντυγχάνω^a: to ask for something with urgency and intensity – 'to plead, to beg, to appeal to, to petition.' ὅτι κατὰ θεὸν ἐντυγχάνει ὑπὲρ ἁγίων 'for (the Spirit) pleads with God on behalf of his people' Ro 8.27; περὶ οὗ ἅπαν τὸ πλῆθος ἐνέτυχον μοι 'about whom all the people appealed to me' Ac 25.24. In translating expressions such as 'to plead' or 'to beg' or 'to appeal to,' the implications of urgency or intensity are often expressed in figurative ways, for example, 'to ask for with the heart exposed' or 'to ask for with crying words' or 'to beg with one's hands outstretched.'

33.170 δέομαι: to ask for with urgency, with the implication of presumed need – 'to plead, to beg.' δέομαί σου, μή με βασανίσῃς 'I beg you, don't punish me' Lk 8.28. See also footnote 33.

33.171 δέησις, εως *f*: (derivative of δέομαι 'to plead, to beg,' 33.170) that which is asked with urgency based on presumed need – 'request, plea, prayer.' μὴ φοβοῦ, Ζαχαρία, διότι εἰσηκούσθη ἡ δέησίς σου 'do not be afraid,

Zechariah! (God) has heard your prayer' Lk 1.13.³²

33.172 ἱκετηρία, ας *f*: that which is being urgently requested by a suppliant – 'plea, supplication.' ὃς ἐν ταῖς ἡμέραις τῆς σαρκὸς αὐτοῦ, δεήσεις τε καὶ ἱκετηρίας 'in his life on earth (Jesus made) his prayers and pleas (to God)' He 5.7.

33.173 ἐπαιτέω; προσαιτέω: to ask for charity – 'to beg.'
ἐπαιτέω: σκάπτειν οὐκ ἰσχύω, ἐπαιτεῖν αἰσχύνομαι 'I am not strong enough to dig, and I am ashamed to beg' Lk 16.3.
προσαιτέω: τυφλὸς ἐκάθητο παρὰ τὴν ὁδὸν προσαιτῶν 'a blind man was sitting and begging by the road' Mk 10.46 (apparatus).

33.174 προσαίτης, ου *m*: (derivative of προσαιτέω 'to beg,' 33.173) one who asks for charity – 'beggar.' οἱ θεωροῦντες αὐτὸν τὸ πρότερον ὅτι προσαίτης ἦν 'those who had seen him before this as a beggar' Jn 9.8.

33.175 προσανατίθεμαι^b: to ask someone for advice – 'to consult with, to ask advice of.' εὐθέως οὐ προσανεθέμην σαρκὶ καὶ αἵματι 'I did not go at once to ask advice of anyone' Ga 1.16. In rendering 'to ask advice of,' one may often employ an expression such as 'to ask what one should do' or 'to ask, What shall I do?'

33.176 ἐπικαλέομαι^a: to call upon someone to do something, normally implying an appeal for aid – 'to call upon, to appeal to, to ask for help.' ἐγὼ δὲ μάρτυρα τὸν θεὸν ἐπικαλοῦμαι 'I appeal to God to be my witness' 2 Cor 1.23.
ἐπικαλέομαι^a also occurs in such expressions as ὃς ἂν ἐπικαλέσηται τὸ ὄνομα κυρίου (Ac 2.21) 'whoever calls upon the name of the Lord,' but the meaning is essentially the same as 'to call upon the Lord,' since τὸ ὄνομα 'the name' may simply be a metonym for 'the Lord.'

---

32 Though δέησις basically means 'that which is asked for urgently,' in the NT it occurs only in connection with pleas made to God, and therefore it is properly translated as 'prayer' (see footnote 33).

33.177 καλῶς ᵉ: a marker of polite request – 'please.' σὺ κάθου ὧδε καλῶς 'please sit here' Jas 2.3. For another interpretation of καλῶς in Jas 2.3, see 87.25.

M Pray ³³ (33.178-33.179)

33.178 εὔχομαι ᵃ; προσεύχομαι; εὐχή ᵃ, ῆς f; προσευχή ᵃ, ῆς f: to speak to or to make requests of God – 'to pray, to speak to God, to ask God for, prayer.' ³⁴

εὔχομαι ᵃ: εὐχόμεθα δὲ πρὸς τὸν θεὸν μὴ ποιῆσαι ὑμᾶς κακὸν μηδέν 'we pray to God that you will do no wrong' 2 Cor 13.7.

προσεύχομαι: ἀνέβη εἰς τὸ ὄρος κατ' ἰδίαν προσεύξασθαι 'he went up a hill by himself to pray' Mt 14.23.

εὐχή ᵃ: ἡ εὐχὴ τῆς πίστεως σώσει τὸν κάμνοντα 'the prayer made in faith will save the sick person' Jas 5.15.

προσευχή ᵃ: ἔσται ὁ οἶκός μου οἶκος προσευχῆς 'my house will be a house of prayer' Lk 19.46.

In some languages there are a number of different terms used for prayer depending upon the nature of the content, for example, requests for material blessing, pleas for spiritual help, intercession for others, thanksgiving, and praise. There may also be important distinctions on the basis of urgency and need. The most generic expression for prayer may simply be 'to speak to God.' It is normally best to avoid an expression which means primarily 'to recite.'

33.179 προσευχή ᵇ, ῆς f: (derivative of προσεύχομαι 'to pray,' 33.178) a place where people customarily meet to pray – 'a place for prayer.' ἐξήλθομεν ἔξω τῆς πύλης παρὰ ποταμὸν οὗ ἐνομίζομεν προσευχὴν εἶναι 'we went out of the city (literally 'outside the gate') to the riverside where we thought there would be a place for prayer' Ac 16.13.

N Question, Answer (33.180-33.188)

33.180 ἐρωτάω ᵃ; ἐπερωτάω ᵃ: to ask for information – 'to ask, to ask a question.' ³⁵

ἐρωτάω ᵃ: ἐφοβοῦντο ἐρωτῆσαι αὐτὸν περὶ τοῦ ῥήματος τούτου 'they were afraid to ask him about this matter' Lk 9.45.

ἐπερωτάω ᵃ: ἐπηρώτα αὐτόν, Τί ὄνομά σοι; 'he asked him, What is your name?' Mk 5.9.

In a number of languages a term such as ἐρωτάω ᵃ or ἐπερωτάω ᵃ implies an introduction of direct discourse, so that in Lk 9.45, for example, it may be necessary to translate 'they were afraid to ask him, What do you mean by what you said?'

33.181 πυνθάνομαι ᵃ: to inquire about something – 'to inquire, to make an inquiry, to ask.' ἐπύθετο οὖν τὴν ὥραν παρ' αὐτῶν ἐν ᾗ κομψότερον ἔσχεν 'he inquired of them what time it was when (his son) got better' Jn 4.52.

33.182 ἐξετάζω ᵇ: to inquire intently, with the implication of careful examination – 'to inquire, to ask.' οὐδεὶς δὲ ἐτόλμα τῶν μαθητῶν ἐξετάσαι αὐτόν, Σὺ τίς εἶ; 'none of his disciples dared to ask him, Who are you?' Jn 21.12.

33.183 ἀποστοματίζω: to question someone with hostile intent – 'to ask hostile questions, to inquire with hostility.' ἤρξαντο οἱ γραμματεῖς καὶ οἱ Φαρισαῖοι δεινῶς ἐνέχειν καὶ ἀποστοματίζειν αὐτὸν περὶ πλειόνων 'the teachers of the Law and the Pharisees began to criticize him bitterly and to ask hostile questions about many things' Lk 11.53.

33.184 ἀποκρίνομαι ᵃ: to respond to a question asking for information – 'to answer, to reply.' ἠρώτησαν αὐτόν, ... Ὁ προφήτης εἶ σύ; καὶ ἀπεκρίθη, Οὔ 'they asked him, ... Are you the prophet? No, he replied' Jn 1.21.

---

33 In addition to the expressions listed in this subdomain, there are others which are often translated 'to pray' or 'prayer,' namely, ἐρωτάω ᵇ (33.161), αἰτέω (33.163), δέομαι (33.170), and δέησις (33.171), used exclusively of urgent requests to God and thus normally translated 'prayer,' though these terms do not mean 'prayer' in and of themselves. The gloss 'prayer' translates their contextual usage.

34 It is possible that εὔχομαι ᵃ and προσεύχομαι differ somewhat in the extent to which focus is upon the person to whom the prayer is addressed, but this cannot be determined from NT usage.

35 There may be some slight difference of meaning between ἐρωτάω ᵃ and ἐπερωτάω ᵃ, but this cannot be determined from existing contexts.

33.185 ἀπόκρισις, εως *f*: (derivative of ἀποκρίνομαι[a] 'to reply,' 33.184) that which is said in response to a question – 'answer, reply.' λέγει τῷ Ἰησοῦ, Πόθεν εἶ σύ; ὁ δὲ Ἰησοῦς ἀπόκρισιν οὐκ ἔδωκεν αὐτῷ 'he said to Jesus, Where do you come from? But Jesus gave him no answer' Jn 19.9.

33.186 ἀνταποκρίνομαι[a]: to respond to a question, with emphasis upon an implied opposition or contradiction – 'to answer, to reply.' οὐκ ἴσχυσαν ἀνταποκριθῆναι πρὸς ταῦτα 'they were not able to reply (to him) about this' Lk 14.6.

33.187 ὑπολαμβάνω[b]: to respond to what has been said (in the NT restricted to responses to questions) – 'to reply, to respond.' εἶπεν πρὸς τὸν Ἰησοῦν, Καὶ τίς ἐστίν μου πλησίον; ὑπολαβὼν ὁ Ἰησοῦς 'he said to Jesus, Who is my neighbor? Jesus responded . . .' Lk 10.29-30.

33.188 προσλέγω: to respond in turn to someone – 'to respond, to reply.' καὶ ὁ Χριστὸς ἐκείνοις προσέλεγεν 'and Christ responded to them' Mk 16.15 (apparatus).

O Inform, Announce[36] (33.189-33.217)

33.189 ἀγγέλλω: to provide otherwise unknown information – 'to tell, to inform.'[37] ἔρχεται Μαριὰμ ἡ Μαγδαληνὴ ἀγγέλουσα τοῖς μαθηταῖς ὅτι Ἑώρακα τὸν κύριον 'so Mary Magdalene came and told the disciples, I have seen the Lord' or '. . . that she had seen the Lord' Jn 20.18.

33.190 κατηχέω[b]: to report in a relatively detailed manner – 'to report, to tell, to in-

form.' γνώσονται πάντες ὅτι ὧν κατήχηνται περὶ σοῦ οὐδέν ἐστιν 'all will know that there is no truth in what they have been told about you' Ac 21.24; περὶ ὧν κατηχήθης λόγων 'concerning those things of which you have been informed' Lk 1.4. It is also possible to understand κατηχέω in Lk 1.4 as systematic teaching (see 33.225).

33.191 προγράφω[b]: to provide information in a vivid manner – 'to describe vividly, to portray.' οἷς κατ' ὀφθαλμοὺς Ἰησοῦς Χριστὸς προεγράφη ἐσταυρωμένος 'you before whose eyes Jesus Christ was portrayed as crucified' Ga 3.1. It would be wrong to assume that προγράφω in Ga 3.1 refers to some kind of theatrical demonstration. The portrayal mentioned here was evidently a vivid verbal description.

33.192 ἐρεύγομαι: to announce in a sudden and emphatic manner (with an implication of 'blurting out') – 'to proclaim, to announce.' ἐρεύξομαι κεκρυμμένα ἀπὸ καταβολῆς κόσμου 'I will announce (to them) things unknown since the creation of the world' Mt 13.35.

33.193 ἀγγελία, ας *f*: (derivative of ἀγγέλλω 'to tell, to inform,' 33.189) the content of what has been announced – 'message, announcement.' ἔστιν αὕτη ἡ ἀγγελία ἣν ἀκηκόαμεν ἀπ' αὐτοῦ 'this is the message that we have heard from him' 1 Jn 1.5

33.194 ἀπόστολος[b], ου *m*: (derivative of ἀποστέλλω[b] 'to send a message,' 15.67) one who is sent with a message – 'messenger.'[38] οὐδὲ ἀπόστολος μείζων τοῦ πέμψαντος αὐτόν 'no messenger is greater than the one who sent him' Jn 13.16.

33.195 ἄγγελος[a], ου *m*: (derivative of ἀγγέλλω 'to tell, to inform,' 33.189) a person who makes an announcement – 'messenger.'[38] ἀπελθόντων δὲ τῶν ἀγγέλων Ἰωάννου ἤρξατο λέγ-

---

36 As will be readily noted, a number of the meanings in this subdomain (*Inform, Announce*) parallel closely meanings in Domain 28 *Know*, particularly in the causative sense of 'to cause to know.' Accordingly, it is difficult to determine in many instances whether the focus of meaning is upon the communicative event or upon the result, namely, the knowledge acquired by the receptors.

37 ἀγγέλλω appears to be more generic in meaning than a term such as ἐμφανίζω[c] (33.208), but it is difficult to indicate in all instances the various aspects of denota-tion and connotation associated with the meanings in this subdomain.

38 ἀπόστολος[b] (33.194) and ἄγγελος[a] (33.195) appear to differ in meaning in that in the case of ἀπόστολος[b] the focus is upon one who is sent, while in the case of ἄγγελος[a] the focus appears to be upon the message which is communicated.

ειν 'after John's messengers had left, (Jesus) began to speak' Lk 7.24.

33.196 σπεκουλάτωρ^a, ορος *m*: a soldier who acts as a courier to carry confidential information – 'courier, messenger.' ἀποστείλας ὁ βασιλεὺς σπεκουλάτορα ἐπέταξεν ἐνέγκαι τὴν κεφαλὴν αὐτοῦ 'the king sent a messenger to arrange to bring his head' Mk 6.27. In Mk 6.27 σπεκουλάτωρ may also have the meaning of 'executioner' (see 20.70).

33.197 ἀναγγέλλω: to provide information, with the possible implication of considerable detail – 'to announce, to inform, to tell.' ἀνήγγειλάν τε ὅσα ὁ θεὸς ἐποίησεν μετ' αὐτῶν 'and they told all that God had done with them' Ac 15.4.

33.198 ἀπαγγέλλω^a: to announce or inform, with possible focus upon the source of information – 'to tell, to inform.' παραγενόμενος ὁ δοῦλος ἀπήγγειλεν τῷ κυρίῳ αὐτοῦ ταῦτα 'the servant went back and told all to his master' Lk 14.21.

33.199 πληρόω^e; πληροφορέω^b: to relate fully the content of a message – 'to proclaim, to tell fully, to proclaim completely.'
πληρόω^e: πεπληρωκέναι τὸ εὐαγγέλιον τοῦ Χριστοῦ 'I have told fully the good news about Christ' Ro 15.19.
πληροφορέω^b: ἵνα δι' ἐμοῦ τὸ κήρυγμα πληροφορηθῇ καὶ ἀκούσωσιν πάντα τὰ ἔθνη 'so that I was able to proclaim completely the message for all the Gentiles to hear' 2 Tm 4.17.

33.200 διασαφέω^b: to inform in detail and with clarity – 'to tell all, to relate fully.' ἐλθόντες διεσάφησαν τῷ κυρίῳ ἑαυτῶν πάντα τὰ γενόμενα 'they went and told their master everything that had happened' Mt 18.31.

33.201 ἐξηγέομαι^a; διηγέομαι; ἐκδιηγέομαι: to provide detailed information in a systematic manner – 'to inform, to relate, to tell fully.'[39]

ἐξηγέομαι^a: μονογενὴς θεὸς . . . ἐκεῖνος ἐξηγήσατο 'the only One who is the same as God . . . he told (us) everything (about him)' Jn 1.18. For another interpretation of ἐξηγέομαι in Jn 1.18, see 28.41.
διηγέομαι: ὑπόστρεφε εἰς τὸν οἶκόν σου, καὶ διηγοῦ ὅσα σοι ἐποίησεν ὁ θεός 'go back to your home and tell them all that God has done for you' Lk 8.39.
ἐκδιηγέομαι: ἐκδιηγούμενοι τὴν ἐπιστροφὴν τῶν ἐθνῶν 'they fully related how the Gentiles had turned (to God)' Ac 15.3.

33.202 ἀνεκδιήγητος, ον: pertaining to that which cannot be fully related or communicated – 'indescribable, beyond words.' χάρις τῷ θεῷ ἐπὶ τῇ ἀνεκδιηγήτῳ αὐτοῦ δωρεᾷ 'let us thank God for his gift which cannot be described with words' 2 Cor 9.15.

33.203 διαγγέλλω^a: to provide specific information (especially with regard to some future contingency) – 'to notify, to give notice of.' εἰσήει εἰς τὸ ἱερόν, διαγγέλλων τὴν ἐκπλήρωσιν τῶν ἡμερῶν τοῦ ἁγνισμοῦ 'then he went into the Temple and gave notice of how many days it would be until the end of the period of purification' Ac 21.26.

33.204 καταγγέλλω; ἐξαγγέλλω: to announce, with focus upon the extent to which the announcement or proclamation extends – 'to proclaim throughout, to announce, to speak out about.'[40]
καταγγέλλω: ἡ πίστις ὑμῶν καταγγέλλεται ἐν ὅλῳ τῷ κόσμῳ 'your faith is proclaimed in the whole world' Ro 1.8.
ἐξαγγέλλω: ὅπως τὰς ἀρετὰς ἐξαγγείλητε 'so that you may proclaim the wonderful acts (of God)' 1 Pe 2.9.

33.205 καταγγελεύς, έως *m*: (derivative of καταγγέλλω 'to proclaim,' 33.204) one who proclaims – 'herald, announcer, proclaimer.' οἱ δέ, Ξένων δαιμονίων δοκεῖ καταγγελεὺς εἶναι

---

39 It is possible that ἐξηγέομαι^a, διηγέομαι, and ἐκδιηγέομαι differ somewhat in emphasis or connotation, but it is impossible to determine this from NT usage.

40 The translation of καταγγέλλω or ἐξαγγέλλω as 'to preach' depends essentially upon the context, in other words, upon the content of what is announced or proclaimed.

'others (said), He seems to be a proclaimer of foreign gods' Ac 17.18.

33.206 κηρύσσω[a]: to announce in a formal or official manner by means of a herald or one who functions as a herald – 'to announce, to proclaim.' εἶδον ἄγγελον ἰσχυρὸν κηρύσσοντα ἐν φωνῇ μεγάλῃ 'I saw a strong angel proclaiming in a loud voice' Re 5.2.

33.207 κηρύσσω[b]; **διαγγέλλω**[b]: to announce extensively and publicly – 'to proclaim, to tell.'
κηρύσσω[b]: ἤρξατο κηρύσσειν ἐν τῇ Δεκαπόλει ὅσα ἐποίησεν αὐτῷ ὁ Ἰησοῦς 'he began to proclaim in Decapolis all that Jesus had done for him' Mk 5.20.
διαγγέλλω[b]: σὺ δὲ ἀπελθὼν διάγγελλε τὴν βασιλείαν τοῦ θεοῦ 'you go and proclaim the kingdom of God' Lk 9.60.

33.208 ἐμφανίζω[c]: to reveal something which is not generally known – 'to tell, to inform, to report.'[41] μηδενὶ ἐκλαλῆσαι ὅτι ταῦτα ἐνεφάνισας πρός με 'tell no one that you have reported this to me' Ac 23.22. For another interpretation of ἐμφανίζω in Ac 23.22, see 28.36.

33.209 μηνύω: to provide information concerning something, with emphasis upon the fact that such information is secret or known only to a select few – 'to inform, to reveal.' ἵνα ἐάν τις γνῷ ποῦ ἐστιν μηνύσῃ 'that if anyone knew where (Jesus) was, he must inform them' Jn 11.57; ὅτι δὲ ἐγείρονται οἱ νεκροὶ καὶ Μωϋσῆς ἐμήνυσεν ἐπὶ τῆς βάτου 'that the dead will rise – even Moses revealed this in the passage concerning the bush' Lk 20.37.

33.210 βαστάζω ὄνομα: (an idiom, literally 'to carry a name') to spread information extensively about a person – 'to make known, to inform.' σκεῦος ἐκλογῆς ἐστίν μοι οὗτος τοῦ βαστάσαι τὸ ὄνομά μου 'he is my chosen instrument to make my name known' or '. . . to inform people about me' Ac 9.15.

41 See footnote 37.

33.211 φάσις, εως *f*; **φήμη, ης** *f*; **ἦχος**[b], **ου** *m*: information concerning a person or an event – 'report, news, word, information.'
φάσις: ζητούντων τε αὐτὸν ἀποκτεῖναι ἀνέβη φάσις τῷ χιλιάρχῳ 'when (the mob) tried to kill him, information was sent to the commander' Ac 21.31.
φήμη: ἐξῆλθεν ἡ φήμη αὕτη εἰς ὅλην τὴν γῆν ἐκείνην 'word about this spread all over that part of the country' Mt 9.26.
ἦχος[b]: ἐξεπορεύετο ἦχος περὶ αὐτοῦ εἰς πάντα τόπον τῆς περιχώρου 'the report about him spread everywhere in that region' Lk 4.37.

33.212 ἀκούω[c]: to receive information about something, normally by word of mouth – 'to receive news, to hear.' ἀκούσαντες οἱ μαθηταὶ αὐτοῦ ἦλθον καὶ ἦραν τὸ πτῶμα αὐτοῦ 'when his disciples received news about this, they came and got his body' Mk 6.29. In Mk 6.29 ἀκούω[c] clearly implies more than mere physiological hearing, for the content of the message is included as a significant element in the meaning of ἀκούω. Compare also ἀκοή[d] (33.213).

33.213 ἀκοή[d], **ῆς** *f*: (derivative of ἀκούω[c] 'to receive news,' 33.212) the content of the news which is heard – 'news, report, information.' ἀπῆλθεν ἡ ἀκοὴ αὐτοῦ εἰς ὅλην τὴν Συρίαν 'the news about him spread throughout the whole country of Syria' Mt 4.24. In a number of languages, however, it is impossible to speak of 'news spreading.' It therefore may be necessary to render Mt 4.24 as 'people throughout the whole country of Syria kept hearing from one another about him.'

33.214 διαφημίζω: to spread information extensively and effectively concerning someone or something – 'to spread information about, to spread the news about.' οἱ δὲ ἐξελθόντες διεφήμισαν αὐτὸν ἐν ὅλῃ τῇ γῇ ἐκείνῃ 'they left and spread the news about him all over that part of the country' Mt 9.31.

33.215 εὐαγγελίζω: to communicate good news concerning something (in the NT a particular reference to the gospel message about Jesus) – 'to tell the good news, to announce the gospel.' ἀρξάμενος ἀπὸ τῆς γραφῆς ταύτης εὐηγγελίσατο αὐτῷ τὸν Ἰησοῦν 'starting from this very passage of Scripture, he told him the good news about Jesus' Ac 8.35; ἀπεστάλην λαλῆσαι πρὸς σὲ καὶ εὐαγγελίσασθαί σοι ταῦτα 'I have been sent to speak to you and tell you this good news' Lk 1.19. In Lk 1.19, however, the reference is to the birth of John the Baptist.

33.216 προευαγγελίζομαι: to spread good news in advance of its happening (in the NT, restricted in reference to the good news about Jesus Christ) – 'to bring the good news ahead of time.' ἡ γραφὴ . . . προευηγγελίσατο τῷ Ἀβραάμ 'the Scripture . . . announced the good news to Abraham ahead of time' Ga 3.8.

33.217 εὐαγγέλιον, ου n: (derivative of εὐαγγελίζω 'to tell the good news,' 33.215) the content of good news (in the NT a reference to the gospel about Jesus) – 'the good news, the gospel.' οὐ γὰρ ἐπαισχύνομαι τὸ εὐαγγέλιον 'for I am not ashamed of the gospel' Ro 1.16. In a number of languages the expression 'the gospel' or 'the good news' must be expressed by a phrase, for example, 'news that makes one happy' or 'information that causes one joy' or 'words that bring smiles' or 'a message that causes the heart to be sweet.'

P Assert, Declare[42] (33.218-33.223)

33.218 φάσκω: to speak about something with certainty – 'to declare, to assert.' ζητήματα . . . περί τινος Ἰησοῦ τεθνηκότος, ὃν ἔφασκεν ὁ Παῦλος ζῆν 'arguments . . . about a certain dead man Jesus, whom Paul declares is alive' Ac 25.19.

33.219 ἐπαγγέλλομαι[b]: to announce something openly and emphatically – 'to assert, to profess.' ὃ πρέπει γυναιξὶν ἐπαγγελλομέναις θεοσέβειαν 'as is proper for women who profess to be religious' 1 Tm 2.10.

33.220 ἀπολέγομαι[b]: to assert opposition to something – 'to denounce.' ἀλλὰ ἀπειπάμεθα

τια kryptia t;hw aĩsx?ynhw 'but we denounced hidden, shameful deeds' 2 Cor 4.2. For another interpretation of ἀπολέγομαι in 2 Cor 4.2, see 13.156.

33.221 ὁμολογέω[c]: to make an emphatic declaration, often public, and at times in response to pressure or an accusation – 'to declare, to assert.' τότε ὁμολογήσω αὐτοῖς ὅτι Οὐδέποτε ἔγνων ὑμᾶς 'then I will declare to them, I never knew you' Mt 7.23; τῆς ἐπαγγελίας ἧς ὡμολόγησεν ὁ θεὸς τῷ Ἀβραάμ 'the promise which God had declared to Abraham' Ac 7.17.

33.222 ἐξηχέομαι: to cause something to sound forth – 'to proclaim.' ἀφ' ὑμῶν γὰρ ἐξήχηται ὁ λόγος τοῦ κυρίου 'you caused the message about the Lord to be proclaimed' 1 Th 1.8.

33.223 μαρτύρομαι[a]; διαμαρτύρομαι[a]: to make a serious declaration on the basis of presumed personal knowledge – 'to declare, to assert, to testify.'[43]
μαρτύρομαι[a]: διότι μαρτύρομαι ὑμῖν ἐν τῇ σήμερον ἡμέρᾳ ὅτι καθαρός εἰμι ἀπὸ τοῦ αἵματος πάντων 'so I testify to you this very day: if any of you should be lost, I am not responsible' Ac 20.26.
διαμαρτύρομαι[a]: διαμαρτυρόμενος τοῖς Ἰουδαίοις εἶναι τὸν Χριστόν Ἰησοῦν 'he testified to the Jews that Jesus is the Christ' Ac 18.5.

Q Teach[44] (33.224-33.250)

33.224 διδάσκω; διδαχή[a], ῆς f; διδασκαλία[a], ας f: to provide instruction in a formal or informal setting – 'to teach, teaching.'
διδάσκω: κύριε, δίδαξον ἡμᾶς προσεύχεσθαι 'Lord, teach us how to pray' Lk 11.1.

---

42 For the series of meanings in Subdomain P *Assert, Declare,* it is often possible to use an expression in receptor languages which means essentially 'to say strongly' or 'to say with confidence' or even 'to know and to say.'

43 It is possible that διαμαρτύρομαι[a] is somewhat stronger and more emphatic than μαρτύρομαι[a], but this cannot be shown from NT contexts.
44 The meanings in the subdomain of *Teach* may be regarded as relating to a process of 'causing someone to learn or to know' and hence overlapping with Domain 27 *Learn* and Domain 28 *Know,* but the meanings in the Subdomain *Teach* involve a more continuous process of formal and informal instruction.

διδαχή^a: ἐν τῇ διδαχῇ αὐτοῦ ἔλεγεν 'as he taught (them), he said' Mk 12.38.

διδασκαλία^a: ὅσα γὰρ προεγράφη, εἰς τὴν ἡμετέραν διδασκαλίαν ἐγράφη 'everything written formerly (in the Scriptures) was written to teach us' Ro 15.4.

The equivalent of 'to teach' in many languages is simply a causative form of a verb meaning 'to learn' or 'to know,' for example, 'to cause to learn' or 'to cause to know.' In choosing a term for 'to teach' it is important to avoid an expression which will denote merely classroom activity.

33.225 κατηχέω^a: to teach in a systematic or detailed manner – 'to instruct, to teach.' οὗτος ἦν κατηχημένος τὴν ὁδὸν τοῦ κυρίου 'this man was instructed in the Way of the Lord' Ac 18.25; περὶ ὧν κατηχήθης λόγων 'concerning the things that you have been taught' Lk 1.4. It is also possible to understand κατηχέω in Lk 1.4 as denoting merely what has been told rather than what has been taught (see κατηχέω^b, 33.190). This distinction is an important one since it implies a quite different relationship of Theophilus to the text of the Gospel of Luke. If Lk 1.4 pertains merely to Theophilus 'being told' something, then one might assume that Theophilus was not a Christian, in which case he may have been a government official to whom the joint publications (the Gospel of Luke and the Acts of the Apostles) would have been directed as a defense of Christianity. On the other hand, if one understands κατηχέω in the sense of 'to be taught' or 'to be instructed,' then one would assume that Theophilus was a Christian who had been instructed in the faith. The relationship of Theophilus to the message would then determine in a number of contexts the difference between 'we' inclusive and 'we' exclusive.

33.226 παιδεύω^a; παιδεία^a, ας *f*: to provide instruction, with the intent of forming proper habits of behavior – 'to teach, to instruct, to train, teaching, instruction.'[45]

παιδεύω^a: ἐπαιδεύθη Μωϋσῆς ἐν πάσῃ σοφίᾳ Αἰγυπτίων 'Moses was trained in all the wisdom of the Egyptians' Ac 7.22.

παιδεία^a: ὠφέλιμος . . . πρὸς παιδείαν τὴν ἐν δικαιοσύνῃ 'useful . . . for instruction in right living' 2 Tm 3.16.

33.227 διδακτός, ή, όν: (derivative of διδάσκω 'to teach,' 33.224) pertaining to that which is taught – 'taught, instructed.' λαλοῦμεν οὐκ ἐν διδακτοῖς ἀνθρωπίνης σοφίας λόγοις 'we do not speak in words taught by human wisdom' 1 Cor 2.13. The expression ἐν διδακτοῖς ἀνθρωπίνης σοφίας λόγοις in 1 Cor 2.13 is semantically complex. One may interpret this to mean 'by means of words used in teaching human wisdom' or 'by means of words concerning human wisdom as it is taught.' Though grammatically διδακτοῖς 'taught' goes with λόγοις 'words,' there is a very close semantic connection between διδακτοῖς and ἀνθρωπίνης σοφίας 'human wisdom.'

33.228 θεοδίδακτος, ον: pertaining to being taught by God – 'taught by God, instructed by God.' αὐτοὶ γὰρ ὑμεῖς θεοδίδακτοί ἐστε εἰς τὸ ἀγαπᾶν ἀλλήλους 'for you yourselves have been taught by God how you should love one another' 1 Th 4.9. In a number of languages the passive expression θεοδίδακτοί ἐστε in 1 Th 4.9 must be rendered in an active form, for example, 'for God himself has taught you how you should love one another.'

33.229 σωφρονίζω: to instruct someone to behave in a wise and becoming manner – 'to teach, to train.' ἵνα σωφρονίζωσιν τὰς νέας 'in order to teach the young women to . . .' Tt 2.4.

33.230 ὑποτίθεμαι: to provide instruction as to what should be done – 'to instruct, to give instructions.' ταῦτα ὑποτιθέμενος τοῖς ἀδελφοῖς καλὸς ἔσῃ διάκονος Χριστοῦ Ἰησοῦ 'if you give these instructions to the fellow believers, you

---

[45] παιδεύω^a and παιδεία^a (33.226) differ in meaning from νουθετέω^a and νουθεσία^a (33.231) and from ἐντρέφω (33.242). παιδεύω^a and παιδεία^a focus upon the forming of proper habits of behavior, while νουθετέω^a and νουθεσία^a focus upon instruction in correct behavior. ἐντρέφω appears to focus more on continuous instruction and training in the area of skill and practical knowledge.

will be a good servant of Christ Jesus' 1 Tm 4.6.

33.231 νουθετέωᵃ; νουθεσίαᵃ, ας *f*: to provide instruction as to correct behavior and belief – 'to instruct, to teach, instruction, teaching.'⁴⁵

νουθετέωᵃ: ἐρωτῶμεν . . . εἰδέναι τοὺς κοπιῶντας ἐν ὑμῖν . . . καὶ νουθετοῦντας ὑμᾶς 'we beg you . . . to pay proper respect to those who work among you . . . and instruct you' 1 Th 5.12.

νουθεσίαᵃ: ἐκτρέφετε αὐτὰ ἐν παιδείᾳ καὶ νουθεσίᾳ κυρίου 'raise them in the discipline and instruction of the Lord' Eph 6.4.

33.232 ἀνατρέφω παρὰ τοὺς πόδας (followed by the genitive): (an idiom, literally 'to be trained at the feet of') to be given extensive and formal instruction by someone – 'to be taught by, to be educated under the direction of.' ἀνατεθραμμένος . . . παρὰ τοὺς πόδας Γαμαλιήλ 'he was educated . . . under the teaching of Gamaliel' Ac 22.3. In a number of languages the closest equivalent of this part of Ac 22.3 is simply 'Gamaliel was his teacher.'

33.233 διδακτικός, ή, όν: (derivative of διδάσκω 'to teach,' 33.224) pertaining to being able to teach – 'able to teach, can teach.' δεῖ οὖν τὸν ἐπίσκοπον ἀνεπίλημπτον εἶναι . . . διδακτικόν 'a church leader must be a man above reproach . . . and he must be able to teach' 1 Tm 3.2.

33.234 ὀρθοτομέω: to give accurate instruction – 'to teach correctly, to expound rightly.' σπούδασον σεαυτὸν . . . ὀρθοτομοῦντα τὸν λόγον τῆς ἀληθείας 'do your best . . . to teach the word of truth correctly' 2 Tm 2.15.

33.235 ἑτεροδιδασκαλέω: to teach that which is different from what should be taught – 'to teach a different doctrine, to teach something different.' ἵνα παραγγείλῃς τισὶν μὴ ἑτεροδιδασκαλεῖν 'that you may order them to stop teaching a different doctrine' 1 Tm 1.3. In rendering ἑτεροδιδασκαλέω in 1 Tm 1.3, it may be necessary to be specific about the particular doctrine which forms the basis of contrast, for example, 'that you may order

them to stop teaching a doctrine which is different from what has already been taught' or '. . . from what I have already taught' or '. . . from what they ought to teach.'

33.236 διδαχήᵇ, ῆς *f*; διδασκαλίαᵇ, ας *f*: (derivatives of διδάσκω 'to teach,' 33.224) the content of what is taught – 'what is taught, doctrine, teaching.'

διδαχήᵇ: πεπληρώκατε τὴν Ἰερουσαλὴμ τῆς διδαχῆς ὑμῶν 'you have filled Jerusalem with your teaching' Ac 5.28.

διδασκαλίαᵇ: κατὰ τὰ ἐντάλματα καὶ διδασκαλίας τῶν ἀνθρώπων 'according to the rules and doctrines of people' Col 2.22.

33.237 παραδίδωμιᶜ: to pass on traditional instruction, often implying over a long period of time – 'to instruct, to teach.' ὑποστρέψαι ἐκ τῆς παραδοθείσης αὐτοῖς ἁγίας ἐντολῆς 'to turn back from the sacred command that had been taught them' 2 Pe 2.21.

33.238 παραλαμβάνωᶠ: to receive traditional instruction – 'to receive instruction from, to be taught by.' ἐγὼ γὰρ παρέλαβον ἀπὸ τοῦ κυρίου, ὃ καὶ παρέδωκα ὑμῖν 'for I received from the Lord what I passed on to you' 1 Cor 11.23.

33.239 παράδοσις, εως *f*: (derivative of παραδίδωμιᶜ 'to instruct,' 33.237) the content of traditional instruction – 'teaching, tradition.' διὰ τί οἱ μαθηταί σου παραβαίνουσιν τὴν παράδοσιν τῶν πρεσβυτέρων; 'why is it that your disciples disobey the tradition of our ancestors?' Mt 15.2.

33.240 πατροπαράδοτος, ον: pertaining to teaching which has been handed down from the ancestors – 'traditions, handed down teaching.' τῆς ματαίας ὑμῶν ἀναστροφῆς πατροπαραδότου 'the futile way of your life handed down from your ancestors' 1 Pe 1.18.

33.241 αἵρεσιςᵇ, εως *f*: the content of teaching which is not true – 'false teaching, untrue doctrine, heresy.' οἵτινες παρεισάξουσιν αἱρέσεις ἀπωλείας 'they will bring in false teachings which are destructive' 2 Pe 2.1.

33.242 ἐντρέφω: to provide instruction and training, with the implication of skill in some area of practical knowledge – 'to train, to teach.' ἐντρεφόμενος τοῖς λόγοις τῆς πίστεως 'trained in the words of faith' 1 Tm 4.6.

33.243 διδάσκαλος, ου *m*: (derivative of διδάσκω 'to teach,' 33.224) one who provides instruction – 'teacher, instructor.' οὐκ ἔστιν μαθητὴς ὑπὲρ τὸν διδάσκαλον 'no pupil is greater than his teacher' Mt 10.24.

33.244 παιδευτής[a], οῦ *m*: (derivative of παιδεύω[a] 'to train,' 33.226) one who provides instruction for the purpose of proper behavior – 'instructor, trainer, teacher.' παιδευτὴν ἀφρόνων 'an instructor for the foolish' Ro 2.20.

33.245 καθηγητής, οῦ *m*: (derivative of καθηγέομαι 'to guide, to explain,' not occurring in the NT) one who provides instruction and guidance – 'teacher, instructor.' μηδὲ κληθῆτε καθηγηταί, ὅτι καθηγητὴς ὑμῶν ἐστιν εἷς ὁ Χριστός 'nor should you be called teachers, because your one and only teacher is the Christ' Mt 23.10.

33.246 ῥαββί (a borrowing from Aramaic): a Jewish teacher and scholar recognized for expertise in interpreting the Jewish Scriptures – 'rabbi, teacher.' καλεῖσθαι ὑπὸ τῶν ἀνθρώπων, Ῥαββί 'to be called "teacher" by people' Mt 23.7.

33.247 ῥαββουνι (an Aramaic transcription): an honorific title for a teacher of the Jewish Scriptures, implying an important personal relationship – 'my teacher.' ὁ δὲ τυφλὸς εἶπεν αὐτῷ, Ῥαββουνι, ἵνα ἀναβλέψω 'and the blind man said to him, My teacher, in order that I may see' Mk 10.51.

33.248 νομοδιδάσκαλος, ου *m*: a person who is skilled in the teaching and interpretation of the law (in the NT referring to the law of the OT) – 'teacher of the Law, expert in the Law.' θέλοντες εἶναι νομοδιδάσκαλοι, μὴ νοοῦντες μήτε ἃ λέγουσιν 'they want to be teachers of the Law, but they do not even understand their own words' 1 Tm 1.7.

33.249 καλοδιδάσκαλος, ου *m* and *f*: one who teaches what is good and morally right – 'teacher of what is good, teacher of what is right.' πρεσβύτιδας . . . καλοδιδασκάλους 'the older women . . . should be ones who teach what is good' Tt 2.3.

33.250 ψευδοδιδάσκαλος, ου *m*: one who teaches falsehoods – 'false teacher, teacher of what is a lie.' ὡς καὶ ἐν ὑμῖν ἔσονται ψευδοδιδάσκαλοι 'and in the same way false teachers will appear among you' 2 Pe 2.1. In rendering ψευδοδιδάσκαλος, it is important to avoid an expression which will simply mean that a person pretends to be a teacher and is not. What is important here is that the individual teaches what is not true.

R Speak Truth, Speak Falsehood (33.251-33.255)

33.251 ἀληθεύω: to communicate what is true – 'to speak the truth, to tell the truth.' ὥστε ἐχθρὸς ὑμῶν γέγονα ἀληθεύων ὑμῖν; 'have I now become your enemy by telling you the truth?' Ga 4.16. In a number of languages it may be difficult to employ a highly abstract term such as 'truth.' Accordingly, one may find it necessary to relate 'truth' in Ga 4.16 to the immediate context, for example, '. . . by telling you what they really want to do' or '. . . what all this really means.'

33.252 τὸ στόμα ἀνοίγω πρός: (an idiom, literally 'to open the mouth to') to speak the complete truth to someone – 'to be completely open with, to conceal nothing from, to speak the whole truth to.' τὸ στόμα ἡμῶν ἀνέῳγεν πρὸς ὑμᾶς 'we spoke the complete truth to you' 2 Cor 6.11.

33.253 ψεύδομαι: to communicate what is false, with the evident purpose of misleading – 'to lie, to tell falsehoods.' ἀλήθειαν λέγω ἐν Χριστῷ, οὐ ψεύδομαι 'what I say is true; I belong to Christ and I do not lie' Ro 9.1. The Greek term ψεύδομαι and the English equivalent 'to lie' involve more than simply telling what is not true, for this could occur without an intent to deceive or mislead. ψεύδομαι, therefore, involves not only the communication of a falsehood but also the intent to deceive.

33.254 ψεῦδος, ους *n*; ψεῦσμα, τος *n*: (derivatives of ψεύδομαι 'to lie,' 33.253) the content of a false utterance – 'lie, falsehood.'
ψεῦδος: πᾶν ψεῦδος ἐκ τῆς ἀληθείας οὐκ ἔστιν 'no lie ever comes from the truth' 1 Jn 2.21.
ψεῦσμα: εἰ δὲ ἡ ἀλήθεια τοῦ θεοῦ ἐν τῷ ἐμῷ ψεύσματι ἐπερίσσευσεν εἰς τὴν δόξαν αὐτοῦ 'and if God's truth abounds to his glory because of my falsehood' Ro 3.7. It may be important in some instances to restructure the semantic relationships in this clause in Ro 3.7, for example, 'if my lie makes God's truth appear more glorious.'

33.255 ψεύστης, ου *m*; ψευδής, ές (derivatives of ψεύδομαι 'to lie,' 33.253); ψευδολόγος, ου *m*: one who utters falsehoods and lies – 'liar.'
ψεύστης: ὅταν λαλῇ τὸ ψεῦδος, ἐκ τῶν ἰδίων λαλεῖ, ὅτι ψεύστης ἐστίν 'when he tells a lie, he is only doing what is natural to him, because he is a liar' Jn 8.44.
ψευδής: καὶ εὗρες αὐτοὺς ψευδεῖς 'and you have found out that they are liars' Re 2.2.
ψευδολόγος: διδασκαλίαις δαιμονίων, ἐν ὑποκρίσει ψευδολόγων 'teachings of demons coming from the deceit of men who are liars' 1 Tm 4.1-2.
Since lying is a universal, there is usually no difficulty in obtaining a satisfactory term for 'liar,' though frequently the equivalent is an idiomatic expression, for example, 'to speak too much,' 'to speak with two tongues,' or 'to speak what is not one's thoughts.'

S Preach, Proclaim (33.256-33.261)

33.256 κηρύσσω^c: to publicly announce religious truths and principles while urging acceptance and compliance – 'to preach.'[46]
πῶς δὲ ἀκούσωσιν χωρὶς κηρύσσοντος; 'how can

they hear if there is no one to preach?' Ro 10.14; τοῖς ἐν φυλακῇ πνεύμασιν πορευθεὶς ἐκήρυξεν 'he went out and preached to those spirits in prison' 1 Pe 3.19. In a number of languages it is impossible to translate κηρύσσω^c without indicating the content of what is preached. Accordingly, one may have such expressions as 'to preach about the good news' or 'to preach about God.'

33.257 προκηρύσσω: to preach in anticipation or in advance – 'to preach beforehand.'
προκηρύξαντος Ἰωάννου πρὸ προσώπου τῆς εἰσόδου αὐτοῦ βάπτισμα μετανοίας 'before his coming, John had preached that people should repent and be baptized' Ac 13.24.

33.258 κήρυγμα, τος *n*: (derivative of κηρύσσω^c 'to preach,' 33.256) the content of what is preached – 'preaching, what is preached.' μετενόησαν εἰς τὸ κήρυγμα Ἰωνᾶ 'they turned from their sins when they heard what Jonah preached' Lk 11.32; εἰ δὲ Χριστὸς οὐκ ἐγήγερται, κενὸν ἄρα καὶ τὸ κήρυγμα ἡμῶν 'if Christ has not been raised from death, then what we have preached is nothing' 1 Cor 15.14.

33.259 κῆρυξ, υκος *m*: (derivative of κηρύσσω^c 'to preach,' 33.256) a person who preaches – 'preacher.' ἐτέθην ἐγὼ κῆρυξ καὶ ἀπόστολος καὶ διδάσκαλος '(God) has appointed me as a preacher, as an apostle, and as a teacher' 2 Tm 1.11.

33.260 λόγος^c, ου *m*: the content of what is preached about Christ or about the good news – 'what is preached, gospel.'[47] ὁ λόγος τοῦ Χριστοῦ 'what is preached concerning Christ' or 'the good news about Christ' Col 3.16; ὁ λόγος ηὔξανεν καὶ ἴσχυεν 'the message about the good news kept spreading and growing stronger' Ac 19.20.

---

46 The referent of κηρύσσω^c (33.256) is essentially similar to that of εὐαγγελίζω (33.215), for both expressions may refer to the content of the Gospel. This does not mean, however, that the meaning of the two expressions is precisely identical.

47 λόγος^c, particularly in contexts such as Col 3.16 and Ac 19.20, represents a highly specialized meaning of λόγος in the NT. Compare Mk 2.2 ἐλάλει αὐτοῖς τὸν λόγον 'he talked to them about the gospel' and Lk 1.2 ὑπηρέται γενόμενοι τοῦ λόγου 'being servants of the good news.'

33.261 θεόπνευστος, ον: pertaining to a communication which has been inspired by God – 'inspired by God, divinely inspired.' πᾶσα γραφὴ θεόπνευστος καὶ ὠφέλιμος πρὸς διδασκαλίαν 'every Scripture divinely inspired and useful for teaching' or 'all Scripture is inspired by God and is useful for teaching' 2 Tm 3.16. In a number of languages it is difficult to find an appropriate term to render 'inspired.' In some instances 'Scripture inspired by God' is rendered as 'Scripture, the writer of which was influenced by God' or '. . . guided by God.' It is important, however, to avoid an expression which will mean 'dictated by God.'

T Witness, Testify (33.262-33.273)

33.262 μαρτυρέω[a]; μαρτυρία[a], ας f; μαρτύριον[a], ου n; ἐπιμαρτυρέω: to provide information about a person or an event concerning which the speaker has direct knowledge – 'to witness.'[48]

μαρτυρέω[a]: αὐτοὶ ὑμεῖς μοι μαρτυρεῖτε ὅτι εἶπον ὅτι Οὐκ εἰμὶ ἐγὼ ὁ Χριστός 'you yourselves can witness that I said, I am not the Messiah' Jn 3.28.

μαρτυρία[a]: οὗτος ἦλθεν εἰς μαρτυρίαν 'he came to witness' Jn 1.7.

μαρτύριον[a]: ἀποβήσεται ὑμῖν εἰς μαρτύριον 'this will be your chance to witness' Lk 21.13.

ἐπιμαρτυρέω: δι' ὀλίγων ἔγραψα, παρακαλῶν καὶ ἐπιμαρτυρῶν ταύτην εἶναι ἀληθῆ χάριν τοῦ θεοῦ 'I write you this brief letter to encourage you and to witness that this is the true grace of God' 1 Pe 5.12.

In a number of languages it is necessary to indicate specifically what is the content of a witness, so that, for example, in Lk 21.13 it may be necessary to say 'this is your chance to witness to the good news' or '. . . to tell about the good news' or '. . . to tell what you yourselves know about the good news.'

33.263 μαρτυρέω[b]: to speak well of a person on the basis of personal experience – 'to speak well of, to approve of.' πάντες ἐμαρτύρουν

αὐτῷ 'they all spoke well of him' Lk 4.22. It is possible that μαρτυρέω in Lk 4.22 should be translated as 'they were well impressed.'

33.264 μαρτυρία[b], ας f; μαρτύριον[b], ου n: (derivatives of μαρτυρέω[a] 'to witness,' 33.262) the content of what is witnessed or said – 'testimony, witness.'

μαρτυρία[b]: ἐζήτουν κατὰ τοῦ Ἰησοῦ μαρτυρίαν 'they tried to find some testimony against Jesus' Mk 14.55.

μαρτύριον[b]: καθὼς τὸ μαρτύριον τοῦ Χριστοῦ ἐβεβαιώθη ἐν ὑμῖν 'the witness about Christ has become so firmly fixed in you' 1 Cor 1.6.

In a number of languages one must specify the content of the witness, and it also may be necessary to indicate the agent who is engaged in the witnessing. For example, in Mk 14.55 it may be necessary to translate 'they tried to find someone who would testify against Jesus' or '. . . say something against Jesus.' In 1 Cor 1.6 it may be necessary to translate 'what we told you from personal experience about Christ has become so firmly fixed in you' or '. . . has become so much a part of you.'

33.265 μαρτυρία[c], ας f (derivative of μαρτυρέω[b] 'to speak well of,' 33.263); ὄνομα[c], τος n: that which is said about a person on the basis of an evaluation of the person's conduct – 'reputation.'

μαρτυρία[c]: δεῖ δὲ καὶ μαρτυρίαν καλὴν ἔχειν ἀπὸ τῶν ἔξωθεν 'he should be a man who has a good reputation among people outside the church' 1 Tm 3.7.

ὄνομα[c]: οἶδά σου τὰ ἔργα, ὅτι ὄνομα ἔχεις ὅτι ζῇς, καὶ νεκρὸς εἶ 'I know what you are doing, that you have the reputation of being alive though you are dead' Re 3.1.

In obtaining a satisfactory equivalent for 'reputation,' it may be necessary to restructure considerably the clause in which a term such as μαρτυρία[c] or ὄνομα[c] occurs. For example, in 1 Tm 3.7 one may translate 'he should be the kind of man that people outside the church say is a good person.' Similarly, in Re 3.1 one may need to translate 'people speak of you as being alive even though you are dead.'

33.266 συμμαρτυρέω: to provide confirming evidence by means of a testimony – 'to sup-

---

48 It is possible that ἐπιμαρτυρέω is somewhat more specific or emphatic in meaning than μαρτυρέω[a], but this cannot be determined from NT contexts.

port by testimony, to provide supporting evidence, to testify in support.' συμμαρτυρούσης αὐτῶν τῆς συνειδήσεως 'their consciences testify in support of this' Ro 2.15. It may be necessary in some languages to translate this phrase in Ro 2.15 as 'their consciences say to them that this is true.'

33.267 ἀμάρτυρος, ον: pertaining to not having a witness – 'without witness.' οὐκ ἀμάρτυρον αὐτὸν ἀφῆκεν ἀγαθουργῶν 'by the good things he does, he did not leave himself without witness' Ac 14.17. In Ac 14.17 it may be rather difficult to introduce what is essentially a double negative, implied by 'not' and 'without.' Accordingly, Ac 14.17 may be rendered as 'by the good things he does, everyone can know about him from experience.'

33.268 συνεπιμαρτυρέω: to join one's witness to that of others – 'to add one's witness to, to witness together with.' συνεπιμαρτυροῦντος τοῦ θεοῦ σημείοις 'God added his witness to theirs by doing signs of power' He 2.4.

33.269 καταμαρτυρέω: to witness against someone or some statement – 'to witness against, to testify against.' οὐκ ἀκούεις πόσα σου καταμαρτυροῦσιν; 'don't you hear all these things they testify against you?' Mt 27.13.

33.270 μάρτυς[a], ρος, dat. pl. σιν m: (derivative of μαρτυρέω[a] 'to witness,' 33.262) a person who witnesses – 'witness, one who testifies.' ἵνα ἐπὶ στόματος δύο μαρτύρων ἢ τριῶν σταθῇ πᾶν ῥῆμα 'in order that everything may be confirmed on the basis of what two or three witnesses say' Mt 18.16.

33.271 ψευδομαρτυρέω: to provide a false or untrue witness – 'to give false witness, to testify falsely.' πολλοὶ γὰρ ἐψευδομαρτύρουν κατ' αὐτοῦ, καὶ ἴσαι αἱ μαρτυρίαι οὐκ ἦσαν 'many gave false witness against him, but their testimonies did not agree' Mk 14.56. A person who gives false witness may deceive in two aspects, (1) in pretending to have been an eye witness to an event and (2) in saying what is not true, but the focal element in ψευδομαρτυρέω is the fact that what is said is not true.

33.272 ψευδομαρτυρία, ας f: (derivative of ψευδομαρτυρέω 'to testify falsely,' 33.271) the content of what is testified falsely – 'false testimony.' ἐζήτουν ψευδομαρτυρίαν κατὰ τοῦ Ἰησοῦ ὅπως αὐτὸν θανατώσωσιν 'they tried to find false testimony against Jesus in order to put him to death' Mt 26.59.

33.273 ψευδόμαρτυς, υρος m: (derivative of ψευδομαρτυρέω 'to testify falsely,' 33.271) one who testifies falsely – 'false witness.' οὐχ εὗρον πολλῶν προσελθόντων ψευδομαρτύρων 'they found nothing, even though many false witnesses came up' Mt 26.60. The focal element in the evidence provided by 'a false witness' is the fact that what is said is not true. It is also possible that such a person has pretended to have been present and thus an eye witness of an event, but that is not the focus of the meaning. In fact, a false witness may have been present but at the same time may later provide false evidence as to what took place. It is possible to render ψευδόμαρτυς in some languages as 'one who pretends to know about something but is really lying in what he says' or 'one who lies about what he pretends to have seen.'

U Profess Allegiance (33.274)

33.274 ὁμολογέω[a]; ὁμολογία, ας f; ἐξομολογέομαι[a]: to express openly one's allegiance to a proposition or person – 'to profess, to confess, confession.'
ὁμολογέω[a]: ὅστις ὁμολογήσει ἐν ἐμοὶ ἔμπροσθεν τῶν ἀνθρώπων, ὁμολογήσω κἀγὼ ἐν αὐτῷ ἔμπροσθεν τοῦ πατρός μου 'whoever confesses me before people, I will confess him before my Father' Mt 10.32.
ὁμολογία: κατέχωμεν τὴν ὁμολογίαν τῆς ἐλπίδος 'let us hold on to the hope we profess' He 10.23.
ἐξομολογέομαι[a]: διὰ τοῦτο ἐξομολογήσομαί σοι ἐν ἔθνεσιν 'therefore I will confess you before the Gentiles' Ro 15.9. For another interpretation of ἐξομολογέομαι in Ro 15.9, see 33.359.

It is often extremely difficult, if not impossible, to translate ὁμολογέω[a], ὁμολογία, and ἐξομολογέομαι[a] by the usual expression for 'confess,' since this would usually imply that one has done something wrong. It is normally necessary, therefore, to employ quite a different type of relationship, usually involving a public utterance and an expression of confidence or allegiance. For example, in Mt 10.32 it may be necessary to translate 'whoever tells people publicly that he is loyal to me, I will tell my Father that I am loyal to that person.' Similarly, in He 10.23 one may translate 'let us hold on to the hope in which we have told people we have such confidence.' Likewise, in Ro 15.9 one may translate 'therefore I will tell the Gentiles how I have put my confidence in you.'

V Admit, Confess, Deny (33.275-33.277)

33.275 ὁμολογέω^b; ἐξομολογέομαι^b: to acknowledge a fact publicly, often in reference to previous bad behavior – 'to admit, to confess.' ὁμολογέω^b: ἐὰν ὁμολογῶμεν τὰς ἁμαρτίας ἡμῶν 'if we confess our sins' 1 Jn 1.9. ἐξομολογέομαι^b: ἐξομολογούμενοι τὰς ἁμαρτίας αὐτῶν 'they confessed their sins' Mt 3.6. In translating Mt 3.6 in some languages, it may be useful to restructure the expression somewhat, for example, 'they admitted to people that they had sinned' or 'they admitted publicly to God . . .'

In Php 2.11 the statement πᾶσα γλῶσσα ἐξομολογήσηται ὅτι κύριος Ἰησοῦς Χριστός ('that everyone may confess that Jesus Christ is Lord') means simply to acknowledge a fact publicly, and in this instance there is no implication of previous bad behavior.

33.276 ὁμολογουμένως: (derivative of ὁμολογέω^b 'to admit,' 33.275) pertaining to what must or should be admitted or acknowledged publicly – 'admittedly, to be admitted, one must admit.' ὁμολογουμένως μέγα ἐστὶν τὸ τῆς εὐσεβείας μυστήριον 'one must admit that the mystery of our religion is great' 1 Tm 3.16.

33.277 ἀρνέομαι^a; ἀπαρνέομαι^a: to say that one does not know about or is in any way related to a person or event – 'to deny.'[49]

---

[49] It is quite possible that ἀπαρνέομαι^a is somewhat more forceful in meaning than ἀρνέομαι^a, but this cannot be demonstrated from NT usage.

ἀρνέομαι^a: ὅστις δ' ἂν ἀρνήσηταί με ἔμπροσθεν τῶν ἀνθρώπων 'whoever shall deny me before people' Mt 10.33; εἶπεν ὁ Ἰησοῦς, Τίς ὁ ἁψάμενός μου; ἀρνουμένων δὲ πάντων 'Jesus asked, Who touched me? But they all denied it' Lk 8.45.

ἀπαρνέομαι^a: πρὶν ἀλέκτορα φωνῆσαι τρὶς ἀπαρνήσῃ με 'before the rooster crows, you will deny me three times' Mt 26.34.

In translating ἀρνέομαι^a and ἀπαρνέομαι^a, one can often use an equivalent phrase such as 'to say that one does not know' or 'to say that one has nothing to do with.'

In denying an event, as in Lk 8.45, it may be possible to translate 'but they all said they knew nothing about it.' It is also possible to deny having done something, and therefore one may translate the response in Lk 8.45 as 'but they all said that they did not do it' or '. . . that they did not touch him.'

W Agree[50] (33.278-33.280)

33.278 ἐξομολογέω: to indicate agreement with a proposition or offer – 'to agree to.' συνέθεντο αὐτῷ ἀργύριον δοῦναι. καὶ ἐξωμολόγησεν 'they offered to pay him money, and he agreed to it' Lk 22.5-6. In some languages one may render 'he agreed to it' by simply saying 'he said, I will do it.'

33.279 ἐπινεύω: to indicate one's approval or agreement, sometimes only by nodding – 'to agree, to consent.' ἐρωτώντων δὲ αὐτῶν ἐπὶ πλείονα χρόνον μεῖναι οὐκ ἐπένευσεν 'they asked him to stay with them a long time, but he would not consent' Ac 18.20.

33.280 ἐπαγγελία^b, ας f: the content of one's agreement or approval – 'agreement, ap-

---

[50] As will be readily noted, there are aspects of the meanings in this subdomain of *Agree* which overlap in part with certain meanings in Domain 31 *Hold a View, Believe, Trust*, particularly those meanings which involve thinking the same as someone else (for example, 31.14-31.25). When the focus seems to be upon the agreement in thought, then the meaning would be classified in Domain 31. If, however, the focus appears to be upon the communication of such agreement, then the meaning is considered as belonging in Domain 33 *Communication*, Subdomain W *Agree*.

proval.' νῦν εἰσιν ἕτοιμοι προσδεχόμενοι τὴν ἀπὸ σοῦ ἐπαγγελίαν 'they are now ready (to do it), and are waiting for your approval' Ac 23.21. In ἐπαγγελία[b] the focus is upon the communication of agreement or approval. One may, therefore, translate 'and are waiting for your approval' in Ac 23.21 as 'and are waiting for a message from you concerning your agreement' or 'and are waiting for word from you as to your approval.'

X Foretell, Tell Fortunes (33.281-33.285)

33.281 προλέγω[b]: to say in advance what is going to happen – 'to tell ahead of time, to predict.' προελέγομεν ὑμῖν ὅτι μέλλομεν θλίβεσθαι 'we told you ahead of time that we were going to be persecuted' 1 Th 3.4.

33.282 προμαρτύρομαι: to state with assurance what is to happen in the future – 'to predict, to foretell.' προμαρτυρόμενον τὰ εἰς Χριστὸν παθήματα 'predicting the sufferings that Christ would have to endure' 1 Pe 1.11.

33.283 προκαταγγέλλω: to announce openly what is to happen in the future – 'to foretell, to predict.' προκατήγγειλεν διὰ στόματος πάντων τῶν προφητῶν παθεῖν τὸν Χριστὸν αὐτοῦ '(God) long ago foretold by means of all the prophets that his Messiah had to suffer' Ac 3.18.

33.284 μαντεύομαι: to function as a more or less professional predicter of future events for the sake of a fee – 'to tell fortunes.' ἥτις ἐργασίαν πολλὴν παρεῖχεν τοῖς κυρίοις αὐτῆς μαντευομένη 'she earned much money for her owners by telling fortunes' Ac 16.16. In Ac 16.16 μαντεύομαι may often be translated as 'for money she told people what was going to happen to them.'

33.285 ἔχω πνεῦμα πύθωνα: (an idiom, literally 'to have a spirit of python,' an appositional construction in Greek) to tell people for pay what would happen to them in the future – 'to be a fortuneteller.' παιδίσκην τινὰ ἔχουσαν πνεῦμα πύθωνα ὑπαντῆσαι ἡμῖν 'we were met

by a slave girl who was a fortuneteller' Ac 16.16.[51]

Y Promise (33.286-33.290)

33.286 ἐπαγγέλλομαι[a]: to announce with certainty as to what one will do – 'to promise.' ἐπηγγείλαντο αὐτῷ ἀργύριον δοῦναι 'they promised to give him money' Mk 14.11.

33.287 προεπαγγέλλομαι: to announce with certainty in advance as to what one will do – 'to promise beforehand.' ὃ προεπηγγείλατο διὰ τῶν προφητῶν αὐτοῦ ἐν γραφαῖς ἁγίαις 'which he promised beforehand through his prophets in the Holy Scriptures' Ro 1.2.

33.288 ἐπάγγελμα, τος n; ἐπαγγελία[a], ας f: (derivatives of ἐπαγγέλλομαι[a] 'to promise,' 33.286) the content of what is promised – 'promise.'[52]
ἐπάγγελμα: δι᾽ ὧν τὰ τίμια καὶ μέγιστα ἡμῖν ἐπαγγέλματα δεδώρηται 'thus he has given us precious and very great promises' 2 Pe 1.4.
ἐπαγγελία[a]: ὁ οὖν νόμος κατὰ τῶν ἐπαγγελιῶν τοῦ θεοῦ; 'does this mean that the Law is against God's promises?' Ga 3.21.

33.289 πίστις[f], εως f: a promise or pledge of faithfulness and loyalty – 'promise, pledge to be faithful.' ἔχουσαι κρίμα ὅτι τὴν πρώτην πίστιν ἠθέτησαν 'guilty of breaking their earlier pledge of faithfulness' 1 Tm 5.12.

33.290 τὰ ὅσια: the divine matters which have been promised – 'divine promises, promises from God.' δώσω ὑμῖν τὰ ὅσια Δαυὶδ τὰ πιστά 'I will give to you the divine promises made to David, promises that can be trusted' Ac 13.34. It is also possible to understand τὰ ὅσια in Ac 13.34 as meaning 'divine decrees' or 'decrees made by God.'

51 The phrase ἔχω πνεῦμα πύθωνα may focus upon the capacity to be a fortuneteller, but the implication is that the individual involved served as a fortuneteller. It is, however, possible to treat this expression in a somewhat different manner, as indicated in 12.48.
52 The meaning of ἐπάγγελμα and ἐπαγγελία[a] focuses primarily upon the content of what is promised, that is to say, what God or someone will do, but the fact of promising is always a relevant element.

Z Threaten (33.291-33.293)

33.291 ἀπειλέω; ἀπειλή, ῆς *f*: to declare that one will cause harm to someone, particularly if certain conditions are not met – 'to threaten, threat.'
ἀπειλέω: πάσχων οὐκ ἠπείλει 'when he suffered, he did not threaten' 1 Pe 2.23.
ἀπειλή: ἀνιέντες τὴν ἀπειλήν 'and stop threatening' Eph 6.9; ἔπιδε ἐπὶ τὰς ἀπειλὰς αὐτῶν 'take notice of the threats they made' Ac 4.29.

Because of the implied reciprocity in ἀπειλέω and ἀπειλή, one may translate 1 Pe 2.23 as 'when he suffered, he did not say he would make them suffer.'

33.292 προσαπειλέομαι: to add to or to extend one's threats – 'to threaten further.' προσαπειλησάμενοι ἀπέλυσαν αὐτούς 'after threatening them further, they set them free' Ac 4.21. It is also possible to understand προσαπειλέομαι in Ac 4.21 as meaning 'to threaten besides.'

33.293 ἐμπνέω ἀπειλῆς: (an idiom, literally 'to breathe out threat') to express dire threats – 'to threaten strongly, to make firm threats.' ὁ δὲ Σαῦλος, ἔτι ἐμπνέων ἀπειλῆς καὶ φόνου εἰς τοὺς μαθητὰς τοῦ κυρίου 'Saul was still making firm threats to kill the disciples of the Lord' Ac 9.1.[53]

A' Advise[54] (33.294-33.298)

33.294 συμβουλεύω: to tell someone what he or she should plan to do – 'to advise, to counsel.' ἦν δὲ Καϊάφας ὁ συμβουλεύσας τοῖς Ἰουδαίοις ὅτι συμφέρει ἕνα ἄνθρωπον ἀποθανεῖν ὑπὲρ τοῦ λαοῦ 'it was Caiaphas who had advised the Jews that it was better that one man die for all the people' Jn 18.14.

[53] The phrase ἀπειλῆς καὶ φόνου is syntactically coordinate but semantically subordinate, in that the content of the threats is to kill the disciples.
[54] Some of the meanings in this subdomain parallel closely Subdomain D *To Intend, To Purpose, To Plan* in Domain 30 *Think*, but the meanings in Subdomain A' focus upon the communication of plans or purposes rather than upon the process of thinking.

33.295 παραινέω: to indicate strongly to someone what he or she should plan to do – 'to advise strongly, to urge.' τὰ νῦν παραινῶ ὑμᾶς εὐθυμεῖν, ἀποβολὴ γὰρ ψυχῆς οὐδεμία ἔσται ἐξ ὑμῶν 'I now strongly advise you to take courage, for no one of you will lose his life' Ac 27.22.

33.296 τίθημι βουλήν: (an idiom, literally 'to put a plan') to suggest a plan of action – 'to advise, to recommend.' οἱ πλείονες ἔθεντο βουλὴν ἀναχθῆναι ἐκεῖθεν 'most of the men advised putting out to sea from there' Ac 27.12.

33.297 σύμβουλος, ου *m*: (derivative of συμβουλεύω 'to advise,' 33.294) one who gives advice – 'adviser.' τίς γὰρ ἔγνω νοῦν κυρίου; ἢ τίς σύμβουλος αὐτοῦ ἐγένετο; 'who knows the mind of the Lord? Who can be his adviser?' Ro 11.34.

33.298 συμβιβάζω[d]: to advise by giving instructions – 'to advise, to instruct.' τίς γὰρ ἔγνω νοῦν κυρίου, ὃς συμβιβάσει αὐτόν; 'who knows the mind of the Lord that he can advise him?' 1 Cor 2.16.

B' Urge, Persuade (33.299-33.306)

33.299 προβιβάζω; προσβιβάζω; παραβιάζομαι: to speak in such a way as to encourage a particular type of behavior or action – 'to urge.'
προβιβάζω: προβιβασθεῖσα ὑπὸ τῆς μητρὸς αὐτῆς, Δός μοι, φησίν 'urged by her mother, she said, Give me . . .' Mt 14.8. It is also possible that προβιβάζω in Mt 14.8 should be interpreted to mean 'to be urged on beforehand' or 'to be put forward.'
προσβιβάζω: ἐκ δὲ τοῦ ὄχλου προσεβίβασαν Ἀλέξανδρον 'some from the crowd urged Alexander' Ac 19.33 (apparatus).
παραβιάζομαι: παρεβιάσαντο αὐτὸν λέγοντες, Μεῖνον μεθ' ἡμῶν 'they urged him saying, Stay with us' Lk 24.29.

33.300 προτρέπομαι: to urge a particular course of action – 'to urge.' προτρεψάμενοι οἱ ἀδελφοὶ ἔγραψαν τοῖς μαθηταῖς ἀποδέξασθαι αὐτόν 'the fellow believers wrote and urged the disciples to receive him' Ac 18.27.

33.301 πείθω^a: to convince someone to believe something and to act on the basis of what is recommended – 'to persuade, to convince.' ἔπεισαν τοὺς ὄχλους ἵνα αἰτήσωνται τὸν Βαραββᾶν 'they persuaded the crowds to ask for Barabbas (to be set free)' Mt 27.20; πείσαντες Βλάστον τὸν ἐπὶ τοῦ κοιτῶνος τοῦ βασιλέως 'they persuaded Blastus, who was in charge of the palace' Ac 12.20.

33.302 ἀναπείθω: to persuade, with the possible implication of resistance and/or for wrong motives or results – 'to persuade, to incite.' παρὰ τὸν νόμον ἀναπείθει οὗτος τοὺς ἀνθρώπους σέβεσθαι τὸν θεόν 'this man incites people to worship God in a way that is against the Law' Ac 18.13.

33.303 πεισμονή, ῆς *f*: (derivative of πείθω^a 'to persuade,' 33.301) the means by which someone is caused to believe – 'that which persuades, the means of convincing.' ἡ πεισμονὴ οὐκ ἐκ τοῦ καλοῦντος ὑμᾶς 'that which persuaded (you) did not come from the one who called you' Ga 5.8. It is also possible to interpret πεισμονή in Ga 5.8 as the actual process of persuasion, in which case πεισμονή would be classified as a nominal form corresponding to πείθω^a (33.301). Such an interpretation would require one to render Ga 5.8 as 'he who called you was not the one who persuaded you.'

33.304 πειθός, ή, όν: (derivative of πείθω^a 'to persuade,' 33.301) pertaining to being able to persuade or convince – 'persuasive, convincing.' ὁ λόγος μου καὶ τὸ κήρυγμά μου οὐκ ἐν πειθοῖς σοφίας λόγοις 'my message and my preaching were not with persuasive words of wisdom' 1 Cor 2.4.

33.305 εὐπειθής, ές: pertaining to being easily persuaded, with the implication of being open to reason or willing to listen – 'one who is easily persuaded, open to reason.' ἡ δὲ ἄνωθεν σοφία . . . ἔπειτα εἰρηνική, ἐπιεικής, εὐπειθής 'the wisdom from above is . . . also peaceful, gentle, and open to reason' Jas 3.17.

33.306 πειθώ, οῦς, dat sg. πειθοῖ *f*: (derivative of πείθω^a 'to persuade,' 33.301) the capacity to persuade or convince – 'persuasive power, convincing ability.' ἐν πειθοῖ σοφίας 'with the persuasive power of (human) wisdom' 1 Cor 2.4 (apparatus).

C' Call (33.307-33.314)

33.307 φωνέω^a; καλέω^c: to communicate directly or indirectly to someone who is presumably at a distance, in order to tell such a person to come – 'to call, to summon.'[55]
φωνέω^a: φωνήσας αὐτὸν εἶπεν αὐτῷ, Τί τοῦτο ἀκούω περὶ σοῦ; '(his master) called him in and said to him, What is this I hear about you?' Lk 16.2.
καλέω^c: ἄνθρωπος ἀποδημῶν ἐκάλεσεν τοὺς ἰδίους δούλους 'a man who was about to leave home on a trip called his servants' Mt 25.14.

33.308 προσφωνέω^c; προσκαλέομαι^a: to call to, with a possible implication of a reciprocal relation – 'to call, to call to.'
προσφωνέω^c: ὅτε ἐγένετο ἡμέρα, προσεφώνησεν τοὺς μαθητὰς αὐτοῦ 'when day came, he called his disciples to him' Lk 6.13.
προσκαλέομαι^a: προσκαλεσάμενος τὸν ὄχλον εἶπεν αὐτοῖς 'he called the crowd to him and said to them' Mt 15.10.

33.309 συγκαλέω: to call persons together, presumably at the reference point of the one who calls – 'to call together.' ἐγένετο δὲ μετὰ ἡμέρας τρεῖς συγκαλέσασθαι αὐτὸν τοὺς ὄντας τῶν Ἰουδαίων πρώτους 'after three days, he called the local Jewish leaders together' Ac 28.17. In some languages it may be almost necessary to indicate something about the place to which people are called. For example, in Ac 28.17 one may translate 'he called the local Jewish leaders together to where he was.'

33.310 παρακαλέω^c: to call to come to where the speaker is – 'to call together to.' διὰ ταύτην οὖν τὴν αἰτίαν παρεκάλεσα ὑμᾶς ἰδεῖν καὶ προσλαλῆσαι 'that is why I called you together to see you and talk with you' Ac 28.20. It is

---

[55] It is possible that φωνέω^a differs from καλέω^c in focusing somewhat more upon the loudness of voice, but this cannot be determined from existing contexts.

also possible to interpret παρακαλέω in Ac 28.20 as meaning 'to request' (see 33.168).

33.311 μετακαλέομαι: to summon someone, with considerable insistence and authority – 'to summon, to tell to come.' καιρὸν δὲ μεταλαβὼν μετακαλέσομαί σε 'and when I have time, I will summon you' Ac 24.25.

33.312 καλέω[d]; κλῆσις[a], εως *f*; προσκαλέομαι[b]: to urgently invite someone to accept responsibilities for a particular task, implying a new relationship to the one who does the calling – 'to call, to call to a task.'[56]
καλέω[d]: εἰς ὃ καὶ ἐκάλεσεν ὑμᾶς διὰ τοῦ εὐαγγελίου ἡμῶν '(God) called you to this through the good news we preached to you' 2 Th 2.14.
κλῆσις[a]: εἰς τὸ εἰδέναι ὑμᾶς τίς ἐστιν ἡ ἐλπὶς τῆς κλήσεως αὐτοῦ 'so that you will know what is the hope to which he has called you' Eph 1.18.
προσκαλέομαι[b]: ὅτι προσκέκληται ἡμᾶς ὁ θεὸς εὐαγγελίσασθαι αὐτούς 'because God has called us to preach the good news to them' or '. . . to the people there' Ac 16.10.
It is rare that one can translate καλέω[d], κλῆσις[a], and προσκαλέομαι[b] as simply 'to call' in the sense of 'to speak to someone at a distance and tell them to come.' For example, in 2 Th 2.14 it may be necessary to render the above clause as 'through the good news we preached, which summoned you to do this.' Similarly, in Ac 16.10 one may translate 'because God has urgently invited us to preach the good news to the people there.'

33.313 κλῆσις[b], εως *f*: the state of having been called to a particular task and/or relation – 'calling.' παρακαλῶ οὖν ὑμᾶς . . . ἀξίως περιπατῆσαι τῆς κλήσεως ἧς ἐκλήθητε 'I ask you then . . . live worthy of your calling to which (God) has called you' Eph 4.1. As in the case of καλέω[d], κλῆσις[a], and προσκαλέομαι[b] (33.312), it may be entirely impossible to use a term in a receptor language which means

literally 'to call.' Therefore, it may be necessary to translate Eph 4.1 as 'I ask you then . . . live worthy of the responsibility which God has urgently invited you to accept' or '. . . live worthy of the task which God has given you to do.'

33.314 κλητός[a], ή, όν: pertaining to having been called – 'called.' κλητὸς ἀπόστολος 'called to be an apostle' Ro 1.1. As in the case of the translation of meanings in 33.312 and 33.313, it may be necessary likewise to make certain semantic adjustments in the translation of κλητός[a]. For example, the phrase in Ro 1.1 may be rendered as 'urgently invited to be an apostle' or even 'summoned and commissioned to be an apostle.'

D' Invite (33.315-33.318)

33.315 καλέω[e]; φωνέω[d]; παρακαλέω[b]: to ask a person to accept offered hospitality – 'to invite.'[57]
καλέω[e]: ὅταν κληθῇς ὑπό τινος εἰς γάμους 'when someone invites you to a wedding feast' Lk 14.8.
φωνέω[d]: ὅταν ποιῇς ἄριστον ἢ δεῖπνον, μὴ φώνει 'when you give a lunch or dinner, do not invite . . .' Lk 14.12.
παρακαλέω[b]: παρεκάλει αὐτὸν εἰσελθεῖν εἰς τὸν οἶκον αὐτοῦ 'he invited him to come to his home' Lk 8.41.

33.316 εἰσκαλέομαι: to invite a person in as a guest – 'to invite in.' εἰσκαλεσάμενος οὖν αὐτοὺς ἐξένισεν 'he invited the men in and entertained them as guests' Ac 10.23.

33.317 ἀντικαλέω: to invite someone in return – 'to invite back.' αὐτοὶ ἀντικαλέσωσίν σε καὶ γένηται ἀνταπόδομά σοι 'they will invite you back and you will be paid for what you did' Lk 14.12.

33.318 κλητός[b], ή, όν: pertaining to having been invited – 'invited.' πολλοὶ γάρ εἰσιν

---

56 It is possible that προσκαλέομαι[b] differs in meaning from καλέω[d] in emphasizing more specifically either the person who is called or the task to which one is called.

57 It is possible that παρακαλέω[b] differs somewhat in meaning from καλέω[e] and φωνέω[d] in implying some greater degree of urging.

κλητοὶ ὀλίγοι δὲ ἐκλεκτοί 'for many are invited, but few are chosen' Mt 22.14. It is possible that this expression in Mt 22.14 was a common popular saying, namely, an adage. There are certain problems in the understanding of this adage in Mt 22.14, for it would seem as though many persons are invited to do something, but few are permitted to do it. Perhaps this should be understood in the sense of 'many are invited to apply, but few are selected.' In this context, of course, both the invitation and the selection would be by God.

E' Insist (33.319-33.322)

33.319 μαρτύρομαι[b]; διαμαρτύρομαι[b]: to be emphatic in stating an opinion or desire – 'to insist.'[58]
μαρτύρομαι[b]: μαρτυρόμενοι εἰς τὸ περιπατεῖν ὑμᾶς ἀξίως τοῦ θεοῦ 'we insisted on your living the kind of life that pleases God' 1 Th 2.12.
διαμαρτύρομαι[b]: ἑτέροις τε λόγοις πλείοσιν διεμαρτύρατο 'with many other words, he insisted' Ac 2.40.

33.320 ἐμβριμάομαι[a]: to state something with sternness – 'to insist sternly.' ἐνεβριμήθη αὐτοῖς ὁ Ἰησοῦς λέγων, Ὁρᾶτε μηδεὶς γινωσκέτω 'Jesus insisted sternly (or '. . . sternly charged them'), Don't tell this to anyone' Mt 9.30.

33.321 διϊσχυρίζομαι: to state something with firmness and certainty – 'to insist firmly, to insist.' ἄλλος τις διϊσχυρίζετο λέγων, Ἐπ' ἀληθείας καὶ οὗτος μετ' αὐτοῦ ἦν 'another man insisted, Without doubt this man was with him' Lk 22.59.

33.322 διαβεβαιόομαι: to state something with confidence and certainty – 'to state with confidence, to insist.' πιστὸς ὁ λόγος, καὶ περὶ τούτων βούλομαί σε διαβεβαιοῦσθαι 'this is a true saying, and I want you to insist on these matters' Tt 3.8.

---

58 It is possible that διαμαρτύρομαι[b] is somewhat more emphatic in connotation than μαρτύρομαι[b], but this cannot be determined from existing contexts.

F' Command, Order (33.323-33.332)

33.323 κελεύω; διαστέλλομαι: to state with force and/or authority what others must do – 'to order, to command.'
κελεύω: ἐκέλευσεν αὐτὸν ὁ κύριος πραθῆναι 'his master ordered him to be sold as a slave' Mt 18.25.
διαστέλλομαι: διεστείλατο αὐτοῖς ἵνα μηδενὶ λέγωσιν 'he ordered them not to speak of it to anyone' Mk 7.36.
In a number of languages the equivalent of 'to order' or 'to command' is 'to speak with strength' or 'to speak strong words' or, in the form of direct discourse, 'to tell others, You must . . .'

33.324 κέλευσμα, τος n: (derivative of κελεύω 'to command,' 33.323) the voicing of a command – 'command, call of command.' ὁ κύριος ἐν κελεύσματι, ἐν φωνῇ ἀρχαγγέλου καὶ ἐν σάλπιγγι θεοῦ, καταβήσεται ἀπ' οὐρανοῦ 'at the word of command, at the sound of the archangel's voice, and at the sound of the trumpet of God, the Lord will come down from heaven' 1 Th 4.16. In a number of languages the expression 'at the word of command' may be rendered as 'when the command is given' or 'when the command is shouted.'

33.325 τάσσω[c]; συντάσσω; προστάσσω[a]; ἐπιτάσσω; διατάσσω[a]: to give detailed instructions as to what must be done – 'to order, to instruct, to tell, to command.'[59]
τάσσω[c]: εἰς τὸ ὄρος οὗ ἐτάξατο αὐτοῖς ὁ Ἰησοῦς 'to the mountain where Jesus had told them to go' Mt 28.16.
συντάσσω: ποιήσαντες καθὼς συνέταξεν αὐτοῖς ὁ Ἰησοῦς 'they did what Jesus had instructed them (to do)' Mt 21.6.
προστάσσω[a]: ἐποίησεν ὡς προσέταξεν αὐτῷ ὁ ἄγγελος 'he did what the angel had told him (to do)' Mt 1.24.
ἐπιτάσσω: παρρησίαν ἔχων ἐπιτάσσειν σοι τὸ ἀνῆκον 'being bold enough to order you to do what should be done' Phm 8.

---

59 The meanings of τάσσω[c], συντάσσω, προστάσσω[a], ἐπιτάσσω, and διατάσσω[a] no doubt differ somewhat, particularly in connotation, but it is not possible to determine this from existing contexts.

διατάσσω^a: διέταξεν αὐτῇ δοθῆναι φαγεῖν 'he ordered them to give her something to eat' Lk 8.55.

33.326 ἐπιταγή^a, ῆς *f*; διαταγή, ῆς *f*; διάταγμα, τος *n*: (derivatives of ἐπιτάσσω and διατάσσω^a 'to order, to instruct,' 33.325) that which has been specifically ordered or commanded – 'order, command, decree, ordinance, instruction.'
ἐπιταγή^a: κατ' ἐπιταγὴν τοῦ αἰωνίου θεοῦ . . . εἰς πάντα τὰ ἔθνη γνωρισθέντος 'by the order of the eternal God . . . it is made known to all nations' Ro 16.26.
διαταγή: οἵτινες ἐλάβετε τὸν νόμον εἰς διαταγὰς ἀγγέλων 'you who received the law on the basis of instructions given by angels' or '. . . on the basis of decrees delivered by angels' Ac 7.53; τῇ τοῦ θεοῦ διαταγῇ ἀνθέστηκεν 'he opposed what God had ordered' Ro 13.2.
διάταγμα: οὐκ ἐφοβήθησαν τὸ διάταγμα τοῦ βασιλέως 'they were not afraid of the king's order' He 11.23.

33.327 ἀπαγγέλλω^b; παραγγέλλω: to announce what must be done – 'to order, to command.'
ἀπαγγέλλω^b: ὁ θεὸς τὰ νῦν ἀπαγγέλλει τοῖς ἀνθρώποις πάντας πανταχοῦ μετανοεῖν 'now God orders all people everywhere to turn away from their evil ways' Ac 17.30 (apparatus).
παραγγέλλω: παραγγέλλει τῷ ὄχλῳ ἀναπεσεῖν ἐπὶ τῆς γῆς 'he ordered the crowd to sit down on the grass' Mk 8.6.

33.328 παραγγελία, ας *f*: (derivative of παραγγέλλω 'to order, to command.' 33.327) an announcement as to what must be done – 'order, instruction, command.' οἴδατε γὰρ τίνας παραγγελίας ἐδώκαμεν ὑμῖν 'for you know the orders we gave you' 1 Th 4.2.

33.329 ἐντέλλομαι: to give definite orders, implying authority or official sanction – 'to command.' ταῦτα ἐντέλλομαι ὑμῖν, ἵνα ἀγαπᾶτε ἀλλήλους 'this is what I command you: love one another' Jn 15.17.

33.330 ἐντολή, ῆς *f*; ἔνταλμα, τος *n*: (derivatives of ἐντέλλομαι 'to command,' 33.329)

that which is authoritatively commanded – 'commandment, order.'
ἐντολή: ἐντολὴν καινὴν δίδωμι ὑμῖν, ἵνα ἀγαπᾶτε ἀλλήλους 'a new commandment I give you: love one another' Jn 13.34.
ἔνταλμα: κατὰ τὰ ἐντάλματα καὶ διδασκαλίας τῶν ἀνθρώπων 'in accordance with the commandments and teachings of people' Col 2.22.

33.331 ἐπιτιμάω^b: to command, with the implication of a threat – 'to command.'
ἐπετίμησεν τῷ ἀνέμῳ καὶ τῷ κλύδωνι τοῦ ὕδατος· καὶ ἐπαύσαντο 'he gave a command to the wind and the stormy water, and they quieted down' Lk 8.24.

33.332 δόγμα^b, τος *n*: an official order or decree – 'order, decree.' ἐξῆλθεν δόγμα παρὰ Καίσαρος Αὐγούστου 'Emperor Augustus sent out an order' Lk 2.1.

G' Law, Regulation, Ordinance (33.333-33.342)

33.333 νόμος^a, ου *m*; δόγμα^a, τος *n*: a formalized rule (or set of rules) prescribing what people must do – 'law, ordinance, rule.'
νόμος^a: ὃς οὐ κατὰ νόμον ἐντολῆς σαρκίνης γέγονεν 'he was not made (a priest) by the law of human decree' He 7.16.
δόγμα^a: παρεδίδοσαν αὐτοῖς φυλάσσειν τὰ δόγματα 'they delivered to them the rules which they were to obey' Ac 16.4.

The difference between 'a law' and 'a command' is that a law is enforced by sanctions from a society, while a command carries only the sanctions of the individual who commands. When, however, the people of Israel accepted the commands of God as the rules which they would follow and enforce, these became their laws.

The occurrence of νόμος two times in Ro 8.2 poses certain problems of both translation and interpretation: ὁ γὰρ νόμος τοῦ πνεύματος τῆς ζωῆς ἐν Χριστῷ Ἰησοῦ ἠλευθέρωσέν σε ἀπὸ τοῦ νόμου τῆς ἁμαρτίας καὶ τοῦ θανάτου 'for the law of the Spirit of life in Christ Jesus freed you from the law which leads to sin and death.' In the second occurrence of νόμος, the meaning is clearly the rules and regulations of the OT law, but in the case of the first occurrence of νόμος, there is no such formulation of decrees. The reference in this instance must therefore be to certain basic principles. If, however, one understands νόμος in the sense of a type of abstract 'governing power,' it is possible that the reference in the phrase νόμος τοῦ πνεύματος τῆς ζωῆς is to this governing power of the Spirit of life which frees one from the law which stipulates sin and death.

33.334 δικαίωμαᵃ, **τος** *n*: (derivative of δικαιόω 'to act justly,' not occurring in the NT) a regulation concerning right or just action – 'regulation, requirement.'[60] οἵτινες τὸ δικαίωμα τοῦ θεοῦ ἐπιγνόντες 'who know the requirements imposed by God' Ro 1.32.

33.335 κανώνᵃ, **όνος** *m*: a rule involving a standard for conduct – 'rule, principle.' ὅσοι τῷ κανόνι τούτῳ στοιχήσουσιν 'as many as follow this rule' Ga 6.16.

33.336 ἔννομοςᵃ, **ον**: (derivative of νόμοςᵃ 'law, rule,' 33.333) pertaining to being in accordance with law – 'legal, in accordance with law.' ἐν τῇ ἐννόμῳ ἐκκλησίᾳ ἐπιλυθήσεται 'it will have to be settled in the legal meeting of citizens' Ac 19.39. In some languages the equivalent of 'legal meeting' would be 'regular meeting' or 'a meeting called by an official' or 'a meeting authorized by an official.'

33.337 νομικός, ή, όν: (derivative of νόμοςᵃ 'law, rule,' 33.333) pertaining to law – 'about the law, about laws.' μάχας νομικὰς περιΐστασο 'avoid fights about laws' Tt 3.9. It is also possible to understand νομικός in Tt 3.9 as specifically the Jewish Law (see νόμοςᵇ, 33.55).

33.338 νομικόςᵃ, **οῦ** *m*: one who is an expert in interpreting religious law (with a probable exception of Tt 3.13 (see 56.37), always in reference to the Jewish Law) – 'interpreter of the Law, expert in the Law.' νομικός τις ἀνέστη ἐκπειράζων αὐτόν 'an expert in the Law came up and tried to test him' or '. . . trap him' Lk 10.25.

33.339 νομοθετέω; νομοθεσία, ας *f*: to give or to establish a law – 'to enact a law, to give a law.'
νομοθετέω: ἥτις ἐπὶ κρείττοσιν ἐπαγγελίαις νενομοθέτηται '(a covenant) which has been given as law based on better promises' He 8.6.
νομοθεσία: ὧν . . . αἱ διαθῆκαι καὶ ἡ νομοθεσία 'to whom belong . . . the covenants and the giving of the Law' Ro 9.4. In Ro 9.4 νομοθεσία refers specifically to the giving of the Jewish Law.
Though in English it is normal to speak of 'giving a law,' such an expression can be entirely misleading, since in some languages 'to give a law' can mean 'to annul a law' in the sense of giving back to people a rule or regulation. A more frequent expression for 'giving a law' may be 'commanding a law' or 'ordering a law.'

33.340 νομοθέτης, ου *m*: (derivative of νομοθετέω 'to give a law,' 33.339) one who gives or enacts laws – 'lawgiver.' εἷς ἐστιν ὁ νομοθέτης καὶ κριτής '(God) is the only lawgiver and judge' Jas 4.12. In a number of languages it is not possible to speak literally of a 'lawgiver' as 'one who gives laws,' for laws seem to be quite distinct from gifts. However, the same meaning is often communicated by somewhat different expressions, for example, 'one who decides what people must do' or 'one who makes a law stand' or 'one who gives strength to a law.'

33.341 νόμος τοῦ ἀνδρός: (an idiom, literally 'law of the man' or 'law of the husband') the law which binds a woman to a man in marriage – 'marriage law.' ἐὰν δὲ ἀποθάνῃ ὁ ἀνήρ, κατήργηται ἀπὸ τοῦ νόμου τοῦ ἀνδρός 'but if her husband dies, she is free from the marriage law' Ro 7.2. It may be especially difficult in some languages to speak of 'being free from the marriage law.' An appropriate equivalent in some languages may be 'she is no longer obliged to remain the wife of the dead man,' but in other languages it is more meaningful

---

60 It is possible that the element of 'just' in the definition of δικαίωμαᵃ is essentially connotative rather than denotative.

to say 'she is then permitted to marry another man.'

33.342 ἔννομος^b, ον: pertaining to being under obligation imposed by law – 'subject to law, under law.' ἀλλ' ἔννομος Χριστοῦ 'but subject to the law of Christ' 1 Cor 9.21. In some languages there is a difficulty involved in rendering ἔννομος by a phrase such as 'under law,' since this may be understood in a sense of 'beneath the law' or 'illegal.' A more common expression would be 'tied to the law' or 'obligated by the law.'

H' Recommend, Propose (33.343-33.346)

33.343 ἵστημι^f: to speak of someone or something as being well qualified or suited for a particular purpose – 'to propose, to recommend.' καὶ ἔστησαν δύο 'and they proposed two persons' Ac 1.23. For another interpretation of ἵστημι in Ac 1.23, see 30.87.

33.344 συνίστημι^a or συνιστάνω^a: to indicate approval of a person or event, with the implication that others adopt the same attitude – 'to recommend.' συνίστημι δὲ ὑμῖν Φοίβην τὴν ἀδελφὴν ἡμῶν 'I recommend to you Phoebe, our sister in Christ' (or 'our fellow believer Phoebe') Ro 16.1; ἀρχόμεθα πάλιν ἑαυτοὺς συνιστάνειν; 'are we beginning to recommend ourselves again?' 2 Cor 3.1.

33.345 συστατικός, ή, όν: (derivative of συνίστημι^a 'to recommend,' 33.344) pertaining to being commended or recommended – 'commendatory, of recommendation.' μὴ χρῄζομεν ὥς τινες συστατικῶν ἐπιστολῶν πρὸς ὑμᾶς 'could it be that, like some other people, we need letters of recommendation to you' 2 Cor 3.1. It may be necessary to restructure considerably the components in an expression such as 'we need letters of recommendation to you,' for example, 'we need letters written to you which recommend us' or '. . . which say, These men are good.'

33.346 τάσσω^d: to propose something to someone – 'to propose, to suggest.' ταξάμενοι δὲ αὐτῷ ἡμέραν ἦλθον πρὸς αὐτόν 'when they

had set a day with him, they came to him' Ac 28.23. It is also possible to understand τάσσω in Ac 28.23 as meaning 'to arrange,' but in Ac 28.23 it would seem that τάσσω implies not only proposing a date but obtaining an agreement.

I' Intercede (33.347-33.348)

33.347 ἐντυγχάνω^b; ἔντευξις, εως f: to speak to someone on behalf of someone else – 'to intercede, intercession.'
ἐντυγχάνω^b: ὃς καὶ ἐντυγχάνει ὑπὲρ ἡμῶν 'who also intercedes on our behalf' Ro 8.34.
ἔντευξις: ἁγιάζεται γὰρ διὰ λόγου θεοῦ καὶ ἐντεύξεως 'for it is made acceptable to God through his word (literally 'God's word') and through your intercession' 1 Tm 4.5.[61]

33.348 ὑπερεντυγχάνω: to intercede on behalf of someone, with specific emphasis upon the fact that what is being done is for the sake of someone else – 'to intercede on behalf of, to intercede for.'[62] τὸ πνεῦμα ὑπερεντυγχάνει στεναγμοῖς ἀλαλήτοις 'the Spirit intercedes with groans that cannot be expressed in words' Ro 8.26.

J' Thanks[63] (33.349-33.353)

33.349 εὐχαριστέω^a; εὐχαριστία, ας f: to express gratitude for benefits or blessings – 'to thank, thanksgiving, thankfulness.'
εὐχαριστέω^a: τί βλασφημοῦμαι ὑπὲρ οὗ ἐγὼ εὐχαριστῶ; 'why should anyone revile me about that for which I thank God?' 1 Cor 10.30.
εὐχαριστία: μετὰ εὐχαριστίας τὰ αἰτήματα ὑμῶν γνωριζέσθω πρὸς τὸν θεόν 'let your requests be made known to God with thanksgiving' Php 4.6.

Thanks is often expressed in highly idioma-

---

61 In a context such as 1 Tm 4.5, ἔντευξις could be classified as a form of prayer and thus occur in Subdomain M *Pray* in this domain.

62 ὑπερεντυγχάνω seems to differ somewhat from ἐντυγχάνω^b and ἔντευξις (33.347) in focusing more attention upon the fact that what is being said is for the special benefit of someone else. This seems to be implied by the prefix ὑπερ-.

63 Compare 25.99-25.101, where attitudes of thankfulness are treated.

tic ways. For example, in some languages one says thank you by saying 'may God pay you.' Such a phrase may be so standardized as to even be used in expressing thankfulness to God himself. In other instances, thankfulness may be expressed as 'you have made my heart warm.'

33.350 χάρις^c, ιτος *f*: an expression of thankfulness – 'thanks.' τῷ δὲ θεῷ χάρις τῷ διδόντι ἡμῖν τὸ νῖκος 'thanks be to God who gives us the victory' 1 Cor 15.57.⁶⁴

33.351 ἐξομολογέομαι^c; ἀνθομολογέομαι: to acknowledge one's thankfulness, restricted in NT usage to contexts in which God is the one being thanked – 'to thank, to give thanks to.'
ἐξομολογέομαι^c: ὁ Ἰησοῦς εἶπεν, Ἐξομολογοῦμαί σοι, πάτερ, κύριε τοῦ οὐρανοῦ καὶ τῆς γῆς 'Jesus said, I thank you, Father, Lord of heaven and earth' Mt 11.25.
ἀνθομολογέομαι: ἀνθωμολογεῖτο τῷ θεῷ 'she gave thanks to God' Lk 2.38.

33.352 εὐχάριστος^b, ον: (derivative of εὐχαριστέω^a 'to thank,' 33.349) pertaining to expressing thanks – 'thankful, thanking, grateful.' εἰς ἣν καὶ ἐκλήθητε ἐν ἑνὶ σώματι· καὶ εὐχάριστοι γίνεσθε 'to which you have been called together in one body; be then thankful' Col 3.15. For another interpretation of εὐχάριστος in Col 3.15, see 25.99.

33.353 ἀχάριστος^b, ον: pertaining to not being thankful – 'unthankful, ungrateful.' αὐτὸς χρηστός ἐστιν ἐπὶ τοὺς ἀχαρίστους καὶ πονηρούς 'he is good to the ungrateful and the wicked' Lk 6.35. For another interpretation of ἀχάριστος in Lk 6.35, see 25.101.

K' Praise (33.354-33.364)

33.354 αἰνέω; αἶνος, ου *m*; αἴνεσις, εως *f*; ἐπαινέω; ἔπαινος^a, ου *m*: to speak of the excellence of a person, object, or event – 'to praise, praise.'

αἰνέω: ἐγένετο σὺν τῷ ἀγγέλῳ πλῆθος στρατιᾶς οὐρανίου αἰνούντων τὸν θεόν 'there appeared with the angel a great army of heaven's angels praising God' Lk 2.13.
αἶνος: πᾶς ὁ λαὸς ἰδὼν ἔδωκεν αἶνον τῷ θεῷ 'when the crowd saw it, they all praised God' Lk 18.43.⁶⁵
αἴνεσις: ἀναφέρωμεν θυσίαν αἰνέσεως διὰ παντὸς τῷ θεῷ 'let us always offer praise as our sacrifice to God' He 13.15.⁶⁵
ἐπαινέω: ἐπήνεσεν ὁ κύριος τὸν οἰκονόμον τῆς ἀδικίας ὅτι φρονίμως ἐποίησεν 'the master of this dishonest manager praised him for doing such a clever thing' Lk 16.8.
ἔπαινος^a: εἰς ἔπαινον δόξης τῆς χάριτος αὐτοῦ 'to the praise of the glory of his grace' Eph 1.6.
In a number of languages praise can only be expressed by direct discourse, and this requires some content which provides the basis for praise. For example, in Lk 2.13 instead of a literal rendering of 'praising God,' it may be necessary to have 'they said, God is wonderful,' and in Lk 16.8 it may be necessary to translate 'the master of this dishonest manager said, You are remarkable for having done such a clever thing.'

33.355 ἔπαινος^b, ου *m*: that which is worthy of or deserves praise – 'something worthy of praise, something praiseworthy.' καὶ εἴ τις ἔπαινος 'and if there is anything praiseworthy' Php 4.8. In some languages the closest equivalent of 'praiseworthy' is 'something which people should praise.'

33.356 εὐλογέω^a; εὐλογία^a, ας *f*; εὐφημία, ας *f*: to speak of something in favorable terms – 'to praise, to speak well of.'
εὐλογέω^a: ἐν αὐτῇ εὐλογοῦμεν τὸν κύριον καὶ πατέρα 'with it we praise the Lord and Father' Jas 3.9.
εὐλογία^a: τῷ καθημένῳ ἐπὶ τῷ θρόνῳ καὶ τῷ ἀρνίῳ ἡ εὐλογία καὶ ἡ τιμή 'to him who sits on

---

64 χάρις^c is a performative expression which communicates thanks by being uttered.

65 The verbs δίδωμι and ἀναφέρω in Lk 18.43 and He 13.15, respectively, serve as what might be called 'empty verbs,' since the semantic content exists in the nouns αἶνος and αἴνεσις. The primary function of δίδωμι and ἀναφέρω in such contexts is to serve as a vehicle for marking case relations (see Domain 90). The same applies to δίδωμι in Lk 17.18 (see 33.357).

the throne, and to the Lamb, be praise and honor' Re 5.13.

εὐφημία: διὰ δόξης καὶ ἀτιμίας, διὰ δυσφημίας καὶ εὐφημίας 'we are honored and disgraced, we are slandered and praised' 2 Cor 6.8.

33.357 δοξάζωᵃ; **δόξα**ᵈ, **ης** *f*: to speak of something as being unusually fine and deserving honor – 'to praise, to glorify, praise.' δοξάζω ᵃ: ὥσπερ οἱ ὑποκριταὶ ποιοῦσιν . . . ὅπως δοξασθῶσιν ὑπὸ τῶν ἀνθρώπων 'like the show-offs do . . . so that people will praise them' Mt 6.2. δόξα ᵈ: οὐχ εὑρέθησαν ὑποστρέψαντες δοῦναι δόξαν τῷ θεῷ εἰ μὴ ὁ ἀλλογενὴς οὗτος; 'why is this foreigner the only one who came back to praise God?' Lk 17.18. ⁶⁵

33.358 μεγαλύνωᵇ: to praise a person in terms of that individual's greatness – 'to praise the greatness of.' ἤκουον γὰρ αὐτῶν λαλούντων γλώσσαις καὶ μεγαλυνόντων τὸν θεόν 'for they heard them speaking with strange sounds and praising God's greatness' Ac 10.46. In a number of languages it is necessary to restructure a statement such as 'praising God's greatness' as a form of direct discourse, for example, 'they said, God is indeed great.'

33.359 ἐξομολογέομαιᵈ: to express praise or honor, with a possible implication of acknowledging the nature of someone or something (occurring in the NT only in quotations from the Septuagint) – 'to praise.' διὰ τοῦτο ἐξομολογήσομαί σοι ἐν ἔθνεσιν 'and so I will praise you among the Gentiles' Ro 15.9. ⁶⁶ This meaning of ἐξομολογέομαι is almost guaranteed by the parallelism of the second line of the quotation in Ro 15.9, but for another interpretation of Ro 15.9, see 33.274.

33.360 εὔφημος, ον: (derivative of εὐφημία 'to praise,' 33.356) pertaining to deserving approval or good reputation – 'worthy of praise,

worthy of approval.' ὅσα προσφιλῆ, ὅσα εὔφημα . . . ταῦτα λογίζεσθε 'fill your minds . . . with those things that are lovely and worthy of praise' Php 4.8. In a number of languages 'worthy of praise' may be rendered as 'what people should praise.'

33.361 ἀχρεῖος, ον: pertaining to being without such qualities as deserve praise or commendation – 'not deserving special praise, not worthy of particular commendation.' δοῦλοι ἀχρεῖοί ἐσμεν, ὃ ὠφείλομεν ποιῆσαι πεποιήκαμεν 'we are servants who do not particularly deserve praise; we have done what we should' Lk 17.10.

33.362 εὐλογητός, ή, όν: (derivative of εὐλογέω ᵃ 'to praise,' 33.356) pertaining to being worthy of praise or commendation – 'one to be praised.' σὺ εἶ ὁ Χριστὸς ὁ υἱὸς τοῦ εὐλογητοῦ; 'are you the Messiah, the Son of the One who should be praised?' Mk 14.61.

33.363 ἀλληλουϊά: (a borrowing from Hebrew, literally 'praise Yahweh') an expression of praise – 'hallelujah, praise God.' ἤκουσα ὡς φωνὴν μεγάλην ὄχλου πολλοῦ ἐν τῷ οὐρανῷ λεγόντων, Ἀλληλουϊά 'I heard what sounded like the voice of a great crowd of people in heaven saying, Praise God' or '. . . Hallelujah' Re 19.1.

33.364 ὡσαννά: (an Aramaic expression meaning 'help, I pray' or 'save, I pray,' but which had become a strictly liturgical formula of praise) a shout of praise or adoration – 'hosanna.' ὡσαννά· εὐλογημένος ὁ ἐρχόμενος ἐν ὀνόματι κυρίου 'hosanna; blessed is the one who comes in the name of the Lord' Mk 11.9; ὡσαννὰ ἐν τοῖς ὑψίστοις 'hosanna in the highest' Mk 11.10; ὡσαννὰ τῷ υἱῷ Δαυίδ 'hosanna to the Son of David' Mt 21.9. In Mt 21.9 ὡσαννὰ τῷ υἱῷ Δαυίδ may also be rendered as 'praise to you, Son of David' or 'we praise you who are the Son of David' or '. . . a descendant of David.'

Though for many early Christians, and especially those of Jewish background, ὡσαννά would be known from its Aramaic background as meaning 'help' or 'save,' nevertheless, its association with liturgical ex-

---

66 It is also possible that ἐξομολογέομαι in Ro 14.11 may mean 'to praise,' but many scholars assume that καὶ πᾶσα γλῶσσα ἐξομολογήσεται τῷ θεῷ should be understood in the sense of 'and everyone will confess God' (see 33.274 and 33.275).

pressions involving praise and exaltation resulted in the expression acquiring quite a different significance; hence, a phrase such as 'hosanna in the highest' became equivalent to 'praise be to God.' For growing numbers of Christians without Jewish background, ὡσαννά probably acquired much the same meaning as it now has in English.

L' Flatter (33.365-33.367)

33.365 θαυμάζω πρόσωπον: (an idiom, literally 'to admire the face') to praise someone, normally in an exaggerated or false manner and with insincere purpose – 'to flatter.'[67] θαυμάζοντες πρόσωπα ὠφελείας χάριν 'they flatter others for their own advantage' Jd 16.

33.366 εὐλογία[b], ας f: excessive praise – 'flattery, flattering talk.' διὰ τῆς χρηστολογίας καὶ εὐλογίας ἐξαπατῶσιν τὰς καρδίας τῶν ἀκάκων 'by their attractive words and flattering talk they deceive the minds of innocent people' Ro 16.18. In some languages flattery is expressed in a descriptive manner, for example, 'to say that a person is wonderful when he really isn't.' Sometimes flattery is expressed idiomatically, for example, 'to use big words about a small person' or 'to call a donkey a man.'

33.367 κολακεία, ας f: praise as a means of gratifying someone's vanity – 'flattering talk, flattery.' οὔτε γάρ ποτε ἐν λόγῳ κολακείας ἐγενήθημεν 'we did not ever come (to you) with flattery' 1 Th 2.5.

M' Boast (33.368-33.373)

33.368 καυχάομαι; καύχημα[a], τος n; καύχησις[a], εως f; ἐγκαυχάομαι; αὐχέω: to express an unusually high degree of confidence in someone or something being exceptionally noteworthy – 'to boast.'[68]

---

67 It is not possible to determine precisely the context from which this idiom is derived, but it would appear that the meaning 'to flatter' is probably the most satisfactory.

68 There are undoubtedly certain connotative differences in these terms for boasting, but this cannot be determined from existing contexts.

καυχάομαι: ὁ καυχώμενος ἐν κυρίῳ καυχάσθω 'whoever boasts must boast of the Lord' 1 Cor 1.31.
καύχημα[a]: οὐ καλὸν τὸ καύχημα ὑμῶν 'your boasting is not right' 1 Cor 5.6.
καύχησις[a]: πᾶσα καύχησις τοιαύτη πονηρά ἐστιν 'all such boasting is wrong' Jas 4.16.
ἐγκαυχάομαι: ὥστε αὐτοὺς ἡμᾶς ἐν ὑμῖν ἐγκαυχάσθαι ἐν ταῖς ἐκκλησίαις τοῦ θεοῦ 'that is why we ourselves boast about you in the churches of God' 2 Th 1.4.
αὐχέω: οὕτως καὶ ἡ γλῶσσα μικρὸν μέλος ἐστὶν καὶ μεγάλα αὐχεῖ 'this is how it is with the tongue: small as it is, it can boast about great things' Jas 3.5.

Whether in any particular context the boasting is legitimate or not depends upon what is boasted about. In a number of languages, however, quite different terms are employed, depending upon the differing degrees of justification for such boasting.

33.369 περπερεύομαι: to praise oneself excessively – 'to be a braggart, to brag.' ἡ ἀγάπη οὐ περπερεύεται 'love does not brag' 1 Cor 13.4.

33.370 κατακαυχάομαι[a]: to boast about something by downgrading something else – 'to boast against, to degrade.' μὴ κατακαυχῶ τῶν κλάδων 'you must not boast and in so doing degrade the branches' Ro 11.18. In many languages it may not be possible to use an expression such as 'to boast against.' Therefore, in rendering μὴ κατακαυχῶ τῶν κλάδων in Ro 11.18 one may use 'you must not say that you are so much better than the branches.' For another interpretation of κατακαυχάομαι in Ro 11.18, see 88.194.

33.371 καύχημα[b], τος n; καύχησις[b], εως f: (derivatives of καυχάομαι 'to boast,' 33.368) the referent of boasting, namely, that which one boasts about – 'what one boasts about.'
καύχημα[b]: καύχημα ὑμῶν ἐσμεν καθάπερ καὶ ὑμεῖς ἡμῶν 'we are what you boast about just as you are what we boast about' 2 Cor 1.14. For another interpretation of καύχημα in 2 Cor 1.14, see 25.203.
καύχηβις[b]: ἡ γὰρ καύχησις ἡμῶν αὕτη ἐστίν 'this is what we boast about' 2 Cor 1.12.

33.372 καύχημα^c, τος *n*: the justification for boasting – 'the right to boast.' ἐὰν γὰρ εὐαγγελίζωμαι, οὐκ ἔστιν μοι καύχημα 'I have no right to boast just because I preach the gospel' 1 Cor 9.16.

33.373 ὑπέρογκος, ον: pertaining to excessive boasting – 'boastful.' τὸ στόμα αὐτῶν λαλεῖ ὑπέρογκα 'their mouths speak boastful words' Jd 16. In some languages the equivalent of 'boastful words' is 'words too big for what one is talking about' or 'puffed up words' or 'swollen words.'

N' Foolish Talk (33.374-33.381)

33.374 φλυαρέω: to speak in such a way as to make no sense, presumably because of ignorance of what is involved – 'to talk nonsense.' λόγοις πονηροῖς φλυαρῶν ἡμᾶς 'he talks nonsense about me with evil words' 3 Jn 10. In some languages 'to talk nonsense' is 'to talk without understanding what one is saying,' but in other instances an equivalent may be 'to talk without anybody being able to understand what one is saying.'

33.375 φλύαρος, ον: (derivative of φλυαρέω 'to talk nonsense,' 33.374) pertaining to talking nonsense – 'one who talks nonsense, gossipy.' φλύαροι καὶ περίεργοι 'they talk nonsense and are busybodies' 1 Tm 5.13. It is possible that in 1 Tm 5.13 φλύαρος should be rendered as 'gossipy' in view of the fact that one who speaks nonsense about someone else is normally gossiping.

33.376 κενοφωνία, ας *f*: talk which lacks significant content – 'foolish talk, empty talk.' τὰς δὲ βεβήλους κενοφωνίας περιΐστασο 'keep away from godless, foolish talk' 2 Tm 2.16. 'Foolish talk' may often be expressed as 'to talk the way fools talk' or 'to talk with a smirk on the face.'

33.377 ματαιολογία, ας *f*: talk which has no beneficial purpose and is thus idle and meaningless – 'idle discussions, meaningless talk.' ὧν τινες ἀστοχήσαντες ἐξετράπησαν εἰς ματαιολογίαν 'some people have turned away from these and have lost their way in meaningless discussions' 1 Tm 1.6.

33.378 ματαιολόγος, ου *m*: (derivative of ματαιολογέω 'to engage in idle talk,' not occurring in the NT) one who engages in empty and idle talk – 'empty talker, foolish babbler.' εἰσὶν γὰρ πολλοὶ καὶ ἀνυπότακτοι, ματαιολόγοι καὶ φρεναπάται 'for there are many rebellious people, empty talkers, and deceivers' Tt 1.10.

33.379 μωρολογία, ας *f*: talk which is both foolish and stupid – 'foolish talk, stupid talk.' αἰσχρότης καὶ μωρολογία ἢ εὐτραπελία, ἃ οὐκ ἀνῆκεν 'nor is it fitting (for you to use) indecent, foolish, or dirty words' Eph 5.4.

33.380 λῆρος, ου *m*: speech which is complete and utter nonsense – 'nonsense, humbug, pure nonsense.' ἐφάνησαν ἐνώπιον αὐτῶν ὡσεὶ λῆρος τὰ ῥήματα ταῦτα 'it seemed to them that these words were pure nonsense' Lk 24.11.

33.381 σπερμολόγος^b, ου *m*: (a figurative expression, literally 'one who picks up seed,' originally a reference to birds picking up seed, but figuratively applied to a person who is an information scavenger) one who is not able to say anything worthwhile in view of his miscellaneous collection of tidbits of information – 'foolish babbler.' τινες ἔλεγον, Τί ἂν θέλοι ὁ σπερμολόγος οὗτος λέγειν; 'some said, What is this foolish babbler trying to say?' Ac 17.18. For another interpretation of σπερμολόγος in Ac 17.18, see 27.19.

O' Complain (33.382-33.386)

33.382 γογγύζω; γογγυσμός, οῦ *m*: to express one's discontent – 'to complain, to grumble, complaint.'
γογγύζω: ἐγόγγυζον οὖν οἱ Ἰουδαῖοι περὶ αὐτοῦ ὅτι εἶπεν 'the Jews started complaining about him because he said . . .' Jn 6.41.
γογγυσμός: ἐγένετο γογγυσμὸς τῶν Ἑλληνιστῶν πρὸς τοὺς Ἑβραίους 'a complaint arose on the part of the Greek-speaking Jews against the native Jews' Ac 6.1. In a number of languages it may be necessary to restructure 'complaint' as a verb rather than as a noun, and therefore this expression in Ac 6.1 may be rendered as 'Greek-speaking Jews complained against what the local Jews were doing.'

33.383 διαγογγύζω: to express discontent in an emphatic way – 'to complain, to grumble.' ἰδόντες πάντες διεγόγγυζον 'all the people who saw it started grumbling' Lk 19.7.

33.384 στενάζω^b: (a figurative extension of meaning of στενάζω^a 'to groan, to sigh,' 25.143) to complain in an intensive and excessive manner – 'to complain strongly.' μὴ στενάζετε, ἀδελφοί, κατ' ἀλλήλων, ἵνα μὴ κριθῆτε 'do not complain against one another, fellow believers, so that you will not be judged' Jas 5.9. It may even be possible to retain something of the figurative meaning of στενάζω in Jas 5.9 by translating 'do not complain with moaning' or 'do not moan and complain against.'

33.385 μομφή, ῆς f: a complaint which implies blame – 'complaint.' χαριζόμενοι ἑαυτοῖς ἐάν τις πρός τινα ἔχῃ μομφήν 'forgive one another whenever any of you has a complaint against someone else' Col 3.13.

33.386 γογγυστής, οῦ m: (derivative of γογγύζω 'to complain,' 33.382) one who has a habit of complaining or grumbling – 'complainer, grumbler.' οὗτοί εἰσιν γογγυσταί, μεμψίμοιροι 'these men are grumblers who blame others' Jd 16.

P' Insult, Slander (33.387-33.403)

33.387 καταλαλέω; καταλαλιά, ᾶς f: to speak against, often involving speaking evil of – 'to speak evil of, to slander, slander.' καταλαλέω: μὴ καταλαλεῖτε ἀλλήλων, ἀδελφοί 'do not speak evil of one another, fellow believers' Jas 4.11. καταλαλιά: κἀγὼ εὑρεθῶ ὑμῖν . . . καταλαλιαί, ψιθυρισμοί 'that I may find among you . . . slander and gossip' 2 Cor 12.20.

33.388 κατάλαλος, ου m: (derivative of καταλαλέω 'to speak evil of,' 33.387) one who engages in speaking against or insulting – 'slanderer, one who insults.' ψιθυριστάς, καταλάλους '(they are) gossipers and slanderers' Ro 1.29-30.

33.389 ὀνειδίζω^a; ὀνειδισμός, οῦ m: to speak disparagingly of a person in a manner which is not justified – 'to insult, insult.' ὀνειδίζω^a: οἱ συνεσταυρωμένοι σὺν αὐτῷ ὠνείδιζον αὐτόν '(the two) who were crucified with him insulted him also' Mk 15.32. ὀνειδισμός: ὀνειδισμοῖς τε καὶ θλίψεσιν θεατριζόμενοι 'you were made a public spectacle by insults and distress' He 10.33.

33.390 ὑβρίζω^b; ἐνυβρίζω: to speak against someone in an insolent and arrogant way – 'to insult.' ὑβρίζω^b: ταῦτα λέγων καὶ ἡμᾶς ὑβρίζεις 'saying these things, you insult us' Lk 11.45. ἐνυβρίζω: καὶ τὸ πνεῦμα τῆς χάριτος ἐνυβρίσας 'and who insults the Spirit of grace' He 10.29.

33.391 ὕβρις^c, εως f: (derivative of ὑβρίζω^b 'to insult,' 33.390) the content of an insulting statement – 'insult.' εὐδοκῶ ἐν ἀσθενείαις, ἐν ὕβρεσιν 'I am content with weaknesses, insults' 2 Cor 12.10. In 2 Cor 12.10 it is not possible to determine whether ὕβρις refers to the content of the slanderous words or to the event of being slandered. For other interpretations of ὕβρις in 2 Cor 12.10, see 88.131 and 20.19.

33.392 ὑβριστής^b, οῦ m: (derivative of ὑβρίζω^b 'to insult,' 33.390) one who insults in an arrogant manner – 'one who insults, insulter.' τὸ πρότερον ὄντα βλάσφημον καὶ διώκτην καὶ ὑβριστήν 'formerly being a defamer, persecutor, and insulter' or 'formerly being one who spoke evil of him, and persecuted and insulted him' 1 Tm 1.13.

33.393 λοιδορέω; λοιδορία, ας f: to speak in a highly insulting manner – 'to slander, to insult strongly, slander, insult.' λοιδορέω: λοιδορούμενοι εὐλογοῦμεν 'when we are slandered, we bless' 1 Cor 4.12. λοιδορία: μὴ ἀποδιδόντες κακὸν ἀντὶ κακοῦ ἢ λοιδορίαν ἀντὶ λοιδορίας 'do not pay back evil with evil or insult with insult' 1 Pe 3.9.⁶⁹

---

69 It is not possible to determine in 1 Pe 3.9 whether λοιδορία denotes specifically the event of insulting or the content of the insult.

33.394 ἀντιλοιδορέω: to answer insults or slander with insulting or slanderous words – 'to insult in return.' ὃς λοιδορούμενος οὐκ ἀντελοιδόρει 'when he was insulted, he did not insult in return' 1 Pe 2.23.

33.395 λοίδορος, ου m: (derivative of λοιδορέω 'to slander,' 33.393) one who engages in slandering – 'slanderer.' οὐ λοίδοροι, οὐχ ἄρπαγες βασιλείαν θεοῦ κληρονομήσουσιν 'no slanderers or violent people will receive the kingdom of God' 1 Cor 6.10.

33.396 ἐκβάλλω τὸ ὄνομα: (an idiom, literally 'to throw out the name') to insult or slander, with a possible implication of a kind of psychological ostracism – 'to insult, to slander.' καὶ ὀνειδίσωσιν καὶ ἐκβάλωσιν τὸ ὄνομα ὑμῶν 'they will insult and slander you' Lk 6.22.

33.397 διάβολοςᶜ, ου m and f: (derivative of διαβάλλω 'to slander,' not occurring in the NT) one who engages in slander – 'slanderer.' γυναῖκας ὡσαύτως σεμνάς, μὴ διαβόλους 'their wives also must be of good character and not slanderers' 1 Tm 3.11. In 1 Tm 3.11 it may be appropriate to render διαβόλους as 'gossipers.'

33.398 δυσφημέω; δυσφημία, ας f: to attribute ill repute or bad reputation to – 'to defame, to slander, slander.'[70]
δυσφημέω: δυσφημούμενοι παρακαλοῦμεν 'when we are defamed, we speak words of encouragement' 1 Cor 4.13.
δυσφημία: διὰ δόξης καὶ ἀτιμίας, διὰ δυσφημίας καὶ εὐφημίας 'we are honored and disgraced, we are slandered and praised' 2 Cor 6.8.

33.399 κακολογέω: to insult in a particularly strong and unjustified manner – 'to revile, to denounce.' ὁ κακολογῶν πατέρα ἢ μητέρα θανάτῳ τελευτάτω 'he who reviles his father or mother must die' Mt 15.4.

33.400 βλασφημέω; βλασφημίαᵃ, ας f: to speak against someone in such a way as to

harm or injure his or her reputation (occurring in relation to persons as well as to divine beings) – 'to revile, to defame, to blaspheme, reviling.'
βλασφημέω: μηδένα βλασφημεῖν 'no one should defame another' Tt 3.2; καὶ μὴ καθὼς βλασφημούμεθα 'and not as I have been reviled' Ro 3.8; τὸ γὰρ ὄνομα τοῦ θεοῦ δι' ὑμᾶς βλασφημεῖται ἐν τοῖς ἔθνεσιν 'for the name of God is reviled by the Gentiles because of you' Ro 2.24; οἱ δὲ παραπορευόμενοι ἐβλασφήμουν αὐτόν 'those who went along reviled him' Mt 27.39.
βλασφημίαᵃ: ψευδομαρτυρίαι, βλασφημίαι 'false witness, reviling' Mt 15.19.
One way in which βλασφημέω and βλασφημίαᵃ were used in speaking of 'defaming God' was by claiming some kind of equality with God. Any such statement was regarded by the Jews of biblical times as being harmful and injurious to the nature of God.

33.401 βλασφημίαᵇ, ας f: (derivative of βλασφημέω 'to blaspheme,' 33.400) the content of a defamation – 'serious insult, blasphemy.' τίς ἐστιν οὗτος ὃς λαλεῖ βλασφημίας; 'who is this who speaks blasphemies?' Lk 5.21.

33.402 βλάσφημος, ον: (derivative of βλασφημέω 'to blaspheme,' 33.400) pertaining to being insulting and slanderous – 'insulting, slanderous, blasphemous.' οὐ φέρουσιν κατ' αὐτῶν παρὰ κυρίου βλάσφημον κρίσιν 'they do not bring against them slanderous condemnation in the presence of the Lord' 2 Pe 2.11; ἀκηκόαμεν αὐτοῦ λαλοῦντος ῥήματα βλάσφημα εἰς Μωϋσῆν καὶ τὸν θεόν 'we have heard him speak blasphemous words against Moses and God' Ac 6.11.

33.403 βλάσφημος, ου m: (derivative of βλασφημέω 'to defame,' 33.400) – 'defamer, blasphemer.' τὸ πρότερον ὄντα βλάσφημον καὶ διώκτην 'formerly being a defamer and persecutor' 1 Tm 1.13. In a number of languages, however, it may be much better to employ verbs as a means of indicating more precisely the object of such activities in 1 Tm 1.13, for example, 'formerly I defamed him and persecuted him.'

---

[70] δυσφημέω and δυσφημία are evidently not as pejorative as λοιδορέω and λοιδορία (33.393).

Q' Gossip (33.404-33.405)

33.404 ψιθυρισμός, οῦ *m*: providing harmful information about a person, often spoken in whispers or in low voice, with the implication that such information is not widely known and therefore should presumably be kept secret – 'gossip.' κἀγὼ εὑρεθῶ ὑμῖν . . . καταλαλιαί, ψιθυρισμοί 'that I may find among you . . . slander and gossip' 2 Cor 12.20.

33.405 ψιθυριστής, οῦ *m*: one who habitually engages in gossip – 'gossiper.' πεπληρωμένους πάσῃ ἀδικίᾳ . . . ψιθυριστάς 'they are filled with all kinds of wickedness . . . they are gossipers' Ro 1.29.

R' Mock, Ridicule (33.406-33.411)

33.406 ἐμπαίζω[a]; ἐμπαιγμός, οῦ *m*; ἐμπαιγμονή, ῆς *f*: to make fun of someone by pretending that he is not what he is or by imitating him in a distorted manner – 'to mock, to ridicule.'
ἐμπαίζω[a]: ἐνέπαιξαν δὲ αὐτῷ καὶ οἱ στρατιῶται 'and even the soldiers mocked him' Lk 23.36.
ἐμπαιγμός: ἕτεροι δὲ ἐμπαιγμῶν καὶ μαστίγων πεῖραν ἔλαβον 'others were mocked and whipped' He 11.36.
ἐμπαιγμονή: ἐλεύσονται ἐπ' ἐσχάτων τῶν ἡμερῶν ἐν ἐμπαιγμονῇ ἐμπαῖκται 'in the last days mockers will come with ridicule' 2 Pe 3.3.

33.407 ἐμπαίκτης, ου *m*: (derivative of ἐμπαίζω[a] 'to mock,' 33.406) one who makes fun of by mocking – 'mocker.' ἐπ' ἐσχάτου τοῦ χρόνου ἔσονται ἐμπαῖκται 'in the last times mockers will come' Jd 18.

33.408 χλευάζω; διαχλευάζω: to make fun of someone by joking or jesting – 'to scoff, to jeer, to joke at.'[71]
χλευάζω: ἀκούσαντες δὲ ἀνάστασιν νεκρῶν οἱ μὲν ἐχλεύαζον 'and when they heard (him speak about) the rising from death, some scoffed (at him)' Ac 17.32.

---

71 It is possible that διαχλευάζω is somewhat more emphatic than χλευάζω, and evidently χλευάζω and διαχλευάζω differ from ἐμπαίζω[a], ἐμπαιγμός, and ἐμπαιγμονή (33.406) in that the principal means of ridicule are verbal.

διαχλευάζω: ἕτεροι δὲ διαχλευάζοντες ἔλεγον ὅτι Γλεύκους μεμεστωμένοι εἰσίν 'others jeered at them, saying, They are drunk' Ac 2.13.

33.409 μυκτηρίζω; ἐκμυκτηρίζω: (figurative extensions of meaning of μυκτηρίζω and ἐκμυκτηρίζω 'to turn up the nose at,' not occurring in the NT) to ridicule in a sneering and contemptuous way – 'to ridicule, to sneer at, to show contempt for.'
μυκτηρίζω: μὴ πλανᾶσθε, θεὸς οὐ μυκτηρίζεται 'do not deceive yourselves; God is not one to be ridiculed' Ga 6.7.
ἐκμυκτηρίζω: οἱ Φαρισαῖοι φιλάργυροι ὑπάρχοντες, καὶ ἐξεμυκτήριζον αὐτόν 'the Pharisees sneered at him because they loved money' Lk 16.14.

33.410 καταγελάω: to make fun of or ridicule by laughing at, but evidently also involving verbal communication – 'to ridicule, to laugh at, to make fun of.' κατεγέλων αὐτοῦ, εἰδότες ὅτι ἀπέθανεν 'they ridiculed him, knowing that she had died' Lk 8.53.

33.411 οὐά: an exclamation of mocking and ridicule – 'aha.' οὐὰ ὁ καταλύων τὸν ναὸν καὶ οἰκοδομῶν ἐν τρισὶν ἡμέραις 'aha, you who are going to destroy the sanctuary and build it up in three days' Mk 15.29. Almost all languages have interjections or exclamatory expressions indicating ridicule. If such does not exist in a language, one can always translate this expression in Mk 15.29 as 'now what about you, you who are going to destroy the sanctuary and in three days build it up again!'

S' Criticize (33.412-33.416)

33.412 διακρίνομαι[c]; ἀνακρίνω[c]: to express disapproval of what someone has done – 'to criticize.'
διακρίνομαι[c]: ὅτε δὲ ἀνέβη Πέτρος εἰς Ἰερουσαλήμ, διεκρίνοντο πρὸς αὐτὸν οἱ ἐκ περιτομῆς 'when Peter went up to Jerusalem, those who insisted on circumcision criticized him' Ac 11.2. It is possible to interpret the meaning of διακρίνομαι in Ac 11.2 as being merely adverse judgment, but since this judgment was clearly voiced, διακρίνομαι implies more than mere judgment. The direct expression of an

adverse judgment may be best rendered in English as 'to criticize.'

ἀνακρίνω^c: ἡ ἐμὴ ἀπολογία τοῖς ἐμὲ ἀνακρίνουσίν ἐστιν αὕτη 'this is my defense to those who criticize me' 1 Cor 9.3. For another interpretation of ἀνακρίνω in 1 Cor 9.3, see 56.12.

33.413 ἀνταποκρίνομαι^b: to express disapproval in return – 'to criticize in return.' μενοῦνγε σὺ τίς εἶ ὁ ἀνταποκρινόμενος τῷ θεῷ; 'but who then are you to criticize God in return?' Ro 9.20.

33.414 μωμάομαι: to find fault with someone by implying blame – 'to criticize, to censure, to find fault with.' ἵνα μὴ μωμηθῇ ἡ διακονία 'we don't want anyone to find fault with our work' 2 Cor 6.3.

33.415 ἀκατάγνωστος, ον; ἀνεπίλημπτος, ον: pertaining to what cannot be criticized – 'above criticism, beyond reproach.'

ἀκατάγνωστος: λόγον ὑγιῆ ἀκατάγνωστον 'sound words which are above criticism' Tt 2.8.

ἀνεπίλημπτος: τηρῆσαί σε τὴν ἐντολὴν ἄσπιλον ἀνεπίλημπτον 'obey the commandment and keep it pure and above reproach' 1 Tm 6.14.

It may be necessary in some languages to restructure ἀκατάγνωστος and ἀνεπίλημπτος as complete clauses, so that instead of 'sound words which are above criticism' in Tt 2.8, one may translate 'sound words which no one can criticize' or '. . . against which no one can say anything.' 'Above reproach' in 1 Tm 6.14 may be rendered as 'in such a way that no one can criticize it.'

33.416 ἀπελεγμός, οῦ m: serious and strong criticism based upon presumed evidence – 'serious criticism, reproach.' τοῦτο κινδυνεύει ἡμῖν τὸ μέρος εἰς ἀπελεγμὸν ἐλθεῖν 'there is danger that this business of ours will be seriously criticized' Ac 19.27.

T' Rebuke (33.417-33.422)

33.417 ἐλέγχω; ἔλεξις, εως f; ἐλεγμός, οῦ m: to state that someone has done wrong, with the implication that there is adequate proof of such wrongdoing – 'to rebuke, to reproach, rebuke, reproach.'

ἐλέγχω: ὁ δὲ Ἡρῴδης ὁ τετραάρχης, ἐλεγχόμενος ὑπ' αὐτοῦ περὶ Ἡρῳδιάδος 'Herod the tetrarch was rebuked by him because of Herodias' Lk 3.19; μᾶλλον δὲ καὶ ἐλέγχετε 'but rather rebuke them' Eph 5.11.[72]

ἔλεγξις: ὃς μισθὸν ἀδικίας ἠγάπησεν ἔλεγξιν δὲ ἔσχεν ἰδίας παρανομίας 'who loved the money he would get for doing wrong and was reproached for his transgression' 2 Pe 2.15-16.

ἐλεγμός: πᾶσα γραφὴ θεόπνευστος καὶ ὠφέλιμος πρὸς διδασκαλίαν, πρὸς ἐλεγμόν 'all Scripture is inspired by God and is useful for teaching, for rebuking' 2 Tm 3.16.

33.418 νουθετέω^b: to admonish someone for having done something wrong – 'to admonish, to rebuke.' παρακαλοῦμεν δὲ ὑμᾶς, ἀδελφοί, νουθετεῖτε τοὺς ἀτάκτους 'we urge you, fellow believers, to admonish the idle' 1 Th 5.14. νουθετέω in 1 Th 5.14 may also be understood in the sense of 'to warn' (see 33.424).

33.419 ἐπιτιμάω^a: to express strong disapproval of someone – 'to rebuke, to denounce.' προσλαβόμενος αὐτὸν ὁ Πέτρος ἤρξατο ἐπιτιμᾶν αὐτῷ 'Peter took him aside and began to rebuke him' Mt 16.22.

33.420 ἐπιπλήσσω: (a figurative extension of meaning of ἐπιπλήσσω 'to strike,' not occurring in the NT) to express strong disapproval as a type of punishment – 'to rebuke, to reproach, to denounce.' πρεσβυτέρῳ μὴ ἐπιπλήξῃς, ἀλλὰ παρακάλει ὡς πατέρα 'do not denounce an older man, but appeal to him as if he were your father' 1 Tm 5.1.

33.421 ἐμβριμάομαι^b: to exhibit irritation or even anger in expressing a harsh reproof – 'to denounce harshly, to scold.' καὶ ἐνεβριμῶντο αὐτῇ 'and they denounced her harshly' Mk 14.5.

---

[72] If the direct object of the verb ἐλέγχω in Eph 5.11 is understood as 'those who have done the fruitless deeds of darkness,' then the meaning is 'rebuke.' However, it is also possible to construe the direct object as being the 'fruitless deeds of darkness,' in which case the meaning of ἐλέγχω would presumably be 'to expose by words.'

33.422 ὀνειδίζω[b]: to reproach someone, with the implication of that individual being evidently to blame – 'to reprimand, to reproach.' τότε ἤρξατο ὀνειδίζειν τὰς πόλεις 'then he began to reprimand the towns' Mt 11.20.

U' Warn (33.423-33.425)

33.423 προλέγω[c]: to tell someone that some future happening is dangerous and may lead to serious consequences – 'to warn.' προλέγω ὑμῖν καθὼς προεῖπον ὅτι οἱ τὰ τοιαῦτα πράσσοντες βασιλείαν θεοῦ οὐ κληρονομήσουσιν 'I warn you now as I have before: those who do these things will not receive the kingdom of God' Ga 5.21.

33.424 νουθετέω[c]; **νουθεσία**[b], **ας** *f*: to advise someone concerning the dangerous consequences of some happening or action – 'to warn, warning.'
νουθετέω[c]: παρακαλοῦμεν δὲ ὑμᾶς, ἀδελφοί, νουθετεῖτε τοὺς ἀτάκτους 'we urge you, Christian brothers, to warn the idle' 1 Th 5.14. νουθετέω in 1 Th 5.14 may also be understood in the sense of 'to admonish' (see 33.418).
νουθεσία[b]: ἐγράφη δὲ πρὸς νουθεσίαν ἡμῶν 'it was written down as a warning for us' 1 Cor 10.11.

33.425 διαμαρτύρομαι[c]: to admonish or instruct with regard to some future happening or action, with the implication of personal knowledge or experience – 'to warn.' ὅπως διαμαρτύρηται αὐτοῖς, ἵνα μὴ καὶ αὐτοὶ ἔλθωσιν εἰς τὸν τόπον τοῦτον τῆς βασάνου 'that he will warn them so that they, at least, will not come to this place of pain' Lk 16.28.

V' Accuse, Blame (33.426-33.434)

33.426 διαβάλλω: to bring a formal or informal complaint, normally to a third person, with the implication that the individual against whom the complaint is made has been guilty of doing something wrong – 'to accuse, to bring charges against.' οὗτος διεβλήθη αὐτῷ ὡς διασκορπίζων τὰ ὑπάρχοντα αὐτοῦ 'he was accused before him (his master) of having wasted his (master's) possessions' Lk 16.1.

33.427 κατηγορέω; ἐγκαλέω: to bring serious charges or accusations against someone, with the possible connotation of a legal or court context – 'to accuse, to bring charges.'[73]
κατηγορέω: μεταξὺ ἀλλήλων τῶν λογισμῶν κατηγορούντων ἢ καὶ ἀπολογουμένων 'conflicting thoughts which either accuse or excuse them' Ro 2.15.
ἐγκαλέω: τίς ἐγκαλέσει κατὰ ἐκλεκτῶν θεοῦ; 'who will bring charges against those whom God has chosen?' Ro 8.33.

33.428 κατηγορία, ας *f*: (derivative of κατηγορέω 'to accuse,' 33.427) the content of the accusation or charge made against someone – 'accusation, charge.' κατὰ πρεσβυτέρου κατηγορίαν μὴ παραδέχου, ἐκτὸς εἰ μὴ ἐπὶ δύο ἢ τριῶν μαρτύρων 'do not listen to an accusation against an elder unless it is brought by two or three witnesses' 1 Tm 5.19. It is possible that in 1 Tm 5.19 κατηγορία may denote either the event of accusing or the content of the accusation. If κατηγορία in 1 Tm 5.19 is understood as the event of accusing, it may be classified with the items in 33.427.

33.429 κατήγωρ, ορος *m*; **κατήγορος, ου** *m*: (derivatives of κατηγορέω 'to accuse,' 33.427) one who brings accusation – 'accuser.'
κατήγωρ: ὅτι ἐβλήθη ὁ κατήγωρ τῶν ἀδελφῶν ἡμῶν 'for the accuser of our Christian brothers has been thrown out' (a reference to the Devil) Re 12.10.
κατήγορος: οἱ κατήγοροι οὐδεμίαν αἰτίαν ἔφερον ὧν ἐγὼ ὑπενόουν πονηρῶν 'his accusers did not charge him with any of the evil crimes that I thought they would' Ac 25.18.

33.430 προαιτιάομαι: to bring charges previously on the basis of presumed blame and guilt – 'to accuse previously.' προῃτιασάμεθα γὰρ Ἰουδαίους τε καὶ Ἕλληνας πάντας ὑφ' ἁμαρτίαν εἶναι 'I have previously accused both Jews and Greeks of being under the power of sin' Ro 3.9.

---

[73] See the corresponding meanings of formal legal charges against someone (Domain 56 *Courts and Legal Procedures*).

33.431 μέμφομαι: to bring accusations against someone on the basis that the person in question is clearly to blame – 'to accuse, to blame.' τί οὖν ἔτι μέμφεται; 'if this is so, how can (God) blame a person?' Ro 9.19;[74] μεμφόμενος γὰρ αὐτοὺς λέγει 'he blamed them and said . . .' He 8.8.

33.432 μεμψίμοιρος, ον: pertaining to a tendency to constantly find fault – 'constantly blaming, fault-finding.' οὗτοί εἰσιν γογγυσταί, μεμψίμοιροι 'these are grumblers, constantly blaming others' Jd 16.

33.433 ἀνέγκλητος, ον: pertaining to one who cannot be accused of anything wrong – 'without accusation.' παραστῆσαι ὑμᾶς ἁγίους καὶ ἀμώμους καὶ ἀνεγκλήτους κατενώπιον αὐτοῦ 'to bring you holy, pure, and without accusations into his presence' Col 1.22. In a number of languages the phrase 'without accusations' must be rendered by a clause, for example, 'in such a way that no one can accuse you of doing wrong' or 'without the possibility of anyone accusing you.'

33.434 συκοφαντέω: to bring false charges against someone, especially with the intent of personal profit – 'to make false charges.' μηδένα διασείσητε μηδὲ συκοφαντήσητε 'do not extort money from people by force and do not bring false charges against them' Lk 3.14. The term συκοφαντέω refers to a practice in which persons could bring charges against an individual and receive a part of the fine or indemnity paid to the court.

W' Defend, Excuse (33.435-33.438)

33.435 ἀπολογέομαι[c]; ἀπολογία[a], ας f: to speak on behalf of oneself or of others against accusations presumed to be false – 'to defend oneself.'
ἀπολογέομαι[c]: ὁ δὲ Ἀλέξανδρος κατασείσας τὴν χεῖρα ἤθελεν ἀπολογεῖσθαι τῷ δήμῳ 'then Alex-

ander motioned with his hand and tried to defend himself before the people' Ac 19.33.
ἀπολογία[a]: ἐν τῇ πρώτῃ μου ἀπολογίᾳ οὐδείς μοι παρεγένετο 'when I first defended myself, no one stood by me' 2 Tm 4.16.

33.436 ἀπολογία[b], ας f: (derivative of ἀπολογέομαι 'to defend oneself,' 33.435) the content of what is said in defense – 'defense, what is said in ·defense, how one defends oneself.' ἡ ἐμὴ ἀπολογία τοῖς ἐμὲ ἀνακρίνουσίν ἐστιν αὕτη 'when people criticize me, this is my defense' 1 Cor 9.3.

33.437 πρόφασις[b], εως f: what is said in defense of a particular action, but without real justification – 'excuse.' νῦν δὲ πρόφασιν οὐκ ἔχουσιν περὶ τῆς ἁμαρτίας αὐτῶν 'they no longer have any excuse for their sin' Jn 15.22. In a number of languages 'to have no excuse' is rendered as 'to not be able to justify' or 'to not be able to give a good reason for.'

33.438 ἀναπολόγητος, ον: pertaining to not being able to defend oneself or to justify one's actions – 'to be without excuse, to have no excuse.' διὸ ἀναπολόγητος εἶ, ὦ ἄνθρωπε πᾶς ὁ κρίνων 'therefore, you, my friend, who pass judgment on others, have no excuse' Ro 2.1.

X' Dispute, Debate[75] (33.439-33.445)

33.439 συμβάλλω[c]: to express differences of opinion in a forceful way, involving alternative opportunities for presenting contrasting viewpoints – 'to debate, to discuss forcefully.' τινὲς δὲ καὶ τῶν Ἐπικουρείων καὶ Στοϊκῶν φιλοσόφων συνέβαλλον αὐτῷ 'certain Epicurean and Stoic teachers debated with him' Ac 17.18.

33.440 συζητέω[a]; συζήτησις, εως f; ζήτημα, τος n; ζήτησις[b], εως f: to express forceful differences of opinion without neces-

---

74 In Ro 9.19 (τί οὖν ἔτι μέμφεται; 'how then can he blame a person?') it is impossible to tell whether there is a direct communication or whether this is merely a statement about God's attitude in regarding a person as guilty.

75 For the various contexts in which meanings in this subdomain occur, it is often difficult to determine the extent of emotional involvement in the statement of differences of opinion. Accordingly, one cannot decide in a number of instances whether the translation should be 'debate' or 'dispute.'

sarily having a presumed goal of seeking a solution – 'to dispute, dispute.'

συζητέω^a: γραμματεῖς συζητοῦντας πρὸς αὐτούς 'some teachers of the Law were disputing with them' Mk 9.14.

συζήτησις: ἀπῆλθον οἱ Ἰουδαῖοι, πολλὴν ἔχοντες ἐν ἑαυτοῖς συζήτησιν 'the Jews departed, disputing strongly among themselves' Ac 28.29 (apparatus).

ζήτημα: εἰ δὲ ζητήματά ἐστιν περὶ λόγου καὶ ὀνόματων καὶ νόμου τοῦ καθ᾽ ὑμᾶς, ὄψεσθε αὐτοί 'since it is a dispute about words and names and your own law, you yourselves must settle it' Ac 18.15.

ζήτησις^b: ἐγένετο οὖν ζήτησις ἐκ τῶν μαθητῶν Ἰωάννου μετὰ Ἰουδαίου περὶ καθαρισμοῦ 'some of John's disciples began disputing with a Jew about the matter of religious washing' Jn 3.25.

33.441 συζητητής, οῦ *m*: (derivative of συζητέω^a 'to debate, to dispute,' 33.440) a person who is skilled in or likely to be involved in expressing strong differences of opinion – 'debater, disputer.' ποῦ σοφός; ποῦ γραμματεύς; ποῦ συζητητὴς τοῦ αἰῶνος τούτου; 'where is the wise person, the scholar, the debater of this world?' 1 Cor 1.20.

33.442 ἐκζήτησις^b, εως *f*: a dispute involving empty speculation – 'idle dispute, meaningless speculation.' αἵτινες ἐκζητήσεις παρέχουσιν μᾶλλον ἢ οἰκονομίαν θεοῦ 'which only produce idle disputes rather than serving God's plan' 1 Tm 1.4. For another interpretation of ἐκζήτησις in 1 Tm 1.4, see 31.33.

33.443 διακατελέγχομαι: to refute completely in a debate – 'to refute, to defeat in debate.' τοῖς Ἰουδαίοις διακατηλέγχετο δημοσίᾳ 'he defeated the Jews in public debate' Ac 18.28.

33.444 διακρίνομαι^b; διάκρισις^b, εως *f*: to dispute with someone on the basis of different judgments – 'to dispute, to debate about, contention, dispute.'

διακρίνομαι^b: τῷ διαβόλῳ διακρινόμενος διελέγετο περὶ τοῦ Μωϋσέως σώματος 'in his dispute with the Devil, he argued about who would have the body of Moses' Jd 9.

διάκρισις^b: μὴ εἰς διακρίσεις διαλογισμῶν 'do not argue about his personal opinions' Ro 14.1.

33.445 ἀντιλογία^a, ας *f*: a dispute involving opposite opinions – 'dispute, contradictory statements.' πάσης αὐτοῖς ἀντιλογίας πέρας εἰς βεβαίωσιν ὁ ὅρκος 'a vow settles all disputes between them' He 6.16.

Y′ Argue, Quarrel (33.446-33.454)

33.446 διαλέγομαι^a; διαλογισμός^c, οῦ *m*: to argue about differences of opinion – 'to argue, to dispute, argument.'

διαλέγομαι^a: διελέχθησαν ἐν τῇ ὁδῷ τίς μείζων 'they argued on the way about who was the greatest' Mk 9.34.

διαλογισμός^c: εἰσῆλθεν δὲ διαλογισμὸς ἐν αὐτοῖς, τὸ τίς ἂν εἴη μείζων αὐτῶν 'they argued which one of them might be the greatest' Lk 9.46.

33.447 ἐρίζω; ἔρις^b, ιδος *f*: to express differences of opinion, with at least some measure of antagonism or hostility – 'to argue, quarrel, dispute.'

ἐρίζω: οὐκ ἐρίσει οὐδὲ κραυγάσει 'he will not argue or shout' Mt 12.19.

ἔρις^b: ὅπου γὰρ ἐν ὑμῖν ζῆλος καὶ ἔρις 'for when there is jealousy among you and you quarrel with one another' 1 Cor 3.3. In a number of contexts in which ἔρις occurs, it is difficult to determine whether there is definite verbal involvement or whether the reference is essentially to a state of rivalry or strife (see 39.22).

33.448 στάσις^b, εως *f*: to engage in intense and emotional expressions of different opinions – 'to quarrel, heated quarrel.' τοῦτο δὲ αὐτοῦ εἰπόντος ἐγένετο στάσις τῶν Φαρισαίων καὶ Σαδδουκαίων 'as soon as he said this, the Pharisees and Sadducees started a heated quarrel' or '. . . started to quarrel vociferously' Ac 23.7.

33.449 φιλονεικία, ας *f*: readiness or desire to argue or quarrel – 'desire to quarrel, readiness to argue, to want to argue, quarrelsomeness.' ἐγένετο δὲ καὶ φιλονεικία ἐν αὐτοῖς, τὸ τίς αὐτῶν δοκεῖ εἶναι μείζων 'they started to argue as to which one of them should be considered the greatest' (literally 'a desire to argue arose among them as to . . .') Lk 22.24.

33.450 φιλόνεικος, ον: pertaining to being desirous of arguing – 'quarrelsome, given to arguing.' εἰ δέ τις δοκεῖ φιλόνεικος εἶναι, ἡμεῖς τοιαύτην συνήθειαν οὐκ ἔχομεν 'if anyone wants to be quarrelsome (about this, the fact is) we do not have such a custom' 1 Cor 11.16.

33.451 παροξυσμός[b], οῦ *m*: a severe argument based on intense difference of opinion – 'sharp argument, sharp difference of opinion.' ἐγένετο δὲ παροξυσμὸς ὥστε ἀποχωρισθῆναι 'they had a sharp argument so that they separated' Ac 15.39.

33.452 διαπαρατριβή, ῆς *f*: to engage in continuous and repeated arguing – 'constant arguing, continuous arguing.' διαπαρατριβαὶ διεφθαρμένων ἀνθρώπων τὸν νοῦν 'constant arguing of those whose minds do not function' 1 Tm 6.5.

33.453 θυμομαχέω[b]: to engage in an angry quarrel with someone – 'to be angry and quarrel, to quarrel angrily.' ἦν δὲ θυμομαχῶν Τυρίοις καὶ Σιδωνίοις 'he was having an angry quarrel with the people of Tyre and Sidon' Ac 12.20. For another interpretation of θυμομαχέω in Ac 12.20, see 88.180.

33.454 λογομαχέω; λογομαχία, ας *f*: to argue or quarrel about the meaning or use of words – 'to quarrel about words, arguing about words.'
λογομαχέω: διαμαρτυρόμενος ἐνώπιον τοῦ θεοῦ μὴ λογομαχεῖν 'give them warning in God's presence not to quarrel over words' 2 Tm 2.14.
λογομαχία: νοσῶν περὶ ζητήσεις καὶ λογομαχίας 'he has an unhealthy desire for arguments and quarrels about words' 1 Tm 6.4.

Z' Oppose, Contradict (33.455-33.458)

33.455 ἀντιλέγω: to speak against something or someone – 'to oppose, to speak in opposition to.' περὶ μὲν γὰρ τῆς αἱρέσεως ταύτης γνωστὸν ἡμῖν ἐστιν ὅτι πανταχοῦ ἀντιλέγεται 'for we do know that everywhere people speak against this party' Ac 28.22.

33.456 ἀντιλογία[b], ας *f*: (derivative of ἀντιλέγω 'to speak against,' 33.455) a contradiction involving a contrary statement or evidence – 'contradiction.' χωρὶς δὲ πάσης ἀντιλογίας 'beyond all contradiction' or 'beyond all doubt' He 7.7.

33.457 ἀντίθεσις, εως *f*: a statement which involves direct contradiction or is logically inconsistent – 'contradiction.' ἐκτρεπόμενος τὰς βεβήλους κενοφωνίας καὶ ἀντιθέσεις τῆς ψευδωνύμου γνώσεως 'avoid godless, foolish talk and the contradictions of what is falsely called knowledge' 1 Tm 6.20.

33.458 ἀναντίρρητος, ον; ἀναντιρρήτως: pertaining to what cannot be spoken against or objected to – 'cannot be denied, without opposition, without objection, indisputable.'
ἀναντίρρητος: ἀναντιρρήτων οὖν ὄντων τούτων δέον ἐστὶν ὑμᾶς κατεσταλμένους ὑπάρχειν 'since these things are not being disputed, you must calm down' Ac 19.36.
ἀναντιρρήτως: διὸ καὶ ἀναντιρρήτως ἦλθον μεταπεμφθείς 'and so when you sent for me, I came without any objection' Ac 10.29.

A'' Prophesy (33.459-33.462)

33.459 προφητεύω: to speak under the influence of divine inspiration, with or without reference to future events – 'to prophesy, to make inspired utterances.' προφήτευσον, τίς ἐστιν ὁ παίσας σε; 'prophesy, Who hit you?' Lk 22.64; ἐπροφήτευσεν ὅτι ἔμελλεν Ἰησοῦς ἀποθνῄσκειν 'he prophesied that Jesus was about to die' Jn 11.51.

33.460 προφητεία[a], ας *f*: an utterance inspired by God – 'inspired utterance, prophecy.' καὶ ἀναπληροῦται αὐτοῖς ἡ προφητεία Ἡσαΐου 'so that the prophecy of Isaiah comes true in their case' Mt 13.14; εἴτε δὲ προφητεῖαι, καταργηθήσονται 'and if there are inspired utterances, they will cease' 1 Cor 13.8. It is possible that προφητεία in 1 Cor 13.8 refers to the action of producing such inspired utterances rather than to the resulting verbal form of the utterances themselves.

33.461 προφητεία^b, ας *f*: the capacity or ability to utter inspired messages – 'to prophesy, ability to prophesy, to be able to speak inspired messages.' καὶ ἐὰν ἔχω προφητείαν 'and if I have the capacity to prophesy' 1 Cor 13.2.[76]

33.462 προφητικός, ή, όν: pertaining to divinely inspired utterances – 'prophetic, of the prophets.' φανερωθέντος δὲ νῦν διά τε γραφῶν προφητικῶν 'being made evident now through the writings of the prophets' Ro 16.26; καὶ ἔχομεν βεβαιότερον τὸν προφητικὸν λόγον 'and we are even more confident of the prophetic word' or '. . . of the message proclaimed by the prophets' 2 Pe 1.19.

B'' Swear, Put Under Oath, Vow (33.463-33.469)

33.463 ὀμνύω or ὄμνυμι; ὅρκος, ου *m*; ὁρκωμοσία, ας *f*: to affirm the truth of a statement by calling on a divine being to execute sanctions against a person if the statement in question is not true (in the case of a deity taking an oath, his divine being is regarded as validating the statement) – 'to swear, to make an oath, oath.'
ὀμνύω: τότε ἤρξατο καταθεματίζειν καὶ ὀμνύειν ὅτι Οὐκ οἶδα τὸν ἄνθρωπον 'then he began to curse and to swear, I do not know the man' Mt 26.74. In Mk 14.71 the same expression occurs with ὀμνύναι (from ὄμνυμι), see 33.472.
ὅρκος: ὅθεν μεθ' ὅρκου ὡμολόγησεν αὐτῇ δοῦναι ὃ ἐὰν αἰτήσηται 'accordingly he promised by swearing that he would give her everything she asked for' Mt 14.7.
ὁρκωμοσία: οἱ μὲν γὰρ χωρὶς ὁρκωμοσίας εἰσὶν ἱερεῖς γεγονότες 'for these became priests without the swearing of an oath' He 7.20.
In a number of languages it is necessary to be quite specific in referring to the swearing of an oath, for example, 'to say something by calling upon God to listen' or 'to state that something is true and asking God to punish if it is not true' or 'to make God responsible for what one has said.'

33.464 ἐπιορκέω^a: to swear that one will do something and then not fulfill the promise – 'to forswear, to break an oath, to swear and fail to keep.' οὐκ ἐπιορκήσεις, ἀποδώσεις δὲ τῷ κυρίῳ τοὺς ὅρκους σου 'do not swear and fail to keep your oath, but fulfill your oaths before the Lord' Mt 5.33. See also 33.465.

33.465 ἐπιορκέω^b: to take an oath that something is true, when in reality one knows that it is false – 'to swear falsely, to perjure oneself.' οὐκ ἐπιορκήσεις, ἀποδώσεις δὲ τῷ κυρίῳ τοὺς ὅρκους σου 'do not swear falsely, but fulfill your oaths before the Lord' Mt 5.33.
In the one occurrence in the NT of ἐπιορκέω (Mt 5.33), it is not possible to determine precisely which meaning is involved, but the emphasis upon fulfilling an oath would seem to point to the meaning of ἐπιορκέω^a (33.464). In either case, it is often necessary to be quite specific about the meaning and to introduce sufficient information into the context so that the specific aspect of either breaking an oath or swearing falsely will be clear.

33.466 ἐπίορκος, ου *m*: (derivative of ἐπιορκέω^b 'to swear falsely,' 33.465) one who swears falsely – 'perjurer.' δικαίῳ νόμος οὐ κεῖται, ἀνόμοις δὲ καὶ . . . ἁμαρτωλοῖς, . . . ἐπιόρκοις 'laws are not made for good people, but for lawbreakers and . . . sinners and . . . perjurers' 1 Tm 1.9-10.

33.467 ὁρκίζω; ἐνορκίζω; ἐξορκίζω: to demand that a person take an oath as to the truth of what is said or as to the certainty that one will carry out the request or command – 'to put under oath, to insist that one take an oath, to require that one swear.'[77]

---

76 It is possible to interpret προφητεία in 1 Cor 13.2 as meaning simply 'to make inspired utterances,' since the verb ἔχω in certain contexts may mean 'to have the capacity to' or 'to be able to.'

77 It is possible that ὁρκίζω, ἐνορκίζω, and ἐξορκίζω differ slightly in meaning, but this cannot be determined on the basis of available contexts.

ὀρκίζω: ὀρκίζω σε τὸν θεόν, μή με βασανίσῃς 'I ask you to swear by the name of God that you will not punish me' Mk 5.7.

ἐνορκίζω: ἐνορκίζω ὑμᾶς τὸν κύριον ἀναγνωσθῆναι τὴν ἐπιστολὴν πᾶσιν τοῖς ἀδελφοῖς 'I ask you to swear by the name of the Lord to read this letter to all the Christian brothers' 1 Th 5.27.

ἐξορκίζω: ἐξορκίζω σε κατὰ τοῦ θεοῦ τοῦ ζῶντος ἵνα ἡμῖν εἴπῃς εἰ σὺ εἶ 'I charge you to swear in the name of the living God to tell us who you are' Mt 26.63.

It is extremely difficult to translate ὀρκίζω, ἐνορκίζω, and ἐξορκίεω in a literal manner, though in some contexts one can say 'I put you under oath,' but in a number of passages the person speaking is imploring and not necessarily in a position to command or insist. Therefore, in a passage such as Mk 5.7, one may render the meaning idiomatically as 'for God's sake, I ask you, do not punish me.' In 1 Th 5.27 one may translate 'in the name of the Lord, I ask you to read this letter to all the Christian brothers,' and in Mt 26.63 one may translate 'in the name of the living God, I charge you, Tell us who you are.'

In most languages one may translate ὀρκίζω, ἐνορκίζω, and ἐξορκίζω by simply adding a causative component to terms meaning 'to swear' or 'to take an oath.' In other words, ὀρκίζω, ἐνορκίζω, and ἐξορκίζω may be rendered as 'to cause a person to say under oath.'

33.468 δίδωμι δόξαν τῷ θεῷ: (an idiom, literally 'to give glory to God') a formula used in placing someone under oath to tell the truth – 'promise before God to tell the truth, swear to tell the truth.' δὸς δόξαν τῷ θεῷ 'promise before God to tell the truth' Jn 9.24.

33.469 εὐχή[b], ῆς f: a promise to God that one will do something, with the implication that failure to act accordingly will result in divine sanctions against the person in question – 'vow.' εἰσὶν ἡμῖν ἄνδρες τέσσαρες εὐχὴν ἔχοντες ἐφ' ἑαυτῶν 'there are four men here who have taken a vow' or 'we have four men who. . .' Ac 21.23. It may, however, be necessary in some languages to be somewhat more specific in rendering 'vow,' so that one may need to translate this expression in Ac 21.23 as 'there are four men here who have promised God that they will do something.'

C'' Bless, Curse (33.470-33.475)

33.470 εὐλογέω[b]; εὐλογία[c], ας f; κατευλογέω: to ask God to bestow divine favor on, with the implication that the verbal act itself constitutes a significant benefit – 'to bless, blessing.'[78]

εὐλογέω[b]: εὐλογεῖτε τοὺς διώκοντας ὑμᾶς 'bless those who persecute you' Ro 12.14.

εὐλογία[c]: ἐκ τοῦ αὐτοῦ στόματος ἐξέρχεται εὐλογία καὶ κατάρα 'from the same mouth come blessing and cursing' Jas 3.10.

κατευλογέω: κατευλόγει τιθεὶς τὰς χεῖρας ἐπ' αὐτά 'he placed his hands on them and blessed them' Mk 10.16.

In a number of languages the closest equivalent of 'to bless' is 'to pray God on behalf of' or 'to ask God to do something good for.'

33.471 καταράομαι; κατάρα[a], ας f: to cause injury or harm by means of a statement regarded as having some supernatural power, often because a deity or supernatural force has been evoked – 'to curse, curse.'

καταράομαι: ἴδε ἡ συκῆ ἣν κατηράσω ἐξήρανται 'look, the fig tree you cursed has died' Mk 11.21.

κατάρα[a]: ἐκ τοῦ αὐτοῦ στόματος ἐξέρχεται εὐλογία καὶ κατάρα 'out of the same mouth come blessing and cursing' Jas 3.10.

33.472 ἀναθεματίζω; καταθεματίζω: to invoke divine harm if what is said is not true or if one does not carry out what has been promised – 'to curse.'[79]

ἀναθεματίζω: ἀναθέματι ἀνεθεματίσαμεν ἑαυτοὺς μηδενὸς γεύσασθαι ἕως οὗ ἀποκτείνωμεν τὸν Παῦλον 'we have cursed ourselves with a curse to taste nothing until we have killed Paul' Ac 23.14; ὁ δὲ ἤρξατο ἀναθεματίζειν καὶ ὀμνύναι 'then he began to curse and to swear'

---

78 It is possible that κατευλογέω is somewhat more emphatic than εὐλογέω[b], but this cannot be determined from existing contexts.

79 It is possible that καταθεματίζω is somewhat stronger in meaning than ἀναθεματίζω, but this cannot be shown from existing contexts.

Mk 14.71. In Mk 14.71 ἀναθεματίζω is in many regards similar in meaning to ὄμνυμι (33.463), but ἀναθεματίζω specifically denotes a curse which was invoked by Peter if what he was saying was not true.

καταθεματίζω: τότε ἤρξατο καταθεματίζειν καὶ ὀμνύειν 'then he began to curse and to swear' Mt 26.74. (See on Mk 14.71 above.)

33.473 ἀρά, ᾶς *f*; κατάρα[b], ας *f*; ἀνάθεμα[a], τος *n*: the content of what is expressed in a curse – 'curse.'

ἀρά: ὧν τὸ στόμα ἀρᾶς καὶ πικρίας γέμει 'their mouths are full of bitter curses' Ro 3.14. It may be difficult or even meaningless to speak of a person's mouth as being 'full of bitter curses,' but one can often say 'they are constantly cursing harshly' or 'speaking heavy curses' or 'constantly uttering harmful curses.'

κατάρα[b]: ὅσοι γὰρ ἐξ ἔργων νόμου εἰσὶν ὑπὸ κατάραν εἰσίν 'these who depend on obeying the Law live under a curse' Ga 3.10.

ἀνάθεμα[a]: ἀναθέματι ἀνεθεματίσαμεν ἑαυτοὺς μηδενὸς γεύσασθαι ἕως οὗ ἀποκτείνωμεν τὸν Παῦλον 'we cursed ourselves with a curse to taste nothing until we have killed Paul' Ac 23.14.

33.474 ἀνάθεμα[b], τος *n*; κατάθεμα, τος *n*; κατάρα[c], ας *f*: that which has been cursed – 'cursed, accursed.'

ἀνάθεμα[b]: ηὐχόμην γὰρ ἀνάθεμα εἶναι 'I would wish that I myself were something accursed' Ro 9.3. It is also possible to translate ἀνάθεμα in Ro 9.3 as 'I would wish that God himself had cursed me.'

κατάθεμα: πᾶν κατάθεμα οὐκ ἔσται ἔτι 'there will no longer be anything which is accursed' Re 22.3.

κατάρα[c]: Χριστὸς . . . γενόμενος ὑπὲρ ἡμῶν κατάρα 'Christ . . . became something accursed for our sake' Ga 3.13.

33.475 ἐπάρατος, ον; ἐπικατάρατος, ον: pertaining to being cursed – 'cursed, accursed.'

ἐπάρατος: ὁ ὄχλος οὗτος ὁ μὴ γινώσκων τὸν νόμον ἐπάρατοί εἰσιν 'this crowd which does not know the Law is accursed' Jn 7.49.

ἐπικατάρατος: ἐπικατάρατος πᾶς ὃς οὐκ ἐμμένει πᾶσιν τοῖς γεγραμμένοις ἐν τῷ βιβλίῳ τοῦ νόμου 'everyone who does not obey everything that is written in the book of the Law is accursed' Ga 3.10.

The occurrences of ἐπάρατος in Jn 7.49 and ἐπικατάρατος in Ga 3.10 imply much more than being cursed by some person. In such contexts, it really means that these individuals have already been condemned by God or are under the threat of such a condemnation.

D'' Non-Verbal Communication (33.476-33.489)

33.476 σύσσημον, ου *n*: a sign which has been previously agreed upon as having a particular meaning or significance – 'signal, sign.' δεδώκει δὲ ὁ παραδιδοὺς αὐτὸν σύσσημον αὐτοῖς 'the one who betrayed him had given them a signal' Mk 14.44. If a language has no specific term for 'signal' or 'sign,' one may indicate the implications of σύσσημον by translating the first part of Mk 14.44 as follows: 'the one who betrayed him told them how he would indicate who Jesus was; he said, The one whom I kiss is the man.'

33.477 σημεῖον, ου *n*: an event which is regarded as having some special meaning – 'sign.' εἰπὲ ἡμῖν . . . τί τὸ σημεῖον τῆς σῆς παρουσίας 'tell us . . . what will be the sign of your coming' Mt 24.3. In translating σημεῖον in Mt 24.3, it may be necessary in some languages to say 'tell us what will happen that will show that you are coming' or 'tell us what we will see that will make us know that you are coming.'

σημεῖον as an event with special meaning was inevitably an unusual or even miraculous type of occurrence, and in a number of contexts σημεῖον may be rendered as 'miracle.' Certainly that is the referent of the occurrence of σημεῖον in Jn 2.23 (πολλοὶ ἐπίστευσαν εἰς τὸ ὄνομα αὐτοῦ, θεωροῦντες αὐτοῦ τὰ σημεῖα ἃ ἐποίει 'many believed in him as they saw the signs he did'). For the Gospel of John, however, a σημεῖον is not simply a miraculous event but something which points to a reality with even greater significance. A strictly literal translation of σημεῖον as 'sign' might mean nothing more than a road sign or a sign on a building, and therefore in some languages σημεῖον in a context such as Jn 2.23

may be rendered as 'a miracle with great meaning.'

33.478 κατασείω: to communicate by means of a sign or signal – 'to make a sign, to give a signal.' κατασείσας δὲ αὐτοῖς τῇ χειρὶ σιγᾶν 'he gave them a signal with his hand to be quiet' Ac 12.17. The rendering of this statement in Ac 12.17 must often be modified depending upon the particular nature of the signal in the receptor language, for example, 'by holding up his hand, he told them to be quiet' or 'he motioned with his hand and they understood they should be quiet.'

33.479 παράσημος, ον: pertaining to being marked with a sign – 'having a sign of, being marked.' ἀνήχθημεν ἐν πλοίῳ . . . ᾿Αλεξανδρίνῳ, παρασήμῳ Διοσκούροις 'we sailed away on an Alexandrian ship marked with the Dioscuri' Ac 28.11. In Ac 28.11 the reference is to the images of the Dioscuri, 'the twin gods,' carved on the prow of the ship. For παράσημον as a noun, see 6.51.

33.480 τέρας, ατος n: an unusual sign, especially one in the heavens, serving to foretell impending events – 'portent, sign.' δώσω τέρατα ἐν τῷ οὐρανῷ ἄνω καὶ σημεῖα ἐπὶ γῆς κάτω 'I will perform portents in the sky above and signs on the earth below' Ac 2.19. In ancient times a portent might consist of a particular arrangement of the planets, an unusual display of northern lights, a conspicuous comet, or a cluster of falling stars. For a discussion of σημεῖον 'sign,' see 33.477.

33.481 στίγμα[b], τος n: something on the surface of an object, for example, line, spot, or scar, without special design but carrying significance – 'mark, scar.'[80] ἐγὼ γὰρ τὰ στίγματα τοῦ ᾿Ιησοῦ ἐν τῷ σώματί μου βαστάζω 'for I carry the marks of Jesus on my body' Ga 6.17. A strictly literal translation of Ga 6.17 might suggest that Paul had the same marks on his hands, feet, and side as Jesus had, but this is evidently not the meaning of the state-

ment in Ga 6.17. It is possible, of course, that since Paul was whipped much the same way that Jesus was whipped, that he would bear such scars on his back, but a more satisfactory rendering of Ga 6.17 would probably be 'for I have on my body scars indicating that I belong to Jesus.' For other interpretations of στίγμα in Ga 6.17, see 8.55 and 90.84.

33.482 χάραγμα[a], τος n: a meaningful mark, whether engraved, imprinted, or branded – 'mark, brand.' οἵτινες . . . οὐκ ἔλαβον τὸ χάραγμα ἐπὶ τὸ μέτωπον 'who . . . have not received the mark (of the beast) on their foreheads' Re 20.4. A strictly literal translation of 'the mark of the beast' might imply 'a picture of the beast' or 'a mark made by the beast.' A more satisfactory indication of the relationship between 'mark' and 'beast' would be 'a mark showing one's relationship to the beast' or 'a mark of loyalty to the beast' or 'a mark of the party of the beast.'

33.483 σφραγίς[c], ῖδος f: the impression of a signet ring or seal, primarily indicating ownership – 'mark, seal.' οἵτινες οὐκ ἔχουσι τὴν σφραγῖδα τοῦ θεοῦ ἐπὶ τῶν μετώπων 'who do not have the mark of God on their foreheads' Re 9.4. One may also translate this clause in Re 9.4 as 'who do not have the mark on their foreheads which shows that they belong to God.'

33.484 σφραγίζω[b]: (derivative of σφραγίς[c] 'mark, seal,' 33.483) to put a mark on something, primarily to indicate ownership but possibly also to mark group identity – 'to mark, to seal.' ἄχρι σφραγίσωμεν τοὺς δούλους τοῦ θεοῦ ἡμῶν ἐπὶ τῶν μετώπων αὐτῶν 'until we have marked with a seal the foreheads of the servants of our God' Re 7.3.

33.485 νεύω; ἐννεύω; διανεύω; κατανεύω: to signal to someone by means of part of the body, especially by means of the head or hands – 'to gesture, to motion, to nod, to beckon.'[81]

---

80 στίγμα[b] differs from στίγμα[a] (8.55) in that the significance of the scar is not the physical object as such but the meaning which the scar carries.

81 There are no doubt certain subtle differences of meaning between νεύω, ἐννεύω, διανεύω, and κατανεύω, but such distinctions are not evident from existing contexts.

νεύω: νεύει οὖν τούτῳ Σίμων Πέτρος πυθέσθαι τίς ἂν εἴη περὶ οὗ λέγει 'Simon Peter motioned to him to ask who it was that he was talking about' Jn 13.24.

ἐννεύω: ἐνένευον δὲ τῷ πατρὶ αὐτοῦ τὸ τί ἂν θέλοι καλεῖσθαι αὐτό 'they made gestures to his father (to ask him) what name he would like the boy to have' Lk 1.62.

διανεύω: αὐτὸς ἦν διανεύων αὐτοῖς 'he made gestures to them' Lk 1.22.

κατανεύω: κατένευσαν τοῖς μετόχοις ἐν τῷ ἑτέρῳ πλοίῳ τοῦ ἐλθόντας συλλαβέσθαι αὐτοῖς 'they motioned to their partners in the other boat to come and help them' Lk 5.7.

In a number of languages it is necessary to be quite specific with regard to the types of gestures or motions by the head or hands and arms. For example, in Jn 13.24 there is an obvious question involved, and this may require in some languages a particular signal by means of the hands or face. The same would be true in the case of Lk 1.62. In Lk 1.22 the gesture would have to be something which would explain or indicate Zechariah's inability to speak, while in Lk 5.7 quite another gesture would no doubt be called for, since the persons involved were at quite a distance from one another.

33.486 ὄναρ *n*; ἐνύπνιον, ου *n*: a dream as a means of communication – 'dream.'[82]
ὄναρ: ἰδοὺ ἄγγελος κυρίου κατ' ὄναρ ἐφάνη αὐτῷ 'behold, an angel of the Lord appeared to him in a dream' Mt 1.20.
ἐνύπνιον: καὶ οἱ πρεσβύτεροι ὑμῶν ἐνυπνίοις ἐνυπνιασθήσονται 'and your old men will dream dreams' Ac 2.17.

In a number of languages there are different terms for 'dream' depending upon the nature of the dream. A frightening dream without

special significance or a dream with erotic implications may be referred to by terms which are quite different from a term referring to a dream which carries important meaning, in other words, a dream which constitutes a type of vision or symbol of some reality.

33.487 ἐνυπνιάζομαι: to experience dreams having the significance of visions – 'to dream.' καὶ οἱ πρεσβύτεροι ὑμῶν ἐνυπνίοις ἐνυπνιασθήσονται 'and your old men will dream dreams' Ac 2.17. For a discussion of some of the problems involved in terms for 'dream,' see 33.486.

33.488 ὅρασις[a], εως *f*; ὅραμα[b], τος *n*; ὀπτασία, ας *f*: an event in which something appears vividly and credibly to the mind, although not actually present, but implying the influence of some divine or supernatural power or agency – 'vision.'
ὅρασις[a]: καὶ οὕτως εἶδον τοὺς ἵππους ἐν τῇ ὁράσει 'and thus I saw the horses in the vision' Re 9.17.
ὅραμα[b]: καὶ εἶδεν ἄνδρα ἐν ὁράματι Ἁνανίαν 'and he saw in a vision a man named Ananias' Ac 9.12.
ὀπτασία: ἐλεύσομαι δὲ εἰς ὀπτασίας καὶ ἀποκαλύψεις κυρίου 'and I will go on to visions and revelations from the Lord' 2 Cor 12.1.

33.489 ἔκστασις[b], εως *f*: a vision accompanied by an ecstatic psychological state – 'ecstatic vision.' ἐγένετο ἐπ' αὐτὸν ἔκστασις 'an ecstatic vision came to him' Ac 10.10. In Ac 11.5, however, where this experience in Ac 10.10 is related, the expression εἶδον ἐν ἐκστάσει ὅραμα ('I saw a vision in a state of ecstasy') is used. It is therefore possible that in Ac 10.10 ἔκστασις refers only to a particular state, but since this statement about the ἔκστασις (used absolutely) introduces the content of the vision, it seems necessary to assume that both the state and the vision are contained in the use of the term ἔκστασις in Ac 10.10.

---

82 The meaning of ὄναρ and ἐνύπνιον could be classified as a psychological state, but their direct connection with communication seems to justify their being included in this domain.

34 Association[1]

Outline of Subdomains

A   Associate (34.1-34.21)
B   Join, Begin to Associate (34.22-34.30)
C   Belong To, Be Included in the Member-ship of, Be Excluded From (34.31-34.39)
D   Limit or Avoid Association (34.40-34.41)
E   Establish or Confirm a Relation (34.42-34.49)
F   Visit (34.50-34.52)
G   Welcome, Receive (34.53-34.56)
H   Show Hospitality (34.57-34.61)
I   Kiss, Embrace (34.62-34.65)
J   Marriage, Divorce (34.66-34.78)

A   Associate[2] (34.1-34.21)

34.1 συναναμίγνυμι; συγχράομαι; συναπάγομαι[b]; ὁμιλία, ας *f*: to associate with one another, normally involving spacial proximity and/or joint activity, and usually implying some kind of reciprocal relation or involvement – 'to associate, to be in the company of, to be involved with, association.'
συναναμίγνυμι: ἔγραφα ὑμῖν ἐν τῇ ἐπιστολῇ μὴ συναναμίγνυσθαι πόρνοις 'I wrote you not to associate with immoral people' 1 Cor 5.9.
συγχράομαι: οὐ γὰρ συγχρῶνται Ἰουδαῖοι Σαμαρίταις 'for Jews do not associate with Samaritans' Jn 4.9. Some scholars interpret συγχράομαι in Jn 4.9 as denoting the use of the same dishes or utensils, so that one may translate this expression in Jn 4.9 as 'Jews do not use dishes together with Samaritans' or 'Jews and Samaritans do not use the same dishes.' Such an interpretation, however, is based upon etymological arguments for which there seems to be no certain justification in general Greek usage.
συναπάγομαι[b]: μὴ τὰ ὑψηλὰ φρονοῦντες ἀλλὰ τοῖς ταπεινοῖς συναπαγόμενοι 'do not be proud, but associate with humble people' Ro 12.16. It is also possible to interpret the phrase τοῖς ταπεινοῖς συναπαγόμενοι in Ro 12.16 as meaning 'share in doing what is humble' (see 41.22).
ὁμιλία: μὴ πλανᾶσθε· Φθείρουσιν ἤθη χρηστὰ ὁμιλίαι κακαί 'do not be fooled: to associate with bad people can ruin a good character' 1 Cor 15.33.

In translating terms referring to association, one may employ a number of different kinds of expressions, for example, 'to have something to do with,' 'to keep company with,' 'to go around with,' 'to join in doing things together,' or 'to become a companion of.' Sometimes association is spoken of in terms of the impression made upon others, for example, 'to be seen often together,' 'to be regarded as close friends,' and even idiomatically as 'to be another person's shadow.'

34.2 προσκαρτερέω[b]: to associate closely and continuously with – 'to stay close to, to associate closely with.' ὁ δὲ Σίμων καὶ αὐτὸς ἐπίστευσεν, καὶ βαπτισθεὶς ἦν προσκαρτερῶν τῷ Φιλίππῳ 'Simon himself also believed and after being baptized, he stayed close to Philip' Ac 8.13.

34.3 διαμένω[a]: to remain in an association for a period of time – 'to remain, to continue.' ὑμεῖς δέ ἐστε οἱ διαμεμενηκότες μετ' ἐμοῦ ἐν τοῖς πειρασμοῖς μου 'but you are the ones who have remained with me during my trials' Lk 22.28.

34.4 συγκοινωνέω: to be associated in some joint activity, with the implication, in some contexts, of a somewhat enduring relation – 'to participate with, to be in partnership with, to associate with.' μὴ συγκοινωνεῖτε τοῖς ἔργοις τοῖς ἀκάρποις τοῦ σκότους 'do not associate with people who do worthless things that belong to darkness' Eph 5.11.

34.5 κοινωνία[a], ας *f*: an association involving close mutual relations and involvement – 'close association, fellowship.' ἵνα καὶ ὑμεῖς κοινωνίαν ἔχητε μεθ' ἡμῶν 'in order that you may have fellowship with us' 1 Jn 1.3; δι' οὗ ἐκλήθητε εἰς κοινωνίαν τοῦ υἱοῦ αὐτοῦ Ἰησοῦ Χριστοῦ 'through whom you were called to

---

1 In Domain 34 *Association*, Subdomains A-E treat the more generic relations, while Subdomains F-J relate to more specific kinds of relations.
2 In Subdomain A *Associate*, the most generic meanings are included.

have fellowship with his Son Jesus Christ' 1 Cor 1.9.

34.6 κοινωνός, οῦ *m*; **συγκοινωνός**[a]**, οῦ** *m*: one who participates with another in some enterprise or matter of joint concern – 'partner, associate, one who joins in with.'[3]
κοινωνός: οἳ ἦσαν κοινωνοὶ τῷ Σίμωνι 'who were partners of Simon' Lk 5.10; εἰ οὖν με ἔχεις κοινωνόν 'if, then, you think of me as your partner' Phm 17; οὐκ ἂν ἤμεθα αὐτῶν κοινωνοὶ ἐν τῷ αἵματι τῶν προφητῶν 'we would not have joined them in killing the prophets' Mt 23.30.
συγκοινωνός[a]: συγκοινωνούς μου τῆς χάριτος πάντας ὑμᾶς ὄντας 'all of you being partners with me in the privilege' Php 1.7.

34.7 μετοχή, ῆς *f*: a relationship involving shared purposes and activity – 'partnership, sharing.' τίς γὰρ μετοχὴ δικαιοσύνῃ καὶ ἀνομίᾳ; 'how can there be a partnership between right and wrong?' 2 Cor 6.14. In 2 Cor 6.14 δικαιοσύνη and ἀνομία refer to 'those who do right' and 'those who do wrong.' In fact, in a number of languages one can only translate this expression in 2 Cor 6.14 as 'how can a person who does right and one who does wrong join in a partnership?' or 'how can one who does right and one who does wrong work together?' In this same verse κοινωνία (see 34.5) has a meaning closely corresponding to μετοχή, and similarly φῶς and σκότος refer respectively to 'those who live in the light' and 'those who live in darkness,' paralleling closely the distinction between δικαιοσύνη and ἀνομία.

34.8 μέτοχος[b]**, ου** *m*: one who shares with someone else as an associate in an enterprise or undertaking – 'companion, partner.' καὶ κατένευσαν τοῖς μετόχοις ἐν τῷ ἑτέρῳ πλοίῳ 'and they signaled to their companions in the other boat' Lk 5.7; διὰ τοῦτο ἔχρισέν σε ὁ θεός, ὁ θεός σου, ἔλαιον ἀγαλλιάσεως παρὰ τοὺς μετόχους σου 'therefore, God, your God, anointed you with the oil of gladness more than he did your companions' He 1.9.

34.9 ἑτεροζυγέω: to be wrongly or poorly matched in an association – 'to be mismatched, to be wrongly matched.' μὴ γίνεσθε ἑτεροζυγοῦντες ἀπίστοις 'do not be wrongly matched with unbelievers' 2 Cor 6.14. It is often necessary to indicate somewhat more precisely the manner in which one may be wrongly matched with others. Accordingly, one can translate 2 Cor 6.14 as 'do not attempt to work together with those who are unbelievers' or 'do not become partners with those who do not believe.'

34.10 συνανάκειμαι: to be associated with others in eating – 'to eat together, to associate in a meal.' πολλοὶ τελῶναι καὶ ἁμαρτωλοὶ ἐλθόντες συνανέκειντο τῷ Ἰησοῦ καὶ τοῖς μαθηταῖς αὐτοῦ 'many tax collectors and outcasts came and associated with Jesus and his disciples in eating' Mt 9.10.[4]

34.11 φίλος, ου *m*: a male person with whom one associates and for whom there is affection or personal regard – 'friend.' φίλε, προσανάβηθι ἀνώτερον 'come on up, friend, to a better place' Lk 14.10; ἵνα μετὰ τῶν φίλων μου εὐφρανθῶ 'for me to have a feast with my friends' Lk 15.29.
   In some languages there are different terms for different grades of friends, that is to say, a difference between intimate friends with whom one constantly shares and those who constitute a somewhat wider circle of persons who are on friendly terms but who are not in the inner circle of intimate relations. The choice of terms for 'friend' will depend, of course, upon individual contexts.

34.12 φίλη, ης *f*: a female person with whom one associates and for whom there is affection or personal regard – 'friend.' καὶ εὑροῦσα συγκαλεῖ τὰς φίλας καὶ γείτονας 'and when she finds it, she calls her friends and neighbors together' Lk 15.9. See discussion at 34.11.

---

3 It is possible that συγκοινωνός[a] is somewhat more emphatic than κοινωνός in focusing upon the joint nature of participation.

4 It is possible, of course, to understand συνανάκειμαι in Mt 9.10 as denoting merely the fact of eating together. However, in NT contexts such as this, the meaning appears to involve more than the mere fact of eating together; it is the association symbolized by eating together which is crucial and therefore constitutes the focal component of meaning.

34.13 χωρέω^d: (a figurative extension of meaning of χωρέω^b 'to have room for,' 80.4) to be friendly disposed toward someone – 'to open one's heart to, to be friendly to.' χωρήσατε ἡμᾶς 'be friendly toward us' 2 Cor 7.2.

34.14 ἀναγκαῖος^b, α, ον: pertaining to a close interpersonal relation – 'close, intimate.' συγκαλεσάμενος τοὺς συγγενεῖς αὐτοῦ καὶ τοὺς ἀναγκαίους φίλους 'having invited his relatives and close friends' Ac 10.24.

34.15 σύντροφος^b, ου m: a close friend on the basis of having been brought up together – 'close friend, intimate friend, friend since childhood.' Μαναήν τε Ἡρῴδου τοῦ τετραάρχου σύντροφος 'Manaen, a close friend of Herod the tetrarch since childhood' Ac 13.1. Some scholars, however, understand σύντροφος in Ac 13.1 as being an instance of σύντροφος^a 'foster brother' (see 10.51).

34.16 ἑταῖρος, ου m: a person who is associated with someone else, though not necessarily involving personal affection (as in the case of φίλος and φίλη, 34.11 and 34.12) – 'companion, friend.' ἑταῖρε, οὐκ ἀδικῶ σε 'friend, I have not cheated you' Mt 20.13; ὁμοία ἐστὶν παιδίοις καθημένοις ἐν ταῖς ἀγοραῖς ἃ προσφωνοῦντα τοῖς ἑταίροις 'like children sitting around in the marketplace and shouting to their companions' Mt 11.16 (apparatus, see Nestle-Aland).

34.17 γνωστός^c, ή, όν: pertaining to being a friend or acquaintance of someone, and thus enjoying certain privileges as a result of such a relation – 'friend, acquaintance.' ὁ δὲ μαθητὴς ἐκεῖνος ἦν γνωστὸς τῷ ἀρχιερεῖ 'that disciple was a friend of the High Priest' Jn 18.15. It is clear that in Jn 18.15 γνωστός implies much more than simply being 'well known by.' To have been simply well known by the High Priest could have been a source of danger for the disciple. It was the fact of a relationship of friendship which made it possible for the disciple to view the proceedings.

34.18 εἰμὶ εἰς τὸν κόλπον: (an idiom, literally 'to be in the bosom of') to be closely and intimately associated, with the implication of strong affection for – 'to be closely involved with, to be close beside.' ὁ ὢν εἰς τὸν κόλπον τοῦ πατρός 'who is close beside the Father' Jn 1.18. In Jn 1.18 one may speak of the Son as 'being at the Father's side' or 'being in closest communion with the Father.'

34.19 συστρατιώτης, ου m: (a figurative extension of meaning of συστρατιώτης 'fellow soldier,' not occurring in the NT) one who serves in arduous tasks or undergoes severe experiences together with someone else – 'one who struggles along with, one who works arduously along with, fellow struggler.' Ἀπφίᾳ τῇ ἀδελφῇ καὶ Ἀρχίππῳ τῷ συστρατιώτῃ ἡμῶν 'to our sister Apphia and our fellow soldier Archippus' Phm 2. A strictly literal translation of συστρατιώτης in Phm 2 might imply that Paul himself was a soldier and therefore, in a sense, a secret agent of some military force. Accordingly, it may be necessary to employ a simile, for example, 'who works like a fellow soldier' or 'one who experiences great hardships along with us.'

34.20 συναγωνίζομαι: to join with someone else in some severe effort – 'to join fervently in, to join vigorously in.' συναγωνίσασθαί μοι ἐν ταῖς προσευχαῖς ὑπὲρ ἐμοῦ πρὸς τὸν θεόν 'to join fervently with me in prayer to God on my behalf' Ro 15.30.

34.21 ὀρφανός^b, οῦ m or f: (a figurative extension of meaning of ὀρφανός^a 'orphan,' 10.40) one who is without associates who may be of sustaining help – 'friendless person, helpless.' οὐκ ἀφήσω ὑμᾶς ὀρφανούς 'I will not leave you helpless' Jn 14.18.

B Join, Begin to Associate (34.22-34.30)

34.22 προσκλίνομαι; κολλάομαι^a; προσκολλάομαι; προσκληρόομαι: to begin an association with someone, whether temporary or permanent – 'to join, to join oneself to, to become a part of.'⁵

---

5 προσκολλάομαι may very well differ from κολλάομαι^a by suggesting a more permanent association, with focus upon reciprocal relations.

προσκλίνομαι: ᾧ προσεκλίθη ἀνδρῶν ἀριθμὸς ὡς τετρακοσίων 'about four hundred men joined him' Ac 5.36.

κολλάομαι[a]: πρόσελθε καὶ κολλήθητι τῷ ἅρματι τούτῳ 'go and join this carriage' Ac 8.29. Though the Greek text of Ac 8.29 says literally 'join this carriage,' in reality, of course, the association is not directly with the carriage, but with the man riding in the carriage. It is therefore necessary in a number of languages to translate κολλήθητι τῷ ἅρματι τούτῳ as 'join the man riding in this carriage.'

προσκολλάομαι: καὶ προσκολληθήσεται πρὸς τὴν γυναῖκα αὐτοῦ 'and he will be joined to his wife' Eph 5.31. In rendering προσκολλάομαι in Eph 5.31, it is necessary to avoid an expression which will refer merely to sexual relations. The focus is upon interpersonal relations rather than upon the sexual act.

προσκληρόομαι: καί τινες ἐξ αὐτῶν ἐπείσθησαν καὶ προσεκληρώθησαν τῷ Παύλῳ καὶ τῷ Σιλᾷ 'and some of them were convinced and joined Paul and Silas' Ac 17.4. προσκληρόομαι in a context such as Ac 17.4 may be rendered as 'to throw in one's lot with' or 'to identify themselves with' or 'to become a part of the same group as.'

34.23 προσέρχομαι[b]: to take the initiative in association with someone – 'to undertake to join with, to seek association with.' ἀθέμιτόν ἐστιν ἀνδρὶ Ἰουδαίῳ κολλᾶσθαι ἢ προσέρχεσθαι ἀλλοφύλῳ 'a Jew is not allowed to join or to seek to associate with a Gentile' Ac 10.28. Though it is also true that Jews were not allowed to continue to associate with Gentiles, the focus of προσέρχομαι[b] appears to be upon the initiative which could not be taken by a Jew in approaching a Gentile in order to be associated in some activity which would be contrary to ritual observances. προσέρχομαι in this context may therefore be rendered in some languages as 'to join arms with a Gentile,' 'to link oneself with a Gentile,' or 'to become a close friend of a Gentile.'

34.24 ἀντέχομαι[a]: to join with and to maintain loyalty to – 'to adhere to.' ἑνὸς ἀνθέξεται καὶ τοῦ ἑτέρου καταφρονήσει 'he will adhere to the one and despise the other' Mt 6.24. The degree of close association suggested by

ἀντέχομαι in Mt 6.24 is sometimes expressed idiomatically as 'to stick oneself to,' 'to glue oneself to,' or 'to become one with.'

34.25 στρέφομαι[d]: to shift one's association to someone else – 'to turn to, to leave and go to, to shift to, to establish a relation with.' στρεφόμεθα εἰς τὰ ἔθνη 'we turn to the Gentiles' Ac 13.46.

34.26 παραπίπτω; ἐκπίπτω[c]; ἀποστρέφομαι[b]; ἀφίσταμαι[b] (and 2nd aorist active): to abandon a former relationship or association, or to dissociate (a type of reversal of beginning to associate) – 'to fall away, to forsake, to turn away.'[6]

παραπίπτω: παραπεσόντας, πάλιν ἀνακαινίζειν εἰς μετάνοιαν 'once they fall away, (it is impossible) to bring them back to repent again' He 6.6.

ἐκπίπτω[c]: τῆς χάριτος ἐξεπέσατε 'you have turned away from the grace (of God)' Ga 5.4. Note, however, that the underlying structure of the expression τῆς χάριτος ἐξεπέσατε really involves 'turning away from God who has shown grace.' For another interpretation of ἐκπίπτω in Ga 5.4, see 90.72.

ἀποστρέφομαι[b]: πολὺ μᾶλλον ἡμεῖς οἱ τὸν ἀπ' οὐρανῶν ἀποστρεφόμενοι 'how much less (shall) we (escape) if we turn away from the one (who speaks) from heaven' He 12.25.

ἀφίσταμαι[b]: ἐν τῷ ἀποστῆναι ἀπὸ θεοῦ ζῶντος 'that he will turn away from the living God' He 3.12.

34.27 μετατίθεμαι ἀπό: (an idiom, literally 'to change from') to abandon an association – 'to turn away from, to abandon one's loyalty to.' θαυμάζω ὅτι οὕτως ταχέως μετατίθεσθε ἀπὸ τοῦ καλέσαντος ὑμᾶς 'I am surprised that thus so quickly you are turning away from the one who called you' Ga 1.6.

34.28 στρέφω[e]: to reject an existing relation of association – 'to reject, to turn away from.' ἔστρεφεν δὲ ὁ θεὸς καὶ παρέδωκεν αὐτοὺς

---

6 The meanings of παραπίπτω, ἐκπίπτω[c], ἀποστρέφομαι[b], and ἀφίσταμαι[b] appear to focus upon the initial aspects of dissociation. As such, they constitute a reversal of the process of joining or beginning to associate.

λατρεύειν τῇ στρατιᾷ τοῦ οὐρανοῦ 'and God rejected them and handed them over to worship the host of heaven' Ac 7.42.

34.29 παρείσακτος, ον: pertaining to joining with someone under false pretenses and motivations – 'falsely pretending, joined falsely.' διὰ δὲ τοὺς παρεισάκτους ψευδαδέλφους 'on account of those who falsely pretended to be fellow believers' Ga 2.4. It is possible that παρείσακτος in Ga 2.4 may be interpreted as a passive in the sense of 'induced to join.'

34.30 παρεισέρχομαι; παρεισδύω: to join surreptitiously with evil intent – 'to slip into a group unnoticed, to join unnoticed.'
παρεισέρχομαι: οἵτινες παρεισῆλθον κατασκοπῆσαι τὴν ἐλευθερίαν ἡμῶν 'who slipped into our group in order to spy on our freedom' Ga 2.4.
παρεισδύω: παρεισέδυσαν γάρ τινες ἄνθρωποι 'for some people have slipped in unnoticed' Jd 4.

C Belong To, Be Included in the Membership of, Be Excluded From (34.31-34.39)

34.31 μετέχω^c: to be included in the membership of a group – 'to belong to.' ἐφ' ὃν γὰρ λέγεται ταῦτα φυλῆς ἑτέρας μετέσχηκεν '(our Lord), of whom these things are said, belonged to a different tribe' He 7.13. In order to express the meaning of 'belonged to a different tribe,' it may be necessary to say 'he had a different tribe name' or 'his tribe was different' or 'he was counted as a member of another tribe.'

34.32 τραπέζης μετέχω: (an idiom, literally 'to share in a table') to belong to a particular religious group as evidenced by ceremonial eating – 'to belong to (a religious group), to eat at the table of.'[7] οὐ δύνασθε τραπέζης κυρίου μετέχειν καὶ τραπέζης δαιμονίων 'you cannot belong to the Lord and belong to demons' 1 Cor 10.21.

34.33 καταριθμέομαι: to be counted as a member of a group – 'to be counted as a member, to be counted as a part, to belong to.' ὅτι κατηριθμημένος ἦν ἐν ἡμῖν 'because he was counted as one of us' Ac 1.17.

34.34 πρόσλημψις, εως *f*: the acceptance of someone into an association – 'acceptance.' τίς ἡ πρόσλημψις εἰ μὴ ζωὴ ἐκ νεκρῶν; 'what is acceptance if not life from the dead?' Ro 11.15. In rendering this expression in Ro 11.15 it may be necessary to indicate clearly the participants involved. For example, one may translate 'what will happen when God accepts them? It will be the same as having risen from the dead' or '. . . will be the resurrection of the dead.'

34.35 παραιτέομαι^c: to refuse to accept one into a particular association – 'to refuse to accept, to reject.' νεωτέρας δὲ χήρας παραιτοῦ 'but do not accept younger widows' 1 Tm 5.11. A strictly literal translation of παραιτέομαι in this context might be misunderstood, since it could suggest that younger widows were to be rejected from membership in the church. It may therefore be necessary to specify the particular relationships by translating 'but do not accept younger widows in the list of those to receive support from the church.'

34.36 ἐκκλείω^b; **ἀφορίζω**^a; **ἐξαίρω**: to exclude or remove someone from an association – 'to exclude, to separate, to get rid of.'
ἐκκλείω^b: ἐκκλεῖσαι ὑμᾶς θέλουσιν 'they no longer want you to relate (to me)' Ga 4.17. It may also be possible to translate this expression in Ga 4.17 as 'they want you to no longer belong (to me), or 'they want you to exclude (me) from your company.'
ἀφορίζω^a: μακάριοί ἐστε . . . ὅταν ἀφορίσωσιν ὑμᾶς . . . ἕνεκα τοῦ υἱοῦ τοῦ ἀνθρώπου 'happy are you . . . when people exclude you from their company . . . because of the Son of Man' Lk 6.22. It is, of course, possible to translate ἀφορίζω in Lk 6.22 as 'not to welcome,' but the emphasis of ἀφορίζω is to exclude from a relationship which has previously existed.

---

[7] It is not possible to determine on the basis of existing evidence whether the expression τραπέζης μετέχω is a genuine idiom or a phrase which is to be taken in a literal sense as referring to the ordinance of Holy Communion in contrast to banqueting in heathen temples.

One may therefore translate Lk 6.22 as 'happy are you . . . when people no longer welcome you in their company . . . because of the Son of Man.' By introducing the temporal element 'no longer,' the fact of exclusion is made clear.

ἐξαίρω: ἐξάρατε τὸν πονηρὸν ἐξ ὑμῶν αὐτῶν 'get rid of the evil one from among yourselves' or 'exclude the evil one from your group' 1 Cor 5.13.

34.37 ἐκπτύω: (a figurative extension of meaning of ἐκπτύω 'to spit out,' not occurring in the NT) to reject, with the implication of a measure of disdain – 'to reject, to have disdain for.' οὐκ ἐξουθενήσατε οὐδὲ ἐξεπτύσατε 'you did not despise or reject (me)' Ga 4.14. In a number of languages 'to reject' is expressed idiomatically as 'to throw away,' 'to push away,' or 'to turn one's back toward.'

34.38 ἀποβολή, ῆς f: the removal of someone from a particular association – 'rejection, elimination.' εἰ γὰρ ἡ ἀποβολὴ αὐτῶν καταλλαγὴ κόσμου 'for if their rejection meant reconciliation for the world' Ro 11.15. In rendering this clause in Ro 11.15, it may be necessary to indicate more specifically the participants and the implied relationships, for example, 'for if their being rejected meant that people in general were reconciled to God.'

34.39 φραγμός^c, οῦ m: (a figurative extension of meaning of φραγμός^a 'fence,' 7.59) that which serves as a means of separation in interpersonal relations – 'that which separates, that which isolates.' τὸ μεσότοιχον τοῦ φραγμοῦ λύσας 'destroying the intervening wall that separates' Eph 2.14. In a number of languages, however, it may be necessary to indicate what or who is separated, and therefore one may need to translate this phrase in Eph 2.14 as '. . . that separates Jews from Gentiles.'

D Limit or Avoid Association (34.40-34.41)

34.40 καταλείπω^c: to cause a particular relationship to cease – 'to leave, to no longer

relate to.' ἀντὶ τούτου καταλείψει ἄνθρωπος τὸν πατέρα καὶ τὴν μητέρα 'on account of this, a man will leave his father and mother' Eph 5.31. In rendering Eph 5.31 it is important to avoid an expression which will suggest abandoning or deserting. It is the limitation of a particular relationship which is involved.

34.41 ἀποτρέπομαι; ἐκκλίνω^a; παραιτέομαι^d; ἀφίσταμαι^c (and 2nd aorist active); στέλλομαι ἀπό: purposely to avoid association with someone – 'to shun, to avoid, to keep away from, to have nothing to do with.'[8]

ἀποτρέπομαι: ἔχοντες μόρφωσιν εὐσεβείας τὴν δὲ δύναμιν αὐτῆς ἠρνημένοι· καὶ τούτους ἀποτρέπου 'they will hold to the outward form of our religion but reject its (real) power. Keep away from these men' 2 Tm 3.5.

ἐκκλίνω^a: σκοπεῖν τοὺς τὰς διχοστασίας . . . ποιοῦντας, καὶ ἐκκλίνετε ἀπ' αὐτῶν 'watch out for those who cause divisions. Keep away from them' Ro 16.17.

παραιτέομαι^d: αἱρετικὸν ἄνθρωπον μετὰ μίαν καὶ δευτέραν νουθεσίαν παραιτοῦ 'give at least two warnings to the man who causes divisions, and then have nothing more to do with him' Tt 3.10.

ἀφίσταμαι^c: ἀπόστητε ἀπὸ τῶν ἀνθρώπων τούτων καὶ ἄφετε αὐτούς 'keep away from these men and let them go on' Ac 5.38.

στέλλομαι ἀπό: στέλλεσθαι ὑμᾶς ἀπὸ παντὸς ἀδελφοῦ ἀτάκτως περιπατοῦντος 'keep away from any fellow believer who lives a lazy life' 2 Th 3.6.

E Establish or Confirm a Relation (34.42-34.49)

34.42 δεξιὰς δίδωμι: (an idiom, literally 'to give right hands') to acknowledge an agreement establishing some relation, normally involving the actual practice of shaking hands – 'to make a covenant, to make an agreement.' δεξιὰς ἔδωκαν ἐμοὶ καὶ Βαρναβᾷ κοινωνίας 'they made a covenant with me and Barnabas as to how they would share the work with us' Ga 2.9.

8 There are probably certain differences of meaning in the terms in 34.41, but without more distinctive contexts, it is difficult to determine the precise areas of meaning.

34.43 διατίθεμαι[b]; διαθήκη[a], ης *f*: to make a solemn agreement involving reciprocal benefits and responsibilities – 'to make a covenant, to covenant together, making of a covenant.'

διατίθεμαι[b]: αὕτη ἡ διαθήκη ἣν διαθήσομαι τῷ οἴκῳ Ἰσραήλ 'this covenant which I will make with the people of Israel' He 8.10; καὶ τῆς διαθήκης ἧς διέθετο ὁ θεὸς πρὸς τοὺς πατέρας ὑμῶν 'and of the covenant which God made with your ancestors' Ac 3.25.

διαθήκη[a]: αὕτη αὐτοῖς ἡ παρ' ἐμοῦ διαθήκη, ὅταν ἀφέλωμαι τὰς ἁμαρτίας αὐτῶν 'I will make this covenant with them when I take away their sins' Ro 11.27.

34.44 διαθήκη[b], ης *f*: the verbal content of an agreement between two persons specifying reciprocal benefits and responsibilities – 'covenant, pact.' ἀνθρώπου κεκυρωμένην διαθήκην οὐδεὶς ἀθετεῖ ἢ ἐπιδιατάσσεται 'no one can break or add to a covenant which is in effect between people' Ga 3.15. In Lk 1.72 ποιῆσαι ἔλεος μετὰ τῶν πατέρων ἡμῶν καὶ μνησθῆναι διαθήκης ἁγίας αὐτοῦ '(God said he) would show mercy to our ancestors and remember his sacred covenant with them,' it is possible that διαθήκη denotes either the making of the covenant (34.43) or the verbal formulation (see 34.44).

In rendering the OT term *brith*, the Septuagint translators employed διαθήκη, literally 'a final will or testament,' in place of συνθήκη 'contract, agreement,' since they evidently wished to emphasize the fact that the initiative for such a covenantal relationship existed with one person rather than being the result of negotiation and compromise.

In many societies, and particularly in tribal ones, a covenant is a very significant bond between persons. It may, in fact, be the most important and lasting interpersonal relationship. It is seldom entered into lightly, for in many societies a covenant binds a person for a lifetime and may even involve willingness to die for the sake of the covenantal relationship.

34.45 ἀσύνθετος, ον: pertaining to not being bound or not regarding oneself as bound by any covenant or agreement – 'not keeping a promise, not abiding by an agreement.'

ἀσυνέτους, ἀσυνθέτους, ἀστόργους 'they have no conscience, they do not keep their promises, and they show no kindness to others' Ro 1.31. It is also possible to translate ἀσύνθετος in Ro 1.31 as 'they feel no obligation to keep their agreements' or 'they do not feel bound to do what they have promised to do.'

34.46 δικαιόω[a]; δικαίωσις[a], εως *f*; δικαιοσύνη[b], ης *f*: to cause someone to be in a proper or right relation with someone else – 'to put right with, to cause to be in a right relationship with.' Some scholars, however, interpret δικαιόω, δικαίωσις, and δικαιοσύνη in the following contexts as meaning 'forensic righteousness,' that it to say, the act of being declared righteous on the basis of Christ's atoning ministry, but it would seem more probable that Paul uses these expressions in the context of the covenant relation rather than in the context of legal procedures.

δικαιόω[a]: δικαιούμενοι δωρεὰν τῇ αὐτοῦ χάριτι διὰ τῆς ἀπολυτρώσεως τῆς ἐν Χριστῷ Ἰησοῦ 'by the free gift of his grace in delivering them through Christ Jesus, they are put right with him' Ro 3.24.

δικαίωσις[a]: ἠγέρθη διὰ τὴν δικαίωσιν ἡμῶν 'he was raised to life in order to put us right with (God)' Ro 4.25.

δικαιοσύνη[b]: δικαιοσύνη γὰρ θεοῦ ἐν αὐτῷ ἀποκαλύπτεται ἐκ πίστεως εἰς πίστιν 'how God puts people right with himself is revealed in it as a matter of faith from beginning to end' Ro 1.17. Some scholars, however, understand the phrase δικαιοσύνη θεοῦ in Ro 1.17 as referring to God's faithfulness to his promises made to Abraham. In other words, the focus would be upon God's moral integrity, but it is difficult to relate this interpretation to the statement about faith in Ro 1.17b.

It may be difficult in some languages to find a succinct expression equivalent to 'to be put right with.' Sometimes the closest equivalent may be 'to be related to as one should be.' In some instances the implication of a right relationship may be expressed by phrases involving 'acceptance.' For example, Ro 3.24 may be expressed as 'by the free gift of God's grace they are accepted by him through Christ Jesus who sets them free.' Similarly, Ro 4.25 is sometimes expressed as 'he was raised to life in order to cause us to be accepted by God.' There are, however, certain dangers involved in terms indicating 'acceptance,' since this might imply God's reluctance to accept people apart from the atoning work of Jesus Christ, while in reality it was God who was in Christ reconciling the world to himself. Therefore, one should clearly avoid a rendering which would seem to suggest different types of motivation in the Godhead.

34.47 δίκαιος[b], α, ον: pertaining to being in a right relationship with someone – 'being in a right relation with, one who has been put right with, righteous.' ὁ δὲ δίκαιος ἐκ πίστεως ζήσεται 'he who is in a right relation with God through faith shall live' or 'he who has been put right with God through faith shall live' Ro 1.17.

34.48 ἀρνέομαι[b]: to deny any relationship of association with someone – 'to deny.' ὁ δὲ ἀρνησάμενός με ἐνώπιον τῶν ἀνθρώπων 'whoever denies me before people' Lk 12.9. In a number of languages one may best translate 'deny' as 'to make manifest not to know.' Accordingly, one may translate the first part of Lk 12.9 as 'whoever shows people that he does not know me' or 'whoever refuses to admit that he does know me.' Denial need not involve some verbal formulation, though in some languages this is the most common practice. See also 33.277.

34.49 ἀπαρνέομαι[c]: to deny strongly, with the implication of rejection – 'to deny, to reject.' ἀπαρνηθήσεται ἐνώπιον τῶν ἀγγέλων τοῦ θεοῦ 'he will be rejected in the presence of the angels of God' Lk 12.9.

F   Visit (34.50-34.52)

34.50 ὁράω[d]; θεάομαι[b]; ἐπισκέπτομαι[b]: to go to see a person on the basis of friendship and with helpful intent – 'to visit, to go to see.'
ὁράω[d]: μεθ' οὗ ἐὰν τάχιον ἔρχηται ὄψομαι ὑμᾶς 'if he comes soon enough, I will have him with me when I visit you' He 13.23.
θεάομαι[b]: ἐλπίζω γὰρ διαπορευόμενος θεάσασθαι

ὑμᾶς 'for I hope to visit you on my way' Ro 15.24.
ἐπισκέπτομαι[b]: καὶ ἐν φυλακῇ καὶ οὐκ ἐπεσκέψασθέ με 'and in prison and you did not visit me' Mt 25.43. For another interpretation of ἐπισκέπτομαι in Mt 25.43, see 35.39.

34.51 ἐπισκοπή[a], ῆς f: the coming of divine power, either for benefit or judgment – 'coming, visitation.' ἀνθ' ὧν οὐκ ἔγνως τὸν καιρὸν τῆς ἐπισκοπῆς σου 'because you did not recognize the time (of God's) coming (to save) you' Lk 19.44; δοξάσωσιν τὸν θεὸν ἐν ἡμέρᾳ ἐπισκοπῆς 'they will praise God on the day of his coming' 1 Pe 2.12. In 1 Pe 2.12 the reference may be to God's coming to rule or his coming in judgment.

34.52 ἱστορέω: to visit, with the purpose of obtaining information – 'to visit and get information.'[9] ἔπειτα μετὰ ἔτη τρία ἀνῆλθον εἰς Ἱεροσόλυμα ἱστορῆσαι Κηφᾶν 'it was three years later that I went to Jerusalem to visit Cephas and get information from him' Ga 1.18. In rendering 'to get information from him' it may be more satisfactory to say 'to learn something from him' or 'to have him tell me what I needed to know.'

G   Welcome, Receive (34.53-34.56)

34.53 προσλαμβάνομαι[e]; παραλαμβάνω[d]; ἀπολαμβάνω[d]; δέχομαι[b]; ἀναδέχομαι[a]; ἀποδέχομαι[a]; ἐπιδέχομαι[a]; εἰσδέχομαι; ὑποδέχομαι; προσδέχομαι[b]; παραδέχομαι[b]: to accept the presence of a person with friendliness – 'to welcome, to receive, to accept, to have as a guest.'[10]

9 ἱστορέω can perhaps best be interpreted as combining two different domains: (1) the domain of *Association* (34) involving visiting and (2) the domain of *Communication* (33) involving the soliciting of information. This is a typical example of a meaning which overlaps two domains.

10 There are no doubt certain contextual constraints involved in the choice of ἀναδέχομαι[a], ἀποδέχομαι[a], ἐπιδέχομαι[a], εἰσδέχομαι, ὑποδέχομαι, προσδέχομαι[b], and παραδέχομαι[b] in the sense that the spacial relationships involved in the welcoming of a guest can be reflected in the prepositional prefixes. For example, in Lk 8.40 the use of ἀποδέχομαι may focus upon the particular source, while ἐπιδέχομαι in 3 Jn 10 may be relevant in view of

προσλαμβάνομαιᶜ: τὸν δὲ ἀσθενοῦντα τῇ πίστει προσλαμβάνεσθε 'you must welcome among you the person who is weak in the faith' Ro 4.1.

παραλαμβάνωᵈ: καὶ οἱ ἴδιοι αὐτὸν οὐ παρέλαβον 'and his own did not receive him' Jn 1.11; μὴ φοβηθῇς παραλαβεῖν Μαρίαν τὴν γυναῖκά σου 'do not fear to accept Mary as your wife' Mt 1.20.

ἀπολαμβάνωᵈ: ὅτι ὑγιαίνοντα αὐτὸν ἀπέλαβεν 'because he received him (back) in sound health' Lk 15.27.

δέχομαιᵇ: ὁ δεχόμενος ὑμᾶς ἐμὲ δέχεται 'whoever receives you, receives me' Mt 10.40.

ἀναδέχομαιᵃ: ὃς ἀναδεξάμενος ἡμᾶς τρεῖς ἡμέρας φιλοφρόνως ἐξένισεν 'he welcomed us and for three days he treated us kindly as his guests' Ac 28.7.

ἀποδέχομαιᵃ: ἐν δὲ τῷ ὑποστρέφειν τὸν Ἰησοῦν ἀπεδέξατο αὐτὸν ὁ ὄχλος 'when Jesus returned (to the other side of the lake), the crowd welcomed him' Lk 8.40.

ἐπιδέχομαιᵃ: οὔτε αὐτὸς ἐπιδέχεται τοὺς ἀδελφούς 'he does not receive the fellow believers' 3 Jn 10.

εἰσδέχομαι: καὶ ἀκαθάρτου μὴ ἅπτεσθε· κἀγὼ εἰσδέξομαι ὑμᾶς 'have nothing to do with what is unclean, and I will receive you' 2 Cor 6.17. In view of the fact that εἰσδέχομαι in 2 Cor 6.17 refers to God's receiving people, it may be necessary to use quite a different expression than one would normally employ in referring to welcoming a guest into the home. In some instances one may use a rather generic expression such as 'to accept,' and this may be expressed idiomatically in some languages as 'to extend my hand to you' or 'to count you as belonging to me.' It is the figurative usage of εἰσδέχομαι in this type of context which may lead to a somewhat different type of rendering.

the fact that the believers are coming to a particular point. προσδέχομαι in Lk 15.2 may suggest a kind of reciprocal relationship which is established with outcasts, and παραδέχομαι in Ac 15.4 may simply point to spacial proximity. However, it would be wrong to insist upon clear distinctions in meaning based on the very limited number of contexts involved. Some of these same distinctions in spacial relations may exist for the set προσλαμβάνομαιᶜ, παραλαμβάνωᵈ, and ἀπολαμβάνωᵈ.

ὑποδέχομαι: γυνὴ δέ τις ὀνόματι Μάρθα ὑπεδέξατο αὐτόν 'a woman named Martha welcomed him (in her home)' Lk 10.38.

προσδέχομαιᵇ: οὗτος ἁμαρτωλοὺς προσδέχεται καὶ συνεσθίει αὐτοῖς 'this man welcomes outcasts and even eats with them' Lk 15.2.

παραδέχομαιᵇ: παραγενόμενοι δὲ εἰς Ἰερουσαλὴμ παρεδέχθησαν ἀπὸ τῆς ἐκκλησίας 'when they arrived in Jerusalem they were welcomed by the church' Ac 15.4; μαστιγοῖ δὲ πάντα υἱὸν ὃν παραδέχεται 'and he disciplines every son whom he accepts' He 12.6.

34.54 δεκτόςᵇ, **ή, όν**: pertaining to being welcomed or acceptable – 'one who is welcomed, one who is acceptable.' ὅτι οὐδεὶς προφήτης δεκτός ἐστιν ἐν τῇ πατρίδι αὐτοῦ 'because no prophet is acceptable in his own hometown' Lk 4.24. In rendering this expression in Lk 4.24 it may be necessary to restructure the relationships somewhat radically, for example, 'because people of a town do not wish to accept one of their fellow townsmen as a prophet.'

34.55 ἀσπάζομαιᶜ: to welcome something or someone, with focus upon the initial greeting – 'to welcome, to accept gladly.' μὴ λαβόντες τὰς ἐπαγγελίας, ἀλλὰ πόρρωθεν αὐτὰς ἰδόντες καὶ ἀσπασάμενοι 'not having received the promises, but from a long way off they saw them and welcomed them' He 11.13. In some languages, however, it may be difficult to speak of 'welcoming promises,' but one can often render this relationship as 'they were happy to know about what had been promised.' For another interpretation of ἀσπάζομαι in He 11.13, see 25.130.

34.56 εἴσοδοςᵇ, **ου** *f*: welcome extended to a person on the occasion of a visit, with probable focus upon the ready acceptance – 'welcome, acceptance.' αὐτοὶ γὰρ περὶ ἡμῶν ἀπαγγέλλουσιν ὁποίαν εἴσοδον ἔσχομεν πρὸς ὑμᾶς 'all those people speak of how you welcomed us when we visited you' 1 Th 1.9.

H Show Hospitality (34.57-34.61)

34.57 ξενίζω; ξενοδοχέω; φιλοξενία, ας *f*; **ξενία**ᵇ, **ας** *f*: to receive and show hospitality to a stranger, that is, someone who is not regarded as a member of the extended family or a close friend – 'to show hospitality, to receive a stranger as a guest, hospitality.'

ξενίζω: ὃς ἀναδεξάμενος ἡμᾶς τρεῖς ἡμέρας φιλοφρόνως ἐξένισεν 'he welcomed us and for three days he treated us kindly as his guests' Ac 28.7.

ξενοδοχέω: εἰ ἐξενοδόχησεν 'if she receives guests' or 'if she is hospitable' 1 Tm 5.10.

φιλοξενία: τὴν φιλοξενίαν διώκοντες 'be eager to show hospitality' Ro 12.13.

ξενία[b]: ἑτοίμαζέ μοι ξενίαν 'prepare hospitality for me' Phm 22. For another interpretation of ξενία in Phm 22, see 7.31. See also footnote 7 in Domain 7.

To receive a stranger as a guest is sometimes expressed idiomatically as 'to let a stranger sit at one's table,' 'to offer a bed to a stranger,' or 'to let a stranger enter one's house.'

34.58 φιλόξενος, ον: pertaining to showing hospitality to strangers – 'to be hospitable.' φιλόξενοι εἰς ἀλλήλους ἄνευ γογγυσμοῦ 'be hospitable to one another without complaining' 1 Pe 4.9.

34.59 πόδας νίπτω: (an idiom, literally 'to wash the feet,' derived from the practice of washing the feet of any guest entering the home) to show sincere and gracious hospitality to someone – 'to be very hospitable to.' εἰ ἁγίων πόδας ἔνιψεν 'if she shows hospitality to God's people' 1 Tm 5.10. It is also possible that the idiom πόδας νίπτω means 'to perform humble duties on behalf of someone' (see 88.58).

34.60 ξένος[b], ου *m*: a person who shows hospitality to guests – 'host.' ἀσπάζεται ὑμᾶς Γάϊος ὁ ξένος μου 'Gaius my host greets you' Ro 16.23. In rendering 'host' it may be necessary to employ a phrase, for example, 'who welcomed and took care of us in his home.'

34.61 καταλύω[e]: to experience the hospitality of someone, with principal focus upon lodging – 'to be a guest.' παρὰ ἁμαρτωλῷ ἀνδρὶ εἰσῆλθεν καταλῦσαι 'this man has gone as a guest to (the home of) a sinner' Lk 19.7; ἵνα

πορευθέντες εἰς τὰς κύκλῳ κώμας καὶ ἀγροὺς καταλύσωσιν καὶ εὕρωσιν ἐπισιτισμόν 'in order that they may go to the villages and hamlets round about and find lodging and food' Lk 9.12.

I Kiss, Embrace[11] (34.62-34.65)

34.62 φιλέω[c]; καταφιλέω; φίλημα, τος *n*: to kiss, either as an expression of greeting or as a sign of special affection and appreciation – 'to kiss.'[12]

φιλέω[c]: ὃν ἂν φιλήσω αὐτός ἐστιν 'the man I kiss is the one' Mt 26.48.

καταφιλέω: προσελθὼν τῷ Ἰησοῦ εἶπεν, Χαῖρε, ῥαββί· καὶ κατεφίλησεν αὐτόν 'he went up to Jesus and said, Hail, Teacher, and kissed him' Mt 26.49; κατεφίλει τοὺς πόδας αὐτοῦ καὶ ἤλειφεν τῷ μύρῳ 'she kissed his feet and poured perfume (on them)' (literally '. . . anointed with perfume') Lk 7.38.

φίλημα: φιλημά μοι οὐκ ἔδωκας 'you did not greet me with a kiss' Lk 7.45.

Since in so many societies kissing is not a form of greeting, it may be necessary to add some kind of classifier to contexts such as Mt 26.48 and Mt 26.49 in order to indicate clearly the intention involved; otherwise, the use of a term meaning merely 'to kiss' might suggest a kind of erotic display. The clause in Mt 26.48 may be translated as 'the man I greet by kissing is the one you want.'

34.63 ἐναγκαλίζομαι: to put one's arms around someone as an expression of affection and concern – 'to embrace, to hug, to put one's arms around.' ἐναγκαλισάμενος αὐτὰ κατευλόγει τιθεὶς τὰς χεῖρας ἐπ' αὐτά 'he put his arms around them and placed his hands on them and blessed them' Mk 10.16. It may be

11 Though it would be possible to classify terms meaning 'kiss, embrace' under Domain 33 *Communication*, such activities do communicate relationships. It seems far more satisfactory to treat them as indicators of interpersonal relations.

12 Though the act of kissing may have different functions, the nature of the event is essentially the same. In some languages, however, a distinction is made between kissing on the cheek and kissing on the lips. Additional distinctions may be made as to whether one is kissing a person of the same sex or of a different sex.

important in some instances to indicate the symbolic value of an embrace by some type of classifying phrase, for example, 'to show his love for by putting his arms around' or 'to embrace to show affection.'

34.64 ἐπιπίπτω ἐπὶ τὸν τράχηλον: (an idiom, literally 'to fall on the neck') to show special affection for by throwing one's arms around a person – 'to hug, to embrace.'[13] ἐπιπεσόντες ἐπὶ τὸν τράχηλον τοῦ Παύλου κατεφίλουν αὐτόν 'they hugged Paul and kissed him goodbye' Ac 20.37. A literal translation of ἐπιπίπτω ἐπὶ τὸν τράχηλον 'to fall on someone's neck' can be seriously misunderstood. In fact, in some languages it is so close to an expression meaning 'to kill' that one should normally avoid any literal rendering. At the same time, it is very important not to employ terms for 'embrace' and 'kiss' in Ac 20.37 which might suggest improper sexual interests.

34.65 συμπεριλαμβάνω: to embrace, as an expression of great concern for someone – 'to embrace, to hug.' καταβὰς δὲ ὁ Παύλος ἐπέπεσεν αὐτῷ καὶ συμπεριλαβών 'but Paul went down and threw himself on him and hugged him' Ac 20.10. In the translation of συμπεριλαμβάνω in Ac 20.10 it is essential to avoid any implication of erotic motivations.

J Marriage, Divorce (34.66-34.78)

34.66 γαμέω; γαμίζω[a]: to enter into a marriage relation, applicable either to a man or to a woman – 'to marry, marriage.'
γαμέω: βούλομαι οὖν νεωτέρας γαμεῖν 'so I would rather that the younger widows get married' 1 Tm 5.14.
γαμίζω[a]: ὥστε καὶ ὁ γαμίζων τὴν ἑαυτοῦ παρθένον καλῶς ποιεῖ, καὶ ὁ μὴ γαμίζων κρεῖσσον ποιήσει 'so the man who marries his betrothed does well, but the one who does not marry does better' 1 Cor 7.38. Some interpreters understand γαμίζω in 1 Cor 7.38 to

mean 'to give in marriage' (see 34.72). See also the discussion at 13.32.

34.67 γάμος[a], ου *m*: the state of being married – 'marriage.'[14] τίμιος ὁ γάμος ἐν πᾶσιν 'marriage should be honored by all' He 13.4.

34.68 γάμος[b], ου *m*: the ceremony associated with becoming married – 'wedding.' βασιλεῖ, ὅστις ἐποίησεν γάμους τῷ υἱῷ αὐτοῦ 'a king who arranged a wedding for his son' Mt 22.2; καὶ ἐπλήσθη ὁ γάμος ἀνακειμένων 'and many were banqueting at the wedding' (literally 'the wedding was filled with those who were banqueting') Mt 22.10.

34.69 γίνομαι ἀνδρί: (an idiom, literally 'to become to a man') to become married to a man – 'to marry.' τοῦ μὴ εἶναι αὐτὴν μοιχαλίδα γενομένην ἀνδρὶ ἑτέρῳ 'she will not be called an adulteress if she marries another' Ro 7.3.

34.70 γυναικὸς ἅπτομαι: (an idiom, literally 'to touch a woman') to marry a woman – 'to marry, to get married.' καλὸν ἀνθρώπῳ γυναικὸς μὴ ἅπτεσθαι 'it is good for a man not to get married' 1 Cor 7.1. It is important to note that this expression in the second part of 1 Cor 7.1 may be either a statement by Paul or a quotation from a letter from the church of Corinth. This fact should be clearly noted in the margin.

34.71 ἐπιγαμβρεύω: to marry the childless widow of one's brother (the so-called levirate marriage; see Dt 25.5-10) – 'to marry.' ἐάν τις ἀποθάνῃ μὴ ἔχων τέκνα, ἐπιγαμβρεύσει ὁ ἀδελφὸς αὐτοῦ τὴν γυναῖκα αὐτοῦ 'if a man who has no children dies, his brother must marry the widow' Mt 22.24.

34.72 γαμίσκω; γαμίζω[b]: to cause a person to become married – 'to give in marriage.'
γαμίσκω: οἱ υἱοὶ τοῦ αἰῶνος τούτου γαμοῦσιν καὶ γαμίσκονται 'the people of our day marry and are given in marriage' Lk 20.34.
γαμίζω[b]: ἐν γὰρ τῇ ἀναστάσει οὔτε γαμοῦσιν

---

13 The idiom ἐπιπίπτω ἐπὶ τὸν τράχηλον would seem to indicate somewhat greater affection and concern than the verb ἐναγκαλίζομαι (34.63).

14 γάμος[a] differs in meaning from γαμέω and γαμίζω[a] (34.66) in denoting the state of being married and not simply the act of entering into a marriage relation.

οὔτε γαμίζονται 'in the resurrection they will not marry or be given in marriage' Mt 22.30.

34.73 συζεύγνυμι: to join two persons in a marriage relationship – 'to cause to be married, to join in marriage.' ὃ οὖν ὁ θεὸς συνέζευξεν ἄνθρωπος μὴ χωριζέτω 'therefore what God has joined together in marriage, man should not separate' Mt 19.6.

34.74 ἁρμόζομαι; μνηστεύομαι: to promise a person for marriage – 'to be engaged, to be promised in marriage.'
ἁρμόζομαι: ἡρμοσάμην γὰρ ὑμᾶς ἑνὶ ἀνδρὶ παρθένον ἁγνήν 'you who are like a pure virgin, I promised you in marriage to one man' 2 Cor 11.2.
μνηστεύομαι: πρὸς παρθένον ἐμνηστευμένην ἀνδρὶ ᾧ ὄνομα Ἰωσήφ '(was sent) to a girl promised in marriage to a man named Joseph' Lk 1.27.
It may be important to note in the margin of a text that in biblical times the act of betrothal was regarded as binding, so that the breaking of a betrothal was legally equivalent to divorce.

34.75 ὕπανδρος, ον: pertaining to being legally bound to a man in marriage – 'married.' ἡ γὰρ ὕπανδρος γυνὴ τῷ ζῶντι ἀνδρὶ δέδεται νόμῳ 'a married woman is bound by the law to her husband as long as he lives' Ro 7.2.

34.76 ἄγαμος, ου f or m: one who is not married – 'unmarried.' λέγω δὲ τοῖς ἀγάμοις καὶ ταῖς χήραις 'to the unmarried and the widows, I say this' 1 Cor 7.8; ἐὰν δὲ καὶ χωρισθῇ, μενέτω ἄγαμος 'if she separates from her husband, let her remain unmarried' 1 Cor 7.11.

34.77 παρθένος[c], ου f or m: a person who has not as yet married (and possibly implying virginity) – 'unmarried person.' περὶ δὲ τῶν παρθένων ἐπιταγὴν κυρίου οὐκ ἔχω 'concerning the unmarried, I do not have a command from the Lord' 1 Cor 7.25. Some scholars interpret παρθένος[c] as referring not only to those who have never married, but also to widows and widowers who have not remarried. The meaning of 'unmarried persons who are not necessarily virgins' is well attested in Greek from classical times.

34.78 ἀφίημι[e]; χωρίζω[b]; ἀπολύω[d]; λύσις, εως f: to dissolve the marriage bond – 'to divorce, to separate.'
ἀφίημι[e]: ἄνδρα γυναῖκα μὴ ἀφιέναι . . . μὴ ἀφιέτω τὸν ἄνδρα 'a husband must not divorce his wife . . . and a wife must not divorce her husband' 1 Cor 7.11, 13.
χωρίζω[b]: εἰ δὲ ὁ ἄπιστος χωρίζεται, χωριζέσθω 'if the one who is not a believer wishes to separate, let him separate' 1 Cor 7.15.
ἀπολύω[d]: ὃς ἂν ἀπολύσῃ τὴν γυναῖκα αὐτοῦ, δότω αὐτῇ ἀποστάσιον 'anyone who divorces his wife must give her a written notice of divorce' Mt 5.31.
λύσις: δέδεσαι γυναικί; μὴ ζήτει λύσιν 'do you have a wife? Then do not try to get a divorce' 1 Cor 7.27.
Expressions for divorce are often based on terms meaning literally 'to send away,' 'to separate from,' or 'to leave one another.' However, in a number of languages idiomatic expressions are employed, for example 'to send him off with his clothes,' 'to untie the knot between them,' or 'to throw away her hearthstones.'
Some persons have attempted to make an important distinction between ἀφίημι in 1 Cor 7.11, 13 and χωρίζω in 1 Cor 7.15 on the assumption that ἀφίημι implies legal divorce, while χωρίζω only relates to separation. Such a distinction, however, seems to be quite artificial.

35 Help, Care For[1]

Outline of Subdomains

A   Help (35.1-35.18)
B   Serve (35.19-35.30)
C   Provide For, Support (35.31-35.35)
D   Care For, Take Care Of (35.36-35.46)
E   Entrust To the Care Of (35.47-35.50)
F   Rear, Bring Up (35.51-35.52)
G   Adopt (35.53)
H   Desert, Forsake (35.54-35.56)

A Help (35.1-35.18)

35.1 ἀντιλαμβάνομαι^a; ἐπιλαμβάνομαι^d; ὑπολαμβάνω^c; συμβάλλομαι; παρίσταμαι^f (and 2nd aorist active); ἀντέχομαι^c; ἐπαρκέω^a; βοηθέω; βοήθεια^a, ας *f*: to assist in supplying what may be needed – 'to help.'[2]
ἀντιλαμβάνομαι^a: πάντα ὑπέδειξα ὑμῖν ὅτι οὕτως κοπιῶντας δεῖ ἀντιλαμβάνεσθαι τῶν ἀσθενούντων 'I have shown you in all things that by working hard in this way we must help the weak' Ac 20.35. As in the case of so many words with the meaning of 'help,' it may be necessary in some instances to use an equivalent phrase, for example, 'to supply people with what they need' or 'to give to people what is necessary' or '. . . what they should have.'
ἐπιλαμβάνομαι^d: οὐ γὰρ δήπου ἀγγέλων ἐπιλαμβάνεται 'for it is clear that it is not the angels that he helps' He 2.16. Though the meaning of 'help' is possible for ἐπιλαμβάνομαι in He 2.16, the more generally accepted interpretation is 'to be concerned with' or 'to take an interest in' (see 30.42).
ὑπολαμβάνω^c: ἡμεῖς οὖν ὀφείλομεν ὑπολαμβάνειν τοὺς τοιούτους 'we then ought to help such people' 3 Jn 8.

συμβάλλομαι: ὃς παραγενόμενος συνεβάλετο πολὺ τοῖς πεπιστευκόσιν διὰ τῆς χάριτος 'when he arrived he was a great help to those who through grace had become believers' Ac 18.27.
παρίσταμαι^f: παραστῆτε αὐτῇ ἐν ᾧ ἂν ὑμῶν χρήζῃ πράγματι 'give her any help she may need from you' Ro 16.2.
ἀντέχομαι^c: ἀντέχεσθε τῶν ἀσθενῶν 'be of help to the weak' 1 Th 5.14.
ἐπαρκέω^a: εἰ θλιβομένοις ἐπήρκεσεν 'if she has helped those in trouble' 1 Tm 5.10.
βοηθέω: εἴ τι δύνῃ, βοήθησον ἡμῖν σπλαγχνισθεὶς ἐφ' ἡμᾶς 'have pity on us and help us if you possibly can' Mk 9.22.
βοήθεια^a: ἵνα λάβωμεν ἔλεος καὶ χάριν εὕρωμεν εἰς εὔκαιρον βοήθειαν 'that we may receive mercy and find grace to help us at the proper time' He 4.16.

35.2 ὠφελέω^a: to provide assistance, with emphasis upon the resulting benefit – 'to help.' ἡ σὰρξ οὐκ ὠφελεῖ οὐδέν 'human nature is of no help' Jn 6.63.

35.3 ἀμύνομαι: to assist by intervening on behalf of, primarily in terms of defense – 'to help.' ἰδών τινα ἀδικούμενον ἠμύνατο καὶ ἐποίησεν ἐκδίκησιν 'when he saw someone being mistreated, he went to his help and took revenge' Ac 7.24.[3]

35.4 ὀνίναμαι: to be the recipient of help or favor – 'to receive help, to receive a benefit, to be favored.' ἐγώ σου ὀναίμην ἐν κυρίῳ 'for the Lord's sake, let me experience a favor from you' or '. . . do me a favor' Phm 20.

35.5 συλλαμβάνομαι; συναντιλαμβάνομαι; συνυπουργέω: to help by joining in an activity or effort – 'to join in helping.'
συλλαμβάνομαι: κατένευσαν τοῖς μετόχοις ἐν τῷ ἑτέρῳ πλοίῳ τοῦ ἐλθόντας συλλαβέσθαι αὐτοῖς

---

1 Domain 35 *Help, Care For* involves primarily those positive aspects of largely interpersonal activity in which people are provided for or supported. In addition, the converse or opposite meanings of 'desert' and 'abandon' are included, primarily in Subdomain H.
2 The various terms noted in 35.1 with a generic meaning of 'help' no doubt possess certain contrastive features of meaning, at least of a connotative type, but there is no specific evidence of this in NT usage.

3 It is possible to interpret ἀμύνομαι in Ac 7.24 as meaning 'to retaliate' or even 'to take revenge,' but this would seem to be a redundant meaning, particularly in view of the following statement, καὶ ἐποίησεν ἐκδίκησιν 'and he took revenge.'

'they motioned to their partners in the other boat to come and help them' Lk 5.7.

συναντιλαμβάνομαι: ὡσαύτως δὲ καὶ τὸ πνεῦμα συναντιλαμβάνεται τῇ ἀσθενείᾳ ἡμῶν 'in the same way the Spirit also comes to help us, weak as we are' (literally '. . . help our weakness') Ro 8.26.

συνυπουργέω: συνυπουργούντων καὶ ὑμῶν ὑπὲρ ἡμῶν τῇ δεήσει 'as you help us by joining us in our prayers' 2 Cor 1.11.

In a number of instances it is not necessary to specify the joint effort or activity, since this is supplied by the context itself as, for example, in Lk 5.7 in which 'coming to help' indicates clearly the joint efforts. But in some languages it may be important to use a specific expression rather than a generic one. Accordingly, 'to come and help them' in Lk 5.7 may be rendered as 'to come and work with them.'

35.6 παραγίνομαι[b]: to come to the assistance of someone – 'to come and help, to be present to help.' οὐδείς μοι παρεγένετο 'no one came to help me' 2 Tm 4.16.

35.7 ἐπικουρία, ας *f*: help, with the possible implication of assistance provided by an ally – 'help.' ἐπικουρίας οὖν τυχὼν τῆς ἀπὸ τοῦ θεοῦ ἄχρι τῆς ἡμέρας ταύτης 'but to this very day I have been helped by God' Ac 26.22.

35.8 ἐπιβλέπω[c]: to provide help, with the implication of having taken special notice of – 'to help, to be concerned with, to look upon and help.' δέομαί σου ἐπιβλέψαι ἐπὶ τὸν υἱόν μου 'I beg you to help my son' Lk 9.38. For another interpretation of ἐπιβλέπω in Lk 9.38, see 30.45.

35.9 ἀντίλημψις, εως *f*: the ability or capacity to help or assist – 'ability to help.' ἔπειτα χαρίσματα ἰαμάτων, ἀντιλήμψεις, κυβερνήσεις 'followed by the gift of healing, or the ability to help others, or to direct them' 1 Cor 12.28.

35.10 βοήθεια[b], ας *f*: (derivative of βοηθέω 'to help,' 35.1) an object which provides help or support – 'support.' βοηθείαις ἐχρῶντο

ὑποζωννύντες τὸ πλοῖον 'they used supports to undergird the ship' Ac 27.17. In a number of languages it may be important to render βοήθεια[b] by something more specific, for example, 'ropes,' as in 'they fastened some ropes tightly around the ship,' since 'ropes' may be the most likely reference in Ac 27.17.

35.11 βοηθός, οῦ *m*: (derivative of βοηθέω 'to help,' 35.1) one who provides help or assistance – 'helper, patron (in the sense of one who supports a person or endeavor).' ὥστε θαρροῦντας ἡμᾶς λέγειν, Κύριος ἐμοὶ βοηθός 'let us be bold, then, and say, The Lord is my helper' He 13.6.

35.12 προΐσταμαι[b]: to be engaged in helping or aiding – 'to be active in helping, to be involved in giving aid.' ἵνα φροντίζωσιν καλῶν ἔργων προΐστασθαι οἱ πεπιστευκότες θεῷ 'so that those who believe in God may fix their attention on being active in providing help' or '. . . in giving aid' Tt 3.8.

35.13 προστάτις, ιδος *f*: (derivative of προΐσταμαι[b] 'to be active in helping,' 35.12) a woman who is active in helping – 'helper, patroness (in the sense of one engaged in supporting an individual or endeavor).' γὰρ αὐτὴ προστάτις πολλῶν ἐγενήθη καὶ ἐμοῦ αὐτοῦ 'for she herself has been a helper to many people and also to me' Ro 16.2.

35.14 παρηγορία[b], ας *f*: that which constitutes a means of help – 'help, assistance.' ἐγενήθησάν μοι παρηγορία 'they have been a help to me' Col 4.11. It is also possible to understand παρηγορία in Col 4.11 as meaning 'comfort' (see 25.155).

35.15 εὐεργέτης, ου *m*: (derivative of εὐεργετέω 'to do good to,' 88.7) a person who provides important help or assistance, often occurring as a title for princes or distinguished persons – 'helper of the people, benefactor.' οἱ βασιλεῖς τῶν ἐθνῶν κυριεύουσιν αὐτῶν καὶ οἱ ἐξουσιάζοντες αὐτῶν εὐεργέται καλοῦνται 'the kings of this world (literally '. . . of the nations') have power over their people, and the rulers are called their benefactors' Lk 22.25.

35.16 παράκλητος[b], ου *m*: (derivative of παρακαλέω 'to call upon to provide help,' not occurring in this specific sense in the NT) one who may be called upon to provide help or assistance – 'helper.'[4] παράκλητον ἔχομεν πρὸς τὸν πατέρα, Ἰησοῦν Χριστὸν δίκαιον 'we have a helper with the Father, even Jesus Christ the righteous one' 1 Jn 2.1.

35.17 καταλείπω[f]: to leave someone without help (possibly in the sense of 'to cease helping') – 'to leave off helping, to leave without help, to not help.' Κύριε, οὐ μέλει σοι ὅτι ἡ ἀδελφή μου μόνην με κατέλιπεν διακονεῖν; 'Lord, aren't you concerned that my sister has left me alone without help to serve?' Lk 10.40.

35.18 ἀποστρέφομαι[c]: to refuse to provide help to someone – 'to refuse to help.' καὶ τὸν θέλοντα ἀπὸ σοῦ δανίσασθαι μὴ ἀποστραφῇς 'do not refuse to help one who wants to borrow from you' Mt 5.42; ἀπεστράφησάν με πάντες οἱ ἐν τῇ Ἀσίᾳ 'all those in Asia refused to help me' 2 Tm 1.15.

B Serve (35.19-35.30)

35.19 θεραπεύω[b]; ὑπηρετέω[a]; διακονέω[a]; διακονία[a], ας *f*: to render assistance or help by performing certain duties, often of a humble or menial nature – 'to serve, to render service, to help, service, help.'
θεραπεύω[b]: οὐδὲ ὑπὸ χειρῶν ἀνθρωπίνων θεραπεύεται προσδεόμενός τινος 'nor does (God) need anything that people can supply by rendering service to him' Ac 17.25.

---

4 The meaning of παράκλητος overlaps considerably with other domains. It certainly involves psychological factors of encouragement and therefore may very well be treated in Domain 25 *Attitudes and Emotions*. There is also a sense in which παράκλητος inevitably involves some communication, and therefore it may fittingly be analyzed in Domain 33 *Communication*. The role of intercession has certain legal implications, and accordingly, παράκλητος is justifiably related to legal procedures in Domain 56 *Courts and Legal Procedures*. It is very rare indeed that any one term in a receptor language will have all of the distinctive features of meaning possessed by παράκλητος, especially in reference to the role of the Holy Spirit (see 12.19).

ὑπηρετέω[a]: Δαυὶδ μὲν γὰρ ἰδίᾳ γενεᾷ ὑπηρετήσας τῇ τοῦ θεοῦ βουλῇ 'for David served God's purposes in his own time' Ac 13.36.
διακονέω[a]: ὁ υἱὸς τοῦ ἀνθρώπου οὐκ ἦλθεν διακονηθῆναι ἀλλὰ διακονῆσαι 'the Son of Man did not come to be served, but to serve' Mt 20.28. In rendering Mt 20.28 it may be necessary to be somewhat more specific about those who serve or are served, for example, 'the Son of Man did not come in order for people to serve him but in order to serve people.'
διακονία[a]: οἶδά σου τὰ ἔργα καὶ τὴν ἀγάπην καὶ τὴν πίστιν καὶ τὴν διακονίαν 'I know what you do, I know your love, your faithfulness, your service' Re 2.19. In rendering 'your service' in Re 2.19, it may be necessary to say 'how you help others' or 'how you serve others.'
In some languages it is essential in communicating the concept of 'service' to introduce a specific reference to 'a servant,' for example, 'to help as a servant' or 'to assist as one who must,' and in some contexts it may be useful to employ a phrase such as 'to help in small things' or 'to do the low tasks.'

35.20 θεράπων, οντος *m*; ὑπηρέτης, ου *m*; διάκονος[a], ου *m* and *f*: (derivatives of θεραπεύω[b], ὑπηρετέω[a], and διακονέω[a] 'to serve,' 35.19) a person who renders service – 'servant.'
θεράπων: Μωϋσῆς μὲν πιστὸς ἐν ὅλῳ τῷ οἴκῳ αὐτοῦ ὡς θεράπων 'Moses was faithful in God's whole house as a servant' He 3.5.
ὑπηρέτης: εἰς τοῦτο γὰρ ὤφθην σοι, προχειρίσασθαί σε ὑπηρέτην 'I have appeared to you to appoint you as (my) servant' Ac 26.16. In the NT ὑπηρέτης is employed to refer to many diverse types of servants, such as attendants to a king, officers of the Sanhedrin, attendants of magistrates, and, especially, in the Gospel of John, Jewish Temple guards.
διάκονος[a]: ἀλλ' ὃς ἐὰν θέλῃ ἐν ὑμῖν μέγας γενέσθαι ἔσται ὑμῶν διάκονος 'if anyone of you wants to be great, he must be the servant of the rest' Mt 20.26.
In rendering θεράπων, ὑπηρέτης, and διάκονος[a] in the sense of 'servant,' it is important to avoid a term which would be too specific, for example, 'one who serves meals' or 'one who works around the house.' It may,

in fact, be necessary to use an expression which means essentially 'helper.'

35.21 διακονία^b, ας *f*: (derivative of διακονέω^a 'to serve,' 35.19) the role or position of serving – 'ministry, task.' ὡς τελειῶσαι τὸν δρόμον μου καὶ τὴν διακονίαν ἣν ἔλαβον παρὰ τοῦ κυρίου 'that I may complete my course of life and my ministry which I received from the Lord' Ac 20.24.

35.22 λειτουργέω^a; λειτουργία^a, ας *f*: to serve, with the implication of more formal or regular service – 'to serve, service.' λειτουργέω^a: ὀφείλουσιν καὶ ἐν τοῖς σαρκικοῖς λειτουργῆσαι αὐτοῖς 'so they ought to serve them with their material things' Ro 15.27. λειτουργία^a: ἵνα ἀναπληρώσῃ τὸ ὑμῶν ὑστέρημα τῆς πρός με λειτουργίας 'to complete what was deficient in your service to me' Php 2.30.

35.23 λειτουργός, οῦ *m*: (derivative of λειτουργέω^a 'to serve,' 35.22) a person who renders special service – 'servant.'⁵ λειτουργοὶ γὰρ θεοῦ εἰσιν εἰς αὐτὸ τοῦτο προσκαρτεροῦντες 'those who devote themselves to this very thing are servants of God' Ro 13.6.

35.24 λειτουργικός, ή, όν: (derivative of λειτουργέω^a 'to serve,' 35.22) pertaining to service – 'serving.' πάντες εἰσὶν λειτουργικὰ πνεύματα 'they are all spirits that render service' He 1.14.

35.25 λειτουργία^b, ας *f*: (derivative of λειτουργέω^a 'to serve,' 35.22) an assignment or role in serving – 'ministry, service.' νυνὶ δὲ διαφορωτέρας τέτυχεν λειτουργίας 'but now he has obtained a more excellent ministry' He 8.6. The meaning of 'ministry' may be expressed in some languages as 'a way of serving.'

35.26 παρεδρεύω: to serve, with the probable implication of continuity and regularity of the service – 'to serve.' οἱ τῷ θυσιαστηρίῳ

---

⁵ The classical Greek meaning of λειτουργός in the sense of a servant of the state assuming public office to be administered at his own expense is completely lacking from NT usage.

παρεδρεύοντες τῷ θυσιαστηρίῳ συμμερίζονται 'those who serve at the sacrifices on the altar get a share of the sacrifices' 1 Cor 9.13.

35.27 δουλεύω^c: to serve, normally in a humble manner and in response to the demands or commands of others – 'to serve.' ἀλλὰ διὰ τῆς ἀγάπης δουλεύετε ἀλλήλοις 'but through love serve one another' Ga 5.13; οὐδεὶς δύναται δυσὶ κυρίοις δουλεύειν 'no one can serve two masters' Mt 6.24. It is possible that in Mt 6.24 δουλεύω should be understood as δουλεύω^a, namely, 'to be a slave' (see 87.79).

35.28 προσκαρτερέω^c: to serve in a close personal relationship – 'to serve personally.' φωνήσας δύο τῶν οἰκετῶν καὶ στρατιώτην εὐσεβῆ τῶν προσκαρτερούντων αὐτῷ 'then he called two of his house servants and a soldier, a religious man who was one of his personal servants' Ac 10.7. The phrase 'his personal servants' can be rendered as 'those who serve just him.'

In Mk 3.9 a literal translation of the phrase ἵνα πλοιάριον προσκαρτερῇ αὐτῷ as 'that a boat may be in personal attendance to him,' may be rather awkward in some languages. A more natural rendering would be '. . . may wait upon him' or '. . . may be ready at hand for him to use.'

35.29 ὀφθαλμοδουλία, ας *f*: to serve with a view to impressing others – 'eyeservice, to serve in order to call attention to oneself.' οἱ δοῦλοι, ὑπακούετε κατὰ πάντα τοῖς κατὰ σάρκα κυρίοις, μὴ ἐν ὀφθαλμοδουλίᾳ . . . ἀλλ' ἐν ἁπλότητι καρδίας 'slaves, obey your human masters in all things, not with eyeservice . . . but with a sincere heart' Col 3.22.

35.30 δουλαγωγέω: to prepare or make something available for service – 'to make ready for service.' ὑπωπιάζω μου τὸ σῶμα καὶ δουλαγωγῶ 'I keep my body under control and make it ready for service' 1 Cor 9.27.

C Provide For, Support (35.31-35.35)

35.31 χορηγέω; ἐπιχορηγέω^a; ἐπιχορηγία, ας *f*: to make available whatever is necessary to help or supply the needs of someone – 'to provide for, to support, to supply the needs of, provision, support.'

χορηγέω and ἐπιχορηγέωᵃ: ὁ δὲ ἐπιχορηγῶν σπόρον τῷ σπείροντι καὶ ἄρτον εἰς βρῶσιν χορηγήσει . . . 'and (God) who supplies seed for the sower and bread to eat, will also supply . . .' 2 Cor 9.10.

ἐπιχορηγία: οἶδα γὰρ ὅτι τοῦτό μοι ἀποβήσεται εἰς σωτηρίαν διὰ τῆς ὑμῶν δεήσεως καὶ ἐπιχορηγίας τοῦ πνεύματος Ἰησοῦ Χριστοῦ 'for I know that because of your prayers and what the Spirit of Jesus Christ will provide for, I shall be set free' Php 1.19.

35.32 ἐπαρκέωᵇ; ὑπηρετέωᵇ; βαστάζωᵈ: to provide continuous and possibly prolonged assistance and help by supplying the needs of someone – 'to provide for, to support.'

ἐπαρκέωᵇ: εἴ τις πιστὴ ἔχει χήρας, ἐπαρκείτω αὐταῖς 'if a woman who is a believer has widows (in her family), she must support them' 1 Tm 5.16.

ὑπηρετέωᵇ: αὐτοὶ γινώσκετε ὅτι ταῖς χρείαις μου καὶ τοῖς οὖσιν μετ' ἐμοῦ ὑπηρέτησαν αἱ χεῖρες αὗται 'you yourselves know that with these hands of mine I have provided for the needs of myself and my companions' Ac 20.34.

βαστάζωᵈ: οὐ σὺ τὴν ῥίζαν βαστάζεις ἀλλὰ ἡ ῥίζα σέ 'you don't support the root; the root supports you' Ro 11.18.⁶

35.33 πληρόωᵈ: to provide for by supplying a complete amount – 'to provide for completely, to supply fully.' πεπλήρωμαι δεξάμενος παρὰ Ἐπαφροδίτου τὰ παρ' ὑμῶν 'I have been fully provided for, now that Epaphroditus has brought me your gifts' Php 4.18. 'To be fully provided for' may be expressed as 'to have all that one needs.'

35.34 προσαναπληρόω: to provide sufficiently in addition (a more emphatic expression than πληρόωᵈ, 35.33) – 'to provide fully.' ὅτι ἡ διακονία τῆς λειτουργίας ταύτης οὐ μόνον ἐστὶν προσαναπληροῦσα τὰ ὑστερήματα τῶν ἁγίων . . . 'for this service you perform not

only supplies the needs of God's people . . .' 2 Cor 9.12.

35.35 προβλέπομαιᵃ: to provide for the needs of others, with the implication of anticipating such a need – 'to provide for.' τοῦ θεοῦ περὶ ἡμῶν κρεῖττόν τι προβλεψαμένου 'for God had provided something better for us' He 11.40. It may be possible to translate προβλέπομαι in He 11.40 as 'to provide for by foreseeing' or '. . . by determining in advance' (see 30.100).

D Care For, Take Care Of⁷ (35.36-35.46)

35.36 θάλπω: to take care of, with the implication of cherishing and concern for – 'to take care of.' οὐδεὶς γάρ ποτε τὴν ἑαυτοῦ σάρκα ἐμίσησεν, ἀλλὰ ἐκτρέφει καὶ θάλπει αὐτήν 'no one ever hates his own body; instead, he feeds it and takes care of it' Eph 5.29. It may be useful in some instances to translate 'and takes care of it' in Eph 5.29 as 'and gives to his own body whatever is needed' or 'and does for himself whatever is necessary.'

35.37 διακονέωᵇ: to take care of, by rendering humble service to – 'to take care of.' πότε σε εἴδομεν πεινῶντα ἢ διψῶντα . . . ἢ ἐν φυλακῇ καὶ οὐ διηκονήσαμέν σοι; 'when did we see you hungry or thirsty . . . or in prison, and we did not take care of you?' Mt 25.44. It may be possible to render 'and we did not take care of you' as 'and we did not give you whatever you needed.'

35.38 διακονίαᶜ, ας f: a procedure for taking care of the needs of people – 'provision for taking care of, arrangement for support.' ὅτι παρεθεωροῦντο ἐν τῇ διακονίᾳ τῇ καθημερινῇ αἱ χῆραι αὐτῶν 'because their widows were being neglected in the arrangement for providing for their needs each day' Ac 6.1. For another interpretation of διακονία in Ac 6.1, see 57.119.

---

6 It is possible to interpret βαστάζω in Ro 11.18 in a more or less literal sense, namely 'to carry' or 'to bear' (see 15.188), but the overall context of Ro 11.18 is figurative.

7 The Subdomain *Care For, Take Care Of* differs from the previous Subdomain *Provide For, Support* in generally emphasizing the personal care and attention involved. Thus, the meanings in this subdomain seem to focus upon the personal concern rather than on supplying needs.

35.39 ἐπισκοπέω[a]; ἐπισκέπτομαι[c]; προνο-έω[b]: to care for or look after, with the implication of continuous responsibility – 'to look after, to take care of, to see to.'

ἐπισκοπέω[a]: ἐπισκοποῦντες μή τις ὑστερῶν ἀπὸ τῆς χάριτος τοῦ θεοῦ 'see to it that no one lacks the benefits of God's kindness' He 12.15. For another interpretation of ἐπισκοπέω in He 12.15, see 30.46.

ἐπισκέπτομαι[c]: ἀσθενὴς καὶ ἐν φυλακῇ καὶ οὐκ ἐπεσκέψασθέ με 'I was sick and in prison but you would not take care of me' Mt 25.43. It is also possible to understand ἐπισκέπτομαι in Mt 25.43 as meaning 'to visit' (see 34.50). πρῶτον ὁ θεὸς ἐπεσκέψατο λαβεῖν ἐξ ἐθνῶν λαὸν τῷ ὀνόματι αὐτοῦ 'God first showed his care for the Gentiles by taking from among them a people for himself' Ac 15.14.

προνοέω[b]: εἰ δέ τις τῶν ἰδίων καὶ μάλιστα οἰκείων οὐ προνοεῖ, τὴν πίστιν ἤρνηται 'if someone does not take care of his relatives, especially the members of his family, he has denied the faith' 1 Tm 5.8.

35.40 ἐπισκοπή[c], ῆς f: (derivative of ἐπισκοπέω[a] 'to take care of,' 35.39) the position of one who has responsibility for the care of someone – 'position of responsibility, position of oversight.' τὴν ἐπισκοπὴν αὐτοῦ λαβέτω ἕτερος 'may someone else take his position of responsibility for the care of (the church)' Ac 1.20. Though in some contexts ἐπισκοπή has been regarded traditionally as a position of authority, in reality the focus is upon the responsibility for caring for others, and in the context of Ac 1.20 the reference is clearly to the responsibility for caring for the church (see 53.69).

35.41 ἀγρυπνέω[b]: to take care of or to look after, with the implication of continuous and wakeful concern for – 'to look after, to take care of.' πείθεσθε τοῖς ἡγουμένοις ὑμῶν καὶ ὑπείκετε, αὐτοὶ γὰρ ἀγρυπνοῦσιν ὑπὲρ τῶν ψυχῶν ὑμῶν 'obey your leaders and follow their orders, for they care for your very person' He 13.17.

35.42 ἐπίστασις[c], εως f: responsibility for oversight based upon authority – 'responsibility for, concern for, care of.' ἡ ἐπίστασίς μοι ἡ καθ' ἡμέραν, ἡ μέριμνα πασῶν τῶν ἐκκλησιῶν 'my daily responsibility and concern for all the churches' 2 Cor 11.28. Though one might regard ἐπίστασις[c] as meaning only the position of authority, nevertheless this authority is expressed in terms of the oversight and care of others. In a sense the meaning of ἐπίστασις in 2 Cor 11.28 is defined by the following appositional phrase, ἡ μέριμνα πασῶν τῶν ἐκκλησιῶν 'concern for all the churches.' For another interpretation of ἐπίστασις in 2 Cor 11.28, see 25.239.

35.43 ἐπίσκοπος[a], ου m: one who has the responsibility of caring for spiritual concerns – 'one responsible for, one who cares for, guardian, keeper.' ἀλλὰ ἐπεστράφητε νῦν ἐπὶ τὸν ποιμένα καὶ ἐπίσκοπον τῶν ψυχῶν ὑμῶν 'but you have now turned to the Shepherd and Keeper of your souls' 1 Pe 2.25. In 1 Pe 2.25 ἐπίσκοπος is applied to Christ, and it no doubt shares certain of the meanings associated with ἐπίσκοπος[b] in 53.71, but the focus in 1 Pe 2.25 is not upon leadership but upon the role of caring for the believers.

35.44 ἐπιμελέομαι[a]; ἐπιμέλεια, ας f: to care for with diligent concern – 'to care for, to take care of, to provide whatever is needed.'

ἐπιμελέομαι[a]: ἤγαγεν αὐτὸν εἰς πανδοχεῖον καὶ ἐπεμελήθη αὐτοῦ 'he took him to an inn where he cared for him' Lk 10.34.

ἐπιμέλεια: ἐπέτρεψεν πρὸς τοὺς φίλους πορευθέντι ἐπιμελείας τυχεῖν 'he allowed him to visit his friends so as to be provided with what he needed' Ac 27.3.

35.45 τρέφω[b]; τροφοφορέω: to take care of, with special reference to supplying necessary nourishment – 'to take care of.'

τρέφω[b]: ὅπου τρέφεται ἐκεῖ καιρὸν καὶ καιροὺς καὶ ἥμισυ καιροῦ ἀπὸ προσώπου τοῦ ὄφεως 'there she will be taken care of for three and a half years, safe from the serpent's attack' or 'the serpent's reach' (literally '. . . the serpent's presence') Re 12.14.

τροφοφορέω: καὶ ὡς τεσσερακονταετῆ χρόνον ἐτροφοφόρησεν αὐτοὺς ἐν τῇ ἐρήμῳ 'and for forty years he took care of them in the desert' Ac 13.18 (apparatus).

35.46 θάπτω τὸν πατέρα μου: (possibly an idiom, literally 'to bury my father') to take care of one's father until his death – 'to take care of a father, to provide for one's father until his death.' ἐπίτρεφόν μοι ἀπελθόντι πρῶτον θάψαι τὸν πατέρα μου 'allow me first to take care of my father until his death' Lk 9.59.

E   Entrust To the Care Of (35.47-35.50)

35.47 παρατίθεμαι[a]: to entrust oneself to the care of someone – 'to entrust oneself to, to commit oneself to the care of.' εἰς χεῖράς σου παρατίθεμαι τὸ πνεῦμά μου 'into your hands I commit my spirit' or 'I give myself into your care' Lk 23.46; παρέθεντο αὐτοὺς τῷ κυρίῳ 'they entrusted themselves to the Lord' Ac 14.23.

35.48 παραθήκη, ης f: that which has been entrusted to the care of someone – 'what is entrusted, what is someone's responsibility to care for.' τὴν παραθήκην φύλαξον 'keep safe what has been entrusted to your care' 1 Tm 6.20; ὅτι δυνατός ἐστιν τὴν παραθήκην μου φυλάξαι 'because he is able to keep what he has entrusted to me' 2 Tm 1.12. It is possible to translate 2 Tm 1.12 as '. . . what I have entrusted to him' referring to Paul's salvation or his life, though such a rendering is less likely. (See also 2 Tm 1.14.)

35.49 κλῆρος[d], ου m: what has been assigned as someone's responsibility to take care of – 'responsibility to care for.' μηδ' ὡς κατακυριεύοντες τῶν κλήρων 'do not lord it over those who are your responsibility to care for' 1 Pe 5.3.

35.50 πιστεύω[d]: to entrust something to the care of someone – 'to entrust to, to put into the care of.' ὅτι ἐπιστεύθησαν τὰ λόγια τοῦ θεοῦ 'because they were entrusted with God's message' or '. . . with God's promises' Ro 3.2. In some languages it may be possible to render this expression in Ro 3.2 as 'because God gave his message to them to take care of' or '. . . to keep,' but one should avoid the implication that the message was simply to be kept by the Jews for themselves.

F   Rear, Bring Up (35.51-35.52)

35.51 τρέφω[c]; ἐκτρέφω[b]; ἀνατρέφω; τεκνοτροφέω: to raise a child to maturity by providing for physical and psychological needs – 'to raise, to rear, to bring up.'[8]

τρέφω[c]: ἦλθεν εἰς Ναζαρά, οὗ ἦν τεθραμμένος 'he went to Nazareth where he had been brought up as a child' Lk 4.16.

ἐκτρέφω[b]: ἐκτρέφετε αὐτὰ ἐν παιδείᾳ καὶ νουθεσίᾳ κυρίου 'raise your children with Christian discipline and instruction' Eph 6.4.

ἀνατρέφω: ἀνεθρέψατο αὐτὸν ἑαυτῇ εἰς υἱόν 'she brought him up as her own son' Ac 7.21.

τεκνοτροφέω: ἐν ἔργοις καλοῖς μαρτυρουμένη, εἰ ἐτεκνοτρόφησεν 'she must have a reputation for good deeds and be a woman who reared her children well' 1 Tm 5.10.

To raise or bring up children may be expressed in a number of different ways, for example, 'to give food to children,' 'to take care of children,' 'to be a parent to children,' 'to cause a child to become an adult,' or 'to make a child become like oneself.'

35.52 τροφός, οῦ f: a person who functions as a substitute for a mother in the process of rearing children – 'nursemaid, nurse (in the British, not American, sense).' ἐγενήθημεν νήπιοι ἐν μέσῳ ὑμῶν ὡς ἐὰν τροφὸς θάλπῃ τὰ ἑαυτῆς τέκνα 'we were as gentle with you as a nurse caring for her children' 1 Th 2.7. It is possible that in 1 Th 2.7 τροφός may mean a mother nursing and rearing her children.

G   Adopt[9] (35.53)

35.53 ἀναιρέομαι; υἱοθεσία, ας f: to formally and legally declare that someone who is not one's own child is henceforth to be treated and cared for as one's own child, including

---

8 There may very well be subtle differences of meaning in the series in 35.51, but there is no direct contextual evidence to support significant distinctions in meaning.

9 It would, of course, be possible to treat *Adopt* under the domain of *Kinship Terms* (10), but since the implications of adoption are so closely related to rearing, bringing up, and caring for, it seems preferable to include this subdomain in Domain 35 *Help, Care For*.

complete rights of inheritance – 'to adopt,
adoption.'

ἀναιρέομαι: ἐκτεθέντος δὲ αὐτοῦ ἀνείλατο αὐτὸν
ἡ θυγάτηρ Φαραὼ 'and when he was put out of
his home, the daughter of Pharaoh adopted
him' Ac 7.21.

υἱοθεσία: προορίσας ἡμᾶς εἰς υἱοθεσίαν διὰ
Ἰησοῦ Χριστοῦ εἰς αὐτόν '(God) had already
decided from the beginning that through
Jesus Christ he would adopt us to be his
children' Eph 1.5.

In a number of languages adoption is
spoken of as 'making a child a son' or 'causing
a child to become a daughter.' In some instances the equivalent expression is merely 'to
treat someone as a son' or '. . . daughter.'

H Desert, Forsake[10] (35.54-35.56)

35.54 ἐγκαταλείπω[b]; ἀνίημι[b]: to desert or
forsake a person and thus leave that individual
uncared for – 'to desert, to forsake.' οὐ μή σε

---

10 Since the process of deserting or forsaking an individual is essentially the converse of helping or caring
for, it seems best to include this subdomain at this point.

ἀνῶ οὐδ' οὐ μή σε ἐγκαταλίπω 'I will never
desert you, and I will never forsake you' He
13.5.

35.55 ἔρημος[c], ον: the state of a person who
has been deserted or forsaken – 'deserted, forsaken.' πολλὰ τὰ τέκνα τῆς ἐρήμου μᾶλλον ἢ τῆς
ἐχούσης τὸν ἄνδρα 'the woman who was
deserted will have more children than the
woman living with her husband' Ga 4.27. In
rendering ἔρημος in Ga 4.27 it may be important to indicate clearly that 'the woman who
was deserted' refers to one who has been
deserted by her husband.

35.56 σαβαχθανι (a translation of an Aramaic word meaning 'you have forsaken me') –
'to forsake.' λεμα σαβαχθανι; τοῦτ' ἔστιν, . . .
ἱνατί με ἐγκατέλιπες; 'lema sabachthani, which
means, . . . Why have you forsaken me?' Mt
27.46. Languages differ appreciably in expressions meaning 'to forsake, to abandon.'
For example, the most appropriate equivalent
in some instances is 'to leave alone' or 'to
leave behind.' In other instances one may
employ a phrase such as 'to leave without
help' or 'to leave and refuse to care for.'

36 Guide, Discipline, Follow

Outline of Subdomains

A Guide, Lead (36.1-36.9)
B Discipline, Train (36.10-36.11)
C Obey, Disobey (36.12-36.30)
D Follow, Be a Disciple (36.31-36.43)

A Guide, Lead[1] (36.1-36.9)

36.1 ἡγέομαι[b]; προΐσταμαι[a]; κατευθύνω;
φέρω[d]; ἄγω[d]: to so influence others as to
cause them to follow a recommended course
of action – 'to guide, to direct, to lead.'

---

1 The meanings in Subdomain A *Guide, Lead* imply a
willingness on the part of others to be led. They also imply a minimum of control on the part of the one guiding
or leading (compare Domain 37 *Control, Rule*).

ἡγέομαι[b]: γινέσθω . . . ὁ ἡγούμενος ὡς ὁ
διακονῶν 'he who takes the lead must be like
the one who serves' or 'he who is the master
must be like one who serves' Lk 22.26;
μνημονεύετε τῶν ἡγουμένων ὑμῶν 'remember
your leaders' or '. . . masters' He 13.7.[2]

προΐσταμαι[a]: προϊσταμένους ὑμῶν ἐν κυρίῳ καὶ
νουθετοῦντας ὑμᾶς 'those who guide you in the
Lord and instruct you' 1 Th 5.12. The phrase
'in the Lord' probably refers to matters concerning Christian life.

κατευθύνω: ὁ δὲ κύριος κατευθύναι ὑμῶν τὰς
καρδίας εἰς τὴν ἀγάπην τοῦ θεοῦ 'may the Lord
lead your hearts to the love for God' 2 Th 3.5.

---

2 Though the basic denotation of ἡγούμενος is 'to
lead,' semantic features of ruling and high status are also
connotatively involved.

φέρω^d: φερόμενοι ἐν τῷ ἁγίῳ πνεύματι 'being guided by the Holy Spirit' Ac 15.29 (apparatus); ἀλλὰ ὑπὸ πνεύματος ἁγίου φερόμενοι ἐλάλησαν 'but being led by the Holy Spirit, they spoke' 2 Pe 1.21.

ἄγω^d: ὅσοι γὰρ πνεύματι θεοῦ ἄγονται 'for as many as are led by the Spirit of God' Ro 8.14.

In some languages it is difficult to distinguish readily between expressions for 'leading' and those which refer to 'ruling' or 'governing,' but it is important to try to distinguish clearly between these two different sets of interpersonal relations. In some languages, the concept of 'leading' can be expressed by 'showing how to' or 'demonstrating how one ought to.' In other languages it is possible to speak of 'leading' as simply 'going ahead of,' but too often such an expression may designate only 'a scout' who goes ahead to see whether things are safe, or it may refer only to a person who insists on his prerogative as the most distinguished person in a group.

36.2 ποιμαίνω^b: (a figurative extension of meaning of ποιμαίνω^a 'to shepherd,' 44.3) to lead, with the implication of providing for – 'to guide and to help, to guide and take care of.' ἐκ σοῦ γὰρ ἐξελεύσεται ἡγούμενος, ὅστις ποιμανεῖ τὸν λαόν μου τὸν Ἰσραήλ 'from you will come a leader who will guide and help my people Israel' Mt 2.6.

36.3 κυβέρνησις, εως f: (derivative of κυβερνάω 'to steer a ship, to guide,' not occurring in the NT) the ability to lead – 'guidance, leadership.' ἔπειτα χαρίσματα ἰαμάτων, ἀντιλήμψεις, κυβερνήσεις 'then those who have the gift of healing, or of helping others, or of leadership' 1 Cor 12.28. 'The gift of leadership' may be expressed in some languages as 'being able to lead others' or 'being able to get others to follow.'

36.4 ὁδηγός^b, οῦ m: one who guides or leads – 'leader, guide.' πέποιθάς τε σεαυτὸν ὁδηγὸν εἶναι τυφλῶν 'you are sure that you are a guide for the blind' Ro 2.19. In Ro 2.19 the context is figurative in the sense that 'the blind' are those who are spiritually blind, and the guidance which they require is a proper

understanding of the truth in terms of how they should behave.

36.5 ἐπίτροπος^b, ου m (derivative of ἐπιτρέπω 'to instruct,' not occurring in the NT); παιδαγωγός, οῦ m: a person who guides, directs, and shows concern for – 'guardian, leader, guide.'

ἐπίτροπος^b: ὑπὸ ἐπιτρόπους ἐστὶν καὶ οἰκονόμους 'he is under the supervision of those who take care of him and manage his affairs' Ga 4.2.

παιδαγωγός: ὁ νόμος παιδαγωγὸς ἡμῶν γέγονεν εἰς Χριστόν 'the Law was our guide to Christ' or '. . . unto the time of Christ' Ga 3.24. In classical times, a παιδαγωγός was a man, usually a slave, whose task it was to conduct a boy to and from school and to supervise and direct his general conduct. He was not a teacher.

It may be difficult to render appropriately ἐπίτροπος^b and παιδαγωγός with a combined meaning of guiding and caring for. It may, in fact, be necessary in some instances to use two verbal expressions, for example, 'to guide and to help' or 'to help by leading' or 'to care for by leading.'

36.6 ἀρχηγός^b, οῦ m: a person who as originator or founder of a movement continues as the leader – 'pioneer leader, founding leader.' τὸν ἀρχηγὸν τῆς σωτηρίας 'their pioneer leader to salvation' He 2.10. In order to indicate clearly the significance of ἀρχηγός in He 2.10, it may be important to employ a translation such as 'who established a way of salvation and leads people to it.' But it is also possible to understand ἀρχηγός in He 2.10 as meaning only the 'initiator' or 'founder' (see 68.2).

36.7 στῦλος^b, ου m: (a figurative extension of meaning of στῦλος^a 'pillar, column,' 7.45) one who is a leader of a group, with the implication of strategic responsibility – 'leader.' οἱ δοκοῦντες στῦλοι εἶναι 'those who seemed to be leaders' Ga 2.9.

36.8 πατήρ^h, πατρός m: (a figurative extension of meaning of πατήρ^a 'father,' 10.14) one who is responsible for having guided another into faith or into a particular pattern of behavior – 'spiritual father, leader in the faith.' ἐὰν γὰρ μυρίους παιδαγωγοὺς ἔχητε ἐν Χριστῷ, ἀλλ' οὐ πολλοὺς πατέρας 'for even if you have ten thousand guardians in Christ, you do not have many spiritual fathers,' or '. . . you have only one spiritual father' 1 Cor 4.15;[3] ὑμεῖς ἐκ τοῦ πατρὸς τοῦ διαβόλου ἐστέ 'you are the children of your spiritual father, the Devil' Jn 8.44.

36.9 πρόδρομος, ου *m*: (a figurative extension of meaning of πρόδρομος 'one who runs on ahead,' not occurring in the NT) one who undergoes an experience in advance of others – 'forerunner.' ὅπου πρόδρομος ὑπὲρ ἡμῶν εἰσῆλθεν Ἰησοῦς 'Jesus has gone in there as the forerunner on our behalf' He 6.20. In rendering πρόδρομος in He 6.20 it is important to avoid an expression which would suggest that Jesus simply 'ran on ahead.' The implication of πρόδρομος in this type of context is that of a precursor, that is to say, one who goes on ahead in order to show the way or to pioneer on behalf of someone else. He 6.20 may therefore be rendered as 'Jesus went on ahead of us in there for our benefit.'

B Discipline, Train (36.10-36.11)

36.10 παιδεύω[b]; παιδεία[b], ας *f*: to train someone in accordance with proper rules of conduct and behavior – 'to discipline, to train, discipline, training.'
παιδεύω[b]: δοῦλον δὲ κυρίου . . . ἐν πραΰτητι παιδεύοντα τοὺς ἀντιδιατιθεμένους 'the Lord's servant . . . must be gentle as he disciplines his opponents' or '. . . those who oppose what he says' 2 Tm 2.24-25.
παιδεία[b]: ἐκτρέφετε αὐτὰ ἐν παιδείᾳ καὶ νουθεσίᾳ κυρίου 'raise your children with the discipline and instruction which comes from the Lord' Eph 6.4.

36.11 γυμνάζω[b]: to experience vigorous training and control, with the implication of increased physical and/or moral strength – 'to train, to undergo discipline.' ὕστερον δὲ καρπὸν εἰρηνικὸν τοῖς δι' αὐτῆς γεγυμνασμένοις ἀποδίδωσιν δικαιοσύνης 'later, however, those who have been disciplined by such punishment reap the peaceful reward of a righteous life' He 12.11. In rendering γυμνάζω in He 12.11 it may be important in some languages to translate 'those who have learned by such punishment' or 'those whose ways have been made right by such punishment' or 'those who because of punishment have learned how they must act.'

C Obey, Disobey (36.12-36.30)

36.12 πείθομαι[a]; πειθαρχέω: to submit to authority or reason by obeying – 'to obey.'
πείθομαι[a]: πείθεσθε τοῖς ἡγουμένοις ὑμῶν καὶ ὑπείκετε 'obey your leaders and submit to them' He 13.17.
πειθαρχέω: πειθαρχήσαντάς μοι μὴ ἀνάγεσθαι ἀπὸ τῆς Κρήτης 'you should have listened to me and not have sailed from Crete' Ac 27.21.

36.13 εὐλαβέομαι[b]: to obey, with the implication of awe and reverence for the source of a command – 'to obey.' εὐλαβηθεὶς κατεσκεύασεν κιβωτόν 'he obeyed (God) and built an ark' He 11.7. For another interpretation of εὐλαβέομαι in He 11.7, see 53.7.

36.14 ἀκούω[e]; ἐπιδέχομαι[b]: to listen or pay attention to a person, with resulting conformity to what is advised or commanded – 'to pay attention to and obey.'[4]
ἀκούω[e]: οὗτός ἐστιν ὁ υἱός μου ὁ ἀγαπητός, ἐν ᾧ εὐδόκησα· ἀκούετε αὐτοῦ 'this is my own dear Son with whom I am well pleased; pay attention to him and obey him' Mt 17.5.
ἐπιδέχομαι[b]: ἀλλ' ὁ φιλοπρωτεύων αὐτῶν Διοτρέφης οὐκ ἐπιδέχεται ἡμᾶς 'but Diotrephes, who loves to be their leader, does not pay attention and do what I say' 3 Jn 9.

---

3 In Greek the expression οὐ πολλοὺς πατέρας clearly seems to be an instance of understatement, and it may therefore be translated as 'only one spiritual father.' The phrase 'in Christ' probably refers to matters concerning Christian life.

4 Both ἀκούω[e] and ἐπιδέχομαι[b] involve an overlapping of domains, for there is an evident factor of perception in 'paying attention,' but also a clear inference of subsequent obedience.

36.15 ὑπακούω^a; ὑπακοή, ῆς f; εἰσακούω^b: to obey on the basis of having paid attention to – 'to obey, obedience.'[5]

ὑπακούω^a: τοῖς πνεύμασι τοῖς ἀκαθάρτοις ἐπιτάσσει, καὶ ὑπακούουσιν αὐτῷ 'he gives orders to the evil spirits and they obey him' Mk 1.27.

ὑπακοή: ἡ γὰρ ὑμῶν ὑπακοὴ εἰς πάντας ἀφίκετο 'everyone has heard of your obedience (to the gospel)' Ro 16.19.

εἰσακούω^b: οὐδ' οὕτως εἰσακούσονταί μου 'even then they will not obey me, (says the Lord)' 1 Cor 14.21.

Terms expressing the concept of 'obedience' may frequently be rendered in some languages as 'to do what one says' or 'to carry out someone's orders.'

36.16 ὑπήκοος, ον: (derivative of ὑπακούω^a 'to obey,' 36.15) pertaining to being obedient – 'obedient.' ἐταπείνωσεν ἑαυτὸν γενόμενος ὑπήκοος μέχρι θανάτου 'he humbled himself and became obedient, even to the point of dying' Php 2.8.

36.17 ἀναπληρόω^e; ἀποπληρόω: to conform to some standard as a means of demonstrating its purpose – 'to obey, to conform to, to submit to.' καὶ οὕτως ἀναπληρώσετε τὸν νόμον τοῦ Χριστοῦ 'and in this way you will obey the law of Christ' Ga 6.2 (... ἀποπληρώσετε ... Ga 6.2 apparatus).

36.18 ὑποτάσσομαι; ὑποταγή, ῆς f; ὑπείκω: to submit to the orders or directives of someone – 'to obey, to submit to, obedience, submission.'

ὑποτάσσομαι: δούλους ἰδίοις δεσπόταις ὑποτάσσεσθαι 'slaves are to obey their masters' Tt 2.9.

ὑποταγή: δοξάζοντες τὸν θεὸν ἐπὶ τῇ ὑποταγῇ τῆς ὁμολογίας ὑμῶν εἰς τὸ εὐαγγέλιον τοῦ Χριστοῦ 'giving glory to God on account of your obedience to the gospel of Christ which you profess' 2 Cor 9.13.

ὑπείκω: πείθεσθε τοῖς ἡγουμένοις ὑμῶν καὶ ὑπείκετε 'obey your leaders and submit to them' He 13.17.

36.19 φυλάσσω^b; τηρέω^c; τήρησις^c, εως f: to continue to obey orders or commandments – 'to obey, to keep commandments, obedience.'

φυλάσσω^b: πάντα ταῦτα ἐφύλαξα 'I have continued to obey all these commandments' Mt 19.20.

τηρέω^c: ἐὰν ἀγαπᾶτέ με, τὰς ἐντολὰς τὰς ἐμὰς τηρήσετε 'if you love me, you will keep my commandments' Jn 14.15.

τήρησις^c: ἀλλὰ τήρησις ἐντολῶν θεοῦ 'but obedience to God's commandments' 1 Cor 7.19.

36.20 τελέω^d: to obey as a means of fulfilling the purpose of a rule or standard – 'to obey, to keep.' ἡ ἐκ φύσεως ἀκροβυστία τὸν νόμον τελοῦσα '(those who) by nature are uncircumcised obey the Law' Ro 2.27. The phrase 'to obey the Law' in Ro 2.27 may be rendered simply as 'to do what the Law says one must do.'

36.21 δογματίζομαι: (derivative of δόγμα^a 'law, rule,' 33.333) to conform to rules and regulations – 'to obey rules.' τί ὡς ζῶντες ἐν κόσμῳ δογματίζεσθε, Μὴ ἅψῃ μηδὲ γεύσῃ 'why do you live as though you belong to this world by obeying rules such as, Don't handle, don't taste' Col 2.20-21.

36.22 δικαιόω^e: to conform to righteous, just commands – 'to obey righteous commands.' πᾶς ὁ λαὸς ἀκούσας καὶ οἱ τελῶναι ἐδικαίωσαν τὸν θεόν 'all the people and the tax collectors heard him, and they obeyed God's righteous commands' Lk 7.29. In some languages it may be difficult to translate literally 'God's righteous commands' in Lk 7.29, especially since the equivalent of 'commands' is often a verb. Accordingly, one may need to translate 'what God commanded, and this was right.'

36.23 ἀπειθέω^a; ἀπείθεια^a, ας f: unwillingness or refusal to comply with the demands of some authority – 'to disobey, disobedience.' ἀπειθέω^a: ὁ δὲ ἀπειθῶν τῷ υἱῷ οὐκ ὄψεται ζωήν 'whoever disobeys the Son will never have life' (literally '... will never see life') Jn 3.36.

---

5 It is possible that there is a subtle distinction in meaning between ὑπακούω^a and εἰσακούω^b in that the former may suggest primarily submission, while εἰσακούω^b may focus more upon attentive listening with resulting obedience.

ἀπείθεια[a]: ἔρχεται ἡ ὀργὴ τοῦ θεοῦ ἐπὶ τοὺς υἱοὺς τῆς ἀπειθείας 'God's wrath comes upon those who do not obey him' Eph 5.6.

36.24 ἀπειθής, ές: (derivative of ἀπειθέω[a] 'to disobey,' 36.23) pertaining to being continuously disobedient – 'disobedient.' ἔσονται γὰρ οἱ ἄνθρωποι φίλαυτοι, φιλάργυροι . . . γονεῦσιν ἀπειθεῖς 'people will be selfish, greedy for money . . . disobedient to their parents' 2 Tm 3.2.

36.25 προάγω[c]: to go beyond established bounds of teaching or instruction, with the implication of failure to obey properly – 'to go beyond bounds, to fail to obey.' πᾶς ὁ προάγων καὶ μὴ μένων ἐν τῇ διδαχῇ τοῦ Χριστοῦ 'anyone who does not remain in the teaching of Christ but goes beyond it' 2 Jn 9.

36.26 ἀνυπότακτος[b], ον: (derivative of ὑποτάσσομαι 'to obey,' 36.18) pertaining to being rebelliously disobedient – 'disobedient, rebellious.' τέκνα ἔχων πιστά, μὴ ἐν κατηγορίᾳ ἀσωτίας ἢ ἀνυπότακτα 'having children that are believers and not having the reputation of being wild and rebellious' Tt 1.6.

36.27 παρακούω[a]; παρακοή, ῆς f; παραιτέομαι[c]: to refuse to listen to and hence to disobey – 'to refuse to listen, to refuse to obey, disobedience.'
παρακούω[a]: ἐὰν δὲ παρακούσῃ αὐτῶν, εἰπὲ τῇ ἐκκλησίᾳ 'if he refuses to listen to them, tell it to the church' Mt 18.17.
παρακοή: ὥσπερ γὰρ διὰ τῆς παρακοῆς τοῦ ἑνὸς ἀνθρώπου ἁμαρτωλοὶ κατεστάθησαν οἱ πολλοί, οὕτως . . . 'just as many people were made sinners as the result of the fact that one man refused to listen, so . . .' Ro 5.19.
παραιτέομαι[c]: βλέπετε μὴ παραιτήσησθε τὸν λαλοῦντα 'be careful then, and do not refuse to listen to him who speaks' He 12.25.
It would be a mistake to translate παρακούω[a], παρακοή, and παραιτέομαι[c] as meaning nothing more than 'not to listen to.' The meaning is clearly 'to refuse to listen to' or 'to refuse to pay attention to,' and hence 'to disobey.' It may therefore be best in a number of instances to translate 'to refuse to obey.'

36.28 παραβαίνω[a]; παράβασις, εως f; παρανομέω; παρέρχομαι[c]: to act contrary to established custom or law, with the implication of intent – 'to disobey, to break the law, to transgress, disobedience, transgression.'
παραβαίνω[a]: διὰ τί οἱ μαθηταί σου παραβαίνουσιν τὴν παράδοσιν τῶν πρεσβυτέρων; 'why is it that your disciples disobey the teaching handed down by our ancestors?' Mt 15.2.
παράβασις: διὰ τῆς παραβάσεως τοῦ νόμου τὸν θεὸν ἀτιμάζεις; 'do you dishonor God by transgressing his law?' Ro 2.23.
παρανομέω: παρανομῶν κελεύεις με τύπτεσθαι 'you break the law by ordering them to strike me' Ac 23.3.
παρέρχομαι[c]: παρέρχεσθε τὴν κρίσιν καὶ τὴν ἀγάπην τοῦ θεοῦ 'you transgress the judgment and love of God' Lk 11.42.
Languages differ appreciably in the way in which they speak of disobeying or transgressing a law. It is rarely possible to speak of 'breaking a law,' since nothing is actually done to the law in the process of transgression, but languages do employ such expressions as 'to tramp on a law,' 'to ridicule a law,' and 'to laugh at a law.' See also discussion at 36.29.

36.29 παραβάτης, ου m: (derivative of παραβαίνω[a] 'to disobey, to break the law,' 36.28) a person who customarily breaks or disobeys the law – 'transgressor.' ἐὰν δὲ παραβάτης νόμου ᾖς 'if you are a transgressor of the Law' Ro 2.25.
For terms involving 'disobedience' or 'transgression,' there are often a number of subtle distinctions reflecting several different types of contrasts. For example, there may be important distinctions between disobeying a person and disobeying a law or custom. A number of languages also make a clear distinction between intentional and unintentional disobedience or transgression. A further distinction may involve repeated activity or consistency of attitude, so that the choice of terms may specify whether a person has consistently disobeyed or has only disobeyed once or twice. A further distinction is sometimes made between disobedience of children or those who are mentally incapacitated and the disobedience of those who

should know better. Accordingly, in the choice of terms for various passages of Scripture it is extremely important to note the distinctive features of meaning; otherwise, much of the emphasis upon disobedience and transgression as stated in the Scriptures may be seriously distorted.

36.30 λύω^e: the failure to conform to a law or regulation, with a possible implication of regarding it as invalid – 'to break (a law), to transgress.' ὃς ἐὰν οὖν λύσῃ μίαν τῶν ἐντολῶν τούτων τῶν ἐλαχίστων 'whoever transgresses one of the least of these commandments' Mt 5.19; ὅτι οὐ μόνον ἔλυεν τὸ σάββατον 'because he not only transgressed the law of the Sabbath' Jn 5.18. See also discussion at 36.29.

D Follow, Be a Disciple (36.31-36.43)

36.31 μαθητεύω^a; ἀκολουθέω^c: to be a follower or a disciple of someone, in the sense of adhering to the teachings or instructions of a leader and in promoting the cause of such a leader – 'to follow, to be a disciple of.'
μαθητεύω^a: ὃς καὶ αὐτὸς ἐμαθητεύθη τῷ Ἰησοῦ 'and he was also a disciple of Jesus' Mt 27.57.
ἀκολουθέω^c: εὐθὺς ἀφέντες τὰ δίκτυα ἠκολούθησαν αὐτῷ 'at once they left their nets and followed him' Mk 1.18.

Though many translators have attempted to employ the metaphorical significance of 'to follow' in the sense of 'to be a disciple of,' there are certain dangers in a number of languages. For example, 'to follow' may often have the connotation of 'to pursue after with evil intent.' In many languages the appropriate equivalent of 'to follow' (in the sense of 'to be a disciple') is literally 'to accompany' or 'to go along with' or 'to be in the group of.'

36.32 παρακολουθέω^a: to conform in one's behavior to a particular system of instruction or teaching – 'to follow, to be a follower of, to conform to.' διδασκαλίας ᾗ παρηκολούθηκας 'teaching which you have followed' 1 Tm 4.6.

36.33 ἐξακολουθέω^a: to conform as a follower in a detailed or dependent manner – 'to follow, to conform to.' οὐ γὰρ σεσοφισμένοις

μύθοις ἐξακολουθήσαντες ἐγνωρίσαμεν ὑμῖν τὴν τοῦ κυρίου ἡμῶν Ἰησοῦ Χριστοῦ δύναμιν καὶ παρουσίαν 'for we did not follow made-up stories in making known to you the powerful coming of our Lord Jesus Christ' 2 Pe 1.16. In some instances it may be necessary to translate ἐξακολουθήσαντες in 2 Pe 1.16 as 'to use' or 'to repeat,' since such expressions may fit the context more satisfactorily.

36.34 πείθομαι^b: to be a disciple or follower of someone, in the sense of having put one's confidence in a leader – 'to be a follower of, to be a disciple of.' πάντες ὅσοι ἐπείθοντο αὐτῷ διελύθησαν 'all of his followers were scattered' Ac 5.36.[6]

36.35 ὀπίσω^b: marker of one who is followed as a leader (occurring with a variety of verbs indicating change of state or movement) – 'after, to follow.' ἴδε ὁ κόσμος ὀπίσω αὐτοῦ ἀπῆλθεν 'look, the whole world is following him' Jn 12.19; εἴ τις θέλει ὀπίσω μου ἐλθεῖν, ἀπαρνησάσθω ἑαυτόν 'if anyone wants to follow me, he must deny himself' Mt 16.24; τοῦ ἀποσπᾶν τοὺς μαθητὰς ὀπίσω αὐτῶν 'in order to draw off disciples to follow them' Ac 20.30; ἤδη γὰρ τινες ἐξετράπησαν ὀπίσω τοῦ Σατανᾶ 'for already some have turned away to follow Satan' 1 Tm 5.15; δεῦτε ὀπίσω μου 'follow after me' Mk 1.17; ἐθαυμάσθη ὅλη ἡ γῆ ὀπίσω τοῦ θηρίου 'the whole earth was amazed and followed the beast' Re 13.3.

36.36 ἀπέρχομαι εἰς τὰ ὀπίσω: (an idiom, literally 'to go back to what lies behind') to cease being a follower or disciple of – 'to no longer be a disciple, to no longer follow.' ἐκ τούτου πολλοὶ ἐκ τῶν μαθητῶν αὐτοῦ ἀπῆλθον εἰς τὰ ὀπίσω 'because of this many of his disciples no longer followed him' Jn 6.66.

---

6 It would be possible to understand πείθομαι in Ac 5.36 as meaning 'those who trust in' or '. . . rely on,' and as such πείθομαι would then be classified along with πείθω^c 'to trust in, to have complete confidence in' (31.82). However, in Ac 5.36 the meaning seems to be much closer to that of μαθητεύω^a and ἀκολουθέω^c (36.31), since in Ac 5.36 the emphasis is upon the relationship of followers to Theudas rather than upon their confidence in or reliance upon him.

36.37 μαθητεύω^b: to cause someone to become a disciple or follower of – 'to make disciples, to cause people to become followers.' πορευθέντες οὖν μαθητεύσατε πάντα τὰ ἔθνη 'go then, to all peoples and make them (my) disciples' Mt 28.19. In rendering μαθητεύω in Mt 28.19 and similar contexts, it is important to avoid the implication of duress or force, that is to say, one should not translate 'force them to be my disciples' or 'compel them to be my disciples.' This might very well be implied in a literal translation of a causative such as 'to make.' In order to avoid a wrong implication of a causative, it may be important to use some such expression as 'convince them to become my disciples' or 'urge them to be my disciples.'

36.38 μαθητής^a, οῦ m: (derivative of μαθητεύω^a 'to follow, to be a disciple of,' 36.31) a person who is a disciple or follower of someone – 'disciple, follower.' τῇ ἐπαύριον πάλιν εἱστήκει ὁ Ἰωάννης καὶ ἐκ τῶν μαθητῶν αὐτοῦ δύο 'the next day John was there again with two of his disciples' Jn 1.35. Though in the NT μαθητής generally refers to men, it is neutral as to sex distinction, and thus in a few instances in the NT also includes women (as in Ac 6.1, πληθυνόντων τῶν μαθητῶν 'the number of disciples kept growing'). In some languages it may be important to indicate clearly the sex distinction, and in those contexts in which the twelve disciples are being referred to, obviously the reference must be to men. However, when the wider group of disciples is referred to, then some indication should be introduced as to the fact that both men and women were involved.

36.39 υἱός^f, οῦ m: (a figurative extension of meaning of υἱός^a 'son,' 10.42) one who is a disciple or follower of someone, with the implication of being like the one whom he follows (a reflection of the Semitic use of υἱός in the expression 'son of') – 'disciple, follower.' καὶ εἰ ἐγὼ ἐν Βεελζεβοὺλ ἐκβάλλω τὰ δαιμόνια, οἱ υἱοὶ ὑμῶν ἐν τίνι ἐκβάλλουσιν; 'and if I drive out demons by the power of Beelzebul, by whose power do your followers drive them out?' Mt 12.27.

In 1 Pe 5.13 the meaning of the expression Μᾶρκος ὁ υἱός μου, literally 'Mark, my son,' may be 'Mark, my disciple' or 'Mark, my follower.' On the other hand, υἱός may simply be a means of referring to a younger person in an affectionate manner (see 9.46).

36.40 τέκνον^c, ου n: a person who looks to another as being, so to speak, a father in the faith and thus becomes a disciple of that person – 'disciple.' ἀκούω τὰ ἐμὰ τέκνα ἐν τῇ ἀληθείᾳ περιπατοῦντα 'I hear that my disciples are walking in accordance with the truth' 3 Jn 4. It is also possible that τέκνον in 3 Jn 4 is to be understood simply as an affectionate way of talking about persons who in one way or another are in a dependent relationship to someone (see 9.46).

36.41 μαθήτρια, ας f: (derivative of μαθητεύω^a 'to follow, to be a disciple of,' 36.31) a disciple who is a woman – 'woman disciple.' ἐν Ἰόππῃ δέ τις ἦν μαθήτρια ὀνόματι Ταβιθά 'in Joppa there was a woman Tabitha who was a disciple' Ac 9.36.

36.42 συμμαθητής, οῦ m: a person who along with someone else is a disciple or follower – 'fellow disciple.' εἶπεν οὖν Θωμᾶς ὁ λεγόμενος Δίδυμος τοῖς συμμαθηταῖς 'then Thomas, called Didymus, said to his fellow disciples' Jn 11.16. The phrase 'his fellow disciples' may be expressed in some languages as 'disciples along with him' or 'those who were disciples even as he was.'

36.43 ἀρνέομαι^c: to refuse to follow someone as a leader – 'to refuse to follow, to refuse to obey, to reject.' τοῦτον τὸν Μωϋσῆν, ὃν ἠρνήσαντο 'this Moses whom they refused to follow' Ac 7.35.

37 Control, Rule

Outline of Subdomains

A Control, Restrain[1] (37.1-37.32)

37.1 δαμάζω; ζωγρέω: to bring under control and to continue to restrain – 'to control, to bring under control, to hold in check.'
δαμάζω: οὐδεὶς ἴσχυεν αὐτὸν δαμάσαι 'no one was able to get control of him' Mk 5.4; πᾶσα γὰρ φύσις θηρίων . . . δαμάζεται . . . τῇ φύσει τῇ ἀνθρωπίνῃ 'all kinds of wild animals . . . can be controlled . . . by people' Jas 3.7.
ζωγρέω: ἐζωγρημένοι ὑπ' αὐτοῦ εἰς τὸ ἐκείνου θέλημα 'having been controlled by him to do his will' 2 Tm 2.26.
In many languages it may be difficult to speak of 'bringing a person under control.' It may therefore be more appropriate to use some such phrase as 'not allow a person to do just what he wants' or 'make a person behave' or 'make a person obey.' In speaking of animals, one may render Jas 3.7 as 'all kinds of wild animals . . . can be made to obey a person.'

37.2 βρόχον ἐπιβάλλω: (an idiom, literally 'to throw a bridle on') to place restrictions upon someone's behavior – 'to restrict, to control, to impose restrictions.' οὐχ ἵνα βρόχον ὑμῖν ἐπιβάλω 'not for the purpose of my putting restrictions on you' 1 Cor 7.35. It may,

however, be important in some languages to express more clearly the intent involved, and therefore one might wish to translate this clause in 1 Cor 7.35 as 'my purpose is not to try to control you' or '. . . to tell you just what you must do.'

37.3 δοῦλος, η, ον: pertaining to a state of being completely controlled by someone or something – 'subservient to, controlled by.' ὥσπερ γὰρ παρεστήσατε τὰ μέλη ὑμῶν δοῦλα τῇ ἀκαθαρσίᾳ καὶ τῇ ἀνομίᾳ εἰς τὴν ἀνομίαν 'for as you presented parts of your body to be subservient to impurity and wickedness for wicked purposes' Ro 6.19. In some languages it may be useful to render δοῦλος in the context of Ro 6.19 as a simile, 'like slaves,' for example, 'for as you surrendered the parts of your body to be like slaves to obey impurity and wickedness' or '. . . to be ordered about by impurity and wickedness.'

37.4 ἐνέχομαι: to be under the control of or to be subject to someone or something – 'to be subject to, to be under the control of.' μὴ πάλιν ζυγῷ δουλείας ἐνέχεσθε 'do not be subject again to the yoke of slavery' Ga 5.1. In a number of languages it is difficult or impossible to maintain the figure of 'yoke.' An equivalent expression may be 'do not become slaves again' or 'do not let people make you slaves again.' Such a bold metaphor, however, must sometimes be changed to a simile: 'do not, as it were, let yourselves be made slaves.'

37.5 ἔνοχος[c], ον: pertaining to being subject to the control of someone or of some institution – 'controlled by, under the control of, subject to.' ὅσοι φόβῳ θανάτου διὰ παντὸς τοῦ ζῆν ἔνοχοι ἦσαν δουλείας 'as many as were subject to slavery because of the fear of death throughout all their lives' He 2.15. In this context one may render ἔνοχοι ἦσαν δουλείας simply as 'slaves' and then render the expression as 'as many as were slaves all their lives because of their fear of death' or '. . . because they were afraid to die.'

37.6 εὐπερίστατος, ον: pertaining to the exertion of tight control – 'being in control of,

---

1 In Subdomain A *Control, Restrain* the focus is upon the controlling of someone else, not of oneself. The meanings of self-control and the lack of such are contained in Domain 88 *Moral and Ethical Qualities and Related Behavior*, Subdomain K.

controlling tightly.' τὴν εὐπερίστατον ἁμαρτίαν 'the sin which controls (us) so tightly' He 12.1.

37.7 ὑπό[b] (with the accusative): a marker of a controlling person, institution, or power – 'under, under the control of, under obligation to.' ἀλλὰ συνέκλεισεν ἡ γραφὴ τὰ πάντα ὑπὸ ἁμαρτίαν 'but the Scripture includes all things under the power of sin' Ga 3.22; ἵνα τοὺς ὑπὸ νόμον ἐξαγοράσῃ 'in order that he may redeem those who are under the Law' or '. . . under obligation to abide by the regulations of the Law' Ga 4.5. It is generally a mistake to render literally the expression τοὺς ὑπὸ νόμον as in Ga 4.5, because 'those who are under the Law' may simply mean 'people who act illegally.'

37.8 ὑπὸ τοὺς πόδας and ὑποκάτω τῶν ποδῶν (idioms, literally 'under the feet of'); ὑποπόδιον τῶν ποδῶν (an idiom, literally 'footstool of the feet'): to be under the complete control of someone – 'under the complete control of.'
ὑπὸ τοὺς πόδας: ἄχρι οὗ θῇ πάντας τοὺς ἐχθροὺς ὑπὸ τοὺς πόδας αὐτοῦ 'until he places all his enemies under his feet' or 'until he completely controls his enemies' 1 Cor 15.25.
ὑποκάτω τῶν ποδῶν: πάντα ὑπέταξας ὑποκάτω τῶν ποδῶν αὐτοῦ 'having put all things under his feet' or 'having put him in control of all things' He 2.8.
ὑποπόδιον τῶν ποδῶν: ἕως ἂν θῶ τοὺς ἐχθρούς σου ὑποπόδιον τῶν ποδῶν σου 'until I put all your enemies under your feet' or 'until I put you in control of your enemies' or 'until I cause you to rule over your enemies' Lk 20.43.
In a number of languages it is simply not possible to preserve the idiom, 'under the feet of,' though in some instances one may use a parallel idiom, for example, 'to stand on,' so that 1 Cor 15.25 might be rendered 'until he stands on all his enemies,' but it is more likely that the idiom in this context is better rendered as 'until he defeats all his enemies.'

37.9 ἐπί[m]: a marker of the object over which someone exercises a control or authority – 'over, with responsibility for.' ὃς ἦν ἐπὶ πάσης τῆς γάζης αὐτῆς 'who is responsible for all her treasury' Ac 8.27; καὶ βασιλεύσει ἐπὶ τὸν οἶκον Ἰακὼβ εἰς τοὺς αἰῶνας 'and he will rule over the people of Jacob forever' Lk 1.33.

37.10 συλαγωγέω: (a figurative extension of meaning of συλαγωγέω 'to carry off as booty or as captive in war,' not occurring in the NT) to take over complete control of a person as one would a captive – 'to control completely, to take control of, to make a captive of.' βλέπετε μή τις ὑμᾶς ἔσται ὁ συλαγωγῶν διὰ τῆς φιλοσοφίας 'see to it that no one gains control over you by human wisdom' Col 2.8. In some languages it is possible to preserve the figurative meaning of συλαγωγέω in Col 2.8 by employing a simile, for example, 'see that no one makes you a kind of captive by human wisdom' or 'see to it that no one uses human wisdom and by this means makes you, so to speak, a captive.'

37.11 περιπίπτω[b]: to become subject to physical control, with the implication of harmful consequences – 'to fall into the hands of, to be seized by.' ἄνθρωπός τις κατέβαινεν ἀπὸ Ἰερουσαλὴμ εἰς Ἰεριχὼ καὶ λῃσταῖς περιέπεσεν 'a man going down from Jerusalem to Jericho fell into the hands of robbers' Lk 10.30. In a number of languages it may be more appropriate to use what may be called 'an active form,' for example, 'robbers seized him.'

37.12 παραδίδωμι εἰς χεῖρας: (an idiom, literally 'to give into the hands') to hand someone over into the control of others – 'to deliver to the control of, to hand over to.' ὁ υἱὸς τοῦ ἀνθρώπου παραδίδοται εἰς χεῖρας ἁμαρτωλῶν 'the Son of Man will be given over into the control of sinners' Mt 26.45. In a context such as Mt 26.45, παραδίδοται εἰς χεῖρας may be rendered as 'will hand him over to be arrested' or 'will cause you to be taken into custody.'

37.13 ἐξουσία[e], ας f: a state of control over someone or something – 'control.' καὶ πραθὲν ἐν τῇ σῇ ἐξουσίᾳ ὑπῆρχεν 'and after it was sold, (the money from the sale) remained under your control' Ac 5.4.

37.14 χείρᵈ, χειρός *f*: (a figurative extension of meaning of χείρᵃ 'hand,' 8.30) a state of control exercised by a person – 'to be in the control of, to be in the power of.' ἐξείλατό με ἐκ χειρὸς Ἡρῴδου 'he rescued me from the control of Herod' Ac 12.11. In some languages it may be necessary to express the meaning of 'control' in the context of Ac 12.11 by a more specific reference to potential action, for example, 'he rescued me and Herod could not do anything to me.'

37.15 παγίςᶜ, ίδος *f*; θήραᵇ, ας *f*: (figurative extensions of meaning of παγίςᵃ and θήραᵃ 'trap,' 6.23 and 6.24) an instrument or means for gaining control, implying an element of surprise – 'means of control, way of trapping.' γενηθήτω ἡ τράπεζα αὐτῶν εἰς παγίδα καὶ εἰς θήραν 'may their feast become a snare to trap them' or 'may their feast become a means of gaining control over them' Ro 11.9. In a number of languages, however, it is possible to reflect something of the figurative meaning of παγίς and θήρα by translating these terms as verbs, for example, 'may they be caught and trapped at their feasts' or 'may their feasts snare and trap them' (see 6.23 and 6.24).

37.16 κρατέωᵇ: to exercise power or force over someone or something – 'to have power over, to control.' καθότι οὐκ ἦν δυνατὸν κρατεῖσθαι αὐτὸν ὑπ' αὐτοῦ 'for it was impossible that it (death) should have power over him' Ac 2.24. See discussion at 37.17.

37.17 ὑπερέχωᵇ; συνέχωᵃ; κατέχωᵈ: to exercise continuous control over someone or something – 'to control, to restrain.'
ὑπερέχωᵇ: ὑποτάγητε . . . βασιλεῖ ὡς ὑπερέχοντι 'submit yourselves . . . to the king who is the one who controls' 1 Pe 2.13.
συνέχωᵃ: ἡ γὰρ ἀγάπη τοῦ Χριστοῦ συνέχει ἡμᾶς 'for Christ's love controls us' 2 Cor 5.14.
κατέχωᵈ: καὶ κατεῖχον αὐτὸν τοῦ μὴ πορεύεσθαι ἀπ' αὐτῶν 'and they tried to keep him from leaving them' Lk 4.42.
There is usually no difficulty in speaking of 'control' if it is performed by a person as in 1 Pe 2.13. However, it may not be possible to speak of 'death' having control, unless the language in question can personify death. In

some instances Ac 2.24 (see 37.16) must be rendered as 'it was impossible for him to continue to be dead,' and in 2 Cor 5.14 'Christ's love controls us' may be rendered as 'the fact that Christ loves us causes us to act as we do.'

37.18 στενοχωρέομαιᵃ: to be under severe limitations or restrictions – 'to live under restrictions, to be restricted, to be confined.' οὐ στενοχωρεῖσθε ἐν ἡμῖν, στενοχωρεῖσθε δὲ ἐν τοῖς σπλάγχνοις ὑμῶν 'you are not restricted by us, but by your own hearts' 2 Cor 6.12. In a number of languages it may be more meaningful to render 2 Cor 6.12 as 'it is not that we impose restrictions on you; it is you yourself who are doing it.' For another interpretation of στενοχωρέομαι in 2 Cor 6.12 as part of an idiom, see 25.54.

37.19 καταλαμβάνωᵈ: to gain control over – 'to overcome, to gain control of.' καὶ ἡ σκοτία αὐτὸ οὐ κατέλαβεν 'and the darkness did not gain control over it' Jn 1.5. It is also possible to understand καταλαμβάνω in Jn 1.5 as meaning 'to understand' (see 32.18).

37.20 βραβεύω: to control the activity of someone, based presumably upon correct judgment and decision – 'to control.' ἡ εἰρήνη τοῦ Χριστοῦ βραβευέτω ἐν ταῖς καρδίαις ὑμῶν 'let the peace of Christ control your thoughts' Col 3.15. In a number of languages it may be difficult to speak of 'the peace of Christ' as 'controlling.' In some instances one may translate this expression in Col 3.15 as 'the peace that Christ provides should show you what you should think.'

37.21 αὐθεντέω: to control in a domineering manner – 'to control, to domineer.' γυναικὶ οὐκ ἐπιτρέπω . . . αὐθεντεῖν ἀνδρός 'I do not allow women . . . to dominate men' 1 Tm 2.12. 'To control in a domineering manner' is often expressed idiomatically, for example, 'to shout orders at,' 'to act like a chief toward,' or 'to bark at.'

37.22 βασιλεύωᵇ: (a figurative extension of meaning of βασιλεύωᵃ 'to rule, to reign as a king,' 37.64) to be in control in an absolute manner – 'to reign, to control completely.'

ἐβασίλευσεν ὁ θάνατος ἀπὸ ᾽Αδὰμ μέχρι Μωϋσέως 'death reigned from the time of Adam to the time of Moses' Ro 5.14. In a number of languages, however, it may be impossible to personify death as being capable of 'reigning' or 'ruling.' Sometimes the equivalent meaning may be expressed as 'from the time of Adam to that of Moses there was no way for people to escape death' or '. . . to die was certain.'

37.23 περικρατής, ές: pertaining to being in control – 'to be in control of, to have under control.' ἰσχύσαμεν μόλις περικρατεῖς γενέσθαι τῆς σκάφης 'we were scarcely able to get the boat under control' Ac 27.16.

37.24 δουλόομαι: (a figurative extension of meaning of δουλόω[a] 'to enslave,' 87.82) to be firmly bound by an obligation or a relationship – 'to be bound, to be under obligation.' οὐ δεδούλωται ὁ ἀδελφὸς ἢ ἡ ἀδελφὴ ἐν τοῖς τοιούτοις 'under such circumstances the believer, whether man or woman, is not bound' or '. . . is not under obligation' or '. . . is free to act' 1 Cor 7.15.

37.25 δουλεύω[b]: (a figurative extension of meaning of δουλεύω[a] 'to be a slave,' 87.79) to be under the control of some influence and to serve the interests of such – 'to be a slave to, to be controlled by.' τοῦ μηκέτι δουλεύειν ἡμᾶς τῇ ἁμαρτίᾳ 'that we might no longer be slaves to sin' Ro 6.6; δουλεύουσιν ἀλλὰ τῇ ἑαυτῶν κοιλίᾳ 'but they serve their own appetites' Ro 16.18. In a number of languages it may be difficult to translate more or less literally 'but they serve their own appetites.' One can, however, often translate this expression in Ro 16.18 as 'but they do just what their own desires told them to do' or 'they do whatever they desired to do.'

37.26 δουλεία, ας f: (a figurative extension of meaning of δουλεία 'slavery,' not occurring in the NT) a state or condition of subservience – 'slavery, subservience.' οὐ γὰρ ἐλάβετε πνεῦμα δουλείας πάλιν εἰς φόβον 'for you did not receive the Spirit that again enslaves you and makes you afraid' or 'for the Spirit that God has given you does not make

you slaves and cause you to be afraid' Ro 8.15.

37.27 δουλόω[b] (a figurative extension of meaning of δουλόω[a] 'to enslave,' 87.82); καταδουλόω (a figurative extension of meaning of καταδουλόω 'to cause a person to be a slave,' not occurring in the NT): to gain control over someone and thus make such an individual subservient to one's own interests – 'to gain control over, to make a slave of, to cause someone to be subservient to, to cause to be like a slave.'

δουλόω[b]: ἐμαυτὸν ἐδούλωσα, ἵνα τοὺς πλείονας κερδήσω 'I made myself a slave in order to win as many as possible' 1 Cor 9.19; ὑπὸ τὰ στοιχεῖα τοῦ κόσμου ἤμεθα δεδουλωμένοι 'we became subjected to the elemental spirits of the universe' or '. . . subjected to rudimentary knowledge' Ga 4.3.

καταδουλόω: οἵτινες παρεισῆλθον κατασκοπῆσαι . . . ἵνα ἡμᾶς καταδουλώσουσιν 'these people have slipped in as spies . . . in order to gain control over us' or '. . . in order that they might make slaves of us' Ga 2.4.

37.28 ἁρπάζω[d]: to gain control over by force – 'to gain control over, to seize, to snatch away.' οὐχ ἁρπάσει τις αὐτὰ ἐκ τῆς χειρός μου 'no one will seize them from my hand,' meaning 'no one will be able to take them away from my control' Jn 10.28. Though in Jn 10.28 ἁρπάζω would appear to be in a literal context in view of the expression ἐκ τῆς χειρός μου 'out of my hand,' nevertheless ἁρπάζω is certainly figurative in meaning and so is χείρ 'hand.'

37.29 αἰχμαλωτίζω[b]: (a figurative extension of meaning of αἰχμαλωτίζω[a] 'to take captive in war,' 55.24) to gain complete control over, either by force or deception – 'to get control of.' οἱ ἐνδύνοντες εἰς τὰς οἰκίας καὶ αἰχμαλωτίζοντες γυναικάρια 'some of them go into homes and get control over helpless women' 2 Tm 3.6.

37.30 χαρίζομαι[d]: to hand someone over into the control of another person, without some reasonable cause – 'to hand over to, to put into the control of someone.' οὐκ ἔστιν ἔθος Ῥωμαίοις χαρίζεσθαί τινα ἄνθρωπον 'it is not the custom of Romans to hand someone over without a cause' Ac 25.16.

37.31 ὑποτάσσω; καταστέλλω: to bring something under the firm control of someone – 'to subject to, to bring under control.'
ὑποτάσσω: κατὰ τὴν ἐνέργειαν τοῦ δύνασθαι αὐτὸν καὶ ὑποτάξαι αὐτῷ τὰ πάντα 'using that power by which he is able to subject all things to him' Php 3.21.
καταστέλλω: καταστείλας δὲ ὁ γραμματεὺς τὸν ὄχλον 'the town secretary got the crowd under control' Ac 19.35.

37.32 ἀνυπότακτος[a], ον; ἀκατάστατος, ον:pertaining to being unable to be controlled by something or someone – 'not controlled by, not subject to, uncontrolled.'
ἀνυπότακτος[a]: οὐδὲν ἀφῆκεν αὐτῷ ἀνυπότακτον 'he left nothing that is not subject to him' He 2.8. It is also possible to restructure this statement in He 2.8 so as to read 'God left nothing that man could not be in control of.' It is also possible to translate this expression as 'and God put him in control over all things.'
ἀκατάστατος: τὴν δὲ γλῶσσαν οὐδεὶς δαμάσαι δύναται ἀνθρώπων· ἀκατάστατον κακόν 'no one can tame a person's tongue; it is an evil which cannot be controlled' Jas 3.8. It is also possible to translate 'it is an evil which cannot be controlled' as 'it is an evil which no one can control' or 'no one can control this evil.'

B Compel, Force[2] (37.33-37.34)

37.33 ἀναγκάζω; δέω[c]: to compel someone to act in a particular manner – 'to compel, to force.'
ἀναγκάζω: εἰ σὺ Ἰουδαῖος ὑπάρχων ἐθνικῶς καὶ οὐχὶ Ἰουδαϊκῶς ζῇς, πῶς τὰ ἔθνη ἀναγκάζεις Ἰουδαΐζειν; 'if you who are a Jew live like a

Gentile and not like a Jew, how can you compel Gentiles to live like Jews?' Ga 2.14.
δέω[c]: καὶ νῦν ἰδοὺ δεδεμένος ἐγὼ τῷ πνεύματι πορεύομαι εἰς Ἰερουσαλήμ 'and now the Spirit compels me to go to Jerusalem' Ac 20.22.
In some instances ἀναγκάζω and δέω[c] may be rendered as 'to cause it to be necessary for.' In other instances a simple causative seems to be the closest equivalent. For example, the last clause of Ga 2.14 may be expressed as 'how can you make Gentiles live like Jews,' and in Ac 20.22 one may translate 'and now the Spirit makes me go to Jerusalem.'

37.34 ἀγγαρεύω: to force civilians to carry a load for some distance (in NT times Roman soldiers had the authority to enforce such service) – 'to compel someone to carry a load, to press someone into service.' ἀγγαρεύουσιν παράγοντά τινα Σίμωνα Κυρηναῖον . . . ἵνα ἄρῃ τὸν σταυρὸν αὐτοῦ 'they pressed into service a passerby, Simon of Cyrene, . . . that he might carry his cross' Mk 15.21.

C Exercise Authority (37.35-37.47)

37.35 ἐξουσία[a], ας f: the right to control or govern over – 'authority to rule, right to control.' ἴσθι ἐξουσίαν ἔχων ἐπάνω δέκα πόλεων 'go with the authority to rule over ten cities' Lk 19.17.

37.36 ἐξουσία[b], ας f: the domain or sphere over which one has authority to control or rule – 'jurisdiction.' σοὶ δώσω τὴν ἐξουσίαν ταύτην ἅπασαν 'I will give to you all of this jurisdiction' Lk 4.6; ἐπιγνοὺς ὅτι ἐκ τῆς ἐξουσίας Ἡρῴδου ἐστίν 'learning that he was from the jurisdiction of Herod' Lk 23.7. In translating ἐξουσία[b] in the sense of 'jurisdiction,' it is often possible simply to use terms such as 'territory' or 'land' or even 'peoples,' as in the case of Lk 4.6.

37.37 ἐξουσία[c], ας f: a means or instrument by which authority is marked or symbolized – 'symbol of authority, symbol of subjection to authority.' ἡ γυνὴ ἐξουσίαν ἔχειν ἐπὶ τῆς κεφαλῆς 'a woman should have on her head a symbol of authority (over her)' 1 Cor 11.10.

2 It would be possible to treat the subdomain entitled *Compel, Force* as an aspect of *Mode* (Domain 71, which involves possibility, probability, and necessity). However, with ἀναγκάζω, δέω[c], and ἀγγαρεύω in the contexts noted in this subdomain, there is a clear indication of force and control.

This passage, however, is subject to a number of different interpretations, as commentaries clearly indicate.

37.38 ἐξουσία[d], ας *f*: one who has the authority to rule or govern – 'an authority, ruler.' ὅταν δὲ εἰσφέρωσιν ὑμᾶς ἐπὶ . . . τὰς ἐξουσίας, μὴ μεριμνήσητε 'when they bring you (to be tried) before . . . the authorities, do not be worried' Lk 12.11.

37.39 οἰκονόμος[b], ου *m*: one who has the authority and responsibility for something – 'one who is in charge of, one who is responsible for, adminstrator, manager.' καὶ οἰκονόμους μυστηρίων θεοῦ 'and those who are responsible for the mysteries of God' 1 Cor 4.1; ὡς καλοὶ οἰκονόμοι ποικίλης χάριτος θεοῦ 'as good managers of God's varied gifts' 1 Pe 4.10.

37.40 ἐπιτροπή, ῆς *f*: the full authority to carry out an assignment or commission – 'authority, complete power.' πορευόμενος εἰς τὴν Δαμασκὸν μετ' ἐξουσίας καὶ ἐπιτροπῆς τῶν ἀρχιερέων 'going to Damascus with authority and complete power from the high priests' Ac 26.12. In Ac 26.12 the combination of ἐξουσία and ἐπιτροπή serves to reinforce the sense of complete authority.

37.41 ἐξουσιαστικός, ή, όν: pertaining to being authoritative – 'authoritative.' τίς ἡ διδαχὴ ἡ κενὴ (=καινή) αὕτη ἡ ἐξουσιαστικὴ αὐτοῦ 'what is this new authoritative teaching of his' Mk 1.27 (apparatus).

37.42 ἐπιταγή[b], ῆς *f*: the right or authority to command – 'right to command, authority to command, authority.' ἔλεγχε μετὰ πάσης ἐπιταγῆς 'rebuke with complete authority' Tt 2.15. It is also possible to translate this expression in Tt 2.15 as 'show that you have every right to command when you rebuke them.'

37.43 κτίσις[e], εως *f*: an instituted authority, with the implication that such an authority has been created or formed – 'authority.' ὑποτάγητε πάσῃ ἀνθρωπίνῃ κτίσει διὰ τὸν κύριον 'for the sake of the Lord, submit yourselves to every human authority' 1 Pe 2.13.[3] The expression 'human authority' may be rendered as 'every person who has the right to rule.' For another interpretation of κτίσις in 1 Pe 2.13, see 42.39.

37.44 ἐπὶ τῆς Μωϋσέως καθέδρας καθίστημι: (an idiom, literally 'to sit upon the seat of Moses') to have the capacity to interpret the Law of Moses with authority – 'to be an authority concerning the Law of Moses.'[4] ἐπὶ τῆς Μωϋσέως καθέδρας ἐκάθισαν οἱ γραμματεῖς καὶ οἱ Φαρισαῖοι 'the teachers of the Law and the Pharisees are authorities in interpreting the Law of Moses' Mt 23.2.

37.45 δέω[d]: to cause someone to be under the authority of someone or something else – 'to restrict, to place under (the jurisdiction of).' ἡ γὰρ ὕπανδρος γυνὴ τῷ ζῶντι ἀνδρὶ δέδεται νόμῳ 'for a married woman is under the law of her husband as long as he lives' Ro 7.2.

37.46 δέω[e]: to exercise authority over something on the basis that it is not legitimate – 'to prohibit, to not allow, to not permit.' ὃ ἐὰν δήσῃς ἐπὶ τῆς γῆς ἔσται δεδεμένον ἐν τοῖς οὐρανοῖς 'what you prohibit on earth will be prohibited in heaven' Mt 16.19. There are a number of different interpretations of the implication of this statement in Mt 16.19, and translators should carefully review this passage in various commentaries.

37.47 λύω[f]: to exercise authority over something on the basis of its being legitimate – 'to permit, to allow.' ὃ ἐὰν λύσῃς ἐπὶ τῆς γῆς ἔσται λελυμένον ἐν τοῖς οὐρανοῖς 'whatever you permit on earth will be permitted in heaven' Mt 16.19. There are a number of different interpretations of the implication of this statement in Mt 16.19, and translators should carefully review this passage in various commentaries.

3 The meaning of κτίσις in 1 Pe 2.13 is by no means certain. Scholarly opinion is seriously divided in view of the obscurity of reference.
4 Since the concept of 'authority' expresses only the manner in which the interpretation of the Law takes place, one may be justified in classifying this idiom under Domain 33 *Communication*.

D Rule, Govern (37.48-37.95)

37.48 ἐξουσιάζω; κατεξουσιάζω: to rule or reign by exercising authority over – 'to rule, to reign.'[5]

ἐξουσιάζω: οἱ ἐξουσιάζοντες αὐτῶν εὐεργέται καλοῦνται 'those who rule over them are called friends of the people' Lk 22.25.

κατεξουσιάζω: καὶ οἱ μεγάλοι κατεξουσιάζουσιν αὐτῶν 'and their great men reign over them' Mt 20.25.

37.49 κρίνω[g]: to rule over people – 'to rule, to govern.' καὶ καθήσεσθε ἐπὶ θρόνων τὰς δώδεκα φυλὰς κρίνοντες τοῦ Ἰσραήλ 'and you will be seated upon thrones, ruling over the twelve tribes of Israel' Lk 22.30. Though it would be possible to understand κρίνω in Lk 22.30 as meaning 'to judge' (see 56.30), the function of the twelve disciples seems to be far greater than that. Furthermore, there seems to be a significant Semitic influence in the meaning of κρίνω, since the corresponding Hebrew term likewise involved far more than merely making judicial decisions.

37.50 κυριεύω; κατακυριεύω[a]: to rule or reign over, with the implication in some contexts of 'lording it over' – 'to rule, to govern, to reign over.'[6]

κυριεύω: οἱ βασιλεῖς τῶν ἐθνῶν κυριεύουσιν αὐτῶν 'the kings of this world (literally 'of the nations') reign over them' Lk 22.25.

κατακυριεύω[a]: οἱ ἄρχοντες τῶν ἐθνῶν κατακυριεύουσιν αὐτῶν 'the rulers of the people reign over them' Mt 20.25.

37.51 κύριος[c], ου m: one who rules or exercises authority over others – 'ruler, master, lord.' οὐδεὶς δύναται δυσὶ κυρίοις δουλεύειν 'no one can serve two masters' Mt 6.24. For the meaning of κύριος as a title for God or for Christ, see 12.9.

37.52 κυριότης[a], ητος f: (derivative of κύριος[c] 'one who rules,' 37.51) a supernatural ruling power – 'ruling power.' εἴτε θρόνοι εἴτε κυριότητες εἴτε ἀρχαὶ εἴτε ἐξουσίαι· τὰ πάντα δι' αὐτοῦ καὶ εἰς αὐτὸν ἔκτισται 'whether rulers or ruling powers or supreme rulers or authorities, all these were created through him and for him' Col 1.16. In general, the series of terms θρόνοι, κυριότητες, ἀρχαί, and ἐξουσίαι in Col 1.16 (as well as in Eph 1.21) are understood as being supernatural cosmic powers, whether angelic or demonic (see 12.44), but it is possible that these should be understood in terms of human rulers.

37.53 ῥάβδος[b], ου f: (a figurative extension of meaning of ῥάβδος 'scepter,' not occurring in the NT) the manner in which a person rules or governs – 'rule, governing.' ἡ ῥάβδος τῆς εὐθύτητος ῥάβδος τῆς βασιλείας σου (literally 'the righteous scepter is the scepter of your kingdom') 'with righteousness you rule over your kingdom' He 1.8. It is rare that a staff constitutes a symbol of power and therefore would have the extended meaning of 'rule.' Accordingly, this expression in He 1.8 must often be rendered as 'the way in which you rule your kingdom will be righteous' or 'you will be righteous as you rule your kingdom.'

37.54 ἄρχω: to rule or govern, with the implication of preeminent position and status – 'to rule, to govern.' ἔσται ἡ ῥίζα τοῦ Ἰεσσαί, καὶ ὁ ἀνιστάμενος ἄρχειν ἐθνῶν 'a descendant of Jesse will come and he will be raised to rule the nations' Ro 15.12.

37.55 ἀρχή[d], ῆς f: the sphere of one's authority or rule – 'sphere of authority, limit of one's rule.' ἀγγέλους τε τοὺς μὴ τηρήσαντας τὴν ἑαυτῶν ἀρχήν 'the angels who did not stay within the sphere of their rule' Jd 6.

37.56 ἄρχων[a], οντος m; ἀρχή[e], ῆς f: (derivatives of ἄρχω 'to rule,' 37.54) one who rules or governs – 'ruler, governor.'

ἄρχων[a]: ταῦτα αὐτοῦ λαλοῦντος αὐτοῖς ἰδοὺ ἄρχων εἷς ἐλθὼν προσκύνει αὐτῷ 'while he was saying these things to them, a certain ruler came and knelt down before him' Mt 9.18.

ἀρχή[e]: ὅταν δὲ εἰσφέρωσιν ὑμᾶς ἐπὶ . . . τὰς

---

5 It is possible that κατεξουσιάζω is somewhat more emphatic in meaning than ἐξουσιάζω, though this cannot be determined from NT contexts.

6 It is possible that κατακυριεύω[a] is somewhat more emphatic in meaning than κυριεύω, but this cannot be determined on the basis of NT usage.

ἀρχὰς . . . μὴ μεριμνήσητε 'when they bring you (to be tried) before . . . the rulers . . . do not be worried' Lk 12.11.

37.57 ποιμαίνω^c: to rule, with the implication of direct personal involvement – 'to rule, to govern.' ποιμανεῖ αὐτοὺς ἐν ῥάβδῳ σιδηρᾷ 'he will rule them with an iron rod' Re 2.27.

37.58 ἡγέομαι^c; ἡγεμονία, ας f: to rule over, with the implication of providing direction and leadership – 'to rule over, to order, to govern, government, rule.'
ἡγέομαι^c: κατέστησεν αὐτὸν ἡγούμενον ἐπ' Αἴγυπτον καὶ ἐφ' ὅλον τὸν οἶκον αὐτοῦ 'he appointed him to rule over Egypt and his whole household' Ac 7.10.
ἡγεμονία: ἐν ἔτει δὲ πεντεκαιδεκάτῳ τῆς ἡγεμονίας Τιβερίου Καίσαρος 'it was the fifteenth year of the rule of the Emperor Tiberius' Lk 3.1.
In a number of languages it may be necessary to express the concept of 'ruling' by some form of 'command,' for example, 'he commands people what they must do' or 'he orders people' or 'he is the chief over people.'

37.59 ἡγεμών^a, όνος m: (derivative of ἡγέομαι^c 'to rule,' 37.58) one who rules, with the implication of preeminent position – 'ruler.' οὐδαμῶς ἐλαχίστη εἶ ἐν τοῖς ἡγεμόσιν Ἰούδα 'you are by no means the least among the rulers of Judah' or '. . . the important places in Judah' Mt 2.6. In the context of Mt 2.6 it is possible to understand 'rulers' as a figurative reference to important places, and therefore one may also translate 'you are by no means the least among the leading cities of Judah.'

37.60 ἡγεμονεύω: (derivative of ἡγεμών^a 'ruler,' 37.59) to be a governor, in the NT restricted to the meaning of a governor of a Roman province – 'to be a governor.' αὕτη ἀπογραφὴ πρώτη ἐγένετο ἡγεμονεύοντος τῆς Συρίας Κυρηνίου 'when this first census took place, Quirinius was governor of Syria' Lk 2.2. The expression 'Quirinius was governor of Syria' may be rendered in some languages as 'Quirinius was the one who commanded all those in the province of Syria' or 'Quirinius gave orders to all those in Syria.'

37.61 δύναμις^d, εως f: one who has the power to rule – 'ruler.' πέπεισμαι . . . οὔτε ἐνεστῶτα οὔτε μέλλοντα οὔτε δυνάμεις . . . ἡμᾶς χωρίσαι ἀπὸ τῆς ἀγάπης τοῦ θεοῦ 'I am convinced that . . . neither the present nor the future nor any ruler . . . can separate us from the love of God' Ro 8.38-39. It is also possible to interpret δύναμις in Ro 8.38-39 as meaning a supernatural power (see 12.44).

37.62 δυνάστης, ου m: (derivative of δύναμις^d 'ruler,' 37.61) one who is in a position of authority to command others – 'official, ruler.' ἀνὴρ Αἰθίοψ εὐνοῦχος δυνάστης Κανδάκης βασιλίσσης Αἰθιόπων 'the man was an Ethiopian, a court official of Candace, the queen of Ethiopia' Ac 8.27 (see also 37.85)[7]; ἣν καιροῖς ἰδίοις δείξει ὁ μακάριος καὶ μόνος δυνάστης 'which at the right time the blessed and only ruler will bring about' 1 Tm 6.15.

37.63 δεσπότης^a, ου m: one who holds complete power or authority over another – 'master, ruler, lord, Lord (as a title for God and for Christ).' ὅσοι εἰσὶν ὑπὸ ζυγὸν δοῦλοι, τοὺς ἰδίους δεσπότας πάσης τιμῆς ἀξίους ἡγείσθωσαν 'those who are slaves under the yoke should regard their masters as deserving all respect' 1 Tm 6.1; δέσποτα, σὺ ὁ ποιήσας τὸν οὐρανὸν καὶ τὴν γῆν 'Lord, you who made heaven and earth' Ac 4.24.[8]

37.64 βασιλεύω^a; βασιλεία^a, ας f: to rule as a king, with the implication of complete authority and the possibility of being able to pass on the right to rule to one's son or near kin – 'to rule, to be a king, to reign, rule, reign.'
βασιλεύω^a: ἀκούσας δὲ ὅτι Ἀρχέλαος βασιλεύει τῆς Ἰουδαίας . . . ἐφοβήθη ἐκεῖ ἀπελθεῖν 'when he heard that Archelaus was king of Judea, . . . he was afraid to settle there' Mt 2.22.

---

7 In Ac 8.27 δυνάστης reinforces the meaning of εὐνοῦχος in the sense of 'court official' (see 37.85).
8 It would also be possible to classify δεσπότης^a meaning 'Lord' along with κύριος^a (12.9) in Domain 12 *Supernatural Beings and Powers*, Subdomain A, in which titles for supernatural beings are included, but δεσπότης in Ac 4.24 appears to be more a descriptive appellative rather than a standardized title.

βασιλεία[a]: τῆς βασιλείας οὐκ αὐτοῦ ἔσται τέλος 'his reign will never end' Lk 1.33.

It is generally a serious mistake to translate the phrase ἡ βασιλεία τοῦ θεοῦ 'the kingdom of God' as referring to a particular area in which God rules. The meaning of this phrase in the NT involves not a particular place or special period of time but the fact of ruling. An expression such as 'to enter the kingdom of God' thus does not refer to 'going to heaven' but should be understood as 'accepting God's rule' or 'welcoming God to rule over.'

37.65 λαμβάνω βασιλείαν: (an idiom, literally 'to take, to receive a rule') to receive from someone else the power or authority to reign as a king – 'to become a king.' ἄνθρωπός τις εὐγενὴς ἐπορεύθη εἰς χώραν μακρὰν λαβεῖν ἑαυτῷ βασιλείαν 'a nobleman went to a faraway country to become king' Lk 19.12.

37.66 συμβασιλεύω: to reign as a king together with someone else – 'to be kings together, to reign with' (used figuratively in 1 Cor 4.8).[9] ὄφελόν γε ἐβασιλεύσατε, ἵνα καὶ ἡμεῖς ὑμῖν συμβασιλεύσωμεν 'I wish you really were kings so that we could be kings together with you' 1 Cor 4.8.

37.67 βασιλεύς, έως m: one who has absolute authority within a particular area and is able to convey this power and authority to a successor (though in NT times, certain kings ruled only with the approval of Roman authorities and had no power to pass on their prerogatives) – 'king.' ἄχρι οὗ ἀνέστη βασιλεὺς ἕτερος ἐπ' Αἴγυπτον ὃς οὐκ ᾔδει τὸν Ἰωσήφ 'at last a different king who had not known Joseph began to rule in Egypt' Ac 7.18.

37.68 βασίλισσα, ης f: a female ruler who has absolute authority within a particular area and who is able to pass on the power to rule to a successor – 'queen.'[10] δυνάστης Κανδάκης

9 Rather than classify συμβασιλεύω as a conventional figurative extension of meaning of an underlying literal sense of 'to reign together,' it seems best to understand this term in 1 Cor 4.8 as merely being used figuratively in a particular context.

10 In certain contexts outside of the NT, βασίλισσα is employed to refer to the wife of a king.

βασιλίσσης Αἰθιόπων 'an official of Candace, the queen of Ethiopia' Ac 8.27. For an analysis of the use of Κανδάκη in Ac 8.27, see 37.77. See also 93.209.

37.69 βασιλικός, ή, όν; βασίλειος, ον: pertaining to a king – 'royal, kingly.'
βασιλικός: ὁ Ἡρῴδης ἐνδυσάμενος ἐσθῆτα βασιλικὴν καὶ καθίσας ἐπὶ τοῦ βήματος 'Herod put on his royal robes and sat on his throne' Ac 12.21.
βασίλειος: ὑμεῖς δὲ γένος ἐκλεκτόν, βασίλειον ἱεράτευμα, ἔθνος ἅγιον 'you are the chosen race, the royal priesthood, the holy nation' 1 Pe 2.9.

The expression 'his royal robes' may be rendered as 'his clothing which he had as king,' and the phrase 'the royal priesthood' may be rendered as 'priests who are like kings.'

37.70 θρόνος[b], ου m: (a figurative extension of meaning of θρόνος[a] 'throne,' 6.112) a ruling power, with the implication of royal status – 'ruler, royal ruler.' εἴτε θρόνοι εἴτε κυριότητες εἴτε ἀρχαὶ εἴτε ἐξουσίαι· τὰ πάντα δι' αὐτοῦ καὶ εἰς αὐτὸν ἔκτισται 'whether rulers or ruling powers or supreme rulers or authorities, all these were created through him and for him' Col 1.16. Most scholars understand θρόνος in Col 1.16 as meaning a supernatural power, whether angelic or demonic (see 12.44), but it is possible that θρόνοι in Col 1.16 means human rulers.

37.71 θρόνος[d], ου m: position of power and authority to rule – 'rule, authority, throne.' δώσει αὐτῷ κύριος ὁ θεὸς τὸν θρόνον Δαυὶδ τοῦ πατρὸς αὐτοῦ 'the Lord God will give him the throne of his father David' or '. . . the power to rule which his father David had' Lk 1.32. There are serious complications in attempting to translate θρόνος in Lk 1.32 literally as 'throne,' since this might refer specifically to the seat on which David earlier sat. It may in fact be necessary to translate this expression in Lk 1.32 as 'the Lord God will cause him to rule in the way in which his ancestor David ruled.'

37.72 θρόνος[e], ου m: the place from which authority or rule is exercised – 'place of authority, place of ruling, throne.' οἶδα ποῦ κατοικεῖς, ὅπου ὁ θρόνος τοῦ Σατανᾶ 'I know where you dwell, where Satan's rule is' Re 2.13; προσερχώμεθα οὖν μετὰ παρρησίας τῷ θρόνῳ τῆς χάριτος 'let us therefore approach with boldness the throne of grace' or '. . . the place from which grace is dispensed' He 4.16. In He 4.16 the phrase τῷ θρόνῳ τῆς χάριτος is clearly a reference to God, and therefore in a number of languages it may be necessary to translate 'let us therefore with boldness approach God, who shows grace.'

37.73 κοσμοκράτωρ^a, ορος *m*: one who rules over the whole world – 'world ruler.' ἔστιν ἡμῖν ἡ πάλη . . . πρὸς τὰς ἀρχάς, πρὸς τὰς ἐξουσίας, πρὸς τοὺς κοσμοκράτορας τοῦ σκότους τούτου 'we are fighting . . . against the rulers and masters, the world rulers of this dark age' Eph 6.12. The expression 'world ruler' should not be understood in terms of merely ruling over the earth as a physical object but of 'ruling over those who are on the earth.' Most scholars, however, interpret κοσμοκράτωρ in Eph 6.12 as meaning a supernatural power (see 12.44), though it is possible to understand κοσμοκράτωρ in this context as meaning a human ruler.

37.74 Καῖσαρ^b, ος *m*: a title for the Roman Emperor – 'the Emperor.' ἔξεστιν δοῦναι κῆνσον Καίσαρι ἢ οὔ; 'is it right to pay taxes to the Emperor or not?' Mt 22.17. In a number of languages it is not easy to distinguish between terms for rulers such as 'governor,' 'king,' and 'emperor.' Sometimes one can only attempt a measure of distinction by indicating relative power or dominion. For example, 'emperor' may be rendered as 'the great ruler' or 'the most important chief of all.'

37.75 ὁ Σεβαστός, οῦ *m*: (derivative of σεβαστός 'revered, worthy of reverence,' not occurring in the NT) a title for the Roman Emperor and denoting his semidivine status – 'the Emperor.' τοῦ δὲ Παύλου ἐπικαλεσαμένου τηρηθῆναι αὐτὸν εἰς τὴν τοῦ Σεβαστοῦ διάγνωσιν 'but Paul appealed to be kept under guard and let the Emperor decide his case' Ac 25.21.

37.76 σεβαστός, ή, όν: (derivative of ὁ Σεβαστός 'the Emperor,' 37.75) pertaining to the Emperor – 'imperial.' παρεδίδουν τόν τε Παῦλον καί τινας ἑτέρους δεσμώτας ἑκατοντάρχῃ ὀνόματι Ἰουλίῳ σπείρης Σεβαστῆς 'they handed Paul and some other prisoners over to Julius, an officer of the imperial regiment' Ac 27.1. The phrase 'the imperial regiment' may be rendered as 'the group of soldiers who protected the Emperor' or '. . . who were under the direct command of the Emperor.'

37.77 Κανδάκη^a, ης *f*: the title of the queen of Ethiopia – 'the Candace, the female ruler of Ethiopia.'¹¹ δυνάστης Κανδάκης βασιλίσσης Αἰθιόπων 'an official of the Candace, queen of Ethiopia' Ac 8.27. For a different interpretation of Κανδάκη in Ac 8.27, see 93.209. See also 37.68.

37.78 τετραάρχης, ου *m*: a ruler with rank and authority lower than that of a king and one who ruled only with the approval of Roman authorities – 'tetrarch, governor of a region.' ἐν ἐκείνῳ τῷ καιρῷ ἤκουσεν Ἡρῴδης ὁ τετραάρχης τὴν ἀκοὴν Ἰησοῦ 'it was at that time that Herod, the tetrarch, heard about Jesus' Mt 14.1.

37.79 τετρααρχέω: to function as a tetrarch (see 37.78) – 'to be a tetrarch, to be the governor of a region.' τετρααρχοῦντος τῆς Γαλιλαίας Ἡρῴδου 'Herod was tetrarch of Galilee' Lk 3.1.

37.80 ἐθνάρχης, ου *m*: a person appointed to rule over a particular area or constituency on behalf of a king – 'ethnarch, official.' ἐν Δαμασκῷ ὁ ἐθνάρχης Ἀρέτα τοῦ βασιλέως ἐφρούρει τὴν πόλιν Δαμασκηνῶν πιάσαι με 'when I was in Damascus the official of King Aretas kept the city under watch in order to arrest me' 2 Cor 11.32.

37.81 Ἀσιάρχης, ου *m*: a high-ranking official in Asia Minor (in an area which is now Turkey) – 'provincial authority, local official.' τινὲς δὲ καὶ τῶν Ἀσιαρχῶν, ὄντες αὐτῷ φιλοι

---

11 It is possible that Κανδάκη was interpreted by persons outside of Ethiopia as being a proper name.

'some of the provincial authorities who were his friends' Ac 19.31.

37.82 ἀνθύπατος, ου *m*: (the Greek equivalent of the Latin proconsul) an official ruling over a province traditionally under the control of the Roman senate – 'proconsul, important official.' ὃς ἦν σὺν τῷ ἀνθυπάτῳ Σεργίῳ Παύλῳ, ἀνδρὶ συνετῷ 'he was associated with the proconsul Sergius Paulus, who was an intelligent man' Ac 13.7.

37.83 ἡγεμών[b]**, όνος** *m*: (the Greek equivalent of the Roman term praefectus) a person who ruled over a minor Roman province – 'prefect, governor.' παρέδωκαν Πιλάτῳ τῷ ἡγεμόνι 'they handed him over to Pilate the governor' Mt 27.2.

37.84 βασιλικός, οῦ *m*: an official directly responsible to a king – 'royal official, official of a king.' ἦν τις βασιλικὸς οὗ ὁ υἱὸς ἠσθένει 'there was an official of the king whose son was sick' Jn 4.46.

37.85 εὐνοῦχος[d]**, ου** *m*: an official of an Oriental court who was entrusted with various important responsibilities and who was also a eunuch – 'court official, eunuch.' ἀποκριθεὶς δὲ ὁ εὐνοῦχος τῷ Φιλίππῳ 'the court official said to Philip' Ac 8.34. In a context such as Ac 8.34, the focus of meaning of εὐνοῦχος[d] seems to be upon the person's official responsibilities and position rather than upon his physical condition. It may therefore be more in keeping with the context to employ an expression such as 'official of the court' or 'important official.' On the other hand, in view of a eunuch's limited acceptance in Jewish religion, the mention of the physical condition would fit Luke's theological purposes well.

37.86 ἐπίτροπος[a]**, ου** *m*: a person in charge of supervising workers – 'foreman.' λέγει ὁ κύριος τοῦ ἀμπελῶνος τῷ ἐπιτρόπῳ αὐτοῦ, Κάλεσον τοὺς ἐργάτας 'the owner of the vineyard said to his foreman, Call the workers' Mt 20.8. The term 'foreman' may be rendered as 'one who commands the workers' or 'one who assigns work to the workers.'

37.87 πρεσβεία, ας *f*: a person who has been given authority to communicate or to act on behalf of a ruler – 'representative, ambassador.'[12] πρεσβείαν ἀποστείλας ἐρωτᾷ τὰ πρὸς εἰρήνην 'he will send representatives and ask for terms of peace' Lk 14.32.

37.88 πρεσβεύω: (derivative of πρεσβεία 'representative,' 37.87) to function as a representative of a ruling authority – 'to be a representative of, to be an ambassador of.'[12] ὑπὲρ Χριστοῦ οὖν πρεσβεύομεν 'we, then, are representatives of Christ' 2 Cor 5.20. It may be possible to render ὑπὲρ Χριστοῦ οὖν πρεσβεύομεν in 2 Cor 5.20 as 'we serve as those who have been delegated by Christ' or 'our work has been specially assigned by Christ.'

37.89 ῥαβδοῦχος, ου *m*: a person responsible for maintaining law and order by preventing and detecting crime and handing offenders over to legal authorities – 'policeman.' ἀπήγγειλαν δὲ τοῖς στρατηγοῖς οἱ ῥαβδοῦχοι τὰ ῥήματα ταῦτα 'the policemen reported these words to the magistrates' Ac 16.38.

37.90 στρατηγός, οῦ *m*: the chief legal official of a city – 'magistrate, ruler of a city.' προσαγαγόντες αὐτοὺς τοῖς στρατηγοῖς εἶπαν, Οὗτοι οἱ ἄνθρωποι ἐκταράσσουσιν ἡμῶν τὴν πόλιν 'they brought them before the magistrates and said, These men are causing trouble in our city' Ac 16.20. In a number of instances στρατηγός may be rendered simply as 'the chief of the town' or 'the ruler of the city.'

37.91 στρατηγὸς τοῦ ἱεροῦ: (a title, literally 'official of the temple') a commander of Jewish soldiers responsible for guarding and maintaining order in the Jewish Temple – 'commander of the Temple guard.' οἱ ἱερεῖς καὶ ὁ στρατηγὸς τοῦ ἱεροῦ καὶ οἱ Σαδδουκαῖοι

12 It is possible to assign the meanings of πρεσβεία (37.87) and πρεσβεύω (37.88) to the domain of *Communication* (33), since communication is an important factor in the function of being a representative. However, the delegated authority and responsibility seem to be more in focus.

'the priests and the captain of the Temple guard and the Sadducees' Ac 4.1. In some contexts, however, a shortened form of this title, namely στρατηγός, is employed if the context indicates clearly that the reference is to the Temple, for example, Lk 22.4.

37.92 πράκτωρ, ορος *m*: an officer of a court responsible for carrying out the orders of a judge – 'bailiff, officer of the court.' ὁ κριτής σε παραδώσει τῷ πράκτορι, καὶ ὁ πράκτωρ σε βαλεῖ εἰς φυλακήν 'the judge will hand you over to the officer, and the officer will put you in jail' Lk 12.58.

37.93 πολιτάρχης, ου *m*: a public official responsible for administrative matters within a town or city and a member of the ruling council of such a political unit – 'city official.' ἔσυρον Ἰάσονα καί τινας ἀδελφοὺς ἐπὶ τοὺς πολιτάρχας 'they dragged Jason and some other fellow believers to the city officials' Ac 17.6.

37.94 γραμματεύς^c, έως *m*: a city official with responsibility for the records of a town or city and apparently certain responsibilities for maintaining law and order – 'town clerk, town secretary.' καταστείλας δὲ ὁ γραμματεὺς τὸν ὄχλον 'and the town clerk got the crowd under control' Ac 19.35.

37.95 ἄρχων τῶν Ἰουδαίων: (a title, literally 'ruler of the Jews') a member of the highest legal, legislative, and judicial body among the Jews – 'a member of the Council.'[13] Νικόδημος ὄνομα αὐτῷ, ἄρχων τῶν Ἰουδαίων 'a man named Nicodemus, a member of the Council' Jn 3.1.

E Assign to a Role or Function (37.96-37.107)

37.96 τάσσω^a; ὁρίζω^b; ἀναδείκνυμι^b; τίθημι^b: to assign someone to a particular task, function, or role – 'to appoint, to designate, to assign, to give a task to.'

τάσσω^a: ἐπίστευσαν ὅσοι ἦσαν τεταγμένοι εἰς ζωὴν αἰώνιον 'those who had been designated for eternal life became believers' Ac 13.48. Though τάσσω in Ac 13.48 has sometimes been interpreted as meaning 'to choose,' there seems to be far more involved than merely a matter of selection, since a relationship is specifically assigned.

ὁρίζω^b: ὁ ὡρισμένος ὑπὸ τοῦ θεοῦ κριτής 'the one designated by God as judge' Ac 10.42.

ἀναδείκνυμι^b: ἀνέδειξεν ὁ κύριος ἑτέρους ἑβδομήκοντα δύο 'the Lord appointed another seventy-two men' Lk 10.1.

τίθημι^b: ἔθηκα ὑμᾶς ἵνα ὑμεῖς ὑπάγητε καὶ καρπὸν φέρητε 'I appointed you to go and bear much fruit' Jn 15.16.

37.97 ἀφορίζω^b: to set aside a person for a particular task or function – 'to appoint, to set apart for.'[14] ἀφορίσατε δή μοι τὸν Βαρναβᾶν καὶ Σαῦλον 'set apart for me Barnabas and Saul' Ac 13.2.

37.98 δίδωμι^e: to assign a person to a task as a particular benefit to others – 'to appoint, to assign (on behalf of).'[15] μετὰ ταῦτα ἔδωκεν κριτάς 'after this he appointed judges (for them)' Ac 13.20. It may be possible in some languages to render δίδωμι in Ac 13.20 as 'he gave them judges,' but more frequently it is necessary to use a phrase such as 'he appointed judges to rule over them.'

37.99 παραλαμβάνω^e: to receive an appointment for a particular ministry – 'to receive an appointment, to receive a task, to be assigned a ministry.' τὴν διακονίαν ἣν παρέλαβες ἐν κυρίῳ 'the ministry which you received in the service of the Lord' Col 4.17.

37.100 μερίζω^d: to assign a particular part or aspect of a function or responsibility – 'to assign a particular responsibility, to give a particular task to, to appoint a particular part

---

13 One may classify ἄρχων τῶν Ἰουδαίων in Domain 11 *Groups and Classes of Persons*, but the phrase ἄρχων τῶν Ἰουδαίων seems to focus primarily upon the authority and status which such a person has, rather than merely upon his being a member of a deliberative body, as in the case of terms such as συνέδριον^a 'city council' (11.79), γερουσία and πρεσβυτέριον^a 'Sanhedrin' (11.83).

14 It is possible that ἀφορίζω^b is somewhat more emphatic in meaning than ὁρίζω^b (37.96).

15 δίδωμι^e seems to imply a benevolent purpose in the action of assigning someone to a role.

to.' κατὰ τὸ μέτρον τοῦ κανόνος οὗ ἐμέρισεν ἡμῖν ὁ θεὸς μέτρου 'according to the limits of the work to which God has appointed us' (literally 'according to the measure of the rule which God has apportioned to us as a measure') 2 Cor 10.13.

37.101 κλῆρος^c, ου *m*: a responsibility, function, or ministry which has been assigned to a person – 'ministry, task.' ἔλαχεν τὸν κλῆρον τῆς διακονίας ταύτης 'he was given a task in this ministry' Ac 1.17. For another interpretation of κλῆρος in Ac 1.17, see 63.18.

37.102 ἐπὶ τὴν κεφαλήν: (an idiom, literally 'upon someone's head') to accept responsibility for some action, often with the implication of blame – 'upon someone's head, responsibility.' τὸ αἷμα ὑμῶν ἐπὶ τὴν κεφαλὴν ὑμῶν literally, 'your blood will be upon your own heads,' meaning 'your destruction will be your own responsibility' Ac 18.6. This statement in Ac 18.6 is no doubt an adage meaning that anything bad which may happen to a person, including one's death, will be one's own responsibility, and therefore no one else is to blame. It is also possible to classify this idiom in Domain 90D. Note that in 37.102 the focus is on the assignment of responsibility.

37.103 χειροτονέω^b: to formally appoint or assign someone to a particular task – 'to appoint, to assign.' χειροτονήσαντες δὲ αὐτοῖς κατ' ἐκκλησίαν πρεσβυτέρους 'in each church they appointed elders for them' Ac 14.23. In Ac 14.23 χειροτονέω may, however, be understood in the meaning of 'to choose or elect to office by the raising of hands' (see 30.101).

37.104 καθίστημι^a; καθίζω^d: to assign to someone a position of authority over others – 'to put in charge of, to appoint, to designate.' καθίστημι^a: κατέστησεν ὁ κύριος ἐπὶ τῆς οἰκετείας αὐτοῦ 'his master placed him in charge of his (other) servants' Mt 24.45. 'To put someone in charge of someone else' may be expressed in a number of languages as 'to give someone the authority to command others' or 'to say to someone, You are to give orders to others.'

καθίζω^d: τοὺς ἐξουθενημένους ἐν τῇ ἐκκλησίᾳ τούτους καθίζετε; 'will you designate those who have no standing in the church?' 1 Cor 6.4. In view of the particular context of 1 Cor 6.4 it may be necessary to indicate more clearly what is involved in such a designation. One may therefore wish to translate as 'are you going to take these matters to be settled by people who have no standing in the church?'

37.105 διατίθεμαι βασιλείαν: (an idiom, literally 'to designate ruling') to designate someone in a somewhat formal or official way for the role of ruling – 'to give the right to rule, to provide with the authority to rule.' κἀγὼ διατίθεμαι ὑμῖν καθὼς διέθετό μοι ὁ πατήρ μου βασιλείαν 'I give you the right to rule just as my Father has given me the right to rule' Lk 22.29. In a number of languages it may be difficult to translate literally 'to give the right to rule.' Often this is expressed by direct discourse, for example, 'to say, You now have the authority to rule' or 'to say, You are now able to command.'

37.106 ποιέω^g: to cause someone to assume a particular type of function – 'to assign to a task, to cause people to assume responsibilities for a task.' ἐποίησεν δώδεκα, οὓς καὶ ἀποστόλους ὠνόμασεν 'he assigned twelve persons whom he also called apostles' Mk 3.14.

37.107 χρίω; χρῖσμα, τος *n*: (figurative extensions of meaning of χρίω and χρῖσμα 'to anoint,' not occurring in the NT) to assign a person to a task, with the implication of supernatural sanctions, blessing, and endowment – 'to anoint, to assign, to appoint, assignment, appointment.'
χρίω: πνεῦμα κυρίου ἐπ' ἐμέ, οὗ εἵνεκεν ἔχρισέν με εὐαγγελίσασθαι πτωχοῖς 'the Spirit of the Lord is upon me; he has appointed me to preach the good news to the poor' Lk 4.18. χρῖσμα: ὑμεῖς χρῖσμα ἔχετε ἀπὸ τοῦ ἁγίου 'you have been anointed by the Holy (Spirit)' 1 Jn 2.20.

It is rare that one can employ a literal rendering of χρίω or χρῖσμα in such contexts as Lk 4.18 and 1 Jn 2.20, since 'to pour oil upon someone' as a means of conveying a supernatural blessing and endowment for a task is culturally very rare. A strictly literal rendering of χρίω or χρῖσμα as 'to pour oil upon' is likely to be interpreted either as an insult or as an event preparatory to setting a person on fire and thus to destroy or to torture. Accordingly, in place of a literal rendering of χρίω or χρῖσμα, it is often necessary to employ some such expression as 'to be appointed by God' or 'to be given a special task by God.'

F Seize, Take into Custody (37.108-37.110)

37.108 καταλαμβάνω^c: to seize and take control of – 'to catch, to seize, to arrest.' οἱ Φαρισαῖοι γυναῖκα ἐπὶ μοιχείᾳ κατειλημμένην 'the Pharisees (brought in) a woman who had been caught committing adultery' Jn 8.3. In a number of languages it may be inappropriate to translate καταλαμβάνω in Jn 8.3 as 'to catch,' since this would imply that the woman was running. A much more satisfactory rendering may be simply 'to arrest' or 'to place under arrest.'

37.109 συλλαμβάνω^a: to seize and to take along with – 'to seize, to catch, to take, to arrest.' ἐπὶ τῇ ἄγρᾳ τῶν ἰχθύων ὧν συνέλαβον 'because of the catch of fish which they have taken' Lk 5.9; Ἰούδα τοῦ γενομένου ὁδηγοῦ τοῖς συλλαβοῦσιν Ἰησοῦν 'Judas, who was the guide of the men who arrested Jesus' Ac 1.16.

37.110 κρατέω^c; ἐπιλαμβάνομαι^b; ἐπιβάλλω τὰς χεῖρας/τὴν χεῖρα (ἐπί) (an idiom, literally 'to lay hands on'); ἐκτείνω τὰς χεῖρας ἐπί (an idiom, literally 'to stretch out hands upon'); πιάζω^b: to take a person into custody for alleged illegal activity – 'to seize, to arrest.'

κρατέω^c: ὁ γὰρ Ἡρῴδης κρατήσας τὸν Ἰωάννην ἔδησεν αὐτὸν καὶ ἐν φυλακῇ ἀπέθετο 'for Herod had ordered John's arrest, and had him tied up and put in prison' Mt 14.3.

ἐπιλαμβάνομαι^b: τότε ἐγγίσας ὁ χιλίαρχος ἐπελάβετο αὐτοῦ καὶ ἐκέλευσεν δεθῆναι ἁλύσεσι δυσί 'then the commander went over to him, arrested him, and ordered him to be tied up with two chains' Ac 21.33.

ἐπιβάλλω τὰς χεῖρας/τὴν χεῖρα (ἐπί): καὶ ἐπέβαλον αὐτοῖς τὰς χεῖρας καὶ ἔθεντο εἰς τήρησιν εἰς τὴν αὔριον 'so they arrested them and put them in jail until the next day' Ac 4.3; ἐζήτουν οὖν αὐτὸν πιάσαι, καὶ οὐδεὶς ἐπέβαλεν ἐπ' αὐτὸν τὴν χεῖρα 'then they tried to seize him, but no one arrested him' Jn 7.30.[16]

ἐκτείνω τὰς χεῖρας ἐπί: οὐκ ἐξετείνατε τὰς χεῖρας ἐπ' ἐμέ 'you did not arrest me' Lk 22.53.

πιάζω^b: ἀπέστειλαν οἱ ἀρχιερεῖς καὶ οἱ Φαρισαῖοι ὑπηρέτας ἵνα πιάσωσιν αὐτόν 'the chief priests and the Pharisees sent some guards to arrest him' Jn 7.32.

G Hand Over, Betray (37.111-37.113)

37.111 παραδίδωμι^b; παρίστημι^e: to deliver a person into the control of someone else, involving either the handing over of a presumably guilty person for punishment by authorities or the handing over of an individual to an enemy who will presumably take undue advantage of the victim – 'to hand over, to turn over to, to betray.'

παραδίδωμι^b: μήποτέ σε παραδῷ ὁ ἀντίδικος τῷ κριτῇ 'so that your opponent may not hand you over to the judge' Mt 5.25; ὁ υἱὸς τοῦ ἀνθρώπου παραδίδοται εἰς χεῖρας ἀνθρώπων, καὶ ἀποκτενοῦσιν αὐτόν 'the Son of Man will be handed over to men who will kill him' Mk 9.31; καὶ ἀπὸ τότε ἐζήτει εὐκαιρίαν ἵνα αὐτὸν παραδῷ 'from then on he was looking for a good chance to betray him' Mt 26.16.

παρίστημι^e: παρέστησαν καὶ τὸν Παῦλον αὐτῷ 'and they turned Paul over to him' Ac 23.33.

As is the case in English, a number of languages make a clear distinction between legitimate handing over of a presumably guilty person to a civil authority and the betrayal of a person in the in-group to someone in the out-group.

37.112 ἔκδοτος, ον: pertaining to being handed over to someone – 'handed over, betrayed.' τοῦτον τῇ ὡρισμένῃ βουλῇ καὶ προγνώ-

---

16 The phrases ἐπιβάλλω τὰς χεῖρας and ἐπιβάλλω τὴν χεῖρα ἐπί also occur with events, and as such focus attention on the beginning of an event, for example, οὐδεὶς ἐπιβαλὼν τὴν χεῖρα ἐπ' ἄροτρον 'no one puts his hand to the plow' or 'no one begins to plow' Lk 9.62. A treatment of this meaning is in 68.6.

σει τοῦ θεοῦ ἔκδοτον 'this one was handed over by the predetermined plan and knowledge of God' Ac 2.23.

37.113 προδότης, ου *m*: (derivative of προδίδωμι 'to betray,' not occurring in the NT) one who delivers without justification a person into the control of someone else – 'betrayer, one who betrays.' ὃς ἐγένετο προδότης 'who became a betrayer' Lk 6.16; οὗ νῦν ὑμεῖς προδόται καὶ φονεῖς ἐγένεσθε 'of whom you became betrayers and murderers' Ac 7.52.

H Imprison (37.114-37.118)

37.114 φυλακίζω; δέω[b]: to confine someone in prison – 'to imprison, imprisonment, to put in jail.'

φυλακίζω: αὐτοὶ ἐπίστανται ὅτι ἐγὼ ἤμην φυλακίζων καὶ δέρων κατὰ τὰς συναγωγὰς τοὺς πιστεύοντας ἐπὶ σέ 'they know well that I imprisoned and beat those in the synagogues who believed in you' Ac 22.19.

δέω[b]: ἦν δὲ ὁ λεγόμενος Βαραββᾶς μετὰ τῶν στασιαστῶν δεδεμένος 'and a man named Barabbas was in prison with rebels' Mk 15.7.

'To imprison a person' is often expressed in somewhat idiomatic forms, for example, 'to be tied inside' or 'to be locked in the dark' or even 'to eat one's food with rats.'

37.115 δεσμός[b]**, οῦ** *m*; **ἅλυσις**[b]**, εως** *f*: (figurative extensions of meaning of δεσμός[a] 'bonds,' 6.14 and ἅλυσις[a] 'chain,' 6.16) the state of being in prison – 'to be in prison, imprisonment.'

δεσμός[b]: ἵνα ὑπὲρ σοῦ μοι διακονῇ ἐν τοῖς δεσμοῖς τοῦ εὐαγγελίου 'that he could help me in your place while I am in prison for the gospel's sake' Phm 13.

ἅλυσις[b]: τοῦ εὐαγγελίου ὑπὲρ οὗ πρεσβεύω ἐν ἁλύσει 'for the sake of the gospel for which I am an ambassador in prison' or '. . . though now I am in prison' Eph 6.19-20.

The state of being a prisoner is often expressed somewhat idiomatically, for example, 'to be tied hand and foot,' 'to be chained like a dog,' or 'to look through iron bars.'

37.116 συνδέομαι: to be in prison along with others – 'to be in prison with, imprisonment

with.' μιμνῄσκεσθε τῶν δεσμίων ὡς συνδεδεμένοι 'remember those who are in prison as though you were in prison with them' He 13.3.

37.117 δέσμιος, ου *m*; **δεσμώτης, ου** *m*: (derivatives of δεσμός[b] 'to be in prison,' 37.115) a person who is under custody in prison – 'prisoner.'

δέσμιος: κατὰ δὲ ἑορτὴν εἰώθει ὁ ἡγεμὼν ἀπολύειν ἕνα τῷ ὄχλῳ δέσμιον ὃν ἤθελον 'at every (Passover) feast the governor was in the habit of setting free any prisoner the crowd asked for' Mt 27.15.

δεσμώτης: παρεδίδουν τόν τε Παῦλον καί τινας ἑτέρους δεσμώτας ἑκατοντάρχῃ 'they handed Paul and some other prisoners over to a Roman officer' Ac 27.1.

37.118 συναιχμάλωτος, ου *m*: one who has been arrested and imprisoned along with someone else – 'fellow prisoner.' ἀσπάσασθε Ἀνδρόνικον καὶ Ἰουνιᾶν τοὺς συγγενεῖς μου καὶ συναιχμαλώτους μου 'greetings to Andronicus and Junias, fellow Jews who were also fellow prisoners with me' Ro 16.7. A strictly literal rendering of συναιχμάλωτος in the sense of 'fellow captive' could be misleading, since it might imply that Paul himself had been a soldier or civilian captured in a war.

I Guard, Watch Over (37.119-37.126)

37.119 φρουρέω; φυλάσσω φυλακάς (an idiom, literally 'to guard a guarding'): to be on one's guard against some eventuality – 'to guard against, to keep under watch, to watch over.'

φρουρέω: ὁ ἐθνάρχης Ἀρέτα τοῦ βασιλέως ἐφρούρει τὴν πόλιν Δαμασκηνῶν πιάσαι με 'the ethnarch under King Aretas kept the city of Damascus under watch in order to arrest me' 2 Cor 11.32.

φυλάσσω φυλακάς: φυλάσσοντες φυλακὰς τῆς νυκτὸς ἐπὶ τὴν ποίμνην αὐτῶν 'guarding their flock during the night' Lk 2.8.

In a number of languages there is a great deal of difference in terminology employed in speaking about guarding an area in order to apprehend someone and guarding a flock of animals for fear of theft from robbers or danger from wild animals.

37.120 φυλάσσω^a: to hold someone in close custody – 'to guard closely.' παραδοὺς τέσσαρσιν τετραδίοις στρατιωτῶν φυλάσσειν αὐτόν 'he was handed over to be guarded by four groups of four soldiers each' Ac 12.4.

37.121 φύλαξ, ακος *m*: one who is responsible for guarding an area or a person – 'guard, sentinel.' καὶ τοὺς φύλακας ἑστῶτας ἐπὶ τῶν θυρῶν 'and the guards standing at the doors' Ac 5.23.

37.122 συνέχω^b; τηρέω^b; τήρησις^a, εως *f*: to continue to hold in custody – 'to guard, to keep watch, custody.'

συνέχω^b: οἱ ἄνδρες οἱ συνέχοντες αὐτὸν ἐνέπαιζον αὐτῷ δέροντες 'the men who were guarding him made fun of him and beat him' Lk 22.63.
τηρέω^b: παραγγείλαντες τῷ δεσμοφύλακι ἀσφαλῶς τηρεῖν αὐτούς 'they ordered the jailer to guard them securely' Ac 16.23.
τήρησις^a: ἐπέβαλον αὐτοῖς τὰς χεῖρας καὶ ἔθεντο εἰς τήρησιν εἰς τὴν αὔριον 'they arrested them and held them in custody until the next day' Ac 4.3.

The act of holding someone in custody or guarding an individual may be expressed as 'standing guard to see that someone will not escape' or 'watching carefully so that one cannot run off' or 'tying someone up so that he cannot leave.'

37.123 φυλακή^b, ῆς *f*: (derivative of φυλάσσω^a 'to guard closely,' 37.120) a place or post for guarding – 'guard post, guard station.' διελθόντες δὲ πρώτην φυλακὴν καὶ δευτέραν ἦλθαν ἐπὶ τὴν πύλην τὴν σιδηρᾶν 'they passed by the first guard post, then the second, and came (at last) to the iron gate' Ac 12.10.

37.124 δεσμοφύλαξ, ακος *m*: a person in charge of guarding a jail or prison – 'jailer, prison guard.' παραγγείλαντες τῷ δεσμοφύλακι ἀσφαλῶς τηρεῖν αὐτούς 'they ordered the jailer to guard them securely' Ac 16.23.

37.125 κατακλείω: to cause a person to be consigned to prison – 'to put into prison, to cause to be put in prison.' πολλούς τε τῶν ἁγίων ἐγὼ ἐν φυλακαῖς κατέκλεισα 'I caused many of the believers to be put in prison' Ac 26.10.

37.126 βασανιστής, οῦ *m*: (derivative of βασανίζω 'to torture,' 38.13) a person serving as a guard in a prison, whose function was to torture prisoners as a phase of judicial examination – 'prison guard, torturer.' ὀργισθεὶς ὁ κύριος αὐτοῦ παρέδωκεν αὐτὸν τοῖς βασανισταῖς ἕως οὗ ἀποδῷ πᾶν τὸ ὀφειλόμενον 'his master was very angry and handed him over to the prison guards until he should pay back the whole amount' Mt 18.34. It is difficult to know in the case of Mt 18.34 if βασανιστής is to be understood in the specific sense of 'torturer' (in which case it could be classified after 38.13) or only in terms of 'prison guard.' The use of βασανιστής in Mt 18.34 may simply be an instance of literary hyperbole. As such it may be possible to translate the expression in Mt 18.34 as 'his master was very angry and handed him over to prison guards to torture him until he should pay back the whole amount.'

J Release, Set Free (37.127-37.138)

37.127 λύω^b; ἀπολύω^c; ἀπαλλάσσω: to release from control, to set free (highly generic meaning applicable to a wide variety of circumstances, including confinement, political domination, sin, sickness) – 'to release, to set free.'[17]

λύω^b: οὐκ ἔδει λυθῆναι ἀπὸ τοῦ δεσμοῦ τούτου τῇ ἡμέρᾳ τοῦ σαββάτου 'should she not be freed from this bond on the Sabbath' Lk 13.16. In a number of languages problems are involved with a somewhat literal translation of λυθῆναι ἀπὸ τοῦ δεσμοῦ τούτου in Lk 13.16 since the expression is highly figurative. The reference, of course, is to the condition of the woman being a cripple. Furthermore, it may not make sense to speak of 'Satan binding' such a person, as in the first part of verse 16. In a number of languages, therefore, one may speak of 'Satan causing the woman to be a cripple,' and then in the latter part of verse

---

17 It is possible that ἀπολύω^c is somewhat more emphatic in meaning than λύω^b in view of the prepositional prefix ἀπο-, but NT contexts are not sufficient to indicate any precise degree of distinction. The same possible distinction also applies to the meanings in 37.128.

16, one may speak of 'causing a person no longer to be a cripple.'

ἀπολύω^c: παιδεύσας οὖν αὐτὸν ἀπολύσω 'I will have him whipped and released' Lk 23.22.

ἀπαλλάσσω: καὶ ἀπαλλάξῃ τούτους, ὅσοι φόβῳ θανάτου διὰ παντὸς τοῦ ζῆν ἔνοχοι ἦσαν δουλείας 'and set free those who were slaves all their lives because of their fear of death' He 2.15.

37.128 λυτρόομαι; λύτρωσις, εως *f*; ἀπολύτρωσις, εως *f*: to release or set free, with the implied analogy to the process of freeing a slave – 'to set free, to liberate, to deliver, liberation, deliverance.'[17]

λυτρόομαι: ἡμεῖς δὲ ἠλπίζομεν ὅτι αὐτός ἐστιν ὁ μέλλων λυτροῦσθαι τὸν Ἰσραήλ 'and we had hoped that he would be the one who was going to liberate Israel' Lk 24.21.

λύτρωσις: ἐλάλει περὶ αὐτοῦ πᾶσιν τοῖς προσδεχομένοις λύτρωσιν Ἰερουσαλήμ 'he spoke about (the child) to all who were waiting for (God) to liberate Jerusalem' Lk 2.38.

ἀπολύτρωσις: ἐν ᾧ ἔχομεν τὴν ἀπολύτρωσιν διὰ τοῦ αἵματος αὐτοῦ 'by his death we are set free' Eph 1.7.

In a number of languages one cannot speak of 'being set free' without specifying the particular manner or circumstances involved. In the case of Lk 24.21, for example, it may be necessary to translate 'to liberate Israel' as 'to cause Israel to be free from foreign control' or '. . . from the power of Rome.' A similar type of translation may be required in Lk 2.38, but in the case of Eph 1.7 it may be necessary to specify 'we are set free from sin' or 'we are set free from our bad desires.'

37.129 λυτρωτής, οῦ *m*: (derivative of λυτρόομαι 'to liberate,' 37.128) a person who liberates or releases others – 'deliverer, liberator.' τοῦτον ὁ θεὸς καὶ ἄρχοντα καὶ λυτρωτὴν ἀπέσταλκεν 'he is the one whom God sent as ruler and liberator' Ac 7.35. The phrase 'ruler and liberator' may, of course, be expressed by a verbal form, for example, 'as one who is to rule over you and to set you free.'

37.130 λύτρον, ου *n*; ἀντίλυτρον, ου *n*: the means or instrument by which release or deliverance is made possible – 'means of release, ransom.'

λύτρον: δοῦναι τὴν ψυχὴν αὐτοῦ λύτρον ἀντὶ πολλῶν 'to give his life as a ransom for many' or 'to die as a means of liberating many' Mt 20.28. 'To liberate many' may be expressed in many languages as 'to cause people to go free' or, in a more idiomatic manner, 'to untie many' or 'to unchain many.'

ἀντίλυτρον: ὁ δοὺς ἑαυτὸν ἀντίλυτρον ὑπὲρ πάντων 'he who gave himself as a ransom for all' 1 Tm 2.6.

37.131 ἀγοράζω^b; ἐξαγοράζω: (figurative extensions of meaning of ἀγοράζω^a 'to buy,' 57.188 and ἐξαγοράζω 'to pay a price,' not occurring in the NT) to cause the release or freedom of someone by a means which proves costly to the individual causing the release – 'to redeem, to set free.'

ἀγοράζω^b: ἠγοράσθητε γὰρ τιμῆς 'for you were redeemed with a price' 1 Cor 6.20.

ἐξαγοράζω: Χριστὸς ἡμᾶς ἐξηγόρασεν ἐκ τῆς κατάρας τοῦ νόμου 'Christ has redeemed us from the curse that the Law brings' Ga 3.13.

A literal rendering of ἀγοράζω^b or ἐξαγοράζω as 'to release by means of paying a price' can be misinterpreted in the sense that Christ actually engaged in some kind of monetary transaction. A literal translation may also lead to the mistaken interpretation, which was widespread in the Middle Ages, that in redeeming the believers God actually paid a price to the Devil. Obviously, ἀγοράζω in 1 Cor 6.20 and ἐξαγοράζω in Ga 3.13 must be understood in a figurative sense.

37.132 ἄφεσις^b, εως *f*: the process of setting free or liberating – 'release, liberty.' ἀπέσταλκέν με κηρύξαι αἰχμαλώτοις ἄφεσιν 'he has sent me to proclaim liberty to the captives' Lk 4.18.

37.133 ἐλευθερία, ας *f*: the state of being free – 'to be free, freedom.' οὗ δὲ τὸ πνεῦμα κυρίου, ἐλευθερία 'where the Spirit of the Lord is present, there is freedom' 2 Cor 3.17. In a number of languages the concept of freedom is expressed as a negation of control or domination, for example, 'where the Spirit of the Lord is present, there is no longer domination' or '. . . a person is not dominated' or '. . . a person does not feel under constraint.'

37.134 ἐλεύθερος[a], α, ον: pertaining to being free – 'free, to be free.' ἐὰν οὖν ὁ υἱὸς ὑμᾶς ἐλευθερώσῃ, ὄντως ἐλεύθεροι ἔσεσθε 'if the Son sets you free, you will be free indeed' Jn 8.36.

37.135 ἐλευθερόω: (derivative of ἐλεύθερος[a] 'free,' 37.134) to cause someone to be set free or to be released – 'to set free, to release.' ἐὰν οὖν ὁ υἱὸς ὑμᾶς ἐλευθερώσῃ, ὄντως ἐλεύθεροι ἔσεσθε 'if the Son sets you free, you will be free indeed' Jn 8.36.

37.136 καταργέομαι[a]: to cause the release from an association with a person or an institution on the basis that the earlier obligation or restriction is no longer relevant or in force – 'to be freed, to be released.' ἐὰν δὲ ἀποθάνῃ ὁ ἀνήρ, κατήργηται ἀπὸ τοῦ νόμου τοῦ ἀνδρός 'if her husband dies, she is free from the law concerning her husband' or 'from the law that bound her to her husband' Ro 7.2. In a number of languages it may be difficult to speak of being freed from a law which stipulates the relationship a woman has to her husband. Accordingly, it may be appropriate to translate this statement in Ro 7.2 as 'if a woman's husband dies, the law no longer ties her to her husband' or even '. . . the law says she is free to marry someone else.'

37.137 ἄνεσις[b], εως f: a partial degree of liberty or freedom – 'some freedom, some liberty.'[18] διαταξάμενος τῷ ἑκατοντάρχῃ τηρεῖσθαι αὐτὸν ἔχειν τε ἄνεσιν 'he ordered the officer in charge to keep him under guard but to give him some freedom' Ac 24.23.

37.138 δικαιόω[d]: to cause to be released from the control of some state or situation involving moral issues – 'to release, to set free.' ὁ γὰρ ἀποθανὼν δεδικαίωται ἀπὸ τῆς ἁμαρτίας 'for when a person dies (to sin), he is released from (the power of) sin' Ro 6.7. In a number of languages the rendering of this expression in Ro 6.7 is extremely difficult; first, because of the figurative meaning of 'to die to sin' and secondly, because of the phrase 'to be released from sin.' It may be necessary to introduce a simile into the first clause and then to restructure considerably the second clause if one cannot speak of 'the power of sin' but must regard sin as exercising some kind of direct control. Accordingly, one may sometimes translate this expression in Ro 6.7 as 'when a person is, as it were, dead as far as sinning is concerned, then sin no longer dominates him' or '. . . then he is not controlled by his desires to sin.'

18 It would also be possible to treat ἄνεσις[b] in Subdomain A *Control, Restrain* on the basis that ἄνεσις[b] would suggest the relaxing of controls.

38 Punish, Reward

Outline of Subdomains

A   Punish (38.1-38.13)
B   Reward, Recompense (38.14-38.20)

A   Punish (38.1-38.13)

38.1 κρίσις[i], εως f: punishment, with the implication of having been judged guilty – 'punishment.' πῶς φύγητε ἀπὸ τῆς κρίσεως τῆς γεέννης; 'how will you escape from punishment in hell?' Mt 23.33. It is also possible, of course, to interpret κρίσις in Mt 23.33 as meaning 'condemnation' (see 56.30), but as such, punishment is certainly implied.

38.2 κολάζω; κόλασις, εως f: to punish, with the implication of resulting severe suffering – 'to punish, punishment.'
κολάζω: ἀδίκους δὲ εἰς ἡμέραν κρίσεως κολαζομένους τηρεῖν 'to keep the wicked under punishment until the day of judgment comes' or '. . . under guard, awaiting punishment on the day of judgment' 2 Pe 2.9.
κόλασις: ἀπελεύσονται οὗτοι εἰς κόλασιν αἰώνιον, οἱ δὲ δίκαιοι εἰς ζωὴν αἰώνιον 'these will

be sent off to eternal punishment, but the righteous (will go) to eternal life' Mt 25.46.

In a number of languages punishment is often expressed as a causative of suffering, that is to say, 'to cause to suffer' or 'to cause to endure harm.' In some languages, however, there are a number of different types of punishment, and clear distinctions must be made between various degrees of punishment as well as between physical versus mental punishment.

38.3 φορέω τὴν μάχαιραν: (an idiom, literally 'to bear the sword') to have the capacity or authority to punish – 'to have the power to punish.' οὐ γὰρ εἰκῇ τὴν μάχαιραν φορεῖ 'for it is not in vain that he has the power to punish' Ro 13.4.

38.4 παιδεύω^c; παιδεία^c, ας *f*: to punish for the purpose of improved behavior – 'to punish, punishment.'
παιδεύω^c: οὐδὲν ἄξιον θανάτου ἐστὶν πεπραγμένον αὐτῷ. παιδεύσας οὖν αὐτὸν ἀπολύσω 'this man has done nothing to deserve death; I will therefore punish him and let him go' Lk 23.15-16.
παιδεία^c: πᾶσα δὲ παιδεία πρὸς μὲν τὸ παρὸν οὐ δοκεῖ χαρᾶς εἶναι ἀλλὰ λύπης 'all punishment seems at the time something not to make (us) glad, but rather sad' He 12.11.

38.5 παιδευτής^b, οῦ *m*: (derivative of παιδεύω^c 'to punish,' 38.4) a person who punishes for constructive purposes – 'punisher, one who punishes.' εἶτα τοὺς μὲν τῆς σαρκὸς ἡμῶν πατέρας εἴχομεν παιδευτὰς καὶ ἐνετρεπόμεθα 'we had our human fathers who punished us and we respected them' He 12.9.

38.6 τιμωρέω; τιμωρία, ας *f*; ἐπιτιμία, ας *f*: to punish, with the implication of causing people to suffer what they deserve – 'to punish, to suffer punishment (with passive construction), punishment.'
τιμωρέω: ἄξων καὶ τοὺς ἐκεῖσε ὄντας δεδεμένους εἰς Ἰερουσαλὴμ ἵνα τιμωρηθῶσιν 'and bring them back in chains to Jerusalem to be punished' Ac 22.5.
τιμωρία: πόσῳ δοκεῖτε χείρονος ἀξιωθήσεται τιμωρίας ὁ τὸν υἱὸν τοῦ θεοῦ καταπατήσας 'just

think how much worse is the punishment he will deserve who despises the Son of God' He 10.29.
ἐπιτιμία: ἱκανὸν τῷ τοιούτῳ ἡ ἐπιτιμία αὕτη ἡ ὑπὸ τῶν πλειόνων 'it is enough for this (offender) that he has been punished in this way by most (of you)' 2 Cor 2.6.

38.7 ζημιόομαι^b: to be punished, with the implication of suffering damage – 'to be punished, to suffer punishment.' εἴ τινος τὸ ἔργον κατακαήσεται, ζημιωθήσεται 'but if anyone's work is burnt up, he will suffer punishment' 1 Cor 3.15. It is also possible to understand ζημιόομαι in 1 Cor 3.15 as meaning simply 'to suffer loss' (see 57.69).

38.8 ἐκδικέω^c; ἐκδίκησις^c, εως *f*; δίκη^a, ης *f*: to punish, on the basis of what is rightly deserved – 'to punish, to cause to suffer, punishment.'
ἐκδικέω^c: ἐν ἑτοίμῳ ἔχοντες ἐκδικῆσαι πᾶσαν παρακοήν '(we will) be ready to punish any act of disobedience' 2 Cor 10.6.
ἐκδίκησις^c: δι' αὐτοῦ πεμπομένοις εἰς ἐκδίκησιν κακοποιῶν 'who have been sent by him to punish the evildoers' 1 Pe 2.14.
δίκη^a: οἵτινες δίκην τίσουσιν ὄλεθρον αἰώνιον 'they will suffer the punishment of eternal destruction' 2 Th 1.9.

38.9 ἔκδικος, ου *m*: (derivative of ἐκδικέω^c 'to punish,' 38.8) a person who punishes – 'punisher.' τὸ μὴ ὑπερβαίνειν ... τὸν ἀδελφὸν αὐτοῦ, διότι ἔκδικος κύριος 'no man should wrong ... his fellow believer, for the Lord will be the punisher' or '... will punish him' 1 Th 4.6.

38.10 ὀργή^b, ῆς *f*: divine punishment based on God's angry judgment against someone – 'to punish, punishment.' μὴ ἄδικος ὁ θεὸς ὁ ἐπιφέρων τὴν ὀργήν; 'God does not do wrong when he punishes (us), does he?' Ro 3.5. Though the focal semantic element in ὀργή^b is punishment, at the same time there is an implication of God's anger because of evil. Therefore, it is possible in some languages to translate this expression in Ro 3.5 as 'God does not do wrong when he is angry and punishes us, does he?'

38.11 μαστιγόω[b]: to punish severely, implying whipping – 'to punish, to punish severely.' μαστιγοῖ δὲ πάντα υἱὸν ὃν παραδέχεται 'he punishes every son whom he receives' He 12.6.

38.12 διχοτομέω[b]: (a figurative extension of meaning of διχοτομέω[a] 'to cut in two,' 19.19) to punish with great severity – 'to punish severely, to punish.' ἥξει ὁ κύριος τοῦ δούλου ἐκείνου ἐν ἡμέρᾳ ᾗ οὐ προσδοκᾷ . . . καὶ διχοτομήσει αὐτόν 'the servant's master will come on a day when he does not expect him . . . and will punish him severely' Mt 24.50-51. It is also possible to understand διχοτομέω in Mt 24.51 and the parallel passage in Lk 12.46 in a strictly literal sense, namely, 'to cut in two' or 'to cut into pieces' (see 19.19).

38.13 βασανίζω; τυμπανίζω: to punish by physical torture or torment – 'to torture, to torment.'
βασανίζω: ἦλθες ὧδε πρὸ καιροῦ βασανίσαι ἡμᾶς; 'have you come here in order to torment us before the right time?' Mt 8.29.
τυμπανίζω: ἄλλοι δὲ ἐτυμπανίσθησαν, οὐ προσδεξάμενοι τὴν ἀπολύτρωσιν 'but others were tortured, having refused deliverance' or '. . . having not received deliverance' He 11.35.[1]

B Reward, Recompense (38.14-38.20)

In this subdomain, *Reward, Recompense,* all the terms may occur in either a positive or a negative sense, that is to say, as a benefit or as a penalty or punishment. Whether the recompense is positive or negative depends upon the context, but the meanings of the terms themselves are neutral in this respect. In the NT itself, however, not all of the terms in question occur in both positive and negative contexts. In most languages, however, it is rare to find terms which are neutral with respect to positive or negative recompense. Therefore, in each context a translator must choose the appropriate expression which will indicate either the positive or negative aspects of the recompense.

38.14 μισθός[b], **οῦ** *m*: a recompense based upon what a person has earned and thus deserves, the nature of the recompense being either positive or negative – 'reward, recompense.' δοῦναι τὸν μισθὸν τοῖς δούλοις σου τοῖς προφήταις 'to give a reward to your servants the prophets' Re 11.18; ὅτι ὁ μισθὸς ὑμῶν πολὺς ἐν τοῖς οὐρανοῖς 'because your reward in heaven is great' Mt 5.12; ἕκαστος δὲ τὸν ἴδιον μισθὸν λήμψεται κατὰ τὸν ἴδιον κόπον 'and each one will receive his own reward in accordance with how he himself has labored' 1 Cor 3.8; ἰδοὺ ἔρχομαι ταχύ, καὶ ὁ μισθός μου μετ' ἐμοῦ 'behold, I come quickly, and my reward is with me' Re 22.12. In the context of Re 22.12, μισθός may be understood as either a positive or negative reward.

38.15 ἀντιμισθία, ας *f*: a recompense based upon what one deserves, either positive or negative, but with special emphasis upon the reciprocal nature of the recompense – 'recompense, exchange.' καὶ τὴν ἀντιμισθίαν ἣν ἔδει τῆς πλάνης αὐτῶν ἐν ἑαυτοῖς ἀπολαμβάνοντες 'and receiving in themselves the recompense they deserve for their wrongdoing' Ro 1.27; τὴν δὲ αὐτὴν ἀντιμισθίαν, ὡς τέκνοις λέγω, πλατύνθητε καὶ ὑμεῖς 'in view of this same reciprocal exchange – I speak to you as children – open your hearts' 2 Cor 6.13.

38.16 ἀποδίδωμι[b]: to recompense someone, whether positively or negatively, depending upon what the individual deserves – 'to reward, to recompense.' ὃς ἀποδώσει ἑκάστῳ κατὰ τὰ ἔργα αὐτοῦ 'who will recompense each person in accordance with what he has done' Ro 2.6.

38.17 μισθαποδοσία, ας *f*: a reward or recompense, whether positive or negative, which has been granted to someone – 'reward, recompense, penalty.' ἀπέβλεπεν γὰρ εἰς τὴν μισθαποδοσίαν 'for he kept looking for the reward' He 11.26; καὶ πᾶσα παράβασις καὶ παρακοὴ ἔλαβεν ἔνδικον μισθαποδοσίαν 'and

1 It is possible that τυμπανίζω implies some special form of torture, but in He 11.35 it is probably employed in a more generic sense.

every trespass and disobedience receives its just penalty' He 2.2.

38.18 μισθαποδότης, ου *m*: one who delivers reward or recompense (whether good or bad) – 'rewarder, recompenser.' ὅτι ἔστιν καὶ τοῖς ἐκζητοῦσιν αὐτὸν μισθαποδότης γίνεται 'that he exists and is the rewarder of those who seek him' He 11.6.

38.19 ἀνταποδίδωμι^b: to cause someone to suffer in turn because of actions which merit such retribution – 'to pay back, to pay in return, to repay, to cause retribution.' ἐμοὶ ἐκδίκησις, ἐγὼ ἀνταποδώσω 'retribution is mine; I will repay' Ro 12.19.

38.20 ἀνταπόδοσις, εως *f*; ἀνταπόδομα^b,

τος *n*: the recompense, whether positive or negative, which is given to someone on the basis of or in exchange for what someone has done – 'recompense, reward for what has been done.'

ἀνταπόδοσις: εἰδότες ὅτι ἀπὸ κυρίου ἀπολήμψεσθε τὴν ἀνταπόδοσιν τῆς κληρονομίας 'knowing that you will receive from the Lord an inheritance as your reward' (literally 'the reward of your inheritance') Col 3.24.

ἀνταπόδομα^b: καὶ εἰς σκάνδαλον καὶ εἰς ἀνταπόδομα αὐτοῖς 'and as something which will make them fall and be the recompense for what they have done' Ro 11.9. In Ro 11.9 one may also justifiably translate ἀνταπόδομα as 'punishment for what they have done,' since the context indicates clearly the negative aspect of the recompense.

39 Hostility, Strife[1]

Outline of Subdomains

1 Domain 39 *Hostility, Strife* involves a number of aspects of interpersonal conflict, including not only generalized opposition and division, but also overt forms of strife, persecution, attack, and conquering. Not included in this set are those meanings which involve actual military operations (see Domain 55). A number of the meanings in the area of hostility have significant psychological implications, and to a considerable extent there is some overlap with Domain 25 *Attitudes and Emotions,* but the meanings included in Domain 39 *Hostility, Strife* also involve overt forms of behavior.

A Opposition, Hostility[2] (39.1-39.12)

39.1 ἀντιτάσσομαι; ἀνθίστημι^a; ἀντίκειμαι; ἀντιδιατίθεμαι; ἐναντιόομαι: to oppose someone, involving not only a psychological attitude but also a corresponding behavior – 'to oppose, to be hostile toward, to show hostility.'[3]

ἀντιτάσσομαι: ἀντιτασσομένων δὲ αὐτῶν καὶ βλασφημούντων 'when they opposed him and said evil things about him' Ac 18.6. It may be that in some languages one can best render ἀντιτάσσομαι in Ac 18.6 as 'to speak against,' though in some languages opposition is often expressed idiomatically as 'to show a sour face toward,' 'to have a mean heart toward,' or 'to turn one's back on.'

ἀνθίστημι^a: κατὰ πρόσωπον αὐτῷ ἀντέστην 'I opposed him to the face' or '. . . openly' (see

2 For a discussion of some of the problems involved in terms for opposition and hostility, see the discussion at 39.12.

3 There are probably certain significant distinctions in meaning in the various verbs listed in 39.1, but on the basis of NT usage it is not possible to determine precisely what these distinctions may be.

83.34) or '. . . in person' (see 83.38) Ga 2.11. In translating this phrase in Ga 2.11 it may be appropriate in some languages to say 'I spoke against him with other people present.'

ἀντίκειμαι: ταῦτα λέγοντος αὐτοῦ κατῃσχύνοντο πάντες οἱ ἀντικείμενοι αὐτῷ 'his answers made all those who opposed him ashamed of themselves' Lk 13.17.

ἀντιδιατίθεμαι: ἐν πραΰτητι παιδεύοντα τοὺς ἀντιδιατιθεμένους 'with gentleness correcting those who oppose him' 2 Tm 2.25.

ἐναντιόομαι: ἐναντιούμενοι καὶ βλασφημοῦντες 'they opposed him and insulted him' Ac 13.45 (apparatus).

39.2 ἀντιστρατεύομαι: (a figurative extension of meaning of ἀντιστρατεύομαι 'to make war against, to fight against,' not occurring in the NT) to actively and strongly oppose – 'to be clearly against, to actively oppose.' βλέπω δὲ ἕτερον νόμον ἐν τοῖς μέλεσίν μου ἀντιστρατευόμενον τῷ νόμῳ τοῦ νοός μου 'I see a different law (at work) in my body, (one which) opposes the law of my mind' or '. . . the law of which my mind approves' Ro 7.23.

39.3 ἐπαίρω τὴν πτέρναν: (an idiom, literally 'to lift one's heel against') to oppose someone by turning against such a person, possibly with focus upon the initial aspect of becoming opposed to – 'to turn against, to oppose.' ὁ τρώγων μου τὸν ἄρτον ἐπῆρεν ἐπ' ἐμὲ τὴν πτέρναν αὐτοῦ 'the one who ate my food turned against me' Jn 13.18. In a number of languages a convenient way of rendering 'to turn against' may be 'to become an enemy of.'

39.4 ἐνέχω[b]: to maintain a state of antagonism or hostility – 'to be against, to be hostile toward.' ἤρξαντο οἱ γραμματεῖς καὶ οἱ Φαρισαῖοι δεινῶς ἐνέχειν 'the teachers of the Law and the Pharisees began to be very hostile' Lk 11.53. In a number of languages hostility is expressed largely in psychological terms, for example, 'to be angry at' or 'to have one's heart curdle against,' but hostility may also be expressed in terms of overt behavior, for example, 'to turn against,' 'to face away from,' or 'to turn one's back on.'

39.5 τάραχος[a]**, ου** *m*: a serious disturbance – 'commotion, serious trouble.' ἐγένετο δὲ κατὰ τὸν καιρὸν ἐκεῖνον τάραχος οὐκ ὀλίγος περὶ τῆς ὁδοῦ 'at that time, serious trouble arose concerning the Way' Ac 19.23.

39.6 ἐναντίος[b]**, α, ον; ὑπεναντίος, α, ον; ἐξ ἐναντίας**[b]: pertaining to being hostile toward – 'hostile, one who is hostile.'[4]

ἐναντίος[b]: θεῷ μὴ ἀρεσκόντων, καὶ πᾶσιν ἀνθρώποις ἐναντίων 'they were displeasing to God and hostile to all people' 1 Th 2.15.

ὑπεναντίος: πυρὸς ζῆλος ἐσθίειν μέλλοντος τοὺς ὑπεναντίους 'the fierce fire which will destroy those who are hostile (toward God)' He 10.27.

ἐξ ἐναντίας[b]: λόγον ὑγιῆ ἀκατάγνωστον, ἵνα ὁ ἐξ ἐναντίας ἐντραπῇ '(use) sound words that cannot be criticized, so that those who are hostile (to you) may be put to shame' Tt 2.8.

39.7 ἐριθεία[b]**, ας** *f*: a feeling of hostility or opposition – 'hostility, being against.' οἱ δὲ ἐξ ἐριθείας τὸν Χριστὸν καταγγέλλουσιν 'but they announce Christ out of a sense of hostility' Php 1.17. It is also possible to understand ἐριθεία in Php 1.17 as meaning 'selfish ambition' or 'rivalry' (see 88.167).

39.8 παροτρύνω; συγκινέω: to stir up hostility against – 'to stir up, to incite to.'

παροτρύνω: οἱ δὲ Ἰουδαῖοι παρώτρυναν τὰς σεβομένας γυναῖκας τὰς εὐσχήμονας 'but the Jews stirred up the devout women of high social standing' Ac 13.50.

συγκινέω: συνεκίνησάν τε τὸν λαὸν καὶ τοὺς πρεσβυτέρους καὶ τοὺς γραμματεῖς 'and they incited the people, the elders, and the teachers of the Law' Ac 6.12.

39.9 ἀντίδικος[b]**, ου** *m*: one who is actively and continuously hostile toward someone – 'adversary, enemy.' ὁ ἀντίδικος ὑμῶν διάβολος ὡς λέων ὠρυόμενος περιπατεῖ 'your adversary, the Devil, roams around like a roaring lion' 1 Pe 5.8.

39.10 ἔχθρα, ας *f*: a state of enmity with someone – 'enmity, being an enemy of.' οὐκ

---

4 It is possible that ὑπεναντίος is somewhat stronger in meaning than ἐναντίος[b], but this cannot be shown from NT contexts.

οἴδατε ὅτι ἡ φιλία τοῦ κόσμου ἔχθρα τοῦ θεοῦ ἐστιν; 'do you not know that being friendly with the world means being at enmity with God?' Jas 4.4.

39.11 ἐχθρός, ά, όν: pertaining to being at enmity with someone – 'being an enemy, in opposition to.' ἐχθροὶ ὄντες κατηλλάγημεν τῷ θεῷ διὰ τοῦ θανάτου τοῦ υἱοῦ αὐτοῦ 'being enemies we were reconciled to God through the death of his Son' Ro 5.10; κατὰ μὲν τὸ εὐαγγέλιον ἐχθροὶ δι' ὑμᾶς 'with respect to the good news, they are enemies for your sake' Ro 11.28.

39.12 ἀλλότριος^c, α, ον: pertaining to being opposed as a result of one's being essentially different – 'to be strongly opposed to, to be an enemy of.' ἐγενήθησαν ἰσχυροὶ ἐν πολέμῳ, παρεμβολὰς ἔκλιναν ἀλλοτρίων 'they became strong in battle and defeated the armies of their enemies' He 11.34.

Meanings involving enmity, hostility, and opposition are frequently idiomatic in nature and are derived primarily from four major experiential sources: (1) psychological attitudes, 'to have one's heart burn against'; (2) gestures, 'to frown against' or 'to refuse to snap fingers' (snapping fingers being a particular form of greeting in various parts of Africa); (3) body stance, 'to stand against'; and (4) movement, 'to turn one's back against' or 'to turn away from.'

B Division (39.13-39.17)

39.13 σχίσμα^b, τος n; διχοστασία, ας f: a division into opposing groups, generally two – 'division, discord.'
σχίσμα^b: σχίσμα οὖν ἐγένετο ἐν τῷ ὄχλῳ δι' αὐτόν 'so there came a division in the crowd because of him' Jn 7.43.
διχοστασία: σκοπεῖν τοὺς τὰς διχοστασίας . . . ποιοῦντας 'watch out for people who cause divisions' Ro 16.17.

In some languages the equivalent of 'causing division' is literally 'to cause two groups in place of one group,' but more frequently the equivalent is expressed in terms of attitudes, for example, 'to cause people to be angry at one another' or 'to cause people not to like one another' or 'to cause people to think of one another as enemies.'

39.14 διαμερίζω^b; διαμερισμός, οῦ m: to be divided into opposing and hostile units – 'to be opposed to, to be against, division, opposition, hostility.'
διαμερίζω^b: ἔσονται γὰρ ἀπὸ τοῦ νῦν πέντε ἐν ἑνὶ οἴκῳ διαμεμερισμένοι, τρεῖς ἐπὶ δυσὶν καὶ δύο ἐπὶ τρισίν 'for from now on a family of five will be divided, three against two and two against three' Lk 12.52.
διαμερισμός: δοκεῖτε ὅτι εἰρήνην παρεγενόμην δοῦναι ἐν τῇ γῇ; οὐχί, λέγω ὑμῖν, ἀλλ' ἢ διαμερισμόν 'do you suppose that I came to bring peace to the world? No, I tell you, but rather division' Lk 12.51.

39.15 πῦρ βάλλω: (an idiom, literally 'to throw fire') to cause discord and contention – 'to cause discord, to cause division.' πῦρ ἦλθον βαλεῖν ἐπὶ τὴν γῆν 'I came to bring division into the world' Lk 12.49. Some translators have preferred to retain the literal rendering of this expression in Lk 12.49, since this seems to be necessary in view of the larger figurative context, which speaks of 'how I wish it were already kindled' (τί θέλω εἰ ἤδη ἀνήφθη). A strictly literal translation may, however, be understood in a completely physical sense, namely, 'to set the world on fire.' There are a number of quite diverse interpretations of the significance of this expression in Lk 12.49. Some have assumed, for example, that it refers to the fire of Pentecost.

39.16 ἀποδιορίζω^a: to cause or instigate divisions between people – 'to cause divisions.' οὗτοί εἰσιν οἱ ἀποδιορίζοντες 'these are the ones who cause divisions' Jd 19. 'To cause divisions' may be expressed in a number of languages in idiomatic ways, for example, 'to cause people to turn their backs on one another' or 'to cause people to no longer speak to one another' or 'to cause people to form parties against one another.' For another interpretation of ἀποδιορίζω in Jd 19, see 30.116.

39.17 αἱρετικός, ή, όν: (derivative of αἵρεσις^c 'division,' 63.27) pertaining to causing divi-

sions – 'divisive, one who causes divisions.'
αἱρετικὸν ἄνθρωπον μετὰ μίαν καὶ δευτέραν
νουθεσίαν παραιτοῦ 'reject a person who causes
divisions after at least two warnings' (literally
'after a first and second warning') or 'give at
least two warnings to the person who causes
divisions, and then have nothing more to do
with him' Tt 3.10.

C Resistance (39.18-39.20)

39.18 ἀνθίστημι[b]; ἀντικαθίστημι; ἀντιπίπτω: to resist by actively opposing pressure
or power – 'to resist.'
ἀνθίστημι[b]: ἵνα δυνηθῆτε ἀντιστῆναι ἐν τῇ ἡμέρᾳ
τῇ πονηρᾷ 'so that you will be able to resist
when the evil day comes' Eph 6.13.
ἀντικαθίστημι: οὔπω μέχρις αἵματος ἀντικατέστητε πρὸς τὴν ἁμαρτίαν ἀνταγωνιζόμενοι 'for
in your struggle against sin you have not yet
resisted to the point of being killed' He 12.4.
ἀντιπίπτω: ὑμεῖς ἀεὶ τῷ πνεύματι τῷ ἁγίῳ
ἀντιπίπτετε 'you always resist the Holy Spirit'
Ac 7.51.
In a number of languages one may appropriately translate 'to resist' in a number of
contexts as 'to fight back against' or 'to oppose in return.' In some contexts, however,
such as Ac 7.51, the meaning may perhaps be
best expressed by a negation, for example,
'you have never been willing to yield to the
Holy Spirit.'

39.19 πρὸς κέντρα λακτίζω: (an idiom,
literally 'to kick against the goad') to react
against authority in such a way as to cause
harm or suffering to oneself – 'to hurt oneself
by reacting against a person or command.'
Σαούλ, τί με διώκεις; σκληρόν σοι πρὸς κέντρα
λακτίζειν 'Saul, why are you persecuting me?
You are hurting yourself by your resistance'
Ac 26.14.

39.20 ὑπομένω[a]: to resist by holding one's
ground – 'to resist, to hold one's ground, to
not be moved.' μακάριος ἀνὴρ ὃς ὑπομένει
πειρασμόν 'happy is the man who holds his
ground when he is tempted' Jas 1.12. For
another interpretation of ὑπομένω in Jas 1.12,
see 68.17.

D Yielding (39.21)

39.21 εἴκω; ἐπιδίδωμι[b]: to give in to a superior power or force – 'to give in to, to surrender, to yield.'
εἴκω: οἷς οὐδὲ πρὸς ὥραν εἴξαμεν 'we did not
give in to them for a minute' (literally '. . . for
an hour') Ga 2.5.
ἐπιδίδωμι[b]: μὴ δυναμένου ἀντοφθαλμεῖν τῷ
ἀνέμῳ ἐπιδόντες ἐφερόμεθα 'since it was impossible to keep (the ship) headed into the
wind, we yielded (to the wind) and were carried along' Ac 27.15.

E Strife, Struggle (39.22-39.32)

39.22 ἔρις[a], ιδος f: conflict resulting from
rivalry and discord – 'strife, discord.'[5] ὅπου
γὰρ ἐν ὑμῖν ζῆλος καὶ ἔρις, οὐχὶ σαρκικοί ἐστε;
'when there is jealousy and strife among you,
doesn't this prove that you are people of this
world?' 1 Cor 3.3. In a number of languages
the type of strife referred to by ἔρις[a] is frequently described as verbal, for example,
'always saying bad things about one another'
or 'never having a good word to say to one
another.' See also 33.447.

39.23 μάχομαι; μάχη, ης f: serious conflict,
either physical or non-physical, but clearly intensive and bitter – 'to clash severely, struggle, fight.'
μάχομαι: τῇ τε ἐπιούσῃ ἡμέρᾳ ὤφθη αὐτοῖς μαχ-
ομένοις καὶ συνήλλασσεν αὐτοὺς εἰς εἰρήνην 'the
next day he saw two men fighting, and he
tried to make peace between them' Ac 7.26;
ἐμάχοντο οὖν πρὸς ἀλλήλους οἱ Ἰουδαῖοι 'then
the Jews clashed severely among themselves'
Jn 6.52.
μάχη: ἐν παντὶ θλιβόμενοι· ἔξωθεν μάχαι, ἔσωθεν φόβοι 'there were troubles everywhere;
struggles with people around us, fears in our
hearts' 2 Cor 7.5.
In order to suggest something of the intensity of conflict in μάχομαι and μάχη, it may be
useful in some instances to employ similes in

---

5 It is possible that in all instances of ἔρις[a] the nature of
the conflict is specifically verbal, and therefore may be
regarded as essentially equivalent to ἔρις[b] 'quarreling'
(33.447).

the rendering of these terms, for example, 'they opposed one another just as though they were actually fighting one another' or 'they are fighting, as it were.'

39.24 ἄμαχος, ον: pertaining to a lack of conflict and contention – 'not contentious, peaceful.' ἐπιεικῆ, ἄμαχον, ἀφιλάργυρον 'gentle, peaceful, without love for money' 1 Tm 3.3.

39.25 μάχαιραᵈ, ης f: (a figurative extension of meaning of μάχαιραᵃ 'sword,' 6.33) a state of discord and strife – 'violence, strife, discord.' οὐκ ἦλθον βαλεῖν εἰρήνην ἀλλὰ μάχαιραν 'I did not come to bring peace but discord' Mt 10.34. For another interpretation of μάχαιρα in Mt 10.34, see 55.6.

39.26 πολεμέωᵇ; πόλεμοςᵇ, ου m: (figurative extensions of meaning of πολεμέωᵃ and πόλεμοςᵃ 'to wage war,' 55.5) to engage in serious and protracted conflict, often involving a series of attacks – 'to fight, to war against.'
πολεμέωᵇ: ζηλοῦτε, καὶ οὐ δύνασθε ἐπιτυχεῖν· μάχεσθε καὶ πολεμεῖτε 'you covet things but you cannot get them, so you clash and fight' Jas 4.2.
πόλεμοςᵇ: πόθεν πόλεμοι καὶ πόθεν μάχαι ἐν ὑμῖν; 'where do (all the) struggles and fights among you come from?' Jas 4.1.

39.27 διαμάχομαι: to fight or contend with, involving severity and thoroughness – 'to protest strongly, to contend with.' τινὲς τῶν γραμματέων τοῦ μέρους τῶν Φαρισαίων διεμάχοντο 'some scribes from the party of the Pharisees protested strongly' Ac 23.9.

39.28 θηριομαχέω: (a figurative extension of meaning of θηριομαχέω 'to be forced to fight with wild animals,' not occurring in the NT) to be in conflict with forceful opposition – 'to be in a serious struggle with, to have to contend with.' εἰ κατὰ ἄνθρωπον ἐθηριομάχησα ἐν Ἐφέσῳ, τί μοι τὸ ὄφελος; 'if I was in serious conflict in Ephesus simply from human motives, what advantage have I gained?' 1 Cor 15.32. Some persons have assumed that θηριομαχέω in 1 Cor 15.32 is to be understood in a literal sense, but this is very unlikely. One can, however, preserve something of the figurative force of this expression by rendering this question in 1 Cor 15.32 as 'if I have, as it were, fought "wild beasts" here in Ephesus simply from human motives, what have I gained?' (TEV). By making a metaphor into a simile one can preserve something of the figurative value of the phrase, while at the same time not introducing possible misunderstanding.

39.29 ἀγωνίζομαιᵃ; ἀγώνᵃ, ῶνος m; πάλη, ης f: to engage in intense struggle, involving physical or nonphysical force against strong opposition – 'to struggle, to fight.'
ἀγωνίζομαιᵃ: εἰ ἐκ τοῦ κόσμου τούτου ἦν ἡ βασιλεία ἡ ἐμή, οἱ ὑπηρέται οἱ ἐμοὶ ἠγωνίζοντο 'if my kingdom belonged to this world, my followers would fight' Jn 18.36.
ἀγώνᵃ: τὸν αὐτὸν ἀγῶνα ἔχοντες οἷον εἴδετε ἐν ἐμοί 'now you can be engaged in the same struggle which you saw I had to struggle' Php 1.30.
πάλη: οὐκ ἔστιν ἡμῖν ἡ πάλη πρὸς αἷμα καὶ σάρκα, ἀλλὰ πρὸς τὰς ἀρχάς 'it is not against human beings that we fight but against spiritual forces' Eph 6.12.
In a number of languages a marked distinction is made between physical fighting and nonphysical contending with someone. It is therefore often impossible to carry over any terminology involving war or physical struggling to contexts in which one is speaking of interpersonal hostility or contention.

39.30 ἐπαγωνίζομαι: to exert intense effort on behalf of something – 'to struggle for.' παρακαλῶν ἐπαγωνίζεσθαι τῇ . . . πίστει 'to encourage you to struggle for the . . . faith' Jd 3.

39.31 ἀνταγωνίζομαι: to engage in an intense struggle against something or someone – 'to struggle against.' οὔπω μέχρις αἵματος ἀντικατέστητε πρὸς τὴν ἁμαρτίαν ἀνταγωνιζόμενοι 'in your struggle against sin you have not yet resisted to the point of being killed' He 12.4. In a number of languages one cannot use a term in He 12.4 which would suggest physical struggle, for essentially this is psychological opposition. In some cases the appropriate equivalent would be 'to do all you can to oppose sin' or 'to do everything possible against evil.'

39.32 θεομάχος, ον: pertaining to fighting against God – 'to fight against God, to be against God, to be an enemy of God.' μήποτε καὶ θεομάχοι εὑρεθῆτε 'lest you find yourselves fighting against God' Ac 5.39. Although the figurative expression 'fighting against God' is an unusual and radical figure of speech, it can often be translated more or less literally, but in some languages such an expression is regarded as both impossible and even ludicrous, and therefore one must employ some such expression as 'to be a constant enemy of God' or 'to be always against God.'

F Revenge (39.33)

39.33 ἐκδικέω[b]; ἐκδίκησις[b], εως f: to repay harm with harm, on the assumption that the initial harm was unjustified and that retribution is therefore called for – 'to pay back, to revenge, to seek retribution, retribution, seeking retribution.'

ἐκδικέω[b]: μὴ ἑαυτοὺς ἐκδικοῦντες, ἀγαπητοί 'never take revenge, my friends' Ro 12.19.

ἐκδίκησις[b]: ἐμοὶ ἐκδίκησις, ἐγὼ ἀνταποδώσω, λέγει κύριος 'the responsibility for seeking retribution is mine; I will pay back, says the Lord' Ro 12.19.

G Rebellion (39.34-39.41)

39.34 ἀνίσταμαι[e]; ἐπανίσταμαι; στάσις[a], εως f; ἐπίστασις[b], εως f; ἀποστασία, ας f; ἀκαταστασία[a], ας f: to rise up in open defiance of authority, with the presumed intention to overthrow it or to act in complete opposition to its demands – 'to rebel against, to revolt, to engage in insurrection, rebellion.'[6]

---

6 It is possible that ἐπανίσταμαι and ἐπίστασις[b], with the prefix ἐπι-, differ in some measure from ἀνίσταμαι[e] and στάσις[a] by virtue of the prefixal element which may suggest action directed specifically toward some object, but there is insufficient contextual evidence to support such distinct meanings. It is also possible that ἀποστασία differs slightly in meaning from ἐπίστασις[b] by virtue of the differences in prefixal formation, but there is insufficient contextual evidence to support such a view.

ἀνίσταμαι[e]: πρὸ γὰρ τούτων τῶν ἡμερῶν ἀνέστη Θευδᾶς . . . καὶ ἐγένοντο εἰς οὐδέν 'some time ago Theudas rebelled . . . but they came to nothing' or '. . . the movement died out' Ac 5.36.

ἐπανίσταμαι: ἐπαναστήσονται τέκνα ἐπὶ γονεῖς καὶ θανατώσουσιν αὐτούς 'children will rise up (or '. . . rebel') against their parents and have them put to death' Mk 13.12.

στάσις[a]: γὰρ κινδυνεύομεν ἐγκαλεῖσθαι στάσεως περὶ τῆς σήμερον 'for there is danger that we will be accused of insurrection in what has happened today' Ac 19.40.

ἐπίστασις[b]: οὔτε . . . εὑρόν με . . . ἐπίστασιν ποιοῦντα ὄχλου 'they did not find me . . . organizing a rebellion of the people' Ac 24.12.

ἀποστασία: ὅτι ἐὰν μὴ ἔλθῃ ἡ ἀποστασία πρῶτον 'for not until the final rebellion takes place' 2 Th 2.3.

ἀκαταστασία[a]: ὅταν δὲ ἀκούσητε πολέμους καὶ ἀκαταστασίας, μὴ πτοηθῆτε 'do not be afraid when you hear of wars and revolts' Lk 21.9. It is possible that ἀκαταστασία in Lk 21.9 denotes merely unsettled conditions, but it is far more likely to carry the meaning of 'insurrections' and 'revolts.'

39.35 ἀντιλογία[c], ας f: rebellion against authority, with special focus upon verbal opposition – 'rebellion, strong opposition, defiance.' καὶ τῇ ἀντιλογίᾳ τοῦ Κόρε 'and (they have been destroyed) by the (kind of) defiance of Korah' Jd 11; ἀναλογίσασθε γὰρ τὸν τοιαύτην ὑπομεμενηκότα ὑπὸ τῶν ἁμαρτωλῶν εἰς ἑαυτὸν ἀντιλογίαν 'think of how he put up with so much defiance on the part of sinners against himself' He 12.3.

39.36 ἀκαταστασία[b], ας f: violent opposition to someone or something, involving mob action – 'riot, being mobbed.'[7] ἐν πληγαῖς, ἐν φυλακαῖς, ἐν ἀκαταστασίαις 'we had been beaten, jailed, and mobbed' 2 Cor 6.5.

39.37 στασιαστής, οῦ m (derivative of στάσις[a] 'insurrection,' 39.34); λῃστής[b], οῦ m: a

---

7 ἀκαταστασία[b] differs from ἀκαταστασία[a] 'revolt, rebellion' (39.34) in that the violent opposition is directed against some person or local circumstance, rather than against governmental authority.

person who engages in insurrection – 'insurrectionist, rebel.'
στασιαστής: Βαραββᾶς μετὰ στασιαστῶν δεδεμένος οἵτινες ἐν τῇ στάσει φόνον πεποιήκεισαν
'Barabbas who was in prison with the rebels
who had committed murder in the uprising'
Mk 15.7.
λῃστής[b]: ἦν δὲ ὁ Βαραββᾶς λῃστής 'and Barabbas was an insurrectionist' Jn 18.40.

39.38 ἐπαίρομαι[a]: (a figurative extension of
meaning of ἐπαίρομαι 'to rise up,' not occurring in the NT) to rise up in opposition against
– 'to rise up against.' καθαιροῦντες καὶ πᾶν
ὕψωμα ἐπαιρόμενον κατὰ τῆς γνώσεως τοῦ θεοῦ
'we pull down every proud obstacle that is
raised up against the knowledge of God'
2 Cor 10.4-5.

39.39 ὑπεραίρομαι[b]: to exalt oneself in pride
against someone or something – 'to rise up in
pride against.' ὁ ἀντικείμενος καὶ ὑπεραιρόμενος
ἐπὶ πάντα λεγόμενον θεόν 'the one opposing
and rising up in pride against any so-called
god' 2 Th 2.4.
ὑπεραίρομαι[b] involves two distinct types of
components: (1) the development of opposition, and (2) the psychological basis for
such opposition, namely, pride. In almost all
instances it will be necessary to represent the
two complementary components by a phrasal
equivalent, for example, 'to be proud and to
rise up against' or 'because of one's pride, to
rise up in opposition to.'

39.40 παραπικραίνω; παραπικρασμός, οῦ
m: to rebel, with the implication of provoking
to anger – 'to rebel, to rebel and provoke to
anger.'
παραπικραίνω: τίνες γὰρ ἀκούσαντες παρεπί-
κραναν; 'for who were those who heard (God's
voice) and yet rebelled (against him)?' He 3.16.
παραπικρασμός: μὴ σκληρύνητε τὰς καρδίας
ὑμῶν ὡς ἐν τῷ παραπικρασμῷ 'do not be stubborn as you were when you rebelled (against
God)' He 3.8.

39.41 ἀναστατόω; ἀφίστημι; διχάζω: to
cause people to rebel against or to reject
authority – 'to incite to revolt, to cause to
rebel.'

ἀναστατόω: οὐκ ἄρα σὺ εἶ ὁ Αἰγύπτιος ὁ πρὸ
τούτων τῶν ἡμερῶν ἀναστατώσας 'then you are
not that Egyptian who some time ago started
a rebellion' Ac 21.38.
ἀφίστημι: ἀπέστησεν λαὸν ὀπίσω αὐτοῦ 'he incited a crowd to follow him in revolt' Ac 5.37.
διχάζω: ἦλθον γὰρ διχάσαι ἄνθρωπον κατὰ τοῦ
πατρὸς αὐτοῦ 'I came to stir up a man in rebellion against his father' Mt 10.35.

H Riot[8] (39.42-39.44)

39.42 θόρυβος[b], ου m; ταραχή[b], ῆς f:
disorderly behavior of people in violent opposition to authority – 'riot.'
θόρυβος[b]: ἔλεγον δέ, Μὴ ἐν τῇ ἑορτῇ, ἵνα μὴ
θόρυβος γένηται ἐν τῷ λαῷ 'we must not do it
during the feast, they said, or the people will
riot' Mt 26.5.
ταραχή[b]: λιμοὶ καὶ ταραχαί 'famines and riots'
Mk 13.8 (apparatus).

39.43 σύγχυσις, εως f; συστροφή[a], ῆς f: disorderly mob revolt, with special implications
of uproar and disturbance – 'uproar, revolt.'
σύγχυσις: ἐπλήσθη ἡ πόλις τῆς συγχύσεως 'the
uproar spread throughout the whole city' (literally 'the city was filled with uproar') Ac
19.29.
συστροφή[a]: μηδενὸς αἰτίου ὑπάρχοντος, περὶ οὗ
οὐ δυνησόμεθα ἀποδοῦναι λόγον περὶ τῆς
συστροφῆς ταύτης 'there is no excuse for all
this uproar and we would not be able to give a
good reason for it' Ac 19.40.
In a number of languages the meaning of
'riot' may be best expressed as 'people
shouting strongly against' or 'people shouting
and fighting against' or 'a mob shouting
against the government.'

**39.44 θορυβέω; ἀνασείω; κινέω[d]; ταράσ-
σω[c]; ἐκταράσσω; ἐπισείω; σαλεύω[b]**: to cause

---

8 In all of the meanings in the subdomain of *Riot*,
there are several significant components: (1) noise or
uproar; (2) disorder and tumult; (3) a relatively large
group; and (4) serious conflicts of interest. Particularly
in view of the components of noise and disorder, the
meanings in this subdomain differ significantly from
those in Subdomain G *Rebellion*.

people to riot against – 'to stir up against, to start a riot, to cause an uproar.'

θορυβέω: ὀχλοποιήσαντες ἐθορύβουν τὴν πόλιν 'they formed a mob and caused an uproar in the city' Ac 17.5.

ἀνασείω: ἀνασείει τὸν λαὸν διδάσκων 'he is starting a riot among the people with his teaching' Lk 23.5.

κινέω^d: ἐκινήθη τε ἡ πόλις ὅλη 'the whole city was set in an uproar' Ac 21.30.

ταράσσω^c: ἐτάραξαν δὲ τὸν ὄχλον 'they caused the crowd to riot' or 'they threw the crowd into an uproar' Ac 17.8.

ἐκταράσσω: οὗτοι οἱ ἄνθρωποι ἐκταράσσουσιν ἡμῶν τὴν πόλιν Ἰουδαῖοι ὑπάρχοντες 'these men are Jews and they are stirring up people in our city' Ac 16.20.

ἐπισείω: ἐπεισείσαντες τοὺς ὄχλους 'they incited the crowds' Ac 14.19 (apparatus).

σαλεύω^b: σαλεύοντες . . . τοὺς ὄχλους 'they incited . . . the crowds' Ac 17.13.

I   Persecution (39.45-39.46)

39.45 διώκω^c; ἐκδιώκω^b; διωγμός, οῦ m: to systematically organize a program to oppress and harass people – 'to persecute, to harass, persecution.'[9]

διώκω^c: μακάριοι οἱ δεδιωγμένοι ἕνεκεν δικαιοσύνης 'happy are those who suffer persecution because they do what God requires' Mt 5.10.

ἐκδιώκω^b: τῶν καὶ τὸν κύριον ἀποκτεινάντων Ἰησοῦν καὶ τοὺς προφήτας, καὶ ἡμᾶς ἐκδιωξάντων 'they killed the Lord Jesus and the prophets, and persecuted us' 1 Th 2.15.[10] For another interpretation of ἐκδιώκω in 1 Th 2.15, see 15.159.

διωγμός: ἐγένετο δὲ ἐν ἐκείνῃ τῇ ἡμέρᾳ διωγμὸς μέγας ἐπὶ τὴν ἐκκλησίαν 'that very day the church began to suffer a cruel persecution' Ac 8.1.

In a number of languages the equivalent of 'to persecute' is simply 'to cause to suffer,' but persecution is also expressed in terms of 'to be mean to' or 'to threaten' or 'to chase from place to place.'

39.46 διώκτης, ου m: (derivative of διώκω^c 'to persecute,' 39.45) a person who engages in persecuting others – 'persecutor.' τὸ πρότερον ὄντα βλάσφημον καὶ διώκτην καὶ ὑβριστήν 'even though in the past I was a person who spoke evil of him, and persecuted him, and insulted him' 1 Tm 1.13.

J   Attack[11] (39.47-39.50)

39.47 ἐφίσταμαι^d (and 2nd aorist active); κατεφίσταμαι (and 2nd aorist active); ἐπέρχομαι^b; ἐπιτίθεμαι^b: to use sudden physical force against someone as the outgrowth of a hostile attitude – 'to attack, to assault.'[12]

ἐφίσταμαι^d: ἐπιστάντες τῇ οἰκίᾳ Ἰάσονος ἐζήτουν αὐτοὺς προαγαγεῖν εἰς τὸν δῆμον 'they attacked the home of Jason, trying to bring them out to the people' Ac 17.5. Although according to the Greek text the attack was made on the home of Jason, the actual objects of the attack were the persons in the home, though the attack may very well have involved battering down the door, and in some languages it may be necessary to make explicit this aspect of the attack.

κατεφίσταμαι: κατεπέστησαν ὁμοθυμαδὸν οἱ Ἰουδαῖοι τῷ Παύλῳ καὶ ἤγαγον αὐτὸν ἐπὶ τὸ βῆμα 'the Jews attacked Paul with one accord and took him into court' Ac 18.12.

ἐπέρχομαι^b: ἐπὰν δὲ ἰσχυρότερος αὐτοῦ ἐπελθὼν νικήσῃ αὐτόν 'but when a stronger man attacks him and defeats him' Lk 11.22.

ἐπιτίθεμαι^b: οὐδεὶς ἐπιθήσεταί σοι τοῦ κακῶσαί

---

9 Some persons have contended that ἐκδιώκω^b is an intensive of διώκω^c with the resulting meaning of 'to persecute harshly.' However, general Greek usage and particularly NT contexts do not seem to bear out any such consistent distinctions in meaning.

10 In a parallel type of context, Lk 11.49 reads ἐξ αὐτῶν ἀποκτενοῦσιν καὶ διώξουσιν 'they will kill some and persecute others,' for which some manuscripts read ἐκδιώξουσιν in place of διώξουσιν.

11 In Subdomain J *Attack*, the sense of 'attack' as organized warfare is not included (for this meaning, see Domain 55 *Military Activities*). In Domain 39 the meanings involve opposition to individuals or groups, but with special emphasis upon hostile attitudes. There is, however, some overlapping with Domain 19 *Physical Impact* and Domain 20 *Violence, Harm, Destroy, Kill*.

12 It is possible that κατεφίσταμαι is somewhat stronger in meaning than ἐφίσταμαι^d, but it is impossible to be certain of such a distinction on the basis of NT contexts.

σε 'no one will assault you to do you harm' Ac 18.10.

In a number of languages the equivalent of 'to attack' is simply 'to start fighting against.' In some languages, however, the equivalent is 'to jump on' or 'to grab to do harm to.'

39.48 καταλαμβάνω[b]: to attack, with the implication of gaining control over – 'to attack, to overpower.' ὅπου ἐὰν αὐτὸν καταλάβῃ ῥήσσει αὐτόν 'whenever (the evil spirit) attacks him, it throws him to the ground' Mk 9.18. The attack upon a person by a demon is often expressed idiomatically, for example, 'to ride a person,' 'to seize a person's mind,' or 'to grab a person's inner life.'

39.49 ἁρπάζω[b]: to attack. with the implication of seizing – 'to attack, to seize.' ὁ λύκος ἁρπάζει αὐτὰ καὶ σκορπίζει 'so the wolf attacks (the sheep) and scatters them' Jn 10.12.

It is also possible that in Mt 11.12 ἁρπάζω is to be understood in the sense of 'attack': βιασταὶ ἁρπάζουσιν αὐτήν 'violent men attack it.'

39.50 συνεπιτίθεμαι; συνεφίσταμαι (and 2nd aorist active): to join in attacking – 'to join in an attack.'
συνεπιτίθεμαι: συνεπέθεντο δὲ καὶ οἱ Ἰουδαῖοι φάσκοντες ταῦτα οὕτως ἔχειν 'the Jews also joined in the attack and said that (all) this was true' Ac 24.9. In Ac 24.9 συνεπιτίθεμαι does not involve physical force but strong verbal opposition. It may therefore be more appropriate to translate 'they opposed him strongly with their words' or 'they spoke very strongly against him.'
συνεφίσταμαι: συνεπέστη ὁ ὄχλος κατ' αὐτῶν 'the crowd joined the attack against them' Ac 16.22.

K Ambush (39.51)

39.51 ἐνεδρεύω[a]; **ἐνέδρα, ας** *f*: to conceal oneself or to proceed secretly, while waiting for an appropriate opportunity to attack – 'to be in an ambush, to make plans for a secret attack, ambush.'
ἐνεδρεύω[a]: σὺ οὖν μὴ πεισθῇς αὐτοῖς· ἐνεδρεύουσιν γὰρ αὐτὸν ἐξ αὐτῶν ἄνδρες πλείους τεσσερά-

κοντα 'but don't listen to them, because there are more than forty men among them who are secretly waiting to attack him' Ac 23.21.
ἐνέδρα: ἀκούσας δὲ ὁ υἱὸς τῆς ἀδελφῆς Παύλου τὴν ἐνέδραν 'and when the son of Paul's sister heard about the ambush' Ac 23.16.

Since ambushing is such a widespread method of warfare and private attack, there is usually little or no difficulty involved in finding an appropriate term and using it in what might be called an anticipatory sense, that is to say, the employment of an ambush despite the fact that it was not finally successful.

L Conquer[13] **(39.52-39.61)**

39.52 καταγωνίζομαι: to gain complete victory over, as the result of a strenuous struggle – 'to conquer, to be victorious over.' οἳ διὰ πίστεως κατηγωνίσαντο βασιλείας 'by faith they conquered kingdoms' He 11.33.

39.53 συντρίβω[c]: (a figurative extension of meaning of συντρίβω[b] 'to crush,' 19.46) to overcome, with the resulting crushing of the power of the opposition – 'to completely overcome, to crush.' ὁ δὲ θεὸς τῆς εἰρήνης συντρίψει τὸν Σατανᾶν 'the God of peace will crush Satan' Ro 16.20.

39.54 πατέω[d]: (a figurative extension of meaning of πατέω[b] 'to trample,' 19.51) to conquer and keep under subjection – 'to conquer, to tread down.' Ἰερουσαλὴμ ἔσται πατουμένη ὑπὸ ἐθνῶν 'Jerusalem will be conquered by the Gentiles' Lk 21.24. For another interpretation of πατέω in Lk 21.24, see 20.22.

39.55 κατακυριεύω[b]: to subject someone or something to a superior force – 'to overpower.' ἐν ᾧ ἦν τὸ πνεῦμα τὸ πονηρὸν κατακυριεύσας ἀμφοτέρων ἴσχυσεν κατ' αὐτῶν '(the man) who had the evil spirit in him overpowered both of them and defeated them' Ac 19.16. In some languages 'to overpower' is 'to fight successfully against' or 'to fight someone and to win.'

13 Subdomain L *Conquer* differs significantly from Subdomain J *Attack* in that the result of the attack is successful and the attacking party gains complete dominance.

39.56 κατισχύω^c: to prevail over something or some person so as to be able to defeat, with the implication that the successful participant has greater strength – 'to defeat, to prevail over.' ἐπὶ ταύτῃ τῇ πέτρᾳ οἰκοδομήσω μου τὴν ἐκκλησίαν, καὶ πύλαι ᾅδου οὐ κατισχύσουσιν αὐτῆς 'on this rock I will build my church and not even death will be able to defeat it' Mt 16.18. In some languages it may be impossible to personify 'death' and thus make it an agent of 'defeating.' However, it is possible to retain some of the figurative meaning involved, at least in some languages, by translating 'and my church will never die out' or 'and my church will never die.'

39.57 νικάω; νίκη, ης *f*; νῖκος, ους *n*: to win a victory over – 'to be victorious over, to be a victor, to conquer, victory.'
νικάω: πᾶν τὸ γεγεννημένον ἐκ τοῦ θεοῦ νικᾷ τὸν κόσμον 'every child of God is victorious over the world' 1 Jn 5.4. In 1 Jn 5.4 'the world' must be understood in terms of the value system of the world. In a number of languages the closest equivalent of 'to be victorious over' is 'to defeat.'
νίκη: αὕτη ἐστὶν ἡ νίκη ἡ νικήσασα τὸν κόσμον, ἡ πίστις ἡμῶν 'this is how we win the victory over the world: with our faith' 1 Jn 5.4.
νῖκος: τῷ δὲ θεῷ χάρις τῷ διδόντι ἡμῖν τὸ νῖκος διὰ τοῦ κυρίου ἡμῶν Ἰησοῦ Χριστοῦ 'thanks be to God who gives us the victory through our Lord Jesus Christ' 1 Cor 15.57.

39.58 ὑπερνικάω: to be completely and overwhelmingly victorious – 'to be completely victorious, to have complete victory over.' ἐν τούτοις πᾶσιν ὑπερνικῶμεν διὰ τοῦ ἀγαπήσαντος ἡμᾶς 'in all these things we have complete victory through him who loved us' Ro 8.37.

39.59 θριαμβεύω^a: (a figurative extension of meaning of θριαμβεύω 'to lead prisoners of war in a victory procession,' not occurring in the NT) to demonstrate one's successful conquest of opposition – 'to triumph over, to be completely victorious over.' ἐδειγμάτισεν ἐν παρρησίᾳ θριαμβεύσας αὐτούς 'he made a public spectacle of them by being completely victorious over them' or '. . . by leading them as captives in his victory procession' Col 2.15. Since the leading of prisoners of war in a victory procession is at the present time a relatively rare cultural phenomenon, it may be impossible to employ such a literal rendering of θριαμβεύω. One may, however, wish to employ a marginal note to indicate the background meaning of θριαμβεύω in this context.

39.60 θριαμβεύω^b: to cause someone to completely triumph over – 'to cause to triumph.' τῷ δὲ θεῷ χάρις τῷ πάντοτε θριαμβεύοντι ἡμᾶς ἐν τῷ Χριστῷ 'but thanks be to God who always caused us to triumph in union with Christ' 2 Cor 2.14. In a number of languages it is difficult to speak of 'triumphing' without indicating the goal of such an event, but in 2 Cor 2.14 there is no specified object over which triumph occurs. It is possible to introduce Satan as the one over whom the believer is victorious (see 2 Cor 2.11). However, it is also possible to understand θριαμβεύω in 2 Cor 2.14 as being essentially similar in meaning to θριαμβεύω^a (39.59) and thus to translate 2 Cor 2.14 as 'for in union with Christ we are always led by God as prisoners in Christ's victorious procession.'

39.61 ἡττάομαι: to experience defeat and subjection – 'to be defeated, to be conquered, to be controlled by.' ᾧ γάρ τις ἥττηται, τούτῳ δεδούλωται 'for a person is a slave of anything that has defeated him' 2 Pe 2.19.
In a number of languages 'to be defeated' is simply 'to be conquered.' In some instances this is expressed as 'to become the prisoner of' or idiomatically 'to be led away by.'

40 Reconciliation, Forgiveness[1]

Outline of Subdomains

A Reconciliation (40.1-40.7)
B Forgiveness (40.8-40.13)

A Reconciliation (40.1-40.7)

40.1 καταλλάσσω; καταλλαγή, ῆς f; ἀπο-καταλλάσσω; συναλλάσσω: to reestablish proper friendly interpersonal relations after these have been disrupted or broken (the componential features of this series of meanings involve (1) disruption of friendly relations because of (2) presumed or real provocation, (3) overt behavior designed to remove hostility, and (4) restoration of original friendly relations) – 'to reconcile, to make things right with one another, reconciliation.'[2]

καταλλάσσω: τὰ δὲ πάντα ἐκ τοῦ θεοῦ τοῦ καταλλάξαντος ἡμᾶς ἑαυτῷ διὰ Χριστοῦ 'all this is done by God who through Christ reconciled us to himself' 2 Cor 5.18.

καταλλαγή: δι' οὗ νῦν τὴν καταλλαγὴν ἐλάβομεν 'through whom we were reconciled (with God)' Ro 5.11.

ἀποκαταλλάσσω: δι' αὐτοῦ ἀποκαταλλάξαι τὰ πάντα εἰς αὐτόν 'through him, (God) reconciled the whole world to himself' Col 1.20.

συναλλάσσω: συνήλλασσεν αὐτοὺς εἰς εἰρήνην 'he tried to make peace between them' Ac 7.26. This is the only instance of συναλλάσσω in the NT, and it has εἰς εἰρήνην added to emphasize peace as the goal, although the feature of making peace between previously hostile individuals is already implicit in the act of reconciliation.

Because of the variety and complexity of the components involved in reconciliation, it is often necessary to use an entire phrase in order to communicate satisfactorily the meanings of the terms in this subdomain. In some languages, however, reconciliation is often spoken of in idiomatic terms, for example, 'to cause to become friends again,' 'to cause to snap fingers again' (a symbol of friendly interpersonal relations in many parts of Africa), 'to cause to be one again,' or 'to take away the separation.' A particularly crucial element in terms for reconciliation is the assigning of responsibility for original guilt in causing the estrangement. Some terms, for example, imply that the individual who initiates reconciliation is by doing so admitting his guilt in causing the estrangement. This, of course, provides a completely untenable meaning for reconciliation in speaking of God reconciling people to himself through Christ. In a number of languages the contextual basis for an expression for reconciliation is often found in terms relating to the reconciliation of husbands and wives. Such expressions fit in well with many contexts in the Scriptures, especially in speaking of reconciliation of people to God, since God is frequently referred to as the husband and the believers as the wife.

40.2 διαλλάσσομαι: to be reconciled to someone – 'to be reconciled, to make peace with.' ὕπαγε πρῶτον διαλλάγηθι τῷ ἀδελφῷ σου 'go at once to be reconciled with your brother' or '. . . with your fellow believer' Mt 5.24.

40.3 ἀπαλλάσσομαι[a]: to settle or come to an agreement with regard to some dispute or issue – 'to settle with, to come to terms with.' ἐν τῇ ὁδῷ δὸς ἐργασίαν ἀπηλλάχθαι ἀπ' αὐτοῦ 'on the way, make an effort to come to an agreement with him' or '. . . to settle the issue with him' Lk 12.58.

40.4 εἰρηνοποιέω: to cause a state of peace or reconciliation between persons – 'to make peace, to make things right.' εἰρηνοποιήσας διὰ τοῦ αἵματος τοῦ σταυροῦ αὐτοῦ '(God) made things right between himself and people

---

1 Domain 40 *Reconciliation, Forgiveness* contains meanings which are generally the converse of meanings found in Domain 39 *Hostility, Strife*. Meanings involving reconciliation have a presuppositional component of opposition and hostility, and it is the process of reconciliation which reverses this presuppositional factor. For meanings involving forgiveness, there is also a presuppositional component of opposition or antagonism which is presumably eliminated by the process of forgiveness.

2 It may be that there are certain subtle distinctions of meaning in the series in 40.1, but there appears to be no contextual indication to justify setting up completely separate meanings.

through (his Son's) death on the cross' Col 1.20. εἰρηνοποιέω is closely related in meaning to the series in 40.1 in that the making of peace or reestablishing peace between persons is a distinctive feature of reconciliation, but the focus in εἰρηνοποιέω seems to be upon the resulting state rather than upon the process.

40.5 εἰρηνοποιός, οῦ *m*: (derivative of εἰρηνοποιέω 'to make peace,' 40.4) a person who restores peace between people – 'peacemaker, one who works for peace.' μακάριοι οἱ εἰρηνοποιοί 'happy are those who work for peace among people' Mt 5.9. Though in Mt 5.9 the cessation of war is by no means excluded, the focus of meaning of εἰρηνοποιός is reconciliation between persons, and not primarily to cause wars to cease.

40.6 μεσίτης[b], ου *m*: a person who acts as a mediator in bringing about reconciliation – 'mediator, one who reconciles.'[3] εἷς καὶ μεσίτης θεοῦ καὶ ἀνθρώπων, ἄνθρωπος Χριστὸς Ἰησοῦς 'there is one mediator between God and people, the man Jesus Christ' 1 Tm 2.5. A mediator may be spoken of in a number of different ways, often idiomatically, for example, 'one who stands in the middle,' 'one who speaks to both,' 'one who cuts palavers,' or 'one who causes arguments to cease.' It is also possible, however, to regard μεσίτης as being related to the process of causing agreement between the parties in question. For this aspect of the meaning of μεσίτης, see 31.22.

40.7 ἄσπονδος, ον: pertaining to being unwilling to be reconciled to others – 'irreconcilable, unwilling to be at peace with others.' ἄστοργοι, ἄσπονδοι, διάβολοι 'unkind, irreconcilable, slanderers' 2 Tm 3.3.

B Forgiveness (40.8-40.13)

40.8 ἀφίημι[f]; ἄφεσις[a], εως *f*; ἀπολύω[e]: to remove the guilt resulting from wrongdoing – 'to pardon, to forgive, forgiveness.'

---

3 Though in μεσίτης[b] there is an important aspect of communication, the focal feature is not primarily communication but reconciliation, and accordingly μεσίτης[b] is considered in this subdomain rather than in one of the subdomains of Domain 33 *Communication*.

ἀφίημι[f]: ἄφες ἡμῖν τὰ ὀφειλήματα ἡμῶν 'forgive us the wrongs that we have done' Mt 6.12. ἄφεσις[a]: τὸ αἷμά μου . . . τὸ περὶ πολλῶν ἐκχυννόμενον εἰς ἄφεσιν ἁμαρτιῶν 'my blood . . . which is poured out for many for the forgiveness of sins' Mt 26.28. ἀπολύω[e]: ἀπολύετε, καὶ ἀπολυθήσεσθε 'forgive and you will be forgiven (by God)' Lk 6.37.

It is extremely important to note that the focus in the meanings of ἀφίημι[f], ἄφεσις[a], and ἀπολύω[e] is upon the guilt of the wrongdoer and not upon the wrongdoing itself. The event of wrongdoing is not undone, but the guilt resulting from such an event is pardoned. To forgive, therefore, means essentially to remove the guilt resulting from wrongdoing.

Some languages make a clear distinction between guilt and sin, and terms for forgiveness are therefore related to guilt and not to the wrongdoing. Therefore, 'to forgive sins' is literally 'to forgive guilt.' Since terms for 'forgiveness' are often literally 'to wipe out,' 'to blot out,' or 'to do away with,' it is obviously not possible to blot out or to wipe out an event, but it is possible to remove or obliterate the guilt.

40.9 ἱλάσκομαι[a]: to forgive, with the focus upon the instrumentality or the means by which forgiveness is accomplished – 'to forgive.' εἰς τὸ ἱλάσκεσθαι τὰς ἁμαρτίας τοῦ λαοῦ 'so that the people's sins would be forgiven' or 'so that God would forgive the people's sins' He 2.17.

40.10 χαρίζομαι[b]: to forgive, on the basis of one's gracious attitude toward an individual – 'to forgive.' χαρίσασθέ μοι τὴν ἀδικίαν ταύτην 'forgive me for being so unfair' 2 Cor 12.13. It may be useful in some instances to translate χαρίζομαι in 2 Cor 12.13 as 'be so kind as to forgive me.'

40.11 ἐπικαλύπτω: (a figurative extension of meaning of ἐπικαλύπτω 'to cover over, to put a covering on,' not occurring in the NT) to cause sin to be forgiven – 'to forgive, to cause forgiveness.' μακάριοι . . . ὧν ἐπεκαλύφθησαν αἱ ἁμαρτίαι 'how happy are . . . those whose sins are forgiven' Ro 4.7.

40.12 ἱλασμός, οῦ *m*; ἱλαστήριον[a], ου *n*: the means by which sins are forgiven – 'the means of forgiveness, expiation.'

ἱλασμός: αὐτὸς ἱλασμός ἐστιν περὶ τῶν ἁμαρτιῶν ἡμῶν '(Christ) himself is the means by which our sins are forgiven' 1 Jn 2.2.

ἱλαστήριον[a]: ὃν προέθετο ὁ θεὸς ἱλαστήριον διὰ τῆς πίστεως 'God offered him as a means by which sins are forgiven through faith (in him)' Ro 3.25.

Though some traditional translations render ἱλαστήριον as 'propitiation,' this involves a wrong interpretation of the term in question. Propitiation is essentially a process by which one does a favor to a person in order to make him or her favorably disposed, but in the NT God is never the object of propitiation since he is already on the side of people. ἱλασμός and ἱλαστήριον[a] denote the means of forgiveness and not propitiation.

40.13 ἱλαστήριον[b], ου *n*: the location or place where sins are forgiven (in traditional translations rendered 'mercy seat') – 'place of forgiveness, place where sins are forgiven.'

ὑπεράνω δὲ αὐτῆς Χερουβὶν δόξης κατασκιάζοντα τὸ ἱλαστήριον 'above the box were the glorious winged creatures spreading their wings over the place where sins are forgiven' He 9.5.

41 Behavior and Related States[1]

Outline of Subdomains

A Behavior, Conduct (41.1-41.24)
B Custom, Tradition (41.25-41.28)
C Particular Patterns of Behavior (41.29-41.43)
D Imitate Behavior (41.44-41.49)
E Change Behavior (41.50-41.54)

A Behavior, Conduct (41.1-41.24)

41.1 γίνομαι[g]: to exist and to conduct oneself, with the particular manner specified by the context – 'to conduct oneself, to behave, conduct.'[2] ὁσίως καὶ δικαίως καὶ ἀμέμπτως ὑμῖν τοῖς πιστεύουσιν ἐγενήθημεν 'our conduct towards you who believe was pure and right and without fault' 1 Th 2.10.

41.2 ζάω[c]: to conduct oneself, with the particular manner specified by the context – 'to live, to conduct oneself, to behave.' πάντες δὲ οἱ θέλοντες εὐσεβῶς ζῆν ἐν Χριστῷ Ἰησοῦ διωχθήσονται 'all who want to live a godly life in Christ Jesus will be persecuted' 2 Tm 3.12. In 2 Tm 3.12 ζάω does not refer to physiological existence, but rather to the manner in which a person behaves or conducts himself in relationship to other persons and to God.

41.3 διάγω; ἀγωγή, ῆς *f*; ἀναστρέφομαι; ἀναστροφή, ῆς *f*: to conduct oneself, with apparent focus upon overt daily behavior – 'to live, to conduct oneself, to behave, behavior, conduct.'[3]

διάγω: ἐν κακίᾳ καὶ φθόνῳ διάγοντες 'we lived in malice and envy' Tt 3.3.

ἀγωγή: σὺ δὲ παρηκολούθησάς μου τῇ διδασκαλίᾳ, τῇ ἀγωγῇ, τῇ προθέσει 'you have followed my teaching, my conduct, and my purpose in life' 2 Tm 3.10.

---

1 Domain 41 *Behavior and Related States* contains a number of meanings which overlap to some extent with other domains. It is not always clear whether a particular term in some contexts refers primarily to psychological attitudes (Domain 25) or relates to more general behavior and related states (Domain 41). Furthermore, in Domain 41 there may be some meanings which could be interpreted as representing moral or ethical qualities (Domain 88), but in Domain 41 the focus is upon the activities themselves and the results of such activities rather than upon the moral or ethical qualities of persons who may be involved.

2 Of all the meanings in Subdomain A *Behavior, Conduct*, γίνομαι[g] is undoubtedly the most generic and implies the widest possible scope of conduct.

3 No doubt there are subtle distinctions in meaning between διάγω, ἀγωγή, ἀναστρέφομαι, and ἀναστροφή, but it is difficult or impossible to determine this from existing contexts.

ἀναστρέφομαι: ἐν χάριτι θεοῦ, ἀνεστράφημεν ἐν τῷ κόσμῳ 'our conduct in the world is by the grace of God' 2 Cor 1.12.

ἀναστροφή: ἠκούσατε γὰρ τὴν ἐμὴν ἀναστροφήν ποτε ἐν τῷ Ἰουδαϊσμῷ 'you have been told of my life when I was devoted to Judaism' Ga 1.13.

41.4 χράομαιᵃ: to conduct oneself in a particular manner with regard to some person – 'to treat, to behave toward.' φιλανθρώπως τε ὁ Ἰούλιος τῷ Παύλῳ χρησάμενος 'Julius treated Paul in a friendly manner' Ac 27.3.

41.5 χράομαιᵇ: to behave or to conduct oneself with respect to certain means – 'to deal with, to have dealings with.' καὶ οἱ χρώμενοι τὸν κόσμον 'and those who have dealings with the world' or 'and those who deal with (the things of) the world' 1 Cor 7.31.

41.6 καταχράομαιᵇ: to conduct oneself in such a way as to become completely occupied by certain means – 'to be fully occupied with.' ὡς μὴ καταχρώμενοι 'as though they are not fully occupied (in dealings with the world)' or '. . . (with things of this world)' 1 Cor 7.31.

41.7 ποιέωᶠ; **προσφέρομαι**: to behave or act in a particular way with respect to someone – 'to behave toward, to deal with, to do to, to act.'
ποιέωᶠ: πάντα οὖν ὅσα ἐὰν θέλητε ἵνα ποιῶσιν ὑμῖν οἱ ἄνθρωποι 'therefore whatsoever you want people to do to you' Mt 7.12; ψευδόμεθα καὶ οὐ ποιοῦμεν τὴν ἀλήθειαν 'we lie and do not act in accordance with the truth' 1 Jn 1.6.
προσφέρομαι: ὡς υἱοῖς ὑμῖν προσφέρεται ὁ θεός 'God behaves toward you as his sons' He 12.7.

41.8 κατάστημα, τος *n*: behavior or conduct, with focus upon the demeanor of an individual – 'behavior, conduct, to behave.' πρεσβύτιδας ὡσαύτως ἐν καταστήματι ἱεροπρεπεῖς '(tell) the older women to behave as women who live a pious life should' Tt 2.3.

41.9 συνοικέω: to conduct oneself in relation to a person with whom one lives – 'to live with, to conduct oneself with.' οἱ ἄνδρες ὁμοί-

ως συνοικοῦντες κατὰ γνῶσιν 'husbands should live with (their wives) thus in accordance with proper understanding' 1 Pe 3.7.

41.10 τρόποςᵇ, **ου** *m*: manner of life, often with focus upon customary acts – 'life, way of life, behavior, manner of life.' μή τις ὑμᾶς ἐξαπατήσῃ κατὰ μηδένα τρόπον 'let no one deceive you in any way of life' 2 Th 2.3; ἀφιλάργυρος ὁ τρόπος 'behavior that is free from the love of money' He 13.5. One may also render this expression in He 13.5 as 'you should not be like people who always love money.'

41.11 περιπατέωᵇ; **πορεύομαι**ᵈ: to live or behave in a customary manner, with possible focus upon continuity of action – 'to live, to behave, to go about doing.'
περιπατέωᵇ: ἐν ἡμῖν τοῖς μὴ κατὰ σάρκα περιπατοῦσιν ἀλλὰ κατὰ πνεῦμα 'among us who live according to the Spirit, not according to human nature' Ro 8.4.
πορεύομαιᵈ: πορευόμενοι ἐν πάσαις ταῖς ἐντολαῖς καὶ δικαιώμασιν τοῦ κυρίου ἄμεμπτοι 'they lived blamelessly in all the commandments and rules of the Lord' Lk 1.6.

41.12 στοιχέω: to live in conformity with some presumed standard or set of customs – 'to live, to behave in accordance with.' εἰ ζῶμεν πνεύματι, πνεύματι καὶ στοιχῶμεν 'if we live because of the Spirit, we should conduct ourselves in accordance with the Spirit' Ga 5.25. In some languages it may be useful to restructure the relationships expressed by the reference to 'the Spirit,' and therefore one may translate this clause in Ga 5.25 as 'since the Spirit has given us life, we should also let him control our lives.'

41.13 ἐκχέομαιᵈ: (a figurative extension of meaning of ἐκχέομαι 'to pour out oneself,' not occurring in the NT) to give oneself completely to some type of behavior – 'to give oneself to, to devote oneself to.' καὶ τῇ πλάνῃ τοῦ Βαλαὰμ μισθοῦ ἐξεχύθησαν 'they gave themselves completely to the kind of deception that Balaam practiced for the sake of money' Jd 11.

41.14 τρέχω^c: to make progress in one's behavior or conduct – 'to behave, to progress.' ἐτρέχετε καλῶς 'you were progressing well' Ga 5.7. It may also be possible to translate ἐτρέχετε καλῶς as 'you were doing better and better.'

41.15 συντρέχω^b: (a figurative extension of meaning of συντρέχω 'to run with,' not occurring in the NT) to be closely associated with others in a particular type of behavior or conduct – 'to join in living, to be closely associated with.' ξενίζονται μὴ συντρεχόντων ὑμῶν εἰς τὴν αὐτὴν τῆς ἀσωτίας ἀνάχυσιν 'they are surprised when you do not join them in the same excess of reckless living' 1 Pe 4.4.

41.16 ὁδός^c, οῦ *f*: (a figurative extension of meaning of ὁδός^a 'road,' 1.99) a customary manner of life or behavior, with probably some implication of goal or purpose – 'way of life, way to live.' ἦλθεν γὰρ Ἰωάννης πρὸς ὑμᾶς ἐν ὁδῷ δικαιοσύνης 'John came to you showing you the way of righteousness' or '. . . the right way to live' Mt 21.32.

41.17 κατευθύνω τοὺς πόδας: (an idiom, literally 'to guide the feet properly') to guide or direct behavior in an appropriate manner – 'to guide, to direct, to make to live.' τοῦ κατευθῦναι τοὺς πόδας ἡμῶν εἰς ὁδὸν εἰρήνης 'to guide our feet into the path of peace' or 'to cause us to live a life of peace' Lk 1.79.

41.18 βιόω; βίος^a, ου *m*; βίωσις, εως *f*: to conduct oneself, with focus upon everyday activity – 'to live, daily life, life, existence.' βιόω: θελήματι θεοῦ τὸν ἐπίλοιπον ἐν σαρκὶ βιῶσαι χρόνον '(you must) live out the rest of your life on earth controlled by God's will' 1 Pe 4.2. βίος^a: ὑπὸ μεριμνῶν καὶ πλούτου καὶ ἡδονῶν τοῦ βίου πορευόμενοι συμπνίγονται 'as they go on living, they are choked by the worries and riches and pleasures of daily life' Lk 8.14. βίωσις: τὴν μὲν οὖν βίωσίν μου τὴν ἐκ νεότητος τὴν ἀπ' ἀρχῆς γενομένην ἐν τῷ ἔθνει μου 'my life I lived from my youth up was spent from the beginning among my own nation' Ac 26.4.

41.19 βιωτικός, ή, όν: (derivative of βιόω 'to live,' 41.18) pertaining to daily life or existence – 'of this life, characteristic of this life, of human existence.' οὐκ οἴδατε ὅτι ἀγγέλους κρινοῦμεν, μήτιγε βιωτικά; 'do you not know that we shall judge the angels? How much more the things of this life?' 1 Cor 6.3.

41.20 ἐργασία^a, ας *f*: (derivative of ἐργάζομαι^a 'to work,' 42.41) to engage in some type of activity or behavior – 'to engage in, to practice, behavior.' ἑαυτοὺς παρέδωκαν τῇ ἀσελγείᾳ εἰς ἐργασίαν ἀκαθαρσίας πάσης 'they gave themselves to vice to practice all kinds of indecency' Eph 4.19.

41.21 ἐργάτης^b, ου *m*: (derivative of ἐργάζομαι^a 'to work,' 42.41) one who characteristically engages in a particular activity – 'worker, one who does, one engaged in.' πάντες ἐργάται ἀδικίας 'all workers of wickedness' or 'all who engage in wickedness' Lk 13.27.

41.22 συναπάγομαι^c: to share in engaging continuously in some activity – 'to share, to share in doing.' μὴ τὰ ὑψηλὰ φρονοῦντες ἀλλὰ τοῖς ταπεινοῖς συναπαγόμενοι 'do not be proud, but share in doing what is humble' Ro 12.16. συναπάγομαι in Ro 12.16 may also be understood as meaning 'to involve oneself with,' and hence one may translate 'do not be proud, but become involved with humble people' or '. . . make friends with humble people.' For this interpretation, see 34.1.

41.23 πραγματεῖαι, ῶν *f*: activities involved in one's behavior or conduct – 'affairs, pursuits.' οὐδεὶς στρατευόμενος ἐμπλέκεται ταῖς τοῦ βίου πραγματείαις 'no soldier gets mixed up in the affairs of daily life' 2 Tm 2.4. In some languages it is possible to translate 'in the affairs of daily life' as 'in what most people must do every day.'

41.24 εἰσέρχομαι καὶ ἐξέρχομαι; εἰσπορεύομαι καὶ ἐκπορεύομαι: (idioms, literally 'to go in and to go out') to live or to conduct oneself in relationship to some community or group – 'to live with, to live among.' εἰσέρχομαι καὶ ἐξέρχομαι: ἐν παντὶ χρόνῳ ᾧ εἰσῆλθεν καὶ ἐξῆλθεν ἐφ' ἡμᾶς ὁ κύριος Ἰησοῦς 'during the whole time that the Lord Jesus lived among us' Ac 1.21.

εἰσπορεύομαι καὶ ἐκπορεύομαι: ἦν μετ' αὐτῶν εἰσπορευόμενος καὶ ἐκπορευόμενος εἰς Ἰερουσαλήμ 'he was living with them in Jerusalem' Ac 9.28.

The semantic focus of these idioms, especially in Ac 1.21 and Ac 9.28, appears to be the manner in which a person conducts himself in relationship to others, but it is possible to imply a certain amount of movement. For example, in Ac 1.21 it is possible to translate 'during the whole time the Lord Jesus travelled about with us,' and in Ac 9.28 one could translate 'Paul stayed with them and went about in Jerusalem.'

B Custom, Tradition (41.25-41.28)

41.25 ἔθος, ους *n*; ἦθος, ους *n*; συνήθεια, ας *f*: a pattern of behavior more or less fixed by tradition and generally sanctioned by the society – 'custom, habit.'
ἔθος: καθὼς ἔθος ἐστὶν τοῖς Ἰουδαίοις ἐνταφιάζειν 'as is the burial custom of the Jews' Jn 19.40.
ἦθος: φθείρουσιν ἤθη χρηστὰ ὁμιλίαι κακαί 'bad companions ruin good habits' 1 Cor 15.33.
συνήθεια: ἡμεῖς τοιαύτην συνήθειαν οὐκ ἔχομεν 'we do not have such a custom' 1 Cor 11.16.
In a number of languages there is no noun for 'custom' or 'habit,' but the same meaning is communicated by verbal aspects or adverbial phrases indicating habitual action. For example, in the case of Jn 19.40 one may translate in some languages 'as is the way in which Jews always bury people,' and for 1 Cor 11.16 one may translate 'this is not what we constantly do.'

41.26 ἐθίζω; εἴωθα: to carry out a custom or tradition – 'to be in the habit of, to carry out a custom, to maintain a tradition.'
ἐθίζω: τοῦ ποιῆσαι αὐτοὺς κατὰ τὸ εἰθισμένον τοῦ νόμου 'that they may carry out the custom of the Law' Lk 2.27.
εἴωθα: κατὰ δὲ ἑορτὴν εἰώθει ὁ ἡγεμὼν ἀπολύειν ἕνα τῷ ὄχλῳ δέσμιον ὃν ἤθελον 'at every Passover feast the governor was in the habit of setting free any prisoner the crowd asked for' Mt 27.15.

41.27 παρατηρέω[b]: to keep or maintain a tradition or custom – 'to observe.' ἡμέρας παρατηρεῖσθε καὶ μῆνας καὶ καιροὺς καὶ ἐνιαυτούς 'you observe days and months and seasons and years' Ga 4.10.

41.28 νομίζομαι: to engage in some activity as a customary practice – 'to practice, to engage in, to take place customarily.' οὗ ἐνομίζετο προσευχὴ εἶναι 'where prayer took place' Ac 16.13 (apparatus). This expression may also be translated as 'where people customarily prayed.'

C Particular Patterns of Behavior (41.29-41.43)

41.29 συσχηματίζομαι: to form or mold one's behavior in accordance with a particular pattern or set of standards – 'to shape one's behavior, to conform one's life.' μὴ συσχηματίζεσθε τῷ αἰῶνι τούτῳ 'do not shape your behavior to the standards of this world' Ro 12.2. In order to express the concept of 'conforming one's life' it may be necessary in some languages to indicate the factor of change, for example, 'to change one's life so that it will be like.'

41.30 τροχιὰς ὀρθὰς ποιέω τοῖς ποσίν: (an idiom, literally 'to make straight wheel tracks for the feet') to live or behave in strict conformance to a predetermined model for behavior – 'to live, to behave, to conduct oneself correctly.' τροχιὰς ὀρθὰς ποιεῖτε τοῖς ποσὶν ὑμῶν 'make straight paths for your feet' or 'live a right life' He 12.13.

41.31 βάρβαρος[c], ον: a pattern of behavior associated with a low cultural level – 'uncivilized, barbarian.' ὅπου οὐκ ἔνι . . . βάρβαρος, Σκύθης, δοῦλος, ἐλεύθερος, ἀλλὰ τὰ πάντα καὶ ἐν πᾶσιν Χριστός 'there are no . . . barbarians, savages, slaves, or free men, but Christ is all and in all' Col 3.11. Regardless of the level of culture or civilization, each ethnic group seems to be able to point to some other group regarded as being uncivilized. In some languages such a group is identified as 'those who live far away' or 'those who do not live in towns' or 'those who are very strange.' In Col 3.11 Σκύθης 'Scythian' (93.583) may represent a state of civilization even lower than that implied by βάρβαρος 'barbarian.'

41.32 Ἰουδαΐζω: to customarily practice Jewish patterns of behavior – 'to live as a Jew, to practice Judaism.' πῶς τὰ ἔθνη ἀναγκάζεις Ἰουδαΐζειν; 'how is it that you force Gentiles to live Jewish?' or 'how can you try to force Gentiles to live Jewish?' Ga 2.14. In some languages an expression such as 'to live Jewish' may be rendered as 'to live just like Jews live' or 'to do the same things that Jews do.'

41.33 Ἰουδαϊσμός, οῦ *m*: the system of Jewish beliefs and customs – 'Judaism, the practice of Judaism, Jewish religion.' προέκοπτον ἐν τῷ Ἰουδαϊσμῷ ὑπὲρ πολλοὺς συνηλικιώτας ἐν τῷ γένει μου 'I was ahead of most fellow Jews of my age in my practice of Judaism' Ga 1.14. In Ga 1.14 Ἰουδαϊσμός may often be rendered as 'Jewish religion' or 'the way in which Jews believe and behave' or 'the ways in which Jews think and do.'

41.34 πολιτεύομαι: to conduct oneself with proper reference to one's obligations in relationship to others, as part of some community – 'to live, to conduct one's life, to live in relation to others.' ἐγὼ πάσῃ συνειδήσει ἀγαθῇ πεπολίτευμαι τῷ θεῷ 'I have lived my life with a clear conscience before God' Ac 23.1.

41.35 ὁδός[d], οῦ *f*: (a figurative extension of meaning of ὁδός[a] 'road, way,' 1.99) behavior in accordance with Christian principles and practices – 'Way, Christian way of life.' ὅπως ἐάν τινας εὕρῃ τῆς ὁδοῦ ὄντας, ἄνδρας τε καὶ γυναῖκας, δεδεμένους ἀγάγῃ εἰς Ἰερουσαλήμ 'so that if he could find any followers of the Way, both men and women, he would be able to arrest them and take them to Jerusalem' Ac 9.2. In a number of languages it is impossible to preserve the figurative meaning of ὁδός in Ac 9.2, and therefore it may be necessary to translate the first part of Ac 9.2 simply as 'so that if he could find any who were followers of Christ' or '. . . those who were Christians.'

41.36 ὀρθοποδέω: to live a life of moral correctness – 'to live right, to live as one ought to.' ὅτε εἶδον ὅτι οὐκ ὀρθοποδοῦσιν πρὸς τὴν ἀλήθειαν 'when I saw that they were not living right, in conformity with the truth' Ga 2.14. ὀρθοποδέω may be translated in a number of languages as 'to live as one should.'

41.37 συναλίζομαι[b]: to live in fellowship with others (a meaning of συναλίζομαι in view of its being regarded as a variant of συναυλίζομαι 'to be with, to stay with,' not occurring in the NT) – 'to live with, to be in fellowship with.' συναλιζόμενος παρήγγειλεν αὐτοῖς 'while they were still together in fellowship, he commanded them' Ac 1.4. συναλίζομαι in the sense of 'to be together in fellowship' fits well in the context of Ac 1.4, but this meaning would seem to be somewhat alien to general Greek usage, and therefore συναλίζομαι is more frequently understood in the context of Ac 1.4 as meaning 'to be eating with' (see 23.13).

41.38 κόσμος[c], ου *m*; αἰών[c], ῶνος *m*: the system of practices and standards associated with secular society (that is, without reference to any demands or requirements of God) – 'world system, world's standards, world.' κόσμος[c]: δι' οὗ ἐμοὶ κόσμος ἐσταύρωται κἀγὼ κόσμῳ 'because of whom the world is crucified to me, and I to the world' Ga 6.14. It may be particularly difficult to speak of the world being crucified, and therefore in a number of languages one must employ a somewhat fuller restructuring, for example, 'because of Christ, the way in which people in this world live is as though it were dead as far as I am concerned, and I am dead, so to speak, as far as the way in which people in this world live.' αἰών[c]: εἴ τις δοκεῖ σοφὸς εἶναι ἐν ὑμῖν ἐν τῷ αἰῶνι τούτῳ, μωρὸς γενέσθω 'if anyone among you thinks that he is a wise man by this world's standards, he should become a fool' 1 Cor 3.18. αἰών in 1 Cor 3.18 may also be rendered as 'by the way in which people in this world think' or 'by the things which people in this world think are right.' In Mk 4.19 the phrase αἱ μέριμναι τοῦ αἰῶνος may be rendered as 'the cares which people in this world have' or 'the way in which people in this world worry about things.'

41.39 κοσμικός[b], ή, όν: (derivative of κόσμος[c] 'world system,' 41.38) pertaining to the system or standards of the world – 'worldly, of the world.' παιδεύουσα ἡμᾶς ἵνα ἀρνησάμενοι τὴν ἀσέβειαν καὶ τὰς κοσμικὰς ἐπιθυμίας 'instructing us to give up ungodly living and worldly desires' Tt 2.12. In Tt 2.12 τὰς κοσμικὰς ἐπιθυμίας may also be rendered as 'the desires which people in this world have,' but in this context the term ἐπιθυμίας should imply wrong desires.

41.40 πνευματικός[c], ή, όν: (derivative of πνεῦμα[a] 'Spirit of God,' 12.18) pertaining to a pattern of life controlled or directed by God's Spirit – 'spiritual, of spiritual conduct, guided by the Spirit.' οὐκ ἠδυνήθην λαλῆσαι ὑμῖν ὡς πνευματικοῖς ἀλλ' ὡς σαρκίνοις 'I could not talk to you as spiritual people, but as worldly people' 1 Cor 3.1.[4]

41.41 ψυχικός[c], ή, όν: (derivative of ψυχή[a] 'inner self,' 26.4) pertaining to behavior which is typical of human nature, in contrast with that which is under the control of God's Spirit – 'unspiritual, worldly, natural.' ψυχικὸς δὲ ἄνθρωπος οὐ δέχεται τὰ τοῦ πνεύματος τοῦ θεοῦ 'a person who is unspiritual cannot receive the gifts that come from God's Spirit' or 'a person who is worldly . . .' 1 Cor 2.14. In a number of languages the equivalent of 'unspiritual' is simply 'one who is not guided by God's Spirit' or 'one who does not live in accordance with God's Spirit.' For another interpretation of ψυχικός in 1 Cor 2.14, see 79.5.

41.42 σάρκινος[d], η, ον; **σαρκικός**[d], ή, όν: (derivatives of σάρξ[f] 'human nature,' 26.7) pertaining to behavior which is typical of human nature, but with special focus upon more base physical desires – 'worldly, base.' σάρκινος[d]: οὐκ ἠδυνήθην λαλῆσαι ὑμῖν ὡς πνευματικοῖς ἀλλ' ὡς σαρκίνοις 'I could not talk

to you as spiritual people, but as worldly people' 1 Cor 3.1. For another interpretation of σάρκινος in 1 Cor 3.1, see 79.4. σαρκικός[d]: παρακαλῶ . . . ἀπέχεσθαι τῶν σαρκικῶν ἐπιθυμιῶν 'I appeal to you . . . not to give in to worldly passions' 1 Pe 2.11. In some languages the expression τῶν σαρκικῶν ἐπιθυμιῶν in 1 Pe 2.11 may be rendered as 'the desires which one's body has' or 'what the body wants.'

41.43 παλαιὸς ἄνθρωπος: (an idiom, literally 'old person' or 'former person') the old or former pattern of behavior, in contrast with a new pattern of behavior which people should conform to – 'old self, old pattern of life.' ἀποθέσθαι ὑμᾶς κατὰ τὴν προτέραν ἀναστροφὴν τὸν παλαιὸν ἄνθρωπον 'to get rid of the old self in accordance with the way you used to conduct yourselves' Eph 4.22. In a number of languages one can best render this expression in Eph 4.22 as 'don't live the way you used to.'

D Imitate Behavior (41.44-41.49)

41.44 μιμέομαι: to behave in the same manner as someone else – 'to imitate, to do as others do.' αὐτοὶ γὰρ οἴδατε πῶς δεῖ μιμεῖσθαι ἡμᾶς 'you yourselves know that you should do just what we did' 2 Th 3.7.

41.45 μιμητής, οῦ m: (derivative of μιμέομαι 'to imitate,' 41.44) one who imitates someone else – 'imitator, one who does what others do.' μιμηταί μου γίνεσθε 'be my imitators' 1 Cor 11.1.

41.46 συμμιμητής, οῦ m: one who joins others as an imitator – 'to join as an imitator, to be an imitator together with others, joint imitator.' συμμιμηταί μου γίνεσθε 'join in being my imitators' Php 3.17.

41.47 περιπατέω τοῖς ἴχνεσιν; στοιχέω τοῖς ἴχνεσιν; ἐπακολουθέω τοῖς ἴχνεσιν: (idioms, literally 'to walk in the tracks' and 'to follow in the tracks') to behave in the same manner as someone else – 'to imitate, to do as others do.' περιπατέω τοῖς ἴχνεσιν: οὐ τῷ αὐτῷ πνεύματι

---

4 It is possible that πνευματικός[c] should be regarded as identical with πνευματικός[a] (12.21), but in 1 Cor 3.1 the focus seems to be upon the pattern of behavior rather than upon the state of having received God's Spirit.

περιεπατήσαμεν; οὐ τοῖς αὐτοῖς ἴχνεσιν; 'do not he and I (literally 'did not we . . .') act from the very same motives and behave in the same way?' 2 Cor 12.18.

στοιχέω τοῖς ἴχνεσιν: ἀλλὰ καὶ τοῖς στοιχοῦσιν τοῖς ἴχνεσιν τῆς . . . πίστεως 'but also because they live the same life of . . . faith' Ro 4.12.

ἐπακολουθέω τοῖς ἴχνεσιν: ἵνα ἐπακολουθήσητε τοῖς ἴχνεσιν αὐτοῦ 'in order that you should live as he did' or 'in order that you should imitate his manner of conduct' 1 Pe 2.21.

41.48 ἐξακολουθέω[b]: to imitate behavior closely (in the NT the imitation involves wrong behavior) – 'to imitate.' καὶ πολλοὶ ἐξακολουθήσουσιν αὐτῶν ταῖς ἀσελγείαις 'and many will imitate their immoral ways' 2 Pe 2.2. An equivalent of this expression in 2 Pe 2.2 may be in some instances 'many will live immoral lives just as they did.'

41.49 προσποιέομαι: to imitate a particular type of behavior as a means of indicating a presumed intent – 'to pretend, to give the impression that, to act as though.' αὐτὸς προσεποιήσατο πορρώτερον πορεύεσθαι 'he acted as though he were going farther' Lk 24.28.

E Change Behavior (41.50-41.54)

41.50 στρέφομαι[c]: to change one's manner of life, with the implication of turning toward God – 'to change one's ways, to turn to God, to repent.' ἐὰν μὴ στραφῆτε καὶ γένησθε ὡς τὰ παιδία, οὐ μὴ εἰσέλθητε εἰς τὴν βασιλείαν τῶν οὐρανῶν 'unless you change your ways and become like children, you will never enter the kingdom of heaven' Mt 18.3. For another interpretation of στρέφομαι in Mt 18.3, see 31.60.

41.51 ἐπιστρέφω[d]; ἐπιστροφή[b], ῆς f: to change one's manner of life in a particular direction, with the implication of turning back to God – 'to change one's ways, to turn to God, repentance.'

ἐπιστρέφω[d]: μήποτε ἐπιστρέφωσιν καὶ ἀφεθῇ αὐτοῖς 'for if they did, they might turn to God and he would forgive them' Mk 4.12.

ἐπιστροφή[b]: ἐκδιηγούμενοι τὴν ἐπιστροφὴν τῶν ἐθνῶν 'they reported how the Gentiles had turned to God' Ac 15.3. For a different interpretation of ἐπιστροφή in Act 15.3, see 31.60.

In a number of languages it is not sufficient to simply translate 'to change one's manner of life,' for this could either be neutral or even suggest a change for the worse. Therefore, it may be necessary in a number of instances to translate 'to change one's way of living as God would want' or 'to change and live like God would want one to live.'

41.52 μετανοέω; μετάνοια, ας f: to change one's way of life as the result of a complete change of thought and attitude with regard to sin and righteousness – 'to repent, to change one's way, repentance.'[5]

μετανοέω: ἐξελθόντες ἐκήρυξαν ἵνα μετανοῶσιν 'they went out and preached that the people should repent' Mk 6.12.

μετάνοια: ἀγνοῶν ὅτι τὸ χρηστὸν τοῦ θεοῦ εἰς μετάνοιάν σε ἄγει; 'do you fail to understand that God is kind because he wants to lead you to repent?' Ro 2.4.

Though in English a focal component of repent is the sorrow or contrition that a person experiences because of sin, the emphasis in μετανοέω and μετάνοια seems to be more specifically the total change, both in thought and behavior, with respect to how one should both think and act. Whether the focus is upon attitude or behavior varies somewhat in different contexts. Compare, for example, Lk 3.8, He 6.1, and Ac 26.20.

41.53 γεννάω ἄνωθεν (an idiom, literally 'to be born again'); παλιγγενεσία[a], ας f: to experience a complete change in one's way of life to what it should be, with the implication of return to a former state or relation – 'to be born again, to experience new birth, rebirth.'

γεννάω ἄνωθεν: ἐὰν μή τις γεννηθῇ ἄνωθεν 'unless a person is born again' Jn 3.3. It is also possible to understand ἄνωθεν in Jn 3.3 as meaning 'from above' or 'from God' (see 84.13), a literary parallel to the phrase ἐκ θεοῦ ἐγεννήθησαν in Jn 1.13. In Jn 3.3, however, Nicodemus understood ἄνωθεν as meaning

---

5 Though it would be possible to classify μετανοέω and μετάνοια in Domain 30 *Think*, the focal semantic feature of these terms is clearly behavioral rather than intellectual.

'again' (see 67.55) and γεννάω as 'physical birth' (see 23.52).

παλιγγενεσία^a: διὰ λουτροῦ παλιγγενεσίας καὶ ἀνακαινώσεως 'new birth and new life by washing' Tt 3.5. The metaphor of 'new birth' is so important in the NT that it should be retained if at all possible. In some languages 'new birth' can be expressed as 'to cause to be born all over again' or 'to have a new life as though one were born a second time.' See also 13.55.

41.54 ἀμετανόητος, ον: pertaining to not being repentant – 'unrepentant, not turning to God, refusing to turn to God.' κατὰ δὲ τὴν σκληρότητά σου καὶ ἀμετανόητον καρδίαν 'but you have a hard and unrepentant heart' Ro 2.5. In a number of languages it is difficult to speak of 'a hard and unrepentant heart.' A more satisfactory equivalent of this expression in Ro 2.5 may be 'but you are stubborn and refuse to repent' or '... refuse to turn to God.'

42 Perform, Do

Outline of Subdomains

A　Function (42.1-42.6)

42.1 ἄγω^e: to be actively performing some function – 'to carry on, to function, to be operative.' εἰ ... ἔχουσι πρός τινα λόγον, ἀγοραῖοι ἄγονται 'if ... they have an accusation against anyone, the courts are functioning' Ac 19.38. In some languages the equivalent of 'the courts are functioning' is 'the courts are open' or 'the judges are on duty' or 'the officials are listening to complaints.'

42.2 ἀργέω: (derivative of ἀργός^a 'idle, not working,' 42.46) to not be functioning – 'to be idle, to not be in force, to not be operative.' οἷς τὸ κρίμα ἔκπαλαι οὐκ ἀργεῖ 'for them the judgment pronounced long ago is not idle' or '... is not without force' 2 Pe 2.3.

42.3 ἐνεργέω^a; ἐνέργεια, ας f: to be engaged in some activity or function, with possible focus upon the energy or force involved – 'to function, to work, to be at work, practice.' ἐνεργέω^a: διὰ τοῦτο αἱ δυνάμεις ἐνεργοῦσιν ἐν αὐτῷ 'this is why these powers are at work in him' Mt 14.2.
ἐνέργεια: δοθείσης μοι κατὰ τὴν ἐνέργειαν τῆς δυνάμεως αὐτοῦ 'given to me in accordance with the working of his power' Eph 3.7.

42.4 ἐνεργέω^b: to cause or make possible a particular function – 'to cause to function, to grant the ability to do.' ὁ δὲ αὐτὸς θεός, ὁ ἐνεργῶν τὰ πάντα ἐν πᾶσιν 'but the same God is the one who causes all these to function in everyone' 1 Cor 12.6. In many instances it is important to specify the references of πάντα and πᾶσιν in 1 Cor 12.6, so that one may translate 'the same God gives the ability to everyone for his or her particular service.'

42.5 πρᾶξις^b, εως f: a function, implying sustained activity and/or responsibility – 'function, task.' τὰ δὲ μέλη πάντα οὐ τὴν αὐτὴν ἔχει πρᾶξιν 'and all these parts have different functions' Ro 12.4. In some languages one may express the meaning of this phrase in Ro 12.4 as 'all these parts help in different ways' or 'all these parts have different work to do.'

42.6 ἀναζάω^b: (a figurative extension of meaning of ἀναζάω^a 'to come back to life,' 23.93) to begin to function, with a possible implication of the suddenness of the action – 'to begin to function, to spring to life, to suddenly be active.' ἐλθούσης δὲ τῆς ἐντολῆς ἡ ἁμαρτία ἀνέζησεν 'but when the commandment came, sin began to function' or '... sprang to life' or '... began to operate' Ro 7.9.[1]

1 It is possible that the prefix ἀνα- in ἀναζάω^b could mean 'to come to life again,' but in this particular context the force of repeated action seems to have been lost.

B Do, Perform (42.7-42.28)

42.7 ποιέω[b]; **ποίησις, εως** *f*: to do or perform (highly generic for almost any type of activity) – 'to do, to act, to carry out, to accomplish, to perform, doing, performance.'

ποιέω[b]: ἀλλ' ὃ μισῶ τοῦτο ποιῶ 'but what I hate, this I do' Ro 7.15;[2] ὃ ποιεῖς ποίησον τάχιον 'what you are going to do, do quickly' Jn 13.27.

ποίησις: οὗτος μακάριος ἐν τῇ ποιήσει αὐτοῦ ἔσται 'this one will be blessed in what he does' Jas 1.25.

42.8 πράσσω[a]; **πρᾶξις**[a], **εως** *f*: to carry out some activity (with possible focus upon the procedures involved) – 'to do, to carry out, to perform, deed.'

πράσσω[a]: οἶδα ὅτι κατὰ ἄγνοιαν ἐπράξατε 'I know that you did this on the basis of ignorance' Ac 3.17. In some languages, however, it may be necessary to translate this expression in Ac 3.17 as 'I know that you did not really understand what you were doing.' οὐ γάρ ἐστιν ἐν γωνίᾳ πεπραγμένον τοῦτο 'for this has not been done in a corner' or '. . . in secret' or '. . . in some isolated place' Ac 26.26.

πρᾶξις[a]: τότε ἀποδώσει ἑκάστῳ κατὰ τὴν πρᾶξιν αὐτοῦ 'then he will repay everyone according to what he has done' Mt 16.27.

42.9 πρᾶγμα[b], **τος** *n*: an activity involving a measure of complexity and responsibility – 'undertaking, task.' ἐν ᾧ ἂν ὑμῶν χρῄζῃ πράγματι 'in whatever undertaking she may need you' Ro 16.2.

42.10 ἕξις, εως *f*: a repeated activity – 'practice, doing again and again, doing repeatedly.'

τῶν διὰ τὴν ἕξιν τὰ αἰσθητήρια γεγυμνασμένα ἐχόντων πρὸς διάκρισιν καλοῦ τε καὶ κακοῦ 'who through practice have their faculties trained to distinguish between good and evil' He 5.14. In a number of languages, however, it may be necessary to restructure this second part of He 5.14 and translate as follows: 'since they have often judged between good and evil,

their abilities to do so are well-trained' or '. . . they are well qualified to do so' or '. . . they can easily and correctly do so.'

42.11 ἔργον[a], **ου** *n*; **ἐνέργημα, τος** *n*: (derivatives of ἐνεργέω[a] 'to function, to work,' 42.3) that which is done, with possible focus on the energy or effort involved – 'act, deed.'

ἔργον[a]: πολλὰ ἔργα καλὰ ἔδειξα ὑμῖν 'I have done many good deeds before you' Jn 10.32.

ἐνέργημα: διαιρέσεις ἐνεργημάτων εἰσίν 'there are diversities of deeds' 1 Cor 12.6.

42.12 ἔργον[c], **ου** *n*: the result of someone's activity or work – 'workmanship, result of what has been done.' οὐ τὸ ἔργον μου ὑμεῖς ἐστε ἐν κυρίῳ; 'are you not the result of what I have done in the Lord?' 1 Cor 9.1.

42.13 καρπός[c], **οῦ** *m*: (a figurative extension of meaning of καρπός[a] 'fruit,' 3.33) the natural result of what has been done – 'deed, activity, result of deeds.' ἀπὸ τῶν καρπῶν αὐτῶν ἐπιγνώσεσθε αὐτούς 'you may know these people by the results of their deeds' or '. . . the results of what they do' Mt 7.16.

42.14 αὐτόφωρος, ον: pertaining to the very act of doing something – 'in the act, in the very activity.' αὕτη ἡ γυνὴ κατείληπται ἐπ' αὐτοφώρῳ μοιχευομένη 'this woman was caught in the very act of committing adultery' Jn 8.4.

42.15 συνεργέω: to engage in an activity together with someone else – 'to work together with, to be active together with.' ἐξελθόντες ἐκήρυξαν πανταχοῦ, τοῦ κυρίου συνεργοῦντος 'they went and preached everywhere and the Lord worked with them' Mk 16.20.

42.16 κοινωνέω[b]: to join with others in some activity – 'to join in doing, to share in doing.' μηδὲ κοινώνει ἁμαρτίαις ἀλλοτρίαις 'do not join in another person's sins' or 'do not join up with others in sinning' 1 Tm 5.22.

42.17 κατεργάζομαι[a]: to do something with success and/or thoroughness – 'to accomplish, to perform successfully, to do thoroughly.' ἅπαντα κατεργασάμενοι στῆναι 'having accomplished everything, to stand' Eph 6.13.

---

2 In Ro 7.15 πράσσω (42.8) and ποιέω seem to be semantically interchangeable, but there may be some subtle stylistic distinction.

42.18 προκόπτω[b]: to progress or advance in some activity – 'to progress, to advance, to accomplish.' ἀλλ' οὐ προκόψουσιν ἐπὶ πλεῖον 'but they will not accomplish much' or 'but they will not get very far' or 'but they will not make much progress' 2 Tm 3.9.

42.19 στέφανος[c], ου *m*: (a figurative extension of meaning of στέφανος[a] 'wreath, crown,' 6.192) a symbol of successful activity – 'crown, symbol of success, sign of accomplishment.' ἀδελφοί μου ἀγαπητοὶ καὶ ἐπιπόθητοι, χαρὰ καὶ στέφανός μου 'my fellow believers, beloved and desired, my joy and crown' Php 4.1.

42.20 ποιητής[a], οῦ *m*: (derivative of ποιέω[b] 'to do,' 42.7) one who does – 'doer.' οἱ ποιηταὶ νόμου δικαιωθήσονται 'these who do what the Law requires will be put right (with God)' Ro 2.13.

42.21 τόπος[c], ου *m*: a role involving activity and responsibility – 'position of service, task.' λαβεῖν τὸν τόπον τῆς διακονίας ταύτης καὶ ἀποστολῆς 'to assume the task of this service and apostleship' Ac 1.25. In some languages the latter part of this expression in Ac 1.25 may be rendered as 'helping in this way and being an apostle' or 'helping in this way as an apostle.' For another interpretation of τόπος in Ac 1.25, see 87.1.

42.22 χρεία[c], ας *f*: an activity which is needed – 'needed task, necessary work.' οὓς καταστήσομεν ἐπὶ τῆς χρείας ταύτης 'whom we will put in charge of this necessary work' Ac 6.3.[3]

42.23 χράομαι[c]: to engage in the activity of making use of something – 'to use, to make use of.' ἀλλ' οὐκ ἐχρησάμεθα τῇ ἐξουσίᾳ ταύτῃ 'but we did not make use of this right' 1 Cor 9.12; ἀλλὰ οἴνῳ ὀλίγῳ χρῶ διὰ τὸν στόμαχον 'but use a little wine for the stomach' 1 Tm 5.23.

42.24 ἀπόχρησις, εως *f*: the activity of using up something – 'being used up, being consumed, consumption.' ἅ ἐστιν πάντα εἰς φθορὰν τῇ ἀποχρήσει 'all of which things are destroyed by being used up' Col 2.22.

42.25 οἰκονομία[a], ας *f*: a task involving management and organization – 'task, commission, responsibility.' εἰ δὲ ἄκων, οἰκονομίαν πεπίστευμαι 'but if not of my own will, I have been entrusted with a responsibility' or 'but since I have not chosen it, I do it as a task entrusted to me' or 'I do it as a matter of duty, because God has entrusted me with this task' 1 Cor 9.17.

42.26 δρόμος[b], ου *m*: (a figurative extension of meaning of δρόμος[a] 'race,' 50.5) a task or function involving continuity, serious effort, and possibly obligation – 'task, mission.' ὡς τελειῶσαι τὸν δρόμον μου 'in order that I may complete my mission' Ac 20.24.

42.27 δαπανάω[c]: (a figurative extension of meaning of δαπανάω[a] 'to spend,' 57.146) to exert great effort in doing something – 'to do anything, to exert great effort.' ἐγὼ δὲ ἥδιστα δαπανήσω . . . ὑπὲρ τῶν ψυχῶν ὑμῶν 'I will gladly do anything I can . . . on your behalf' 2 Cor 12.15. It is possible, however, that δαπανάω in 2 Cor 12.15 should be understood in the literal sense and hence rendered 'I will be glad to spend all I have on your behalf' (see 57.146).

42.28 ἐκδαπανάω: (a figurative extension of meaning of ἐκδαπανάω 'to spend completely,' not occurring in the NT) to do anything and everything to the limit of one's capacity – 'to give oneself completely for, to do anything and everything.' ἐγὼ δὲ ἥδιστα δαπανήσω καὶ ἐκδαπανηθήσομαι ὑπὲρ τῶν ψυχῶν ὑμῶν 'I will gladly do anything and even be completely exhausted on your behalf' 2 Cor 12.15.[4] If one wishes to preserve something of the underlying figurative meaning of this part of 2 Cor 12.15, one may translate 'I will gladly spend everything and be completely spent on your behalf.'

---

3 It is possible that in Ac 6.3 χρεία should be understood simply in terms of task or responsibility.

4 In 2 Cor 12.15 it is clear that ἐκδαπανάω is to be understood in a more intensive sense that δαπανάω[c] (42.27).

C Make, Create (42.29-42.40)

42.29 ποιέω^c: to produce something new, with the implication of using materials already in existence (in contrast with κτίζω 'to create,' 42.35) – 'to make, to fashion.' λέγων τοῖς κατοικοῦσιν ἐπὶ τῆς γῆς ποιῆσαι εἰκόνα τῷ θηρίῳ 'told all the people of the world (literally 'told the inhabitants of the earth') to make an image in honor of the beast' Re 13.14.

42.30 ποίημα, τος n: (derivative of ποιέω^c 'to make,' 42.29) that which is made – 'product, what is made.' αὐτοῦ γάρ ἐσμεν ποίημα 'we are what he has made' Eph 2.10.

42.31 πλάσσω^a: to fashion or form an object – 'to form, to fashion, to make, to mold.' Ἀδὰμ γὰρ πρῶτος ἐπλάσθη, εἶτα Εὕα 'God formed Adam first and then Eve' 1 Tm 2.13.

42.32 χειροποίητος, ον: pertaining to what has been made by someone – 'man-made, made by human hands.' ἀλλ' οὐχ ὁ ὕψιστος ἐν χειροποιήτοις κατοικεῖ 'but the Most High God does not live in (houses) built by human hands' Ac 7.48.

42.33 ἀχειροποίητος, ον: pertaining to what has not been made by someone – 'not made by human hands, not man-made.' ἔχομεν οἰκίαν ἀχειροποίητον αἰώνιον ἐν τοῖς οὐρανοῖς 'we have an everlasting home in the heavens not made by human hands' 2 Cor 5.1.

42.34 οἰκοδομή^b, ῆς f: the construction of something, with focus on the event of building up or on the result of such an event – 'to build up, to construct, construction.' εἰς οἰκοδομὴν τοῦ σώματος τοῦ Χριστοῦ 'in order to build up the body of Christ' Eph 4.12; θεοῦ οἰκοδομή ἐστε 'you are God's construction' 1 Cor 3.9. In 1 Cor 3.9 the phrase θεοῦ οἰκοδομή has been interpreted by many as 'a dwelling place for God' (see 7.1), but it is more likely that the Christian is regarded as the result of God's activity, that is to say, the believer is 'God's construction' or 'that which God has made.' οἰκοδομή in 2 Cor 5.1 (οἰκοδομὴν ἐκ θεοῦ ἔχομεν 'we have a construction from God') may be regarded as having essentially

the same meaning as in 1 Cor 3.9, though the reference here is to the glorified body.

42.35 κτίζω; κτίσις^a, εως f: to make or create something which has not existed before – 'to create, creation' (in the NT, used exclusively of God's activity in creation). κτίζω: ἀποκεκρυμμένου ἀπὸ τῶν αἰώνων ἐν τῷ θεῷ τῷ τὰ πάντα κτίσαντι 'hidden through the past ages in God who created all things' Eph 3.9. κτίσις^a: θλῖψις οἵα οὐ γέγονεν τοιαύτη ἀπ' ἀρχῆς κτίσεως 'trouble such as has not happened since the beginning of creation' or '. . . the beginning when God created the world' Mk 13.19.

42.36 καταρτίζω^c: to create, with the implication of putting into proper condition – 'to create, to make.' πίστει νοοῦμεν κατηρτίσθαι τοὺς αἰῶνας ῥήματι θεοῦ 'by faith we understand that the universe was created by the word of God' or '. . . God created the world by the words he spoke' He 11.3.

42.37 καταβολή, ῆς f: creation, particularly of the world, with focus upon the beginning phase of founding – 'creation.' κληρονομήσατε τὴν ἡτοιμασμένην ὑμῖν βασιλείαν ἀπὸ καταβολῆς κόσμου 'receive the kingdom which has been prepared for you since the creation of the world' Mt 25.34.

42.38 κτίσις^b, εως f; κτίσμα, τος n: that which has been created – 'creation, creature, what has been created.' κτίσις^b: ἐλάτρευσαν τῇ κτίσει παρὰ τὸν κτίσαντα 'they worshiped what has been created instead of the one who created' Ro 1.25. κτίσμα: ἀπέθανεν τὸ τρίτον τῶν κτισμάτων τῶν ἐν τῇ θαλάσσῃ 'a third of the creatures of the sea died' Re 8.9.

42.39 κτίσις^d, εως f: (derivative of κτίζω 'to create,' 42.35) a human institution or social structure as something which has been created – 'institution, structure.' ὑποτάγητε πάσῃ ἀνθρωπίνῃ κτίσει διὰ τὸν κύριον 'be subject to every human institution on account of the Lord' 1 Pe 2.13. It is possible that κτίσις in 1 Pe 2.13 may have the implication of 'authorized institution.' It might even be possible to render χτίσις in such a context as 'authority' (compare χτίσις^e in 37.43).

42.40 χτίστης, ου *m*: (derivative of χτίζω 'to create,' 42.35) one who creates – 'creator.' πιστῷ χτίστῃ παρατιθέσθωσαν τὰς ψυχὰς αὐτῶν 'they should entrust themselves completely to their Creator' 1 Pe 4.19.

D Work, Toil⁵ (42.41-42.50)

42.41 ἐργάζομαι^a; ποιέω^d: to engage in an activity involving considerable expenditure of effort – 'to work, to labor.'
ἐργάζομαι^a: ὕπαγε σήμερον ἐργάζου ἐν τῷ ἀμπελῶνι 'go, work in the vineyard today' Mt 21.28.
ποιέω^d: οὗτοι οἱ ἔσχατοι μίαν ὥραν ἐποίησαν 'these last ones have worked for only one hour' Mt 20.12.

42.42 ἔργον^b, ου *n*: that which one normally does – 'work, task.' δοὺς τοῖς δούλοις αὐτοῦ τὴν ἐξουσίαν, ἑκάστῳ τὸ ἔργον αὐτοῦ 'giving the responsibility to his servants, to each one his particular work (to do)' Mk 13.34.

42.43 ἐργάτης^a, ου *m*: (derivative of ἐργάζομαι^a 'to work,' 42.41) one who works – 'worker.' ἄξιος γὰρ ὁ ἐργάτης τοῦ μισθοῦ αὐτοῦ 'for the workman is worthy of his pay' Lk 10.7.

42.44 συνεργός, οῦ *m*: one who works together with someone else – 'fellow worker.' ἀσπάζεται ὑμᾶς Τιμόθεος ὁ συνεργός μου 'Timothy, my fellow worker, sends you his greetings' Ro 16.21.

42.45 σύζυγος, ου *m*: one who is closely linked with another in some activity – 'fellow worker.'⁶ ἐρωτῶ καὶ σέ, γνήσιε σύζυγε, συλλαμβάνου αὐταῖς 'you, too, my faithful fellow

---

5 In Subdomain D *Work, Toil*, the implication is that a certain amount of physical effort and energy must be involved.
6 σύζυγος seems to differ in meaning from συνεργός 'fellow worker' (42.44) in implying a closer relationship with greater sharing of responsibility.

worker, I want you to help these women' Php 4.3. Some scholars, however, interpret σύζυγος in Php 4.3 as being a proper name.

42.46 ἀργός^a, ή, όν: pertaining to not working – 'idle, not working.' εἶδεν ἄλλους ἑστῶτας ἐν τῇ ἀγορᾷ ἀργούς 'he saw some men standing in the marketplace and not working' Mt 20.3.

42.47 κοπιάω^a; κόπος^a, ου *m*: to engage in hard work, implying difficulties and trouble – 'hard work, toil, to work hard, to toil, to labor.' κοπιάω^a: δι' ὅλης νυκτὸς κοπιάσαντες οὐδὲν ἐλάβομεν 'we worked hard all night long and caught nothing' Lk 5.5.
κόπος^a: ἐν κόπῳ καὶ μόχθῳ 'in hard work and toil' 2 Th 3.8.

42.48 μόχθος, ου *m*: hard work, implying unusual exertion of energy and effort – 'hard labor, toil.' ἐν κόπῳ καὶ μόχθῳ 'in hard work and toil' 2 Th 3.8.

42.49 πόνος^b, ου *m*: hard work, implying accompanying pain and distress – 'hard work, burdensome labor.' μαρτυρῶ γὰρ αὐτῷ ὅτι ἔχει πολὺν πόνον ὑπὲρ ὑμῶν 'I (can personally) testify to his hard work for you' Col 4.13.

42.50 συναθλέω: to toil together with someone in a struggle, implying opposition and/or competition – 'to labor alongside of, to toil with.' αἵτινες ἐν τῷ εὐαγγελίῳ συνήθλησάν μοι 'they have labored with me to spread the gospel' Php 4.3.

E Craft, Trade (42.51-42.53)

42.51 τέχνη, ης *f*: an activity involving specialized training and skill – 'craft, occupation.' ἦσαν γὰρ σκηνοποιοὶ τῇ τέχνῃ 'for they were tentmakers by craft' Ac 18.3. In a number of languages there is no special term for 'craft,' but an equivalent of this clause in Ac 18.3 may be rendered as 'for their work was making tents' or 'they earned money making tents' or 'they customarily made tents.'

42.52 ὁμότεχνος, ον: pertaining to joint activity in some occupation or craft – 'of the same trade, of the same craft, involved in the same occupation, having the same kind of work.' διὰ τὸ ὁμότεχνον εἶναι ἔμενεν παρ' αὐτοῖς καὶ ἠργάζετο 'because they were of the same craft, he stayed and worked with them' Ac 18.3.

42.53 τεχνίτης, ου *m*: one who customarily engages in a particular craft or occupation – 'craftsman.' πᾶς τεχνίτης πάσης τέχνης οὐ μὴ εὑρεθῇ ἐν σοὶ ἔτι 'no craftsman of any occupation will ever be found in you again' Re 18.22.

43 Agriculture

43.1 γεωργέω: to engage in agriculture or gardening – 'to cultivate land, to farm, to garden.' τίκτουσα βοτάνην εὔθετον ἐκείνοις δι' οὓς καὶ γεωργεῖται 'which grows plants that are useful to those for whom it is cultivated' He 6.7.

43.2 γεωργός, οῦ *m*: (derivative of γεωργέω 'to cultivate land,' 43.1) one who engages in agriculture or gardening – 'farmer, gardener.' ἐξέδετο αὐτὸν γεωργοῖς, καὶ ἀπεδήμησεν 'he rented (the vineyard) to farmers and left home on a trip' Mt 21.33.

43.3 σκάπτω[b]: to dig into the ground, specifically in connection with turning over the earth for agricultural or gardening purposes – 'to till the ground, to dig.' σκάψω περὶ αὐτὴν καὶ βάλω κόπρια 'I will dig around it and apply fertilizer' Lk 13.8; σκάπτειν οὐκ ἰσχύω 'I am not strong enough to dig' or 'to work the soil' Lk 16.3. For another interpretation of σκάπτω in Lk 16.3, see 19.55.

43.4 ἀροτριάω: to plow, as a means of preparing land for sowing – 'to plow, to use a plow.' τίς δὲ ἐξ ὑμῶν δοῦλον ἔχων ἀροτριῶντα 'suppose one of you has a servant who is plowing' Lk 17.7. In biblical times plows did not turn over the soil but were used simply to break the surface, seldom to a depth of more than about ten inches (or 25 centimeters).

43.5 φυτεύω: to plant, used primarily in relation to vines, bushes, and trees – 'to plant.' τίς φυτεύει ἀμπελῶνα καὶ τὸν καρπὸν αὐτοῦ οὐκ ἐσθίει; 'who plants a vineyard and does not eat its fruit?' 1 Cor 9.7.

43.6 σπείρω: to scatter seed over tilled ground – 'to sow.'[1] ἐν τῷ σπείρειν αὐτὸν ἃ μὲν ἔπεσεν παρὰ τὴν ὁδόν 'as he was sowing, some of the seed fell along the path' Mt 13.4. In many languages there is a problem of translating σπείρω literally as 'to scatter seed,' since this is interpreted as an exceedingly wasteful manner of sowing, but unless one translates more or less literally and then provides some explanatory footnote, the parable loses much of its significance for many cultures.

43.7 σπόριμα, ων *n*: (derivative of σπείρω 'to sow,' 43.6) grain growing in a field – 'standing grain, grain fields.' παραπορεύεσθαι διὰ τῶν σπορίμων 'to go through the grain fields' Mk 2.23. In a number of languages there are distinct terms for various stages of growth of grain, and in view of the context of the account in Mk 2.23 and parallel passages, it is important to indicate that the grain was essentially ripe.

43.8 ἐπισπείρω: to sow in addition to a previous sowing – 'to sow in addition, to sow on top of.' ἦλθεν αὐτοῦ ὁ ἐχθρὸς καὶ ἐπέσπειρεν ζιζάνια ἀνὰ μέσον τοῦ σίτου 'an enemy came and sowed weeds where the wheat was' Mt 13.25.

43.9 ποτίζω[b]: to provide water for plants – 'to water, to irrigate.' ἐγὼ ἐφύτευσα, Ἀπολλῶς ἐπότισεν, ἀλλὰ ὁ θεὸς ηὔξανεν 'I did the planting, Apollos watered, but God made it grow' 1 Cor 3.6. In a number of languages one can-

---

1 In Mk 4.26 the phrase σπόρον βάλλω (literally 'to throw seed') has the same meaning as σπείρω.

not speak of 'watering a plant,' but one may 'water the ground' or 'cause the ground to drink' or 'make the ground muddy.'

43.10 ἐγκεντρίζω: to insert a shoot or bud into a growing plant – 'to graft, to bud.' σὺ δὲ ἀγριέλαιος ὢν ἐνεκεντρίσθης ἐν αὐτοῖς 'you who are a wild olive tree have been grafted into them' Ro 11.17. Since grafting is not known in some cultures, it may be important to employ a descriptive phrase, for example, 'to cause a small twig of one tree to grow in another,' but such a descriptive phrase must almost always be accompanied by a descriptive marginal note, for example, 'to take a bud or twig from one tree and insert it under the bark of another tree so that it will grow.'

43.11 ἐκριζόω: to remove a plant, including its roots – 'to uproot, to pull out by the roots.' πᾶσα φυτεία ἣν οὐκ ἐφύτευσεν ὁ πατήρ μου ὁ οὐράνιος ἐκριζωθήσεται 'every plant which my Father in heaven did not plant will be pulled up' Mt 15.13.

43.12 καθαίρωᵇ: to cut away or cut back unproductive branches or to cut back productive branches so they can produce better – 'to take away, to prune, to cut off.' πᾶν τὸ καρπὸν φέρον καθαίρει αὐτό 'every (branch) that bears fruit, he prunes it' Jn 15.2. In Jn 15.2 the verb καθαίρω involves a play on two different meanings. The one meaning involves pruning of a plant, while the other meaning involves a cleansing process (79.49). This play on two meanings of καθαίρω serves to highlight the meanings of καθαρός as 'clean' (79.48) or 'pure' (53.29) in Jn 15.3.

43.13 ἀμάω: to cut down grass or grain in a field – 'to mow.' ὁ μισθὸς τῶν ἐργατῶν τῶν ἀμησάντων τὰς χώρας ὑμῶν 'the wages of the laborers who mowed your fields' Jas 5.4. In biblical times mowing would have been done by means of a scythe or sickle, instruments with curved blades especially appropriate for cutting grass or standing grain.

43.14 θερίζω: θερισμόςᵃ, οῦ m: to cut ripe grain and to gather bundles of such grain together – 'to reap, to harvest, harvest, reaping.'

θερίζω: θερίζεις ὃ οὐκ ἔσπειρας 'you harvest what you did not plant' Lk 19.21.
θερισμόςᵃ: ἄφετε συναυξάνεσθαι ἀμφότερα ἕως τοῦ θερισμοῦ 'let them both grow together until harvest' Mt 13.30.²

43.15 καρπόςᵇ, οῦ m; θερισμόςᵇ, οῦ m: that which is harvested – 'harvest, crop, fruit, grain.'
καρπόςᵇ: ὁ θερίζων μισθὸν λαμβάνει καὶ συνάγει καρπόν 'he who reaps is being paid, and he gathers the harvest' Jn 4.36.
θερισμόςᵇ: ὁ μὲν θερισμὸς πολύς, οἱ δὲ ἐργάται ὀλίγοι 'the harvest is plentiful, but the workers are few' Lk 10.2.

43.16 θεριστής, οῦ m: (derivative of θερίζω 'to harvest,' 43.14) a person who gathers in a crop – 'reaper, harvester.' ἐν καιρῷ τοῦ θερισμοῦ ἐρῶ τοῖς θερισταῖς 'when the time of harvest comes, I will say to the reapers' Mt 13.30. In a number of languages there is no specific term for 'reapers,' and therefore it may be necessary in Mt 13.30 to say '. . . I will say to those who are working in the fields' or '. . . who are cutting down the grain.'

43.17 βάλλω τὸ δρέπανον (an idiom, literally 'to throw a sickle'); ἀποστέλλω τὸ δρέπανον and πέμπω τὸ δρέπανον (idioms, literally 'to send a sickle'): to begin to harvest a crop by cutting ripe grain with a sickle – 'to use a sickle, to swing a sickle, to begin to harvest.'
βάλλω τὸ δρέπανον: ἔβαλεν ὁ ἄγγελος τὸ δρέπανον αὐτοῦ εἰς τὴν γῆν 'the angel swung his sickle on the earth' Re 14.19.
ἀποστέλλω τὸ δρέπανον: εὐθὺς ἀποστέλλει τὸ δρέπανον 'immediately he begins to harvest the grain' Mk 4.29.
πέμπω τὸ δρέπανον: πέμψον τὸ δρέπανόν σου καὶ θέρισον, ὅτι ἦλθεν ἡ ὥρα θερίσαι 'use your sickle and harvest, because the time to harvest has come' Re 14.15. In Re 14.15 and 19 these idioms occur in figurative contexts, and therefore it may be necessary in some languages to

---

2 In Mt 13.30 there is a semantic component of time involved in θερισμός, but the process of harvesting is more focal than the temporal element.

speak of 'harvesting' rather than using a phrase which mentions the literal use of a sickle.

43.18 τρυγάω: to pick or gather ripe fruit (especially used of grapes) – 'to pick, to gather.'[3] οὐδὲ ἐκ βάτου σταφυλὴν τρυγῶσιν 'they do not gather a bunch of grapes from a thorn bush' Lk 6.44.

43.19 ἀλοάω: to separate grain from the husks of plants, either by beating or by being tread on by farm animals – 'to thresh, to tread out.' βοῦν ἀλοῶντα οὐ φιμώσεις 'do not tie up the mouth of an ox when it is treading out the grain' 1 Tm 5.18. In a number of societies the idea of having animals tread out grain seems

---

3 In Greek usage τρυγάω seems to be an agricultural term in contrast with τίλλω (18.9) and συλλέγω (18.10).

---

to be extremely wasteful and unsanitary, but there is no way of avoiding a translation of such passages in a more or less literal fashion; otherwise, there is no meaning to the context. It may also be important to provide some type of marginal note to explain more clearly what was involved.

43.20 κηπουρός, οῦ *m*: one who takes care of a garden or orchard – 'gardener.' ἐκείνη δοκοῦσα ὅτι ὁ κηπουρός ἐστιν λέγει αὐτῷ 'she thought he was the gardener, so she asked him' Jn 20.15.

43.21 ἀμπελουργός, οῦ *m*: one who takes care of a vineyard – 'vinedresser, vineyard worker.' συκῆν εἶχέν τις πεφυτευμένην ἐν τῷ ἀμπελῶνι αὐτοῦ . . . εἶπεν δὲ πρὸς τὸν ἀμπελουργόν 'a man had a fig tree growing in his vineyard . . . and he said to his vinedresser' Lk 13.6-7.

44 Animal Husbandry, Fishing

44.1 βόσκω[b]: to herd animals so as to provide them with adequate pasture and to take care of what other needs may be involved – 'to take care of, to herd, to look after.' ἔπεμψεν αὐτὸν εἰς τοὺς ἀγροὺς αὐτοῦ βόσκειν χοίρους 'he sent him to his fields to look after the pigs' Lk 15.15; λέγει αὐτῷ, Βόσκε τὰ ἀρνία μου 'he said to him, Take care of my lambs' Jn 21.15. For another interpretation of βόσκω in Jn 21.15, see 23.10.

44.2 σιτευτός[a], ή, όν; σιτιστός, ή, όν: pertaining to being well fed on grain and hence fattened – 'fat, fattened, grain-fattened.' σιτευτός[a]: ἔθυσεν ὁ πατήρ σου τὸν μόσχον τὸν σιτευτόν 'your father slaughtered the grain-fattened calf' Lk 15.27. In Lk 15.27 σιτευτός may, however, mean 'valuable' or 'prize.' This would simply be an extended meaning of σιτευτός in view of the resulting condition or value of a grain-fed animal. For this interpretation of σιτευτός in Lk 15.27, see 65.8. σιτιστός: οἱ ταῦροί μου καὶ τὰ σιτιστὰ τεθυμένα 'my bulls and grain-fed animals have been slaughtered' Mt 22.4.

44.3 ποιμαίνω[a]: to herd and tend flocks of sheep or goats – 'to shepherd, to take care of, to tend, to pasture.' λέγει αὐτῷ, Ποίμαινε τὰ πρόβατά μου 'he said to him, Shepherd my sheep' or '. . . Take care of my sheep' Jn 21.16. In a number of cultures sheep are not herded or taken care of; they serve primarily as scavengers, and therefore it may be necessary to introduce some type of marginal note, especially in passages which have figurative significance.

44.4 ποιμήν[a], ἑνος *m*: (derivative of ποιμαίνω[a] 'to take care of sheep or goats,' 44.3) one who takes care of sheep or goats – 'shepherd.' ἐρριμμένοι ὡσεὶ πρόβατα μὴ ἔχοντα ποιμένα 'dejected like sheep without a shepherd' Mt 9.36.

44.5 ἀρχιποίμην, ενος *m*: the head shepherd who directs the activities of other shepherds – 'chief shepherd, head shepherd' (in its only NT occurrence, a figurative reference to Christ). καὶ φανερωθέντος τοῦ ἀρχιποίμενος κομιεῖσθε τὸν ἀμαράντινον τῆς δόξης στέφανον 'and when the Chief Shepherd appears, you will receive the glorious crown which will never lose its brightness' 1 Pe 5.4.[1]

44.6 κημόω; φιμόω[a]: to put something over or around the mouths of animals so as to prevent them from eating – 'to muzzle, to keep from eating.'

κημόω: οὐ κημώσεις βοῦν ἀλοῶντα 'do not muzzle the ox that treads out the grain' 1 Cor 9.9.

φιμόω[a]: βοῦν ἀλοῶντα οὐ φιμώσεις 'do not muzzle the ox that treads out the grain' 1 Tm 5.18.

In some languages it may be necessary to employ some type of descriptive equivalent of 'to muzzle,' for example, 'do not tie the mouth of the ox so that it cannot eat' or 'do not cover the mouth of the ox so that it cannot eat.'

44.7 ἁλιεύω: to catch fish, whether by means of a line or by a net – 'to fish.' λέγει αὐτοῖς

Σίμων Πέτρος, Ὑπάγω ἁλιεύειν 'Simon Peter said to them, I am going fishing' Jn 21.3.[2]

44.8 ἀμφιβάλλω: to cast a net in order to catch fish – 'to cast a fishnet.' εἶδεν . . . ἀμφιβάλλοντας ἐν τῇ θαλάσσῃ 'he saw . . . them casting a fishnet into the sea' Mk 1.16. The net implied in the use of the verb ἀμφιβάλλω was probably a circular net which had small weights on its edge and which could be thrown by a single person.

44.9 συγκλείω: to catch in a net (animals or fish) – 'to catch, to net.' συνέκλεισαν πλῆθος ἰχθύων πολύ 'they caught a large number of fish' Lk 5.6.

44.10 ἁλιεύς, έως *m*: one whose occupation is to catch fish – 'fisherman.' βάλλοντας ἀμφίβληστρον εἰς τὴν θάλασσαν· ἦσαν γὰρ ἁλιεῖς 'throwing their net into the sea, for they were fishermen' Mt 4.18.

44.11 ἅλωσις, εως *f*: the capture or catching of animals – 'capture, to be caught.' γεγεννημένα φυσικὰ εἰς ἅλωσιν καὶ φθοράν 'born to be caught and killed' 2 Pe 2.12.

---

1 The occurrence of ἀρχιποίμην 'chief shepherd' in 1 Pe 5.4 is an excellent example of figurative usage. There is no indication that by the time 1 Peter was written ἀρχιποίμην had acquired the conventional meaning of a title designating Christ as one who had principal responsibility for believers. The meaning of ἀρχιποίμην, therefore, is simply 'chief shepherd,' but the reference is to Christ in a function which does not involve the literal care of sheep.

2 In the last part of Jn 21.3 πιάζω 'to seize, to catch' (18.3) is used of catching fish, but this usage should be subsumed under the broader meaning of 'to seize.'

45 Building, Constructing

45.1 οἰκοδομέω[a]; **κατασκευάζω**[b]: to make or erect any kind of construction – 'to build, to construct.'[1]

οἰκοδομέω[a]: ὁμοιωθήσεται ἀνδρὶ φρονίμῳ, ὅστις ᾠκοδόμησεν αὐτοῦ τὴν οἰκίαν ἐπὶ τὴν πέτραν 'will be like a wise man who built his house on the rock' Mt 7.24.

κατασκευάζω[b]: πᾶς γὰρ οἶκος κατασκευάζεται ὑπό τινος 'for every house is built by someone' He 3.4.

---

1 It is possible that in some contexts κατασκευάζω[b] differs from οἰκοδομέω[a] in implying that a construction is being readied for some special purpose.

45.2 πήγνυμι; ἐπιτελέω[c]: to set up or erect a construction, often used in connection with tents – 'to set up, to erect, to put up.'

πήγνυμι: τῆς σκηνῆς τῆς ἀληθινῆς, ἣν ἔπηξεν ὁ κύριος 'in the real tent which was put up by the Lord' He 8.2.

ἐπιτελέω[c]: Μωϋσῆς μέλλων ἐπιτελεῖν τὴν σκηνήν 'when Moses was about to set up the tent' He 8.5.

45.3 ἀνοικοδομέω: to rebuild something which has been destroyed – 'to rebuild, to restore.' τὰ κατεσκαμμένα αὐτῆς ἀνοικοδομήσω 'I will rebuild its ruins' Ac 15.16.

45.4 ἀνορθόω^a: to build something up again after it has fallen – 'to restore, to build up again.' καὶ ἀνορθώσω αὐτήν 'and I will build it up again' Ac 15.16.

45.5 ἐποικοδομέω^a: to build or construct something on some specified location – 'to build upon.' θεμέλιον ἔθηκα, ἄλλος δὲ ἐποικοδομεῖ 'I laid the foundation and another man is building upon it' 1 Cor 3.10.[2]

45.6 συνοικοδομοῦμαι: to be built together with some other object or objects – 'to be built together.' ὑμεῖς συνοικοδομεῖσθε εἰς κατοικητήριον τοῦ θεοῦ 'you are being built together into a dwelling place of God' Eph 2.22. The context of Eph 2.22 is, of course, figurative.

45.7 οἰκοδόμος, ου *m*: (derivative of οἰκοδομέω^a 'to build,' 45.1) one who builds – 'builder' (normally referring to builders of houses and other types of relatively large constructions). ὁ λίθος ὁ ἐξουθενηθεὶς ὑφ᾽ ὑμῶν τῶν οἰκοδόμων, ὁ γενόμενος εἰς κεφαλὴν γωνίας 'the stone that you builders despised turned out to be the most important stone' Ac 4.11.

45.8 δημιουργός, οῦ *m*: one who creates a construction, involving both design and building (often used in reference to divine activity) – 'builder.' πόλιν, ἧς τεχνίτης καὶ

2 In 1 Cor 3.10 ἐποικοδομέω is clearly *used* in a figurative sense, since the context itself is figurative, but the meanings of ἐποικοδομέω and θεμέλιον are to be understood in their normal sense.

δημιουργὸς ὁ θεός 'the city, whose skilled craftsman and builder is God' He 11.10.

45.9 τέκτων, ονος *m*: one who uses various materials (wood, stone, and metal) in building – 'builder, carpenter.' οὐχ οὗτός ἐστιν ὁ τοῦ τέκτονος υἱός; 'isn't he the carpenter's son?' Mt 13.55. There is every reason to believe that in biblical times one who was regarded as a τέκτων would be skilled in the use of wood and stone and possibly even metal.

45.10 ἀρχιτέκτων, ονος *m*: one who is a master or expert builder – 'expert builder, master builder.' ὡς σοφὸς ἀρχιτέκτων θεμέλιον ἔθηκα 'as a wise master builder, I laid a foundation' 1 Cor 3.10.

45.11 ἀποστεγάζω: to take the roof off of a house – 'to remove the roof, to unroof.' ἀπεστέγασαν τὴν στέγην ὅπου ἦν 'they took off the roof where he was' Mk 2.4. In Mk 2.4 ἀποστεγάζω refers to only a part of the roof, and therefore in a number of languages it may be necessary to translate as 'they made a hole in the roof.' In view of the type of houses built in Palestine in NT times, the roof no doubt would have been flat, held up by heavy beams over which were laid planks or sticks and then covered with sun-baked clay.

45.12 κονιάω: to apply whitewash to a surface – 'to whitewash.' παρομοιάζετε τάφοις κεκονιαμένοις 'you are like whitewashed tombs' Mt 23.27. For many languages the closest equivalent of the phrase 'whitewashed tombs' is simply 'tombs that have been painted white.'

46 Household Activities

46.1 οἰκονομέω; οἰκονομία^c, ας *f*: to manage and provide for a household – 'to manage a household, to run a household, to be in charge of a household.' ἀπόδος τὸν λόγον τῆς οἰκονομίας σου, οὐ γὰρ δύνῃ ἔτι οἰκονομεῖν 'give an account of your management of the household, for you can no longer be in charge

of my household' Lk 16.2. In biblical times a household would consist of more than the nuclear family, that is to say, more than simply husband, wife, and children, for servants, slaves, and permanent hired workers living with the family would be regarded as a part of the total household.

46.2 οἰκοδεσποτέω: to command and give leadership to a household – 'to direct a household, to manage a home.'[1] βούλομαι οὖν νεωτέρας γαμεῖν, τεκνογονεῖν, οἰκοδεσποτεῖν 'I would rather that the younger widows get married, have children, and manage their homes' 1 Tm 5.14.

46.3 οἰκουργός, όν: one who works in the home – 'one who takes care of the home, homemaker.' σώφρονας, ἁγνάς, οἰκουργοὺς ἀγαθάς '(how the younger women should be) sensible, chaste, good homemakers' Tt 2.5.

46.4 οἰκονόμος[a], ου m: one who is in charge of running a household – 'manager of a household, steward.' ἄνθρωπός τις ἦν πλούσιος ὃς εἶχεν οἰκονόμον . . . διασκορπίζων τὰ ὑπάρχοντα αὐτοῦ 'there was a rich man who had a manager of his household . . . wasting his master's money' Lk 16.1. It may be necessary in some languages to indicate that οἰκονόμος[a] was a person hired to engage in a particular activity, and therefore in Lk 16.1 it may be necessary to say 'there was a rich man who had hired a man to manage his household.'

46.5 οἰκέτης, ου m: a servant in a household – 'house servant, household servant, personal servant.' φωνήσας δύο τῶν οἰκετῶν 'he called two of his personal servants' Ac 10.7.

46.6 οἰκετεία, ας f; θεραπεία[b], ας f: the group of servants working in a particular household – 'the household servants.'
οἰκετεία: ὃν κατέστησεν ὁ κύριος ἐπὶ τῆς οἰκετείας αὐτοῦ 'whom the master has placed in charge of the household servants' Mt 24.45.
θεραπεία[b]: ὃν καταστήσει ὁ κύριος ἐπὶ τῆς θεραπείας αὐτοῦ 'whom the master will put in charge of his household servants' Lk 12.42.

46.7 ἀρχιτρίκλινος, ου m: the head servant in charge of all those who served at meals or feasts – 'head steward.' ἀντλήσατε νῦν καὶ

φέρετε τῷ ἀρχιτρικλίνῳ 'draw some out and take it to the head steward' Jn 2.8. It is also possible that ἀρχιτρίκλινος in Jn 2.8 refers to the master of ceremonies or the toastmaster at the feast.

46.8 θυρωρός, οῦ m and f: one who guards the door giving access to a house or building – 'doorkeeper.' εἶπεν τῇ θυρωρῷ καὶ εἰσήγαγεν τὸν Πέτρον 'he spoke to the doorkeeper and brought Peter inside' Jn 18.16.

46.9 στρώννυμι[b]: to fit out or arrange a room in a suitable manner (that is, to provide it with necessary furniture) – 'to furnish, to arrange.' κἀκεῖνος ὑμῖν δείξει ἀνάγαιον μέγα ἐστρωμένον 'he will show you a large upstairs room all furnished' Lk 22.12.[2]

46.10 στρώννυμι[c]: to prepare a bed, either for sleeping or making it up after it has been used – 'to make one's bed.' ἀνάστηθι καὶ στρῶσον σεαυτῷ 'get up and make your bed up' Ac 9.34.[2]

46.11 ὑπακούω[b]: to respond to someone knocking or calling at a door – 'to answer the door.' κρούσαντος δὲ αὐτοῦ τὴν θύραν τοῦ πυλῶνος προσῆλθεν παιδίσκη ὑπακοῦσαι ὀνόματι Ῥόδη 'he knocked at the outside door and a servant girl named Rhoda came to answer it' Ac 12.13.

46.12 παρασκευάζω: to prepare or cook a meal – 'to prepare a meal, to get a meal ready.' παρασκευαζόντων δὲ αὐτῶν ἐγένετο ἐπ' αὐτὸν ἔκστασις 'while they were busy preparing the meal, he had a vision' Ac 10.10.

46.13 διακονέω[c]; διακονία[d], ας f: to serve food and drink to those who are eating – 'to serve, to wait upon.'
διακονέω[c]: ἀφῆκεν αὐτὴν ὁ πυρετός, καὶ διηκόνει αὐτοῖς 'the fever left her and she began to serve them' Mk 1.31.
διακονία[d]: ἡ δὲ Μάρθα περιεσπᾶτο περὶ πολλὴν

---

1 It is possible that in some contexts οἰκονομέω, οἰκονομία[c] (46.1), and οἰκοδεσποτέω are essentially equivalent in meaning, though οἰκοδεσποτέω probably differs connotatively in emphasizing commanding or being the head of a household.

2 It is possible to argue that στρώννυμι (and the corresponding form στρωννύω) has only the base meaning 'to spread something out' (as in Mt 21.8; see 16.22), but this term seems to be used in an absolute sense in rather highly diverse contexts, and therefore one is justified in setting up more than one distinct meaning.

διαχονίαν 'Martha was upset over all the serving (she had to do)' Lk 10.40.

46.14 ἀρτύω: to add condiments to food – 'to season.' ἐὰν δὲ καὶ τὸ ἅλας μωρανθῇ, ἐν τίνι ἀρτυθήσεται 'if the salt loses its taste, there is no way to season it (again)' Lk 14.34. In rendering Lk 14.34 it may be necessary to translate ἀρτυθήσεται as 'to cause it to taste like salt again' or 'to cause it to taste right again.'

46.15 ὀπτός, ή, όν: pertaining to being roasted, baked, or broiled – 'broiled, baked.' οἱ δὲ ἐπέδωκαν αὐτῷ ἰχθύος ὀπτοῦ μέρος 'they gave him a piece of broiled fish' Lk 24.42. In a number of languages it is necessary to make a distinction as to whether something is cooked over an open fire or in an enclosed area such as an oven. Furthermore, cooking over an open fire frequently involves a distinction as to whether the cooking is by means of active flames or simply the result of hot coals.

46.16 ἀλήθω: to grind grain in a mill – 'to grind grain.' ἔσονται δύο ἀλήθουσαι ἐπὶ τὸ αὐτό 'two will be grinding grain at the same place' Lk 17.35. In Lk 17.35 and also in Mt 24.41 the reference is evidently to a hand mill, which was normally operated by two women working together. In societies in which such mills are not known, translators have frequently substituted the process of pounding grain by means of a mortar and pestle.

46.17 διϋλίζω: to filter or strain out substances from a liquid – 'to strain out, to filter out.' οἱ διϋλίζοντες τὸν κώνωπα τὴν δὲ κάμηλον καταπίνοντες 'those who filter out a gnat but swallow a camel' Mt 23.24.

46.18 σινιάζω: to sift by shaking in a sieve – 'to sift.' ὁ Σατανᾶς ἐξητήσατο ὑμᾶς τοῦ σινιάσαι ὡς τὸν σῖτον 'Satan has received permission to sift you like wheat' Lk 22.31.[3] The expression ὑμᾶς τοῦ σινιάσαι ὡς τὸν σῖτον in Lk 22.31 is clearly a type of figurative usage and in many languages must be translated as 'to test you' or 'to test you so as to separate the good from the bad.' In some languages, however, it may be more satisfactory to shift the figure from sifting to winnowing and hence translate 'to winnow you like a farmer who separates the wheat from the chaff.'

46.19 σαρόω: to sweep by using a broom – 'to sweep.' οὐχὶ ἅπτει λύχνον καὶ σαροῖ τὴν οἰκίαν 'will she not light a lamp and sweep the house' Lk 15.8.

---

3 In Lk 22.31 the expression ὑμᾶς τοῦ σινιάσαι ὡς τὸν σῖτον 'to sift you like wheat' is semantically complex, for σινιάσαι ὡς τὸν σῖτον 'to sift like wheat' must be taken in a literal sense, but when used with the object ὑμᾶς 'you' (plural), obviously it is not wheat which is involved, but persons, and therefore the meaning must relate to some type of testing of actions and/or motivations. It is impossible to determine whether the expression σινιάσαι ὡς τὸν σῖτον had actually become an established idiom.

47 Activities Involving Liquids or Masses

Outline of Subdomains

A Movement of Liquids or Masses (47.1-47.7)

47.1 ἀντλέω: to draw a liquid, normally water, from a container or well – 'to draw water.' λέγει αὐτοῖς, Ἀντλήσατε νῦν 'he said to them, Draw it out now' Jn 2.8.

47.2 βάλλω[d]: to cause a liquid to pour – 'to pour.' οὐδὲ βάλλουσιν οἶνον νέον εἰς ἀσκοὺς παλαιούς 'they do not pour new wine into old wineskins' Mt 9.17.

47.3 χεράννυμι[b]: to pour something out – 'to pour, to pour out.' ἐκ τοῦ οἴνου τοῦ θυμοῦ τοῦ θεοῦ τοῦ κεχερασμένου ἀκράτου ἐν τῷ ποτηρίῳ τῆς ὀργῆς αὐτοῦ 'from the wine of the wrath of God poured out undiluted into the cup of his anger' Re 14.10. Since κεράννυμι normally means 'to mix,' it is possible to interpret the participial form κεκερασμένου in Re 14.10 as meaning 'to be mixed' (see 63.9), but this would seem to contradict in some measure the following adjective ἄκρατος 'full strength, pure' (79.99).

47.4 ἐκχέωᵃ: to cause to pour out – 'to pour out.' ὑπάγετε καὶ ἐκχέετε τὰς ἑπτὰ φιάλας τοῦ θυμοῦ τοῦ θεοῦ εἰς τὴν γῆν 'go and pour out the seven vials of the wrath of God upon the earth' Re 16.1.

47.5 καταχέω: to cause to pour down on – 'to pour on, to pour over.' συντρίψασα τὴν ἀλάβαστρον κατέχεεν αὐτοῦ τῆς κεφαλῆς 'she broke the alabaster container and poured (the perfume) on his head' Mk 14.3.

47.6 ἐπιχέω: to cause to pour on or flow on – 'to pour on.' κατέδησεν τὰ τραύματα αὐτοῦ ἐπιχέων ἔλαιον καὶ οἶνον 'he bound up his wounds, pouring on oil and wine' Lk 10.34.

47.7 πρόσχυσις, εως *f*: the act of pouring something on or against something – 'pouring' (or possibly 'sprinkling'). πίστει πεποίηκεν τὸ πάσχα καὶ τὴν πρόσχυσιν τοῦ αἵματος 'by faith he established the Passover and the pouring of blood' He 11.28. Since in most contexts this act of πρόσχυσις τοῦ αἵματος is spoken of as 'sprinkling,' it may be preferable to employ 'sprinkling' in He 11.28, since πρόσχυσις may have acquired a generic sense which would include the specific act of sprinkling. See also 47.16.

B Use of Liquids (47.8-47.13)

47.8 πλύνω: to wash an object which is not a body or part of a body – 'to wash, to clean.' οἱ δὲ ἁλιεῖς ἀπ' αὐτῶν ἀποβάντες ἔπλυνον τὰ δίκτυα 'the fishermen left their boats and went to wash their nets' Lk 5.2.

47.9 νίπτω: to wash a part of a body, usually the hands or feet – 'to wash.' καὶ ἤρξατο νίπτειν τοὺς πόδας τῶν μαθητῶν 'and he began to wash the disciples' feet' Jn 13.5.

47.10 ἀπονίπτω: to wash off a part of the body – 'to wash off, to wash.' λαβὼν ὕδωρ ἀπενίψατο τὰς χεῖρας ἀπέναντι τοῦ ὄχλου 'he took some water and washed his hands in front of the crowd' Mt 27.24.

47.11 βάπτω; ἐμβάπτω: to dip an object in a liquid – 'to dip in.'¹
βάπτω: πέμψον Λάζαρον ἵνα βάψῃ τὸ ἄκρον τοῦ δακτύλου αὐτοῦ ὕδατος 'send Lazarus so he may dip the end of his finger in water' Lk 16.24.
ἐμβάπτω: ὁ ἐμβαπτόμενος μετ' ἐμοῦ εἰς τὸ τρύβλιον 'he who dips with me into the bowl' Mk 14.20.

47.12 λούω: to wash the body – 'to bathe, to wash.' ἐγένετο . . . ἀσθενήσασαν αὐτὴν ἀποθανεῖν· λούσαντες δὲ ἔθηκαν αὐτὴν ἐν ὑπερῴῳ 'she got sick and died; and her body was washed and laid in a room upstairs' Ac 9.37.

47.13 ἄνιπτος, ον: pertaining to not being washed – 'not washed, unwashed.' τὸ δὲ ἀνίπτοις χερσὶν φαγεῖν 'to eat with unwashed hands' Mt 15.20.

C Application and Removal of Liquids or Masses (47.14-47.18)

47.14 ἀλείφω: to anoint with a liquid, normally oil or perfume – 'to anoint.' ἐλαίῳ τὴν κεφαλήν μου οὐκ ἤλειψας· αὕτη δὲ μύρῳ ἤλειψεν τούς πόδας μου 'you did not anoint my head with oil, but she anointed my feet with perfume' Lk 7.46.

47.15 ἐγχρίω; ἐπιχρίω: to smear or rub on substances such as salve or oil – 'to put on, to smear on, to rub on, to anoint.'²
ἐγχρίω: ἀγοράσαι . . . καὶ κολλούριον ἐγχρῖσαι τοὺς ὀφθαλμούς σου ἵνα βλέπῃς 'buy . . . also some salve to put on your eyes that you may see' Re 3.18.

---

1 It is possible that ἐμβάπτω differs in meaning from βάπτω in specifying somewhat more clearly the factor of something being in something else.
2 It is possible that ἐγχρίω and ἐπιχρίω differ slightly in meaning in that ἐγχρίω refers primarily to smearing something in and ἐπιχρίω to smearing on, although both terms seem to be related to essentially the same process.

ἐπιχρίω: πηλὸν ἐποίησεν καὶ ἐπέχρισέν μου τοὺς ὀφθαλμούς 'he made some mud and rubbed it on my eyes' Jn 9.11.

47.16 ῥαίνω; ῥαντίζω[a]; ῥαντισμός, οῦ *m*: to sprinkle a liquid upon something – 'to sprinkle, sprinkling.'
ῥαίνω: ἱμάτιον ῥεραμμένον αἵματι 'a garment sprinkled with blood' Re 19.13 (apparatus).
ῥαντίζω[a]: τὸν λαὸν ἐράντισεν 'he sprinkled the people' He 9.19.[3]
ῥαντισμός: εἰς ὑπακοὴν καὶ ῥαντισμὸν αἵματος Ἰησοῦ Χριστοῦ 'unto obedience and the sprinkling of the blood of Jesus Christ' 1 Pe

3 In view of the religious significance of such sprinkling, this meaning of ῥαντίζω, as well as other meanings in the set, could be classified under Domain 53 *Religious Activities* (see 53.32).

1.2. In a number of languages it may be important to restructure somewhat this elliptical phrase so as to translate 'to obey Jesus Christ and be sprinkled by his blood' or '. . . be purified by his blood.'

47.17 περιραίνω; περιραντίζω: to sprinkle around on – 'to sprinkle, to sprinkle around.'
περιραίνω: ἱμάτιον περιρεραμμένον αἵματι 'a garment sprinkled with blood' Re 19.13 (apparatus).
περιραντίζω: ἱμάτιον περιρεραντισμένον αἵματι 'a garment sprinkled with blood' Re 19.13 (apparatus).

47.18 ἐξαλείφω[a]: to remove a liquid by wiping off – 'to wipe away.' καὶ ἐξαλείψει ὁ θεὸς πᾶν δάκρυον ἐκ τῶν ὀφθαλμῶν αὐτῶν 'and God will wipe away every tear from their eyes' Re 7.17.

48 Activities Involving Cloth

48.1 ξαίνω: to comb wool as an initial step in the making of wool thread – 'to comb wool.' οὐ ξαίνουσιν οὐδὲ νήθουσιν οὐδὲ κοπιῶσιν 'they do not comb wool, spin, or work hard' Mt 6.28 (apparatus).[1]

48.2 νήθω: to make yarn by twisting fibers together as one of the steps in making cloth – 'to spin.' κατανοήσατε τὰ κρίνα πῶς αὐξάνει· οὐ κοπιᾷ οὐδὲ νήθει 'look how the wild flowers grow; they do not work or spin' Lk 12.27.

48.3 ὑφαίνω: to interlace threads to form a fabric – 'to weave.' οὔτε νήθει οὔτε ὑφαίνει 'they do not spin and they do not weave' Lk 12.27 (apparatus).

48.4 ὑφαντός, ή, όν: (derivative of ὑφαίνω 'to weave,' 48.3) pertaining to being woven –

1 In Mt 6.28 the Sinaiticus manuscript has an interesting reading, οὐ ξένουσιν (= οὐ ξαίνουσιν), thus providing three processes or activities involving cloth rather than two. However, in view of the relatively limited support for this reading, most translators follow the text which has αὐξάνουσιν 'they grow.'

'woven.' ἦν δὲ ὁ χιτὼν ἄραφος, ἐκ τῶν ἄνωθεν ὑφαντὸς δι' ὅλου 'and the robe was seamless, woven as one piece throughout' Jn 19.23. In a number of languages it may be best to translate the last part of Jn 19.23 as simply 'it was only one piece of cloth' or 'it was not made by sewing pieces of cloth together.'

48.5 ἐπιράπτω: to stitch or sew pieces of cloth together – 'to sew on, to sew to.' οὐδεὶς ἐπίβλημα ῥάκους ἀγνάφου ἐπιράπτει ἐπὶ ἱμάτιον παλαιόν 'no one sews a piece of new cloth on to an old garment' Mk 2.21. This statement in Mk 2.21 may seem entirely senseless in some societies, since it is a familiar practice to sew new cloth on an old garment; in fact, garments may be so patched that it is difficult to determine what was the original piece of cloth. It may, therefore, be important to have some type of marginal explanation.

48.6 ἄραφος, ον: (derivative of ῥάπτω 'to sew together,' not occurring in the NT) pertaining to being without a seam, that is, without being sewn together – 'seamless, without a seam.' ἦν δὲ ὁ χιτὼν ἄραφος 'and the robe was without a seam' or 'the robe consisted of a single piece of cloth' Jn 19.23. In some languages it may be necessary to describe such a seamless robe as 'his robe was woven as just one piece of cloth.'

48.7 γναφεύς, έως *m*: one who cards, cleans, and/or bleaches cloth – 'bleacher, fuller.' τὰ ἱμάτια αὐτοῦ ἐγένετο στίλβοντα λευκὰ λίαν οἷα γναφεὺς ἐπὶ τῆς γῆς οὐ δύναται οὕτως λευκᾶναι 'his clothes became very shining white, so white as no bleacher on earth could make them' Mk 9.3. In Mk 9.3 the reference is obviously to the process of bleaching, but a γναφεύς also was engaged in the cleaning of cloth as well as carding it, a process by which the nap of cloth was somewhat raised and made soft by being combed with bristles.

48.8 ἄγναφος, ον: pertaining to an unshrunken condition of cloth, that is, before it has been washed and dried – 'unshrunken, not as yet shrunken.' οὐδεὶς δὲ ἐπιβάλλει ἐπίβλημα ῥάκους ἀγνάφου 'but no one puts on a patch of unshrunken cloth' Mt 9.16.

49 Activities Involving Clothing and Adorning

49.1 ἐνδύω; ἐνδιδύσκω; ἱματίζω: to put on clothes, without implying any particular article of clothing – 'to clothe, to dress, to put on.'
ἐνδύω: τακτῇ δὲ ἡμέρᾳ ὁ Ἡρῴδης ἐνδυσάμενος ἐσθῆτα βασιλικὴν καὶ καθίσας ἐπὶ τοῦ βήματος 'on a chosen day Herod put on his royal robes and sat on his throne' Ac 12.21.
ἐνδιδύσκω: ἄνθρωπος δέ τις ἦν πλούσιος, καὶ ἐνεδιδύσκετο πορφύραν καὶ βύσσον 'there was once a rich man who dressed in purple and fine linen' Lk 16.19.
ἱματίζω: θεωροῦσιν τὸν δαιμονιζόμενον καθήμενον ἱματισμένον καὶ σωφρονοῦντα 'they saw the man who had been demon possessed sitting (there), clothed and in his right mind' Mk 5.15.

49.2 ἐπενδύομαι: to put a garment on over existing clothing – 'to put on over, to put on an additional garment.' τὸ οἰκητήριον ἡμῶν τὸ ἐξ οὐρανοῦ ἐπενδύσασθαι ἐπιποθοῦντες 'desiring to have our home which is in heaven put on over us as clothes' 2 Cor 5.2.

49.3 ἀμφιάζω[a]; ἀμφιέννυμι[a]; περιβάλλω[a]: to put on clothes, implying the clothing being completely around – 'to clothe.' See also 49.5.
ἀμφιάζω[a]: εἰ δὲ ἐν ἀγρῷ τὸν χόρτον . . . ὁ θεὸς οὕτως ἀμφιέζει, πόσῳ μᾶλλον ὑμᾶς 'if this is how God clothes the wild grass . . . how much more (will he clothe) you' Lk 12.28.[1]

ἀμφιέννυμι[a]: εἰ δὲ τὸν χόρτον τοῦ ἀγροῦ . . . ὁ θεὸς οὕτως ἀμφιέννυσιν, οὐ πολλῷ μᾶλλον ὑμᾶς 'if this is how God clothes the wild grass . . . how much more (will he clothe) you' Mt 6.30.[1]
περιβάλλω[a]: λέγω δὲ ὑμῖν ὅτι οὐδὲ Σολομὼν ἐν πάσῃ τῇ δόξῃ αὐτοῦ περιεβάλετο ὡς ἓν τούτων 'I tell you that not even Solomon in all his glory was clothed as beautifully as one of these (flowers)' Mt 6.29.

49.4 περίκειμαι: to have in a position around oneself – 'to have around, to wear.' ἕνεκεν γὰρ τῆς ἐλπίδος τοῦ Ἰσραὴλ τὴν ἅλυσιν ταύτην περίκειμαι 'for on account of Israel's hope I wear these chains' Ac 28.20.

49.5 ἀμφιάζω[b]; ἀμφιέννυμι[b]; περιβάλλω[b]: to put on clothing to adorn the outward form of something – 'to clothe, to adorn.'[2] For the relevant contexts, see 49.3.

1 Manuscripts alternate frequently between ἀμφιάζω and ἀμφιέννυμι, which appear to be closely related synonyms.
2 As is evident from the contexts cited in 49.3, ἀμφιάζω, ἀμφιέννυμι, and περιβάλλω occur not only in the sense of putting on clothes but in the more generic sense of adorning the outward appearance of something, for these verbs may occur not only with persons who are literally clothed but also with plants which are made attractive.

49.6 σπαργανόω: to wrap a child in swaddling clothes (long strips of cloth) – 'to clothe in strips of cloth, to wrap up in strips of cloth, to wrap in cloths.' ἐσπαργάνωσεν αὐτὸν καὶ ἀνέκλινεν αὐτὸν ἐν φάτνῃ 'she wrapped him in cloths and laid him in a manger' Lk 2.7.

49.7 περίθεσις, εως f: the act of putting on or around and the resultant wearing – 'to put on, to wear, wearing.' περιθέσεως χρυσίων 'the wearing of gold jewelry' 1 Pe 3.3.

49.8 ζώννυμι[b] or ζωννύω: to dress oneself, including the fastening of one's belt as the final act in dressing – 'to dress.' ὅτε ἦς νεώτερος, ἐζώννυες σεαυτὸν καὶ περιεπάτεις ὅπου ἤθελες 'when you were young, you used to dress yourself and go anywhere you wanted to' Jn 21.18.[3]

49.9 ἐγκομβόομαι: to dress oneself, with the implication of clothing which is tied on – 'to dress.' πάντες δὲ ἀλλήλοις τὴν ταπεινοφροσύνην ἐγκομβώσασθε 'all of you should dress yourselves with humility toward one another' 1 Pe 5.5. In 1 Pe 5.5 ἐγκομβόομαι is used figuratively, and one may render it as 'to show' or 'to demonstrate.'[4]

49.10 λαμβάνω[j]: to put on an article of clothing – 'to put on.' ὅτε οὖν ἔνιψεν τοὺς πόδας αὐτῶν καὶ ἔλαβεν τὰ ἱμάτια αὐτοῦ καὶ ἀνέπεσεν πάλιν 'after he had washed their feet, he put on his outer garment again and returned to the table' Jn 13.12.[5]

49.11 φορέω; ἔνδυσις, εως f: to put on and to wear clothes – 'to wear, to dress.'

φορέω: οἱ τὰ μαλακὰ φοροῦντες ἐν τοῖς οἴκοις τῶν βασιλέων εἰσίν 'people who dress in luxurious clothes live in palaces' Mt 11.8.
ἔνδυσις: οὐχ ὁ ἔξωθεν . . . ἐνδύσεως ἱματίων κόσμος 'not the outward . . . adornment through the wearing of clothes' 1 Pe 3.3.

49.12 καταστολή, ῆς f: clothing as a symbol of behavior – 'manner of dress.' γυναῖκας ἐν καταστολῇ κοσμίῳ μετὰ αἰδοῦς καὶ σωφροσύνης κοσμεῖν ἑαυτάς 'women should dress themselves in a proper manner with modesty and good sense' or 'women should be modest and sensible about the clothes they wear and dress properly' 1 Tm 2.9.

49.13 ἔχω[d]: to wear clothes – 'to wear.' ὁ Ἰωάννης εἶχεν τὸ ἔνδυμα αὐτοῦ ἀπὸ τριχῶν καμήλου 'John wore clothes made of camel's hair' Mt 3.4.[6]

49.14 ζώννυμι[a] or ζωννύω; διαζώννυμι: to tuck up or hold a garment firmly in place by wrapping a belt, girdle, or piece of cloth around it – 'to gird, to fasten one's belt, to wear a narrow band of cloth around the waist (compare ζώνη 'belt, girdle,' 6.178), to tie around the waist.'[7]
ζώννυμι[a]: ζῶσαι καὶ ὑπόδησαι τὰ σανδάλιά σου 'put on your belt and put on your shoes' Ac 12.8.
διαζώννυμι: λαβὼν λέντιον διέζωσεν ἑαυτόν 'he took a towel and tied it around his waist' Jn 13.4.

49.15 περιζώννυμαι: to have a belt or sash around oneself – 'to gird oneself, to be girded, to be tied around.'[8] ὅμοιον υἱὸν ἀνθρώπου, ἐνδεδυμένον ποδήρη καὶ περιεζωσμένον πρὸς τοῖς μαστοῖς ζώνην χρυσᾶν 'looking like a man

---

3 In Jn 21.18 ζώννυμι involves more than the fastening of one's belt or putting a sash around the waist. Accordingly, it differs in meaning from ζώννυμι[a] (49.14).

4 There seems to be no evidence that ἐγκομβόομαι in 1 Pe 5.5 has acquired a conventional figurative meaning.

5 One might argue that λαμβάνω in Jn 13.12 should have merely the common meaning of 'taking' (18.1) or 'receiving' (57.125), but in this context there is more involved than merely taking along an outer garment. The reference is clearly to the act of putting on the outer garment. It might be possible to explain this unusual sense of λαμβάνω in Jn 13.12 as being based upon some kind of ellipsis.

6 One might argue that ἔχω in Mt 3.4 means merely 'to possess' (57.1), but obviously there is more in the context of Mt 3.4 than just possessing certain types of clothing. What is relevant is the habitual wearing of such clothing.

7 It is possible that διαζώννυμι is somewhat more forceful in meaning than ζώννυμι[a], but this cannot be determined from existing contexts.

8 περιζώννυμαι appears to differ in meaning from ζώννυμι[a] (49.14) primarily in emphasizing the fact of a strip of cloth being around the middle part of the body.

dressed in a long robe and girded around his chest with a gold band' Re 1.13.

49.16 κατακαλύπτομαι; κατὰ κεφαλῆς ἔχω (an idiom, literally 'to have down on the head'): to wear a covering over one's head – 'to have one's head covered, to cover one's head.'
κατακαλύπτομαι: εἰ γὰρ οὐ κατακαλύπτεται γυνή 'for if a woman does not have her head covered' 1 Cor 11.6.
κατὰ κεφαλῆς ἔχω: πᾶς ἀνὴρ προσευχόμενος ἢ προφητεύων κατὰ κεφαλῆς ἔχων 'any man who prays or prophesies with his head covered' 1 Cor 11.4.

49.17 ὑποδέομαι: to put on and wear footwear (shoes, boots, or sandals) – 'to put on, to tie on, to wear (footwear).' ὑποδεδεμένους σανδάλια 'putting on sandals' Mk 6.9.

49.18 ἐκδύω: to remove clothing from the body (as a reverse process of ἐνδύω 'to put on,' 49.1) – 'to take off clothes, to strip off.' ἐκδύσαντες αὐτὸν χλαμύδα κοκκίνην περιέθηκαν αὐτῷ 'they stripped off his clothes and put a scarlet robe on him' Mt 27.28.

49.19 ἀποβάλλωᵃ: to remove a piece of clothing quickly and cast it aside – 'to throw off, to remove and throw aside.' ὁ δὲ ἀποβαλὼν τὸ ἱμάτιον αὐτοῦ 'he threw off his cloak' Mk 10.50.

49.20 ἀπεκδύομαι; ἀπέκδυσις, εως *f*: to take off or strip off clothing – 'to undress, to disrobe, stripping off.'
ἀπεκδύομαι: ἀπεκδυσάμενος τὰς ἀρχὰς καὶ τὰς ἐξουσίας ἐδειγμάτισεν ἐν παρρησίᾳ 'he stripped off the clothing of the rulers and authorities and made them a public spectacle' Col 2.15. ἀπεκδύομαι in Col 2.15 appears to be a case of figurative usage, but it may refer to the stripping away of weapons and hence the removal of authority and power.
ἀπέκδυσις (a case of figurative usage found only in Col 2.11): ἐν τῇ ἀπεκδύσει τοῦ σώματος τῆς σαρκός 'by the stripping off of the (sinful) body' Col 2.11.

49.21 τίθημιᶜ: to remove or take off clothing – 'to remove, to take off.' ἐγείρεται ἐκ τοῦ δείπ-

νου καὶ τίθησιν τὰ ἱμάτια 'he got up from the meal and took off his outer garment' Jn 13.4.⁹

49.22 γυμνόςᵃ, **ή, όν**: pertaining to wearing no clothing or being very scantily clothed – 'naked.' πότε σε εἴδομεν . . . γυμνὸν ἢ ἀσθενῆ ἢ ἐν φυλακῇ καὶ οὐ διηκονήσαμέν σοι; 'when did we ever see you . . . naked or sick or in prison and we would not help you?' Mt 25.44; ὁ δὲ καταλιπὼν τὴν σινδόνα γυμνὸς ἔφυγεν 'he left the linen cloth behind and ran away naked' Mk 14.52.

49.23 γυμνότης, ητος *f*: the state of being naked or only scantily clothed – 'nakedness.' τίς ἡμᾶς χωρίσει ἀπὸ τῆς ἀγάπης τοῦ Χριστοῦ; θλῖψις . . . ἢ γυμνότης ἢ κίνδυνος ἢ μάχαιρα; 'shall tribulation . . . or nakedness or peril or death . . . separate us from the love of Christ?' Ro 8.35. In the context of Ro 8.35 'nakedness' refers to poverty.

49.24 γυμνιτεύω: to dress in worn-out, ragged clothing – 'to wear ragged clothing, to wear rags, to be poorly clothed.' ἄχρι τῆς ἄρτι ὥρας καὶ πεινῶμεν καὶ διφῶμεν καὶ γυμνιτεύομεν 'to this very hour we go hungry and thirsty; we are wearing ragged clothing' 1 Cor 4.11.

49.25 κομάω: to wear long hair as part of one's attire – 'to have long hair, to appear with long hair, to wear long hair.' γυνὴ δὲ ἐὰν κομᾷ δόξα αὐτῇ ἐστιν 'if a women wears long hair, it is a pride for her' 1 Cor 11.15. In a number of languages it may be necessary to translate κομάω as 'to let one's hair grow long' or 'not to cut one's hair.'

49.26 ἐμπλοκή, ῆς *f*: fashionable braiding (of the hair) – 'braiding.' ὁ ἔξωθεν ἐμπλοκῆς τριχῶν . . . κόσμος 'the outward adorning by the elaborate braiding of the hair' 1 Pe 3.3. In a number of languages it is possible to employ as an equivalent of ἐμπλοκῆς τριχῶν in 1 Pe 3.3 'elaborate hairdo' or 'fancy way in which the hair is combed.'

9 This seemingly unusual use of τίθημι with τὰ ἱμάτια in Jn 13.4 parallels the use of λαμβάνω in the sense of 'putting on a garment' in Jn 13.12 (see 49.10 and footnote 5).

49.27 πλέκω: to interlace strands, either by braiding or weaving – 'to braid, to weave.' πλέξαντες ἀκάνθινον στέφανον 'weaving a crown of thorn branches' Mk 15.17.

49.28 πλέγμα, τος n: anything which is intertwined or interlaced, either woven or braided – 'woven object, braided (hair).' μὴ ἐν πλέγμασιν καὶ χρυσίῳ 'not with braids and gold' (a reference to elaborate adorning) 1 Tm 2.9.

49.29 χρυσόομαι: to be adorned with gold objects – 'to be adorned with gold, to be dressed with gold, to be covered with gold adornments.' ἡ γυνὴ ἦν περιβεβλημένη πορφυροῦν καὶ κόκκινον, καὶ κεχρυσωμένη χρυσίῳ καὶ λίθῳ τιμίῳ 'the woman was dressed in purple and scarlet and adorned with gold ornaments and precious stones' Re 17.4. In Re 17.4 the phrase κεχρυσωμένη χρυσίῳ involves semantic redundancy or what one may also speak of as semantic reinforcement.

50 Contests and Play

50.1 ἀγωνίζομαι[b]: to compete in an athletic contest, with emphasis on effort – 'to compete, to struggle.' πᾶς δὲ ὁ ἀγωνιζόμενος πάντα ἐγκρατεύεται 'everyone who competes in an athletic contest exercises self-control in all things' 1 Cor 9.25.

50.2 ἀθλέω: to engage in an athletic contest, with emphasis upon competition – 'to compete.' ἐὰν δὲ καὶ ἀθλῇ τις, οὐ στεφανοῦται ἐὰν μὴ νομίμως ἀθλήσῃ 'one who competes in an athletic game cannot win the prize unless he competes according to the rules' 2 Tm 2.5.

50.3 ἄθλησις[a], εως f: struggle against opposition – 'struggle, conflict.' πολλὴν ἄθλησιν ὑπεμείνατε παθημάτων 'you endured much struggle in your sufferings' He 10.32. It is also possible to interpret ἄθλησις in He 10.32 as meaning 'challenge' (see 74.13).

50.4 ἀγών[b], ῶνος m: a race involving competition and struggle – 'race.' δι᾽ ὑπομονῆς τρέχωμεν τὸν προκείμενον ἡμῖν ἀγῶνα 'let us run with determination the race that lies before us' He 12.1.

50.5 δρόμος[a], ου m: the course that one follows in a race – 'course, race.' τὸν δρόμον τετέλεκα 'I have finished the race' 2 Tm 4.7. The context of 2 Tm 4.7 is figurative.

50.6 πυκτεύω: to fight with fists, frequently in reference to boxing – 'to box.' οὕτως πυκτεύω ὡς οὐκ ἀέρα δέρων 'I box in such a way as not to beat the air' 1 Cor 9.26. This sole occurrence of πυκτεύω in the NT is in a figurative context.

50.7 γυμνασία, ας f: to engage in physical exercise as a way of improving the body – 'physical exercise.' ἡ γὰρ σωματικὴ γυμνασία πρὸς ὀλίγον ἐστὶν ὠφέλιμος 'for physical exercise has some value to it' 1 Tm 4.8.

50.8 παίζω: to engage in an activity for the sake of amusement and/or recreation – 'to play.' ἐκάθισεν ὁ λαὸς φαγεῖν καὶ πεῖν, καὶ ἀνέστησαν παίζειν 'the people sat down to eat and drink and got up to play' 1 Cor 10.7. The specific reference of παίζω in 1 Cor 10.7 is probably to dancing, but some scholars interpret παίζω in this context as a euphemism for sex.

51 Festivals

51.1 ἑορτάζω: to celebrate a festival or feast – 'to celebrate, to observe a feast, to participate in a festival.' ἑορτάζωμεν . . . ἐν ἀζύμοις 'let us celebrate . . . with unleavened bread' 1 Cor 5.8.

51.2 ἑορτή, ῆς *f*: the events associated with the celebration of a festival or feast – 'festival, feast, celebration.' ἀγόρασον ὧν χρείαν ἔχομεν εἰς τὴν ἑορτήν '(go and) buy what we need for the feast' Jn 13.29.

Though various celebrations of the Jewish religious year have traditionally been called 'feasts,' it would be wrong to use a term which would suggest gluttony or wasteful abundance of food. The emphasis should be upon the ceremonial character of the eating rather than upon the extent of what was eaten. Therefore, it may be better in a number of languages to use terms referring to 'celebrations' or 'festivals,' since the festivities of such gatherings were far more important than the feasting.

51.3 εὐφραίνομαι[b]: to celebrate an occasion, with the implication of happiness and joy – 'to celebrate.' εὐφρανθῆναι δὲ καὶ χαρῆναι ἔδει 'it was necessary to celebrate and be glad' Lk 15.32; εὐφραίνοντο ἐν τοῖς ἔργοις τῶν χειρῶν αὐτῶν 'they celebrated because of what their hands had performed' Ac 7.41. For another interpretation of εὐφραίνομαι in Ac 7.41, see 25.122.

51.4 πανήγυρις, εως *f*: a gathering for a happy, joyous festivity – 'celebration, festivity, joyous festival.' προσεληλύθατε . . . πανηγύρει 'you have come to . . . the joyous festival' He 12.22. For the punctuation problem in translating the total context of He 12.22, see commentaries.

51.5 νεομηνία, ας *f*: a festivity associated with the appearance of the new moon – 'new moon festival.' μὴ οὖν τις ὑμᾶς κρινέτω . . . ἑορτῆς ἢ νεομηνίας 'let no one evaluate you (or 'judge you') in regard to . . . celebrations or new moon festivals' or 'let no one take you to task over the observance of . . . celebrations or new moon festivals' Col 2.16.

51.6 πάσχα[a] *n*: the Jewish festival commemorating the deliverance of Jews from Egypt – 'Passover festival, Passover.' ἔστιν δὲ συνήθεια ὑμῖν ἵνα ἕνα ἀπολύσω ὑμῖν ἐν τῷ πάσχα 'according to your custom, I always set free a prisoner for you during the Passover' Jn 18.39. In some languages the term πάσχα has been borrowed in one form or another, but frequently it is necessary to have some qualifying statement to identify this festival, for example, 'a festival to celebrate the passing over of the angel' or 'a festival to celebrate deliverance from Egypt.'

51.7 πάσχα[b] *n*: a Passover meal eaten in connection with the Passover festival (see 51.6) – 'Passover meal.' καὶ ἡτοίμασαν τὸ πάσχα 'and they prepared the Passover meal' or 'they prepared the food to be eaten in celebrating the Passover' Mt 26.19.

51.8 πεντηκοστή, ῆς *f*: a Jewish harvest festival celebrated on the fiftieth day after Passover – 'Pentecost.' ἔσπευδεν γὰρ εἰ δυνατὸν εἴη αὐτῷ τὴν ἡμέραν τῆς πεντηκοστῆς γενέσθαι εἰς Ἱεροσόλυμα 'he was in a hurry to arrive in Jerusalem, if at all possible, by the day of Pentecost' Ac 20.16. In most languages the festival of Pentecost is identified simply by a borrowed term based on the Greek expression πεντηκοστή. Some languages, however, use a phrase such as 'the festival of the fiftieth day,' and then in a footnote explain the fact that this was a harvest or thanksgiving festival occurring fifty days after Passover.

51.9 ἐγκαίνια, ων *n*: a Jewish festival commemorating the rededication of the Temple in the time of Judas Maccabaeus in 165 B.C. – 'the festival of dedication of the Temple.' ἐγένετο τότε τὰ ἐγκαίνια ἐν τοῖς Ἱεροσολύμοις 'the time came to celebrate the dedication of the Temple in Jerusalem' Jn 10.22. It may be possible to speak of this Festival of Dedication as 'the festival to celebrate the time when the Temple was again made pure and ready for worship.'

51.10 σκηνοπηγία, ας *f*: a Jewish festival commemorating God's provision during the

529

wanderings in the wilderness – 'festival of the tabernacles' or 'celebration of the tents.' ἦν δὲ ἐγγὺς ἡ ἑορτὴ τῶν Ἰουδαίων ἡ σκηνοπηγία 'the Jewish Festival of the Tents was near' Jn 7.2. In some languages it may be useful to speak of the Festival of Tents as 'the festival when people lived in tents.'

51.11 νηστεία^c, ας *f*: a Jewish festival celebrating the forgiveness of sins on the day of atonement – 'festival of the atonement, day to commemorate the atonement of sin.'[1] ὄντος ἤδη ἐπισφαλοῦς τοῦ πλοὸς διὰ τὸ καὶ τὴν νηστεί-

1 The festival of νηστεία involved avoidance of certain foods (compare νηστεία^a 'fast,' 53.65) but not complete abstinence from food.

αν ἤδη παρεληλυθέναι 'it became dangerous to continue the voyage, for by now the Day of Atonement was already past' Ac 27.9. The Day of Atonement in the Jewish calendar occurs in the fall, a time which is particularly dangerous to small ships in the Mediterranean. In biblical times, small merchant ships normally stayed in a harbor over the winter months.

51.12 γενέσια, ων *n*: a celebration or a festivity marking the anniversary of someone's birth – 'birthday celebration, birthday festival.' γενεσίοις δὲ γενομένοις τοῦ Ἡρῴδου ὠρχήσατο ἡ θυγάτηρ τῆς Ἡρῳδιάδος 'at Herod's birthday celebration, the daughter of Herodias danced' Mt 14.6.

52 Funerals and Burial

52.1 κόπτομαι; κοπετός, οῦ *m*: to beat the breast and lament as an expression of sorrow – 'to mourn, to lament, to beat the breast, mourning, lamentation.'[1]

κόπτομαι: ἔκλαιον δὲ πάντες καὶ ἐκόπτοντο αὐτήν 'everyone (there) was crying and mourning for her' Lk 8.52.

κοπετός: συνεκόμισαν δὲ τὸν Στέφανον ἄνδρες εὐλαβεῖς καὶ ἐποίησαν κοπετὸν μέγαν ἐπ' αὐτῷ 'some devout men buried Stephen, making loud lamentation over him' Ac 8.2.

In a number of languages it is entirely impossible to use an expression such as 'to beat the breast' in referring to mourning or grief, since 'to beat the breast' is often employed as a gesture of self-congratulation or pride in accomplishment. In a number of instances the closest equivalent of 'to beat the breast' is 'to beat the head' or even 'to pull out the hair.'

52.2 θρηνέω^c: to wail and lament for the dead, implying a ritualized form of mourning

1 The meanings of κόπτομαι and κοπετός in Domain 52 differ from related meanings in Domain 23 *Physiological Processes and States* and Domain 25 *Attitudes and Emotions,* since the expressions of grief in Lk 8.52 and Ac 8.2 reflect a kind of ritualized and institutionalized form of mourning.

at funerals – 'to wail, to lament.'[2] ἠκολούθει δὲ αὐτῷ πολὺ πλῆθος τοῦ λαοῦ καὶ γυναικῶν αἳ ἐκόπτοντο καὶ ἐθρήνουν αὐτόν 'a very large crowd followed him, among whom were some women who beat the breast and lamented' Lk 23.27. For another interpretation of θρηνέω in Lk 23.27, see 25.141.

52.3 ὀδυρμός, οῦ *m*: ritualized wailing and crying as an expression of grief and sorrow at funerals – 'wailing, lamenting.'[2] φωνὴ ἐν Ῥαμὰ ἠκούσθη, κλαυθμὸς καὶ ὀδυρμὸς πολύς 'a sound is heard in Ramah, crying and great lamentation' Mt 2.18.

52.4 θάπτω: to bury a dead person – 'to bury.' ἀπέθανεν δὲ καὶ ὁ πλούσιος καὶ ἐτάφη 'finally (literally 'and also') the rich man died and was buried' Lk 16.22.

52.5 συγκομίζω: (a euphemistic figurative extension of meaning of συγκομίζω 'to bring

2 ὀδυρμός (52.3) apparently differs in meaning from θρηνέω^c (52.2) in being less institutionalized and focusing somewhat more upon the wailing at funerals, while θρηνέω^b denotes the singing of a dirge, see 33.115. See also 33.116 and 25.141. The meanings in Domain 52 differ in that they reflect ritualized wailing.

in a harvest,' not occurring in the NT) to carry out arrangements for burial – 'to bury.' συνεκόμισαν δὲ τὸν Στέφανον ἄνδρες εὐλαβεῖς 'some devout men buried Stephen' Ac 8.2.

52.6 ἐνταφιάζω; ἐνταφιασμός, οῦ *m*: to prepare a body for burial – 'to prepare for burial, preparation for burial.'[3]
ἐνταφιάζω: ἔδησαν αὐτὸ ὀθονίοις μετὰ τῶν ἀρωμάτων, καθὼς ἔθος ἐστὶν τοῖς Ἰουδαίοις ἐνταφιάζειν 'they wrapped the body in linen cloths with spices, as is the custom of the Jews in preparing (a body) for burial' Jn 19.40.
ἐνταφιασμός: προέλαβεν μυρίσαι τὸ σῶμά μου εἰς τὸν ἐνταφιασμόν 'she was anointing my body beforehand as a preparation for burial' Mk 14.8.

52.7 προστίθημι πρὸς τοὺς πατέρας αὐτοῦ: (a Semitic idiom, literally 'to place with his fathers') to carry out a burial procedure – 'to bury.' ἐκοιμήθη καὶ προσετέθη πρὸς τοὺς

---

3 It is also possible to interpret ἐνταφιάζω and ἐνταφιασμός as the actual process of burial.

πατέρας αὐτοῦ 'he died and was buried' Ac 13.36.

52.8 συνθάπτω: to bury someone along with someone else – 'to bury together with.' συνετάφημεν οὖν αὐτῷ διὰ τοῦ βαπτίσματος εἰς τὸν θάνατον 'by our baptism, then, we were buried with him and shared in his death' Ro 6.4. In Ro 6.4 συνθάπτω is used figuratively, since it evidently had not already acquired a conventional figurative meaning. In a number of languages it is necessary to mark this figurative usage by means of a simile, for example, 'we were, so to speak, buried with him.'

52.9 ταφή, ῆς *f*: a place for burying – 'burial place.' ἠγόρασαν ἐξ αὐτῶν τὸν ἀγρὸν τοῦ κεραμέως εἰς ταφὴν τοῖς ξένοις 'they used the money to buy the Potter's Field as a burial place for foreigners' Mt 27.7. It is also possible to understand ταφή in the context of Mt 27.7 as a reference to the process of burial, and one may therefore translate Mt 27.7 as 'they used the money to buy the Potter's Field to bury foreigners.'

53 Religious Activities[1]

Outline of Subdomains

A Religious Practice (53.1-53.15)
B Offering, Sacrifice (53.16-53.27)
C Purify, Cleanse (53.28-53.32)
D Defiled, Unclean, Common (53.33-53.40)
E Baptize (53.41-53.43)
F Dedicate, Consecrate (53.44-53.52)
G Worship, Reverence (53.53-53.64)
H Fasting (53.65)
I Roles and Functions (53.66-53.95)
J Magic (53.96-53.101)
K Exorcism (53.102-53.103)
L Sacrilege (53.104-53.105)

A Religious Practice (53.1-53.15)

53.1 θρησκεία, ας *f*; εὐσέβεια[a], ας *f*; θεοσέβεια, ας *f*: appropriate beliefs and

devout practice of obligations relating to supernatural persons and powers – 'religion, piety.'
θρησκεία: μὴ χαλιναγωγῶν γλῶσσαν αὐτοῦ ἀλλὰ ἀπατῶν καρδίαν αὐτοῦ, τούτου μάταιος ἡ θρησκεία 'if he does not control his tongue, he deceives himself, and his religion is worthless' Jas 1.26.
εὐσέβεια[a]: ὁμολογουμένως μέγα ἐστὶν τὸ τῆς εὐσεβείας μυστήριον 'without any doubt, the secret of (our) religion is great' 1 Tm 3.16.
θεοσέβεια: ὃ πρέπει γυναιξὶν ἐπαγγελλομέναις

---

1 Domain 53 *Religious Activities* includes a number of aspects of religious behavior, including primarily attitudes, roles, rituals, and related states. It is closely related to Domain 12 *Supernatural Beings and Powers* and to Domain 88 *Moral and Ethical Qualities and Related Behavior*.

θεοσέβειαν 'as is proper for women who proclaim their religion' 1 Tm 2.10.

In a number of languages there is no specific term equivalent to 'religion,' but one may always speak of this phase of culture by some phrase such as 'how to act toward God' or 'what one does to placate spirits' or 'how one worships.'

53.2 δεισιδαιμονία, ας *f*: a set of beliefs concerning deity, with the implication of corresponding behavior – 'religion.' ζητήματα δέ τινα περὶ τῆς ἰδίας δεισιδαιμονίας εἶχον πρὸς αὐτόν 'they had some arguments with him about their own religion' Ac 25.19.

53.3 δεισιδαίμων, ον: pertaining to being religious – 'religious.' δεισιδαιμονεστέρους ὑμᾶς θεωρῶ 'I perceive that you are very religious people' Ac 17.22. δεισιδαίμων may occur in either a good or a bad sense; that is to say, it may mean either 'very religious' or 'superstitious,' although the meaning of 'superstitious' is primarily a later development in the meaning of this word. In Ac 17.22 there seems every reason to believe that Paul was using the term in a positive sense.

53.4 δικαιοσύνη^c, ης *f*: observances or practices required by one's religion – 'religious observances, religious requirements.' προσέχετε δὲ τὴν δικαιοσύνην ὑμῶν μὴ ποιεῖν ἔμπροσθεν τῶν ἀνθρώπων 'be careful not to perform your religious observances in public' Mt 6.1. It is also possible to understand δικαιοσύνη in Mt 6.1 as meaning 'alms' (see 57.111).

53.5 εὐσέβεια^b, ας *f*: behavior reflecting correct religious beliefs and attitudes – 'piety, godliness.' ἵνα ἤρεμον καὶ ἡσύχιον βίον διάγωμεν ἐν πάσῃ εὐσεβείᾳ καὶ σεμνότητι 'that we may live a quiet and peaceful life in entire godliness and with modesty' 1 Tm 2.2. In a number of languages εὐσέβεια in 1 Tm 2.2 may be appropriately translated as 'to live as God would have us live' or 'to live as God has told us we should live.'

53.6 εὐσεβής, ές; εὐσεβῶς; θεοσεβής, ές; ἱεροπρεπής, ές; θρησκός, όν: pertaining to being devoted to a proper expression of religious beliefs – 'devout, pious, religious.'[2]

εὐσεβής: εὐσεβὴς καὶ φοβούμενος τὸν θεὸν σὺν παντὶ τῷ οἴκῳ αὐτοῦ 'a devout and God-fearing person together with all his family' Ac 10.2.

εὐσεβῶς: σωφρόνως καὶ δικαίως καὶ εὐσεβῶς ζήσωμεν ἐν τῷ νῦν αἰῶνι 'that we may live sensibly, uprightly, and in a devout manner in this world' Tt 2.12.

θεοσεβής: ἐάν τις θεοσεβὴς ᾖ καὶ τὸ θέλημα αὐτοῦ ποιῇ τούτου ἀκούει 'if a person is devout and does his (God's) will, (God) will listen to him' Jn 9.31.

ἱεροπρεπής: πρεσβύτιδας ὡσαύτως ἐν καταστήματι ἱεροπρεπεῖς 'similarly, the older women should conduct themselves as devout persons' Tt 2.3.

θρησκός: εἴ τις δοκεῖ θρησκὸς εἶναι, μὴ χαλιναγωγῶν γλῶσσαν αὐτοῦ . . . τούτου μάταιος ἡ θρησκεία 'if anyone thinks he is pious, but does not control his tongue . . . his piety is worthless' Jas 1.26.

In a number of languages the concept of 'living a godly life' may be best expressed as 'to live as God would have one live' or 'to live like one should who believes in God' or 'to always do what God requires.' In some languages, however, the only equivalent is 'to live a good life' or 'to live always doing good to others.' The shift from the focus upon religious belief to good living or being good to others results from the fact that in some religious systems there is little or no connection between religious beliefs and moral behavior.

53.7 εὐλαβέομαι^a; εὐλάβεια, ας *f*: to show reverent regard for – 'to reverence, reverent regard for, reverence.'

εὐλαβέομαι^a: εὐλαβηθεὶς κατεσκεύασεν κιβωτόν 'with reverent regard for (God), he built an ark' He 11.7.

εὐλάβεια: εἰσακουσθεὶς ἀπὸ τῆς εὐλαβείας 'he was heard for his reverence (toward God)' He 5.7.

In εὐλαβέομαι^a and εὐλάβεια there is also a certain element of awe, which may be interpreted in some instances as implying even

---

2 There are no doubt certain subtle differences of meaning in this series, but it is difficult to define these distinctions on the basis of existing contexts.

fear. The implication of such reverent fear or awe is, of course, obedience, and some scholars prefer to interpret the use of these terms in He 11.7 and He 5.7 as meaning 'to obey' (see 36.13) or 'obedience.'

53.8 εὐλαβής, ές: pertaining to being reverent toward God – 'reverent, pious.' ὁ ἄνθρωπος οὗτος δίκαιος καὶ εὐλαβής 'this man was righteous and pious' Lk 2.25.

53.9 ἱερός, ά, όν: pertaining to being appropriate for the expression of worship and reverence – 'holy.' ὅτι ἀπὸ βρέφους τὰ ἱερὰ γράμματα οἶδας 'because from the time you were a child, you have known the Holy Scriptures' or '. . . the holy writings' 2 Tm 3.15; οἱ τὰ ἱερὰ ἐργαζόμενοι 'those engaged in holy activities' or 'those engaged in activities involving worship' 1 Cor 9.13. In 1 Cor 9.13 the reference of the expression οἱ τὰ ἱερὰ ἐργαζόμενοι is the activities in the Temple involving the performance of various rituals. In a number of languages, however, it is difficult to speak of 'holy writings' or 'holy activities.' In some instances one may use an expression which refers to positive taboo, that is to say, something which has been dedicated exclusively to the service of God, but in other languages it may be necessary to use some phrase which identifies objects or activities as being 'appropriate for worship' or 'characteristic of worship' or 'involved in worship.'

53.10 ἀσεβέω; ἀσέβεια, ας f: to live in a manner contrary to proper religious beliefs and practice – 'to live in an ungodly manner, godlessness.'
ἀσεβέω: περὶ πάντων τῶν ἔργων . . . ὧν ἠσέβησαν 'of all their deeds . . . which they have done by their ungodly living' Jd 15.
ἀσέβεια: ἐλέγξαι πᾶσαν ψυχὴν περὶ πάντων τῶν ἔργων ἀσεβείας αὐτῶν 'to condemn everyone for their deeds of godlessness' or '. . . for all they did when they acted in a godless way' or '. . . all they did when they acted without any regard for God' Jd 15.

53.11 ἀσεβής, ές: pertaining to living without regard for religious belief or practice – 'ungodly.' κατὰ καιρὸν ὑπὲρ ἀσεβῶν ἀπέθανεν 'at the right time, he died for the ungodly' Ro 5.6.

53.12 ἐθελοθρησκία, ας f: a set of religious beliefs and practices resulting from one's own desires and initiative – 'self-imposed religion, religion thought up by oneself.' ἅτινά ἐστιν λόγον μὲν ἔχοντα σοφίας ἐν ἐθελοθρησκίᾳ 'these (rules) appear to have an air of wisdom in the self-imposed religion' Col 2.23.

53.13 λειτουργέω[b]; λειτουργία[c], ας f: to perform religious rites as part of one's religious duties or as the result of one's role – 'to perform religious duties, to carry out religious rites.'[3]
λειτουργέω[b]: πᾶς μὲν ἱερεὺς ἔστηκεν καθ' ἡμέραν λειτουργῶν 'every priest stands day by day performing his religious rites' He 10.11.
λειτουργία[c]: ἐγένετο ὡς ἐπλήσθησαν αἱ ἡμέραι τῆς λειτουργίας αὐτοῦ ἀπῆλθεν εἰς τὸν οἶκον αὐτοῦ 'when his period to perform the religious rites (in the Temple) was over, he went back home' Lk 1.23.

53.14 λατρεύω; λατρεία, ας f: to perform religious rites as a part of worship – 'to perform religious rites, to worship, to venerate, worship.'[3]
λατρεύω: μετὰ ταῦτα ἐξελεύσονται καὶ λατρεύσουσίν μοι ἐν τῷ τόπῳ τούτῳ 'afterward they will come out (of that country) and will worship me in this place' Ac 7.7.
λατρεία: εἶχε μὲν οὖν καὶ ἡ πρώτη δικαιώματα λατρείας 'now, the first (covenant) indeed had rules for worship' He 9.1.

53.15 ἐμβατεύω: The meaning of ἐμβατεύω, which occurs only once in the NT, namely in Col 2.18, is obscure. It may mean more or less literally 'to set foot upon' or 'to enter' or possibly 'to come into possession of.' It may also mean 'to enter into' in the sense of to go into detail in treating a subject, but it seems

---

3 In general Greek usage, λειτουργέω and λειτουργία denote service performed by an individual, free of charge, on behalf of the state. This meaning is not found in the NT. In the NT λειτουργέω[b] and λειτουργία[c] (53.13) are less specifically religious in connotation than λατρεύω and λατρεία (53.14).

more likely that ἐμβατεύω in Col 2.18 is a technical term derived from the mystery religions, and it could be interpreted in the phrase ἃ ἑόρακεν ἐμβατεύων as meaning 'who enters the sanctuary which he saw in ecstasy' or 'taking his stand on what he has seen in the mysteries.' In view of the context, which speaks of someone being puffed up without cause, one might also render this Greek phrase as 'by what he saw when he was initiated.' For further data on this semantically difficult term, see *A Greek-English Lexicon of the New Testament,* University of Chicago Press, second edition by Gingrich and Danker.

B   Offering, Sacrifice (53.16-53.27)

53.16 προσφορά, ᾶς *f*: that which is offered to God in religious activity – 'offering, sacrifice.' οὐκέτι προσφορὰ περὶ ἁμαρτίας 'an offering to take away sins is no longer needed' He 10.18.

53.17 ἀναφέρω^c: to offer up someone or something as a sacrifice (a technical term in the sacrificial system) – 'to offer, to offer up, to make an offering.' ἀνενέγκας Ἰσαὰκ τὸν υἱὸν αὐτοῦ ἐπὶ τὸ θυσιαστήριον 'having offered up his son Isaac upon the altar' Jas 2.21.

53.18 ἀνάθημα, τος *n*: that which is dedicated exclusively to the service of deity – 'offering.' τινων λεγόντων περὶ τοῦ ἱεροῦ, ὅτι λίθοις καλοῖς καὶ ἀναθήμασιν κεκόσμηται 'when some remarked about the Temple – how beautiful it is with its stones and offerings' (literally 'that it was adorned with beautiful stones and offerings') Lk 21.5.

53.19 θύω^a: to slaughter an animal in a ritual manner as a sacrifice to deity – 'to sacrifice, to make a sacrifice.' ταύρους καὶ στέμματα ἐπὶ τοὺς πυλῶνας ἐνέγκας σὺν τοῖς ὄχλοις ἤθελεν θύειν 'he brought bulls and flowers to the gate, and he and the crowds wanted to make a sacrifice' Ac 14.13.

53.20 θυσία, ας *f*; σφάγιον, ου *n*: that which is offered as a sacrifice – 'sacrifice.'
θυσία: παρέδωκεν ἑαυτὸν ὑπὲρ ἡμῶν προσφορὰν καὶ θυσίαν τῷ θεῷ 'he gave himself for us as an offering and sacrifice to God' Eph 5.2.

σφάγιον: μὴ σφάγια καὶ θυσίας προσηνέγκατέ μοι 'it was not to me that you offered slain animals and sacrifices' Ac 7.42. The terms σφάγια and θυσίας semantically reinforce one another and are here combined essentially for emphasis.

53.21 ἱερόθυτος, ον: pertaining to being sacrificed to a deity – 'what has been sacrificed, having been sacrificed to a deity.' ἐὰν δέ τις ὑμῖν εἴπῃ, Τοῦτο ἱερόθυτόν ἐστιν, μὴ ἐσθίετε 'if someone says to you, This food is something which has been sacrificed to a deity, do not eat it' 1 Cor 10.28.

In some cultures sacrificing is not practiced, and even the idea of killing an animal as a gift to a deity seems not only strange but even abhorrent. In such languages no special term is to be found for sacrifice, and it may therefore be necessary to use a phrase such as 'to kill an animal and give it to God' or 'to kill an animal in honor of God.' In such cases, however, it is obviously necessary to have some kind of supplementary note or glossary statement which will attempt to explain the significance and function of sacrifice in the Bible.

53.22 κορβᾶν (a borrowing from Hebrew): that which has been set aside as a gift to be given later to God, but which is still at the disposal of the owner – 'gift to God, offering, corban.' ὑμεῖς δὲ λέγετε, Ἐὰν εἴπῃ ἄνθρωπος τῷ πατρὶ ἢ τῇ μητρί, Κορβᾶν . . . οὐκέτι ἀφίετε αὐτὸν οὐδὲν ποιῆσαι τῷ πατρὶ ἢ τῇ μητρί 'you teach that if a person says to his father or mother, This is corban . . . he is excused from helping his father or mother' Mk 7.11-12. In some languages it is important to translate 'corban' as 'what I have promised to later give to God.'

53.23 ἀπαρχή^a, ῆς *f*: the first portion of something which has been set aside and offered to God before the rest of the substance or objects can be used – 'first portion, first offering.' εἰ δὲ ἡ ἀπαρχὴ ἁγία, καὶ τὸ φύραμα 'if the first offering (or 'first portion') is consecrated, then so is the whole loaf' Ro 11.16.

53.24 ὁλοκαύτωμα, τος *n*: an animal which has been sacrificed to God and completely

burned up on the altar – 'whole burnt offering.' ὁλοκαυτώματα καὶ περὶ ἁμαρτίας οὐκ
εὐδόκησας 'you are not pleased with the offering of animals burned whole to take away
sins' He 10.6.

53.25 θυμιάω; θυμίαμα[b], τος *n*: to burn
aromatic substances as an offering to God –
'to offer incense, to burn incense, incense offering.'
θυμιάω: ἔλαχε τοῦ θυμιᾶσαι 'he was chosen by
lot to burn the incense offering' Lk 1.9.
θυμίαμα[b]: πᾶν τὸ πλῆθος ἦν τοῦ λαοῦ προσευχόμενον ἔξω τῇ ὥρᾳ τοῦ θυμιάματος 'all the
people were praying outside during the hour
of the incense offering' Lk 1.10.

53.26 ἄρτοι τῆς προθέσεως: (an idiom,
literally 'bread of the placing forth') bread
which was set out as an offering in the
presence of God in the Tabernacle and later
in the Temple – 'bread offered to God, consecrated bread.' εἰσῆλθεν εἰς τὸν οἶκον τοῦ θεοῦ
καὶ τοὺς ἄρτους τῆς προθέσεως ἔφαγον 'he went
into the house of God, and they ate the bread
that had been offered to God' Mt 12.4. In
some languages ἄρτοι τῆς προθέσεως is rendered as 'bread placed before God' or 'bread
placed in the presence of God.'

53.27 σπένδω: to pour out an offering as an
act of worship or ritual observance – 'to pour
a libation, to pour out an offering.' ἀλλὰ εἰ καὶ
σπένδομαι ἐπὶ τῇ θυσίᾳ 'but if I am to be
poured out as an offering upon the sacrifice'
Php 2.17. In some languages it may be almost
meaningless to speak of 'a person being
poured out,' and therefore it may be more appropriate to translate this expression in Php
2.17 as 'but if my blood is to be poured out
upon the sacrifice.' In Php 2.17 and in 2 Tm
4.6 (the other occurrence of σπένδω in the
NT), the contexts are highly figurative.

C Purify, Cleanse (53.28-53.32)

53.28 καθαρίζω[b]; καθαρότης, ητος *f*;
καθαρισμός, οῦ *m*: to cleanse from ritual contamination or impurity – 'to cleanse, to
purify, purification.'
καθαρίζω[b]: ἃ ὁ θεὸς ἐκαθάρισεν σὺ μὴ κοίνου 'do

not consider unclean what God has made
clean' Ac 10.15. In Ac 10.15 the cleansing obviously involves not physical cleansing, but
ritual cleansing, that is to say, the elimination
of so-called negative taboo or ritual defilement.

ἐκαθαρίσθη αὐτοῦ ἡ λέπρα 'his leprosy was
cleansed' Mt 8.3. The cleansing or healing of
leprosy involved religious, physiological, and
sociological implications. Since leprosy was
regarded as a defilement and hence made a
person ritually unacceptable, it also meant ex-
communication from normal social life. The
removal of leprosy was regarded as an important religious matter, and the healing had to
be verified by the priests before an individual
was regarded as ritually cleansed. In a number
of languages, however, it is quite impossible
to speak of 'cleansing a leper,' for this would
mean only 'giving a bath to a leper.' Accordingly, it may be essential to say 'to heal a
leper' or 'to cure a leper' or even 'to make a
person's leprosy disappear.' In such instances
it is usually essential to have some kind of
marginal note or glossary explanation so as to
indicate the religious implications of leprosy
and the resulting ritual defilement.

καθαρότης: εἰ γὰρ τὸ αἷμα . . . ῥαντίζουσα τοὺς
κεκοινωμένους ἁγιάζει πρὸς τὴν τῆς σαρκὸς
καθαρότητα πόσῳ μᾶλλον . . . 'for if blood
. . . sprinkled on the people who are ritually
unclean, dedicates them to the service of God
in order to make them ritually acceptable
(literally 'for the purification of their bodies'),
how much more . . .' He 9.13.

καθαρισμός: ἐγένετο οὖν ζήτησις ἐκ τῶν μαθητῶν
Ἰωάννου μετὰ Ἰουδαίου περὶ καθαρισμοῦ 'then
some of John's disciples began arguing with a
Jew about the matter of purification' Jn 3.25.

The set of terms having the stem καθαρ- appears to focus upon the elimination of ritual
impurities. From an anthropological standpoint, this means the elimination of ritual
contamination, or, in other words, negative
taboo. This series of terms with the stem
καθαρ- appears to contrast with ἁγνίζω[a] and
ἁγνισμός 'to purify' (53.30), which involve not
only the elimination of ritual defilement, but
imply a positive state of dedication to God or
ritual acceptability. Terms such as ἁγιάζω[a],
ἁγιασμός, ἁγιωσύνη[b], and ἅγιος[b] (53.44-46)

focus upon a positive state of consecration and dedication to God and may be regarded as reflecting the acquisition of so-called positive taboo, that is to say, a state of holiness.

53.29 καθαρός[b], **ά, όν**: pertaining to being ritually clean or pure – 'clean, pure.' πλὴν τὰ ἐνόντα δότε ἐλεημοσύνην, καὶ ἰδοὺ πάντα καθαρὰ ὑμῖν ἐστιν 'but give what is (in your cups and plates) to the poor (literally 'as charity') and everything will be clean for you' Lk 11.41. In Lk 11.41 καθαρός may be rendered in some languages as 'pure in the eyes of God' or even 'right in the eyes of God.'

In a number of languages there is simply no relationship between physical cleanness and ritual acceptability or purity. Accordingly, it may be necessary to render καθαρός in Lk 11.41 and similar contexts as 'acceptable to God' or 'good in God's eyes' or 'good as God thinks.'

53.30 ἁγνίζω[a]; **ἁγνισμός, οῦ** *m*: to purify and cleanse ritually and thus acquire a state of ritual acceptability – 'to purify, purification.' ἁγνίζω[a]: ἀνέβησαν πολλοὶ εἰς Ἰεροσόλυμα ἐκ τῆς χώρας πρὸ τοῦ πάσχα ἵνα ἁγνίσωσιν ἑαυτούς 'many people went up from the country to Jerusalem before the Passover, to purify themselves' Jn 11.55. ἁγνισμός: διαγγέλλων τὴν ἐκπλήρωσιν τῶν ἡμερῶν τοῦ ἁγνισμοῦ 'he gave notice of how many days it would be until the end of the purification' Ac 21.26.

53.31 βαπτίζω[a]; **καταβαπτίζω; βαπτισμός**[a], **οῦ** *m*: to wash (in some contexts, possibly by dipping into water), with a view to making objects ritually acceptable – 'to wash, to purify, washing, purification.' βαπτίζω[a]: ἀπ' ἀγορᾶς ἐὰν μὴ βαπτίσωνται οὐκ ἐσθίουσιν 'nor do they eat anything that comes from the market unless they wash it' Mk 7.4. It is also possible to understand βαπτίσωνται in Mk 7.4 as a middle form meaning 'to wash themselves.' καταβαπτίζω: See Mk 7.4 apparatus. βαπτισμός[a]: καὶ ἄλλα πολλά ἐστιν ἃ παρέλαβον κρατεῖν, βαπτισμοὺς ποτηρίων καὶ ξεστῶν καὶ χαλκίων καὶ κλινῶν 'and they follow many other rules which they have received such as

to wash cups, pots, copper bowls and beds' Mk 7.4.

There is some doubt as to the precise extent to which βαπτίζω, καταβαπτίζω, and βαπτισμός in Mk 7.4 involve ritual cleansing, but the context would seem to imply this, particularly in view of the relationship of such washing to the rules followed by Jews in general and Pharisees in particular.

53.32 ῥαντίζω[b]: to cleanse and purify by means of sprinkling – 'to cleanse, to purify.' ἐὰν μὴ ῥαντίσωνται οὐκ ἐσθίουσιν 'if they do not cleanse themselves, they do not eat' Mk 7.4 (apparatus).

D Defile, Unclean, Common (53.33-53.40)

53.33 κοινόω[a]; **βεβηλόω**: to cause something to become unclean, profane, or ritually unacceptable – 'to make unclean, to defile, to profane.'[4] κοινόω[a]: πάντα ταῦτα τὰ πονηρὰ ἔσωθεν ἐκπορεύεται καὶ κοινοῖ τὸν ἄνθρωπον 'all these evil things come from inside a person and make him unclean' Mk 7.23. βεβηλόω: ὃς καὶ τὸ ἱερὸν ἐπείρασεν βεβηλῶσαι 'he also tried to defile the Temple' Ac 24.6.

In a number of languages it is quite impossible to translate literally the concept of 'unclean,' for physical cleanliness and ritual acceptability are completely unrelated. In some languages it is necessary to translate κοινόω[a] or βεβηλόω as 'to take away its holiness' or 'to make something unacceptable to God.' In many cultures one must express this concept as involving so-called negative taboo.

53.34 μιαίνω[b]; **μολύνω**[b]: to cause something to be ceremonially impure, with the implication of serious defilement – 'to defile, to stain.' μιαίνω[b]: αὐτοὶ οὐκ εἰσῆλθον εἰς τὸ πραιτώριον, ἵνα μὴ μιανθῶσιν 'they themselves did not go

---

4 βεβηλόω may differ significantly from κοινόω[a] in denoting a more serious degree of defilement, but this cannot be readily determined from existing contexts.

inside the governor's palace in order not to be defiled' Jn 18.28.

μολύνω^b: οὗτοί εἰσιν οἳ μετὰ γυναικῶν οὐκ ἐμολύνθησαν 'these are those who have not been defiled with women' Re 14.4; καὶ ἡ συνείδησις αὐτῶν ἀσθενὴς οὖσα μολύνεται 'and their conscience, being weak, is defiled' or 'their conscience is weak and they feel defiled' 1 Cor 8.7.

53.35 μολυσμός, οῦ *m*: a state of defilement, involving both religious and moral aspects – 'defilement, to be defiled.' καθαρίσωμεν ἑαυτοὺς ἀπὸ παντὸς μολυσμοῦ σαρκὸς καὶ πνεύματος 'let us purify ourselves from every defilement of the body and the spirit' or '. . . of everything which might defile the body and the spirit' 2 Cor 7.1. In a number of languages, religious defilement is expressed as 'badness in God's sight.' In some instances, this same concept may be expressed idiomatically as 'ugliness of the heart.'

53.36 ἀμίαντος, ον: (derivative of μιαίνω^b 'to defile,' 53.34, with the addition of the negative prefix ἀ-) pertaining to not being ritually defiled, with implications of accompanying moral defilement – 'undefiled, untainted.' θρησκεία καθαρὰ καὶ ἀμίαντος παρὰ τῷ θεῷ καὶ πατρὶ αὕτη ἐστίν 'this is what God the Father considers to be pure and untainted religion' Jas 1.27.

53.37 ἀλίσγημα, τος *n*: that which has been ritually defiled – 'a thing defiled.' ἐπιστεῖλαι αὐτοῖς τοῦ ἀπέχεσθαι τῶν ἀλισγημάτων τῶν εἰδώλων 'to write a letter (telling) them to abstain from things defiled by idols' Ac 15.20.

53.38 τὸ βδέλυγμα τῆς ἐρημώσεως: (a fixed phrase derived from Hebrew, literally 'the detestable thing of desolation') an abomination (either an object or an event) which defiles a holy place and thus causes it to be abandoned and left desolate – 'an abomination which desolates, a horrible thing which defiles.' ὅταν οὖν ἴδητε τὸ βδέλυγμα τῆς ἐρημώσεως . . . ἑστὸς ἐν τόπῳ ἁγίῳ 'when you see the desolating abomination . . . standing in the holy place' Mt 24.15. In translating βδέλυγμα, it may be necessary in some

languages to use a phrase such as 'that which God detests' or 'that which God hates' or even 'that which causes God's anger.' The term ἐρημώσεως may then be translated as 'that which causes people to abandon' or 'that which causes something to be deserted.' The entire phrase may then be translated in some languages as 'that which God detests and which causes something to be abandoned' or 'left desolate.'

53.39 κοινός^b, ή, όν; ἀκάθαρτος, ον: pertaining to being ritually unacceptable, either as the result of defilement or because of the very nature of the object itself (for example, ritually unacceptable animals) – 'defiled, ritually unclean.' οὐδέποτε ἔφαγον πᾶν κοινὸν καὶ ἀκάθαρτον 'I have never eaten anything defiled and ritually unclean' Ac 10.14. It is possible that there is some subtle distinction in meaning, particularly on a connotative level, between κοινός^b and ἀκάθαρτος in Ac 10.14, but it is difficult to determine the precise differences of meaning on the basis of existing contexts. The two terms are probably used in Ac 10.14 primarily for the sake of emphasis.

53.40 κοινόω^b: to call or to regard something as common or defiled – 'to call something common, to regard something as defiled.' ἃ ὁ θεὸς ἐκαθάρισεν σὺ μὴ κοίνου 'those things which God has purified, you should not regard as defiled' Ac 10.15.

E Baptize (53.41-53.43)

53.41 βαπτίζω^b; βάπτισμα, τος *n*; βαπτισμός^b, οῦ *m*: to employ water in a religious ceremony designed to symbolize purification and initiation on the basis of repentance – 'to baptize, baptism.'[5]
βαπτίζω^b: ἐγὼ ἐβάπτισα ὑμᾶς ὕδατι 'I baptized you with water' Mk 1.8; βαπτισθήτω ἕκαστος

---

5 βαπτίζω^b and βαπτισμός^b should not be confused in meaning with βαπτίζω^a and βαπτισμός^a 'to wash, to purify' (53.31). Both sets of meanings involve purification, but only βαπτίζω^b and βαπτισμός^b involve initiation into a religious community.

ὑμῶν ἐπὶ τῷ ὀνόματι Ἰησοῦ Χριστοῦ 'each one of you should be baptized into the name of Jesus Christ' Ac 2.38.

βάπτισμα: κηρύσσων βάπτισμα μετανοίας '(John) preached the baptism of repentance' or '. . . turn away from your sins and be baptized' Mk 1.4.

βαπτισμός[b]: μετανοίας ἀπὸ νεκρῶν ἔργων, καὶ πίστεως ἐπὶ θεόν, βαπτισμῶν διδαχῆς 'the turning away from useless works, believing in God, teaching about baptisms' He 6.1-2.

According to the *Didache* (early second century) different forms of baptism were practiced in the early church, but with evident preference given to immersion.

The baptism practiced by John the Baptist would seem to reflect far more the Jewish pattern of ritual washing than the type of baptism employed by Christians, which constituted a symbol of initiation into the Christian community on the basis of belief in and loyalty to Jesus Christ as Lord and Savior. There seems, however, to be no reason to employ a different expression for baptism in the case of John than in the case of the early Christians. Most translators actually employ a transliterated form of the Greek term βαπτίζω, but in some languages this is both awkward as well as inappropriate, especially if another term or expression has already been employed and is widely accepted by groups practicing various types or forms of baptism. In some languages, for example, one may employ an expression such as 'to enter the water' or 'to undergo the ritual involving water.' Such expressions do not necessarily imply the quantity of water nor the particular means by which water is applied.

53.42 βαπτιστής, οῦ *m*: (derivative of βαπτίζω[b] 'to baptize,' 53.41) one who baptizes – 'baptizer.' ἐν δὲ ταῖς ἡμέραις ἐκείναις παραγίνεται Ἰωάννης ὁ βαπτιστὴς κηρύσσων ἐν τῇ ἐρήμῳ τῆς Ἰουδαίας 'in those days John the baptizer appeared, preaching in the wilderness of Judea' Mt 3.1.

53.43 λουτρόν, οῦ *n*: ceremonial washing referring to baptism – 'washing, baptism.' ἵνα αὐτὴν ἁγιάσῃ καθαρίσας τῷ λουτρῷ τοῦ ὕδατος ἐν ῥήματι 'in order to dedicate it, having purified it by the washing of water by the word' Eph 5.26. In Eph 5.26 the phrase τῷ λουτρῷ τοῦ ὕδατος has been generally interpreted as a reference to baptism, since the literal washing of an object by means of water would not be a means of ritual purification in the sense in which the church would be dedicated or consecrated to God. Similarly, in Tt 3.5, λουτρόν has generally been regarded as referring to baptism.

F Dedicate, Consecrate (53.44-53.52)

53.44 ἁγιάζω[a]; ἁγιασμός, οῦ *m*: to dedicate to the service of and to loyalty to deity – 'to consecrate, consecration, to dedicate to God, dedication.'

ἁγιάζω[a]: τῇ ἐκκλησίᾳ τοῦ θεοῦ τῇ οὔσῃ ἐν Κορίνθῳ, ἡγιασμένοις ἐν Χριστῷ Ἰησοῦ 'to the church of God which is in Corinth, consecrated to him in union with Christ Jesus' 1 Cor 1.2.

ἁγιασμός: εἰρήνην διώκετε μετὰ πάντων, καὶ τὸν ἁγιασμόν, οὗ χωρὶς οὐδεὶς ὄψεται τὸν κύριον 'pursue peace with all persons, and consecration, without which no one will see the Lord' He 12.14.

Though in certain contexts ἁγιάζω[a] and ἁγιασμός suggest resulting moral behavior, the emphasis is not upon a manner of life but upon religious activity and observances which reflect one's dedication or consecration to God. Accordingly, in 1 Cor 1.2 one may translate ἁγιάζω as 'who have given themselves to God' or 'who serve God with a whole heart.'

53.45 ἁγιωσύνη[b], ης *f*; ὁσιότης[b], ητος *f*: the state resulting from being dedicated to the service of God – 'dedication, consecration.'

ἁγιωσύνη[b]: εἰς τὸ στηρίξαι ὑμῶν τὰς καρδίας ἀμέμπτους ἐν ἁγιωσύνῃ ἔμπροσθεν τοῦ θεοῦ 'so that he may strengthen your heart to be blameless in consecration before God' 1 Th 3.13.

ὁσιότης[b]: ἐν ὁσιότητι καὶ δικαιοσύνῃ ἐνώπιον αὐτοῦ πάσαις ταῖς ἡμέραις ἡμῶν 'to be dedicated and righteous (literally 'in dedication and righteousness') before him all the days of our life' Lk 1.75. For another interpretation of ὁσιότης in Lk 1.75, see 88.25.

53.46 ἅγιος^b, α, ον; ὅσιος^b, α, ον: pertaining to being dedicated or consecrated to the service of God – 'devout, godly, dedicated.'

ἅγιος^b: ἐφοβεῖτο τὸν Ἰωάννην, εἰδὼς αὐτὸν ἄνδρα δίκαιον καὶ ἅγιον 'he feared John because he knew that John was a good and holy man' Mk 6.20.

ὅσιος^b: οὐδὲ δώσεις τὸν ὅσιόν σου ἰδεῖν διαφθοράν 'you will not allow your devoted one to suffer decay' Ac 2.27.

In some languages it is essential to distinguish between ἅγιος and ὅσιος when these refer to God (see 88.24) and when they refer to persons or objects which have been consecrated to the service of God. It is both theoretically and practically advantageous to make a significant distinction in meaning on the basis of these contextual differences which occur in the Greek NT. It is not difficult to translate ἅγιος and ὅσιος by expressions meaning 'dedicated to God,' 'devout,' 'pious,' etc., but it may be extremely difficult to translate ἅγιος and ὅσιος when applied to God. In some languages one can only use an expression such as 'he who is truly God' or 'he who is in every respect God.'

53.47 ἀνόσιος, ον: pertaining to what is not consecrated or devoted to God – 'unholy, impious, godless.' δικαίω νόμος οὐ κεῖται, ἀνόμοις δὲ καὶ . . . ἁμαρτωλοῖς, ἀνοσίοις 'the law is not for the righteous, but for lawbreakers . . . sinners and the godless' 1 Tm 1.9.

53.48 ἑαυτὸν δίδωμι: (an idiom, literally 'to give oneself') to dedicate oneself to some activity in a completely willing manner, usually implying service on behalf of someone or something – 'to give oneself to, to dedicate oneself to.' ἑαυτοὺς ἔδωκαν πρῶτον τῷ κυρίῳ καὶ ἡμῖν διὰ θελήματος θεοῦ 'they gave themselves first to the Lord and to us by God's will' 2 Cor 8.5.

53.49 βαπτίζω^c: (a figurative extension of meaning of βαπτίζω^b 'to baptize,' 53.41) to cause someone to have a highly significant religious experience involving special manifestations of God's power and presence – 'to baptize.' αὐτὸς δὲ βαπτίσει ὑμᾶς ἐν πνεύματι ἁγίῳ 'but he will baptize you with the Holy

Spirit' Mk 1.8; αὐτὸς ὑμᾶς βαπτίσει ἐν πνεύματι ἁγίῳ καὶ πυρί 'but he will baptize you with the Holy Spirit and fire' Mt 3.11.⁶

53.50 τελειόω^c: to admit into or initiate into faith (possibly based on technical usage in the mystery religions) – 'to admit into, to initiate.' οὐχ ὅτι ἤδη ἔλαβον ἢ ἤδη τετελείωμαι 'not that I have already attained or that I have already become an initiate' Php 3.12. It is important that in Php 3.12 τελειόω is to be understood in the sense of a functional stage of religious attainment. For another interpretation of τελειόω in Php 3.12, see 68.31.

53.51 περιτέμνω; περιτομή, ῆς f: to cut off the foreskin of the male genital organ as a religious rite involving consecration and ethnic identification – 'to circumcise, circumcision.'

περιτέμνω: ὅσοι θέλουσιν εὐπροσωπῆσαι ἐν σαρκί, οὗτοι ἀναγκάζουσιν ὑμᾶς περιτέμνεσθαι 'those who want to show off about external matters are the ones who are trying to force you to be circumcised' Ga 6.12.

περιτομή: διὰ τοῦτο Μωϋσῆς δέδωκεν ὑμῖν τὴν περιτομήν 'Moses therefore gave you circumcision' Jn 7.22.

In the case of societies which practice circumcision, there is normally a perfectly satisfactory term to designate this type of operation, though it may not have any religious significance but only be a part of puberty ritual. For societies which do not practice circumcision or are not well acquainted with such a practice, a term which specifically describes the operation may be both offensive and vulgar. It may therefore be necessary to use a borrowing or to employ a somewhat obscure term such as 'to cut around' and then to explain the specific meaning of the term or phrase in a glossary.

Even in the case of societies which practice circumcision, there may be problems in comprehension of the significance of such an act, and these difficulties may require marginal

---

6 In Mt 3.11 'fire' is generally regarded as a reference to the experience of Pentecost, but it is possible to understand 'fire' in this context as referring to judgment.

notes. If, for example, a society practices circumcision only in connection with puberty
rites, it may seem inexplicable that Jesus
would have been circumcised on the eighth
day after his birth (Lk 2.21). In many societies
such an act would seem to be either a deed of
extreme cruelty to a baby or a sign of mature
sexuality in an infant.

53.52 ἐπισπάομαι: (a technical, and medical
term) to pull the foreskin over the end of the
penis as a means of concealing former circumcision – 'to conceal circumcision, to extend
the foreskin.' μὴ ἐπισπάσθω 'do not conceal
the circumcision' 1 Cor 7.18.
   A literal and descriptive rendering of ἐπισπάομαι could prove to be quite vulgar in
some languages. Furthermore, such a practice
might seem to be medically impossible or absurd, so that in general, translators have used
some such expression as 'do not conceal the
circumcision' or 'do not change the circumcision to appear like uncircumcision,' but often
some additional marginal note is required if
people are to understand satisfactorily what is
involved.

G Worship, Reverence (53.53-53.64)

53.53 σέβομαι; σεβάζομαι; εὐσεβέω[a]: to express in attitude and ritual one's allegiance to
and regard for deity – 'to worship, to venerate.'
σέβομαι: παρὰ τὸν νόμον ἀναπείθει οὗτος τοὺς
ἀνθρώπους σέβεσθαι τὸν θεόν 'this man tried to
persuade people to worship God in a way that
is against the law' Ac 18.13.
σεβάζομαι: καὶ ἐσεβάσθησαν καὶ ἐλάτρευσαν τῇ
κτίσει παρὰ τὸν κτίσαντα 'and worshiped and
venerated what has been created instead of the
Creator' Ro 1.25.
εὐσεβέω[a]: ὃ οὖν ἀγνοοῦντες εὐσεβεῖτε, τοῦτο ἐγὼ
καταγγέλλω ὑμῖν 'what you worship, even
though you do not know it, is what I (now)
proclaim to you' Ac 17.23.
   In a number of languages worship is expressed in an idiomatic manner, for example,
'to bow down before,' 'to lower one's head
before,' 'to raise one's arms to,' 'to sing to,'
'to honor.' It is important in selecting an expression for worship to employ a term or

phrase which will include various aspects of
worship.

53.54 σέβασμα[a], τος *n*: (derivative of σεβάζομαι 'to worship,' 53.53) a place of worship – 'sanctuary.' ἀναθεωρῶν τὰ σεβάσματα
ὑμῶν 'looking at your sanctuaries' Ac 17.23.
For another interpretation of σέβασμα in Ac
17.23, see 53.55.

53.55 σέβασμα[b], τος *n*: (derivative of σεβάζομαι 'to worship,' 53.53) an object which
is worshiped – 'object of worship.' ἀναθεωρῶν
τὰ σεβάσματα ὑμῶν 'looking at your objects of
worship' Ac 17.23. For another interpretation
of σέβασμα in Ac 17.23, see 53.54.

53.56 προσκυνέω[a]: to express by attitude and
possibly by position one's allegiance to and
regard for deity – 'to prostrate oneself in worship, to bow down and worship, to worship.'[7]
εἴδομεν γὰρ αὐτοῦ τὸν ἀστέρα ἐν τῇ ἀνατολῇ καὶ
ἤλθομεν προσκυνῆσαι αὐτῷ 'for we saw his star
in the east and we came to worship him' Mt
2.2.

53.57 προσκυνητής, οῦ *m*: (derivative of
προσκυνέω[a] 'to worship,' 53.56) one who worships – 'worshiper.' ὅτε οἱ ἀληθινοὶ προσ-
κυνηταὶ προσκυνήσουσιν τῷ πατρὶ ἐν πνεύματι
καὶ ἀληθείᾳ 'when the real worshipers will
worship the Father in spirit and in truth' Jn
4.23.

53.58 φοβέομαι[c]: (a figurative extension of
meaning of φοβέομαι[a] 'to fear,' 25.252) to have
profound reverence and respect for deity,
with the implication of awe bordering on fear
– 'to reverence, to worship.' καὶ τὸ ἔλεος αὐτοῦ
εἰς γενεὰς καὶ γενεὰς τοῖς φοβουμένοις αὐτόν
'and his mercy for generation after generation
to those who have reverence for him' Lk 1.50.
   In Ac 13.16 the phrase οἱ φοβούμενοι τὸν
θεόν, literally 'those who fear God,' is essentially a technical phrase to identify non-Jews
who worshiped the God of the Jews. These

---

7 προσκυνέω[a] appears to differ somewhat in meaning
from σέβομαι, σεβάζομαι, and εὐσεβέω[a] 'to worship'
(53.53) in emphasizing more the semantic component of
position or attitude involved in worship.

would have been Gentiles who were 'God fearers' or 'worshipers of God.'

53.59 φόβος^d, ου *m*; δέος, ους *n*: profound respect and awe for deity – 'reverence, awe.' φόβος^d: καὶ πορευομένη τῷ φόβῳ τοῦ κυρίου 'and (the church) lived in reverence for the Lord' Ac 9.31. δέος: λατρεύωμεν . . . μετὰ εὐλαβείας καὶ δέους 'let us worship . . . with reverence and awe' He 12.28.

53.60 ἀφόβως^c: pertaining to being without reverence or awe for God – 'without reverence, shamelessly.' συνευωχούμενοι ἀφόβως 'carousing without reverence for God' or 'carrying on shamelessly' Jd 12. It is also possible that ἀφόβως in Jd 12 should be understood as simply 'being without fear' or 'boldly' (25.253). For another interpretation of ἀφόβως in Jd 12, see 88.151.

53.61 κάμπτω τὸ γόνυ: (a Semitic idiom, literally 'the knee bends' or '. . . bows') to bend or bow the knee as a symbol of religious devotion – 'to worship, to bow before.'[8] ἐμοὶ κάμψει πᾶν γόνυ 'every knee will bow to me' or 'everyone will worship me' Ro 14.11.

53.62 ὀνομάζω τὸ ὄνομα κυρίου: (an idiom, literally 'to name the name of the Lord') to employ the name of the Lord as evidence that one worships the Lord – 'to say that one belongs to the Lord' or 'to declare that one is a worshiper of the Lord.' ἀποστήτω ἀπὸ ἀδικίας πᾶς ὁ ὀνομάζων τὸ ὄνομα κυρίου 'whoever says that he belongs to the Lord must turn away from wrongdoing' 2 Tm 2.19.

53.63 εἰδωλολατρία, ας *f*: the worship of idols – 'idolatry.' φεύγετε ἀπὸ τῆς εἰδωλολατρίας 'keep away from the worship of idols' 1 Cor 10.14.

---

[8] One may also interpret the idiom κάμπτω τὸ γόνυ as consisting of a metonymy in the case of τὸ γόνυ (in other words, 'knee' as a substitute for 'person'). Accordingly, κάμπτω 'to bend' or 'to bow' could then be interpreted as meaning simply 'to worship.'

53.64 εἰδωλολάτρης, ου *m*: a person who worships idols – 'idolater, worshiper of idols.' μηδὲ εἰδωλολάτραι γίνεσθε 'do not be worshipers of idols' 1 Cor 10.7.

H Fasting (53.65)

53.65 νηστεύω; νηστεία^a, ας *f*: to go without food for a set time as a religious duty – 'to fast, fasting.' νηστεύω: οἱ δὲ μαθηταί σου οὐ νηστεύουσιν 'but your disciples do not fast at all' Mt 9.14. νηστεία^a: νηστείαις καὶ δεήσεσιν λατρεύουσα νύκτα καὶ ἡμέραν 'day and night she worshiped (God), fasting and praying' Lk 2.37.

I Roles and Functions (53.66-53.95)

53.66 διακονέω^d: to serve God in some special way, such as a deacon – 'to be a deacon, to minister to.' οὗτοι δὲ δοκιμαζέσθωσαν πρῶτον, εἶτα διακονείτωσαν ἀνέγκλητοι ὄντες 'they should be tested first, and then, if they prove blameless, they should serve as deacons' 1 Tm 3.10.

It seems quite evident that διακονέω^d involved a number of different functions as persons served others, especially in connection with relief to the poor. In some instances it may be best to translate διακονέω^d as 'to have responsibility to help others' or 'to be responsible to take care of the needs of believers.'

53.67 διάκονος^b, ου *m* and *f*: one who serves as a deacon, with responsibility to care for the needs of believers – 'deacon, one who helps the believers.' συνίστημι δὲ ὑμῖν Φοίβην τὴν ἀδελφὴν ἡμῶν, οὖσαν καὶ διάκονον τῆς ἐκκλησίας τῆς ἐν Κεγχρεαῖς 'I recommend to you our sister Phoebe who is a deacon in the church at Cenchreae' Ro 16.1; διακόνους ὡσαύτως σεμνούς 'deacons should be of good character' 1 Tm 3.8.

53.68 εὐπάρεδρον, ου *n*: devoted service to God – 'devoted to, devoted service of, devotion.' εὐπάρεδρον τῷ κυρίῳ ἀπερισπάστως 'devoted service to the Lord without distraction' 1 Cor 7.35.

53.69 ἐπισκοπή^b, ῆς *f*: a religious role involving both service and leadership – 'office, position, ministry as church leader.' τὴν ἐπισκοπὴν αὐτοῦ λαβέτω ἕτερος 'let someone else take his office' Ac 1.20; εἴ τις ἐπισκοπῆς ὀρέγεται, καλοῦ ἔργου ἐπιθυμεῖ 'if a man is eager to fulfill a ministry as a church leader, he desires an excellent work' 1 Tm 3.1. See discussion at 53.71. For a more probable interpretation of ἐπισκοπή in Ac 1.20, see 35.40.

53.70 ἐπισκοπέω[c]: to have responsibility for the care of someone, implying a somewhat official responsibility within a congregation – 'to minister unto, to be responsible, to care for.' ποιμάνατε τὸ ἐν ὑμῖν ποίμνιον τοῦ θεοῦ, ἐπισκοποῦντες μὴ ἀναγκαστῶς 'be shepherds of the flock of God committed to you, being responsible for the care of such and not as a matter of obligation' 1 Pe 5.2. It is possible, however, that ἐπισκοπέω in 1 Pe 5.2 is not to be understood as designating some official responsibility but merely as a role of helping and serving (see 35.39).

53.71 ἐπίσκοπος[b], ου m: one who serves as a leader in a church – 'church leader.' δεῖ γὰρ τὸν ἐπίσκοπον ἀνέγκλητον εἶναι ὡς θεοῦ οἰκονόμον 'since he is in charge of God's work, the church leader should be without fault' Tt 1.7. For ἐπίσκοπος in 1 Pe 2.25, see 35.43.

In translating ἐπισκοπή[b] (53.69), ἐπισκοπέω[c] (53.70), or ἐπίσκοπος[b], it is important to try to combine the concepts of both service and leadership, in other words, the responsibility of caring for the needs of a congregation as well as directing the activities of the membership. In some translations an equivalent may be 'helper and leader.'

53.72 ποιμήν[b], ένος m: (a figurative extension of meaning of ποιμήν[a] 'shepherd,' 44.4) one who is responsible for the care and guidance of a Christian congregation – 'pastor, minister.' αὐτὸς ἔδωκεν τοὺς μὲν ἀποστόλους, τοὺς δὲ προφήτας, τοὺς δὲ εὐαγγελιστάς, τοὺς δὲ ποιμένας καὶ διδασκάλους 'he appointed some to be apostles, some to be prophets, some to be evangelists, others to be pastors and teachers' Eph 4.11. Note that in Eph 4.11 there are four classes of persons, not five, for the last class involves two complementary roles, that of pastor and teacher,

in other words, to guide and help a congregation as well as to teach.

53.73 ἀποστολή, ῆς f: the role of one who has been commissioned and sent as a special messenger – 'apostleship, to be an apostle, to be a special messenger.' δι' οὗ ἐλάβομεν χάριν καὶ ἀποστολήν 'through whom I received the privilege of being an apostle' Ro 1.5. See also ἀπόστολος[a] (53.74).

53.74 ἀπόστολος[a], ου m: one who fulfills the role of being a special messenger (generally restricted to the immediate followers of Jesus Christ, but also extended, as in the case of Paul, to other early Christians active in proclaiming the message of the gospel) – 'apostle, special messenger.' Παῦλος δοῦλος Χριστοῦ Ἰησοῦ, κλητὸς ἀπόστολος 'Paul, a servant of Christ Jesus, called (by God) to be an apostle' Ro 1.1. The relationship of an apostle to Jesus Christ is sometimes expressed as 'being Christ's messenger' or 'being a special messenger of Jesus Christ.' In such a phrase, the term 'special' refers to having been commissioned by Jesus Christ for a particular task or role.

53.75 ψευδαπόστολος, ου m: one who claims to be an apostle but is not – 'false apostle.' οἱ γὰρ τοιοῦτοι ψευδαπόστολοι, ἐργάται δόλιοι 'those people are false apostles who lie about their work' 2 Cor 11.13.

53.76 εὐαγγελιστής, οῦ m: one who announces the gospel – 'evangelist.' εἰσελθόντες εἰς τὸν οἶκον Φιλίππου τοῦ εὐαγγελιστοῦ . . . ἐμείναμεν παρ' αὐτῷ 'we went to the home of the evangelist Philip . . . and stayed with him' Ac 21.8. Though the term εὐαγγελιστής indicates only an individual who 'announces the gospel,' early usage would suggest that this was often a person who went from place to place announcing the good news.

53.77 πρεσβύτερος[b], ου m: a person of responsibility and authority in matters of socio-religious concerns, both in Jewish and Christian societies – 'elder.' ὅπου οἱ γραμματεῖς καὶ οἱ πρεσβύτεροι συνήχθησαν 'where the teachers of the Law and the elders had gathered together' Mt 26.57; ἀπὸ δὲ τῆς Μιλήτου πέμψας εἰς "Εφεσον μετεκαλέσατο τοὺς πρεσβυτέρους τῆς ἐκκλησίας 'he sent a message from Miletus to Ephesus asking the elders of the church to meet him' Ac 20.17. In some languages πρεσβύτεροςᵇ is best rendered as 'older leaders,' but in other languages the more appropriate term would be the equivalent of 'counselor,' since it would be assumed that counselors would be older than the average person in a group as well as having authority to lead and direct activities.

53.78 συμπρεσβύτερος, ου *m*: one who is an elder along with others – 'fellow elder.' πρεσβυτέρους οὖν ἐν ὑμῖν παρακαλῶ ὁ συμπρεσβύτερος 'I appeal to the elders among you, (I who am) an elder along with you' 1 Pe 5.1.

53.79 προφήτης, ου *m*: one who proclaims inspired utterances on behalf of God – 'prophet, inspired preacher.'⁹ τοῦτο δὲ ὅλον γέγονεν ἵνα πληρωθῇ τὸ ῥηθὲν ὑπὸ κυρίου διὰ τοῦ προφήτου 'all this happened in order to make come true what the Lord had said through the prophet' Mt 1.22; κατῆλθέν τις ἀπὸ τῆς Ἰουδαίας προφήτης ὀνόματι "Αγαβος 'a prophet by the name of Agabus came down from Judea' Ac 21.10.
There is a tendency in a number of languages to translate προφήτης only in the sense of 'one who foretells the future,' but foretelling the future was only a relatively minor aspect of the prophet's function, though gradually it became more important. Patristic authors defined the function of a prophet mainly in terms of foretelling the future. In New Testament times, however, the focus was upon the inspired utterance proclaimed on behalf of and on the authority of God. Accordingly, in a number of languages it is more appropriate to translate προφήτης as 'one who speaks for God.'

53.80 προφῆτις, ιδος *f*: a woman who proclaims inspired utterances on behalf of God – 'prophetess, inspired preacher.'⁹ ἦν "Αννα

9 Even in the NT, the role of the προφήτης had become recognized as a special function, and therefore it should not be equated with preaching (33.256-259) in general.

προφῆτις 'there was a prophetess named Anna' Lk 2.36.

53.81 ψευδοπροφήτης, ου *m*: one who claims to be a prophet and is not and thus proclaims what is false – 'false prophet.' πολλοὶ ψευδοπροφῆται ἐγερθήσονται καὶ πλανήσουσιν πολλούς 'many false prophets will appear and fool many people' Mt 24.11.

53.82 Χριστόςᵃ, οῦ *m*; Μεσσίας, ου *m*: (literally 'one who has been anointed') in the NT, titles for Jesus as the Messiah – 'Christ, Messiah' (but in many contexts, and especially without an article, Χριστός becomes a part of the name of Jesus, see 93.387).
Χριστόςᵃ: ἐπυνθάνετο παρ' αὐτῶν ποῦ ὁ Χριστὸς γεννᾶται 'he inquired where the Messiah was to be born' Mt 2.4.
Μεσσίας: οἶδα ὅτι Μεσσίας ἔρχεται, ὁ λεγόμενος Χριστός 'I know that the Messiah, the one called Christ, will come' Jn 4.25.
In a number of languages Χριστός (or Μεσσίας) as a reference to the Messiah, occurs in a transliterated form based either on Χριστός in Greek or on *Messiah* in Hebrew. However, in some languages an attempt is made to represent the significance of the terms Χριστός and Μεσσίας by translating 'God's appointed one' or 'God's specially chosen one' or 'the expected one,' in the sense of one to whom everyone was looking for help and deliverance.

53.83 ἀντίχριστος, ου *m*: one who is opposed to Christ, in the sense of usurping the role of Christ – 'antichrist.' καθὼς ἠκούσατε ὅτι ἀντίχριστος ἔρχεται, καὶ νῦν ἀντίχριστοι πολλοὶ γεγόνασιν 'since you have heard that the antichrist has come, and now there are many antichrists' 1 Jn 2.18. The term ἀντίχριστος appears to have become increasingly equivalent to a proper name as the personification of all that was opposed to and contrary to the role and ministry of Christ.

53.84 ψευδόχριστος, ου *m*: one who claims to be the Christ or the Messiah but is not – 'false Christ, false Messiah.' ἐγερθήσονται γὰρ ψευδόχριστοι καὶ ψευδοπροφῆται . . . ὥστε πλανῆσαι . . . τοὺς ἐκλεκτούς 'false Messiahs

and false prophets will appear . . . to deceive
. . . God's chosen people' Mt 24.24.

53.85 ἱερουργέω; ἱερατεύω: to serve as a
priest in the performance of religious rites
and duties – 'to serve as a priest, to be a
priest.'
ἱερουργέω: εἰς τὰ ἔθνη, ἱερουργοῦντα τὸ εὐαγγέλιον τοῦ θεοῦ 'I serve as a priest by bringing
the good news from God to the Gentiles' Ro
15.16.
ἱερατεύω: ἐγένετο δὲ ἐν τῷ ἱερατεύειν . . . ἔναντι τοῦ θεοῦ 'he was doing his work as a priest
. . . before God' Lk 1.8.
  In contrast with the prophet who speaks to
people on behalf of God, the priest is often
defined as one who represents the people
before God. In reality, however, the priest is
one who is primarily engaged in religious
ritual and ceremony in contrast with the
prophet, whose primary activity is involved in
proclaiming a message. In societies in which
there is no organized priesthood and where
there are only medicine men or shamans, it
has often been possible to translate ἱερουργέω
and ἱερατεύω as simply 'to be God's shaman.'
Whether such an expression can be used
depends very largely upon the connotations
associated with shamanism.

53.86 ἱερατεία, ας *f*; ἱεράτευμα, τος *n*;
ἱερωσύνη, ης *f*: the role of being a priest –
'priesthood, to be a priest.'
ἱερατεία: τὴν ἱερατείαν λαμβάνοντες ἐντολὴν ἔχουσιν ἀποδεκατοῦν τὸν λαὸν κατὰ τὸν νόμον
'those who are priests are commanded to collect a tenth from the people in accordance
with the Law' He 7.5.
ἱεράτευμα: εἰς ἱεράτευμα ἅγιον, ἀνενέγκαι
πνευματικὰς θυσίας '(where) you will serve as
holy priests to offer spiritual sacrifices' 1 Pe
2.5.
ἱερωσύνη: μετατιθεμένης γὰρ τῆς ἱερωσύνης ἐξ
ἀνάγκης καὶ νόμου μετάθεσις γίνεται 'when the
role of the priest is changed, there also
necessarily has to be a change of the law' He
7.12.

53.87 ἱερεύς, έως *m*: (derivative of ἱερουργέω
or ἱερατεύω 'to serve as a priest,' 53.85) one
who performs religious rites and duties on
behalf of others – 'priest.' ὅ τε ἱερεὺς τοῦ Διὸς
. . . ἤθελεν θύειν 'the priest of the god Zeus
. . . wanted to offer sacrifice' Ac 14.13.

53.88 ἀρχιερεύς[a], έως *m*: a principal priest,
in view of belonging to one of the highpriestly
families – 'chief priest.' ἀπέστειλαν οἱ ἀρχιερεῖς
καὶ οἱ Φαρισαῖοι ὑπηρέτας ἵνα πιάσωσιν αὐτόν
'the Pharisees and the chief priests sent some
guards to arrest him' Jn 7.32. In a number of
languages 'chief priests' are referred to simply
as 'big priests' or 'important priests.'

53.89 ἀρχιερεύς[b], έως *m*: the principal
member among the chief priests – 'high
priest, most important priest.' ἤγαγον πρὸς
Ἅνναν πρῶτον . . . ὃς ἦν ἀρχιερεὺς τοῦ
ἐνιαυτοῦ ἐκείνου 'they took him first to Annas
. . . who was high priest that year' Jn 18.13.

53.90 ἀρχιερατικός, όν: (derivative of ἀρχιερεύς[b] 'high priest,' 53.89) pertaining to the
high priest – 'highpriestly, of the high priest.'
ὅσοι ἦσαν ἐκ γένους ἀρχιερατικοῦ 'others who
were members of the family of the high priest'
Ac 4.6.

53.91 Λευίτης, ου *m*: a member of the tribe
of Levi and having the responsibility to serve
as an assistant to Jewish priests – 'a Levite.'
ἀπέστειλαν πρὸς αὐτὸν οἱ Ἰουδαῖοι ἐξ Ἱεροσολύμων ἱερεῖς καὶ Λευίτας ἵνα ἐρωτήσωσιν αὐτόν
'the Jews in Jerusalem sent priests and Le-
vites to him to ask him' Jn 1.19. In most languages Λευίτης has simply been transliterated,
but in other languages it is rendered as 'assistant priest,' especially in those contexts in
which religious activity is involved.

53.92 Λευιτικός, ή, όν: (derivative of Λευί
'Levi, son of Jacob,' 93.231) pertaining to being a descendant of Levi – 'Levitical, of Levi.'
εἰ μὲν οὖν τελείωσις διὰ τῆς Λευιτικῆς ἱερωσύνης
ἦν 'if, then, there had been perfection through
the Levitical priesthood' He 7.11. The phrase
'through the Levitical priesthood' may be
rendered in some languages as 'by those
priests who were descended from Levi.'

53.93 ἀρχισυνάγωγος, ου *m*: one who is the
head of and who directs the affairs of a

synagogue – 'president of a synagogue, leader of a synagogue.' ὁ ἀρχισυνάγωγος, ἀγανακτῶν ὅτι τῷ σαββάτῳ ἐθεράπευσεν ὁ Ἰησοῦς 'the president of the synagogue was angry that Jesus had healed (the woman) on a Sabbath' Lk 13.14.

53.94 γραμματεύς[a], έως *m*: a recognized expert in Jewish law (including both canonical and traditional laws and regulations) – 'one who is learned in the Law, expert in the Law' or '. . . Law of Moses.' πῶς λέγουσιν οἱ γραμματεῖς ὅτι ὁ Χριστὸς υἱὸς Δαυίδ ἐστιν; 'how can the experts of the Law say that the Messiah will be the descendant of David?' Mk 12.35.

53.95 νεωκόρος, ου *m*: one who had responsibility to tend to and to guard a temple – 'temple-keeper.' τίς γάρ ἐστιν ἀνθρώπων ὃς οὐ γινώσκει τὴν Ἐφεσίων πόλιν νεωκόρον οὖσαν τῆς μεγάλης Ἀρτέμιδος 'everyone knows that the city of Ephesus is the keeper of the temple of the great Artemis' Ac 19.35. In Ac 19.35 νεωκόρος is used in a somewhat figurative sense, since it is the city of Ephesus itself which is regarded as being the keeper of the temple.

J Magic (53.96-53.101)

53.96 μαγεύω; μαγεία, ας *f*: to practice magic, presumably by invoking supernatural powers – 'to practice magic, to employ witchcraft, magic.'
μαγεύω: ἀνήρ δέ τις ὀνόματι Σίμων προϋπῆρχεν ἐν τῇ πόλει μαγεύων καὶ ἐξιστάνων τὸ ἔθνος τῆς Σαμαρείας 'in that city lived a man named Simon who for some time had astounded the Samaritans with his magic' Ac 8.9.
μαγεία: προσεῖχον δὲ αὐτῷ διὰ τὸ ἱκανῷ χρόνῳ ταῖς μαγείαις ἐξεστακέναι αὐτούς 'he had astounded them with his magic for such a long time that they paid close attention to him' Ac 8.11.

53.97 μάγος[b], ου *m*: (derivative of μαγεύω 'to practice magic,' 53.96) one who practices magic and witchcraft – 'magician.' ἀνθίστατο δὲ αὐτοῖς Ἐλύμας ὁ μάγος 'Elymas the magician opposed them' Ac 13.8.

53.98 βασκαίνω[a]: to bewitch a person, frequently by use of the evil eye and with evil intent – 'to bewitch, to practice magic on.' ὦ ἀνόητοι Γαλάται, Τίς ὑμᾶς ἐβάσκανεν 'you foolish Galatians, who bewitched you' Ga 3.1. βασκαίνω[a] differs from μαγεύω 'to practice magic' (53.96) in that the former involves the use of so-called 'black magic,' but for a different interpretation of βασκαίνω in Ga 3.1, see 88.159.

53.99 περίεργος, ου *m*: the use of magic based on superstition – 'magic, witchcraft.' ἱκανοὶ δὲ τῶν τὰ περίεργα πραξάντων συνενέγκαντες τὰς βίβλους κατέκαιον 'many of those who had practiced witchcraft brought their books together and burned them' Ac 19.19.

53.100 φαρμακεία, ας *f*; φάρμακον, ου *n*: the use of magic, often involving drugs and the casting of spells upon people – 'to practice magic, to cast spells upon, to engage in sorcery, magic, sorcery.'
φαρμακεία: ἐν τῇ φαρμακείᾳ σου ἐπλανήθησαν πάντα τὰ ἔθνη 'with your magic spells you deceived all the peoples (of the world)' Re 18.23.
φάρμακον: οὐ μετενόησαν ἐκ τῶν φόνων αὐτῶν οὔτε ἐκ τῶν φαρμάκων αὐτῶν 'they did not repent of their murders nor of their magic' Re 9.21.
φαρμακεία and the variant φάρμακον (as in Re 9.21) differ from the preceding terms (53.96-53.99) in that the focus is upon the use of certain potions or drugs and the casting of spells.

53.101 φάρμακος, ου *m*: (derivative of φαρμακεία 'to practice magic, to engage in sorcery,' 53.100) one who uses magic and sorcery – 'sorcerer.' ἔξω οἱ κύνες καὶ οἱ φάρμακοι καὶ οἱ πόρνοι καὶ οἱ φονεῖς 'outside (the city) are the perverts, the sorcerers, the immoral, and the murderers' Re 22.15.

K Exorcism (53.102-53.103)

53.102 ἐκβάλλω[e]: to cause a demon to no longer possess or control a person – 'to cast out, to make go out, to exorcise.' οἱ δὲ Φαρισαῖοι ἔλεγον, Ἐν τῷ ἄρχοντι τῶν δαιμονίων ἐκβάλλει τὰ δαιμόνια 'but the Pharisees said, By the prince of the demons he casts out demons' Mt 9.34; καὶ δαιμόνια πολλὰ ἐξέβαλεν 'and he cast out many demons' Mk 1.34. The process of exorcism is expressed in different languages in a number of diverse ways, for example, 'to make leave,' 'to chase away,' 'to force to run,' 'to destroy,' 'to overpower,' or 'to kill.'

53.103 ἐξορκιστής, οῦ *m*: one who drives out evil spirits, usually by invoking supernatural persons or powers or by the use of magic formulas – 'exorcist, one driving out evil spirits.' ἐπεχείρησαν δέ τινες καὶ τῶν περιερχομένων Ἰουδαίων ἐξορκιστῶν ὀνομάζειν . . . κυρίου Ἰησοῦ 'some Jews who travelled around and drove out evil spirits also tried to use the name . . . of the Lord Jesus (to do it)' Ac 19.13.

L Sacrilege (53.104-53.105)

53.104 ἱεροσυλέω[b]: to commit sacrilege by doing harm or damage to sacred objects in temples – 'to commit sacrilege, to desecrate.' ὁ βδελυσσόμενος τὰ εἴδωλα ἱεροσυλεῖς; 'you who detest idols, do you commit sacrilege?' or '. . . commit sacrilege by damaging temples?' Ro 2.22. In biblical times the damaging of valuable objects in a temple was more than simply a criminal act, since it involved a serious breach of respect for supernatural beings. Accordingly, doing harm to sacred objects in a temple would be regarded as a particularly godless deed. For another interpretation of ἱεροσυλέω in Ro 2.22, see 57.241.

53.105 ἱερόσυλος, ου *m*: one who commits sacrilege by damaging sacred objects in temples – 'desecrator, one who commits sacrilege.' ἠγάγετε γὰρ τοὺς ἄνδρας τούτους οὔτε ἱεροσύλους οὔτε βλασφημοῦντας τὴν θεὸν ἡμῶν 'for you have brought these men who are neither desecrators nor ones who speak evil of our goddess' Ac 19.37. For another interpretation of ἱερόσυλος in Ac 19.37, see 57.242.

54 Maritime Activities[1]

54.1 πλέω; πλοῦς, πλοός, acc. πλοῦν *m*: the movement of a boat or ship through the water, either rowed or blown by the wind – 'to sail, sailing.'
πλέω: πλεόντων δὲ αὐτῶν ἀφύπνωσεν 'while they were sailing, he fell asleep' Lk 8.23.
πλοῦς: ὄντος ἤδη ἐπισφαλοῦς τοῦ πλοός 'sailing had already become dangerous' Ac 27.9.

54.2 βραδυπλοέω: to move slowly by boat – 'to sail slowly.' ἐν ἱκαναῖς δὲ ἡμέραις βραδυπλοοῦντες 'we sailed slowly for several days' Ac 27.7.

54.3 εὐθυδρομέω: to follow a straight course to one's destination or goal – 'to sail a straight course, to sail straight to.' ἀναχθέντες δὲ ἀπὸ Τρῳάδος εὐθυδρομήσαμεν εἰς Σαμοθρᾴκην 'we left by ship from Troas and sailed straight across to Samothrace' Ac 16.11.

54.4 ἀνάγομαι: to begin to go by boat – 'to

---

1 Domain 54 *Maritime Activities* involves those activities relating to ships and to persons who perform various functions with regard to ships.

In this domain there are a number of technical, nautical terms which may seem to have quite arbitrary meanings; nevertheless, one must recognize that for all seagoing peoples there are almost always a number of specialized terms representing various ways in which movement over water is distinguished by specialized lexical units. Other languages may also have a number of highly specialized terms based upon local nautical ex-

perience. For example, in Aymara, a language spoken around Lake Titicaca in South America, there are different terms depending upon the direction, distance, and type of land to which a boat may be going. For example, one term may designate crossing the lake as a whole, while another may only mean crossing a bay or going from one promontory to another. Still other terms are used for following a shoreline. For translations into languages spoken by people who are relatively unfamiliar with navigation by water, it may be necessary to use rather extensive descriptive equivalents.

set sail, to put out to sea.' ἀναχθέντες δὲ ἀπὸ τῆς Πάφου 'they set sail from Paphos' Ac 13.13. In some languages a distinction is made in putting out to sea based upon whether the boat goes out from a beach and thus passes through waves or whether it goes out to sea from a harbor. In the various contexts of the book of Acts it is preferable to use a term which implies a harbor, while in contexts which speak of the Sea of Galilee, movement would normally be from a beach (see 54.5).

54.5 ἐπανάγω^b: to leave the shore for a point out in the water or in the direction of open water – 'to put out to open water, to go away from the shore.' ἠρώτησεν αὐτὸν ἀπὸ τῆς γῆς ἐπαναγαγεῖν ὀλίγον 'he asked him to put out to open water a little off the shore' Lk 5.3.

54.6 ἐκπλέω: to sail out of an area – 'to sail out of port, to sail away from.' ἡμεῖς δὲ ἐξεπλεύσαμεν μετὰ τὰς ἡμέρας τῶν ἀζύμων ἀπὸ Φιλίππων 'we sailed from Philippi after the Feast of Unleavened Bread' Ac 20.6.

54.7 ἀποπλέω: to sail away from a point – 'to sail away, to sail from.' ἐκεῖθέν τε ἀπέπλευσαν εἰς Κύπρον 'they sailed from there to Cyprus' Ac 13.4.

54.8 παραλέγομαι: (a technical, nautical term) to sail along beside some object – 'to sail along the coast, to sail along the shore.' παρελέγοντο τὴν Κρήτην 'they sailed along the coast of Crete' Ac 27.13.

54.9 παραπλέω: to sail to and beyond a particular point – 'to sail past, to sail by.' κεκρίκει γὰρ ὁ Παῦλος παραπλεῦσαι τὴν Ἔφεσον 'Paul decided to sail on by Ephesus' Ac 20.16.

54.10 ὑποπλέω; ὑποτρέχω: to sail or move along beside some object which provides a degree of protection or shelter – 'to sail under the shelter of; to sail on, protected by.'
ὑποπλέω: κἀκεῖθεν ἀναχθέντες ὑπεπλεύσαμεν τὴν Κύπρον 'we set sail from there and sailed on the sheltered side of Cyprus' Ac 27.4.
ὑποτρέχω: νησίον δέ τι ὑποδραμόντες καλούμενον Καῦδα 'we sailed under the protection of a small island called Cauda' Ac 27.16.

54.11 διαπλέω: to sail through an area from one side to the other – 'to sail across.' τό τε πέλαγος τὸ κατὰ τὴν Κιλικίαν καὶ Παμφυλίαν διαπλεύσαντες 'we had sailed across the open sea off the coast of Cilicia and Pamphylia' Ac 27.5.

54.12 παραβάλλω: (a technical, nautical term) to sail up to or near – 'to approach, to arrive at, to sail to.' παρεβάλομεν εἰς Σάμον 'we approached Samos' or 'we arrived at Samos' Ac 20.15.

54.13 καταπλέω: to sail down to a coast – 'to sail toward shore, to approach a shore.' κατέπλευσαν εἰς τὴν χώραν τῶν Γερασηνῶν 'they sailed over to the territory of the Gerasenes' Lk 8.26.

54.14 συμπληρόομαι^a: (a technical, nautical term) to be swamped with water while sailing in a boat – 'to be swamped, to have a boat filling rapidly with water.' καὶ συνεπληροῦντο καὶ ἐκινδύνευον 'and they were being swamped with water and were in danger' Lk 8.23.

54.15 κατέρχομαι^b; κατάγομαι: (technical, nautical terms) to go by ship toward the shore – 'to arrive at land, to put in at.'
κατέρχομαι^b: κατελθὼν εἰς Καισάρειαν 'when he arrived at Caesarea' Ac 18.22.
κατάγομαι: τῇ τε ἑτέρᾳ κατήχθημεν εἰς Σιδῶνα 'the next day we arrived at Sidon' Ac 27.3.

54.16 κατάγω^b: to cause a boat to put in at a shore or to land – 'to put in at, to land, to bring to shore.' καταγαγόντες τὰ πλοῖα ἐπὶ τὴν γῆν 'they brought the boats onto the beach' Lk 5.11.

54.17 ἐξωθέω^b: the movement of a ship being driven ashore – 'to run aground, to run a ship onto a beach.' κόλπον δέ τινα κατενόουν ἔχοντα αἰγιαλὸν εἰς ὃν ἐβουλεύοντο εἰ δύναιντο ἐξῶσαι τὸ πλοῖον 'they noticed a bay with a beach and decided that if possible, they would run the ship aground there' Ac 27.39.²

2 In Ac 27.39 a few manuscripts read ἐκσῶσαι, perhaps not aor inf of ἐκσῴζω (see 21.18), but rather a misspelling for ἐξῶσαι due to homophony.

54.18 ἐπικέλλω: (a technical, nautical term) to cause a ship to run up onto or against a shore – 'to run aground.' περιπεσόντες δὲ εἰς τόπον διθάλασσον ἐπέκειλαν τὴν ναῦν 'but the ship hit a sandbank and went aground' (literally 'but striking a sandbank they ran the ship aground') Ac 27.41. In some instances it may be necessary to translate ἐπικέλλω as 'they caused the ship to get stuck in the sand' or '. . . in the mud.'

54.19 ἐκπίπτω[b]: (a technical, nautical term) to drift off or be blown off one's course and hence run aground – 'to run aground, to be blown off course and run aground.' φοβούμενοί τε μή που κατὰ τραχεῖς τόπους ἐκπέσωμεν 'we were afraid that we would run aground on the rocky coast' Ac 27.29.

54.20 προσορμίζομαι: to moor a ship in a safe place, either by anchor or possibly by drawing up on a beach – 'to moor, to anchor, to tie up.' ἦλθον εἰς Γεννησαρὲτ καὶ προσωρμίσθησαν 'they came to land at Gennesaret, where they tied up the boat' Mk 6.53.

54.21 εὐθύνω[b]: to steer a ship on its course – 'to pilot a ship, to steer a course.' ὅπου ἡ ὁρμὴ τοῦ εὐθύνοντος βούλεται 'wherever the will of the person who pilots it wants (it to go)' Jas 3.4. In a number of languages the equivalent of 'piloting a ship' is 'to hold the rudder' or 'to hold the wheel' (referring to the wheel which controls the position of the rudder).

54.22 κατέχω εἰς: (a nautical idiom, literally 'to control toward') to control the movement of a ship to a particular point – 'to steer, to head for.' κατεῖχον εἰς τὸν αἰγιαλόν 'they steered it toward the beach' Ac 27.40.

54.23 βολίζω: to use a rope with a lead weight attached to it in order to measure the depth of water – 'to take soundings, to heave the lead, to drop a plummet.' βολίσαντες εὗρον ὀργυιὰς εἴκοσι 'they took soundings and found that the water was one hundred and twenty feet deep' or '. . . about forty meters deep' or '. . . twenty fathoms deep' Ac 27.28.

54.24 περιαιρέω[b]: (a technical, nautical term) to raise the anchor in preparation for departing – 'to lift anchor, to sail off.' ὅθεν περιελόντες κατηντήσαμεν εἰς Ῥήγιον 'from there we lifted anchor and arrived at Rhegium' or 'from there we sailed off . . .' Ac 28.13.

54.25 ὑποζώννυμι: (a technical, nautical term) to brace a ship – 'to fasten ropes around, to brace.' ὑποζωννύντες τὸ πλοῖον 'they fastened ropes around the ship' Ac 27.17.

54.26 ναυαγέω: to experience or suffer shipwreck – 'to be shipwrecked.' τρὶς ἐναυάγησα 'three times I suffered shipwreck' 2 Cor 11.25.

In some languages it is necessary to specify the particular cause of a shipwreck, for example, 'the ship struck a rock or reef' or 'the ship sank because of a storm' or 'the ship collided with another ship and sank.' In view of the context of 2 Cor 11.25, it is probably best to select an expression which would refer to a ship sinking because of a storm, though obviously one cannot be certain.

54.27 ὁ ἐπὶ τόπον πλέων: one who frequently travels by sea – 'sea traveller, sea merchant.'[3] πᾶς κυβερνήτης καὶ πᾶς ὁ ἐπὶ τόπον πλέων . . . ἀπὸ μακρόθεν ἔστησαν 'all ship captains and sea travellers . . . stood a long way off' Re 18.17.

54.28 κυβερνήτης, ου m: one who commands a ship – 'captain of a ship.' ὁ δὲ ἑκατοντάρχης τῷ κυβερνήτῃ καὶ τῷ ναυκλήρῳ μᾶλλον ἐπείθετο ἢ τοῖς ὑπὸ Παύλου λεγομένοις 'the army officer was more convinced by what the captain and the owner of the ship said, than by what Paul said' Ac 27.11. In some languages a captain is simply 'the chief of a ship' or 'one who commands the sailors.'

54.29 ναύκληρος, ου m: one who owns a ship – 'ship owner.' For an illustrative example, see Ac 27.11 in 54.28.

3 There are considerable differences of opinion as to the meaning of the expression ὁ ἐπὶ τόπον πλέων. It may denote merely passengers, but it probably has a more specialized meaning. Some prefer to interpret it as meaning 'one who sails along the coast.'

54.30 ναύτης, ου *m*: one who works on a ship – 'sailor.' τῶν δὲ ναυτῶν ζητούντων φυγεῖν ἐκ τοῦ πλοίου καὶ χαλασάντων τὴν σκάφην εἰς τὴν θάλασσαν 'the sailors tried to escape from the ship and lowered the boat into the sea' Ac 27.30. In some languages the equivalent of ναύτης is 'one who handles the ropes' or 'one who works on a boat.'

55 Military Activities

Outline of Subdomains

A   To Arm (55.1)
B   To Fight (55.2-55.6)
C   Army (55.7-55.13)
D   Soldiers, Officers (55.14-55.22)
E   Prisoners of War (55.23-55.25)

A   To Arm (55.1)

55.1 καθοπλίζω: to arm completely with weapons – 'to arm fully.' ὅταν ὁ ἰσχυρὸς καθωπλισμένος φυλάσσῃ τὴν ἑαυτοῦ αὐλήν, ἐν εἰρήνῃ ἐστὶν τὰ ὑπάρχοντα αὐτοῦ 'when a strong man who is fully armed guards his house, his belongings are safe' Lk 11.21. In some languages the equivalent of 'to be fully armed' is 'to have all the weapons one needs to defend oneself' or 'to have the weapons needed in order to be safe.'

B   To Fight (55.2-55.6)

55.2 ἐγείρομαι^c: to go to war against – 'to rise up in arms against, to make war against.' ἐγερθήσεται γὰρ ἔθνος ἐπ' ἔθνος 'one country will make war against another country' Mk 13.8.

55.3 ὑπαντάω^b: to oppose in battle – 'to meet in battle, to face in battle.' πρῶτον βουλεύσεται εἰ δυνατός ἐστιν ἐν δέκα χιλιάσιν ὑπαντῆσαι τῷ μετὰ εἴκοσι χιλιάδων ἐρχομένῳ ἐπ' αὐτόν 'he will first decide if he is strong enough with ten thousand men to face in battle the one who comes against him with twenty thousand men' Lk 14.31.

55.4 στρατεύομαι^a; στρατεία, ας *f*: to engage in war or battle as a soldier – 'to battle, to fight, to engage in war, warfare.'

στρατεύομαι^a: ταύτην τὴν παραγγελίαν παρατίθεμαί σοι . . . ἵνα στρατεύῃ ἐν αὐταῖς τὴν καλὴν στρατείαν 'this command I entrust to you . . . that by these (weapons) you may wage the good battle' 1 Tm 1.18.

στρατεία: τὰ γὰρ ὅπλα τῆς στρατείας ἡμῶν οὐ σαρκικὰ ἀλλὰ δυνατὰ τῷ θεῷ 'the weapons we use in our battle are not the world's but God's powerful weapons' 2 Cor 10.4.

στρατεύομαι^a and στρατεία in 1 Tm 1.18 and 2 Cor 10.4 are used figuratively, and it may be essential to mark this figurative usage as a type of simile. For example, in 1 Tm 1.18 στρατεύομαι may be rendered as 'you may, so to speak, wage the good battle' or 'it is like you are fighting.' Similarly, in 2 Cor 10.4 στρατεία may be rendered as 'in what is like a battle for us.'

55.5 πολεμέω^a; πόλεμος^a, ου *m*: to engage in open warfare – 'to wage war, war, fighting.'

πολεμέω^a: ὁ Μιχαὴλ καὶ οἱ ἄγγελοι αὐτοῦ τοῦ πολεμῆσαι μετὰ τοῦ δράκοντος 'Michael and his angels waged war against the dragon' Re 12.7.

πόλεμος^a: μελλήσετε δὲ ἀκούειν πολέμους καὶ ἀκοὰς πολέμων 'you are going to hear of wars and rumors of war' Mt 24.6.

55.6 μάχαιρα^b, ης *f*; ῥομφαία^b, ας *f* (figurative extensions of meaning of μάχαιρα^a 'sword,' 6.33, and ῥομφαία^a 'broad sword,' 6.32) – 'war, fighting, conflict.'

μάχαιρα^b: οὐκ ἦλθον βαλεῖν εἰρήνην ἀλλὰ μάχαιραν 'I did not come to bring peace, but conflict' Mt 10.34. For another interpretation of μάχαιρα in Mt 10.34, see 39.25.

ῥομφαία^b: ἀποκτεῖναι ἐν ῥομφαίᾳ καὶ ἐν λιμῷ καὶ ἐν θανάτῳ 'to kill with war, famine, and disease' Re 6.8. It is possible that ῥομφαία in Re 6.8 should be understood in its literal meaning of 'broad sword' (see 6.32).

C Army (55.7-55.13)

55.7 στρατόπεδον, ου *n*; στράτευμα[a], τος *n*: a large organized group of soldiers – 'army.' στρατόπεδον: ὅταν δὲ ἴδητε κυκλουμένην ὑπὸ στρατοπέδων Ἰερουσαλήμ 'when you see Jerusalem surrounded by armies' Lk 21.20.[1] στράτευμα[a]: εἶδον τὸ θηρίον καὶ τοὺς βασιλεῖς τῆς γῆς καὶ τὰ στρατεύματα αὐτῶν συνηγμένα ποιῆσαι τὸν πόλεμον 'then I saw the beast and the kings of the earth and their armies gathered to make war' Re 19.19.

55.8 λεγιών, ῶνος *f*: a Roman army unit of about six thousand soldiers – 'legion, army.' ἢ δοκεῖς ὅτι οὐ δύναμαι παρακαλέσαι τὸν πατέρα μου, καὶ παραστήσει μοι ἄρτι πλείω δώδεκα λεγιῶνας ἀγγέλων; 'don't you know that I could call on my Father and at once he would send me more than twelve legions of angels?' Mt 26.53. The expression 'twelve legions of angels' indicates a very large group of angels; accordingly, the meaning may be rendered as 'many, many angels' or 'thousands of angels.'

55.9 σπεῖρα, ης *f*: a Roman military unit of about six hundred soldiers, though only a part of such a cohort was often referred to as a cohort – 'cohort, band of soldiers.' Κορνήλιος, ἑκατοντάρχης ἐκ σπείρης τῆς καλουμένης Ἰταλικῆς 'Cornelius, a captain of the cohort called The Italian' Ac 10.1; Ἰούδας λαβὼν τὴν σπεῖραν καὶ ἐκ τῶν ἀρχιερέων καὶ ἐκ τῶν Φαρισαίων ὑπηρέτας ἔρχεται ἐκεῖ 'Judas came there with a group of soldiers and some temple guards sent by the chief priests and Pharisees' Jn 18.3.

55.10 στράτευμα[b], τος *n*: a small detachment of soldiers – 'some soldiers, a few soldiers, a small group of soldiers.' ἐξουθενήσας δὲ αὐτὸν καὶ ὁ Ἡρῴδης σὺν τοῖς στρατεύμασιν αὐτοῦ καὶ ἐμπαίξας 'Herod and some of his soldiers made fun of him and treated him with contempt' Lk 23.11; ἐκέλευσεν τὸ στράτευμα καταβὰν ἁρπάσαι αὐτόν 'he commanded a group of soldiers to go down and seize him' Ac 23.10.

55.11 τετράδιον, ου *n*: a detachment of four soldiers – 'squad, group of four soldiers.' ἔθετο εἰς φυλακήν, παραδοὺς τέσσαρσιν τετραδίοις στρατιωτῶν φυλάσσειν αὐτόν 'he was put in jail where he was handed over to be guarded by four groups of four soldiers each' Ac 12.4.

55.12 πραιτώριον[b], ου *n*: a detachment of soldiers serving as the palace guard – 'group of soldiers, palace guard.' ὥστε τοὺς δεσμούς μου φανεροὺς ἐν Χριστῷ γενέσθαι ἐν ὅλῳ τῷ πραιτωρίῳ καὶ τοῖς λοιποῖς πᾶσιν 'so that all the palace guard and all others recognize that my being in prison is because of Christ' Php 1.13.

55.13 κουστωδία, ας *f*: a group of soldiers serving as a guard – 'guard.' ἔχετε κουστωδίαν· ὑπάγετε ἀσφαλίσασθε ὡς οἴδατε 'take a guard; go and guard (the grave) as well as you know how' Mt 27.65.

D Soldiers, Officers (55.14-55.22)

55.14 στρατοπέδαρχος, ου *m*: one in command of a military camp – 'camp commander.' παρέδωκε τοὺς δεσμίους τῷ στρατοπεδάρχῳ 'he turned the prisoners over to the camp commander' Ac 28.16 (apparatus).

55.15 χιλίαρχος, ου *m*: a military officer, normally in command of a thousand soldiers – 'commanding officer, general, chiliarch.' ἡ οὖν σπεῖρα καὶ ὁ χιλίαρχος καὶ οἱ ὑπηρέται τῶν Ἰουδαίων συνέλαβον τὸν Ἰησοῦν 'the cohort with their commanding officer and the Jewish guards arrested Jesus' Jn 18.12.

55.16 κεντυρίων, ωνος *m*; ἑκατόνταρχος or ἑκατοντάρχης, ου *m*: a Roman officer in command of about one hundred men – 'centurion, captain.' κεντυρίων: ὁ κεντυρίων ὁ παρεστηκὼς ἐξ ἐναντίας αὐτοῦ 'the centurion who was standing there in front of it' Mk 15.39. ἑκατόνταρχος: προσῆλθεν αὐτῷ ἑκατόνταρχος παρακαλῶν αὐτόν 'a centurion met him and begged for help' Mt 8.5. For ἑκατοντάρχης, see Ac 10.1. In a number of languages, centurion can very readily be rendered by a phrase such as 'a

1 It is possible that στρατόπεδον in Lk 21.20 refers specifically to Roman legions.

commander of a hundred soldiers,' but in many instances the closest natural equivalent is simply 'captain.'

55.17 στρατιώτης, ου *m*: a person of ordinary rank in an army – 'soldier.' τότε οἱ στρατιῶται τοῦ ἡγεμόνος παραλαβόντες τὸν Ἰησοῦν εἰς τὸ πραιτώριον 'then the governor's soldiers took Jesus into the palace' Mt 27.27.

In some languages the normal equivalent of στρατιώτης would be 'one who carries a gun,' but such an expression would be completely anachronistic. Some translators have attempted to substitute a phrase such as 'one who carries a sword,' but this has failed in most cases since it suggests merely individual violence instead of organized warfare. It may therefore be important to use a phrase such as 'one who fights under command' or 'one who is charged by the rulers to fight.'

55.18 στρατεύομαι[b]: (derivative of στρατιώτης 'soldier,' 55.17) to engage in military activity as a soldier – 'to serve as a soldier, to be a soldier.' ἐπηρώτων δὲ αὐτὸν καὶ στρατευόμενοι λέγοντες, Τί ποιήσωμεν καὶ ἡμεῖς; 'some soldiers also asked him, What shall we do?' Lk 3.14.

55.19 στρατολογέω[a]: to cause someone to be a soldier – 'to enlist soldiers.' οὐδεὶς στρατευόμενος ἐμπλέκεται ταῖς τοῦ βίου πραγματείαις, ἵνα τῷ στρατολογήσαντι ἀρέσῃ 'no soldier gets himself mixed up in civilian life, because he must please the man who enlisted him' 2 Tm 2.4. In some languages it may be necessary to specify somewhat more clearly the relationship involved in 'to enlist soldiers.' For example, the last part of 2 Tm 2.4 may be rendered as 'because he must please the one who caused him to be a soldier' or '. . . who got him to be a soldier' or '. . . who induced him to be a soldier for him.' For another interpretation of στρατολογέω in 2 Tm 2.4, see 55.20.

55.20 στρατολογέω[b]: to be a commanding officer of a group of soldiers – 'to be an army commander, to be an army officer.' οὐδεὶς στρατευόμενος ἐμπλέκεται ταῖς τοῦ βίου πραγματείαις, ἵνα τῷ στρατολογήσαντι ἀρέσῃ 'no soldier gets himself mixed up in civilian life, because he must please his army officer' 2 Tm 2.4. For another interpretation of στρατολογέω in 2 Tm 2.4, see 55.19.

55.21 ἱππεύς, έως *m*; **ἱππικόν, οῦ** *n*: a soldier who fights on horseback – 'horseman, cavalryman.'
ἱππεύς: τῇ δὲ ἐπαύριον ἐάσαντες τοὺς ἱππεῖς ἀπέρχεσθαι σὺν αὐτῷ ὑπέστρεψαν εἰς τὴν παρεμβολήν 'the next day (the soldiers) returned to the camp and let the horsemen go on with him' Ac 23.32.
ἱππικόν: ὁ ἀριθμὸς τῶν στρατευμάτων τοῦ ἱππικοῦ δισμυριάδες μυριάδων 'the number of the cavalry soldiers was two hundred million' Re 9.16.

55.22 δεξιολάβος, ου *m*: a soldier armed with a spear – 'spearman.' ἑτοιμάσατε στρατιώτας διακοσίους ὅπως πορευθῶσιν ἕως Καισαρείας, καὶ ἱππεῖς ἑβδομήκοντα καὶ δεξιολάβους διακοσίους 'get two hundred soldiers ready to go to Caesarea along with seventy horsemen and two hundred spearmen' Ac 23.23.

E Prisoners of War (55.23-55.25)

55.23 αἰχμαλωσία, ας *f*: the state of being taken as a prisoner of war and kept a captive – 'captivity.' εἴ τις εἰς αἰχμαλωσίαν, εἰς αἰχμαλωσίαν ὑπάγει 'if anyone is meant for captivity, he (will) go into captivity' Re 13.10. In a number of languages it may be necessary to render 'captivity' in terms of 'being a captive,' and therefore this expression in Re 13.10 may be rendered as 'if anyone is meant to become a captive, he will indeed become a captive.'

55.24 αἰχμαλωτίζω[a]; **αἰχμαλωτεύω**: to cause someone to become a prisoner of war – 'to make captive, to take captive, to capture someone in war.'
αἰχμαλωτίζω[a]: πεσοῦνται στόματι μαχαίρης καὶ αἰχμαλωτισθήσονται εἰς τὰ ἔθνη πάντα 'they will be killed by the sword and taken captive to all countries' Lk 21.24.
αἰχμαλωτεύω: ἀναβὰς εἰς ὕψος ᾐχμαλώτευσεν αἰχμαλωσίαν 'when he went up to the very heights, he took many captives with him' Eph 4.8. In Eph 4.8 αἰχμαλωσία 'captivity' (55.23) is added redundantly to αἰχμαλωτεύω due to

Semitic usage. The combination of words simply means 'to take many captives.'

55.25 αἰχμάλωτος, ου *m*: one who has been taken captive in war – 'captive, prisoner of war.' ἀπέσταλκέν με κηρύξαι αἰχμαλώτοις

ἄφεσιν 'he has sent me to proclaim liberty to the captives' Lk 4.18. In Lk 4.18 αἰχμάλωτος occurs on two levels: (1) in the literal sense of 'being a captive of war' and (2) in the broader sense of referring to all those who are oppressed by foreign domination.

56 Courts and Legal Procedures[1]

Outline of Subdomains

A   Court of Justice (56.1)
B   Lawsuit, Case (56.2-56.3)
C   Accusation (56.4-56.11)
D   Judicial Hearing, Inquiry (56.12-56.19)
E   Judge, Condemn, Acquit (56.20-56.34)
F   Obtain Justice (56.35)
G   Attorney, Lawyer (56.36-56.37)
H   Lead Off to Punishment (56.38)

A   Court of Justice (56.1)

56.1 ἀγοραῖος[b], ου *m*; κριτήριον[a], ου *n*; κρίσις[c], εως *f*; ἡμέρα[e], ας *f*: a court of justice for determining guilt or innocence – 'court, court of justice.'[2]

ἀγοραῖος[b]: εἰ μὲν οὖν Δημήτριος καὶ οἱ σὺν αὐτῷ τεχνῖται ἔχουσι πρός τινα λόγον, ἀγοραῖοι ἄγονται 'if Demetrius and his workers have an accusation against someone, the courts are open' Ac 19.38.

κριτήριον[a]: οὐχ οἱ πλούσιοι καταδυναστεύουσιν ὑμῶν, καὶ αὐτοὶ ἕλκουσιν ὑμᾶς εἰς κριτήρια; 'is it not the rich who oppress you and drag you into court?' Jas 2.6.

κρίσις[c]: ὃς δ᾽ ἂν φονεύσῃ, ἔνοχος ἔσται τῇ κρίσει 'anyone who commits murder will be brought to court' Mt 5.21.[3]

ἡμέρα[e]: ἐμοὶ δὲ εἰς ἐλάχιστόν ἐστιν ἵνα ὑφ᾽ ὑμῶν ἀνακριθῶ ἢ ὑπὸ ἀνθρωπίνης ἡμέρας 'I am not at all concerned about being judged by you or by any human court' 1 Cor 4.3.

For languages which do not have technical terms for a court, it is usually possible to use some such phrase as 'to be brought before a judge' or 'to have judges decide one's case.'

B   Lawsuit, Case (56.2-56.3)

56.2 πρᾶγμα[c], τος *n*; κριτήριον[b], ου *n*; κρίμα[e], τος *n*: legal action taken in a court of law against someone – 'lawsuit, case, legal action.'[4]

πρᾶγμα[c]: τολμᾷ τις ὑμῶν πρᾶγμα ἔχων πρὸς τὸν ἕτερον κρίνεσθαι ἐπὶ τῶν ἀδίκων; 'if one of you has a case against another (Christian brother), how dare he go before heathen judges?' 1 Cor 6.1.

κριτήριον[b]: εἰ ἐν ὑμῖν κρίνεται ὁ κόσμος, ἀνάξιοί ἐστε κριτηρίων ἐλαχίστων; 'if you are to judge the world, are you not capable of small cases?' 1 Cor 6.2.

κρίμα[e]: ἤδη μὲν οὖν ὅλως ἥττημα ὑμῖν ἐστιν ὅτι κρίματα ἔχετε μεθ᾽ ἑαυτῶν 'the very fact that you have lawsuits among yourselves shows that you have failed completely' 1 Cor 6.7.

In most languages there are technical terms for lawsuits or cases in court, but where these do not exist, one may always use a descriptive phrase, for example, 'to accuse someone before a judge' or 'to argue against someone in court' or 'to say in court that someone has done a person harm.'

---

1 The legal procedures described in Domain 56 apply not only to human institutions and activities but also to corresponding judicial procedures in heaven.

2 There are no doubt certain subtle differences of meaning in these terms, especially in their connotations, but it is not possible to specify the difference on the basis of existing contexts.

3 In Mt 5.21 κρίσις probably refers to a local court of justice.

4 It is possible that πρᾶγμα[c] is somewhat more generic in meaning than κριτήριον[b] or κρίμα[e], but it is difficult to determine this from existing contexts.

56.3 εὐνοέω^c: to settle a case out of court – 'to settle with.' ἴσθι εὐνοῶν τῷ ἀντιδίκῳ σου ταχύ 'go settle with your accuser quickly' Mt 5.25. For other interpretations of εὐνοέω in Mt 5.25, see 30.23 and 31.20.

C Accusation⁵ (56.4-56.11)

56.4 αἰτία^b, ας *f*: (a technical, legal term) the basis of or grounds for an accusation in court – 'cause, case, basis for an accusation.' ἐγὼ οὐδεμίαν εὑρίσκω ἐν αὐτῷ αἰτίαν 'I find in him no reason for an accusation' Jn 18.38. For another interpretation of αἰτία in Jn 18.38, see 88.315.

In rendering αἰτία^b as 'basis for an accusation,' one may sometimes speak of 'a reason for accusing someone' or 'why someone should be accused of something bad.'

56.5 αἰτίωμα, τος *n*; αἰτία^c, ας *f*: the content of legal charges brought against someone – 'accusation, charge, complaint.'

αἰτίωμα: πολλὰ καὶ βαρέα αἰτιώματα καταφέροντες ἃ οὐκ ἴσχυον ἀποδεῖξαι 'they made many serious charges against (him) which they were not able to prove' Ac 25.7.

αἰτία^c: ἐπέθηκαν ἐπάνω τῆς κεφαλῆς αὐτοῦ τὴν αἰτίαν αὐτοῦ γεγραμμένην 'above his head they put the written notice of the accusation against him' Mt 27.37.

56.6 ἔγκλημα, τος *n*: (a technical, legal term) a formal indictment or accusation brought against someone – 'indictment, accusation, case.' τόπον τε ἀπολογίας λάβοι περὶ τοῦ ἐγκλήματος 'and might receive an opportunity for a defense against the indictment' Ac 25.16.

56.7 λόγος^j, ου *m*: a formal declaration of charges against someone in court – 'charges, accusation, declaration of wrongdoing.' εἰ μὲν οὖν Δημήτριος καὶ οἱ σὺν αὐτῷ τεχνῖται ἔχουσι πρός τινα λόγον 'if Demetrius and his workers

---

5 In this subdomain it is not always possible to determine accurately some of the subtle distinctions in meaning (particularly on a connotative level) between αἰτία^b (56.4), αἰτίωμα (56.5), αἰτία^c (56.5), ἔγκλημα (56.6), and λόγος^j (56.7).

---

have an accusation against someone' Ac 19.38.

56.8 ἐμφανίζω^d: to make a formal report before authorities on a judicial matter – 'to bring charges, to accuse formally.' οἵτινες ἐνεφάνισαν τῷ ἡγεμόνι κατὰ τοῦ Παύλου 'they brought before the governor charges against Paul' Ac 24.1; περὶ οὗ γενομένου μου εἰς Ἱεροσόλυμα ἐνεφάνισαν οἱ ἀρχιερεῖς καὶ οἱ πρεσβύτεροι τῶν Ἰουδαίων 'when I was in Jerusalem the chief priests and elders of the Jews brought charges against him' Ac 25.15.

56.9 ἐκζητέω^b: to charge someone with a crime or offense – 'to charge, to bring charges against.' ἵνα ἐκζητηθῇ τὸ αἷμα πάντων τῶν προφητῶν τὸ ἐκκεχυμένον ἀπὸ καταβολῆς κόσμου ἀπὸ τῆς γενεᾶς ταύτης 'in order that the people of this generation may be charged with the death of all of the prophets from the time of the creation of the world' Lk 11.50.

56.10 κατὰ λόγον ἀνέχομαι: (an idiom, literally 'to accept in accordance with a charge') to accept a complaint against someone for a legal review – 'to accept a complaint in court, to admit a complaint to judgment.' κατὰ λόγον ἂν ἀνεσχόμην ὑμῶν 'I would formally accept your complaint' Ac 18.14. It is also possible to understand the expression κατὰ λόγον ἀνέχομαι in Ac 18.14 not as an idiom, but as meaning 'to be reasonably patient with.' See 25.171 and 89.18.

56.11 ἀντίδικος^a, ου *m*: one who brings an accusation against someone – 'accuser, plaintiff.' ἴσθι εὐνοῶν τῷ ἀντιδίκῳ σου ταχύ 'go settle with your accuser quickly' Mt 5.25.

D Judicial Hearing, Inquiry (56.12-56.19)

56.12 ἀνακρίνω^b; ἀνάκρισις, εως *f*: to conduct a judicial inquiry – 'to investigate in court, to hear a case, to interrogate, to question.'

ἀνακρίνω^b: ἰδοὺ ἐγὼ ἐνώπιον ὑμῶν ἀνακρίνας οὐθὲν εὗρον ἐν τῷ ἀνθρώπῳ τούτῳ αἴτιον 'now, I conducted a judicial inquiry in your presence and I found nothing that this man is guilty of'

Lk 23.14; Ἡρῴδης δὲ ἐπιζητήσας αὐτὸν καὶ μὴ εὑρὼν ἀνακρίνας τοὺς φύλακας ἐκέλευσεν ἀπαχθῆναι 'Herod looked for him and when he did not find him, he interrogated (or 'he questioned') the guards and commanded them to be led away to punishment' Ac 12.19; ἡ ἐμὴ ἀπολογία τοῖς ἐμὲ ἀνακρίνουσίν ἐστιν αὕτη 'this is my defense to those who hear my case' 1 Cor 9.3. The use of ἀνακρίνω in 1 Cor 9.3 does not imply necessarily the strictly legal procedures of a courtroom. It is also possible to interpret ἀνακρίνω in 1 Cor 9.3 as meaning 'to criticize' or 'to judge' (see 33.412).

ἀνάκρισις: ὅπως τῆς ἀνακρίσεως γενομένης σχῶ τί γράψω 'so that after investigating his case, I may have something to write' Ac 25.26.

56.13 ἀκούω[g]; διακούω: to give a judicial hearing in a legal matter – 'to hear a case, to provide a legal hearing, to hear a case in court.'[6]

ἀκούω[g]: μὴ ὁ νόμος ἡμῶν κρίνει τὸν ἄνθρωπον ἐὰν μὴ ἀκούσῃ πρῶτον παρ' αὐτοῦ καὶ γνῷ τί ποιεῖ; 'according to our Law we cannot condemn a man before a legal hearing to find out what he has done, can we?' Jn 7.51.

διακούω: διακούσομαί σου, ἔφη, ὅταν καὶ οἱ κατήγοροί σου παραγένωνται 'I will hear your case, he said, when your accusers arrive' Ac 23.35.

In some languages the most satisfactory way of speaking about 'a court hearing' is to describe the relationship between the principal participants. This may sometimes be done by translating 'for a judge to listen to an accuser and a defender.'

56.14 ἐπερωτάω[c]: to attempt in a legal or semi-legal procedure to know the truth about a matter, normally by interrogation – 'to question, to interrogate, to try to learn.' ἐπηρώτησεν αὐτὸν ὁ ἡγεμὼν λέγων, Σὺ εἶ ὁ βασιλεὺς τῶν Ἰουδαίων; 'the governor attempted to learn the truth of the matter from him, saying, Are you the king of the Jews?' Mt 27.11.

56.15 ἐπικαλέομαι[b]: to claim one's legal right to have a case reviewed by a higher tribunal – 'to appeal one's case, to appeal to a higher court.' ἀπολελύσθαι ἐδύνατο ὁ ἄνθρωπος οὗτος εἰ μὴ ἐπεκέκλητο Καίσαρα 'this man could have been released if he had not appealed to the Emperor' Ac 26.32. The second clause in Ac 26.32 may also be rendered in a number of languages as 'if he had not asked for the Emperor to listen to his case' or '. . . to judge the accusations against him.'

56.16 ἀνετάζω: to interrogate a defendant during a judicial hearing, often by means of torture or lashing – 'to interrogate, to examine.' εὐθέως οὖν ἀπέστησαν ἀπ' αὐτοῦ οἱ μέλλοντες αὐτὸν ἀνετάζειν 'at once the men who were about to interrogate him drew back from him' Ac 22.29; εἴπας μάστιξιν ἀνετάζεσθαι αὐτὸν ἵνα ἐπιγνῷ δι' ἣν αἰτίαν οὕτως ἐπεφώνουν αὐτῷ 'he told them to examine him by flogging to learn why they (the Jews) were screaming like this against him' Ac 22.24. In the Roman legal system it was customary to use various forms of physical torture in order to extract confessions from persons who were not Romans and who had been charged with serious crimes, particularly crimes against the state.

56.17 ὑπόδικος, ον: pertaining to being subject to justifying behavior before a court of justice – 'answerable to, liable to judgment.' ἵνα πᾶν στόμα φραγῇ καὶ ὑπόδικος γένηται πᾶς ὁ κόσμος τῷ θεῷ 'to silence everyone and make the whole world answerable to God' Ro 3.19.

56.18 ἀναβάλλω: to adjourn a court proceeding until a later time – 'to adjourn a hearing, to stop a hearing and put it off until later.' ἀνεβάλετο δὲ αὐτοὺς ὁ Φῆλιξ, ἀκριβέστερον εἰδὼς τὰ περὶ τῆς ὁδοῦ 'then Felix, who was well informed about the Way, adjourned their hearing' Ac 24.22.

56.19 ἀκατάκριτος, ον: pertaining to not having gone through a judicial hearing, with the implication of not having been condemned – 'without trial.' εἰ ἄνθρωπον Ῥωμαῖον καὶ ἀκατάκριτον ἔξεστιν ὑμῖν μαστίζειν; 'is it lawful for you to whip a Roman citizen who has not been tried for any crime?' Ac 22.25.

---

6 ἀκούω[g] and διακούω apparently differ somewhat in meaning from ἀνακρίνω[b] (56.12) in that the former two seem to be more neutral in connotation and do not appear to imply later condemnation.

E Judge, Condemn, Acquit
(56.20-56.34)

56.20 κρίνω^e; κρίσις^a, εως *f*; κρίμα^a, τος *n*: to decide a question of legal right or wrong, and thus determine the innocence or guilt of the accused and assign appropriate punishment or retribution – 'to decide a legal question, to act as a judge, making a legal decision, to arrive at a verdict, to try a case' (in the passive 'to stand trial').[7]

κρίνω^e: σὺ κάθη κρίνων με κατὰ τὸν νόμον 'you sit (there) to judge me according to the Law' Ac 23.3; εἶπεν οὖν αὐτοῖς ὁ Πιλᾶτος, Λάβετε αὐτὸν ὑμεῖς, καὶ κατὰ τὸν νόμον ὑμῶν κρίνατε αὐτόν 'Pilate said to them, Take him yourselves and try him according to your law' Jn 18.31; ἕως πότε, ὁ δεσπότης ὁ ἅγιος καὶ ἀληθινός, οὐ κρίνεις καὶ ἐκδικεῖς τὸ αἷμα ἡμῶν ἐκ τῶν κατοικούντων ἐπὶ τῆς γῆς; 'almighty Lord, holy and true! How long will it be until you judge the people on earth and punish them for killing us?' or '. . . avenge our blood?' Re 6.10.

κρίσις^a: ἀνεκτότερον ἔσται γῆ Σοδόμων καὶ Γομόρρων ἐν ἡμέρα κρίσεως ἢ τῇ πόλει ἐκείνῃ 'on the day when he judges, he will show more mercy to the people of Sodom and Gomorrah than to the people of that town' Mt 10.15.

κρίμα^a: διαλεγομένου δὲ αὐτοῦ περὶ δικαιοσύνης καὶ ἐγκρατείας καὶ τοῦ κρίματος τοῦ μέλλοντος 'but as he went on discussing about goodness, self-control, and the coming day when (God) will judge everyone' Ac 24.25.

The process of legal judging is often expressed idiomatically. In Africa, one of the standard phrases for judging is 'to cut a palaver,' but other expressions in other languages may be 'to find guilt,' 'to point the finger at wrong,' or 'to untangle strife.'

56.21 διαγινώσκω^b; διάγνωσις, εως *f*: to make a judgment on legal matters, with the implication of thorough examination – 'to decide a case, to arrive at a verdict after examination.'

διαγινώσκω^b: εἶπας, ῞Οταν Λυσίας ὁ χιλίαρχος καταβῇ διαγνώσομαι τὰ καθ' ὑμᾶς 'I will decide your case, he told them, when the commander Lysias arrives' Ac 24.22.

διάγνωσις: τοῦ δὲ Παύλου ἐπικαλεσαμένου τηρηθῆναι αὐτὸν εἰς τὴν τοῦ Σεβαστοῦ διάγνωσιν 'when Paul made his appeal to be held over for the Emperor to decide his case' Ac 25.21.

56.22 κρίμα^b, τος *n*; κρίσις^b, εως *f*: (derivatives of κρίνω^e 'to judge legal cases,' 56.20) the authority or right to judge guilt or innocence – 'the right to judge, the authority to judge.'

κρίμα^b: κρίμα ἐδόθη αὐτοῖς 'they were given the authority to judge' Re 20.4.

κρίσις^b: τὴν κρίσιν πᾶσαν δέδωκεν τῷ υἱῷ 'he has given the right to judge to his Son' Jn 5.22.

56.23 κριτικός, ή, όν: (derivative of κρίνω^e 'to judge legal cases,' 56.20) pertaining to the ability or capacity to judge legal cases – 'able to judge, to have the capacity to judge.'

κριτικὸς ἐνθυμήσεων καὶ ἐννοιῶν καρδίας 'able to judge the desires and thoughts of people's hearts' He 4.12.

56.24 κρίσις^d, εως *f*; κρίμα^c, τος *n*: the legal decision rendered by a judge, whether for or against the accused – 'verdict, sentence, judgment.'

κρίσις^d: ἔνδειγμα τῆς δικαίας κρίσεως τοῦ θεοῦ 'here is the proof that God's verdict is just' 2 Th 1.5; ἡ κρίσις ἡ ἐμὴ δικαία ἐστίν 'my judgment is just' Jn 5.30.

κρίμα^c: τὸ . . . κρίμα ἐξ ἑνὸς εἰς κατάκριμα 'the . . . verdict followed one (offense) and brought condemnation' Ro 5.16.

56.25 κρίσις^f, εως *f*: the administration of justice – 'justice, fairness.' ἕως ἂν ἐκβάλῃ εἰς νῖκος τὴν κρίσιν 'until he causes justice to triumph' Mt 12.20. It may be difficult to speak of 'justice triumphing,' and so in some languages it may be necessary to translate 'so that all accusations are judged justly' or 'so that everyone receives what he should' or 'until all judgments are just.'

---

7 κρίνω^e, κρίσις^a, and κρίμα^a often appear in contexts referring to the judgment of God, particularly in reference to the so-called 'end times,' but the limited differences in semantic components of meaning in contexts referring to God's judgment do not warrant setting up a separate set of meanings.

56.26 ἀπόκριμα, τος *n*: an official decision, frequently involving a legal verdict – 'decision, verdict.' αὐτοὶ ἐν ἑαυτοῖς τὸ ἀπόκριμα τοῦ θανάτου ἐσχήκαμεν 'we felt that the sentence of death had been passed against us' 2 Cor 1.9. In 2 Cor 1.9 ἀπόκριμα is used figuratively; no actual official decision had been made, but in view of all of the difficulties which Paul and his colleagues had suffered, it seemed as though such an official decision had been rendered.

56.27 δικαιοκρισία, ας *f*: a right or just verdict or judgment – 'right judgment, just verdict.' θησαυρίζεις σεαυτῷ ὀργὴν ἐν ἡμέρᾳ ὀργῆς καὶ ἀποκαλύψεως δικαιοκρισίας τοῦ θεοῦ 'you are making your own punishment even greater on the day when God's wrath and right verdict will be revealed' Ro 2.5.

56.28 κριτής, οῦ *m*; δικαστής, οῦ *m*: one who presides over a court session and pronounces judgment – 'judge.'
κριτής: ἀπόκειταί μοι ὁ τῆς δικαιοσύνης στέφανος, ὃν ἀποδώσει μοι ὁ κύριος ἐν ἐκείνῃ τῇ ἡμέρᾳ, ὁ δίκαιος κριτής 'the crown of righteousness is waiting for me, which the Lord, the righteous judge, will give me on that day' 2 Tm 4.8.
δικαστής: τίς σε κατέστησεν ἄρχοντα καὶ δικαστὴν ἐφ' ἡμῶν; 'who made you ruler and judge over us?' Ac 7.27.[8]

56.29 ἄρχων[b], οντος *m*: a minor government official serving as a judge – 'official, judge.' ὡς γὰρ ὑπάγεις μετὰ τοῦ ἀντιδίκου σου ἐπ' ἄρχοντα 'if someone brings a lawsuit against you and takes you to the judge' Lk 12.58. Though in Lk 12.58 ἄρχων has essentially the same reference as κριτής and δικαστής (56.28), the meaning differs in that ἄρχων represents government authority functioning in judgment on cases.

56.30 κρίνω[f]; κρίσις[e], εως *f*; κρίμα[d], τος *n*: to judge a person to be guilty and liable to

punishment – 'to judge as guilty, to condemn, condemnation.'[9]
κρίνω[f]: μὴ ὁ νόμος ἡμῶν κρίνει τὸν ἄνθρωπον ἐὰν μὴ ἀκούσῃ πρῶτον παρ' αὐτοῦ καὶ γνῷ τί ποιεῖ; 'does our Law permit a man to be condemned before a legal hearing to find out what he has done?' Jn 7.51.
κρίσις[e]: ἤτω δὲ ὑμῶν τὸ Ναὶ ναὶ καὶ τὸ Οὒ οὔ, ἵνα μὴ ὑπὸ κρίσιν πέσητε 'let your "yes" be yes, and your "no" be no, or you will be condemned' Jas 5.12.
κρίμα[d]: οἷς τὸ κρίμα ἔκπαλαι οὐκ ἀργεῖ, καὶ ἡ ἀπώλεια αὐτῶν οὐ νυστάζει 'their condemnation has long been hanging over them, and their destruction has not been sleeping' 2 Pe 2.3.

56.31 κατακρίνω; κατάκρισις, εως *f*; κατάκριμα, τος *n*; καταδικάζω; καταδίκη, ης *f*: to judge someone as definitely guilty and thus subject to punishment – 'to condemn, to render a verdict of guilt, condemnation.'[10]
κατακρίνω: οἱ δὲ πάντες κατέκριναν αὐτὸν ἔνοχον εἶναι θανάτου 'they all decided he was guilty and worthy of death' Mk 14.64; ἵνα μὴ σὺν τῷ κόσμῳ κατακριθῶμεν 'so that we shall not be condemned together with the world' 1 Cor 11.32.
κατάκρισις: εἰ γὰρ τῇ διακονίᾳ τῆς κατακρίσεως δόξα 'if the service by which people are condemned was glorious' 2 Cor 3.9.
κατάκριμα: τὸ . . . κρίμα ἐξ ἑνὸς εἰς κατάκριμα 'the . . . verdict followed one (offense) and brought condemnation' Ro 5.16.
καταδικάζω: οὐκ ἂν κατεδικάσατε τοὺς ἀναιτίους 'you would not condemn people who are not guilty' Mt 12.7.

9 One might argue that the meaning of κρίνω, κρίσις, and κρίμα in the cited contexts is only 'to make a judgment' and that the negative or adverse character of the judgment depends entirely on the context. However, the frequency of the occurrence of κρίνω, κρίσις, and κρίμα in the specific sense of adverse judgment or verdict of guilt is such as to justify setting up two different meanings, one involving simply the process of rendering a legal judgment (56.20) and the other, the process of legal condemnation (56.30).

10 The series κατακρίνω, κατάκρισις, and κατάκριμα probably differs slightly in meaning from καταδικάζω and καταδίκη in that the first series focuses more upon the actual process of judging rather than upon the verdict, but it is not possible to determine this from existing NT contexts.

8 It is possible that in Ac 7.27 δικαστής is more an arbitrator than a person with legal authority. Accordingly, in Ac 7.27 δικαστής might be rendered as 'one who decides differences between us' (see Subdomain G in Domain 30).

καταδίκη: αἰτούμενοι κατ' αὐτοῦ καταδίκην 'they asked that he be condemned' Ac 25.15.

56.32 ὑπὸ κρίσιν πίπτω: (an idiom, literally 'to fall under judgment') to be condemned for acting contrary to laws and regulations – 'to be condemned, to suffer condemnation, to be judged guilty.' ἵνα μὴ ὑπὸ κρίσιν πέσητε 'in order that you may not be condemned' Jas 5.12. In this context the condemnation refers to God's judgment.

56.33 ἡμέρα σφαγῆς: (an idiom, literally 'day of slaughter') a time of destructive judgment – 'day of condemnation.' ἐθρέψατε τὰς καρδίας ὑμῶν ἐν ἡμέρᾳ σφαγῆς 'you have nourished your hearts for the day of condemnation' Jas 5.5. The reference of the phrase ἡμέρα σφαγῆς in Jas 5.5 is the destructive judgment of God, but it is possible that σφαγῆς should be interpreted in a more literal sense of 'destruction' rather than mere condemnation.

56.34 δικαιόω^c; δικαίωσις^b, εως *f*; δικαίωμα^c, τος *n*: the act of clearing someone of transgression – 'to acquit, to set free, to remove guilt, acquittal.'
δικαιόω^c: ἀπὸ πάντων ὧν οὐκ ἠδυνήθητε ἐν νόμῳ Μωϋσέως δικαιωθῆναι 'from all (the sins) from which the Law of Moses could not set you free' Ac 13.38.
δικαίωσις^b: δι' ἑνὸς δικαιώματος εἰς πάντας ἀνθρώπους εἰς δικαίωσιν ζωῆς 'the righteous act of one man sets all people free and gives them life' Ro 5.18.
δικαίωμα^c: τὸ δὲ χάρισμα ἐκ πολλῶν παραπτωμάτων εἰς δικαίωμα 'but the gift after so many sins is acquittal' Ro 5.16.
    In a number of languages the process of acquittal takes the form of a direct statement, for example, 'to say, You are not guilty' or '. . ., You no longer have sin' or, as expressed idiomatically in some instances, '. . ., Sin is no longer on your head' or '. . ., Your sins are now given back to you.'

F Obtain Justice (56.35)

56.35 ἐκδικέω^a; ἐκδίκησις^a, εως *f*: to give justice to someone who has been wronged – 'to give someone justice.'

ἐκδικέω^a: ἐκδίκησόν με ἀπὸ τοῦ ἀντιδίκου μου 'give me justice against my opponent' Lk 18.3.
ἐκδίκησις^a: ὁ δὲ θεὸς οὐ μὴ ποιήσῃ τὴν ἐκδίκησιν τῶν ἐκλεκτῶν αὐτοῦ τῶν βοώντων αὐτῷ ἡμέρας καὶ νυκτός; 'will God not give justice to his own people who cry to him for help day and night?' Lk 18.7.[11]

G Attorney, Lawyer (56.36-56.37)

56.36 ῥήτωρ, ορος *m*:['] one who speaks in court as an attorney or advocate (either for the prosecution or for the defense) – 'lawyer, attorney, advocate.' κατέβη ὁ ἀρχιερεὺς Ἀνανίας μετὰ πρεσβυτέρων τινῶν καὶ ῥήτορος Τερτύλλου τινός 'the high priest Ananias went with some elders and a lawyer (named) Tertullus' Ac 24.1.

56.37 νομικός^b, οῦ *m*: a specialist in civil law – 'lawyer.' Ζηνᾶν τὸν νομικὸν καὶ Ἀπολλῶν σπουδαίως πρόπεμψον 'do all you can to send Zenas the lawyer and Apollos on their way' Tt 3.13. It is possible that νομικός in Tt 3.13 may have designated an expert in interpreting religious law (see 33.338) rather than a general legal practitioner.

H Lead Off to Punishment (56.38)

56.38 ἀπάγω^b: to lead a person away for punishment after being sentenced, frequently employed in a context of putting a condemned person to death – 'to lead off (to punishment or to death).' μὴ εὑρὼν ἀνακρίνας τοὺς φύλακας ἐκέλευσεν ἀπαχθῆναι 'when he did not find him, he interrogated the guards and commanded them to be led off for punishment' Ac 12.19. For another interpretation of ἀπάγω in Ac 12.19, see 20.65.

---

11 It is difficult to determine whether ἐκδίκησις in Lk 18.7 should be interpreted as a state of justice or the activity of giving justice. One might assume that the activity is represented by the verb ποιέω and that ἐκδίκησις then denotes the resulting state, but it is also possible to understand ποιέω as a kind of 'empty verb,' which simply marks a case relationship between the agent (ὁ θεός) and the primary activity in ἐκδίκησις.

57 Possess, Transfer, Exchange[1]

Outline of Subdomains

A Have, Possess, Property, Owner (57.1-57.21)

57.1 ἔχω^a; κατέχω^c; κατάσχεσις^a, εως *f*: to have or possess objects or property (in the technical sense of having control over the use of such objects)[2] – 'to have, to own, to possess, to belong to.'[3]

ἔχω^a: οὐκ ἔχομεν ὧδε εἰ μὴ πέντε ἄρτους 'we have nothing here except five loaves of bread' Mt 14.17; τίς γυνὴ δραχμὰς ἔχουσα δέκα 'there was a woman who had ten drachmas' Lk 15.8. ἔχω^a may also occur in an absolute construction where the objects possessed are not explicitly mentioned in the context: τῷ γὰρ ἔχοντι παντὶ δοθήσεται 'for to everyone who has will something be given' Mt 25.29.

κατέχω^c: ὡς μηδὲν ἔχοντες καὶ πάντα κατέχοντες 'we seem to have nothing but we really possess everything' 2 Cor 6.10.

κατάσχεσις^a: δοῦναι αὐτῷ εἰς κατάσχεσιν αὐτήν 'to give it to him as a possession' Ac 7.5.

57.2 γίνομαι^f; ὑπάρχω^d: to belong to someone – 'to belong to, to have.'[4]

γίνομαι^f: ἐὰν γένηταί τινι ἀνθρώπῳ ἑκατὸν πρόβατα 'if a hundred sheep belong to a man' Mt 18.12.

ὑπάρχω^d: ὑπῆρχεν χωρία τῷ πρώτῳ τῆς νήσου 'fields which belonged to the chief of the island' Ac 28.7.

57.3 ἐπιβάλλω^d: to belong to or to come to belong to, with the possible implication of by right or by inheritance – 'to belong to.' δός μοι τὸ ἐπιβάλλον μέρος τῆς οὐσίας 'give me the share of the property that belongs to me' Lk 15.12.

57.4 ἴδιος^a, α, ον: pertaining to being the exclusive property of someone – 'one's own,

---

1 Domain 57 comprises the meanings of events and related states involving ownership or possession of objects, whether temporary or permanent, movable or immovable, tangible or intangible. The meanings of 'to own' or 'to possess' may imply merely having something in one's own control, that is, 'at one's disposal for use.' Possession often involves the more formal sense of ownership as a socially recognized right to use (exclusively or partially exclusively) by the owner, and accordingly, non-owners are forbidden such use.

In this domain there are numerous states and events, together with certain associated derivatives (affected, agentive, experiencer, locative, etc.). The meanings involving complex activities or commercial exchange, together with their associated states and derivatives, are also included.

2 Ownership usually entails to a greater or lesser degree the social sanctions of the right by the owner to use the object in question and the obligation by non-owners to recognize that right and to desist from such usage.

3 This meaning of 'have/possess' contrasts with 'hold, grasp' (Domain 18), the whole/part relation (Domain 63), to be in a relationship to (Domain 89), to be in a state or condition (Domain 13), and to have authority, power, or control over persons or objects, either sociologically or physically (Domain 37).

4 It would also be possible to classify the meaning of γίνομαι^f and ὑπάρχω^d as belonging to the domain of *Relations* (89), especially if one regards the occurrence of the dative of the possessor with γίνομαι^f and ὑπάρχω^d as being an integral element in the meaning.

one's property.'⁵ οὐδὲ εἷς τι τῶν ὑπαρχόντων αὐτῷ ἔλεγεν ἴδιον εἶναι, ἀλλ' ἦν αὐτοῖς ἅπαντα κοινά 'no one said that any of his property was his own, but they shared with one another everything they had' Ac 4.32; ἕκαστος γὰρ τὸ ἴδιον δεῖπνον προλαμβάνει ἐν τῷ φαγεῖν 'for as you eat, each one goes ahead with his own meal' 1 Cor 11.21.

57.5 περιούσιοςᵃ, ον: pertaining to being a special or a distinctive possession of someone – 'one's private possession, one's special possession.'⁶ καθαρίσῃ ἑαυτῷ λαὸν περιούσιον 'to make us a pure people who belong to him alone' Tt 2.14. For another interpretation of περιούσιος in Tt 2.14, see 58.48.

57.6 μετέχωᵃ: to share in the possession of something – 'to share in, to have a share of.' ὁ ἀλοῶν ἐπ' ἐλπίδι τοῦ μετέχειν 'the one who reaps does so in hope of having a share (of the crop)' 1 Cor 9.10.

57.7 συμμερίζομαι: to share in something by having an appropriate part – 'to share in, to have a part of together with others.' οἱ τῷ θυσιαστηρίῳ παρεδρεύοντες τῷ θυσιαστηρίῳ συμμερίζονταϊ 'those who offer sacrifices on the altar have a share of what is sacrificed' 1 Cor 9.13.

57.8 συμμέτοχος, ου *m*: (derivative of συμμετέχω 'to share in the possession of something,' not occurring in the NT) one who shares in a possession or a relationship – 'sharer, partner.' συμμέτοχα τῆς ἐπαγγελίας ἐν Χριστῷ Ἰησοῦ 'partners in the promise made through Christ Jesus' Eph 3.6.

---

5 τὰ ἴδια is a substantivized form of ἴδιοςᵃ, occurring only in the neuter plural and meaning 'one's own possessions,' as in Lk 18.28, ἰδοὺ ἡμεῖς ἀφέντες τὰ ἴδια ἠκολουθήσαμέν σοι 'look, we have left all our possessions to follow you.' Some scholars, however, interpret τὰ ἴδια in this passage to mean 'one's own home.' In Jn 1.11, εἰς τὰ ἴδια ἦλθεν 'he came into his own possessions,' it is possible to understand τὰ ἴδια in the sense of 'his own nation.'
6 It is possible to classify this meaning of περιούσιος as a kind of relation (see Domain 89) rather than as possession, but the reference is typical of possessive relationships.

57.9 κοινόςᵃ, ή, όν: pertaining to sharing with someone else in a possession or a relationship implying mutual interest – 'shared, mutual, common.' Τίτῳ γνησίῳ τέκνῳ κατὰ κοινὴν πίστιν '(I write) to Titus, my true son in (our) mutual faith' or '. . . in the faith that we have in common' Tt 1.4. Since the emphasis in Tt 1.4 is upon the fact that Paul and Titus have the same faith, one may also translate as '. . . the faith that you and I have' or '. . . the faith we both believe in.'

57.10 συγκοινωνόςᵇ, οῦ *m*: one who shares jointly with someone else in a possession or relationship, with emphasis upon that which is in common – 'sharer, partner, one who shares in.' ἵνα συγκοινωνὸς αὐτοῦ γένωμαι 'in order that I might become one who shares in it' (that is, '. . . in the gospel') 1 Cor 9.23.

57.11 κτήτωρ, ορος *m*: (derivative of κτάομαι 'to acquire,' 57.58) one who owns or possesses property – 'owner.' ὅσοι γὰρ κτήτορες χωρίων ἢ οἰκιῶν ὑπῆρχον, πωλοῦντες 'those who were owners of fields or houses would sell them' Ac 4.34.

57.12 κύριοςᵇ, ου *m*: one who owns and controls property, including especially servants and slaves, with important supplementary semantic components of high status and respect – 'owner, master, lord.' κύριος πάντων ὤν '(even) though he is owner of everything' Ga 4.1; λυόντων δὲ αὐτῶν τὸν πῶλον εἶπαν οἱ κύριοι αὐτοῦ πρὸς αὐτούς 'as they were untying the colt, its owners spoke to them' Lk 19.33; οὐκ ἔστιν δοῦλος μείζων τοῦ κυρίου αὐτοῦ 'no slave is greater than his master' Jn 13.16.

57.13 δεσπότηςᵇ, ου *m*: one who owns and/or controls the activities of slaves, servants, or subjects, with the implication of absolute, and in some instances, arbitrary jurisdiction – 'owner, master, lord.' ἡγιασμένον, εὔχρηστον τῷ δεσπότῃ 'dedicated and useful to his master' 2 Tm 2.21.

57.14 οἰκοδεσπότης, ου *m*: one who owns and manages a household, including family, servants, and slaves – 'master of the household.' ἄνθρωπος ἦν οἰκοδεσπότης ὅστις ἐφύτευσεν ἀμπελῶνα 'there was a master of a household who planted a vineyard' Mt 21.33.

57.15 κτῆμα, τος *n*: (derivative of κτάομαι 'to acquire,' 57.58) that which is owned or possessed (usually land) – 'property, possession.' ἦν γὰρ ἔχων κτήματα πολλά 'for he had many possessions' Mt 19.22.

57.16 ὕπαρξις, εως *f* (derivative of ὑπάρχω[d] 'to belong to,' 57.2); τὰ ὑπάρχοντα (neuter plural participle of ὑπάρχω[d] 'to belong to,' 57.2): that which constitutes someone's possession – 'possessions, property.'[7]
ὕπαρξις: τὰ κτήματα καὶ τὰς ὑπάρξεις ἐπίπρασκον 'they would sell their property and possessions' Ac 2.45.[8]
τὰ ὑπάρχοντα: ἐπὶ πᾶσιν τοῖς ὑπάρχουσιν αὐτοῦ καταστήσει αὐτόν 'he will place him over all his property' Mt 24.47.

57.17 τὰ παρόντα: (derivative of πάρειμι[a] 'to be present,' 85.23) what one has on hand as available for use – 'what one has, possessions.' ἀρκούμενοι τοῖς παροῦσιν 'be content with what you have' He 13.5.

57.18 βίος[b], ου *m*: (semantic derivative of βίος[a] 'life,' 41.18) the resources which one has as a means of living – 'possessions, property, livelihood.' αὕτη δὲ ἐκ τῆς ὑστερήσεως αὐτῆς πάντα ὅσα εἶχεν ἔβαλεν, ὅλον τὸν βίον αὐτῆς 'but she, as poor as she was, put in all she had – (she gave) all she had to live on' Mk 12.44; ὁ δὲ διεῖλεν αὐτοῖς τὸν βίον 'so he divided the property between them' Lk 15.12; ἡ ἀλαζονεία τοῦ βίου, οὐκ ἔστιν ἐκ τοῦ πατρός 'the pride in worldly possessions is not from the Father' 1 Jn 2.16.

57.19 οὐσία, ας *f*: (derivative of εἰμί[c] 'to exist,' 13.69) that which exists as property and wealth – 'property, wealth.' πάτερ, δός μοι τὸ ἐπιβάλλον μέρος τῆς οὐσίας 'father, give me now my share of the property' Lk 15.12. In most contexts in which οὐσία occurs in non-biblical Greek, the reference is to considerable possessions or wealth, and accordingly it would be appropriate in Lk 15.12 to speak of 'estate.'

57.20 σκεῦος[c], ους *n* (occurring only in the plural): objects which are possessed – 'goods, belongings, household furnishings.' οὐ δύναται οὐδεὶς εἰς τὴν οἰκίαν τοῦ ἰσχυροῦ εἰσελθὼν τὰ σκεύη αὐτοῦ διαρπάσαι 'no one can break into a strong man's house and take away his belongings' Mk 3.27.

57.21 οἰκία[c], ας *f*; οἶκος[d], ου *m*: (figurative extensions of meaning of οἰκία[a] and οἶκος[a] 'house,' 7.3 and 7.2) possessions associated with a house and household – 'property, possessions.'
οἰκία[c]: οἱ κατεσθίοντες τὰς οἰκίας τῶν χηρῶν 'they take away from widows all that they possess' Mk 12.40. It is also possible in Mk 12.40 to understand τὰς οἰκίας as meaning specifically 'houses.'
οἶκος[d]: κατέστησεν αὐτὸν ἡγούμενον ἐπ' Αἴγυπτον καὶ ἐφ' ὅλον τὸν οἶκον αὐτοῦ 'he made him governor over Egypt and over all his property' Ac 7.10. The rendering 'property' seems to be far more justified by the context and by general usage than the more common meaning of 'household' (see 10.8).

B Have Sufficient (57.22-57.24)

57.22 χορέννυμι[b]: to have enough, often with the implication of even more than enough – 'to have enough, to be satiated.' χορεσθέντες δὲ τροφῆς 'when you have eaten enough' Ac 27.38; ἤδη κεχορεσμένοι ἐστέ 'you already have enough' 1 Cor 4.8. This first statement in 1 Cor 4.8 is probably to be understood ironically, and therefore it may be readily translated as a question, for example, 'do you already have everything you need?' or as a statement referring to what the people of Corinth evidently presumed, for example,

---

7 ὕπαρξις and τὰ ὑπάρχοντα are similar in meaning to κτῆμα (57.15) but are probably more generic in reference and more formal in connotation.

8 It is possible that in Ac 2.45 τὰ κτήματα (see 57.15) refers to real estate (in accordance with later usage of κτῆμα) and that τὰς ὑπάρξεις refers to possessions in general, but the combination of the two expressions may simply be used for emphasis, thus specifying the extent of the possessions in question or the fact that all types of possessions were brought.

'you think you already have all you need.' For another interpretation of χορέννυμι in 1 Cor 4.8, see 25.80.

57.23 πλεονάζω[d]: to have more than enough to meet one's needs – 'to have more than enough, to have too much.' ὁ τὸ πολὺ οὐκ ἐπλεόνασεν 'the one who (gathered) much did not have anything extra' or '. . . did not have too much' 2 Cor 8.15.

57.24 περισσεύω[c]: to have such an abundance as to be more than sufficient – 'to have (much) more than enough, to have an overabundance.' πόσοι μίσθιοι τοῦ πατρός μου περισσεύονται ἄρτων 'all my father's workers have much more than they can eat' Lk 15.17.

C Be Rich, Be Wealthy[9] (57.25-57.35)

57.25 πλουτέω[a]: to have considerably more than what would be regarded as the norm in a society – 'to be rich, to be wealthy, well-to-do.' πλουτοῦντας ἐξαπέστειλεν κενούς 'he has sent away empty those who are rich' Lk 1.53.

57.26 πλούσιος[a], α, ον: pertaining to being rich – 'rich, wealthy, well-to-do.' ὀψίας δὲ γενομένης ἦλθεν ἄνθρωπος πλούσιος ἀπὸ Ἀριμαθαίας 'when it was evening, a rich man from Arimathea arrived' Mt 27.57.

57.27 εὐπορέομαι: to be financially well off – 'to have plenty, to be rich, to be well off.' τῶν δὲ μαθητῶν καθὼς εὐπορεῖτό τις ὥρισαν ἕκαστος αὐτῶν εἰς διακονίαν πέμψαι τοῖς κατοικοῦσιν ἐν τῇ Ἰουδαίᾳ ἀδελφοῖς 'so the disciples agreed to make a contribution for the relief of their Christian brothers in Judea, each one to do this in accordance with how well off he was' Ac 11.29. It may be useful in some languages to translate εὐπορέομαι in Ac 11.29 as 'each one was to do this in proportion as he had more than he needed' or '. . . in proportion to the amount of possessions which he owned.'

57.28 πλουτέω[b]: to prosper to the point of being rich – 'to become rich, to become wealthy, to prosper.' οἱ ἔμποροι τούτων, οἱ πλουτήσαντες ἀπ᾽ αὐτῆς 'the businessmen (literally 'the traders in these (wares). . .') who became rich from doing business in that (city)' Re 18.15. In some instances it may be useful to translate 'to become wealthy' as 'he soon possessed much' or even 'he was no longer poor, but rich.' By introducing 'poor' in contrast with 'rich,' one may identify a change of state.

57.29 πλουτίζω[a]: to cause someone to become rich – 'to enrich, to make rich, to cause to become rich.' ἐν παντὶ πλουτιζόμενοι εἰς πᾶσαν ἁπλότητα 'he will always make you rich enough to be generous at all times' 2 Cor 9.11. The causative in πλουτίζω may sometimes be expressed by a verb meaning 'to help,' for example, 'will help you become rich.'

57.30 πλοῦτος[a], ου m and n: an abundance of possessions exceeding the norm of a particular society and often with a negative connotation – 'wealth, riches, abundance.' ἡ ἀπάτη τοῦ πλούτου καὶ αἱ περὶ τὰ λοιπὰ ἐπιθυμίαι εἰσπορευόμεναι συμπνίγουσιν τὸν λόγον 'the deception of riches and all other kinds of desires crowd in and choke the message' Mk 4.19; ὁ πλοῦτος ὑμῶν σέσηπεν 'your riches have rotted away' Jas 5.2. 'Your riches' may be expressed by means of a descriptive phrase, for example, 'all the many things you possess.'

57.31 χρῆμα[a], τος n: economic resources, usually implying an abundance of such assets – 'riches, wealth, abundance.' πῶς δυσκόλως οἱ τὰ χρήματα ἔχοντες εἰς τὴν βασιλείαν τοῦ θεοῦ εἰσελεύσονται 'how hard it will be for those who are rich to enter the kingdom of God' Mk 10.23.

57.32 εὐπορία[a], ας f: the result of having acquired wealth – 'prosperity.' ἄνδρες, ἐπίστασθε ὅτι ἐκ ταύτης τῆς ἐργασίας ἡ εὐπορία ἡμῖν ἐστιν 'men, you know our prosperity comes from this work' Ac 19.25. It may also be convenient to translate this clause in Ac 19.25 as 'you

---

9 For the contrasting subdomain, see Subdomain F *Be Poor, Be Needy, Poverty* (57.49-57.54).

know that this work we do makes us rich.' For another interpretation of εὐπορία in Ac 19.25, see 57.201.

57.33 τὰ ἀγαθά (occurring only in the plural): possessions which provide material benefits, usually used with reference to movable or storable possessions rather than real estate – 'goods, possessions.' καὶ ἐρῶ τῇ ψυχῇ μου, Ψυχή, ἔχεις πολλὰ ἀγαθὰ κείμενα εἰς ἔτη πολλά 'then I will say to myself, Self, you have all the goods you need for many years' Lk 12.19. It may also be possible to translate Lk 12.19 as 'you have all you need to live well for many years.'

57.34 μαμωνᾶς, ᾶ m (an Aramaic word): wealth and riches, with a strongly negative connotation – 'worldly wealth, riches.' ἐγὼ ὑμῖν λέγω, ἑαυτοῖς ποιήσατε φίλους ἐκ τοῦ μαμωνᾶ τῆς ἀδικίας 'so I tell you: make friends for yourselves with unrighteous worldly wealth' Lk 16.9; οὐ δύνασθε θεῷ δουλεύειν καὶ μαμωνᾷ 'you cannot serve God and riches' Lk 16.13.

57.35 τιμιότης, ητος f: (derivative of τίμιος[a] 'valuable, precious,' 65.2) a large quantity of costly, valuable possessions – 'wealth, riches.' ἐν ᾗ ἐπλούτησαν πάντες οἱ ἔχοντες τὰ πλοῖα ἐν τῇ θαλάσσῃ ἐκ τῆς τιμιότητος αὐτῆς '(she is a city) where all who have ships sailing the seas became rich on her wealth' Re 18.19. 'Wealth' may usually be rendered by 'the many valuable possessions.'

D Treasure (57.36)

57.36 γάζα, ης f: a number of possessions and valuables constituting an important and official asset of a political entity – 'treasury.' ὃς ἦν ἐπὶ πάσης τῆς γάζης αὐτῆς 'who was in charge of all her treasury' Ac 8.27.

E Need, Lack[10] (57.37-57.48)

57.37 ὑστερέω[a]; ὑστέρησις, εως f: to be

lacking in what is essential or needed – 'to lack, to be in need of, to be in want.'[11] ὑστερέω[a]: ὅτε ἀπέστειλα ὑμᾶς ἄτερ βαλλαντίου καὶ πήρας καὶ ὑποδημάτων, μή τινος ὑστερήσατε; 'when I sent you out that time without purse, bag, and shoes, did you lack anything?' Lk 22.35; παρὼν πρὸς ὑμᾶς καὶ ὑστερηθεὶς οὐ κατενάρκησα οὐθενός 'and during the time I was with you I did not burden anyone for help when I was in need' 2 Cor 11.9; περιῆλθον ἐν μηλωταῖς, ἐν αἰγείοις δέρμασιν, ὑστερούμενοι 'they went around in skins of sheep or goats; they were in need' He 11.37.
ὑστέρησις: οὐχ ὅτι καθ᾽ ὑστέρησιν 'not because of any lack' Php 4.11; αὕτη δὲ ἐκ τῆς ὑστερήσεως αὐτῆς πάντα ὅσα εἶχεν ἔβαλεν 'but even though she was in need, she gave everything she had' Mk 12.44.

57.38 ὑστέρημα[a], τος n: (derivative of ὑστερέω[a] 'to be lacking,' 57.37) that which is lacking in what is essential or needed – 'what is lacking, what is needed.'[11] ἐν τῷ νῦν καιρῷ τὸ ὑμῶν περίσσευμα εἰς τὸ ἐκείνων ὑστέρημα 'the plenty which you have at this time should make up for what they lack' 2 Cor 8.14; τὸ γὰρ ὑστέρημά μου προσανεπλήρωσαν οἱ ἀδελφοί 'the fellow believers supplied the things I was lacking' 2 Cor 11.9; αὕτη δὲ ἐκ τοῦ ὑστερήματος αὐτῆς πάντα τὸν βίον ὃν εἶχεν ἔβαλεν 'but she from what she lacked gave all that she had to live on' Lk 21.4.
  In a number of languages the expression of 'lack' may be indicated as 'not to have enough' or 'not to possess what one needs' or 'not to have what one should have.'

57.39 χρῄζω: to lack something which is necessary and particularly needed – 'to need, to lack, to be without.' οἶδεν γὰρ ὁ πατὴρ ὑμῶν ὁ οὐράνιος ὅτι χρῄζετε τούτων ἀπάντων 'your Father in heaven knows you have need of all

---

10 Subdomain E differs from Subdomain F in that the former focuses upon a significant lack of something but does not necessarily imply poverty or destitution.

11 As will be readily noted, the terms ὑστερέω[a] (57.37), ὑστέρησις (57.37), and ὑστέρημα[a] (57.38) occur in contexts implying various degrees of lack, so that in certain contexts one may appropriately translate these terms as 'in dire need,' 'to be poor,' or even 'to be poverty stricken,' but there seems to be no semantically justifiable means by which one may clearly distinguish degrees of lack.

these things' Mt 6.32; ἐγερθεὶς δώσει αὐτῷ ὅσων χρῄζει 'he will get up and give him everything he needs' Lk 11.8.

57.40 χρεία[a], ας *f*: (derivative of χρῄζω 'to lack,' 57.39) that which is lacking and particularly needed – 'need, lack, what is needed.' ταῖς χρείαις τῶν ἁγίων κοινωνοῦντες 'sharing with the fellow believers what they need' Ro 12.13; ἀγόρασον ὧν χρείαν ἔχομεν εἰς τὴν ἑορτήν 'buy what we need for the feast' Jn 13.29; ὁ δὲ θεός μου πληρώσει πᾶσαν χρείαν ὑμῶν 'my God will supply everything you need' Php 4.19.

57.41 ἐλαττονέω: to possess too little of some substance – 'to have too little, to have less.' καὶ ὁ τὸ ὀλίγον οὐκ ἠλαττόνησεν 'and he who (gathered) little did not have too little' 2 Cor 8.15.

57.42 κενός[a], ή, όν: pertaining to being without anything – 'without anything, empty, empty-handed.' καὶ ἀπέστειλαν κενόν 'and sent him back without anything' Mk 12.3; καὶ πλουτοῦντας ἐξαπέστειλεν κενούς 'and sent the rich away empty-handed' Lk 1.53.

57.43 λείπω[a]: to not possess something which is necessary – 'to not have, to be in need of, to lack.' ἐὰν ἀδελφὸς ἢ ἀδελφὴ γυμνοὶ ὑπάρχωσιν καὶ λειπόμενοι τῆς ἐφημέρου τροφῆς 'if there is a fellow believer, man or woman, who needs clothes and has nothing to eat each day' Jas 2.15; ἐν μηδενὶ λειπόμενοι 'lacking in nothing' Jas 1.4.

57.44 λείπω[b]: to be lacking in the sense of not being in someone's possession – 'to be lacking, to not be possessed.'[12] ἔτι ἕν σοι λείπει 'one thing more you still lack' Lk 18.22. For another interpretation of λείπω in Lk 18.22, see 71.33.

57.45 προσδέομαι: to need or lack something further or in addition – 'to be in need of

something more, to lack something additional.' οὐδὲ ὑπὸ χειρῶν ἀνθρωπίνων θεραπεύεται προσδεόμενός τινος 'nor does he need anything more that people can supply by working for him' Ac 17.25. One may also render Ac 17.25 as 'there is nothing that he needs that people can supply by working for him.'

57.46 ἐκλείπω[a]: to change to a state in which something is lacking or insufficient – 'to give out, to fail.'[13] ἑαυτοῖς ποιήσατε φίλους ἐκ τοῦ μαμωνᾶ τῆς ἀδικίας, ἵνα ὅταν ἐκλίπῃ δέξωνται ὑμᾶς εἰς τὰς αἰωνίους σκηνάς 'make friends for yourselves with unrighteous worldly wealth, so that when it gives out you will be welcomed in the eternal home' Lk 16.9. 'To give out' may be expressed as 'to no longer exist' or 'no longer to have any.'

57.47 ἀποστερέω[b]: to cause someone not to possess something – 'to deprive of.' ἀπεστερημένων τῆς ἀληθείας 'being deprived of the truth' 1 Tm 6.5. Though the resulting state of ἀποστερέω[b] may be the mere absence of something, nevertheless the implication is that some activity has taken place to cause a person no longer to possess something. This meaning may then be expressed in some languages as 'to have something taken away from someone.'

57.48 ἐπιτήδειος, α, ον: pertaining to being needed or necessary for some particular purpose – 'needed, necessary, essential.'[14] μὴ δῶτε δὲ αὐτοῖς τὰ ἐπιτήδεια τοῦ σώματος 'but you don't give them the things their bodies need' Jas 2.16.

---

13 It would be possible to interpret ἐκλείπω[a] as a change in a state of existence, and hence it could be treated as a negation of existence (Domain 13), but one could also analyze the meaning of ἐκλείπω[a] as a negation of quantity and thus treat it in Domain 59.

14 In view of the more general meaning of ἐπιτήδειος in non-biblical Greek, one could classify ἐπιτήδειος under Domain 71 *Mode*, since the focus in so many contexts outside of the Scriptures is upon suitability and fitness, but in the one occurrence in the NT, namely Jas 2.16, the element of lack is focal, namely, poverty as a more or less continuous state of lack of needed possessions.

12 It would also be possible to treat λείπω[b] in Domain 13 as an instance of non-existence of a possession.

F Be Poor, Be Needy, Poverty[15]
(57.49-57.54)

57.49 πενιχρός, ά, όν: pertaining to the lack of the essential means of livelihood – 'poor, needy.'[16] εἶδεν δέ τινα χήραν πενιχρὰν βάλλουσαν ἐκεῖ λεπτὰ δύο 'he also saw a very poor widow dropping in two little copper coins' Lk 21.2.

57.50 πένης, ητος *m*: a person who is poor and must live sparingly, but probably not as destitute as a person spoken of as πτωχός[a] (57.53) – 'poor, needy.' ἔδωκεν τοῖς πένησιν 'he gave to the poor' 2 Cor 9.9.

57.51 ἐνδεής, ές: pertaining to lacking what is needed or necessary for existence – 'poor, needy.' οὐδὲ γὰρ ἐνδεής τις ἦν ἐν αὐτοῖς 'there was no one in the group who was in need' Ac 4.34. ἐνδεής is similar in meaning to πτωχός[a] (57.53), but the focus seems to be more upon a severe lack of needed resources rather than upon a state of poverty and destitution.

57.52 πτωχεία, ας *f*: a state of having insufficient possessions – 'poverty, destitution.' ἡ περισσεία τῆς χαρᾶς αὐτῶν καὶ ἡ κατὰ βάθους πτωχεία αὐτῶν ἐπερίσσευσεν εἰς τὸ πλοῦτος τῆς ἁπλότητος αὐτῶν 'the abundance of their joy and the depths of their poverty resulted in an outpouring of extreme generosity' 2 Cor 8.2.

57.53 πτωχός[a], ή, όν: pertaining to being poor and destitute, implying a continuous state – 'poor, destitute.' εἰσέλθῃ δὲ καὶ πτωχὸς ἐν ῥυπαρᾷ ἐσθῆτι 'but there comes in also a poor man in ragged clothing' Jas 2.2. See comments at 57.51.

Since in all societies there are poor people, there is no difficulty involved in finding a suitable expression to designate such persons, but in some languages idiomatic phrases are

used, for example, 'those who walk in rags' or 'those whose ribs are always showing.'

57.54 πτωχεύω: to change to a state of poverty – 'to become poor.'[17] δι' ὑμᾶς ἐπτώχευσεν πλούσιος ὤν 'although (Christ) was rich, he became poor for your sake' 2 Cor 8.9. In some languages it may be inappropriate to translate literally 'rich' and 'poor,' since these may have highly specific meanings and inappropriate connotations for the context of 2 Cor 8.9. Therefore, it may be necessary to translate 'although Christ had previously possessed very much, he became one who possessed nothing and he did this for your sake.'

G Take, Obtain, Gain, Lose[18]
(57.55-57.70)

57.55 λαμβάνω[b]: to acquire possession of something – 'to take, to acquire, to obtain.'[19] καὶ τῷ θέλοντί σοι κριθῆναι καὶ τὸν χιτῶνά σου λαβεῖν, ἄφες αὐτῷ καὶ τὸ ἱμάτιον 'if anyone wants to sue you in court to take your shirt, let him have your coat as well' Mt 5.40. In some languages 'take' in Mt 5.40 may be best rendered as 'go away with' or 'put it on as his own.'

57.56 καταλαμβάνω[a]: to acquire, with the implication of significant effort – 'to acquire, to attain, to obtain, to take.' οὕτως τρέχετε ἵνα καταλάβητε 'run, then, in such a way as to take (the prize)' 1 Cor 9.24.

57.57 κατάσχεσις[b], εως *f*: the act of taking possession of something – 'to take possession, to obtain.' ἐν τῇ κατασχέσει τῶν ἐθνῶν 'took

---

15 Subdomain F differs from the preceding Subdomain E in that the state of lack is more continuous and results in a lower social status as a result of a person being economically dependent.

16 The term πενιχρός appears to be more or less equivalent in meaning to πτωχός[a] (57.53) except for the fact that it is more likely to occur in poetic, literary contexts.

17 Outside of NT usage πτωχεύω means simply 'to be poor,' but in the NT πτωχεύω is used only figuratively in referring to Christ's incarnation.

18 The meanings in this subdomain involve a transfer of possessions but without necessarily the implication of exchange (see Subdomain J). Accordingly, meanings dealing with giving and receiving; buying and selling; earning, hiring, and paying are treated under other subdomains. Subdomain G also contrasts with Domain 18 involving holding and grasping.

19 λαμβάνω[b] in the sense of 'to acquire' is highly generic.

possession of what belonged to the nations' Ac 7.45.

57.58 κτάομαι: to acquire possession of something – 'to get, to acquire, to gain.'[20] ἀποδεκατῶ πάντα ὅσα κτῶμαι 'I give a tenth of everything I gain' Lk 18.12; μὴ κτήσησθε χρυσὸν μηδὲ ἄργυρον μηδὲ χαλκόν 'do not acquire gold, silver, or bronze' Mt 10.9.

57.59 ζητέω[g]: to try to obtain something from someone – 'to try to obtain, to attempt to get, to seek.' ζητοῦντες παρ' αὐτοῦ σημεῖον 'to try to get a sign from him' or 'to try to get him to perform a sign' Mk 8.11.[21] For another interpretation of ζητέω in Mk 8.11, see 33.167.

57.60 ἐπιτυγχάνω[a]: to acquire or gain what is sought after – 'to acquire, to obtain, to attain.' ζηλοῦτε, καὶ οὐ δύνασθε ἐπιτυχεῖν 'you strongly desire things, but you cannot obtain (them)' Jas 4.2; οὕτως μακροθυμήσας ἐπέτυχεν τῆς ἐπαγγελίας 'he was patient, and so he obtained what (God) had promised' He 6.15; τί οὖν; ὃ ἐπιζητεῖ Ἰσραήλ, τοῦτο οὐκ ἐπέτυχεν 'what then? The people of Israel did not obtain what they were looking for' Ro 11.7. It is also possible to interpret ἐπιτυγχάνω in certain contexts as being essentially equivalent to the experiencer of an event and thus equivalent to τυγχάνω (see 90.61).

57.61 περιποιέομαι: to acquire possession of something, with the probable component of considerable effort – 'to acquire, to achieve, to win.' ποιμαίνειν τὴν ἐκκλησίαν τοῦ θεοῦ, ἣν περιεποιήσατο διὰ τοῦ αἵματος τοῦ ἰδίου 'be shepherds of the church of God, which he ac-quired by means of his own Son's death' Ac 20.28; οἱ γὰρ καλῶς διακονήσαντες βαθμὸν ἑαυτοῖς καλὸν περιποιοῦνται 'those who do a good work win for themselves a good standing' 1 Tm 3.13.

57.62 περιποίησις[b], εως f: (derivative of περιποιέομαι 'to acquire,' 57.61) that which is acquired, presumably with considerable effort – 'possessions, property.' λαὸς εἰς περιποίησιν 'a people that has become (God's own) posses-sion' 1 Pe 2.9; ἀλλὰ εἰς περιποίησιν σωτηρίας διὰ τοῦ κυρίου ἡμῶν Ἰησοῦ Χριστοῦ 'but for the possession of salvation through our Lord Jesus Christ' 1 Th 5.9. For another inter-pretation of περιποίησις in 1 Th 5.9, see 90.74.

57.63 κλείς[b], κλειδός f: (a figurative exten-sion of meaning of κλείς[a] 'key,' 6.220) a means of acquiring something – 'the means of, the key to.' ὅτι ἤρατε τὴν κλεῖδα τῆς γνώσεως 'because you have taken the key to knowl-edge' Lk 11.52. One may also translate this expression in Lk 11.52 as 'you have kept to yourselves the key to knowledge' or '. . . the means by which one may gain understand-ing.'

57.64 εὐοδόομαι[b]: (a figurative extension of meaning of εὐοδόομαι 'to travel along a good road,' not occurring in the NT) to be suc-cessful in acquiring profit or gain – 'to pros-per, to gain in business, to gain by work.' ἕκαστος ὑμῶν παρ' ἑαυτῷ τιθέτω θησαυρίζων ὅ τι ἐὰν εὐοδῶται 'each of you must put aside some money, in proportion to what he has earned' 1 Cor 16.2.

57.65 πράσσω[b]; λαμβάνω[d]: to collect what is due (normally in terms of taxes and interest), with the possible implication of extortion (as in Lk 3.13) – 'to receive (interest), to collect (taxes).'
πράσσω[b]: κἀγὼ ἐλθὼν σὺν τόκῳ ἂν αὐτὸ ἔπραξα 'then I would have collected it with interest when I returned' Lk 19.23; μηδὲν πλέον παρὰ τὸ διατεταγμένον ὑμῖν πράσσετε 'do not collect more than you have been authorized' Lk 3.13. λαμβάνω[d]: προσῆλθον οἱ τὰ δίδραχμα λαμ-βάνοντες τῷ Πέτρῳ 'those who collect the two-drachma tax came to Peter' Mt 17.24.

---

20 In several contexts κτάομαι refers to the acquiring of some possession or benefit by means of payment of money, as in Ac 8.20 (τὴν δωρεὰν τοῦ θεοῦ ἐνόμισας διὰ χρημάτων κτᾶσθαι 'you thought you could acquire God's gift with money'), but κτάομαι in itself does not mean 'to buy' but simply 'to acquire,' and if the reference is to buying, then the context must indicate the use of money as a means of acquisition.

21 In Mk 8.11 what is sought is a 'sign,' but obviously this implies that Jesus would have to perform a sign. Nevertheless, the event of producing a sign may be regarded as something which is obtained or acquired.

57.66 λογεία, ας *f*: the act of collecting contributions, especially those involving voluntary response – 'collection.' ἵνα μὴ ὅταν ἔλθω τότε λογεῖαι γίνωνται 'so that there will be no need to collect contributions of money when I come' 1 Cor 16.2. In some instances it may be important to translate λογεία as 'to receive gifts of money,' but the focus is upon the activity of the person or persons engaged in obtaining the contributions. This may be expressed in some instances as 'to go from one person to another to receive their contributions.'

57.67 ἀπόλλυμι[b]: to fail to obtain a valued object – 'to not obtain, to fail to get.' οὐ μὴ ἀπολέσῃ τὸν μισθὸν αὐτοῦ 'he certainly won't fail to get his reward' Mt 10.42.

57.68 ἀπόλλυμι[c]: to lose something which one already possesses – 'to lose.' τίς γυνὴ δραχμὰς ἔχουσα δέκα, ἐὰν ἀπολέσῃ δραχμὴν μίαν 'suppose a woman who has ten silver coins loses one of them' Lk 15.8. ἀπόλλυμι in the sense of losing what one already possesses may be analyzed basically as 'not to have that which one has previously had.' There is, however, no suggestion in ἀπόλλυμι[c] as to the particular type of circumstances involved in the loss, whether, for example, from neglect, by accident, or as the result of some external force. It is also possible to interpret ἀπόλλυμι in Lk 15.8 as 'to not know where something is' (see 27.29).

57.69 ζημιόομαι[a]; ζημία, ας *f*: to suffer the loss of something which one has previously possessed, with the implication that the loss involves considerable hardship or suffering – 'to suffer loss, to forfeit.' ζημιόομαι[a]: δι᾽ ὃν τὰ πάντα ἐζημιώθην 'for the sake of whom I have suffered the loss of all things' Php 3.8; ἐὰν τὸν κόσμον ὅλον κερδήσῃ τὴν δὲ ψυχὴν αὐτοῦ ζημιωθῇ 'if he gains the whole world and loses his life' Mt 16.26. ζημία: πολλῆς ζημίας οὐ μόνον τοῦ φορτίου καὶ τοῦ πλοίου ἀλλὰ καὶ τῶν ψυχῶν ἡμῶν 'great loss not only of the cargo and the ship but also of our lives' Ac 27.10.[22]

22 ζημία may be interpreted either as the process of losing or as that which is lost.

57.70 ἀποτάσσομαι[c]: to willingly give up or set aside what one possesses – 'to give up, to part with one's possessions.' πᾶς ἐξ ὑμῶν ὃς οὐκ ἀποτάσσεται πᾶσιν τοῖς ἑαυτοῦ ὑπάρχουσιν οὐ δύναται εἶναί μου μαθητής 'none of you can be my disciple unless he gives up everything he has' Lk 14.33.

H Give[23] (57.71-57.124)

57.71 δίδωμι[a]; δόσις[a], εως *f*: to give an object, usually implying value – 'to give, giving.'
δίδωμι[a]: κλάσας ἔδωκεν τοῖς μαθηταῖς τοὺς ἄρτους 'he broke the loaves and gave them to the disciples' Mt 14.19.
δόσις[a]: οὐδεμία μοι ἐκκλησία ἐκοινώνησεν εἰς λόγον δόσεως καὶ λήμψεως εἰ μὴ ὑμεῖς μόνοι 'not one church shared with me in the matter of giving and receiving, except you only' Php 4.15.[24]

57.72 δότης, ου *m*: (derivative of δίδωμι[a] 'to give,' 57.71) the one who gives – 'giver.' ἱλαρὸν γὰρ δότην ἀγαπᾷ ὁ θεός 'for God loves a cheerful giver' 2 Cor 9.7.

57.73 δόσις[b], εως *f*; δόμα, τος *n*: (derivatives of δίδωμι[a] 'to give,' 57.71) that which is given – 'gift.'
δόσις[b]: πᾶσα δόσις ἀγαθὴ καὶ πᾶν δώρημα τέλειον ἄνωθέν ἐστιν 'every good gift and every perfect gift comes from above' Jas 1.17.
δόμα: οὐχ ὅτι ἐπιζητῶ τὸ δόμα 'it isn't that I'm trying to get the gift' Php 4.17.

57.74 προδίδωμι: to give in advance of some other event – 'to give beforehand, to give in advance, to give first.' ἢ τίς προέδωκεν αὐτῷ; 'who has ever given (God) something first?'

23 Subdomain H *Give* involves the transfer of some object or benefit from one person to another with the initiative resting with the person who gives and without incurring an obligation on the part of a receiver to reciprocate. Furthermore, the giving of such an object or benefit does not imply remuneration for a previous exchange. For the meanings in Subdomain H, the focus is on the initiative and activity of the former possessor.
24 It is possible to interpret the phrase εἰς λόγον δόσεως καὶ λήμψεως as meaning 'in the calculation of debit and credit,' in which case δόσις would be analyzed as being in Subdomain T of Domain 57.

Ro 11.35. It is possible to render Ro 11.35 as 'who has ever given God something before God gave something.?'

57.75 ἐπιδίδωμι[a]: to give, with the implication of motion toward the receiver – 'to give to, to deliver to.' ἢ καὶ αἰτήσει ᾠόν, ἐπιδώσει αὐτῷ σκορπίον; 'if he requests an egg, will he give him a scorpion?' Lk 11.12.

57.76 ἀναδίδωμι: to hand over or to deliver to (especially in reference to letters), with the possible implication of a somewhat formal activity – 'to hand over, to deliver.' ἀναδόντες τὴν ἐπιστολὴν τῷ ἡγεμόνι 'they delivered the letter to the governor' Ac 23.33.

57.77 παραδίδωμι[a]: to hand over to or to convey something to someone, particularly a right or an authority – 'to give over, to hand over.' ὅτι ἐμοὶ παραδέδοται καὶ ᾧ ἐὰν θέλω δίδωμι αὐτήν 'because this has been handed over to me and I give it to whomever I wish' Lk 4.6. In some languages, however, it is impossible to speak of 'handing over authority.' In some instances one may use a causative expression, for example, 'to cause someone to have.'

57.78 προστίθημι[b]; ἐπιτίθεμαι[a]: to place something at the disposal of someone else – 'to give, to provide, to grant.'
προστίθημι[b]: πλὴν ζητεῖτε τὴν βασιλείαν αὐτοῦ, καὶ ταῦτα προστεθήσεται ὑμῖν 'instead, be concerned with his kingdom, and all these things will be given to you' or '. . . and he will provide you with these things' Lk 12.31.
ἐπιτίθεμαι[a]: ἐπέθεντο τὰ πρὸς τὰς χρείας 'they provided those things that were necessary' Ac 28.10.

57.79 ἀναπληρόω[b]: to provide what has been lacking – 'to provide what is lacking, to make up for.' ὅτι τὸ ὑμέτερον ὑστέρημα οὗτοι ἀνεπλήρωσαν 'because these made up for your absence' 1 Cor 16.17.

57.80 προσφέρω[c]: to present something to someone, often involving actual physical transport of the object in question – 'to bring to, to present to.' ἀνοίξαντες τοὺς θησαυροὺς αὐτῶν προσήνεγκαν αὐτῷ δῶρα 'they opened their bags and presented him with gifts' Mt 2.11.

57.81 παρίστημι[d]: to make something available to someone without necessarily involving actual change of ownership – 'to make available, to provide, to present to.' κτήνη τε παραστῆσαι ἵνα ἐπιβιβάσαντες τὸν Παῦλον 'provide some horses for Paul to ride on' Ac 23.24; παραστῆσαι τὰ σώματα ὑμῶν θυσίαν ζῶσαν 'offer yourselves as a living sacrifice (to God)' Ro 12.1; ὑμᾶς ἑνὶ ἀνδρὶ παρθένον ἁγνὴν παραστῆσαι τῷ Χριστῷ 'present you as a holy virgin to one man, namely, Christ' 2 Cor 11.2.

57.82 τίθημι (παρὰ or πρὸς) τοὺς πόδας: (an idiom, literally 'to put at someone's feet') to present something to someone who is reckoned as having superior status or position – 'to turn over to, to put at someone's disposal.' ἐνέγκας μέρος τι παρὰ τοὺς πόδας τῶν ἀποστόλων ἔθηκεν 'he brought a part of it and turned it over to the apostles' Ac 5.2; ἔθηκεν πρὸς τοὺς πόδας τῶν ἀποστόλων 'he turned (the money) over to the apostles' Ac 4.37.

57.83 δωρέομαι: to give an object or benefit to someone, with the probable implication of greater formality than in the case of δίδωμι[a] (57.71) – 'to give, to bestow, to grant.' ἐδωρήσατο τὸ πτῶμα τῷ Ἰωσήφ 'he granted Joseph the body' Mk 15.45.

57.84 δώρημα, τος n; δωρεά, ᾶς f; δῶρον[a], ου n: (derivatives of δωρέομαι 'to give, to grant,' 57.83) that which is given or granted – 'gift, present.'
δώρημα: πᾶν δώρημα τέλειον ἄνωθέν ἐστιν 'every perfect gift comes from above' Jas 1.17.
δωρεά: λήμψεσθε τὴν δωρεὰν τοῦ ἁγίου πνεύματος 'you will receive (God's) gift, the Holy Spirit' Ac 2.38.
δῶρον[a]: δῶρα πέμψουσιν ἀλλήλοις 'they will send presents to one another' Re 11.10; ἄφες ἐκεῖ τὸ δῶρόν σου ἔμπροσθεν τοῦ θυσιαστηρίου 'leave there your gift before the altar of sacrifice' Mt 5.24. Since δῶρον in Mt 5.24 refers specifically to the sacrifice, it may be useful to translate this phrase as 'leave there your sacrifice before the altar.'

57.85 δωρεάν[a]: (derivative of δωρέομαι 'to give,' 57.83) pertaining to being freely given – 'without cost, as a free gift, without paying.' οὐδὲ δωρεὰν ἄρτον ἐφάγομεν παρά τινος 'we didn't eat anyone's bread without paying for it' 2 Th 3.8.

57.86 δωροφορία, ας *f*: the bringing of a gift or present – 'bringing of gifts.' ἡ δωροφορία μου ἡ εἰς Ἰερουσαλὴμ εὐπρόσδεκτος τοῖς ἁγίοις γένηται 'that my bringing of gifts to Jerusalem may be acceptable to God's people (there)' Ro 15.31 (apparatus).

57.87 σφραγίζω[c]: to arrange to give something to someone in a secure manner – 'to turn over to in a secure way, to give in a secure manner.' σφραγισάμενος αὐτοῖς τὸν καρπὸν τοῦτον 'and having turned over to them in a secure way this contribution' Ro 15.28. For a somewhat different interpretation of σφραγίζω in Ro 15.28, see 15.189.

57.88 κλῆρος[b], **ου** *m*: that which is given as a rightful possession (often in the sense of an inheritance) – 'possession, what is possessed.' εὐχαριστοῦντες τῷ πατρὶ τῷ ἱκανώσαντι ὑμᾶς εἰς τὴν μερίδα τοῦ κλήρου τῶν ἁγίων 'giving thanks to the Father who has made you capable of having a share in what the people of God possess' Col 1.12.

57.89 διαμερίζω[a]; **μερίζω**[b]; **μερισμός**[b], **οῦ** *m*: to distribute objects to a series of persons – 'to distribute, to give to each in turn, distribution.' διαμερίζω[a]: τὰ κτήματα καὶ τὰς ὑπάρξεις ἐπίπρασκον καὶ διεμέριζον αὐτὰ πᾶσιν καθότι ἄν τις χρείαν εἶχεν 'they would sell their property and possessions and distribute the money among all according to what each needed' Ac 2.45. μερίζω[b]: τοὺς δύο ἰχθύας ἐμέρισεν πᾶσιν 'he divided the two fish among them all' Mk 6.41. μερισμός[b]: πνεύματος ἁγίου μερισμοῖς κατὰ τὴν αὐτοῦ θέλησιν 'by (gifts) of the Holy Spirit distributed according to his will' He 2.4.

57.90 μερίζω[c]: to give to someone a part of something – 'to give, to give a part of.' ᾧ καὶ

δεκάτην ἀπὸ πάντων ἐμέρισεν Ἀβραάμ 'to whom Abraham gave a tithe of everything' He 7.2.

57.91 διαιρέω; διαίρεσις[a], **εως** *f*: to divide and distribute to persons on the basis of certain implied distinctions or differences – 'to divide, to distribute, division, distribution.' διαιρέω: ὁ δὲ διεῖλεν αὐτοῖς τὸν βίον 'so he divided his property between them' Lk 15.12. διαίρεσις[a]: διαιρέσεις δὲ χαρισμάτων εἰσίν, τὸ δὲ αὐτὸ πνεῦμα 'there are distributions of spiritual gifts, but the same Spirit' 1 Cor 12.4. In 1 Cor 12.4 it is also possible to interpret διαίρεσις as meaning 'difference' or 'variety' (see 58.39).

57.92 μετρέω[b]: to give a measured portion to someone – 'to give, to apportion.' ἐν ᾧ μέτρῳ μετρεῖτε μετρηθήσεται ὑμῖν 'the measure you give will be the measure you get' Mk 4.24. It is possible to interpret this expression in Mk 4.24 (and also in Mt 7.2) as used in a more figurative sense, for example, 'he will deal with you in the manner that you deal with others.'

57.93 ἀντιμετρέω: to give a measured portion to someone in repayment – 'to repay, to return, to pay back.' ᾧ γὰρ μέτρῳ μετρεῖτε ἀντιμετρηθήσεται ὑμῖν 'the measure you used in dealing (with others) is the one (God) will use in paying you back' Lk 6.38.

57.94 διαδίδωμι: to give something to a series of persons – 'to give out, to distribute.' εὐχαριστήσας διέδωκεν τοῖς ἀνακειμένοις 'he gave thanks and distributed (the bread) to those who were seated' Jn 6.11.

57.95 σκορπίζω[b]: (a figurative extension of meaning of σκορπίζω[a] 'to scatter,' 15.135) to give or distribute generously or in abundance – 'to give generously, to distribute generously.' ἐσκόρπισεν. ἔδωκεν τοῖς πένησιν 'he distributed generously, he gave to the poor' 2 Cor 9.9.[25] In a number of languages 'to give

25 In view of the fact that σκορπίζω in 2 Cor 9.9 is a quotation based on the rendering of the Hebrew text of Ps 112.9, it is possible that σκορπίζω is only used figuratively in this context.

generously' may simply be rendered as 'to give much often,' but one may sometimes employ such figurative expressions as 'to give from a full heart' or 'to give without holding back a thing.'

57.96 μεταδίδωμι: to share with someone else what one has – 'to share, to give.' ὁ ἔχων δύο χιτῶνας μεταδότω τῷ μὴ ἔχοντι 'a person who has two shirts must share with another who doesn't have any' Lk 3.11.

57.97 εὐμετάδοτος, ον: pertaining to being generous in sharing – 'liberal, generous in sharing.' ἀγαθοεργεῖν, πλουτεῖν ἐν ἔργοις καλοῖς, εὐμεταδότους εἶναι '(command them) to be good, to be rich in good works, and to be generous in sharing with others' 1 Tm 6.18.

57.98 κοινωνέω[a]; κοινωνία[b], ας f: to share one's possessions, with the implication of some kind of joint participation and mutual interest – 'to share.'
κοινωνέω[a]: κοινωνείτω δὲ ὁ κατηχούμενος τὸν λόγον τῷ κατηχοῦντι ἐν πᾶσιν ἀγαθοῖς 'the man who is being taught the Christian message should share all the good things he has with his teacher' Ga 6.6.
κοινωνία[b]: μετὰ πολλῆς παρακλήσεως δεόμενοι ἡμῶν τὴν χάριν καὶ τὴν κοινωνίαν τῆς διακονίας τῆς εἰς τοὺς ἁγίους 'they urgently pleaded with us for the privilege of sharing in this service to the people of God' 2 Cor 8.4.

57.99 ἔχω κοινός: (an idiom, literally 'to have in common') to share with one another equitably – 'to share, to share with one another.' εἶχον ἅπαντα κοινά 'they shared all their belongings with one another' Ac 2.44. The mutuality of sharing may be expressed in some languages as 'each person shared with all of the rest' or 'each person gave to the others and received from the others.'

57.100 κοινωνικός, ή, όν: (derivative of κοινωνέω[a] 'to share,' 57.98) pertaining to willing and ready sharing – 'ready to share.' εὐμεταδότους εἶναι, κοινωνικούς 'to be liberal and ready in sharing' 1 Tm 6.18.

57.101 κοινωνία[c], ας f: (derivative of κοινωνέω[a] 'to share,' 57.98) that which is

readily shared – 'willing gift, ready contribution.' εὐδόκησαν γὰρ Μακεδονία καὶ Ἀχαΐα κοινωνίαν τινὰ ποιήσασθαι εἰς τοὺς πτωχοὺς τῶν ἁγίων τῶν ἐν Ἰερουσαλήμ 'Macedonia and Achaia were happy to make a willing contribution to the poor among God's people in Jerusalem' Ro 15.26.

57.102 χαρίζομαι[a]: to give or grant graciously and generously, with the implication of good will on the part of the giver – 'to give, to grant, to bestow generously.'[26] ἐχαρίσατο αὐτῷ τὸ ὄνομα τὸ ὑπὲρ πᾶν ὄνομα 'he bestowed on him a name that is greater than any other name' Php 2.9; τῷ δὲ Ἀβραὰμ δι' ἐπαγγελίας κεχάρισται ὁ θεός 'but because of his promise God graciously gave it to Abraham' Ga 3.18; πῶς οὐχὶ καὶ σὺν αὐτῷ τὰ πάντα ἡμῖν χαρίσεται 'how will he not also, along with him, graciously give us all things' Ro 8.32; ἐλπίζω γὰρ ὅτι διὰ τῶν προσευχῶν ὑμῶν χαρισθήσομαι ὑμῖν 'for I hope that through your prayers I shall be given to you' Phm 22.[27]

57.103 χάρις[b], ιτος f; χάρισμα, τος n: (derivatives of χαρίζομαι[a] 'to give graciously and generously,' 57.102) that which is given freely and generously – 'gift, gracious gift.'
χάρις[b]: τούτους πέμψω ἀπενεγκεῖν τὴν χάριν ὑμῶν εἰς Ἰερουσαλήμ 'I will send these men to convey your gracious gift to Jerusalem' 1 Cor 16.3. χάρις[b] may also occur in contexts in which the meaning of 'generous gift' may imply the purpose of gaining some favor or benefit. In Ac 24.27 (θέλων τε χάριτα καταθέσθαι τοῖς Ἰουδαίοις ὁ Φῆλιξ 'Felix wanted to be offered a generous gift by the Jews') the impli-

26 In the classification of χαρίζομαι[a] there is obviously a problem of what might be called 'fuzzy sets,' since these meanings may involve not only the transfer of actual objects but may often refer equally well to more generalized activities in which one person treats another graciously and generously (see 88.66). As such, these meanings could very well be classified under certain aspects of Domain 25 *Attitudes and Emotions*, though there seems to be no clear-cut distinction. Rather, there seems to be a gradient from one aspect of meaning to another.
27 The form of χαρίζομαι in Phm 22 may best be understood as a passive in contrast with the middle forms of χαρίζομαι which occur with an active sense.

cation is that of 'a bribe,' but probably spoken of euphemistically here as 'a gift.'

χάρισμα: ἵνα τι μεταδῶ χάρισμα ὑμῖν πνευματικόν 'in order that I might share with you some spiritual gift' Ro 1.11; τὸ δὲ χάρισμα τοῦ θεοῦ ζωὴ αἰώνιος ἐν Χριστῷ Ἰησοῦ τῷ κυρίῳ ἡμῶν 'but the gracious gift of God is eternal life in Christ Jesus our Lord' Ro 6.23.

57.104 πλουτέωᶜ: (a figurative extension of meaning of πλουτέωᵇ 'to become rich,' 57.28) to give generously of one's wealth – 'to be generous, to give of one's wealth.' πλουτῶν εἰς πάντας τοὺς ἐπικαλουμένους αὐτόν 'giving generously to all those who call upon him' Ro 10.12.

57.105 εὐλογίαᶜ, ας f: (derivative of εὐλογέωᵇ 'to bless,' 33.470) that which is bestowed or given as a blessing or benefit – 'gift, blessing, contribution.' ταύτην ἑτοίμην εἶναι οὕτως ὡς εὐλογίαν καὶ μὴ ὡς πλεονεξίαν 'then it will be ready as a gift, not as one grudgingly given' 2 Cor 9.5.

57.106 ἁπλότηςᵇ, ητος f: an act of generosity – 'generosity, liberality, to act in a generous manner.' ὁ μεταδιδοὺς ἐν ἁπλότητι 'the person who shares should do it generously' Ro 12.8.

57.107 ἁπλοῦςᵇ, ῆ, οῦν; ἁπλῶς: pertaining to willing and generous giving – 'generous, generously, liberal.'

ἁπλοῦςᵇ: ἐὰν οὖν ᾖ ὁ ὀφθαλμός σου ἁπλοῦς, ὅλον τὸ σῶμά σου φωτεινὸν ἔσται 'if you (literally 'your eye') are generous, then your whole body will be filled with light' Mt 6.22. In Mt 6.22 and the corresponding passage in Lk 11.34, most scholars understand ἁπλοῦς in the sense of 'to be healthy' or 'to be sound' (see 23.132).

ἁπλῶς: αἰτείτω παρὰ τοῦ διδόντος θεοῦ πᾶσιν ἁπλῶς 'let that person ask from God, who gives to all generously' Jas 1.5.

57.108 ὀφθαλμὸς πονηρόςᵇ: (an idiom, literally 'evil eye') to be stingy – 'stingy, miserly.' ἢ ὁ ὀφθαλμός σου πονηρός ἐστιν ὅτι ἐγὼ ἀγαθός εἰμι; 'or are you stingy because I am good?' Mt 20.15. It is also possible that ὀφθαλμὸς πονηρός in Mt 20.15 is to be

understood in the sense of 'jealous,' see 88.165. See also 23.149.

57.109 ἀγαθωσύνηᵇ, ης f: the act of generous giving, with the implication of its relationship to goodness – 'to be generous, generosity.' ὁ δὲ καρπὸς τοῦ πνεύματός ἐστιν ἀγάπη, χαρά . . . ἀγαθωσύνη 'but the Spirit produces love, joy . . . and generosity' Ga 5.22.[28]

57.110 ἀγαθόςᶜ, ή, όν: pertaining to being generous, with the implication of its relationship to goodness – 'generous.' ὁ ὀφθαλμός σου πονηρός ἐστιν ὅτι ἐγὼ ἀγαθός εἰμι; 'or are you jealous because I am generous?' Mt 20.15.[29]

57.111 δικαιοσύνηᵈ, ης f; ἐλεημοσύνηᵃ, ης f: to give to those in need as an act of mercy – 'acts of charity, alms, giving to the needy.'

δικαιοσύνηᵈ: προσέχετε δὲ τὴν δικαιοσύνην ὑμῶν μὴ ποιεῖν ἔμπροσθεν τῶν ἀνθρώπων 'be careful not to do your giving to the needy in public' Mt 6.1. It is also possible to interpret δικαιοσύνη in Mt 6.1 as 'religious observances' (see 53.4).

ἐλεημοσύνηᵃ: αἱ προσευχαί σου καὶ αἱ ἐλεημοσύναι σου ἀνέβησαν εἰς μνημόσυνον ἔμπροσθεν τοῦ θεοῦ 'your prayers and acts of charity have gone up as a memorial before God' Ac 10.4.

57.112 ἐλεημοσύνηᵇ, ης f: (semantic derivative of ἐλεημοσύνηᵃ 'giving to the needy,' 57.111) that which is given to help the needy – 'gift, money given to the needy, charity donation.' τοῦ αἰτεῖν ἐλεημοσύνην παρὰ τῶν εἰσπορευομένων εἰς τὸ ἱερόν 'he begged for donations from people who were going into the Temple' Ac 3.2. In some languages the closest equivalent of ἐλεημοσύνη in Ac 3.2 is simply 'money.'

57.113 ψωμίζωᵇ: (a figurative extension of meaning of ψωμίζωᵃ 'to feed, to give to eat,' 23.5) to give away or dole out, with the probable implication of bit by bit – 'to give away,

---

28 ἀγαθωσύνη in Ga 5.22 may also be understood as 'goodness' (see 88.1).

29 ἀγαθός in Mt 20.15 may also be understood as meaning 'good' (see 88.1).

to dole out.' κἄν ψωμίσω πάντα τὰ ὑπάρχοντά μου 'if I give away everything I own' or 'if I give to others all I have' 1 Cor 13.3.

57.114 ἀποδεκατόω^a; δεκατόομαι: to give a tenth of one's income – 'to give a tenth, to tithe.'
ἀποδεκατόω^a: ἀποδεκατοῦτε τὸ ἡδύοσμον καὶ τὸ πήγανον καὶ πᾶν λάχανον 'you give (to God) a tenth of mint, rue, and all the other herbs' Lk 11.42.
δεκατόομαι: Λευὶ ὁ δεκάτας λαμβάνων δεδεκά-τωται 'Levi, who receives the tenth, paid the tenth' He 7.9. In He 7.9 it may be important to indicate clearly that it was not Levi himself who received the tenth but his descendants. Therefore, one may render the latter part of He 7.9 as 'Levi, whose descendants collect the tenth, also paid it.'

57.115 ἀποδεκατόω^b; δεκατόω: to cause someone to pay a tenth – 'to collect tithes, to exact tithes from.'
ἀποδεκατόω^b: ἐντολὴν ἔχουσιν ἀποδεκατοῦν τὸν λαὸν κατὰ τὸν νόμον 'they are commanded by Law to collect the tenth from the people' He 7.5.
δεκατόω: δεδεκάτωκεν Ἀβραάμ 'he collected one tenth from Abraham' He 7.6.
In a number of languages there are problems involved in speaking of 'a tenth,' and accordingly there are difficulties in formulating expressions about 'tithing.' In some languages one may speak of 'a tenth' as 'one part of ten parts' or 'one part together with nine parts.' 'To tithe' may be rendered as 'from ten parts to pay one part' or 'to pay one part and to keep nine parts.'

57.116 παρατίθημι: to give or to provide for, with the implication of placing something in front of a person, normally food – 'to give food to, to provide with food.' οὐκ ἔχω ὃ παραθήσω αὐτῷ 'I don't have any food to give him' Lk 11.6.

57.117 τιμάω^c: to provide aid or financial assistance, with the implication that this is an appropriate means of showing respect – 'to give assistance to, to provide for the needs of as a sign of respect, to support and honor.'

χήρας τίμα τὰς ὄντως χήρας 'support and honor those widows who really are left alone' 1 Tm 5.3.

57.118 ὀψώνιον^b, ου *n*: money which is needed for living expenses – 'money for support, money to live on.' ἄλλας ἐκκλησίας ἐσύλησα λαβὼν ὀψώνιον πρὸς τὴν ὑμῶν διακονίαν 'I robbed other churches by receiving money for support from them so as to serve you' 2 Cor 11.8. ὀψώνιον in 2 Cor 11.8 may be rendered as 'money on which to live' or 'money for food and lodging.'

57.119 διακονία^c, ας *f*: (semantic derivative of διακονία^a 'to serve,' 35.19) money given to help someone in need – 'contribution, help, support.' παρεθεωροῦντο ἐν τῇ διακονίᾳ τῇ καθημερινῇ αἱ χῆραι αὐτῶν '(they said that) their widows were being neglected in the daily distribution of money for support' Ac 6.1. For another interpretation of διακονία in Ac 6.1, see 35.38.

57.120 βραβεῖον, ου *n*: a gift received as a prize or reward as the result of having won in a competition – 'prize, reward.' οἱ ἐν σταδίῳ τρέχοντες πάντες μὲν τρέχουσιν, εἷς δὲ μαμβάνει τὸ βραβεῖον 'in a race all the runners take part in it, but only one of them wins the prize' 1 Cor 9.24. In some contexts βραβεῖον refers not to a physical prize or reward but to a spiritual benefit, as in Php 3.14 (τὸ βραβεῖον τῆς ἄνω κλήσεως τοῦ ξεοῦ ἐν Χριστῷ Ἰησοῦ 'the prize which is God's call through Jesus Christ to the life above').

57.121 στέφανος^b, ου *m*: a prize or reward given as the result of outstanding performance – 'prize, reward.' δώσω σοι τὸν στέφανον τῆς ζωῆς 'I will give to you the prize of life' Re 2.10. In Re 2.10 the relationship between τὸν στέφανον and τῆς ζωῆς is one of apposition, for the prize consists of life. Essentially the same relationship exists in the construction ἀπόκειταί μοι ὁ τῆς δικαιοσύνης στέφανος 'the prize of righteousness awaits me' 2 Tm 4.8. In this case the prize is 'being declared righteous' or 'being put right with God.'

57.122 στεφανόω^a: (derivative of στέφανος^b 'prize, reward,' 57.121) to cause someone to receive a prize or reward as the result of excellence in competition – 'to give a prize, to provide a reward.' οὐ στεφανοῦται ἐὰν μὴ νομίμως ἀθλήσῃ 'he will not receive the prize unless he competes according to the rules' 2 Tm 2.5.

57.123 διατίθεμαι^a: to dispose of one's property by means of a will – 'to make a will.' ἐπεὶ μήποτε ἰσχύει ὅτε ζῇ ὁ διαθέμενος 'for (a will) is not in force while the one who has made the will is still alive' He 9.17. 'To make a will' may be rendered as 'to write out a will' or 'to say who is to receive one's property after one dies.'

57.124 διαθήκη^c, ης *f*: (derivative of διατίθεμαι^a 'to make a will,' 57.123) a legal document by which property is transferred by the deceased to an heir or heirs – 'will, testament.' ὅπου γὰρ διαθήκη, θάνατον ἀνάγκη φέρεσθαι τοῦ διαθεμένου 'where there is a will, it has to be proved that the one who made it has died' He 9.16.

I   Receive[30] (57.125-57.141)

57.125 δέχομαι^a; λαμβάνω^c; λῆμψις, εως *f*: to receive or accept an object or benefit for which the initiative rests with the giver, but the focus of attention in the transfer is upon the receiver – 'to receive, receiving, to accept.'[31]
δέχομαι^a: ἡμεῖς οὔτε γράμματα περὶ σοῦ ἐδεξάμεθα ἀπὸ τῆς Ἰουδαίας 'we didn't even receive letters about you from Judea' Ac 28.21; πεπλήρωμαι δεξάμενος παρὰ Ἐπαφροδίτου τὰ παρ' ὑμῶν 'I am amply supplied, now that I have received from Epaphroditus the gifts you sent' Php 4.18.
λαμβάνω^c: ὁ θέλων λαβέτω ὕδωρ ζωῆς δωρεάν

---

30 In Subdomain I *Receive*, the meanings involve a transfer of objects or benefits in which the focus is upon the activity or experience of the receiver.

31 There may be some subtle distinction in meaning between δέχομαι^a on the one hand and λαμβάνω^c and λῆμψις on the other, in that the latter set of meanings may imply more active participation on the part of the one who receives or takes the gift, but this cannot be determined from existing contexts.

'accept the water of life as a gift, whoever wants it' Re 22.17.
λῆμψις: οὐδεμία μοι ἐκκλησία ἐκοινώνησεν εἰς λόγον δόσεως καὶ λήμψεως εἰ μὴ ὑμεῖς μόνοι 'not one church shared with me in the matter of giving and receiving, except you only' Php 4.15.

57.126 κομίζομαι^a: to receive as a type of compensation – 'to receive, to obtain.' φανερωθέντος τοῦ ἀρχιποίμενος κομιεῖσθε τὸν ἀμαράντινον τῆς δόξης στέφανον 'when the Chief Shepherd appears, you will receive the glorious crown which will never lose its brightness' 1 Pe 5.4.

57.127 λαγχάνω^a: to receive, with the implication that the process is related somehow to divine will or favor – 'to receive.' ἔλαχεν τὸν κλῆρον τῆς διακονίας ταύτης 'he received a share in this ministry' Ac 1.17; τοῖς ἰσότιμον ἡμῖν λαχοῦσιν πίστιν ἐν δικαιοσύνῃ τοῦ θεοῦ ἡμῶν καὶ σωτῆρος Ἰησοῦ Χριστοῦ 'to those who through the righteousness of our God and Savior Jesus Christ have received a faith as precious as ours' 2 Pe 1.1. It is, however, possible to interpret λαγχάνω in Ac 1.17 and in 2 Pe 1.1 as referring to the process of divine choice and thus translate as 'be chosen to have.'

57.128 ἀπολαμβάνω^a: to receive, with probable focus upon the source – 'to receive from, to obtain, to receive.' ἀπέλαβες τὰ ἀγαθά σου ἐν τῇ ζωῇ σου 'in your lifetime you received all the good things' Lk 16.25.

57.129 μεταλαμβάνω^a; μετάλημψις, εως *f*: to receive as one's share in or as one's part of – 'to receive a share in, to have a share of.'
μεταλαμβάνω^a: τὸν κοπιῶντα γεωργὸν δεῖ πρῶτον τῶν καρπῶν μεταλαμβάνειν 'the farmer who has done the hard work should have the first share of the harvest' 2 Tm 2.6; μετελάμβανον τροφῆς ἐν ἀγαλλιάσει καὶ ἀφελότητι καρδίας 'sharing food with glad and humble hearts' Ac 2.46.
μετάλημψις: ἃ ὁ θεὸς ἔκτισεν εἰς μετάλημψιν 'which God created for people to share in' 1 Tm 4.3. In 1 Tm 4.3 the reference of μετάλημψιν is to the activity of eating, and

therefore one may translate as 'which God created for people to eat,' but one should not mistake the reference of μετάλημψιν for the meaning of the term.

57.130 διαδέχομαι: to succeed someone as the owner of a particular object or possession – 'to receive from, to receive in turn.' ἡ σκηνὴ . . . ἣν . . . διαδεξάμενοι οἱ πατέρες ἡμῶν 'the tent . . . which . . . our ancestors received from (their forefathers)' Ac 7.44-45.

57.131 κληρονομέω[a]: to receive something of considerable value which has not been earned – 'to receive, to be given, to gain possession of.' μακάριοι οἱ πραεῖς, ὅτι αὐτοὶ κληρονομήσουσιν τὴν γῆν 'happy are those who are gentle; they shall receive the land' or '. . . what God promised' Mt 5.5; μιμηταὶ δὲ τῶν διὰ πίστεως καὶ μακροθυμίας κληρονομούντων τὰς ἐπαγγελίας 'but imitators of those who through faith and patience received what had been promised' He 6.12.

57.132 κληρονομία[a], ας f: (derivative of κληρονομέω[a] 'to gain as a possession,' 57.131) a valuable possession which has been received – 'possession.' οὐκ ἔδωκεν αὐτῷ κληρονομίαν ἐν αὐτῇ 'he did not give him any part of it as his own possession' Ac 7.5.

57.133 κληρονόμος[a], ου m: (derivative of κληρονομέω[a] 'to gain as a possession,' 57.131) one who receives something as a gift – 'one who receives, one who comes into possession of, receiver, heir.' κληρονόμους τῆς βασιλείας 'those who will receive the kingdom' Jas 2.5.[32]

57.134 συγκληρονόμος, ου m: one who receives a possession together with someone

else – 'one who also receives, receiver, fellow heir.' κληρονόμοι μὲν θεοῦ, συγκληρονόμοι δὲ Χριστοῦ 'heirs of God and fellow heirs with Christ' Ro 8.17. It is essential in rendering κληρονόμος (57.133) or συγκληρονόμος to avoid any implication of being an 'heir' to anyone who has died. The focus is upon receiving an unearned gift. In the biblical sense 'heirs of God' are those who will receive the blessings that God has for his people.

57.135 κατακληρονομέω: (derivative of κληρονομέω[a] 'to receive, to be given,' 57.131) to cause someone to receive something of value as a gift – 'to make someone the recipient of a valuable gift.' κατεκληρονόμησεν τὴν γῆν αὐτῶν 'he caused (his people) to receive their land' Ac 13.19.

57.136 ἀπολαμβάνω[b]; κομίζομαι[b]: to receive back something which one has previously possessed or its equivalent – 'to get back, to receive back, to be paid back.'
ἀπολαμβάνω[b]: ἁμαρτωλοὶ ἁμαρτωλοῖς δανίζουσιν ἵνα ἀπολάβωσιν τὰ ἴσα 'even sinners lend to sinners to get back the same amount' Lk 6.34.
κομίζομαι[b]: ἐλθὼν ἐγὼ ἐκομισάμην ἂν τὸ ἐμὸν σὺν τόκῳ 'I would have received it all back with interest when I returned' Mt 25.27.

57.137 ἀπέχω[a]: to receive something in full, with the implication that all that is due has been paid – 'to receive in full, to be paid in full.' ἀπέχουσιν τὸν μισθὸν αὐτῶν 'they have been paid in full' Mt 6.2. It may also be possible to translate the final part of Mt 6.2 as 'they have received all that is coming to them' or '. . . all that they deserve.'

57.138 κληρονομέω[b]: to receive a possession or benefit as a gift from someone who has died, generally a parent – 'to inherit, to receive from a deceased parent.' οὐ γὰρ μὴ κληρονομήσει ὁ υἱὸς τῆς παιδίσκης μετὰ τοῦ υἱοῦ τῆς ἐλευθέρας 'for the son of the slave woman will not inherit the father's property with the son of the free woman' Ga 4.30. In some languages the process of inheritance must be made rather explicit, so that 'he will inherit the property' must be expressed as 'he will

---

32 It is possible to interpret κληρονόμος in Jas 2.5 (and particularly in Tt 3.7, ἵνα δικαιωθέντες τῇ ἐκείνου χάριτι κληρονόμοι γενηθῶμεν κατ᾽ ἐλπίδα ζωῆς αἰωνίου 'so that by his grace we might be put right with God and come into possession of the eternal life we hope for,' in which the gift is eternal life) as identifying essentially a future experiencer, but with the additional components of the experience being valuable and not having been worked for. In this respect κληρονόμος overlaps between Subdomain I *Receive* in Domain 57 and Domain 93 *Case*.

become owner of the property which his father said he should have.'

57.139 κληρονόμος[b], ου *m*: (derivative of κληρονομέω[b] 'to inherit,' 57.138) the person who inherits possessions – 'heir.' οὗτός ἐστιν ὁ κληρονόμος 'this is the heir to the property' Mk 12.7.

57.140 κληρονομία[b], ας *f*: (derivative of κληρονομέω[b] 'to inherit,' 57.138) that which is received from a deceased person – 'inheritance.' διδάσκαλε, εἰπὲ τῷ ἀδελφῷ μου μερίσασθαι μετ' ἐμοῦ τὴν κληρονομίαν 'teacher, tell my brother to divide with me the inheritance' Lk 12.13. In Lk 12.13 it may also be possible to render κληρονομία as 'the property our father left us' or 'the property which our father said should be given to us.'

57.141 ἀπόβλητος, ον: (derivative of ἀποβάλλω 'to reject,' not occurring in the NT) that which is to be rejected – 'something to be rejected.' καὶ οὐδὲν ἀπόβλητον μετὰ εὐχαριστίας λαμβανόμενον 'nothing received with thanksgiving is to be rejected' 1 Tm 4.4. The closest equivalent of ἀπόβλητος in a number of languages is 'something to be thrown away' or 'something to refuse.'

J Exchange (57.142-57.145)

57.142 ἀλλάσσω[b]; μεταλλάσσω[a]: to exchange one thing for another – 'to exchange, to substitute.'[33]
ἀλλάσσω[b]: ἤλλαξαν τὴν δόξαν τοῦ ἀφθάρτου θεοῦ ἐν ὁμοιώματι εἰκόνος φθαρτοῦ ἀνθρώπου 'they exchanged the glory of immortal God for an image in the likeness of mortal man' Ro 1.23.
μεταλλάσσω[a]: οἵτινες μετήλλαξαν τὴν ἀλήθειαν τοῦ θεοῦ ἐν τῷ ψεύδει 'who exchanged the truth of God for a lie' Ro 1.25. In rendering μεταλλάσσω in Ro 1.25 it is essential to avoid anything which might mean 'to change something into.' It is the substitution of one thing

for another; hence, 'exchange' rather than 'change' is the correct gloss.

57.143 ἀντάλλαγμα, τος *n*: (derivative of ἀνταλλάσσω 'to exchange,' not occurring in the NT) that which is exchanged or given in exchange – 'something given in exchange.' τί γὰρ δοῖ ἄνθρωπος ἀντάλλαγμα τῆς ψυχῆς αὐτοῦ; 'what would a person give as a means of exchange for his life?' or '. . . in payment for his life' Mk 8.37.

57.144 συνάγω[c]: to convert property or goods into money – 'to convert into money, to turn into money.' μετ' οὐ πολλὰς ἡμέρας συναγαγὼν πάντα 'after a short time, he turned everything into money' Lk 15.13.

57.145 ἀντί[e]: a marker of an exchange relation – 'for, in place of.' ὃς ἀντὶ βρώσεως μιᾶς ἀπέδοτο τὰ πρωτοτόκια ἑαυτοῦ 'who for a single meal gave up his rights as the first-born son' He 12.16.

K Spend, Waste (57.146-57.151)

57.146 δαπανάω[a]: to pay out money (or other assets) as a means of obtaining benefits or in payment for benefits – 'to spend, to pay out, to pay expenses.' πολλὰ παθοῦσα ὑπὸ πολλῶν ἰατρῶν καὶ δαπανήσασα τὰ παρ' αὐτῆς πάντα 'she had been treated by many doctors and had spent all her money' Mk 5.26; δαπάνησον ἐπ' αὐτοῖς 'pay their expenses' Ac 21.24; ἐγὼ δὲ ἥδιστα δαπανήσω καὶ ἐκδαπανηθήσομαι ὑπὲρ τῶν ψυχῶν ὑμῶν 'I will gladly spend all I have and even give myself in order to help you' 2 Cor 12.15. For another interpretation of δαπανάω in 2 Cor 12.15, see 42.27.

57.147 προσδαπανάω: to pay out or spend in addition – 'to spend in addition.' ὅ τι ἂν προσδαπανήσῃς ἐγὼ ἐν τῷ ἐπανέρχεσθαί με ἀποδώσω σοι 'when I come back this way, I will pay you back whatever you spend in addition (to the two denarii)' Lk 10.35.

57.148 προσαναλίσκω: to spend excessively – 'to spend a lot, to spend much.' ἥτις ἰατροῖς προσαναλώσασα ὅλον τὸν βίον 'she had spent all her living on doctors' Lk 8.43.

---

[33] μεταλλάσσω[a] may focus somewhat more emphatically than ἀλλάσσω[b] on the substitution of one thing for another.

57.149 δαπανάωᵇ: to spend completely, with the implication of uselessly, and therefore, to waste – 'to spend completely, to waste.' διότι κακῶς αἰτεῖσθε, ἵνα ἐν ταῖς ἡδοναῖς ὑμῶν δαπανήσητε 'because you ask with bad intentions in order to waste them on your own pleasures' Jas 4.3. In some languages 'to waste' may be expressed as 'to use up and to get no benefit' or 'to have, but for no purpose.'

57.150 κατεσθίωᵈ: (a figurative extension of meaning of κατεσθίωᵃ 'to eat up, to consume,' 23.11) to spend or use up excessively and uselessly – 'to consume, to waste.' ὁ υἱός σου οὗτος ὁ καταφαγών σου τὸν βίον μετὰ πορνῶν 'this son of yours wasted all your property on prostitutes' Lk 15.30.

57.151 διασκορπίζωᵇ: (a figurative extension of meaning of διασκορπίζωᵃ 'to scatter,' 15.136) to spend foolishly and to no purpose – 'to squander, to waste.' ἐκεῖ διεσκόρπισεν τὴν οὐσίαν αὐτοῦ ζῶν ἀσώτως 'there he wasted his money in reckless living' Lk 15.13.

L Pay, Price, Cost (57.152-57.171)

57.152 δίδωμιᶠ: to pay or remunerate with money or other valuables – 'to pay, to remunerate.' ἐπηγγείλαντο αὐτῷ ἀργύριον δοῦναι 'they promised to pay him money' Mk 14.11; ἔδωκαν αὐτὰ εἰς τὸν ἀγρὸν τοῦ κεραμέως 'they paid the money to buy the potter's field' Mt 27.10; ἵνα ἀπὸ τοῦ καρποῦ τοῦ ἀμπελῶνος δώσουσιν αὐτῷ 'in order that they might pay him (his share) from what the vineyard produced' Lk 20.10.

57.153 ἀποδίδωμιᵃ: to make a payment, with the implication of such a payment being in response to an incurred obligation – 'to pay, to render.'³⁴ κάλεσον τοὺς ἐργάτας καὶ ἀπόδος αὐτοῖς τὸν μισθόν 'call the workers and pay them their wages' Mt 20.8; οἵτινες ἀποδώσουσιν αὐτῷ τοὺς καρποὺς ἐν τοῖς καιροῖς αὐτῶν 'they will pay him his share of the harvest at

the right time' Mt 21.41; ἀπόδοτε οὖν τὰ Καίσαρος Καίσαρι καὶ τὰ τοῦ θεοῦ τῷ θεῷ 'render to Caesar what are his and to God what are his' Mt 22.21; οὐ μὴ ἐξέλθῃς ἐκεῖθεν ἕως ἂν ἀποδῷς τὸν ἔσχατον κοδράντην 'there you will stay (literally 'you will never come out from there') until you pay the last penny (of your fine)' Mt 5.26.

57.154 ἀνταποδίδωμιᵃ: to pay something back to someone as the result of an incurred obligation – 'to repay, to pay back, to give back.'³⁵ ἢ τίς προέδωκεν αὐτῷ, καὶ ἀνταποδοθήσεται αὐτῷ; 'who has ever given him anything, so that he had to pay it back?' Ro 11.35; μακάριος ἔσῃ, ὅτι οὐκ ἔχουσιν ἀνταποδοῦναί σοι 'you will be blessed, because they are not able to pay you back (with an invitation)' Lk 14.14.

57.155 ἀνταπόδομαᵃ, τος n: (derivative of ἀνταποδίδωμιᵃ 'to repay,' 57.154) that which is repaid – 'repayment.' μήποτε καὶ αὐτοὶ ἀντικαλέσωσίν σε καὶ γένηται ἀνταπόδομά σοι 'lest they invite you in turn and you get repaid' Lk 14.12.

57.156 ἀποτίνω: (a technical, legal term) to pay compensation for damages or costs – 'to pay back, to remunerate.' ἐγὼ ἀποτίσω 'I will remunerate you' Phm 19. It is also possible to translate this expression in Phm 19 as 'I will pay you for any loss which you have had.'

57.157 στρέφωᵈ: to return a payment – 'to pay back, to return a payment.' μεταμεληθεὶς ἔστρεψεν τὰ τριάκοντα ἀργύρια 'he repented and paid back the thirty silver coins' or '. . . returned the thirty silver coins' Mt 27.3. It is possible to interpret στρέφω in Mt 27.3 as simply meaning 'to bring back' or 'to take back' (see 15.195).

57.158 ἵστημιᵈ: to pay, possibly in the sense of to weigh out or to count out a sum of money – 'to pay.' οἱ δὲ ἔστησαν αὐτῷ τριάκοντα

---

34 ἀποδίδωμιᵃ occurs with a very wide range of types of transfer, for example, wages, proceeds, taxes, debts, and rewards.

35 The implication of a return payment is somewhat more emphatic in ἀνταποδίδωμιᵃ than in ἀποδίδωμιᵃ (57.153).

ἀργύρια 'they paid him thirty silver coins' Mt 26.15.[36]

57.159 ἀφυστερέω: to not pay someone for what is owed – 'to withhold payment, to not pay.' ὁ μισθὸς τῶν ἐργατῶν τῶν ἀμησάντων τὰς χώρας ὑμῶν ὁ ἀπεστερημένος 'you have withheld the wages of the men who work in your fields' Jas 5.4.

57.160 δαπάνη, ης f: (derivative of δαπανάω[a] 'to spend,' 57.146) the amount spent or to be spent in procuring some object or benefit – 'cost, expense.' τίς γὰρ ἐξ ὑμῶν θέλων πύργον οἰκοδομῆσαι οὐχὶ πρῶτον καθίσας ψηφίζει τὴν δαπάνην; 'if one of you is planning to build a tower, will he not sit down first and figure out what it will cost?' Lk 14.28.

57.161 τιμή[c], ῆς f: the amount of money or property regarded as representing the value or price of something – 'amount, price, cost.' ἐνοσφίσατο ἀπὸ τῆς τιμῆς 'he kept back (some money) from the price (received)' Ac 5.2; ἔλαβον τὰ τριάκοντα ἀργύρια τὴν τιμὴν τοῦ τετιμημένου ὃν ἐτιμήσαντο ἀπὸ υἱῶν Ἰσραήλ 'they took the thirty silver coins, the price the people of Israel had agreed to pay for him' Mt 27.9; τιμῆς ἠγοράσθητε 'you have been bought with a price' 1 Cor 7.23. It would be wrong to assume that τιμή in 1 Cor 7.23 necessarily means 'a high price.' The notion 'high' comes from the contextual reference to the death of Christ. In 1 Cor 7.23, however, the implication is that a price was set and that the payment has been made. If the passive expression in 1 Cor 7.23 must be made active, one may translate as 'Christ bought you with a price' or 'Christ paid for you.'

57.162 κεφάλαιον[b], ου n: a sum of money – 'some money, price.' ἀπεκρίθη δὲ ὁ χιλίαρχος, Ἐγὼ πολλοῦ κεφαλαίου τὴν πολιτείαν ταύτην ἐκτησάμην 'but the chiliarch answered, I bought this citizenship with a large sum of money' Ac 22.28.

57.163 ἐκ[m]: a marker of price – 'with, by means of.' συμβούλιον δὲ λαβόντες ἠγόρασαν ἐξ αὐτῶν τὸν ἀγρὸν τοῦ κεραμέως 'and after consulting on the matter, they bought with the money (literally 'with them') the potter's field' Mt 27.7.

57.164 ἀδάπανος, ον: pertaining to there being no charge or expenditure – 'free of charge, without cost.' ἵνα εὐαγγελιζόμενος ἀδάπανον θήσω τὸ εὐαγγέλιον 'that in preaching the good news I may offer the gospel free of charge' or '. . . without charging for it' 1 Cor 9.18.

57.165 τιμάω[b]: to determine an amount to be used in paying for something – 'to set a price on, to determine the cost.' ἔλαβον τὰ τριάκοντα ἀργύρια, τὴν τιμὴν τοῦ τετιμημένου ὃν ἐτιμήσαντο ἀπὸ υἱῶν Ἰσραήλ 'they took the thirty silver coins, the price set on him by the people of Israel' Mt 27.9. It would also be possible to translate 'the price set on him by the people of Israel' as 'the amount the people of Israel had agreed to pay for him.'

57.166 ὀψώνιον[a], ου n: the payment made to soldiers as ration money – 'pay, compensation.' ἀρκεῖσθε τοῖς ὀψωνίοις ὑμῶν 'be satisfied with your pay' Lk 3.14.

57.167 τιμή[d], ῆς f: compensation given for special service, with the implication that this is a way by which honor or respect may be shown – 'compensation, pay, honorarium.' οἱ καλῶς προεστῶτες πρεσβύτεροι διπλῆς τιμῆς ἀξιούσθωσαν, μάλιστα οἱ κοπιῶντες ἐν λόγῳ 'the elders who do good work as leaders should be considered worthy of receiving double compensation, especially those who work hard at preaching' 1 Tm 5.17. τιμή[d] in the sense of 'compensation' is related in meaning to τιμάω[c] 'to support, to provide for' (57.117) and τιμή[c] 'cost' (57.161), but in 1 Tm 5.17 it is also possible to understand τιμή in the sense of τιμή[a] 'honor, respect' (87.4), and therefore one may speak of the elders as 'receiving double honor.'

---

36 It is possible to interpret ἵστημι in Mt 26.15 as meaning only 'to offer,' but in view of the statement in Mt 27.3 (see 57.157) it is evident that the money was actually paid rather than merely offered, though the actual payment could have occurred after the betrayal.

57.168 ἀμοιβή, ῆς *f*: that which is given as a means of recompense or repayment – 'recompense, repayment.' ἀμοιβὰς ἀποδιδόναι τοῖς προγόνοις 'to make repayment to their parents and grandparents' (literally 'their ancestors') 1 Tm 5.4. One may also translate 'repayment to their parents and grandparents' as 'to pay back to their parents and grandparents for what these have done for them' or 'to help their parents and grandparents because of what these have done to help them.'

57.169 ἱκανόν, οῦ *n*: the amount of money required to release someone who has been held in custody – 'bond, bail, the amount of money required for release.' λαβόντες τὸ ἱκανὸν παρὰ τοῦ Ἰάσονος καὶ τῶν λοιπῶν ἀπέλυσαν αὐτούς '(the authorities) made Jason and the others pay the required amount of money and then set them free' Ac 17.9. It may be necessary in a number of languages to be very specific about the meaning of ἱκανόν, for example, 'the amount of money which had to be paid in order for someone to be released from arrest.'

57.170 ἀρραβών, ῶνος *m*: the first or initial payment of money or assets, as a guarantee for the completion of a transaction or pledge (in the NT ἀρραβών is used only figuratively in referring to the Holy Spirit as the pledge or guarantee of the blessings promised by God) – 'first installment, downpayment, pledge, guarantee.'[37] ἐσφραγίσθητε τῷ πνεύματι τῆς ἐπαγγελίας τῷ ἁγίῳ, ὅ ἐστιν ἀρραβὼν τῆς κληρονομίας ἡμῶν 'you have been sealed by the Holy Spirit which he promised and which is the first installment of what we shall receive' Eph 1.13-14.

57.171 ἀπαρχή[c], ῆς *f*: (a figurative extension of meaning of ἀπαρχή[a] 'first portion,' 53.23) a foretaste and pledge of blessings to come – 'foretaste, pledge, foretaste and pledge.' αὐτοὶ τὴν ἀπαρχὴν τοῦ πνεύματος ἔχοντες ἡμεῖς 'we

who have the Spirit as a foretaste and pledge (of blessings to come)' Ro 8.23. In many respects ἀπαρχή[c] parallels closely the meaning of ἀρραβών (57.170).

M Hire, Rent Out (57.172-57.177)

57.172 μισθόομαι: to arrange for services by an offer to pay compensation or salary – 'to hire.' ὅτι οὐδεὶς ἡμᾶς ἐμισθώσατο 'it is because no one hired us' Mt 20.7.

57.173 μισθός[a], οῦ *m*: (derivative of μισθόομαι 'to hire,' 57.172) the amount offered for services or paid for work done – 'pay, wages.' ἄξιος γὰρ ὁ ἐργάτης τοῦ μισθοῦ αὐτοῦ 'the worker should be given his pay' Lk 10.7.

57.174 μίσθιος, ου *m*; μισθωτός, οῦ *m*: (derivatives of μισθόομαι 'to hire,' 57.172) a person who has been hired to perform a particular service or work – 'hired worker, hired person.'[38]
μίσθιος: πόσοι μίσθιοι τοῦ πατρός μου περισσεύονται ἄρτων 'all my father's hired workers have more than they can eat' Lk 15.17.
μισθωτός: ὁ μισθωτὸς καὶ οὐκ ὢν ποιμήν 'the hired man, who is not a shepherd' Jn 10.12.

57.175 μίσθωμα, τος *n*: (derivative of μισθόομαι 'to hire,' 57.172) that which has been hired or rented (but in the NT occurring only in reference to a rented dwelling) – 'hired, rented.' ἐνέμεινεν δὲ διετίαν ὅλην ἐν ἰδίῳ μισθώματι 'for two years he lived there in a place he rented for himself' Ac 28.30. In some languages one may speak of 'rent' as 'money paid in order to stay in a place.' This may be necessary in order to distinguish such payments from a payment made to purchase something.

57.176 ὑποβάλλω: to hire a person to act in a particular way, often involving dishonest activities – 'to hire, to bribe, to induce.' τότε

---

[37] It is possible that in the NT ἀρραβών has already been generalized in meaning and thus signifies simply 'that which guarantees.'

[38] μίσθιος and μισθωτός involve two sets of components, one focusing upon the work which such a person does and the other upon the fact that the individual in question is paid. This means that μίσθιος and μισθωτός could justifiably be classified either in Domain 42 *Perform, Do* or in Domain 57.

ὑπέβαλον ἄνδρας λέγοντας ὅτι Ἀκηκόαμεν αὐτοῦ λαλοῦντος ῥήματα βλάσφημα εἰς Μωϋσῆν καὶ τὸν θεόν 'then they hired men to say, We have heard him speak blasphemy against Moses and God' Ac 6.11.

57.177 ἐκδίδομαι: to permit the use of property or assets in exchange for remuneration – 'to let out, to lease, to rent out.' ἄνθρωπός τις ἐφύτευσεν ἀμπελῶνα, καὶ ἐξέδοτο αὐτὸν γεωργοῖς 'a man planted a vineyard and rented it out to tenants' Lk 20.9. In some languages it may be necessary to specify quite clearly the implications of 'renting out land,' for example, 'he let farmers grow crops on his land in exchange for a part of the harvest.'

N Tax, Tribute (57.178-57.185)

57.178 τελέω^c: to pay tax or tribute (used absolutely or with a noun complement meaning 'tax' or 'tribute') – 'to pay taxes, to pay customs duty.' διὰ τοῦτο γὰρ καὶ φόρους τελεῖτε 'this is the reason that you pay taxes' Ro 13.6; ὁ διδάσκαλος ὑμῶν οὐ τελεῖ τὰ δίδραχμα; 'does your teacher pay the two-drachma tax?' Mt 17.24.

57.179 τέλος^c, ους n: payments customarily due a governmental authority – 'duty, tax, revenue.' οἱ βασιλεῖς τῆς γῆς ἀπὸ τίνων λαμβάνουσιν τέλη ἢ κῆνσον; 'but from whom do the kings of earth collect duties or taxes?' Mt 17.25. The term τέλος^c differs from κῆνσος (57.180) in being somewhat more generic in meaning. In certain contexts τέλος^c may refer to various kinds of direct taxes, customs duties, and tribute money, but in contexts such as Mt 17.25 in which κῆνσος also occurs, τέλος probably refers primarily to customs duties, while κῆνσος refers to a direct poll tax upon all adult males.

57.180 κῆνσος, ου m (a borrowing from Latin): a tax paid by each adult male to the government – 'tax, poll tax' (see discussion at 57.179). ἔξεστιν δοῦναι κῆνσον Καίσαρι ἢ οὔ; 'is it lawful to pay tax to the Emperor or not?' Mk 12.14.

57.181 δίδραχμον, ου n: a tax of two drachmas required of each male Jew each year as a kind of Temple tax – 'Temple tax, two-drachma tax.' ὁ διδάσκαλος ὑμῶν οὐ τελεῖ τὰ δίδραχμα; 'does not your teacher pay the Temple tax?' Mt 17.24. The two-drachma coin referred to in Mt 17.24 was approximately equivalent to two denarii. The meaning of δίδραχμον is treated here in Domain 57 rather than in Domain 6 (where the value of other coins is discussed) since the focus of the meaning of δίδραχμον is the required Temple tax rather than the value or form of the coin itself.

57.182 φόρος, ου m: a payment made by the people of one nation to another, with the implication that this is a symbol of submission and dependence – 'tribute tax.' ἔξεστιν ἡμᾶς Καίσαρι φόρον δοῦναι ἢ οὔ; 'is it lawful for us to pay the tribute tax to the Emperor or not?' Lk 20.22; κωλύοντα φόρους Καίσαρι διδόναι 'he told them not to pay the tribute tax to the Emperor' Lk 23.2.

57.183 τελώνιον, ου n: (derivative of τελέω^c 'to pay taxes,' 57.178) a place where taxes or revenue was collected from those entering a town to sell produce – 'revenue office, tax office.' ἐθεάσατο τελώνην ὀνόματι Λευὶν καθήμενον ἐπὶ τὸ τελώνιον 'he saw a tax collector named Levi, sitting at the place where revenue was collected' Lk 5.27. In the ancient world taxes were primarily of two types: (1) a head tax on each individual (which was relatively small) and (2) revenue or tribute paid for goods and produce brought into an area for sale. The latter was essentially a kind of 'sales tax,' but paid by the seller who obviously increased the prices of goods accordingly.

57.184 τελώνης, ου m: (derivative of τελέω^c 'to pay taxes,' 57.178) one who collects taxes for the government – 'tax collector, revenue officer.' διὰ τί μετὰ τῶν τελωνῶν καὶ ἁμαρτωλῶν ἐσθίετε καὶ πίνετε; 'why do you eat and drink with tax collectors and outcasts?' Lk 5.30. Since Jews who farmed the taxes for the Romans (that is to say, who paid Roman authorities for the privilege of collecting taxes) were considered traitors to their own people, the term τελώνης has strongly negative connotations in the NT. In any translation of the

Gospels it may be especially important to have an adequate marginal note designed to explain the basis for the hostility which many people had toward tax collectors.

57.185 ἀρχιτελώνης, ου *m*: chief tax collector, in the sense of one who controlled activities of certain other tax collectors – 'chief tax collector, director of tax collectors.' ἀνὴρ ὀνόματι καλούμενος Ζακχαῖος, καὶ αὐτὸς ἦν ἀρχιτελώνης καὶ αὐτὸς πλούσιος 'a man named Zacchaeus, a chief tax collector who was rich' Lk 19.2. It is also possible to understand ἀρχιτελώνης as meaning a principal or important tax collector rather than one who controlled the activities of other tax collectors.

O Sell, Buy, Price (57.186-57.188)

57.186 πωλέω; πιπράσκω; ἀποδίδομαι: to dispose of property or provide services in exchange for money or other valuable considerations – 'to sell.'
πωλέω: ὕπαγε ὅσα ἔχεις πώλησον 'go and sell all you have' Mk 10.21; πορεύεσθε μᾶλλον πρὸς τοὺς πωλοῦντας καὶ ἀγοράσατε ἑαυταῖς 'go, instead, to those who sell and buy (oil) for yourselves' Mt 25.9.
πιπράσκω: διὰ τί τοῦτο τὸ μύρον οὐκ ἐπράθη τριακοσίων δηναρίων καὶ ἐδόθη πτωχοῖς; 'why wasn't this perfume sold for three hundred denarii and given to the poor?' Jn 12.5.
ἀποδίδομαι: εἰπέ μοι, εἰ τοσούτου τὸ χωρίον ἀπέδοσθε; 'tell me, Did you sell the property for this amount?' Ac 5.8.
πιπράσκω and ἀποδίδομαι may also be used to refer to selling a person into slavery. Note, for example, πιπράσκω in Mt 18.25 (ἐκέλευσεν αὐτὸν ὁ κύριος πραθῆναι 'his master ordered him to be sold as a slave') and ἀποδίδομαι in Ac 7.9 (οἱ πατριάρχαι ζηλώσαντες τὸν Ἰωσὴφ ἀπέδοντο εἰς Αἴγυπτον 'the patriarchs were jealous of Joseph and sold him to be a slave in Egypt'). In a number of languages, however, it may be important to use a distinctive term for selling a person into slavery. In fact, it may be necessary to describe the event rather explicitly, for example, 'to receive money for handing a person over to someone else to be a slave.'
In Ro 7.14 πιπράσκω is used figuratively in the phrase πεπραμένος ὑπὸ τὴν ἁμαρτίαν 'sold as a slave to sin,' in the sense that sin is personified as the master.

57.187 ἀνδραποδιστής, οῦ *m*: one who sells persons as slaves, including one who kidnaps persons and sells them – 'slave dealer, kidnapper.' ἀρσενοκοίταις, ἀνδραποδισταῖς, ψεύσταις 'sexual perverts, kidnappers (or 'slave dealers'), liars' 1 Tm 1.10.

57.188 ἀγοράζω[a]; ὠνέομαι: to acquire possessions or services in exchange for money – 'to buy, to purchase.'
ἀγοράζω[a]: ἀπερχομένων δὲ αὐτῶν ἀγοράσαι ἦλθεν ὁ νυμφίος 'while they were gone to buy (some oil), the bridegroom arrived' Mt 25.10.
ὠνέομαι: ἐτέθησαν ἐν τῷ μνήματι ᾧ ὠνήσατο Ἀβραὰμ τιμῆς ἀργυρίου παρὰ τῶν υἱῶν Ἐμμὼρ 'they were buried in a grave which Abraham had bought from the tribe of Hamor for a sum of money' Ac 7.16.

P Earn, Gain, Do Business (57.189-57.208)

57.189 κερδαίνω[a]; ποιέω[h]: to gain by means of one's activity or investment – 'to earn, to gain, to make a profit.'
κερδαίνω[a]: ἐμπορευσόμεθα καὶ κερδήσομεν 'we shall go into business and make a profit' Jas 4.13; ἠργάσατο ἐν αὐτοῖς καὶ ἐκέρδησεν ἄλλα πέντε 'he invested his money (literally 'he did business with them') and earned another five' Mt 25.16; τί γὰρ ὠφελεῖται ἄνθρωπος κερδήσας τὸν κόσμον ὅλον ἑαυτὸν δὲ ἀπολέσας ἢ ζημιωθείς; 'what will a person accomplish if he gains the whole world but is himself lost or must suffer for it?' Lk 9.25.
ποιέω[h]: ἡ μνᾶ σου . . . ἐποίησεν πέντε μνᾶς 'your mina . . . has earned five minas' Lk 19.18. In many languages, however, it may be quite impossible to speak of 'one mina has earned five minas' or even 'one coin has earned five coins.' It may be necessary to turn this into an expression involving a human agent, for example, 'I have earned five minas with the one that you gave me.'

57.190 τὸν ἑαυτοῦ ἄρτον ἐσθίω: (an idiom, literally 'to eat one's own bread') to earn a living by one's own efforts – 'to earn a living, to earn a livelihood.' ἵνα μετὰ ἡσυχίας ἐργαζόμενοι τὸν ἑαυτῶν ἄρτον ἐσθίωσιν 'in order that they may live calmly and work to earn their living' 2 Th 3.12.

57.191 προσεργάζομαι: to earn or to gain something in addition – 'to make more, to earn in addition.' ἡ μνᾶ σου δέκα προσηργάσατο μνᾶς 'your one mina has earned in addition ten minas' Lk 19.16. As in the case of Lk 19.18 (see 57.189), it may be necessary to change the form of expression so as to introduce a personal agent, for example, 'I have earned ten minas with the one you gave me.' In some languages it may be necessary to say 'I did business with the one mina and now I have ten' or '. . . it has become ten minas.'

57.192 κέρδος, ους n: (derivative of κερδαίνωᵃ 'to earn, to gain,' 57.189) that which is gained or earned – 'gain, profit.' οἵτινες ὅλους οἴκους ἀνατρέπουσιν διδάσκοντες ἃ μὴ δεῖ αἰσχροῦ κέρδους χάριν 'they are upsetting whole families by teaching what they should not, for the shameful purpose of gain' Tt 1.11.
κέρδος in the sense of 'gain' is not restricted, however, to monetary gain or profit. It may refer to any kind of benefit or advantage, for example, ἐμοὶ γὰρ τὸ ζῆν Χριστὸς καὶ τὸ ἀποθανεῖν κέρδος 'for me life is Christ, and death is a gain' Php 1.21.

57.193 ἐργασίαᶜ, ας f: to make a profit from one's business or activity – 'to make money, profit.' ἰδόντες δὲ οἱ κύριοι αὐτῆς ὅτι ἐξῆλθεν ἡ ἐλπὶς τῆς ἐργασίας αὐτῶν 'when her owners realized that their hope of making money was gone' Ac 16.19.

57.194 πορισμός, οῦ m: a means of gaining a profit or wealth – 'profit, gain, wealth.' νομιζόντων πορισμὸν εἶναι τὴν εὐσέβειαν 'they think that religion is a way to gain wealth' 1 Tm 6.5. In 1 Tm 6.6 πορισμός is used with an extended meaning of advantage or benefit, but the context shows clearly that this is a rather unusual and perhaps somewhat forced extension of meaning.

57.195 διαπραγματεύομαι: to profit from engaging in commerce and trade – 'to earn, to profit.' ἵνα γνοῖ τί διεπραγματεύσαντο 'in order to find out how much they had earned' Lk 19.15.

57.196 ἐμπορεύομαιᵃ; ἐμπορία, ας f: to carry on a business involving buying and selling – 'to be in business, to engage in a business, to trade, business.'
ἐμπορεύομαιᵃ: ποιήσομεν ἐκεῖ ἐνιαυτὸν καὶ ἐμπορευσόμεθα καὶ κερδήσομεν 'we will spend a year there and go into business and make (much) money' Jas 4.13.
ἐμπορία: οἱ δὲ ἀμελήσαντες ἀπῆλθον, ὃς μὲν εἰς τὸν ἴδιον ἀγρόν, ὃς δὲ ἐπὶ τὴν ἐμπορίαν αὐτοῦ 'they were not interested and went away, one to his farm, another to his business' Mt 22.5.

57.197 πραγματεύομαι: to be engaged in some kind of business, generally buying and selling – 'to do business, to be involved in business.' ἔδωκεν αὐτοῖς δέκα μνᾶς καὶ εἶπεν πρὸς αὐτούς, Πραγματεύσασθε ἐν ᾧ ἔρχομαι 'he gave them ten coins and told them, Do business with these while I am gone' Lk 19.13.

57.198 ἐργάζομαιᵇ; ἐργασίαᵇ, ας f: to be involved in business, with focus upon the work which is involved – 'to do business, to trade, work, business.'
ἐργάζομαιᵇ: πορευθεὶς ὁ τὰ πέντε τάλαντα λαβὼν ἠργάσατο ἐν αὐτοῖς καὶ ἐκέρδησεν ἄλλα πέντε 'the one who had received the five coins went and traded with them and earned another five' Mt 25.16.
ἐργασίαᵇ: ἐπίστασθε ὅτι ἐκ ταύτης τῆς ἐργασίας ἡ εὐπορία ἡμῖν ἐστιν 'realize that our prosperity comes from this business' Ac 19.25.

57.199 μέροςᵉ, ους n: a particular kind of business activity or occupation – 'business, occupation, endeavor.' οὐ μόνον δὲ τοῦτο κινδυνεύει ἡμῖν τὸ μέρος εἰς ἀπελεγμὸν ἐλθεῖν 'not only is there danger that this business of ours will get a bad name' Ac 19.27.

57.200 πορείαᵇ, ας f: business pursuits, with the implication of extensive activity and journeys required – 'pursuit of business,

business endeavors, business activity.' οὕτως καὶ ὁ πλούσιος ἐν ταῖς πορείαις αὐτοῦ μαρανθήσεται 'in the same way the rich man will be destroyed while pursuing his business' Jas 1.11.

57.201 εὐπορία[b], ας *f:* an easy means of gaining a profit from one's business or trade – 'good business, easy way of making a living.' ἐκ ταύτης τῆς ἐργασίας ἡ εὐπορία ἡμῖν ἐστιν 'from this occupation we have an easy way of making a living' or 'for us, this occupation is good business' Ac 19.25. For another interpretation of εὐπορία in Ac 19.25, see 57.32.

57.202 καπηλεύω: to engage in retail business, with the implication of deceptiveness and greedy motives – 'to peddle for profit, to huckster.' οὐ γάρ ἐσμεν ὡς οἱ πολλοὶ καπηλεύοντες τὸν λόγον τοῦ θεοῦ 'we are not like so many others who peddle God's message' 2 Cor 2.17.

57.203 ἔμπορος, ου *m:* (derivative of ἐμπορεύομαι[a] 'to be in business,' 57.196) one who is engaged in commerce and trade – 'merchant, trader.' οἱ ἔμποροι τῆς γῆς ἐκ τῆς δυνάμεως τοῦ στρήνους αὐτῆς ἐπλούτησαν 'the merchants of the world grew rich from her unrestrained lust' Re 18.3.

57.204 πορφυρόπωλις, ιδος *f:* a woman who specialized in selling purple cloth – 'dealer in purple cloth.' γυνὴ ὀνόματι Λυδία, πορφυρόπωλις 'a woman named Lydia, who was a dealer in purple cloth' Ac 16.14.

57.205 κολλυβιστής, οῦ *m*; κερματιστής, οῦ *m:* one who exchanges currency, either in terms of different types of currency or different values of the same currency – 'moneychanger.'
κολλυβιστής: τῶν κολλυβιστῶν ἐξέχεεν τὸ κέρμα καὶ τὰς τραπέζας ἀνέτρεψεν 'he overturned the tables of the moneychangers and scattered their coins' Jn 2.15.
κερματιστής: εὗρεν ἐν τῷ ἱερῷ . . . τοὺς κερματιστὰς καθημένους 'in the Temple he found . . . the moneychangers sitting (at their tables)' Jn 2.14.

57.206 ἐμπόριον, ου *n:* (derivative of ἐμπορεύομαι[a] 'to engage in a business,' 57.196) a place for engaging in business – 'marketplace' (but see ἀγορά, 57.207). μὴ ποιεῖτε τὸν οἶκον τοῦ πατρός μου οἶκον ἐμπορίου 'do not make my Father's house a marketplace' Jn 2.16.

57.207 ἀγορά, ᾶς *f:* a commercial center with a number of places for doing business – 'market, marketplace, business center.' ἀπ' ἀγορᾶς ἐὰν μὴ βαπτίσωνται οὐκ ἐσθίουσιν 'they do not eat anything that comes from the market unless they wash it' Mk 7.4; διελέγετο μὲν . . . ἐν τῇ ἀγορᾷ κατὰ πᾶσαν ἡμέραν 'he had discussions . . . every day in the marketplace' Ac 17.17.

ἀγορά differs in meaning from ἐμπόριον (57.206) in that the focus is upon a commercial center involving a number of places for doing business. The term ἐμπόριον may be used to refer to the same type of geographical location, but the focus is upon the activity and not the place.

57.208 μάκελλον, ου *n:* an area in a city or town where meat was sold – 'meat market' (μάκελλον would normally be a particular part of the ἀγορά, 57.207). πᾶν τὸ ἐν μακέλλῳ πωλούμενον ἐσθίετε 'you are free to eat anything sold in the meat market' 1 Cor 10.25.

Q Lend, Loan, Interest, Borrow, Bank (57.209-57.218)

57.209 δανείζω: to lend money, normally with the expectation of receiving the same amount in return plus interest – 'to make a loan, to lend money.' ἁμαρτωλοὶ ἁμαρτωλοῖς δανίζουσιν ἵνα ἀπολάβωσιν τὰ ἴσα 'even sinners give loans to sinners and hope to get back the same amount' Lk 6.34. In Lk 6.34 it is possible that no interest payment is involved, in which case the meaning is similar to that of κίχρημι 'to lend' (57.214).

57.210 δάνειον, ου *n:* (derivative of δανείζω 'to lend money,' 57.209) that which has been loaned – 'loan, debt.' τὸ δάνειον ἀφῆκεν αὐτῷ 'he cancelled his debt' Mt 18.27.

57.211 δανιστής, οῦ *m:* (derivative of δανείζω 'to lend money,' 57.209) a person whose business it is to lend money to others at an interest rate – 'moneylender.' δύο χρεοφειλέται ἦσαν δανιστῇ τινι 'there were two men who owed money to a moneylender' Lk 7.41.

57.212 τόκος, ου *m*: the interest on money that has been loaned – 'interest.' κἀγὼ ἐλθὼν σὺν τόκῳ ἂν αὐτὸ ἔπραξα 'then I would have received it back with interest when I returned' Lk 19.23.

57.213 δανείζομαι: to borrow money, normally with the implication of interest to be paid – 'to borrow money.' τὸν θέλοντα ἀπὸ σοῦ δανίσασθαι μὴ ἀποστραφῇς 'do not turn your back on the person who wishes to borrow from you' Mt 5.42. It is possible, however, that in Mt 5.42 interest on the loan is not involved.

57.214 κίχρημι: to give something to someone for use, with the expectation that the same or its equivalent will be returned – 'to lend.' χρῆσόν μοι τρεῖς ἄρτους 'lend me three loaves of bread' Lk 11.5.

57.215 τράπεζα^c, ης *f*: a place where money is kept or managed or where credit is established – 'bank.' διὰ τί οὐκ ἔδωκάς μου τὸ ἀργύριον ἐπὶ τράπεζαν; 'why didn't you put my money in the bank?' Lk 19.23.

57.216 τραπεζίτης, ου *m*: (derivative of τράπεζα^c 'bank,' 57.215) a person who manages or works in a bank – 'banker.' ἔδει σε οὖν βαλεῖν τὰ ἀργύριά μου τοῖς τραπεζίταις 'you should have deposited my money with the bankers' Mt 25.27.

57.217 τίθημι^e; βάλλω^h; δίδωμι^g: to deposit money with a banker, with the intent of earning interest – 'to deposit, to put in a bank.'
τίθημι^e: αἴρεις ὃ οὐκ ἔθηκας 'you withdraw what you did not deposit' Lk 19.21.
βάλλω^h: ἔδει σε οὖν βαλεῖν τὰ ἀργύριά μου τοῖς τραπεζίταις 'you ought to have deposited my money with bankers' Mt 25.27.
δίδωμι^g: καὶ διὰ τί οὐκ ἔδωκάς μου τὸ ἀργύριον ἐπὶ τράπεζαν; 'why didn't you put my money in the bank?' Lk 19.23.

57.218 αἴρω^d: to withdraw money from a bank – 'to withdraw.' αἴρεις ὃ οὐκ ἔθηκας 'you withdraw what you did not deposit' Lk 19.21.

R Owe, Debt, Cancel (57.219-57.223)

57.219 ὀφείλω^a: to be under obligation to make a payment as the result of having previously received something of value – 'to owe, to be in debt.' ὃς ὤφειλεν αὐτῷ ἑκατὸν δηνάρια 'who owed him a hundred denarii' Mt 18.28; εἰ δέ τι ἠδίκησέν σε ἢ ὀφείλει 'if he has done you any wrong or owes you anything' Phm 18.

57.220 προσοφείλω: to owe something to someone in return, implying a reciprocal relationship – 'to owe in return, to likewise owe.' ὅτι καὶ σεαυτόν μοι προσοφείλεις 'that you even owe yourself to me in return' Phm 19.

57.221 ὀφειλή^a, ῆς *f*; ὀφείλημα^a, τος *n*: (derivatives of ὀφείλω^a 'to owe,' 57.219) that which is owed – 'debt, amount owed.'
ὀφειλή^a: ἀπόδοτε πᾶσιν τὰς ὀφειλάς 'pay them all the amount you owe' Ro 13.7.
ὀφείλημα^a: τῷ δὲ ἐργαζομένῳ ὁ μισθὸς οὐ λογίζεται κατὰ χάριν ἀλλὰ κατὰ ὀφείλημα 'the wages of a man who works are not regarded as a gift but as what is owed to him' Ro 4.4. It is also possible to understand ὀφείλημα in Ro 4.4 as meaning 'obligation' (see 71.26).

57.222 ὀφειλέτης^a, ου *m* (derivative of ὀφείλω^a 'to owe,' 57.219); χρεοφειλέτης, ου *m*: a person who is in debt – 'debtor.'
ὀφειλέτης^a: προσηνέχθη αὐτῷ εἷς ὀφειλέτης μυρίων ταλάντων 'one man who was a debtor to him for ten thousand talents was brought in' Mt 18.24.
χρεοφειλέτης: δύο χρεοφειλέται ἦσαν δανιστῇ τινι 'there were two men who were debtors to a moneylender' Lk 7.41.

57.223 ἀφίημι^g; χαρίζομαι^c: to release a person from the obligation of repaying what is owed – 'to cancel a debt, to forgive a debt.'
ἀφίημι^g: τὸ δάνειον ἀφῆκεν αὐτῷ 'he cancelled his debt from the loan' Mt 18.27; πᾶσαν τὴν ὀφειλὴν ἐκείνην ἀφῆκά σοι 'I forgave you that entire debt' Mt 18.32.

χαρίζομαι^c: μὴ ἐχόντων αὐτῶν ἀποδοῦναι ἀμφοτέροις ἐχαρίσατο 'neither of them could pay him back, so he cancelled the debts of both' Lk 7.42.

S Be a Financial Burden (57.224-57.225)

57.224 ἐπιβαρέω; καταναρκάω: to be a financial burden to someone by requiring too much support – 'to burden, to be a financial burden to.'
ἐπιβαρέω: νυκτὸς καὶ ἡμέρας ἐργαζόμενοι πρὸς τὸ μὴ ἐπιβαρῆσαί τινα ὑμῶν 'working day and night in order not to be a burden to any of you' 1 Th 2.9.
καταναρκάω: καὶ παρὼν πρὸς ὑμᾶς καὶ ὑστερηθεὶς οὐ κατενάρκησα οὐθενός 'while I was with you, I did not burden anyone for support when I was in need' 2 Cor 11.9.

57.225 ἀβαρής, ές: (a figurative extension of meaning of ἀβαρής 'to be light in weight,' not occurring in the NT) pertaining to not being financially burdensome to anyone – 'not being financially burdensome.' ἀβαρῆ ἐμαυτὸν ὑμῖν ἐτήρησα καὶ τηρήσω 'I kept myself and will keep myself from being a financial burden to you' 2 Cor 11.9.

T Keep Records (57.226-57.231)

57.226 ἐλλογέω^b or ἐλλογάω: to charge to an account – 'to charge.' εἰ δέ τι ἠδίκησέν σε ἢ ὀφείλει, τοῦτο ἐμοὶ ἐλλόγα 'if he has done you any wrong or owes you anything, charge it to my account' Phm 18.

57.227 λογίζομαι^d: to keep records of commercial accounts, involving both debits and credits – 'to put into one's account, to charge one's account, to regard as an account.' τῷ δὲ ἐργαζομένῳ ὁ μισθὸς οὐ λογίζεται κατὰ χάριν ἀλλὰ κατὰ ὀφείλημα 'to a person who has worked, the wage is not regarded (or 'not credited to his account') as a gift but as a debt to be paid' (or 'a debt owed to him') Ro 4.4.

57.228 λόγος^f, ου m: a record of assets and liabilities – 'account, credit, debit.' ἠθέλησεν συνᾶραι λόγον μετὰ τῶν δούλων αὐτοῦ 'he

wanted to check on his servants' accounts' Mt 18.23; ἐπιζητῶ τὸν καρπὸν τὸν πλεονάζοντα εἰς λόγον ὑμῶν 'I seek the results which will increase the amount of your account' (or '. . . to your credit') Php 4.17. The phrase εἰς λόγον in Php 4.17 is a technical expression referring to the settlement of an account and indicates that this is a credit to the account. Accordingly, one may properly translate λόγον as 'the amount of an account.'

57.229 συναίρω: to settle or check on accounts with someone – 'to check on accounts, to settle accounts.' ἀρξαμένου δὲ αὐτοῦ συναίρειν 'as he began to check on accounts' Mt 18.24.

57.230 διακονέω τραπέζαις: (an idiom, literally 'to serve tables') to be responsible for financial aspects of an enterprise – 'to handle finances.' οὐκ ἀρεστόν ἐστιν ἡμᾶς καταλείψαντας τὸν λόγον τοῦ θεοῦ διακονεῖν τραπέζαις 'it is not right that we should give up preaching the word of God to handle finances' Ac 6.2. It is also possible to interpret the phrase διακονέω τραπέζαις not as an idiom but simply as 'to wait on tables, to serve meals' (see 23.26 and 46.13), but even so the context relates to caring for needs.

57.231 οἰκονόμος τῆς πόλεως: (an idiom, literally 'manager of a city') one who is in charge of the finances of a city – 'city treasurer.' ἀσπάζεται ὑμᾶς Ἔραστος ὁ οἰκονόμος τῆς πόλεως 'Erastus, the city treasurer, sends you his greetings' Ro 16.23.

U Steal, Rob³⁹ (57.232-57.248)

57.232 κλέπτω; κλέμμα, τος n; κλοπή, ῆς f: to take secretly and without permission the property of someone else – 'to steal, theft.'
κλέπτω: μήποτε ἐλθόντες οἱ μαθηταὶ αὐτοῦ κλέψωσιν αὐτόν 'lest his disciples come and steal him' Mt 27.64; μὴ θησαυρίζετε ὑμῖν θησαυροὺς ἐπὶ τῆς γῆς . . . ὅπου κλέπται

---

39 Though in Subdomain U *Steal, Rob* there are frequently semantic elements of physical impact (Domain 19) and destruction (Domain 20), the element of transfer of possession seems to be far more focal, and therefore this subdomain is included in Domain 57.

διορύσσουσιν καὶ κλέπτουσιν 'don't store up your treasure on earth ... for thieves will break in and steal it' Mt 6.19.

κλέμμα: οὐ μετενόησαν ... ἐκ τῶν κλεμμάτων αὐτῶν 'they didn't repent ... of their stealing' Re 9.21.

κλοπή: ἔσωθεν γὰρ ἐκ τῆς καρδίας τῶν ἀνθρώπων ... ἐκπορεύονται κλοπαί 'it is from within a person's heart ... that stealing takes place' Mk 7.21.

57.233 κλέπτης, ου *m*: (derivative of κλέπτω 'to steal,' 57.232) a person who steals – 'thief.' κλέπτης ἦν 'he was a thief' Jn 12.6.

57.234 συλάω: to take by force that which belongs to someone else (often used of taking spoils of war, but occurring in the NT only figuratively of Paul's accepting financial support from some churches in order to help others) – 'to rob.' ἄλλας ἐκκλησίας ἐσύλησα λαβὼν ὀψώνιον πρὸς τὴν ὑμῶν διακονίαν 'I robbed other churches by receiving money for support from them so as to serve you' 2 Cor 11.8.[40]

57.235 ἁρπάζω[c]; **ἁρπαγμός**[a], **οῦ** *m*; **ἁρπαγή**[a], **ῆς** *f*: to forcefully take something away from someone else, often with the implication of a sudden attack – 'to rob, to carry off, to plunder, to forcefully seize.' ἁρπάζω[c]: πῶς δύναταί τις εἰσελθεῖν εἰς τὴν οἰκίαν τοῦ ἰσχυροῦ καὶ τὰ σκεύη αὐτοῦ ἁρπάσαι 'no one can break into a strong man's house and carry off his belongings' Mt 12.29. ἁρπαγμός[a]: ὃς ἐν μορφῇ θεοῦ ὑπάρχων οὐχ ἁρπαγμὸν ἡγήσατο τὸ εἶναι ἴσα θεῷ 'he always had the nature of God and did not think that becoming equal with God was something to be taken by force' Php 2.6. This interpretation of Php 2.6 reflects the position of Jesus after the incarnation and the fact that he had no thought of trying to become equal with God because he already possessed all of the qualities of deity. Some traditional translations have rendered the latter part of Php 2.6 as 'did not think it robbery to be equal with God,' but see 57.236.

---

40 It seems quite clear that in 2 Cor 11.8 Paul uses συλάω in a highly figurative sense and thus not with a conventionalized metaphorical value.

ἁρπαγή[a]: τὴν ἁρπαγὴν τῶν ὑπαρχόντων ὑμῶν μετὰ χαρᾶς προσεδέξασθε 'you endured the plundering of your belongings with gladness' He 10.34.

57.236 ἁρπαγμός[b], **οῦ** *m*: that which is to be held on to forcibly – 'something to hold by force, something to be forcibly retained.' ὃς ἐν μορφῇ θεοῦ ὑπάρχων οὐχ ἁρπαγμὸν ἡγήσατο τὸ εἶναι ἴσα θεῷ 'he always had the nature of God and did not consider that remaining equal with God was something to be held on to forcibly' Php 2.6 (compare the rendering of ἁρπαγμός[a] in 57.235). Since ἁρπαγμός may mean not only 'to grasp something forcefully which one does not have' (57.235) but also 'to retain by force what one possesses,' it is possible to translate Php 2.6 in two quite different ways. This second interpretation of ἁρπαγμός presumes the position of Jesus prior to the incarnation and hence his willingness to experience the kenosis or 'emptying' of his divine prerogatives. In any translation of Php 2.6 it is important that both possible renderings be clearly indicated, one in the text and the other in the margin.

57.237 ἁρπαγή[b], **ῆς** *f*: (derivative of ἁρπαγή[a] 'to plunder,' 57.235) that which is taken by force or plundered – 'plunder, booty.' ἔσωθεν δὲ γέμουσιν ἐξ ἁρπαγῆς 'but inside they are full of what has been taken by violence' Mt 23.25.

57.238 διαρπάζω: to plunder something thoroughly or completely – 'to plunder, to rob.' τότε τὴν οἰκίαν αὐτοῦ διαρπάσει 'then he will plunder his house' Mk 3.27. In some languages one may render 'plunder' as 'to carry off all that one can.'

57.239 ἅρπαξ, αγος *m*: (derivative of ἁρπάζω[a] 'to carry off by force,' 57.235) one who carries off the possessions of another by force – 'robber, plunderer.' οὐχ ἅρπαγες βασιλείαν θεοῦ κληρονομήσουσιν 'robbers will not inherit the kingdom of God' 1 Cor 6.10; ὅτι οὐκ εἰμὶ ὥσπερ οἱ λοιποὶ τῶν ἀνθρώπων, ἅρπαγες, ἄδικοι, μοιχοί 'that I am not like other people, robbers, unjust, adulterers' Lk 18.11. For an interpretation of ἅρπαξ as an adjective in Lk 18.11, see 25.25.

57.240 ληστής[a], οῦ *m*: (derivative of ληστεύω 'to practice robbery, piracy,' not occurring in the NT) one who robs by force and violence – 'robber, highwayman.' ἄνθρωπός τις κατέβαινεν ἀπὸ Ἰερουσαλὴμ εἰς Ἰεριχὼ καὶ λῃσταῖς περιέπεσεν 'a certain man came down from Jerusalem to Jericho and was attacked by robbers' Lk 10.30.

57.241 ἱεροσυλέω[a]: to take by force or stealth objects from a temple – 'to rob temples.' ὁ βδελυσσόμενος τὰ εἴδωλα ἱεροσυλεῖς; 'you who abhor idols, do you not rob temples?' Ro 2.22. It is also possible to interpret ἱεροσυλέω in Ro 2.22 as meaning 'to commit sacrilege,' in the sense of doing harm or damage to sacred objects in temples (see 53.104).

57.242 ἱερόσυλος, ου *m*: one who robs temples – 'temple robber.' ἠγάγετε γὰρ τοὺς ἄνδρας τούτους οὔτε ἱεροσύλους οὔτε βλασφημοῦντας τὴν θεὸν ἡμῶν 'for you have brought these men who are neither temple robbers nor ones who speak evil of our goddess' Ac 19.37. For another interpretation of ἱερόσυλος in Ac 19.37, see 53.105.

57.243 σκῦλα, ων *n*: that which is taken away by force, particularly in the case of war – 'booty, spoils, plunder.' τὰ σκῦλα αὐτοῦ διαδίδωσιν 'he divides up the booty he has taken' Lk 11.22.

57.244 ἀκροθίνιον, ου *n* (usually in the plural): the best part of the booty, particularly that which is offered to deity – 'the best of the booty, the finest spoils, the most valuable plunder.' ᾧ καὶ δεκάτην Ἀβραὰμ ἔδωκεν ἐκ τῶν ἀκροθινίων ὁ παρτιάρχης 'to whom Abraham the patriarch gave a tenth of the best of the booty' He 7.4.

57.245 διασείω: to extort money by force or threat of violence – 'to extort, to take money by violence.' μηδένα διασείσητε 'don't take money from anyone by force' Lk 3.14.

57.246 νοσφίζομαι: to misappropriate funds for one's own benefit – 'to misappropriate funds for oneself, to embezzle.' καὶ νοσφίσασθαι ἀπὸ τῆς τιμῆς τοῦ χωρίου 'and to keep back for yourself some of the price of the property' Ac 5.3.

57.247 κατεσθίω[c]: (a figurative extension of meaning of κατεσθίω[a] 'to eat up, to consume,' 23.11) to take over by dishonest means the property of someone else – 'to appropriate dishonestly, to rob.' οἱ κατεσθίοντες τὰς οἰκίας τῶν χηρῶν 'they rob widows of their homes' Mk 12.40.

57.248 ἀποστερέω[a]: to take something from someone by means of deception or trickery – 'to defraud, to deprive by deception.' μὴ ἀποστερήσῃς 'do not defraud' Mk 10.19.

58 Nature, Class, Example

Outline of Subdomains

A Nature, Character (58.1-58.13)
B Appearance as an Outward Manifestation of Form (58.14-58.18)
C Basic Principles or Features Defining the Nature of Something (58.19-58.20)
D Class, Kind (58.21-58.30)
E Same or Equivalent Kind or Class (58.31-58.35)

F Different Kind or Class (58.36-58.46)
G Distinctive, Unique (58.47-58.53)
H Unusual, Different From the Ordinary (58.54-58.57)
I Pattern, Model, Example, and Corresponding Representation (58.58-58.62)
J Archetype, Corresponding Type (Antitype) (58.63-58.69)
K New, Old (primarily non-temporal) (58.70-58.75)

A Nature, Character (58.1-58.13)

58.1 ὑπόστασις[a], εως *f*: the essential or basic nature of an entity – 'substance, nature, essence, real being.' ὃς ὢν . . . χαρακτὴρ τῆς ὑποστάσεως αὐτοῦ 'who is . . . the exact representation of his real being' or '. . . nature' He 1.3. In some languages there is no ready lexical equivalent of 'real being' or 'nature.' Therefore, one may express this concept in He 1.3 as 'who is . . . just like what he really is.'

58.2 μορφή[a], ῆς *f*: the nature or character of something, with emphasis upon both the internal and external form – 'nature, character.' ὃς ἐν μορφῇ θεοῦ ὑπάρχων 'he always had the very nature of God' Php 2.6; μορφὴν δούλου λαβών 'he took on the nature of a servant' Php 2.7. In view of the lack of a closely corresponding lexical unit such as 'nature,' it may be necessary to restructure the form of Php 2.7 as 'he became truly a servant.'

58.3 μόρφωσις, εως *f*: the embodiment of the essential features and qualities of something – 'embodiment, full content, essential features.' ἔχοντα τὴν μόρφωσιν τῆς γνώσεως καὶ τῆς ἀληθείας ἐν τῷ νόμῳ 'having the essential features of knowledge and truth in the Law' Ro 2.20. In some languages there may not be a substantive corresponding to 'features' or 'essential features.' It may therefore be important to restructure this expression in Ro 2.20 as 'to possess correctly the knowledge and truth in the Law' or 'to truly possess the knowledge and truth in the Law' or even 'in the Law to know fully the truth.'

58.4 μορφόω: (derivative of μορφή[a] 'nature, character,' 58.2) to cause something to have a certain form or nature – 'to form the nature of.' μέχρις οὗ μορφωθῇ Χριστὸς ἐν ὑμῖν 'until Christ's nature is formed in you' Ga 4.19. It may be possible in some languages to render Ga 4.19 as 'until you become like Christ was' or '. . . like Christ is.'

58.5 σύμμορφος, ον: pertaining to that which has a similar form or nature – 'similar in

form, of the same form.' προώρισεν συμμόρφους τῆς εἰκόνος τοῦ υἱοῦ αὐτοῦ 'he set them apart in order that they might be similar in form to the nature of his Son' Ro 8.29; σύμμορφον τῷ σώματι τῆς δόξης αὐτοῦ 'of the same form as his glorious body' Php 3.21.

In the case of Ro 8.29 it may be necessary in some languages to translate 'he set them apart in order that they might be like his Son,' and in Php 3.21 it may be necessary in some languages to translate 'having a glorious body like his.'

58.6 συμμορφίζομαι: to come to be similar in form to something else – 'to share in having the likeness of, to take on the same form as, to become like.' συμμορφιζόμενος τῷ θανάτῳ αὐτοῦ 'to come to be similar in form to him in his death' Php 3.10. In some languages a more appropriate equivalent of this expression in Php 3.10 may be 'to come to be like him in his death' or 'to die in a manner similar to his death.'

58.7 σχῆμα[a], τος *n*: the form or nature of something, with special reference to its outer form or structure – 'form, nature, structure.' παράγει γὰρ τὸ σχῆμα τοῦ κόσμου τούτου 'the form of this world is passing away' 1 Cor 7.31. In 1 Cor 7.31 σχῆμα does not refer to the physical form of the earth but to the way of life in the world. The reference is primarily to culture rather than to physical form. It is possible, therefore, to render this expression in 1 Cor 7.31 as 'the way of life in this world is passing away.'

58.8 φύσις[a], εως *f*: the nature of something as the result of its natural development or condition – 'nature.' τοῖς φύσει μὴ οὖσιν θεοῖς 'beings who by nature are not gods' Ga 4.8; θείας κοινωνοὶ φύσεως 'sharers in the divine nature' 2 Pe 1.4.

For languages in which there is no ready equivalent to the lexical term 'nature,' it may be possible to render the expression in Ga 4.8 as 'beings who are really not gods,' and in 2 Pe 1.4 one may translate 'to share in what God is like' or 'to be like God in certain ways.'

58.9 φυσικός, ή, όν; φυσικῶς: pertaining to that which is in accordance with the nature or character of something – 'natural, naturally, by nature, by instinct.'

φυσικός: μετήλλαξαν τὴν φυσικὴν χρῆσιν εἰς τὴν παρὰ φύσιν 'they changed the use which is in accordance with nature to that which is contrary to nature' Ro 1.26. For some languages the equivalent of 'being in accordance with nature' is simply 'being as it should be.' ζῶα γεγεννημένα φυσικὰ εἰς ἅλωσιν καὶ φθοράν 'natural creatures born to be caught and killed' 2 Pe 2.12. In place of an expression such as 'natural creatures' a more appropriate equivalent in some languages is simply 'animals.'

φυσικῶς: ὅσα δὲ φυσικῶς ὡς τὰ ἄλογα ζῶα ἐπίστανται 'which they know by instinct, like wild animals' Jd 10.

58.10 σάρξ[g], σαρκός f: human nature, particularly in reference to the physical aspect of human life – 'human nature, physical nature of people.' κατὰ σάρκα γεγέννηται 'was born in accordance with the physical aspect of human nature' Ga 4.23. In some languages one may more appropriately translate this phrase in Ga 4.23 as 'was born like any person is' or 'was born like people are normally born.'

58.11 πλάσσω[b]: to give a particular form to something – 'to form, to mold.' μὴ ἐρεῖ τὸ πλάσμα τῷ πλάσαντι, Τί με ἐποίησας οὕτως; 'will what is formed say to the one who formed it, Why did you make me this way?' Ro 9.20.

58.12 πλάσμα, τος n: (derivative of πλάσσω[b] 'to form,' 58.11) that which is formed or molded – 'what is formed.' μὴ ἐρεῖ τὸ πλάσμα τῷ πλάσαντι, Τί με ἐποίησας οὕτως; 'will what is formed say to the one who formed it, Why did you make me this way?' Ro 9.20.

58.13 σπέρμα[c], τος n: a derivative and imparted nature – 'nature, something of the nature of.' πᾶς ὁ γεγεννημένος ἐκ τοῦ θεοῦ ἁμαρτίαν οὐ ποιεῖ, ὅτι σπέρμα αὐτοῦ ἐν αὐτῷ μένει 'everyone who is born of God does not commit sin, because God's nature is in him' 1 Jn 3.9. If in some languages it is not possible to speak literally of 'God's nature,' it may still

be possible to render the second clause in 1 Jn 3.9 as 'because something of what God is like is in him' or 'because he has in himself something of what God is like.'

B Appearance as an Outward Manifestation of Form (58.14-58.18)

58.14 εἶδος[a], ους n; εἰδέα, ας f: appearance as the form of that which is seen – 'form, appearance.'

εἶδος[a]: καὶ ἐγένετο ἐν τῷ προσεύχεσθαι αὐτὸν τὸ εἶδος τοῦ προσώπου αὐτοῦ ἕτερον 'while he was praying, his face changed in its appearance' Lk 9.29. One may also translate this expression in Lk 9.29 as 'while he was praying, his face became different' or '. . . his face was seen as different' or '. . . he didn't look the same.'

εἰδέα: ἦν δὲ ἡ εἰδέα αὐτοῦ ὡς ἀστραπή 'his appearance was like lightning' Mt 28.3. In some languages a strictly literal translation of Mt 28.3 might be misinterpreted to mean that there was something jagged about the outline of Jesus' appearance. The focus, of course, is upon the brightness, and therefore it may be important to translate 'his appearance was bright like lightning.'

58.15 μορφή[b], ῆς f: a visual form of something – 'visual form, appearance.' ἐφανερώθη ἐν ἑτέρᾳ μορφῇ 'he appeared in a different form' Mk 16.12.

58.16 μεταμορφόομαι[b]: to take on a different physical form or appearance – 'to change in appearance.' μετεμορφώθη ἔμπροσθεν αὐτῶν 'his appearance was changed in their presence' Mk 9.2. In some instances it may be more appropriate to render this expression in Mk 9.2 as 'as they watched, he appeared different.'

58.17 σχῆμα[b], τος n: appearance as an element of outward form – 'appearance, form.' καὶ σχήματι εὑρεθεὶς ὡς ἄνθρωπος 'and his appearance was seen to be that of a person' or '. . . like that of a person' (literally 'and in appearance he attained to being a person') Php 2.7.

58.18 μετασχηματίζω^a: to cause a change in the form of something – 'to change, to change from one form into another.' ὃς μετασχηματίσει τὸ σῶμα τῆς ταπεινώσεως ἡμῶν σύμμορφον τῷ σώματι τῆς δόξης αὐτοῦ 'who will change our weak bodies into the form of his glorious body' Php 3.21.

C Basic Principles or Features Defining the Nature of Something (58.19-58.20)

58.19 στοιχεῖα^c, ων n: basic principles which underlie the nature of something – 'basic principles, elementary concepts.' πάλιν χρείαν ἔχετε τοῦ διδάσκειν ὑμᾶς τινὰ τὰ στοιχεῖα τῆς ἀρχῆς τῶν λογίων τοῦ θεοῦ 'again you have need of someone to teach you the basic principles about the elementary aspects of God's message' He 5.12. In some languages it may be extremely difficult to find the lexical equivalents of 'the basic principles about the elementary aspects.' In Greek this represents highly generic vocabulary, and in many languages the closest equivalent is 'how to understand the simple truths.' Therefore, this expression in He 5.12 may be rendered as 'again you have need for someone to teach you how to understand the simple truths about God's message.'

58.20 ἀρχή^g, ῆς f: elementary and preliminary aspects defining the nature of something – 'elementary aspect, simple truth.' ἀφέντες τὸν τῆς ἀρχῆς τοῦ Χριστοῦ λόγον 'leaving the message concerning the elementary aspects of Christ' or '. . . the simple truths about Christ' He 6.1. Compare also the occurrence of ἀρχή^g in He 5.12 in which it serves to reinforce the meaning of στοιχεῖα (see 58.19).

D Class, Kind (58.21-58.30)

58.21 τάξις^c, εως f: kind or type of entity, implying a contrast-comparison to other similar entities – 'kind, type.' σὺ ἱερεὺς εἰς τὸν αἰῶνα κατὰ τὴν τάξιν Μελχισέδεκ 'you are a priest forever in accordance with the kind of priest that Melchizedek was' or '. . . like Melchizedek' He 5.6. It is possible that τάξις in He 5.6 refers to a kind of priest on the basis of being in a particular grouping or order of priests, but there seems to be no reference to any higher rank or position.

58.22 ὄνομα^d, τος n: category or kind, based upon an implied designation for a class of entities – 'category of, being of the type that.' ὃς γὰρ ἂν ποτίσῃ ὑμᾶς ποτήριον ὕδατος ἐν ὀνόματι ὅτι Χριστοῦ ἐστε 'whoever gives you a drink under the category that you belong to Christ' or '. . . in view of the kind of person you are, namely, that you belong to Christ' Mk 9.41; ὁ δεχόμενος προφήτην εἰς ὄνομα προφήτου 'whoever receives a prophet within the category of his being a prophet' or '. . . because he is a prophet' or '. . . as a prophet' Mt 10.41.

58.23 γένος^c, ους n: a category or class based upon an implied derivation and/or lineage – 'kind, type.' ἐκ παντὸς γένους συναγαγούσῃ 'gathering (fish) of every kind' Mt 13.47; τοσαῦτα εἰ τύχοι γένη φωνῶν εἰσιν ἐν κόσμῳ 'there are perhaps a great many kinds of languages in the world' 1 Cor 14.10.

58.24 φύσις^b, εως f: a class of entities based on physiological and genetic similarity – 'kind, class, species.' πᾶσα γὰρ φύσις θηρίων τε καὶ πετεινῶν ἑρπετῶν τε καὶ ἐναλίων δαμάζεται καὶ δεδάμασται τῇ φύσει τῇ ἀνθρωπίνῃ 'every kind of wild animal, bird, reptile, and fish can be tamed and has been tamed by people' (literally '. . . humankind') Jas 3.7.[1]

58.25 τύπος^f, ου m: a kind or class, implying a relationship to some model or pattern – 'kind, class, type.' γράψας ἐπιστολὴν ἔχουσαν τὸν τύπον τοῦτον 'having written a letter of the following type' or '. . . of this kind' or '. . . a letter like this' Ac 23.25. For another interpretation of τύπος in Ac 23.25, see 90.28.

58.26 υἱός^h, οῦ m; γέννημα^b, τος n; τέκνον^f, ου n: a kind or class of persons, with the implication of possessing certain derived characteristics – 'son of, offspring of, child of, kind of, one who has the characteristics of, person of.'

---

1 There is clearly a play on the use of the term φύσις at the beginning and at the end of Jas 3.7.

υἱός^h: οἱ υἱοὶ τοῦ αἰῶνος τούτου 'people of this age' (in the sense of the kind of people typical of this age) Lk 16.8.

γέννημα^b: γεννήματα ἐχιδνῶν 'offspring of vipers' (in the sense of the kind of people who are like vipers) Mt 3.7. For another interpretation of γέννημα in Mt 3.7, see 23.53.

τέκνον^f: τέκνα ὑ ακοῆς 'children of obedience' (in the sense of the kind of people who obey) 1 Pe 1.14.

58.27 ἐγκρίνω: to classify by judging something to be in a particular category or class – 'to classify.' οὐ γὰρ τολμῶμεν ἐγκρῖναι ἢ συγκρῖναι ἑαυτούς τισιν τῶν ἑαυτοὺς συνιστανόντων 'for we would not dare to classify ourselves or compare ourselves with those who rate themselves so highly' 2 Cor 10.12. In 2 Cor 10.12 there is evidently a play on the meanings of ἐγκρῖναι and συγκρῖναι (see συγκρίνω^a, 64.6).

58.28 πᾶς^c, πᾶσα, πᾶν: a totality of kinds or sorts – 'every kind of, all sorts of.' πᾶσαν νόσον καὶ πᾶσαν μαλακίαν 'every kind of disease or weakness' Mt 4.23; πᾶν ἁμάρτημα 'every kind of sin' 1 Cor 6.18.

58.29 πολυτρόπως^a: pertaining to that which occurs in many kinds of ways – 'in many ways.' πολυτρόπως πάλαι ὁ θεὸς λαλήσας τοῖς πατράσιν 'in many ways God spoke in earlier times to the ancestors' He 1.1. For another interpretation of πολυτρόπως in He 1.1, see 89.82.

58.30 ποταπός, ή, όν; ὁποῖος, α, ον; ποῖος^b, α, ον; οἷος^b, α, ον: interrogative references to class or kind – 'what sort of, what kind of.'
ποταπός: ἐγίνωσκεν ἂν τίς καὶ ποταπὴ ἡ γυνὴ ἥτις ἅπτεται αὐτοῦ 'he would know who and what sort of woman she is who is touching him' Lk 7.39; διελογίζετο ποταπὸς εἴη ὁ ἀσπασμὸς οὗτος 'she wondered what sort of greeting this was' Lk 1.29.
ὁποῖος: ἐπελάθετο ὁποῖος ἦν 'he forgets what sort of person he is' Jas 1.24; ὁποῖοί ποτε ἦσαν οὐδέν μοι διαφέρει 'what sort of people they were makes no difference to me' Ga 2.6.
ποῖος^b: ποίῳ δὲ σώματι ἔρχονται; 'and with what sort of body will they come?' 1 Cor

15.35; τοῦτο δὲ ἔλεγεν σημαίνων ποίῳ θανάτῳ ἤμελλεν ἀποθνῄσκειν 'he said this to show what sort of death he was going to die' Jn 12.33.
οἷος^b: ὑγιὴς ἐγίνετο οἵῳ δήποτ' οὖν κατείχετο νοσήματι 'was made well from whatever disease he had' Jn 5.4 (apparatus).

E Same or Equivalent Kind or Class[2] (58.31-58.35)

58.31 αὐτός^a, ή, ό (occurring with the article): pertaining to that which is identical to something – 'same.' προσηύξατο τὸν αὐτὸν λόγον εἰπών 'he prayed, saying the same thing' Mk 14.39; οὐχὶ καὶ οἱ τελῶναι τὸ αὐτὸ ποιοῦσιν; 'do not even the tax collectors do the same thing?' Mt 5.46.

58.32 ἰσότης, ητος f: the state of being equal – 'equality' (in the sense of having equal features or characteristics). ἀλλ' ἐξ ἰσότητος 'but as a matter of equality' 2 Cor 8.13.

58.33 ἴσος, η, ον: pertaining to that which is equal, either in number, size, quality, or characteristics – 'equal, equivalent, same.' τὸ μῆκος καὶ τὸ πλάτος καὶ τὸ ὕψος αὐτῆς ἴσα ἐστίν 'the length and breadth and height of it are the same' Re 21.16; ἴσον ἑαυτὸν ποιῶν τῷ θεῷ 'making himself equal with God' Jn 5.18.

58.34 ἰσότιμος, ον: pertaining to that which is of equal significance or value – 'equal to, of the equivalent kind as.' τοῖς ἰσότιμον ἡμῖν . . . πίστιν 'faith . . . of a kind equivalent to ours' or 'faith . . . of the same kind as ours' 2 Pe 1.1.

58.35 εἰκών^b, όνος f: that which has the same form as something else – 'same form, likeness.' καὶ καθὼς ἐφορέσαμεν τὴν εἰκόνα τοῦ χοϊκοῦ, φορέσομεν καὶ τὴν εἰκόνα τοῦ ἐπουρανίου 'since we bear the likeness of that which is

---

2 Subdomain E *Same or Equivalent Kind or Class* does not contain meanings related to comparison, since these meanings have been organized in a separate domain, *64 Comparison*. There are, of course, a number of points at which Domains 58 and 64 tend to coincide and even to overlap, but in view of the greater specificity of the contextual references in Domain 64, it seems better to classify these meanings in a separate domain.

typical of the earth, we will also bear the likeness of that which is typical of heaven' 1 Cor 15.49. Since the expressions τοῦ χοϊκοῦ and τοῦ ἐπουρανίου refer to individuals, it is much more satisfactory to translate 1 Cor 15.49 as 'just as we have the likeness of the man made of earth, so we will have the likeness of the Man from heaven.'

In 1 Cor 15.49 εἰκών designates similarity in class or kind, while in Ro 1.23 εἰκών indicates a fashioned object (see 6.96).

F Different Kind or Class (58.36-58.46)

58.36 ἄλλος[a], η, ο; ἄλλως; ἕτερος[a], α, ον; ἑτέρως: pertaining to that which is different in kind or class from all other entities – 'different, differently, other than.'[3]

ἄλλος[a]: οὐ πᾶσα σὰρξ ἡ αὐτὴ σάρξ, ἀλλὰ ἄλλη μὲν ἀνθρώπων, ἄλλη δὲ σὰρξ κτηνῶν, ἄλλη δὲ σὰρξ πτηνῶν, ἄλλη δὲ ἰχθύων 'not all flesh is the same flesh, but there is one type of flesh of humans, another of animals, another of birds, and another of fish' or 'not all flesh is the same, for there is one kind for people, a different kind for animals, a different kind for birds, and a different kind for fish' 1 Cor 15.39.

ἄλλως: καὶ τὰ ἄλλως ἔχοντα κρυβῆναι οὐ δύνανται 'those that are different cannot remain hidden' 1 Tm 5.25.

ἕτερος[a]: ἐν ἑτέρα μορφῇ 'in a different form' Mk 16.12; ἀλλὰ ἑτέρα ·μὲν ἡ τῶν ἐπουρανίων δόξα, ἑτέρα δὲ ἡ τῶν ἐπιγείων 'but the beauty of the heavenly is different from the beauty of the earthly' 1 Cor 15.40.

ἑτέρως: ἑτέρως φρονεῖτε 'you think differently' Php 3.15.

58.37 ἄλλος[b], η, ο; ἕτερος[b], α, ον: pertaining to that which is other than some other

---

3 Some persons have assumed that the distinction between ἄλλος and ἕτερος is simply a difference between what is another in a series and that which is significantly different in kind, but such a distinction cannot be confirmed from existing contexts, though there may be this type of distinction implied in Ga 1.6-7 in which 'another kind of gospel' is rejected on the basis that there is 'no other gospel.' Note, however, that both ἄλλος and ἕτερος also occur in the meaning of 'another, which is not the same' (see 58.37).

item implied or identified in a context – 'other, another.'[3]

ἄλλος[b]: μή πως ἄλλοις κηρύξας αὐτὸς ἀδόκιμος γένωμαι 'so that I myself will not be rejected after having proclaimed the message to others' 1 Cor 9.27; δι' ἄλλης ὁδοῦ ἀνεχώρησαν 'they went home by another route' Mt 2.12.

ἕτερος[b]: ἐν τῷ ἑτέρῳ πλοίῳ 'in the other boat' Lk 5.7; ἕτερος δὲ τῶν μαθητῶν 'another of the disciples' Mt 8.21; καὶ πάλιν ἑτέρα γραφὴ λέγει 'and again another (passage of) Scripture says . . .' Jn 19.37.

58.38 παρεκτός: pertaining to being different and in addition to something else, with the implication of something being external to central concerns – 'besides, additional.' χωρὶς τῶν παρεκτὸς ἡ ἐπίστασίς μοι ἡ καθ' ἡμέραν, ἡ μέριμνα πασῶν τῶν ἐκκλησιῶν 'quite apart from other matters the daily pressure and concern which I have for all the churches' 2 Cor 11.28.

58.39 διαίρεσις[b], εως f: a state of difference in the nature of objects or events, with the implication of significant variety – 'difference, variety.' διαιρέσεις δὲ χαρισμάτων εἰσίν, τὸ δὲ αὐτὸ πνεῦμα 'and there are differences of gifts, but the same Spirit' 1 Cor 12.4. It is also possible to interpret διαίρεσις in 1 Cor 12.4 as the allotment or apportionment of such spiritual gifts (see 57.91).

58.40 διάφορος, ον: pertaining to that which is different – 'different, varied.' ἔχοντες δὲ χαρίσματα κατὰ τὴν χάριν τὴν δοθεῖσαν ἡμῖν διάφορα 'having differing gifts according to the grace which has been given to us' Ro 12.6; μόνον ἐπὶ βρώμασιν καὶ πόμασιν καὶ διαφόροις βαπτισμοῖς 'only concerning food, drink, and various purification ceremonies' He 9.10.

58.41 διαφέρω[c]: to be different from someone or something – 'to differ from, to be different from.' ἀστὴρ γὰρ ἀστέρος διαφέρει ἐν δόξῃ 'one star differs from another in beauty' 1 Cor 15.41.

58.42 διαστολή, ῆς f: a clear or marked distinction – 'difference, distinction.' διαστολὴ Ἰουδαίου τε καὶ Ἕλληνος 'a distinction between a Jew and a Greek' or '. . . a Gentile'

Ro 10.12; ἐὰν διαστολὴν τοῖς φθόγγοις μὴ δῷ 'if they do not produce a clear distinction in their tones' 1 Cor 14.7.

58.43 ἀλλάσσω[a]: to cause a difference by altering the character or nature of something – 'to change, to alter, to make different.' καὶ ἀλλάξει τὰ ἔθη ἃ παρέδωκεν ἡμῖν Μωϋσῆς 'and he will alter the customs which Moses handed down to us' Ac 6.14.

58.44 παραλλαγή, ῆς *f*: a change or variation in the nature or character of something – 'change.' παρ' ᾧ οὐκ ἔνι παραλλαγή 'in whom there is not a single change' Jas 1.17.

58.45 ποικίλος, η, ον: pertaining to that which exists in a variety of kinds – 'of various kinds, diversified.' ἔχοντας ποικίλαις ... βασάνοις 'having various kinds of ... torments' Mt 4.24; ποικίλης χάριτος θεοῦ 'the grace of God that shows itself in various ways' 1 Pe 4.10.

58.46 πολυποίκιλος, ον: pertaining to that which is different in a number of ways – 'many and diverse, manifold, many-sided.' ἡ πολυποίκιλος σοφία τοῦ θεοῦ 'the wisdom of God in its many different forms' Eph 3.10.

G Distinctive, Unique (58.47-58.53)

58.47 ἴδιος[b], α, ον: pertaining to that which is peculiar or distinctive to some entity – 'peculiar, distinctive.' ἕκαστον γὰρ δένδρον ἐκ τοῦ ἰδίου καρποῦ γινώσκεται 'every tree is known by its own particular kind of fruit' Lk 6.44; παρέβη Ἰούδας πορευθῆναι εἰς τὸν τόπον τὸν ἴδιον 'Judas left to go to his own particular place' Ac 1.25.

58.48 περιούσιος[b], ον: pertaining to that which is peculiar or special about some entity – 'peculiar, special.' καὶ καθαρίσῃ ἑαυτῷ λαὸν περιούσιον 'and purify for himself a special people' Tt 2.14. For another interpretation of περιούσιος in Tt 2.14, see 57.5.

58.49 τοιόσδε, άδε, όνδε: pertaining to being of such a kind, often with the implication of a degree of uniqueness or distinctiveness – 'of such a kind, distinctive, special.' φωνῆς ἐνεχθείσης αὐτῷ τοιᾶσδε ὑπὸ τῆς μεγαλοπρεποῦς δόξης 'a very special voice having come to him from the Sublime Glory' 2 Pe 1.17.

58.50 μόνος[a], η, ον: the only entity in a class – 'only one, alone.' κἀγὼ ὑπελείφθην μόνος 'I am the only one left' Ro 11.3; καὶ τὴν δόξαν τὴν παρὰ τοῦ μόνου θεοῦ οὐ ζητεῖτε 'you do not seek praise from the one who alone is God' Jn 5.44.

58.51 μόνος[b], η, ον; κατὰ μόνας (an idiom, literally 'throughout only places'): the only item of a class in a place – 'alone, all by oneself.'

μόνος[b]: καὶ ἐν τῷ γενέσθαι τὴν φωνὴν εὑρέθη Ἰησοῦς μόνος 'when the voice stopped, Jesus was there alone' Lk 9.36.

κατὰ μόνας: καὶ ὅτε ἐγένετο κατὰ μόνας 'and when he was alone' Mk 4.10; καὶ ἐγένετο ἐν τῷ εἶναι αὐτὸν προσευχόμενον κατὰ μόνας συνῆσαν αὐτῷ οἱ μαθηταί 'and it happened that while he was praying alone, the disciples came to him' Lk 9.18.

58.52 μονογενής, ές: pertaining to what is unique in the sense of being the only one of the same kind or class – 'unique, only.' τὸν υἱὸν τὸν μονογενῆ ἔδωκεν 'he gave his only Son' Jn 3.16; τὸν υἱὸν αὐτοῦ τὸν μονογενῆ ἀπέσταλκεν ὁ θεός 'God sent his only Son' 1 Jn 4.9; τὸν μονογενῆ προσέφερεν ὁ τὰς ἐπαγγελίας ἀναδεξάμενος 'he who had received the promises presented his only son' or '. . . was ready to offer his only son' He 11.17. Abraham, of course, did have another son, Ishmael, and later sons by Keturah, but Isaac was a unique son in that he was a son born as the result of certain promises made by God. Accordingly, he could be called a μονογενής son, since he was the only one of his kind.

58.53 ἀγαπητός[b], ή, όν: pertaining to one who is the only one of his or her class, but at the same time is particularly loved and cherished – 'only, only dear.' οὗτός ἐστιν ὁ υἱός μου ὁ ἀγαπητός 'this is my one dear Son' Mt 3.17.[4]

4 ἀγαπητός in this sense is typical of a term which shares significant components from two different seman-

H Unusual, Different From the Ordinary (58.54-58.57)

58.54 ἄτοπος[b], ον: pertaining to that which is unusual, and generally with the implication of harmful or dangerous – 'unusual, unusual and bad.' μηδὲν ἄτοπον εἰς αὐτὸν γινόμενον 'nothing unusual happened to him' Ac 28.6.

58.55 γνωστός[f], ή, όν: pertaining to that which is unusual in the sense of being extraordinary – 'unusual, extraordinary.' γνωστὸν σημεῖον γέγονεν δι᾽ αὐτῶν πᾶσιν τοῖς κατοικοῦσιν Ἰερουσαλὴμ φανερόν 'all the inhabitants of Jerusalem know that this extraordinary miracle has taken place as a result of what they did' or '. . . they performed this extraordinary miracle' Ac 4.16. For another interpretation of γνωστός in Ac 4.16, see 28.32.

58.56 παράδοξος[b], ον: pertaining to that which is unusual in the sense of contrary to expectations – 'unusual, remarkable.' εἴδομεν παράδοξα σήμερον 'we have seen a remarkable miracle' Lk 5.26. For another interpretation of παράδοξος in Lk 5.26, see 31.44.

58.57 περισσός[b], ή, όν: pertaining to that which is exceptional in the sense of being more than what is expected – 'exceptional, outstanding, remarkable, unusual.' τί περισσὸν ποιεῖτε; 'what exceptional thing have you done?' (literally 'do you do?') Mt 5.47.

I Pattern, Model, Example, and Corresponding Representation[5] (58.58-58.62)

58.58 τύπος[c], ου *m*: a visual form designed to be imitated or copied – 'model, pattern.' ποιῆσαι αὐτὴν κατὰ τὸν τύπον ὃν ἑωράκει 'to make it according to the model which he had

tic domains. In the context of Mt 3.17 the focus seems clearly to be upon the distinctive and unique elements of meaning, but it would be entirely wrong to rule out the supplementary component of being loved and cherished (see ἀγαπητός[a], 25.45).

5 In this subdomain the patterns, models, or examples may be elements to be imitated and thus to a certain extent constitute standards, or they may suggest that which is to be avoided and hence indirectly constitute warnings.

seen' Ac 7.44; ποιήσεις πάντα κατὰ τὸν τύπον τὸν δειχθέντα σοι ἐν τῷ ὄρει 'you will make all these things according to the model which was shown to you on the mountain' He 8.5.

58.59 τύπος[d], ου *m*; ὑποτύπωσις, εως *f*; ὑπογραμμός, οῦ *m*; ὑπόδειγμα, τος *n*: a model of behavior as an example to be imitated or to be avoided – 'model, example.'

τύπος[d]: σκοπεῖτε τοὺς οὕτω περιπατοῦντας καθὼς ἔχετε τύπον ἡμᾶς 'pay attention to those who follow the example that we have set for you' Php 3.17; ταῦτα δὲ τύποι ἡμῶν ἐγενήθησαν, εἰς τὸ μὴ εἶναι ἡμᾶς ἐπιθυμητὰς κακῶν, καθὼς κἀκεῖνοι ἐπεθύμησαν 'and these have become examples for us so that we would not desire evil things as they did' 1 Cor 10.6.

ὑποτύπωσις: πρὸς ὑποτύπωσιν τῶν μελλόντων πιστεύειν ἐπ᾽ αὐτῷ 'as an example to those who would later believe in him' 1 Tm 1.16; ὑποτύπωσιν ἔχε ὑγιαινόντων λόγων ὧν παρ᾽ ἐμοῦ ἤκουσας 'hold to the example of sound teaching which you have heard from me' 2 Tm 1.13.

ὑπογραμμός: ὑμῖν ὑπολιμπάνων ὑπογραμμὸν ἵνα ἐπακολουθήσητε τοῖς ἴχνεσιν αὐτοῦ 'leaving you an example in order that you would follow in his footsteps' 1 Pe 2.21.

ὑπόδειγμα: ὑπόδειγμα γὰρ ἔδωκα ὑμῖν ἵνα καθὼς ἐγὼ ἐποίησα ὑμῖν καὶ ὑμεῖς ποιῆτε 'for I have given you an example in order that you should do even as I have done to you' Jn 13.15.

58.60 τυπικῶς: pertaining to that which serves as a model or example – 'example, model.' ταῦτα δὲ τυπικῶς συνέβαινεν ἐκείνοις 'these things happened to them as examples' 1 Cor 10.11.

58.61 εἰκών[c], όνος *f*: that which represents something else in terms of basic form and features – 'representation, pattern.' ὁ νόμος . . . οὐκ αὐτὴν τὴν εἰκόνα τῶν πραγμάτων 'the Law . . . is not the representation itself of the real things' He 10.1.

58.62 χαρακτήρ, ῆρος *m*: a representation as an exact reproduction of a particular form or structure – 'exact representation.' ὃς ὢν ἀπαύγασμα τῆς δόξης καὶ χαρακτὴρ τῆς ὑποστάσεως αὐτοῦ 'who is the reflection of his glory and the exact representation of his being' He 1.3.

J Archetype, Corresponding Type (Antitype) (58.63-58.69)

58.63 τύπος^e, ου *m*; παραβολή^b, ῆς *f*: a model or example which anticipates or precedes a later realization – 'archetype, figure, foreshadow, symbol.'

τύπος^e: Ἀδάμ, ὅς ἐστιν τύπος τοῦ μέλλοντος 'Adam, who was a figure of one who was to come' Ro 5.14.

παραβολή^b: ἥτις παραβολὴ εἰς τὸν καιρὸν τὸν ἐνεστηκότα 'which is a symbol of the present time' He 9.9. In a number of languages it may be difficult to find a lexical unit equivalent to 'symbol,' but one can often employ a relatively close paraphrase. For example, in referring to certain aspects of the tabernacle as being a παραβολή, one may render the first clause of He 9.9 as 'this says something to us about the present time.' In other languages one may sometimes use a term which means 'picture,' for example, 'this is a picture for the present time' or 'this contains some meaning for the present time.'

58.64 πατήρ^g, πατρός *m*; μήτηρ^b, τρός *f*: (figurative extensions of meaning of πατήρ^a 'father,' 10.14, and μήτηρ^a 'mother,' 10.16) an archetype anticipating a later reality and suggesting a derivative relationship – 'archetype, father, spiritual father, mother, spiritual mother.'[6]

πατήρ^g: εἰς τὸ εἶναι αὐτὸν πατέρα πάντων τῶν πιστευόντων 'so that he could be the father of all those who believe' Ro 4.11.

μήτηρ^b: ἡ δὲ ἄνω Ἰερουσαλὴμ ἐλευθέρα ἐστίν, ἥτις ἐστὶν μήτηρ ἡμῶν 'but the heavenly Jerusalem is free and she is our mother' Ga 4.26.

58.65 σκιά^c, ᾶς *f*: a faint archetype which foreshadows a later reality – 'foreshadow,

faint prototype, shadow.' ἅ ἐστιν σκιὰ τῶν μελλόντων 'which are a shadow of things to come' Col 2.17.

58.66 σῶμα^e, τος *n*: an entity which corresponds to an archetype or foreshadowing – 'reality, corresponding reality.' τὸ δὲ σῶμα τοῦ Χριστοῦ 'but the reality is Christ' Col 2.17.

58.67 εἰμί^g: to belong to a particular class – 'to be.' αὐτὸς ἦν ἀρχιτελώνης 'he was a chief tax collector' Lk 19.2; θεὸς ἦν ὁ λόγος 'the Word was God' Jn 1.1. In Jn 1.1 θεός obviously is a unique member of a class, and therefore syntactically this would appear to be a case of complete identification. One can, however, translate 'the Word was God' but not 'God was the Word.'

58.68 συστοιχέω; εἰμί^h: to correspond to something else in certain significant features – 'to correspond to, to stand for, to be a figure of, to represent.'

συστοιχέω: τὸ δὲ Ἀγὰρ . . . συστοιχεῖ δὲ τῇ νῦν Ἰερουσαλήμ 'Hagar . . . is a figure of the present Jerusalem' or '. . . corresponds to . . .' Ga 4.25; Σινᾶ ὄρος . . . συστοιχεῖ δὲ τῇ νῦν Ἰερουσαλήμ 'Mount Sinai . . . corresponds to the present Jerusalem' Ga 4.25 (apparatus). In a number of languages συστοιχέω in a context such as Ga 4.25 may be best rendered as 'points to' or 'is really talking about,' so that one may render this expression in Ga 4.25 as 'Mount Sinai . . . really points to the present Jerusalem' or 'Hagar . . . really points to the present Jerusalem.' The full form of Ga 4.25 may be rendered as 'Hagar, who stands for Mount Sinai in Arabia, represents the present Jerusalem.'

εἰμί^h: τὸ δὲ Ἀγὰρ Σινᾶ ὄρος ἐστὶν ἐν τῇ Ἀραβίᾳ 'Hagar stands for Mount Sinai in Arabia' or 'Hagar represents Mount Sinai in Arabia' Ga 4.25.

58.69 ἀντίτυπος, ον: pertaining to that which corresponds in form and structure to something else, either as an anticipation of a later reality or as a fulfillment of a prior type – 'correspondence, antitype, representation, fulfillment.' ὃ καὶ ὑμᾶς ἀντίτυπον νῦν σῴζει βάπτισμα 'which corresponds to baptism which

---

6 πατήρ and μήτηρ in this figurative sense do not differ essentially in meaning. The choice of either πατήρ or μήτηρ depends entirely upon the contextual referent which serves as the original example or archetype.

now saves you' 1 Pe 3.21; χειροποίητα . . . ἅγια . . . ἀντίτυπα τῶν ἀληθινῶν 'a sanctuary . . . made with hands . . . corresponding to the true sanctuary' He 9.24.

K New, Old (primarily non-temporal)[7] (58.70-58.75)

58.70 καινότης^c, ητος *f*: the state of being new and different, with the implication of superiority – 'newness.' οὕτως καὶ ἡμεῖς ἐν καινότητι ζωῆς περιπατήσωμεν 'so that we might walk in newness of life' Ro 6.4.[8]

58.71 καινός^b, ή, όν; νέος^b, α, ον: pertaining to that which is new or recent and hence superior to that which is old – 'new.'[9]
καινός^b: καινοὺς δὲ οὐρανοὺς καὶ γῆν καινήν 'new heavens and new earth' 2 Pe 3.13.
νέος^b: καὶ ἐνδυσάμενοι τὸν νέον τὸν ἀνακαινούμενον εἰς ἐπίγνωσιν 'and putting on the new self which is made new in knowledge' Col 3.10.

58.72 ἀνακαίνωσις, εως *f*; ἀνακαινόω^a; ἀνανεόω: to cause something to become new and different, with the implication of becoming superior – 'to make new, renewal.'
ἀνακαίνωσις: ἀλλὰ μεταμορφοῦσθε τῇ ἀνακαινώσει τοῦ νοός 'but be transformed by the renewal of the mind' Ro 12.2.
ἀνακαινόω^a: καὶ ἐνδυσάμενοι τὸν νέον τὸν ἀνακαινούμενον εἰς ἐπίγνωσιν 'and put on the new self which is made new in knowledge' Col 3.10.
ἀνανεόω: ἀνανεοῦσθαι δὲ τῷ πνεύματι τοῦ νοὸς ὑμῶν literally, 'to be made new in the spirit of your mind,' but more accurately, 'to be made new in your spirit and mind' Eph 4.23.

58.73 πρόσφατος, ον: pertaining to what is new and recent, in the sense of not previously existing – 'new, recent, new and different.' ἐνεκαίνισεν ἡμῖν ὁδὸν πρόσφατον καὶ ζῶσαν 'he inaugurated for us a new and living way' He 10.20.

58.74 παλαιότης^b, ητος *f*: the state of that which is old, obsolete, and hence inferior and unsatisfactory (in contrast with that which is either καινός^b or νέος^b 'new,' 58.71) – 'old, obsolete, old way.' ὥστε δουλεύειν ἡμᾶς ἐν καινότητι πνεύματος καὶ οὐ παλαιότητι γράμματος 'so that we may serve in the newness of the Spirit and not in the old way of the written law' Ro 7.6. For a somewhat different interpretation of παλαιότης in Ro 7.6, see 67.100.[10]

58.75 παλαιός^c, ά, όν: pertaining to that which is old, obsolete, and hence inferior – 'old.' ὁ παλαιὸς ἡμῶν ἄνθρωπος συνεσταυρώθη 'our old self was crucified with (him)' Ro 6.6.

---

7 Though it might appear that Subdomain K *New, Old* would belong to the abstract domain of *Time* (67), the contrast in this subdomain is essentially between items which are different or the same in terms of class membership; and if different, then good; and if the same, then obsolete and unsatisfactory. The temporal components of meaning are strictly secondary or even tertiary.

8 Though in Ro 6.4 the focal semantic component is upon the distinctive superiority of the 'newness,' there are contexts in which καινότης is primarily temporal in significance (see 67.101).

9 Some persons see in the use of καινός in contrast with νέος a distinction based upon that which is novel and different in contrast with that which is young and recent. Though this distinction may be applicable to certain contexts and is more in accordance with classical usage, it is not possible to find in all occurrences of καινός and νέος this type of distinction.

10 Whether παλαιότης in Ro 7.6 is to be classified in Domain 58 or in Domain 67 *Time* depends upon which of the principal features of meaning seems to be focal. Judgments may obviously differ.

59 Quantity[1]

A   Many, Few (Countables) (59.1-59.10)

59.1 πολύς^a, πολλή, πολύ, gen. πολλοῦ, ῆς, οῦ: a relatively large quantity of objects or events – 'many, a great deal of, a great number of.' τῷ σῷ ὀνόματι δυνάμεις πολλὰς ἐποιήσαμεν 'in your name we did many mighty deeds' Mt 7.22; ἑτέροις τε λόγοις πλείοσιν 'in many more words' Ac 2.40. In translating 'in many more words' it is necessary in some languages to employ a verb of speaking, for example, 'in speaking more.' ὁ Χριστὸς ὅταν ἔλθῃ μὴ πλείονα σημεῖα ποιήσει ὧν οὗτος ἐποίησεν; 'when Christ comes, will he do more miracles than this one does?' Jn 7.31; ἵνα τοὺς πλείονας κερδήσω 'in order that I might gain more persons' 1 Cor 9.19.

59.2 ἱκανός^e, ή, όν: a considerable number of objects or events, probably implying what could be expected under the circumstances – 'considerable, many, quite a number of.' οὗ ἦσαν ἱκανοὶ συνηθροισμένοι καὶ προσευχόμενοι 'where many were gathered together and praying' Ac 12.12.

59.3 ὀλίγος^a, η, ον; ἐλάσσων^a, ον: a relatively small quantity on any dimension – 'few, less.'
ὀλίγος^a: ὁ μὲν θερισμὸς πολύς, οἱ δὲ ἐργάται

ὀλίγοι 'a large harvest, but few workers' Mt 9.37.
ἐλάσσων^a: χήρα . . . μὴ ἔλαττον ἐτῶν ἑξήκοντα γεγονυῖα 'any widow . . . not less than sixty years old' 1 Tm 5.9.

59.4 βραχύς^a, εῖα, ύ: a relatively small number of objects or events, probably implying less than expected – 'few, limited number of.' διὰ βραχέων ἐπέστειλα ὑμῖν 'I have written to you a few words' (literally '. . . by means of a few words') He 13.22. In a number of languages the equivalent of a small or limited number of objects is expressed by a negative attribution to an expression of large quantity, so that 'few' becomes 'not many.' For another interpretation of διὰ βραχέων in He 13.22, see 67.106.

59.5 πόσος^a, η, ον: interrogative of quantity of objects or events, usually implying a considerable amount – 'how many.' πόσους ἄρτους ἔχετε; 'how many loaves do you have?' Mt 15.34.

59.6 τοσοῦτος^a, -αύτη, -οῦτον: pertaining to a quantity of objects or events considerably beyond normal expectations – 'so many, this many.' ἀλλὰ ταῦτα τί ἐστιν εἰς τοσούτους; 'but what are these for so many people?' Jn 6.9.

59.7 ὅσος^a, η, ον: pertaining to a comparative quantity of objects or events – 'as many as, as much as.' ὅσοι δὲ ἔλαβον αὐτόν 'as many as received him' Jn 1.12.

59.8 τὸ πλεῖστον: the largest number of objects or events possible under the circumstances – 'the most, not more than.' δύο ἢ τὸ πλεῖστον τρεῖς 'two or, at the most, three' 1 Cor 14.27.

59.9 πλῆθος^a, ους *n*: a large number of countable objects or events, with the probable implication of some type of grouping – 'large number of, a multitude of.' καλύψει πλῆθος ἁμαρτιῶν '(love) covers a multitude of sins' Jas 5.20; καθὼς τὰ ἄστρα τοῦ οὐρανοῦ τῷ πλήθει 'as many as the stars in heaven in number' He 11.12.

---

1 This domain of *Quantity* does not include size of objects, since the latter is treated in Domain 79 *Features of Objects*.

59.10 πλήρηςᶜ, ες: pertaining to a particularly large number of objects or events – 'very many, numerous.' αὕτη ἦν πλήρης ἔργων ἀγαθῶν 'she had done very many good deeds' Ac 9.36.

B Much, Little (Masses, Collectives, Extensions) (59.11-59.22)

59.11 πολύςᵇ, πολλή, πολύ, gen. πολλοῦ, ῆς, οῦ: a relatively large quantity – 'much, great, extensive.' ἦν δὲ χόρτος πολὺς ἐν τῷ τόπῳ 'there was much grass there' Jn 6.10; πολύς τε ἀριθμὸς ὁ πιστεύσας 'a great number of people believed' Ac 11.21; πολὺν ἤδη χρόνον ἔχει '(the man) had already been (sick) for a long time' Jn 5.6; καὶ συνάγεται πρὸς αὐτὸν ὄχλος πλεῖστος 'and a very large crowd came to him' Mk 4.1.

59.12 ἱκανόςᶠ, ή, όν: a relatively large quantity, probably implying what could be expected under the circumstances – 'large, considerable, extensive.' ἀργύρια ἱκανὰ ἔδωκαν τοῖς στρατιώταις 'they gave a considerable sum of money to the soldiers' Mt 28.12; τῶν μαθητῶν αὐτοῦ καὶ ὄχλου ἱκανοῦ 'his disciples and a large crowd' Mk 10.46; χρόνῳ ἱκανῷ οὐκ ἐνεδύσατο ἱμάτιον 'he had gone for a considerable time without clothes' Lk 8.27.

59.13 ὀλίγοςᶜ, η, ον: a relatively small quantity – 'little, small amount.' οἴνῳ ὀλίγῳ χρῶ διὰ τὸν στόμαχον 'take a little wine to help your digestion' 1 Tm 5.23; εἰδὼς ὅτι ὀλίγον καιρὸν ἔχει 'he knows he has only a little time' Re 12.12; ἠρώτησεν αὐτὸν ἀπὸ τῆς γῆς ἐπαναγαγεῖν ὀλίγον 'he asked him to push off a little from the shore' Lk 5.3.

59.14 βραχύςᵇ, εῖα, ύ: a relatively small quantity or extent, probably implying less than expected – 'little, small amount of.' ἵνα ἕκαστος βραχύ τι λάβῃ 'for everyone to have even a little' Jn 6.7; μετὰ βραχὺ ἕτερος ἰδὼν αὐτόν 'after a little (while), another noticed him' Lk 22.58; βραχὺ δὲ διαστήσαντες 'having gone a little further' Ac 27.28. For βραχύ τι in He 2.7, see 78.43.

59.15 μικρόςᵃ, ά, όν: pertaining to a particularly limited quantity – 'little, few, limited

amount of.' μὴ φοβοῦ, τὸ μικρὸν ποίμνιον 'do not fear, little flock' Lk 12.32. In Lk 12.32 ποίμνιον must be regarded as a collective, but in a number of languages it may be necessary to shift the expression to include potential countables, for example, 'do not fear, you who are like just a few sheep.' προελθὼν μικρόν 'going forward a little' Mt 26.39.

59.16 κατωτέρω: pertaining to a lesser amount or extent – 'less, under.' πάντας τοὺς παῖδας τοὺς ἐν Βηθλέεμ καὶ ἐν πᾶσι τοῖς ὁρίοις αὐτῆς ἀπὸ διετοῦς καὶ κατωτέρω 'all the children in Bethlehem and all the nearby regions from two years of age and less' or '. . . from two years of age and under' Mt 2.16.

59.17 πόσοςᵇ, η, ον: interrogative of quantity – 'how much, how extensive.' πόσον ὀφείλεις τῷ κυρίῳ μου; 'how much do you owe my master?' Lk 16.5. In a number of languages it may be necessary in Lk 16.5 to employ an expression relating to countable objects, for example, 'how many pieces of money do you owe my master?' (see 59.5).

59.18 τοσοῦτοςᵇ, -αύτη, -οῦτον: pertaining to a quantity considerably beyond normal expectations – 'so much, so great, such a large.' μιᾷ ὥρα ἠρημώθη ὁ τοσοῦτος πλοῦτος 'in one hour she lost so much wealth' Re 18.17; χορτάσαι ὄχλον τοσοῦτον 'to feed such a large crowd' Mt 15.33; ἐν Δαυὶδ λέγων μετὰ τοσοῦτον χρόνον 'saying through David so much later' He 4.7.

59.19 ὅσοςᵇ, η, ον: pertaining to a comparison of a quantity – 'as much as, as long as.' ὅσον ἤθελον 'as much as they wanted' Jn 6.11; ὁ νόμος κυριεύει τοῦ ἀνθρώπου ἐφ' ὅσον χρόνον ζῇ 'the law has dominion over a person as long as he or she lives' Ro 7.1.

59.20 πολλαπλασίων, ον, gen. ονος: a quantity many times greater than normally expected – 'many times as much, many times greater than.' ἀπολάβῃ πολλαπλασίονα ἐν τῷ καιρῷ τούτῳ 'he will receive many times more in this present age' Lk 18.30.

59.21 ἕωςᵉ: the extent of a quantity – 'as much as, up to.' ὅ τι ἐάν με αἰτήσῃς δώσω σοι ἕως ἡμίσους τῆς βασιλείας μου 'whatever you ask I will give you, up to half of my kingdom' Mk 6.23. In a number of languages it may be necessary to restructure somewhat the expression 'up to half of my kingdom,' for example, 'I will give you half of my kingdom but not more than half.'

59.22 μέγας[a], μεγάλη, μέγα: a large quantity, involving extent – 'much, big, great, extensive.' ἔστιν δὲ πορισμὸς μέγας ἡ εὐσέβεια μετὰ αὐταρκείας 'godliness with contentment is great gain' 1 Tm 6.6.

C All, Any, Each, Every (Totality) (59.23-59.34)

59.23 πᾶς[a], πᾶσα, πᾶν; ἅπας, ασα, αν (alternative form of πᾶς):[2] the totality of any object, mass, collective, or extension – 'all, every, each, whole.' τότε οἱ μαθηταὶ πάντες ἀφέντες αὐτὸν ἔφυγον 'then all the disciples left him and ran away' Mt 26.56; ἦλθεν ὁ κατακλυσμὸς καὶ ἦρεν ἅπαντας 'the flood came and swept them all away' Mt 24.39; ὥρμησεν πᾶσα ἡ ἀγέλη κατὰ τοῦ κρημνοῦ 'the whole herd rushed down the side of the cliff' Mt 8.32; οὕτως πᾶς Ἰσραὴλ σωθήσεται 'this is how all Israel will be saved' Ro 11.26; σοὶ δώσω τὴν ἐξουσίαν ταύτην ἅπασαν 'I will give to you all this power' Lk 4.6; ὁ . . . πᾶς νόμος 'the whole Law' Ga 5.14; πάντα γὰρ ὑμῶν ἐστιν 'for everything is yours' 1 Cor 3.21.

59.24 πᾶς[b], πᾶσα, πᾶν: any one of a totality – 'any, anyone, anything.' ἐὰν δύο συμφωνήσωσιν ἐξ ὑμῶν ἐπὶ τῆς γῆς περὶ παντὸς πράγματος οὗ ἐὰν αἰτήσωνται 'whenever two of you on earth agree about anything you pray for' Mt 18.19; εἰ ἔξεστιν ἀνθρώπῳ ἀπολῦσαι τὴν γυναῖκα αὐτοῦ κατὰ πᾶσαν αἰτίαν; 'is a man allowed to divorce his wife for any reason?' Mt 19.3.

59.25 ἀμφότεροι[a], αι, α: the totality of two – 'both.' τυφλὸς δὲ τυφλὸν ἐὰν ὁδηγῇ, ἀμφό-

τεροι εἰς βόθυνον πεσοῦνται 'when one blind man leads another, they both fall into a ditch' Mt 15.14. In a number of languages ἀμφότεροι may be rendered as 'the two.'

59.26 ἀμφότεροι[b], αι, α: all of a few (three or more) – 'all, everyone.' κατακυριεύσας ἀμφοτέρων ἴσχυσεν κατ' αὐτῶν 'he attacked them and overcame them all' Ac 19.16. It is clear that in Ac 19.16 ἀμφότεροι must refer to the seven sons of a Jewish high priest named Sceva.

59.27 ἕκαστος, η, ον: each one of a totality in a distributive sense – 'each.' ἑκάστῳ στρατιώτῃ μέρος 'one part for each soldier' Jn 19.23.

59.28 παμπληθεί: the totality of a relatively large group – 'all together.' ἀνέκραγον δὲ παμπληθεὶ λέγοντες, Αἶρε τοῦτον 'the whole crowd cried out, Kill him' Lk 23.18.

59.29 ὅλος[b], η, ον: a totality as a complete unit – 'whole, complete, entire.' οἵτινες ὅλους οἴκους ἀνατρέπουσιν 'they are upsetting whole families' Tt 1.11.

59.30 ὁλόκληρος, ον: a totality, with special emphasis upon the entity as a whole – 'whole, entire.' καὶ ὁλόκληρον ὑμῶν τὸ πνεῦμα καὶ ἡ ψυχὴ καὶ τὸ σῶμα ἀμέμπτως . . . τηρηθείη 'and may he keep . . . your entire being, spirit, soul, and body, without blame' 1 Th 5.23. In a number of languages it may be difficult to speak of 'your entire being.' A substitute expression in 1 Th 5.23 may be 'yourselves as one person.'

59.31 πλήρης[b], ες: a totality which has been brought to completion – 'whole, complete, full.' ἀλλὰ μισθὸν πλήρη ἀπολάβητε 'but receive your full reward' 2 Jn 8.

59.32 πλήρωμα[b], τος n: a total quantity, with emphasis upon completeness – 'full number, full measure, fullness, completeness, totality.' ἄχρις οὗ τὸ πλήρωμα τῶν ἐθνῶν εἰσέλθῃ 'until the complete number of the Gentiles comes (to God)' Ro 11.25; ὅτι ἐν αὐτῷ κατοικεῖ πᾶν τὸ πλήρωμα τῆς θεότητος σωματικῶς 'for the totality of the divine nature lives in him

2 In Attic Greek ἅπας occurs after consonants and πᾶς after vowels, but this distinction is not maintained in the NT, and there is insufficient evidence to indicate any significant distinction in meaning, though some persons have believed that ἅπας is somewhat more emphatic.

(Christ) in bodily form' Col 2.9. In a number of languages it may be difficult to use a generic expression such as 'totality.' As a result, this clause in Col 2.9 must often be completely restructured, for example, 'for Christ is completely like God' or 'for just what God is, that is exactly what Christ is.'

59.33 πληρόω^b; ἀναπληρόω^a: to make something total or complete – 'to make complete, to complete the number of.'
πληρόω^b: ἕως πληρωθῶσιν καὶ οἱ σύνδουλοι αὐτῶν καὶ οἱ ἀδελφοὶ αὐτῶν 'until the number of their fellow servants and fellow believers would be complete' Re 6.11; ἵνα τὸ δικαίωμα τοῦ νόμου πληρωθῇ ἐν ἡμῖν 'so that the requirements of the Law may be completely met by us' or 'so that we may do all that the Law requires' or '. . . everything the Law requires' Ro 8.4.
ἀναπληρόω^a: εἰς τὸ ἀναπληρῶσαι αὐτῶν τὰς ἁμαρτίας 'to complete the total number of their sins' 1 Th 2.16. For another interpretation of ἀναπληρόω in 1 Th 2.16, see 68.27.

59.34 ἀνταναπληρόω: to complete something by adding what is still lacking – 'to fill up, to complete, to make complete.' καὶ ἀνταναπληρῶ τὰ ὑστερήματα τῶν θλίψεων τοῦ Χριστοῦ ἐν τῇ σαρκί μου ὑπὲρ τοῦ σώματος αὐτοῦ, ὅ ἐστιν ἡ ἐκκλησία 'and I am completing what still remains of Christ's physical sufferings on behalf of his body, which is the church' Col 1.24.

D Full, Empty[3] **(59.35-59.43)**

59.35 πλήρης^a, ες: a quantity of space completely occupied by something – 'full.' τὸ περισσεῦον τῶν κλασμάτων ἦραν, ἑπτὰ σπυρίδας πλήρεις 'they took up seven baskets full of pieces left over' Mt 15.37.

59.36 πλήρωμα^a, τος n: a quantity which fills a space – 'that which fills, contents.' ἡ γῆ καὶ τὸ πλήρωμα αὐτῆς 'the earth and everything that is in it' or '. . . that fills it' 1 Cor

10.26. In a number of languages, however, it is not possible to translate 1 Cor 10.26 as either 'everything that is in it' or '. . . that fills it,' for this would refer to that which is on the inside of the earth. Accordingly, it may be necessary to render this expression in 1 Cor 10.26 as 'the earth and everything that is on it' or '. . . everything that is all over it.' ἦραν . . . δώδεκα κοφίνων πληρώματα 'they gathered . . . twelve baskets full' Mk 6.43.

59.37 πληρόω^a: (derivative of πλήρης^a 'full,' 59.35) to cause something to become full – 'to fill.' ἣν ὅτε ἐπληρώθη 'when (the net) was full' Mt 13.48; ἦχος . . . ἐπλήρωσεν ὅλον τὸν οἶκον 'a sound . . . filled the whole house' Ac 2.2.

59.38 πίμπλημι^a: to cause something to be completely full – 'to fill completely, to fill up.' λαβὼν σπόγγον πλήσας τε ὄξους 'taking a sponge, he filled it with sour wine' Mt 27.48. In a number of languages one cannot speak of 'filling a sponge,' and it may be necessary to render this expression in Mt 27.48 as 'to make a sponge completely wet with cheap wine.' καὶ ἔπλησαν ἀμφότερα τὰ πλοῖα 'and they filled both boats' Lk 5.7.

59.39 μεστός^a, ή, όν: pertaining to a quantity that fills a space beyond expectations or appropriateness – 'very full.' τὸ δίκτυον . . . μεστὸν ἰχθύων μεγάλων 'the net . . . very full of big fish' Jn 21.11.

59.40 μεστόω: (derivative of μεστός^a 'very full,' 59.39) to cause a space to be exceptionally full – 'to fill, to cause to bulge.' γλεύχους μεμεστωμένοι εἰσίν 'they are full of new wine' or 'they are drunk' Ac 2.13. In many instances one cannot speak of persons being 'full of new wine.' It is, however, possible in Ac 2.13 to say 'they have drunk a great deal of new wine.'

59.41 γέμω: to be full of some substance or objects – 'to be full of, to contain.' ἔσωθεν δὲ γέμουσιν ὀστέων νεκρῶν καὶ πάσης ἀκαθαρσίας 'but inside they are full of dead people's bones and all kinds of filth' Mt 23.27; τὸ δὲ ἔσωθεν ὑμῶν γέμει ἁρπαγῆς καὶ πονηρίας 'but within you are full of violence and evil' Lk 11.39. In

3 In Subdomain D *Full, Empty,* quantity is related primarily to space.

Lk 11.39 there is a mixed figure of speech, and as a result γέμω may be interpreted as indicating a degree of intensity.

59.42 γεμίζω: to fill an object with a substance (normally used of masses) – 'to fill.' γεμίσατε τὰς ὑδρίας ὕδατος 'fill these water jars with water' Jn 2.7.

59.43 σχολάζω^b: to be empty, with special reference to a dwelling – 'to be empty, to be vacant.' καὶ ἐλθὸν εὑρίσκει σχολάζοντα σεσαρωμένον καὶ κεκοσμημένον 'and he went and found it empty, swept, and fixed up' Mt 12.44.

E Enough, Sufficient (59.44-59.47)

59.44 ἱκανός^d, ή, όν: pertaining to a quantity which is adequate for a particular purpose – 'enough, sufficient.' κύριε, ἰδοὺ μάχαιραι ὧδε δύο. ὁ δὲ εἶπεν αὐτοῖς, Ἱκανόν ἐστιν 'here are two swords, Lord. It is enough, he answered' Lk 22.38.

59.45 ἀρκετός, ή, όν: pertaining to what is sufficient for some purpose and accordingly resulting in satisfaction – 'sufficient, adequate.'[4] ἀρκετὸν τῇ ἡμέρᾳ ἡ κακία αὐτῆς 'sufficient for the day are its troubles' Mt 6.34; ἀρκετὸς γὰρ ὁ παρεληλυθὼς χρόνος 'the time in the past is sufficient' 1 Pe 4.3; ἀρκετὸν τῷ μαθητῇ ἵνα γένηται ὡς ὁ διδάσκαλος αὐτοῦ 'it is sufficient for a pupil to be like his teacher' Mt 10.25.

59.46 ἀρκέω: to be sufficient or adequate for a particular purpose, with the implication of leading to satisfaction – 'to be sufficient, to be adequate, to be enough.' οὐ μὴ ἀρκέσῃ ἡμῖν καὶ ὑμῖν 'there is not enough for you and us both' Mt 25.9.

59.47 ἀπέχω^c: to mark the point at which the duration of a state or process is enough – 'to be enough, to be sufficient.' καθεύδετε τὸ

λοιπὸν καὶ ἀναπαύεσθε; ἀπέχει 'are you still sleeping and resting? Enough!' Mk 14.41. In a number of languages the equivalent of 'enough!' would be 'that is the end' or 'you must stop sleeping now.'

F Abundance, Excess, Sparing (59.48-59.61)

59.48 πλεονάζω^c: to exist or be in abundance – 'to be in abundance, to have in abundance.' ταῦτα γὰρ ὑμῖν ὑπάρχοντα καὶ πλεονάζοντα 'for if you have these in abundance' 2 Pe 1.8. The two participial forms, ὑπάρχοντα (see 57.2) and πλεονάζοντα, are coalesced in the translation as 'have . . . in abundance.' In a number of languages the equivalent of this expression in 2 Pe 1.8 might be 'if you have a great many of these' or 'for if these are big with you.'

59.49 ὑπερπλεονάζω; ὑπερπερισσεύω^a: to be more abundant than a given quantity – 'to be more than, to be more abundant.'
ὑπερπλεονάζω: ὑπερεπλεόνασεν δὲ ἡ χάρις τοῦ κυρίου ἡμῶν 'but the grace of our Lord was more abundant' 1 Tm 1.14. In a number of languages it may be difficult to indicate the overabundance of grace in 1 Tm 1.14, since there is nothing in the context to provide a basis for comparison. Accordingly, the closest equivalent may be 'but the grace of our Lord was very, very much.'
ὑπερπερισσεύω^a: ὑπερεπερίσσευσεν ἡ χάρις 'grace abounds even more' Ro 5.20. For another interpretation of ὑπερπερισσεύω in Ro 5.20, see 78.34.

59.50 ἐκχέω^c: (a figurative extension of meaning of ἐκχέω^a 'to pour out,' 47.4) to cause to exist in an abundance – 'to give in abundance, to bestow generously.' ἐξέχεεν τοῦτο ὃ ὑμεῖς καὶ βλέπετε καὶ ἀκούετε 'he has bestowed on us in abundance what you see and hear' Ac 2.33.[5]

59.51 περισσός^c, ή, όν: pertaining to a quantity so abundant as to be considerably more

---

4 It is possible to derive ἀρκετός from the verb ἀρκέω 'to be sufficient' (59.46), and ἀρκετός could then be defined as 'that which ought to be sufficient and hence leading to satisfaction.'

5 It is possible that ἐκχέω in Ac 2.33 denotes only 'to cause to exist.' However, it seems more likely that the figurative force of ἐκχέω implies an abundance of that which exists.

than what one would expect or anticipate – 'that which is more than, more than enough, beyond the norm, abundantly, superfluous.'[6] ἐγὼ ἦλθον ἵνα ζωὴν ἔχωσιν καὶ περισσὸν ἔχωσιν 'I came that they might have life and have it abundantly' Jn 10.10; περὶ μὲν γὰρ τῆς διακονίας τῆς εἰς τοὺς ἁγίους περισσόν μοί ἐστιν τὸ γράφειν ὑμῖν 'it is superfluous for me to write to you concerning help for the people of God' 2 Cor 9.1. For another interpretation of περισσός in 2 Cor 9.1, see 71.40.

59.52 περισσεύω[a]: (derivative of περισσός[c] 'abundant,' 59.51) to be or exist in abundance, with the implication of being considerably more than what would be expected – 'to abound, to be in abundance, to be a lot of, to exist in a large quantity, to be left over.' ὅτι καθὼς περισσεύει τὰ παθήματα τοῦ Χριστοῦ εἰς ἡμᾶς 'for as the sufferings of Christ abound in us' 2 Cor 1.5. In a number of languages it is extremely difficult to find an equivalent of 'to abound.' Moreover, it is not at all easy to find an expression of quantity which seems to go satisfactorily with 'the sufferings of Christ.' In some languages the closest equivalent of this expression in 2 Cor 1.5 may be 'for just as we suffer a great deal, even as Christ suffered.' It would be wrong, however, to use an expression for 'suffering' which would suggest vicarious suffering. αἱ μὲν οὖν ἐκκλησίαι . . . ἐπερίσσευον τῷ ἀριθμῷ καθ' ἡμέραν 'the churches . . . grew in numbers every day' Ac 16.5. The rendering of περισσεύω in Ac 16.5 as 'to grow' results from the expression τῷ ἀριθμῷ. In a number of languages the equivalent would be 'the number of people in the churches increased every day' or 'how many believers there were was more and more each day.' περισσεύοντες ἐν τῷ ἔργῳ τοῦ κυρίου πάντοτε 'being very much occupied in the work of the Lord always' 1 Cor 15.58; συναγάγετε τὰ περισσεύσαντα κλάσματα 'gather up the pieces that are left over' or '. . . that have been more than enough' Jn 6.12.

6 A close comparison with Domain 78 *Degree*, Subdomain B *More Than, Less Than* will indicate how closely related are the meanings of degree and those of quantity. In fact, in a number of instances, the same expressions may be interpreted either as quantity or as degree.

59.53 περίσσευμα, τος *n*; περισσεία[a], ας *f*: (derivatives of περισσεύω[a] 'to abound,' 59.52) that which exists in an abundance – 'abundance, a great deal of.'
περίσσευμα: ἐν τῷ νῦν καιρῷ τὸ ὑμῶν περίσσευμα 'since you have an abundance at this time' 2 Cor 8.14; ἦραν περισσεύματα κλασμάτων ἑπτὰ σπυρίδας 'they took up seven baskets full of pieces left over' Mk 8.8.
περισσεία[a]: διὸ ἀποθέμενοι πᾶσαν ῥυπαρίαν καὶ περισσείαν κακίας 'so get rid of every filthy habit and the abundance of wickedness' Jas 1.21.

59.54 περισσεύω[b]: to cause something to exist in an abundance – 'to provide in abundance, to provide a great deal of, to cause to be abundant.' τῆς χάριτος αὐτοῦ, ἧς ἐπερίσσευσεν εἰς ἡμᾶς 'his grace which he provided in abundance for us' or '. . . which he caused us to have abundantly' or '. . . which he caused us to have very much of' Eph 1.7-8. In some languages, however, it may be very strange to speak of having or receiving an abundance of grace. The closest equivalent for Eph 1.7-8 may be 'grace which he caused us to experience abundantly' or 'grace which he showed to us in an abundant way.'

59.55 κόσμος[g], ου *m*: (a figurative extension of meaning of κόσμος[a] 'world, universe,' 1.1) a great sum of something, implying an almost incredible totality – 'a world of, a tremendous amount of.' ἡ γλῶσσα πῦρ, ὁ κόσμος τῆς ἀδικίας 'the tongue is a fire, a world of evil' Jas 3.6. In some languages the phrase ὁ κόσμος τῆς ἀδικίας may be rendered as 'the very symbol of evil,' 'a sign of what is truly evil,' or 'what is completely evil.'

59.56 ἐπ' εὐλογίαις: (an idiom, literally 'on the basis of blessings') a large amount of something, with the implication of blessing or benefit – 'large amount, abundant amount, abundance.' ὁ σπείρων ἐπ' εὐλογίαις ἐπ' εὐλογίαις καὶ θερίσει 'the one who plants an abundance will reap an abundance' 2 Cor 9.6. In translating 2 Cor 9.6 it may be necessary to indicate clearly the objects which form the abundance, for example, 'the one who plants a great deal of grain will reap a very large crop.'

59.57 πλούσιος^b, α, ον; πλουσίως^a: pertaining to that which exists in a large amount, with the implication of its being valuable – 'in large amount, in abundance, rich, richly.'
πλούσιος^b: ὁ δὲ θεὸς πλούσιος ὢν ἐν ἐλέει 'but God's mercy is so abundant' Eph 2.4.⁷
πλουσίως^a: ἠλπικέναι . . . ἐπὶ θεῷ τῷ παρέχοντι ἡμῖν πάντα πλουσίως εἰς ἀπόλαυσιν 'to place their hope . . . in God who gives us in abundance all good things to enjoy' 1 Tm 6.17.

59.58 πλουτέω^d: to have a large amount of something which has value – 'to be rich in, to have a great deal of.' πλουτεῖν ἐν ἔργοις καλοῖς 'to have an abundance of good works' or 'to be rich in good works' or 'to do many good works' 1 Tm 6.18.

59.59 πλουτίζω^b: to cause someone to have an abundance of that which is of value or worth – 'to make rich in, to cause to have an abundance of.' ἐν παντὶ ἐπλουτίσθητε 'you have become rich in all things' 1 Cor 1.5. In 1 Cor 1.5 the final phrase, ἐν παντὶ λόγῳ καὶ πάσῃ γνώσει, indicates that the abundance refers to both the quantity of messages and the knowledge.

59.60 ἁδρότης, ητος f: an abundant amount, with the implication of generosity – 'abundance, generous gift.' στελλόμενοι τοῦτο μή τις ἡμᾶς μωμήσηται ἐν τῇ ἁδρότητι ταύτῃ τῇ διακονουμένῃ ὑφ' ἡμῶν 'we are being careful not to stir up any complaints about the way we handle this generous gift' 2 Cor 8.20.

59.61 φειδομένως: pertaining to what is done in a limited, sparing manner and of negligible quantity or extent – 'sparingly, in a limited manner.' ὁ σπείρων φειδομένως φειδομένως καὶ θερίσει 'the one who sows sparingly will reap sparingly' 2 Cor 9.6. In 2 Cor 9.6 φειδομένως is obviously in contrast with the phrase ἐπ' εὐλογίαις 'abundantly' (59.56). It may, however, be necessary to indicate clearly the nature of that which is sown or reaped

---

⁷ πλούσιος in Eph 2.4 may be interpreted either as degree or extent; in other words, in terms of the intensity of God's expression of mercy or in the extent of occasions in which God shows mercy.

sparingly, for example, 'the one who plants only a small amount of seed will have only a very small harvest.'

G Increase, Decrease (59.62-59.71)

59.62 αὐξάνω^a and αὔξω: to increase in the extent of or in the instances of an activity or state – 'to increase, to grow, to spread, to extend.' αὐξανόμενοι τῇ ἐπιγνώσει τοῦ θεοῦ 'you will grow in your knowledge of God' Col 1.10. If one assumes that ἐπίγνωσις in Col 1.10 is to be understood in the sense of 'knowledge about' (see 28.18), then one may translate this expression as 'you will know more and more about God,' but if ἐπίγνωσις is to be understood in the sense of 'to experience knowledge' (see 28.2), one may render the phrase as 'you will know God more and more' or 'you will come to know more and more what God does.' ὁ λόγος ηὔξανεν καὶ ἴσχυεν 'the message (about the Good News) kept spreading and growing stronger' Ac 19.20; ἐν ᾧ πᾶσα οἰκοδομὴ συναρμολογουμένη αὔξει εἰς ναὸν ἅγιον ἐν κυρίῳ 'in whom the whole building is held together and extends into (or 'increases until it becomes') a sacred temple in the Lord' Eph 2.21.

59.63 αὐξάνω^b: to cause something to increase – 'to cause to increase, to increase.' αὐξήσει τὰ γενήματα τῆς δικαιοσύνης ὑμῶν 'he will increase the harvest of your righteousness' or '. . . the harvest resulting from your generosity' or '. . . the result of your generosity' 2 Cor 9.10.

59.64 προκόπτω^c: to cause a significant increase in some quantity – 'to increase, to advance.' ἐπὶ πλεῖον γὰρ προκόψουσιν ἀσεβείας 'for they will greatly increase godlessness' 2 Tm 2.16. This expression in 2 Tm 2.16 may be rendered in some languages as 'they cause people to be more and more godless' or '. . . to do what God does not want them to do.'

59.65 ἐπισωρεύω: (a figurative extension of meaning of ἐπισωρεύω 'to heap up,' not occurring in the NT) to significantly increase the number of something – 'to greatly increase, to heap up.' ἑαυτοῖς ἐπισωρεύσουσιν διδασκάλους 'they will greatly increase for themselves the number of teachers' 2 Tm 4.3.

59.66 κολλάομαι . . . ἄχρι τοῦ οὐρανοῦ: (an idiom, literally 'to cling to heaven') to increase enormously the number of something, with the implication of reaching the attention of God – 'to increase greatly, to reach to high heaven.' ὅτι ἐκολλήθησαν αὐτῆς αἱ ἁμαρτίαι ἄχρι τοῦ οὐρανοῦ 'because her sins reached to heaven' or 'because her sins became very, very many' Re 18.5.

59.67 πλεονάζω^a: to increase considerably the extent of an activity or state, with the implication of the result being an abundance – 'to increase considerably, to become more and more, to multiply.' οὗ δὲ ἐπλεόνασεν ἡ ἁμαρτία 'but where sin increased' Ro 5.20. It may be difficult in some languages to speak of 'sin increasing,' but in Ro 5.20 one can say 'where people sinned more and more.' ἡ χάρις πλεονάσασα διὰ τῶν πλειόνων 'grace reaching more and more people' 2 Cor 4.15. In 2 Cor 4.15 the increase would be in the instances of God's grace extending to more and more people.

59.68 πληθύνω^a: to increase greatly in number or extent – 'to grow, to increase greatly, to multiply.' ἐπληθύνετο ὁ ἀριθμὸς τῶν μαθητῶν ἐν Ἰερουσαλὴμ σφόδρα 'the number of disciples in Jerusalem grew larger and larger' Ac 6.7. It may be difficult to speak of 'a number growing' in some languages, so that one may need to translate this expression in Ac 6.7 as 'the disciples in Jerusalem became more and more' or 'there were more and more disciples in Jerusalem.' διὰ τὸ πληθυνθῆναι τὴν ἀνομίαν 'such will be the increase of evil' Mt 24.12. It may be difficult, if not impossible, to speak of 'evil increasing' as in Mt 24.12, but one can usually speak of a greater number of instances of doing evil, and therefore one may translate 'more and more people will be doing what is evil.' ὁ δὲ λόγος τοῦ θεοῦ ηὔξανεν καὶ ἐπληθύνετο 'the word of God increased and multiplied' Ac 12.24. A literal rendering of Ac 12.24 may be impossible in many languages, for a strictly literal rendering would im-

ply that somehow the message from God 'got bigger,' which may mean in some languages 'resulted in lies.' The meaning is, of course, that more and more people accepted God's word as true.

59.69 πληθύνω^b: to cause an increase in the number of objects – 'to increase, to cause an increase, to multiply.' εἰ μὴν εὐλογῶν εὐλογήσω σε καὶ πληθύνων πληθυνῶ σε 'I will certainly bless you and cause the number of your descendants to increase' He 6.14. In He 6.14 it is essential in most languages to specify what is increased. A strictly literal translation such as 'to cause you to increase' would simply mean 'to cause you to get big.' The reference is clearly to Abraham's descendants, and it is usually essential to make this reference clear.

59.70 διπλόω: to cause a quantity to be twice as much – 'to double, to cause twice as much as.' διπλώσατε τὰ διπλᾶ κατὰ τὰ ἔργα αὐτῆς 'pay her back twice as much as she has done' Re 18.6.⁸

59.71 κολοβόω: to cause something to be reduced in number or extent – 'to shorten, to decrease, to reduce in number.' διὰ δὲ τοὺς ἐκλεκτοὺς κολοβωθήσονται αἱ ἡμέραι ἐκεῖναι 'but because of the elect, those days will be shortened' Mt 24.22. There may be difficulties involved in a strictly literal rendering of 'those days will be shortened,' for it might appear that each day would become shorter rather than that the number of days would be decreased. Therefore, one must render this expression in Mt 24.22 in a number of languages as 'those days will be fewer.'

H Add, Subtract (59.72-59.76)

59.72 προστίθημι^a; ἐπιτίθημι^b; προσανατίθεμαι^a: to add something to an existing quantity – 'to add.'

---

8 It would be possible to interpret διπλόω with τὰ διπλᾶ as indicating intensity rather than extent of either punishment or instances of punishment.

προστίθημιª: προσέθηκεν καὶ τοῦτο ἐπὶ πᾶσιν 'he added this also to all (his other misdeeds)' Lk 3.20.

ἐπιτίθημιᵇ: ἐάν τις ἐπιθῇ ἐπ' αὐτά 'if anyone adds anything to them' Re 22.18.

προσανατίθεμαιª: ἐμοὶ γὰρ οἱ δοκοῦντες οὐδὲν προσανέθεντο 'for those who were of repute added nothing to me' or '. . . made no new suggestions' Ga 2.6.

In a number of languages it is not at all difficult to speak of 'adding things,' but to add events may provide some special difficulties in restructuring. For example, in Lk 3.20 it may be important to translate as 'he had done many other bad things, but he also did this,' and in Ga 2.6 it may be helpful to translate 'for those who were of repute did not say that I should do anything more than I was doing.'

59.73 ἐπιδιατάσσομαι: to add to, with the implication of some reorganization or rearrangement – 'to add to, to introduce something new.' διαθήκην οὐδεὶς ἀθετεῖ ἢ ἐπιδιατάσσεται 'no one can break that covenant or add anything to it' Ga 3.15. In some languages the equivalent of 'adding something to a covenant' would be rendered as 'to say that one must also do something else to fulfill the covenant.'

59.74 ἐπιχορηγέωᵇ: to provide something in addition to what already exists – 'to add.' ἐπιχορηγήσατε ἐν τῇ πίστει ὑμῶν τὴν ἀρετήν 'add goodness to your faith' 2 Pe 1.5.

59.75 ἔτιᵇ: the state of something being in addition to what already exists – 'in addition, besides.' παράλαβε μετὰ σοῦ ἔτι ἕνα ἢ δύο 'take one or two other persons with you in addition' Mt 18.16; . . . καὶ τοὺς ἀδελφοὺς καὶ τὰς ἀδελφάς, ἔτι τε καὶ τὴν ψυχὴν ἑαυτοῦ '. . . his brothers and his sisters and himself as well' Lk 14.26. The sequence ἔτι τε καί in Lk 14.26 is clearly emphatic, so that one might well render the expression ἔτι τε καὶ τὴν ψυχὴν ἑαυτοῦ as 'and he himself as well.'

59.76 παρά¹: the state of being less than a given number or quantity – 'less, minus.' τεσσεράκοντα παρὰ μίαν 'forty (lashes) minus one' 2 Cor 11.24. In a number of languages it may seem strange as well as illogical to speak of 'forty lashes minus one.' Accordingly, one may translate 'thirty-nine lashes' in 2 Cor 11.24.

60 Number¹

Outline of Subdomains

A Number, Countless (60.1-60.9)
B One, Two, Three, Etc. (Cardinals) (60.10-60.45)
C First, Second, Third, Etc. (Ordinals) (60.46-60.61)
D Half, Third, Fourth (Fractional Part) (60.62-60.66)
E Once, Twice, Three Times, Etc. (Cardinals of Time) (60.67-60.74)
F Double, Four Times As Much, Etc. (Multiples) (60.75-60.78)
G Pair, Group (Numbered Collectives) (60.79-60.80)

1 Languages differ considerably not only in the system used for numbering but also in the extent of the system. For the most part, numbering systems are either based on human extremities (the fingers and toes) or upon what is called 'the blanket count,' a system involving folds. The system based on human extremities more often than not consists of fundamental units of ten, that is to say, units based upon the counting of the fingers. In some languages, however, a system of twenty has been employed, so that a unit of twenty may even have the name of 'a person.' Therefore, a designation such as 'five persons' equals one hundred. Within any numbering system there may be numerous irregularities and shifts, so that one may employ either addition or subtraction. As a result, the number eleven may be 'ten plus one,' while nineteen may be 'twenty minus one.' Languages which use the so-called 'blanket system' often count as one, two, and then three becomes 'two plus one,' while four is 'two doubled.' Five then becomes 'doubled two plus one'; six becomes 'doubled two plus two,' etc. Languages which employ this blanket system, however, normally do not have a very extended system of number-

A Number, Countless (60.1-60.9)

60.1 ἀριθμός^a, οῦ *m*: any cardinal number – 'number.' ὁ ἀριθμὸς αὐτοῦ ἑξακόσιοι ἑξήκοντα ἕξ 'his number was 666' Re 13.18. It may be important to add a marginal note to Re 13.18 to indicate that the number 666 was actually derived from adding up the numerical values of the letters of a name.

60.2 ἀριθμός^b, οῦ *m*: the sum or total of a numbered quantity – 'number, total sum.' ἐπληθύνετο ὁ ἀριθμὸς τῶν μαθητῶν 'the number of the disciples increased' Ac 6.7; ἐγενήθη ὁ ἀριθμὸς τῶν ἀνδρῶν ὡς χιλιάδες πέντε 'the number of men was about five thousand' Ac 4.4.

60.3 ἀριθμέω: (derivative of ἀριθμός^a 'number,' 60.1) to employ numbers in determining a quantity – 'to count, to number.'[2] αἱ τρίχες τῆς κεφαλῆς πᾶσαι ἠριθμημέναι εἰσίν 'all the hairs of the head are numbered' Mt 10.30; ὄχλος πολύς, ὃν ἀριθμῆσαι αὐτὸν οὐδεὶς ἐδύνατο

---

ing. Even some languages which use the fingers or toes may be quite limited in numbering, so that specific numbers may not go to more than ten or twenty, after which there may be a series of terms indicating various large, indefinite numbers of items. Such strictly limited systems for numbering are typical, of course, of so-called 'primitive peoples,' but once such people come in contact with more complex and developed societies, they rapidly extend their numbering systems and often simply take over a numbering system from a dominant language in the area.

In a number of languages all numbers specify the class of objects being counted. For example, all animate beings may be in one class, all plants in another, all lumpy objects in still another class, all liquids with still a separate designation, and the same would be true of such classes of objects as dry masses, long/ slender, flat/round, and flat objects with corners, etc. Sometimes the forms of the numbers are the same for all classes, but there is a bound affix associated with the numerals in order to designate the class of objects being counted. In other instances there are completely different number systems for different kinds of objects. All of these matters must be carefully considered in any translation of the Scriptures, particularly in contexts in which new material or spiritual items are being counted or numbered.

2 ἀριθμέω could be classified as a type of mental activity, but since its derivational base is in this domain of *Number*, it seems better to retain it here, as is normally the case with semantic derivatives.

'a great multitude which no one was able to count' Re 7.9.

60.4 ψηφίζω^a; συμψηφίζω: to count up or calculate a total – 'to count, to calculate, to add up, to figure out.'
ψηφίζω^a: ψηφίζει τὴν δαπάνην 'he calculates the cost' Lk 14.28; ψηφισάτω τὸν ἀριθμὸν τοῦ θηρίου 'let him add up the number of the beast' Re 13.18. This process of 'adding up the number of the beast' involved calculating the total based upon the numerical values of each of the letters of the name. For another interpretation of ψηφίζω in Re 13.18, see 32.15.
συμψηφίζω: συνεψήφισαν τὰς τιμὰς αὐτῶν 'they calculated the value of them' Ac 19.19.

60.5 συγκαταψηφίζομαι: to be counted as belonging to a particular group – 'to be counted.' συγκατεψηφίσθη μετὰ τῶν ἕνδεκα ἀποστόλων 'he was counted as one of the eleven apostles' Ac 1.26.

60.6 ἀναρίθμητος, ον: pertaining to what cannot be counted – 'countless, innumerable, beyond counting.' ὡς ἡ ἄμμος ἡ παρὰ τὸ χεῖλος τῆς θαλάσσης ἡ ἀναρίθμητος 'as countless as the sand along the edge of the sea' He 11.12. In a number of languages the equivalent of 'countless' is 'so many that no one can count' or 'so many that there are no numbers left.'

60.7 μυρίος, α, ον: pertaining to what is extremely numerous – 'very very many, innumerable, countless.' μυρίους παιδαγωγούς 'countless guardians' 1 Cor 4.15. It would be possible to interpret μυρίους in 1 Cor 4.15 as meaning literally 'ten thousand' (see 60.45), but the evident intent in this context is to emphasize the indefinitely large number rather than any specific quantity.

60.8 μυριάς^b, άδος *f*: a very large indefinite number – 'countless, innumerable, many many.' μυριάσιν ἀγγέλων 'countless angels' He 12.22.

60.9 δισμυριάδες μυριάδων: an indefinitely large number (even greater than μυριάς^b, 60.8) – 'countless, incalculable, great number of.' δισμυριάδες μυριάδων 'countless' or 'an enormous number' Re 9.16. Though it is possible to understand δισμυριάδες μυριάδων in Re 9.16 as meaning 'two hundred million' (literally 20 000 × 10 000), the evident intent of the text is to emphasize the extreme number rather than to specify some large quantity.

B   One, Two, Three, Etc. (Cardinals) (60.10-60.45)

60.10 εἷς^a, μία, ἕν: one, in contrast to more than one – 'one.' ὅστις σε ἀγγαρεύσει μίλιον ἕν 'whoever forces you to carry a pack one mile' Mt 5.41; οὕτως οἱ πολλοὶ ἕν σῶμά ἐσμεν 'though many, we form one body' Ro 12.5.

60.11 δύο, gen. and acc. δύο, dat. δυσίν – 'two.' δύο δαιμονιζόμενοι 'two possessed of demons' Mt 8.28. In a number of languages it is not possible to use numbers as pronominal substitutes for specific references to animate or inanimate objects. Accordingly, in Mt 8.28 one must often translate as 'two men possessed by demons.'

60.12 τρεῖς, τρία, gen. τριῶν, dat. τρισίν – 'three.' τὰ τρία ταῦτα 'these are three' 1 Cor 13.13.

60.13 τέσσαρες, neut. τέσσαρα, gen. τεσσάρων – 'four.' ἐκ τῶν τεσσάρων ἀνέμων 'from the four winds' or 'from the four directions' Mt 24.31. In a number of languages the equivalent of 'from the four winds' or 'from the four directions' is simply 'from every direction.' The Greek expression does not mean from only four specific directions, but rather from every direction.

60.14 πέντε – 'five.' πέντε γὰρ ἄνδρας ἔσχες 'for you have had five husbands' Jn 4.18.

60.15 ἕξ – 'six.' μεθ' ἡμέρας ἕξ 'after six days' Mt 17.1.

60.16 ἑπτά – 'seven.' παραλαμβάνει μεθ' ἑαυτοῦ ἑπτὰ ἕτερα πνεύματα 'he takes along with him seven other spirits' Mt 12.45; Ἰωάννης ταῖς ἑπτὰ ἐκκλησίαις ταῖς ἐν τῇ Ἀσίᾳ 'John to the seven churches that are in Asia' Re 1.4. In ancient times, seven was regarded as a par-

ticularly important sacred number, and this is especially relevant in a number of passages in the book of Revelation.

60.17 ὀκτώ – 'eight.' κιβωτοῦ, εἰς ἥν ὀλίγοι, τοῦτ' ἔστιν ὀκτὼ ψυχαί, διεσώθησαν δι' ὕδατος 'an ark, into which a few, that is eight persons, were saved through water' 1 Pe 3.20; ὅτε ἐπλήσθησαν ἡμέραι ὀκτώ 'when eight days had passed' or 'a week later' Lk 2.21. To designate a week, the normal practice in NT times was to speak of 'eight days,' since in a series both the first and the last days were counted. The equivalent in many languages would be simply 'after seven days had passed.'

60.18 ἐννέα – 'nine.' οἱ δὲ ἐννέα ποῦ; 'but where are the nine?' Lk 17.17. In Lk 17.17 there is a significant ellipsis, and so in some languages one may wish to translate 'where are the other nine persons?' or '. . . nine men?'

60.19 δέκα – 'ten.' οἱ δέκα ἠγανάκτησαν περὶ τῶν δύο ἀδελφῶν 'the ten became angry with the two brothers' Mt 20.24.

60.20 ἕνδεκα – 'eleven.' οἱ δὲ ἕνδεκα μαθηταὶ ἐπορεύθησαν εἰς τὴν Γαλιλαίαν 'the eleven disciples went to Galilee' Mt 28.16.

60.21 δώδεκα – 'twelve.' γυνὴ αἱμορροῦσα δώδεκα ἔτη 'a woman who had suffered hemorrhaging for twelve years' Mt 9.20.

60.22 δεκατέσσαρες – 'fourteen.' ἀπὸ Ἀβραὰμ ἕως Δαυὶδ γενεαὶ δεκατέσσαρες 'from Abraham to David, fourteen generations' Mt 1.17. It is possible that δεκατέσσαρες in Mt 1.17 has a symbolic meaning in view of its being equivalent to twice seven. Others have suggested that the number fourteen is derived from the value of the name David based on the numerical values of the consonants in the Hebrew form of the name. This may explain certain of the irregularities in the listing of the generations.

60.23 δεκαπέντε – 'fifteen.' ὡς ἀπὸ σταδίων δεκαπέντε 'about fifteen stades' (about 2 775 meters or 'somewhat more than two kilometers' or 'less than two miles') Jn 11.18.

60.24 δεκαοκτώ – 'eighteen.' ἐκεῖνοι οἱ δεκαοκτὼ ἐφ᾽ οὓς ἔπεσεν ὁ πύργος 'those eighteen on whom the tower fell' Lk 13.4.

60.25 εἴκοσι – 'twenty.' τῷ μετὰ εἴκοσι χιλιάδων ἐρχομένῳ ἐπ᾽ αὐτόν 'one who is coming against him with twenty thousand' Lk 14.31.

60.26 τριάκοντα – 'thirty.' αὐτὸς ἦν Ἰησοῦς ἀρχόμενος ὡσεὶ ἐτῶν τριάκοντα 'when Jesus began (his work), he was about thirty years old' Lk 3.23.

60.27 τεσσεράκοντα – 'forty.' τεσσεράκοντα καὶ ἓξ ἔτεσιν οἰκοδομήθη ὁ ναὸς οὗτος 'it has taken forty-six years to build this Temple' Jn 2.20.

60.28 πεντήκοντα – 'fifty.' ὁ δὲ ἕτερος πεντήκοντα 'the other (owed him) fifty (denarii)' Lk 7.41.

60.29 ἑξήκοντα – 'sixty.' σταδίους ἑξήκοντα ἀπὸ Ἰερουσαλήμ 'sixty stades from Jerusalem' (a distance of approximately eleven kilometers or about seven miles) Lk 24.13; ὃ δὲ ἑξήκοντα 'and some sixty' (a reference to the seed which produced grain) Mt 13.8. Note that ἑξήκοντα in Mt 13.8 is not ἑξηκόντακις 'sixty times.' The evident meaning here is that some of the seeds grew into plants which produced as many as a hundred seeds; others grew into plants which produced sixty seeds; and still others, only thirty seeds.

60.30 ἑβδομήκοντα – 'seventy.' ἀνέδειξεν ὁ κύριος ἑτέρους ἑβδομήκοντα δύο 'the Lord chose another seventy-two' Lk 10.1.

60.31 ὀγδοήκοντα – 'eighty.' αὐτὴ χήρα ἕως ἐτῶν ὀγδοήκοντα τεσσάρων 'this widow was eighty-four years old' Lk 2.37.

60.32 ἐνενήκοντα – 'ninety.' οὐχὶ ἀφήσει τὰ ἐνενήκοντα ἐννέα ἐπὶ τὰ ὄρη; 'would he not leave the ninety-nine on the mountains?' Mt 18.12.

60.33 ἑκατόν – 'one hundred.' ἐὰν γένηταί τινι ἀνθρώπῳ ἑκατὸν πρόβατα 'if a man has a hundred sheep' Mt 18.12.

60.34 διακόσιοι, αι, α – 'two hundred.' ἀγοράσωμεν δηναρίων διακοσίων ἄρτους; 'shall we buy two hundred denarii-worth of bread?' Mk 6.37.

60.35 τριακόσιοι, αι, α – 'three hundred.' ἐπάνω δηναρίων τριακοσίων 'more than three hundred denarii' Mk 14.5.

60.36 τετρακόσιοι, αι, α – 'four hundred.' ἀνδρῶν ἀριθμὸς ὡς τετρακοσίων 'a number of men, about four hundred' Ac 5.36.

60.37 πεντακόσιοι, αι, α – 'five hundred.' ὁ εἷς ὤφειλεν δηνάρια πεντακόσια 'one owed five hundred denarii' Lk 7.41.

60.38 ἑξακόσιοι, αι, α – 'six hundred.' ὁ ἀριθμὸς αὐτοῦ ἑξακόσιοι ἑξήκοντα ἕξ 'his number was 666' Re 13.18. This symbolic number would result from the total of the numerical values of the letters of the person's name.

60.39 χίλιοι, αι, α – 'thousand.' προφητεύσουσιν ἡμέρας χιλίας διακοσίας ἑξήκοντα 'they will prophesy 1 260 days' Re 11.3.

60.40 δισχίλιοι, αι, α – 'two thousand.' ὡς δισχίλιοι 'about two thousand' (the number of pigs drowned in the lake) Mk 5.13.

60.41 τρισχίλιοι, αι, α – 'three thousand.' προσετέθησαν ἐν τῇ ἡμέρᾳ ἐκείνῃ ψυχαὶ ὡσεὶ τρισχίλιαι 'about three thousand people were added on that day' ('added' in the sense of added to the membership of the believing community) Ac 2.41.

60.42 τετρακισχίλιοι, αι, α – 'four thousand.' οἱ δὲ ἐσθίοντες ἦσαν τετρακισχίλιοι ἄνδρες 'those who ate were four thousand men' Mt 15.38.

60.43 πεντακισχίλιοι, αι, α – 'five thousand.' ἦσαν ἄνδρες ὡσεὶ πεντακισχίλιοι 'they were about five thousand men' Mt 14.21.

60.44 ἑπτακισχίλιοι, αι, α – 'seven thousand.' κατέλιπον ἐμαυτῷ ἑπτακισχιλίους ἄνδρας 'seven thousand men remained to me' Ro 11.4.

60.45 μύριοι, αι, α; μυριάς[a], άδος f – 'ten thousand.'
μύριοι: εἷς ὀφειλέτης μυρίων ταλάντων 'someone who owed ten thousand talents' Mt 18.24.
μυριάς[a]: ἀργυρίου μυριάδας πέντε 'fifty thousand pieces of silver' Ac 19.19.

C First, Second, Third, Etc. (Ordinals)[3] (60.46-60.61)

60.46 πρῶτος[a], η, ον; α: first in a series involving time, space, or set – 'first.'
πρῶτος[a]: πρῶτος ἐξ ἀναστάσεως νεκρῶν 'first to rise from the dead' Ac 26.23; προσελθὼν τῷ πρώτῳ 'he came to the first (son)' Mt 21.28; ἤρξατο λέγειν πρὸς τοὺς μαθητὰς αὐτοῦ πρῶτον 'he began to speak first to his disciples' Lk 12.1; σκηνὴ γὰρ κατεσκευάσθη ἡ πρώτη 'for the first tent was put up' He 9.2. In He 9.2 πρῶτος must, however, be understood in the sense of the outer tent, which was the first one to which a person came in entering the sanctuary.
α (occurring only in titles of NT writings): πρὸς Κορινθίους α 'First Letter to the Corinthians'; Ἰωάννου α 'First Epistle of John.'

60.47 πρότερος[b], α, ον: first, with the implication of emphasis, frequently in reference to time – 'the first time.' εὐηγγελισάμην ὑμῖν τὸ πρότερον 'I announced to you the good news the first time' Ga 4.13. It is also possible to understand πρότερος in this context as meaning 'earlier, formerly' (see 67.18).

60.48 πρώτως: first in a temporal sequence – 'for the first time.' χρηματίσαι τε πρώτως ἐν Ἀντιοχείᾳ τοὺς μαθητὰς Χριστιανούς 'and it was in Antioch that the believers were first called Christians' Ac 11.26.

60.49 δεύτερος[a], α, ον; β: second in a series involving either time, space, or set – 'second, in the second place, secondly.'
δεύτερος[a]: ὁμοίως καὶ ὁ δεύτερος καὶ ὁ τρίτος 'and likewise also the second and the third' Mt 22.26; δευτέρα δὲ ὁμοία αὐτῇ 'and the second is like it' (referring to commandments) Mt 22.39; πάλιν ἐκ δευτέρου ἀπελθὼν προσηύξατο 'again, a second time, he went away and prayed' Mt 26.42.
β (occurring only in the titles of NT writings): πρὸς Κορινθίους β 'Second Letter to the Corinthians'; πρὸς Τιμόθεον β 'Second Letter to Timothy.'

60.50 τρίτος, η, ον; γ: third in a series involving either time, space, or set – 'third.'
τρίτος: ἕως τρίτου οὐρανοῦ 'up to the third heaven' 2 Cor 12.2; τῇ ἡμέρᾳ τῇ τρίτῃ 'on the third day' Lk 18.33; τρίτην ὥραν 'third hour' or 'nine o'clock in the morning' Mt 20.3; ἔρχεται τὸ τρίτον 'he went the third time' Mk 14.41.[4]
γ (occurring only in titles of NT writings): Ἰωάννου γ 'Third Letter of John.'

60.51 τέταρτος, η, ον: fourth in a series involving either time, space, or set – 'fourth.' τετάρτη δὲ φυλακῇ τῆς νυκτός 'in the fourth watch of the night' or 'between three and six o'clock in the morning' Mt 14.25.

60.52 πέμπτος, η, ον: fifth in a series involving either time, space, or set – 'fifth.' ἤνοιξεν τὴν πέμπτην σφραγῖδα 'he opened the fifth seal' Re 6.9.

60.53 ἕκτος, η, ον: sixth in a series involving either time, space, or set – 'sixth.' ἐν δὲ τῷ μηνὶ τῷ ἕκτῳ 'in the sixth month' Lk 1.26.

---

3 It would be possible to classify all ordinals as involving essentially sequence, and they could therefore be combined with Domain 61 *Sequence*. However, the specific numerical value of sequential items seems to be sufficiently focal as to warrant the classification of ordinals in this series of numerals. See also comments on 60.55.

4 Though τὸ τρίτον functions in an adverbial sense, there seems to be no reason to set up a separate meaning of τρίτος as referring only to a temporal sequence. The interpretation of τρίτος in terms of time or space is a factor of the context. When objects are involved, ordinals simply mark position in a spacial sequence; when events are involved, ordinals simply mark position in a temporal sequence.

60.54 ἕβδομος, η, ον: seventh in a series involving either time, space, or set – 'seventh.' ἕβδομος ἀπὸ ᾽Αδὰμ ᾽Ενώχ 'Enoch, the seventh from Adam' Jd 14;[5] ὥραν ἑβδόμην 'the seventh hour' or 'one o'clock in the afternoon' Jn 4.52.

60.55 ὄγδοος, η, ον: eighth in a series involving either time, space, or set – 'eighth.' ἐν τῇ ἡμέρᾳ τῇ ὀγδόῃ 'on the eighth day' Lk 1.59; ὄγδοον Νῶε δικαιοσύνης κήρυκα ἐφύλαξεν 'he preserved Noah, the preacher of righteousness, as the eighth' 2 Pe 2.5. In a number of languages one does not speak of 'the eighth' as being the eighth item in a set. Often it is far more usual to say 'one together with seven others.' This same system may apply to all ordinals in a language.

60.56 ἔνατος, η, ον: ninth in a series involving either time, space, or set – 'ninth.' ἐνάτην ὥραν 'the ninth hour' or 'three o'clock in the afternoon' Mt 20.5; ὁ ἔνατος τοπάζιον 'the ninth, topaz' Re 21.20.

60.57 δέκατος, η, ον: tenth in a series involving either time, space, or set – 'tenth.' ὥρα ἦν ὡς δεκάτη 'it was about the tenth hour' or '. . . four o'clock in the afternoon' Jn 1.39.

60.58 ἐνδέκατος, η, ον: eleventh in a series involving either time, space, or set – 'eleventh.' περὶ τὴν ἑνδεκάτην ὥραν 'at the eleventh hour' or 'at five o'clock in the afternoon' Mt 20.9.

60.59 δωδέκατος, η, ον: twelfth in a series involving either time, space, or set – 'twelfth.' ὁ δωδέκατος ἀμέθυστος 'the twelfth, amethyst' Re 21.20.

60.60 τεσσαρεσκαιδέκατος, η, ον: fourteenth in a series involving either time, space, or set

---

5 In the more general manner of counting an ordinal series, ἕβδομος in Jd 14 would really refer to the 'sixth descendant from Adam.' In the Hebrew system of counting, Adam himself would be counted as part of the series, and hence the use in Jd 14 of ἕβδομος rather than ἕκτος.

– 'fourteenth.' τεσσαρεσκαιδεκάτη νύξ 'the fourteenth night' Ac 27.27.

60.61 πεντεκαιδέκατος, η, ον: fifteenth in a series involving time, space, or set – 'fifteenth.' ἐν ἔτει δὲ πεντεκαιδεκάτῳ τῆς ἡγεμονίας Τιβερίου Καίσαρος 'in the fifteenth year of the reign of the Emperor Tiberius' Lk 3.1.

D Half, Third, Fourth (Fractional Part) (60.62-60.66)

60.62 ἥμισυς, εια, υ, gen. ἡμίσους: one half of an object, series, or mass – 'half.' ἰδοὺ τὰ ἡμίσιά μου τῶν ὑπαρχόντων, κύριε, τοῖς πτωχοῖς δίδωμι 'behold, Lord, I will give to the poor half of my possessions' Lk 19.8.

60.63 τρίτον, ου n: a third part of an object, series, or mass – 'third, third part.' τὸ τρίτον τῶν δένδρων 'a third of the trees' Re 8.7; καὶ τὸ τρίτον τῆς γῆς κατεκάη 'and a third of the earth was consumed by fire' Re 8.7. In a number of languages a fractional part of something is referred to by means of ordinal numbers. For example, 'a third of the trees' would be rendered as 'every third tree,' and 'a third of the earth was consumed by fire' would be rendered as 'the third part of the earth was consumed by fire' or 'having divided the earth into three parts, one part was destroyed by fire.'

60.64 τέταρτον, ου n: a fourth part of an object, series, or mass – 'fourth, fourth part.' τὸ τέταρτον τῆς γῆς 'the fourth part of the earth' Re 6.8. For a discussion of some of the translational problems involved, see 60.63.

60.65 δέκατον, ου n: a tenth part of an object, series, or mass – 'tenth, tenth part.' τὸ δέκατον τῆς πόλεως ἔπεσεν 'the tenth of the city fell' Re 11.13. In rendering 'the tenth of the city fell' in Re 11.13, it may be necessary in some languages to say 'for every ten buildings, one building fell' or 'every tenth building in the city collapsed.'

60.66 δεκάτη, ης f: (derivative of δέκατον 'tenth part,' 60.65) a tenth of a substance being offered for some distinctive purpose –

'tenth.' ᾧ καὶ δεκάτην ἀπὸ πάντων ἐμέρισεν Ἀβραάμ 'to whom Abraham divided and gave a tenth of everything' (referring to booty of war) He 7.2; καὶ ὧδε μὲν δεκάτας ἀποθνῄσκοντες ἄνθρωποι λαμβάνουσιν 'and here men who die receive the tenth' He 7.8.

E Once, Twice, Three Times, Etc. (Cardinals of Time)⁶ (60.67-60.74)

60.67 ἅπαξ ᵃ; ἐφάπαξ ᵃ: a single occurrence – 'once, one time.'⁷
ἅπαξ ᵃ: ἅπαξ ἐλιθάσθην 'I was stoned once' 2 Cor 11.25.
ἐφάπαξ ᵃ: ἔπειτα ὤφθη ἐπάνω πεντακοσίοις ἀδελφοῖς ἐφάπαξ 'then he appeared once to more than five hundred (of our) fellow believers' 1 Cor 15.6. For another interpretation of ἐφάπαξ in 1 Cor 15.6, see 67.34.

60.68 ἅπαξ ᵇ; ἐφάπαξ ᵇ: a single occurrence to the exclusion of any other similar occurrence – 'once and for all, once and never again.'⁷
ἅπαξ ᵇ: νυνὶ δὲ ἅπαξ ἐπὶ συντελείᾳ τῶν αἰώνων 'and now once and for all at the end of the ages' He 9.26; τῇ ἅπαξ παραδοθείσῃ τοῖς ἁγίοις πίστει 'the faith given once and for all to God's people' Jd 3.
ἐφάπαξ ᵇ: τῇ ἁμαρτίᾳ ἀπέθανεν ἐφάπαξ 'he died to sin once and for all' Ro 6.10. In a number of languages the equivalent of 'once and for all' is simply 'once and not again' or 'once and not twice.'

60.69 δίς: two occurrences – 'twice.' νηστεύω δὶς τοῦ σαββάτου 'I fast twice during the week' Lk 18.12.

60.70 ἅπαξ καὶ δίς: (an idiom, literally 'once and twice') an indefinite low number, but more than once – 'more than once, several times.' ἅπαξ καὶ δὶς εἰς τὴν χρείαν μοι ἐπέμψατε

'you provided for my need several times' Php 4.16.

60.71 τρίς: three occurrences – 'thrice, three times.' τρὶς ἀπαρνήσῃ με 'three times you will deny me' Mt 26.34.

60.72 πεντάκις: five occurrences – 'five times.' ὑπὸ Ἰουδαίων πεντάκις τεσσεράκοντα παρὰ μίαν ἔλαβον 'five times I was given the thirty-nine lashes by the Jews' 2 Cor 11.24. See 59.76.

60.73 ἑπτάκις: seven occurrences – 'seven times.' ἕως ἑπτάκις 'as many as seven times' Mt 18.21; καὶ ἐὰν ἑπτάκις τῆς ἡμέρας ἁμαρτήσῃ εἰς σέ 'even if he sins seven times a day against you' Lk 17.4. It is also possible to understand ἑπτάκις in these contexts as referring to a relatively large number, that is, more than one would expect from the context.

60.74 ἑβδομηκοντάκις ᵃ: seventy occurrences – 'seventy times.' ἕως ἑβδομηκοντάκις ἑπτά 'up to seventy-seven times' Mt 18.22. For another interpretation of ἑβδομηκοντάκις in Mt 18.22, see 60.77.

F Double, Four Times As Much, Etc. (Multiples) (60.75-60.78)

60.75 διπλοῦς, ῆ, οῦν: twice the quantity – 'twice as much, double.' οἱ καλῶς προεστῶτες πρεσβύτεροι διπλῆς τιμῆς ἀξιούσθωσαν 'those elders who do good work should be regarded as worthy of double honor' or more probably '. . . double pay' 1 Tm 5.17; ποιεῖτε αὐτὸν υἱὸν γεέννης διπλότερον ὑμῶν 'you make him twice as much the son of gehenna as yourselves' Mt 23.15; καὶ διπλώσατε τὰ διπλᾶ κατὰ τὰ ἔργα αὐτῆς 'and pay her back double for what she has done' Re 18.6.
It is possible that in some contexts διπλοῦς does not mean precisely 'twice as much' but simply 'much more.' For example, in Re 18.6 it may be appropriate to translate 'pay her back much more for what she has done.'

60.76 τετραπλοῦς, ῆ, οῦν: four times as much in quantity – 'four times, four times as much.' ἀποδίδωμι τετραπλοῦν 'I will pay back four times as much' Lk 19.8.

---

6 The meanings in this subdomain are applicable primarily to time and therefore could be classified under Domain 67 *Time;* however, they also occur as elements in multiple units. Since the predominant element in this series of meanings is numerical rather than temporal, they are classified at this point.
7 It is possible that ἐφάπαξ is somewhat more emphatic in meaning than ἅπαξ, but this cannot be determined from existing NT contexts.

60.77 ἑβδομηκοντάκις[b]: seventy multiples of a quantity – 'seventy times.' ἕως ἑβδομηκοντάκις ἑπτά 'seventy times seven' (a total of 490 times) Mt 18.22. One should not, however, interpret ἑβδομηκοντάκις ἑπτά as referring to a specific number, such as 490, but simply an unusually large number with symbolic significance of being totally adequate or complete.[8] For another interpretation of ἑβδομηκοντάκις in Mt 18.22, see 60.74.

60.78 ἑκατονταπλασίων, ον: one hundred times as much in quantity – 'a hundred times, a hundred times as much.' ἐποίησεν καρπὸν ἑκατονταπλασίονα 'it produced a hundred times as much grain' Lk 8.8.

8 It is also possible that ἑβδομηκοντάκις ἑπτά in Mt 18.22 is a shortened form for ἑβδομηκοντάκις ἑπτάκις, which would mean 'seventy times seven times,' but this is, of course, essentially equivalent to ἑβδομηκοντάκις ἑπτά.

G   Pair, Group (Numbered Collectives) (60.79-60.80)

60.79 ζεῦγος, ους n: a collective of two – 'pair, team.' ζεῦγος τρυγόνων 'a pair of turtledoves' Lk 2.24; ζεύγη βοῶν 'a team of oxen' Lk 14.19.

60.80 χιλιάς, άδος f – 'a group of a thousand.' εἰ δυνατός ἐστιν ἐν δέκα χιλιάσιν ὑπαντῆσαι 'if he is able to fight with ten battalions of a thousand each' Lk 14.31. Normally, however, ἐν δέκα χιλιάσιν is simply translated as 'with ten thousand soldiers.' χιλιάδες χιλιάδων 'thousands upon thousands' Re 5.11. In Re 5.11 the implication is that each group consists of a thousand each, but the expression 'thousands upon thousands' is really a way of emphasizing the enormous number. In a number of languages the equivalent would be 'millions' or 'an exceedingly large number.'

61 Sequence[1]

61.1 καθεξῆς: a sequence of one after another in time, space, or logic – 'in order, in sequence, one after another.' διερχόμενος καθεξῆς τὴν Γαλατικὴν χώραν καὶ Φρυγίαν 'going from one place to another in Galatia and Phrygia' Ac 18.23; καθεξῆς σοι γράψαι 'to write to you in sequence' or '. . . in an orderly manner' Lk 1.3; πάντες δὲ οἱ προφῆται ἀπὸ Σαμουὴλ καὶ τῶν καθεξῆς 'all the prophets from Samuel and those that followed in order' Ac 3.24. The expression 'from Samuel' in Ac 3.24 seems to include Samuel. Therefore, one may also render Ac 3.24 as 'Samuel and all the prophets who came after him.'

61.2 ἀπὸ μιᾶς: (an idiom, literally 'from one') a sequence of single units, one after another – 'one after another, one by one.' καὶ ἤρξαντο ἀπὸ μιᾶς πάντες παραιτεῖσθαι 'and they all began to make excuses, one after the other' Lk 14.18.

61.3 τάξις[a], εως f: an ordered or arranged sequence – 'in order, in a sequence.' ἐγένετο δὲ ἐν τῷ ἱερατεύειν αὐτὸν ἐν τῇ τάξει τῆς ἐφημερίας αὐτοῦ 'it happened while he was serving as a priest in the order of his division' Lk 1.8.

61.4 ἀνὰ μέρος: (an idiom, literally 'up to a part' or 'according to a part') a series in which each element follows in strict succession – 'in turn, in succession, one after another.' εἴτε γλώσσῃ τις λαλεῖ, κατὰ δύο ἢ τὸ πλεῖστον τρεῖς, καὶ ἀνὰ μέρος 'if anyone speaks in a tongue, two or three at the most (should speak), and one after another' 1 Cor 14.27.

61.5 τροχός[a], οῦ m: (a figurative extension of meaning of τροχός 'wheel,' not occurring in the NT) an ordered series of events, involving repeated patterns – 'course, pattern.' τὸν

1 This domain involves sequence of a non-numerical nature. Some of the meanings in this domain are rather similar to those occurring in the domain relating to various relations, both coordinate and dependent (Domain 89).

τροχὸν τῆς γενέσεως 'the course of existence' Jas 3.6.[2] For another interpretation of τροχός in Jas 3.6, see 67.83.

61.6 ἀνώτερον[a]: pertaining to preceding in a written or spoken series – 'preceding, above.' ἀνώτερον λέγων 'referring to what has just been said' or 'in saying the above' or 'in saying the preceding' He 10.8.

61.7 ἄλφα *n*: the first in a series, with implications of significance or importance – 'alpha, the first, the beginning.' ἐγώ εἰμι τὸ Ἄλφα καὶ τὸ Ὦ 'I am the alpha and the omega' Re 1.8. This expression is explained in some manuscripts as 'the beginning and the end' and in others as 'the first and the last' and in Re 22.13 as both 'the first and the last' and 'the beginning and the end.' The combination of alpha and omega in secular literature came to designate the entire universe and all kinds of divine and demonic powers, so that in Revelation this title could refer to Christ's dominion over the universe. In the use of such an expression as 'the alpha and the omega,' there is obviously also an important element of status.

61.8 ἀπαρχή[b], ῆς *f*: the first of a set, often in relation to something being given – 'first.' ἀπαρχὴ τῶν κεκοιμημένων 'the first of those who have fallen asleep' 1 Cor 15.20.

61.9 οὕτως[a] or οὕτω (a rarely occurring variant): with reference to that which precedes – 'so, thus, in this way.' καὶ διδάξῃ οὕτως τοὺς ἀνθρώπους 'and teaches men thus' Mt 5.19; οὕτως οὖν καὶ ἐν τῷ νῦν καιρῷ λεῖμμα κατ' ἐκλογὴν χάριτος γέγονεν 'and so it is then, even at the present time, there is a number left of those who have been chosen because of (God's) grace' Ro 11.5; ἐὰν ἀφῶμεν αὐτὸν οὕτως 'if we let him do thus' (that is, in accordance with what he had been doing, namely, performing various miracles) Jn 11.48; οὕτω σε δεῖ καὶ εἰς Ῥώμην μαρτυρῆσαι 'in this way you must also witness in Rome' Ac 23.11.

61.10 οὕτως[b]: referring to that which follows (compare 61.9) – 'the following, as follows.' οὕτως γὰρ γέγραπται διὰ τοῦ προφήτου· καὶ σύ, Βηθλέεμ γῆ Ἰούδα 'for the following has been written by the prophet: And you, Bethlehem, in the land of Judah . . .' Mt 2.5-6; ἡ δὲ ἐκ πίστεως δικαιοσύνη οὕτως λέγει 'the righteousness that is derived from faith says the following . . .' Ro 10.6.

61.11 διάδοχος, ου *m*: one who succeeds another in a position or responsibility – 'successor.' ἔλαβεν διάδοχον ὁ Φῆλιξ Πόρκιον Φῆστον 'Felix was succeeded by Porcius Festus' Ac 24.27.

61.12 δευτερόπρωτος, ον: a term of doubtful meaning, occurring only in Lk 6.1 in manuscripts of the Byzantine tradition, and normally omitted in critical texts; one possible meaning is 'the second after the first,' but in relationship to the word σάββατον, the reference is uncertain.

61.13 ἔσχατος[a], η, ον: pertaining to being the last in a series of objects or events – 'last, final, finally.' γίνεται τὰ ἔσχατα τοῦ ἀνθρώπου ἐκείνου χείρονα τῶν πρώτων 'the last state of that man becomes worse than the first' Mt 12.45; ἕως ἂν ἀποδῷς τὸν ἔσχατον κοδράντην 'until you pay the last small piece of money' Mt 5.26; ἐγώ εἰμι ὁ πρῶτος καὶ ὁ ἔσχατος 'I am the first and the last' Re 1.17.

61.14 λοιπόν[c] or τὸ λοιπόν: an addition which serves as the last item in a series and marks a degree of finality or a conclusion – 'finally, in summary, at last, beyond that.' λοιπὸν οὐκ οἶδα 'beyond that I do not know' 1 Cor 1.16; λοιπόν, ἀδελφοί, χαίρετε 'finally, Christian brothers, rejoice' 2 Cor 13.11; τὸ λοιπόν, ἀδελφοί, ὅσα ἐστὶν ἀληθῆ 'finally, Christian brothers, whatever is true' Php 4.8.

61.15 πέρας[b], ατος *n*: the end point of a process, implying a conclusion of a matter – 'end, conclusion.' καὶ πάσης αὐτοῖς ἀντιλογίας πέρας εἰς βεβαίωσιν ὁ ὅρκος 'and in all their disputes, an oath constitutes the conclusion for establishing (evidence)' He 6.16. In a number of

2 The expression τὸν τροχὸν τῆς γενέσεως in Jas 3.6 is similar in meaning to the lexical units found in Domain 41, Subdomain B *Custom, Tradition.*

languages it may be necessary to restructure this statement in He 6.16, for example, 'when people are contradicting one another, an oath serves to confirm what is said and to put an end to the dispute.'

61.16 ὕστερος[a], α, ον: pertaining to being final in a series, but probably not as emphatic as ἔσχατος[a] 'last,' 61.13 – 'last, final, finally.' ὕστερον δὲ ἀπέστειλεν πρὸς αὐτοὺς τὸν υἱὸν αὐτοῦ 'and finally, he sent to them his son' Mt 21.37; ὕστερον δὲ πάντων ἀπέθανεν ἡ γυνή 'and last of all, the woman died' Mt 22.27; ἐν ὑστέροις καιροῖς 'in the last times' 1 Tm 4.1.

61.17 τὸ τέλος: (an idiom, literally 'the end') a marker of a conclusion to what has preceded, but not necessarily the conclusion of a text – 'finally, in conclusion.' τὸ δὲ τέλος πάντες ὁμόφρονες 'finally, all should be of the same mind' 1 Pe 3.8.

61.18 Ω (the last letter of the Greek alphabet): the last in an inclusive series beginning with ἄλφα (61.7), implying an all-inclusive sphere of authority and high status – 'omega, the last, the end.' ἐγώ εἰμι τὸ Ἄλφα καὶ τὸ Ω 'I am the alpha and the omega' Re 1.8. For a discussion of the relationship of Ω to ἄλφα and its different translations, see 61.7.

61.19 ἀπέραντος, ον: pertaining to a series which has no end – 'without limits, endless.' μηδὲ προσέχειν μύθοις καὶ γενεαλογίαις ἀπεράντοις 'not to occupy themselves with myths and endless genealogies' 1 Tm 1.4. In a number of languages 'endless' is rendered as 'it cannot be counted' or 'there is never a last one.'

62 Arrange, Organize

Outline of Subdomains

A Put Together, Arrange (of physical objects) (62.1-62.2)
B Organize (of events and states) (62.3-62.9)

A Put Together, Arrange (of physical objects) (62.1-62.2)

62.1 συναρμολογέομαι: to fit together in a coherent and compatible manner – 'to fit together, to be joined together.'[1] ἐν ᾧ πᾶσα οἰκοδομὴ συναρμολογουμένη 'in whom the whole structure is joined together' or '... fits together' Eph 2.21; πᾶν τὸ σῶμα συναρμολογούμενον 'all (the different parts of) the body fit together' Eph 4.16.

62.2 συγκεράννυμι: to cause parts to fit together in an overall arrangement – 'to put together, to compose, to structure.' ὁ θεὸς συνεκέρασεν τὸ σῶμα 'God has put the body together' or '... has structured the body' 1 Cor 12.24.

B Organize (of events and states) (62.3-62.9)

62.3 ἀνατάσσομαι: to organize a series of items – 'to organize (a report), to arrange, to compile, to put together.' ἐπειδήπερ πολλοὶ ἐπεχείρησαν ἀνατάξασθαι διήγησιν περὶ τῶν πεπληροφορημένων ἐν ἡμῖν πραγμάτων 'as many have undertaken to compile a report about the things that have taken place among us' Lk 1.1.

62.4 ἐπιδιορθόω: to cause matters to be ordered in the correct manner – 'to set right, to correct, to put into order.' ἀπέλιπόν σε ἐν Κρήτῃ, ἵνα τὰ λείποντα ἐπιδιορθώσῃ 'I left you in Crete for you to put in order the things that still needed doing' Tt 1.5.

62.5 διόρθωσις[a], εως f: a corrected new

---

1 The meaning 'to be joined together' does not suggest that συναρμολογέομαι is to be understood as a causative passive. The reference is simply to the state of being joined together.

order, implying a change from an earlier state – 'new order, improvement.' μέχρι καιροῦ διορθώσεως 'as until the time of the new order' He 9.10, but see 62.6 for the generally preferred interpretation.

62.6 διόρθωσις[b], εως *f*: the process of establishing a new order – 'to establish a new order, forming a new order, reformation.' μέχρι καιροῦ διορθώσεως 'until the time when he will establish a new order' or '. . . will reform all things' He 9.10, but see 62.5.

62.7 τάξις[b], εως *f*; **τάγμα**, τος *n*: a proper and correct order – 'right order, good order, in order, in an orderly manner.' τάξις[b]: πάντα δὲ εὐσχημόνως καὶ κατὰ τάξιν γινέσθω 'everything must be done in a proper and orderly manner' 1 Cor 14.40; χαίρων καὶ βλέπων ὑμῶν τὴν τάξιν 'rejoicing to see your orderliness' Col 2.5. In Col 2.5 τάξις may refer to the orderly manner in which the church at Colossae conducted its affairs or carried on its worship.

τάγμα: ἕκαστος δὲ ἐν τῷ ἰδίῳ τάγματι 'each in his own order' 1 Cor 15.23.

62.8 διατάσσω[b]: to arrange matters in a particular manner – 'to arrange for, to plan.' οὕτως γὰρ διατεταγμένος ἦν μέλλων αὐτὸς πεζεύειν 'for he had arranged matters in this way since he was going there by foot' Ac 20.13.

62.9 προστάσσω[b]: to arrange in a prescribed manner – 'to prescribe, to arrange for.' ὁρίσας προστεταγμένους καιρούς 'having set limits to prescribed times' or 'having fixed beforehand the prescribed periods of time' Ac 17.26. In some languages it may be important to recast to some extent the rendering of the second part of Ac 17.26 so as to combine both place and time, for example, 'he set limits to the time and determined the places they would dwell.'

63 Whole, Unite, Part, Divide

Outline of Subdomains

A Whole (63.1-63.4)
B Unite (63.5-63.8)
C Mix (63.9-63.12)
D Part (63.13-63.20)
E Remnant (63.21-63.22)
F Divide (63.23-63.27)
G Separate (63.28-63.31)

A Whole[1] (63.1-63.4)

63.1 ὅλος[a], η, ον: pertaining to being whole, complete, or entire, with focus on unity – 'whole, all, complete, entire.' ὅλη ἡ πόλις 'the

entire city' Mk 1.33; δι' ὅλης νυκτός 'through the entire night' Lk 5.5; ἡ πίστις ὑμῶν καταγγέλλεται ἐν ὅλῳ τῷ κόσμῳ 'your faith has been made known throughout the whole world' Ro 1.8.

63.2 πᾶς[d], πᾶσα, πᾶν (with the definite article): pertaining to being entire or whole, with focus on the totality – 'entire, whole, total.' πάσῃ τῇ κτίσει 'the entire creation' Mk 16.15; πάσῃ τῇ γῇ 'all the earth' Ro 9.17; πᾶσαν τὴν ὀφειλὴν ἐκείνην ἀφῆκά σοι 'I forgave you that entire debt' Mt 18.32.

63.3 ἑνότης, ητος *f*: a state of oneness – 'unity, oneness.' τηρεῖν τὴν ἑνότητα τοῦ πνεύματος 'to keep the unity of the Spirit' or '. . . the unity which the Spirit causes' Eph 4.3; καταντήσωμεν οἱ πάντες εἰς τὴν ἑνότητα τῆς πίστεως 'we shall all attain to that oneness in our faith' Eph 4.13. In some languages it may be strange to speak of 'that oneness in our faith.' The closest equivalent may be 'we

---

1 There is a significant overlap in Subdomain A *Whole* with Domain 59 *Quantity*, Subdomain C *All, Any, Each, Every (Totality)*. Some of the same terms may focus either upon the quantity involved or the entirety, and in a number of contexts it is not possible to determine which particular aspect of meaning is in focus.

believe just as though we were all one person' or 'we believe in one and the same way.'

63.4 εἷςᶜ, μία, ἕν: that which is united as one in contrast with being divided or consisting of separate parts – 'one.' καὶ ἔσονται οἱ δύο εἰς σάρκα μίαν 'and the two shall become one flesh' Mt 19.5; ὁ δὲ θεὸς εἷς ἐστιν 'but God is one' Ga 3.20. This phrase in Ga 3.20 is a reference to the fact that God of the Scriptures is defined as a unit and not as being characterized by numerous manifestations or realizations.

B Unite (63.5-63.8)

63.5 συμβιβάζωᵃ: to bring together into a unit – 'to bring together, to cause to be a unit, to unite, to combine.' τὸ σῶμα . . . συμβιβαζόμενον διὰ πάσης ἁφῆς 'the body . . . united by means of every ligament' Eph 4.16; συμβιβασθέντες ἐν ἀγάπῃ 'united in love' Col 2.2.

63.6 συνίστημιᶜ or συνιστάνω: to bring together or hold together something in its proper or appropriate place or relationship – 'to hold together.' τὰ πάντα ἐν αὐτῷ συνέστηκεν 'in him all things hold together' Col 1.17. In Col 1.17 it may not be easy to indicate clearly the relationship of the phrase 'in him' to the rest of the expression, namely, 'all things hold together.' Some translations have expanded the expression 'in him' to 'in union with him' or 'in view of the fact that we are joined together with him.' It is also possible to understand ἐν αὐτῷ as indicating agent, so that this expression in Col 1.17 may mean 'by means of him all things hold together.'

63.7 σύνδεσμοςᵇ, ου m: that which combines or brings objects and/or events together – 'to bring together, to bind together, to unite.' τὴν ἀγάπην, ὅ ἐστιν σύνδεσμος τῆς τελειότητος 'love, which binds all things together in perfect unity' or 'love, which perfectly binds all things together' Col 3.14.

63.8 ἀνακεφαλαιόω: to bring everything together in terms of some unifying principle or person – 'to bring together.' ἀνακεφαλαιώσασθαι τὰ πάντα ἐν τῷ Χριστῷ 'to bring everything together in Christ' Eph 1.10; ἐν τῷ λόγῳ τούτῳ ἀνακεφαλαιοῦται, ἐν τῷ Ἀγαπήσεις τὸν πλησίον σου ὡς σεαυτόν 'it is brought together in this one statement, Love your neighbor as yourself' Ro 13.9.

C Mix (63.9-63.12)

63.9 κεράννυμιᵃ: to mix substances, normally liquids – 'to mix.' ἐν τῷ ποτηρίῳ ᾧ ἐκέρασεν κεράσατε αὐτῇ διπλοῦν 'in the cup in which she has mixed, mix her a double portion' Re 18.6; τοῦ οἴνου τοῦ θυμοῦ τοῦ θεοῦ τοῦ κεκερασμένου ἀκράτου 'of the wine of the wrath of God mixed at full strength' Re 14.10. Note that in the process of mixing, the various substances become a single mass, and the constituent parts are indistinguishable. For another interpretation of κεράννυμι in Re 14.10, see 47.3.

63.10 μίγνυμι: to mix or mingle, either of liquids or solids, often involving substances which do not normally go together – 'to mix, to mingle.' οἶνον μετὰ χολῆς μεμιγμένον 'wine mixed with gall' Mt 27.34; ὧν τὸ αἷμα Πιλᾶτος ἔμιξεν μετὰ τῶν θυσιῶν αὐτῶν 'whose blood Pilate mingled with their sacrifices' Lk 13.1. This statement in Lk 13.1 must be understood figuratively, and it can often be best translated as 'Pilate caused them to be killed while they were offering sacrifices to God' or 'Pilate ordered them to be slain while they were sacrificing.'

63.11 μίγμα, τος n: (derivative of μίγνυμι 'to mix, to mingle,' 63.10) that which has been mixed – 'mixture.' μίγμα σμύρνης καὶ ἀλόης 'a mixture of myrrh and aloes' Jn 19.39.

63.12 φύραμαᵇ, τος n: (derivative of φυράω 'to mix substances such as flour, either with other dry substances or with water,' not occurring in the NT) that which is mixed or kneaded – 'mixture, batch of dough.' ἐκκαθάρατε τὴν παλαιὰν ζύμην, ἵνα ἦτε νέον φύραμα 'get rid of the old yeast so that you may be a fresh batch of dough' 1 Cor 5.7.

D Part (63.13-63.20)

63.13 μερίςᵃ, ίδος f: part or portion, with the possible implication of a division or significant distinction – 'share, portion.' οὐκ ἔστιν σοι μερὶς οὐδὲ κλῆρος ἐν τῷ λόγῳ τούτῳ 'you have no share or part in this matter' Ac 8.21; τὴν μερίδα τοῦ κλήρου τῶν ἁγίων 'a share in the inheritance of the people of God' Col 1.12; τίς μερὶς πιστῷ μετὰ ἀπίστου; 'what does a believer share with an unbeliever?' 2 Cor 6.15.

63.14 μέρος[a], ους *n*: a part in contrast with a whole – 'part, aspect, feature.' μοι τὸ ἐπιβάλλον μέρος τῆς οὐσίας 'the part of the property that belongs to me' Lk 15.12; τὸ δεδοξασμένον ἐν τούτῳ τῷ μέρει 'that which was glorious in this aspect' 2 Cor 3.10.

63.15 ἐκ μέρους; ἀπὸ μέρους[a]: (idioms, literally 'from a part') the state of being part of something – 'being part of, as a part of, in part, partially.'
ἐκ μέρους: ὑμεῖς δέ ἐστε σῶμα Χριστοῦ καὶ μέλη ἐκ μέρους 'you are the body of Christ and each member is a part of it' or '. . . and each one is a part of the body' 1 Cor 12.27.
ἀπὸ μέρους[a]: καθὼς καὶ ἐπέγνωτε ἡμᾶς ἀπὸ μέρους 'even as you partially understand us' 2 Cor 1.14.

63.16 κατὰ μέρος: (an idiom, literally 'in accordance with a part') pertaining to an activity which proceeds part by part – 'in detail, one item after another.' περὶ ὧν οὐκ ἔστιν νῦν λέγειν κατὰ μέρος 'there is now no time to speak of these matters in detail' He 9.5.

63.17 μέλος[b], ους *n*: a part as a member of a unit – 'member' (based on the figure of the relationship of parts to the body). μέλη ἐσμὲν τοῦ σώματος αὐτοῦ 'we are members of his body' Eph 5.30; καθ' εἷς ἀλλήλων μέλη 'members in relationship to one another' Ro 12.5.

63.18 κλῆρος[c], ου *m*: a share or portion which has been assigned or granted – 'part, share.' κλῆρον ἐν τοῖς ἡγιασμένοις 'a share among those who are sanctified' Ac 26.18; ἔλαχεν τὸν κλῆρον τῆς διακονίας ταύτης 'he had been granted a part in this ministry' Ac 1.17. For another interpretation of κλῆρος in Ac 1.17, see 37.101.

63.19 πολυμερῶς[a]: pertaining to that which occurs in many parts – 'fragmentary, in many parts.' πολυμερῶς καὶ πολυτρόπως πάλαι ὁ θεὸς λαλήσας τοῖς πατράσιν 'in many parts and in many ways God spoke in early times to the ancestors' He 1.1. It is also possible to interpret πολυμερῶς in He 1.1 as referring to many different occasions, and therefore it may be translated as 'often' or 'many times' (67.11). For yet another interpretation of πολυμερῶς in He 1.1, see 89.81.

63.20 ἐκ[i]; ἀπό[d]: markers of a part of a whole, whether consisting of countables or of mass – 'one of, one among, a part of.'
ἐκ[i]: ἀληθῶς καὶ σὺ ἐξ αὐτῶν εἶ 'surely you are one of them' Mt 26.73.
ἀπό[d]: ἵνα παρὰ τῶν γεωργῶν λάβῃ ἀπὸ τῶν καρπῶν τοῦ ἀμπελῶνος 'in order to receive from the farmers a part of the produce of the vineyard' Mk 12.2.

E Remnant[2] (63.21-63.22)

63.21 λοιπός, ή, όν; ἐπίλοιπος, ον; κατάλοιπος, ον: pertaining to the part of a whole which remains or continues, and thus constitutes the rest of the whole – 'rest, remaining, what remains, other.'[3]
λοιπός: τῶν λοιπῶν φωνῶν 'the remaining blasts' Re 8.13; οἱ λοιποὶ τῶν ἀνθρώπων 'the rest of the people' Re 9.20.
ἐπίλοιπος: τὸν ἐπίλοιπον . . . χρόνον 'the rest of . . . the time' 1 Pe 4.2.
κατάλοιπος: ὅπως ἂν ἐκζητήσωσιν οἱ κατάλοιποι τῶν ἀνθρώπων τὸν κύριον 'so that the rest of mankind would seek the Lord' Ac 15.17.

63.22 λεῖμμα, τος *n*; ὑπόλειμμα, τος *n*: a relatively small part which continues to exist – 'remnant, small part.'
λεῖμμα: ἐν τῷ νῦν καιρῷ λεῖμμα κατ' ἐκλογὴν χάριτος γέγονεν 'at the present time there is a small number of those (whom God has) chosen by his grace' Ro 11.5.

2 The meanings in Subdomain E *Remnant* are part of a whole which has caused to continue in a state or to exist in contrast with the other parts of the whole.
3 There may be certain distinctions in meaning in λοιπός, ἐπίλοιπος, and κατάλοιπος, but these cannot be readily determined from existing contexts.

ὑπόλειμμα: τὸ ὑπόλειμμα σωθήσεται 'the remnant will be saved' Ro 9.27.

F   Divide (63.23-63.27)

63.23 μερίζω[a]; διαμερίζω[c]: to divide into separate parts – 'to divide, to disunite, division, separation.'[4]

μερίζω[a]: μερίσασθαι μετ' ἐμοῦ τὴν κληρονομίαν 'to divide with me the inheritance' Lk 12.13; μεμέρισται ὁ Χριστός; 'has Christ been divided?' 1 Cor 1.13; πᾶσα βασιλεία μερισθεῖσα καθ' ἑαυτῆς 'every kingdom divided against itself' Mt 12.25.

διαμερίζω[c]: διαμεριζόμεναι γλῶσσαι ὡσεὶ πυρός 'divided tongues as of fire' Ac 2.3. For another interpretation of διαμερίζω in Ac 2.3 (as middle, not passive), see 15.140.

63.24 μερισμός[a], οῦ _m_: the point at which parts divide or meet – 'the point of division, the point of meeting.' ἄχρι μερισμοῦ ψυχῆς καὶ πνεύματος 'to the point where soul and spirit meet' or '. . . come together' He 4.12.

63.25 μεριστής, οῦ _m_: (derivative of μερίζω[a] 'to divide,' 63.23) one who divides – 'divider.' τίς με κατέστησεν κριτὴν ἢ μεριστήν; 'who made me a judge or divider?' Lk 12.14.

63.26 σχίζω[b]: to split or divide into two parts – 'to divide, to split, to tear in two.' αἱ πέτραι ἐσχίσθησαν 'the rocks were split' Mt 27.51; ἐσχίσθη δὲ τὸ καταπέτασμα τοῦ ναοῦ μέσον 'the curtain of the sanctuary was split down the middle' Lk 23.45.

63.27 αἵρεσις[c], εως _f_: a division of people into different and opposing sets – 'division, separate group.' δεῖ γὰρ καὶ αἱρέσεις ἐν ὑμῖν εἶναι 'for it is necessary that divisions exist among you' or 'the existence of divisions among you is inevitable' 1 Cor 11.19.

G   Separate[5] (63.28-63.31)

63.28 ἀφορίζω[c]: to separate into two or more parts or groups, often by some intervening space – 'to separate, to set one apart from another.' καὶ ἀφορίσει αὐτοὺς ἀπ' ἀλλήλων, ὥσπερ ὁ ποιμὴν ἀφορίζει τὰ πρόβατα ἀπὸ τῶν ἐρίφων 'and he set them apart from one another as a shepherd separates the sheep from the goats' Mt 25.32.

63.29 χωρίζω[a]: to separate objects by introducing considerable space or isolation – 'to separate, to isolate one from another.' κεχωρισμένος ἀπὸ τῶν ἁμαρτωλῶν 'separated from sinners' He 7.26. This phrase in He 7.26 may also imply the exultation of Christ to the heavenly world. τίς ἡμᾶς χωρίσει ἀπὸ τῆς ἀγάπης τοῦ Χριστοῦ; 'who will be able to separate us from the love of Christ?' Ro 8.35.

63.30 ἀποχωρίζομαι[b]: to separate more or less definitively one from another (evidently somewhat more emphatic in meaning than χωρίζω[a] 'to separate,' 63.29) – 'to separate definitely, to go one's own way, to split up.' ὥστε ἀποχωρισθῆναι αὐτοὺς ἀπ' ἀλλήλων 'so that they each went their own way one from another' Ac 15.39; καὶ ὁ οὐρανὸς ἀπεχωρίσθη 'and the heaven split open' Re 6.14. For another interpretation of ἀποχωρίζομαι in Re 6.14, see 15.14.

63.31 χωρίς[b]: pertaining to something which occurs separately or by itself – 'separately, by itself.' οὐ μετὰ τῶν ὀθονίων κείμενον ἀλλὰ χωρίς 'not lying with the linen cloths but lying off by itself' Jn 20.7.

---

4 It is possible that διαμερίζω[c] differs in meaning from μερίζω[a] in being somewhat more emphatic, but this cannot be readily determined from existing contexts.

5 Subdomain G _Separate_ differs from Subdomain F _Divide_ either in space or in class of the items involved.

64 Comparison[1]

64.1 οἷος[a], α, ον; ὅμοιος, α, ον; ὁμοίως: pertaining to being similar to something else in some respect – 'like, such as, likewise, similar.'[2]

οἷος[a]: θλῖψις μεγάλη οἵα οὐ γέγονεν ἀπ' ἀρχῆς κόσμου ἕως τοῦ νῦν 'great tribulation such as has not taken place from the beginning of the world until now' Mt 24.21; λευκὰ λίαν οἷα γναφεὺς ἐπὶ τῆς γῆς οὐ δύναται οὕτως λευκᾶναι 'very white, such as no fuller on earth could make them so white' Mk 9.3.

ὅμοιος: ἀλλὰ ὅμοιος αὐτῷ ἐστιν 'but he is like him' Jn 9.9; καὶ ὁ καθήμενος ὅμοιος ὁράσει λίθῳ ἰάσπιδι 'and he who sits (on the throne) is like in appearance to a jasper stone' (perhaps in the sense of 'colorful radiance') Re 4.3; ἐὰν φανερωθῇ ὅμοιοι αὐτῷ ἐσόμεθα 'when he appears, we shall be like him' 1 Jn 3.2.

ὁμοίως: καὶ ὁ ἔχων βρώματα ὁμοίως ποιείτω 'and whoever has food, let him do likewise' Lk 3.11; ὁμοίως καὶ ὁ δεύτερος καὶ ὁ τρίτος, ἕως τῶν ἑπτά 'similarly, also the second and the third, until the seven (brothers)' Mt 22.26.

64.2 τοιοῦτος[a], αὕτη, οὗτον: pertaining to being like some identified entity or event – 'such, like such, like that.' καὶ οἶδα τὸν τοιοῦτον ἄνθρωπον 'and I know a person like that' 2 Cor 12.3; καὶ γὰρ ὁ πατὴρ τοιούτους ζητεῖ τοὺς προσκυνοῦντας αὐτόν 'for the Father seeks persons like that to worship him' Jn 4.23; θλῖψις οἵα οὐ γέγονεν τοιαύτη ἀπ' ἀρχῆς κτίσεως 'tribulation such as has not happened in this way from the beginning of the world'

Mk 13.19;[3] τοῦτο λογιζέσθω ὁ τοιοῦτος, ὅτι οἷοί ἐσμεν τῷ λόγῳ δι' ἐπιστολῶν ἀπόντες, τοιοῦτοι καὶ παρόντες τῷ ἔργῳ 'such a person should understand this; namely, what we say in letters while absent will be such as we will do when we are present' 2 Cor 10.11.

64.3 ὁμοιότης, ητος *f*; ὁμοίωμα[a], τος *n*; ὁμοίωσις, εως *f*: the state of being similar to something – 'similarity, likeness, being similar.'

ὁμοιότης: πεπειρασμένον δὲ κατὰ πάντα καθ' ὁμοιότητα χωρὶς ἁμαρτίας 'but was tempted in everything in a way similar (to us) but without sin' He 4.15; κατὰ τὴν ὁμοιότητα Μελχισέδεκ ἀνίσταται ἱερεὺς ἕτερος 'another priest has appeared in the likeness of Melchizedek' or '. . . similar to Melchizedek' He 7.15.

ὁμοίωμα[a]: εἰ γὰρ σύμφυτοι γεγόναμεν τῷ ὁμοιώματι τοῦ θανάτου αὐτοῦ 'for if we have become one with him in the likeness of his death' or '. . . in dying as he died' Ro 6.5; καὶ ἤλλαξαν τὴν δόξαν τοῦ ἀφθάρτου θεοῦ ἐν ὁμοιώματι εἰκόνος φθαρτοῦ ἀνθρώπου καὶ πετεινῶν καὶ τετραπόδων καὶ ἑρπετῶν 'they changed the glory of the immortal God into the likeness of a mortal person and of birds, four-footed beasts, and serpents' Ro 1.23; ἐν ὁμοιώματι ἀνθρώπων γενόμενος 'appearing in human likeness' or 'coming to be like a person' Php 2.7.

ὁμοίωσις: καταρώμεθα τοὺς ἀνθρώπους τοὺς καθ' ὁμοίωσιν θεοῦ γεγονότας 'we curse people who are in the likeness of God' Jas 3.9.

64.4 ὁμοιόω[a]; ἀφομοιόω; ἔοικα: to be like or similar to something else – 'to be like, to resemble, to be similar to.'

ὁμοιόω[a]: οἱ θεοὶ ὁμοιωθέντες ἀνθρώποις κατέβησαν πρὸς ἡμᾶς 'the gods resembling men have come down to us' Ac 14.11; ὁμοιώθη ἡ βασιλεία τῶν οὐρανῶν ἀνθρώπῳ σπείραντι καλὸν σπέρμα ἐν τῷ ἀγρῷ αὐτοῦ 'the kingdom of heaven is like a man who sowed good seed in his field' Mt 13.24.

---

1 The meanings in Domain 64 *Comparison* might well be included within Domain 58 *Nature, Class, Example*. A subdomain such as *Similarity* could well be added after Subdomain E *Same or Equivalent Kind or Class*. However, the meanings in Domain 64 seem to be more specificallly matters of comparison rather than focusing on the nature or character of the entities or processes involved.

There is also a problem involved in this set of meanings in that in some contexts it would seem appropriate to speak of something being 'same' rather than simply 'similar.' Unfortunately, in English the term *same* does not mean 'identical with' but merely 'closely resembling.'

2 οἷος[a] differs from ὅμοιος and ὁμοίως only in its syntactic function.

3 In Mk 13.19 τοιαύτη serves to make more emphatic the comparison already stated in οἵα.

ἀφομοιόω: ἀφωμοιωμένος δὲ τῷ υἱῷ τοῦ θεοῦ 'being similar to the Son of God' or 'resembling the Son of God' He 7.3.

ἔοικα: ὁ γὰρ διακρινόμενος ἔοικεν κλύδωνι θαλάσσης 'for the one who doubts is like a wave on the sea' Jas 1.6; οὗτος ἔοικεν ἀνδρὶ κατανοοῦντι τὸ πρόσωπον τῆς γενέσεως αὐτοῦ ἐν ἐσόπτρῳ 'such a person is like a man who sees his own face in a mirror' Jas 1.23.

64.5 ὁμοιόω[b]: to consider something to be like something else – 'to compare.'[4] τίνι ὁμοιώσω τὴν βασιλείαν τοῦ θεοῦ; 'to what shall I liken the kingdom of God?' or 'to what shall I compare the kingdom of God?' Lk 13.20; πῶς ὁμοιώσωμεν τὴν βασιλείαν τοῦ θεοῦ; 'how shall we compare the kingdom of God?' Mk 4.30.

64.6 συγκρίνω[a]: to judge whether something is like something else – 'to judge the degree of similarity, to compare.'[4] οὐ γὰρ τολμῶμεν ἐγκρῖναι ἢ συγκρῖναι ἑαυτούς τισιν τῶν ἑαυτοὺς συνιστανόντων 'for we do not dare to classify ourselves or compare ourselves with those who rate themselves so highly' 2 Cor 10.12.

64.7 παρόμοιος, ον: pertaining to being closely similar to – 'resembling closely, much alike, very similar.' καὶ παρόμοια τοιαῦτα πολλὰ ποιεῖτε 'you do many other such similar things' Mk 7.13.

64.8 παρομοιάζω: to be very much like something – 'to resemble closely, to be very similar to, to be just like.' ὅτι παρομοιάζετε τάφοις κεκονιαμένοις 'because you are just like white-washed graves' Mt 23.27.

64.9 παραπλήσιος, α, ον; παραπλησίως: pertaining to being similar in the sense of almost equivalent to – 'very similar, closely resembling, almost the same as.'

παραπλήσιος: καὶ γὰρ ἠσθένησεν παραπλήσιον θανάτῳ 'for he was so sick he was almost the same as dead' or '. . . he almost died' Php 2.27.

παραπλησίως: καὶ αὐτὸς παραπλησίως μετέσχεν τῶν αὐτῶν 'and he became very much like them' He 2.14.

64.10 συμφωνέω[b]: to be sufficiently like something as to fit or match – 'to be like, to match.' καὶ τῷ παλαιῷ οὐ συμφωνήσει τὸ ἐπίβλημα τὸ ἀπὸ τοῦ καινοῦ 'and the patch (taken) from the new (cloth) will not match the old' Lk 5.36.

64.11 ὅμως[b]: pertaining to being, at least in some respects, similar – 'similarly, likewise.' ὅμως ἀνθρώπου κεκυρωμένην διαθήκην οὐδεὶς ἀθετεῖ 'similarly, no one invalidates a covenant which has been duly authorized by someone' Ga 3.15. For another interpretation of ὅμως in Ga 3.15, see 89.74.

64.12 ὡς[a]; **ὡσεί**[a]: relatively weak markers of a relationship between events or states – 'as, like.'[5]

ὡς[a]: ἡμέρα κυρίου ὡς κλέπτης ἐν νυκτὶ οὕτως ἔρχεται 'the day of the Lord comes like a thief in the night' 1 Th 5.2; γενηθήτω σοι ὡς θέλεις 'may it happen to you as you wish' Mt 15.28; τί ἔτι κἀγὼ ὡς ἁμαρτωλὸς κρίνομαι; 'why then am I still judged as a sinner?' Ro 3.7.

ὡσεί[a]: εἶδεν τὸ πνεῦμα τοῦ θεοῦ καταβαῖνον ὡσεὶ περιστεράν 'he saw the Spirit of God come down as a dove' Mt 3.16; καὶ ἐγένετο ὡσεὶ νεκρός 'and he became as dead' Mk 9.26.

64.13 ὥσπερ; ὡσπερεί: somewhat more emphatic markers of similarity between events and states – 'as, just as.'[6]

ὥσπερ: ὥσπερ γὰρ ἄνθρωπος ἀποδημῶν 'for as in the case of a man who goes away on a trip' Mt 25.14; ὥσπερ γὰρ ἦν Ἰωνᾶς ἐν τῇ κοιλίᾳ τοῦ

---

4 In a number of languages there is relatively little difficulty in finding an adequate lexical expression for 'being like' or 'being similar to'; however, it is often much more difficult to find a satisfactory equivalent for the process of 'comparing.' In many instances the equivalent expression is somewhat paraphrastic, for example, 'to see things together,' 'to set things alongside of one another,' 'to measure things against one another,' or 'to say how similar things are.'

5 Though ὡσεί literally consists of ὡς and εἰ ('as if'), in most cases all or at least most of the conditional aspect of the meaning has been lost.

6 In general it seems that forms which include the enclitic -περ are somewhat more emphatic, but this is not always possible to establish on the basis of evidently contrastive contexts.

κήτους τρεῖς ἡμέρας καὶ τρεῖς νύκτας 'for just as Jonah was in the belly of the big fish three days and three nights' Mt 12.40; ὥσπερ οἱ ὑποκριταὶ ποιοῦσιν ἐν ταῖς συναγωγαῖς καὶ ἐν ταῖς ῥύμαις 'as the hypocrites do in the synagogues and on the street corners' Mt 6.2. ὡσπερεί: ἔσχατον δὲ πάντων ὡσπερεὶ τῷ ἐκτρώματι ὤφθη κἀμοί 'and last of all he appeared to me as one who was born at the wrong time' or '. . . as one whose birth was abnormal' 1 Cor 15.8.

64.14 καθά; καθώς^c; καθό^a: markers of similarity in events and states, with the possible implication of something being in accordance with something else – 'just as, in comparison to.'
καθά: καθὰ συνέταξέν μοι κύριος 'just as the Lord had ordered me' Mt 27.10.
καθώς^c: καθὼς γὰρ ἐγένετο Ἰωνᾶς τοῖς Νινευίταις σημεῖον 'for just as Jonah became a sign to the Ninevites' Lk 11.30; καθὼς ἠγάπησέν με ὁ πατήρ 'the same way as the Father loved me' Jn 15.9.
καθό^a: τί προσευξώμεθα καθὸ δεῖ οὐκ οἴδαμεν 'we do not know what we should pray for as we ought to' Ro 8.26.

64.15 καθάπερ; καθώσπερ: emphatic markers of comparison between events and states – 'just as, precisely as.'[7]
καθάπερ: μηδὲ γογγύζετε, καθάπερ τινὲς αὐτῶν ἐγόγγυσαν 'do not grumble as some of them grumbled' 1 Cor 10.10; καθάπερ καὶ Δαυὶδ λέγει τὸν μακαρισμὸν τοῦ ἀνθρώπου ᾧ ὁ θεὸς λογίζεται δικαιοσύνην χωρὶς ἔργων 'just as also

7 It may be of interest to note that in Greek NT manuscripts καθάπερ and καθώσπερ are often alternative forms.
As in the case of ὥσπερ and ὡσπερεί (64.13) in contrast with ὡς^a and ὡσεί^a (64.12), so καθάπερ and καθώσπερ appear to be somewhat more emphatic than καθά and καθώς^c (64.14).

David spoke of the blessedness of a person to whom God reckons righteousness apart from works' Ro 4.6.
καθώσπερ: ἀλλὰ καλούμενος ὑπὸ τοῦ θεοῦ, καθώσπερ καὶ Ἀαρών 'but he is called by God just as even Aaron was' He 5.4.

64.16 ὡσαύτως: a marker of similarity which approximates identity – 'just as, in the same way, in like manner.' πάλιν δὲ ἐξελθὼν περὶ ἕκτην καὶ ἐνάτην ὥραν ἐποίησεν ὡσαύτως 'and again going out at the sixth and the ninth hour, he did the same thing' Mt 20.5; ὁ δεύτερος ἔλαβεν αὐτήν, καὶ ἀπέθανεν μὴ καταλιπὼν σπέρμα· καὶ ὁ τρίτος ὡσαύτως 'the second one took her (as wife), but died without having an offspring, and the third likewise' or '. . . and the third experienced the same' Mk 12.21; ὡσαύτως καὶ τὸ ποτήριον μετὰ τὸ δειπνῆσαι 'and similarly after the meal (he took) the cup' 1 Cor 11.25.

64.17 πρός^q: a marker of that which is compared to something else – 'with, in comparison with, to be compared to.' οὐκ ἄξια τὰ παθήματα τοῦ νῦν καιροῦ πρὸς τὴν μέλλουσαν δόξαν 'the sufferings of this time are not really (or '. . . are not worthy') to be compared with the future glory' Ro 8.18.

64.18 ἤ^b: a marker of comparison – 'than.' ἀνεκτότερον ἔσται γῇ Σοδόμων καὶ Γομόρρων ἐν ἡμέρᾳ κρίσεως ἢ τῇ πόλει ἐκείνῃ 'it will be easier for the land of Sodom and Gomorrah in the day of judgment than for that city' Mt 10.15.

64.19 ἤπερ: an emphatic marker of comparison – 'than, indeed than.' ἠγάπησαν γὰρ τὴν δόξαν τῶν ἀνθρώπων μᾶλλον ἤπερ τὴν δόξαν τοῦ θεοῦ 'for they love the praise of people rather than the praise that comes from God' Jn 12.43.

65 Value[1]

A Valuable, Lacking in Value[2] (65.1-65.16)

65.1 τιμή[b], ῆς f: the worth or merit of some object, event, or state – 'worth, value.' καὶ ἃ δοκοῦμεν ἀτιμότερα εἶναι τοῦ σώματος, τούτοις τιμὴν περισσοτέραν περιτίθεμεν 'the (parts) of the body which we regard as being less valuable, to these we accord special value' or '... we think of as being exceptionally valuable' 1 Cor 12.23. In some languages the equivalent of 'value' is almost always in terms of 'importance.' This is particularly true if one is speaking of objects which are normally not bought and sold. Accordingly, one may render this particular expression in 1 Cor 12.23 as 'those parts of the body which we think of as not being so important, to these we grant particular importance' or '... we consider as being very important.' It is also possible to interpret τιμή in 1 Cor 12.23 as a degree of honor or appreciation (see τιμή[a], 87.4).

65.2 τίμιος[a], α, ον; ἔντιμος[a], ον: pertaining to being of considerable value or worth – 'valuable, precious.'

τίμιος[a]: δι᾽ ὧν τὰ τίμια καὶ μέγιστα ἡμῖν ἐπαγγέλματα δεδώρηται 'in this way he has given us valuable and very important promises' 2 Pe 1.4; χρυσόν, ἄργυρον, λίθους τιμίους 'gold, silver, valuable stones' 1 Cor 3.12. It is possible to interpret λίθους τιμίους in 1 Cor 3.12 as a unit, meaning 'precious stones' (see 2.29), but in this figurative context of a foundation, the reference may very well be more general.

ἔντιμος[a]: λίθον ζῶντα, ὑπὸ ἀνθρώπων μὲν ἀποδεδοκιμασμένον παρὰ δὲ θεῷ ἐκλεκτὸν ἔντιμον 'the living stone rejected by men but chosen as valuable by God' 1 Pe 2.4.

65.3 βαρύτιμος, ον; πολύτιμος, ον; πολυτελής, ές: pertaining to being of great value or worth, implying in some contexts a monetary scale – 'valuable, expensive.'

βαρύτιμος: προσῆλθεν αὐτῷ γυνὴ ἔχουσα ἀλάβαστρον μύρου βαρυτίμου 'a woman came to him with an alabaster jar of very expensive perfume' Mt 26.7.

πολύτιμος: εὑρὼν δὲ ἕνα πολύτιμον μαργαρίτην 'and when he finds a very precious pearl' Mt 13.46. Though it is possible to understand πολύτιμος in Mt 13.46 as meaning 'expensive,' the reference may be far more general, in other words, 'a valuable pearl' in the sense of a pearl having exceptionally fine characteristics. ἵνα τὸ δοκίμιον ὑμῶν τῆς πίστεως πολυτιμότερον χρυσίου ... εὑρέθη ... 'that your faith which has much more value than

---

1 Meanings involving *Value* always imply some type of scale or scales and can often be stated in terms of a medium of exchange. In other words, values imply what a person might be willing to give in order to acquire or retain some possession. The value of something, however, may be stated indirectly in terms of time, energy, or other possessions.

In dealing with various meanings involving *Value*, there is a danger in equating values which seem at least superficially to be similar in meaning. For example, one might be tempted to equate the meanings of 'valuable' and 'expensive,' but 'expensive' relates to high price and may in some contexts simply suggest that the object in question costs far more than it is worth.

Another danger in dealing with meanings of *Value* is to assume that nominal and adjectival forms are essentially equivalent in meaning, but this is by no means always the case. For example, to state that 'the table is valuable' means that on a scale of worth the table in question is relatively high, that is to say, considerably greater than the average for other objects of the same class which could be placed on such a scale. On the other hand, the expression 'the value of the table' does not necessarily imply that the table in question is valuable. In fact, the table in question may not have any great worth, so that in the nominal form one is only talking about a scale and is not implying a particular location on a scale.

2 For Subdomain A *Valuable, Lacking in Value* there are often several implied scales, and one might define these as essentially 'general well-being,' involving possibly prosperity, happiness, and social acceptance.

gold, when tested, . . . may be found . . .' (literally 'that the testing of your faith . . . may be found . . .') 1 Pe 1.7.

πολυτελής: τοῦ πραέως καὶ ἡσυχίου πνεύματος, ὅ ἐστιν ἐνώπιον τοῦ θεοῦ πολυτελές 'of a gentle and quiet spirit which is of great value in God's sight' 1 Pe 3.4; ἀλάβαστρον μύρου νάρδου πιστικῆς πολυτελοῦς 'an alabaster jar of very expensive perfume made of pure nard' Mk 14.3.

65.4 ὑπερέχω[a]: to be of surpassing or exceptional value – 'to be exceptionally valuable, to surpass in value, to be better.' ἡγοῦμαι πάντα ζημίαν εἶναι διὰ τὸ ὑπερέχον τῆς γνώσεως Χριστοῦ Ἰησοῦ τοῦ κυρίου μου 'I consider everything to be loss for the sake of that which is of surpassing value, namely, the knowledge of Christ Jesus my Lord' Php 3.8; ἀλλὰ τῇ ταπεινοφροσύνῃ ἀλλήλους ἡγούμενοι ὑπερέχοντας ἑαυτῶν 'but in humility considering others as better than yourselves' Php 2.3.

65.5 δοξάζομαι: to be of exceptional value, with the implication of being particularly praiseworthy – 'to be wonderful, to be glorious.' ἀγαλλιᾶσθε χαρᾷ ἀνεκλαλήτῳ καὶ δεδοξασμένῃ 'rejoice with glorious joy which cannot be put into words' or 'rejoice with unspeakable and glorious joy' 1 Pe 1.8.

65.6 διαφέρω[d]: to be of considerable value, in view of having certain distinctive characteristics – 'to be valuable, to have worth.' οὐχ ὑμεῖς μᾶλλον διαφέρετε αὐτῶν; 'are you not much more valuable than these (birds)?' Mt 6.26; εἰς τὸ δοκιμάζειν ὑμᾶς τὰ διαφέροντα 'so that you will be able to choose those things that are more valuable' Php 1.10.

65.7 πιότης[b], ητος f: (a figurative extension of meaning of πιότης[a] 'fatness,' 3.59) a rich, valuable substance – 'richness, value.' συγκοινωνὸς τῆς ῥίζης τῆς πιότητος τῆς ἐλαίας 'sharing in the valuable root of the olive' or 'sharing in the rich tradition of Judaism' Ro 11.17.[3] For

another interpretation of πιότης in Ro 11.17, see 3.59.

65.8 σιτευτός[b], ή, όν: pertaining to being valuable or prized on the basis of its being well fed and fat (occurring in reference to a calf) – 'valuable, prize.' ἔθυσεν ὁ πατήρ σου τὸν μόσχον τὸν σιτευτόν 'your father slaughtered the prize calf' Lk 15.27. For another interpretation of σιτευτός in Lk 15.27, see 44.2.

65.9 ὑψηλός[c], ή, όν: pertaining to being regarded as of particular value, implying evident comparison with other items – 'very valuable, of exceptional value.' ὅτι τὸ ἐν ἀνθρώποις ὑψηλὸν βδέλυγμα ἐνώπιον τοῦ θεοῦ 'for that which is considered by people as being of great value is abhorrent in God's sight' Lk 16.15. For another interpretation of ὑψηλός in Lk 16.15, see 88.208.

65.10 θησαυρός[c], οῦ m: that which is of exceptional value and kept safe – 'treasure, wealth, riches.' καὶ ἕξεις θησαυρὸν ἐν οὐρανοῖς 'and you will have riches in heaven' Mt 19.21.

65.11 θησαυρίζω[a] (derivative of θησαυρός[c] 'treasure,' 65.10); ἀποθησαυρίζω: to keep safe that which is of great value – 'to treasure up, to keep safe.'
θησαυρίζω[a]: θησαυρίζετε δὲ ὑμῖν θησαυροὺς ἐν οὐρανῷ 'treasure up for yourselves riches in heaven' Mt 6.20.
ἀποθησαυρίζω: ἀποθησαυρίζοντας ἑαυτοῖς θεμέλιον καλὸν εἰς τὸ μέλλον 'treasuring up for yourselves a good foundation for the future' 1 Tm 6.19. There are certain problems involved in the combination of ἀποθησαυρίζοντας and θεμέλιον, for this would constitute a type of mixed metaphor. In some languages, therefore, it may be useful to speak of θεμέλιον in 1 Tm 6.19 as 'a help' or even as 'something valuable.'

65.12 δοκιμή[c], ῆς f: the proven or evident worth of someone or something – 'value,

3 It is difficult to determine whether the expression συγκοινωνὸς τῆς ῥίζης τῆς πιότητος τῆς ἐλαίας in Ro 11.17 should be interpreted merely as an instance of an extended figurative use of related terms, or whether πιότης should be understood in a metaphorical sense of 'value'

or 'wealth,' which it had already acquired in secular literature. If πιότης is to be understood in a figurative sense, then one is likewise justified in regarding ῥίζα in the figurative sense of 'tradition' and ἐλαία in this context as being a direct reference to Judaism.

worth.' τὴν δὲ δοκιμὴν αὐτοῦ γινώσκετε, ὅτι ὡς πατρὶ τέκνον σὺν ἐμοὶ ἐδούλευσεν εἰς τὸ εὐαγγέλιον 'you know his value in that he has worked with me for the sake of the gospel like a son serving his father' Php 2.22.

65.13 ἀδόκιμος[b], ον: pertaining to having been proven worthless – 'of no value, value-less, worth nothing.' ἐκφέρουσα δὲ ἀκάνθας καὶ τριβόλους ἀδόκιμος καὶ κατάρας ἐγγύς 'if it grows thorns and weeds, it is worth nothing and close to being cursed' He 6.8.

65.14 ἀπώλεια[b], ας f: an action demonstrating complete disregard for the value of something – 'waste, ruin.' εἰς τί ἡ ἀπώλεια αὕτη τοῦ μύρου γέγονεν; 'what was the purpose for wasting the perfume?' Mk 14.4. In the context of Mk 14.4 the understanding of ἀπώλεια in the literal sense of 'destruction' (see 20.31) does not seem to be adequate. The following verse concerning the three hundred denarii would seem to indicate that it was disregard for the value of something rather than destroying the perfume. In fact, the use of the perfume would not have been a matter of destroying. Accordingly, an equivalent of 'waste' seems to be far more satisfactory. In some languages the equivalent of this question in Mk 14.4 is 'why did she not think about the value of the perfume?'

65.15 κοινός[c], ή, όν: pertaining to being of little value, in view of being ordinary and common – 'of little value, relatively worthless.' τὸ αἷμα τῆς διαθήκης κοινὸν ἡγησάμενος ἐν ᾧ ἡγιάσθη 'who treats the blood of the covenant which made him pure as being of little value' He 10.29.

65.16 πτωχός[c], ή, όν: pertaining to being of inadequate or insufficient value – 'of little or no value, relatively worthless.' πῶς ἐπιστρέφετε πάλιν ἐπὶ τὰ ἀσθενῆ καὶ πτωχὰ στοιχεῖα 'how do you want to turn back to those weak and worthless ruling spirits' Ga 4.9. It is possible that πτωχός in Ga 4.9 refers to the contrast with that which is beneficial or useful, in which case the meaning of πτωχός in this context would be classified in Subdomain D *Useful, Useless* (65.30-65.39).

B Worthy, Not Worthy[4] (65.17-65.19)

65.17 ἄξιος[a], α, ον; ἀξίως[a]: pertaining to having a relatively high degree of comparable merit or worth – 'worthy, comparable, of comparable value, worthily.'

ἄξιος[a]: λογίζομαι γὰρ ὅτι οὐκ ἄξια τὰ παθήματα τοῦ νῦν καιροῦ πρὸς τὴν μέλλουσαν δόξαν ἀποκαλυφθῆναι εἰς ἡμᾶς 'for I consider that the sufferings of this era (or 'this world') are not worthy (or 'are not of comparable value') to be compared with the future glory to be revealed to us' Ro 8.18; μηδὲν δὲ ἄξιον θανάτου 'and nothing worthy of death' Ac 23.29.

ἀξίως[a]: περιπατῆσαι ἀξίως τοῦ κυρίου 'live in a manner worthy of the Lord' or '. . . worthy of your relationship to the Lord' Col 1.10.

65.18 ἀξιόω[a]; καταξιόω: to consider something of a comparable merit or worth – 'to regard as worthy of, to consider as meriting, to regard as being valuable for.'[5]

ἀξιόω[a]: οἱ καλῶς προεστῶτες πρεσβύτεροι διπλῆς τιμῆς ἀξιούσθωσαν 'the elders who do good work as leaders should be considered worthy of double pay' 1 Tm 5.17; διὸ οὐδὲ ἐμαυτὸν ἠξίωσα πρὸς σὲ ἐλθεῖν 'and accordingly I do not regard myself as worthy of coming to you' Lk 7.7. It is possible that in Lk 7.7 the focus is upon social status, and in many languages the equivalent would be 'I do not think of myself as being important enough to

---

4 Subdomain B *Worthy, Not Worthy* must not be confused with the meaning of 'worth,' since 'worthy' or 'not worthy' refers to a correspondence to some position on a scale and thus suggests a comparable value, whether positive or negative. To say that a person is 'worthy of his pay' suggests that his activities or characteristics correspond to a scalar point which deserves remuneration. In a negative context one may also speak of a person being 'worthy of death,' that is to say, the behavior is judged as corresponding to the penalty of death. In this subdomain there is often the implication of an obligation, so that terms meaning 'worthy' or 'not worthy' refer indirectly to what should or should not happen. In this respect there is an evident overlapping in meaning with Domain 71 *Mode*.

5 ἀξιόω[a] and καταξιόω are semantically complex in that they involve an intellectual activity as well as an abstract of merit or worth. Accordingly, these meanings may be justifiably classified under Domain 30 *Think*, Subdomain G *To Distinguish, To Evaluate, To Judge*. These meanings are typical instances of semantic overlapping.

come to you.' In some languages the idea of 'not being important enough' may be rendered figuratively as 'being too small a person.'

καταξιόω: ἐπορεύοντο χαίροντες ἀπὸ προσώπου τοῦ συνεδρίου ὅτι κατηξιώθησαν ὑπὲρ τοῦ ὀνόματος ἀτιμασθῆναι 'they left the Council full of joy that God had considered them (literally '. . . that they were considered') worthy to suffer disgrace for the name (of Jesus)' Ac 5.41.

65.19 ἀνάξιος, ον; ἀναξίως[a]: pertaining to not corresponding to a comparable merit or worth – 'not being worthy, not meriting, unworthily.'

ἀνάξιος: εἰ ἐν ὑμῖν κρίνεται ὁ κόσμος, ἀνάξιοί ἐστε κριτηρίων ἐλαχίστων; 'if you are to judge the world, are you not worthy to judge small matters?' 1 Cor 6.2.

ἀναξίως[a]: ὃς ἂν ἐσθίῃ τὸν ἄρτον ἢ πίνῃ τὸ ποτήριον τοῦ κυρίου ἀναξίως 'anyone who eats the Lord's bread and drinks from his cup without being worthy' 1 Cor 11.27. For another interpretation of ἀναξίως in 1 Cor 11.27, see 66.7.

C Good, Bad[6] (65.20-65.29)

65.20 ἀγαθός[b], ή, όν: pertaining to having the proper characteristics or performing the expected function in a fully satisfactory way – 'good, nice, pleasant.' μνήσθητι ὅτι ἀπέλαβες τὰ ἀγαθά σου ἐν τῇ ζωῇ σου 'remember that

---

6 Values implied in Subdomain C *Good, Bad* may involve a number of different scales. For example, in speaking of a book as being 'good,' one may refer to its being well written, having an interesting content, or being relaxing and entertaining. Similarly, in speaking of food as 'good,' one may refer either to its nutritious content or to its being tasty. The particular scales depend largely upon the expectations of a particular culture. The upper end of any such scale involves a positive attitude toward presumably desirable features and the lower end of the scale would imply a contrary evaluation. It would be wrong to conclude that anything which could be legitimately translated as 'good' in some context would automatically fit into this subdomain. For example, in 1 Cor 14.12 it would be possible to render πρὸς τὴν οἰκοδομὴν τῆς ἐκκλησίας ζητεῖτε as 'seek what is for the good of the church,' but οἰκοδομή clearly indicates a particular kind of 'good' in that the result js building up and strengthening the church.

you received good things during your life' Lk 16.25; πᾶν δένδρον ἀγαθὸν καρποὺς καλοὺς ποιεῖ 'every good tree produces fine fruit' Mt 7.17; ἔπεσεν εἰς τὴν γῆν τὴν ἀγαθήν 'it fell into good soil' or '. . . fertile soil' Lk 8.8.

65.21 κρείττων[a], ον or κρείσσων: pertaining to being superior to something else in characteristics or function – 'better, superior.' ἐπεισαγωγὴ δὲ κρείττονος ἐλπίδος 'the provision of a better hope' He 7.19; ὁ μὴ γαμίζων κρεῖσσον ποιήσει 'he who does not marry will do better' 1 Cor 7.38.

65.22 καλός[b], ή, όν: pertaining to having acceptable characteristics or functioning in an agreeable manner, often with the focus on outward form or appearance – 'good, fine.' πᾶν δένδρον ἀγαθὸν καρποὺς καλοὺς ποιεῖ 'every good tree produces fine fruit' Mt 7.17.

65.23 καλῶς[b]; εὖ[b]; εὖγε; βέλτιον: pertaining to events which measure up to their intended purpose – 'fine, well, good, excellent, well done.' In the following contexts, καλῶς, εὖ, and εὖγε occur in highly elliptical constructions.

καλῶς[b]: καλῶς, διδάσκαλε, ἐπ' ἀληθείας εἶπες 'well done, Teacher. It is true as you say' Mk 12.32.

εὖ[b]: εὖ, δοῦλε ἀγαθὲ καὶ πιστέ 'well done, good and faithful servant' Mt 25.21.

εὖγε: εὖγε, ἀγαθὲ δοῦλε 'fine, you are a good servant' Lk 19.17.

βέλτιον: βέλτιον σὺ γινώσκεις 'you know very well' 2 Tm 1.18.

65.24 πρῶτος[d], η, ον: pertaining to being superior in value to all other items of the same class – 'best.' ταχὺ ἐξενέγκατε στολὴν τὴν πρώτην 'quickly bring the best robe' Lk 15.22.

65.25 χρηστός[a], ή, όν: pertaining to being superior for a particular purpose or use – 'fine, better.' οὐδεὶς πιὼν παλαιὸν θέλει νέον· λέγει γάρ, Ὁ παλαιὸς χρηστός ἐστιν 'no one wants new (wine) after drinking old (wine), for he says, Old (wine) is better' Lk 5.39. In a number of languages it may be necessary to translate Lk 5.39 as 'the old wine tastes better' or 'the old wine is fine to the taste' or, in an idiomatic expression, 'the old wine makes the tongue dance.'

65.26 κακός[b], **ή, όν**: pertaining to being harsh and difficult – 'bad, harsh, difficult.' καὶ Λάζαρος ὁμοίως τὰ κακά 'and Lazarus likewise (experienced) the bad things' Lk 16.25. In a number of languages one cannot speak of 'experiencing bad things'; rather, one must say in Lk 16.25 'suffered a great deal' or 'always lived with difficulty' or 'always had troubles.'

65.27 πονηρός[b], **ά, όν**: pertaining to possessing a serious fault and consequently being worthless – 'bad, worthless.' οὐ δύναται δένδρον ἀγαθὸν καρποὺς πονηρούς 'a good tree cannot bear bad fruit' Mt 7.18. In a number of languages one must speak of 'bad fruit' in the context of Mt 7.18 as 'fruit which does not taste good.' It is often wrong to use an expression such as 'rotten fruit,' since a good tree may produce fruit which rots as a result of being overly ripe.

65.28 σαπρός[a], **ά, όν**: pertaining to being of poor or bad quality and hence of little or no value (particularly in reference to plants, either in the sense of seriously diseased or of seedling stock, that is, not budded or grafted) – 'bad, diseased' and possibly 'seedling.' οὐδὲ δένδρον σαπρὸν καρποὺς καλοὺς ποιεῖν 'a bad tree cannot bear good fruit' Mt 7.18.

Some scholars have suggested that σαπρός in Mt 7.18 really refers to a seedling, that is to say, a tree which has grown up completely from seed rather than being budded or grafted. Seedling trees often produce tasteless or even bitter fruit. By its very nature, such a tree cannot produce good fruit and is, therefore, considered to be of no value.

65.29 ἥσσων[b], **ον; χείρων**[b], **ον**: pertaining to being less satisfactory than something else – 'worse.'
ἥσσων[b]: οὐκ ἐπαινῶ ὅτι οὐκ εἰς τὸ κρεῖσσον ἀλλὰ εἰς τὸ ἧσσον συνέρχεσθε 'I do not praise you since your (church) meetings are not for the better but for the worse' 1 Cor 11.17.
χείρων[b]: γίνεται τὰ ἔσχατα τοῦ ἀνθρώπου ἐκείνου χείρονα τῶν πρώτων 'the last state of that man is worse than the first' Lk 11.26.

D Useful, Useless[7] (65.30-65.39)

65.30 χρήσιμος, η, ον: pertaining to having a valid use or function – 'useful, use.' μὴ λογομαχεῖν, ἐπ' οὐδὲν χρήσιμον 'do not fight over words; it is of no use' 2 Tm 2.14. In some languages, χρήσιμος in 2 Tm 2.14 may be expressed as 'helpful.' For example, 'it is of no use' may then be rendered as 'it isn't helpful' or 'it does not help.'

65.31 εὔχρηστος, ον: pertaining to being of positive or good use – 'useful, valuable.' τόν ποτέ σοι ἄχρηστον νυνὶ δὲ καὶ σοὶ καὶ ἐμοὶ εὔχρηστον 'at one time he was of no use to you, but now he is useful both to you and to me' Phm 11.

65.32 εὔθετος[b], **ον**: pertaining to being capable of being put to a useful purpose – 'useful, of value.' οὔτε εἰς γῆν οὔτε εἰς κοπρίαν εὔθετόν ἐστιν 'it is of no use to the soil, not even to the dung heap' Lk 14.35.

65.33 ἄχρεῖος[a], **ον; ἄχρηστος, ον**: pertaining to not being useful – 'useless, not useful, worthless.'
ἄχρεῖος[a]: καὶ τὸν ἀχρεῖον δοῦλον ἐκβάλετε εἰς τὸ σκότος τὸ ἐξώτερον 'and throw this useless servant into the outer darkness' Mt 25.30.
ἄχρηστος: τόν ποτέ σοι ἄχρηστον νυνὶ δὲ καὶ σοὶ καὶ ἐμοὶ εὔχρηστον 'at one time he was of no use to you, but now he is useful both to you and to me' Phm 11. In a number of languages usefulness or lack of usefulness can only be expressed in terms of a verb meaning 'to help,' so that in Phm 11 it may be necessary to translate 'at one time he did not help you at all and now he can help both you and me.'

65.34 ἄκαρπος[b], **ον**: pertaining to being useless, in the sense of being unproductive – 'useless, unproductive.' μὴ συγκοινωνεῖτε τοῖς ἔργοις τοῖς ἀκάρποις τοῦ σκότους 'have nothing

---

7 Subdomain D *Useful, Useless* refers essentially to objects or events which are beneficial. To some extent there is an overlapping with the following Subdomain E *Advantageous, Not Advantageous,* but this latter domain refers essentially to that which is useful under special circumstances and often implies a shift in a scale of benefit or usefulness.

to do with people who do unproductive things that belong to the darkness' Eph 5.11.

65.35 ἀνεύθετος, ον: pertaining to something which should not or cannot be used – 'unusable.' ἀνευθέτου δὲ τοῦ λιμένος ὑπάρχοντος πρὸς παραχειμασίαν 'and because the harbor could not be used for wintering' or '. . . for staying there during the winter' Ac 27.12.

65.36 ἀργός^d, ή, όν: pertaining to being useless, in the sense of accomplishing nothing – 'useless.' ὅτι ἡ πίστις χωρὶς τῶν ἔργων ἀργή ἐστιν 'that faith apart from works is useless' Jas 2.20.

65.37 μάταιος, α, ον; ματαιότης, ητος f: pertaining to being useless on the basis of being futile and lacking in content – 'useless, futile, empty, futility.'
μάταιος: μὴ χαλιναγωγῶν γλῶσσαν αὐτοῦ . . . τούτου μάταιος ἡ θρησκεία 'if he does not control his tongue . . . his religion is futile' Jas 1.26.
ματαιότης: μηκέτι ὑμᾶς περιπατεῖν καθὼς καὶ τὰ ἔθνη περιπατεῖ ἐν ματαιότητι τοῦ νοὸς αὐτῶν 'do not live any longer like the heathen whose thoughts are useless' Eph 4.17.

65.38 ματαιόομαι: to become useless and hence worthless – 'to become futile, to become worthless, to become nonsense.' ἐματαιώθησαν ἐν τοῖς διαλογισμοῖς αὐτῶν 'their thoughts became worthless' or 'their reasoning became nonsense' (literally, 'they became worthless in their reasoning') Ro 1.21.

65.39 νεκρός^b, ά, όν: pertaining to being utterly useless, with the implication of total lack of purport – 'useless, futile, vain.' καθαριεῖ τὴν συνείδησιν ἡμῶν ἀπὸ νεκρῶν ἔργων 'will cleanse our conscience from useless rituals' He 9.14.

E Advantageous, Not Advantageous[8] (65.40-65.51)

65.40 ὄφελος, ους n; ὠφέλιμος, ον: pertaining to a benefit to be derived from some object, event, or state – 'advantage, benefit, beneficial.'
ὄφελος: τί τὸ ὄφελος, ἀδελφοί μου, ἐὰν πίστιν λέγῃ τις ἔχειν, ἔργα δὲ μὴ ἔχῃ; 'what advantage is it, my fellow believers, for a person to say, I have faith, if his actions do not prove it?' Jas 2.14.
ὠφέλιμος: ἡ γὰρ σωματικὴ γυμνασία πρὸς ὀλίγον ἐστὶν ὠφέλιμος 'physical exercise is beneficial to a small extent' 1 Tm 4.8.
  In a number of languages the equivalent of 'benefit' or 'beneficial' is often 'that which helps.' Accordingly, in 1 Tm 4.8 one may render ἡ γὰρ σωματικὴ γυμνασία πρὸς ὀλίγον ἐστὶν ὠφέλιμος as 'physical exercise helps to a small extent' or 'if one exercises one's body, that helps a little.'

65.41 ὠφέλεια, ας f: the state of having acquired an advantage or benefit – 'advantage, benefit.' τίς ἡ ὠφέλεια τῆς περιτομῆς; 'what is the advantage of being circumcised?' Ro 3.1.

65.42 ἐξαγοράζομαι τὸν καιρόν^a: (an idiom, literally 'to buy out the time') to take full advantage of any opportunity – 'to make good use of every opportunity, to take advantage of every chance.' ἐν σοφίᾳ περιπατεῖτε πρὸς τοὺς ἔξω, τὸν καιρὸν ἐξαγοραζόμενοι 'be wise in the way you act toward nonbelievers, taking advantage of every opportunity' Col 4.5. The implication of this statement in Col 4.5 is taking advantage of every opportunity to manifest the reality of one's faith.

65.43 καλός^c, ή, όν: pertaining to providing some special or superior benefit – 'advantageous, better.' καλόν σοί ἐστιν εἰσελθεῖν εἰς τὴν ζωὴν κυλλὸν ἢ χωλόν, ἢ δύο χεῖρας ἢ δύο πόδας ἔχοντα βληθῆναι εἰς τὸ πῦρ τὸ αἰώνιον 'it is to your advantage to enter life without a hand or foot rather than to keep both hands and feet and be thrown into the eternal fire' Mt 18.8.

65.44 λυσιτελεῖ; συμφέρω^b: to be of an advantage to someone – 'to be advantageous, to be better off, to be to someone's advantage.' λυσιτελεῖ: λυσιτελεῖ αὐτῷ εἰ λίθος μυλικὸς

---

[8] Subdomain E *Advantageous, Not Advantageous,* as already indicated in footnote 7, normally implies particular circumstances and a shift in one direction or another in a scale of value.

περίκειται περὶ τὸν τράχηλον αὐτοῦ καὶ ἔρριπται εἰς τὴν θάλασσαν 'it would be to his advantage if a millstone were tied around his neck and he were thrown into the sea' or 'he would be better off if a millstone were tied around his neck . . .' Lk 17.2.

συμφέρω[b]: οὐδὲ λογίζεσθε ὅτι συμφέρει ὑμῖν ἵνα εἷς ἄνθρωπος ἀποθάνῃ ὑπὲρ τοῦ λαοῦ 'you don't realize that it is to your advantage to have one man die for the people' Jn 11.50; οὐδὲν ὑπεστειλάμην τῶν συμφερόντων 'I did not hold back anything that would be advantageous (to you)' Ac 20.20.

In a number of languages the idea of 'advantage' implies some comparison, either a benefit which is greater than someone else has or a benefit which makes one's later state better off than the previous state. For example, in the case of Jn 11.50 one may translate 'don't you realize that if one man dies for the people, then you are much better off.'

65.45 σύμφορον, ου *n*: that which constitutes an advantage – 'advantage, benefit.' τοῦτο δὲ πρὸς τὸ ὑμῶν αὐτῶν σύμφορον λέγω 'I am saying this for the purpose of its being a benefit to you' 1 Cor 7.35.

65.46 περισσός[a], ή, όν: pertaining to causing a decided or distinct advantage – 'special advantage, of greater benefit.' τί οὖν τὸ περισσὸν τοῦ Ἰουδαίου; 'what special advantage do the Jews have?' Ro 3.1.

65.47 περισσεύω[f]; προέχομαι; προκατέχομαι: to experience superior benefit or advantage, implying some type of comparison – 'to have a greater benefit, to experience a superior advantage.'

περισσεύω[f]: οὔτε ἐὰν φάγωμεν περισσεύομεν 'if we do eat, we will have no special advantage' 1 Cor 8.8.

προέχομαι, προκατέχομαι: τί οὖν; προεχόμεθα; 'well then, do we have an advantage superior (to that of others)?' Ro 3.9. See Ro 3.9 (apparatus) for προκατέχομαι.

In indicating 'a superior advantage' it may be necessary to be quite specific about the basis for the comparison. For example, in 1 Cor 8.8 it may be necessary to translate as 'if we do eat, we will be no better off than if we

did not eat,' and in Ro 3.9 one may translate 'what then; are we decidedly better off than the others are?'

65.48 ἀντιλαμβάνομαι[c]: to experience a benefit from someone – 'to enjoy a benefit, to be benefited.' ὅτι πιστοί εἰσιν καὶ ἀγαπητοὶ οἱ τῆς εὐεργεσίας ἀντιλαμβανόμενοι 'because those who are benefited by their good work are believers and persons whom they love' 1 Tm 6.2. For another interpretation of ἀντιλαμβάνομαι in 1 Tm 6.2, see 25.79.

65.49 ἀλυσιτελής, ές: pertaining to being of no advantage – 'of no advantage, without special benefit.' ἀλυσιτελὲς γὰρ ὑμῖν τοῦτο 'and that would not be of any advantage to you' or 'and that would not be of any special benefit to you' He 13.17.

65.50 ἀνωφελής[a], ές: pertaining to not offering any special benefit – 'without advantage, of no special benefit.' ἀθέτησις μὲν γὰρ γίνεται προαγούσης ἐντολῆς διὰ τὸ αὐτῆς ἀσθενὲς καὶ ἀνωφελές 'the old rule, then, is set aside, because it was weak and of no special benefit' He 7.18.

65.51 ὑστερέω[b]: to be lacking in any special benefit or advantage – 'to lack benefits, to lack an advantage.' οὔτε ἐὰν μὴ φάγωμεν ὑστερούμεθα 'if we do not eat, we shall not be lacking in any advantage' 1 Cor 8.8.

F Important, Unimportant[9] (65.52-65.57)

65.52 πρῶτος[e], η, ον: pertaining to exceeding everything else in importance – 'most important.' ποία ἐστὶν ἐντολὴ πρώτη πάντων; 'what is the most important commandment of all?' Mk 12.28. In some languages 'most important' is expressed by a negative comparison, for example, 'the commandment that nothing else surpasses' or 'the commandment than which nothing else is greater' or '. . . of more value.'

9 The meanings in Subdomain F *Important, Unimportant* focus upon the value involved and not the status. Compare Domain 87 *Status*.

65.53 μέγιστος, η, ον: pertaining to being extremely important – 'very important, extremely important.' τὰ τίμια καὶ μέγιστα ἡμῖν ἐπαγγέλματα δεδώρηται 'valuable and very important promises have been given to us' 2 Pe 1.4.

65.54 πρό^c: marker of primary importance – 'more important than, of greatest importance, above.' πρὸ πάντων δέ, ἀδελφοί μου, μὴ ὀμνύετε 'more important than all else, my fellow believers, do not use an oath' Jas 5.12; πρὸ πάντων τὴν εἰς ἑαυτοὺς ἀγάπην ἐκτενῆ ἔχοντες 'more important than everything else, earnestly love one another' 1 Pe 4.8.

65.55 βαρύς^c, εῖα, ύ: pertaining to being important in view of substantive character – 'important, significant.' καὶ ἀφήκατε τὰ βαρύτερα τοῦ νόμου 'and you set aside the more important things in the Law' Mt 23.23.

65.56 ἐν βάρει εἰμί: (an idiom, literally 'to be in weight,' see 86.1) to insist on one's importance or worth – 'to insist on one's worth, to claim one's importance.' δυνάμενοι ἐν βάρει εἶναι 'we could have insisted on our importance' 1 Th 2.7. It is possible to interpret ἐν βάρει εἰμί as denoting a person's status, and accordingly, one could classify this idiom in Domain 87 *Status*, but it is also possible to interpret this expression in 1 Th 2.7 as the demands which could be placed upon persons, and therefore one could translate as 'we could have made demands on you.' Such a translation would imply the relationship of authority, and the meaning could be classified in Domain 37 *Control, Rule*.

65.57 ἐλάχιστος^b, η, ον: pertaining to being of the least importance – 'of least importance, of very little importance.' ὃς ἐὰν οὖν λύσῃ μίαν τῶν ἐντολῶν τούτων τῶν ἐλαχίστων 'whoever disobeys one of these least commandments' or '. . . one of these least important commandments' Mt 5.19.

66 Proper, Improper[1]

66.1 πρέπει; καθήκει; ἀνήκει: to be fitting or right, with the implication of possible moral judgment involved – 'to be fitting, to be right.'
πρέπει: πλεονεξία μηδὲ ὀνομαζέσθω ἐν ὑμῖν, καθὼς πρέπει 'it is not fitting that greed should even be mentioned among you' Eph 5.3.
καθήκει: οὐ γὰρ καθῆκεν αὐτὸν ζῆν 'it is not right that this man should live' Ac 22.22.
ἀνήκει: καὶ αἰσχρότης καὶ μωρολογία ἢ εὐτραπελία, ἃ οὐκ ἀνῆκεν 'nor is it fitting for you to use obscene, foolish, or dirty words' Eph 5.4.

66.2 καλός^d, ή, όν: pertaining to being fitting and at the same time probably good – 'fitting, good.' Πέτρος λέγει τῷ Ἰησοῦ, Ῥαββί, καλόν ἐστιν ἡμᾶς ὧδε εἶναι 'Peter said to Jesus, Teacher, it is good that we are here' Mk 9.5.

66.3 εὔθετος^a, ον: pertaining to being fitting or appropriate, with the probable implication of usable – 'fit, suitable, usable.' οὐδεὶς ἐπιβαλὼν τὴν χεῖρα ἐπ' ἄροτρον καὶ βλέπων εἰς τὰ ὀπίσω εὔθετός ἐστιν τῇ βασιλείᾳ τοῦ θεοῦ 'no one who puts his hand to the plow and looks back is fit for the kingdom of God' Lk 9.62.

66.4 εὐσχημόνως^b: pertaining to being proper, with the implication of pleasing – 'proper.' πάντα δὲ εὐσχημόνως καὶ κατὰ τάξιν γινέσθω 'everything must be done in a proper and orderly way' 1 Cor 14.40.

66.5 δίκαιος^c, α, ον: pertaining to being proper or right in the sense of being fully justified – 'proper, right.' ἐστιν δίκαιον ἐμοὶ τοῦτο φρονεῖν ὑπὲρ πάντων ὑμῶν 'it is proper for me to feel this way about all of you' Php 1.7.

---

1 Domain 66 *Proper, Improper* implies a norm or standard by which events or circumstances are judged. Generally, such a standard or set of standards is implicit within any one culture.

66.6 ἄξιος^b, α, ον; ἀξίως^b: pertaining to being fitting or proper in corresponding to what should be expected – 'proper, properly, fitting, worthy of, correspond to.'

ἄξιος^b: ἄξια τῆς μετανοίας ἔργα πράσσοντας 'doing those things which are appropriate for repentance' or '. . . which correspond to one's having repented' Ac 26.20.

ἀξίως^b: ἀξίως περιπατῆσαι τῆς κλήσεως ἧς ἐκλήθητε 'live a life that corresponds to the standard (God) set when he called you' Eph 4.1.

66.7 ἀναξίως^b: pertaining to being proper in not corresponding to what should happen – 'improperly, in an improper manner.' ὃς ἂν ἐσθίῃ τὸν ἄρτον ἢ πίνῃ τὸ ποτήριον τοῦ κυρίου ἀναξίως 'anyone who eats the Lord's bread and drinks from his cup in an improper manner' 1 Cor 11.27. For another interpretation of ἀναξίως in 1 Cor 11.27, see 65.19.

66.8 ἀρεστός^b, ή, όν: pertaining to being proper or right, with the implication of desirable – 'proper, right.' οὐκ ἀρεστόν ἐστιν ἡμᾶς καταλείψαντας τὸν λόγον τοῦ θεοῦ 'it is not right for us to neglect the preaching of God's word' Ac 6.2.

66.9 δεκτός^c, ή, όν: pertaining to being appropriate or fitting, with the implication of being favorable – 'appropriate, proper.' καιρῷ δεκτῷ ἐπήκουσά σου 'at the appropriate time I heard you' 2 Cor 6.2.

66.10 κόσμιος^b, ον: pertaining to being proper or suitable in terms of being attractive – 'proper, suitable.' γυναῖκας ἐν καταστολῇ κοσμίῳ 'women in proper clothing' 1 Tm 2.9. For another interpretation of κόσμιος in 1 Tm 2.9, see 88.48.

66.11 πλείων^c, πλεῖον or πλέον: pertaining to being more appropriate or fitting – 'more appropriate, better, more acceptable.' πίστει πλείονα θυσίαν Ἄβελ παρὰ Κάϊν προσήνεγκεν τῷ θεῷ 'by faith Abel offered to God a sacrifice which was more fitting than Cain's' He 11.4.

66.12 ἀναίδεια, ας f: a lack of sensitivity to what is proper – 'insolence, audacity, impudence, shamelessness.' διά γε τὴν ἀναίδειαν αὐτοῦ ἐγερθεὶς δώσει αὐτῷ ὅσων χρῄζει 'but he will get up and give what he needs because of his insolence (in keeping on asking)' or '. . . because he lacks a sense of what is proper' Lk 11.8.

67 Time¹

Outline of Subdomains

I. Points of Time (67.1-67.77)

A A Point of Time without Reference to Other Points of Time: Time, Occasion, Ever, Often (67.1-67.16)
B A Point of Time with Reference to Other Points of Time: Before, Long Ago, Now, At the Same Time, When, About, After (67.17-67.64)
C A Point of Time with Reference to Duration of Time: Beginning, End (67.65-67.72)
D A Point of Time with Reference to Units of Time: Daybreak, Midday, Midnight, Late (67.73-67.77)

II. Duration of Time (67.78-67.141)

E Duration of Time without Reference to Points or Units of Time: Time, Spend Time, Always, Eternal, Old, Immediately, Young (67.78-67.117)
F Duration of Time with Reference to

---

1 Abstracts of *Time* may be classified in several different ways, but three principal features, namely, points of time, duration, and units of time, seem to be the most significant and diagnostic. There is considerable overlapping and intersection between these categories, as may be noted in the outline of subdomains, but the focal component of meaning in each instance relates specifically to one or another of these primary categories.

Some Point of Time: Until, Delay, Still, From (67.118-67.135)

G Duration of Time with Reference to Some Unit of Time: During, In, While, Throughout (67.136-67.141)

III. Units of Time (67.142-67.208)

H Indefinite Units of Time: Age, Lifetime, Interval, Period (67.142-67.162)

I Definite Units of Time: Year, Month, Week, Day, Hour (67.163-67.200)

J Units of Time with Reference to Other Units or Points of Time: Yesterday, Today, Next Day (67.201-67.208)

I. Points of Time[2] (67.1-67.77)

A A Point of Time without Reference to Other Points of Time: Time, Occasion, Ever, Often (67.1-67.16)

67.1 καιρός[a], οῦ *m*; χρόνος[b], ου *m*; ὥρα[a], ας *f*: points of time consisting of occasions for particular events – 'time, occasion.'

καιρός[a]: καὶ ἐν καιρῷ τοῦ θερισμοῦ ἐρῶ τοῖς θερισταῖς 'and when the time of the harvest comes, I will say to the reapers' Mt 13.30.

χρόνος[b]: καθὼς δὲ ἤγγιζεν ὁ χρόνος τῆς ἐπαγγελίας ἧς ὡμολόγησεν ὁ θεός 'and when the time drew near for God to keep his promise' Ac 7.17.

ὥρα[a]: ἤγγικεν ἡ ὥρα καὶ ὁ υἱὸς τοῦ ἀνθρώπου παραδίδοται 'the time has come for the Son of Man to be handed over' Mt 26.45.[3]

In a number of languages there is no general term for 'time' or 'occasion.' In some contexts it is simply not necessary to have

2 The feature of *Points of Time* should not be understood to mean that the temporal period is to be regarded as instantaneous or of particularly short duration. Temporal events always involve some element of duration, but they may be regarded as consisting essentially of a single point of time.

3 Some terms which designate a unit of time in their so-called literal meanings may also have the meaning of point of time, as in the case of ὥρα, which in Mt 26.45 is essentially an indicator of a point of time, but in 67.148, it is treated as a unit of time. The same may occur in the case of ἡμέρα, which as a unit of time is treated in 67.142, but in the expression 'day of the Lord' it indicates essentially a point of time.

such a term. For example, in rendering Mt 13.30 one may translate 'when the harvest comes, I will say to the reapers' or 'when people begin to harvest, I will say to the reapers.' In other contexts, a term which normally refers to some unit is employed in a generic sense, as in the case of Greek ὥρα which means literally 'hour' but is frequently used as a generic expression for a point of time, as in Mt 8.13. In Ac 7.17 χρόνος may often be rendered by a generic expression such as 'day,' for example, 'when it was almost the day for God to keep his promise.' In the case of Mt 26.45, the nearness of the time may be indicated as 'very soon the Son of Man will be handed over.'

Though it seems quite ordinary in English for one to speak of 'time coming' or '. . . drawing near,' this type of figurative usage is impossible in many languages. The equivalent may be simply 'will soon be' or 'is about to happen.' The expression οὔπω ἥκει ἡ ὥρα μου (literally 'my time has not yet come') in Jn 2.4 denotes that it is not yet the occasion for a particular event (see καιρός in Jn 7.8 and compare Jn 7.10) but that it will soon be. In these contexts the expression may be rendered as 'there is still time' or 'I will soon do it.' In Jn 7.30 and 8.20 (οὔπω ἐληλύθει ἡ ὥρα αὐτοῦ 'his time has not yet come') the reference is to the occasion of his eventual arrest, implying that it will indeed happen.

67.2 προθεσμία, ας *f*: some point of time selected in advance – 'set time, designated time.' ὑπὸ ἐπιτρόπους ἐστὶν καὶ οἰκονόμους ἄχρι τῆς προθεσμίας τοῦ πατρός 'to take care of him and manage his affairs until the time set by his father' Ga 4.2.

67.3 ὡραῖος[b], α, ον: pertaining to a point of time which is particularly appropriate – 'timely, happening at the right time.' ὡς ὡραῖοι οἱ πόδες τῶν εὐαγγελιζομένων τὰ ἀγαθά 'how timely is the coming of messengers who bring good news' Ro 10.15. It is also possible to interpret ὡραῖος in Ro 10.15 as implying something which is fine (see 79.10).

67.4 εὐκαιρέω[a]: to experience an appropriate occasion for some activity – 'to have an appropriate time for, to have an occasion to, to have a chance to.' καὶ οὐδὲ φαγεῖν εὐκαίρουν 'and they didn't have time to eat' Mk 6.31; ἐλεύσεται δὲ ὅταν εὐκαιρήσῃ 'and he will go when he has a chance' or '. . . when it is a favorable occasion' or '. . . when he has an opportunity to do so' 1 Cor 16.12.

67.5 εὐκαιρία, ας *f*: a favorable occasion for some event – 'opportunity, good occasion, favorable time.' ἀπὸ τότε ἐζήτει εὐκαιρίαν ἵνα αὐτὸν παραδῷ 'from then on he sought a favorable opportunity to betray him' Mt 26.16.

67.6 εὔκαιρος, ον; εὐκαίρως: pertaining to being a favorable occasion for some event – 'favorable, good.'
εὔκαιρος: γενομένης ἡμέρας εὐκαίρου ὅτε Ἡρῴδης τοῖς γενεσίοις αὐτοῦ δεῖπνον ἐποίησεν 'a favorable time occurred when Herod gave a banquet in celebration of his birthday' Mk 6.21.
εὐκαίρως: καὶ ἐζήτει πῶς αὐτὸν εὐκαίρως παραδοῖ 'and he sought how he might betray him at an opportune time' Mk 14.11.

67.7 ἀκαιρέομαι: to not have a favorable opportunity to do something – 'to lack an opportunity, to have no chance to.' ἠκαιρεῖσθε δέ 'but you had no opportunity' Php 4.10.

67.8 ἀκαίρως: pertaining to the lack of a favorable opportunity for doing something – 'unfavorable, when the time is not right.' κήρυξον τὸν λόγον, ἐπίστηθι εὐκαίρως ἀκαίρως 'proclaim the message; keep doing so whether the opportunity is favorable or not' 2 Tm 4.2.

67.9 ποτέ[a]; πώποτε; δήποτε: an indefinite point of time or occasion – 'ever, at any time, at some time.'
ποτέ[a]: τίς στρατεύεται ἰδίοις ὀψωνίοις ποτέ; 'who ever paid his own expenses as a soldier in the army?' or 'who has ever served as a soldier at his own expense?' 1 Cor 9.7; ἄγουσιν αὐτὸν πρὸς τοὺς Φαρισαίους τόν ποτε τυφλόν 'they brought to the Pharisees the one who had been blind' Jn 9.13. In Jn 9.13 ποτέ may be rendered as 'had been,' but the meaning is simply indefinite reference to time.
πώποτε: θεὸν οὐδεὶς ἑώρακεν πώποτε 'no one has ever seen God' Jn 1.18.

δήποτε: ὑγιὴς ἐγίνετο οἵῳ δήποτ' οὖν κατείχετο νοσήματι 'he was cured from whatever disease he ever had' Jn 5.4 (apparatus).

67.10 μήποτε[a]; μηδέποτε; οὐδέποτε: an indefinite negated point of time – 'never, not ever, at no time.'
μήποτε[a]: μήποτε ἰσχύει ὅτε ζῇ ὁ διαθέμενος '(a will) never goes into effect as long as the one who made it is alive' He 9.17.
μηδέποτε: πάντοτε μανθάνοντα καὶ μηδέποτε εἰς ἐπίγνωσιν ἀληθείας ἐλθεῖν δυνάμενα 'always trying to learn and yet never able to come to know the truth' 2 Tm 3.7.
οὐδέποτε: οὐδέποτε ἐλάλησεν οὕτως ἄνθρωπος 'nobody has ever talked the way this man does' Jn 7.46.

67.11 πολλά; πολλάκις; πολυμερῶς[b]: a number of related points of time – 'often, many times.'
πολλά: διὰ τί ἡμεῖς καὶ οἱ Φαρισαῖοι νηστεύομεν πολλά, οἱ δὲ μαθηταί σου οὐ νηστεύουσιν; 'why is it that we and the Pharisees fast often, but your disciples do not fast at all?' Mt 9.14.
πολλάκις: ᾔδει δὲ καὶ Ἰούδας . . . τὸν τόπον, ὅτι πολλάκις συνήχθη Ἰησοῦς ἐκεῖ μετὰ τῶν μαθητῶν αὐτοῦ 'Judas knew . . . the place because many times Jesus had met there with his disciples' Jn 18.2.
πολυμερῶς[b]: πολυμερῶς καὶ πολυτρόπως πάλαι ὁ θεὸς λαλήσας τοῖς πατράσιν 'in the past God spoke to our ancestors many times and in many ways' He 1.1. It is also possible to understand πολυμερῶς as meaning 'in many ways' and thus being essentially synonymous to πολυτρόπως[a] (58.29). Some scholars, however, understand πολυμερῶς in the sense of 'fragmentary' (see 63.19). For yet another interpretation of πολυμερῶς in He 1.1, see 89.81.

67.12 πυκνός, ή, όν; πυκνά: pertaining to a number of related points of time occurring with limited intervals – 'often, frequent, so often.'
πυκνός: οἴνῳ ὀλίγῳ χρῶ διὰ τὸν στόμαχον καὶ τὰς πυκνάς σου ἀσθενείας 'take a little wine to help your digestion, since you are sick so often' 1 Tm 5.23.
πυκνά: οἱ μαθηταὶ Ἰωάννου νηστεύουσιν πυκνά

καὶ δεήσεις ποιοῦνται 'the disciples of John fast frequently and offer up prayers' Lk 5.33.

67.13 πυκνότερον: pertaining to a number of related points of time occurring with short intervals and probably somewhat more emphatic than πυκνός, πυκνά (67.12) – 'so often, very often, as often as possible.' διὸ καὶ πυκνότερον αὐτὸν μεταπεμπόμενος ὡμίλει αὐτῷ 'and for this reason he would call for him as often as possible, and talk with him' Ac 24.26. It is possible to understand πυκνότερον in Ac 24.26 as a comparative form of the stem πυκνο-, but it is also possible that any comparative force may have been lost and thus πυκνότερον would not be significantly different in meaning from πυκνά (67.12).

67.14 ποσάκις: a number of related points of time, occurring in interrogative or exclamatory contexts – 'how often, so often.' κύριε, ποσάκις ἁμαρτήσει εἰς ἐμὲ ὁ ἀδελφός μου 'Lord, how often can my brother sin against me' Mt 18.21.

67.15 διὰ παντός[a]: (an idiom, literally 'through all') a number of related points of time, occurring at regular intervals – 'regularly, periodically.' εἰς μὲν τὴν πρώτην σκηνὴν διὰ παντὸς εἰσίασιν οἱ ἱερεῖς τὰς λατρείας ἐπιτελοῦντες 'the priests go into the outer tent regularly to perform their duties' He 9.6.

67.16 πρός[1]: a marker of a point of time, probably implying proximity – 'at.' πᾶσα δὲ παιδεία πρὸς μὲν τὸ παρὸν οὐ δοκεῖ χαρᾶς εἶναι ἀλλὰ λύπης 'every punishment at the time does not seem to be a matter of happiness but of grief' He 12.11.

B   A Point of Time with Reference to Other Points of Time: Before, Long Ago, Now, At the Same Time, When, About, After (67.17-67.64)

67.17 πρό[b]; πρίν or πρὶν ἤ; ἄχρι οὗ[a]: a point of time prior to another point of time – 'before, previous.'

πρό[b]: οἶδεν γὰρ ὁ πατὴρ ὑμῶν ὧν χρείαν ἔχετε πρὸ τοῦ ὑμᾶς αἰτῆσαι αὐτόν 'your Father knows what you need before you ask him' Mt 6.8.

πρίν or πρὶν ἤ: ἐν ταύτῃ τῇ νυκτὶ πρὶν ἀλέκτορα φωνῆσαι τρὶς ἀπαρνήσῃ με 'before the rooster crows tonight, you will say three times that you do not know me' Mt 26.34; σὺ σήμερον ταύτῃ τῇ νυκτὶ πρὶν ἢ δὶς ἀλέκτορα φωνῆσαι τρίς με ἀπαρνήσῃ 'before the rooster crows twice tonight, you will say three times that you do not know me' Mk 14.30.

ἄχρι οὗ[a]: ἄχρι δὲ οὗ ἡμέρα ἤμελλεν γίνεσθαι 'just before it began to dawn' Ac 27.33.

67.18 πρῶτος[b], η, ον; πρῶτον; πρότερος[a], α, ον; πρότερον: pertaining to a point of time earlier in a sequence – 'before, former, formerly.'[4]

πρῶτος[b]: ἔσται ἡ ἐσχάτη πλάνη χείρων τῆς πρώτης 'this last lie would be even worse than the former one' Mt 27.64.

πρῶτον: γινώσκετε ὅτι ἐμὲ πρῶτον ὑμῶν μεμίσηκεν 'remember that (the world) hated me before it hated you' Jn 15.18.

πρότερος[a]: ὑμᾶς κατὰ τὴν προτέραν ἀναστροφήν 'you live as (you did) formerly' Eph 4.22.

πρότερον: μὴ συσχηματιζόμενοι ταῖς πρότερον . . . ἐπιθυμίαις 'do not be shaped by those desires you had formerly' 1 Pe 1.14.

67.19 πρὸ προσώπου: (an idiom, literally 'before the face,' equivalent in meaning to πρό[b] 'before,' 67.17, but a somewhat more elaborate phrase rhetorically) a point of time, possibly only a short time before another point of time – 'before, previous.' προκηρύξαντος Ἰωάννου πρὸ προσώπου τῆς εἰσόδου 'before the coming (of Jesus), John preached' Ac 13.24.

67.20 ἤδη: a point of time preceding another point of time and implying completion – 'already.' μή μοι κόπους πάρεχε· ἤδη ἡ θύρα κέκλεισται 'don't bother me; my door is already locked' Lk 11.7; ἤδη δὲ ἡ ἀξίνη πρὸς τὴν ῥίζαν τῶν δένδρων κεῖται 'the axe lies already at the roots of the trees' Mt 3.10. Note that the subsequent point of time in Lk 11.7 and Mt 3.10 is the act of speaking.

---

4 It would be possible to classify meanings such as 'before' and 'former' as a matter of sequence (Domain 61), but the meanings in this series do not point to the first item in a sequence but simply to a point of time prior to some other point.

67.21 ἐγγίζω^b: the occurrence of a point of time close to a subsequent point of time – 'to approach, to come near, to approximate.' ὅτε δὲ ἤγγισεν ὁ καιρὸς τῶν καρπῶν 'when the time for the harvest came near' Mt 21.34. Though in many languages time may be expressed in terms of space, as in speaking of 'time coming near,' in other languages this may not be at all possible. Accordingly, this clause in Mt 21.34 may need to be translated as 'it was about time to harvest' or 'when it was about time to gather the grapes.'

67.22 πάλαι^c: a point of time preceding another point of time and implying completion, but with a longer interval of time than in the case of ἤδη (67.20) – 'already, already for some time.' προσκαλεσάμενος τὸν κεντυρίωνα ἐπηρώτησεν αὐτὸν εἰ πάλαι ἀπέθανεν '(Pilate) called the army officer and asked him if (Jesus) had died already' Mk 15.44. The use of πάλαι in Mk 15.44 would seem to suggest that Jesus' death had taken place considerably sooner than what Pilate had thought would happen. In trying to render the implication of πάλαι^c, it may be possible to translate Mk 15.44 as 'Pilate called the army officer and asked him if Jesus had indeed already died.'

67.23 προσφάτως: pertaining to a point of time preceding another point of time, but with a relatively short interval – 'recently.' εὑρών τινα Ἰουδαῖον . . . προσφάτως ἐληλυθότα ἀπὸ τῆς Ἰταλίας 'he met a Jew . . . who had recently come from Italy' Ac 18.2. For languages which do not have an adverb meaning 'recently,' one can always introduce an equivalent approximate statement in Ac 18.2, for example, 'he met a Jew who only a few days before had come from Italy.' One cannot be certain as to the interval of time, but a phrase such as 'a few days before' can be a satisfactory equivalent.

67.24 πάλαι^a; ἔκπαλαι^a; παλαιός^c, ά, όν: pertaining to a point of time preceding another point of time, with an interval of considerable length – 'long ago, of long ago.'[5]

5 It is possible that ἔκπαλαι^a is somewhat more emphatic than πάλαι^a, but this cannot be determined from existing contexts.

πάλαι^a: πάλαι ὁ θεὸς λαλήσας τοῖς πατράσιν ἐν τοῖς προφήταις 'long ago God spoke to our ancestors through the prophets' He 1.1.
ἔκπαλαι^a: οὐρανοὶ ἦσαν ἔκπαλαι καὶ γῆ . . . συνεστῶσα τῷ τοῦ θεοῦ λόγῳ 'long ago . . . God spoke . . . and the heavens and earth . . . were created' 2 Pe 3.5.

References to a point of time preceding another point of time may express a relationship to an event in the discourse or to the time of the discourse itself. In He 1.1 πάλαι^a marks a point of time long before the actual writing of this Letter to the Hebrews. The same is true of ἔκπαλαι in 2 Pe 3.5. In some languages it is necessary to indicate clearly whether the interval is (1) between a prior time and the event mentioned in the discourse or (2) between a prior time and the discourse itself. For example, in He 1.1 it may be necessary to translate 'long ago before now God spoke to our ancestors through the prophets' or 'long ago before now that I am writing . . .'

παλαιός^c: ἐπὶ τῇ ἀναγνώσει τῆς παλαιᾶς διαθήκης 'in the reading of the covenant of long ago' 2 Cor 3.14. Though in some translations τῆς παλαιᾶς διαθήκης is rendered as 'the old covenant,' it is important to distinguish in the meanings of 'old' between that which has lasted for a long time and that which comes from a period long ago. It is the latter meaning which is relevant in this context.

67.25 ἀπ᾽ αἰῶνος: (an idiom, literally 'from an age') a point of time preceding another point of time, with a very long interval between (more emphatic than πάλαι^a, ἔκπαλαι^a, 67.24) – 'long ago, very long ago.' ἐλάλησεν διὰ στόματος τῶν ἁγίων ἀπ᾽ αἰῶνος προφητῶν αὐτοῦ 'long ago (God) spoke by means of his holy prophets' Lk 1.70. Some persons have concluded that ἀπ᾽ αἰῶνος must be understood in the sense of 'from an earlier age,' but there seems to be no justification for reading a dispensational implication into this idiomatic expression.

67.26 ἀφ᾽ ἡμερῶν ἀρχαίων: (an idiom, literally 'from ancient days') a point of time preceding another point of time, with a considerable interval – 'long ago, some time ago.'

ὑμεῖς ἐπίστασθε ὅτι ἀφ' ἡμερῶν ἀρχαίων ἐν ὑμῖν ἐξελέξατο ὁ θεός 'you know that sometime ago God chose from among you' Ac 15.7. This reference to Peter having been chosen by God sometime before to bring the gospel to the Gentiles can hardly be regarded as a reference to ancient times, though some persons understand this to mean that God's decision was made at the beginning of time. The usage of ἀφ' ἡμερῶν ἀρχαίων is probably designed to emphasize the established nature of God's decision for Peter to take the gospel to the Gentiles beginning with the centurion Cornelius. The fact that this was relatively early in the development of the church may also serve to explain the use of the idiom.

67.27 πρεσβύτερος[b], α, ον: pertaining to a person who has lived in ancient times, that is to say, at a point long before the point of time of the discourse itself (πρεσβύτερος[b] may also carry the implication of prestige) – 'of ancient times.' ἐν ταύτῃ γὰρ ἐμαρτυρήθησαν οἱ πρεσβύτεροι 'for by this, those of ancient times won (God's) approval' He 11.2.

67.28 καινότερον: pertaining to a point of time preceding another point of time, with a relatively short interval and with the implication of something different – 'latest, newest.' εἰς οὐδὲν ἕτερον ηὐκαίρουν ἢ λέγειν τι ἢ ἀκούειν τι καινότερον 'they were used to spending their time in nothing other than telling or hearing the latest thing' Ac 17.21.

67.29 προφθάνω: to do something at a point of time which immediately precedes another point of time – 'to be ahead of, to anticipate, to be in advance.' προέφθασεν αὐτὸν ὁ Ἰησοῦς λέγων 'Jesus spoke to him first' Mt 17.25. It would also be possible to render this expression in Mt 17.25 as 'Jesus spoke to Simon before Simon could speak to him.'

67.30 πότε; ποτέ[b]; ὁπότε; ὅτε[a]; ὅταν[b]: a point of time which is roughly simultaneous to or overlaps with another point of time – 'when.'
πότε: εἰπὲ ἡμῖν πότε ταῦτα ἔσται 'tell us when this will happen' Mt 24.3.
ποτέ[b]: σύ ποτε ἐπιστρέψας στήρισον τοὺς ἀδελ-

φούς σου 'when you turn back, you must strengthen your fellow believers' Lk 22.32.
ὁπότε: ὃ ἐποίησεν Δαυὶδ ὅτε ἐπείνασεν αὐτὸς καὶ οἱ μετ' αὐτοῦ ὄντες 'what David did when he and his men were hungry' Lk 6.3.
ὅτε[a]: ὅτε ἐτέλεσεν ὁ Ἰησοῦς τοὺς λόγους τούτους ἐξεπλήσσοντο οἱ ὄχλοι 'when Jesus finished saying these things, the crowds were amazed' Mt 7.28.
ὅταν[b]: ὅταν ἤνοιξεν τὴν σφραγῖδα τὴν ἑβδόμην 'when the seventh seal was opened' Re 8.1.[6]

67.31 ὅταν[a]; ἐπάν: an indefinite point or points of time, which may be roughly simultaneous to or overlap with another point of time (ὅταν[a] and ἐπάν may also imply some degree of uncertainty) – 'whenever, when.'
ὅταν[a]: μακάριοί ἐστε ὅταν ὀνειδίσωσιν ὑμᾶς . . . ἕνεκεν ἐμοῦ 'happy are you whenever people insult you . . . because of me' or '. . . because you are my followers' Mt 5.11.
ἐπάν: ἐπὰν δὲ εὕρητε ἀπαγγείλατέ μοι 'and when you find him, let me know' Mt 2.8.

67.32 ἐάν[b]: a point of time which is somewhat conditional and simultaneous with another point of time – 'when, when and if.' κἀγὼ ἐὰν ὑψωθῶ ἐκ τῆς γῆς, πάντας ἑλκύσω πρὸς ἐμαυτόν 'when I am lifted up from earth, I will draw all people to me' Jn 12.32.

67.33 κατά[g]; ἐπί[s]; ἐν[s]; ἐκ[k]; καθώς[d]: markers of a point of time which is simultaneous to or overlaps with another point of time – 'when, at the time of.'[7]
κατά[g]: κατὰ τὴν ἡμέραν τοῦ πειρασμοῦ ἐν τῇ ἐρήμῳ 'at the time of the testing in the desert' He 3.8.
ἐπί[s]: ἐπὶ Ἀβιαθὰρ ἀρχιερέως 'when Abiathar was the high priest' Mk 2.26; ἀνέβαινον εἰς τὸ

6 It is possible that ὅταν occurs in Re 8.1 because of the prophetic nature of the context, so that in reality, though the verb is in the past tense, the reference is ultimately to a future event which is indefinite in time. If this is the case, then ὅταν[b] may simply be classified with ὅταν[a] (67.31).

7 The difference in meaning between the set κατά[g], ἐπί[s], ἐν[s], ἐκ[k], and καθώς[d] and the set πότε, ποτέ[b], ὁπότε, ὅτε[a], and ὅταν[b] (67.30) is largely a matter of class meanings, but there may be certain subtle rhetorical differences as well.

ἱερὸν ἐπὶ τὴν ὥραν τῆς προσευχῆς 'he went into the Temple at the time of prayer' Ac 3.1.

ἐνˢ: ἐν τῷ γενέσθαι τὴν φωνὴν εὑρέθη Ἰησοῦς μόνος 'when the voice stopped (or 'when the voice had spoken'), Jesus was (there) all alone' (literally 'when the voice occurred . . .') Lk 9.36.

ἐκᵏ: προσηύξατο ἐκ τρίτου τὸν αὐτὸν λόγον εἰπών 'he prayed the third time saying the same words' Mt 26.44.

καθώςᵈ: καθὼς δὲ ἤγγιζεν ὁ χρόνος τῆς ἐπαγγελίας 'when the time (for fulfilling) of the promise drew near' Ac 7.17.

67.34 ἅμαᵃ; ἐφάπαξᶜ: a point of time which is emphatically simultaneous with another point of time – 'at the same time.'

ἅμαᵃ: ἅμα καὶ ἐλπίζων ὅτι χρήματα δοθήσεται αὐτῷ ὑπὸ τοῦ Παύλου 'at the same time he was hoping that Paul would give him some money' Ac 24.26.

ἐφάπαξᶜ: ἔπειτα ὤφθη ἐπάνω πεντακοσίοις ἀδελφοῖς ἐφάπαξ 'then he appeared to more than five hundred (of our) fellow believers at the same time' 1 Cor 15.6. For another interpretation of ἐφάπαξ in 1 Cor 15.6, see 60.67.

67.35 κατάʰ; περίᶜ: markers of a point of time which is approximately simultaneous to another point of time – 'about.'

κατάʰ: κατὰ δὲ τὸ μεσονύκτιον Παῦλος καὶ Σιλᾶς προσευχόμενοι ὕμνουν τὸν θεόν 'about midnight Paul and Silas were praying and singing hymns to God' Ac 16.25.

περίᶜ: περὶ μεσημβρίαν ἐξαίφνης ἐκ τοῦ οὐρανοῦ περιαστράψαι φῶς ἱκανὸν περὶ ἐμέ 'about midday a bright light suddenly flashed from the sky around me' Ac 22.6.

67.36 ὅτανᶜ; ὁσάκις ἐάν; ἡνίκα ἄν; ἡνίκα ἐάν: indefinite and multiple points of time, simultaneous with other corresponding points of time – 'whenever, as often as.'

ὅτανᶜ: τὰ πνεύματα τὰ ἀκάθαρτα, ὅταν αὐτὸν ἐθεώρουν, προσέπιπτον αὐτῷ 'whenever the evil spirits saw him, they fell down before him' Mk 3.11.

ὁσάκις ἐάν: τοῦτο ποιεῖτε, ὁσάκις ἐὰν πίνητε, εἰς τὴν ἐμὴν ἀνάμνησιν 'as often as you drink it, do it in memory of me' 1 Cor 11.25.

ἡνίκα ἄν: ἡνίκα ἂν ἀναγινώσκηται Μωϋσῆς 'whenever they read the Law of Moses' 2 Cor 3.15.

ἡνίκα ἐάν: ἡνίκα δὲ ἐὰν ἐπιστρέψῃ πρὸς κύριον 'whenever a person turns to the Lord' 2 Cor 3.16.

67.37 τὸ παρόν: a specific time corresponding to some other time – 'the present, that which exists at any time.' πᾶσα δὲ παιδεία πρὸς μὲν τὸ παρὸν οὐ δοκεῖ χαρᾶς εἶναι ἀλλὰ λύπης 'all punishment seems at the time not a matter of joy but of sadness' He 12.11.

67.38 νῦνᵃ or νυνίᵃ (a variant form of νῦνᵃ); ἄρτιᵃ: a point of time simultaneous with the event of the discourse itself – 'now.'

νῦνᵃ: νῦν μὲν λύπην ἔχετε· πάλιν δὲ ὄψομαι ὑμᾶς 'now you are sad, but I will see you again' Jn 16.22; περὶ ὧν νυνὶ κατηγοροῦσίν μου 'concerning those things of which they are now accusing me' Ac 24.13.

ἄρτιᵃ: βλέπομεν γὰρ ἄρτι δι' ἐσόπτρου ἐν αἰνίγματι 'what we see now is like a dim image in a mirror' 1 Cor 13.12.

67.39 νῦνᵇ or νυνίᵇ (a variant form of νῦνᵇ); ἄρτιᵇ: a time shortly before or shortly after the time of the discourse – 'just now, presently.'

νῦνᵇ: νῦν ἐζήτουν σε λιθάσαι οἱ Ἰουδαῖοι 'the Jews were just now trying to stone you' Jn 11.8; νυνὶ δὲ πορεύομαι εἰς Ἰερουσαλήμ 'presently I am going to Jerusalem' Ro 15.25.

ἄρτιᵇ: ἡ θυγάτηρ μου ἄρτι ἐτελεύτησεν 'my daughter has just died' Mt 9.18.

67.40 ἤδη ποτέ: (an idiom, literally 'already sometime') a time simultaneous with the discourse but in relationship to preceding time – 'already now, now at last, now at length.' εἴ πως ἤδη ποτὲ εὐοδωθήσομαι ἐν τῷ θελήματι τοῦ θεοῦ ἐλθεῖν πρὸς ὑμᾶς 'somehow now at last I might have the opportunity to come to you by the will of God' Ro 1.10.

67.41 ἐνίσταμαιᵇ (and perfect active): to be simultaneous with the time of the discourse – 'present, to be present.' ὅπως ἐξέληται ἡμᾶς ἐκ τοῦ αἰῶνος τοῦ ἐνεστῶτος πονηροῦ 'in order to set us free from this present evil age' Ga 1.4.

67.42 ἡ ἄρτι ὥρα: (an idiom, literally 'the present hour') an emphatic reference to a point of time which is simultaneous with another point of time – 'at this very moment, at this very time.' ἄχρι τῆς ἄρτι ὥρας καὶ πεινῶμεν 'until this very time we go hungry' 1 Cor 4.11.

67.43 δεῦρο[b]: a point of time simultaneous with another point of time, but with the possible implication of a particular set of circumstances – 'now, the present time.' προεθέμην ἐλθεῖν πρὸς ὑμᾶς, καὶ ἐκωλύθην ἄχρι τοῦ δεῦρο 'I intended to come to you, but until now I have been prevented (from doing so)' Ro 1.13.[8]

67.44 εἶτα[a]; ἔπειτα; μετέπειτα: a point of time following another point – 'then, afterwards, later.'[9]
εἶτα[a]: Ἀδὰμ γὰρ πρῶτος ἐπλάσθη, εἶτα Εὕα 'Adam was created first, and then Eve' 1 Tm 2.13.
ἔπειτα: ἔπειτα ὤφθη ἐπάνω πεντακοσίοις ἀδελφοῖς 'later he appeared to more than five hundred of his followers' 1 Cor 15.6.
μετέπειτα: ἴστε γὰρ ὅτι καὶ μετέπειτα θέλων κληρονομῆσαι τὴν εὐλογίαν 'you know that later he wanted to receive his (father's) blessing' He 12.17.

67.45 ἐπειδή[b]; ὡς[d]: a point of time which is prior to another point of time, with the possible implication in some contexts of reason or cause – 'when.'
ἐπειδή[b]: ἐπειδὴ ἐπλήρωσεν πάντα τὰ ῥήματα αὐτοῦ . . . εἰσῆλθεν 'and when he had finished saying all these things . . . he went' Lk 7.1.
ὡς[d]: ὡς δὲ ἐγεύσατο ὁ ἀρχιτρίκλινος τὸ ὕδωρ οἶνον γεγενημένον . . . φωνεῖ 'and when the man in charge of the feast tasted the water which had turned into wine . . . he called' Jn 2.9; τὰ δὲ λοιπὰ ὡς ἂν ἔλθω διατάξομαι 'as for the other matters, I will settle them when I come' 1 Cor 11.34.

67.46 πόρρωθεν[a]: from a point of time considerably prior to another point of time – 'far ahead of time, long before.' μὴ λαβόντες τὰς ἐπαγγελίας, ἀλλὰ πόρρωθεν αὐτὰς ἰδόντες 'not having received those things that had been promised, but long before they recognized them' He 11.13. It is also possible to interpret πόρρωθεν in He 11.13 as meaning 'from afar' or 'from a great distance' (see 83.31).

67.47 τότε; κἀκεῖθεν[b]: a point of time subsequent to another point of time – 'then.'
τότε: τότε ἐάν τις ὑμῖν εἴπῃ, Ἰδοὺ ὧδε ὁ Χριστός, ἤ, Ὧδε, μὴ πιστεύσητε 'then, if anyone says to you, Look, here is the Messiah, or, There he is, do not believe him' Mt 24.23; διαλλάγηθι τῷ ἀδελφῷ σου, καὶ τότε ἐλθὼν πρόσφερε τὸ δῶρόν σου 'make peace with your brother, and then come back and offer your gift (to God)' Mt 5.24.
κἀκεῖθεν[b]: κἀκεῖθεν ᾐτήσαντο βασιλέα, καὶ ἔδωκεν αὐτοῖς ὁ θεὸς τὸν Σαούλ 'then they asked for a king, and God gave them Saul' Ac 13.21.

67.48 μετά[g]: a marker of a point of time closely associated with a prior point of time – 'after.' καὶ μετὰ τρεῖς ἡμέρας ἀναστῆναι 'and to arise after three days' (that is, 'on the third day,' since both the first and the last days of such a set were counted) Mk 8.31; μετὰ ταῦτα ἦλθεν ὁ Ἰησοῦς καὶ οἱ μαθηταὶ αὐτοῦ εἰς τὴν Ἰουδαίαν γῆν 'after this, Jesus and his disciples went to the province of Judea' Jn 3.22. In a number of languages there is no convenient preposition-like word such as 'after,' but one can render the expression in Jn 3.22 as 'these things happened, and then Jesus and his disciples went to the province of Judea.'

67.49 ἄχρι[b]: a point of time which is subsequent to a duration and simultaneous with another point of time – 'later, until after.' ἤλθομεν πρὸς αὐτοὺς εἰς τὴν Τρῳάδα ἄχρι ἡμερῶν πέντε 'five days later we joined them in Troas' Ac 20.6.

67.50 δεύτερος[b], α, ον; ὕστερος[b], α, ον: pertaining to a subsequent event, but not necessarily the second in a series – 'afterward, later.'

---

8 The implications of δεῦρο in Ro 1.13 may reflect the spacial meaning of δεῦρο[a] 'here' (see 84.24).
9 It is possible that μετέπειτα suggests a somewhat longer interval of time or it may be merely a stylistic variant of ἔπειτα.

δεύτερος[b]: λαὸν ἐκ γῆς Αἰγύπτου σώσας τὸ δεύτερον τοὺς μὴ πιστεύσαντας ἀπώλεσεν 'he saved the people (of Israel) from the land of Egypt, but afterward destroyed those that did not believe' Jd 5.

ὕστερος[b]: ὁ δὲ ἀποκριθεὶς εἶπεν, Οὐ θέλω, ὕστερον δὲ μεταμεληθεὶς ἀπῆλθεν 'I don't want to, he answered, but later he changed his mind and went' Mt 21.29.

67.51 ὀψέ[c]: a point of time subsequent to another point of time, with the implication of relative lateness – 'after.' ὀψὲ δὲ σαββάτων, τῇ ἐπιφωσκούσῃ εἰς μίαν σαββάτων 'after the Sabbath, as the first day of the week was dawning' Mt 28.1.

67.52 ἐν τῷ (καθ)εξῆς: (an idiom, literally 'in the next') a point of time subsequent to another point of time, but with the implication of an ordered sequence – 'later, next.' καὶ ἐγένετο ἐν τῷ καθεξῆς καὶ αὐτὸς διώδευεν κατὰ πόλιν καὶ κώμην 'later he made a trip through towns and villages' Lk 8.1; ἐγένετο ἐν τῷ ἑξῆς ἐπορεύθη εἰς πόλιν καλουμένην Ναΐν 'next he went to a town called Nain' Lk 7.11.

67.53 εὐθύς; εὐθέως: a point of time immediately subsequent to a previous point of time (the actual interval of time differs appreciably, depending upon the nature of the events and the manner in which the sequence is interpreted by the writer) – 'immediately, right away, then.'
εὐθύς: καὶ εὐθὺς ἐκ τῆς συναγωγῆς ἐξελθόντες 'and immediately they left the synagogue' or 'then they left . . .' Mk 1.29; καὶ εὐθὺς τοῖς σάββασιν εἰσελθὼν εἰς τὴν συναγωγὴν ἐδίδασκεν 'and immediately on the Sabbath he went into the synagogue and taught' Mk 1.21. εὐθύς probably implies what was done on the immediately following Sabbath. Accordingly, one may translate this expression in Mk 1.21 as 'and on the next Sabbath he went into the synagogue and taught.'
εὐθέως: εὐθέως δὲ μετὰ τὴν θλῖψιν τῶν ἡμερῶν ἐκείνων, ὁ ἥλιος σκοτισθήσεται 'immediately after the trouble of those days, the sun will grow dark' Mt 24.29; ἐλπίζω δὲ εὐθέως σε ἰδεῖν 'I hope to see you right away' 3 Jn 14. It is impossible to determine from the context

whether εὐθέως in 3 Jn 14 should be understood as referring to a very short lapse of time and therefore be rendered as 'very soon,' or whether it refers to the very next event which is relevant to the total context.

67.54 μεταξύ[c]: a point of time which is subsequent in order to a previous point of time – 'next.' παρεκάλουν εἰς τὸ μεταξὺ σάββατον 'they invited (them) for the next Sabbath' Ac 13.42.

67.55 ἄνωθεν[b]; πάλιν[a]; εἰς τὸ πάλιν: a subsequent point of time involving repetition – 'again.'
ἄνωθεν[b]: οἷς πάλιν ἄνωθεν δουλεύειν θέλετε 'whom you want to serve as slaves all over again' Ga 4.9.
In Jn 3.3 ἄνωθεν involves a play on the two distinct meanings of the word, namely, ἄνωθεν[b] 'again' and ἄνωθεν[a] 'from above' (see 84.13). For the idiom γεννάω ἄνωθεν, see 41.53.
πάλιν[a]: εἶτα πάλιν ἐπέθηκεν τὰς χεῖρας ἐπὶ τοὺς ὀφθαλμοὺς αὐτοῦ 'then he again placed his hands on the man's eyes' Mk 8.25.
εἰς τὸ πάλιν: ἐὰν ἔλθω εἰς τὸ πάλιν οὐ φείσομαι 'when I come again, I will not spare anyone' or '. . . nobody will escape punishment' 2 Cor 13.2.

67.56 ταχύ[a]; ταχέως[b]; ταχινός[b], ή, όν; ἐν τάχει: pertaining to a point of time subsequent to another point of time (either an event in the discourse or the time of the discourse itself), with emphasis upon the relatively brief interval between the two points of time – 'soon, very soon.'
ταχύ[a]: οὐδεὶς γάρ ἐστιν ὃς ποιήσει δύναμιν ἐπὶ τῷ ὀνόματί μου καὶ δυνήσεται ταχὺ κακολογῆσαί με 'no one performing a miracle in my name will be able soon afterward to say bad things about me' Mk 9.39.
ταχέως[b]: ἐλπίζω δὲ ἐν κυρίῳ Ἰησοῦ Τιμόθεον ταχέως πέμψαι ὑμῖν 'I trust in the Lord Jesus that I will be able to send Timothy to you soon' Php 2.19.
ταχινός[b]: εἰδὼς ὅτι ταχινή ἐστιν ἡ ἀπόθεσις τοῦ σκηνώματός μου 'I know that I shall soon put off this mortal body' 2 Pe 1.14.
ἐν τάχει: δεῖξαι τοῖς δούλοις αὐτοῦ ἃ δεῖ γενέσθαι

ἐν τάχει 'to show his servants what must happen soon' Re 22.6.

67.57 ὡς τάχιστα: a point of time subsequent to another point of time, with an interval as brief as possible – 'as soon as possible, very soon.' λαβόντες ἐντολὴν πρὸς τὸν Σιλᾶν καὶ τὸν Τιμόθεον ἵνα ὡς τάχιστα ἔλθωσιν πρὸς αὐτόν 'with instructions from him that Silas and Timothy join him as soon as possible' Ac 17.15. In some languages the equivalent of 'as soon as possible' would involve a verb meaning 'to hurry' or 'to do something quickly.' Accordingly, Ac 17.15 may be rendered as 'with instructions from him that Silas and Timothy hurry to join him.'

67.58 αὔριον[b]; ἐπὶ θύραις (an idiom, literally 'at the doors'); πρὸ θυρῶν (an idiom, literally 'before the doors'): a point of time subsequent to another point of time and indicating imminence, that is to say, the subsequent event is regarded as almost begun – 'soon, very soon.'
αὔριον[b]: φάγωμεν καὶ πίωμεν, αὔριον γὰρ ἀποθνήσκομεν 'let us eat and drink for soon we (will) die' 1 Cor 15.32.
ἐπὶ θύρας: ὅταν ἴδητε πάντα ταῦτα, γινώσκετε ὅτι ἐγγύς ἐστιν ἐπὶ θύραις 'when you see all these things, you will know it will happen soon' Mt 24.33.
πρὸ θυρῶν: ὁ κριτὴς πρὸ τῶν θυρῶν ἕστηκεν 'the Judge is coming soon' (literally, '. . . standing at the doors') Jas 5.9.

67.59 δι' ἡμερῶν: (an idiom, literally 'through days') a point of time subsequent to another point of time after an interval of a few days – 'a few days later.' εἰσελθὼν πάλιν εἰς Καφαρναοὺμ δι' ἡμερῶν 'a few days later he came back to Capernaum' Mk 2.1.

67.60 δι' ἐτῶν: (an idiom, literally 'through years') a point of time subsequent to another point of time after an interval of some years – 'some years later.' δι' ἐτῶν δὲ πλειόνων ἐλεημοσύνας ποιήσων εἰς τὸ ἔθνος μου παρεγενόμην καὶ προσφοράς 'after a number of years I went to take some money to my own people and to make offerings' Ac 24.17.

67.61 ἐγγύς[b]: a point of time subsequent to

another point of time, but relatively close – 'near.' ἐγγὺς ἦν τὸ πάσχα τῶν Ἰουδαίων 'the Jewish Feast of Passover was near' Jn 2.13.

67.62 μέλλω[a]: to occur at a point of time in the future which is subsequent to another event and closely related to it – 'to be about to.' δύνασθε πιεῖν τὸ ποτήριον ὃ ἐγὼ μέλλω πίνειν; 'can you drink the cup that I am about to drink?' Mt 20.22.

67.63 ἐφίσταμαι[e] (and perfect active); ἐνίσταμαι[c] (and perfect active): to occur with high probability at a point of time just subsequent to another point of time – 'imminent, impending.'
ἐφίσταμαι[e]: ὁ καιρὸς τῆς ἀναλύσεώς μου ἐφέστηκεν 'the time of my departure is very near' 2 Tm 4.6.
ἐνίσταμαι[c]: νομίζω οὖν τοῦτο καλὸν ὑπάρχειν διὰ τὴν ἐνεστῶσαν ἀνάγκην 'I think that this is better, due to the impending distress' 1 Cor 7.26.

67.64 παρίσταμαι[d] (and perfect active); ἄγω[f]: to occur at a particular or expected time – 'to take place, to be, to occur.'
παρίσταμαι[d]: ὅτι παρέστηκεν ὁ θερισμός 'for the harvest has come' Mk 4.29.
ἄγω[f]: τρίτην ταύτην ἡμέραν ἄγει ἀφ' οὗ ταῦτα ἐγένετο 'it is now the third day since these things happened' Lk 24.21. For another interpretation of ἄγω in Lk 24.21, see 67.79.

C A Point of Time with Reference to Duration of Time: Beginning, End (67.65-67.72)

67.65 ἀρχή[b], ῆς f; ἄρχομαι[b]: a point of time at the beginning of a duration – 'beginning, to begin.'
ἀρχή[b]: ἐν ἀρχῇ ἦν ὁ λόγος 'in the beginning was the Word' or 'before the world was created, the Word (already) existed' or 'at a time in the past when there was nothing . . .' Jn 1.1.
ἄρχομαι[b]: ἀρξάμενος ἀπὸ τοῦ βαπτίσματος Ἰωάννου 'beginning from the time of John's baptizing' Ac 1.22. It is also possible to understand this expression in Ac 1.22 as 'beginning from the time of John's baptizing (him).'

67.66 τέλος^a, ους *n*; συντέλεια, ας *f*: a point of time marking the end of a duration – 'end.'

τέλος^a: κηρυχθήσεται τοῦτο τὸ εὐαγγέλιον τῆς βασιλείας . . . πᾶσιν τοῖς ἔθνεσιν, καὶ τότε ἥξει τὸ τέλος 'this good news about the kingdom will be preached . . . to all mankind, and then the end will come' Mt 24.14; ἔφθασεν δὲ ἐπ' αὐτοὺς ἡ ὀργὴ εἰς τέλος 'and in the end wrath has come down on them' or 'and wrath has at last come down on them' 1 Th 2.16. There are serious problems involved in rendering τέλος^a in Mt 24.14 and in similar contexts. In a number of languages one simply cannot say 'the end will come'; rather, it may be necessary to say 'that is the finish' or 'everything is finished.' In the context of Mt 24.14, however, it may be best to translate 'God will finish everything.' The phrase εἰς τέλος in 1 Th 2.16 may also be understood as an idiomatic expression involving a degree of completeness (see 78.47).

συντέλεια: οὕτως ἔσται ἐν τῇ συντελείᾳ τοῦ αἰῶνος 'so it will be at the end of the age' Mt 13.40. As in the case of a number of expressions involving 'end,' it may be important to use a verb meaning 'to finish,' for example, 'so it will be like that when the age finishes' or '. . . when there isn't any more of the age.'

67.67 τελέω^b; συντελέω^c: (derivatives of τέλος^a and συντέλεια 'end,' 67.66) to occur or happen at the end of a duration – 'to end, to come to an end.'

τελέω^b: ἄχρι τελεσθῇ τὰ χίλια ἔτη 'until the thousand years came to an end' Re 20.3.

συντελέω^c: ὡς δὲ ἔμελλον αἱ ἑπτὰ ἡμέραι συντελεῖσθαι 'when the seven days were about to come to an end' Ac 21.27.

67.68 ἔκβασις^a, εως *f*: (a figurative extension of meaning of ἔκβασις 'way out of,' not occurring in the NT) the end point of a duration, but often with the implication of outcome or result – 'end.' ὧν ἀναθεωροῦντες τὴν ἔκβασιν τῆς ἀναστροφῆς 'of whom you have observed the end of their life' He 13.7. For another interpretation of ἔκβασις in He 13.7, see 89.39.

67.69 πλήρωμα^c, τος *n*; ἐκπλήρωσις, εως *f*: the totality of a period of time, with the im-

plication of proper completion – 'end, completion.'[10]

πλήρωμα^c: ὅτε δὲ ἦλθεν τὸ πλήρωμα τοῦ χρόνου 'when the complete time finally came' Ga 4.4.

ἐκπλήρωσις: τὴν ἐκπλήρωσιν τῶν ἡμερῶν τοῦ ἁγνισμοῦ 'the completion of the period of purification' Ac 21.26.

67.70 πίμπλαμαι^a; πληρόομαι^a; συμπληρόομαι^b: to come to the end of a period of time, with the implication of the completion of an implied purpose or plan – 'to complete, to come to an end.'[10]

πίμπλαμαι^a: ἐγένετο ὡς ἐπλήσθησαν αἱ ἡμέραι τῆς λειτουργίας αὐτοῦ 'when his period of service was complete' Lk 1.23.

πληρόομαι^a: καὶ πληρωθέντων ἐτῶν τεσσεράκοντα 'after forty years were completed' or '. . . came to an end' Ac 7.30.

συμπληρόομαι^b: ἐγένετο δὲ ἐν τῷ συμπληροῦσθαι τὰς ἡμέρας τῆς ἀναλήμψεως αὐτοῦ 'as the days were completed for him to be taken up (to heaven)' Lk 9.51.

In a number of languages it may be difficult to speak of a period of time being 'complete.' In Lk 1.23 one may often translate as 'when he had finished his period of service' or even 'when he had done his work.' In the case of Ac 7.30, the expression 'after forty years were completed' may be rendered in some languages as 'after forty years were passed' or 'when forty years had happened.'

67.71 ἐξαρτίζω^a: to cause a duration to come to an end – 'to bring to an end, to end.' ὅτε δὲ ἐγένετο ἡμᾶς ἐξαρτίσαι τὰς ἡμέρας 'when we brought that time to an end' or 'when our time with them was over' Ac 21.5.

67.72 συντέμνω: to cause a duration to come to an abrupt end, with the implication of

---

10 In a number of contexts it is difficult to determine whether the meanings in 67.69 and 67.70 are primarily temporal or aspectual. If the meaning in any one context seems to focus upon the completion of an activity, then the meaning should be classified as aspectual (Domain 68 *Aspect*), but if the emphasis would seem to be primarily upon the end point of an activity, then one may legitimately classify these meanings as being temporal.

sooner than expected – 'to cut short, to shorten, to bring to an end.' λόγον γὰρ συντελῶν καὶ συντέμνων ποιήσει κύριος ἐπὶ τῆς γῆς 'for the Lord will act upon the earth by settling accounts and by cutting short (the time)' Ro 9.28. There are a number of different opinions with regard to the meaning of συντέμνω in Ro 9.28. Translators are accordingly encouraged to consult commentaries and to provide for significantly different interpretations in translations.

D A Point of Time with Reference to Units of Time: Daybreak, Midday, Midnight, Late (67.73-67.77)

67.73 αὐγή, ῆς f; ὄρθρος[b], ου m: the point of time when the day begins – 'daybreak, sunrise, dawn.'[11]

αὐγή: ἐφ' ἱκανόν τε ὁμιλήσας ἄχρι αὐγῆς οὕτως ἐξῆλθεν 'after talking with them for a long time until dawn, he left' Ac 20.11.

ὄρθρος[b]: τῇ δὲ μιᾷ τῶν σαββάτων ὄρθρου βαθέως ἐπὶ τὸ μνῆμα ἦλθον 'at early dawn on the first day of the week they went to the grave' Lk 24.1; εἰσῆλθον ὑπὸ τὸν ὄρθρον εἰς τὸ ἱερὸν 'at daybreak they entered the Temple' Ac 5.21.

67.74 μεσημβρία[a], ας f: the midpoint of a day – 'noon, midday.' πορεύου κατὰ μεσημβρίαν ἐπὶ τὴν ὁδὸν τὴν καταβαίνουσαν ἀπὸ Ἰερουσαλὴμ εἰς Γάζαν 'about noon, go on the road that goes from Jerusalem to Gaza' Ac 8.26. In a number of languages μεσημβρία[a] may be rendered as 'when the sun is high' or 'when the sun is above one's head' or 'just as the sun starts down.' For another interpretation of μεσημβρία in Ac 8.26, see 82.4.

67.75 μεσονύκτιον, ου n: the midpoint of the night – 'midnight.' τίς ἐξ ὑμῶν ἕξει φίλον καὶ πορεύσεται πρὸς αὐτὸν μεσονυκτίου 'suppose one of you should go to a friend's house at midnight' Lk 11.5. In some languages μεσονύκτιον may be rendered as 'when the

night is half over' or 'when the night is cut in half.'

67.76 ὀψέ[a]; ὄψιος, α, ον: pertaining to a point near the end of a day (normally after sunset but before night) – 'late, late in the day.'

ὀψέ[a]: ὅταν ὀψὲ ἐγένετο, ἐξεπορεύοντο ἔξω τῆς πόλεως 'when it became late, they went out of the city' Mk 11.19. It is also possible to understand ὀψέ in Mk 11.19 as indicating a period of time, namely 'evening' (see 67.197).

ὄψιος: ὀψίας ἤδη οὔσης τῆς ὥρας, ἐξῆλθεν εἰς Βηθανίαν 'since it was already late, he went out to Bethany' Mk 11.11.

67.77 ὥρα πολλή: (an idiom, literally 'much hour') a point of time relatively late in view of the circumstances (late in the afternoon or in the evening) – 'late, very late.' ἔρημός ἐστιν ὁ τόπος, καὶ ἤδη ὥρα πολλή 'this place is lonely and it is very late' Mk 6.35.

II. Duration of Time (67.78-67.141)

E Duration of Time without Reference to Points or Units of Time: Time, Spend Time, Always, Eternal, Old, Immediately, Young (67.78-67.117)

67.78 χρόνος[a], ου m; καιρός[b], οῦ m: an indefinite unit of time (the actual extent of time being determined by the context) – 'time, period of time.'[12]

χρόνος[a]: ποιήσαντες δὲ χρόνον ἀπελύθησαν 'after spending some time there, they were sent off' Ac 15.33.

καιρός[b]: εἰδὼς ὅτι ὀλίγον καιρὸν ἔχει 'for he knows that he has only a little time left' Re 12.12.

67.79 χρονοτριβέω; ἄγω[g]: to experience a duration of time – 'to spend time.'

χρονοτριβέω: ὅπως μὴ γένηται αὐτῷ χρονοτριβῆσαι ἐν τῇ Ἀσίᾳ 'so as not to spend any

11 There may be slight differences of meaning between αὐγή and ὄρθρος[b] in that αὐγή focuses primarily upon light and ὄρθρος[b] perhaps on the early part of dawn, but this cannot be determined precisely from existing contexts.

12 χρόνος[a] and καιρός[b] denote essentially a duration of time, but without specified limits. One may, however, speak of a duration as simply 'a period of time,' but this does not imply a unit such as 'hour,' 'year,' or 'generation.'

time in the province of Asia' Ac 20.16. In a number of languages χρονοτριβέω may be best rendered as 'to remain for a time' or idiomatically as 'to sit for a time.'

ἄγω[g]: τρίτην ταύτην ἡμέραν ἄγει ἀφ' οὗ ταῦτα ἐγένετο '(Jesus) is spending the third day since these things happened' Lk 24.21. For another interpretation of ἄγω in Lk 24.21, see 67.64.

67.80 εὐκαιρέω[b]: to spend time in an enjoyable and profitable manner – 'to spend time, to enjoy spending time.' εἰς οὐδὲν ἕτερον ηὐκαίρουν ἢ λέγειν τι ἢ ἀκούειν τι καινότερον 'enjoyed spending their time on nothing else than saying or hearing the latest thing' Ac 17.21.

67.81 σχολάζω[a]: to engage actively and earnestly in some activity over a period of time – 'to give time to, to devote oneself to.' ἵνα σχολάσητε τῇ προσευχῇ 'in order to give time to prayer' 1 Cor 7.5.

67.82 χρονίζω[b]: to spend a considerable period of time in a state or activity – 'to spend a long time in, to stay a long time.' ἐθαύμαζον ἐν τῷ χρονίζειν ἐν τῷ ναῷ αὐτόν 'they were wondering why he was spending such a long time in the Temple' Lk 1.21.

67.83 τροχός[b], οῦ *m*: (a figurative extension of meaning of τροχός 'wheel,' not occurring in the NT) a period of time of indefinite length, characterized by recurring events or patterns – 'course, cycle.' φλογίζουσα τὸν τροχὸν τῆς γενέσεως 'it sets on fire the cycle of our existence' Jas 3.6. In some languages τὸν τροχὸν τῆς γενέσεως may be best rendered as 'the very way in which we live' or 'the manner of our life.' For another interpretation of τροχός in Jas 3.6, see 61.5.

67.84 διαγίνομαι; διΐσταμαι[c] (and 2nd aorist active): to mark the passage of time – 'to pass, passage.'
διαγίνομαι: διαγενομένου τοῦ σαββάτου 'after the Sabbath day had passed' Mk 16.1.
διΐσταμαι[c]: διαστάσης ὡσεὶ ὥρας μιᾶς 'about an hour later' or 'after an hour had passed' Lk 22.59.

67.85 παρέρχομαι[e]; παροίχομαι: to mark the passage of time, with focus upon completion – 'to pass, to have passed, past.'
παρέρχομαι[e]: οὐ μὴ παρέλθῃ ἡ γενεὰ αὕτη ἕως ἂν πάντα ταῦτα γένηται 'this generation will not pass until all these things happen' or 'this age will not pass . . .' Mt 24.34. In Mt 24.34 it may be important to distinguish carefully between γενεά meaning 'people' (11.4) and γενεά meaning 'time' (67.144), since this will undoubtedly influence the way in which the temporal reference of παρέρχομαι[e] is represented. If one understands generation in the sense of 'people,' then one may translate 'these people living now will not die until all these things happen.'
παροίχομαι: ὃς ἐν ταῖς παρῳχημέναις γενεαῖς εἴασεν πάντα τὰ ἔθνη πορεύεσθαι ταῖς ὁδοῖς αὐτῶν 'in past generations he allowed all peoples to go their own way' Ac 14.16.

67.86 ἀεί; διὰ παντός[b] (an idiom, literally 'through all'): duration of time, either continuous or episodic, but without limits – 'always, constantly, continually.'
ἀεί: ὡς λυπούμενοι ἀεὶ δὲ χαίροντες 'although saddened, we are always glad' 2 Cor 6.10.
διὰ παντός[b]: διὰ παντὸς βλέπουσι τὸ πρόσωπον τοῦ πατρός μου 'they are always in the presence of my Father' Mt 18.10.
In some languages there may be problems involved in rendering ἀεί or διὰ παντός[b], since there may be a basic distinction between (a) continuous activity and (b) activity which may be defined as 'episodic' in that it regularly recurs in related episodes. For example, in 2 Cor 6.10 the fact of being glad may be related specifically to the occasions of being saddened, while in Mt 18.10 the focus of meaning is probably upon the continuous nature of the relation.

67.87 ἐχθὲς καὶ σήμερον καὶ εἰς τοὺς αἰῶνας: (an idiom, literally 'yesterday, today, and forever') an unlimited extension of time, from the past into the future – 'always, eternally, past and present and future.' Ἰησοῦς Χριστὸς ἐχθὲς καὶ σήμερον ὁ αὐτός, καὶ εἰς τοὺς αἰῶνας 'Jesus Christ is eternally the same' or 'Jesus Christ is the same in the past, in the present, and in the future' He 13.8.

67.88 πάντοτε; ἑκάστοτε: duration of time, with reference to a series of occasions – 'always, at all times, on every occasion.'

πάντοτε: οὐκ ἀφῆκέν με μόνον, ὅτι ἐγὼ τὰ ἀρεστὰ αὐτῷ ποιῶ πάντοτε 'he has not left me alone because I always do what pleases him' Jn 8.29; πάντοτε μνείαν σου ποιούμενος ἐπὶ τῶν προσευχῶν μου 'every time I pray, I mention you' Phm 4.

ἑκάστοτε: σπουδάσω δὲ καὶ ἑκάστοτε ἔχειν ὑμᾶς μετὰ τὴν ἐμὴν ἔξοδον τὴν τούτων μνήμην ποιεῖσθαι 'I will do my best to provide a way for you to remember these matters at all times after my death' 2 Pe 1.15.

67.89 μακρός[a], ά, όν; μακροχρόνιος, ον; ἐν μεγάλῳ (an idiom, literally 'in great'); ἐπὶ πολύ (an idiom, literally 'upon much'): pertaining to a relatively long duration of time – 'long, long time, for some time.'

μακρός[a]: προφάσει μακρὰ προσεύχονται 'they make a show by praying a long time' Lk 20.47.

μακροχρόνιος: ἔσῃ μακροχρόνιος ἐπὶ τῆς γῆς 'you may live a long time in the land' Eph 6.3.

ἐν μεγάλῳ: εὐξαίμην . . . ἐν ὀλίγῳ καὶ ἐν μεγάλῳ . . . πάντας . . . γενέσθαι τοιούτους ὁποῖος καὶ ἐγώ εἰμι 'my prayer is that . . . all of you . . . might become what I am . . . whether in a short time or in a long time' Ac 26.29.

ἐπὶ πολύ: ἐπὶ πολὺ δὲ αὐτῶν προσδοκώντων καὶ θεωρούντων μηδὲν ἄτοπον εἰς αὐτὸν γινόμενον 'for some time these waited and saw that nothing strange was happening to him' Ac 28.6.

67.90 ἄνωθεν[c]: duration of time for a relatively long period in the past – 'for a long time.' προγινώσκοντές με ἄνωθεν 'they have known me previously for a long time' Ac 26.5; κἀμοὶ παρηκολουθηκότι ἄνωθεν πᾶσιν ἀκριβῶς 'since I have carefully studied all these matters for a long time' Lk 1.3.

67.91 ἐφ' ἱκανόν: (an idiom, literally 'upon enough') duration of time for a considerable period, with the focus upon sufficiency of time – 'during a considerable period of time, for a long time.' ἐφ' ἱκανόν τε ὁμιλήσας ἄχρι αὐγῆς οὕτως ἐξῆλθεν 'after talking to them for a considerable period of time until sunrise, he left' Ac 20.11.

67.92 ἡμέρα ἐξ ἡμέρας: (an idiom, literally 'day out of day') a relatively long period of time – 'for a long time, for quite a while, day after day.' ἡμέραν ἐξ ἡμέρας ψυχὴν δικαίαν ἀνόμοις ἔργοις ἐβασάνιζεν 'for a long time his righteous soul was tormented by (their) evil deeds' (literally '. . . he tormented his righteous soul . . .') 2 Pe 2.8.

67.93 ἡμέρας τεσσεράκοντα καὶ νύκτας τεσσεράκοντα or, in the shortened form, ἡμέρας τεσσεράκοντα: possibly a symbolic temporal expression denoting a relatively long period of time – 'a long time.' νηστεύσας ἡμέρας τεσσεράκοντα καὶ νύκτας τεσσεράκοντα ὕστερον ἐπείνασεν 'after spending a long time without food, he was hungry' Mt 4.2.

Most translations render ἡμέρας τεσσεράκοντα καὶ νύκτας τεσσεράκοντα as either 'forty days and forty nights' or 'forty days,' though it is possible, in view of the symbolic meaning of the number 'forty,' that this expression is to be understood as meaning a long period of time.

67.94 ἔτη τεσσεράκοντα: possibly a symbolic temporal expression denoting a very long period of time – 'a very long time.' ποιήσας τέρατα καὶ σημεῖα . . . ἐν τῇ ἐρήμῳ ἔτη τεσσεράκοντα 'performing miracles and wonders . . . in the desert for a very long time' Ac 7.36. Though most translations render ἔτη τεσσεράκοντα as 'forty years,' the expression probably is to be understood as meaning an unusually long period of time. See also discussion at 67.93.

67.95 εἰς τὸ διηνεκές; εἰς αἰῶνα or εἰς τὸν αἰῶνα or εἰς τοὺς αἰῶνας or the more elaborate expressions εἰς ἡμέραν αἰῶνος; εἰς παντὰς τοὺς αἰῶνας; εἰς τὸν αἰῶνα τοῦ αἰῶνος/τῶν αἰώνων; εἰς τοὺς αἰῶνας τῶν αἰώνων; εἰς τὸ παντελές[a]: unlimited duration of time, with particular focus upon the future – 'always, forever, forever and ever, eternally.'

εἰς τὸ διηνεκές: μένει ἱερεὺς εἰς τὸ διηνεκές 'he remains a priest forever' He 7.3.

εἰς αἰῶνα (and related forms): εἰς αἰῶνα τετήρηται 'has been reserved forever' Jd 13; ὁ Χριστὸς μένει εἰς τὸν αἰῶνα 'the Messiah will remain forever' Jn 12.34; ᾧ ἐστιν ἡ δόξα καὶ τὸ κράτος εἰς τοὺς αἰῶνας τῶν αἰώνων 'to him belong the glory and the power forever and ever' 1 Pe 4.11; αὐτῷ ἡ δόξα . . . εἰς πάσας τὰς γενεὰς τοῦ αἰῶνος τῶν αἰώνων 'to him be the glory . . . for all ages forever and ever' Eph 3.21. See also Lk 1.33; 2 Pe 3.18; Jd 25; He 1.8. The more elaborate expressions employing αἰών are somewhat more emphatic in meaning and are to be found especially in the solemn style of doxologies.

εἰς τὸ παντελές[a]: σῴζειν εἰς τὸ παντελὲς δύναται 'he is able to save forever' He 7.25. For another interpretation of εἰς τὸ παντελές in He 7.25, see 78.47.

67.96 ἀΐδιος, ον; αἰώνιος, ον: pertaining to an unlimited duration of time – 'eternal.'[13] ἀΐδιος: ἥ τε ἀΐδιος αὐτοῦ δύναμις καὶ θειότης 'his eternal power and divine nature' Ro 1.20. αἰώνιος: βληθῆναι εἰς τὸ πῦρ τὸ αἰώνιον 'be thrown into the eternal fire' Mt 18.8; τοῦ αἰωνίου θεοῦ 'of the eternal God' Ro 16.26.

The most frequent use of αἰώνιος in the NT is with ζωή 'life,' for example, ἵνα πᾶς ὁ πιστεύων ἐν αὐτῷ ἔχῃ ζωὴν αἰώνιον 'so that everyone who believes in him may have eternal life' Jn 3.15. In combination with ζωή there is evidently not only a temporal element, but also a qualitative distinction. In such contexts, αἰώνιος evidently carries certain implications associated with αἰώνιος in relationship to divine and supernatural attributes. If one translates 'eternal life' as simply 'never dying,' there may be serious misunderstandings, since persons may assume that 'never dying' refers only to physical existence rather than to 'spiritual death.' Accordingly, some translators have rendered 'eternal life' as 'unending real life,' so as to introduce a qualitative distinction.

67.97 παλαιός[a], ά, όν: pertaining to having existed continuously for a relatively long time – 'old.' οὐδεὶς βάλλει οἶνον νέον εἰς ἀσκοὺς παλαιούς 'no one pours new wine into old wineskins' Mk 2.22. παλαιός[a] in a context involving wineskins focuses upon the use of

such wineskins over a long period of time, and therefore it may be necessary in some languages to translate 'used wineskins' or 'wineskins which have been used for a long time.'

67.98 ἀρχαῖος, α, ον: pertaining to having existed for a long time in the past, with the possible implication of such existence from the beginning of an event or state – 'for a long time, from the beginning, ancient.' Μνάσωνί τινι Κυπρίῳ, ἀρχαίῳ μαθητῇ 'Mnason from Cyprus, who was a disciple for a very long time' or '. . . from the beginning' Ac 21.16; ὁ ὄφις ὁ ἀρχαῖος 'the ancient serpent' Re 12.9; ἠκούσατε ὅτι ἐρρέθη τοῖς ἀρχαίοις 'you have heard that it was said by the men of ancient times' Mt 5.21.

67.99 προβαίνω ἐν ἡμέραις: (an idiom, literally 'to advance in days') to be quite advanced in age – 'to be old.' καὶ ἀμφότεροι προβεβηκότες ἐν ταῖς ἡμέραις αὐτῶν ἦσαν 'and they were both old' Lk 1.7.

67.100 παλαιότης[a], ητος f: the state of being old, with the implication of obsolescence – 'oldness, old, being obsolete.' ὥστε δουλεύειν ἡμᾶς ἐν καινότητι πνεύματος καὶ οὐ παλαιότητι γράμματος 'so that we may serve in the newness of the Spirit and not in the old way of the written document' Ro 7.6. For a somewhat different interpretation of παλαιότης in Ro 7.6, see 58.74.

67.101 καινότης[a], ητος f: the state of being relatively recent, with the implication of being appropriately contemporary – 'newness.' ὥστε δουλεύειν ἡμᾶς ἐν καινότητι πνεύματος καὶ οὐ παλαιότητι γράμματος 'so that we may serve in the newness of the Spirit and not in the old way of the written document' Ro 7.6.

67.102 μείζων[c], ον; πρεσβύτερος[a], α, ον: pertaining to the older of two objects – 'older.' μείζων[c]: ὁ μείζων δουλεύσει τῷ ἐλάσσονι 'the older will serve the younger' Ro 9.12. In some languages 'the older will serve the younger' must be rendered as 'the one who was born first will serve the one who was born later.' πρεσβύτερος[a]: ἦν δὲ ὁ υἱὸς αὐτοῦ ὁ πρεσβύτερος

---

13 There is no real distinction in meaning between the terms ἀΐδιος and αἰώνιος. The term ἀΐδιος, however, is in certain respects a somewhat more technical expression, particularly popular among philosophers.

ἐν ἀγρῷ 'his older son was (out) in the field' Lk 15.25.

67.103 παλαιόω: to cause to become old and obsolete, and hence no longer valid – 'to make old, to make out of date.' ἐν τῷ λέγειν Καινὴν πεπαλαίωκεν τὴν πρώτην 'by speaking of a new covenant, he has made the first one out of date' He 8.13.

67.104 παλαιόομαι: to become old, with the implication of becoming obsolete and/or useless – 'to become old, to deteriorate.' πάντες ὡς ἱμάτιον παλαιωθήσονται 'they will all grow old like clothes' He 1.11. In some languages it may be useful to translate παλαιόομαι in He 1.11 as 'they will become old and worn out.'

67.105 γηράσκω: to become old in age (referring to living beings) – 'to grow old, to become old.' ὅταν δὲ γηράσῃς . . . ἄλλος σε . . . οἴσει ὅπου οὐ θέλεις 'when you become old . . . someone else will take you where you do not want to go' Jn 21.18.[14]

67.106 ἐν ὀλίγῳ[a]; δι' ὀλίγων; πρὸς ὀλίγον; διὰ βραχέων; μικρός[d], ά, όν: pertaining to a relatively brief extent of time – 'a little while, for a little while, a short time, brief, briefly.'[15]
ἐν ὀλίγῳ[a]: ἐν ὀλίγῳ με πείθεις Χριστιανὸν ποιῆσαι 'you think you will make me a Christian in a short time' Ac 26.28. It is also possible to interpret ἐν ὀλίγῳ in Ac 26.28 as meaning 'easily' or 'without difficulty' (see 22.41).
δι' ὀλίγων: δι' ὀλίγων ἔγραψα 'I have written you briefly' 1 Pe 5.12. In some languages it may be best to translate this phrase in 1 Pe 5.12 as 'I have written a brief letter.'
πρὸς ὀλίγον: ἀτμὶς γάρ ἐστε ἡ πρὸς ὀλίγον

14 It is also possible to treat γηράσκω in Domain 23 *Physiological Events,* but the focus in Jn 21.18 seems to be more upon duration of time than upon a physiological state.

15 The series of expressions indicating relative shortness of time may very well differ slightly, at least in connotative meaning, but on the basis of existing NT contexts it is not possible to determine significant denotative differences. The phrases in this series may be technically regarded as idioms, but functionally they are better classed as 'frozen phrases,' which act essentially like morphological units.

φαινομένη 'you are like a thin fog which appears for a little while' Jas 4.14.
διὰ βραχέων: διὰ βραχέων ἐπέστειλα ὑμῖν 'for I have written to you briefly' He 13.22. In He 13.22 the phrase διὰ βραχέων may refer to the act of sending the communication or the amount of time required to receive the communication, that is to say, to read the communication or to hear it read. For another interpretation of διὰ βραχέων in He 13.22, see 59.4.
μικρός[d]: τί ἐστιν τοῦτο ὃ λέγει, τὸ μικρόν; 'what does he mean by a little while?' or '. . . by the expression, a little while?' Jn 16.18.

67.107 μικρὸν ὅσον ὅσον: (an idiom, literally 'little, how much, how much') a relatively short time, with emphasis upon the certainty of the brief period – 'very soon, in a very short while.' ἔτι γὰρ μικρὸν ὅσον ὅσον, ὁ ἐρχόμενος ἥξει 'just a very little while longer and he who is coming will come' He 10.37.

67.108 συντόμως: pertaining to a relatively brief period of time, implying some measure of reduction or shortening – 'briefly, in a short time.' παρακαλῶ ἀκοῦσαί σε ἡμῶν συντόμως τῇ σῇ ἐπιεικείᾳ 'I urge you to kindly listen to us briefly' or '. . . to our brief report' Ac 24.4.

67.109 πρόσκαιρος, ον; πρὸς καιρόν; πρὸς καιρὸν ὥρας; ἀπὸ μέρους[b] (an idiom, literally 'from a part'); παραυτίκα: pertaining to a relatively short period of time, with emphasis upon the temporary nature of the event or state – 'not long, temporary, for a little while, for a while.'
πρόσκαιρος: οὐκ ἔχει δὲ ῥίζαν ἐν ἑαυτῷ ἀλλὰ πρόσκαιρός ἐστιν 'but it does not sink deep in them, and so they don't last long' Mt 13.21.
πρὸς καιρόν: οἳ πρὸς καιρὸν πιστεύουσιν 'they believe only for a while' Lk 8.13.
πρὸς καιρὸν ὥρας: ἀπορφανισθέντες ἀφ' ὑμῶν πρὸς καιρὸν ὥρας 'when we were separated from you for a little while' 1 Th 2.17.
ἀπὸ μέρους[b]: ἐὰν ὑμῶν πρῶτον ἀπὸ μέρους ἐμπλησθῶ 'to go there after I have enjoyed (visiting) you for a while' Ro 15.24.
παραυτίκα: τὸ γὰρ παραυτίκα ἐλαφρὸν τῆς θλίψεως ἡμῶν 'for our affliction is not hard to bear and it is only temporary' 2 Cor 4.17.

67.110 ταχύς, εῖα, ύ; ταχύᵇ (adv); ταχέωςᵃ; ταχινόςᵃ, ή, όν; τάχιον: pertaining to a very short extent of time – 'quickly, hurriedly, swift, speedy.'

ταχύς: ἔστω δὲ πᾶς ἄνθρωπος ταχὺς εἰς τὸ ἀκοῦσαι 'everyone must be quick to listen' Jas 1.19.

ταχύᵇ: ὡς ἤκουσεν ἠγέρθη ταχὺ καὶ ἤρχετο πρὸς αὐτόν 'when she heard this, she quickly got up and went out to meet him' Jn 11.29. In Jn 11.29 ταχύ probably refers to the short period of time between Mary's hearing about Jesus and her getting up to go out to meet him. It is, of course, also possible to interpret ταχύ in Jn 11.29 as referring to the rapidity of Mary's movement in getting up and going out to meet Jesus.

ταχέωςᵃ: θαυμάζω ὅτι οὕτως ταχέως μετατίθεσθε ἀπὸ τοῦ καλέσαντος ὑμᾶς 'I am surprised that you are so quickly deserting the one who called you' Ga 1.6. In Ga 1.6 ταχέως refers clearly to the relatively brief period of time before the Galatians abandoned their earlier convictions.

ταχινόςᵃ: ἐπάγοντες ἑαυτοῖς ταχινὴν ἀπώλειαν 'bring upon themselves a swift destruction' 2 Pe 2.1. In 2 Pe 2.1 ταχινός may refer to the swift nature of the destruction or to the fact that destruction comes after a relatively brief period of time.

τάχιον: ὃ ποιεῖς ποίησον τάχιον 'what you are about to do, do it quickly' Jn 13.27. Again, the emphasis is upon the brief period of time before Judas is to do what he had set out to do.

67.111 τάχος, ους *n*: a very brief period of time – 'a very short while, quickly (in combination with the preposition ἐν).' σπεῦσον καὶ ἔξελθε ἐν τάχει ἐξ Ἰερουσαλήμ 'hurry, and leave Jerusalem quickly' Ac 22.18. In Ac 22.18 τάχος evidently refers to a brief period of time before fulfilling the admonition to leave Jerusalem.

67.112 ὀξύςᵇ, εῖα, ύ: pertaining to a very short period of time, with the probable implication of special haste – 'quick, swift.' ὀξεῖς οἱ πόδες αὐτῶν ἐκχέαι αἷμα 'they are quick to hurt and kill' (literally, 'their feet are swift in shedding blood') Ro 3.15. It would also be

possible to understand ὀξεῖς οἱ πόδες αὐτῶν 'their feet are swift' as being an idiom, but ὀξύς occurs frequently in non-biblical Greek with the meaning of 'quick, swift, soon.' In Ro 3.15 οἱ πόδες αὐτῶν is a metonymic expression meaning 'the people,' so that it is not simply the feet that are swift to shed blood, but it is the people who are quick to kill.

67.113 αἰφνίδιος, ον; ἐξαίφνης; ἐξάπινα; ἐξαυτῆς; ἄφνω; ἄρτιᶜ; παραχρῆμα: pertaining to an extremely short period of time between a previous state or event and a subsequent state or event – 'suddenly, at once, immediately' (in a number of contexts there is the implication of unexpectedness, but this seems to be a derivative of the context as a whole and not a part of the meaning of the lexical items).

αἰφνίδιος: ἐπιστῇ ἐφ' ὑμᾶς αἰφνίδιος ἡ ἡμέρα ἐκείνη 'that Day may come on you suddenly' Lk 21.34.

ἐξαίφνης: ἐξαίφνης ἐγένετο σὺν τῷ ἀγγέλῳ πλῆθος στρατιᾶς οὐρανίου 'suddenly a great army of heaven's angels appeared with the angel' Lk 2.13.

ἐξάπινα: ἐξάπινα περιβλεψάμενοι οὐκέτι οὐδένα εἶδον 'they immediately looked around but did not see anybody' Mk 9.8.

ἐξαυτῆς: ὃς ἐξαυτῆς παραλαβὼν στρατιώτας καὶ ἑκατοντάρχας κατέδραμεν ἐπ' αὐτούς 'at once he took some soldiers and officers and rushed down to them' Ac 21.32.

ἄφνω: ἄφνω δὲ σεισμὸς ἐγένετο μέγας 'suddenly there was a violent earthquake' Ac 16.26.

ἄρτιᶜ: παραστήσει μοι ἄρτι πλείω δώδεκα λεγιῶνας ἀγγέλων 'at once he would send me more than twelve armies of angels' Mt 26.53.

παραχρῆμα: ἀφῆκεν αὐτήν· παραχρῆμα δὲ ἀναστᾶσα διηκόνει αὐτοῖς '(the fever) left her and she got up at once and began to wait upon them' Lk 4.39.

67.114 ἐν ῥιπῇ ὀφθαλμοῦ: (an idiom, literally 'in the blinking of an eye') an extremely short duration of time – 'quickly, suddenly.' ἐν ῥιπῇ ὀφθαλμοῦ, ἐν τῇ ἐσχάτῃ σάλπιγγι 'suddenly, when the last trumpet sounds' 1 Cor 15.52. For another interpretation of the phrase ἐν ῥιπῇ ὀφθαλμοῦ, see 16.5.

67.115 νέος^a, α, ον; καινός^a, ή, όν: pertaining to having been in existence for only a short time – 'new, recent.'

νέος^a: οὐδεὶς βάλλει οἶνον νέον εἰς ἀσκοὺς παλαιούς 'no one pours new wine into old wineskins' Mk 2.22.

καινός^a: ἀλλὰ οἶνον νέον εἰς ἀσκοὺς καινούς 'but new wine must be poured in new wineskins' Mk 2.22.

67.116 νέος^c, α, ον; μικρός^f, ά, όν; ἐλάσσων^c, ον: pertaining to a living being who is relatively young, often the younger of two objects – 'young, younger.'

νέος^c: εἶπεν ὁ νεώτερος αὐτῶν τῷ πατρί 'the younger one said to his father' Lk 15.12.

μικρός^f: καὶ Μαρία ἡ Ἰακώβου τοῦ μικροῦ 'and Mary the mother of James the younger' Mk 15.40. It is possible, however, that μικρός in Mk 15.40 denotes small size rather than being younger (see 81.13).

ἐλάσσων^c: ὁ μείζων δουλεύσει τῷ ἐλάσσονι 'the older will serve the younger' Ro 9.12.

67.117 εἰς^o: a marker of an extent of time – 'for, in, at.' ἔχεις πολλὰ ἀγαθὰ κείμενα εἰς ἔτη πολλά 'you have many good things stored up for many years' Lk 12.19; ἔφθασεν δὲ ἐπ' αὐτοὺς ἡ ὀργὴ εἰς τέλος 'but punishment has come upon them at the end' 1 Th 2.16. For another interpretation of εἰς τέλος in 1 Th 2.16 (as an idiom), see 78.47.

F   Duration of Time with Reference to Some Point of Time: Until, Delay, Still, From (67.118-67.135)

67.118 συστέλλω^a; κλίνω^c; προκόπτω^d: to extend in time, with focus upon the end point – 'to draw near, to draw to a close.'

συστέλλω^a: ὁ καιρὸς συνεσταλμένος ἐστίν 'the time is coming to an end' 1 Cor 7.29.

κλίνω^c: ἡ δὲ ἡμέρα ἤρξατο κλίνειν 'when the day was coming to an end' Lk 9.12. For another interpretation of κλίνω in Lk 9.12, see 68.51.

προκόπτω^d: ἡ νὺξ προέκοψεν 'the night is nearly over' Ro 13.12.

67.119 ἕως^a or ἕως ὅτου^a or ἕως οὗ^a; ἄχρι^a or ἄχρις οὗ^a or ἄχρι οὗ^b; μέχρι^a or μέχρις οὗ;

εἰς^q: the continuous extent of time up to a point – 'until, to, at last, at length.'[16]

ἕως^a: προῆγεν αὐτοὺς ἕως ἐλθὼν ἐστάθη ἐπάνω οὗ ἦν τὸ παιδίον '(the star) went ahead of them until it came and stopped over the place where the child was' or 'went ahead of them. At length it came . . .' Mt 2.9; πῶς συνέχομαι ἕως ὅτου τελεσθῇ 'how distressed I am until it is over' Lk 12.50; ἕως οὗ ἔτεκεν υἱόν 'until she gave birth to a son' Mt 1.25.

ἄχρι^a: ὁμιλήσας ἄχρι αὐγῆς 'he talked with them until sunrise' Ac 20.11; τὸν θάνατον τοῦ κυρίου καταγγέλλετε, ἄχρις οὗ ἔλθῃ 'you proclaim the death of the Lord until he comes' 1 Cor 11.26; δεῖ γὰρ αὐτὸν βασιλεύειν ἄχρι οὗ θῇ πάντας τοὺς ἐχθροὺς ὑπὸ τοὺς πόδας αὐτοῦ 'for he (Christ) must rule until he (God) defeats all enemies' 1 Cor 15.25; ἄχρι οὗ ἀνέστη βασιλεὺς ἕτερος 'at last another king arose' Ac 7.18.

μέχρι^a: διεφημίσθη ὁ λόγος οὗτος παρὰ Ἰουδαίοις μέχρι τῆς σήμερον 'that report was spread around by the Jews until this day' Mt 28.15; οὐ μὴ παρέλθῃ ἡ γενεὰ αὕτη μέχρις οὗ ταῦτα πάντα γένηται 'this generation will not pass away until all these things take place' Mk 13.30.

εἰς^q: ὁ δὲ ὑπομείνας εἰς τέλος οὗτος σωθήσεται 'he who remains to the end will be saved' Mt 10.22; εἰς τέλος ἠγάπησεν αὐτούς 'he loved them to the end' Jn 13.1. For an interpretation of εἰς τέλος in Jn 13.1 as an idiom, see 78.47.

The phrase εἰ μὴ ὅταν is often translated as 'until' (for example, μηδενὶ ἃ εἶδον διηγήσωνται, εἰ μὴ ὅταν ὁ υἱὸς τοῦ ἀνθρώπου ἐκ νεκρῶν ἀναστῇ 'not to tell anybody what they have seen until the Son of Man has risen from death' Mk 9.9), but this phrase may be analyzed as meaning 'if it is not when,' an expression which is semantically equivalent to 'until.'

67.120 παρατείνω^a: to extend a period of time – 'to prolong.' παρέτεινέν τε τὸν λόγον μέχρι μεσονυκτίου 'and prolonged his speech until midnight' Ac 20.7. For another interpretation of παρατείνω in Ac 20.7, see 68.21.

---

16 ἕως, ἄχρι, and μέχρι frequently occur with a postposed marker of indefinite temporal reference: οὗ, occurring with all three markers, and ὅτου with ἕως.

67.121 μέλλω^c: to extend time unduly, with the implication of lack of decision – 'to wait, to delay.' νῦν τί μέλλεις; ἀναστὰς βάπτισαι 'what are you waiting for? Get up and be baptized' Ac 22.16.

67.122 χρονίζω^a: to extend a state or an event beyond an expected time – 'to be late.' χρονίζοντος δὲ τοῦ νυμφίου 'because the bridegroom was late' Mt 25.5.

67.123 βραδύς, εῖα, ύ: pertaining to an extended period of time, with the implication of being slow to do something – 'slow, dilatory.' ἔστω . . . βραδὺς εἰς τὸ λαλῆσαι, βραδὺς εἰς ὀργήν 'be . . . slow to speak and slow to become angry' Jas 1.19.

67.124 βραδύνω; βραδύτης, ητος f: (derivatives of βραδύς 'slow,' 67.123) to extend a period of time, with the implication of slowness and/or delay – 'to be slow, to delay.' βραδύνω: ἐλπίζων ἐλθεῖν πρός σε ἐν τάχει· ἐὰν δὲ βραδύνω 'I hope to come and see you soon, but if I delay' 1 Tm 3.14-15. βραδύτης: οὐ βραδύνει κύριος τῆς ἐπαγγελίας, ὥς τινες βραδύτητα ἡγοῦνται 'the Lord is not slow to do what he has promised, as some people count it to be slowness' 2 Pe 3.9.

67.125 ὀκνέω: to extend a period of time, with the implication of lack of activity – 'to delay.' μὴ ὀκνήσῃς διελθεῖν ἕως ἡμῶν 'do not delay to come to us' Ac 9.38.

67.126 μακροθυμέω^b: to extend a period of time on the basis of a particular mental attitude – 'to be slow to, to delay in.' καὶ μακροθυμεῖ ἐπ' αὐτοῖς; 'and will he be slow to help them?' Lk 18.7.

67.127 ἀναβολή, ῆς f: to extend a period of time by postponing an event – 'to put off, to postpone.' ἀναβολὴν μηδεμίαν ποιησάμενος τῇ ἐξῆς καθίσας ἐπὶ τοῦ βήματος 'I did not postpone, but on the very next day I sat in judgment court' Ac 25.17.

67.128 ἀκμήν; ἔτι^a; τὸ λοιπόν^b: extension of time up to and beyond an expected point – 'still, yet.'

ἀκμήν: ἀκμὴν καὶ ὑμεῖς ἀσύνετοί ἐστε; 'are you still without understanding?' Mt 15.16.
ἔτι^a: ἔτι αὐτοῦ λαλοῦντος ἰδοὺ Ἰούδας εἷς τῶν δώδεκα ἦλθεν 'he was still speaking when Judas, one of the twelve, arrived' Mt 26.47.
τὸ λοιπόν^b: καθεύδετε τὸ λοιπὸν καὶ ἀναπαύεσθε; 'are you still sleeping and resting?' Mt 26.45. Some manuscripts have λοιπόν instead of τὸ λοιπόν in Mt 26.45.

67.129 οὔπω; οὐδέπω; μήπω; μηδέπω: the negation of extending time up to and beyond an expected point – 'not yet, still not.'
οὔπω: ἔλεγεν αὐτοῖς, Οὔπω συνίετε; 'he said to them, Are you still without understanding?' Mk 8.21.
οὐδέπω: οὐδέπω γὰρ ᾔδεισαν τὴν γραφήν 'they still did not understand the scripture' Jn 20.9.
μήπω: μήπω πεφανερῶσθαι τὴν τῶν ἁγίων ὁδόν 'the way into the Most Holy Place has not yet been opened' He 9.8.
μηδέπω: περὶ τῶν μηδέπω βλεπομένων 'about things he could not yet see' He 11.7.

67.130 οὐκέτι; μηκέτι: the extension of time up to a point but not beyond – 'no longer.'
οὐκέτι: οὐκέτι εἰμὶ ἄξιος κληθῆναι υἱός σου 'I am no longer fit to be called your son' Lk 15.19.
μηκέτι: τοῦ μηκέτι δουλεύειν ἡμᾶς τῇ ἁμαρτίᾳ 'so that we should no longer be the slaves of sin' Ro 6.6.

67.131 ἐκ^l; ἀπό^h: markers of the extent of time from a point in the past – 'since, from.'
ἐκ^l: εἶδεν ἄνθρωπον τυφλὸν ἐκ γενετῆς 'he saw a man who had been blind from birth' Jn 9.1.
ἀπό^h: ἐσώθη ἡ γυνὴ ἀπὸ τῆς ὥρας ἐκείνης 'the woman became well from that moment' Mt 9.22; τρίτην ταύτην ἡμέραν ἄγει ἀφ' οὗ ταῦτα ἐγένετο 'this is now the third day since these things happened' Lk 24.21.[17]

67.132 ἔκπαλαι^b: an extensive period of time from a point in the past – 'since a long time, for a long time.' οἷς τὸ κρίμα ἔκπαλαι οὐκ ἀργεῖ 'their judge has been ready since a long time' 2 Pe 2.3.

17 The phrase ἀφ' οὗ 'since' is best interpreted as an elliptical expression in which the relative pronoun οὗ refers to a specific temporal element or to an elliptical one, as occurs in a number of instances.

67.133 ἐκ τοῦ αἰῶνος; ἀπὸ τῶν αἰώνων; πρὸ παντὸς τοῦ αἰῶνος; πρὸ χρόνων αἰωνίων; χρόνοις αἰωνίοις: an exceedingly long period of time from an assumed beginning up to the present – 'since all time, from all ages past, from the beginning of time.'

ἐκ τοῦ αἰῶνος: ἐκ τοῦ αἰῶνος οὐκ ἠκούσθη ὅτι ἠνέῳξέν τις ὀφθαλμοὺς τυφλοῦ γεγεννημένου 'from the beginning of time it has never been heard that someone opened the eyes of a man born blind' Jn 9.32.

ἀπὸ τῶν αἰώνων: τὸ μυστήριον τὸ ἀποκεκρυμμένον ἀπὸ τῶν αἰώνων καὶ ἀπὸ τῶν γενεῶν 'the secret which he hid since all ages past from mankind' Col 1.26.

πρὸ παντὸς τοῦ αἰῶνος: θεῷ . . . ἐξουσία πρὸ παντὸς τοῦ αἰῶνος 'to God . . . be the authority since all ages past' Jd 25.

πρὸ χρόνων αἰωνίων: χάριν, τὴν δοθεῖσαν ἡμῖν ἐν Χριστῷ Ἰησοῦ πρὸ χρόνων αἰωνίων 'he gave this grace to us in Christ Jesus from all ages past' 2 Tm 1.9.

χρόνοις αἰωνίοις: ἀποκάλυψιν μυστηρίου χρόνοις αἰωνίοις σεσιγημένου 'the revelation of the secret truth which was hidden from the beginning of time' Ro 16.25.

67.134 τὸ λοιπόν[a]: an extent of time beginning with the time of a discourse – 'from now on, henceforth.' τὸ λοιπὸν ἵνα καὶ οἱ ἔχοντες γυναῖκας ὡς μὴ ἔχοντες ὦσιν 'from now on married men should live as though they were not married' 1 Cor 7.29. In a number of languages τὸ λοιπόν in a context such as 1 Cor 7.29 may be expressed as 'from today' or 'beginning today.'

67.135 τὸ μέλλον: unlimited extent of time beginning with the time of the discourse – 'the future.' ἀποθησαυρίζοντας ἑαυτοῖς θεμέλιον καλὸν εἰς τὸ μέλλον 'will store up for themselves a treasure which will be a solid foundation for the future' 1 Tm 6.19.

G Duration of Time with Reference to Some Unit of Time: During, In, While, Throughout (67.136-67.141)

67.136 ἐν[t]; διά[i]; ἐπί[t]: markers of the extent of time within a unit – 'during, in the course of, within, for.'

ἐν[t]: λύσατε τὸν ναὸν τοῦτον καὶ ἐν τρισὶν ἡμέραις ἐγερῶ αὐτόν 'tear down this Temple and within three days I will build it again' Jn 2.19; ἐν τῷ σπείρειν αὐτὸν ἃ μὲν ἔπεσεν παρὰ τὴν ὁδόν 'as he scattered the seed (in the field), some of it fell along the path' Mt 13.4.

διά[i]: ἄγγελος δὲ κυρίου διὰ νυκτὸς ἀνοίξας τὰς θύρας τῆς φυλακῆς 'but during the night an angel of the Lord opened the prison gates' Ac 5.19.

ἐπί[t]: ὃς ὤφθη ἐπὶ ἡμέρας πλείους τοῖς συναναβᾶσιν αὐτῷ ἀπὸ τῆς Γαλιλαίας εἰς Ἰερουσαλήμ 'he appeared for many days to those who had gone with him from Galilee to Jerusalem' Ac 13.31.

67.137 μεσόω: to be in the middle of a period of time – 'to be in the middle of, to have something half over.' ἤδη δὲ τῆς ἑορτῆς μεσούσης ἀνέβη Ἰησοῦς εἰς τὸ ἱερόν 'when the feast was already half over, Jesus went up into the Temple' or 'already in the middle of the festival, Jesus went up into the Temple' Jn 7.14.

67.138 ἐν τῷ μεταξύ: (an idiom, literally 'in the between') an extent of time within another unit or extension of time – 'in the meantime, meanwhile.' ἐν τῷ μεταξὺ ἠρώτων αὐτὸν οἱ μαθηταὶ λέγοντες 'in the meantime his disciples were begging him saying . . .' Jn 4.31.

67.139 ὡς[e]; ὅτε[b]; ὅταν[d]; ἕως[b] or ἕως ὅτου[b] or ἕως οὗ[b]; ἐν ᾧ; ὅσος[d], η, ον; ἄχρις οὗ[b]: an extent of time of the same length as another extent or unit of time – 'as long as, while.'

ὡς[e]: περιπατεῖτε ὡς τὸ φῶς ἔχετε 'as long as you have the light, live your lives' Jn 12.35.

ὅτε[b]: ὅτε γὰρ ἦμεν ἐν τῇ σαρκί, τὰ παθήματα τῶν ἁμαρτιῶν . . . εἰς τὸ καρποφορῆσαι τῷ θανάτῳ 'for as long as we lived according to our human nature, our sinful desires . . . produced death' Ro 7.5.

ὅταν[d]: ὅταν ἐν τῷ κόσμῳ ὦ, φῶς εἰμι τοῦ κόσμου 'while I am in the world, I am the light of the world' Jn 9.5.

ἕως[b]: ἠνάγκασεν τοὺς μαθητὰς αὐτοῦ ἐμβῆναι εἰς τὸ πλοῖον . . . ἕως αὐτὸς ἀπολύει τὸν ὄχλον 'he made his disciples get into the boat . . . while he sent the crowd away' Mk 6.45; ἴσθι εὐνοῶν τῷ ἀντιδίκῳ σου ταχὺ ἕως ὅτου εἶ μετ' αὐτοῦ ἐν τῇ ὁδῷ 'come to terms quickly with your opponent while you are with him on the way' Mt 5.25; ἕως οὗ ἀπολύσῃ τοὺς ὄχλους 'while he sent the people away' Mt 14.22.

ἐν ᾧ: μὴ δύνανται οἱ υἱοὶ τοῦ νυμφῶνος ἐν ᾧ ὁ νυμφίος μετ' αὐτῶν ἐστιν νηστεύειν; 'as long as the bridegroom is with them, the wedding guests cannot fast, can they?' Mk 2.19.

ὅσος^d: μὴ δύνανται οἱ υἱοὶ τοῦ νυμφῶνος πενθεῖν ἐφ' ὅσον μετ' αὐτῶν ἐστιν ὁ νυμφίος; 'as long as the bridegroom is with them, the wedding guests cannot be sad, can they?' Mt 9.15; ὅσον χρόνον ἔχουσιν τὸν νυμφίον μετ' αὐτῶν οὐ δύνανται νηστεύειν 'as long as the bridegroom is with them, they will not fast' Mk 2.19; γυνὴ δέδεται ἐφ' ὅσον χρόνον ζῇ ὁ ἀνὴρ αὐτῆς 'a woman is not free as long as her husband lives' 1 Cor 7.39. The additon of ἐπί (degree, 78.51) and/or χρόνος (time, 67.78) reinforces this meaning of ὅσος.

ἄχρις οὗ^b: παρακαλεῖτε ἑαυτοὺς καθ' ἑκάστην ἡμέραν, ἄχρις οὗ τὸ Σήμερον καλεῖται 'you must help one another each day as long as the term "today" applies' He 3.13.

67.140 διά^j: a marker of an extent of time of the same length as another extent of time, with emphasis upon totality – 'throughout.' δι' ὅλης νυκτὸς κοπιάσαντες οὐδὲν ἐλάβομεν 'we worked hard throughout the night and caught nothing' Lk 5.5.

67.141 πάλαι^b: a considerable and continuous extent of time in the past – 'all this time, all that time.' πάλαι δοκεῖτε ὅτι ὑμῖν ἀπολογούμεθα; 'do you think that all this time we have been defending ourselves before you?' 2 Cor 12.19.

III. Units of Time (67.142-67.208)

H Indefinite Units of Time: Age, Lifetime, Interval, Period (67.142-67.162)

67.142 ἡμέρα^c, ας f: an indefinite unit of time (whether grammatically singular or plural), but not particularly long (note the contrast with αἰών^a 'age,' 67.143, and γενεά^d 'age,' 67.144) – 'time, period.' ἐγένετο ὡς ἐπλήσθησαν αἱ ἡμέραι τῆς λειτουργίας αὐτοῦ 'when his period of service (in the Temple)

was over' Lk 1.23. In a number of languages there is no specific term such as 'period' referring to an indefinite extent of time. One can, however, render Lk 1.23 as 'when he no longer had to serve in the Temple' or 'when he had finished the days when he served in the Temple.'

67.143 αἰών^a, ῶνος m: a unit of time as a particular stage or period of history – 'age, era.' οὐκ ἀφεθήσεται αὐτῷ οὔτε ἐν τούτῳ τῷ αἰῶνι οὔτε ἐν τῷ μέλλοντι 'he will not be forgiven, not in this age, neither in the following' Mt 12.32. In a number of languages there is no specific term for 'age' or 'era.' The closest approximation in the context of Mt 12.32 may be 'not in these many years and not in the many years which will follow.'

In 1 Tm 1.17 (τῷ δὲ βασιλεῖ τῶν αἰώνων literally, 'to the king of the ages') the genitive phrase τῶν αἰώνων is better understood as an abstract of unlimited extent of time, and accordingly, one may translate more accurately as 'the eternal king.' Compare 67.95.

67.144 γενεά^d, ᾶς f: an indefinite period of time, but in close relationship to human existence and in some contexts, a period of time about the length of a generation – 'age, epoch.' ὃς ἐν ταῖς παρῳχημέναις γενεαῖς εἴασεν πάντα τὰ ἔθνη πορεύεσθαι ταῖς ὁδοῖς αὐτῶν 'in the past ages he allowed all peoples to go their own way' Ac 14.16. It is, of course, possible in Ac 14.16 that the reference should be to 'generations' in the sense of periods of time.

67.145 καιρός^c, οῦ m: an indefinite period of time, but probably with the implication of the relation of a period to a particular state of affairs – 'age, era.' ἐὰν μὴ λάβῃ ἑκατονταπλασίονα νῦν ἐν τῷ καιρῷ τούτῳ 'and would not receive a hundred times as much now in this present era' Mk 10.30.

67.146 ἐνιαυτός^b, οῦ m: a unit of time of indefinite length, possibly somewhat shorter than αἰών^a 'age' (67.143) but of a relatively uncertain reference – 'age, era, time.' κηρύξαι ἐνιαυτὸν κυρίου δεκτόν 'to announce the favorable time of the Lord' (that is to say, an era in which the Lord bestows his favor) Lk 4.19.

67.147 παλιγγενεσία^b, ας *f*: an era involving the renewal of the world (with special reference to the time of the Messiah) – 'new age, Messianic age.' ἐν τῇ παλιγγενεσίᾳ, ὅταν καθίσῃ ὁ υἱὸς τοῦ ἀνθρώπου ἐπὶ θρόνου δόξης αὐτοῦ 'when the Son of Man sits on his glorious throne in the new age' Mt 19.28.

67.148 ὥρα^b, ας *f*: an indefinite unit of time which is relatively short – 'a while.' ὑμεῖς δὲ ἠθελήσατε ἀγαλλιαθῆναι πρὸς ὥραν ἐν τῷ φωτὶ αὐτοῦ 'and you were willing to enjoy his light for a while' Jn 5.35. For languages which have no term for an indefinite unit of time which is relatively short, it may be necessary to approximate the time span in the context, for example, 'for several months' or possibly 'for a year or so.'

67.149 στιγμή, ῆς *f*; ἄτομος, ον: an extremely short unit of time – 'moment, flash, instant.'
στιγμή: ἔδειξεν αὐτῷ πάσας τὰς βασιλείας τῆς οἰκουμένης ἐν στιγμῇ χρόνου 'he showed him all the kingdoms of the world in a moment of time' Lk 4.5.[18]
ἄτομος: πάντες δὲ ἀλλαγησόμεθα, ἐν ἀτόμῳ 'in an instant we shall all be changed' 1 Cor 15.51-52.

67.150 διάστημα, τος *n*: a unit of time between specified events – 'interval.' ἐγένετο δὲ ὡς ὡρῶν τριῶν διάστημα καὶ ἡ γυνὴ . . . εἰσῆλθεν 'and after an interval of about three hours, his wife . . . came in' Ac 5.7. In a number of languages it is not necessary to have a term such as 'interval,' for if one says 'after about three hours,' the meaning of 'interval' is implied.

67.151 ἡλικία^a, ας *f*: the period of time when a person is alive – 'span of life, lifetime, age.' τίς δὲ ἐξ ὑμῶν μεριμνῶν δύναται προσθεῖναι ἐπὶ τὴν ἡλικίαν αὐτοῦ πῆχυν ἕνα; 'which one of you by worrying can add a single day to his lifetime?' Mt 6.27. In Mt 6.27 ἡλικία may also denote height (see 81.4). If one understands ἡλικία in Mt 6.27 as time, then obviously some adjustment needs to be made to the

18 In Lk 4.5 χρόνος is added somewhat redundantly.

meaning of πῆχυς 'cubit' (81.25). For many languages the most appropriate term is one which means 'day,' but it would also be possible to use some other unit of length if this would clearly imply an impossibility.

67.152 βρέφος^b, ους *n*: the period of time when one is very young – 'childhood (probably implying a time when a child is still nursing), infancy.'[19] ὅτι ἀπὸ βρέφους . . . οἶδας 'you know . . . that ever since your childhood' 2 Tm 3.15.

67.153 παιδιόθεν: the period from the time a person is a child until the time of the context – 'since childhood.'[19] πόσος χρόνος ἐστὶν ὡς τοῦτο γέγονεν αὐτῷ; ὁ δὲ εἶπεν, Ἐκ παιδιόθεν 'how long has he been like this? He said, Since childhood' Mk 9.21. In παιδιόθεν, the stem παιδιο- would suggest an age somewhat older than in the case of βρέφος^b 'infancy' (67.152). παιδιόθεν, accordingly, would probably refer to a period of time which begins after a child has been weaned.

67.154 νεότης, ητος *f*: a period of time when one is young – 'youth, being young.'[19] μηδείς σου τῆς νεότητος καταφρονείτω 'let no one look down on your being young' or 'let no one despise your youth' 1 Tm 4.12.

67.155 νεωτερικός, ή, όν: pertaining to the period of time when one is an adolescent – 'belonging to youth, youthful, youth.'[19] τὰς δὲ νεωτερικὰς ἐπιθυμίας φεῦγε 'avoid the passions of youth' 2 Tm 2.22.

67.156 ἡλικία^b, ας *f*: the period of life when one is mature and at one's prime – 'prime, of age, mature.'[19] αὐτὸν ἐρωτήσατε, ἡλικίαν ἔχει 'ask him; he is of age' or '. . . he is an adult' Jn 9.21; καὶ παρὰ καιρὸν ἡλικίας 'though she was past her prime' He 11.11. Normally the

19 The meanings of terms in 67.152-67.158 could almost be treated equally well in Domain 23 *Physiological Events*, since these could be regarded as simply derivatives of physiological states. However, the focus of meaning in the respective contexts seems to be more upon a particular period of time rather than upon a physiological state or condition.

phrase παρὰ καιρὸν ἡλικίας would refer to a woman beyond menopause.

67.157 γῆρας, ως or ους, dat. γήρει n: the period of advanced age, normally of a person beyond his or her prime – 'old age.'[19] αὐτὴ συνείληφεν υἱὸν ἐν γήρει αὐτῆς 'she herself has received a son in her old age' Lk 1.36.

67.158 ὑπέρακμος, ον: pertaining to being of an age beyond the prime of life (in 1 Cor 7.36 a reference to a woman beyond the normal marriageable age) – 'past one's prime, past marriageable age.'[19] ἐὰν ᾖ ὑπέρακμος 'if she is past marriageable age' or 'if she has passed the right age to marry' 1 Cor 7.36.

67.159 συνηλικιώτης, ου m: a person who is of one's own age – 'contemporary.' καὶ προέκοπτον ἐν τῷ Ἰουδαϊσμῷ ὑπὲρ πολλοὺς συνηλικιώτας 'and in Judaism I surpassed many contemporaries' Ga 1.14.

67.160 εἰς[p]: a marker of a unit of time – 'on, at, for.' παρεκάλουν εἰς τὸ μεταξὺ σάββατον 'they invited (them) for the next Sabbath' Ac 13.42.

67.161 ὑπό[e]: a marker of the approximate time of a period (a rare usage) – 'about, at.' εἰσῆλθον ὑπὸ τὸν ὄρθρον εἰς τὸ ἱερὸν καὶ ἐδίδασκον 'they went into the Temple about dawn and taught' Ac 5.21.

67.162 πρός[k]: a marker of a period of time occurring before a subsequent period, and implying anticipation – 'to, toward.' ὅτι πρὸς ἑσπέραν ἐστίν 'because it is toward evening' or '. . . it is almost evening' or '. . . it is nearly evening' Lk 24.29.

I Definite Units of Time: Year, Month, Week, Day, Hour (67.163-67.200)

67.163 θέρος, ους n: the warmest period of the year and primarily the season for the growth of vegetation – 'summer.' ὅταν προβάλωσιν ἤδη, βλέποντες ἀφ' ἑαυτῶν γινώσκετε ὅτι ἤδη ἐγγὺς τὸ θέρος ἐστίν 'when you see that (the trees) are putting out leaves, you know that summer is near' Lk 21.30. In some areas

of the Tropics, there are difficulties involved in arriving at a satisfactory term for θέρος. It may not be possible, for example, to use a term 'the warm season,' since that may refer to the end of a dry season just before the rains begin. Normally, therefore, one can equate θέρος with 'the rainy season,' but a context such as Lk 21.30 may be difficult, for one would not normally say 'when you see that the trees are putting out leaves, you know that the rainy season is near,' for trees normally do not put out the leaves until after the rainy season has begun. It may, therefore, be necessary to render Lk 21.30 as 'when you see the trees putting out leaves, you know that the time for growth is near' or '. . . the time for trees to produce fruit.'

67.164 φθινοπωρινός, ή, όν: pertaining to the latter part of autumn – 'late autumn.' οὗτοί εἰσιν . . . δένδρα φθινοπωρινὰ ἄκαρπα 'they are like . . . trees in late autumn without any fruit' Jd 12. The use of φθινοπωρινός in Jd 12 should not be understood to imply that the fruit has already been picked, but rather that the trees in question have not produced fruit at all, and even in late autumn there is no productivity.

67.165 χειμών[a], ῶνος m: the coldest season of the year – 'winter.' σπούδασον πρὸ χειμῶνος ἐλθεῖν 'do your best to come before winter' 2 Tm 4.21. In a number of languages it may be important to translate χειμών[a] as simply 'the time of the cold rains.' Such rains may actually occur during the growing season or as a part of the rainy season. In semi-tropical areas, however, the cold rains do normally occur in what is regarded as the winter, while the warm rains occur in the summer. See also discussion at 67.163.

67.166 παραχειμάζω; παραχειμασία, ας f: to experience the winter season – 'to spend the winter, to be in a place during the winter.' παραχειμάζω: εἴ πως δύναιντο καταντήσαντες εἰς Φοίνικα παραχειμάσαι 'to try to reach Phoenix to spend the winter there' Ac 27.12. παραχειμασία: ἀνευθέτου δὲ τοῦ λιμένος ὑπάρχοντος πρὸς παραχειμασίαν 'the harbor was not a good one in which to spend the winter' Ac 27.12.

67.167 ἔτος, ους *n*: a unit of time involving a complete cycle of seasons – 'year.' ὅτε ἐγένετο ἐτῶν δώδεκα 'when he was twelve years old' Lk 2.42. In a number of languages, years are described in terms of repeated seasons. For example, some languages would speak of 'twelve years' as being 'twelve winters' or 'twelve summers,' while in other languages one might have an expression such as 'twelve rainy seasons' or 'twelve returns of the sun.'

67.168 ἐνιαυτός[a], οῦ *m*: the period of a complete year (similar in meaning to ἔτος 'year,' 67.167, but with the focus upon duration) – 'one-year period, one year.' πορευσόμεθα εἰς τήνδε τὴν πόλιν καὶ ποιήσομεν ἐκεῖ ἐνιαυτόν 'we will travel to a certain city where we will spend a year' Jas 4.13.

67.169 διετία, ας *f*: a period of two successive years – 'a two-year period.' ἐνέμεινεν δὲ διετίαν ὅλην ἐν ἰδίῳ μισθώματι 'for a period of two full years he lived there in a place he rented for himself' Ac 28.30.

67.170 διετής, ές: pertaining to having existed for two years – 'two years old.' διετοῦς καὶ κατωτέρω 'two years old and under' Mt 2.16. This expression in Mt 2.16 may be rendered in some languages as 'children who were two years old and those who were not yet two years old.'

67.171 τριετία, ας *f*: a period of three successive years – 'a three-year period, for three years.' μνημονεύοντες ὅτι τριετίαν . . . οὐκ ἐπαυσάμην . . . νουθετῶν ἕνα ἕκαστον 'remember that . . . I did not cease . . . teaching everyone . . . for a period of three years' Ac 20.31.

67.172 τεσσερακονταετής, ές: pertaining to a period of forty years – 'forty years.' ὡς δὲ ἐπληροῦτο αὐτῷ τεσσερακονταετὴς χρόνος 'when he was about forty years old' Ac 7.23; ὡς τεσσερακονταετῆ χρόνον ἐτροποφόρησεν αὐτοὺς ἐν τῇ ἐρήμῳ 'he took care of them in the desert for about forty years' Ac 13.18.

67.173 ἑκατονταετής, ές: pertaining to a period of a hundred years – 'hundred years.'

ἑκατονταετής που ὑπάρχων 'he was almost a hundred years old' Ro 4.19.

67.174 μήν, μηνός *m*: a period of time measured by a complete cycle in the phases of the moon – 'month.' περιέκρυβεν ἑαυτὴν μῆνας πέντε 'she kept herself in seclusion for five months' Lk 1.24. In a number of languages the equivalent of 'month' is simply 'moon,' so that one would translate this expression in Lk 1.24 as 'she kept herself in seclusion for five moons.'

67.175 τρίμηνον, ου *n*: a period of three months – 'for three months.'[20] πίστει Μωϋσῆς γεννηθεὶς ἐκρύβη τρίμηνον ὑπὸ τῶν πατέρων αὐτοῦ 'by faith, after Moses was born, he was hidden by his parents for three months' He 11.23.

67.176 τετράμηνος, ου *f*: a period of four months – 'for four months.'[20] οὐχ ὑμεῖς λέγετε ὅτι Ἔτι τετράμηνός ἐστιν καὶ ὁ θερισμὸς ἔρχεται; 'don't you have a saying, In four months the harvest comes?' Jn 4.35.

67.177 σάββατον[b], ου *n*: a period of seven days – 'week.' νηστεύω δὶς τοῦ σαββάτου 'I fast two days a week' Lk 18.12; τῇ δὲ μιᾷ τῶν σαββάτων 'on the first day of the week' Jn 20.1. In some languages it may be better to render Lk 18.12 as simply 'for every seven days, I fast two days.' For the expression 'the first day of the week,' there may be a number of complications, especially since in present-day usage Monday is often regarded as 'the first day of the week.' For the NT, of course, the Sabbath Day, or 'Saturday,' marked the seventh day of the week and the next day would be regarded as 'the first day of the week,' namely, Sunday.

67.178 ἡμέρα[a], ας *f*: according to Hebrew reckoning (as reflected in the NT), a period of time beginning at sunset and ending at the

---

20 For both items 67.175 and 67.176 it is, of course, also possible to speak of 'months' as 'moons.' Compare 67.174.

following sunset – 'day.' ἓξ ἡμέραι εἰσὶν ἐν αἷς δεῖ ἐργάζεσθαι 'there are six days in which we should work' Lk 13.14.

67.179 νυχθήμερον, ου *n*: a period consisting of a night and a day (essentially similar in meaning to ἡμέρα[a] 'day,' 67.178, but somewhat more explicit and emphatic) – 'a night and a day.' τρὶς ἐναυάγησα, νυχθήμερον ἐν τῷ βυθῷ πεποίηκα 'I have been in three shipwrecks; I have spent a night and a day in the deep waters of the sea' 2 Cor 11.25.

67.180 δευτεραῖος, α, ον: pertaining to the second of two days – 'on the second day.' δευτεραῖοι ἤλθομεν εἰς Ποτιόλους 'on the second day we came to Puteoli' Ac 28.13. Some persons have interpreted δευτεραῖος as a period of two days, so that one may translate 'after two days we came to Puteoli.' Though general Greek usage does not seem to substantiate this meaning for δευτεραῖος, the context of Ac 28.13 may involve a span of two days.

67.181 τεταρταῖος, α, ον: pertaining to the fourth in a series of days – 'on the fourth day.' τεταρταῖος γάρ ἐστιν 'for it is the fourth day' or '(he has been dead) four days' Jn 11.39.

67.182 ὀκταήμερος, ον: pertaining to taking place on the eighth in a series of days – 'on the eighth day.' περιτομῇ ὀκταήμερος 'circumcised on the eighth day' Php 3.5. Since in NT times the counting of days involved numbering both the first and the last day in a series, ὀκταήμερος may be rendered as 'a week later' or 'seven days later.' Compare ἡμέραι ὀκτώ 'eight days' (Lk 2.21) as being equivalent to one week; see discussion at 60.17.

67.183 καθημερινός, ή, όν; ἐφήμερος, ον; ἐπιούσιος[a], ον: pertaining to recurring on a daily basis – 'daily, on each day.'
καθημερινός: ὅτι παρεθεωροῦντο ἐν τῇ διακονίᾳ τῇ καθημερινῇ αἱ χῆραι αὐτῶν '(saying) that their widows were being neglected in the daily distribution of funds' Ac 6.1.
ἐφήμερος: λειπόμενοι τῆς ἐφημέρου τροφῆς 'they don't have enough to eat each day' Jas 2.15.
ἐπιούσιος[a]: τὸν ἄρτον ἡμῶν τὸν ἐπιούσιον δὸς ἡμῖν σήμερον 'give us each day our daily bread' Mt 6.11. For another interpretation of ἐπιούσιος in Mt 6.11, see 67.206.

It is also possible to understand ἐπιούσιος in Mt 6.11 as meaning 'necessary for existence' or 'that which is needed for each day' or 'that which is needed for the following day' or '. . . for the future.' One reason for the difficulties involved in determining the meaning of ἐπιούσιος is the fact that, as Origen stated, it may very well have been coined by the Gospel writers.

67.184 σάββατον[a], ου *n*: the seventh or last day of the week (religiously the most important since it was consecrated to the worship of God) – 'Sabbath, Saturday.' ποιοῦσιν ὃ οὐκ ἔξεστιν ποιεῖν ἐν σαββάτῳ 'they do what is not allowed to do on the Sabbath' Mt 12.2; ἐὰν ἐμπέσῃ τοῦτο τοῖς σάββασιν εἰς βόθυνον 'if (your sheep) falls into a deep hole on the Sabbath' Mt 12.11.

67.185 σαββατισμός, οῦ *m*: (derivative of σάββατον[a], 67.184) a special religiously significant period for rest and worship – 'a Sabbath rest, a period of rest.' ἀπολείπεται σαββατισμὸς τῷ λαῷ τοῦ θεοῦ 'there still remains for God's people a period of rest' He 4.9.

67.186 ἡμέρα[b], ας *f*: the daylight period between sunrise and sunset (divided into twelve hours) – 'day.' ἡμᾶς δεῖ ἐργάζεσθαι . . . ἕως ἡμέρα ἐστίν· ἔρχεται νὺξ ὅτε οὐδεὶς δύναται ἐργάζεσθαι 'we must work . . . as long as it is day; the night comes when no one can work' Jn 9.4.

67.187 πρωΐ; πρωΐα, ας *f*; ὄρθρος[a], ου *m*: the early part of the daylight period – 'early morning.'
πρωΐ: πείθων τε αὐτοὺς περὶ τοῦ Ἰησοῦ . . . ἀπὸ πρωΐ ἕως ἑσπέρας 'he tried to convince them about Jesus . . . from early morning till evening' Ac 28.23.
πρωΐα: πρωΐας δὲ γενομένης συμβούλιον ἔλαβον πάντες 'in the early morning they all made their plan against him' Mt 27.1.
ὄρθρος[a]: ὄρθρου δὲ πάλιν παρεγένετο εἰς τὸ ἱερόν 'in the early morning he went back to the Temple' Jn 8.2.

67.188 πρωϊνός, ή, όν: pertaining to early morning – 'of the early morning.' δώσω αὐτῷ τὸν ἀστέρα τὸν πρωϊνόν 'I will give to him the early morning star' Re 2.28.

67.189 ὀρθρινός, ή, όν: pertaining to being early in the morning – 'early in the morning.' γενόμεναι ὀρθριναὶ ἐπὶ τὸ μνημεῖον 'early in the morning the women went to the grave' Lk 24.22.

67.190 ὀρθρίζω: (derivative of ὄρθρος[a] 'early morning,' 67.187) to get up early in the morning and go about one's affairs – 'to get up early, to get up early and go.' πᾶς ὁ λαὸς ὤρθριζεν πρὸς αὐτὸν ἐν τῷ ἱερῷ ἀκούειν αὐτοῦ 'all the people would get up early in the morning and go to the Temple to listen to him' (literally '. . . go to him in the Temple to listen to him') Lk 21.38.

67.191 ἑσπέρα, ας f: a period from late in the afternoon until darkness – 'evening' (contrast 67.197). μεῖνον μεθ᾽ ἡμῶν, ὅτι πρὸς ἑσπέραν ἐστίν 'stay with us, for it is getting towards evening' Lk 24.29.

67.192 νύξ[a], νυκτός f: the period between sunset and sunrise – 'night.' φυλάσσοντες φυλακὰς τῆς νυκτὸς ἐπὶ τὴν ποίμνην 'keeping watch over their flocks during the night' Lk 2.8.

67.193 ἔννυχα: pertaining to the period between sunset and sunrise – 'at night, in the night.' καὶ πρωῒ ἔννυχα λίαν ἀναστὰς ἐξῆλθεν 'and early in the morning while it was still dark (literally 'and early morning, very much at night') he rose and went out' Mk 1.35. In some languages it may be necessary to translate ἔννυχα λίαν in Mk 1.35 as 'before sunrise' or 'long before daylight' or 'before the heavens open.'

67.194 αὐλίζομαι: to lodge in a place during the night – 'to spend the night.' ἐξῆλθεν ἔξω τῆς πόλεως εἰς Βηθανίαν, καὶ ηὐλίσθη ἐκεῖ 'he went out of the city to Bethany and spent the night there' Mt 21.17.

67.195 διανυκτερεύω: to continue in an activity or state during the night – 'to spend the night.' καὶ ἦν διανυκτερεύων ἐν τῇ προσευχῇ τοῦ θεοῦ 'and spent the night praying to God' Lk 6.12.

67.196 φυλακή[c], ῆς f: one of four periods of time into which the night was divided (during which time certain assigned persons would be on the lookout) – 'watch, a fourth of the night.' περὶ τετάρτην φυλακὴν τῆς νυκτὸς ἔρχεται πρὸς αὐτοὺς περιπατῶν ἐπὶ τῆς θαλάσσης 'it was about the fourth watch that he came to them walking on the lake' Mk 6.48. In general, φυλακή in the NT refers to one of four periods into which the night was divided, based on the Roman custom of dividing the night into four equal periods or watches. In Mt 24.43 and Lk 12.38, however, it is possible that the reference is to three night watches, as was typical among Hebrews and Greeks.

67.197 ὀψία, ας f; ὀψέ[b]: the period after sunset and before darkness – 'evening' (contrast 67.191).
ὀψία: ὀψίας δὲ γενομένης, ὅτε ἔδυ ὁ ἥλιος 'when evening came, after the sun had set' Mk 1.32.
ὀψέ[b]: ἢ ὀψὲ ἢ μεσονύκτιον ἢ ἀλεκτοροφωνίας ἢ πρωΐ 'it may be in the evening, at midnight, when the cock crows, or early in the morning' Mk 13.35.

67.198 ἀλεκτοροφωνία, ας f: the name of the third Roman watch during the night, called 'cockcrow' (see φυλακή[c] 'watch,' 67.196) – 'before dawn, when the cock crows.' ἢ ὀψὲ ἢ μεσονύκτιον ἢ ἀλεκτοροφωνίας ἢ πρωΐ 'it may be in the evening, at midnight, when the cock crows, or early in the morning' Mk 13.35.

67.199 ὥρα[c], ας f: the twelfth part of a day, measured from sunrise to sunset (in any one day the hours would be of equal length, but would vary somewhat depending on the time of the year) – 'hour.' ἐχθὲς ὥραν ἑβδόμην ἀφῆκεν αὐτὸν ὁ πυρετός 'yesterday at the seventh hour, the fever left him' Jn 4.52. Since the hours were counted beginning at sunrise, the seventh hour would be approximately one o'clock in the afternoon. For other references to numbered hours, see 60.50, 60.56, 60.57, and 60.58.

67.200 ἡμίωρον, ου *n*: a period of half an hour – 'half an hour.' ἐγένετο σιγὴ ἐν τῷ οὐρανῷ ὡς ἡμίωρον 'there was silence in heaven for about half an hour' Re 8.1.

J Units of Time with Reference to Other Units or Points of Time: Yesterday, Today, Next Day (67.201-67.208)

67.201 παρασκευή, ῆς *f*: a day on which preparations were made for a sacred or feast day – 'day of preparation, Friday.' τῇ δὲ ἐπαύριον, ἥτις ἐστὶν μετὰ τὴν παρασκευήν, συνήχθησαν 'on the next day, the day after the day of preparation, they met' or 'the next day, which was a Sabbath, they met' Mt 27.62. The identification of παρασκευή with Friday became so traditional that it eventually came to be the present-day Greek term for 'Friday.'

67.202 προσάββατον, ου *n*: the day immediately before the Sabbath – 'the day before the Sabbath, Friday.' ἐπεὶ ἦν παρασκευή, ὅ ἐστιν προσάββατον, ἐλθὼν Ἰωσήφ 'because it was the preparation day, that is, the day before the Sabbath, Joseph went ...' Mk 15.42-43.

67.203 ἐχθές: a day prior to the time of a discourse – 'yesterday.' μὴ ἀνελεῖν με σὺ θέλεις ὃν τρόπον ἀνεῖλες ἐχθὲς τὸν Αἰγύπτιον; 'do you want to kill me just as you killed the Egyptian yesterday?' Ac 7.28.

67.204 πέρυσι: a year prior to the year of a discourse – 'last year.' Ἀχαΐα παρεσκεύασται ἀπὸ πέρυσι '(the believers in) Achaia have been ready to help since last year' 2 Cor 9.2.

67.205 σήμερον: the same day as the day of a discourse – 'today.' ὕπαγε σήμερον ἐργάζου ἐν τῷ ἀμπελῶνι 'go work in the vineyard today' Mt 21.28.

67.206 ἐπιούσιος[b], ον: pertaining to a day which is the same as the day of a discourse – 'today, for today.' τὸν ἄρτον ἡμῶν τὸν ἐπιούσιον δὸς ἡμῖν σήμερον 'give us today the food we need for today' Mt 6.11. For several other meanings of ἐπιούσιος, see 67.183.

67.207 αὔριον[a]: a day following the day of a discourse – 'tomorrow.' μὴ οὖν μεριμνήσητε εἰς τὴν αὔριον 'do not worry about tomorrow' Mt 6.34.

67.208 τῇ ἑξῆς; τῇ ἐπαύριον; τῇ ἐπιούσῃ; τῇ ἐχομένῃ; τῇ ἑτέρᾳ: a day immediately following a previous day – 'the next day, on the next day.'[21]
τῇ ἑξῆς: τῇ δὲ ἑξῆς εἰς τὴν Ῥόδον 'the next day (we came) to Rhodes' or '. . . (we reached) Rhodes' Ac 21.1.
τῇ ἐπαύριον: τῇ ἐπαύριον βλέπει τὸν Ἰησοῦν ἐρχόμενον πρὸς αὐτόν 'the next day he saw Jesus coming to him' Jn 1.29.
τῇ ἐπιούσῃ: τῇ δὲ ἐπιούσῃ εἰσῄει ὁ Παῦλος σὺν ἡμῖν πρὸς Ἰάκωβον 'the next day Paul went with us to (see) James' Ac 21.18.
τῇ ἐχομένῃ: δεῖ με σήμερον καὶ αὔριον καὶ τῇ ἐχομένῃ πορεύεσθαι 'I must be on my way today, tomorrow, and the next day' Lk 13.33.
τῇ ἑτέρᾳ: τῇ δὲ ἑτέρᾳ παρεβάλομεν εἰς Σάμον, τῇ δὲ ἐχομένῃ ἤλθομεν εἰς Μίλητον 'the following day we came to Samos and the next day we reached Miletus' Ac 20.15.

---

21 Rather than treat these phrases as lexical units, one can interpret them as elliptical expressions with the omission of the dative of ἡμέρα[a] 'day' (67.178).

68 Aspect[1]

Outline of Subdomains

A Begin, Start (68.1-68.10)
B Continue (68.11-68.21)
C Complete, Finish, Succeed (68.22-68.33)
D Cease, Stop (68.34-68.57)
E Try, Attempt (68.58-68.62)
F Do Intensely or Extensively (68.63-68.78)
G Rapidity, Suddenness (68.79-68.82)

Since most of the terms whose meanings are included in this domain are verbs, it may appear strange to regard the meanings as merely aspects of action rather than as events or actions in and of themselves. This is particularly true since most persons are accustomed to thinking of a principal verb in an English sentence as denoting action rather than being merely an aspect of the action occurring in the verb complement. In a number of languages, however, the various aspects included in this domain turn out to be adverbial clitics or affixes attached to verbs. They do not designate events but characterize them in terms of various aspects.

A Begin, Start[2] (68.1-68.10)

68.1 ἄρχομαι[a]; ἀρχή[a], ῆς f: to initiate an action, process, or state of being – 'to begin, to commence, beginning.'
ἄρχομαι[a]: ἀπὸ τότε ἤρξατο ὁ 'Ιησοῦς κηρύσσειν 'from that time Jesus began to preach (his message)' Mt 4.17. ἄρχομαι[a] may also be used in an absolute sense in which the related activity is merely implied: αὐτὸς ἦν 'Ιησοῦς ἀρχόμενος ὡσεὶ ἐτῶν τριάκοντα 'when Jesus

---

1 Meanings involving aspect normally relate to events, but they may also be applicable to states of being, as, for example, in items 68.11 and 68.57.
2 γίνομαι in the sense of 'to become' often refers to the initial aspect of adopting a new role, and it may therefore be translated 'to begin,' though there is far more involved in γίνομαι than merely the aspect of initiating an event or state, since it serves primarily to identify a change of state or role. In 1 Jn 2.18, ἀντίχριστοι πολλοὶ γεγόνασιν may be rendered as 'many have begun to oppose Christ,' and in Col 1.23, ἐγενόμην ἐγὼ Παῦλος διάκονος may be rendered as 'I began serving Christ.' For a treatment of γίνομαι in the sense of 'to become,' see 13.48.

---

began, he was about thirty years old' Lk 3.23. In rendering Lk 3.23, it may be useful to translate as 'when Jesus began his ministry, he was about thirty years old.'
ἀρχή[a]: ἀρχὴ τοῦ εὐαγγελίου 'Ιησοῦ Χριστοῦ 'the beginning of the good news about Jesus Christ' Mk 1.1. It would also be possible to treat ἀρχή in Mk 1.1 as indicating sequence (Domain 61), so that the contents of verse 1 could be regarded as a type of title for the following section. It seems far better, however, to regard ἀρχή in Mk 1.1 as being closely related to what immediately follows in verse 2, so that one may translate 'the good news about Jesus Christ the Son of God began as the prophet Isaiah had written . . .'

68.2 ἀρχηγός[a], οῦ m: one who causes something to begin – 'initiator, founder, originator.' τὸν ἀρχηγὸν τῆς σωτηρίας 'the founder of salvation' or 'the one who institutes salvation' He 2.10. For another interpretation of ἀρχηγός in He 2.10, see 36.6.

68.3 ἐνάρχομαι: to begin in a particular state or relationship – 'to begin, to commence.' ἐναρξάμενοι πνεύματι 'you began by (God's) Spirit' Ga 3.3.

68.4 προενάρχομαι: to begin an activity previously – 'to begin previously.' ἵνα καθὼς προενήρξατο οὕτως 'since he had earlier begun his work' 2 Cor 8.6.

68.5 ἐπιβάλλω[f]: to begin an activity, with special emphasis upon the inception or possibly the suddenness with which the event takes place – 'to begin.' ἐπιβαλὼν ἔκλαιεν 'he began to cry' Mk 14.72. It would also be possible to understand ἐπιβάλλω in Mk 14.72 as meaning 'when he thought of it' or 'when he reflected on it' (see 30.7).

68.6 ἐπιβάλλω τὴν χεῖρα ἐπ' ἄροτρον καὶ βλέπω εἰς τὰ ὀπίσω: (a Semitic idiom, literally 'one who puts his hand to the plow and looks back') to begin some activity requiring close attention but then to change one's mind about proceeding – 'to start to do something and then to hesitate, to begin but have second thoughts about continuing.' οὐδεὶς ἐπιβαλὼν τὴν χεῖρα ἐπ' ἄροτρον καὶ βλέπων εἰς τὰ ὀπίσω εὔθετός ἐστιν τῇ βασιλείᾳ τοῦ θεοῦ 'no one who puts his hand to the plow and then keeps looking back is of any use for the kingdom of God' or 'no one who begins and then has second thoughts is of any use for the kingdom of God' Lk 9.62. It is probably best to regard the phrase ἐπιβαλὼν τὴν χεῖρα ἐπ' ἄροτρον καὶ βλέπων εἰς τὰ ὀπίσω as a part of a traditional saying referring to anyone who has second thoughts about undertaking some new or different enterprise, but the particular manner in which this is adapted to a statement concerning 'the kingdom of God' makes its strictly idiomatic structure somewhat doubtful.

68.7 εἰσέρχομαι^c; ἐφίσταμαι^f (and perfect active): to begin, with the focus upon the initial stages of an activity – 'to begin, to commence.'

εἰσέρχομαι^c: εἰσῆλθεν δὲ διαλογισμὸς ἐν αὐτοῖς 'an argument began among them' or 'they began to argue' Lk 9.46. In the first clause of Lk 9.46, it is clear that the event is to be found in the noun διαλογισμός, while the verb εἰσῆλθεν merely contributes an aspect of the event.

ἐφίσταμαι^f: διὰ τὸν ὑετὸν τὸν ἐφεστῶτα 'because it began to rain' or 'because the rain started' Ac 28.2. It is also possible to interpret ἐφίσταμαι in Ac 28.2 as meaning 'to be imminent' (see 67.63).

68.8 ἀναζωπυρέω: (a figurative extension of meaning of ἀναζωπυρέω 'to rekindle a fire,' not occurring in the NT) to cause something to begin again – 'to reactivate, to cause to begin to be active again.' ἀναζωπυρεῖν τὸ χάρισμα τοῦ θεοῦ 'to rekindle the gift of God' 2 Tm 1.6. It may also be possible to translate ἀναζωπυρέω in 2 Tm 1.6 as 'to cause to take on new life.' A few translators have used an expression such as 'to keep alive the gift,' primarily in order to avoid the impression that Timothy had in some measure departed from his earlier dedication to the gospel.

68.9 ἐπεγείρω: to cause to begin and to intensify an activity – 'to stir up, to commence.'

ἐπήγειραν διωγμὸν ἐπὶ τὸν Παῦλον καὶ Βαρναβᾶν 'they stirred up persecution against Paul and Barnabas' Ac 13.50.

68.10 ἐπεισαγωγή, ῆς f: the process of causing something to begin – 'introduction, to begin.' ἐπεισαγωγὴ δὲ κρείττονος ἐλπίδος 'but the introduction of a better hope' He 7.19.

B Continue (68.11-68.21)

68.11 μένω^d; διαμένω^b; ἐπιμένω^b; προσμένω^b; ἐμμένω^b; παραμένω^b: to continue in an activity or state – 'to continue, to remain in, to keep on.'

μένω^d: μὴ μένων ἐν τῇ διδαχῇ τοῦ Χριστοῦ 'one not remaining in the teaching of Christ' 2 Jn 9; ὁ ἀγαπῶν τὸν ἀδελφὸν αὐτοῦ ἐν τῷ φωτὶ μένει 'he who loves his fellow believer remains in the light' 1 Jn 2.10.

διαμένω^b: αὐτὸς ἦν διανεύων αὐτοῖς, καὶ διέμενεν κωφός 'he made signs to them and remained unable to speak' or '. . . remained dumb' Lk 1.22.

ἐπιμένω^b: ὡς δὲ ἐπέμενον ἐρωτῶντες αὐτόν, ἀνέκυψεν καὶ εἶπεν αὐτοῖς 'when they kept on questioning him, he straightened up and spoke to them' Jn 8.7. It is also possible to understand ἐπιμένω in Jn 8.7 as continuing in a place (see ἐπιμένω^a, 85.55), and therefore one may translate 'as they stood there.'

προσμένω^b: προσμένει ταῖς δεήσεσιν καὶ ταῖς προσευχαῖς νυκτὸς καὶ ἡμέρας 'she continues in prayer and supplications day and night' 1 Tm 5.5. It is possible that προσμένω^b differs from ἐπιμένω^b in focusing upon the continuity or extent of time involved.

ἐμμένω^b: ὅτι αὐτοὶ οὐκ ἐνέμειναν ἐν τῇ διαθήκῃ μου 'because they did not continue in my covenant' He 8.9. In He 8.9 the implication of 'to continue in a covenant' is to adhere to the articles or stipulations of a covenant. Accordingly one may render He 8.9 as 'because they did not remain faithful to my covenant.' In παρακαλοῦντες ἐμμένειν τῇ πίστει 'encourage them to remain true to the faith' Ac 14.22, it is also possible to translate the expression 'to remain true to the faith' as 'to continue to believe.'

παραμένω^b: γεγονότες ἱερεῖς διὰ τὸ θανάτῳ κωλύεσθαι παραμένειν 'because they were hindered by death from continuing their work as priests' He 7.23.

68.12 ἐκτενής[a], ές; ἐκτενῶς[a]: (derivatives of ἐκτείνω 'to stretch out,' 16.19) pertaining to an unceasing activity, normally involving a degree of intensity and/or perseverance – 'without ceasing, continuously, constantly.'
ἐκτενής[a]: πρὸ πάντων τὴν εἰς ἑαυτοὺς ἀγάπην ἐκτενῆ ἔχοντες 'above everything, love one another without ceasing' 1 Pe 4.8. For another interpretation of ἐκτενής in 1 Pe 4.8, see 25.71.
ἐκτενῶς[a]: προσευχὴ δὲ ἦν ἐκτενῶς γινομένη ὑπὸ τῆς ἐκκλησίας πρὸς τὸν θεὸν περὶ αὐτοῦ 'the people in the church were praying constantly to God for him' Ac 12.5. For another interpretation of ἐκτενῶς in Ac 12.5, see 25.71.

68.13 προστίθεμαι[a]: to continue, with focus upon the next element – 'to continue, to proceed to.' ἀκουόντων δὲ αὐτῶν ταῦτα προσθεὶς εἶπεν παραβολήν 'while they were listening to this, he continued and told them a parable' Lk 19.11.

68.14 ἐφίσταμαι[g] (and 2nd aorist active): to continue in an activity in spite of presumed opposition – 'to continue, to persist in.' κήρυξον τὸν λόγον, ἐπίστηθι εὐκαίρως ἀκαίρως 'preach the word; and do it with persistence whether or not the circumstances are favorable' 2 Tm 4.2.

68.15 ἐκκρέμαμαι[b]: (a figurative extension of meaning of ἐκκρέμαμαι 'to hang from,' not occurring in the NT) to persist in doing something – 'to continue intently, to persist in.' ὁ λαὸς γὰρ ἅπας ἐξεκρέματο αὐτοῦ ἀκούων 'for all the people kept listening eagerly to him' Lk 19.48. For another interpretation of ἐκκρέμαμαι in Lk 19.48, see 30.34.

68.16 ἐπίκειμαι[d]: to keep on doing something with presumed insistence – 'to keep on, to continue insisting, to persist in.' οἱ δὲ ἐπέκειντο φωναῖς μεγάλαις 'but they kept on shouting with loud voices' Lk 23.23.

68.17 ὑπομένω[c]: to continue in an activity or state despite resistance and opposition – 'to continue, to remain, to endure.' μακάριος ἀνὴρ ὃς ὑπομένει πειρασμόν 'happy is the man who experiences temptation and still continues (to trust)' Jas 1.12. For another interpretation of ὑπομένω in Jas 1.12, see 39.20.

68.18 διανύω[b]: to continue, with the implication of movement – 'to continue, to proceed.' ἡμεῖς δὲ τὸν πλοῦν διανύσαντες ἀπὸ Τύρου 'and we continued our voyage from Tyre' Ac 21.7. For another interpretation of διανύω in Ac 21.7, see 68.25.

68.19 συνέχομαι[c]; προσέχω[d]: to continue with close attention and devotion – 'to continue to give oneself to, to continue to apply oneself to.'
συνέχομαι[c]: συνείχετο τῷ λόγῳ ὁ Παῦλος 'Paul continued to give himself to (preaching) the word' Ac 18.5.
προσέχω[d]: οὐδεὶς προσέσχηκεν τῷ θυσιαστηρίῳ 'no one (of his tribe) gave himself continuously to the ministry of the altar' He 7.13. It would also be possible to render this portion of He 7.13 as 'no one of his tribe served continuously as priest.'

68.20 μελετάω[c]; εἰμὶ ἐν (an idiom, literally 'to be in'): to continue to perform certain activities with care and concern – 'to practice, to continue to do, to cultivate.' ταῦτα μελέτα, ἐν τούτοις ἴσθι, ἵνα σου ἡ προκοπὴ φανερὰ ᾖ πᾶσιν 'practice these things and give yourself to them in order that your progress may be seen by all' 1 Tm 4.15. The construction in 1 Tm 4.15, in which ταῦτα μελέτα and ἐν τούτοις ἴσθι appear to be essentially synonymous reinforcements one of the other, would appear to fully justify combining these expressions as essentially equivalent in meaning, but for another interpretation of μελετάω in 1 Tm 4.15, see 30.20.

68.21 παρατείνω[b]: to cause an event to continue beyond an expected period of time – 'to prolong, to stretch out, to keep on.' ὁ Παῦλος διελέγετο αὐτοῖς . . . παρέτεινέν τε τὸν λόγον μέχρι μεσονυκτίου 'Paul spoke to the people . . . and prolonged his speech until midnight' or '. . . he kept on speaking until midnight'

Ac 20.7. For another interpretation of παρατείνω in Ac 20.7, see 67.120.[3]

C Complete, Finish, Succeed (68.22-68.33)

68.22 τελέω[a]; ἐκτελέω; ἀποτελέω; ἐπιτελέω[a]; συντελέω[a]; τελειόω[c]: to bring an activity to a successful finish – 'to complete, to finish, to end, to accomplish.'[4]

τελέω[a]: ὅταν τελέσωσιν τὴν μαρτυρίαν αὐτῶν 'when they finish proclaiming their message' Re 11.7; ἄχρι τελεσθῶσιν αἱ ἑπτὰ πληγαὶ τῶν ἑπτὰ ἀγγέλων 'until the seven plagues brought by the seven angels had come to an end' Re 15.8.

ἐκτελέω: ἵνα μήποτε θέντος αὐτοῦ θεμέλιον καὶ μὴ ἰσχύοντος ἐκτελέσαι 'so that he will not be able to finish (building the tower), after having laid the foundation' Lk 14.29.

ἀποτελέω: ἡ δὲ ἁμαρτία ἀποτελεσθεῖσα ἀποκύει θάνατον 'sin, when it has completed its action, produces death' Jas 1.15; ἰάσεις ἀποτελῶ σήμερον καὶ αὔριον 'I am completing cures today and tomorrow' Lk 13.32. It is also possible to translate ἀποτελέω in Lk 13.32 as 'am performing,' but the focus evidently is upon the completion of a series of such healings. The final phrase of Lk 13.32, καὶ τῇ τρίτῃ τελειοῦμαι 'and on the third day I will be finished,' points to a possible distinction between ἀποτελέω and τελειόω, in which the first apparently serves to mark the end of a particular series, while the second points to the completion of anything and everything involved.

ἐπιτελέω[a]: ὁ ἐναρξάμενος ἐν ὑμῖν ἔργον ἀγαθὸν ἐπιτελέσει ἄχρι ἡμέρας Χριστοῦ Ἰησοῦ '(God), who began (this) good work in you, will carry it on until it is finished in the day of Christ Jesus' Php 1.6.

σύντελέω[a]: συντελέσας πάντα πειρασμὸν ὁ διάβολος ἀπέστη ἀπ' αὐτοῦ ἄχρι καιροῦ 'when the Devil finished tempting him in every way, he left him for a while' Lk 4.13; λόγον γὰρ συντελῶν 'for he will accomplish what he has said' Ro 9.28. It is also possible to render this phrase in Ro 9.28 as 'for he will settle the account,' the implication being that he will accomplish what he has said he would do.

τελειόω[c]: ὡς τελειῶσαι τὸν δρόμον μου καὶ τὴν διακονίαν ἣν ἔλαβον παρὰ τοῦ κυρίου Ἰησοῦ 'if only I may finish the race and complete the task the Lord Jesus has given me' Ac 20.24.

68.23 τέλειος[d], α, ον: pertaining to that which is fully accomplished or finished – 'complete, finished.' ἡ δὲ ὑπομονὴ ἔργον τέλειον ἐχέτω 'but be sure that patience completes its work' Jas 1.4.

68.24 τελειωτής, οῦ m: one who makes possible the successful completion of something – 'one who completes, perfecter.' ἀφορῶντες εἰς τὸν τῆς πίστεως ἀρχηγὸν καὶ τελειωτὴν Ἰησοῦν 'looking to Jesus, the one who initiates and completes faith' or 'looking to Jesus on whom (our) faith depends from beginning to end' He 12.2.

68.25 διανύω[a]: to complete an activity, normally involving movement – 'to complete, to finish.' ἡμεῖς δὲ τὸν πλοῦν διανύσαντες ἀπὸ Τύρου κατηντήσαμεν εἰς Πτολεμαΐδα 'but after completing the voyage from Tyre, we arrived at Ptolemais' Ac 21.7. For another interpretation of διανύω in Ac 21.7, see 68.18.

68.26 πληρόω[c]: to finish an activity after having done everything involved – 'to finish, to complete.' Βαρναβᾶς δὲ καὶ Σαῦλος ὑπέστρεψαν εἰς Ἰερουσαλὴμ πληρώσαντες τὴν διακονίαν 'Barnabas and Saul finished their mission and returned to Jerusalem' Ac 12.25 (note the textual problem of εἰς).

68.27 ἀναπληρόω[f]: to bring something to completion, with emphasis upon the process – 'to bring to completion, to cause to be complete.' εἰς τὸ ἀναπληρῶσαι αὐτῶν τὰς ἁμαρτίας πάντοτε 'to the point of bringing to comple-

---

3 παρατείνω in Ac 20.7 is a typical instance in which a meaning may be interpreted either as an aspect of an event or as a marker of temporal extension.

4 There are no doubt certain subtle distinctions, particularly of emphasis, in the series τελέω[a], ἐκτελέω, ἀποτελέω, ἐπιτελέω[a], συντελέω[a], and τελειόω[c], but it is not possible to determine with precision the particular distinctions on the basis of existing contexts, though possibly ἐκτελέω and ἀποτελέω emphasize more finality, while ἐπιτελέω[a] may focus upon the resulting purpose.

tion the sins (that they had) always (committed)' 1 Th 2.16. For another interpretation of ἀναπληρόω in 1 Th 2.16, see 59.33.

68.28 ἀπαρτισμός, οῦ *m*: the completion of an activity, with the implication of the result being fully satisfactory – 'to complete, to finish, completion.' ψηφίζει τὴν δαπάνην, εἰ ἔχει εἰς ἀπαρτισμόν 'he figures out the cost (to see) if he has (enough money) to finish (building)' Lk 14.28.

68.29 κρατέω^c: to be able to complete or finish, presumably despite difficulties – 'to accomplish, to do successfully, to carry out.' δόξαντες τῆς προθέσεως κεκρατηκέναι 'thinking that they could carry out their purpose' Ac 27.13.

68.30 εὐοδόομαι^c: to be successful in accomplishing some activity or event – 'to complete, to succeed in.' εἴ πως ἤδη ποτὲ εὐοδωθήσομαι ἐν τῷ θελήματι τοῦ θεοῦ ἐλθεῖν πρὸς ὑμᾶς 'whether somehow I might now at last succeed by the will of God in coming to you' Ro 1.10.

68.31 τελειόω^d: to be completely successful in accomplishing some goal or attaining some state – 'to be completely successful, to succeed fully.' οὐχ ὅτι ἤδη ἔλαβον ἢ ἤδη τετελείωμαι 'not that I have already reached (the goal) or have already been completely successful' Php 3.12. For another interpretation of τελειόω in Php 3.12, see 53.50.

68.32 πληροφορέω^c: to fully accomplish one's task – 'to perform one's complete duty, to finish fully one's task, to accomplish satisfactorily.' τὴν διακονίαν σου πληροφόρησον 'fulfill completely your service (to God)' or '. . . your ministry' 2 Tm 4.5.

68.33 ὠφελέω^b: to be successful in accomplishing some goal, with the implication that such might be useful – 'to accomplish, to do.' ἰδὼν δὲ ὁ Πιλᾶτος ὅτι οὐδὲν ὠφελεῖ 'when Pilate saw that he was accomplishing nothing' or, idiomatically, '. . . getting nowhere' Mt 27.24.

D Cease, Stop (68.34-68.57)

68.34 παύομαι; ἀνάπαυσις^a, εως *f*: to cease from an activity in which one is engaged – 'to cease, to stop.'
παύομαι: ὡς δὲ ἐπαύσατο λαλῶν, εἶπεν πρὸς τὸν Σίμωνα 'when he ceased speaking, he said to Simon' Lk 5.4. A literal rendering of Lk 5.4, however, may suggest a contradiction in some languages, since the initial clause implies a cessation of speech, while the principal clause indicates that Jesus spoke to Simon. It may be possible in some languages to use two entirely different words for speaking, one referring to speaking to a large group, and the second indicating a direct communication with a single person.
ἀνάπαυσις^a: ἀνάπαυσιν οὐκ ἔχουσιν ἡμέρας καὶ νυκτὸς λέγοντες 'day and night they never stopped saying . . .' Re 4.8. It is possible that ἀνάπαυσις in Re 4.8 should be interpreted as a period of cessation, but such a meaning would only be derivative of this particular context.

68.35 ἐάω ἕως: (an idiom, literally 'to leave off until') to cease from what one is doing, with the implication of strong admonition – 'stop, quit, cease.' ἐᾶτε ἕως τούτου 'stop this' Lk 22.51.

68.36 διαλείπω; ἐκλείπω^c; ἐγκαταλείπω^c: to cease from an activity which has gone on for some time – 'to cease, to stop, to forsake.'
διαλείπω: αὕτη δὲ ἀφ' ἧς εἰσῆλθον οὐ διέλιπεν καταφιλοῦσά μου τοὺς πόδας 'she has not stopped kissing my feet since I came' Lk 7.45.
ἐκλείπω^c: ἐγὼ δὲ ἐδεήθην περὶ σοῦ ἵνα μὴ ἐκλίπῃ ἡ πίστις σου 'I have prayed for you, so that you will not stop trusting' Lk 22.32; τοῦ ἡλίου ἐκλιπόντος 'the sun stopped shining' Lk 23.45. In this phrase in Lk 23.45 there is an evident ellipsis of an expression meaning 'to shine.'
ἐγκαταλείπω^c: μὴ ἐγκαταλείποντες τὴν ἐπισυναγωγήν 'not forsaking assembling together' He 10.25.

68.37 ἀποτίθεμαι^b: (a figurative extension of meaning of ἀποτίθεμαι^a 'to put away,' 85.44) to cease doing what one is accustomed to doing – 'to stop, to cease.' ἀποθέσθαι ὑμᾶς κατὰ τὴν προτέραν ἀναστροφήν 'stop living the way you did formerly' Eph 4.22.

68.38 μεθίσταμαι: to cease from a state or function, with the implication of transfer or removal – 'to cease.' ὅταν μετασταθῶ ἐκ τῆς οἰκονομίας 'when I cease being in charge' or '. . . managing' Lk 16.4. See also 13.64 (passive of μεθίστημι[b]).

68.39 παραβαίνω[b]: (a figurative extension of meaning of παραβαίνω 'to go aside,' not occurring in the NT) to cease by removing oneself from some activity or position – 'to cease, to stop, to give up.' τῆς διακονίας ταύτης καὶ ἀποστολῆς, ἀφ᾽ ἧς παρέβη Ἰούδας 'this ministry and service as an apostle, which Judas ceased to perform' Ac 1.25. In Ac 1.25 διακονίας and ἀποστολῆς are the events to which παρέβη is related as aspect.

68.40 ἀπογίνομαι[a]: (a figurative extension of meaning of ἀπογίνομαι 'to die,' not occurring in the NT) to cease, with a complete and abrupt change – 'to cease, to stop.' ταῖς ἁμαρτίαις ἀπογενόμενοι 'having stopped sinning' or 'ceased sinning' 1 Pe 2.24. It is possible that in the translation of this phrase in 1 Pe 2.24 one might wish to preserve the figurative form and translate as 'dying to sin.' For another interpretation of ἀπογίνομαι in 1 Pe 2.24, see 74.27.

68.41 ἐκκλίνω[c]: to cease doing something, with the implication of engaging in some alternative – 'to cease, to stop.' ἐκκλινάτω δὲ ἀπὸ κακοῦ 'cease doing what is bad' 1 Pe 3.11.

68.42 ἵσταμαι[d]; κοπάζω: to cease, in reference to some type of movement – 'to cease, to stop.'
ἵσταμαι[d]: παραχρῆμα ἔστη ἡ ῥύσις τοῦ αἵματος αὐτῆς 'suddenly the flow of her blood stopped' Lk 8.44; καὶ ἐκέλευσεν στῆναι τὸ ἅρμα 'and he ordered the carriage to stop' Ac 8.38.
κοπάζω: ἀναβάντων αὐτῶν εἰς τὸ πλοῖον ἐκόπασεν ὁ ἄνεμος 'they got into the boat and the wind stopped blowing' Mt 14.32. Languages may differ considerably in expressions relating to the ceasing of wind, for example, 'the wind died,' 'the wind stood still,' 'the wind refused to move,' or 'the wind could not be felt.'

68.43 ἀνίημι[c]; ἀφίημι[i]; περιαιρέω[d]: to stop doing something, with the implication of complete cessation – 'to give up, to stop, to quit.'
ἀνίημι[c]: ἀνιέντες τὴν ἀπειλήν 'stop using threats' Eph 6.9.
ἀφίημι[i]: τὴν ἀγάπην σου τὴν πρώτην ἀφῆκες 'you have stopped loving me (as you did) at first' Re 2.4.
περιαιρέω[d]: λοιπὸν περιῃρεῖτο ἐλπὶς πᾶσα τοῦ σώζεσθαι ἡμᾶς 'we finally stopped hoping at all that we would be saved' Ac 27.20.

68.44 ἀποστρέφω[e]: (a figurative extension of meaning of ἀποστρέφω 'to cause to turn back from,' not occurring in the NT) to cease doing something, with the implication of rejection – 'to stop, to cease, to reject.' καὶ ἀπὸ μὲν τῆς ἀληθείας τὴν ἀκοὴν ἀποστρέφουσιν 'and they will stop listening to the truth' 2 Tm 4.4; ἐν τῷ ἀποστρέφειν ἕκαστον ἀπὸ τῶν πονηριῶν ὑμῶν 'by each of you stopping your evil ways' Ac 3.26. For another interpretation of ἀποστρέφω in Ac 3.26, see 31.70.

68.45 φράσσω: to cause something to cease (used with special reference to speech) – 'to cause to cease, to stop.' ἡ καύχησις αὕτη οὐ φραγήσεται εἰς ἐμὲ ἐν τοῖς κλίμασιν τῆς Ἀχαΐας 'as far as I am concerned, this boasting will not be stopped in the regions of Achaia' 2 Cor 11.10.

68.46 παύω; καταπαύω[c]: to cause something or someone to cease from some activity or state – 'to cause to cease, to make stop.'[5]
παύω: παυσάτω τὴν γλῶσσαν ἀπὸ κακοῦ 'make the tongue cease (speaking) evil' 1 Pe 3.10.
καταπαύω[c]: κατέπαυσαν τοὺς ὄχλους τοῦ μὴ θύειν αὐτοῖς 'they made the crowds stop sacrificing to them' Ac 14.18.

68.47 ἀφαιρέω[b]: to cause to cease, implying that someone is no longer permitted to enjoy or participate in some state or activity – 'to take away (from), to cause to no longer do.' ἀφελεῖ ὁ θεὸς τὸ μέρος αὐτοῦ ἀπὸ τοῦ ξύλου τῆς

---

5 It is possible that καταπαύω[c] should be understood as being somewhat more emphatic in meaning than παύω.

ζωῆς καὶ ἐκ τῆς πόλεως τῆς ἁγίας 'God will take away his share in the tree of life and in the holy city' Re 22.19; Μαριὰμ γὰρ τὴν ἀγαθὴν μερίδα ἐξελέξατο ἥτις οὐκ ἀφαιρεθήσεται αὐτῆς 'Mary has chosen the right thing and it will not be taken away from her' Lk 10.42; ὁ κύριός μου ἀφαιρεῖται τὴν οἰκονομίαν ἀπ' ἐμοῦ 'my master will take away from me my job as overseer' Lk 16.3.

68.48 θανατόω^b (a figurative extension of meaning of θανατόω^a 'to put to death,' 20.65); νεκρόω (a figurative extension of meaning of νεκρόω 'to put to death,' not occurring in the NT): to cease completely from activity, with the implication of extreme measures taken to guarantee such a cessation – 'to stop completely, to cease completely.'⁶
θανατόω^b: εἰ δὲ πνεύματι τὰς πράξεις τοῦ σώματος θανατοῦτε 'if by the Spirit you completely cease to do what the body wants' Ro 8.13. It is possible that in rendering this expression in Ro 8.13 one may desire to retain the figure of speech and therefore translate 'if by the Spirit you put to death the works of the body.'
νεκρόω: νεκρώσατε οὖν τὰ μέλη τὰ ἐπὶ τῆς γῆς 'therefore cease completely the earthly activities' Col 3.5.

68.49 πίπτω^f: (a figurative extension of meaning of πίπτω^a 'to fall,' 15.118) to cease, with the possible implication of failure – 'to stop, to cease, to fail.' ἡ ἀγάπη οὐδέποτε πίπτει 'love never ceases' 1 Cor 13.8. For another interpretation of πίπτω in 1 Cor 13.8, see 75.7.

68.50 μεταλλάσσω^b: to cease one activity and to start something else in exchange – 'to cease and to start, to exchange.' αἵ τε γὰρ θήλειαι αὐτῶν μετήλλαξαν τὴν φυσικὴν χρῆσιν εἰς τὴν παρὰ φύσιν 'for their women ceased engaging in the natural function and started

---

6 In certain instances, particularly in the case of θανατόω^b and νεκρόω, it is difficult to determine whether the figurative meanings involved have become conventionalized or whether they represent what may be called figurative usage, in other words, new figures of speech which no doubt had become somewhat conventional for the Christian community.

doing that which is contrary to nature' Ro 1.26.

68.51 κλίνω^d: to begin to come to an end, with particular reference to the period of a day (a figurative meaning dependent upon the position of the sun) – 'to begin to end.' ἡ δὲ ἡμέρα ἤρξατο κλίνειν 'when the day was about to end' Lk 9.12. For another interpretation of κλίνω in Lk 9.12, see 67.118.

68.52 σβέννυμι^b: (a figurative extension of meaning of σβέννυμι^a 'to extinguish a fire,' 14.70) to cause a fervent activity to cease – 'to stop, to quench.' τὸ πνεῦμα μὴ σβέννυτε 'do not stop the activity of the Spirit' 1 Th 5.19. Though the particular activity of the Spirit is not overtly indicated in the context of 1 Th 5.19, the book as a whole contains sufficient reference to the activity of the Spirit so as to indicate what is involved.

68.53 ὑποστέλλω^b; ὑποστολή, ῆς f: to cease doing something of presumed positive value because of adverse circumstances or fear – 'to cease, to stop, to give up doing.'
ὑποστέλλω^b: ὑπέστελλεν καὶ ἀφώριζεν ἑαυτόν 'he stopped and held himself aloof' Ga 2.12. It is also possible to translate this clause in Ga 2.12 as 'he withdrew and separated himself.' οὐ γὰρ ὑπεστειλάμην τοῦ μὴ ἀναγγεῖλαι πᾶσαν τὴν βουλὴν τοῦ θεοῦ ὑμῖν 'for I have not ceased to announce to you the whole purpose of God' Ac 20.27. For another interpretation of ὑποστέλλω in Ac 20.27, see 13.160.
ὑποστολή: ἡμεῖς δὲ οὐκ ἐσμὲν ὑποστολῆς εἰς ἀπώλειαν 'but we will not cease believing and so be lost' He 10.39. In He 10.39 ὑποστολῆς serves as an aspect of an implied πίστις, which occurs in He 10.38.

68.54 ἐκ^j: a marker of the aspect of cessation – 'from.' ἵνα ἀναπαήσονται ἐκ τῶν κόπων αὐτῶν 'in order that they might cease from their labor' or '. . . cease toiling' Re 14.13.

68.55 ἀδιάλειπτος, ον; ἀδιαλείπτως: pertaining to not ceasing from some continuous activity – 'not ceasing, not stopping, unceasingly, continuously.'
ἀδιάλειπτος: ὡς ἀδιάλειπτον ἔχω τὴν περὶ σοῦ

μνείαν 'as I unceasingly remember you' 2 Tm 1.3.

ἀδιαλείπτως: ἡμεῖς εὐχαριστοῦμεν τῷ θεῷ ἀδιαλείπτως 'we give thanks unceasingly to God' 1 Th 2.13.

68.56 ἀκατάπαυστος, ον: pertaining to not ceasing from some activity – 'never ceasing, not stopping.' ὀφθαλμοὺς ἔχοντες μεστοὺς μοιχαλίδος καὶ ἀκαταπαύστους ἁμαρτίας 'with their eyes always looking for adultery, they never stop sinning' 2 Pe 2.14.

68.57 ἀφθαρσία[b], ας f: a continuous state or process, with the implication that the state or process in question is not interrupted by death – 'unceasing, always, eternally, undying.' ἡ χάρις μετὰ πάντων τῶν ἀγαπώντων τὸν κύριον ἡμῶν Ἰησοῦν Χριστὸν ἐν ἀφθαρσίᾳ 'grace be with all those who love our Lord Jesus Christ unceasingly' Eph 6.24. A number of scholars, however, insist that ἀφθαρσία in Eph 6.24 must be understood in the sense of 'immortality' or 'eternity' as a temporal expression, but one which can be rendered as 'with undying love.'

E Try, Attempt (68.58-68.62)

68.58 πειράζω[d]; πειράομαι; πεῖραν λαμβάνω (an idiom, literally 'to take an attempt')[7]: to attempt to do something, with the implication of not succeeding – 'to try, to attempt.'
πειράζω[d]: παραγενόμενος δὲ εἰς Ἰερουσαλὴμ ἐπείραζεν κολλᾶσθαι τοῖς μαθηταῖς 'so he went to Jerusalem and tried to join the disciples' Ac 9.26.
πειράομαι: ἕνεκα τούτων με Ἰουδαῖοι συλλαβόμενοι ὄντα ἐν τῷ ἱερῷ ἐπειρῶντο διαχειρίσασθαι 'it was for this reason that the Jews seized me while I was in the Temple and tried to kill me' Ac 26.21.
πεῖραν λαμβάνω: ἧς πεῖραν λαβόντες οἱ Αἰγύπτιοι κατεπόθησαν 'when the Egyptians tried to do it, they were drowned' He 11.29.
In a number of languages expressions such

as πειράζω[d], πειράομαι, and πεῖραν λαμβάνω may be expressed as 'to start to do something, but not be able to' or 'to think that one can do something, but discover it is impossible.'

68.59 ἐπιχειρέω: to undertake to do something, but not necessarily without success – 'to try, to undertake.' ἐπεχείρησαν δέ τινες καὶ τῶν περιερχομένων Ἰουδαίων ἐξορκιστῶν ὀνομάζειν ἐπὶ τοὺς ἔχοντας τὰ πνεύματα τὰ πονηρὰ τὸ ὄνομα τοῦ κυρίου Ἰησοῦ 'some Jews who travelled and drove out evil spirits also undertook to use the name of the Lord Jesus to do this' Ac 19.13.

68.60 ζητέω[e]: to seek to do something, but without success – 'to seek to do, to try.' ἄνδρες φέροντες ἐπὶ κλίνης ἄνθρωπον ὃς ἦν παραλελυμένος, καὶ ἐζήτουν αὐτὸν εἰσενεγκεῖν 'men were carrying a paralyzed man on a bed and they attempted to take him into (the house)' Lk 5.18.

68.61 τρέχω[b]: to try to do something (employed in the absolute construction) – 'to try, to attempt to do.' ἄρα οὖν οὐ τοῦ θέλοντος οὐδὲ τοῦ τρέχοντος 'therefore, indeed, it is not a matter of what one wishes nor of what one attempts to do' Ro 9.16.

68.62 δίδωμι ἐργασίαν: (an idiom, literally 'to give energy') to do one's best in attempting to accomplish something – 'to do one's best, to try very hard to.' ἐν τῇ ὁδῷ δὸς ἐργασίαν ἀπηλλάχθαι ἀπ' αὐτοῦ 'on the way do your best to be reconciled with him' or '. . . to come to an agreement with him' Lk 12.58.

F Do Intensely or Extensively (68.63-68.78)

68.63 σπουδάζω[b]; σπουδή[b], ῆς f: to do something with intense effort and motivation – 'to work hard, to do one's best, to endeavor.'
σπουδάζω[b]: σπουδάζοντες τηρεῖν τὴν ἑνότητα τοῦ πνεύματος 'do your best to preserve the unity which the Spirit gives' Eph 4.3.
σπουδή[b]: ὁ προϊστάμενος ἐν σπουδῇ 'whoever has authority must work hard' Ro 12.8.

---

7 The phrase πεῖραν λαμβάνω may be regarded as a so-called 'low-grade idiom,' or λαμβάνω may be regarded as a relatively 'empty term' which serves primarily to mark case relations. See Domain 90, footnote 17.

68.64 σπουδὴν πᾶσαν παρεισφέρω: (an idiom, literally 'to bring every effort to') to do one's very best in attempting to do something – 'to do one's best, to make every effort to, to try as hard as possible.' σπουδὴν πᾶσαν παρεισενέγκαντες ἐπιχορηγήσατε ἐν τῇ πίστει ὑμῶν τὴν ἀρετήν 'do your very best to add goodness to your faith' 2 Pe 1.5. In some languages it may be almost impossible to speak of 'adding goodness to faith.' However, an appropriate equivalent of this expression in 2 Pe 1.5 may be 'do your best to be good as well as to believe.'

68.65 σπουδαίως^a: (derivative of σπουδή^b 'to endeavor,' 68.63) pertaining to intense effort in accomplishing some goal – 'making an effort to, doing one's best.' Ζηνᾶν τὸν νομικὸν καὶ Ἀπολλῶν σπουδαίως πρόπεμψον 'do your best to help Zenas the lawyer and Apollos to get started on their travels' Tt 3.13.

68.66 διώκω^d: (a figurative extension of meaning of διώκω^a 'to pursue,' 15.158) to do something with intense effort and with definite purpose or goal – 'to do with effort, to strive toward.' ὅτι ἔθνη τὰ μὴ διώκοντα δικαιοσύνην κατέλαβεν δικαιοσύνην 'that the nations who did not strive for righteousness obtained righteousness' Ro 9.30; τὴν φιλοξενίαν διώκοντες 'strive to be friendly to strangers' Ro 12.13.

68.67 προΐσταμαι^c (and 2nd aorist, perfect active): to engage in something with intense devotion – 'to strive for, to devote oneself to.' οἱ ἡμέτεροι καλῶν ἔργων προΐστασθαι 'our people should strive to do what is good' Tt 3.14.[8]

68.68 προσκαρτερέω^a; προσκαρτέρησις, εως f: to continue to do something with intense effort, with the possible implication of despite difficulty – 'to devote oneself to, to keep on, to persist in.'
προσκαρτερέω^a: τῇ προσευχῇ προσκαρτεροῦντες 'devote yourselves to prayer' Ro 12.12.
προσκαρτέρησις: εἰς αὐτὸ ἀγρυπνοῦντες ἐν πάσῃ προσκαρτερήσει καὶ δεήσει περὶ πάντων τῶν

---

8 It is possible to analyze the use of προΐσταμαι in Tt 3.14 as being a matter of case relations (Domain 90).

ἁγίων 'for this reason, be alert and always keep on praying for all God's people' Eph 6.18.

68.69 τάσσω^c: to do something with devotion, with the possible implication of systematic, regular activity – 'to do with devotion, to give oneself to.' εἰς διακονίαν τοῖς ἁγίοις ἔταξαν ἑαυτούς 'they gave themselves to helping God's people' 1 Cor 16.15.

68.70 προηγέομαι^a: to do something with eagerness – 'to do with eagerness.' τῇ τιμῇ ἀλλήλους προηγούμενοι 'showing eagerness in honoring one another' Ro 12.10. For another interpretation of προηγέομαι in Ro 12.10, see 78.35.

68.71 ἐπισχύω: to do something with persistence, implying both continuity and strong effort – 'to persist in, to insist on.' οἱ δὲ ἐπίσχυον λέγοντες 'they persisted in saying . . .' Lk 23.5.

68.72 ἀσκέω: to engage in some activity, with both continuity and effort – 'to do one's best, to endeavor.' ἀσκῶ ἀπρόσκοπον συνείδησιν ἔχειν πρὸς τὸν θεὸν καὶ τοὺς ἀνθρώπους διὰ παντός 'I always do my best to have a clear conscience before God and people' Ac 24.16.

68.73 ἐξαγοράζομαι τὸν καιρόν^b: (an idiom, literally 'to redeem the time') to do something with intensity and urgency (used absolutely) – 'to work urgently, to redeem the time.' ἐξαγοραζόμενοι τὸν καιρόν, ὅτι αἱ ἡμέραι πονηραί εἰσιν 'do everything with urgency, because the days are evil' Eph 5.16. It is also possible to interpret ἐξαγοράζομαι τὸν καιρόν in Eph 5.16 as 'to take full advantage of every opportunity' (see 65.42).

68.74 ἀγωνίζομαι^c: to strive to do something with great intensity and effort – 'to make every effort to, to do everything possible to, to strain oneself to.' ἀγωνίζεσθε εἰσελθεῖν διὰ τῆς στενῆς θύρας 'make every effort to enter through the narrow door' Lk 13.24.

68.75 ἐκχέομαι^b: to give oneself over completely to some activity or state – 'to give oneself over to, to plunge into, to commit oneself totally to.' καὶ τῇ πλάνῃ τοῦ Βαλαὰμ μισθοῦ ἐξεχύθησαν 'they gave themselves over completely to the error of Balaam for the sake of money' Jd 11.

68.76 σωρεύομαι: (a figurative extension of meaning of σωρεύω 'to heap up,' see 25.199) to be engaged intensively and extensively in some activity – 'to be given over to doing, to be fully engaged in.' αἰχμαλωτίζοντες γυναικάρια σεσωρευμένα ἁμαρτίαις 'gaining control over weak women given over to sins' 2 Tm 3.6. It is possible to interpret the usage of σωρεύομαι in 2 Tm 3.6 as referring to a state of being 'burdened by sins' or 'burdened by the guilt of sin.'

68.77 μεστός^c, ή, όν: pertaining to being extensively engaged in some activity or attitude – 'to be full of, to be constantly engaged in.' αὐτοὶ μεστοί ἐστε ἀγαθωσύνης 'you yourselves are full of goodness' or 'you yourselves are constantly engaged in doing good' Ro 15.14.

68.78 ὑπερεκτείνω: to engage in an activity beyond some implied limit, whether in intensity or extent – 'to overextend, to stretch out beyond, to overstep a limit.' οὐ γὰρ ὡς μὴ ἐφικνούμενοι εἰς ὑμᾶς ὑπερεκτείνομεν ἑαυτούς, ἄχρι γὰρ καὶ ὑμῶν ἐφθάσαμεν ἐν τῷ εὐαγγελίῳ τοῦ Χριστοῦ 'for since you are within those limits, we were not going beyond them when we came to you with the good news about Christ' 2 Cor 10.14. There are significant differences of opinion with regard to the interpretation of 2 Cor 10.14, and these differences should no doubt be reflected in marginal notes.

G Rapidity, Suddenness (68.79-68.82)

68.79 σπουδάζω^a; σπουδή^a, ῆς f; σπεύδω^a: to do something hurriedly, with the implication of associated energy – 'to hasten to, to hurry to, to do quickly.'[9]
σπουδάζω^a: σπούδασον ἐλθεῖν πρός με εἰς Νικόπολιν 'hurry to join me in Nicopolis' Tt 3.12.
σπουδή^a: εἰσελθοῦσα εὐθὺς μετὰ σπουδῆς πρὸς τὸν βασιλέα 'at once the girl hurried in to the king' or '. . . went in hurriedly to the king' Mk 6.25.
σπεύδω^a: ἔσπευδεν . . . γενέσθαι εἰς Ἱεροσόλυμα 'he was in a hurry . . . to arrive in Jerusalem' Ac 20.16. For another interpretation of σπεύδω in Ac 20.16, see 25.74.

68.80 σπεύδω^b: to cause something to happen soon – 'to cause to happen soon, to hurry up.' σπεύδοντας τὴν παρουσίαν τῆς τοῦ θεοῦ ἡμέρας 'making the day of God come soon' or 'hurrying up the day of God' 2 Pe 3.12. It is also possible to render this meaning of σπεύδω in 2 Pe 3.12 as 'doing your best to cause . . .'

68.81 ῥήγνυμι^c: to do something rapidly and with considerable energy or effort – 'to break forth with, to burst into.' ῥῆξον καὶ βόησον, ἡ οὐκ ὠδίνουσα 'break forth with shouts, you who never felt the pains of childbirth' Ga 4.27. For another interpretation of ῥήγνυμι in Ga 4.27, see 33.85.

68.82 ὅρμημα, τος n: an event involving sudden force and possible violence – 'sudden violence, sudden force.' οὕτως ὁρμήματι βληθήσεται Βαβυλὼν ἡ μεγάλη πόλις 'and so with sudden violence the great city of Babylon will be thrown down' Re 18.21.

9 The meanings in this series (68.79) may very well be classified under Domain 67 *Time*, implying either that the period of time before beginning the event is a brief one or that the event itself takes place in a brief period of time. There is, however, a factor of energy involved in these terms, and therefore it seems legitimate to consider this additional factor as justifying the classification of these meanings as aspectual.

69 Affirmation, Negation[1]

Outline of Subdomains

A   Affirmation (69.1)

69.1 ναί: an affirmative response to questions or statements or an emphatic affirmation of a statement – 'yes, yes it is true that, yes it is so, sure, indeed.' πιστεύετε ὅτι δύναμαι τοῦτο ποιῆσαι; λέγουσιν αὐτῷ, Ναί, κύριε 'do you believe I am able to do this? They said to him, Yes, Lord' Mt 9.28; ἡ δὲ εἶπεν, Ναί, κύριε, καὶ γὰρ τὰ κυνάρια . . . 'she said, It is true, sir, but even the dogs . . .' Mt 15.27; ναί, ἔρχομαι ταχύ 'yes, indeed, I am coming soon' Re 22.20.

B   Negation (69.2-69.6)

69.2 οὔ: a negative response to questions or statements or an emphatic negation of a statement – 'no.' ὁ δέ φησιν, Οὔ 'and he said, No' Mt 13.29; ἤτω δὲ ὑμῶν . . . τὸ Οὔ οὔ 'let your . . . no be no' Jas 5.12.

69.3 οὐ[a] (or οὐκ or οὐχ); μή[a]: markers of negative propositions – 'not.'[2]

οὐ[a]: οὐ δύνασθε θεῷ δουλεύειν καὶ μαμωνᾷ 'you cannot serve God and mammon' Mt 6.24; οὐ πᾶς ὁ λέγων μοι, Κύριε κύριε 'not everyone who calls me Lord, Lord' Mt 7.21.

μή[a]: ὁ μὴ ὢν μετ' ἐμοῦ κατ' ἐμοῦ ἐστιν 'anyone who is not with me is against me' Mt 12.30; λέγοντες μὴ εἶναι ἀνάστασιν 'the ones saying that people will not rise from death' Mt 22.23.

69.4 οὐχί[a]: a marker of a somewhat more emphatically negativized proposition – 'not, not indeed.' τί γέγονεν ὅτι ἡμῖν μέλλεις ἐμφανίζειν σεαυτὸν καὶ οὐχὶ τῷ κόσμῳ; 'how can it be that you will reveal yourself to us and not to the world?' Jn 14.22.

69.5 οὐ μή[a]: a marker of emphatic negation – 'by no means, certainly not.'[3] ἰῶτα ἓν ἢ μία κεραία οὐ μὴ παρέλθῃ ἀπὸ τοῦ νόμου 'the smallest detail of the Law will certainly not be done away with' Mt 5.18.

69.6 οὐδαμῶς; μηδαμῶς: markers of strongly emphatic negation – 'no indeed, by no means, most certainly not.'
οὐδαμῶς: οὐδαμῶς ἐλαχίστη εἶ ἐν τοῖς ἡγεμόσιν Ἰούδα 'by no means are you the least among the leading cities of Judah' Mt 2.6.
μηδαμῶς: ὁ δὲ Πέτρος εἶπεν, Μηδαμῶς 'then Peter said, No, indeed' Ac 10.14.[4]

C   Negation Combined with Clitics[5] (69.7-69.10)

69.7 οὐδέ[a]; μηδέ[a]: combinations of the nega-

---

1 In all languages negation is generally the so-called 'marked category,' that is to say, positive statements do not require some special lexical item in order to indicate that they are affirmative in nature. There is, however, in Greek one affirmative particle, namely, ναί (69.1).

2 οὐ[a] and μή[a] are lexically equivalent in meaning, but they have a syntactic distribution which may be said to give them certain distinctions in so-called 'class meaning.' However, since these differences are based upon syntactic distributions, such distinctions in meaning are beyond the scope of this type of lexical analysis. The form οὐ, of course, tends to occur primarily in indicative clauses, while μή occurs generally in non-indicative clauses.

3 The combination οὐ μή[a] may be regarded technically as a type of idiom in that the two negations do not cancel each other out, but constitute an emphatic negation.

4 μηδαμῶς rather than οὐδαμῶς occurs in Ac 10.14 since this would be a correct response to a previous imperative form.

5 The forms occurring in Subdomain C *Negation Combined with Clitics* are not to be regarded as compounds, but as combinations of abstracts and clitics which are structurally distinct from the negation. They are dealt with here simply because they form a so-called phonological word, but structurally the two parts are independent.

tive particles οὐᵃ or μήᵃ 'not,' 69.3, and the postpositive conjunction δέᵃ 'and,' 89.94 – 'and not, nor, neither.'

οὐδέᵃ: κλέπται οὐ διορύσσουσιν οὐδὲ κλέπτουσιν 'thieves cannot break in nor can they steal' Mt 6.20; οὐ σπείρουσιν οὐδὲ θερίζουσιν 'they do not plant seeds nor do they gather a harvest' Mt 6.26.

μηδέᵃ: τὸ καθόλου μὴ φθέγγεσθαι μηδὲ διδάσκειν ἐπὶ τῷ ὀνόματι τοῦ Ἰησοῦ 'under no condition (were they) to speak or teach in the name of Jesus' Ac 4.18.

69.8 οὐδέᵇ; μηδέᵇ: combinations of the negative particles οὐᵃ or μήᵃ 'not,' 69.3, and the postpositional particle δέ 'even,' not occurring as such as an independent graphic unit – 'not even.'

οὐδέᵇ: οὐδὲ Σολομὼν . . . περιεβάλετο ὡς ἓν τούτων 'not even Solomon . . . was dressed like one of them' Mt 6.29.

μηδέᵇ: πορνεία δὲ καὶ ἀκαθαρσία πᾶσα ἢ πλεονεξία μηδὲ ὀνομαζέσθω ἐν ὑμῖν 'sexual immorality and any kind of impurity or greed should not even be mentioned among you' Eph 5.3.

69.9 οὔτε; μήτε: markers of coordinate negativized expressions (combinations of the negative particles οὐᵃ or μήᵃ 'not,' 69.3, and the postpositive conjunction τέᵃ 'and,' 89.95) – 'neither . . . nor.'[6]

οὔτε: ὅπου οὔτε σὴς οὔτε βρῶσις ἀφανίζει 'where neither moth nor tarnish destroys' Mt 6.20.

μήτε: ἀνεθεμάτισαν ἑαυτοὺς λέγοντες μήτε φαγεῖν μήτε πιεῖν 'they vowed that they would neither eat nor drink' Ac 23.12.

69.10 μήγε: a combination of the negative particle μήᵃ, 69.3, and the somewhat emphatic postpositional particle γέ, 91.6; these are often written separately – 'though not, no indeed.' εἰ δὲ μήγε (or μή γε) ῥήγνυνται οἱ ἀσκοί 'but if not, the wineskins burst' or 'otherwise, the wineskins burst' Mt 9.17.

D   Markers for an Affirmative Response to Questions[7] (69.11-69.13)

69.11 οὐᵇ (or οὐκ or οὐχ): markers of an affirmative response to a question. οὐκ ἀκούεις πόσα σου καταμαρτυροῦσιν; 'didn't you hear all the things they accuse you of?' Mt 27.13.[8]

69.12 οὐχίᵇ; οὐκοῦν: markers of a somewhat more emphatic affirmative response.

οὐχίᵇ: οὐχὶ καὶ οἱ τελῶναι τὸ αὐτὸ ποιοῦσιν; 'even the tax collectors do that, do they not?' Mt 5.46.

οὐκοῦν: οὐκοῦν βασιλεὺς εἶ σύ; 'are you not a king?' Jn 18.37.

69.13 οὐ μήᵇ: a marker of a strongly emphatic affirmative response to a question. τὸ ποτήριον ὃ δέδωκέν μοι ὁ πατὴρ οὐ μὴ πίω αὐτό; 'will I not drink the cup which my Father has given me?' Jn 18.11.

E   Markers for a Negative Response to Questions[9] (69.14-69.16)

69.14 ἆρα: a marker of a negative response to questions, usually implying anxiety or impatience – 'indeed, then, ever.'[10] ἆρα εὑρήσει τὴν πίστιν; 'will he find faith?' Lk 18.8; ἆρα Χριστὸς ἁμαρτίας διάκονος; 'is Christ then a servant of sin?' Ga 2.17.

---

7 The use of a negative marker in questions designed for an affirmative response (that is, those indicating agreement) is far more complex than might appear to be the case. In reality, the negative markers οὐᵇ (69.11), οὐχίᵇ (69.12), and οὐ μήᵇ (69.13) are designed to elicit agreement with the intent of the question, even though it is seemingly negatively posed. It is this complex form which gives rise to different ways in which agreement is signaled in different languages. In most Indo-European languages agreement is signaled by the answer meaning 'yes,' but in some languages the same agreement is indicated by 'no' as a kind of echo of the negative particle. The converse exists for negative responses, that is, those indicating disagreement.

8 In a number of languages, however, an affirmative response to such a question would be indicated by a negative particle, so that the answer to the question in Mt 27.13 would be 'no.'

9 See footnote 7.

10 In English it is difficult to provide a direct translation of ἆρα in this sense, though other languages may have a regularly corresponding particle with essentially the same significance.

---

6 In some instances οὔτε or μήτε may serve as the first element in a negativized series.

In order to attempt to do some justice to the occurrence of the particle ἄρα, one may introduce a variety of terms which make a question somewhat more emphatically negative. In the case of Lk 18.8 one might translate 'will he indeed find faith?' In the case of Ga 2.17 one might translate 'how, then, could Christ ever be a servant of sin?'

69.15 μή^b: a marker of a negative response to a question. μή τινος ὑστερήσατε; 'you didn't lack anything, did you?' Lk 22.35. [11]

11 A question such as μή τινος ὑστερήσατε; (Lk 22.35) actually suggests agreement with the equivalent of a negative statement, 'you did not lack anything.' It is for this reason that in some languages the response to this type of question is with a positive particle meaning 'yes.'

69.16 μήτι: a marker of a somewhat more emphatic negative response. μήτι συλλέγουσιν ἀπὸ ἀκανθῶν σταφυλάς; 'thorn bushes do not bear grapes, do they?' Mt 7.16; μήτι οὗτός ἐστιν ὁ Χριστός; 'he couldn't be the Messiah, could he?' Jn 4.29. Some persons have argued that the occurrence of μήτι in Jn 4.29 is contradictory, since it would appear from the context that the individuals posing the question regarded Jesus as a possible Messiah. On the other hand, asking the question in this form would have certainly fit the circumstances in which there was strong opposition to anyone claiming that Jesus was the Messiah. This form of the question would have avoided an overt commitment, while at the same time indicating people's evident interest and concern.

70 Real, Unreal[1]

70.1 ὅλως^b: pertaining to reality, with the implication of being generally known – 'actually, really.'[2] ὅλως ἀκούεται ἐν ὑμῖν πορνεία 'it is actually reported that there is sexual immorality among you' 1 Cor 5.1.

70.2 ὄντως: pertaining to actual existence – 'really, certainly, truly.'[2] χήρας τίμα τὰς ὄντως χήρας 'show respect for those who are really widows' 1 Tm 5.3.

70.3 ἀληθής^b, ές; ἀληθινός^a, ή, όν; ἀληθῶς: pertaining to being real and not imaginary – 'real, really, true, truly.'[2]
ἀληθής^b: ἡ γὰρ σάρξ μου ἀληθής ἐστιν βρῶσις 'for my flesh is real food' Jn 6.55. The figurative or symbolic sense of this statement does not, of course, take away from its reality.
ἀληθινός^a: ἵνα γινώσκωσιν σὲ τὸν μόνον ἀληθινὸν θεόν 'that they may know you, the only one who is really God' Jn 17.3. In some languages

1 In Domain 70 *Real, Unreal*, the contrast is between that which actually happened and that which people may have thought or imagined took place.
2 It would seem that the meanings of items 70.1-70.4 do reflect certain subtle differences, but it is not at all easy to determine precisely how they differ.

'the only one who is really God' can only be expressed as 'the only God who exists' or 'who is God and there are no other gods.'
ἀληθῶς: ἀληθῶς θεοῦ υἱὸς εἶ 'you are truly the Son of God' Mt 14.33; ἴδε ἀληθῶς Ἰσραηλίτης ἐν ᾧ δόλος οὐκ ἔστιν 'here is a real Israelite in whom there is nothing false' Jn 1.47.

70.4 ἐν ἀληθείᾳ; ἐπ' ἀληθείας; κατ' ἀλήθειαν: (idioms, literally 'in truth,' 'upon truth,' and 'according to truth') pertaining to being a real or actual event or state – 'actually, really.'[2]
ἐν ἀληθείᾳ: καὶ τὴν ὁδὸν τοῦ θεοῦ ἐν ἀληθείᾳ διδάσκεις 'you really teach the way of God' Mt 22.16; ἵνα ὦσιν καὶ αὐτοὶ ἡγιασμένοι ἐν ἀληθείᾳ 'in order that these may be truly dedicated' Jn 17.19.
ἐπ' ἀληθείας: συνήχθησαν γὰρ ἐπ' ἀληθείας ἐν τῇ πόλει ταύτῃ 'for they really came together in this city' Ac 4.27.
κατ' ἀλήθειαν: τὸ κρίμα τοῦ θεοῦ ἐστιν κατὰ ἀλήθειαν ἐπὶ τοὺς τὰ τοιαῦτα πράσσοντας 'the judgment of God is upon those who actually did such things' Ro 2.2.

70.5 φέρω^j: to present evidence that something has actually happened – 'to show something happened, to demonstrate something was real.' ὅπου γὰρ διαθήκη, θάνατον ἀνάγκη φέρεσθαι τοῦ διαθεμένου 'where there is a will, it is necessary to show that the one who made the will has actually died' He 9.16. In rendering φέρω in He 9.16, it may be necessary to redistribute the semantic components even as in the case of the English translation, for example, 'to show . . . actually . . .'

70.6 κυρόω[b]: to cause someone to recognize the reality of something – 'to show something to be real, to make something real.' διὸ παρακαλῶ ὑμᾶς κυρῶσαι εἰς αὐτὸν ἀγάπην 'therefore, I urge you to show that your love for

him is real' or '. . . that you actually do love him' 2 Cor 2.8.

70.7 σωματικῶς[b]: pertaining to being real (in the sense of material) in contrast with being symbolic – 'in reality, really.' ἐν αὐτῷ κατοικεῖ πᾶν τὸ πλήρωμα τῆς θεότητος σωματικῶς 'in him exists the complete content of deity in a real form' Col 2.9. For another interpretation of σωματικῶς in Col 2.9, see 8.2.

70.8 ἔγγυος, ου *m*: one who guarantees the reality of something – 'the guarantee, guarantor.' κρείττονος διαθήκης γέγονεν ἔγγυος Ἰησοῦς 'Jesus has become the guarantor of the better covenant' He 7.22.

71 Mode

Mode consists of the evaluation of events in relation to such factors as possibility, probability, contingency, obligation, necessity, and inevitability. One of the principal difficulties involved in analyzing model meanings is that contexts do not always make clear what features of these factors are involved. For example, it may be impossible in the case of obligation to determine whether this arises out of self-interest or reflects a moral code or is the result of external pressure. Similarly, distinctions in possibility may in some instances result from the nature of the physical universe, and in other instances, from the capacity of an individual. Furthermore, a number of contexts are so ambivalent as to make it difficult to decide what modal features are involved. But perhaps one can best classify the principal distinctions of *Mode* in terms of the following subdomains:

Outline of Subdomains

A   Possible, Impossible (71.1-71.10)

71.1 εἰμί[f]; **ἔξεστι**[a]: to mark an event as being possible in a highly generic sense – 'to be possible.'
εἰμί[f]: οὐκ ἔστιν νῦν λέγειν κατὰ μέρος 'it is not possible now to discuss (these things) in detail' He 9.5. In He 9.5 one cannot determine precisely those factors which make it impossible for the author to be more precise. It may be simply the urgency of other matters or the limitations of space or even the inappropriateness of such considerations for the topic under consideration. In some languages, however, one must be somewhat more specific, for a strictly literal translation might imply that the author of the Epistle to the Hebrews was simply incapable of producing a detailed analysis. This would, of course, be quite contradictory to the implication of the statement in He 9.5 and the scope of the wider context.
ἔξεστι[a]: ἐξὸν εἰπεῖν μετὰ παρρησίας πρὸς ὑμᾶς περὶ τοῦ πατριάρχου Δαυίδ 'it is possible to speak to you with confidence concerning the patriarch David' Ac 2.29. In Ac 2.29 the possibility of speaking confidently about David evidently is based upon well-known facts.

71.2 δυνατός[a], **ή, όν**: pertaining to being possible, with the implication of power or ability to alter or control circumstances – 'possible.' πάτερ μου, εἰ δυνατόν ἐστιν, παρελθάτω ἀπ' ἐμοῦ τὸ ποτήριον τοῦτο 'my Father, if it is possible, take this cup away from me' Mt 26.39.

71.3 ἀδυνατεῖ; ἀδύνατος[b], **ον**: pertaining to being impossible, presumably because of a lack of power to alter or control circumstances – 'impossible.'

ἀδυνατεῖ: ὅτι οὐκ ἀδυνατήσει παρὰ τοῦ θεοῦ πᾶν ῥῆμα 'for there is not a thing that God cannot do' Lk 1.37. In view of the double negation in Lk 1.37, it is often better to translate it as a positive statement, for example, 'God can do anything.'

ἀδύνατος[b]: ἀδύνατον ψεύσασθαι τὸν θεόν 'it is impossible for God to lie' He 6.18;[1] ἀδύνατον γὰρ τοὺς . . . παραπεσόντας, πάλιν ἀνακαινίζειν εἰς μετάνοιαν 'for it is impossible . . . to bring back to repent those who have abandoned their faith' He 6.4-6. In He 6.4 the use of ἀδύνατον seems to be an instance of hyperbole in view of the warnings against apostasy (see He 5.11-6.12). Therefore, one may translate ἀδύνατον in He 6.4 as 'it is extremely difficult to.' TEV introduces a rhetorical question to express strong doubt, "for how can those who abandon their faith be brought back to repent again?"

71.4 ἐνδέχεται: to be possible, in the sense of being fully in accord with human experience – 'to be possible, to be thinkable.' οὐκ ἐνδέχεται προφήτην ἀπολέσθαι ἔξω Ἰερουσαλήμ 'it is not possible that a prophet would die outside Jerusalem' or 'it is unthinkable that a prophet would die outside Jerusalem' Lk 13.33.[2]

1 This statement in He 6.18 may provide certain philosophical problems in view of the doctrine of the absoluteness of God, but no doubt the writer of Hebrews makes this statement in view of the presumed nature of God himself.

2 Even though one may translate Lk 13.33 as 'it is unthinkable,' it does not necessarily follow that one should classify this in Domain 30 Think. The meaning of 'unthinkable' is simply a derivative from the concept of impossibility.

71.5 ἀνένδεκτος, ον: pertaining to not being possible, in the sense of not being in accord with human experience – 'impossible.' ἀνένδεκτόν ἐστιν τοῦ τὰ σκάνδαλα μὴ ἐλθεῖν 'it is impossible that things which cause people to sin should not happen' Lk 17.1. In view of the double negation in Lk 17.1, it may be better to translate 'things that make people fall into sin are bound to happen.' The derivative meaning of ἀνένδεκτος in the context of Lk 17.1 is thus a matter of inevitability as based upon human experience (see 71.38).

71.6 τόπος[c], **ου** *m*: the possibility of some occasion or opportunity – 'possibility, chance, opportunity.' τόπον τε ἀπολογίας λάβοι περὶ τοῦ ἐγκλήματος 'to receive the possibility of defending oneself concerning the accusation' or 'to have the opportunity of defense with regard to the accusation' Ac 25.16; μετανοίας γὰρ τόπον οὐχ εὗρεν 'for he did not find the possibility of repenting (of what he had done)' He 12.17.

71.7 ἄρα[b]: marker of the possibility of something being true – 'possible.' τίς ἄρα οὗτός ἐστιν 'who can this one possibly be' Mk 4.41; τίς ἄρα ἐστὶν ὁ πιστὸς δοῦλος 'who can possibly be the faithful servant' Mt 24.45.

71.8 ἄν[b]; **ἐάν**[c]: markers of the possibility of any number of occurrences of some event – '-ever' (wherever, whatever, whoever, however).

ἄν[b]: ὅπου ἂν εἰσεπορεύετο εἰς κώμας ἢ εἰς πόλεις 'wherever he went into villages and towns' Mk 6.56; ὃς ἂν ὀμόσῃ ἐν τῷ ναῷ 'whoever swears by the Temple' Mt 23.16.

ἐάν[c]: ἵνα ὑμεῖς με προπέμψητε οὗ ἐὰν πορεύωμαι 'in order that you may send me on to wherever I am going' 1 Cor 16.6.

71.9 ἀνοίγω θύραν: (an idiom, literally 'to open a door') to make possible some opportunity – 'to make it possible.' ἵνα ὁ θεὸς ἀνοίξῃ ἡμῖν θύραν τοῦ λόγου 'in order that God may make it possible for us to preach the word' Col 4.3; ὅτι ἤνοιξεν τοῖς ἔθνεσιν θύραν πίστεως 'because he made it possible for the Gentiles to have faith' Ac 14.27.

71.10 τυχόν: (the neuter participle of τυγχάνω 'to happen,' not occurring in the NT) pertaining to the possible occurrence of an event or state – 'perhaps, possibly.' πρὸς ὑμᾶς δὲ τυχὸν παραμενῶ ἢ καὶ παραχειμάσω 'I may perhaps spend some time with you, possibly even the whole winter' 1 Cor 16.6.

B Probable, Improbable (71.11-71.13)

71.11 ἴσως: pertaining to an event having a high degree of probability – 'probably, likely.' πέμψω τὸν υἱόν μου τὸν ἀγαπητόν· ἴσως τοῦτον ἐντραπήσονται 'I will send my own son, whom I love; they are likely to respect him' Lk 20.13. In view of the misjudgment implied in Lk 20.13, a number of translators have rendered ἴσως as simply 'perhaps' or 'maybe,' though the Greek term ἴσως would certainly imply a considerably higher degree of hope for a successful outcome.

71.12 τάχα: pertaining to a low probability of occurrence – 'perhaps, possibly, maybe.' ὑπὲρ γὰρ τοῦ ἀγαθοῦ τάχα τις καὶ τολμᾷ ἀποθανεῖν 'it may be that someone might dare to die for a good person' Ro 5.7.

71.13 εἰ τύχοι: (an idiom, literally 'if it should happen') a marker of a degree of probability – 'probably.' τοσαῦτα εἰ τύχοι γένη φωνῶν εἰσιν ἐν κόσμῳ 'as many different kinds of languages as there probably are in the world' 1 Cor 14.10.

C Certain, Uncertain[3] (71.14-71.20)

71.14 ἄν[a]: (in combination with a past tense, as part of the apodosis of a conditional sentence) pertaining to being certain, in view of particular circumstances of a condition

---

3 A number of terms involving certainty or uncertainty are treated in Domain 70 *Real, Unreal.* The meanings listed here in Domain 71 seem to be only modal and lack the additional features characteristic of the meanings in Domain 70. It is important to note, however, that elements of certainty and uncertainty are frequently expressed in Greek by subjunctive and optative grammatical modes, an area of semantics beyond the scope of this dictionary.

---

contrary to fact – 'would.'[4] οὗτος εἰ ἦν προφήτης, ἐγίνωσκεν ἄν 'if this person were a prophet, he would know' Lk 7.39.

71.15 βέβαιος[a], α, ον: pertaining to being certain, on the basis of being well established – 'certain, sure.' εἰς τὸ εἶναι βεβαίαν τὴν ἐπαγγελίαν 'in order for the promise to be certain' Ro 4.16.

71.16 πάντως[a]: pertaining to being in every respect certain – 'certainly, really, doubtless, no doubt.' πάντως φονεύς ἐστιν ὁ ἄνθρωπος οὗτος 'certainly this man is a murderer' Ac 28.4; πάντως ἀκούσονται ὅτι ἐλήλυθας 'they will no doubt hear that you have come' Ac 21.22.

71.17 πιστός[c], ή, όν: pertaining to being sure, with the implication of being fully trustworthy – 'sure.' δώσω ὑμῖν τὰ ὅσια Δαυὶδ τὰ πιστά 'I will give you the sacred and sure (blessings promised) to David' Ac 13.34.

71.18 μήποτε[b]: pertaining to not being certain – 'can be, might be, whether perhaps.' μήποτε ἀληθῶς ἔγνωσαν οἱ ἄρχοντες ὅτι οὗτός ἐστιν ὁ Χριστός; 'can it be that the leaders really know that he is the Messiah?' Jn 7.26; διαλογιζομένων πάντων ἐν ταῖς καρδίαις αὐτῶν περὶ τοῦ Ἰωάννου, μήποτε αὐτὸς εἴη ὁ Χριστός 'all began to wonder as to whether John might be the Messiah' Lk 3.15.

71.19 ἄρα[c]: a degree of uncertainty – 'perhaps.' τί ἄρα ὁ Πέτρος ἐγένετο 'what had perhaps happened to Peter' Ac 12.18.

71.20 ἀδηλότης, ητος f: the uncertainty of some event or state – 'uncertainty.' μηδὲ ἠλπικέναι ἐπὶ πλούτου ἀδηλότητι 'not to put one's hope in the uncertainty of riches' 1 Tm 6.17.

D Should, Ought (71.21-71.33)

71.21 δεῖ[b]: to be something which should be done as the result of compulsion, whether in-

---

4 The meaning of 'certainty' in this type of conditional sentence cannot be attributed solely to ἄν but to the combination of ἄν with certain tense forms. This is a typical case of a combined lexical and syntactic meaning.

ternal (as a matter of duty) or external (law, custom, and circumstances) – 'should, ought, to have to do.' οὐκ ἔδει καὶ σὲ ἐλεῆσαι τὸν σύνδουλόν σου, ὡς κἀγὼ σὲ ἠλέησα; 'should you not have shown mercy to your fellow servant as I showed mercy to you?' Mt 18.33; ταῦτα δὲ ἔδει ποιῆσαι '(you) ought to do these things' Mt 23.23; ἔδει δὲ αὐτὸν διέρχεσθαι διὰ τῆς Σαμαρείας 'he had to go through Samaria' Jn 4.4; τὸ γὰρ ἅγιον πνεῦμα διδάξει ὑμᾶς ἐν αὐτῇ τῇ ὥρᾳ ἃ δεῖ εἰπεῖν 'for the Holy Spirit will teach you at that time what you should say' Lk 12.12; ἔδει μέν, ὦ ἄνδρες, πειθαρχήσαντάς μοι μὴ ἀνάγεσθαι ἀπὸ τῆς Κρήτης 'men, you should have listened to me and not sailed from Crete' Ac 27.21.

71.22 χρή: that which should be or happen, with the implication of propriety – 'should, ought.' οὐ χρή . . . ταῦτα οὕτως γίνεσθαι 'this should not happen' Jas 3.10.

71.23 χρεία^b, ας *f*: that which should be or happen, with the implication of need or lack to be made up – 'need, what should be.' πάλιν χρείαν ἔχετε τοῦ διδάσκειν ὑμᾶς τινά 'yet you need to have someone to teach you' He 5.12.

71.24 ὀφειλή^b, ῆς *f*: that which ought to be done as a matter of duty or social obligation – 'what one should do, duty.' τῇ γυναικὶ ὁ ἀνὴρ τὴν ὀφειλὴν ἀποδιδότω, ὁμοίως δὲ καὶ ἡ γυνὴ τῷ ἀνδρί 'the husband should fulfill his marital duty to his wife and likewise the wife to her husband' 1 Cor 7.3.

71.25 ὀφείλω^c: to be obligatory in view of some moral or legal requirement – 'ought, to be under obligation.' κατὰ τὸν νόμον ὀφείλει ἀποθανεῖν 'according to the law, he ought to die' Jn 19.7; μηδενὶ μηδὲν ὀφείλετε 'let no one be under obligation to anyone' Ro 13.8.

71.26 ὀφείλημα^b, τος *n*: that which one must do out of a sense of duty or as the result of commitment – 'obligation.' ὁ μισθὸς οὐ λογίζεται κατὰ χάριν ἀλλὰ κατὰ ὀφείλημα 'the wages are not reckoned as a gift but as an obligation' Ro 4.4. For another interpretation of ὀφείλημα in Ro 4.4, see 57.221.

71.27 ὀφειλέτης^b, ου *m*: (derivative of ὀφείλω^c 'to be under obligation,' 71.25) one who is obligated to do something – 'one who is obliged to, one who is obligated to, one who must.' ὀφειλέτης ἐστὶν ὅλον τὸν νόμον ποιῆσαι 'he must obey the whole Law' Ga 5.3.

71.28 ὄφελον: that which ought to be if one only had one's wish – 'would that.' καὶ ὄφελόν γε ἐβασιλεύσατε 'and would that you really were kings' or 'would that you really were ruling' 1 Cor 4.8; ὄφελον ἀνείχεσθέ μου μικρόν τι ἀφροσύνης 'would that you would grant me a little bit of foolishness' 2 Cor 11.1. In a number of languages it may be preferable to translate ὄφελον as simply an expression of wishing. Therefore, 2 Cor 11.1 might be rendered as 'I wish you would grant me a bit of foolishness' or 'I wish you would tolerate a bit of foolishness on my part.'

71.29 εὐσεβέω^b: to fulfill one's socio-religious obligations – 'to fulfill one's duties, to complete one's religious duty.' μανθανέτωσαν πρῶτον τὸν ἴδιον οἶκον εὐσεβεῖν 'they should first learn to carry out their religious duties toward their own family' 1 Tm 5.4.

71.30 ἀνάγκη^b, ης *f*: an obligation of a compelling nature – 'complete obligation, necessary obligation.' ἀνάγκη γάρ μοι ἐπίκειται 'I have a necessary obligation' 1 Cor 9.16; ἵνα μὴ ὡς κατὰ ἀνάγκην τὸ ἀγαθόν σου ᾖ ἀλλὰ κατὰ ἑκούσιον 'in order that your helpfulness may not be based on obligation but on willingness' Phm 14.

71.31 ἀναγκαστῶς: (derivative of ἀνάγκη^b 'complete obligation,' 71.30) pertaining to being obligatory on the basis of being imposed – 'out of obligation, ought to.' μὴ ἀναγκαστῶς ἀλλὰ ἑκουσίως 'not as a matter of obligation but willingly' 1 Pe 5.2.

71.32 ἔξεστι^b: to be obligatory – 'must, ought to' (with a negative particle, 'ought not to'). οἱ μαθηταί σου ποιοῦσιν ὃ οὐκ ἔξεστιν ποιεῖν ἐν σαββάτῳ 'your disciples are doing what they ought not to do on the Sabbath' Mt 12.2.

71.33 λείπω^c: to be a continuing obligation – 'still ought to, still need to.' ἔτι ἕν σοι λείπει 'one thing you still ought to do' Lk 18.22. For another interpretation of λείπω in Lk 18.22, see 57.44.

E Necessary, Unnecessary (71.34-71.40)

71.34 δεῖ[a]: to be that which must necessarily take place, often with the implication of inevitability – 'to be necessary, must.' δέον ἐστὶν ὑμᾶς κατεσταλμένους ὑπάρχειν 'it is necessary for you to calm down' Ac 19.36; ὅταν δὲ ἀκούσητε πολέμους καὶ ἀκοὰς πολέμων, μὴ θροεῖσθε· δεῖ γενέσθαι 'don't be troubled when you hear (the noise) of battles (close by) and news of battles (far away); such things must happen' Mk 13.7. It is impossible to tell in a context such as Mk 13.7 whether δεῖ implies mere inevitability of an event or whether the events are somehow part of the plan and purpose of God. The latter interpretation could only be derived from broader theological implications and not from the meaning of δεῖ itself.

71.35 ὀφείλω[b]: to be necessary or indispensable, with the implication of a contingency – 'must, have to, it is necessary.' ἐπεὶ ὠφείλετε ἄρα ἐκ τοῦ κόσμου ἐξελθεῖν 'since you would have to get out of the world completely' 1 Cor 5.10.

71.36 μέλλω[b]: to be inevitable, with respect to future developments – 'must be, has to be.' οὕτως καὶ ὁ υἱὸς τοῦ ἀνθρώπου μέλλει πάσχειν ὑπ᾽ αὐτῶν 'in the same way the Son of Man must also be mistreated by them' Mt 17.12. In a number of languages there is a problem involved in speaking of what is necessary or inevitable in the future, for a distinction is made between that which is purely impersonal or physical and that which is the result of some person's purpose, intent, or activity. As in the case of δεῖ in Mk 13.7 (71.34), it is

impossible in the case of μέλλω in Mt 17.12 to determine whether the reference is merely to an inevitable future event ('bound to happen') or whether this is part of the plan and purpose of God. In order to avoid a wrong interpretation of Mt 17.12, it may therefore be useful to translate as 'in the same way the Son of Man will most certainly be mistreated by them.'

71.37 ἀπόκειμαι[c]: to be necessary in view of something being inevitable – 'to be necessary, must.' ἀπόκειται τοῖς ἀνθρώποις ἅπαξ ἀποθανεῖν 'everyone must die once' He 9.27.

71.38 ἀνάγκη[c], **ης** *f*: necessity as a law of human experience – 'inevitability, what is bound to be, to have to be.' ἀνάγκη γὰρ ἐλθεῖν τὰ σκάνδαλα, πλὴν οὐαὶ τῷ ἀνθρώπῳ δι᾽ οὗ τὸ σκάνδαλον ἔρχεται 'things that cause people to sin are bound to happen, but how terrible for the one who causes them' Mt 18.7.

71.39 ἀναγκαῖος[a], **α, ον**; **ἐπάναγκες**: pertaining to being necessary and indispensable to the occurrence of some event – 'necessary, indispensable.'
ἀναγκαῖος[a]: ὑμῖν ἦν ἀναγκαῖον πρῶτον λαληθῆναι τὸν λόγον τοῦ θεοῦ 'it was necessary that the word of God should be spoken first to you' Ac 13.46.
ἐπάναγκες: ἔδοξεν γὰρ τῷ πνεύματι τῷ ἁγίῳ καὶ ἡμῖν μηδὲν πλέον ἐπιτίθεσθαι ὑμῖν βάρος πλὴν τούτων τῶν ἐπάναγκες 'for the Holy Spirit and we have agreed not to put any burden on you beside these indispensable (rules)' Ac 15.28.

71.40 περισσός[d], **ή, όν**: pertaining to being unnecessary in view of being superfluous – 'unnecessary, not required.' περισσόν μοί ἐστιν τὸ γράφειν ὑμῖν 'it is not necessary for me to write to you' 2 Cor 9.1. For another interpretation of περισσός in 2 Cor 9.1, see 59.51.

72 True, False

A True, False[2] (72.1-72.11)

72.1 ἀληθής[a], ές; ἀληθινός[b], ή, όν: pertaining to being in accordance with historical fact – 'true, truth.'
ἀληθής[a]: τοῦτο ἀληθὲς εἴρηκας 'you have told the truth' Jn 4.18. In a number of languages 'the truth' may be rendered simply as 'what really is' or 'what is so' or 'what has happened.'
ἀληθινός[b]: καὶ ἀληθινὴ αὐτοῦ ἐστιν ἡ μαρτυρία 'and his witness is true' Jn 19.35.

72.2 ἀλήθεια, ας f: the content of that which is true and thus in accordance with what actually happened – 'truth.' εἶπεν αὐτῷ πᾶσαν τὴν ἀλήθειαν 'she told him the whole truth' Mk 5.33. In Jn 8.32 ἀλήθεια is used to refer to the revelation of God that Jesus brings or, perhaps, to Jesus himself for what he actually is as the revelation of God.

72.3 φωτισμός[a], οῦ m: (a figurative extension of meaning of φωτισμός 'light,' not occurring in the NT) that which has been revealed as true – 'truth, revealed truth.' εἰς τὸ μὴ αὐγάσαι τὸν φωτισμὸν τοῦ εὐαγγελίου τῆς δόξης τοῦ Χριστοῦ 'so that they will not see the truth of the good news about the glory of Christ' 2 Cor 4.4.

72.4 παρίστημι[f]; παρατίθεμαι[b]: to establish evidence to show that something is true – 'to show to be true, to present evidence of truth, to prove.'

---

1 It would be possible to treat the two subdomains as distinct units, but they are brought together under the title *True, False* since they relate in somewhat different ways to historical fact.

2 Subdomain A *True, False* not only involves consistency with external facts but often implies positive or negative moral values. In this subdomain 'false' usually suggests intention to deceive. Meanings which involve the telling of falsehoods are treated in Domain 33 *Communication*, Subdomain R.

παρίστημι[f]: οὐδὲ παραστῆσαι δύνανταί σοι περὶ ὧν νυνὶ κατηγοροῦσίν μου 'nor can they present you with evidence that the accusations they now bring against me are true' Ac 24.13.
παρατίθεμαι[b]: διανοίγων καὶ παρατιθέμενος ὅτι τὸν Χριστὸν ἔδει παθεῖν 'he explained (the Scriptures) and presented evidence that the Messiah had to suffer' Ac 17.3.

72.5 ἐπιδείκνυμι[b]; ἀποδείκνυμι[c]: to demonstrate that something is true – 'to show to be true, to prove.'
ἐπιδείκνυμι[b]: ἐπιδεικνὺς διὰ τῶν γραφῶν εἶναι τὸν Χριστόν, Ἰησοῦν 'proving from the Scriptures that Jesus is the Messiah' Ac 18.28.
ἀποδείκνυμι[c]: πολλὰ καὶ βαρέα αἰτιώματα καταφέροντες ἃ οὐκ ἴσχυον ἀποδεῖξαι 'they made many serious charges (against him) which they were not able to prove' Ac 25.7.

72.6 ἀμήν: strong affirmation of what is declared – 'truly, indeed, it is true that.' ἀμὴν γὰρ λέγω ὑμῖν 'for I tell you the truth' Mt 5.18; ὅς ἐστιν εὐλογητὸς εἰς τοὺς αἰῶνας· ἀμήν 'who is to be praised forever; indeed, this is true' Ro 1.25; ἀμὴν ἀμὴν λέγω ὑμῖν, ὄψεσθε τὸν οὐρανὸν ἀνεῳγότα καὶ τοὺς ἀγγέλους τοῦ θεοῦ ἀναβαίνοντας καὶ καταβαίνοντας ἐπὶ τὸν υἱὸν τοῦ ἀνθρώπου 'I am telling you the solemn truth: you will see heaven opened and the angels of God ascending and descending upon the Son of Man' Jn 1.51.

72.7 δοκιμή[b], ῆς f: that which causes something to be known as true or genuine, in the sense of being what it appears to be – 'evidence, proof of genuineness, evidence for the fact that.' ἐπεὶ δοκιμὴν ζητεῖτε τοῦ ἐν ἐμοὶ λαλοῦντος Χριστοῦ 'since you seek proof of the fact that Christ speaks through me' 2 Cor 13.3.

72.8 ἔλεγχος, ου m: the evidence, normally based on argument or discussion, as to the truth or reality of something – 'proof, verification, evidence for.' πραγμάτων ἔλεγχος οὐ βλεπομένων 'a proof of the things we cannot see' or 'evidence that what we cannot see really exists' He 11.1.

72.9 δολόω: to cause something to be or to become false as the result of deception or distortion – 'to cause to be false, to distort.' μηδὲ δολοῦντες τὸν λόγον τοῦ θεοῦ 'and not distorting the word of God' 2 Cor 4.2.

72.10 κενός^c, ή, όν: pertaining to being untrue in view of lacking truth – 'untrue, lacking in truth.' κενὸν ἄρα καὶ τὸ κήρυγμα ἡμῶν 'our preaching is then untrue' 1 Cor 15.14. For other interpretations of κενός in 1 Cor 15.14, see 89.53 and 89.64.

72.11 πλαστός, ή, όν: (derivative of πλάσσω^a 'to form, to make,' 42.31) pertaining to being false in view of being made-up or fabricated – 'false, made-up, invented.' ἐν πλεονεξίᾳ πλαστοῖς λόγοις ὑμᾶς ἐμπορεύσονται 'in their greed they will cheat you by (telling you) made-up stories' 2 Pe 2.3.

B Accurate, Inaccurate[3] (72.12-72.22)

72.12 καλῶς^c: pertaining to being accurate and right, with a possible implication of being commendable – 'accurate, correctly, right.' καλῶς ἐπροφήτευσεν περὶ ὑμῶν Ἡσαΐας 'Isaiah rightly prophesied about you' or 'Isaiah was right when he prophesied about you' Mt 15.7.

72.13 ὀρθῶς: pertaining to conforming closely to an accepted norm or standard – 'correct, correctly.' ὁ δὲ εἶπεν αὐτῷ, Ὀρθῶς ἔκρινας 'your answer is correct, (Jesus) said to him' Lk 7.43.

72.14 ὑγιής^b, ές: pertaining to being accurate, as well as useful and beneficial – 'right, accurate, sound.' λόγον ὑγιῆ ἀκατάγνωστον 'sound words that cannot be criticized' Tt 2.8.[4]

---

3 Subdomain B *Accurate, Inaccurate* involves consistency with external facts (as in the case of Subdomain A *True, False*), but in Subdomain B there are additional features of detail and completeness of evidence. In the case of Subdomain B there is an almost total lack of positive or negative moral implications.

4 ὑγιής^b covers a relatively wide range of meaning, but in Tt 2.8 the focal element appears to be 'that which is right.'

72.15 ὑγιαίνω^b: (derivative of ὑγιής^b 'right, accurate,' 72.14) to be correct in one's views, with the implication of such a state being positively valued – 'to be correct, to be sound, to be accurate.' ἔλεγχε αὐτοὺς ἀποτόμως, ἵνα ὑγιαίνωσιν ἐν τῇ πίστει 'rebuke them sharply that they might be correct in their faith' Tt 1.13.

72.16 ἐπανόρθωσις, εως f: to cause something to be or to become correct, with the implication of a previous condition of faults or failures – 'to correct, correcting faults.' πᾶσα γραφὴ . . . ὠφέλιμος . . . πρὸς ἐπανόρθωσιν 'all Scripture . . . is useful . . . for correcting faults' 2 Tm 3.16.

72.17 διόρθωμα, τος n: the result of having corrected a wrong or bad situation – 'reform.' καὶ διορθωμάτων γινομένων τῷ ἔθνει τούτῳ 'and reforms have been instituted for the sake of this nation' Ac 24.2. In some languages 'reforms' may be rendered as 'changes from bad to good' or 'making things what they should be' or 'causing new good customs.'

72.18 νομίμως: pertaining to being correct according to rules and regulations – 'correctly, according to the rules.' καλὸς ὁ νόμος ἐάν τις αὐτῷ νομίμως χρῆται 'the Law is good if one uses it correctly' 1 Tm 1.8.

72.19 ἀκριβῶς; ἀκριβής, ές: pertaining to strict conformity to a norm or standard, involving both detail and completeness – 'accurate, accurately, strict, strictly.'
ἀκριβῶς: ἐδίδασκεν ἀκριβῶς τὰ περὶ τοῦ Ἰησοῦ 'he taught accurately the facts about Jesus' Ac 18.25.
ἀκριβής: κατὰ τὴν ἀκριβεστάτην αἵρεσιν τῆς ἡμετέρας θρησκείας ἔζησα 'I have lived as a member of the strictest party of our religion' Ac 26.5.

72.20 ἀκρίβεια, ας f: strict conformity to a norm or standard, involving both detail and completeness – 'strictness, strict conformance to, accurateness.' πεπαιδευμένος κατὰ ἀκρίβειαν τοῦ πατρῴου νόμου 'I received instruction in strict conformance to the Law of our ancestors' or 'the instruction I received was to conform strictly to the Law of our ancestors' Ac 22.3.

72.21 ἀργός^e, ή, όν: pertaining to showing indifference as to whether something is as it should be – 'careless, indifferent.' πᾶν ῥῆμα ἀργὸν ὃ λαλήσουσιν οἱ ἄνθρωποι ἀποδώσουσιν περὶ αὐτοῦ λόγον ἐν ἡμέρᾳ κρίσεως 'on the day of judgment everyone will have to give account of every careless word he has ever spoken' Mt 12.36. It is also possible to inter-pret ἀργός in Mt 12.36 as meaning 'without thought' (30.44), 'worthless,' or even 'useless' (65.36).

72.22 κακῶς^c; κακός^d, ή, όν: pertaining to being incorrect or inaccurate, with the possible implication of also being reprehensible – 'incorrect, wrong.' εἰ κακῶς ἐλάλησα, μαρτύρησον περὶ τοῦ κακοῦ 'if I have said something wrong, confirm that it is wrong' Jn 18.23.

73 Genuine, Phony

73.1 γνήσιος, α, ον; γνησίως: pertaining to possessing purported good character or quality – 'genuine, real.'
γνήσιος: τὸ τῆς ὑμετέρας ἀγάπης γνήσιον δοκιμάζων 'trying to find out how genuine your love is' 2 Cor 8.8.
γνησίως: ὅστις γνησίως τὰ περὶ ὑμῶν μεριμνήσει 'who genuinely cares about you' Php 2.20.

73.2 ἀληθινός^c, ή, όν: pertaining to being what something should be – 'genuine, sincere, true.' προσερχώμεθα μετὰ ἀληθινῆς καρδίας 'let us come near with a sincere heart' He 10.22.

73.3 δοκίμιον^b, ου n: genuineness on the basis of having been tested – 'genuineness, genuine.' ἵνα τὸ δοκίμιον ὑμῶν τῆς πίστεως . . . εὑρεθῇ 'so as to prove that your faith is genuine' 1 Pe 1.7.

73.4 δόκιμος^b, ον: pertaining to being genuine on the basis of testing – 'genuine, sincere.' ἀσπάσασθε Ἀπελλῆν τὸν δόκιμον ἐν Χριστῷ 'greet Apelles (whose faith) in Christ is genuine' Ro 16.10.

73.5 λογικός, ή, όν: pertaining to being genuine, in the sense of being true to the real and essential nature of something – 'rational, genuine, true.' τὴν λογικὴν λατρείαν ὑμῶν 'this is your true worship' Ro 12.1; ὡς ἀρτιγέννητα βρέφη τὸ λογικὸν ἄδολον γάλα ἐπιποθήσατε 'as newborn babes you drank the true, unadulter-ated milk' 1 Pe 2.2. Since in 1 Pe 2.2 the context is figurative, some translators have preferred to render λογικός as 'spiritual,' so as to make the reference not literal but figurative.

73.6 τέλειος^b, α, ον: pertaining to being truly and completely genuine – 'genuine, true.' ἀλλ' ἡ τελεία ἀγάπη ἔξω βάλλει τὸν φόβον 'but genuine love casts out fear' or '. . . eliminates fear' or 'one who truly loves no longer fears' 1 Jn 4.18.

73.7 τελειόω^b: to cause to be truly and completely genuine – 'make genuine, make true, make completely real.' ἀληθῶς ἐν τούτῳ ἡ ἀγάπη τοῦ θεοῦ τετελείωται 'truly in this person the love of God is made real' 1 Jn 2.5. For another interpretation of τελειόω in 1 Jn 2.5, see 88.38.

73.8 ἀνυπόκριτος, ον: pertaining to being genuine and sincere, and hence lacking in pretense or show – 'genuine, sincere.' εἰς φιλαδελφίαν ἀνυπόκριτον 'to the point of genuine love for fellow believers' 1 Pe 1.22.[1]

73.9 σφραγίς^e, ῖδος f: that which confirms or

1 It is possible to interpret ἀνυπόκριτος in 1 Pe 1.22 as being simply the negative state of hypocrisy and thus semantically neutral, but there seems to be an important positive element and therefore ἀνυπόκριτος is classified here under *Genuine*, rather than in Domain 88, Subdomain C'.

attests to the genuineness of something – 'certification, validation, proof, evidence of genuineness.' ἡ γὰρ σφραγίς μου τῆς ἀποστολῆς ὑμεῖς ἐστε 'you are the certification for my being an apostle' or 'you show clearly that I am an apostle' 1 Cor 9.2.

74 Able, Capable

74.1 δύναμις[a], εως *f*: the ability to perform a particular activity or to undergo some experience – 'ability, capability.' καθ᾽ ὑπερβολὴν ὑπὲρ δύναμιν ἐβαρήθημεν 'we were under great pressure far beyond our ability (to endure)' 2 Cor 1.8. In a number of languages the equivalent of 'ability' in 2 Cor 1.8 may be expressed simply by a modal such as 'can,' for example, 'far beyond what we can endure.'

74.2 δυνατός[b], ή, όν: (derivative of δύναμις[a] 'ability,' 74.1) pertaining to having the ability to perform some function – 'able, can.' βουλεύσεται εἰ δυνατός ἐστιν ἐν δέκα χιλιάσιν ὑπαντῆσαι τῷ μετὰ εἴκοσι χιλιάδων ἐρχομένῳ ἐπ᾽ αὐτόν 'he will decide whether he is able with ten thousand men to face one who is coming out against him with twenty thousand men' Lk 14.31; ἵνα δυνατὸς ᾖ καὶ παρακαλεῖν 'in order that he may be able to encourage (others)' Tt 1.9. For another interpretation of δυνατός in Tt 1.9, see 74.4.

74.3 ὁ δυνατός: (derivative of δυνατός[b] 'able, can,' 74.2; a title for God, literally 'the one who is able') one who is capable of doing anything – 'the Mighty One, Mighty God, the Almighty.' ὅτι ἐποίησέν μοι μεγάλα ὁ δυνατός 'because the Mighty One has done great things for me' Lk 1.49.

74.4 δυνατός[c], ή, όν: pertaining to having special competence in performing some function – 'particularly capable, expert, competent.' δυνατὸς ὢν ἐν ταῖς γραφαῖς 'particularly competent in the Scriptures' or 'expert in interpreting the Scriptures' Ac 18.24; ἵνα δυνατὸς ᾖ καὶ παρακαλεῖν ἐν τῇ διδασκαλίᾳ τῇ ὑγιαινούσῃ 'in order to be specially competent to encourage (others) by sound teaching' Tt 1.9. For another interpretation of δυνατός in Tt 1.9, see 74.2.

74.5 δύναμαι; δυνατέω: (derivatives of δύναμις[a] 'ability,' 74.1) to be able to do or to experience something – 'can, to be able to.'
δύναμαι: οὐδεὶς δύναται δυσὶ κυρίοις δουλεύειν 'no one can serve two masters' Mt 6.24.
δυνατέω: σταθήσεται δέ, δυνατεῖ γὰρ ὁ κύριος στῆσαι αὐτόν 'he will succeed, because the Lord is able to make him succeed' Ro 14.4.

74.6 δυναμόω; ἐνδυναμόω: (derivatives of δύναμαι 'to be able,' 74.5) to cause someone to have the ability to do or to experience something – 'to make someone able, to give capability to, to enable, to strengthen, to empower.'
δυναμόω: ἐν πάσῃ δυνάμει δυναμούμενοι κατὰ τὸ κράτος τῆς δόξης αὐτοῦ 'being strengthened with all power according to his glorious might' Col 1.11.
ἐνδυναμόω: πάντα ἰσχύω ἐν τῷ ἐνδυναμοῦντί με 'I can do all things by the one who makes me able' or 'I am able to face anything by the one who makes me able (to do it)' Php 4.13; ἀλλ᾽ ἐνεδυναμώθη τῇ πίστει 'but he was enabled by faith' Ro 4.20.

74.7 ἐνδυναμόομαι: to become able to do something – 'to become able, to become capable.' Σαῦλος δὲ μᾶλλον ἐνεδυναμοῦτο 'Saul became all the more able' Ac 9.22; τοῦ λοιποῦ ἐνδυναμοῦσθε ἐν κυρίῳ καὶ ἐν τῷ κράτει τῆς ἰσχύος αὐτοῦ 'finally, in union with the Lord become capable by means of his great strength' Eph 6.10.

74.8 ἰσχύς[a], ύος *f*: exceptional capability, with the probable implication of personal potential – 'capability, strength.' ἀγαπήσεις κύριον τὸν θεόν σου . . . ἐξ ὅλης τῆς ἰσχύος σου 'love the Lord your God . . . with all your strength' or '. . . with your whole being' Mk 12.30. In a number of languages the expression 'to love the Lord with one's strength,' in the sense of physical strength, is meaningless, and therefore it may be necessary to translate 'love the Lord your God as completely as you can.' It is important to note that in a passage such as Mk 12.30 the terms in the series καρδία, ψυχή, διάνοια, and ἰσχύς do not refer to completely different parts or aspects of human personality; rather, the four are combined to emphasize the totality of the individual. In some languages the equivalent way of expressing this comprehensive aspect of personality is 'to love him completely with all you feel and all you think.'

74.9 ἰσχύω[a]: (derivative of ἰσχύς[a] 'capability,' 74.8) to have special personal ability to do or experience something – 'to be able to, to have the strength to, to be very capable of.'[1] πολλοί, . . . ζητήσουσιν εἰσελθεῖν καὶ οὐκ ἰσχύσουσιν 'many people . . . will try to go in, but they will not be able to' Lk 13.24; πάντα ἰσχύω ἐν τῷ ἐνδυναμοῦντί με 'I am able to face all conditions by the one who makes me able (to do it)' Php 4.13.

74.10 ἐξισχύω; κατισχύω[a]: to be completely capable of doing or experiencing something – 'to be completely able, to be fully able.'
ἐξισχύω: ἵνα ἐξισχύσητε καταλαβέσθαι σὺν πᾶσιν τοῖς ἁγίοις 'that you, together with all God's people, may be fully able to understand . . .' Eph 3.18.
κατισχύω[a]: ἵνα κατισχύσητε ἐκφυγεῖν ταῦτα πάντα τὰ μέλλοντα γίνεσθαι 'that you may be completely able to escape all that is about to happen' Lk 21.36. For another interpretation of κατισχύω in Lk 21.36, see 79.64.

74.11 κατακαυχάομαι[c]: to have greater power or potential than – 'to be more powerful than, to triumph over.' κατακαυχᾶται ἔλεος κρίσεως 'mercy is more powerful than judg-

ment' or 'mercy triumphs over judgment' Jas 2.13. The reference to 'mercy' and 'judgment' in Jas 2.13 must be related to God's mercy and judgment. In a number of languages it is not possible to personify mercy and judgment, and therefore one must relate these two expressions to God, for example, 'the extent to which God shows mercy is even more than the way in which he judges' or 'God shows mercy even more than he judges.'

74.12 ἔχω[e]: to possess the capacity to do something – 'to be able to, to have the capacity to.' σπουδάσω δὲ καὶ ἑκάστοτε ἔχειν ὑμᾶς μετὰ τὴν ἐμὴν ἔξοδον τὴν τούτων μνήμην ποιεῖσθαι 'and I will make every effort to see that after my departure you will always be able to remember these things' 2 Pe 1.15; κοπιάτω ἐργαζόμενος ταῖς ἰδίαις χερσὶν τὸ ἀγαθόν, ἵνα ἔχῃ μεταδιδόναι τῷ χρείαν ἔχοντι 'let him start working to earn an honest living for himself in order to be able to help the one in need' Eph 4.28.

74.13 ἄθλησις[b], εως f: a test of someone's capability to resist or to respond to some difficulty – 'challenge.' πολλὴν ἄθλησιν ὑπεμείνατε παθημάτων 'in your sufferings you stood up to the great challenge' He 10.32. For another interpretation of ἄθλησις in He 10.32, see 50.3.

74.14 σθενόω: to cause someone to be or to become more able or capable, with the implication of a contrast with weakness – 'to make more able, to strengthen.' αὐτὸς καταρτίσει, στηρίξει, σθενώσει 'he will restore, strengthen, and make (you) stronger' 1 Pe 5.10. The terms στηρίζω (see 74.19) and σθενόω in 1 Pe 5.10 are very similar in meaning and serve primarily to intensify the meaning of making persons more able to engage in or to undergo certain experiences.

74.15 οἰκοδομέω[b]; ἐποικοδομέω[b]; οἰκοδομή[c], ῆς f: to increase the potential of someone or something, with focus upon the process involved – 'to strengthen, to make more able, to build up.'
οἰκοδομέω[b]: οἰκοδομουμένη καὶ πορευομένη τῷ

---

1 Note that ἰσχύω[a] may occur without a verb complement, thus making possible a translation such as 'to be able to do' or 'to be able to prevail' as in Re 12.8 (καὶ οὐκ ἴσχυσεν 'and he was not able to prevail'). In some languages, however, it may be better to render this expression in Re 12.8 as 'he was defeated.'

φόβῳ τοῦ κυρίου 'built up and living in reverence for the Lord' Ac 9.31.

ἐποικοδομέω[b]: ἐποικοδομοῦντες ἑαυτοὺς τῇ
ἁγιωτάτῃ ὑμῶν πίστει 'build yourselves up on
your most holy faith' or '. . . by means of your
most holy faith' Jd 20.

οἰκοδομή[c]: κατὰ τὴν ἐξουσίαν ἣν ὁ κύριος ἔδωκέν μοι, εἰς οἰκοδομὴν καὶ οὐκ εἰς καθαίρεσιν
'according to the authority which the Lord
has given me to build you up, not to tear you
down' or '. . . to strengthen and not to
weaken' 2 Cor 13.10.

74.16 καθαίρεσις[b], εως *f*: to cause someone
or something to be less able or to lose capacity
– 'to weaken, to tear down, to make less able.'
κατὰ τὴν ἐξουσίαν ἣν ὁ κύριος ἔδωκέν μοι, εἰς
οἰκοδομὴν καὶ οὐκ εἰς καθαίρεσιν 'according to
the authority which the Lord has given me to
build you up, not to tear you down' or '. . . to
strengthen and not to weaken' 2 Cor 13.10.

74.17 βεβαιόομαι: to increase in inner
strength, with the implication of greater firmness of character or attitude – 'to receive more
inner strength, to be strengthened in one's
heart.' ἐποικοδομούμενοι ἐν αὐτῷ καὶ βε-
βαιούμενοι τῇ πίστει 'built up in him and
receiving more inner strength in your faith' or
'. . . becoming stronger in your faith' Col 2.7.

74.18 ῥιζόομαι: to become strengthened,
with focus upon the source of such strength –
'to be strengthened, to be rooted in.' ἐρριζω-
μένοι καὶ ἐποικοδομούμενοι ἐν αὐτῷ 'being
strengthened and built up in him' Col 2.7.

74.19 στηρίζω[a]; ἐπιστηρίζω; στερεόω[b]: to
cause someone to become stronger in the
sense of more firm and unchanging in attitude
or belief – 'to strengthen, to make more firm.'
στηρίζω[a]: σύ ποτε ἐπιστρέψας στήρισον τοὺς
ἀδελφούς σου 'when you turn back, you must
strengthen your brothers' or '. . . your fellow
disciples' Lk 22.32.
ἐπιστηρίζω: ἐπιστηρίζοντες τὰς ψυχὰς τῶν
μαθητῶν 'they strengthened the believers' Ac
14.22.
στερεόω[b]: αἱ μὲν οὖν ἐκκλησίαι ἐστερεοῦντο τῇ
πίστει 'so the churches were strengthened in
the faith' Ac 16.5.

74.20 στερέωμα, τος *n*; στηριγμός[b], οῦ *m*: a
state of firm, inner strength – 'firm position,
being firm in, firmness, steadfastness.'
στερέωμα: ὑμῶν τὴν τάξιν καὶ τὸ στερέωμα τῆς
εἰς Χριστὸν πίστεως ὑμῶν 'your orderliness and
steadfastness in your faith in Christ' Col 2.5.
στηριγμός[b]: ἐκπέσητε τοῦ ἰδίου στηριγμοῦ 'fall
from your firm position' 2 Pe 3.17. For
another interpretation of στηριγμός in 2 Pe
3.17, see 21.13.

74.21 στερεός[b], ά, όν: pertaining to being
firm and steadfast in one's attitudes or beliefs
– 'to be firm, to be strong.' ᾧ ἀντίστητε στε-
ρεοὶ τῇ πίστει 'be strong in your faith and
resist him' 1 Pe 5.9.

74.22 ἀδύνατος[a], ον: pertaining to not being
able to do or experience something – 'incapable, not being able.' ὀφείλομεν δὲ ἡμεῖς οἱ
δυνατοὶ τὰ ἀσθενήματα τῶν ἀδυνάτων βαστάζειν
'but we who are capable ought to bear the
weaknesses of those who are not capable' Ro
15.1. In Ro 15.1 οἱ δυνατοί refers to capability
with respect to faith and τῶν ἀδυνάτων refers,
conversely, to those who are incapable with
respect to faith. In some languages, therefore,
it may be possible to use a similar biblical
phrase, 'weak in the faith.' τις ἀνὴρ ἀδύνατος ἐν
Λύστροις τοῖς ποσὶν ἐκάθητο 'in Lystra there
was (see 85.63) a man who was unable to use
his feet' Ac 14.8. In many languages the
appropriate equivalent of Ac 14.8 would be
'but in Lystra there was a man who was crippled.'

74.23 ἀσθένεια[a], ας *f*: a state of incapacity to
do or experience something – 'incapacity,
weakness, limitation.' ἥδιστα οὖν μᾶλλον καυ-
χήσομαι ἐν ταῖς ἀσθενείαις μου 'I am happy
then to be proud of my weaknesses' 2 Cor
12.9b; ἡ γὰρ δύναμις ἐν ἀσθενείᾳ τελεῖται
'power is made complete in weakness' 2 Cor
12.9a. A literal rendering of this expression in
2 Cor 12.9 may not be meaningful, and in fact
can be quite misleading. δύναμις is best interpreted as 'God's power' and ἀσθένεια as the
weakness which Paul experienced. Therefore,
one may be able to translate as 'my power is
greatest when you are weak' (see Today's
English Version).

74.24 ἀσθένημα, τος *n*: (derivative of ἀσθενέω[a] 'to be weak,' 74.26) an instance of weakness or limited capacity – 'weakness, case of weakness.' ὀφείλομεν δὲ ἡμεῖς οἱ δυνατοὶ τὰ ἀσθενήματα τῶν ἀδυνάτων βαστάζειν 'we who are capable ought to bear the weaknesses of those who are not capable' Ro 15.1. In some languages it may be appropriate to translate τὰ ἀσθενήματα as 'times when they are weak.'

74.25 ἀσθενής[a], ές: (derivative of ἀσθένεια[a] 'weakness,' 74.23) pertaining to a state of limited capacity to do or be something – 'weak, unable.' ἐγενόμην τοῖς ἀσθενέσιν ἀσθενής 'to those who are weak (in faith), I became weak' or 'I became weak to those who are weak' 1 Cor 9.22.

74.26 ἀσθενέω[a]: to be in a state of incapacity or weakness – 'to be weak, to be unable to, to be limited in.' τὸν δὲ ἀσθενοῦντα τῇ πίστει προσλαμβάνεσθε 'welcome the one who is weak in faith' Ro 14.1. In some languages it may be better to translate this expression in Ro 14.1 as 'welcome those who have only a little faith.' τὸ γὰρ ἀδύνατον τοῦ νόμου, ἐν ᾧ ἠσθένει διὰ τῆς σαρκός 'for what the Law could not do in that it was weak because of human nature' Ro 8.3.

74.27 ἀποθνῄσκω[c] (a figurative extension of meaning of ἀποθνῄσκω[a] 'to die,' 23.99); ἀπο-γίνομαι[b] (a figurative extension of meaning of ἀπογίνομαι 'to die,' not occurring in the NT): to be unable to respond or react to any impulse or desire – 'to be dead to, to not respond to, to have no part in.'

ἀποθνῄσκω[c]: ἀπεθάνομεν τῇ ἁμαρτίᾳ 'we have died to sin' Ro 6.2.

ἀπογίνομαι[b]: ἵνα ταῖς ἁμαρτίαις ἀπογενόμενοι τῇ δικαιοσύνῃ ζήσωμεν 'in order that having died to sin we may live to righteousness' 1 Pe 2.24. For another interpretation of ἀπογίνομαι in 1 Pe 2.24, see 68.40.

In a number of languages it is extremely difficult to speak of 'dying to sin.' In some instances one can preserve the figurative meaning by an expression such as 'to be like dead as far as desiring to sin' or 'to be like a corpse as far as temptations to sin are concerned.'

74.28 νεκρός[c], ά, όν: pertaining to being unable to respond to any impulse or to perform some function – 'unable, ineffective, dead, powerless.' ὄντας ἡμᾶς νεκροὺς τοῖς παραπτώμασιν συνεζωοποίησεν τῷ Χριστῷ 'we who were dead because of our sins, (God) brought to life through Christ' Eph 2.5. Since the reference in Eph 2.5 (see also Eph 2.1) is to matters relating to God, one may translate 'we who were unable to respond to matters relating to God because of our sins . . .' or 'we who were spiritually dead . . .'

75 Adequate, Qualified[1]

75.1 ἱκανότης, ητος *f*: the state of being adequate or qualified for something – 'adequacy, qualification.' ἀλλ' ἡ ἱκανότης ἡμῶν ἐκ τοῦ θεοῦ 'but our adequacy comes from God' 2 Cor 3.5.

75.2 ἱκανός[c], ή, όν: (derivative of ἱκανότης 'adequacy,' 75.1) pertaining to being adequate for something – 'adequate, qualified.' καὶ πρὸς ταῦτα τίς ἱκανός; 'and who is adequate for these things?' 2 Cor 2.16.

75.3 ἱκανόω: (derivative of ἱκανός[c] 'adequate,' 75.2) to cause someone or something to be adequate for something – 'to make sufficient, to make adequate, to cause to be qualified.' ὃς καὶ ἱκάνωσεν ἡμᾶς διακόνους καινῆς διαθήκης 'who makes us adequate to be servants of the new covenant' 2 Cor 3.6.

75.4 ἄρτιος, α, ον: pertaining to being qualified to perform some function – 'qualified, proficient.' ἵνα ἄρτιος ᾖ ὁ τοῦ θεοῦ ἄνθρωπος 'in

---

1 It would be possible to combine Domain 75 *Adequate, Qualified* with Domain 74 *Able, Capable*, for the meanings are closely related. However, the meanings in Domain 75 seem to relate to a particular measure of capability or adequacy rather than being relatively unqualified as to degree of capability, which is more characteristic of the meanings in Domain 74.

order that the man of God may be qualified' 2 Tm 3.17.

75.5 ἐξαρτίζω[b]; καταρτίζω[a]; κατάρτισις, εως *f*; καταρτισμός, οῦ *m*: to make someone completely adequate or sufficient for something – 'to make adequate, to furnish completely, to cause to be fully qualified, adequacy.'

ἐξαρτίζω[b]: πρὸς πᾶν ἔργον ἀγαθὸν ἐξηρτισμένος 'completely qualified for every good deed' 2 Tm 3.17.

καταρτίζω[a]: κατηρτισμένος δὲ πᾶς ἔσται ὡς ὁ διδάσκαλος αὐτοῦ 'everyone who is thoroughly qualified will be like his teacher' Lk 6.40. In this context, however, it may be useful to translate κατηρτισμένος as 'one who has been fully trained.'

κατάρτισις: τοῦτο καὶ εὐχόμεθα, τὴν ὑμῶν κατάρτισιν 'and for this we pray, namely, your becoming fully qualified' 2 Cor 13.9.

καταρτισμός: πρὸς τὸν καταρτισμὸν τῶν ἁγίων εἰς ἔργον διακονίας 'in order to make God's people fully qualified for work in (his) service' or '. . . for (this) work of service' Eph 4.12.

75.6 αὐτάρκεια[b], ας *f*: a state of adequacy or sufficiency – 'what is adequate, what is sufficient, what is needed, adequacy.' πάντοτε πᾶσαν αὐτάρκειαν ἔχοντες 'always having complete sufficiency' 2 Cor 9.8. In a number of languages the equivalent of this expression in 2 Cor 9.8 may be 'always having all that you need' or, stated negatively, 'not lacking in anything.'

75.7 πίπτω[j]; ἐκπίπτω[e]: (figurative extensions of meaning of πίπτω[a] 'to fall,' 15.118, and ἐκπίπτω[a] 'to fall out or from,' 15.120) to become inadequate for some function – 'to become inadequate, to fail.'

πίπτω[j]: ἡ ἀγάπη οὐδέποτε πίπτει 'love never fails' or, stated positively, 'love is always sufficient' or 'love is always adequate for anything' 1 Cor 13.8. For another interpretation of πίπτω in 1 Cor 13.8, see 68.49.

ἐκπίπτω[e]: οὐχ οἷον δὲ ὅτι ἐκπέπτωκεν ὁ λόγος τοῦ θεοῦ 'not that the word of God has failed' or '. . . is inadequate' or '. . . cannot do what it is supposed to do' Ro 9.6.

76 Power, Force

76.1 δύναμις[b], εως *f*: the potentiality to exert force in performing some function – 'power.' ἀλλὰ λήμψεσθε δύναμιν ἐπελθόντος τοῦ ἁγίου πνεύματος ἐφ' ὑμᾶς 'but you shall receive power when the Holy Spirit has come upon you' Ac 1.8.

76.2 μεγαλειότης[b], ητος *f*: a manifestation of great power – 'mighty power, mighty act.' ἐξεπλήσσοντο δὲ πάντες ἐπὶ τῇ μεγαλειότητι τοῦ θεοῦ 'all the people were amazed at the mighty power of God' Lk 9.43.

76.3 χείρ[c], χειρός *f* (a figurative extension of meaning of χείρ[a] 'hand,' 8.30); βραχίων, ονος *m* (a figurative extension of meaning of βραχίων 'arm,' not occurring in the NT); δάκτυλος[b], ου *m* (a figurative extension of meaning of δάκτυλος[a] 'finger,' 8.34): power as an expression of the activity of a person or supernatural being – 'power.'[1]

χείρ[c]: καὶ γὰρ χεὶρ κυρίου ἦν μετ' αὐτοῦ 'for the power of the Lord was with him' Lk 1.66; οὐχὶ ἡ χείρ μου ἐποίησεν ταῦτα πάντα; 'did not my power do all these things?' or 'did not I use my power to do . . .?' Ac 7.50.

βραχίων: ἐποίησεν κράτος ἐν βραχίονι αὐτοῦ 'he performed a great deed by his power' Lk 1.51.

δάκτυλος[b]: εἰ δὲ ἐν δακτύλῳ θεοῦ ἐγὼ ἐκβάλλω τὰ δαιμόνια 'but if by the power of God I cast out demons' Lk 11.20.

In some languages there is no abstract term

---

1 It is possible that χείρ[c], βραχίων, and δάκτυλος[b] in the figurative sense of 'power of an individual' differ somewhat in meaning one from the other, but it is impossible to determine this on the basis of existing contexts.

for 'power.' The equivalent of doing something by the power of someone is 'someone makes it possible to do' or, in a figurative sense, 'someone gives strength to do.'

76.4 δεξιά^b, ᾶς *f*: (a figurative extension of meaning of δεξιά^a 'right hand,' 8.32) power, with the added implication of authority – 'power.' τῇ δεξιᾷ οὖν τοῦ θεοῦ ὑψωθείς 'therefore he was raised up by the power of God' Ac 2.33.

76.5 βραχίων ὑψηλός: (an idiom, literally 'exalted arm' or 'lifted up arm') great power, with the implication of an exalted quality – 'great power, exalted power, marvelous power.' μετὰ βραχίονος ὑψηλοῦ ἐξήγαγεν αὐτοὺς ἐξ αὐτῆς '(God) brought them out of there by his great power' Ac 13.17.

76.6 κράτος^a, ους *n*: the power to rule or control – 'power, might.' τὸν τὸ κράτος ἔχοντα τοῦ θανάτου 'the one who has power over death' He 2.14.

76.7 κράτος^b, ους *n*; δύναμις^c, εως *f*: a deed manifesting great power, with the implication of some supernatural force – 'mighty deed, miracle.'
κράτος^b: ἐποίησεν κράτος ἐν βραχίονι αὐτοῦ 'he did a mighty deed by his power' Lk 1.51.
δύναμις^c: ἄνδρα ἀποδεδειγμένον ἀπὸ τοῦ θεοῦ εἰς ὑμᾶς δυνάμεσι καὶ τέρασι 'a man manifested to you by God by means of mighty deeds and wonders' Ac 2.22.

76.8 μεγαλεῖον, ου *n*: a deed of importance and power – 'mighty act, great deed.' ἀκούομεν λαλούντων αὐτῶν ταῖς ἡμετέραις γλώσσαις τὰ μεγαλεῖα τοῦ θεοῦ 'we hear them speaking in our own languages about the great deeds of God' or '. . . the great things which God has done' Ac 2.11.
    In some contexts it is not possible to distinguish readily between τέρας (33.480), σημεῖον (33.477), κράτος^b (76.7), δύναμις^c (76.7), and μεγαλεῖον, for all may refer to miraculous events, and in a number of instances these terms are used in pairs, primarily to emphasize rather than to distinguish different kinds of miraculous events. All of these

expressions may indicate a supernatural component with important religious implications, especially since the performance of such miracles implies divine power.

76.9 κραταιός, ά, όν: (derivative of κράτος^a 'power,' 76.6) pertaining to being powerful or mighty – 'powerful, mighty.' ταπεινώθητε οὖν ὑπὸ τὴν κραταιὰν χεῖρα τοῦ θεοῦ 'humble yourselves, then, under God's mighty power' 1 Pe 5.6. In 1 Pe 5.6 χείρ is, of course, to be interpreted as power (see 76.3).

76.10 κραταιόομαι^b: (derivative of κραταιός 'powerful,' 76.9) to become strong psychologically – 'to become strong, to become powerful.' ἐκραταιοῦτο πνεύματι 'he became strong in spirit' or 'he developed in spirit' Lk 1.80; κραταιωθῆναι διὰ τοῦ πνεύματος αὐτοῦ εἰς τὸν ἔσω ἄνθρωπον 'to become strengthened through his Spirit in the inner person' Eph 3.16; ἀνδρίζεσθε, κραταιοῦσθε 'be brave, be strong' 1 Cor 16.13. In 1 Cor 16.13 κραταιόομαι must be understood in a non-physical sense. The implication is that the believer is to be sufficiently strong as to be able to dominate any evil influence.

76.11 ἰσχυρός^a, ά, όν: pertaining to having power – 'powerful, strong.' τὰ ἀσθενῆ τοῦ κόσμου ἐξελέξατο ὁ θεὸς ἵνα καταισχύνῃ τὰ ἰσχυρά 'God chose the weak things of the world in order to put to shame the powerful' 1 Cor 1.27.

76.12 ἐξουσία^f, ας *f*: the power to do something, with or without an added implication of authority – 'power.' ἡ γὰρ ἐξουσία τῶν ἵππων ἐν τῷ στόματι αὐτῶν ἐστιν καὶ ἐν ταῖς οὐραῖς αὐτῶν 'the power of the horses is in their mouths and in their tails' Re 9.19; ἔχειν ἐξουσίαν ἐκβάλλειν τὰ δαιμόνια 'to have the power to drive out demons' Mk 3.15. It is also possible to understand ἐξουσία in Mk 3.15 as meaning 'authority,' and in a number of instances it is difficult to determine whether the focus is upon the power which an individual has or a granted authority to do something which naturally implies strength or power (see 37.35-37.38).

76.13 δόξα^c, ης *f*: a manifestation of power characterized by glory – 'glorious power, amazing might.' ὥσπερ ἠγέρθη Χριστὸς ἐκ νεκρῶν διὰ τῆς δόξης τοῦ πατρός 'just as Christ was raised from the dead by the glorious power of the Father' Ro 6.4. In some languages the aspect of 'glorious' may be expressed as 'that which causes wonder' or 'that which causes people to marvel.'

76.14 ἀρετή^b, ῆς *f*: a manifestation of power characterized by excellence – 'wonderful act, powerful deed, wonderful deed.' ὅπως τὰς ἀρετὰς ἐξαγγείλητε 'so that you may proclaim the wonderful deeds (of God)' 1 Pe 2.9.

76.15 σκληρός^b, ά, όν: pertaining to being powerful or strong – 'strong, powerful.' ὑπὸ ἀνέμων σκληρῶν ἐλαυνόμενα 'driven by powerful winds' Jas 3.4. For another interpretation of σκληρός in Jas 3.4, see 20.3.

76.16 κέρας^c, ατος *n*: (a figurative extension of meaning of κέρας^a 'horn,' 8.17) power of unusual significance – 'power, mighty power.' καὶ ἤγειρεν κέρας σωτηρίας ἡμῖν 'and he raised up for us a power of salvation' Lk 1.69. In Lk 1.69 the reference of the phrase κέρας σωτηρίας is to the role of the Messiah, and accordingly one may often best render this phrase as 'mighty Savior' or 'powerful Savior.'

76.17 ἐπίκειμαι^c: to possess power or sanction – 'to be in force, to have power over.' δικαιώματα σαρκὸς μέχρι καιροῦ διορθώσεως ἐπικείμενα 'outward regulations are in force until the establishment of a new order' He 9.10. In some languages the concept of 'being in force' may be expressed simply as 'to work' or 'to do what they are supposed to do' or 'to be in control.' For another interpretation of ἐπίκειμαι in He 9.10, see 13.73.

76.18 κυρόω^a: to invest something with power or force – 'to give force to, to validate.' κεκυρωμένην διαθήκην οὐδεὶς ἀθετεῖ 'no one sets aside an agreement which has been put into force' or 'no one sets aside a covenant which has been validated' Ga 3.15. In order to express the meaning of this phrase in Ga 3.15, it may be necessary in some languages to make more specific the arrangements involv-

ed, for example, 'if people have signed an agreement, no one can disregard it' or 'if an agreement has been confirmed, no one can say it does not exist' or, as in some languages, 'if an agreement has been tied, no one can untie it.'

76.19 προκυρόω: to cause to be in force in advance – 'to authorize in advance, to establish in advance, to validate in advance.' διαθήκην προκεκυρωμένην ὑπὸ τοῦ θεοῦ 'covenant established in advance by God' Ga 3.17. In some languages an equivalent of this expression in Ga 3.17 may be 'God tied the covenant in advance.'

76.20 ἵστημι^b: to acknowledge the validity of something – 'to uphold, to maintain, to accept the validity of.' ἀλλὰ νόμον ἱστάνομεν 'but we uphold the Law' Ro 3.31.

76.21 ἵστημι^c: to establish as validated and in force – 'to establish, to authorize, to put into force.' τὴν ἰδίαν δικαιοσύνην ζητοῦντες στῆσαι 'seeking to establish their own righteousness' or '. . . their own way of being put right with God' Ro 10.3; ἀναιρεῖ τὸ πρῶτον ἵνα τὸ δεύτερον στήσῃ 'he does away with the first in order to establish the second' He 10.9. In rendering this expression in He 10.9 it may be necessary to indicate what is involved in 'the first' and 'the second.' The contrast is between the OT system of sacrifices and the sacrifice of Christ.

76.22 ἀναιρέω^b: to remove or withdraw the validation of something – 'to abolish, to invalidate, to do away with.' ἀναιρεῖ τὸ πρῶτον ἵνα τὸ δεύτερον στήσῃ 'he does away with the first in order to establish the second' He 10.9. See 76.21.

76.23 καταλύω^d: to completely invalidate something which has been in force – 'to do away with, to invalidate, to make invalid.' μὴ νομίσητε ὅτι ἦλθον καταλῦσαι τὸν νόμον 'do not think that I have come to do away with the Law' Mt 5.17.

76.24 ἀθετέω^b; ἀθέτησις^a, εως *f*: to refuse to recognize the validity of something – 'to reject, to regard as invalid, annulment.'

ἀθετέω^b: οἱ δὲ Φαρισαῖοι καὶ οἱ νομικοὶ τὴν βουλὴν τοῦ θεοῦ ἠθέτησαν εἰς ἑαυτούς 'the Pharisees and the interpreters of the Law rejected the plan of God for themselves' Lk 7.30; ἀθετήσας τις νόμον Μωϋσέως 'anyone who rejects the Law of Moses' He 10.28. In He 10.28 the rejection may express itself in disobedience.
ἀθέτησις^a: ἀθέτησις μὲν γὰρ γίνεται προαγούσης ἐντολῆς 'for the earlier commandment has been set aside' He 7.18.

76.25 ἀκυρόω; περιφρονέω: to refuse to recognize the force or power of something – 'to invalidate the authority of, to reject, to disregard.'
ἀκυρόω: ἠκυρώσατε τὸν λόγον τοῦ θεοῦ διὰ τὴν παράδοσιν ὑμῶν 'you have disregarded the command of God for the sake of your traditions' Mt 15.6; ἀκυροῦντες τὸν λόγον τοῦ θεοῦ τῇ παραδόσει ὑμῶν ᾗ παρεδώκατε 'disregarding what God has said (or '. . . the command of God') by means of your tradition which you pass on (to others)' Mk 7.13. In both Mt 15.6 and Mk 7.13 the emphasis is upon the fact that people had regarded traditions as having greater authority than the word of God.

περιφρονέω: μηδείς σου περιφρονείτω 'let no one invalidate your authority' Tt 2.15.

76.26 καταργέω^c: to render ineffective the power or force of something – 'to invalidate, to abolish, to cause not to function.' τὸν νόμον τῶν ἐντολῶν ἐν δόγμασιν καταργήσας 'to abolish the Law of commandments consisting of regulations' Eph 2.15; ἵνα τὰ ὄντα καταργήσῃ 'in order to abolish those things that are' 1 Cor 1.28. In rendering this expression in 1 Cor 1.28 it may be quite necessary to stipulate the reference to τὰ ὄντα, and in this context the contrast between τὰ ὄντα and τὰ μὴ ὄντα may perhaps be best expressed as 'those things that are not regarded as important in order to abolish those that are regarded as important.' The rendering of these expressions depends, of course, upon the manner in which the preceding context from verse 26 is rendered.

76.27 κενόω^a: to take away the power or significance of something – 'to cause to lose power, to cause to be emptied of power, to make powerless.' ἵνα μὴ κενωθῇ ὁ σταυρὸς τοῦ Χριστοῦ 'in order that the cross of Christ may not be deprived of its power' 1 Cor 1.17.

77 Ready, Prepared

77.1 ἑτοιμασία, ας f: a state of being ready for action – 'readiness to, being ready to.' ἐν ἑτοιμασίᾳ τοῦ εὐαγγελίου τῆς εἰρήνης 'in readiness (to proclaim) the good news of peace' Eph 6.15.

77.2 ἕτοιμος, η, ον; ἑτοίμως: pertaining to a state of readiness – 'ready, prepared.'
ἕτοιμος: ἀνάγαιον μέγα ἐστρωμένον ἕτοιμον 'a large, upstairs room, arranged and ready' Mk 14.15.
ἑτοίμως: τρίτον τοῦτο ἑτοίμως ἔχω ἐλθεῖν πρὸς ὑμᾶς 'this is the third time I have been ready to come to visit you' 2 Cor 12.14.

77.3 ἑτοιμάζω: (derivative of ἑτοιμασία 'readiness,' 77.1) to cause to be ready – 'to

make ready, to prepare.' τὸ ἄριστόν μου ἡτοίμακα 'I have made ready my feast' or 'my feast is ready' Mt 22.4; ἀλλ' οἷς ἡτοίμασται ὑπὸ τοῦ πατρός μου 'but for those for whom it has been made ready by my Father' or 'but for whom it has been prepared by my Father' Mt 20.23.

77.4 προετοιμάζω; προκαταρτίζω: to make ready or prepare in advance – 'to make ready in advance, to prepare in advance.'
προετοιμάζω: ἃ προητοίμασεν εἰς δόξαν 'whom he has made ready in advance to receive (his) glory' Ro 9.23.
προκαταρτίζω: ἵνα προέλθωσιν εἰς ὑμᾶς καὶ προκαταρτίσωσιν τὴν προεπηγγελμένην εὐλογίαν ὑμῶν 'in order that they might go ahead to

you and make ready the gift which you have promised in advance' 2 Cor 9.5.

77.5 περιζώννυμαι τὴν ὀσφύν: (an idiom, literally 'to gird up the loins') to cause oneself to be in a state of readiness – 'to get ready, to prepare oneself.' στῆτε οὖν περιζωσάμενοι τὴν ὀσφὺν ὑμῶν ἐν ἀληθείᾳ 'stand ready with truth' Eph 6.14. In the context of Eph 6.14, however, it may be useful to preserve the extended figure of readiness for warfare beginning with Eph 6.13 and extending through verse 17.

77.6 κατασκευάζω[a]; κατεργάζομαι[d]: to cause to be thoroughly prepared – 'to prepare, to make ready.'
κατασκευάζω[a]: ἑτοιμάσαι κυρίῳ λαὸν κατεσκευασμένον 'make ready for the Lord a people thoroughly prepared' Lk 1.17.
κατεργάζομαι[d]: ὁ δὲ κατεργασάμενος ἡμᾶς εἰς αὐτὸ τοῦτο θεός 'God who has prepared us for this' 2 Cor 5.5.

77.7 κατασκευάζω τὴν ὁδόν: (an idiom, literally 'to prepare the road') to cause circumstances to be ready or propitious for some event – 'to make ready for, to prepare for, to prepare the way for.' ὃς κατασκευάσει τὴν ὁδόν σου ἔμπροσθέν σου 'who will prepare your way before you' or 'who will make everything ready for you' Mt 11.10. In some languages it

may be better to render this expression in Mt 11.10 as 'who will arrange everything for you.'

77.8 ἐπισκευάζομαι; παρασκευάζομαι: to be or to become ready for some purpose – 'to be ready, to make ready, to become ready, to prepare.'
ἐπισκευάζομαι: μετὰ δὲ τὰς ἡμέρας ταύτας ἐπισκευασάμενοι ἀνεβαίνομεν εἰς Ἱεροσόλυμα 'after those days we got ready and went up to Jerusalem' Ac 21.15.
παρασκευάζομαι: τίς παρασκευάσεται εἰς πόλεμον; 'who will make ready for battle?' or 'who will prepare for war?' 1 Cor 14.8.

77.9 ἀπαρασκεύαστος, ον: pertaining to being not prepared – 'unprepared, not ready.' ἐὰν ἔλθωσιν σὺν ἐμοὶ Μακεδόνες καὶ εὕρωσιν ὑμᾶς ἀπαρασκευάστους 'if those of Macedonia should come with me and find you unprepared' or '. . . find you as yet not ready' 2 Cor 9.4.

77.10 ὁπλίζομαι: (a figurative extension of meaning of ὁπλίζομαι 'to arm oneself,' not occurring in the NT) to prepare, with focus upon the process of equipping – 'to prepare, to make ready.' ὑμεῖς τὴν αὐτὴν ἔννοιαν ὁπλίσασθε 'prepare yourselves with the same insight' or 'get ready by having the same understanding' 1 Pe 4.1.

78 Degree[1]

Outline of Subdomains

A Much, Little (Positive-Negative Degree) (78.1-78.27)
B More Than, Less Than (Comparative Degree) (78.28-78.39)
C About, Approximately, Almost, Hardly (Approximate Degree) (78.40-78.43)
D Completely, Enough (Completive Degree) (78.44-78.50)
E Up To, As Much As, To the Degree That (Marked Extent of Degree) (78.51-78.53)

A Much, Little (Positive-Negative Degree) (78.1-78.27)

78.1 λίαν: generalized, positive degree – 'very.' ἐθυμώθη λίαν 'he became very angry' Mt 2.16.

1 Expressions of *Degree* specify positions with relationship to scales such as size, intelligence, speed, and quantity. Expressions of *Degree* generally involve such semantic elements as 'very,' 'great,' 'exceedingly,' 'hardly,' and 'excessively' as applied to various scales, for example, 'very fat,' 'exceedingly fast,' 'highly intelligent,' and

78.2 μέγας^b, μεγάλη, μέγα; μεγάλως; μέγεθος, ους *n*: the upper range of a scale of extent, with the possible implication of importance in relevant contexts – 'great, greatly, greatness, to a great degree, intense, terrible.'
μέγας^b: δυνάμει μεγάλη 'with great power' Ac 4.33; καῦμα μέγα 'great heat' or 'intense heat' Re 16.9.
μεγάλως: ἐχάρην δὲ ἐν κυρίῳ μεγάλως 'I rejoice in the Lord greatly' Php 4.10. In a number of languages the expression of intense degree associated with some activity or state is expressed by means of a verb, not an adverb, so that one may render Php 4.10 literally as 'I am-intense joyous in the Lord,' in which the form 'am-intense' is an attempt to represent a verb expression in such a language.
μέγεθος: τὸ ὑπερβάλλον μέγεθος τῆς δυνάμεως αὐτοῦ 'his exceedingly great power' Eph 1.19. In Eph 1.19 there are two expressions of degree, ὑπερβάλλον (treated in 78.33) and μέγεθος, which, though syntactically the head of the phrase, is semantically an expression of degree with δύναμις^b 'power' (76.1).

78.3 πολύς^c, πολλή, πολύ, gen. πολλοῦ, ῆς, οῦ: the upper range of a scale of extent, but probably somewhat less than for μέγας^b, μεγάλως, and μέγεθος (78.2) – 'great, greatly, much, a great deal.' ἠγάπησεν πολύ 'the great love she has shown' Lk 7.47; τὸ πολὺ αὐτοῦ ἔλεος 'his great mercy' 1 Pe 1.3; πολλὰ σπαράξας 'caused him to convulse severely' Mk 9.26; καὶ πολλὰ ἐπετίμα αὐτοῖς 'and he sternly warned them' Mk 3.12. In Mk 3.12 πολλά indicates only degree, but it may be rendered in English as 'sternly' because part of the meaning of ἐπετίμα may be appropriately transferred to the adverbial attributive so as

'great quantity.' Some expressions of *Degree* also include other implied scales. For example, the expression τὸ πλοῦτος τῆς ἁπλότητος αὐτῶν, literally 'the richness of their generosity' (2 Cor 8.2), involves an expression of degree in τὸ πλοῦτος, so that one may render this expression as 'their great generosity' (see 78.15). At the same time, there is also the implication of value.
In Mt 15.22 the adverb κακῶς in the statement ἡ θυγάτηρ μου κακῶς δαιμονίζεται 'my daughter is grievously demon-possessed' functions to indicate the severity of the degree of demon possession, but it also has the implication of the negative element of harm (see 78.17).

to express the extent and nature of the warning. In Ac 21.40 the phrase πολλῆς δὲ σιγῆς γενομένης refers to the fact that the crowd became very quiet. πολλῆς clearly indicates the degree of quietness, though in many languages one cannot speak of something being 'very quiet'; on the contrary, such a state can only be described in terms of the absence of noise, for example, 'when nobody was saying anything.'

78.4 οὕτως^c or οὕτω (a rarely occurring variant): a relatively high degree, presumably in keeping with the context – 'so, so much.' οὕτως ἀνόητοί ἐστε; 'are you so foolish?' Ga 3.3; οὕτω φοβερὸν ἦν τὸ φανταζόμενον 'the sight was so terrifying' He 12.21.

78.5 αὐξάνομαι: to increase in the degree of a state – 'to increase, to grow.' ἐλπίδα δὲ ἔχοντες αὐξανομένης τῆς πίστεως ὑμῶν 'hoping that your faith may grow' 2 Cor 10.15. It would be possible to interpret αὐξάνομαι in 2 Cor 10.15 as being quantitative, but with an expression of state such as πίστις, intensity of degree seems to be more appropriate. In a number of languages, however, it may be necessary to render this expression in 2 Cor 10.15 as 'hoping that you may trust more and more.'

78.6 ὑπεραυξάνω: to increase exceedingly in the degree of a state – 'to increase greatly.' ὅτι ὑπεραυξάνει ἡ πίστις ὑμῶν 'because your faith has increased exceedingly' 2 Th 1.3.

78.7 μάλιστα: a very high point on a scale of extent – 'very much, especially, particularly, exceptionally.' ὀδυνώμενοι μάλιστα ἐπὶ τῷ λόγῳ ᾧ εἰρήκει 'they were especially sad at the words he had spoken' Ac 20.38.²

78.8 ὀλίγος^b, η, ον: a relatively low point on a scale of extent – 'little, to a small degree, slight.' ᾧ δὲ ὀλίγον ἀφίεται, ὀλίγον ἀγαπᾷ 'but whoever has been forgiven little, shows only a little love' Lk 7.47. The first ὀλίγον in Lk 7.47 is an expression of quantity (see 59.13),

2 Though μάλιστα is a superlative in form, it does not always carry a superlative meaning.

while the second ὀλίγον indicates degree. Accordingly, in some languages it may be necessary to translate Lk 7.47 as 'but whoever has been forgiven only a few things loves only a little bit.' τάραχος οὐκ ὀλίγος ἐν τοῖς στρατιώταις 'not a little confusion among the guards' Ac 12.18. In a number of languages, however, it is impossible to speak of 'not a little' (a case of litotes or purposeful understatement). The appropriate equivalent in Ac 12.18 would be simply 'there was great confusion among the guards' or 'the guards were intensely disturbed' or 'the guards were in tremendous confusion.'

78.9 μικρός^c, ά, όν: a very low point on a scale of extent – 'little, very little.' μικρὰν ἔχεις δύναμιν 'you have little power' Re 3.8. In Re 3.8 it would seem that μικρός might very well be classified as indicating quantity (see 59.15), but it is probably better understood as indicating the extent of a state of being powerful, expressed in a number of languages in a negative form, for example, 'you are not very powerful.'

78.10 ἐλαφρός^b, ά, όν: a strictly limited point on the lower part of a scale of extent – 'limited, light, not intense.' τὸ γὰρ παραυτίκα ἐλαφρὸν τῆς θλίψεως ἡμῶν 'for our temporary, limited suffering' 2 Cor 4.17.

78.11 μετρίως: a moderate degree of some activity or state – 'moderately, to a moderate extent.' ἤγαγον δὲ τὸν παῖδα ζῶντα, καὶ παρεκλήθησαν οὐ μετρίως 'they took the young man home alive and were greatly comforted' Ac 20.12. In Ac 20.12 the phrase οὐ μετρίως, literally 'not to a moderate degree,' is equivalent to a strong positive statement, namely 'greatly' or 'to a great extent.'

78.12 ἐκ μέτρου: (an idiom, literally 'from measure') a scalar point marking considerable limitation in the extent of some activity – 'sparingly, in a limited way.' οὐ γὰρ ἐκ μέτρου δίδωσιν τὸ πνεῦμα 'for he does not give the Spirit sparingly' Jn 3.34. In a number of languages this expression in Jn 3.34 may be appropriately rendered as 'he doesn't hold back at all when he gives the Spirit' or 'he gives the Spirit in an abundant way.'

78.13 ὡς^j; πόσος^c, η, ον; ἡλίκος^b, η, ον: a relatively high point on a scale involving exclamation – 'how, very, how great, how much, intense, severe.'

ὡς^j: ὡς ὡραῖοι οἱ πόδες τῶν εὐαγγελιζομένων τὰ ἀγαθά 'how wonderful is the coming of those who bring good news' Ro 10.15.

πόσος^c: τὸ σκότος πόσον 'how great must the darkness be!' Mt 6.23.

ἡλίκος^b: ἡλίκον ἀγῶνα ἔχω 'how great a struggle I have' Col 2.1. In a number of languages the equivalent of ἡλίκον ἀγῶνα ἔχω in Col 2.1 would be 'I struggle very much indeed.'

In a number of languages an expression of high degree in an exclamation can only be reproduced as an expression of intensive degree in a non-exclamatory form. For example, the statement in Mt 6.23 'how great must the darkness be!' must be rendered in a number of languages as 'the darkness is very, very intense' or 'it is very, very dark there.'

78.14 ἱκανός^b, ή, όν: a relatively high point on a scale of extent – 'great, intense, bright (in relationship to light).' φῶς ἱκανόν 'a bright light' Ac 22.6;[3] ἱκανὸν τῷ τοιούτῳ ἡ ἐπιτιμία 'the punishment for such a person is extensive' 2 Cor 2.6. It is also possible to understand ἱκανός in 2 Cor 2.6 as 'sufficiency' (see 78.50).

78.15 πλοῦτος^b, ου m and n; πλουσίως^b: a high point on any scale and having the implication of value as well as abundance – 'great, abundant, abundantly, greatly, extremely.'

πλοῦτος^b: τὸ πλοῦτος τῆς χάριτος αὐτοῦ 'his very great grace' Eph 1.7. In a number of languages, however, this expression in Eph 1.7 would need to be translated as 'he is very, very kind.' τὸ πλοῦτος τῆς ἁπλότητος αὐτῶν 'their great generosity' 2 Cor 8.2; ὁ πλοῦτος τῆς δόξης τῆς κληρονομίας αὐτοῦ 'his very wonderful inheritance' Eph 1.18. Though syntactically ὁ πλοῦτος is the nominal head of this phrase in Eph 1.18, semantically ὁ

---

3 ἱκανός as an expression of degree also occurs with the meaning of 'enough' (see 78.50), but the meaning of 'enough' or 'sufficient' would not be appropriate in Ac 22.6.

πλοῦτος indicates the extent of the δόξα, and δόξα, in turn, clarifies the nature of the κληρονομία.

πλουσίως[b]: οὗ ἐξέχεεν ἐφ᾿ ἡμᾶς πλουσίως '(the Holy Spirit) whom he poured out upon us abundantly' Tt 3.6. In a number of languages it is impossible to preserve the figurative meaning of ἐκχέω in Tt 3.6; therefore, one must render this expression as 'whom God caused us to have in an extensive manner' or 'whom God caused us to have very much of.'
οὕτως γὰρ πλουσίως ἐπιχορηγηθήσεται ὑμῖν ἡ εἴσοδος 'for thus you have been granted entrance in an abundant manner' 2 Pe 1.11.

78.16 ἰσχυρός[c], ά, όν: a high point on a scale of extent and with the implication of strength involved in the activity or state – 'great, greatly, intense, severe.' λιμὸς ἰσχυρά 'a severe famine' Lk 15.14; ἰσχυρὰν παράκλησιν ἔχωμεν 'we were greatly encouraged' He 6.18.

78.17 κακῶς[d]: a high point on a scale of extent and implying harm and seriousness of the state – 'seriously, severely, grievously, dangerously.' ἡ θυγάτηρ μου κακῶς δαιμονίζεται 'my daughter is grievously demon-possessed' Mt 15.22.

78.18 εὐτόνως: a relatively high point on a scale of extent and implying tension and opposition – 'vigorously, vehemently, strong.'[4] εὐτόνως κατηγοροῦντες αὐτοῦ 'made strong accusations against him' Lk 23.10; εὐτόνως γὰρ τοῖς Ἰουδαίοις διακατηλέγχετο 'for he refuted the Jews vigorously' Ac 18.28.

78.19 σφόδρα; σφοδρῶς: a very high point on a scale of extent and in many contexts implying vehemence or violence – 'exceedingly, greatly, violently, terrible.'
σφόδρα: ἐχάρησαν χαρὰν μεγάλην σφόδρα 'they rejoiced exceedingly with great joy' or 'they rejoiced even more exceedingly' Mt 2.10; ἦν γὰρ πλούσιος σφόδρα 'he was exceedingly rich' Lk 18.23; ὅτι μεγάλη ἐστὶν ἡ πληγὴ αὐτῆς σφόδρα 'because it was such a very terrible plague' Re 16.21.

4 In the case of εὐτόνως, the aspect of degree is well balanced by the qualitative aspect of the meaning.

σφοδρῶς: σφοδρῶς δὲ χειμαζομένων ἡμῶν 'we were beaten violently by the storm' Ac 27.18.

78.20 ἐκ περισσοῦ: (an idiom, literally 'from excess') an extremely high point on a scale of extent and implying excess – 'exceedingly, extremely, decidedly, excessively.' λίαν ἐκ περισσοῦ ἐν ἑαυτοῖς ἐξίσταντο 'they were exceedingly amazed' Mk 6.51. In Mk 6.51 both λίαν (78.1) and ἐκ περισσοῦ are expressions of degree and they reinforce one another.

78.21 καλῶς[f]: a positive degree (and even more emphatic in the comparative form κάλλιον) with an implication of correctness – 'certainly, very well.' ὡς καὶ σὺ κάλλιον ἐπιγινώσκεις 'and also you certainly know' Ac 25.10.

78.22 βάθος[c], ους n; κατὰ βάθους (an idiom, literally 'according to depth'); βαθύς[b], εῖα, ύ: an extreme point on a scale of extent – 'extremely, exceedingly great, very very.'
βάθος[c]: ὦ βάθος πλούτου καὶ σοφίας καὶ γνώσεως θεοῦ 'how exceedingly great are God's riches, wisdom, and knowledge' Ro 11.33.
κατὰ βάθους: ἡ κατὰ βάθους πτωχεία αὐτῶν 'even though they were extremely poor' 2 Cor 8.2.
βαθύς[b]: τῇ δὲ μιᾷ τῶν σαββάτων ὄρθρου βαθέως 'on the first day of the week, exceedingly early in the morning' Lk 24.1; καταφερόμενος ὕπνῳ βαθεῖ 'having become exceptionally sleepy' Ac 20.9.

78.23 βάρος[b], ους n: a high point on a scale of extent and often implying importance and value – 'tremendous, very great.' βάρος δόξης 'tremendous glory' 2 Cor 4.17.

78.24 δεινῶς: an extreme point on a scale involving negative values – 'terribly, bitterly.' δεινῶς βασανιζόμενος 'suffering terribly' Mt 8.6; ἤρξαντο οἱ γραμματεῖς καὶ οἱ Φαρισαῖοι δεινῶς ἐνέχειν 'the scribes and Pharisees began to criticize (him) terribly' or '. . . bitterly' or '. . . in a violent manner' Lk 11.53.

78.25 ζῆλος[c], ου m and ους n: a high point on a scale of extent and implying intensity of

involvement – 'extremely, intensely, fierce.'
φοβερὰ δέ τις ἐκδοχὴ κρίσεως καὶ πυρὸς ζῆλος 'a
fearful expectancy of judgment and fierce fire'
He 10.27.

78.26 ἀνάχυσις, εως *f*: (a figurative extension of meaning of ἀνάχυσις 'flood,' not occurring in the NT) an extremely high point on a
scale of extent and implying an excess of
something with negative value – 'excessive,
extreme.' τῆς ἀσωτίας ἀνάχυσιν 'excessive
dissipation' 1 Pe 4.4. In some languages the
equivalent of this phrase in 1 Pe 4.4 is 'they
lived very bad lives' or 'there was nothing bad
that they didn't do.'

78.27 εἰς τὰ ἄμετρα: (an idiom, literally 'into that which is not measured') a point on a
scale going beyond what is expected – 'excessive, beyond measure.' ἡμεῖς δὲ οὐκ εἰς τὰ
ἄμετρα καυχησόμεθα 'we will not boast beyond
certain limits' 2 Cor 10.13. In a number of
languages one can perhaps best render this
statement in 2 Cor 10.13 as 'we will not boast
too much' or 'we will boast only so much.'

B   More Than, Less Than (Comparative Degree)[5] (78.28-78.39)

78.28 πλείων[b], πλεῖον or πλέον; μείζων[a],
ον; μᾶλλον[a]: a degree which surpasses in
some manner a point on an explicit or implicit
scale of extent – 'more, more than, to a
greater degree, even more.'[6]
πλείων[b]: τίς οὖν αὐτῶν πλεῖον ἀγαπήσει αὐτόν;
'therefore, which one will love him more?' Lk
7.42.

5 In this subdomain of *Comparative Degree*, the lexical
units in question have meanings which imply some type
of comparison, which is either overt or covert within the
immediate context. What is significant about these
meanings is that they all imply a degree which is beyond
or below a norm. This domain, however, does not treat
all the comparative forms of adjectives and adverbs, but
only those expressions of degree which mark a comparative element in scales involving events and states.
6 It is possible that μείζων as an expression of degree
differs somewhat in meaning from πλείων[b], even as in
the positive degree a distinction seems to occur between
μέγας[b] (78.2) and πολύς[c] (78.3). In the comparative
forms, however, it seems difficult to substantiate this
type of distinction.

μείζων[a]: οἱ δὲ μεῖζον ἔκραξαν 'but they shouted
even more loudly' Mt 20.31; μείζονα ταύτης
ἀγάπην οὐδεὶς ἔχει 'no one has greater love
than this' Jn 15.13.
μᾶλλον[a]: μᾶλλον ἐφοβήθη 'he was even more
afraid' Jn 19.8; μακάριόν ἐστιν μᾶλλον διδόναι ἢ
λαμβάνειν 'it is more blessed to give than to
receive' Ac 20.35.

78.29 παρά[k]; ὑπέρ[e]: a degree which is beyond
that of a compared scale of extent – 'more
than, to a greater degree than, beyond.'
παρά[k]: ἁμαρτωλοὶ παρὰ πάντας τοὺς Γαλιλαίους
'worse sinners than all the other Galileans' Lk
13.2.
ὑπέρ[e]: οὐκ ἐάσει ὑμᾶς πειρασθῆναι ὑπὲρ ὃ
δύνασθε 'he will not allow you to be tested
beyond your power (to resist)' 1 Cor 10.13;
ὑπὲρ ἐγώ 'I, even more' or 'I, to an even
greater degree' 2 Cor 11.23.

78.30 ἐπάνω[b]: a degree which is significantly
in excess of some amount – 'more than, in excess of.' ἔπειτα ὤφθη ἐπάνω πεντακοσίοις
ἀδελφοῖς ἐφάπαξ 'since he was seen at one time
by more than five hundred fellow believers'
1 Cor 15.6.

78.31 περισσεία[b], ας *f*; ἐκπερισσῶς; περισσῶς; περισσεύω[d]; περισσότερος, α, ον;
περισσοτέρως: a degree which is considerably
in excess of some point on an implied or explicit scale of extent – 'very great, excessive,
extremely, emphatic, surpassing, all the more,
much greater.'
περισσεία[b]: ἡ περισσεία τῆς χαρᾶς αὐτῶν 'their
joy was very great' 2 Cor 8.2.
ἐκπερισσῶς: ὁ δὲ ἐκπερισσῶς ἐλάλει 'he
answered even more emphatically' Mk 14.31.
περισσῶς: οἱ δὲ περισσῶς ἔκραζον 'they shouted
at the top of their voices' Mt 27.23; περισσῶς
τε ἐμμαινόμενος 'extremely furious' Ac 26.11.
περισσεύω[d]: ἐὰν μὴ περισσεύσῃ ὑμῶν ἡ
δικαιοσύνη πλεῖον τῶν γραμματέων 'unless
your righteousness is much greater than that
of the scribes' Mt 5.20; προσεύχομαι, ἵνα ἡ
ἀγάπη ὑμῶν ἔτι μᾶλλον καὶ μᾶλλον περισσεύῃ 'I
pray that your love may keep on growing
more and more' Php 1.9. In Php 1.9 it is clear
that μᾶλλον καὶ μᾶλλον (see 78.28) serves to
emphasize the degree expressed in περισσεύῃ.

ἵνα περισσεύητε μᾶλλον 'in that you might do so even more' 1 Th 4.1. The verb περισσεύητε in 1 Th 4.1 may be regarded as a kind of substitute verb referring to περιπατεῖτε and indicating essentially a matter of degree. This is, of course, further reinforced by μᾶλλον (78.28).

περισσότερος: τῇ περισσοτέρᾳ λύπῃ καταποθῇ 'he may be overwhelmed by excessive sorrow' 2 Cor 2.7.

περισσοτέρως: περισσοτέρως μᾶλλον ἐχάρημεν 'we rejoiced even more greatly' 2 Cor 7.13.

78.32 περισσεύω[e]; πλεονάζω[b]: to cause an increase in the degree of some experience or state – 'to cause to be intense, to cause to be more, to cause to grow.'[7] ὑμᾶς δὲ ὁ κύριος πλεονάσαι καὶ περισσεύσαι τῇ ἀγάπῃ εἰς ἀλλήλους καὶ εἰς πάντας 'may the Lord greatly increase your love for one another and for all' 1 Th 3.12. It would seem that πλεονάσαι and περισσεύσαι in 1 Th 3.12 simply reinforce the meaning of intense degree. It is assumed that these two expressions are not completely synonymous, but it is difficult to determine precisely how they may contrast. It may simply be that περισσεύσαι is somewhat more emphatic.

78.33 ὑπερβάλλω; ὑπερβολή, ῆς *f*: a degree which exceeds extraordinarily a point on an implied or overt scale of extent – 'extraordinary, extreme, supreme, far more, much greater, to a far greater degree.'[8]
ὑπερβάλλω: τὸ ὑπερβάλλον πλοῦτος τῆς χάριτος αὐτοῦ 'the extraordinary greatness of his grace' Eph 2.7. In this expression in Eph 2.7, both ὑπερβάλλον and πλοῦτος (78.15) serve as expressions of degree; ὑπερβάλλον indicates an implied comparison, while πλοῦτος suggests not only a high degree of something, but also value.

---

7 It is possible that περισσεύω[e] differs somewhat from πλεονάζω[b] in intensity, implying perhaps an overabundance of something, but it is difficult to confirm such a distinction on the basis of existing texts.
8 It is difficult to determine the extent to which this set of meanings (78.33) differs from those in 78.31, but a number of contexts for the terms in 78.33 would seem to imply something even beyond what is indicated in the series containing the base περισσ- (78.31).

ὑπερβολή: ἡ ὑπερβολὴ τῆα δυνάμεως ᾖ ττῦ θεοῦ 'the extraordinary power belongs to God' 2 Cor 4.7; καθ' ὑπερβολὴν ἐδίωκον τὴν ἐκκλησίαν 'I persecuted the church to an extreme degree' Ga 1.13; καθ' ὑπερβολὴν εἰς ὑπερβολὴν . . . δόξης 'glory . . . beyond all comparison' 2 Cor 4.17; καθ' ὑπερβολὴν ὁδὸν ὑμῖν δείκνυμι 'I show you a far better way' 1 Cor 12.31.

There are obviously a number of problems involved in attempting to render an expression of extraordinary degree, but it is sometimes possible to express such a degree by building up a series of intensive markers. For example, in Eph 2.7 one might translate τὸ ὑπερβάλλον πλοῦτος τῆς χάριτος αὐτοῦ as 'his very, very great grace,' and in 2 Cor 4.7 one might render ἡ ὑπερβολὴ τῆς δυνάμεως ᾖ τοῦ θεοῦ as 'God has very, very great power.' Such expressions, however, may not do full justice to the intensity of degree expressed in ὑπερβάλλω and ὑπερβολή, since in a number of languages the closest equivalent might be something involving figurative meanings. For example, τὸ ὑπερβάλλον πλοῦτος τῆς χάριτος αὐτοῦ in Eph 2.7 might be rendered as 'he is gracious beyond anything we can imagine,' and in 2 Cor 4.7 ἡ ὑπερβολὴ τῆς δυνάμεως ᾖ τοῦ θεοῦ may be rendered as 'God has power beyond any words to describe.'

78.34 ὑπερεκπερισσοῦ; ὑπερπερισσεύω[b]; ὑπερπερισσῶς; ὑπερβαλλόντως; ὑπερλίαν: an extraordinary degree, involving a considerable excess over what would be expected (this series differs from the series in 78.31 primarily in emphasizing the excessive degree) – 'extreme, extremely, to an extreme degree, to a very great degree.'
ὑπερεκπερισσοῦ: ὑπερεκπερισσοῦ δεόμενοι 'praying with extreme earnestness' 1 Th 3.10.
ὑπερπερισσεύω[b]: ὑπερπερισσεύομαι τῇ χαρᾷ 'I am exceedingly joyful' 2 Cor 7.4; οὗ δὲ ἐπλεόνασεν ἡ ἁμαρτία, ὑπερεπερίσσευσεν ἡ χάρις 'where sin increased, grace was even more' Ro 5.20. Though it is possible to interpret ὑπερπερισσεύω in Ro 5.20 as referring simply to quantity (see 59.49), it is better to interpret it as expressing degree. χάρις itself indicates the activity of God in showing favor, and ὑπερπερισσεύω is simply an expression of abundant degree involved in such an activity.

ὑπερπερισσῶς: ὑπερπερισσῶς ἐξεπλήσσοντο 'they were extremely amazed' Mk 7.37.

ὑπερβαλλόντως: ἐν πληγαῖς ὑπερβαλλόντως 'whipped excessively' 2 Cor 11.23.

ὑπερλίαν: λογίζομαι γὰρ μηδὲν ὑστερηκέναι τῶν ὑπερλίαν ἀποστόλων 'for I reckon that I am in no respect inferior to those "very much apostles" ' or '. . . those very special apostles' or '. . . those very exceptional apostles' 2 Cor 11.5. In order that something of the irony of the phrase τῶν ὑπερλίαν ἀποστόλων may be indicated, one may wish to follow the example of Today's English Version and translate "I do not think that I am the least bit inferior to those very special so-called 'apostles' of yours!"

78.35 προηγέομαι[b]: to exhibit a type of behavior far above the norm – 'to excel, to do exceedingly.' τῇ τιμῇ ἀλλήλους προηγούμενοι 'excelling in honoring one another' Ro 12.10. In Ro 12.10 προηγέομαι serves primarily to indicate the degree of showing honor. One could therefore translate this expression as 'honor one another to an exceptional degree.' For another interpretation of προηγέομαι in Ro 12.10, see 68.70.

78.36 τηλικοῦτος[b], αὕτη, οὗτο: a degree which is comparable to some other expression of degree – 'so great, that great, so much.' τηλικοῦτος σεισμὸς οὕτω μέγας 'so great was that earthquake' Re 16.18. In a number of languages the closest equivalent of this expression in Re 16.18 may be 'that earthquake was indeed very great.'

78.37 πύρωσις[c], εως f: (a figurative extension of meaning of πύρωσις[a] 'burning,' 14.63) an exceptionally intense degree of some experience, with the implication of suffering – 'intense, intensity, exceptional degree of.' μὴ ξενίζεσθε τῇ ἐν ὑμῖν πυρώσει πρὸς πειρασμὸν ὑμῖν γινομένῃ 'do not be surprised at the intense trials which are happening to you' or '. . . the intensity of the trials . . .' 1 Pe 4.12. For another interpretation of πύρωσις in 1 Pe 4.12, see 24.91.

78.38 ἥσσων[a], ον, gen. ονος: a degree which is lower than what would be expected in the

context – 'less, to a lesser degree.' εἰ περισσοτέρως ὑμᾶς ἀγαπῶν, ἧσσον ἀγαπῶμαι; 'shall I be loved to a lesser extent if I have loved you so very much?' 2 Cor 12.15.

78.39 ψύχομαι: (a figurative extension of meaning of ψύχομαι 'to become cold,' not occurring in the NT) to diminish significantly in intensity – 'to diminish greatly, to become cold.' ψυγήσεται ἡ ἀγάπη τῶν πολλῶν 'the love of many will greatly diminish' Mt 24.12.

C About, Approximately, Almost, Hardly (Approximate Degree) (78.40-78.43)

78.40 πού[b]; σχεδόν: a degree which falls just short of some point on a scale of extent – 'almost, nearly, about.'

πού[b]: ἑκατονταετής που ὑπάρχων 'he was almost a hundred years old' Ro 4.19. In some languages this expression in Ro 4.19 may be accurately represented by a translation meaning literally 'he lacked only a little of being a hundred years old.'

σχεδόν: σχεδὸν πᾶσα ἡ πόλις συνήχθη 'almost everyone in town came' Ac 13.44. The equivalent of this expression in Ac 13.44 in some languages is 'all the people in the town came, but some did not' or 'only a few of the people in town didn't come.'

78.41 ὀλίγως; μόλις[a] or μόγις: a degree which almost equals some point on a scale of extent, but not quite – 'barely, just, scarcely, with difficulty, hardly.'[9]

ὀλίγως: τοὺς ὀλίγως ἀποφεύγοντας 'those who are barely beginning to escape' 2 Pe 2.18. In a number of languages it may be difficult to render the degree 'which just falls short of the precise extent.' For example, in the case of 2 Pe 2.18 an equivalent of τοὺς ὀλίγως ἀποφεύγοντας may be 'those who were just starting to escape.'

μόλις[a] or μόγις: μόλις κατέπαυσαν τοὺς ὄχλους τοῦ μὴ θύειν αὐτοῖς 'they could scarcely keep

---

9 μόλις and μόγις are often regarded as alternative forms of the same lexical unit. The form μόγις appears to be preferred in later prose.

the crowds from offering a sacrifice to them'
Ac 14.18. For another interpretation of μόλις
in Ac 14.18, see 22.33. μόγις ἀποχωρεῖ ἀπ'
αὐτοῦ '(the spirit) scarcely leaves him' Lk
9.39.

78.42 ὡςⁱ; ὡσεί^b: a degree which approximates a point on a scale of extent, either
above or below – 'about, approximately.'
ὡςⁱ: ἀριθμὸς τῶν ἀνδρῶν ὡς χιλιάδες πέντε 'the
number of men came to about five thousand'
Ac 4.4.
ὡσεί^b: ὡσεὶ λίθου βολήν 'about a stone's throw'
Lk 22.41.

78.43 βραχύ τι: a degree of indefinite approximation – 'somewhat, about.' ἠλάττωσας
αὐτὸν βραχύ τι παρ' ἀγγέλους 'having caused
him to be somewhat less than the angels' He
2.7. In He 2.7 (a quotation from Ps 8.6) the
expression βραχύ τι as a lexical unit refers to
rank. However, He 2.8-9 suggests that the
writer of Hebrews probably interpreted βραχύ
as meaning a small quantity (see 59.14) and as
referring to time in the sense of a 'little
(while).' For τι, according to this interpretation, see 92.12.

D Completely, Enough (Completive Degree) (78.44-78.50)

78.44 πᾶς^c, πᾶσα, πᾶν gen. παντός, πάσης,
παντός; ὅλος^c, η, ον; ὅλως^a; καθόλου; ὅρος,
ου *m*: a degree of totality or completeness –
'complete, completely, totally, totality.'[10]
πᾶς^c: μετὰ παρρησίας πάσης λαλεῖν τὸν λόγον
σου 'to speak your message with complete
boldness' Ac 4.29; πάσης ἀποδοχῆς ἄξιος
'worthy to be completely accepted' 1 Tm 4.9;
μετὰ πάσης ἐπιταγῆς 'using your full authority' Tt 2.15.
ὅλος^c: ὁ λελουμένος . . . ἔστιν καθαρὸς ὅλος
'whoever has bathed . . . is completely clean'
Jn 13.10.
ὅλως^a: ὅλως ἥττημα ὑμῖν ἐστιν '(shows that)

you have completely failed' 1 Cor 6.7; ἐγὼ δὲ
λέγω ὑμῖν μὴ ὀμόσαι ὅλως 'but I say to you,
Do not swear at all' Mt 5.34. In Mt 5.34 ὅλως
should not be interpreted as a qualifier of
ὀμόσαι 'to swear,' for this is not a matter of
'not swearing completely,' but ὅλως is a
degree attributive of the proposition 'do not
swear.' In a number of languages the closest
equivalent is 'do not ever swear' or 'under no
circumstances whatsoever make an oath.'
καθόλου (occurring only in Ac 4.18 in a
negative expression): τὸ καθόλου μὴ φθέγγεσθαι 'do not speak at all' Ac 4.18.
ὅρος: ὁ ὅρος τῶν ἐτῶν 'the total number of the
years' (literally 'the totality of the years') Mk
16.14-15 (apparatus).

78.45 μεστός^b, ή, όν: a degree of completeness, with the implication of abundance
– 'full of, completely, very, totally.' μεστὴ
ἐλέους καὶ καρπῶν ἀγαθῶν 'entirely merciful
and engaged in good deeds' Jas 3.17; ἔσωθεν δέ
ἐστε μεστοὶ ὑποκρίσεως καὶ ἀνομίας 'within you
are completely hypocritical and lawless' Mt
23.28. In a number of languages it is simply
not possible to speak of a person being 'full of'
some quality or 'full of' some type of activity.
Accordingly, one must often restructure the
semantic relationships so as to indicate that
one is 'completely' of a certain nature or 'entirely' engaged in some activity. In fact, in
some languages this may be expressed
negatively in the case of Mt 23.28 as 'within
there is nothing but hypocrisy and lawlessness.' In the case of Jas 3.17 one can often express the meaning in terms of habitual activity, for example, 'always merciful and doing
good things.'

78.46 πίμπλαμαι^b; πληρόομαι^b: to experience a complete degree of involvement in
some event or state – 'to be completely, to be
entirely, to be full of, to be totally.'
πίμπλαμαι^b: ἐπλήσθησαν φόβου 'they were
completely fearful' Lk 5.26; ἐπλήσθησαν θάμβους 'they were completely surprised' Ac
3.10. In both Lk 5.26 and Ac 3.10 πίμπλαμαι
simply emphasizes a particular degree of the
following state. The words φόβου and θάμβους
are semantically the crucial elements in the
expressions, and the verb πίμπλαμαι merely

---

10 There may very well be certain significant differences of meaning in this series of degree expressions,
but this is difficult, if not impossible, to determine from
existing contexts.

indicates the degree. The same semantic relationships exist in the case of πληρόομαι in the following example from Ac 13.52.

πληρόομαι[b]: οἵ τε μαθηταὶ ἐπληροῦντο χαρᾶς 'the disciples were completely joyful' Ac 13.52.

78.47 τέλος[d], ους *n*; εἰς τὸ παντελές[b]; ὁλοτελής, ές; τελείως; εἰς τέλος (an idiom, literally 'into end'): a degree of completeness, with the possible implication of purpose or result – 'completely, totally, entirely, wholly.'

τέλος[d]: ἐλπίζω δὲ ὅτι ἕως τέλους ἐπιγνώσεσθε 'I hope that you will come to understand completely' 2 Cor 1.13. It is also possible to understand the phrase ἕως τέλους in the temporal sense of 'to the end' (see 67.66).

εἰς τὸ παντελές[b]: σῴζειν εἰς τὸ παντελὲς δύναται 'he is able to save completely' He 7.25. It is also possible to understand the phrase εἰς τὸ παντελές as meaning 'forever' (see 67.95). μὴ δυναμένη ἀνακύψαι εἰς τὸ παντελές 'she could not straighten up completely' Lk 13.11. It is possible to translate this expression in Lk 13.11 as 'she could not straighten up at all.' The difference of interpretation in Lk 13.11 depends upon the scope of the phrase εἰς τὸ παντελές. If this phrase qualifies the negation, then the rendering is 'she could not straighten up at all,' but if the phrase εἰς τὸ παντελές qualifies just ἀνακύψαι, then the appropriate meaning would be 'she could not straighten up completely.'

ὁλοτελής: ὁ θεὸς τῆς εἰρήνης ἁγιάσαι ὑμᾶς ὁλοτελεῖς 'may the God of peace sanctify you completely' 1 Th 5.23.

τελείως: τελείως ἐλπίσατε ἐπὶ τὴν φερομένην ὑμῖν χάριν 'set your hope completely on the blessing brought to you' 1 Pe 1.13.

εἰς τέλος: ἔφθασεν δὲ ἐπ' αὐτοὺς ἡ ὀργὴ εἰς τέλος 'wrath has come down completely upon them' or 'wrath in full measure has come down upon them' 1 Th 2.16. It is also possible to understand τέλος in the expression εἰς τέλος in 1 Th 2.16 as a temporal expression, with εἰς (67.117) as a marker of an extent of time, so that this passage may be rendered as 'and in the end wrath has come down on them' or 'and wrath has at last come down on them,' see 67.66. In this context ὀργή may very well be translated as 'punishment' (38.10), and in

many languages it is necessary to indicate the agent of such punishment. The same ambiguity with εἰς τέλος occurs in Jn 13.1 in the clause εἰς τέλος ἠγάπησεν αὐτούς, meaning 'he loved them completely' or 'he loved them to the end,' see 67.119.

78.48 ἐκ . . . εἰς . . .: (an idiomatic frame, literally 'from . . . to . . .') a degree of totality emphasizing exclusiveness or the elimination of other possibilities – 'completely, entirely, exclusively a matter of.' δικαιοσύνη γὰρ θεοῦ ἐν αὐτῷ ἀποκαλύπτεται ἐκ πίστεως εἰς πίστιν 'for God's righteousness is revealed in it as exclusively a matter of faith' or 'the way God has put people right with himself is revealed in it as a matter of faith from beginning to end' Ro 1.17; οἷς μὲν ὀσμὴ ἐκ θανάτου εἰς θάνατον, οἷς δὲ ὀσμὴ ἐκ ζωῆς εἰς ζωήν 'on the one hand, to those (who are being lost) it is a stench which is completely a matter of death, but to those (who are being saved) it is a fragrance which is completely a matter of life' 2 Cor 2.16.

78.49 μέρος[f], ους *n*: a degree which is only part of some totality – 'partially, to some degree, part, partly.'[11] μέρος τι πιστεύω 'I believe this to some degree' 1 Cor 11.18; τὸ ἐκ μέρους καταργηθήσεται 'that which exists only in part will disappear' 1 Cor 13.10.

78.50 ἱκανός[a], ή, όν: a degree which is sufficient – 'enough, sufficient.'[12] ἱκανὸν τῷ τοιούτῳ ἡ ἐπιτιμία 'the punishment is sufficient for such a person' 2 Cor 2.6. In some languages one can express the concept of sufficiency in 2 Cor 2.6 by introducing a negative, for example, 'it is not necessary to punish such a person more.' For another interpretation of ἱκανός in 2 Cor 2.6, see 78.14.

---

11 μέρος[f] is incorporated at this point in Subdomain D *Completely, Enough* since it serves as a semantic opposite to the meanings involved in πᾶς[c] (78.44), τέλος[d] (78.47), and ὅλος[c] (78.44).

12 Compare ἱκανός[b] meaning 'a relatively high point on a scale of extent' (78.14) and also ἱκανός[e] (59.2) and ἱκανός[f] (59.12) referring to quantity.

E Up To, As Much As, To the Degree That (Marked Extent of Degree) (78.51-78.53)

78.51 ἕως^d; μέχρι^c or μέχρις; εἰς^j; ἐπί^r; πρός^m: a degree extending to a particular point as marked by the context – 'to the point of, to the extent of, to the degree that, up to.'

ἕως^d: περίλυπός ἐστιν ἡ ψυχή μου ἕως θανάτου 'my soul is very sorrowful, even to the point of death' Mt 26.38. In a number of languages it is difficult to express in a succinct manner a degree which reaches to a particular point. The same meaning, however, may often be expressed in a somewhat different form. For example, in Mt 26.38 one may translate 'my soul is very sorrowful; it is just as though I were dying.'

μέχρι^c or μέχρις: κακοπαθῶ μέχρι δεσμῶν ὡς κακοῦργος 'I am suffering to the point of being chained like a criminal' 2 Tm 2.9; οὔπω μέχρις αἵματος ἀντικατέστητε 'you have not yet resisted to the point of death' or '. . . of shedding your blood' He 12.4.

εἰς^j: ἐν ὑμῖν μεγαλυνθῆναι . . . εἰς περισσείαν 'to be increased among you . . . to the point of being much more' 2 Cor 10.15. In 2 Cor 10.15 περισσείαν itself indicates a superabundant degree of something (see 78.31), while εἰς marks a degree up to such a point. One may say, therefore, that semantically εἰς serves to reinforce the meaning of περισσείαν.

ἐπί^r: καὶ ἐμέτρησεν τὴν πόλιν τῷ καλάμῳ ἐπὶ σταδίων δώδεκα χιλιάδων 'and he measured the city with the reed to the extent of twelve thousand stadia' Re 21.16; ἀλλ' ἵνα μὴ ἐπὶ πλεῖον διανεμηθῇ εἰς τὸν λαόν 'but in order that it might not spread even further among the people' Ac 4.17. See also Ro 11.13 in 78.52.

πρός^m: πρὸς φθόνον ἐπιποθεῖ τὸ πνεῦμα ὃ κατῴκισεν ἐν ἡμῖν 'the spirit that dwells within us desires to the point of jealousy' or 'the spirit that dwells within us is filled with fierce desires' or '. . . intense desires' Jas 4.5.

78.52 ὅσος^c, η, ον; τοσοῦτος^c, αὕτη, οὗτον: a degree of correlative extent – 'to the degree that, to the same degree, as much as.'

ὅσος^c: διαφορωτέρας τέτυχεν λειτουργίας, ὅσῳ καὶ κρείττονός ἐστιν διαθήκης μεσίτης '(Christ) has obtained a ministry which is as much more excellent than the old as the covenant he mediates is better' He 8.6. One may also render this expression in He 8.6 as 'Christ's ministry is better than the old to the same degree that the covenant he mediates is better.' ὅσον δὲ αὐτοῖς διεστέλλετο, αὐτοὶ μᾶλλον περισσότερον ἐκήρυσσον 'but as much as he commanded them (not to speak about it), the more they proclaimed (it)' Mk 7.36; ἐφ' ὅσον μὲν οὖν εἰμι ἐγὼ ἐθνῶν ἀπόστολος 'as much as I am an apostle to the Gentiles' Ro 11.13. In Ro 11.13 ὅσον is strengthened by ἐπί, see 78.51.

τοσοῦτος^c: ὅσα ἐδόξασεν αὐτὴν καὶ ἐστρηνίασεν, τοσοῦτον δότε αὐτῇ βασανισμὸν καὶ πένθος 'give her as much suffering and grief as the glory and luxury she gave herself' Re 18.7. It is also possible to render this portion of Re 18.7 as 'to the degree that she glorified herself and lived in luxury, to that same degree give her torment and sorrow.' τοσούτῳ κρείττων γενόμενος τῶν ἀγγέλων ὅσῳ διαφορώτερον παρ' αὐτοὺς κεκληρονόμηκεν ὄνομα 'to the degree that he inherited a name superior to them, to that extent is he greater than the angels' He 1.4.

Expressions involving correspondence of degrees must often be rather considerably restructured. For example, in the first part of Re 18.7 one may translate in some languages 'she honored herself very much and lived in great luxury, and so give her very much suffering and grief.' In the case of He 1.4, one may translate 'God gave his Son a name that was more important than the name of the angels; therefore, God's Son is greater than the angels.'

78.53 καθό^b; καθώς^a; καθότι^b: in accordance with a degree as specified by the context – 'to the degree that, just as.'

καθό^b: καθὸ κοινωνεῖτε τοῖς τοῦ Χριστοῦ παθήμασιν χαίρετε 'to the degree that you share Christ's sufferings, rejoice' 1 Pe 4.13.

καθώς^a: καθὼς εὐπορεῖτό τις 'each one to the degree that he was able' Ac 11.29.

καθότι^b: διεμέριζον αὐτὰ πᾶσιν καθότι ἄν τις χρείαν εἶχεν 'they divided these among all to the extent that anyone had need' or '. . . in proportion to anyone's need' Ac 2.45.

There may be a number of problems of

restructuring in rendering the relationship between clauses marked by καθό[b], καθώς[a], and καθότι[b]. For example, in the case of 1 Pe 4.13 it may be necessary to translate 'how much you share Christ's sufferings is how much you can rejoice.'

79 Features of Objects[1]

Outline of Subdomains

A   Physical (Material), Spiritual (79.1-79.3)
B   Natural (Human), Spiritual (79.4-79.6)
C   Solid, Liquid (79.7-79.8)
D   Beautiful, Ugly (79.9-79.17)
E   Glorious (79.18-79.23)
F   Transparent, Opaque (Obscure) (79.24-79.25)
G   Color (79.26-79.38)
H   Sweet, Bitter, Tasteless (79.39-79.44)
I   Fragrance, Odor (79.45-79.47)
J   Clean, Dirty (79.48-79.56)
K   Spotted, Spotless (79.57-79.59)
L   Blemished, Unblemished (79.60-79.61)
M   Strong, Weak (79.62-79.69)
N   Hot, Lukewarm, Cold (79.70-79.77)
O   Wet, Dry (79.78-79.83)
P   Uneven (Rough), Level (Smooth) (79.84-79.87)
Q   Straight, Crooked (79.88-79.90)
R   Two-Dimensional and Three-Dimensional Shapes (79.91-79.94)
S   Sharp (79.95-79.96)
T   Pure, Unadulterated, Undiluted (79.97-79.99)
U   Soft, Tender (79.100-79.101)
V   Male, Female (79.102-79.103)
W   Shapes (79.104-79.109)
X   Open, Closed (79.110-79.113)
Y   Covered Over (79.114-79.117)
Z   Wrapped (79.118-79.119)
A' Rolled Up (79.120-79.122)
B' Large, Small (79.123-79.128)
C' Perfect (79.129)

A   Physical (Material), Spiritual[2] (79.1-79.3)

79.1 σαρκικός[b], ή, όν: pertaining to being material or physical, with the possible implication of inferior – 'material, physical.' ἐν τοῖς σαρκικοῖς λειτουργῆσαι αὐτοῖς 'to serve them with material blessings' Ro 15.27. It is possible that σαρκικός in Ro 15.27 refers to blessings for the body, but the context would seem to imply blessings of greater significance than those designed only for a person's body.

79.2 ψυχικός[a], ή, όν: pertaining to being material or physical, especially in relation to life processes – 'physical, natural.' σπείρεται σῶμα ψυχικόν 'when sown, it is a physical body' 1 Cor 15.44. In some languages, however, it is impossible to translate σπείρεται in 1 Cor 15.44 as 'sown,' and one must therefore translate this expression as 'when buried, it is a physical body.'

79.3 πνευματικός[d], ή, όν: pertaining to not being physical – 'not physical, not material, spiritual.' ἐγείρεται σῶμα πνευματικόν 'when it is raised, it will be a spiritual body' or 'it will not be a physical body' 1 Cor 15.44. In some languages the concept of 'spiritual body' can only be expressed negatively as 'the body will not have flesh and bones' or 'the body will not be a regular body.'

B   Natural (Human), Spiritual (79.4-79.6)

79.4 σάρκινος[c], η, ον; σαρκικός[c], ή, όν: pertaining to the natural, physical characteristics

---

1 Domain 79 *Features of Objects* includes certain states resulting from events, since they affect materially the appearance or nature of the objects involved (see Subdomains X-A').

2 The opposite of 'physical' or 'material' is not merely 'non-material.' From the biblical standpoint it is the 'spiritual' which contrasts with the 'physical.'

of persons and often including their characteristic behavior – 'natural, human.'[3]

σάρκινος^c: οὐκ ἐν πλαξὶν λιθίναις ἀλλ' ἐν πλαξὶν καρδίαις σαρκίναις 'not on stone tablets but on the tablets of human hearts' 2 Cor 3.3; οὐκ ἠδυνήθην λαλῆσαι ὑμῖν ὡς πνευματικοῖς ἀλλ' ὡς σαρκίνοις 'I was not able to speak to you as to spiritual persons but as to ordinary human beings' or '. . . as people of this world' 1 Cor 3.1. For another interpretation of σάρκινος in 1 Cor 3.1, see 41.42.

σαρκικός^c: ἔτι γὰρ σαρκικοί ἐστε 'for you are still like people of this world' or '. . . ordinary human beings' 1 Cor 3.3.[4]

79.5 ψυχικός^b, ή, όν: pertaining to human nature (possibly contrasting with σάρκινος^c and σαρκικός^c 'natural, human,' 79.4, in focusing somewhat more on so-called higher endowments of personality) – 'natural, human.' ψυχικὸς δὲ ἄνθρωπος οὐ δέχεται τὰ τοῦ πνεύματος τοῦ θεοῦ 'but the natural person does not receive the things of the Spirit of God' 1 Cor 2.14. For another interpretation of ψυχικός in 1 Cor 2.14, see 41.41.

79.6 πνευματικός^c, ή, όν: pertaining to being supernatural and having its ultimate source in God – 'spiritual, supernatural.' πάντες τὸ αὐτὸ πνευματικὸν ἔπιον πόμα· ἔπινον γὰρ ἐκ πνευματικῆς ἀκολουθούσης πέτρας 'all drank the same spiritual drink; for they drank from the spiritual rock which accompanied them' 1 Cor 10.4. In a number of languages this meaning of πνευματικός can only be reflected by a phrase such as 'which comes from God' or 'provided by God.'

C Solid, Liquid (79.7-79.8)

79.7 στερεός^a, ά, όν: pertaining to being solid or firm in contrast with that which is

soft or liquid – 'solid, firm.' τελείων δέ ἐστιν ἡ στερεὰ τροφή 'solid food, on the other hand, is for adults' He 5.14; ὁ μέντοι στερεὸς θεμέλιος τοῦ θεοῦ ἕστηκεν 'but the solid foundation that God has laid stands' or '. . . remains firm' 2 Tm 2.19.

79.8 τήκομαι: to become liquid, either by melting or condensation – 'to become liquid, to melt.' στοιχεῖα καυσούμενα τήκεται 'the heavenly bodies will melt in the heat' or 'will melt by burning' 2 Pe 3.12.

D Beautiful, Ugly (79.9-79.17)

79.9 καλός^e, ή, όν: pertaining to being beautiful or attractive in terms of outward form or shape, often implying a corresponding fine value – 'beautiful, fine.' λίθοις καλοῖς καὶ ἀναθήμασιν κεχόσμηται 'it was decorated with beautiful stones and offerings' Lk 21.5.

79.10 ὡραῖος^a, α, ον: pertaining to being beautiful, often with the implication of appropriateness – 'beautiful, lovely.' τάφοις κεχονιαμένοις, οἵτινες ἔξωθεν μὲν φαίνονται ὡραῖοι 'whitewashed tombs, which look beautiful on the outside' Mt 23.27.

79.11 ἀστεῖος, α, ον: pertaining to being beautiful or attractive in terms of being well-formed – 'beautiful, attractive.' εἶδον ἀστεῖον τὸ παιδίον 'they saw that he was a beautiful child' He 11.23.

79.12 κοσμέω; κόσμος^e, ου m: to cause something to be beautiful by decorating – 'to beautify, to adorn, to decorate, adornment, adorning.'
κοσμέω: λίθοις καλοῖς καὶ ἀναθήμασιν κεχόσμηται 'it was decorated with beautiful stones and offerings' Lk 21.5; οὕτως γάρ ποτε καὶ αἱ ἅγιαι γυναῖκες . . . ἐκόσμουν ἑαυτάς 'for the devout women of the past . . . used to adorn themselves in this way' 1 Pe 3.5.
κόσμος^e: ὁ ἔξωθεν ἐμπλοκῆς τριχῶν καὶ περιθέσεως χρυσίων ἢ ἐνδύσεως ἱματίων κόσμος 'the outward adorning consisting of the braiding of hair, the wearing of gold jewelry, or dressing up' 1 Pe 3.3. For another interpretation of κόσμος in 1 Pe 3.3, see 6.188.

---

3 In a number of contexts it is difficult to determine whether the focus of σάρκινος^c and σαρκικός^c is upon the natural, physical characteristics or upon the tendency to behave in a particular way. In any event, resulting behavior is always implied.

4 The close proximity of σάρκινος and σαρκικός in the context of 1 Cor 3.1-3 would seem to indicate that there is little, if any, difference in meaning.

79.13 εὐπρέπεια, ας *f*; εὐσχημοσύνη, ης *f*: a state of beauty or fine appearance, with the implication of being attractive and well-suited – 'beauty, attractiveness, loveliness.'

εὐπρέπεια: τὸ ἄνθος αὐτοῦ ἐξέπεσεν καὶ ἡ εὐπρέπεια τοῦ προσώπου αὐτοῦ ἀπώλετο 'its bloom falls off and its attractiveness is destroyed' Jas 1.11.

εὐσχημοσύνη: τὰ ἀσχήμονα ἡμῶν εὐσχημοσύνην περισσοτέραν 'our unseemly parts (acquire) more than ordinary seemliness' 1 Cor 12.23.

79.14 μεγαλοπρεπής, ές: pertaining to being unusually attractive and beautiful – 'very wonderful, sublime.' φωνῆς ἐνεχθείσης αὐτῷ τοιᾶσδε ὑπὸ τῆς μεγαλοπρεποῦς δόξης 'a voice having come to him from the One who is supremely glorious' or '. . . wondrously glorious' or '. . . from the Glorious One who is sublimely so' 2 Pe 1.17. For μεγαλοπρεπής as part of a title, see 12.6.

79.15 εὐσχήμων[a], ον, gen ονος: pertaining to having an attractive form – 'attractive, presentable.' τὰ δὲ εὐσχήμονα ἡμῶν οὐ χρείαν ἔχει '(special attention which) the more presentable parts of our (body) do not need' 1 Cor 12.24.

79.16 ἀσχήμων, ον: pertaining to being unattractive or unseemly – 'unattractive, ugly, unpresentable.' ἃ . . . τοῦ σώματος . . . τὰ ἀσχήμονα ἡμῶν 'the parts of our body . . . which are not presentable' or 'which are unseemly' 1 Cor 12.23.

79.17 ἀφανίζω[b]: to cause something to be unattractive or unsightly – 'to make unsightly, to disfigure, to make ugly.' ἀφανίζουσιν γὰρ τὰ πρόσωπα αὐτῶν 'for they make their faces unsightly' Mt 6.16.

E Glorious (79.18-79.23)

79.18 δόξα[a], ης *f*: the quality of splendid, remarkable appearance – 'glory, splendor.' οὐδὲ Σολομὼν ἐν πάσῃ τῇ δόξῃ αὐτοῦ περιεβάλετο ὡς ἓν τούτων 'even Solomon in all his splendor was not arrayed like one of these' Mt 6.29; καὶ πᾶσα δόξα αὐτῆς ὡς ἄνθος 'and all its splendor as a flower' 1 Pe 1.24.

79.19 ἔνδοξος[a], ον: pertaining to being splendid or glorious – 'glorious, splendid, wonderful, in splendor.' οἱ ἐν ἱματισμῷ ἐνδόξῳ 'the ones in splendid raiment' Lk 7.25; ἵνα παραστήσῃ αὐτὸς ἑαυτῷ ἔνδοξον τὴν ἐκκλησίαν 'in order that he might present to himself the church in all its splendor' Eph 5.27.

79.20 λαμπρός[c], ά, όν: pertaining to being brilliant or splendid, though with the possible implication of ostentatious or superficial – 'splendid, glamorous.' πάντα τὰ λιπαρὰ καὶ τὰ λαμπρὰ ἀπώλετο ἀπὸ σοῦ 'all your splendid and glamorous things are gone' Re 18.14. See note at 79.21.

79.21 λιπαρός[c], ά, όν: pertaining to being splendid, with the implication of luxurious – 'splendid, luxurious, glamorous.' πάντα τὰ λιπαρὰ καὶ τὰ λαμπρὰ ἀπώλετο ἀπὸ σοῦ 'all your splendid and glamorous things are gone' Re 18.14. In Re 18.14 λαμπρός (79.20) and λιπαρός serve primarily to reinforce one another.

79.22 ἐπιφανής, ές: pertaining to being glorious or wonderful, in view of being conspicuous and self-evident – 'glorious, wonderful, marvelous.' πρὶν ἐλθεῖν ἡμέραν κυρίου τὴν μεγάλην καὶ ἐπιφανῆ 'before the great and wonderful day of the Lord appears' Ac 2.20.

79.23 ἀμαράντινος, η, ον; ἀμάραντος, ον: pertaining to not losing the wonderful, pristine character of something – 'unfading, not losing brightness, retaining its wonderful character.'

ἀμαράντινος: κομιεῖσθε τὸν ἀμαράντινον τῆς δόξης στέφανον 'you will receive a glorious crown which will not lose its brightness' 1 Pe 5.4.

ἀμάραντος: εἰς κληρονομίαν ἄφθαρτον καὶ ἀμίαντον καὶ ἀμάραντον 'for an inheritance which will not decay and spoil and fade away' or '. . . lose its wonderfulness' 1 Pe 1.4.

F Transparent, Opaque (Obscure) (79.24-79.25)

79.24 διαυγής, ές: pertaining to possessing such physical properties as can be seen through – 'transparent.' χρυσίον καθαρὸν ὡς ὕαλος διαυγής 'pure gold, transparent as glass' Re 21.21.

79.25 λαμπρός^b, ά, όν: pertaining to being clear and also bright – 'bright, sparkling.' ποταμὸν ὕδατος ζωῆς λαμπρὸν ὡς κρύσταλλον 'a river of the water of life, sparkling like crystal' Re 22.1.

G Color (79.26-79.38)

79.26 μέλας, αινα, αν – 'black, dark color.' ἰδοὺ ἵππος μέλας 'there was a black horse' Re 6.5; ὁ ἥλιος ἐγένετο μέλας 'the sun became black' Re 6.12.

Expressions for a number of terms for color differ on the basis of the object which is designated as having such a color. For example, a term for black as applied to a horse may be a different term from what one would use in speaking of a black box.

79.27 λευκός^a, ή, όν – 'white, light color.' αἱ τρίχες λευκαὶ ὡς ἔριον λευκόν, ὡς χιών 'his hair was white as wool or as snow' Re 1.14.

The term λευκός also occurs in Jn 4.35 in speaking of fields being 'white for the harvest,' but in a number of languages it would be quite impossible to use the same term for the ripe condition of a harvest as in the case of the color of wool or snow. Furthermore, there may be a serious difficulty in speaking of wool as being 'white,' since in many parts of the world, wool is not regarded as being particularly white.

79.28 λευκαίνω: to cause something to become white – 'to make white, to whiten.' λευκὰ λίαν οἷα γναφεὺς ἐπὶ τῆς γῆς οὐ δύναται οὕτως λευκᾶναι 'whiter than any bleacher on earth could make (them) white' Mk 9.3; ἔπλυναν τὰς στολὰς αὐτῶν καὶ ἐλεύκαναν αὐτὰς ἐν τῷ αἵματι τοῦ ἀρνίου 'washed their robes and made them white in the blood of the Lamb' Re 7.14. This statement in Re 7.14 may raise numerous difficulties for receptors, since blood would not be regarded as an instrument for making anything white. It may be necessary, therefore, to introduce a marginal note explaining the figurative language and suggesting the rendering 'to make them pure.'

79.29 κόκκινος, η, ον – 'scarlet, red.' χλαμύδα κοκκίνην περιέθηκαν αὐτῷ 'they put a scarlet robe on him' Mt 27.28. In Mt 27.28 'scarlet robe' may have implied high military rank.

79.30 ἐρυθρός, ά, όν – 'red.' διέβησαν τὴν Ἐρυθρὰν Θάλασσαν 'they crossed the Red Sea' He 11.29. In a number of languages it may be necessary to use a term in He 11.29 which means 'reddish,' since an expression meaning 'bright red' might seem entirely inappropriate in speaking of a body of water.

79.31 πυρρός, ά, όν – 'fiery red' (probably with a tinge of yellow or orange). ἐξῆλθεν ἄλλος ἵππος πυρρός 'another horse came out, a fiery red one' Re 6.4. As in other instances of color terms, it may be necessary in Re 6.4 to use an expression which is particularly applicable to a horse. δράκων μέγας πυρρός 'a huge, red dragon' Re 12.3.

79.32 πυρράζω – 'to be fiery red.' πυρράζει γὰρ ὁ οὐρανός 'because the sky is fiery red' Mt 16.2.

79.33 πύρινος, η, ον – 'fiery red.' ἔχοντας θώρακας πυρίνους 'they had breastplates which were fiery red' Re 9.17. One may also render 'fiery red' as 'red like fire' or 'the color of fire.'

79.34 χλωρός^a, ά, όν – 'light green, green' (typical of plants).⁵ ἀνακλῖναι . . . ἐπὶ τῷ χλωρῷ χόρτῳ 'sit down . . . on the green grass' Mk 6.39.

79.35 χλωρός^b, ά, όν – 'pale greenish gray' (evidently regarded as typical of a corpse, since the color is used as a symbol of death).⁵

---

5 It is difficult to determine whether χλωρός should be regarded as having two different meanings or whether the meaning should be regarded as covering a range of color from light green through greenish yellow and greenish gray, but for the practical purposes of highlighting certain differences in color, two meanings of χλωρός are listed here (79.34 and 79.35).

ἰδοὺ ἵππος χλωρός 'there was a pale-colored horse' Re 6.8.

79.36 θειώδης, ες – 'sulfureous yellow, yellow as sulfur.' θώρακας . . . θειώδεις 'breastplates . . . yellow as sulfur' Re 9.17. Note that in Re 9.17 the three colors parallel three plagues, fire, smoke, and sulfur, and it may therefore be useful to translate the latter part of Re 9.17 as 'they had breastplates red as fire, blue as sapphire, and yellow as sulfur.' See also 79.37.

79.37 ὑακίνθινος, η, ον: pertaining to being the color of the flower hyacinth (see 2.41), probably a shade of blue – 'blue.' ἔχοντας θώρακας . . . ὑακινθίνους 'they had breastplates . . . blue as hyacinth' Re 9.17. Since in some languages the flower hyacinth may not be as well known as precious stones such as sapphire and turquoise, it may be possible to render Re 9.17 as 'blue as sapphire' or 'blue as turquoise.' The justification for this is simply that the Greek term ὑακίνθινος had become primarily a designation for color.

79.38 πορφυροῦς, ᾶ, οῦν – 'purple' (having the symbolic value of royal status). ἱμάτιον πορφυροῦν περιέβαλον αὐτόν 'they put a purple robe on him' Jn 19.2. In Jn 19.2 the use of πορφυροῦς may refer more to the symbolic value of the color than to the color itself. Therefore, it may be important to include some marginal note indicating the significance of the color.

H Sweet, Bitter, Tasteless (79.39-79.44)

79.39 γλυκύς, εῖα, ύ: pertaining to being sweet in contrast with being bitter or salty – 'sweet, fresh, not bitter, good.' ἐν τῷ στόματί σου ἔσται γλυκὺ ὡς μέλι 'in your mouth it will be sweet as honey' Re 10.9; μήτι ἡ πηγὴ ἐκ τῆς αὐτῆς ὀπῆς βρύει τὸ γλυκὺ καὶ τὸ πικρόν 'no spring pours out sweet and bitter water from the same opening' Jas 3.11. In a number of languages it would be somewhat misleading to speak of 'sweet water,' since this would suggest water to which sugar or some other sweet substance had been added. The equivalent in Jas 3.11 may be 'fresh water' or

'good water' in contrast with 'bad water', or 'not bitter water' in contrast with 'bitter water.'

79.40 πικρία[a], ας f: with a bitter taste – 'bitterness, bitter' (occurring only in the idiom χολὴ πικρίας). εἰς γὰρ χολὴν πικρίας καὶ σύνδεσμον ἀδικίας ὁρῶ σε ὄντα 'for I see that you are full of bitter envy and are a prisoner of sin' Ac 8.23. As a part of the idiom εἰς χολὴν πικρίας εἰμί, πικρίας is to be understood in a literal sense, but the idiom as such means to be particularly envious or resentful of someone (see 88.166).

79.41 πικρός[a], ά, όν: pertaining to being bitter or pungent – 'bitter, pungent.' μήτι ἡ πηγὴ ἐκ τῆς αὐτῆς ὀπῆς βρύει τὸ γλυκὺ καὶ τὸ πικρόν 'no spring pours out sweet and bitter water from the same opening' Jas 3.11.

79.42 πικραίνω: to cause something to become bitter – 'to make bitter.' πικρανεῖ σου τὴν κοιλίαν 'it will make your stomach bitter' or 'it will become bitter in your stomach' Re 10.9; ὅτι ἐπικράνθησαν 'because (the water) had turned bitter' Re 8.11.

79.43 ἄψινθος[b], ου m and f: the taste of wormwood, a bitter-tasting herb used as a cure for intestinal worms – 'bitter, bitter like wormwood' (compare 3.21). ἐγένετο τὸ τρίτον τῶν ὑδάτων εἰς ἄψινθον 'a third of the waters turned bitter' or '. . . became like wormwood' Re 8.11. As already noted in 3.21, the meaning of ἄψινθος in Re 8.11 is not that the waters turned into a particular plant but that the waters came to be as bitter as the plant in question.

79.44 μωραίνομαι[b]: to become insipid or tasteless – 'to become tasteless, to lose taste.' δὲ τὸ ἅλας μωρανθῇ 'but the salt loses its taste' Mt 5.13. In Mt 5.13 μωραίνομαι is equivalent to ἄναλος (5.27), that is to say, to be without a salt taste. Pure salt cannot actually lose its taste, but the sodium chloride of impure salt can be leached out, especially in humid weather, and the remaining substance is accordingly tasteless. See also discussion at 5.25.

I Fragrance, Odor (79.45-79.47)

79.45 ὀσμή, ῆς *f*: the scent or odor of a substance, whether agreeable or disagreeable – 'smell, scent, odor.' ἡ δὲ οἰκία ἐπληρώθη ἐκ τῆς ὀσμῆς τοῦ μύρου 'the smell of the perfume filled the house' Jn 12.3.

79.46 εὐωδία, ας *f*: a pleasant or sweet-smelling odor – 'aroma, fragrance.' ὀσμὴν εὐωδίας, θυσίαν δεκτήν, εὐάρεστον τῷ θεῷ 'they are like a sweet-smelling fragrance, an offering acceptable to God' Php 4.18. Since the reference in Php 4.18 is to a sacrifice, the use of εὐωδία may seem strange, if not contradictory, in many languages, since the odor from burning flesh is normally not regarded as being fragrant or pleasant. It may therefore be necessary to include a marginal note to explain this usage.

79.47 ὄζω: to cause a foul-smelling odor – 'to stink, to have a bad smell.' ἤδη ὄζει, τεταρταῖος γάρ ἐστιν '(the body) already stinks, for he (has been buried) four days' Jn 11.39.

J Clean, Dirty (79.48-79.56)

79.48 καθαρός[a], ά, όν: pertaining to not being dirty – 'clean.' ὁ λελουμένος . . . ἔστιν καθαρὸς ὅλος 'whoever has taken a bath . . . is completely clean' Jn 13.10; καὶ τὸ ἐκτὸς αὐτοῦ καθαρόν 'then the outside (of the cup) will be clean too' Mt 23.26.

79.49 καθαρίζω[a]; καθαίρω[a]: to cause something to become clean – 'to make clean, to cleanse, to clean.'
καθαρίζω[a]: καθαρίζετε τὸ ἔξωθεν τοῦ ποτηρίου καὶ τῆς παροψίδος 'you clean the outside of the cup and plate' Mt 23.25.
καθαίρω[a]: πᾶν τὸ καρπὸν φέρον καθαίρει αὐτό 'every (branch) that bears fruit he cleanses' Jn 15.2. In Jn 15.2 the meaning of καθαίρω may also be understood as 'to prune branches' (see 43.12), thus playing on two distinct meanings of καθαίρω.

79.50 ἐκκαθαίρω: to make clean by removing that which is unclean – 'to clean out, to clean away.' ἐκκαθάρατε τὴν παλαιὰν ζύμην 'clean out the old yeast' 1 Cor 5.7. In 1 Cor 5.7 ἐκκαθαίρω is used in a complex figurative expression and may often be better rendered as 'to get rid of' or 'to remove.'

79.51 διακαθαίρω; διακαθαρίζω: to clean out or to clean off thoroughly – 'to clean, to clean off, to clean thoroughly, to clean out.'
διακαθαίρω: οὗ τὸ πτύον ἐν τῇ χειρὶ αὐτοῦ διακαθᾶραι τὴν ἅλωνα αὐτοῦ 'his winnowing shovel is in his hand to thoroughly clean what he has threshed' Lk 3.17.
διακαθαρίζω: οὗ τὸ πτύον ἐν τῇ χειρὶ αὐτοῦ, καὶ διακαθαριεῖ τὴν ἅλωνα αὐτοῦ 'his winnowing shovel is in his hand, and he will thoroughly clean what he has threshed' Mt 3.12.

79.52 ῥυπαρός[a], ά, όν: pertaining to being dirty or filthy – 'dirty, filthy.' εἰσέλθῃ δὲ καὶ πτωχὸς ἐν ῥυπαρᾷ ἐσθῆτι 'and a poor man in dirty clothes also comes' Jas 2.2. In Jas 2.2 the emphasis of ῥυπαρός is not upon clothes being ragged as one might expect in the case of a poor man, but upon the clothes being filthy and thus the basis for greater offense and avoidance.

79.53 περικάθαρμα, τος *n*; **περίψημα, τος** *n*: rubbish, resulting from the process of cleansing – 'offscourings, garbage, scum, rubbish.' ὡς περικαθάρματα τοῦ κόσμου ἐγενήθημεν, πάντων περίψημα, ἕως ἄρτι 'we have become like this world's garbage; we are now the scum of all things' 1 Cor 4.13.[6]

79.54 ἀκαθαρσία[b], ας *f*: any substance which is filthy or dirty – 'filth, dirt, rubbish.' ἔσωθεν δὲ γέμουσιν ὀστέων νεκρῶν καὶ πάσης ἀκαθαρσίας 'but inside they are full of dead people's bones and all kinds of filth' Mt 23.27.

79.55 ῥύπος, ου *m*: dirt as refuse in contrast with soil – 'dirt, refuse.' οὐ σαρκὸς ἀπόθεσις ῥύπου 'it is not a matter of getting rid of bodily dirt' or '. . . getting rid of dirt that is on the body' 1 Pe 3.21.

---

6 In 1 Cor 4.13 περικάθαρμα and περίψημα appear to be typical instances of figurative usage.

79.56 μολύνω[a]: to cause something to become dirty or soiled – 'to soil, to make dirty.' ἃ οὐκ ἐμόλυναν τὰ ἱμάτια αὐτῶν 'who have not soiled their garments' Re 3.4.

K Spotted, Spotless (79.57-79.59)

79.57 σπίλος, ου *m*; σπιλάς[b], άδος *f*: that which constitutes an unwanted spot or stain upon something – 'spot, stain.'
σπίλος: ἔνδοξον τὴν ἐκκλησίαν, μὴ ἔχουσαν σπίλον ἢ ῥυτίδα 'the church in all its splendor, without spot or wrinkle' Eph 5.27.
σπιλάς[b]: οὗτοί εἰσιν οἱ ἐν ταῖς ἀγάπαις ὑμῶν σπιλάδες 'they are like dirty spots on your fellowship meals' Jd 12. It is also possible that in Jd 12 σπιλάς means an 'unseen danger,' in that it may refer to a rock which is mostly or completely covered by the sea (see 21.5).

79.58 σπιλόω: to cause a spot or stain upon something – 'to spot, to stain.' μισοῦντες καὶ τὸν ἀπὸ τῆς σαρκὸς ἐσπιλωμένον χιτῶνα 'but hate their very clothes, stained by their sinful lusts' Jd 23.

79.59 ἄσπιλος[a], ον: pertaining to having no spot or stain – 'spotless, without stain.' ὡς ἀμνοῦ ἀμώμου καὶ ἀσπίλου 'like a lamb without defect or spot' 1 Pe 1.19.

L Blemished, Unblemished (79.60-79.61)

79.60 μῶμος, ου *m*: that which constitutes a defect or blemish, either in the physical or moral sense – 'blemish, spot, defect.' σπίλοι καὶ μῶμοι ἐντρυφῶντες ἐν ταῖς ἀπάταις αὐτῶν συνευωχούμενοι ὑμῖν 'while enjoying their deceitful ways, they are spots and blemishes as they join you in your meals' 2 Pe 2.13. The context of 2 Pe 2.13 is highly figurative, and the occurrence of μῶμος may be regarded as an instance of figurative usage.

79.61 ἄμωμος[a], ον: pertaining to having no defect or blemish – 'without defect, without blemish.' ὡς ἀμνοῦ ἀμώμου καὶ ἀσπίλου 'like a lamb without defect or spot' 1 Pe 1.19. In 1 Pe 1.19 the overall context is figurative, but

the immediate meaning must be regarded as literal.

M Strong, Weak (79.62-79.69)

79.62 ἰσχύς[b], ύος *f*: the quality of physical strength – 'strength.' ἐξ ἰσχύος ἧς χορηγεῖ ὁ θεός 'with the strength which God provides' 1 Pe 4.11.

79.63 ἰσχυρός[b], ά, όν: pertaining to being physically strong and vigorous – 'strong, vigorous.' ὅταν ὁ ἰσχυρὸς καθωπλισμένος φυλάσσῃ τὴν ἑαυτοῦ αὐλήν 'when a strong man who is fully armed guards his house' Lk 11.21.

79.64 ἰσχύω[b]; κατισχύω[b]: to be physically strong enough for some purpose – 'to be strong enough to, to be able to, to have the strength to.'
ἰσχύω[b]: σκάπτειν οὐκ ἰσχύω 'I am not strong enough to dig' Lk 16.3.
κατισχύω[b]: ἵνα κατισχύσητε ἐκφυγεῖν ταῦτα πάντα τὰ μέλλοντα γίνεσθαι 'in order that you may be strong enough to escape all these things that are going to take place' Lk 21.36. For another interpretation of κατισχύω in Lk 21.36, see 74.10.

79.65 ἐνισχύω[b]: to regain one's physical strength after a temporary loss of it – 'to regain strength.' λαβὼν τροφὴν ἐνίσχυσεν 'after he had eaten, his strength came back' Ac 9.19. It may, however, be impossible to say in some languages 'his strength came back,' because this would seem to imply a kind of personification of 'strength.' Therefore, it may be necessary to translate this phrase in Ac 9.19 as 'after he had eaten, he became strong again' or '. . . he was no longer weak.'

79.66 ἐνισχύω[a]: to cause someone to regain strength after a temporary loss – 'to strengthen again, to cause strength to return.' ὤφθη δὲ αὐτῷ ἄγγελος ἀπ' οὐρανοῦ ἐνισχύων αὐτόν 'an angel from heaven appeared to him to strengthen him' Lk 22.43.

79.67 στερεόομαι: to be physically strong and vigorous – 'to be strong, to become strong.' παραχρῆμα δὲ ἐστερεώθησαν αἱ βάσεις αὐτοῦ καὶ τὰ σφυδρά 'and immediately his feet and ankles became strong' Ac 3.7.

79.68 στερεόω[a]: to make physically strong – 'to make strong, to strengthen.' ἐστερέωσεν τὸ ὄνομα αὐτοῦ 'his name made him strong' or 'the power of Christ's name made him strong' Ac 3.16. In a number of languages one cannot speak of a name doing anything or even the 'power of a name' accomplishing some goal. Since in Greek the use of ὄνομα 'name' is essentially a metonym for the person, it is often necessary to translate an expression such as is in Ac 3.16 as 'Christ made him strong' or 'Jesus made him strong.' Such an expression, however, should not imply that this was a miracle performed directly by Jesus, either before or immediately after the resurrection.

79.69 ἀσθενής[c], ές: pertaining to being physically weak – 'weak.' ὡς ἀσθενεστέρῳ σκεύει τῷ γυναικείῳ ἀπονέμοντες τιμήν 'respecting the female as the weaker object' 1 Pe 3.7. Such a literal translation of this expression in 1 Pe 3.7, however, may be misleading, for in general τῷ γυναικείῳ is interpreted as a reference to one's wife. Therefore, one may translate as 'treating with respect one's wife as the physically weaker partner' or '. . . as of the weaker sex.' ἡ δὲ παρουσία τοῦ σώματος ἀσθενής 'weak in physical appearance' or 'appearing physically weak' or 'appearing weak in body' 2 Cor 10.10.

N Hot, Lukewarm, Cold[7] (79.70-79.77)

79.70 θέρμη, ης f: a state of a relatively high degree of heat – 'heat.' ἔχιδνα ἀπὸ τῆς θέρμης ἐξελθοῦσα 'a snake came out on account of the heat' or '. . . because it was hot' or '. . . because the fire was hot' Ac 28.3.

---

7 In Subdomain N *Hot, Lukewarm, Cold* of Domain 79 and in Subdomain H *Burning* of Domain 14 there are two series of meanings involving heat. In Domain 14, however, the focus is upon the physical events rather than upon states or conditions of particular objects or circumstances. There is, however, a certain degree of overlapping.

79.71 ζεστός, ή, όν: pertaining to being hot, often associated with boiling – 'hot.' ὅτι οὔτε ψυχρὸς εἶ οὔτε ζεστός 'that you are neither cold nor hot' Re 3.15. In Re 3.15 the usage is figurative; ζεστός in the sense of a favorable attitude towards something seems not to have been a conventionalized meaning. In a number of languages the contrast between 'hot' and 'cold' may refer primarily to sex or anger, in which case the contrast is certainly not appropriate for Re 3.15. It may therefore be necessary in many instances to use an equivalent such as 'for or against' or 'friendly to or hostile toward.'

79.72 πυρόω: to cause to be hot, as of fire – 'to heat, to make fiery hot.' οἱ πόδες αὐτοῦ ὅμοιοι χαλκολιβάνῳ ὡς ἐν καμίνῳ πεπυρωμένης 'his feet were like brass made fiery hot in a furnace' or '. . . in a forge' Re 1.15.

79.73 θερμαίνομαι: to cause oneself to become warm – 'to warm oneself.' καὶ ἰδοῦσα τὸν Πέτρον θερμαινόμενον 'when she saw Peter warming himself' Mk 14.67; θερμαίνεσθε καὶ χορτάζεσθε 'warm yourselves and eat well' Jas 2.16. In some languages a literal meaning of 'to warm oneself' would mean 'to increase in anger,' and therefore it may be necessary in a case such as Mk 14.67 to say simply 'when she saw Peter there near the fire.'

79.74 χλιαρός, ά, όν: pertaining to being somewhere between hot and cold – 'lukewarm, tepid.' ὅτι χλιαρὸς εἶ καὶ οὔτε ζεστὸς οὔτε ψυχρός, μέλλω σε ἐμέσαι ἐκ τοῦ στόματός μου 'because you are lukewarm and neither hot nor cold, I will spew you out of my mouth' or '. . . I will spit you out of my mouth' Re 3.16.

79.75 ψῦχος, ους n: pertaining to being cold, as of weather conditions – 'cold.' διὰ τὸν ὑετὸν τὸν ἐφεστῶτα καὶ διὰ τὸ ψῦχος 'it had started to rain and was cold' Ac 28.2; ὅτι ψῦχος ἦν 'it was cold' Jn 18.18.

79.76 καταψύχω: to cause something to become cool – 'to make cool, to cool.' καὶ καταψύξῃ τὴν γλῶσσάν μου 'and to cool my tongue' Lk 16.24. In some languages it may be necessary to render this expression in Lk 16.24 as 'to cause my tongue to feel cool.'

79.77 ψυχρός, ά, όν: pertaining to being cold, as of objects and masses – 'cold.' ὅτι οὔτε ψυχρὸς εἶ οὔτε ζεστός 'that you are neither cold nor hot' Re 3.15 (see discussion at 79.71); ὃς ἂν ποτίσῃ ἕνα τῶν μικρῶν τούτων ποτήριον ψυχροῦ μόνον 'whoever gives even a drink of cold water to one of the least of these' Mt 10.42.

O Wet, Dry (79.78-79.83)

79.78 ὑγρός, ά, όν: pertaining to being wet or moist – 'wet, moist, green (in reference to wood).' εἰ ἐν τῷ ὑγρῷ ξύλῳ ταῦτα ποιοῦσιν 'if such things as these are done when the wood is moist' or '. . . green' Lk 23.31.

79.79 βρέχω^c: to make something wet or moist – 'to wet, to make wet, to moisten.' κλαίουσα, τοῖς δάκρυσιν ἤρξατο βρέχειν τοὺς πόδας αὐτοῦ 'crying, she began wetting his feet with her tears' Lk 7.38. In a number of languages a clear distinction is made in the use of terms which imply different quantities of moisture, and one must make certain that the choice of a term in Lk 7.38 is in keeping with this context of crying and moistening by means of tears.

79.80 ξηρός^a, ά, όν: pertaining to being dry – 'dry, withered.' ἐν τῷ ξηρῷ τί γένηται; 'what will it be like when (the wood) is dry?' Lk 23.31; διέβησαν τὴν Ἐρυθρὰν Θάλασσαν ὡς διὰ ξηρᾶς γῆς 'they crossed the Red Sea as if on dry ground' He 11.29.

79.81 ξηραίνομαι^a: (derivative of ξηρός^a 'dry,' 79.80) to become dry – 'to dry up.' ἐξηράνθη τὸ ὕδωρ 'the river dried up' Re 16.12; ἐβλήθη ἔξω ὡς τὸ κλῆμα καὶ ἐξηράνθη 'it is thrown out like a branch and dries up' Jn 15.6; καὶ εὐθὺς ἐξηράνθη ἡ πηγὴ τοῦ αἵματος αὐτῆς 'and immediately the flow of her blood dried up' Mk 5.29. It may be more appropriate in a number of languages to translate this clause in Mk 5.29 as 'and immediately her menstrual bleeding stopped.'

79.82 ξηραίνω: to cause something to become dry – 'to dry out, to dry up, to wither.'

ἀνέτειλεν γὰρ ὁ ἥλιος σὺν τῷ καύσωνι καὶ ἐξήρανεν τὸν χόρτον 'for the sun comes up with its heat and withers the grass' Jas 1.11.

79.83 ἐκμάσσω: to cause something to become dry by wiping with a dry substance – 'to wipe dry.' καὶ ταῖς θριξὶν τῆς κεφαλῆς αὐτῆς ἐξέμασσεν 'then she dried (his feet) with her hair' Lk 7.38; καὶ ἐκμάσσειν τῷ λεντίῳ ᾧ ἦν διεζωσμένος 'and to dry them with the towel around his waist' Jn 13.5.

P Uneven (Rough), Level (Smooth) (79.84-79.87)

79.84 τραχύς, εῖα, ύ: pertaining to being uneven and rough, as of terrain – 'rough.' αἱ τραχεῖαι εἰς ὁδοὺς λείας 'the rough places made smooth' Lk 3.5; φοβούμενοί τε μή που κατὰ τραχεῖς τόπους ἐκπέσωμεν 'we were afraid that we would run aground on the rocky coast' Ac 27.29.

79.85 πεδινός, ή, όν: pertaining to being level or flat, in contrast with what is steep or uneven – 'level.' ἔστη ἐπὶ τόπου πεδινοῦ, καὶ ὄχλος πολὺς μαθητῶν αὐτοῦ 'he stood on a level place with a great many of his disciples' Lk 6.17.

79.86 λεῖος, α, ον: pertaining to being level or smooth (that is, without rough or uneven contours) – 'smooth, level.' αἱ τραχεῖαι εἰς ὁδοὺς λείας 'the rough places made smooth' Lk 3.5.

79.87 ταπεινόω^b: to cause something to become level – 'to level off, to make level.' καὶ πᾶν ὄρος καὶ βουνὸς ταπεινωθήσεται 'and every mountain and hill will be leveled off' Lk 3.5. One might argue that ταπεινόω in Lk 3.5 is to be understood as 'to be brought low,' but in contrast with πληρωθήσεται, which refers to filling up valleys, ταπεινωθήσεται should perhaps be understood as referring to 'leveling off' mountains and hills. For this other interpretation of ταπεινόω in Lk 3.5, see 81.7.

Q Straight, Crooked (79.88-79.90)

79.88 ὀρθός, ή, όν; εὐθύς^a, εῖα, ύ, gen. έως:

pertaining to being straight in contrast to what is crooked – 'straight, direct.'[8]

ὀρθός: τροχιὰς ὀρθὰς ποιεῖτε τοῖς ποσὶν ὑμῶν 'keep walking on straight paths' He 12.13. The context of He 12.13 is, of course, figurative.

εὐθύς[a]: εὐθείας ποιεῖτε τὰς τρίβους αὐτοῦ 'make a straight path for him (to travel)' Mt 3.3.

79.89 εὐθύνω[a]: to make something straight – 'to cause to be straight, to make straight, to straighten.' εὐθύνατε τὴν ὁδὸν κυρίου 'make a straight path for the Lord (to travel)' Jn 1.23. In a number of languages a distinction is made between making some object straight and straightening out a road. The first meaning may be equivalent to 'bending something straight,' while the latter meaning may be literally 'to avoid the curves.'

79.90 σκολιός[a], ά, όν: pertaining to being crooked or winding – 'winding, crooked.' καὶ ἔσται τὰ σκολιὰ εἰς εὐθείαν 'the crooked (roads) must be made straight' Lk 3.5.

R Two-Dimensional and Three-Dimensional Shapes (79.91-79.94)

79.91 τετράγωνος, ον: pertaining to having four equal sides and four right angles – 'square.' ἡ πόλις τετράγωνος κεῖται 'the city was square' Re 21.16.

79.92 φύραμα[a], τος n: a three-dimensional object with irregular rounding contours – 'lump.' ἢ οὐκ ἔχει ἐξουσίαν ὁ κεραμεὺς τοῦ πηλοῦ ἐκ τοῦ αὐτοῦ φυράματος ποιῆσαι 'or doesn't the potter have the power to make from the same lump of clay . . .' Ro 9.21.

79.93 πρόσωπον[c], ου n: the two-dimensional surface of an object – 'surface, face.' ἐπεισελεύσεται γὰρ ἐπὶ πάντας τοὺς καθημένους ἐπὶ πρόσωπον πάσης τῆς γῆς 'for it will come upon all those who inhabit the entire earth' Lk 21.35. In a number of cases one does not

translate πρόσωπον in the sense of 'surface' since it is an implied component of other terms. For example, the phrase 'on the earth' implies the surface of the earth.

79.94 δίστομος, ον: pertaining to having two edges, with particular reference to a sword – 'double-edged.' καὶ ἐκ τοῦ στόματος αὐτοῦ ῥομφαία δίστομος ὀξεῖα ἐκπορευομένη 'and a sharp, two-edged sword coming out of his mouth' Re 1.16.

S Sharp (79.95-79.96)

79.95 ὀξύς[a], εῖα, ύ: pertaining to having a thin cutting edge – 'sharp.' ἐν τῇ χειρὶ αὐτοῦ δρέπανον ὀξύ 'a sharp sickle in his hand' Re 14.14; ῥομφαία δίστομος ὀξεῖα 'a sharp two-edged sword' Re 1.16.

79.96 τομός, ή, όν: pertaining to having the capacity to cut efficiently – 'cutting, sharp.' τομώτερος ὑπὲρ πᾶσαν μάχαιραν δίστομον 'sharper than any two-edged sword' He 4.12.

T Pure, Unadulterated, Undiluted (79.97-79.99)

79.97 πιστικός, ή, όν: pertaining to being pure, with the possible implication of a quality which can be trusted – 'pure.'[9] μύρου νάρδου πιστικῆς πολυτίμου 'a very expensive perfume made of pure nard' Jn 12.3.

79.98 ἄδολος, ον: pertaining to being pure, with the implication of not being adulterated – 'unadulterated, pure.' τὸ λογικὸν ἄδολον γάλα ἐπιποθήσατε 'thirsty for the pure, spiritual milk' 1 Pe 2.2.

79.99 ἄκρατος, ον: pertaining to being pure in the sense of not being diluted and hence at full strength – 'at full strength, undiluted, pure.' καὶ αὐτὸς πίεται ἐκ τοῦ οἴνου τοῦ θυμοῦ τοῦ θεοῦ τοῦ κεκερασμένου ἀκράτου 'and he will drink from the wine of the wrath of God poured out at full strength' Re 14.10.

---

8 In earlier Greek ὀρθός meant 'straight up and down' while εὐθύς meant 'straight on the horizontal plane,' but this distinction has not always been preserved in Koine Greek.

9 Scholarly opinion is divided as to the derivation of πιστικός, but πιστικός was associated with πίστις by some later writers, and it was then interpreted to mean 'genuine, unadulterated.'

U   Soft, Tender (79.100-79.101)

79.100 μαλακός[a], ή, όν: pertaining to being soft to the touch – 'soft, delicate, luxurious.' ἄνθρωπον ἐν μαλακοῖς ἱματίοις ἠμφιεσμένον 'a man dressed up in luxurious clothes' Lk 7.25.

79.101 ἀπαλός, ή, όν: pertaining to being tender (yielding readily to pressure) – 'tender.' ὅταν ἤδη ὁ κλάδος αὐτῆς γένηται ἀπαλός 'whenever its branch becomes tender' Mt 24.32.

V   Male, Female (79.102-79.103)

79.102 ἄρσην, εν, gen. ενος: the male of any living creature – 'male, man.' ἄρσεν καὶ θῆλυ ἐποίησεν αὐτούς 'he made them male and female' Mt 19.4; οἱ ἄρσενες ἀφέντες τὴν φυσικὴν χρῆσιν τῆς θηλείας 'males giving up natural sexual relations with females' Ro 1.27.

79.103 θῆλυς, εια, υ: the female of any living creature – 'female, woman.' ἄρσεν καὶ θῆλυ ἐποίησεν αὐτούς 'he made them male and female' Mt 19.4; αἵ τε γὰρ θήλειαι αὐτῶν μετήλλαξαν τὴν φυσικὴν χρῆσιν εἰς τὴν παρὰ φύσιν 'their women pervert the natural use of their sex into that which is contrary to nature' Ro 1.26.

W   Shapes (79.104-79.109)

79.104 ἄκρον[b], ου n: the tip or top of a pointed object – 'tip, top.' προσεκύνησεν ἐπὶ τὸ ἄκρον τῆς ῥάβδου αὐτοῦ 'he bowed in worship on the top of his walking stick' He 11.21; βάψῃ τὸ ἄκρον τοῦ δακτύλου αὐτοῦ ὕδατος 'to dip the tip of his finger in some water' Lk 16.24.

79.105 κέρας[b], ατος n: a projection at the corner of an object – 'projection, corner.' φωνὴν μίαν ἐκ τῶν τεσσάρων κεράτων τοῦ θυσιαστηρίου τοῦ χρυσοῦ 'a voice coming from the four corners of the golden altar' Re 9.13.

79.106 ἀρχή[h], ῆς f: the corner of a two-dimensional object, such as a sheet of cloth – 'corner.' ὀθόνην μεγάλην τέσσαρσιν ἀρχαῖς καθιέμενον 'a large sheet being lowered by its four corners' Ac 10.11.

79.107 γωνία, ας f: the corner of an area or construction, either an inside corner or an outside corner – 'corner.' ἐν ταῖς γωνίαις τῶν πλατειῶν . . . προσεύχεσθαι 'to pray . . . on the street corners' Mt 6.5; ἑστῶτας ἐπὶ τὰς τέσσαρας γωνίας τῆς γῆς 'standing on the four corners of the earth' Re 7.1. This expression in Re 7.1 must be rendered in some languages as 'standing at the end of the earth in four different directions' or 'standing at the four horizons of the earth.' οὐ γάρ ἐστιν ἐν γωνίᾳ πεπραγμένον τοῦτο 'this thing was not done in a corner' (a reference to something which was not done in secret) Ac 26.26.

79.108 μέρος[b], ους n (always plural): an area at the side of an object – 'side.' βάλετε εἰς τὰ δεξιὰ μέρη τοῦ πλοίου τὸ δίκτυον 'throw your net out on the right side of the boat' Jn 21.6.

79.109 στόμα[c], τος n: (a figurative extension of meaning of στόμα[a] 'mouth,' 8.19) the sharp edge of a weapon – 'sharp edge, cutting edge.' πεσοῦνται στόματι μαχαίρης 'they died by the sword' or literally 'they fell by the edge of the sword' Lk 21.24. For a discussion of στόμα μαχαίρης, see 6.33.

X   Open, Closed (79.110-79.113)

79.110 ἀνοίγω; διανοίγω[a]: to cause something to be open – 'to open, to make open.'[10] ἀνοίγω: οὐκ ἤνοιξεν τὸν πυλῶνα 'she did not open the outer door' Ac 12.14; κρούετε, καὶ ἀνοιγήσεται ὑμῖν 'knock and it will be opened to you' Mt 7.7. This entire expression in Mt 7.7 is, of course, to be understood in a figurative sense. τάφος ἀνεῳγμένος ὁ λάρυγξ αὐτῶν 'their throat is an open tomb' Ro 3.13. διανοίγω[a]: λέγει αὐτῷ, Εφφαθα, ὅ ἐστιν, Διανοίχθητι Mk 7.34. See also discussion at 79.111.

79.111 εφφαθα (an Aramaic word) – 'be opened.' λέγει αὐτῷ, Εφφαθα, ὅ ἐστιν, Διανοίχθητι 'he said to him, Ephphatha, which

---

10 It is possible that διανοίγω[a] is somewhat more emphatic than ἀνοίγω.

means, Be opened' Mk 7.34. The Aramaic word εφφαθα, together with the Greek interpretation 'be opened,' may still be relatively meaningless in the context of Mk 7.34 since it refers to the capacity for hearing. In a number of languages one does not speak of a deaf person as 'one whose ears are closed.' The most appropriate equivalent may simply be 'be able to hear' or even 'now you can hear.'

79.112 κλείω: to cause something to be shut – 'to shut, to make shut, to close.' καὶ ἐκλείσθη ἡ θύρα 'and the door was closed' Mt 25.10; τὸ δεσμωτήριον εὕρομεν κεκλεισμένον ἐν πάσῃ ἀσφαλείᾳ 'we found the jail shut tightly' Ac 5.23. In some languages the equivalent of this expression in Ac 5.23 would be 'we found the jail securely locked.'

79.113 ἀποκλείω: to close off an area, and in the process of doing so, to exclude – 'to close off, to shut.' ἀφ' οὗ ἂν ἐγερθῇ ὁ οἰκοδεσπότης καὶ ἀποκλείσῃ τὴν θύραν, καὶ ἄρξησθε ἔξω ἑστάναι καὶ κρούειν τὴν θύραν 'when the master of the house gets up and closes the door, then you on the outside will begin to knock at the door' Lk 13.25.

Y Covered Over (79.114-79.117)

79.114 καλύπτω[a]: to cause something to be covered over and hence not visible – 'to cover, to cover over.' οὐδεὶς δὲ λύχνον ἅψας καλύπτει αὐτὸν σκεύει 'no one takes a lamp and covers it with a bowl' Lk 8.16; τότε ἄρξονται λέγειν . . . τοῖς βουνοῖς, Καλύψατε ἡμᾶς 'then they will begin to say . . . to the hills, Cover us' Lk 23.30.

79.115 περικαλύπτω: to cover by putting something around – 'to cover, to cover around.' καὶ ἤρξαντό τινες ἐμπτύειν αὐτῷ καὶ περικαλύπτειν αὐτοῦ τὸ πρόσωπον 'and some began to spit on him and to cover his face' Mk 14.65.

79.116 ἀκατακάλυπτος, ον: pertaining to not being covered – 'uncovered.' ἡ προφητεύουσα ἀκατακαλύπτῳ τῇ κεφαλῇ 'or prophesying with her head uncovered' 1 Cor 11.5.

79.117 ἀνακαλύπτω: to cause something to be uncovered – 'to unveil, to remove a veil, to uncover.' ἡμεῖς δὲ πάντες ἀνακεκαλυμμένῳ προσώπῳ τὴν δόξαν κυρίου κατοπτριζόμενοι 'we all reflect the glory of the Lord with uncovered faces' or '. . . unveiled faces' 2 Cor 3.18. The symbolic significance of ἀνακεκαλυμμένῳ προσώπῳ 'unveiled face' in 2 Cor 3.18 needs to be understood only in terms of the preceding discussion in 2 Cor 3.13-15.

Z Wrapped (79.118-79.119)

79.118 ἐνειλέω; ἐντυλίσσω[a]; καταδέω: to enclose an object by winding something about or around it – 'to wrap, to bandage.'
ἐνειλέω: καθελὼν αὐτὸν ἐνείλησεν τῇ σινδόνι 'having taken him down, he wrapped him in a sheet' Mk 15.46.
ἐντυλίσσω[a]: καθελὼν ἐνετύλιξεν αὐτὸ σινδόνι 'having taken down (the body), he wrapped it in a sheet' Lk 23.53.
καταδέω: προσελθὼν κατέδησεν τὰ τραύματα αὐτοῦ 'he went over to him and bandaged his wounds' Lk 10.34.

79.119 συστέλλω[c]: to wrap up an object, with the implication of getting it ready to remove – 'to wrap up, to make a bundle of.' ἀναστάντες δὲ οἱ νεώτεροι συνέστειλαν αὐτὸν καὶ ἐξενέγκαντες ἔθαψαν 'the young men came in, wrapped him up, and carried him out for burial' Ac 5.6. For another interpretation of συστέλλω in Ac 5.6, see 15.200.

A' Rolled Up (79.120-79.122)

79.120 ἐλίσσω; ἐντυλίσσω[b]; πτύσσω: to cause something to be in the shape of a roll – 'to roll up, to make into a roll.'[11]
ἐλίσσω: καὶ ὁ οὐρανὸς ἀπεχωρίσθη ὡς βιβλίον ἐλισσόμενον 'and the sky disappeared like a rolled-up scroll' or '. . . like a scroll being rolled up' Re 6.14.
ἐντυλίσσω[b]: καὶ τὸ σουδάριον, ὃ ἦν ἐπὶ τῆς

---

11 There may very well be some significant difference of meaning in the series of terms in 79.120, but it is impossible to determine this on the basis of existing contexts.

κεφαλῆς αὐτοῦ, οὐ μετὰ τῶν ὀθονίων κείμενον ἀλλὰ χωρὶς ἐντετυλιγμένον εἰς ἕνα τόπον 'and the cloth which had been about his head was not lying with the linen cloths but was rolled up and lying in a separate place' Jn 20.7.
πτύσσω: πτύξας τὸ βιβλίον 'he rolled up the scroll' or 'he rolled up the book' Lk 4.20.

79.121 ἕλιγμα, τος *n*: (derivative of ἑλίσσω 'to roll up,' 79.120) that which has been rolled up in the form of a package – 'package, bundle, rolled-up object.' φέρων ἕλιγμα σμύρνης καὶ ἀλόης 'bringing a bundle of myrrh and aloes' Jn 19.39 (apparatus).

79.122 ἀναπτύσσω: to cause something to be unrolled – 'to unroll a scroll, to unroll (a book in the form of) a scroll.' ἀναπτύξας τὸ βιβλίον εὗρεν τὸν τόπον οὗ ἦν γεγραμμένον 'having unrolled the book of the scroll, he found the passage where it was written' Lk 4.17.

B' Large, Small (79.123-79.128)

79.123 μέγας^c, μεγάλη, μέγα: a large size, relative to the norm for the class of objects in question – 'large, big, great.' προσκυλίσας λίθον μέγαν τῇ θύρᾳ 'he rolled a large stone across the entrance' Mt 27.60; ἦν δὲ ἐκεῖ . . . ἀγέλη χοίρων μεγάλη 'a large herd of pigs . . . was nearby' Mk 5.11; ἅλυσιν μεγάλην ἐπὶ τὴν χεῖρα αὐτοῦ 'a big chain in his hand' Re 20.1.

79.124 μεγαλύνω^a: to cause to be large – 'to make big, to make large, to enlarge.' μεγαλύνουσιν τὰ κράσπεδα 'they make their tassels big' Mt 23.5. It is possible to interpret the large size of the tassels as referring primarily to the length of the tassels and, therefore, to translate as 'they make their tassels long.'

However, it seems more likely that the reference includes all dimensions.

79.125 μικρός^b, ά, όν; ἐλάχιστος^a, η, ον: a small size, relative to the norm for the class of objects in question – 'small, little.'
μικρός^b: ὃ μικρότερον . . . πάντων τῶν σπερμάτων 'the smallest . . . of all seeds' Mt 13.32.
ἐλάχιστος^a (superlative of μικρός): μετάγεται ὑπὸ ἐλαχίστου πηδαλίου 'it can be steered by a very small rudder' Jas 3.4. Note that in the case of a Greek superlative such as ἐλάχιστος, the meaning is not 'the smallest' but simply 'very small.' This is typical of many uses of the superlative in Greek.

79.126 πηλίκος^a, η, ον: an interrogative of large size – 'how large, what large.' ἴδετε πηλίκοις ὑμῖν γράμμασιν ἔγραφα 'see with what large letters I am writing to you' Ga 6.11.

79.127 ἡλίκος^a, η, ον: an interrogative of size occurring in indirect questions – 'how extensive, how large, how small.' ἰδοὺ ἡλίκον πῦρ ἡλίκην ὕλην ἀνάπτει 'see how large a forest can be set on fire by such a small flame' Jas 3.5.

79.128 τηλικοῦτος^a, αὕτη, οῦτο: a reference to the size of something (occurring rarely in an absolute sense) – 'so large, so great.' τὰ πλοῖα, τηλικαῦτα ὄντα 'the ships, being so large' Jas 3.4.

C' Perfect (79.129)

79.129 τέλειος^c, α, ον: pertaining to having no defect whatsoever – 'perfect.' διὰ τῆς μείζονος καὶ τελειοτέρας σκηνῆς 'through the greater and more perfect tent' He 9.11.

80 Space

Outline of Subdomains

A   Space, Place (80.1-80.4)
B   Limits, Boundaries of Space (80.5-80.7)

A   Space, Place (80.1-80.4)

80.1 τόπος^a, ου *m*: an area of any size, regarded in certain contexts as a point in space – 'space, place, room.' διότι οὐκ ἦν αὐτοῖς τόπος ἐν τῷ καταλύματι 'because there was no space for them in the inn' Lk 2.7; καὶ ἔτι τόπος ἐστίν 'and there is still space' Lk 14.22; οἱ ἄνδρες τοῦ τόπου ἐκείνου ἀπέστειλαν εἰς ὅλην τὴν περίχωρον ἐκείνην 'the men of that place sent into all the surrounding area' Mt 14.35; ἐν τῷ τόπῳ οὗ ἐρρέθη αὐτοῖς, Οὐ λαός μου ὑμεῖς 'in the place where it was said to them, You are not my people' Ro 9.26. In Jn 11.48 (ἀροῦσιν ἡμῶν τὸν τόπον 'they will destroy our place') the reference is to the Temple in Jerusalem.

80.2 κανών^b, όνος *m*: an area of activity, defined geographically and functionally – 'area, sphere, territory.' οὐκ ἐν ἀλλοτρίῳ κανόνι εἰς τὰ ἕτοιμα καυχήσασθαι 'and shall not have to boast of work already done in another person's area' 2 Cor 10.16.

80.3 βῆμα ποδός: (an idiom, literally 'a step of a foot,' a distance of approximately two and a half feet or a little less than a meter) an extremely limited or restricted space – 'a square yard, a square meter.' καὶ οὐκ ἔδωκεν αὐτῷ κληρονομίαν ἐν αὐτῇ οὐδὲ βῆμα ποδός 'and he did not give him any part of the inheritance, not even a square yard of it' or 'not even a square foot of it' or 'not even a square meter of it' Ac 7.5.[1]

[1] Despite certain differences in size, in some languages the closest natural equivalent of the phrase βῆμα ποδός is

80.4 χωρέω^b: to be a quantity of space – 'to have room for, to be space for, to contain.' οὐδ' αὐτὸν οἶμαι τὸν κόσμον χωρῆσαι τὰ γραφόμενα βιβλία 'I suppose the whole world (literally 'the world itself') would not be large enough to contain the books that would be written' Jn 21.25; χωροῦσαι ἀνὰ μετρητὰς δύο ἢ τρεῖς 'holding between twenty and thirty gallons' Jn 2.6; ὥστε μηκέτι χωρεῖν μηδὲ τὰ πρὸς τὴν θύραν 'so that there was no longer any room, even around the door' Mk 2.2.

B   Limits, Boundaries of Space (80.5-80.7)

80.5 ὁροθεσία, ας *f*: established or fixed boundaries – 'limits, fixed limits.' τὰς ὁροθεσίας τῆς κατοικίας αὐτῶν 'fixed limits of the places where they would live' Ac 17.26.

80.6 πέρας^a, ατος *n*: limit as the distant end of a space – 'end, limit.' εἰς τὰ πέρατα τῆς οἰκουμένης τὰ ῥήματα αὐτῶν 'their words reached to the ends of the earth' Ro 10.18.

80.7 ἄκρον^a, ου *n*: the extreme limit of a space – 'extreme boundary, final limit, end.' ἐπισυνάξουσιν τοὺς ἐκλεκτοὺς αὐτοῦ . . . ἀπ' ἄκρων οὐρανῶν ἕως τῶν ἄκρων αὐτῶν 'they will gather his chosen people . . . from one extreme end of the world to the other' Mt 24.31.

simply 'a square foot,' while in other languages employing the metric system, a phrase such as 'a square meter' would be more appropriate. Some languages, however, may employ expressions such as 'the measure of an arm's length' or 'the ground of one stride.' The focal point in Ac 7.5 is not so much the specific measurement, but rather the very limited space.

81 Spacial Dimensions

Outline of Subdomains

A Measure, To Measure (81.1-81.2)
B High, Low, Deep (81.3-81.11)
C Long, Short, Far (81.12-81.14)
D Narrow, Wide (81.15-81.19)
E Specific Measures of Volume (81.20-81.24)
F Specific Measures of Length (81.25-81.29)

A Measure, To Measure (81.1-81.2)

81.1 μέτρον, ου *n*: a unit of measurement, either of length or volume – 'measure.' μέτρον ἀνθρώπου, ὅ ἐστιν ἀγγέλου 'the unit of measurement used by a person, that is, by an angel' Re 21.17; ᾧ γὰρ μέτρῳ μετρεῖτε 'for in accordance with the measure which you use in measuring' Lk 6.38. Some languages do not have a generic term for 'measure,' but they may express the concept by a phrase meaning 'how one knows how big something is' or '. . . how long something is.' In other words, it is necessary to use expressions involving specific dimensions.

81.2 μετρέωᵃ: to determine the measurement of something – 'to measure.' καὶ ἐμέτρησεν τὴν πόλιν 'and he measured the city' Re 21.16. In some languages one may best translate this expression in Re 21.16 as 'the angel learned how big the city was' or, as in other languages, 'the angel walked the size of the city.'

B High, Low, Deep (81.3-81.11)

81.3 ὕψοςᵃ, **ους** *n*: the measurement of height – 'height.' καὶ τὸ ὕψος αὐτῆς ἴσα ἐστίν 'and the height of it was the same' Re 21.16; τί τὸ πλάτος καὶ μῆκος καὶ ὕψος καὶ βάθος 'what is the width and length and height and depth' Eph 3.18. In Eph 3.18 the four different dimensions of space are used figuratively in the sense of 'that which is all-encompassing.'

81.4 ἡλικίαᶜ, **ας** *f*: height as the dimension of stature of an animate object – 'height, stature.' ὅτι τῇ ἡλικίᾳ μικρὸς ἦν 'because he was short in stature' Lk 19.3.

81.5 ὑψόωᵃ: to cause something to become high – 'to raise up, to lift up.' καθὼς Μωϋσῆς ὕψωσεν τὸν ὄφιν 'as Moses lifted up the serpent' Jn 3.14.[1]

81.6 ὑψηλόςᵃ, **ή**, **όν**: pertaining to being high – 'high, tall.' παραλαμβάνει αὐτὸν ὁ διάβολος εἰς ὄρος ὑψηλὸν λίαν 'the Devil took him to the top of a very high mountain' Mt 4.8.[2]

81.7 ταπεινόωᵃ: to cause something to become low in height – 'to make low.' πᾶν ὄρος καὶ βουνὸς ταπεινωθήσεται 'all hills and mountains shall be made low' Lk 3.5. For another (probably preferred) interpretation of Lk 3.5, see 79.87.

81.8 βάθοςᵃ, **ους** *n*: the distance beneath a surface – 'depth, deep.' εὐθέως ἐξανέτειλεν διὰ τὸ μὴ ἔχειν βάθος γῆς 'and it immediately dried up because there was no depth of soil' or '. . . because the soil was not deep' Mt 13.5. In some languages it may be best to say 'because there was not much soil.'

81.9 βάθοςᵇ, **ους** *n*: a place that is deep – 'deep place, deep water.' ἐπανάγαγε εἰς τὸ βάθος 'take (the boat) farther out to the deep water' Lk 5.4.

81.10 βαθύςᵃ, **εῖα**, **ύ**: pertaining to being considerably below a surface – 'deep.' οὔτε ἄντλημα ἔχεις καὶ τὸ φρέαρ ἐστὶν βαθύ 'you don't have a bucket and the well is deep' Jn 4.11.

81.11 βαθύνω: to cause to be deep – 'to make deep, to go deep.' ὃς ἔσκαψεν καὶ ἐβάθυνεν 'who dug and went down deep' or 'who dug deep' Lk 6.48.

---

1 The focus of meaning of ὑψόω in Jn 3.14 is on the final position and not on the movement itself.
2 It is possible in Mt 4.8 to interpret ὑψηλός as being a physical feature of the mountain, namely, a 'tall mountain,' rather than being the top of a mountain which was in a high chain of mountains.

C Long, Short, Far (81.12-81.14)

81.12 μῆκος, ους *n*: the measurement of length – 'length.' καὶ τὸ μῆκος αὐτῆς ὅσον καὶ τὸ πλάτος 'and the length of it was as much as the breadth' Re 21.16.

81.13 μικρός^c, ά, όν: pertaining to being short, in a horizontal or vertical dimension – 'short.' ὅτι τῇ ἡλικίᾳ μικρὸς ἦν 'because he was short in stature' Lk 19.3; προελθὼν μικρόν 'he went a short distance' Mt 26.39.

81.14 μακρός^b, ά, όν: pertaining to being far from some point of reference – 'distant, far.' ὁ νεώτερος υἱὸς ἀπεδήμησεν εἰς χώραν μακράν 'the younger son went off into a distant country' or 'the younger son went to a country which was far away' Lk 15.13.

D Narrow, Wide (81.15-81.19)

81.15 πλάτος, ους *n*: the measurement of width – 'width, breadth.' τὸ μῆκος αὐτῆς ὅσον καὶ τὸ πλάτος 'its length was as great as its breadth' or 'it was as long as it was wide' Re 21.16.

81.16 πλατύς, εῖα, ύ: pertaining to being wide – 'wide, broad.' πλατεῖα ἡ πύλη 'the gate is wide' Mt 7.13. In Mt 7.13 πύλη seems to refer to the gateway (in other words, to the space) rather than to the gate as an object. (See 7.48.)

81.17 πλατύνω: to cause something to be wide – 'to widen, to broaden, to make broad.' πλατύνουσιν γὰρ τὰ φυλακτήρια αὐτῶν 'they broaden their phylacteries' Mt 23.5.

81.18 εὐρύχωρος, ον: pertaining to being broad and spacious, with the implication of agreeable and pleasant – 'spacious, broad.' καὶ εὐρύχωρος ἡ ὁδός 'and the road is spacious' or '. . . broad' Mt 7.13.

81.19 στενός, ή, όν: pertaining to being narrow or restricted – 'narrow.' ἀγωνίζεσθε εἰσελθεῖν διὰ τῆς στενῆς θύρας 'do your best to go in through the narrow door' Lk 13.24; εἰσέλθατε διὰ τῆς στενῆς πύλης 'go in through the narrow gateway' Mt 7.13.

E Specific Measures of Volume³ (81.20-81.24)

81.20 βάτος^b, ου *m*: a Hebrew liquid measure of between eight and nine gallons or approximately 35 liters – 'bath.' ἑκατὸν βάτους ἐλαίου 'one hundred baths of olive oil' Lk 16.6. Because of the possible symbolic numerical values used in the Parable of the Dishonest Steward, it is important to retain the numerals, while making some adjustment in the case of the term βάτος. Accordingly, one may speak of 'one hundred barrels of olive oil' or 'one hundred containers of olive oil' or 'one hundred large jars of olive oil.'

81.21 κόρος, ου *m*: a Hebrew dry measure for grain, flour, etc., of between ten and twelve bushels or about 390 liters – 'cor.' ἑκατὸν κόρους σίτου 'a hundred cors of wheat' Lk 16.7. In order to reflect more accurately the total quantity involved, one is justified in English to employ an expression such as 'a thousand bushels of wheat.' An equivalent metric unit could be thirty metric tons.⁴

81.22 μετρητής, οῦ *m*: a liquid measure of about nine gallons or forty liters – 'measure.' χωροῦσαι ἀνὰ μετρητὰς δύο ἢ τρεῖς 'holding between twenty and thirty gallons' or '. . . between 80 and 120 liters' Jn 2.6.

81.23 σάτον, ου *n*: the Hebrew measure for grain, about a peck and a half or somewhat less than one-half bushel (a bushel consists of four pecks) or approximately twelve liters in the metric system – 'saton, measure, batch.' ἣν λαβοῦσα γυνὴ ἐνέκρυψεν εἰς ἀλεύρου σάτα τρία 'the woman takes it and mixes it with a batch of flour' Mt 13.33. In Mt 13.33 the precise amount of flour is not important.

3 The meaning of the term μόδιος as a unit of measurement is not included in this subdomain, for in the only texts in which it occurs in the NT, namely Mt 5.15, Mk 4.21, and Lk 11.33, it designates an artifact and is not a measure of volume (see 6.151).

4 Though in the Greek text of Lk 16.7 the number of cors is given as 'a hundred,' it may not be particularly important to preserve the numeral as in the previous item (Lk 16.6 in 81.20), for at least in English the expression 'a thousand' may have a similar symbolic significance of 'a huge amount.'

What is important is to provide some type of measurement which will indicate a considerable quantity.

81.24 χοῖνιξ, ιχος *f*: a dry measure of approximately one quart or one liter – 'quart.' χοῖνιξ σίτου δηναρίου, καὶ τρεῖς χοίνικες κριθῶν δηναρίου 'a quart of wheat for a day's wages and three quarts of barley for a day's wages' Re 6.6. The Greek text of Re 6.6 has literally 'denarius' (see 6.75), but it is preferable in translating Re 6.6 to relate a denarius to its buying power in terms of a day's wages for an average worker.

F Specific Measures of Length (81.25-81.29)

81.25 πῆχυς, εως *m*: traditionally the distance from the elbow to the end of the fingers, about eighteen inches or one-half meter – 'cubit, eighteen inches, half meter.' οὐ γὰρ ἦσαν μακρὰν ἀπὸ τῆς γῆς ἀλλὰ ὡς ἀπὸ πηχῶν διακοσίων 'not very far from land, about 200 cubits' or '. . . about 100 yards' or '. . . about 100 meters' Jn 21.8; τίς δὲ ἐξ ὑμῶν μεριμνῶν δύναται προσθεῖναι ἐπὶ τὴν ἡλικίαν αὐτοῦ πῆχυν ἕνα; 'who of you by worrying is able to add a half meter to his stature?' Mt 6.27. The interpretation of πῆχυς in Mt 6.27 as a measurement of stature rather than length of life may be justified as an instance of literary hyperbole or exaggeration. Most modern translations, however, interpret πῆχυς in this context as a reference to length of life rather than as a measurement of height (see discussion under ἡλικία[a] in 67.151).

81.26 ὀργυιά, ᾶς *f*: traditionally the measurement of a man's arms stretched out horizontally, reckoned at approximately six feet or 1.85 meters and used as a technical, nautical term to measure the depth of water – 'fathom.' βολίσαντες εὗρον ὀργυιὰς εἴκοσι 'they found the depth of the water to be twenty fathoms' or '. . . about forty meters' Ac 27.28. If one adopts a metric system, the later expression in Ac 27.28, namely, ὀργυιὰς δεκαπέντε 'fifteen fathoms,' may be rendered as 'about thirty meters.'

81.27 στάδιος, ου *m*: a measure of distance of about 600 feet or 185 meters – 'stade' (but normally adapted to familiar measurements of distance). τὸ δὲ πλοῖον ἤδη σταδίους πολλοὺς ἀπὸ τῆς γῆς ἀπεῖχεν 'the boat was already a number of stades away from land' or '. . . was quite a distance from land' Mt 14.24; ἐληλακότες οὖν ὡς σταδίους εἴκοσι πέντε ἢ τριάκοντα 'then having gone some twenty-five or thirty stades' or 'having gone about three or four miles' or '. . . about five or six kilometers' Jn 6.19.

81.28 σαββάτου ὁδός: a Sabbath day's journey, somewhat over half a mile and about one kilometer – 'half a mile, one kilometer, Sabbath journey.' ὅ ἐστιν ἐγγὺς Ἰερουσαλὴμ σαββάτου ἔχον ὁδόν 'which is near Jerusalem, about a half a mile away' Ac 1.12.

81.29 μίλιον, ου *n*: a Roman mile, consisting of a thousand paces and equivalent to somewhat less than an English mile but equal to about one kilometer and a half – 'mile, kilometer.' ὅστις σε ἀγγαρεύσει μίλιον ἕν 'whoever forces you to carry his pack one mile' Mt 5.41. In translating Mt 5.41 in the metric system, it would be better to simply say 'whoever forces you to carry his pack one kilometer' rather than to attempt more specific distance, namely 'a kilometer and a half.'

82 Spacial Orientations

Outline of Subdomains

A North, South, East, West (82.1-82.6)
B Left, Right, Straight Ahead, Opposite (82.7-82.12)

A North, South, East, West (82.1-82.6)

82.1 ἀνατολή[b], ῆς *f* – 'east' (as the direction of the rising sun). ἥξουσιν ἀπὸ ἀνατολῶν καὶ δυσμῶν 'people will come from the east and the west' Lk 13.29. See the discussion at 82.3.

82.2 δύσις, εως *f*; δυσμή, ῆς *f* – 'west' (as the direction of the setting sun).
δύσις: αὐτὸς ὁ Ἰησοῦς ἀπὸ ἀνατολῆς καὶ ἄχρι δύσεως ἐξαπέστειλεν δι' αὐτῶν τὸ . . . κήρυγμα 'Jesus himself sent out through them the . . . message from east to west' Mk 16 shorter ending.
δυσμή: ἀπὸ νότου πυλῶνες τρεῖς, καὶ ἀπὸ δυσμῶν πυλῶνες τρεῖς 'three gates on the south and three gates on the west' Re 21.13. See the discussion at 82.3.

82.3 βορρᾶς, ᾶ *m* – 'north.' ἥξουσιν . . . ἀπὸ βορρᾶ καὶ νότου 'people will come . . . from the north and the south' Lk 13.29.

In most languages east and west are related to the rising or setting sun, although in some languages there may be some local geographical feature which serves as a marker of direction, for example, the location of a particular mountain, the ocean, or a river. For north, some languages employ 'to the left of the rising sun,' that is to say, the direction is oriented in terms of the left hand of a person facing toward the rising sun. Similarly, south would be 'to the right of the rising sun.'

82.4 νότος[a], ου *m*; μεσημβρία[b], ας *f* – 'south.'
νότος[a]: ἥξουσιν . . . ἀπὸ βορρᾶ καὶ νότου 'people will come . . . from the north and the south' Lk 13.29.
μεσημβρία[b]: πορεύου κατὰ μεσημβρίαν 'go toward the south' Ac 8.26. It is also possible to interpret κατὰ μεσημβρίαν in Ac 8.26 as

meaning 'about noon,' since μεσημβρία is a normal expression for 'midday' or 'noon' (see 67.74). See also the discussion at 82.3.

82.5 χῶρος, ου *m* – 'northwest.' λιμένα τῆς Κρήτης βλέποντα κατὰ λίβα καὶ κατὰ χῶρον 'a harbor in Crete that faces southwest and northwest' or perhaps '. . . northeast and southeast' Ac 27.12. The difference in expression is due to designating the directions of the wind either as the direction from which the wind comes or the direction toward which the wind blows. See commentaries.

In rendering directions which are not cardinal points, one may often use a variety of expressions, for example, 'between north and west' or 'from the north a little west' or 'to the north of west.' A high percentage of languages designate directions by reference to the rising and setting of the sun. Accordingly, Ac 27.12 may be rendered as 'a harbor that is open to the sea to the left of the setting sun and to the right of the setting sun.'

82.6 λίψ, acc. λίβα *m* – 'southwest.' λιμένα τῆς Κρήτης βλέποντα κατὰ λίβα καὶ κατὰ χῶρον 'a harbor in Crete that faces southwest and northwest' or perhaps '. . . northeast and southeast' Ac 27.12.

As in the case of the intermediate direction 'northwest' (82.5), one may also express 'southwest' in some languages as 'a little south of west' or 'toward the south, but actually somewhat west' or 'veering to the right of south.'

B Left, Right, Straight Ahead, Opposite (82.7-82.12)

82.7 ἀριστερός[a], ά, όν; εὐώνυμος, ον: pertaining to being to the left of some point of reference – 'left, left side.'
ἀριστερός[a]: εἷς σου ἐκ δεξιῶν καὶ εἷς ἐξ ἀριστερῶν καθίσωμεν 'let us sit (with you), one at your right and one at your left' Mk 10.37. For another interpretation of ἀριστερός as part of an idiom in Mk 10.37, see 87.35.
εὐώνυμος: τὸ δὲ καθίσαι ἐκ δεξιῶν μου καὶ ἐξ

εὐωνύμων οὐκ ἔστιν ἐμὸν τοῦτο δοῦναι 'it is not for me to choose who will sit on my right and on my left' Mt 20.23.

In 2 Cor 6.7 the phrase ὅπλον ἀριστερόν, literally 'lefthand weapon,' refers to a weapon used by the left hand and therefore a defensive weapon, while ὅπλον δεξιόν, literally 'weapon for the right hand,' refers to an offensive weapon.

82.8 δεξιός, ά, όν: pertaining to being to the right of some point of reference – 'right, right side.' βάλετε εἰς τὰ δεξιὰ μέρη τοῦ πλοίου τὸ δίκτυον 'throw your net out on the right side of the boat' Jn 21.6; εἷς σου ἐκ δεξιῶν καὶ εἷς ἐξ ἀριστερῶν καθίσωμεν 'let us sit (with you), one at your right and one at your left' Mk 10.37. For another interpretation of δεξιός as part of an idiom in Mark 10.37, see 87.34.

82.9 ἀντοφθαλμέω: to face straight ahead – 'to face into' (for example, the wind). μὴ

δυναμένου ἀντοφθαλμεῖν τῷ ἀνέμῳ 'since (the ship) was not able to face into the wind' Ac 27.15.

82.10 βλέπω^g: (a figurative extension of meaning of βλέπω^a 'to see,' 24.7) to be oriented in a particular direction – 'facing.' λιμένα τῆς Κρήτης βλέποντα κατὰ λίβα καὶ κατὰ χῶρον 'a harbor in Crete facing southwest and northwest' Ac 27.12.

82.11 ἐναντίος^a, α, ον: pertaining to being oriented in the direction opposite to a movement – 'against.' ἦν γὰρ ὁ ἄνεμος ἐναντίος αὐτοῖς 'for the wind was against them' or 'the wind was blowing against them' Mk 6.48.

82.12 φέρω^e: to be oriented in the direction of a movement – 'to lead to, to lead into.' ἦλθαν ἐπὶ τὴν πύλην τὴν σιδηρᾶν τὴν φέρουσαν εἰς τὴν πόλιν 'they came to the iron gate leading into the city' Ac 12.10.

83 Spacial Positions[1]

Outline of Subdomains

A   Here, There (83.1-83.4)
B   Where, Somewhere, Everywhere (83.5-83.8)
C   Among, Between, In, Inside (83.9-83.17)
D   Around, About, Outside (83.18-83.22)
E   At, Beside, Near, Far (83.23-83.32)
F   In Front Of, Face To Face, In Back Of, Behind (83.33-83.41)
G   Opposite, Over Against, Across From, Offshore From (83.42-83.45)
H   On, Upon, On the Surface Of (83.46-83.47)
I   Above, Below (83.48-83.54)
J   Beyond, On the Other Side Of (83.55-83.56)

A Here, There[2] (83.1-83.4)

83.1 ὧδε^a; ἐνθάδε: a position relatively near the speaker, writer, or viewpoint person – 'here.'
ὧδε^a: οὐκ ἔστιν ὧδε, ἠγέρθη γάρ 'he is not here, for he is risen' Mt 28.6; οὐ γὰρ ἔχομεν ὧδε μένουσαν πόλιν 'there is no permanent city for us here (on earth)' He 13.14; ἀνάβα ὧδε, καὶ δείξω σοι ἃ δεῖ γενέσθαι μετὰ ταῦτα 'come up here and I will show you what must happen hereafter' Re 4.1.
ἐνθάδε: ἔχετέ τι βρώσιμον ἐνθάδε; 'do you have anything to eat here?' Lk 24.41; οἱ τὴν οἰκουμένην ἀναστατώσαντες οὗτοι καὶ ἐνθάδε πάρεισιν 'those who have turned the world upside down have come here too' Ac 17.6; ὕπαγε

---

1 In Domain 83 'position' is to be understood as the location or place of a person or thing at a given time. It has nothing to do with stance, which is treated in Domain 17.

2 The spacial positions of 'here' and 'there' relate to the event of the discourse and normally involve the speaker or writer as the point of orientation. In some instances, however, it is the so-called 'viewpoint character' who constitutes the point of orientation.

φώνησον τὸν ἄνδρα σου καὶ ἐλθὲ ἐνθάδε 'go call your husband and come here' Jn 4.16.

Though ὧδε[a] and ἐνθάδε may seem to be rendered in some contexts as 'to here' or 'hither,' the semantic component of movement is not found in ὧδε[a] or ἐνθάδε, but in other words in the context indicating movement.

83.2 ἐκεῖ; ἐκεῖσε; ἐκείνης: a position relatively far from the speaker, writer, or viewpoint person – 'there, at that place.'[3]

ἐκεῖ: καθίσατε αὐτοῦ ἕως οὗ ἀπελθὼν ἐκεῖ προσεύξωμαι 'sit here while I go over there and pray' Mt 26.36.

ἐκεῖσε: ἐκεῖσε γὰρ τὸ πλοῖον ἦν ἀποφορτιζόμενον τὸν γόμον 'for there the ship was to unload its cargo' Ac 21.3; ἄξων καὶ τοὺς ἐκεῖσε ὄντας δεδεμένους εἰς Ἰερουσαλήμ 'to lead those who were there to Jerusalem in chains' Ac 22.5.

ἐκείνης: ἵνα ἴδῃ αὐτόν, ὅτι ἐκείνης ἤμελλεν διέρχεσθαι 'in order that he might see him because he was going to pass there' or '. . . along that way' Lk 19.4.

83.3 αὐτοῦ: a position either near or far from the speaker, writer, or viewpoint character – 'here, there.' εἰσίν τινες τῶν αὐτοῦ ἑστηκότων 'there are some of those standing here' Lk 9.27; κἀκείνους κατέλιπεν αὐτοῦ 'he left them there' Ac 18.19.

83.4 ἀλλαχοῦ: a position other than the one in the immediate context – 'elsewhere.' ἄγωμεν ἀλλαχοῦ 'let us go elsewhere' Mk 1.38.

B Where, Somewhere, Everywhere (83.5-83.8)

83.5 ὅπου[a]; οὗ[a]: a reference to a position in space (often used with ἐάν or ἄν 'ever,' 71.8, to mark an indefinite and unrestricted position in space) – 'where, wherever.'

ὅπου[a]: τὸν Ἰησοῦν ἀπήγαγον πρὸς Καϊάφαν τὸν ἀρχιερέα, ὅπου οἱ γραμματεῖς καὶ οἱ πρεσβύτεροι συνήχθησαν 'they took Jesus to Caiaphas, the High Priest, where the teachers of the Law

---

3 As in the case of ὧδε[a] and ἐνθάδε (83.1), the semantic component of movement is not necessarily found in ἐκεῖ, ἐκεῖσε, and ἐκείνης.

and the elders had gathered together' Mt 26.57; ἀκολουθήσω σοι ὅπου ἐὰν ἀπέρχῃ 'I will follow you wherever you go' Mt 8.19; οὗτοι οἱ ἀκολουθοῦντες τῷ ἀρνίῳ ὅπου ἂν ὑπάγῃ 'these are the ones who follow the Lamb wherever he goes' Re 14.4.

οὗ[a]: ἦλθεν εἰς Ναζαρά, οὗ ἦν τεθραμμένος 'he went to Nazareth, where he had been brought up' or '. . . where he had grown up' Lk 4.16.

83.6 ποῦ[a]: an interrogative reference to a position – 'where?' ποῦ ἐστιν ὁ τεχθεὶς βασιλεὺς τῶν Ἰουδαίων; 'where is the one born (to be) king of the Jews?' Mt 2.2; εἰπέ μοι ποῦ ἔθηκας αὐτόν 'tell me where you have put him' Jn 20.15; κύριε, ποῦ ὑπάγεις; 'where are you going, Lord?' Jn 13.36.

83.7 πού[a]: an indefinite position in space – 'somewhere.' διεμαρτύρατο δέ πού τις λέγων 'as it says somewhere (in the Scriptures)' or literally 'as someone testified somewhere, saying' He 2.6; φοβούμενοί τε μή που κατὰ τραχεῖς τόπους ἐκπέσωμεν 'we were afraid that we would land somewhere on a rocky place' Ac 27.29.

83.8 πανταχῇ; πανταχοῦ; πάντοθεν[b]; πάντῃ: all possible positions – 'everywhere, anywhere, all over.'

πανταχῇ: πάντας πανταχῇ διδάσκων 'teaching all people everywhere' Ac 21.28.

πανταχοῦ: νῦν παραγγέλλει τοῖς ἀνθρώποις πάντας πανταχοῦ μετανοεῖν 'now he commands all people everywhere to repent' Ac 17.30.

πάντοθεν[b]: περικεκαλυμμένην πάντοθεν χρυσίῳ 'covered everywhere with gold' or 'covered all over with gold' He 9.4.

πάντῃ: πάντῃ τε καὶ πανταχοῦ ἀποδεχόμεθα 'we acknowledge (this) anywhere and everywhere' Ac 24.3. The expression πάντῃ τε καὶ πανταχοῦ in Ac 24.3 is repetitive for the sake of emphasis. Some scholars, however, interpret πάντῃ in Ac 24.3 as 'at all times,' in which case Ac 24.3 would be a rare example of this meaning of πάντῃ in Greek.

C Among, Between, In, Inside (83.9-83.17)

83.9 μέσος[a], η, ον; ἀνὰ μέσον[a]; ἐντός[a]; ἐν[b]; μετά[h]; εἰς[e]; ἐπί[c]; πρός[d]; παρά[b]: a position within an area determined by other objects and distributed among such objects – 'among, with.'[4]

μέσος[a]:[5] μέσος ὑμῶν ἔστηκεν ὃν ὑμεῖς οὐκ οἴδατε 'among you stands one you do not know' Jn 1.26; ἀφοριοῦσιν τοὺς πονηροὺς ἐκ μέσου τῶν δικαίων 'gather the evil from among the good' Mt 13.49; ἐν μέσῳ ὑμῶν 'in your midst' 1 Th 2.7.[6]

ἀνὰ μέσον[a]: ἐπέσπειρεν ζιζάνια ἀνὰ μέσον τοῦ σίτου 'he sowed weeds among the wheat' Mt 13.25.

ἐντός[a]: ἡ βασιλεία τοῦ θεοῦ ἐντὸς ὑμῶν ἐστιν 'the kingdom of God is among you' or '. . . in your midst' Lk 17.21. For another interpretation of ἐντός in Lk 17.21, see discussion at 26.1.

ἐν[b]: προφήτης μέγας ἠγέρθη ἐν ἡμῖν 'a great prophet has appeared among us' Lk 7.16.

μετά[h]: τί ζητεῖτε τὸν ζῶντα μετὰ τῶν νεκρῶν; 'why do you seek the living among the dead?' Lk 24.5.

εἰς[c]: ὁ δὲ εἰς τὰς ἀκάνθας σπαρείς 'the seed that fell among thorns' Mt 13.22; ἀλλ' ἵνα μὴ ἐπὶ πλεῖον διανεμηθῇ εἰς τὸν λαόν 'but in order to keep this from spreading further among the people' Ac 4.17.

ἐπί[c]: χρόνῳ ᾧ εἰσῆλθεν καὶ ἐξῆλθεν ἐφ' ἡμᾶς ὁ κύριος Ἰησοῦς 'the time during which the Lord Jesus went in and out among us' or '. . . went about with us' Ac 1.21.

πρός[d]: αἱ ἀδελφαὶ αὐτοῦ οὐχὶ πᾶσαι πρὸς ἡμᾶς εἰσιν; 'are not all his sisters among us?' Mt 13.56.

παρά[b]: διεφημίσθη ὁ λόγος οὗτος παρὰ Ἰουδαίοις 'this account was spread among the Jews' Mt 28.15.

---

4 There are no doubt certain subtle distinctions in the meanings of the terms in 83.9. For example, πρός[d] may suggest some kind of interaction or response and παρά[b] may focus upon association, but it is difficult, if not impossible, on the basis of existing contexts to define precisely the differences in meaning.

5 In some contexts the meanings of μέσος[a] (83.9) and μέσος[b] (83.10) may be said to overlap, or the situation may be such as to provide two different interpretations. For example, in Mt 10.16 'sheep in the midst of wolves' may mean that the sheep are completely surrounded by wolves or that the wolves intermingle with the sheep.

6 One can perhaps best interpret the relationship between ἐν and μέσῳ in the phrase ἐν μέσῳ in 1 Th 2.7 as one of redundant reinforcing, since ἐν can also be understood in the sense of 'among, with.'

83.10 μέσος[b], η, ον; ἀνὰ μέσον[b]: a position in the middle of an area (either an object in the midst of other objects or an area in the middle of a larger area) – 'in the middle, in the midst.'

μέσος[b]:[5] τὸ δὲ πλοῖον ἤδη ἦν εἰς μέσον τῆς θαλάσσης 'the ship was already in the middle of the lake' Mt 14.24 (apparatus); περιαφάντων δὲ πῦρ ἐν μέσῳ τῆς αὐλῆς 'a fire had been lit in the center of the courtyard' Lk 22.55; ὠρχήσατο . . . ἐν τῷ μέσῳ 'danced . . . in the middle (of the whole group)' Mt 14.6; ἐσχίσθη δὲ τὸ καταπέτασμα τοῦ ναοῦ μέσον 'the curtain in the Temple was torn in two in the middle' Lk 23.45.

ἀνὰ μέσον[b]: τὸ ἀρνίον τὸ ἀνὰ μέσον τοῦ θρόνου 'the Lamb in the midst of the throne' or 'the Lamb in the middle of the throne area' Re 7.17.

83.11 μεταξύ[a]: a position defined by the location of two objects, one on each side – 'between.' τοῦ ἀπολομένου μεταξὺ τοῦ θυσιαστηρίου καὶ τοῦ οἴκου 'who was killed between the altar and the Temple' Lk 11.51; κοιμώμενος μεταξὺ δύο στρατιωτῶν 'he was sleeping between two guards' Ac 12.6.

83.12 κατά[e]: a variety of positions distributed throughout an area or among a number of objects – 'throughout, among.'[7] τοὺς κατὰ τὰ ἔθνη πάντας Ἰουδαίους 'all the Jews who are among the Gentiles' Ac 21.21; ἡ μὲν οὖν ἐκκλησία καθ' ὅλης τῆς Ἰουδαίας καὶ Γαλιλαίας καὶ Σαμαρείας 'the church throughout all of Judea, Galilee, and Samaria' Ac 9.31; διήρχοντο κατὰ τὰς κώμας εὐαγγελιζόμενοι 'they travelled throughout the villages, preaching the good news' Lk 9.6.

83.13 ἔσω; ἐν[a]; εἰς[d]: a position defined as being within certain limits – 'inside, within, in.'[8]

---

7 κατά[e] differs in meaning from μέσος[a], ἀνὰ μέσον[a], ἐντός[a], ἐν[b], μετά[h], εἰς[c], ἐπί[c], πρός[d], and παρά[b] (83.9) in that the focus of meaning is upon distribution rather than upon inclusion within any defined area or set.

8 In contexts where an accompanying expression designates movement into an area, ἐν[a] and εἰς[d] may be rendered as 'into.'

ἔσω: ἀνοίξαντες δὲ ἔσω οὐδένα εὕρομεν 'when we opened (the gate), we did not find anyone inside' Ac 5.23; εἰσελθὼν ἔσω 'he went into (the courtyard)' Mt 26.58.

ἐν[a]: ὃς τὴν κατοίκησιν εἶχεν ἐν τοῖς μνήμασιν 'who lived in the tombs' Mk 5.3. Some translations render Mk 5.3 as 'he lived among the graves,' but it is likely that the Greek expression refers to living within relatively elaborate tombs. κηρύσσων ἐν τῇ ἐρήμῳ τῆς Ἰουδαίας 'preaching in the desert of Judea' Mt 3.1; ὅτι οὕτως διαλογίζονται ἐν ἑαυτοῖς 'because they were reasoning this way within themselves' Mk 2.8. In Mk 2.8 it is also possible to understand the phrase ἐν ἑαυτοῖς as meaning 'among themselves' (see ἐν[b], 83.9). ἔγραψα ὑμῖν ἐν τῇ ἐπιστολῇ 'I wrote to you in the letter' 1 Cor 5.9. It may not be possible in some languages to speak of a part of a document as being 'in' something. It may, therefore, be necessary to render this expression in 1 Cor 5.9 as 'part of what I wrote to you about was . . .'

εἰς[d]: τὰ παιδία μου μετ' ἐμοῦ εἰς τὴν κοίτην εἰσίν 'my children are with me in bed' Lk 11.7; πρῶτον δὲ ἐπίτρεψόν μοι ἀποτάξασθαι τοῖς εἰς τὸν οἶκόν μου 'but first let me say goodbye to those in my home' Lk 9.61.

83.14 καρδία[b], ας f: (a figurative extension of meaning of καρδία 'heart,' not occurring in the NT in its literal sense) a location deep within a larger area – 'depths, far inside.' ἐν τῇ καρδίᾳ τῆς γῆς τρεῖς ἡμέρας καὶ τρεῖς νύκτας 'three days and nights in the depths of the earth' or '. . . far within the earth' Mt 12.40.

83.15 ἐσώτερος, α, ον: pertaining to a position within an area – 'inner, far within.' ἔβαλεν αὐτοὺς εἰς τὴν ἐσωτέραν φυλακήν 'he threw them into the inner cell' Ac 16.24; εἰς τὸ ἐσώτερον τοῦ καταπετάσματος 'into the inner sanctuary' or 'into the inner part of the curtained-off area' He 6.19.

83.16 ἔσωθεν[b]: the inner surface of an object – 'within, on the inside.' βιβλίον γεγραμμένον ἔσωθεν καὶ ὄπισθεν 'a scroll written on the inside and on the outside' Re 5.1; οὐχ ὁ ποιήσας τὸ ἔξωθεν καὶ τὸ ἔσωθεν ἐποίησεν; 'did not he who made the outside also make the inside?' Lk 11.40.

83.17 ἐντός[b]: pertaining to being within an area – 'the contents of, that which is inside.' καθάρισον πρῶτον τὸ ἐντὸς τοῦ ποτηρίου 'clean what is inside the cup first' Mt 23.26. It is also possible, though not probable, to understand ἐντός in Mt 23.26 as the inside surface itself rather than the contents.

D Around, About, Outside (83.18-83.22)

83.18 περί[a]; πέριξ: a position or a series of positions around an area, but not necessarily involving complete encirclement – 'around.'
περί[a]: Σόδομα καὶ Γόμορρα καὶ αἱ περὶ αὐτὰς πόλεις 'Sodom and Gomorrah and the towns around them' Jd 7; ζώνην δερματίνην περὶ τὴν ὀσφὺν αὐτοῦ 'a leather belt around his waist' Mt 3.4.
πέριξ: τὸ πλῆθος τῶν πέριξ πόλεων Ἰερουσαλήμ 'the crowd from the towns around Jerusalem' Ac 5.16.

83.19 κύκλῳ; κυκλόθεν[a]: a position completely encircling an area or object – 'around, in a circle.'
κύκλῳ: καὶ περιῆγεν τὰς κώμας κύκλῳ 'then he went to the villages around there' Mk 6.6; περιβλεψάμενος τοὺς περὶ αὐτὸν κύκλῳ καθημένους 'looking around at those seated around him in a circle' Mk 3.34; κύκλῳ τοῦ θρόνου 'in a circle around the throne' Re 4.6.
κυκλόθεν[a]: ἶρις κυκλόθεν τοῦ θρόνου 'around the throne there was a rainbow' Re 4.3; κυκλόθεν τοῦ θρόνου θρόνους εἴκοσι τέσσαρες 'in a circle around the throne were twenty-four other thrones' Re 4.4.

83.20 ἔξω[a]; ἔξωθεν[b]; ἐκτός[a]: a position not contained within a particular area – 'outside, apart from.'
ἔξω[a]: ἡ μήτηρ καὶ οἱ ἀδελφοὶ αὐτοῦ εἱστήκεισαν ἔξω 'his mother and his brothers stood outside' Mt 12.46; ἐξήλθομεν ἔξω τῆς πύλης παρὰ ποταμόν 'we went outside the gate to the riverside' Ac 16.13. It is also possible to understand ἔξω in Ac 16.13 as involving extension (see 84.27).
ἔξωθεν[b]: ἡ ληνὸς ἔξωθεν τῆς πόλεως 'the winepress outside the city' Re 14.20.
ἐκτός[a]: εἴτε ἐκτὸς τοῦ σώματος οὐκ οἶδα 'whether outside of the body, I do not know' 2 Cor 12.2.

83.21 ἔξωθεν^c; ἐκτός^b; ὄπισθεν^c: the outside surface of an object – 'on the outside, outside of.'

ἔξωθεν^c: τάφοις κεκονιαμένοις, οἵτινες ἔξωθεν μὲν φαίνονται ὡραῖοι 'whitewashed tombs which look fine on the outside' Mt 23.27; καθαρίζετε τὸ ἔξωθεν τοῦ ποτηρίου καὶ τῆς παροψίδος 'you clean the outside of your cup and plate' Mt 23.25.

ἐκτός^b: καὶ τὸ ἐκτὸς αὐτοῦ καθαρόν 'then the outside of the (cup will be) clean' Mt 23.26.

ὄπισθεν^c: βιβλίον γεγραμμένον ἔσωθεν καὶ ὄπισθεν 'a scroll written on the inside and on the outside' Re 5.1.

The manner in which ἔξωθεν^c, ἐκτός^b, and ὄπισθεν^c may be rendered in particular contexts depends very largely upon what is being spoken about. For example, ἔξωθεν in 1 Pe 3.3 refers to the outward aids employed in making oneself beautiful, but instead of speaking of such objects as being 'on the surface' or 'on the outside,' it may be necessary to speak of 'those things which one puts on the body' or 'what one wears.'

83.22 κυκλόθεν^b: a position on the total outside surface of a three-dimensional object – 'outside, on the outside.' κυκλόθεν καὶ ἔσωθεν γέμουσιν ὀφθαλμῶν 'they were covered with eyes on the outside and on the inside' Re 4.8.

E At, Beside, Near, Far (83.23-83.32)

83.23 ἐπί^b; ἐν^d: a position in proximity to or in the immediate vicinity of an object or other position – 'at, by.'

ἐπί^b: καθήμενον ἐπὶ τὸ τελώνιον 'sitting at the place of customs' Mt 9.9; ἔσθητε καὶ πίνητε ἐπὶ τῆς τραπέζης μου 'you will eat and drink at my table' Lk 22.30; ἐφανέρωσεν ἑαυτὸν πάλιν ὁ Ἰησοῦς τοῖς μαθηταῖς ἐπὶ τῆς θαλάσσης τῆς Τιβεριάδος 'Jesus showed himself once more to his disciples at Lake Tiberias' Jn 21.1; ἰδοὺ ἔστηκα ἐπὶ τὴν θύραν καὶ κρούω 'behold, I stand at the door and knock' Re 3.20.

ἐν^d: καθίσας ἐν δεξιᾷ αὐτοῦ 'seated him at his right hand' Eph 1.20. See also 87.36 for the idiom involved in this expression in Eph 1.20.

83.24 πρός^c: a position near another location or object, often with the implication of facing toward – 'at, by.' ὁ δὲ Πέτρος εἱστήκει πρὸς τῇ θύρᾳ ἔξω 'Peter stayed outside at the gate' Jn 18.16; ἦν ὅλη ἡ πόλις ἐπισυνηγμένη πρὸς τὴν θύραν 'all the people gathered at the door' Mk 1.33; ἔθαψαν πρὸς τὸν ἄνδρα αὐτῆς 'they buried her beside her husband' Ac 5.10.

83.25 παρά^a: a position near another location or object, usually with the implication of being alongside or close to – 'at, by, alongside, beside.' εἱστήκεισαν δὲ παρὰ τῷ σταυρῷ τοῦ Ἰησοῦ 'standing beside Jesus' cross' Jn 19.25; ἔστησεν αὐτὸ παρ᾽ ἑαυτῷ 'he stood him at his side' Lk 9.47; δύο τυφλοὶ καθήμενοι παρὰ τὴν ὁδόν 'two blind men who were sitting beside the road' Mt 20.30; τῇ τε ἡμέρᾳ τῶν σαββάτων ἐξήλθομεν ἔξω τῆς πύλης παρὰ ποταμὸν οὗ ἐνομίζομεν προσευχὴν εἶναι 'on the Sabbath we went out of the city gate to a place beside the river where we thought there would be a place of prayer' Ac 16.13.[9]

83.26 ἐγγύς^a: a position relatively close to another position – 'near, nearby.' ἐν Αἰνὼν ἐγγὺς τοῦ Σαλείμ 'in Aenon near Salem' Jn 3.23.

83.27 πλησίον^a: a position quite close to another position, with the possible implication of being contiguous – 'quite near, nearby.' πλησίον τοῦ χωρίου ὃ ἔδωκεν Ἰακώβ 'close by the field that Jacob had given' Jn 4.5.

83.28 ἆσσον: a position extremely close to another position – 'very near, as close as possible.' ἆσσον παρελέγοντο τὴν Κρήτην 'they sailed as close as possible along (the coast of) Crete' Ac 27.13.

83.29 ἐχόμενος, η, ον: (a participial form of ἔχω^a 'to have,' 57.1) a position contiguous to another position – 'neighboring.' εἰς τὰς ἐχομένας κωμοπόλεις 'to the neighboring villages' Mk 1.38.

---

9 Rather than set up a special meaning of παρά as 'to a point beside,' it seems far better to understand παρά in Ac 16.13 as meaning simply 'beside' and to assume an ellipsis of some verb of movement which could be readily omitted in view of the preceding ἐξήλθομεν.

83.30 μακράν; μακρόθεν: a position at a relatively great distance from another position – 'far, at a distance, some distance away, far away.'[10]

μακράν: ἔτι δὲ αὐτοῦ μακρὰν ἀπέχοντος 'he was still a long way from home' Lk 15.20; ἐγὼ εἰς ἔθνη μακρὰν ἐξαποστελῶ σε 'I will send you far away to the Gentiles' Ac 22.21; ὑμῖν γάρ ἐστιν ἡ ἐπαγγελία καὶ τοῖς τέκνοις ὑμῶν καὶ πᾶσιν τοῖς εἰς μακράν 'for the promise is to you and to your children and to all who are far away' Ac 2.39. For εἰς in Ac 2.39, see 84.16.

μακρόθεν: ὁ δὲ τελώνης μακρόθεν ἑστώς 'but the tax collector stood at a distance' Lk 18.13; εἰστήκεισαν δὲ πάντες οἱ γνωστοὶ αὐτῷ ἀπὸ μακρόθεν 'all those who knew him stood at a distance' Lk 23.49; ὁ δὲ Πέτρος ἠκολούθει μακρόθεν 'Peter followed at a distance' Lk 22.54; ἀπὸ μακρόθεν θεωροῦσαι 'looking on from a distance' Mt 27.55.

83.31 πόρρω; πόρρωθεν[b]: a position at a relatively great distance, with the possible implication of comparison – 'far away, at a distance, a long way off.'[11]

πόρρω: ἔτι αὐτοῦ πόρρω ὄντος 'while he was still a long way off' Lk 14.32.

πόρρωθεν[b]: οἳ ἔστησαν πόρρωθεν, καὶ αὐτοὶ ἦραν φωνὴν λέγοντες 'they stood at a distance and shouted' Lk 17.12-13; ἀλλὰ πόρρωθεν αὐτὰς ἰδόντες καὶ ἀσπασάμενοι 'but from a long way off they saw and welcomed them' He 11.13. In He 11.13 πόρρωθεν may be interpreted as time (see 67.46), but it is perhaps more satisfactorily interpreted as implying some visionary experience and hence a matter of space.

83.32 πορρώτερον: a position at an even greater distance than πόρρω 'far away' (83.31) – 'further, farther.'[12] αὐτὸς προσεποιήσατο

πορρώτερον πορεύεσθαι 'he acted as if he were going farther' Lk 24.28.

F In Front Of, Face To Face, In Back Of, Behind (83.33-83.41)

83.33 ἔμπροσθεν[a]; ἐνώπιον[a]; ἐναντίον[a]; ἔναντι[a]; κατενώπιον[a]; πρό[a]; πρόσωπον[f], ου n: a position in front of an object, whether animate or inanimate, which is regarded as having a spacial orientation of front and back – 'in front of, before.'[13]

ἔμπροσθεν[a]: ἄφες ἐκεῖ τὸ δῶρόν σου ἔμπροσθεν τοῦ θυσιαστηρίου 'leave your gift there in front of the altar' Mt 5.24; ὁ δὲ Ἰησοῦς ἐστάθη ἔμπροσθεν τοῦ ἡγεμόνος 'Jesus stood before the governor' Mt 27.11; ἐξῆλθεν ἔμπροσθεν πάντων 'he went away in front of everyone' or '. . . while they all watched' Mk 2.12.

ἐνώπιον[a]: ἰδοὺ ἀνὴρ ἔστη ἐνώπιόν μου 'suddenly a man stood in front of me' Ac 10.30; ἐγώ εἰμι Γαβριὴλ ὁ παρεστηκὼς ἐνώπιον τοῦ θεοῦ 'I am Gabriel, who stands before God' Lk 1.19.

ἐναντίον[a]: ὡς ἀμνὸς ἐναντίον τοῦ κείραντος αὐτὸν ἄφωνος 'like a lamb dumb before its shearer' Ac 8.32.

ἔναντι[a]: ἱερατεύειν . . . ἔναντι τοῦ θεοῦ 'serving as a priest . . . before God' Lk 1.8.

κατενώπιον[a]: κατενώπιον τῆς δόξης αὐτοῦ ἀμώμους ἐν ἀγαλλιάσει 'faultless and joyful before his glorious presence' Jd 24.

πρό[a]: ἑστάναι τὸν Πέτρον πρὸ τοῦ πυλῶνος 'Peter stood in front of the gate' Ac 12.14.

πρόσωπον[f]: τῶν ἐθνῶν ὧν ἐξῶσεν ὁ θεὸς ἀπὸ προσώπου τῶν πατέρων ἡμῶν 'the nations that God drove out in front of our ancestors' (literally '. . . from the face of our ancestors') Ac 7.45; ἀπέστειλεν αὐτοὺς . . . πρὸ προσώπου αὐτοῦ 'he sent them out . . . (to go) ahead of him' Lk 10.1.

83.34 κατ' ὀφθαλμούς (an idiom, literally 'according to eyes'); κατὰ πρόσωπον[a] (an idiom, literally 'according to face'): a position in front of an object, with the implication of

---

10 μακρόθεν may differ somewhat from μακράν in emphasizing the separation of one location from another, but such a distinction is not always borne out in the various contexts.

11 It is possible that πόρρωθεν[b] differs in meaning from πόρρω in emphasizing the degree of separation, but this cannot be determined from existing contexts.

12 πορρώτερον may be regarded simply as a comparative form of πόρρω, and hence πορρώτερον could be combined with πόρρω and πόρρωθεν[b] in 83.31.

13 There are no doubt certain slight differences of meaning in this series (83.33), but such distinctions cannot be readily determined from existing contexts.

direct sight – 'in front of, before, to the face of, in the presence of.'

κατ' ὀφθαλμούς: οἷς κατ' ὀφθαλμοὺς Ἰησοῦς Χριστὸς προεγράφη ἐσταυρωμένος 'before whom Jesus Christ was depicted as crucified' Ga 3.1.

κατὰ πρόσωπον^a: ὃ ἡτοίμασας κατὰ πρόσωπον πάντων τῶν λαῶν 'which you prepared in the presence of all peoples' Lk 2.31.

83.35 ἐπί^d: a position before, with the implication of a relationship of authority – 'before.' Καίσαρα ἐπικέκλησαι, ἐπὶ Καίσαρα πορεύσῃ 'you appeal to Caesar, you will go before Caesar' Ac 25.12; ἐπὶ ἡγεμόνας δὲ καὶ βασιλεῖς ἀχθήσεσθε 'you will be brought before governors and kings' Mt 10.18.

83.36 ἔμπροσθεν^b: a position on the front surface of an object – 'in front, on the front.' γέμοντα ὀφθαλμῶν ἔμπροσθεν καὶ ὄπισθεν 'full of eyes in front and in back' or '. . . on the front and on the back' Re 4.6.

83.37 πρόσωπον πρὸς πρόσωπον: (an idiom, literally 'face to face') the position of one person facing another, with the implication of direct, personal interaction – 'face to face.' τότε δὲ πρόσωπον πρὸς πρόσωπον 'but then face to face' 1 Cor 13.12. The implication of this idiom in 1 Cor 13.12 is that there will be clear understanding, and in some languages it is necessary to shift somewhat the figurative expression. For example, it may be necessary to render this passage as 'how we now understand is like seeing a dim image in a mirror, but then we shall understand as clearly as though we were seeing face to face' or '. . . as though we were seeing something directly.'

83.38 κατὰ πρόσωπον^b: (an idiom, literally 'according to face') the position of one person facing another, with or without the implication of opposition – 'face to face, in person, to one's face.' πρὶν ἢ ὁ κατηγορούμενος κατὰ πρόσωπον ἔχοι τοὺς κατηγόρους 'before he has met his accusers face to face' Ac 25.16; κατὰ πρόσωπον αὐτῷ ἀντέστην 'I opposed him to his face' Ga 2.11; ὃς κατὰ πρόσωπον μὲν ταπεινὸς ἐν ὑμῖν '(I) who am mild when with you in person' 2 Cor 10.1.

83.39 στόμα πρὸς στόμα: (an idiom, literally 'mouth to mouth') the position of persons facing one another and engaged in discussion – 'face to face, person to person.' γενέσθαι πρὸς ὑμᾶς καὶ στόμα πρὸς στόμα λαλῆσαι 'to visit you and talk to you face to face' 2 Jn 12.

83.40 ὀπίσω^a: a position behind an object or other position – 'behind, in back of.' στᾶσα ὀπίσω παρὰ τοὺς πόδας αὐτοῦ 'she stood at his feet behind him' Lk 7.38; ἤκουσα ὀπίσω μου φωνὴν μεγάλην 'I heard a loud voice behind me' Re 1.10.

83.41 ὄπισθεν^b: a position on the back surface of an object – 'the back of, in back of, on the back of.' γέμοντα ὀφθαλμῶν ἔμπροσθεν καὶ ὄπισθεν 'covered with eyes in front and in back' Re 4.6.

G Opposite, Over Against, Across From, Offshore From[14] (83.42-83.45)

83.42 ἀπέναντι^a; κατέναντι^a; ἐξ ἐναντίας^a: a position over against an object or other position – 'opposite, in front of, before, across from, in the presence of.'

ἀπέναντι^a: ἔδωκεν αὐτῷ τὴν ὁλοκληρίαν ταύτην ἀπέναντι πάντων ὑμῶν 'made him well like this before you all' Ac 3.16; ἀπενίψατο τὰς χεῖρας ἀπέναντι τοῦ ὄχλου 'he washed his hands in front of the crowd' Mt 27.24.

κατέναντι^a: πορεύεσθε εἰς τὴν κώμην τὴν κατέναντι ὑμῶν 'go into the village opposite you' Mt 21.2; τὸ ὄρος τῶν Ἐλαιῶν κατέναντι τοῦ ἱεροῦ 'the Mount of Olives, across from the Temple' Mk 13.3; ὡς ἐξ εἰλικρινείας . . . κατέναντι θεοῦ . . . λαλοῦμεν 'we speak . . . with sincerity . . . in God's presence' 2 Cor 2.17.[15]

ἐξ ἐναντίας^a: παρεστηκὼς ἐξ ἐναντίας αὐτοῦ 'standing there opposite (the cross)' Mk 15.39.

---

14 The meanings in this subdomain differ from those of the previous subdomains in emphasizing the contrast of position.

15 It is possible, as in the case of 2 Cor 2.17, for the implication of contrast to be somewhat neutralized in particular contexts.

83.43 πέραν; ἀντιπέρα: a position opposite another position, with something intervening – 'opposite, across from, on the other side of.'

πέραν: ἀπῆλθεν ὁ Ἰησοῦς πέραν τῆς θαλάσσης τῆς Γαλιλαίας 'Jesus went back to the other side of Lake Galilee' Jn 6.1; εὑρόντες αὐτὸν πέραν τῆς θαλάσσης 'they found him on the other side of the lake' Jn 6.25; πέραν τοῦ Ἰορδάνου '(the land) on the other side of the Jordan' Mt 4.25.

ἀντιπέρα: κατέπλευσαν εἰς τὴν χώραν τῶν Γερασηνῶν, ἥτις ἐστὶν ἀντιπέρα τῆς Γαλιλαίας 'they went to the country of the Gergesenes, which is across from Galilee' or '. . . across the lake from Galilee' Lk 8.26.

83.44 ἄντικρυς; κατά[f]: a position directly opposite and implying some space between – 'opposite, off, offshore from.'

ἄντικρυς: κατηντήσαμεν ἄντικρυς Χίου 'we arrived off Chios' Ac 20.15. This expression in Ac 20.15 may be rendered in a number of languages as 'we arrived near Chios.'

κατά[f]: τό τε πέλαγος τὸ κατὰ τὴν Κιλικίαν καὶ Παμφυλίαν διαπλεύσαντες 'we crossed over the sea off Cilicia and Pamphylia' Ac 27.5;[16] γενόμενοι κατὰ τὴν Κνίδον 'we arrived off Cnidus' Ac 27.7.

83.45 κατά[d]: the position of an object oriented toward a particular direction – 'facing, toward.' λιμένα τῆς Κρήτης βλέποντα κατὰ λίβα καὶ κατὰ χῶρον 'a harbor of Crete facing toward the southwest and northwest' Ac 27.12; πορεύου κατὰ μεσημβρίαν 'go toward the south' Ac 8.26; κατὰ σκοπὸν διώκω 'I run straight toward the goal' Php 3.14. For κατὰ σκοπὸν διώκω as an idiom, see 89.56.

H On, Upon, On the Surface Of (83.46-83.47)

83.46 ἐπί[a]: a position on a surface of an object, whether vertical or horizontal, and in contact with the object – 'on, upon.'

16 It is possible that κατά in Ac 27.5 refers to a position parallel with the coast and possibly involving a type of extension.

περιπατῶν ἐπὶ τῆς θαλάσσης 'walking on the water' Mk 6.48; διεχειρίσασθε κρεμάσαντες ἐπὶ ξύλου 'you killed him by nailing him upon a cross' Ac 5.30; ἐπὶ τὰς κεφαλὰς αὐτῶν στεφάνους χρυσοῦς '(wearing) gold crowns on their heads' Re 4.4; ἐπέταξεν αὐτοῖς ἀνακλῖναι πάντας συμπόσια συμπόσια ἐπὶ τῷ χλωρῷ χόρτῳ 'he ordered them all to recline in groups on the green grass' Mk 6.39; πόθεν τούτους δυνήσεταί τις ὧδε χορτάσαι ἄρτων ἐπ' ἐρημίας; 'where on this desert can anyone (find enough) food to feed these people?' Mk 8.4; ἵνα μὴ μείνῃ ἐπὶ τοῦ σταυροῦ τὰ σώματα 'in order that the bodies would not remain on the crosses' Jn 19.31; οὐ μὴ ἀφεθῇ ὧδε λίθος ἐπὶ λίθον 'here one stone will not be left on another' Mt 24.2.

83.47 ἐν[c]; εἰς[c]: a position on the surface of an area – 'on, at.'

ἐν[c]: κατὰ τὸν τύπον τὸν δειχθέντα σοι ἐν τῷ ὄρει 'according to the pattern you were shown on the mountain' He 8.5; φιλοῦσιν . . . ἐν ταῖς γωνίαις τῶν πλατειῶν ἑστῶτες προσεύχεσθαι 'they love . . . to stand up and pray on the street corners' Mt 6.5; οὐκ ἐν πλαξὶν λιθίναις ἀλλ' ἐν πλαξὶν καρδίαις σαρκίναις 'not on tablets of stone but on tablets of the human heart' 2 Cor 3.3. In a number of languages it may be quite impossible to speak of 'tablets of the human heart.' An equivalent may be 'in the human heart' or 'in people's hearts.' In some languages, however, it may be necessary to substitute 'mind,' for example, 'in people's minds.'

εἰς[c]: καὶ ἐμπτύσαντες εἰς αὐτὸν ἔλαβον τὸν κάλαμον καὶ ἔτυπτον εἰς τὴν κεφαλὴν αὐτοῦ 'and spit on him and took a reed and beat him on the head' Mt 27.30; ὅστις σε ῥαπίζει εἰς τὴν δεξιὰν σιαγόνα σου 'whoever hits you on the right cheek' Mk 5.39.

I Above, Below (83.48-83.54)

83.48 ἄνω[a]: a position above, often with the point of orientation left implicit – 'up, above.' ἐγὼ ἐκ τῶν ἄνω εἰμί 'I am from above' Jn 8.23; δώσω τέρατα ἐν τῷ οὐρανῷ ἄνω 'I will perform miracles in the sky above' Ac 2.19; καὶ ἐγέμισαν αὐτὰς ἕως ἄνω 'and they filled them up to the top' Jn 2.7. In Jn 2.7 ἄνω could be defined as that position above the point where liquid would normally be when an object was full.

83.49 ὑπεράνω^a; ἐπάνω^a: a position above another, whether or not in contact – 'above, over, on, upon.'

ὑπεράνω^a: ὑπεράνω δὲ αὐτῆς Χερουβὶν δόξης κατασκιάζοντα τὸ ἱλαστήριον 'above it the glorious cherubim overshadowing the place of atonement' He 9.5.

ἐπάνω^a: ἐπέθηκαν ἐπάνω τῆς κεφαλῆς αὐτοῦ τὴν αἰτίαν αὐτοῦ γεγραμμένην 'they placed above his head the written accusation against him' Mt 27.37; πατεῖν ἐπάνω ὄφεων καὶ σκορπίων 'you can walk on snakes and scorpions' Lk 10.19; ἀπεκύλισεν τὸν λίθον καὶ ἐκάθητο ἐπάνω αὐτοῦ 'he rolled away the stone and sat upon it' Mt 28.2.

83.50 ὑψηλότερος, α, ον (comparative of ὑψηλός^a 'high,' 81.6): a position above another, on the basis of being higher – 'above, higher than.' ὑψηλότερος τῶν οὐρανῶν γενόμενος 'being above the heavens' He 7.26.

83.51 ὑπό^a; ὑποκάτω^a: a position below another position or object – 'under.'

ὑπό^a: ὄντα ὑπὸ τὴν συκῆν εἶδόν σε 'I saw you when you were under the fig tree' Jn 1.48; μήτι ἔρχεται ὁ λύχνος ἵνα ὑπὸ τὸν μόδιον τεθῇ 'does anyone ever bring in a lamp and put it under a container' Mk 4.21.

ὑποκάτω^a: καὶ τὰ κυνάρια ὑποκάτω τῆς τραπέζης ἐσθίουσιν ἀπὸ τῶν ψιχίων τῶν παιδίων 'even the dogs under the table eat the children's leftovers' Mk 7.28; εἶδόν σε ὑποκάτω τῆς συκῆς 'I saw you when you were under the fig tree' Jn 1.50.

83.52 ὑποκάτω^b: a position on the undersurface of an object – 'under, on.' ἐκτινάξατε τὸν χοῦν τὸν ὑποκάτω τῶν ποδῶν ὑμῶν 'shake off the dust under your feet' or '. . . on your feet' Mk 6.11.

83.53 κάτω^a: a position immediately or directly below a point of orientation, which is often left implicit – 'below.' ὑμεῖς ἐκ τῶν κάτω ἐστέ 'you are from below' Jn 8.23; δώσω . . . σημεῖα ἐπὶ τῆς γῆς κάτω 'I will perform . . . marvels on the earth below' Ac 2.19. In a number of languages it is not possible to speak of something 'below' without indicating precisely what is involved, but in the case of Ac 2.19 it would be irrelevant to say 'marvels on the earth below the sky.' Therefore, one may perhaps most satisfactorily translate this expression in Ac 2.19 as 'marvels here on the earth.'

83.54 κατώτερος, α, ον: pertaining to being in a position below a point of orientation – 'low, lower.' κατέβη εἰς τὰ κατώτερα μέρη τῆς γῆς 'he went down into the lower parts of the earth' Eph 4.9. See discussion at 1.18.

J Beyond, On the Other Side Of (83.55-83.56)

83.55 ἐπέκεινα; ὑπερέκεινα: a position farther away than a reference point – 'beyond, farther away.'

ἐπέκεινα: μετοικιῶ ὑμᾶς ἐπέκεινα Βαβυλῶνος 'I will send you away (or '. . . deport you') beyond Babylon' Ac 7.43.

ὑπερέκεινα: εἰς τὰ ὑπερέκεινα ὑμῶν εὐαγγελίσασθαι 'to preach the good news in countries beyond you' 2 Cor 10.16.

83.56 μετάⁱ: a position farther away and behind some object – 'beyond, behind.' μετὰ δὲ τὸ δεύτερον καταπέτασμα 'behind the second veil' He 9.3.

84 Spacial Extensions[1]

Outline of Subdomains

A Extension From a Source (84.1-84.15)
B Extension To a Goal (84.16-84.28)
C Extension Along a Path (84.29-84.33)

A Extension From a Source (84.1-84.15)

84.1 νομή[b], ῆς f: (a figurative extension of meaning of νομή[a] 'pasture,' 1.98) extension of an area – 'extension, extend, spread, increase.' ὁ λόγος αὐτῶν ὡς γάγγραινα νομὴν ἕξει 'their teaching will spread like a cancer' 2 Tm 2.17.

84.2 διανέμω: to cause the spread or extension of something – 'to spread (a report).' ἀλλ' ἵνα μὴ ἐπὶ πλεῖον διανεμηθῇ εἰς τὸν λαόν 'but in order that this may not spread further among the people' Ac 4.17.

84.3 ἀπό[c]: extension from or away from a source – 'from, away from.' εἰς πάντα τὰ ἔθνη – ἀρξάμενοι ἀπὸ Ἰερουσαλήμ 'to all nations, beginning from Jerusalem' Lk 24.47; σημεῖον ἀπὸ τοῦ οὐρανοῦ 'a sign from heaven' Mk 8.11;[2] ὡς ἀπὸ σταδίων δεκαπέντε 'about fifteen stades away' Jn 11.18;[3] οὓς δὲ ἐπί τινων τῶν ἀπὸ τοῦ πλοίου 'and others on some of the things which came from the ship' Ac 27.44.

84.4 ἐκ[a]: extension from an area or space, usually with the implication of removal out of a delimited area – 'from, out from, out of.' σημεῖον ἐκ τοῦ οὐρανοῦ 'a sign from heaven' Mt 16.1;[2] αἱ γυναῖκες, αἵτινες ἦσαν συνεληλυθυῖαι ἐκ τῆς Γαλιλαίας αὐτῷ 'women who had followed him from Galilee' Lk 23.55.

84.5 παρά[c] (with the genitive case[4]): extension from a source which is actively involved in an activity or relation – 'from.' ὁ ὢν παρὰ τοῦ θεοῦ 'he is from God' or 'he comes from God' Jn 6.46; ἐξῆλθεν δόγμα παρὰ Καίσαρος Αὐγούστου 'a decree went out from Caesar Augustus' Lk 2.1; δύναμις παρ' αὐτοῦ ἐξήρχετο 'power was going out from him' Lk 6.19.

84.6 πόθεν[a]: extension from a source, with an incorporated interrogative point of reference – 'from where?, whence?, where?' πόθεν ἡμῖν . . . ἄρτοι τοσοῦτοι; 'where will we find . . . enough food?' Mt 15.33; οἶδα πόθεν ἦλθον καὶ ποῦ ὑπάγω 'I know where I came from and where I am going' Jn 8.14.

84.7 πάντοθεν[a]: extension from a source, involving all possible points – 'from everywhere, from all directions.' ἤρχοντο πρὸς αὐτὸν πάντοθεν 'they came to him from everywhere' Mk 1.45; συνέξουσίν σε πάντοθεν 'they will close in on you from every side' Lk 19.43.

84.8 ἀλλαχόθεν: extension from a source which is different – 'from elsewhere, from some other way.' μὴ εἰσερχόμενος διὰ τῆς θύρας . . . ἀλλὰ ἀναβαίνων ἀλλαχόθεν 'does not enter by the door, . . . but climbs in from some other way' Jn 10.1.

84.9 ἔνθεν; ἐντεῦθεν[a]: extension from a source, with the point of reference near the speaker – 'from here.'
ἔνθεν: διαβῆναι ἔνθεν 'to cross over from here' Lk 16.26.
ἐντεῦθεν[a]: βάλε σεαυτὸν ἐντεῦθεν κάτω 'throw yourself down from here' Lk 4.9.[5]

---

1 The meanings in Domain 84 *Spacial Extensions* may imply movement, but usually in a redundant manner. The actual movement is generally found in verb or noun expressions, which frequently incorporate redundantly the corresponding lexical units as prefixes.
2 In Mk 8.11 (see 84.3) and Mt 16.1 (see 84.4) there is a clear overlap of reference between ἀπό[c] and ἐκ[a].
3 In Jn 11.18 ἀπό with a statement of measurement may be analyzed as marking the extent of the measurement from a particular point.

4 The occurrence of a preposition with a particular case relationship may be described as an instance of a noncontiguous semantic unit in which both features join in signaling the meaning. But it is also possible to analyze such a relationship as one in which a case suffix marks the particular meaning which may be assigned to a preposition.
5 ἐντεῦθεν also occurs in the fixed phrase ἐντεῦθεν καὶ ἐντεῦθεν meaning 'on each side' as in Jn 19.18, καὶ μετ' αὐτοῦ ἄλλους δύο ἐντεῦθεν καὶ ἐντεῦθεν 'and with him two

84.10 ἐκεῖθεν and κἀκεῖθεν[a] (a contraction of καὶ ἐκεῖθεν): extension from a source which is away from the speaker – 'from there, from that place.' καὶ προβὰς ἐκεῖθεν 'and going on from there' Mt 4.21; παράγων ὁ Ἰησοῦς ἐκεῖθεν 'Jesus left that place' Mt 9.9; κἀκεῖθεν ἀπέπλευσαν 'and from there they sailed' Ac 14.26.

84.11 ὅθεν[a]: extension from a source to which the element ὁ- refers – 'from where, from there, from which.'[6] εἰς τὸν οἶκόν μου ἐπιστρέψω ὅθεν ἐξῆλθον 'I will go back to my house from which I left' Mt 12.44; ὅθεν περιελόντες 'from there we sailed on' Ac 28.13.

84.12 ὄπισθεν[a]: extension from a source which is behind – 'from behind, behind.' προσελθοῦσα ὄπισθεν 'she came up from behind (Jesus)' Mt 9.20; κράζει ὄπισθεν ἡμῶν 'she is crying out behind us' Mt 15.23.

84.13 ἄνωθεν[a]: extension from a source which is above – 'from above, from the top of.' ἦν δεδομένον σοι ἄνωθεν 'it was given to you from above' Jn 19.11; ἐσχίσθη εἰς δύο ἀπ' ἄνωθεν ἕως κάτω 'torn in two from top to bottom' Mk 15.38; ἐκ τῶν ἄνωθεν ὑφαντὸς δι' ὅλου 'woven from the top in one piece' Jn 19.23; ὁ ἄνωθεν ἐρχόμενος ἐπάνω πάντων ἐστίν 'he who comes from above is far above all' Jn 3.31. In Jn 3.31 the reference of ἄνωθεν is obviously heaven, and in many languages it is essential to translate 'he who comes from heaven is far above all.' ἐὰν μή τις γεννηθῇ ἄνωθεν 'unless someone is born from above' Jn 3.3. In Jn 3.3 ἄνωθεν may also mean 'again' (see 67.55). For ἄνωθεν as part of an idiom, see 41.53.

84.14 ἔσωθεν[a]: extension from a source which is inside – 'from inside.' κἀκεῖνος ἔσωθεν ἀποκριθείς 'and he answers from inside' Lk 11.7.

84.15 ἔξωθεν[a]: extension from a source which is outside – 'from outside.' πᾶν τὸ ἔξωθεν εἰσπορευόμενον εἰς τὸν ἄνθρωπον οὐ δύναται αὐτὸν κοινῶσαι 'nothing that goes into a person from the outside can defile him' Mk 7.18.

B Extension To a Goal (84.16-84.28)

84.16 εἰς[a]: extension toward a special goal – 'to, toward, in the direction of.'[7] ἤρχοντο εἰς τὸ μνημεῖον 'they went to the tomb' Jn 20.3; ὅτε ἤγγισαν εἰς Ἱεροσόλυμα 'as they drew near to Jerusalem' Mt 21.1.

84.17 ἐπί[e]: extension toward a goal, usually implying reaching the goal – 'to, toward, in the direction of.'[7] γενόμεναι ὀρθριναὶ ἐπὶ τὸ μνημεῖον 'they went at dawn to the tomb' Lk 24.22; ἐπὶ δὲ τὸν Ἰησοῦν ἐλθόντες 'but when they came to Jesus' Jn 19.33; ἀνήχθημεν ἐπὶ τὴν Ἆσσον 'we sailed to Assos' Ac 20.13.

84.18 πρός[a]: extension toward a goal, with the probability of some type of implied interaction or reciprocity – 'to.' ἀνέπεμψεν αὐτὸν πρὸς Ἡρῴδην 'he sent him to Herod' Lk 23.7; πορεύεσθε δὲ μᾶλλον πρὸς τὰ πρόβατα τὰ ἀπολωλότα οἴκου Ἰσραήλ 'go instead to the lost sheep of the people of Israel' Mt 10.6.

84.19 ἕως[c]; ἄχρι[c]; μέχρι[b]: extension up to or as far as a goal – 'to, up to, as far as.'[8] ἕως[c]: διέλθωμεν δὴ ἕως Βηθλέεμ 'let us go to Bethlehem' Lk 2.15; ὁ δὲ Πέτρος ἠκολούθει αὐτῷ . . . ἕως τῆς αὐλῆς 'Peter followed him . . . as far as the courtyard' Mt 26.58. ἄχρι[c]: διελθόντες δὲ ὅλην τὴν νῆσον ἄχρι Πάφου 'they went all the way across the island to Paphos' Ac 13.6; ἄχρι τῶν χαλινῶν τῶν ἵππων 'up to the bridles of the horses' Re 14.20. μέχρι[b]: ἀπὸ Ἰερουσαλὴμ . . . μέχρι τοῦ Ἰλ-

---

others, one on each side.' The phrase ἐντεῦθεν καὶ ἐντεῦθεν may be interpreted as representing two different extensions from the same reference point. In Jn 19.18 the position of Jesus constitutes the reference point.

6 It would also be possible to classify ὅθεν[a] as a relative pronoun in Domain 92 *Discourse Referentials*.

7 In the meaning of extension toward a goal, εἰς[a] (84.16) and ἐπί[e] (84.17) overlap considerably. It is, of course, possible to argue that ἐπί implies being on or at a point, while εἰς defines entering into an area related to some point, but such a distinction would seem to be arbitrary.

8 It is probable that ἕως[c], ἄχρι[c], and μέχρι[b] differ slightly in meaning, but this cannot be readily determined from existing contexts.

λυρικοῦ '(travelled) from Jerusalem . . . to Il-lyricum' Ro 15.19.

84.20 ἐπί^f: extension to a goal, with implied contact on a horizontal surface – 'on, onto.' πεσὼν ἐπὶ τῆς γῆς 'he fell on the ground' Mk 9.20; ἐκάθισεν ἐπὶ βήματος 'he sat down on the judge's seat' Jn 19.13.

84.21 κατά^a: extension to a goal, normally down – 'down, down to, downward.' Λευίτης γενόμενος κατὰ τὸν τόπον 'a Levite, coming down to the place' Lk 10.32. In going from Jerusalem to Jericho, the movement would be downhill.

84.22 εἰς^b; ἐν^f: extension toward a goal which is inside of an area – 'into.'
εἰς^b: εἰσῆλθεν εἰς τὸ μνημεῖον 'he entered into the tomb' Jn 20.6; ἐμβάντι αὐτῷ εἰς τὸ πλοῖον 'he got into the boat' Mt 8.23.
ἐν^f: ἄγγελος γὰρ κυρίου κατὰ καιρὸν κατέβαινεν ἐν τῇ κολυμβήθρᾳ 'an angel of the Lord from time to time went down into the pool' Jn 5.4 (apparatus).

84.23 πρός^b: extension toward a goal, involving presumed contact and reaction – 'against.' μήποτε προσκόψῃς πρὸς λίθον τὸν πόδα σου 'in order that you do not dash your foot against a stone' Mt 4.6; σκληρόν σοι πρὸς κέντρα λακτίζειν 'it is hard on you to kick against the goad' Ac 26.14.[9]

84.24 δεῦρο^a; δεῦτε (with plural subject): extension toward a goal at or near the speaker and implying movement – 'here, hither, come here.'[10]
δεῦρο^a: δεῦρο ἀκολούθει μοι 'come here and follow me' Mt 19.21; Λάζαρε, δεῦρο ἔξω 'Lazarus, come out here' Jn 11.43.

9 The expression πρὸς κέντρα λακτίζειν 'to kick against the goad' is an idiom (see 39.19), but within the idiom πρός is to be understood in the sense of 'against.' The meaning of the idiom is to oppose, in one way or another, a dominant force.
10 δεῦρο^a and δεῦτε may be regarded (particularly in their absolute usage) as semantic hybrids in that they are adverbial in form, but in certain contexts they involve not only extension toward a goal near the speaker but actual movement.

δεῦτε: δεῦτε ἴδετε τὸν τόπον 'come here and see the place' Mt 28.6.

84.25 ἄνω^b: extension toward a goal which is up or above – 'up, upwards, toward above.' ὁ δὲ Ἰησοῦς ἦρεν τοὺς ὀφθαλμοὺς ἄνω καὶ εἶπεν 'Jesus looked up and said' Jn 11.41; ῥίζα πικρίας ἄνω φύουσα 'a bitter plant that grows up' He 12.15.

84.26 κάτω^b: extension toward a goal which is down or below – 'down, down to, below to.' βάλε σεαυτὸν κάτω 'throw yourself down to (the ground)' Mt 4.6; ὁ δὲ Ἰησοῦς κάτω κύψας τῷ δακτύλῳ κατέγραφεν εἰς τὴν γῆν 'Jesus bent down and wrote on the ground with his finger' Jn 8.6.

84.27 ἔξω^b: extension to a goal which is outside of a presumed area – 'out, outside, away.' τὸν ἐρχόμενον πρὸς ἐμὲ οὐ μὴ ἐκβάλω ἔξω 'I will never turn away anyone who comes to me' Jn 6.37; τὰ δὲ σαπρὰ ἔξω ἔβαλον 'the worthless ones are thrown away' Mt 13.48.

84.28 σκοπός, οῦ *m*: that toward which movement or activity is directed – 'goal.' κατὰ σκοπὸν διώκω εἰς τὸ βραβεῖον 'I press toward the goal for the prize' Php 3.14. The context of σκοπός in Php 3.14 is highly figurative, and in some languages it may be better rendered as 'what I seek to achieve' or 'what I wish to accomplish.' For σκοπός in the idiom κατὰ σκοπὸν διώκω, see 89.56.

C Extension Along a Path (84.29-84.33)

84.29 διά^g (with the genitive): extension through an area or object – 'through.' ἐπορεύθη ὁ Ἰησοῦς . . . διὰ τῶν σπορίμων 'Jesus was walking . . . through the wheatfields' Mt 12.1. This expression in Mt 12.1 does not mean, however, that Jesus and his disciples were actually trampling on the ripened grain. They were probably following a path which led through the wheatfields; otherwise, the reaction of those who saw the event would certainly have been somewhat different. παρεπορεύοντο διὰ τῆς Γαλιλαίας 'they went on through Galilee' Mk 9.30. It is not possible to determine from the context of Mk 9.30

whether Jesus entered Galilee, went through Galilee and then went out of Galilee, an extension which is often implied by διά. Compare, for example, the expression 'through Macedonia' in Ac 20.3: ἐγένετο γνώμης τοῦ ὑποστρέφειν διὰ Μακεδονίας 'he decided to go back through Macedonia.' κάμηλον διὰ τρυπήματος ῥαφίδος διελθεῖν 'a camel to go through the eye of a needle' Mt 19.24.

84.30 κατά[b]: extension along a path or road, implying movement – 'along, on.' μηδένα κατὰ τὴν ὁδὸν ἀσπάσησθε 'don't (stop to) greet anyone on the road' Lk 10.4. Translated literally into some languages, this command in Lk 10.4 could be seriously misunderstood, since it would imply complete lack of courtesy and friendliness. What is implied, of course, is the avoidance of long, involved greetings and discussions, which often lead to the acceptance of time-consuming hospitality. ἐνέδραν ποιοῦντες ἀνελεῖν αὐτὸν κατὰ τὴν ὁδόν 'they made a plot to kill him on the way' Ac 25.3; ἡμέρας μέσης κατὰ τὴν ὁδόν 'it was along the road at midday' Ac 26.13.

84.31 κατά[c]: extension in every direction throughout an area – 'throughout.' γνωστὸν δὲ ἐγένετο καθ᾽ ὅλης τῆς Ἰόππης 'it became known throughout Joppa' Ac 9.42; ἀπῆλθεν καθ᾽ ὅλην τὴν πόλιν 'he went throughout the entire city' Lk 8.39.

84.32 διά[h] (with the genitive): an extension along a particular route – 'along.' ὥστε μὴ ἰσχύειν τινὰ παρελθεῖν διὰ τῆς ὁδοῦ ἐκείνης 'so that no one was able to pass along that road' Mt 8.28.[11]

84.33 ἀπάγω[e]: to mark an extension along a route – 'to extend to, to lead to, to lead from, to go.' εὐρύχωρος ἡ ὁδὸς ἡ ἀπάγουσα εἰς τὴν ἀπώλειαν 'the road is easy that leads to destruction' Mt 7.13. Though the context of Mt 7.13 is figurative, ἀπάγω should be interpreted in the specific sense of marking a route from one place to another.

11 It is possible to interpret διά in Mt 8.28 as being a blend of two meanings, namely, extension along a path and passage through an area (see 84.29).

85 Existence in Space[1]

Outline of Subdomains

A   Be in a Place (85.1-85.31)
B   Put, Place (85.32-85.54)
C   Remain, Stay (85.55-85.64)
D   Leave in a Place (85.65-85.66)
E   Dwell, Reside (85.67-85.85)

A   Be in a Place (85.1-85.31)

85.1 εἰμί[e]: to be in a place – 'to be.' ἐν τοῖς τοῦ πατρός μου δεῖ εἶναί με 'I had to be in my Father's house' Lk 2.49. Some persons have understood the expression ἐν τοῖς τοῦ πατρός μου in Lk 2.49 to refer to 'the affairs of my Father.' ἐν ἐκείνῃ τῇ ἡμέρᾳ ὃς ἔσται ἐπὶ τοῦ δώματος 'in that day, whoever is on the rooftop' Lk 17.31; ἐν ἐκείναις ταῖς ἡμέραις πάλιν πολλοῦ ὄχλου ὄντος 'in those days again there was a large crowd' Mk 8.1.

85.2 σύνειμι[b]: to be together with someone – 'to be with.' συνῆσαν αὐτῷ οἱ μαθηταί 'the disciples were with him' Lk 9.18.

85.3 κεῖμαι[b]: to be in a place, frequently in the sense of 'being contained in' or 'resting on' – 'to be, to lie.' σκεῦος ἔκειτο ὄξους μεστόν 'a bowl was there, full of cheap wine' Jn 19.29; πόλις . . . ἐπάνω ὄρους κειμένη 'a city . . . that is on a hill' Mt 5.14; λίθιναι ὑδρίαι ἓξ κατὰ τὸν καθαρισμὸν τῶν Ἰουδαίων κείμεναι

1 The meanings in Domain 85 are complex in that they involve both events or states and spacial positions. These meanings could, of course, be readily grouped with other domains relating to events, but in view of the focus upon spacial relations, it has seemed preferable to place them together with other spacial domains, namely, Domains 80-84.

'six stone jars sitting there in accordance with the practice of purification of the Jews' Jn 2.6.

85.4 ἐπίκειμαιᵃ: to be in a place on something – 'to be on, to lie on.' καὶ ὀψάριον ἐπικείμενον 'and fish lying on (the coals)' Jn 21.9.

85.5 περίκειμαιᵃ: to be located around some object or area – 'to be around, to surround.' τοσοῦτον ἔχοντες περικείμενον ἡμῖν νέφος μαρτύρων 'having such a large crowd of witnesses around us' He 12.1.

85.6 γίνομαιʰ: to be in a place, with the possible implication of having come to be in such a place – 'to be (in a place).' πῶς μεθ' ὑμῶν τὸν πάντα χρόνον ἐγενόμην 'how I was with you all the time' Ac 20.18.

85.7 γίνομαιⁱ; **παραγίνομαι**ᶜ: to come to be in a place – 'to come to be, to appear, to be in a place.'
γίνομαιⁱ: ἐξαίφνης ἐγένετο σὺν τῷ ἀγγέλῳ πλῆθος στρατιᾶς οὐρανίου 'suddenly there appeared with the angel a multitude of heavenly forces' Lk 2.13.
παραγίνομαιᶜ: ἐν δὲ ταῖς ἡμέραις ἐκείναις παραγίνεται Ἰωάννης ὁ βαπτιστὴς κηρύσσων ἐν τῇ ἐρήμῳ 'in those days John the Baptist appeared preaching in the wilderness' Mt 3.1.

85.8 ἵσταμαιᶜ (and 2nd aorist active): to be in a location, with the possible implication of standing but with the focus upon location – 'to be.' εἰσίν τινες τῶν ὧδε ἑστώτων οἵτινες οὐ μὴ γεύσωνται θανάτου ἕως . . . 'there are some here who will not die until . . .' Mt 16.28.

85.9 κατέχωᵉ: to come to occupy a particular place – 'to come to be in a place, to occupy.' τότε ἄρξῃ μετὰ αἰσχύνης τὸν ἔσχατον τόπον κατέχειν 'then with embarrassment you will begin to occupy the last place' Lk 14.9.

85.10 ἥκωᵇ: to be in a place, as the result of having arrived – 'to be here, to be there.' ἐγὼ γὰρ ἐκ τοῦ θεοῦ ἐξῆλθον καὶ ἥκω 'for I have come from God and am here' Jn 8.42. For another interpretation of ἥκω in Jn 8.42, see 15.84.

85.11 ἐπισκέπτομαιᵈ: to be present, with the implication of concern – 'to be present to help, to be on hand to aid.'[2] ἐπεσκέψατο ὁ θεὸς τὸν λαὸν αὐτοῦ 'God has come to help his people' Lk 7.16.

85.12 παρατυγχάνω: to happen to be in a place – 'to happen to be, to be by chance.' τοὺς παρατυγχάνοντας 'those who happened to be there' Ac 17.17.

85.13 παρίσταμαιᵇ (and 2nd aorist active); **ἐφίσταμαι**ᵇ (and 2nd aorist active): to be in proximity to something – 'to be near, to be at, to be nearby.'
παρίσταμαιᵇ: μετὰ μικρὸν πάλιν οἱ παρεστῶτες ἔλεγον τῷ Πέτρῳ 'a little while later those nearby accused Peter again' Mk 14.70;[3] ὁ δὲ κύριός μοι παρέστη 'but the Lord was with me' 2 Tm 4.17.[4]
ἐφίσταμαιᵇ: καὶ αὐτὸς ἤμην ἐφεστώς 'I myself was nearby' Ac 22.20; ἄνδρες δύο ἐπέστησαν αὐταῖς ἐν ἐσθῆτι ἀστραπτούσῃ 'two men in dazzling garments were there by them' Lk 24.4. For another interpretation of ἐφίσταμαι in Lk 24.4, see 17.5.

85.14 παρίστημιᵃ: to cause to be in a place – 'to present (oneself), to cause to be.' οἷς καὶ παρέστησεν ἑαυτὸν ζῶντα 'to whom he presented himself alive' Ac 1.3.

85.15 συνομορέω: to be at a place which is next to something else – 'to be next to, to border on.' οὗ ἡ οἰκία ἦν συνομοροῦσα τῇ συναγωγῇ 'his house was next to the synagogue' Ac 18.7. In a number of languages the concept of 'being next to' may be best expressed as 'there was no space between.'

85.16 ἀπέχωᵇ: to be at some distance away from – 'to be away from, to be off from.' ἔτι δὲ

---

2 ἐπισκέπτομαι is typical of a so-called complex semantic unit, since it involves both presence and purpose, namely, to aid or help.
3 It would also be possible to classify παρίσταμαι in Mk 14.70 as a matter involving primarily stance (compare παρίσταμαιᵃ 'to stand near,' 17.3).
4 It is also valid to classify παρίσταμαι in 2 Tm 4.17 as meaning 'to be on hand to help' (see 35.1).

αὐτοῦ μακρὰν ἀπέχοντος 'he was still a long way from (home)' Lk 15.20.

85.17 ἀπορφανίζω: (a figurative extension of meaning of ἀπορφανίζω 'to cause to be an orphan,' not occurring in the NT) to cause someone to be spacially separated, with the implication of additional emotional deprivation – 'to separate and to deprive.' ἀπορφανισθέντες ἀφ' ὑμῶν πρὸς καιρὸν ὥρας 'separated from you for a time' or 'separated and deprived of your company for a time' 1 Th 2.17.

85.18 παρίσταμαι^c (and 2nd aorist active): to be in front of something, presumably facing it – 'to be in front of, to stand before.' καίσαρί σε δεῖ παραστῆναι 'you must stand before the emperor' Ac 27.24. The actual body stance in translating παρίσταμαι^c is not crucial to the meaning; the focus in Ac 27.24 is simply upon the position in front of the emperor.

85.19 ἔνειμι: to be inside an area or object – 'to be inside' (in the participial forms, 'what is inside, contents'). τὰ ἐνόντα δότε ἐλεημοσύνην 'give as alms what is in (your plates and cups)' Lk 11.41.

85.20 ἐνδημέω: to be in a place where one rightfully or normally belongs – 'to be at home, to fit in a place.' ἐνδημῆσαι πρὸς τὸν κύριον 'to be at home with the Lord' 2 Cor 5.8.

85.21 ἐκδημέω: to be absent from a place where one rightfully or normally belongs – 'to be absent, to be away from.' ἐνδημοῦντες ἐν τῷ σώματι ἐκδημοῦμεν ἀπὸ τοῦ κυρίου 'when we are at home in the body, we are absent from the Lord' 2 Cor 5.6.

85.22 ἀπόδημος, ον: pertaining to being away from where one usually resides – 'to be away from home, to be away on a journey.'⁵ ἄνθρωπος ἀπόδημος 'a man who is away on a journey' Mk 13.34.

85.23 πάρειμι^a; παράκειμαι: to be present at a particular time and place – 'to be present, to be here, to be there, to be at hand.'⁶ πάρειμι^a: παρῆσαν δέ τινες ἐν αὐτῷ τῷ καιρῷ 'at that time, some persons were present' Lk 13.1. παράκειμαι: τὸ κακὸν παράκειται 'evil is present' Ro 7.21.

85.24 ἀναπληρόω^d: to occupy a designated place – 'to occupy, to be in.' ὁ ἀναπληρῶν τὸν τόπον τοῦ ἰδιώτου 'who occupies the place of an ordinary person' 1 Cor 14.16. It is possible, however, to understand ἀναπληρόω in 1 Cor 14.16 as specifically referring to fulfilling a particular function. One could therefore translate this phrase in 1 Cor 14.16 as 'one who takes part in the service as an ordinary person.'

85.25 παρουσία^a, ας f: the presence of an object at a particular place – 'presence, being at hand, to be in person.' ἡ δὲ παρουσία τοῦ σώματος 'when he is with us in person' (literally '. . . his bodily presence') 2 Cor 10.10.

85.26 πρόσωπον^c, ου n: (a figurative extension of meaning of πρόσωπον^a 'face,' 8.18) the personal presence of an individual at a particular place – 'presence, being at a place.' πληρώσεις με εὐφροσύνης μετὰ τοῦ προσώπου σου 'with your presence you will fill me with joy' Ac 2.28.

85.27 ἄπειμι^b: to be absent from a place at a particular time – 'to be absent.' διὰ τοῦτο ταῦτα ἀπὼν γράφω 'this is why I write this while I am absent (from you)' 2 Cor 13.10.

85.28 ἀπουσία, ας f: the state of being absent – 'being absent, absence, being away from.' μὴ ὡς ἐν τῇ παρουσίᾳ μου μόνον ἀλλὰ νῦν πολλῷ μᾶλλον ἐν τῇ ἀπουσίᾳ μου 'not as in my presence only, but now much more so in my absence' Php 2.12.

85.29 ὑστέρημα^b, τος n: absence as an element of lack or deficiency – 'absence, not be-

---

5 It would also be possible to treat ἀπόδημος as derivatively related to ἀποδημέω 'to leave home on a journey' (15.47).

6 πάρειμι^a and παράκειμαι are semantically complex in that they involve both temporal and spacial factors.

ing present.' τὸ ὑμέτερον ὑστέρημα οὗτοι ἀνεπλήρωσαν 'they have made up for your absence' 1 Cor 16.17.

85.30 συμπάρειμι: to be in a place together with others – 'to be with, to be present with.' καὶ πάντες οἱ συμπαρόντες ἡμῖν 'and all who are with us' Ac 25.24.

85.31 ἔμφυτος, ον: (a figurative extension of meaning of ἔμφυτος 'to be implanted,' not occurring in the NT) to be permanently in a place, with the implication of development – 'placed in, permanently established in, implanted.' δέξασθε τὸν ἔμφυτον λόγον τὸν δυνάμενον σῶσαι τὰς ψυχὰς ὑμῶν 'you received the word which is implanted (within you) and which is able to save your souls' Jas 1.21.

B Put, Place (85.32-85.54)

85.32 τίθημι[a]: to put or place in a particular location – 'to put, to place.'[7] οὐδεὶς λύχνον ἅψας . . . τίθησιν οὐδὲ ὑπὸ τὸν μόδιον 'no one lights a lamp and . . . puts it under a container' Lk 11.33; κατὰ μίαν σαββάτου ἕκαστος ὑμῶν παρ' ἑαυτῷ τιθέτω 'on the first day of every week each one of you should put aside (some money)' 1 Cor 16.2.

85.33 δίδωμι[d]: to put or place an object, with the implication of some type of transfer of location or possession – 'to put.' δότε δακτύλιον εἰς τὴν χεῖρα αὐτοῦ 'put a ring on his hand' Lk 15.22.

85.34 βάλλω[e]: to put or place some object or mass in a location, with the possible implication of force in some contexts – 'to put, to cause to be put.' τῶν ἵππων τοὺς χαλινοὺς εἰς τὰ στόματα βάλλομεν 'we put bits into the mouths of horses' Jas 3.3; ἔβαλεν αὐτὸν εἰς φυλακήν 'he had him thrown into jail' Mt 18.30; βάλλουσιν οἶνον νέον εἰς ἀσκοὺς καινούς 'they put new wine into new wineskins' Mt 9.17c.

---

7 In this subdomain τίθημι[a] is by far the most generic expression.

85.35 ἐμβάλλω: to put or throw into a place – 'to put into, to throw into.' φοβήθητε τὸν μετὰ τὸ ἀποκτεῖναι ἔχοντα ἐξουσίαν ἐμβαλεῖν εἰς τὴν γέενναν 'fear the one who after killing has the power to put (you) into hell' Lk 12.5. Despite the use of the verb ἐμβάλλω in Lk 12.5, the focus of meaning is not so much upon the act of throwing or hurling but rather upon the act of causing someone to be in a particular place.

85.36 βλητέος, α, ον: pertaining to being obligatorily put or placed – 'must be put, necessary to be put.' οἶνον νέον εἰς ἀσκοὺς καινοὺς βλητέον 'new wine must be put in new wineskins' Lk 5.38.

85.37 ῥίπτω[b]: to put or place something down, with the possible implication of rapidity of action – 'to put down, to place down.' ἑτέρους πολλούς, καὶ ἔρριψαν αὐτοὺς παρὰ τοὺς πόδας αὐτοῦ 'many other (sick people), whom they placed at his feet' Mt 15.30.

85.38 στηρίζω[b]: to put or place something firmly in a location – 'to cause to be fixed, to establish in a place.' μεταξὺ ἡμῶν . . . χάσμα μέγα ἐστήρικται 'there is a great chasm fixed . . . between us' Lk 16.26.

85.39 περιτίθημι[a]; παρεμβάλλω: to place something around an object or area – 'to put around, to surround.'
περιτίθημι[a]: καὶ φραγμὸν αὐτῷ περιέθηκεν 'and put a fence around it' Mt 21.33.
παρεμβάλλω: παρεμβαλοῦσιν οἱ ἐχθροί σου χάρακά σοι 'your enemies will surround you with barricades' Lk 19.43.

85.40 ἵστημι[a]: to cause to be in a place, with or without the accompanying feature of standing position – 'to put, to place, to set, to make stand, to be there.' ἀγαγόντες δὲ αὐτοὺς ἔστησαν ἐν τῷ συνεδρίῳ 'they brought them in and made them stand before the council' Ac 5.27; ἔστησάν τε μάρτυρας ψευδεῖς λέγοντας 'false witnesses were there who said . . .' Ac 6.13; προσκαλεσάμενος παιδίον ἔστησεν αὐτὸ ἐν μέσῳ αὐτῶν 'calling a child, he placed him in the midst of them' Mt 18.2. As may be seen from the preceding three contexts, ἵστημι[a] may very well imply a standing position, but what is in focus is not the stance but the location.

85.41 χωρίζω[d]: to cause to be at a distance – 'to remove at a distance, to separate considerably.' ἐχωρίσθη πρὸς ὥραν ἵνα αἰώνιον αὐτὸν ἀπέχῃς 'separated from you for a time in order that you might have him back permanently' Phm 15.

85.42 φέρω[g]: to put or place an object by moving it to a particular point – 'to put, to place.' φέρε τὸν δάκτυλόν σου ὧδε 'put your finger here' Jn 20.27.[8]

85.43 ἐξαιρέω: to take something out of its place – 'to take out, to remove.' ἔξελε αὐτὸν καὶ βάλε ἀπὸ σοῦ 'take it out and throw it away from you' Mt 5.29.

85.44 ἀποτίθεμαι[a]; ἀφαιρέω[a]: to put or take something away from its normal location – 'to put away, to put out of the way, to remove.'[9] ἀποτίθεμαι[a]: ἔδησεν αὐτὸν καὶ ἐν φυλακῇ ἀπέθετο 'have him tied up and put in prison' Mt 14.3. The semantic element of 'out of the way' is implied in the activity of 'putting in prison.' οἱ μάρτυρες ἀπέθεντο τὰ ἱμάτια αὐτῶν παρὰ τοὺς πόδας νεανίου 'the witnesses put their clothes at a young man's feet' Ac 7.58. ἀφαιρέω[a]: ἐάν τις ἀφέλῃ ἀπὸ τῶν λόγων τοῦ βιβλίου τῆς προφητείας ταύτης 'if anyone takes away from the words of this book of prophecy' or 'if anyone removes any words from this book of prophecy' Re 22.19; καὶ ἀφεῖλεν τὸ οὖς αὐτοῦ τὸ δεξιόν 'and he removed his right ear' Lk 22.50. In the context of Lk 22.50

it may be far more appropriate to translate 'and he cut off his right ear.'

85.45 ἀφίημι[c]: to let something be put behind in a place – 'to leave, to leave behind.' οἱ δὲ εὐθέως ἀφέντες τὰ δίκτυα 'they immediately left the nets' Mt 4.20.

85.46 ἐκτίθημι: to put or place something out of an area – 'to put out of.' ἐκτεθέντος δὲ αὐτοῦ 'and when he was put out of (his home)' Ac 7.21.

85.47 ἔκθετος, ον: (derivative of ἐκτίθημι 'to put out of,' 85.46) pertaining to being put out and hence exposed (with particular reference to abandoned children) – 'exposed, abandoned.' τοῦ ποιεῖν τὰ βρέφη ἔκθετα αὐτῶν εἰς τὸ μὴ ζῳογονεῖσθαι 'to expose their infants so that they would not live' Ac 7.19.

85.48 συνάγω[b]: to collect and put in a safe place – 'to store, to keep in a place.' ὅτι οὐκ ἔχω ποῦ συνάξω τοὺς καρπούς μου 'because I do not have a place where I can store my crops' Lk 12.17.[10]

85.49 καταβάλλομαι: to put or place something down, with the implication of permanence – 'to put down, to lay.' μὴ πάλιν θεμέλιον καταβαλλόμενοι 'we should not lay again the foundation' He 6.1.[11]

85.50 ἐγκρύπτω: to put into, with the implication of the substance no longer being visible – 'to put into, to hide in.' γυνὴ ἐνέκρυψεν εἰς ἀλεύρου σάτα τρία 'a woman puts it into a bushel of flour' Mt 13.33.

85.51 ἐπιτίθημι[a]; ἐπίθεσις, εως f; ἐπιβάλλω[b]: to place something on something – 'to put on, to place on, to lay on.' ἐπιτίθημι[a]: ἐπέθηκαν αὐτῷ τὸν σταυρόν 'they put on him the cross' Lk 23.26.

---

8 It is possible that the occurrence of φέρω in Jn 20.27 should be classified merely as an instance of 'bringing' or 'carrying,' but the focus seems to be far more upon placement at a particular location. The element of movement appears to be entirely secondary.

9 It would also be possible to classify the meanings of ἀποτίθεμαι[a] and ἀφαιρέω[a] in Domain 15 *Linear Movement*, but in a number of contexts the focus seems not to be primarily upon the movement but upon the removal from a particular location. In other words, the focus is upon the absence of an object from a place rather than the movement involved in removal.

10 συνάγω in Lk 12.17 is another instance of a complex semantic structure involving not only the gathering together of material but the proper provision for it in some location. In Lk 12.17 the focus seems to be upon the storage rather than the process of harvesting.

11 The context of καταβάλλομαι in He 6.1 is, of course, figurative.

ἐπίθεσις: μετὰ ἐπιθέσεως τῶν χειρῶν τοῦ πρεσβυτερίου 'after the elders had laid their hands (on you)' 1 Tm 4.14.

ἐπιβάλλω^b: οὐδεὶς δὲ ἐπιβάλλει ἐπίβλημα ῥάκους ἀγνάφου ἐπὶ ἱματίῳ παλαιῷ 'no one puts a patch of unshrunken cloth on an old garment' Mt 9.16.

85.52 ἀποστρέφω^c: to cause something to be in a place where it was formerly – 'to return, to put back.' ἀπόστρεφον τὴν μάχαιράν σου εἰς τὸν τόπον αὐτῆς 'put your sword back in its place' Mt 26.52.

85.53 ἀπόκειμαι^a: to put something away for safekeeping – 'to store, to put away in a place.' ἡ μνᾶ σου ἣν εἶχον ἀποκειμένην ἐν σουδαρίῳ 'your mina which I put away for safekeeping in a napkin' Lk 19.20.

85.54 περίκειμαι^b: to lie or be placed around – 'to be placed around, to be put around.' λυσιτελεῖ αὐτῷ εἰ λίθος μυλικὸς περίκειται περὶ τὸν τράχηλον αὐτοῦ 'it will be better for him if a millstone is placed around his neck' Lk 17.2. In Lk 17.2 there is a problem involved in placing a millstone around a person's neck, for millstones normally had no such hole through which a head might be placed. Therefore, it is usually necessary to translate this expression in Lk 17.2 as 'to have a millstone hung around one's neck' or 'to hang a millstone to a person's neck.'

C   Remain, Stay (85.55-85.64)

85.55 μένω^a; ἐμμένω^a; ἐπιμένω^a; καταμένω: to remain in the same place over a period of time – 'to remain, to stay.'[12]

μένω^a: ἐκεῖ μένετε ἕως ἂν ἐξέλθητε ἐκεῖθεν 'stay there until you leave that place' Mk 6.10; ἐὰν μὴ οὗτοι μείνωσιν ἐν τῷ πλοίῳ 'if these (sailors) don't stay on the ship' Ac 27.31.

12 There may be slight nuances of meaning in the various terms in this series, but such distinctions cannot be clearly determined from existing contexts, especially since the prefixes are redundant with other expressions of space.

ἐμμένω^a: ἐνέμεινεν δὲ διετίαν ὅλην ἐν ἰδίῳ μισθώματι 'for two full years he stayed in a place he rented for himself' Ac 28.30.

ἐπιμένω^a: ἐπιμενῶ δὲ ἐν Ἐφέσῳ 'but I will stay (here) in Ephesus' 1 Cor 16.8.

καταμένω: οὗ ἦσαν καταμένοντες '(the room) where they were staying' Ac 1.13.

85.56 παραμένω^a: to stay in a place together with someone – 'to stay with, to remain with.' πρὸς ὑμᾶς δὲ τυχὸν παραμενῶ 'I shall probably stay (some time) with you' 1 Cor 16.6; καὶ παραμενῶ πᾶσιν ὑμῖν 'and I will remain with all of you' Php 1.25. In Php 1.25 παραμενῶ contrasts to some extent with μενῶ. The implication, in this particular context at least, is that the purpose of remaining is to serve the interests or needs of the believers in Philippi. It is also possible that some of this implication of serving may be found in 1 Cor 16.6.

85.57 ὑπομένω^b: to stay longer in a place than one is expected to – 'to stay behind, to remain longer than.' ὑπέμεινεν Ἰησοῦς ὁ παῖς ἐν Ἱερουσαλήμ 'the boy Jesus stayed behind in Jerusalem' Lk 2.43; ὑπέμεινάν τε ὅ τε Σιλᾶς καὶ ὁ Τιμόθεος ἐκεῖ 'both Silas and Timothy stayed on there' Ac 17.14.

85.58 ἀναπαύομαι^b: to remain in a place, with the implication of continuing to rest – 'to remain, to abide.' ἵνα ἀναπαύσονται ἔτι χρόνον μικρόν 'continue to abide for yet a short time' Re 6.11.

85.59 προσμένω^a; ἐπέχω^d: to stay or remain in a place beyond some point of time – 'to stay on, to remain.'

προσμένω^a: ὁ δὲ Παῦλος ἔτι προσμείνας 'Paul stayed on there' Ac 18.18; παρεκάλεσά σε προσμεῖναι ἐν Ἐφέσῳ 'I want you to stay on in Ephesus' 1 Tm 1.3.

ἐπέχω^d: αὐτὸς ἐπέσχεν χρόνον εἰς τὴν Ἀσίαν 'he himself stayed on for a time in Asia' Ac 19.22.

85.60 μένω^b; ἀναμένω; περιμένω; προσδέχομαι^c; ἐκδέχομαι^a: to remain in a place and/or state, with expectancy concerning a future event – 'to await, to wait for.'[13]

μένω[b]: οὗτοι δὲ προελθόντες ἔμενον ἡμᾶς ἐν Τρῳάδι 'these went ahead and waited for us in Troas' Ac 20.5.

ἀναμένω: ἀναμένειν τὸν υἱὸν αὐτοῦ ἐκ τῶν οὐρανῶν 'to wait for his Son from heaven' 1 Th 1.10.

περιμένω: ἀλλὰ περιμένειν τὴν ἐπαγγελίαν τοῦ πατρός 'but to wait for the promise from the Father' Ac 1.4.

προσδέχομαι[c]: ὃς καὶ αὐτὸς ἦν προσδεχόμενος τὴν βασιλείαν τοῦ θεοῦ 'he was one who was waiting for the kingdom of God' Mk 15.43.

ἐκδέχομαι[a]: ἐκδεχομένων τὴν τοῦ ὕδατος κίνησιν 'waiting for the movement of the water' Jn 5.3 (apparatus).

85.61 διατρίβω: to remain or stay in a place, with the implication of some type of activity – 'to remain, to stay.' ἱκανὸν μὲν οὖν χρόνον διέτριψαν 'they stayed (there) for a long time' Ac 14.3; ἦμεν δὲ ἐν ταύτῃ τῇ πόλει διατρίβοντες ἡμέρας τινάς 'we spent several days in that city' Ac 16.12.

85.62 ἀφίημι[d]: to permit something to continue in a place – 'to let remain, to leave.' οὐ μὴ ἀφεθῇ ὧδε λίθος ἐπὶ λίθον 'here not one stone will be left on another' Mt 24.2.

85.63 καθίζω[c]; κάθημαι[b]: to remain for some time in a place, often with the implication of a settled situation – 'to remain, to stay, to reside, to inhabit, to be, to settle.' καθίζω[c]: ὑμεῖς δὲ καθίσατε ἐν τῇ πόλει ἕως . . . 'but you must stay in the city until . . .' Lk 24.49; ἐκάθισεν δὲ ἐνιαυτὸν καὶ μῆνας ἕξ 'he stayed (there) a year and a half' Ac 18.11.
κάθημαι[b]: ἐπεισελεύσεται γὰρ ἐπὶ πάντας τοὺς καθημένους ἐπὶ πρόσωπον πάσης τῆς γῆς 'for it will come upon all those who inhabit the entire earth' Lk 21.35; τις ἀνὴρ ἀδύνατος ἐν Λύστροις τοῖς ποσὶν ἐκάθητο 'in Lystra there was a man who was unable to use his feet' Ac 14.8.

85.64 ἀγραυλέω: to spend time outdoors, with the possible implication of living outdoors – 'to remain outdoors.' ποιμένες ἦσαν ἐν τῇ χώρᾳ τῇ αὐτῇ ἀγραυλοῦντες 'there were shepherds in that place staying out in the fields' Lk 2.8.

D Leave in a Place[14] **(85.65-85.66)**

85.65 ἀπολείπω[a]; καταλείπω[b]: to cause or permit something to remain in a place and to go away (with or without implying purpose) – 'to leave, to leave behind, to abandon.'
ἀπολείπω[a]: τὸν φαιλόνην ὃν ἀπέλιπον ἐν Τρῳάδι . . . φέρε 'bring my coat that I left in Troas' 2 Tm 4.13. In a number of languages it is necessary to make a distinction between that which is left behind by accident and that which is left behind with intent or purpose. It is impossible to tell in the context of 2 Tm 4.13 whether or not Paul's action was purposeful , but if one must make a decision, it would be preferable to imply purpose, since Paul could have indicated the accidental nature of the event by the use of terms meaning 'to lose' or 'to forget.' τούτου χάριν ἀπέλιπόν σε ἐν Κρήτῃ 'for this reason I left you in Crete' Tt 1.5.
καταλείπω[b]: ὁ δὲ καταλιπὼν τὴν σινδόνα γυμνὸς ἔφυγεν 'he ran away naked, leaving the linen cloth behind' Mk 14.52.

85.66 περιλείπομαι; ὑπολείπομαι: to be left behind, with the implication of continuing to exist – 'to be left behind, to be left, to remain.'
περιλείπομαι: ἡμεῖς οἱ ζῶντες οἱ περιλειπόμενοι εἰς τὴν παρουσίαν τοῦ κυρίου 'we who are alive and left behind at the time of the Lord's appearing' or 'we who are still alive when the Lord comes' 1 Th 4.15.
ὑπολείπομαι: κἀγὼ ὑπελείφθην μόνος 'and I alone am left' Ro 11.3.

---

13 There are probably certain subtle distinctions of meaning in this set. The terms containing the stem μεν- probably focus more upon location, while with the stem δεχ- the focus may be more upon anticipation, but there is no consistent patterning on the basis of this type of distinction.

14 It is also possible to analyze the meanings in Subdomain D as involving the result of a movement away from an object or location, but in a number of contexts the focus seems to be upon the continuation of an object in a particular location rather than the movement away from such an object or location.

E Dwell, Reside[15] (85.67-85.85)

85.67 οἰκέω[a]: to live or dwell in a place – 'to live, to dwell.' αὕτη συνευδοκεῖ οἰκεῖν μετ' αὐτοῦ '(if) she agrees to go on living with him' 1 Cor 7.12; φῶς οἰκῶν ἀπρόσιτον 'he lives in light that no one can approach' 1 Tm 6.16.

85.68 οἰκητήριον, ου *n*: (derivative of οἰκέω[a] 'to dwell,' 85.67) a place in which one may dwell – 'dwelling place, home.' ἀγγέλους τε τοὺς ... ἀπολιπόντας τὸ ἴδιον οἰκητήριον 'angels who ... abandoned their own dwelling place' Jd 6; τὸ οἰκητήριον ἡμῶν τὸ ἐξ οὐρανοῦ ἐπενδύσασθαι ἐπιποθοῦντες 'our desire is to have our dwelling place which is in heaven put on over us' 2 Cor 5.2.

85.69 κατοικέω: to live or dwell in a place in an established or settled manner – 'to live, to dwell, to reside.' μὴ ἔστω ὁ κατοικῶν ἐν αὐτῇ 'may no one live in his house' Ac 1.20. This quotation from Ps 69.25 normally requires a literal rendering, but the entire passage is figurative.

85.70 κατοικία, ας *f*; κατοίκησις, εως *f*; κατοικητήριον, ου *n*: (derivatives of κατοικέω 'to dwell,' 85.69) a place of dwelling, whether an object or area – 'dwelling place, dwelling.'[16]
κατοικία: τὰς ὁροθεσίας τῆς κατοικίας αὐτῶν 'the limits of the place where they would dwell' Ac 17.26.
κατοίκησις: ὃς τὴν κατοίκησιν εἶχεν ἐν τοῖς μνήμασιν 'who had a place to dwell among the tombs' or 'who lived in the tombs' Mk 5.3.
κατοικητήριον: ἐγένετο κατοικητήριον δαιμονίων 'has become a dwelling place of demons' Re 18.2; εἰς κατοικητήριον τοῦ θεοῦ ἐν πνεύματι 'into a place where God dwells through his Spirit' Eph 2.22.

85.71 παροικέω[a]: to live or dwell temporari-

ly in a place as a stranger – 'to dwell temporarily, to be a foreigner.' σὺ μόνος παροικεῖς Ἰερουσαλήμ 'are you the only person living for a time in Jerusalem' or 'are you the only stranger living in Jerusalem' Lk 24.18.

85.72 ἐγκατοικέω: to live or dwell among – 'to live among, to dwell among.' ὁ δίκαιος ἐγκατοικῶν ἐν αὐτοῖς ἡμέραν ἐξ ἡμέρας 'that good man lived among them day after day' 2 Pe 2.8.

85.73 οἰκέω[b] (a figurative extension of meaning of οἰκέω[a] 'to live,' 85.67); ἐνοικέω (a figurative extension of meaning of ἐνοικέω 'to live in,' not occurring in the NT): to remain in a place defined psychologically or spiritually – 'to be in, to live in, to dwell in, to reside in.'
οἰκέω[b]: εἴπερ πνεῦμα θεοῦ οἰκεῖ ἐν ὑμῖν 'if the Spirit of God dwells in you' Ro 8.9; ἡ οἰκοῦσα ἐν ἐμοὶ ἁμαρτία 'the sin that resides in me' Ro 7.17.
ἐνοικέω: ὁ λόγος τοῦ Χριστοῦ ἐνοικείτω ἐν ὑμῖν πλουσίως 'let the message of Christ dwell richly in you' Col 3.16; πίστεως, ἥτις ἐνῴκησεν πρῶτον ἐν τῇ μάμμῃ σου Λωΐδι καὶ τῇ μητρί σου Εὐνίκῃ 'faith, which resided first in your grandmother Lois and your mother Eunice' 2 Tm 1.5.

85.74 περιοικέω: to live near and around – 'to live all around, to be neighbors, to live nearby.' καὶ ἐγένετο ἐπὶ πάντας φόβος τοὺς περιοικοῦντας αὐτούς 'and all those who lived around there became fearful' Lk 1.65.

85.75 σκηνόω; ἐπισκηνόω: to come to dwell in a place defined psychologically or spiritually (with the possible implication in some contexts of a temporary arrangement) – 'to take up residence, to come to reside, to come to dwell.'
σκηνόω: σκηνώσει μετ' αὐτῶν 'he will come to dwell with them' Re 21.3; ὁ λόγος σὰρξ ἐγένετο καὶ ἐσκήνωσεν ἐν ἡμῖν 'the Word became a human being and dwelt among us' Jn 1.14.
ἐπισκηνόω: ἵνα ἐπισκηνώσῃ ἐπ' ἐμὲ ἡ δύναμις τοῦ Χριστοῦ 'that the power of Christ may come to dwell in me' 2 Cor 12.9.

---

15 The meanings in this subdomain differ from those in Subdomain C *Remain, Stay* since they imply the carrying on of those activities characteristic of residing or dwelling in a place.
16 There are no doubt certain subtle distinctions between the meanings of the terms in this set, but this cannot be determined from existing NT contexts.

In all of these contexts, σκηνόω and ἐπι-σκηνόω are essentially figurative in meaning, for they deal with spiritual existence and residence rather than human residence or dwelling. In translating one should, in so far as possible, try to preserve this important figurative relationship, since it expresses one of the most significant ways in which spiritual and human existence can be combined. In some languages, however, it may be necessary to employ an expression which means simply 'to be in' or 'to continue with,' since expressions for 'living' or 'dwelling' may be based upon terms which are too specific in meaning, for example, 'to eat from the same pot' or 'to enter by the same door.'

85.76 μονή, ῆς *f*: a place where one may remain or dwell – 'place, dwelling place.' ἐν τῇ οἰκίᾳ τοῦ πατρός μου μοναὶ πολλαί εἰσιν 'in my Father's house are many dwelling places' Jn 14.2; ἐλευσόμεθα καὶ μονὴν παρ' αὐτῷ ποιησόμεθα 'I will come and live with him' (literally '. . . and make my dwelling place with him') Jn 14.23.

85.77 σκήνωμα[b]**, τος** *n*: (derivative of σκηνόω 'to take up residence,' 85.75) a place where one may dwell, with the possible implication in certain contexts of something which is of temporary duration – 'dwelling place, temporary dwelling place.' εὑρεῖν σκήνωμα τῷ οἴκῳ Ἰακώβ 'to provide a dwelling place for the people of Jacob' Ac 7.46. An alternative reading of this expression in Ac 7.46 has θεῷ for οἴκῳ, see 7.8 and the consequent translation 'a house for the God of Jacob.' ταχινή ἐστιν ἡ ἀπόθεσις τοῦ σκηνώματός μου 'I shall soon put off this temporary dwelling place' or 'I shall soon no longer live in my body' 2 Pe 1.14. For another interpretation of σκήνωμα in 2 Pe 1.14, see 8.5.

85.78 ἐπιδημέω; παροικέω[b]: to dwell more or less permanently in a place which is not one's own country – 'to sojourn, to live as a foreigner.' (Compare related meanings in 11.77.)
ἐπιδημέω: Ἀθηναῖοι δὲ πάντες καὶ οἱ ἐπιδημοῦντες ξένοι 'all the citizens of Athens and the foreigners who live there' Ac 17.21.

παροικέω[b]: πίστει παρῴκησεν εἰς γῆν . . . ὡς ἀλλοτρίαν 'by faith he lived in the country . . . as though he were a foreigner' He 11.9.

85.79 παροικία, ας *f*: (derivative of παροικέω[b] 'to sojourn,' 85.78) the time or occasion of one's living in a place as a foreigner – 'time of residence, stay.' ἐν τῇ παροικίᾳ ἐν γῇ Αἰγύπτου 'during the time they lived as foreigners in the land of Egypt' Ac 13.17.

85.80 ἀστατέω[b]: to not have a place of residence – 'to be homeless, to be without residence.' κολαφιζόμεθα καὶ ἀστατοῦμεν 'we are buffeted about and have no place of residence' 1 Cor 4.11. For another interpretation of ἀστατέω in 1 Cor 4.11, see 15.25.

85.81 ἐμπεριπατέω: (a figurative extension of meaning of ἐμπεριπατέω 'to walk about among,' not occurring in the NT) to live or dwell among – 'to live among, to be with.' ἐνοικήσω ἐν αὐτοῖς καὶ ἐμπεριπατήσω 'I will make my home with them and live among them' 2 Cor 6.16.

85.82 κατοικίζω: (a figurative extension of meaning of κατοικίζω 'to cause to dwell,' not occurring in the NT) to cause to be in a place defined psychologically or spiritually – 'to put within, to cause to dwell.' τὸ πνεῦμα ὃ κατῴκισεν ἐν ἡμῖν 'the spirit that (God) caused to dwell in us' or '. . . put within us' Jas 4.5.

85.83 μετοικίζω; μετοικεσία, ας *f*: to cause someone to change a place of habitation – 'to resettle, to move to another place, to deport, deportation.'
μετοικίζω: μετῴκισεν αὐτὸν εἰς τὴν γῆν ταύτην '(God) made him move to this country' Ac 7.4; μετοικιῶ ὑμᾶς ἐπέκεινα Βαβυλῶνος 'I will deport you beyond Babylon' Ac 7.43.
μετοικεσία: μετὰ δὲ τὴν μετοικεσίαν Βαβυλῶνος 'after the deportation to Babylon' Mt 1.12.

85.84 ἔρημος[a]**, ον**: pertaining to an absence of residents or inhabitants in a place – 'uninhabited, deserted.' γενηθήτω ἡ ἔπαυλις αὐτοῦ ἔρημος 'may his house become uninhabited' Ac 1.20; ἀφίεται ὑμῖν ὁ οἶκος ὑμῶν ἔρημος 'your house will be left uninhabited' Mt 23.38.

85.85 φυλακή[d], ῆς *f*: a place for wild animals and evil spirits to dwell – 'haunt, lair, dwelling place.' καὶ φυλακὴ παντὸς πνεύματος ἀκαθάρτου καὶ φυλακὴ παντὸς ὀρνέου ἀκαθάρτου καὶ φυλακὴ παντὸς θηρίου ἀκαθάρτου 'and a haunt for every unclean spirit, every unclean bird, and every unclean wild animal' Re 18.2.

86 Weight

Outline of Subdomains

A   Heavy, Light (86.1-86.3)
B   Pound, Talent (Specific Units of Weight) (86.4-86.5)

A Heavy, Light (86.1-86.3)

86.1 βαρύς[a], εῖα, ύ: pertaining to being relatively heavy – 'heavy, burdensome.' δεσμεύουσιν δὲ φορτία βαρέα καὶ δυσβάστακτα καὶ ἐπιτιθέασιν ἐπὶ τοὺς ὤμους τῶν ἀνθρώπων 'they fix heavy loads that are hard to carry and tie them on people's backs' Mt 23.4. Although the meaning of βαρύς in Mt 23.4 is literal, the entire expression is figurative, and so it may be necessary in some languages to say 'they fix up heavy loads, so to speak, and tie them on people's backs.'

86.2 ἐλαφρός[a], ά, όν: pertaining to being relatively light in weight – 'light, not heavy.' τὸ φορτίον μου ἐλαφρόν ἐστιν 'my burden is light' Mt 11.30. Though in Mt 11.30 ἐλαφρός can be understood in a literal sense, the entire statement in this verse is, of course, figurative. Therefore, one can also interpret ἐλαφρός in Mt 11.30 as figurative (see 22.38). Note, however, that the phrase ὁ . . . ζυγός μου does not refer to something which Christ carries but to something which he places upon his followers. The same is true of the phrase τὸ φορτίον μου 'my burden,' which is the burden he gives to his disciples or servants.

86.3 κουφίζω: to cause something to weigh less – 'to lighten, to make less heavy.' ἐκούφιζον τὸ πλοῖον ἐκβαλλόμενοι τὸν σῖτον εἰς τὴν θάλασσαν 'they lightened the ship by throwing the wheat into the sea' Ac 27.38.

B Pound, Talent (Specific Units of Weight) (86.4-86.5)

86.4 λίτρα, ας *f*: a Roman pound, weighing about twelve ounces or about 325 grams – 'pound, pint.' ἡ οὖν Μαριὰμ λαβοῦσα λίτραν μύρου 'then Mary took a pound of perfume' Jn 12.3. In speaking of perfume in Jn 12.3 it may be far better to indicate quantity rather than weight, and therefore one may translate 'then Mary took a pint of perfume.' In translating λίτρα in the NT, one need not identify the pound as being 'a Roman pound.' It is better to employ a common term for pound (normally weighing sixteen ounces) or to provide a rounded-off equivalent of the amount in metric units, for example, three hundred grams or one-half liter.

86.5 ταλαντιαῖος, α, ον: pertaining to weighing a talent or 125 Roman pounds of twelve ounces each or approximately ninety pounds (English weight) or forty kilograms – 'weighing a talent.' χάλαζα μεγάλη ὡς ταλαντιαία 'great stones of hail, each weighing some ninety pounds' Re 16.21. It may, however, be better to use in Re 16.21 an expression with a more general sense, for example, 'great stones of hail weighing almost a hundred pounds' or '. . . forty kilos.'

87 Status[1]

Outline of Subdomains

A Position, Rank (87.1-87.3)
B Honor or Respect in Relation to Status (87.4-87.18)
C High Status or Rank (including persons of high status) (87.19-87.57)
D Low Status or Rank (including persons of low status) (87.58-87.75)
E Slave, Free (87.76-87.86)

A Position, Rank (87.1-87.3)

87.1 τόπος[d], **ου** *m*: the position of a person within a group, implying a particular role or type of activity – 'position, role.' λαβεῖν τὸν τόπον τῆς διακονίας ταύτης καὶ ἀποστολῆς 'to take this position of service (literally 'the position of this service') as an apostle' Ac 1.25. In a number of languages the equivalent of this expression in Ac 1.25 may be simply 'to undertake the work of an apostle' or 'to be an apostle in serving.' For another interpretation of τόπος in Ac 1.25, involving a shift in focus, see 42.21.

87.2 κλῆσις[c], **εως** *f*: the station in life or social role which one has – 'station, role.' ἕκαστος ἐν τῇ κλήσει ᾗ ἐκλήθη ἐν ταύτῃ μενέτω 'everyone should remain in the station of life in which he was called' 1 Cor 7.20. In this context, κλῆσις refers to the status or role of being either a slave or a free person. In a number of languages this expression in 1 Cor 7.20 can be best translated as 'everyone should continue to be the same kind of person that he was when he was called.' Such an expression must, of course, refer to one's posi-

tion in society and in the total social structure, not to particular aspects of moral or immoral behavior.

87.3 βαθμός, οῦ *m*: a standing in society implying rank or status – 'standing, rank, status.' οἱ γὰρ καλῶς διακονήσαντες βαθμὸν ἑαυτοῖς καλὸν περιποιοῦνται 'those who do a good work win for themselves a good standing' 1 Tm 3.13.

B Honor or Respect in Relation to Status (87.4-87.18)

87.4 τιμή[a], **ῆς** *f*; **δόξα**[e], **ης** *f*: honor as an element in the assignment of status to a person – 'honor, respect, status.'
τιμή[a]: προφήτης ἐν τῇ ἰδίᾳ πατρίδι τιμὴν οὐκ ἔχει 'a prophet has no honor in his own country' Jn 4.44.
δόξα[e]: τότε ἔσται σοι δόξα ἐνώπιον πάντων τῶν συνανακειμένων 'this will bring you honor in the presence of all the other guests' Lk 14.10.

87.5 κλέος, ους *n*: a good reputation as an index of status – 'honor, fame, good reputation.' ποῖον γὰρ κλέος εἰ ἁμαρτάνοντες καὶ κολαφιζόμενοι ὑπομενεῖτε; 'for what honor is there in enduring the beatings you deserve for having done wrong?' 1 Pe 2.20.

87.6 τίμιος[b], **α, ον**; **ἔντιμος**[b], **ον**; **ἔνδοξος**[b], **ον**: pertaining to high status, involving both honor and respect – 'honored, respected.'
τίμιος[b]: νομοδιδάσκαλος τίμιος παντὶ τῷ λαῷ 'a teacher of the Law (who was) respected by all the people' Ac 5.34.
ἔντιμος[b]: καὶ τοὺς τοιούτους ἐντίμους ἔχετε 'and show respect to all such persons' Php 2.29.
ἔνδοξος[b]: ὑμεῖς ἔνδοξοι, ἡμεῖς δὲ ἄτιμοι 'you are honored; we are dishonored' 1 Cor 4.10.

87.7 δόκιμος[c], **ον**: pertaining to being respected on the basis of proven worth – 'respected, honored.' εὐάρεστος τῷ θεῷ καὶ δόκιμος τοῖς ἀνθρώποις 'pleasing to God and respected by people' Ro 14.18. In a number of languages, meanings such as those of τίμιος[b], ἔντιμος[b], ἔνδοξος[b] (87.6), and δόκιμος[c]

---

1 In any analysis of *Status* a number of factors must be taken into account, for example, wealth, power, authority, fame, respect, occupation, and birth. Furthermore, there are a number of semantic domains in which status is highly significant, though secondary to rank and role. For example, there are numerous ranks or priestly functionaries in religion, but these are treated under *Religious Activities* (Domain 53). The same is true of persons with various military ranks or statuses which are treated in *Military Activities* (Domain 55).

may be rendered by a type of clause involving people's attitudes toward an individual, for example, 'one who people think is great' or 'one of whom everyone approves' or 'one to whom everyone looks up.'

87.8 τιμάωᵃ; **δοξάζω**ᵇ: to attribute high status to someone by honoring – 'to honor, to respect.'
τιμάωᵃ: τίμα τὸν πατέρα καὶ τὴν μητέρα 'honor your father and mother' Mt 15.4; ὁ μὴ τιμῶν τὸν υἱὸν οὐ τιμᾷ τὸν πατέρα 'the one who does not honor the Son does not honor the Father' Jn 5.23.
δοξάζωᵇ: ἔστιν ὁ πατήρ μου ὁ δοξάζων με 'the one who honors me is my Father' Jn 8.54; ὅπως δοξασθῶσιν ὑπὸ τῶν ἀνθρώπων 'so that they may be honored by the people' Mt 6.2.

87.9 ἐνδοξάζομαι: to be the object of great honor – 'to receive honor, to be honored.' ὅπως ἐνδοξασθῇ τὸ ὄνομα τοῦ κυρίου ἡμῶν Ἰησοῦ ἐν ὑμῖν 'so that the name of our Lord Jesus may receive honor from you' 2 Th 1.12.

87.10 συνδοξάζομαι: to receive great honor together with someone else – 'to be honored together with, to be exalted together with.' εἴπερ συμπάσχομεν ἵνα καὶ συνδοξασθῶμεν 'if we suffer together with (him), we will also receive honor together with (him)' Ro 8.17.

87.11 ἐντρέπομαι: to show respect to a person on the basis of his high status – 'to respect, to show respect.' πέμψω τὸν υἱόν μου τὸν ἀγαπητόν· ἴσως τοῦτον ἐντραπήσονται 'I will send my own dear son; surely they will respect him' Lk 20.13. In a number of languages the showing of respect is referred to by a number of figurative expressions, for example, 'to bow before,' 'to kneel before,' 'to crouch before,' or 'to stand appalled in the presence of.'

87.12 οἶδαᵉ; **φρονέω**ᵈ: to acknowledge the high status of a person or event – 'to honor, to show honor to, to respect.'
οἶδαᵉ: ἐρωτῶμεν δὲ ὑμᾶς, ἀδελφοί, εἰδέναι τοὺς κοπιῶντας ἐν ὑμῖν 'we beg you, Christian brothers, to respect those who work among you' 1 Th 5.12.

φρονέωᵈ: ὁ φρονῶν τὴν ἡμέραν κυρίῳ φρονεῖ 'one who respects a certain day shows his respect for the Lord' Ro 14.6.

87.13 στεφανόωᵇ: (a figurative extension of meaning of στεφανόω 'to crown' or 'to put a victory wreath on,' not occurring in the NT with this meaning) to show particular honor to a person as the result of some type of victory – 'to honor, to exalt.' βλέπομεν Ἰησοῦν διὰ τὸ πάθημα τοῦ θανάτου δόξῃ καὶ τιμῇ ἐστεφανωμένον 'we see Jesus exalted with glory and honor because of the death he suffered' He 2.9.

87.14 φοβέομαιᵇ; **τρέμω**ᶜ: to have such awe or respect for a person as to involve a measure of fear – 'to fear, to show great reverence for, to show great respect for.'
φοβέομαιᵇ: κριτής τις ἦν ἔν τινι πόλει τὸν θεὸν μὴ φοβούμενος καὶ ἄνθρωπον μὴ ἐντρεπόμενος 'there was a judge in a certain town who neither feared God nor had any respect for people' Lk 18.2.
τρέμωᶜ: τολμηταί, αὐθάδεις, δόξας οὐ τρέμουσιν 'they are bold and arrogant and show no respect at all for the glorious beings' 2 Pe 2.10. For another interpretation of τρέμω in 2 Pe 2.10, see 25.259.
In a number of languages there are serious problems involved in speaking of 'fearing God,' for this might imply merely 'to be scared of God' as though God were some kind of bogeyman. If there is a term with the meaning of 'awe' (perhaps in a phrase such as 'to stand in awe of'), this may be an adequate equivalent. In some instances awe is expressed idiomatically as 'to stand with one's heart in one's throat' or 'to be in someone's presence with one's heart beating fast.'

87.15 μεγαλύνωᶜ: to show respect to a person on the basis of the importance of such an individual – 'to pay special respect to, to hold in high honor, to regard as important.' ἀλλ' ἐμεγάλυνεν αὐτοὺς ὁ λαός 'even though the people held them in great honor' Ac 5.13.

87.16 ὑπερυψόω: to regard a person as being exceptionally honored in view of high status – 'to give exceptional honor.' διὸ καὶ ὁ θεὸς αὐτὸν ὑπερύψωσεν 'therefore God gave him exceptional honor' Php 2.9.

87.17 ἐπιβλέπω^d: to regard a person as deserving special respect – 'to pay special respect to, to look upon as being someone to be honored.' ἐπιβλέψητε δὲ ἐπὶ τὸν φοροῦντα τὴν ἐσθῆτα τὴν λαμπράν 'if you pay special respect to the well-dressed man' Jas 2.3. For another interpretation of ἐπιβλέπω in Jas 2.3, see 24.12.

87.18 πρωτοκλισία, ας *f*; **πρωτοκαθεδρία, ας** *f*: a position or place of particular importance, implying special status to the person occupying it – 'place of honor, seat of honor, best seat, best place.' φιλοῦσιν δὲ τὴν πρωτοκλισίαν ἐν τοῖς δείπνοις καὶ τὰς πρωτοκαθεδρίας ἐν ταῖς συναγωγαῖς 'they love the best places at feasts and the seats of honor in the synagogues' Mt 23.6.

C High Status or Rank (including persons of high status) (87.19-87.57)

87.19 ὕψος^c, **ους** *n*; **ἐξοχή, ῆς** *f*: a position of high status – 'high position, high rank, prominence.'

ὕψος^c: καυχάσθω δὲ ὁ ἀδελφὸς ὁ ταπεινὸς ἐν τῷ ὕψει αὐτοῦ 'let the humble Christian brother rejoice in his high position' or '. . . when (God) lifts him to a high position' Jas 1.9.

ἐξοχή: εἰσελθόντων εἰς τὸ ἀκροατήριον σύν τε χιλιάρχοις καὶ ἀνδράσιν τοῖς κατ' ἐξοχὴν τῆς πόλεως 'entered the audience hall with the military chiefs and the prominent men of the city' Ac 25.23.

87.20 ὑψόω^b: to cause someone to have high status – 'to give high position to, to exalt.' καὶ ὕψωσεν ταπεινούς 'and he gave high position to the lowly' Lk 1.52; τοῦτον ὁ θεὸς ἀρχηγὸν καὶ σωτῆρα ὕψωσεν τῇ δεξιᾷ αὐτοῦ 'God exalted him to his right side as Leader and Savior' Ac 5.31.

87.21 μεγαλωσύνη^a, **ης** *f*; **μεγαλειότης**^a, **ητος** *f*: a state of greatness or importance – 'prominence, greatness, importance.'

μεγαλωσύνη^a: μόνῳ θεῷ . . . δόξα μεγαλωσύνη κράτος 'to the only God . . . glory, prominence, might' Jd 25.

μεγαλειότης^a: καὶ καθαιρεῖσθαι τῆς μεγαλειότητος αὐτῆς 'and that her greatness will be destroyed' Ac 19.27.

87.22 μέγας^d, **μεγάλη, μέγα**: pertaining to being great in terms of status – 'great, important.' οὗτος μέγας κληθήσεται ἐν τῇ βασιλείᾳ τῶν οὐρανῶν 'he will make him great in the kingdom of heaven' Mt 5.19.

87.23 δόξα^f, **ης** *f*: a state of being great and wonderful – 'greatness, glory.' δείκνυσιν αὐτῷ πάσας τὰς βασιλείας τοῦ κόσμου καὶ τὴν δόξαν αὐτῶν 'he showed him all the kingdoms of earth and their greatness' Mt 4.8; οὐδὲ Σολομὼν ἐν πάσῃ τῇ δόξῃ αὐτοῦ 'nor Solomon in all his greatness' or '. . . glorious greatness' Lk 12.27.

87.24 δοξάζω^c: to cause someone to have glorious greatness – 'to make gloriously great, to glorify.' καὶ νῦν δόξασόν με σύ, πάτερ 'and now, Father, glorify me' or '. . . give me that glorious greatness' Jn 17.5. In some languages the equivalent of this expression in Jn 17.5 may be 'raise me up high' or 'give me great glory in the eyes of.'

87.25 καλός^f, **ή, όν; καλῶς**^d: pertaining to having high status, with the possible implication of its attractiveness – 'high, important, fine.'

καλός^f: δεῖ δὲ καὶ μαρτυρίαν καλὴν ἔχειν ἀπὸ τῶν ἔξωθεν 'he should be a man who has a high reputation among the people outside (the church)' 1 Tm 3.7.

καλῶς^d: σὺ κάθου ὧδε καλῶς 'have this best seat here' Jas 2.3. It is also possible that καλῶς in Jas 2.3 has the meaning of a polite invitation, translatable as 'please!' (see 33.177).

87.26 ὑπεροχή, ῆς *f*: a state of high rank or position, with the implication in some contexts of being too high or excessive – 'high status, high sounding, pompous.' ὑπὲρ βασιλέων καὶ πάντων τῶν ἐν ὑπεροχῇ ὄντων 'for kings and all others who are in high position' 1 Tm 2.2; ὑπεροχὴν λόγου ἢ σοφίας 'high-sounding words or wisdom' 1 Cor 2.1.

87.27 εὐγενής^a, **ές**: pertaining to having high status, with the possible implication of special family relations contributing to such status – 'high status, important.' οὐ πολλοὶ σοφοὶ κατὰ σάρκα, οὐ πολλοὶ δυνατοί, οὐ πολλοὶ εὐγενεῖς 'few of you were wise by nature or powerful or of high status' 1 Cor 1.26. In this one occurrence of εὐγενής[a] in the NT, it is somewhat unlikely, though not impossible, that hereditary status is involved.

87.28 κρείττων[b], ον, gen. ονος; μείζων[b], ον: pertaining to having a higher status in comparison to something else – 'better, greater, superior to.'
κρείττων[b]: τοσούτῳ κρείττων γενόμενος τῶν ἀγγέλων 'having been made so much greater than the angels' He 1.4.
μείζων[b]: οὐκ ἐγήγερται ἐν γεννητοῖς γυναικῶν μείζων Ἰωάννου τοῦ βαπτιστοῦ 'none has arisen among those born of women who is greater than John the Baptist' Mt 11.11.

87.29 ἀνώτερον[b]: pertaining to being qualitatively superior in view of being in a higher or better position – 'higher, better.' ἀνάπεσε εἰς τὸν ἔσχατον τόπον, ἵνα ὅταν ἔλθῃ ὁ κεκληκώς σε ἐρεῖ σοι, Φίλε, προσανάβηθι ἀνώτερον 'sit in the lowest place so that when your host comes to you he will say, Come on up, my friend, to a higher place' Lk 14.10.

87.30 ὑπέρ[f]: a marker of status which is superior to another status – 'above, superior to.' οὐκ ἔστιν μαθητὴς ὑπὲρ τὸν διδάσκαλον 'a pupil is not above his teacher' Mt 10.24.

87.31 ἐπάνω[c]; ὑπεράνω[b]: a marker of superior status, suggesting an additional factor of degree – 'far above, considerably superior to.'
ἐπάνω[c]: ὁ ἄνωθεν ἐρχόμενος ἐπάνω πάντων ἐστίν 'he who comes from heaven is far above all' Jn 3.31. (See discussion at 84.13.)
ὑπεράνω[b]: ὑπεράνω πάσης ἀρχῆς καὶ ἐξουσίας καὶ δυνάμεως καὶ κυριότητος 'far above all rulers, authorities, powers, and lords' Eph 1.21.

87.32 πηλίκος[b], η, ον: pertaining to a correlative degree of high status – 'how great, how important.' θεωρεῖτε δὲ πηλίκος οὗτος ᾧ καὶ δεκάτην Ἀβραὰμ ἔδωκεν 'you see, then,

how great he was to whom Abraham gave a tenth' He 7.4.

87.33 εὐσχήμων[b], ον, gen. ονος: pertaining to having special prestige or honor – 'esteemed, honored.' Ἰωσὴφ ὁ ἀπὸ Ἀριμαθαίας εὐσχήμων βουλευτής 'Joseph of Arimathea, an esteemed member of the council' Mk 15.43.

87.34 ἐκ δεξιῶν καθίζω: (an idiom, literally 'to sit on the right side of') to be in a position of high status – 'to sit on the right side of, to be granted high position.' ἵνα εἷς σου ἐκ δεξιῶν . . . καθίσωμεν 'in order that one of us may sit on your right side' or 'in order that one of us may be specially honored' Mk 10.37. Compare the use of ἀριστερός in 87.35 and see the discussion of Mk 10.37 there. For another interpretation of δεξιός in Mk 10.37, see 82.8.

87.35 ἐξ ἀριστερῶν καθίζω: (an idiom, literally 'to sit on the left side of') to be in a position of high status, but less than in the case of the right side (compare 87.34) – 'to be given somewhat less high status, to sit on the left side of.' ἵνα . . . εἷς ἐξ ἀριστερῶν καθίσωμεν 'in order that . . . the other one might sit on your left side' or 'in order that . . . the other of us may be honored but in a somewhat less extensive manner' Mk 10.37. (Compare the use of δεξιός in 87.34.) In a number of languages the equivalent of this entire expression in Mk 10.37 would be 'in order that one of us may be number one and the other may be number two in your kingdom' or 'in order that one of us may be your first officer and the other your second officer in your kingdom.' For another interpretation of ἀριστερός in Mk 10.37, see 82.7.

87.36 καθίζω ἐν δεξιᾷ: (an idiom, literally 'to cause to sit at the right hand') to seat at the right hand of someone as an expression of assigning special importance or high status to such an individual – 'to seat at the right side, to give a special place of honor to.' καθίσας ἐν δεξιᾷ αὐτοῦ ἐν τοῖς ἐπουρανίοις 'and gave him a special place of honor in the heavenly world' Eph 1.20.

87.37 αὐξάνω[d]: to increase in status – 'to become more important, to enjoy greater respect or honor.' ἐκεῖνον δεῖ αὐξάνειν, ἐμὲ δὲ ἐλαττοῦσθαι 'he must become more important while I become less important' Jn 3.30. In some languages the increase or decrease of respect or honor must be expressed idiomatically, for example, 'he must become more of a chief while I become more of a follower' or 'he must become a big man while I become a small man.'

87.38 ἐξεγείρωᶜ: to cause someone to have a higher position and status – 'to give higher status to, to raise up, to exalt.' εἰς αὐτὸ τοῦτο ἐξήγειρά σε 'for this very reason I raised you up' Ro 9.17. For another interpretation of ἐξεγείρω in Ro 9.17, see 13.83.

87.39 ἀνάστασιςᵇ, εως f: a process of change from a lower to a higher status (note the contrast with πτῶσιςᵇ 'a falling,' 87.75) – 'to rise, to rise up, rising up.' κεῖται εἰς πτῶσιν καὶ ἀνάστασιν πολλῶν ἐν τῷ Ἰσραήλ '(this child) is set (by God) for the falling and rising up of many in Israel' Lk 2.34. ἀνάστασις in Lk 2.34 may also be interpreted merely as a change for the better (see 13.60).

Reversals of rank and status are a frequent theme in the declaration of the prophets, and this becomes particularly significant in the Magnificat (see Lk 1.46-55).

87.40 οἱ μεγάλοι (only in the plural): persons of important or high status – 'important persons, great men.' καὶ οἱ μεγάλοι αὐτῶν κατεξουσιάζουσιν αὐτῶν 'and their great men rule over them' Mk 10.42.

87.41 μεγιστάν, ᾶνος m (occurring regularly in the plural): a person of particularly great importance and high status – 'very important person, great person.' δεῖπνον ἐποίησεν τοῖς μεγιστᾶσιν αὐτοῦ 'he gave a banquet for the important persons (in his court)' Mk 6.21.

87.42 οἱ δοκοῦντες: those who have a reputation of being important or are generally recognized as being important – 'important persons, influential persons, prominent persons.' ἀνεθέμην αὐτοῖς τὸ εὐαγγέλιον ὃ κηρύσσω ἐν τοῖς ἔθνεσιν, κατ' ἰδίαν δὲ τοῖς δοκοῦσιν 'in a private meeting with the prominent persons, I

explained to them the gospel message that I preach to the Gentiles' Ga 2.2.

87.43 οἱ δυνατοί: important persons, based upon their power or influence – 'important, influential.' οἱ οὖν ἐν ὑμῖν, φησίν, δυνατοὶ συγκαταβάντες εἴ τί ἐστιν ἐν τῷ ἀνδρὶ ἄτοπον κατηγορείτωσαν αὐτοῦ 'let your important persons go (to Caesarea) with me, he said, and accuse the man if he has done anything wrong' Ac 25.5.

87.44 ἰσχυρόςᵈ, α, ον: pertaining to high status, probably on the basis of significant personal capacity – 'powerful, great.' οἱ πλούσιοι καὶ οἱ ἰσχυροὶ . . . ἔκρυψαν ἑαυτούς 'the rich and the great . . . hid themselves' Re 6.15.

87.45 πρῶτοςᶜ, η, ον: pertaining to being of high rank, with the implication of special prominence and status – 'great, prominent, important, foremost.' Ἡρῴδης . . . δεῖπνον ἐποίησεν . . . τοῖς πρώτοις τῆς Γαλιλαίας 'Herod . . . gave a feast . . . for the important people of Galilee' Mk 6.21; ὃς ἂν θέλη ἐν ὑμῖν εἶναι πρῶτος 'whoever among you wishes to be important' or '. . . to have first rank' Mt 20.27.

87.46 πρωτεύω: to be in the first position, with the implication of high rank and prominence – 'to be the first, to have superior status.' ἵνα γένηται ἐν πᾶσιν αὐτὸς πρωτεύων 'in order that he might have first place in all things' Col 1.18.

87.47 πρωτότοκοςᶜ, ον: pertaining to existing superior to all else of the same or related class – 'superior to, above all.' πρωτότοκος πάσης κτίσεως 'existing superior to all creation' Col 1.15. For another interpretation of πρωτότοκος in Col 1.15, see 13.79; see also discussion at 10.43.

87.48 πατήρᶜ, πατρός m: a title for a person of high rank – 'father, the honorable, excellency.' καὶ πατέρα μὴ καλέσητε ὑμῶν 'do not call anyone among you, Your excellency' or '. . . Father' or '. . . Your honor' Mt 23.9.

87.49 εἰμί τις: (an idiom, literally 'to be someone') to be an important person – 'to be great, to be important.' πρὸ γὰρ τούτων τῶν ἡμερῶν ἀνέστη Θευδᾶς, λέγων εἶναί τινα ἑαυτόν 'some time ago Theudas rose up claiming that he was a great person' Ac 5.36.

87.50 ἐπιστάτης, ου *m*: a person of high status, particularly in view of a role of leadership – 'leader, master.' ἐπιστάτα, δι' ὅλης νυκτὸς κοπιάσαντες οὐδὲν ἐλάβομεν 'Master, we worked hard all night long and caught nothing' Lk 5.5.

87.51 κεφαλή[b], ῆς *f*: (a figurative extension of meaning of κεφαλή[a] 'head,' 8.10) one who is of supreme or pre-eminent status, in view of authority to order or command – 'one who is the head of, one who is superior to, one who is supreme over.' ὅς ἐστιν ἡ κεφαλή, Χριστός 'who is the head, (even) Christ' Eph 4.15; παντὸς ἀνδρὸς ἡ κεφαλὴ ὁ Χριστός ἐστιν, κεφαλὴ δὲ γυναικὸς ὁ ἀνήρ, κεφαλὴ δὲ τοῦ Χριστοῦ ὁ θεός 'Christ is supreme over every man, the husband is supreme over his wife, and God is supreme over Christ' 1 Cor 11.3.

87.52 πρωτοστάτης, ου *m*: a person of top rank in view of leadership – 'leader, ringleader.' εὑρόντες . . . τοῦτον . . . πρωτοστάτην τε τῆς τῶν Ναζωραίων αἱρέσεως 'we found . . . him . . . to be the ringleader of the party of the Nazarenes' Ac 24.5.

87.53 κύριος[d], ου *m*: a title of respect used in addressing or speaking of a man – 'sir, mister.' οἱ δοῦλοι τοῦ οἰκοδεσπότου εἶπον αὐτῷ, Κύριε, οὐχὶ καλὸν σπέρμα ἔσπειρας ἐν τῷ σῷ ἀγρῷ; 'the landowner's servants said to him, Sir, was it not good seed you sowed in your field?' Mt 13.27.

87.54 κυρία, ας *f*: a title of respect used in addressing or speaking of a woman – 'lady, dear lady.' ὁ πρεσβύτερος ἐκλεκτῇ κυρίᾳ καὶ τοῖς τέκνοις αὐτῆς 'the elder (writes) to you, dear lady, and to your children' 2 Jn 1. It is likely, however, that κυρία in 2 Jn 1 refers to the church as a lady.

87.55 κράτιστος, η, ον: pertaining to having noble status, with the implication of power and authority, often employed as a title – 'ex-cellency, most excellent, your honor.' ἀποδεχόμεθα, κράτιστε Φῆλιξ 'most excellent Felix, we welcome (your reforms)' Ac 24.3.

87.56 τῷ ἰδίῳ κυρίῳ στήκει ἢ πίπτει: (an idiom, literally 'to his own master he stands or falls,' probably a familiar adage) whether one maintains one's status or relationship to a master depends on the master's judgment or evaluation – 'honor or disgrace depends on the person whom one serves.' τῷ ἰδίῳ κυρίῳ στήκει ἢ πίπτει 'it is up to his own master whether a person stands or falls' or 'only his master decides whether he stands or falls' or '. . . succeeds or fails' or '. . . is honored or disgraced' Ro 14.4.

87.57 φαντασία, ας *f*: a pompous ceremony, implying a cheap display of high status – 'pomp and ceremony, pompous display.' τῇ οὖν ἐπαύριον ἐλθόντος τοῦ Ἀγρίππα καὶ τῆς Βερνίκης μετὰ πολλῆς φαντασίας 'then the next day Agrippa and Bernice came with great pomp and ceremony' Ac 25.23.

D Low Status or Rank (including persons of low status) (87.58-87.75)

87.58 μικρός[g], ά, όν: pertaining to being of low or unimportant status – 'low, unimportant' (in contrast with μέγας[d] 'great, important,' 87.22). ᾧ προσεῖχον πάντες ἀπὸ μικροῦ ἕως μεγάλου 'everyone there from the least to the greatest paid close attention to him' Ac 8.10; ὁ δὲ μικρότερος ἐν τῇ βασιλείᾳ τῶν οὐρανῶν μείζων αὐτοῦ ἐστιν 'but he who is least in the kingdom of heaven is greater than he is' Mt 11.11.

87.59 ἀγενής, ές; ἄσημος, ον: pertaining to being obscure or insignificant, with the possible implication of lacking in noble descent – 'low, insignificant, inferior.'
ἀγενής: τὰ ἀγενῆ τοῦ κόσμου . . . ἐξελέξατο ὁ θεός 'God chose . . . what was inferior in (the eyes of) the world' 1 Cor 1.28.
ἄσημος: Ταρσεὺς τῆς Κιλικίας, οὐκ ἀσήμου πόλεως πολίτης 'a person of Tarsus in Cilicia, a citizen of a not insignificant city' Ac 21.39. In a number of languages, however, it would be important to avoid the double negative in

Ac 21.39 (despite the effectiveness of the litotes in Greek) by translating 'a citizen of an important city.'

87.60 ταπείνωσις^b, εως *f*: the state of low status, with the probable implication of humility – 'low status, low estate, humility.' ἐπέβλεψεν ἐπὶ τὴν ταπείνωσιν τῆς δούλης αὐτοῦ 'he has looked upon the low status of his bondservant' Lk 1.48.

87.61 ταπεινός^c, ή, όν: pertaining to having low and humble status – 'lowly, humble.' καθεῖλεν δυνάστας ἀπὸ θρόνων καὶ ὕψωσεν ταπεινούς 'he brought down the mighty from their thrones and gave high position to the lowly' Lk 1.52.

87.62 ταπεινόω^c: to cause someone to be in a low status – 'to make humble, to bring down low.' ὅστις δὲ ὑψώσει ἑαυτὸν ταπεινωθήσεται 'whoever exalts himself will be humbled' Mt 23.12.

87.63 ταπεινόομαι: to live in circumstances regarded as characteristic of low status – 'to live in humble circumstances, to live like those of low status.' οἶδα καὶ ταπεινοῦσθαι, οἶδα καὶ περισσεύειν 'I know how to live in humble circumstances and what it is to have more than enough' Php 4.12. In a number of languages ταπεινόομαι in Php 4.12 may be rendered as 'to live like poor people.'

87.64 ὄχλος^b, ου *m*; λαός^d, οῦ *m*: the common people, in contrast with those who are rich, leaders, and/or authorities in the society, often with the implication of disdain and low esteem – 'common people, rabble.' ὄχλος^b: ὁ ὄχλος οὗτος ὁ μὴ γινώσκων τὸν νόμον ἐπάρατοί εἰσιν 'the common people who do not know the Law are damned' Jn 7.49. λαός^d: ἵνα μὴ θόρυβος γένηται ἐν τῷ λαῷ 'that there might not be a riot among the common people' Mt 26.5.

In a number of languages the equivalent of 'the common people' is 'the poor people,' but in some languages an equivalent depends upon geographical location, for example, 'those who live on the edge of town' (the opposite situation from what exists in most present-day metropolitan centers). In still other languages 'the common people' may be designated in terms of lack of status, for example, 'those who have no position' or 'those whom the rich do not greet' or 'those before whom no one ever bows.'

87.65 ὑστερέω^c: to be in a state of low status – 'to be inferior, to lack honor.' τῷ ὑστερουμένῳ περισσοτέραν δοὺς τιμήν 'he gave greater honor to the parts that are inferior' or '. . . to the parts that are lacking in honor' 1 Cor 12.24.

87.66 ἔσχατος^b, η, ον; ἐλάχιστος^c, η, ον: pertaining to being of the lowest status – 'lowest, least important, last.' ἔσχατος^b: ὅταν κληθῇς πορευθεὶς ἀνάπεσε εἰς τὸν ἔσχατον τόπον 'when you are invited (to a feast), go and take the last place' Lk 14.10. ἐλάχιστος^c: ἐφ' ὅσον ἐποιήσατε ἑνὶ τούτων τῶν ἀδελφῶν μου τῶν ἐλαχίστων, ἐμοὶ ἐποιήσατε 'whenever you did this for one of the least important of these brothers of mine, you did it for me' Mt 25.40.

87.67 ἐλάσσων^b, ον: pertaining to being of less status than something else – 'lesser.' χωρὶς δὲ πάσης ἀντιλογίας τὸ ἔλαττον ὑπὸ τοῦ κρείττονος εὐλογεῖται 'without any doubt, that which is of lesser status is blessed by the one of greater status' He 7.7.

87.68 ἐλαττόω: to cause something to have less status or rank – 'to cause to be less.' ἠλάττωσας αὐτὸν βραχύ τι παρ' ἀγγέλους 'having caused him to be somewhat less than angels' He 2.7.

87.69 ἐλαττόομαι: to decrease in status or rank – 'to become less important' (compare αὐξάνω^d 'to become more important,' 87.37). ἐκεῖνον δεῖ αὐξάνειν, ἐμὲ δὲ ἐλαττοῦσθαι 'he must become more important while I become less important' Jn 3.30.

87.70 κενόω^b: to completely remove or eliminate elements of high status or rank by eliminating all privileges or prerogatives associated with such status or rank – 'to empty oneself, to divest oneself of position.' ἑαυτὸν ἐκένωσεν 'he emptied himself' Php 2.7.

87.71 ἀτιμία, ας *f*: a state of dishonor or disrespect as a negative of τιμή[a] 'honor, respect' (87.4) – 'dishonor, disrespect.' ὃ μὲν εἰς τιμὴν σκεῦος, ὃ δὲ εἰς ἀτιμίαν 'the one an object of honor, the other an object of dishonor' Ro 9.21.

87.72 ἄτιμος, ον: pertaining to being of low status on the basis of not having honor or respect – 'lacking in honor, dishonored.' ὑμεῖς ἔνδοξοι, ἡμεῖς δὲ ἄτιμοι 'you are honored; we are dishonored' 1 Cor 4.10.

87.73 ὄνειδος, ους *n*: a low status characterized by public disgrace – 'disgrace.' ἐπεῖδεν ἀφελεῖν ὄνειδός μου ἐν ἀνθρώποις 'he took notice of me to take away my public disgrace' Lk 1.25.

87.74 ἀτιμάζω[b]: to cause someone to have low status involving dishonor and disrespect – 'to cause to be dishonored, to cause to suffer dishonor.' χαίροντες . . . ὅτι κατηξιώθησαν ὑπὲρ τοῦ ὀνόματος ἀτιμασθῆναι 'full of joy . . . that he had considered them worthy to suffer dishonor for the name (of Jesus)' Ac 5.41. In a number of languages the equivalent of 'causing someone to be dishonored' is expressed idiomatically, for example, 'to cause someone to be laughed at' or 'to cause people to wag their heads at someone' or 'to cause people to turn away from someone.'

87.75 πτῶσις[b], εως *f*: (a figurative extension of meaning of πτῶσις 'fall,' not occurring in the NT) radical change toward a lower status (note the contrast with ἀνάστασις[b] 'rising up,' 87.39) – 'a falling.' κεῖται εἰς πτῶσιν καὶ ἀνάστασιν πολλῶν ἐν τῷ Ἰσραήλ '(this child) is set (by God) for the falling and rising up of many in Israel' Lk 2.34. For somewhat different interpretations of πτῶσις in Lk 2.34, see 20.50 and 13.59.

E Slave, Free (87.76-87.86)

87.76 δοῦλος, ου *m*: one who is a slave in the sense of becoming the property of an owner (though in ancient times it was frequently possible for a slave to earn his freedom) – 'slave, bondservant.' λέγω . . . τῷ δούλῳ μου,

Ποίησον τοῦτο, καὶ ποιεῖ 'I say . . . to my slave, Do this, and he does it' Mt 8.9.

When Paul speaks of himself as a slave of Jesus Christ or of God in Ro 1.1, Ga 1.10, and Tt 1.1, the term δοῦλος focuses attention primarily upon his belonging to Christ or to God. There are probably also important positive overtones, since in some languages of the ancient Middle East a phrase meaning 'slave of the king' or 'servant of the king' had become the title of an important person in the government. For a discussion of certain further implications of the term δοῦλος, see the discussion at 87.81.

87.77 παῖς[c], παιδός *m* and *f*: a slave, possibly serving as a personal servant and thus with the implication of kindly regard – 'slave.' ἀλλὰ εἰπὲ λόγῳ, καὶ ἰαθήτω ὁ παῖς μου 'just give the order and my slave will get well' Lk 7.7.

87.78 σῶμα[d], τος *n*: a slave as property to be sold, with the probable implicaton of commerce – 'slave.' οὐδεὶς ἀγοράζει οὐκέτι, γόμον . . . ἵππων . . . σωμάτων 'no one buys their goods any longer . . . their horses . . . slaves' Re 18.11-13.

87.79 δουλεύω[a]: to be a slave of someone – 'to be a slave.' οὐδενὶ δεδουλεύκαμεν πώποτε 'we have never been anyone's slaves' Jn 8.33.

87.80 εἰμὶ ὑπὸ ζυγόν: (an idiom, literally 'to be under a yoke') to be in a state of slavery – 'to be a slave.' ὅσοι εἰσὶν ὑπὸ ζυγὸν δοῦλοι 'those who are slaves' 1 Tm 6.1. In 1 Tm 6.1 ὑπὸ ζυγόν is redundant in that it simply emphasizes the status of being a slave.

87.81 σύνδουλος, ου *m*: one who is a fellow slave or a slave alongside another slave – 'fellow slave.' ἐξελθὼν δὲ ὁ δοῦλος ἐκεῖνος εὗρεν ἕνα τῶν συνδούλων αὐτοῦ 'that slave went out and met one of his fellow slaves' Mt 18.28.

In some languages there is a very strong negative connotation in any word meaning 'slave,' for it may suggest 'vile person' or even 'foreigner,' since in a number of areas only foreigners were made slaves. It may therefore be necessary to use a term for slave which is more or less equivalent to 'servant,' 'one who works without pay,' 'one who must work without pay,' or 'bondservant.'

87.82 δουλόωᵃ: to cause someone to become a slave – 'to enslave, to make a slave of someone.' καὶ δουλώσουσιν αὐτό 'and they will make slaves of them' Ac 7.6. In Ac 7.6 αὐτό refers to the preceding τὸ σπέρμα αὐτοῦ 'his descendants.'

87.83 δούλη, ης *f*; **παιδίσκη, ης** *f*: a female slave – 'slave girl, slave woman.'[2]
δούλη: ἐπέβλεψεν ἐπὶ τὴν ταπείνωσιν τῆς δούλης αὐτοῦ 'he had regard for the humble state of his slave girl' or possibly 'he had regard for the humble state of his slave woman' Lk 1.48.
παιδίσκη: οὐκ ἐσμὲν παιδίσκης τέκνα ἀλλὰ τῆς ἐλευθέρας 'we are not children of a slave woman but of a free woman' Ga 4.31.

87.84 ἐλεύθεροςᵇ, **α, ον**: pertaining to a person who is not a slave, either one who has

never been a slave or one who was a slave formerly but is no longer – 'free person, free man.' ὁ ἐλεύθερος κληθεὶς δοῦλός ἐστιν Χριστοῦ 'a free person who has been called by Christ is his slave' 1 Cor 7.22; πῶς σὺ λέγεις ὅτι Ἐλεύθεροι γενήσεσθε; 'how can you then say, You will become free people?' Jn 8.33.

87.85 ἀπελεύθερος, ου *m*: a person who has previously been a slave but is now released from slavery – 'freedman, free person.' ὁ γὰρ ἐν κυρίῳ κληθεὶς δοῦλος ἀπελεύθερος κυρίου ἐστίν 'for a slave who has been called by the Lord is the Lord's freedman' or '. . . free person' 1 Cor 7.22.

87.86 Λιβερτῖνος, ου *m*: (a Latin name) a group of people, presumably Jews, who had been slaves but later obtained their freedom; their synagogue was also known by the same name – 'free man.' ἀνέστησαν δέ τινες τῶν ἐκ τῆς συναγωγῆς τῆς λεγομένης Λιβερτίνων 'some men opposed him; they were (members) of the synagogue of the Free Men as it was called' Ac 6.9.

---

2 παιδίσκη probably refers to someone younger than would be the case for δούλη.

88 Moral and Ethical Qualities and Related Behavior[1]

Outline of Subdomains[2]

A   Goodness (88.1-88.11)
B   Just, Righteous (88.12-88.23)
C   Holy, Pure (88.24-88.35)
D   Perfect, Perfection (88.36-88.38)
E   Honesty, Sincerity (88.39-88.45)
F   Modesty, Propriety (88.46-88.50)
G   Humility (88.51-88.58)
H   Gentleness, Mildness (88.59-88.65)
I   Kindness, Harshness (88.66-88.74)
J   Mercy, Merciless (88.75-88.82)
K   Self-Control, Lack of Self-Control (88.83-88.92)
L   Sensible Behavior, Senseless Behavior (88.93-88.99)
M   Mature Behavior (88.100-88.101)
N   Peaceful Behavior (88.102-88.104)

1 Domain 88 *Moral and Ethical Qualities and Related Behavior* overlaps in certain respects with Domain 41 *Behavior and Related States*. The basic reason for such overlapping of semantic elements is that all moral and ethical qualities are in one way or another related to the manner in which people conduct themselves. In Domain 88, however, the focus is upon the moral and ethical qualities of states and behavior. In Domain 41 the focus is upon behavior which is either ethically neutral or does not imply ethical aspects. There is also a degree to which Domain 88 overlaps with Domains 36-40, since moral and ethical elements almost inevitably involve certain interpersonal relations. Domain 88 is unusually large, primarily because moral and ethical qualities and their consequent behavior figure so largely in the content of the NT.
2 In most domains it seems best to treat positive and negative features in as close a proximity as possible. In this domain, however, it has seemed better in general to treat the positive qualities first and then the set of corresponding negative qualities, though there are a number of exceptions primarily because of the related lexical bases.

O   Bad, Evil, Harmful, Damaging
     (88.105-88.125)
P   Treat Badly (88.126-88.134)
Q   Act Harshly (88.135-88.138)
R   Act Lawlessly (88.139-88.143)
S   Exploit (88.144-88.148)
T   Act Shamefully (88.149-88.151)
U   Mislead, Lead Astray, Deceive
     (88.152-88.159)
V   Envy, Jealousy (88.160-88.166)
W   Resentful, Hold a Grudge Against
     (88.167-88.170)
X   Anger, Be Indignant With
     (88.171-88.191)
Y   Despise, Scorn, Contempt
     (88.192-88.197)
Z   Hate, Hateful (88.198-88.205)
A'   Arrogance, Haughtiness, Pride
     (88.206-88.222)
B'   Stubbornness (88.223-88.226)
C'   Hypocrisy, Pretense (88.227-88.237)
D'   Show Favoritism, Prejudice
     (88.238-88.242)
E'   Being a Busybody (88.243-88.245)
F'   Laziness, Idleness (88.246-88.251)
G'   Extravagant Living, Intemperate Living
     (88.252-88.255)
H'   Impurity (88.256-88.261)
I'   Licentiousness, Perversion
     (88.262-88.270)
J'   Sexual Misbehavior (88.271-88.282)
K'   Drunkenness (88.283-88.288)
L'   Sin, Wrongdoing, Guilt (88.289-88.318)

A Goodness (88.1-88.11)

88.1 ἀγαθός^a, ή, όν; ἀγαθωσύνη^a, ης *f*: positive moral qualities of the most general nature – 'good, goodness, good act.'

ἀγαθός^a: τί ἀγαθὸν ποιήσω ἵνα σχῶ ζωὴν αἰώνιον; 'what good thing must I do to receive eternal life?' Mt 19.16.

ἀγαθωσύνη^a: πέπεισμαι . . . ὅτι καὶ αὐτοὶ μεστοί ἐστε ἀγαθωσύνης 'I am sure . . . that you are full of goodness' Ro 15.14. In a number of languages there is no abstract term such as 'goodness.' Since goodness implies some type of activity involving others, one must frequently use a verb expression, for example, 'to be good to' or 'to benefit.' The qualification 'full of' in Ro 15.14 must likewise be

restructured in a number of languages so as to indicate the fact that one always engages in doing good, for example, 'that you are always doing good to people.'

88.2 ἄκακος^a, ον: pertaining to being without fault and hence guileless – 'without fault, guileless, innocent.' ὅσιος, ἄκακος, ἀμίαντος, κεχωρισμένος ἀπὸ τῶν ἁμαρτωλῶν 'holy, guileless, undefiled, set apart from sinners' He 7.26. In He 7.26 ἄκακος has a far more positive meaning than merely 'not being bad.' In other words, the negation of κακός^a 'bad' (88.106) does not produce a term which is merely morally neutral, but it designates something of a clearly positive character.[3]

88.3 ἀγαθοποιέω; ἀγαθοποιΐα, ας *f*; ἀγαθοεργέω: to engage in doing what is good – 'to do good, to perform good deeds, good works.'

ἀγαθοποιέω: εἰ ἀγαθοποιοῦντες καὶ πάσχοντες ὑπομενεῖτε 'if you endure suffering when you have done good' 1 Pe 2.20.

ἀγαθοποιΐα: πιστῷ κτίστῃ παρατιθέσθωσαν τὰς ψυχὰς αὐτῶν ἐν ἀγαθοποιΐᾳ 'let them entrust themselves to their faithful Creator by the good deeds they do' 1 Pe 4.19.

ἀγαθοεργέω: ἀγαθοεργεῖν, πλουτεῖν ἐν ἔργοις καλοῖς 'to do good, to be rich in good works' 1 Tm 6.18.

88.4 καλός^a, ή, όν; καλῶς^a: pertaining to a positive moral quality, with the implication of being favorably valued – 'good, fine, praiseworthy.'

καλός^a: ὁ ποιμὴν ὁ καλὸς τὴν ψυχὴν αὐτοῦ τίθησιν ὑπὲρ τῶν προβάτων 'the good shepherd is willing to die for the sheep' Jn 10.11.

καλῶς^a: ζηλοῦσιν ὑμᾶς οὐ καλῶς 'they have a deep concern for you, but their intentions are not good' Ga 4.17.

88.5 καλοποιέω: to do that which has a positive moral quality and which would nor-

---

3 There is a certain parallel to ἄκακος in the English expression 'not bad,' which in many contexts indicates something which is positively good. In fact, with certain intonation the expression 'not bad' may actually have a stronger positive designation than 'good.'

mally produce a favorable response – 'to do good.' ὑμεῖς δέ, ἀδελφοί, μὴ ἐγκακήσητε καλοποιοῦντες 'but you, fellow believers, must not get tired of doing good' 2 Th 3.13.

88.6 εὖª: that which is good in the sense of beneficial – 'good, beneficial.' ὅταν θέλητε δύνασθε αὐτοῖς εὖ ποιῆσαι 'whenever you want to, you can do good to them' Mk 14.7.

88.7 εὐεργετέω; εὐεργεσία, ας f; εὐποιΐα, ας f: to do that which is good and beneficial to someone – 'to do good, good deed.'
εὐεργετέω: ὃς διῆλθεν εὐεργετῶν 'who went everywhere doing good' Ac 10.38.
εὐεργεσία: ἀνακρινόμεθα ἐπὶ εὐεργεσίᾳ ἀνθρώπου ἀσθενοῦς 'we are being questioned about a good deed done to a lame man' Ac 4.9.
εὐποιΐα: τῆς δὲ εὐποιΐας καὶ κοινωνίας μὴ ἐπιλανθάνεσθε 'do not forget to do good and to share with one another' He 13.16.

88.8 ἀγαθοποιός, οῦ m: (derivative of ἀγαθοποιέω 'to do good,' 88.3) one who customarily does good – 'one who does good, one who benefits others.' εἰς ἐκδίκησιν κακοποιῶν ἔπαινον δὲ ἀγαθοποιῶν 'to punish the evildoers and praise those who do good' 1 Pe 2.14.

88.9 χρηστόςᵇ, ή, όν: pertaining to being useful and benevolent – 'good, useful, suitable.' φθείρουσιν ἤθη χρηστὰ ὁμιλίαι κακαί 'bad companions ruin good habits' 1 Cor 15.33.

88.10 χρηστότηςª, ητος f: an event or activity which is useful or benevolent – 'that which is useful, what is benevolent, benevolence.' οὐκ ἔστιν ὁ ποιῶν χρηστότητα, οὐκ ἔστιν ἕως ἑνός 'no one does what is useful, not even one' Ro 3.12. In the case of χρηστόςᵇ (88.9) and χρηστότηςª, an equivalent often contains an expression meaning 'to help.' For example, the expression 'what is useful' is often rendered as 'that which helps people' or 'that which proves good for people.'

88.11 ἀρετήª, ῆς f: the quality of moral excellence – 'outstanding goodness, virtue.' εἴ τις ἀρετὴ καὶ εἴ τις ἔπαινος 'if there is any moral excellence and if there is (reason for) praise' Php 4.8; τοῦ καλέσαντος ἡμᾶς ἰδίᾳ δόξῃ καὶ ἀρετῇ 'one who has called us to (share in) his own glory and moral excellence' 2 Pe 1.3. It is possible, however, that ἀρετή in 2 Pe 1.3 denotes the manifestation of (divine) power (see 76.14).

B Just, Righteous (88.12-88.23)

88.12 δίκαιοςª, α, ον: pertaining to being in accordance with what God requires – 'righteous, just.' Ἰωσὴφ δὲ ὁ ἀνὴρ αὐτῆς, δίκαιος ὢν 'Joseph, her husband, was a righteous man' Mt 1.19.

88.13 δικαιοσύνηª, ης f: the act of doing what God requires – 'righteousness, doing what God requires, doing what is right.' μακάριοι οἱ δεδιωγμένοι ἕνεκεν δικαιοσύνης 'happy are those who suffer persecution because of their doing what God requires' Mt 5.10.

88.14 δικαίωμαᵇ, τος n: an act which is in accordance with what God requires – 'righteous act.' οὕτως καὶ δι' ἑνὸς δικαιώματος εἰς πάντας ἀνθρώπους εἰς δικαίωσιν ζωῆς 'in the same way the one righteous act sets all people free and gives them life' Ro 5.18.

88.15 ἔνδικος, ον; δικαίως: pertaining to being right as the result of being justified and deserved – 'right, just.'
ἔνδικος: ὧν τὸ κρίμα ἔνδικόν ἐστιν 'their condemnation is right' Ro 3.8.
δικαίως: ἡμεῖς μὲν δικαίως, ἄξια γὰρ ὧν ἐπράξαμεν ἀπολαμβάνομεν 'our (sentence) is right, for we are getting what we deserve for what we did' Lk 23.41.

88.16 δικαιόωᵇ: to demonstrate that something is morally right – 'to show to be right, to prove to be right.' ὅπως ἂν δικαιωθῇς ἐν τοῖς λόγοις σου 'you must be shown to be right when you speak' Ro 3.4.

88.17 εὐθύςᵇ, εῖα, ύ: pertaining to being just and right – 'just, right, upright.' ἡ γὰρ καρδία σου οὐκ ἔστιν εὐθεῖα ἔναντι τοῦ θεοῦ 'for your heart is not right before God' Ac 8.21.

88.18 εὐθεῖα ὁδός: (an idiom, literally 'a straight road') the right or correct pattern of behavior – 'right way, correct manner of life, just way of life.' καταλείποντες εὐθεῖαν ὁδόν 'having left the right way of life' 2 Pe 2.15.

88.19 εὐθύτης, ητος f: the quality of uprightness – 'righteousness, righteous, uprightness.' ἡ ῥάβδος τῆς εὐθύτητος ῥάβδος τῆς βασιλείας σου 'the scepter of your kingdom is a righteous scepter' He 1.8. In a number of languages it makes no sense to speak of a 'righteous scepter,' and therefore this expression in He 1.8 may be better rendered as 'you will rule righteously' or 'the way in which you rule is just.'

88.20 ἄδικος, ον; ἀδίκως: pertaining to not being right or just – 'unjust, unjustly, unrighteous.' ἄδικος: μὴ ἄδικος ὁ θεὸς ὁ ἐπιφέρων τὴν ὀργήν; 'is God unjust when he punishes (us)?' Ro 3.5. ἀδίκως: χάρις εἰ . . . ὑποφέρει τις λύπας πάσχων ἀδίκως '(God) will bless if . . . one endures the pain of suffering unjustly' 1 Pe 2.19.

88.21 ἀδικία, ας f: an activity which is unjust – 'unjust deed, unrighteousness, doing what is unjust.' ἀπόστητε ἀπ' ἐμοῦ, πάντες ἐργάται ἀδικίας 'get away from me, all you workers of what is unjust' Lk 13.27.

88.22 ἀδικέω[b]: to do that which is unjust or unrighteous – 'to act unjustly, to do what is wrong.' Ἰουδαίους οὐδὲν ἠδίκησα, ὡς καὶ σὺ κάλλιον ἐπιγινώσκεις 'I have done nothing wrong to the Jews, as you also very well know' Ac 25.10.

88.23 ἀδίκημα, τος n: (derivative of ἀδικέω[b] 'to act unjustly,' 88.22) what is done in an unrighteous or unjust manner – 'unrighteous act, crime.' αὐτοὶ οὗτοι εἰπάτωσαν τί εὗρον ἀδίκημα στάντος μου 'let these men themselves tell what unrighteous act they found me guilty of' Ac 24.20.

C Holy, Pure (88.24-88.35)

88.24 ἅγιος[a], α, ον; ὅσιος[a], α, ον; ὁσίως: pertaining to being holy in the sense of superior moral qualities and possessing certain essentially divine qualities in contrast with what is human – 'holy, pure, divine.'[4]
ἅγιος[a]: κατὰ τὸν καλέσαντα ὑμᾶς ἅγιον καὶ αὐτοὶ ἅγιοι ἐν πάσῃ ἀναστροφῇ γενήθητε, διότι γέγραπται ὅτι Ἅγιοι ἔσεσθε, ὅτι ἐγὼ ἅγιός εἰμι 'be holy in all that you do, just as he who called you is holy, because it is written, Be holy because I am holy' 1 Pe 1.15-16.
ὅσιος[a]: κύριε . . . ὅτι μόνος ὅσιος 'Lord . . . for you alone are holy' Re 15.4.
ὁσίως: ὁσίως καὶ δικαίως καὶ ἀμέμπτως ὑμῖν τοῖς πιστεύουσιν ἐγενήθημεν 'our conduct toward you who believe was holy and right and without fault' 1 Th 2.10.

88.25 ἁγιωσύνη[a], ης f; ἁγιότης, ητος f; ὁσιότης[a], ητος f: the quality of holiness as an expression of the divine in contrast with the human – 'holiness, divine quality.'
ἁγιωσύνη[a]: τοῦ ὁρισθέντος υἱοῦ θεοῦ ἐν δυνάμει κατὰ πνεῦμα ἁγιωσύνης 'as to his divine being, he was shown with great power to be the Son of God' Ro 1.4.
ἁγιότης: εἰς τὸ μεταλαβεῖν τῆς ἁγιότητος αὐτοῦ 'so that we may share his holiness' He 12.10.
ὁσιότης[a]: ἐν ὁσιότητι καὶ δικαιοσύνῃ ἐνώπιον αὐτοῦ πάσαις ταῖς ἡμέραις ἡμῶν 'to be holy and righteous before him all the days of our life' Lk 1.75. For another interpretation of ὁσιότης in Lk 1.75, see 53.45.

88.26 ἁγιάζω[b]: to cause someone to have the quality of holiness – 'to make holy.'[5] αὐτὸς δὲ ὁ θεὸς τῆς εἰρήνης ἁγιάσαι ὑμᾶς ὁλοτελεῖς 'may God himself who gives (us) peace make you holy in every way' 1 Th 5.23; καὶ ὁ ἅγιος ἁγιασθήτω ἔτι 'whoever is holy must keep on being holy' Re 22.11.

88.27 ἁγιάζω[c]: to feel reverence for or to honor as holy – 'to hallow, to regard as holy, to honor as holy.' ἁγιασθήτω τὸ ὄνομά σου

---

4 There may be certain subtle distinctions in these two sets of meanings, those with the stem ἁγ- and those with the stem ὁσ-, but this cannot be determined with any degree of certainty from existing contexts.
5 Note that ἁγιάζω[b] denotes the causing of a quality of holiness in contrast with ἁγιάζω[a] (53.44) which means the dedication of someone to the service of or loyalty to deity.

'hallowed be your name' or 'may your name be honored as holy' Mt 6.9. In a number of languages it is impossible to employ an expression such as 'your name' as a reference for God himself. Therefore, it may be necessary to translate this expression in Mt 6.9 as 'may you be reverenced as holy' or even 'may you be acknowledged as God.'

88.28 ἁγνός, ή, όν: pertaining to being without moral defect or blemish and hence pure – 'pure, without defect.' ἐποπτεύσαντες τὴν ἐν φόβῳ ἁγνὴν ἀναστροφὴν ὑμῶν 'for they will see how pure and reverent your conduct is' 1 Pe 3.2.

88.29 ἁγνεία, ας f; ἁγνότης, ητος f: the quality of moral purity – 'to be without moral defect, purity.'
ἁγνεία: τύπος γίνου τῶν πιστῶν ἐν λόγῳ, ἐν ἀναστροφῇ, ἐν ἀγάπῃ, ἐν πίστει, ἐν ἁγνείᾳ 'be an example for the believers in your speech, conduct, love, faith, and purity' 1 Tm 4.12.
ἁγνότης: ἐν παντὶ συνίσταντες ἑαυτοὺς ὡς θεοῦ διάκονοι . . . ἐν ἁγνότητι 'in everything we do we show that we are God's servants . . . by our purity' 2 Cor 6.4-6.
In a number of languages the meaning of ἁγνεία and ἁγνότης is expressed idiomatically, for example, 'to have a clean heart,' 'to not have other thoughts,' or 'to not cover up one's real desires.'

88.30 ἁγνίζω^b; ἀπολούω (a figurative extension of meaning of ἀπολούω 'wash off, wash away,' not occurring in the NT): to cause a state of moral purity – 'to purify, to cause to be pure.'
ἁγνίζω^b: ἁγνίζει ἑαυτὸν καθὼς ἐκεῖνος ἁγνός ἐστιν 'he purifies himself even as that one is pure' 1 Jn 3.3; ἁγνίσατε καρδίας 'purify your hearts' Jas 4.8. In a number of languages this phrase in Jas 4.8 may be expressed idiomatically as 'get rid of all your bad desires.'
ἀπολούω: βάπτισαι καὶ ἀπόλουσαι τὰς ἁμαρτίας σου ἐπικαλεσάμενος τὸ ὄνομα αὐτοῦ 'be baptized and have your sins purified by asking the Lord to help you' Ac 22.16; ἀλλὰ ἀπελούσασθε, ἀλλὰ ἡγιάσθητε 'but you have been purified, you have been made holy' 1 Cor 6.11.

88.31 ῥαντίζομαι τὴν καρδίαν: (an idiom, literally 'to be sprinkled in the heart') to be purified from moral failure – 'to have one's heart made pure, to be purified in one's heart, to be pure.' ῥεραντισμένοι τὰς καρδίας ἀπὸ συνειδήσεως πονηρᾶς 'to have hearts purified from a guilty conscience' He 10.22.

88.32 ἀκέραιος, ον: pertaining to being without a mixture of evil and hence to being pure – 'pure, untainted.' θέλω δὲ ὑμᾶς σοφοὺς εἶναι εἰς τὸ ἀγαθόν, ἀκεραίους δὲ εἰς τὸ κακόν 'I want you to be wise about what is good and untainted with what is evil' Ro 16.19.

88.33 ἄσπιλος^b, ον: (a figurative extension of meaning of ἄσπιλος^a 'spotless, without stain,' 79.59) pertaining to being without that which might mar one's moral character – 'morally spotless, pure.' σπουδάσατε ἄσπιλοι καὶ ἀμώμητοι 'do your best to be pure and blameless' 2 Pe 3.14.

88.34 ἄμωμος^b, ον: pertaining to being without fault and hence morally blameless – 'blameless, without fault, faultless, perfect.' ἁγίους καὶ ἀμώμους κατενώπιον αὐτοῦ 'holy and perfect before him' or 'holy and faultless before him' Eph 1.4; τέκνα θεοῦ ἄμωμα μέσον γενεᾶς σκολιᾶς 'faultless children of God in the midst of a perverted generation (of people)' Php 2.15.

88.35 ἀμώμητος, ον: pertaining to not being subject to blame and hence morally irreproachable – 'blameless, without blame, being one who cannot be blamed.' σπουδάσατε ἄσπιλοι καὶ ἀμώμητοι 'do your best to be pure and blameless' 2 Pe 3.14.

D Perfect, Perfection (88.36-88.38)

88.36 τέλειος^a, α, ον: pertaining to being perfect in the sense of not lacking any moral quality – 'perfect.' εἴ τις ἐν λόγῳ οὐ πταίει, οὗτος τέλειος ἀνήρ 'if someone never makes a mistake in what he says, he is a perfect man' Jas 3.2; ἔσεσθε οὖν ὑμεῖς τέλειοι ὡς ὁ πατὴρ ὑμῶν ὁ οὐράνιος τέλειός ἐστιν 'therefore be perfect even as your heavenly Father is perfect' Mt 5.48. Compare the meaning of τέλειος^e 'mature' in 88.100.

88.37 τελειότης^b, ητος *f*: a state of perfection, implying some process of maturity – 'perfection, perfect.' ἐπὶ πᾶσιν δὲ τούτοις τὴν ἀγάπην, ὅ ἐστιν σύνδεσμος τῆς τελειότητος 'in addition to all these, love, which is the bond of perfection' or '. . . which produces perfect unity' or '. . . which binds all things together in perfect unity' Col 3.14.

88.38 τελειόω^a; τελείωσις^a, εως *f*: to make perfect in the moral sense – 'to make perfect, to perfect, causing perfection.'
τελειόω^a: οὐδέποτε δύναται τοὺς προσερχομένους τελειῶσαι 'it is not ever able to make perfect those who come (to God)' He 10.1; ἀληθῶς ἐν τούτῳ ἡ ἀγάπη τοῦ θεοῦ τετελείωται 'truly in this person the love of God is made perfect' 1 Jn 2.5. For another interpretation of τελειόω in 1 Jn 2.5, see 73.7.
τελείωσις^a: εἰ μὲν οὖν τελείωσις διὰ τῆς Λευιτικῆς ἱερωσύνης ἦν 'then, perfection was obtainable through the Levitical priesthood' or 'if the Levitical priesthood could cause perfection' He 7.11.

E Honesty, Sincerity[6] (88.39-88.45)

88.39 ἀληθής^c, ές: pertaining to being truthful and honest – 'truthful, honest, a person of integrity.' οἴδαμεν ὅτι ἀληθὴς εἶ 'we know that you are an honest man' Mt 22.16. In a number of languages one must translate ἀληθής in Mt 22.16 as 'you always say what is true.'

88.40 ἀψευδής, ές: pertaining to not speaking falsehood – 'truthful.' ἣν ἐπηγγείλατο ὁ ἀψευδὴς θεός 'God who is truthful promised this' Tt 1.2.

88.41 εἰλικρινής, ές: pertaining to being sincere in the sense of having pure motivation – 'sincere, without hidden motives.' ἵνα ἦτε εἰλικρινεῖς καὶ ἀπρόσκοποι εἰς ἡμέραν Χριστοῦ 'that you may be sincere and without blame on the day of Christ' Php 1.10.[7]

88.42 εἰλικρίνεια, ας *f*: the quality of sincerity as an expression of pure or unadulterated motives – 'sincerity, purity of motives.' ἐν ἀζύμοις εἰλικρινείας καὶ ἀληθείας '(the bread) that has no yeast, (the bread) of sincerity and truth' or '(bread) without yeast, representing sincerity and truth' or '. . . which stands for sincerity and truth' 1 Cor 5.8; ὡς ἐξ εἰλικρινείας, ἀλλ' ὡς ἐκ θεοῦ κατέναντι θεοῦ ἐν Χριστῷ λαλοῦμεν 'but because God has sent us, we speak with sincerity in his presence, as (servants of) Christ' 2 Cor 2.17.

88.43 ἀφθορία, ας *f*: the quality of integrity as an expression of moral soundness – 'integrity, sincerity.' ἐν τῇ διδασκαλίᾳ ἀφθορίαν 'integrity in teaching' or 'teaching the whole truth' Tt 2.7.

88.44 ἁπλότης^a, ητος *f*: the quality of sincerity as an expression of singleness of purpose or motivation – 'sincerity, purity of motive.' ὑπακούετε κατὰ πάντα τοῖς κατὰ σάρκα κυρίοις . . . ἐν ἁπλότητι καρδίας 'obey your human masters in all things . . . with sincerity of heart' or '. . . with a heart which seeks only one purpose' Col 3.22.

88.45 ἁγνῶς: pertaining to purity of motives – 'sincerely, out of pure motives, sincere motives.' οἱ δὲ ἐξ ἐριθείας τὸν Χριστὸν καταγγέλλουσιν, οὐχ ἁγνῶς 'but these proclaim Christ out of contentiousness, not as a result of sincere motives' Php 1.17.

F Modesty, Propriety (88.46-88.50)

88.46 σεμνότης, ητος *f*: behavior which is befitting, implying a measure of dignity leading to respect – 'propriety, befitting behavior.' διάγωμεν ἐν πάσῃ εὐσεβείᾳ καὶ σεμνότητι 'that we may live in entire godliness and propriety' 1 Tm 2.2. In some languages

---

6 Certain meanings in this subdomain overlap to a certain extent with the domain of *Communication* (33), since honesty and sincerity so frequently involve some kinds of communication.

7 It is possible that in Php 1.10 εἰλικρινής is to be understood in the sense of moral purity and hence 'with clean lives' or 'without fault.'

'propriety' is best expressed as 'to act in the right way' or 'to act as one ought.'

88.47 σεμνός, ή, όν: pertaining to appropriate, befitting behavior and implying dignity and respect – 'honorable, worthy of respect, of good character.' διακόνους ὡσαύτως σεμνούς 'helpers should be of good character' or 'deacons . . .' 1 Tm 3.8.

88.48 κόσμιος[a], ον: pertaining to being modest in the sense of moderate and well-ordered – 'modest, well-ordered, moderate, becoming.' δεῖ οὖν τὸν ἐπίσκοπον . . . νηφάλιον, σώφρονα, κόσμιον 'the church leader must be . . . sober, self-controlled, moderate' 1 Tm 3.2; ἐν καταστολῇ κοσμίῳ 'in modest apparel' 1 Tm 2.9. For another interpretation of κόσμιος in 1 Tm 2.9, see 66.10.

88.49 αἰδώς, οῦς f: the quality of modesty, with the implication of resulting respect – 'modesty.' γυναῖκας ἐν καταστολῇ κοσμίῳ μετὰ αἰδοῦς καὶ σωφροσύνης κοσμεῖν ἑαυτάς 'that women dress themselves in becoming clothing, modestly, and properly' 1 Tm 2.9.

88.50 εὐσχημόνως[a]: pertaining to being a fitting or becoming manner of behavior – 'in a becoming manner, decently, with propriety.' ὡς ἐν ἡμέρᾳ εὐσχημόνως περιπατήσωμεν 'let us conduct ourselves in a becoming manner as (people who live) in (the light of) day' Ro 13.13.

G Humility (88.51-88.58)

88.51 ταπείνωσις[a], εως f: the quality of unpretentious behavior, suggesting a total lack of arrogance or pride – 'humility, humble behavior.' καυχάσθω . . . ὁ δὲ πλούσιος ἐν τῇ ταπεινώσει αὐτοῦ 'let the rich . . . boast . . . in his humility' Jas 1.9-10. In some languages humility is expressed indirectly by an idiomatic phrase, for example, 'to live without strutting' or 'to walk without wanting to be noticed.'

88.52 ταπεινός[b], ή, όν: pertaining to being unpretentious in one's behavior – 'humble.' ὅτι πραΰς εἰμι καὶ ταπεινὸς τῇ καρδίᾳ 'for I am

gentle and humble in spirit' Mt 11.29. In some languages the expression 'humble in spirit' or 'humble in heart' may be expressed as 'speaking only soft words' or 'without shouting at others.'

88.53 ταπεινοφροσύνη, ης f: the quality of humility – 'humble attitude, humility, without arrogance.' δουλεύων τῷ κυρίῳ μετὰ πάσης ταπεινοφροσύνης καὶ δακρύων 'with all humility and tears I served the Lord' or '. . . I did my work as the Lord's servant' Ac 20.19; ἐν ταπεινοφροσύνῃ καὶ θρησκείᾳ τῶν ἀγγέλων 'in false humility and the worship of angels' Col 2.18. The rendering of ταπεινοφροσύνη in Col 2.18 as 'false humility' is justified in terms of the context, but there is nothing in the word ταπεινοφροσύνη itself which means 'false.' It would be possible to render ταπεινοφροσύνη in Col 2.18 as 'subjection to,' and one might render the entire expression as 'in abject worship of angels.' In other languages 'false humility' may be rendered as 'just pretending to be humble' or 'appearing to be humble but really being proud.'

88.54 ταπεινόφρων, ον, gen. ονος: pertaining to having the attitude of humility – 'humble.' εὔσπλαγχνοι, ταπεινόφρονες 'have compassion and be humble in your attitudes (toward one another)' 1 Pe 3.8.

88.55 ἀφελότης, ητος f: humility associated with simplicity of life – 'humility, humbleness, simplicity.' μετελάμβανον τροφῆς ἐν ἀγαλλιάσει καὶ ἀφελότητι καρδίας 'eating their food with gladness and humbleness of heart' Ac 2.46.

88.56 ταπεινόω[d]: (derivative of ταπεινός[b] 'humble,' 88.52) to cause someone to be or to become humble – 'to make humble, to humble.' ὅστις οὖν ταπεινώσει ἑαυτὸν ὡς τὸ παιδίον τοῦτο, οὗτός ἐστιν ὁ μείζων ἐν τῇ βασιλείᾳ τῶν οὐρανῶν 'he who humbles himself like this child is the greatest in the kingdom of heaven' Mt 18.4. A strictly literal rendering of 'he who humbles himself' could be misunderstood as 'one who despises himself' or 'one who has no regard for himself.' In the context of Mt 18.4 it is often important to use an idiomatic expression which will adequately convey the meaning, for example, 'one who causes his heart to bow down' or even 'one who makes his heart small.'

88.57 πτωχὸς τῷ πνεύματι: (an idiom, literally 'poor in spirit') pertaining to one who is humble with regard to his own capacities (in the one NT occurrence, namely Mt 5.3, this humility is in relationship to God) – 'to be humble.' μακάριοι οἱ πτωχοὶ τῷ πνεύματι 'happy are those who are humble before God' Mt 5.3. A literal translation of πτωχὸς τῷ πνεύματι may lead to serious misunderstanding, since 'poor in spirit' is likely to mean either 'lacking in the Holy Spirit' or 'lacking in ambition or drive.' In order to indicate clearly that this poverty or need is related in some way to spiritual realities, one may translate 'happy are those who recognize their need of God.'

88.58 πόδας νίπτω[b]: (an idiom, literally 'to wash the feet') to show humility by doing humble tasks – 'to act humbly, to behave in a humble manner.' εἰ ἁγίων πόδας ἔνιψεν 'if she performs humble duties for fellow believers' 1 Tm 5.10. For another interpretation of πόδας νίπτω in 1 Tm 5.10, see 34.59.

H Gentleness, Mildness (88.59-88.65)

88.59 πραΰτης, ητος f; πραϋπαθία, ας f: gentleness of attitude and behavior, in contrast with harshness in one's dealings with others – 'gentleness, meekness, mildness.' πραΰτης: μετὰ πάσης ταπεινοφροσύνης καὶ πραΰτητος 'be always humble and meek' Eph 4.2. πραϋπαθία: δίωκε . . . ὑπομονήν, πραϋπαθίαν 'strive for . . . endurance and gentleness' 1 Tm 6.11.

In a number of languages 'gentleness' is often expressed as a negation of harshness, so that 'gentleness' may often by rendered as 'not being harsh with people,' but gentleness may also be expressed in some instances in an idiomatic manner, for example, 'always speaking softly to' or 'not raising one's voice.'

88.60 πραΰς, πραεῖα, πραΰ: pertaining to being gentle and mild – 'mild, gentle, meek.'

καὶ μάθετε ἀπ' ἐμοῦ, ὅτι πραΰς εἰμι 'and learn from me because I am gentle' Mt 11.29.

88.61 ἤπιος, α, ον: pertaining to being gentle, with the implication of kindness – 'gentle, kind.' δοῦλον δὲ κυρίου οὐ δεῖ μάχεσθαι, ἀλλὰ ἤπιον εἶναι πρὸς πάντας 'the Lord's servant must not quarrel; he must be gentle toward all' 2 Tm 2.24.

88.62 ἐπιείκεια, ας f: the quality of gracious forbearing – 'gentleness, graciousness, forbearance.' παρακαλῶ ἀκοῦσαί σε ἡμῶν συντόμως τῇ σῇ ἐπιεικείᾳ 'I beg you by your forbearance to listen to our brief account' Ac 24.4; παρακαλῶ ὑμᾶς διὰ τῆς πραΰτητος καὶ ἐπιεικείας τοῦ Χριστοῦ 'I beg you by the meekness and gentleness of Christ' 2 Cor 10.1.

88.63 ἐπιεικής, ές: pertaining to being gracious and forbearing – 'gentle, gracious, forbearing.' μηδένα βλασφημεῖν, ἀμάχους εἶναι, ἐπιεικεῖς 'not to speak evil of anyone, nor to be quarrelsome, but to be forbearing' Tt 3.2.

88.64 ταπεινός[d], ή, όν: pertaining to being meek, with the implication of low status – 'gentle, meek and mild.' ὃς κατὰ πρόσωπον μὲν ταπεινὸς ἐν ὑμῖν 'I who am meek when present among you' 2 Cor 10.1.

88.65 μετριοπαθέω: to be gentle in one's attitude toward someone – 'to deal gently with, to be gently disposed toward.' μετριοπαθεῖν δυνάμενος τοῖς ἀγνοοῦσιν καὶ πλανωμένοις 'being able to deal gently with those who are ignorant and make mistakes' He 5.2.

I Kindness, Harshness (88.66-88.74)

88.66 χαριτόω; χάρις[a], ιτος f: to show kindness to someone, with the implication of graciousness on the part of the one showing such kindness – 'to show kindness, to manifest graciousness toward, kindness, graciousness, grace.' χαριτόω: κεχαριτωμένη, ὁ κύριος μετὰ σοῦ 'the Lord is with you, you to whom (the Lord) has shown kindness' Lk 1.28; ἧς ἐχαρίτωσεν ἡμᾶς ἐν τῷ ἠγαπημένῳ 'which he has graciously shown us in the one he loves' Eph 1.6.

χάρις[a]: ἐξῆλθεν παραδοθεὶς τῇ χάριτι τοῦ κυρίου ὑπὸ τῶν ἀδελφῶν 'he left, being commended by the brothers to the kindness of the Lord' Ac 15.40.

It is important to note that kindness in English indicates an activity in which an individual is kind to someone; it is essentially an event involving a particular quality. The same is true of χάρις in Ac 15.40, for this is not a mere gracious disposition, but an expectation of the Lord's showing kindness.

88.67 χρηστεύομαι; χρηστότης[b], ητος f: to provide something beneficial for someone as an act of kindness – 'to act kindly, to be kind, kindness.'
χρηστεύομαι: ἡ ἀγάπη μακροθυμεῖ, χρηστεύεται 'love is patient and acts kindly' 1 Cor 13.4.
χρηστότης[b]: ἐνδύσασθε οὖν . . . χρηστότητα, ταπεινοφροσύνην, πραΰτητα 'you must put on therefore . . . kindness, humility, gentleness' Col 3.12.

88.68 χρηστός[c], ή, όν: (derivative of χρηστεύομαι 'to act kindly,' 88.67) pertaining to being kind – 'kind, gracious.' τὸ χρηστὸν τοῦ θεοῦ εἰς μετάνοιάν σε ἄγει 'God is kind because he wants to lead you to repent' Ro 2.4. In a number of languages the equivalent of 'God is kind' is 'God is good to' or 'God does what is good for.'

88.69 εὐλογέω[c]; ἐνευλογέω: to provide benefits, often with the implication of certain supernatural factors involved – 'to act kindly toward, to bless.'
εὐλογέω[c]: εὐλογητὸς ὁ θεὸς καὶ πατὴρ τοῦ κυρίου ἡμῶν Ἰησοῦ Χριστοῦ, ὁ εὐλογήσας ἡμᾶς 'let us praise the God and Father of our Lord Jesus Christ, for he has acted kindly toward us' Eph 1.3. In Eph 1.3 there is an obvious play on the words εὐλογητός and εὐλογήσας. The term εὐλογητός designates 'the one to be praised' (see 33.362), but εὐλογήσας designates 'blessing.'
ἐνευλογέω: ἐνευλογηθήσονται ἐν σοὶ πάντα τὰ ἔθνη 'through you he will act kindly toward all the people on earth' Ga 3.8.

88.70 εὐλογία[d], ας f: (derivative of εὐλογέω[c] 'to bless,' 88.69) the content of the act of

blessing – 'blessing, benefit.' πρὸς ὑμᾶς ἐν πληρώματι εὐλογίας Χριστοῦ ἐλεύσομαι 'I shall come to you with a full measure of the blessing from Christ' Ro 15.29. In Ro 15:29 this blessing is something which Christ has extended to Paul, in other words, a type of special favor granted to Paul by Christ.

88.71 φιλανθρωπία[b], ας f: to show friendly concern for someone – 'friendliness, kindness.' οἵ τε βάρβαροι παρεῖχον οὐ τὴν τυχοῦσαν φιλανθρωπίαν ἡμῖν 'the natives there showed us unusual kindness' Ac 28.2.

88.72 φιλανθρώπως; φιλοφρόνως: pertaining to friendly concern and kindness toward someone – 'kindly, in a friendly way.'
φιλανθρώπως: φιλανθρώπως τε ὁ Ἰούλιος τῷ Παύλῳ χρησάμενος ἐπέτρεψεν πρὸς τοὺς φίλους πορευθέντι 'Julius treated Paul kindly and allowed him to go and see his friends' Ac 27.3.
φιλοφρόνως: ὃς ἀναδεξάμενος ἡμᾶς τρεῖς ἡμέρας φιλοφρόνως ἐξένισεν 'he welcomed us and for three days he treated us kindly as his guests' Ac 28.7.

88.73 ἀποτομία, ας f: to act harshly toward someone – 'to show harshness, to act harshly, to be harsh, harshness.' ἐπὶ μὲν τοὺς πεσόντας ἀποτομία, ἐπὶ δὲ σὲ χρηστότης θεοῦ, ἐὰν ἐπιμένῃς τῇ χρηστότητι 'God is harsh toward those who have fallen, but kind to you if you continue in his kindness' Ro 11.22.

88.74 ἀποτόμως: (derivative of ἀποτομία 'to show harshness,' 88.73) pertaining to acting or dealing harshly with someone – 'harshly.' ἵνα παρὼν μὴ ἀποτόμως χρήσωμαι κατὰ τὴν ἐξουσίαν ἣν ὁ κύριος ἔδωκέν μοι 'so that when I arrive, I will not have to deal harshly (with you) in using the authority the Lord gave me' 2 Cor 13.10. In some languages the equivalent of ἀποτομία (88.73) or ἀποτόμως is a negative expression combined with showing kindness, and therefore one may translate 'to refuse to show kindness.' In a number of circumstances, however, the equivalent of ἀποτομία or ἀποτόμως is a highly idiomatic expression, for example, 'to refuse to look at,' 'to frown upon,' or 'to push aside.'

J Mercy, Merciless (88.75-88.82)

88.75 ἱλάσκομαι[b]: to show compassion and concern for someone in difficulty, despite that person's having committed a moral offense – 'to show mercy, to show compassion.' ὁ θεός, ἱλάσθητί μοι τῷ ἁμαρτωλῷ 'O, God, have mercy on me, a sinner' Lk 18.13. In rendering ἱλάσκομαι in Lk 18.13 it is inadequate simply to indicate an attitude on the part of God. Having mercy or showing compassion must involve some act of kindness or concern.

88.76 ἐλεάω or ἐλεέω; ἔλεος, ους n: to show kindness or concern for someone in serious need – 'to show mercy, to be merciful toward, to have mercy on, mercy.'
ἐλεάω: ἐλέησόν με, κύριε, υἱὸς Δαυίδ 'have mercy on me, Sir, Son of David' Mt 15.22.
ἔλεος: ὁ δὲ θεὸς πλούσιος ὢν ἐν ἐλέει 'but God is rich in mercy' Eph 2.4.

88.77 ἵλεως, ων; ἐλεήμων, ον, gen. ονος: (derivatives of ἐλεάω and ἔλεος 'to show mercy,' 88.76) pertaining to showing mercy – 'merciful.'
ἵλεως: ἵλεως ἔσομαι ταῖς ἀδικίαις αὐτῶν 'I will be merciful on their transgressions' He 8.12.
ἐλεήμων: μακάριοι οἱ ἐλεήμονες, ὅτι αὐτοὶ ἐλεηθήσονται 'happy are those who are merciful (to others), for they will receive mercy' Mt 5.7.

88.78 ἵλεώς σοι: (an idiom, literally 'mercy to you') a highly elliptical expression equivalent in meaning to the statement 'may God be merciful to you in sparing you from having to undergo some experience' – 'God forbid it, may it not happen.' ἵλεώς σοι, κύριε 'may it not happen to you, Lord' Mt 16.22.

88.79 ἐλεεινός, ή, όν: pertaining to being deserving of pity in view of one's miserable condition – 'pitiable, miserable.' ἐλεεινότεροι πάντων ἀνθρώπων ἐσμέν 'we are the most pitiable of all people' or 'we deserve more pity than anyone else' 1 Cor 15.19.

88.80 οἰκτίρω; οἰκτιρμός, οῦ m: to show mercy and concern, with the implication of sensitivity and compassion – 'to have mercy, to show compassion, mercy, tender compassion.'

οἰκτίρω: οἰκτιρήσω ὃν ἂν οἰκτίρω 'I will have mercy on whom I have mercy' Ro 9.15.
οἰκτιρμός: ἐνδύσασθε . . . σπλάγχνα οἰκτιρμοῦ, χρηστότητα 'you must put on . . . feelings of tender compassion and kindness' Col 3.12.

88.81 οἰκτίρμων, ον: (derivative of οἰκτίρω 'to have mercy,' 88.80) pertaining to showing mercy or compassion – 'merciful, compassionate.' γίνεσθε οἰκτίρμονες καθὼς καὶ ὁ πατὴρ ὑμῶν οἰκτίρμων ἐστίν 'be merciful, just as your Father is merciful' Lk 6.36. In a number of languages expressions involving showing mercy or being merciful are expressed in highly idiomatic ways, for example, 'to show one's heart toward,' 'to feel in one's stomach for,' 'to have one's heart go out toward,' or 'to treat as a loving child.'

88.82 ἀνέλεος, ον; ἀνελεήμων, ον: pertaining to the lack of mercy or the refusal to be merciful – 'merciless, unmerciful.'
ἀνέλεος: ἡ γὰρ κρίσις ἀνέλεος τῷ μὴ ποιήσαντι ἔλεος 'for he will be unmerciful when he judges the person who has not shown mercy' Jas 2.13.
ἀνελεήμων: ἀσυνέτους, ἀσυνθέτους, ἀστόργους, ἀνελεήμονας 'they are without understanding, disloyal, unloving, and merciless' Ro 1.31.
The meaning of ἀνέλεος and ἀνελεήμων is often expressed in highly idiomatic ways, for example, 'to refuse to look at,' 'to turn one's back on,' or 'to refuse to hear a person's cries for help.'

K Self-Control, Lack of Self-Control (88.83-88.92)

88.83 ἐγκρατεύομαι; ἐγκράτεια, ας f: to exercise complete control over one's desires and actions – 'to control oneself, to exercise self-control, self-control.'
ἐγκρατεύομαι: πᾶς δὲ ὁ ἀγωνιζόμενος πάντα ἐγκρατεύεται 'everyone who competes in an athletic contest (or 'in the games') exercises self-control in all things' 1 Cor 9.25.
ἐγκράτεια: διαλεγομένου δὲ αὐτοῦ περὶ δικαιοσύνης καὶ ἐγκρατείας 'he went on discussing goodness and the exercising of self-control' Ac 24.25.
An adequate rendering of the expression 'to

exercise self-control' may require an idiomatic equivalent, for example, 'to hold oneself in,' 'to command oneself,' 'to be a chief of oneself,' 'to make one's heart be oedient,' 'to command one's own desires,' 'to be the master of what one wants,' or 'to say No to one's body.' (Compare ἀκρασία 'lack of self-control,' 88.91 and ἀκρατής 'lacking in self-control,' 88.92.)

88.84 ἐγκρατής, ές: (derivative of ἐγκρατεύ-ομαι 'to exercise self-control,' 88.83) pertaining to exercising self-control – 'self-controlled.' δεῖ γὰρ τὸν ἐπίσκοπον . . . ὅσιον, ἐγκρατῆ 'the church leader should be . . . consecrated and self-controlled' Tt 1.7-8.

88.85 χαλιναγωγέω: (a figurative extension of meaning of χαλιναγωγέω 'to control with bit or bridle,' not occurring in the NT) to exercise close control over some function – 'to control, to exercise self-control.' μὴ χαλιναγω-γῶν γλῶσσαν αὐτοῦ . . . τούτου μάταιος ἡ θρησκεία 'the religion . . . of one who does not control his tongue . . . is worthless' Jas 1.26. In some languages the expression μὴ χαλι-ναγωγῶν γλῶσσαν αὐτοῦ in Jas 1.26 may be rendered as 'one who does not tell his tongue what to say' or 'one who cannot tie his tongue down' or 'one who cannot stop his talking.'

88.86 νήφωᵇ: (a figurative extension of meaning of νήφω 'to be sober,' in the sense of not being drunk, probably not occurring in the NT) to behave with restraint and moderation, thus not permitting excess – 'to be self-controlled, to be restrained, to be moderate in one's behavior, to be sober.' σὺ δὲ νῆφε ἐν πᾶσιν 'you must keep control of yourself in all circumstances' 2 Tm 4.5; οἱ μεθυσκόμενοι νυκτὸς μεθύουσιν· ἡμεῖς δὲ ἡμέρας ὄντες νή-φωμεν 'those who are drunk get drunk in the night; we belong to the day and we should be sober' 1 Th 5.7-8. It is possible that in 1 Th 5.8 νήφω means lack of drunkenness, but most scholars interpret the use of νήφω in the NT as applying to a broader range of soberness or sobriety, namely, restraint and moderation which avoids excess in passion, rashness, or confusion. For another interpretation of νήφω in 1 Th 5.8, as well as in 1 Th 5.6, see 30.25.

88.87 νηφάλιος, α, ον: (derivative of νήφωᵇ 'to be restrained,' 88.86) pertaining to behaving in a sober, restrained manner – 'sober, restrained.' ἐπίσκοπον . . . νηφάλιον, σώφρονα, κόσμιον 'a church leader . . . must be sober, self-controlled, and orderly' 1 Tm 3.2. In a number of languages νηφάλιος may be idiomatically rendered as 'one who holds himself in' or 'one who always has a halter on himself.'

88.88 γυμνάζωᵃ: to control oneself by thorough discipline – 'to discipline oneself, to keep oneself disciplined.' γύμναζε δὲ σεαυτὸν πρὸς εὐσέβειαν 'keep yourself disciplined for a godly life' 1 Tm 4.7. In a number of languages the equivalent of 'to discipline oneself' is literally 'to make oneself obey.' This may sometimes be expressed idiomatically as 'to command one's heart.'

88.89 ὑπωπιάζωᵇ: (a figurative extension of meaning of ὑπωπιάζω 'to strike the eye,' not occurring in the NT) to keep one's body under complete control, with the implication of rough treatment given to the body, possibly as an aspect of discipline (a meaning evidently taken from the language of prize-fighting) – 'to keep under control, to exercise self-control.' ὑπωπιάζω μου τὸ σῶμα καὶ δουλαγωγῶ 'I keep my body under control and make it ready for service' 1 Cor 9.27.

88.90 ἀφειδία, ας f: severe self-control, suggesting an ascetic and unsparing attitude – 'severe self-control, harsh control over.' ἔχον-τα σοφίας ἐν ἐθελοθρησκίᾳ καὶ ταπεινοφροσύνῃ καὶ ἀφειδίᾳ σώματος 'having wisdom in self-made religion and humility and severe self-control of the body' Col 2.23.

88.91 ἀκρασία, ας f: to fail to exercise self-control – 'lack of self-control, failure to control oneself.' ἵνα μὴ πειράζῃ ὑμᾶς ὁ Σατανᾶς διὰ τὴν ἀκρασίαν ὑμῶν 'so that you may not be tempted by Satan because of your lack of self-control' 1 Cor 7.5.

88.92 ἀκρατής, ές: (derivative of ἀκρασία 'lack of self-control,' 88.91) pertaining to lacking self-control – 'uncontrolled, lacking in self-control.' ἐνστήσονται καιροὶ χαλεποί· ἔσονται γὰρ οἱ ἄνθρωποι φίλαυτοι . . . διάβολοι, ἀκρατεῖς 'difficult times will come, for people will be greedy . . . slanderers, lacking in self-control' 2 Tm 3.1-3.

L Sensible Behavior, Senseless Behavior[8] (88.93-88.99)

88.93 σωφρονισμός[b], οῦ *m*; σωφροσύνη[b], ης *f*: to behave in a sensible manner, with the implication of thoughtful awareness of what is best – 'moderation, sensibility.'
σωφρονισμός[b]: πνεῦμα . . . ἀγάπης καὶ σωφρονισμοῦ '(his) Spirit . . . (fills us) with love and moderation' 2 Tm 1.7. For another interpretation of σωφρονισμός in 2 Tm 1.7, see 32.34.
σωφροσύνη[b]: ἐν πίστει καὶ ἀγάπῃ καὶ ἁγιασμῷ μετὰ σωφροσύνης 'in faith and love and holiness with sensibility' 1 Tm 2.15.

88.94 σώφρων, ον, gen. ονος; σωφρόνως: (derivatives of the stem σωφρο- 'to behave in a sensible manner,' 88.93) pertaining to being sensible and moderate in one's behavior – 'sensible, sensibly, moderate, moderately.'
σώφρων: πρεσβύτας νηφαλίους εἶναι, σεμνούς, σώφρονας 'the older men should be sober, proper, sensible' Tt 2.2.
σωφρόνως: ἵνα . . . σωφρόνως καὶ δικαίως καὶ εὐσεβῶς ζήσωμεν 'that . . . we may live sensibly, uprightly, and godly' Tt 2.12.
In a number of languages terms such as σωφρονισμός[b] (88.93), σωφροσύνη[b] (88.93), σώφρων, and σωφρόνως may be rendered as 'to have right thoughts about what one should do' or 'to let one's mind guide one's body.'

88.95 μὴ ὑπὲρ ἃ γέγραπται: (an idiom, literally 'not above what is written') to act sensibly in not violating written rules and traditions – 'to act sensibly in keeping with rules, to observe rules properly.' ἵνα ἐν ἡμῖν μάθητε τὸ Μὴ ὑπὲρ ἃ γέγραπται 'so that you may learn from us what it means to live according to the rules' or 'what the saying means, Observe the rules' 1 Cor 4.6.

88.96 ἀσωτία, ας *f*: behavior which shows lack of concern or thought for the consequences of an action – 'senseless deeds, reckless deeds, recklessness.' μὴ μεθύσκεσθε οἴνῳ, ἐν ᾧ ἐστιν ἀσωτία 'do not get drunk with wine, for that results in reckless deeds' Eph 5.18. In some languages ἀσωτία in Eph 5.18 may be rendered as 'what one does without being able to think about it' or 'what one does when the mind is absent.'

88.97 ἀσώτως: (derivative of ἀσωτία 'senseless deeds,' 88.96) pertaining to senseless, reckless behavior – 'senselessly, recklessly.' ἀπεδήμησεν εἰς χώραν μακράν, καὶ ἐκεῖ διεσκόρπισεν τὴν οὐσίαν αὐτοῦ ζῶν ἀσώτως 'he went to a far-off country where he wasted his money by living recklessly' Lk 15.13. In a number of languages 'to live recklessly' is 'to live without thinking' or 'to live without being concerned.'

88.98 προπετής, ές: pertaining to impetuous and reckless behavior – 'reckless, impetuous.' δέον ἐστὶν ὑμᾶς κατεσταλμένους ὑπάρχειν καὶ μηδὲν προπετὲς πράσσειν 'so then, you must calm down and not do anything reckless' Ac 19.36. In some instances it may be possible to translate προπετής in Ac 19.36 as 'without thinking' or 'without counting the cost.'

88.99 ἐλαφρία, ας *f*: behavior characterized by caprice and instability – 'fickleness.' τοῦτο οὖν βουλόμενος μήτι ἄρα τῇ ἐλαφρίᾳ ἐχρησάμην; 'in planning this, did I act in fickleness?' 2 Cor 1.17. In some instances ἐλαφρία may be rendered in 2 Cor 1.17 as 'not thinking about what I was doing' or 'not keeping the same thoughts about what I was doing.'

M Mature Behavior[8] (88.100-88.101)

88.100 τέλειος[c], α, ον: pertaining to being mature in one's behavior – 'mature, grown-up.' εἰς ἄνδρα τέλειον, εἰς μέτρον ἡλικίας τοῦ πληρώματος τοῦ Χριστοῦ 'to the mature person, to the measure of the stature of the fullness of Christ' Eph 4.13. It is also possible

---

8 Several of the meanings in Subdomains L and M could be classified in Domain 25 *Attitudes and Emotions* or Domain 41 *Behavior and Related States,* but where the focal element of meaning implies moral action or behavior, it seems best to treat such meanings here.

to interpret τέλειος in Eph 4.13 as meaning 'perfect' (see 88.36). In Mt 5.48 it is possible that τέλειος also means maturity of behavior, but it is usually interpreted as 'being perfect,' since the comparison is made with God (see 88.36).

88.101 τελειότης^a, ητος *f*: maturity in thought and behavior – 'maturity.' διὸ ἀφέντες τὸν τῆς ἀρχῆς τοῦ Χριστοῦ λόγον ἐπὶ τὴν τελειότητα φερώμεθα 'therefore leaving aside teaching concerning first principles relating to Christ, let us move forward to matters of maturity' or '. . . mature teaching' He 6.1.

N Peaceful Behavior (88.102-88.104)

88.102 εἰρηνεύω: to live in peace with others – 'to behave peacefully, to live in peace.' εἰρηνεύετε ἐν ἀλλήλοις 'live in peace with one another' Mk 9.50. In some languages the equivalent of 'live in peace' is a negation of fighting, for example, 'do not fight' or 'do not constantly quarrel.'

88.103 ἡσυχάζω^b; ἡσυχία^c, ας *f*: to live in a quiet, peaceful, mild manner – 'to live a quiet life, peaceful living.'
ἡσυχάζω^b: καὶ φιλοτιμεῖσθαι ἡσυχάζειν 'make it your aim to live a quiet life' 1 Th 4.11.
ἡσυχία^c: ἵνα μετὰ ἡσυχίας ἐργαζόμενοι 'in order that they should live quiet lives and work' 2 Th 3.12. For another interpretation of ἡσυχία in 2 Th 3.12, focusing on the circumstances involved, see 22.43.

88.104 ἡσύχιος, ον; ἤρεμος: pertaining to a quiet, peaceful existence or attitude – 'quiet, peaceful.'
ἡσύχιος: τοῦ πραέως καὶ ἡσυχίου πνεύματος 'of a gentle and quiet spirit' or 'of a gentle and peaceful disposition' 1 Pe 3.4.
ἤρεμος: ἵνα ἤρεμον καὶ ἡσύχιον βίον διάγωμεν 'that we may live a quiet and peaceful life' 1 Tm 2.2.

O Bad, Evil, Harmful, Damaging (88.105-88.125)

88.105 κακία^a, ας *f*: the quality of wickedness, with the implication of that which is harmful and damaging – 'wickedness, evil, badness.' μηδὲ ἐν ζύμῃ κακίας καὶ πονηρίας 'not with the yeast of evil and wickedness' 1 Cor 5.8.

88.106 κακός^a, ή, όν; κακῶς^a: pertaining to being bad, with the implication of harmful and damaging – 'bad, evil, harmful, harshly.'
κακός^a: κακοὺς κακῶς ἀπολέσει αὐτούς 'he will harshly destroy those bad men' Mt 21.41.
κακῶς^a: ἄρχοντα τοῦ λαοῦ σου οὐκ ἐρεῖς κακῶς 'you must not speak in an evil manner about the ruler of your people' Ac 23.5. The implication in Ac 23.5 is that one must not speak in such a way as 'to cause harm to.'

88.107 χείρων, ον: (comparative of κακός^a 'bad,' 88.106) pertaining to being worse in the sense of being harmful and damaging – 'worse, very bad.' πονηροὶ δὲ ἄνθρωποι καὶ γόητες προκόψουσιν ἐπὶ τὸ χεῖρον 'evil men and impostors will keep on going from bad to worse' 2 Tm 3.13.

88.108 πονηρία, ας *f*: an evil, wicked nature – 'wickedness.' πρὸς τὰ πνευματικὰ τῆς πονηρίας ἐν τοῖς ἐπουρανίοις 'against those spiritual forces of wickedness in heavenly realms' Eph 6.12. In a number of languages one can speak of 'a wicked nature' as 'one who is bent on doing what is wicked' or 'one who habitually does what is wicked.' For the total expression in Eph 6.12 as a title, see 12.44.

88.109 πονηρίαι, ων *f* (always in the plural): deeds which are wicked and evil – 'wicked deeds, doing evil things.' μοιχεῖαι, πλεονεξίαι, πονηρίαι 'adultery, greediness, evil deeds' Mk 7.22.

88.110 πονηρός^a, ά, όν: pertaining to being morally corrupt and evil – 'immoral, evil, wicked.' ὅταν . . . εἴπωσιν πᾶν πονηρὸν καθ' ὑμῶν 'when . . . they tell all kinds of evil things against you' Mt 5.11. In translating Mt 5.11 it is important to indicate that the words spoken are not evil in themselves, but the content of what is spoken involves attributing evil and wicked deeds to the followers of Jesus. It may, therefore, be necessary to say in some languages 'when men speak against you by saying that you have done wicked deeds.'

88.111 ἀδόκιμοςᵃ, **ον; ἄτοπος**ᵃ, **ον:** pertaining to not being in accordance with what is right, appropriate, or fitting – 'not fitting, what should not be done, bad.'
ἀδόκιμοςᵃ: παρέδωκεν αὐτοὺς ὁ θεὸς εἰς ἀδόκιμον νοῦν, ποιεῖν τὰ μὴ καθήκοντα 'God has given them over to corrupted minds so that they do the things they should not do' Ro 1.28.
ἄτοποςᵃ: οὗτος δὲ οὐδὲν ἄτοπον ἔπραξεν 'but he has done nothing bad' Lk 23.41.

88.112 κακοποιέωᵃ: to do that which is evil or wrong – 'to do evil, to do wrong.' ἔξεστιν τοῖς σάββασιν ἀγαθὸν ποιῆσαι ἢ κακοποιῆσαι; 'what is one allowed to do on the Sabbath? To do good or to do evil?' Mk 3.4. For another interpretation of κακοποιέω in Mk 3.4, see 20.12.

88.113 κακοήθεια, **ας** *f:* an evil disposition leading one to habitually engage in malicious acts – 'evil disposition, malice.' μεστοὺς φθόνου φόνου ἔριδος δόλου κακοηθείας 'they are full of jealousy, murder, fighting, deceit and malice' Ro 1.29.

88.114 κακοποιός, **οῦ** *m;* **κακοῦργος**, **ου** *m:* one who customarily engages in doing what is bad – 'wrongdoer, evildoer, bad person.'
κακοποιός: ἐν ᾧ καταλαλοῦσιν ὑμῶν ὡς κακοποιῶν 'when they accuse you of being evildoers' 1 Pe 2.12.
κακοῦργος: ἤγοντο δὲ καὶ ἕτεροι κακοῦργοι δύο 'they took two others also, both of them evildoers' Lk 23.32.

88.115 βέβηλος, **ον:** pertaining to being profane in the sense of worldly or godless – 'worldly, godless.' τοὺς δὲ βεβήλους καὶ γραώδεις μύθους παραιτοῦ 'have nothing to do with worldly and foolish legends' 1 Tm 4.7.

88.116 φαῦλος, **η**, **ον:** pertaining to being evil in the sense of moral baseness – 'mean, bad, evil.' πᾶς γὰρ ὁ φαῦλα πράσσων μισεῖ τὸ φῶς 'anyone who does mean things hates the light' Jn 3.20.

88.117 ἀσθενήςᵇ, **ές:** pertaining to being morally weak and hence incapable of doing good – 'morally weak, without moral strength.' ἔτι γὰρ Χριστὸς ὄντων ἡμῶν ἀσθενῶν ἔτι κατὰ καιρὸν ὑπὲρ ἀσεβῶν ἀπέθανεν 'for while we were still morally weak, Christ died for the wicked at the right time' Ro 5.6. It is also possible to understand ἀσθενής in Ro 5.6 as a helpless condition rather than moral weakness (see 22.3).

88.118 ἁμαρτίαᵇ, **ας** *f:* a state of sinfulness as an integral element of someone's nature – 'sinfulness, being evil.' ἐν ἁμαρτίαις σὺ ἐγεννήθης ὅλος 'you were born completely in sinfulness' or 'from birth you have been evil' Jn 9.34. The implication of this statement made in criticism of Jesus in Jn 9.34 was that he had not adhered rigorously to all the conventional requirements of the OT law as interpreted by the Pharisees.

88.119 θηρίονᶜ, **ου** *n:* (a figurative extension of meaning of θηρίονᵇ '(wild) animal,' 4.4) a bad person, in the sense of being both harmful and dangerous – 'bad person, wicked person, evil beast.' Κρῆτες ἀεὶ ψεῦσται, κακὰ θηρία 'Cretans are always liars and wicked beasts' Tt 1.12. The translation of θηρίονᶜ as merely 'wild animal' may be seriously misunderstood in some languages, since speaking of a person as 'a wild animal' might be a compliment based upon the idea of strength and courage. It may, therefore, be necessary to use some such expression as 'dangerous animal' or 'harmful wild animal.'

88.120 ἀλώπηξᵇ, **εκος** *f:* (a figurative extension of meaning of ἀλώπηξᵃ 'fox,' 4.10) a wicked person, probably with the implication of being cunning and treacherous – 'wicked person, cunning person, fox.' εἴπατε τῇ ἀλώπεκι ταύτῃ 'tell that fox' (a reference to Herod) Lk 13.32. Some scholars, however, suggest that ἀλώπηξ in Lk 13.32 may imply 'worthlessness.'
Rendering ἀλώπηξ in Lk 13.32 by a term meaning 'fox' may sometimes be misleading, since in some cultures the fox is regarded as a particularly wise animal, and therefore referring to a person as a fox may be a compliment. A local term for 'fox' may have other connotations which are quite undesirable. For example, in some languages a term for fox is used

to designate a male or female prostitute, usually of the lowest grade.

88.121 λύκος[b], ου *m*: (a figurative extension of meaning of λύκος[a] 'wolf,' 4.11) a person who is particularly vicious and dangerous – 'vicious person, fierce wolf, fierce person.' εἰσελεύσονται . . . λύκοι βαρεῖς εἰς ὑμᾶς 'fierce wolves will come among you' or 'vicious men will do you harm' Ac 20.29. In situations where wolves are not known, it may be possible to translate Ac 20.29 as 'men like fierce animals will come among you.' In some instances λύκος in Ac 20.29 has been rendered as 'fierce, wild dogs.'

88.122 κύων[b], κυνός, dat. pl. κυσί *m*: (a figurative extension of meaning of κύων[a] 'dog,' 4.34) a particularly bad person, perhaps specifically one who ridicules what is holy – 'bad person, dog.' βλέπετε τοὺς κύνας 'beware of the dogs' Php 3.2. It is also possible that κύων in Php 3.2 may be interpreted as meaning 'pervert' (see 88.282).

A term for 'dog' may have quite a different connotation than it does in English. For example, to call a person 'a dog' in some languages is to compliment him for his faithfulness, but in other languages it may be merely a way of attributing promiscuous sexual behavior.

88.123 ἔχιδνα[b], ης *f* (a figurative extension of meaning of ἔχιδνα[a] 'viper,' 4.53); ὄφις[b], εως *m* (a figurative extension of meaning of ὄφις[a] 'snake,' 4.52): a dangerous and despised person – 'evil person, viper, snake.'
ἔχιδνα[b]: γεννήματα ἐχιδνῶν, πῶς δύνασθε ἀγαθὰ λαλεῖν πονηροὶ ὄντες; 'you brood of vipers, how can you say good things when you are evil?' Mt 12.34.
ὄφις[b]: ὄφεις γεννήματα ἐχιδνῶν, πῶς φύγητε ἀπὸ τῆς κρίσεως τῆς γεέννης; 'you snakes and brood of vipers, how do you (expect to) escape from being condemned to hell?' Mt 23.33.

One must exercise due caution in rendering ἔχιδνα in Mt 12.34 and ὄφις in Mt 23.33, since in some cultures snakes are regarded as being particularly wise and clever, and therefore an expression such as 'brood of vipers' could be a compliment. In some languages important

distinctions are made between different types of snakes, and therefore connotations may vary considerably.

88.124 διάβολος[d], ου *m*: (a figurative extension of meaning of διάβολος[a] 'Devil,' 12.34) a wicked person who has a number of characteristics typical of the Devil – 'a devil.' ἐξ ὑμῶν εἷς διάβολός ἐστιν 'one of you is a devil' Jn 6.70. In some languages it would not be possible to translate Jn 6.70 literally as 'one of you is a devil.' The closest equivalent in such circumstances may be a simile, for example, 'one of you is just like the Devil.' For another interpretation of διάβολος in Jn 6.70, see 12.37.

88.125 σκότος[b], ους *n*; σκοτία[b], ας *f*: (figurative extensions of meaning of σκότος[a] and σκοτία[a] 'darkness,' 14.53) the realm of sin and evil – 'evil world, realm of evil, darkness.'
σκότος[b]: ὃς ἐρρύσατο ἡμᾶς ἐκ τῆς ἐξουσίας τοῦ σκότους 'he rescued us from the power of darkness' or '. . . the power of sin' Col 1.13. It is possible that in Col 1.13 σκότος[b] is a figurative reference to the Devil or Satan, since ἐκ τῆς ἐξουσίας τοῦ σκότους is in a parallel relationship with τὴν βασιλείαν τοῦ υἱοῦ τῆς ἀγάπης αὐτοῦ.
σκοτία[b]: ὁ δὲ μισῶν τὸν ἀδελφὸν αὐτοῦ ἐν τῇ σκοτίᾳ ἐστίν 'he who hates his brother is in darkness' or '. . . in the realm of evil' 1 Jn 2.11.

P Treat Badly[9] **(88.126-88.134)**

88.126 κακουχέω; καταπονέω: to cause someone to suffer ill treatment – 'to mistreat, to ill-treat, to cause to suffer.'
κακουχέω: περιῆλθον . . . ὑστερούμενοι, θλιβόμενοι, κακουχούμενοι 'they went around . . . poor, persecuted, and mistreated' He 11.37.
καταπονέω: ἐποίησεν ἐκδίκησιν τῷ καταπονου-

---

9 Subdomain P *Treat Badly* contains a number of meanings which to an extent overlap with certain meanings in Domain 19 *Physical Impact,* but in Subdomain P *Treat Badly* the behavior is more generalized rather than specifically physical and immediate.

μένω 'he went to help the man who was being ill-treated' Ac 7.24.

88.127 ἀτιμάζωᵃ: to treat someone in a shameful and dishonorable manner – 'to treat shamefully, to mistreat.' κἀκεῖνον ἐκεφαλίωσαν καὶ ἠτίμασαν 'they beat him over the head and treated him shamefully' Mk 12.4. It is often possible to translate ἀτιμάζω in Mk 12.4 as 'to make him suffer the way he should not.'

88.128 ἀδικέωᶜ: to mistreat by acting unjustly toward someone – 'to act unjustly toward, to mistreat.' οὐκ ἀδικῶ σε· οὐχὶ δηναρίου συνεφώνησάς μοι; 'I have not mistreated you. Did you not agree with me to work for a silver coin?' Mt 20.13. It is also possible to understand ἀδικέω in Mt 20.13 as 'to act unjustly toward,' see 88.22.

88.129 ἐπηρεάζω: to mistreat, with the implication of threats and abuse – 'to mistreat.' προσεύχεσθε περὶ τῶν ἐπηρεαζόντων ὑμᾶς 'pray for those who mistreat you' Lk 6.28.

88.130 ὑβρίζωᵃ: to maltreat in an insolent manner – 'to maltreat, to mistreat with insolence.' οἱ δὲ λοιποὶ κρατήσαντες τοὺς δούλους αὐτοῦ ὕβρισαν καὶ ἀπέκτειναν 'others grabbed the servants, mistreated them, and even killed them' Mt 22.6. In a number of contexts ὑβρίζω seems to combine not only the maltreatment of persons but the attitude of insolence on the part of the one who maltreats another. Therefore, it may be useful in some instances to employ a double expression, for example, 'to look down upon and to maltreat.'

88.131 ὕβριςᵃ, εως f: to be insolently mistreated – 'maltreatment, insolence and mistreatment.' εὐδοκῶ ἐν ἀσθενείαις, ἐν ὕβρεσιν, ἐν ἀνάγκαις 'I am content with weaknesses, mistreatment, hardships' 2 Cor 12.10. It is also possible to understand ὕβρις in 2 Cor 12.10 as actual physical violence (see 20.19) or as insults (see 33.391).

88.132 ὑβριστής, οῦ m: (derivative of ὑβρίζωᵃ 'to mistreat with insolence,' 88.130) one who maltreats others with insolence – 'insolent person, insolent and violent.' θεοστυγεῖς,

ὑβριστάς, ὑπερηφάνους 'hateful to God, insolent, proud' Ro 1.30. It is important to recognize in the term ὑβριστής more than merely an attitude of pride, for ὑβρίζω implies an attitude of superiority which results in mistreatment of and violent acts against others.

88.133 ἐξουδενέω: to ill-treat someone with contempt – 'to ill-treat, to ill-treat and look down upon.' τὸν υἱὸν τοῦ ἀνθρώπου ἵνα πολλὰ πάθῃ καὶ ἐξουδενηθῇ 'the Son of Man will suffer much and be ill-treated' Mk 9.12. Because of the complex nature of the meaning of ἐξουδενέω, it is often possible to translate the term with a semantic doublet, for example, 'to look down upon and to ill-treat.' This double meaning can be readily derived from the literal rendering 'to regard as nothing.'

88.134 ἑσσόομαι: to experience worse treatment – 'to be treated worse, to suffer more.' τί γάρ ἐστιν ὃ ἡσσώθητε ὑπὲρ τὰς λοιπὰς ἐκκλησίας 'how were you treated any worse than the other churches' 2 Cor 12.13.

Q Act Harshly (88.135-88.138)

88.135 σκληρόςᶜ, ά, όν: pertaining to being harsh or possibly cruel in one's behavior – 'harsh, cruel.' περὶ πάντων τῶν σκληρῶν ὧν ἐλάλησαν 'for all the harsh words they have spoken' Jd 15. In a number of languages σκληρός in Jd 15 may be translated as 'words that cause pain' or idiomatically as 'words that are like daggers.'

88.136 σκληρόςᵈ, ά, όν: pertaining to being hard and demanding in one's behavior – 'hard, severe, demanding.' ἔγνων σε ὅτι σκληρὸς εἶ ἄνθρωπος, θερίζων ὅπου οὐκ ἔσπειρας 'I know that you are a demanding man, for you reap a harvest where you did not plant' Mt 25.24.

88.137 πλήκτης, ου m: a person who is pugnacious and demanding – 'bully, violent person.' μὴ πάροινον, μὴ πλήκτην 'not a drunkard or a bully' 1 Tm 3.3.

88.138 αὐστηρός, ά, όν: pertaining to being exacting, with a possible implication of being severe in either a favorable or unfavorable sense – 'exacting, severe.' ἐφοβούμην γάρ σε, ὅτι ἄνθρωπος αὐστηρὸς εἶ, αἴρεις ὃ οὐκ ἔθηκας 'I was afraid because you are a severe man; you take what is not yours' Lk 19.21.

R Act Lawlessly (88.139-88.143)

88.139 ἀνομία, ας *f*: to behave with complete disregard for the laws or regulations of a society – 'to live lawlessly, lawlessness, lawless living.' συλλέξουσιν ἐκ τῆς βασιλείας αὐτοῦ πάντα τὰ σκάνδαλα καὶ τοὺς ποιοῦντας τὴν ἀνομίαν 'they will gather up out of his kingdom all who cause people to sin and those who live in lawlessness' Mt 13.41. In some languages one may translate ἀνομία in Mt 13.41 as 'to live as though there were no laws,' 'to refuse completely to obey the laws,' or 'to live as one who despises all laws.'

88.140 ἄνομος[a], **ον**: (derivative of ἀνομία 'to live lawlessly,' 88.139) pertaining to living without regard to law, in the sense of refusing to obey laws – 'lawless.' διὰ χειρὸς ἀνόμων προσπήξαντες ἀνείλατε 'you killed him by having him nailed to the cross by lawless men' Ac 2.23.

88.141 ἄθεσμος, ον: pertaining to refusing to be subjected to legal requirements – 'lawless, unruly, not complying with law.' καταπονούμενον ὑπὸ τῆς τῶν ἀθέσμων ἐν ἀσελγείᾳ ἀναστροφῆς 'who was troubled by the licentious conduct of lawless people' 2 Pe 2.7.

88.142 παρανομία, ας *f*: behavior which is contrary to law – 'lawless act, evil doing.' ἔλεγξιν δὲ ἔσχεν ἰδίας παρανομίας 'and he was rebuked for his evil doing' 2 Pe 2.16.

88.143 ἀθέμιτος[b], **ον**: pertaining to being bad and disgusting on the basis of not being allowed – 'disgusting, bad.'[10] πότοις, καὶ

---

10 Though ἀθέμιτος may be regarded as meaning literally 'pertaining to what is not allowed' (13.144), it acquires by association not only the meaning of 'lawless' (a meaning which is possibly applicable to 1 Pe 4.3) but also 'disgusting' or 'wanton' in connection with idol worship. Such a semantic development is typical of what often happens when meanings shift from an objective to a subjective orientation.

ἀθεμίτοις εἰδωλολατρίαις 'drinking parties and disgusting worship of idols' 1 Pe 4.3.

S Exploit (88.144-88.148)

88.144 πλεονεκτέω; πλεονεξία[b], **ας** *f*: to take advantage of someone, usually as the result of a motivation of greed – 'to take advantage of, to exploit, exploitation.'
πλεονεκτέω: τὸ μὴ ὑπερβαίνειν καὶ πλεονεκτεῖν ἐν τῷ πράγματι τὸν ἀδελφὸν αὐτοῦ 'in this matter, then, no one should do wrong to his brother or take advantage of him' 1 Th 4.6.
πλεονεξία[b]: ὡς εὐλογίαν καὶ μὴ ὡς πλεονεξίαν 'as something you want to do and not because you are being taken advantage of' 2 Cor 9.5.[11] It is also possible to understand πλεονεξία in 2 Cor 9.5 as referring to 'compulsion.'

88.145 κατεσθίω[e]: (a figurative extension of meaning of κατεσθίω[a] 'to eat up,' 23.11) to take total advantage of someone – 'to exploit completely, to take complete advantage of.' ἀνέχεσθε γὰρ εἴ τις ὑμᾶς καταδουλοῖ, εἴ τις κατεσθίει 'you will tolerate anyone who gets control of you or takes complete advantage of you' 2 Cor 11.20.

88.146 λαμβάνω[g]: (a figurative extension of meaning of λαμβάνω[a] 'to take hold,' 18.1) to take advantage of someone by trickery or deception – 'to exploit by deception, to take advantage of by trickery.' εἴ τις λαμβάνει 'if someone exploits (you) by deception' 2 Cor 11.20.

88.147 κατασοφίζομαι: to exploit by means of craftiness and cunning, implying false arguments – 'to exploit with cunning, to take advantage of in a cunning manner.' οὗτος κατασοφισάμενος τὸ γένος ἡμῶν ἐκάκωσεν τοὺς πατέρας ἡμῶν 'he cunningly exploited our people and was cruel to our ancestors' Ac 7.19. It is also possible to render κατασοφίζομαι in Ac 7.19 as 'to take advantage of by clever words' or 'to persuade by sweet talk.'

---

11 Though in 2 Cor 9.5 one may translate μὴ ὡς πλεονεξίαν as 'not because you are being taken advantage of,' the meaning of πλεονεξία is essentially active and may also be rendered as 'not because someone is exploiting you.'

88.148 ἐμπορεύομαι^b: to take advantage of someone by implying that what is offered is more valuable than it is – 'to exploit, to exploit by deception, to cheat.' ἐν πλεονεξίᾳ πλαστοῖς λόγοις ὑμᾶς ἐμπορεύσονται 'in their greed (these false teachers) will exploit you by telling you made-up stories' 2 Pe 2.3.¹²

T Act Shamefully (88.149-88.151)

88.149 ἀσχημονέω; ἀσχημοσύνη^a, ης *f*; αἰσχύνη^c, ης *f*; αἰσχρότης, ητος *f*: to act in defiance of social and moral standards, with resulting disgrace, embarrassment, and shame – 'to act shamefully, indecent behavior, shameful deed.'

ἀσχημονέω: ἡ ἀγάπη . . . οὐκ ἀσχημονεῖ, οὐ ζητεῖ τὰ ἑαυτῆς 'love . . . never behaves shamefully and does not seek its own interests' 1 Cor 13.4-5.

ἀσχημοσύνη^a: ἄρσενες ἐν ἄρσεσιν τὴν ἀσχημοσύνην κατεργαζόμενοι 'men do shameful deeds with each other' Ro 1.27.

αἰσχύνη^c: κύματα ἄγρια θαλάσσης ἐπαφρίζοντα τὰς ἑαυτῶν αἰσχύνας 'they are like wild waves of the sea with their shameful deeds showing up like foam' Jd 13.

αἰσχρότης: αἰσχρότης καὶ μωρολογία ἢ εὐτραπελία, ἃ οὐκ ἀνῆκεν 'indecent behavior, foolish and dirty talk are not fitting for you' Eph 5.4.

Behavior involving disgrace, embarrassment, and shame is often expressed in an idiomatic manner, for example, 'to bury one's face,' 'to hide one's eyes,' or 'to feel stabbed by people's eyes.' Since shame is seemingly a universal type of feeling, there is usually no difficulty involved in obtaining a satisfactory equivalent.

88.150 αἰσχρός, ά, όν: pertaining to behaving in a disgraceful or shameful manner – 'disgraceful, shameful.' εἰ δὲ αἰσχρὸν γυναικὶ τὸ κείρασθαι ἢ ξυρᾶσθαι, κατακαλυπτέσθω 'since it is shameful for a woman to shave or cut her hair, she should cover her head' 1 Cor 11.6.

88.151 ἀφόβως^b: pertaining to disgraceful behavior which shows no regard or fear for social sanctions – 'disgracefully, shamefully.' οὗτοί εἰσιν οἱ ἐν ταῖς ἀγάπαις ὑμῶν σπιλάδες συνευωχούμενοι ἀφόβως 'with their shameless feasting they are like dirty spots in your fellowship meals' Jd 12. For another interpretation of ἀφόβως in Jd 12, see 53.60.

U Mislead, Lead Astray, Deceive¹³ (88.152-88.159)

88.152 ἀπάγω^d: to cause someone to depart from correct behavior – 'to lead astray, to mislead, to deceive.' ὅτε ἔθνη ἦτε πρὸς τὰ εἴδωλα τὰ ἄφωνα ὡς ἂν ἤγεσθε ἀπαγόμενοι 'while you were still heathen, you were controlled by dead idols who led you astray' 1 Cor 12.2.

88.153 παραλογίζομαι: to deceive by arguments or false reasons – 'to deceive.' μηδεὶς ὑμᾶς παραλογίζηται ἐν πιθανολογίᾳ 'let no one deceive you with false arguments' Col 2.4.

88.154 δολιόω; δόλος, ου *m*: to deceive by using trickery and falsehood – 'to deceive, to trick into, treachery.'

δολιόω: ταῖς γλώσσαις αὐτῶν ἐδολιοῦσαν 'with their tongues they keep deceiving' Ro 3.13.

δόλος: συνεβουλεύσαντο ἵνα τὸν Ἰησοῦν δόλῳ κρατήσωσιν 'they made plans to arrest Jesus by means of treachery' Mt 26.4.

88.155 δόλιος, α, ον: (derivative of δολιόω 'to deceive,' 88.154) pertaining to using treachery in order to deceive – 'deceitful, treacherous.' οἱ γὰρ τοιοῦτοι ψευδαπόστολοι, ἐργάται δόλιοι, μετασχηματιζόμενοι εἰς ἀποστόλους Χριστοῦ 'they are false apostles, deceitful workers, disguising themselves as apostles of Christ' 2 Cor 11.13.

88.156 ἐμπαίζω^b: to trick someone into thinking or doing something and thus to make

---

12 In contexts outside the NT ἐμπορεύομαι may refer to the process of selling cheap merchandise at a high price, and accordingly the feature of exaggerating the value of something is evidently an important component of meaning of ἐμπορεύομαι in 2 Pe 2.3.

13 A number of terms dealing with various forms of deception are treated in Domain 31, Subdomain B *Hold a Wrong View, Be Mistaken* (31.8-31.13), in which the meanings focus primarily upon the intellectual processes, though there are often implications of resulting wrong behavior.

a fool of such a person – 'to trick, to make a fool of.' τότε Ἡρῴδης ἰδὼν ὅτι ἐνεπαίχθη ὑπὸ τῶν μάγων 'when Herod realized that the wise men had tricked him' Mt 2.16. In Mt 2.16 ἐμπαίζω would seem to carry two closely related meanings, namely 'to deceive' and also 'to make a fool of,' and therefore it may be quite appropriate to translate this portion of Mt 2.16 as 'when Herod realized that the wise men had deceived him and made a fool of him.'

88.157 κυβεία, ας f: trickery that results from craftiness (κυβεία literally refers to dice playing) – 'trickery, craftiness.' τῆς διδασκαλίας ἐν τῇ κυβείᾳ τῶν ἀνθρώπων 'of the teaching given through the trickery of people' Eph 4.14.

88.158 μεθοδεία, ας f: crafty scheming with the intent to deceive – 'deceit, scheming.' πρὸς τὸ δύνασθαι ὑμᾶς στῆναι πρὸς τὰς μεθοδείας τοῦ διαβόλου 'so that you can stand up against the Devil's scheming' Eph 6.11.

88.159 βασκαίνω[b]: to deceive a person by devious and crafty means, with the possibility of a religious connotation in view of the literal meaning 'to bewitch' (see 53.98) – 'to deceive, to bewitch, to beguile.' ὦ ἀνόητοι Γαλάται, τίς ὑμᾶς ἐβάσκανεν 'you foolish Galatians, who has deceived you' Ga 3.1. It is also possible that βασκαίνω in Ga 3.1 is to be understood literally in the sense of bewitching by means of black magic (see 53.98).

V Envy, Jealousy[14] (88.160-88.166)

88.160 φθόνος, ου m: a state of ill will toward someone because of some real or presumed advantage experienced by such a person – 'envy, jealousy.' τινὲς μὲν καὶ διὰ φθόνον καὶ ἔριν . . . τὸν Χριστὸν κηρύσσουσιν 'some people . . . preach Christ . . . because of envy and rivalry' Php 1.15. Expressions for 'envy' or 'jealousy'

14 A number of meanings in Subdomain V *Envy, Jealousy* involve a measure of resentment, but this is not as focal a feature as it is in the set of meanings in Subdomain W *Resentful, Hold a Grudge Against* (88.167-88.170).

are often idiomatic, for example, 'the heart burns' or 'the stomach is hot.'

88.161 φθονέω: to experience a feeling of ill will due to real or presumed advantage experienced by someone else – 'to be envious, to be jealous.' μὴ γινώμεθα κενόδοξοι, ἀλλήλους προκαλούμενοι, ἀλλήλοις φθονοῦντες 'we must not be proud or irritate one another or be jealous of one another' Ga 5.26.

88.162 ζῆλος[b], ου m and ους n: a particularly strong feeling of resentment and jealousy against someone – 'envy, jealousy, resentment.' ἰδόντες δὲ οἱ Ἰουδαῖοι τοὺς ὄχλους ἐπλήσθησαν ζήλου 'when the Jews saw the crowds, they were filled with jealousy' Ac 13.45.

88.163 ζηλόω[d]: to experience strong envy and resentment against someone – 'to be jealous, to be envious.' ζηλώσαντες δὲ οἱ Ἰουδαῖοι καὶ προσλαβόμενοι τῶν ἀγοραίων ἄνδρας τινὰς πονηρούς 'but the Jews were jealous and gathered some worthless loafers from the street' Ac 17.5.

88.164 παραζηλόω: to cause someone to feel strong jealousy or resentment against someone – 'to make jealous, to cause to be envious.' ἐγὼ παραζηλώσω ὑμᾶς ἐπ' οὐκ ἔθνει 'I will make you jealous of the people who are not a real nation' Ro 10.19.

88.165 ὀφθαλμὸς πονηρός[a]: (an idiom, literally 'evil eye') a feeling of jealousy and resentment because of what someone else has or does – 'jealous(y).' ὀφθαλμὸς πονηρός, βλασφημία . . . πάντα ταῦτα τὰ πονηρὰ ἔσωθεν ἐκπορεύεται 'jealousy, slander . . . all these evil things come from within' Mk 7.22-23; ἢ ὁ ὀφθαλμός σου πονηρός ἐστιν ὅτι ἐγὼ ἀγαθός εἰμι; 'or are you jealous because I am generous?' Mt 20.15. It is also possible to understand ὀφθαλμὸς πονηρός in Mt 20.15 as meaning 'stinginess,' see 57.108. See also 23.149.

88.166 εἰς χολὴν πικρίας εἰμί: (an idiom, literally 'to be in the gall of bitterness') to be particularly envious or resentful of someone

– 'to be very jealous, to be terribly envious, to be bitterly envious.' εἰς γὰρ χολὴν πικρίας καὶ σύνδεσμον ἀδικίας ὁρῶ σε ὄντα 'for I see that you are full of bitter envy (or 'are bitterly envious') and are a prisoner of sin' Ac 8.23.

W Resentful, Hold a Grudge Against (88.167-88.170)

88.167 ἐριθεία[a], ας *f*: a feeling of resentfulness based upon jealousy and implying rivalry – 'selfish ambition, rivalry, resentfulness.' τοῖς δὲ ἐξ ἐριθείας καὶ ἀπειθοῦσι τῇ ἀληθείᾳ 'others are selfishly ambitious and reject what is right' Ro 2.8; οἱ δὲ ἐξ ἐριθείας τὸν Χριστὸν καταγγέλλουσιν 'others proclaim Christ out of a feeling of rivalry' Php 1.17. For another interpretation of ἐριθεία in Php 1.17, see 39.7.

The meaning of 'rivalry' may be expressed as 'wanting to be better than someone else' or 'wanting to make people think they are better.' The meaning of 'selfish ambition' may be rendered as 'what they do is just to make themselves look bigger' or 'what they do is just for themselves.'

88.168 ἐρεθίζω[a]: to cause someone to feel resentment – 'to make resentful, to make someone bitter.' μὴ ἐρεθίζετε τὰ τέκνα ὑμῶν 'do not cause your children to become resentful' Col 3.21.

88.169 ἐνέχω[a]: to feel resentful because of what someone has done – 'to be resentful against, to have a grudge against.' ἡ δὲ Ἡρῳδιὰς ἐνεῖχεν αὐτῷ 'so Herodias held a grudge against him' Mk 6.19.

88.170 πικρός[b], ά, όν: (a figurative extension of meaning of πικρός[a] 'bitter,' 79.41) pertaining to feeling resentful – 'resentful.' εἰ δὲ ζῆλον πικρὸν ἔχετε 'but if you are resentfully jealous' or 'if you are jealous and resentful' or 'if you have jealousy and resentment' Jas 3.14.

X Anger, Be Indignant With (88.171-88.191)

88.171 χολάω: to have a strong feeling of displeasure and antagonism as the result of some real or supposed wrong – 'to be very angry, to be full of anger.' ἐμοὶ χολᾶτε ὅτι ὅλον ἄνθρωπον ὑγιῆ ἐποίησα ἐν σαββάτῳ; 'why are you angry with me because I made a man completely well on the Sabbath?' Jn 7.23. In a number of languages expressions for 'anger' are highly idiomatic, for example, 'his abdomen burned against,' 'to be bitter toward,' or 'to become red against.'

88.172 προσοχθίζω: to feel strong irritation because of what someone has done – 'to be provoked, to be angry.' τίσιν δὲ προσώχθισεν τεσσεράκοντα ἔτη; 'with whom was he provoked for forty years?' He 3.17.

88.173 ὀργή[a], ῆς *f*: a relative state of anger – 'anger, fury.' ἐπαίροντας ὁσίους χεῖρας χωρὶς ὀργῆς καὶ διαλογισμοῦ 'who can lift up holy hands (to pray) without anger or argument' 1 Tm 2.8. In a number of languages it is impossible to speak of 'anger' without indicating against whom the anger exists. For example, in 1 Tm 2.8 it might be possible to say 'to pray without anger against anyone' or 'to pray without being angry at anyone.'

88.174 ὀργίζομαι: to be relatively angry – 'to be full of anger, to be furious, to be angry.' πᾶς ὁ ὀργιζόμενος τῷ ἀδελφῷ αὐτοῦ 'whoever is angry with his brother' Mt 5.22.

88.175 ὀργίλος, η, ον: pertaining to a tendency to become angry – 'angry, quick-tempered, given to anger.' δεῖ γὰρ τὸν ἐπίσκοπον . . . μὴ ὀργίλον 'the overseer of the church must . . . not be quick-tempered' Tt 1.7.

88.176 παροργισμός, οῦ *m*: a state of being quite angry and upset at something – 'anger, being provoked.' ὁ ἥλιος μὴ ἐπιδυέτω ἐπὶ τῷ παροργισμῷ ὑμῶν 'do not stay angry all day' (literally 'do not let the sun go down upon your anger') Eph 4.26.

88.177 παροργίζω: (derivative of παροργισμός 'anger,' 88.176) to cause someone to become provoked or quite angry – 'to cause to be provoked, to make angry.' ἐπ' ἔθνει ἀσυνέτῳ παροργιῶ ὑμᾶς 'I will make you angry with a nation of foolish people' Ro 10.19.

88.178 θυμός[a], οῦ *m*: a state of intense anger, with the implication of passionate outbursts – 'anger, fury, wrath, rage.' ἐπλήσθησαν πάντες θυμοῦ ἐν τῇ συναγωγῇ ἀκούοντες ταῦτα 'all the people in the synagogue were filled with anger when they heard this' Lk 4.28. In a number of contexts θυμός[a] is combined with ὀργή[a] (88.173) in such a manner that the meaning of one simply heightens the intensity or significance of the other, as in Ro 2.8, τοῖς δὲ ἐξ ἐριθείας καὶ ἀπειθοῦσι τῇ ἀληθείᾳ πειθομένοις δὲ τῇ ἀδικίᾳ, ὀργὴ καὶ θυμός 'and to those who out of jealousy reject the truth and adhere to evil, there will be fury and anger.' But in a number of languages it is necessary to specify who experiences such anger or fury, and therefore it may be necessary to translate 'God will be furious and angry against them.' The fury and anger of God is generally interpreted in terms of 'divine retribution and punishment.'

88.179 θυμόομαι: (derivative of θυμός[a] 'anger,' 88.178) to be extremely angry, even to the point of being in a rage – 'to be extremely angry.' τότε Ἡρῴδης ἰδὼν ὅτι ἐνεπαίχθη ὑπὸ τῶν μάγων ἐθυμώθη λίαν 'then when Herod saw that he had been tricked by the wise men, he was extremely angry' Mt 2.16. In some instances it may be possible to speak of 'being extremely angry' as 'to be so angry as not to be able to think.'

88.180 θυμομαχέω: to be extremely angry, with the implication of violence – 'to be violently angry, to be furious.' ἦν δὲ θυμομαχῶν Τυρίοις 'he was furious with the people of Tyre' Ac 12.20. For another interpretation of θυμομαχέω in Ac 12.20, see 33.453.

88.181 διαπρίομαι: (a figurative extension of meaning of διαπρίομαι 'to be sawn through,' not occurring in the NT) to be angry to the point of rage – 'to be furious, to be enraged.' οἱ δὲ ἀκούσαντες διεπρίοντο καὶ ἐβούλοντο ἀνελεῖν αὐτούς 'when they heard this, they were furious and planned to put them to death' Ac 5.33.

88.182 ἐμμαίνομαι: to be so furiously angry with someone as to be almost out of one's mind – 'to be enraged, to be infuriated, to be insanely angry.' περισσῶς τε ἐμμαινόμενος αὐτοῖς ἐδίωκον ἕως καὶ εἰς τὰς ἔξω πόλεις 'I was so infuriated with them that I even went to foreign cities to persecute them' Ac 26.11. In some instances it may be possible to render ἐμμαίνομαι in Ac 26.11 as 'to be so angry as to be like an insane person.'

88.183 ἄνοια[b], ας *f*: a state of such extreme anger as to suggest an incapacity to use one's mind – 'extreme fury, great rage.' αὐτοὶ δὲ ἐπλήσθησαν ἀνοίας 'they were extremely furious' Lk 6.11.

88.184 βρύχω τοὺς ὀδόντας[b]: (an idiom, literally 'to grind one's teeth') to express and manifest intense anger – 'to be furious.' ἔβρυχον τοὺς ὀδόντας ἐπ' αὐτόν 'they were furious at him' Ac 7.54. As noted in 23.41, it is possible to understand the expression βρύχω τοὺς ὀδόντας in both a literal as well as a figurative sense. The persons may very well have 'ground their teeth' as a sign of their anger and fury, so that a statement about what such persons did could be true in a literal as well as in a figurative sense.

88.185 φρυάσσω: to show insolent anger – 'to rave, to be incensed.' ἱνατί ἐφρύαξαν ἔθνη 'why are the nations raving' Ac 4.25. φρυάσσω evidently combines not only anger but a considerable measure of opposition, both verbal and nonverbal.

88.186 ἀγανάκτησις, εως *f*: a state of strong opposition and displeasure against someone or something judged to be wrong – 'indignation, anger.' πόσην κατειργάσατο ὑμῖν σπουδήν, ἀλλὰ ἀπολογίαν, ἀλλὰ ἀγανάκτησιν 'it caused such earnestness in you, such eagerness to prove your innocence, such indignation' 2 Cor 7.11.

88.187 ἀγανακτέω: (derivative of ἀγανάκτησις 'indignation,' 88.186) to be indignant against what is judged to be wrong – 'to be indignant, to be angry with.' καὶ ἀκούσαντες οἱ δέκα ἤρξαντο ἀγανακτεῖν περὶ Ἰακώβου καὶ Ἰωάννου 'and when the ten heard this, they began to be indignant with James and John' Mk 10.41.

88.188 προκαλέομαι: to cause provocation or irritation in someone – 'to provoke, to irritate.' μὴ γινώμεθα κενόδοξοι, ἀλλήλους προκαλούμενοι, ἀλλήλοις φθονοῦντες 'we must not be proud or provoke one another or be jealous of one another' Ga 5.26.

88.189 παροξύνομαι: to be provoked or upset at someone or something involving severe emotional concern – 'to be provoked, to be upset.' ἡ ἀγάπη . . . οὐ παροξύνεται 'love . . . is not upset' 1 Cor 13.4-5; παρωξύνετο τὸ πνεῦμα αὐτοῦ ἐν αὐτῷ θεωροῦντος κατείδωλον οὖσαν τὴν πόλιν 'his spirit was greatly upset (literally 'upset within him') when he noticed how full of idols the city was' Ac 17.16. In some languages the expression 'to be greatly upset' must be rendered idiomatically as 'his heart was eating him' or 'his stomach was hot.'

88.190 διαπονέομαι: to be strongly irked or provoked at something or someone – 'to be irked, to be provoked, to become angry.' διαπονούμενοι διὰ τὸ διδάσκειν αὐτοὺς τὸν λαόν 'being provoked that they were teaching the people' Ac 4.2; διαπονηθεὶς δὲ Παῦλος 'Paul became provoked' Ac 16.18.

88.191 ἔα: an exclamatory particle indicating surprise, indignation, or anger – 'ah.' ἔα, τί ἡμῖν καὶ σοί 'ah! What do you want with us' Lk 4.34. If another language does not have a fully satisfactory particle expressing surprise, indignation, or anger, it is probably best to leave this particle untranslated, as, for example, in a number of translations into English which make no attempt to introduce a corresponding emotive particle.

Y Despise, Scorn, Contempt (88.192-88.197)

88.192 καταφρονέω: to feel contempt for someone or something because it is thought to be bad or without value – 'to despise, to scorn, to look down on.' καὶ τῆς μακροθυμίας καταφρονεῖς 'and do you have contempt for (God's) patience' Ro 2.4; ὁρᾶτε μὴ καταφρονήσητε ἑνὸς τῶν μικρῶν τούτων 'see that you do not despise one of these little ones' Mt 18.10.

In a number of languages the equivalent of 'to despise' is 'to think that something has no value' or 'to reckon something as being worthless.'

88.193 καταφρονητής, οῦ *m*: (derivative of καταφρονέω 'to despise,' 88.192) one who customarily feels contempt for something or someone – 'one who feels contempt, scoffer.' ἴδετε, οἱ καταφρονηταί 'look, you scoffers' Ac 13.41. The equivalent of 'scoffer' may be 'one who always talks against' or 'one who thinks nothing is ever any good.'

88.194 κατακαυχάομαι[b]: to despise, with the implication of regarding oneself as superior – 'to despise, to look down on.' μὴ κατακαυχῶ τῶν κλάδων 'you should not despise the branches' (meaning 'those who had been broken off like branches') Ro 11.18. For another interpretation of κατακαυχάομαι in Ro 11.18, see 33.370.

88.195 ἐξουθενέω: to despise someone or something on the basis that it is worthless or of no value – 'to despise.' ὅτι εἰσὶν δίκαιοι καὶ ἐξουθενοῦντας τοὺς λοιπούς 'and they were righteous and despised everyone else' Lk 18.9; ὁ ἐσθίων τὸν μὴ ἐσθίοντα μὴ ἐξουθενείτω 'the one who eats should not despise the one who does not eat' Ro 14.3.

88.196 καταπατέω[b]: (a figurative extension of meaning of καταπατέω[a] 'to trample on,' 19.52) to thoroughly despise someone or something – 'to despise, to treat with complete disdain.' ὁ τὸν υἱὸν τοῦ θεοῦ καταπατήσας 'he who shows utter disdain for the Son of God' He 10.29.

88.197 ὀλιγωρέω: to regard something or someone as of little value – 'to look down on, to have contempt for, to make light of, to despise.' μὴ ὀλιγώρει παιδείας κυρίου 'do not make light of correction coming from the Lord' He 12.5.

Z Hate, Hateful (88.198-88.205)

88.198 μισέω: to dislike strongly, with the implication of aversion and hostility – 'to hate, to detest.' οἱ δὲ πολῖται αὐτοῦ ἐμίσουν αὐτόν 'and his fellow countrymen hated him' Lk 19.14. Expressions for 'hatred' frequently involve idiomatic phrases, for example, 'to kill in the heart' or 'to spit at someone in the heart.'

88.199 κακία^c, ας *f*: a feeling of hostility and strong dislike, with a possible implication of desiring to do harm – 'hateful feeling.' σὺν πάσῃ κακίᾳ 'together with every hateful feeling' Eph 4.31.

88.200 κακόω τὴν ψυχὴν κατά: (an idiom, literally 'to cause a person's attitude to be bad against') to cause someone to have hostile feelings of dislike toward someone – 'to turn someone against, to cause to dislike.' ἐκάκωσαν τὰς ψυχὰς τῶν ἐθνῶν κατὰ τῶν ἀδελφῶν 'they turned the Gentiles against the fellow believers' Ac 14.2.

88.201 πικρία^b, ας *f*: (a figurative extension of meaning of πικρία^a 'bitter taste,' 79.40) a state of sharp, intense resentment or hate – 'bitter resentment, spite, bitterness.' ὧν τὸ στόμα ἀρᾶς καὶ πικρίας γέμει 'whose mouth is full of curses and bitter resentment' Ro 3.14; πᾶσα πικρία καὶ θυμὸς . . . ἀρθήτω 'get rid of . . . all bitterness and anger' Eph 4.31.

88.202 πικραίνομαι: (derivative of πικρία^b 'bitterness,' 88.201) to have bitter resentment or hatred toward someone else – 'to be embittered, to have bitter hate.' οἱ ἄνδρες, ἀγαπᾶτε τὰς γυναῖκας καὶ μὴ πικραίνεσθε πρὸς αὐτάς 'husbands, love your wives, and do not be bitterly hateful toward them' Col 3.19.

88.203 ἀποστυγέω: to have a strong dislike for someone or something, implying repulsion and desire for avoidance – 'to hate, to despise.' ἀποστυγοῦντες τὸ πονηρόν, κολλώμενοι τῷ ἀγαθῷ 'hate what is evil; hold on to what is good' Ro 12.9.

88.204 στυγητός, ή, όν: pertaining to being hated or regarded as worthy of being hated – 'hated.' ἦμεν γάρ ποτε καὶ ἡμεῖς ἀνόητοι . . . στυγητοί 'for we ourselves were once foolish . . . and hated' Tt 3.3.

88.205 θεοστυγής, ές: pertaining to hatred for God – 'hating God, one who hates God.' θεοστυγεῖς 'haters of God' Ro 1.30. It is possible, though unlikely, that θεοστυγής in Ro 1.30 could be interpreted as 'those whom God hates.'

A' Arrogance, Haughtiness, Pride (88.206-88.222)

88.206 αὐθάδης, ες: pertaining to being arrogant as the result of self-will and stubbornness – 'arrogant, self-willed.' μὴ αὐθάδη, μὴ ὀργίλον 'not arrogant, not quick-tempered' Tt 1.7. In a number of languages 'arrogant' may be expressed as 'thinking one is so much better than everyone else' or 'always looking down on other people' or 'always saying, I am better.'

88.207 ὕψωμα^c, τος *n*: (a figurative extension of meaning of ὕψωμα 'height,' not occurring in the NT) an exaggerated evaluation of what one is or of what one has done – 'conceit, pride, arrogance.' καὶ πᾶν ὕψωμα ἐπαιρόμενον κατὰ τῆς γνώσεως τοῦ θεοῦ 'and all arrogance that raises itself up against the knowledge of God' 2 Cor 10.5.

88.208 ὑψηλός^d, ή, όν: pertaining to being arrogant or proud – 'arrogant, proud.' ὅτι τὸ ἐν ἀνθρώποις ὑψηλὸν βδέλυγμα ἐνώπιον τοῦ θεοῦ 'because that which people are proud of is an abomination in the sight of God' or 'arrogance among people is detestable before God' Lk 16.15. The phrase τὸ ἐν ἀνθρώποις ὑψηλόν may be rendered in some languages as 'that which people think is great' or 'that which people think is very good indeed.' For another interpretation of ὑψηλός in Lk 16.15, see 65.9.

88.209 ὑψηλοφρονέω; ὑψηλὰ φρονέω: to have an arrogant, haughty attitude – 'to be haughty, to be arrogant.'
ὑψηλοφρονέω: τοῖς πλουσίοις ἐν τῷ νῦν αἰῶνι παράγγελλε μὴ ὑψηλοφρονεῖν 'command those who are rich in this life not to be haughty' 1 Tm 6.17. The meaning of 'to be haughty' may be expressed in a number of languages as 'to regard oneself as better than anyone else.'

ὑψηλὰ φρονέω: μὴ ὑψηλὰ φρόνει, ἀλλὰ φοβοῦ 'do not be proud of it, but be afraid' Ro 11.20.

88.210 ὑπερφρονέω: to have an unwarranted pride in oneself or in one's accomplishments – 'to be conceited, to be arrogant, to be proud, to think highly of oneself.' μὴ ὑπερφρονεῖν παρ' ὃ δεῖ φρονεῖν 'do not think of yourselves more highly than you ought to think' or 'do not have an exaggerated opinion of your importance' Ro 12.3.

88.211 ὑπεραίρομαι[a]: to become puffed up with pride, with the probable implication of being disparaging toward others – 'to be overly proud, to be puffed up with pride, to feel overly self-confident.' ἵνα μὴ ὑπεραίρωμαι 'in order that I would not be puffed up with pride' 2 Cor 12.7.

88.212 ἐπαίρομαι[b]: to become haughty in one's attitude toward others – 'to be haughty, to be arrogant.' ἀνέχεσθε γὰρ εἴ τις ὑμᾶς . . . λαμβάνει, εἴ τις ἐπαίρεται 'you will tolerate anyone who . . . takes advantage of you or who behaves haughtily toward you' 2 Cor 11.20.

88.213 ὑπερηφανία, ας f: a state of ostentatious pride or arrogance bordering on insolence – 'pride, arrogance, haughtiness.' βλασφημία, ὑπερηφανία, ἀφροσύνη 'slander, haughtiness, folly' Mk 7.22.

88.214 ὑπερήφανος, ον: pertaining to being ostentatiously proud – 'arrogant, haughty, contemptuous.' ὁ θεὸς ὑπερηφάνοις ἀντιτάσσεται, ταπεινοῖς δὲ δίδωσιν χάριν 'God resists the haughty but gives grace to the humble' Jas 4.6.

88.215 φυσίωσις, εως f: (a figurative extension of meaning of φυσίωσις 'inflation,' not occurring in the NT) an inflated, puffed up, exaggerated view of one's own importance – 'pride, arrogance, feeling of self-importance.' ψιθυρισμοί, φυσιώσεις, ἀκαταστασίαι 'gossip, arrogance, and disorder' 2 Cor 12.20.

88.216 φυσιόομαι: (a figurative extension of meaning of φυσιόω 'to puff up, to inflate,' not

occurring in the NT) to be puffed up with pride – 'to be proud, to be haughty.' μὴ εἷς ὑπὲρ τοῦ ἑνὸς φυσιοῦσθε κατὰ τοῦ ἑτέρου 'none (of you) should be proud of one person and despise another' (literally '. . . one person against another') 1 Cor 4.6.

88.217 φυσιόω: (a figurative extension of meaning of φυσιόω 'to puff up, to inflate,' not occurring in the NT) to cause someone to be proud, arrogant, or haughty – 'to make proud, to make arrogant, to make haughty.' ἡ γνῶσις φυσιοῖ, ἡ δὲ ἀγάπη οἰκοδομεῖ 'such knowledge makes a person haughty, but love builds up' 1 Cor 8.1.

88.218 τυφόομαι: (a figurative extension of meaning of τυφόομαι 'to be crazy, to be demented,' not occurring in the NT) to be so arrogant as to be practically demented – 'to be insanely arrogant, to be extremely proud, to be very arrogant.' ἵνα μὴ τυφωθεὶς εἰς κρίμα ἐμπέσῃ 'otherwise he will become extremely proud and be condemned' 1 Tm 3.6.

88.219 ἀλαζονεία, ας f: a state of pride or arrogance, but with the implication of complete lack of basis for such an attitude – 'false arrogance, pretentious pride, boastful haughtiness.' νῦν δὲ καυχᾶσθε ἐν ταῖς ἀλαζονείαις ὑμῶν 'but now you are boasting in your pretentious pride' Jas 4.16. 'Pretentious pride' may be rendered as 'constantly talking about how great oneself is.'

88.220 ἀλαζών, όνος m: (derivative of ἀλαζονεία 'pretentious pride,' 88.219) one who is pretentiously proud and given to bragging about it – 'braggart, arrogant person.' ἔσονται γὰρ οἱ ἄνθρωποι φίλαυτοι, φιλάργυροι, ἀλαζόνες 'for there will be people who are lovers of themselves, lovers of money, braggarts' 2 Tm 3.2. In a number of languages an arrogant person is described figuratively as 'one who speaks big words about himself' or 'one whose mouth is too big for his body.'

88.221 κενοδοξία, ας f: a state of pride which is without basis or justification – 'empty pride, cheap pride, vain pride.' μηδὲν κατ' ἐριθείαν μηδὲ κατὰ κενοδοξίαν '(do) nothing

from selfish ambition or from empty pride'
Php 2.3.

88.222 κενόδοξος, ον: pertaining to being
proud without basis or justification – 'falsely
proud.' μὴ γινώμεθα κενόδοξοι 'we should not
become falsely proud' Ga 5.26. It is often
possible to render 'to be falsely proud' as 'to
be proud when there is no reason to be proud'
or 'to be proud even when there is nothing to
be proud of.'

B' Stubbornness (88.223-88.226)

88.223 σκληρότης, ητος f: a stubborn attitude with regard to any change in behavior
– 'stubbornness.' κατὰ δὲ τὴν σκληρότητά σου
καὶ ἀμετανόητον καρδίαν 'because of your stubbornness and unrepentant heart' Ro 2.5. In a
number of languages stubbornness may be
described as 'refusing to change' or 'refusing
to think differently.' In some instances stubbornness may be expressed idiomatically as
'one's heart only sees one thing' or 'one's
heart is blind' or 'one who always says No.'

**88.224 σκληροτράχηλος, ον; σκληροκαρ-
δία, ας f; ἀπερίτμητος καρδία καὶ τοῖς
ὠσίν** (an idiom, literally 'uncircumcised in
heart and ears'): pertaining to being obdurate
and obstinate – 'stubborn, completely un-
yielding.'[15]
σκληροτράχηλος and ἀπερίτμητος καρδία καὶ
τοῖς ὠσίν: σκληροτράχηλοι καὶ ἀπερίτμητοι
καρδίαις καὶ τοῖς ὠσίν 'stubborn and obstinate
in your thinking and understanding' Ac 7.51.
σκληροκαρδία: Μωϋσῆς πρὸς τὴν σκληροκαρδίαν
ὑμῶν ἐπέτρεψεν ὑμῖν ἀπολῦσαι τὰς γυναῖκας
ὑμῶν 'Moses gave you permission to divorce
your wives because you were so obstinate' Mt
19.8.
    In the contexts illustrated by σκληροτράχ-
ηλος, ἀπερίτμητος καρδία καὶ τοῖς ὠσίν, and
σκληροκαρδία, the focus of the stubbornness
and obstinacy is the unwillingness to be
taught or to understand.

---

15 The series of expressions in 88.224 appears to differ somewhat in intensity from σκληρότης 'stubbornness'
(88.223).

88.225 σκληρύνομαι: to be stubborn, in the
sense of refusing to believe – 'to be stubborn,
to be obstinate.' τινες ἐσκληρύνοντο καὶ ἠπεί-
θουν 'they were stubborn and would not believe' Ac 19.9.

88.226 σκληρύνω: to cause to be stubborn
and obstinate, especially with regard to the
truth – 'to make stubborn, to make obstinate.'
ὃν δὲ θέλει σκληρύνει 'whom he wishes to, he
makes stubborn' Ro 9.18.
    In the expression σκληρύνω τὰς καρδίας 'to
cause the hearts to be obstinate' in He 3.8, 15
and 4.7, καρδία must be understood as 'the inner self' (see 26.3) and as such the addition of
καρδία merely reinforces the meaning of the
verb σκληρύνω.

C' Hypocrisy, Pretense (88.227-88.237)

88.227 ὑποκρίνομαι; ὑπόκρισις, εως f: to
give an impression of having certain purposes
or motivations, while in reality having quite
different ones – 'to pretend, to act hypocritically, pretense, hypocrisy.'
ὑποκρίνομαι: ἀπέστειλαν ἐγκαθέτους ὑποκρινομένους ἑαυτοὺς δικαίους εἶναι, ἵνα ἐπιλάβωνται
αὐτοῦ λόγου 'they sent spies who pretended to
be righteous in order to trap him in some
statement' Lk 20.20.
ὑπόκρισις: ὁ δὲ εἰδὼς αὐτῶν τὴν ὑπόκρισιν εἶπεν
αὐτοῖς, Τί με πειράζετε; 'he saw through their
hypocrisy and said, Why are you trying to
trap me?' Mk 12.15.
    In a number of languages ὑποκρίνομαι and
ὑπόκρισις are expressed in idiomatic ways, for
example, 'to have two faces,' 'to have two
tongues,' 'to be two people,' or 'to have two
hearts.'

88.228 ὑποκριτής, οῦ m: (derivative of ὑποκρίνομαι 'to pretend,' 88.227) one who pretends to be other than he really is – 'hypocrite, pretender, one who acts hypocritically.'
ὅταν δὲ νηστεύητε, μὴ γίνεσθε ὡς οἱ ὑποκριταὶ
σκυθρωποί 'when you fast, do not put on a sad
face like the hypocrites' Mt 6.16.

88.229 συνυποκρίνομαι: to act hypocritically
along with others – 'to pretend together, to
join in hypocrisy.' συνυπεκρίθησαν αὐτῷ καὶ οἱ

λοιποὶ Ἰουδαῖοι 'other Jews also joined him in this hypocrisy' Ga 2.13.

88.230 πρόφασις[a], εως *f*: to pretend to be engaged in a particular activity – 'to pretend, pretense.' χαλασάντων τὴν σκάφην εἰς τὴν θάλασσαν προφάσει ὡς ἐκ πρῴρης ἀγκύρας μελλόντων ἐκτείνειν 'they lowered the boat into the water and pretended that they were going to put out some anchors from the front of the ship' Ac 27.30.

88.231 ἀρνέομαι[f]: to behave in a way which is untrue to one's real self, in a sense of denying certain valid aspects of one's personality – 'to be false to oneself, to be untrue to oneself.' ἐκεῖνος πιστὸς μένει, ἀρνήσασθαι γὰρ ἑαυτὸν οὐ δύναται 'he remains faithful, for he cannot be false to himself' 2 Tm 2.13. It is possible in some languages to translate 'he cannot be false to himself' in 2 Tm 2.13 as 'he cannot be different from what he really is' or 'he cannot be otherwise than good.'

88.232 γόης, ητος *m*: one who habitually fools or deceives people through pretense – 'impostor, hypocrite.' πονηροὶ δὲ ἄνθρωποι καὶ γόητες προκόψουσιν ἐπὶ τὸ χεῖρον 'evil men and impostors will go from bad to worse' 2 Tm 3.13.

88.233 ἔρχομαι ἐν ἐνδύμασιν προβάτων: (an idiom, literally 'to come in sheep's clothing') to pretend to be harmless when in reality one is dangerous and destructive – 'to pretend to be good, to act hypocritically, to come in sheep's clothing.' προσέχετε ἀπὸ τῶν ψευδοπροφητῶν, οἵτινες ἔρχονται πρὸς ὑμᾶς ἐν ἐνδύμασιν προβάτων, ἔσωθεν δέ εἰσιν λύκοι ἅρπαγες 'watch out for false prophets who come to you in sheep's clothing, but in reality are greedy wolves' Mt 7.15. In many languages it is possible to retain the idiom ἔρχομαι ἐν ἐνδύμασιν προβάτων, since the context seems to explain rather clearly what is meant. However, in a number of languages it may be necessary to translate ἔρχομαι ἐν ἐνδύμασιν προβάτων as 'to come looking like sheep' or 'to come looking as innocent as sheep.'

88.234 τοῖχος κεχονιαμένος: (an idiom, literally 'whitewashed wall') one who pre-

tends to be one thing, while in reality he is something quite different – 'hypocrite, impostor.' τύπτειν σε μέλλει ὁ θεός, τοῖχε κεχονιαμένε 'God will strike you, you impostor' Ac 23.3.

88.235 δίλογος, ον: pertaining to contradictory behavior based upon pretense or hypocrisy – 'double-tongued, two-faced, hypocritical.' διακόνους ὡσαύτως σεμνούς, μὴ διλόγους 'church helpers must be good and not be two-faced' 1 Tm 3.8. In some languages the equivalent of δίλογος is 'to speak in two directions' or 'to cover one's thoughts by means of one's words.'

88.236 εὐπροσωπέω: to make a good showing, particularly with regard to outward appearances – 'to wish to show off, to make a good showing.' ὅσοι θέλουσιν εὐπροσωπῆσαι ἐν σαρκί, οὗτοι ἀναγκάζουσιν ὑμᾶς περιτέμνεσθαι 'those who force you to be circumcised are those who wish to make a good showing in external matters' (literally, '. . . in the flesh') Ga 6.12.

88.237 ζύμη[b], ης *f*: (a figurative extension of meaning of ζύμη[a] 'yeast,' 5.11) hypocritical behavior, probably implying hidden attitudes and motivations – 'hypocrisy, pretense.' βλέπετε ἀπὸ τῆς ζύμης τῶν Φαρισαίων καὶ τῆς ζύμης Ἡρῴδου 'beware of the hypocrisy of the Pharisees and the hypocrisy of Herod' Mk 8.15; προσέχετε ἑαυτοῖς ἀπὸ τῆς ζύμης, ἥτις ἐστὶν ὑπόκρισις, τῶν Φαρισαίων 'guard yourselves from the pretense of the Pharisees which is hypocrisy' Lk 12.1.

In Mt 16.6 the ζύμη of the Pharisees and the Sadducees is equated with their teaching, but the context would indicate clearly that this was a type of hypocritical teaching, since the religious leaders said one thing but did something quite different.

In 1 Corinthians 5.6-7 there is an extended figurative reference to ζύμη. At first, ζύμη must be understood in the literal sense (as in Domain 5), yet ζύμη in verse 7 refers to wrong behavior. It is important, however, to try to preserve the continuity of the figurative reference, and for that reason the phrase παλαιὰ ζύμη is sometimes translated as 'the old yeast of sin.' It is difficult to know to what extent there may be a reference at this point to the hypocrisy which accompanies legalistic behavior.

D' Show Favoritism, Prejudice (88.238-88.242)

88.238 προσωπολημπτέω; προσωπολημ-ψία, ας *f*; λαμβάνω πρόσωπον (an idiom, literally 'to accept a face'): to make unjust distinctions between people by treating one person better than another – 'to show favoritism, to be partial, partiality.'
προσωπολημπτέω: εἰ δὲ προσωπολημπτεῖτε, ἁμαρτίαν ἐργάζεσθε 'if you treat one person better than another, you are guilty of sin' Jas 2.9.
προσωπολημψία: οὐ γάρ ἐστιν προσωπολημψία παρὰ τῷ θεῷ 'God shows no favoritism' Ro 2.11.
λαμβάνω πρόσωπον: διδάσκεις καὶ οὐ λαμβάνεις πρόσωπον 'you teach and do not show partiality' Lk 20.21.
'To show favoritism' or 'to be partial' is expressed in an idiomatic manner in some languages, for example, 'to look only upon a person's face,' 'to call a sparrow a chicken,' or 'to give one's clansman the best piece of meat.'

88.239 προσωπολήμπτης, ου *m*: (derivative of προσωπολημπτέω 'to show favoritism,' 88.238) one who unjustly treats one person better than another – 'one who shows favoritism, a respecter of persons.' καταλαμβάνομαι ὅτι οὐκ ἔστιν προσωπολήμπτης ὁ θεός 'I realize that God does not show favoritism (in dealing with people)' Ac 10.34.

88.240 ἀπροσωπολήμπτως: pertaining to behaving in an unprejudiced manner – 'impartially, in an impartial manner.' πατέρα ἐπικαλεῖσθε τὸν ἀπροσωπολήμπτως κρίνοντα κατὰ τὸ ἑκάστου ἔργον 'you address him as Father who judges people impartially according to what each one has done' 1 Pe 1.17.

88.241 πρόσκλισις, εως *f*: a decided and unjustified preference for something or someone – 'prejudice, partiality.' διαμαρτύρομαι . . .

μηδὲν ποιῶν κατὰ πρόσκλισιν 'I call upon you . . . not to show prejudice in anything you do' 1 Tm 5.21.

88.242 ἀδιάκριτος, ον: pertaining to not being prejudiced – 'impartial, free from prejudice.' ἡ δὲ ἄνωθεν σοφία πρῶτον μὲν ἁγνή ἐστιν . . . ἀδιάκριτος, ἀνυπόκριτος 'but the wisdom from above is first of all pure . . . free from prejudice and hypocrisy' Jas 3.17.

E' Being a Busybody (88.243-88.245)

88.243 περιεργάζομαι: to meddle in the affairs of someone else – 'to be a busybody.' μηδὲν ἐργαζομένους ἀλλὰ περιεργαζομένους 'who do nothing but meddle in the affairs of others' 2 Th 3.11. In some languages one may speak of a busybody as 'one who puts his spoon in someone else's cup' or 'one who always tells another how to buy and sell.'

88.244 περίεργος[a], ου *m*: pertaining to meddling in someone else's business – '(being a) busybody, meddling.' ἀλλὰ καὶ φλύαροι καὶ περίεργοι 'but they are gossips and busybodies' 1 Tm 5.13.

88.245 ἀλλοτριεπίσκοπος, ου *m*: one who busies himself in the affairs of others in an unwarranted manner – 'busybody, meddler.' μὴ γάρ τις ὑμῶν πασχέτω ὡς φονεὺς ἢ κλέπτης ἢ κακοποιὸς ἢ ὡς ἀλλοτριεπίσκοπος 'none of you should suffer punishment as a murderer, thief, evildoer, or as a meddler in others' affairs' 1 Pe 4.15.

F' Laziness, Idleness (88.246-88.251)

88.246 ἀτακτέω: to refuse being engaged in the efforts of work – 'to do nothing, to be idle, to be lazy.' οὐκ ἠτακτήσαμεν ἐν ὑμῖν . . . ἐργαζόμενοι πρὸς τὸ μὴ ἐπιβαρῆσαί τινα ὑμῶν 'we were not lazy when we were with you . . . we kept working so as not to be an expense to any of you' 2 Th 3.7-8. Traditional translations have often interpreted ἀτακτέω in an etymological sense of 'not being ordered' and hence with a meaning of 'to behave in a disorderly manner,' but this is quite contrary to the context.

88.247 ἄτακτος, ον; ἀτάκτως: (derivatives of ἀτακτέω 'to do nothing,' 88.246) pertaining to refusing to work – 'idle, lazy, lazily.'
ἄτακτος: παρακαλοῦμεν δὲ ὑμᾶς, ἀδελφοί, νουθετεῖτε τοὺς ἀτάκτους 'we urge you, brothers, warn those who are lazy' 1 Th 5.14.
ἀτάκτως: στέλλεσθαι ὑμᾶς ἀπὸ παντὸς ἀδελφοῦ ἀτάκτως περιπατοῦντος 'keep away from all brothers who are living lazily' 2 Th 3.6. For a discussion of ἀτακτέω in the related context of 2 Th 3.7, see 88.246.

88.248 ἀργός[b], ή, όν: pertaining to habitually refusing to work (probably with a more unfavorable connotation than in the case of ἄτακτος, 88.247) – 'lazy, good-for-nothing.'
Κρῆτες ἀεὶ ψεῦσται, κακὰ θηρία, γαστέρες ἀργαί 'Cretans are always liars, wicked beasts, lazy gluttons' Tt 1.12.

88.249 νωθρός, ά, όν: pertaining to being sluggish or slow to become involved in some activity – 'lazy.' ἐνδείκνυσθαι σπουδὴν πρὸς τὴν πληροφορίαν τῆς ἐλπίδος ἄχρι τέλους, ἵνα μὴ νωθροὶ γένησθε 'keep up your eagerness to the end so that what you hope for will come true and do not become lazy' He 6.11-12.

88.250 ὀκνηρός[a], ά, όν: pertaining to shrinking from or hesitating to engage in something worthwhile, possibly implying lack of ambition – 'lazy, lacking in ambition.' τῇ σπουδῇ μὴ ὀκνηροί 'not lacking in zeal' Ro 12.11.

88.251 ἀγοραῖος[a], ου m: (derivative of ἀγορά 'marketplace,' 57.207) a person who habitually idles in the marketplace – 'loafer, bum.' προσλαβόμενοι τῶν ἀγοραίων ἄνδρας τινὰς πονηροὺς καὶ ὀχλοποιήσαντες 'they gathered some wicked loafers and formed a mob' Ac 17.5.

G' Extravagant Living, Intemperate Living (88.252-88.255)

88.252 σπαταλάω: to indulge oneself excessively in satisfying one's own appetites and desires – 'to live indulgently.' ἐτρυφήσατε ἐπὶ τῆς γῆς καὶ ἐσπαταλήσατε 'you lived here on earth with intemperance and indulgence' Jas 5.5.

88.253 τρυφάω; ἐντρυφάω; τρυφή, ῆς f: to live a life of luxury, usually associated with intemperate feasting and drinking – 'to revel, to carouse, to live a life of luxury.'
τρυφάω: ἐτρυφήσατε ἐπὶ τῆς γῆς καὶ ἐσπαταλήσατε 'you lived here on earth with intemperance and indulgence' Jas 5.5.
ἐντρυφάω and τρυφή: ἡδονὴν ἡγούμενοι τὴν ἐν ἡμέρᾳ τρυφήν, σπίλοι καὶ μῶμοι ἐντρυφῶντες ἐν ταῖς ἀπάταις αὐτῶν συνευωχούμενοι ὑμῖν 'pleasure for them is revelling in the daytime; they are stains and blemishes, behaving extravagantly in their deceptions as they feast with you' 2 Pe 2.13.

88.254 στρηνιάω; στρῆνος, ους n: to live sensually by gratifying the senses with sexual immorality – 'to live sensually, to live intemperately, lust, sensual living.'
στρηνιάω: κλαύσουσιν καὶ κόψονται ἐπ' αὐτὴν οἱ βασιλεῖς τῆς γῆς οἱ μετ' αὐτῆς πορνεύσαντες καὶ στρηνιάσαντες 'the kings of the earth who shared in her immorality and intemperate living will cry and wail' Re 18.9.
στρῆνος: καὶ οἱ ἔμποροι τῆς γῆς ἐκ τῆς δυνάμεως τοῦ στρήνους αὐτῆς ἐπλούτησαν 'and the merchants of the earth grew rich from her overwhelming lust' Re 18.3.

88.255 λαμπρῶς: pertaining to living in ostentatious luxury – 'luxuriously, with ostentation, showing off.' ἐνεδιδύσκετο πορφύραν καὶ βύσσον εὐφραινόμενος καθ' ἡμέραν λαμπρῶς 'he dressed in fine clothes (literally 'in purple cloth') and rejoiced in living luxuriously every day' Lk 16.19. The equivalent of λαμπρῶς in the sense of 'luxuriously' may be rendered in a number of languages as 'richly' or 'with things which cost a great deal' or 'with more possessions than one can count.'

H' Impurity (88.256-88.261)

88.256 ῥυπαρία, ας f: a state of moral impurity and filth – 'moral impurity, moral filth, filthiness.' ἀποθέμενοι πᾶσαν ῥυπαρίαν καὶ περισσείαν κακίας 'put aside all moral filthiness and remaining wickedness' Jas 1.21.

88.257 ῥυπαρός[b], ά, όν: pertaining to being morally impure or filthy – 'morally impure, morally filthy, morally perverted.' ὁ ῥυπαρὸς ῥυπανθήτω ἔτι 'whoever is morally filthy must go on being filthy' Re 22.11.

It would be a mistake to assume that physical filth is necessarily related to moral impurity. Hence, one cannot simply take a word meaning 'dirty' and presume that it may carry the figurative significance of moral depravity or impurity. The equivalent in some languages is 'moral degenerate,' 'stained with badness,' 'spotted with evil,' or 'has sin on him like leprous spots.'

88.258 ῥυπαίνομαι: to live in a degenerate manner – 'to live in moral filth, to live a completely bad life.' ὁ ῥυπαρὸς ῥυπανθήτω ἔτι 'whoever is morally filthy must go on being filthy' Re 22.11.

88.259 μίασμα, τος n; μιασμός, οῦ m: a state of being tainted or stained by evil – 'impurity, impure, tainted, evil, defilement.'
μίασμα: εἰ γὰρ ἀποφυγόντες τὰ μιάσματα τοῦ κόσμου 'if they have escaped the defilement of the world' 2 Pe 2.20.
μιασμός: μάλιστα δὲ τοὺς ὀπίσω σαρκὸς ἐν ἐπιθυμίᾳ μιασμοῦ πορευομένους 'especially those who follow their impure bodily lusts' 2 Pe 2.10.

88.260 μιαίνω[a]: to cause someone to be morally tainted or defiled – 'to defile, to contaminate, to cause to be morally filthy.' τοῖς δὲ μεμιαμμένοις καὶ ἀπίστοις οὐδὲν καθαρόν 'to those who are defiled and unbelieving, nothing is pure' Tt 1.15.

88.261 ἀκαθαρσία[a], ας f: the state of moral impurity, especially in relationship to sexual sin – 'impurity, immorality, filthiness.' παρέδωκεν αὐτοὺς ὁ θεὸς ἐν ταῖς ἐπιθυμίαις τῶν καρδιῶν αὐτῶν εἰς ἀκαθαρσίαν 'God has given them over to do the immoral things their hearts desire' Ro 1.24.

Ι' Licentiousness, Perversion (88.262-88.270)

88.262 πλάνη[c], ης f: behavior which deviates seriously from that which is morally correct – 'perversion.' τὴν ἀντιμισθίαν ἣν ἔδει τῆς πλάνης αὐτῶν ἐν ἑαυτοῖς ἀπολαμβάνοντες 'they receive in themselves the punishment they deserve for their perversion' Ro 1.27. In a number of languages πλάνη in Ro 1.27 may be rendered as 'what people do which is completely wrong' or '. . . what is very wrong indeed.'

88.263 ἀχρειόομαι: to engage in behavior which is totally wrong and harmful – 'to go wrong, to become perverse.' πάντες ἐξέκλιναν, ἅμα ἠχρεώθησαν 'they have all turned away; they have all gone wrong' Ro 3.12.

88.264 ἀποστρέφω[b]; διαστρέφω[b]: to cause someone to depart from correct behavior and thus engage in serious wrongdoing – 'to lead astray, to pervert, to mislead.'
ἀποστρέφω[b]: προσηνέγκατέ μοι τὸν ἄνθρωπον τοῦτον ὡς ἀποστρέφοντα τὸν λαόν 'you brought this man to me and said that he was misleading the people' Lk 23.14. For another interpretation of ἀποστρέφω in Lk 23.14, see 31.70.
διαστρέφω[b]: ὦ γενεὰ ἄπιστος καὶ διεστραμμένη 'unbelieving and perverted generation' Mt 17.17; τοῦτον εὕραμεν διαστρέφοντα τὸ ἔθνος ἡμῶν 'we caught this man perverting our people' Lk 23.2. For another interpretation of διαστρέφω in Lk 23.2, see 31.71. In rendering διαστρέφω as 'to pervert,' one should not understand the meaning in terms of 'sexual perversion.' In speaking of 'perverting our people' in Lk 23.2, it would be better in most languages to translate 'to cause our people to go astray' or 'to cause them to do what they certainly should not do.'

88.265 ἐκστρέφομαι: to have departed from the patterns of correct behavior and thus to have become corrupt – 'to be corrupt, to have become corrupt.' εἰδὼς ὅτι ἐξέστραπται ὁ τοιοῦτος 'you know that such a person has become corrupt' Tt 3.11.

88.266 φθείρω[c]; διαφθείρω[b]; καταφθείρω: to cause someone to become perverse or depraved, as a type of moral destruction – 'to deprave, to pervert, to ruin, to cause the moral ruin of.'[16]

---

16 It is possible that διαφθείρω[b] and καταφθείρω are somewhat more emphatic in meaning than φθείρω[c].

φθείρω^c: ἔκρινεν τὴν πόρνην τὴν μεγάλην ἥτις ἔφθειρεν τὴν γῆν ἐν τῇ πορνείᾳ αὐτῆς 'he condemned the great harlot who was leading the world into moral ruin with her immorality' Re 19.2.

διαφθείρω^b: διαφθεῖραι τοὺς διαφθείροντας τὴν γῆν 'to destroy those who ruin the earth' or '. . . cause the earth to be depraved' Re 11.18; διαπαρατριβαὶ διεφθαρμένων ἀνθρώπων τὸν νοῦν 'constant arguments from those whose minds are depraved' 1 Tm 6.5.

καταφθείρω: ἄνθρωποι κατεφθαρμένοι τὸν νοῦν 'people with depraved minds' 2 Tm 3.8.

88.267 φθορά^c, ᾶς *f*: a state of moral corruption and depravity – 'moral corruption, depravity.' αὐτοὶ δοῦλοι ὑπάρχοντες τῆς φθορᾶς 'they themselves are slaves of moral corruption' 2 Pe 2.19. In some languages 'slaves of moral corruption' in 2 Pe 2.19 may be expressed as 'their immoral desires make slaves of them' or '. . . cause them to be slaves.'

88.268 σκολιός^b, ά, όν: (a figurative extension of meaning of σκολιός^a 'crooked,' 79.90) pertaining to being unscrupulous and dishonest – 'crooked, unscrupulous, dishonest.' σώθητε ἀπὸ τῆς γενεᾶς τῆς σκολιᾶς ταύτης 'save yourselves from this crooked generation' Ac 2.40.

88.269 πανοῦργος, ον: pertaining to being crafty and sly (literally 'one who is ready to do anything') – 'scoundrel, crafty fellow.' ὑπάρχων πανοῦργος δόλῳ ὑμᾶς ἔλαβον 'being a crafty person, I took you in by deceit' 2 Cor 12.16.

88.270 πανουργία, ας *f*: trickery involving evil cunning – 'craftiness, treachery.' ὡς ὁ ὄφις ἐξηπάτησεν Εὔαν ἐν τῇ πανουργίᾳ αὐτοῦ 'as the snake deceived Eve by its treachery' 2 Cor 11.3.

J' Sexual Misbehavior (88.271-88.282)

88.271 πορνεύω; ἐκπορνεύω; πορνεία, ας *f*: to engage in sexual immorality of any kind, often with the implication of prostitution – 'to engage in illicit sex, to commit fornication, sexual immorality, fornication, prostitution.' πορνεύω: ὁ δὲ πορνεύων εἰς τὸ ἴδιον σῶμα

ἁμαρτάνει 'the person who commits immorality sins against his own body' 1 Cor 6.18.

ἐκπορνεύω: ὡς Σόδομα καὶ Γόμορρα . . . ἐκπορνεύσασαι 'they committed sexual immorality . . . like Sodom and Gomorrah' Jd 7. πορνεία: τοῦτο γάρ ἐστιν θέλημα τοῦ θεοῦ, ὁ ἁγιασμὸς ὑμῶν, ἀπέχεσθαι ὑμᾶς ἀπὸ τῆς πορνείας 'this is God's will (for you; he wants you) to be consecrated to him and to abstain from sexual immorality' 1 Th 4.3. In some NT contexts πορνεία may refer specifically to incest.

88.272 ἀσέλγεια, ας *f*: behavior completely lacking in moral restraint, usually with the implication of sexual licentiousness – 'licentious behavior, extreme immorality.' μὴ μετανοησάντων ἐπὶ τῇ ἀκαθαρσίᾳ καὶ πορνείᾳ καὶ ἀσελγείᾳ ᾗ ἔπραξαν 'they have not repented of the filthy things they have done, their immorality and licentious deeds' 2 Cor 12.21. In some languages the equivalent of 'licentious behavior' would be 'to live like a dog' or 'to act like a goat' or 'to be a rooster,' in each instance pertaining to promiscuous sexual behavior.

88.273 κοίτη^c, ης *f*: to engage in immoral sexual excess – 'sexual immorality, lasciviousness.'[17] ὡς ἐν ἡμέρᾳ εὐσχημόνως περιπατήσωμεν, μὴ κώμοις καὶ μέθαις, μὴ κοίταις 'let us conduct ourselves properly as people who live in the light of day; no orgies and drunkenness, no sexual immorality' Ro 13.13.

88.274 πόρνος, ου *m*: one who engages in sexual immorality, whether a man or a woman, and in some contexts, distinguished from an adulterer or adulteress – 'a sexually immoral person.' ἔγραψα ὑμῖν ἐν τῇ ἐπιστολῇ μὴ συναναμίγνυσθαι πόρνοις 'in the letter that I wrote you I told you not to associate with sexually immoral people' 1 Cor 5.9.

88.275 πόρνη, ης *f*: a woman who practices sexual immorality as a profession – 'prostitute.' λέγω ὑμῖν ὅτι οἱ τελῶναι καὶ αἱ πόρναι

---

17 κοίτη^c 'sexual immorality' is a peripheral extension of meaning of κοίτη^b 'sexual relations' (see 23.62). This is due to a process of semantic narrowing.

προάγουσιν ὑμᾶς εἰς τὴν βασιλείαν τοῦ θεοῦ 'I tell you, the tax collectors and the prostitutes are going into the kingdom of God ahead of you' Mt 21.31. Since prostitution is an almost universal behavioral trait, it is not difficult to obtain terms for such a person or activity. The difficulty is usually involved in selecting a term which will not be vulgar. Expressions for a prostitute are often idiomatic, for example, 'one who acts like a she-dog,' 'one who sells her vulva,' 'one who sells herself,' or 'one who receives any man.'

88.276 μοιχεύω; μοιχάομαι; μοιχεία, ας *f*: sexual intercourse of a man with a married woman other than his own spouse – 'to commit adultery, adultery.' From the standpoint of the NT, adultery was normally defined in terms of the married status of the woman involved in any such act. In other words, sexual intercourse of a married man with an unmarried woman would usually be regarded as πορνεία 'fornication' (88.271), but sexual intercourse of either an unmarried or a married man with someone else's wife was regarded as adultery, both on the part of the man as well as the woman. In view of the married status of the woman being the determining factor in μοιχεύω, μοιχάομαι, μοιχεία, and related terms (88.277-278) there is a significant contrast with πορνεύω and related expressions (88.271). πορνεύω, however, may be regarded as more generic in meaning, and thus in certain contexts including adultery.
μοιχεύω: πᾶς ὁ ἀπολύων τὴν γυναῖκα αὐτοῦ καὶ γαμῶν ἑτέραν μοιχεύει 'any man who divorces his wife and marries another woman commits adultery' Lk 16.18. The parallel expression in Mt 5.32 is somewhat different: πᾶς ὁ ἀπολύων τὴν γυναῖκα αὐτοῦ παρεκτὸς λόγου πορνείας ποιεῖ αὐτὴν μοιχευθῆναι, usually rendered as 'anyone who divorces his wife for any cause other than fornication makes her guilty of committing adultery,' presumably on the implication that she would marry someone else, as is implied in the final clause of Mt 5.32.
μοιχάομαι: ἐὰν αὐτὴ ἀπολύσασα τὸν ἄνδρα αὐτῆς γαμήσῃ ἄλλον μοιχᾶται 'if a woman divorces her husband and marries another man, she commits adultery' Mk 10.12.
μοιχεία: ἐκ τῆς καρδίας τῶν ἀνθρώπων οἱ διαλογισμοὶ οἱ κακοὶ ἐκπορεύονται, πορνεῖαι, κλοπαί, φόνοι, μοιχεῖαι 'from the hearts of people come evil reasonings which lead to sexual immorality, theft, murder, adultery' Mk 7.21-22.

88.277 μοιχός, οῦ *m*: (derivative of μοιχεύω 'to commit adultery,' 88.276) a person who commits adultery, specifically referring to males, but also including females in generic contexts – 'adulterer, adulteress.' οὔτε μοιχοὶ . . . βασιλείαν θεοῦ κληρονομήσουσιν 'no adulterers . . . will receive God's kingdom' 1 Cor 6.9-10.

88.278 μοιχαλίς, ίδος *f*: (derivative of μοιχεύω 'to commit adultery,' 88.276) a woman who commits adultery – 'adulteress.' ἄρα οὖν ζῶντος τοῦ ἀνδρὸς μοιχαλὶς χρηματίσει ἐὰν γένηται ἀνδρὶ ἑτέρῳ 'so then, if she lives with another man while her husband is alive, she will be called an adulteress' Ro 7.3.

88.279 ἀπέρχομαι ὀπίσω σαρκὸς ἑτέρας: (an idiom, literally 'to go after strange flesh') to engage in unnatural sexual intercourse – 'have homosexual intercourse.' ὡς Σόδομα καὶ Γόμορρα . . . ἀπελθοῦσαι ὀπίσω σαρκὸς ἑτέρας 'they committed homosexual intercourse . . . like the people of Sodom and Gomorrah' Jd 7. Though in some societies homosexuality is extremely rare, there are always ways of talking about it, though frequently the expressions may seem to be quite vulgar.

88.280 ἀρσενοκοίτης, ου *m*: a male partner in homosexual intercourse – 'homosexual.' οὐκ οἴδατε ὅτι . . . οὔτε μοιχοὶ οὔτε μαλακοὶ οὔτε ἀρσενοκοῖται . . . βασιλείαν θεοῦ κληρονομήσουσιν 'don't you know that . . . no adulterers or homosexuals . . . will receive the kingdom of God' 1 Cor 6.9-10. It is possible that ἀρσενοκοίτης in certain contexts refers to the active male partner in homosexual intercourse in contrast with μαλακός[b], the passive male partner (88.281).

88.281 μαλακός[b], οῦ *m*: the passive male partner in homosexual intercourse – 'homosexual.' For a context of μαλακός[b], see 1 Cor 6.9-10 in 88.280. As in Greek, a number of other languages also have entirely distinct terms for the active and passive roles in homosexual intercourse.

88.282 χύων^c, χυνός, dat. pl. χυσί *m*: (a figurative extension of meaning of χύων^a 'dog,' 4.34) one who is a sexual pervert or possibly one who is sexually promiscuous – 'pervert.' ἔξω οἱ χύνες χαὶ οἱ φάρμαχοι χαὶ οἱ πόρνοι 'but outside are the perverts, those who practice magic, and the immoral' Re 22.15. It is also possible, however, that in Re 22.15 χύων means 'a wicked person' who might have complete contempt for what is holy, a meaning which parallels the significance of the adage in Mt 7.6 (see 88.122).

K' Drunkenness[18] **(88.283-88.288)**

88.283 μεθύω^a; μέθη, ης *f*: to become drunk on alcoholic beverages – 'to be drunk, drunkenness.'
μεθύω^a: οὐ γὰρ ὡς ὑμεῖς ὑπολαμβάνετε οὗτοι μεθύουσιν 'these men are not drunk as you suppose' Ac 2.15.
μέθη: ἐν ἡμέρα εὐσχημόνως περιπατήσωμεν, μὴ χώμοις χαὶ μέθαις 'let us conduct ourselves properly as people who live in the light of day; no orgies, no drunkenness' Ro 13.13.

88.284 οἰνοφλυγία, ας *f*: drunkenness, implying the consumption of a large quantity of wine – 'drunkenness.' πεπορευμένους ἐν ἀσελγείαις, ἐπιθυμίαις, οἰνοφλυγίαις 'your lives were spent in licentiousness, lust, drunkenness' 1 Pe 4.3.

88.285 μεθύσχομαι: to become intoxicated – 'to get drunk.' μὴ μεθύσχεσθε οἴνω, ἐν ᾧ ἐστιν ἀσωτία 'do not get drunk with wine, for this means reckless living' Eph 5.18.

88.286 χραιπάλη, ης *f*: drunken behavior which is completely without moral restraint – 'drunken dissipation.' μήποτε βαρηθῶσιν ὑμῶν αἱ χαρδίαι ἐν χραιπάλη χαὶ μέθη 'do not let yourselves become occupied with drunken dissipation and inebriety' Lk 21.34. In a number of languages it may be possible to translate χραιπάλη as 'bad things people do when they are very drunk.'

88.287 χῶμος, ου *m*; πότος, ου *m*: drinking parties involving unrestrained indulgence in alcoholic beverages and accompanying immoral behavior – 'orgy, revelling, carousing.'
χῶμος: ἐν ἡμέρα εὐσχημόνως περιπατήσωμεν, μὴ χώμοις χαὶ μέθαις 'let us conduct ourselves properly as people who live in the light of day; no orgies, no drunkenness' Ro 13.13.
πότος: πεπορευμένους ἐν ἀσελγείαις, ἐπιθυμίαις, οἰνοφλυγίαις, χώμοις, πότοις 'your lives were spent in licentiousness, lust, drunkenness, orgies, revelling' 1 Pe 4.3.

88.288 μέθυσος, ου *m*; οἰνοπότης, ου *m*; πάροινος, ου *m*: a person who habitually drinks too much and thus becomes a drunkard – 'drunkard, heavy drinker.'
μέθυσος: οὐ μέθυσοι, οὐ λοίδοροι, οὐχ ἅρπαγες βασιλείαν θεοῦ κληρονομήσουσιν 'people who are drunkards or who slander others or are swindlers will not receive God's kingdom' 1 Cor 6.10.
οἰνοπότης: ἰδοὺ ἄνθρωπος φάγος χαὶ οἰνοπότης 'look at this man; he is a glutton and a drunkard' Lk 7.34.[19]
πάροινος: μὴ αὐθάδη, μὴ ὀργίλον, μὴ πάροινον 'he must not be arrogant, quick-tempered, or a drunkard' Tt 1.7.[19]

L' Sin, Wrongdoing, Guilt[20] **(88.289-88.318)**

88.289 ἁμαρτάνω; ἁμαρτία^a, ας *f*: to act contrary to the will and law of God – 'to sin, to engage in wrongdoing, sin.'
ἁμαρτάνω: πορεύσομαι πρὸς τὸν πατέρα μου χαὶ ἐρῶ αὐτῷ, Πάτερ, ἥμαρτον εἰς τὸν οὐρανὸν χαὶ ἐνώπιόν σου 'I will get up and go to my father

---

18 People in the ancient Mediterranean world were not acquainted with the distillation of alcoholic beverages; their alcohol-containing drinks involved fermented fruit juice (primarily of grapes) and grain.

19 Though the compounds πάροινος and οἰνοπότης contain the stem οἰνο- 'wine,' these derivatives do not necessarily restrict the type of alcoholic beverage consumed.
20 The meaning of 'guilt' is included in this subdomain as a state resulting from sinful behavior.

and say, Father, I have sinned against God and against you' Lk 15.18.

ἁμαρτία[a]: μηδὲ κοινώνει ἁμαρτίαις ἀλλοτρίαις 'take no part in the sins of others' or 'do not join others in sinning' 1 Tm 5.22.

88.290 ἁμάρτημα, τος *n*: that which someone has done in violating the will and law of God – 'sin, wrongdoing.' διὰ τὴν πάρεσιν τῶν προγεγονότων ἁμαρτημάτων 'because he overlooked their sins previously committed' Ro 3.25.

88.291 πταίω: (a figurative extension of meaning of πταίω 'to stumble,' not occurring in the NT) to fail to keep the law (of God) – 'to stumble, to err, to sin.' ὅστις γὰρ ὅλον τὸν νόμον τηρήσῃ, πταίσῃ δὲ ἐν ἑνί, γέγονεν πάντων ἔνοχος 'whoever keeps the whole law, yet sins in one point, has become guilty of all' Jas 2.10; λέγω οὖν, μὴ ἔπταισαν ἵνα πέσωσιν; 'I ask, then, when they sinned, did they fall to ruin?' Ro 11.11.

88.292 ἄπταιστος, ον: pertaining to not having failed to keep the law (of God) – 'free from stumbling, free from sinning.' τῷ δὲ δυναμένῳ φυλάξαι ὑμᾶς ἀπταίστους 'to him who is able to keep you free from sinning' Jd 24.

88.293 προαμαρτάνω: to sin previously or in the past – 'to sin previously, to have sinned.' πενθήσω πολλοὺς τῶν προημαρτηκότων καὶ μὴ μετανοησάντων 'I shall mourn over many who have sinned in the past and have not repented' 2 Cor 12.21.

88.294 ἁμαρτωλός, όν: (derivative of ἁμαρτάνω 'to sin,' 88.289) pertaining to sinful behavior – 'sinful, sinning.' ἐν τῇ γενεᾷ ταύτῃ τῇ μοιχαλίδι καὶ ἁμαρτωλῷ 'in this unfaithful and sinful generation' Mk 8.38.

88.295 ἁμαρτωλός, οῦ *m*: (derivative of ἁμαρτάνω 'to sin,' 88.289) a person who customarily sins – 'sinner, outcast.' οὐκ ἦλθον καλέσαι δικαίους ἀλλὰ ἁμαρτωλούς 'I have not come to call righteous people, but sinners' Mk 2.17. In contexts such as Mk 2.17, Mt 9.10, Lk 15.2, etc., ἁμαρτωλός may refer to persons who were irreligious in the sense of

having no concern for observing the details of the Law. Such people were often treated as social outcasts.

88.296 ὑπερβαίνω: to transgress the will and law of God by going beyond prescribed limits – 'to transgress, to sin against.' τὸ μὴ ὑπερβαίνειν καὶ πλεονεκτεῖν ἐν τῷ πράγματι τὸν ἀδελφὸν αὐτοῦ 'in this matter, then, no man should sin against his Christian brother or take advantage of him' 1 Th 4.6.

88.297 παράπτωμα, τος *n*: what a person has done in transgressing the will and law of God by some false step or failure – 'transgression, sin.'[21] ὃς παρεδόθη διὰ τὰ παραπτώματα ἡμῶν 'who was handed over because of our transgressions' Ro 4.25; ἐὰν δὲ μὴ ἀφῆτε τοῖς ἀνθρώποις, οὐδὲ ὁ πατὴρ ὑμῶν ἀφήσει τὰ παραπτώματα ὑμῶν 'if you do not forgive others, your Father will not forgive your transgressions' Mt 6.15.

88.298 ὀφείλω[d]: to commit a sin against someone and thus to incur moral debt – 'to sin against, to offend.' ἀφίομεν παντὶ ὀφείλοντι ἡμῖν 'we forgive everyone who sins against us' Lk 11.4.

88.299 ὀφείλημα[c], τος *n*: (derivative of ὀφείλω[d] 'to sin against,' 88.298) the moral debt incurred as the result of sin – 'offense, sin, transgression, guilt.' ἄφες ἡμῖν τὰ ὀφειλήματα ἡμῶν 'forgive us our sins' Mt 6.12.[22]

88.300 ὀφειλέτης[c], ου *m*: (derivative of ὀφείλω[d] 'to sin against,' 88.298) one who commits sin and thus incurs a moral debt – 'sinner, offender.' ὡς καὶ ἡμεῖς ἀφήκαμεν τοῖς ὀφειλέταις ἡμῶν 'as we forgive those who sin against us' Mt 6.12.

---

21 παράπτωμα is used in a number of contexts in a way in which it appears to be equivalent in meaning to ἁμάρτημα (88.290) or ἁμαρτία[a] (88.289), but it is possible that παράπτωμα focuses more upon unpremeditated violation of God's will and law.

22 Some scholars interpret ὀφείλημα in Mt 6.12 as referring literally to debts, since they believe the statement refers to the actual forgiveness of debts in the idealized jubilee year in the Jewish Law.

88.301 ῥᾳδιουργία, ας *f*; ῥᾳδιούργημα, τος *n*: to violate moral principles by acting in an unscrupulous manner – 'wrongdoing, unscrupulousness.'

ῥᾳδιουργία: ὦ πλήρης παντὸς δόλου καὶ πάσης ῥᾳδιουργίας 'you, who are full of all deceit and all wrongdoing' Ac 13.10.

ῥᾳδιούργημα: εἰ μὲν ἦν ἀδίκημά τι ἢ ῥᾳδιούργημα πονηρόν 'if this were a matter of some crime or serious unscrupulousness' Ac 18.14.

ῥᾳδιουργία and ῥᾳδιούργημα may often be rendered simply as 'doing what one should not do.' These terms also may often be translated merely as 'cheating.'

88.302 ἀγνόημα, τος *n*: sin which is committed as the result of ignorance – 'to sin through ignorance, to sin without knowing that one has sinned.' ὃ προσφέρει ὑπὲρ ἑαυτοῦ καὶ τῶν τοῦ λαοῦ ἀγνοημάτων 'which he offers (to God) on behalf of himself and for the sin which the people have committed without knowing they were sinning' He 9.7.

88.303 δελεάζω: to lure or entice someone to sin (compare δέλεαρ 'bait,' not occurring in the NT) – 'to lead astray, to lure into sin.' ἕκαστος δὲ πειράζεται ὑπὸ τῆς ἰδίας ἐπιθυμίας ἐξελκόμενος καὶ δελεαζόμενος 'a person is tempted when he is drawn away and enticed by his own evil desires' Jas 1.14. δελεάζω may often be translated as 'to make sinning look attractive' or 'to make sin taste good' or 'to wave sin in front of a person's nose.'

88.304 σκανδαλίζω[b]: (a figurative extension of meaning of σκανδαλίζω 'to cause to stumble,' not occurring in the NT) to cause to sin, with the probable implication of providing some special circumstances which contribute to such behavior – 'to cause to sin.' εἰ δὲ ὁ ὀφθαλμός σου ὁ δεξιὸς σκανδαλίζει σε, ἔξελε αὐτὸν καὶ βάλε ἀπὸ σοῦ 'if your right eye causes you to sin, take it out and throw it away' Mt 5.29.

88.305 σκανδαλίζομαι[b]: to fall into sin, with the implication of certain contributing circumstances – 'to sin, to fall into sin.' τίς σκανδαλίζεται, καὶ οὐκ ἐγὼ πυροῦμαι; 'who falls into sin without my being greatly distressed?' 2 Cor 11.29.

88.306 σκάνδαλον[b], ου *n*: (a figurative extension of meaning of σκάνδαλον[a] 'trap,' 6.25) that which or one who causes someone to sin – 'that which causes someone to sin, one who causes someone to sin.' συλλέξουσιν ἐκ τῆς βασιλείας αὐτοῦ πάντα τὰ σκάνδαλα καὶ τοὺς ποιοῦντας τὴν ἀνομίαν 'they will gather up out of his kingdom all who cause people to sin and those who live lawlessly' Mt 13.41.

88.307 πρόσκομμα[c], τος *n*; προσκοπή[c], ῆς *f*: that which provides an opportunity or occasion for causing someone to sin – 'that which causes someone to sin' or 'that which provides an occasion for someone to sin.'

πρόσκομμα[c]: βλέπετε δὲ μή πως ἡ ἐξουσία ὑμῶν αὕτη πρόσκομμα γένηται τοῖς ἀσθενέσιν 'be careful not to let your freedom of action (literally 'this freedom of yours') make those who are weak in the faith fall into sin' 1 Cor 8.9.

προσκοπή[c]: μηδεμίαν ἐν μηδενὶ διδόντες προσκοπήν 'giving to no one in anything a cause to sin' 2 Cor 6.3. For other interpretations of προσκοπή in 2 Cor 6.3, see 22.14 and 25.183.

88.308 πειράζω[c]; ἐκπειράζω[c]; πειρασμός[b], οῦ *m*: to endeavor or attempt to cause someone to sin – 'to tempt, to trap, to lead into temptation, temptation.'

πειράζω[c]: ἦν ἐν τῇ ἐρήμῳ τεσσεράκοντα ἡμέρας πειραζόμενος ὑπὸ τοῦ Σατανᾶ 'he stayed for forty days in the desert and Satan tried to make him sin' Mk 1.13. In translating expressions involving tempting or trying, it is necessary in a number of languages to indicate clearly whether or not the temptations succeeded. Therefore, it may not be sufficient in Mk 1.13 to simply say 'Satan tempted him'; in fact, in some instances it may be necessary to make the failure of the temptation quite specific, for example, 'Satan tried to make Jesus sin, but was not successful.'

ἐκπειράζω[c]: νομικός τις ἀνέστη ἐκπειράζων αὐτόν 'a certain teacher of the Law came up and tried to catch him (saying something wrong)' Lk 10.25. It is also possible to understand ἐκπειράζω in Lk 10.25 as merely a process of testing (see 27.46) or of trying to trap (see 27.31).

πειρασμός[b]: συντελέσας πάντα πειρασμὸν ὁ

διάβολος ἀπέστη ἀπ' αὐτοῦ ἄχρι καιροῦ 'when the Devil completely finished tempting (Jesus), he left him for a while' Lk 4.13.

88.309 ἀπείραστος, ον: pertaining to not being able to be tempted – 'unable to be tempted, one who cannot be tempted.' ὁ γὰρ θεὸς ἀπείραστός ἐστιν κακῶν 'God cannot be tempted by evil' Jas 1.13. There may be some difficulties involved in rendering the passive expression in Jas 1.13, but it is often possible to restructure this as an active expression with an indefinite person made the subject, for example, 'no one can tempt God to do what is bad.' It is also possible to shift the meaning slightly in terms of desire or will and thus say 'God would never want to do what is evil.'

88.310 ἁμαρτία^c, ας *f*: the moral consequence of having sinned – 'guilt, sin.' τὸ αἷμα Ἰησοῦ τοῦ υἱοῦ αὐτοῦ καθαρίζει ἡμᾶς ἀπὸ πάσης ἁμαρτίας 'the death of Jesus his Son makes us clean from every sin' (or 'from all our guilt') 1 Jn 1.7; ἄφεσιν ἁμαρτιῶν 'the forgiveness of sins' Mt 26.28; ἀναστὰς βάπτισαι καὶ ἀπόλουσαι τὰς ἁμαρτίας σου ἐπικαλεσάμενος τὸ ὄνομα αὐτοῦ 'stand up, be baptized, and have your sins purified by praying to him' (literally 'by calling upon his name,' see 33.176) Ac 22.16; μετανοήσατε οὖν καὶ ἐπιστρέψατε εἰς τὸ ἐξαλειφθῆναι ὑμῶν τὰς ἁμαρτίας 'therefore, repent, turn to (God) so that your sins may be wiped away' or '. . . forgiven' Ac 3.19.

A number of languages make a clear distinction between the active event of committing sin and the resulting moral effect of guilt, so that one must speak of 'committing sin' but 'forgiving guilt.' This is often required in some languages since a term meaning 'to forgive' is literally 'to wipe away,' 'to erase,' 'to blot out,' or 'to return to someone.' The actual event of sinning often does not fit with such verb expressions, since it is not the event itself which is eliminated but the moral consequences of such an event, namely, the guilt.

88.311 ἀναμάρτητος, ον: pertaining to being without guilt – 'guiltless, sinless.' εἶπεν αὐτοῖς, Ὁ ἀναμάρτητος ὑμῶν πρῶτος ἐπ' αὐτὴν βαλέτω λίθον 'he said to them, Whichever one of you is guiltless may throw the first stone at her' (literally 'may be the first to throw a stone at her') Jn 8.7.

88.312 ἔνοχος^a, ον: pertaining to being guilty for having done wrong (primarily a legal term) – 'guilty, liable.' ἔνοχος ἔσται τοῦ σώματος καὶ τοῦ αἵματος τοῦ κυρίου 'he will be guilty of sin against the Lord's body and blood' 1 Cor 11.27. In some languages the equivalent of 'being guilty' is expressed in terms of the justification for an accusation. Accordingly, this expression in 1 Cor 11.27 may be rendered as 'he can rightly be accused of sinning against the Lord's body and blood.'

88.313 ἔνοχος^b, ον: pertaining to being guilty and thus deserving some particular penalty – 'guilty and deserving, guilty and punishable by.' οἱ δὲ ἀποκριθέντες εἶπαν, Ἔνοχος θανάτου ἐστίν 'they answered, He is guilty and deserves death' Mt 26.66; οἱ δὲ πάντες κατέκριναν αὐτὸν ἔνοχον εἶναι θανάτου 'they all condemned him as being guilty and punishable by death' Mk 14.64.

88.314 πονηρός^c, ά, όν: pertaining to guilt resulting from an evil deed – 'guilty.' ῥεραντισμένοι τὰς καρδίας ἀπὸ συνειδήσεως πονηρᾶς 'with hearts that have been made clean from a guilty conscience' (literally 'having been cleansed as to our hearts . . .') He 10.22. In a number of languages it would be entirely misleading to speak of 'a guilty conscience,' for this would seem to imply that there is something sinful about the conscience itself. In reality, it is the conscience that says that a person is guilty, and therefore it may be necessary to translate He 10.22 as 'with hearts that have been purified from a condition in which their conscience has said that they are guilty.'

88.315 αἴτιον^b, ου *n*; αἰτία^d, ας *f*: guilt as a basis or reason for condemnation – 'guilt, wrongdoing, reason for condemning.'
αἴτιον^b: ὁ δὲ Πιλᾶτος εἶπεν πρὸς τοὺς ἀρχιερεῖς καὶ τοὺς ὄχλους, Οὐδὲν εὑρίσκω αἴτιον ἐν τῷ ἀνθρώπῳ τούτῳ 'Pilate said to the chief priests and to the crowds, I find no guilt in this man' Lk 23.4.
αἰτία^d: λέγει αὐτοῖς, Ἐγὼ οὐδεμίαν εὑρίσκω ἐν αὐτῷ αἰτίαν 'he said to them, I can find no

guilt in him' Jn 18.38. It is also possible to understand αἰτία in Jn 18.38 as 'reason for legal accusation,' as noted in 56.4.

88.316 ἀναίτιος, ον; ἀθῷος, ον: pertaining to not being guilty of wrongdoing – 'guiltless, innocent.'
ἀναίτιος: ὅτι τοῖς σάββασιν οἱ ἱερεῖς ἐν τῷ ἱερῷ τὸ σάββατον βεβηλοῦσιν καὶ ἀναίτιοί εἰσιν 'because on the Sabbath the priests in the Temple break the Sabbath (law), yet they are not guilty' Mt 12.5.
ἀθῷος: ἥμαρτον παραδοὺς αἷμα ἀθῷον 'I have sinned by betraying an innocent man to death' Mt 27.4.

88.317 ἄμεμπτος, ον; ἀμέμπτως: pertaining to being without fault or blame – 'blameless, without blame, innocent, guiltless.'
ἄμεμπτος: πορευόμενοι ἐν πάσαις ταῖς ἐντολαῖς καὶ δικαιώμασιν τοῦ κυρίου ἄμεμπτοι 'they lived without blame, obeying all the rules and commandments of the Lord' Lk 1.6.
ἀμέμπτως: ὡς ὁσίως καὶ δικαίως καὶ ἀμέμπτως ὑμῖν τοῖς πιστεύουσιν ἐγενήθημεν 'that our conduct toward you who believe was pure and right and without blame' 1 Th 2.10.

88.318 ἀπρόσκοπος[a], ον: pertaining to being blameless in view of not having given offense – 'blameless, without blame.' ἀσκῶ ἀπρόσκοπον συνείδησιν ἔχειν πρὸς τὸν θεὸν καὶ τοὺς ἀνθρώπους 'I do my best to live blameless before God and people' Ac 24.16. In a number of languages the concept of 'being blameless' as in 88.317 and 88.318 can only be expressed by a verbal expression involving some measure of complaint. For example, the expression in Ac 24.16 may be rendered as 'I do my best to live in such a way that neither God nor people can blame me' or '. . . can complain against me.'

89 Relations[1]

Outline of Subdomains

A Relation (89.1)
B Dependency (89.2)
C Derivation (89.3)
D Specification (89.4-89.7)
E Relations Involving Correspondence (Isomorphisms) (89.8-89.11)
F Basis (89.12-89.14)
G Cause and/or Reason (89.15-89.38)
H Result (89.39-89.54)
I Purpose (89.55-89.64)
J Condition (89.65-89.70)
K Concession (89.71-89.75)

L Means (89.76-89.78)
M Attendant Circumstances (89.79-89.80)
N Manner (89.81-89.86)
O Sequential Addition (89.87-89.89)
P Distribution (89.90-89.91)
Q Addition (89.92-89.104)
R Linkage (89.105)
S Equivalence (89.106)
T Association (89.107-89.119)
U Dissociation (89.120-89.122)
V Combinative Relation (89.123)
W Contrast (89.124-89.138)
X Alternative Relation (89.139-89.140)
Y Substance (89.141-89.142)
Z Mediation (89.143)

1 Domain 89 *Relations* includes a number of quite diverse relations between events and/or objects designated primarily by particles such as prepositions and conjunctions. Subdomains B-N are generally regarded as subordinate, while the following subdomains are usually treated as coordinate, but this distinction is largely based upon syntactic structures rather than upon semantic relations. In many languages there is no such corresponding set of syntactic distinctions.

A Relation (89.1)

89.1 αἰτία[e], ας f: a relation existing between two or more objects or events – 'relation.' εἰ οὕτως ἐστὶν ἡ αἰτία τοῦ ἀνθρώπου μετὰ τῆς γυναικός, οὐ συμφέρει γαμῆσαι 'if that is the relation between a man and a woman, it is better not to marry' Mt 19.10.

B Dependency (89.2)

89.2 κρέμαμαι[b]: to be in a relation of dependency upon something – 'to depend upon.' ἐν ταύταις ταῖς δυσὶν ἐντολαῖς ὅλος ὁ νόμος κρέμαται καὶ οἱ προφῆται 'the entire Law and the Prophets depend on these two commandments' Mt 22.40. In a number of languages dependency as in Mt 22.40 may be expressed as 'to hang on' or 'to be tied together by' or 'only have meaning because of.'

C Derivation (89.3)

89.3 ἐκ[h]: a marker of the source from which someone or something is physically or psychologically derived – 'from.' ὁ ὢν ἐκ τοῦ θεοῦ τὰ ῥήματα τοῦ θεοῦ ἀκούει 'he who is from God obeys the words of God' Jn 8.47; ὅσοι ἦσαν ἐκ γένους ἀρχιερατικοῦ 'as many as were of the family of the high priest' Ac 4.6; Ἅννα . . . ἐκ φυλῆς Ἀσήρ 'Anna . . . from the tribe of Asher' Lk 2.36.

D Specification (89.4-89.7)

89.4 κατά[m]: a marker of a specific element bearing a relation to something else – 'in relation to, with regard to.' τοῦ γενομένου ἐκ σπέρματος Δαυὶδ κατὰ σάρκα 'with regard to his body (or 'with regard to his physical nature . . .'), being of the lineage of David' Ro 1.3.

89.5 ἐν[k]; **ἐν μέρει** (an idiom, literally 'in part'); **ὅπου**[d]: markers of an area of activity which bears some relation to something else – 'in, about, in the case of, with regard to.'
ἐν[k]: ὁ δὲ θεὸς πλούσιος ὢν ἐν ἐλέει 'God being rich in mercy' Eph 2.4; ἐν μηδενὶ λειπόμενοι 'lacking in nothing' Jas 1.4.
ἐν μέρει: μὴ οὖν τις ὑμᾶς κρινέτω . . . ἐν πόσει ἢ ἐν μέρει ἑορτῆς 'let no one judge you . . . about what you drink or about a festival' Col 2.16.
ὅπου[d]: ὅπου γὰρ διαθήκη, θάνατον ἀνάγκη φέρεσθαι τοῦ διαθεμένου 'in the case of a will, it is necessary to show that the one who made the will has actually died' He 9.16.

89.6 περί[g]: a marker of a relation, usually involving content or topic – 'in relation to, with regard to, concerning.' ἀναβαίνειν . . . εἰς Ἰε-ρουσαλὴμ περὶ τοῦ ζητήματος τούτου 'go up . . . to Jerusalem in relation to this question' Ac 15.2.

89.7 πρός[n]: a marker of a relation involving potential interaction – 'with regard to, with, between . . . and.' ἢ τίς κοινωνία φωτὶ πρὸς σκότος; 'or what kind of fellowship can there be between light and darkness?' 2 Cor 6.14; οἱ δὲ εἶπαν, Τί πρὸς ἡμᾶς; 'and they said, What does that have to do with us?' Mt 27.4.

E Relations Involving Correspondences (Isomorphisms) (89.8-89.11)

89.8 κατά[k]: a marker of a relation involving similarity of process – 'in accordance with, in relation to.' ὅτε ἐπλήσθησαν αἱ ἡμέραι τοῦ καθαρισμοῦ αὐτῶν κατὰ τὸν νόμον Μωϋσέως 'when the days of their purification had been completed in accordance with the Law of Moses' Lk 2.22; καὶ τότε ἀποδώσει ἑκάστῳ κατὰ τὴν πρᾶξιν αὐτοῦ 'and then he will reward each person in accordance with his deeds' Mt 16.27.

89.9 πρός[j]: a marker of a relation involving correspondence, with the probable implication of some element of reciprocity – 'in accordance with, according to, in line with.' μὴ ἑτοιμάσας ἢ ποιήσας πρὸς τὸ θέλημα αὐτοῦ δαρήσεται πολλάς '(the servant who) did not get ready or act in accordance with his (master's) desire will be whipped much' Lk 12.47; ὅτι οὐκ ὀρθοποδοῦσιν πρὸς τὴν ἀλήθειαν τοῦ εὐαγγελίου 'that they were not walking in line with the truth of the gospel' Ga 2.14.

89.10 ἀναλογία, ας *f*: a relation of proportion – 'in relation to, in proportion to.' εἴτε προφητείαν κατὰ τὴν ἀναλογίαν τῆς πίστεως 'if prophecy, then in accordance with the proportion of faith' Ro 12.6. It is also possible to understand ἀναλογία in Ro 12.6 as meaning 'in agreement with,' but this meaning likewise involves a degree of isomorphic relationship.

89.11 μετασχηματίζω[b]: to relate something to something else on the basis of certain correspondences – 'to apply to, to regard as applicable to.' ταῦτα . . . μετεσχημάτισα εἰς ἐμαυτὸν καὶ 'Απολλῶν δι' ὑμᾶς 'these things I have applied to myself and to Apollos for your sake' 1 Cor 4.6.

F   Basis (89.12-89.14)

89.12 θεμέλιον[b], ου *n*: (a figurative extension of meaning of θεμέλιον[a] 'foundation,' 7.41) the basis for some action or event – 'basis, foundation.' μὴ πάλιν θεμέλιον καταβαλλόμενοι μετανοίας ἀπὸ νεκρῶν ἔργων 'not again establishing a basis for repentance from dead works' or '. . . useless works' He 6.1; ἀποθησαυρίζοντας ἑαυτοῖς θεμέλιον καλὸν εἰς τὸ μέλλον 'treasuring up for themselves a fine basis for the future' 1 Tm 6.19.

89.13 ἐπί[q]: a marker of the basis of some event – 'on the basis of, in view of.' ἵνα ἐπὶ στόματος δύο μαρτύρων ἢ τριῶν σταθῇ πᾶν ῥῆμα 'so that everything may be established on the basis of what two or three witnesses say' Mt 18.16.

89.14 νή: a marker of the basis for an oath or strong declaration – 'on the basis of, by virtue of.' νὴ τὴν ὑμετέραν καύχησιν '(I say this) on the basis of (my) pride in you' 1 Cor 15.31. Because of the elliptical nature of this expression in 1 Cor 15.31, the semantic implications of νή are often omitted, or the implication of νή is introduced by employing an overt declaration, as in Today's English Version, "The pride I have in you, in our life in union with Christ Jesus our Lord, makes me declare this."

G   Cause and/or Reason[2] (89.15-89.38)

89.15 αἰτία[a], ας *f*; αἴτιον[a], ου *n*; αἴτιος, ου *m*: reason or cause for an event or state – 'reason, cause, source, because of.'

---

2 Though in some languages a very important distinction is made between an external physical cause of an event and the reason for an event based upon a decision by a conscious being, this distinction is not made lexically in Greek, and there are numerous contexts in which one may interpret the relation as either cause or reason or a blend of the two.

αἰτία[a]: διὰ ταύτην οὖν τὴν αἰτίαν παρεκάλεσα ὑμᾶς ἰδεῖν καὶ προσλαλῆσαι 'therefore, for this reason I have asked to see you and to talk with you' Ac 28.20.

αἴτιον[a]: μηδενὸς αἰτίου ὑπάρχοντος 'there being no cause' Ac 19.40.

αἴτιος: ἐγένετο πᾶσιν τοῖς ὑπακούουσιν αὐτῷ αἴτιος σωτηρίας αἰωνίου 'he became the source of eternal salvation for all those who obey him' He 5.9.

89.16 ἀρχή[c], ῆς *f*: one who or that which constitutes an initial cause – 'first cause, origin.' ἡ ἀρχὴ τῆς κτίσεως τοῦ θεοῦ 'the origin of what God has created' Re 3.14. It is also possible to understand ἀρχή in Re 3.14 as meaning 'ruler' (see 37.56).

89.17 ῥίζα[c], ης *f*: (a figurative extension of meaning of ῥίζα[a] 'root,' 3.47) that which constitutes a basic source or reason for an event or state – 'source, cause, reason.' ῥίζα γὰρ πάντων τῶν κακῶν ἐστιν ἡ φιλαργυρία 'for the love of money is the cause of all evil' 1 Tm 6.10. In a number of languages this passage in 1 Tm 6.10 must be structurally modified, for example, 'because people love money, they do all those bad things.'

89.18 λόγος[g], ου *m*: a reason, with the implication of some verbal formulation – 'reason.' πυνθάνομαι οὖν τίνι λόγῳ μετεπέμψασθέ με; 'I ask, therefore, for what reason did you send for me?' Ac 10.29; πᾶς ὁ ἀπολύων τὴν γυναῖκα αὐτοῦ παρεκτὸς λόγου πορνείας 'everyone who divorces his wife except for the reason of adultery' Mt 5.32; παντὶ τῷ αἰτοῦντι ὑμᾶς λόγον περὶ τῆς ἐν ὑμῖν ἐλπίδος 'to everyone who asks you the reason for your hope' 1 Pe 3.15.

89.19 ἄλογος[b], ον: pertaining to not providing a reason or cause, in view of something being contrary to reason – 'unreasonable, without basis, absurd.' ἄλογον γάρ μοι δοκεῖ 'it seems unreasonable to me' Ac 25.27. In some languages the equivalent of 'being unreasonable' is 'being something which people should not think.' Note that ἄλογος[b] refers to that which is contrary to proper reasoning, while ἄλογος[a] (30.12) pertains to a lack of capacity to reason.

89.20 δωρεάν^b; εἰκῇ^a: pertaining to there being no cause or legitimate reason – 'without cause, without reason, for no reason.'

δωρεάν^b: ἐμίσησάν με δωρεάν 'they hated me for no reason' Jn 15.25.

εἰκῇ^a: εἰκῇ φυσιούμενος 'being puffed up for no reason' Col 2.18.

89.21 αὐτόματος, η, ον: pertaining to being self-caused (or possibly, without evident cause) – 'without any cause, without something to cause it, by itself.'[3] ἥτις αὐτομάτη ἠνοίγη αὐτοῖς '(the gate) opened for them by itself' Ac 12.10. In some languages one can only express 'opened . . . by itself' in Ac 12.10 by 'opened . . . nobody made it open.'

89.22 ἀφορμή^b, ῆς f: an unwarranted reason for some event – 'unwarranted reason, excuse.' ἵνα ἐκκόψω τὴν ἀφορμὴν τῶν θελόντων ἀφορμήν 'in order that I may remove the excuse of those who wish an excuse' 2 Cor 11.12.

89.23 γάρ^a: a marker of cause or reason between events, though in some contexts the relation is often remote or tenuous – 'for, because.' αὐτὸς γὰρ ἐγίνωσκεν τί ἦν ἐν τῷ ἀνθρώπῳ 'for he knew what was in people' Jn 2.25; ἔφυγον ἀπὸ τοῦ μνημείου, εἶχεν γὰρ αὐτὰς τρόμος καὶ ἔκστασις 'they ran from the tomb, for they were trembling and amazed' Mk 16.8.

89.24 ἀντί^c: a marker of reason, with the possible implication of purpose – 'because, for this reason, for the purpose of.' ἀντὶ τούτου καταλείψει ἄνθρωπος τὸν πατέρα καὶ τὴν μητέρα 'because of this, a man will leave his father and mother' Eph 5.31.

89.25 ἀπόⁱ; ἐκ^b; ὅθεν^b; παρά^j: markers of cause or reason, with focus upon the source – 'because of.'[4]

3 It is difficult to determine whether αὐτόματος focuses primarily upon an event taking place because of the action of an object itself or whether the implication is that there is no evident cause.

4 No doubt the meanings in this series differ somewhat, but it is not possible on the basis of the contexts now available to determine precisely what designative or associative features of meaning may be involved.

ἀπόⁱ: οὐκ ἠδύνατο ἀπὸ τοῦ ὄχλου 'he was not able to because of the crowd' Lk 19.3; οἱ πλουτήσαντες ἀπ' αὐτῆς 'those who had become rich because of her' Re 18.15. In Re 18.15 the reference to the city of Babylon is not primarily an indication of agency so much as a reference to what Babylon did in purchasing and consuming so many luxury items. οὐκ ἐνέβλεπον ἀπὸ τῆς δόξης τοῦ φωτὸς ἐκείνου 'I was not able to see because of the brightness of that light' Ac 22.11.

ἐκ^b: ἐκ τούτου πολλοὶ ἐκ τῶν μαθητῶν αὐτοῦ ἀπῆλθον 'because of this, many of his followers went away' Jn 6.66; ἐκ τούτου ὁ Πιλᾶτος ἐζήτει ἀπολῦσαι αὐτόν 'because of this, Pilate sought to release him' Jn 19.12.

ὅθεν^b: ὅθεν μεθ' ὅρκου ὡμολόγησεν 'since he had promised with an oath' Mt 14.7.

παρά^j: οὐ παρὰ τοῦτο οὐκ ἔστιν ἐκ τοῦ σώματος 'not because of that would it not be a part of the body' 1 Cor 12.15.

89.26 διά^f; διότι^a; ὑπό^d; ἐν^q: markers of cause or reason, with focus upon instrumentality, either of objects or events – 'because of, on account of, by reason of.'

διά^f: μὴ δυναμένου δὲ αὐτοῦ γνῶναι τὸ ἀσφαλὲς διὰ τὸν θόρυβον 'he was not able to find out exactly (what happened) because of the confusion' Ac 21.34; διὰ τί μετὰ τῶν τελωνῶν καὶ ἁμαρτωλῶν ἐσθίει ὁ διδάσκαλος ὑμῶν; 'for what reason does your teacher eat with tax collectors and outcasts?' Mt 9.11; διὰ τὸ μὴ ἔχειν βάθος 'because it had no depth' Mt 13.5; ἀπέλυσεν δὲ τὸν διὰ στάσιν καὶ φόνον βεβλημένον εἰς φυλακήν 'he released the one who had been put into prison because of a riot and murder' Lk 23.25.

διότι^a: διότι οὐκ ἦν αὐτοῖς τόπος ἐν τῷ καταλύματι 'because there was no room for them in the inn' Lk 2.7; οὐχ ηὑρίσκετο διότι μετέθηκεν αὐτὸν ὁ θεός 'he was not found because God had taken him' He 11.5.

ὑπό^d: ὑπὸ μεριμνῶν καὶ πλούτου καὶ ἡδονῶν τοῦ βίου πορευόμενοι συμπνίγονται 'as they go on living, they are choked by the worries and riches and pleasures of daily life' Lk 8.14; ἕκαστος δὲ πειράζεται ὑπὸ τῆς ἰδίας ἐπιθυμίας 'but each one is tempted because of his own desires' Jas 1.14.

ἐν^q: ἐν τούτῳ πιστεύομεν ὅτι ἀπὸ θεοῦ ἐξῆλθες

'because of this we believe that you came from God' Jn 16.30; ἔφυγεν δὲ Μωϋσῆς ἐν τῷ λόγῳ τούτῳ 'because of this report, Moses fled' Ac 7.29.

89.27 ἐπί[n]: a marker of cause or reason as the basis for a subsequent event or state – 'because of, on the basis of.' ἡ δὲ ἐπὶ τῷ λόγῳ διεταράχθη 'she was greatly disturbed because of what was said' Lk 1.29; ἐξεπλήσσοντο οἱ ὄχλοι ἐπὶ τῇ διδαχῇ αὐτοῦ 'the crowds were amazed because of the way in which he taught' Mt 7.28.

89.28 ὑπέρ[e]: a marker of cause or reason, often with the implication of something which has been beneficial – 'because of, in view of.' τὰ δὲ ἔθνη ὑπὲρ ἐλέους δοξάσαι τὸν θεόν 'and the nations to praise God because of his mercy' Ro 15.9; τί βλασφημοῦμαι ὑπὲρ οὗ ἐγὼ εὐχαριστῶ; 'why should I be criticized because of something I give thanks for?' 1 Cor 10.30.

89.29 χάριν[a]: a marker of a reason, often with the implication of an underlying purpose – 'because of, by reason of.' οὗ χάριν λέγω σοι, ἀφέωνται αἱ ἁμαρτίαι αὐτῆς αἱ πολλαί 'because of this I tell you that her many sins are forgiven' Lk 7.47; καὶ χάριν τίνος ἔσφαξεν αὐτόν; 'and for what reason did he murder him?' 1 Jn 3.12.

89.30 εἰ[b]: a marker of cause or reason on the basis that an actual case is regarded formally as a supposition – 'since, because.' εἰ δὲ ἀπεθάνομεν σὺν Χριστῷ, πιστεύομεν ὅτι καὶ συζήσομεν αὐτῷ 'and since we died with Christ, we believe that we shall also live with him' Ro 6.8; εἰ δὲ τὸν χόρτον τοῦ ἀγροῦ . . . ὁ θεὸς οὕτως ἀμφιέννυσιν 'and since God clothes thus . . . the grass of the field' Mt 6.30. In English it is possible to translate εἰ in passages such as Ro 6.8 and Mt 6.30 as either 'if' or 'since,' for the conjunction 'if' may also refer to an actual event as a supposition. In a number of languages, however, it is impossible to translate 'if God so clothes the grass of the field,' for this would imply serious doubt as to whether God actually does perform such an activity. It may therefore be necessary in such languages to translate quite specifically 'because' or 'since.'

89.31 ἕνεκεν[a] (also εἵνεκεν) or ἕνεκα[a]: a marker of cause or reason, often with the implication of purpose in the sense of 'for the sake of' – 'on account of, because of.' μακάριοι οἱ δεδιωγμένοι ἕνεκεν δικαιοσύνης 'happy are those who are persecuted because of righteousness' Mt 5.10; εἵνεκεν τῆς ὑπερβαλλούσης δόξης 'on account of the greater glory' or 'on account of the more exceeding glory' 2 Cor 3.10; ἕνεκα τούτου καταλείψει ἄνθρωπος τὸν πατέρα καὶ τὴν μητέρα 'on account of this, a man will leave his father and mother' Mt 19.5.

89.32 ἐπεί; ἐπειδή[a]; ἐπειδήπερ: markers of cause or reason, often with the implication of a relevant temporal element – 'because, since, for, inasmuch as.'[5]
ἐπεί: πᾶσαν τὴν ὀφειλὴν ἐκείνην ἀφῆκά σοι, ἐπεὶ παρεκάλεσάς με 'I forgave you all that debt, since you asked me to' Mt 18.32; ἐπεὶ ἔδει αὐτὸν πολλάκις παθεῖν 'since (otherwise) he would have had to suffer many times' He 9.26.
ἐπειδή[a]: ἐπειδὴ φίλος μου παρεγένετο ἐξ ὁδοῦ πρός με 'because a friend of mine who was on a trip has just come to me' Lk 11.6.
ἐπειδήπερ: ἐπειδήπερ πολλοὶ ἐπεχείρησαν ἀνατάξασθαι διήγησιν 'inasmuch as many have undertaken to prepare an account' Lk 1.1.

89.33 ὅτι[b]; καθότι[a]: markers of cause or reason, based on an evident fact – 'because, since, for, in view of the fact that.'
ὅτι[b]: οὐκ ἤθελεν παρακληθῆναι, ὅτι οὐκ εἰσίν 'she would not be comforted, because they were not (that is, they were no longer living)' Mt 2.18; ὅτι ἑώρακάς με πεπίστευκας; 'because you see me, do you believe?' Jn 20.29.
καθότι[a]: καθότι ἦν ἡ Ἐλισάβετ στεῖρα 'in view of the fact that Elizabeth was barren' Lk 1.7; καθότι οὐκ ἦν δυνατὸν κρατεῖσθαι αὐτὸν ὑπ'

---

5 In this series ἐπειδή[a] may be more emphatic than ἐπεί and the conjunction ἐπειδήπερ even more emphatic than ἐπειδή[a].

αὐτοῦ 'because it was not possible for him to be held by it' Ac 2.24.

89.34 καθώς[b]: a marker of cause or reason, often with the implication of some implied comparison – 'inasmuch as, because.' καθὼς ἔδωκας αὐτῷ ἐξουσίαν πάσης σαρκός 'inasmuch as you have given him authority over all mankind' Jn 17.2; καθὼς οὐκ ἐδοκίμασαν τὸν θεὸν ἔχειν ἐν ἐπιγνώσει 'inasmuch as they refused to keep God in their consciousness' Ro 1.28.

89.35 ὅπου[c]: a marker of cause or reason, with special reference to a set of relevant circumstances – 'whereas, since.' ὅπου γὰρ ἐν ὑμῖν ζῆλος καὶ ἔρις 'for whereas there is jealousy and strife among you' 1 Cor 3.3.

89.36 περί[d]: a marker of cause or reason as an implied content of speaking – 'for, on account of, because.' αἰνεῖν τὸν θεὸν φωνῇ μεγάλῃ περὶ πασῶν ὧν εἶδον δυνάμεων 'to praise God with loud voices because of all the miracles they saw' Lk 19.37. One may also interpret περί in Lk 19.37 as being primarily a matter of specification (see 89.6). As in a number of instances in this domain, markers may have more than one semantic function.

89.37 ὡς[f]: a marker of cause or reason, implying the special nature of the circumstances – 'on the grounds that, because.' οὐχ ὡς τοῦ ἔθνους μου ἔχων τι κατηγορεῖν 'not because I had any charge to bring against my people' Ac 28.19; ὡς πάντα ἡμῖν τῆς θείας δυνάμεως αὐτοῦ . . . δεδωρημένης 'because his divine power has given us everything' 2 Pe 1.3.

89.38 πόθεν[c]; **ἱνατί**; **λεμα** (an Aramaic expression): interrogative expressions of reason – 'why.'
πόθεν[c]: πόθεν μοι τοῦτο ἵνα ἔλθῃ ἡ μήτηρ τοῦ κυρίου μου πρὸς ἐμέ; 'why does it happen to me that the mother of my Lord comes to me?' Lk 1.43.
ἱνατί: ἔκκοψον οὖν αὐτήν· ἱνατί καὶ τὴν γῆν καταργεῖ; 'cut it down, then! Why should it also use up the soil?' or '. . . make the soil useless?' Lk 13.7.
λεμα: ηλι ηλι λεμα σαβαχθανι; 'my God, my God, why have you forsaken me?' Mt 27.46.

H Result[6] (89.39-89.54)

89.39 ἔκβασις[b], **εως** *f*: the outcome of an event or state – 'result, outcome.' τὴν ἔκβασιν τῆς ἀναστροφῆς 'the outcome of one's life' He 13.7. It is also possible to understand ἔκβασις in He 13.7 as meaning 'the end' of one's life (see 67.68).

89.40 τέλος[b], **ους** *n*: the result of an event or process, with special focus upon the final state or condition – 'outcome, result, end.' ἐκάθητο μετὰ τῶν ὑπηρετῶν ἰδεῖν τὸ τέλος 'he sat with the servants to see the result' Mt 26.58. In some languages τέλος in Mt 26.58 may be rendered simply as 'what would happen' or 'what would finally happen.' τὸ γὰρ τέλος ἐκείνων θάνατος 'for the result of those things is death' Ro 6.21.

89.41 ἀποβαίνω εἰς: (an idiom, literally 'to go away into') to result in a state – 'to result in, to lead to.' οἶδα γὰρ ὅτι τοῦτό μοι ἀποβήσεται εἰς σωτηρίαν 'for I know that this will lead to my release' Php 1.19.

89.42 ὀψώνιον[c], **ου** *n*: (a figurative extension of meaning of ὀψώνιον[a] 'a soldier's wages,' 57.166) the end result from some activity, viewed as something which one receives in return – 'wages, result.' τὰ γὰρ ὀψώνια τῆς ἁμαρτίας θάνατος 'for the result of sin is death' Ro 6.23.

89.43 ἔρχομαι εἰς: (an idiom, literally 'to come into') to result in a state – 'to result in, to end up being.' κινδυνεύει ἡμῖν τὸ μέρος εἰς ἀπελεγμὸν ἐλθεῖν 'there is a danger that our business will end up getting a bad name' Ac 19.27.

89.44 πρός[i]: a marker of result, with focus upon the end point – 'result in, end in, have as a consequence.' αὕτη ἡ ἀσθένεια οὐκ ἔστιν πρὸς θάνατον 'the final outcome of this illness

---

6 *Result* (Subdomain H) and *Purpose* (Subdomain I) may in some cases be regarded as more or less the two faces of the same coin. Result may view an event on the basis of what has happened, and purpose may view the same event in terms of its future potentiality.

is not death' or 'this illness will not end in death' Jn 11.4.

89.45 ἀντί^d: a marker of result, with the implication of something being in return for something else – 'therefore, so then.' ἀνθ' ὧν ὅσα ἐν τῇ σκοτίᾳ εἴπατε ἐν τῷ φωτὶ ἀκουσθήσεται 'so then, whatever you say in the dark will be heard in the light' Lk 12.3.

89.46 ἄρα^a: a marker of result as an inference from what has preceded (frequently used in questions and in the result clause of conditional sentences) – 'so, then, consequently, as a result.' οὐδὲν ἄρα νῦν κατάκριμα 'so, then, there is now no condemnation' Ro 8.1; τίς ἄρα μείζων ἐστὶν ἐν τῇ βασιλείᾳ τῶν οὐρανῶν; 'who, then, is greater in the kingdom of heaven?' Mt 18.1; εἰ δὲ ἐν πνεύματι θεοῦ ἐγὼ ἐκβάλλω τὰ δαιμόνια, ἄρα ἔφθασεν ἐφ' ὑμᾶς ἡ βασιλεία τοῦ θεοῦ 'but if I cast out demons by the Spirit of God, then the kingdom of God has come upon you' Mt 12.28.

89.47 διό; διόπερ: relatively emphatic markers of result, usually denoting the fact that the inference is self-evident – 'therefore, for this reason, for this very reason, so then.'[7,8]
διό: διὸ ἐκλήθη ὁ ἀγρὸς ἐκεῖνος Ἀγρὸς Αἵματος 'therefore, that field was called Field of Blood' Mt 27.8; διὸ καὶ τὸ γεννώμενον ἅγιον κληθήσεται, υἱὸς θεοῦ 'for this reason the holy child will be called the Son of God' Lk 1.35.
διόπερ: διόπερ εἰ βρῶμα σκανδαλίζει τὸν ἀδελφόν μου, οὐ μὴ φάγω κρέα εἰς τὸν αἰῶνα 'therefore, if meat causes offense to my fellow believer, I will never eat meat' 1 Cor 8.13; διόπερ, ἀγαπητοί μου, φεύγετε ἀπὸ τῆς εἰδωλολατρίας 'so then, my dear friends, keep away from the worship of idols' 1 Cor 10.14.

89.48 εἰς^g; ἐν^r: markers of result, with the probable implication of a preceding process –

'with the result that, so that as a result, to cause.'
εἰς^g: εἰς τὸ εἶναι αὐτοὺς ἀναπολογήτους 'so that as a result they are without excuse' Ro 1.20; εἰς τὸ καταξιωθῆναι ὑμᾶς τῆς βασιλείας τοῦ θεοῦ 'as a result you will be worthy of the kingdom of God' 2 Th 1.5. It is also possible to interpret εἰς in this construction of 2 Th 1.5 as purpose (see εἰς^f, 89.57). ὅτι τὸ χρηστὸν τοῦ θεοῦ εἰς μετάνοιάν σε ἄγει 'because the kindness of God leads you to repent' Ro 2.4. It would be possible to interpret εἰς . . . ἄγω in Ro 2.4 as being purely an expression of cause since ἄγω^g (see 36.1) also involves a component of cause, and therefore one may interpret the expression εἰς μετάνοιάν σε ἄγει as 'it causes you to repent.' In either case, however, εἰς marks a resulting event or state. καὶ εἰς ἀπώλειαν ὑπάγει 'and he goes to destruction' Re 17.8.
ἐν^r: ἐπιστρέψαι καρδίας πατέρων ἐπὶ τέκνα καὶ ἀπειθεῖς ἐν φρονήσει δικαίων 'to turn the hearts of the fathers toward their children and to cause the disobedient to have the mind of the righteous' Lk 1.17. In some languages this expression in Lk 1.17 may be rendered as 'to cause the disobedient people to think like the righteous.'

89.49 ἵνα^b: a marker of result, though in some cases implying an underlying or indirect purpose – 'so as a result, that, so that.' τίς ἥμαρτεν, οὗτος ἢ οἱ γονεῖς αὐτοῦ, ἵνα τυφλὸς γεννηθῇ; 'who sinned, this man or his parents, so that he was born blind?' Jn 9.2. In some languages it is difficult to mark a result clause in a context such as Jn 9.2. This may be done, however, by restructuring the statement as 'he was born blind; therefore, who sinned? Did this man sin or did his parents sin?'

89.50 οὖν^a; μενοῦν^b: markers of result, often implying the conclusion of a process of reasoning – 'so, therefore, consequently, accordingly, then, so then.'
οὖν^a: πᾶς οὖν ὅστις ἀκούει μου τοὺς λόγους τούτους 'therefore, everyone who hears these words of mine' Mt 7.24; συνήγαγον οὖν, καὶ ἐγέμισαν δώδεκα κοφίνους κλασμάτων 'therefore they gathered and filled twelve baskets with pieces' Jn 6.13.

---

7 Since the result is stated as an inference based upon what has preceded, one may translate this expression of result as 'for this reason' or 'for this very reason.' What precedes constitutes the reason, but the result may be effectively introduced by referring back to the reason.
8 διόπερ may be regarded as somewhat more emphatic than διό.

μενοῦν[b]: μενοῦν μακάριοι οἱ ἀκούοντες τὸν λόγον τοῦ θεοῦ καὶ φυλάσσοντες 'therefore, truly blessed are (or 'happy are . . .') those who hear the word of God and obey it' Lk 11.28. For other interpretations of μενοῦν in Lk 11.28, see 89.128 and 91.8.

89.51 τοίνυν; τοιγαροῦν: emphatic markers of result, often associated with exhortation – 'for this very reason, therefore, hence, therefore indeed, so then.'

τοίνυν: τοίνυν ἀπόδοτε τὰ Καίσαρος Καίσαρι 'therefore give to Caesar the things that belong to Caesar' Lk 20.25; τοίνυν ἐξερχώμεθα πρὸς αὐτὸν ἔξω τῆς παρεμβολῆς 'so then, let us go out to him outside the camp' He 13.13.

τοιγαροῦν: τοιγαροῦν . . . δι' ὑπομονῆς τρέχωμεν τὸν προκείμενον ἡμῖν ἀγῶνα 'so then . . . let us run with patience the race that lies before us' He 12.1; τοιγαροῦν ὁ ἀθετῶν οὐκ ἄνθρωπον ἀθετεῖ ἀλλὰ τὸν θεόν 'so then, whoever rejects (this teaching) is not rejecting man but God' 1 Th 4.8.

89.52 ὡς[h]; ὥστε[a]: markers of result, often in contexts implying an intended or indirect purpose[9] – 'therefore, (so) accordingly, as a result, so that, so then, and so.'

ὡς[h]: ὡς ὤμοσα ἐν τῇ ὀργῇ μου 'accordingly, I swore in my anger' or 'so that as a result, I swore in my anger' He 3.11.

ὥστε[a]: ὥστε ἔξεστιν τοῖς σάββασιν καλῶς ποιεῖν 'so it is permitted to do good on the Sabbath' Mt 12.12; σεισμὸς μέγας ἐγένετο ἐν τῇ θαλάσσῃ, ὥστε τὸ πλοῖον καλύπτεσθαι ὑπὸ τῶν κυμάτων 'a great storm took place on the lake so that the boat was covered with the waves' Mt 8.24; ὥστε, ἀδελφοί μου ἀγαπητοί, ἑδραῖοι γίνεσθε 'so then, my dear Christian brothers, stand firm' 1 Cor 15.58; τὸ πάσχα ἡμῶν ἐτύθη Χριστός· ὥστε ἑορτάζωμεν 'Christ our Passover Lamb has been sacrificed, and so let us celebrate' 1 Cor 5.7-8.

89.53 κενός[c], ή, όν: pertaining to being lacking in results – 'without result, without effect.' ἡ χάρις αὐτοῦ ἡ εἰς ἐμὲ οὐ κενὴ ἐγενήθη 'his grace was not without effect in me' 1 Cor

15.10; τὴν εἴσοδον ἡμῶν τὴν πρὸς ὑμᾶς ὅτι οὐ κενὴ γέγονεν 'our visit to you was not without results' 1 Th 2.1; εἰ δὲ Χριστὸς οὐκ ἐγήγερται, κενὸν ἄρα καὶ τὸ κήρυγμα ἡμῶν 'if Christ has not been raised from the dead, our message is indeed without any result' 1 Cor 15.14. In 1 Cor 15.14, however, one may understand purpose rather than result, and hence one can translate 'our message is indeed without purpose,' see 89.64. For yet another interpretation of κενός in 1 Cor 15.14, see 72.10.

89.54 εἰκῇ[b]; μάτην: pertaining to being without any result – 'in vain, to no avail, with no result.'

εἰκῇ[b]: φοβοῦμαι ὑμᾶς μή πως εἰκῇ κεκοπίακα εἰς ὑμᾶς 'I am afraid that my work among you will be without results' Ga 4.11. In a number of languages an expression such as 'to be without results' may be rendered as 'will accomplish nothing' or 'will be as though it had never happened.'

μάτην: μάτην δὲ σέβονταί με 'but they worship me in vain' or 'it is no use for them to worship me' Mt 15.9.

I   Purpose[6] (89.55-89.64)

89.55 τέλος[c], ους *n*: the purpose of an event or state, viewed in terms of its result – 'purpose, intent, goal.' τὸ δὲ τέλος τῆς παραγγελίας ἐστὶν ἀγάπη ἐκ καθαρᾶς καρδίας 'the purpose of the order is love from a pure heart' 1 Tm 1.5.

89.56 κατὰ σκοπὸν διώκω: (an idiom, literally 'to pursue to a goal, to press toward a goal') to strive energetically for some purpose – 'to strive toward a goal, to press on with the purpose of.' κατὰ σκοπὸν διώκω εἰς τὸ βραβεῖον 'I press toward the goal for the prize' or 'I strive for the purpose of the prize' Php 3.14.

89.57 εἰς[f]: a marker of intent, often with the implication of expected result – 'for the purpose of, in order to.' εἰς τὸ καταξιωθῆναι ὑμᾶς τῆς βασιλείας τοῦ θεοῦ 'for the purpose of your becoming worthy of the kingdom of God' 2 Th 1.5. It is also possible to interpret εἰς in this construction of 2 Th 1.5 as result (see εἰς[g], 89.48). προσένεγκον τὸ δῶρον ὃ προσέταξεν

---

9 The purpose in such instances is not, however, an aspect of the meaning of ὥστε, but is derived from the context.

6 See page 782.

Μωϋσῆς, εἰς μαρτύριον αὐτοῖς 'take the offering which Moses prescribed, in order to provide proof for them' Mt 8.4; εἰς τοῦτο ἐλήλυθα εἰς τὸν κόσμον 'for this purpose I came into the world' Jn 18.37; φῶς εἰς ἀποκάλυψιν ἐθνῶν 'light to serve as a revelation to the Gentiles' Lk 2.32.

89.58 ἕνεκεν[b] or ἕνεκα[b]: a marker of purpose, with the frequent implication of some underlying reason – 'in order that, for the sake of, for.' ἕνεκεν τοῦ φανερωθῆναι τὴν σπουδὴν ὑμῶν 'in order that your zeal might be made known' 2 Cor 7.12; καὶ οἱ πλείους οὐκ ᾔδεισαν τίνος ἕνεκα συνεληλύθεισαν 'and most of them did not know for what they had come together' or '. . . why they had come together' Ac 19.32.

89.59 ἵνα[a]; ὅπως[b]: markers of purpose for events and states (sometimes occurring in highly elliptical contexts) – 'in order to, for the purpose of, so that.'[10]
ἵνα[a]: μήτι ἔρχεται ὁ λύχνος ἵνα ὑπὸ τὸν μόδιον τεθῇ ἢ ὑπὸ τὴν κλίνην; 'does anyone ever bring in a lamp in order to put it under a measuring bowl or under a bed?' Mk 4.21; ὃν ἔπεμψα πρὸς ὑμᾶς εἰς αὐτὸ τοῦτο ἵνα γνῶτε τὰ περὶ ἡμῶν 'whom I sent to you for the very purpose that you might know our circumstances' Eph 6.22; ἀλλ' ἵνα μαρτυρήσῃ περὶ τοῦ φωτός 'but (this happened) in order that he could witness concerning the light' Jn 1.8.
ὅπως[b]: ὅπως δοξασθῶσιν ὑπὸ τῶν ἀνθρώπων 'in order that they will be honored by people' Mt 6.2; ὅπως ἀναβλέψῃς καὶ πλησθῇς πνεύματος ἁγίου 'in order that you might see and be filled with the Holy Spirit' Ac 9.17; δεήθητε ὑμεῖς ὑπὲρ ἐμοῦ πρὸς τὸν κύριον ὅπως μηδὲν ἐπέλθῃ ἐπ' ἐμὲ ὧν εἰρήκατε 'pray to the Lord on my behalf, so that nothing of what you have said will come upon me' Ac 8.24.

---

10 ἵνα[a] and ὅπως[b] seem to have similar meanings and in some contexts appear to be substituted one for the other for stylistic purposes. It is, of course, possible that even in the meaning of purpose ὅπως[b] suggests something of the manner or way in which the purpose is to be realized, but it is impossible on the basis of existing contexts to make a clear distinction between ἵνα[a] and ὅπως[b] when they serve as markers of purpose.

89.60 ἐπί[o]; πρός[h]; χάριν[b]: markers of purpose, pointing to the goal of an event or state – 'for the purpose of, for the sake of, in order to.'
ἐπί[o]: κτισθέντες ἐν Χριστῷ Ἰησοῦ ἐπὶ ἔργοις ἀγαθοῖς 'created in Christ Jesus for the purpose of good works' Eph 2.10; ἰδὼν δὲ πολλοὺς τῶν Φαρισαίων καὶ Σαδδουκαίων ἐρχομένους ἐπὶ τὸ βάπτισμα αὐτοῦ 'seeing many of the Pharisees and Sadducees coming to be baptized by him' Mt 3.7.
πρός[h]: αὐτὸς ἦν ὁ πρὸς τὴν ἐλεημοσύνην καθήμενος ἐπὶ τῇ Ὡραίᾳ Πύλῃ 'he was the one who sat at the Beautiful Gate for the purpose of receiving alms' Ac 3.10; πρὸς τὴν ἔνδειξιν τῆς δικαιοσύνης αὐτοῦ 'in order to demonstrate his righteousness' Ro 3.26.
χάριν[b]: τούτου χάριν κάμπτω τὰ γόνατά μου πρὸς τὸν πατέρα 'for this purpose I bow my knees to the Father' Eph 3.14; τούτου χάριν ἐγὼ Παῦλος ὁ δέσμιος τοῦ Χριστοῦ Ἰησοῦ 'for this purpose I, Paul, am a prisoner of Christ Jesus' Eph 3.1. One may also interpret τούτου χάριν as expressing reason in both Eph 3.1 and Eph 3.14, with a link from verse 1 to verse 14 after the digression in Eph 3.2-13 (see 89.29). τί οὖν ὁ νόμος; τῶν παραβάσεων χάριν προσετέθη 'what, then, was the purpose of the Law? It was added in order to show what wrongdoing is' Ga 3.19.

89.61 ὡς[g]; ὥστε[b]: markers of purpose, with the implication that what has preceded serves as a means – 'then, in order to, so that.'
ὡς[g]: εἰσῆλθον εἰς κώμην Σαμαριτῶν, ὡς ἑτοιμάσαι αὐτῷ 'they went into a village of Samaria in order to get things ready for him' Lk 9.52.
ὥστε[b]: ἔδωκεν αὐτοῖς ἐξουσίαν πνευμάτων ἀκαθάρτων ὥστε ἐκβάλλειν αὐτά 'he gave them power over unclean spirits in order to cast them out' Mt 10.1.

89.62 μή[c]; μήποτε[c]; μή πως: markers of negative purpose, often with the implication of apprehension – 'in order that . . . not, so that . . . not, lest.'
μή[c]: μή τις ἐκκολυμβήσας διαφύγῃ 'in order that none would swim out and escape' Ac 27.42.
μήποτε[c]: μήποτε προσκόψῃς πρὸς λίθον τὸν πόδα

σου 'in order that you will not hurt your foot on a stone' Mt 4.6; μήποτε καὶ θεομάχοι εὑρεθῆτε 'so that you may not be found fighting against God' Ac 5.39; μήποτε καταπατήσουσιν αὐτοὺς ἐν τοῖς ποσὶν αὐτῶν 'in order that they will not tramp them down with their feet' Mt 7.6.

μή πως: μή πως ἄλλοις κηρύξας αὐτὸς ἀδόκιμος γένωμαι 'in order that I myself may not be found unworthy after having preached to others' 1 Cor 9.27; βλέπετε δὲ μή πως ἡ ἐξουσία ὑμῶν αὕτη πρόσκομμα γένηται τοῖς ἀσθενέσιν 'but see to it that your freedom (literally 'this freedom of yours') does not become a cause of offense to those who are weak (in the faith)' 1 Cor 8.9.

89.63 εἰκῇᶜ; δωρεάνᶜ: pertaining to being without purpose – 'for no purpose, without purpose.'

εἰκῇᶜ: οὐ γὰρ εἰκῇ τὴν μάχαιραν φορεῖ 'he does not carry the sword for no purpose' Ro 13.4.

δωρεάνᶜ: ἄρα Χριστὸς δωρεὰν ἀπέθανεν 'then Christ died for no purpose' Ga 2.21.

89.64 κενόςᵈ, ή, όν; κενῶς: pertaining to being totally without purpose – 'in vain, for no purpose.'

κενόςᵈ: εἰ δὲ Χριστὸς οὐκ ἐγήγερται, κενὸν ἄρα καὶ τὸ κήρυγμα ἡμῶν 'if Christ has not been raised, our message is indeed in vain' 1 Cor 15.14. For other interpretations of κενός in 1 Cor 15.14, see 72.10 and 89.53.

κενῶς: ἢ δοκεῖτε ὅτι κενῶς ἡ γραφὴ λέγει 'or do you think that what the Scripture says is for no purpose' Jas 4.5.

J Condition (89.65-89.70)

89.65 εἰᵃ: a marker of a condition, real or hypothetical, actual or contrary to fact – 'if.' εἰ υἱὸς εἶ τοῦ θεοῦ 'if you (really) are the Son of God' Mt 4.3; εἰ οὐ δύναται τοῦτο παρελθεῖν 'if it is not possible for this to pass' Mt 26.42; εἰ ἐν Τύρῳ καὶ Σιδῶνι ἐγένοντο αἱ δυνάμεις 'if these miracles had taken place in Tyre and Sidon' Mt 11.21; εἰ ἔγνως ἐν τῇ ἡμέρᾳ ταύτῃ καὶ σὺ τὰ πρὸς εἰρήνην 'if you only knew in this day what is needed for peace' Lk 19.42.

89.66 εἴπερ: an emphatic marker of condition – 'if indeed, if after all.' εἴπερ ἄρα νεκροὶ

οὐκ ἐγείρονται 'if after all the dead really do not arise' 1 Cor 15.15.

89.67 ἐάνᵃ: a marker of condition, with the implication of reduced probability – 'if.' ἐὰν θέλῃς δύνασαί με καθαρίσαι 'if you want to, you are able to cleanse me' Mk 1.40; ἐὰν γὰρ ἀγαπήσητε τοὺς ἀγαπῶντας ὑμᾶς 'therefore, if you love those who love you' Mt 5.46; οὐ στεφανοῦται ἐὰν μὴ νομίμως ἀθλήσῃ 'he does not win the prize unless he competes according to the rules' 2 Tm 2.5.

89.68 ἐάνπερ: an emphatic marker of condition, with the implication of reduced probability – 'if indeed, if surely.' καὶ τοῦτο ποιήσομεν ἐάνπερ ἐπιτρέπῃ ὁ θεός 'and we will do this if indeed God permits' He 6.3; ἐάνπερ τὴν ἀρχὴν τῆς ὑποστάσεως μέχρι τέλους βεβαίαν κατάσχωμεν 'if indeed we hold firmly to the end the confidence (we had) at the beginning' He 3.14.

89.69 εἴτε . . . εἴτε: (normally a doublet, but in 1 Cor 14.27 occurring singly) a double or multiple marker of condition (equivalent in meaning to εἰᵃ 'if,' 89.65) – 'if . . . if, whether . . . or.' εἴτε δὲ θλιβόμεθα . . . εἴτε παρακαλούμεθα 'if we are in difficulty . . . if we are encouraged' 2 Cor 1.6; εἴτε Παῦλος εἴτε Ἀπολλῶς εἴτε Κηφᾶς εἴτε κόσμος εἴτε ζωὴ εἴτε θάνατος . . . 'whether Paul or Apollos or Cephas or the world or life or death . . .' 1 Cor 3.22; εἴτε γλώσσῃ τις λαλεῖ 'if someone speaks in a tongue' 1 Cor 14.27.

89.70 πότερον: a marker of an indirect condition – 'whether, if.' γνώσεται περὶ τῆς διδαχῆς πότερον ἐκ τοῦ θεοῦ ἐστιν ἢ ἐγὼ ἀπ' ἐμαυτοῦ λαλῶ 'he will know about the teaching, whether it is from God or whether I speak on my own authority' Jn 7.17.

K Concession (89.71-89.75)

89.71 καίπερ: a marker of concession – 'although, though, even though.' καίπερ ὢν υἱὸς ἔμαθεν . . . τὴν ὑπακοήν 'even though he was (God's) Son, he learned . . . to be obedient' He 5.8; μελλήσω ἀεὶ ὑμᾶς ὑπομιμνήσκειν περὶ τούτων, καίπερ εἰδότας 'I will always remind you of these matters, even though you already know them' 2 Pe 1.12.

In some languages concession is marked not by a particle attached to the so-called concessive clause, but by marking an unexpected contrast in the related clause. For example, the expression in He 5.8 may be rendered in some languages as 'he was God's Son, but nevertheless he learned to be obedient,' and the expression in 2 Pe 1.12 may be rendered as 'you already know these matters, but nevertheless I will always remind you of them.'

89.72 καίτοι; καίτοιγε: markers of concession, with the probable implication of an additional component of contrast – 'although, even though, and yet.'
καίτοι: εἴρηκεν . . . καίτοι τῶν ἔργων ἀπὸ καταβολῆς κόσμου γενηθέντων 'he said this . . . even though his work was finished from the time he created the world' He 4.3; ὃς ἐν ταῖς παρῳχημέναις γενεαῖς εἴασεν πάντα τὰ ἔθνη πορεύεσθαι ταῖς ὁδοῖς αὐτῶν· καίτοι οὐκ ἀμάρτυρον αὐτὸν ἀφῆκεν ἀγαθουργῶν 'who in times past allowed all peoples to go their own way, and yet he has not left himself without witnesses (to his nature) by the good things he does' Ac 14.16-17.
καίτοιγε: καίτοιγε Ἰησοῦς αὐτὸς οὐκ ἐβάπτιζεν 'although Jesus himself did not actually baptize anyone' Jn 4.2.

89.73 κἄν (καί + ἐάν): an emphatic marker of concession – 'even if, even though.' κἄν ἐγὼ μαρτυρῶ περὶ ἐμαυτοῦ, ἀληθής ἐστιν ἡ μαρτυρία μου 'even if I do testify on my own behalf, what I say is true' Jn 8.14; ὁ πιστεύων εἰς ἐμὲ κἄν ἀποθάνῃ ζήσεται 'whoever believes in me will live even though he dies' Jn 11.25.

89.74 ὅμωςᵃ: a marker of concession, with the possible implication of an added aspect of similarity – 'although, though.' ὅμως ἀνθρώπου . . . διαθήκην οὐδεὶς ἀθετεῖ 'although it is only a human . . . will, no one annuls it' Ga 3.15; ὅμως τὰ ἄψυχα φωνὴν διδόντα, εἴτε αὐλὸς εἴτε κιθάρα 'although the flute and harp are lifeless, they give a sound . . .' 1 Cor 14.7.
The interpretation of ὅμως in Ga 3.15 and 1 Cor 14.7 as indicating concession is doubtful, and it may be preferable to understand ὅμως in these contexts as meaning 'likewise' or

'similarly,' for example, 'similarly, in the case of a human will, no one annuls it' and 'similarly, in the case of a flute or harp, lifeless instruments which produce a sound' (see 64.11).

89.75 ὅμως μέντοι: a marker of an implied clause of concession – 'nevertheless, and yet.'[11] ὅμως μέντοι καὶ ἐκ τῶν ἀρχόντων πολλοὶ ἐπίστευσαν εἰς αὐτόν 'and yet even many of the rulers believed in him' Jn 12.42.

L Means (89.76-89.78)

89.76 εἰςʰ; ἐνᵖ; διάᶜ: markers of the means by which one event makes another event possible – 'by means of, through, by.'[12]
εἰςʰ: οἵτινες ἐλάβετε τὸν νόμον εἰς διαταγὰς ἀγγέλων 'you who received the Law through arrangements made by angels' or 'you who received the Law handed down by angels' Ac 7.53.
ἐνᵖ: ὡς ἐγνώσθη αὐτοῖς ἐν τῇ κλάσει τοῦ ἄρτου 'how he became known to them by the breaking of bread' Lk 24.35.
διάᶜ: ἣν περιεποιήσατο διὰ τοῦ αἵματος τοῦ ἰδίου 'which he made his own through his own blood' Ac 20.28. The term 'blood' in Ac 20.28 is a figurative expression designating the event of sacrificial death (see 23.107). καὶ ἀποκαταλλάξῃ τοὺς ἀμφοτέρους ἐν ἑνὶ σώματι τῷ θεῷ διὰ τοῦ σταυροῦ 'and he reconciled both in one body to God through the cross' Eph 2.16. In Eph 2.16 'cross' refers to the sacrificial death of Christ. ἡγιασμένοι ἐσμὲν διὰ τῆς προσφορᾶς τοῦ σώματος Ἰησοῦ Χριστοῦ ἐφάπαξ 'we have been made holy through the offering of the body of Jesus Christ once for all' He 10.10.

11 An expression meaning 'nevertheless' normally presupposes a concessive clause, for example, 'although one would not have expected it, nevertheless . . .,' and implies a circumstance contrary to expectation. Some languages do not have a conjunction marking a concessive clause but do have a particle or phrase for a resultant clause, for example, 'he did not work; nevertheless he was paid,' which is equivalent to 'although he did not work, he was paid.'
12 There are probably certain subtle distinctions between the use of διάᶜ in contrast with εἰςʰ or ἐνᵖ as markers of means, but this cannot be clearly determined from existing contexts.

89.77 ἐκ^c: a marker of means as constituting a source – 'by means of, from.' αἵτινες διηκόνουν αὐτοῖς ἐκ τῶν ὑπαρχόντων αὐταῖς 'who served them from their possessions' or '. . . by means of their possessions' Lk 8.3; ἑαυτοῖς ποιήσατε φίλους ἐκ τοῦ μαμωνᾶ τῆς ἀδικίας 'make for yourselves friends by means of the wealth of this wicked world' (literally 'by means of unrighteous mammon' or '. . . by means of unrighteous riches') Lk 16.9. Some scholars have interpreted ἐκ in Lk 16.9 as ἐκ^g 'apart from' (see 89.121). This requires the reading of ἐκλίπητε (found in a few late manuscripts) for ἐκλίπῃ in Lk 16.9b.

89.78 μετά^k: a marker of means, with the probable additional implication of attendant circumstance (see μετά^d 'with,' 89.79) – 'by means of, with, through.' πληρώσεις με εὐφροσύνης μετὰ τοῦ προσώπου σου 'you will fill me with joy by means of your presence' Ac 2.28. In Ac 2.28 πρόσωπον is a figurative designation for the presence of a person (see 85.26).

M Attendant Circumstances[13] (89.79-89.80)

89.79 μετά^d: a marker of circumstances which contribute significantly to the context of the principal event – 'with, in.'[14] καὶ τότε ἄρξῃ μετὰ αἰσχύνης τὸν ἔσχατον τόπον κατέχειν 'and then with embarrassment you will go and take the lowest place' or 'and then you will be embarrassed and have to sit in the lowest place' Lk 14.9; πορευόμενος εἰς τὴν Δαμασκὸν μετ' ἐξουσίας καὶ ἐπιτροπῆς τῆς τῶν ἀρχιερέων 'going to Damascus, having the authority and orders from the chief priests' Ac 26.12; ἠσφαλίσαντο τὸν τάφον σφραγίσαντες

τὸν λίθον μετὰ τῆς κουστωδίας 'having put a seal on the stone, they (left) a guard to make the tomb secure' Mt 27.66.

89.80 ἐν^h: a marker of attendant circumstances, often with the implication of means – 'with, while at the same time.'[14] ἄχρι γὰρ καὶ ὑμῶν ἐφθάσαμεν ἐν τῷ εὐαγγελίῳ τοῦ Χριστοῦ 'for we had already (or 'we were the first to') come to you bringing the good news about Christ' 2 Cor 10.14; οἶδα δὲ ὅτι ἐρχόμενος πρὸς ὑμᾶς ἐν πληρώματι εὐλογίας Χριστοῦ ἐλεύσομαι 'I know that in coming to you I shall come with a full measure of the blessing of Christ' Ro 15.29.

N Manner (89.81-89.86)

89.81 πολυμερῶς^c: pertaining to a number of different manners in which something may be done – 'in many ways, in many different ways.' πολυμερῶς καὶ πολυτρόπως πάλαι ὁ θεὸς λαλήσας τοῖς πατράσιν ἐν τοῖς προφήταις 'in the past God spoke to our ancestors in a great many different ways through the prophets' He 1.1. In the case of this meaning of πολυμερῶς, the terms πολυτρόπως (see 89.82) and πολυμερῶς may be regarded as mutually reinforcing, but for different interpretations of πολυμερῶς in He 1.1, see 63.19 and 67.11.

89.82 πολυτρόπως^b: pertaining to occurring in many ways or manners – 'in many ways.' πολυτρόπως πάλαι ὁ θεὸς λαλήσας τοῖς πατράσιν 'in many ways God spoke in earlier times to the ancestors' He 1.1. For another interpretation of πολυτρόπως in He 1.1, see 58.29.

89.83 τρόπος^a, ου *m*: the manner in which something is done – 'manner, way.' μή τις ὑμᾶς ἐξαπατήσῃ κατὰ μηδένα τρόπον 'do not let anyone deceive you in any way' 2 Th 2.3.

89.84 ἐν^j: a marker of the manner in which an event occurs – 'with.'[15] ὁ μεταδιδοὺς ἐν

---

13 The category of *Attendant Circumstances* is very similar to both *Means* (Subdomain L) and *Manner* (Subdomain N). An expression of attendant circumstances supplies a significant aspect of a complex event, and in some contexts it may also suggest how something may have been brought about or even something of the manner in which an event takes place, but its primary function is simply to state a context in which the principal event is to be understood.

14 Attendant circumstances are often expressed in English by participial or gerund phrases.

15 Manner is expressed in a number of different ways in diverse languages. In English it is often expressed by means of a phrase introduced by 'with,' but the appropriate equivalent in some contexts is simply an adverb. Often, however, an entire clause or additional complete sentence is required.

ἁπλότητι 'one who shares with others (should do so) with generosity' or '. . . generously' Ro 12.8. In some languages it may be better to restructure this statement in Ro 12.8 and translate 'one should be generous in sharing with others.'

89.85 ἐκ[c]: a marker of manner, often with the implication of source – 'with, from.' ἕκαστος καθὼς προῄρηται τῇ καρδίᾳ, μὴ ἐκ λύπης ἢ ἐξ ἀνάγκης 'each one (should give) as he has decided, not with regret or out of a sense of duty' 2 Cor 9.7.

89.86 ὅπως[a]; **καθώς**[e]; **ὡς**[c]; **πόθεν**[b]: markers of an event indicating how something took place – 'how, in what manner.'
ὅπως[a]: ὅπως τε παρέδωκαν αὐτὸν οἱ ἀρχιερεῖς καὶ οἱ ἄρχοντες ἡμῶν εἰς κρίμα θανάτου 'and how our chief priests and rulers handed him over to be condemned to death' Lk 24.20.[16]
καθώς[e]: Συμεὼν ἐξηγήσατο καθὼς πρῶτον ὁ θεὸς ἐπεσκέψατο λαβεῖν ἐξ ἐθνῶν λαὸν τῷ ὀνόματι αὐτοῦ 'Simon explained how God first showed his care for the Gentiles by taking from them a people to belong to him' (literally, '. . . for his name') Ac 15.14.
ὡς[c]: ἐξηγοῦντο τὰ ἐν τῇ ὁδῷ καὶ ὡς ἐγνώσθη αὐτοῖς 'they explained what had happened on the road and how he became known to them' Lk 24.35.
πόθεν[b]: καὶ πόθεν αὐτοῦ ἐστιν υἱός; 'then how is he his son?' Mk 12.37.

O Sequential Addition (89.87-89.89)

89.87 καί[b]; **δέ**[b]: markers of a sequence of closely related events – 'and, and then.'
καί[b]: εἰσῆλθον ὑπὸ τὸν ὄρθρον εἰς τὸ ἱερὸν καὶ ἐδίδασκον 'at dawn they entered the Temple and taught' Ac 5.21.
δέ[b]: Ἀβραὰμ ἐγέννησεν τὸν Ἰσαάκ, Ἰσαὰκ δὲ ἐγέννησεν τὸν Ἰακώβ 'Abraham was the father of Isaac and Isaac was the father of Jacob' Mt 1.2.

89.88 τέ[b]: a marker of a close relationship between sequential events or states – 'and,

and then.' κατενύγησαν τὴν καρδίαν, εἶπόν τε πρὸς τὸν Πέτρον 'they were deeply troubled and said to Peter' Ac 2.37.

89.89 προστίθεμαι[b]: to mark an immediately following event – 'to proceed to.' ἰδὼν δὲ ὅτι ἀρεστόν ἐστιν τοῖς Ἰουδαίοις προσέθετο συλλαβεῖν καὶ Πέτρον 'seeing that it pleased the Jews, he proceeded to arrest Peter' Ac 12.3.

P Distribution[17] (89.90-89.91)

89.90 κατά[l]: a marker of distributive relations, whether of place, time, or number – 'throughout, from . . . to, . . . after . . .' καὶ ἔσονται λιμοὶ καὶ σεισμοὶ κατὰ τόπους 'there will be famines and earthquakes in place after place' Mt 24.7; Σαῦλος δὲ ἐλυμαίνετο τὴν ἐκκλησίαν κατὰ τοὺς οἴκους εἰσπορευόμενος 'Saul was trying to destroy the church by going from house to house' Ac 8.3; καὶ ἐπορεύοντο οἱ γονεῖς αὐτοῦ κατ' ἔτος εἰς Ἰερουσαλήμ 'and his parents went to Jerusalem year after year' Lk 2.41; καθ' ἡμέραν ἐν τῷ ἱερῷ ἐκαθεζόμην διδάσκων 'day after day I sat in the Temple teaching' Mt 26.55; ἤρξαντο λυπεῖσθαι καὶ λέγειν αὐτῷ εἷς κατὰ εἷς 'they began to be sad and say to him, one after another' Mk 14.19.

89.91 ἀνά: (in combination with numerable objects) a marker of distributive relations involving numerable objects – 'each, apiece, sets of.' οἱ περὶ τὴν ἑνδεκάτην ὥραν ἔλαβον ἀνὰ δηνάριον 'those who came to work at the eleventh hour received a denarius each' or '. . . received a denarius apiece' Mt 20.9; ἀπέστειλεν αὐτοὺς ἀνὰ δύο δύο 'he sent them out two by two' Lk 10.1; κατακλίνατε αὐτοὺς κλισίας ὡσεὶ ἀνὰ πεντήκοντα 'seat them in groups of about fifty each' Lk 9.14.

Q Addition (89.92-89.104)

89.92 καί[a]: a marker of coordinate relations – 'and.' Ἰάκωβος καὶ Ἰωσὴφ καὶ Σίμων καὶ

---

16 It is also possible to interpret this clause in Lk 24.20 as representing the content of a verb of speaking.

17 Distributive relations involve place, time, and number. Though in many languages it may be important to distinguish clearly between these three types of distribution, they are semantically similar.

Ἰούδας 'James and Joseph and Simon and Judas' Mt 13.55; χάρις ὑμῖν καὶ εἰρήνη ἀπὸ θεοῦ πατρὸς ἡμῶν καὶ κυρίου Ἰησοῦ Χριστοῦ 'grace to you and peace from God our Father and the Lord Jesus Christ' Ro 1.7; κεκένωται ἡ πίστις καὶ κατήργηται ἡ ἐπαγγελία 'faith means nothing and the promise is ineffectual' Ro 4.14.

89.93 καί°: a marker of an additive relation which is not coordinate – 'and, and also, also, in addition, even.' ὅστις σε ῥαπίζει εἰς τὴν δεξιὰν σιαγόνα σου, στρέφον αὐτῷ καὶ τὴν ἄλλην 'whoever strikes you on your right cheek, turn also the other cheek to him' Mt 5.39; ἀπήγγειλαν πάντα καὶ τὰ τῶν δαιμονιζομένων 'they told everything and also what had happened to the men with the demons' Mt 8.33.[18]

89.94 δέ^a: a marker of an additive relation, but with the possible implication of some contrast – 'and.' Παῦλος δοῦλος θεοῦ, ἀπόστολος δὲ Ἰησοῦ Χριστοῦ 'Paul, a servant of God and an apostle of Jesus Christ' Tt 1.1.

89.95 τέ^a: a marker of a close relationship between coordinate, nonsequential items – 'and.' ἐν ἀγάπῃ πνεύματί τε πραΰτητος 'in love and the spirit of gentleness' 1 Cor 4.21.

89.96 ἀλλά^b: a marker of a series of coordinate relations which are contrastive with a previously identified event or state – 'and.' πόσην κατειργάσατο ὑμῖν σπουδήν, ἀλλὰ ἀπολογίαν, ἀλλὰ ἀγανάκτησιν, ἀλλὰ φόβον 'how earnest it has made you, and how eager to prove your innocence, and such indignation, and such alarm ...' 2 Cor 7.11.

89.97 πάλιν^b: a marker of an additive relation involving repetition – 'and, also, again.' πάλιν λέγει, Εὐφράνθητε, ἔθνη ... καὶ πάλιν,

Αἰνεῖτε ... τὸν κύριον ... καὶ πάλιν Ἡσαΐας λέγει 'also it says, Rejoice, Gentiles ... and again, Praise ... the Lord ... and again, Isaiah says ...' Ro 15.10-12; καὶ πάλιν ἑτέρα γραφὴ λέγει 'and also another Scripture says' Jn 19.37; οἱ δὲ πάλιν ἔκραξαν, Σταύρωσον αὐτόν 'they again shouted, Crucify him' Mk 15.13.[19]

89.98 λοιπόν^d: a marker of an additional comment closely related to what has preceded – 'furthermore, also.' ὧδε λοιπὸν ζητεῖται ἐν τοῖς οἰκονόμοις ἵνα πιστός τις εὑρεθῇ 'furthermore, in this case it is required of stewards that they be found trustworthy' 1 Cor 4.2.

89.99 περαιτέρω: a marker of something in addition to what is already implied in the context – 'in addition, further.' εἰ δέ τι περαιτέρω ἐπιζητεῖτε 'but if you want anything in addition' or '... more than what I have just mentioned' Ac 19.39.

89.100 εἶτα^b: a marker of an addition which has just been specified in the context – 'besides this, furthermore.' εἶτα τοὺς μὲν τῆς σαρκὸς ἡμῶν πατέρας εἴχομεν παιδευτάς 'besides this, we have earthly fathers to discipline us' He 12.9.

89.101 ἐπί^l: a marker of an addition to what already exists, but with the possible implication of something more significant – 'in addition to, and.' ἐπὶ πᾶσιν δὲ τούτοις τὴν ἀγάπην 'love in addition to all these' or 'and to all these (add) love' Col 3.14.

89.102 καί ... καί; τε ... καί; τε καί: markers of a totality of two closely related elements – 'both ... and.' καί ... καί: φοβεῖσθε δὲ μᾶλλον τὸν δυνάμενον καὶ ψυχὴν καὶ σῶμα ἀπολέσαι ἐν γεέννῃ 'but fear rather the one who is able to destroy both soul and body in hell' Mt 10.28; ἀλλὰ λέγω

---

18 In Mt 8.33 the phrase καὶ τὰ τῶν δαιμονιζομένων is semantically a part of what was told. It is not, however, coordinate but dependent, in that it forms only a part of the entire account. From the standpoint of the people who announced what had happened, the focus was evidently upon the loss of the herd of pigs, and the healing of the demoniacs was an additional, less important factor. Accordingly, one must treat καί in this structure as being a marker of a non-coordinate relation.

19 There are certain difficulties involved in the interpretation of πάλιν in Mk 15.13, for this is the first instance in this Marcan context in which reference is made to the crowd's shouting. The introduction of πάλιν may be the result of harmonization, or it could mean 'they shouted back.' It is also possible to interpret πάλιν in the sense of 'and in turn they shouted.' One may, however, assume a first occurrence of such a shout in verse 11.

ὑμῖν ὅτι καὶ Ἡλίας ἐλήλυθεν, καὶ ἐποίησαν αὐτῷ ὅσα ἤθελον 'but I tell you, Elijah has both come and they have done to him whatever they wanted' Mk 9.13. This double use of καί, however, may merely reflect a Semitic tendency.

τε . . . καί: ὅ τε στρατηγὸς τοῦ ἱεροῦ καὶ οἱ ἀρχιερεῖς 'both the captain of the temple guards and the chief priests' Ac 5.24.

τε καί: δῶρά τε καὶ θυσίας 'both gifts and sacrifices' He 5.1; δεήσεις τε καὶ ἱκετηρίας 'both prayers and requests' He 5.7.

89.103 τε . . . τε: markers of a closely related coordinate set – 'as . . . so, not only . . . but also.' ἐάν τε οὖν ζῶμεν ἐάν τε ἀποθνήσκωμεν 'so, not only if we live, but also if we die' Ro 14.8; μάρτυρα ὧν τε εἶδές με ὧν τε ὀφθήσομαί σοι 'witness not only of what you have seen of me, but also of what I will show you' Ac 26.16; τοῦ βαστάσαι τὸ ὄνομά μου ἐνώπιον ἐθνῶν τε καὶ βασιλέων υἱῶν τε Ἰσραήλ 'to make my name known not only to Gentiles and kings but also to the people of Israel' Ac 9.15.

89.104 μέν . . . δέ[a]: markers of two or more items which are additively related and thematically parallel – 'some . . . others, first . . . then.' ὃ μὲν ἑκατόν, ὃ δὲ ἑξήκοντα, ὃ δὲ τριάκοντα 'some had a hundred (grains), others sixty, and others thirty' Mt 13.8; πρῶτον μὲν ἑρμηνευόμενος βασιλεὺς δικαιοσύνης ἔπειτα δὲ καὶ βασιλεὺς Σαλήμ 'first interpreted King of Righteousness and then also King of Salem' He 7.2.

R Linkage[20] (89.105)

89.105 σύν[b]: a marker of linkage between objects or between events, but without specify-

ing the precise positional or functional relation – 'with, on, together with, at.' καθῆκαν αὐτὸν σὺν τῷ κλινιδίῳ εἰς τὸ μέσον ἔμπροσθεν τοῦ Ἰησοῦ 'they let him down on his bed in the middle of those in front of Jesus' Lk 5.19; ἀλλὰ ποιήσει σὺν τῷ πειρασμῷ καὶ τὴν ἔκβασιν τοῦ δύνασθαι ὑπενεγκεῖν 'but together with the trial he makes also a way of escape, namely, being able to endure' 1 Cor 10.13; ἐγὼ ἐκομισάμην ἂν τὸ ἐμὸν σὺν τόκῳ 'I would receive mine together with interest' Mt 25.27.

S Equivalence (89.106)

89.106 τοῦτ' ἔστιν; ὅ ἐστιν: markers of an explanation or a clarification in the same or a different language – 'that is, that means.'
τοῦτ' ἔστιν: κοιναῖς χερσίν, τοῦτ' ἔστιν ἀνίπτοις, ἐσθίουσιν τοὺς ἄρτους 'they were eating their food with unclean hands, that is, with unwashed hands' Mk 7.2; οὐκ οἰκεῖ ἐν ἐμοί, τοῦτ' ἔστιν ἐν τῇ σαρκί μου, ἀγαθόν 'good does not live in me, that is, in my human nature' Ro 7.18.
ὅ ἐστιν: Βοανηργές, ὅ ἐστιν Υἱοὶ Βροντῆς 'Boanerges, which means Men of Thunder' Mk 3.17. In some languages one must make more specific the interpretation of a term in another language. For example, in Mk 3.17 it may be necessary to translate 'Boanerges, which in another language means Men of Thunder' or 'Boanerges, for which we would say, Men of Thunder.'

T Association (89.107-89.119)

89.107 σύν[a]: a marker of an associative relation, often involving joint participation in some activity – 'with, together with.'[21] ὁ δὲ Λάζαρος εἷς ἦν ἐκ τῶν ἀνακειμένων σὺν αὐτῷ 'and Lazarus was one of those with him at the

---

20 Subdomain R *Linkage* differs from Subdomain Q *Addition* in that the items involved are not merely added one to another but are linked in some positional or functional relationship. However, the positions or functions are not clearly stipulated, even though the context may make clear what is actually involved. The meanings in this subdomain also differ from those in Subdomain T *Association* in that the manner of association is not specified but the fact of some connection or linkage is marked.

21 The semantic domains of σύν[a] (89.107) and μετά[a] (89.108) overlap considerably, for in a number of instances essentially the same referential relationship can be expressed either by σύν[a] or by μετά[a]. However, in contexts involving hostility and combat, opposing forces may be spoken of as fighting against one another with μετά[a]. In this type of context the preposition σύν[a] would not be appropriate, since it would suggest those fighting on the same side, not on opposite sides of the conflict.

table' Jn 12.2; ἐρχόμεθα καὶ ἡμεῖς σὺν σοί 'we also will go with you' Jn 21.3.

89.108 μετά[a]: a marker of an associative relation, usually with the implication of being in the company of – 'with, in the company of, together with.'[21] τότε προσῆλθεν αὐτῷ ἡ μήτηρ τῶν υἱῶν Ζεβεδαίου μετὰ τῶν υἱῶν αὐτῆς 'then the mother of the sons of Zebedee went to him with her sons' Mt 20.20; ὅταν αὐτὸ πίνω μεθ' ὑμῶν καινόν 'when I drink it with you new' Mt 26.29. In a number of languages the equivalent of μετά in such contexts as Mt 20.20 and Mt 26.29 requires considerable restructuring. For example, in Mt 20.20 one may need to translate 'then the mother of the sons of Zebedee went to him and her two sons went along.' In Mt 26.29 it may be necessary to translate 'when I drink it new and you also will be drinking it.' ἐγὼ μεθ' ὑμῶν εἰμι πάσας τὰς ἡμέρας 'I am with you always' Mt 28.20.

89.109 μετά[b]: a marker of association, involving instruments relevant to an event – 'with, having.' ὄχλος πολὺς μετὰ μαχαιρῶν καὶ ξύλων 'a large crowd with swords and clubs' Mt 26.47; ἔρχεται ἐκεῖ μετὰ φανῶν καὶ λαμπάδων καὶ ὅπλων 'he went there with torches, lanterns, and arms' Jn 18.3.

89.110 περί[f]: a marker of association, involving accompaniment – 'with, in company of.' οἱ περὶ Παῦλον ἦλθον εἰς Πέργην τῆς Παμφυλίας 'Paul and those with him went to Perga of Pamphylia' Ac 13.13. Note that οἱ περὶ Παῦλον does not mean 'those who were with Paul,' but it includes Paul and those with him.

89.111 παρά[i]: a marker of association, with the implication of proximity to the so-called viewpoint character – 'with.' ἐρωτᾷ αὐτὸν Φαρισαῖος ὅπως ἀριστήσῃ παρ' αὐτῷ 'a Pharisee asked him whether he would eat with him' Lk 11.37.

89.112 πρός[g]: a marker of association, often with the implication of interrelationships – 'with, before.' εἰρήνην ἔχομεν πρὸς τὸν θεόν 'we have peace with God' Ro 5.1; καὶ ὁ λόγος ἦν πρὸς τὸν θεόν 'the Word was with God' Jn 1.1; παρρησίαν ἔχομεν πρὸς τὸν θεόν 'we have confidence before God' 1 Jn 3.21.

89.113 κατά[n]: a marker of association, involving common, cultural, or ethnic elements – 'with, among' (but often expressed by so-called possessive forms). ὡς καί τινες τῶν καθ' ὑμᾶς ποιητῶν εἰρήκασιν 'as even some of your poets have said' Ac 17.28; μάλιστα γνώστην ὄντα σε πάντων τῶν κατὰ Ἰουδαίους ἐθῶν τε καὶ ζητημάτων 'particularly because you know all the customs of the Jews and the disputes' Ac 26.3.

89.114 ἅμα[b]: a marker of association, involving additional items affected by some event – 'together with, in addition.' μήποτε συλλέγοντες τὰ ζιζάνια ἐκριζώσητε ἅμα αὐτοῖς τὸν σῖτον 'in order that when you gather up the tares you may not also root up the wheat together with them' Mt 13.29.

89.115 μεταξύ[b]: a marker of an exclusive association – 'between . . . and.' μεταξὺ σοῦ καὶ αὐτοῦ μόνου 'between yourself and him alone' or 'just between yourselves' Mt 18.15; καὶ οὐθὲν διέκρινεν μεταξὺ ἡμῶν τε καὶ αὐτῶν 'he made no difference between us and them' Ac 15.9.

89.116 ὁμοῦ: a marker of association, based on similarity of activity or state – 'together.' ἵνα ὁ σπείρων ὁμοῦ χαίρῃ καὶ ὁ θερίζων 'so that the sower and the reaper may rejoice together' Jn 4.36; ἔτρεχον δὲ οἱ δύο ὁμοῦ 'the two were running together' Jn 20.4; ἦσαν πάντες ὁμοῦ ἐπὶ τὸ αὐτό 'they were all together in one place' Ac 2.1.

89.117 σύμφυτος, ον: pertaining to being closely associated in a similar experience – 'to be like, to be one with.' εἰ γὰρ σύμφυτοι γεγόναμεν τῷ ὁμοιώματι τοῦ θανάτου αὐτοῦ 'for if we are one with him in dying as he died' Ro 6.5.

89.118 κοινός[d], **ή, όν**: pertaining to being in common between two or more persons – 'in common.' περὶ τῆς κοινῆς ἡμῶν σωτηρίας 'about our common salvation' or 'about the salvation which we have in common' Jd 3. It is also possible to understand κοινός in Jd 3 as κοινός[a] 'shared, mutual,' see 57.9.

89.119 ἐν[g]: a marker of close personal association – 'in, one with, in union with, joined closely to.' ὅτι ἐν ἐμοὶ ὁ πατὴρ κἀγὼ ἐν τῷ πατρί 'that the Father is in me and I am in the Father' Jn 10.38; μείνατε ἐν ἐμοί, κἀγὼ ἐν ὑμῖν 'remain in me and I (will remain) in you' Jn 15.4; εἴπερ πνεῦμα θεοῦ οἰκεῖ ἐν ὑμῖν 'because the Spirit of God dwells in you' Ro 8.9; ὑμεῖς ὃ ἠκούσατε ἀπ' ἀρχῆς ἐν ὑμῖν μενέτω 'let what you heard from the beginning remain in you' 1 Jn 2.24; ζῇ δὲ ἐν ἐμοὶ Χριστός 'but Christ lives in me' Ga 2.20.

U Dissociation (89.120-89.122)

89.120 ἄνευ; ἄτερ; χωρίς[a]: markers of negatively linked elements – 'without, not with, no relationship to, apart from, independent of.'[22]

ἄνευ: ἓν ἐξ αὐτῶν οὐ πεσεῖται ἐπὶ τὴν γῆν ἄνευ τοῦ πατρὸς ὑμῶν 'not a single one of them falls to the ground without your Father' Mt 10.29. The phrase ἄνευ τοῦ πατρὸς ὑμῶν in Mt 10.29 is elliptical, for it presumes some type of involvement by God in such an event. Some have interpreted the phrase ἄνευ τοῦ πατρὸς ὑμῶν as meaning 'without your Father's consent,' while others interpret it as meaning 'without your Father's knowledge.' The particular manner or mode of involvement by God must depend upon the broader context and not upon the meaning of ἄνευ. φιλόξενοι εἰς ἀλλήλους ἄνευ γογγυσμοῦ 'practice hospitality toward one another without complaining' 1 Pe 4.9; διὰ τῆς τῶν γυναικῶν ἀναστροφῆς ἄνευ λόγου κερδηθήσονται 'they may be won without a word by the behavior of their wives' 1 Pe 3.1. The phrase ἄνευ λόγου in 1 Pe 3.1 is semantically equivalent to an event, for it means essentially 'without their saying a word' or 'without them saying anything.'

---

22 It appears impossible to find a significant distinction between ἄνευ and ἄτερ. It may be that χωρίς[a] differs from ἄνευ and ἄτερ in focusing upon a greater degree of separation or lack of involvement.

ἄτερ: ἐζήτει εὐκαιρίαν τοῦ παραδοῦναι αὐτὸν ἄτερ ὄχλου αὐτοῖς 'he looked for a favorable opportunity to betray him to them without the people' Lk 22.6. The phrase ἄτερ ὄχλου may be interpreted to mean 'without the people knowing about it' or 'in the absence of the multitude.'

χωρίς[a]: χωρὶς αὐτοῦ ἐγένετο οὐδὲ ἕν 'not one thing came into existence without him' Jn 1.3. It would be wrong to restructure Jn 1.3 to read 'he made everything in all creation,' for in the Scriptures God is spoken of as the Creator, but the creation was done 'through the Word.' If one must restructure Jn 1.3, it may be possible to say 'he was involved in everything that was created' or 'he took part in creating everything.' τὸ σῶμα χωρὶς πνεύματος νεκρόν ἐστιν 'the body without the spirit is dead' Jas 2.26; πάντα ποιεῖτε χωρὶς γογγυσμῶν καὶ διαλογισμῶν 'do everything without complaining and arguing' Php 2.14; οὔτε γυνὴ χωρὶς ἀνδρὸς οὔτε ἀνὴρ χωρὶς γυναικός 'nor is woman without man, nor man without woman' 1 Cor 11.11. In 1 Cor 11.11 χωρίς does not specify the particular relationship but only indicates the lack of relationship or involvement. This, of course, is negated by οὔτε, so that one may translate this portion of 1 Cor 11.11 as 'nor is woman without some relationship to man, nor is man without some relationship to woman.' In view of the overall context, one may then render the passage simply as 'woman is not independent of man, nor is man independent of woman.' In some languages, however, it may be necessary to speak of 'wife' and 'husband,' since terms for 'man' or 'woman' may be wrongly interpreted in a strictly erotic sense. Because of the double negation in the rendering of 1 Cor 11.11, in some languages it may be necessary to employ a positive equivalent, for example, 'woman is dependent on man and man is dependent on woman' or 'a wife is dependent on her husband and a husband is dependent on his wife.' ᾧ ὁ θεὸς λογίζεται δικαιοσύνην χωρὶς ἔργων 'whom God accepts as righteous apart from (any) works' Ro 4.6. The expression 'apart from any works' in Ro 4.6 may be rendered in some languages as 'and what a person does, does not count' or 'and this is not because of what one does.'

89.121 ἐκᵍ; ἐκτός ᵈ: markers of dissociation in the sense of being 'independent from' someone or something – 'from, free from, apart from, independent of.'

ἐκᵍ: ἵνα τηρήσῃς αὐτοὺς ἐκ τοῦ πονηροῦ 'in order that you may keep them separate from the evil one' Jn 17.15; ἐλεύθερος γὰρ ὢν ἐκ πάντων 'for I am free from all' 1 Cor 9.19. In 1 Cor 9.19 it may be valuable to relate the first part of the verse to what immediately follows, for example, 'for I am not a slave of anyone, but I make myself a slave to everyone' or 'though I am not anyone's slave, I serve everyone.'

ἐκτός ᵈ: πᾶν ἁμάρτημα ὃ ἐὰν ποιήσῃ ἄνθρωπος ἐκτὸς τοῦ σώματός ἐστιν 'every sin which a person does is independent of the body' 1 Cor 6.18.

89.122 ἀπό ᵃ: a marker of dissociation, implying a rupture from a former association – 'from, separated from.' ηὐχόμην γὰρ ἀνάθεμα εἶναι αὐτὸς ἐγὼ ἀπὸ τοῦ Χριστοῦ 'for I would pray to be cursed and thus myself be separated from Christ' Ro 9.3.

V Combinative Relation (89.123)

89.123 μετά ᶜ: a marker of a relation in which one thing is combined with another – 'with, combined with.' ἔδωκαν αὐτῷ πιεῖν οἶνον μετὰ χολῆς μεμιγμένον 'they gave him wine mixed with gall to drink' Mt 27.34; ὧν τὸ αἷμα Πιλᾶτος ἔμιξεν μετὰ τῶν θυσιῶν αὐτῶν 'whose blood Pilate mixed with their sacrifices' Lk 13.1. This expression in Lk 13.1 must be understood in a figurative sense, for it refers to the act of Pilate killing the people while they were sacrificing. ἀγάπη μετὰ πίστεως 'love with faith' or 'love combined with faith' Eph 6.23. In some languages this expression in Eph 6.23 can only be expressed as 'love and trust at the same time.' ἐν πίστει καὶ ἀγάπῃ καὶ ἁγιασμῷ μετὰ σωφροσύνης 'with faith and love and holiness with modesty' 1 Tm 2.15. In 1 Tm 2.15 modesty is in a combinative relation with faith, love, and holiness and not merely with holiness. In languages in which such expressions are normally translated by verbs, one may render the final clause of 1 Tm 2.15 as 'if she continues to trust and love and to be holy while at the same time showing modesty.'

W Contrast (89.124-89.138)

89.124 δέ ᶜ: a marker of contrast – 'but, on the other hand.' πολλοὶ γάρ εἰσιν κλητοὶ ὀλίγοι δὲ ἐκλεκτοί 'many are invited, but few are chosen' Mt 22.14; ὡς δὲ ἀνέβησαν οἱ ἀδελφοὶ αὐτοῦ εἰς τὴν ἑορτήν, τότε καὶ αὐτὸς ἀνέβη 'but after his brothers went to the feast, he also went' Jn 7.10.

89.125 ἀλλά ᵃ: a marker of more emphatic contrast (as compared with δέ ᶜ, 89.124) – 'but, instead, on the contrary.' οὐκ ἦλθον καταλῦσαι ἀλλὰ πληρῶσαι 'I have not come to do away (with them), but to give (their teachings) full sense' Mt 5.17; τὸ παιδίον οὐκ ἀπέθανεν ἀλλὰ καθεύδει 'the child is not dead but is sleeping' Mk 5.39.

ἀλλά also occurs with μᾶλλον and ἤ in more emphatic phrases marking contrast: ἀλλὰ μᾶλλον δουλευέτωσαν 'on the contrary, they are to serve (them) even better' 1 Tm 6.2; οὐχί, λέγω ὑμῖν, ἀλλ᾽ ἢ διαμερισμόν 'not (peace), I tell you, but rather division' Lk 12.51.

89.126 μᾶλλον ᵇ: a marker of contrast indicating an alternative – 'on the contrary, instead, but rather.' καὶ ὑμεῖς πεφυσιωμένοι ἐστέ, καὶ οὐχὶ μᾶλλον ἐπενθήσατε; 'you have become proud, but on the contrary, should you not be exceedingly sad?' 1 Cor 5.2; νῦν δὲ γνόντες θεόν, μᾶλλον δὲ γνωσθέντες ὑπὸ θεοῦ 'but now (that you) know God, but rather, are known by God' Ga 4.9.

89.127 οὖν ᶜ: a marker of relatively weak contrast – 'but.' οὐκ ἐπίστευσαν οὖν οἱ Ἰουδαῖοι περὶ αὐτοῦ ὅτι ἦν τυφλός 'but the Jews did not believe that he was blind' Jn 9.18. In a context such as Jn 9.18, ὅτι may also serve as a type of transition.

89.128 μενοῦν ᵃ; μενοῦνγε: relatively emphatic markers of contrast – 'but, on the contrary, on the other hand.'

μενοῦν ᵃ: μενοῦν μακάριοι οἱ ἀκούοντες τὸν λόγον τοῦ θεοῦ καὶ φυλάσσοντες 'on the contrary, those who hear the word of God and keep it are happy' or '. . . fortunate' Lk 11.28. For other interpretations of μενοῦν in Lk 11.28, see 89.50 and 91.8.

μενοῦνγε: μενοῦνγε σὺ τίς εἶ ὁ ἀνταποκρινόμενος τῷ θεῷ; 'on the contrary, who are you to talk back to God?' Ro 9.20.

89.129 πάλιν^c: a marker of contrast, with the implication of a sequence – 'on the other hand, but in turn, however.' πάλιν γέγραπται 'on the other hand, it is written' Mt 4.7; λογιζέσθω πάλιν ἐφ' ἑαυτοῦ 'but let him remind himself' 2 Cor 10.7.

89.130 μέντοι; πλήν: markers of contrast, implying the validity of something irrespective of other considerations – 'but, nevertheless, except.'
μέντοι: παρακύψας βλέπει κείμενα τὰ ὀθόνια, οὐ μέντοι εἰσῆλθεν 'he bent over and saw the linen clothes lying (there), but he did not go in' Jn 20.5; ὁ μέντοι στερεὸς θεμέλιος τοῦ θεοῦ ἕστηκεν 'nevertheless, the solid foundation that God has made stands firm' 2 Tm 2.19.
πλήν: ἀνάγκη γὰρ ἐλθεῖν τὰ σκάνδαλα, πλὴν οὐαὶ τῷ ἀνθρώπῳ δι' οὗ τὸ σκάνδαλον ἔρχεται 'offenses must come, but woe to the person on whose account they occur' or 'such things will always happen; nevertheless, how terrible for the one who causes them' Mt 18.7; πλὴν οὐχ ὡς ἐγὼ θέλω ἀλλ' ὡς σύ 'nevertheless, not as I wish, but as you wish' Mt 26.39.

89.131 εἰ μή: a marker of contrast by designating an exception – 'except that, but, however, instead, but only.' ὃ οὐκ ἔστιν ἄλλο· εἰ μή τινές εἰσιν οἱ ταράσσοντες ὑμᾶς 'not that there is another (gospel), except that there are some who trouble you' Ga 1.7; ὃ οὐκ ἐξὸν ἦν αὐτῷ φαγεῖν οὐδὲ τοῖς μετ' αὐτοῦ, εἰ μὴ τοῖς ἱερεῦσιν μόνοις 'it was not lawful for him or the ones with him to eat, but instead, for the priests only' Mt 12.4.

89.132 παρά^h: a marker of contrast by means of an alternative – 'rather than, instead of.' ἐσεβάσθησαν καὶ ἐλάτρευσαν τῇ κτίσει παρὰ τὸν κτίσαντα 'they worship and serve what (God has) created instead of the Creator' Ro 1.25. In a number of languages an alternative contrast must be expressed by a positive-negative sequence. For example, in Ro 1.25 one may translate 'they worship and serve what God

has created; they do not worship and serve the Creator himself.'

89.133 ἀντί^a: a marker of an alternative serving as a contrast – 'instead.' ἀντὶ τοῦ λέγειν ὑμᾶς, Ἐὰν ὁ κύριος θελήσῃ 'instead, you should say, If the Lord wills' Jas 4.15; ἀντὶ ἰχθύος ὄφιν αὐτῷ ἐπιδώσει; 'will he give him a snake instead of a fish?' Lk 11.11.

89.134 τοὐναντίον: a marker of an alternative serving as an emphatic contrast – 'on the contrary, rather, instead.' μὴ ἀποδιδόντες κακὸν ἀντὶ κακοῦ . . . τοὐναντίον δὲ εὐλογοῦντες 'do not pay back evil with evil . . . instead, pay back with a blessing' 1 Pe 3.9.

89.135 ἔτι^c: a marker of contrast, involving something contrary to expectation – 'nevertheless.' τί οὖν ἔτι μέμφεται; 'nevertheless, how then can anyone be blamed?' Ro 9.19.

89.136 μέν . . . δέ^b; μέντοι . . . δέ; μέν . . . ἀλλά; μέν . . . πλήν: markers of sets of items in contrast with one another – 'on the one hand . . . but on the other hand.'
μέν . . . δέ^b: ἐγὼ μὲν ὑμᾶς βαπτίζω ἐν ὕδατι εἰς μετάνοιαν· ὁ δὲ ὀπίσω μου ἐρχόμενος . . . ὑμᾶς βαπτίσει ἐν πνεύματι ἁγίῳ καὶ πυρί 'I baptize you with water for repentance, but the one who will come after me . . . will baptize you with the Holy Spirit and fire' Mt 3.11.
μέντοι . . . δέ: εἰ μέντοι νόμον τελεῖτε βασιλικὸν . . . εἰ δὲ προσωπολημπτεῖτε 'if indeed on the one hand you fulfill the royal law . . . but if on the other hand you show partiality' Jas 2.8-9.
μέν . . . ἀλλά: πάντα μὲν καθαρά, ἀλλὰ κακὸν τῷ ἀνθρώπῳ τῷ διὰ προσκόμματος ἐσθίοντι 'on the one hand all (foods) are ritually pure (or 'may be eaten'), but on the other hand it is wrong to eat anything that will cause someone else to fall into sin' Ro 14.20.
μέν . . . πλήν: ὁ υἱὸς μὲν τοῦ ἀνθρώπου κατὰ τὸ ὡρισμένον πορεύεται πλὴν οὐαὶ τῷ ἀνθρώπῳ ἐκείνῳ δι' οὗ παραδίδοται 'the Son of Man will die in accordance with what has been decided, but woe to that man by whom he is betrayed' Lk 22.22.

89.137 παρά^g: a marker of that which is contrary to what should be or to expectation – 'contrary to, opposed, not in accordance.'

σκοπεῖν τοὺς τὰς διχοστασίας καὶ τὰ σκάνδαλα παρὰ τὴν διδαχὴν ἣν ὑμεῖς ἐμάθετε ποιοῦντας 'look out for those who cause dissensions and difficulties which are contrary to the teaching which you have learned' Ro 16.17; αἵ τε γὰρ θήλειαι αὐτῶν μετήλλαξαν τὴν φυσικὴν χρῆσιν εἰς τὴν παρὰ φύσιν 'for their women have changed the natural use for that which is contrary to nature' or '. . . the way people should not act' or '. . . the way in which people were not made to behave' Ro 1.26.

89.138 ἐκτός^c: a marker of a contrast involving an exception – 'except, as an exception.' οὐδὲν ἐκτὸς λέγων ὧν τε οἱ προφῆται ἐλάλησαν μελλόντων γίνεσθαι καὶ Μωϋσῆς 'saying nothing except what the prophets and Moses said was going to happen' Ac 26.22; μείζων δὲ ὁ προφητεύων ἢ ὁ λαλῶν γλώσσαις, ἐκτὸς εἰ μὴ διερμηνεύῃ 'the one who prophesies is of greater value than the one who speaks in tongues, except when there is someone to interpret' 1 Cor 14.5.

X Alternative Relation (89.139-89.140)

89.139 ἤ^a: a marker of an alternative – 'or.' ὅτι οὐ δύνασαι μίαν τρίχα λευκὴν ποιῆσαι ἢ μέλαιναν 'because you are not able to make one hair white or black' Mt 5.36.

89.140 ἤ . . . ἤ; ἤτοι . . . ἤ: markers of double alternatives – 'either . . . or.' ἤ . . . ἤ: ἢ γὰρ τὸν ἕνα μισήσει καὶ τὸν ἕτερον ἀγαπήσει, ἢ ἑνὸς ἀνθέξεται καὶ τοῦ ἑτέρου καταφρονήσει 'for either he will hate the one

and love the other or he will be loyal to one and despise the other' Mt 6.24. ἤτοι . . . ἤ: δοῦλοί ἐστε ᾧ ὑπακούετε, ἤτοι ἁμαρτίας εἰς θάνατον ἢ ὑπακοῆς εἰς δικαιοσύνην 'you are slaves of what you obey, either of sin which leads to death or obedience which leads to righteousness' Ro 6.16.

Y Substance (89.141-89.142)

89.141 ἐν^l: a marker of that of which something consists – 'in, of, consisting of.' Ἰακὼβ τὸν πατέρα αὐτοῦ καὶ πᾶσαν τὴν συγγένειαν ἐν ψυχαῖς ἑβδομήκοντα πέντε 'Jacob his father and the whole family, consisting of seventy-five persons' Ac 7.14; τὸν νόμον τῶν ἐντολῶν ἐν δόγμασιν καταργήσας 'having abolished the Law of commandments consisting of rules' Eph 2.15.

89.142 ἐκ^m; ἀπό^e: markers of the substance of which something consists or out of which it is made – 'of, consisting of, out of, made of.' ἐκ^m: καὶ πλέξαντες στέφανον ἐξ ἀκανθῶν ἐπέθηκαν ἐπὶ τῆς κεφαλῆς αὐτοῦ 'and having woven a crown made of thorns, they put it on his head' Mt 27.29. ἀπό^e: τὸ ἔνδυμα αὐτοῦ ἀπὸ τριχῶν καμήλου 'his garment made of the hair of a camel' Mt 3.4.

Z Mediation (89.143)

89.143 ἀνὰ μέσον^c: a marker of mediation – 'between, among.' ὃς δυνήσεται διακρῖναι ἀνὰ μέσον τοῦ ἀδελφοῦ αὐτοῦ 'who can settle a dispute between fellow believers' 1 Cor 6.5.

90 Case

Traditionally, case has been treated almost solely in terms of the so-called case endings on nouns, pronouns, and adjectives, though some persons have related case to the voice in verbs, namely, active, middle, and passive. In Domain 90, however, case is defined in terms of *the relation of participants to events or states,* and such participants may be in a number of different case relations, for example, agents, causative agents, instruments, experiencers, participants who may be benefited, those directly affected, and those who are viewpoint participants in events or states. This domain, however, does not deal with the relations marked by affixation, but by words, primarily prepositions and verbs.

In the following description of case relations, there are two principal ways in which cases are formally marked by lexical units. First, there are a number of different prepositions which are employed to mark quite diverse case relations. Second, there are quite a few verbs which serve as markers of case relations, but in many instances these verbs also carry additional semantic components. As such, the verbs function in a complex manner, since they belong essentially to two different sets of semantic domains. As will be readily noted, in some instances the verbs have lost almost all of the meaning normally associated with their so-called central or literal significance. In other instances, a considerable amount of the literal meaning is still retained, while the verb serves the additional function of marking a case relation.

Outline of Subdomains

A Agent, Personal or Nonpersonal, Causative or Immediate, Direct or Indirect (90.1-90.7)
B Instrument (90.8-90.13)
C Source of Event or Activity (90.14-90.16)
D Responsibility (90.17-90.19)
E Viewpoint Participant (90.20)
F Content (90.21-90.28)
G Guarantor Participant with Oaths (90.29-90.30)
H Opposition (90.31-90.35)
I Benefaction (90.36-90.42)
J Reason Participant (90.43-90.44)
K Agent of a Numerable Event (90.45-90.50)
L Agent in a Causative Role Marked by Verbs (90.51-90.55)
M Experiencer (90.56-90.84)
N To Cause to Experience (90.85-90.97)

A Agent, Personal or Nonpersonal, Causative or Immediate, Direct or Indirect (90.1-90.7)

90.1 ὑπό^c (with the genitive): a marker of agent or force, whether person or event – 'by.' ἦν ἐν τῇ ἐρήμῳ τεσσεράκοντα ἡμέρας πειραζόμενος ὑπὸ τοῦ Σατανᾶ 'he was in the desert for forty days being tempted by Satan' Mk 1.13; ἱκανὸν τῷ τοιούτῳ ἡ ἐπιτιμία αὕτη ἡ ὑπὸ τῶν πλειόνων 'this punishment by the majority is enough for this person' 2 Cor 2.6; βασανιζόμενον ὑπὸ τῶν κυμάτων 'tossed about by the waves' Mt 14.24; κάλαμον ὑπὸ ἀνέμου σαλευόμενον 'a reed shaken by the wind' Lk 7.24; ἱνατί γὰρ ἡ ἐλευθερία μου κρίνεται ὑπὸ ἄλλης συνειδήσεως 'for why is my freedom judged by someone else's conscience' 1 Cor 10.29.

In a number of languages it is difficult, if not impossible, to use a so-called passive expression which introduces an agent by means of a preposition. It may, therefore, be necessary in a number of instances to make the agent the subject of the sentence or clause. For example, Mk 1.13 may be restructured as 'Satan tempted Jesus when Jesus was in the desert for forty days.'

90.2 σὺν χειρί (followed by the genitive): (an idiom, literally 'with the hand of') a marker of an associated agent – 'by, with the help of.' λυτρωτὴν ἀπέσταλκεν σὺν χειρὶ ἀγγέλου τοῦ ὀφθέντος αὐτῷ ἐν τῇ βάτῳ 'he accomplished deliverance with the help of an angel who appeared to him in the bush' Ac 7.35.

90.3 παρά^c (with the genitive or dative): a marker of potential agent – 'by, for, with.' παρὰ ἀνθρώποις τοῦτο ἀδύνατόν ἐστιν, παρὰ δὲ θεῷ πάντα δυνατά 'for people this is not possible, but for God all things are possible' Mt 19.26. In some languages, however, it may be necessary to restructure such a relation as 'people cannot do everything, but God can do anything.' ὅτι οὐκ ἀδυνατήσει παρὰ τοῦ θεοῦ πᾶν ῥῆμα 'because there is nothing impossible with God' or 'because there is nothing that God cannot do' Lk 1.37.

90.4 διά^a (with the genitive): a marker of intermediate agent, with implicit or explicit causative agent – 'through, by.' τὸ ῥηθὲν ὑπὸ κυρίου διὰ τοῦ προφήτου λέγοντος 'that which was spoken by the Lord through the prophet' Mt 1.22; πιστὸς ὁ θεὸς δι' οὗ ἐκλήθητε 'God is faithful through whom you were called' 1 Cor 1.9. It is somewhat unusual to find διά with the genitive used in a context such as 1 Cor

1.9, since it is normally the calling which is 'by God' (with ὑπό) rather than 'through God' (with διά). πάντα δι᾽ αὐτοῦ ἐγένετο 'all things came into existence through him' Jn 1.3.

90.5 ἐπί[u] (with the accusative): a marker of agent, with the added implication of effect upon the agent – 'by.' ἐπιστεύθη τὸ μαρτύριον ἡμῶν ἐφ᾽ ὑμᾶς 'our witness was believed by you' 2 Th 1.10. It is possible that in 2 Th 1.10 there is a double relation marked by ἐπί, for it may be construed as marking the affected participant with τὸ μαρτύριον and at the same time the agent participant with ἐπιστεύθη. It is this double role which may account for the use of ἐπί rather than ὑπό, which would clearly mark a relation with ἐπιστεύθη, or πρός, which would indicate clearly a relation with μαρτύριον.

90.6 ἐν[n] (with the dative): a marker of agent, often with the implication of an agent being used as an instrument, and in some instances relating to general behavior rather than to some specific event – 'by, from.' εἰ ἐν ὑμῖν κρίνεται ὁ κόσμος 'if the world is to be judged by you' 1 Cor 6.2; ἐν αὐτῷ ἐκτίσθη τὰ πάντα ἐν τοῖς οὐρανοῖς καὶ ἐπὶ τῆς γῆς 'all things in heaven and on earth were made by him' Col 1.16; ἵνα ἐν ἡμῖν μάθητε 'in order that you might learn from us' 1 Cor 4.6; τὸν αὐτὸν ἀγῶνα ἔχοντες οἷον εἴδετε ἐν ἐμοὶ καὶ νῦν ἀκούετε ἐν ἐμοί 'having the same struggle which you saw me engaged in, and which you now hear that I am engaged in' Php 1.30.

90.7 ἀπό[f] (with the genitive): a marker of agent which may also be regarded as a source – 'by, from.'[1] Ἰωσὴφ δὲ ὁ ἐπικληθεὶς Βαρναβᾶς ἀπὸ τῶν ἀποστόλων 'Joseph, who was called Barnabas by the apostles' Ac 4.36; οὔτε ζητοῦντες ἐξ ἀνθρώπων δόξαν, οὔτε ἀφ᾽ ὑμῶν οὔτε ἀπ᾽ ἄλλων 'neither seeking to be honored by people, neither by you nor by others' or 'neither seeking glory from people, neither from you nor from others' 1 Th 2.6. The expression ζητοῦντες . . . δόξαν in 1 Th 2.6 clearly indicates an event of 'seeking to be honored' or 'seeking to be given glory.' In such an instance, ἀπό serves to mark not only the agent but also a source.

B Instrument[2] (90.8-90.13)

90.8 διά[b] (with the genitive): a marker of the instrument by which something is accomplished – 'by means of, through, with.' γράφειν οὐκ ἐβουλήθην διὰ χάρτου καὶ μέλανος 'I would rather not write with paper and ink' 2 Jn 12.

90.9 ἐπί[i] (with the dative): a marker of instrument as the basis for some event – 'by, by means of.' οὐκ ἐπ᾽ ἄρτῳ μόνῳ ζήσεται ὁ ἄνθρωπος, ἀλλ᾽ ἐπὶ παντὶ ῥήματι ἐκπορευομένῳ διὰ στόματος θεοῦ 'a person shall not live by bread alone, but by every word that comes from the mouth of God' Mt 4.4.

90.10 ἐν[i] (with the dative): a marker of an immediate instrument – 'by, with.' εἰ πατάξομεν ἐν μαχαίρῃ; 'shall we strike with a sword?' Lk 22.49; εἰ δυνατός ἐστιν ἐν δέκα χιλιάσιν ὑπαντῆσαι τῷ μετὰ εἴκοσι χιλιάδων ἐρχομένῳ ἐπ᾽ αὐτόν 'whether he is able with ten thousand (soldiers) to withstand someone coming against him with twenty thousand (soldiers)' Lk 14.31.

---

1 In most instances ἀπό as a marker of agent involves communication, but an expression such as occurs in Mt 20.20 may very well give rise to the use of ἀπό in the double sense of both agent and source of communication. In the phrase αἰτοῦσά τι ἀπ᾽ αὐτοῦ 'seeking something from him,' the immediate response would have been a communication of a promise, so that the ἀπό would clearly reflect not only the immediate agent of the promise but the ultimate source for the requested benefit.

2 The category of *Means* (89.76-89.78) involves a relation between two events while the category of *Instrument* includes objects which are employed in some activity or event. However, it is sometimes difficult to distinguish clearly between these two categories. For example, in Mt 4.4 (see 90.9) the statement 'a person shall not live by bread alone' would appear to mean that 'bread' is to be understood as instrument. On a deeper level of analysis, however, the term ἄρτος 'bread' is only a metonym for 'the eating of food.' Therefore, what on a surface level appears to be instrument is on a deeper level a matter of means. See also 90.56.

90.11 ἀπό^g (with the genitive): a marker of instrument which serves as a source of information or reason – 'by, from.' ἀπὸ δὲ τῆς συκῆς μάθετε τὴν παραβολήν 'learn a parable from the fig tree' Mt 24.32.

90.12 ἐκ^d (with the genitive): a marker of instrument, with the added implication of result – 'by, as a result of.' χρυσίον πεπυρωμένον ἐκ πυρός 'gold refined by fire' Re 3.18; πολλοὶ τῶν ἀνθρώπων ἀπέθανον ἐκ τῶν ὑδάτων 'many people died of the water' Re 8.11.

90.13 χράομαι^d; καταχράομαι^a: to make use of instruments – 'to use, to employ, with.'³
χράομαι^d: ἣν ἄραντες βοηθείαις ἐχρῶντο ὑποζωννύντες τὸ πλοῖον 'having pulled it (the boat) aboard, they used ropes tied tightly around the ship' or '. . . they girded the ship with ropes' Ac 27.17. In Ac 27.17 βοηθεία is best regarded as a technical nautical term for supports (ropes or cables) used in aiding a ship in danger (see 35.10).
καταχράομαι^a: εἰς τὸ μὴ καταχρήσασθαι τῇ ἐξουσίᾳ μου ἐν τῷ εὐαγγελίῳ 'so as not to employ my rights in proclaiming the good news' 1 Cor 9.18.

C Source of Event or Activity (90.14-90.16)

90.14 παρά^d (with the genitive): a marker of the agentive source of an activity, though often remote and indirect – 'from, by, of.' χάρις ἔλεος εἰρήνη παρὰ θεοῦ πατρός 'grace, mercy, peace from God the Father' 2 Jn 3; ἵνα παρὰ τῶν γεωργῶν λάβῃ ἀπὸ τῶν καρπῶν τοῦ ἀμπελῶνος 'in order to receive from the farmers some of the fruit of the vineyard' Mk 12.2; πῶς σὺ Ἰουδαῖος ὢν παρ' ἐμοῦ πεῖν αἰτεῖς γυναικὸς Σαμαρίτιδος οὔσης; 'how is it that you being a Jew ask for a drink from me, a Samaritan woman?' Jn 4.9; τοῦ αἰτεῖν ἐλεημοσύνην παρὰ τῶν εἰσπορευομένων εἰς τὸ ἱερόν 'to ask alms of those who were going into the Temple' Ac 3.2.

90.15 ἀπό^b (with the genitive): a marker of source of an implied event – 'from, by.' τὸν θέλοντα ἀπὸ σοῦ δανίσασθαι μὴ ἀποστραφῇς 'do not turn away from the one who wishes to borrow from you' Mt 5.42. In Mt 5.42 ἀπό also marks the one who would be the agent of loaning.

90.16 ἐκ^f (with the genitive): a marker of the source of an activity or state, with the implication of something preceding from or out of the source – 'from, by.' Ῥεβέκκα ἐξ ἑνὸς κοίτην ἔχουσα, Ἰσαὰκ τοῦ πατρὸς ἡμῶν 'Rebecca became pregnant by our forefather Isaac' Ro 9.10; οὔτε ζητοῦντες ἐξ ἀνθρώπων δόξαν 'neither seeking praise from people' 1 Th 2.6; ὅτι ἔκρινεν ὁ θεὸς τὸ κρίμα ὑμῶν ἐξ αὐτῆς 'because God condemned her for what she did to you' Re 18.20.

D Responsibility (90.17-90.19)

90.17 ἐπί^g (with the accusative): a marker of the one upon whom responsibility falls – 'on, upon.' ἔλθῃ ἐφ' ὑμᾶς πᾶν αἷμα δίκαιον 'responsibility for the murder of all innocent people will come upon you' Mt 23.35; τὸ αἷμα αὐτοῦ ἐφ' ἡμᾶς καὶ ἐπὶ τὰ τέκνα ἡμῶν 'let the responsibility for his death be upon us and upon our children' Mt 27.25. See also 37.102.

90.18 ἐπιρίπτω ἐπί: (an idiom, literally 'to throw upon' or 'to cast upon') to cause responsibility for something to be upon someone – 'to put responsibility on, to make responsible for.' πᾶσαν τὴν μέριμναν ὑμῶν ἐπιρίψαντες ἐπ' αὐτόν 'put upon him all responsibility for your cares' or 'make him responsible for all your worries' 1 Pe 5.7. For another explanation of this expression in 1 Pe 5.7 taking τὴν μέριμναν ἐπιρίπτω ἐπί as an idiom, see 25.250.

90.19 ἀπό^j (with the genitive): a marker of one who is responsible for an event or state – 'by, on (the basis of), of, upon.' ἀπ' ἐμαυτοῦ οὐκ ἐλήλυθα 'I didn't come on my own' or 'I am not the one who is responsible for my coming' Jn 7.28; τί δὲ καὶ ἀφ' ἑαυτῶν οὐ κρίνετε τὸ δίκαιον; 'why don't you accept responsibility for judging what is right?' or 'why do you

---

³ It may be that χράομαι^d differs from καταχράομαι^a in intensity.

not take it upon yourselves to judge what is right?' Lk 12.57.

E   Viewpoint Participant[4] (90.20)

90.20 παρά[f] (with the dative); πρός[o] (with the accusative); ἔμπροσθεν[c]; ἐναντίον[b]; ἔναντι[b]; κατέναντι[b]; ἐνώπιον[b]; κατενώπιον[b] (except for παρά[f] and πρός[o], all with the genitive): marking a participant whose viewpoint is relevant to an event – 'in the sight of, in the opinion of, in the judgment of.'[5]

παρά[f]: οὐ γὰρ οἱ ἀκροαταὶ νόμου δίκαιοι παρὰ τῷ θεῷ 'for it is not the hearers of the Law who are righteous in God's sight' Ro 2.13.

πρός[o]: ἀπρόσκοπον συνείδησιν ἔχειν πρὸς τὸν θεὸν καὶ τοὺς ἀνθρώπους 'to have a clear conscience before God and people' Ac 24.16.

ἔμπροσθεν[c]: ὅτι οὕτως εὐδοκία ἐγένετο ἔμπροσθέν σου 'for thus it was good in your sight' Mt 11.26.

ἐναντίον[b]: ἦσαν δὲ δίκαιοι ἀμφότεροι ἐναντίον τοῦ θεοῦ 'they both lived righteous lives in God's sight' Lk 1.6.

ἔναντι[b]: ἡ γὰρ καρδία σου οὐκ ἔστιν εὐθεῖα ἔναντι τοῦ θεοῦ 'your heart is not right in God's sight' Ac 8.21.

κατέναντι[b]: κατέναντι θεοῦ ἐν Χριστῷ λαλοῦμεν 'we speak (as those who) in the sight of God (are) in Christ' 2 Cor 12.19.

ἐνώπιον[b]: ἓν ἐξ αὐτῶν οὐκ ἔστιν ἐπιλελησμένον ἐνώπιον τοῦ θεοῦ 'not one of them is forgotten in the sight of God' Lk 12.6; ἥμαρτον εἰς τὸν οὐρανὸν καὶ ἐνώπιόν σου 'I have sinned against heaven and in your sight' Lk 15.18. It is also possible to interpret ἐνώπιον in Lk 12.6 as a marker of agent (90A) as in TEV "not one of them is forgotten by God."

κατενώπιον[b]: εἶναι ἡμᾶς ἁγίους καὶ ἀμώμους κατενώπιον αὐτοῦ 'so that we would be judged holy and without fault in his sight' Eph 1.4.[6]

F   Content (90.21-90.28)

90.21 ὅτι[a]; διότι[b]; ὡς[b]: markers of discourse content, whether direct or indirect – 'that, the fact that.'

ὅτι[a]: ἀλλὰ ἔχω κατὰ σοῦ ὅτι τὴν ἀγάπην σου τὴν πρώτην ἀφῆκες 'but I have against you the fact that you have left your first love' Re 2.4; ἡμεῖς δὲ ἠλπίζομεν ὅτι αὐτός ἐστιν ὁ μέλλων λυτροῦσθαι τὸν Ἰσραήλ 'but we hoped that he would be the one who would deliver Israel' Lk 24.21; ὑμεῖς λέγετε ὅτι Βλασφημεῖς 'you say, You blaspheme' Jn 10.36; ἐλπίζω δὲ ὅτι γνώσεσθε ὅτι ἡμεῖς οὐκ ἐσμὲν ἀδόκιμοι 'I hope that you know that we are not failures' or '. . . not persons who have been tested and found wanting' 2 Cor 13.6; καὶ τότε ὁμολογήσω αὐτοῖς ὅτι Οὐδέποτε ἔγνων ὑμᾶς 'and then I will tell them, I never knew you' Mt 7.23.

διότι[b]: ἐφ' ἐλπίδι διότι καὶ αὐτὴ ἡ κτίσις ἐλευθερωθήσεται ἀπὸ τῆς δουλείας τῆς φθορᾶς 'in the hope that the creation itself will be freed from bondage to corruption' Ro 8.20-21 (apparatus). In Ro 8.21 διότι appears to be simply a variant of ὅτι with essentially the same meaning, though some scholars have interpreted διότι in this context as meaning 'because' (see διότι[a], 89.26).

ὡς[b]: μάρτυς γάρ μου ὁ θεός, ὡς ἐπιποθῶ πάντας ὑμᾶς 'God is my witness that I have a deep feeling for all of you' Php 1.8.

The marking of direct and indirect discourse varies greatly from language to language. In some instances there is no marker at all; in other cases one marker precedes and another follows. In still other instances a repetition of an expression of speaking occurs at the end of a quotation, whether direct or indirect. In a number of languages written usage differs appreciably from spoken usage, because intonation so often marks introduced discourse in the spoken form of a language.

---

4 It would be possible to classify the meanings of the markers in Subdomain E as belonging to Domain 30 *Think*, but the mental activity involved is not focal. Accordingly, it seems far more satisfactory to consider this relation as a matter of case rather than one of some specific intellectual judgment or opinion.

5 There are undoubtedly certain subtle distinctions of meaning associated with the various markers in 90.20, but it is impossible to determine those differences on the basis of existing contexts.

6 It would also be possible to understand κατενώπιον in Eph 1.4 as the presence of God (see κατενώπιον[a], 83.33).

90.22 ἵνα^c: a marker of the content of discourse, particularly if and when purpose is implied – 'that.'[7] παρεκάλουν αὐτὸν ἵνα μόνον ἅψωνται τοῦ κρασπέδου τοῦ ἱματίου αὐτοῦ 'they begged him to let the sick at least touch the edge of his cloak' Mt 14.36; ἐκήρυξαν ἵνα μετανοῶσιν 'they preached that the people should repent' Mk 6.12; ἡ δὲ γυνὴ ἵνα φοβῆται τὸν ἄνδρα 'and every wife should respect her husband' Eph 5.33. An expression of command is implicit in this passage in Eph 5.33, and therefore one may interpret this clause with ἵνα as being a matter of content.

90.23 ἐπί^p (with the genitive); εἰςⁱ (with the accusative); ἐν^u (with the dative): markers of content as a means of specifying a particular referent – 'concerning, with respect to, with reference to, about, in.'
ἐπί^p: οὐ λέγει, Καὶ τοῖς σπέρμασιν, ὡς ἐπὶ πολλῶν 'it does not say, And to the descendants, as a reference to many' Ga 3.16; βαπτισθήτω ἕκαστος ὑμῶν ἐπὶ τῷ ὀνόματι Ἰησοῦ Χριστοῦ 'each one of you must be baptized in (or 'with respect to') the name of Jesus Christ' Ac 2.38.
εἰςⁱ: Δαυὶδ γὰρ λέγει εἰς αὐτόν 'for David spoke concerning him' Ac 2.25; θέλω δὲ ὑμᾶς σοφοὺς εἶναι εἰς τὸ ἀγαθόν 'but I want you to be wise concerning what is good' Ro 16.19; βαπτίζοντες αὐτοὺς εἰς τὸ ὄνομα τοῦ πατρὸς καὶ τοῦ . . . 'and baptize them in the name of the Father and the . . .' Mt 28.19.
ἐν^u: ἐν τῷ ὀνόματι Ἰησοῦ Χριστοῦ βαπτισθῆναι 'to be baptized in the name of Jesus Christ' Ac 10.48.

90.24 περί^b (with the genitive); ὑπέρ^b (with the genitive): markers of general content, whether of a discourse or mental activity – 'concerning, about, of.'[8]

---

7 In a number of instances, a marker of direct discourse is not represented in translation, particularly if what is indirect discourse in the Greek text is rendered as direct discourse.
8 The general equivalence in meaning of περί and ὑπέρ in contexts introducing content can be readily seen from the tendency for scribes to interchange these terms in manuscripts. However, there may be certain subtle distinctions in meaning, but these cannot be determined from existing contexts.

περί^b: γνώσεται περὶ τῆς διδαχῆς 'he will know concerning the teaching' Jn 7.17; εὐθὺς λέγουσιν αὐτῷ περὶ αὐτῆς 'immediately they spoke to him about her' Mk 1.30.
ὑπέρ^b: οὗτός ἐστιν ὑπὲρ οὗ ἐγὼ εἶπον 'this is the one concerning whom I spoke' Jn 1.30; πολλή μοι καύχησις ὑπὲρ ὑμῶν 'my great confidence concerning you' 2 Cor 7.4; ἡ ἐλπὶς ἡμῶν βεβαία ὑπὲρ ὑμῶν 'our hope concerning you is firm' 2 Cor 1.7.

90.25 πρός^f (with the accusative): a marker of content, particularly when persons are involved and/or the context suggests some type of response being made – 'about, to.' ἔγνωσαν γὰρ ὅτι πρὸς αὐτοὺς τὴν παραβολὴν εἶπεν 'for they knew that he spoke the parable about them' Mk 12.12; καὶ οὐκ ἀπεκρίθη αὐτῷ πρὸς οὐδὲ ἓν ῥῆμα 'and he didn't answer to a single charge' Mt 27.14; ἐάν τις πρός τινα ἔχῃ μομφήν 'if anyone has a complaint about anyone' Col 3.13. For a different interpretation of πρός in Mk 12.12 and Col 3.13, see 90.33.

90.26 εἰ^c: a marker of an indirect question as content – 'whether, if, that.' εἰ ἁμαρτωλός ἐστιν οὐκ οἶδα 'I do not know whether he is a sinner' Jn 9.25; ὁ δὲ Πιλᾶτος ἐθαύμασεν εἰ ἤδη τέθνηκεν 'Pilate was amazed that he had already died' Mk 15.44. In Mk 15.44 the use of εἰ would suggest that Pilate questioned whether Jesus had actually died. οὐδὲν ἐκτὸς λέγων ὧν τε οἱ προφῆται ἐλάλησαν μελλόντων γίνεσθαι καὶ Μωϋσῆς, εἰ παθητὸς ὁ Χριστός 'saying nothing other than what the prophets and Moses said about what was going to happen, namely, that the Messiah would suffer' Ac 26.22-23.

90.27 ἔχωⁱ; περιέχω^a: markers of designations of content – 'to have, to contain.'
ἔχωⁱ: γράψας ἐπιστολὴν ἔχουσαν τὸν τύπον τοῦτον 'writing a letter containing this content' Ac 23.25.
περιέχω^a: γράψαντες ἐπιστολὴν διὰ χειρὸς αὐτῶν περιέχουσαν τάδε 'writing a letter through them having these (words)' Ac 15.23 (apparatus).

90.28 τύπος^g, ου *m*: the content of a discourse or a document – 'content.' γράψας ἐπιστολὴν ἔχουσαν τὸν τύπον τοῦτον 'writing a letter having this content' Ac 23.25. For another interpretation of τύπος in Ac 23.25, see 58.25.

G Guarantor Participant with Oaths (90.29-90.30)

90.29 κατά[j] (with the genitive): a marker of a supernatural person or force called upon to guarantee the carrying out of an oath or vow – 'by, in the name of.' ἐξορκίζω σε κατὰ τοῦ θεοῦ τοῦ ζῶντος 'I adjure you by the living God' or 'I put you under oath to the living God' Mt 26.63; ὤμοσεν καθ' ἑαυτοῦ 'he swore by himself' He 6.13.

Depending upon the context, it may be necessary to be quite specific in some languages in marking the relations between swearing and the supernatural power invoked to guarantee the fulfillment of an oath. For example, in swearing that something is true, it may be necessary to translate 'I swear that this is true and call upon God to punish me if it is not true,' or if the swearing involves a promise, then one may translate 'I promise to do this, but if I do not, may God punish me.'

90.30 ἐν[o] (with the dative); εἰς[n] (with the dative): markers of objects which serve as symbolic substitutes for supernatural persons or powers presumed to act as guarantors of compliance with oaths – 'by.' μήτε ἐν τῷ οὐρανῷ, ὅτι θρόνος ἐστὶν τοῦ θεοῦ· μήτε ἐν τῇ γῇ, ὅτι ὑποπόδιόν ἐστιν τῶν ποδῶν αὐτοῦ· μήτε εἰς Ἱεροσόλυμα, ὅτι πόλις ἐστὶν τοῦ μεγάλου βασιλέως· μήτε ἐν τῇ κεφαλῇ σου ὀμόσῃς, ὅτι οὐ δύνασαι μίαν τρίχα λευκὴν ποιῆσαι ἢ μέλαιναν 'not by heaven, because it is God's throne; nor by the earth, because it is his footstool; nor by Jerusalem, because it is the city of the great King; nor should you swear by your head, because you cannot make a single hair white or black' Mt 5.34b-36.

H Opposition (90.31-90.35)

90.31 κατά[j] (with the genitive): a marker of opposition, with the possible implication of antagonism – 'against, in opposition to, in conflict with.' στρατεύονται κατὰ τῆς ψυχῆς 'they fight against the soul' 1 Pe 2.11;

ἐξαλείψας τὸ καθ' ἡμῶν χειρόγραφον 'cancelling the record against us' Col 2.14; καὶ εἴπωσιν πᾶν πονηρὸν καθ' ὑμῶν 'and speak all kinds of evil against you' Mt 5.11; οἵτινες ἐνεφάνισαν τῷ ἡγεμόνι κατὰ τοῦ Παύλου 'who appeared before the governor (with accusations) against Paul' Ac 24.1.

90.32 μετά[f] (with the genitive): a marker of opposition and conflict, implying interaction – 'against, with.' πολεμήσω μετ' αὐτῶν ἐν τῇ ῥομφαίᾳ τοῦ στόματός μου 'I will fight against them with the sword of my mouth' Re 2.16; ὅτι κρίματα ἔχετε μεθ' ἑαυτῶν 'because you have legal disputes against one another' 1 Cor 6.7.

90.33 πρός[p] (with the accusative): a marker of opposition, with the probable implication of a reaction or response to a previous event – 'against.' ἔγνωσαν γὰρ ὅτι πρὸς αὐτοὺς τὴν παραβολὴν εἶπεν 'for they knew that he spoke this parable against them' Mk 12.12; ἐάν τις πρός τινα ἔχῃ μομφήν 'if anyone has any blame against anyone' Col 3.13. For another interpretation of πρός in Mk 12.12 and Col 3.13, see 90.25.

90.34 ἐπί[j] (with the accusative or dative): a marker of opposition in a judicial or quasi-judicial context – 'against.' ὡς ἐπὶ λῃστὴν ἐξήλθατε μετὰ μαχαιρῶν καὶ ξύλων 'did you come out with swords and clubs as against a thief' Mt 26.55; ἐπαναστήσονται τέκνα ἐπὶ γονεῖς καὶ θανατώσουσιν αὐτούς 'children will rise up against their parents and cause them to be put to death' Mt 10.21; τρεῖς ἐπὶ δυσὶν καὶ δύο ἐπὶ τρισίν 'three against two and two against three' Lk 12.52.

90.35 ἀπέναντι[b] (with the genitive): a marker of opposition or hostility, with the implication that something is done in place of something else – 'against.' οὗτοι πάντες ἀπέναντι τῶν δογμάτων Καίσαρος πράσσουσι 'all these act against the decrees of Caesar' or '. . . of the Emperor' Ac 17.7.

I Benefaction (90.36-90.42)

90.36 ὑπέρ[a] (with the genitive): a marker of a participant who is benefited by an event or on whose behalf an event takes place – 'for, on behalf of, for the sake of.' ὅς ἐστιν πιστὸς ὑπὲρ ὑμῶν διάκονος τοῦ Χριστοῦ 'who is a faithful servant of Christ on your behalf' Col 1.7; ἵνα εἷς ἄνθρωπος ἀποθάνῃ ὑπὲρ τοῦ λαοῦ 'in order that one person might die on behalf of the nation' Jn 11.50; δεήσεις, προσευχάς, ἐντεύξεις, εὐχαριστίας, ὑπὲρ πάντων ἀνθρώπων 'petitions, prayers, intercession and thanksgiving on behalf of all people' 1 Tm 2.1; τοῦ δόντος ἑαυτὸν ὑπὲρ τῶν ἁμαρτιῶν ἡμῶν 'he who gave himself on behalf of our sins' Ga 1.4. In a number of languages, one cannot speak of 'doing something on behalf of sins'; only a person can be benefited by an event, and therefore one must translate 'who gave himself on behalf of us who had sinned' in Ga 1.4. See also 90.39.

90.37 ἀντί[b] (with the genitive): a marker of a participant who is benefited by an event, usually with the implication of some type of exchange or substitution involved – 'for, on behalf of.' ἐκεῖνον λαβὼν δὸς αὐτοῖς ἀντὶ ἐμοῦ καὶ σοῦ 'take (a coin) and give it to them for me and you' Mt 17.27.

90.38 διά[d] (with the accusative): a marker of a participant who is benefited by an event or for whom an event occurs – 'for the sake of, for, on behalf of, for the benefit of.' τὸ σάββατον διὰ τὸν ἄνθρωπον ἐγένετο καὶ οὐχ ὁ ἄνθρωπος διὰ τὸ σάββατον 'the Sabbath was made for the benefit of mankind and not mankind for the benefit of the Sabbath' Mk 2.27.

90.39 περί[e] (with the genitive): a marker of events which are indirectly involved in a beneficial activity – 'on behalf of.' ὅτι καὶ Χριστὸς ἅπαξ περὶ ἁμαρτιῶν ἔπαθεν 'because Christ once for all suffered on behalf of sins' 1 Pe 3.18. A strictly literal translation of this expression in 1 Pe 3.18 could be extremely misleading in some languages, since it would imply that Christ's suffering in some way benefited or enhanced sins. Accordingly, it is necessary in a number of languages to translate as 'because Christ once for all suffered for the sake of people who had sinned.'

Note a similar use of ὑπέρ in Ga 1.4 (see 90.36).

90.40 ἐπί[k] (with the dative): a marker of persons benefited by an event, with the implication of their being in a dependent relationship – 'for.' δαπάνησον ἐπ' αὐτοῖς ἵνα ξυρήσονται τὴν κεφαλήν 'make a payment for their expenses, in order that they may shave their heads' Ac 21.24.

90.41 εἰς[m] (with the accusative): a marker of persons benefited by an event, with the implication of something directed to them – 'for, on behalf of.' περὶ δὲ τῆς λογείας τῆς εἰς τοὺς ἁγίους 'concerning the collection made on behalf of the people of God' 1 Cor 16.1; τὴν κοινωνίαν τῆς διακονίας τῆς εἰς τοὺς ἁγίους 'a share in helping the people of God' 2 Cor 8.4. In both 1 Cor 16.1 and 2 Cor 8.4 there is clearly an ellipsis of an event of 'sending' such help to and on behalf of God's people.

90.42 μετά[j] (with the genitive): a marker of association in which one party acts or exists for the benefit of another – 'with, on the same side as.' ὁ μὴ ὢν μετ' ἐμοῦ κατ' ἐμοῦ ἐστιν 'he who is not with me is against me' Mt 12.30. In Mt 12.30 there is an implied event.

J   Reason Participant[9] (90.43-90.44)

90.43 ἕνεκεν[c] or ἕνεκα[c] (with the genitive): a marker of a participant constituting the reason for an event – 'because of, for the sake of.' εἴπωσιν πᾶν πονηρὸν καθ' ὑμῶν ψευδόμενοι ἕνεκεν ἐμοῦ 'they will say all kinds of evil things against you falsely because of me' Mt 5.11; ἐκβάλωσιν τὸ ὄνομα ὑμῶν ὡς πονηρὸν ἕνεκα τοῦ υἱοῦ τοῦ ἀνθρώπου 'they regard you as evil because of the Son of Man' Lk 6.22; ὃς δ' ἂν ἀπολέσῃ τὴν ψυχὴν αὐτοῦ ἕνεκεν ἐμοῦ εὑρήσει αὐτήν 'whoever loses his life because of me shall find it' Mt 16.25; ἕνεκεν γὰρ τῆς

---

9 The subdomain entitled *Reason Participant* include[s] markers of a person who constitutes the reason for a p[ar]ticular event. Reason is also an important element in [do]main 89, but there the relation is between two eve[nts] which one constitutes the reason for anoth[er] 89.15-89.38). In Domain 90, it is simply a parti[cipant in] the event who constitutes the reason.

ἐλπίδος τοῦ Ἰσραὴλ τὴν ἅλυσιν ταύτην περί-κειμαι 'because of him for whom the people of Israel hope, I wear this chain' or '. . . I am bound in chains' Ac 28.20. In Ac 28.20 there is an ellipsis of a reference to the person who is the object of the hope.

90.44 διάᵉ (with the accusative): a marker of a participant constituting the cause or reason for an event or state – 'because of, on account of, for this reason.' καὶ ἔσεσθε μισούμενοι ὑπὸ πάντων διὰ τὸ ὄνομά μου 'you will be hated by everyone because of me' (literally '. . . because of my name') Mt 10.22; ἔδησεν αὐτὸν ἐν φυλακῇ διὰ Ἡρῳδιάδα 'he put him in jail be-cause of Herodias' Mk 6.17. In Mk 6.17 Herodias clearly constituted the reason or cause for Herod putting John in prison, but there is a sense in which διὰ Ἡρῳδιάδα may also indicate Herod's purpose in trying to please Herodias, and therefore one may translate 'for the sake of Herodias' (see διάᵈ, 90.38).

K   Agent of a Numerable Event[10] (90.45-90.50)

90.45 ποιέωᵃ: a marker of an agent relation with a numerable event – 'to do, to perform, to practice, to make.' διδάσκων καὶ πορείαν ποιούμενος εἰς Ἱεροσόλυμα 'teaching as he made a journey to Jerusalem' Lk 13.22; οἱ μαθηταὶ Ἰωάννου νηστεύουσιν πυκνὰ καὶ δεήσεις ποιοῦνται 'John's disciples often fast and pray' Lk 5.33; τῷ σῷ ὀνόματι δυνάμεις πολλὰς ἐποιήσαμεν 'in your name we did many

10 In this subdomain agents are not marked by prepositions but by what may be called 'empty verbs,' which are syntactically focal to the clause in question but ⸋ semantically focal, that is to say, the focal event oc- ⸋he form of an accompanying substantive which ⸋gular or plural; hence numerable. Compare, ⸋, the English phrases *he spoke* and *he made a* ⸋*ve three speeches*, in which the verb forms ⸋ are semantically empty and serve primari- ⸋e relation between the subject and the ⸋l substantive *speech*. ⸋d in the translations of various passages ⸋mpty verbs, there is frequently no ⸋ling lexical item representing the ⸋ion. This is because the semantic ⸋mpanying substantive.

miracles' Mt 7.22; πίστει πεποίηκεν τὸ πάσχα 'by faith he performed the Passover' He 11.28.

90.46 ἀποδίδωμιᵈ: a marker of an agent rela-tion with a numerable event, with the prob-able implication of some transfer involved – 'to make, to perform, to do, to give.' οἱ ἄνθρω-ποι ἀποδώσουσιν περὶ αὐτοῦ λόγον ἐν ἡμέρᾳ κρίσεως 'people will have to account for it in the day of judgment' Mt 12.36; καὶ δυνάμει μεγάλῃ ἀπεδίδουν τὸ μαρτύριον οἱ ἀπόστολοι τῆς ἀναστάσεως τοῦ κυρίου Ἰησοῦ 'and with great power the apostles witnessed to the resurrec-tion of the Lord Jesus' Ac 4.33.

90.47 ἐργάζομαιᶜ; κατεργάζομαιᵇ: markers of an agent relation with numerable events, with the probable implication of comprehen-siveness – 'to do, to make, to perform.'
ἐργάζομαιᶜ: ὁ φοβούμενος αὐτὸν καὶ ἐργαζόμενος δικαιοσύνην 'who reveres him and does what is right' Ac 10.35.
κατεργάζομαιᵇ: ἄρσενες ἐν ἄρσεσιν τὴν ἀσχημο-σύνην κατεργαζόμενοι 'men with men doing shameless deeds' Ro 1.27; ἐπὶ πᾶσαν ψυχὴν ἀνθρώπου τοῦ κατεργαζομένου τὸ κακόν 'on everyone who does evil' Ro 2.9.

90.48 λαμβάνωᵏ: a marker of an agent rela-tion with numerable events, with the implica-tion of having assumed some initiative – 'to do, to make.' συμβούλιον δὲ λαβόντες ἠγόρασαν . . . τὸν ἀγρὸν τοῦ κεραμέως 'having consulted they bought . . . a potter's field' Mt 27.7.

90.49 προλαμβάνωᵇ: a marker of an agent relation with numerable events, with the im-plication of some prior or unexpected time factor – 'to do in advance, to make before, to undertake ahead of time.' προέλαβεν μυρίσαι τὸ σῶμά μου 'she anointed my body ahead of time' Mk 14.8.

90.50 ἀφίημιˡ: a marker of an agent relation with numerable events, with the implication of something which proceeds from an agent – 'to produce, to make, to give.' ὁ δὲ Ἰησοῦς ἀφεὶς φωνὴν μεγάλην ἐξέπνευσεν 'Jesus gave a loud cry and died' or 'with a loud cry, Jesus died' Mk 15.37.

L Agent in a Causative Role Marked by Verbs[11] **(90.51-90.55)**

90.51 δίδωμι[h]; ἔχω[h]: markers of a causative relation, with otherwise almost empty semantic content – 'to cause, to bring about, to produce.'

δίδωμι[h]: τοῦ δοῦναι γνῶσιν σωτηρίας τῷ λαῷ αὐτοῦ 'to cause his people to know about deliverance' Lk 1.77.

ἔχω[h]: οὕτως καὶ ἡ πίστις, ἐὰν μὴ ἔχῃ ἔργα 'and so faith, if it does not produce action' or '. . . cause someone to do something' Jas 2.17.

90.52 διεγείρω[b]: a marker of a causative relation, with the implication of a significant change in state – 'to cause.' διεγείρειν ὑμᾶς ἐν ὑπομνήσει 'to cause you to remember' 2 Pe 1.13.

90.53 κινέω[e]: a marker of a causative relation, with the implication of significant activity – 'to cause.' κινοῦντα στάσεις πᾶσιν τοῖς Ἰουδαίοις 'causing riots among all the Jews' Ac 24.5.

90.54 ἀπονέμω: a marker of a causative relation, with the implication of something deserved – 'to cause, to show, to assign to.' ἀπονέμοντες τιμήν, ὡς καὶ συγκληρονόμοις χάριτος ζωῆς 'showing (them) respect, since they received jointly with you the gift of life' 1 Pe 3.7.

90.55 ἐρεθίζω[b]; παροξυσμός[a], οῦ [m]: markers of a causative relation, with the implication of stimulating a change in motivation or attitude – 'to cause, encouragement.'

ἐρεθίζω[b]: τὸ ὑμῶν ζῆλος ἠρέθισεν τοὺς πλείονας 'your eagerness has caused most of them (to want to help)' 2 Cor 9.2.[12] The relevant action

in 2 Cor 9.2b comes from the immediately preceding statements in 2 Cor 9.1-2a.

παροξυσμός[a]: καὶ κατανοῶμεν ἀλλήλους εἰς παροξυσμὸν ἀγάπης καὶ καλῶν ἔργων 'and let us be concerned with one another in order to encourage love and good works' or '. . . to cause people to love and to do good' He 10.24.[12]

M Experiencer[13] **(90.56-90.84)**

90.56 ἐν[m]: a marker of an experiencer of an event – 'in relation to, with respect to, to.'[14] ἐποίησαν ἐν αὐτῷ ὅσα ἠθέλησαν 'they did to him as they pleased' Mt 17.12; καλὸν ἔργον ἠργάσατο ἐν ἐμοί 'she has done a fine thing to me' Mk 14.6; πᾶς οὖν ὅστις ὁμολογήσει ἐν ἐμοὶ ἔμπροσθεν τῶν ἀνθρώπων 'therefore everyone who confesses me before people' Mt 10.32; οὐκ ἔγραφα δὲ ταῦτα ἵνα οὕτως γένηται ἐν ἐμοί 'I have not written these things in order that this might happen to me' 1 Cor 9.15; ἀποκαλύψαι τὸν υἱὸν αὐτοῦ ἐν ἐμοί 'to reveal his Son to me' Ga 1.16. It is also possible to interpret the relation expressed by ἐν in Ga 1.16 as indicating agent or instrument for example, 'to reveal his Son by me' or '. . . through my life' (compare ἐν as an expression of agent in

its more common meaning (see 88.168). But in 2 Cor 9.2 it may also represent an instance in which the original meaning of a term has been largely lost or at least reduced to primarily a marker of causative relation. It appears likely that παροξυσμός in He 10.24 has also been largely reduced to a marker of a causative relation, in other words, 'to cause people to love and to do good,' but since in this instance there seems to be some focus upon the psychological factors involved, one may translate παροξυσμός as 'to encourage'.

13 The experiencer of an event is most commonly marked morphologically by a passive form of a verb or by a so-called 'object case form' (principally accusative). Experiencers may also be marked lexically in two principal ways: (1) by certain prepositions such as ἐν, ἐπί, πρός, εἰς, μετά, and (2) by a number of event words (usually verbs), some of which may have lost most of their so-called literal meaning and thus serve primarily as markers of case and a number which serve not only to mark case but also contribute certain supplementary features of meaning.

14 As will be noted in a number of instances markers of experiencer relations, there may be no l[·] item in a translation which specifically correspo[·] such a marker.

---

11 In this subdomain the event terms (usually verbs) which mark a causative role may retain some significant semantic components of their more or less literal meanings, but their primary function in marking case is to indicate a causative relation between the agent and an event or state.

12 In the case of 2 Cor 9.2 it is difficult to know precisely how much meaning to attach to ἐρεθίζω in the sense of 'to encourage' or 'to motivate.' It is possible that ἐρεθίζω retains in this context a considerable amount of

90.6 and instrument in 90.10), or even means (ἐν ἐμοί referring to his behavior) as in 89.76.

90.57 ἐπί[h]: a marker of the experiencer, often with the implication of an action by a superior force or agency – 'to, at, on.' προσέχετε ἑαυτοῖς ἐπὶ τοῖς ἀνθρώποις τούτοις τί μέλλετε πράσσειν 'be careful what you are about to do to these men' Ac 5.35; ἐθεώρουν τὰ σημεῖα ἃ ἐποίει ἐπὶ τῶν ἀσθενούντων 'they had seen the miracles which he did to those who were sick' Jn 6.2; ὀνομάζειν ἐπὶ τοὺς ἔχοντας τὰ πνεύματα τὰ πονηρὰ τὸ ὄνομα τοῦ κυρίου Ἰησοῦ 'to pronounce the name of the Lord Jesus on those possessed of evil spirits' Ac 19.13; ἦλθεν δὲ λιμὸς ἐφ' ὅλην τὴν Αἴγυπτον 'a famine came on all Egypt' Ac 7.11.

90.58 πρός[e]: a marker of an experiencer of an event, with the implication that the participant may then be in some dyadic relation – 'with, to.' τῆς διαθήκης ἧς διέθετο ὁ θεὸς πρὸς τοὺς πατέρας ὑμῶν 'the covenant which God made with your ancestors' Ac 3.25; ἐργαζώμεθα τὸ ἀγαθὸν πρὸς πάντας 'we should do good to everyone' Ga 6.10.

90.59 εἰς[i]: a marker of an involved experiencer – 'to, toward, for.' τὸ κήρυγμα Ἰησοῦ Χριστοῦ . . . εἰς πάντα τὰ ἔθνη γνωρισθέντος 'the proclamation about Jesus Christ . . . has been made known to all nations' Ro 16.25-26; συνίστησιν δὲ τὴν ἑαυτοῦ ἀγάπην εἰς ἡμᾶς ὁ θεός 'but God demonstrates his love toward us' Ro 5.8; τὸ φρόνημα τῆς σαρκὸς ἔχθρα εἰς θεόν 'the human way of thinking is hostile to God' Ro 8.7; ἐραυνῶντες εἰς τίνα ἢ ποῖον καιρόν 'trying to find out whom it would be and at what time (he would come)' 1 Pe 1.11. It is possible to translate 1 Pe 1.11 as 'trying to find out when the time would be ˬˬ how it would come' by interpreting εἰς in ˬˬ11 as εἰς[i] (90.23) and ποῖον as ποῖος[b]

ˬˬ ˬˬ[e]: a marker of the experiencer of ˬˬith the added implication of association, to.' ἡ χάρις τοῦ κυρίου Ἰησοῦ ˬˬgrace of our Lord Jesus be with ˬˬ3; ἔσται μεθ' ἡμῶν χάρις ἔλεος ˬˬ πατρός, καὶ παρὰ Ἰησοῦ

Χριστοῦ τοῦ υἱοῦ τοῦ πατρός 'may God the Father and Jesus Christ his Son grant us grace, mercy, and peace' 2 Jn 3.[15]

90.61 τυγχάνω; ἐπιτυγχάνω[b]: to experience some happening (generally neutral in connotation) – 'to experience, to have happen to.'

τυγχάνω: πολλῆς εἰρήνης τυγχάνοντες διὰ σοῦ 'experiencing much peace through you' Ac 24.2; ἵνα καὶ αὐτοὶ σωτηρίας τύχωσιν τῆς ἐν Χριστῷ Ἰησοῦ 'in order that even these might experience the salvation which is through Jesus Christ' 2 Tm 2.10; ἵνα κρείττονος ἀναστάσεως τύχωσιν 'so that they may experience a better resurrection' He 11.35; δυνάμεις τε οὐ τὰς τυχούσας 'unusual miracles' (literally 'miracles not experienced') Ac 19.11.

ἐπιτυγχάνω[b]: ὃ ἐπιζητεῖ Ἰσραήλ, τοῦτο οὐκ ἐπέτυχεν, ἡ δὲ ἐκλογὴ ἐπέτυχεν 'what the people of Israel sought, this they did not experience, but the chosen ones did experience it' Ro 11.7. For another interpretation of ἐπιτυγχάνω in Ro 11.7, see 57.60.

90.62 κατατίθεμαι: to experience, with the implication of something having been bestowed upon – 'to gain, to obtain, to experience.' θέλων τε χάριτα καταθέσθαι τοῖς Ἰουδαίοις 'and wanting to gain favor with the Jews' Ac 24.27. In some languages it may be more natural to translate as 'and wanting the Jews to show him goodwill' or 'and hoping that the Jews would like him.'

90.63 λαμβάνω[h]; ἀπολαμβάνω[e]; ἐπιλαμβάνομαι[f]; μεταλαμβάνω[b]: to experience some event or state, often with the implication of something negatively valued – 'to undergo, to experience.'[16]

---

15 In 2 Jn 3 χάρις, ἔλεος, and εἰρήνη refer to the events which are experienced by ἡμῶν.

16 There are no doubt certain subtle distinctions of meaning in this series of related expressions in 90.63, but it is difficult to determine the precise distinctions on the basis of existing contexts.

As in the case of a number of verbs which mark an experiencer relation, an equivalent translation consists simply of a passive form of a verb related to the noun complement. For example, in the case of Jn 7.23, one might very well translate 'if a person is circumcised on the Sabbath.'

λαμβάνω[h]: εἰ περιτομὴν λαμβάνει ἄνθρωπος ἐν σαββάτῳ 'if a person undergoes circumcision on the Sabbath' Jn 7.23; διὰ τοῦτο λήμφεσθε περισσότερον κρίμα 'on account of this you will be judged more severely' Mt 23.14 (apparatus); δι' οὗ νῦν τὴν καταλλαγὴν ἐλάβομεν 'through whom we now have received reconciliation' Ro 5.11; ἕτεροι δὲ ἐμπαιγμῶν καὶ μαστίγων πεῖραν ἔλαβον 'some experienced mocking and whipping' He 11.36.[17]

ἀπολαμβάνω[c]: ἄξια γὰρ ὧν ἐπράξαμεν ἀπολαμβάνομεν 'for we are experiencing what we deserve as the result of what we did' Lk 23.41; τὴν ἀντιμισθίαν ἣν ἔδει τῆς πλάνης αὐτῶν ἐν ἑαυτοῖς ἀπολαμβάνοντες 'receiving punishment which they deserve for their wrongdoing' Ro 1.27.

ἐπιλαμβάνομαι[f]: ἐπιλαβοῦ τῆς αἰωνίου ζωῆς 'experience eternal life' 1 Tm 6.12. In this expression in 1 Tm 6.12, ἐπιλαβοῦ no doubt also suggests some activity associated with the state of eternal life.

μεταλαμβάνω[b]: γῆ . . . μεταλαμβάνει εὐλογίας ἀπὸ τοῦ θεοῦ 'the earth . . . experiences blessings from God' He 6.7.

90.64 φέρω[h]: to experience an event or state which may be burdensome or difficult – 'to experience, to bear up under, to undergo.' τὸν ὀνειδισμὸν αὐτοῦ φέροντες 'experiencing his shame' or '. . . the shame which he bore' He 13.13.

90.65 ἔχω[f]; συνέχομαι[a]: to experience a state or condition, generally involving duration – 'to experience, to have.'
ἔχω[f]: ταῦτα λελάληκα ὑμῖν ἵνα ἐν ἐμοὶ εἰρήνην ἔχητε 'I have told you these things so that you might experience peace in me' Jn 16.33; ἵνα αὐτοῦ ἅψωνται ὅσοι εἶχον μάστιγας 'in order that as many as had diseases might touch him' Mk 3.10.
συνέχομαι[a]: προσήνεγκαν αὐτῷ πάντας τοὺς κακῶς ἔχοντας 'they brought to him all those who were sick' Mt 4.24; ἐγένετο δὲ τὸν πατέρα τοῦ Ποπλίου πυρετοῖς καὶ δυσεντερίῳ συνεχό-

μενον κατακεῖσθαι 'Publius's father was in bed, sick with fever and dysentery' Ac 28.8.

90.66 πάσχω[b]: to undergo an experience, usually difficult, and normally with the implication of physical or psychological suffering – 'to experience, to suffer.' μηδὲν φοβοῦ ἃ μέλλεις πάσχειν 'fear none of those things which you are going to experience' or '. . . to suffer' Re 2.10; τοσαῦτα ἐπάθετε εἰκῇ 'you experience so many things in vain' Ga 3.4.

The first statement in Ga 3.4 is generally interpreted as referring to the valuable experiences which the Galatians had in receiving the Spirit on the basis of hearing and believing. Some scholars, however, understand πάσχω in Ga 3.4 as referring to difficult experiences resulting from those who opposed this new faith in Jesus Christ.

90.67 ἀπέχω[d]: to experience an event to the limit of what one could expect – 'to experience all one deserves.' ὅτι ἀπέχετε τὴν παράκλησιν ὑμῶν 'because you have experienced all the comfort you are going to get' Lk 6.24.

90.68 ὑπέχω: to experience something to which a person is subjected – 'to be subjected to, to experience, to undergo, to suffer.' πρόκεινται δεῖγμα πυρὸς αἰωνίου δίκην ὑπέχουσαι 'they exist as an example by being subjected to the punishment of eternal fire' Ju 7.

90.69 περιέχω[b]: (a figurative extension of meaning of περιέχω 'to surround,' not occurring in the NT) to experience an emotion or mood in an overwhelming manner – 'to experience, to be seized by, to have happen to.' θάμβος γὰρ περιέσχεν αὐτόν 'for he was seized with amazement' Lk 5.9.[18]

90.70 εἰσέρχομαι[d]; εὑρίσκω[d]: to begin to experience an event or state – 'to begin to

---

17 In He 11.36 πεῖραν 'trial' is semantically redundant in that ἐμπαιγμῶν and μαστίγων contain by implication the semantic components of πεῖραν. See Domain 68, footnote 7.

18 The expression θάμβος γὰρ περιέσχεν αὐτόν in Lk 5.9 is a clear example of a syntactic structure being formally the converse of the semantic structure. One may say 'amazement seized him,' but clearly it is the person who experiences the amazement.

experience, to come into an experience, to attain.'

εἰσέρχομαι[d]: προσεύχεσθε μὴ εἰσελθεῖν εἰς πειρασμόν 'pray that you will not begin to experience temptation' or '. . . trial' Lk 22.40; καλόν ἐστίν σε κυλλὸν εἰσελθεῖν εἰς τὴν ζωὴν ἢ τὰς δύο χεῖρας ἔχοντα ἀπελθεῖν εἰς τὴν γέενναν 'it is better for you to come to experience (true) life with one hand than to keep two hands and end up in Gehenna' Mk 9.43.

εὑρίσκω[d]: εὑρήσετε ἀνάπαυσιν ταῖς ψυχαῖς ὑμῶν 'you will begin to experience rest for yourselves' Mt 11.29; αἰωνίαν λύτρωσιν εὑράμενος 'he attained eternal salvation' or '. . . deliverance' He 9.12; ὃς εὗρεν χάριν ἐνώπιον τοῦ θεοῦ 'who attained favor in the sight of God' or 'on whom God looked with favor' Ac 7.46.

90.71 πίπτω[k]; περιπίπτω[c]; ἐμπίπτω[b]: to experience somewhat suddenly that which is difficult or bad – 'to come to experience, to experience, to encounter, to be beset by.'

πίπτω[k]: ἵνα μὴ ὑπὸ κρίσιν πέσητε 'in order that you might not experience condemnation' Jas 5.12.

περιπίπτω[c]: πᾶσαν χαρὰν ἡγήσασθε . . . ὅταν πειρασμοῖς περιπέσητε ποικίλοις 'consider yourselves fortunate . . . when you experience all kinds of trials' Jas 1.2.

ἐμπίπτω[b]: τοῦ ἐμπεσόντος εἰς τοὺς λῃστάς 'of the one who is beset by robbers' or 'who suddenly found himself attacked by robbers' Lk 10.36; ἵνα μὴ τυφωθεὶς εἰς κρίμα ἐμπέσῃ τοῦ διαβόλου 'in order that he may not be puffed up and thus experience the condemnation meted out to the Devil' 1 Tm 3.6.

90.72 ἐκπίπτω[f]: to no longer experience a state or condition – 'to be outside of, to experience no longer.' τῆς χάριτος ἐξεπέσατε 'you no longer experienced (God's) grace' Ga 5.4. For another interpretation of ἐκπίπτω in Ga 5.4, see 34.26.

90.73 περιπείρω: to experience something which is adverse and severe – 'to undergo, to experience.' ἑαυτοὺς περιέπειραν ὀδύναις πολλαῖς 'they have caused themselves to experience severe grief' 1 Tm 6.10.

90.74 περιποίησις[a], εως f: the experience of an event or state which has been acquired –

'experience, to experience.' ἀλλὰ εἰς περιποίησιν σωτηρίας 'but for the purpose of experiencing salvation' 1 Th 5.9. For another interpretation of περιποίησις in 1 Th 5.9, see 57.62.

90.75 ἀναδέχομαι[b]: to experience something as the recipient of an event – 'to experience, to receive.' ὁ τὰς ἐπαγγελίας ἀναδεξάμενος 'the one who had received the promises' He 11.17.[19]

90.76 πράσσω[c]: to experience events and to also engage in them – 'to experience, to fare.' ἵνα δὲ εἰδῆτε καὶ ὑμεῖς τὰ κατ᾽ ἐμέ, τί πράσσω 'in order that you also may have news concerning me as to how I am faring' or '. . . as to how I am getting along' or '. . . as to how I am making out' Eph 6.21.[20]

90.77 τίνω: to experience something bad, often in retribution for some wrongdoing – 'to suffer, to experience retribution.' οἵτινες δίκην τίσουσιν ὄλεθρον αἰώνιον 'they will receive the punishment of being destroyed forever' 2 Th 1.9.

90.78 γεύομαι[c]: (a figurative extension of meaning of γεύομαι[a] 'to taste,' 24.72) to experience, probably focusing on personal involvement – 'to experience.' εἰσίν τινες τῶν ὧδε ἑστώτων οἵτινες οὐ μὴ γεύσωνται θανάτου 'there are some here who will not experience death' Mt 16.28; γευσαμένους τε τῆς δωρεᾶς τῆς ἐπουρανίου 'they have experienced the heavenly gifts' He 6.4.

90.79 ὁράω[e] (a figurative extension of meaning of ὁράω[a] 'to see,' 24.1); θεωρέω[c] (a figurative extension of meaning of θεωρέω[a] 'to

19 Though one may render ἀναδέχομαι in He 11.17 as 'to receive,' in reality the receiver is simply the individual who experiences either the event of promising or the content of the promises as expressed through subsequent events.

20 This meaning of πράσσω is particularly complex because it certainly is not restricted merely to what one is actually overtly engaged in doing. At the same time one must recognize that the meaning is not merely to undergo experiences. It is this particularly complex aspect of the meaning of πράσσω which is perhaps best reflected in 'how I am faring' or 'how I am making out.'

observe,' 24.14): to experience an event or state, normally in negative expressions indicating what one will not experience – 'to experience, to undergo.'

ὁράω^e: ὁ δὲ ἀπειθῶν τῷ υἱῷ οὐκ ὄψεται ζωήν 'one who does not obey the Son will not experience life' Jn 3.36; πίστει Ἐνὼχ μετετέθη τοῦ μὴ ἰδεῖν θάνατον 'it was faith that kept Enoch from experiencing death' He 11.5.

θεωρέω^c: ἐάν τις τὸν ἐμὸν λόγον τηρήσῃ, θάνατον οὐ μὴ θεωρήσῃ εἰς τὸν αἰῶνα 'if anyone obeys my word, he will never experience death' Jn 8.51.

90.80 βαστάζω^e: to undergo a grievous, difficult experience – 'to undergo, to suffer.' ὁ δὲ ταράσσων ὑμᾶς βαστάσει τὸ κρίμα 'the one who is upsetting you will suffer condemnation' Ga 5.10.

90.81 ἐμπλέκομαι: (a figurative extension of meaning of ἐμπλέκομαι 'to become entangled,' not occurring in the NT) to become so involved in some activity as to experience severe restrictions as to what one can do – 'to become involved.' οὐδεὶς στρατευόμενος ἐμπλέκεται ταῖς τοῦ βίου πραγματείαις 'no one who is a soldier becomes involved in the affairs of civilian life' 2 Tm 2.4.[21]

90.82 ἐκχέομαι^c: (a figurative extension of meaning of ἐκχέομαι^a 'to flow out,' 14.18) to be involved in experiencing something in an abundant manner – 'to fully experience, to become fully involved.' τῇ πλάνῃ τοῦ Βαλαὰμ μισθοῦ ἐξεχύθησαν 'they became fully involved in Balaam's error for pay' or 'they have plunged into Balaam's error for the sake of money' Jd 11.

90.83 ἔχω μέρος ἐν: (an idiom, literally 'to have a part in') to experience along with others – 'to experience together with, to share

in experiencing.' ὁ ἔχων μέρος ἐν τῇ ἀναστάσει τῇ πρώτῃ 'one who experiences along with others the first resurrection' Re 20.6.

90.84 βαστάζω στίγματα: (an idiom, literally 'to bear marks') to undergo experiences which mark one as the slave of some master – 'to bear the marks of a slave, to experience being the slave of.' ἐγὼ γὰρ τὰ στίγματα τοῦ Ἰησοῦ ἐν τῷ σώματί μου βαστάζω 'for I bear in my body marks which indicate I belong to Jesus' or '. . . that I am the slave of Jesus' Ga 6.17.[22] See also 8.55 and 33.481.

N To Cause to Experience (90.85–90.97)

90.85 λαμβάνωⁱ: to cause to experience, normally implying something grievous – 'to make experience.' καὶ οἱ ὑπηρέται ῥαπίσμασιν αὐτὸν ἔλαβον 'and the guards slapped him' (literally 'made him experience slapping') Mk 14.65. It is, of course, possible to understand λαμβάνω in Mk 14.65 in a more or less literal sense (see 18.1) and thus to translate this expression as 'the guards took him and slapped him.'

90.86 τίθημι^g: to cause someone to experience, with the implication of subjecting a person to something – 'to make experience, to subject to.' οὐκ ἔθετο ἡμᾶς ὁ θεὸς εἰς ὀργήν 'God did not subject us to (suffering) his anger' 1 Th 5.9.

90.87 ἐπιτίθημι^c: to subject someone to a particular experience, normally by the use of force – 'to subject to.' πληγὰς ἐπιθέντες ἀπῆλθον ἀφέντες ἡμιθανῆ 'having beaten him, they went away, leaving him half dead' Lk 10.30; πολλάς τε ἐπιθέντες αὐτοῖς πληγὰς ἔβαλον εἰς φυλακήν 'having beaten them thoroughly, they threw them into prison' Ac 16.23; ἐπιθήσει ὁ θεὸς ἐπ' αὐτὸν τὰς πληγὰς τὰς

---

21 As in the case of πράσσω^d (90.76 and footnote 20), ἐμπλέκομαι in 2 Tm 2.4 involves both action and experiencing. One may say, therefore, that ἐμπλέκομαι in such a context is semantically complex in that it really belongs to two different semantic domains. Here, however, the condition of the soldier seems to be more in focus than his activity, and for that reason ἐμπλέκομαι is classified in this subdomain.

22 It is difficult to know the extent to which βαστάζω στίγματα should be regarded as an idiom. It is possible to understand this expression to mean that Paul had the scars from wounds which were similar to those of Jesus, but it seems far better to understand this in a more figurative sense, despite the fact that one cannot determine precisely the extent to which such a phrase has become a standardized idiom.

γεγραμμένας ἐν τῷ βιβλίῳ τούτῳ 'God will subject him to the plagues described in this book' Re 22.18. In Re 22.18, there is obviously a play on two different meanings of ἐπιτίθημι, 'to add to' and 'to subject to.' In the preceding clause ἐάν τις ἐπιθῇ ἐπ' αὐτά, the meaning is clearly 'if anyone adds to these' (see ἐπιτίθημι[b], 59.72), but in the second clause there is both the addition as well as the subjection of a person to punishment.

90.88 πέμπω[d]: to cause someone to experience an event or state from outside the area of normal influences – 'to cause to experience, to send upon.' καὶ διὰ τοῦτο πέμπει αὐτοῖς ὁ θεὸς ἐνέργειαν πλάνης 'and on account of this, God causes them to experience a deceptive power' or '. . . sends upon them a powerful deception' or '. . . a power that will deceive' 2 Th 2.11.

90.89 ἐκχέω[d]: (a figurative extension of meaning of ἐκχέω[a] 'to pour out,' 47.4) to cause someone to experience something in an abundant or full manner – 'to cause to fully experience.' ὅτι ἡ ἀγάπη τοῦ θεοῦ ἐκκέχυται ἐν ταῖς καρδίαις ἡμῶν 'because our hearts have been made to fully experience the love of God' (literally 'because the love of God has been poured out into our hearts') Ro 5.5.

90.90 δίδωμι[i]: to cause people to undergo some experience, with the probable implication of something which is in retribution for something done – 'to cause, to make experience.' διδόντος ἐκδίκησιν τοῖς μὴ εἰδόσιν θεόν 'to punish those who ignore God' 2 Th 1.8.

90.91 παρέχω[c]: to cause someone to experience something, with the possible implication of a duration – 'to cause to, to cause to experience, to give.' κόπους μοι μηδεὶς παρεχέτω 'let no one give me trouble' or '. . . cause me trouble' Ga 6.17. See also 13.127.

90.92 κομίζω[b]: to cause someone to experience something on the basis of what that person has already done – 'to cause to experience in return, to cause to suffer for, to cause to experience in proportion to, to be repaid for.' ὁ γὰρ ἀδικῶν κομίσεται ὃ ἠδίκησεν 'for the one who has done wrong will be caused to suffer for what he has done' Col 3.25; ἵνα κομίσηται ἕκαστος τὰ διὰ τοῦ σώματος πρὸς ἃ ἔπραξεν 'in order that each one may be repaid in proportion to those things which he has done in his bodily life' 2 Cor 5.10.

90.93 εἰσφέρω[b]: to cause someone to enter into a particular event or state – 'to cause to, to bring in to, to lead to.' καὶ μὴ εἰσενέγκῃς ἡμᾶς εἰς πειρασμόν 'and do not lead us to trial' or 'do not cause us to be tested' Mt 6.13.

90.94 ἐπιφέρω: to cause someone to experience something, with the implication of imposed authority – 'to bring upon, to impose upon.' μὴ ἄδικος ὁ θεὸς ὁ ἐπιφέρων τὴν ὀργήν; 'God doesn't do wrong, does he, when he punishes us?' or '. . . when he causes us to experience his anger?' Ro 3.5.

90.95 βυθίζω[b]: (a figurative extension of meaning of βυθίζω[a] 'to cause to sink,' 15.115) to cause someone to experience serious consequences – 'to cause, to bring upon, to pull down to.' αἵτινες βυθίζουσιν τοὺς ἀνθρώπους εἰς ὄλεθρον καὶ ἀπώλειαν 'which cause people ruin and destruction' 1 Tm 6.9.

90.96 αἴρω ἀπό: (an idiom, literally 'to take from') to cause someone to no longer experience something – 'to take away from, to remove from.' ἀρθήσεται ἀφ' ὑμῶν ἡ βασιλεία τοῦ θεοῦ 'the kingdom of God will be taken from you' Mt 21.43.

90.97 παραφέρω τὸ ποτήριον . . . ἀπό: (an idiom, literally 'to take the cup . . . from') to cause someone to not undergo some trying experience – 'to cause someone not to experience, to take the cup from.' παρένεγκε τὸ ποτήριον τοῦτο ἀπ' ἐμοῦ 'take this cup of suffering from me' or 'do not make me undergo this suffering' Mk 14.36.

91 Discourse Markers [1]

Outline of Subdomains

A   Markers of Transition (91.1-91.5)
B   Markers of Emphasis (91.6-91.12)
C   Prompters of Attention (91.13)
D   Marker of Direct Address (91.14)
E   Markers of Identificational and Explanatory Clauses (Epexegetical) (91.15)

A Markers of Transition [2] (91.1-91.5)

91.1 γάρ[b]: a marker of a new sentence, but often best left untranslated or reflected in the use of 'and' or the conjunctive adverb 'then.' ὁ δὲ ἔφη, Τί γὰρ κακὸν ἐποίησεν; 'and he said, What bad thing has he done?' Mt 27.23. It is possible that in Mt 27.23 the conjunction γάρ reflects Pilate's attempt to reason with the crowd demanding Jesus' crucifixion, but γάρ serves primarily to highlight the significance of the question rather than to provide a reason.

91.2 ἀλλά[c]: a marker of transition, with a slightly adversative implication in some contexts, often best left untranslated – 'and, yet.' οὕτως δὲ φιλοτιμούμενον εὐαγγελίζεσθαι οὐχ ὅπου ὠνομάσθη Χριστός, ἵνα μὴ ἐπ' ἀλλότριον θεμέλιον οἰκοδομῶ, ἀλλὰ καθὼς γέγραπται 'my ambition has always been to proclaim the good news in places where Christ has not been heard of, so as not to build on a foundation laid by someone else. As the Scripture says, . . .' or '. . . else, but as the Scripture says, . . .' Ro 15.20-21. In Ro 15.21 there is certainly no adversative value in the conjunction ἀλλά; if anything, it would only mark

some underlying reason, but again it seems best to leave ἀλλά untranslated and to regard it simply as a transitional marker.

91.3 μέν[a]: a marker of linkage in discourse – 'and, so' but often left untranslated. τὰ μὲν σημεῖα τοῦ ἀποστόλου κατειργάσθη ἐν ὑμῖν ἐν πάσῃ ὑπομονῇ 'the miracles showing that I am an apostle were performed among you with complete patience' 2 Cor 12.12.

91.4 νυνὶ δέ: a marker of a summary statement – 'and so, accordingly, meanwhile' or left untranslated. νυνὶ δὲ μένει πίστις, ἐλπίς, ἀγάπη 'now remain faith, hope, and love' 1 Cor 13.13.

91.5 γίνομαι[j]: a marker of new information, either concerning participants in an episode or concerning the episode itself (occurring normally in the formulas ἐγένετο δέ or καὶ ἐγένετο) – 'there was, and it happened that' or, as often, left untranslated. ἐγένετο ἄνθρωπος ἀπεσταλμένος παρὰ θεοῦ 'there was a man sent from God' Jn 1.6; ἐγένετο δὲ τῇ ἑξῆς ἡμέρᾳ κατελθόντων αὐτῶν ἀπὸ τοῦ ὄρους 'and it happened on the sixth day as they were going down from the mountain' Lk 9.37. [3]

B Markers of Emphasis (91.6-91.12)

91.6 μέν[b]; **γέ**; **δή**: markers of relatively weak emphasis – 'then, indeed' or frequently not translated but possibly reflected in the word order.
μέν[b]: ὡς οὖν ἤκουσεν ὅτι ἀσθενεῖ, τότε μὲν ἔμεινεν ἐν ᾧ ἦν τόπῳ δύο ἡμέρας 'when he received news that (Lazarus) was sick, he then stayed where he was for two more days' Jn 11.6; ἤδη μὲν οὖν ὅλως ἥττημα ὑμῖν ἐστιν 'indeed, then, there is complete failure on your

---

1 In certain respects discourse markers parallel the markers of coordinate and subordinate relations (Domain 89). This is particularly true of the markers of transition, but the discourse markers in this domain have lost most or all of their coordinating or subordinating features.
2 In a number of contexts, the following markers of transition are perhaps best left untranslated, since they serve more to indicate merely a new sentence or a new paragraph rather than to carry significant features of coordinate or subordinate relations.

3 ἐγένετο δέ and καὶ ἐγένετο occur frequently in the Gospels, especially in Luke, as markers of transition, and in a number of languages they are equivalent to a new paragraph. Note the following passages especially: Lk 5.1, 12, 17; 6.1, 6, 12; 7.11; 8.1, 22; 9.18, 28, 37, 51.

part' or 'therefore there is indeed a complete lack on your part' 1 Cor 6.7.

γέ: διά γε τὸ παρέχειν μοι κόπον τὴν χήραν ταύτην 'because of all the trouble this woman is giving me' Lk 18.5.

δή: ἀφορίσατε δή μοι τὸν Βαρναβᾶν καὶ Σαῦλον εἰς τὸ ἔργον ὃ προσκέκλημαι αὐτούς 'set apart for me, then, Barnabas and Saul to do the work for which I have called them' Ac 13.2.

91.7 δήπου; οὖν[b]: markers of somewhat greater emphasis (in comparison with μέν[b], γέ, and δή, 91.6) – 'surely, indeed, then.'

δήπου: οὐ γὰρ δήπου ἀγγέλων ἐπιλαμβάνεται 'for it is surely not angels that he helps' He 2.16.

οὖν[b]: τί οὖν ἐστιν Ἀπολλῶς; 'who, then, is Apollos?' 1 Cor 3.5.

91.8 εἰ μήν; μενοῦν[c]: markers of considerable emphasis (in comparison with δήπου and οὖν[b], 91.7) – 'surely, certainly.'

εἰ μήν: λέγων, Εἰ μὴν εὐλογῶν εὐλογήσω σε καὶ πληθύνων πληθυνῶ σε 'he said, I will certainly bless you with blessings and multiply you abundantly' He 6.14.

μενοῦν[c]: μενοῦν μακάριοι οἱ ἀκούοντες τὸν λόγον τοῦ θεοῦ καὶ φυλάσσοντες 'indeed happy are those who hear the word of God and keep it' or '. . . obey it' Lk 11.28. For other interpretations of μενοῦν in Lk 11.28, see 89.50 and 89.128.

91.9 μήτιγε: a marker of emphasis, involving some degree of contrast and/or comparison – 'how much more.' οὐκ οἴδατε ὅτι ἀγγέλους κρινοῦμεν, μήτιγε βιωτικά; 'you do know, don't you, that we shall judge angels? How much more the things of this life?' 1 Cor 6.3.

91.10 πάντως[b]; **ἰδού**[b]: markers of strong emphasis, indicating complete validation of what is said – 'indeed, certainly, at all, at least, in any event.'

πάντως[b]: ἢ δι' ἡμᾶς πάντως λέγει; 'or did he not indeed mean us?' 1 Cor 9.10.

ἰδού[b]: ἣν ἔδησεν ὁ Σατανᾶς ἰδοὺ δέκα καὶ ὀκτὼ ἔτη 'whom Satan bound indeed for eighteen years' Lk 13.16.

91.11 ἀλλά[d]: a marker of contrastive emphasis – 'certainly, emphatically.' εἰ καὶ πάντες σκανδαλισθήσονται, ἀλλ' οὐκ ἐγώ 'even if all others become offended, I most emphatically will not be' Mk 14.29; εἰ γὰρ σύμφυτοι γεγόναμεν τῷ ὁμοιώματι τοῦ θανάτου αὐτοῦ, ἀλλὰ καὶ τῆς ἀναστάσεως ἐσόμεθα 'for since we have become one with him in dying as he did, we shall certainly in the same way be one with him in being raised to life as he was' Ro 6.5.[4]

91.12 καί[d]: a marker of emphasis, involving surprise and unexpectedness – 'then, indeed, how is it then, yet.' καὶ σὺ ἔρχῃ πρός με; 'how is it then that you come to me?' Mt 3.14; καὶ τίς δύναται σωθῆναι; 'who then can possibly be saved?' Mk 10.26; ἐπεθύμησαν ἰδεῖν ἃ βλέπετε καὶ οὐκ εἶδαν 'they desired to see what you see, yet they didn't see it' Mt 13.17.

C Prompters of Attention (91.13)

91.13 ἰδού[a]; **ἴδε**; **ἄγε**: prompters of attention, which serve also to emphasize the following statement – 'look, listen, pay attention, come now, then.'

ἰδού[a]: ἰδοὺ ἐξῆλθεν ὁ σπείρων σπεῖραι 'listen, there was a man who went out to sow' Mk 4.3.

ἴδε: ἴδε ἐγὼ Παῦλος λέγω ὑμῖν 'listen, I, Paul, tell you' Ga 5.2; ἴδε νῦν ἠκούσατε τὴν βλασφημίαν 'listen, you have just now heard the blasphemy' Mt 26.65.

ἄγε: ἄγε νῦν οἱ λέγοντες 'now, pay attention, you who say' Jas 4.13.

D Marker of Direct Address (91.14)

91.14 ὦ: a marker of direct address (functionally equivalent to the traditional vocative) – 'O' or left untranslated. ὦ ἀνόητοι Γαλάται, τίς ὑμᾶς ἐβάσκανεν; 'O, foolish Galatians, who has bewitched you?' or 'foolish Galatians, who has bewitched you?' or 'you foolish Galatians, who has bewitched you?' Ga 3.1.

---

4 In Ro 6.5 one must reckon with considerable ellipsis in the Greek text.

E   **Markers of Identificational and Explanatory Clauses (Epexegetical)**[5] **(91.15)**

91.15 ὅτι[c]; ἵνα[d]: markers of identificational and explanatory clauses – 'that, namely, that is, namely that.'

ὅτι[c]: αὕτη δέ ἐστιν ἡ κρίσις, ὅτι τὸ φῶς ἐλήλυθεν εἰς τὸν κόσμον καὶ ἠγάπησαν οἱ ἄνθρωποι μᾶλλον τὸ σκότος ἢ τὸ φῶς 'this is the judgment, namely, that the light has come into the

5 Markers of identificational and explanatory clauses (epexegetical) do not enter into the internal syntactic structure of the clauses which they mark.

world and people love the darkness rather than the light' Jn 3.19; αὕτη ἐστὶν ἡ μαρτυρία, ὅτι ζωὴν αἰώνιον ἔδωκεν ἡμῖν ὁ θεός 'this is the witness; namely, that God has given us eternal life' 1 Jn 5.11.

ἵνα[d]: μείζονα ταύτης ἀγάπην οὐδεὶς ἔχει, ἵνα τις τὴν ψυχὴν αὐτοῦ θῇ ὑπὲρ τῶν φίλων αὐτοῦ 'no one has greater love than this; namely, that he gives his life on behalf of his friends' Jn 15.13; συμφέρει γάρ σοι ἵνα ἀπόληται ἓν τῶν μελῶν σου καὶ μὴ ὅλον τὸ σῶμά σου βληθῇ εἰς γέενναν 'it is better for you that you lose one of the parts of your body rather than having your whole body thrown into hell' Mt 5.29.

92 Discourse Referentials[1]

Outline of Subdomains[2]

1 In addition to the referentials included in Domain 92 *Discourse Referentials*, certain others could be added, for example, ὧδε[a] 'here' (83.1) and ἐκεῖ 'there' (83.2), but the semantic features of space are primary. Similarly, ὅσος could be treated as one of the discourse referentials, but it is already subsumed under the domain of *Quantity* (see 59.19) in view of its primary semantic feature. Domain 92 *Discourse Referentials* is restricted to those lexical items in which the primary feature is referential, and hence the domain includes only personal pronouns (first, second and third person), those referentials indicating reflexive, reciprocal, interrogative, relative, and demonstrative relations, and the emphatic adjunct.

2 As will be readily noted in the listing of the subdomains, the pronominal structure of Greek may be regarded as non-orthogonal. This is particularly apparent in the plural reference of reciprocals and reflexives and in the relationship of the relative and demonstrative pronouns for all persons.

A   **Speaker (92.1-92.3)**

92.1 ἐγώ, ἐμοῦ or μου, ἐμοί or μοι, ἐμέ or με: a reference to the speaker (with an added feature of emphasis in the form ἐγώ) – 'I, I indeed.' ἐγὼ καὶ ὁ πατὴρ ἕν ἐσμεν 'the Father and I are one' Jn 10.30; ἐγὼ δὲ λέγω ὑμῖν 'but I tell you' or 'I am the one telling you' Mt 5.22; τίς μου ἥψατο; 'who touched me?' Mk 5.31.

The terminology 'first, second, and third persons' reflects the normal order in Greek in which the so-called first person always occurred first in any listing of participants. The second person would be in the second position, and similarly, the third person would be in a third relative position. To preserve that order in English, however, could imply impoliteness, and it is for that reason that it is preferable to translate Jn 10.30 as 'the Father and I are one.'

92.2 ἐμός, ή, όν: pertaining to a speaker – 'my, mine, of me.' ἡ βασιλεία ἡ ἐμὴ οὐκ ἔστιν ἐκ τοῦ κόσμου τούτου 'my kingdom is not of this world' Jn 18.36; οὐκ ἔστιν ἐμὸν τοῦτο δοῦναι 'it is not mine to give' Mt 20.23.

92.3 ἐμαυτοῦ, ῆς: a reflexive reference to the first person singular within the immediate context – 'myself, me.' οὐδὲ ἐμαυτὸν ἠξίωσα 'I did not consider myself worthy' Lk 7.7; γὰρ ἐγὼ ἄνθρωπός εἰμι ὑπὸ ἐξουσίαν, ἔχων ὑπ' ἐμαυτὸν στρατιώτας 'for I am a man under authority, having soldiers under me' Mt 8.9. For the plural, see 92.25.

B Speaker and Those Associated with the Speaker (exclusive and inclusive)[3] (92.4-92.5)

92.4 ἡμεῖς, ἡμῶν, ἡμῖν, ἡμᾶς: a reference to the speaker or writer and those associated with him or her, either including or excluding the audience (with an added feature of emphasis in the form ἡμεῖς) – 'we, us.' διὰ τί ἡμεῖς καὶ οἱ Φαρισαῖοι νηστεύομεν πολλά 'why is it that we and the Pharisees fast often?' Mt 9.14; εἰπὲ ἡμῖν παρρησία 'tell us openly' Jn 10.24; ἰδοὺ ἡμεῖς ἀφήκαμεν πάντα καὶ ἠκολουθήκαμέν σοι 'look, we have left everything and followed you' Mk 10.28.

92.5 ἡμέτερος, α, ον: pertaining to the speaker or writer and those associated with him or her, either including or excluding the audience – 'our, of us, ours.' εἰς τὴν ἡμετέραν διδασκαλίαν ἐγράφη 'it was written for our instruction' Ro 15.4; κατὰ τὸν ἡμέτερον νόμον ἐβουλήθημεν ἀνελεῖν 'we wished to judge him according to our law' Ac 24.6 (apparatus).

C Receptor, Receptors[4] (92.6-92.10)

92.6 σύ, σοῦ or σου, σοί or σοι, σέ or σε: a reference to a receptor of a message (with an added feature of emphasis in the form σύ) – 'you.' σὺ δὲ ὅταν προσεύχῃ 'but when you pray' Mt 6.6; λέγω σοι 'I am telling you' Lk 12.59.

92.7 ὑμεῖς, ὑμῶν, ὑμῖν, ὑμᾶς: a reference to the receptors of a message, whether oral or

3 The so-called inclusive first person plural includes the audience to which a speaker or writer is addressing a communication. The exclusive first person plural excludes the audience but includes those who are in one way or another associated with the speaker or writer.
4 In speaking of the second person reference, it is general to use terminology such as 'hearer, hearers,' but since such individuals can also constitute an audience to whom a communication is written, we have chosen to use here 'receptor, receptors.'

written (with an added feature of emphasis in the form ὑμεῖς) – 'you, your.' ἡμεῖς μωροὶ . . . ὑμεῖς δὲ φρόνιμοι 'we are foolish . . . but you are wise' 1 Cor 4.10; ἡ πίστις ὑμῶν 'your faith' Ro 1.8.

92.8 σός, σή, σόν: pertaining to a receptor – 'your, of you.' ὁ λόγος ὁ σὸς ἀλήθειά ἐστιν 'your word is truth' Jn 17.17; τὴν δὲ ἐν τῷ σῷ ὀφθαλμῷ δοκὸν οὐ κατανοεῖς 'you do not recognize the beam in your own eye' Mt 7.3.

92.9 ὑμέτερος, α, ον: pertaining to receptors – 'your, yours, of you.' τὸν λόγον . . . τὸν ὑμέτερον 'your . . . teaching' Jn 15.20; τὸ ὑμέτερον ὑστέρημα 'that which is lacking in you' 1 Cor 16.17; ὑμετέρα ἐστὶν ἡ βασιλεία τοῦ θεοῦ 'the kingdom of God is yours' Lk 6.20.

92.10 σεαυτοῦ, ῆς: a reflexive reference to a receptor noted in the immediate context – 'yourself, of you, your.' καὶ νῦν δόξασόν με σύ, πάτερ, παρὰ σεαυτῷ τῇ δόξῃ 'and now, Father, glorify me with your own glory' Jn 17.5; εἰ υἱὸς εἶ τοῦ θεοῦ, βάλε σεαυτὸν κάτω 'if you are the Son of God, cast yourself down' Mt 4.6. For the plural, see 92.25.

D Whom or What Spoken or Written About (92.11-92.25)

92.11 αὐτός[b], ή, ό: a reference to a definite person or persons spoken or written about (with an added feature of emphasis in the nominative forms) – 'he, him, she, her, it, they, them.' αὐτὸς γὰρ σώσει τὸν λαὸν αὐτοῦ ἀπὸ τῶν ἁμαρτιῶν αὐτῶν 'for he will save his people from their sins' Mt 1.21; καὶ οὗτος μὴν ἕκτος ἐστὶν αὐτῇ τῇ καλουμένῃ στείρᾳ 'and this was the sixth month for her who was called barren' Lk 1.36; αὐτῶν τὴν συνείδησιν 'their conscience' 1 Cor 8.12; καὶ κρατήσας τῆς χειρὸς τοῦ παιδίου λέγει αὐτῇ 'and taking the child by the hand, he said to her' Mk 5.41.

92.12 τις[a], τι: a reference to someone or something indefinite, spoken or written about – 'someone, something, anyone, a, anything.' ἐάν τις ὑμῖν εἴπῃ τι 'if anyone says anything to you' Mt 21.3; καὶ ἤλπιζέν τι σημεῖον ἰδεῖν 'and he hoped to see a sign' Lk 23.8.

92.13 τις^b, τι (occurring only in a predicate position): a reference to someone or something of prominence or distinction – 'someone important, something important.' πρὸ γὰρ τούτων τῶν ἡμερῶν ἀνέστη Θευδᾶς, λέγων εἶναί τινα ἑαυτόν 'sometime ago Theudas appeared claiming that he was somebody important' Ac 5.36. For a treatment of τις^b as part of an idiom in Ac 5.36, see 87.49.

92.14 τίς, τί: an interrogative reference to someone or something – 'who? what?' τί ἔτι χρείαν ἔχομεν μαρτύρων; 'what further need do we have of witnesses?' Mk 14.63; τίς ἐστιν ὁ παίσας σε; 'who is it that struck you?' Mt 26.68; τίνα λέγουσιν οἱ ἄνθρωποι εἶναι τὸν υἱὸν τοῦ ἀνθρώπου; 'who do people say the Son of Man is?' Mt 16.13.

92.15 τί: an interrogative reference to reason – 'why? for what reason?' τί καὶ ἡμεῖς κινδυνεύομεν πᾶσαν ὥραν; 'why should we run risks every hour?' or 'why should we continually be in danger?' 1 Cor 15.30. The expression τί ἐμοὶ καὶ σοί (literally 'what for me and you?') in Jn 2.4 is an adage meaning 'for what reason are you saying or doing this to me?' In some languages it may be preferable to translate Jn 2.4 as 'why do you ask me this?' In Mk 1.24 one may translate 'what do you want with us?'

92.16 πῶς: an interrogative reference to means – 'how? by what means?' πῶς σὺ Ἰουδαῖος ὢν παρ' ἐμοῦ πεῖν αἰτεῖς γυναικὸς Σαμαρίτιδος οὔσης; 'how is it that you being a Jew are asking a drink from me, a Samaritan woman?' Jn 4.9; πῶς οὖν ἠνεῴχθησάν σου οἱ ὀφθαλμοί; 'how then were your eyes opened?' or 'how then did you become able to see?' Jn 9.10.

92.17 ὅπως^c: a reference to an indefinite means – 'how, somehow.' ὅπως τε παρέδωκαν αὐτὸν οἱ ἀρχιερεῖς καὶ οἱ ἄρχοντες ἡμῶν εἰς κρίμα θανάτου 'and how your chief priests and rulers handed him over to be condemned to death' Lk 24.20.

92.18 ὅστις, ἥτις, ὅ τι: a reference to an indefinite entity, event, or state – 'whoever, whichever, whatever' (though often translated as 'who, which, or what,' since these pronouns in English are often indefinite in meaning). ὅστις γὰρ ἂν ποιήσῃ τὸ θέλημα τοῦ πατρός μου τοῦ ἐν οὐρανοῖς 'for whoever does the will of my Father who is in heaven' Mt 12.50; οἵτινες ἐθεραπεύοντο ἅπαντες 'who were all healed' Ac 5.16.

92.19 δεῖνα m and f: a reference to an entity which one cannot or does not wish to make explicit (in the NT only a reference to a man) – 'certain, somebody.' ὑπάγετε εἰς τὴν πόλιν πρὸς τὸν δεῖνα καὶ εἴπατε αὐτῷ 'go into the city to a man and say to him' Mt 26.18. Though in many translations δεῖνα is translated as 'certain,' this can give a wrong impression since it would imply that the individual is known to the parties involved or has been identified by the context.

92.20 ἀλλότριος^a, α, ον: a reference to what belongs to someone else – 'belonging to another, belonging to someone else.' εἰ ἐν τῷ ἀλλοτρίῳ πιστοὶ οὐκ ἐγένεσθε 'if you are not faithful in what belongs to someone else' Lk 16.12.

92.21 ἴδιος^c, α, ον: a reference to each one individually – 'individually, separately.' διαιροῦν ἰδίᾳ ἑκάστῳ καθὼς βούλεται 'distributing to each one individually as he wishes' 1 Cor 12.11.

92.22 εἷς^b, μία, ἕν: a reference to a single, indefinite person or thing (sometimes reinforced by the indefinite reference τις^a, 92.12) – 'a, one.' προσελθὼν εἷς γραμματεὺς εἶπεν αὐτῷ 'a teacher of the Law came and said to him' Mt 8.19; ἐπάταξεν εἷς τις ἐξ αὐτῶν τοῦ ἀρχιερέως τὸν δοῦλον 'one of them struck the high priest's slave' Lk 22.50.

92.23 οὐδείς, οὐδεμία, οὐδέν; μηδείς, μηδεμία, μηδέν: a negative reference to an entity, event, or state – 'no one, none, nothing.'
οὐδείς: οὐδεὶς προφήτης δεκτός ἐστιν ἐν τῇ πατρίδι αὐτοῦ 'no prophet is accepted in his own hometown' Lk 4.24; οὐδεὶς δύναται δυσὶ κυρίοις δουλεύειν 'no one can serve two mas-

ters' Mt 6.24; Ἰουδαίους οὐδὲν ἠδίκησα 'I have done no wrong to the Jews' Ac 25.10.

μηδείς: διὰ τὸ μηδεμίαν αἰτίαν θανάτου ὑπάρχειν ἐν ἐμοί 'on account of the fact that I have done nothing worthy of being put to death' Ac 28.18; ἀκούοντες μὲν τῆς φωνῆς μηδένα δὲ θεωροῦντες 'hearing the sound but seeing no one' Ac 9.7; μηδὲν ὠφεληθεῖσα ἀλλὰ μᾶλλον εἰς τὸ χεῖρον ἐλθοῦσα 'not having been helped in any respect but rather became worse' Mk 5.26; ὅρα μηδενὶ εἴπῃς 'see that you tell no one' Mt 8.4; μηδὲν αἴρωσιν εἰς ὁδόν 'take nothing for the journey' Mk 6.8. Though in English one may readily say 'tell no one' or 'take nothing,' in a number of languages the negation must be related to the verb and not to a pronominal object. Accordingly, it may be necessary to translate as 'do not tell anyone' or 'do not take anything.'

92.24 ὁ, ἡ, τό (pl. οἱ, αἱ, τά): a reference to an entity, event, or state, clearly identified by the linguistic or non-linguistic context of the utterance – 'the, he, she, it.'[5] τοῦ γὰρ καὶ γένος ἐσμέν 'for we are also his offspring' Ac 17.28; τὸ γὰρ ἅγιον πνεῦμα διδάξει ὑμᾶς 'for the Holy Spirit will teach you' Lk 12.12; παντὸς ἀκούοντος τὸν λόγον τῆς βασιλείας 'everyone who hears the message about the kingdom' Mt 13.19.

92.25 ἑαυτοῦ, ῆς, οῦ: in the singular, a reflexive reference to a person or thing spoken or written about,[6] and in the plural, a reflexive reference to any and all persons or things involved as subjects of the clause (including first, second and third persons) – 'himself, herself, itself, ourselves, yourselves, themselves.' περιέκρυβεν ἑαυτὴν μῆνας πέντε 'she hid herself for five months' Lk 1.24; ὁ δὲ πλεῖστος ὄχλος ἔστρωσαν ἑαυτῶν τὰ ἱμάτια ἐν τῇ ὁδῷ 'a great crowd of people spread their cloaks on the road' Mt 21.8; ἡμεῖς καὶ αὐτοὶ ἐν ἑαυτοῖς

5 In this semantic analysis, no distinction is made between the articular and the pronominal use of ὁ, ἡ, τό. In the articular construction, ὁ, ἡ, or τό simply occurs together with a substantive, while in the pronominal usage, there is no combined substantive, since the substantive is fully understood from the context.
6 For the first and second person singulars, see 92.3 and 92.10, respectively.

στενάζομεν υἱοθεσίαν ἀπεκδεχόμενοι 'we ourselves groan within ourselves, waiting to be adopted as sons' Ro 8.23; ἀρχόμεθα πάλιν ἑαυτοὺς συνιστάνειν; 'are we beginning again to commend ourselves?' 2 Cor 3.1; ὥστε μαρτυρεῖτε ἑαυτοῖς ὅτι υἱοί ἐστε τῶν φονευσάντων τοὺς προφήτας 'so that you testify concerning yourselves that you are the sons of those who murdered the prophets' Mt 23.31; προσέχετε ἑαυτοῖς ἐπὶ τοῖς ἀνθρώποις τούτοις τί μέλλετε πράσσειν 'take care as to what you are about to do to these men' Ac 5.35.

E Reciprocal Reference (92.26)

92.26 ἀλλήλων, οις, ους; ἑαυτῶν: a reciprocal reference between entities – 'each other, one another.'

ἀλλήλων: καθ' εἷς ἀλλήλων μέλη 'individually members of one another' Ro 12.5; μὴ καταλαλεῖτε ἀλλήλων 'do not slander one another' Jas 4.11; τοῦτο δέ ἐστιν συμπαρακληθῆναι ἐν ὑμῖν διὰ τῆς ἐν ἀλλήλοις πίστεως ὑμῶν τε καὶ ἐμοῦ 'what I mean is that both you and I will be encouraged while among you, you by my faith and I by yours' Ro 1.12; ἐφοβήθησαν φόβον μέγαν, καὶ ἔλεγον πρὸς ἀλλήλους 'they became very much afraid and said to one another' Mk 4.41.

ἑαυτῶν: οἱ δὲ περισσῶς ἐξεπλήσσοντο λέγοντες πρὸς ἑαυτούς 'and they were completely astonished, saying to one another' Mk 10.26; χαριζόμενοι ἑαυτοῖς 'forgiving one another' Eph 4.32.

F Relative Reference (92.27-92.28)

92.27 ὅς, ἥ, ὅ: a relative reference to any entity, event, or state, either occurring overtly in the immediate context or clearly implied in the discourse or setting – 'who, which, what, the one who, that which.' ὁ ἀστὴρ ὃν εἶδον 'the star which they saw' Mt 2.9; τίς δέ ἐστιν οὗτος περὶ οὗ ἀκούω τοιαῦτα; 'and who is this concerning whom I heard these things?' Lk 9.9; ὃς οὐ λαμβάνει τὸν σταυρὸν αὐτοῦ καὶ ἀκολουθεῖ ὀπίσω μου, οὐκ ἔστιν μου ἄξιος 'the one who does not take up his cross and follow behind me is not worthy of me' Mt 10.38; ἀλλ' ἰδοὺ ἔρχεται μετ' ἐμὲ οὗ οὐκ εἰμὶ ἄξιος τὸ ὑπόδημα τῶν ποδῶν λῦσαι 'but behold, there is coming after me one whose shoelaces I am not worthy to untie' Ac 13.25.

92.28 οὖᵇ; ὅπουᵇ; ποῦᵇ: a relative reference to a set of circumstances – 'where, in which.'

οὖᵇ: οὗ δὲ οὐκ ἔστιν νόμος, οὐδὲ παράβασις 'where there is no law, there is no transgression' Ro 4.15.

ὅπουᵇ: ὅπου οὐκ ἔνι Ἕλλην καὶ Ἰουδαῖος 'where there is neither Greek nor Jew' or 'in which there is neither Greek nor Jew' Col 3.11.

ποῦᵇ (interrogative): ποῦ οὖν ἡ καύχησις; 'where, then, can we boast?' or 'under what circumstances can we boast?' Ro 3.27.

G Demonstrative or Deictic Reference (92.29-92.36)

92.29 οὗτος, αὕτη, τοῦτο: a reference to an entity regarded as a part of the discourse setting,[7] with pejorative meaning in certain contexts[8] – 'this, this one.' οὗτός ἐστιν ὁ υἱός μου 'this is my Son' Mt 3.17; οὗτος ἦν ἐν ἀρχῇ πρὸς τὸν θεόν 'this was in the beginning with God' Jn 1.2; τοῦτο γινώσκετε ὅτι ἤγγικεν ἡ βασιλεία τοῦ θεοῦ 'know this, that the kingdom of God has come near' Lk 10.11; τοῦτο ἀληθὲς εἴρηκας 'this that you have said is true' Jn 4.18; ἢ καὶ ὡς οὗτος ὁ τελώνης 'or even like this tax collector' Lk 18.11; ὅτε δὲ ὁ υἱός σου οὗτος ὁ καταφαγών σου τὸν βίον μετὰ πορνῶν ἦλθεν 'but when this son of yours, who wasted your property with prostitutes, came' Lk 15.30.

92.30 ἐκεῖνος, η, ο: a reference to an entity regarded as relatively absent in terms of the discourse setting – 'that, that one.'[9] ἐκεῖνον λαβὼν δὸς αὐτοῖς ἀντὶ ἐμοῦ καὶ σοῦ 'take that and give it to them for you and me' Mt 17.27; ὁ ποιήσας με ὑγιῆ ἐκεῖνός μοι εἶπεν 'that one who made me well said to me' Jn 5.11;

---

[7] The reference in the discourse may be to that which precedes or follows.

[8] The pejorative meaning of οὗτος depends primarily upon the total context and not upon οὗτος as such.

[9] In some contexts, for example, Mk 16.10, the implication of absence in a discourse setting becomes relatively weak. In a number of contexts both οὗτος (92.29) and ἐκεῖνος (92.30) may be translated by personal pronouns such as he, she, it, they.

ἀνεκτότερον ἔσται γῇ Σοδόμων καὶ Γομόρρων ἐν ἡμέρᾳ κρίσεως ἢ τῇ πόλει ἐκείνῃ 'it will be easier for the land of Sodom and Gomorrah in the day of judgment than for that city' Mt 10.15; ἐν δὲ ταῖς ἡμέραις ἐκείναις παραγίνεται Ἰωάννης ὁ βαπτιστὴς κηρύσσων ἐν τῇ ἐρήμῳ τῆς Ἰουδαίας 'in those days John the Baptist came preaching in the desert of Judea' Mt 3.1; ἐκείνη πορευθεῖσα ἀπήγγειλεν τοῖς μετ' αὐτοῦ 'she (literally 'that one') went and told his companions' Mk 16.10.

92.31 τοιοῦτοςᵇ, αὕτη, οὗτον: a reference to that which is of such a kind as is identified in the context – 'of such a kind, of a kind such as this.' καὶ οἶδα τὸν τοιοῦτον ἄνθρωπον 'and I know a man such as this' or '. . . of this kind' 2 Cor 12.3.

92.32 ὅδεᵃ, ἥδε, τόδε: a reference to an entity regarded as relatively present in terms of the discourse setting, whether preceding or following – 'this, he, she, it, they.'[10] γυνὴ δέ τις ὀνόματι Μάρθα ὑπεδέξατο αὐτόν. καὶ τῇδε ἦν ἀδελφὴ καλουμένη Μαριάμ 'a woman by the name of Martha received him, and she had a sister named Mary' Lk 10.38-39; τάδε λέγει τὸ πνεῦμα τὸ ἅγιον, Τὸν ἄνδρα οὗ ἐστιν ἡ ζώνη αὕτη οὕτως δήσουσιν ἐν Ἰερουσαλὴμ οἱ Ἰουδαῖοι 'the Holy Spirit says this: The Jews in Jerusalem will tie up in this way the man who owns this belt' Ac 21.11.

92.33 ὅδεᵇ, ἥδε, τόδε: a reference to indefinite alternatives – 'such and such, this or that.' σήμερον ἢ αὔριον πορευσόμεθα εἰς τήνδε τὴν πόλιν 'today or tomorrow we will go to this or that town' Jas 4.13.

92.34 ἐντεῦθενᵇ: a reference to reason or source – 'from this.' οὐκ ἐντεῦθεν, ἐκ τῶν ἡδονῶν ὑμῶν τῶν στρατευομένων ἐν τοῖς μέλεσιν ὑμῶν 'is it not from this, namely, from your desires which are at war within you' (a reference to an occasion or set of circumstances regarded as present) Jas 4.1.

92.35 ὧδεᶜ: a reference to a present object, event, or state in terms of its relevance to the

---

[10] Much of the earlier meaning of ὅδε in the sense of 'here' is lost in NT usage.

discourse – 'in this, in this case, in the case of.' ὧδε λοιπὸν ζητεῖται ἐν τοῖς οἰκονόμοις ἵνα πιστός τις εὑρεθῇ 'moreover, in this case what is sought in any manager is that he be found faithful' 1 Cor 4.2; καὶ ὧδε μὲν δεκάτας ἀποθνήσκοντες ἄνθρωποι λαμβάνουσιν 'and in this case (of the priests) those who received the tenth were persons who die' He 7.8.

92.36 ποῖος[a], α, ον: a reference to one among several objects, events, or states – 'which, which one, which sort of.' ποία ἐντολὴ μεγάλη ἐν τῷ νόμῳ; 'which is the greatest commandment in the Law?' Mt 22.36.

H Emphatic Adjunct (92.37)

92.37 αὐτός[c], ή, ό: a marker of emphasis by calling attention to the distinctiveness of the

lexical unit with which it occurs (used for all persons, genders, and numbers) – '-self, -selves' (for example, myself, yourself, yourselves, ourselves, himself, herself, itself, themselves).[11] πέπεισμαι δέ, ἀδελφοί μου, καὶ αὐτὸς ἐγὼ περὶ ὑμῶν 'my fellow believers, I myself am persuaded concerning you' Ro 15.14; αὐτὸς Δαυὶδ εἶπεν ἐν τῷ πνεύματι τῷ ἁγίῳ 'David himself spoke by means of the Holy Spirit' Mk 12.36.

11 Note the overlap between αὐτός[b] (92.11) and αὐτός[c] (92.37). αὐτός[b] serves essentially as a reference to the third person, both singular and plural, and only in the nominative form does it carry emphasis. This could very well be classified as an instance of αὐτός[c]. In the oblique cases there is no such emphasis. On the other hand, αὐτός[c] may be an adjunct to any lexical unit in an oblique case and, as such, carries emphasis.

93 Names of Persons and Places[1]

Outline of Subdomains

A Persons (93.1-93.388)
B Places (93.389-93.615)

A Persons[2] (93.1-93.388)

93.1 Ἀαρών m: the elder brother of Moses and Israel's first high priest – 'Aaron' (Ac 7.40).

1 As in the case of other domains, derivatives are listed with their semantic bases, so that Ῥωμαῖος 'Roman' (93.562) is listed with Ῥώμη 'Rome' (93.563). Even in those instances in which there happens to be no corresponding base in the New Testament text, derivatives of places are nevertheless listed with the names of places even though they may refer to an individual belonging to such a place. For example, Ἀλεξανδρεύς 'an Alexandrian' is listed in Subdomain B *Places* (93.402).
   In addition to the listing of the Greek name for either persons or places, there is a brief identification and at least one reference where the name occurs. For geographical place names, a listing of the map and the quadrants on the map are given.
   2 Under the category of *Persons* are included individuals, ethnic names, and certain supernatural powers

93.2 Ἀβαδδών m: the Hebrew name for the ruling angel in Hell – 'Abaddon' meaning 'Destroyer' (Re 9.11). See 93.32.

93.3 Ἄβελ m: the second son of Adam and Eve and the brother of Cain – 'Abel' (Mt 23.35).

93.4 Ἀβιά m: (1) a person in the genealogy of Jesus (Mt 1.7); (2) a founder of a class of priests (Lk 1.5) – 'Abijah.'

93.5 Ἀβιαθάρ m: a priest to David – 'Abiathar' (Mk 2.26).

93.6 Ἀβιούδ m: a person in the genealogy of Jesus – 'Abiud' (Mt 1.13).

93.7 Ἀβραάμ m: the patriarch of the Israelite nation and father of the faithful – 'Abraham' (Lk 1.73).

generally regarded as personified. In addition, there are, as usual, a number of derivatives of both persons and places.

93.8 ″Αγαβος, ου *m*: a Christian prophet from Judea – 'Agabus' (Ac 11.28).

93.9 'Αγάρ *f*: the handmaid of Sarah and the concubine of Abraham and mother of Ishmael – 'Hagar' (Ga 4.24, 25).

93.10 'Αγρίππας, α *m*: Herod Agrippa II (Ac 25.26), the son of Herod Agrippa I (see Ac 12.1) – 'Agrippa.'

93.11 'Αδάμ *m*: ancestor of the human race – 'Adam' (Lk 3.38; 1 Tm 2.13).

93.12 'Αδδί *m*: a person in the genealogy of Jesus – 'Addi' (Lk 3.28).

93.13 'Αδμίν *m*: a person in the genealogy of Jesus – 'Admin' (Lk 3.33).

93.14 'Αζώρ *m*: a person in the genealogy of Jesus – 'Azor' (Mt 1.13, 14).

93.15 Αἰνέας, ου *m*: a person who was healed by Peter – 'Aeneas' (Ac 9.33, 34).

93.16 'Ακύλας, acc. αν *m*: a friend of Paul and the husband of Priscilla – 'Aquila' (Ac 18.2).

93.17 'Αλέξανδρος, ου *m*: (1) the son of Simon of Cyrene (Mk 15.21); (2) a member of the high-priestly family (Ac 4.6); (3) a Jew of Ephesus (Ac 19.33); (4) a false teacher in the church (1 Tm 1.20); (5) a coppersmith and opponent of Paul (2 Tm 4.14) – 'Alexander.' Some scholars have suggested that 4 and 5 refer to the same person, but this is by no means certain.

93.18 'Αλμεί *m*: a person in the genealogy of Jesus – 'Almi' (Lk 3.33, apparatus).

93.19 'Αλφαῖος, ου *m*: (1) the father of 'Ιάκωβος 3 (Mt 10.3); (2) the father of Λευί 1 (Mk 2.14) – 'Alphaeus.'

93.20 'Αμιναδάβ *m*: a person in the genealogy of Jesus – 'Amminadab' (Mt 1.4; Lk 3.33). Compare 'Αμιναδάμ (Lk 3.33, apparatus).

93.21 'Αμπλιᾶτος, ου *m*: a person greeted in Ro 16.8 – 'Ampliatus.'

93.22 'Αμών or 'Αμμών *m*: a person in the genealogy of Jesus – 'Amon' or 'Ammon' (Mt 1.10, apparatus).

93.23 'Αμώς *m*: (1) the father of Josiah (Mt 1.10); (2) the father of Ματταθίας 1 (Lk 3.25) – 'Amos.'

93.24 'Ανανίας, ου *m*: (1) the husband of Sapphira (Ac 5.1); (2) a Christian in Damascus (Ac 9.10); (3) a Jewish high priest (Ac 23.2) – 'Ananias.'

93.25 'Ανδρέας, ου *m*: the brother of Simon Peter and one of the twelve apostles – 'Andrew' (Jn 1.40).

93.26 'Ανδρόνικος, ου *m*: a person greeted in Ro 16.7 – 'Andronicus.'

93.27 ″Αννα, ας *f*: a prophetess – 'Anna' (Lk 2.36).

93.28 ″Αννας, α *m*: a Jewish high priest – 'Annas' (Lk 3.2; Jn 18.24).

93.29 'Αντιπᾶς, ᾶ *m*: a martyr in Pergamum – 'Antipas' (Re 2.13).

93.30 'Αουλία: an alternative form of 'Ιουλία, 93.175 (Ro 16.15, apparatus).

93.31 'Απελλῆς, οῦ *m*: a person greeted in Ro 16.10 – 'Apelles.'

93.32 'Απολλύων, ονος *m*: the Greek name for the ruling angel in Hell – 'Apollyon' meaning 'Destroyer' (Re 9.11). See 93.2.

93.33 'Απολλῶς, gen. and acc. ῶ *m*: a Christian of Alexandria who worked in Ephesus and Corinth – 'Apollos' (Ac 18.24; 19.1).

93.34 'Απφία, ας *f*: a Christian woman, probably the wife of Philemon – 'Apphia' (Phm 2).

93.35 'Αράμ *m*: a person in the genealogy of

Jesus – 'Aram' (Mt 1.3, 4; Lk 3.33, apparatus).

93.36 Ἀρέτας, α *m*: a king of Nabatean Arabia – 'Aretas' (2 Cor 11.32).

93.37 Ἀρηί: an alternative form of Ἀρνί, 93.41 (Lk 3.33, apparatus).

93.38 Ἀρίσταρχος, ου *m*: a companion of Paul – 'Aristarchus' (Ac 20.4; Phm 24).

93.39 Ἀριστόβουλος, ου *m*: a person whose family is greeted in Ro 16.10 – 'Aristobulus.'

93.40 Ἀρμίν: an alternative form of Ἀδμίν, 93.13 (Lk 3.33, apparatus).

93.41 Ἀρνί *m*: a person in the genealogy of Jesus – 'Arni' (Lk 3.33).

93.42 Ἀρτεμᾶς, ᾶ *m*: a friend of Paul – 'Artemas' (Tt 3.12).

93.43 Ἄρτεμις, ιδος *f*: a Greek goddess worshiped especially in Asia Minor – 'Artemis' (Ac 19.28).

93.44 Ἀρφαξάδ *m*: a person in the genealogy of Jesus – 'Arphaxad' (Lk 3.36).

93.45 Ἀρχέλαος, ου *m*: the son of Herod I – 'Archelaus' (Mt 2.22).

93.46 Ἄρχιππος, ου *m*: a Christian in Colossae – 'Archippus' (Col 4.17).

93.47 Ἀσά: an alternative form of Ἀσάφ, 93.48 (Mt 1.7, 8, apparatus).

93.48 Ἀσάφ *m*: a person in the genealogy of Jesus – 'Asaph' (Mt 1.7, 8).

93.49 Ἀσήρ *m*: a son of Jacob and ancestor of an Israelite tribe – 'Asher' (Lk 2.36; Re 7.6).

93.50 Ἀσσά: an alternative form of Ἀσάφ, 93.48 (Mt 1.7-8 apparatus).

93.51 Ἀσύγκριτος, ου *m*: a person greeted in Ro 16.14 – 'Asyncritus.'

93.52 Αὔγουστος, ου *m*: a Latin title given to Emperor Octavian and equivalent to a proper name – 'Augustus' (Lk 2.1).

93.53 Ἀχάζ *m*: a person in the genealogy of Jesus – 'Ahaz' (Mt 1.9).

93.54 Ἀχαϊκός, οῦ *m*: a Christian at Corinth – 'Achaicus' (1 Cor 16.17).

93.55 Ἀχίμ *m*: a person in the genealogy of Jesus – 'Achim' (Mt 1.14).

93.56 Βάαλ *m*: a Semitic deity – 'Baal' (Ro 11.4).

93.57 Βαλαάμ *m*: a sorcerer and prophet summoned by Balak to curse Israel – 'Balaam' (Re 2.14).

93.58 Βαλάκ *m*: a king of Moab involved with Balaam – 'Balak' (Re 2.14).

93.59 Βαραββᾶς, ᾶ *m*: a prisoner released by Pilate at the request of the Jews during the trial of Jesus – 'Barabbas' (Mt 27.16).

93.60 Βαράκ *m*: an Israelite general – 'Barak' (He 11.32).

93.61 Βαραχίας, ου *m*: the father of a man killed in the Temple – 'Barachiah' (Mt 23.35).

93.62 Βαρθολομαῖος, ου *m*: one of the twelve apostles – 'Bartholomew' (Mt 10.3).

93.63 Βαριησοῦς, οῦ *m*: a false prophet – 'Bar-Jesus' (Ac 13.6).

93.64 Βαριωνᾶ or Βαριωνᾶς, ᾶ *m*: the family name of the apostle Simon Peter – 'Bar-Jona' or 'Bar-Jonas' (Mt 16.17).

93.65 Βαρναβᾶς, ᾶ *m*: an additional name of a certain Joseph, a Levite from Cyprus who was an associate of Paul – 'Barnabas' (Ac 4.36; 13.43).

93.66 Βαρσαββᾶς, ᾶ *m*: (1) the family name of a certain Joseph (often called Justus) who was one of two candidates for the place of

Judas Iscariot (Ac 1.23); (2) the family name of a certain Judas who was appointed as a companion of Paul (Ac 15.22) – 'Barsabbas.'

93.67 Βαρτιμαῖος, ου *m*: a blind man – 'Bartimaeus' (Mk 10.46).

93.68 Βεελζεβούλ *m*: the name of the Devil as the prince of the demons – 'Beelzebul' (Lk 11.15).

93.69 Βελιάρ *m*: a name given to the Devil or to the Antichrist – 'Belial' (2 Cor 6.15).

93.70 Βενιαμίν or Βενιαμείν *m*: a son of Jacob and ancestor of an Israelite tribe – 'Benjamin' (Ac 13.21; Re 7.8).

93.71 Βερνίκη, ης *f*: the daughter of Herod Agrippa I and sister of Herod Agrippa II – 'Bernice' (Ac 25.13).

93.72 Βέρος, ου *m*: a person mentioned in some manuscripts of Ac 20.4 – 'Berus.'

93.73 Βεωορσόρ: an alternative form of Βεώρ, 93.74 (2 Pe 2.15, apparatus).

93.74 Βεώρ *m*: the father of Balaam – 'Beor' (2 Pe 2.15, apparatus). Most manuscripts read Βοσόρ (93.80) in 2 Pe 2.15.

93.75 Βηρεύς, έως *m*: a person greeted in Ro 16.15 (apparatus) – 'Bereus.'

93.76 Βλάστος, ου *m*: a court official of Herod Agrippa I – 'Blastus' (Ac 12.20).

93.77 Βοανηργές: a nickname given by Jesus to the sons of Zebedee – 'Boanerges' meaning 'Sons of Thunder' (Mk 3.17).

93.78 Βόες *m*: a person in the genealogy of Jesus – 'Boaz' (Mt 1.5).

93.79 Βόος *m*: an alternative form of Βόες (93.78) – 'Boaz' (Lk 3.32).

93.80 Βοσόρ *m*: the father of Balaam – 'Bosor' (2 Pe 2.15). Βοσόρ is the reading in most NT manuscripts for Βεώρ (Nu 22.5); see

93.74. Βοσύρ is an incidental variant spelling (2 Pe 2.15, apparatus).

93.81 Γαβριήλ *m*: an archangel – 'Gabriel' (Lk 1.19).

93.82 Γάδ *m*: a son of Jacob and ancestor of an Israelite tribe – 'Gad' (Re 7.5).

93.83 Γάϊος, ου *m*: (1) a Macedonian companion of Paul (Ac 19.29); (2) a Christian from Derbe (Ac 20.4); (3) a man from Corinth who was baptized by Paul (Ro 16.23; 1 Cor 1.14); (4) the recipient of 3 John (3 Jn 1) – 'Gaius.'

93.84 Γαλλίων, ωνος *m*: a Roman proconsul of Achaia – 'Gallio' (Ac 18.12).

93.85 Γαμαλιήλ *m*: a renowned Pharisee in Jerusalem – 'Gamaliel' (Ac 5.34).

93.86 Γεδεών *m*: a military leader and hero of Israel – 'Gideon' (He 11.32).

93.87 Γώγ *m*: a cryptic name to designate an enemy to be conquered by the Messiah – 'Gog' (Re 20.8).

93.88 Δαδδαῖος: an alternative form of Θαδδαῖος, 93.150 (Mk 3.18, apparatus).

93.89 Δάμαρις, ιδος *f*: an Athenian woman converted by Paul – 'Damaris' (Ac 17.34).

93.90 Δανιήλ *m*: a major OT prophet – 'Daniel' (Mt 24.15).

93.91 Δαυίδ *m*: a king of Israel and an ancestor in the genealogy of Jesus – 'David' (Lk 1.27; Ro 1.3).

93.92 Δημᾶς, ᾶ *m*: a companion of Paul – 'Demas' (Col 4.14).

93.93 Δημήτριος, ου *m*: (1) a silversmith in Ephesus (Ac 19.24); (2) a church leader (3 Jn 12) – 'Demetrius.'

93.94 Δία: the accusative form of the word Ζεύς (93.138).

93.95 Δίδυμος, ου *m*: the Greek name of the apostle Thomas (93.155) – 'Didymus' meaning 'Twin' (Jn 11.16).

93.96 Διονύσιος, ου *m*: an Athenian and a member of the Areopagus who was converted by Paul – 'Dionysius' (Ac 17.34).

93.97 Διός: the genitive form of the word Ζεύς (93.138).

93.98 Διόσκουροι, ων *m*: a joint name for Castor and Pollux, pagan deities of an Alexandrian ship – 'Dioscuri' meaning 'heavenly twins' (Ac 28.11).

93.99 Διοτρέφης, ους *m*: a Christian who is criticized in 3 Jn 9 – 'Diotrephes.'

93.100 Δονεῖ *m*: a person in the genealogy of Jesus – 'Doni' (Lk 3.33, apparatus).

93.101 Δορκάς, άδος *f*: a Christian woman in Joppa who was known for charitable works; her Aramaic name was Ταβιθά (93.355) – 'Dorcas' meaning 'gazelle, deer' (Ac 9.36).

93.102 Δρούσιλλα, ης *f*: the youngest daughter of Herod Agrippa I who was married to Felix the procurator – 'Drusilla' (Ac 24.24).

93.103 Ἔβερ *m*: a person in the genealogy of Jesus – 'Eber' (Lk 3.35).

93.104 Ἑβραϊκός, ή, όν: (derivative of Ἑβραῖος 'a Hebrew,' 93.105) pertaining to the Hebrews – 'Hebrew' (Lk 23.38, apparatus). The addition of γράμμασιν in some manuscripts literally applies to Hebrew letters, though the reference seems to be to the language, probably Aramaic. In Ac 21.40, 22.2 and 26.14 a peculiar form of Ἑβραϊκός, ή, όν occurs, namely, Ἑβραΐδι. Some scholars, however, explain it as from Ἑβραΐς, ΐδος *f* relating it to Ἑβραῖος, ου *m* (93.105).

93.105 Ἑβραῖος, ου *m*: the oldest ethnic name for a Jew or the Jewish people – 'a Hebrew' (Php 3.5).

93.106 Ἐζεκίας, ου *m*: a person in the genealogy of Jesus – 'Hezekiah' (Mt 1.9, 10).

93.107 Ἐλεάζαρ *m*: a person in the genealogy of Jesus – 'Eleazar' (Mt 1.15).

93.108 Ἐλιακίμ *m*: (1) the son of Abiud in the genealogy of Jesus (Mt 1.13); (2) son of Melea in the genealogy of Jesus (Lk 3.30) – 'Eliakim.'

93.109 Ἐλιέζερ *m*: a person in the genealogy of Jesus – 'Eliezer' (Lk 3.29).

93.110 Ἐλιούδ *m*: a person in the genealogy of Jesus – 'Eliud' (Mt 1.14, 15).

93.111 Ἐλισάβετ *f*: the wife of Zechariah the priest, and mother of John the Baptist – 'Elizabeth' (Lk 1.5, 57).

93.112 Ἐλισαῖος, ου *m*: a major OT prophet – 'Elisha' (Lk 4.27).

93.113 Ἐλμαδάμ *m*: a person in the genealogy of Jesus – 'Elmadam' (Lk 3.28).

93.114 Ἐλύμας, α *m*: a magician of Cyprus – 'Elymas' (Ac 13.8).

93.115 Ἐμμανουήλ *m*: a name attributed to Jesus Christ – 'Emmanuel' (Mt 1.23).

93.116 Ἐμμώρ *m*: a man from whose sons Abraham bought a burial place – 'Hamor' (Ac 7.16).

93.117 Ἐνώς *m*: a person in the genealogy of Jesus – 'Enos' (Lk 3.38).

93.118 Ἐνώχ *m*: a person in the genealogy of Jesus and an example of obedience and faith – 'Enoch' (Lk 3.37; He 11.5).

93.119 Ἐπαίνετος, ου *m*: the first Christian in Asia Minor – 'Epaenetus' (Ro 16.5).

93.120 Ἐπαφρᾶς, ᾶ, *m*: a Christian of Colossae – 'Epaphras' (Col 1.7).

93.121 Ἐπαφρόδιτος, ου *m*: a messenger

sent to Paul from the Philippian church – 'Epaphroditus' (Php 2.25).

93.122 Ἔραστος, ου *m*: (1) a companion of Paul (Ac 19.22); (2) a city treasurer (Ro 16.23) – 'Erastus.'

93.123 Ἑρμᾶς, ᾶ *m*: a person greeted in Ro 16.14 – 'Hermas.'

93.124 Ἑρμῆς, οῦ *m*: (1) a Greek god (Ac 14.12); (2) a person greeted in Ro 16.14 – 'Hermes.'

93.125 Ἑρμογένης, ους *m*: a Christian from Asia Minor – 'Hermogenes' (2 Tm 1.15).

93.126 Ἐσλί *m*: a person in the genealogy of Jesus – 'Esli' (Lk 3.25).

93.127 Ἐσρώμ *m*: a person in the genealogy of Jesus – 'Hezron' (Mt 1.3; Lk 3.33).

93.128 Εὔα, ας *f*: ancestor of the human race – 'Eve' (1 Tm 2.13).

93.129 Εὔβουλος, ου *m*: a Christian who sent greetings in 2 Tm 4.21 – 'Eubulus.'

93.130 Εὐνίκη, ης *f*: the mother of Timothy – 'Eunice' (2 Tm 1.5).

93.131 Εὐοδία, ας *f*: a Christian woman in the church of Philippi – 'Euodia' (Php 4.2).

93.132 Εὔτυχος, ου *m*: a young man who fell out of a window in Troas – 'Eutychus' (Ac 20.9).

93.133 Ζαβουλών[a] *m*: a son of Jacob and ancestor of an Israelite tribe – 'Zebulun' (Re 7.8).

93.134 Ζακχαῖος, ου *m*: a chief tax collector of Jericho – 'Zacchaeus' (Lk 19.2).

93.135 Ζάρα *m*: a person in the genealogy of Jesus – 'Zerah' (Mt 1.3).

93.136 Ζαχαρίας, ου *m*: (1) a priest who was the father of John the Baptist (Lk 1.13); (2) an OT prophet killed in the Temple (Mt 23.35) – 'Zechariah.'

93.137 Ζεβεδαῖος, ου *m*: the father of the apostles James and John – 'Zebedee' (Mt 4.21).

93.138 Ζεύς, gen. Διός, acc. Δία *m*: the chief Greek deity – 'Zeus' (Ac 14.12).

93.139 Ζηνᾶς, acc ᾶν *m*: a Christian lawyer – 'Zenas' (Tt 3.13).

93.140 Ζοροβαβέλ *m*: a governor in postexilic Jerusalem who was mentioned in the genealogy of Jesus – 'Zerubbabel' (Mt 1.12; Lk 3.27).

93.141 Ἡλί *m*: a person in the genealogy of Jesus – 'Heli' (Lk 3.23).

93.142 Ἡλίας, ου *m*: a major OT prophet – 'Elijah' (Lk 1.17).

93.143 Ἤρ *m*: a person in the genealogy of Jesus – 'Er' (Lk 3.28).

93.144 Ἡρῴδης, ου *m*: (1) Herod I, known as Herod the Great (Mt 2.1); (2) Herod Antipas, son of Herod I, who had John the Baptist executed (Mt 14.1); (3) Herod Agrippa I, grandson of Herod I (Ac 12.1) – 'Herod.'

93.145 Ἡρῳδιάς, άδος *f*: a granddaughter of Herod I and wife of Herod Antipas – 'Herodias' (Mk 6.17; Mt 14.3).

93.146 Ἡρῳδίων, ωνος *m*: a person greeted in Ro 16.11 – 'Herodion.'

93.147 Ἡσαΐας, ου *m*: a major OT prophet – 'Isaiah' (Mt 3.3; Jn 1.23).

93.148 Ἡσαῦ *m*: a son of Isaac and the elder twin brother of Jacob – 'Esau' (He 11.20).

93.149 Θαδαῖος: an alternative form of Θαδδαῖος, 93.150 (Mk 3.18, apparatus).

93.150 Θαδδαῖος, ου *m*: one of the twelve apostles – 'Thaddaeus' (Mt 10.3). See also 93.227.

93.151 Θαμάρ *f*: the daughter-in-law of Judah in the genealogy of Jesus – 'Tamar' (Mt 1.3).

93.152 Θάρα *m*: the father of Abraham in the genealogy of Jesus – 'Terah' (Lk 3.34).

93.153 Θεόφιλος, ου *m*: an important Christian to whom the books of Luke and Acts were dedicated – 'Theophilus' (Lk 1.3; Ac 1.1).

93.154 Θευδᾶς, ᾶ *m*: a Jewish insurrectionist – 'Theudas' (Ac 5.36).

93.155 Θωμᾶς, ᾶ *m*: one of the twelve apostles – 'Thomas' (Mt 10.3). See also 93.95.

93.156 Ἰάϊρος, ου *m*: a synagogue official – 'Jairus' (Mk 5.22).

93.157 Ἰακώβ *m*: (1) the patriarch Jacob, a son of Isaac (Mt 1.2); (2) the father of Ἰωσήφ 2 in the genealogy of Jesus (Mt 1.15) – 'Jacob.'

93.158 Ἰάκωβος, ου *m*: (1) one of the twelve apostles and the son of Zebedee and brother of John (Mt 4.21); (2) a brother of Jesus (Mt 13.55); (3) the son of Alphaeus and one of the twelve apostles (Mt 10.3); (4) the son of Μαρία 4 (Mt 27.56) and called 'the younger' in Mk 15.40; (5) the father of Judas, one of the twelve apostles (Lk 6.16); (6) a tax collector called James rather than Levi (Mk 2.14, apparatus) – 'James.' Some scholars consider 3 and 4 to be the same person.

93.159 Ἰαμβρῆς *m*: an Egyptian sorcerer who together with Jannes opposed Moses before Pharaoh – 'Jambres' (2 Tm 3.8).

93.160 Ἰανναί *m*: a person in the genealogy of Jesus – 'Jannai' (Lk 3.24).

93.161 Ἰάννης *m*: an Egyptian sorcerer who together with Jambres opposed Moses before Pharaoh – 'Jannes' (2 Tm 3.8).

93.162 Ἰάρετ *m*: the father of Enoch in the genealogy of Jesus – 'Jared' (Lk 3.37).

93.163 Ἰάσων, ονος *m*: (1) the host of Paul and Silas in Thessalonica (Ac 17.5); (2) a person who sends greetings in Ro 16.21 – 'Jason.'

93.164 Ἰεζάβελ *f*: King Ahab's notorious queen – 'Jezebel' (Re 2.20).

93.165 Ἰερεμίας, ου *m*: a major OT prophet – 'Jeremiah' (Mt 2.17).

93.166 Ἰεσσαί *m*: the father of King David in the genealogy of Jesus – 'Jesse' (Lk 3.32).

93.167 Ἰεφθάε *m*: one of the judges of Israel – 'Jephthah' (He 11.32).

93.168 Ἰεχονίας, ου *m*: a king of Judah mentioned in the genealogy of Jesus – 'Jechoniah' (Mt 1.11).

93.169 Ἰησοῦς, οῦ *m*: (1) Jesus Christ of Nazareth (Mt 1.1); (2) an additional name assigned to Barabbas (Mt 27.16, 17, apparatus); (3) the son of Eliezer mentioned in the genealogy of Jesus (Lk 3.29); (4) an additional name assigned to Justus, a companion of Paul (Col 4.11); (5) Joshua, the successor of Moses (Ac 7.45; He 4.8) – 'Jesus, Joshua.' 'Jesus' is a Greek transliteration for the Hebrew name Joshua.

93.170 Ἰουδαία, ης *f*: (derivative of Ἰούδαςᵃ 'Judah,' 93.173, and Ἰούδαςᶜ 'Judah,' 93.488)[3] the ethnic name of a woman belonging to the Jewish nation – 'a Jewess' (Ac 24.24).

93.171 Ἰουδαϊκός, ή, όν; Ἰουδαϊκῶς: (derivatives of Ἰουδαῖος 'a Jew,' 93.172) pertaining to the Jewish nation – 'Jewish' (Tt 1.14; Ga 2.14).

93.172 Ἰουδαῖος, ου *m*: (derivative of Ἰούδαςᵃ 'Judah,' 93.173, and Ἰούδαςᶜ 'Judah,' 93.488)[3] the ethnic name of a person who belongs to the Jewish nation – 'a Jew' (Mk

---

3 These derivatives relate historically both to the proper name of the person Judah and also to the locality which derived its name from the tribal entity.

7.3). In NT usage the reference of the term οἱ Ἰουδαῖοι may be either the Jewish people as such, the inhabitants of Jerusalem and environs, the authorities in Jerusalem, or even the people hostile to Jesus.

93.173 Ἰούδας[a], α *m*: (1) Judas Iscariot, the betrayer of Jesus and one of the twelve apostles (Mt 10.4); (2) Judas the son of James, and one of the twelve apostles (Lk 6.16); (3) Judas, a brother of Jesus (Mt 13.55); (4) Judas, Paul's host in Damascus (Ac 9.11); (5) Judas, called Barsabbas, a leading Christian in Jerusalem and a companion of Paul (Ac 15.22); (6) Judas, a revolutionary leader (Ac 5.37); (7) Judah, a person in the genealogy of Jesus (Lk 3.30); (8) Judah, a son of Jacob in the genealogy of Jesus and an ancestor of an Israelite tribe (Mt 1.2; Re 7.5) – 'Judas' or 'Judah.'

93.174 Ἰούδας[b], α *m*: the tribe Judah – 'Judah' (He 7.14).

93.175 Ἰουλία, ας *f*: a person greeted in Ro 16.15 – 'Julia.'

93.176 Ἰούλιος, ου *m*: a Roman centurion – 'Julius' (Ac 27.1).

93.177 Ἰουνία, ας *f*: an alternative form of Ἰουλία, 93.175 – 'Junia' (Ro 16.15, apparatus).

93.178 Ἰουνιᾶς, ᾶ *m*: a Jewish Christian greeted in Ro 16.7 – 'Junias.'

93.179 Ἰοῦστος, ου *m*: (1) an additional name of Joseph Barsabbas, one of two candidates for the place of Judas Iscariot (Ac 1.23); (2) an additional name of Titius, a Jewish proselyte (Ac 18.7); (3) Jesus called Justus, a companion of Paul (Col 4.11) – 'Justus.'

93.180 Ἰσαάκ *m*: a son of Abraham and father of Jacob and Esau – 'Isaac' (He 11.17).

93.181 Ἰσκαριώθ or Ἰσκαρι(ι)ώτης, ου *m*: an identifying name (probably based on a place name, see 93.496) of Judas, the betrayer of Jesus – 'Iscariot' (Mk 3.19 and 3.19, apparatus).

93.182 Ἰσραήλ *m*: (1) the patriarch Jacob (Ro 9.6); (2) the nation of Israel (Mt 2.6); (3) a figurative reference to Christians as the true Israel (Ga 6.16) – 'Israel.'

93.183 Ἰσραηλίτης, ου *m*: (derivative of Ἰσραήλ 2 in 93.182) the ethnic name of a person belonging to the nation of Israel – 'Israelite' (Ac 2.22).

93.184 Ἰσσαχάρ *m*: a son of Jacob and ancestor of an Israelite tribe – 'Issachar' (Re 7.7).

93.185 Ἰωαθάμ *m*: a person in the genealogy of Jesus – 'Jotham' (Mt 1.9).

93.186 Ἰωακείμ *m*: a person in the genealogy of Jesus – 'Jehoiakim' (Mt 1.11, apparatus).

93.187 Ἰωανάν *m*: a person in the genealogy of Jesus – 'Joanan' (Lk 3.27).

93.188 Ἰωάννα, ας *f*: the wife of Chuza, an official of Herod Antipas – 'Joanna' (Lk 8.3).

93.189 Ἰωαννᾶς and Ἰωανᾶς, ᾶ *m*: alternative forms for Ἰωάννης 5 – 'Jonas' (Jn 1.42, apparatus).

93.190 Ἰωάννης, ου *m*: (1) John the Baptist (Mt 3.1); (2) one of the twelve apostles and the son of Zebedee and brother of James (Mk 1.19); (3) the author of the book of Revelation (Re 1.1); (4) a companion of Paul who was also called Mark (Ac 12.12); (5) the father of Peter and Andrew (Jn 1.42); (6) a member of the Sanhedrin (Ac 4.6) – 'John.' Some persons consider 2 and 3 to be the same.

93.191 Ἰώβ *m*: the central figure of the book of Job – 'Job' (Jas 5.11).

93.192 Ἰωβήδ *m*: a person in the genealogy of Jesus – 'Obed' (Mt 1.5; Lk 3.32).

93.193 Ἰωδά *m*: a person in the genealogy of Jesus – 'Joda' (Lk 3.26).

93.194 Ἰωήλ *m*: an OT prophet – 'Joel' (Ac 2.16).

93.195 Ἰωνάθας, ου *m*: an alternative form for Ἰωάννης 6 – 'Jonathas' (Ac 4.6, apparatus).

93.196 Ἰωνάμ *m*: a person in the genealogy of Jesus – 'Jonam' (Lk 3.30).

93.197 Ἰωνᾶς, ᾶ *m*: (1) an OT prophet (Mt 12.39-41); (2) an alternative form for Ἰωάννης 5 (Jn 1.42, apparatus) – 'Jonah.'

93.198 Ἰωράμ *m*: a king of Judah mentioned in the genealogy of Jesus – 'Joram' (Mt 1.8).

93.199 Ἰωρίμ *m*: a person in the genealogy of Jesus – 'Jorim' (Lk 3.29).

93.200 Ἰωσαφάτ *m*: a king of Judah mentioned in the genealogy of Jesus – 'Jehoshaphat' (Mt 1.8).

93.201 Ἰωσῆς, ῆ or ῆτος *m*: (1) a brother of Jesus (Mk 6.3, see Ἰωσήφ 4); (2) a brother of James the younger (Mk 15.40) – 'Joses.'

93.202 Ἰωσήφ *m*: (1) a son of Jacob and ancestor of an Israelite tribe (Jn 4.5; Re 7.8); (2) the husband of Mary the mother of Jesus (Mt 1.16); (3) a person from Arimathea who was a member of the Sanhedrin (Mt 27.57); (4) a brother of Jesus (Mt 13.55); (5) a Levite from Cyprus, also called Barnabas (Ac 4.36); (6) a man whose family name was Barsabbas and who was also called Justus; he was one of two candidates for the place of Judas Iscariot (Ac 1.23); (7) a son of Μαρία 4 (Mt 27.56); (8) and (9) persons mentioned in the genealogy of Jesus (Lk 3.24, 30) – 'Joseph.'

93.203 Ἰωσήχ *m*: a person in the genealogy of Jesus – 'Josech' (Lk 3.26).

93.204 Ἰωσίας, ου *m*: a king of Judah mentioned in the genealogy of Jesus – 'Josiah' (Mt 1.10).

93.205 Καϊάφας, α *m*: the high priest who played a prominent role in the condemnation of Jesus – 'Caiaphas' (Mt 26.3; Jn 18.13).

93.206 Κάϊν *m*: the first son of Adam and Eve and the brother of Abel – 'Cain' (He 11.4).

93.207 Καϊνάμ *m*: (1) the son of Arphaxad in the genealogy of Jesus (Lk 3.36); (2) the son of Enos in the genealogy of Jesus (Lk 3.37) – 'Cainan.'

93.208 Καῖσαρᵃ, ος *m*: the Greek transcription for a Latin word used as a name and title for a Roman emperor – 'Caesar' (Mt 22.21).

93.209 Κανδάκηᵇ, ης *f*: interpreted by some as the name of the queen of Ethiopia – 'Candace' (Ac 8.27), but see 37.77.

93.210 Κάρπος, ου *m*: a Christian of Troas – 'Carpus' (2 Tm 4.13).

93.211 Κηφᾶς, ᾶ *m*: the Aramaic equivalent of the Greek name Πέτρος 'Peter' (93.296) – 'Cephas' meaning 'Rock' (Jn 1.42; 1 Cor 1.12).

93.212 Κίς *m*: the father of King Saul – 'Kish' (Ac 13.21).

93.213 Κλαυδία, ας *f*: a Christian woman who sent greetings in 2 Tm 4.21 – 'Claudia.'

93.214 Κλαύδιος, ου *m*: (1) Tiberius Claudius Nero Germanicus (contrast 93.359), a Roman emperor (Ac 11.28); (2) Claudius Lysias, a Roman officer in Jerusalem (Ac 23.26) – 'Claudius.'

93.215 Κλεοπᾶς, ᾶ *m*: a believer whom Jesus met on the road to Emmaus – 'Cleopas' (Lk 24.18).

93.216 Κλήμης, εντος *m*: a member of the church at Philippi – 'Clement' (Php 4.3).

93.217 Κλωπᾶς, ᾶ *m*: the husband of Μαρία 5, one of the women at the crucifixion – 'Clopas' (Jn 19.25).

93.218 Κόρε *m*: the leader of a rebellion against Moses – 'Korah' (Jd 11).

93.219 Κορνήλιος, ου *m*: a Roman centurion to whom Peter ministered – 'Cornelius' (Ac 10.1).

93.220 Κούαρτος, ου *m*: a Christian who sent greetings in Ro 16.23 – 'Quartus.'

93.221 Κρήσκης, εντος *m*: a companion of Paul – 'Crescens' (2 Tm 4.10).

93.222 Κρίσπος, ου *m*: a leader of the synagogue in Corinth – 'Crispus' (Ac 18.8).

93.223 Κυρήνιος, ου *m*: the imperial governor of Syria – 'Quirinius' (Lk 2.2).

93.224 Κωσάμ *m*: a person in the genealogy of Jesus – 'Cosam' (Lk 3.28).

93.225 Λάζαρος, ου *m*: (1) the brother of Mary 2 and Martha (Jn 11.1); (2) a beggar in a parable (Lk 16.20) – 'Lazarus.'

93.226 Λάμεχ *m*: the father of Noah in the genealogy of Jesus – 'Lamech' (Lk 3.36).

93.227 Λεββαῖος, ου *m*: one of the twelve apostles, generally regarded as being the same as Thaddaeus (93.150) – 'Lebbaeus' (Mt 10.3, apparatus).

93.228 Λεββεδαῖος, ου *m*: an alternative form of Λεββαῖος, 93.227 – 'Lebbedaeus' (Mt 10.3, apparatus).

93.229 Λεγιών, ῶνος *m*: the name of a host of demons – 'Legion' (Mk 5.9).

93.230 Λευεί and Λευή(ς): alternative forms of Λευί 1, see 93.231 (Mk 2.14, apparatus; 3.18, apparatus).

93.231 Λευί, acc. ίν *m*: (1) a tax collector and one of the twelve apostles, generally regarded as being the same as Matthew, 93.244 (Lk 5.27); (2) a son of Jacob and ancestor of an Israelite tribe (He 7.9; Re 7.7); (3) the son of Μελχί 1 in the genealogy of Jesus (Lk 3.24); (4) the son of Συμεών 5 in the genealogy of Jesus (Lk 3.29) – 'Levi.'

93.232 Λευίς: an alternative form of Λευί 1, see 93.231 (Lk 5.29).

93.233 Λίνος, ου *m*: a Christian who sent greetings in 2 Tm 4.21 – 'Linus.'

93.234 Λουκᾶς, ᾶ *m*: a companion of Paul who is generally regarded as the author of Luke and the Acts of the Apostles – 'Luke' (2 Tm 4.11).

93.235 Λούκιος, ου *m*: (1) a teacher and prophet at Antioch (Ac 13.1); (2) a person sending greetings in Ro 16.21 – 'Lucius.'

93.236 Λυδία, ας *f*: a woman merchant of purple cloth from Thyatira who was converted by Paul – 'Lydia' (Ac 16.14).

93.237 Λυσανίας, ου *m*: a tetrarch of Abilene – 'Lysanias' (Lk 3.1).

93.238 Λυσίας, ου *m*: Claudius Lysias, a Roman officer in Jerusalem – 'Lysias' (Ac 23.26). See 93.214.

93.239 Λωΐς, ΐδος *f*: the grandmother of Timothy – 'Lois' (2 Tm 1.5).

93.240 Λώτ *m*: the nephew of Abraham – 'Lot' (Lk 17.28).

93.241 Μάαθ *m*: a person in the genealogy of Jesus – 'Maath' (Lk 3.26).

93.242 Μαγδαληνή, ῆς *f*: (derivative of Μαγδαλά 93.523) the attributive name of Μαρία 3, a woman of Magdala – 'Magdalene' (Mt 27.56).

93.243 Μαγώγ *m*: a cryptic name to designate an enemy to be conquered by the Messiah – 'Magog' (Re 20.8).

93.244 Μαθθαῖος or Ματθαῖος, ου *m*: a tax collector and one of the twelve apostles, generally regarded as being the same as Λευί 1, see 93.231 – 'Matthew' (Mt 10.3).

93.245 Μαθθάτ or Ματθάτ *m*: (1) the father of Eli in the genealogy of Jesus (Lk 3.24); (2) the father of Jorim in the genealogy of Jesus (Lk 3.29) – 'Matthat.'

93.246 Μαθθίας or Ματθίας, ου *m*: the person elected to take the place of the apostle Judas Iscariot – 'Matthias' (Ac 1.26).

93.247 Μαθουσαλά *m*: a person in the genealogy of Jesus – 'Methuselah' (Lk 3.37).

93.248 Μαλελεήλ *m*: a person in the genealogy of Jesus – 'Maleleel' (Lk 3.37).

93.249 Μάλχος, ου *m*: the high priest's slave whom Peter wounded – 'Malchus' (Jn 18.10).

93.250 Μαναήν *m*: a prophet and teacher in the church at Antioch – 'Manaen' (Ac 13.1).

93.251 Μανασσῆς, ῆ (gen and acc) *m*: (1) a son of Ἰωσήφ 1 and ancestor of an Israelite tribe (Re 7.6); (2) a person in the genealogy of Jesus (Mt 1.10) – 'Manasseh.'

93.252 Μάρθα, ας *f*: a sister of Mary 2 and Lazarus 1 of Bethany – 'Martha' (Jn 11.1).

93.253 Μαρία, ας *f*: (1) the mother of Jesus Christ (Mt 1.18); (2) a sister of Martha and Lazarus 1 (Jn 11.1); (3) Mary Magdalene, a follower of Jesus (Mt 27.56); (4) the mother of Ἰάκωβος 4 and Ἰωσήφ 7 (Mt 27.56); (5) the wife of Clopas (Jn 19.25); (6) the mother of John Mark (Ac 12.12); (7) a person greeted in Ro 16.6 – 'Mary.'

93.254 Μαριάμ *f*: an alternative form of Μαρία 1, 93.253 (Lk 1.27).

93.255 Μᾶρκος, ου *m*: a companion of Paul who was also called John – 'Mark' (Ac 12.12).

93.256 Ματθάν *m*: a person in the genealogy of Jesus – 'Matthan' (Mt 1.15).

93.257 Ματταθά *m*: a person in the genealogy of Jesus – 'Mattatha' (Lk 3.31).

93.258 Ματταθίας, ου *m*: (1) the son of Amos in the genealogy of Jesus (Lk 3.25); (2) the son of Semein in the genealogy of Jesus (Lk 3.26) – 'Mattathias.'

93.259 Μελεά *m*: a person in the genealogy of Jesus – 'Melea' (Lk 3.31).

93.260 Μελχί *m*: (1) the father of Λευί 3 in the genealogy of Jesus (Lk 3.24); (2) the father of Neri in the genealogy of Jesus (Lk 3.28); (3) the father of Aminadam in the genealogy of Jesus (Lk 3.33, apparatus) – 'Melchi.'

93.261 Μελχισέδεκ *m*: a king of Salem and priest of the Most High God in the time of Abraham – 'Melchizedek' (He 7.1).

93.262 Μεννά *m*: a person in the genealogy of Jesus – 'Menna' (Lk 3.31).

93.263 Μιχαήλ *m*: the name of the chief angel – 'Michael' (Jd 9).

93.264 Μνάσων, ωνος *m*: a Christian from Cyprus – 'Mnason' (Ac 21.16).

93.265 Μολόχ or Μόλοχ *m*: the name of a Canaanite god – 'Moloch' (Ac 7.43).

93.266 Μωϋσῆς, έως *m*: the leader of the Israelites out of Egypt and the lawgiver – 'Moses' (Mt 8.4).

93.267 Ναασσών *m*: a person in the genealogy of Jesus – 'Nahshon' (Mt 1.4; Lk 3.32).

93.268 Ναγγαί *m*: a person in the genealogy of Jesus – 'Naggai' (Lk 3.25).

93.269 Ναθάμ *m*: a person in the genealogy of Jesus – 'Nathan' (Lk 3.31).

93.270 Ναθαναήλ *m*: a disciple of Jesus – 'Nathanael' (Jn 21.2).

93.271 Ναιμάν *m*: a Syrian army commander healed by Elisha – 'Naaman' (Lk 4.27).

93.272 Ναούμ *m*: a person in the genealogy of Jesus – 'Nahum' (Lk 3.25).

93.273 Νάρκισσος, ου *m*: a person whose household is greeted in Ro 16.11 – 'Narcissus.'

93.274 Ναχώρ *m*: a person in the genealogy of Jesus – 'Nahor' (Lk 3.34).

93.275 Νεφθαλίμ[a] *m*: a son of Jacob and ancestor of an Israelite tribe – 'Naphtali' (Re 7.6).

93.276 Νηρεύς, έως *m*: a person greeted in Ro 16.15 – 'Nereus.'

93.277 Νηρί *m*: a person in the genealogy of Jesus – 'Neri' (Lk 3.27).

93.278 Νήφα: an alternative form of Νύμφα, 93.284 (Col 4.15, apparatus).

93.279 Νίγερ *m*: an additional name of Συμεών 4, the prophet – 'Niger' (Ac 13.1).

93.280 Νικάνωρ, ορος *m*: one of the seven helpers in the church in Jerusalem – 'Nicanor' (Ac 6.5).

93.281 Νικόδημος, ου *m*: a member of the Sanhedrin who spoke with Jesus – 'Nicodemus' (Jn 3.1).

93.282 Νικολαΐτης, ου *m*: (derivative of Νικόλαος 1, see 93.283) a follower of Nicolaus 1 – 'Nicolaitan' (Re 2.6).

93.283 Νικόλαος, ου *m*: (1) the founder of a sect (not occurring in the NT, but see 93.282); (2) one of the seven helpers in the church in Jerusalem (Ac 6.5) – 'Nicolaus.'

93.284 Νύμφα, ας *f* or Νυμφᾶς, ᾶ *m*: a Christian woman or man mentioned in Col 4.15 (text and apparatus) – 'Nympha' or 'Nymphas.'

93.285 Νῶε *m*: a preacher of repentance who built an ark – 'Noah' (Lk 3.36; 17.26).

93.286 'Οζίας, ου *m*: a Hebrew king in the genealogy of Jesus – 'Uzziah' (Mt 1.8, 9).

93.287 'Ολυμπᾶς, ᾶ *m*: a person greeted in Ro 16.15 – 'Olympas.'

93.288 'Ονήσιμος, ου *m*: a slave of Philemon – 'Onesimus' (Col 4.9; Phm 10).

93.289 'Ονησίφορος, ου *m*: a Christian mentioned in 2 Tm 1.16 and 4.19 – 'Onesiphorus.'

93.290 Οὐρβανός, οῦ *m*: a person greeted in Ro 16.9 – 'Urbanus.'

93.291 Οὐρίας, ου *m*: a man whose wife is referred to in the genealogy of Jesus – 'Uriah' (Mt 1.6).

93.292 Παρμενᾶς, ᾶ *m*: one of the seven helpers in the church in Jerusalem – 'Parmenas' (Ac 6.5).

93.293 Πατροβᾶς, ᾶ *m*: a person greeted in Ro 16.14 – 'Patrobas.'

93.294 Παῦλος, ου *m*: (1) an apostle of Jesus Christ whose Hebrew name was Saul (Ro 1.1); (2) Sergius Paulus, the governor of Cyprus (Ac 13.7) – 'Paul, Paulus.'

93.295 Περσίς, ίδος *f*: a person greeted in Ro 16.12 – 'Persis.'

93.296 Πέτρος, ου *m*: the Greek name of the leader of the twelve apostles, who was also called Cephas and whose name was originally Simon – 'Peter' (Mt 10.2).

93.297 Πιλᾶτος, ου *m*: a procurator of Judea who gave the order for the crucifixion of Jesus – 'Pilate' (Mk 15.15).

93.298 Πόντιος, ου *m*: an additional name for Pilate – 'Pontius' (Lk 3.1).

93.299 Πόπλιος, ου *m*: the principal authority on the island of Malta – 'Publius' (Ac 28.7).

93.300 Πόρκιος, ου *m*: Porcius Festus, the successor to Felix as procurator of Palestine – 'Porcius' (Ac 24.27). See 93.376.

93.301 Πούδης, εντος *m*: a Christian who sent greetings in 2 Tm 4.21 – 'Pudens.'

93.302 Πρίσκα, ης *f* or Πρίσκιλλα, ης *f*: the wife of Aquila – 'Prisca' or 'Priscilla' (Ro 16.3; Ac 18.2).

93.303 Πρόχορος, ου *m*: one of the seven helpers in the church in Jerusalem – 'Prochorus' (Ac 6.5).

93.304 Πύθιος, ου *m*: a person mentioned in some manuscripts of Ac 20.4 – 'Pythius.'

93.305 Πύρρος, ου *m*: a companion of Paul – 'Pyrrhus' (Ac 20.4).

93.306 Ῥαάβ *f*: an alternative form of Ῥαχάβ, 93.309, a harlot in Jericho saved by the Israelite spies (He 11.31; Jas 2.25).

93.307 Ῥαγαύ *m*: a person in the genealogy of Jesus – 'Reu' (Lk 3.35).

93.308 Ῥαιφάν *m*: a pagan God – 'Rephan' (Ac 7.43).

93.309 Ῥαχάβ *f*: a woman of Jericho mentioned in the genealogy of Jesus – 'Rahab' (Mt 1.5). See 93.306.

93.310 Ῥαχήλ *f*: the wife of Jacob – 'Rachel' (Mt 2.18).

93.311 Ῥεβέκκα, ας *f*: the wife of Isaac – 'Rebecca' (Ro 9.10).

93.312 Ῥησά *m*: a person in the genealogy of Jesus – 'Rhesa' (Lk 3.27).

93.313 Ῥοβοάμ *m*: a Hebrew king in the genealogy of Jesus – 'Rehoboam' (Mt 1.7).

93.314 Ῥόδη, ης *f*: a maidservant in the house of Μαρία 6 – 'Rhoda' (Ac 12.13).

93.315 Ῥουβήν *m*: the oldest son of Jacob and ancestor of an Israelite tribe – 'Reuben' (Re 7.5).

93.316 Ῥούθ *f*: the wife of Boaz in the genealogy of Jesus – 'Ruth' (Mt 1.5).

93.317 Ῥοῦφος, ου *m*: (1) a son of Σίμων 4 of Cyrene (Mk 15.21); (2) a person greeted in Ro 16.13 – 'Rufus.'

93.318 Σαδώκ *m*: a person in the genealogy of Jesus – 'Zadok' (Mt 1.14).

93.319 Σαλά *m*: (1) the father of Boaz in the genealogy of Jesus (Lk 3.32); (2) the father of Eber in the genealogy of Jesus (Lk 3.35) – 'Shelah.'

93.320 Σαλαθιήλ *m*: a person in the genealogy of Jesus – 'Salathiel' (Mt 1.12; Lk 3.27).

93.321 Σαλήμ[b] *f*: the expression βασιλεὺς Σαλήμ 'king of Salem' (He 7.1, 2) may be interpreted as 'king of peace,' and as such it may be regarded as an honorific name. It is also possible that Σαλήμ refers to a place (see 93.566).

93.322 Σαλμάν: an alternative form of Σαλά 1, see 93.319 (Lk 3.32, apparatus).

93.323 Σαλμών *m*: a person in the genealogy of Jesus –'Salmon' (Mt 1.4, 5; Lk 3.32, apparatus).

93.324 Σαλώμη, ης *f*: a Galilean woman who followed Jesus – 'Salome' (Mk 15.40; 16.1).

93.325 Σαμουήλ *m*: a major OT prophet – 'Samuel' (Ac 13.20; He 11.32).

93.326 Σαμψών *m*: one of the judges of Israel – 'Samson' (He 11.32).

93.327 Σαούλ *m*: (1) the Hebrew name of the apostle Paul (Ac 9.4); (2) the first king of Israel (Ac 13.21) – 'Saul.'

93.328 Σάπφιρα, ης *f*: the wife of Ἀνανίας 1 – 'Sapphira' (Ac 5.1).

93.329 Σάρρα, ας *f*: the wife of Abraham – 'Sarah' (Ro 4.19).

93.330 Σατανᾶς[b], ᾶ *m*: (a borrowing from Hebrew and Aramaic meaning literally 'adversary') the usual proper name of the Devil – 'Satan' (Ac 26.18). See also 12.34.

93.331 Σαῦλος, ου *m*: an alternative form of Σαούλ, 93.327, the Hebrew name of the apostle Paul (Ac 7.58).

93.332 Σειλεᾶς: an alternative form of Σιλᾶς, 93.339 (Ac 15.34, apparatus).

93.333 Σεκοῦνδος, ου *m*: a Christian of Thessalonica who was a companion of Paul – 'Secundus' (Ac 20.4).

93.334 Σεμεΐν *m*: a person in the genealogy of Jesus – 'Semein' (Lk 3.26).

93.335 Σέργιος, ου *m*: Sergius Paulus, the governor of Cyprus – 'Sergius' (Ac 13.7).

93.336 Σερούχ *m*: a person in the genealogy of Jesus – 'Serug' (Lk 3.35).

93.337 Σήθ *m*: a person in the genealogy of Jesus – 'Seth' (Lk 3.38).

93.338 Σήμ *m*: a person in the genealogy of Jesus – 'Shem' (Lk 3.36).

93.339 Σιλᾶς, ᾶ *m*: a Christian in the Jerusalem church and an associate of Paul – 'Silas' (Ac 15.22).

93.340 Σιλουανός, οῦ *m*: generally regarded as the same person as Σιλᾶς (93.339) – 'Silvanus' (1 Th 1.1).

93.341 Σίμων, ωνος *m*: (1) Simon Peter, one of the twelve apostles (Mt 4.18); (2) Simon the Zealot, one of the twelve apostles (Lk 6.15); (3) a brother of Jesus (Mt 13.55); (4) Simon of Cyrene, who carried the cross of Jesus (Mt 27.32); (5) the father of Judas Iscariot (Jn 6.71); (6) a tanner in Joppa (Ac 9.43); (7) a magician of Samaria (Ac 8.9); (8) a leper (Mt 26.6); (9) a Pharisee (Lk 7.40) – 'Simon.'

93.342 Σκαριότα, Σκαριώθ, and Σκαριώτης: alternative forms of Ἰσκαριώθ and Ἰσκαριώτης, 93.181 (Jn 13.26, apparatus; Mk 3.19, apparatus; Mt 10.4, apparatus).

93.343 Σκευᾶς, ᾶ *m*: a Jewish high priest – 'Sceva' (Ac 19.14).

93.344 Σολομών, ῶνος *m* and Σολομῶν, ῶντος *m*: the son and successor of David – 'Solomon' (Mt 6.29; Ac 3.11).

93.345 Σουσάννα, ης *f*: a follower of Jesus – 'Susanna' (Lk 8.3).

93.346 Στάχυς, υος *m*: a person greeted in Ro 16.9 – 'Stachys.'

93.347 Στεφανᾶς, ᾶ *m*: a Christian of Corinth – 'Stephanas' (1 Cor 1.16).

93.348 Στέφανος, ου *m*: one of the seven helpers in the church in Jerusalem and the first Christian martyr – 'Stephen' (Ac 6.5; 7.59).

93.349 Συμεών *m*: (1) one form of the apostle Peter's Aramaic name (Ac 15.14); (2) a son of Jacob and ancestor of an Israelite tribe (Re 7.7); (3) an elderly man of Jerusalem (Lk 2.25, 34); (4) a Christian prophet at Antioch who was also called Niger (Ac 13.1); (5) a person in the genealogy of Jesus (Lk 3.30) – 'Simeon.'

93.350 Συντύχη, ης *f*: a Christian woman in the church of Philippi – 'Syntyche' (Php 4.2).

93.351 Συχέμ[a] *m*: the son of Hamor – 'Shechem' (Ac 7.16, apparatus).

93.352 Σώπατρος, ου *m*: a Christian in Beroea – 'Sopater' (Ac 20.4).

93.353 Σωσθένης, ους *m*: (1) a leader of a synagogue in Corinth (Ac 18.17); (2) a Christian of Corinth (1 Cor 1.1) – 'Sosthenes.' Many scholars consider 1 and 2 to be the same person.

93.354 Σωσίπατρος, ου *m*: a person who sends greetings in Ro 16.21 – 'Sosipater.'

93.355 Ταβιθά *f*: the Aramaic name of a Christian woman in Joppa whose name was interpreted as Δορκάς (93.101) – 'Tabitha' (Ac 9.36).

93.356 Ταδδαῖον: an alternative form of Θαδδαῖος, 93.150 (Mk 3.18, apparatus).

93.357 Τέρτιος, ου *m*: a person who sends greetings in Ro 16.22 – 'Tertius.'

93.358 Τέρτυλλος, ου *m*: an attorney who accused Paul before Felix – 'Tertullus' (Ac 24.1).

93.359 Τιβέριος, ου *m*: the Roman emperor Tiberius Claudius Caesar Augustus – 'Tiberius' (Lk 3.1). Contrast 93.214.

93.360 Τιμαῖος, ου *m*: the father of Bartimaeus – 'Timaeus' (Mk 10.46).

93.361 Τιμόθεος, ου *m*: a friend and co-worker of Paul – 'Timothy' (Ac 16.1; Ro 16.21).

93.362 Τίμων, ωνος *m*: one of the seven helpers in the church in Jerusalem – 'Timon' (Ac 6.5).

93.363 Τίτιος, ου *m*: a Jewish proselyte in Corinth whose additional name was Justus – 'Titius' (Ac 18.7). See 93.179.

93.364 Τίτος, ου *m*: (1) a friend and companion of Paul (Tt 1.4); (2) an alternative form of Τίτιος, 93.363 (Ac 18.7, apparatus) – 'Titus.'

93.365 Τρόφιμος, ου *m*: a Christian of Ephesus and companion of Paul – 'Trophimus' (Ac 20.4).

93.366 Τρύφαινα, ης *f*: a person greeted in Ro 16.12 – 'Tryphaena.'

93.367 Τρυφῶσα, ης *f*: a person greeted in Ro 16.12 – 'Tryphosa.'

93.368 Τύραννος, ου *m*: an Ephesian in whose hall Paul lectured – 'Tyrannus' (Ac 19.9).

93.369 Τύχικος, ου *m*: a leader from the province of Asia who was associated with Paul – 'Tychicus' (Ac 20.4; Eph 6.21; Col 4.7).

93.370 Ὑμέναιος, ου *m*: a person who defected from true faith – 'Hymenaeus' (1 Tm 1.20; 2 Tm 2.17).

93.371 Φάλεκ *m*: a person in the genealogy of Jesus – 'Peleg' (Lk 3.35).

93.372 Φανουήλ *m*: the father of Anna the prophetess – 'Phanuel' (Lk 2.36).

93.373 Φαραώ *m*: a title used as a proper name of the Egyptian king – 'Pharaoh' (Ac 7.10).

93.374 Φάρες *m*: a person in the genealogy of Jesus – 'Perez' (Mt 1.3; Lk 3.33).

93.375 Φῆλιξ, ικος *m*: a procurator of Palestine – 'Felix' (Ac 23.24).

93.376 Φῆστος, ου *m*: Porcius Festus, the successor to Felix as procurator of Palestine – 'Festus' (Ac 24.27). See 93.300.

93.377 Φιλήμων, ονος *m*: a convert and friend of Paul – 'Philemon' (Phm 1).

93.378 Φίλητος, ου *m*: a false teacher in the church – 'Philetus' (2 Tm 2.17).

93.379 Φίλιππος, ου *m*: (1) one of the twelve apostles (Mt 10.3); (2) a son of Herod the Great and brother of Herod Antipas (Lk 3.1); (3) one of the seven helpers in the church in Jerusalem (Ac 6.5); (4) the first husband of Herodias (Mt 14.3; Mk 6.17) – 'Philip.'

93.380 Φιλόλογος, ου *m*: a person greeted in Ro 16.15 – 'Philologus.'

93.381 Φλέγων, οντος *m*: a person greeted in Ro 16.14 – 'Phlegon.'

93.382 Φοίβη, ης *f*: a deaconess of the church commended in Ro 16.1 – 'Phoebe.'

93.383 Φορτουνᾶτος, ου *m*: a Christian of Corinth – 'Fortunatus' (1 Cor 16.17).

93.384 Φύγελος, ου *m*: a Christian in Asia who with Hermogenes turned his back on Paul – 'Phygelus' (2 Tm 1.15).

93.385 Χλόη, ης *f*: a person whose family members reported to Paul about divisions in the church in Corinth – 'Chloe' (1 Cor 1.11).

93.386 Χουζᾶς, ᾶ *m*: the husband of Joanna, a follower of Jesus – 'Chuza' (Lk 8.3).

93.387 Χριστός[b], οῦ *m*: (the Greek translation of the Hebrew and Aramaic word 'Messiah') a proper name for Jesus – 'Christ' (Mt 27.17). See also 53.82.

93.388 Ὡσηέ *m*: a prophet of Israel – 'Hosea' (Ro 9.25).

B Places (93.389-93.615)

93.389 Ἀβιληνή, ῆς *f*: a territory around the city of Abila, northwest of Damascus and ruled over by Lysanias – 'Abilene' (Lk 3.1), Map 2 E-1.

93.390 Ἀδραμυττηνός, ή όν: (derivative of Ἀδραμύττιον 'Adramyttium,' not occurring in the NT) pertaining to Adramyttium, a seaport in Mysia (Map 4 E-2) – 'of Adramyttium' (Ac 27.2).

93.391 Ἀδρίας, ου *m* – 'Adriatic Sea' (Ac 27.27), Map 4 B-2.

93.392 Ἄζωτος, ου *f*: a city on the coast of southern Palestine – 'Azotus' (Ac 8.40), Map 2 A-6, the Ashdod of the OT, Map 1 A-6.

93.393 Ἀθῆναι, ῶν *f*: a principal city of Greece – 'Athens' (Ac 17.15), Maps 3 A-1 and 4 D-3.

93.394 Ἀθηναῖος, α, ον: (derivative of Ἀθῆναι 'Athens,' 93.393) pertaining to Athens – 'Athenian' (Ac 17.22).

93.395 Ἀθηναῖος, ου *m*: (derivative of Ἀθῆναι 'Athens,' 93.393) a person who lives in or is a native of Athens – 'an Athenian' (Ac 17.21).

93.396 Αἰγύπτιος, α, ον: (derivative of Αἴγυπτος 'Egypt,' 93.398) pertaining to Egypt – 'Egyptian' (Ac 7.22).

93.397 Αἰγύπτιος, ου *m*: (derivative of Αἴγυπτος 'Egypt,' 93.398) a person who is a native of Egypt – 'an Egyptian' (Ac 7.24).

93.398 Αἴγυπτος, ου *f* – 'Egypt' (Mt 2.13; Ac 7.36), Maps 3 B-4 and 4 F-5.

93.399 Αἰθίοψ, οπος *m*: (derivative of Αἰθιωπία 'Ethiopia,' not occurring in the NT) a person who is a native of Ethiopia – 'an Ethiopian' (Ac 8.27).

93.400 Αἰνών *f*: a place where John the Baptist was baptizing – 'Aenon' (Jn 3.23), Map 2 C-4.

93.401 Ἀκελδαμάχ: (an Aramaic term meaning 'field of blood') a piece of land, probably south of the valley of Hinnom outside Jerusalem, which was bought with Judas's money – 'Akeldama' (Ac 1.19).

93.402 Ἀλεξανδρεύς, έως *m*: (derivative of Ἀλεξανδρία 'Alexandria,' not occurring in the NT) a person who lives in or is a native of Alexandria (Map 4 F-5) – 'an Alexandrian' (Ac 18.24).

93.403 Ἀλεξανδρῖνος, η, ον: (derivative of Ἀλεξανδρία 'Alexandria,' not occurring in the NT) pertaining to Alexandria (Map 4 F-5) – 'Alexandrian' (Ac 27.6).

93.404 Ἀμφίπολις, εως *f*: the capital of southeast Macedonia – 'Amphipolis' (Ac 17.1), Map 4 D-2.

93.405 Ἀντιόχεια, ας *f*: (1) a city in Syria (Ac 11.26), Map 4 G-3; (2) a city in Pisidia (Ac 13.14), Map 4 F-2 – 'Antioch.'

93.406 Ἀντιοχεύς, έως *m*: (derivative of Ἀντιόχεια 'Antioch,' 93.405) a person who lives in or is a native of Antioch – 'an Antiochean' (Ac 6.5).

93.407 Ἀντιπατρίς, ίδος *f*: a city in Judea – 'Antipatris' (Ac 23.31), Maps 2 B-5 and 4 G-4.

93.408 Ἀπολλωνία, ας *f*: a city in Macedonia – 'Apollonia' (Ac 17.1), Map 4 D-2.

93.409 Ἀππίου Φόρον: a market town south of Rome – 'Forum of Appius' (Ac 28.15), Map 4 A-1.

93.410 Ἀραβία, ας *f* – 'Arabia' (Ga 4.25, probably a reference to the Sinai Peninsula), Maps 2 E-4, 3 E-4, and 4 H-4.

93.411 Ἄραψ, βος *m*: (derivative of Ἀραβία 'Arabia,' 93.410) a person who is a native of Arabia – 'an Arab' (Ac 2.11).

93.412 Ἄρειος Πάγος[a] *m*: (literally 'hill of Mars') the location of an Athenian court, traditionally associated with a rocky hill close to the Acropolis, though probably located in the marketplace at the foot of the hill – 'Areopagus' (Ac 17.19, 22). For another interpretation of Ἄρειος Πάγος in Ac 17.19, 22, see 11.81.

93.413 Ἀριμαθαία, ας *f*: a city in Judea – 'Arimathea' (Lk 23.51), Map 2 B-5.

93.414 Ἁρμαγεδών: a cryptic place name designating the territory which will be the scene of the final battle of the forces of good and evil – 'Armageddon' (Re 16.16).

93.415 Ἀσία, ας *f*: the Roman province of Asia, primarily the western part of present-day Turkey – 'Asia' (Ac 2.9), Map 4 E-2.

93.416 Ἀσιανός, οῦ *m*: (derivative of Ἀσία 'Asia,' 93.415) a person who is a native of Asia – 'an Asian' (Ac 20.4).

93.417 Ἄσσος, ου *f*: a city of Mysia – 'Assos' (Ac 20.13), Map 4 E-2.

93.418 Ἀττάλεια, ας *f*: a seaport in Pamphylia – 'Attalia' (Ac 14.25), Map 4 F-3.

93.419 Ἀχαΐα, ας *f*: a Roman province including the most important parts of Greece – 'Achaia' (Ac 18.27; 2 Cor 1.1), Map 4 C-2.

93.420 Βαβυλών, ῶνος *f*: the capital of Babylonia – 'Babylon' (Mt 1.11; Ac 7.43), Map 3 F-3. Βαβυλών also occurs as a symbol of demonic world power (Re 14.8; 16.19).

93.421 Βελζεθά: an alternative form of Βηθζαθά, 93.430 (Jn 5.2, apparatus).

93.422 Βέροια, ας *f*: a city in Macedonia – 'Beroea' (Ac 17.10), Map 4 C-2.

93.423 Βεροιαῖος, ου *m*: (derivative of Βέροια 'Beroea,' 93.422) a person who lives in or is a native of Beroea – 'a Beroean' (Ac 20.4).

93.424 Βηδσαϊδάν: an alternative form of Βηθσαϊδά, 93.432 (Jn 5.2, apparatus).

93.425 Βηζαθά: an alternative form of Βηθζαθά, 93.430 (Jn 5.2, apparatus).

93.426 Βηθαβαρά *f*: a place of uncertain location – 'Bethabara' (Jn 1.28, apparatus).

93.427 Βηθανία, ας *f*: (1) a village on the Mount of Olives (Jn 11.1), Map 2 C-6; (2) a place on the east side of the Jordan where John baptized (Jn 1.28) – 'Bethany.'

93.428 Βηθαραβά: an alternative form of Βηθαβαρά, 93.426 (Jn 1.28, apparatus).

93.429 Βηθεσδά *f*: an alternative form of Βηθζαθά (93.430) – 'Bethesda' (Jn 5.2, apparatus).

93.430 Βηθζαθά *f*: a pool in the northeast part of Old Jerusalem – 'Bethzatha' (Jn 5.2).

93.431 Βηθλέεμ *f*: a town south of Jerusalem – 'Bethlehem' (Mt 2.1), Maps 1 C-6 and 2 C-6.

93.432 Βηθσαϊδά *f*: a place northeast of the Lake of Galilee – 'Bethsaida' (Mt 11.21; Lk 9.10; Jn 1.44), Map 2 D-3.

93.433 Βηθφαγή *f*: a village near Jerusalem, perhaps east of Bethany – 'Bethphage' (Mk 11.1).

93.434 Βησσαϊδά: an alternative form of Βηθσαϊδά, 93.432 (Jn 5.2, apparatus).

93.435 Βιθαρά: an alternative form of Βηθαβαρά, 93.426 (Jn 1.28, apparatus).

93.436 Βιθυνία, ας *f*: a province in northern Asia Minor – 'Bithynia' (Ac 16.7), Map 4 F-2.

93.437 Γαββαθα: the Aramaic name for a paved area outside the residence of Pontius Pilate and the setting for the public trial of Jesus – 'Gabbatha' (Jn 19.13). See 7.71.

93.438 Γαδαρηνός, οῦ *m*: (derivative of

Γάδαρα 'Gadara,' not occurring in the NT) a person who lives in or is a native of Gadara (Map 2 D-4) – 'a Gadarene' (Mt 8.28).

93.439 Γάζα, ης *f*: a city in southwest Palestine on a principal road to Egypt – 'Gaza' (Ac 8.26), Maps 1 A-7, 2 A-7, and 3 C-4.

93.440 Γαζαρηνός: an alternative form of Γαδαρηνός, 93.438 (Mt 8.28, apparatus).

93.441 Γαλάτης, ου *m*: (derivative of Γαλατία 'Galatia,' 93.442) a person who is a native of Galatia – 'a Galatian' (Ga 3.1).

93.442 Γαλατία, ας *f*: a district in the Roman province of Asia – 'Galatia' (Ga 1.2; 1 Cor 16.1), Map 4 F-2, 4 G-2.

93.443 Γαλατικός, ή, όν: (derivative of Γαλατία 'Galatia,' 93.442) pertaining to Galatia – 'Galatian' (Ac 18.23).

93.444 Γαλιλαία, ας *f*: (1) a district in the northern part of Palestine (Lk 5.17; 17.11; Mt 21.11); (2) the Lake of Galilee, also called Tiberias and Gennesaret (Mt 15.29; Mk 1.16) – 'Galilee,' Map 2 C-3, 2 D-3, 4 G-4.

93.445 Γαλιλαῖος, ου *m*: (derivative of Γαλιλαία 'Galilee,' 93.444) a person who is a native of Galilee – 'a Galilean' (Lk 13.1).

93.446 Γαλλία, ας *f*: an alternative form of Γαλατία, 93.442 (2 Tm 4.10, apparatus).

93.447 Γαύδη: an alternative form of Καῦδα, 93.497 (Ac 27.16, apparatus).

93.448 Γεθσημανί: a garden at the foot of the Mount of Olives – 'Gethsemane' (Mt 26.36).

93.449 Γεννησαρέτ *f*: (1) a fertile plain south of Capernaum (Mk 6.53); (2) a name for the Lake of Galilee, also called the Lake of Tiberias (Lk 5.1) – 'Gennesaret.'

93.450 Γερασηνός, οῦ *m*: (derivative of Γέρασα 'Gerasa,' not occurring in the NT) a person who lives in or is a native of Gerasa, a city in Peraea, east of the Jordan (Map 2 D-5) – 'a Gerasene' (Mk 5.1).

93.451 Γεργεσηνός, οῦ *m*: (derivative of Γέργεσα 'Gergesa,' not occurring in the NT) a person who lives in or is a native of Gergesa (Map 2 D-3) – 'a Gergesene' (Mt 8.28, apparatus).

93.452 Γερσινός: an alternative form of Γεργεσηνός, 93.451 (Mt 8.28, apparatus).

93.453 Γολγοθᾶ, acc. ᾶν *f*: the Aramaic name of a hill near Jerusalem where executions took place – 'Golgotha' (Mt 27.33). See also 8.11.

93.454 Γόμορρα, ας *f* and ων *n*: a city located at the southern part of the Dead Sea and destroyed because of its evil – 'Gomorrah' (2 Pe 2.6).

93.455 Γύλλιον: an alternative form of Τρωγύλλιον, 93.600 (Ac 20.15, apparatus).

93.456 Δαλμανουθά *f*: a place of uncertain location near the western shore of the Lake of Galilee – 'Dalmanutha' (Mk 8.10).

93.457 Δαλματία, ας *f*: the southern part of Illyricum – 'Dalmatia' (2 Tm 4.10), Map 4 B-1.

93.458 Δαμασκηνός, οῦ *m*: (derivative of Δαμασκός 'Damascus,' 93.459) a person who lives in or is a native of Damascus – 'a Damascene' (2 Cor 11.32).

93.459 Δαμασκός, οῦ *f*: the capital of Syria – 'Damascus' (Ac 9.2; 2 Cor 11.32; Ga 1.17), Maps 1 E-1, 2 E-1, 3 D-3, and 4 H-4.

93.460 Δεκάπολις, εως *f*: a league of ten cities in a region east of the Jordan – 'Decapolis' (Mt 4.25; Mk 5.20), Map 2 D-5.

93.461 Δερβαῖος, ου *m*: (derivative of Δέρβη 'Derbe,' 93.462) a person who lives in or is a native of Derbe – 'a Derbean' (Ac 20.4).

93.462 Δέρβη, ης *f*: a city in Lycaonia – 'Derbe' (Ac 14.6), Map 4 F-3.

93.463 Δουβέριος, ου *m*: (derivative of Δόβηρος 'Doberus,' not occurring in the NT) a person who lives in or is a native of Doberus, a city in Macedonia – 'a Doberian' (Ac 20.4, apparatus).

93.464 Ἔγυπτος: an alternative form of Αἴγυπτος 'Egypt,' 93.398 (Ac 7.18, apparatus).

93.465 Ἐλαμίτης, ου *m*: (alternative form of Ἐλυμαῖος, derivative of Ἐλυμαίς 'Elumais' or 'Elam,' not occurring in the NT) a person who is a native of Elam (Map 3 G-3) – 'an Elamite' (Ac 2.9).

93.466 Ἑλλάς, άδος *f* – 'Greece' (Ac 20.2), Map 4 C-3.

93.467 Ἐμμαοῦς *f*: a village in Judea, not far from Jerusalem – 'Emmaus' (Lk 24.13), Map 2 B-6.

93.468 Εὐφράτης, ου *m*: a river in Mesopotamia – 'Euphrates' (Re 9.14), Maps 3 E-3 and 4 H-2.

93.469 Ἐφέσιος, α, ον: (derivative of Ἔφεσος 'Ephesus,' 93.471) pertaining to Ephesus – 'Ephesian' (Ac 19.35).

93.470 Ἐφέσιος, ου *m*: (derivative of Ἔφεσος 'Ephesus,' 93.471) a person who lives in or is a native of Ephesus – 'an Ephesian' (Ac 21.29).

93.471 Ἔφεσος, ου *f*: a seaport in the western part of the Roman province of Asia – 'Ephesus' (Ac 18.19; 1 Cor 15.32; 1 Tm 1.3), Maps 3 B-2 and 4 E-3.

93.472 Ἐφραίμ *m*: a city of uncertain location – 'Ephraim' (Jn 11.54), Map 2 C-6.

93.473 Ζαβουλών[b] *m*: the territory of the tribe of Zebulun – 'Zebulun' (Mt 4.13), Maps 1 C-3 and 2 C-3.

93.474 Θεσσαλονικεύς, έως *m*: (derivative of Θεσσαλονίκη 'Thessalonica,' 93.475) a person who lives in or is a native of Thessalonica – 'a Thessalonian' (1 Th 1.1).

93.475 Θεσσαλονίκη, ης *f*: a city of Macedonia – 'Thessalonica' (Ac 17.1; Php 4.16), Map 4 D-2.

93.476 Θυάτειρα or Θυάτιρα, ων *n*: a city in Lydia – 'Thyatira' (Ac 16.14; Re 2.18), Map 4 E-2.

93.477 Ἰδουμαία, ας *f*: a mountainous region south of Judea (Edom of the OT) – 'Idumea' (Mk 3.8), Map 2 B-7.

93.478 Ἱεράπολις, εως *f*: a city in Phrygia – 'Hierapolis' (Col 4.13), Map 4 E-2.

93.479 Ἱεριχώ *f*: a city in Judea, not far from the north end of the Dead Sea – 'Jericho' (Mk 10.46; Lk 18.35), Maps 1 C-6, 1i C-1, and 2 C-6.

93.480 Ἱεροσόλυμα *f* and ων *n* and Ἱερουσαλήμ *f*: (1) the city of Jerusalem, including its inhabitants (Mk 3.8; Jn 1.19; Ac 5.28), Maps 1 C-6, 1i A-1, 2 C-6, 3 C-4, and 4 G-4; (2) the heavenly Jerusalem of the future (Ga 4.25; He 12.22; Re 3.12) – 'Jerusalem.'

93.481 Ἱεροσολυμίτης, ου *m*: (derivative of Ἱεροσόλυμα 'Jerusalem,' 93.480) an inhabitant of Jerusalem – 'a person from Jerusalem' (Mk 1.5).

93.482 Ἰκόνιον, ου *n*: a city in Lycaonia – 'Iconium' (Ac 13.51), Map 4 F-2.

93.483 Ἰλλυρικόν, οῦ *n*: a district to the north of Macedonia – 'Illyricum' (Ro 15.19), Map 4 C-1.

93.484 Ἰόππη, ης *f*: a seaport on the coast of Palestine – 'Joppa' or 'Jaffa' (Ac 9.36), Maps 1 B-5, 2 B-5, and 3 C-4.

93.485 Ἰορδάνης, ου *m* – 'Jordan River' (Mt 3.6; Lk 3.3), Maps 1 D-5 and 2 D-5.

93.486 Ἰουδαία, ας *f*: (1) the southern part of Palestine (Mt 2.1; Lk 1.65), Map 2 C-6; (2) the wider region occupied by the Jewish nation (Ac 10.37; 26.20; Mt 19.1) – 'Judea.'

93.487 Ἰουδαῖος, α, ον: (derivative of Ἰουδαία 'Judea,' 93.486) pertaining to Judea – 'Judean' (Mk 1.5).

93.488 Ἰούδας^c, α *m*: the territory of the tribe of Judah – 'Judah' (Mt 2.6), Map 1 C-6.

93.489 Ἰταλία, ας *f* – 'Italy' (Ac 18.2; He 13.24), Map 4 A-1.

93.490 Ἰταλικός, ή, όν: (derivative of Ἰταλία 'Italy,' 93.489) pertaining to Italy – 'Italian' (Ac 10.1).

93.491 Ἰτουραῖος, α, ον: (derivative of Ἰτυραία 'Ituraea,' not occurring in the NT) pertaining to Ituraea (Map 2 D-2) – 'Ituraean' (Lk 3.1).

93.492 Καισάρεια, ας *f*: (1) Caesarea on the coast of Palestine, south of Mount Carmel (Ac 8.40; 25.1), Maps 2 B-4 and 4 G-4; (2) Caesarea Philippi (Καισάρεια τῆς Φιλίππου) at the foot of Mount Hermon (Mt 16.13; Mk 8.27), Map 2 D-2 – 'Caesarea, Caesarea Philippi.' See also 93.605.

93.493 Καλοὶ Λιμένες, ων *m*: a bay on the south coast of Crete – 'Fair Havens' (Ac 27.8), Map 4 D-4.

93.494 Κανά *f*: a city in Galilee – 'Cana' (Jn 2.1), Map 2 C-3.

93.495 Καππαδοκία, ας *f*: a province in the interior of Asia Minor – 'Cappadocia' (Ac 2.9; 1 Pe 1.1), Map 4 G-2.

93.496 Καρυῶτος: a place in southern Judea – 'Carioth' or 'Kerioth' (Jn 6.71, apparatus; 13.2, apparatus).

93.497 Καῦδα: a small island south of Crete – 'Cauda' (Ac 27.16), Map 4 D-4.

93.498 Καφαρναούμ *f*: a city on the Lake of Galilee – 'Capernaum' (Mt 4.13; Mk 1.21; Jn 2.12), Map 2 D-3.

93.499 Κεγχρεαί, ῶν *f*: a seaport of the city of Corinth – 'Cenchreae' (Ac 18.18; Ro 16.1), Map 4 D-3.

93.500 Κεδρών *m*: a valley between Jerusalem and the Mount of Olives – 'Kidron' (Jn 18.1).

93.501 Κιλικία, ας *f*: a province in the southeast corner of Asia Minor – 'Cilicia' (Ac 6.9; Ga 1.21), Map 4 G-3.

93.502 Κλαῦδα, Κλαύδη, Κλαύδιον, Κλάδιν: alternative forms of Καῦδα, 93.497 (Ac 27.16, apparatus).

93.503 Κνίδος, ου *f*: a peninsula on the southwest coast of Asia Minor – 'Cnidus' (Ac 27.7), Map 4 E-3.

93.504 Κολοσσαί, ῶν *f*: a city in Phrygia in Asia Minor – 'Colossae' (Col 1.2), Map 4 E-3.

93.505 Κορίνθιος, ου *m*: (derivative of Κόρινθος 'Corinth,' 93.506) a person who lives in or is a native of Corinth – 'a Corinthian' (2 Cor 6.11).

93.506 Κόρινθος, ου *f*: a city in Greece – 'Corinth' (Ac 18.1; 1 Cor 1.2; 2 Tm 4.20), Map 4 D-3.

93.507 Κρής, ητός *m*: (derivative of Κρήτη 'Crete,' 93.508) a person who is a native of Crete – 'a Cretan' (Ac 2.11).

93.508 Κρήτη, ης *f*: an island south of Greece – 'Crete' (Ac 27.7; Tt 1.5), Maps 3 A-2 and 4 D-3.

93.509 Κύπριος, ου *m*: (derivative of Κύπρος 'Cyprus,' 93.510) a person who is a native of Cyprus – 'a Cyprian' (Ac 21.16).

93.510 Κύπρος, ου *f*: an island off the south coast of Asia Minor – 'Cyprus' (Ac 13.4), Maps 3 C-3 and 4 G-3.

93.511 Κυρηναῖος, ου *m*: (derivative of Κυρήνη 'Cyrene,' 93.512) a person who lives in or is a native of Cyrene – 'a Cyrenian' (Mk 15.21).

93.512 Κυρήνη, ης *f*: a city on the coast of north Africa – 'Cyrene' (Ac 2.10), Map 4 C-4.

93.513 Κώς, Κῶ, acc. Κῶ *f*: an island in the Aegean Sea – 'Cos' (Ac 21.1), Map 4 E-3.

93.514 Λαοδίκεια, ας *f*: a city in Phrygia in Asia Minor – 'Laodicea' (Col 2.1; Re 3.14), Map 4 E-2.

93.515 Λαοδικεύς, έως *m*: (derivative of Λαοδίκεια 'Laodicea,' 93.514) a person who lives in or is a native of Laodicea – 'a Laodicean' (Col 4.16).

93.516 Λασαία, ας *f*: a city on the south coast of the island of Crete – 'Lasea' (Ac 27.8), Map 4 D-4.

93.517 Λιβύη, ης *f*: a district in north Africa – 'Libya' (Ac 2.10), Maps 3 A-4 and 4 D-5.

93.518 Λύδδα, ας, acc. Λύδδα *f*: a city southeast of Joppa – 'Lydda' (Ac 9.38), Map 2 B-6.

93.519 Λυκαονία, ας *f*: a province in the interior of Asia Minor – 'Lycaonia' (Ac 14.6), Map 4 F-2.

93.520 Λυκία, ας *f*: a projection on the south coast of Asia Minor – 'Lycia' (Ac 27.5), Map 4 E-3.

93.521 Λύστρα, dat. οις, acc. αν *f* and *n*: a city in Lycaonia in Asia Minor – 'Lystra' (Ac 14.6; 16.1; 2 Tm 3.11), Map 4 F-2.

93.522 Μαγαδάν *f* or Μαγαδά or Μαγεδάν: a place of uncertain location on the Lake of Galilee – 'Magadan' (Mt 15.39; Mk 8.10, apparatus).

93.523 Μαγδαλά *f*: a town on the west side of the Lake of Galilee – 'Magdala,' Map 2 C-3. Μαγδαλά occurs only in the apparatus of the UBS Greek New Testament (Mt 15.39), but see Μαγδαληνή (93.242).

93.524 Μαγδαλάν, Μαγεδάλ, and Μελεγαδά: alternative forms of Μαγαδάν, 93.522, and Μαγδαλά, 93.523 (Mt 15.39, apparatus; Mk 8.10, apparatus).

93.525 Μαγεδά: probably an alternative of Μαγαδάν, 93.522, though designated as a mountain in Mk 8.10, apparatus.

93.526 Μαδιάμ *m*: a region in the Sinai peninsula and nearby Arabia – 'Midian' (Ac 7.29), Map 3 C-4.

93.527 Μακεδονία, ας *f*: a Roman province in Greece – 'Macedonia' (Ac 16.9; 2 Cor 2.13; Php 4.15), Map 4 C-2.

93.528 Μακεδών, όνος *m*: (derivative of Μακεδονία 'Macedonia,' 93.527) a person who is a native of Macedonia – 'a Macedonian' (2 Cor 9.2).

93.529 Μελίτη, ης *f*: an island located south of Sicily – 'Malta' (Ac 28.1), Map 4 A-3.

93.530 Μεσοποταμία, ας *f*: the valley of the Euphrates and Tigris rivers – 'Mesopotamia' (Ac 2.9), Map 3 E-2.

93.531 Μῆδος, ου *m*: (derivative of Μηδία 'Media,' not occurring in the NT) a person who is a native of Media (Map 3 G-3) – 'a Mede' (Ac 2.9).

93.532 Μίλητος, ου *f*: a seaport city on the west coast of Asia Minor – 'Miletus' (2 Tm 4.20; Ac 20.15), Map 4 E-3.

93.533 Μιτυλήνη, ης *f*: the chief city on the island of Lesbos in the Aegean Sea – 'Mitylene' (Ac 20.14), Map 4 E-2.

93.534 Μύρα, ων *n*: a city on the south coast of Lycia in Asia Minor – 'Myra' (Ac 27.5), Map 4 F-3.

93.535 Μυσία, ας *f*: a province in northwest Asia Minor – 'Mysia' (Ac 16.7), Map 4 E-2.

93.536 Ναζαρά or Ναζαρέθ or Ναζαρέτ *f*: a town in the south central part of Galilee – 'Nazareth' (Mt 4.13; 21.11; Lk 2.4; Mk 1.9), Map 2 C-3.

93.537 Ναζαρηνός, οῦ *m*: (derivative of Ναζαρέθ 'Nazareth,' 93.536) a person who lives in or is a native of Nazareth – 'a Nazarene' (Mk 1.24). Ναζορηνός, Ναζωρηνός, and Ναζωρινός (Mk 10.47, apparatus) are incidental alternative spellings.

93.538 Ναζωραῖος, ου *m*: an alternative form of Ναζαρηνός, 93.537 (Mt 2.23; Lk 18.37).

93.539 Ναΐν *f*: a city in southern Galilee – 'Nain' (Lk 7.11), Map 2 C-4.

93.540 Ναραῖος: an alternative form of Ναζωραῖος, 93.538 (Mk 10.47, apparatus).

93.541 Νέα Πόλις *f*: the harbor of Philippi in Macedonia – 'Neapolis' (Ac 16.11), Map 4 D-2.

93.542 Νεφθαλίμ[b] *m*: the territory of the tribe of Naphtali – 'Naphtali' (Mt 4.13), Maps 1 C-3 and 2 C-3.

93.543 Νικόπολις, εως *f*: a city on the west coast of Greece – 'Nicopolis' (Tt 3.12), Map 4 C-2.

93.544 Νινευίτης, ου *m*: (derivative of Νινευή 'Nineveh,' not occurring in the NT) a person who lives in or is a native of Nineveh (Map 3 E-2) – 'a Ninevite' (Mt 12.41).

93.545 Παμφυλία, ας *f*: a province in the southern part of Asia Minor – 'Pamphylia' (Ac 2.10), Map 4 F-3.

93.546 Πάρθος, ου *m*: (derivative of Παρθία 'Parthia,' not occurring in the NT) a person who is a native of Parthia, a region southeast of Media – 'a Parthian' (Ac 2.9).

93.547 Πάταρα, ων *n*: a city in Lycia on the southwest coast of Asia Minor – 'Patara' (Ac 21.1), Map 4 E-3.

93.548 Πάτμος, ου *m*: a small, rocky island in the Aegean Sea – 'Patmos' (Re 1.9), Map 4 E-3.

93.549 Πάφος, ου *f*: a city on the southwest coast of the island of Cyprus – 'Paphos' (Ac 13.6), Map 4 F-3.

93.550 Πέργαμος, ου *f* or Πέργαμον, ου *n*: an important city in northwest Asia Minor – 'Pergamum' (Re 2.12), Map 4 E-2.

93.551 Πέργη, ης *f*: a city in Pamphylia, near the south coast of Asia Minor – 'Perga' (Ac 13.14), Map 4 F-3.

93.552 Πισιδία, ας *f*: a region in central Asia Minor – 'Pisidia' (Ac 14.24), Map 4 F-2.

93.553 Πισίδιος, α, ον: (derivative of Πισιδία 'Pisidia,' 93.552) pertaining to Pisidia – 'Pisidian' (Ac 13.14).

93.554 Ποντικός, ή, όν: (derivative of Πόντος 'Pontus,' 93.555) pertaining to Pontus – 'Pontian' (Ac 18.2).

93.555 Πόντος, ου *m*: a region in northeast Asia Minor – 'Pontus' (Ac 2.9; 1 Pe 1.1), Map 4 G-1.

93.556 Ποτίολοι, ων *m*: a city on the coast of Italy, south of Rome – 'Puteoli' (Ac 28.13), Map 4 A-1.

93.557 Πτολεμαΐς, ΐδος *f*: a seaport on the coast of Palestine (called Acco in OT times) – 'Ptolemais' (Ac 21.7), Maps 2 B-3 and 4 G-4.

93.558 Ῥαμά *f*: a city north of Jerusalem – 'Ramah' (Mt 2.18), Maps 1 C-6 and li A-1.

93.559 Ῥήγιον, ου *n*: a city on a promontory in the south of Italy – 'Rhegium' (Ac 28.13), Map 4 B-2.

93.560 Ῥόδος, ου *f*: an island off the southwest coast of Asia Minor – 'Rhodes' (Ac 21.1), Maps 3 B-2 and 4 E-3.

93.561 Ῥωμαϊκός, ή, όν: (derivative of Ῥωμαῖος 'a Roman,' 93.562) pertaining to the Romans – 'Roman' (Lk 23.38, apparatus). The addition of the word γράμμασιν in some manuscripts literally applies to Roman letters, though the reference seems to be to the Roman language, Latin.

93.562 Ῥωμαῖος, ου *m*: (derivative of Ῥώμη

'Rome,' 93.563) a person who lives in or is a native of Rome or a citizen of the Roman Empire – 'a Roman' (Ac 2.10; 22.25).

93.563 Ῥώμη, ης *f*: the capital city of the Roman Empire – 'Rome' (Ac 18.2; Ro 1.7), Map 4 A-1.

93.564 Σαλαμίς, ῖνος *f*: a city on the southeast coast of Cyprus – 'Salamis' (Ac 13.5), Map 4 G-3.

93.565 Σαλείμ or Σαλίμ *n*: a place in northern Samaria (location uncertain) – 'Salim' (Jn 3.23), Map 2 C-4.

93.566 Σαλήμ[a] *f*: a place of which Melchizedek was king – 'Salem' (He 7.1, 2). See also 93.321.

93.567 Σαλμώνη, ης *f*: a promontory on the northeast corner of Crete – 'Salmone' (Ac 27.7), Map 4 E-3.

93.568 Σαμάρεια, ας *f*: (1) a region in the central part of Palestine (Jn 4.4; Lk 17.11), Map 2 C-4; (2) the principal city of Samaria (Ac 8.5), Map 1 C-5 – 'Samaria.'

93.569 Σαμαρίτης, ου *m*: (derivative of Σαμάρεια 'Samaria,' 93.568) a person who is a native of Samaria – 'a Samaritan' (Lk 17.16).

93.570 Σαμαρῖτις, ιδος *f*: (derivative of Σαμάρεια 'Samaria,' 93.568) a woman who is a native of Samaria – 'a Samaritan woman' (Jn 4.9).

93.571 Σαμοθράκη, ης *f*: an island in the northern Aegean Sea – 'Samothrace' (Ac 16.11), Map 4 E-2.

93.572 Σάμος, ου *f*: an island off the west coast of Asia Minor – 'Samos' (Ac 20.15), Map 4 E-3.

93.573 Σάρδεις, εων *f*: a city in western Asia Minor – 'Sardis' (Re 3.1), Maps 3 B-2 and 4 E-2.

93.574 Σάρεπτα, ων *n*: a city on the coast of Phoenicia between Tyre and Sidon – 'Zarephath' (Lk 4.26), Maps 1 C-1 and 2 C-1.

93.575 Σαρών, ῶνος *m*: the plain along the coast of Palestine – 'Sharon' (Ac 9.35), Maps 1 B-4 and 2 B-4.

93.576 Σελεύκεια, ας *f*: the port city of Antioch in Syria – 'Seleucia' (Ac 13.4), Map 4 G-3.

93.577 Σιδών, ῶνος *f*: a city on the coast of Phoenicia – 'Sidon' (Mt 11.21; Mk 3.8), Maps 1 C-1, 2 C-1, 3 D-3, and 4 G-4.

93.578 Σιδώνιος, α, ον: (derivative of Σιδών 'Sidon,' 93.577) pertaining to Sidon – 'Sidonian' (Lk 4.26).

93.579 Σιδώνιος, ου *m*: (derivative of Σιδών 'Sidon,' 93.577) a person who lives in or is a native of Sidon – 'a Sidonian' (Ac 12.20).

93.580 Σιλωάμ *m*: the name for a system of water supply in Jerusalem; the pool of Siloam was probably the basin into which the water flowed – 'Siloam' (Jn 9.7; Lk 13.4).

93.581 Σινᾶ *n*: a rocky mountain on the peninsula of Sinai – '(Mount) Sinai' (Ac 7.30; Ga 4.24), Map 3 C-5.

93.582 Σιών *f*: (1) Mount Zion, a hill within the city of Jerusalem (Re 14.1); (2) the city of Jerusalem together with its people, particularly in poetic discourse (Mt 21.5; Jn 12.15); see also 11.66 – 'Zion.'

93.583 Σκύθης, ου *m*: (derivative of Σκυθία 'Scythia,' not occurring in the NT) a person who is a native of Scythia, a region north of the Black Sea, and regarded by the Greco-Roman world as utterly pagan and uncivilized – 'Scythian' (Col 3.11).

93.584 Σμύρνα, ης *f*: a city on the west coast of Asia Minor – 'Smyrna' (Re 2.8), Map 4 E-2.

93.585 Σόδομα, ων *n*: a city located at the southern part of the Dead Sea and destroyed because of its evil – 'Sodom' (2 Pe 2.6).

93.586 Σπανία, ας *f*: a country at the western end of the Mediterranean Sea – 'Spain' (Ro 15.24).

93.587 Στογύλιον and Στρογγύλιον: alternative forms of Τρωγύλλιον, 93.600 (Ac 20.15, apparatus).

93.588 Συράκουσαι, ῶν *f*: a city on the east coast of Sicily – 'Syracuse' (Ac 28.12), Map 4 A-3.

93.589 Συρία, ας *f*: a region to the north and east of Palestine and known as Aram in OT times – 'Syria' (Mt 4.24; Ac 18.18), Maps 3 D-3 and 4 H-3.

93.590 Σύρος, ου *m*: (derivative of Συρία 'Syria,' 93.589) a person who is a native of Syria – 'a Syrian' (Lk 4.27).

93.591 Συροφοινίκισσα, ης *f*: (derivative of Συροφοινικία 'Syro-Phoenicia,' not occurring in the NT) a woman who is a native of Syro-Phoenicia (Map 2 C-2) – 'a Syrophoenician woman' (Mk 7.26). See also discussion at 10.1.

93.592 Σύρτις, εως *f*: two shallow and treacherous Mediterranean gulfs along the north African coastline – 'the Syrtis' (Ac 27.17), Map 4 B-5.

93.593 Συχάρ *f*: a city in Samaria – 'Sychar' (Jn 4.5), Map 2 C-5.

93.594 Συχέμ[b] *f*: a city in Samaria – 'Shechem' (Ac 7.16), Maps 1 C-5 and 2 C-5.

93.595 Ταρσεύς, έως *m*: (derivative of Ταρσός 'Tarsus,' 93.596) a person who lives in or is a native of Tarsus – 'a person from Tarsus' (Ac 9.11).

93.596 Ταρσός, οῦ *f*: the capital of Cilicia in southeast Asia Minor – 'Tarsus' (Ac 9.30; 11.25), Map 4 G-3.

93.597 Τιβεριάς, άδος *f*: (1) a city on the west shore of the Lake of Galilee (Jn 6.23),

Map 2 C-3; (2) the Lake of Tiberias, also known as the Lake of Galilee (Jn 21.1) – 'Tiberias.'

93.598 Τραχωνῖτις, ιδος *f*: a district to the south of Damascus – 'Trachonitis' (Lk 3.1), Map 2 E-2.

93.599 Τρῳάς, άδος *f*: a city and region in the northwest corner of Asia Minor – 'Troas' (Ac 20.6; 2 Cor 2.12), Map 4 D-2.

93.600 Τρωγύλλιον, ου *n*: a promontory and town south of Ephesus in Asia Minor – 'Trogyllium' (Ac 20.15, apparatus), Map 4 E-3.

93.601 Τύριος, ου *m*: (derivative of Τύρος 'Tyre,' 93.602) a person who lives in or is a native of Tyre – 'a Tyrian' (Ac 12.20).

93.602 Τύρος, ου *f*: a city on the Phoenician coast – 'Tyre' (Mt 11.21; Lk 6.17), Maps 1 C-2, 2 C-2, 3 C-3, and 4 G-4.

93.603 Φιλαδέλφεια, ας *f*: a city in the west central part of Asia Minor – 'Philadelphia' (Re 3.7), Map 4 E-2.

93.604 Φιλιππήσιος, ου *m*: (derivative of Φίλιπποι 'Philippi,' 93.605) a person who lives in or is a native of Philippi – 'a Philippian' (Php 4.15).

93.605 Φίλιπποι, ων *m*: a city in Macedonia – 'Philippi' (Ac 16.12; Php 1.1), Map 4 D-1. For Καισάρεια τῆς Φιλίππου 'Caesarea Philippi,' see 93.492.

93.606 Φοινίκη, ης *f*: an area along the seacoast to the west and north of Palestine – 'Phoenicia' (Ac 11.19; 21.2), Map 4 G-4.

93.607 Φοῖνιξ, ικος *m*: a seaport on the south coast of Crete – 'Phoenix' (Ac 27.12), Map 4 D-4.

93.608 Φόρον, ου *n*: see Ἀππίου Φόρον (93.409).

93.609 Φρυγία, ας *f*: a district in central

Asia Minor – 'Phrygia' (Ac 2.10; 16.6), Map 4 E-2.

93.610 Χαλδαῖος, ου *m*: (derivative of Χαλδαία 'Chaldea,' not occurring in the NT) a person who is a native of Chaldea (Map 3 F-4) – 'a Chaldean' (Ac 7.4).

93.611 Χανάαν *f*: the land west of the Jordan – 'Canaan' (Ac 7.11), Map 3 C-3.

93.612 Χαναναῖος, α, ον: (derivative of Χανάαν 'Canaan,' 93.611) pertaining to Canaan – 'Canaanite' (Mt 15.22).

93.613 Χαρράν *f*: a city in Mesopotamia – 'Haran' (Ac 7.2, 4), Map 3 D-2.

93.614 Χίος, ου *f*: an island, with a city of the same name, in the Aegean Sea – 'Chios' (Ac 20.15), Map 4 D-2.

93.615 Χοραζίν *f*: a city in Galilee – 'Chorazin' (Mt 11.21; Lk 10.13), Map 2 D-3.

ABBREVIATIONS

NEW TESTAMENT BOOKS

Mt	*Matthew*	1, 2 Th	*1, 2 Thessalonians*
Mk	*Mark*	1, 2 Tm	*1, 2 Timothy*
Lk	*Luke*	Tt	*Titus*
Jn	*John*	Phm	*Philemon*
Ac	*Acts*	He	*Hebrews*
Ro	*Romans*	Jas	*James*
1, 2 Cor	*1, 2 Corinthians*	1, 2 Pe	*1, 2 Peter*
Ga	*Galatians*	1, 2, 3 Jn	*1, 2, 3 John*
Eph	*Ephesians*	Jd	*Jude*
Php	*Philippians*	Re	*Revelation*
Col	*Colossians*		

OTHER ABBREVIATIONS

acc	*accusative*	NEB	*New English Bible*
act	*active*	neut	*neuter*
adj	*adjective*	nom	*nominative*
adv	*adverb*	NT	*New Testament*
alt	*alternative*	opt	*optative*
aor	*aorist*	OT	*Old Testament*
dat	*dative*	pass	*passive*
f	*feminine*	perf	*perfect*
fem	*feminine*	pf	*perfect*
fn	*footnote*	pl	*plural*
fut	*future*	plpf	*pluperfect*
gen	*genitive*	pres	*present*
impf	*imperfect*	ptc	*participle*
impv	*imperative*	RSV	*Revised Standard Version*
ind	*indicative*	sg	*singular*
inf	*infinitive*	subj	*subjunctive*
m	*masculine*	TEV	*Today's English Version*
masc	*masculine*	UBS	*United Bible Societies*
midd	*middle*	unaugm	*unaugmented*
n	*neuter*		

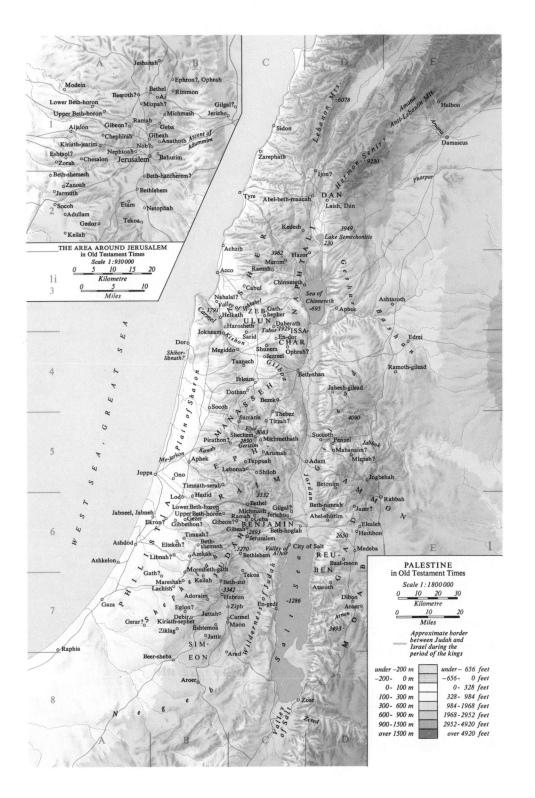

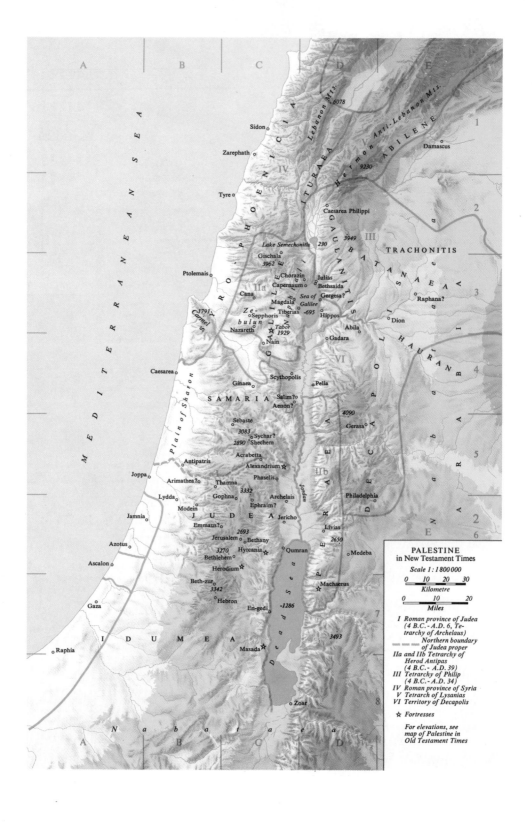

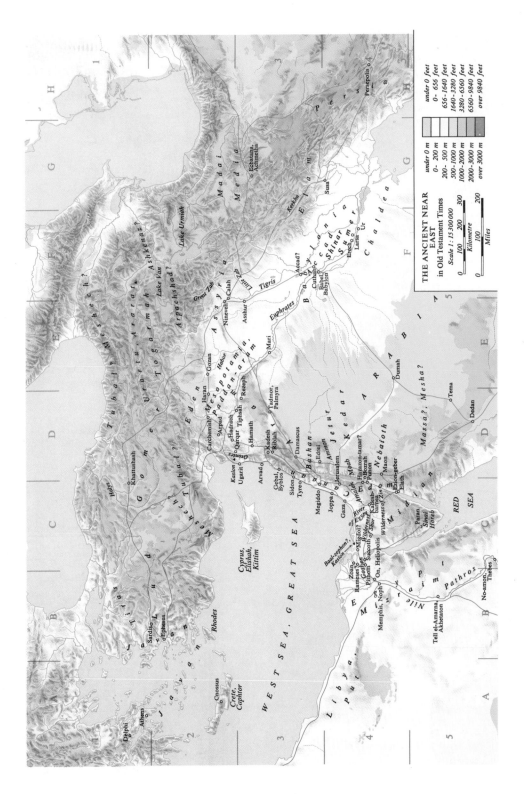

THE ANCIENT NEAR
EAST
in Old Testament Times

Scale 1: 15 300 000

0	100	200	300
Kilometre			

0	100	200
Miles		

	under 0 m	under 0 feet
	0- 200 m	0- 656 feet
	200- 500 m	656-1640 feet
	500-1000 m	1640-3280 feet
	1000-2000 m	3280-6560 feet
	2000-3000 m	6560-9840 feet
	over 3000 m	over 9840 feet

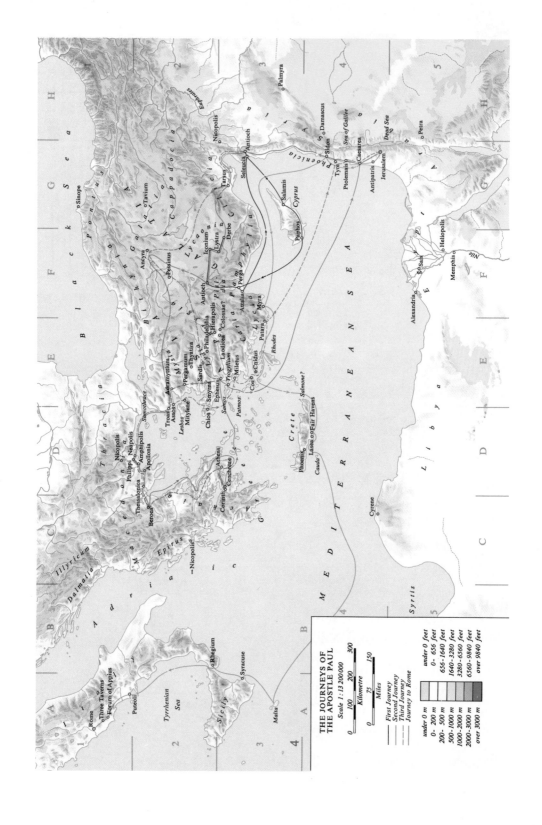

THE JOURNEYS OF
THE APOSTLE PAUL

Scale 1:13 200 000

Kilometre
0   100   200   300

Miles
0   75   150

— — — First Journey
———— Second Journey
———— Third Journey
- - - - Journey to Rome

	under 0 feet	under 0 m
	0– 656 feet	0– 200 m
	656–1640 feet	200– 500 m
	1640–3280 feet	500–1000 m
	3280–6560 feet	1000–2000 m
	6560–9840 feet	2000–3000 m
	over 9840 feet	over 3000 m